SC 1977

5410

BYRON
POETICAL WORKS

Oxford University Press, Ely House, London W. 1

GLASGOW NEW YORK TORONTO MELBOURNE WELLINGTON
CAPE TOWN SALISBURY IBADAN NAIROBI DAR ES SALAAM LUSAKA ADDIS ABABA
BOMBAY CALCUTTA MADRAS KARACHI LAHORE DACCA
KUALA LUMPUR SINGAPORE HONG KONG TOKYO

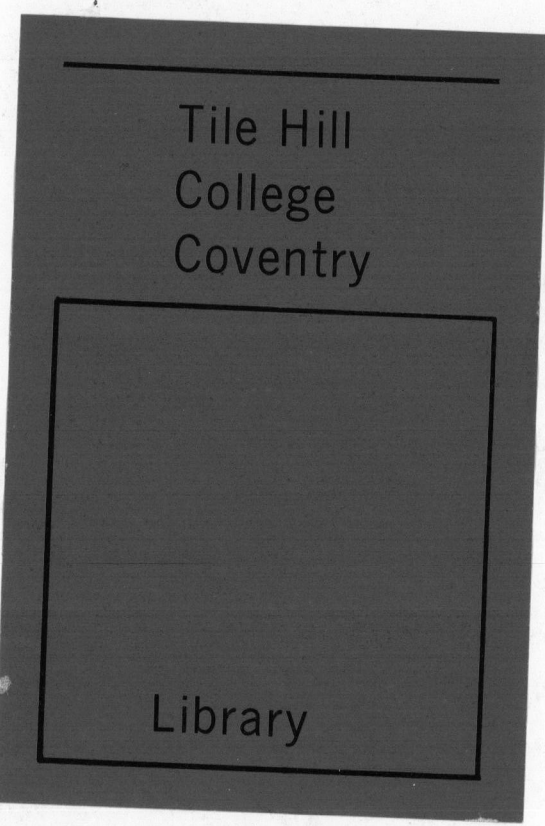

BYRON
POETICAL WORKS

EDITED BY FREDERICK PAGE
A NEW EDITION, CORRECTED BY JOHN JUMP

LONDON
OXFORD UNIVERSITY PRESS
NEW YORK TORONTO

GEORGE GORDON, LORD BYRON

Born, London   22 *January* 1788
Died, Missolonghi, Greece   19 *April* 1824

An edition of the Poetical Works of Lord Byron was first published in the Oxford Standard Authors series in July 1904; *reprinted* 1906, 1909 1911, 1912, 1914, 1917, 1921, 1923, 1926, 1928, 1929, 1933, 1935 *and* 1939. *A reset edition was first printed in* 1945, *and reprinted in* 1950, 1952, 1957, 1960, 1961, 1964, 1966, 1967 (*twice*), *and* 1969.

  This third edition was first published in Oxford Paperbacks in 1970 *and reprinted in Oxford Standard Authors in* 1970.

© Copyright O.U.P. 1970

19 254118 8

CONTENTS

CONTENTS

CONTENTS

CONTENTS

CONTENTS

A NOTE ON THE THIRD EDITION

In revising the text of the Oxford Standard Authors *Byron* for reprinting and publication in the present format, I have respected the previous editor's preferences with regard to such accidental features as spelling, punctuation, italicization, and the use of initial capitals. He italicizes and capitalizes, and occasionally punctuates, rather more lightly than does E. H. Coleridge in what is still the standard edition (*The Works of Lord Byron: Poetry*, 7 vols., London, 1898-1904); and he adopts a small number of more modern spellings, such as 'control' for 'controul'. Many of these minor differences merely reflect divergent editorial tastes on matters to which the poet himself was relatively indifferent.

My chief aim in the time available to me as reviser has been to remove substantive errors by reference to the edition of *Don Juan* by T. G. Steffan and W. W. Pratt (4 vols., Austin, Texas, and Edinburgh, 1957) and to the texts of the other poems as edited by E. H. Coleridge. In addition, I have corrected a few minor misprints and have taken the opportunity of adding to the present text of *Don Juan* the fragment of a seventeenth canto which was evidently not available to my predecessor. But it has not been practicable to insert in *Cain* the three-and-a-half lines following I.i.163 in which Lucifer foretells the Atonement:

> perhaps he'll make
> One day a Son unto himself—as he
> Gave you a father—and if he so doth,
> Mark me! that Son will be a sacrifice!

All the early editions omitted these, but E. H. Coleridge restored them to the text from the manuscript.

Coleridge also prints some shorter pieces—mostly juvenile verses and *jeux d'esprit*—which do not appear in the Oxford Standard Authors *Byron*, and he provides fuller versions of a few of the *jeux d'esprit* which do appear there. None of this material is of major importance, and it has not been added in the present edition.

University of Manchester, 1969

JOHN D. JUMP

HOURS OF IDLENESS

A SERIES OF POEMS ORIGINAL AND TRANSLATED

[*First published in 1807*]

' Virginibus puerisque canto.'—HORACE, lib. iii, Ode 1.
' Μήτ' ἄρ με μάλ' αἴνεε, μήτε τι νείκει.'—HOMER, *Iliad*, x. 249.
' He whistled as he went, for want of thought.'—DRYDEN.

PREFACE TO THE FIRST EDITION

IN submitting to the public eye the following collection, I have not only to combat the difficulties that writers of verse generally encounter, but may incur the charge of presumption for obtruding myself on the world, when, without doubt, I might be, at my age, more usefully employed.

These productions are the fruits of the lighter hours of a young man who has lately completed his nineteenth year. As they bear the internal evidence of a boyish mind, this is, perhaps, unnecessary information. Some few were written during the disadvantages of illness and depression of spirits: under the former influence, 'CHILDISH RECOLLECTIONS,' in particular, were composed. This consideration, though it cannot excite the voice of praise, may at least arrest the arm of censure. A considerable portion of these poems has been privately printed, at the request and for the perusal of my friends. I am sensible that the partial and frequently injudicious admiration of a social circle is not the criterion by which poetical genius is to be estimated, yet 'to do greatly' we must 'dare greatly'; and I have hazarded my reputation and feelings in publishing this volume. I have 'passed the Rubicon,' and must stand or fall by the 'cast of the die.' In the latter event I shall submit without a murmur; for, though not without solicitude for the fate of these effusions, my expectations are by no means sanguine. It is probable that I may have dared much and done little; for, in the words of Cowper, 'it is one thing to write what may please our friends, who, because they are such, are apt to be a little biassed in our favour, and another to write what may please everybody; because they who have no connexion, or even knowledge of the author, will be sure to find fault if they can.' To the truth of this, however, I do not wholly subscribe; on the contrary, I feel convinced that these trifles will not be treated with injustice. Their merit, if they possess any, will be liberally allowed; their numerous faults, on the other hand, cannot expect that favour which has been denied to others of maturer years, decided character, and far greater ability.

I have not aimed at exclusive originality, still less have I studied any particular model for imitation; some translations are given, of which many are paraphrastic. In the original pieces there may appear a casual coincidence with authors whose works I have been accustomed to read; but I have not been guilty of intentional plagiarism. To produce anything entirely new, in an age so fertile in rhyme, would be a Herculean task, as every subject has already been treated to its utmost extent. Poetry, however, is not my primary vocation; to divert the dull moments of indisposition, or the monotony of a vacant hour, urged me 'to this sin': little can be expected from so unpromising a muse. My wreath, scanty as it must be, is all I shall derive from these productions; and I shall never attempt to replace its fading leaves, or pluck a single additional sprig from groves where I am, at best, an intruder. Though accustomed, in my younger days, to rove a careless mountaineer on the Highlands of Scotland, I have not, of late years, had the benefit of such pure air, or so elevated a residence, as might enable me to enter the lists with genuine bards, who have enjoyed both these advantages. But they derive considerable fame, and a few not less profit, from their productions; while I shall expiate my rashness as an interloper, certainly without the latter, and in all probability with a very slight share of the former. I leave to others 'virûm volitare per ora.' I look to the few who will hear with patience, 'dulce est desipere in loco.' To the former worthies I resign, without repining, the hope of immortality, and content myself with the not very magnificent prospect of ranking amongst 'the mob of gentlemen who write';—my readers must determine whether I dare say 'with ease,' or the honour of a posthumous page in 'The Catalogue of Royal and Noble Authors,'—a work to which the Peerage is under infinite obligations, inasmuch as many names of considerable length, sound, and antiquity, are thereby rescued from the obscurity which unluckily overshadows several voluminous productions of their illustrious bearers.

With slight hopes, and some fears, I publish this first and last attempt. To the dictates of young ambition may be ascribed many actions more criminal and equally absurd. To a few of my own age the contents may afford amusement; I trust they will, at least, be found harmless. It is highly improbable, from my situation and pursuits hereafter, that I should ever obtrude myself a second time on the public; nor even, in the very doubtful event of present indulgence, shall I be tempted to commit a future trespass of the same nature. The opinion of Dr. Johnson on the poems of a noble relation of mine*, 'That when a man of rank appeared in the character of an author, he deserved to have his merit handsomely allowed,' can have little weight with verbal, and still less with periodical, censors; but were it otherwise, I should be loth to avail myself of the privilege, and would rather incur the bitterest censure of anonymous criticism, than triumph in honours granted solely to a title.

* The Earl of Carlisle, whose works have long received the meed of public applause, to which, by their intrinsic worth, they were well entitled.

TO

THE RIGHT HONOURABLE FREDERICK, EARL OF CARLISLE,

KNIGHT OF THE GARTER, ETC., ETC.,

THE SECOND EDITION OF THESE POEMS IS INSCRIBED,

BY HIS OBLIGED WARD AND AFFECTIONATE KINSMAN,

THE AUTHOR.

ON THE DEATH OF A YOUNG LADY

Cousin to the Author, and very dear to him.

HUSH'D are the winds, and still the even-
    ing gloom,
    Not e'en a zephyr wanders through the
    grove,
Whilst I return, to view my Margaret's
    tomb,
    And scatter flowers on the dust I love.

Within this narrow cell reclines her clay,
    That clay, where once such animation
    beam'd;   6
The King of Terrors seized her as his
    prey,
    Not worth nor beauty have her life re-
    deem'd.

Oh! could that King of Terrors pity feel,
    Or Heaven reverse the dread decree of
    fate,   10
Not here the mourner would his grief re-
    veal,
    Not here the muse her virtues would
    relate.

But wherefore weep? Her matchless
    spirit soars
Beyond where splendid shines the orb
    of day;
And weeping angels lead her to those
    bowers   15
    Where endless pleasures virtuous deeds
    repay.

And shall presumptuous mortals Heaven
    arraign,
    And, madly, godlike Providence ac-
    cuse?
Ah! no, far fly from me attempts so
    vain:—
    I'll ne'er submission to my God
    refuse.   20

Yet is remembrance of those virtues dear,
    Yet fresh the memory of that beauteous
    face;
Still they call forth my warm affection's
    tear,
    Still in my heart retain their wonted
    place.

1802.

TO E—

LET Folly smile, to view the names
    Of thee and me in friendship twined;
Yet Virtue will have greater claims
    To love, than rank with vice combined.

And though unequal is thy fate,   5
    Since title deck'd my higher birth!
Yet envy not this gaudy state;
    Thine is the pride of modest worth.

Our souls at least congenial meet,
    Nor can thy lot my rank disgrace;   10
Our intercourse is not less sweet,
    Since worth of rank supplies the
    place.

November 1802.

TO D—

IN thee I fondly hoped to clasp
    A friend whom death alone could sever;
Till envy, with malignant grasp,
    Detach'd thee from my breast for ever.

True, she has forced thee from my
    breast,   5
    Yet in my heart thou keep'st thy seat;
There, there thine image still must rest,
    Until that heart shall cease to beat.

And when the grave restores her dead,
    When life again to dust is given,   10
On thy dear breast I'll lay my head—
    Without thee where would be my
    heaven?

February 1803.

EPITAPH ON A BELOVED FRIEND

'Αστὴρ πρὶν μὲν ἔλαμπες ἐνὶ ζωοῖσιν ἑῷος.
LAERT.

OH, Friend! for ever loved, for ever dear!
What fruitless tears have bathed thy
    honour'd bier!
What sighs re-echo'd to thy parting breath,
Whilst thou wast struggling in the pangs
    of death!
Could tears retard the tyrant in his
    course;   5
Could sighs avert his dart's relentless
    force;
Could youth and virtue claim a short
    delay,
Or beauty charm the spectre from his
    prey;
Thou still hadst lived to bless my aching
    sight,
Thy comrade's honour and thy friend's
    delight.   10
If yet thy gentle spirit hover nigh
The spot where now thy mouldering
    ashes lie,
Here wilt thou read, recorded on my
    heart,
A grief too deep to trust the sculptor's art.
No marble marks thy couch of lowly
    sleep,   15
But living statues there are seen to weep;
Affliction's semblance bends not o'er thy
    tomb,
Affliction's self deplores thy youthful
    doom.
What though thy sire lament his failing
    line,
A father's sorrows cannot equal mine!
Though none, like thee, his dying hour
    will cheer,   21
Yet other offspring soothe his anguish
    here:
But who with me shall hold thy former
    place?
Thine image what new friendship can
    efface?
Ah, none!—a father's tears will cease to
    flow,   25
Time will assuage an infant brother's woe;
To all, save one, is consolation known,
While solitary friendship sighs alone.
1803.

A FRAGMENT

WHEN, to their airy hall, my fathers' voice
Shall call my spirit, joyful in their choice;
When, poised upon the gale, my form
    shall ride,
Or, dark in mist, descend the mountain's
    side;
Oh! may my shade behold no sculptured
    urns,   5
To mark the spot where earth to earth
    returns!

No lengthen'd scroll, no praise-encum-
    ber'd stone;
My epitaph shall be my name alone:
If *that* with honour fail to crown my clay,
Oh! may no other fame my deeds repay!
That, only *that*, shall single out the spot;
By that remember'd, or with that forgot.
1803.

ON LEAVING NEWSTEAD ABBEY

'Why dost thou build the hall, son of the winged
days? Thou lookest from thy tower to-day: yet
a few years, and the blast of the desert comes, it
howls in thy empty court.'—OSSIAN.

THROUGH thy battlements, Newstead,
    the hollow winds whistle;
Thou, the hall of my fathers, art gone
    to decay;
In thy once smiling garden, the hemlock
    and thistle
Have choked up the rose which late
    bloom'd in the way.

Of the mail-cover'd Barons, who proudly
    to battle   5
Led their vassals from Europe to
    Palestine's plain,
The escutcheon and shield, which with
    every blast rattle,
Are the only sad vestiges now that remain.

No more doth old Robert, with harp-
    stringing numbers,
Raise a flame in the breast for the war-
    laurell'd wreath;   10
Near Askalon's towers, John of Horistan
    slumbers,
Unnerved is the hand of his minstrel by
    death.

Paul and Hubert, too, sleep in the valley
    of Cressy;
For the safety of Edward and England
    they fell:
My fathers! the tears of your country re-
    dress ye;   15
How you fought, how you died, still her
    annals can tell.

On Marston, with Rupert, 'gainst traitors
    contending,
Four brothers enrich'd with their blood
    the bleak field;
For the rights of a monarch their country
    defending,
Till death their attachment to royalty
    seal'd.   20

Shades of heroes, farewell! your descen-
    dant, departing
From the seat of his ancestors, bids you
    adieu!

3

Abroad, or at home, your remembrance
        imparting
    New courage, he'll think upon glory
        and you.

Though a tear dim his eye at this sad
        separation,   25
    'Tis nature, not fear, that excites his
        regret;
Far distant he goes, with the same emula-
        tion,
    The fame of his fathers he ne'er can
        forget.

That fame, and that memory, still will he
        cherish;
    He vows that he ne'er will disgrace
        your renown: 30
Like you will he live, or like you will he
        perish;
    When decay'd, may he mingle his dust
        with your own!

                                          1803.

LINES

WRITTEN IN 'LETTERS OF AN ITALIAN NUN
AND AN ENGLISH GENTLEMAN: BY J. J.
ROUSSEAU: FOUNDED ON FACTS.'

'AWAY, away, your flattering arts
May now betray some simpler hearts;
And you will smile at their believing,
And they shall weep at their deceiving.'

ANSWER TO THE FOREGOING, ADDRESSED TO
MISS ——.

Dear, simple girl, those flattering arts,
From which thou'dst guard frail female
        hearts,
Exist but in imagination,—
Mere phantoms of thine own creation;
For he who views that witching grace, 5
That perfect form, that lovely face,
With eyes admiring, oh! believe me,
He never wishes to deceive thee:
Once in thy polish'd mirror glance,
Thou'lt there descry that elegance   10
Which from our sex demands such praises,
But envy in the other raises:
Then he who tells thee of thy beauty,
Believe me, only does his duty;
Ah! fly not from the candid youth;   15
It is not flattery,—'tis truth.

                                      July 1804.

ADRIAN'S ADDRESS TO HIS
SOUL WHEN DYING

[ANIMULA! vagula, blandula,
Hospes comesque corporis,
Quæ nunc abibis in loca—
Pallidula, rigida, nudula,
Nec, ut soles, dabis jocos?]

AH! gentle, fleeting, wav'ring sprite,
Friend and associate of this clay!
    To what unknown region borne,

Wilt thou now wing thy distant flight?
No more with wonted humour gay,   5
    But pallid, cheerless, and forlorn.

TRANSLATION FROM
CATULLUS

AD LESBIAM

EQUAL to Jove that youth must be—
Greater than Jove he seems to me—
Who, free from Jealousy's alarms,
Securely views thy matchless charms.
That cheek, which ever dimpling glows, 5
That mouth, from whence such music
        flows,
To him, alike, are always known,
Reserved for him, and him alone.
Ah! Lesbia! though 'tis death to me,
I cannot choose but look on thee;   10
But, at the sight, my senses fly;
I needs must gaze, but, gazing, die;
Whilst trembling with a thousand fears,
Parch'd to the throat my tongue adheres,
My pulse beats quick, my breath heaves
        short,   15
My limbs deny their slight support,
Cold dews my pallid face o'erspread,
With deadly languor droops my head,
My ears with tingling echoes ring,
And life itself is on the wing;   20
My eyes refuse the cheering light,
Their orbs are veil'd in starless night:
Such pangs my nature sinks beneath,
And feels a temporary death.

TRANSLATION OF THE EPITAPH
ON VIRGIL AND TIBULLUS

BY DOMITIUS MARSUS

HE who sublime in epic numbers roll'd,
    And he who struck the softer lyre of
        love,
By Death's unequal hand alike controll'd,
    Fit comrades in Elysian regions move!

IMITATION OF TIBULLUS

'Sulpicia ad Cerinthum.'—Lib. iv.

CRUEL Cerinthus! does the fell disease
Which racks my breast your fickle bosom
        please?
Alas! I wish'd but to o'ercome the pain,
That I might live for love and you again;
But now I scarcely shall bewail my fate:
By death alone I can avoid your hate.

TRANSLATION FROM
CATULLUS

[Lugete, Veneres, Cupidinesque, &c.]

YE Cupids, droop each little head,
Nor let your wings with joy be spread;
My Lesbia's favourite bird is dead,
    Whom dearer than her eyes she loved:

4

For he was gentle, and so true,　　5
Obedient to her call he flew,
No fear, no wild alarm he knew,
　　But lightly o'er her bosom moved:

And softly fluttering here and there,
He never sought to cleave the air,　　10
But chirrup'd oft, and, free from care,
Tuned to her ear his grateful strain.
Now having pass'd the gloomy bourne
From whence he never can return,
His death and Lesbia's grief I mourn,　　15
　　Who sighs, alas! but sighs in vain.

Oh! curst be thou, devouring grave!
Whose jaws eternal victims crave,
From whom no earthly power can save,
　　For thou hast ta'en the bird away:　　20
From thee my Lesbia's eyes o'erflow,
Her swollen cheeks with weeping glow;
Thou art the cause of all her woe,
　　Receptacle of life's decay.

IMITATED FROM CATULLUS

TO ELLEN

OH! might I kiss those eyes of fire,
A million scarce would quench desire:
Still would I steep my lips in bliss,
And dwell an age on every kiss:
Nor then my soul should sated be;　　5
Still would I kiss and cling to thee:
Nought should my kiss from thine dissever;
Still would we kiss and kiss for ever;
E'en though the numbers did exceed
The yellow harvest's countless seed.　　10
To part would be a vain endeavour:
Could I desist?—ah! never—never!

TRANSLATION FROM HORACE

[Justum et tenacem propositi virum, &c.]

THE man of firm and noble soul
No factious clamours can control;
No threat'ning tyrant's darkling brow
　　Can swerve him from his just intent:
Gales the warring waves which plough,
　　By Auster on the billows spent,　　6
To curb the Adriatic main,
Would awe his fix'd, determined mind in
　　vain.

Ay, and the red right arm of Jove,
Hurtling his lightnings from above,　　10
With all his terrors there unfurl'd,
　　He would unmoved, unawed, behold.
The flames of an expiring world,
　　Again in crashing chaos roll'd,
In vast promiscuous ruin hurl'd,　　15
Might light his glorious funeral pile:
Still dauntless 'midst the wreck of earth
　　he'd smile.

FROM ANACREON

[Θέλω λέγειν 'Ατρείδας, κ. τ. λ.]

I WISH to tune my quivering lyre
To deeds of fame and notes of fire;
To echo, from its rising swell,
How heroes fought and nations fell,
When Atreus' sons advanced to war,
Or Tyrian Cadmus roved afar;　　6
But still, to martial strains unknown,
My lyre recurs to love alone.
Fired with the hope of future fame,
I seek some nobler hero's name;　　10
The dying chords are strung anew,
To war, to war, my harp is due:
With glowing strings, the epic strain
To Jove's great son I raise again;
Alcides and his glorious deeds,　　15
Beneath whose arm the Hydra bleeds,
All, all in vain; my wayward lyre
Wakes silver notes of soft desire.
Adieu, ye chiefs renown'd in arms!
Adieu the clang of war's alarms!　　20
To other deeds my soul is strung,
And sweeter notes shall now be sung;
My harp shall all its powers reveal,
To tell the tale my heart must feel;
Love, love alone, my lyre shall claim,
In songs of bliss and sighs of flame.　　26

FROM ANACREON

[Μεσονυκτίοις ποθ' ὥραις, κ. τ. λ.]

'TWAS now the hour when Night had
　　driven
Her car half round yon sable heaven;
Boötes, only, seem'd to roll
His arctic charge around the pole;
While mortals, lost in gentle sleep,　　5
Forgot to smile, or ceased to weep:
At this lone hour the Paphian boy,
Descending from the realms of joy,
Quick to my gate directs his course,
And knocks with all his little force.　　10
My visions fled, alarm'd I rose,—
'What stranger breaks my blest repose?'
'Alas!' replies the wily child,
In faltering accents sweetly mild,
'A hapless infant here I roam,　　15
Far from my dear maternal home.
Oh! shield me from the wintry blast!
The nightly storm is pouring fast.
No prowling robber lingers here.
A wandering baby who can fear?'　　20
I heard his seeming artless tale,
I heard his sighs upon the gale:
My breast was never pity's foe,
But felt for all the baby's woe.
I drew the bar, and by the light　　25
Young Love, the infant, met my sight;
His bow across his shoulders flung,
And thence his fatal quiver hung
(Ah! little did I think the dart
Would rankle soon within my heart).　　30

5

With care I tend my weary guest,
His little fingers chill my breast;
His glossy curls, his azure wing,
Which droop with nightly showers,
   I wring;   34
His shivering limbs the embers warm;
And now reviving from the storm,
Scarce had he felt his wonted glow,
Than swift he seized his slender bow:—
'I fain would know, my gentle host,'
He cried, 'if this its strength has lost; 40
I fear, relax'd with midnight dews,
The strings their former aid refuse.'
With poison tipt, his arrow flies,
Deep in my tortured heart it lies: 44
Then loud the joyous urchin laugh'd:—
'My bow can still impel the shaft:
'Tis firmly fix'd, thy sighs reveal it;
Say, courteous host, canst thou not feel
   it?'

FROM THE PROMETHEUS VINCTUS OF ÆSCHYLUS

[Μηδάμ' ὁ πάντα νέμων, κ. τ. λ.]

GREAT Jove, to whose almighty throne
  Both gods and mortals homage pay,
Ne'er may my soul thy power disown,
  Thy dread behests ne'er disobey.
Oft shall the sacred victim fall   5
  In sea-girt Ocean's mossy hall;
My voice shall raise no impious strain
'Gainst him who rules the sky and azure
  main.

How different now thy joyless fate,
  Since first Hesione thy bride,   10
When placed aloft in godlike state,
  The blushing beauty by thy side,
Thou sat'st, while reverend Ocean
  smiled,
And mirthful strains the hours beguiled;
The Nymphs and Tritons danced
  around,   15
Nor yet thy doom was fix'd, nor Jove
  relentless frown'd.

               HARROW, Dec. 1, 1804.

TO EMMA

SINCE now the hour is come at last,
  When you must quit your anxious
   lover;
Since now our dream of bliss is past,
  One pang, my girl, and all is over.

Alas! that pang will be severe,   5
  Which bids us part to meet no more;
Which tears me far from one so dear,
  Departing for a distant shore.

Well! we have pass'd some happy hours,
  And joy will mingle with our tears; 10
When thinking on these ancient towers,
  The shelter of our infant years;

Where from this Gothic casement's
  height,
  We view'd the lake, the park, the dell,
And still, though tears obstruct our sight,
  We lingering look a last farewell, 16

O'er fields through which we used to run,
  And spend the hours in childish play;
O'er shades where, when our race was
  done,
  Reposing on my breast you lay; 20

Whilst I, admiring, too remiss,
  Forgot to scare the hovering flies,
Yet envied every fly the kiss
  It dared to give your slumbering eyes:

See still the little painted bark, 25
  In which I row'd you o'er the lake;
See there, high waving o'er the park,
  The elm I clamber'd for your sake.

These times are past—our joys are gone,
  You leave me, leave this happy vale;
These scenes I must retrace alone: 31
  Without thee what will they avail?

Who can conceive, who has not proved,
  The anguish of a last embrace?
When, torn from all you fondly loved,
  You bid a long adieu to peace. 36

This is the deepest of our woes,
  For this these tears our cheeks bedew;
This is of love the final close,
  Oh, God! the fondest, last adieu! 40

TO M. S. G.

WHENE'ER I view those lips of thine,
  Their hue invites my fervent kiss;
Yet I forego that bliss divine,
  Alas! it were unhallow'd bliss.

Whene'er I dream of that pure breast, 5
  How could I dwell upon its snows!
Yet is the daring wish represt,
  For that—would banish its repose.

A glance from thy soul-searching eye
  Can raise with hope, depress with fear;
Yet I conceal my love,—and why? 11
  I would not force a painful tear.

I ne'er have told my love, yet thou
  Hast seen my ardent flame too well;
And shall I plead my passion now, 15
  To make thy bosom's heaven a hell?

No! for thou never canst be mine,
  United by the priest's decree:
By any ties but those divine,
  Mine, my beloved, thou ne'er shalt be.

Then let the secret fire consume, 21
  Let it consume, thou shalt not know:
With joy I court a certain doom,
  Rather than spread its guilty glow.

I will not ease my tortured heart   25
  By driving dove-eyed peace from thine;
Rather than such a sting impart,
  Each thought presumptuous I resign.

Yes! yield those lips, for which I'd brave   30
  More than I here shall dare to tell;
Thy innocence and mine to save,—
  I bid thee now a last farewell.

Yes! yield that breast, to seek despair,
  And hope no more thy soft embrace;
Which to obtain my soul would dare   35
  All, all reproach, but thy disgrace.

At least from guilt shalt thou be free,
  No matron shall thy shame reprove;
Though cureless pangs may prey on me,
  No martyr shalt thou be to love.   40

TO CAROLINE

THINK'ST thou I saw thy beauteous eyes,
  Suffused in tears, implore to stay;
And heard unmoved thy plenteous sighs,
  Which said far more than words can say?

Though keen the grief thy tears exprest,   5
  When love and hope lay both o'er-
    thrown,
Yet still, my girl, this bleeding breast
  Throbb'd with deep sorrow as thine
    own.

But when our cheeks with anguish glow'd,
  When thy sweet lips were join'd to mine,
The tears that from my eyelids flow'd   11
  Were lost in those which fell from thine.

Thou couldst not feel my burning cheek,
  Thy gushing tears had quench'd its
    flame;
And as thy tongue essay'd to speak,   15
  In signs alone it breathed my name.

And yet, my girl, we weep in vain,
  In vain our fate in sighs deplore;
Remembrance only can remain,—
  But that will make us weep the more.

Again, thou best beloved, adieu!   21
  Ah! if thou canst, o'ercome regret;
Nor let thy mind past joys review,—
  Our only hope is to forget!

TO CAROLINE

WHEN I hear you express an affection so
  warm,
Ne'er think, my beloved, that I do not
  believe;
For your lip would the soul of suspicion
  disarm,
  And your eye beams a ray which can
  never deceive.

Yet still this fond bosom regrets, while
  adoring,   5
  That love, like the leaf, must fall into
  the sere;
That age will come on, when remembrance, deploring,
  Contemplates the scenes of her youth
  with a tear;

That the time must arrive, when, no
  longer retaining
  Their auburn, those locks must wave
  thin to the breeze,   10
When a few silver hairs of those tresses
  remaining,
  Prove nature a prey to decay and
  disease.

'Tis this, my beloved, which spreads
  gloom o'er my features,
  Though I ne'er shall presume to
  arraign the decree
Which God has proclaim'd as the fate of
  his creatures,   15
  In the death which one day will deprive
  you of me.

Mistake not, sweet sceptic, the cause of
  emotion,
  No doubt can the mind of your lover
  invade;
He worships each look with such faithful
  devotion,
  A smile can enchant, or a tear can dissuade.   20

But as death, my beloved, soon or late
  shall o'ertake us,
  And our breasts, which alive with such
  sympathy glow,
Will sleep in the grave till the blast shall
  awake us,
  When calling the dead, in earth's
  bosom laid low,—

Oh! then let us drain, while we may,
  draughts of pleasure,   25
  Which from passion like ours must un-
  ceasingly flow;
Let us pass round the cup of love's bliss
  in full measure,
  And quaff the contents as our nectar
  below.

1805.

TO CAROLINE

OH! when shall the grave hide for ever my
  sorrow?
Oh! when shall my soul wing her flight
  from this clay?
The present is hell, and the coming to-
  morrow
  But brings, with new torture, the curse
  of to-day.

7

From my eye flows no tear, from my lips
    flow no curses,   5
  I blast not the fiends who have hurl'd
    me from bliss;
For poor is the soul which bewailing re-
    hearses
  Its querulous grief, when in anguish
    like this.

Was my eye, 'stead of tears, with red fury
    flakes bright'ning,
  Would my lips breathe a flame which
    no stream could assuage,   10
On our foes should my glance launch in
    vengeance its lightning,
  With transport my tongue give a loose
    to its rage.

But now tears and curses, alike unavailing,
  Would add to the souls of our tyrants
    delight;
Could they view us our sad separation be-
    wailing,   15
  Their merciless hearts would rejoice at
    the sight.

Yet still, though we bend with a feign'd
    resignation,
  Life beams not for us with one ray that
    can cheer;
Love and hope upon earth bring no more
    consolation;
  In the grave is our hope, for in life is
    our fear.   20

Oh! when, my adored, in the tomb will
    they place me,
  Since, in life, love and friendship for
    ever are fled?
If again in the mansion of death I
    embrace thee,
  Perhaps they will leave unmolested the
    dead.

                    1805.

STANZAS TO A LADY, WITH THE POEMS OF CAMOËNS

This votive pledge of fond esteem,
  Perhaps, dear girl! for me thou'lt prize;
It sings of Love's enchanting dream,
  A theme we never can despise.

Who blames it but the envious fool,   5
  The old and disappointed maid;
Or pupil of the prudish school,
  In single sorrow doom'd to fade?

Then read, dear girl! with feeling read,
  For thou wilt ne'er be one of those;
To thee in vain I shall not plead   11
  In pity for the poet's woes.

He was in sooth a genuine bard;
  His was no faint, fictitious flame.
Like his, may love be thy reward,   15
  But not thy hapless fate the same.

THE FIRST KISS OF LOVE

'Α βάρβιτος δὲ χορδαῖς
"Ερωτα μοῦνον ἠχεῖ.—ANACREON.

Away with your fictions of flimsy
    romance;
  Those tissues of falsehood which folly
    has wove!
Give me the mild beam of the soul-
    breathing glance,
  Or the rapture which dwells on the
    first kiss of love.

Ye rhymers, whose bosoms with phantasy
    glow,   5
  Whose pastoral passions are made for
    the grove;
From what blest inspiration your sonnets
    would flow,
  Could you ever have tasted the first kiss
    of love!

If Apollo should e'er his assistance re-
    fuse,
  Or the Nine be disposed from your
    service to rove,   10
Invoke them no more, bid adieu to the
    muse,
  And try the effect of the first kiss of
    love.

I hate you, ye cold compositions of art!
  Though prudes may condemn me, and
    bigots reprove,
I court the effusions that spring from the
    heart,   15
  Which throbs with delight to the first
    kiss of love.

Your shepherds, your flocks, those fan-
    tastical themes,
  Perhaps may amuse, yet they never can
    move:
Arcadia displays but a region of dreams:
  What are visions like these to the first
    kiss of love?   20

Oh! cease to affirm that man, since his
    birth,
  From Adam till now, has with wretched-
    ness strove,
Some portion of paradise still is on earth,
  And Eden revives in the first kiss of
    love.

When age chills the blood, when our plea-
    sures are past—   25
  For years fleet away with the wings of
    the dove—
The dearest remembrance will still be the
    last,
  Our sweetest memorial the first kiss of
    love.

ON A CHANGE OF MASTERS
AT A GREAT PUBLIC SCHOOL

WHERE are those honours, Ida! once your
    own,
When Probus fill'd your magisterial
    throne?
As ancient Rome, fast falling to disgrace,
Hail'd a barbarian in her Cæsar's place,
So you, degenerate, share as hard a fate,
And seat Pomposus where your Probus
    sate.   6
Of narrow brain, yet of a narrower soul,
Pomposus holds you in his harsh control;
Pomposus, by no social virtue sway'd,
With florid jargon, and with vain parade;
With noisy nonsense, and new-fangled
    rules,   11
Such as were ne'er before enforced in
    schools.
Mistaking pedantry for learning's laws,
He governs, sanction'd but by self-applause;
With him the same dire fate attending
    Rome,   15
Ill-fated Ida! soon must stamp your doom;
Like her o'erthrown, for ever lost to fame,
No trace of science left you, but the name.
                      July 1805.

TO THE DUKE OF DORSET

DORSET! whose early steps with mine
    have stray'd,
Exploring every path of Ida's glade;
Whom still affection taught me to defend,
And made me less a tyrant than a friend,
Though the harsh custom of our youth-
    ful band   5
Bade *thee* obey, and gave *me* to command;
Thee, on whose head a few short years
    will shower
The gift of riches and the pride of power;
E'en now a name illustrious is thine own,
Renown'd in rank, nor far beneath the
    throne.   10
Yet, Dorset, let not this seduce thy soul
To shun fair science, or evade control,
Though passive tutors, fearful to dispraise
The titled child, whose future breath may
    raise,   14
View ducal errors with indulgent eyes,
And wink at faults they tremble to
    chastise.
    When youthful parasites, who bend the
    knee
To wealth, their golden idol, not to thee,—
And even in simple boyhood's opening dawn
Some slaves are found to flatter and to
    fawn,—   20
When these declare, 'that pomp alone
    should wait
On one by birth predestined to be great;
That books were only meant for drudging
    fools,

That gallant spirits scorn the common
    rules;'
Believe them not;—they point the path to
    shame,   25
And seek to blast the honours of thy
    name.
Turn to the few in Ida's early throng,
Whose souls disdain not to condemn the
    wrong;
Or if, amidst the comrades of thy youth,
None dare to raise the sterner voice of
    truth,   30
Ask thine own heart; 'twill bid thee, boy,
    forbear;
For *well* I know that virtue lingers there.
    Yes! I have mark'd thee many a passing
    day,
But now new scenes invite me far away;
Yes! I have mark'd within that generous
    mind   35
A soul, if well matured, to bless mankind;
Ah! though myself by nature haughty,
    wild,
Whom Indiscretion hail'd her favourite
    child;
Though every error stamps me for her
    own,
And dooms my fall, I fain would fall
    alone;   40
Though my proud heart no precept now
    can tame,
I love the virtues which I cannot claim.
    'Tis not enough, with other sons of
    power,
To gleam the lambent meteor of an hour;
To swell some peerage page in feeble
    pride,   45
With long-drawn names that grace no
    page beside;
Then share with titled crowds the com-
    mon lot—
In life just gazed at, in the grave forgot;
While nought divides thee from the vulgar
    dead,
Except the dull cold stone that hides thy
    head,   50
The mouldering 'scutcheon, or the
    herald's roll,
That well-emblazon'd but neglected scroll,
Where lords, unhonour'd, in the tomb
    may find
One spot, to leave a worthless name
    behind.
There sleep, unnoticed as the gloomy
    vaults   55
That veil their dust, their follies, and their
    faults,
A race, with old armorial lists o'erspread,
In records destined never to be read.
Fain would I view thee, with prophetic
    eyes,
Exalted more among the good and wise,
A glorious and a long career pursue,   61
As first in rank, the first in talent too:

Spurn every vice, each little meanness
   shun;
Not Fortune's minion, but her noblest son.
   Turn to the annals of a former day; 65
Bright are the deeds thine earlier sires dis-
   play.
One, though a courtier, lived a man of
   worth,
And call'd, proud boast! the British
   drama forth.
Another view, not less renown'd for wit;
Alike for courts, and camps, or senates
   fit; 70
Bold in the field, and favour'd by the
   Nine;
In every splendid part ordain'd to shine;
Far, far distinguish'd from the glittering
   throng,
The pride of princes, and the boast of song.
Such were thy fathers; thus preserve their
   name; 75
Not heir to titles only, but to fame.
The hour draws nigh, a few brief days will
   close,
To me, this little scene of joys and woes;
Each knell of Time now warns me to re-
   sign
Shades where Hope, Peace, and Friend-
   ship all were mine: 80
Hope, that could vary like the rainbow's
   hue,
And gild their pinions as the moments flew;
Peace, that reflection never frown'd away,
By dreams of ill to cloud some future day;
Friendship, whose truth let childhood only
   tell; 85
Alas! they love not long, who love so well.
To these adieu! nor let me linger o'er
Scenes hail'd, as exiles hail their native
   shore,
Receding slowly through the dark-blue
   deep,
Beheld by eyes that mourn, yet cannot
   weep. 90
   Dorset, farewell! I will not ask one part
Of sad remembrance in so young a heart;
The coming morrow from thy youthful
   mind
Will sweep my name, nor leave a trace be-
   hind.
And yet, perhaps, in some maturer year,
Since chance has thrown us in the self-
   same sphere, 96
Since the same senate, nay, the same
   debate,
May one day claim our suffrage for the
   state,
We hence may meet, and pass each other
   by,
With faint regard, or cold and distant
   eye. 100
For me, in future, neither friend nor foe,
A stranger to thyself, thy weal or woe,
With thee no more again I hope to trace

The recollection of our early race;
No more, as once, in social hours rejoice,
Or hear, unless in crowds, thy well-known
   voice: 106
Still, if the wishes of a heart untaught
To veil those feelings which perchance
   it ought,
If these—but let me cease the lengthen'd
   strain,—
Oh! if these wishes are not breathed in
   vain, 110
The guardian seraph who directs thy fate
Will leave thee glorious, as he found thee
   great.

1805.

FRAGMENT

WRITTEN SHORTLY AFTER THE
MARRIAGE OF MISS CHAWORTH

HILLS of Annesley, bleak and barren,
   Where my thoughtless childhood stray'd,
How the northern tempests, warring,
   Howl above thy tufted shade!

Now no more, the hours beguiling, 5
   Former favourite haunts I see;
Now no more my Mary smiling
   Makes ye seem a heaven to me.

1805.

GRANTA

A MEDLEY

Ἀργυρέαις λόγχαισι μάχου καὶ πάντα κρατήσεις.

OH! could Le Sage's demon's gift
   Be realized at my desire,
This night my trembling form he'd lift
   To place it on St. Mary's spire.

Then would, unroof'd, old Granta's halls
   Pedantic inmates full display; 6
Fellows who dream on lawn or stalls,
   The price of venal votes to pay.

Then would I view each rival wight,
   Petty and Palmerston survey; 10
Who canvass there with all their might,
   Against the next elective day.

Lo! candidates and voters lie
   All lull'd in sleep, a goodly number;
A race renown'd for piety, 15
   Whose conscience won't disturb their
   slumber.

Lord H——, indeed, may not demur:
   Fellows are sage, reflecting men:
They know preferment can occur
   But very seldom,—now and then. 20

They know the Chancellor has got
   Some pretty livings in disposal:
Each hopes that one may be his lot,
   And therefore smiles on his proposal.

Now from the soporific scene   25
  I'll turn mine eye, as night grows later,
To view, unheeded and unseen,
  The studious sons of Alma Mater.

There, in apartments small and damp,
  The candidate for college prizes   30
Sits poring by the midnight lamp;
  Goes late to bed, yet early rises.

He surely well deserves to gain them,
  With all the honours of his college,
Who, striving hardly to obtain them,   35
  Thus seeks unprofitable knowledge:

Who sacrifices hours of rest
  To scan precisely metres Attic;
Or agitates his anxious breast
  In solving problems mathematic: 40

Who reads false quantities in Seale,
  Or puzzles o'er the deep triangle;
Deprived of many a wholesome meal;
  In barbarous Latin doom'd to wrangle:

Renouncing every pleasing page   45
  From authors of historic use;
Preferring to the letter'd sage
  The square of the hypothenuse.

Still, harmless are these occupations,
  That hurt none but the hapless student,
Compared with other recreations,   51
  Which bring together the imprudent;

Whose daring revels shock the sight,
  When vice and infamy combine,
When drunkenness and dice invite,   55
  As every sense is steep'd in wine.

Not so the methodistic crew,
  Who plans of reformation lay:
In humble attitude they sue,
  And for the sins of others pray: 60

Forgetting that their pride of spirit,
  Their exultation in their trial,
Detracts most largely from the merit
  Of all their boasted self-denial.   64

'Tis morn:—from these I turn my sight.
  What scene is this which meets the eye?
A numerous crowd, array'd in white,
  Across the green in numbers fly.

Loud rings in air the chapel bell,
  'Tis hush'd:—what sounds are these I
    hear?   70
The organ's soft celestial swell
  Rolls deeply on the list'ning ear.

To this is join'd the sacred song,
  The royal minstrel's hallow'd strain;
Though he who hears the music long   75
  Will never wish to hear again.

Our choir would scarcely be excused,
  Even as a band of raw beginners;
All mercy now must be refused
  To such a set of croaking sinners.   80

If David, when his toils were ended,
  Had heard these blockheads sing
    before him,
To us his psalms had ne'er descended,—
  In furious mood he would have tore 'em.

The luckless Israelites, when taken   85
  By some inhuman tyrant's order,
Were ask'd to sing, by joy forsaken,
  On Babylonian river's border.

Oh! had they sung in notes like these,
  Inspired by stratagem or fear,   90
They might have set their hearts at ease,
  The devil a soul had stay'd to hear.

But if I scribble longer now,
  The deuce a soul will stay to read;
My pen is blunt, my ink is low;   95
  'Tis almost time to stop, indeed.

Therefore, farewell, old Granta's spires!
  No more, like Cleofas, I fly;
No more, thy theme my muse inspires;
  The reader's tired, and so am I.   100
                          1806.

ON A DISTANT VIEW OF THE VILLAGE AND SCHOOL OF HARROW ON THE HILL

Oh! mihi præteritos referat si Jupiter annos.—
                    VIRGIL.

YE scenes of my childhood, whose loved
    recollection
  Embitters the present, compared with
    the past;
Where science first dawn'd on the powers
    of reflection,
  And friendships were form'd, too
    romantic to last;

Where fancy yet joys to retrace the resem-
    blance   5
  Of comrades, in friendship and mischief
    allied;
How welcome to me your ne'er fading re-
    membrance,
  Which rests in the bosom, though
    hope is denied!

Again I revisit the hills where we sported,
  The streams where we swam, and the
    fields where we fought;   10
The school where, loud warn'd by the
    bell, we resorted,
  To pore o'er the precepts by pedagogues
    taught.

11

Again I behold where for hours I have
    ponder'd,
  As reclining, at eve, on yon tombstone
    I lay;
Or round the steep brow of the church-
    yard I wander'd,   15
  To catch the last gleam of the sun's
    setting ray.

I once more view the room, with spec-
    tators surrounded,
  Where, as Zanga, I trod on Alonzo
    o'erthrown;
While, to swell my young pride, such ap-
    plauses resounded,
  I fancied Mossop himself was out-
    shone: 20

Or, as Lear, I pour'd forth the deep impre-
    cation,
  By my daughters of kingdom and
    reason deprived;
Till, fired by loud plaudits and self-adula-
    tion,
  I regarded myself as a Garrick revived.

Ye dreams of my boyhood, how much I
    regret you!   25
  Unfaded your memory dwells in my
    breast;
Though sad and deserted, I ne'er can
    forget you:
  Your pleasures may still be in fancy
    possest.

To Ida full oft may remembrance restore
    me,
  While fate shall the shades of the future
    unroll!   30
Since darkness o'ershadows the prospect
    before me,
  More dear is the beam of the past to my
    soul!

But if, through the course of the years
    which await me,
  Some new scene of pleasure should
    open to view,
I will say, while with rapture the thought
    shall elate me,   35
  'Oh! such were the days which my
    infancy knew.'

                    1806.

TO M—

Oh! did those eyes, instead of fire,
  With bright but mild affection shine,
Though they might kindle less desire,
  Love, more than mortal, would be thine.

For thou art form'd so heavenly fair,   5
  Howe'er those orbs may wildly beam,
We must admire, but still despair;
  That fatal glance forbids esteem.

When Nature stamp'd thy beauteous birth,
  So much perfection in thee shone,   10
She fear'd that, too divine for earth,
  The skies might claim thee for their own:

Therefore, to guard her dearest work,
  Lest angels might dispute the prize,
She bade a secret lightning lurk   15
  Within those once celestial eyes.

These might the boldest sylph appal,
  When gleaming with meridian blaze;
Thy beauty must enrapture all;
  But who can dare thine ardent gaze?   20

'Tis said that Berenice's hair
  In stars adorns the vault of heaven;
But they would ne'er permit thee there,
  Thou wouldst so far outshine the seven.

For did those eyes as planets roll,   25
  Thy sister-lights would scarce appear:
E'en suns, which systems now control,
  Would twinkle dimly through their
    sphere.

                    1806.

TO WOMAN

Woman! experience might have told me
That all must love thee who behold thee:
Surely experience might have taught
Thy firmest promises are nought;
But, placed in all thy charms before me,
All I forget, but to adore thee.   6
Oh memory! thou choicest blessing
When join'd with hope, when still possess-
    ing;
But how much cursed by every lover
When hope is fled and passion's over.   10
Woman, that fair and fond deceiver,
How prompt are striplings to believe her!
How throbs the pulse when first we view
The eye that rolls in glossy blue,
Or sparkles black, or mildly throws   15
A beam from under hazel brows!
How quick we credit every oath,
And hear her plight the willing troth!
Fondly we hope 'twill last for aye,
When, lo! she changes in a day.   20
This record will for ever stand,
'Woman, thy vows are traced in sand.'

TO M. S. G.

When I dream that you love me, you'll
    surely forgive;
  Extend not your anger to sleep;
For in visions alone your affection can
    live,—
  I rise, and it leaves me to weep.

Then, Morpheus! envelope my faculties
    fast,   5
  Shed o'er me your languor benign;
Should the dream of to-night but re-
    semble the last,
  What rapture celestial is mine!

They tell us that slumber, the sister of
    death,
Mortality's emblem is given;   10
To fate how I long to resign my frail breath
    If this be a foretaste of heaven!

Ah! frown not, sweet lady, unbend your
    soft brow,
    Nor deem me too happy in this;   14
If I sin in my dream, I atone for it now,
    Thus doom'd but to gaze upon bliss.

Though in visions, sweet lady, perhaps
    you may smile,
    Oh! think not my penance deficient!
When dreams of your presence my
    slumbers beguile,
    To awake will be torture sufficient.   20

TO MARY

ON RECEIVING HER PICTURE

THIS faint resemblance of thy charms,
    Though strong as mortal art could give,
My constant heart of fear disarms,
    Revives my hopes, and bids me live.

Here I can trace the locks of gold   5
    Which round thy snowy forehead wave,
The cheeks which sprung from beauty's
    mould,
    The lips which made me beauty's slave.

Here I can trace—ah, no! that eye,
    Whose azure floats in liquid fire,   10
Must all the painter's art defy,
    And bid him from the task retire.

Here I behold its beauteous hue;
    But where's the beam so sweetly stray-
    ing,
Which gave a lustre to its blue,   15
    Like Luna o'er the ocean playing?

Sweet copy! far more dear to me,
    Lifeless, unfeeling as thou art,
Than all the living forms could be,
    Save her who placed thee next my heart.

She placed it, sad, with needless fear,   21
    Lest time might shake my wavering
    soul,
Unconscious that her image there
    Held every sense in fast control.

Through hours, through years, through
    time, 'twill cheer;   25
    My hope, in gloomy moments, raise;
In life's last conflict 'twill appear,
    And meet my fond expiring gaze.

TO LESBIA

LESBIA! since far from you I've ranged,
    Our souls with fond affection glow not;
You say 'tis I, not you, have changed.
    I'd tell you why,—but yet I know not.

Your polish'd brow no cares have crost;
    And, Lesbia! we are not much older
Since, trembling, first my heart I lost,
    Or told my love, with hope grown
    bolder.

Sixteen was then our utmost age,
    Two years have lingering pass'd away,
    love!   10
And now new thoughts our minds engage,
    At least I feel disposed to stray, love!

'Tis I that am alone to blame,
    I, that am guilty of love's treason;
Since your sweet breast is still the same,   15
    Caprice must be my only reason.

I do not, love! suspect your truth,
    With jealous doubt my bosom heaves
    not;
Warm was the passion of my youth,
    One trace of dark deceit it leaves not.

No, no, my flame was not pretended;   21
    For, oh! I loved you most sincerely;
And—though our dream at last is
    ended—
    My bosom still esteems you dearly.

No more we meet in yonder bowers;   25
    Absence has made me prone to roving;
But older, firmer hearts than ours,
    Have found monotony in loving.

Your cheek's soft bloom is unimpair'd,
    New beauties still are daily bright'ning,
Your eye for conquest beams prepared,
    The forge of love's resistless lightning.

Arm'd thus, to make their bosoms bleed,
    Many will throng to sigh like me, love!
More constant they may prove, indeed;
    Fonder, alas! they ne'er can be, love!

LINES ADDRESSED TO A
YOUNG LADY

[As the author was discharging his pistols in
a garden, two ladies passing near the spot were
alarmed by the sound of a bullet hissing near
them; to one of whom the following stanzas were
addressed the next morning.]

DOUBTLESS, sweet girl! the hissing lead,
    Wafting destruction o'er thy charms,
And hurtling o'er thy lovely head,
    Has fill'd that breast with fond alarms.

Surely some envious demon's force,   5
    Vex'd to behold such beauty here,
Impell'd the bullet's viewless course,
    Diverted from its first career.

Yes! in that nearly fatal hour   9
    The ball obey'd some hell-born guide;
But Heaven, with interposing power,
    In pity turn'd the death aside.

Yet, as perchance one trembling tear
  Upon that thrilling bosom fell;
Which I, th' unconscious cause of fear, 15
  Extracted from its glistening cell:

Say, what dire penance can atone
  For such an outrage done to thee?
Arraign'd before thy beauty's throne,
  What punishment wilt thou decree?

Might I perform the judge's part, 21
  The sentence I should scarce deplore;
It only would restore a heart
  Which but belong'd to thee before.

The least atonement I can make 25
  Is to become no longer free;
Henceforth I breathe but for thy sake,
  Thou shalt be all in all to me.

But thou, perhaps, may'st now reject
  Such expiation of my guilt; 30
Come then, some other mode elect;
  Let it be death, or what thou wilt.

Choose then, relentless! and I swear
  Nought shall thy dread decree prevent;
Yet hold—one little word forbear! 35
  Let it be aught but banishment.

LOVE'S LAST ADIEU

'Αεὶ δ' ἀεί με φεύγει.—ANACREON.

THE roses of love glad the garden of life,
  Though nurtured 'mid weeds dropping
    pestilent dew,
Till time crops the leaves with unmerciful knife,
  Or prunes them for ever, in love's last
    adieu!

In vain with endearments we soothe the
    sad heart, 5
  In vain do we vow for an age to be true;
The chance of an hour may command us
    to part,
  Or death disunite us in love's last adieu!

Still Hope, breathing peace through the
    grief-swollen breast,
  Will whisper, 'Our meeting we yet may
    renew:' 10
With this dream of deceit half our
    sorrow's represt,
  Nor taste we the poison of love's last adieu!

Oh! mark you yon pair: in the sunshine
    of youth
  Love twined round their childhood his
    flowers as they grew; 14
They flourish awhile in the season of truth,
  Till chill'd by the winter of love's last
    adieu!

Sweet lady! why thus doth a tear steal its
    way
  Down a cheek which outrivals thy
    bosom in hue?
Yet why do I ask?—to distraction a prey,
  Thy reason has perish'd with love's last
    adieu! 20

Oh! who is yon misanthrope, shunning
    mankind?
  From cities to caves of the forest he flew:
There, raving, he howls his complaint to
    the wind;
  The mountains reverberate love's last
    adieu!

Now hate rules a heart which in love's
    easy chains 25
  Once passion's tumultuous blandishments knew;
Despair now inflames the dark tide of his
    veins;
  He ponders in frenzy on love's last
    adieu!

How he envies the wretch with a soul
    wrapt in steel!
  His pleasures are scarce, yet his
    troubles are few, 30
Who laughs at the pang that he never can
    feel,
  And dreads not the anguish of love's
    last adieu!

Youth flies, life decays, even hope is
    o'ercast;
  No more with love's former devotion
    we sue:
He spreads his young wing, he retires
    with the blast; 35
  The shroud of affection is love's last
    adieu!

In this life of probation for rapture divine,
  Astrea declares that some penance is
    due;
From him who has worshipp'd at love's
    gentle shrine,
  The atonement is ample in love's last
    adieu! 40

Who kneels to the god, on his altar of
    light
  Must myrtle and cypress alternately
    strew:
His myrtle, an emblem of purest delight;
  His cypress, the garland of love's last
    adieu!

DAMÆTAS

IN law an infant, and in years a boy,
In mind a slave to every vicious joy;
From every sense of shame and virtue
    wean'd;
In lies an adept, in deceit a fiend;

Versed in hypocrisy, while yet a child; 5
Fickle as wind, of inclinations wild;
Woman his dupe, his heedless friend a
    tool;
Old in the world, though scarcely broke
    from school;
Damætas ran through all the maze of sin,
And found the goal when others just
    begin: 10
Even still conflicting passions shake his
    soul,
And bid him drain the dregs of pleasure's
    bowl;
But, pall'd with vice, he breaks his former
    chain,
And what was once his bliss appears his
    bane.

And, lest my precepts be displeasing 41
To those who think remonstrance teasing:
At once I'll tell thee our opinion
Concerning woman's soft dominion:
Howe'er we gaze with admiration 45
On eyes of blue or lips carnation,
Howe'er the flowing locks attract us,
Howe'er those beauties may distract us,
Still fickle, we are prone to rove,
These cannot fix our souls to love; 50
It is not too severe a stricture
To say they form a pretty picture;
But wouldst thou see the secret chain
Which binds us in your humble train,
To hail you queens of all creation, 55
Know, in a word, 'tis ANIMATION.

TO MARION

MARION! why that pensive brow?
What disgust to life hast thou?
Change that discontented air;
Frowns become not one so fair.
'Tis not love disturbs thy rest, 5
Love's a stranger to thy breast;
He in dimpling smiles appears,
Or mourns in sweetly timid tears,
Or bends the languid eyelid down,
But shuns the cold forbidding frown. 10
Then resume thy former fire,
Some will love, and all admire;
While that icy aspect chills us,
Nought but cool indifference thrills us.
Wouldst thou wandering hearts beguile, 16
Smile at least, or seem to smile.
Eyes like thine were never meant
To hide their orbs in dark restraint.
Spite of all thou fain wouldst say,
Still in truant beams they play. 20
Thy lips—but here my modest Muse
Her impulse chaste must needs refuse:
She blushes, curt'sies, frowns,—in short
    she
Dreads lest the subject should transport
    me;
And flying off in search of reason, 25
Brings prudence back in proper season.
All I shall therefore say (whate'er
I think, is neither here nor there)
Is, that such lips, of looks endearing,
Were form'd for better things than sneer-
    ing: 30
Of soothing compliments divested,
Advice at least's disinterested;
Such is my artless song to thee,
From all the flow of flattery free;
Counsel like mine is as a brother's, 35
My heart is given to some others;
That is to say, unskill'd to cozen,
It shares itself among a dozen.

Marion, adieu! oh, pr'ythee slight not
This warning, though it may delight not;

TO A LADY

WHO PRESENTED TO THE AUTHOR A LOCK
OF HAIR BRAIDED WITH HIS OWN, AND
APPOINTED A NIGHT IN DECEMBER TO
MEET HIM IN THE GARDEN

THESE locks, which fondly thus entwine,
In firmer chains our hearts confine,
Than all th' unmeaning protestations,
Which swell with nonsense love orations.
Our love is fix'd, I think we've proved it;
Nor time, nor place, nor art have moved it;
Then wherefore should we sigh and whine,
With groundless jealousy repine,
With silly whims and fancies frantic,
Merely to make our love romantic? 10
Why should you weep like Lydia Lan-
    guish,
And fret with self-created anguish?
Or doom the lover you have chosen,
On winter nights to sigh half frozen;
In leafless shades to sue for pardon, 15
Only because the scene's a garden?
For gardens seem, by one consent,
Since Shakspeare set the precedent,
Since Juliet first declared her passion,
To form the place of assignation. 20
Oh! would some modern muse inspire,
And seat her by a sea-coal fire;
Or had the bard at Christmas written,
And laid the scene of love in Britain,
He surely, in commiseration, 25
Had changed the place of declaration.
In Italy I've no objection;
Warm nights are proper for reflection;
But here our climate is so rigid,
That love itself is rather frigid: 30
Think on our chilly situation,
And curb this rage for imitation;
Then let us meet, as oft we've done,
Beneath the influence of the sun;
Or, if at midnight I must meet you, 35
Within your mansion let me greet you:
There we can love for hours together,
Much better, in such snowy weather,
Than placed in all th' Arcadian groves
That ever witness'd rural loves; 40

Then, if my passion fail to please,
Next night I'll be content to freeze;
No more I'll give a loose to laughter
But curse my fate for ever after.

OSCAR OF ALVA

A TALE

How sweetly shines through azure skies,
  The lamp of heaven on Lora's shore;
Where Alva's hoary turrets rise,
  And hear the din of arms no more!

But often has yon rolling moon   5
  On Alva's casques of silver play'd;
And view'd, at midnight's silent noon,
  Her chiefs in gleaming mail array'd:

And on the crimson'd rocks beneath,
  Which scowl o'er ocean's sullen flow,
Pale in the scatter'd ranks of death, 11
  She saw the gasping warrior low;

While many an eye which ne'er again
  Could mark the rising orb of day,
Turn'd feebly from the gory plain, 15
  Beheld in death her fading ray.

Once to those eyes the lamp of Love,
  They blest her dear propitious light;
But now she glimmer'd from above,
  A sad, funereal torch of night. 20

Faded is Alva's noble race,
  And gray her towers are seen afar;
No more her heroes urge the chase,
  Or roll the crimson tide of war.

But who was last of Alva's clan? 25
  Why grows the moss on Alva's stone?
Her towers resound no steps of man,
  They echo to the gale alone.

And when that gale is fierce and high,
  A sound is heard in yonder hall; 30
It rises hoarsely through the sky,
  And vibrates o'er the mould'ring wall.

Yes, when the eddying tempest sighs,
  It shakes the shield of Oscar brave;
But there no more his banners rise, 35
  No more his plumes of sable wave.

Fair shone the sun on Oscar's birth,
  When Angus hail'd his eldest born;
The vassals round their chieftain's hearth
  Crowd to applaud the happy morn. 40

They feast upon the mountain deer,
  The pibroch raised its piercing note;
To gladden more their highland cheer,
  The strains in martial numbers float:

And they who heard the war-notes wild
  Hoped that one day the pibroch's strain
Should play before the hero's child
  While he should lead the tartan train.

Another year is quickly past,
  And Angus hails another son; 50
His natal day is like the last,
  Nor soon the jocund feast was done.

Taught by their sire to bend the bow,
  On Alva's dusky hills of wind, 54
The boys in childhood chased the roe,
  And left their hounds in speed behind.

But ere their years of youth are o'er,
  They mingle in the ranks of war;
They lightly wheel the bright claymore,
  And send the whistling arrow far. 60

Dark was the flow of Oscar's hair,
  Wildly it stream'd along the gale;
But Allan's locks were bright and fair,
  And pensive seem'd his cheek, and pale.

But Oscar own'd a hero's soul, 65
  His dark eye shone through beams of truth;
Allan had early learn'd control,
  And smooth his words had been from youth.

Both, both were brave; the Saxon spear
  Was shiver'd oft beneath their steel; 70
And Oscar's bosom scorn'd to fear,
  But Oscar's bosom knew to feel;

While Allan's soul belied his form,
  Unworthy with such charms to dwell:
Keen as the lightning of the storm, 75
  On foes his deadly vengeance fell.

From high Southannon's distant tower
  Arrived a young and noble dame;
With Kenneth's lands to form her dower,
  Glenalvon's blue-eyed daughter came;

And Oscar claim'd the beauteous bride,
  And Angus on his Oscar smiled: 82
It soothed the father's feudal pride
  Thus to obtain Glenalvon's child.

Hark to the pibroch's pleasing note! 85
  Hark to the swelling nuptial song!
In joyous strains the voices float,
  And still the choral peal prolong.

See how the heroes' blood-red plumes
  Assembled wave in Alva's hall; 90
Each youth his varied plaid assumes,
  Attending on their chieftain's call.

It is not war their aid demands,
  The pibroch plays the song of peace;
To Oscar's nuptials throng the bands, 95
  Nor yet the sounds of pleasure cease.

But where is Oscar? sure 'tis late:
  Is this a bridegroom's ardent flame?
While thronging guests and ladies wait,
  Nor Oscar nor his brother came. 100

At length young Allan join'd the bride;
  'Why comes not Oscar?' Angus said:
'Is he not here?' the youth replied;
  'With me he roved not o'er the glade:

'Perchance, forgetful of the day,   105
  'Tis his to chase the bounding roe;
Or ocean's waves prolong his stay;
  Yet Oscar's bark is seldom slow.'

'Oh, no!' the anguish'd sire rejoin'd,
  'Nor chase, nor wave, my boy delay;
Would he to Mora seem unkind?   111
  Would aught to her impede his way?

'Oh, search, ye chiefs! oh, search around!
  Allan, with these through Alva fly;
Till Oscar, till my son is found,   115
  Haste, haste, nor dare attempt reply.'

All is confusion—through the vale
  The name of Oscar hoarsely rings,
It rises on the murmuring gale,
  Till night expands her dusky wings;

It breaks the stillness of the night,   121
  But echoes through her shades in vain;
It sounds through morning's misty light,
  But Oscar comes not o'er the plain.

Three days, three sleepless nights, the
    Chief   125
  For Oscar search'd each mountain cave:
Then hope is lost; in boundless grief,
  His locks in gray-torn ringlets wave.

'Oscar! my son!—thou God of heaven,
  Restore the prop of sinking age!   130
Or if that hope no more is given,
  Yield his assassin to my rage.

'Yes, on some desert rocky shore
  My Oscar's whiten'd bones must lie;
Then grant, thou God! I ask no more,
  With him his frantic sire may die!   136

'Yet he may live,—away, despair!
  Be calm, my soul! he yet may live;
T' arraign my fate, my voice forbear!
  O God! my impious prayer forgive.

'What, if he live for me no more,   141
  I sink forgotten in the dust,
The hope of Alva's age is o'er:
  Alas! can pangs like these be just?'

Thus did the hapless parent mourn,   145
  Till Time, which soothes severest woe,
Had bade serenity return
  And made the tear-drop cease to flow.

For still some latent hope survived   149
  That Oscar might once more appear;
His hope now droop'd and now revived,
  Till Time had told a tedious year.

Days roll'd along, the orb of light
  Again had run his destined race;
No Oscar bless'd his father's sight,   155
  And sorrow left a fainter trace.

For youthful Allan still remain'd,
  And now his father's only joy:
And Mora's heart was quickly gain'd,
  For beauty crown'd the fair-hair'd boy.

She thought that Oscar low was laid,
  And Allan's face was wondrous fair;
If Oscar lived, some other maid
  Had claim'd his faithless bosom's care.

And Angus said, if one year more   165
  In fruitless hope was pass'd away,
His fondest scruples should be o'er,
  And he would name their nuptial day.

Slow roll'd the moons, but blest at last
  Arrived the dearly destined morn: 170
The year of anxious trembling past,
  What smiles the lovers' cheeks adorn!

Hark to the pibroch's pleasing note!
  Hark to the swelling nuptial song!
In joyous strains the voices float,   175
  And still the choral peal prolong.

Again the clan, in festive crowd,
  Throng through the gate of Alva's hall;
The sounds of mirth re-echo loud,
  And all their former joy recall.   180

But who is he, whose darken'd brow
  Glooms in the midst of general mirth?
Before his eyes' far fiercer glow
  The blue flames curdle o'er the hearth.

Dark is the robe which wraps his form,
  And tall his plume of gory red;   186
His voice is like the rising storm,
  But light and trackless is his tread.

'Tis noon of night, the pledge goes round,
  The bridegroom's health is deeply
    quaff'd;   190
With shouts the vaulted roofs resound,
  And all combine to hail the draught.

Sudden the stranger-chief arose,
  And all the clamorous crowd are
    hush'd;   194
And Angus' cheek with wonder glows,
  And Mora's tender bosom blush'd.

'Old man!' he cried, 'this pledge is done;
  Thou saw'st 'twas duly drank by me;
It hail'd the nuptials of thy son:
  Now will I claim a pledge from thee.

'While all around is mirth and joy,   201
  To bless thy Allan's happy lot,
Say, hadst thou ne'er another boy?
  Say, why should Oscar be forgot?'

17

'Alas!' the hapless sire replied, 205
  The big tear starting as he spoke,
'When Oscar left my hall, or died,
  This aged heart was almost broke.

'Thrice has the earth revolved her course
  Since Oscar's form has bless'd my
    sight; 210
And Allan is my last resource,
  Since martial Oscar's death or flight.'

''Tis well,' replied the stranger stern,
  And fiercely flash'd his rolling eye;
'Thy Oscar's fate I fain would learn; 215
  Perhaps the hero did not die.

'Perchance, if those whom most he
    loved
  Would call, thy Oscar might return;
Perchance the chief has only roved;
  For him thy beltane yet may burn. 220

'Fill high the bowl the table round,
  We will not claim the pledge by stealth;
With wine let every cup be crown'd;
  Pledge me departed Oscar's health.'

'With all my soul,' old Angus said, 225
  And fill'd his goblet to the brim:
'Here's to my boy! alive or dead,
  I ne'er shall find a son like him.'

'Bravely, old man, this health has sped;
  But why does Allan trembling stand?
Come, drink remembrance of the dead,
  And raise thy cup with firmer hand.'

The crimson glow of Allan's face
  Was turn'd at once to ghastly hue;
The drops of death each other chase 235
  Adown in agonizing dew.

Thrice did he raise the goblet high,
  And thrice his lips refused to taste;
For thrice he caught the stranger's eye
  On his with deadly fury placed. 240

'And is it thus a brother hails
  A brother's fond remembrance here?
If thus affection's strength prevails,
  What might we not expect from fear?'

Roused by the sneer, he raised the bowl,
  'Would Oscar now could share our
    mirth!' 246
Internal fear appall'd his soul;
  He said, and dash'd the cup to earth.

''Tis he! I hear my murderer's voice!'
  Loud shrieks a darkly gleaming form.
'A murderer's voice!' the roof replies,
  And deeply swells the bursting storm.

The tapers wink, the chieftains shrink,
  The stranger's gone,—amidst the crew,
A form was seen in tartan green, 255
  And tall the shade terrific grew.

His waist was bound with a broad belt
    round,
  His plume of sable stream'd on high;
But his breast was bare, with the red
    wounds there, 259
  And fix'd was the glare of his glassy eye.

And thrice he smiled, with his eye so wild,
  On Angus bending low the knee;
And thrice he frown'd on a chief on the
    ground, 263
  Whom shivering crowds with horror see.

The bolts loud roll from pole to pole,
  The thunders through the welkin ring,
And the gleaming form, through the mist
    of the storm,
  Was borne on high by the whirlwind's
    wing.

Cold was the feast, the revel ceased.
  Who lies upon the stony floor? 270
Oblivion press'd old Angus' breast,
  At length his life-pulse throbs once
    more.

'Away, away! let the leech essay
  To pour the light on Allan's eyes:'
His sand is done,—his race is run,— 275
  Oh! never more shall Allan rise!

But Oscar's breast is cold as clay,
  His locks are lifted by the gale;
And Allan's barbed arrow lay 279
  With him in dark Glentanar's vale.

And whence the dreadful stranger came,
  Or who, no mortal wight can tell; 282
But no one doubts the form of flame,
  For Alva's sons knew Oscar well.

Ambition nerved young Allan's hand,
  Exulting demons wing'd his dart;
While Envy waved her burning brand,
  And pour'd her venom round his heart.

Swift is the shaft from Allan's bow;
  Whose streaming life-blood stains his
    side? 290
Dark Oscar's sable crest is low,
  The dart has drunk his vital tide.

And Mora's eye could Allan move,
  She bade his wounded pride rebel:
Alas! that eyes which beam'd with love
  Should urge the soul to deeds of hell.

Lo! seest thou not a lonely tomb 297
  Which rises o'er a warrior dead?
It glimmers through the twilight gloom;
  Oh! that is Allan's nuptial bed. 300

Far, distant far, the noble grave
  Which held his clan's great ashes stood;
And o'er his corse no banners wave,
  For they were stain'd with kindred blood.

What minstrel gray, what hoary bard,
　　Shall Allan's deeds on harp-strings raise?
The song is glory's chief reward,
　　But who can strike a murderer's praise?

Unstrung, untouch'd, the harp must stand,　309
　　No minstrel dare the theme awake;
Guilt would benumb his palsied hand,
　　His harp in shuddering chords would break.

No lyre of fame, no hallow'd verse,
　　Shall sound his glories high in air:
A dying father's bitter curse,　315
　　A brother's death-groan echoes there.

THE EPISODE OF NISUS AND EURYALUS

A PARAPHRASE FROM THE ÆNEID, LIB. IX

Nisus, the guardian of the portal, stood,
Eager to gild his arms with hostile blood;
Well skill'd in fight the quivering lance to wield,
Or pour his arrows through th' embattled field:
From Ida torn, he left his sylvan cave,　5
And sought a foreign home, a distant grave.
To watch the movements of the Daunian host,
With him Euryalus sustains the post;
No lovelier mien adorn'd the ranks of Troy,
And beardless bloom yet graced the gallant boy;　10
Though few the seasons of his youthful life,
As yet a novice in the martial strife,
'Twas his, with beauty, valour's gifts to share—
A soul heroic, as his form was fair;
These burn with one pure flame of generous love;　15
In peace, in war, united still they move;
Friendship and glory form their joint reward;
And now combined they hold their nightly guard.

'What god,' exclaim'd the first, 'instils this fire?
Or, in itself a god, what great desire?　20
My labouring soul, with anxious thought oppress'd,
Abhors this station of inglorious rest;
The love of fame with this can ill accord,
Be 't mine to seek for glory with my sword.
Seest thou yon camp, with torches twinkling dim,　25
Where drunken slumbers wrap each lazy limb?
Where confidence and ease the watch disdain,
And drowsy Silence holds her sable reign?
Then hear my thought:—In deep and sullen grief
Our troops and leaders mourn their absent chief:　30
Now could the gifts and promised prize be thine
(The deed, the danger, and the fame be mine),
Were this decreed, beneath yon rising mound,
Methinks, an easy path perchance were found;
Which past, I speed my way to Pallas' walls,　35
And lead Æneas from Evander's halls.'

With equal ardour fired, and warlike joy,
His glowing friend address'd the Dardan boy:—

'These deeds, my Nisus, shalt thou dare alone?
Must all the fame, the peril, be thine own?　40
Am I by thee despised, and left afar,
As one unfit to share the toils of war?
Not thus his son the great Opheltes taught;
Not thus my sire in Argive combats fought;
Not thus, when Ilion fell by heavenly hate,
I track'd Æneas through the walks of fate:　46
Thou know'st my deeds, my breast devoid of fear,
And hostile life-drops dim my gory spear.
Here is a soul with hope immortal burns,
And life, ignoble life, for *glory* spurns.
Fame, fame is cheaply earn'd by fleeting breath:　51
The price of honour is the sleep of death.'

Then Nisus:—'Calm thy bosom's fond alarms:
Thy heart beats fiercely to the din of arms.
More dear thy worth and valour than my own,　55
I swear by him who fills Olympus' throne!
So may I triumph, as I speak the truth,
And clasp again the comrade of my youth!
But should I fall,—and he who dares advance
Through hostile legions must abide by chance,—　60
If some Rutulian arm, with adverse blow,
Should lay the friend, who ever loved thee, low,
Live thou, such beauties I would fain preserve,
Thy budding years a lengthen'd term deserve.

When humbled in the dust, let some one
be,   65
Whose gentle eyes will shed one tear for
me;
Whose manly arm may snatch me back
by force,
Or wealth redeem from foes my captive corse;
Or, if my destiny these last deny,
If in the spoiler's power my ashes lie, 70
Thy pious care may raise a simple tomb,
To mark thy love, and signalize my doom.
Why should thy doting wretched mother
weep
Her only boy, reclined in endless sleep?
Who, for thy sake, the tempest's fury
dared,   75
Who, for thy sake, war's deadly peril shared;
Who braved what woman never braved
before,
And left her native for the Latian shore.'

'In vain you damp the ardour of my
soul,'
Replied Euryalus; 'it scorns control! 80
Hence, let us haste!'—their brother
guards arose,
Roused by their call, nor court again
repose;
The pair, buoy'd up on Hope's exulting
wing,
Their stations leave, and speed to seek the
king.

Now o'er the earth a solemn stillness ran,
And lull'd alike the cares of brute and
man;   86
Save where the Dardan leaders nightly
hold
Alternate converse, and their plans un-
fold.
On one great point the council are agreed,
An instant message to their prince de-
creed;   90
Each lean'd upon the lance he well could
wield,
And poised with easy arm his ancient
shield;
When Nisus and his friend their leave
request
To offer something to their high behest.
With anxious tremors, yet unawed by
fear,   95
The faithful pair before the throne appear:
Iulus greets them; at his kind command,
The elder first address'd the hoary band.

'With patience' (thus Hyrtacides began)
'Attend, nor judge from youth our humble
plan.   100
Where yonder beacons half expiring beam,
Our slumbering foes of future conquest
dream,
Nor heed that we a secret path have
traced,
Between the ocean and the portal placed.

Beneath the covert of the blackening
smoke,   105
Whose shade securely our design will
cloak!
If you, ye chiefs, and fortune will allow,
We'll bend our course to yonder moun-
tain's brow,
Where Pallas' walls at distance meet the
sight,
Seen o'er the glade, when not obscured by
night: 110
Then shall Æneas in his pride return,
When hostile matrons raise their off-
spring's urn;
And Latian spoils and purpled heaps of
dead
Shall mark the havoc of our hero's tread.
Such is our purpose, not unknown the
way;   115
Where yonder torrent's devious waters
stray,
Oft have we seen, when hunting by the
stream,
The distant spires above the valleys
gleam.'

Mature in years, for sober wisdom
famed,
Moved by the speech, Alethes here ex-
claim'd,—   120
'Ye parent gods! who rule the fate of
Troy,
Still dwells the Dardan spirit in the boy;
When minds like these in striplings thus ye
raise,
Yours is the godlike act, be yours the
praise;
In gallant youth, my fainting hopes
revive,   125
And Ilion's wonted glories still survive.'
Then in his warm embrace the boys he
press'd,
And, quivering, strain'd them to his aged
breast;
With tears the burning cheek of each be-
dew'd,
And, sobbing, thus his first discourse re-
new'd: 130
'What gift, my countrymen, what martial
prize,
Can we bestow, which you may not de-
spise?
Our deities the first best boon have
given—
Internal virtues are the gift of Heaven.
What poor rewards can bless your deeds
on earth,   135
Doubtless await such young, exalted
worth.
Æneas and Ascanius shall combine
To yield applause far, far surpassing mine.'

Iulus then:—'By all the powers above!
By those Penates who my country love!

20

By hoary Vesta's sacred fane, I swear,　141
My hopes are all in you, ye generous pair!
Restore my father to my grateful sight,
And all my sorrows yield to one delight.
Nisus! two silver goblets are thine own,
Saved from Arisba's stately domes o'er-
　thrown!　146
My sire secured them on that fatal day,
Nor left such bowls an Argive robber's
　prey:
Two massy tripods, also, shall be thine;
Two talents polish'd from the glittering
　mine;　150
An ancient cup, which Tyrian Dido gave,
While yet our vessels press'd the Punic
　wave:
But when the hostile chiefs at length bow
　down,
When great Æneas wears Hesperia's
　crown,
The casque, the buckler, and the fiery steed
Which Turnus guides with more than
　mortal speed,　156
Are thine; no envious lot shall then be
　cast,
I pledge my word, irrevocably past:
Nay more, twelve slaves, and twice six
　captive dames,
To soothe thy softer hours with amorous
　flames,　160
And all the realms which now the Latins
　sway,
The labours of to-night shall well repay.
But thou, my generous youth, whose
　tender years
Are near my own, whose worth my heart
　reveres,
Henceforth affection, sweetly thus begun,
Shall join our bosoms and our souls in
　one;　166
Without thy aid, no glory shall be mine;
Without thy dear advice, no great design;
Alike through life esteem'd, thou godlike
　boy,
In war my bulwark, and in peace my joy.'

To him Euryalus:—'No day shall
　shame　171
The rising glories which from this I claim.
Fortune may favour, or the skies may
　frown,
But valour, spite of fate, obtains renown.
Yet, ere from hence our eager steps de-
　part,　175
One boon I beg, the nearest to my heart:
My mother, sprung from Priam's royal
　line,
Like thine ennobled, hardly less divine,
Nor Troy nor king Acestes' realms re-
　strain　179
Her feeble age from dangers of the main:
Alone she came, all selfish fears above,
A bright example of maternal love,
Unknown the secret enterprise I brave,

Lest grief should bend my parent to the
　grave;
From this alone no fond adieus I seek,
No fainting mother's lips have press'd my
　cheek;　186
By gloomy night and thy right hand I vow
Her parting tears would shake my pur-
　pose now:
Do thou, my prince, her failing age sustain,
In thee her much-loved child may live
　again;　190
Her dying hours with pious conduct bless,
Assist her wants, relieve her fond distress:
So dear a hope must all my soul inflame,
To rise in glory, or to fall in fame.'
Struck with a filial care so deeply felt,　195
In tears at once the Trojan warriors melt;
Faster than all, Iulus' eyes o'erflow!
Such love was his, and such had been his
　woe.
'All thou hast ask'd, receive,' the prince
　replied;
'Nor this alone, but many a gift beside,
To cheer thy mother's years shall be my
　aim,　201
Creusa's style but wanting to the dame.
Fortune an adverse wayward course may
　run,
But bless'd thy mother in so dear a son.
Now, by my life!—my sire's most sacred
　oath—　205
To thee I pledge my full, my firmest troth,
All the rewards which once to thee were
　vow'd,
If thou shouldst fall, on her shall be be-
　stow'd.'
Thus spoke the weeping prince, then forth
　to view
A gleaming falchion from the sheath he
　drew;　210
Lycaon's utmost skill had graced the steel,
For friends to envy and for foes to feel:
A tawny hide, the Moorish lion's spoil,
Slain 'midst the forest, in the hunter's toil,
Mnestheus to guard the elder youth be-
　stows,　215
And old Alethes' casque defends his
　brows.
Arm'd, thence they go, while all th' as-
　sembled train,
To aid their cause, implore the gods in vain.
More than a boy, in wisdom and in grace,
Iulus holds amidst the chiefs his place:
His prayer he sends; but what can prayers
　avail,　221
Lost in the murmurs of the sighing gale?

The trench is pass'd, and, favour'd by
　the night,
Through sleeping foes they wheel their
　wary flight.
When shall the sleep of many a foe be o'er?
Alas! some slumber who shall wake no
　more!　226

21

Chariots and bridles, mix'd with arms, are
   seen;
And flowing flasks, and scatter'd troops
   between:
Bacchus and Mars to rule the camp com-
   bine;
A mingled chaos this of war and wine.
'Now,' cries the first, 'for deeds of blood
   prepare,   231
With me the conquest and the labour share:
Here lies our path; lest any hand arise,
Watch thou, while many a dreaming
   chieftain dies:
I'll carve our passage through the heed-
   less foe,   235
And clear thy road with many a deadly
   blow.'
His whispering accents then the youth re-
   press'd,
And pierced proud Rhamnes through his
   panting breast:
Stretch'd at his ease, th' incautious king
   reposed;
Debauch, and not fatigue, his eyes had
   closed: 240
To Turnus dear, a prophet and a prince,
His omens more than augur's skill evince;
But he, who thus foretold the fate of all,
Could not avert his own untimely fall.
Next Remus' armour-bearer, hapless, fell,
And three unhappy slaves the carnage
   swell;   246
The charioteer along his courser's sides
Expires, the steel his sever'd neck divides;
And, last, his lord is number'd with the
   dead:
Bounding convulsive, flies the gasping
   head;   250
From the swoll'n veins the blackening tor-
   rents pour;
Stain'd is the couch and earth with clot-
   ting gore.
Young Lamyrus and Lamus next expire,
And gay Serranus, fill'd with youthful fire;
Half the long night in childish games was
   pass'd;   255
Lull'd by the potent grape, he slept at last:
Ah! happier far had he the morn survey'd,
And till Aurora's dawn his skill display'd.

In slaughter'd folds, the keepers lost in
   sleep,
His hungry fangs a lion thus may steep;
'Mid the sad flock, at dead of night he
   prowls,   261
With murder glutted, and in carnage
   rolls:
Insatiate still, through teeming herds he
   roams,
In seas of gore the lordly tyrant foams.

Nor less the other's deadly vengeance
   came,   265
But falls on feeble crowds without a name;

His wound unconscious Fadus scarce can
   feel,
Yet wakeful Rhæsus sees the threatening
   steel;
His coward breast behind a jar he hides,
And vainly in the weak defence confides;
Full in his heart, the falchion search'd his
   veins,   271
The reeking weapon bears alternate stains;
Through wine and blood, commingling as
   they flow,
One feeble spirit seeks the shades below.
Now where Messapus dwelt they bend
   their way,   275
Whose fires emit a faint and trembling
   ray;
There, unconfined, behold each grazing
   steed,
Unwatch'd, unheeded, on the herbage
   feed:
Brave Nisus here arrests his comrade's
   arm,
Too flush'd with carnage, and with
   conquest warm: 280
'Hence let us haste, the dangerous path
   is pass'd;
Full foes enough to-night have breathed
   their last:
Soon will the day those eastern clouds
   adorn;
Now let us speed, nor tempt the rising
   morn.'

What silver arms, with various art em-
   boss'd,   285
What bowls and mantles in confusion
   toss'd,
They leave regardless! yet one glittering
   prize
Attracts the younger hero's wandering
   eyes;
The gilded harness Rhamnes' coursers
   felt,
The gems which stud the monarch's
   golden belt: 290
This from the pallid corse was quickly
   torn,
Once by a line of former chieftains worn.
Th' exulting boy the studded girdle wears,
Messapus' helm his head in triumph
   bears;
Then from the tents their cautious steps
   they bend,   295
To seek the vale where safer paths extend.

Just at this hour, a band of Latian
   horse
To Turnus' camp pursue their destined
   course:
While the slow foot their tardy march delay,
The knights, impatient, spur along the
   way: 300

Three hundred mail-clad men, by Volscens
led,
To Turnus with their master's promise
sped:
Now they approach the trench, and view
the walls,
When, on the left, a light reflection falls;
The plunder'd helmet, through the
waning night,   305
Sheds forth a silver radiance, glancing
bright.
Volscens with question loud the pair
alarms:—
'Stand, stragglers! stand! why early thus
in arms?
From whence! to whom?'—He meets
with no reply;
Trusting the covert of the night, they fly:
The thicket's depth with hurried pace
they tread,   311
While round the wood the hostile squad-
ron spread.

  With brakes entangled, scarce a path
between,
Dreary and dark appears the sylvan
scene:
Euryalus his heavy spoils impede,   315
The boughs and winding turns his steps
mislead;
But Nisus scours along the forest's maze
To where Latinus' steeds in safety graze,
Then backward o'er the plain his eyes
extend,   319
On every side they seek his absent friend.
'O God! my boy,' he cries, 'of me bereft,
In what impending perils art thou left!'
Listening he runs—above the waving trees,
Tumultuous voices swell the passing
breeze;
The war-cry rises, thundering hoofs
around   325
Wake the dark echoes of the trembling
ground.
Again he turns, of footsteps hears the
noise;
The sound elates, the sight his hope de-
stroys:
The hapless boy a ruffian train surround,
While lengthening shades his weary way
confound;   330
Him with loud shouts the furious knights
pursue,
Struggling in vain, a captive to the crew.
What can his friend 'gainst thronging
numbers dare?
Ah! must he rush his comrade's fate to
share?
What force, what aid, what stratagem
essay,   335
Back to redeem the Latian spoiler's prey?
His life a votive ransom nobly give,
Or die with him for whom he wish'd to
live?

Poising with strength his lifted lance on
high,
On Luna's orb he cast his frenzied eye:—
'Goddess serene, transcending every star!
Queen of the sky, whose beams are seen
afar!   342
By night heaven owns thy sway, by day
the grove,
When, as chaste Dian, here thou deign'st
to rove;
If e'er myself, or sire, have sought to
grace   345
Thine altars with the produce of the chase,
Speed, speed my dart to pierce yon vaunt-
ing crowd,
To free my friend, and scatter far the
proud.'
Thus having said, the hissing dart he
flung;
Through parted shades the hurtling
weapon sung;   350
The thirsty point in Sulmo's entrails lay,
Transfix'd his heart, and stretch'd him on
the clay:
He sobs, he dies,—the troop in wild
amaze,
Unconscious whence the death, with
horror gaze.
While pale they stare, through Tagus'
temples riven,   355
A second shaft with equal force is driven:
Fierce Volscens rolls around his lowering
eyes;
Veil'd by the night, secure the Trojan
lies.
Burning with wrath, he view'd his soldiers
fall.
'Thou youth accurst, thy life shall pay for
all!'   360
Quick from the sheath his flaming glaive
he drew,
And, raging, on the boy defenceless flew.
Nisus no more the blackening shade con-
ceals,
Forth, forth he starts, and all his love
reveals;
Aghast, confused, his fears to madness
rise,   365
And pour these accents, shrieking as he
flies:
'Me, me,—your vengeance hurl on me
alone;
Here sheathe the steel, my blood is all
your own,
Ye starry spheres! thou conscious Heaven!
attest!
He could not—durst not—lo! the guile
confest!   370
All, all was mine,—his early fate suspend;
He only loved too well his hapless friend:
Spare, spare, ye chiefs! from him your
rage remove;
His fault was friendship, all his crime was
love.'

He pray'd in vain; the dark assassin's
   sword   375
Pierced the fair side, the snowy bosom
   gored;
Lowly to earth inclines his plume-clad
   crest,
And sanguine torrents mantle o'er his
   breast:
As some young rose, whose blossom
   scents the air,
Languid in death, expires beneath the
   share;   380
Or crimson poppy, sinking with the shower,
Declining gently, falls a fading flower;
Thus, sweetly drooping, bends his lovely
   head,
And lingering beauty hovers round the
   dead.

But fiery Nisus stems the battle's tide,
Revenge his leader, and despair his guide;
Volscens he seeks amidst the gathering
   host,   387
Volscens must soon appease his comrade's
   ghost;
Steel, flashing, pours on steel, foe crowds
   on foe;
Rage nerves his arm, fate gleams in every
   blow;   390
In vain beneath unnumber'd wounds he
   bleeds,
Nor wounds, nor death, distracted Nisus
   heeds;
In viewless circles wheel'd, his falchion flies,
Nor quits the hero's grasp till Volscens
   dies:
Deep in his throat its end the weapon found,
The tyrant's soul fled groaning through
   the wound.   396
Thus Nisus all his fond affection proved—
Dying, revenged the fate of him he loved;
Then on his bosom sought his wonted
   place,
And death was heavenly in his friend's
   embrace!   400

Celestial pair! if aught my verse can
   claim,
Wafted on Time's broad pinion, yours is
   fame!
Ages on ages shall your fate admire,
No future day shall see your names
   expire,
While stands the Capitol, immortal dome!
And vanquish'd millions hail their em-
   press, Rome!   406

TRANSLATION FROM THE
MEDEA OF EURIPIDES

['Ἔρωτες ὑπὲρ μὲν ἄγαν, κ. τ. λ.]

WHEN fierce conflicting passions urge
   The breast where love is wont to glow,
What mind can stem the stormy surge
   Which rolls the tide of human woe?

The hope of praise, the dread of shame,
   Can rouse the tortured breast no more;
The wild desire, the guilty flame,
   Absorbs each wish it felt before.

But if affection gently thrills
   The soul by purer dreams possest,   10
The pleasing balm of mortal ills
   In love can soothe the aching breast:
If thus thou comest in disguise,
   Fair Venus! from thy native heaven,
What heart unfeeling would despise   15
   The sweetest boon the gods have given?

But never from thy golden bow
   May I beneath the shaft expire!
Whose creeping venom, sure and slow,
   Awakes an all-consuming fire: 20
Ye racking doubts! ye jealous fears!
   With others wage internal war;
Repentance, source of future tears,
   From me be ever distant far!

May no distracting thoughts destroy   25
   The holy calm of sacred love!
May all the hours be wing'd with joy,
   Which hover faithful hearts above!
Fair Venus! on thy myrtle shrine
   May I with some fond lover sigh,   30
Whose heart may mingle pure with mine—
   With me to live, with me to die!

My native soil! beloved before,
   Now dearer as my peaceful home,
Ne'er may I quit thy rocky shore,   35
   A hapless banish'd wretch to roam!
This very day, this very hour,
   May I resign this fleeting breath!
Nor quit my silent humble bower;   39
   A doom to me far worse than death.

Have I not heard the exile's sigh,
   And seen the exile's silent tear,
Through distant climes condemn'd to fly,
   A pensive weary wanderer here?
Ah! hapless dame! no sire bewails,   45
   No friend thy wretched fate deplores,
No kindred voice with rapture hails
   Thy steps within a stranger's doors.

Perish the fiend whose iron heart,
   To fair affection's truth unknown,   50
Bids her he fondly loved depart,
   Unpitied, helpless, and alone!
Who ne'er unlocks with silver key
   The milder treasures of his soul,—
May such a friend be far from me,   55
   And ocean's storms between us roll!

THOUGHTS SUGGESTED BY
A COLLEGE EXAMINATION

HIGH in the midst, surrounded by his
   peers,
MAGNUS his ample front sublime uprears:

24

Placed on his chair of state, he seems a god,
While Sophs and Freshmen tremble at
   his nod.
As all around sit wrapt in speechless gloom,
His voice in thunder shakes the sounding
   dome;   6
Denouncing dire reproach to luckless
   fools,
Unskill'd to plod in mathematic rules.

Happy the youth in Euclid's axioms
   tried,
Though little versed in any art beside; 10
Who, scarcely skill'd an English line to
   pen,
Scans Attic metres with a critic's ken.
What, though he knows not how his
   fathers bled,
When civil discord piled the fields with
   dead,
When Edward bade his conquering bands
   advance,   15
Or Henry trampled on the crest of France,
Though marvelling at the name of
   Magna Charta,
Yet well he recollects the laws of Sparta;
Can tell what edicts sage Lycurgus made,
While Blackstone's on the shelf neglected
   laid;   20
Of Grecian dramas vaunts the deathless
   fame,
Of Avon's bard remembering scarce the
   name.

Such is the youth whose scientific pate
Class-honours, medals, fellowships, await;
Or even, perhaps, the declamation prize,
If to such glorious height he lifts his
   eyes.   26
But lo! no common orator can hope
The envied silver cup within his scope.
Not that our heads much eloquence
   require,
Th' ATHENIAN'S glowing style, or Tully's
   fire.   30
A manner clear or warm is useless, since
We do not try by speaking to convince.
Be other orators of pleasing proud,—
We speak to please ourselves, not move
   the crowd:
Our gravity prefers the muttering tone,
A proper mixture of the squeak and
   groan: 36
No borrow'd grace of action must be seen;
The slightest motion would displease the
   Dean;
Whilst every staring graduate would
   prate
Against what he could never imitate.   40

The man who hopes t' obtain the promised cup
Must in one posture stand, and ne'er look
   up;

Nor stop, but rattle over every word—
No matter what, so it can *not* be heard.
Thus let him hurry on, nor think to rest:
Who speaks the fastest's sure to speak the
   best;   46
Who utters most within the shortest space
May safely hope to win the wordy race.

The sons of science these, who, thus
   repaid,
Linger in ease in Granta's sluggish shade;
Where on Cam's sedgy banks supine they
   lie,   51
Unknown, unhonour'd live, unwept-for
   die:
Dull as the pictures which adorn their
   halls,
They think all learning fix'd within their
   walls:
In manners rude, in foolish forms pre-
   cise,   55
All modern arts affecting to despise;
Yet prizing Bentley's, Brunck's, or Por-
   son's note,
More than the verse on which the critic
   wrote:
Vain as their honours, heavy as their
   ale,
Sad as their wit, and tedious as their
   tale;   60
To friendship dead, though not untaught
   to feel
When Self and Church demand a bigot
   zeal.
With eager haste they court the lord of
   power,
Whether 'tis Pitt or Petty rules the hour;
To him, with suppliant smiles, they bend
   the head,   65
While distant mitres to their eyes are
   spread.
But should a storm o'erwhelm him with
   disgrace,
They'd fly to seek the next who fill'd his
   place.
Such are the men who learning's treasures
   guard!
Such is their practice, such is their reward!
This much, at least, we may presume to
   say—   71
The premium can't exceed the price they
   pay.

                            1806.

TO A BEAUTIFUL QUAKER

SWEET girl! though only once we met,
That meeting I shall ne'er forget;
And though we ne'er may meet again,
Remembrance will thy form retain.
I would not say, 'I love,' but still   5
My senses struggle with my will:
In vain, to drive thee from my breast,
My thoughts are more and more represt;

In vain I check the rising sighs,
Another to the last replies: 10
Perhaps this is not love, but yet
Our meeting I can ne'er forget.

What though we never silence broke,
Our eyes a sweeter language spoke;
The tongue in flattering falsehood deals,
And tells a tale it never feels: 16
Deceit the guilty lips impart,
And hush the mandates of the heart;
But soul's interpreters, the eyes,
Spurn such restraint, and scorn disguise.
As thus our glances oft conversed,   21
And all our bosoms felt rehearsed,
No spirit, from within, reproved us,
Say rather, ''twas the spirit moved us.'
Though what they utter'd I repress,   25
Yet I conceive thou'lt partly guess;
For as on thee my memory ponders,
Perchance to me thine also wanders.
This for myself, at least, I'll say,
Thy form appears through night, through
    day;   30
Awake, with it my fancy teems;
In sleep, it smiles in fleeting dreams;
The vision charms the hours away,
And bids me curse Aurora's ray
For breaking slumbers of delight   35
Which make me wish for endless night.
Since, oh! whate'er my future fate,
Shall joy or woe my steps await,
Tempted by love, by storms beset,
Thine image I can ne'er forget.   40

Alas! again no more we meet,
No more our former looks repeat;
Then let me breathe this parting prayer,
The dictate of my bosom's care:
'May Heaven so guard my lovely quaker,
That anguish never can o'ertake her;   46
That peace and virtue ne'er forsake her,
But bliss be aye her heart's partaker!
Oh! may the happy mortal, fated
To be, by dearest ties, related,   50
For her each hour new joys discover,
And lose the husband in the lover!
May that fair bosom never know
What 'tis to feel the restless woe
Which stings the soul, with vain regret,   55
Of him who never can forget!'

THE CORNELIAN

No specious splendour of this stone
   Endears it to my memory ever;
With lustre only once it shone,
   And blushes modest as the giver.   4

Some, who can sneer at friendship's ties,
   Have, for my weakness, oft reproved
   me;
Yet still the simple gift I prize,
   For I am sure the giver loved me.

He offer'd it with downcast look,
   As fearful that I might refuse it;   10
I told him, when the gift I took,
   My only fear should be to lose it.

This pledge attentively I view'd,
   And sparkling as I held it near,
Methought one drop the stone bedew'd,
   And ever since I've loved a tear.   16

Still, to adorn his humble youth,
   Nor wealth nor birth their treasures
    yield;
But he who seeks the flowers of truth
   Must quit the garden for the field.   20

'Tis not the plant uprear'd in sloth,
   Which beauty shows, and sheds per-
    fume;
The flowers which yield the most of both
   In Nature's wild luxuriance bloom.

Had Fortune aided Nature's care,   25
   For once forgetting to be blind,
His would have been an ample share,
   If well proportion'd to his mind.

But had the goddess clearly seen,   29
   His form had fix'd her fickle breast;
Her countless hoards would his have been,
   And none remain'd to give the rest.

AN OCCASIONAL PROLOGUE

DELIVERED PREVIOUS TO THE PERFOR-
MANCE OF 'THE WHEEL OF FORTUNE' AT
A PRIVATE THEATRE

SINCE the refinement of this polish'd age
Has swept immoral raillery from the stage;
Since taste has now expunged licentious
   wit,
Which stamp'd disgrace on all an author
   writ;
Since now to please with purer scenes we
   seek,   5
Nor dare to call the blush from Beauty's
   cheek;
Oh! let the modest Muse some pity claim,
And meet indulgence, though she find not
   fame.
Still, not for her alone we wish respect,
Others appear more conscious of defect;
To-night no veteran Roscii you behold,
In all the arts of scenic action old;   12
No Cooke, no Kemble, can salute here,
No Siddons draw the sympathetic tear;
To-night you throng to witness the *début*
Of embryo actors, to the Drama new:
Here, then, our almost unfledged wings we
   try;   17
Clip not our pinions ere the birds can fly:
Failing in this our first attempt to soar,
Drooping, alas! we fall to rise no more.

Not one poor trembler only fear betrays
Who hopes, yet almost dreads, to meet
   your praise,
But all our dramatis personæ wait
In fond suspense this crisis of their fate.
No venal views our progress can retard, 25
Your generous plaudits are our sole re-
   ward.
For these, each Hero all his power displays,
Each timid Heroine shrinks before your
   gaze.
Surely the last will some protection find;
None to the softer sex can prove unkind:
While Youth and Beauty form the female
   shield, 31
The sternest censor to the fair must yield.
Yet, should our feeble efforts nought avail,
Should, after all, our best endeavours fail,
Still let some mercy in your bosoms live,
And, if you can't applaud, at least forgive.

ON THE DEATH OF MR. FOX

THE FOLLOWING ILLIBERAL IMPROMPTU APPEARED IN A MORNING PAPER

'OUR nation's foes lament on Fox's death,
But bless the hour when PITT resign'd his
   breath:
These feelings wide, let sense and truth
   unclue,
We give the palm where Justice points its
   due.'

TO WHICH THE AUTHOR OF THESE PIECES SENT THE FOLLOWING REPLY

OH factious viper! whose envenom'd
   tooth
Would mangle still the dead, perverting
   truth;
What though our 'nation's foes' lament
   the fate,
With generous feeling, of the good and great,
Shall dastard tongues essay to blast the
   name 5
Of him whose meed exists in endless fame?
When PITT expired in plenitude of power,
Though ill success obscured his dying hour,
Pity her dewy wings before him spread,
For noble spirits 'war not with the dead:'
His friends, in tears, a last sad requiem
   gave, 11
As all his errors slumber'd in the grave;
He sunk, an Atlas bending 'neath the
   weight
Of cares o'erwhelming our conflicting
   state:
When, lo! a Hercules in Fox appear'd, 15
Who for a time the ruin'd fabric rear'd:
He, too, is fall'n, who Britain's loss
   supplied,
With him our fast reviving hopes have
   died;
Not one great people only raise his urn,
All Europe's far-extended regions mourn.

'These feelings wide, let sense and truth
   unclue, 21
To give the palm where Justice points its
   due;'
Yet let not canker'd Calumny assail,
Or round our statesman wind her gloomy
   veil.
Fox! o'er whose corse a mourning world
   must weep, 25
Whose dear remains in honour'd marble
   sleep;
For whom, at last, e'en hostile nations
   groan,
While friends and foes alike his talents own;
Fox shall in Britain's future annals shine,
Nor e'en to PITT the patriot's palm resign;
Which Envy, wearing Candour's sacred
   mask, 31
For PITT, and PITT alone, has dared to
   ask.

THE TEAR

'O lachrymarum fons, tenero sacros
  Ducentium ortus ex animo; quater
    Felix! in imo qui scatentem
      Pectore te, pia Nympha, sensit.'—GRAY.

WHEN Friendship or Love our sympathies
   move,
When Truth in a glance should appear,
The lips may beguile with a dimple or
   smile,
But the test of affection 's a Tear.

Too oft is a smile but the hypocrite's wile,
To mask detestation or fear; 6
Give me the soft sigh, whilst the soul-
   telling eye
Is dimm'd for a time with a Tear.

Mild Charity's glow, to us mortals below,
Shows the soul from barbarity clear; 10
Compassion will melt where this virtue is
   felt,
And its dew is diffused in a Tear.

The man doom'd to sail with the blast of
   the gale,
Through billows Atlantic to steer,
As he bends o'er the wave which may
   soon be his grave, 15
The green sparkles bright with a Tear.

The soldier braves death for a fanciful
   wreath
In Glory's romantic career;
But he raises the foe when in battle laid
   low,
And bathes every wound with a Tear.

If with high-bounding pride he return to
   his bride, 21
Renouncing the gore-crimson'd spear,
All his toils are repaid when, embracing
   the maid,
From her eyelid he kisses the Tear.

Sweet scene of my youth! seat of Friend-
   ship and Truth, 25
  Where love chased each fast-fleeting
   year,
Loth to leave thee, I mourn'd, for a last
   look I turn'd,
  But thy spire was scarce seen through a
   Tear.

Though my vows I can pour to my Mary
   no more,
  My Mary to Love once so dear, 30
In the shade of her bower I remember the
   hour
  She rewarded those vows with a Tear.

By another possest, may she live ever blest!
  Her name still my heart must revere:
With a sigh I resign what I once thought
   was mine, 35
  And forgive her deceit with a Tear.

Ye friends of my heart, ere from you I de-
   part,
  This hope to my breast is most near:
If again we shall meet in this rural retreat,
  May we meet, as we part, with a Tear.

When my soul wings her flight to the
   regions of night, 41
  And my corse shall recline on its bier,
As ye pass by the tomb where my ashes
   consume,
  Oh! moisten their dust with a Tear.

May no marble bestow the splendour of
   woe 45
  Which the children of vanity rear;
No fiction of fame shall blazon my name.
  All I ask—all I wish—is a Tear.
             October 26, 1806.

REPLY TO SOME VERSES OF J. M. B. PIGOT, ESQ., ON THE CRUELTY OF HIS MISTRESS

WHY, Pigot, complain of this damsel's dis-
   dain,
  Why thus in despair do you fret?
For months you may try, yet, believe me,
   a sigh
  Will never obtain a coquette.

Would you teach her to love? for a time
   seem to rove; 5
  At first she may frown in a pet;
But leave her awhile, she shortly will
   smile,
  And then you may kiss your coquette.

For such are the airs of these fanciful
   fairs,
  They think all our homage a debt: 10
Yet a partial neglect soon takes an effect,
  And humbles the proudest coquette.

Dissemble your pain, and lengthen your
   chain,
  And seem her hauteur to regret;
If again you shall sigh, she no more will
   deny, 15
  That yours is the rosy coquette.

If still, from false pride, your pangs she
   deride,
  This whimsical virgin forget;
Some other admire, who will melt with
   your fire,
  And laugh at the little coquette. 20

For me, I adore some twenty or more,
  And love them most dearly; but yet,
Though my heart they enthral, I'd aban-
   don them all,
  Did they act like your blooming
   coquette.

No longer repine, adopt this design, 25
  And break through her slight-woven
   net;
Away with despair, no longer forbear
  To fly from the captious coquette.

Then quit her, my friend! your bosom defend,
  Ere quite with her snares you're beset;
Lest your deep-wounded heart, when in-
   censed by the smart, 31
  Should lead you to curse the coquette.
             October 27, 1806.

TO THE SIGHING STREPHON

YOUR pardon, my friend, if my rhymes
   did offend;
  Your pardon, a thousand times o'er:
From friendship I strove your pangs to
   remove,
  But, I swear, I will do so no more.

Since your beautiful maid your flame has
   repaid, 5
  No more I your folly regret;
She's now most divine, and I bow at the
   shrine
  Of this quickly reformed coquette.

Yet still, I must own, I should never have
   known
  From your verses what else she deserved; 10
Your pain seem'd so great, I pitied your
   fate,
  As your fair was so devilish reserved.

Since the balm-breathing kiss of this
   magical miss
  Can such wonderful transports produce;
Since the 'world you forget, when your
   lips once have met,' 15
  My counsel will get but abuse.

You say, 'When I rove, I know nothing
    of love;'
'Tis true, I am given to range;
If I rightly remember, I've loved a good
    number,
    Yet there's pleasure, at least, in a change.

I will not advance, by the rules of ro-
    mance,   21
    To humour a whimsical fair;
Though a smile may delight, yet a frown
    won't affright,
    Or drive me to dreadful despair.

While my blood is thus warm I ne'er shall
    reform,   25
    To mix in the Platonists' school;
Of this I am sure, was my passion so pure,
    Thy mistress would think me a fool.

And if I should shun every woman for one,
    Whose image must fill my whole
    breast—   30
Whom I must prefer, and sigh but for
    her—
    What an insult 'twould be to the rest!

Now, Strephon, good bye, I cannot deny
    Your passion appears most absurd;
Such love as you plead is pure love in-
    deed,   35
    For it only consists in the word.

TO ELIZA

ELIZA, what fools are the Mussulman sect,
    Who to woman deny the soul's future
    existence!
Could they see thee, Eliza, they'd own
    their defect,
    And this doctrine would meet with a
    general resistance.

Had their prophet possess'd half an atom
    of sense,   5
    He ne'er would have woman from para-
    dise driven;
Instead of his houris, a flimsy pretence,
    With woman alone he had peopled his
    heaven.

Yet still, to increase your calamities more,
    Not content with depriving your bodies
    of spirit,   10
He allots one poor husband to share
    amongst four!—
    With souls you'd dispense; but this
    last, who could bear it?

His religion to please neither party is
    made;
    On husbands 'tis hard, to the wives
    most uncivil;
Still I can't contradict, what so oft has
    been said,   15
    'Though women are angels, yet wed-
    lock's the devil.'

LACHIN Y GAIR

AWAY, ye gay landscapes, ye gardens of
    roses!
    In you let the minions of luxury rove;
Restore me the rocks, where the snow-
    flake reposes,
    Though still they are sacred to freedom
    and love:
Yet, Caledonia, beloved are thy moun-
    tains,   5
    Round their white summits though
    elements war;
Though cataracts foam 'stead of smooth-
    flowing fountains,
    I sigh for the valley of dark Loch na Garr.

Ah! there my young footsteps in infancy
    wander'd;
    My cap was the bonnet, my cloak was
    the plaid;   10
On chieftains long perish'd my memory
    ponder'd,
    As daily I strode through the pine-
    cover'd glade;
I sought not my home till the day's dying
    glory
    Gave place to the rays of the bright
    polar star;
For fancy was cheer'd by traditional
    story,   15
    Disclosed by the natives of dark Loch
    na Garr.

'Shades of the dead! have I not heard
    your voices
    Rise on the night-rolling breath of the
    gale?'
Surely the soul of the hero rejoices,
    And rides on the wind, o'er his own
    Highland vale.   20
Round Loch na Garr while the stormy
    mist gathers,
    Winter presides in his cold icy car:
Clouds there encircle the forms of my
    fathers;
    They dwell in the tempests of dark
    Loch na Garr.

'Ill-starr'd, though brave, did no visions
    foreboding   25
    Tell you that fate had forsaken your
    cause?'
Ah! were you destined to die at Cullo-
    den,
    Victory crown'd not your fall with ap-
    plause:
Still were you happy in death's earthy
    slumber,
    You rest with your clan in the caves of
    Braemar;   30
The pibroch resounds, to the piper's loud
    number,
    Your deeds on the echoes of dark Loch
    na Garr.

Years have roll'd on, Loch na Garr,
  since I left you,
Years must elapse ere I tread you again:
Nature of verdure and flow'rs has bereft
  you,   35
  Yet still are you dearer than Albion's
    plain.
England! thy beauties are tame and
  domestic
  To one who has roved o'er the mountains
    afar:
Oh for the crags that are wild and
  majestic!
  The steep frowning glories of dark
    Loch na Garr.   40

TO ROMANCE

PARENT of golden dreams, Romance!
  Auspicious queen of childish joys,
Who lead'st along, in airy dance,
  Thy votive train of girls and boys;
At length, in spells no longer bound,   5
  I break the fetters of my youth;
No more I tread thy mystic round,
  But leave thy realms for those of Truth.

And yet 'tis hard to quit the dreams
  Which haunt the unsuspicious soul, 10
Where every nymph a goddess seems,
  Whose eyes through rays immortal roll;
While Fancy holds her boundless reign,
  And all assume a varied hue;
When virgins seem no longer vain, 15
  And even woman's smiles are true.

And must we own thee but a name,
  And from thy hall of clouds descend?
Nor find a sylph in every dame,
  A Pylades in every friend? 20
But leave at once thy realms of air
  To mingling bands of fairy elves;
Confess that woman's false as fair,
  And friends have feeling for—them-
    selves!

With shame I own I've felt thy sway; 25
  Repentant, now thy reign is o'er,
No more thy precepts I obey,
  No more on fancied pinions soar.
Fond fool! to love a sparkling eye,
  And think that eye to truth was dear;
To trust a passing wanton's sigh, 31
  And melt beneath a wanton's tear!

Romance! disgusted with deceit,
  Far from thy motley court I fly,
Where Affectation holds her seat, 35
  And sickly Sensibility;
Whose silly tears can never flow
  For any pangs excepting thine;
Who turns aside from real woe,
  To steep in dew thy gaudy shrine. 40

Now join with sable Sympathy,
  With cypress crown'd, array'd in weeds,
Who heaves with thee her simple sigh,
  Whose breast for every bosom bleeds;
And call thy sylvan female choir, 45
  To mourn a swain for ever gone,
Who once could glow with equal fire,
  But bends not now before thy throne.

Ye genial nymphs, whose ready tears
  On all occasions swiftly flow; 50
Whose bosoms heave with fancied fears,
  With fancied flames and phrensy glow;
Say, will you mourn my absent name,
  Apostate from your gentle train?
An infant bard at least may claim 55
  From you a sympathetic strain.

Adieu, fond race! a long adieu!
  The hour of fate is hovering nigh,
E'en now the gulf appears in view,
  Where unlamented you must lie: 60
Oblivion's blackening lake is seen,
  Convulsed by gales you cannot weather;
Where you, and eke your gentle queen,
  Alas! must perish altogether.

ANSWER TO SOME ELEGANT VERSES SENT BY A FRIEND TO THE AUTHOR, COMPLAINING THAT ONE OF HIS DESCRIPTIONS WAS RATHER TOO WARMLY DRAWN

'But if any old lady, knight, priest, or physician,
  Should condemn me for printing a second edi-
  tion;
If good Madam Squintum my work should abuse,
  May I venture to give her a smack of my muse?'
                  New Bath Guide.

CANDOUR compels me, BECHER! to com-
  mend
The verse which blends the censor with
  the friend.
Your strong yet just reproof extorts ap-
  plause
From me, the heedless and imprudent
  cause.
For this wild error which pervades my
  strain,   5
I sue for pardon,—must I sue in vain?
The wise sometimes from Wisdom's ways
  depart:
Can youth then hush the dictates of the
  heart?
Precepts of prudence curb, but can't
  control,
The fierce emotions of the flowing soul. 10
When Love's delirium haunts the glowing
  mind,
Limping Decorum lingers far behind:
Vainly the dotard mends her prudish pace,
Outstrip and vanquish'd in the mental
  chase.

The young, the old, have worn the chains
of love;   15
Let those they ne'er confined my lay re-
prove:
Let those whose souls contemn the pleas-
ing power
Their censures on the hapless victim
shower.
Oh! how I hate the nerveless, frigid song,
The ceaseless echo of the rhyming throng,
Whose labour'd lines in chilling numbers
flow,   21
To paint a pang the author ne'er can
know!
The artless Helicon I boast is youth;—
My lyre, the heart; my muse, the simple
truth.
Far be 't from me the 'virgin's mind' to
'taint':   25
Seduction's dread is here no slight re-
straint.
The maid whose virgin breast is void of
guile,
Whose wishes dimple in a modest smile,
Whose downcast eye disdains the wanton
leer,
Firm in her virtue's strength, yet not
severe—   30
She whom a conscious grace shall thus
refine
Will ne'er be 'tainted' by a strain of
mine.
But for the nymph whose premature
desires
Torment her bosom with unholy fires,
No net to snare her willing heart is
spread;   35
She would have fallen, though she ne'er
had read.
For me, I fain would please the chosen
few,
Whose souls, to feeling and to nature true,
Will spare the childish verse, and not de-
stroy
The light effusions of a heedless boy.   40
I seek not glory from the senseless crowd;
Of fancied laurels I shall ne'er be proud;
Their warmest plaudits I would scarcely
prize,
Their sneers or censures I alike despise.
     November 26, 1806.

ELEGY ON NEWSTEAD ABBEY

'It is the voice of years that are gone! they roll
before me with all their deeds.'—OSSIAN.

NEWSTEAD! fast-falling, once-resplendent
dome!
  Religion's shrine! repentant HENRY's
pride!
Of warriors, monks, and dames the cloister'd tomb,
  Whose pensive shades around thy
ruins glide,

Hail to thy pile! more honour'd in thy
fall   5
  Than modern mansions in their pillar'd
state;
Proudly majestic frowns thy vaulted hall,
  Scowling defiance on the blasts of fate.

No mail-clad serfs, obedient to their lord,
  In grim array the crimson cross de-
mand;   10
Or gay assemble round the festive board
  Their chief's retainers, an immortal
band:

Else might inspiring Fancy's magic eye
  Retrace their progress through the
lapse of time,
Marking each ardent youth, ordain'd to
die,   15
  A votive pilgrim in Judea's clime.

But not from thee, dark pile! departs the
chief;
  His feudal realm in other regions lay:
In thee the wounded conscience courts
relief,
  Retiring from the garish blaze of day.

Yes! in thy gloomy cells and shades profound   21
  The monk abjured a world he ne'er
could view;
Or blood-stain'd guilt repenting solace
found,
  Or innocence from stern oppression flew.

A monarch bade thee from that wild
arise,   25
  Where Sherwood's outlaws once were
wont to prowl;
And Superstition's crimes, of various
dyes,
  Sought shelter in the priest's protecting
cowl.

Where now the grass exhales a murky
dew,
  The humid pall of life-extinguish'd
clay,   30
In sainted fame the sacred fathers grew,
  Nor raised their pious voices but to pray.

Where now the bats their wavering wings
extend
  Soon as the gloaming spreads her
waning shade,
The choir did oft their mingling vespers
blend,   35
  Or matin orisons to Mary paid.

Years roll on years; to ages, ages yield;
  Abbots to abbots, in a line, succeed;
Religion's charter their protecting shield,
  Till royal sacrilege their doom decreed.

One holy HENRY rear'd the Gothic walls,
  And bade the pious inmates rest in
    peace;   42
Another HENRY the kind gift recalls,
  And bids devotion's hallow'd echoes
    cease.

Vain is each threat or supplicating prayer;
  He drives them exiles from their blest
    abode,   46
To roam a dreary world in deep despair—
  No friend, no home, no refuge, but
    their God.

Hark how the hall, resounding to the
    strain,
  Shakes with the martial music's novel
    din!   50
The heralds of a warrior's haughty reign,
  High crested banners wave thy walls
    within.

Of changing sentinels the distant hum,
  The mirth of feasts, the clang of
    burnish'd arms,
The braying trumpet and the hoarser
    drum,   55
  Unite in concert with increased alarms.

An abbey once, a regal fortress now,
  Encircled by insulting rebel powers,
War's dread machines o'erhang thy
    threat'ning brow,
  And dart destruction in sulphureous
    showers.   60

Ah vain defence! the hostile traitor's siege,
  Though oft repulsed, by guile o'er-
    comes the brave;
His thronging foes oppress the faithful
    liege,
  Rebellion's reeking standards o'er him
    wave.   64

Not unavenged the raging baron yields;
  The blood of traitors smears the purple
    plain;
Unconquer'd still, his falchion there he
    wields,
  And days of glory yet for him remain.

Still in that hour the warrior wish'd to
    strew
  Self-gather'd laurels on a self-sought
    grave;   70
But Charles' protecting genius hither flew,
  The monarch's friend, the monarch's
    hope, to save.

Trembling, she snatch'd him from th'
    unequal strife,
  In other fields the torrent to repel;
For nobler combats, here, reserved his life,
  To lead the band where godlike FALK-
    LAND fell.   76

From thee, poor pile! to lawless plunder
    given,
  While dying groans their painful re-
    quiem sound,
Far different incense now ascends to
    heaven,
  Such victims wallow on the gory
    ground.   80

There many a pale and ruthless robber's
    corse,
  Noisome and ghast, defiles thy sacred
    sod;
O'er mingling man, and horse commix'd
    with horse,
  Corruption's heap, the savage spoilers
    trod.

Graves, long with rank and sighing weeds
    o'erspread,   85
  Ransack'd, resign perforce their mortal
    mould:
From ruffian fangs escape not e'en the
    dead,
  Raked from repose in search of buried
    gold.

Hush'd is the harp, unstrung the warlike
    lyre,
  The minstrel's palsied hand reclines in
    death;   90
No more he strikes the quivering chords
    with fire,
  Or sings the glories of the martial
    wreath.

At length the sated murderers, gorged
    with prey,
  Retire: the clamour of the fight is o'er;
Silence again resumes her awful sway, 95
  And sable Horror guards the massy
    door.

Here Desolation holds her dreary court:
  What satellites declare her dismal reign!
Shrieking their dirge, ill-omen'd birds
    resort,   99
  To flit their vigils in the hoary fane.

Soon a new morn's restoring beams dispel
  The clouds of anarchy from Britain's
    skies;
The fierce usurper seeks his native hell,
  And Nature triumphs as the tyrant dies.

With storms she welcomes his expiring
    groans;   105
  Whirlwinds, responsive, greet his
    labouring breath;
Earth shudders as her caves receive his
    bones,
  Loathing the offering of so dark a
    death.

The legal ruler now resumes the helm,
  He guides through gentle seas the prow
    of state; 110
Hope cheers, with wonted smiles, the
    peaceful realm,
  And heals the bleeding wounds of
    wearied hate.

The gloomy tenants, Newstead! of thy
    cells,
  Howling, resign their violated nest;
Again the master on his tenure dwells,
  Enjoy'd, from absence, with enraptured
    zest. 116

Vassals, within thy hospitable pale,
  Loudly carousing, bless their lord's
    return;
Culture again adorns the gladdening vale,
  And matrons, once lamenting, cease to
    mourn. 120

A thousand songs on tuneful echo float,
  Unwonted foliage mantles o'er the
    trees;
And hark! the horns proclaim a mellow
    note,
  The hunters' cry hangs lengthening on
    the breeze.

Beneath their coursers' hoofs the valleys
    shake: 125
  What fears, what anxious hopes, attend
    the chase!
The dying stag seeks refuge in the lake;
  Exulting shouts announce the finish'd
    race.

Ah happy days! too happy to endure!
  Such simple sports our plain forefathers
    knew: 130
No splendid vices glitter'd to allure;
  Their joys were many, as their cares
    were few.

From these descending, sons to sires
    succeed;
  Time steals along, and Death uprears
    his dart;
Another chief impels the foaming steed,
  Another crowd pursue the panting
    hart. 136

Newstead! what saddening change of
    scene is thine!
  Thy yawning arch betokens slow decay;
The last and youngest of a noble line
  Now holds thy mouldering turrets in
    his sway. 140

Deserted now, he scans thy gray worn
    towers;
  Thy vaults, where dead of feudal ages
    sleep;

Thy cloisters, pervious to the wintry
    showers;
  These, these he views, and views them
    but to weep.

Yet are his tears no emblem of regret:
  Cherish'd affection only bids them
    flow. 146
Pride, hope, and love forbid him to forget,
  But warm his bosom with impassion'd
    glow.

Yet he prefers thee to the gilded domes
  Or gewgaw grottos of the vainly great,
Yet lingers 'mid thy damp and mossy
    tombs, 151
  Nor breathes a murmur 'gainst the will
    of fate.

Haply thy sun, emerging, yet may shine,
  Thee to irradiate with meridian ray;
Hours splendid as the past may still be
    thine, 155
  And bless thy future as thy former day.

CHILDISH RECOLLECTIONS

'I cannot but remember such things were,
And were most dear to me.'

When slow Disease, with all her host of
    pains,
Chills the warm tide which flows along
    the veins;
When Health, affrighted, spreads her rosy
    wing,
And flies with every changing gale of
    spring; 4
Not to the aching frame alone confined,
Unyielding pangs assail the drooping
    mind:
What grisly forms, the spectre-train of woe,
Bid shuddering Nature shrink beneath
    the blow,
With Resignation wage relentless strife,
While Hope retires appall'd, and clings to
    life! 10
Yet less the pang when, through the
    tedious hour,
Remembrance sheds around her genial
    power,
Calls back the vanish'd days to rapture
    given,
When love was bliss, and Beauty form'd
    our heaven;
Or, dear to youth, portrays each childish
    scene, 15
Those fairy bowers, where all in turn have
    been.
As when through clouds that pour the
    summer storm
The orb of day unveils his distant form,
Gilds with faint beams the crystal dews of
    rain,
And dimly twinkles o'er the watery plain;

Thus, while the future dark and cheerless
   gleams,   21
The sun of memory, glowing through my
   dreams,
Though sunk the radiance of his former
   blaze,
To scenes far distant points his paler rays;
Still rules my senses with unbounded sway,
The past confounding with the present day.

Oft does my heart indulge the rising
   thought,   27
Which still recurs, unlook'd for and un-
   sought;
My soul to Fancy's fond suggestion yields,
And roams romantic o'er her airy fields.
Scenes of my youth, developed, crowd to
   view,   31
To which I long have bade a last adieu!
Seats of delight, inspiring youthful themes;
Friends lost to me for aye, except in
   dreams;   34
Some who in marble prematurely sleep,
Whose forms I now remember but to weep;
Some who yet urge the same scholastic
   course
Of early science, future fame the source;
Who, still contending in the studious race,
In quick rotation fill the senior place. 40
These with a thousand visions now unite,
To dazzle, though they please, my aching
   sight.

IDA! blest spot, where Science holds her
   reign,
How joyous once I join'd thy youthful
   train!
Bright in idea gleams thy lofty spire, 45
Again I mingle with thy playful quire;
Our tricks of mischief, every childish game,
Unchanged by time or distance, seem the
   same;
Through winding paths along the glade, I
   trace
The social smile of every welcome face; 50
My wonted haunts, my scenes of joy or
   woe,
Each early boyish friend, or youthful foe,
Our feuds dissolved, but not my friendship
   past,—
I bless the former, and forgive the last.
Hours of my youth! when, nurtured in my
   breast,   55
To love a stranger, friendship made me
   blest,—
Friendship, the dear peculiar bond of
   youth,
When every artless bosom throbs with
   truth,
Untaught by worldly wisdom how to feign,
And check each impulse with prudential
   rein;   60
When all we feel, our honest souls dis-
   close—
In love to friends, in open hate to foes;

No varnish'd tales the lips of youth repeat,
No dear-bought knowledge purchased by
   deceit,
Hypocrisy, the gift of lengthen'd years, 65
Matured by age, the garb of prudence
   wears.
When now the boy is ripen'd into man,
His careful sire chalks forth some wary
   plan;
Instructs his son from candour's path to
   shrink,
Smoothly to speak, and cautiously to think;
Still to assent, and never to deny— 71
A patron's praise can well reward the lie:
And who, when Fortune's warning voice is
   heard,
Would lose his opening prospects for a word,
Although against that word his heart rebel,
And truth indignant all his bosom swell.

Away with themes like this! not mine
   the task   77
From flattering friends to tear the hateful
   mask;
Let keener bards delight in satire's sting;
My fancy soars not on Detraction's wing:
Once, and but once, she aim'd a deadly
   blow,   81
To hurl defiance on a secret foe;
But when that foe, from feeling or from
   shame,
The cause unknown, yet still to me the
   same,
Warn'd by some friendly hint, perchance,
   retired,   85
With this submission all her rage expired.
From dreaded pangs that feeble foe to save,
She hush'd her young resentment, and for-
   gave;
Or, if my muse a pedant's portrait drew,
POMPOSUS' virtues are but known to few:
I never fear'd the young usurper's nod,
And he who wields must sometimes feel the
   rod.   92
If since on Granta's failings, known to all
Who share the converse of a college hall,
She sometimes trifled in a lighter strain,
'Tis past, and thus she will not sin again;
Soon must her early song for ever cease,
And all may rail when I shall rest in peace.

Here first remember'd be the joyous
   band,
Who hail'd me chief, obedient to com-
   mand;   100
Who join'd with me in every boyish
   sport—
Their first adviser, and their last resort;
Nor shrunk beneath the upstart pedant's
   frown,
Or all the sable glories of his gown;
Who, thus transplanted from his father's
   school—   105
Unfit to govern, ignorant of rule—

Succeeded him, whom all unite to praise,
The dear preceptor of my early days!
PROBUS, the pride of science, and the boast,
To IDA now, alas! for ever lost,   110
With him, for years, we search'd the classic
        page,
And fear'd the master, though we loved
        the sage:
Retired at last, his small yet peaceful seat
From learning's labour is the blest retreat.
POMPOSUS fills his magisterial chair;   115
POMPOSUS governs,—but, my muse, for-
        bear:
Contempt, in silence, be the pedant's lot;
His name and precepts be alike forgot;
No more his mention shall my verse de-
        grade,—
To him my tribute is already paid.   120

High through those elms, with hoary
        branches crown'd,
Fair IDA'S bower adorns the landscape
        round;
There Science, from her favour'd seat,
        surveys
The vale where rural Nature claims her
        praise;
To her awhile resigns her youthful train,
Who move in joy, and dance along the
        plain;   126
In scatter'd groups each favour'd haunt
        pursue,
Repeat old pastimes, and discover new;
Flush'd with his rays, beneath the noon-
        tide sun,
In rival bands, between the wickets run,
Drive o'er the sward the ball with active
        force,   131
Or chase with nimble feet its rapid course.
But these with slower steps direct their way,
Where Brent's cool waves in limpid cur-
        rents stray;
While yonder few search out some green
        retreat   135
And arbours shade them from the summer
        heat:
Others, again, a pert and lively crew,
Some rough and thoughtless stranger
        placed in view,
With frolic quaint their antic jests expose,
And tease the grumbling rustic as he goes;
Nor rest with this, but many a passing fray
Tradition treasures for a future day: 142
"Twas here the gather'd swains for
        vengeance fought,
And here we earn'd the conquest dearly
        bought;
Here have we fled before superior might,
And here renew'd the wild tumultuous
        fight.'   146
While thus our souls with early passions
        swell,
In lingering tones resounds the distant
        bell,

Th' allotted hour of daily sport is o'er,
And Learning beckons from her temple's
        door.   150
No splendid tablets grace her simple hall,
But ruder records fill the dusky wall;
There, deeply carved, behold! each tyro's
        name
Secures its owner's academic fame;
Here mingling view the names of sire and
        son—   155
The one long graved, the other just begun:
These shall survive alike when son and sire
Beneath one common stroke of fate expire;
Perhaps their last memorial these alone,
Denied in death a monumental stone,   160
Whilst to the gale in mournful cadence
        wave
The sighing weeds that hide their nameless
        grave.
And here my name, and many an early
        friend's,
Along the wall in lengthen'd line extends.
Though still our deeds amuse the youthful
        race,   165
Who tread our steps, and fill our former
        place,
Who young obey'd their lords in silent
        awe,
Whose nod commanded, and whose voice
        was law;
And now, in turn, possess the reins of
        power,
To rule, the little tyrants of an hour; 170
Though sometimes, with the tales of
        ancient day,
They pass the dreary winter's eve away—
'And thus our former rulers stemm'd the
        tide,
And thus they dealt the combat side by
        side;
Just in this place the mouldering walls
        they scaled,   175
Nor bolts nor bars against their strength
        avail'd;
Here PROBUS came, the rising fray to
        quell,
And here he falter'd forth his last fare-
        well;
And here one night abroad they dared to
        roam,
While bold POMPOSUS bravely stay'd at
        home;'   180
While thus they speak, the hour must soon
        arrive,
When names of these, like ours, alone
        survive:
Yet a few years, one general wreck will
        whelm
The faint remembrance of our fairy realm.

Dear honest race! though now we meet
        no more,   185
One last long look on what we were
        before—

Our first kind greetings, and our last
   adieu—
Drew tears from eyes unused to weep with
   you.
Through splendid circles, fashion's gaudy
   world,
Where folly's glaring standard waves un-
   furl'd,   190
I plunged to drown in noise my fond regret,
And all I sought or hoped was to forget.
Vain wish! if chance some well-remember'd
   face,
Some old companion of my early race,
Advanced to claim his friend with honest
   joy,   195
My eyes, my heart, proclaim'd me still a
   boy;
The glittering scene, the fluttering groups
   around,
Were quite forgotten when my friend was
   found;
The smiles of beauty—(for, alas! I've
   known
What 'tis to bend before Love's mighty
   throne)—   200
The smiles of beauty, though those smiles
   were dear,
Could hardly charm me, when that friend
   was near;
My thoughts bewilder'd in the fond sur-
   prise,
The woods of IDA danced before my eyes;
I saw the sprightly wand'rers pour along,
I saw and join'd again the joyous throng;
Panting, again I traced her lofty grove,
And friendship's feelings triumph'd over
   love.   208

   Yet why should I alone with such de-
      light
Retrace the circuit of my former flight?
Is there no cause beyond the common claim
Endear'd to all in childhood's very name?
Ah! sure some stronger impulse vibrates
   here,
Which whispers friendship will be doubly
   dear
To one who thus for kindred hearts must
   roam,   215
And seek abroad the love denied at home.
Those hearts, dear IDA, have I found in
   thee—
A home, a world, a paradise to me.
Stern Death forbade my orphan youth to
   share   219
The tender guidance of a father's care.
Can rank, or e'en a guardian's name supply
The love which glistens in a father's eye?
For this can wealth or title's sound atone,
Made, by a parent's early loss, my own?
What brother springs a brother's love to
   seek?   225
What sister's gentle kiss has prest my
   cheek?

For me how dull the vacant moments rise,
To no fond bosom link'd by kindred ties!
Oft in the progress of some fleeting dream
Fraternal smiles collected round me seem;
While still the visions to my heart are
   prest,   231
The voice of love will murmur in my rest:
I hear—I wake—and in the sound rejoice;
I hear again,—but, ah! no brother's voice.
A hermit, 'midst of crowds, I fain must
   stray   235
Alone, though thousand pilgrims fill the
   way;
While these a thousand kindred wreaths
   entwine,
I cannot call one single blossom mine:
What then remains? in solitude to groan,
To mix in friendship, or to sigh alone.
Thus must I cling to some endearing hand,
And none more dear than IDA's social
   band.

   Alonzo! best and dearest of my friends,
Thy name ennobles him who thus com-
   mends;
From this fond tribute thou canst gain no
   praise;   245
The praise is his who now that tribute pays.
Oh! in the promise of thy early youth,
If hope anticipate the words of truth,
Some loftier bard shall sing thy glorious
   name,   249
To build his own upon thy deathless fame.
Friend of my heart, and foremost of the list
Of those with whom I lived supremely
   blest,
Oft have we drain'd the font of ancient
   lore;
Though drinking deeply, thirsting still the
   more.
Yet, when confinement's lingering hour
   was done,   255
Our sports, our studies, and our souls were
   one:
Together we impell'd the flying ball;
Together waited in our tutor's hall;
Together join'd in cricket's manly toil,
Or shared the produce of the river's spoil;
Or, plunging from the green declining
   shore,   261
Our pliant limbs the buoyant billows bore;
In every element, unchanged, the same,
All, all that brothers should be, but the
   name.

   Nor yet are you forgot, my jocund boy!
DAVUS, the harbinger of childish joy;
For ever foremost in the ranks of fun,
The laughing herald of the harmless pun;
Yet with a breast of such materials made—
Anxious to please, of pleasing half afraid—
Candid and liberal, with a heart of steel
In danger's path, though not untaught to
   feel.

Still I remember, in the factious strife,
The rustic's musket aim'd against my life:
High pois'd in air the massy weapon
hung, 275
A cry of horror burst from every tongue;
Whilst I, in combat with another foe,
Fought on, unconscious of th' impending
blow;
Your arm, brave boy, arrested his career—
Forward you sprung, insensible to fear;
Disarm'd and baffled by your conquering
hand, 281
The grovelling savage roll'd upon the sand:
An act like this, can simple thanks repay?
Or all the labours of a grateful lay? 284
Oh no! whene'er my breast forgets the deed,
That instant, Davus, it deserves to bleed.

Lycus! on me thy claims are justly great:
Thy milder virtues could my muse relate,
To thee alone, unrivall'd, would belong
The feeble efforts of my lengthen'd song.
Well canst thou boast, to lead in senates
fit, 291
A Spartan firmness with Athenian wit:
Though yet in embryo these perfections
shine,
Lycus! thy father's fame will soon be
thine.
Where learning nurtures the superior
mind, 295
What may we hope from genius thus re-
fined!
When time at length matures thy growing
years,
How wilt thou tower above thy fellow
peers!
Prudence and sense, a spirit bold and free,
With honour's soul, united beam in thee.

Shall fair Euryalus pass by unsung?
From ancient lineage, not unworthy
sprung:
What though one sad dissension bade us
part?
That name is yet embalm'd within my heart;
Yet at the mention does that heart re-
bound, 305
And palpitate, responsive to the sound.
Envy dissolved our ties, and not our will:
We once were friends,—I'll think we are
so still.
A form unmatch'd in nature's partial
mould,
A heart untainted, we in thee behold:
Yet not the senate's thunder thou shalt
wield, 311
Nor seek for glory in the tented field;
To minds of ruder texture these be given—
Thy soul shall nearer soar its native
heaven.
Haply, in polish'd courts might be thy seat,
But that thy tongue could never forge
deceit: 316

The courtier's supple bow and sneering
smile,
The flow of compliment, the slippery
wile,
Would make that breast with indignation
burn,
And all the glittering snares to tempt thee
spurn. 320
Domestic happiness will stamp thy fate;
Sacred to love, unclouded e'er by hate;
The world admire thee, and thy friends
adore;
Ambition's slave alone would toil for
more. 324

Now last, but nearest of the social band,
See honest, open, generous Cleon stand;
With scarce one speck to cloud the pleas-
ing scene,
No vice degrades that purest soul serene.
On the same day our studious race begun,
On the same day our studious race was
run; 330
Thus side by side we pass'd our first career,
Thus side by side we strove for many a
year;
At last concluded our scholastic life,
We neither conquer'd in the classic strife:
As speakers each supports an equal name,
And crowds allow to both a partial fame:
To soothe a youthful rival's early pride,
Though Cleon's candour would the palm
divide,
Yet candour's self compels me now to own
Justice awards it to my friend alone. 340

Oh! friends regretted, scenes for ever
dear,
Remembrance hails you with her warmest
tear!
Drooping, she bends o'er pensive Fancy's
urn,
To trace the hours which never can return;
Yet with the retrospection loves to dwell,
And soothe the sorrows of her last fare-
well! 346
Yet greets the triumph of my boyish mind,
As infant laurels round my head were
twined,
When Probus' praise repaid my lyric song,
Or placed me higher in the studious
throng; 350
Or when my first harangue received
applause,
His sage instruction the primeval cause,
What gratitude to him my soul possest,
While hope of dawning honours fill'd my
breast!
For all my humble fame, to him alone
The praise is due, who made that fame my
own. 356
Oh! could I soar above these feeble lays,
These young effusions of my early days,

To him my muse her noblest strain would
   give:
The song might perish, but the theme
   might live.   360
Yet why for him the needless verse essay?
His honour'd name requires no vain dis-
   play:
By every son of grateful IDA blest,
It finds an echo in each youthful breast;
A fame beyond the glories of the proud,
Or all the plaudits of the venal crowd.

IDA! not yet exhausted is the theme,
Nor closed the progress of my youthful
   dream.
How many a friend deserves the grateful
   strain!
What scenes of childhood still unsung re-
   main!   370
Yet let me hush this echo of the past,
This parting song, the dearest and the last;
And brood in secret o'er those hours of
   joy,
To me a silent and a sweet employ,   374
While future hope and fear alike unknown,
I think with pleasure on the past alone;
Yes, to the past alone my heart confine,
And chase the phantom of what once was
   mine.

IDA! still o'er thy hills in joy preside,
And proudly steer through time's eventful
   tide;   380
Still may thy blooming sons thy name
   revere,
Smile in thy bower, but quit thee with a
   tear,—
That tear, perhaps, the fondest which will
   flow,
O'er their last scene of happiness be-
   low.   384
Tell me, ye hoary few, who glide along,
The feeble veterans of some former throng,
Whose friends, like autumn leaves by tem-
   pests whirl'd,
Are swept for ever from this busy world;
Revolve the fleeting moments of your
   youth,
While Care has yet withheld her venom'd
   tooth;   390
Say if remembrance days like these endears
Beyond the rapture of succeeding years?
Say, can ambition's fever'd dream bestow
So sweet a balm to soothe your hours of
   woe?
Can treasures, hoarded for some thankless
   son,   395
Can royal smiles, or wreaths by slaughter
   won,
Can stars or ermine, man's maturer toys
(For glittering baubles are not left to boys),
Recall one scene so much beloved to view,
As those where Youth her garland twined
   for you?   400

Ah, no! amidst the gloomy calm of age
You turn with faltering hand life's varied
   page;
Peruse the record of your days on earth,
Unsullied only where it marks your birth;
Still lingering pause above each chequer'd
   leaf,   405
And blot with tears the sable lines of grief;
Where Passion o'er the theme her mantle
   threw,
Or weeping Virtue sigh'd a faint adieu;
But bless the scroll which fairer words
   adorn,
Traced by the rosy finger of the morn;
When Friendship bow'd before the shrine
   of Truth,   411
And Love, without his pinion, smiled on
   Youth.

ANSWER TO A BEAUTIFUL POEM

ENTITLED 'THE COMMON LOT'

MONTGOMERY! true, the common lot
   Of mortals lies in Lethe's wave;
Yet some shall never be forgot,
   Some shall exist beyond the grave.

'Unknown the region of his birth,'   5
   The hero rolls the tide of war;
Yet not unknown his martial worth,
   Which glares a meteor from afar.

His joy or grief, his weal or woe,
   Perchance may 'scape the page of fame;
Yet nations now unborn will know   11
   The record of his deathless name.

The patriot's and the poet's frame
   Must share the common tomb of all:
Their glory will not sleep the same;   15
   That will arise, though empires fall.

The lustre of a beauty's eye
   Assumes the ghastly stare of death;
The fair, the brave, the good must die,
   And sink the yawning grave beneath.

Once more the speaking eye revives,   21
   Still beaming through the lover's strain;
For Petrarch's Laura still survives:
   She died, but ne'er will die again.

The rolling seasons pass away,   25
   And Time, untiring, waves his wing;
Whilst honour's laurels ne'er decay,
   But bloom in fresh, unfading spring.

All, all must sleep in grim repose,
   Collected in the silent tomb;   30
The old and young, with friends and foes,
   Fest'ring alike in shrouds, consume.

The mouldering marble lasts its day,
   Yet falls at length an useless fane;
To ruin's ruthless fangs a prey,   35
   The wrecks of pillar'd pride remain.

What, though the sculpture be destroy'd,
  From dark oblivion meant to guard;
A bright renown shall be enjoy'd
  By those whose virtues claim reward.

Then do not say the common lot   41
  Of all lies deep in Lethe's wave;
Some few who ne'er will be forgot
  Shall burst the bondage of the grave.
                                    1806.

TO A LADY

WHO PRESENTED THE AUTHOR WITH THE
VELVET BAND WHICH BOUND HER TRESSES

THIS Band, which bound thy yellow hair,
  Is mine, sweet girl! thy pledge of love;
It claims my warmest, dearest care,
  Like relics left of saints above.

Oh! I will wear it next my heart;   5
  'Twill bind my soul in bonds to thee:
From me again 'twill ne'er depart,
  But mingle in the grave with me.

The dew I gather from thy lip
  Is not so dear to me as this;   10
That I but for a moment sip,
  And banquet on a transient bliss:

This will recall each youthful scene,
  E'en when our lives are on the wane;
The leaves of Love will still be green   15
  When Memory bids them bud again.

Oh! little lock of golden hue,
  In gently waving ringlet curl'd,
By the dear head on which you grew,
  I would not lose you for a world.   20

Not though a thousand more adorn
  The polish'd brow where once you shone,
Like rays which gild a cloudless morn,
  Beneath Columbia's fervid zone.

> 1806. [First published, 1832, as
> a single poem, though the last two
> stanzas are apparently indepen-
> dent of the first four.]

LINES

ADDRESSED TO THE REV. J. T. BECHER, ON
HIS ADVISING THE AUTHOR TO MIX MORE
WITH SOCIETY

DEAR Becher, you tell me to mix with man-
    kind;
  I cannot deny such a precept is wise;
But retirement accords with the tone of my
    mind:
  I will not descend to a world I despise.

Did the senate or camp my exertions re-
    quire,   5
  Ambition might prompt me, at once, to
    go forth;
When infancy's years of probation expire,
  Perchance I may strive to distinguish
    my birth.

The fire in the cavern of Etna conceal'd
  Still mantles unseen in its secret recess;
At length, in a volume terrific reveal'd,
  No torrent can quench it, no bounds
    can repress.   12

Oh! thus, the desire in my bosom for fame
  Bids me live but to hope for posterity's
    praise.
Could I soar with the phœnix on pinions
    of flame,   15
  With him I would wish to expire in the
    blaze.

For the life of a Fox, of a Chatham the
    death,
  What censure, what danger, what woe
    would I brave!
Their lives did not end when they yielded
    their breath;
  Their glory illumines the gloom of
    their grave.   20

Yet why should I mingle in Fashion's full
    herd?
  Why crouch to her leaders, or cringe to
    her rules?
Why bend to the proud, or applaud the
    absurd?
  Why search for delight in the friendship
    of fools?

I have tasted the sweets and the bitters of
    love;   25
  In friendship I early was taught to
    believe;
My passion the matrons of prudence reprove;
  I have found that a friend may profess,
    yet deceive.

To me what is wealth?—it may pass in an
    hour,
  If tyrants prevail, or if Fortune should
    frown: 30
To me what is title?—the phantom of
    power;
  To me what is fashion?—I seek but re-
    nown.

Deceit is a stranger as yet to my soul:
  I still am unpractised to varnish the
    truth:
Then why should I live in a hateful con-
    trol?   35
  Why waste upon folly the days of my
    youth?
                                    1806.

REMEMBRANCE

'TIS done!—I saw it in my dreams;
No more with Hope the future beams;
  My days of happiness are few:
Chill'd by misfortune's wintry blast,
My dawn of life is overcast;   5
  Love, Hope, and Joy, alike adieu!
  Would I could add Remembrance too!
                    1806. [First published, 1832.]

THE DEATH OF CALMAR AND ORLA

AN IMITATION OF MACPHERSON'S OSSIAN

DEAR are the days of youth! Age dwells on their remembrance through the mist of time. In the twilight he recalls the sunny hours of morn. He lifts his spear with trembling hand. 'Not thus feebly did I raise the steel before my fathers!' Past is the race of heroes. But their fame rises on the harp; their souls ride on the wings of the wind; they hear the sound through the sighs of the storm, and rejoice in their hall of clouds! Such is Calmar. The gray stone marks his narrow house. He looks down from eddying tempests: he rolls his form in the whirlwind, and hovers on the blast of the mountain.

In Morven dwelt the chief; a beam of war to Fingal. His steps in the field were marked in blood. Lochlin's sons had fled before his angry spear; but mild was the eye of Calmar; soft was the flow of his yellow locks: they streamed like the meteor of the night. No maid was the sigh of his soul: his thoughts were given to friendship,—to dark-haired Orla, destroyer of heroes! Equal were their swords in battle; but fierce was the pride of Orla:—gentle alone to Calmar. Together they dwelt in the cave of Oithona.

From Lochlin, Swaran bounded o'er the blue waves. Erin's sons fell beneath his might. Fingal roused his chiefs to combat. Their ships cover the ocean. Their hosts throng on the green hills. They come to the aid of Erin.

Night rose in clouds. Darkness veils the armies: but the blazing oaks gleam through the valley. The sons of Lochlin slept: their dreams were of blood. They lift the spear in thought, and Fingal flies. Not so the host of Morven. To watch was the post of Orla. Calmar stood by his side. Their spears were in their hands. Fingal called his chiefs: they stood around. The king was in the midst. Gray were his locks, but strong was the arm of the king. Age withered not his powers. 'Sons of Morven,' said the hero, 'to-morrow we meet the foe. But where is Cuthullin, the shield of Erin? He rests in the halls of Tura; he knows not of our coming. Who will speed through Lochlin to the hero, and call the chief to arms? The path is by the swords of foes; but many are my heroes. They are thunderbolts of war. Speak, ye chiefs! Who will arise?'

'Son of Trenmor! mine be the deed,' said dark-haired Orla, 'and mine alone. What is death to me? I love the sleep of the mighty, but little is the danger. The sons of Lochlin dream. I will seek car-borne Cuthullin. If I fall, raise the song of bards; and lay me by the stream of Lubar.' —'And shalt thou fall alone?' said fair-haired Calmar. 'Wilt thou leave thy friend afar? Chief of Oithona! not feeble is my arm in fight. Could I see thee die, and not lift the spear? No, Orla! ours has been the chase of the roebuck, and the feast of shells; ours be the path of danger: ours has been the cave of Oithona; ours be the narrow dwelling on the banks of Lubar.' 'Calmar,' said the chief of Oithona, 'why should thy yellow locks be darkened in the dust of Erin? Let me fall alone. My father dwells in his hall of air: he will rejoice in his boy; but the blue-eyed Mora spreads the feast for her son in Morven. She listens to the steps of the hunter on the heath, and thinks it is the tread of Calmar. Let her not say, "Calmar has fallen by the steel of Lochlin: he died with gloomy Orla, the chief of the dark brow." Why should tears dim the azure eye of Mora? Why should her voice curse Orla, the destroyer of Calmar? Live, Calmar! Live to raise my stone of moss; live to revenge me in the blood of Lochlin. Join the song of bards above my grave. Sweet will be the song of death to Orla, from the voice of Calmar. My ghost shall smile on the notes of praise.' 'Orla,' said the son of Mora, 'could I raise the song of death to my friend? Could I give his fame to the winds? No, my heart would speak in sighs: faint and broken are the sounds of sorrow. Orla! our souls shall hear the song together. One cloud shall be ours on high: the bards will mingle the names of Orla and Calmar.'

They quit the circle of the chiefs. Their steps are to the host of Lochlin. The dying blaze of oak dim twinkles through the night. The northern star points the path to Tura. Swaran, the king, rests on his lonely hill. Here the troops are mixed: they frown in sleep; their shields beneath their heads. Their swords gleam at distance in heaps. The fires are faint; their embers fail in smoke. All is hushed; but the gale sighs on the rocks above. Lightly wheel the heroes through the slumbering band. Half the journey is past, when Mathon, resting on his shield, meets the eye of Orla. It rolls in flame, and glistens through the shade. His spear is raised on high. 'Why dost thou bend thy brow, chief of Oithona?' said fair-haired Calmar: 'we are in the midst of foes. Is this a time for delay?' 'It is a time for vengeance,' said Orla of the gloomy brow. 'Mathon of Lochlin sleeps: seest thou his spear? Its point is dim with the gore of my father. The blood of Mathon shall reek on mine; but shall I slay him sleeping, son of Mora?

No! he shall feel his wound: my fame shall not soar on the blood of slumber. Rise, Mathon, rise! The son of Conna calls; thy life is his; rise to combat.' Mathon starts from sleep; but did he rise alone? No: the gathering chiefs bound on the plain. 'Fly! Calmar, fly!' said dark-haired Orla. 'Mathon is mine. I shall die in joy: but Lochlin crowds around. Fly through the shade of night.' Orla turns. The helm of Mathon is cleft; his shield falls from his arm: he shudders in his blood. He rolls by the side of the blazing oak. Strumon sees him fall: his wrath rises: his weapon glitters on the head of Orla: but a spear pierced his eye. His brain gushes through the wound, and foams on the spear of Calmar. As roll the waves of the Ocean on two mighty barks of the north, so pour the men of Lochlin on the chiefs. As, breaking the surge in foam, proudly steer the barks of the north, so rise the chiefs of Morven on the scattered crests of Lochlin. The din of arms came to the ear of Fingal. He strikes his shield; his sons throng around; the people pour along the heath. Ryno bounds in joy. Ossian stalks in his arms. Oscar shakes the spear. The eagle wing of Fillan floats on the wind. Dreadful is the clang of death! many are the widows of Lochlin! Morven prevails in its strength.

Morn glimmers on the hills: no living foe is seen; but the sleepers are many; grim they lie on Erin. The breeze of ocean lifts their locks; yet they do not awake. The hawks scream above their prey.

Whose yellow locks wave o'er the breast of a chief? Bright as the gold of the stranger, they mingle with the dark hair of his friend. 'Tis Calmar: he lies on the bosom of Orla. Theirs is one stream of blood. Fierce is the look of the gloomy Orla. He breathes not; but his eye is still a flame. It glares in death unclosed. His hand is grasped in Calmar's; but Calmar lives! he lives, though low. 'Rise,' said the king, 'rise, son of Mora: 'tis mine to heal the wounds of heroes. Calmar may yet bound on the hills of Morven.'

'Never more shall Calmar chase the deer of Morven with Orla,' said the hero. 'What were the chase to me alone? Who should share the spoils of battle with Calmar? Orla is at rest! Rough was thy soul, Orla! yet soft to me as the dew of morn. It glared on others in lightning: to me a silver beam of night. Bear my sword to blue-eyed Mora; let it hang in my empty hall. It is not pure from blood: but it could not save Orla. Lay me with my friend. Raise the song when I am dark!'

They are laid by the stream of Lubar. Four gray stones mark the dwelling of Orla and Calmar. When Swaran was bound, our sails rose on the blue waves. The winds gave our barks to Morven:—the bards raised the song.

'What form rises on the roar of clouds? Whose dark ghost gleams on the red streams of tempests? His voice rolls on the thunder. 'Tis Orla, the brown chief of Oithona. He was unmatched in war. Peace to thy soul, Orla! thy fame will not perish. Nor thine, Calmar! Lovely wast thou, son of blue-eyed Mora; but not harmless was thy sword. It hangs in thy cave. The ghosts of Lochlin shriek around its steel. Hear thy praise, Calmar! It dwells on the voice of the mighty. Thy name shakes on the echoes of Morven. Then raise thy fair locks, son of Mora. Spread them on the arch of the rainbow; and smile through the tears of the storm.'

L'AMITIÉ EST L'AMOUR
SANS AILES

WHY should my anxious breast repine,
  Because my youth is fled?
Days of delight may still be mine;
  Affection is not dead.
In tracing back the years of youth,   5
One firm record, one lasting truth,
  Celestial consolation brings;
Bear it, ye breezes, to the seat,
Where first my heart responsive beat,—
  'Friendship is Love without his wings!'

Through few, but deeply chequer'd years,
  What moments have been mine!   12
Now half obscured by clouds of tears,
  Now bright in rays divine;
Howe'er my future doom be cast,   15
My soul, enraptured with the past,
  To one idea fondly clings;
Friendship! that thought is all thine own,
Worth worlds of bliss, that thought alone—
  'Friendship is Love without his wings!'

Where yonder yew-trees lightly wave   21
  Their branches on the gale,
Unheeded heaves a simple grave,
  Which tells the common tale;
Round this unconscious schoolboys stray,
Till the dull knell of childish play   26
  From yonder studious mansion rings;
But here whene'er my footsteps move,
My silent tears too plainly prove
  'Friendship is Love without his wings!'

Oh, Love! before thy glowing shrine   31
  My early vows were paid;
My hopes, my dreams, my heart was thine,
  But these are now decay'd;
For thine are pinions like the wind,   35
No trace of thee remains behind,

Except, alas! thy jealous stings.
Away, away! delusive power,
Thou shalt not haunt my coming hour;
  Unless, indeed, without thy wings. 40

Seat of my youth! thy distant spire
  Recalls each scene of joy;
My bosom glows with former fire,—
  In mind again a boy.
Thy grove of elms, thy verdant hill, 45
Thy every path delights me still,
  Each flower a double fragrance flings;
Again, as once, in converse gay,
Each dear associate seems to say,
  'Friendship is Love without his wings!'

My Lycus! wherefore dost thou weep?
  Thy falling tears restrain; 52
Affection for a time may sleep,
  But, oh, 'twill wake again.
Think, think, my friend, when next we
    meet, 55
Our long-wish'd interview, how sweet!
  From this my hope of rapture springs;
While youthful hearts thus fondly swell,
Absence, my friend, can only tell,
  'Friendship is Love without his wings!'

In one, and one alone deceived, 61
  Did I my error mourn?
No—from oppressive bonds relieved,
  I left the wretch to scorn.
I turn'd to those my childhood knew,
With feelings warm, with bosoms true,
  Twined with my heart's according
    strings;
And till those vital chords shall break,
For none but these my breast shall wake
  Friendship, the power deprived of
    wings! 70

Ye few! my soul, my life is yours,
  My memory and my hope;
Your worth a lasting love insures,
  Unfetter'd in its scope; 74
From smooth deceit and terror sprung
With aspect fair and honey'd tongue,
  Let Adulation wait on kings;
With joy elate, by snares beset,
We, we, my friends, can ne'er forget
  'Friendship is Love without his wings!'

Fictions and dreams inspire the bard 81
  Who rolls the epic song;
Friendship and truth be my reward—
  To me no bays belong;
If laurell'd Fame but dwells with lies, 85
Me the enchantress ever flies,
  Whose heart and not whose fancy sings;
Simple and young, I dare not feign;
Mine be the rude yet heartfelt strain, 89
  'Friendship is Love without his wings!'

December 1806.
[First published, 1832.]

THE PRAYER OF NATURE

FATHER of Light! great God of Heaven!
  Hear'st thou the accents of despair?
Can guilt like man's be e'er forgiven?
  Can vice atone for crimes by prayer?

Father of Light, on thee I call! 5
  Thou seest my soul is dark within;
Thou who canst mark the sparrow's fall,
  Avert from me the death of sin.

No shrine I seek, to sects unknown;
  Oh, point to me the path of truth! 10
Thy dread omnipotence I own;
  Spare, yet amend, the faults of youth.

Let bigots rear a gloomy fane,
  Let superstition hail the pile, 14
Let priests, to spread their sable reign,
  With tales of mystic rites beguile.

Shall man confine his Maker's sway
  To Gothic domes of mouldering stone?
Thy temple is the face of day;
  Earth, ocean, heaven, thy boundless
    throne. 20

Shall man condemn his race to hell,
  Unless they bend in pompous form?
Tell us that all, for one who fell,
  Must perish in the mingling storm?

Shall each pretend to reach the skies, 25
  Yet doom his brother to expire,
Whose soul a different hope supplies,
  Or doctrines less severe inspire?

Shall these, by creeds they can't expound,
  Prepare a fancied bliss or woe? 30
Shall reptiles, grovelling on the ground,
  Their great Creator's purpose know?

Shall those, who live for self alone,
  Whose years float on in daily crime—
Shall they by Faith for guilt atone, 35
  And live beyond the bounds of Time?

Father! no prophet's laws I seek,—
  Thy laws in Nature's works appear;—
I own myself corrupt and weak,
  Yet will I pray, for thou wilt hear! 40

Thou, who canst guide the wandering star
  Through trackless realms of æther's
    space;
Who calm'st the elemental war,
  Whose hand from pole to pole I trace:

Thou, who in wisdom placed me here,
  Who, when thou wilt, canst take me
    hence, 46
Ah! whilst I tread this earthly sphere,
  Extend to me thy wide defence.

To Thee, my God, to thee I call!
  Whatever weal or woe betide, 50
By thy command I rise or fall,
  In thy protection I confide.

If, when this dust to dust's restored,
  My soul shall float on airy wing,
How shall thy glorious name adored 55
  Inspire her feeble voice to sing!

But, if this fleeting spirit share
  With clay the grave's eternal bed,
While life yet throbs I raise my prayer,
  Though doom'd no more to quit the
    dead. 60

To Thee I breathe my humble strain,
  Grateful for all thy mercies past,
And hope, my God, to thee again
  This erring life may fly at last.
          December 29, 1806.
      [First published, 1830.]

TO EDWARD NOEL LONG, ESQ.

'Nil ego contulerim jucundo sanus amico.'—HOR.

DEAR LONG, in this sequester'd scene,
  While all around in slumber lie,
The joyous days which ours have been
  Come rolling fresh on Fancy's eye;
Thus if amidst the gathering storm, 5
While clouds the darken'd noon deform,
Yon heaven assumes a varied glow,
I hail the sky's celestial bow,
Which spreads the sign of future peace,
And bids the war of tempests cease. 10
Ah! though the present brings but pain
I think those days may come again;
Or if, in melancholy mood,
Some lurking envious fear intrude,
To check my bosom's fondest thought,
  And interrupt the golden dream, 16
I crush the fiend with malice fraught,
  And still indulge my wonted theme.
Although we ne'er again can trace,
  In Granta's vale, the pedant's lore; 20
Nor through the groves of Ida chase
  Our raptured visions as before,
Though Youth has flown on rosy pinion,
And Manhood claims his stern dominion,
Age will not every hope destroy, 25
But yield some hours of sober joy.

Yes, I will hope that Time's broad wing
Will shed around some dews of spring:
But if his scythe must sweep the flowers
Which bloom among the fairy bowers,
Where smiling youth delights to dwell,
And hearts with early rapture swell;
If frowning Age, with cold control,
Confines the current of the soul,
Congeals the tear of Pity's eye, 35
Or checks the sympathetic sigh,
Or hears unmoved misfortune's groan,
And bids me feel for self alone;

Oh! may my bosom never learn
  To soothe its wonted heedless flow, 40
Still, still despise the censor stern,
  But ne'er forget another's woe.
Yes, as you knew me in the days
O'er which Remembrance yet delays,
Still may I rove, untutor'd, wild, 45
And even in age at heart a child.

Though now on airy visions borne,
  To you my soul is still the same.
Oft has it been my fate to mourn,
  And all my former joys are tame. 50
But, hence! ye hours of sable hue!
  Your frowns are gone, my sorrows o'er:
By every bliss my childhood knew,
  I'll think upon your shade no more.
Thus, when the whirlwind's rage is past,
  And caves their sullen roar enclose,
We heed no more the wintry blast,
  When lull'd by zephyr to repose.

Full often has my infant Muse
  Attuned to love her languid lyre; 60
But now, without a theme to choose,
  The strains in stolen sighs expire.
My youthful nymphs, alas! are flown;
  E—— is a wife, and C—— a mother,
And Carolina sighs alone, 65
  And Mary's given to another;
And Cora's eye, which roll'd on me,
  Can now no more my love recall:
In truth, dear LONG, 'twas time to flee;
  For Cora's eye will shine on all. 70
And though the sun, with genial rays,
His beams alike to all displays,
And every lady's eye's a *sun*,
These last should be confined to one. 74
The soul's meridian don't become her,
Whose sun displays a general *summer*!
Thus faint is every former flame,
And passion's self is now a name.
As, when ebbing flames are low,
  The aid which once improved their
    light, 80
And bade them burn with fiercer glow,
  Now quenches all their sparks in night;
Thus has it been with passion's fires,
  As many a boy and girl remembers,
While all the force of love expires, 85
  Extinguish'd with the dying embers.

But now, dear LONG, 'tis midnight's
    noon,
And clouds obscure the watery moon,
Whose beauties I shall not rehearse,
Described in every stripling's verse; 90
For why should I the path go o'er,
Which every bard has trod before?
Yet ere yon silver lamp of night
  Has thrice perform'd her stated round,
Has thrice retraced her path of light, 95
  And chased away the gloom profound,

I trust that we, my gentle friend,
Shall see her rolling orbit wend
Above the dear-loved peaceful seat,
Which once contain'd our youth's re-
   treat;   100
And then with those our childhood knew
We'll mingle in the festive crew;
While many a tale of former day
Shall wing the laughing hours away;
And all the flow of souls shall pour   105
The sacred intellectual shower,
Nor cease till Luna's waning horn
Scarce glimmers through the mist of
   morn.

TO A LADY

OH! had my fate been join'd with thine,
  As once this pledge appear'd a token,
These follies had not then been mine,
  For then my peace had not been broken.

To thee these early faults I owe,   5
  To thee, the wise and old reproving:
They know my sins, but do not know
  'Twas thine to break the bonds of
    loving.

For once my soul, like thine, was pure,
  And all its rising fires could smother;
But now thy vows no more endure,   11
  Bestow'd by thee upon another;

Perhaps his peace I could destroy,
  And spoil the blisses that await him;
Yet let my rival smile in joy,   15
  For thy dear sake I cannot hate him.

Ah! since thy angel form is gone,
  My heart no more can rest with any;
But what it sought in thee alone,
  Attempts, alas! to find in many.   20

Then fare thee well, deceitful maid!
  'Twere vain and fruitless to regret thee;
Nor hope nor memory yield their aid,
  But pride may teach me to forget thee.

Yet all this giddy waste of years,   25
  This tiresome round of palling pleasures;
These varied loves, these matrons' fears,
  These thoughtless strains to passion's
    measures—

If thou wert mine, had all been hush'd:—
  This cheek, now pale from early riot,
With passion's hectic ne'er had flushed,
  But bloom'd in calm domestic quiet.

Yes, once the rural scene was sweet,   33
  For Nature seem'd to smile before thee;
And once my breast abhorr'd deceit,—
  For then it beat but to adore thee.

But now I seek for other joys: 37
  To think would drive my soul to mad-
    ness;
In thoughtless throngs and empty noise
  I conquer half my bosom's sadness.

Yet, even in these a thought will steal
  In spite of every vain endeavour,—
And fiends might pity what I feel,—
  To know that thou art lost for ever.

I WOULD I WERE A CARELESS CHILD

I WOULD I were a careless child,
  Still dwelling in my Highland cave,
Or roaming through the dusky wild,
  Or bounding o'er the dark blue wave;
The cumbrous pomp of Saxon pride   5
  Accords not with the freeborn soul,
Which loves the mountain's craggy side,
  And seeks the rocks where billows
    roll.

Fortune! take back these cultured lands,
  Take back this name of splendid sound!
I hate the touch of servile hands,   11
  I hate the slaves that cringe around.
Place me among the rocks I love,
  Which sound to Ocean's wildest roar;
I ask but this—again to rove   15
  Through scenes my youth hath known
    before.

Few are my years, and yet I feel
  The world was ne'er design'd for me:
Ah! why do dark'ning shades conceal
  The hour when man must cease to be?
Once I beheld a splendid dream,   21
  A visionary scene of bliss:
Truth!—wherefore did thy hated beam
  Awake me to a world like this?

I loved—but those I loved are gone;   25
  Had friends—my early friends are fled:
How cheerless feels the heart alone,
  When all its former hopes are dead!
Though gay companions o'er the bowl
  Dispel awhile the sense of ill;   30
Though pleasure stirs the maddening soul,
  The heart—the heart—is lonely still.

How dull! to hear the voice of those
  Whom rank or chance, whom wealth or
    power,
Have made, though neither friends nor
    foes,   35
  Associates of the festive hour.
Give me again a faithful few,
  In years and feelings still the same,
And I will fly the midnight crew,   39
  Where boist'rous joy is but a name.

And woman, lovely woman! thou,
  My hope, my comforter, my all!
How cold must be my bosom now,
  When e'en thy smiles begin to pall!
Without a sigh would I resign   45
  This busy scene of splendid woe,
To make that calm contentment mine,
  Which virtue knows, or seems to
    know.

Fain would I fly the haunts of men—
  I seek to shun, not hate mankind;   50
My breast requires the sullen glen,
  Whose gloom may suit a darken'd
    mind.
Oh! that to me the wings were given
  Which bear the turtle to her nest!
Then would I cleave the vault of
    heaven,   55
  To flee away, and be at rest.

WHEN I ROVED A YOUNG HIGHLANDER

When I roved a young Highlander o'er
  the dark heath,
  And climb'd thy steep summit, oh
    Morven of snow!
To gaze on the torrent that thunder'd
  beneath,
  Or the mist of the tempest that gather'd
    below,   4
Untutor'd by science, a stranger to fear,
  And rude as the rocks where my in-
    fancy grew,
No feeling, save one, to my bosom was
  dear;
  Need I say, my sweet Mary, 'twas
    centred in you?

Yet it could not be love, for I knew not
  the name,—
  What passion can dwell in the heart of
    a child?   10
But still I perceive an emotion the same
  As I felt, when a boy, on the crag-
    cover'd wild:
One image alone on my bosom impress'd,
  I loved my bleak regions, nor panted
    for new;
And few were my wants, for my wishes
  were bless'd;   15
  And pure were my thoughts, for my
    soul was with you.

I arose with the dawn; with my dog as my
  guide,
  From mountain to mountain I bounded
    along;
I breasted the billows of Dee's rushing
  tide,
  And heard at a distance the High-
    lander's song: 20

At eve, on my heath-cover'd couch of re-
  pose,
  No dreams, save of Mary, were spread
    to my view;
And warm to the skies my devotions arose,
  For the first of my prayers was a bless-
    ing on you.

I left my bleak home, and my visions are
  gone;   25
  The mountains are vanish'd, my youth
    is no more;
As the last of my race, I must wither alone,
  And delight but in days I have wit-
    ness'd before:
Ah! splendour has raised but embitter'd
  my lot;
  More dear were the scenes which my
    infancy knew: 30
Though my hopes may have fail'd, yet
  they are not forgot;
  Though cold is my heart, still it lingers
    with you.

When I see some dark hill point its crest
  to the sky,
  I think of the rocks that o'ershadow
    Colbleen;
When I see the soft blue of a love-speaking
  eye,   35
  I think of those eyes that endear'd the
    rude scene;
When, haply, some light-waving locks I
  behold,
  That faintly resemble my Mary's in hue,
I think on the long, flowing ringlets of
  gold,
  The locks that were sacred to beauty,
    and you.   40

Yet the day may arrive when the moun-
  tains once more
  Shall rise to my sight in their mantles of
    snow:
But while these soar above me, unchanged
  as before,
  Will Mary be there to receive me?—ah,
    no!
Adieu, then, ye hills, where my childhood
  was bred!   45
  Thou sweet flowing Dee, to thy waters
    adieu!
No home in the forest shall shelter my
  head,—
  Ah! Mary, what home could be mine but
    with you?

TO GEORGE, EARL DELAWARR

Oh! yes, I will own we were dear to each
  other;
  The friendships of childhood, though
    fleeting, are true;
The love which you felt was the love of a
  brother,
  Nor less the affection I cherish'd for you.

But Friendship can vary her gentle do-
  minion; 5
  The attachment of years in a moment
    expires:
Like Love, too, she moves on a swift-
  waving pinion,
  But glows not, like Love, with un-
    quenchable fires.

Full oft have we wander'd through Ida
  together,
  And blest were the scenes of our youth,
    I allow: 10
In the spring of our life, how serene is the
  weather!
  But winter's rude tempests are gathering
    now.

No more with affection shall memory
  blending,
  The wonted delights of our childhood
    retrace:
When pride steels the bosom, the heart is
  unbending, 15
  And what would be justice appears a
    disgrace.

However, dear George, for I still must
  esteem you;
  The few whom I love I can never up-
    braid:
The chance which has lost may in future
  redeem you,
  Repentance will cancel the vow you
    have made. 20

I will not complain, and though chill'd is
  affection,
  With me no corroding resentment shall
    live:
My bosom is calm'd by the simple reflec-
  tion,
  That both may be wrong, and that both
    should forgive.

You knew that my soul, that my heart, my
  existence, 25
  If danger demanded, were wholly your
    own;
You knew me unalter'd by years or by dis-
  tance,
  Devoted to love and to friendship alone.

You knew,—but away with the vain retro-
  spection!
  The bond of affection no longer endures;
Too late you may droop o'er the fond
  recollection, 31
  And sigh for the friend who was for-
    merly yours.

For the present, we part,—I will hope not
  for ever;
  For time and regret will restore you at
    last:

To forget our dissension we both should
  endeavour, 35
  I ask no atonement, but days like the
    past.

TO THE EARL OF CLARE

'Tu semper amoris
Sis memor, et cari comitis ne abscedat imago.'
                         VAL FLAC.

FRIEND of my youth! when young we
  roved,
Like striplings, mutually beloved,
  With friendship's purest glow,
The bliss which wing'd those rosy hours
Was such as pleasure seldom showers 5
  On mortals here below.

The recollection seems alone
Dearer than all the joys I've known,
  When distant far from you: 9
Though pain, 'tis still a pleasing pain,
To trace those days and hours again,
  And sigh again, adieu!

My pensive memory lingers o'er
Those scenes to be enjoy'd no more,
  Those scenes regretted ever; 15
The measure of our youth is full,
Life's evening dream is dark and dull,
  And we may meet—ah! never!

As when one parent spring supplies
Two streams which from one fountain
  rise, 20
  Together join'd in vain;
How soon, diverging from their source,
Each, murmuring, seeks another course,
  Till mingled in the main!

Our vital streams of weal or woe, 25
Though near, alas! distinctly flow,
  Nor mingle as before:
Now swift or slow, now black or clear,
Till death's unfathom'd gulf appear,
  And both shall quit the shore. 30

Our souls, my friend! which once supplied
One wish, nor breathed a thought beside,
  Now flow in different channels:
Disdaining humbler rural sports,
'Tis yours to mix in polish'd courts, 35
  And shine in fashion's annals;

'Tis mine to waste on love my time,
Or vent my reveries in rhyme,
  Without the aid of reason;
For sense and reason (critics know it) 40
Have quitted every amorous poet,
  Nor left a thought to seize on.

Poor LITTLE! sweet, melodious bard!
Of late esteem'd it monstrous hard
  That he, who sang before all,— 45
He who the lore of love expanded,—
By dire reviewers should be branded
  As void of wit and moral.

And yet, while Beauty's praise is thine,
Harmonious favourite of the Nine! 50
　Repine not at thy lot.
Thy soothing lays may still be read,
When Persecution's arm is dead,
　And critics are forgot.

Still I must yield those worthies merit, 55
Who chasten, with unsparing spirit,
　Bad rhymes, and those who write them;
And though myself may be the next
By critic sarcasm to be vext,
　I really will not fight them. 60

Perhaps they would do quite as well
To break the rudely sounding shell
　Of such a young beginner:
He who offends at pert nineteen,
Ere thirty may become, I ween, 65
　A very harden'd sinner.

Now, Clare, I must return to you;
And, sure, apologies are due:
　Accept, then, my concession.
In truth, dear Clare, in fancy's flight 70
I soar along from left to right;
　My muse admires digression.

I think I said 'twould be your fate
To add one star to royal state;—
　May regal smiles attend you! 75
And should a noble monarch reign,
You will not seek his smiles in vain,
　If worth can recommend you.

Yet since in danger courts abound,
Where specious rivals glitter round, 80
　From snares may saints preserve you;
And grant your love or friendship ne'er
From any claim a kindred care,
　But those who best deserve you!

Not for a moment may you stray 85
From truth's secure, unerring way!
　May no delights decoy!
O'er roses may your footsteps move,
Your smiles be ever smiles of love,
　Your tears be tears of joy! 90

Oh! if you wish that happiness
Your coming days and years may bless,
　And virtues crown your brow;
Be still as you were wont to be,
Spotless as you've been known to me,— 96
　Be still as you are now.

And though some trifling share of praise,
To cheer my last declining days,
　To me were doubly dear;
Whilst blessing your beloved name 100
I'd waive at once a *poet's* fame,
　To prove a *prophet* here.

LINES WRITTEN BENEATH AN ELM IN THE CHURCHYARD OF HARROW

Spot of my youth! whose hoary branches sigh,
Swept by the breeze that fans thy cloudless sky;
Where now alone I muse, who oft have trod,
With those I loved, thy soft and verdant sod;
With those who, scatter'd far, perchance deplore, 5
Like me, the happy scenes they knew before:
Oh! as I trace again thy winding hill,
Mine eyes admire, my heart adores thee still,
Thou drooping Elm! beneath whose boughs I lay,
And frequent mused the twilight hours away; 10
Where, as they once were wont, my limbs recline,
But, ah! without the thoughts which then were mine:
How do thy branches, moaning to the blast,
Invite the bosom to recall the past,
And seem to whisper, as they gently swell,
'Take, while thou canst, a lingering, last farewell!' 16

When fate shall chill, at length, this fever'd breast,
And calm its cares and passions into rest,
Oft have I thought, 'twould soothe my dying hour,—
If aught may soothe when life resigns her power,— 20
To know some humble grave, some narrow cell,
Would hide my bosom where it loved to dwell;
With this fond dream, methinks 'twere sweet to die—
And here it linger'd, here my heart might lie;
Here might I sleep where all my hopes arose, 25
Scene of my youth, and couch of my repose;
For ever stretch'd beneath this mantling shade,
Press'd by the turf where once my childhood play'd;
Wrapt by the soil that veils the spot I loved,
Mix'd with the earth o'er which my footsteps moved; 30
Blest by the tongues that charm'd my youthful ear,
Mourn'd by the few my soul acknowledged here;
Deplored by those in early days allied,
And unremember'd by the world beside.

September 2, 1807.

47

OCCASIONAL PIECES

1807—1824

THE ADIEU

WRITTEN UNDER THE IMPRESSION THAT THE
AUTHOR WOULD SOON DIE

ADIEU, thou Hill! where early joy
    Spread roses o'er my brow;
Where Science seeks each loitering boy
    With knowledge to endow.
Adieu, my youthful friends or foes,   5
Partners of former bliss or woes;
    No more through Ida's paths we stray;
Soon must I share the gloomy cell,
Whose ever-slumbering inmates dwell
    Unconscious of the day.   10

Adieu, ye hoary Regal Fanes,
    Ye spires of Granta's vale,
Where Learning robed in sable reigns,
    And Melancholy pale.
Ye comrades of the jovial hour,   15
Ye tenants of the classic bower,
    On Cama's verdant margin placed,
Adieu! while memory still is mine,
For, offerings on Oblivion's shrine,
    These scenes must be effaced.   20

Adieu, ye mountains of the clime
    Where grew my youthful years;
Where Loch na Garr in snows sublime
    His giant summit rears.
Why did my childhood wander forth   25
From you, ye regions of the North,
    With sons of pride to roam?
Why did I quit my Highland cave,
Mar's dusky heath, and Dee's clear wave,
    To seek a Sotheron home!   30

Hall of my Sires! a long farewell—
    Yet why to thee adieu?
Thy vaults will echo back my knell,
    Thy towers my tomb will view:
The faltering tongue which sung thy fall,
And former glories of thy Hall,   36
    Forgets its wonted simple note—
But yet the Lyre retains the strings,
And sometimes, on Æolian wings,
    In dying strains may float.   40

Fields, which surround yon rustic cot,
    While yet I linger here,
Adieu! you are not now forgot,
    To retrospection dear.   44
Streamlet! along whose rippling surge
My youthful limbs were wont to urge,
    At noontide heat, their pliant course;
Plunging with ardour from the shore,
Thy springs will lave these limbs no more,
    Deprived of active force.   50

And shall I here forget the scene,
    Still nearest to my breast?
Rocks rise and rivers roll between
    The spot which passion blest;
Yet, Mary, all thy beauties seem   55
Fresh as in Love's bewitching dream,
    To me in smiles display'd;
Till slow disease resigns his prey
To Death, the parent of decay,
    Thine image cannot fade.   60

And thou, my Friend! whose gentle love
    Yet thrills my bosom's chords,
How much thy friendship was above
    Description's power of words!
Still near my breast thy gift I wear   65
Which sparkled once with Feeling's tear,
    Of Love the pure, the sacred gem;
Our souls were equal, and our lot
In that dear moment quite forgot;
    Let Pride alone condemn!   70

All, all is dark and cheerless now!
    No smile of Love's deceit
Can warm my veins with wonted glow,
    Can bid Life's pulses beat:
Not e'en the hope of future fame   75
Can wake my faint, exhausted frame,
    Or crown with fancied wreaths my
        head.
Mine is a short inglorious race,—
To humble in the dust my face,
    And mingle with the dead.   80

Oh Fame! thou goddess of my heart;
    On him who gains thy praise,
Pointless must fall the Spectre's dart,
    Consumed in Glory's blaze;
But me she beckons from the earth,   85
My name obscure, unmark'd my birth,
    My life a short and vulgar dream:
Lost in the dull, ignoble crowd,
My hopes recline within a shroud,
    My fate is Lethe's stream.   90

When I repose beneath the sod,
    Unheeded in the clay,
Where once my playful footsteps trod,
    Where now my head must lay,
The meed of Pity will be shed   95
In dew-drops o'er my narrow bed,
    By nightly skies, and storms alone;
No mortal eye will deign to steep
With tears the dark sepulchral deep
    Which hides a name unknown.   100

Forget this world, my restless sprite,
  Turn, turn thy thoughts to Heaven:
There must thou soon direct thy flight,
  If errors are forgiven.
To bigots and to sects unknown,   105
Bow down beneath the Almighty's Throne;
  To Him address thy trembling prayer:
He, who is merciful and just,
Will not reject a child of dust,
  Although his meanest care.   110

Father of Light! to Thee I call;
  My soul is dark within:
Thou who canst mark the sparrow's fall,
  Avert the death of sin.
Thou, who canst guide the wandering star,
Who calm'st the elemental war,   116
  Whose mantle is yon boundless sky,
My thoughts, my words, my crimes for-
    give:
And, since I soon must cease to live,
  Instruct me how to die.   120
          1807. [First published, 1832.]

TO A VAIN LADY

AH! heedless girl! why thus disclose
  What ne'er was meant for other ears:
Why thus destroy thine own repose
  And dig the source of future tears?

Oh, thou wilt weep, imprudent maid,   5
  While lurking envious foes will smile,
For all the follies thou hast said
  Of those who spoke but to beguile.

Vain girl! thy ling'ring woes are nigh,
  If thou believ'st what striplings say:
Oh, from the deep temptation fly,   11
  Nor fall the specious spoiler's prey.

Dost thou repeat, in childish boast,
  The words man utters to deceive?
Thy peace, thy hope, thy all is lost,   15
  If thou canst venture to believe.

While now amongst thy female peers
  Thou tell'st again the soothing tale,
Canst thou not mark the rising sneers
  Duplicity in vain would veil?   20

These tales in secret silence hush,
  Nor make thyself the public gaze:
What modest maid without a blush
  Recounts a flattering coxcomb's praise?

Will not the laughing boy despise   25
  Her who relates each fond conceit—
Who, thinking Heaven is in her eyes,
  Yet cannot see the slight deceit?

For she who takes a soft delight
  These amorous nothings in revealing,
Must credit all we say or write,   31
  While vanity prevents concealing.

Cease, if you prize your beauty's reign!
  No jealousy bids me reprove:
One, who is thus from nature vain,   35
  I pity, but I cannot love.
            January 15, 1807.
          [First published, 1832.]

TO ANNE

OH, Anne, your offences to me have been
      grievous:
  I thought from my wrath no atonement
      could save you:
But woman is made to command and de-
      ceive us—
  I look'd in your face, and I almost for-
      gave you.

I vow'd I could ne'er for a moment re-
      spect you,   5
  Yet thought that a day's separation was
      long;
When we met, I determined again to sus-
      pect you—
  Your smile soon convinced me suspi-
      cion was wrong.

I swore, in a transport of young indigna-
      tion,
  With fervent contempt evermore to dis-
      dain you: 10
I saw you—my anger became admiration;
  And now, all my wish, all my hope's to
      regain you.

With beauty like yours, oh, how vain the
      contention!
  Thus lowly I sue for forgiveness before
      you;
At once to conclude such a fruitless dis-
      sension,   15
  Be false, my sweet Anne, when I cease
      to adore you!
            January 16, 1807.
          [First published, 1832.]

TO THE SAME

OH, say not, sweet Anne, that the Fates
      have decreed
  The heart which adores you should
      wish to dissever;
Such Fates were to me most unkind ones
      indeed,—
  To bear me from love and from beauty
      for ever.

Your frowns, lovely girl, are the Fates
      which alone   5
  Could bid me from fond admiration
      refrain;
By these, every hope, every wish were
      o'erthrown,
  Till smiles should restore me to rapture
      again.

As the ivy and oak, in the forest entwined,
  The rage of the tempest united must
  weather; 10
My love and my life were by nature de-
  sign'd
  To flourish alike, or to perish together.

Then say not, sweet Anne, that the Fates
  have decreed
  Your lover should bid you a lasting
  adieu;
Till Fate can ordain that his bosom shall
  bleed, 15
  His soul, his existence, are centred in
  you.

  1807. [First published, 1832.]

TO THE AUTHOR OF A SONNET

BEGINNING ' "SAD IS MY VERSE," YOU SAY,
  "AND YET NO TEAR" '

THY verse is 'sad' enough, no doubt:
  A devilish deal more sad than witty!
Why we should weep I can't find out,
  Unless for *thee* we weep in pity.

Yet there is one I pity more; 5
  And much, alas! I think he needs it;
For he, I'm sure, will suffer sore,
  Who, to his own misfortune, reads it.

Thy rhymes, without the aid of magic,
  May *once* be read—but never after:
Yet their effect's by no means tragic, 11
  Although by far too dull for laughter.

But would you make our bosoms bleed,
  And of no common pang complain—
If you would make us weep again, 15
  Tell us, you'll read them o'er again.

  March 8, 1807.
  [First published, 1832.]

ON FINDING A FAN

IN one who felt as once he felt,
  This might, perhaps, have fann'd the
  flame;
But now his heart no more will melt,
  Because that heart is not the same.

As when the ebbing flames are low, 5
  The aid which once improved their
  light,
And bade them burn with fiercer glow,
  Now quenches all their blaze in night.

Thus has it been with passion's fires—
  As many a boy and girl remembers—
While every hope of love expires, 11
  Extinguish'd with the dying embers.

The *first*, though not a spark survive,
  Some careful hand may teach to burn;
The *last*, alas! can ne'er survive; 15
  No touch can bid its warmth return.

Or, if it chance to wake again,
  Not always doom'd its heat to smother,
It sheds (so wayward fates ordain)
  Its former warmth around another. 20
  1807. [First published, 1832.]

FAREWELL TO THE MUSE

THOU Power! who hast ruled me through
  infancy's days,
  Young offspring of fancy, 'tis time we
  should part;
Then rise on the gale this the last of my
  lays,
  The coldest effusion which springs from
  my heart.

This bosom, responsive to rapture no
  more, 5
  Shall hush thy wild notes, nor implore
  thee to sing;
The feelings of childhood, which taught
  thee to soar,
  Are wafted far distant on Apathy's
  wing.

Though simple the themes of my rude
  flowing Lyre,
  Yet even these themes are departed for
  ever; 10
No more beam the eyes which my dream
  could inspire,
  My visions are flown, to return,—alas!
  never.

When drain'd is the nectar which gladdens
  the bowl,
  How vain is the effort delight to prolong!
When cold is the beauty which dwelt in
  my soul, 15
  What magic of Fancy can lengthen my
  song?

Can the lips sing of Love in the desert
  alone,
  Of kisses and smiles which they now
  must resign?
Or dwell with delight on the hours that
  are flown?
  Ah, no! for those hours can no longer
  be mine. 20

Can they speak of the friends that I lived
  but to love?
  Ah, surely affection ennobles the strain!
But how can my numbers in sympathy
  move,
  When I scarcely can hope to behold
  them again?

Can I sing of the deeds which my Fathers
  have done, 25
  And raise my loud harp to the fame of
  my Sires?

For glories, like theirs, oh, how faint is my
tone!
For Heroes' exploits how unequal my
fires!

Untouch'd, then, my Lyre shall reply to
the blast—
'Tis hush'd; and my feeble endeavours
are o'er;   30
And those who have heard it will pardon
the past,
When they know that its murmurs shall
vibrate no more.

And soon shall its wild erring notes be
forgot,
Since early affection and love is o'ercast:
Oh! blest had my fate been, and happy
my lot,   35
Had the first strain of love been the
dearest, the last.

Farewell, my young Muse! since we now
can ne'er meet;
If our songs have been languid, they
surely are few;
Let us hope that the present at least will
be sweet—
The present—which seals our eternal
Adieu.   40

1807. [First published, 1832.]

TO AN OAK AT NEWSTEAD

YOUNG Oak! when I planted thee deep in
the ground,
I hoped that thy days would be longer
than mine;
That thy dark-waving branches would
flourish around,
And ivy thy trunk with its mantle entwine.

Such, such was my hope, when in infancy's
years,   5
On the land of my fathers I rear'd thee
with pride;
They are past, and I water thy stem with
my tears,—
Thy decay not the weeds that surround
thee can hide.

I left thee, my Oak, and, since that fatal
hour,
A stranger has dwelt in the hall of my
sire;   10
Till manhood shall crown me, not mine is
the power,
But his, whose neglect may have bade
thee expire.

Oh! hardy thou wert—even now little care
Might revive thy young head, and thy
wounds gently heal:

But thou wert not fated affection to
share—   15
For who could suppose that a stranger
would feel!

Ah, droop not, my Oak! lift thy head for
a while;
Ere twice round yon Glory this planet
shall run,
The hand of thy Master will teach thee to
smile,
When Infancy's years of probation are
done.   20

Oh, live then, my Oak! tow'r aloft from
the weeds,
That clog thy young growth, and assist
thy decay,
For still in thy bosom are life's early seeds,
And still may thy branches their beauty
display.

Oh! yet, if maturity's years may be thine,
Though I shall lie low in the cavern of
death,   26
On thy leaves yet the day-beam of ages
may shine,
Uninjured by time, or the rude winter's
breath.

For centuries still may thy boughs lightly
wave
O'er the corse of thy lord in thy canopy
laid;   30
While the branches thus gratefully shelter
his grave,
The chief who survives may recline in
thy shade.

And as he, with his boys, shall revisit this
spot,
He will tell them in whispers more softly
to tread.
Oh! surely, by these I shall ne'er be forgot;   35
Remembrance still hallows the dust of
the dead.

And here, will they say, when in life's
glowing prime,
Perhaps he has pour'd forth his young
simple lay,
And here must he sleep, till the moments
of time
Are lost in the hours of Eternity's day.

1807. [First published, 1832.]

ON REVISITING HARROW

HERE once engaged the stranger's view
Young Friendship's record simply
traced;
Few were her words,—but yet, though
few,
Resentment's hand the line defaced.

Deeply she cut—but not erased,   5
  The characters were still so plain,
That Friendship once return'd, and
    gazed,—
  Till Memory hail'd the words again.

Repentance placed them as before;   9
  Forgiveness join'd her gentle name;
So fair the inscription seem'd once more,
  That Friendship thought it still the
    same.

Thus might the Record now have been;
  But, ah, in spite of Hope's endeavour,
Or Friendship's tears, Pride rush'd be-
    tween,   15
  And blotted out the line for ever.
                    September 1807.

EPITAPH ON JOHN ADAMS, OF SOUTHWELL

A CARRIER, WHO DIED OF DRUNKENNESS

JOHN ADAMS lies here, of the parish of
  Southwell,
A *Carrier* who *carried* his can to his mouth
  well:
He *carried* so much, and he *carried* so fast,
He could *carry* no more—so was *carried*
  at last;
For, the liquor he drank, being too much
  for one,   5
He could not *carry* off,—so he's now
  carri-on.
                    September 1807.

TO MY SON

THOSE flaxen locks, those eyes of blue,
Bright as thy mother's in their hue;
Those rosy lips, whose dimples play
And smile to steal the heart away,
Recall a scene of former joy,   5
And touch thy father's heart, my Boy!

And thou canst lisp a father's name—
Ah, William, were thine own the same,—
No self-reproach—but, let me cease—
My care for thee shall purchase peace; 10
Thy mother's shade shall smile in joy,
And pardon all the past, my Boy!

Her lowly grave the turf has prest,
And thou hast known a stranger's breast;
Derision sneers upon thy birth,   15
And yields thee scarce a name on earth;
Yet shall not these one hope destroy,—
A Father's heart is thine, my Boy!

Why, let the world unfeeling frown,
Must I fond Nature's claim disown? 20
Ah, no—though moralists reprove,
I hail thee, dearest child of love,
Fair cherub, pledge of youth and joy—
A Father guards thy birth, my Boy!

Oh, 'twill be sweet in thee to trace, 25
Ere age has wrinkled o'er my face,
Ere half my glass of life is run,
At once a brother and a son;
And all my wane of years employ
In justice done to thee, my Boy!   30

Although so young thy heedless sire,
Youth will not damp parental fire;
And, wert thou still less dear to me,
While Helen's form revives in thee,
The breast which beat to former joy, 35
Will ne'er desert its pledge, my Boy!
        1807. [First published, 1830.]

FAREWELL! IF EVER FONDEST PRAYER

FAREWELL! if ever fondest prayer
  For other's weal avail'd on high,
Mine will not all be lost in air,
  But waft thy name beyond the sky. 4
'Twere vain to speak, to weep, to sigh:
  Oh! more than tears of blood can tell,
When wrung from guilt's expiring eye,
  Are in that word—Farewell!—Fare-
    well!

These lips are mute, these eyes are dry;
  But in my breast and in my brain, 10
Awake the pangs that pass not by,
  The thought that ne'er shall sleep again.
My soul nor deigns nor dares complain,
  Though grief and passion there rebel;
I only know we loved in vain— 15
  I only feel—Farewell!—Farewell!
                    1808.

BRIGHT BE THE PLACE OF THY SOUL

BRIGHT be the place of thy soul!
  No lovelier spirit than thine
E'er burst from its mortal control
  In the orbs of the blessed to shine.

On earth thou wert all but divine, 5
  As thy soul shall immortally be;
And our sorrow may cease to repine,
  When we know that thy God is with
    thee.

Light be the turf of thy tomb!
  May its verdure like emeralds be: 10
There should not be the shadow of gloom
  In aught that reminds us of thee.

Young flowers and an evergreen tree
  May spring from the spot of thy rest:
But nor cypress nor yew let us see; 15
  For why should we mourn for the blest?
                    1808.

WHEN WE TWO PARTED

WHEN we two parted
  In silence and tears,
Half broken-hearted
  To sever for years,
Pale grew thy cheek and cold,   5
  Colder thy kiss;
Truly that hour foretold
  Sorrow to this.

The dew of the morning
  Sunk chill on my brow—   10
It felt like the warning
  Of what I feel now.
Thy vows are all broken,
  And light is thy fame:
I hear thy name spoken,   15
  And share in its shame.

They name thee before me,
  A knell to mine ear;
A shudder comes o'er me—
  Why wert thou so dear?   20
They know not I knew thee,
  Who knew thee too well:—
Long, long shall I rue thee,
  Too deeply to tell.

In secret we met—   25
  In silence I grieve,
That thy heart could forget,
  Thy spirit deceive.
If I should meet thee
  After long years,   30
How should I greet thee?
  With silence and tears.

          1808.

TO A YOUTHFUL FRIEND

FEW years have pass'd since thou and I
  Were firmest friends, at least in name,
And childhood's gay sincerity
  Preserved our feelings long the same.

But now, like me, too well thou know'st
  What trifles oft the heart recall;   6
And those who once have loved the most
  Too soon forget they loved at all.

And such the change the heart displays,
  So frail is early friendship's reign,   10
A month's brief lapse, perhaps a day's,
  Will view thy mind estranged again.

If so, it never shall be mine
  To mourn the loss of such a heart;   14
The fault was Nature's fault, not thine,
  Which made thee fickle as thou art.

As rolls the ocean's changing tide,
  So human feelings ebb and flow;
And who would in a breast confide
  Where stormy passions ever glow?   20

It boots not that, together bred,
  Our childish days were days of joy:
My spring of life has quickly fled;
  Thou, too, hast ceased to be a boy.

And when we bid adieu to youth,   25
  Slaves to the specious world's control,
We sigh a long farewell to truth;
  That world corrupts the noblest soul.

Ah, joyous season! when the mind
  Dares all things boldly but to lie;   30
When thought ere spoke is unconfined,
  And sparkles in the placid eye.

Not so in Man's maturer years,
  When Man himself is but a tool;   34
When interest sways our hopes and fears,
  And all must love and hate by rule.

With fools in kindred vice the same,
  We learn at length our faults to blend;
And those, and those alone, may claim
  The prostituted name of friend.   40

Such is the common lot of man:
  Can we then 'scape from folly free?
Can we reverse the general plan,
  Nor be what all in turn must be?

No; for myself, so dark my fate   45
  Through every turn of life hath been;
Man and the world so much I hate,
  I care not when I quit the scene.

But thou, with spirit frail and light,
  Wilt shine awhile, and pass away;   50
As glow-worms sparkle through the night,
  But dare not stand the test of day.

Alas! whenever folly calls
  Where parasites and princes meet
(For cherish'd first in royal halls,   55
  The welcome vices kindly greet),

Ev'n now thou'rt nightly seen to add
  One insect to the fluttering crowd;
And still thy trifling heart is glad   59
  To join the vain and court the proud.

There dost thou glide from fair to fair,
  Still simpering on with eager haste,
As flies along the gay parterre
  That taint the flowers they scarcely taste.

But say, what nymph will prize the flame
  Which seems, as marshy vapours move,
To flit along from dame to dame,   67
  An ignis-fatuus gleam of love?

What friend for thee, howe'er inclined,
  Will deign to own a kindred care?   70
Who will debase his manly mind,
  For friendship every fool may share?

In time forbear; amidst the throng
  No more so base a thing be seen;
No more so idly pass along;   75
  Be something, anything, but—mean.
                           1808.

LINES INSCRIBED UPON A CUP FORMED FROM A SKULL

START not—nor deem my spirit fled;
  In me behold the only skull,
From which, unlike a living head,
  Whatever flows is never dull.

I lived, I loved, I quaff'd, like thee: 5
  I died: let earth my bones resign;
Fill up—thou canst not injure me;
  The worm hath fouler lips than thine.

Better to hold the sparkling grape,
  Than nurse the earth-worm's slimy
    brood;   10
And circle in the goblet's shape
  The drink of gods, than reptile's food.

Where once my wit, perchance, hath shone,
  In aid of others' let me shine;
And when, alas! our brains are gone, 15
  What nobler substitute than wine?

Quaff while thou canst: another race,
  When thou and thine, like me, are sped,
May rescue thee from earth's embrace,
  And rhyme and revel with the dead.

Why not? since through life's little day
  Our heads such sad effects produce;
Redeem'd from worms and wasting clay,
  This chance is theirs, to be of use.
               Newstead Abbey, 1808.

WELL! THOU ART HAPPY

WELL! thou art happy, and I feel
  That I should thus be happy too;
For still my heart regards thy weal
  Warmly, as it was wont to do.   4

Thy husband's blest—and 'twill impart
  Some pangs to view his happier lot:
But let them pass—Oh! how my heart
  Would hate him if he loved thee not!

When late I saw thy favourite child, 9
  I thought my jealous heart would break;
But when the unconscious infant smiled,
  I kiss'd it for its mother's sake. 12

I kiss'd it,—and repress'd my sighs
  Its father in its face to see;
But then it had its mother's eyes, 15
  And they were all to love and me.

Mary, adieu! I must away:
  While thou art blest I'll not repine;
But near thee I can never stay; 19
  My heart would soon again be thine.

I deem'd that time, I deem'd that pride,
  Had quench'd at length my boyish
    flame;
Nor knew, till seated by thy side,
  My heart in all,—save hope,—the same.

Yet was I calm: I knew the time   25
  My breast would thrill before thy look;
But now to tremble were a crime—
  We met,—and not a nerve was shook.

I saw thee gaze upon my face,
  Yet meet with no confusion there: 30
One only feeling could'st thou trace;
  The sullen calmness of despair.

Away! away! my early dream
  Remembrance never must awake:
Oh! where is Lethe's fabled stream? 35
  My foolish heart, be still, or break.
                  November 2, 1808.

INSCRIPTION ON THE MONUMENT OF A NEWFOUNDLAND DOG

WHEN some proud son of man returns to
    earth,
Unknown to glory, but upheld by birth,
The sculptor's art exhausts the pomp of
    woe,
And storied urns record who rest below:
When all is done, upon the tomb is seen,
Not what he was, but what he should
    have been: 6
But the poor dog, in life the firmest friend,
The first to welcome, foremost to defend,
Whose honest heart is still his master's
    own,
Who labours, fights, lives, breathes for
    him alone,   10
Unhonour'd falls, unnoticed all his worth,
Denied in heaven the soul he held on earth,
While man, vain insect! hopes to be for-
    given,
And claims himself a sole exclusive heaven.
Oh man! thou feeble tenant of an hour,
Debased by slavery, or corrupt by power,
Who knows thee well must quit thee with
    disgust,   17
Degraded mass of animated dust!
Thy love is lust, thy friendship all a cheat,
Thy smiles hypocrisy, thy words deceit!
By nature vile, ennobled but by name,
Each kindred brute might bid thee blush
    for shame.
Ye! who perchance behold this simple urn,
Pass on—it honours none you wish to
    mourn:
To mark a friend's remains these stones
    arise;   25
I never knew but one,—and here he lies.
          Newstead Abbey, *November* 30, 1808.

TO A LADY

ON BEING ASKED MY REASON FOR QUITTING
ENGLAND IN THE SPRING

WHEN Man, expell'd from Eden's bowers,
  A moment linger'd near the gate,
Each scene recall'd the vanish'd hours,
  And bade him curse his future fate.

But, wandering on through distant climes,
  He learnt to bear his load of grief; 6
Just gave a sigh to other times,
  And found in busier scenes relief.

Thus, lady! will it be with me,
  And I must view thy charms no more;
For, while I linger, near to thee, 11
  I sigh for all I knew before.

In flight I shall be surely wise,
  Escaping from temptation's snare;
I cannot view my paradise 15
  Without the wish of dwelling there.

December 2, 1808.

REMIND ME NOT, REMIND ME NOT

REMIND me not, remind me not,
  Of those beloved, those vanish'd hours,
When all my soul was given to thee;
  Hours that may never be forgot,
Till time unnerves our vital powers, 5
  And thou and I shall cease to be.

Can I forget—canst thou forget,
  When playing with thy golden hair,
How quick thy fluttering heart did
    move?
Oh! by my soul, I see thee yet, 10
  With eyes so languid, breast so fair,
And lips, though silent, breathing
    love.

When thus reclining on my breast,
  Those eyes threw back a glance so sweet,
As half reproach'd yet raised desire,
And still we near and nearer prest, 16
  And still our glowing lips would meet,
As if in kisses to expire.

And then those pensive eyes would close,
  And bid their lids each other seek, 20
Veiling the azure orbs below;
While their long lashes' darken'd gloss
  Seem'd stealing o'er thy brilliant cheek,
Like raven's plumage smooth'd on
    snow.

I dreamt last night our love return'd, 25
  And, sooth to say, that very dream
    Was sweeter in its phantasy,
Than if for other hearts I burn'd,
  For eyes that ne'er like thine could
    beam
    In rapture's wild reality. 30

Then tell me not, remind me not,
  Of hours which, though for ever gone,
    Can still a pleasing dream restore,
Till thou and I shall be forgot, 34
  And senseless, as the mouldering stone
    Which tells that we shall be no more.

THERE WAS A TIME, I NEED NOT NAME

THERE was a time, I need not name,
  Since it will ne'er forgotten be,
When all our feelings were the same
  As still my soul hath been to thee.

And from that hour when first thy tongue
  Confess'd a love which equall'd mine,
Though many a grief my heart hath
    wrung, 7
  Unknown, and thus unfelt, by thine,

None, none hath sunk so deep as this—
  To think how all that love hath flown;
Transient as every faithless kiss, 11
  But transient in thy breast alone.

And yet my heart some solace knew,
  When late I heard thy lips declare,
In accents once imagined true, 15
  Remembrance of the days that were.

Yes! my adored, yet most unkind!
  Though thou wilt never love again,
To me 'tis doubly sweet to find
  Remembrance of that love remain. 20

Yes! 'tis a glorious thought to me,
  Nor longer shall my soul repine,
Whate'er thou art or e'er shalt be,
  Thou hast been dearly, solely mine.

AND WILT THOU WEEP WHEN I AM LOW?

AND wilt thou weep when I am low?
  Sweet lady! speak those words again:
Yet if they grieve thee, say not so—
  I would not give that bosom pain.

My heart is sad, my hopes are gone, 5
  My blood runs coldly through my
    breast;
And when I perish, thou alone
  Wilt sigh above my place of rest.

And yet, methinks, a gleam of peace
  Doth through my cloud of anguish
    shine: 10
And for a while my sorrows cease,
  To know thy heart hath felt for mine.

Oh lady! blessed be that tear—
  It falls for one who cannot weep;
Such precious drops are doubly dear 15
  To those whose eyes no tear may steep.

Sweet lady! once my heart was warm
  With every feeling soft as thine;
But beauty's self hath ceased to charm
  A wretch created to repine.   20

Yet wilt thou weep when I am low?
  Sweet lady! speak those words again:
Yet if they grieve thee, say not so—
  I would not give that bosom pain.

FILL THE GOBLET AGAIN

A SONG

FILL the goblet again! for I never before
Felt the glow which now gladdens my
    heart to its core;
Let us drink!—who would not?—since,
    through life's varied round,
In the goblet alone no deception is found.

I have tried in its turn all that life can
    supply;   5
I have bask'd in the beam of a dark rolling
    eye;
I have loved!—who has not?—but what
    heart can declare
That pleasure existed while passion was
    there?

In the days of my youth, when the heart's
    in its spring,
And dreams that affection can never take
    wing,   10
I had friends!—who has not?— but what
    tongue will avow,
That friends, rosy wine! are so faithful as
    thou?

The heart of a mistress some boy may
    estrange,
Friendship shifts with the sunbeam—thou
    never canst change;
Thou grow'st old—who does not?— but
    on earth what appears,   15
Whose virtues, like thine, still increase
    with its years?

Yet if blest to the utmost that love can
    bestow,
Should a rival bow down to our idol
    below,
We are jealous!—who 's not?—thou hast
    no such alloy;
For the more that enjoy thee, the more
    we enjoy.   20

Then the season of youth and its vanities
    past,
For refuge we fly to the goblet at last;
There we find—do we not?—in the flow
    of the soul,
That truth, as of yore, is confined to the
    bowl.

When the box of Pandora was opened on
    earth,   25
And Misery's triumph commenced over
    Mirth,
Hope was left,—was she not?—but the
    goblet we kiss,
And care not for Hope, who are certain
    of bliss.

Long life to the grape! for when summer
    is flown,
The age of our nectar shall gladden our
    own: 30
We must die—who shall not?—May our
    sins be forgiven,
And Hebe shall never be idle in heaven.

STANZAS TO A LADY, ON LEAVING ENGLAND

'TIS done—and shivering in the gale
The bark unfurls her snowy sail;
And whistling o'er the bending mast,
Loud sings on high the fresh'ning blast;
And I must from this land be gone,   5
Because I cannot love but one.

But could I be what I have been,
And could I see what I have seen—
Could I repose upon the breast
Which once my warmest wishes blest—
I should not seek another zone   11
Because I cannot love but one.

'Tis long since I beheld that eye
Which gave me bliss or misery;
And I have striven, but in vain,   15
Never to think of it again:
For though I fly from Albion,
I still can only love but one.

As some lone bird, without a mate,
My weary heart is desolate;   20
I look around, and cannot trace
One friendly smile or welcome face,
And ev'n in crowds am still alone,
Because I cannot love but one.

And I will cross the whitening foam,   25
And I will seek a foreign home;
Till I forget a false fair face,
I ne'er shall find a resting-place;
My own dark thoughts I cannot shun,
But ever love, and love but one.   30

The poorest, veriest wretch on earth
Still finds some hospitable hearth,
Where friendship's or love's softer glow
May smile in joy or soothe in woe;
But friend or leman I have none,   35
Because I cannot love but one.

I go—but wheresoe'er I flee
There's not an eye will weep for me;
There's not a kind congenial heart,
Where I can claim the meanest part; 40
Nor thou, who hast my hopes undone,
Wilt sigh, although I love but one.

To think of every early scene,
Of what we are, and what we've been,
Would whelm some softer hearts with
    woe— 45
But mine, alas! has stood the blow:
Yet still beats on as it begun,
And never truly loves but one.

And who that dear loved one may be,
Is not for vulgar eyes to see; 50
And why that early love was cross'd,
Thou know'st the best, I feel the most:
But few that dwell beneath the sun
Have loved so long, and loved but one.

I've tried another's fetters too, 55
With charms perchance as fair to view;
And I would fain have loved as well,
But some unconquerable spell
Forbade my bleeding breast to own
A kindred care for aught but one. 60

'Twould soothe to take one lingering view,
And bless thee in my last adieu;
Yet wish I not those eyes to weep
For him that wanders o'er the deep; 64
His home, his hope, his youth are gone,
Yet still he loves, and loves but one.
                    1809.

LINES TO MR. HODGSON

WRITTEN ON BOARD THE LISBON PACKET

Huzza! Hodgson, we are going,
  Our embargo's off at last;
Favourable breezes blowing
  Bend the canvas o'er the mast.
From aloft the signal's streaming, 5
  Hark! the farewell gun is fired;
Women screeching, tars blaspheming,
  Tell us that our time's expired.
      Here's a rascal
      Come to task all, 10
  Prying from the custom-house,
      Trunks unpacking,
      Cases cracking,
  Not a corner for a mouse
'Scapes unsearch'd amid the racket, 15
Ere we sail on board the Packet.

Now our boatmen quit their mooring,
  And all hands must ply the oar;
Baggage from the quay is lowering,
  We're impatient, push from shore. 20
'Have a care! that case holds liquor—
  Stop the boat—I'm sick—oh Lord!'

'Sick, ma'am, damme, you'll be sicker
Ere you've been an hour on board.'
      Thus are screaming 25
      Men and women,
  Gemmen, ladies, servants, Jacks;
      Here entangling,
      All are wrangling,
  Stuck together close as wax.— 30
Such the general noise and racket,
Ere we reach the Lisbon Packet.

Now we've reach'd her, lo! the captain,
  Gallant Kidd, commands the crew;
Passengers their berths are clapt in, 35
  Some to grumble, some to spew.
'Heyday! call you that a cabin?
  Why 'tis hardly three feet square:
Not enough to stow Queen Mab in—
  Who the deuce can harbour there?' 40
      'Who, sir? plenty—
      Nobles twenty
  Did at once my vessel fill.'—
      'Did they? Jesus,
      How you squeeze us! 45
  Would to God they did so still:
Then I'd scape the heat and racket
Of the good ship, Lisbon Packet.'

Fletcher! Murray! Bob! where are you?
  Stretch'd along the deck like logs—
Bear a hand, you jolly tar, you! 51
  Here's a rope's end for the dogs.
Hobhouse muttering fearful curses,
  As the hatchway down he rolls,
Now his breakfast, now his verses, 55
  Vomits forth—and damns our souls.
      'Here's a stanza
      On Braganza—
  Help!'—'A couplet?'—'No, a cup
      Of warm water—' 60
      'What's the matter?'
  'Zounds! my liver's coming up:
I shall not survive the racket
Of this brutal Lisbon Packet.'

Now at length we're off for Turkey, 65
  Lord knows when we shall come back!
Breezes foul and tempests murky
  May unship us in a crack.
But, since life at most a jest is,
  As philosophers allow, 70
Still to laugh by far the best is,
  Then laugh on—as I do now.
      Laugh at all things,
      Great and small things,
  Sick or well, at sea or shore; 75
      While we're quaffing,
      Let's have laughing—
  Who the devil cares for more?—
Some good wine! and who would lack it,
Ev'n on board the Lisbon Packet? 80
        Falmouth Roads, *June* 30, 1809.
        [First published, 1830.]

OCCASIONAL PIECES

TO FLORENCE

Oh Lady! when I left the shore,
   The distant shore which gave me birth,
I hardly thought to grieve once more
   To quit another spot on earth:

Yet here, amidst this barren isle,   5
   Where panting Nature droops the head,
Where only thou art seen to smile,
   I view my parting hour with dread.

Though far from Albin's craggy shore,
   Divided by the dark-blue main;   10
A few, brief, rolling seasons o'er,
   Perchance I view her cliffs again:

But wheresoe'er I now may roam,
   Through scorching clime, and varied
      sea,   14
Though Time restore me to my home,
   I ne'er shall bend mine eyes on thee:

On thee, in whom at once conspire
   All charms which heedless hearts can
      move,
Whom but to see is to admire,   19
   And, oh! forgive the word—to love.

Forgive the word, in one who ne'er
   With but a word can more offend;
And since thy heart I cannot share,
   Believe me, what I am, thy friend.

And who so cold as look on thee,   25
   Thou lovely wand'rer, and be less?
Nor be, what man should ever be,
   The friend of Beauty in distress?

Ah! who would think that form had past
   Through Danger's most destructive
      path,   30
Had braved the death-wing'd tempest's
      blast,
   And 'scaped a tyrant's fiercer wrath?

Lady! when I shall view the walls
   Where free Byzantium once arose,
And Stamboul's Oriental halls   35
   The Turkish tyrants now enclose;

Though mightiest in the lists of fame,
   That glorious city still shall be;
On me 'twill hold a dearer claim,
   As spot of thy nativity: 40

And though I bid thee now farewell,
   When I behold that wondrous scene,
Since where thou art I may not dwell,
   'Twill soothe to be where thou hast
      been.
          September 1809.

LINES WRITTEN IN AN ALBUM, AT MALTA

As o'er the cold sepulchral stone
   Some name arrests the passer-by;
Thus, when thou view'st this page alone,
   May mine attract thy pensive eye!

And when by thee that name is read,   5
   Perchance in some succeeding year,
Reflect on me as on the dead,
   And think my heart is buried here.
          September 14, 1809.

STANZAS COMPOSED DURING A THUNDER-STORM

Chill and mirk is the nightly blast,
   Where Pindus' mountains rise,
And angry clouds are pouring fast
   The vengeance of the skies.

Our guides are gone, our hope is lost,   5
   And lightnings, as they play,
But show where rocks our path have crost,
   Or gild the torrent's spray.

Is yon a cot I saw, though low?
   When lightning broke the gloom—   10
How welcome were its shade!—ah, no!
   'Tis but a Turkish tomb.

Through sounds of foaming waterfalls,
   I hear a voice exclaim—
My way-worn countryman, who calls   15
   On distant England's name.

A shot is fired—by foe or friend?
   Another—'tis to tell
The mountain-peasants to descend,
   And lead us where they dwell.   20

Oh! who in such a night will dare
   To tempt the wilderness?
And who 'mid thunder-peals can hear
   Our signal of distress?

And who that heard our shouts would
      rise   25
   To try the dubious road?
Nor rather deem from nightly cries
   That outlaws were abroad.

Clouds burst, skies flash, oh, dreadful
      hour!
   More fiercely pours the storm!   30
Yet here one thought has still the power
   To keep my bosom warm.

While wandering through each broken
      path,
   O'er brake and craggy brow;
While elements exhaust their wrath,   35
   Sweet Florence, where art thou?

Not on the sea, not on the sea,
　Thy bark hath long been gone:
Oh, may the storm that pours on me
　Bow down my head alone!　　　　40

Full swiftly blew the swift Siroc,
　When last I press'd thy lip;
And long ere now, with foaming shock
　Impell'd thy gallant ship.

Now thou art safe; nay, long ere now
　Hast trod the shore of Spain;　　46
'Twere hard if aught so fair as thou
　Should linger on the main.

And since I now remember thee
　In darkness and in dread,　　　50
As in those hours of revelry
　Which mirth and music sped;

Do thou, amid the fair white walls,
　If Cadiz yet be free,
At times from out her latticed halls　55
　Look o'er the dark blue sea;

Then think upon Calypso's isles,
　Endear'd by days gone by;
To others give a thousand smiles,
　To me a single sigh.　　　　　　60

And when the admiring circle mark
　The paleness of thy face,
A half-form'd tear, a transient spark
　Of melancholy grace,

Again thou'lt smile, and blushing shun
　Some coxcomb's raillery,　　　66
Nor own for once thou thought'st on one,
　Who ever thinks on thee.

Though smile and sigh alike are vain,
　When sever'd hearts repine,　　70
My spirit flies o'er mount and main,
　And mourns in search of thine.

STANZAS WRITTEN IN PASSING 'THE AMBRACIAN GULF

Through cloudless skies, in silvery sheen,
　Full beams the moon on Actium's
　　coast:
And on these waves, for Egypt's queen,
　The ancient world was won and lost.

And now upon the scene I look,　　5
　The azure grave of many a Roman;
Where stern Ambition once forsook
　His wavering crown to follow woman.

Florence! whom I will love as well
　As ever yet was said or sung　　10
(Since Orpheus sang his spouse from hell),
　Whilst thou art fair and I am young;

Sweet Florence! those were pleasant times,
　When worlds were staked for ladies'
　　eyes:　　　　　　　　　　　14
Had bards as many realms as rhymes,
　Thy charms might raise new Antonies.

Though Fate forbids such things to be,
　Yet, by thine eyes and ringlets curl'd!
I cannot lose a world for thee,
　But would not lose thee for a world.
　　　　　　　　　　　　Nov. 14, 1809.

THE SPELL IS BROKE, THE CHARM IS FLOWN!

WRITTEN AT ATHENS, JANUARY 16, 1810

The spell is broke, the charm is flown!
　Thus is it with life's fitful fever:
We madly smile when we should groan:
　Delirium is our best deceiver.

Each lucid interval of thought　　　5
　Recalls the woes of Nature's charter;
And he that acts as wise men ought,
　But lives, as saints have died, a martyr.

WRITTEN AFTER SWIMMING FROM SESTOS TO ABYDOS

If, in the month of dark December,
　Leander, who was nightly wont
(What maid will not the tale remember?)
　To cross thy stream, broad Hellespont!

If, when the wintry tempest roar'd,　5
　He sped to Hero, nothing loth,
And thus of old thy current pour'd,
　Fair Venus! how I pity both!

For *me*, degenerate modern wretch,
　Though in the genial month of May,
My dripping limbs I faintly stretch,　11
　And think I've done a feat to-day.

But since he cross'd the rapid tide,
　According to the doubtful story,
To woo,—and—Lord knows what be-
　　side,　　　　　　　　　　　15
　And swam for Love, as I for Glory;

'Twere hard to say who fared the best:
　Sad mortals! thus the gods still plague
　　you!
He lost his labour, I my jest;　　　19
　For he was drown'd, and I've the ague.
　　　　　　　　　　　　May 9, 1810.

LINES IN THE TRAVELLERS' BOOK AT ORCHOMENUS

IN THIS BOOK A TRAVELLER HAD WRITTEN:—

'Fair Albion, smiling, sees her son depart
To trace the birth and nursery of art:
Noble his object, glorious is his aim;
He comes to Athens, and he writes his
　name.'

OCCASIONAL PIECES

BENEATH WHICH LORD BYRON INSERTED THE FOLLOWING:—

THE modest bard, like many a bard un-
　known,
Rhymes on our names, but wisely hides
　his own;
But yet, whoe'er he be, to say no worse,
His name would bring more credit than
　his verse.

1810.

MAID OF ATHENS, ERE WE PART

Ζωή μου, σᾶς ἀγαπῶ.

MAID of Athens, ere we part,
Give, oh give me back my heart!
Or, since that has left my breast,
Keep it now, and take the rest!
Hear my vow before I go,　　　　5
Ζωή μου, σᾶς ἀγαπῶ.

By those tresses unconfined,
Woo'd by each Ægean wind;
By those lids whose jetty fringe
Kiss thy soft cheeks' blooming tinge;
By those wild eyes like the roe,　　11
Ζωή μου, σᾶς ἀγαπῶ.

By that lip I long to taste;
By that zone-encircled waist;
By all the token-flowers that tell　15
What words can never speak so well;
By love's alternate joy and woe,
Ζωή μου, σᾶς ἀγαπῶ.

Maid of Athens! I am gone:
Think of me, sweet! when alone.　　20
Though I fly to Istambol,
Athens holds my heart and soul:
Can I cease to love thee? No!
Ζωή μου, σᾶς ἀγαπῶ.

Athens, 1810.

TRANSLATION OF THE NURSE'S DOLE IN THE MEDEA OF EURIPIDES

OH how I wish that an embargo
Had kept in port the good ship Argo!
Who, still unlaunch'd from Grecian docks,
Had never pass'd the Azure rocks;
But now I fear her trip will be a　　5
Damn'd business for my Miss Medea,
&c. &c.

June 1810.

MY EPITAPH

YOUTH, Nature, and relenting Jove,
To keep my lamp *in* strongly strove;
But Romanelli was so stout,
He beat all three—and *blew* it *out.*

Oct. 1810.

SUBSTITUTE FOR AN EPITAPH

KIND Reader! take your choice to cry or
　laugh;
Here HAROLD lies—but where's his Epi-
　taph?
If such you seek, try Westminster, and
　view
Ten thousand just as fit for him as you.

Athens.

LINES WRITTEN BENEATH A PICTURE

DEAR object of defeated care!
Though now of Love and thee bereft,
To reconcile me with despair,
Thine image and my tears are left.

'Tis said with Sorrow Time can cope;　5
But this I feel can ne'er be true:
For by the death-blow of my Hope
My Memory immortal grew.

Athens, *January* 1811.

TRANSLATION OF THE FAMOUS GREEK WAR SONG

Δεῦτε παῖδες τῶν Ἑλλήνων.

SONS of the Greeks, arise!
　The glorious hour's gone forth,
And, worthy of such ties,
　Display who gave us birth.

CHORUS.

Sons of Greeks! let us go　　　　5
In arms against the foe,
Till their hated blood shall flow
In a river past our feet.

Then manfully despising
　The Turkish tyrant's yoke,　　　10
Let your country see you rising,
　And all her chains are broke.
Brave shades of chiefs and sages,
　Behold the coming strife!
Hellénes of past ages,　　　　　15
　Oh, start again to life!
At the sound of my trumpet, breaking
　Your sleep, oh, join with me!
And the seven-hill'd city seeking,
　Fight, conquer, till we're free.　20

Sons of Greeks, &c.

Sparta, Sparta, why in slumbers
　Lethargic dost thou lie?
Awake, and join thy numbers
　With Athens, old ally!
Leonidas recalling,　　　　　　25
　That chief of ancient song,
Who saved ye once from falling,
　The terrible! the strong!

Who made that bold diversion
In old Thermopylæ,   30
And warring with the Persian
To keep his country free;
With his three hundred waging
The battle, long he stood,
And like a lion raging,   35
Expired in seas of blood.

Sons of Greeks, &c.

TRANSLATION OF THE ROMAIC SONG

"Μπένω μες' τὸ περιβόλι
Ὡραιοτάτη Χαηδή," κ.τ.λ.

I ENTER thy garden of roses,
Beloved and fair Haidée,
Each morning where Flora reposes,
For surely I see her in thee.
Oh, Lovely! thus low I implore thee,   5
Receive this fond truth from my
tongue,
Which utters its song to adore thee,
Yet trembles for what it has sung;
As the branch, at the bidding of Nature,
Adds fragrance and fruit to the tree,
Through her eyes, through her every
feature,   11
Shines the soul of the young Haidée.

But the loveliest garden grows hateful
When Love has abandon'd the bowers;
Bring me hemlock—since mine is un-
grateful,   15
That herb is more fragrant than flowers.
The poison, when pour'd from the chalice,
Will deeply embitter the bowl;
But when drunk to escape from thy malice,
The draught shall be sweet to my soul.
Too cruel! in vain I implore thee   21
My heart from these horrors to save:
Will nought to my bosom restore thee?
Then open the gates of the grave.

As the chief who to combat advances   25
Secure of his conquest before,
Thus thou, with those eyes for thy lances,
Hast pierced through my heart to its
core.
Ah, tell me, my soul! must I perish
By pangs which a smile would dispel?
Would the hope, which thou once bad'st
me cherish,   31
For torture repay me too well?
Now sad is the garden of roses,
Beloved but false Haidée!
There Flora all wither'd reposes,   35
And mourns o'er thine absence with me.
1811.

ON PARTING

THE kiss, dear maid! thy lip has left
Shall never part from mine,
Till happier hours restore the gift
Untainted back to thine.

Thy parting glance, which fondly beams,
An equal love may see: 6
The tear that from thine eyelid streams
Can weep no change in me.

I ask no pledge to make me blest
In gazing when alone;   10
Nor one memorial for a breast,
Whose thoughts are all thine own.

Nor need I write—to tell the tale
My pen were doubly weak:
Oh! what can idle words avail,   15
Unless the heart could speak?

By day or night, in weal or woe,
That heart, no longer free,
Must bear the love it cannot show,
And silent ache for thee.   20

March 1811.

EPITAPH FOR JOSEPH BLACKETT, LATE POET AND SHOEMAKER

STRANGER! behold, interr'd together,
The *souls* of learning and of leather.
Poor Joe is gone, but left his *all:*
You'll find his relics in a *stall.*
His works were neat, and often found   5
Well stitch'd, and with *morocco* bound.
Tread lightly—where the bard is laid
He cannot mend the shoe he made;
Yet is he happy in his hole,
With verse immortal as his *sole.*   10
But still to business he held fast,
And stuck to Phœbus to the last.
Then who shall say so good a fellow
Was only 'leather and prunella?'
For character—he did not lack it;   15
And if he did, 'twere shame to 'Black it.'

Malta, May 16, 1811.

FAREWELL TO MALTA

ADIEU, ye joys of La Valette!
Adieu, sirocco, sun, and sweat!
Adieu, thou palace rarely enter'd!
Adieu, ye mansions where—I've ventured!
Adieu, ye cursed streets of stairs!   5
(How surely he who mounts you swears!)
Adieu, ye merchants often failing!
Adieu, thou mob for ever railing!
Adieu, ye packets—without letters!
Adieu, ye fools—who ape your betters!
Adieu, thou damned'st quarantine,   11
That gave me fever, and the spleen!
Adieu, that stage which makes us yawn,
Sirs,
Adieu, his Excellency's dancers!
Adieu to Peter—whom no fault's in,   15
But could not teach a colonel waltzing!
Adieu, ye females fraught with graces!
Adieu, red coats, and redder faces!
Adieu, the supercilious air
Of all that strut 'en militaire'!   20

OCCASIONAL PIECES

I go—but God knows when, or why,
To smoky towns and cloudy sky,
To things (the honest truth to say)
As bad—but in a different way.

Farewell to these, but not adieu,   25
Triumphant sons of truest blue!
While either Adriatic shore,
And fallen chiefs, and fleets no more,
And nightly smiles, and daily dinners,
Proclaim you war and woman's winners.
Pardon my Muse, who apt to prate is,
And take my rhyme—because 'tis 'gratis.'

And now I've got to Mrs. Fraser,
Perhaps you think I mean to praise her—
And were I vain enough to think   35
My praise was worth this drop of ink,
A line—or two—were no hard matter,
As here, indeed, I need not flatter:
But she must be content to shine
In better praises than in mine,   40
With lively air, and open heart,
And fashion's ease, without its art;
Her hours can gaily glide along,
Nor ask the aid of idle song.

And now, O Malta! since thou'st got us,
Thou little military hothouse!   46
I'll not offend with words uncivil,
And wish thee rudely at the Devil,
But only stare from out my casement,
And ask, for what is such a place meant?
Then, in my solitary nook,   51
Return to scribbling, or a book,
Or take my physic while I'm able
(Two spoonfuls hourly by the label),
Prefer my nightcap to my beaver,   55
And bless the gods I've got a fever.

May 26, 1811.
[First published, 1816.]

TO DIVES

A FRAGMENT

UNHAPPY DIVES! in an evil hour
'Gainst Nature's voice seduced to deeds
accurst!
Once Fortune's minion, now thou feel'st
her power;
Wrath's vial on thy lofty head hath
burst.   4
In Wit, in Genius, as in Wealth the first,
How wondrous bright thy blooming morn
arose!
But thou wert smitten with th' unhallow'd
thirst
Of crime un-named, and thy sad noon
must close
In scorn, and solitude unsought, the worst
of woes.

1811. [First published, 1832.]

ON MOORE'S LAST OPERATIC FARCE, OR FARCICAL OPERA

GOOD plays are scarce,
So Moore writes farce:
The poet's fame grows brittle—
We knew before
That *Little*'s Moore,   5
But now 'tis *Moore* that's *little*.

September 14, 1811.
[First published, 1830.]

EPISTLE TO A FRIEND

IN ANSWER TO SOME LINES EXHORTING THE
AUTHOR TO BE CHEERFUL, AND TO 'BAN-
ISH CARE'

'OH! banish care'—such ever be
The motto of *thy* revelry!
Perchance of *mine*, when wassail nights
Renew those riotous delights,
Wherewith the children of Despair   5
Lull the lone heart, and 'banish care.'
But not in morn's reflecting hour,
When present, past, and future lower,
When all I loved is changed or gone,   9
Mock with such taunts the woes of one,
Whose every thought—but let them pass—
Thou know'st I am not what I was.
But, above all, if thou wouldst hold
Place in a heart that ne'er was cold,
By all the powers that men revere,   15
By all unto thy bosom dear,
Thy joys below, thy hopes above,
Speak—speak of anything but love.

'Twere long to tell, and vain to hear,
The tale of one who scorns a tear;   20
And there is little in that tale
Which better bosoms would bewail.
But mine has suffer'd more than well
'Twould suit philosophy to tell.
I've seen my bride another's bride,—   25
Have seen her seated by his side,—
Have seen the infant, which she bore,
Wear the sweet smile the mother wore,
When she and I in youth have smiled,
As fond and faultless as her child;   30
Have seen her eyes, in cold disdain,
Ask if I felt no secret pain;
And *I* have acted well my part,
And made my cheek belie my heart,
Return'd the freezing glance she gave,
Yet felt the while *that* woman's slave;—
Have kiss'd, as if without design,
The babe which ought to have been mine,
And show'd, alas! in each caress
Time had not made me love the less.   40

But let this pass—I'll whine no more,
Nor seek again an eastern shore;
The world befits a busy brain,—
I'll hie me to its haunts again.

62

But if, in some succeeding year,   45
When Britain's 'May is in the sere,'
Thou hear'st of one whose deepening crimes
Suit with the sablest of the times,
Of one, whom love nor pity sways,
Nor hope of fame, nor good men's praise;
One, who in stern ambition's pride,   51
Perchance not blood shall turn aside;
One rank'd in some recording page
With the worst anarchs of the age,
Him wilt thou *know*—and *knowing* pause,
Nor with the *effect* forget the cause.   56

Newstead Abbey, *Oct.* 11, 1811.
[First published, 1830.]

TO THYRZA

WITHOUT a stone to mark the spot,
    And say, what Truth might well have said,
By all, save one, perchance forgot,
    Ah! wherefore art thou lowly laid?

By many a shore and many a sea   5
    Divided, yet beloved in vain;
The past, the future fled to thee,
    To bid us meet—no—ne'er again!

Could this have been—a word, a look,
    That softly said, 'We part in peace,'
Had taught my bosom how to brook,   11
    With fainter sighs, thy soul's release.

And didst thou not, since Death for thee
    Prepared a light and pangless dart,
Once look on him thou ne'er shalt see,
    Who held, and holds thee in his heart?

Oh! who like him had watch'd thee here?
    Or sadly mark'd thy glazing eye,
In that dread hour ere death appear,
    When silent sorrow fears to sigh,   20

Till all was past? But when no more
    'Twas thine to reck of human woe,
Affection's heart-drops, gushing o'er,
    Had flow'd as fast—as now they flow.

Shall they not flow, when many a day
    In these, to me, deserted towers,   26
Ere call'd but for a time away,
    Affection's mingling tears were ours?

Ours too the glance none saw beside;
    The smile none else might understand;
The whisper'd thought of hearts allied,
    The pressure of the thrilling hand;   32

The kiss, so guiltless and refined,
    That Love each warmer wish forbore;
Those eyes proclaim'd so pure a mind,
    Even Passion blush'd to plead for more.

The tone, that taught me to rejoice,
    When prone, unlike thee, to repine;
The song, celestial from thy voice,
    But sweet to me from none but thine;

The pledge we wore—I wear it still,   41
    But where is thine?—Ah! where art thou?
Oft have I borne the weight of ill,
    But never bent beneath till now!

Well hast thou left in life's best bloom
    The cup of woe for me to drain.   46
If rest alone be in the tomb,
    I would not wish thee here again.

But if in worlds more blest than this
    Thy virtues seek a fitter sphere,   50
Impart some portion of thy bliss,
    To wean me from mine anguish here.

Teach me—too early taught by thee!
    To bear, forgiving and forgiven:
On earth thy love was such to me;   55
    It fain would form my hope in heaven!

October 11, 1811.

AWAY, AWAY, YE NOTES OF WOE!

AWAY, away, ye notes of woe!
    Be silent, thou once soothing strain,
Or I must flee from hence—for, oh!
    I dare not trust those sounds again.
To me they speak of brighter days—   5
    But lull the chords, for now, alas!
I must not think, I may not gaze,
    On what I am—on what I was.

The voice that made those sounds more sweet
    Is hush'd, and all their charms are fled
And now their softest notes repeat   11
    A dirge, an anthem o'er the dead!
Yes, Thyrza! yes, they breathe of thee,
    Beloved dust! since dust thou art;
And all that once was harmony   15
    Is worse than discord to my heart!

'Tis silent all!—but on my ear
    The well remember'd echoes thrill;
I hear a voice I would not hear,   19
    A voice that now might well be still:
Yet oft my doubting soul 'twill shake;
    Even slumber owns its gentle tone,
Till consciousness will vainly wake
    To listen, though the dream be flown.

Sweet Thyrza! waking as in sleep,   25
    Thou art but now a lovely dream;
A star that trembled o'er the deep,
    Then turn'd from earth its tender beam.
But he who through life's dreary way
    Must pass, when heaven is veil'd in wrath,   30
Will long lament the vanish'd ray
    That scatter'd gladness o'er his path.

December 6, 1811.

63   D

ONE STRUGGLE MORE, AND I AM FREE

ONE struggle more, and I am free
　From pangs that rend my heart in twain;
One last long sigh to love and thee,
　Then back to busy life again.
It suits me well to mingle now　　5
　With things that never pleased before!
Though every joy is fled below,
　What future grief can touch me more?

Then bring me wine, the banquet bring;
　Man was not form'd to live alone:　10
I'll be that light, unmeaning thing
　That smiles with all, and weeps with
　　none.
It was not thus in days more dear,
　It never would have been, but thou
Hast fled, and left me lonely here;　15
　Thou'rt nothing—all are nothing now.

In vain my lyre would lightly breathe!
　The smile that sorrow fain would wear
But mocks the woe that lurks beneath,
　Like roses o'er a sepulchre.　　20
Though gay companions o'er the bowl
　Dispel awhile the sense of ill:
Though pleasure fires the maddening soul,
　The heart,—the heart is lonely still!

On many a lone and lovely night　25
　It sooth'd to gaze upon the sky;
For then I deem'd the heavenly light
　Shone sweetly on thy pensive eye:
And oft I thought at Cynthia's noon,
　When sailing o'er the Ægean wave,
'Now Thyrza gazes on that moon'—
　Alas, it gleam'd upon her grave!　32

When stretch'd on fever's sleepless bed,
　And sickness shrunk my throbbing
　　veins,
'Tis comfort still,' I faintly said,　35
　'That Thyrza cannot know my pains:'
Like freedom to the time-worn slave,
　A boon 'tis idle then to give,
Relenting Nature vainly gave
　My life, when Thyrza ceased to live!

My Thyrza's pledge in better days,　41
　When love and life alike were new!
How different now thou meet'st my gaze!
　How tinged by time with sorrow's hue!
The heart that gave itself with thee　45
　Is silent—ah, were mine as still!
Though cold as e'en the dead can be,
　It feels, it sickens with the chill.

Thou bitter pledge! thou mournful token!
　Though painful, welcome to my breast!
Still, still preserve that love unbroken,
　Or break the heart to which thou'rt
　　press'd.

Time tempers love, but not removes,
　More hallow'd when its hope is fled:
Oh! what are thousand living loves　55
　To that which cannot quit the dead?

EUTHANASIA

WHEN Time, or soon or late, shall bring
　The dreamless sleep that lulls the dead,
Oblivion! may thy languid wing
　Wave gently o'er my dying bed!

No band of friends or heirs be there,　5
　To weep, or wish, the coming blow:
No maiden with dishevelled hair,
　To feel, or feign, decorous woe.

But silent let me sink to earth,
　With no officious mourners near:　10
I would not mar one hour of mirth,
　Nor startle friendship with a tear.

Yet Love, if Love in such an hour
　Could nobly check its useless sighs,
Might then exert its latest power　15
　In her who lives, and him who dies.

'Twere sweet, my Psyche! to the last
　Thy features still serene to see:
Forgetful of its struggles past,
　E'en Pain itself should smile on thee.

But vain the wish—for Beauty still　21
　Will shrink, as shrinks the ebbing
　　breath;
And women's tears, produced at will,
　Deceive in life, unman in death.

Then lonely be my latest hour,　25
　Without regret, without a groan;
For thousands Death hath ceas'd to lower,
　And pain been transient or unknown.

'Ay, but to die, and go,' alas!
　Where all have gone, and all must go!
To be the nothing that I was　31
　Ere born to life and living woe!

Count o'er the joys thine hours have seen,
　Count o'er thy days from anguish free,
And know, whatever thou hast been,　35
　'Tis something better not to be.

AND THOU ART DEAD, AS YOUNG AND FAIR

'Heu, quanto minus est cum reliquis versari
quam tui meminisse!'

AND thou art dead, as young and fair
　As aught of mortal birth;
And form so soft, and charms so rare,
　Too soon return'd to Earth!

Though Earth received them in her bed 5
And o'er the spot the crowd may tread
  In carelessness or mirth,
There is an eye which could not brook
A moment on that grave to look.

I will not ask where thou liest low, 10
  Nor gaze upon the spot;
There flowers or weeds at will may grow,
  So I behold them not:
It is enough for me to prove
That what I loved, and long must love,
  Like common earth can rot; 16
To me there needs no stone to tell,
'Tis Nothing that I loved so well.

Yet did I love thee to the last
  As fervently as thou, 20
Who didst not change through all the past,
  And canst not alter now.
The love where Death has set his seal,
Nor age can chill, nor rival steal,
  Nor falsehood disavow: 25
And, what were worse, thou canst not see
Or wrong, or change, or fault in me.

The better days of life were ours;
  The worst can be but mine:
The sun that cheers, the storm that lowers,
  Shall never more be thine. 31
The silence of that dreamless sleep
I envy now too much to weep;
  Nor need I to repine,
That all those charms have pass'd away
I might have watch'd through long decay.

The flower in ripen'd bloom unmatch'd
  Must fall the earliest prey;
Though by no hand untimely snatch'd,
  The leaves must drop away: 40
And yet it were a greater grief
To watch it withering, leaf by leaf,
  Than see it pluck'd to-day;
Since earthly eye but ill can bear
To trace the change to foul from fair.

I know not if I could have borne 46
  To see thy beauties fade;
The night that follow'd such a morn
  Had worn a deeper shade:
Thy day without a cloud hath pass'd, 50
And thou wert lovely to the last;
  Extinguish'd, not decay'd;
As stars that shoot along the sky
Shine brightest as they fall from high.

As once I wept, if I could weep, 55
  My tears might well be shed,
To think I was not near to keep
  One vigil o'er thy bed;
To gaze, how fondly! on thy face,
To fold thee in a faint embrace, 60
  Uphold thy drooping head;
And show that love, however vain,
Nor thou nor I can feel again.

Yet how much less it were to gain,
  Though thou hast left me free, 65
The loveliest things that still remain,
  Than thus remember thee!
The all of thine that cannot die
Through dark and dread Eternity
  Returns again to me, 70
And more thy buried love endears
Than aught except its living years.

February 1812.

IF SOMETIMES IN THE HAUNTS OF MEN

IF sometimes in the haunts of men
  Thine image from my breast may fade,
The lonely hour presents again
  The semblance of thy gentle shade:
And now that sad and silent hour 5
  Thus much of thee can still restore,
And sorrow unobserved may pour
  The plaint she dare not speak before.

Oh, pardon that in crowds awhile
  I waste one thought I owe to thee, 10
And self-condemn'd, appear to smile,
  Unfaithful to thy memory:
Nor deem that memory less dear,
  That then I seem not to repine;
I would not fools should overhear 15
  One sigh that should be wholly *thine*.

If not the goblet pass unquaff'd,
  It is not drain'd to banish care;
The cup must hold a deadlier draught,
  That brings a Lethe for despair. 20
And could Oblivion set my soul
  From all her troubled visions free,
I'd dash to earth the sweetest bowl
  That drown'd a single thought of thee.

For wert thou vanish'd from my mind, 25
  Where could my vacant bosom turn?
And who would then remain behind
  To honour thine abandon'd Urn?
No, no—it is my sorrow's pride
  That last dear duty to fulfil: 30
Though all the world forget beside,
  'Tis meet that I remember still.

For well I know, that such had been
  Thy gentle care for him, who now 34
Unmourn'd shall quit this mortal scene,
  Where none regarded him, but thou:
And, oh! I feel in *that* was given
  A blessing never meant for me;
Thou wert too like a dream of Heaven
  For earthly Love to merit thee. 40

March 14, 1812.

FROM THE FRENCH

ÆGLE, beauty and poet, has two little crimes;
  She makes her own face, and does not make her rhymes.

OCCASIONAL PIECES

ON A CORNELIAN HEART WHICH WAS BROKEN

ILL-FATED Heart! and can it be,
　That thou should'st thus be rent in
　　twain?
Have years of care for thine and thee
　Alike been all employ'd in vain?

Yet precious seems each shatter'd part,
　And every fragment dearer grown,　6
Since he who wears thee feels thou art
　A fitter emblem of *his own*.

March 16, 1812.

LINES TO A LADY WEEPING

WEEP, daughter of a royal line,
　A Sire's disgrace, a realm's decay;
Ah! happy if each tear of thine
　Could wash a father's fault away!

Weep—for thy tears are Virtue's tears—
　Auspicious to these suffering isles;　6
And be each drop in future years
　Repaid thee by thy people's smiles!

March 1812.

THE CHAIN I GAVE

FROM THE TURKISH

THE chain I gave was fair to view,
　The lute I added sweet in sound;
The heart that offer'd both was true,
　And ill deserved the fate it found.

These gifts were charm'd by secret spell,
　Thy truth in absence to divine;　6
And they have done their duty well,—
　Alas! they could not teach thee thine.

That chain was firm in every link,
　But not to bear a stranger's touch;　10
That lute was sweet—till thou could'st
　　think
In other hands its notes were such.

Let him who from thy neck unbound
　The chain which shiver'd in his grasp,
Who saw that lute refuse to sound,　15
　Restring the chords, renew the clasp.

When thou wert changed, they alter'd too;
　The chain is broke, the music mute.
'Tis past—to them and thee adieu—
　False heart, frail chain, and silent lute.

LINES WRITTEN ON A BLANK LEAF OF 'THE PLEASURES OF MEMORY'

ABSENT or present, still to thee,
　My friend, what magic spells belong!
As all can tell, who share, like me,
　In turn thy converse and thy song.　4

But when the dreaded hour shall come
　By Friendship ever deem'd too nigh,
And 'MEMORY' o'er her Druid's tomb
　Shall weep that aught of thee can die,

How fondly will she then repay
　Thy homage offer'd at her shrine,　10
And blend, while ages roll away,
　Her name immortally with *thine!*

April 19, 1812.

ADDRESS, SPOKEN AT THE OPENING OF DRURY-LANE THEATRE

SATURDAY, OCTOBER 10, 1812

IN one dread night our city saw, and sigh'd,
Bow'd to the dust, the Drama's tower of
　pride;
In one short hour beheld the blazing fane,
Apollo sink, and Shakspeare cease to
　reign.

Ye who beheld, (oh! sight admired and
　mourn'd,　5
Whose radiance mock'd the ruin it
　adorn'd!)
Through clouds of fire the massy frag-
　ments riven,
Like Israel's pillar, chase the night from
　heaven;
Saw the long column of revolving flames
Shake its red shadow o'er the startled
　Thames,　10
While thousands, throng'd around the
　burning dome,
Shrank back appall'd, and trembled for
　their home,
As glared the volumed blaze, and ghastly
　shone
The skies, with lightnings awful as their
　own,　14
Till blackening ashes and the lonely wall
Usurp'd the Muse's realm, and mark'd
　her fall;
Say—shall this new, nor less aspiring pile,
Rear'd where once rose the mightiest in
　our isle,
Know the same favour which the former
　knew,
A shrine for Shakspeare—worthy him
　and *you?*　20

Yes—it shall be—the magic of that
　name
Defies the scythe of time, the torch of
　flame;
On the same spot still consecrates the
　scene,
And bids the Drama *be* where she hath
　been:
This fabric's birth attests the potent
　spell—　25
Indulge our honest pride, and say, *How
　well!*

As soars this fane to emulate the last,
Oh! might we draw our omens from the
    past,
Some hour propitious to our prayers may
    boast
Names such as hallow still the dome we
    lost.   30
On Drury first your Siddons' thrilling art
O'erwhelm'd the gentlest, storm'd the
    sternest heart.
On Drury, Garrick's latest laurels grew;
Here your last tears retiring Roscius drew,
Sigh'd his last thanks, and wept his last
    adieu: 35
But still for living wit the wreaths may
    bloom,
That only waste their odours o'er the
    tomb.
Such Drury claim'd and claims—nor you
    refuse
One tribute to revive his slumbering
    muse;
With garlands deck your own Menander's
    head,   40
Nor hoard your honours idly for the dead.
Dear are the days which made our annals
    bright,
Ere Garrick fled, or Brinsley ceased to
    write.
Heirs to their labours, like all high-born
    heirs,
Vain of *our* ancestry as they of *theirs*;
While thus Remembrance borrows Ban-
    quo's glass   46
To claim the sceptred shadows as they
    pass,
And we the mirror hold, where imaged
    shine
Immortal names, emblazon'd on our line,
Pause—ere their feebler offspring you
    condemn,   50
Reflect how hard the task to rival them!

Friends of the stage! to whom both
    Players and Plays
Must sue alike for pardon or for praise,
Whose judging voice and eye alone direct
The boundless power to cherish or reject;
If e'er frivolity has led to fame,   56
And made us blush that you forbore to
    blame;
If e'er the sinking stage could condescend
To soothe the sickly taste it dare not mend,
All past reproach may present scenes re-
    fute,   60
And censure, wisely loud, be justly mute!
Oh! since your fiat stamps the Drama's
    laws,
Forbear to mock us with misplaced ap-
    plause;
So pride shall doubly nerve the actor's
    powers,
And reason's voice be echo'd back by
    ours!   65

This greeting o'er, the ancient rule
    obey'd,
The Drama's homage by her herald paid,
Receive *our* welcome too, whose every
    tone
Springs from our hearts, and fain would
    win your own.
The curtain rises—may our stage unfold
Scenes not unworthy Drury's days of old!
Britons our judges, Nature for our guide,
Still may *we* please—long, long may *you*
    preside.   73

PARENTHETICAL ADDRESS

BY DR. PLAGIARY

Half stolen, with acknowledgments, to be spoken
in an inarticulate voice by Master P. at the opening of the next new theatre. Stolen parts marked
with the inverted commas of quotation—thus
'——'.

'WHEN energising objects men pursue,'
Then Lord knows what is writ by Lord
    knows who.
'A modest monologue you here survey,'
Hiss'd from the theatre the 'other day,'
As if Sir Fretful wrote 'the slumberous'
    verse,   5
And gave his son 'the rubbish' to re-
    hearse.
'Yet at the thing you'd never be amazed,'
Knew you the rumpus which the author
    raised,
'Nor even here your smiles would be re-
    prest,'
Knew you these lines—the badness of the
    best,   10
'Flame! fire! and flame!' (words borrowed
    from Lucretius,)
'Dread metaphors which open wounds'
    like issues!
'And sleeping pangs awake—and—but
    away'
(Confound me if I know what next to say).
'Lo Hope reviving re-expands her wings,'
And Master G—— recites what Dr. Busby
    sings!—   16
'If mighty things with small we may com-
    pare,'
(Translated from the grammar for the
    fair!)
Dramatic 'spirit drives a conquering car,'
And burn'd poor Moscow like a tub of
    'tar.'   20
'This spirit Wellington has shown in
    Spain,'
To furnish melodrames for Drury Lane.
'Another Marlborough points to Blen-
    heim's story,'
And George and I will dramatise it for ye.

'In arts and sciences our isle hath
    shone'   25
(This deep discovery is mine alone).

'Oh British poesy, whose powers inspire'
My verse—or I'm a fool—and Fame's a
    liar,
'Thee we invoke, your sister arts implore'
With 'smiles,' and 'lyres,' and 'pencils,'
    and much more.   30
These, if we win the Graces, too, we gain
Disgraces, too! 'inseparable train!'
'Three who have stolen their witching
    airs from Cupid'
(You all know what I mean, unless you're
    stupid):
'Harmonious throng' that I have kept *in
    petto*   35
Now to produce in a '*divine sestetto*'!!
'While Poesy,' with these delightful doxies,
'Sustains her part' in all the 'upper'
    boxes!
'Thus lifted gloriously, you'll soar along,'
Borne in the vast balloon of Busby's
    song;   40
'Shine in your farce, masque, scenery,
    and play'
(For this last line George had a holiday).
'Old Drury never, never soar'd so high,'
So says the manager, and so say I.
'But hold, you say, this self-complacent
    boast;'   45
Is this the poem which the public lost?
'True—true—that lowers at once our
    mounting pride;'
But lo:—the papers print what you
    deride.
''Tis ours to look on you—you hold the
    prize,'
'Tis *twenty guineas*, as they advertise! 50
'A double blessing your rewards impart'—
I wish I had them, then, with all my heart.
'Our *twofold* feeling *owns* its twofold
    cause,'
Why son and I both beg for your applause.
'When in your fostering beams you bid
    us live,'   55
My next subscription list shall say how
    much you give!
                         October 1812.

VERSES FOUND IN A SUMMER-HOUSE AT HALES-OWEN

When Dryden's fool, 'unknowing what
    he sought,'
His hours in whistling spent, 'for want of
    thought,'
This guiltless oaf his vacancy of sense
Supplied, and amply too, by innocence:
Did modern swains, possess'd of Cymon's
    powers,   5
In Cymon's manner waste their leisure
    hours,
Th' offended guests would not, with blush-
    ing, see
These fair green walks disgraced by in-
    famy.

Severe the fate of modern fools, alas!
When vice and folly mark them as they
    pass.   10
Like noxious reptiles o'er the whiten'd
    wall,
The filth they leave still points out where
    they crawl.

REMEMBER THEE! REMEMBER THEE!

Remember thee! remember thee!
    Till Lethe quench life's burning stream
Remorse and shame shall cling to thee,
    And haunt thee like a feverish dream!

Remember thee! Ay, doubt it not.   5
    Thy husband too shall think of thee!
By neither shalt thou be forgot,
    Thou *false* to him, thou *fiend* to me!

TO TIME

Time! on whose arbitrary wing
    The varying hours must flag or fly,
Whose tardy winter, fleeting spring,
    But drag or drive us on to die—

Hail thou! who on my birth bestow'd
    Those boons to all that know thee
    known;   6
Yet better I sustain thy load,
    For now I bear the weight alone.

I would not one fond heart should share
    The bitter moments thou hast given;
And pardon thee, since thou could'st
    spare   11
    All that I loved, to peace or heaven.

To them be joy or rest, on me
    Thy future ills shall press in vain;
I nothing owe but years to thee,   15
    A debt already paid in pain.

Yet even that pain was some relief,
    It felt, but still forgot thy power:
The active agony of grief   19
    Retards, but never counts the hour.

In joy I've sigh'd to think thy flight
    Would soon subside from swift to
    slow;
Thy cloud could overcast the light,
    But could not add a night to woe;

For then, however drear and dark, 25
    My soul was suited to thy sky;
One star alone shot forth a spark
    To prove thee—not Eternity.

That beam hath sunk, and now thou art
    A blank; a thing to count and curse,
Through each dull tedious trifling part,
    Which all regret, yet all rehearse. 32

One scene even thou canst not deform;
  The limit of thy sloth or speed
When future wanderers bear the storm
  Which we shall sleep too sound to
    heed;   36

And I can smile to think how weak
  Thine efforts shortly shall be shown,
When all the vengeance thou canst wreak
  Must fall upon—a nameless stone.

TRANSLATION OF A ROMAIC LOVE SONG

Ah! Love was never yet without
  The pang, the agony, the doubt,
Which rends my heart with ceaseless sigh,
While day and night roll darkling by.

Without one friend to hear my woe,   5
I faint, I die beneath the blow.
That Love had arrows well I knew;
Alas! I find them poison'd too.

Birds, yet in freedom, shun the net
Which Love around your haunts hath set;
Or, circled by his fatal fire,   11
Your hearts shall burn, your hopes expire.

A bird of free and careless wing
Was I through many a smiling spring;
But caught within the subtle snare,   15
I burn, and feebly flutter there.

Who ne'er have loved, and loved in vain,
Can neither feel nor pity pain,
The cold repulse, the look askance,
The lightning of Love's angry glance. 20

In flattering dreams I deem'd thee mine;
Now hope, and he who hoped, decline;
Like melting wax, or withering flower,
I feel my passion, and thy power.

My light of life! ah, tell me why   25
That pouting lip, and alter'd eye?
My bird of love! my beauteous mate!
And art thou changed, and canst thou
    hate?

Mine eyes like wintry streams o'erflow:
What wretch with me would barter woe?
My bird! relent: one note could give
A charm to bid thy lover live.   32

My curdling blood, my madd'ning brain,
In silent anguish I sustain;
And still thy heart, without partaking
One pang, exults—while mine is breaking.

Pour me the poison; fear not thou!
Thou canst not murder more than now:
I've lived to curse my natal day,
And Love, that thus can lingering slay.

My wounded soul, my bleeding breast,
Can patience preach thee into rest?   42
Alas! too late, I dearly know
That joy is harbinger of woe.

THOU ART NOT FALSE, BUT THOU ART FICKLE

Thou art not false, but thou art fickle,
  To those thyself so fondly sought;
The tears that thou hast forced to trickle
  Are doubly bitter from that thought:
'Tis this which breaks the heart thou
    grievest,   5
Too well thou lov'st—too soon thou
    leavest.

The wholly false the heart despises,
  And spurns deceiver and deceit;
But she who not a thought disguises,
  Whose love is as sincere as sweet,—
When she can change who loved so truly,
It feels what mine has felt so newly. 12

To dream of joy and wake to sorrow
  Is doom'd to all who love or live;
And if, when conscious on the morrow,
  We scarce our fancy can forgive,   16
That cheated us in slumber only,
To leave the waking soul more lonely,

What must they feel whom no false vision,
  But truest, tenderest passion warm'd?
Sincere, but swift in sad transition; 21
  As if a dream alone had charm'd?
Ah! sure such grief is fancy's scheming,
And all thy change can be but dreaming!

ON BEING ASKED WHAT WAS THE 'ORIGIN OF LOVE'

The 'Origin of Love!'—Ah, why
  That cruel question ask of me,
When thou may'st read in many an eye
  He starts to life on seeing thee?

And should'st thou seek his *end* to
    know: 5
  My heart forebodes, my fears foresee,
He'll linger long in silent woe;
  But live—until I cease to be.

REMEMBER HIM WHOM PASSION'S POWER

Remember him whom passion's power
  Severely, deeply, vainly proved:
Remember thou that dangerous hour,
  When neither fell, though both were
    loved.   4

That yielding breast, that melting eye,
  Too much invited to be bless'd:
That gentle prayer, that pleading sigh,
  The wilder wish reproved, repress'd.

Oh! let me feel that all I lost
  But saved thee all that conscience
    fears;   10
And blush for every pang it cost
  To spare the vain remorse of years.

69

Yet think of this when many a tongue,
  Whose busy accents whisper blame,
Would do the heart that loved thee
    wrong,   15
  And brand a nearly blighted name.

Think that, whate'er to others, thou
  Hast seen each selfish thought subdued:
I bless thy purer soul even now,
  Even now, in midnight solitude.   20

Oh, God! that we had met in time,
  Our hearts as fond, thy hand more free;
When thou hadst loved without a crime,
  And I been less unworthy thee!

Far may thy days, as heretofore,   25
  From this our gaudy world be past!
And that too bitter moment o'er,
  Oh! may such trial be thy last.

This heart, alas! perverted long,   29
  Itself destroy'd might there destroy;
To meet thee in the glittering throng,
  Would wake Presumption's hope of
    joy.

Then to the things whose bliss or woe,
  Like mine, is wild and worthless all,
That world resign—such scenes forego,
  Where those who feel must surely fall.

Thy youth, thy charms, thy tenderness,
  Thy soul from long seclusion pure;
From what even here hath pass'd, may
    guess
  What there thy bosom must endure.

Oh! pardon that imploring tear,   41
  Since not by Virtue shed in vain,
My frenzy drew from eyes so dear;
  For me they shall not weep again.

Though long and mournful must it be,
  The thought that we no more may
    meet;   46
Yet I deserve the stern decree,
  And almost deem the sentence sweet.

Still, had I loved thee less, my heart
  Had then less sacrificed to thine; 50
It felt not half so much to part
  As if its guilt had made thee mine.
                                   1813.

ON LORD THURLOW'S POEMS

WHEN Thurlow this damn'd nonsense sent
(I hope I am not violent),
Nor men nor gods knew what he meant.

And since not even our Rogers' praise
To common sense his thoughts could
    raise—   5
Why *would* they let him print his lays?

.   .   .   .   .

To me, divine Apollo, grant—O!
Hermilda's first and second canto,
I'm fitting up a new portmanteau;

And thus to furnish decent lining,   10
My own and others' bays I'm twining,—
So, gentle Thurlow, throw me thine in.

TO LORD THURLOW

'I lay my branch of laurel down,
Then thus to form Apollo's crown,
Let every other bring his own.'
        Lord Thurlow's lines to Mr. Rogers

'*I lay my branch of laurel down.*'

THOU 'lay thy branch of *laurel* down!'
  Why, what thou'st stole is not enow;
And, were it lawfully thine own,
  Does Rogers want it most, or thou?
Keep to thyself thy wither'd bough,   5
  Or send it back to Doctor Donne:
Were justice done to both, I trow,
  He'd have but little, and thou—none.

'*Then thus to form Apollo's crown.*'

A crown! why, twist it how you will,
Thy chaplet must be foolscap still.   10
When next you visit Delphi's town,
  Inquire amongst your fellow-lodgers,
They'll tell you Phœbus gave his crown,
  Some years before your birth, to Rogers.

'*Let every other bring his own.*'

When coals to Newcastle are carried,
  And owls sent to Athens, as wonders,
From his spouse when the Regent's un-
    married,   17
  Or Liverpool weeps o'er his blunders;
When Tories and Whigs cease to quarrel,
  When Castlereagh's wife has an heir,
Then Rogers shall ask us for laurel,
  And thou shalt have plenty to spare.

TO THOMAS MOORE

WRITTEN THE EVENING BEFORE HIS VISIT
TO MR. LEIGH HUNT IN HORSEMONGER
LANE GAOL, MAY 19, 1813

OH you, who in all names can tickle the town,
Anacreon, Tom Little, Tom Moore, or
    Tom Brown,
For hang me if I know of which you
    may most brag,
Your Quarto two-pounds, or your Two-
    penny Post Bag;

.   .   .   .   .

But now to my letter—to *yours* 'tis an
    answer—   5
To-morrow be with me, as soon as you
    can, sir,
All ready and dress'd for proceeding to
    spunge on
(According to compact) the wit in the
    dungeon—

Pray Phœbus at length our political ma-
lice
May not get us lodgings within the same
palace! 10
I suppose that to-night you're engaged
with some codgers,
And for Sotheby's Blues have deserted
Sam Rogers;
And I, though with cold I have nearly
my death got,
Must put on my breeches, and wait on
the Heathcote;
But to-morrow, at four, we will both
play the *Scurra*, 15
And you'll be Catullus, the Regent
Mamurra.

[First published in 1830.]

IMPROMPTU, IN REPLY TO A FRIEND

WHEN, from the heart where Sorrow sits,
Her dusky shadow mounts too high,
And o'er the changing aspect flits,
And clouds the brow, or fills the eye;
Heed not that gloom, which soon shall
sink: 5
My thoughts their dungeon know too
well;
Back to my breast the wanderers shrink,
And droop within their silent cell.

September 1813.

SONNET, TO GENEVRA

THINE eyes' blue tenderness, thy long
fair hair,
And the wan lustre of thy features—
caught
From contemplation—where serenely
wrought,
Seems Sorrow's softness charm'd from
its despair—
Have thrown such speaking sadness in
thine air, 5
That—but I know thy blessed bosom
fraught
With mines of unalloy'd and stainless
thought—
I should have deem'd thee doom'd to
earthly care.
With such an aspect, by his colours blent,
When from his beauty-breathing pen-
cil born 10
(Except that *thou* hast nothing to repent),
The Magdalen of Guido saw the
morn—
Such seem'st thou—but how much more
excellent!
With nought Remorse can claim—nor
Virtue scorn.

December 17, 1813.

SONNET, TO THE SAME

THY cheek is pale with thought, but not
from woe,
And yet so lovely, that if Mirth could
flush
Its rose of whiteness with the brightest
blush,
My heart would wish away that ruder
glow:
And dazzle not thy deep-blue eyes—but,
oh! 5
While gazing on them sterner eyes will
gush,
And into mine my mother's weakness
rush,
Soft as the last drops round heaven's
airy bow.
For, through thy long dark lashes low
depending,
The soul of melancholy Gentleness
Gleams like a seraph from the sky de-
scending, 11
Above all pain, yet pitying all distress;
At once such majesty with sweetness
blending,
I worship more, but cannot love thee
less.

December 17, 1813.

FROM THE PORTUGUESE

'TU MI CHAMAS'

IN moments to delight devoted,
'My life!' with tenderest tone, you cry;
Dear words! on which my heart had doted,
If youth could neither fade nor die.

To death even hours like these must roll,
Ah! then repeat those accents never;
Or change 'my life!' into 'my soul!'
Which, like my love, exists for ever.

ANOTHER VERSION

YOU call me still your *life*.—Oh! change
the word—
Life is as transient as the inconstant
sigh:
Say rather I'm your soul; more just that
name,
For, like the soul, my love can never die.

THE DEVIL'S DRIVE

AN UNFINISHED RHAPSODY

THE Devil return'd to hell by two,
And he stay'd at home till five;
When he dined on some homicides done
in *ragoût*,
And a rebel or so in an *Irish* stew,
And sausages made of a self-slain Jew—
And bethought himself what next to do,
'And,' quoth he, 'I'll take a drive. 7
I walk'd in the morning, I'll ride to-night;
In darkness my children take most delight,
And I'll see how my favourites thrive,

71

'And what shall I ride in?' quoth Lucifer
    then—
  'If I follow'd my taste, indeed,
I should mount in a waggon of wounded
    men,
  And smile to see them bleed.
But these will be furnish'd again and
    again,   15
  And at present my purpose is speed;
To see my manor as much as I may,
  And watch that no souls shall be poach'd
    away.

'I have a state-coach at Carlton House,
  A chariot in Seymour Place;   20
But they're lent to two friends, who
    make me amends,
  By driving my favourite pace:
And they handle their reins with such
    a grace,
  I have something for both at the end of
    their race.

'So now for the earth to take my chance:'
  Then up to the earth sprung he;   26
And making a jump from Moscow to
    France,
  He stepp'd across the sea,
And rested his hoof on a turnpike road,
  No very great way from a bishop's
    abode.   30

But first as he flew, I forgot to say
That he hover'd a moment upon his way,
  To look upon Leipsic plain;
And so sweet to his eye was its sulphury
    glare,
And so soft to his ear was the cry of
    despair,   35
  That he perch'd on a mountain of
    slain;
And he gazed with delight from its grow-
    ing height,
  Nor often on earth had he seen such a
    sight,
    Nor his work done half as well:
For the field ran so red with the blood of
    the dead,   40
  That it blush'd like the waves of hell!
Then loudly, and wildly, and long laugh'd
    he:
  'Methinks they have here little need of
    me!'   43

.   .   .   .   .

But the softest note that soothed his ear
  Was the sound of a widow sighing;
And the sweetest sight was the icy tear,
Which horror froze in the blue eye clear
  Of a maid by her lover lying—
As round her fell her long fair hair;
  And she look'd to heaven with that
    frenzied air,   50
Which seem'd to ask if a God were there!
And, stretch'd by the wall of a ruin'd hut,

With its hollow cheek, and eyes half shut,
  A child of famine dying:
And the carnage begun, when resistance
    is done,   55
  And the fall of the vainly flying!

.   .   .   .   .

But the Devil has reach'd our cliffs so
    white,
  And what did he there, I pray?
If his eyes were good, he but saw by
    night
  What we see every day: 60
But he made a tour, and kept a journal
Of all the wondrous sights nocturnal,
And he sold it in shares to the *Men* of
    the *Row*,
Who bid pretty well—but they *cheated*
    him, though!

The Devil first saw, as he thought, the
    Mail,   65
  Its coachman and his coat;
So instead of a pistol he cock'd his tail,
  And seized him by the throat:
'Aha!' quoth he, 'what have we here?
'Tis a new barouche, and an ancient
    peer!'   70

So he sat him on his box again,
  And bade him have no fear,
But be true to his club, and stanch to
    his rein,
  His brothel, and his beer;
'Next to seeing a lord at the council
    board,   75
  I would rather see him here.'

.   .   .   .   .

The Devil gat next to Westminster,
  And he turn'd to 'the room' of the
    Commons;
But he heard, as he purposed to enter in
    there,
  That 'the Lords' had received a sum-
    mons;   80
And he thought, as a '*quondam* aristocrat,'
He might peep at the peers, though to
  hear them were flat;
And he walk'd up the house so like one
    of our own,
That they say that he stood pretty near
    the throne.

He saw the Lord Liverpool seemingly
    wise,   85
  The Lord Westmoreland certainly
    silly,
And Johnny of Norfolk—a man of some
    size—
  And Chatham, so like his friend Billy;
And he saw the tears in Lord Eldon's
    eyes,
  Because the Catholics would *not* rise,
  In spite of his prayers and his prophe-
    cies;   91

And he heard—which set Satan himself
    a staring—
A certain Chief Justice say something
    like *swearing*.
And the Devil was shock'd—and quoth
    he, 'I must go,
For I find we have much better manners
    below: 95
If thus he harangues when he passes my
    border,
I shall hint to friend Moloch to call him
    to order.'

WINDSOR POETICS

Lines composed on the occasion of His Royal
  Highness the Prince Regent being seen standing
  between the coffins of Henry VIII and Charles I,
  in the royal vault at Windsor.

FAMED for contemptuous breach of sac-
    red ties,
By headless Charles see heartless Henry
    lies;
Between them stands another sceptred
    thing—
It moves, it reigns—in all but name, a
    king: 4

Charles to his people, Henry to his wife,
—In him the double tyrant starts to life:
Justice and death have mix'd their dust
    in vain,
Each royal vampire wakes to life again.
Ah, what can tombs avail!—since these
    disgorge
The blood and dust of both—to mould
    a George.   10

ODE TO NAPOLEON
BUONAPARTE

'Expende Annibalem:—quot libras in duce
    summo
Invenies?'—JUVENAL, *Sat.* x.

'The Emperor Nepos was acknowledged by the
Senate, by the Italians, and by the Provincials of
Gaul; his moral virtues, and military talents,
were loudly celebrated; and those who derived
any private benefit from his government announced in prophetic strains the restoration of
public felicity. . . . By this shameful abdication,
he protracted his life a few years, in a very ambiguous state, between an Emperor and an
Exile, till ———.'—GIBBON'S *Decline and Fall*,
vol. vi, p. 220.

I

'TIS done—but yesterday a King!
    And arm'd with Kings to strive—
And now thou art a nameless thing:
    So abject—yet alive!
Is this the man of thousand thrones,
Who strew'd our earth with hostile bones,
    And can he thus survive?
Since he, miscall'd the Morning Star,
Nor man nor fiend hath fallen so far.

II

Ill-minded man! why scourge thy kind
    Who bow'd so low the knee?
By gazing on thyself grown blind,
    Thou taught'st the rest to see.
With might unquestion'd,—power to
    save,—
Thine only gift hath been the grave
    To those that worshipp'd thee;
Nor till thy fall could mortals guess
Ambition's less than littleness!

III

Thanks for that lesson—It will teach
    To after-warriors more
Than high Philosophy can preach,
    And vainly preach'd before.
That spell upon the minds of men
Breaks never to unite again,
    That led them to adore
Those Pagod things of sabre sway
With fronts of brass, and feet of clay.

IV

The triumph and the vanity,
    The rapture of the strife—
The earthquake voice of Victory,
    To thee the breath of life;
The sword, the sceptre, and that sway
Which man seem'd made but to obey,
    Wherewith renown was rife—
All quell'd!—Dark Spirit! what must be
The madness of thy memory!

V

The Desolator desolate!
    The Victor overthrown!
The Arbiter of others' fate
    A Suppliant for his own!
Is it some yet imperial hope
That with such change can calmly cope?
    Or dread of death alone?
To die a prince—or live a slave—
Thy choice is most ignobly brave!

VI

He who of old would rend the oak,
    Dream'd not of the rebound:
Chain'd by the trunk he vainly broke—
    Alone—how look'd he round?
Thou, in the sternness of thy strength,
An equal deed hast done at length,
    And darker fate hast found:
He fell, the forest prowlers' prey;
But thou must eat thy heart away!

VII

The Roman, when his burning heart
    Was slaked with blood of Rome,
Threw down the dagger—dared depart,
    In savage grandeur, home—

OCCASIONAL PIECES

He dared depart in utter scorn
Of men that such a yoke had borne,
  Yet left him such a doom!
His only glory was that hour
Of self-upheld abandon'd power.

VIII

The Spaniard, when the lust of sway
  Had lost its quickening spell,
Cast crowns for rosaries away,
  An empire for a cell;
A strict accountant of his beads,
A subtle disputant on creeds,
  His dotage trifled well:
Yet better had he neither known
A bigot's shrine, nor despot's throne.

IX

But thou—from thy reluctant hand
  The thunderbolt is wrung—
Too late thou leav'st the high command
  To which thy weakness clung;
All Evil Spirit as thou art,
It is enough to grieve the heart
  To see thine own unstrung;
To think that God's fair world hath been
The footstool of a thing so mean;

X

And Earth hath spilt her blood for him,
  Who thus can hoard his own!
And Monarchs bow'd the trembling limb,
  And thank'd him for a throne!
Fair Freedom! we may hold thee dear,
When thus thy mightiest foes their fear
  In humblest guise have shown.
Oh! ne'er may tyrant leave behind
A brighter name to lure mankind!

XI

Thine evil deeds are writ in gore,
  Nor written thus in vain—
Thy triumphs tell of fame no more,
  Or deepen every stain:
If thou hadst died as honour dies,
Some new Napoleon might arise,
  To shame the world again—
But who would soar the solar height,
To set in such a starless night?

XII

Weigh'd in the balance, hero dust
  Is vile as vulgar clay;
Thy scales, Mortality! are just
  To all that pass away:
But yet methought the living great
Some higher sparks should animate,
  To dazzle and dismay:
Nor deem'd Contempt could thus make
    mirth
Of these, the Conquerors of the earth.

XIII

And she, proud Austria's mournful
    flower,
  Thy still imperial bride;
How bears her breast the torturing hour?
  Still clings she to thy side?
Must she too bend, must she too share
Thy late repentance, long despair,
  Thou throneless Homicide?
If still she loves thee, hoard that gem,—
'Tis worth thy vanish'd diadem!

XIV

Then haste thee to thy sullen Isle,
  And gaze upon the sea;
That element may meet thy smile—
  It ne'er was ruled by thee!
Or trace with thine all idle hand
In loitering mood upon the sand
  That Earth is now as free!
That Corinth's pedagogue hath now
Transferr'd his by-word to thy brow.

XV

Thou Timour! in his captive's cage
  What thoughts will there be thine,
While brooding in thy prison'd rage?
  But one—'The world was mine!'
Unless, like he of Babylon,
All sense is with thy sceptre gone,
  Life will not long confine
That spirit pour'd so widely forth—
So long obey'd—so little worth!

XVI

Or, like the thief of fire from heaven,
  Wilt thou withstand the shock?
And share with him, the unforgiven,
  His vulture and his rock!
Foredoom'd by God—by man accurst,
And that last act, though not thy worst,
  The very Fiend's arch mock;
He in his fall preserved his pride,
And, if a mortal, had as proudly died!

XVII

There was a day—there was an hour,
  While earth was Gaul's—Gaul thine—
When that immeasurable power
  Unsated to resign
Had been an act of purer fame
Than gathers round Marengo's name,
  And gilded thy decline,
Through the long twilight of all time,
Despite some passing clouds of crime.

XVIII

But thou forsooth must be a king,
  And don the purple vest,
As if that foolish robe could wring
  Remembrance from thy breast.

74

Where is that faded garment? where
The gewgaws thou wert fond to wear,
  The star, the string, the crest?
Vain froward child of empire! say,
Are all thy playthings snatched away?

XIX

Where may the wearied eye repose
  When gazing on the Great;
Where neither guilty glory glows,
  Nor despicable state?
Yes—one—the first—the last—the best—
The Cincinnatus of the West,
  Whom envy dared not hate,
Bequeath'd the name of Washington,
To make man blush there was but one!

STANZAS FOR MUSIC

I SPEAK not, I trace not, I breathe not
    thy name,
There is grief in the sound, there is guilt
    in the fame:
But the tear which now burns on my
    cheek may impart
The deep thoughts that dwell in that
    silence of heart.

Too brief for our passion, too long for
    our peace,   5
Were those hours—can their joy or their
    bitterness cease?
We repent, we abjure, we will break from
    our chain,—
We will part, we will fly to—unite it
    again!

Oh! thine be the gladness, and mine be
    the guilt!
Forgive me, adored one!—forsake, if
    thou wilt;—   10
But the heart which is thine shall expire
    undebased,
And *man* shall not break it—whatever
    thou mayst.

And stern to the haughty, but humble to
    thee,
This soul, in its bitterest blackness, shall
    be;
And our days seem as swift, and our
    moments more sweet,   15
With thee by my side, than with worlds
    at our feet.

One sigh of thy sorrow, one look of thy
    love,
Shall turn me or fix, shall reward or re-
    prove;
And the heartless may wonder at all I
    resign—
Thy lip shall reply, not to them, but to
    mine.   20
                              May 1814.

ADDRESS INTENDED TO BE RE-CITED AT THE CALEDONIAN MEETING

WHO hath not glow'd above the page
    where fame
Hath fix'd high Caledon's unconquer'd
    name;
The mountain-land which spurn'd the
    Roman chain,
And baffled back the fiery-crested Dane,
Whose bright claymore and hardihood
    of hand   5
No foe could tame—no tyrant could
    command?
That race is gone—but still their children
    breathe,
And glory crowns them with redoubled
    wreath:
O'er Gael and Saxon mingling banners
    shine,
And, England! add their stubborn
    strength to thine.   10
The blood which flow'd with Wallace
    flows as free,
But now 'tis only shed for fame and thee!
Oh! pass not by the northern veteran's
    claim,
But give support—the world hath given
    him fame!

The humbler ranks, the lowly brave, who
    bled   15
While cheerly following where the mighty
    led—
Who sleep beneath the undistinguish'd sod
Where happier comrades in their tri-
    umph trod,
To us bequeath—'tis all their fate allows—
The sireless offspring and the lonely
    spouse: 20
She on high Albyn's dusky hills may raise
The tearful eye in melancholy gaze,
Or view, while shadowy auguries disclose
The Highland Seer's anticipated woes,
The bleeding phantom of each martial
    form   25
Dim in the cloud, or darkling in the
    storm;
While sad, she chants the solitary song,
The soft lament for him who tarries
    long—
For him, whose distant relics vainly crave
The Coronach's wild requiem to the
    brave!   30

'Tis Heaven—not man—must charm
    away the woe,
Which bursts when Nature's feelings
    newly flow;
Yet tenderness and time may rob the tear
Of half its bitterness for one so dear;
A nation's gratitude perchance may
    spread   35
A thornless pillow for the widow'd head;

May lighten well her heart's maternal
care,
And wean from penury the soldier's
heir.

May 1814.

FRAGMENT OF AN EPISTLE TO THOMAS MOORE

'WHAT say *I?*'—not a syllable further in
prose;
I'm your man 'of all measures,' dear
Tom,—so here goes!
Here goes, for a swim on the stream of
old Time,
On those buoyant supporters, the blad-
ders of rhyme,
If our weight breaks them down, and we
sink in the flood,   5
We are smother'd, at least, in respectable
mud,
Where the Divers of Bathos lie drown'd
in a heap,
And Southey's last Pæan has pillow'd his
sleep;
That 'Felo de se,' who, half drunk with
his malmsey,
Walk'd out of his depth and was lost in
a calm sea,   10
Singing 'Glory to God' in a spick and
span stanza,
The like (since Tom Sternhold was
choked) never man saw.

The papers have told you, no doubt,
of the fusses,
The fêtes, and the gapings to get at these
Russes,—
Of his Majesty's suite, up from coach-
man to Hetman,   15
And what dignity decks the flat face of
the great man.
I saw him, last week, at two balls and a
party,—
For a prince, his demeanour was rather
too hearty.
You know *we* are used to quite different
graces,
.   .   .   .   .   .

The Czar's look, I own, was much
brighter and brisker,   20
But then he is sadly deficient in whisker;
And wore but a starless blue coat, and in
kersey-
-mere breeches whisk'd round, in a waltz
with the Jersey,
Who lovely as ever, seem'd just as delighted
With Majesty's presence as those she
invited.   25
.   .   .   .   .   .
.   .   .   .   .   .

June 1814.

CONDOLATORY ADDRESS TO SARAH, COUNTESS OF JERSEY

ON THE PRINCE REGENT'S RETURNING HER
PICTURE TO MRS. MEE

WHEN the vain triumph of the imperial
lord,
Whom servile Rome obey'd, and yet
abhorr'd,
Gave to the vulgar gaze each glorious
bust,
That left a likeness of the brave or
just;   4
What most admired each scrutinising eye
Of all that deck'd that passing pageantry?
What spread from face to face that
wondering air?
The thought of Brutus—for his was not
there!
That absence proved his worth,—that
absence fix'd
His memory on the longing mind, un-
mix'd;   10
And more decreed his glory to endure,
Than all a gold Colossus could secure.
If thus, fair Jersey, our desiring gaze
Search for thy form, in vain and mute
amaze,
Amidst those pictured charms, whose
loveliness,   15
Bright though they be, thine own had
render'd less:
If he, that vain old man, whom truth
admits
Heir of his father's crown, and of his wits,
If his corrupted eye, and wither'd heart,
Could with thy gentle image bear to part;
That tasteless shame be *his*, and ours the
grief,   21
To gaze on Beauty's band without its
chief:
Yet comfort still one selfish thought
imparts,
We lose the portrait, but preserve our
hearts.
What can his vaulted gallery now
disclose?   25
A garden with all flowers—except the
rose;—
A fount that only wants its living stream;
A night, with every star, save Dian's
beam.
Lost to our eyes the present forms shall
be,
That turn from tracing them to dream of
thee;   30
And more on that recall'd resemblance
pause,
Than all he *shall* not force on our
applause.
Long may thy yet meridian lustre
shine,
With all that Virtue asks of Homage
thine:

The symmetry of youth, the grace of
    mien,   35
The eye that gladdens, and the brow
    serene;
The glossy darkness of that clustering
    hair,
Which shades, yet shows that forehead
    more than fair!
Each glance that wins us, and the life that
    throws
A spell which will not let our looks re-
    pose,   40
But turn to gaze again, and find anew
Some charm that well rewards another
    view.
These are not lessen'd, these are still as
    bright,
Albeit too dazzling for a dotard's sight;
And those must wait till ev'ry charm is
    gone,   45
To please the paltry heart that pleases
    none;—
That dull cold sensualist, whose sickly eye
In envious dimness pass'd thy portrait by;
Who rack'd his little spirit to combine
Its hate of *Freedom's* loveliness, and
    thine.   50

August 1814.

ELEGIAC STANZAS ON THE DEATH OF SIR PETER PARKER, BART.

THERE is a tear for all that die,
    A mourner o'er the humblest grave;
But nations swell the funeral cry,
    And Triumph weeps above the brave.

For them is Sorrow's purest sigh   5
    O'er Ocean's heaving bosom sent:
In vain their bones unburied lie,
    All earth becomes their monument!

A tomb is theirs on every page,
    An epitaph on every tongue: 10
The present hours, the future age,
    For them bewail, to them belong.

For them the voice of festal mirth
    Grows hush'd, *their name* the only
    sound;
While deep Remembrance pours to
    Worth   15
    The goblet's tributary round.

A theme to crowds that knew them not,
    Lamented by admiring foes,
Who would not share their glorious lot?
    Who would not die the death they
    chose?   20

And, gallant Parker! thus enshrined
    Thy life, thy fall, thy fame shall be;
And early valour, glowing, find
    A model in thy memory.

But there are breasts that bleed with
    thee   25
    In woe, that glory cannot quell;
And shuddering hear of victory,
    Where one so dear, so dauntless, fell.

Where shall they turn to mourn thee less?
    When cease to hear thy cherish'd name?
Time cannot teach forgetfulness,   31
    While Grief's full heart is fed by Fame.

Alas! for them, though not for thee,
    They cannot choose but weep the more;
Deep for the dead the grief must be,   35
    Who ne'er gave cause to mourn before.

October 1814.

TO BELSHAZZAR

BELSHAZZAR! from the banquet turn,
    Nor in thy sensual fulness fall;
Behold! while yet before thee burn
    The graven words, the glowing wall,
Many a despot men miscall   5
    Crown'd and anointed from on high;
But thou, the weakest, worst of all—
    Is it not written, thou must die?

Go! dash the roses from thy brow—
    Grey hairs but poorly wreathe with
    them;   10
Youth's garlands misbecome thee now,
    More than thy very diadem,
Where thou hast tarnish'd every gem:—
    Then throw the worthless bauble by,
Which, worn by thee, ev'n slaves con-
    temn;   15
    And learn like better men to die!

Oh! early in the balance weigh'd,
    And ever light of word and worth,
Whose soul expired ere youth decay'd,
    And left thee but a mass of earth.   20
To see thee moves the scorner's mirth:
    But tears in Hope's averted eye
Lament that even thou hadst birth—
    Unfit to govern, live, or die.

HEBREW MELODIES

ADVERTISEMENT

THE subsequent poems were written at the request of my friend, the Hon. Douglas Kinnaird,
for a Selection of Hebrew Melodies, and have been
published, with the music, arranged by Mr. Bra-
ham and Mr. Nathan.

January, 1815.

SHE WALKS IN BEAUTY

I

SHE walks in beauty, like the night
    Of cloudless climes and starry skies;
And all that's best of dark and bright
    Meet in her aspect and her eyes:
Thus mellow'd to that tender light
    Which heaven to gaudy day denies.

II

One shade the more, one ray the less,
　Had half impair'd the nameless grace
Which waves in every raven tress,
　Or softly lightens o'er her face;
Where thoughts serenely sweet express
　How pure, how dear their dwelling-
　　place.

III

And on that cheek, and o'er that brow,
　So soft, so calm, yet eloquent,
The smiles that win, the tints that glow,
　But tell of days in goodness spent,
A mind at peace with all below,
　A heart whose love is innocent!

THE HARP THE MONARCH MINSTREL SWEPT

I

THE harp the monarch minstrel swept,
　The King of men, the loved of Heaven,
Which Music hallow'd while she wept
　O'er tones her heart of hearts had given,
Redoubled be her tears, its chords are
　　riven!
It soften'd men of iron mould,
　It gave them virtues not their own;
No ear so dull, no soul so cold,
　That felt not, fired not to the tone,
　Till David's lyre grew mightier than his
　　throne!

II

It told the triumphs of our King,
　It wafted glory to our God;
It made our gladden'd valleys ring,
　The cedars bow, the mountains nod;
Its sound aspired to heaven and there
　abode!
Since then, though heard on earth no
　more,
　Devotion and her daughter Love
Still bid the bursting spirit soar
　To sounds that seem as from above,
In dreams that day's broad light can
　not remove.

IF THAT HIGH WORLD

I

IF that high world, which lies beyond
　Our own, surviving Love endears;
If there the cherish'd heart be fond,
　The eye the same, except in tears—
How welcome those untrodden spheres!
　How sweet this very hour to die!
To soar from earth and find all fears
　Lost in thy light—Eternity!

II

It must be so: 'tis not for self
　That we so tremble on the brink;
And striving to o'erleap the gulf,
　Yet cling to Being's severing link.
Oh! in that future let us think
　To hold each heart the heart that shares;
With them the immortal waters drink,
　And soul in soul grow deathless theirs!

THE WILD GAZELLE

I

THE wild gazelle on Judah's hills
　Exulting yet may bound,
And drink from all the living rills
　That gush on holy ground:
Its airy step and glorious eye
May glance in tameless transport by:—

II

A step as fleet, an eye more bright,
　Hath Judah witness'd there;
And o'er her scenes of lost delight
　Inhabitants more fair.
The cedars wave on Lebanon,
But Judah's statelier maids are gone!

III

More blest each palm that shades those
　plains
　Than Israel's scatter'd race;
For, taking root, it there remains
　In solitary grace:
It cannot quit its place of birth,
It will not live in other earth.

IV

But we must wander witheringly,
　In other lands to die;
And where our fathers' ashes be,
　Our own may never lie:
Our temple hath not left a stone,
And Mockery sits on Salem's throne.

OH! WEEP FOR THOSE

I

OH! weep for those that wept by Babel's
　stream,
Whose shrines are desolate, whose land a
　dream;
Weep for the harp of Judah's broken
　shell;
Mourn—where their God hath dwelt the
　godless dwell!

II

And where shall Israel lave her bleeding
　feet?
And when shall Zion's songs again seem
　sweet?
And Judah's melody once more rejoice
The hearts that leap'd before its heavenly
　voice?

III

Tribes of the wandering foot and weary
  breast,
How shall ye flee away and be at rest!
The wild-dove hath her nest, the fox his
  cave,
Mankind their country—Israel but the
  grave!

ON JORDAN'S BANKS

I

ON Jordan's banks the Arab's camels
  stray,
On Sion's hill the False One's votaries
  pray,
The Baal-adorer bows on Sinai's steep—
Yet there—even there—Oh God! thy
  thunders sleep:

II

There—where thy finger scorch'd the tab-
  let stone!
There—where thy shadow to thy people
  shone!
Thy glory shrouded in its garb of fire:
Thyself—none living see and not expire!

III

Oh! in the lightning let thy glance appear;
Sweep from his shiver'd hand the oppres-
  sor's spear!
How long by tyrants shall thy land be trod?
How long thy temple worshipless, Oh God?

JEPHTHA'S DAUGHTER

I

SINCE our Country, our God—Oh, my
  Sire!
Demand that thy Daughter expire;
Since thy triumph was bought by thy
  vow—
Strike the bosom that's bared for thee now!

II

And the voice of my mourning is o'er,
And the mountains behold me no more:
If the hand that I love lay me low,
There cannot be pain in the blow!

III

And of this, oh, my Father! be sure—
That the blood of thy child is as pure
As the blessing I beg ere it flow,
And the last thought that soothes me be-
  low.

IV

Though the virgins of Salem lament,
Be the judge and the hero unbent!
I have won the great battle for thee,
And my Father and Country are free!

V

When this blood of thy giving hath gush'd,
When the voice that thou lovest is hush'd,
Let my memory still be thy pride,
And forget not I smiled as I died!

OH! SNATCH'D AWAY IN BEAUTY'S BLOOM

I

OH! snatch'd away in beauty's bloom,
On thee shall press no ponderous tomb;
  But on thy turf shall roses rear
  Their leaves, the earliest of the year;
And the wild cypress wave in tender
  gloom:

II

And oft by yon blue gushing stream
  Shall Sorrow lean her drooping head,
And feed deep thought with many a
  dream,
  And lingering pause and lightly tread;
Fond wretch! as if her step disturb'd
  the dead!

III

Away! we know that tears are vain,
  That death nor heeds nor hears distress:
Will this unteach us to complain?
  Or make one mourner weep the less?
And thou—who tell'st me to forget,
Thy looks are wan, thine eyes are wet.

MY SOUL IS DARK

I

My soul is dark—Oh! quickly string
  The harp I yet can brook to hear;
And let thy gentle fingers fling
  Its melting murmurs o'er mine ear.
If in this heart a hope be dear,
  That sound shall charm it forth again:
If in these eyes there lurk a tear,
'Twill flow, and cease to burn my brain.

II

But bid the strain be wild and deep,
  Nor let thy notes of joy be first:
I tell thee, minstrel, I must weep,
  Or else this heavy heart will burst;
For it hath been by sorrow nursed,
  And ached in sleepless silence long;
And now 'tis doom'd to know the worst,
  And break at once—or yield to song.

I SAW THEE WEEP

I

I SAW thee weep—the big bright tear
  Came o'er that eye of blue;
And then methought it did appear
  A violet dropping dew;

OCCASIONAL PIECES

I saw thee smile—the sapphire's blaze
  Beside thee ceased to shine;
It could not match the living rays
  That fill'd that glance of thine.

II

As clouds from yonder sun receive
  A deep and mellow dye,
Which scarce the shade of coming eve
  Can banish from the sky,
Those smiles unto the moodiest mind
  Their own pure joy impart;
Their sunshine leaves a glow behind
  That lightens o'er the heart.

THY DAYS ARE DONE

I

THY days are done, thy fame begun;
  Thy country's strains record
The triumphs of her chosen Son,
  The slaughters of his sword!
The deeds he did, the fields he won,
  The freedom he restored!

II

Though thou art fall'n, while we are free
  Thou shalt not taste of death!
The generous blood that flow'd from thee
  Disdain'd to sink beneath:
Within our veins its currents be,
  Thy spirit on our breath!

III

Thy name, our charging hosts along,
  Shall be the battle-word!
Thy fall, the theme of choral song
  From virgin voices pour'd!
To weep would do thy glory wrong:
  Thou shalt not be deplored.

SAUL

I

THOU whose spell can raise the dead,
  Bid the prophet's form appear.
'Samuel, raise thy buried head!
  King, behold the phantom seer!'
Earth yawn'd; he stood the centre of a
    cloud: 5
Light changed its hue, retiring from his
    shroud.
Death stood all glassy in his fixed eye;
His hand was wither'd, and his veins were
    dry;
His foot, in bony whiteness, glitter'd there,
Shrunken and sinewless, and ghastly bare;
From lips that moved not and unbreath-
    ing frame,   11
Like cavern'd winds, the hollow accents
    came.
Saul saw, and fell to earth, as falls the oak,
At once, and blasted by the thunder-
    stroke.

II

'Why is my sleep disquieted?   15
Who is he that calls the dead?
Is it thou, O King? Behold,
Bloodless are these limbs, and cold:
Such are mine; and such shall be
Thine to-morrow, when with me:
Ere the coming day is done,   21
Such shalt thou be, such thy son.
Fare thee well, but for a day,
Then we mix our mouldering clay.
Thou, thy race, lie pale and low,   25
Pierced by shafts of many a bow;
And the falchion by thy side
To thy heart thy hand shall guide:
Crownless, breathless, headless fall,
Son and sire, the house of Saul!'   30

SONG OF SAUL BEFORE HIS LAST BATTLE

I

WARRIORS and chiefs! should the shaft or
    the sword
Pierce me in leading the host of the Lord,
Heed not the corse, though a king's, in
    your path:
Bury your steel in the bosoms of Gath!

II

Thou who art bearing my buckler and bow,
Should the soldiers of Saul look away from
    the foe,
Stretch me that moment in blood at thy feet!
Mine be the doom which they dared not
    to meet.

III

Farewell to others, but never we part,
Heir to my royalty, son of my heart!
Bright is the diadem, boundless the sway,
Or kingly the death, which awaits us to-day!

'ALL IS VANITY, SAITH THE PREACHER'

I

FAME, wisdom, love, and power were mine,
  And health and youth possess'd me;
My goblets blush'd from every vine,
  And lovely forms caress'd me;
I sunn'd my heart in beauty's eyes,
  And felt my soul grow tender;
All earth can give, or mortal prize,
  Was mine of regal splendour.

II

I strive to number o'er what days
  Remembrance can discover,
Which all that life or earth displays
  Would lure me to live over.
There rose no day, there roll'd no hour
  Of pleasure unembitter'd;
And not a trapping deck'd my power
  That gall'd not while it glitter'd.

III

The serpent of the field, by art
  And spells, is won from harming;
But that which coils around the heart,
  Oh! who hath power of charming?
It will not list to wisdom's lore,
  Nor music's voice can lure it;
But there it stings for evermore
  The soul that must endure it.

WHEN COLDNESS WRAPS THIS SUFFERING CLAY

I

WHEN coldness wraps this suffering clay,
  Ah! whither strays the immortal mind?
It cannot die, it cannot stay,
  But leaves its darken'd dust behind.
Then, unembodied, doth it trace
  By steps each planet's heavenly way?
Or fill at once the realms of space,
  A thing of eyes, that all survey?

II

Eternal, boundless, undecay'd,
  A thought unseen, but seeing all,
All, all in earth or skies display'd,
  Shall it survey, shall it recall:
Each fainter trace that memory holds
  So darkly of departed years,
In one broad glance the soul beholds,
  And all, that was, at once appears.

III

Before Creation peopled earth,
  Its eye shall roll through chaos back;
And where the farthest heaven had birth,
  The spirit trace its rising track.
And where the future mars or makes,
  Its glance dilate o'er all to be,
While sun is quench'd or system breaks,
  Fix'd in its own eternity.

IV

Above or Love, Hope, Hate, or Fear,
  It lives all passionless and pure:
An age shall fleet like earthly year;
  Its years as moments shall endure.
Away, away, without a wing,
  O'er all, through all, its thought shall fly,
A nameless and eternal thing,
  Forgetting what it was to die.

VISION OF BELSHAZZAR

I

THE King was on his throne,
  The Satraps throng'd the hall:
A thousand bright lamps shone
  O'er that high festival.

A thousand cups of gold,
  In Judah deem'd divine—
Jehovah's vessels hold
  The godless Heathen's wine!

II

In that same hour and hall,
  The fingers of a hand
Came forth against the wall,
  And wrote as if on sand:
The fingers of a man;—
  A solitary hand
Along the letters ran,
  And traced them like a wand.

III

The monarch saw, and shook,
  And bade no more rejoice;
All bloodless wax'd his look,
  And tremulous his voice.
'Let the men of lore appear,
  The wisest of the earth,
And expound the words of fear,
  Which mar our royal mirth.'

IV

Chaldea's seers are good,
  But here they have no skill;
And the unknown letters stood
  Untold and awful still.
And Babel's men of age
  Are wise and deep in lore;
But now they were not sage,
  They saw—but knew no more.

V

A captive in the land,
  A stranger and a youth,
He heard the king's command,
  He saw that writing's truth.
The lamps around were bright.
  The prophecy in view;
He read it on that night,—
  The morrow proved it true.

VI

'Belshazzar's grave is made,
  His kingdom pass'd away,
He, in the balance weigh'd,
  Is light and worthless clay;
The shroud his robe of state,
  His canopy the stone;
The Mede is at his gate!
  The Persian on his throne!'

SUN OF THE SLEEPLESS!

SUN of the sleepless! melancholy star!
Whose tearful beam glows tremulously far,
That show'st the darkness thou canst not dispel,
How like art thou to joy remember'd well!

So gleams the past, the light of other
    days,   5
Which shines, but warms not with its
    powerless rays;
A night-beam Sorrow watcheth to behold,
Distinct, but distant—clear—but, oh how
    cold!

WERE MY BOSOM AS FALSE AS THOU DEEM'ST IT TO BE

I

WERE my bosom as false as thou deem'st
    it to be,
I need not have wander'd from far Galilee;
It was but abjuring my creed to efface
The curse which, thou say'st, is the crime
    of my race.

II

If the bad never triumph, then God is with
    thee!
If the slave only sin, thou art spotless
    and free!
If the Exile on earth is an Outcast on high,
Live on in thy faith, but in mine I will die.

III

I have lost for that faith more than thou
    canst bestow,
As the God who permits thee to prosper
    doth know;
In his hand is my heart and my hope—
    and in thine
The land and the life which for him I
    resign.

HEROD'S LAMENT FOR MARIAMNE

I

OH, Mariamne! now for thee
    The heart for which thou bled'st is
    bleeding;
Revenge is lost in agony,
    And wild remorse to rage succeeding.
Oh, Mariamne! where art thou?
    Thou canst not hear my bitter pleading:
Ah! could'st thou—thou would'st pardon
    now,
    Though Heaven were to my prayer un-
    heeding.

II

And is she dead?—and did they dare
    Obey my frenzy's jealous raving?
My wrath but doom'd my own despair:
    The sword that smote her's o'er me
    waving.—
But thou art cold, my murder'd love!
    And this dark heart is vainly craving
For her who soars alone above,
    And leaves my soul unworthy saving.

III

She's gone, who shared my diadem;
    She sunk, with her my joys entombing;
I swept that flower from Judah's stem,
    Whose leaves for me alone were bloom-
    ing;
And mine's the guilt, and mine the hell,
    This bosom's desolation dooming;
And I have earn'd those tortures well,
    Which unconsumed are still consum-
    ing!

ON THE DAY OF THE DESTRUCTION OF JERUSALEM BY TITUS

I

FROM the last hill that looks on thy once
    holy dome,
I beheld thee, oh Sion! when render'd to
    Rome:
'Twas thy last sun went down, and the
    flames of thy fall
Flash'd back on the last glance I gave to
    thy wall.

II

I look'd for thy temple, I look'd for my
    home,
And forgot for a moment my bondage to
    come;
I beheld but the death-fire that fed on thy
    fane,
And the fast-fetter'd hands that made
    vengeance in vain.

III

On many an eve, the high spot whence I
    gazed
Had reflected the last beam of day as it
    blazed;
While I stood on the height, and beheld
    the decline
Of the rays from the mountain that shone
    on thy shrine.

IV

And now on that mountain I stood on
    that day,
But I mark'd not the twilight beam melt-
    ing away;
Oh! would that the lightning had glared
    in its stead,
And the thunderbolt burst on the con-
    queror's head!

V

But the gods of the Pagan shall never pro-
    fane
The shrine where Jehovah disdain'd not
    to reign;
And scatter'd and scorn'd as thy people
    may be,
Our worship, oh Father! is only for thee.

BY THE RIVERS OF BABYLON WE SAT DOWN AND WEPT

I

We sat down and wept by the waters
  Of Babel, and thought of the day
When our foe, in the hue of his slaughters,
  Made Salem's high places his prey;
And ye, oh her desolate daughters!
  Were scatter'd all weeping away.

II

While sadly we gazed on the river
  Which roll'd on in freedom below,
They demanded the song: but, oh never
  That triumph the stranger shall know!
May this right hand be wither'd for ever,
  Ere it string our high harp for the foe!

III

On the willow that harp is suspended,
  Oh Salem! its sound should be free;
And the hour when thy glories were ended
  But left me that token of thee:
And ne'er shall its soft tones be blended
  With the voice of the spoiler by me!

THE DESTRUCTION OF SENNACHERIB

I

The Assyrian came down like the wolf on
    the fold,
And his cohorts were gleaming in purple
    and gold;
And the sheen of their spears was like
    stars on the sea,
When the blue wave rolls nightly on deep
    Galilee.

II

Like the leaves of the forest when Summer
    is green,
That host with their banners at sunset
    were seen:
Like the leaves of the forest when Autumn
    hath blown,
That host on the morrow lay wither'd and
    strown.

III

For the Angel of Death spread his wings
    on the blast,
And breathed in the face of the foe as he
    pass'd;
And the eyes of the sleepers wax'd deadly
    and chill,
And their hearts but once heaved, and for
    ever grew still!

IV

And there lay the steed with his nostril
    all wide,
But through it there roll'd not the breath
    of his pride;

And the foam of his gasping lay white on
    the turf,
And cold as the spray of the rock-beating
    surf.

V

And there lay the rider distorted and pale,
With the dew on his brow, and the rust
    on his mail:
And the tents were all silent, the banners
    alone,
The lances unlifted, the trumpet unblown.

VI

And the widows of Ashur are loud in
    their wail,
And the idols are broke in the temple of
    Baal;
And the might of the Gentile, unsmote
    by the sword,
Hath melted like snow in the glance of the
    Lord!

A SPIRIT PASS'D BEFORE ME

FROM JOB

I

A spirit pass'd before me: I beheld
The face of immortality unveil'd—
Deep sleep came down on every eye save
    mine—
And there it stood,—all formless—but
    divine:
Along my bones the creeping flesh did
    quake;
And as my damp hair stiffen'd, thus it
    spake:

II

'Is man more just than God? Is man more
    pure
Than he who deems even Seraphs in-
    secure?
Creatures of clay—vain dwellers in the
    dust!
The moth survives you, and are ye more
    just?
Things of a day! you wither ere the night,
Heedless and blind to Wisdom's wasted
    light!'   _____

STANZAS FOR MUSIC

There be none of Beauty's daughters
  With a magic like thee;
And like music on the waters
  Is thy sweet voice to me:
When, as if its sound were causing   5
The charmed ocean's pausing,
The waves lie still and gleaming
And the lull'd winds seem dreaming:

83

And the midnight moon is weaving
　Her bright chain o'er the deep;　10
Whose breast is gently heaving,
　As an infant's asleep:
So the spirit bows before thee,
To listen and adore thee;
With a full but soft emotion,　15
Like the swell of Summer's ocean.

STANZAS FOR MUSIC

'O Lachrymarum fons, tenero sacros
Ducentium ortus ex animo: quater
Felix! in imo qui scatentem
Pectore te, pia Nympha, sensit.'
GRAY's *Poemata.*

THERE's not a joy the world can give like
　that it takes away,
When the glow of early thought declines
　in feeling's dull decay;
'Tis not on youth's smooth cheek the
　blush alone, which fades so fast,
But the tender bloom of heart is gone, ere
　youth itself be past.

Then the few whose spirits float above the
　wreck of happiness　5
Are driven o'er the shoals of guilt or
　ocean of excess:
The magnet of their course is gone, or
　only points in vain
The shore to which their shiver'd sail shall
　never stretch again.

Then the mortal coldness of the soul like
　death itself comes down;
It cannot feel for others' woes, it dare not
　dream its own;　10
That heavy chill has frozen o'er the foun-
　tain of our tears,
And though the eye may sparkle still, 'tis
　where the ice appears.

Though wit may flash from fluent lips,
　and mirth distract the breast,
Through midnight hours that yield no
　more their former hope of rest;
'Tis but as ivy-leaves around the ruin'd
　turret wreath,　15
All green and wildly fresh without, but
　worn and grey beneath.

Oh could I feel as I have felt,—or be what
　I have been,
Or weep as I could once have wept o'er
　many a vanish'd scene;
As springs in deserts found seem sweet,
　all brackish though they be,
So, midst the wither'd waste of life, those
　tears would flow to me.　20

March 1815.

ON NAPOLEON'S ESCAPE FROM ELBA

ONCE fairly set out on his party of pleasure,
Taking towns at his liking, and crowns
　at his leisure,
From Elba to Lyons and Paris he goes,
Making *balls for* the ladies, and *bows to*
　his foes.

March 27, 1815.

ODE FROM THE FRENCH

I

WE do not curse thee, Waterloo!
Though Freedom's blood thy plain bedew;
There 'twas shed, but is not sunk—
Rising from each gory trunk,
Like the water-spout from ocean,　5
With a strong and growing motion—
It soars, and mingles in the air,
With that of lost Labédoyère—
With that of him whose honour'd grave
Contains the 'bravest of the brave.'　10
A crimson cloud it spreads and glows,
But shall return to whence it rose;
When 'tis full 'twill burst asunder—
Never yet was heard such thunder
As then shall shake the world with won-
　der—　15
Never yet was seen such lightning
As o'er heaven shall then be bright'ning!
Like the Wormwood Star foretold
By the sainted Seer of old,
Show'ring down a fiery flood,　20
Turning rivers into blood.

II

The Chief has fallen, but not by you,
Vanquishers of Waterloo!
When the soldier citizen
Sway'd not o'er his fellow-men—　25
Save in deeds that led them on
Where Glory smiled on Freedom's son—
Who, of all the despots banded,
　With that youthful chief competed?
Who could boast o'er France defeated,
Till lone Tyranny commanded?　31
Till, goaded by ambition's sting,
The Hero sunk into the King?
Then he fell:—so perish all,
Who would men by man enthral!　35

III

And thou, too, of the snow-white plume!
Whose realm refused thee ev'n a tomb;
Better hadst thou still been leading
France o'er hosts of hirelings bleeding,
Than sold thyself to death and shame
For a meanly royal name;　41
Such as he of Naples wears,
Who thy blood-bought title bears.
Little didst thou deem, when dashing
　On thy war-horse through the ranks,
　Like a stream which burst its banks,
While helmets cleft, and sabres clashing,

Shone and shiver'd fast around thee—
Of the fate at last which found thee:
Was that haughty plume laid low   50
By a slave's dishonest blow?
Once—as the moon sways o'er the tide,
It roll'd in air, the warrior's guide;
Through the smoke-created night
Of the black and sulphurous fight,   55
The soldier raised his seeking eye
To catch that crest's ascendancy,—
And, as it onward rolling rose,
So moved his heart upon our foes.
There, where death's brief pang was
        quickest,   60
And the battle's wreck lay thickest,
Strew'd beneath the advancing banner
Of the eagle's burning crest—
(There with thunder-clouds to fan her,
  Who could then her wing arrest—   65
    Victory beaming from her breast?)
While the broken line enlarging
    Fell, or fled along the plain;
There be sure was Murat charging!
    There he ne'er shall charge again!   70

IV

O'er glories gone the invaders march,
Weeps Triumph o'er each levell'd arch—
But let Freedom rejoice,
With her heart in her voice;
But, her hand on her sword,   75
Doubly shall she be adored;
France hath twice too well been taught
The 'moral lesson' dearly bought—
Her safety sits not on a throne,
With Capet or Napoleon!   80
But in equal rights and laws,
Hearts and hands in one great cause—
Freedom, such as God hath given
Unto all beneath his heaven,
With their breath, and from their birth,
Though guilt would sweep it from the
        earth;   86
With a fierce and lavish hand
Scattering nations' wealth like sand;
Pouring nations' blood like water,
In imperial seas of slaughter!   90

V

But the heart and the mind,
And the voice of mankind,
Shall arise in communion—
And who shall resist that proud union?
The time is past when swords subdued—
Man may die—the soul's renew'd: 96
Even in this low world of care
Freedom ne'er shall want an heir;
Millions breathe but to inherit
Her for ever bounding spirit—   100
When once more her hosts assemble,
Tyrants shall believe and tremble—
Smile they at this idle threat?
Crimson tears will follow yet.

FROM THE FRENCH

I

MUST thou go, my glorious Chief,
    Sever'd from thy faithful few?
Who can tell thy warrior's grief,
    Maddening o'er that long adieu?
Woman's love, and friendship's zeal,
    Dear as both have been to me—
What are they to all I feel,
    With a soldier's faith for thee?

II

Idol of the soldier's soul!
    First in fight, but mightiest now;
Many could a world control;
    Thee alone no doom can bow.
By thy side for years I dared
    Death; and envied those who fell,
When their dying shout was heard,
    Blessing him they served so well.

III

Would that I were cold with those,
    Since this hour I live to see;
When the doubts of coward foes
    Scarce dare trust a man with thee,
Dreading each should set thee free!
    Oh! although in dungeons pent,
All their chains were light to me,
    Gazing on thy soul unbent.

IV

Would the sycophants of him
    Now so deaf to duty's prayer,
Were his borrow'd glories dim,
    In his native darkness share?
Were that world this hour his own,
    All thou calmly dost resign,
Could he purchase with that throne
    Hearts like those which still are thine?

V

My chief, my king, my friend, adieu!
    Never did I droop before;
Never to my sovereign sue,
    As his foes I now implore:
All I ask is to divide
    Every peril he must brave;
Sharing by the hero's side
    His fall, his exile, and his grave.

ON THE STAR OF 'THE LEGION
OF HONOUR'

[FROM THE FRENCH]

STAR of the brave!—whose beam hath
        shed
Such glory o'er the quick and dead—
Thou radiant and adored deceit!
Which millions rush'd in arms to greet,
Wild meteor of immortal birth;   5
Why rise in Heaven to set on Earth?

85

Souls of slain heroes form'd thy rays;
Eternity flash'd through thy blaze;
The music of thy martial sphere
Was fame on high and honour here;   10
And thy light broke on human eyes,
Like a volcano of the skies.

Like lava roll'd thy stream of blood,
And swept down empires with its flood;
Earth rock'd beneath thee to her base,
As thou didst lighten through all space;
And the shorn Sun grew dim in air,
And set while thou wert dwelling there.

Before thee rose, and with thee grew,
A rainbow of the loveliest hue   20
Of three bright colours, each divine,
And fit for that celestial sign;
For Freedom's hand had blended them,
Like tints in an immortal gem.

One tint was of the sunbeam's dyes;   25
One, the blue depth of Seraph's eyes;
One, the pure Spirit's veil of white
Had robed in radiance of its light:
The three so mingled did beseem
The texture of a heavenly dream.   30

Star of the brave! thy ray is pale,
And darkness must again prevail!
But, oh thou Rainbow of the free!
Our tears and blood must flow for thee.
When thy bright promise fades away,   35
Our life is but a load of clay.

And Freedom hallows with her tread
The silent cities of the dead;
For beautiful in death are they
Who proudly fall in her array;   40
And soon, oh Goddess! may we be
For evermore with them or thee!

NAPOLEON'S FAREWELL

[FROM THE FRENCH]

I

FAREWELL to the Land where the gloom
of my Glory
Arose and o'ershadow'd the earth with
her name—
She abandons me now—but the page of
her story,
The brightest or blackest, is fill'd with my
fame.
I have warr'd with a world which vanquish'd me only
When the meteor of conquest allured me
too far;
I have coped with the nations which dread
me thus lonely,
The last single Captive to millions in war.

II

Farewell to thee, France! when thy diadem crown'd me,
I made thee the gem and the wonder of
earth,
But thy weakness decrees I should leave
as I found thee,
Decay'd in thy glory, and sunk in thy
worth.
Oh! for the veteran hearts that were
wasted
In strife with the storm, when their battles
were won—
Then the Eagle, whose gaze in that moment was blasted,
Had still soar'd with eyes fix'd on victory's
sun!

III

Farewell to thee, France!—but when
Liberty rallies
Once more in thy regions, remember me
then,—
The violet still grows in the depth of thy
valleys;
Though wither'd, thy tear will unfold it
again—
Yet, yet, I may baffle the hosts that sur-
round us,
And yet may thy heart leap awake to my
voice—
There are links which must break in the
chain that has bound us,
Then turn thee and call on the Chief of
thy choice!

DOMESTIC PIECES

1816

FARE THEE WELL

'Alas! they had been friends in youth;
But whispering tongues can poison truth;
And constancy lives in realms above;
And life is thorny; and youth is vain;
And to be wroth with one we love,
Doth work like madness in the brain;

.   .   .   .   .

But never either found another
To free the hollow heart from paining—
They stood aloof, the scars remaining,
Like cliffs which had been rent asunder;
A dreary sea now flows between,
But neither heat, nor frost, nor thunder,
Shall wholly do away, I ween,
The marks of that which once hath been.'
COLERIDGE'S *Christabel.*

FARE thee well! and if for ever,
Still for ever, fare thee well:
Even though unforgiving, never
'Gainst thee shall my heart rebel.

Would that breast were bared before thee
Where thy head so oft hath lain.   6
While that placid sleep came o'er thee
Which thou ne'er canst know again;

Would that breast, by thee glanced over,
  Every inmost thought could show! 10
Then thou wouldst at last discover
  'Twas not well to spurn it so.

Though the world for this commend
    thee—
  Though it smile upon the blow,
Even its praises must offend thee, 15
  Founded on another's woe:

Though my many faults defaced me,
  Could no other arm be found,
Than the one which once embraced me,
  To inflict a cureless wound? 20

Yet, oh yet, thyself deceive not;
  Love may sink by slow decay,
But by sudden wrench, believe not
  Hearts can thus be torn away:

Still thine own its life retaineth, 25
  Still must mine, though bleeding, beat;
And the undying thought which paineth
  Is—that we no more may meet.

These are words of deeper sorrow
  Than the wail above the dead; 30
Both shall live, but every morrow
  Wake us from a widow'd bed.

And when thou wouldst solace gather,
  When our child's first accents flow,
Wilt thou teach her to say 'Father!' 35
  Though his care she must forego?

When her little hands shall press thee,
  When her lip to thine is press'd,
Think of him whose prayer shall bless
    thee,
  Think of him thy love had bless'd! 40

Should her lineaments resemble
  Those her never more may'st see,
Then thy heart will softly tremble
  With a pulse yet true to me. 44

All my faults perchance thou knowest,
  All my madness none can know;
All my hopes, where'er thou goest,
  Wither, yet with *thee* they go.

Every feeling hath been shaken; 49
  Pride, which not a world could bow,
Bows to thee—by thee forsaken,
  Even my soul forsakes me now:

But 'tis done—all words are idle—
  Words from me are vainer still;
But the thoughts we cannot bridle 55
  Force their way without the will.

Fare thee well! thus disunited,
  Torn from every nearer tie,
Sear'd in heart, and lone, and blighted,
  More than this I scarce can die. 60
              March 17, 1816.

A SKETCH

'Honest—honest Iago!
If that thou be'st a devil, I cannot kill thee.'
                    SHAKSPEARE.

BORN in the garret, in the kitchen bred,
Promoted thence to deck her mistress' head;
Next—for some gracious service un-
    express'd,
And from its wages only to be guess'd—
Raised from the toilette to the table,—
    where 5
Her wondering betters wait behind her
    chair.
With eye unmoved, and forehead un-
    abash'd,
She dines from off the plate she lately
    wash'd.
Quick with the tale, and ready with the lie,
The genial confidante, and general spy,
Who could, ye gods! her next employ-
    ment guess— 11
An only infant's earliest governess!
She taught the child to read, and taught
    so well,
That she herself, by teaching, learn'd to
    spell.
An adept next in penmanship she grows,
As many a nameless slander deftly shows:
What she had made the pupil of her art,
None know—but that high Soul secured
    the heart,
And panted for the truth it could not hear,
With longing breast and undeluded ear.
Foil'd was perversion by that youthful
    mind, 21
Which Flattery fool'd not, Baseness could
    not blind,
Deceit infect not, near Contagion soil,
Indulgence weaken, nor Example spoil,
Nor master'd Science tempt her to look
    down 25
On humbler talents with a pitying frown,
Nor Genius swell, nor Beauty render vain,
Nor Envy ruffle to retaliate pain,
Nor Fortune change, Pride raise, nor
    Passion bow,
Nor virtue teach austerity—till now. 30
Serenely purest of her sex that live,
But wanting one sweet weakness—to for-
    give,
Too shock'd at faults her soul can never
    know,
She deems that all could be like her be-
    low:
Foe to all vice, yet hardly Virtue's friend,
For Virtue pardons those she would
    amend. 36

But to the theme, now laid aside too
    long,
The baleful burthen of this honest song,
Though all her former functions are no
    more,
She rules the circle which she served before.

If mothers—none know why—before her
    quake;   41
If daughters dread her for the mothers'
    sake;
If early habits—those false links, which
    bind
At times the loftiest to the meanest
    mind—
Have given her power too deeply to instil
The angry essence of her deadly will; 46
If like a snake she steal within your
    walls,
Till the black slime betray her as she
    crawls;
If like a viper to the heart she wind,
And leave the venom there she did not
    find;   50
What marvel that this hag of hatred works
Eternal evil latent as she lurks,
To make a Pandemonium where she
    dwells,
And reign the Hecate of domestic hells?
Skill'd by a touch to deepen scandal's
    tints   55
With all the kind mendacity of hints,
While mingling truth with falsehood,
    sneers with smiles,
A thread of candour with a web of
    wiles:
A plain blunt show of briefly-spoken
    seeming,
To hide her bloodless heart's soul-
    harden'd scheming;   60
A lip of lies; a face form'd to conceal,
And, without feeling, mock at all who
    feel:
With a vile mask the Gorgon would dis-
    own,—
A cheek of parchment, and an eye of
    stone.
Mark, how the channels of her yellow
    blood   65
Ooze to her skin, and stagnate there to
    mud,
Cased like the centipede in saffron mail,
Or darker greenness of the scorpion's
    scale—
(For drawn from reptiles only may we
    trace
Congenial colours in that soul or face)—
Look on her features! and behold her
    mind   71
As in a mirror of itself defined:
Look on the picture! deem it not o'er-
    charged—
There is no trait which might not be en-
    larged:
Yet true to 'Nature's journeymen,' who
    made   75
This monster when their mistress left off
    trade—
This female dog-star of her little sky,
Where all beneath her influence droop or
    die.

Oh! wretch without a tear—without a
    thought,
Save joy above the ruin thou hast
    wrought—   80
The time shall come, nor long remote,
    when thou
Shalt feel far more than thou inflictest
    now;
Feel for thy vile self-loving self in vain,
And turn thee howling in unpitied pain.
May the strong curse of crush'd affections
    light   85
Back on thy bosom with reflected blight!
And make thee in thy leprosy of mind
As loathsome to thyself as to mankind!
Till all thy self-thoughts curdle into hate,
Black—as thy will for others would cre-
    ate: 90
Till thy hard heart be calcined into dust,
And thy soul welter in its hideous crust.
Oh, may thy grave be sleepless as the bed,
The widow'd couch of fire, that thou hast
    spread!
Then, when thou fain wouldst weary
    Heaven with prayer,   95
Look on thine earthly victims—and des-
    pair!
Down to the dust!—and, as thou rott'st
    away,
Even worms shall perish on thy poisonous
    clay.
But for the love I bore, and still must bear,
To her thy malice from all ties would
    tear—   100
Thy name—thy human name—to every eye
The climax of all scorn should hang on
    high,
Exalted o'er thy less abhorr'd compeers—
And festering in the infamy of years.

                 March 29, 1816.

ENDORSEMENT TO THE DEED OF SEPARATION

IN THE APRIL OF 1816

A YEAR ago, you swore, fond she!
    'To love, to honour,' and so forth:
Such was the vow you pledged to me,
    And here's exactly what 'tis worth.

STANZAS TO AUGUSTA

I

WHEN all around grew drear and dark,
    And reason half withheld her ray—
And hope but shed a dying spark
    Which more misled my lonely way;

II

In that deep midnight of the mind,
    And that internal strife of heart,
When dreading to be deem'd too kind,
    The weak despair—the cold depart;

III

When fortune changed—and love fled far,
  And hatred's shafts flew thick and fast,
Thou wert the solitary star
  Which rose and set not to the last.

IV

Oh! blest be thine unbroken light!
  That watch'd me as a seraph's eye,
And stood between me and the night,
  For ever shining sweetly nigh.

V

And when the cloud upon us came,
  Which strove to blacken o'er thy ray—
Then purer spread its gentle flame,
  And dash'd the darkness all away.

VI

Still may thy spirit dwell on mine,
  And teach it what to brave or brook—
There's more in one soft word of thine
  Than in the world's defied rebuke.

VII

Thou stood'st, as stands a lovely tree,
  That still unbroke, though gently bent,
Still waves with fond fidelity
  Its boughs above a monument.

VIII

The winds might rend—the skies might pour,
  But there thou wert—and still wouldst be
Devoted in the stormiest hour
  To shed thy weeping leaves o'er me.

IX

But thou and thine shall know no blight,
  Whatever fate on me may fall;
For heaven in sunshine will requite
  The kind—and thee the most of all.

X

Then let the ties of baffled love
  Be broken—thine will never break;
Thy heart can feel—but will not move;
  Thy soul, though soft, will never shake.

XI

And these, when all was lost beside,
  Were found and still are fix'd in thee;—
And bearing still a breast so tried,
  Earth is no desert—ev'n to me.

STANZAS TO AUGUSTA

I

THOUGH the day of my destiny's over,
  And the star of my fate hath declined,
Thy soft heart refused to discover
  The faults which so many could find;
Though thy soul with my grief was acquainted,
  It shrunk not to share it with me,
And the love which my spirit hath painted
  It never hath found but in *thee*.

II

Then when nature around me is smiling,
  The last smile which answers to mine,
I do not believe it beguiling,
  Because it reminds me of thine;
And when winds are at war with the ocean,
  As the breasts I believed in with me,
If their billows excite an emotion,
  It is that they bear me from *thee*.

III

Though the rock of my last hope is shiver'd,
  And its fragments are sunk in the wave,
Though I feel that my soul is deliver'd
  To pain—it shall not be its slave.
There is many a pang to pursue me:
  They may crush, but they shall not contemn;
They may torture, but shall not subdue me;
  'Tis of *thee* that I think—not of them.

IV

Though human, thou didst not deceive me,
  Though woman, thou didst not forsake,
Though loved, thou forborest to grieve me,
  Though slander'd, thou never couldst shake;
Though trusted, thou didst not disclaim me,
  Though parted, it was not to fly,
Though watchful, 'twas not to defame me,
  Nor, mute, that the world might belie.

V

Yet I blame not the world, nor despise it,
  Nor the war of the many with one;
If my soul was not fitted to prize it,
  'Twas folly not sooner to shun:
And if dearly that error hath cost me,
  And more than I once could foresee,
I have found that, whatever it lost me,
  It could not deprive me of *thee*.

VI

From the wreck of the past, which hath perish'd,
  Thus much I at least may recall,
It hath taught me that what I most cherish'd
  Deserved to be dearest of all:
In the desert a fountain is springing,
  In the wide waste there still is a tree,
And a bird in the solitude singing,
  Which speaks to my spirit of *thee*.

July 24, 1816.

EPISTLE TO AUGUSTA

I

My sister! my sweet sister! if a name
Dearer and purer were, it should be
    thine;
Mountains and seas divide us, but I
    claim
No tears, but tenderness to answer
    mine:
Go where I will, to me thou art the
    same—
A loved regret which I would not re-
    sign,
There yet are two things in my des-
    tiny,—
A world to roam through, and a home
    with thee.

II

The first were nothing—had I still the
    last,
It were the haven of my happiness;
But other claims and other ties thou
    hast,
And mine is not the wish to make
    them less.
A strange doom is thy father's son's,
    and past
Recalling, as it lies beyond redress;
Reversed for him our grandsire's fate
    of yore,—
He had no rest at sea, nor I on shore.

III

If my inheritance of storms hath been
In other elements, and on the rocks
Of perils, overlook'd or unforeseen,
I have sustain'd my share of worldly
    shocks,
The fault was mine; nor do I seek to
    screen
My errors with defensive paradox;
I have been cunning in mine overthrow,
The careful pilot of my proper woe.

IV

Mine were my faults, and mine be their
    reward.
My whole life was a contest, since the
    day
That gave me being, gave me that which
    marr'd
The gift,—a fate, or will, that walk'd
    astray;
And I at times have found the struggle
    hard,
And thought of shaking off my bonds
    of clay:
But now I fain would for a time sur-
    vive,
If but to see what next can well arrive.

V

Kingdoms and empires in my little day
I have outlived, and yet I am not old;
And when I look on this, the petty spray
Of my own years of trouble, which have
    roll'd
Like a wild bay of breakers, melts away:
Something—I know not what—does
    still uphold
A spirit of slight patience;—not in vain,
Even for its own sake, do we purchase
    pain.

VI

Perhaps the workings of defiance stir
Within me—or perhaps a cold despair,
Brought on when ills habitually recur,—
Perhaps a kinder clime, or purer air,
(For even to this may change of soul
    refer,
And with light armour we may learn to
    bear,)
Have taught me a strange quiet, which
    was not
The chief companion of a calmer lot.

VII

I feel almost at times as I have felt
In happy childhood; trees, and flowers,
    and brooks,
Which do remember me of where I dwelt
Ere my young mind was sacrificed to
    books,
Come as of yore upon me, and can melt
My heart with recognition of their
    looks;
And even at moments I could think I see
Some living thing to love—but none like
    thee.

VIII

Here are the Alpine landscapes which
    create
A fund for contemplation;—to admire
Is a brief feeling of a trivial date;
But something worthier do such scenes
    inspire:
Here to be lonely is not desolate,
For much I view which I could most
    desire,
And, above all, a lake I can behold
Lovelier, not dearer, than our own of old.

IX

Oh that thou wert but with me!—but
    I grow
The fool of my own wishes, and forget
The solitude which I have vaunted so
Has lost its praise in this but one regret;
There may be others which I less may
    show;—
I am not of the plaintive mood, and yet
I feel an ebb in my philosophy,
And the tide rising in my alter'd eye.

X

I did remind thee of our own dear Lake,
By the old Hall which may be mine no
more.
Leman's is fair; but think not I forsake
The sweet remembrance of a dearer
shore:
Sad havoc Time must with my memory
make,
Ere *that* or *thou* can fade these eyes
before;
Though, like all things which I have
loved, they are
Resign'd for ever, or divided far.

XI

The world is all before me; I but ask
Of Nature that with which she will
comply—
It is but in her summer's sun to bask,
To mingle with the quiet of her sky,
To see her gentle face without a mask,
And never gaze on it with apathy.
She was my early friend, and now shall
be
My sister—till I look again on thee.

XII

I can reduce all feelings but this one;
And that I would not;—for at length I
see
Such scenes as those wherein my life
begun.
The earliest—even the only paths for
me—
Had I but sooner learnt the crowd to
shun,
I had been better than I now can be;
The passions which have torn me would
have slept;
I had not suffer'd, and *thou* hadst not
wept.

XIII

With false Ambition what had I to do?
Little with Love, and least of all with
Fame;
And yet they came unsought, and with
me grew,
And made me all which they can make
—a name.
Yet this was not the end I did pursue;
Surely I once beheld a nobler aim.
But all is over—I am one the more
To baffled millions which have gone be-
fore.

XIV

And for the future, this world's future
may
From me demand but little of my care;
I have outlived myself by many a day;
Having survived so many things that
were;

My years have been no slumber, but
the prey
Of ceaseless vigils; for I had the share
Of life which might have fill'd a cen-
tury,
Before its fourth in time had pass'd me by.

XV

And for the remnant which may be to
come
I am content; and for the past I feel
Not thankless,—for within the crowded
sum
Of struggles, happiness at times would
steal,
And for the present, I would not be-
numb
My feelings further.—Nor shall I con-
ceal
That with all this I still can look around,
And worship Nature with a thought pro-
found.

XVI

For thee, my own sweet sister, in thy
heart
I know myself secure, as thou in mine;
We were and are—I am, even as thou
art—
Beings who ne'er each other can resign;
It is the same, together or apart,
From life's commencement to its slow
decline
We are entwined—let death come slow
or fast,
The tie which bound the first endures the
last!

THE DREAM

I

OUR life is two-fold: Sleep hath its own
world,
A boundary between the things misnamed
Death and existence: Sleep hath its own
world,
And a wide realm of wild reality.
And dreams in their development have
breath,   5
And tears, and tortures, and the touch of
joy;
They leave a weight upon our waking
thoughts,
They take a weight from off our waking
toils,
They do divide our being; they become
A portion of ourselves as of our time,
And look like heralds of eternity;   11
They pass like spirits of the past,—they
speak
Like Sibyls of the future: they have
power—
The tyranny of pleasure and of pain;

They make us what we were not—what
   they will,   15
And shake us with the vision that's gone
   by,
The dread of vanish'd shadows—Are they
   so?
Is not the past all shadow?—What are
   they?
Creations of the mind?—The mind can
   make
Substance, and people planets of its own
With beings brighter than have been, and
   give   21
A breath to forms which can outlive all
   flesh.
I would recall a vision which I dream'd
Perchance in sleep—for in itself a thought,
A slumbering thought, is capable of years,
And curdles a long life into one hour.

II

I saw two beings in the hues of youth
Standing upon a hill, a gentle hill,
Green and of mild declivity, the last
As 'twere the cape of a long ridge of such,
Save that there was no sea to lave its base,
But a most living landscape, and the wave
Of woods and corn-fields, and the abodes
   of men   33
Scatter'd at intervals, and wreathing
   smoke
Arising from such rustic roofs;—the hill
Was crown'd with a peculiar diadem   36
Of trees, in circular array, so fix'd,
Not by the sport of nature, but of man:
These two, a maiden and a youth, were
   there   39
Gazing—the one on all that was beneath
Fair as herself—but the boy gazed on her;
And both were young, and one was beauti-
   ful:
And both were young—yet not alike in
   youth.
As the sweet moon on the horizon's verge,
The maid was on the eve of womanhood;
The boy had fewer summers, but his heart
Had far outgrown his years, and to his
   eye   47
There was but one beloved face on earth,
And that was shining on him: he had
   look'd
Upon it till it could not pass away;   50
He had no breath, no being, but in hers;
She was his voice; he did not speak to her,
But trembled on her words; she was his
   sight,
For in her eye follow'd hers, and saw with
   hers,
Which colour'd all his objects:—he had
   ceased   55
To live within himself; she was his life,
The ocean to the river of his thoughts,
Which terminated all: upon a tone,

A touch of hers, his blood would ebb and
   flow,
And his cheek change tempestuously—
   his heart   60
Unknowing of its cause of agony.
But she in these fond feelings had no share:
Her sighs were not for him; to her he was
Even as a brother—but no more; 'twas
   much,
For brotherless she was, save in the name
Her infant friendship had bestow'd on
   him;   66
Herself the solitary scion left
Of a time-honour'd race.—It was a name
Which pleased him, and yet pleased him
   not—and why?
Time taught him a deep answer—when
   she loved   70
Another; even *now* she loved another,
And on the summit of that hill she stood
Looking afar if yet her lover's steed
Kept pace with her expectancy, and flew.

III

A change came o'er the spirit of my
   dream.   75
There was an ancient mansion, and be-
   fore
Its walls there was a steed caparison'd;
Within an antique Oratory stood
The Boy of whom I spake;—he was alone,
And pale, and pacing to and fro: anon
He sate him down, and seized a pen, and
   traced   81
Words which I could not guess of; then
   he lean'd
His bow'd head on his hands, and shook
   as 'twere
With a convulsion—then arose again,
And with his teeth and quivering hands
   did tear   85
What he had written, but he shed no tears,
And he did calm himself, and fix his brow
Into a kind of quiet: as he paused,
The Lady of his love re-entered there;
She was serene and smiling then, and yet
She knew she was by him beloved,—she
   knew,   91
For quickly comes such knowledge, that
   his heart
Was darken'd with her shadow, and she
   saw
That he was wretched, but she saw not all.
He rose, and with a cold and gentle grasp
He took her hand; a moment o'er his face
A tablet of unutterable thoughts   97
Was traced, and then it faded, as it came;
He dropp'd the hand he held, and with
   slow steps
Retired, but not as bidding her adieu,
For they did part with mutual smiles; he
   pass'd   101
From out the massy gate of that old Hall,

And mounting on his steed he went his
　　way;
And ne'er repass'd that hoary threshold
　more.

IV

A change came o'er the spirit of my
　dream.　　　　　　　　　　　　105
The Boy was sprung to manhood: in the
　wilds
Of fiery climes he made himself a home,
And his soul drank their sunbeams: he
　was girt
With strange and dusky aspects; he was
　not　　　　　　　　　　　　　　109
Himself like what he had been; on the sea
And on the shore he was a wanderer.
There was a mass of many images
Crowded like waves upon me, but he was
A part of all; and in the last he lay
Reposing from the noontide sultriness,
Couch'd among fallen columns, in the
　shade　　　　　　　　　　　　　116
Of ruin'd walls that had survived the
　names
Of those who rear'd them; by his sleeping
　side
Stood camels grazing, and some goodly
　steeds　　　　　　　　　　　　119
Were fasten'd near a fountain; and a man
Clad in a flowing garb did watch the while,
While many of his tribe slumber'd around:
And they were canopied by the blue sky,
So cloudless, clear, and purely beautiful,
That God alone was to be seen in heaven.

V

A change came o'er the spirit of my dream.
The Lady of his love was wed with One
Who did not love her better:—in her
　home,
A thousand leagues from his,—her native
　home,　　　　　　　　　　　　129
She dwelt, begirt with growing Infancy,
Daughters and sons of Beauty,—but be-
　hold!
Upon her face there was the tint of grief,
The settled shadow of an inward strife,
And an unquiet drooping of the eye,
As if its lid were charged with unshed
　tears.　　　　　　　　　　　　135
What could her grief be?—she had all she
　loved,
And he who had so loved her was not
　there
To trouble with bad hopes, or evil wish,
Or ill-repress'd affliction, her pure thoughts.
What could her grief be?—she had loved
　him not,　　　　　　　　　　　140
Nor given him cause to deem himself be-
　loved,
Nor could he be a part of that which
　prey'd
Upon her mind—a spectre of the past.

VI

A change came o'er the spirit of my
　dream.
The Wanderer was return'd.—I saw him
　stand　　　　　　　　　　　　145
Before an Altar—with a gentle bride;
Her face was fair, but was not that which
　made
The Starlight of his Boyhood;—as he
　stood
Even at the altar, o'er his brow there came
The self-same aspect, and the quivering
　shock　　　　　　　　　　　　150
That in the antique Oratory shook
His bosom in its solitude; and then—
As in that hour—a moment o'er his face
The tablet of unutterable thoughts
Was traced,—and then it faded as it
　came,　　　　　　　　　　　　155
And he stood calm and quiet, and he
　spoke
The fitting vows, but heard not his own
　words,
And all things reel'd around him; he
　could see
Not that which was, nor that which should
　have been—
But the old mansion, and the accustom'd
　hall,　　　　　　　　　　　　160
And the remember'd chambers, and the
　place,
The day, the hour, the sunshine, and the
　shade,
All things pertaining to that place and
　hour,
And her who was his destiny,—came back
And thrust themselves between him and
　the light:　　　　　　　　　　165
What business had they there at such a
　time?

VII

A change came o'er the spirit of my
　dream.
The Lady of his love:—Oh! she was
　changed
As by the sickness of the soul; her mind
Had wander'd from its dwelling, and her
　eyes　　　　　　　　　　　　170
They had not their own lustre, but the
　look
Which is not of the earth; she was become
The queen of a fantastic realm; her
　thoughts
Were combinations of disjointed things;
And forms impalpable and unperceived
Of others' sight familiar were to hers.　176
And this the world calls frenzy; but the
　wise
Have a far deeper madness, and the glance
Of melancholy is a fearful gift;
What is it but the telescope of truth?　180
Which strips the distance of its fantasies,

And brings life near in utter nakedness,
Making the cold reality too real!

VIII

A change came o'er the spirit of my
    dream.
The Wanderer was alone as heretofore,
The beings which surrounded him were
    gone,   186
Or were at war with him; he was a mark
For blight and desolation, compass'd
    round
With Hatred and Contention; Pain was
    mix'd   189
In all which was served up to him, until,
Like to the Pontic monarch of old days,
He fed on poisons, and they had no power,
But were a kind of nutriment; he lived
Through that which had been death to
    many men,
And made him friends of mountains:
    with the stars   195
And the quick Spirit of the Universe
He held his dialogues; and they did teach
To him the magic of their mysteries;
To him the book of Night was open'd
    wide,
And voices from the deep abyss reveal'd
A marvel and a secret—Be it so.   201

IX

My dream was past; it had no further
    change.
It was of a strange order, that the doom
Of these two creatures should be thus
    traced out
Almost like a reality—the one   205
To end in madness—both in misery.

July 1816.

LINES ON HEARING THAT LADY BYRON WAS ILL

AND thou wert sad—yet I was not with
    thee;
And thou wert sick, and yet I was not
    near;
Methought that joy and health alone
    could be
Where I was *not*—and pain and sorrow
    here!
And is it thus?—it is as I foretold,   5
And shall be more so; for the mind
    recoils
Upon itself, and the wreck'd heart lies
    cold,
While heaviness collects the shatter'd
    spoils.
It is not in the storm nor in the strife
We feel benumb'd, and wish to be no
    more,   10
But in the after-silence on the shore,
When all is lost, except a little life.

I am too well avenged!—but 'twas my right;
Whate'er my sins might be, *thou* wert
    not sent
To be the Nemesis who should requite—
Nor did Heaven choose so near an
    instrument.   16
Mercy is for the merciful!—if thou
Hast been of such, 'twill be accorded now.
Thy nights are banish'd from the realms
    of sleep!—
Yes! they may flatter thee, but thou
    shalt feel   20
A hollow agony which will not heal,
For thou art pillow'd on a curse too deep;
Thou hast sown in my sorrow, and must
    reap
The bitter harvest in a woe as real!
I have had many foes, but none like thee;
For 'gainst the rest myself I could de-
    fend,   26
And be avenged, or turn them into
    friend;
But thou in safe implacability
Hadst nought to dread—in thy own
    weakness shielded,
And in my love, which hath but too much
    yielded,   30
And spared, for thy sake, some I should
    not spare;
And thus upon the world—trust in thy
    truth,
And the wild fame of my ungovern'd
    youth—
On things that were not, and on things
    that are—   34
Even upon such a basis hast thou built
A monument, whose cement hath been
    guilt!
The moral Clytemnestra of thy lord,
And hew'd down, with an unsuspected
    sword,
Fame, peace, and hope—and all the better
    life,
Which, but for this cold treason of thy
    heart,   40
Might still have risen from out the grave
    of strife,
And found a nobler duty than to part.
But of thy virtues didst thou make a vice,
Trafficking with them in a purpose cold,
For present anger, and for future
    gold—   45
And buying others' grief at any price.
And thus once enter'd into crooked ways,
The earthly truth, which was thy proper
    praise,
Did not still walk beside thee—but at
    times,
And with a breast unknowing its own
    crimes,   50
Deceit, averments incompatible,
Equivocations, and the thoughts which
    dwell
In Janus-spirits—the significant eye

Which learns to lie with silence—the pre-
text   54
Of prudence, with advantages annex'd—
The acquiescence in all things which tend,
No matter how, to the desired end—
  All found a place in thy philosophy.
The means were worthy, and the end is
won—
I would not do by thee as thou hast done!
              September 1816.

DARKNESS

I HAD a dream, which was not all a dream.
The bright sun was extinguish'd, and the
stars
Did wander darkling in the eternal space,
Rayless, and pathless, and the icy earth
Swung blind and blackening in the moon-
less air;   5
Morn came and went—and came, and
brought no day,
And men forgot their passions in the dread
Of this their desolation; and all hearts
Were chill'd into a selfish prayer for light:
And they did live by watchfires—and the
thrones,   10
The palaces of crowned kings—the huts,
The habitations of all things which dwell,
Were burnt for beacons; cities were con-
sumed,
And men were gather'd round their blaz-
ing homes
To look once more into each other's face;
Happy were those who dwelt within the
eye   16
Of the volcanos, and their mountain-torch:
A fearful hope was all the world contain'd;
Forests were set on fire—but hour by hour
They fell and faded—and the crackling
trunks   20
Extinguish'd with a crash—and all was
black.
The brows of men by the despairing light
Wore an unearthly aspect, as by fits
The flashes fell upon them; some lay down
And hid their eyes and wept; and some
did rest   25
Their chins upon their clenched hands,
and smiled;
And others hurried to and fro, and fed
Their funeral piles with fuel, and look'd up
With mad disquietude on the dull sky,   29
The pall of a past world; and then again
With curses cast them down upon the dust,
And gnash'd their teeth and howl'd: the
wild birds shriek'd
And, terrified, did flutter on the ground,
And flap their useless wings; the wildest
brutes
Came tame and tremulous; and vipers
crawl'd   35
And twined themselves among the multi-
tude,

Hissing, but stingless—they were slain for
food.
And War, which for a moment was no
more,
Did glut himself again:—a meal was
bought
With blood, and each sate sullenly apart
Gorging himself in gloom: no love was
left;   41
All earth was but one thought—and that
was death
Immediate and inglorious; and the pang
Of famine fed upon all entrails—men
Died, and their bones were tombless as
their flesh;   45
The meagre by the meagre were devour'd,
Even dogs assail'd their masters, all save
one,
And he was faithful to a corse, and kept
The birds and beasts and famish'd men
at bay,
Till hunger clung them, or the dropping
dead   50
Lured their lank jaws; himself sought out
no food,
But with a piteous and perpetual moan,
And a quick desolate cry, licking the hand
Which answer'd not with a caress—he
died.
The crowd was famish'd by degrees; but
two   55
Of an enormous city did survive,
And they were enemies: they met beside
The dying embers of an altar-place
Where had been heap'd a mass of holy
things
For an unholy usage; they raked up,   60
And shivering scraped with their cold
skeleton hands
The feeble ashes, and their feeble breath
Blew for a little life, and made a flame
Which was a mockery; then they lifted up
Their eyes as it grew lighter, and beheld
Each other's aspects—saw, and shriek'd,
and died—   66
Even of their mutual hideousness they
died,
Unknowing who he was upon whose brow
Famine had written Fiend. The world
was void,
The populous and the powerful was a
lump,   70
Seasonless, herbless, treeless, manless,
lifeless,
A lump of death—a chaos of hard clay.
The rivers, lakes, and ocean all stood still,
And nothing stirr'd within their silent
depths;
Ships sailorless lay rotting on the sea,   75
And their masts fell down piecemeal: as
they dropp'd
They slept on the abyss without a surge—
The waves were dead; the tides were in
their grave,

The moon, their mistress, had expired
    before;
The winds were wither'd in the stagnant
    air,   80
And the clouds perish'd; Darkness had
    no need
Of aid from them—She was the Universe.

                 Diodati, *July* 1816.

MONODY ON THE DEATH

OF

THE RIGHT HON. R. B. SHERIDAN

SPOKEN AT DRURY-LANE THEATRE

WHEN the last sunshine of expiring day
In summer's twilight weeps itself away,
Who hath not felt the softness of the hour
Sink on the heart, as dew along the flower?
With a pure feeling which absorbs and
    awes   5
While Nature makes that melancholy
    pause,
Her breathing moment on the bridge
    where Time
Of light and darkness forms an arch sub-
    lime,
Who hath not shared that calm, so still
    and deep,
The voiceless thought which would not
    speak but weep,   10
A holy concord, and a bright regret,
A glorious sympathy with suns that set?
'Tis not harsh sorrow, but a tenderer woe,
Nameless, but dear to gentle hearts below,
Felt without bitterness, but full and clear,
A sweet dejection, a transparent tear, 16
Unmix'd with worldly grief or selfish stain,
Shed without shame, and secret without
    pain.

Even as the tenderness that hour instils
When Summer's day declines along the
    hills,   20
So feels the fulness of our heart and eyes
When all of Genius which can perish dies.
A mighty Spirit is eclipsed—a Power
Hath pass'd from day to darkness—to
    whose hour
Of light no likeness is bequeath'd—no
    name,   25
Focus at once of all the rays of Fame!
The flash of Wit, the bright Intelligence,
The beam of Song, the blaze of Eloquence,
Set with their Sun, but still have left be-
    hind   29
The enduring produce of immortal Mind;
Fruits of a genial morn, and glorious noon,
A deathless part of him who died too soon.
But small that portion of the wondrous
    whole,
These sparkling segments of that circling
    soul,

Which all embraced, and lighten'd over
    all,   35
To cheer, to pierce, to please, or to appal.
From the charm'd council to the festive
    board,
Of human feelings the unbounded lord;
In whose acclaim the loftiest voices vied,
The praised, the proud, who made his
    praise their pride.   40
When the loud cry of trampled Hindostan
Arose to Heaven in her appeal from man,
His was the thunder, his the avenging rod,
The wrath—the delegated voice of God!
Which shook the nations through his lips,
    and blazed   45
Till vanquish'd senates trembled as they
    praised.

And here, oh! here, where yet all
    young and warm,
The gay creations of his spirit charm,
The matchless dialogue, the deathless wit,
Which knew not what it was to intermit;
The glowing portraits, fresh from life, that
    bring   51
Home to our hearts the truth from which
    they spring;
These wondrous beings of his fancy,
    wrought
To fulness by the fiat of his thought,
Here in their first abode you still may
    meet,   55
Bright with the hues of his Promethean
    heat;
A halo of the light of other days,
Which still the splendour of its orb be-
    trays.

But should there be to whom the fatal
    blight   59
Of failing Wisdom yields a base delight,
Men who exult when minds of heavenly
    tone
Jar in the music which was born their own,
Still let them pause—ah! little do they
    know
That what to them seem'd Vice might be
    but Woe.   64
Hard is his fate on whom the public gaze
Is fix'd for ever to detract or praise;
Repose denies her requiem to his name,
And Folly loves the martyrdom of Fame.
The secret enemy whose sleepless eye
Stands sentinel, accuser, judge, and spy,
The foe, the fool, the jealous, and the vain,
The envious who but breathe in others'
    pain,   72
Behold the host! delighting to deprave,
Who track the steps of Glory to the grave,
Watch every fault that daring Genius owes
Half to the ardour which its birth bestows,
Distort the truth, accumulate the lie,
And pile the pyramid of Calumny!   78

These are his portion—but if join'd to
  these
Gaunt Poverty should league with deep
  Disease,   80
If the high Spirit must forget to soar,
And stoop to strive with Misery at the
  door,
To soothe Indignity—and face to face
Meet sordid Rage, and wrestle with Dis-
  grace,
To find in Hope but the renew'd caress,
The serpent-fold of further Faithless-
  ness:—   86
If such may be the ills which men assail,
What marvel if at last the mightiest fail?
Breasts to whom all the strength of feeling
  given
Bear hearts electric—charged with fire
  from Heaven,   90
Black with the rude collision, inly torn,
By clouds surrounded, and on whirl-
  winds borne,
Driven o'er the lowering atmosphere that
  nurst
Thoughts which have turn'd to thunder—
  scorch, and burst.

But far from us and from our mimic
  scene   95
Such things should be—if such have ever
  been;
Ours be the gentler wish, the kinder task,
To give the tribute Glory need not ask,
To mourn the vanish'd beam, and add
  our mite   99
Of praise in payment of a long delight.
Ye Orators! whom yet our councils yield,
Mourn for the veteran Hero of your field!
The worthy rival of the wondrous *Three!*
Whose words were sparks of Immortality!
Ye Bards! to whom the Drama's muse is
  dear,   105
He was your Master—emulate him *here!*
Ye men of wit and social eloquence!
He was your brother—bear his ashes
  hence!
While Powers of mind almost of bound-
  less range,
Complete in kind, as various in their
  change,   110
While Eloquence, Wit, Poesy, and Mirth,
That humbler Harmonist of care on
  Earth,
Survive within our souls—while lives our
  sense
Of pride in Merit's proud pre-eminence,
Long shall we seek his likeness, long in
  vain,   115
And turn to all of him which may remain,
Sighing that nature form'd but one such
  man,
And broke the die—in moulding Sheri-
  dan!

           Diodati, July 17, 1816.

CHURCHILL'S GRAVE

A FACT LITERALLY RENDERED

I STOOD beside the grave of him who
  blazed
The comet of a season, and I saw
The humblest of all sepulchres, and gazed
With not the less of sorrow and of awe
On that neglected turf and quiet stone,
With name no clearer than the names un-
  known,   6
Which lay unread around it; and I ask'd
The Gardener of that ground, why it
  might be
That for this plant strangers his memory
  task'd,
Through the thick deaths of half a cen-
  tury?   10
And thus he answer'd—'Well, I do not
  know
Why frequent travellers turn to pilgrims
  so;
He died before my day of Sextonship,
And I had not the digging of this grave.'
And is this all? I thought—and do we rip
The veil of Immortality, and crave
I know not what of honour and of light
Through unborn ages, to endure this
  blight,   18
So soon, and so successless? As I said,
The Architect of all on which we tread,
For Earth is but a tombstone, did essay,
To extricate remembrance from the clay,
Whose minglings might confuse a New-
  ton's thought,
Were it not that all life must end in one,
Of which we are but dreamers;—as he
  caught,   25
As 'twere the twilight of a former Sun,
Thus spoke he,—'I believe the man of
  whom
You wot, who lies in this selected tomb,
Was a most famous writer in his day,
And therefore travellers step from out
  their way   30
To pay him honour,—and myself whate'er
Your honour pleases:'—then most
  pleased I shook
From out my pocket's avaricious nook
Some certain coins of silver, which as
  'twere
Perforce I gave this man, though I could
  spare   35
So much but inconveniently:—Ye smile,
I see ye, ye profane ones! all the while,
Because my homely phrase the truth
  would tell.
You are the fools, not I—for I did dwell
With a deep thought, and with a soften'd
  eye,   40
On that old Sexton's natural homily,
In which there was Obscurity and Fame—
The Glory and the Nothing of a Name.

           Diodati, 1816.

OCCASIONAL PIECES
PROMETHEUS

I

Titan! to whose immortal eyes
  The sufferings of mortality,
  Seen in their sad reality,
Were not as things that gods despise;
What was thy pity's recompense?   5
A silent suffering, and intense;
The rock, the vulture, and the chain,
All that the proud can feel of pain,
The agony they do not show,
The suffocating sense of woe,   10
  Which speaks but in its loneliness,
And then is jealous lest the sky
Should have a listener, nor will sigh
  Until its voice is echoless.

II

Titan! to thee the strife was given   15
  Between the suffering and the will,
  Which torture where they cannot kill;
And the inexorable Heaven,
And the deaf tyranny of Fate,
The ruling principle of Hate,   20
Which for its pleasure doth create
The things it may annihilate,
Refused thee even the boon to die:
The wretched gift eternity   24
Was thine—and thou hast borne it well.
All that the Thunderer wrung from thee
Was but the menace which flung back
On him the torments of thy rack;
The fate thou didst so well foresee,
But would not to appease him tell;   30
And in thy Silence was his Sentence,
And in his Soul a vain repentance,
And evil dread so ill dissembled,
That in his hand the lightnings trembled.

III

Thy Godlike crime was to be kind,   35
  To render with thy precepts less
  The sum of human wretchedness,
And strengthen Man with his own mind;
But baffled as thou wert from high,
Still in thy patient energy,   40
In the endurance, and repulse
  Of thine impenetrable Spirit,
Which Earth and Heaven could not con-
    vulse,
  A mighty lesson we inherit:
Thou art a symbol and a sign   45
  To Mortals of their fate and force;
Like thee, Man is in part divine,
  A troubled stream from a pure source;
And Man in portions can foresee
His own funereal destiny;   50
His wretchedness, and his resistance,
And his sad unallied existence:
To which his Spirit may oppose
Itself—and equal to all woes,
  And a firm will, and a deep sense,   55

Which even in torture can descry
  Its own concenter'd recompense,
Triumphant where it dares defy,
And making Death a Victory.

Diodati, July 1816.

A FRAGMENT

Could I remount the river of my years
To the first fountain of our smiles and
    tears,
I would not trace again the stream of
    hours
Between their outworn banks of wither'd
    flowers,
But bid it flow as now—until it glides   5
Into the number of the nameless tides.

      .   .   .   .

What is this Death?—a quiet of the heart?
The whole of that of which we are a part?
For life is but a vision—what I see
Of all which lives alone is life to me,   10
And being so—the absent are the dead,
Who haunt us from tranquillity, and
    spread
A dreary shroud around us, and invest
With sad remembrances our hours of rest.
  The absent are the dead—for they are
      cold,   15
And ne'er can be what once we did behold;
And they are changed, and cheerless,—
    or if yet
The unforgotten do not all forget,
Since thus divided—equal must it be
If the deep barrier be of earth, or sea;   20
It may be both—but one day end it must
In the dark union of insensate dust.
  The under-earth inhabitants—are they
But mingled millions decomposed to clay?
The ashes of a thousand ages spread   25
Wherever man has trodden or shall tread?
Or do they in their silent cities dwell
Each in his incommunicative cell?
Or have they their own language? and a
    sense
Of breathless being?—darken'd and in-
    tense   30
As midnight in her solitude?—Oh Earth!
Where are the past?—and wherefore had
    they birth?
The dead are thy inheritors—and we
But bubbles on thy surface; and the
    key
Of thy profundity is in the grave,   35
The ebon portal of thy peopled cave,
Where I would walk in spirit, and behold
Our elements resolved to things untold,
And fathom hidden wonders, and ex-
    plore
The essence of great bosoms now no
    more.   40

      .   .   .   .

Diodati, July 1816.

SONNET TO LAKE LEMAN

ROUSSEAU—Voltaire—our   Gibbon—and
    De Staël—
    Leman! these names are worthy of thy
        shore,
    Thy shore of names like these! wert
        thou no more,
Their memory thy remembrance would
    recall: 4
To them thy banks were lovely as to all,
    But they have made them lovelier, for
        the lore
    Of mighty minds doth hallow in the core
Of human hearts the ruin of a wall
    Where dwelt the wise and wondrous;
        but by *thee*
How much more, Lake of Beauty! do we
    feel,   10
    In sweetly gliding o'er thy crystal sea,
The wild glow of that not ungentle zeal,
    Which of the heirs of immortality
Is proud, and makes the breath of glory
    real!

                            Diodati, *July* 1816.

STANZAS FOR MUSIC*

I

BRIGHT be the place of thy soul!
    No lovelier spirit than thine
E'er burst from its mortal control,
    In the orbs of the blessed to shine.
On earth thou wert all but divine,
    As thy soul shall immortally be;
And our sorrow may cease to repine
    When we know that thy God is with
        thee.

II

Light be the turf of thy tomb!
    May its verdure like emeralds be!
There should not be the shadow of gloom
    In aught that reminds us of thee.
Young flowers and an evergreen tree
    May spring from the spot of thy rest:
But not cypress nor yew let us see;
    For why should we mourn for the blest?

A VERY MOURNFUL BALLAD ON THE SIEGE AND CONQUEST OF ALHAMA

*Which, in the Arabic language, is to the
    following purport*

I

THE Moorish King rides up and down,
Through Granada's royal town;
From Elvira's gate to those
Of Bivarambla on he goes.
            Woe is me, Alhama!

* [See also p. 52.]

II

Letters to the monarch tell
How Alhama's city fell:
In the fire the scroll he threw,
And the messenger he slew.
            Woe is me, Alhama!

III

He quits his mule, and mounts his horse,
And through the street directs his course;
Through the street of Zacatin
To the Alhambra spurring in.
            Woe is me, Alhama!

IV

When the Alhambra walls he gain'd,
On the moment he ordain'd
That the trumpet straight should sound
With the silver clarion round.
            Woe is me, Alhama!

V

And when the hollow drums of war
Beat the loud alarm afar,
That the Moors of town and plain
Might answer to the martial strain.
            Woe is me, Alhama!

VI

Then the Moors, by this aware,
That bloody Mars recall'd them there,
One by one, and two by two,
To a mighty squadron grew.
            Woe is me, Alhama!

VII

Out then spake an aged Moor
In these words the king before,
'Wherefore call on us, oh King?
What may mean this gathering?'
            Woe is me, Alhama!

VIII

'Friends! ye have, alas! to know
Of a most disastrous blow;
That the Christians, stern and bold,
Have obtain'd Alhama's hold.'
            Woe is me, Alhama!

IX

Out then spake old Alfaqui,
With his beard so white to see,
'Good King! thou art justly served,
Good King! this thou hast deserved.
            Woe is me, Alhama!

X

'By thee were slain, in evil hour,
The Abencerrage, Granada's flower;
And strangers were received by thee
Of Cordova the Chivalry.
Woe is me, Alhama!

XI

'And for this, oh King! is sent
On thee a double chastisement:
Thee and thine, thy crown and realm,
One last wreck shall overwhelm.
Woe is me, Alhama!

XII

'He who holds no laws in awe,
He must perish by the law;
And Granada must be won,
And thyself with her undone.'
Woe is me, Alhama!

XIII

Fire flash'd from out the old Moor's eyes,
The Monarch's wrath began to rise,
Because he answer'd, and because
He spake exceeding well of laws.
Woe is me, Alhama!

XIV

'There is no law to say such things
As may disgust the ear of kings:'—
Thus, snorting with his choler, said
The Moorish King, and doom'd him dead.
Woe is me, Alhama!

XV

Moor Alfaqui! Moor Alfaqui!
Though thy beard so hoary be,
The King hath sent to have thee seized,
For Alhama's loss displeased.
Woe is me, Alhama!

XVI

And to fix thy head upon
High Alhambra's loftiest stone;
That this for thee should be the law,
And others tremble when they saw.
Woe is me, Alhama!

XVII

'Cavalier, and man of worth!
Let these words of mine go forth!
Let the Moorish Monarch know,
That to him I nothing owe.
Woe is me, Alhama!

XVIII

'But on my soul Alhama weighs,
And on my inmost spirit preys;

And if the King his land hath lost,
Yet others may have lost the most.
Woe is me, Alhama!

XIX

'Sires have lost their children, wives
Their lords, and valiant men their lives!
One what best his love might claim
Hath lost, another wealth, or fame.
Woe is me, Alhama!

XX

'I lost a damsel in that hour,
Of all the land the loveliest flower;
Doubloons a hundred I would pay,
And think her ransom cheap that day.'
Woe is me, Alhama!

XXI

And as these things the old Moor said,
They sever'd from the trunk his head;
And to the Alhambra's wall with speed
'Twas carried, as the King decreed.
Woe is me, Alhama!

XXII

And men and infants therein weep
Their loss, so heavy and so deep;
Granada's ladies, all she rears
Within her walls, burst into tears.
Woe is me, Alhama!

XXIII

And from the windows o'er the walls
The sable web of mourning falls;
The King weeps as a woman o'er
His loss, for it is much and sore.
Woe is me, Alhama!

STANZAS FOR MUSIC

I

THEY say that Hope is happiness;
But genuine Love must prize the past,
And Memory wakes the thoughts that
bless:
They rose the first—they set the last;

II

And all that Memory loves the most
Was once our only Hope to be,
And all that Hope adored and lost
Hath melted into Memory.

III

Alas! it is delusion all:
The future cheats us from afar,
Nor can we be what we recall,
Nor dare we think on what we are.

TRANSLATION FROM VITTORELLI

ON A NUN

Sonnet composed in the name of a father, whose daughter had recently died shortly after her marriage; and addressed to the father of her who had lately taken the veil.

OF two fair virgins, modest, though ad-
    mired,
  Heaven made us happy; and now,
    wretched sires,
  Heaven for a nobler doom their worth
    desires,
And gazing upon *either*, *both* required.
Mine, while the torch of Hymen newly
    fired   5
  Becomes extinguish'd, soon—too soon
    —expires:
But thine, within the closing grate re-
    tired,
  Eternal captive, to her God aspires.
But *thou* at least from out the jealous door,
  Which shuts between your never-meet-
    ing eyes,   10
  May'st hear her sweet and pious voice
    once more:
I to the marble, where *my* daughter lies,
  Rush,—the swoln flood of bitterness
    I pour,
  And knock, and knock, and knock—
    but none replies.

ON THE BUST OF HELEN BY CANOVA

IN this beloved marble view,
  Above the works and thoughts of man,
What Nature *could*, but *would not*, do,
  And Beauty and Canova *can*!
Beyond imagination's power,   5
  Beyond the Bard's defeated art,
With immortality her dower,
  Behold the *Helen* of the *heart*!

November 1816.

SONG FOR THE LUDDITES

I

As the Liberty lads o'er the sea
Bought their freedom, and cheaply, with
    blood,
    So we, boys, we
Will *die* fighting, or *live* free,
And down with all kings but King Ludd!

II

When the web that we weave is com-
    plete,
And the shuttle exchanged for the sword,
  We will fling the winding sheet
  O'er the despot at our feet,
And dye it deep in the gore he has pour'd.

III

Though black as his heart its hue,
Since his veins are corrupted to mud,
    Yet this is the dew
    Which the tree shall renew
Of Liberty, planted by Ludd!

December 1816.

VERSICLES

I READ the 'Christabel';
    Very well:
I read the 'Missionary';
    Pretty—very
I tried at 'Ilderim';   5
    Ahem!
I read a sheet of 'Marg'ret of *Anjou*';
    Can you?
I turn'd a page of Scott's 'Waterloo';
    Pooh! pooh!   10
I look'd at Wordsworth's milk-white
    'Rylstone Doe';
    Hillo!
  &c. &c. &c.

March 1817.

SO, WE'LL GO NO MORE A ROVING

I

So, we'll go no more a roving
  So late into the night,
Though the heart be still as loving,
  And the moon be still as bright.

II

For the sword outwears its sheath,
  And the soul wears out the breast,
And the heart must pause to breathe,
  And love itself have rest.

III

Though the night was made for loving,
  And the day returns too soon,
Yet we'll go no more a roving
  By the light of the moon.

1817.

TO THOMAS MOORE

WHAT are you doing now,
  Oh Thomas Moore?
What are you doing now,
  Oh Thomas Moore?
Sighing or suing now,   5
Rhyming or wooing now,
Billing or cooing now,
  Which, Thomas Moore?

But the Carnival's coming,
  Oh Thomas Moore!   10
The Carnival's coming,
  Oh Thomas Moore!

Masking and humming,
Fifing and drumming,
Guitarring and strumming,   15
Oh Thomas Moore!

TO MR. MURRAY

To hook the reader, you, John Murray,
  Have publish'd 'Anjou's Margaret,'
Which won't be sold off in a hurry
  (At least, it has not been as yet);
And then, still further to bewilder 'em, 5
Without remorse, you set up 'Ilderim;'
  So mind you don't get into debt,
Because as how, if you should fail,
These books would be but baddish bail.

And mind you do *not* let escape   10
  These rhymes to Morning Post or Perry,
Which would be *very* treacherous—
  very,
And get me into such a scrape!
For, firstly, I should have to sally,
  All in my little boat, against a *Galley;*
And, should I chance to slay the Assyrian
  wight, 16
Have next to combat with the female
  knight.

March 25, 1817.

TO THOMAS MOORE

I

My boat is on the shore,
  And my bark is on the sea;
But, before I go, Tom Moore,
  Here's a double health to thee!

II

Here's a sigh to those who love me,
  And a smile to those who hate;
And, whatever sky's above me,
  Here's a heart for every fate.

III

Though the ocean roar around me,
  Yet it still shall bear me on;
Though a desert should surround me,
  It hath springs that may be won.

IV

Were't the last drop in the well,
  As I gasp'd upon the brink,
Ere my fainting spirit fell,
  'Tis to thee that I would drink.

V

With that water, as this wine,
  The libation I would pour
Should be—peace with thine and mine,
  And a health to thee, Tom Moore.

July 1817.

EPISTLE FROM MR. MURRAY TO DR. POLIDORI

DEAR Doctor, I have read your play,
Which is a good one in its way,—
Purges the eyes and moves the bowels,
And drenches handkerchiefs like towels
With tears, that, in a flux of grief, 5
Afford hysterical relief
To shatter'd nerves and quicken'd pulses,
Which your catastrophe convulses.

I like your moral and machinery;
Your plot, too, has such scope for scen-
  ery: 10
Your dialogue is apt and smart:
The play's concoction full of art;
Your hero raves, your heroine cries,
All stab, and everybody dies.
In short, your tragedy would be 15
The very thing to hear and see:
And for a piece of publication,
If I decline on this occasion,
It is not that I am not sensible
To merits in themselves ostensible, 20
But—and I grieve to speak it—plays
Are drugs—mere drugs, sir—now-a-days.
I had a heavy loss by 'Manuel,'—
Too lucky if it prove not annual,—
And Sotheby, with his 'Orestes,' 25
(Which, by the by, the author's best is,)
Has lain so very long on hand,
That I despair of all demand.
I've advertised, but see my books,
Or only watch my shopman's looks;—
Still Ivan, Ina, and such lumber, 31
My back-shop glut, my shelves encumber.

There's Byron too, who once did better,
Has sent me, folded in a letter,
A sort of—it's no more a drama 35
Than Darnley, Ivan, or Kehama:
So alter'd since last year his pen is,
I think he's lost his wits at Venice.
In short, sir, what with one and t'other,
I dare not venture on another. 40
I write in haste; excuse each blunder;
The coaches through the street so thun-
  der!
My room's so full—we've Gifford here
Reading MS., with Hookham Frere,
Pronouncing on the nouns and particles
Of some of our forthcoming Articles. 46

The Quarterly—Ah, sir, if you
Had but the genius to review!—
A smart critique upon St. Helena,
Or if you only would but tell in a 50
Short compass what——but to resume:
As I was saying, sir, the room—
The room's so full of wits and bards,
Crabbes, Campbells, Crokers, Freres, and
  Wards,

And others, neither bards nor wits:—
My humble tenement admits   56
All persons in the dress of gent,
From Mr. Hammond to Dog Dent.

A party dines with me to-day,
All clever men, who make their way;
Crabbe, Malcolm, Hamilton, and Chan-
   trey,   61
Are all partakers of my pantry.
They're at this moment in discussion
On poor De Staël's late dissolution.
Her book, they say, was in advance—
Pray Heaven, she tell the truth of France!
Thus run our time and tongues away;—
But, to return, sir, to your play:
Sorry, sir, but I cannot deal,
Unless 'twere acted by O'Neill;   70
My hands so full, my head so busy,
I'm almost dead, and always dizzy;
And so, with endless truth and hurry,
Dear Doctor, I am yours,
            JOHN MURRAY.
            August 1817.

EPISTLE TO MR. MURRAY

My dear Mr. Murray,
You're in a damn'd hurry,
   To set up this ultimate Canto;
But (if they don't rob us)
You'll see Mr. Hobhouse   5
   Will bring it safe in his portmanteau.

For the Journal you hint of,
As ready to print off,
   No doubt you do right to commend it;
But as yet I have writ off   10
The devil a bit of
   Our 'Beppo:'—when copied, I'll send
      it.

Then you've Sotheby's Tour,—
No great things, to be sure,—
   You could hardly begin with a less
      work;   15
For the pompous rascallion,
Who don't speak Italian
   Nor French, must have scribbled by
      guess work.

You can make any loss up
With 'Spence' and his gossip,   20
   A work which must surely succeed;
Then Queen Mary's Epistle-craft,
With the new 'Fytte' of 'Whistlecraft,'
   Must make people purchase and read.

Then you've General Gordon,   25
Who girded his sword on,
   To serve with a Muscovite master
And help him to polish
A nation so owlish,
   They thought shaving their beards a
      disaster.   30

For the man, 'poor and shrewd,'
With whom you'd conclude
   A compact without more delay,
Perhaps some such pen is
Still extant in Venice;   35
   But please, sir, to mention *your pay*.
          Venice, *January* 8, 1818.

TO MR. MURRAY

STRAHAN, Tonson, Lintot of the times,
Patron and publisher of rhymes,
For thee the bard up Pindus climbs,
      My Murray.

To thee, with hope and terror dumb,   5
The unfledged MS. authors come;
Thou printest all—and sellest some—
      My Murray.

Upon thy table's baize so green
The last new Quarterly is seen,—   10
But where is thy new Magazine,
      My Murray?

Along thy sprucest bookshelves shine
The works thou deemest most divine—
The 'Art of Cookery,' and mine,   15
      My Murray.

Tours, Travels, Essays, too, I wist,
And Sermons, to thy mill bring grist;
And then thou hast the 'Navy List,'
      My Murray.   20

And Heaven forbid I should conclude
Without 'the Board of Longitude,'
Although this narrow paper would,
      My Murray.
          Venice, *March* 25, 1818.

ON THE BIRTH OF
JOHN WILLIAM RIZZO HOPPNER

HIS father's sense, his mother's grace,
   In him, I hope, will always fit so;
With—still to keep him in good case—
   The health and appetite of Rizzo.
          February 1818.

ODE ON VENICE

I

OH Venice! Venice! when thy marble walls
   Are level with the waters, there shall be
A cry of nations o'er thy sunken halls,
   A loud lament along the sweeping sea!
If I, a northern wanderer, weep for thee,
What should thy sons do?—anything but
      weep: 6
And yet they only murmur in their sleep.
In contrast with their fathers—as the
      slime,
The dull green ooze of the receding deep,
Is with the dashing of the spring-tide foam
That drives the sailor shipless to his home,

Are they to those that were; and thus they
creep,   12
Crouching and crab-like, through their
sapping streets.
Oh! agony—that centuries should reap
No mellower harvest! Thirteen hundred
years   15
Of wealth and glory turn'd to dust and
tears;
And every monument the stranger meets,
Church, palace, pillar, as a mourner
greets;
And even the Lion all subdued appears,
And the harsh sound of the barbarian
drum,   20
With dull and daily dissonance, repeats
The echo of thy tyrant's voice along
The soft waves, once all musical to song,
That heaved beneath the moonlight with
the throng
Of gondolas—and to the busy hum   25
Of cheerful creatures, whose most sinful
deeds
Were but the overbeating of the heart,
And flow of too much happiness, which
needs
The aid of age to turn its course apart
From the luxuriant and voluptuous flood
Of sweet sensations, battling with the
blood.   31
But these are better than the gloomy
errors,
The weeds of nations in their last decay,
When Vice walks forth with her unsoften'd
terrors,
And Mirth is madness, and but smiles to
slay;   35
And Hope is nothing but a false delay,
The sick man's lightning half an hour ere
death,
When Faintness, the last mortal birth of
Pain,
And apathy of limb, the dull beginning
Of the cold staggering race which Death
is winning,   40
Steals vein by vein and pulse by pulse away;
Yet so relieving the o'er-tortured clay,
To him appears renewal of his breath,
And freedom the mere numbness of his
chain;   44
And then he talks of life, and how again
He feels his spirit soaring—albeit weak,
And of the fresher air, which he would
seek:
And as he whispers knows not that he
gasps,
That his thin finger feels not what it clasps,
And so the film comes o'er him, and the
dizzy   50
Chamber swims round and round, and
shadows busy,
At which he vainly catches, flit and gleam,
Till the last rattle chokes the strangled
scream,

And all is ice and blackness,—and the
earth
That which it was the moment ere our
birth.   55

II

There is no hope for nations!—Search the
page
Of many thousand years—the daily
scene,
The flow and ebb of each recurring age,
The everlasting *to be* which *hath been*,
Hath taught us nought, or little: still
we lean   60
On things that rot beneath our weight,
and wear
Our strength away in wrestling with the
air:
For 'tis our nature strikes us down: the
beasts
Slaughter'd in hourly hecatombs for feasts
Are of as high an order—they must go
Even where their driver goads them,
though to slaughter.   66
Ye men, who pour your blood for kings
as water,
What have they given your children in re-
turn?
A heritage of servitude and woes,
A blindfold bondage, where your hire is
blows.   70
What! do not yet the red-hot plough-
shares burn,
O'er which you stumble in a false ordeal,
And deem this proof of loyalty the *real;*
Kissing the hand that guides you to your
scars,
And glorying as you tread the glowing
bars?   75
All that your sires have left you, all that
Time
Bequeaths of free, and History of sublime,
Spring from a different theme! Ye see and
read,
Admire and sigh, and then succumb and
bleed!
Save the few spirits who, despite of all,
And worse than all, the sudden crimes
engender'd   81
By the down-thundering of the prison-
wall,
And thirst to swallow the sweet waters
tender'd,
Gushing from Freedom's fountains, when
the crowd,
Madden'd with centuries of drought, are
loud,   85
And trample on each other to obtain
The cup which brings oblivion of a chain
Heavy and sore, in which long yoked they
plough'd
The sand,—or if there sprung the yellow
grain,

'Twas not for them, their necks were too
 much bow'd,   90
And their dead palates chew'd the cud of
 pain:
Yes! the few spirits, who, despite of deeds
Which they abhor, confound not with the
 cause
Those momentary starts from Nature's
 laws,
Which, like the pestilence and earthquake,
 smite   95
But for a term, then pass, and leave the
 earth
With all her seasons to repair the blight
With a few summers, and again put forth
Cities and generations—fair, when free—
For, Tyranny, there blooms no bud for
 thee!   100

III

Glory and Empire! once upon these
 towers
 With Freedom—godlike Triad! how you
  sate!
The league of mightiest nations, in those
 hours
 When Venice was an envy, might abate,
 But did not quench her spirit; in her
  fate   105
All were enwrapp'd: the feasted monarchs
 knew
 And loved their hostess, nor could learn
  to hate,
Although they humbled—with the kingly
 few
The many felt, for from all days and climes
She was the voyager's worship; even her
 crimes   110
Were of the softer order—born of Love,
She drank no blood, nor fatten'd on the
 dead,
But gladden'd where her harmless con-
 quests spread;
For these restored the Cross, that from
 above
Hallow'd her sheltering banners, which
 incessant   115
Flew between earth and the unholy Cres-
 cent,
Which, if it waned and dwindled, Earth
 may thank
The city it has clothed in chains, which
 clank
Now, creaking in the ears of those who
 owe
The name of Freedom to her glorious
 struggles;   120
Yet she but shares with them a common
 woe,
And call'd the 'kingdom' of a conquering
 foe,
But knows what all—and, most of all, we
 know—
With what set gilded terms a tyrant juggles!

IV

The name of Commonwealth is past and
 gone   125
 O'er the three fractions of the groaning
  globe;
Venice is crush'd, and Holland deigns to
 own
 A sceptre, and endures the purple robe;
If the free Switzer yet bestrides alone
His chainless mountains, 'tis but for a
 time,   130
For tyranny of late is cunning grown,
And in its own good season tramples down
The sparkles of our ashes. One great
 clime,
Whose vigorous offspring by dividing ocean
Are kept apart and nursed in the devotion
Of Freedom, which their fathers fought
 for, and   136
Bequeath'd—a heritage of heart and hand,
And proud distinction from each other
 land,
Whose sons must bow them at a monarch's
 motion,
As if his senseless sceptre were a wand
Full of the magic of exploded science—
Still one great clime, in full and free de-
 fiance,   142
Yet rears her crest, unconquer'd and sub-
 lime,
Above the far Atlantic!—She has taught
Her Esau-brethren that the haughty flag,
The floating fence of Albion's feebler crag,
May strike to those whose red right hands
 have bought   147
Rights cheaply earn'd with blood. Still,
 still, for ever,
Better, though each man's life-blood were
 a river,
That it should flow, and overflow, than
 creep   150
Through thousand lazy channels in our
 veins,
Damm'd like the dull canal with locks and
 chains,
And moving, as a sick man in his sleep,
Three paces, and then faltering: better be
Where the extinguish'd Spartans still are
 free,   155
In their proud charnel of Thermopylæ,
Than stagnate in our marsh,—or o'er the
 deep
Fly, and one current to the ocean add,
One spirit to the souls our fathers had,
One freeman more, America, to thee!

STANZAS TO THE PO

RIVER, that rollest by the ancient walls,
 Where dwells the lady of my love, when
  she
Walks by thy brink, and there perchance
 recalls
 A faint and fleeting memory of me;

OCCASIONAL PIECES

What if thy deep and ample stream should
  be   5
  A mirror of my heart, where she may
    read
The thousand thoughts I now betray to thee,
  Wild as thy wave, and headlong as thy
    speed!

What do I say—a mirror of my heart?
  Are not thy waters sweeping, dark, and
    strong?   10
Such as my feelings were and are, thou art;
  And such as thou art were my passions
    long.

Time may have somewhat tamed them,—
    not for ever;
  Thou overflow'st thy banks, and not for
    aye   14
Thy bosom overboils, congenial river!
  Thy floods subside, and mine have sunk
    away:

But left long wrecks behind, and now again,
  Borne on our old unchanged career, we
    move:
Thou tendest wildly onwards to the main,
  And I—to loving *one* I should not love.

The current I behold will sweep beneath
  Her native walls, and murmur at her
    feet;   22
Her eyes will look on thee, when she shall
    breathe
  The twilight air, unharm'd by summer's
    heat.

She will look on thee,—I have look'd on
    thee,   25
  Full of that thought: and, from that
    moment, ne'er
Thy waters could I dream of, name, or see
  Without the inseparable sigh for her!

Her bright eyes will be imaged in thy
    stream,
  Yes! they will meet the wave I gaze on
    now: 30
Mine cannot witness, even in a dream,
  That happy wave repass me in its flow!

The wave that bears my tears returns no
    more:
  Will she return by whom that wave shall
    sweep?—
Both tread thy banks, both wander on
    thy shore,   35
  I by thy source, she by the dark-blue
    deep.

But that which keepeth us apart is not
  Distance, nor depth of wave, nor space
    of earth,
But the distraction of a various lot,
  As various as the climates of our birth.

A stranger loves the lady of the land,   41
  Born far beyond the mountains, but his
    blood
Is all meridian, as if never fann'd
  By the black wind that chills the polar
    flood.

My blood is all meridian; were it not,   45
  I had not left my clime, nor should I be,
In spite of tortures ne'er to be forgot,
  A slave again of love,—at least of thee.

'Tis vain to struggle—let me perish
    young—   49
  Live as I lived, and love as I have loved;
To dust if I return, from dust I sprung,
  And then, at least, my heart can ne'er
    be moved.

April 1819.

SONNET TO GEORGE THE FOURTH

ON THE REPEAL OF LORD EDWARD FITZGERALD'S FORFEITURE

To be the father of the fatherless,
  To stretch the hand from the throne's
    height, and raise
  His offspring, who expired in other days
To make thy sire's sway by a kingdom
    less,—
This is to be a monarch, and repress   5
  Envy into unutterable praise.
Dismiss thy guard, and trust thee to such
    traits,
For who would lift a hand, except to bless?
Were it not easy, sir, and is't not sweet
  To make thyself beloved? and to be
Omnipotent by mercy's means? for thus
  Thy sovereignty would grow but more
    complete: 12
A despot thou, and yet thy people free,
  And by the heart, not hand, enslaving us.

Bologna, *August* 12, 1819.

EPIGRAM

FROM THE FRENCH OF RULHIÈRES

If, for silver or for gold,
  You could melt ten thousand pimples
  Into half a dozen dimples,
Then your face we might behold,   4
  Looking, doubtless, much more snugly;
  Yet even *then* 'twould be damned ugly.

August 12, 1819.

STANZAS

COULD Love for ever
Run like a river,
And Time's endeavour
  Be tried in vain—
No other pleasure   5
With this could measure;
And like a treasure
  We'd hug the chain.

But since our sighing
Ends not in dying,   10
And, form'd for flying,
  Love plumes his wing;
Then for this reason
Let's love a season;
But let that season be only Spring.   15

When lovers parted
Feel broken-hearted,
And, all hopes thwarted,
  Expect to die;
A few years older,   20
Ah! how much colder
They might behold her
  For whom they sigh!
When link'd together,
In every weather,   25
They pluck Love's feather
  From out his wing—
He'll stay for ever,
But sadly shiver
Without his plumage, when past the Spring.

Like chiefs of Faction,   31
His life is action—
A formal paction
  That curbs his reign,
Obscures his glory,   35
Despot no more, he
Such territory
  Quits with disdain.
Still, still advancing,
With banners glancing,   40
His power enhancing,
  He must move on—
Repose but cloys him,
Retreat destroys him,
Love brooks not a degraded throne.   45

Wait not, fond lover!
Till years are over,
And then recover
  As from a dream.
While each bewailing   50
The other's failing,
With wrath and railing,
  All hideous seem—
While first decreasing,
Yet not quite ceasing,   55
Wait not till teasing
  All passion blight:
If once diminish'd,
Love's reign is finish'd—
Then part in friendship—and bid good-   60
  night.

So shall Affection
To recollection
The dear connexion
  Bring back with joy:
You had not waited   65
Till, tired or hated,
Your passions sated
  Began to cloy.

Your last embraces
Leave no cold traces—   70
The same fond faces
  As through the past:
And eyes, the mirrors
Of your sweet errors,
Reflect but rapture—not least though last. 75

True, separations   76
Ask more than patience;
What desperations
  From such have risen!
But yet remaining,   80
What is't but chaining
Hearts which, once waning,
  Beat 'gainst their prison?
Time can but cloy love
And use destroy love: 85
The winged boy, Love,
  Is but for boys—
You'll find it torture,
Though sharper, shorter,
To wean, and not wear out your joys.

                                        1819

ON MY WEDDING-DAY

HERE'S a happy new year! but with reason
  I beg you'll permit me to say—
Wish me *many* returns of the *season*,
  But as *few* as you please of the day.
                                January 2, 1820.

EPITAPH FOR WILLIAM PITT

WITH death doom'd to grapple,
  Beneath this cold slab, he
Who lied in the Chapel
  Now lies in the Abbey.
                                January 1820.

EPIGRAM

IN digging up your bones, Tom Paine,
  Will. Cobbett has done well:
You visit him on earth again,
  He'll visit you in hell.
                                January 1820.

STANZAS

WHEN a man hath no freedom to fight
    for at home,
  Let him combat for that of his neigh-
    bours;
Let him think of the glories of Greece and
    of Rome,
  And get knock'd on the head for his
    labours.
To do good to mankind is the chivalrous
    plan,   5
  And is always as nobly requited;
Then battle for freedom wherever you can,
  And, if not shot or hang'd, you'll get
    knighted.
                                November 1820.

OCCASIONAL PIECES

EPIGRAM

THE world is a bundle of hay,
    Mankind are the asses who pull;
Each tugs it a different way,
    And the greatest of all is John Bull.

THE CHARITY BALL

WHAT matter the pangs of a husband and
        father,
If his sorrows in exile be great or be small,
So the Pharisee's glories around her she
        gather,
And the saint patronizes her 'charity
        ball!'

What matters—a heart which, though
    faulty, was feeling,   5
Be driven to excesses which once could
    appal—
That the sinner should suffer is only fair
    dealing,
As the saint keeps her charity back for
    'the ball'!

EPIGRAM

ON THE BRAZIERS' COMPANY HAVING RE-
SOLVED TO PRESENT AN ADDRESS TO
QUEEN CAROLINE

THE braziers, it seems, are determined to pass
An address, and present it themselves all
    in brass;—
A superfluous pageant—for, by the Lord
    Harry!
They'll find where they're going much
    more than they carry.

EPIGRAM ON MY WEDDING-DAY

TO PENELOPE

THIS day, of all our days, has done
    The worst for me and you:—
'Tis just *six* years since we were *one*,
    And *five* since we were *two*.
                                January 2, 1821.

ON MY THIRTY-THIRD BIRTHDAY

JANUARY 22, 1821

THROUGH life's dull road, so dim and dirty,
I have dragg'd to three-and-thirty.
What have these years left to me?
Nothing—except thirty-three.

MARTIAL, LIB. I, EPIG. I

'Hic est, quem legis, ille, quem requiris,
    Toto notus in orbe Martialis,' &c.

HE unto whom thou art so partial,
Oh, reader! is the well-known Martial,
The Epigrammatist: while living,
Give him the fame thou wouldst be giving;
So shall he hear, and feel, and know it— 5
Post-obits rarely reach a poet.

BOWLES AND CAMPBELL

To the tune of 'Why, how now, saucy jade?'

WHY, how now, saucy Tom?
    If you thus must ramble,
I will publish some
    Remarks on Mister Campbell.

ANSWER

WHY, how now, Billy Bowles?   5
    Sure the priest is maudlin!
(*To the public*) How can you, d—n your
    souls?
Listen to his twaddling?
                                February 22, 1821.

EPIGRAMS

OH, Castlereagh! thou art a patriot now;
Cato died for his country, so didst thou:
He perish'd rather than see Rome en-
    slaved,
Thou cutt'st thy throat that Britain may
    be saved!

So Castlereagh has cut his throat!—The
    worst
Of this is,—that his own was not the first.

So *He* has cut his throat at last!—He!
    Who?
The man who cut his country's long ago.

EPITAPH

POSTERITY will ne'er survey
    A nobler grave than this:
Here lie the bones of Castlereagh:
    Stop, traveller——

JOHN KEATS

WHO kill'd John Keats?
    'I,' says the Quarterly,
    So savage and Tartarly;
    ''Twas one of my feats.'

Who shot the arrow?   5
    'The poet-priest Milman
    (So ready to kill man),
    Or Southey, or Barrow.'
                                July 1821.

THE CONQUEST

[This fragment was found amongst Lord Byron's
papers after his departure from Genoa for
Greece.]

THE Son of Love and Lord of War I sing;
    Him who bade England bow to Nor-
        mandy,
And left the name of conqueror more
    than king
    To his unconquerable dynasty.

108

Not fann'd alone by Victory's fleeting
    wing,   5
He rear'd his bold and brilliant throne
    on high:
The Bastard kept, like lions, his prey fast,
    And Britain's bravest victor was the
    last.

March 8–9, 1823.

TO MR. MURRAY

For Orford and for Waldegrave
You give much more than me you gave;
Which is not fairly to behave,
        My Murray.

Because if a live dog, 'tis said,   5
Be worth a lion fairly sped,
A *live lord* must be worth *two* dead,
        My Murray.

And if, as the opinion goes,   9
Verse hath a better sale than prose,—
Certes, I should have more than those,
        My Murray.

But now this sheet is nearly cramm'd,
So, if *you will*, *I* shan't be shamm'd,
And if you *won't*, *you* may be damn'd,
        My Murray.   16

THE IRISH AVATAR

'And Ireland, like a bastinadoed elephant,
kneeling to receive the paltry rider.'—Curran.

Ere the daughter of Brunswick is cold in
    her grave,
    And her ashes still float to their home
    o'er the tide,
Lo! George the triumphant speeds over
    the wave,
    To the long-cherish'd isle which he
    loved like his—bride!

True, the great of her bright and brief era
    are gone,   5
    The rainbow-like epoch where Freedom
    could pause
For the few little years, out of centuries
    won,
    Which betray'd not, or crush'd not, or
    wept not her cause.

True, the chains of the Catholic clank o'er
    his rags,
    The castle still stands, and the senate 's
    no more,   10
And the famine which dwelt on her free-
    domless crags
    Is extending its steps to her desolate
    shore.

To her desolate shore—where the emi-
    grant stands
    For a moment to gaze ere he flies from
    his hearth;

Tears fall on his chain, though it drops
    from his hands,   15
    For the dungeon he quits is the place of
    his birth.

But he comes! the Messiah of royalty
    comes!
    Like a goodly Leviathan roll'd from the
    waves;
Then receive him as best such an advent
    becomes,
    With a legion of cooks, and an army of
    slaves!   20

He comes in the promise and bloom of
    threescore,
    To perform in the pageant the sove-
    reign's part—
But long live the shamrock, which sha-
    dows him o'er!
    Could the green in his *hat* be transferr'd
    to his *heart* !

Could that long-wither'd spot but be ver-
    dant again,   25
    And a new spring of noble affections
    arise—
Then might freedom forgive thee this
    dance in thy chain,
    And this shout of thy slavery which sad-
    dens the skies.

Is it madness or meanness which clings to
    thee now?
    Were he God—as he is but the com-
    monest clay,   30
With scarce fewer wrinkles than sins on
    his brow—
    Such servile devotion might shame him
    away.

Ay, roar in his train! let thine orators lash
    Their fanciful spirits to pamper his
    pride—
Not thus did thy Grattan indignantly flash
    His soul o'er the freedom implored and
    denied.   36

Ever glorious Grattan! the best of the
    good!
    So simple in heart, so sublime in the rest!
With all which Demosthenes wanted en-
    dued,
    And his rival or victor in all he possess'd.

Ere Tully arose in the zenith of Rome,
    Though unequall'd, preceded, the task
    was begun—   42
But Grattan sprung up like a god from the
    tomb
    Of ages, **the first, last, the saviour, the**
    one !

With the skill of an Orpheus to soften the
   brute;   45
  With the fire of Prometheus to kindle
    mankind;
Even Tyranny listening sate melted or
   mute,
  And Corruption shrunk scorch'd from
    the glance of his mind.

But back to our theme! Back to despots
   and slaves!
  Feasts furnish'd by Famine! rejoicings
    by Pain!   50
True freedom but *welcomes*, while slavery
   still *raves*,
  When a week's saturnalia hath loosen'd
    her chain.

Let the poor squalid splendour thy wreck
   can afford
  (As the bankrupt's profusion his ruin
    would hide),
Gild over the palace, Lo! Erin, thy lord!
  Kiss his foot with thy blessing, his bless-
    ings denied!   56

Or *if* freedom past hope be extorted at last,
  If the idol of brass find his feet are of
    clay,
Must what terror or policy wring forth be
   class'd
  With what monarchs ne'er give, but as
    wolves yield their prey?   60

Each brute hath its nature; a king's is to
   reign,—
  To *reign !* in that word see, ye ages, com-
    prised
The cause of the curses all annals contain,
  From Cæsar the dreaded to George the
    despised!

Wear, Fingal, thy trapping! O'Connell,
   proclaim   65
  His accomplishments! *Hist !!!* and thy
    country convince
Half an age's contempt was an error of
   fame,
  And that 'Hal is the rascaliest, sweet-
    est *young* prince!'

Will thy yard of blue riband, poor Fingal,
   recall
  The fetters from millions of Catholic
    limbs?   70
Or, has it not bound thee the fastest of all
  The slaves, who now hail their betrayer
    with hymns?

Ay! 'Build him a dwelling!' let each give
   his mite!
  Till, like Babel, the new royal dome
    hath arisen!

Let thy beggars and helots their pittance
   unite—   75
  And a palace bestow for a poor-house
    and prison!

Spread—spread, for Vitellius, the royal
   repast,
  Till the gluttonous despot be stuff'd to
    the gorge!
And the roar of his drunkards proclaim
   him at last
  The fourth of the fools and oppressors
    call'd 'George!'   80

Let the tables be loaded with feasts till they
   groan!
  Till they *groan* like thy people, through
    ages of woe!
Let the wine flow around the old Bac-
   chanal's throne,
  Like their blood which has flow'd, and
    which yet has to flow.

But let not *his* name be thine idol alone—
  On his right hand behold a Sejanus
    appears!   86
Thine own Castlereagh! let him still be
   thine own!
  A wretch never named but with curses
    and jeers!

Till now, when the isle which should blush
   for his birth,
  Deep, deep as the gore which he shed
    on her soil,   90
Seems proud of the reptile which crawl'd
   from her earth,
  And for murder repays him with shouts
    and a smile.

Without one single ray of her genius, with-
   out
  The fancy, the manhood, the fire of her
    race—
The miscreant who well might plunge Erin
   in doubt   95
  If *she* ever gave birth to a being so base.

If she did—let her long-boasted proverb
   be hush'd,
  Which proclaims that from Erin no
    reptile can spring—
See the cold-blooded serpent, with venom
   full flush'd,
  Still warming its folds in the breast of a
    king!   100

Shout, drink, feast, and flatter! Oh! Erin,
   how low
  Wert thou sunk by misfortune and
    tyranny, till
Thy welcome of tyrants hath plunged thee
   below
  The depth of thy deep in a deeper gulf
    still!

My voice, though but humble, was raised
   for thy right,   105
  My vote, as a freeman's, still voted thee
    free,
This hand, though but feeble, would arm
   in thy fight,
  And this heart, though outworn, had a
    throb still for *thee*!

Yes, I loved thee and thine, though thou
   art not my land,
  I have known noble hearts and great
    souls in thy sons,   110
And I wept with the world, o'er the patriot
   band
  Who are gone, but I weep them no
    longer as once.

For happy are they now reposing afar,—
  Thy Grattan, thy Curran, thy Sheridan,
    all
Who, for years, were the chiefs in the
   eloquent war,   115
And redeem'd, if they have not retarded,
   thy fall.

Yes, happy are they in their cold English
   graves!
  Their shades cannot start to thy shouts
    of to-day—
Nor the steps of enslavers and chain-kiss-
   ing slaves
  Be stamp'd in the turf o'er their fetter-
    less clay.   120

Till now I had envied thy sons and their
   shore,
  Though their virtues were hunted, their
    liberties fled;
There was something so warm and sublime
   in the core
  Of an Irishman's heart, that I envy—
    thy *dead*.

Or, if aught in my bosom can quench for
   an hour   125
  My contempt for a nation so servile,
    though sore,
Which though trod like the worm will not
   turn upon power,
  'Tis the glory of Grattan, and genius of
    Moore!

            September 1821.

STANZAS WRITTEN ON THE ROAD BETWEEN FLORENCE AND PISA

OH, talk not to me of a name great in
   story;
The days of our youth are the days of our
   glory;
And the myrtle and ivy of sweet two-and-
   twenty
Are worth all your laurels, though ever so
   plenty.

What are garlands and crowns to the brow
   that is wrinkled?   5
'Tis but as a dead flower with May-dew
   besprinkled.
Then away with all such from the head
   that is hoary!
What care I for the wreaths that can *only*
   give glory!

Oh FAME!—if I e'er took delight in thy
   praises,
'Twas less for the sake of thy high-sound-
   ing phrases,   10
Than to see the bright eyes of the dear one
   discover,
She thought that I was not unworthy to
   love her.

There chiefly I sought thee, *there* only I
   found thee;
Her glance was the best of the rays that
   surround thee;
When it sparkled o'er aught that was
   bright in my story,   15
I knew it was love, and I felt it was glory.
            November, 1821.

STANZAS TO A HINDOO AIR

OH! my lonely—lonely—lonely—Pillow!
Where is my lover? where is my lover?
Is it his bark which my dreary dreams discover?
Far—far away! and alone along the
   billow?

Oh! my lonely—lonely—lonely—Pillow!   5
Why must my head ache where his gentle
   brow lay?
How the long night flags lovelessly and
   slowly,
And my head droops over thee like the
   willow!

Oh! thou, my sad and solitary Pillow!
Send me kind dreams to keep my heart
   from breaking,   10
In return for the tears I shed upon thee
   waking;
  Let me not die till he comes back o'er
    the billow.

Then if thou wilt—no more my *lonely*
   Pillow,
In one embrace let these arms again enfold
   him,
And then expire of the joy—but to behold
   him!   15
  Oh! my lone bosom!—oh! my lonely
    Pillow!

OCCASIONAL PIECES

IMPROMPTU

BENEATH Blessington's eyes
The reclaimed Paradise
Should be free as the former from evil;
    But if the new Eve
    For an Apple should grieve,   5
What mortal would not play the Devil?

                    1823.

TO THE COUNTESS OF BLESSINGTON

YOU have ask'd for a verse:—the request
    In a rhymer 'twere strange to deny;
But my Hippocrene was but my breast,
    And my feelings (its fountain) are dry.

Were I now as I was, I had sung   5
    What Lawrence has painted so well;
But the strain would expire on my tongue,
    And the theme is too soft for my shell.

I am ashes where once I was fire,
    And the bard in my bosom is dead;
What I loved I now merely admire,   11
    And my heart is as grey as my head.

My life is not dated by years—
    There are moments which act as a
        plough;
And there is not a furrow appears   15
    But is deep in my soul as my brow.

Let the young and the brilliant aspire
    To sing what I gaze on in vain;
For sorrow has torn from my lyre   19
    The string which was worthy the strain.

ON THIS DAY I COMPLETE MY THIRTY-SIXTH YEAR

          MISSOLONGHI, Jan. 22, 1824.

'Tis time this heart should be unmoved,
    Since others it hath ceased to move:
Yet, though I cannot be beloved,
    Still let me love!

My days are in the yellow leaf;   5
    The flowers and fruits of love are gone;
The worm, the canker, and the grief
    Are mine alone!

The fire that on my bosom preys
    Is lone as some volcanic isle;   10
No torch is kindled at its blaze—
    A funeral pile.

The hope, the fear, the jealous care,
    The exalted portion of the pain
And power of love, I cannot share,   15
    But wear the chain.

But 'tis not *thus*—and 'tis not *here*—
    Such thoughts should shake my soul,
        nor *now*,
Where glory decks the hero's bier,
    Or binds his brow.   20

The sword, the banner, and the field,
    Glory and Greece, around me see!
The Spartan, borne upon his shield,
    Was not more free.

Awake! (not Greece—she *is* awake!)   25
    Awake, my spirit! Think through *whom*
Thy life-blood tracks its parent lake,
    And then strike home!

Tread those reviving passions down,
    Unworthy manhood!—unto thee   30
Indifferent should the smile or frown
    Of beauty be.

If thou regrett'st thy youth, *why live?*
    The land of honourable death
Is here:—up to the field, and give   35
    Away thy breath!

Seek out—less often sought than found—
    A soldier's grave, for thee the best;
Then look around, and choose thy ground,
    And take thy rest.   40

SATIRES

ENGLISH BARDS AND SCOTCH REVIEWERS

A SATIRE

'I had rather be a kitten, and cry mew!
Than one of these same metre ballad-mongers.'
                                        SHAKSPEARE.
'Such shameless bards we have; and yet 'tis true,
There are as mad, abandon'd critics too.'—POPE.

PREFACE*

ALL my friends, learned and unlearned, have urged me not to publish this Satire with my name. If I were to be 'turned from the career of my humour by quibbles quick, and paper bullets of the brain,' I should have complied with their counsel. But I am not to be terrified by abuse, or bullied by reviewers, with or without arms. I can safely say that I have attacked none personally, who did not commence on the offensive. An author's works are public property: he who purchases may judge, and publish his opinion if he pleases; and the authors I have endeavoured to commemorate may do by me as I have done by them. I dare say they will succeed better in condemning my scribblings, than in mending their own. But my object is not to prove that I can write well, but, if possible, to make others write better.

As the poem has met with far more success than I expected, I have endeavoured in this edition to make some additions and alterations, to render it more worthy of public perusal.

In the first edition of this satire, published anonymously, fourteen lines on the subject of Bowles's Pope were written by, and inserted at the request of, an ingenious friend of mine†, who has now in the press a volume of poetry. In the present edition they are erased, and some of my own substituted in their stead; my only reason for this being that which I conceive would operate with any other person in the same manner,—a determination not to publish with my name any production which was not entirely and exclusively my own composition.

With‡ regard to the real talents of many of the poetical persons whose performances are mentioned or alluded to in the following pages, it is presumed by the author that there can be little difference of opinion in the public at large; though, like other sectaries, each has his separate tabernacle of proselytes, by whom his abilities are over-rated, his faults overlooked, and his metrical canons received without scruple and without consideration. But the unquestionable possession of considerable genius by several of the writers here censured renders their mental prostitution more to be regretted. Imbecility may be pitied, or, at worst, laughed at and forgotten: perverted powers demand the most decided reprehension. No one can wish more than the author that some known and able writer had undertaken their exposure; but Mr. Gifford has devoted himself to Massinger, and, in the absence of the regular physician, a country practitioner may, in cases of absolute necessity, be allowed to prescribe his nostrum to prevent the extension of so deplorable an epidemic, provided there be no quackery in his treatment of the malady. A caustic is here offered; as it is to be feared nothing short of actual cautery can recover the numerous patients afflicted with the present prevalent and distressing *rabies* for rhyming.—As to the Edinburgh Reviewers, it would indeed require an Hercules to crush the Hydra; but if the author succeeds in merely 'bruising one of the heads of the serpent,' though his own hand should suffer in the encounter, he will be amply satisfied.

STILL must I hear?—shall hoarse Fitz-
        gerald bawl
His creaking couplets in a tavern hall,
And I not sing, lest, haply, Scotch reviews
Should dub me scribbler, and denounce
        my muse?
Prepare for rhyme—I'll publish, right or
        wrong: 5
Fools are my theme, let satire be my song.

Oh! nature's noblest gift—my grey
        goose-quill!
Slave of my thoughts, obedient to my will,
Torn from thy parent bird to form a pen,
That mighty instrument of little men!

The pen! foredoom'd to aid the mental
        throes   11
Of brains that labour, big with verse or
        prose,
Though nymphs forsake, and critics may
        deride,
The lover's solace, and the author's pride.
What wits, what poets dost thou daily
        raise!   15
How frequent is thy use, how small thy
        praise!
Condemn'd at length to be forgotten
        quite,
With all the pages which 'twas thine to
        write.

* This preface was written for the second edition, and printed with it. The noble author had left this country previous to the publication of that edition, and is not yet returned.—*Note to the fourth edition*, 1811.
† [Mr. Hobhouse.]   ‡ [Here the preface to the first edition commenced.]

But thou, at least, mine own especial pen!
Once laid aside, but now assumed again,
Our task complete, like Hamet's shall be
  free;   21
Though spurn'd by others, yet beloved by
  me:
Then let us soar to-day; no common theme,
No eastern vision, no distemper'd dream
Inspires—our path, though full of thorns,
  is plain;   25
Smooth be the verse, and easy be the
  strain.

When Vice triumphant holds her sov'-
  reign sway,
Obey'd by all who nought beside obey;
When Folly, frequent harbinger of crime,
Bedecks her cap with bells of every clime:
When knaves and fools combined o'er all
  prevail,   31
And weigh their justice in a golden scale;
E'en then the boldest start from public
  sneers,
Afraid of shame, unknown to other fears,
More darkly sin, by satire kept in awe,
And shrink from ridicule, though not
  from law.   36

Such is the force of wit! but not belong
To me the arrows of satiric song;
The royal vices of our age demand
A keener weapon, and a mightier hand.
Still there are follies, e'en for me to chase,
And yield at least amusement in the race:
Laugh when I laugh, I seek no other fame;
The cry is up, and scribblers are my game.
Speed, Pegasus!—ye strains of great and
  small,   45
Ode, epic, elegy, have at you all!
I too can scrawl, and once upon a time
I pour'd along the town a flood of rhyme,
A schoolboy freak, unworthy praise or
  blame;
I printed—older children do the same. 50
'Tis pleasant, sure, to see one's name in
  print;
A book's a book, although there's nothing
  in't.
Not that a title's sounding charm can save
Or scrawl or scribbler from an equal
  grave:
This Lambe must own, since his patrician
  name   55
Fail'd to preserve the spurious farce from
  shame.
No matter, George continues still to write,
Though now the name is veil'd from pub-
  lic sight.
Moved by the great example, I pursue
The self-same road, but make my own
  review: 60
Not seek great Jeffrey's, yet, like him,
  will be
Self-constituted judge of poesy.

A man must serve his time to every trade
Save censure—critics all are ready made.
Take hackney'd jokes from Miller, got by
  rote,   65
With just enough of learning to misquote;
A mind well skill'd to find or forge a fault;
A turn for punning, call it Attic salt;
To Jeffrey go, be silent and discreet,
His pay is just ten sterling pounds per
  sheet: 70
Fear not to lie, 'twill seem a sharper hit;
Shrink not from blasphemy, 'twill pass for
  wit;
Care not for feeling—pass your proper
  jest,
And stand a critic, hated yet caress'd.

And shall we own such judgment? no
  —as soon   75
Seek roses in December—ice in June;
Hope constancy in wind, or corn in chaff;
Believe a woman or an epitaph,
Or any other thing that's false, before
You trust in critics, who themselves are
  sore;   80
Or yield one single thought to be misled
By Jeffrey's heart, or Lambe's Bœotian
  head.
To these young tyrants, by themselves
  misplaced,
Combined usurpers on the throne of taste;
To these, when authors bend in humble
  awe,   85
And hail their voice as truth, their word
  as law—
While these are censors, 'twould be sin to
  spare;
While such are critics, why should I for-
  bear?
But yet, so near all modern worthies run,
'Tis doubtful whom to seek, or whom to
  shun;   90
Nor know we when to spare, or where to
  strike,
Our bards and censors are so much alike.

Then should you ask me, why I venture
  o'er
The path which Pope and Gifford trod be-
  fore;
If not yet sicken'd, you can still proceed:
Go on; my rhyme will tell you as you read.
'But hold!' exclaims a friend, 'here's some
  neglect: 97
This—that—and t'other line seem in-
  correct.'
What then? the self-same blunder Pope
  has got,
And careless Dryden—'Ay, but Pye has
  not:'—   100
Indeed!—'tis granted, faith!—but what
  care I?
Better to err with Pope, than shine with
  Pye.

Time was, ere yet in these degenerate
   days
Ignoble themes obtain'd mistaken praise,
When sense and wit with poesy allied,
No fabled graces, flourish'd side by side;
From the same fount their inspiration
   drew,   107
And, rear'd by taste, bloom'd fairer as they
   grew.
Then, in this happy isle, a Pope's pure
   strain
Sought the rapt soul to charm, nor sought
   in vain;   110
A polish'd nation's praise aspired to claim,
And raised the people's, as the poet's
   fame.
Like him great Dryden pour'd the tide of
   song,
In stream less smooth, indeed, yet doubly
   strong.
Then Congreve's scenes could cheer, or
   Otway's melt—   115
For nature then an English audience felt.
But why these names, or greater still, re-
   trace,
When all to feebler bards resign their
   place?
Yet to such times our lingering looks are
   cast,
When taste and reason with those times
   are past.   120
Now look around, and turn each trifling
   page,
Survey the precious works that please the
   age;
This truth at least let satire's self allow,
No dearth of bards can be complain'd of
   now.
The loaded press beneath her labour
   groans,   125
And printers' devils shake their weary
   bones;
While Southey's epics cram the creaking
   shelves,
And Little's lyrics shine in hot-press'd
   twelves.
Thus saith the Preacher: 'Nought beneath
   the sun
Is new,' yet still from change to change
   we run: 130
What varied wonders tempt us as they
   pass!
The cow-pox, tractors, galvanism, and
   gas,
In turns appear, to make the vulgar stare,
Till the swoln bubble bursts—and all is
   air!
Nor less new schools of Poetry arise,
Where dull pretenders grapple for the
   prize: 136
O'er taste awhile these pseudo-bards pre-
   vail;
Each country book-club bows the knee to
   Baal,

And, hurling lawful genius from the
   throne,
Erects a shrine and idol of its own;   140
Some leaden calf—but whom it matters
   not,
From soaring Southey down to grovelling
   Stott.

Behold! in various throngs the scrib-
   bling crew,
For notice eager, pass in long review:
Each spurs his jaded Pegasus apace,   145
And rhyme and blank maintain an equal
   race;
Sonnets on sonnets crowd, and ode on
   ode;
And tales of terror jostle on the road;
Immeasurable measures move along;
For simpering folly loves a varied song,
To strange mysterious dulness still the
   friend,   151
Admires the strain she cannot compre-
   hend.
Thus Lays of Minstrels—may they be the
   last!—
On half-strung harps whine mournful to
   the blast.
While mountain spirits prate to river
   sprites,   155
That dames may listen to the sound at
   nights;
And goblin brats, of Gilpin Horner's brood,
Decoy young border-nobles through the
   wood,
And skip at every step, Lord knows how
   high,
And frighten foolish babes, the Lord
   knows why;   160
While high-born ladies in their magic cell,
Forbidding knights to read who cannot
   spell,
Despatch a courier to a wizard's grave,
And fight with honest men to shield a
   knave.

Next view in state, proud prancing on
   his roan,   165
The golden-crested haughty Marmion,
Now forging scrolls, now foremost in the
   fight,
Not quite a felon, yet but half a knight,
The gibbet or the field prepared to grace;
A mighty mixture of the great and base.
And think'st thou, Scott! by vain conceit
   perchance,   171
On public taste to foist thy stale romance,
Though Murray with his Miller may com-
   bine
To yield thy muse just half-a-crown per
   line?
No! when the sons of song descend to
   trade,   175
Their bays are sear, their former laurels
   fade.

Let such forego the poet's sacred name,
Who rack their brains for lucre, not for
    fame:
Still for stern Mammon may they toil in
    vain!
And sadly gaze on gold they cannot gain!
Such be their meed, such still the just re-
    ward   181
Of prostituted muse and hireling bard!
For this we spurn Apollo's venal son,
And bid a long 'good night to Marmion.'

These are the themes that claim our
    plaudits now;   185
These are the bards to whom the muse
    must bow;
While Milton, Dryden, Pope, alike forgot,
Resign their hallow'd bays to Walter Scott.

The time has been, when yet the muse
    was young,
When Homer swept the lyre, and Maro
    sung,   190
An epic scarce ten centuries could claim,
While awe-struck nations hail'd the magic
    name:
The work of each immortal bard appears
The single wonder of a thousand years.
Empires have moulder'd from the face of
    earth,   195
Tongues have expired with those who gave
    them birth,
Without the glory such a strain can give,
As even in ruin bids the language live.
Not so with us, though minor bards, content
On one great work a life of labour spent:
With eagle pinion soaring to the skies,
Behold the ballad-monger Southey rise!
To him let Camoëns, Milton, Tasso yield,
Whose annual strains, like armies, take
    the field.
First in the ranks see Joan of Arc advance,
The scourge of England and the boast of
    France!   206
Though burnt by wicked Bedford for a
    witch,
Behold her statue placed in glory's niche;
Her fetters burst, and just released from
    prison,   209
A virgin phœnix from her ashes risen.
Next see tremendous Thalaba come on,
Arabia's monstrous, wild, and wondrous son:
Domdaniel's dread destroyer, who o'er-
    threw
More mad magicians than the world e'er
    knew.   214
Immortal hero! all thy foes o'ercome,
For ever reign—the rival of Tom Thumb!
Since startled metre fled before thy face,
Well wert thou doom'd the last of all thy
    race!   218
Well might triumphant genii bear thee
    hence,
Illustrious conqueror of common sense!

Now, last and greatest, Madoc spreads
    his sails,   221
Cacique in Mexico, and prince in Wales;
Tells us strange tales, as other travellers
    do,
More old than Mandeville's, and not so
    true.
Oh! Southey! Southey! cease thy varied
    song!   225
A bard may chant too often and too long:
As thou art strong in verse, in mercy,
    spare!
A fourth, alas! were more than we could
    bear.
But if, in spite of all the world can say,
Thou still wilt verseward plod thy weary
    way;   230
If still in Berkley ballads most uncivil,
Thou wilt devote old women to the devil,
The babe unborn thy dread intent may
    rue:
'God help thee,' Southey, and thy readers
    too.

Next comes the dull disciple of thy
    school,   235
That mild apostate from poetic rule,
The simple Wordsworth, framer of a lay
As soft as evening in his favourite May,
Who warns his friend 'to shake off toil
    and trouble,
And quit his books, for fear of growing
    double;'   240
Who, both by precept and example, shows
That prose is verse, and verse is merely
    prose;
Convincing all, by demonstration plain,
Poetic souls delight in prose insane;
And Christmas stories tortured into
    rhyme   245
Contain the essence of the true sublime.
Thus, when he tells the tale of Betty Foy,
The idiot mother of 'an idiot boy';
A moon-struck, silly lad, who lost his way,
And, like his bard, confounded night with
    day;   250
So close on each pathetic part he dwells,
And each adventure so sublimely tells,
That all who view the 'idiot in his glory'
Conceive the bard the hero of the story.

Shall gentle Coleridge pass unnoticed
    here,   255
To turgid ode and tumid stanza dear?
Though themes of innocence amuse him
    best,
Yet still obscurity's a welcome guest.
If Inspiration should her aid refuse   259
To him who takes a pixy for a muse,
Yet none in lofty numbers can surpass
The bard who soars to elegise an ass.
So well the subject suits his noble mind,
He brays the laureat of the long-ear'd
    kind.

Oh! wonder-working Lewis! monk, or
  bard,   265
Who fain wouldst make Parnassus a
  churchyard!
Lo! wreaths of yew, not laurel, bind thy
  brow,
Thy muse a sprite, Apollo's sexton thou!
Whether on ancient tombs thou tak'st thy
  stand,
By gibb'ring spectres hail'd, thy kindred
  band;   270
Or tracest chaste descriptions on thy page,
To please the females of our modest age;
All hail, M. P.! from whose infernal brain
Thin-sheeted phantoms glide, a grisly
  train;
At whose command 'grim women' throng
  in crowds,   275
And kings of fire, of water, and of clouds,
With 'small gray men,' 'wild yagers,' and
  what not,
To crown with honour thee and Walter
  Scott;
Again all hail! if tales like thine may
  please,
St. Luke alone can vanquish the disease;
Even Satan's self with thee might dread to
  dwell,   281
And in thy skull discern a deeper hell.

Who in soft guise, surrounded by a choir
Of virgins melting, not to Vesta's fire,
With sparkling eyes, and cheek by passion
  flush'd,   285
Strikes his wild lyre, whilst listening dames
  are hush'd?
'Tis Little! young Catullus of his day,
As sweet, but as immoral, in his lay!
Grieved to condemn, the muse must still
  be just,
Nor spare melodious advocates of lust.
Pure is the flame which o'er her altar
  burns;   291
From grosser incense with disgust she
  turns:
Yet kind to youth, this expiation o'er,
She bids thee 'mend thy line and sin no
  more.'

For thee, translator of the tinsel song,
To whom such glittering ornaments be-
  long,   296
Hibernian Strangford! with thine eyes of
  blue,
And boasted locks of red or auburn hue,
Whose plaintive strain each love-sick miss
  admires,
And o'er harmonious fustian half expires,
Learn, if thou canst, to yield thine author's
  sense,   301
Nor vend thy sonnets on a false pretence.
Think'st thou to gain thy verse a higher
  place,
By dressing Camoëns in a suit of lace?

Mend, Strangford! mend thy morals and
  thy taste;   305
Be warm, but pure; be amorous, but be
  chaste;
Cease to deceive; thy pilfer'd harp restore,
Nor teach the Lusian bard to copy Moore.

Behold!—ye tarts!—one moment spare
  the text—
Hayley's last work, and worst—until his
  next;   310
Whether he spin poor couplets into plays,
Or damn the dead with purgatorial praise,
His style in youth or age is still the same,
For ever feeble and for ever tame.
Triumphant first see 'Temper's Triumphs'
  shine!   315
At least I'm sure they triumph'd over mine.
Of 'Music's Triumphs,' all who read may
  swear
That luckless music never triumph'd there.

Moravians, rise! bestow some meet re-
  ward
On dull devotion—Lo! the Sabbath bard,
Sepulchral Grahame, pours his notes sub-
  lime   321
In mangled prose, nor e'en aspires to
  rhyme;
Breaks into blank the Gospel of St. Luke,
And boldly pilfers from the Pentateuch;
And, undisturb'd by conscientious qualms,
Perverts the Prophets, and purloins the
  Psalms.   326

Hail, Sympathy! thy soft idea brings
A thousand visions of a thousand things,
And shows, still whimpering through three-
  score of years,
The maudlin prince of mournful sonnet-
  eers.   330
And art thou not their prince, harmonious
  Bowles!
Thou first, great oracle of tender souls?
Whether thou sing'st with equal ease, and
  grief,
The fall of empires, or a yellow leaf;
Whether thy muse most lamentably tells
What merry sounds proceed from Oxford
  bells,   336
Or, still in bells delighting, finds a friend
In every chime that jingled from Ostend;
Ah! how much juster were thy muse's hap,
If to thy bells thou wouldst but add a cap!
Delightful Bowles! still blessing and still
  blest,   341
All love thy strain, but children like it
  best.
'Tis thine, with gentle Little's moral song,
To soothe the mania of the amorous
  throng!
With thee our nursery damsels shed their
  tears,   345
Ere miss as yet completes her infant years:

But in her teens thy whining powers are
vain;
She quits poor Bowles for Little's purer
strain.
Now to soft themes thou scornest to con-
fine   349
The lofty numbers of a harp like thine;
'Awake a louder and a loftier strain,'
Such as none heard before, or will again!
Where all Discoveries jumbled from the
flood,
Since first the leaky ark reposed in mud,
By more or less, are sung in every book,
From Captain Noah down to Captain
Cook.   356
Nor this alone; but, pausing on the road,
The bard sighs forth a gentle episode;
And gravely tells—attend, each beauteous
miss!—
When first Madeira trembled to a kiss.
Bowles! in thy memory let this precept
dwell,   361
Stick to thy sonnets, man!—at least they
sell.
But if some new-born whim, or larger
bribe,
Prompt thy crude brain, and claim thee for
a scribe;
If chance some bard, though once by
dunces fear'd,   365
Now, prone in dust, can only be revered;
If Pope, whose fame and genius, from the
first,
Have foil'd the best of critics, needs the
worst,
Do thou essay: each fault, each failing
scan;
The first of poets was, alas! but man.
Rake from each ancient dunghill every
pearl,   371
Consult Lord Fanny, and confide in Curll;
Let all the scandals of a former age
Perch on thy pen, and flutter o'er thy page;
Affect a candour which thou canst not
feel,   375
Clothe envy in the garb of honest zeal;
Write, as if St. John's soul could still in-
spire,
And do from hate what Mallet did for hire.
Oh! hadst thou lived in that congenial
time,
To rave with Dennis, and with Ralph to
rhyme;   380
Throng'd with the rest around his living
head,
Not raised thy hoof against the lion dead;
A meet reward had crown'd thy glorious
gains,
And link'd thee to the Dunciad for thy
pains.

Another epic! Who inflicts again   385
More books of blank upon the sons of
men?

Bœotian Cottle, rich Bristowa's boast,
Imports old stories from the Cambrian
coast,
And sends his goods to market—all alive!
Lines forty thousand, cantos twenty-five?
Fresh fish from Helicon! who'll buy,
who'll buy?   391
The precious bargain's cheap—in faith,
not I.
Your turtle-feeder's verse must needs be
flat,
Though Bristol bloat him with the ver-
dant fat;
If Commerce fills the purse, she clogs the
brain,   395
And Amos Cottle strikes the lyre in vain.
In him an author's luckless lot behold,
Condemn'd to make the books which once
he sold.
Oh, Amos Cottle!—Phœbus! what a name
To fill the speaking trump of future
fame!—   400
Oh, Amos Cottle! for a moment think
What meagre profits spring from pen and ink!
When thus devoted to poetic dreams,
Who will peruse thy prostituted reams?
Oh! pen perverted! paper misapplied!
Had Cottle still adorn'd the counter's side,
Bent o'er the desk, or, born to useful toils,
Been taught to make the paper which he
soils,   408
Plough'd, delved, or plied the oar with
lusty limb,
He had not sung of Wales, nor I of him.

As Sisyphus against the infernal steep
Rolls the huge rock whose motions ne'er
may sleep,
So up thy hill, ambrosial Richmond,
heaves
Dull Maurice all his granite weight of
leaves: 414
Smooth, solid monuments of mental pain!
The petrifactions of a plodding brain,
That, ere they reach the top, fall lumbering
back again.

With broken lyre, and cheek serenely
pale,
Lo! sad Alcæus wanders down the vale;
Though fair they rose, and might have
bloom'd at last,   420
His hopes have perish'd by the northern
blast:
Nipp'd in the bud by Caledonian gales,
His blossoms wither as the blast prevails!
O'er his lost works let *classic* Sheffield
weep;
May no rude hand disturb their early
sleep!   425

Yet say! why should the bard at once
resign
His claim to favour from the sacred Nine?

For ever startled by the mingled howl
Of northern wolves, that still in darkness
    prowl;
A coward brood, which mangle as they
    prey,   430
By hellish instinct, all that cross their way;
Aged or young, the living or the dead,
No mercy find—these harpies must be fed.
Why do the injured unresisting yield
The calm possession of their native field?
Why tamely thus before their fangs re-
    treat,   436
Nor hunt the blood-hounds back to Ar-
    thur's Seat?

    Health to immortal Jeffrey! once, in
        name,
England could boast a judge almost the
    same;
In soul so like, so merciful, yet just,   440
Some think that Satan has resign'd his trust,
And given the spirit to the world again,
To sentence letters, as he sentenced men.
With hand less mighty, but with heart as
    black,
With voice as willing to decree the rack;
Bred in the courts betimes, though all that
    law   446
As yet hath taught him is to find a flaw;
Since well instructed in the patriot school
To rail at party, though a party tool,
Who knows, if chance his patrons should
    restore   450
Back to the sway they forfeited before,
His scribbling toils some recompense may
    meet,
And raise this Daniel to the judgment-seat?
Let Jeffreys' shade indulge the pious hope,
And greeting thus, present him with a
    rope: 455
'Heir to my virtues! man of equal mind!
Skill'd to condemn as to traduce mankind,
This cord receive, for thee reserved with
    care,
To wield in judgment, and at length to
    wear.'

    Health to great Jeffrey! Heaven pre-
        serve his life,   460
To flourish on the fertile shores of Fife,
And guard it sacred in its future wars,
Since authors sometimes seek the field of
    Mars!
Can none remember that eventful day,
That ever-glorious, almost fatal fray,
When Little's leadless pistol met his eye,
And Bow-street myrmidons stood laugh-
    ing by?
Oh, day disastrous! on her firm-set rock,
Dunedin's castle felt a secret shock;
Dark roll'd the sympathetic waves of
    Forth,   470
Low groan'd the startled whirlwinds of
    the north;

Tweed ruffled half his waves to form a tear,
The other half pursued its calm career;
Arthur's steep summit nodded to its base,
The surly Tolbooth scarcely kept her
    place.   475
The Tolbooth felt—for marble sometimes
    can,
On such occasions, feel as much as man—
The Tolbooth felt defrauded of his charms,
If Jeffrey died, except within her arms:
Nay last, not least, on that portentous
    morn,   480
The sixteenth story, where himself was
    born,
His patrimonial garret, fell to ground,
And pale Edina shudder'd at the sound;
Strew'd were the streets around with milk-
    white reams,
Flow'd all the Canongate with inky
    streams;   485
This of his candour seem'd the sable dew,
That of his valour show'd the bloodless
    hue;
And all with justice deem'd the two com-
    bined
The mingled emblems of his mighty mind.
But Caledonia's goddess hover'd o'er
The field, and saved him from the wrath
    of Moore;   491
From either pistol snatch'd the vengeful
    lead,
And straight restored it to her favourite's
    head;
That head, with greater than magnetic
    power,
Caught it, as Danaë caught the golden
    shower,   495
And, though the thickening dross will
    scarce refine,
Augments its ore, and is itself a mine.
'My son,' she cried, 'ne'er thirst for gore
    again,
Resign the pistol and resume the pen;
O'er politics and poesy preside,   500
Boast of thy country, and Britannia's
    guide!
For long as Albion's heedless sons submit,
Or Scottish taste decides on English wit,
So long shall last thine unmolested reign,
Nor any dare to take thy name in vain.
Behold, a chosen band shall aid thy plan,
And own thee chieftain of the critic clan.
First in the oat-fed phalanx shall be seen
The travell'd thane, Athenian Aberdeen.
Herbert shall wield Thor's hammer, and
    sometimes,   510
In gratitude, thou'lt praise his rugged
    rhymes.
Smug Sidney too thy bitter page shall seek,
And classic Hallam, much renown'd for
    Greek;
Scott may perchance his name and in-
    fluence lend,   514
And paltry Pillans shall traduce his friend;

While gay Thalia's luckless votary, Lambe,
Damn'd like the devil, devil-like will
  damn,
Known be thy name, unbounded be thy
  sway!
Thy Holland's banquets shall each toil re-
  pay;
While grateful Britain yields the praise she
  owes   520
To Holland's hirelings and to learning's
  foes.
Yet mark one caution ere thy next Review
Spread its light wings of saffron and of
  blue,
Beware lest blundering Brougham destroy
  the sale,
Turn beef to bannocks, cauliflowers to
  kail.'   525
Thus having said, the kilted goddess kiss'd
Her son, and vanish'd in a Scottish mist.

Then prosper, Jeffrey! pertest of the train
Whom Scotland pampers with her fiery
  grain!
Whatever blessing waits a genuine Scot,
In double portion swells thy glorious lot;
For thee Edina culls her evening sweets,
And showers their odours on thy candid
  sheets,
Whose hue and fragrance to thy work
  adhere—
This scents its pages, and that gilds its rear.
Lo! blushing Itch, coy nymph, enamour'd
  grown,   536
Forsakes the rest, and cleaves to thee
  alone;
And, too unjust to other Pictish men,
Enjoys thy person, and inspires thy pen!

Illustrious Holland! hard would be his
  lot,   540
His hirelings mention'd, and himself for-
  got!
Holland, with Henry Petty at his back,
The whipper-in and huntsman of the pack.
Blest be the banquets spread at Holland
  House,
Where Scotchmen feed, and critics may
  carouse!   545
Long, long beneath that hospitable roof
Shall Grub-street dine, while duns are kept
  aloof.
See honest Hallam lay aside his fork,
Resume his pen, review his Lordship's
  work,   549
And, grateful for the dainties on his plate,
Declare his landlord can at least translate!
Dunedin! view thy children with delight,
They write for food—and feed because
  they write:
And lest, when heated with the unusual
  grape,
Some glowing thoughts should to the press
  escape,   555

And tinge with red the female reader's
  cheek,
My lady skims the cream of each critique;
Breathes o'er the page her purity of soul,
Reforms each error, and refines the whole.

Now to the Drama turn—Oh! motley
  sight!   560
What precious scenes the wondering eyes
  invite!
Puns, and a prince within a barrel pent,
And Dibdin's nonsense yield complete
  content.
Though now, thank Heaven! the Roscio-
  mania's o'er,
And full-grown actors are endured once
  more;   565
Yet what avail their vain attempts to
  please,
While British critics suffer scenes like
  these;
While Reynolds vents his 'dammes!'
  'poohs!' and 'zounds!'
And common-place and common sense
  confounds?
While Kenney's 'World'—ah! where is
  Kenney's wit?—   570
Tires the sad gallery, lulls the listless pit;
And Beaumont's pilfer'd Caratach affords
A tragedy complete in all but words?
Who but must mourn, while these are all
  the rage,
The degradation of our vaunted stage!
Heavens! is all sense of shame and talent
  gone?   576
Have we no living bard of merit?—none!
Awake, George Colman! Cumberland,
  awake!
Ring the alarum bell! let folly quake!
Oh, Sheridan! if aught can move thy
  pen,   580
Let Comedy assume her throne again;
Abjure the mummery of German schools;
Leave new Pizarros to translating fools;
Give, as thy last memorial to the age,
One classic drama, and reform the stage.
Gods! o'er those boards shall Folly rear her
  head,   586
Where Garrick trod, and Siddons lives to
  tread?
On those shall Farce display Buffoon'ry's
  mask,
And Hook conceal his heroes in a cask?
Shall sapient managers new scenes pro-
  duce   590
From Cherry, Skeffington, and Mother
  Goose?
While Shakspeare, Otway Massinger,
  forgot,
On stalls must moulder, or in closets
  rot?
Lo! with what pomp the daily prints pro-
  claim
The rival candidates for Attic fame! 595

In grim array though Lewis' spectres rise,
Still Skeffington and Goose divide the
    prize.
And sure *great* Skeffington must claim our
    praise,
For skirtless coats and skeletons of plays
Renown'd alike; whose genius ne'er con-
    fines   600
Her flight to garnish Greenwood's gay
    designs;
Nor sleeps with 'Sleeping Beauties,' but
    anon
In five facetious acts comes thundering on,
While poor John Bull, bewilder'd with the
    scene
Stares, wondering what the devil it can
    mean;   605
But as some hands applaud, a venal few!
Rather than sleep, why John applauds it
    too.

Such are we now. Ah! wherefore should
    we turn
To what our fathers were, unless to
    mourn?
Degenerate Britons! are ye dead to shame,
Or, kind to dulness, do you fear to blame?
Well may the nobles of our present race
Watch each distortion of a Naldi's face;
Well may they smile on Italy's buffoons,
And worship Catalani's pantaloons,   615
Since their own drama yields no fairer trace
Of wit than puns, of humour than grimace.

Then let Ausonia, skill'd in every art
To soften manners, but corrupt the heart,
Pour her exotic follies o'er the town,
To sanction Vice, and hunt Decorum
    down: 621
Let wedded strumpets languish o'er Des-
    hayes,
And bless the promise which his form dis-
    plays;
While Gayton bounds before th' enrap-
    tured looks   624
Of hoary marquises and stripling dukes:
Let high-born lechers eye the lively Présle
Twirl her light limbs, that spurn the need-
    less veil;
Let Angiolini bare her breast of snow,
Wave the white arm, and point the pliant
    toe;
Collini trill her love-inspiring song,   630
Strain her fair neck, and charm the listen-
    ing throng!
Whet not your scythe, suppressors of our
    vice!
Reforming saints! too delicately nice!
By whose decrees, our sinful souls to save,
No Sunday tankards foam, no barbers
    shave;   635
And beer undrawn, and beards unmown,
    display
Your holy reverence for the Sabbath-day.

Or hail at once the patron and the pile
Of vice and folly, Greville and Argyle!
Where yon proud palace, Fashion's hal-
    low'd fane,   640
Spreads wide her portals for the motley
    train,
Behold the new Petronius of the day,
Our arbiter of pleasure and of play!
There the hired eunuch, the Hesperian
    choir,   644
The melting lute, the soft lascivious lyre,
The song from Italy, the step from
    France,
The midnight orgy, and the mazy dance,
The smile of beauty, and the flush of
    wine,
For fops, fools, gamesters, knaves, and
    lords combine:
Each to his humour—Comus all allows;
Champaign, dice, music, or your neigh-
    bour's spouse.   651
Talk not to us, ye starving sons of trade!
Of piteous ruin, which ourselves have
    made;
In plenty's sunshine Fortune's minions
    bask,
Nor think of poverty, except 'en masque,'
When for the night some lately titled ass
Appears the beggar which his grandsire
    was.   657
The curtain dropp'd, the gay burletta o'er,
The audience take their turn upon the
    floor;
Now round the room the circling dow'gers
    sweep,   660
Now in loose waltz the thin-clad daughters
    leap;
The first in lengthen'd line majestic swim,
The last display the free unfetter'd limb!
Those for Hibernia's lusty sons repair
With art the charms which nature could
    not spare;   665
These after husbands wing their eager
    flight,
Nor leave much mystery for the nuptial
    night.

Oh! blest retreats of infamy and ease,
Where, all forgotten but the power to
    please,
Each maid may give a loose to genial
    thought,   670
Each swain may teach new systems, or be
    taught:
There the blithe youngster, just return'd
    from Spain,
Cuts the light pack, or calls the rattling
    main;
The jovial caster's set, and seven's the
    nick,
Or—done!—a thousand on the coming
    trick!   675
If, mad with loss, existence 'gins to tire,
And all your hope or wish is to expire,

Here's Powell's pistol ready for your
    life,
And, kinder still, two Pagets for your
    wife;   679
Fit consummation of an earthly race
Begun in folly, ended in disgrace;
While none but menials o'er the bed of
    death,
Wash thy red wounds, or watch thy waver-
    ing breath:
Traduced by liars, and forgot by all,
The mangled victim of a drunken brawl,
To live like Clodius, and like Falkland
    fall.   686

    Truth! rouse some genuine bard, and
    guide his hand
To drive this pestilence from out the land.
E'en I—least thinking of a thoughtless
    throng,
Just skill'd to know the right and choose
    the wrong,   690
Freed at that age when reason's shield is
    lost,
To fight my course through passion's
    countless host,
Whom every path of pleasure's flowery
    way
Has lured in turn, and all have led astray—
E'en I must raise my voice, e'en I must
    feel   695
Such scenes, such men, destroy the public
    weal:
Although some kind, censorious friend
    will say,
'What art thou better, meddling fool, than
    they?'
And every brother rake will smile to see
That miracle, a moralist in me.   700
No matter—when some bard in virtue
    strong,
Gifford perchance, shall raise the chasten-
    ing song,
Then sleep my pen for ever! and my voice
Be only heard to hail him, and rejoice;
Rejoice, and yield my feeble praise, though
    I   705
May feel the lash that Virtue must apply.

    As for the smaller fry, who swarm in
    shoals,
From silly Hafiz up to simple Bowles,
Why should we call them from their dark
    abode,
In broad St. Giles's or in Tottenham-
    road?   710
Or (since some men of fashion nobly dare
To scrawl in verse) from Bond-street or the
    Square?
If things of ton their harmless lays indite,
Most wisely doom'd to shun the public
    sight,   714
What harm? in spite of every critic elf,
Sir T. may read his stanzas to himself;

Miles Andrews still his strength in coup-
    lets try,
And live in prologues, though his dramas
    die:
Lords too are bards, such things at times
    befall,   719
And 'tis some praise in peers to write at all.
Yet, did or taste or reason sway the times
Ah! who would take their titles with their
    rhymes?
Roscommon! Sheffield! with your spirits
    fled,
No future laurels deck a noble head;
No muse will cheer, with renovating smile,
The paralytic puling of Carlisle.   726
The puny schoolboy and his early lay
Men pardon, if his follies pass away;
But who forgives the senior's ceaseless
    verse,
Whose hairs grow hoary as his rhymes
    grow worse?   730
What heterogeneous honours deck the
    peer!
Lord, rhymester, petit-maître, and pamph-
    leteer!
So dull in youth, so drivelling in his
    age,
His scenes alone had damn'd our sinking
    stage;
But managers for once cried, 'Hold,
    enough!'   735
Nor drugg'd their audience with the tragic
    stuff.
Yet at their judgment let his lordship
    laugh,
And case his volumes in congenial calf;
Yes! doff that covering, where morocco
    shines,
And hang a calf-skin on those recreant
    lines.   740

    With you, ye Druids! rich in native lead,
Who daily scribble for your daily bread;
With you I war not: Gifford's heavy hand
Has crush'd, without remorse, your nu-
    merous band.   744
On 'all the talents' vent your venal spleen;
Want is your plea, let pity be your screen.
Let monodies on Fox regale your crew,
And Melville's Mantle prove a blanket
    too!
One common Lethe waits each hapless
    bard,
And, peace be with you! 'tis your best re-
    ward.   750
Such damning fame as Dunciads only give
Could bid your lines beyond a morning
    live;
But now at once your fleeting labours
    close,
With names of greater note in blest re-
    pose.   754
Far be't from me unkindly to upbraid
The lovely Rosa's prose in masquerade,

Whose strains, the faithful echoes of her
   mind,
Leave wondering comprehension far be-
   hind.
Though Crusca's bards no more our
   journals fill,
Some stragglers skirmish round the col-
   umns still;   760
Last of the howling host which once was
   Bell's,
Matilda snivels yet, and Hafiz yells;
And Merry's metaphors appear anew,
Chain'd to the signature of O. P. Q.

When some brisk youth, the tenant of a
   stall,   765
Employs a pen less pointed than his awl,
Leaves his snug shop, forsakes his store
   of shoes,
St. Crispin quits, and cobbles for the
   muse,
Heavens! how the vulgar stare! how
   crowds applaud!
How ladies read, and literati laud!   770
If chance some wicked wag should pass
   his jest,
'Tis sheer ill-nature—don't the world
   know best?
Genius must guide when wits admire the
   rhyme,
And Capel Lofft declares 'tis quite sub-
   lime.
Hear, then, ye happy sons of needless
   trade!   775
Swains! quit the plough, resign the useless
   spade!
Lo! Burns and Bloomfield, nay, a greater
   far,
Gifford was born beneath an adverse
   star,
Forsook the labours of a servile state,
Stemm'd the rude storm, and triumph'd
   over fate;   780
Then why no more? if Phœbus smiled on
   you,
Bloomfield! why not on brother Nathan
   too?
Him too the mania, not the muse, has
   seized;
Not inspiration, but a mind diseased:
And now no boor can seek his last abode,
No common be enclosed without an ode.
Oh! since increased refinement deigns to
   smile
On Britain's sons, and bless our genial
   isle,   788
Let poesy go forth, pervade the whole,
Alike the rustic, and mechanic soul!
Ye tuneful cobblers! still your notes pro-
   long,
Compose at once a slipper and a song;
So shall the fair your handywork peruse,
Your sonnets sure shall please—perhaps
   your shoes.

May Moorland weavers boast Pindaric
   skill,   795
And tailors' lays be longer than their
   bill!
While punctual beaux reward the grateful
   notes,
And pay for poems—when they pay for
   coats.

To the famed throng now paid the trib-
   ute due,
Neglected genius! let me turn to you.
Come forth, oh Campbell! give thy talents
   scope;   801
Who dares aspire if thou must cease to
   hope?
And thou, melodious Rogers! rise at
   last,
Recall the pleasing memory of the
   past;
Arise! let blest remembrance still in-
   spire,   805
And strike to wonted tones thy hallow'd
   lyre;
Restore Apollo to his vacant throne,
Assert thy country's honour and thine
   own.
What! must deserted Poesy still weep
Where her last hopes with pious Cowper
   sleep?   810
Unless, perchance, from his cold bier she
   turns,
To deck the turf that wraps her minstrel,
   Burns!
No! though contempt hath mark'd the
   spurious brood,
The race who rhyme from folly, or for
   food,
Yet still some genuine sons 'tis hers to
   boast,   815
Who, least affecting, still affect the most:
Feel as they write, and write but as they
   feel—
Bear witness Gifford, Sotheby, Macneil.

'Why slumbers Gifford?' once was
   ask'd in vain;   819
Why slumbers Gifford? let us ask again.
Are there no follies for his pen to purge?
Are there no fools whose backs demand
   the scourge?
Are there no sins for satire's bard to
   greet?
Stalks not gigantic Vice in every street?
Shall peers or princes tread pollution's
   path,   825
And 'scape alike the law's and muse's
   wrath?
Nor blaze with guilty glare through future
   time,
Eternal beacons of consummate crime?
Arouse thee, Gifford! be thy promise
   claim'd,   829
Make bad men better, or at least ashamed.

Unhappy White! while life was in its
   spring,
And thy young muse just waved her joy-
   ous wing,
The spoiler swept that soaring lyre away,
Which else had sounded an immortal lay.
Oh! what a noble heart was here un-
   done, 835
When Science' self destroy'd her favourite
   son!
Yes, she too much indulged thy fond pur-
   suit,
She sow'd the seeds, but death has reap'd
   the fruit.
'Twas thine own genius gave the final
   blow,
And help'd to plant the wound that laid
   thee low: 840
So the struck eagle, stretch'd upon the
   plain,
No more through rolling clouds to soar
   again,
View'd his own feather on the fatal dart,
And wing'd the shaft that quiver'd in his
   heart;
Keen were his pangs, but keener far to
   feel 845
He nursed the pinion which impell'd the
   steel;
While the same plumage that had warm'd
   his nest
Drank the last life-drop of his bleeding
   breast.

There be who say, in these enlighten'd
   days, 849
That splendid lies are all the poet's praise;
That strain'd invention, ever on the wing,
Alone impels the modern bard to sing:
'Tis true, that all who rhyme—nay, all who
   write,
Shrink from that fatal word to genius—
   trite;
Yet Truth sometimes will lend her noblest
   fires, 855
And decorate the verse herself inspires:
This fact in Virtue's name let Crabbe
   attest;
Though nature's sternest painter, yet the
   best.

And here let Shee and Genius find a
   place,
Whose pen and pencil yield an equal
   grace; 860
To guide whose hand the sister arts com-
   bine,
And trace the poet's or the painter's line;
Whose magic touch can bid the canvas
   glow,
Or pour the easy rhyme's harmonious
   flow; 864
While honours, doubly merited, attend
The poet's rival, but the painter's friend.

Blest is the man who dares approach
   the bower
Where dwelt the muses at their natal hour;
Whose steps have press'd, whose eye has
   mark'd afar,
The clime that nursed the sons of song and
   war, 870
The scenes which glory still must hover
   o'er,
Her place of birth, her own Achaian shore.
But doubly blest is he whose heart ex-
   pands
With hallow'd feelings for those classic
   lands; 874
Who rends the veil of ages long gone by,
And views their remnants with a poet's eye!
Wright! 'twas thy happy lot at once to view
Those shores of glory, and to sing them
   too;
And sure no common muse inspired thy
   pen 879
To hail the land of gods and godlike men.

And you, associate bards! who snatch'd
   to light
Those gems too long withheld from
   modern sight;
Whose mingling taste combined to cull the
   wreath
Where Attic flowers Aonion odours
   breathe, 884
And all their renovated fragrance flung
To grace the beauties of your native
   tongue;
Now let those minds, that nobly could
   transfuse
The glorious spirit of the Grecian muse,
Though soft the echo, scorn a borrow'd
   tone:
Resign Achaia's lyre, and strike your own.

Let these, or such as these, with just
   applause, 891
Restore the muse's violated laws;
But not in flimsy Darwin's pompous
   chime,
That mighty master of unmeaning rhyme,
Whose gilded cymbals, more adorn'd than
   clear, 895
The eye delighted, but fatigued the ear;
In show the simple lyre could once sur-
   pass,
But now, worn down, appear in native
   brass;
While all his train of hovering sylphs
   around
Evaporate in similes and sound: 900
Him let them shun, with him let tinsel
   die:
False glare attracts, but more offends the
   eye.

Yet let them not to vulgar Wordsworth
   stoop,
The meanest object of the lowly group,

Whose verse, of all but childish prattle
void, 905
Seems blessed harmony to Lamb and
Lloyd:
Let them—but hold, my muse, nor dare to
teach
A strain far, far beyond thy humble reach:
The native genius with their being given
Will point the path, and peal their notes to
heaven. 910

And thou, too, Scott! resign to minstrels
rude
The wilder slogan of a border feud:
Let others spin their meagre lines for
hire;
Enough for genius, if itself inspire!
Let Southey sing, although his teeming
muse, 915
Prolific every spring, be too profuse:
Let simple Wordsworth chime his childish
verse,
And brother Coleridge lull the babe at
nurse;
Let spectre-mongering Lewis aim, at most,
To rouse the galleries, or to raise a ghost;
Let Moore still sigh; let Strangford steal
from Moore, 921
And swear that Camoëns sang such notes
of yore;
Let Hayley hobble on, Montgomery rave,
And godly Grahame chant a stupid
stave:
Let sonneteering Bowles his strains re-
fine, 925
And whine and whimper to the fourteenth
line;
Let Stott, Carlisle, Matilda, and the
rest
Of Grub Street, and of Grosvenor Place
the best,
Scrawl on, till death release us from the
strain,
Or Common Sense assert her rights
again. 930
But thou, with powers that mock the aid
of praise,
Shouldst leave to humbler bards ignoble
lays:
Thy country's voice, the voice of all the
nine,
Demand a hallow'd harp—that harp is
thine.
Say! will not Caledonia's annals yield
The glorious record of some nobler
field, 936
Than the wild foray of a plundering
clan,
Whose proudest deeds disgrace the name
of man?
Or Marmion's acts of darkness, fitter
food
For Sherwood's outlaw tales of Robin
Hood? 940

Scotland! still proudly claim thy native
bard,
And be thy praise his first, his best reward!
Yet not with thee alone his name should
live,
But own the vast renown a world can
give:
Be known, perchance, when Albion is no
more, 945
And tell the tale of what she was before;
To future times her faded fame recall,
And save her glory, though his country
fall.

Yet what avails the sanguine poet's
hope,
To conquer ages, and with time to
cope? 950
New eras spread their wings, new nations
rise,
And other victors fill the applauding skies;
A few brief generations fleet along,
Whose sons forget the poet and his song:
E'en now, what once-loved minstrels
scarce may claim 955
The transient mention of a dubious name!
When fame's loud trump hath blown its
noblest blast,
Though long the sound, the echo sleeps
at last;
And glory, like the phœnix midst her
fires, 959
Exhales her odours, blazes, and expires.

Shall hoary Granta call her sable sons,
Expert in science, more expert at
puns?
Shall these approach the muse? ah, no!
she flies,
Even from the tempting ore of Seaton's
prize;
Though printers condescend the press to
soil 965
With rhyme by Hoare, and epic blank by
Hoyle:
Not him whose page, if still upheld by
whist,
Requires no sacred theme to bid us
list.
Ye! who in Granta's honours would sur-
pass,
Must mount her Pegasus, a full-grown
ass; 970
A foal well worthy of her ancient dam,
Whose Helicon is duller than her Cam.

There Clarke, still striving piteously 'to
please,'
Forgetting doggrel leads not to degrees,
A would-be satirist, a hired buffoon, 975
A monthly scribbler of some low lam-
poon,

Condemn'd to drudge, the meanest of the mean,
And furbish falsehoods for a magazine,
Devotes to scandal his congenial mind;
Himself a living libel on mankind.   980

Oh! dark asylum of a Vandal race!
At once the boast of learning, and disgrace!
So lost to Phœbus, that nor Hodgson's verse
Can make thee better, nor poor Hewson's worse.
But where fair Isis rolls her purer wave,
The partial muse delighted loves to lave;   986
On her green banks a greener wreath she wove,
To crown the bards that haunt her classic grove:
Where Richards wakes a genuine poet's fires,
And modern Britons glory in their sires.

For me, who, thus unask'd, have dared to tell   991
My country what her sons should know too well,
Zeal for her honour bade me here engage
The host of idiots that infest her age;
No just applause her honour'd name shall lose,   995
As first in freedom, dearest to the muse.
Oh! would thy bards but emulate thy fame,
And rise more worthy, Albion, of thy name!
What Athens was in science, Rome in power,
What Tyre appear'd in her meridian hour,   1000
'Tis thine at once, fair Albion! to have been—
Earth's chief dictatress, ocean's lovely queen:
But Rome decay'd, and Athens strew'd the plain,
And Tyre's proud piers lie shatter'd in the main:
Like these, thy strength may sink, in ruin hurl'd,   1005
And Britain fall, the bulwark of the world.
But let me cease, and dread Cassandra's fate,
With warning ever scoff'd at, till too late;
To themes less lofty still my lay confine,
And urge thy bards to gain a name like thine.   1010

Then, hapless Britain! be thy rulers blest,
The senate's oracles, the people's jest!

Still hear thy motley orators dispense
The flowers of rhetoric, though not of sense,
While Canning's colleagues hate him for his wit,   1015
And old dame Portland fills the place of Pitt.

Yet once again, adieu! ere this the sail
That wafts me hence is shivering in the gale;
And Afric's coast and Calpe's adverse height,
And Stamboul's minarets must greet my sight: 1020
Thence shall I stray through beauty's native clime,
Where Kaff is clad in rocks, and crown'd with snows sublime.
But should I back return, no tempting press
Shall drag my journal from the desk's recess;
Let coxcombs, printing as they come from far,   1025
Snatch his own wreath of ridicule from Carr;
Let Aberdeen and Elgin still pursue
The shade of fame through regions of virtù;
Waste useless thousands on their Phidian freaks,
Misshapen monuments and maim'd antiques;   1030
And make their grand saloons a general mart
For all the mutilated blocks of art:
Of Dardan tours let dilettanti tell,
I leave topography to rapid Gell;
And, quite content, no more shall interpose   1035
To stun the public ear—at least with prose.

Thus far I've held my undisturb'd career,
Prepared for rancour, steel'd 'gainst selfish fear:
This thing of rhyme I ne'er disdain'd to own—
Though not obtrusive, yet not quite unknown: 1040
My voice was heard again, though not so loud,
My page, though nameless, never disavow'd;
And now at once I tear the veil away:—
Cheer on the pack! the quarry stands at bay,
Unscared by all the din of Melbourne House,   1045
By Lambe's resentment, or by Holland's spouse,

126

By Jeffrey's harmless pistol, Hallam's
	rage,
Edina's brawny sons and brimstone
	page.
Our men in buckram shall have blows
	enough,
And feel they too are 'penetrable
	stuff':						1050
And though I hope not hence unscathed
	to go,
Who conquers me shall find a stubborn
	foe.
The time hath been, when no harsh sound
	would fall
From lips that now may seem imbued with
	gall;
Nor fools nor follies tempt me to
	despise						1055
The meanest thing that crawl'd beneath
	my eyes:
But now, so callous grown, so changed
	since youth,
I've learn'd to think, and sternly speak the
	truth;
Learn'd to deride the critic's starch de-
	cree,
And break him on the wheel he meant for
	me;						1060
To spurn the rod a scribbler bids me
	kiss,
Nor care if courts and crowds applaud or
	hiss:
Nay more, though all my rival rhymesters
	frown,
I too can hunt a poetaster down;
And, arm'd in proof, the gauntlet cast at
	once						1065
To Scotch marauder, and to southern
	dunce.
Thus much I've dared; if my incondite
	lay
Hath wrong'd these righteous times, let
	others say;
This, let the world, which knows not how
	to spare,					1069
Yet rarely blames unjustly, now declare.

POSTSCRIPT TO THE SECOND EDITION

I HAVE been informed, since the present edition
went to the press, that my trusty and well-beloved
cousins, the Edinburgh Reviewers, are preparing
a most vehement critique on my poor, gentle, *unresisting* Muse, whom they have already so be-
devilled with their ungodly ribaldry:

'Tantæne animis cœlestibus iræ!'

I suppose I must say of Jeffrey as Sir Andrew
Aguecheek saith, 'An I had known he was so cunning of fence, I had seen him damned ere I had
fought him.' What a pity it is that I shall be
beyond the Bosphorus before the next number has
passed the Tweed! But I yet hope to light my pipe
with it in Persia.

My northern friends have accused me, with justice, of personality towards their great literary
anthropophagus, Jeffrey; but what else was to be
done with him and his dirty pack, who feed by
'lying and slandering,' and slake their thirst by
'evil speaking'? I have adduced facts already well
known, and of Jeffrey's mind I have stated my free
opinion, nor has he thence sustained any injury;
—what scavenger was ever soiled by being pelted
with mud? It may be said that I quit England
because I have censured there 'persons of honour
and wit about town'; but I am coming back again,
and their vengeance will keep hot till my return.
Those who know me can testify that my motives
for leaving England are very different from fears,
literary or personal: those who do not, may one
day be convinced. Since the publication of this
thing, my name has not been concealed; I have
been mostly in London, ready to answer for my
transgressions, and in daily expectation of sundry
cartels; but, alas! 'the age of chivalry is over,' or,
in the vulgar tongue, there is no spirit now-a-days.

There is a youth ycleped Hewson Clarke (sub-
audi *esquire*), a sizer of Emanuel College, and, I
believe, a denizen of Berwick-upon-Tweed, whom
I have introduced in these pages to much better
company than he has been accustomed to meet;
he is, notwithstanding, a very sad dog, and for no
reason that I can discover, except a personal
quarrel with a bear, kept by me at Cambridge to
sit for a fellowship, and whom the jealousy of his
Trinity contemporaries prevented from success,
has been abusing me, and, what is worse, the
defenceless innocent above mentioned, in 'The
Satirist,' for one year and some months. I am
utterly unconscious of having given him any provocation; indeed, I am guiltless of having heard
his name, till coupled with 'The Satirist.' He has
therefore no reason to complain, and I dare say
that, like Sir Fretful Plagiary, he is rather *pleased*
than otherwise. I have now mentioned all who
have done me the honour to notice me and mine,
that is, my bear and my book, except the editor of
'The Satirist,' who, it seems, is a gentleman—God
wot! I wish he could impart a little of his gentility
to his subordinate scribblers. I hear that Mr.
Jerningham is about to take up the cudgels for his
Mæcenas, Lord Carlisle. I hope not: he was one
of the few, who, in the very short intercourse I had
with him, treated me with kindness when a boy;
and whatever he may say or do, 'pour on, I will
endure.' I have nothing further to add, save a
general note of thanksgiving to readers, pur-
chasers, and publishers, and, in the words of Scott,
I wish

'To all and each a fair good night,
	And rosy dreams and slumbers light.'

HINTS FROM HORACE

BEING AN ALLUSION IN ENGLISH VERSE TO THE EPISTLE 'AD PISONES,
DE ARTE POETICA,' AND INTENDED AS A SEQUEL TO 'ENGLISH BARDS
AND SCOTCH REVIEWERS'

——'Ergo fungar vice cotis, acutum
Reddere quae ferrum valet, exsors ipsa secandi'
HOR. *De Arte Poet.*

'Rhymes are difficult things—they are stubborn things, sir.'
FIELDING'S *Amelia.*

ATHENS: CAPUCHIN CONVENT,
March 12, 1811.

WHO would not laugh, if Lawrence, hired
to grace
His costly canvas with each flatter'd face,
Abused his art, till Nature, with a blush,
Saw cits grow centaurs underneath his
brush?
Or, should some limner join, for show or
sale, 5
A maid of honour to a mermaid's tail?
Or low Dubost—as once the world has
seen—
Degrade God's creatures in his graphic
spleen?
Not all that forced politeness, which de-
fends
Fools in their faults, could gag his grin-
ning friends. 10
Believe me, Moschus, like that picture
seems
The book which, sillier than a sick man's
dreams,
Displays a crowd of figures incomplete,
Poetic nightmares, without head or feet.

Poets and painters, as all artists know,
May shoot a little with a lengthen'd bow;
We claim this mutual mercy for our task,
And grant in turn the pardon which we
ask;
But make not monsters spring from gen-
tle dams—
Birds breed not vipers, tigers nurse not
lambs. 20

A labour'd, long exordium, sometimes
tends
(Like patriot speeches) but to paltry ends;
And nonsense in a lofty note goes down,
As pertness passes with a legal gown:
Thus many a bard describes in pompous
strain 25
The clear brook babbling through the
goodly plain:
The groves of Granta, and her Gothic
halls,
King's Coll., Cam's stream, stain'd win-
dows, and old walls:
Or, in advent'rous numbers, neatly aims
To paint a rainbow, or—the river Thames.

You sketch a tree, and so perhaps may
shine— 31
But daub a shipwreck like an alehouse
sign;
You plan a *vase*—it dwindles to a *pot*;
Then glide down Grub-street—fasting and
forgot;
Laugh'd into Lethe by some quaint Re-
view, 35
Whose wit is never troublesome till—true.

In fine, to whatsoever you aspire,
Let it at least be simple and entire.

The greater portion of the rhyming
tribe
(Give ear, my friend, for thou hast been a
scribe)
Are led astray by some peculiar lure. 40
I labour to be brief—become obscure;

Humano capiti cervicem pictor equinam
Iungere si velit, et varias inducere plumas,
Undique collatis membris, ut turpiter atrum
Desinat in piscem mulier formosa superne:
Spectatum admissi risum teneatis, amici? 5
Credite, Pisones, isti tabulae fore librum
Persimilem, cuius, velut aegri somnia, vanae
Fingentur species; ut nec pes nec caput uni
Reddatur formae. Pictoribus atque poëtis
Quidlibet audendi semper fuit aequa potestas.
Scimus, et hanc veniam petimusque damusque
vicissim; 11
Sed non ut placidis coëant immitia; non ut
Serpentes avibus geminentur, tigribus agni.
Incoeptis gravibus plerumque et magna pro-
fessis,

Purpureus, late qui splendeat, unus et alter 15
Assuitur pannus; cum lucus et ara Dianae,
Et properantis aquae per amoenos ambitus
agros,
Aut flumen Rhenum, aut pluvius describitur
arcus.
Sed nunc non erat his locus: et fortasse cupres-
sum 19
Scis simulare: quid hoc, si fractis enatat exspes
Navibus, aere dato qui pingitur? amphora
coepit
Institui; currente rota cur urceus exit?
Denique sit quod vis, simplex duntaxat et unum.
Maxima pars vatum, pater et iuvenes patre
digni,
Decipimur specie recti. Brevis esse laboro, 25

128

One falls while following elegance too
    fast;
Another soars, inflated with bombast;
Too low a third crawls on, afraid to fly,
He spins his subject to satiety;   46
Absurdly varying, he at last engraves
Fish in the woods, and boars beneath the
    waves!

Unless your care's exact, your judgment
    nice,
The flight from folly leads but into vice;
None are complete, all wanting in some
    part,   51
Like certain tailors, limited in art.
For galligaskins Slowshears is your man;
But coats must claim another artisan.
Now this to me, I own, seems much the
    same   55
As Vulcan's feet to bear Apollo's frame;
Or, with a fair complexion, to expose
Black eyes, black ringlets, but—a bottle
    nose!

Dear authors! suit your topics to your
    strength,
And ponder well your subject and its
    length;   60
Nor lift your load before you're quite
    aware
What weight your shoulders will, or will
    not, bear.
But lucid Order, and Wit's siren voice,
Await the poet, skilful in his choice;
With native eloquence he soars along,
Grace in his thoughts, and music in his
    song.   66

Let judgment teach them wisely to com-
    bine
With future parts the now omitted line:
This shall the author choose, or that re-
    ject,   69
Precise in style, and cautious to select;

Nor slight applause will candid pens afford
To him who furnishes a wanting word.
Then fear not, if 'tis needful, to produce
Some term unknown, or obsolete in use,
(As Pitt has furnish'd us a word or two,
Which lexicographers declined to do;)
So you indeed, with care,—(but be con-
    tent
To take this license rarely)—may in-
    vent.
New words find credit in these latter days,
If neatly grafted on a Gallic phrase.   80
What Chaucer, Spenser did, we scarce
    refuse
To Dryden's or to Pope's maturer muse.
If you can add a little, say why not,
As well as William Pitt, and Walter Scott?
Since they, by force of rhyme and force of
    lungs,   85
Enrich'd our island's ill-united tongues;
'Tis then—and shall be—lawful to present
Reform in writing, as in parliament.

As forests shed their foliage by degrees,
So fade expressions which in season
    please;   90
And we and ours, alas! are due to fate,
And works and words but dwindle to a
    date.
Though as a monarch nods, and com-
    merce calls,
Impetuous rivers stagnate in canals;
Though swamps subdued, and marshes
    drain'd, sustain   95
The heavy ploughshare and the yellow
    grain,
And rising ports along the busy shore
Protect the vessel from old Ocean's roar,
All, all, must perish; but, surviving last,
The love of letters half preserves the past.
True, some decay, yet not a few revive;
Though those shall sink, which now
    appear to thrive,   102

Obscurus fio: sectantem levia, nervi
Deficiunt animique: professus grandia, turget:
Serpit humi, tutus nimium, timidusque pro-
    cellae:
Qui variare cupit rem prodigialiter unam,
Delphinum sylvis appingit, fluctibus aprum. 30
In vitium ducit culpae fuga, si caret arte.
Aemilium circa ludum faber unus et ungues
Exprimet, et molles imitabitur aere capillos;
Infelix operis summa, quia ponere totum
Nesciet. Hunc ego me, si quid componere
    curem,   35
Non magis esse velim, quam pravo vivere naso,
Spectandum nigris oculis nigroque capillo.
    Sumite materiam vestris, qui scribitis, aequam
Viribus; et versate diu quid ferre recusent   39
Quid valeant humeri. Cui lecta potenter erit res,
Nec facundia deseret hunc nec lucidus ordo.
    Ordinis haec virtus erit et venus, aut ego fallor,
Ut iam nunc dicat, iam nunc debentia dici
Pleraque differat, et praesens in tempus omittat;
    In verbis etiam tenuis cautusque serendis: 45
Hoc amet, hoc spernat promissi carminis auctor.
Dixeris egregie, notum si callida verbum

Reddiderit iunctura novum. Si forte necesse est
Indiciis monstrare recentibus abdita rerum,
Fingere cinctutis non exaudita Cethegis   50
Continget; dabiturque licentia sumpta pudenter;
Et nova fictaque nuper habebunt verba fidem, si
Graeco fonte cadant, parce detorta. Quid autem
Caecilio Plautoque dabit Romanus, ademptum
Virgilio Varioque? ego cur, acquirere pauca 55
Si possum, invideor; cum lingua Catonis et Enni
Sermonem patrium ditaverit, et nova rerum
Nomina protulerit? Licuit, semperque licebit,
Signatum praesente nota producere nomen. 59
    Ut silvae foliis pronos mutantur in annos;
Prima cadunt: ita verborum vetus interit aetas,
Et iuvenum ritu florent modo nata, vigentque.
Debemur morti nos, nostraque: sive receptus
Terra Neptunus classes Aquilonibus arcet,
Regis opus; sterilisque diu palus, aptaque remis
Vicinas urbes alit, et grave sentit aratrum: 66
Seu cursum mutavit iniquum frugibus amnis,
Doctus iter melius; mortalia facta peribunt:
Nedum sermonum stet honos, et gratia vivax.
Multa renascentur, quae iam cecidere; cadent-
    que,   70

As custom arbitrates, whose shifting
    sway
Our life and language must alike obey.

The immortal wars which gods and
    angels wage,   105
Are they not shown in Milton's sacred
    page?
His strain will teach what numbers best
    belong
To themes celestial told in epic song.

The slow, sad stanza will correctly
    paint
The lover's anguish, or the friend's com-
    plaint.   110
But which deserves the laurel—rhyme or
    blank?
Which holds on Helicon the higher rank?
Let squabbling critics by themselves dis-
    pute
This point, as puzzling as a Chancery
    suit.

Satiric rhyme first sprang from selfish
    spleen.   115
You doubt—see Dryden, Pope, St. Pat-
    rick's dean.

Blank verse is now, with one consent,
    allied
To Tragedy, and rarely quits her side.
Though mad Almanzor rhymed in Dry-
    den's days,   119
No sing-song hero rants in modern plays;
While modest Comedy her verse fore-
    goes
For jest and *pun* in very middling prose.
Not that our Bens or Beaumonts show the
    worse,
Or lose one point, because they wrote in
    verse.
But so Thalia pleases to appear,   125
Poor virgin! damn'd some twenty times
    a year!

Whate'er the scene, let this advice have
    weight:—
Adapt your language to your hero's state.
At times Melpomene forgets to groan,
And brisk Thalia takes a serious tone;
Nor unregarded will the act pass by   131
Where angry Townly lifts his voice on
    high.
Again our Shakspeare limits verse to
    kings,
When common prose will serve for com-
    mon things;
And lively Hal resigns heroic ire,   135
To 'hollowing Hotspur' and the sceptred
    sire.

'Tis not enough, ye bards, with all your
    art,
To polish poems; they must touch the
    heart:
Where'er the scene be laid, whate'er the
    song,
Still let it bear the hearer's soul along;
Command your audience or to smile or
    weep,   141
Whiche'er may please you—anything but
    sleep.
The poet claims our tears; but, by his
    leave,
Before I shed them, let me see him grieve.

If banish'd Romeo feign'd nor sigh nor
    tear,   145
Lull'd by his languor, I should sleep or
    sneer.
Sad words, no doubt, become a serious
    face,
And men look angry in the proper place.
At double meanings folks seem wondrous
    sly,
And sentiment prescribes a pensive eye;
For nature form'd at first the inward
    man,   151
And actors copy nature—when they can.

Quae nunc sunt in honore vocabula, si volet
    usus.
Quem penes arbitrium est, et ius, et norma
    loquendi.
  Res gestae regumque ducumque et tristia bella,
Quo scribi possent numero, monstravit Ho-
    merus.
  Versibus impariter iunctis querimonia pri-
    mum: 75
Post etiam inclusa est voti sententia compos.
Quis tamen exiguos elegos emiserit auctor,
Grammatici certant, et adhuc sub iudice lis est.
  Archilochum proprio rabies armavit iambo;
Hunc socci cepere pedem grandesque cothurni,
Alternis aptum sermonibus, et populares   81
Vincentem strepitus, et natum rebus agendis.
  Musa dedit fidibus divos, puerosque deorum,
Et pugilem victorem, et equum certamine pri-
    mum,
Et iuvenum curas, et libera vina referre.   85
  Descriptas servare vices, operumque colores,
Cur ego, si nequeo ignoroque, poeta salutor?

Cur nescire, pudens prave, quam discere malo?
  Versibus exponi tragicis res comica non vult;
Indignatur item privati, ac prope socco   90
Dignis carminibus narrari coena Thyestae.
Singula quaeque locum teneant sortita decenter
Interdum tamen et vocem comoedia tollit,
Iratusque Chremes tumido delitigat ore:
Et tragicus plerumque dolet sermone pedestri.
Telephus et Peleus, cum pauper et exul, uterque
Proicit ampullas, et sesquipedalia verba,   97
Si curat cor spectantis tetigisse querela.
  Non satis est pulchra esse poemata; dulcia
    sunto,
Et quocunque volent, animum auditoris agunto.
Ut ridentibus arrident, ita flentibus adsunt 101
Humani vultus; si vis me flere dolendum est
Primum ipsi tibi; tunc tua me infortunia laedent,
Telephe, vel Peleu; male si mandata loqueris
Aut dormitabo, aut ridebo: tristia moestum
Vultum verba decent; iratum, plena minarum;
Ludentem, lasciva; severum, seria dictu.   107
Format enim natura prius nos intus ad omnem

She bids the beating heart with rapture
   bound,
Raised to the stars, or levell'd with the
   ground;   154
And for expression's aid, 'tis said, or sung,
She gave our mind's interpreter—the
   tongue,
Who, worn with use, of late would fain
   dispense
(At least in theatres) with common sense;
O'erwhelm with sound the boxes, gallery,
   pit,   159
And raise a laugh with anything—but wit.

To skilful writers it will much import,
Whence spring their scenes, from common
   life or court;
Whether they seek applause by smile or
   tear,
To draw a 'Lying Valet,' or a 'Lear,'
A sage, or rakish youngster wild from
   school,   165
A wandering 'Peregrine,' or plain 'John
   Bull,'
All persons please when nature's voice
   prevails,
Scottish or Irish, born in Wilts or Wales.

Or follow common fame, or forge a
   plot;   169
Who cares if mimic heroes lived or not?
One precept serves to regulate the scene:—
Make it appear as if it *might* have *been.*

If some Drawcansir you aspire to draw,
Present him raving, and above all law:
If female furies in your scheme are
   plann'd,   175
Macbeth's fierce dame is ready to your
   hand;
For tears and treachery, for good and evil,
Constance, King Richard, Hamlet, and
   the Devil!
But if a new design you dare essay, 179
And freely wander from the beaten way,

True to your characters, till all be past,
Preserve consistency from first to last.

'Tis hard to venture where our betters
   fail,
Or lend fresh interest to a twice-told tale;
And yet, perchance, 'tis wiser to prefer
A hackney'd plot, than choose a new, and
   err;   186
Yet copy not too closely, but record,
More justly, thought for thought than
   word for word;
Nor trace your prototype through narrow
   ways,
But only follow where he merits praise.

For you, young bard! whom luckless
   fate may lead   191
To tremble on the nod of all who read,
Ere your first score of cantos time unrolls,
Beware—for God's sake, don't begin like
   Bowles!
'Awake a louder and a loftier strain,'—
And pray, what follows from his boiling
   brain?—   196
He sinks to Southey's level in a trice,
Whose epic mountains never fail in mice!
Not so of yore awoke your mighty sire
The temper'd warblings of his master-
   lyre;   200
Soft as the gentle breathing of the lute,
'Of man's first disobedience and the fruit'
He speaks, but, as his subject swells along,
Earth, Heaven, and Hades echo with the
   song.
Still to the midst of things he hastens on,
As if we witness'd all already done; 206
Leaves on his path whatever seems too
   mean
To raise the subject, or adorn the scene;
Gives, as each page improves upon the
   sight,
Not smoke from brightness, but from
   darkness—light;   210

Fortunarum habitum; iuvat, aut impellit ad
   iram;
Aut ad humum moerore gravi deducit, et angit;
Post effert animi motus interprete lingua. 111
Si dicentis erunt fortunis absona dicta,
Romani tollent equites, peditesque cachinnum.
   Intererit multum, Davusne loquatur an heros;
Maturusne senex, an adhuc florente iuventa
Fervidus; an matrona potens, an sedula nutrix;
Mercatorne vagus, cultorne virentis agelli;
Colchus an Assyrius; Thebis nutritus, an Argis.
   Aut famam sequere, aut sibi convenientia
   finge,   119
Scriptor. Honoratum si forte reponis Achillem;
Impiger, iracundus, inexorabilis, acer,
Iura neget sibi nata, nihil non arroget armis.
Sit Medea ferox invictaque; flebilis Ino;
Perfidus Ixion; Io vaga; tristis Orestes. 124
Si quid inexpertum scenae committis, et audes
Personam formare novam: servetur ad imum
Qualis ab incepto processerit, et sibi constet.
   Difficile est proprie communia dicere: tuque
Rectius Iliacum carmen deducis in actus,

Quam si proferres ignota indictaque primus.
Publica materies privati iuris erit, si 131
Nec circa vilem patulumque moraberis orbem;
Nec verbum verbo curabis reddere fidus
Interpres, nec desilies imitator in arctum
Unde pedem proferre pudor vetet, aut operis lex.
Nec sic incipies, ut scriptor Cyclicus olim: 136
'Fortunam Priami cantabo, et nobile bellum.'
Quid dignum tanto feret hic promissor hiatu?
Parturiunt montes: nascetur ridiculus mus.
Quanto rectius hic, qui nil molitur inepte! 140
'Dic mihi, Musa, virum, captae post tempora
   Troiae,
Qui mores hominum multorum vidit, et urbes.'
Non fumum ex fulgore, sed ex fumo dare lucem
Cogitat, ut speciosa dehinc miracula promat,
Antiphaten, Scyllamque, et cum Cyclope Cha-
   rybdin.   145
Nec reditum Diomedis ab interitu Meleagri,
Nec gemino bellum Troianum orditur ab ovo.
Semper ad eventum festinat; et in medias res
Non secus ac notas, auditorem rapit, et quae
Desperat tractata nitescere posse, relinquit: 150

HINTS FROM HORACE

And truth and fiction with such art compounds,
We know not where to fix their several bounds.
If you would please the public, deign to hear
What soothes the many-headed monster's ear:
If your heart triumph when the hands of all   215
Applaud in thunder at the curtain's fall,
Deserve those plaudits—study nature's page,
And sketch the striking traits of every age;
While varying man and varying years unfold
Life's little tale, so oft, so vainly told;   220
Observe his simple childhood's dawning days,
His pranks, his prate, his playmates, and his plays;
Till time at length the mannish tyro weans,
And prurient vice outstrips his tardy teens!

Behold him Freshman! forced no more to groan   225
O'er Virgil's devilish verses and his own;
Prayers are too tedious, lectures too abstruse,
He flies from Tavell's frown to 'Fordham's Mews';
(Unlucky Tavell! doom'd to daily cares
By pugilistic pupils, and by bears,)   230
Fines, tutors, tasks, conventions threat in vain,
Before hounds, hunters, and Newmarket plain.
Rough with his elders, with his equals rash,
Civil to sharpers, prodigal of cash;
Constant to nought—save hazard and a whore,   235
Yet cursing both—for both have made him sore;
Unread (unless, since books beguile disease,
The p—x becomes his passage to degrees);
Fool'd, pillaged, dunn'd, he wastes his term away,
And unexpell'd, perhaps, retires M.A.;

Master of arts! as *hells* and *clubs* proclaim,   241
Where scarce a blackleg bears a brighter name!

Launch'd into life, extinct his early fire,
He apes the selfish prudence of his sire;
Marries for money, chooses friends for rank,   245
Buys land, and shrewdly trusts not to the Bank;
Sits in the Senate; gets a son and heir;
Sends him to Harrow, for himself was there.
Mute, though he votes, unless when call'd to cheer,
His son's so sharp—he'll see the dog a peer!   250

Manhood declines—age palsies every limb;
He quits the scene—or else the scene quits him;
Scrapes wealth, o'er each departing penny grieves,
And avarice seizes all ambition leaves;
Counts cent. per cent., and smiles, or vainly frets,   255
O'er hoards diminish'd by young Hopeful's debts;
Weighs well and wisely what to sell or buy,
Complete in all life's lessons—but to die;
Peevish and spiteful, doting, hard to please,
Commending every time, save times like these;   260
Crazed, querulous, forsaken, half forgot,
Expires unwept—is buried—let him rot!

But from the Drama let me not digress,
Nor spare my precepts, though they please you less.
Though woman weep, and hardest hearts are stirr'd,   265
When what is done is rather seen than heard,
Yet many deeds preserved in history's page
Are better told than acted on the stage;

Atque ita mentitur, sic veris falsa remiscet,
Primo ne medium, medio ne discrepet imum.
  Tu, quid ego et populus mecum desideret,
  audi.
Si plausoris eges aulaea manentis, et usque
Sessuri, donec cantor, Vos plaudite, dicat;   155
Aetatis cuiusque notandi sunt tibi mores,
Mobilibusque decor naturis dandus et annis.
Reddere qui voces iam scit puer, et pede certo
Signat humum; gestit paribus colludere, et iram
Colligit ac ponit temere, et mutatur in horas.
  Imberbus iuvenis, tandem custode remoto,
Gaudet equis canibusque, et aprici gramine
  campi;
Cereus in vitium flecti, monitoribus asper,
Utilium tardus provisor, prodigus aeris,

Sublimis, cupidusque, et amata relinquere pernix.   165
  Conversis studiis, aetas animusque virilis
Quaerit opes et amicitias, inservit honori;
Commisisse cavet quod mox mutare laboret.
  Multa senem circumveniunt incommoda; vel
  quod   169
Quaerit, et inventis miser abstinet, ac timet uti;
Vel quod res omnes timide gelideque ministrat,
Dilator, spe longus, iners, avidusque futuri,
Difficilis, querulus, laudator temporis acti
Se puero, castigator censorque minorum.   174
Multa ferunt anni venientes commoda secum,
Multa recedentes adimunt. Ne forte seniles
Mandentur iuveni partes, pueroque viriles,
Semper in adiunctis, aevoque morabimur aptis.

132

The ear sustains what shocks the timid eye,
And horror thus subsides to sympathy.
True Briton all beside, I here am French—
Bloodshed 'tis surely better to retrench;
The gladiatorial gore we teach to flow
In tragic scene disgusts, though but in show;
We hate the carnage while we see the trick, 275
And find small sympathy in being sick.
Not on the stage the regicide Macbeth
Appals an audience with a monarch's death;
To gaze when sable Hubert threats to sear
Young Arthur's eyes, can *ours* or *nature* bear? 280
A halter'd heroine Johnson sought to slay—
We saved Irene, but half damn'd the play,
And (Heaven be praised!) our tolerating times
Stint metamorphoses to pantomimes;
And Lewis' self, with all his sprites, would quake 285
To change Earl Osmond's negro to a snake!
Because, in scenes exciting joy or grief,
We loathe the action which exceeds belief:
And yet, God knows! what may not authors do,
Whose postscripts prate of dyeing 'heroines blue?' 290

Above all things, *Dan* Poet, if you can,
Eke out your acts, I pray, with mortal man,
Nor call a ghost, unless some cursed scrape
Must open ten trap-doors for your escape.
Of all the monstrous things I'd fain forbid, 295
I loathe an opera worse than Dennis did;
Where good and evil persons, right or wrong,
Rage, love, and aught but moralise, in song.
Hail, last memorial of our foreign friends,
Which Gaul allows, and still Hesperia lends! 300
Napoleon's edicts no embargo lay
On whores, spies, singers, wisely shipp'd away.
Our giant capital, whose squares are spread
Where rustics earn'd, and now may beg, their bread,
In all iniquity is grown so nice, 305
It scorns amusements which are not of price.

Hence the pert shopkeeper, whose throbbing ear
Aches with orchestras which he pays to hear,
Whom shame, not sympathy, forbids to snore,
His anguish doubling by his own 'encore';
Squeezed in 'Fop's Alley,' jostled by the beaux, 311
Teased with his hat, and trembling for his toes;
Scarce wrestles through the night, nor tastes of ease,
Till the dropp'd curtain gives a glad release:
Why this, and more, he suffers—can ye guess?— 315
Because it costs him dear, and makes him dress!

So prosper eunuchs from Etruscan schools;
Give us but fiddlers, and they're sure of fools!
Ere scenes were play'd by many a reverend clerk,
(What harm, if David danced before the ark?) 320
In Christmas revels, simple country folks
Were pleased with morrice-mumm'ry and coarse jokes.
Improving years, with things no longer known,
Produced blithe Punch and merry Madame Joan, 324
Who still frisk on with feats so lewdly low,
'Tis strange Benvolio suffers such a show;
Suppressing peer! to whom each vice gives place,
Oaths, boxing, begging,—all, save rout and race.

Farce follow'd Comedy, and reach'd her prime,
In ever-laughing Foote's fantastic time:
Mad wag! who pardon'd none, nor spared the best, 331
And turn'd some very serious things to jest.
Nor church nor state escaped his public sneers,
Arms nor the gown, priests, lawyers, volunteers:
'Alas, poor Yorick!' now for ever mute!
Whoever loves a laugh must sigh for Foote. 336

Aut agitur res in scenis, aut acta refertur.
Segnius irritant animos demissa per aurem 180
Quam quae sunt oculis subiecta fidelibus, et quae
Ipse sibi tradit spectator. Non tamen intus
Digna geri promes in scenam; multaque tolles
Ex oculis, quae mox narret facundia praesens.
Ne pueros coram populo Medea trucidet; 185
Aut humana palam coquat exta nefarius Atreus;
Aut in avem Progne vertatur, Cadmus in anguem.
Quodcunque ostendis mihi sic, incredulus odi.

Neve minor, neu sit quinto productior actu
Fabula, quae posci vult, et spectata reponi. 190
Nec deus intersit, nisi dignus vindice nodus
Inciderit, ...
  Ex noto fictum carmen sequar, ut sibi quivis 240
Speret idem: sudet multum frustraque laboret
Ausus idem: tantum series iuncturaque pollet;
Tantum de medio sumtis accedit honoris.
Silvis deducti caveant, me iudice, Fauni,

We smile, perforce, when histrionic scenes
Ape the swoln dialogue of kings and queens,
When 'Chrononhotonthologos must die,'
And Arthur struts in mimic majesty.

Moschus! with whom once more I hope to sit,   341
And smile at folly, if we can't at wit;
Yes, friend! for thee I'll quit my cynic cell,
And bear Swift's motto, 'Vive la bagatelle!'
Which charm'd our days in each Aegean clime,   345
As oft at home, with revelry and rhyme,
Then may Euphrosyne, who sped the past,
Soothe thy life's scenes, nor leave thee in the last;
But find in thine, like pagan Plato's bed,
Some merry manuscript of mimes, when dead.   350

Now to the Drama let us bend our eyes,
Where fetter'd by whig Walpole low she lies;
Corruption foil'd her, for she fear'd her glance;
Decorum left her for an opera dance!
Yet Chesterfield, whose polished pen inveighs   355
'Gainst laughter, fought for freedom to our plays;
Uncheck'd by megrims of patrician brains,
And damning dulness of lord chamberlains.
Repeal that act! again let Humour roam
Wild o'er the stage—we've time for tears at home.   360
Let 'Archer' plant the horns on 'Sullen's' brows,
And 'Estifania' gull her 'Copper' spouse;
The moral's scant—but that may be excused,
Men go not to be lectured, but amused.
He whom our plays dispose to good or ill
Must wear a head in want of Willis' skill;
Ay, but Macheath's example—psha!—no more!   367
It form'd no thieves—the thief was form'd before;
And, spite of puritans and Collier's curse,
Plays make mankind no better, and no worse.   370
Then spare our stage, ye methodistic men!
Nor burn damn'd Drury if it rise again.

But why to brain-scorch'd bigots thus appeal?
Can heavenly mercy dwell with earthly zeal?   374
For times of fire and faggot let them hope!
Times dear alike to puritan or pope.
As pious Calvin saw Servetus blaze,
So would new sects on newer victims gaze.
E'en now the songs of Solyma begin;   379
Faith cants, perplex'd apologist of sin!
While the Lord's servant chastens whom he loves,
And Simeon kicks, where Baxter only 'shoves.'

Whom nature guides, so writes, that every dunce,
Enraptured, thinks to do the same at once;
But after inky thumbs and bitten nails,
And twenty scatter'd quires, the coxcomb fails.   386

Let Pastoral be dumb; for who can hope
To match the youthful eclogues of our Pope?
Yet his and Phillips' faults, of different kind,   389
For art too rude, for nature too refined,
Instruct how hard the medium 'tis to hit
'Twixt too much polish and too coarse a wit.

A vulgar scribbler, certes, stands disgraced
In this nice age, when all aspire to taste;
The dirty language, and the noisome jest,
Which pleased in Swift of yore, we now detest;   396
Proscribed not only in the world polite,
But even too nasty for a city knight!

Peace to Swift's faults! his wit hath made them pass,
Unmatch'd by all, save matchless Hudibras!   400
Whose author is perhaps the first we meet,
Who from our couplet lopp'd two final feet;
Nor less in merit than the longer line,
This measure moves a favourite of the Nine.
Though at first view eight feet may seem in vain   405
Form'd, save in ode, to bear a serious strain,

Ne, velut innati triviis, ac pene forenses,   245
Aut nimium teneris iuvenentur versibus unquam,
Aut immunda crepent, ignominiosaque dicta.
Offenduntur enim, quibus est equus, et pater, et res:
Nec, si quid fricti ciceris probat et nucis emtor,
Aequis accipiunt animis, donantve corona.
  Syllaba longa brevi subiecta vocatur iambus,
Pes citus: unde etiam trimetris accrescere iussit

Nomen iambeis, cum senos redderet ictus,
Primus ad extremum similis sibi: non ita pridem,
Tardior ut paulo graviorque veniret ad aures,
Spondeos stabiles in iura paterna recepit   256
Commodus et patiens; non ut de sede secunda
Cederet aut quarta socialiter. Hic et in Acci
Nobilibus trimetris apparet rarus, et Enni.
In scenam missos magno cum pondere versus,
Aut operae celeris nimium, curaque carentis,
Aut ignoratae premit artis crimine turpi.   262

Yet Scott has shown our wondering isle of late
This measure shrinks not from a theme of weight,
And, varied skilfully, surpasses far   409
Heroic rhyme, but most in love and war,
Whose fluctuations, tender or sublime,
Are curb'd too much by long-recurring rhyme.

But many a skilful judge abhors to see,
What few admire—irregularity.
This some vouchsafe to pardon; but 'tis hard   415
When such a word contents a British bard.

And must the bard his glowing thoughts confine,
Lest censure hover o'er some faulty line?
Remove whate'er a critic may suspect,
To gain the paltry suffrage of '*correct*'?
Or prune the spirit of each daring phrase,
To fly from error, not to merit praise?

Ye, who seek finish'd models, never cease,
By day and night, to read the works of Greece.
But our good fathers never bent their brains   425
To heathen Greek, content with native strains.
The few who read a page, or used a pen,
Were satisfied with Chaucer and old Ben;
The jokes and numbers suited to their taste
Were quaint and careless, anything but chaste;   430
Yet whether right or wrong the ancient rules,
It will not do to call our fathers fools!
Though you and I, who eruditely know
To separate the elegant and low,   434
Can also, when a hobbling line appears,
Detect with fingers, in default of ears.

In sooth I do not know, or greatly care
To learn, who our first English strollers were;

Or if, till roofs received the vagrant art,
Our Muse, like that of Thespis, kept a cart;   440
But this is certain, since our Shakspeare's days,
There's pomp enough, if little else, in plays;
Nor will Melpomene ascend her throne
Without high heels, white plume, and Bristol stone.

Old comedies still meet with much applause,   445
Though too licentious for dramatic laws;
At least, we moderns, wisely, 'tis confest,
Curtail, or silence, the lascivious jest.

Whate'er their follies, and their faults beside,
Our enterprising bards pass nought untried;   450
Nor do they merit slight applause who choose
An English subject for an English muse,
And leave to minds which never dare invent
French flippancy and German sentiment.
Where is that living language which could claim   455
Poetic more, as philosophic, fame,
If all our bards, more patient of delay,
Would stop, like Pope, to polish by the way?

Lords of the quill, whose critical assaults
O'erthrow whole quartos with their quires of faults,   460
Who soon detect, and mark where'er we fail,
And prove our marble with too nice a nail!
Democritus himself was not so bad;
He only *thought*, but *you* would make, us mad!

But truth to say, most rhymers rarely guard   465
Against that ridicule they deem so hard;
In person negligent, they wear, from sloth,
Beards of a week, and nails of annual growth;

Non quivis videt immodulata poemata iudex;
Et data Romanis venia est indigna poetis.
Idcirco vager, scribamque licenter? an omnes
Visuros peccata putem mea; tutus, et intra
Spem veniae cautus? vitavi denique culpam,
Non laudem merui. Vos exemplaria Graeca
Nocturna versate manu, versate diurna.
At vestri proavi Plautinos et numeros et   270
Laudavere sales; nimium patienter utrumque,
Ne dicam stulte, mirati; si modo ego et vos
Scimus inurbanum lepido seponere dicto,
Legitimumque sonum digitis callemus et aure.
  Ignotum tragicae genus invenisse Camoena
Dicitur, et plaustris vexisse poemata Thespis,
Quae canerent agerentque peruncti faecibus
  ora.   277
Post hunc personae pallaeque repertor honestae

Aeschylus, et modicis instravit pulpita tignis,
Et docuit magnumque loqui, nitique cothurno.
  Successit vetus his comoedia, non sine multa
Laude; sed in vitium libertas excidit, et vim
Dignam lege regi; lex est accepta; chorusque
Turpiter obticuit, sublato iure nocendi.
  Nil intentatum nostri liquere poetae;   285
Nec minimum meruere decus, vestigia Graeca
Ausi deserere, et celebrare domestica facta;
Vel qui praetextas, vel qui docuere togatas.
Nec virtute foret clarisve potentius armis,
Quam lingua, Latium, si non offenderet unum-
quemque poetarum limae labor, et mora. Vos, o
Pompilius sanguis, carmen reprehendite, quod
  non   292
Multa dies et multa litura coercuit, atque
Praesectum decies non castigavit ad unguem.

HINTS FROM HORACE

Reside in garrets, fly from those they
 meet,
And walk in alleys, rather than the street.

With little rhyme, less reason, if you
 please, 471
The name of poet may be got with ease,
So that not tuns of helleboric juice
Shall ever turn your head to any use;
Write but like Wordsworth, live beside a
 Lake, 475
And keep your bushy locks a year from
 Blake;
Then print your book, once more return
 to town,
And boys shall hunt your bardship up and
 down.

Am I not wise, if such some poets' plight,
To purge in spring—like Bayes—before
 I write? 480
If this precaution soften'd not my bile,
I know no scribbler with a madder style;
But since (perhaps my feelings are too
 nice)
I cannot purchase fame at such a price,
I'll labour gratis as a grinder's wheel,
And, blunt myself, give edge to others'
 steel, 486
Nor write at all, unless to teach the art
To those rehearsing for the poet's part;
From Horace show the pleasing paths of
 song,
And from my own example—what is
 wrong. 490

Though modern practice sometimes
 differs quite,
'Tis just as well to think before you write;
Let every book that suits your theme be
 read,
So shall you trace it to the fountain-head.

He who has learn'd the duty which he
 owes 495

To friends and country, and to pardon foes;
Who models his deportment as may best
Accord with brother, sire, or stranger guest;
Who takes our laws and worship as they are,
Nor roars reform for senate, church, and
 bar; 500
In practice, rather than loud precept, wise,
Bids not his tongue, but heart, philoso-
 phise:
Such is the man the poet should rehearse,
As joint exemplar of his life and verse.

Sometimes a sprightly wit, and tale well
 told, 505
Without much grace, or weight, or art,
 will hold
A longer empire o'er the public mind
Than sounding trifles, empty, though refined.

Unhappy Greece! thy sons of ancient
 days
The muse may celebrate with perfect
 praise, 510
Whose generous children narrow'd not
 their hearts
With commerce, given alone to arms and
 arts.
Our boys (save those whom public schools
 compel
To 'long and short' before they're taught
 to spell) 514
From frugal fathers soon imbibe by rote,
'A penny saved, my lad, 's a penny got.'
Babe of a city birth! from sixpence take
The third, how much will the remainder
 make?—
'A groat.'—'Ah, bravo! Dick hath done
 the sum!
He'll swell my fifty thousand to a plum.'

They whose young souls receive this
 rust betimes, 521
'Tis clear, are fit for anything but rhymes;

Ingenium misera quia fortunatius arte 295
Credit, et excludit sanos Helicone poetas
Democritus; bona pars non ungues ponere
 curat,
Non barbam; secreta petit loca, balnea vitat.
Nanciscetur enim pretium nomenque poetae,
Si tribus Anticyris caput insanabile nunquam
Tonsori Licino commiserit. O ego laevus, 301
Qui purgor bilem sub verni temporis horam!
Non alius faceret meliora poemata: verum
Nil tanti est: ergo fungar vice cotis, acutum
Reddere quae ferrum valet, exsors ipsa secandi:
Munus et officium, nil scribens ipse, docebo;
Unde parentur opes; quid alat formetque
 poetam;
Quid deceat, quid non; quo virtus, quo ferat
 error. 308
 Scribendi recte sapere est et principium et fons.
Rem tibi Socraticae poterunt ostendere chartae:
Verbaque provisam rem non invita sequentur:
Qui didicit patriae quid debeat, et quid amicis;

Quo sic amore parens, quo frater amandus, et
 hospes;
Quod sit conscripti, quod iudicis officium; quae
Partes in bellum missi ducis; ille profecto 315
Reddere personae scit convenientia cuique.
Respicere exemplar vitae morumque iubebo
Doctum imitatorem, et vivas hinc ducere voces.
 Interdum speciosa locis morataque recte
Fabula, nullius veneris, sine pondere et arte,
Valdius oblectat populum, meliusque moratur,
Quam versus inopes rerum, nugaeque canorae.
 Graiis ingenium, Graiis dedit ore rotundo
Musa loqui, praeter laudem nullius avaris.
Romani pueri longis rationibus assem 325
Discunt in partes centum diducere: dicat
Filius Albini, Si de quincunce remota est
Uncia, quid superat? poteras dixisse—Triens. Eu!
Rem poteris servare tuam. Redit uncia: quid
 fit? 329
Semis. An haec animos aerugo et cura peculi
Cum semel imbuerit, speramus carmina fingi

136

And Locke will tell you, that the father's
 right
Who hides all verses from his children's
 sight;   524
For poets (says this sage, and many more,)
Make sad mechanics with their lyric lore;
And Delphi now, however rich of old,
Discovers little silver, and less gold,
Because Parnassus, though a mount di-
 vine,
Is poor as Irus, or an Irish mine. 530

Two objects always should the poet
 move,
Or one or both,—to please or to improve.
Whate'er you teach, be brief, if you design
For our remembrance your didactic line;
Redundance places memory on the rack,
For brains may be o'erloaded, like the
 back.   536

Fiction does best when taught to look
 like truth,
And fairy fables bubble none but youth:
Expect no credit for too wondrous tales,
Since Jonas only springs alive from
 whales!   540

Young men with aught but elegance
 dispense;
Maturer years require a little sense.
To end at once:—that bard for all is fit
Who mingles well instruction with his wit;
For him reviews shall smile, for him o'er-
 flow   545
The patronage of Paternoster-row;
His book, with Longman's liberal aid,
 shall pass
(Who ne'er despises books that bring him
 brass);
Through three long weeks the taste of
 London lead,
And cross St. George's Channel and the
 Tweed.   550

But everything has faults, nor is 't un-
 known
That harps and fiddles often lose their tone,
And wayward voices, at their owner's call,
With all his best endeavours, only squall;
Dogs blink their covey, flints withhold the
 spark,   555
And double-barrels (damn them!) miss
 their mark.

Where frequent beauties strike the
 reader's view,
We must not quarrel for a blot or two;
But pardon equally to books or men,
The slips of human nature, and the pen.

Yet if an author, spite of foe or friend,
Despises all advice too much to mend,
But ever twangs the same discordant string,
Give him no quarter, howsoe'er he sing.
Let Havard's fate o'ertake him, who, for
 once,   565
Produced a play too dashing for a dunce:
At first none deem'd it his; but when his
 name
Announced the fact—what then?—it lost
 its fame.
Though all deplore when Milton deigns to
 doze,
In a long work 'tis fair to steal repose.

As pictures, so shall poems be; some
 stand   571
The critic eye, and please when near at
 hand;
But others at a distance strike the sight;
This seeks the shade, but that demands
 the light,
Nor dreads the connoisseur's fastidious
 view,   575
But, ten times scrutinised, is ten times new.

Parnassian pilgrims! ye whom chance or
 choice
Hath led to listen to the Muse's voice,

Posse linenda cedro, et levi servanda cupresso?
 Aut prodesse volunt, aut delectare poetae;
Aut simul et iucunda et idonea dicere vitae. 334
Quidquid praecipies, esto brevis: ut cito dicta
Percipiant animi dociles, teneantque fideles.
Omne supervacuum pleno de pectore manat.
 Ficta voluptatis causa sint proxima veris:
Nec, quodcunque volet, poscat sibi fabula credi:
Neu pransae Lamiae vivum puerum extrahat
 alvo.   340
 Centuriae seniorum agitant expertia frugis:
Celsi praetereunt austera poemata Rhamnes.
Omne tulit punctum, qui miscuit utile dulci:
Lectorem delectando pariterque monendo. 344
Hic meret aera liber Sosiis; hic et mare transit,
Et longum noto scriptori prorogat aevum.
 Sunt delicta tamen, quibus ignovisse velimus:
Nam neque chorda sonum reddit quem vult
 manus et mens,
Poscentique gravem persaepe remittit acutum;
Nec semper feriet quodcunque minabitur arcus.

Verum ubi plura nitent in carmine, non ego
 paucis   351
Offendar maculis, quas aut incuria fudit,
Aut humana parum cavit natura. Quid ergo est?
Ut scriptor si peccat idem librarius usque,
Quamvis est monitus, venia caret; ut citharoedus
Ridetur, chorda qui semper oberrat eadem:
Sic mihi, qui multum cessat, fit Choerilus ille,
Quem bis terve bonum cum risu miror; et idem
Indignor, quandoque bonus dormitat Homerus.
Verum operi longo fas est obrepere somnum.
 Ut pictura, poesis: erit quae, si propius stes,
Te capiat magis; et quaedam, si longius abstes:
Haec amat obscurum; volet haec sub luce videri,
Iudicis argutum quae non formidat acumen:
Haec placuit semel; haec decies repetita placebit.
 O maior iuvenum, quamvis et voce paterna
Fingeris ad rectum, et per te sapis, hoc tibi
 dictum   367
Tolle memor: certis medium et tolerabile rebus
Recte concedi: consultus iuris, et actor

Receive this counsel, and be timely wise;
Few reach the summit which before you
  lies.   580
Our church and state, our courts and
  camps, concede
Reward to very moderate heads indeed!
In these plain common sense will travel
  far;
All are not Erskines who mislead the bar:
But poesy between the best and worst
No medium knows; you must be last or
  first;   586
For middling poets' miserable volumes
Are damn'd alike by gods, and men, and
  columns.

Again, my Jeffrey!—as that sound in-
  spires,   589
How wakes my bosom to its wonted fires!
Fires, such as gentle Caledonians feel
When Southrons writhe upon their critic
  wheel,
Or mild Eclectics, when some, worse than
  Turks,
Would rob poor Faith to decorate 'good
  works.'
Such are the genial feelings thou canst
  claim—   595
My falcon flies not at ignoble game.
Mightiest of all Dunedin's beasts of chase!
For thee my Pegasus would mend his pace.
Arise, my Jeffrey! or my inkless pen 599
Shall never blunt its edge on meaner men;
Till thee or thine mine evil eye discerns,
Alas! 'I cannot strike at wretched kernes.'
Inhuman Saxon! wilt thou then resign
A muse and heart by choice so wholly
  thine?
Dear d——d contemner of my schoolboy
  songs,   605
Hast thou no vengeance for my man-
  hood's wrongs?
If unprovoked thou once could bid me
  bleed,
Hast thou no weapon for my daring deed?
What! not a word!—and am I then so low?
Wilt thou forbear, who never spared a
  foe?   610
Hast thou no wrath, or wish to give it vent?
No wit for nobles, dunces by descent?
No jest on 'minors,' quibbles on a name,
Nor one facetious paragraph of blame?

Is it for this on Ilion I have stood, 615
And thought of Homer less than Holy-
  rood!
On shore of Euxine or Aegean sea,
My hate, untravell'd, fondly turn'd to thee.
Ah! let me cease: in vain my bosom burns,
From Corydon unkind Alexis turns: 620
Thy rhymes are vain; thy Jeffrey then
  forego,
Nor woo that anger which he will not
  show.
What then?—Edina starves some lanker
  son,
To write an article thou canst not shun;
Some less fastidious Scotchman shall be
  found,   625
As bold in Billingsgate, though less re-
  nown'd.

As if at table some discordant dish
Should shock our optics, such as frogs for
  fish;
As oil in lieu of butter men decry, 629
And poppies please not in a modern pie;
If all such mixtures then be half a crime,
We must have excellence to relish rhyme.
Mere roast and boil'd no epicure invites;
Thus poetry disgusts, or else delights.

Who shoot not flying rarely touch a
  gun: 635
Will he who swims not to the river run?
And men unpractised in exchanging
  knocks
Must go to Jackson ere they dare to box.
Whate'er the weapon, cudgel, fist, or foil,
None reach expertness without years of
  toil;   640
But fifty dunces can, with perfect ease,
Tag twenty thousand couplets, when they
  please.
Why not?—shall I, thus qualified to sit
For rotten boroughs, never show my wit?
Shall I, whose fathers with the quorum
  sate,   645
And lived in freedom on a fair estate;
Who left me heir, with stables, kennels,
  packs,
To all their income, and to—twice its tax;
Whose form and pedigree have scarce a
  fault,
Shall I, I say, suppress my Attic salt? 650

Causarum mediocris abest virtute diserti 370
Messalae, nec scit quantum Cascellius Aulus:
Sed tamen in pretio est: mediocribus esse poetis
Non homines, non di, non concessere columnae.
Ut gratas inter mensas symphonia discors,
Et crassum unguentum, et Sardo cum melle
  papaver   375
Offendunt, poterat duci quia coena sine istis;
Sic animis natum inventumque poema iuvandis,
Si paulum a summo decessit, vergit ad imum.
  Ludere qui nescit, campestribus abstinet
armis,

Indoctusque pilae, discive, trochive, quiescit,
Ne spissae risum tollant impune coronae: 381
Qui nescit, versus tamen audet fingere!—Quid-
  ni?
Liber et ingenuus praesertim census equestrem
Summam nummorum, vitioque remotus ab
  omni.
Tu nihil invita dices faciesve Minerva: 385
Id tibi iudicium est, ea mens: si quid tamen olim
Scripseris, in Metii descendat iudicis aures,
Et patris, et nostras, nonumque prematur in
annum,

Thus think 'the mob of gentlemen;' but
you, 651
Besides all this, must have some genius
too.
Be this your sober judgment, and a rule,
And print not piping hot from Southey's
school,
Who (ere another Thalaba appears) 655
I trust will spare us for at least nine
years.
And hark 'ye, Southey! pray—but don't be
vex'd—
Burn all your last three works—and half
the next.
But why this vain advice? once published,
books
Can never be recall'd—from pastry-
cooks! 660
Though 'Madoc,' with 'Pucelle,' instead
of punk,
May travel back to Quito—on a trunk!

Orpheus, we learn from Ovid and Lem-
priere,
Led all wild beasts but women by the
ear;
And had he fiddled at the present hour,
We'd seen the lions waltzing in the
Tower; 666
And old Amphion, such were minstrels
then,
Had built St. Paul's without the aid of
Wren.
Verse too was justice, and the bards of
Greece
Did more than constables to keep the
peace; 670
Abolish'd cuckoldom with much ap-
plause,
Call'd county meetings, and enforced the
laws,
Cut down crown influence with reforming
scythes,
And served the church—without demand-
ing tithes;
And hence, throughout all Hellas and the
East, 675
Each poet was a prophet and a priest,
Whose old-establish'd board of joint con-
trols
Included kingdoms in the cure of souls.

Next rose the martial Homer, Epic's
prince,
And fighting's been in fashion ever since;
And old Tyrtæus, when the Spartans
warr'd, 681
(A limping leader, but a lofty bard,)
Though wall'd Ithome had resisted long,
Reduced the fortress by the force of song.

When oracles prevail'd, in times of old,
In song alone Apollo's will was told.
Then if your verse is what all verse should
be,
And gods were not ashamed on't, why
should we?

The Muse, like mortal females, may be
woo'd; 689
In turns she'll seem a Paphian, or a prude;
Fierce as a bride when first she feels af-
fright,
Mild as the same upon the second night;
Wild as the wife of alderman or peer,
Now for his grace, and now a grenadier!
Her eyes beseem, her heart belies, her
zone, 695
Ice in a crowd, and lava when alone.

If verse be studied with some show of
art,
Kind Nature always will perform her part;
Though without genius, and a native vein
Of wit, we loathe an artificial strain, 700
Yet art and nature join'd will win the prize,
Unless they act like us and our allies.

The youth who trains to ride, or run a
race,
Must bear privations with unruffled face,
Be call'd to labour when he thinks to
dine, 705
And, harder still, leave wenching and his
wine.
Ladies who sing, at least who sing at sight,
Have follow'd music through her farthest
flight;
But rhymers tell you neither more nor less,
'I've got a pretty poem for the press';
And that's enough; then write and print so
fast:— 711
If Satan take the hindmost, who'd be last?

Membranis intus positis: delere licebit 389
Quod non edideris; nescit vox missa reverti.
 Sylvestres homines sacer interpresque deorum
Caedibus et victu foedo deterruit Orpheus:
Dictus ob hoc lenire tigres, rabidosque leones:
Dictus et Amphion, Thebanae conditor arcis,
Saxa movere sono testudinis, et prece blanda
Ducere quo vellet: fuit haec sapientia quondam,
Publica privatis secernere, sacra profanis:
Concubitu prohibere vago; dare iura maritis;
Oppida moliri; leges incidere ligno. 399
Sic honor et nomen divinis vatibus atque
Carminibus venit. Post hos insignis Homerus
Tyrtaeusque mares animos in Martia bella

Versibus exacuit; dictae per carmina sortes:
Et vitae monstrata via est: et gratia regum
Pieriis tentata modis: ludusque repertus, 405
Et longorum operum finis: ne forte pudori
Sit tibi Musa lyrae solers, et cantor Apollo.
 Natura fieret laudabile carmen, an arte,
Quaesitum est: ego nec studium sine divite vena,
Nec rude quid possit video ingenium: alterius sic
Altera poscit opem res, et coniura amice. 411
Qui studet optatam cursu contingere metam,
Multa tulit fecitque puer; sudavit et alsit;
Abstinuit Venere et vino; qui Pythia cantat
Tibicen, didicit prius, extimuitque magistrum.
Nunc satis est dixisse: ego mira poemata pango:

They storm the types, they publish, one
   and all,
They leap the counter, and they leave the
   stall.
Provincial maidens, men of high com-
   mand,   715
Yea, baronets have ink'd the bloody hand!
Cash cannot quell them; Pollio play'd this
   prank,
(Then Phoebus first found credit in a bank!)
Not all the living only, but the dead,
Fool on, as fluent as an Orpheus' head;
Damn'd all their days, they posthumously
   thrive, •   721
Dug up from dust, though buried when
   alive!
Reviews record this epidemic crime,
Those Books of Martyrs to the rage for
   rhyme,   724
Alas! woe worth the scribbler! often seen
In Morning Post or Monthly Magazine.
There lurk his earlier lays; but soon, hot
   press'd,
Behold a quarto!—Tarts must tell the rest.
Then leave, ye wise, the lyre's precarious
   chords   729
To muse-mad baronets, or madder lords,
Or country Crispins, now grown some-
   what stale,
Twin Doric minstrels, drunk with Doric
   ale!
Hark to those notes, narcotically soft!
The cobbler-laureats sing to Capel Lofft!
Till, lo! that modern Midas, as he hears,
Adds an ell growth to his egregious ears!

There lives one druid, who prepares in
   time   737
'Gainst future feuds his poor revenge of
   rhyme;
Racks his dull memory, and his duller
   muse,
To publish faults which friendship should
   excuse.   740
If friendship's nothing, self-regard might
   teach
More polish'd usage of his parts of speech.
But what is shame, or what is aught to
   him?
He vents his spleen, or gratifies his whim..
Some fancied slight has roused his lurk-
   ing hate,   745
Some folly cross'd, some jest, or some
   debate;
Up to his den Sir Scribbler hies, and soon
The gather'd gall is voided in lampoon.

Perhaps at some pert speech you've dared
   to frown,
Perhaps your poem may have pleased the
   town: 750
If so, alas! 'tis nature in the man—
May Heaven forgive you, for he never can!
Then be it so; and may his withering bays
Bloom fresh in satire, though they fade in
   praise!
While his lost songs no more shall steep
   and stink,   755
The dullest, fattest weeds on Lethe's brink,
But springing upwards from the sluggish
   mould,
Be (what they never were before) be—sold!
Should some rich bard (but such a mon-
   ster now,   759
In modern physics, we can scarce allow),
Should some pretending scribbler of the
   court,
Some rhyming peer—there's plenty of the
   sort—
All but one poor dependent priest with-
   drawn,
(Ah! too regardless of his chaplain's
   yawn!)   764
Condemn the unlucky curate to recite
Their last dramatic work by candle-light,
How would the preacher turn each rueful
   leaf,
Dull as his sermons, but not half so brief!
Yet, since 'tis promised at the rector's
   death,
He'll risk no living for a little breath.
Then spouts and foams, and cries at every
   line,   771
(The Lord forgive him!) 'Bravo! grand!
   divine!'
Hoarse with those praises (which, by
   flatt'ry fed,
Dependence barters for her bitter bread),
He strides and stamps along with creaking
   boot;   775
Till the floor echoes his emphatic foot,
Then sits again, then rolls his pious eye,
As when the dying vicar will not die!
Nor feels, forsooth, emotion at his
   heart;—   779
But all dissemblers overact their part.

Ye, who aspire to 'build the lofty rhyme,'
Believe not all who laud your false 'sub-
   lime;'
But if some friend shall hear your work,
   and say,
'Expunge that stanza, lop that line away,'

Occupet extremum scabies; mihi turpe relinqui
   est,   407
Et, quod non didici, sane nescire fateri.

   ·   ·   ·   ·

   —— Si carmina condes,   436
Nunquam te fallant animi sub vulpe latentes.
Quintilio si quid recitares, Corrige, sodes,
Hoc (aiebat) et hoc: melius te posse negares,
Bis terque expertum frustra, delere iubebat,

Et male tornatos incudi reddere versus.   441
Si defendere delictum quam vertere malles,
Nullum ultra verbum, aut operam insumebat
   inanem,
Quin sine rivali teque et tua solus amares.
   Vir bonus et prudens versus reprehendet
   inertes;   445
Culpabit duros; incomptis allinet atrum
Transverso calamo signum; ambitiosa recidet

And, after fruitless efforts, you return
Without amendment, and he answers,
   'Burn!'   786
That instant throw your paper in the fire,
Ask not his thoughts, or follow his desire;
But if (true bard!) you scorn to con-
   descend,
And will not alter what you can't defend,
If you will breed this bastard of your
   brains,   791
We'll have no words—I've only lost my
   pains.

Yet, if you only prize your favourite
   thought,
As critics kindly do, and authors ought;
If your cool friend annoy you now and
   then,   795
And cross whole pages with his plaguy
   pen;
No matter, throw your ornaments aside,—
Better let him than all the world deride.
Give light to passages too much in shade,
Nor let a doubt obscure one verse you've
   made;   800
Your friend's a 'Johnson,' not to leave
   one word,
However trifling, which may seem absurd;
Such erring trifles lead to serious ills,
And furnish food for critics, or their quills.

As the Scotch fiddle, with its touching
   tune,   805
Or the sad influence of the angry moon,
All men avoid bad writers' ready tongues,
As yawning waiters fly Fitzscribble's
   lungs;
Yet on he mouths—ten minutes—tedious
   each   809
As prelate's homily, or placeman's speech;
Long as the last years of a lingering lease,
When riot pauses until rents increase.
While such a minstrel, muttering fustian,
   strays
O'er hedge and ditch, through unfre-
   quented ways,

If by some chance he walks into a well,
And shouts for succour with stentorian
   yell,   816
'A rope! help, Christians, as ye hope for
   grace!'
Nor woman, man, nor child will stir a
   pace;
For there his carcass he might freely fling,
From frenzy, or the humour of the thing.
Though this has happen'd to more bards
   than one;   821
I'll tell you Budgell's story,—and have
   done.

Budgell, a rogue and rhymester, for no
   good,
(Unless his case be much misunderstood,)
When teased with creditors' continual
   claims,   825
'To die like Cato,' leapt into the Thames!
And therefore be it lawful through the
   town
For any bard to poison, hang, or drown.
Who saves the intended suicide receives
Small thanks from him who loathes the
   life he leaves;   830
And, sooth to say, mad poets must not
   lose
The glory of that death they freely choose.

Nor is it certain that some sorts of verse
Prick not the poet's conscience as a curse;
Dosed with vile drams on Sunday he was
   found,   835
Or got a child on consecrated ground!
And hence is haunted with a rhyming
   rage—
Fear'd like a bear just bursting from his
   cage.
If free, all fly his versifying fit,
Fatal at once to simpleton or wit: 840
But *him*, unhappy! whom he seizes,—*him*
He flays with recitation limb by limb;
Probes to the quick where'er he makes his
   breach,
And gorges like a lawyer—or a leech.

Ornamenta; parum claris lucem dare coget;
Arguet ambigue dictum; mutanda notabit;
Fiet Aristarchus: nec dicet, Cur ego amicum
Offendam in nugis? hae nugae seria ducent
In mala derisum semel exceptumque sinistre.
  Ut mala quem scabies aut morbus regius
   urget,
Aut fanaticus error et iracunda Diana,   454
Vesanum tetigisse timent fugiuntque poetam,
Qui sapiunt; agitant pueri, incautique sequuntur.
Hic, dum sublimis versus ructatur, et errat,
Si veluti merulis intentus decidit auceps
In puteum, foveamve; licet, Succurrite, longum
Clamet, Io cives! non sit qui tollere curet. 460
Si quis curet opem ferre, et demittere funem,
Qui scis an prudens huc se deiecerit, atque

Servari nolit? dicam: Siculique poetae
Narrabo interitum. Deus immortalis haberi
Dum cupit Empedocles, ardentem frigidus Aet-
  nam   465
Insiluit. Sit ius liceatque perire poetis:
Invitum qui servat, idem facit occidenti.
Nec semel hoc fecit; nec, si retractus erit,
  iam
Fiet homo, et ponet famosae mortis amorem.
Nec satis apparet cur versus factitet; utrum
Minxerit in patrios cineres, an triste bidental
Moverit incestus: certe furit, ac velut ursus,
Obiectos caveae valuit si frangere clathros, 473
Indoctum doctumque fugat recitator acerbus.
Quem vero arripuit, tenet, occiditque legendo,
Non missura cutem, nisi plena cruoris, hirudo.

THE CURSE OF MINERVA

——'Pallas te hoc vulnere, Pallas
Immolat, et poenam scelerato ex sanguine sumit.'
Aeneid, lib. xii.

ATHENS: CAPUCHIN CONVENT,
March 17, 1811.

SLOW sinks, more lovely ere his race be run,
Along Morea's hills the setting sun;
Not, as in northern climes, obscurely bright,
But one unclouded blaze of living light;
O'er the hush'd deep the yellow beam he throws, 5
Gilds the green wave that trembles as it glows;
On old Aegina's rock and Hydra's isle
The god of gladness sheds his parting smile;
O'er his own regions lingering loves to shine,
Though there his altars are no more divine. 10
Descending fast, the mountain-shadows kiss
Thy glorious gulf, unconquer'd Salamis!
Their azure arches through the long expanse,
More deeply purpled, meet his mellowing glance,
And tenderest tints, along their summits driven, 15
Mark his gay course, and own the hues of heaven;
Till, darkly shaded from the land and deep,
Behind his Delphian rock he sinks to sleep.

On such an eve his palest beam he cast
When, Athens! here thy wisest look'd his last, 20
How watch'd thy better sons his farewell ray,
That closed their murder'd sage's latest day!
Not yet—not yet—Sol pauses on the hill,
The precious hour of parting lingers still;
But sad his light to agonising eyes, 25
And dark the mountain's once delightful dyes:
Gloom o'er the lovely land he seem'd to pour,
The land where Phoebus never frown'd before;
But ere he sunk below Cithaeron's head,
The cup of woe was quaff'd—the spirit fled; 30
The soul of him that scorn'd to fear or fly,
Who lived and died as none can live or die.

But, lo! from high Hymettus to the plain
The queen of night asserts her silent reign;
No murky vapour, herald of the storm,
Hides her fair face, or girds her glowing form, 36
With cornice glimmering as the moonbeams play,
There the white column greets her grateful ray,
And bright around, with quivering beams beset,
Her emblem sparkles o'er the minaret:
The groves of olive scatter'd dark and wide, 41
Where meek Cephisus sheds his scanty tide,
The cypress saddening by the sacred mosque,
The gleaming turret of the gay kiosk,
Near Theseus' fane, yon solitary palm; 46
All, tinged with varied hues, arrest the eye;
And dull were his that pass'd them heedless by.

Again the Aegean, heard no more afar,
Lulls his chafed breast from elemental war: 50
Again his waves in milder tints unfold
Their long expanse of sapphire and of gold,
Mix'd with the shades of many a distant isle
That frown, where gentler ocean deigns to smile. 54

As thus, within the walls of Pallas' fane,
I mark'd the beauties of the land and main,
Alone, and friendless, on the magic shore,
Whose arts and arms but live in poets' lore;
Oft as the matchless dome I turn'd to scan,
Sacred to gods, but not secure from man,
The past return'd, the present seem'd to cease, 61
And Glory knew no clime beyond her Greece!

Hours roll'd along, and Dian's orb on high
Had gain'd the centre of her softest sky;
And yet unwearied still my footsteps trod
O'er the vain shrine of many a vanish'd god: 66
But chiefly, Pallas! thine, when Hecate's glare,
Check'd by thy columns, fell more sadly fair

142

O'er the chill marble, where the startling
   tread
Thrills the lone heart like echoes from the
   dead. 70
Long had I mused, and treasured every
   trace
The wreck of Greece recorded of her race,
When, lo! a giant form before me strode,
And Pallas hail'd me in her own abode!

Yes, 'twas Minerva's self; but, ah! how
   changed, 75
Since o'er the Dardan field in arms she
   ranged!
Not such as erst, by her divine command,
Her form appear'd from Phidias' plastic
   hand:
Gone were the terrors of her awful brow,
Her idle aegis bore no Gorgon now; 80
Her helm was dinted, and the broken lance
Seem'd weak and shaftless e'en to mortal
   glance;
The olive branch, which still she deign'd to
   clasp,
Shrunk from her touch, and wither'd in her
   grasp;
And, ah! though still the brightest of the
   sky, 85
Celestial tears bedimm'd her large blue
   eye:
Round the rent casque her owlet circled
   slow,
And mourn'd his mistress with a shriek of
   woe!

'Mortal!'—'twas thus she spake—'that
   blush of shame 89
Proclaims thee Briton, once a noble name;
First of the mighty, foremost of the free,
Now honour'd *less* by all, and *least* by me:
Chief of thy foes shall Pallas still be found.
Seek'st thou the cause of loathing?—look
   around. 94
Lo! here, despite of war and wasting fire,
I saw successive tyrannies expire.
'Scaped from the ravage of the Turk and
   Goth,
Thy country sends a spoiler worse than
   both.
Survey this vacant, violated fane; 99
Recount the relics torn that yet remain:
These Cecrops placed, *this* Pericles
   adorn'd,
That Adrian rear'd when drooping Sci-
   ence mourn'd.
What more I owe let gratitude attest—
Know, Alaric and Elgin did the rest.
That all may learn from whence the
   plunderer came, 105
The insulted wall sustains his hated name:
For Elgin's fame thus grateful Pallas
   pleads,
Below, his name—above, behold his
   deeds!

Be ever hail'd with equal honour here
The Gothic monarch and the Pictish peer:
Arms gave the first his right, the last had
   none, 111
But basely stole what less barbarians won.
So when the lion quits his fell repast,
Next prowls the wolf, the filthy jackal last:
Flesh, limbs, and blood the former make
   their own, 115
The last poor brute securely gnaws the
   bone.
Yet still the gods are just, and crimes are
   cross'd:
See here what Elgin won, and what he lost!
Another name with *his* pollutes my shrine:
Behold where Dian's beams disdain to
   shine! 120
Some retribution still might Pallas claim,
When Venus half avenged Minerva's
   shame.'

She ceased awhile, and thus I dared
   reply,
To soothe the vengeance kindling in her
   eye:
'Daughter of Jove! in Britain's injured
   name, 125
A true-born Briton may the deed disclaim.
Frown not on England; England owns
   him not:
Athena, no! thy plunderer was a Scot.
Ask'st thou the difference? From fair
   Phyle's towers
Survey Bœotia;—Caledonia's ours. 130
And well I know within that bastard land
Hath Wisdom's goddess never held com-
   mand;
A barren soil, where Nature's germs, con-
   fined
To stern sterility, can stint the mind;
Whose thistle well betrays the niggard
   earth, 135
Emblem of all to whom the land gives
   birth;
Each genial influence nurtured to resist;
A land of meanness, sophistry, and mist.
Each breeze from foggy mount and
   marshy plain
Dilutes with drivel every drizzly brain,
Till, burst at length, each wat'ry head o'er-
   flows, 141
Foul as their soil, and frigid as their
   snows.
Then thousand schemes of petulance and
   pride
Despatch her scheming children far and
   wide:
Some east, some west, some everywhere
   but north, 145
In quest of lawless gain, they issue forth.
And thus—accursed be the day and year!
She sent a Pict to play the felon here.
Yet Caledonia claims some native worth,
As dull Bœotia gave a Pindar birth; 150

So may her few, the letter'd and the brave,
Bound to no clime, and victors of the grave,
Shake off the sordid dust of such a land,
And shine like children of a happier
    strand;
As once, of yore, in some obnoxious
    place,   155
Ten names (if found) had saved a wretched
    race.'

  'Mortal!' the blue-eyed maid resumed,
    'once more
Bear back my mandate to thy native shore.
Though fallen, alas! this vengeance yet is
    mine,
To turn my counsels far from lands like
    thine.   160
Hear then in silence Pallas' stern behest;
Hear and believe, for time will tell the rest.

  'First on the head of him who did this
    deed
My curse shall light,—on him and all his
    seed: 164
Without one spark of intellectual fire,
Be all the sons as senseless as the sire:
If one with wit the parent brood disgrace,
Believe him bastard of a brighter race:
Still with his hireling artists let him prate,
And Folly's praise repay for Wisdom's
    hate;   170
Long of their patron's gusto let them tell,
Whose noblest, *native* gusto is—to sell:
To sell, and make—may shame record the
    day!—
The state receiver of his pilfer'd prey.
Meantime, the flattering, feeble dotard,
    West,   175
Europe's worst dauber, and poor Britain's
    best,
With palsied hand shall turn each model
    o'er,
And own himself an infant of fourscore.
Be all the bruisers cull'd from all St. Giles',
That art and nature may compare their
    styles;   180
While brawny brutes in stupid wonder
    stare,
And marvel at his lordship's "stone shop"
    there.
Round the throng'd gate shall sauntering
    coxcombs creep,
To lounge and lucubrate, to prate and
    peep;
While many a languid maid, with longing
    sigh,   185
On giant statues casts the curious eye;
The room with transient glance appears to
    skim
Yet marks the mighty back and length of
    limb;
Mourns o'er the difference of *now* and *then*;
Exclaims, "These Greeks indeed were
    proper men!"   190

Draws slight comparisons of *these* with
    those,
And envies Laïs all her Attic beaux.
When shall a modern maid have swains
    like these!
Alas! Sir Harry is no Hercules!   194
And last of all, amidst the gaping crew,
Some calm spectator, as he takes his view,
In silent indignation mix'd with grief,
Admires the plunder, but abhors the thief.
Oh, loath'd in life, nor pardon'd in the
    dust,
May hate pursue his sacrilegious lust!
Link'd with the fool that fired the Ephe-
    sian dome,   201
Shall vengeance follow far beyond the
    tomb,
And Eratostratus and Elgin shine
In many a branding page and burning line;
Alike reserved for aye to stand accursed,
Perchance the second blacker than the
    first.   206

  'So let him stand, through ages yet un-
    born,
Fix'd statue on the pedestal of Scorn;
Though not for him alone revenge shall
    wait,
But fits thy country for her coming fate:
Hers were the deeds that taught her law-
    less son   211
To do what oft Britannia's self had done.
Look to the Baltic—blazing from afar,
Your old ally yet mourns perfidious war.
Not to such deeds did Pallas lend her aid,
Or break the compact which herself had
    made;   216
Far from such councils, from the faithless
    field
She fled—but left behind her Gorgon
    shield;
A fatal gift that turn'd your friends to
    stone,
And left lost Albion hated and alone.

  'Look to the East, where Ganges'
    swarthy race   221
Shall shake your tyrant empire to its base;
Lo! there Rebellion rears her ghastly head,
And glares the Nemesis of native dead;
Till Indus rolls a deep purpureal flood
And claims his long arrear of northern
    blood.   226
So may ye perish! Pallas, when she gave
Your free-born rights, forbade ye to en-
    slave.

  'Look on your Spain!—she clasps the
    hand she hates,
But boldly clasps, and thrusts you from
    her gates.   230
Bear witness, bright Barossa! thou canst tell
Whose were the sons that bravely fought
    and fell.

But Lusitania, kind and dear ally,   233
Can spare a few to fight, and sometimes fly.
Oh glorious field! by Famine fiercely won,
The Gaul retires for once, and all is done!
But when did Pallas teach, that one re-
   treat
Retrieved three long olympiads of defeat?

'Look last at home—ye love not to look
   there;   239
On the grim smile of comfortless despair:
Your city saddens: loud though Revel
   howls,
Here Famine faints, and yonder Rapine
   prowls.
See all alike of more or less bereft;
No misers tremble when there's nothing
   left.
"Blest paper credit;" who shall dare to
   sing?   245
It clogs like lead Corruption's weary wing.
Yet Pallas pluck'd each premier by the ear,
Who gods and men alike disdain'd to hear;
But one, repentant o'er a bankrupt state,
On Pallas calls,—but calls, alas! too late:
Then raves for * *; to that Mentor bends,
Though he and Pallas never yet were
   friends.   252
Him senates hear, whom never yet they
   heard,
Contemptuous once, and now no less ab-
   surd.
So, once of yore, each reasonable frog
Swore faith and fealty to his sovereign
   "log".   256
Thus hail'd your rulers their patrician
   clod,
As Egypt chose an onion for a god.

'Now fare ye well! enjoy your little hour;
Go, grasp the shadow of your vanish'd
   power;   260
Gloss o'er the failure of each fondest
   scheme;
Your strength a name, your bloated wealth
   a dream.
Gone is that gold, the marvel of mankind,
And pirates barter all that 's left behind.
No more the hirelings, purchased near and
   far,   265
Crowd to the ranks of mercenary war.
The idle merchant on the useless quay
Droops o'er the bales no bark may bear
   away;
Or, back returning, sees rejected stores
Rot piecemeal on his own encumber'd
   shores: 270
The starved mechanic breaks his rusting
   loom,
And desperate mans him 'gainst the com-
   ing doom.
Then in the senate of your sinking state
Show me the man whose counsels may
   have weight.

Vain is each voice where tones could once
   command;   275
E'en factions cease to charm a factious
   land:
Yet jarring sects convulse a sister isle,
And light with maddening hands the mutual pile.

''Tis done, 'tis past, since Pallas warns
   in vain;
The Furies seize her abdicated reign:
Wide o'er the realm they wave their kind-
   ling brands,   281
And wring her vitals with their fiery hands.
But one convulsive struggle still re-
   mains,
And Gaul shall weep ere Albion wear her
   chains.
The banner'd pomp of war, the glittering
   files,   285
O'er whose gay trappings stern Bellona
   smiles;
The brazen trump, the spirit-stirring drum,
That bid the foe defiance ere they come;
The hero bounding at his country's call,
The glorious death that consecrates his
   fall,   290
Swell the young heart with visionary
   charms,
And bid it antedate the joys of arms.
But know, a lesson you may yet be taught,
With death alone are laurels cheaply
   bought:
Not in the conflict Havoc seeks delight,
His day of mercy is the day of fight.   296
But when the field is fought, the battle
   won,
Though drench'd with gore, his woes are
   but begun:
His deeper deeds as yet ye know by name;
The slaughter'd peasant and the ravish'd
   dame,   300
The rifled mansion and the foe-reap'd
   field,
Ill suit with souls at home, untaught to
   yield.
Say with what eye along the distant down
Would flying burghers mark the blazing
   town?
How view the column of ascending flames
Shake his red shadow o'er the startled
   Thames?   306
Nay, frown not, Albion! for the torch was
   thine
That lit such pyres from Tagus to the
   Rhine:
Now should they burst on thy devoted
   coast,
Go, ask thy bosom who deserves them
   most.   310
The law of heaven and earth is life for
   life,
And she who raised, in vain regrets, the
   strife.'

THE WALTZ

AN APOSTROPHIC HYMN

'Qualis in Eurotae ripis, aut per iuga Cynthi,
Exercet Diana choros.'—VIRGIL.

'Such on Eurota's banks, or Cynthia's height,
Diana seems: and so she charms the sight,
When in the dance the graceful goddess leads
The quire of nymphs, and overtops their heads.'
DRYDEN'S VIRGIL.

TO THE PUBLISHER

SIR,

I AM a country gentleman of a midland county. I might have been a parliament man for a certain borough; having had the offer of as many votes as General T. at the general election in 1812*. But I was all for domestic happiness; as, fifteen years ago, on a visit to London, I married a middle-aged maid of honour. We lived happily at Hornem Hall last season, when my wife and I were invited by the Countess of Waltzaway (a distant relation of my spouse) to pass the winter in town. Thinking no harm, and our girls being come to a marriageable (or, as they call it, *marketable*) age, and having besides a Chancery suit inveterately entailed upon the family estate, we came up in our old chariot,—of which, by the by, my wife grew so much ashamed in less than a week, that I was obliged to buy a second-hand barouche, of which I might mount the box, Mrs. H. says, if I could drive, but never see the inside—that place being reserved for the Honourable Augustus Tiptoe, her partner-general and opera-knight. Hearing great praises of Mrs. H.'s dancing (she was famous for birthnight minuets in the latter end of the last century), I unbooted, and went to a ball at the Countess's, expecting to see a country dance, or at most, cotillons, reels, and all the old paces to the newest tunes. But, judge of my surprise, on arriving, to see poor dear Mrs. Hornem with her arms half round the loins of a huge hussar-looking gentleman I never set eyes on before; and his, to say truth, rather more than half round her waist, turning round and round to a d——d see-saw up-and-down sort of tune, that reminded me of the 'Black Joke,' only more '*affettuoso*,' till it made me quite giddy with wondering they were not so. By-and-by they stopped a bit, and I thought they would sit or fall down:—but no; with Mrs. H.'s hand on his shoulder, '*quam familiariter*†,' (as Terence said, when I was at school,) they walked about a minute, and then at it again, like two cock-chafers spitted on the same bodkin. I asked what all this meant, when, with a loud laugh, a child no older than our Wilhelmina (a name I never heard but in the Vicar of Wakefield, though her mother would call her after the Princess of Swappenbach,) said, 'Lord! Mr. Hornem, can't you see they're valtzing?' or waltzing (I forget which); and then up she got, and her mother and sister, and away they went, and round-abouted it till supper-time. Now that I know what it is, I like it of all things, and so does Mrs. H. (though I have broken my shins, and four times overturned Mrs. Hornem's maid, in practising the preliminary steps in a morning). Indeed, so much do I like it, that having a turn for rhyme, tastily displayed in some election ballads, and songs in honour of all the victories (but till lately I have had little practice in that way), I sat down, and with the aid of William Fitzgerald, Esq., and a few hints from Dr. Busby, (whose recitations I attend, and am monstrous fond of Master Busby's manner of delivering his father's| late successful 'Drury Lane Address,') I composed the following hymn, wherewithal to make my sentiments known to the public; whom, nevertheless, I heartily despise, as well as the critics.

I am, Sir, yours, &c. &c.,
HORACE HORNEM.

MUSE of the many-twinkling feet! whose charms
Are now extended up from legs to arms;
Terpsichore!—too long misdeem'd a maid—
Reproachful term—bestow'd but to upbraid—
Henceforth in all the bronze of brightness shine, 5
The least a vestal of the virgin Nine.
Far be from thee and thine the name of prude:
Mock'd, yet triumphant; sneer'd at, unsubdued;

Thy legs must move to conquer as they fly, 10
If but thy coats are reasonably high;
Thy breast—if bare enough—requires no shield;
Dance forth—*sans armour* thou shalt take the field,
And own—impregnable to *most* assaults,
Thy not too lawfully begotten 'Waltz.'

Hail, nimble nymph! to whom the young hussar, 15
The whisker'd votary of waltz and war,
His night devotes, despite of spur and boots;
A sight unmatch'd since Orpheus and his brutes:

---

* State of the poll (last day) 5.
† My Latin is all forgotten, if a man can be said to have forgotten what he never remembered; but I bought my title-page motto of a Catholic priest for a three-shilling bank token, after much haggling for the even sixpence. I grudged the money to a Papist, being all for the memory of Perceval and 'No Popery,' and quite regretting the downfall of the pope, because we can't burn him any more.

Hail, spirit-stirring Waltz!—beneath whose
   banners
A modern hero fought for modish man-
   ners;   20
On Hounslow's heath to rival Wellesley's
   fame,
Cock'd, fired, and miss'd his man—but
   gain'd his aim;
Hail, moving muse! to whom the fair one's
   breast
Gives all it can, and bids us take the rest.
Oh! for the flow of Busby, or of Fitz, 25
The latter's loyalty, the former's wits,
To 'energise the object I pursue,'
And give both Belial and his dance their
   due!

Imperial Waltz! imported from the
   Rhine
(Famed for the growth of pedigrees and
   wine),   30
Long be thine import from all duty free,
And hock itself be less esteem'd than thee;
In some few qualities alike—for hock
Improves our cellar—*thou* our living
   stock.
The head to hock belongs—thy subtler
   art   35
Intoxicates alone the heedless heart:
Through the full veins thy gentler poison
   swims,
And wakes to wantonness the willing
   limbs.

Oh, Germany! how much to thee we
   owe,
As heaven-born Pitt can testify below,
Ere cursed confederation made thee
   France's,   41
And only left us thy d—d debts and
   dances!
Of subsidies and Hanover bereft,
We bless thee still—for George the Third
   is left!
Of kings the best—and last, not least in
   worth,   45
For graciously begetting George the
   Fourth.
To Germany, and highnesses serene,
Who owe us millions—don't we owe the
   queen?
To Germany, what owe we not besides?
So oft bestowing Brunswickers and
   brides;
Who paid for vulgar, with her royal blood,
Drawn from the stem of each Teutonic
   stud: 52
Who sent us—so be pardon'd all her
   faults—
A dozen dukes, some kings, a queen—and
   Waltz.

But peace to her—her emperor and diet,
Though now transferr'd to Buonaparte's
   'fiat!'   56

Back to my theme—O Muse of motion!
   say,
How first to Albion found thy Waltz her
   way!

Borne on the breath of hyperborean
   gales,
From Hamburg's port (while Hamburg
   yet had *mails*),   60
Ere yet unlucky Fame—compell'd to creep
To snowy Gottenburg—was chill'd to
   sleep;
Or, starting from her slumbers, deign'd
   arise,
Heligoland! to stock thy mart with lies;
While unburnt Moscow yet had news to
   send,   65
Nor owed her fiery exit to a friend,
She came—Waltz came—and with her
   certain sets
Of true despatches, and as true gazettes:
Then flamed of Austerlitz the blest des-
   patch,
Which 'Moniteur' nor 'Morning Post'
   can match;   70
And—almost crush'd beneath the glorious
   news—
Ten plays, and forty tales of Kotzebue's;
One envoy's letters, six composers' airs,
And loads from Frankfort and from
   Leipsic fairs;   74
Meiner's four volumes upon womankind,
Like Lapland witches to insure a wind,
Brunck's heaviest tome for ballast, and,
   to back it,
Of Heyné, such as should not sink the
   packet.

Fraught with this cargo—and her fair-
   est freight,   79
Delightful Waltz, on tiptoe for a mate,
The welcome vessel reach'd the genial
   strand,
And round her flock'd the daughters of the
   land.
Not decent David, when, before the ark,
His grand pas-seul excited some remark;
Not love-lorn Quixote, when his Sancho
   thought   85
The knight's fandango friskier than it
   ought;
Not soft Herodias, when, with winning
   tread,
Her nimble feet danced off another's
   head;
Not Cleopatra on her galley's deck,
Display'd so much of *leg*, or more of
   neck,   90
Than thou, ambrosial Waltz, when first
   the moon
Beheld thee twirling to a Saxon tune!

To you, ye husbands of ten years! whose
   brows
Ache with the annual tributes of a spouse;

THE WALTZ

To you of nine years less, who only bear
The budding sprouts of those that you
    shall wear,   96
With added ornaments around them roll'd
Of native brass, or law-awarded gold;
To you, ye matrons, ever on the watch
To mar a son's, or make a daughter's
    match;   100
To you, ye children of—whom chance
    accords—
Always the ladies, and *sometimes* their
    lords;
To you, ye single gentlemen, who seek
Torments for life, or pleasures for a week;
As Love or Hymen your endeavours
    guide,   105
To gain your own, or snatch another's
    bride:—
To one and all the lovely stranger came,
And every ball-room echoes with her
    name.

  Endearing Waltz!—to thy more melting
    tune
Bow Irish jig and ancient rigadoon.   110
Scotch reels, avaunt! and country-dance,
    forego
Your future claims to each fantastic toe!
Waltz—Waltz alone—both legs and arms
    demands,
Liberal of feet, and lavish of her hands;
Hands which may freely range in public
    sight   115
Where ne'er before—but—pray 'put out
    the light.'
Methinks the glare of yonder chandelier
Shines much too far—or I am much too
    near;
And true, though strange—Waltz whis-
    pers this remark,   119
'My slippery steps are safest in the dark!'
But here the Muse with due decorum halts,
And lends her longest petticoat to Waltz.

  Observant travellers of every time!   123
Ye quartos publish'd upon every clime!
O say, shall dull Romaika's heavy round,
Fandango's wriggles, or Bolero's bound;
Can Egypt's Almas—tantalising group—
Columbia's caperers to the warlike
    whoop—
Can aught from cold Kamschatka to Cape
    Horn
With Waltz compare, or after Waltz be
    borne?   130
Ah, no! from Morier's pages down to
    Galt's,
Each tourist pens a paragraph for 'Waltz.'

  Shades of those belles whose reign be-
    gan of yore,
With George the Third's—and ended long
    before!—
Though in your daughters' daughters yet
    you thrive,   135

Burst from your lead, and be yourselves
    alive!
Back to the ball-room speed your spectred
    host,
Fool's Paradise is dull to that you lost.
No treacherous powder bids conjecture
    quake;
No stiff-starch'd stays make meddling
    fingers ache;   140
(Transferr'd to those ambiguous things
    that ape
Goats in their visage, women in their
    shape;)
No damsel faints when rather closely
    press'd,
But more caressing seems when most ca-
    ress'd,
Superfluous hartshorn, and reviving salts,
Both banish'd by the sovereign cordial
    'Waltz.'   146

  Seductive Waltz!—though on thy native
    shore
Even Werter's self proclaim'd thee half a
    whore;
Werter—to decent vice though much in-
    clined,
Yet warm, not wanton; dazzled, but not
    blind—   150
Though gentle Genlis, in her strife with
    Staël,
Would even proscribe thee from a Paris
    ball;
The fashion hails—from countesses to
    queens,
And maids and valets waltz behind the
    scenes;
Wide and more wide thy witching circle
    spreads,   155
And turns—if nothing else—at least our
    heads;
With thee even clumsy cits attempt to
    bounce,
And cockneys practise what they can't
    pronounce.
Gods! how the glorious theme my strain
    exalts,
And rhyme finds partner rhyme in praise
    of 'Waltz!'   160

  Blest was the time Waltz chose for her
    début;
The court, the Regent, like herself were
    new;
New face for friends, for foes some new
    rewards;
New ornaments for black and royal
    guards;
New laws to hang the rogues that roar'd
    for bread;   165
New coins (most new) to follow those that
    fled;
New victories—nor can we prize them less,
Though Jenky wonders at his own success;
New wars, because the old succeed so well,

148

That most survivors envy those who fell;
New mistresses—no, old—and yet 'tis
　　true,　　　　　　　　　　　　　171
Though they be *old*, the *thing* is something
　　new;
Each new, quite new—(except some
　　ancient tricks),
New white-sticks, gold-sticks, broom-
　　sticks, all new sticks!
With vests or ribands—deck'd alike in hue,
New troopers strut, new turncoats blush
　　in blue:
So saith the muse: my——, what say you?
Such was the time when Waltz might best
　　maintain
Her new preferments in this novel reign;
Such was the time, nor ever yet was such;
Hoops are *no more*, and petticoats *not
　　much*;　　　　　　　　　　　　181
Morals and minuets, virtue and her stays,
And tell-tale powder—all have had their
　　days.
The ball begins—the honours of the house
First duly done by daughter or by spouse,
Some potentate—or royal or serene—
With Kent's gay grace, or sapient Glos-
　　ter's mien,
Leads forth the ready dame, whose rising
　　flush
Might once have been mistaken for a blush,
From where the garb just leaves the
　　bosom free,　　　　　　　　　190
That spot where hearts were once sup-
　　posed to be;
Round all the confines of the yielded waist,
The strangest hand may wander undis-
　　placed;
The lady's in return may grasp as much
As princely paunches offer to her touch.
Pleased round the chalky floor how well
　　they trip,　　　　　　　　　　196
One hand reposing on the royal hip;
The other to the shoulder no less royal
Ascending with affection truly loyal!
Thus front to front the partners move or
　　stand,　　　　　　　　　　　　200
The foot may rest, but none withdraw the
　　hand;
And all in turn may follow in their rank,
The Earl of—Asterisk—and Lady—
　　Blank;
Sir—Such-a-one—with those of fashion's
　　host,
For whose blest surnames—vide 'Morn-
　　ing Post.'　　　　　　　　　　205
(Or if for that impartial print too late,
Search Doctors' Commons six months
　　from my date)—
Thus all and each, in movement swift or
　　slow,
The genial contact gently undergo;
Till some might marvel, with the modest
　　Turk,　　　　　　　　　　　　210
If 'nothing follows all this palming work?'

True, honest Mirza!—you may trust my
　　rhyme—
Something does follow at a fitter time;
The breast thus publicly resign'd to man,
In private may resist him—if it can.　215

O ye who loved our grandmothers of
　　yore,
Fitzpatrick, Sheridan, and many more!
And thou, my prince! whose sovereign
　　taste and will
It is to love the lovely beldames still!
Thou ghost of Queensberry! whose judg-
　　ing sprite　　　　　　　　　　220
Satan may spare to peep a single night,
Pronounce—if ever in your days of bliss
Asmodeus struck so bright a stroke as this;
To teach the young ideas how to rise,
Flush in the cheek, and languish in the
　　eyes:　　　　　　　　　　　　225
Rush to the heart, and lighten through
　　the frame,
With half-told wish, and ill-dissembled
　　flame,
For prurient nature still will storm the
　　breast—
Who, tempted thus, can answer for the
　　rest?　　　　　　　　　　　　229

But ye—who never felt a single thought
For what our morals are to be, or ought;
Who wisely wish the charms you view to
　　reap,
Say—would you make those beauties
　　quite so cheap?
Hot from the hands promiscuously ap-
　　plied,
Round the slight waist, or down the glow-
　　ing side,　　　　　　　　　　235
Where were the rapture then to clasp the
　　form
From this lewd grasp and lawless contact
　　warm?
At once love's most endearing thought
　　resign,
To press the hand so press'd by none but
　　thine;　　　　　　　　　　　　239
To gaze upon that eye which never met
Another's ardent look without regret;
Approach the lip which all, without re-
　　straint,
Come near enough—if not to touch—to
　　taint;
If such thou lovest—love her then no
　　more,
Or give—like her—caresses to a score;
Her mind with these is gone, and with it
　　go　　　　　　　　　　　　　246
The little left behind it to bestow.

Voluptuous Waltz! and dare I thus
　　blaspheme?
Thy bard forgot thy praises were his
　　theme.

Terpsichore, forgive!—at every ball 250
My wife *now* waltzes—and my daughters
  shall;
My son—(or stop—'tis needless to inquire—
These little accidents should ne'er tran-
  spire;

Some ages hence our genealogic tree
Will wear as green a bough for him as
  me)— 255
Waltzing shall rear, to make our name
  amends,
Grandsons for me—in heirs to all his
  friends.

THE BLUES

A LITERARY ECLOGUE

'Nimium ne crede colori.'—VIRGIL.

O trust not, ye beautiful creatures, to hue,
Though your *hair* were as *red* as your *stockings* are *blue*.

ECLOGUE THE FIRST

London.—Before the Door of a Lecture Room.

Enter TRACY, *meeting* INKEL.

Ink. YOU'RE too late.
Tra.   Is it over?
Ink.   Nor will be this hour.
But the benches are cramm'd like a garden in flower,
With the pride of our belles, who have made it the fashion;
So, instead of 'beaux arts,' we may say 'la *belle* passion'
For learning, which lately has taken the lead in 5
The world, and set all the fine gentlemen reading.
Tra. I know it too well, and have worn out my patience
With studying to study your new publications.
There's Vamp, Scamp, and Mouthy, and Wordswords and Co.
With their damnable——
Ink. Hold, my good friend, do you know 10
Whom you speak to?
Tra.   Right well, boy, and so does 'the Row:'
You're an author—a poet—
Ink.   And think you that I
Can stand tamely in silence, to hear you decry
The Muses?
Tra. Excuse me: I meant no offence
To the Nine; though the number who make some pretence 15
To their favours is such——but the subject to drop,
I am just piping hot from a publisher's shop,
(Next door to the pastry-cook's; so that when I

Cannot find the new volume I wanted to buy
On the bibliopole's shelves, it is only two paces, 20
As one finds every author in one of those places:)
Where I just had been skimming a charming critique,
So studded with wit, and so sprinkled with Greek!
Where your friend—you know who—has just got such a thrashing,
That it is, as the phrase goes, extremely '*refreshing.*' 25
What a beautiful word!
Ink.   Very true; 'tis so soft
And so cooling—they use it a little too oft;
And the papers have got it at last—but no matter.
So they've cut up our friend then?
Tra.   Not left him a tatter—
Not a rag of his present or past reputation, 30
Which they call a disgrace to the age and the nation.
Ink. I'm sorry to hear this! for friendship, you know——
Our poor friend!—but I thought it would terminate so.
Our friendship is such, I'll read nothing to shock it.
You don't happen to have the Review in your pocket? 35
Tra. No; I left a round dozen of authors and others
(Very sorry, no doubt, since the cause is a brother's)
All scrambling and jostling, like so many imps,
And on fire with impatience to get the next glimpse.
Ink. Let us join them.
Tra.   What, won't you return to the lecture? 40

Ink. Why the place is so cramm'd,
  there's no room for a spectre.
Besides, our friend Scamp is to-day so
  absurd——
  Tra. How can you know that till you
    hear him?
Ink.   I heard
Quite enough; and, to tell you the truth,
  my retreat
Was from his vile nonsense, no less than
  the heat.   45
  Tra. I have had no great loss then?
  Ink.   Loss!—such a palaver!
I'd inoculate sooner my wife with the
  slaver
Of a dog when gone rabid, than listen two
  hours
To the torrent of trash which around him
  he pours,
Pump'd up with such effort, disgorged
  with such labour,
That——come—do not make me speak
  ill of one's neighbour.
  Tra. I make you!
  Ink.   Yes, you! I said nothing until
You compell'd me, by speaking the
  truth——
  Tra.   *To speak ill!*
Is that your deduction?
  Ink.   When speaking of Scamp ill,
I certainly *follow, not set* an example. 55
The fellow's a fool, an impostor, a
  zany.
  Tra. And the crowd of to-day shows
    that one fool makes many.
But we two will be wise.
  Ink.   Pray, then, let us retire.
  Tra. I would, but——
  Ink.   There must be attraction much
    higher
Than Scamp, or the Jew's harp he nick-
  names his lyre,   60
To call *you* to this hotbed.
  Tra.   I own it—'tis true—
A fair lady——
  Ink.   A spinster?
  Tra.   Miss Lilac.
  Ink.   The Blue!
The heiress!
  Tra.   The angel!
  Ink.   The devil! why, man,
Pray get out of this hobble as fast as you
  can.
You wed with Miss Lilac! 'twould be
  your perdition: 65
She's a poet, a chymist, a mathematician.
  Tra. I say she's an angel.
  Ink.   Say rather an *angle*.
If you and she marry, you'll certainly
  wrangle.
I say she's a Blue, man, as blue as the
  ether.
  Tra. And is that any cause for not
    coming together?   70

Ink. Humph! I can't say I know any
  happy alliance
Which has lately sprung up from a wed-
  lock with science.
She's so learned in all things, and fond
  of concerning
Herself in all matters connected with
  learning,
That——
  Tra. What?
  Ink.   I perhaps may as well hold my
    tongue;   75
But there's five hundred people can tell
  you you're wrong.
  Tra. You forget Lady Lilac's as rich as
    a Jew.
  Ink. Is it miss or the cash of mamma
    you pursue?
  Tra. Why, Jack, I'll be frank with you
    —something of both.
The girl's a fine girl.
  Ink.   And you feel nothing loth
To her good lady-mother's reversion; and
  yet   81
Her life is as good as your own, I will bet.
  Tra. Let her live, and as long as she
    likes; I demand
Nothing more than the heart of her
  daughter and hand.
  Ink. Why that heart's in the ink-
    stand—that hand on the pen.   85
  Tra. A propos—Will you write me a
    song now and then?
  Ink. To what purpose?
  Tra.   You know, my dear friend,
    that in prose
My talent is decent, as far as it goes;
But in rhyme——
  Ink.   You're a terrible stick, to be sure.
  Tra. I own it: and yet, in these times,
    there's no lure   90
For the heart of the fair like a stanza or
  two;
And so, as I can't, will you furnish a few?
  Ink. In your name?
  Tra.   In my name. I will copy
    them out,
To slip into her hand at the very next rout.
  Ink. Are you so far advanced as to
    hazard this?
  Tra.   Why,
Do you think me subdued by a Blue-
  stocking's eye,   96
So far as to tremble to tell her in rhyme
What I've told her in prose, at the least,
  as sublime?
  Ink. As sublime! If it be so, no need of
    my Muse.
  Tra. But consider, dear Inkel, she's
    one of the 'Blues.'   100
  Ink. As sublime!—Mr. Tracy—I've
    nothing to say.
Stick to prose—As sublime!!—but I wish
  you good day.

Tra. Nay, stay, my dear fellow—con-
sider—I'm wrong;
I own it; but, prithee, compose me the
song.
Ink. As sublime!!
Tra. I but used the expression in haste.
Ink. That may be, Mr. Tracy, but
shows damn'd bad taste. 106
Tra. I own it—I know it—acknow-
ledge it—what
Can I say to you more?
Ink. I see what you'd be at:
You disparage my parts with insidious
abuse,
Till you think you can turn them best to
your own use. 110
Tra. And is that not a sign I respect
them?
Ink. Why that
To be sure makes a difference.
Tra. I know what is what:
And you, who're a man of the gay world
no less
Than a poet of t'other, may easily guess
That I never could mean, by a word, to
offend 115
A genius like you, and moreover, my
friend.
Ink. No doubt; you by this time should
know what is due
To a man of——but come—let us shake
hands.
Tra. You knew,
And you *know*, my dear fellow, how
heartily I
Whatever you publish, am ready to buy.
Ink. That's my bookseller's business;
I care not for sale; 121
Indeed the best poems at first rather fail.
There were Renegade's epics, and
Botherby's plays,
And my own grand romance——
Tra. Had its full share of praise.
I myself saw it puff'd in the 'Old Girl's
Review.' 125
Ink. What Review?
Tra. 'Tis the English 'Journal
de Trevoux;'
A clerical work of our Jesuits at home.
Have you never yet seen it?
Ink. That pleasure's to come.
Tra. Make haste then.
Ink. Why so?
Tra. I have heard people say
That it threaten'd to give up the *ghost*
t'other day. 130
Ink. Well, that is a sign of some *spirit.*
Tra. No doubt.
Shall you be at the Countess of Fiddle-
come's rout?
Ink. I've a card, and shall go: but at
present, as soon
As friend Scamp shall be pleased to step
down from the moon

(Where he seems to be soaring in search
of his wits), 135
And an interval grants from his lecturing
fits,
I'm engaged to the Lady Bluebottle's
collation,
To partake of a luncheon and learn'd
conversation:
'Tis a sort of reunion for Scamp, on the days
Of his lecture, to treat him with cold
tongue and praise. 140
And I own, for my own part, that 'tis not
unpleasant.
Will you go? There's Miss Lilac will also
be present.
Tra. That 'metal's attractive.'
Ink. No doubt—to the pocket.
Tra. You should rather encourage my
passion than shock it.
But let us proceed; for I think by the
hum—— 145
Ink. Very true; let us go, then, before
they can come,
Or else we'll be kept here an hour at their
levee,
On the rack of cross questions, by all the
blue bevy.
Hark! Zounds, they'll be on us; I know
by the drone
Of old Botherby's spouting ex-cathedrâ
tone. 150
Ay! there he is at it. Poor Scamp! better
join
Your friends, or he'll pay you back in
your own coin.
Tra. All fair; 'tis but lecture for lecture.
Ink. That's clear.
But for God's sake let's go, or the Bore
will be here.
Come, come: nay, I'm off. [*Exit* INKEL.
Tra. You are right, and I'll follow;
'Tis high time for a '*Sic me servavit
Apollo.*' 156
And yet we shall have the whole crew on
our kibes,
Blues, dandies, and dowagers, and second-
hand scribes,
All flocking to moisten their exquisite
throttles
With a glass of Madeira at Lady Blue-
bottle's. [*Exit* TRACY.

ECLOGUE THE SECOND

An Apartment in the House of LADY
BLUEBOTTLE.—*A Table prepared.*

SIR RICHARD BLUEBOTTLE *solus.*

WAS there ever a man who was married so
sorry?
Like a fool, I must needs do the thing in
a hurry.
My life is reversed, and my quiet destroy'd;

My days, which once pass'd in so gentle a
    void,
Must now, every hour of the twelve, be
    employ'd;   5
The twelve, do I say?—of the whole
    twenty-four,
Is there one which I dare call my own any
    more?
What with driving and visiting, dancing,
    and dining,
What with learning, and teaching, and
    scribbling, and shining
In science and art, I'll be cursed if I
    know   10
Myself from my wife; for although we
    are two,
Yet she somehow contrives that all things
    shall be done
In a style which proclaims us eternally
    one.
But the thing of all things which distresses
    me more
Than the bills of the week (though they
    trouble me sore)   15
Is the numerous, humorous, backbiting
    crew
Of scribblers, wits, lecturers, white, black,
    and blue,
Who are brought to my house as an inn, to
    my cost—
For the bill here, it seems, is defray'd by
    the host—
No pleasure! no leisure! no thought for
    my pains,   20
But to hear a vile jargon which addles my
    brains;
A smatter and chatter, glean'd out of re-
    views,
By the rag, tag, and bobtail, of those they
    call 'BLUES;'
A rabble who know not—But soft, here
    they come!
Would to God I were deaf! as I'm not,
    I'll be dumb.   25

Enter LADY BLUEBOTTLE, MISS LILAC,
    LADY BLUEMOUNT, MR. BOTHERBY, IN-
    KEL, TRACY, MISS MAZARINE, *and*
    others, *with* SCAMP *the Lecturer*, &c. &c.

  Lady Blueb. Ah! Sir Richard, good
    morning: I've brought you some
    friends.
  Sir Rich. [*bows, and afterwards aside.*]
    If friends, they're the first.
  Lady Blueb. But the luncheon attends.
I pray ye be seated, '*sans cérémonie*.'
Mr. Scamp, you're fatigued; take your
    chair there next me.   [*They all sit.*
  Sir Rich. [*aside.*] If he does, his fatigue
    is to come.
  Lady Blueb.   Mr. Tracy—   30
Lady   Bluemount—Miss   Lilac—be
    pleased, pray, to place ye;

And you, Mr. Botherby—
  Both.   Oh, my dear Lady,
I obey.
  Lady Blueb. Mr. Inkel, I ought to up-
    braid ye:
You were not at the lecture.
  Ink.   Excuse me, I was;
But the heat forced me out in the best
    part—alas!   35
And when——
  Lady Blueb. To be sure it was broiling;
    but then
You have lost such a lecture!
  Both.   The best of the ten.
  Tra. How can you know that? there are
    two more.
  Both.   Because
I defy him to beat this day's wondrous
    applause.
The very walls shook.
  Ink.   Oh, if that be the test,
I allow our friend Scamp has this day done
    his best.   41
Miss Lilac, permit me to help you;—a
    wing?
  Miss Lil. No more, sir, I thank you.
    Who lectures next spring?
  Both. Dick Dunder.
  Ink.   That is, if he lives.
  Miss Lil.   And why not?
  Ink. No reason whatever, save that he's
    a sot.   45
Lady Bluemount! a glass of Madeira?
  Lady Bluem.   With pleasure.
  Ink. How does your friend Words-
    words, that Windermere treasure?
Does he stick to his lakes, like the leeches
    he sings,
And their gatherers, as Homer sung war-
    riors and kings?
  Lady Bluem. He has just got a place.
  Ink.   As a footman?
  Lady Bluem.   For shame!
Nor profane with your sneers so poetic a
    name.   51
  Ink. Nay, I meant him no evil, but
    pitied his master;
For the poet of pedlars 'twere, sure, no
    disaster
To wear a new livery; the more, as 'tis
    not
The first time he has turn'd both his creed
    and his coat.   55
  Lady Bluem. For shame! I repeat. If
    Sir George could but hear——
  Lady Blueb. Never mind our friend
    Inkel; we all know, my dear,
'Tis his way.
  Sir Rich. But this place——
  Ink.   Is perhaps like friend Scamp's,
A lecturer's.
  Lady Bluem. Excuse me—'tis one in the
    'Stamps':
He is made a collector.

Tra.   Collector!
Sir Rich.   How?
Miss Lil.   What?
Ink. I shall think of him oft when I buy
  a new hat: 61
There his works will appear——
Lady Bluem. Sir, they reach to the
  Ganges.
Ink. I shan't go so far—I can have them
  at Grange's.
Lady Bluem. Oh fie!
Miss Lil.   And for shame!
Lady Bluem.   You're too bad.
Both.   Very good!
Lady Bluem. How good?
Lady Blueb. He means nought—'tis his
  phrase.
Lady Bluem.   He grows rude.
Lady Blueb. He means nothing; nay, ask
  him.   66
Lady Bluem. Pray, Sir! did you mean
What you say?
Ink. Never mind if he did: 'twill be seen
That whatever he means won't alloy what
  he says.
Both. Sir?
Ink. Pray be content with your por-
  tion of praise;   69
'Twas in your defence.
Both. If you please, with submission,
I can make out my own.
Ink.   It would be your perdition.
While you live, my dear Botherby, never
  defend
Yourself or your works; but leave both to
  a friend.
A propos—Is your play then accepted at
  last?
Both. At last?
Ink. Why I thought—that's to say—
  there had pass'd   75
A few green-room whispers, which hinted,
  —you know
That the taste of the actors at best is so
  so.
Both. Sir, the green-room's in rapture,
  and so's the Committee.
Ink. Ay—yours are the plays for ex-
  citing our 'pity
And fear,' as the Greek says: for 'purging
  the mind,'   80
I doubt if you'll leave us an equal be-
  hind.
Both. I have written the prologue, and
  meant to have pray'd
For a spice of your wit in an epilogue's
  aid.
Ink. Well, time enough yet, when the
  play's to be play'd.   84
Is it cast yet?
Both. The actors are fighting for parts,
As is usual in that most litigious of arts.
Lady Blueb. We'll all make a party, and
  go the *first* night.

Tra. And you promised the epilogue,
  Inkel.
Ink.   Not quite.
However, to save my friend Botherby
  trouble,
I'll do what I can, though my pains must
  be double.   90
Tra. Why so?
Ink.   To do justice to what goes before.
Both. Sir, I'm happy to say, I've no
  fears on that score.
Your parts, Mr. Inkel, are——
Ink.   Never mind *mine*;
Stick to those of your play, which is quite
  your own line.
Lady Bluem. You're a fugitive writer, I
  think, sir, of rhymes?   95
Ink. Yes, ma'am; and a fugitive reader
  sometimes.
On Wordswords, for instance, I seldom
  alight,
Or on Mouthey, his friend, without taking
  to flight.
Lady Bluem. Sir, your taste is too com-
  mon; but time and posterity
Will right these great men, and this age's
  severity   100
Become its reproach.
Ink.   I've no sort of objection,
So I'm not of the party to take the infec-
  tion.
Lady Blueb. Perhaps you have doubts
  that they ever will *take?*
Ink. Not at all; on the contrary, those
  of the lake
Have taken already, and still will con-
  tinue   105
To take—what they can, from a groat to
  a guinea,
Of pension or place;—but the subject's a
  bore.
Lady Bluem. Well, sir, the time's
  coming.
Ink.   Scamp! don't you feel sore?
What say you to this?
Scamp.   They have merit, I own;
Though their system's absurdity keeps it
  unknown.   110
Ink. Then why not unearth it in one of
  your lectures?
Scamp. It is only time past which comes
  under my strictures.
Lady Blueb. Come, a truce with all
  tartness;—the joy of my heart
Is to see Nature's triumph o'er all that is
  art.
Wild Nature!—Grand Shakspeare!
Both.   And down Aristotle! 115
Lady Bluem. Sir George thinks exactly
  with Lady Bluebottle:
And my Lord Seventy-four, who protects
  our dear Bard,
And who gave him his place, has the
  greatest regard

For the poet, who, singing of pedlars and
asses,
Has found out the way to dispense with
Parnassus.   120
Tra. And you, Scamp!—
Scamp.   I needs must confess I'm
embarrass'd.
Ink. Don't call upon Scamp, who's
already so harass'd
With old *schools*, and new *schools*, and no
schools, and all *schools*.
Tra. Well, one thing is certain, that
some must be fools.
I should like to know who.
Ink.   And I should not be sorry   125
To know who are *not*:—it would save us
some worry.
Lady Blueb. A truce with remark, and
let nothing control
This 'feast of our reason, and flow of the
soul.'
Oh! my dear Mr. Botherby! sympathise!
—I
Now feel such a rapture, I'm ready to
fly,   130
I feel so elastic—'*so buoyant—so buoy-
ant!*'
Ink. Tracy! open the window.
Tra.   I wish her much joy on't.
Both. For God's sake, my Lady Blue-
bottle, check not
This gentle emotion, so seldom our lot
Upon earth. Give it way: 'tis an impulse
which lifts   135
Our spirits from earth; the sublimest of
gifts;
For which poor Prometheus was chain'd
to his mountain:
'Tis the source of all sentiment—feeling's
true fountain;
'Tis the Vision of Heaven upon Earth: 'tis
the gas
Of the soul: 'tis the seizing of shades as
they pass,   140
And making them substance: 'tis something divine:—
Ink. Shall I help you, my friend, to a
little more wine?

Both. I thank you; not any more, sir,
till I dine.
Ink. A propos—Do you dine with Sir
Humphry to-day?
Tra. I should think with *Duke* Humphry
was more in your way.   145
Ink. It might be of yore; but we authors
now look
To the Knight, as a landlord, much more
than the Duke.
The truth is, each writer now quite at his
ease is,
And (except with his publisher) dines
where he pleases.
But 'tis now nearly five, and I must to the
Park.   150
Tra. And I'll take a turn with you
there till 'tis dark.
And you, Scamp—
Scamp. Excuse me! I must to my notes,
For my lecture next week.
Ink.   He must mind whom he quotes
Out of 'Elegant Extracts.'
Lady Blueb.   Well, now we break
up;
But remember Miss Diddle invites us to
sup.   155
Ink. Then at two hours past midnight
we all meet again,
For the sciences, sandwiches, hock, and
champagne!
Tra. And the sweet lobster salad!
Both.   I honour that meal;
For 'tis then that our feelings most
genuinely—feel.
Ink. True; feeling is truest *then*, far
beyond question: 160
I wish to the gods 'twas the same with
digestion!
Lady Blueb. Pshaw!—never mind that;
for one moment of feeling
Is worth—God knows what.
Ink.   'Tis at least worth concealing
For itself, or what follows——But here
comes your carriage.
Sir Rich. [aside.] I wish all these people
were d——d with *my* marriage!   165
                              [*Exeunt.*

THE VISION OF JUDGMENT

BY

QUEVEDO REDIVIVUS

SUGGESTED BY THE COMPOSITION SO ENTITLED BY THE AUTHOR OF 'WAT TYLER'

> 'A Daniel come to judgment! yea, a Daniel!
> I thank thee, Jew, for teaching me that word.'

PREFACE

It hath been wisely said, that 'One fool makes many;' and it hath been poetically observed—

> 'That fools rush in where angels fear to tread.'—POPE.

If Mr. Southey had not rushed in where he had no business, and where he never was before, and never will be again, the following poem would not have been written. It is not impossible that it may be as good as his own, seeing that it cannot, by any species of stupidity, natural or acquired, be *worse*. The gross flattery, the dull impudence, the renegado intolerance, and impious cant, of the poem by the author of 'Wat Tyler,' are something so stupendous as to form the sublime of himself—containing the quintessence of his own attributes.

So much for his poem—a word on his preface. In this preface it has pleased the magnanimous Laureate to draw the picture of a supposed 'Satanic School,' the which he doth recommend to the notice of the legislature; thereby adding to his other laurels the ambition of those of an informer. If there exists anywhere, except in his imagination, such a School, is he not sufficiently armed against it by his own intense vanity? The truth is, that there are certain writers whom Mr. S. imagines, like Scrub, to have 'talked of *him;* for they laughed consumedly.'

I think I know enough of most of the writers to whom he is supposed to allude, to assert, that they, in their individual capacities, have done more good, in the charities of life, to their fellow-creatures, in any one year, than Mr. Southey has done harm to himself by his absurdities in his whole life; and this is saying a great deal. But I have a few questions to ask.

1stly, Is Mr. Southey the author of 'Wat Tyler'?

2ndly, Was he not refused a remedy at law by the highest judge of his beloved England, because it was a blasphemous and seditious publication?

3rdly, Was he not entitled by William Smith, in full parliament, 'a rancorous renegado'?

4thly, Is he not poet laureate, with his own lines on Martin the regicide staring him in the face?

And, 5thly, Putting the four preceding items together, with what conscience dare *he* call the attention of the laws to the publications of others, be they what they may?

I say nothing of the cowardice of such a proceeding, its meanness speaks for itself; but I wish to touch upon the *motive*, which is neither more nor less than that Mr. S. has been laughed at a little in some recent publications, as he was of yore in the 'Anti-jacobin,' by his present patrons. Hence all this 'skimble-scamble stuff' about 'Satanic,' and so forth. However, it is worthy of him—'*qualis ab incepto.*'

If there is anything obnoxious to the political opinions of a portion of the public in the following poem, they may thank Mr. Southey. He might have written hexameters, as he has written everything else, for aught that the writer cared—had they been upon another subject. But to attempt to canonise a monarch, who, whatever were his household virtues, was neither a successful nor a patriot king,— inasmuch as several years of his reign passed in war with America and Ireland, to say nothing of the aggression upon France,—like all other exaggeration, necessarily begets opposition. In whatever manner he may be spoken of in this new 'Vision,' his *public* career will not be more favourably transmitted by history. Of his private virtues (although a little expensive to the nation) there can be no doubt.

With regard to the supernatural personages treated of, I can only say that I know as much about them, and (as an honest man) have a better right to talk of them than Robert Southey. I have also treated them more tolerantly. The way in which that poor insane creature, the Laureate, deals about his judgments in the next world, is like his own judgment in this. If it was not completely ludicrous, it would be something worse. I don't think that there is much more to say at present.

QUEVEDO REDIVIVUS.

P.S.—It is possible that some readers may object, in these objectionable times, to the freedom with which saints, angels, and spiritual persons discourse in this 'Vision.' But, for precedents upon such points, I must refer him to Fielding's 'Journey from this World to the next,' and to the Visions of myself, the said Quevedo, in Spanish or translated. The reader is also requested to observe, that no doctrinal tenets are insisted upon or discussed; that the person of the Deity is carefully withheld from sight, which is more than can be said for the Laureate, who hath thought proper to make him talk, not 'like a school-divine,' but like the unscholarlike Mr. Southey. The whole action passes on the outside of heaven; and Chaucer's 'Wife of Bath,' Pulci's 'Morgante Maggiore,' Swift's 'Tale of a Tub,' and the other works above referred to, are cases in point of the freedom with which saints, &c. may be permitted to converse in works not intended to be serious.

Q. R.

*** Mr. Southey being, as he says, a good Christian and vindictive, threatens, I understand, a reply to this our answer. It is to be hoped that his visionary faculties will in the mean time have acquired a little more judgment, properly so called: otherwise he will get himself into new dilemmas. These apostate jacobins furnish rich rejoinders. Let him take a specimen. Mr. Southey laudeth grievously 'one Mr. Landor,' who cultivates much private renown in the shape of Latin verses; and not long ago, the poet laureate dedicated to him, it appeareth, one of his fugitive lyrics, upon the strength of a poem called '*Gebir*.' Who could suppose, that in this same Gebir the aforesaid Savage Landor (for such is his grim cognomen) putteth into the infernal regions no less a person than the hero of his friend Mr. Southey's heaven,—yea, even George the Third! See also how personal Savage becometh, when he hath a mind. The following is his portrait of our late gracious sovereign:

(Prince Gebir having descended into the infernal regions, the shades of his royal ancestors are, at his request, called up to his view; and he exclaims to his ghostly guide)—

'Aroar, what wretch that nearest us? what wretch
Is that with eyebrows white and slanting brow?
Listen! him yonder who, bound down supine,
Shrinks yelling from that sword there, engine-hung.
He too amongst my ancestors! I hate
The despot, but the dastard I despise.
Was he our countryman?'
                              'Alas, O king!
Iberia bore him, but the breed accurst
Inclement winds blew blighting from north-east.'
'He was a warrior then, nor fear'd the gods?'
'Gebir, he fear'd the demons, not the gods,
Though them indeed his daily face adored;
And was no warrior, yet the thousand lives
Squander'd, as stones to exercise a sling,
And the tame cruelty and cold caprice—
Oh madness of mankind! address'd, adored!'
                              Gebir, p. 28.

I omit noticing some edifying Ithyphallics of Savagius, wishing to keep the proper veil over them, if his grave but somewhat indiscreet worshipper will suffer it; but certainly these teachers of 'great moral lessons' are apt to be found in strange company.

I

SAINT PETER sat by the celestial gate:
  His keys were rusty, and the lock was
    dull,
So little trouble had been given of late;
  Not that the place by any means was full,
But since the Gallic era 'eighty-eight'
  The devils had ta'en a longer, stronger
    pull,
And 'a pull altogether,' as they say
At sea—which drew most souls another
    way.

II

The angels all were singing out of tune,
  And hoarse with having little else to do,
Excepting to wind up the sun and moon,
  Or curb a runaway young star or two,
Or wild colt of a comet, which too soon
  Broke out of bounds o'er th' ethereal
    blue,
Splitting some planet with its playful tail,
As boats are sometimes by a wanton
    whale.

III

The guardian seraphs had retired on high,
  Finding their charges past all care
    below;

Terrestrial business fill'd nought in the sky
  Save the recording angel's black bureau;
Who found, indeed, the facts to multiply
  With such rapidity of vice and woe,
That he had stripp'd off both his wings in
    quills,
And yet was in arrear of human ills.

IV

His business so augmented of late years,
  That he was forced, against his will no
    doubt,
(Just like those cherubs, earthly ministers,)
  For some resource to turn himself
    about,
And claim the help of his celestial peers,
  To aid him ere he should be quite worn
    out
By the increased demand for his remarks:
Six angels and twelve saints were named
    his clerks.

V

This was a handsome board—at least for
    heaven;
  And yet they had even then enough to do,
So many conquerors' cars were daily
    driven,
  So many kingdoms fitted up anew;

157

THE VISION OF JUDGMENT

Each day too slew its thousands six or
    seven,
    Till at the crowning carnage, Waterloo,
They threw their pens down in divine
    disgust—
The page was so besmear'd with blood and
    dust.

VI

This by the way; 'tis not mine to record
    What angels shrink from: even the very
    devil
On this occasion his own work abhorr'd,
    So surfeited with the infernal revel:
Though he himself had sharpen'd every
    sword,
    It almost quench'd his innate thirst of
    evil.
(Here Satan's sole good work deserves
    insertion—
'Tis, that he has both generals in rever-
    sion.)

VII

Let's skip a few short years of hollow
    peace,
    Which peopled earth no better, hell as
    wont,
And heaven none—they form the tyrant's
    lease,
    With nothing but new names subscribed
    upon't;
'Twill one day finish: meantime they in-
    crease,
    'With seven heads and ten horns,' and
    all in front,
Like Saint John's foretold beast; but ours
    are born
Less formidable in the head than horn.

VIII

In the first year of freedom's second dawn
    Died George the Third; although no
    tyrant, one
Who shielded tyrants, till each sense with-
    drawn
    Left him nor mental nor external sun:
A better farmer ne'er brush'd dew from
    lawn,
    A worse king never left a realm undone!
He died—but left his subjects still be-
    hind,
One half as mad—and t'other no less
    blind.

IX

He died! his death made no great stir on
    earth:
    His burial made some pomp; there was
    profusion
Of velvet, gilding, brass, and no great
    dearth
    Of aught but tears—save those shed by
    collusion.

For these things may be bought at their
    true worth;
    Of elegy there was the due infusion—
Bought also; and the torches, cloaks, and
    banners,
Heralds, and relics of old Gothic manners,

X

Form'd a sepulchral melodrame. Of all
    The fools who flock'd to swell or see the
    show,
Who cared about the corpse? The funeral
    Made the attraction, and the black the
    woe.
There throbb'd not there a thought which
    pierced the pall;
    And when the gorgeous coffin was laid
    low,
It seem'd the mockery of hell to fold
The rottenness of eighty years in gold.

XI

So mix his body with the dust! It might
    Return to what it *must* far sooner, were
The natural compound left alone to fight
    Its way back into earth, and fire, and
    air;
But the unnatural balsams merely blight
    What nature made him at his birth, as
    bare
As the mere million's base unmummied
    clay—
Yet all his spices but prolong decay.

XII

He's dead—and upper earth with him has
    done;
    He's buried; save the undertaker's bill,
Or lapidary scrawl, the world is gone
    For him, unless he left a German will:
But where's the proctor who will ask his
    son?
    In whom his qualities are reigning still,
Except that household virtue, most un-
    common,
Of constancy to a bad, ugly woman.

XIII

'God save the king!' It is a large economy
    In God to save the like; but if he will
Be saving, all the better; for not one am I
    Of those who think damnation better
    still:
I hardly know too if not quite alone am I
    In this small hope of bettering future ill
By circumscribing, with some slight re-
    striction,
The eternity of hell's hot jurisdiction.

XIV

I know this is unpopular; I know
    'Tis blasphemous; I know one may be
    damn'd
For hoping no one else may e'er be so;

I know my catechism; I know we're
cramm'd
With the best doctrines till we quite o'erflow;
I know that all save England's church
have shamm'd,
And that the other twice two hundred
churches
And synagogues have made a *damn'd* bad
purchase.

XV

God help us all! God help me too! I am,
God knows, as helpless as the devil can
wish,
And not a whit more difficult to damn,
Than is to bring to land a late-hook'd
fish,
Or to the butcher to purvey the lamb;
Not that I'm fit for such a noble dish,
As one day will be that immortal fry
Of almost everybody born to die.

XVI

Saint Peter sat by the celestial gate,
And nodded o'er his keys; when, lo!
there came
A wondrous noise he had not heard of
late—
A rushing sound of wind, and stream,
and flame;
In short, a roar of things extremely great,
Which would have made aught save a
saint exclaim;
But he, with first a start and then a wink,
Said, 'There's another star gone out, I
think!'

XVII

But ere he could return to his repose,
A cherub flapp'd his right wing o'er his
eyes—
At which St. Peter yawn'd, and rubb'd his
nose:
'Saint porter,' said the angel, 'prithee
rise!'
Waving a goodly wing, which glow'd, as
glows
An earthly peacock's tail, with heavenly
dyes:
To which the saint replied, 'Well, what's
the matter?
'Is Lucifer come back with all this
clatter?'

XVIII

'No,' quoth the cherub; 'George the
Third is dead.'
'And who *is* George the Third?' replied
the apostle,
'*What George? what Third?*' 'The king
of England,' said
The angel. 'Well! he won't find kings
to jostle

Him on his way; but does he wear his
head?
Because the last we saw here had a
tustle,
And ne'er would have got into heaven's
good graces,
Had he not flung his head in all our faces.

XIX

'He was, if I remember, king of France;
That head of his, which could not keep
a crown
On earth, yet ventured in my face to
advance
A claim to those of martyrs—like my
own:
If I had had my sword, as I had once
When I cut ears off, I had cut him down;
But having but my *keys*, and not my
brand,
I only knock'd his head from out his hand.

XX

'And then he set up such a headless howl,
That all the saints came out and took
him in;
And there he sits by St. Paul, cheek by
jowl;
That fellow Paul—the parvenù! The
skin
Of St. Bartholomew, which makes his
cowl
In heaven, and upon earth redeem'd
his sin,
So as to make a martyr, never sped
Better than did this weak and wooden
head.

XXI

'But had it come up here upon its shoul-
ders,
There would have been a different tale
to tell:
The fellow-feeling in the saint's beholders
Seems to have acted on them like a spell,
And so this very foolish head heaven
solders
Back on its trunk: it may be very well,
And seems the custom here to overthrow
Whatever has been wisely done below.'

XXII

The angel answer'd, 'Peter! do not pout:
The king who comes has head and all
entire,
And never knew much what it was about—
He did as doth the puppet—by its wire,
And will be judged like all the rest, no
doubt:
My business and your own is not to
inquire
Into such matters, but to mind our cue—
Which is to act as we are bid to do.'

159

G

THE VISION OF JUDGMENT

XXIII

While thus they spake, the angelic cara-
van,
  Arriving like a rush of mighty wind,
Cleaving the fields of space, as doth the
    swan
  Some silver stream (say Ganges, Nile,
    or Inde,
Or Thames, or Tweed), and 'midst them
    an old man
  With an old soul, and both extremely
    blind,
Halted before the gate, and in his shroud
Seated their fellow traveller on a cloud.

XXIV

But bringing up the rear of this bright host
  A Spirit of a different aspect waved
His wings, like thunder-clouds above some
    coast
  Whose barren beach with frequent
    wrecks is paved;
His brow was like the deep when tempest-
    toss'd;
  Fierce and unfathomable thoughts en-
    graved
Eternal wrath on his immortal face,
And *where* he gazed a gloom pervaded
    space.

XXV

As he drew near, he gazed upon the gate
  Ne'er to be enter'd more by him or Sin,
With such a glance of supernatural hate,
  As made Saint Peter wish himself with-
    in;
He potter'd with his keys at a great rate,
  And sweated through his apostolic skin:
Of course his perspiration was but ichor,
Or some such other spiritual liquor.

XXVI

The very cherubs huddled all together,
  Like birds when soars the falcon; and
    they felt
A tingling to the tip of every feather,
  And form'd a circle like Orion's belt
Around their poor old charge; who scarce
    knew whither
  His guards had led him, though they
    gently dealt
With royal manes (for by many stories,
And true, we learn the angels all are
    Tories).

XXVII

As things were in this posture, the gate flew
  Asunder, and the flashing of its hinges
Flung over space an universal hue
  Of many-colour'd flame, until its tinges
Reach'd even our speck of earth, and
    made a new
  Aurora borealis spread its fringes

O'er the North Pole; the same seen, when
    ice-bound,
By Captain Parry's crew, in 'Melville's
    Sound.'

XXVIII

And from the gate thrown open issued
    beaming
  A beautiful and mighty Thing of Light,
Radiant with glory, like a banner stream-
    ing
  Victorious from some world-o'erthrow-
    ing fight:
My poor comparisons must needs be
    teeming
  With earthly likenesses, for here the
    night
Of clay obscures our best conceptions,
    saving
Johanna Southcote, or Bob Southey
    raving.

XXIX

'Twas the archangel Michael; all men
    know
  The make of angels and archangels,
    since
There's scarce a scribbler has not one to
    show,
  From the fiends' leader to the angels'
    prince;
There also are some altar-pieces, though
  I really can't say that they much evince
One's inner notions of immortal spirits;
But let the connoisseurs explain *their*
    merits.

XXX

Michael flew forth in glory and in good;
  A goodly work of him from whom all
    glory
And good arise; the portal past—he stood;
  Before him the young cherubs and
    saints hoary—
(I say *young*, begging to be understood
  By looks, not years; and should be very
    sorry
To state, they were not older than St.
    Peter,
But merely that they seem'd a little
    sweeter).

XXXI

The cherubs and the saints bow'd down
    before
  That arch-angelic hierarch, the first
Of essences angelical, who wore
  The aspect of a god; but this ne'er
    nursed
Pride in his heavenly bosom, in whose core
  No thought, save for his Master's
    service, durst
Intrude, however glorified and high;
He knew him but the viceroy of the sky.

XXXII

He and the sombre, silent Spirit met—
    They knew each other both for good
      and ill;
Such was their power, that neither could
    forget
    His former friend and future foe; but still
There was a high, immortal, proud regret
    In either's eye, as if 'twere less their will
Than destiny to make the eternal years
Their date of war, and their 'champ clos'
    the spheres.

XXXIII

But here they were in neutral space: we
    know
    From Job, that Satan hath the power to
      pay
A heavenly visit thrice a year or so;
    And that the 'sons of God', like those
      of clay,
Must keep him company; and we might
    show
    From the same book, in how polite a
      way
The dialogue is held between the Powers
Of Good and Evil—but 'twould take up
    hours.

XXXIV

And this is not a theologic tract,
    To prove with Hebrew and with Arabic,
If Job be allegory or a fact,
    But a true narrative; and thus I pick
From out the whole but such and such an
    act
    As sets aside the slightest thought of
      trick.
'Tis every tittle true, beyond suspicion,
And accurate as any other vision.

XXXV

The spirits were in neutral space, before
    The gate of heaven; like eastern thres-
      holds is
The place where Death's grand cause is
    argued o'er,
    And souls despatch'd to that world or
    to this;
And therefore Michael and the other wore
    A civil aspect: though they did not kiss,
Yet still between his Darkness and his
    Brightness
There pass'd a mutual glance of great
    politeness.

XXXVI

The Archangel bow'd, not like a modern
    beau,
    But with a graceful Oriental bend,
Pressing one radiant arm just where below
    The heart in good men is supposed to
    tend;
He turn'd as to an equal, not too low,

But kindly; Satan met his ancient friend
With more hauteur, as might an old
    Castilian
Poor noble meet a mushroom rich civilian.

XXXVII

He merely bent his diabolic brow
    An instant; and then raising it, he stood
In act to assert his right or wrong, and show
    Cause why King George by no means
    could or should
Make out a case to be exempt from woe
    Eternal, more than other kings, endued
With better sense and hearts, whom
    history mentions,
Who long have 'paved hell with their good
    intentions.'

XXXVIII

Michael began: 'What wouldst thou with
    this man,
    Now dead, and brought before the
    Lord? What ill
Hath he wrought since his mortal race began,
    That thou canst claim him? Speak! and
    do thy will,
If it be just: if in this earthly span
    He hath been greatly failing to fulfil
His duties as a king and mortal, say,
And he is thine; if not, let him have way.'

XXXIX

'Michael!' replied the Prince of Air, 'even
    here,
    Before the Gate of him thou servest,
    must
I claim my subject: and will make appear
    That as he was my worshipper in dust,
So shall he be in spirit, although dear
    To thee and thine, because nor wine nor
    lust
Were of his weaknesses; yet on the throne
He reign'd o'er millions to serve me alone.

XL

'Look to *our* earth, or rather *mine;* it was,
    Once, more thy master's: but I triumph
    not
In this poor planet's conquest; nor, alas!
    Need he thou servest envy me my lot:
With all the myriads of bright worlds
    which pass
    In worship round him, he may have
    forgot
Yon weak creation of such paltry things:
I think few worth damnation save their
    kings,—

XLI

'And these but as a kind of quit-rent, to
    Assert my right as lord: and even had
I such an inclination, 'twere (as you
    Well know) superfluous; they are grown
    so bad,

THE VISION OF JUDGMENT

That hell has nothing better left to do
   Than leave them to themselves: so much
     more mad
And evil by their own internal curse,
Heaven cannot make them better, nor I
   worse.

XLII

'Look to the earth, I said, and say again:
   When this old, blind, mad, helpless,
     weak, poor worm
Began in youth's first bloom and flush to
   reign,
   The world and he both wore a different
     form,
And much of earth and all the watery plain
   Of ocean call'd him king: through many
     a storm
His isles had floated on the abyss of time;
For the rough virtues chose them for their
   clime.

XLIII

'He came to his sceptre young; he leaves
   it old:
   Look to the state in which he found his
     realm,
And left it; and his annals too behold,
   How to a minion first he gave the helm;
How grew upon his heart a thirst for gold,
   The beggar's vice, which can but over-
     whelm
The meanest hearts; and for the rest, but
   glance
Thine eye along America and France.

XLIV

''Tis true, he was a tool from first to last
   (I have the workmen safe); but as a tool
So let him be consumed. From out the
   past
   Of ages, since mankind have known the
     rule
Of monarchs—from the bloody rolls
   amass'd
   Of sin and slaughter—from the Cæsar's
     school,
Take the worst pupil; and produce a reign
More drench'd with gore, more cumber'd
   with the slain.

XLV

'He ever warr'd with freedom and the
   free:
   Nations as men, home subjects, foreign
     foes,
So that they utter'd the word "Liberty!"
   Found George the Third their first
     opponent. Whose
History was ever stain'd as his will be
   With national and individual woes?
I grant his household abstinence; I grant
His neutral virtues, which most monarchs
   want;

XLVI

'I know he was a constant consort;
   own
   He was a decent sire, and middling
     lord.
All this is much, and most upon a throne;
   As temperance, if at Apicius' board,
Is more than at an anchorite's supper
   shown.
   I grant him all the kindest can accord;
And this was well for him, but not for
   those
Millions who found him what oppression
   chose.

XLVII

'The New World shook him off; the Old
   yet groans
   Beneath what he and his prepared, if
     not
Completed: he leaves heirs on many
   thrones
   To all his vices, without what begot
Compassion for him—his tame virtues;
   drones
   Who sleep, or despots who have now
     forgot
A lesson which shall be re-taught them,
   wake
Upon the thrones of earth; but let them
   quake!

XLVIII

'Five millions of the primitive, who hold
   The faith which makes ye great on
     earth, implored
A *part* of that vast *all* they held of old,—
   Freedom to worship—not alone your
     Lord,
Michael, but you, and you, Saint Peter!
   Cold
   Must be your souls, if you have not
     abhorr'd
The foe to Catholic participation
In all the license of a Christian nation.

XLIX

'True! he allow'd them to pray God; but
   as
   A consequence of prayer, refused the
     law
Which would have placed them upon the
   same base
   With those who did not hold the saints
     in awe.'
But here Saint Peter started from his
   place,
   And cried, 'You may the prisoner with-
     draw:
Ere heaven shall ope her portals to this
   Guelph,
While I am guard, may I be damn'd my-
   self!

L

'Sooner will I with Cerberus exchange
    My office (and *his* is no sinecure)
Than see this royal Bedlam bigot range
    The azure fields of heaven, of that be
        sure!'
'Saint!' replied Satan, 'you do well to
        avenge
    The wrongs he made your satellites
        endure;
And if to this exchange you should be
        given,
I'll try to coax *our* Cerberus up to heaven!'

LI

Here Michael interposed: 'Good saint!
        and devil!
    Pray, not so fast; you both outrun dis-
        cretion.
Saint Peter! you were wont to be more
        civil!
    Satan! excuse this warmth of his ex-
        pression,
And condescension to the vulgar's level:
    Even saints sometimes forget them-
        selves in session.
Have you got more to say?'—'No.'—'If
        you please,
I'll trouble you to call your witnesses.'

LII

Then Satan turn'd and waved his swarthy
        hand,
    Which stirr'd with its electric qualities
Clouds farther off than we can understand,
    Although we find him sometimes in our
        skies;
Infernal thunder shook both sea and land
    In all the planets, and hell's batteries
Let off the artillery, which Milton men-
        tions
As one of Satan's most sublime inventions.

LIII

This was a signal unto such damn'd souls
    As have the privilege of their damnation
Extended far beyond the mere controls
    Of worlds past, present, or to come; no
        station
Is theirs particularly in the rolls
    Of hell assign'd; but where their inclina-
        tion
Or business carries them in search of
        game,
They may range freely—being damn'd the
        same.

LIV

They're proud of this—as very well they
        may,
    It being a sort of knighthood, or gilt key
Stuck in their loins; or like to an 'entré'
    Up the back stairs, or such free-
        masonry.
I borrow my comparisons from clay,
    Being clay myself. Let not those spirits
        be
Offended with such base low likenesses;
    We know their posts are nobler far than
        these.

LV

When the great signal ran from heaven to
        hell—
    About ten million times the distance
        reckon'd
From our sun to its earth, as we can tell
    How much time it takes up, even to a
        second,
For every ray that travels to dispel
    The fogs of London, through which,
        dimly beacon'd,
The weathercocks are gilt some thrice a
        year,
If that the *summer* is not too severe:

LVI

I say that I can tell—'twas half a minute;
    I know the solar beams take up more
        time
Ere, pack'd up for their journey, they
        begin it;
    But then their telegraph is less sublime,
And if they ran a race, they would not win
        it
    'Gainst Satan's couriers bound for their
        own clime.
The sun takes up some years for every ray
To reach its goal—the devil not half a
        day.

LVII

Upon the verge of space, about the size
    Of half-a-crown, a little speck appear'd
(I've seen a something like it in the skies
    In the Ægean, ere a squall); it near'd,
And, growing bigger, took another guise,
    Like an aërial ship it tack'd, and steer'd,
Or *was* steer'd (I am doubtful of the
        grammar
Of the last phrase, which makes the stanza
        stammer;—

LVIII

But take your choice): and then it grew a
        cloud;
    And so it was—a cloud of witnesses.
But such a cloud! No land e'er saw a
        crowd
    Of locusts numerous as the heavens saw
        these;
They shadow'd with their myriads space;
        their loud
    And varied cries were like those of wild
        geese
(If nations may be liken'd to a goose),
And realised the phrase of 'hell broke
        loose.'

LIX

Here crash'd a sturdy oath of stout John Bull,
  Who damn'd away his eyes as heretofore:
There Paddy brogued 'By Jasus!'—
  'What's your wull?'
The temperate Scot exclaim'd: the French ghost swore
In certain terms I shan't translate in full,
  As the first coachman will; and 'midst the war,
The voice of Jonathan was heard to express,
'*Our* president is going to war, I guess.'

LX

Besides there were the Spaniard, Dutch, and Dane;
  In short, an universal shoal of shades,
From Otaheite's isle to Salisbury Plain,
  Of all climes and professions, years and trades,
Ready to swear against the good king's reign,
  Bitter as clubs in cards are against spades:
All summon'd by this grand 'subpœna,' to
Try if kings mayn't be damn'd like me or you.

LXI

When Michael saw this host, he first grew pale,
  As angels can; next, like Italian twilight,
He turn'd all colours—as a peacock's tail,
  Or sunset streaming through a Gothic skylight
In some old abbey, or a trout not stale,
  Or distant lightning on the horizon *by* night,
Or a fresh rainbow, or a grand review
Of thirty regiments in red, green, and blue.

LXII

Then he address'd himself to Satan: 'Why—
  My good old friend, for such I deem you, though
Our different parties make us fight so shy,
  I ne'er mistake you for a *personal* foe;
Our difference is *political*, and I
  Trust that, whatever may occur below,
You know my great respect for you: and this
Makes me regret whate'er you do amiss—

LXIII

'Why, my dear Lucifer, would you abuse
  My call for witnesses? I did not mean
That you should half of earth and hell produce;

'Tis even superfluous, since two honest, clean,
True testimonies are enough: we lose
  Our time, nay, our eternity, between
The accusation and defence: if we
Hear both, 'twill stretch our immortality.'

LXIV

Satan replied, 'To me the matter is
  Indifferent, in a personal point of view:
I can have fifty better souls than this
  With far less trouble than we have gone through
Already; and I merely argued his
  Late majesty of Britain's case with you
Upon a point of form: you may dispose
Of him; I've kings enough below, God knows!'

LXV

Thus spoke the Demon (late call'd 'multi-faced'
  By multo-scribbling Southey). 'Then we'll call
One or two persons of the myriads placed
  Around our congress, and dispense with all
The rest,' quoth Michael: 'Who may be so graced
  As to speak first? there's choice enough—who shall
It be?' Then Satan answer'd, 'There are many;
But you may choose Jack Wilkes as well as any.'

LXVI

A merry, cock-eyed, curious-looking sprite
  Upon the instant started from the throng,
Dress'd in a fashion now forgotten quite;
  For all the fashions of the flesh stick long
By people in the next world; where unite
  All the costumes since Adam's, right or wrong,
From Eve's fig-leaf down to the petticoat,
Almost as scanty, of days less remote.

LXVII

The spirit look'd around upon the crowds
  Assembled, and exclaim'd, 'My friends of all
The spheres, we shall catch cold amongst these clouds;
  So let's to business: why this general call?
If those are freeholders I see in shrouds,
  And 'tis for an election that they bawl,
Behold a candidate with unturn'd coat!
Saint Peter, may I count upon your vote?'

LXVIII

'Sir,' replied Michael, 'you mistake; these things
  Are of a former life, and what we do
Above is more august; to judge of kings
  Is the tribunal met: so now you know.'
'Then I presume those gentlemen with wings,'
  Said Wilkes, 'are cherubs; and that soul below
Looks much like George the Third, but to my mind
  A good deal older—Bless me! is he blind?'

LXIX

'He is what you behold him, and his doom
  Depends upon his deeds,' the Angel said;
'If you have aught to arraign in him, the tomb
  Gives licence to the humblest beggar's head
To lift itself against the loftiest.'—'Some,'
  Said Wilkes, 'don't wait to see them laid in lead,
For such a liberty—and I, for one,
Have told them what I thought beneath the sun.'

LXX

'*Above* the sun repeat, then, what thou hast
  To urge against him,' said the Archangel. 'Why,'
Replied the spirit, 'since old scores are past,
  Must I turn evidence? In faith, not I.
Besides, I beat him hollow at the last,
  With all his Lords and Commons: in the sky
I don't like ripping up old stories, since
His conduct was but natural in a prince.

LXXI

'Foolish, no doubt, and wicked, to oppress
  A poor unlucky devil without a shilling;
But then I blame the man himself much less
  Than Bute and Grafton, and shall be unwilling
To see him punish'd here for their excess,
  Since they were both damn'd long ago, and still in
Their place below: for me, I have forgiven,
And vote his "habeas corpus" into heaven.'

LXXII

'Wilkes,' said the Devil, 'I understand all this;
  You turn'd to half a courtier ere you died,
And seem to think it would not be amiss
  To grow a whole one on the other side

Of Charon's ferry; you forget that *his*
  Reign is concluded; whatsoe'er betide,
He won't be sovereign more: you've lost your labour,
For at the best he will but be your neighbour.

LXXIII

'However, I knew what to think of it,
  When I beheld you in your jesting way,
Flitting and whispering round about the spit
  Where Belial, upon duty for the day,
With Fox's lard was basting William Pitt,
  His pupil; I knew what to think, I say:
That fellow even in hell breeds farther ills;
I'll have him *gagg'd*—'twas one of his own bills.

LXXIV

'Call Junius!' From the crowd a shadow stalk'd,
  And at the name there was a general squeeze,
So that the very ghosts no longer walk'd
  In comfort, at their own aërial ease,
But were all ramm'd, and jamm'd (but to be balk'd,
  As we shall see), and jostled hands and knees,
Like wind compress'd and pent within a bladder,
Or like a human colic, which is sadder.

LXXV

The shadow came—a tall, thin, grey-hair'd figure,
  That look'd as it had been a shade on earth;
Quick in its motions, with an air of vigour,
  But nought to mark its breeding or its birth;
Now it wax'd little, then again grew bigger,
  With now an air of gloom, or savage mirth;
But as you gazed upon its features, they
Changed every instant—to *what*, none could say.

LXXVI

The more intently the ghosts gazed, the less
  Could they distinguish whose the features were;
The Devil himself seem'd puzzled even to guess;
  They varied like a dream—now here, now there;
And several people swore from out the press,
  They knew him perfectly; and one could swear
He was his father: upon which another
Was sure he was his mother's cousin's brother:

LXXVII

Another, that he was a duke, or knight,
   An orator, a lawyer, or a priest,
A nabob, a man-midwife; but the wight
   Mysterious changed his countenance at
      least
As oft as they their minds; though in full
      sight
   He stood, the puzzle only was increased;
The man was a phantasmagoria in
Himself—he was so volatile and thin.

LXXVIII

The moment that you had pronounced
      him one,
   Presto! his face changed, and he was
      another;
And when that change was hardly well put
      on,
   It varied, till I don't think his own
      mother
(If that he had a mother) would her son
   Have known, he shifted so from one to
      t'other;
Till guessing from a pleasure grew a task,
At this epistolary 'Iron Mask.'

LXXIX

For sometimes he like Cerberus would
      seem—
   'Three gentlemen at once' (as sagely
      says
Good Mrs. Malaprop); then you might
      deem
   That he was not even one; now many
      rays
Were flashing round him; and now a thick
      steam
   Hid him from sight—like fogs on Lon-
      don days:
Now Burke, now Tooke, he grew to
      people's fancies,
And certes often like Sir Philip Francis.

LXXX

I've an hypothesis—'tis quite my own;
   I never let it out till now, for fear
Of doing people harm about the throne,
   And injuring some minister or peer,
On whom the stigma might perhaps be
      blown;
   It is—my gentle public, lend thine ear!
'Tis, that what Junius we are wont to call
Was really, truly, nobody at all.

LXXXI

I don't see wherefore letters should not be
   Written without hands, since we daily
      view
Them written without heads; and books,
      we see,
   Are fill'd as well without the latter too:
And really till we fix on somebody

For certain sure to claim them as his
      due,
   Their author, like the Niger's mouth, will
      bother
The world to say if there be mouth or
      author.

LXXXII

'And who and what art thou?' the Arch-
      angel said.
   'For that you may consult my title-
      page,'
Replied this mighty shadow of a shade:
   'If I have kept my secret half an age,
I scarce shall tell it now.'—'Canst thou
      upbraid,'
   Continued Michael, 'George Rex, or
      allege
Aught further?' Junius answer'd, 'You
      had better
First ask him for his answer to my letter:

LXXXIII

'My charges upon record will outlast
   The brass of both his epitaph and tomb.'
'Repent'st thou not,' said Michael, 'of
      some past
   Exaggeration? something which may
      doom
Thyself if false, as him if true? Thou wast
   Too bitter—is it not so?—in thy gloom
Of passion?'—'Passion!' cried the phan-
      tom dim,
'I loved my country, and I hated him.

LXXXIV

'What I have written, I have written: let
   The rest be on his head or mine!' So
      spoke
Old 'Nominis Umbra'; and while speak-
      ing yet,
   Away he melted in celestial smoke.
Then Satan said to Michael, 'Don't forget
   To call George Washington, and John
      Horne Tooke,
And Franklin;'—but at this time there
      was heard
A cry for room, though not a phantom
      stirr'd.

LXXXV

At length with jostling, elbowing, and the
      aid
   Of cherubim appointed to that post,
The devil Asmodeus to the circle made
   His way, and look'd as if his journey
      cost
Some trouble. When his burden down he
      laid,
   'What's this?' cried Michael; 'why,
      'tis not a ghost?'
'I know it,' quoth the incubus; 'but he
Shall be one, if you leave the affair to
me.

LXXXVI

'Confound the renegado! I have sprain'd
My left wing, he's so heavy; one would
think
Some of his works about his neck were
chain'd.
But to the point; while hovering o'er
the brink
Of Skiddaw (where as usual it still rain'd),
I saw a taper, far below me, wink,
And stooping, caught this fellow at a
libel—
No less on history than the Holy Bible.

LXXXVII

'The former is the devil's scripture, and
The latter yours, good Michael: so the
affair
Belongs to all of us, you understand.
I snatch'd him up just as you see him
there,
And brought him off for sentence out of
hand:
I've scarcely been ten minutes in the
air—
At least a quarter it can hardly be:
I dare say that his wife is still at tea.'

LXXXVIII

Here Satan said, 'I know this man of old,
And have expected him for some time
here;
A sillier fellow you will scarce behold,
Or more conceited in his petty sphere:
But surely it was not worth while to fold
Such trash below your wing, Asmodeus
dear:
We had the poor wretch safe (without
being bored
With carriage) coming of his own accord.

LXXXIX

'But since he's here, let's see what he has
done.'
'Done!' cried Asmodeus, 'he antici-
pates
The very business you are now upon,
And scribbles as if head clerk to the
Fates.
Who knows to what his ribaldry may run,
When such an ass as this, like Balaam's,
prates?'
'Let's hear,' quoth Michael, 'what he has
to say:
You know we're bound to that in every
way.'

XC

Now the bard, glad to get an audience,
which
By no means often was his case below,
Began to cough, and hawk, and hem, and
pitch
His voice into that awful note of woe

To all unhappy hearers within reach
Of poets when the tide of rhyme's in
flow;
But stuck fast with his first hexameter,
Not one of all whose gouty feet would stir.

XCI

But ere the spavin'd dactyls could be
spurr'd
Into recitative, in great dismay
Both cherubim and seraphim were heard
To murmur loudly through their long
array;
And Michael rose ere he could get a word
Of all his founder'd verses under way,
And cried, 'For God's sake stop, my
friend! 'twere best—
Non Di, non homines—you know the rest.'

XCII

A general bustle spread throughout the
throng,
Which seem'd to hold all verse in detes-
tation;
The angels had of course enough of song
When upon service; and the generation
Of ghosts had heard too much in life, not
long
Before, to profit by a new occasion;
The monarch, mute till then, exclaim'd,
'What! what!
Pye come again? No more—no more of
that!'

XCIII

The tumult grew; an universal cough
Convulsed the skies, as during a debate,
When Castlereagh has been up long
enough
(Before he was first minister of state,
I mean—the *slaves hear now*); some cried
'Off, off!'
As at a farce; till, grown quite desperate,
The bard Saint Peter pray'd to interpose
(Himself an author) only for his prose.

XCIV

The varlet was not an ill-favour'd knave;
A good deal like a vulture in the face,
With a hook nose and a hawk's eye, which
gave
A smart and sharper-looking sort of
grace
To his whole aspect, which, though rather
grave,
Was by no means so ugly as his case;
But that, indeed, was hopeless as can be,
Quite a poetic felony '*de se*.'

XCV

Then Michael blew his trump, and still'd
the noise
With one still greater, as is yet the mode
On earth besides; except some grumbling
voice,

167

THE VISION OF JUDGMENT

Which now and then will make a slight
    inroad
Upon decorous silence, few will twice
    Lift up their lungs when fairly over-
      crow'd;
And now the bard could plead his own bad
    cause,
With all the attitudes of self-applause.

XCVI

He said—(I only give the heads)—he said,
    He meant no harm in scribbling; 'twas
      his way
Upon all topics; 'twas, besides, his bread,
    Of which he butter'd both sides; 'twould
      delay
Too long the assembly (he was pleased to
    dread),
    And take up rather more time than a
      day,
To name his works—he would but cite a
    few—
'Wat Tyler'—'Rhymes on Blenheim'—
    'Waterloo.'

XCVII

He had written praises of a regicide;
    He had written praises of all kings what-
      ever;
He had written for republics far and wide,
    And then against them bitterer than ever;
For pantisocracy he once had cried
    Aloud, a scheme less moral than 'twas
      clever;
Then grew a hearty anti-jacobin—
Had turn'd his coat—and would have
    turn'd his skin.

XCVIII

He had sung against all battles, and again
    In their high praise and glory; he had
      call'd
Reviewing 'the ungentle craft,' and then
    Become as base a critic as e'er crawl'd—
Fed, paid, and pamper'd by the very men
    By whom his muse and morals had been
      maul'd:
He had written much blank verse, and
    blanker prose,
And more of both than anybody knows.

XCIX

He had written Wesley's life:—here turn-
    ing round
To Satan, 'Sir, I'm ready to write yours,
In two octavo volumes, nicely bound,
    With notes and preface, all that most
      allures
The pious purchaser; and there's no
    ground
    For fear, for I can choose my own re-
      viewers:
So let me have the proper documents,
That I may add you to my other saints.'

C

Satan bow'd, and was silent. 'Well, if you,
    With amiable modesty, decline
My offer, what says Michael? There are
    few
    Whose memoirs could be render'd more
      divine.
Mine is a pen of all work; not so new
    As it was once, but I would make you
      shine
Like your own trumpet. By the way, my
    own
Has more of brass in it, and is as well
    blown.

CI

'But talking about trumpets, here's my
    Vision!
    Now you shall judge, all people; yes,
      you shall
Judge with my judgment, and by my de-
    cision
    Be guided who shall enter heaven or fall.
I settle all these things by intuition,
    Times present, past, to come, heaven,
      hell, and all,
Like King Alfonso. When I thus see
    double,
I save the Deity some worlds of trouble.'

CII

He ceased, and drew forth an MS.; and no
    Persuasion on the part of devils, saints,
Or angels, now could stop the torrent; so
    He read the first three lines of the con-
      tents;
But at the fourth, the whole spiritual show
    Had vanish'd, with variety of scents,
Ambrosial and sulphureous, as they
    sprang,
Like lightning, off from his 'melodious
    twang.'

CIII

Those grand heroics acted as a spell:
    The angels stopp'd their ears and plied
      their pinions;
The devils ran howling, deafen'd, down to
    hell;
    The ghosts fled, gibbering, for their own
      dominions—
(For 'tis not yet decided where they dwell,
    And I leave every man to his opinions);
Michael took refuge in his trump—but, lo!
His teeth were set on edge, he could not
    blow!

CIV

Saint Peter, who has hitherto been known
    For an impetuous saint, upraised his
      keys,
And at the fifth line knock'd the poet
    down;
    Who fell like Phaeton, but more at ease,

Into his lake, for there he did not drown;
A different web being by the Destinies
Woven for the Laureate's final wreath,
whene'er
Reform shall happen either here or there.

In his own den, to scrawl some 'Life' or
'Vision,'
As Welborn says—'the devil turn'd pre-
cisian.'

CV

He first sank to the bottom—like his
works,
But soon rose to the surface—like him-
self;
For all corrupted things are buoy'd like
corks,
By their own rottenness, light as an elf,
Or wisp that flits o'er a morass: he lurks,
It may be, still, like dull books on a shelf,

CVI

As for the rest, to come to the conclusion
Of this true dream, the telescope is gone
Which kept my optics free from all de-
lusion,
And show'd me what I in my turn have
shown;
All I saw farther, in the last confusion,
Was, that King George slipp'd into
heaven for one;
And when the tumult dwindled to a calm,
I left him practising the hundredth psalm.

THE AGE OF BRONZE

OR,

CARMEN SECULARE ET ANNUS HAUD MIRABILIS

'Impar *Congressus* Achilli.'

I

THE 'good old times'—all times when old
are good—
Are gone; the present might be if they
would;
Great things have been, and are, and
greater still
Want little of mere mortals but their will:
A wider space, a greener field, is given
To those who play their 'tricks before high
heaven.'   6
I know not if the angels weep, but men
Have wept enough—for what?—to weep
again!

II

All is exploded—be it good or bad.   9
Reader! remember when thou wert a lad,
Then Pitt was all; or, if not all, so much,
His very rival almost deem'd him such.
We, we have seen the intellectual race
Of giants stand, like Titans, face to face—
Athos and Ida, with a dashing sea   15
Of eloquence between, which flow'd all free,
As the deep billows of the Ægean roar
Betwixt the Hellenic and the Phrygian
shore.
But where are they—the rivals! a few feet
Of sullen earth divide each winding sheet.
How peaceful and how powerful is the
grave,   21
Which hushes all! a calm, unstormy wave,
Which oversweeps the world. The theme
is old
Of 'dust to dust;' but half its tale untold.

Time tempers not its terrors—still the
worm   25
Winds its cold folds, the tomb preserves
its form,
Varied above, but still alike below;
The urn may shine, the ashes will not glow,
Though Cleopatra's mummy cross the sea
O'er which from empire she lured An-
thony;   30
Though Alexander's urn a show be grown
On shores he wept to conquer, though un-
known—
How vain, how worse than vain, at length
appear
The madman's wish, the Macedonian's
tear!
He wept for worlds to conquer—half the
earth   35
Knows not his name, or but his death, and
birth,
And desolation; while his native Greece
Hath all of desolation, save its peace.
He 'wept for worlds to conquer'! he who
ne'er
Conceived the globe, he panted not to
spare!   40
With even the busy Northern Isle un-
known,
Which holds his urn, and never knew his
throne.

III

But where is he, the modern, mightier far,
Who, born no king, made monarchs draw
his car;

169

The new Sesostris, whose unharness'd
    kings,   45
Freed from the bit, believe themselves
    with wings,
And spurn the dust o'er which they crawl'd
    of late,
Chain'd to the chariot of the chieftain's
    state?
Yes! where is he, the champion and the
    child
Of all that's great or little, wise or wild;
Whose game was empires, and whose
    stakes were thrones;   51
Whose table earth—whose dice were
    human bones?
Behold the grand result in yon lone isle,
And, as thy nature urges, weep or smile.
Sigh to behold the eagle's lofty rage   55
Reduced to nibble at his narrow cage;
Smile to survey the queller of the nations
Now daily squabbling o'er disputed
    rations;
Weep to perceive him mourning, as he
    dines,
O'er curtail'd dishes and o'er stinted
    wines;   60
O'er petty quarrels upon petty things.
Is this the man who scourged or feasted
    kings?
Behold the scales in which his fortune
    hangs,
A surgeon's statement, and an earl's
    harangues!   64
A bust delayed, a book refused, can shake
The sleep of him who kept the world
    awake.
Is this indeed the tamer of the great,
Now slave of all could tease or irritate—
The paltry gaoler and the prying spy,
The staring stranger with his note-book
    nigh?   70
Plunged in a dungeon he had still been
    great;
How low, how little was this middle state,
Between a prison and a palace, where
How few could feel for what he had to
    bear!
Vain his complaint,—my lord presents his
    bill,   75
His food and wine were doled out duly still;
Vain was his sickness, never was a clime
So free from homicide—to doubt's a
    crime;
And the stiff surgeon, who maintain'd his
    cause,
Hath lost his place, and gain'd the world's
    applause.   80
But smile—though all the pangs of brain
    and heart
Disdain, defy, the tardy aid of art;
Though, save the few fond friends and
    imaged face
Of that fair boy his sire shall ne'er em-
    brace,

None stand by his low bed—though even
    the mind   85
Be wavering, which long awed and awes
    mankind:
Smile—for the fetter'd eagle breaks his
    chain,
And higher worlds than this are his again.

IV

How, if that soaring spirit still retain
A conscious twilight of his blazing reign,
How must he smile, on looking down, to
    see   91
The little that he was and sought to be!
What though his name a wider empire
    found
Than his ambition, though with scarce a
    bound;   94
Though first in glory, deepest in reverse,
He tasted empire's blessings and its curse;
Though kings, rejoicing in their late escape
From chains, would gladly be their tyrant's
    ape;
How must he smile, and turn to yon lone
    grave,
The proudest sea-mark that o'ertops the
    wave!   100
What though his gaoler, duteous to the
    last,
Scarce deem'd the coffin's lead could keep
    him fast,
Refusing one poor line along the lid,
To date the birth and death of all it hid;
That name shall hallow the ignoble shore,
A talisman to all save him who bore: 106
The fleets that sweep before the eastern
    blast
Shall hear their sea-boys hail it from the
    mast;
When Victory's Gallic column shall but
    rise,   109
Like Pompey's pillar, in a desert's skies,
The rocky isle that holds or held his dust,
Shall crown the Atlantic like the hero's
    bust,
And mighty nature o'er his obsequies
Do more than niggard envy still denies.
But what are these to him? Can glory's
    lust   115
Touch the freed spirit or the fetter'd dust?
Small care hath he of what his tomb con-
    sists;
Nought if he sleeps—nor more if he exists:
Alike the better-seeing shade will smile
On the rude cavern of the rocky isle,   120
As if his ashes found their latest home
In Rome's Pantheon or Gaul's mimic
    dome.
He wants not this; but France shall feel
    the want
Of this last consolation, though so scant:
Her honour, fame, and faith demand his
    bones,   125
To rear above a pyramid of thrones;

Or carried onward in the battle's van,
To form, like Guesclin's dust, her talis-
man.
But be it as it is—the time may come
His name shall beat the alarm, like Ziska's
drum.   130

V

Oh heaven! of which he was in power a
feature;
Oh earth! of which he was a noble
creature;
Thou isle! to be remember'd long and
well,
That saw'st the unfledged eaglet chip his
shell!
Ye Alps, which view'd him in his dawning
flights   135
Hover, the victor of a hundred fights!
Thou Rome, who saw'st thy Cæsar's
deeds outdone!
Alas! why pass'd he too the Rubicon—
The Rubicon of man's awaken'd rights,
To herd with vulgar kings and parasites?
Egypt! from whose all dateless tombs
arose   141
Forgotten Pharaohs from their long re-
pose,
And shook within their pyramids to hear
A new Cambyses thundering in their ear;
While the dark shades of forty ages stood
Like startled giants by Nile's famous
flood;   146
Or from the pyramid's tall pinnacle
Beheld the desert peopled, as from hell,
With clashing hosts, who strew'd the
barren sand,
To re-manure the uncultivated land!
Spain! which, a moment mindless of the
Cid,   151
Beheld his banner flouting thy Madrid!
Austria! which saw thy twice-ta'en
capital
Twice spared to be the traitress of his fall!
Ye race of Frederic!—Frederics but in
name   155
And falsehood—heirs to all except his
fame:
Who, crush'd at Jena, crouch'd at Berlin,
fell
First, and but rose to follow! Ye who
dwell
Where Kosciusko dwelt, remembering yet
The unpaid amount of Catherine's bloody
debt!   160
Poland! o'er which the avenging angel
pass'd,
But left thee as he found thee, still a waste,
Forgetting all thy still enduring claim,
Thy lotted people and extinguish'd name,
Thy sigh for freedom, thy long-flowing
tear,   165
That sound that crashes in the tyrant's
ear—

Kosciusko! On—on—on—the thirst of
war
Gasps for the gore of serfs and of their
Czar.
The half barbaric Moscow's minarets
Gleam in the sun, but 'tis a sun that sets!
Moscow! thou limit of his long career,
For which rude Charles had wept his
frozen tear   172
To see in vain—he saw thee—how? with
spire
And palace fuel to one common fire.
To this the soldier lent his kindling match,
To this the peasant gave his cottage
thatch,   176
To this the merchant flung his hoarded
store,
The prince his hall—and Moscow was no
more!
Sublimest of volcanos! Etna's flame
Pales before thine, and quenchless Hecla's
tame;   180
Vesuvius shows his blaze, an usual sight
For gaping tourists, from his hackney'd
height:
Thou stand'st alone unrivall'd, till the fire
To come, in which all empires shall expire!

Thou other element! as strong and stern,
To teach a lesson conquerors will not
learn!—   186
Whose icy wing flapp'd o'er the faltering foe,
Till fell a hero with each flake of snow:
How did thy numbing beak and silent fang
Pierce, till hosts perish'd with a single
pang!   190
In vain shall Seine look up along his banks
For the gay thousands of his dashing
ranks!
In vain shall France recall beneath her vines
Her youth—their blood flows faster than
her wines;   194
Or stagnant in their human ice remains
In frozen mummies on the Polar plains.
In vain will Italy's broad sun awaken
Her offspring chill'd; its beams are now
forsaken.
Of all the trophies gather'd from the war,
What shall return? the conqueror's broken
car!   200
The conqueror's yet unbroken heart!
Again
The horn of Roland sounds, and not in
vain.
Lutzen, where fell the Swede of victory,
Beholds him conquer, but, alas! not die:
Dresden surveys three despots fly once
more   205
Before their sovereign,—sovereign as be-
fore;
But there exhausted Fortune quits the
field,
And Leipsic's treason bids the unvan-
quish'd yield;

171

The Saxon jackal leaves the lion's side
To turn the bear's, and wolf's, and fox's
  guide;   210
And backward to the den of his despair
The forest monarch shrinks, but finds no
  lair!

  Oh ye! and each, and all! Oh France!
  who found
Thy long fair fields plough'd up as hostile
  ground,   214
Disputed foot by foot, till treason, still
His only victor, from Montmartre's hill
Look'd down o'er trampled Paris! and
  thou Isle,
Which seest Etruria from thy ramparts
  smile,
Thou momentary shelter of his pride,
Till woo'd by danger, his yet weeping
  bride!   220
Oh, France! retaken by a single march,
Whose path was through one long tri-
  umphal arch!
Oh, bloody and most bootless Waterloo!
Which proves how fools may have their
  fortune too,
Won half by blunder, half by treachery:
Oh, dull Saint Helen! with thy gaoler
  nigh—   226
Hear! hear Prometheus from his rock
  appeal
To earth, air, ocean, all that felt or feel
His power and glory, all who yet shall hear
A name eternal as the rolling year;   230
He teaches them the lesson taught so long,
So oft, so vainly—learn to do no wrong!
A single step into the right had made
This man the Washington of worlds be-
  tray'd: 234
A single step into the wrong has given
His name a doubt to all the winds of
  heaven;
The reed of Fortune, and of thrones the
  rod,
Of Fame the Moloch or the demigod;
His country's Cæsar, Europe's Hannibal,
Without their decent dignity of fall.   240
Yet Vanity herself had better taught
A surer path even to the fame he sought,
By pointing out on history's fruitless page
Ten thousand conquerors for a single sage.
While Franklin's quiet memory climbs to
  heaven,   245
Calming the lightning which he thence hath
  riven,
Or drawing from the no less kindled earth
Freedom and peace to that which boasts
  his birth;
While Washington's a watchword, such
  as ne'er
Shall sink while there's an echo left to air:
While even the Spaniard's thirst of gold
  and war   251
Forgets Pizarro to shout Bolivar!

Alas! why must the same Atlantic wave
Which wafted freedom gird a tyrant's
  grave—
The king of kings, and yet of slaves the
  slave,   255
Who burst the chains of millions to re-
  new
The very fetters which his arm broke
  through,
And crush'd the rights of Europe and his
  own,
To flit between a dungeon and a throne?

VI

But 'twill not be—the spark's awaken'd—
  lo!   260
The swarthy Spaniard feels his former
  glow;
The same high spirit which beat back the
  Moor
Through eight long ages of alternate gore
Revives—and where? in that avenging
  clime
Where Spain was once synonymous with
  crime,   265
Where Cortes and Pizarro's banner flew,
The infant world redeems her name of
  'New.'
'Tis the *old* aspiration breathed afresh,
To kindle souls within degraded flesh,
Such as repulsed the Persian from the
  shore   270
Where Greece *was*—No! she still is Greece
  once more.
One common cause makes myriads of one
  breast,
Slaves of the East, or helots of the West:
On Andes' and on Athos' peaks un-
  furl'd,
The self-same standard streams o'er either
  world: 275
The Athenian wears again Harmodius'
  sword;
The Chili chief abjures his foreign lord;
The Spartan knows himself once more a
  Greek,
Young Freedom plumes the crest of each
  cacique;
Debating despots, hemm'd on either
  shore,   280
Shrink vainly from the roused Atlantic's
  roar;
Through Calpe's strait the rolling tides
  advance,
Sweep slightly by the half-tamed land of
  France,
Dash o'er the old Spaniard's cradle, and
  would fain
Unite Ausonia to the mighty main: 285
But driven from thence awhile, yet not for
  aye,
Break o'er th' Ægean, mindful of the day
Of Salamis!—there, there the waves arise,
Not to be lull'd by tyrant victories.

Lone, lost, abandon'd in their utmost
   need   290
By Christians, unto whom they gave their
   creed,
The desolated lands, the ravaged isle,
The foster'd feud encouraged to beguile,
The aid evaded, and the cold delay,
Prolong'd but in the hope to make a
   prey;—   295
These, these shall tell the tale, and Greece
   can show
The false friend worse than the infuriate
   foe.
But this is well: Greeks only should free
   Greece,
Not the barbarian, with his mask of peace.
How should the autocrat of bondage be
The king of serfs, and set the nations free?
Better still serve the haughty Mussulman,
Than swell the Cossaque's prowling
   caravan;
Better still toil for masters, than await,
The slave of slaves, before a Russian
   gate,—   305
Number'd by hordes, a human capital,
A live estate, existing but for thrall,
Lotted by thousands, as a meet reward
For the first courtier in the Czar's regard;
While their immediate owner never tastes
His sleep, *sans* dreaming of Siberia's
   wastes: 311
Better succumb even to their own despair,
And drive the camel than purvey the bear.

VII

But not alone within the hoariest clime
Where Freedom dates her birth with that
   of Time,   315
And not alone where, plunged in night, a
   crowd
Of Incas darken to a dubious cloud,
The dawn revives: renown'd, romantic
   Spain
Holds back the invader from her soil
   again.
Not now the Roman tribe nor Punic
   horde   320
Demand her fields as lists to prove the
   sword;
Not now the Vandal or the Visigoth
Pollute the plains, alike abhorring both;
Nor old Pelayo on his mountain rears
The warlike fathers of a thousand years.
That seed is sown and reap'd, as oft the
   Moor   326
Sighs to remember on his dusky shore.
Long in the peasant's song or poet's page
Has dwelt the memory of Abencerrage;
The Zegri, and the captive victors, flung
Back to the barbarous realm from whence
   they sprung.   331
But these are gone—their faith, their
   swords, their sway,
Yet left more anti-christian foes than they;

The bigot monarch, and the butcher priest,
The Inquisition, with her burning feast,
The faith's red 'auto,' fed with human
   fuel,   336
While sate the catholic Moloch, calmly
   cruel,
Enjoying, with inexorable eye,
That fiery festival of agony!
The stern or feeble sovereign, one or both
By turns; the haughtiness whose pride was
   sloth;   341
The long degenerate noble; the debased
Hidalgo, and the peasant less disgraced,
But more degraded; the unpeopled realm;
The once proud navy which forgot the
   helm;   345
The once impervious phalanx disarray'd;
The idle forge that form'd Toledo's blade;
The foreign wealth that flow'd on ev'ry
   shore,
Save hers who earn'd it with the natives'
   gore;
The very language which might vie with
   Rome's,   350
And once was known to nations like
   their homes,
Neglected or forgotten:—such was Spain;
But such she is not, nor shall be again.
These worst, these *home* invaders, felt and
   feel
The new Numantine soul of old Castile;
Up! up again! undaunted Tauridor! 356
The bull of Phalaris renews his roar;
Mount, chivalrous Hidalgo! not in vain
Revive the cry!—'Iago! and close Spain!'
Yes, close her with your armed bosoms
   round,   360
And form the barrier which Napoleon
   found,—
The exterminating war, the desert plain,
The streets without a tenant, save the slain;
The wild sierra, with its wilder troop
Of vulture-plumed guerrillas, on the stoop
For their incessant prey; the desperate
   wall   366
Of Saragossa, mightiest in her fall;
The man nerved to a spirit, and the maid
Waving her more than Amazonian blade;
The knife of Arragon, Toledo's steel; 370
The famous lance of chivalrous Castile:
The unerring rifle of the Catalan;
The Andalusian courser in the van;
The torch to make a Moscow of Madrid;
And in each heart the spirit of the Cid:—
Such have been, such shall be, such are.
   Advance,   376
And win—not Spain! but thine own free-
   dom, France!

VIII

But lo! a Congress! What! that hallow'd
   name
Which freed the Atlantic! May we hope
   the same

For outworn Europe? With the sound
          arise,   380
Like Samuel's shade to Saul's monarchic
          eyes,
The prophets of young Freedom, sum-
          mon'd far
From climes of Washington and Bolivar;
Henry, the forest-born Demosthenes,
Whose thunder shook the Philip of the
          seas;   385
And stoic Franklin's energetic shade,
Robed in the lightnings which his hand
          allay'd;
And Washington, the tyrant-tamer, wake,
To bid us blush for these old chains, or
          break.
But who compose this senate of the few
That should redeem the many? Who
          renew   391
This consecrated name, till now assign'd
To councils held to benefit mankind?
Who now assemble at the holy call?
The blest Alliance, which says three are
          all!   395
An earthly trinity! which wears the shape
Of heaven's, as man is mimick'd by the ape.
A pious unity! in purpose one—
To melt three fools to a Napoleon.
Why, Egypt's gods were rational to these;
Their dogs and oxen knew their own
          degrees,   401
And, quiet in their kennel or their shed,
Cared little, so that they were duly fed;
But these, more hungry, must have some-
          thing more—
The power to bark and bite, to toss and
          gore.   405
Ah, how much happier were good Æsop's
          frogs
Than we! for ours are animated logs,
With ponderous malice swaying to and fro,
And crushing nations with a stupid blow;
All duly anxious to leave little work   410
Unto the revolutionary stork.

IX

Thrice blest Verona! since the holy three
With their imperial presence shine on
          thee!
Honour'd by them, thy treacherous site
          forgets
The vaunted tomb of 'all the Capulets';
Thy Scaligers—for what was 'Dog the
          Great,'   416
'Can Grande,' (which I venture to tran-
          slate,)
To these sublimer pugs? Thy poet too,
Catullus, whose old laurels yield to new;
Thine amphitheatre, where Romans sate;
And Dante's exile shelter'd by thy gate;
Thy good old man, whose world was all
          within
Thy wall, nor knew the country held him in;

Would that the royal guests it girds about
Were so far like, as never to get out!   425
Ay, shout! inscribe! rear monuments of
          shame,
To tell Oppression that the world is tame!
Crowd to the theatre with loyal rage,
The comedy is not upon the stage;
The show is rich in ribandry and stars,
Then gaze upon it through thy dungeon
          bars;   431
Clap thy permitted palms, kind Italy,
For thus much still thy fetter'd hands are
          free!

X

Resplendent sight! Behold the coxcomb
          Czar,
The autocrat of waltzes and of war!   435
As eager for a plaudit as a realm,
And just as fit for flirting as the helm;
A Calmuck beauty with a Cossack wit,
And generous spirit, when 'tis not frost-
          bit;
Now half dissolving to a liberal thaw, 440
But harden'd back whene'er the morning's
          raw;
With no objection to true liberty,
Except that it would make the nations
          free.
How well the imperial dandy prates of
          peace!
How fain, if Greeks would be his slaves,
          free Greece!   445
How nobly gave he back the Poles their
          Diet,
Then told pugnacious Poland to be quiet!
How kindly would he send the mild
          Ukraine,
With all her pleasant Pulks, to lecture
          Spain!
How royally show off in proud Madrid
His goodly person, from the South long
          hid!   451
A blessing cheaply purchased, the world
          knows,
By having Muscovites for friends or foes.
Proceed, thou namesake of great Philip's
          son!
La Harpe, thine Aristotle, beckons on;
And that which Scythia was to him of
          yore   456
Find with thy Scythians on Iberia's shore.
Yet think upon, thou somewhat aged
          youth,
Thy predecessor on the banks of Pruth;
Thou hast to aid thee, should his lot be
          thine,   460
Many an old woman, but no Catherine.
Spain, too, hath rocks, and rivers, and
          defiles—
The bear may rush into the lion's toils.
Fatal to Goths are Xeres' sunny fields;
Think'st thou to thee Napoleon's victor
          yields?   465

Better reclaim thy deserts, turn thy swords
To ploughshares, shave and wash thy
    Bashkir hordes,
Redeem thy realms from slavery and the
    knout,
Than follow headlong in the fatal route,
To infest the clime whose skies and laws
    are pure   470
With thy foul legions. Spain wants no
    manure:
Her soil is fertile, but she feeds no foe:
Her vultures, too, were gorged not long ago;
And wouldst thou furnish them with
    fresher prey?   474
Alas! thou wilt not conquer, but purvey.
I am Diogenes, though Russ and Hun
Stand between mine and many a myriad's
    sun;
But were I not Diogenes, I'd wander
Rather a worm than *such* an Alexander!
Be slaves who will, the cynic shall be
    free;   480
His tub hath tougher walls than Sinopè:
Still will he hold his lantern up to scan
The face of monarchs for an 'honest man.'

XI

And what doth Gaul, the all-prolific land
Of *ne plus ultra* ultras and their band
Of mercenaries? and her noisy chambers
And tribune, which each orator first
    clambers
Before he finds a voice, and when 'tis
    found,
Hears 'the lie' echo for his answer round?
Our British Commons sometimes deign to
    'hear!'   490
A Gallic senate hath more tongue than ear;
Even Constant, their sole master of debate,
Must fight next day his speech to vindicate.
But this costs little to true Franks, who'd
    rather   494
Combat than listen, were it to their father.
What is the simple standing of a shot,
To listening long, and interrupting not?
Though this was not the method of old
    Rome,
When Tully fulmined o'er each vocal
    dome,
Demosthenes has sanction'd the trans-
    action,   500
In saying eloquence meant 'Action,
    action!'

XII

But where's the monarch? hath he dined?
    or yet
Groans beneath indigestion's heavy debt?
Have revolutionary pâtés risen,
And turn'd the royal entrails to a prison?
Have discontented movements stirr'd the
    troops?   506
Or have *no* movements follow'd traitorous
    soups?

Have Carbonaro cooks not carbonadoed
Each course enough! or doctors dire dis-
    suaded   509
Repletion? Ah! in thy dejected looks
I read all France's treason in her cooks!
Good classic Louis! is it, canst thou say,
Desirable to be the 'Desiré'?
Why wouldst thou leave calm Hartwell's
    green abode,
Apician table, and Horatian ode,   515
To rule a people who will not be ruled,
And love much rather to be scourged than
    school'd?
Ah! thine was not the temper or the taste
For thrones; the table sees thee better
    placed:
A mild Epicurean, form'd, at best,   520
To be a kind host and as good a guest,
To talk of letters, and to know by heart
One *half* the poet's, *all* the gourmand's
    art:
A scholar always, now and then a wit,
And gentle when digestion may permit;—
But not to govern lands enslaved or free;
The gout was martyrdom enough for thee.

XIII

Shall noble Albion pass without a phrase
From a bold Briton in her wonted praise?
'Arts, arms, and George, and glory, and
    the isles,   530
And happy Britain, wealth, and Free-
    dom's smiles,
White cliffs, that held invasion far aloof,
Contented subjects, all alike tax-proof,
Proud Wellington, with eagle beak so
    curl'd,
That nose, the hook where he suspends
    the world!   535
And Waterloo, and trade, and——(hush!
    not yet
A syllable of imposts or of debt)——
And ne'er (enough) lamented Castlereagh,
Whose penknife slit a goose-quill t' other
    day—
And "pilots who have weather'd every
    storm"—   540
(But, no, not even for rhyme's sake, name
    Reform).'
These are the themes thus sung so oft
    before,
Methinks we need not sing them any more;
Found in so many volumes far and
    near,
There's no occasion you should find them
    here.   545
Yet something may remain perchance to
    chime
With reason, and what's stranger still,
    with rhyme.
Even this thy genius, Canning! may per-
    mit,
Who, bred a statesman, still wast born a
    wit,

And never, even in that dull House,
  couldst tame   550
To unleaven'd prose thine own poetic
  flame;
Our last, our best, our only orator,
Even I can praise thee—Tories do no
  more:
Nay, not so much;—they hate thee, man,
  because
Thy spirit less upholds them than it awes.
The hounds will gather to their huntsman's
  hollo,   556
And where he leads the duteous pack will
  follow;
But not for love mistake their yelling cry;
Their yelp for game is not an eulogy;
Less faithful far than the four-footed
  pack,   560
A dubious scent would lure the bipeds
  back,
Thy saddle-girths are not yet quite secure,
Nor royal stallion's feet extremely sure;
The unwieldy old white horse is apt at last
To stumble, kick, and now and then stick
  fast   565
With his great self and rider in the mud;
But what of that? the animal shows blood.

XIV

Alas, the country! how shall tongue or pen
Bewail her now _un_country gentlemen?
The last to bid the cry of warfare cease,
The first to make a malady of peace. 571
For what were all these country patriots
  born?
To hunt, and vote, and raise the price of
  corn?
But corn, like every mortal thing, must fall,
Kings, conquerors, and markets most of
  all.   575
And must ye fall with every ear of grain?
Why would you trouble Buonaparté's
  reign?
He was your great Triptolemus; his vices
Destroy'd but realms, and still maintain'd
  your prices;   579
He amplified to every lord's content
The grand agrarian alchymy, high _rent_.
Why did the tyrant stumble on the Tartars,
And lower wheat to such desponding
  quarters?
Why did you chain him on yon isle so lone?
The man was worth much more upon his
  throne.   585
True, blood and treasure boundlessly were
  spilt,
But what of that? the Gaul may bear the
  guilt;
But bread was high, the farmer paid his
  way,
And acres told upon the appointed day.
But where is now the goodly audit ale?
The purse-proud tenant, never known to
  fail?   591

The farm which never yet was left on
  hand?
The marsh reclaim'd to most improving
  land?
The impatient hope of the expiring lease?
The doubling rental? What an evil's
  peace!   595
In vain the prize excites the ploughman's
  skill,
In vain the Commons pass their patriot
  bill;
The _landed interest_—(you may understand
The phrase much better leaving out the
  land)—
The land self-interest groans from shore to
  shore,   600
For fear that plenty should attain the poor.
Up, up again, ye rents! exalt your notes,
Or else the ministry will lose their votes,
And patriotism, so delicately nice,
Her loaves will lower to the market price;
For ah! 'the loaves and fishes,' once so
  high,   606
Are gone—their oven closed, their ocean
  dry,
And nought remains of all the millions
  spent,
Excepting to grow moderate and content.
They who are not so, _had_ their turn—and
  turn   610
About still flows from Fortune's equal
  urn;
Now let their virtue be its own reward,
And share the blessings which themselves
  prepared.
See these inglorious Cincinnati swarm,
Farmers of war, dictators of the farm;
Their ploughshare was the sword in hire-
  ling hands,   616
Their fields manured by gore of other
  lands;
Safe in their barns, these Sabine tillers sent
Their brethren out to battle—why? for
  rent!
Year after year they voted cent. per cent.,
Blood, sweat, and tear-wrung millions—
  why? for rent!   621
They roar'd, they dined, they drank, they
  swore they meant
To die for England—why then live?—for
  rent!
The peace has made one general malcon-
  tent
Of these high-market patriots; war was
  rent!   625
Their love of country, millions all mis-
  spent,
How reconcile? by reconciling rent!
And will they not repay the treasures lent?
No: down with everything, and up with
  rent!
Their good, ill, health, wealth, joy, or dis-
  content,   630
Being, end, aim, religion—rent, rent, rent!

Thou sold'st thy birthright, Esau! for a
mess;
Thou shouldst have gotten more, or eaten
less;
Now thou hast swill'd thy pottage, thy
demands
Are idle; Israel says the bargain stands.
Such, landlords! was your appetite for
war,   636
And gorged with blood, you grumble at a
scar!
What! would they spread their earthquake
even o'er cash?
And when land crumbles, bid firm paper
crash?
So rent may rise, bid bank and nation
fall,   640
And found on 'Change a *Fundling* Hos-
pital?
Lo, Mother Church, while all religion
writhes,
Like Niobe, weeps o'er her offspring,
Tithes;
The prelates go to—where the saints have
gone,   644
And proud pluralities subside to one;
Church, state, and faction wrestle in the
dark,
Toss'd by the deluge in their common ark.
Shorn of her bishops, banks, and divi-
dends,
Another Babel soars—but Britain ends.
And why? to pamper the self-seeking
wants,   650
And prop the hill of these agrarian ants.
'Go to these ants, thou sluggard, and be
wise;'
Admire their patience through each sacri-
fice,
Till taught to feel the lesson of their pride,
The price of taxes and of homicide;   655
Admire their justice, which would fain
deny
The debt of nations:—pray, *who made it
high?*

xv

Or turn to sail between those shifting
rocks,
The new Symplegades—the crushing
Stocks,
Where Midas might again his wish be-
hold   660
In real paper or imagined gold.
That magic palace of Alcina shows
More wealth than Britain ever had to lose,
Were all her atoms of unleaven'd ore,
And all her pebbles from Pactolus' shore.
There Fortune plays, while Rumour holds
the stake,   666
And the world trembles to bid brokers
break.
How rich is Britain! not indeed in mines,
Or peace or plenty, corn or oil, or wines;

No land of Canaan, full of milk and
honey,   670
Nor (save in paper shekels) ready money:
But let us not to own the truth refuse,
Was ever Christian land so rich in Jews?
Those parted with their teeth to good
King John,
And now, ye kings! they kindly draw your
own;   675
All states, all things, all sovereigns they
control,
And waft a loan 'from Indus to the pole.'
The banker, broker, baron, brethren,
speed
To aid these bankrupt tyrants in their need.
Nor these alone; Columbia feels no less
Fresh speculations follow each success;
And philanthropic Israel deigns to drain
Her mild per-centage from exhausted
Spain.
Not without Abraham's seed can Russia
march;
'Tis gold, not steel, that rears the con-
queror's arch.   685
Two Jews, a chosen people, can command
In every realm their scripture-promised
land:—
Two Jews keep down the Romans, and up-
hold
The accursed Hun, more brutal than of
old: 689
Two Jews—but not Samaritans—direct
The world, with all the spirit of their sect.
What is the happiness of earth to them?
A congress forms their 'New Jerusalem,'
Where baronies and orders both invite—
Oh, holy Abraham! dost thou see the
sight?   695
Thy followers mingling with these royal
swine,
Who spit not 'on their Jewish gaberdine,'
But honour them as portion of the show—
(Where now, oh Pope! is thy forsaken
toe?
Could it not favour Judah with some
kicks?   700
Or has it ceased to 'kick against the
pricks?')
On Shylock's shore behold them stand
afresh,
To cut from nations' hearts their 'pound
of flesh.'

xvi

Strange sight this Congress! destined to
unite   704
All that's incongruous, all that's opposite.
I speak not of the sovereigns—they're
alike,
A common coin as ever mint could strike;
But those who sway the puppets, pull the
strings,
Have more of motley than their heavy
kings.

Jews, authors, generals, charlatans, com-
bine,   710
While Europe wonders at the vast design:
There Metternich, power's foremost para-
site,
Cajoles; there Wellington forgets to fight;
There Chateaubriand forms new books of
martyrs;
And subtle Greeks intrigue for stupid
Tartars;   715
There Montmorenci, the sworn foe to
charters,
Turns a diplomatist of great éclat,
To furnish articles for the 'Débats;'
Of war so certain—yet not quite so sure
As his dismissal in the 'Moniteur.'   720
Alas! how could his cabinet thus err!
Can peace be worth an ultra-minister?
He falls indeed, perhaps to rise again,
'Almost as quickly as he conquer'd Spain.'

XVII

Enough of this—a sight more mournful
woos   725
The averted eye of the reluctant muse.
The imperial daughter, the imperial bride,
The imperial victim—sacrifice to pride;
The mother of the hero's hope, the boy,
The young Astyanax of modern Troy;   730
The still pale shadow of the loftiest queen
That earth has yet to see, or e'er hath seen;
She flits amidst the phantoms of the hour,
The theme of pity, and the wreck of power.
Oh, cruel mockery! Could not Austria
spare   735
A daughter? What did France's widow
there?
Her fitter place was by St. Helen's wave,
Her only throne is in Napoleon's grave.
But, no—she still must hold a petty reign,
Flank'd by her formidable chamberlain;
The martial Argus, whose not hundred
eyes   741
Must watch her through these paltry page-
antries.
What though she share no more, and
shared in vain,
A sway surpassing that of Charlemagne,
Which swept from Moscow to the south-
ern seas!   745
Yet still she rules the pastoral realm of
cheese,

Where Parma views the traveller resort,
To note the trappings of her mimic court.
But she appears! Verona sees her shorn
Of all her beams—while nations gaze and
mourn—   750
Ere yet her husband's ashes have had time
To chill in their inhospitable clime;
(If e'er those awful ashes can grow cold;—
But no,—their embers soon will burst the
mould;)
She comes!—the Andromache (but not
Racine's,   755
Nor Homer's,)—Lo! on Pyrrhus' arm she
leans!
Yes! the right arm, yet red from Water-
loo,
Which cut her lord's half-shatter'd sceptre
through,
Is offer'd and accepted? Could a slave
Do more? or less?—and he in his new
grave!   760
Her eye, her cheek, betray no inward
strife,
And the ex-empress grows as ex a wife!
So much for human ties in royal breasts!
Why spare men's feelings, when their own
are jests?

XVIII

But, tired of foreign follies, I turn home,
And sketch the group—the picture's yet
to come,   766
My muse 'gan weep, but, ere a tear was
spilt,
She caught Sir William Curtis in a kilt!
While throng'd the chiefs of every High-
land clan
To hail their brother, Vich Ian Alder-
man!   770
Guildhall grows Gael, and echoes with
Erse roar,
While all the Common Council cry 'Clay-
more!'
To see proud Albyn's tartans as a belt
Gird the gross sirloin of a city Celt,
She burst into a laughter so extreme,   775
That I awoke—and lo! it was no dream!

Here, reader, will we pause:—if there's no
harm in
This first—you'll have, perhaps, a second
'Carmen.'

CHILDE HAROLD'S PILGRIMAGE

A ROMAUNT

L'UNIVERS est une espèce de livre, dont on n'a lu que la première page quand on n'a vu que son pays. J'en ai feuilleté un assez grand nombre, que j'ai trouvé également mauvaises. Cet examen ne m'a point été infructueux. Je haïssais ma patrie. Toutes les impertinences des peuples divers, parmi lesquels j'ai vécu, m'ont réconcilié avec elle. Quand je n'aurais tiré d'autre bénéfice de mes voyages que celui-là, je n'en regretterais ni les frais ni les fatigues.—LE COSMOPOLITE.

PREFACE TO THE FIRST AND SECOND CANTOS

THE following poem was written, for the most part, amidst the scenes which it attempts to describe. It was begun in Albania; and the parts relative to Spain and Portugal were composed from the author's observations in those countries. Thus much it may be necessary to state for the correctness of the descriptions. The scenes attempted to be sketched are in Spain, Portugal, Epirus, Acarnania, and Greece. There, for the present, the poem stops; its reception will determine whether the author may venture to conduct his readers to the capital of the East, through Ionia and Phrygia: these two cantos are merely experimental.

A fictitious character is introduced for the sake of giving some connexion to the piece; which, however, makes no pretension to regularity. It has been suggested to me by friends, on whose opinions I set a high value, that in this fictitious character, 'Childe Harold,' I may incur the suspicion of having intended some real personage: this I beg leave, once for all, to disclaim—Harold is the child of imagination, for the purpose I have stated. In some very trivial particulars, and those merely local, there might be grounds for such a notion; but in the main points, I should hope, none whatever.

It is almost superfluous to mention that the appellation 'Childe,' as 'Childe Waters,' 'Childe Childers,' &c., is used as more consonant with the old structure of versification which I have adopted. The 'Good Night,' in the beginning of the first canto, was suggested by 'Lord Maxwell's Good Night,' in the Border Minstrelsy, edited by Mr. Scott.

With the different poems which have been published on Spanish subjects, there may be found some slight coincidence in the first part, which treats of the Peninsula, but it can only be casual; as, with the exception of a few concluding stanzas, the whole of this poem was written in the Levant.

The stanza of Spenser, according to one of our most successful poets, admits of every variety. Dr. Beattie makes the following observation:—'Not long ago, I began a poem in the style and stanza of Spenser, in which I propose to give full scope to my inclination, and be either droll or pathetic, descriptive or sentimental, tender or satirical, as the humour strikes me; for, if I mistake not, the measure which I have adopted admits equally of all these kinds of composition'.*—Strengthened in my opinion by such authority, and by the example of some in the highest order of Italian poets, I shall make no apology for attempts at similar variations in the following composition; satisfied that if they are unsuccessful, their failure must be in the execution, rather than in the design, sanctioned by the practice of Ariosto, Thomson, and Beattie.

LONDON, February, 1812.

ADDITION TO THE PREFACE

I HAVE now waited till almost all our periodical journals have distributed their usual portion of criticism. To the justice of the generality of their criticisms I have nothing to object: it would ill become me to quarrel with their very slight degree of censure, when, perhaps, if they had been less kind they had been more candid. Returning, therefore, to all and each my best thanks for their liberality, on one point alone shall I venture an observation. Amongst the many objections justly urged to the very indifferent character of the 'vagrant Childe' (whom, notwithstanding many hints to the contrary, I still maintain to be a fictitious personage), it has been stated, that, besides the anachronism, he is very *unknightly*, as the times of the Knights were times of Love, Honour, and so forth. Now, it so happens that the good old times, when 'l'amour du bon vieux tems, l'amour antique,' flourished, were the most profligate of all possible centuries. Those who have any doubts on this subject may consult Sainte-Palaye, *passim*, and more particularly vol. ii. p. 69. The vows of chivalry were no better kept than any other vows whatsoever; and the songs of the Troubadours were not more decent, and certainly were much less refined, than those of Ovid. The 'Cours d'amour, parlemens d'amour, ou de courtesie et de gentilesse' had much more of love than of courtesy or gentleness. See Rolland on the same subject with Sainte-Palaye. Whatever other objection may be urged to that most unamiable personage Childe Harold, he was so far perfectly knightly in his attributes—'No waiter, but a knight templar†.' By the by, I fear that Sir Tristrem and Sir Lancelot were no better than they should be, although very poetical personages and true knights 'sans peur,' though not 'sans reproche.' If the story of the institution of the 'Garter' be not a fable, the knights of that order have for several centuries borne the badge of a Countess of Salisbury, of indifferent memory. So much for chivalry. Burke need not have regretted that its days are over, though Marie-Antoinette was quite as chaste as most of those in whose honour lances were shivered, and knights unhorsed.

Before the days of Bayard, and down to those of Sir Joseph Banks (the most chaste and celebrated of ancient and modern times), few exceptions will be found to this statement; and I fear a little investigation will teach us not to regret these monstrous mummeries of the middle ages.

I now leave 'Childe Harold' to live his day, such as he is; it had been more agreeable, and certainly

* Beattie's Letters.   † The Rovers, or the Double Arrangement.

more easy, to have drawn an amiable character. It had been easy to varnish over his faults, to make him do more and express less, but he never was intended as an example, further than to show, that early perversion of mind and morals leads to satiety of past pleasures and disappointment in new ones, and that even the beauties of nature and the stimulus of travel (except ambition, the most powerful of all excitements) are lost on a soul so constituted, or rather misdirected. Had I proceeded with the poem, this character would have deepened as he drew to the close; for the outline which I once meant to fill up for him was, with some exceptions, the sketch of a modern Timon, perhaps a poetical Zeluco.

LONDON, 1813.

TO IANTHE

Not in those climes where I have late
    been straying,
Though Beauty long hath there been
    matchless deem'd;
Not in those visions to the heart dis-
    playing
Forms which it sighs but to have only
    dream'd,
Hath aught like thee in truth or fancy
    seem'd: 5
Nor, having seen thee, shall I vainly seek
To paint those charms which varied as
    they beam'd—
To such as see thee not my words were
    weak;
To those who gaze on thee what language
    could they speak?

Ah! may'st thou ever be what now thou
    art,   10
Nor unbeseem the promise of thy spring,
As fair in form, as warm yet pure in
    heart,
Love's image upon earth without his
    wing,
And guileless beyond Hope's imagining!
And surely she who now so fondly rears
Thy youth, in thee, thus hourly bright-
    ening,   16
Beholds the rainbow of her future years,
Before whose heavenly hues all sorrow
    disappears.

Young Peri of the West!—'tis well for me
My years already doubly number thine;
My loveless eye unmoved may gaze on
    thee,   21
And safely view thy ripening beauties
    shine;

Happy, I ne'er shall see them in decline;
Happier, that while all younger hearts
    shall bleed,
Mine shall escape the doom thine eyes
    assign   25
To those whose admiration shall succeed,
But mix'd with pangs to Love's even love-
    liest hours decreed.

Oh! let that eye, which, wild as the
    Gazelle's,
Now brightly bold or beautifully shy,
Wins as it wanders, dazzles where it
    dwells,   30
Glance o'er this page, nor to my verse
    deny
That smile for which my breast might
    vainly sigh
Could I to thee be ever more than friend:
This much, dear maid, accord; nor
    question why
To one so young my strain I would
    commend,   35
But bid me with my wreath one matchless
    lily blend.

Such is thy name with this my verse
    entwined;
And long as kinder eyes a look shall cast
On Harold's page, Ianthe's here en-
    shrined
Shall thus be first beheld, forgotten last:
My days once number'd, should this
    homage past   41
Attract thy fairy fingers near the lyre
Of him who hail'd thee loveliest, as
    thou wast,
Such is the most my memory may de-
    sire;
Though more than Hope can claim, could
    Friendship less require?   45

CHILDE HAROLD'S PILGRIMAGE

CANTO THE FIRST

I

Oh, thou! in Hellas deem'd of heavenly
    birth,
Muse! form'd or fabled at the minstrel's
    will!
Since shamed full oft by later lyres on
    earth,
Mine dares not call thee from thy sacred
    hill:

Yet there I've wander'd by thy vaunted
    rill;
Yes! sigh'd o'er Delphi's long deserted
    shrine,
Where, save that feeble fountain, all is
    still;
Nor mote my shell awake the weary
    Nine
To grace so plain a tale—this lowly lay of
    mine.

II

Whilome in Albion's isle there dwelt a
    youth,
Who ne in virtue's ways did take de-
    light;
But spent his days in riot most uncouth,
And vex'd with mirth the drowsy ear of
    Night.
Ah me! in sooth he was a shameless
    wight,
Sore given to revel and ungodly glee;
Few earthly things found favour in his
    sight
Save concubines and carnal companie,
And flaunting wassailers of high and low
    degree.

III

Childe Harold was he hight:—but
    whence his name
And lineage long, it suits me not to say;
Suffice it, that perchance they were of
    fame,
And had been glorious in another day:
But one sad losel soils a name for aye,
However mighty in the olden time;
Nor all that heralds rake from coffin'd
    clay,
Nor florid prose, nor honeyed lies of
    rhyme,
Can blazon evil deeds, or consecrate a
    crime.

IV

Childe Harold bask'd him in the noon-
    tide sun,
Disporting there like any other fly;
Nor deem'd before his little day was
    done
One blast might chill him into misery.
But long ere scarce a third of his pass'd
    by,
Worse than adversity the Childe befell;
He felt the fulness of satiety:
Then loathed he in his native land to
    dwell,
Which seem'd to him more lone than
    Eremite's sad cell.

V

For he through Sin's long labyrinth had
    run,
Nor made atonement when he did
    amiss,
Had sigh'd to many though he loved but
    one,
And that loved one, alas! could ne'er
    be his.
Ah, happy she! to 'scape from him
    whose kiss
Had been pollution unto aught so chaste;
Who soon had left her charms for
    vulgar bliss,

And spoil'd her goodly lands to gild his
    waste,
Nor calm domestic peace had ever deign'd
    to taste.

VI

And now Childe Harold was sore sick
    at heart,
And from his fellow bacchanals would
    flee;
'Tis said, at times the sullen tear would
    start,
But Pride congeal'd the drop within his ee:
Apart he stalk'd in joyless reverie,
And from his native land resolved to go,
And visit scorching climes beyond the
    sea;
With pleasure drugg'd, he almost long'd
    for woe,
And e'en for change of scene would seek
    the shades below.

VII

The Childe departed from his father's
    hall:
It was a vast and venerable pile;
So old, it seemèd only not to fail,
Yet strength was pillar'd in each massy
    aisle.
Monastic dome! condemn'd to uses vile!
Where Superstition once had made her
    den
Now Paphian girls were known to sing
    and smile;
And monks might deem their time was
    come agen,
If ancient tales say true, nor wrong these
    holy men.

VIII

Yet oft-times in his maddest mirthful
    mood
Strange pangs would flash along Childe
    Harold's brow
As if the memory of some deadly feud
Or disappointed passion lurk'd below:
But this none knew, nor haply cared to
    know;
For his was not that open, artless soul
That feels relief by bidding sorrow flow,
Nor sought he friend to counsel or
    condole,
Whate'er this grief mote be, which he
    could not control.

IX

And none did love him: though to hall
    and bower
He gather'd revellers from far and near,
He knew them flatt'rers of the festal
    hour;
The heartless parasites of present cheer.

Yea! none did love him—not his lemans
  dear—
But pomp and power alone are woman's
  care,
And where these are light Eros finds a
  feere;
Maidens, like moths, are ever caught by
  glare,
And Mammon wins his way where
  Seraphs might despair.

X

Childe Harold had a mother—not for-
  got,
Though parting from that mother he
  did shun;
A sister whom he loved, but saw her not
Before his weary pilgrimage begun:
If friends he had, he bade adieu to
  none.
Yet deem not thence his breast a breast
  of steel:
Ye, who have known what 'tis to dote
  upon
A few dear objects, will in sadness feel
Such partings break the heart they fondly
  hope to heal.

XI

His house, his home, his heritage, his
  lands,
The laughing dames in whom he did
  delight,
Whose large blue eyes, fair locks, and
  snowy hands,
Might shake the saintship of an an-
  chorite,
And long had fed his youthful appetite;
His goblets brimm'd with every costly
  wine,
And all that mote to luxury invite,
Without a sigh he left, to cross the
  brine,
And traverse Paynim shores, and pass
  Earth's central line.

XII

The sails were fill'd, and fair the light
  winds blew,
As glad to waft him from his native
  home;
And fast the white rocks faded from his
  view,
And soon were lost in circumambient
  foam:
And then, it may be, of his wish to roam
Repented he, but in his bosom slept
The silent thought, nor from his lips did
  come
One word of wail, whilst others sate and
  wept,
And to the reckless gales unmanly moan-
  ing kept.

XIII

But when the sun was sinking in the sea
He seized his harp, which he at times
  could string,
And strike, albeit with untaught melody,
When deem'd he no strange ear was
  listening:
And now his fingers o'er it he did fling,
And tuned his farewell in the dim
  twilight.
While flew the vessel on her snowy wing,
And fleeting shores receded from his
  sight,
Thus to the elements he pour'd his last
  'Good Night.'

1

ADIEU, adieu! my native shore
  Fades o'er the waters blue;
The night-winds sigh, the breakers roar,
  And shrieks the wild sea-mew.
Yon sun that sets upon the sea
  We follow in his flight;
Farewell awhile to him and thee,
  My native Land—Good Night!

2

A few short hours and he will rise
  To give the morrow birth;
And I shall hail the main and skies,
  But not my mother earth.
Deserted is my own good hall,
  Its hearth is desolate;
Wild weeds are gathering on the wall;
  My dog howls at the gate.

3

'Come hither, hither, my little page!
  Why dost thou weep and wail?
Or dost thou dread the billows' rage,
  Or tremble at the gale?
But dash the tear-drop from thine eye;
  Our ship is swift and strong:
Our fleetest falcon scarce can fly
  More merrily along.'

4

'Let winds be shrill, let waves roll high,
  I fear not wave nor wind:
Yet marvel not, Sir Childe, that I
  Am sorrowful in mind;
For I have from my father gone,
  A mother whom I love,
And have no friend, save these alone,
  But thee—and one above.

5

'My father bless'd me fervently,
  Yet did not much complain;
But sorely will my mother sigh
  Till I come back again.'—
'Enough, enough, my little lad!
  Such tears become thine eye;
If I thy guileless bosom had,
  Mine own would not be dry.

6

'Come hither, hither, my staunch yeoman,
  Why dost thou look so pale?
Or dost thou dread a French foeman?
  Or shiver at the gale?'—
'Deem'st thou I tremble for my life?
  Sir Childe, I'm not so weak;
But thinking on an absent wife
  Will blanch a faithful cheek.

7

'My spouse and boys dwell near thy hall,
  Along the bordering lake,
And when they on their father call,
  What answer shall she make?'—
'Enough, enough, my yeoman good,
  Thy grief let none gainsay;
But I, who am of lighter mood,
  Will laugh to flee away.'

8

For who would trust the seeming sighs
  Of wife or paramour?
Fresh feeres will dry the bright blue eyes
  We late saw streaming o'er.
For pleasures past I do not grieve,
  Nor perils gathering near;
My greatest grief is that I leave
  No thing that claims a tear.

9

And now I'm in the world alone,
  Upon the wide, wide sea:
But why should I for others groan,
  When none will sigh for me?
Perchance my dog will whine in vain,
  Till fed by stranger hands;
But long ere I come back again
  He'd tear me where he stands.

10

With thee, my bark, I'll swiftly go
  Athwart the foaming brine;
Nor care what land thou bear'st me to,
  So not again to mine.
Welcome, welcome, ye dark-blue waves!
  And when you fail my sight,
Welcome, ye deserts and ye caves!
  My native Land—Good Night!

XIV

On, on the vessel flies, the land is gone,
And winds are rude in Biscay's sleepless
  bay.
Four days are sped, but with the fifth,
  anon,
New shores descried make every bosom
  gay;
And Cintra's mountain greets them on
  their way,
And Tagus dashing onward to the deep,
His fabled golden tribute bent to pay;

And soon on board the Lusian pilots
  leap,
And steer 'twixt fertile shores where yet
  few rustics reap.

XV

Oh, Christ! it is a goodly sight to see
What Heaven hath done for this delicious land:
What fruits of fragrance blush on every
  tree!
What goodly prospects o'er the hills
  expand!
But man would mar them with an impious hand:
And when the Almighty lifts his fiercest
  scourge
'Gainst those who most transgress his
  high command,
With treble vengeance will his hot
  shafts urge
Gaul's locust host, and earth from fellest
  foemen purge.

XVI

What beauties doth Lisboa first unfold!
Her image floating on that noble tide,
Which poets vainly pave with sands of
  gold,
But now whereon a thousand keels did
  ride
Of mighty strength, since Albion was
  allied,
And to the Lusians did her aid afford:
A nation swoln with ignorance and
  pride,
Who lick yet loathe the hand that waves
  the sword
To save them from the wrath of Gaul's
  unsparing lord.

XVII

But whoso entereth within this town,
That, sheening far, celestial seems to be,
Disconsolate will wander up and down,
'Mid many things unsightly to strange
  ee;
For hut and palace show like filthily:
The dingy denizens are rear'd in dirt;
Ne personage of high or mean degree
Doth care for cleanness of surtout or
  shirt;
Though shent with Egypt's plague, un-
  kempt, unwash'd, unhurt.

XVIII

Poor, paltry slaves! yet born 'midst
  noblest scenes—
Why, Nature, waste thy wonders on
  such men?
Lo! Cintra's glorious Eden intervenes
In variegated maze of mount and glen.

Ah me! what hand can pencil guide, or
pen,
To follow half on which the eye dilates
Through views more dazzling unto
mortal ken
Than those whereof such things the bard
relates,
Who to the awe-struck world unlock'd
Elysium's gates?

XIX

The horrid crags, by toppling convent
crown'd,
The cork-trees hoar that clothe the
shaggy steep,
The mountain-moss by scorching skies
imbrown'd,
The sunken glen, whose sunless shrubs
must weep,
The tender azure of the unruffled deep,
The orange tints that gild the greenest
bough,
The torrents that from cliff to valley leap,
The vine on high, the willow branch
below,
Mix'd in one mighty scene, with varied
beauty glow.

XX

Then slowly climb the many-winding
way,
And frequent turn to linger as you go,
From loftier rocks new loveliness survey,
And rest ye at 'Our Lady's house of
woe;'
Where frugal monks their little relics
show,
And sundry legends to the stranger tell:
Here impious men have punish'd been,
and lo!
Deep in yon cave Honorius long did
dwell,
In hope to merit Heaven by making earth
a Hell.

XXI

And here and there, as up the crags you
spring,
Mark many rude-carved crosses near
the path:
Yet deem not these devotion's offering—
These are memorials frail of murderous
wrath:
For wheresoe'er the shrieking victim
hath
Pour'd forth his blood beneath the
assassin's knife,
Some hand erects a cross of mouldering
lath;
And grove and glen with thousand such
are rife
Throughout this purple land, where law
secures not life.

XXII

On sloping mounds, or in the vale beneath,
Are domes where whilome kings did
make repair;
But now the wild flowers round them
only breathe;
Yet ruin'd splendour still is lingering
there.
And yonder towers the Prince's palace
fair:
There thou too, Vathek! England's
wealthiest son,
Once form'd thy Paradise, as not aware
When wanton Wealth her mightiest
deeds hath done,
Meek Peace voluptuous lures was ever
wont to shun.

XXIII

Here didst thou dwell, here schemes of
pleasure plan,
Beneath yon mountain's ever beauteous
brow:
But now, as if a thing unblest by
Man,
Thy fairy dwelling is as lone as thou!
Here giant weeds a passage scarce allow
To halls deserted, portals gaping wide:
Fresh lessons to the thinking bosom,
how
Vain are the pleasaunces on earth sup-
plied;
Swept into wrecks anon by Time's un-
gentle tide!

XXIV

Behold the hall where chiefs were late
convened!
Oh! dome displeasing unto British
eye!
With diadem hight foolscap, lo! a fiend,
A little fiend that scoffs incessantly,
There sits in parchment robe array'd,
and by
His side is hung a seal and sable scroll,
Where blazon'd glare names known to
chivalry,
And sundry signatures adorn the roll,
Whereat the Urchin points and laughs
with all his soul.

XXV

Convention is the dwarfish demon
styled
That foil'd the knights in Marialva's
dome:
Of brains (if brains they had) he them
beguiled,
And turned a nation's shallow joy to
gloom.
Here Folly dash'd to earth the victor's
plume,

And Policy regain'd what arms had lost:
For chiefs like ours in vain may laurels
　　bloom!
Woe to the conqu'ring, not the con-
　　quer'd host,
Since baffled Triumph droops on Lusi-
　　tania's coast!

XXVI

And ever since that martial synod met,
Britannia sickens, Cintra! at thy name;
And folks in office at the mention fret,
And fain would blush, if blush they
　　could, for shame.
How will posterity the deed proclaim!
Will not our own and fellow nations sneer,
To view these champions cheated of
　　their fame,
By foes in fight o'erthrown, yet victors
　　here,
Where Scorn her finger points through
　　many a coming year?

XXVII

So deem'd the Childe, as o'er the moun-
　　tains he
Did take his way in solitary guise:
Sweet was the scene, yet soon he thought
　　to flee,
More restless than the swallow in the
　　skies:
Though here awhile he learn'd to mora-
　　lize,
For Meditation fix'd at times on him;
And conscious Reason whisper'd to
　　despise
His early youth, misspent in maddest
　　whim;
But as he gazed on truth his aching eyes
　　grew dim.

XXVIII

To horse! to horse! he quits, for ever
　　quits
A scene of peace, though soothing to
　　his soul:
Again he rouses from his moping fits,
But seeks not now the harlot and the
　　bowl.
Onward he flies, nor fix'd as yet the goal
Where he shall rest him on his pilgrim-
　　age;
And o'er him many changing scenes
　　must roll
Ere toil his thirst for travel can assuage,
Or he shall calm his breast, or learn ex-
　　perience sage.

XXIX

Yet Mafra shall one moment claim delay,
Where dwelt of yore the Lusians' luck-
　　less queen;
And church and court did mingle their
　　array,
And mass and revel were alternate seen;

Lordlings and freres—ill-sorted fry I
　　ween!
But here the Babylonian whore hath
　　built
A dome, where flaunts she in such
　　glorious sheen,
That men forget the blood which she
　　hath spilt,
And bow the knee to Pomp that loves to
　　varnish guilt.

XXX

O'er vales that teem with fruits, roman-
　　tic hills,
(Oh, that such hills upheld a free-born
　　race!)
Whereon to gaze the eye with joyaunce
　　fills,
Childe Harold wends through many a
　　pleasant place.
Though sluggards deem it but a foolish
　　chase,
And marvel men should quit their easy
　　chair,
The toilsome way, and long, long
　　league to trace,
Oh! there is sweetness in the mountain
　　air,
And life, that bloated Ease can never hope
　　to share.

XXXI

More bleak to view the hills at length
　　recede,
And, less luxuriant, smoother vales ex-
　　tend;
Immense horizon-bounded plains succeed!
Far as the eye discerns, withouten end,
Spain's realms appear whereon her
　　shepherds tend
Flocks, whose rich fleece right well the
　　trader knows—
Now must the pastor's arm his lambs
　　defend:
For Spain is compass'd by unyielding
　　foes,
And all must shield their all, or share Sub-
　　jection's woes.

XXXII

Where Lusitania and her Sister meet,
Deem ye what bounds the rival realms
　　divide?
Or ere the jealous queens of nations
　　greet,
Doth Tayo interpose his mighty tide?
Or dark Sierras rise in craggy pride?
Or fence of art, like China's vasty
　　wall?—
Ne barrier wall, ne river deep and wide,
Ne horrid crags, nor mountains dark
　　and tall,
Rise like the rocks that part Hispania's
　　land from Gaul:

XXXIII

But these between a silver streamlet
glides,
And scarce a name distinguisheth the
brook,
Though rival kingdoms press its verdant
sides.
Here leans the idle shepherd on his
crook,
And vacant on the rippling waves doth
look,
That peaceful still 'twixt bitterest foemen flow;
For proud each peasant as the noblest
duke:
Well doth the Spanish hind the difference know
'Twixt him and Lusian slave, the lowest of
the low.

XXXIV

But ere the mingling bounds have far
been pass'd,
Dark Guadiana rolls his power along
In sullen billows, murmuring and vast,
So noted ancient roundelays among.
Whilome upon his banks did legions
throng
Of Moor and Knight, in mailèd splen-
dour drest:
Here ceased the swift their race, here
sunk the strong;
The Paynim turban and the Christian crest
Mix'd on the bleeding stream, by floating
hosts oppress'd.

XXXV

Oh, lovely Spain! renown'd, romantic
land!
Where is that standard which Pelagio
bore,
When Cava's traitor-sire first call'd the
band
That dyed thy mountain streams with
Gothic gore?
Where are those bloody banners which
of yore
Waved o'er thy sons, victorious to the
gale,
And drove at last the spoilers to their
shore?
Red gleam'd the cross, and waned the
crescent pale,
While Afric's echoes thrill'd with Moorish
matrons' wail.

XXXVI

Teems not each ditty with the glorious
tale?
Ah! such, alas! the hero's amplest fate!
When granite moulders and when
records fail,
A peasant's plaint prolongs his dubious
date.

Pride! bend thine eye from heaven to
thine estate,
See how the Mighty shrink into a song!
Can Volume, Pillar, Pile preserve thee
great?
Or must thou trust Tradition's simple
tongue,
When Flattery sleeps with thee, and History does thee wrong?

XXXVII

Awake, ye sons of Spain! awake! ad-
vance!
Lo! Chivalry, your ancient goddess,
cries,
But wields not, as of old, her thirsty lance,
Nor shakes her crimson plumage in the
skies:
Now on the smoke of blazing bolts she
flies,
And speaks in thunder through yon en-
gine's roar:
In every peal she calls—'Awake! arise!'
Say, is her voice more feeble than of
yore,
When her war-song was heard on Anda-
lusia's shore?

XXXVIII

Hark! heard you not those hoofs of
dreadful note?
Sounds not the clang of conflict on the
heath?
Saw ye not whom the reeking sabre
smote,
Nor saved your brethren ere they sank
beneath
Tyrants and tyrants' slaves? the fires of
death,
The bale-fires flash on high:—from rock
to rock
Each volley tells that thousands cease
to breathe:
Death rides upon the sulphury Siroc,
Red Battle stamps his foot, and nations
feel the shock.

XXXIX

Lo! where the Giant on the mountain
stands,
His blood-red tresses deep'ning in the
sun,
With death-shot glowing in his fiery
hands,
And eye that scorcheth all it glares
upon;
Restless it rolls, now fix'd, and now anon
Flashing afar,—and at his iron feet
Destruction cowers, to mark what deeds
are done;
For on this morn three potent nations
meet,
To shed before his shrine the blood he
deems most sweet.

186

XL

By Heaven! it is a splendid sight to see
(For one who hath no friend, no brother
    there)
Their rival scarfs of mix'd embroidery,
Their various arms that glitter in the air!
What gallant war-hounds rouse them
    from their lair,
And gnash their fangs, loud yelling for
    the prey!
All join the chase, but few the triumph
    share;
The Grave shall bear the chiefest prize
    away,
And Havoc scarce for joy can number
    their array.

XLI

Three hosts combine to offer sacrifice;
Three tongues prefer strange orisons
    on high;
Three gaudy standards flout the pale
    blue skies;
The shouts are France, Spain, Albion,
    Victory!
The foe, the victim, and the fond ally
That fights for all, but ever fights in vain,
Are met—as if at home they could not
    die—
To feed the crow on Talavera's plain,
And fertilize the field that each pretends
    to gain.

XLII

There shall they rot—Ambition's hon-
    our'd fools!
Yes, Honour decks the turf that wraps
    their clay!
Vain Sophistry! in these behold the
    tools,
The broken tools, that tyrants cast away
By myriads, when they dare to pave their
    way
With human hearts—to what?—a
    dream alone.
Can despots compass aught that hails
    their sway?
Or call with truth one span of earth their
    own,
Save that wherein at last they crumble
    bone by bone?

XLIII

Oh, Albuera! glorious field of grief!
As o'er thy plain the Pilgrim prick'd his
    steed,
Who could foresee thee, in a space so
    brief,
A scene where mingling foes should
    boast and bleed!
Peace to the perish'd! may the warrior's
    meed
And tears of triumph their reward pro-
    long!

Till others fall where other chieftains
    lead
Thy name shall circle round the gaping
    throng,
And shine in worthless lays the theme of
    transient song.

XLIV

Enough of battle's minions! let them
    play
Their game of lives, and barter breath
    for fame:
Fame that will scarce reanimate their
    clay,
Though thousands fall to deck some
    single name.
In sooth 'twere sad to thwart their noble
    aim
Who strike, blest hirelings! for their
    country's good,
And die, that living might have proved
    her shame;
Perish'd, perchance, in some domestic
    feud,
Or in a narrower sphere wild Rapine's
    path pursued.

XLV

Full swiftly Harold wends his lonely
    way
Where proud Sevilla triumphs unsub-
    dued:
Yet is she free—the spoiler's wish'd-for
    prey!
Soon, soon shall Conquest's fiery foot
    intrude,
Blackening her lovely domes with traces
    rude.
Inevitable hour! 'Gainst fate to strive
Where Desolation plants her famish'd
    brood
Is vain, or Ilion, Tyre, might yet sur-
    vive,
And Virtue vanquish all, and murder
    cease to thrive.

XLVI

But all unconscious of the coming
    doom,
The feast, the song, the revel here a-
    bounds;
Strange modes of merriment the hours
    consume,
Nor bleed these patriots with their
    country's wounds;
Nor here War's clarion, but Love's re-
    beck sounds;
Here Folly still his votaries inthrals;
And young-eyed Lewdness walks her
    midnight rounds;
Girt with the silent crimes of Capitals,
Still to the last kind Vice clings to the
    tott'ring walls.

XLVII

Not so the rustic—with his trembling
    mate
He lurks, nor casts his heavy eye afar,
Lest he should view his vineyard desolate,
Blasted below the dun hot breath of war.
No more beneath soft Eve's consenting
    star
Fandango twirls his jocund castanet:
Ah, monarchs! could ye taste the mirth
    ye mar,
Not in the toils of Glory would ye fret;
The hoarse dull drum would sleep, and
    Man be happy yet!

XLVIII

How carols now the lusty muleteer?
Of love, romance, devotion is his lay,
As whilome he was wont the leagues to
    cheer,
His quick bells wildly jingling on the
    way?
No! as he speeds, he chants 'Vivā el
    Rey!'
And checks his song to execrate Godoy,
The royal wittol Charles, and curse the
    day
When first Spain's queen beheld the
    black-eyed boy,
And gore-faced Treason sprung from her
    adulterate joy.

XLIX

On yon long, level plain, at distance
    crown'd
With crags, whereon those Moorish
    turrets rest,
Wide scatter'd hoof-marks dint the
    wounded ground;
And, scathed by fire, the greensward's
    darken'd vest
Tells that the foe was Andalusia's guest:
Here was the camp, the watch-flame,
    and the host,
Here the bold peasant storm'd the
    dragon's nest;
Still does he mark it with triumphant
    boast;
And points to yonder cliffs, which oft
    were won and lost.

L

And whomsoe'er along the path you
    meet
Bears in his cap the badge of crimson
    hue,
Which tells you whom to shun and
    whom to greet.
Woe to the man that walks in public
    view
Without of loyalty this token true:
Sharp is the knife, and sudden is the
    stroke;

And sorely would the Gallic foeman rue,
If subtle poniards, wrapt beneath the
    cloke,
Could blunt the sabre's edge, or clear the
    cannon's smoke.

LI

At every turn Morena's dusky height
Sustains aloft the battery's iron load;
And, far as mortal eye can compass
    sight,
The mountain-howitzer, the broken
    road,
The bristling palisade, the fosse o'er-
    flow'd,
The station'd bands, the never-vacant
    watch,
The magazine in rocky durance stow'd,
The holster'd steed beneath the shed of
    thatch,
The ball-piled pyramid, the ever-blazing
    match,

LII

Portend the deeds to come:—but he
    whose nod
Has tumbled feebler despots from their
    sway,
A moment pauseth ere he lifts the rod;
A little moment deigneth to delay:
Soon will his legions sweep through
    these their way;
The West must own the Scourger of the
    world.
Ah! Spain! how sad will be thy reckon-
    ing day,
When soars Gaul's Vulture, with his
    wings unfurl'd,
And thou shalt view thy sons in crowds to
    Hades hurl'd.

LIII

And must they fall? the young, the
    proud, the brave,
To swell one bloated Chief's unwhole-
    some reign?
No step between submission and a grave?
The rise of rapine and the fall of Spain?
And doth the Power that man adores
    ordain
Their doom, nor heed the suppliant's
    appeal?
Is all that desperate Valour acts in vain?
And Counsel sage, and patriotic Zeal,
The Veteran's skill, Youth's fire, and
    Manhood's heart of steel?

LIV

Is it for this the Spanish maid, aroused,
Hangs on the willow her unstrung guitar,
And, all unsex'd, the Anlace hath
    espoused,
Sung the loud song, and dared the deed
    of war?

And she, whom once the semblance of a scar
Appall'd, an owlet's 'larum chill'd with dread,
Now views the column-scattering bay'-net jar,
The falchion flash, and o'er the yet warm dead
Stalks with Minerva's step where Mars might quake to tread.

LV

Ye who shall marvel when you hear her tale,
Oh! had you known her in her softer hour,
Mark'd her black eye that mocks her coal-black veil,
Heard her light, lively tones in Lady's bower,
Seen her long locks that foil the painter's power,
Her fairy form, with more than female grace,
Scarce would you deem that Saragoza's tower
Beheld her smile in Danger's Gorgon face,
Thin the closed ranks, and lead in Glory's fearful chase.

LVI

Her lover sinks—she sheds no ill-timed tear;
Her chief is slain—she fills his fatal post;
Her fellows flee—she checks their base career;
The foe retires—she heads the sallying host:
Who can appease like her a lover's ghost?
Who can avenge so well a leader's fall?
What maid retrieve when man's flush'd hope is lost?
Who hang so fiercely on the flying Gaul,
Foil'd by a woman's hand, before a batter'd wall?

LVII

Yet are Spain's maids no race of Amazons,
But form'd for all the witching arts of love:
Though thus in arms they emulate her sons,
And in the horrid phalanx dare to move,
'Tis but the tender fierceness of the dove,
Pecking the hand that hovers o'er her mate:
In softness as in firmness far above
Remoter females, famed for sickening prate;
Her mind is nobler sure, her charms perchance as great.

LVIII

The seal Love's dimpling finger hath impress'd
Denotes how soft that chin which bears his touch:
Her lips, whose kisses pout to leave their nest,
Bid man be valiant ere he merit such:
Her glance how wildly beautiful! how much
Hath Phœbus woo'd in vain to spoil her cheek,
Which glows yet smoother from his amorous clutch!
Who round the North for paler dames would seek?
How poor their forms appear! how languid, wan, and weak!

LIX

Match me, ye climes! which poets love to laud;
Match me, ye harems of the land! where now
I strike my strain, far distant, to applaud
Beauties that ev'n a cynic must avow;
Match me those Houries, whom ye scarce allow
To taste the gale lest Love should ride the wind,
With Spain's dark-glancing daughters—deign to know,
There your wise Prophet's paradise we find,
His black-eyed maids of Heaven, angelically kind.

LX

Oh, thou Parnassus! whom I now survey,
Not in the phrensy of a dreamer's eye,
Not in the fabled landscape of a lay,
But soaring snow-clad through thy native sky,
In the wild pomp of mountain majesty!
What marvel if I thus essay to sing?
The humblest of thy pilgrims passing by
Would gladly woo thine Echoes with his string,
Though from thy heights no more one Muse will wave her wing.

LXI

Oft have I dream'd of Thee! whose glorious name
Who knows not, knows not man's divinest lore:
And now I view thee, 'tis, alas! with shame
That I in feeblest accents must adore.
When I recount thy worshippers of yore

I tremble, and can only bend the knee;
Nor raise my voice, nor vainly dare to
soar,
But gaze beneath thy cloudy canopy
In silent joy to think at last I look on Thee!

LXII

Happier in this than mightiest bards
have been,
Whose fate to distant homes confined
their lot,
Shall I unmoved behold the hallow'd
scene,
Which others rave of, though they know
it not?
Though here no more Apollo haunts his
grot,
And thou, the Muses' seat, art now their
grave,
Some gentle spirit still pervades the spot,
Sighs in the gale, keeps silence in the cave,
And glides with glassy foot o'er yon melo-
dious wave.

LXIII

Of thee hereafter.—Ev'n amidst my
strain
I turn'd aside to pay my homage here;
Forgot the land, the sons, the maids of
Spain;
Her fate, to every freeborn bosom dear;
And hail'd thee, not perchance without
a tear.
Now to my theme—but from thy holy
haunt
Let me some remnant, some memorial
bear;
Yield me one leaf of Daphne's deathless
plant,
Nor let thy votary's hope be deem'd an
idle vaunt.

LXIV

But ne'er didst thou, fair Mount, when
Greece was young,
See round thy giant base a brighter choir,
Nor e'er did Delphi, when her priestess
sung
The Pythian hymn with more than mor-
tal fire,
Behold a train more fitting to inspire
The song of love, than Andalusia's
maids,
Nurst in the glowing lap of soft desire:
Ah! that to these were given such peace-
ful shades
As Greece can still bestow, though Glory
fly her glades.

LXV

Fair is proud Seville; let her country
boast
Her strength, her wealth, her site of
ancient days;

But Cadiz, rising on the distant coast,
Calls forth a sweeter, though ignoble
praise.
Ah, Vice! how soft are thy voluptuous
ways!
While boyish blood is mantling, who
can 'scape
The fascination of thy magic gaze?
A Cherub-hydra round us dost thou
gape,
And mould to every taste thy dear delusive
shape.

LXVI

When Paphos fell by Time—accursed
Time!
The Queen who conquers all must yield
to thee—
The Pleasures fled, but sought as warm
a clime;
And Venus, constant to her native sea,
To nought else constant, hither deign'd
to flee,
And fix'd her shrine within these walls
of white;
Though not to one dome circumscribeth
she
Her worship, but, devoted to her rite,
A thousand altars rise, for ever blazing
bright.

LXVII

From morn till night, from night till
startled Morn
Peeps blushing on the revel's laughing
crew,
The song is heard, the rosy garland
worn;
Devices quaint, and frolics ever new,
Tread on each other's kibes. A long
adieu
He bids to sober joy that here sojourns:
Nought interrupts the riot, though in
lieu
Of true devotion monkish incense
burns,
And love and prayer unite, or rule the hour
by turns.

LXVIII

The Sabbath comes, a day of blessed
rest:
What hallows it upon this Christian
shore?
Lo! it is sacred to a solemn feast:
Hark! heard you not the forest-mon-
arch's roar?
Crashing the lance, he snuffs the spouting gore
Of man and steed, o'erthrown beneath
his horn;
The throng'd arena shakes with shouts
for more;

Yells the mad crowd o'er entrails freshly
    torn,
Nor shrinks the female eye, nor ev'n affects
    to mourn.

LXIX

The seventh day this; the jubilee of man.
London! right well thou know'st the
    day of prayer:
Then thy spruce citizen, wash'd artisan,
And smug apprentice gulp their weekly
    air:
Thy coach of hackney, whiskey, one-
    horse chair,
And humblest gig through sundry sub-
    urbs whirl;
To Hampstead, Brentford, Harrow
    make repair;
Till the tired jade the wheel forgets to
    hurl,
Provoking envious gibe from each pedes-
    trian churl.

LXX

Some o'er thy Thamis row the ribbon'd
    fair,
Others along the safer turnpike fly;
Some Richmond-hill ascend, some scud
    to Ware,
And many to the steep of Highgate hie.
Ask ye, Bœotian shades! the reason
    why?
'Tis to the worship of the solemn Horn,
Grasp'd in the holy hand of Mystery,
In whose dread name both men and
    maids are sworn,
And consecrate the oath with draught, and
    dance till morn.

LXXI

All have their fooleries—not alike are
    thine,
Fair Cadiz, rising o'er the dark blue sea!
Soon as the matin bell proclaimeth nine,
Thy Saint-adorers count the rosary:
Much is the VIRGIN teased to shrive
    them free
(Well do I ween the only virgin there)
From crimes as numerous as her beads-
    men be;
Then to the crowded circus forth they
    fare:
Young, old, high, low, at once the same
    diversion share.

LXXII

The lists are oped, the spacious area
    clear'd,
Thousands on thousands piled are
    seated round;
Long ere the first loud trumpet's note is
    heard,
Ne vacant space for lated wight is
    found:

Here dons, grandees, but chiefly dames
    abound,
Skill'd in the ogle of a roguish eye,
Yet ever well inclined to heal the wound;
None through their cold disdain are
    doom'd to die,
As moon-struck bards complain, by
    Love's sad archery.

LXXIII

Hush'd is the din of tongues—on gallant
    steeds,
With milk-white crest, gold spur, and
    light-poised lance,
Four cavaliers prepare for venturous
    deeds,
And lowly bending to the lists advance;
Rich are their scarfs, their chargers
    featly prance;
If in the dangerous game they shine to-
    day,
The crowd's loud shout and ladies' lovely
    glance,
Best prize of better acts, they bear
    away,
And all that kings or chiefs e'er gain their
    toils repay.

LXXIV

In costly sheen and gaudy cloak array'd,
But all afoot, the light-limb'd Matadore
Stands in the centre, eager to invade
The lord of lowing herds; but not be-
    fore
The ground, with cautious tread, is tra-
    versed o'er,
Lest aught unseen should lurk to thwart
    his speed:
His arms a dart, he fights aloof, nor
    more
Can man achieve without the friendly
    steed—
Alas! too oft condemn'd for him to bear
    and bleed.

LXXV

Thrice sounds the clarion; lo! the signal
    falls,
The den expands, and Expectation mute
Gapes round the silent circle's peopled
    walls.
Bounds with one lashing spring the
    mighty brute,
And, wildly staring, spurns, with sound-
    ing foot,
The sand, nor blindly rushes on his
    foe:
Here, there, he points his threatening
    front, to suit
His first attack, wide waving to and fro
His angry tail; red rolls his eye's dilated
    glow.

LXXVI

Sudden he stops; his eye is fix'd: away,
Away, thou heedless boy! prepare the spear:
Now is thy time to perish, or display
The skill that yet may check his mad career.
With well-timed croupe the nimble coursers veer;
On foams the bull, but not unscathed he goes;
Streams from his flank the crimson torrent clear:
He flies, he wheels, distracted with his throes;
Dart follows dart; lance, lance; loud bellowings speak his woes.

LXXVII

Again he comes; nor dart nor lance avail,
Nor the wild plunging of the tortured horse;
Though man and man's avenging arms assail,
Vain are his weapons, vainer is his force.
One gallant steed is stretch'd a mangled corse;
Another, hideous sight! unseam'd appears,
His gory chest unveils life's panting source;
Though death-struck, still his feeble frame he rears;
Staggering, but stemming all, his lord unharm'd he bears.

LXXVIII

Foil'd, bleeding, breathless, furious to the last,
Full in the centre stands the bull at bay,
Mid wounds, and clinging darts, and lances brast,
And foes disabled in the brutal fray;
And now the Matadores around him play,
Shake the red cloak and poise the ready brand:
Once more through all he bursts his thundering way—
Vain rage! the mantle quits the conynge hand,
Wraps his fierce eye—'tis past—he sinks upon the sand!

LXXIX

Where his vast neck just mingles with the spine,
Sheathed in his form the deadly weapon lies.
He stops—he starts—disdaining to decline:
Slowly he falls, amidst triumphant cries,

Without a groan, without a struggle dies.
The decorated car appears—on high
The corse is piled—sweet sight for vulgar eyes—
Four steeds that spurn the rein, as swift as shy,
Hurl the dark bulk along, scarce seen in dashing by.

LXXX

Such the ungentle sport that oft invites
The Spanish maid, and cheers the Spanish swain.
Nurtured in blood betimes, his heart delights
In vengeance, gloating on another's pain.
What private feuds the troubled village stain!
Though now one phalanx'd host should meet the foe,
Enough, alas! in humble homes remain,
To meditate 'gainst friends the secret blow,
For some slight cause of wrath whence life's warm stream must flow.

LXXXI

But Jealousy has fled: his bars, his bolts,
His wither'd centinel, Duenna sage!
And all whereat the generous soul revolts,
Which the stern dotard deem'd he could encage,
Have pass'd to darkness with the vanish'd age.
Who late so free as Spanish girls were seen
(Ere War uprose in his volcanic rage),
With braided tresses bounding o'er the green,
While on the gay dance shone Night's lover-loving Queen?

LXXXII

Oh! many a time and oft, had Harold loved,
Or dream'd he loved, since rapture is a dream;
But now his wayward bosom was unmoved,
For not yet had he drunk of Lethe's stream;
And lately had he learn'd with truth to deem
Love has no gift so grateful as his wings:
How fair, how young, how soft soe'er he seem,
Full from the fount of Joy's delicious springs
Some bitter o'er the flowers its bubbling venom flings.

LXXXIII

Yet to the beauteous form he was not
    blind,
Though now it moved him as it moves
    the wise:
Not that Philosophy on such a mind
E'er deign'd to bend her chastely-awful
    eyes:
But Passion raves herself to rest, or flies;
And Vice, that digs her own voluptuous
    tomb,
Had buried long his hopes, no more to
    rise:
Pleasure's pall'd victim! life-abhorring
    gloom
Wrote on his faded brow curst Cain's un-
    resting doom.

LXXXIV

Still he beheld, nor mingled with the
    throng;
But view'd them not with misanthropic
    hate:
Fain would he now have join'd the
    dance, the song;
But who may smile that sinks beneath
    his fate:
Nought that he saw his sadness could
    abate:
Yet once he struggled 'gainst the de-
    mon's sway,
And as in Beauty's bower he pensive
    sate,
Pour'd forth his unpremeditated lay,
To charms as fair as those that soothed
    his happier day.

TO INEZ

1

Nay, smile not at my sullen brow;
    Alas! I cannot smile again:
Yet Heaven avert that ever thou
    Shouldst weep, and haply weep in vain.

2

And dost thou ask what secret woe
    I bear, corroding joy and youth?
And wilt thou vainly seek to know
    A pang, ev'n thou must fail to soothe?

3

It is not love, it is not hate,
    Nor low Ambition's honours lost,
That bids me loathe my present state,
    And fly from all I prized the most:

4

It is that weariness which springs
    From all I meet, or hear, or see:
To me no pleasure Beauty brings;
    Thine eyes have scarce a charm for me.

5

It is that settled, ceaseless gloom
    The fabled Hebrew wanderer bore;
That will not look beyond the tomb,
    But cannot hope for rest before.

6

What Exile from himself can flee?
    To zones though more and more remote,
Still, still pursues, where'er I be,
    The blight of life—the demon Thought.

7

Yet others rapt in pleasure seem,
    And taste of all that I forsake;
Oh! may they still of transport dream,
    And ne'er, at least like me, awake!

8

Through many a clime 'tis mine to go,
    With many a retrospection curst;
And all my solace is to know,
    Whate'er betides, I've known the worst.

9

What is that worst? Nay, do not ask—
    In pity from the search forbear:
Smile on—nor venture to unmask
    Man's heart, and view the Hell that's
    there.

LXXXV

Adieu, fair Cadiz! yea, a long adieu!
Who may forget how well thy walls have
    stood?
When all were changing, thou alone
    wert true,
First to be free, and last to be subdued:
And if amidst a scene, a shock so rude,
Some native blood was seen thy streets
    to dye
A traitor only fell beneath the feud:
Here all were noble, save Nobility!
None hugg'd a conqueror's chain, save
    fallen Chivalry!

LXXXVI

Such be the sons of Spain, and strange
    her fate!
They fight for freedom who were never
    free,
A Kingless people for a nerveless state;
Her vassals combat when their chief-
    tains flee,
True to the veriest slaves of Treachery:
Fond of a land which gave them nought
    but life,
Pride points the path that leads to
    Liberty;
Back to the struggle, baffled in the strife,
War, war is still the cry, 'War even to the
    knife!'

LXXXVII

Ye, who would more of Spain and Span-
iards know,
Go, read whate'er is writ of bloodiest
strife:
Whate'er keen Vengeance urged on
foreign foe
Can act, is acting there against man's
life:
From flashing scimitar to secret knife,
War mouldeth there each weapon to his
need—
So may he guard the sister and the wife,
So may he make each curst oppressor
bleed—
So may such foes deserve the most re-
morseless deed!

LXXXVIII

Flows there a tear of pity for the dead?
Look o'er the ravage of the reeking
plain;
Look on the hands with female slaughter
red;
Then to the dogs resign the unburied
slain,
Then to the vulture let each corse remain,
Albeit unworthy of the prey-bird's
maw;
Let their bleach'd bones, and blood's
unbleaching stain,
Long mark the battle-field with hideous
awe:
Thus only may our sons conceive the
scenes we saw!

LXXXIX

Nor yet, alas! the dreadful work is done;
Fresh legions pour adown the Pyrenees:
It deepens still, the work is scarce begun,
Nor mortal eye the distant end foresees.
Fall'n nations gaze on Spain; if freed,
she frees
More than her fell Pizarros once en-
chain'd:
Strange retribution! now Columbia's
ease
Repairs the wrongs that Quito's sons
sustain'd,
While o'er the parent clime prowls Mur-
der unrestrain'd.

XC

Not all the blood at Talavera shed,
Not all the marvels of Barossa's fight,
Not Albuera lavish of the dead,
Have won for Spain her well-asserted
right.
When shall her Olive-Branch be free
from blight?
When shall she breathe her from the
blushing toil?

How many a doubtful day shall sink in
night,
Ere the Frank robber turn him from his
spoil,
And Freedom's stranger-tree grow native
of the soil!

XCI

And thou, my friend!—since unavail-
ing woe
Bursts from my heart, and mingles with
the strain—
Had the sword laid thee with the mighty
low,
Pride might forbid e'en Friendship to
complain:
But thus unlaurel'd to descend in vain,
By all forgotten, save the lonely breast,
And mix unbleeding with the boasted
slain,
While Glory crowns so many a meaner
crest!
What hadst thou done to sink so peacefully
to rest?

XCII

Oh, known the earliest, and esteem'd the
most!
Dear to a heart where nought was left so
dear!
Though to my hopeless days for ever
lost,
In dreams deny me not to see thee here!
And Morn in secret shall renew the
tear
Of Consciousness awaking to her
woes,
And Fancy hover o'er thy bloodless
bier,
Till my frail frame return to whence it
rose,
And mourn'd and mourner lie united in
repose.

XCIII

Here is one fytte of Harold's pilgrim-
age:
Ye who of him may further seek to
know,
Shall find some tidings in a future
page,
If he that rhymeth now may scribble
moe.
Is this too much? stern Critic! say not
so:
Patience! and ye shall hear what he be-
held
In other lands, where he was doom'd to
go:
Lands that contain the monuments of
Eld,
Ere Greece and Grecian arts by barbarous
hands were quell'd.

CANTO THE SECOND

I

COME, blue-eyed maid of heaven!—but
  thou, alas!
Didst never yet one mortal song in-
  spire—
Goddess of Wisdom! here thy temple
  was,
And is, despite of war and wasting fire,
And years, that bade thy worship to
  expire:
But worse than steel, and flame, and
  ages slow,
Is the dread sceptre and dominion dire
Of men who never felt the sacred glow
That thoughts of thee and thine on polish'd
  breasts bestow.

II

Ancient of days! august Athena! where,
Where are thy men of might? thy grand
  in soul?
Gone—glimmering through the dream
  of things that were:
First in the race that led to Glory's goal,
They won, and pass'd away—is this the
  whole?
A schoolboy's tale, the wonder of an
  hour!
The warrior's weapon and the sophist's
  stole
Are sought in vain, and o'er each moul-
  dering tower,
Dim with the mist of years, gray flits the
  shade of power.

III

Son of the morning, rise! approach you
  here!
Come—but molest not yon defenceless
  urn:
Look on this spot—a nation's sepulchre!
Abode of gods, whose shrines no longer
  burn.
Even gods must yield—religions take
  their turn:
'Twas Jove's—'tis Mahomet's—and
  other creeds
Will rise with other years, till man shall
  learn
Vainly his incense soars, his victim
  bleeds
Poor child of Doubt and Death, whose
  hope is built on reeds.

IV

Bound to the earth, he lifts his eye to
  heaven—
Is't not enough, unhappy thing! to
  know
Thou art? Is this a boon so kindly
  given,
That being, thou wouldst be again, and
  go,
Thou know'st not, reck'st not, to what
  region, so
On earth no more, but mingled with the
  skies?
Still wilt thou dream on future joy and
  woe?
Regard and weigh yon dust before it
  flies:
That little urn saith more than thousand
  homilies.

V

Or burst the vanish'd Hero's lofty
  mound;
Far on the solitary shore he sleeps:
He fell, and falling nations mourn'd
  around;
But now not one of saddening thousands
  weeps,
Nor warlike worshipper his vigil keeps
Where demi-gods appear'd, as records
  tell.
Remove yon skull from out the scatter'd
  heaps:
Is that a temple where a God may dwell?
Why ev'n the worm at last disdains her
  shatter'd cell!

VI

Look on its broken arch, its ruin'd wall,
Its chambers desolate, and portals foul:
Yes, this was once Ambition's airy hall,
The dome of Thought, the palace of the
  Soul:
Behold through each lack-lustre, eyeless
  hole,
The gay recess of Wisdom and of Wit,
And Passion's host, that never brook'd
  control:
Can all saint, sage, or sophist ever writ,
People this lonely tower, this tenement re-
  fit?

VII

Well didst thou speak, Athena's wisest
  son!
'All that we know is, nothing can be
  known.'
Why should we shrink from what we
  cannot shun?
Each hath his pang, but feeble sufferers
  groan
With brain-born dreams of evil all their
  own.
Pursue what Chance or Fate proclaimeth best;
Peace waits us on the shores of Acheron:
There no forced banquet claims the
  sated guest,
But Silence spreads the couch of ever
  welcome rest.

VIII

Yet if, as holiest men have deem'd,
   there be
A land of souls beyond that sable shore,
To shame the doctrine of the Sadducee
And sophists, madly vain of dubious
   lore;
How sweet it were in concert to adore
With those who made our mortal la-
   bours light!
To hear each voice we fear'd to hear no
   more!
Behold each mighty shade reveal'd to
   sight,
The Bactrian, Samian sage, and all who
   taught the right!

IX

There, thou!—whose love and life to-
   gether fled,
Have left me here to love and live in
   vain—
Twined with my heart, and can I deem
   thee dead
When busy Memory flashes on my
   brain?
Well—I will dream that we may meet
   again,
And woo the vision to my vacant breast:
If aught of young Remembrance then
   remain,
Be as it may Futurity's behest,
For me 'twere bliss enough to know thy
   spirit blest!

X

Here let me sit upon this massy stone,
The marble column's yet unshaken
   base;
Here, son of Saturn! was thy fav'rite
   throne:
Mightiest of many such! Hence let me
   trace
The latent grandeur of thy dwelling-
   place.
It may not be: nor ev'n can Fancy's eye
Restore what Time hath labour'd to de-
   face.
Yet these proud pillars claim no passing
   sigh;
Unmoved the Moslem sits, the light Greek
   carols by.

XI

But who, of all the plunderers of yon
   fane
On high, where Pallas linger'd, loth to
   flee
The latest relic of her ancient reign;
The last, the worst, dull spoiler, who was
   he?
Blush, Caledonia! such thy son could
   be!

England! I joy no child he was of
   thine:
Thy free-born men should spare what
   once was free;
Yet they could violate each saddening
   shrine,
And bear these altars o'er the long-
   reluctant brine.

XII

But most the modern Pict's ignoble
   boast,
To rive what Goth, and Turk, and Time
   hath spared:
Cold as the crags upon his native coast,
His mind as barren and his heart as
   hard,
Is he whose head conceived, whose hand
   prepared,
Aught to displace Athena's poor re-
   mains:
Her sons, too weak the sacred shrine to
   guard,
Yet felt some portion of their mother's
   pains,
And never knew, till then, the weight of
   Despot's chains.

XIII

What! shall it e'er be said by British
   tongue,
Albion was happy in Athena's tears?
Though in thy name the slaves her
   bosom wrung,
Tell not the deed to blushing Europe's
   ears;
The ocean queen, the free Britannia,
   bears
The last poor plunder from a bleeding
   land:
Yes, she, whose gen'rous aid her name
   endears,
Tore down those remnants with a
   harpy's hand,
Which envious Eld forbore, and tyrants
   left to stand.

XIV

Where was thine Ægis, Pallas! that ap-
   pall'd
Stern Alaric and Havoc on their way?
Where Peleus' son? whom Hell in vain
   enthrall'd,
His shade from Hades upon that dread
   day
Bursting to light in terrible array!
What! could not Pluto spare the chief
   once more,
To scare a second robber from his prey?
Idly he wander'd on the Stygian shore,
Nor now preserved the walls he loved to
   shield before.

XV

Cold is the heart, fair Greece! that looks
      on thee,
Nor feels as lovers o'er the dust they
      loved;
Dull is the eye that will not weep to see
Thy walls defaced, thy mouldering
      shrines removed
By British hands, which it had best be-
      hoved
To guard those relics ne'er to be re-
      stored.
Curst be the hour when from their isle
      they roved,
And once again thy hapless bosom
      gored,
And snatch'd thy shrinking Gods to
      northern climes abhorr'd!

XVI

But where is Harold? shall I then forget
To urge the gloomy wanderer o'er the
      wave?
Little reck'd he of all that men regret;
No loved-one now in feign'd lament
      could rave;
No friend the parting hand extended
      gave,
Ere the cold stranger pass'd to other
      climes:
Hard is his heart whom charms may not
      enslave;
But Harold felt not as in other times,
And left without a sigh the land of war and
      crimes.

XVII

He that has sail'd upon the dark blue
      sea
Has view'd at times, I ween, a full fair
      sight:
When the fresh breeze is fair as breeze
      may be,
The white sail set, the gallant frigate
      tight;
Masts, spires, and strand retiring to the
      right,
The glorious main expanding o'er the
      bow,
The convoy spread like wild swans in
      their flight,
The dullest sailer wearing bravely now,
So gaily curl the waves before each dash-
      ing prow.

XVIII

And oh, the little warlike world within!
The well-reeved guns, the netted can-
      opy,
The hoarse command, the busy hum-
      ming din,
When, at a word, the tops are mann'd
      on high:

Hark, to the Boatswain's call, the cheer-
      ing cry!
While through the seaman's hand the
      tackle glides;
Or schoolboy Midshipman that, stand-
      ing by,
Strains his shrill pipe as good or ill be-
      tides,
And well the docile crew that skilful
      urchin guides.

XIX

White is the glassy deck, without a stain,
Where on the watch the staid Lieutenant
      walks:
Look on that part which sacred doth re-
      main
For the lone chieftain, who majestic
      stalks,
Silent and fear'd by all—not oft he talks
With aught beneath him, if he would
      preserve
That strict restraint, which broken, ever
      balks
Conquest and fame: but Britons rarely
      swerve
From law, however stern, which tends
      their strength to nerve.

XX

Blow! swiftly blow, thou keel-compel-
      ling gale!
Till the broad sun withdraws his lessen-
      ing ray;
Then must the pennant-bearer slacken
      sail,
That lagging barks may make their lazy
      way.
Ah! grievance sore, and listless dull de-
      lay,
To waste on sluggish hulks the sweetest
      breeze!
What leagues are lost, before the dawn
      of day,
Thus loitering pensive on the willing seas,
The flapping sail haul'd down to halt for
      logs like these!

XXI

The moon is up; by Heaven, a lovely eve!
Long streams of light o'er dancing
      waves expand;
Now lads on shore may sigh, and maids
      believe:
Such be our fate when we return to land!
Meantime some rude Arion's restless
      hand
Wakes the brisk harmony that sailors
      love;
A circle there of merry listeners stand,
Or to some well-known measure featly
      move,
Thoughtless, as if on shore they still were
      free to rove.

XXII

Through Calpe's straits survey the steepy
  shore;
Europe and Afric on each other gaze!
Lands of the dark-eyed Maid and dusky
  Moor
Alike beheld beneath pale Hecate's blaze:
How softly on the Spanish shore she
  plays,
Disclosing rock, and slope, and forest
  brown,
Distinct, though darkening with her
  waning phase;
But Mauritania's giant shadows frown,
From mountain-cliff to coast descending
  sombre down.

XXIII

'Tis night, when Meditation bids us
  feel
We once have loved, though love is at an
  end:
The heart, lone mourner of its baffled
  zeal,
Though friendless now, will dream it
  had a friend.
Who with the weight of years would
  wish to bend,
When Youth itself survives young Love
  and Joy?
Alas! when mingling souls forget to
  blend,
Death hath but little left him to destroy!
Ah! happy years! once more who would
  not be a boy?

XXIV

Thus bending o'er the vessel's laving
  side,
To gaze on Dian's wave-reflected
  sphere,
The soul forgets her schemes of hope
  and pride,
And flies unconscious o'er each backward year.
None are so desolate but something
  dear,
Dearer than self, possesses or possess'd
A thought, and claims the homage of a
  tear;
A flashing pang! of which the weary
  breast
Would still, albeit in vain, the heavy heart
  divest.

XXV

To sit on rocks, to muse o'er flood and
  fell,
To slowly trace the forest's shady scene,
Where things that own not man's dominion dwell,
And mortal foot hath ne'er or rarely
  been;

To climb the trackless mountain all
  unseen,
With the wild flock that never needs a
  fold;
Alone o'er steeps and foaming falls to
  lean;
This is not solitude; 'tis but to hold
Converse with Nature's charms, and view
  her stores unroll'd.

XXVI

But midst the crowd, the hum, the shock
  of men,
To hear, to see, to feel, and to possess,
And roam along, the world's tired deni-
  zen,
With none who bless us, none whom we
  can bless;
Minions of splendour shrinking from
  distress!
None that, with kindred consciousness
  endued,
If we were not, would seem to smile the
  less,
Of all that flatter'd, follow'd, sought,
  and sued;
This is to be alone; this, this is solitude!

XXVII

More blest the life of godly eremite,
Such as on lonely Athos may be seen,
Watching at eve upon the giant height,
Which looks o'er waves so blue, skies so
  serene,
That he who there at such an hour hath
  been
Will wistful linger on that hallow'd spot;
Then slowly tear him from the 'witching
  scene,
Sigh forth one wish that such had been
  his lot,
Then turn to hate a world he had almost
  forgot.

XXVIII

Pass we the long, unvarying course, the
  track
Oft trod, that never leaves a trace behind;
Pass we the calm, the gale, the change,
  the tack,
And each well-known caprice of wave
  and wind;
Pass we the joys and sorrows sailors
  find,
Coop'd in their winged sea-girt citadel;
The foul, the fair, the contrary, the
  kind,
As breezes rise and fall and billows
  swell,
Till on some jocund morn—lo, land! and
  all is well.

XXIX

But not in silence pass Calypso's isles,
The sister tenants of the middle deep;
There for the weary still a haven smiles,
Though the fair goddess long hath
    ceased to weep,
And o'er her cliffs a fruitless watch to
    keep
For him who dared prefer a mortal
    bride:
Here, too, his boy essay'd the dreadful
    leap
Stern Mentor urged from high to yon-
    der tide;
While thus of both bereft, the nymph-
    queen doubly sigh'd.

XXX

Her reign is past, her gentle glories gone:
But trust not this: too easy youth, be-
    ware!
A mortal sovereign holds her dangerous
    throne,
And thou mayst find a new Calypso
    there.
Sweet Florence! could another ever
    share
This wayward, loveless heart, it would
    be thine:
But check'd by every tie, I may not dare
To cast a worthless offering at thy shrine,
Nor ask so dear a breast to feel one pang
    for mine.

XXXI

Thus Harold deem'd, as on that lady's
    eye
He look'd, and met its beam without a
    thought
Save admiration glancing harmless by:
Love kept aloof, albeit not far remote,
Who knew his votary often lost and
    caught,
But knew him as his worshipper no
    more,
And ne'er again the boy his bosom
    sought:
Since now he vainly urged him to adore,
Well deem'd the little God his ancient
    sway was o'er.

XXXII

Fair Florence found, in sooth with some
    amaze,
One who, 'twas said, still sigh'd to all
    he saw,
Withstand, unmoved, the lustre of her
    gaze,
Which others hail'd with real or mimic
    awe,
Their hope, their doom, their punish-
    ment, their law;
All that gay Beauty from her bondsmen
    claims:

And much she marvell'd that a youth so
    raw
Nor felt, nor feign'd at least, the oft-told
    flames,
Which, though sometimes they frown, yet
    rarely anger dames.

XXXIII

Little knew she that seeming marble
    heart,
Now mask'd in silence or withheld by
    pride,
Was not unskilful in the spoiler's art,
And spread its snares licentious far and
    wide;
Nor from the base pursuit had turn'd
    aside,
As long as aught was worthy to pursue:
But Harold on such arts no more relied;
And had he doted on those eyes so blue,
Yet never would he join the lover's
    whining crew.

XXXIV

Not much he kens, I ween, of woman's
    breast,
Who thinks that wanton thing is won by
    sighs;
What careth she for hearts when once
    possess'd?
Do proper homage to thine idol's eyes;
But not too humbly, or she will despise
Thee and thy suit, though told in
    moving tropes:
Disguise ev'n tenderness, if thou art
    wise;
Brisk Confidence still best with woman
    copes:
Pique her and soothe in turn, soon Passion
    crowns thy hopes.

XXXV

'Tis an old lesson; Time approves it
    true,
And those who know it best deplore it
    most;
When all is won that all desire to woo,
The paltry prize is hardly worth the
    cost:
Youth wasted, minds degraded, honour
    lost,
These are thy fruits, successful Passion!
    these!
If, kindly cruel, early hope is crost,
Still to the last it rankles, a disease,
Not to be cured when love itself forgets to
    please.

XXXVI

Away! nor let me loiter in my song,
For we have many a mountain-path to
    tread,
And many a varied shore to sail along,
By pensive Sadness, not by Fiction,
    led—

Climes, fair withal as ever mortal head
Imagined in its little schemes of thought;
Or e'er in new Utopias were ared,
To teach man what he might be, or he
ought;
If that corrupted thing could ever such be
taught.

XXXVII

Dear Nature is the kindest mother still,
Though always changing in her aspect
mild;
From her bare bosom let me take my
fill,
Her never-wean'd, though not her
favour'd child.
Oh! she is fairest in her features wild,
Where nothing polish'd dares pollute
her path:
To me by day or night she ever smiled,
Though I have mark'd her when none
other hath,
And sought her more and more, and loved
her best in wrath.

XXXVIII

Land of Albania! where Iskander rose,
Theme of the young, and beacon of the
wise,
And he his namesake, whose oft-baffled
foes
Shrunk from his deeds of chivalrous
emprize:
Land of Albania! let me bend mine eyes
On thee, thou rugged nurse of savage
men!
The cross descends, thy minarets arise,
And the pale crescent sparkles in the
glen,
Through many a cypress grove within each
city's ken.

XXXIX

Childe Harold sail'd, and pass'd the
barren spot,
Where sad Penelope o'erlook'd the
wave;
And onward view'd the mount, not yet
forgot,
The lover's refuge, and the Lesbian's
grave.
Dark Sappho! could not verse immortal
save
That breast imbued with such immortal
fire?
Could she not live who life eternal gave?
If life eternal may await the lyre,
That only Heaven to which Earth's child-
ren may aspire.

XL

'Twas on a Grecian autumn's gentle eve
Childe Harold hail'd Leucadia's cape
afar;

A spot he longed to see, nor cared to
leave:
Oft did he mark the scenes of vanish'd
war,
Actium, Lepanto, fatal Trafalgar;
Mark them unmoved, for he would not
delight
(Born beneath some remote inglorious
star)
In themes of bloody fray, or gallant
fight,
But loathed the bravo's trade, and laughed
at martial wight.

XLI

But when he saw the evening star above
Leucadia's far-projecting rock of woe,
And hail'd the last resort of fruitless
love,
He felt, or deem'd he felt, no common
glow:
And as the stately vessel glided slow
Beneath the shadow of that ancient
mount,
He watch'd the billows' melancholy
flow,
And, sunk albeit in thought as he was
wont,
More placid seem'd his eye, and smooth
his pallid front.

XLII

Morn dawns: and with it stern Albania's
hills,
Dark Suli's rocks, and Pindus' inland
peak,
Robed half in mist, bedew'd with snowy
rills,
Array'd in many a dun and purple
streak,
Arise; and, as the clouds along them
break,
Disclose the dwelling of the mountaineer;
Here roams the wolf, the eagle whets his
beak,
Birds, beasts of prey, and wilder men
appear,
And gathering storms around convulse the
closing year.

XLIII

Now Harold felt himself at length
alone,
And bade to Christian tongues a long
adieu;
Now he adventured on a shore unknown,
Which all admire, but many dread to
view:
His breast was arm'd 'gainst fate, his
wants were few;

Peril he sought not, but ne'er shrank to
    meet:
The scene was savage, but the scene was
    new;
This made the ceaseless toil of travel
    sweet,
Beat back keen winter's blast, and wel-
    comed summer's heat.

XLIV

Here the red cross, for still the cross is
    here,
Though sadly scoff'd at by the circum-
    cised,
Forgets that pride to pamper'd priest-
    hood dear;
Churchman and votary alike de-
    spised.
Foul Superstition! howsoe'er disguised,
Idol, saint, virgin, prophet, crescent,
    cross,
For whatsoever symbol thou art prized,
Thou sacerdotal gain, but general loss!
Who from true worship's gold can
    separate thy dross?

XLV

Ambracia's gulf behold, where once was
    lost
A world for woman, lovely, harmless
    thing!
In yonder rippling bay, their naval
    host
Did many a Roman chief and Asian
    king
To doubtful conflict, certain slaughter
    bring:
Look where the second Cæsar's trophies
    rose:
Now, like the hands that rear'd them,
    withering,
Imperial anarchs, doubling human
    woes!
GOD! was thy globe ordain'd for such to
    win and lose?

XLVI

From the dark barriers of that rugged
    clime,
Ev'n to the centre of Illyria's vales,
Childe Harold pass'd o'er many a
    mount sublime,
Through lands scarce noticed in historic
    tales;
Yet in famed Attica such lovely dales
Are rarely seen; nor can fair Tempe
    boast
A charm they know not; loved Par-
    nassus fails,
Though classic ground and consecrated
    most,
To match some spots that lurk within this
    lowering coast.

XLVII

He pass'd bleak Pindus, Acherusia's
    lake,
And left the primal city of the land,
And onwards did his further journey
    take
To greet Albania's chief, whose dread
    command
Is lawless law; for with a bloody hand
He sways a nation, turbulent and bold;
Yet here and there some daring moun-
    tain-band
Disdain his power, and from their rocky
    hold
Hurl their defiance far, nor yield, unless to
    gold.

XLVIII

Monastic Zitza! from thy shady brow,
Thou small but favour'd spot of holy
    ground!
Where'er we gaze, around, above, be-
    low,
What rainbow tints, what magic charms
    are found!
Rock, river, forest, mountain, all
    abound,
And bluest skies that harmonise the
    whole:
Beneath, the distant torrent's rushing
    sound
Tells where the volumed cataract doth
    roll
Between those hanging rocks, that shock
    yet please the soul.

XLIX

Amidst the grove that crowns yon
    tufted hill,
Which, were it not for many a mountain
    nigh
Rising in lofty ranks, and loftier still,
Might well itself be deem'd of dignity,
The convent's white walls glisten fair on
    high:
Here dwells the caloyer, nor rude is
    he,
Nor niggard of his cheer; the passer
    by
Is welcome still; nor heedless will he
    flee
From hence, if he delight kind Nature's
    sheen to see.

L

Here in the sultriest season let him rest,
Fresh is the green beneath those aged
    trees;
Here winds of gentlest wing will fan his
    breast,
From heaven itself he may inhale the
    breeze:

The plain is far beneath—oh! let him
seize
Pure pleasure while he can; the scorching ray
Here pierceth not, impregnate with
disease:
Then let his length the loitering pilgrim
lay,
And gaze, untired, the morn, the noon,
the eve away.

LI

Dusky and huge, enlarging on the sight,
Nature's volcanic amphitheatre,
Chimæra's alps extend from left to
right:
Beneath, a living valley seems to stir;
Flocks play, trees wave, streams flow,
the mountain-fir
Nodding above; behold black Acheron!
Once consecrated to the sepulchre.
Pluto! if this be hell I look upon,
Close shamed Elysium's gates, my shade
shall seek for none.

LII

Ne city's towers pollute the lovely view;
Unseen is Yanina, though not remote,
Veil'd by the screen of hills: here men
are few,
Scanty the hamlet, rare the lonely cot:
But, peering down each precipice, the
goat
Browseth; and, pensive o'er his scatter'd
flock,
The little shepherd in his white capote
Doth lean his boyish form along the
rock,
Or in his cave awaits the tempest's short-
lived shock.

LIII

Oh! where, Dodona! is thine aged
grove,
Prophetic fount, and oracle divine?
What valley echoed the response of
Jove?
What trace remaineth of the Thunder-
er's shrine?
All, all forgotten—and shall man repine
That his frail bonds to fleeting life are
broke?
Cease, fool! the fate of gods may well
be thine:
Wouldst thou survive the marble or the
oak?
When nations, tongues, and worlds must
sink beneath the stroke!

LIV

Epirus' bounds recede, and mountains
fail;
Tired of up-gazing still, the wearied eye
Reposes gladly on as smooth a vale

As ever Spring yclad in grassy dye:
Ev'n on a plain no humble beauties lie,
Where some bold river breaks the long
expanse,
And woods along the banks are waving
high,
Whose shadows in the glassy waters
dance,
Or with the moonbeam sleep in midnight's
solemn trance.

LV

The sun had sunk behind vast Tomerit,
And Laos wide and fierce came roaring
by;
The shades of wonted night were
gathering yet,
When, down the steep banks winding
warily,
Childe Harold saw, like meteors in the
sky,
The glittering minarets of Tepalen,
Whose walls o'erlook the stream; and
drawing nigh,
He heard the busy hum of warrior-men
Swelling the breeze that sigh'd along the
lengthening glen.

LVI

He pass'd the sacred Haram's silent
tower,
And underneath the wide o'erarching
gate
Survey'd the dwelling of this chief of
power,
Where all around proclaim'd his high
estate.
Amidst no common pomp the despot
sate,
While busy preparation shook the
court,
Slaves, eunuchs, soldiers, guests, and
santons wait;
Within, a palace, and, without, a fort:
Here men of every clime appear to make
resort.

LVII

Richly caparison'd, a ready row
Of armed horse, and many a warlike
store,
Circled the wide-extending court below;
Above, strange groups adorn'd the
corridore;
And oft-times through the area's echo-
ing door,
Some high-capp'd Tartar spurr'd his
steed away:
The Turk, the Greek, the Albanian, and
the Moor,
Here mingled in their many-hued array,
While the deep war-drum's sound an-
nounced the close of day.

LVIII

The wild Albanian kirtled to his knee,
With shawl-girt head and ornamented
    gun,
And gold-embroider'd garments, fair to
    see;
The crimson-scarfèd men of Macedon;
The Delhi with his cap of terror on,
And crooked glaive; the lively, supple
    Greek;
And swarthy Nubia's mutilated son;
The bearded Turk, that rarely deigns to
    speak,
Master of all around, too potent to be
    meek,

LIX

Are mix'd conspicuous: some recline in
    groups,
Scanning the motley scene that varies
    round;
There some grave Moslem to devotion
    stoops,
And some that smoke, and some that
    play, are found;
Here the Albanian proudly treads the
    ground;
Half whispering there the Greek is
    heard to prate;
Hark! from the mosque the nightly
    solemn sound,
The Muezzin's call doth shake the
    minaret,
'There is no god but God!—to prayer—
    lo! God is great!'

LX

Just at this season Ramazani's fast
Through the long day its penance did
    maintain:
But when the lingering twilight hour
    was past,
Revel and feast assumed the rule again:
Now all was bustle, and the menial train
Prepared and spread the plenteous
    board within;
The vacant gallery now seem'd made in
    vain,
But from the chambers came the
    mingling din,
As page and slave anon were passing out
    and in.

LXI

Here woman's voice is never heard:
    apart,
And scarce permitted, guarded, veil'd,
    to move,
She yields to one her person and her
    heart,
Tamed to her cage, nor feels a wish to
    rove:
For, not unhappy in her master's love,
And joyful in a mother's gentlest cares,
Blest cares! all other feelings far above!
Herself more sweetly rears the babe she
    bears,
Who never quits the breast, no meaner
    passion shares.

LXII

In marble-paved pavilion, where a
    spring
Of living water from the centre rose,
Whose bubbling did a genial freshness
    fling,
And soft voluptuous couches breathed
    repose,
ALI reclined, a man of war and woes:
Yet in his lineaments ye cannot trace,
While Gentleness her milder radiance
    throws
Along that aged venerable face,
The deeds that lurk beneath, and stain him
    with disgrace.

LXIII

It is not that yon hoary lengthening
    beard
Ill suits the passions which belong to
    youth;
Love conquers age—so Hafiz hath
    averr'd,
So sings the Teian, and he sings in
    sooth—
But crimes that scorn the tender voice
    of ruth,
Beseeming all men ill, but most the man
In years, have mark'd him with a tiger's
    tooth;
Blood follows blood, and, through their
    mortal span,
In bloodier acts conclude those who with
    blood began.

LXIV

'Mid many things most new to ear and
    eye
The pilgrim rested here his weary feet,
And gazed around on Moslem luxury,
Till quickly wearied with that spacious
    seat
Of Wealth and Wantonness, the choice
    retreat
Of sated Grandeur from the city's noise:
And were it humbler, it in sooth were
    sweet;
But Peace abhorreth artificial joys,
And Pleasure, leagued with Pomp, the
    zest of both destroys.

LXV

Fierce are Albania's children, yet they
    lack
Not virtues, were those virtues more
    mature.

Where is the foe that ever saw their back?
Who can so well the toil of war endure?
Their native fastnesses not more secure
Than they in doubtful time of troublous
    need:
Their wrath how deadly! but their
    friendship sure,
When Gratitude or Valour bids them bleed
Unshaken rushing on where'er their chief
    may lead.

LXVI

Childe Harold saw them in their chief-
    tain's tower
Thronging to war in splendour and
    success;
And after view'd them, when, within
    their power,
Himself awhile the victim of distress;
That saddening hour when bad men
    hotlier press:
But these did shelter him beneath their
    roof,
When less barbarians would have
    cheer'd him less,
And fellow-countrymen have stood
    aloof—
In aught that tries the heart how few
    withstand the proof!

LXVII

It chanced that adverse winds once
    drove his bark
Full on the coast of Suli's shaggy shore,
When all around was desolate and dark;
To land was perilous, to sojourn more;
Yet for a while the mariners forbore,
Dubious to trust where treachery might
    lurk:
At length they ventured forth, though
    doubting sore
That those who loathe alike the Frank
    and Turk
Might once again renew their ancient
    butcher-work.

LXVIII

Vain fear! the Suliotes stretch'd the
    welcome hand,
Led them o'er rocks and past the dan-
    gerous swamp,
Kinder than polish'd slaves, though not
    so bland,
And piled the hearth, and wrung their
    garments damp,
And fill'd the bowl, and trimm'd the
    cheerful lamp,
And spread their fare; though homely,
    all they had:
Such conduct bears Philanthropy's rare
    stamp:
To rest the weary and to soothe the sad,
Doth lesson happier men, and shames at
    least the bad.

LXIX

It came to pass, that when he did address
Himself to quit at length this mountain-
    land,
Combined marauders half-way barr'd
    egress,
And wasted far and near with glaive and
    brand;
And therefore did he take a trusty band
To traverse Acarnania's forest wide,
In war well season'd, and with labours
    tann'd,
Till he did greet white Achelous' tide,
And from his further bank Ætolia's wolds
    espied.

LXX

Where lone Utraikey forms its circling
    cove,
And weary waves retire to gleam at
    rest,
How brown the foliage of the green hill's
    grove,
Nodding at midnight o'er the calm bay's
    breast,
As winds come lightly whispering from
    the west,
Kissing, not ruffling, the blue deep's
    serene:—
Here Harold was received a welcome
    guest;
Nor did he pass unmoved the gentle
    scene,
For many a joy could he from Night's soft
    presence glean.

LXXI

On the smooth shore the night-fires
    brightly blazed,
The feast was done, the red wine circling
    fast,
And he that unawares had there ygazed
With gaping wonderment had stared
    aghast;
For ere night's midmost, stillest hour
    was past,
The native revels of the troop began;
Each Palikar his sabre from him cast,
And bounding hand in hand, man link'd
    to man,
Yelling their uncouth dirge, long daunced
    the kirtled clan.

LXXII

Childe Harold at a little distance stood
And view'd, but not displeased, the
    revelrie,
Nor hated harmless mirth, however
    rude:
In sooth, it was no vulgar sight to
    see
Their barbarous, yet their not indecent,
    glee;

And, as the flames along their faces
　　gleam'd,
Their gestures nimble, dark eyes flash-
　　ing free,
The long wild locks that to their girdles
　　stream'd,
While thus in concert they this lay half
　　sang, half screamed:—

1

TAMBOURGI! Tambourgi! thy 'larum afar
Gives hope to the valiant, and promise of
　　war;
All the sons of the mountains arise at the
　　note,
Chimariot, Illyrian, and dark Suliote!

2

Oh! who is more brave than a dark Suliote,
In his snowy camese and his shaggy
　　capote?
To the wolf and the vulture he leaves his
　　wild flock,
And descends to the plain like the stream
　　from the rock.

3

Shall the sons of Chimari, who never
　　forgive
The fault of a friend, bid an enemy live?
Let those guns so unerring such vengeance
　　forego?
What mark is so fair as the breast of a foe?

4

Macedonia sends forth her invincible race;
For a time they abandon the cave and the
　　chase;
But those scarfs of blood-red shall be
　　redder, before
The sabre is sheathed and the battle is o'er.

5

Then the pirates of Parga that dwell by the
　　waves,
And teach the pale Franks what it is to be
　　slaves,
Shall leave on the beach the long galley
　　and oar,
And track to his covert the captive on
　　shore.

6

I ask not the pleasures that riches supply,
My sabre shall win what the feeble must
　　buy;
Shall win the young bride with her long
　　flowing hair,
And many a maid from her mother shall
　　tear.

7

I love the fair face of the maid in her
　　youth,
Her caresses shall lull me, her music shall
　　soothe;
Let her bring from the chamber her many-
　　toned lyre,
And sing us a song on the fall of her sire.

8

Remember the moment when Previsa fell,
The shrieks of the conquer'd, the con-
　　queror's yell;
The roofs that we fired, and the plunder
　　we shared,
The wealthy we slaughter'd, the lovely we
　　spared.

9

I talk not of mercy, I talk not of fear;
He neither must know who would serve
　　the Vizier:
Since the days of our prophet the Crescent
　　ne'er saw
A chief ever glorious like Ali Pashaw.

10

Dark Muchtar his son to the Danube is
　　sped,
Let the yellow-hair'd Giaours view his
　　horse-tail with dread;
When his Delhis come dashing in blood
　　o'er the banks,
How few shall escape from the Muscovite
　　ranks!

11

Selictar! unsheathe then our chief's scimi-
　　tar;
Tambourgi! thy 'larum gives promise of
　　war.
Ye mountains, that see us descend to the
　　shore,
Shall view us as victors, or view us no
　　more!

LXXIII

Fair Greece! sad relic of departed worth!
Immortal, though no more; though
　　fallen, great!
Who now shall lead thy scatter'd child-
　　ren forth,
And long accustom'd bondage un-
　　create?
Not such thy sons who whilome did
　　await,
The hopeless warriors of a willing doom,
In bleak Thermopylæ's sepulchral
　　strait—
Oh! who that gallant spirit shall re-
　　sume,
Leap from Eurotas' banks, and call thee
　　from the tomb?

LXXIV

Spirit of freedom! when on Phyle's brow
Thou sat'st with Thrasybulus and his train,
Couldst thou forebode the dismal hour which now
Dims the green beauties of thine Attic plain?
Not thirty tyrants now enforce the chain,
But every carle can lord it o'er thy land;
Nor rise thy sons, but idly rail in vain,
Trembling beneath the scourge of Turkish hand;
From birth till death enslaved; in word, in deed, unmann'd.

LXXV

In all save form alone, how changed! and who
That marks the fire still sparkling in each eye,
Who would but deem their bosoms burn'd anew
With thy unquenchèd beam, lost Liberty!
And many dream withal the hour is nigh
That gives them back their fathers' heritage:
For foreign arms and aid they fondly sigh,
Nor solely dare encounter hostile rage,
Or tear their name defiled from Slavery's mournful page.

LXXVI

Hereditary bondsmen! know ye not
Who would be free themselves must strike the blow?
By their right arms the conquest must be wrought?
Will Gaul or Muscovite redress ye? no!
True, they may lay your proud despoilers low,
But not for you will Freedom's altars flame.
Shades of the Helots! triumph o'er your foe!
Greece! change thy lords, thy state is still the same;
Thy glorious day is o'er, but not thy years of shame.

LXXVII

The city won for Allah from the Giaour,
The Giaour from Othman's race again may wrest;
And the Serai's impenetrable tower
Receive the fiery Frank, her former guest;
Or Wahab's rebel brood, who dared divest

The prophet's tomb of all its pious spoil,
May wind their path of blood along the West;
But ne'er will freedom seek this fated soil,
But slave succeed to slave through years of endless toil.

LXXVIII

Yet mark their mirth—ere lenten days begin,
That penance which their holy rites prepare
To shrive from man his weight of mortal sin,
By daily abstinence and nightly prayer:
But ere his sackcloth garb Repentance wear,
Some days of joyaunce are decreed to all,
To take of pleasaunce each his secret share,
In motley robe to dance at masking ball,
And join the mimic train of merry Carnival.

LXXIX

And whose more rife with merriment than thine,
Oh Stamboul! once the empress of their reign?
Though turbans now pollute Sophia's shrine,
And Greece her very altars eyes in vain:
(Alas! her woes will still pervade my strain!)
Gay were her minstrels once, for free her throng,
All felt the common joy they now must feign,
Nor oft I've seen such sight, nor heard such song,
As woo'd the eye, and thrill'd the Bosphorus along.

LXXX

Loud was the lightsome tumult on the shore,
Oft Music changed, but never ceased her tone,
And timely echo'd back the measured oar,
And rippling waters made a pleasant moan:
The Queen of tides on high consenting shone,
And when a transient breeze swept o'er the wave,
'Twas, as if darting from her heavenly throne,
A brighter glance her form reflected gave,
Till sparkling billows seem'd to light the banks they lave.

LXXXI

Glanced many a light caique along the
  foam,
Danced on the shore the daughters of
  the land,
No thought had man or maid of rest or
  home,
While many a languid eye and thrilling
  hand
Exchanged the look few bosoms may
  withstand,
Or gently prest, return'd the pressure
  still:
Oh Love! young Love! bound in thy
  rosy band,
Let sage or cynic prattle as he will,
These hours, and only these, redeem Life's
  years of ill!

LXXXII

But, midst the throng in merry mas-
  querade,
Lurk there no hearts that throb with
  secret pain,
Even through the closest searment half
  betray'd?
To such the gentle murmurs of the main
Seem to re-echo all they mourn in vain;
To such the gladness of the gamesome
  crowd
Is source of wayward thought and stern
  disdain:
How do they loathe the laughter idly
  loud,
And long to change the robe of revel for
  the shroud!

LXXXIII

This must he feel, the true-born son of
  Greece,
If Greece one true-born patriot still can
  boast:
Not such as prate of war, but skulk in
  peace,
The bondsman's peace, who sighs for
  all he lost,
Yet with smooth smile his tyrant can
  accost,
And wield the slavish sickle, not the
  sword:
Ah! Greece! they love thee least who
  owe thee most—
Their birth, their blood, and that sub-
  lime record
Of hero sires, who shame thy now de-
  generate horde!

LXXXIV

When riseth Lacedemon's hardihood,
When Thebes Epaminondas rears again,
When Athens' children are with hearts
  endued,
When Grecian mothers shall give birth
  to men.

Then may'st thou be restored; but not
  till then.
A thousand years scarce serve to form
  a state;
An hour may lay it in the dust: and
  when
Can man its shatter'd splendour renovate,
Recall its virtues back, and vanquish Time
  and Fate?

LXXXV

And yet how lovely in thine age of woe,
Land of lost gods and godlike men, art
  thou!
Thy vales of evergreen, thy hills of snow,
Proclaim thee Nature's varied favourite
  now:
Thy fanes, thy temples to thy surface
  bow,
Commingling slowly with heroic earth,
Broke by the share of every rustic
  plough:
So perish monuments of mortal birth,
So perish all in turn, save well-recorded
  Worth;

LXXXVI

Save where some solitary column
  mourns
Above its prostrate brethren of the
  cave;
Save where Tritonia's airy shrine adorns
Colonna's cliff, and gleams along the
  wave;
Save o'er some warrior's half-forgotten
  grave,
Where the gray stones and unmolested
  grass
Ages, but not oblivion, feebly brave;
While strangers only not regardless
  pass,
Lingering like me, perchance, to gaze, and
  sigh 'Alas!'

LXXXVII

Yet are thy skies as blue, thy crags as
  wild;
Sweet are thy groves, and verdant are
  thy fields,
Thine olive ripe as when Minerva
  smiled,
And still his honey'd wealth Hymettus
  yields;
There the blithe bee his fragrant fortress
  builds,
The freeborn wanderer of thy moun-
  tain-air;
Apollo still thy long, long summer gilds,
Still in his beam Mendeli's marbles
  glare;
Art, Glory, Freedom fail, but Nature still
  is fair.

LXXXVIII

Where'er we tread 'tis haunted, holy
  ground;
No earth of thine is lost in vulgar mould,
But one vast realm of wonder spreads
  around,
And all the Muse's tales seem truly told,
Till the sense aches with gazing to be-
  hold
The scenes our earliest dreams have
  dwelt upon;
Each hill and dale, each deepening glen
  and wold
Defies the power which crush'd thy
  temples gone:
Age shakes Athena's tower, but spares
  gray Marathon.

LXXXIX

The sun, the soil, but not the slave, the
  same;
Unchanged in all except its foreign
  lord;
Preserves alike its bounds and bound-
  less fame
The Battle-field, where Persia's victim
  horde
First bow'd beneath the brunt of Hellas'
  sword,
As on the morn to distant Glory dear,
When Marathon became a magic word;
Which utter'd, to the hearer's eye
  appear
The camp, the host, the fight, the con-
  queror's career,

XC

The flying Mede, his shaftless broken
  bow;
The fiery Greek, his red pursuing spear;
Mountains above, Earth's, Ocean's
  plain below;
Death in the front, Destruction in the
  rear!
Such was the scene—what now remain-
  eth here?
What sacred trophy marks the hallow'd
  ground,
Recording Freedom's smile and Asia's
  tear?
The rifled urn, the violated mound,
The dust thy courser's hoof, rude stranger!
  spurns around.

XCI

Yet to the remnants of thy splendour
  past
Shall pilgrims, pensive, but unwearied,
  throng;
Long shall the voyager, with th' Ionian
  blast,
Hail the bright clime of battle and of
  song;

Long shall thine annals and immortal
  tongue
Fill with thy fame the youth of many a
  shore;
Boast of the aged! lesson of the young!
Which sages venerate and bards adore,
As Pallas and the Muse unveil their awful
  lore.

XCII

The parted bosom clings to wonted
  home,
If aught that's kindred cheer the wel-
  come hearth;
He that is lonely, hither let him roam,
And gaze complacent on congenial
  earth.
Greece is no lightsome land of social
  mirth:
But he whom Sadness sootheth may
  abide,
And scarce regret the region of his
  birth,
When wandering slow by Delphi's
  sacred side,
Or gazing o'er the plains where Greek and
  Persian died.

XCIII

Let such approach this consecrated
  land,
And pass in peace along the magic
  waste;
But spare its relics—let no busy hand
Deface the scenes, already how defaced!
Not for such purpose were these altars
  placed:
Revere the remnants nations once
  revered:
So may our country's name be undis-
  graced,
So may'st thou prosper where thy youth
  was rear'd,
By every honest joy of love and life endear'd!

XCIV

For thee, who thus in too protracted
  song
Hast soothed thine idlesse with in-
  glorious lays,
Soon shall thy voice be lost amid the
  throng
Of louder minstrels in these later days:
To such resign the strife for fading
  bays—
Ill may such contest now the spirit move
Which heeds nor keen reproach nor
  partial praise,
Since cold each kinder heart that might
  approve,
And none are left to please when none are
  left to love.

XCV

Thou too art gone, thou loved and
    lovely one!
Whom youth and youth's affections
    bound to me;
Who did for me what none beside have
    done,
Nor shrank from one albeit unworthy
    thee.
What is my being? thou hast ceased to
    be!
Nor staid to welcome here thy wanderer
    home,
Who mourns o'er hours which we no
    more shall see—
Would they had never been, or were to
    come!
Would he had ne'er return'd to find fresh
    cause to roam!

XCVI

Oh! ever loving, lovely, and beloved!
How selfish Sorrow ponders on the past,
And clings to thoughts now better far
    removed!
But Time shall tear thy shadow from
    me last.
All thou couldst have of mine, stern
    Death! thou hast;
The parent, friend, and now the more
    than friend;
Ne'er yet for one thine arrows flew so
    fast,
And grief with grief continuing still to
    blend,
Hath snatch'd the little joy that life had
    yet to lend.

XCVII

Then must I plunge again into the
    crowd,
And follow all that Peace disdains to
    seek?
Where Revel calls, and Laughter, vainly
    loud,
False to the heart, distorts the hollow
    cheek,
To leave the flagging spirit doubly weak;
Still o'er the features, which perforce
    they cheer,
To feign the pleasure or conceal the
    pique;
Smiles form the channel of a future tear,
Or raise the writhing lip with ill-dis-
    sembled sneer.

XCVIII

What is the worst of woes that wait on
    age?
What stamps the wrinkle deeper on the
    brow?
To view each loved one blotted from
    life's page,
And be alone on earth, as I am now.

Before the Chastener humbly let me
    bow,
O'er hearts divided and o'er hopes
    destroy'd:
Roll on, vain days! full reckless may ye
    flow,
Since Time hath reft whate'er my soul
    enjoy'd,
And with the ills of Eld mine earlier years
    alloy'd.

CANTO THE THIRD

'Afin que cette application vous forçât à penser
à autre chose; il n'y a en vérité de remède que
celui-là et le temps.'—*Lettre du Roi de Prusse à
D'Alembert, Sept.* 7, 1776.

I

Is thy face like thy mother's, my fair
    child!
ADA! sole daughter of my house and
    heart?
When last I saw thy young blue eyes
    they smiled,
And then we parted,—not as now we
    part,
But with a hope.—
        Awaking with a start,
The waters heave around me; and on
    high
The winds lift up their voices: I depart,
Whither I know not; but the hour's
    gone by,
When Albion's lessening shores could
    grieve or glad mine eye.

II

Once more upon the waters! yet once
    more!
And the waves bound beneath me as a
    steed
That knows his rider. Welcome to their
    roar!
Swift be their guidance, wheresoe'er it
    lead!
Though the strain'd mast should quiver
    as a reed,
And the rent canvas fluttering strew the
    gale,
Still must I on; for I am as a weed,
Flung from the rock, on Ocean's foam
    to sail
Where'er the surge may sweep, the tem-
    pest's breath prevail.

III

In my youth's summer I did sing of One,
The wandering outlaw of his own dark
    mind;
Again I seize the theme, then but begun,
And bear it with me, as the rushing wind
Bears the cloud onwards: in that Tale
    I find

The furrows of long thought, and dried-
    up tears,
Which, ebbing, leave a sterile track
    behind,
O'er which all heavily the journeying
    years
Plod the last sands of life,—where not a
    flower appears.

IV

Since my young days of passion—joy,
    or pain,
Perchance my heart and harp have lost
    a string,
And both may jar: it may be, that in vain
I would essay as I have sung to sing.
Yet, though a dreary strain, to this I
    cling;
So that it wean me from the weary dream
Of selfish grief or gladness—so it fling
Forgetfulness around me—it shall seem
To me, though to none else, a not un-
    grateful theme.

V

He, who grown aged in this world of woe,
In deeds, not years, piercing the depths
    of life,
So that no wonder waits him; nor below
Can love or sorrow, fame, ambition,
    strife,
Cut to his heart again with the keen knife
Of silent, sharp endurance: he can tell
Why thought seeks refuge in lone caves,
    yet rife
With airy images, and shapes which
    dwell
Still unimpair'd, though old, in the soul's
    haunted cell.

VI

'Tis to create, and in creating live
A being more intense, that we endow
With form our fancy, gaining as we
    give
The life we image, even as I do now.
What am I? Nothing: but not so art
    thou,
Soul of my thought! with whom I
    traverse earth,
Invisible but gazing, as I glow
Mix'd with thy spirit, blended with thy
    birth,
And feeling still with thee in my crush'd
    feelings' dearth.

VII

Yet must I think less wildly:—I *have*
    thought
Too long and darkly, till my brain
    became,
In its own eddy boiling and o'er-
    wrought,
A whirling gulf of phantasy and flame:

And thus, untaught in youth my heart
    to tame,
My springs of life were poison'd. 'Tis
    too late!
Yet am I changed; though still enough
    the same
In strength to bear what time cannot
    abate,
And feed on bitter fruits without accusing
    Fate.

VIII

Something too much of this:—but now
    'tis past,
And the spell closes with its silent seal.
Long absent HAROLD re-appears at last;
He of the breast which fain no more
    would feel,
Wrung with the wounds which kill not,
    but ne'er heal;
Yet Time, who changes all, had alter'd
    him
In soul and aspect as in age: years steal
Fire from the mind as vigour from the
    limb;
And life's enchanted cup but sparkles near
    the brim.

IX

His had been quaff'd too quickly, and
    he found
The dregs were wormwood; but he fill'd
    again,
And from a purer fount, on holier
    ground,
And deem'd its spring perpetual; but in
    vain!
Still round him clung invisibly a chain
Which gall'd for ever, fettering though
    unseen,
And heavy though it clank'd not; worn
    with pain,
Which pined although it spoke not, and
    grew keen,
Entering with every step he took through
    many a scene.

X

Secure in guarded coldness, he had
    mix'd
Again in fancied safety with his kind,
And deem'd his spirit now so firmly fix'd
And sheath'd with an invulnerable
    mind,
That, if no joy, no sorrow lurk'd behind;
And he, as one, might 'midst the many
    stand
Unheeded, searching through the crowd
    to find
Fit speculation; such as in strange land
He found in wonder-works of God and
    Nature's hand.

XI

But who can view the ripen'd rose, nor
  seek
To wear it? who can curiously behold
The smoothness and the sheen of
  beauty's cheek,
Nor feel the heart can never all grow
  old?
Who can contemplate Fame through
  clouds unfold
The star which rises o'er her steep, nor
  climb?
Harold, once more within the vortex,
  roll'd
On with the giddy circle, chasing Time,
Yet with a nobler aim than in his youth's
  fond prime.

XII

But soon he knew himself the most
  unfit
Of men to herd with Man; with whom
  he held
Little in common; untaught to submit
His thoughts to others, though his soul
  was quell'd
In youth by his own thoughts; still un-
  compell'd,
He would not yield dominion of his mind
To spirits against whom his own rebell'd;
Proud though in desolation; which
  could find
A life within itself, to breathe without
  mankind.

XIII

Where rose the mountains, there to him
  were friends;
Where roll'd the ocean, thereon was his
  home;
Where a blue sky, and glowing clime,
  extends,
He had the passion and the power to
  roam;
The desert, forest, cavern, breaker's
  foam,
Were unto him companionship; they
  spake
A mutual language, clearer than the
  tome
Of his land's tongue, which he would
  oft forsake
For Nature's pages glass'd by sunbeams
  on the lake.

XIV

Like the Chaldean, he could watch the
  stars,
Till he had peopled them with beings
  bright
As their own beams; and earth, and
  earthborn jars,
And human frailties, were forgotten
  quite:

Could he have kept his spirit to that
  flight
He had been happy; but this clay will
  sink
Its spark immortal, envying it the light
To which it mounts, as if to break the
  link
That keeps us from yon heaven which
  woos us to its brink.

XV

But in Man's dwellings he became a
  thing
Restless and worn, and stern and weari-
  some,
Droop'd as a wild-born falcon with
  clipt wing,
To whom the boundless air alone were
  home:
Then came his fit again, which to o'ercome,
As eagerly the barr'd-up bird will beat
His breast and beak against his wiry
  dome
Till the blood tinge his plumage, so the
  heat
Of his impeded soul would through his
  bosom eat.

XVI

Self-exiled Harold wanders forth again,
With nought of hope left, but with less
  of gloom;
The very knowledge that he lived in vain,
That all was over on this side the tomb,
Had made Despair a smilingness assume,
Which, though 'twere wild,—as on the
  plunder'd wreck
When mariners would madly meet their
  doom
With draughts intemperate on the
  sinking deck,—
Did yet inspire a cheer, which he forbore
  to check.

XVII

Stop!—for thy tread is on an Empire's
  dust!
An Earthquake's spoil is sepulchred
  below!
Is the spot mark'd with no colossal
  bust?
Nor column trophied for triumphal
  show?
None; but the moral's truth tells simpler
  so,
As the ground was before, thus let it
  be;—
How that red rain hath made the harvest
  grow!
And is this all the world has gain'd by
  thee,
Thou first and last of fields! king-making
  Victory?

XVIII

And Harold stands upon this place of skulls,
The grave of France, the deadly Waterloo!
How in an hour the power which gave annuls
Its gifts, transferring fame as fleeting too!
In 'pride of place' here last the eagle flew,
Then tore with bloody talon the rent plain,
Pierced by the shaft of banded nations through;
Ambition's life and labours all were vain;
He wears the shatter'd links of the world's broken chain.

XIX

Fit retribution! Gaul may champ the bit
And foam in fetters;—but is Earth more free?
Did nations combat to make *One* submit;
Or league to teach all kings true sovereignty?
What! shall reviving Thraldom again be
The patch'd-up idol of enlighten'd days?
Shall we, who struck the Lion down, shall we
Pay the Wolf homage? proffering lowly gaze
And servile knees to thrones? No; *prove* before ye praise!

XX

If not, o'er one fallen despot boast no more!
In vain fair cheeks were furrow'd with hot tears
For Europe's flowers long rooted up before
The trampler of her vineyards; in vain years
Of death, depopulation, bondage, fears,
Have all been borne, and broken by the accord
Of roused-up millions; all that most endears
Glory, is when the myrtle wreathes a sword
Such as Harmodius drew on Athens' tyrant lord.

XXI

There was a sound of revelry by night,
And Belgium's capital had gather'd then
Her Beauty and her Chivalry, and bright
The lamps shone o'er fair women and brave men;
A thousand hearts beat happily; and when
Music arose with its voluptuous swell,
Soft eyes look'd love to eyes which spake again,
And all went merry as a marriage bell;
But hush! hark! a deep sound strikes like a rising knell!

XXII

Did ye not hear it?—No; 'twas but the wind,
Or the car rattling o'er the stony street;
On with the dance! let joy be unconfined;
No sleep till morn, when Youth and Pleasure meet
To chase the glowing Hours with flying feet—
But hark!—that heavy sound breaks in once more,
As if the clouds its echo would repeat;
And nearer, clearer, deadlier than before!
Arm! Arm! it is—it is—the cannon's opening roar!

XXIII

Within a window'd niche of that high hall
Sate Brunswick's fated chieftain; he did hear
That sound the first amidst the festival,
And caught its tone with Death's prophetic ear;
And when they smiled because he deem'd it near,
His heart more truly knew that peal too well
Which stretch'd his father on a bloody bier,
And roused the vengeance blood alone could quell;
He rush'd into the field, and, foremost fighting, fell.

XXIV

Ah! then and there was hurrying to and fro,
And gathering tears, and tremblings of distress,
And cheeks all pale, which but an hour ago
Blush'd at the praise of their own loveliness;
And there were sudden partings, such as press
The life from out young hearts, and choking sighs
Which ne'er might be repeated; who could guess
If ever more should meet those mutual eyes,
Since upon night so sweet such awful morn could rise!

XXV

And there was mounting in hot haste: the steed,
The mustering squadron, and the clattering car,
Went pouring forward with impetuous speed,
And swiftly forming in the ranks of war;
And the deep thunder peal on peal afar;
And near, the beat of the alarming drum
Roused up the soldier ere the morning star;
While throng'd the citizens with terror dumb,
Or whispering, with white lips—'The foe! they come! they come!'

XXVI

And wild and high the 'Cameron's gathering' rose!
The war-note of Lochiel, which Albyn's hills
Have heard, and heard, too, have her Saxon foes:—
How in the noon of night that pibroch thrills,
Savage and shrill! But with the breath which fills
Their mountain-pipe, so fill the mountaineers
With the fierce native daring which instils
The stirring memory of a thousand years,
And Evan's, Donald's fame rings in each clansman's ears!

XXVII

And Ardennes waves above them her green leaves,
Dewy with nature's tear-drops as they pass,
Grieving, if aught inanimate e'er grieves,
Over the unreturning brave,—alas!
Ere evening to be trodden like the grass
Which now beneath them, but above shall grow
In its next verdure, when this fiery mass
Of living valour, rolling on the foe
And burning with high hope shall moulder cold and low.

XXVIII

Last noon beheld them full of lusty life,
Last eve in Beauty's circle proudly gay,
The midnight brought the signal-sound of strife,
The morn the marshalling in arms,—the day
Battle's magnificently stern array!

The thunder-clouds close o'er it, which when rent
The earth is cover'd thick with other clay,
Which her own clay shall cover, heap'd and pent,
Rider and horse,—friend, foe,—in one red burial blent!

XXIX

Their praise is hymn'd by loftier harps than mine:
Yet one I would select from that proud throng,
Partly because they blend me with his line,
And partly that I did his sire some wrong,
And partly that bright names will hallow song;
And his was of the bravest, and when shower'd
The death-bolts deadliest the thinn'd files along,
Even where the thickest of war's tempest lower'd,
They reach'd no nobler breast than thine, young gallant Howard!

XXX

There have been tears and breaking hearts for thee,
And mine were nothing had I such to give;
But when I stood beneath the fresh green tree,
Which living waves where thou didst cease to live,
And saw around me the wide field revive
With fruits and fertile promise, and the Spring
Came forth her work of gladness to contrive,
With all her reckless birds upon the wing,
I turn'd from all she brought to those she could not bring.

XXXI

I turn'd to thee, to thousands, of whom each
And one as all a ghastly gap did make
In his own kind and kindred, whom to teach
Forgetfulness were mercy for their sake;
The Archangel's trump, not Glory's, must awake
Those whom they thirst for; though the sound of Fame
May for a moment soothe, it cannot slake
The fever of vain longing, and the name
So honour'd but assumes a stronger, bitterer claim.

XXXII

They mourn, but smile at length; and, smiling, mourn;
The tree will wither long before it fall;
The hull drives on, though mast and sail be torn;
The roof-tree sinks, but moulders on the hall
In massy hoariness; the ruin'd wall
Stands when its wind-worn battlements are gone;
The bars survive the captive they enthral;
The day drags through, though storms keep out the sun;
And thus the heart will break, yet brokenly live on

XXXIII

Even as a broken mirror, which the glass
In every fragment multiplies; and makes
A thousand images of one that was,
The same, and still the more, the more it breaks;
And thus the heart will do which not forsakes,
Living in shatter'd guise; and still, and cold,
And bloodless, with its sleepless sorrow aches,
Yet withers on till all without is old,
Showing no visible sign, for such things are untold.

XXXIV

There is a very life in our despair,
Vitality of poison,—a quick root
Which feeds these deadly branches; for it were
As nothing did we die; but Life will suit
Itself to Sorrow's most detested fruit,
Like to the apples on the Dead Sea's shore,
All ashes to the taste: Did man compute
Existence by enjoyment, and count o'er
Such hours 'gainst years of life,—say, would he name threescore?

XXXV

The Psalmist number'd out the years of man:
They are enough: and if thy tale be *true*,
Thou, who didst grudge him even that fleeting span,
More than enough, thou fatal Waterloo!
Millions of tongues record thee, and anew
Their children's lips shall echo them, and say—

'Here, where the sword united nations drew,
Our countrymen were warring on that day!'
And this is much, and all which will not pass away.

XXXVI

There sunk the greatest, nor the worst of men,
Whose spirit, antithetically mixt,
One moment of the mightiest, and again
On little objects with like firmness fixt;
Extreme in all things! hadst thou been betwixt,
Thy throne had still been thine, or never been;
For daring made thy rise as fall: thou seek'st
Even now to re-assume the imperial mien,
And shake again the world, the Thunderer of the scene!

XXXVII

Conqueror and captive of the earth art thou!
She trembles at thee still, and thy wild name
Was ne'er more bruited in men's minds than now
That thou art nothing, save the jest of Fame,
Who woo'd thee once, thy vassal, and became
The flatterer of thy fierceness, till thou wert
A god unto thyself; nor less the same
To the astounded kingdoms all inert,
Who deem'd thee for a time whate'er thou didst assert.

XXXVIII

Oh, more or less than man—in high or low,
Battling with nations, flying from the field;
Now making monarchs' necks thy footstool, now
More than thy meanest soldier taught to yield;
An empire thou couldst crush, command, rebuild,
But govern not thy pettiest passion, nor,
However deeply in men's spirits skill'd,
Look through thine own, nor curb the lust of war,
Nor learn that tempted Fate will leave the loftiest star.

XXXIX

Yet well thy soul hath brook'd the
    turning tide
With that untaught innate philosophy,
Which, be it wisdom, coldness, or deep
    pride,
Is gall and wormwood to an enemy.
When the whole host of hatred stood
    hard by,
To watch and mock thee shrinking, thou
    hast smiled
With a sedate and all-enduring eye;—
When Fortune fled her spoil'd and
    favourite child,
He stood unbow'd beneath the ills upon
    him piled.

XL

Sager than in thy fortunes; for in them
Ambition steel'd thee on too far to show
That just habitual scorn, which could
    contemn
Men and their thoughts; 'twas wise to
    feel, not so
To wear it ever on thy lip and brow,
And spurn the instruments thou wert to
    use
Till they were turn'd unto thine over-
    throw:
'Tis but a worthless world to win or
    lose;
So hath it proved to thee, and all such lot
    who choose.

XLI

If, like a tower upon a headland rock,
Thou hadst been made to stand or fall
    alone,
Such scorn of man had help'd to brave
    the shock;
But men's thoughts were the steps which
    paved thy throne,
Their admiration thy best weapon
    shone;
The part of Philip's son was thine, not
    then
(Unless aside thy purple had been
    thrown)
Like stern Diogenes to mock at men;
For sceptred cynics earth were far too
    wide a den.

XLII

But quiet to quick bosoms is a hell,
And *there* hath been thy bane; there is
    a fire
And motion of the soul which will not
    dwell
In its own narrow being, but aspire
Beyond the fitting medium of desire;
And, but once kindled, quenchless ever-
    more,
Preys upon high adventure, nor can tire

Of aught but rest; a fever at the core,
Fatal to him who bears, to all who ever
    bore.

XLIII

This makes the madmen who have made
    men mad
By their contagion; Conquerors and
    Kings,
Founders of sects and systems, to whom
    add
Sophists, Bards, Statesmen, all un-
    quiet things
Which stir too strongly the soul's secret
    springs,
And are themselves the fools to those
    they fool;
Envied, yet how unenviable! what stings
Are theirs! One breast laid open were
    a school
Which would unteach mankind the lust
    to shine or rule:

XLIV

Their breath is agitation, and their life
A storm whereon they ride, to sink at
    last,
And yet so nursed and bigoted to strife,
That should their days, surviving perils
    past,
Melt to calm twilight, they feel overcast
With sorrow and supineness, and so die;
Even as a flame unfed, which runs to
    waste
With its own flickering, or a sword laid
    by,
Which eats into itself, and rusts inglori-
    ously.

XLV

He who ascends to mountain-tops, shall
    find
The loftiest peaks most wrapt in clouds
    and snow;
He who surpasses or subdues mankind,
Must look down on the hate of those
    below.
Though high *above* the sun of glory
    glow,
And far *beneath* the earth and ocean
    spread,
Round him are icy rocks, and loudly
    blow
Contending tempests on his naked head,
And thus reward the toils which to those
    summits led.

XLVI

Away with these! true Wisdom's world
    will be
Within its own creation, or in thine,
Maternal Nature! for who teems like
    thee,
Thus on the banks of thy majestic Rhine?

There Harold gazes on a work divine,
A blending of all beauties; streams and
  dells,
Fruit, foliage, crag, wood, cornfield,
  mountain, vine,
And chiefless castles breathing stern
  farewells
From gray but leafy walls, where Ruin
  greenly dwells.

XLVII

And there they stand, as stands a lofty
  mind,
Worn, but unstooping to the baser
  crowd,
All tenantless, save to the crannying
  wind,
Or holding dark communion with the
  cloud.
There was a day when they were young
  and proud;
Banners on high, and battles pass'd
  below;
But they who fought are in a bloody
  shroud,
And those which waved are shredless
  dust ere now,
And the bleak battlements shall bear no
  future blow.

XLVIII

Beneath these battlements, within those
  walls,
Power dwelt amidst her passions; in
  proud state
Each robber chief upheld his armed
  halls,
Doing his evil will, nor less elate
Than mightier heroes of a longer date.
What want these outlaws conquerors
  should have
But history's purchased page to call
  them great?
A wider space, an ornamented grave?
Their hopes were not less warm, their
  souls were full as brave.

XLIX

In their baronial feuds and single fields,
What deeds of prowess unrecorded died!
And Love, which lent a blazon to their
  shields,
With emblems well devised by amorous
  pride,
Through all the mail of iron hearts
  would glide;
But still their flame was fierceness, and
  drew on
Keen contest and destruction near
  allied,
And many a tower for some fair mischief
  won,
Saw the discolour'd Rhine beneath its
  ruin run.

L

But Thou, exulting and abounding
  river!
Making thy waves a blessing as they
  flow
Through banks whose beauty would
  endure for ever
Could man but leave thy bright creation
  so,
Nor its fair promise from the surface
  mow
With the sharp scythe of conflict,—then
  to see
Thy valley of sweet waters, were to know
Earth paved like Heaven; and to seem
  such to me,
Even now what wants thy stream?—that
  it should Lethe be.

LI

A thousand battles have assail'd thy
  banks,
But these and half their fame have pass'd
  away,
And Slaughter heap'd on high his
  weltering ranks;
Their very graves are gone, and what
  are they?
Thy tide wash'd down the blood of
  yesterday,
And all was stainless, and on thy clear
  stream
Glass'd, with its dancing light, the sunny
  ray;
But o'er the blacken'd memory's blighting dream
Thy waves would vainly roll, all sweeping
  as they seem.

LII

Thus Harold inly said, and pass'd along,
Yet not insensible to all which here
Awoke the jocund birds to early song
In glens which might have made even
  exile dear:
Though on his brow were graven lines
  austere,
And tranquil sternness, which had ta'en
  the place
Of feelings fierier far but less severe,
Joy was not always absent from his face,
But o'er it in such scenes would steal with
  transient trace.

LIII

Nor was all love shut from him, though
  his days
Of passion had consumed themselves to
  dust.
It is in vain that we would coldly gaze
On such as smile upon us; the heart
  must
Leap kindly back to kindness, though
  disgust

Hath wean'd it from all worldlings:
   thus he felt,
For there was soft remembrance, and
   sweet trust
In one fond breast, to which his own
   would melt,
And in its tenderer hour on that his bosom
   dwelt.

LIV

And he had learn'd to love,—I know not
   why,
For this in such as him seems strange
   of mood,—
The helpless looks of blooming infancy,
Even in its earliest nurture; what sub-
   dued,
To change like this, a mind so far im-
   bued
With scorn of man, it little boots to
   know;
But thus it was; and though in solitude
Small power the nipp'd affections have
   to grow,
In him this glow'd when all beside had
   ceased to glow.

LV

And there was one soft breast, as hath
   been said,
Which unto his was bound by stronger
   ties
Than the church links withal; and,
   though unwed,
That love was pure, and, far above dis-
   guise,
Had stood the test of mortal enmities
Still undivided, and cemented more
By peril, dreaded most in female eyes;
But this was firm, and from a foreign
   shore
Well to that heart might his these absent
   greetings pour!

1

The castled crag of Drachenfels
Frowns o'er the wide and winding
   Rhine,
Whose breast of waters broadly swells
Between the banks which bear the vine,
And hills all rich with blossom'd trees,
And fields which promise corn and
   wine,
And scatter'd cities crowning these,
Whose far white walls along them
   shine,
Have strew'd a scene, which I should
   see
With double joy wert *thou* with me.

2

And peasant girls, with deep blue eyes,
And hands which offer early flowers,
Walk smiling o'er this paradise;
Above, the frequent feudal towers

Through green leaves lift their walls
   of gray;
And many a rock which steeply lowers,
And noble arch in proud decay,
Look o'er this vale of vintage-bowers;
But one thing want these banks of
   Rhine,—
Thy gentle hand to clasp in mine!

3

I send the lilies given to me;
Though long before thy hand they
   touch,
I know that they must wither'd be,
But yet reject them not as such;
For I have cherish'd them as dear,
Because they yet may meet thine eye,
And guide thy soul to mine even here,
When thou behold'st them drooping
   nigh,
And know'st them gather'd by the
   Rhine,
And offer'd from my heart to thine!

4

The river nobly foams and flows,
The charm of this enchanted ground,
And all its thousand turns disclose
Some fresher beauty varying round:
The haughtiest breast its wish might
   bound
Through life to dwell delighted here;
Nor could on earth a spot be found
To nature and to me so dear,
Could thy dear eyes in following mine
Still sweeten more these banks of
   Rhine!

LVI

By Coblentz, on a rise of gentle ground,
There is a small and simple pyramid,
Crowning the summit of the verdant
   mound;
Beneath its base are heroes' ashes hid,
Our enemy's—but let not that forbid
Honour to Marceau! o'er whose early
   tomb
Tears, big tears, gush'd from the rough
   soldier's lid,
Lamenting and yet envying such a doom,
Falling for France, whose rights he battled
   to resume.

LVII

Brief, brave, and glorious was his young
   career,—
His mourners were two hosts, his friends
   and foes;
And fitly may the stranger lingering here
Pray for his gallant spirit's bright repose;
For he was Freedom's champion, one of
   those,

The few in number, who had not o'er-
      stept
The charter to chastise which she be-
      stows
On such as wield her weapons; he had
      kept
The whiteness of his soul, and thus men
      o'er him wept.

LVIII

Here Ehrenbreitstein, with her shatter'd
      wall
Black with the miner's blast, upon her
      height
Yet shows of what she was, when shell
      and ball
Rebounding idly on her strength did
      light:
A tower of victory! from whence the
      flight
Of baffled foes was watch'd along the
      plain:
But Peace destroy'd what War could
      never blight,
And laid those proud roofs bare to Sum-
      mer's rain—
On which the iron shower for years had
      pour'd in vain.

LIX

Adieu to thee, fair Rhine! How long
      delighted
The stranger fain would linger on his
      way!
Thine is a scene alike where souls
      united
Or lonely Contemplation thus might
      stray;
And could the ceaseless vultures cease
      to prey
On self-condemning bosoms, it were
      here,
Where Nature, nor too sombre nor too
      gay,
Wild but not rude, awful yet not austere,
Is to the mellow Earth as Autumn to the
      year.

LX

Adieu to thee again! a vain adieu!
There can be no farewell to scene like
      thine;
The mind is colour'd by thy every hue;
And if reluctantly the eyes resign
Their cherish'd gaze upon thee, lovely
      Rhine!
'Tis with the thankful glance of parting
      praise;
More mighty spots may rise, more glar-
      ing shine,
But none unite in one attaching maze
The brilliant, fair, and soft,—the glories
      of old days.

LXI

The negligently grand, the fruitful bloom
Of coming ripeness, the white city's
      sheen,
The rolling stream, the precipice's
      gloom,
The forest's growth, and Gothic walls
      between,
The wild rocks shaped as they had
      turrets been,
In mockery of man's art; and these
      withal
A race of faces happy as the scene,
Whose fertile bounties here extend to all,
Still springing o'er thy banks, though Em-
      pires near them fall.

LXII

But these recede. Above me are the
      Alps,
The palaces of Nature, whose vast walls
Have pinnacled in clouds their snowy
      scalps,
And throned Eternity in icy halls
Of cold sublimity, where forms and falls
The avalanche—the thunderbolt of
      snow!
All that expands the spirit, yet appals,
Gather around these summits, as to
      show
How Earth may pierce to Heaven, yet
      leave vain man below.

LXIII

But ere these matchless heights I dare to
      scan,
There is a spot should not be pass'd in
      vain,—
Morat! the proud, the patriot field!
      where man
May gaze on ghastly trophies of the
      slain,
Nor blush for those who conquer'd on
      that plain;
Here Burgundy bequeath'd his tombless
      host,
A bony heap, through ages to remain,
Themselves their monument;—the Sty-
      gian coast
Unsepulchred they roam'd, and shriek'd
      each wandering ghost.

LXIV

While Waterloo with Cannæ's carnage
      vies,
Morat and Marathon twin names shall
      stand;
They were true Glory's stainless vic-
      tories,
Won by the unambitious heart and hand
Of a proud, brotherly, and civic band,
All unbought champions in no princely
      cause

Of vice-entail'd Corruption; they no land
Doom'd to bewail the blasphemy of laws
Making kings' rights divine, by some
　Draconic clause.

LXV

By a lone wall a lonelier column rears
A gray and grief-worn aspect of old
　days;
'Tis the last remnant of the wreck of
　years,
And looks as with the wild-bewilder'd
　gaze
Of one to stone converted by amaze,
Yet still with consciousness; and there
　it stands
Making a marvel that it not decays,
When the coeval pride of human hands,
Levell'd Adventicum, hath strew'd her
　subject lands.

LXVI

And there—oh! sweet and sacred be the
　name!—
Julia—the daughter, the devoted—gave
Her youth to Heaven; her heart, be-
　neath a claim
Nearest to Heaven's, broke o'er a
　father's grave.
Justice is sworn 'gainst tears, and hers
　would crave
The life she lived in; but the judge was
　just,
And then she died on him she could not
　save.
Their tomb was simple, and without a
　bust,
And held within their urn one mind, one
　heart, one dust.

LXVII

But these are deeds which should not
　pass away,
And names that must not wither, though
　the earth
Forgets her empires with a just decay,
The enslavers and the enslaved, their
　death and birth;
The high, the mountain-majesty of worth
Should be, and shall, survivor of its woe,
And from its immortality look forth
In the sun's face, like yonder Alpine
　snow,
Imperishably pure beyond all things
　below.

LXVIII

Lake Leman woos me with its crystal
　face,
The mirror where the stars and moun-
　tains view
The stillness of their aspect in each trace
Its clear depth yields of their far height
　and hue:

There is too much of man here, to look
　through
With a fit mind the might which I be-
　hold;
But soon in me shall Loneliness renew
Thoughts hid, but not less cherish'd
　than of old,
Ere mingling with the herd had penn'd me
　in their fold.

LXIX

To fly from, need not be to hate, mankind:
All are not fit with them to stir and toil,
Nor is it discontent to keep the mind
Deep in its fountain, lest it overboil
In the hot throng, where we become the
　spoil
Of our infection, till too late and long
We may deplore and struggle with the
　coil,
In wretched interchange of wrong for
　wrong
Midst a contentious world, striving where
　none are strong.

LXX

There, in a moment we may plunge our
　years
In fatal penitence, and in the blight
Of our own soul turn all our blood to tears,
And colour things to come with hues of
　Night;
The race of life becomes a hopeless flight
To those that walk in darkness: on the
　sea
The boldest steer but where their ports
　invite;
But there are wanderers o'er Eternity
Whose bark drives on and on, and an-
　chor'd ne'er shall be.

LXXI

Is it not better, then, to be alone,
And love Earth only for its earthly sake?
By the blue rushing of the arrowy
　Rhone,
Or the pure bosom of its nursing lake,
Which feeds it as a mother who doth
　make
A fair but froward infant her own care,
Kissing its cries away as these awake;—
Is it not better thus our lives to wear,
Than join the crushing crowd, doom'd to
　inflict or bear?

LXXII

I live not in myself, but I become
Portion of that around me; and to me
High mountains are a feeling, but the
　hum
Of human cities torture: I can see
Nothing to loathe in nature, save to be

A link reluctant in a fleshly chain,
Class'd among creatures, when the soul
   can flee,
And with the sky, the peak, the heaving
   plain
Of ocean, or the stars, mingle, and not in
   vain.

LXXIII

And thus I am absorb'd, and this is life:
I look upon the peopled desert past,
As on a place of agony and strife,
Where, for some sin, to sorrow I was
   cast,
To act and suffer, but remount at last
With a fresh pinion; which I feel to
   spring,
Though young, yet waxing vigorous as
   the blast
Which it would cope with, on delighted
   wing,
Spurning the clay-cold bonds which round
   our being cling.

LXXIV

And when, at length, the mind shall be
   all free
From what it hates in this degraded
   form,
Reft of its carnal life, save what shall be
Existent happier in the fly and worm,—
When elements to elements conform,
And dust is as it should be, shall I not
Feel all I see, less dazzling, but more
   warm?
The bodiless thought? the Spirit of each
   spot?
Of which, even now, I share at times the
   immortal lot?

LXXV

Are not the mountains, waves, and
   skies, a part
Of me and of my soul, as I of them?
Is not the love of these deep in my heart
With a pure passion? should I not con-
   temn
All objects, if compared with these? and
   stem
A tide of suffering, rather than forego
Such feelings for the hard and worldly
   phlegm
Of those whose eyes are only turn'd
   below,
Gazing upon the ground, with thoughts
   which dare not glow?

LXXVI

But this is not my theme; and I return
To that which is immediate, and require
Those who find contemplation in the
   urn,
To look on One, whose dust was once
   all fire,

A native of the land where I respire
The clear air for a while—a passing
   guest,
Where he became a being,—whose
   desire
Was to be glorious; 'twas a foolish
   quest,
The which to gain and keep, he sacrificed
   all rest.

LXXVII

Here the self-torturing sophist, wild
   Rousseau,
The apostle of affliction, he who threw
Enchantment over passion, and from
   woe
Wrung overwhelming eloquence, first
   drew
The breath which made him wretched;
   yet he knew
How to make madness beautiful, and
   cast
O'er erring deeds and thoughts a
   heavenly hue
Of words, like sunbeams, dazzling as
   they past
The eyes, which o'er them shed tears feel-
   ingly and fast.

LXXVIII

His love was passion's essence:—as a
   tree
On fire by lightning, with ethereal flame
Kindled he was, and blasted; for to
   be
Thus, and enamour'd, were in him the
   same.
But his was not the love of living
   dame,
Nor of the dead who rise upon our
   dreams,
But of ideal beauty, which became
In him existence, and o'erflowing teems
Along his burning page, distemper'd
   though it seems.

LXXIX

This breathed itself to life in Julie, *this*
Invested her with all that's wild and
   sweet;
This hallow'd, too, the memorable kiss
Which every morn his fever'd lip would
   greet,
From hers, who but with friendship his
   would meet;
But to that gentle touch through brain
   and breast
Flash'd the thrill'd spirit's love-devour-
   ing heat;
In that absorbing sigh perchance more
   blest
Than vulgar minds may be with all they
   seek possest.

LXXX

His life was one long war with self-
sought foes,
Or friends by him self-banish'd; for his
mind
Had grown Suspicion's sanctuary, and
chose,
For its own cruel sacrifice, the kind,
'Gainst whom he raged with fury
strange and blind.
But he was phrensied,—wherefore, who
may know?
Since cause might be which skill could
never find;
But he was phrensied by disease or
woe,
To that worst pitch of all, which wears a
reasoning show.

LXXXI

For then he was inspired, and from him
came,
As from the Pythian's mystic cave of
yore,
Those oracles which set the world in
flame,
Nor ceased to burn till kingdoms were
no more:
Did he not this for France? which lay
before
Bow'd to the inborn tyranny of years?
Broken and trembling to the yoke she
bore,
Till by the voice of him and his compeers
Roused up to too much wrath, which
follows o'ergrown fears?

LXXXII

They made themselves a fearful monu-
ment!
The wreck of old opinions—things
which grew,
Breathed from the birth of time: the
veil they rent,
And what behind it lay, all earth shall
view.
But good with ill they also overthrew,
Leaving but ruins, wherewith to rebuild
Upon the same foundation, and renew
Dungeons and thrones, which the same
hour refill'd
As heretofore, because ambition was self-
will'd.

LXXXIII

But this will not endure, nor be endured!
Mankind have felt their strength, and
made it felt.
They might have used it better, but,
allured
By their new vigour, sternly have they
dealt
On one another; pity ceased to melt

With her once natural charities. But
they,
Who in oppression's darkness caved
had dwelt,
They were not eagles, nourish'd with
the day;
What marvel then, at times, if they mistook their prey?

LXXXIV

What deep wounds ever closed without
a scar?
The heart's bleed longest, and but heal
to wear
That which disfigures it; and they who
war
With their own hopes, and have been
vanquish'd, bear
Silence, but not submission: in his lair
Fix'd Passion holds his breath, until the
hour
Which shall atone for years; none need
despair:
It came, it cometh, and will come,—the
power
To punish or forgive—in *one* we shall be
slower.

LXXXV

Clear, placid Leman! thy contrasted
lake,
With the wild world I dwelt in, is a
thing
Which warns me, with its stillness, to
forsake
Earth's troubled waters for a purer
spring.
This quiet sail is as a noiseless wing
To waft me from distraction; once I
loved
Torn ocean's roar, but thy soft murmuring
Sounds sweet as if a Sister's voice reproved,
That I with stern delights should e'er have
been so moved.

LXXXVI

It is the hush of night, and all between
Thy margin and the mountains, dusk,
yet clear,
Mellow'd and mingling, yet distinctly
seen,
Save darken'd Jura, whose capt heights
appear
Precipitously steep; and drawing near,
There breathes a living fragrance from
the shore,
Of flowers yet fresh with childhood; on
the ear
Drops the light drip of the suspended
oar,
Or chirps the grasshopper one good-night
carol more:

LXXXVII

He is an evening reveller, who makes
His life an infancy, and sings his fill;
At intervals, some bird from out the
brakes
Starts into voice a moment, then is still.
There seems a floating whisper on the hill,
But that is fancy, for the starlight dews
All silently their tears of love instil,
Weeping themselves away, till they infuse
Deep into nature's breast the spirit of her
hues.

LXXXVIII

Ye stars! which are the poetry of heaven!
If in your bright leaves we would read
the fate
Of men and empires,—'tis to be for-
given,
That in our aspirations to be great,
Our destinies o'erleap their mortal state,
And claim a kindred with you; for ye are
A beauty and a mystery, and create
In us such love and reverence from afar,
That fortune, fame, power, life, have
named themselves a star.

LXXXIX

All heaven and earth are still—though
not in sleep,
But breathless, as we grow when feeling
most;
And silent, as we stand in thoughts too
deep:—
All heaven and earth are still: From the
high host
Of stars, to the lull'd lake and mountain-
coast,
All is concenter'd in a life intense,
Where not a beam, nor air, nor leaf is lost,
But hath a part of being, and a sense
Of that which is of all Creator and defence.

XC

Then stirs the feeling infinite, so felt
In solitude, where we are *least* alone;
A truth, which through our being then
doth melt,
And purifies from self: it is a tone,
The soul and source of music, which
makes known
Eternal harmony, and sheds a charm
Like to the fabled Cytherea's zone,
Binding all things with beauty;—
'twould disarm
The spectre Death, had he substantial
power to harm.

XCI

Not vainly did the early Persian make
His altar the high places, and the peak
Of earth-o'ergazing mountains, and
thus take
A fit and unwall'd temple, there to seek
The Spirit, in whose honour shrines are
weak,
Uprear'd of human hands. Come, and
compare
Columns and idol-dwellings, Goth or
Greek,
With Nature's realms of worship, earth
and air,
Nor fix on fond abodes to circumscribe
thy pray'r!

XCII

The sky is changed!—and such a change!
Oh night,
And storm, and darkness, ye are won-
drous strong,
Yet lovely in your strength, as is the light
Of a dark eye in woman! Far along,
From peak to peak, the rattling crags
among
Leaps the live thunder! Not from one
lone cloud,
But every mountain now hath found a
tongue,
And Jura answers, through her misty
shroud,
Back to the joyous Alps, who call to her
aloud!

XCIII

And this is in the night:—Most glorious
night!
Thou wert not sent for slumber! let me
be
A sharer in thy fierce and far delight,—
A portion of the tempest and of thee!
How the lit lake shines, a phosphoric
sea,
And the big rain comes dancing to the
earth!
And now again 'tis black,—and now,
the glee
Of the loud hills shakes with its moun-
tain-mirth,
As if they did rejoice o'er a young earth-
quake's birth.

XCIV

Now, where the swift Rhone cleaves his
way between
Heights which appear as lovers who
have parted
In hate, whose mining depths so inter-
vene,
That they can meet no more, though
broken-hearted;
Though in their souls, which thus each
other thwarted,
Love was the very root of the fond rage
Which blighted their life's bloom, and
then departed:
Itself expired, but leaving them an age
Of years all winters,—war within them-
selves to wage.

XCV

Now, where the quick Rhone thus hath
    cleft his way,
The mightiest of the storms hath ta'en
    his stand:
For here, not one, but many, make their
    play,
And fling their thunder-bolts from hand
    to hand,
Flashing and cast around; of all the
    band,
The brightest through these parted hills
    hath fork'd
His lightnings,—as if he did under-
    stand,
That in such gaps as desolation work'd,
There the hot shaft should blast whatever
    therein lurk'd.

XCVI

Sky, mountains, river, winds, lake,
    lightnings! ye!
With night, and clouds, and thunder,
    and a soul
To make these felt and feeling, well may
    be
Things that have made me watchful; the
    far roll
Of your departing voices, is the knoll
Of what in me is sleepless,—if I rest.
But where of ye, O tempests! is the
    goal?
Are ye like those within the human
    breast?
Or do ye find, at length, like eagles, some
    high nest?

XCVII

Could I embody and unbosom now
That which is most within me,—could
    I wreak
My thoughts upon expression, and thus
    throw
Soul, heart, mind, passions, feelings,
    strong or weak,
All that I would have sought, and all I
    seek,
Bear, know, feel, and yet breathe—into
    one word,
And that one word were Lightning, I
    would speak;
But as it is, I live and die unheard,
With a most voiceless thought, sheathing
    it as a sword.

XCVIII

The morn is up again, the dewy morn,
With breath all incense, and with cheek
    all bloom,
Laughing the clouds away with playful
    scorn,
And living as if earth contain'd no
    tomb,—

And glowing into day: we may resume
The march of our existence: and thus I,
Still on thy shores, fair Leman! may find
    room
And food for meditation, nor pass by
Much, that may give us pause, if ponder'd
    fittingly.

XCIX

Clarens! sweet Clarens, birthplace of
    deep Love!
Thine air is the young breath of passion-
    ate thought;
Thy trees take root in Love; the snows
    above,
The very Glaciers have his colours
    caught,
And sun-set into rose-hues sees them
    wrought
By rays which sleep there lovingly: the
    rocks,
The permanent crags, tell here of Love,
    who sought
In them a refuge from the worldly
    shocks,
Which stir and sting the soul with hope
    that woos, then mocks.

C

Clarens! by heavenly feet thy paths are
    trod,—
Undying Love's, who here ascends a
    throne
To which the steps are mountains;
    where the god
Is a pervading life and light,—so shown
Not on those summits solely, nor alone
In the still cave and forest; o'er the flower
His eye is sparkling, and his breath hath
    blown,
His soft and summer breath, whose
    tender power
Passes the strength of storms in their most
    desolate hour.

CI

All things are here of *him;* from the
    black pines,
Which are his shade on high, and the
    loud roar
Of torrents, where he listeneth, to the
    vines
Which slope his green path downward
    to the shore,
Where the bow'd waters meet him, and
    adore,
Kissing his feet with murmurs; and the
    wood,
The covert of old trees, with trunks all
    hoar,
But light leaves, young as joy, stands
    where it stood,
Offering to him, and his, a populous soli-
    tude.

CII

A populous solitude of bees and birds,
And fairy-form'd and many-colour'd
    things,
Who worship him with notes more
    sweet than words,
And innocently open their glad wings,
Fearless and full of life: the gush of
    springs,
And fall of lofty fountains, and the bend
Of stirring branches, and the bud which
    brings
The swiftest thought of beauty, here ex-
    tend,
Mingling, and made by Love, unto one
    mighty end.

CIII

He who hath loved not, here would learn
    that lore,
And make his heart a spirit; he who
    knows
That tender mystery, will love the more;
For this is Love's recess, where vain
    men's woes,
And the world's waste, have driven him
    far from those,
For 'tis his nature to advance or die;
He stands not still, but or decays, or
    grows
Into a boundless blessing, which may vie
With the immortal lights, in its eternity!

CIV

'Twas not for fiction chose Rousseau
    this spot,
Peopling it with affections; but he found
It was the scene which Passion must
    allot
To the Mind's purified beings; 'twas the
    ground
Where early Love his Psyche's zone
    unbound,
And hallow'd it with loveliness: 'tis
    lone,
And wonderful, and deep, and hath a
    sound,
And sense, and sight of sweetness; here
    the Rhone
Hath spread himself a couch, the Alps
    have rear'd a throne.

CV

Lausanne! and Ferney! ye have been
    the abodes
Of names which unto you bequeath'd a
    name;
Mortals, who sought and found, by
    dangerous roads,
A path to perpetuity of fame:
They were gigantic minds, and their
    steep aim
Was, Titan-like, on daring doubts to pile

Thoughts which should call down thun-
    der, and the flame
Of Heaven again assail'd, if Heaven the
    while
On man and man's research could deign
    do more than smile.

CVI

The one was fire and fickleness, a child
Most mutable in wishes, but in mind
A wit as various,—gay, grave, sage, or
    wild,—
Historian, bard, philosopher, combined;
He multiplied himself among mankind,
The Proteus of their talents: But his own
Breathed most in ridicule,—which, as
    the wind,
Blew where it listed, laying all things
    prone,—
Now to o'erthrow a fool, and now to shake
    a throne.

CVII

The other, deep and slow, exhausting
    thought,
And hiving wisdom with each studious
    year,
In meditation dwelt, with learning
    wrought,
And shaped his weapon with an edge
    severe,
Sapping a solemn creed with solemn sneer;
The lord of irony,—that master-spell,
Which stung his foes to wrath, which
    grew from fear,
And doom'd him to the zealot's ready
    Hell,
Which answers to all doubts so eloquently
    well.

CVIII

Yet, peace be with their ashes,—for by
    them,
If merited, the penalty is paid;
It is not ours to judge,—far less con-
    demn;
The hour must come when such things
    shall be made
Known unto all, or hope and dread
    allay'd
By slumber, on one pillow, in the dust,
Which, thus much we are sure, must lie
    decay'd;
And when it shall revive, as is our trust,
'Twill be to be forgiven, or suffer what is
    just.

CIX

But let me quit man's works, again to
    read
His Maker's, spread around me, and
    suspend
This page, which from my reveries I
    feed,
Until it seems prolonging without end.

The clouds above me to the white Alps
   tend,
And I must pierce them, and survey
   whate'er
May be permitted, as my steps I bend
To their most great and growing region,
   where
The earth to her embrace compels the
   powers of air.

CX

Italia! too, Italia! looking on thee,
Full flashes on the soul the light of ages,
Since the fierce Carthaginian almost
   won thee,
To the last halo of the chiefs and sages
Who glorify thy consecrated pages;
Thou wert the throne and grave of em-
   pires; still,
The fount at which the panting mind
   assuages
Her thirst of knowledge, quaffing there
   her fill,
Flows from the eternal source of Rome's
   imperial hill.

CXI

Thus far have I proceeded in a theme
Renew'd with no kind auspices:—to feel
We are not what we have been, and to
   deem
We are not what we should be, and to
   steel
The heart against itself; and to conceal,
With a proud caution, love, or hate, or
   aught,—
Passion or feeling, purpose, grief or
   zeal,—
Which is the tyrant spirit of our thought,
Is a stern task of soul:—No matter,—it is
   taught.

CXII

And for these words, thus woven into
   song,
It may be that they are a harmless wile,—
The colouring of the scenes which fleet
   along,
Which I would seize, in passing, to be-
   guile
My breast, or that of others, for a while.
Fame is the thirst of youth, but I am not
So young as to regard men's frown or
   smile,
As loss or guerdon of a glorious lot;
I stood and stand alone,—remember'd or
   forgot.

CXIII

I have not loved the world, nor the world
   me;
I have not flatter'd its rank breath, nor
   bow'd
To its idolatries a patient knee,

Nor coin'd my cheek to smiles, nor cried
   aloud
In worship of an echo; in the crowd
They could not deem me one of such; I
   stood
Among them, but not of them; in a
   shroud
Of thoughts which were not their
   thoughts, and still could,
Had I not filed my mind, which thus itself
   subdued.

CXIV

I have not loved the world, nor the world
   me,—
But let us part fair foes; I do believe,
Though I have found them not, that
   there may be
Words which are things, hopes which
   will not deceive,
And virtues which are merciful, nor
   weave
Snares for the failing; I would also deem
O'er others' griefs that some sincerely
   grieve;
That two, or one, are almost what they
   seem,
That goodness is no name, and happiness
   no dream.

CXV

My daughter! with thy name this song
   begun;
My daughter! with thy name thus much
   shall end;
I see thee not, I hear thee not, but none
Can be so wrapt in thee; thou art the
   friend
To whom the shadows of far years extend:
Albeit my brow thou never shouldst behold,
My voice shall with thy future visions
   blend,
And reach into thy heart, when mine is
   cold,
A token and a tone, even from thy father's
   mould.

CXVI

To aid thy mind's development, to watch
Thy dawn of little joys, to sit and see
Almost thy very growth, to view thee
   catch
Knowledge of objects,—wonders yet to
   thee!
To hold thee lightly on a gentle knee,
And print on thy soft cheek a parent's
   kiss,—
This, it should seem, was not reserved
   for me;
Yet this was in my nature: as it is,
I know not what is there, yet something
   like to this.

CXVII

Yet, though dull Hate as duty should be
    taught,
I know that thou wilt love me; though
    my name
Should be shut from thee, as a spell still
    fraught
With desolation, and a broken claim:
Though the grave closed between us,—
    'twere the same,
I know that thou wilt love me; though
    to drain
My blood from out thy being were an
    aim,
And an attainment,—all would be in
    vain,—
Still thou wouldst love me, still that more
    than life retain.

CXVIII

The child of love, though born in bitter-
    ness,
And nurtured in convulsion. Of thy sire
These were the elements, and thine no
    less.
As yet such are around thee, but thy fire
Shall be more temper'd, and thy hope
    far higher.
Sweet be thy cradled slumbers! O'er the
    sea
And from the mountains where I now
    respire,
Fain would I waft such blessing upon
    thee,
As, with a sigh, I deem thou might'st have
    been to me.

CANTO THE FOURTH

'Visto ho Toscana, Lombardia, Romagna,
    Quel Monte che divide, e quel che serra
Italia, e un mare e l' altro, che la bagna.'
                    Ariosto, Satira iii.

TO

JOHN HOBHOUSE, ESQ., A.M., F.R.S.,
&c. &c. &c.

VENICE, *January* 2, 1818.

MY DEAR HOBHOUSE,

AFTER an interval of eight years between the
composition of the first and last cantos of Childe
Harold, the conclusion of the poem is about to be
submitted to the public. In parting with so old a
friend, it is not extraordinary that I should recur to
one still older and better,—to one who has beheld
the birth and death of the other, and to whom I am
far more indebted for the social advantages of an
enlightened friendship, than—though not ungrateful—I can, or could be, to Childe Harold, for any
public favour reflected through the poem on the
poet,—to one, whom I have known long and accompanied far, whom I have found wakeful over
my sickness and kind in my sorrow, glad in my
prosperity and firm in my adversity, true in counsel
and trusty in peril,—to a friend often tried and
never found wanting;—to yourself.

In so doing, I recur from fiction to truth; and in
dedicating to you in its complete, or at least concluded state, a poetical work which is the longest,
the most thoughtful and comprehensive of my
compositions, I wish to do honour to myself by
the record of many years' intimacy with a man of
learning, of talent, of steadiness, and of honour.
It is not for minds like ours to give or to receive
flattery; yet the praises of sincerity have ever been
permitted to the voice of friendship; and it is not
for you, nor even for others, but to relieve a heart
which has not elsewhere, or lately, been so much
accustomed to the encounter of good-will as to
withstand the shock firmly, that I thus attempt to
commemorate your good qualities, or rather the
advantages which I have derived from their exertion. Even the recurrence of the date of this letter,
the anniversary of the most unfortunate day of my
past existence*, but which cannot poison my future
while I retain the resource of your friendship, and
of my own faculties, will henceforth have a more
agreeable recollection for both, inasmuch as it will
remind us of this my attempt to thank you for an
indefatigable regard, such as few men have experienced, and no one could experience without thinking better of his species and of himself.

It has been our fortune to traverse together, at
various periods, the countries of chivalry, history,
and fable—Spain, Greece, Asia Minor, and Italy;
and what Athens and Constantinople were to us
a few years ago, Venice and Rome have been more
recently. The poem also, or the pilgrim, or both,
have accompanied me from first to last; and perhaps it may be a pardonable vanity which induces
me to reflect with complacency on a composition
which in some degree connects me with the spot
where it was produced, and the objects it would
fain describe; and however unworthy it may be
deemed of those magical and memorable abodes,
however short it may fall of our distant conceptions and immediate impressions, yet as a mark of
respect for what is venerable, and of feeling for
what is glorious, it has been to me a source of
pleasure in the production, and I part with it with
a kind of regret, which I hardly suspected that
events could have left me for imaginary objects.

With regard to the conduct of the last canto,
there will be found less of the pilgrim than in any
of the preceding, and that little slightly, if at all,
separated from the author speaking in his own
person. The fact is, that I had become weary of
drawing a line which every one seemed determined
not to perceive: like the Chinese in Goldsmith's
'Citizen of the World,' whom nobody would believe to be a Chinese, it was in vain that I asserted,
and imagined that I had drawn, a distinction
between the author and the pilgrim; and the very
anxiety to preserve this difference, and disappointment at finding it unavailing, so far crushed my
efforts in the composition, that I determined to
abandon it altogether—and have done so. The
opinions which have been, or may be, formed on
that subject are *now* a matter of indifference; the
work is to depend on itself, and not on the writer;
and the author, who has no resources in his own
mind beyond the reputation, transient or permanent, which is to arise from his literary efforts,
deserves the fate of authors.

In the course of the following canto it was my
intention, either in the text or in the notes, to have
touched upon the present state of Italian literature,
and perhaps of manners. But the text, within the
limits I proposed, I soon found hardly sufficient

* His marriage.

for the labyrinth of external objects, and the consequent reflections; and for the whole of the notes, excepting a few of the shortest, I am indebted to yourself, and these were necessarily limited to the elucidation of the text.

It is also a delicate, and no very grateful task, to dissert upon the literature and manners of a nation so dissimilar; and requires an attention and impartiality which would induce us—though perhaps no inattentive observers, nor ignorant of the language or customs of the people amongst whom we have recently abode—to distrust, or at least defer our judgment, and more narrowly examine our information. The state of literary, as well as political party, appears to run, or to *have* run, so high, that for a stranger to steer impartially between them is next to impossible. It may be enough, then, at least for my purpose, to quote from their own beautiful language—'Mi pare che in un paese tutto poetico, che vanta la lingua la più nobile ed insieme la più dolce, tutte tutte le vie diverse si possono tentare, e che sinche la patria di Alfieri e di Monti non ha perduto l' antico valore, in tutte essa dovrebbe essere la prima.' Italy has great names still—Canova, Monti, Ugo Foscolo, Pindemonte, Visconti, Morelli, Cicognara, Albrizzi, Mezzofanti, Mai, Mustoxidi, Aglietti, and Vacca, will secure to the present generation an honourable place in most of the departments of Art, Science, and Belles Lettres; and in some the very highest—Europe—the World—has but one Canova.

It has been somewhere said by Alfieri, that 'La pianta uomo nasce più robusta in Italia che in qualunque altra terra—e che gli stessi atroci delitti che vi si commettono ne sono una prova.' Without subscribing to the latter part of his proposition, a dangerous doctrine, the truth of which may be disputed on better grounds, namely, that the Italians are in no respect more ferocious than their neighbours, that man must be wilfully blind, or ignorantly heedless, who is not struck with the extraordinary capacity of this people, or, if such a word be admissible, their *capabilities*, the facility of their acquisitions, the rapidity of their conceptions, the fire of their genius, their sense of beauty, and, amidst all the disadvantages of repeated revolutions, the desolation of battles, and the despair of ages, their still unquenched 'longing after immortality,'—the immortality of independence. And when we ourselves, in riding round the walls of Rome, heard the simple lament of the labourers' chorus, 'Roma! Roma! Roma! Roma non è più come era prima!' it was difficult not to contrast this melancholy dirge with the bacchanal roar of the songs of exultation still yelled from the London taverns, over the carnage of Mont St. Jean, and the betrayal of Genoa, of Italy, of France, and of the world, by men whose conduct you yourself have exposed in a work worthy of the better days of our history. For me,—

'Non movero mai corda
Ove la turba di sue ciance assorda.'

What Italy has gained by the late transfer of nations, it were useless for Englishmen to inquire, till it becomes ascertained that England has acquired something more than a permanent army and a suspended Habeas Corpus; it is enough for them to look at home. For what they have done abroad, and especially in the South, 'Verily they *will have* their reward,' and at no very distant period.

Wishing you, my dear Hobhouse, a safe and agreeable return to that country whose real welfare can be dearer to none than to yourself, I dedicate to you this poem in its completed state; and repeat once more how truly I am ever

Your obliged and affectionate friend,

BYRON.

I

I STOOD in Venice, on the Bridge of Sighs;
A palace and a prison on each hand:
I saw from out the wave her structures rise
As from the stroke of the enchanter's wand:
A thousand years their cloudy wings expand
Around me, and a dying Glory smiles
O'er the far times, when many a subject land
Look'd to the winged Lion's marble piles,
Where Venice sate in state, throned on her hundred isles!

II

She looks a sea Cybele, fresh from ocean,
Rising with her tiara of proud towers
At airy distance, with majestic motion,
A ruler of the waters and their powers:
And such she was;—her daughters had their dowers
From spoils of nations, and the exhaustless East
Pour'd in her lap all gems in sparkling showers.
In purple was she robed, and of her feast
Monarchs partook, and deem'd their dignity increased.

III

In Venice Tasso's echoes are no more,
And silent rows the songless gondolier;
Her palaces are crumbling to the shore,
And music meets not always now the ear:
Those days are gone—but Beauty still is here.
States fall, arts fade—but Nature doth not die,
Nor yet forget how Venice once was dear,
The pleasant place of all festivity,
The revel of the earth, the masque of Italy!

IV

But unto us she hath a spell beyond
Her name in story, and her long array
Of mighty shadows, whose dim forms despond
Above the dogeless city's vanish'd sway;

227

Ours is a trophy which will not decay
With the Rialto; Shylock and the Moor,
And Pierre, cannot be swept or worn
　away—
The keystones of the arch! though all
　were o'er,
For us repeopled were the solitary shore.

V

The beings of the mind are not of clay;
Essentially immortal, they create
And multiply in us a brighter ray
And more beloved existence: that which
　Fate
Prohibits to dull life, in this our state
Of mortal bondage, by these spirits
　supplied,
First exiles, then replaces what we hate;
Watering the heart whose early flowers
　have died,
And with a fresher growth replenishing
　the void.

VI

Such is the refuge of our youth and age,
The first from Hope, the last from
　Vacancy;
And this wan feeling peoples many a
　page,
And, may be, that which grows beneath
　mine eye:
Yet there are things whose strong reality
Outshines our fairy-land; in shape and
　hues
More beautiful than our fantastic sky,
And the strange constellations which
　the Muse
O'er her wild universe is skilful to diffuse:

VII

I saw or dream'd of such,—but let them
　go,—
They came like truth, and disappear'd
　like dreams;
And whatsoe'er they were—are now but
　so:
I could replace them if I would; still
　teems
My mind with many a form which aptly
　seems
Such as I sought for, and at moments
　found;
Let these too go—for waking Reason
　deems
Such overweening phantasies unsound,
And other voices speak, and other sights
　surround.

VIII

I've taught me other tongues, and in
　strange eyes
Have made me not a stranger; to the
　mind
Which is itself, no changes bring sur-
　prise;

Nor is it harsh to make, nor hard to
　find
A country with—ay, or without man-
　kind;
Yet was I born where men are proud to
　be,—
Not without cause; and should I leave
　behind
The inviolate island of the sage and
　free,
And seek me out a home by a remoter
　sea,

IX

Perhaps I loved it well: and should I
　lay
My ashes in a soil which is not mine,
My spirit shall resume it—if we may
Unbodied choose a sanctuary. I twine
My hopes of being remember'd in my
　line
With my land's language: if too fond
　and far
These aspirations in their scope in-
　cline,—
If my fame should be, as my fortunes
　are,
Of hasty growth and blight, and dull
　Oblivion bar

X

My name from out the temple where the
　dead
Are honour'd by the nations—let it be—
And light the laurels on a loftier head!
And be the Spartan's epitaph on me—
'Sparta hath many a worthier son than
　he.'
Meantime I seek no sympathies, nor
　need;
The thorns which I have reap'd are of
　the tree
I planted: they have torn me, and I
　bleed:
I should have known what fruit would
　spring from such a seed.

XI

The spouseless Adriatic mourns her
　lord;
And, annual marriage now no more re-
　new'd,
The Bucentaur lies rotting unrestored,
Neglected garment of her widowhood!
St. Mark yet sees his lion where he
　stood
Stand, but in mockery of his wither'd
　power,
Over the proud Place where an Emperor
　sued,
And monarchs gazed and envied in the
　hour
When Venice was a queen with an un-
　equall'd dower.

XII

The Suabian sued, and now the Austrian
  reigns—
An Emperor tramples where an Emper-
  or knelt;
Kingdoms are shrunk to provinces, and
  chains
Clank over sceptred cities; nations melt
From power's high pinnacle, when they
  have felt
The sunshine for a while, and downward
  go
Like Lauwine loosen'd from the moun-
  tain's belt;
Oh for one hour of blind old Dandolo!
Th' octogenarian chief, Byzantium's con-
  quering foe.

XIII

Before St. Mark still glow his steeds of
  brass,
Their gilded collars glittering in the sun;
But is not Doria's menace come to pass?
Are they not bridled?—Venice, lost and
  won,
Her thirteen hundred years of freedom
  done,
Sinks, like a seaweed, unto whence she
  rose!
Better be whelm'd beneath the waves,
  and shun,
Even in destruction's depth, her foreign
  foes,
From whom submission wrings an in-
  famous repose.

XIV

In youth she was all glory,—a new Tyre;
Her very by-word sprung from victory,
The 'Planter of the Lion,' which
  through fire
And blood she bore o'er subject earth
  and sea;
Though making many slaves, herself
  still free,
And Europe's bulwark 'gainst the Otto-
  mite;
Witness Troy's rival, Candia! Vouch
  it, ye
Immortal waves that saw Lepanto's
  fight!
For ye are names no time nor tyranny can
  blight.

XV

Statues of glass—all shiver'd—the long
  file
Of her dead Doges are declined to dust;
But where they dwelt, the vast and
  sumptuous pile
Bespeaks the pageant of their splendid
  trust;
Their sceptre broken, and their sword
  in rust,

Have yielded to the stranger: empty
  halls,
Thin streets, and foreign aspects, such
  as must
Too oft remind her who and what en-
  thrals,
Have flung a desolate cloud o'er Venice'
  lovely walls.

XVI

When Athens' armies fell at Syracuse,
And fetter'd thousands bore the yoke
  of war,
Redemption rose up in the Attic Muse,
Her voice their only ransom from afar:
See! as they chant the tragic hymn, the
  car
Of the o'ermaster'd victor stops, the
  reins
Fall from his hands, his idle scimitar
Starts from its belt—he rends his cap-
  tive's chains,
And bids him thank the bard for freedom
  and his strains.

XVII

Thus, Venice, if no stronger claim were
  thine,
Were all thy proud historic deeds forgot,
Thy choral memory of the Bard divine,
Thy love of Tasso, should have cut the
  knot
Which ties thee to thy tyrants; and thy lot
Is shameful to the nations,—most of all,
Albion! to thee: the Ocean queen should
  not
Abandon Ocean's children; in the fall
Of Venice think of thine, despite thy
  watery wall.

XVIII

I loved her from my boyhood; she to me
Was as a fairy city of the heart,
Rising like water-columns from the sea,
Of joy the sojourn, and of wealth the
  mart;
And Otway, Radcliffe, Schiller, Shak-
  speare's art,
Had stamp'd her image in me, and even
  so,
Although I found her thus, we did not
  part;
Perchance even dearer in her day of woe,
Than when she was a boast, a marvel, and
  a show.

XIX

I can repeople with the past—and of
The present there is still for eye and
  thought,
And meditation chasten'd down,
  enough;
And more, it may be, than I hoped or
  sought;

And of the happiest moments which
    were wrought
Within the web of my existence, some
From thee, fair Venice! have their col-
    ours caught:
There are some feelings Time cannot be-
    numb,
Nor Torture shake, or mine would now be
    cold and dumb.

XX

But from their nature will the Tannen
    grow
Loftiest on loftiest and least shelter'd
    rocks,
Rooted in barrenness, where nought
    below
Of soil supports them 'gainst the Alpine
    shocks
Of eddying storms; yet springs the
    trunk, and mocks
The howling tempest, till its height and
    frame
Are worthy of the mountains from
    whose blocks
Of bleak, gray granite into life it came,
And grew a giant tree;—the mind may
    grow the same.

XXI

Existence may be borne, and the deep
    root
Of life and sufferance make its firm
    abode
The bare and desolated bosoms: mute
The camel labours with the heaviest
    load,
And the wolf dies in silence,—not be-
    stow'd
In vain should such example be; if they,
Things of ignoble or of savage mood,
Endure and shrink not, we of nobler
    clay
May temper it to bear,—it is but for a
    day.

XXII

All suffering doth destroy, or is de-
    stroy'd,
Even by the sufferer; and, in each event,
Ends:—Some, with hope replenish'd
    and rebuoy'd,
Return to whence they came—with like
    intent,
And weave their web again; some,
    bow'd and bent,
Wax gray and ghastly, withering ere
    their time,
And perish with the reed on which they
    leant;
Some seek devotion, toil, war, good or
    crime,
According as their souls were form'd to
    sink or climb.

XXIII

But ever and anon of griefs subdued
There comes a token like a scorpion's
    sting,
Scarce seen, but with fresh bitterness
    imbued;
And slight withal may be the things
    which bring
Back on the heart the weight which it
    would fling
Aside for ever: it may be a sound—
A tone of music—summer's eve—or
    spring—
A flower—the wind—the ocean—which
    shall wound,
Striking the electric chain wherewith we
    are darkly bound;

XXIV

And how and why we know not, nor can
    trace
Home to its cloud this lightning of the
    mind,
But feel the shock renew'd, nor can
    efface
The blight and blackening which it
    leaves behind,
Which out of things familiar, un-
    design'd,
When least we deem of such, calls up to
    view
The spectres whom no exorcism can
    bind,—
The cold, the changed, perchance the
    dead—anew,
The mourn'd, the loved, the lost—too
    many! yet how few!

XXV

But my soul wanders; I demand it
    back
To meditate amongst decay, and stand
A ruin amidst ruins; there to track
Fall'n states and buried greatness, o'er
    a land
Which *was* the mightiest in its old com-
    mand,
And *is* the loveliest, and must ever be
The master-mould of Nature's heavenly
    hand;
Wherein were cast the heroic and the
    free,
The beautiful, the brave, the lords of earth
    and sea,

XXVI

The commonwealth of kings, the men
    of Rome!
And even since, and now, fair Italy!
Thou art the garden of the world, the
    home
Of all Art yields, and Nature can
    decree;

Even in thy desert, what is like to thee?
Thy very weeds are beautiful, thy waste
More rich than other climes' fertility;
Thy wreck a glory, and thy ruin graced
With an immaculate charm which cannot
be defaced.

XXVII

The moon is up, and yet it is not night;
Sunset divides the sky with her; a sea
Of glory streams along the Alpine
height
Of blue Friuli's mountains; Heaven is
free
From clouds, but of all colours seems
to be,—
Melted to one vast Iris of the West,—
Where the Day joins the past Eternity,
While, on the other hand, meek Dian's
crest
Floats through the azure air—an island of
the blest!

XXVIII

A single star is at her side, and reigns
With her o'er half the lovely heaven; but
still
Yon sunny sea heaves brightly, and re-
mains
Roll'd o'er the peak of the far Rhætian
hill,
As Day and Night contending were,
until
Nature reclaim'd her order:—gently
flows
The deep-dyed Brenta, where their hues
instil
The odorous purple of a new-born rose,
Which streams upon her stream, and
glass'd within it glows,

XXIX

Fill'd with the face of heaven, which,
from afar,
Comes down upon the waters; all its
hues,
From the rich sunset to the rising star,
Their magical variety diffuse:
And now they change; a paler shadow
strews
Its mantle o'er the mountains; parting
day
Dies like the dolphin, whom each pang
imbues
With a new colour as it gasps away—
The last still loveliest,—till—'tis gone—
and all is gray.

XXX

There is a tomb in Arqua;—rear'd in
air,
Pillar'd in their sarcophagus, repose
The bones of Laura's lover: here repair
Many familiar with his well-sung woes,

The pilgrims of his genius. He arose
To raise a language, and his land reclaim
From the dull yoke of her barbaric foes:
Watering the tree which bears his lady's
name
With his melodious tears, he gave himself
to fame.

XXXI

They keep his dust in Arqua, where he
died;
The mountain-village where his latter
days
Went down the vale of years; and 'tis
their pride—
An honest pride—and let it be their
praise,
To offer to the passing stranger's gaze
His mansion and his sepulchre; both
plain
And venerably simple, such as raise
A feeling more accordant with his strain
Than if a pyramid form'd his monumental
fane.

XXXII

And the soft quiet hamlet where he dwelt
Is one of that complexion which seems
made
For those who their mortality have felt,
And sought a refuge from their hopes
decay'd
In the deep umbrage of a green hill's
shade,
Which shows a distant prospect far away
Of busy cities, now in vain display'd,
For they can lure no further; and the ray
Of a bright sun can make sufficient
holiday,

XXXIII

Developing the mountains, leaves, and
flowers,
And shining in the brawling brook,
whereby,
Clear as its current, glide the sauntering
hours
With a calm languor, which, though to
the eye
Idlesse it seem, hath its morality.
If from society we learn to live,
'Tis solitude should teach us how to die;
It hath no flatterers; vanity can give
No hollow aid; alone—man with his God
must strive:

XXXIV

Or, it may be, with demons, who impair
The strength of better thoughts, and
seek their prey
In melancholy bosoms, such as were
Of moody texture from their earliest
day,

And loved to dwell in darkness and dismay,
Deeming themselves predestined to a doom
Which is not of the pangs that pass away;
Making the sun like blood, the earth a tomb,
The tomb a hell, and hell itself a murkier gloom.

XXXV

Ferrara! in thy wide and grass-grown streets,
Whose symmetry was not for solitude,
There seems as 'twere a curse upon the seats
Of former sovereigns, and the antique brood
Of Este, which for many an age made good
Its strength within thy walls, and was of yore
Patron or tyrant, as the changing mood
Of petty power impell'd, of those who wore
The wreath which Dante's brow alone had worn before.

XXXVI

And Tasso is their glory and their shame.
Hark to his strain! and then survey his cell!
And see how dearly earn'd Torquato's fame,
And where Alfonso bade his poet dwell:
The miserable despot could not quell
The insulted mind he sought to quench, and blend
With the surrounding maniacs, in the hell
Where he had plunged it. Glory without end
Scatter'd the clouds away; and on that name attend

XXXVII

The tears and praises of all time; while thine
Would rot in its oblivion—in the sink
Of worthless dust, which from thy boasted line
Is shaken into nothing—but the link
Thou formest in his fortunes bids us think
Of thy poor malice, naming thee with scorn:
Alfonso! how thy ducal pageants shrink
From thee! if in another station born,
Scarce fit to be the slave of him thou madest to mourn:

XXXVIII

Thou! form'd to eat, and be despised, and die,
Even as the beasts that perish, save that thou
Hadst a more splendid trough and wider sty:
He! with a glory round his furrow'd brow,
Which emanated then, and dazzles now,
In face of all his foes, the Cruscan quire,
And Boileau, whose rash envy could allow
No strain which shamed his country's creaking lyre,
That whetstone of the teeth—monotony in wire!

XXXIX

Peace to Torquato's injured shade! 'twas his
In life and death to be the mark where Wrong
Aim'd with her poison'd arrows,—but to miss.
Oh, victor unsurpass'd in modern song!
Each year brings forth its millions; but how long
The tide of generations shall roll on,
And not the whole combined and countless throng
Compose a mind like thine? though all in one
Condensed their scatter'd rays, they would not form a sun.

XL

Great as thou art, yet parallel'd by those,
Thy countrymen, before thee born to shine,
The Bards of Hell and Chivalry: first rose
The Tuscan father's Comedy Divine;
Then, not unequal to the Florentine,
The southern Scott, the minstrel who call'd forth
A new creation with his magic line,
And, like the Ariosto of the North,
Sang ladye-love and war, romance and knightly worth.

XLI

The lightning rent from Ariosto's bust
The iron crown of laurel's mimick'd leaves;
Nor was the ominous element unjust,
For the true laurel-wreath which Glory weaves
Is of the tree no bolt of thunder cleaves,
And the false semblance but disgraced his brow;
Yet still, if fondly Superstition grieves,
Know, that the lightning sanctifies below
Whate'er it strikes;—yon head is doubly sacred now.

XLII

Italia! oh Italia! thou who hast
The fatal gift of beauty, which became
A funeral dower of present woes and
    past,
On thy sweet brow is sorrow plough'd
    by shame,
And annals graved in characters of
    flame.
Oh, God! that thou wert in thy naked-
    ness
Less lovely or more powerful, and
    couldst claim
Thy right, and awe the robbers back,
    who press
To shed thy blood, and drink the tears of
    thy distress;

XLIII

Then might'st thou more appal; or, less
    desired,
Be homely and be peaceful, undeplored
For thy destructive charms; then, still
    untired,
Would not be seen the armed torrents
    pour'd
Down the deep Alps; nor would the
    hostile horde
Of many-nation'd spoilers from the Po
Quaff blood and water; nor the stran-
    ger's sword
Be thy sad weapon of defence, and so,
Victor or vanquish'd, thou the slave of
    friend or foe.

XLIV

Wandering in youth, I traced the path
    of him,
The Roman friend of Rome's least-
    mortal mind,
The friend of Tully: as my bark did
    skim
The bright blue waters with a fanning
    wind,
Came Megara before me, and behind
Ægina lay, Piræus on the right,
And Corinth on the left; I lay re-
    clined
Along the prow, and saw all these unite
In ruin, even as he had seen the desolate
    sight;

XLV

For Time hath not rebuilt them, but
    uprear'd
Barbaric dwellings on their shatter'd
    site,
Which only make more mourn'd and
    more endear'd
The few last rays of their far-scatter'd
    light,
And the crush'd relics of their vanish'd
    might.

The Roman saw these tombs in his own
    age,
These sepulchres of cities, which excite
Sad wonder, and his yet surviving page
The moral lesson bears, drawn from such
    pilgrimage.

XLVI

That page is now before me, and on
    mine
His country's ruin added to the mass
Of perish'd states he mourn'd in their
    decline,
And I in desolation: all that *was*
Of then destruction *is*; and now, alas!
Rome—Rome imperial, bows her to the
    storm,
In the same dust and blackness, and we
    pass
The skeleton of her Titanic form,
Wrecks of another world, whose ashes still
    are warm.

XLVII

Yet, Italy! through every other land
Thy wrongs should ring, and shall, from
    side to side;
Mother of Arts! as once of arms; thy
    hand
Was then our guardian, and is still our
    guide;
Parent of our religion! whom the wide
Nations have knelt to for the keys of
    heaven!
Europe, repentant of her parricide,
Shall yet redeem thee, and, all backward
    driven,
Roll the barbarian tide, and sue to be for-
    given.

XLVIII

But Arno wins us to the fair white walls,
Where the Etrurian Athens claims and
    keeps
A softer feeling for her fairy halls.
Girt by her theatre of hills, she reaps
Her corn, and wine, and oil, and Plenty
    leaps
To laughing life, with her redundant
    horn.
Along the banks where smiling Arno
    sweeps
Was modern Luxury of Commerce
    born,
And buried Learning rose, redeem'd to a
    new morn.

XLIX

There, too, the Goddess loves in stone,
    and fills
The air around with beauty; we inhale
The ambrosial aspect, which, beheld,
    instils
Part of its immortality; the veil

233

Of heaven is half undrawn; within the pale
We stand, and in that form and face behold
What Mind can make, when Nature's self would fail;
And to the fond idolaters of old
Envy the innate flash which such a soul could mould:

L

We gaze and turn away, and know not where,
Dazzled and drunk with beauty, till the heart
Reels with its fulness; there—for ever there—
Chain'd to the chariot of triumphal Art,
We stand as captives, and would not depart.
Away!—there need no words nor terms precise,
The paltry jargon of the marble mart,
Where Pedantry gulls Folly—we have eyes:
Blood, pulse, and breast confirm the Dardan Shepherd's prize.

LI

Appear'dst thou not to Paris in this guise?
Or to more deeply blest Anchises? or,
In all thy perfect Goddess-ship, when lies
Before thee thy own vanquish'd Lord of War?
And gazing in thy face as toward a star,
Laid on thy lap, his eyes to thee upturn,
Feeding on thy sweet cheek! while thy lips are
With lava kisses melting while they burn,
Shower'd on his eyelids, brow, and mouth, as from an urn?

LII

Glowing, and circumfused in speechless love,
Their full divinity inadequate
That feeling to express, or to improve,
The gods become as mortals, and man's fate
Has moments like their brightest; but the weight
Of earth recoils upon us;—let it go!
We can recall such visions, and create,
From what has been, or might be, things which grow
Into thy statue's form, and look like gods below.

LIII

I leave to learned fingers, and wise hands,
The artist and his ape, to teach and tell
How well his connoisseurship understands

The graceful bend, and the voluptuous swell:
Let these describe the undescribable:
I would not their vile breath should crisp the stream
Wherein that image shall for ever dwell;
The unruffled mirror of the loveliest dream
That ever left the sky on the deep soul to beam.

LIV

In Santa Croce's holy precincts lie
Ashes which make it holier, dust which is
Even in itself an immortality,
Though there were nothing save the past, and this,
The particle of those sublimities
Which have relapsed to chaos: here repose
Angelo's, Alfieri's bones, and his,
The starry Galileo, with his woes;
Here Machiavelli's earth return'd to whence it rose.

LV

These are four minds, which, like the elements,
Might furnish forth creation:—Italy!
Time, which hath wrong'd thee with ten thousand rents
Of thine imperial garment, shall deny,
And hath denied, to every other sky,
Spirits which soar from ruin: thy decay
Is still impregnate with divinity,
Which gilds it with revivifying ray;
Such as the great of yore, Canova is to-day.

LVI

But where repose the all Etruscan three—
Dante, and Petrarch, and, scarce less than they,
The Bard of Prose, creative spirit! he
Of the Hundred Tales of love—where did they lay
Their bones, distinguish'd from our common clay
In death as life? Are they resolved to dust,
And have their country's marbles nought to say?
Could not her quarries furnish forth one bust?
Did they not to her breast their filial earth entrust?

LVII

Ungrateful Florence! Dante sleeps afar,
Like Scipio, buried by the upbraiding shore;
Thy factions, in their worse than civil war,
Proscribed the bard whose name for evermore

Their children's children would in vain
  adore
With the remorse of ages; and the crown
Which Petrarch's laureate brow su-
  premely wore,
Upon a far and foreign soil had grown,
His life, his fame, his grave, though rifled—
  not thine own.

LVIII

Boccaccio to his parent earth bequeath'd
His dust,—and lies it not her great
  among,
With many a sweet and solemn requiem
  breathed
O'er him who form'd the Tuscan's siren
  tongue?
That music in itself, whose sounds are
  song,
The poetry of speech? No;—even his
  tomb
Uptorn, must bear the hyæna bigot's
  wrong,
No more amidst the meaner dead find
  room,
Nor claim a passing sigh, because it told
  for *whom*!

LIX

And Santa Croce wants their mighty
  dust;
Yet for this want more noted, as of
  yore
The Cæsar's pageant, shorn of Brutus'
  bust,
Did but of Rome's best Son remind her
  more:
Happier Ravenna! on thy hoary shore,
Fortress of falling empire! honour'd
  sleeps
The immortal exile;—Arqua, too, her
  store
Of tuneful relics proudly claims and
  keeps,
While Florence vainly begs her banish'd
  dead and weeps.

LX

What is her pyramid of precious stones?
Of porphyry, jasper, agate, and all hues
Of gem and marble, to encrust the bones
Of merchant-dukes? the momentary
  dews
Which, sparkling to the twilight stars,
  infuse
Freshness in the green turf that wraps
  the dead,
Whose names are mausoleums of the
  Muse,
Are gently prest with far more reverent
  tread
Than ever paced the slab which paves the
  princely head.

LXI

There be more things to greet the heart
  and eyes
In Arno's dome of Art's most princely
  shrine,
Where Sculpture with her rainbow sis-
  ter vies;
There be more marvels yet—but not for
  mine;
For I have been accustom'd to entwine
My thoughts with Nature rather in the
  fields,
Than Art in galleries; though a work
  divine
Calls for my spirit's homage, yet it yields
Less than it feels, because the weapon
  which it wields

LXII

Is of another temper, and I roam
By Thrasimene's lake, in the defiles
Fatal to Roman rashness, more at
  home;
For there the Carthaginian's warlike
  wiles
Come back before me, as his skill be-
  guiles
The host between the mountains and the
  shore,
Where Courage falls in her despairing
  files,
And torrents, swoll'n to rivers with their
  gore,
Reek through the sultry plain, with legions
  scatter'd o'er,

LXIII

Like to a forest fell'd by mountain winds;
And such the storm of battle on this
  day,
And such the frenzy, whose convulsion
  blinds
To all save carnage, that, beneath the
  fray,
An earthquake reel'd unheededly away!
None felt stern Nature rocking at his
  feet,
And yawning forth a grave for those
  who lay
Upon their bucklers for a winding-
  sheet;
Such is the absorbing hate when warring
  nations meet!

LXIV

The Earth to them was as a rolling bark
Which bore them to Eternity; they saw
The Ocean round, but had no time to
  mark
The motions of their vessel; Nature's
  law,
In them suspended, reck'd not of the
  awe

Which reigns when mountains tremble, and the birds
Plunge in the clouds for refuge, and withdraw
From their down-toppling nests; and bellowing herds
Stumble o'er heaving plains, and man's dread hath no words.

LXV

Far other scene is Thrasimene now;
Her lake a sheet of silver, and her plain
Rent by no ravage save the gentle plough;
Her aged trees rise thick as once the slain
Lay where their roots are; but a brook hath ta'en—
A little rill of scanty stream and bed—
A name of blood from that day's sanguine rain;
And Sanguinetto tells ye where the dead
Made the earth wet, and turn'd the unwilling waters red.

LXVI

But thou, Clitumnus! in thy sweetest wave
Of the most living crystal that was e'er
The haunt of river nymph, to gaze and lave
Her limbs where nothing hid them, thou dost rear
Thy grassy banks whereon the milk-white steer
Grazes; the purest god of gentle waters!
And most serene of aspect, and most clear;
Surely that stream was unprofaned by slaughters,
A mirror and a bath for Beauty's youngest daughters!

LXVII

And on thy happy shore a Temple still,
Of small and delicate proportion, keeps,
Upon a mild declivity of hill,
Its memory of thee; beneath it sweeps
Thy current's calmness; oft from out it leaps
The finny darter with the glittering scales,
Who dwells and revels in thy glassy deeps;
While, chance, some scatter'd water-lily sails
Down where the shallower wave still tells its bubbling tales.

LXVIII

Pass not unblest the Genius of the place!
If through the air a zephyr more serene
Win to the brow, 'tis his; and if ye trace
Along his margin a more eloquent green,
If on the heart the freshness of the scene
Sprinkle its coolness, and from the dry dust
Of weary life a moment lave it clean
With Nature's baptism,—'tis to him ye must
Pay orisons for this suspension of disgust.

LXIX

The roar of waters!—from the headlong height
Velino cleaves the wave-worn precipice;
The fall of waters! rapid as the light
The flashing mass foams shaking the abyss;
The hell of waters! where they howl and hiss,
And boil in endless torture; while the sweat
Of their great agony, wrung out from this
Their Phlegethon, curls round the rocks of jet
That guard the gulf around, in pitiless horror set,

LXX

And mounts in spray the skies, and thence again
Returns in an unceasing shower, which round,
With its unemptied cloud of gentle rain,
Is an eternal April to the ground,
Making it all one emerald:—how profound
The gulf! and how the giant element
From rock to rock leaps with delirious bound,
Crushing the cliffs, which, downward worn and rent
With his fierce footsteps, yield in chasms a fearful vent

LXXI

To the broad column which rolls on, and shows
More like the fountain of an infant sea
Torn from the womb of mountains by the throes
Of a new world, than only thus to be
Parent of rivers, which flow gushingly,
With many windings, through the vale:—Look back!
Lo! where it comes like an eternity,
As if to sweep down all things in its track,
Charming the eye with dread,—a matchless cataract,

LXXII

Horribly beautiful! but on the verge,
From side to side, beneath the glittering morn,
An Iris sits, amidst the infernal surge,
Like Hope upon a death-bed, and, unworn

Its steady dyes, while all around is torn
By the distracted waters, bears serene
Its brilliant hues with all their beams
  unshorn:
Resembling, 'mid the torture of the
  scene,
Love watching Madness with unalterable
  mien.

LXXIII

Once more upon the woody Apennine,
The infant Alps, which—had I not be-
  fore
Gazed on their mightier parents, where
  the pine
Sits on more shaggy summits, and where
  roar
The thundering Lauwine—might be
  worshipp'd more;
But I have seen the soaring Jungfrau rear
Her never-trodden snow, and seen the
  hoar
Glaciers of bleak Mont Blanc both far
  and near,
And in Chimari heard the thunder-hills of
  fear,

LXXIV

Th' Acroceraunian mountains of old
  name;
And on Parnassus seen the eagles fly
Like spirits of the spot, as 'twere for
  fame,
For still they soared unutterably high:
I've look'd on Ida with a Trojan's eye;
Athos, Olympus, Ætna, Atlas, made
These hills seem things of lesser dignity,
All, save the lone Soracte's height, dis-
  play'd
Not *now* in snow, which asks the lyric
  Roman's aid

LXXV

For our remembrance, and from out the
  plain
Heaves like a long-swept wave about to
  break,
And on the curl hangs pausing: not in
  vain
May he, who will, his recollections rake,
And quote in classic raptures, and awake
The hills with Latian echoes; I abhorr'd
Too much, to conquer for the poet's
  sake,
The drill'd dull lesson, forced down
  word by word
In my repugnant youth, with pleasure to
  record

LXXVI

Aught that recalls the daily drug which
  turn'd
My sickening memory; and, though
  Time hath taught

My mind to meditate what then it
  learn'd,
Yet such the fix'd inveteracy wrought
By the impatience of my early thought,
That, with the freshness wearing out
  before
My mind could relish what it might have
  sought,
If free to choose, I cannot now restore
Its health; but what it then detested, still
  abhor.

LXXVII

Then farewell, Horace; whom I hated so,
Not for thy faults, but mine; it is a curse
To understand, not feel thy lyric flow,
To comprehend, but never love thy verse:
Although no deeper Moralist rehearse
Our little life, nor Bard prescribe his art,
Nor livelier Satirist the conscience
  pierce,
Awakening without wounding the
  touch'd heart,
Yet fare thee well—upon Soracte's ridge
  we part.

LXXVIII

Oh Rome! my country! city of the soul!
The orphans of the heart must turn to
  thee,
Lone mother of dead empires! and con-
  trol
In their shut breasts their petty misery.
What are our woes and sufferance? Come
  and see
The cypress, hear the owl, and plod your
  way
O'er steps of broken thrones and tem-
  ples, Ye!
Whose agonies are evils of a day—
A world is at our feet as fragile as our clay.

LXXIX

The Niobe of nations! there she stands,
Childless and crownless, in her voiceless
  woe;
An empty urn within her wither'd hands,
Whose holy dust was scatter'd long ago;
The Scipios' tomb contains no ashes
  now;
The very sepulchres lie tenantless
Of their heroic dwellers: dost thou flow,
Old Tiber! through a marble wilderness?
Rise, with thy yellow waves, and mantle
  her distress.

LXXX

The Goth, the Christian, Time, War,
  Flood, and Fire,
Have dealt upon the seven-hill'd city's
  pride;
She saw her glories star by star expire,
And up the steep barbarian monarchs
  ride,

237

Where the car climb'd the Capitol; far
   and wide
Temple and tower went down, nor left a
   site:
Chaos of ruins! who shall trace the
   void,
O'er the dim fragments cast a lunar
   light,
And say, 'here was, or is,' where all is
   doubly night?

LXXXI

The double night of ages, and of her,
Night's daughter, Ignorance, hath wrapt
   and wrap
All round us: we but feel our way to
   err:
The ocean hath his chart, the stars their
   map,
And Knowledge spreads them on her
   ample lap;
But Rome is as the desert, where we
   steer
Stumbling o'er recollections; now we
   clap
Our hands, and cry 'Eureka!' it is
   clear—
When but some false mirage of ruin rises
   near.

LXXXII

Alas! the lofty city! and alas!
The trebly hundred triumphs! and the
   day
When Brutus made the dagger's edge
   surpass
The conqueror's sword in bearing fame
   away!
Alas, for Tully's voice, and Virgil's lay,
And Livy's pictured page!—but these
   shall be
Her resurrection; all beside—decay.
Alas, for Earth, for never shall we see
That brightness in her eye she bore when
   Rome was free!

LXXXIII

Oh thou, whose chariot roll'd on Fortune's wheel,
Triumphant Sylla! Thou, who didst subdue
Thy country's foes ere thou wouldst
   pause to feel
The wrath of thy own wrongs, or reap
   the due
Of hoarded vengeance till thine eagles
   flew
O'er prostrate Asia;—thou, who with
   thy frown
Annihilated senates—Roman, too,
With all thy vices, for thou didst lay
   down
With an atoning smile a more than earthly
   crown—

LXXXIV

The dictatorial wreath—couldst thou
   divine
To what would one day dwindle that
   which made
Thee more than mortal? and that so supine
By aught than Romans Rome should
   thus be laid?
She who was named Eternal, and array'd
Her warriors but to conquer—she who
   veil'd
Earth with her haughty shadow, and
   display'd,
Until the o'er-canopied horizon fail'd,
Her rushing wings—Oh! she who was Al-
   mighty hail'd!

LXXXV

Sylla was first of victors; but our own,
The sagest of usurpers, Cromwell!—he
Too swept off senates while he hew'd the
   throne
Down to a block—immortal rebel! See
What crimes it costs to be a moment free,
And famous through all ages! but be-
   neath
His fate the moral lurks of destiny;
His day of double victory and death
Beheld him win two realms, and, happier,
   yield his breath.

LXXXVI

The third of the same moon whose former course
Had all but crown'd him, on the self-
   same day
Deposed him gently from his throne of
   force,
And laid him with the earth's preceding
   clay.
And show'd not Fortune thus how fame
   and sway,
And all we deem delightful, and consume
Our souls to compass through each
   arduous way,
Are in her eyes less happy than the
   tomb?
Were they but so in man's, how different
   were his doom!

LXXXVII

And thou, dread statue! yet existent in
The austerest form of naked majesty,
Thou who beheldest, 'mid the assassins'
   din,
At thy bathed base the bloody Cæsar lie,
Folding his robe in dying dignity,
An offering to thine altar from the queen
Of gods and men, great Nemesis! did he
   die,
And thou, too, perish, Pompey? have ye
   been
Victors of countless kings, or puppets of
   a scene?

LXXXVIII

And thou, the thunder-stricken nurse of
  Rome!
She-wolf! whose brazen-imaged dugs
  impart
The milk of conquest yet within the
  dome
Where, as a monument of antique art,
Thou standest:—Mother of the mighty
  heart,
Which the great founder suck'd from
  thy wild teat,
Scorch'd by the Roman Jove's ethereal
  dart,
And thy limbs black with lightning—
  dost thou yet
Guard thine immortal cubs, nor thy fond
  charge forget?

LXXXIX

Thou dost; but all thy foster-babes are
  dead—
The men of iron: and the world hath
  rear'd
Cities from out their sepulchres: men bled
In imitation of the things they fear'd,
And fought and conquer'd, and the
  same course steer'd,
At apish distance; but as yet none have,
Nor could, the same supremacy have
  near'd,
Save one vain man, who is not in the grave,
But, vanquish'd by himself, to his own
  slaves a slave—

XC

The fool of false dominion—and a kind
Of bastard Cæsar, following him of old
With steps unequal; for the Roman's
  mind
Was modell'd in a less terrestrial mould,
With passions fiercer, yet a judgment cold,
And an immortal instinct which re-
  deem'd
The frailties of a heart so soft, yet bold,
Alcides with the distaff now he seem'd
At Cleopatra's feet,—and now himself he
  beam'd,

XCI

And came—and saw—and conquer'd!
  But the man
Who would have tamed his eagles down
  to flee,
Like a train'd falcon, in the Gallic van,
Which he, in sooth, long led to victory,
With a deaf heart, which never seem'd
  to be
A listener to itself, was strangely framed;
With but one weakest weakness—
  vanity,
Coquettish in ambition, still he aim'd—
At what? can he avouch, or answer what
  he claim'd?

XCII

And would be all or nothing—nor could
  wait
For the sure grave to level him; few years
Had fix'd him with the Cæsars in his fate,
On whom we tread: For *this* the con-
  queror rears
The arch of triumph and for this the tears
And blood of earth flow on as they have
  flow'd,
An universal deluge, which appears
Without an ark for wretched man's abode,
And ebbs but to reflow! Renew thy rain-
  bow, God!

XCIII

What from this barren being do we reap?
Our senses narrow, and our reason frail,
Life short, and truth a gem which loves
  the deep,
And all things weigh'd in custom's fals-
  est scale;
Opinion an omnipotence,—whose veil
Mantles the earth with darkness, until
  right
And wrong are accidents, and men
  grow pale
Lest their own judgments should become
  too bright,
And their free thoughts be crimes, and
  earth have too much light.

XCIV

And thus they plod in sluggish misery,
Rotting from sire to son, and age to age,
Proud of their trampled nature, and so
  die,
Bequeathing their hereditary rage
To the new race of inborn slaves, who
  wage
War for their chains, and rather than
  be free,
Bleed gladiator-like, and still engage
Within the same arena where they see
Their fellows fall before, like leaves of the
  same tree.

XCV

I speak not of men's creeds—they rest
  between
Man and his Maker—but of things
  allow'd,
Averr'd, and known, and daily, hourly
  seen—
The yoke that is upon us doubly bow'd,
And the intent of tyranny avow'd,
The edict of Earth's rulers, who are
  grown
The apes of him who humbled once the
  proud,
And shook them from their slumbers
  on the throne:
Too glorious, were this all his mighty arm
  had done.

XCVI

Can tyrants but by tyrants conquer'd be,
And Freedom find no champion and no
child
Such as Columbia saw arise when she
Sprung forth a Pallas, arm'd and un-
defiled?
Or must such minds be nourish'd in the
wild,
Deep in the unpruned forest, 'midst the
roar
Of cataracts, where nursing Nature
smiled
On infant Washington? Has Earth no
more
Such seeds within her breast, or Europe
no such shore?

XCVII

But France got drunk with blood to
vomit crime,
And fatal have her Saturnalia been
To Freedom's cause, in every age and
clime;
Because the deadly days which we have
seen,
And vile Ambition, that built up be-
tween
Man and his hopes an adamantine wall,
And the base pageant last upon the
scene,
Are grown the pretext for the eternal
thrall
Which nips life's tree, and dooms man's
worst—his second fall.

XCVIII

Yet, Freedom! yet thy banner, torn, but
flying,
Streams like the thunder-storm *against*
the wind;
Thy trumpet voice, though broken now
and dying,
The loudest still the tempest leaves be-
hind;
Thy tree hath lost its blossoms, and the
rind,
Chopp'd by the axe, looks rough and
little worth,
But the sap lasts,—and still the seed
we find
Sown deep, even in the bosom of the
North;
So shall a better spring less bitter fruit
bring forth.

XCIX

There is a stern round tower of other
days,
Firm as a fortress, with its fence of stone,
Such as an army's baffled strength de-
lays,
Standing with half its battlements alone,

And with two thousand years of ivy
grown,
The garland of eternity, where wave
The green leaves over all by time o'erthrown;—
What was this tower of strength? within
its cave
What treasure lay so lock'd, so hid?—A
woman's grave.

C

But who was she, the lady of the
dead,
Tomb'd in a palace? Was she chaste
and fair?
Worthy a king's, or more—a Roman's
bed?
What race of chiefs and heroes did she
bear?
What daughter of her beauties was the
heir?
How lived, how loved, how died she?
Was she not
So honoured—and conspicuously there,
Where meaner relics must not dare to
rot,
Placed to commemorate a more than mor-
tal lot?

CI

Was she as those who love their lords, or
they
Who love the lords of others? such have
been
Even in the olden time, Rome's annals
say.
Was she a matron of Cornelia's mien,
Or the light air of Egypt's graceful
queen,
Profuse of joy—or 'gainst it did she war,
Inveterate in virtue? Did she lean
To the soft side of the heart, or wisely
bar
Love from amongst her griefs?—for such
the affections are.

CII

Perchance she died in youth: it may be,
bow'd
With woes far heavier than the ponder-
ous tomb
That weigh'd upon her gentle dust, a
cloud
Might gather o'er her beauty, and a
gloom
In her dark eye, prophetic of the doom
Heaven gives its favourites—early
death; yet shed
A sunset charm around her, and illume
With hectic light, the Hesperus of the
dead,
Of her consuming cheek the autumnal
leaf-like red.

CIII

Perchance she died in age—surviving all,
Charms, kindred, children—with the
    silver gray
On her long tresses, which might yet re-
    call,
It may be, still a something of the day
When they were braided, and her proud
    array
And lovely form were envied, praised,
    and eyed
By Rome—But whither would Conjec-
    ture stray?
Thus much alone we know—Metella
    died,
The wealthiest Roman's wife: Behold his
    love or pride!

CIV

I know not why—but standing thus by
    thee
It seems as if I had thine inmate known,
Thou Tomb! and other days come back
    on me
With recollected music, though the tone
Is changed and solemn, like the cloudy
    groan
Of dying thunder on the distant wind;
Yet could I seat me by this ivied stone
Till I had bodied, forth the heated mind,
Forms from the floating wreck which Ruin
    leaves behind;

CV

And from the planks, far shatter'd o'er
    the rocks,
Built me a little bark of hope, once more
To battle with the ocean and the shocks
Of the loud breakers, and the ceaseless
    roar
Which rushes on the solitary shore
Where all lies founder'd that was ever
    dear:
But could I gather from the wave-worn
    store
Enough for my rude boat, where should
    I steer?
There woos no home, nor hope, nor life,
    save what is here.

CVI

Then let the winds howl on! their har-
    mony
Shall henceforth be my music, and the
    night
The sound shall temper with the owlets'
    cry,
As I now hear them, in the fading light
Dim o'er the bird of darkness' native
    site,
Answering each other on the Palatine,
With their large eyes, all glistening gray
    and bright,

And sailing pinions.—Upon such a
    shrine
What are our petty griefs?—let me not
    number mine.

CVII

Cypress and ivy, weed and wallflower
    grown,
Matted and mass'd together, hillocks
    heap'd
On what were chambers, arch crush'd,
    column strown
In fragments, choked up vaults, and
    frescos steep'd
In subterranean damps, where the owl
    peep'd,
Deeming it midnight:—Temples, baths,
    or halls?
Pronounce who can; for all that Learn-
    ing reap'd
From her research hath been, that these
    are walls—
Behold the Imperial Mount! 'tis thus the
    mighty falls.

CVIII

There is the moral of all human tales;
'Tis but the same rehearsal of the past,
First Freedom, and then Glory—when
    that fails,
Wealth, vice, corruption,—barbarism
    at last.
And History, with all her volumes vast,
Hath but *one* page,—'tis better writ-
    ten here
Where gorgeous Tyranny hath thus
    amass'd
All treasures, all delights, that eye or ear,
Heart, soul, could seek, tongue ask—
    Away with words! draw near,

CIX

Admire, exult, despise, laugh, weep,—
    for here
There is such matter for all feeling:—
    Man!
Thou pendulum betwixt a smile and tear,
Ages and realms are crowded in this span,
This mountain, whose obliterated plan
The pyramid of empires pinnacled,
Of Glory's gewgaws shining in the van
Till the sun's rays with added flame were
    fill'd!
Where are its golden roofs? where those
    who dared to build?

CX

Tully was not so eloquent as thou,
Thou nameless column with the buried
    base!
What are the laurels of the Cæsar's
    brow?
Crown me with ivy from his dwelling-
    place.

Whose arch or pillar meets me in the
face,
Titus or Trajan's? No—'tis that of
Time:
Triumph, arch, pillar, all he doth dis-
place
Scoffing; and apostolic statues climb
To crush the imperial urn, whose ashes
slept sublime,

CXI

Buried in air, the deep blue sky of
Rome,
And looking to the stars: they had con-
tain'd
A spirit which with these would find a
home,
The last of those who o'er the whole
earth reign'd,
The Roman globe, for after none sus-
tain'd,
But yielded back his conquests:—he
was more
Than a mere Alexander, and, unstain'd
With household blood and wine, serene-
ly wore
His sovereign virtues—still we Trajan's
name adore.

CXII

Where is the rock of Triumph, the high
place
Where Rome embraced her heroes?
where the steep
Tarpeian? fittest goal of Treason's race,
The promontory whence the Traitor's
Leap
Cured all ambition. Did the conquerors
heap
Their spoils here? Yes; and in yon field
below,
A thousand years of silenced factions
sleep—
The Forum, where the immortal accents
glow,
And still the eloquent air breathes—burns
with Cicero!

CXIII

The field of freedom, faction, fame, and
blood:
Here a proud people's passions were
exhaled,
From the first hour of empire in the bud
To that when further worlds to conquer
fail'd;
But long before had Freedom's face
been veil'd,
And Anarchy assumed her attributes;
Till every lawless soldier who assail'd
Trod on the trembling senate's slavish
mutes,
Or raised the venal voice of baser prosti-
tutes.

CXIV

Then turn we to her latest tribune's name,
From her ten thousand tyrants turn to
thee,
Redeemer of dark centuries of shame—
The friend of Petrarch—hope of Italy—
Rienzi! last of Romans! While the tree
Of freedom's wither'd trunk puts forth
a leaf
Even for thy tomb a garland let it be—
The forum's champion, and the people's
chief—
Her new-born Numa thou—with reign,
alas! too brief.

CXV

Egeria! sweet creation of some heart
Which found no mortal resting-place
so fair
As thine ideal breast; whate'er thou art
Or wert,—a young Aurora of the air,
The nympholepsy of some fond despair;
Or, it might be, a beauty of the earth,
Who found a more than common votary
there
Too much adoring; whatsoe'er thy birth,
Thou wert a beautiful thought, and softly
bodied forth.

CXVI

The mosses of thy fountain still are
sprinkled
With thine Elysian water-drops; the face
Of cave-guarded spring with years
unwrinkled,
Reflects the meek-eyed genius of the
place,
Whose green, wild margin now no more
erase
Art's works; nor must the delicate
waters sleep,
Prison'd in marble—bubbling from the
base
Of the cleft statue, with a gentle leap
The rill runs o'er—and round—fern, flowers,
and ivy creep,

CXVII

Fantastically tangled: the green hills
Are clothed with early blossoms,
through the grass
The quick-eyed lizard rustles, and the
bills
Of summer-birds sing welcome as ye
pass;
Flowers fresh in hue, and many in their
class,
Implore the pausing step, and with their
dyes,
Dance in the soft breeze in a fairy mass;
The sweetness of the violet's deep blue
eyes,
Kiss'd by the breath of heaven, seems
colour'd by its skies.

CXVIII

Here didst thou dwell, in this enchanted
cover,
Egeria! thy all heavenly bosom beating
For the far footsteps of thy mortal lover;
The purple Midnight veil'd that mystic
meeting
With her most starry canopy, and seat-
ing
Thyself by thine adorer, what befell?
This cave was surely shaped out for the
greeting
Of an enamour'd Goddess, and the cell
Haunted by holy Love—the earliest oracle!

CXIX

And didst thou not, thy breast to his
replying,
Blend a celestial with a human heart;
And Love, which dies as it was born, in
sighing,
Share with immortal transports? could
thine art
Make them indeed immortal, and impart
The purity of heaven to earthly joys,
Expel the venom and not blunt the
dart—
The dull satiety which all destroys—
And root from out the soul the deadly
weed which cloys?

CXX

Alas! our young affections run to waste,
Or water but the desert; whence arise
But weeds of dark luxuriance, tares of
haste,
Rank at the core, though tempting to the
eyes,
Flowers whose wild odours breathe but
agonies,
And trees whose gums are poisons; such
the plants
Which spring beneath her steps as
Passion flies
O'er the world's wilderness, and vainly
pants
For some celestial fruit forbidden to our
wants.

CXXI

Oh, Love! no habitant of earth thou
art—
An unseen seraph, we believe in thee,—
A faith whose martyrs are the broken
heart,—
But never yet hath seen, nor e'er shall see
The naked eye, thy form, as it should be;
The mind hath made thee, as it peopled
heaven,
Even with its own desiring phantasy,
And to a thought such shape and image
given,
As haunts the unquench'd soul—parch'd,
wearied, wrung, and riven.

CXXII

Of its own beauty is the mind diseased,
And fevers into false creation:—where,
Where are the forms the sculptor's soul
hath seiz'd?
In him alone. Can Nature show so fair?
Where are the charms and virtues which
we dare
Conceive in boyhood and pursue as
men,
The unreach'd Paradise of our despair,
Which o'er-informs the pencil and the
pen,
And overpowers the page where it would
bloom again?

CXXIII

Who loves, raves—'tis youth's frenzy
—but the cure
Is bitterer still, as charm by charm un-
winds
Which robed our idols, and we see too
sure
Nor worth nor beauty dwells from out
the mind's
Ideal shape of such; yet still it binds
The fatal spell, and still it draws us on,
Reaping the whirlwind from the oft-
sown winds;
The stubborn heart, its alchemy begun,
Seems ever near the prize—wealthiest
when most undone.

CXXIV

We wither from our youth, we gasp
away—
Sick—sick; unfound the boon, unslaked
the thirst,
Though to the last, in verge of our decay,
Some phantom lures, such as we sought
at first—
But all too late,—so are we doubly curst.
Love, fame, ambition, avarice—'tis
the same,
Each idle, and all ill, and none the
worst—
For all are meteors with a different name,
And Death the sable smoke where van-
ishes the flame.

CXXV

Few—none—find what they love or
could have loved,
Though accident, blind contact, and the
strong
Necessity of loving, have removed
Antipathies—but to recur, ere long,
Envenom'd with irrevocable wrong;
And Circumstance, that unspiritual god
And miscreator, makes and helps along
Our coming evils with a crutch-like rod,
Whose touch turns Hope to dust,—the
dust we all have trod.

CXXVI

Our life is a false nature: 'tis not in
The harmony of things,—this hard de-
cree,
This uneradicable taint of sin,
This boundless upas, this all-blasting
tree,
Whose root is earth, whose leaves and
branches be
The skies which rain their plagues on
men like dew—
Disease, death, bondage—all the woes
we see,
And worse, the woes we see not—which
throb through
The immedicable soul, with heart-aches
ever new.

CXXVII

Yet let us ponder boldly—'tis a base
Abandonment of reason to resign
Our right of thought—our last and only
place
Of refuge; this, at least, shall still be
mine:
Though from our birth the faculty
divine
Is chain'd and tortured—cabin'd,
cribb'd, confined,
And bred in darkness, lest the truth
should shine
Too brightly on the unprepared mind,
The beam pours in, for time and skill will
couch the blind.

CXXVIII

Arches on arches! as it were that Rome,
Collecting the chief trophies of her
line,
Would build up all her triumphs in one
dome,
Her Coliseum stands; the moonbeams
shine
As 'twere its natural torches, for divine
Should be the light which streams here
to illume
This long-explored but still exhaustless
mine
Of contemplation; and the azure gloom
Of an Italian night, where the deep skies
assume

CXXIX

Hues which have words, and speak to
ye of heaven,
Floats o'er this vast and wondrous
monument,
And shadows forth its glory. There is
given
Unto the things of earth, which Time
hath bent,
A spirit's feeling, and where he hath
leant

His hand, but broke his scythe, there is
a power
And magic in the ruin'd battlement,
For which the palace of the present hour
Must yield its pomp, and wait till ages are
its dower.

CXXX

Oh Time! the beautifier of the dead,
Adorner of the ruin, comforter
And only healer when the heart hath bled;
Time! the corrector where our judg-
ments err,
The test of truth, love—sole philosopher,
For all beside are sophists—from thy
thrift,
Which never loses though it doth defer—
Time, the avenger! unto thee I lift
My hands, and eyes, and heart, and crave
of thee a gift:

CXXXI

Amidst this wreck, where thou hast
made a shrine
And temple more divinely desolate,
Among thy mightier offerings here are
mine,
Ruins of years, though few, yet full of
fate:
If thou hast ever seen me too elate,
Hear me not; but if calmly I have borne
Good, and reserved my pride against the
hate
Which shall not whelm me, let me not
have worn
This iron in my soul in vain—shall *they*
not mourn?

CXXXII

And thou, who never yet of human
wrong
Left the unbalanced scale, great Nemesis!
Here, where the ancient paid thee homage long—
Thou who didst call the Furies from the
abyss,
And round Orestes bade them howl and
hiss
For that unnatural retribution—just,
Had it but been from hands less near—
in this
Thy former realm, I call thee from the
dust!
Dost thou not hear my heart?—Awake!
thou shalt, and must.

CXXXIII

It is not that I may not have incurr'd
For my ancestral faults or mine the
wound
I bleed withal, and, had it been conferr'd
With a just weapon, it had flow'd unbound;

But now my blood shall not sink in the
      ground;
To thee I do devote it—*thou* shalt take
The vengeance, which shall yet be
      sought and found,
Which if *I* have not taken for the sake—
But let that pass—I sleep, but thou shalt
      yet awake.

CXXXIV

And if my voice break forth, 'tis not that
      now
I shrink from what is suffer'd: let him
      speak
Who hath beheld decline upon my brow,
Or seen my mind's convulsion leave it
      weak;
But in this page a record will I seek.
Not in the air shall these my words dis-
      perse,
Though I be ashes; a far hour shall
      wreak
The deep prophetic fulness of this verse,
And pile on human heads the mountain
      of my curse!

CXXXV

That curse shall be Forgiveness.—Have
      I not—
Hear me, my mother Earth! behold it,
      Heaven!
Have I not had to wrestle with my lot?
Have I not suffer'd things to be forgiven?
Have I not had my brain sear'd, my
      heart riven,
Hopes sapp'd, name blighted, Life's
      life lied away?
And only not to desperation driven,
Because not altogether of such clay
As rots into the souls of those whom I
      survey.

CXXXVI

From mighty wrongs to petty perfidy
Have I not seen what human things
      could do?
From the loud roar of foaming calumny
To the small whisper of the as paltry few,
And subtler venom of the reptile crew,
The Janus glance of whose significant eye,
Learning to lie with silence, would *seem*
      true,
And without utterance, save the shrug
      or sigh,
Deal round to happy fools its speechless
      obloquy.

CXXXVII

But I have lived, and have not lived in
      vain:
My mind may lose its force, my blood its
      fire,
And my frame perish even in conquer-
      ing pain;

But there is that within me which shall tire
Torture and Time, and breathe when I
      expire;
Something unearthly, which they deem
      not of,
Like the remember'd tone of a mute lyre,
Shall on their soften'd spirits sink, and
      move
In hearts all rocky now the late remorse of
      love.

CXXXVIII

The seal is set.—Now welcome, thou
      dread power!
Nameless, yet thus omnipotent, which
      here
Walk'st in the shadow of the midnight
      hour
With a deep awe, yet all distinct from
      fear;
Thy haunts are ever where the dead
      walls rear
Their ivy mantles, and the solemn scene
Derives from thee a sense so deep and
      clear
That we become a part of what has been,
And grow unto the spot, all-seeing but
      unseen.

CXXXIX

And here the buzz of eager nations ran,
In murmur'd pity, or loud-roar'd ap-
      plause,
As man was slaughter'd by his fellow-
      man.
And wherefore slaughter'd? wherefore,
      but because
Such were the bloody Circus' genial
      laws,
And the imperial pleasure.—Wherefore
      not?
What matters where we fall to fill the
      maws
Of worms—on battle-plains or listed
      spot?
Both are but theatres—where the chief
      actors rot.

CXL

I see before me the Gladiator lie:
He leans upon his hand—his manly
      brow
Consents to death, but conquers agony,
And his droop'd head sinks gradually
      low—
And through his side the last drops, ebb-
      ing slow
From the red gash, fall heavy, one by
      one,
Like the first of a thunder-shower; and
      now
The arena swims around him—he is
      gone,
Ere ceased the inhuman shout which hail'd
      the wretch who won.

245

CXLI

He heard it, but he heeded not—his eyes
Were with his heart, and that was far
    away;
He reck'd not of the life he lost nor prize,
But where his rude hut by the Danube
    lay,
There were his young barbarians all at
    play,
There was their Dacian mother—he,
    their sire,
Butcher'd to make a Roman holiday—
All this rush'd with his blood—Shall he
    expire
And unavenged? Arise! ye Goths, and glut
    your ire!

CXLII

But here, where Murder breathed her
    bloody steam;
And here, where buzzing nations choked
    the ways,
And roar'd or murmur'd like a moun-
    tain stream
Dashing or winding as its torrent strays;
Here, where the Roman million's blame
    or praise
Was death or life, the playthings of a
    crowd,
My voice sounds much—and fall the
    stars' faint rays
On the arena void—seats crush'd—
    walls bow'd—
And galleries, where my steps seem echoes
    strangely loud.

CXLIII

A ruin—yet what ruin! from its mass
Walls, palaces, half-cities, have been
    rear'd;
Yet oft the enormous skeleton ye pass,
And marvel where the spoil could have
    appear'd.
Hath it indeed been plunder'd, or but
    clear'd?
Alas! developed, opens the decay,
When the colossal fabric's form is near'd:
It will not bear the brightness of the day,
Which streams too much on all—years—
    man—have reft away.

CXLIV

But when the rising moon begins to
    climb
Its topmost arch, and gently pauses
    there;
When the stars twinkle through the
    loops of time,
And the low night-breeze waves along
    the air
The garland-forest, which the gray walls
    wear,
Like laurels on the bald first Cæsar's
    head;

When the light shines serene but doth
    not glare,
Then in this magic circle raise the dead:
Heroes have trod this spot—'tis on their
    dust ye tread.

CXLV

'While stands the Coliseum, Rome shall
    stand;
'When falls the Coliseum, Rome shall
    fall;
'And when Rome falls—the World.'
    From our own land
Thus spake the pilgrims o'er this mighty
    wall
In Saxon times, which we are wont to call
Ancient; and these three mortal things
    are still
On their foundations, and unalter'd all;
Rome and her Ruin past Redemption's
    skill,
The World, the same wide den—of thieves,
    or what ye will.

CXLVI

Simple, erect, severe, austere, sublime—
Shrine of all saints and temple of all
    gods,
From Jove to Jesus—spared and blest
    by time;
Looking tranquillity, while falls or nods
Arch, empire, each thing round thee,
    and man plods
His way through thorns to ashes—
    glorious dome!
Shalt thou not last? Time's scythe and
    tyrants' rods
Shiver upon thee—sanctuary and home
Of art and piety—Pantheon!—pride of
    Rome!

CXLVII

Relic of nobler days, and noblest arts!
Despoil'd yet perfect, with thy circle
    spreads
A holiness appealing to all hearts—
To art a model; and to him who treads
Rome for the sake of ages, Glory sheds
Her light through thy sole aperture; to
    those
Who worship, here are altars for their
    beads;
And they who feel for genius may repose
Their eyes on honour'd forms, whose busts
    around them close.

CXLVIII

There is a dungeon, in whose dim drear
    light
What do I gaze on? Nothing: Look
    again!
Two forms are slowly shadow'd on my
    sight—
Two insulated phantoms of the brain:

It is not so; I see them full and plain—
An old man, and a female young and
fair,
Fresh as a nursing mother, in whose
vein
The blood is nectar:—but what doth
she there,
With her unmantled neck, and bosom
white and bare?

CXLIX

Full swells the deep pure fountain of
young life,
Where *on* the heart and *from* the heart
we took
Our first and sweetest nurture, when the
wife,
Blest into mother, in the innocent look,
Or even the piping cry of lips that brook
No pain and small suspense, a joy per-
ceives
Man knows not, when from out its
cradled nook
She sees her little bud put forth its
leaves—
What may the fruit be yet? I know not—
Cain was Eve's.

CL

But here youth offers to old age the
food,
The milk of his own gift: it is her
sire
To whom she renders back the debt of
blood
Born with her birth. No; he shall not
expire
While in those warm and lovely veins
the fire
Of health and holy feeling can provide
Great Nature's Nile, whose deep stream
rises higher
Than Egypt's river: from that gentle
side
Drink, drink and live, old man! Heaven's
realm holds no such tide.

CLI

The starry fable of the milky way
Has not thy story's purity; it is
A constellation of a sweeter ray,
And sacred Nature triumphs more in
this
Reverse of her decree, than in the
abyss
Where sparkle distant worlds:—Oh,
holiest nurse!
No drop of that clear stream its way
shall miss
To thy sire's heart, replenishing its
source
With life, as our freed souls rejoin the
universe.

CLII

Turn to the mole which Hadrian rear'd
on high,
Imperial mimic of old Egypt's piles,
Colossal copyist of deformity
Whose travell'd phantasy from the far
Nile's
Enormous model, doom'd the artist's
toils
To build for giants, and for his vain
earth,
His shrunken ashes, raise this dome:
How smiles
The gazer's eye with philosophic mirth,
To view the huge design which sprung
from such a birth!

CLIII

But lo! the dome—the vast and won-
drous dome,
To which Diana's marvel was a cell—
Christ's mighty shrine above his mar-
tyr's tomb!
I have beheld the Ephesian's miracle;—
Its columns strew the wilderness, and
dwell
The hyæna and the jackal in their shade;
I have beheld Sophia's bright roofs
swell
Their glittering mass i' the sun, and have
survey'd
Its sanctuary the while the usurping Mos-
lem pray'd;

CLIV

But thou, of temples old, or altars new,
Standest alone, with nothing like to
thee—
Worthiest of God, the holy and the true.
Since Zion's desolation, when that He
Forsook his former city, what could be,
Of earthly structures, in his honour
piled,
Of a sublimer aspect? Majesty,
Power, Glory, Strength, and Beauty all
are aisled
In this eternal ark of worship undefiled.

CLV

Enter: its grandeur overwhelms thee
not;
And why? It is not lessen'd; but thy
mind,
Expanded by the genius of the spot,
Has grown colossal, and can only find
A fit abode wherein appear enshrined
Thy hopes of immortality; and thou
Shalt one day, if found worthy, so de-
fined,
See thy God face to face, as thou dost
now
His Holy of Holies, nor be blasted by his
brow.

CLVI

Thou movest, but increasing with the
    advance,
Like climbing some great Alp, which
    still doth rise,
Deceived by its gigantic elegance;
Vastness which grows, but grows to
    harmonise—
All musical in its immensities;
Rich marbles, richer painting—shrines
    where flame
The lamps of gold—and haughty dome
    which vies
In air with Earth's chief structures,
    though their frame
Sits on the firm-set ground, and this the
    clouds must claim.

CLVII

Thou seest not all; but piecemeal thou
    must break,
To separate contemplation, the great
    whole;
And as the ocean many bays will make
That ask the eye—so here condense thy
    soul
To more immediate objects, and control
Thy thoughts until thy mind hath got by
    heart
Its eloquent proportions, and unroll
In mighty graduations, part by part,
The glory which at once upon thee did not
    dart,

CLVIII

Not by its fault—but thine: Our out-
    ward sense
Is but of gradual grasp—and as it is
That what we have of feeling most in-
    tense
Outstrips our faint expression; even so
    this
Outshining and o'erwhelming edifice
Fools our fond gaze, and greatest of the
    great
Defies at first our Nature's littleness,
Till, growing with its growth, we thus
    dilate
Our spirits to the size of that they contem-
    plate.

CLIX

Then pause, and be enlighten'd; there is
    more
In such a survey than the sating gaze
Of wonder pleased, or awe which would
    adore
The worship of the place, or the mere
    praise
Of art and its great masters, who could
    raise
What former time, nor skill, nor thought
    could plan;
The fountain of sublimity displays

Its depth, and thence may draw the
    mind of man
Its golden sands, and learn what great
    conceptions can.

CLX

Or, turning to the Vatican, go see
Laocoön's torture dignifying pain—
A father's love and mortal's agony
With an immortal's patience blending:
    —Vain
The struggle; vain, against the coiling
    strain
And gripe, and deepening of the dra-
    gon's grasp,
The old man's clench; the long en-
    venom'd chain
Rivets the living links,—the enormous
    asp
Enforces pang on pang, and stifles gasp on
    gasp.

CLXI

Or view the Lord of the unerring bow,
The God of life, and poesy, and light—
The Sun in human limbs array'd, and
    brow
All radiant from his triumph in the fight;
The shaft hath just been shot—the
    arrow bright
With an immortal's vengeance; in his
    eye
And nostril beautiful disdain, and might
And majesty, flash their full lightnings
    by,
Developing in that one glance the Deity.

CLXII

But in his delicate form—a dream of
    Love,
Shaped by some solitary nymph, whose
    breast
Long'd for a deathless lover from above,
And madden'd in that vision—are ex-
    prest
All that ideal beauty ever bless'd
The mind with in its most unearthly
    mood,
When each conception was a heavenly
    guest—
A ray of immortality—and stood
Starlike, around, until they gather'd to a
    god!

CLXIII

And if it be Prometheus stole from
    Heaven
The fire which we endure, it was repaid
By him to whom the energy was given
Which this poetic marble hath array'd
With an eternal glory—which, if made
By human hands, is not of human
    thought;

And Time himself hath hallow'd it, nor laid
One ringlet in the dust—nor hath it caught
A tinge of years, but breathes the flame with which 'twas wrought.

CLXIV

But where is he, the Pilgrim of my song,
The being who upheld it through the past?
Methinks he cometh late and tarries long.
He is no more—these breathings are his last;
His wanderings done, his visions ebbing fast,
And he himself as nothing:—if he was
Aught but a phantasy, and could be class'd
With forms which live and suffer—let that pass—
His shadow fades away into Destruction's mass,

CLXV

Which gathers shadow, substance, life, and all
That we inherit in its mortal shroud,
And spreads the dim and universal pall
Through which all things grow phantoms; and the cloud
Between us sinks and all which ever glow'd,
Till Glory's self is twilight, and displays
A melancholy halo scarce allow'd
To hover on the verge of darkness; rays
Sadder than saddest night, for they distract the gaze.

CLXVI

And send us prying into the abyss,
To gather what we shall be when the frame
Shall be resolved to something less than this
Its wretched essence; and to dream of fame,
And wipe the dust from off the idle name
We never more shall hear,—but never more,
Oh, happier thought! can we be made the same:
It is enough in sooth that once we bore
These fardels of the heart—the heart whose sweat was gore.

CLXVII

Hark! forth from the abyss a voice proceeds,
A long low distant murmur of dread sound,
Such as arises when a nation bleeds

With some deep and immedicable wound;
Through storm and darkness yawns the rending ground,
The gulf is thick with phantoms, but the chief
Seems royal still, though with her head discrown'd,
And pale, but lovely, with maternal grief
She clasps a babe, to whom her breast yields no relief.

CLXVIII

Scion of chiefs and monarchs, where art thou?
Fond hope of many nations, art thou dead?
Could not the grave forget thee, and lay low
Some less majestic, less beloved head?
In the sad midnight, while thy heart still bled,
The mother of a moment, o'er thy boy,
Death hush'd that pang for ever: with thee fled
The present happiness and promised joy
Which fill'd the imperial isles so full it seem'd to cloy.

CLXIX

Peasants bring forth in safety.—Can it be,
Oh thou that wert so happy, so adored!
Those who weep not for kings shall weep for thee,
And Freedom's heart, grown heavy, cease to hoard
Her many griefs for ONE; for she had pour'd
Her orisons for thee, and o'er thy head
Beheld her Iris.—Thou, too, lonely lord,
And desolate consort—vainly wert thou wed!
The husband of a year! the father of the dead!

CLXX

Of sackcloth was thy wedding garment made;
Thy bridal's fruit is ashes: in the dust
The fair-hair'd Daughter of the Isles is laid,
The love of millions! How we did intrust
Futurity to her! and, though it must
Darken above our bones, yet fondly deem'd
Our children should obey her child, and bless'd
Her and her hoped-for seed, whose promise seem'd
Like stars to shepherds' eyes:—'twas but a meteor beam'd.

CLXXI

Woe unto us, not her; for she sleeps
well:
The fickle reek of popular breath, the
tongue
Of hollow counsel, the false oracle,
Which from the birth of monarchy hath
rung
Its knell in princely ears, till the o'er-
stung
Nations have arm'd in madness, the
strange fate
Which tumbles mightiest sovereigns,
and hath flung
Against their blind omnipotence a
weight
Within the opposing scale, which crushes
soon or late,—

CLXXII

These might have been her destiny; but
no,
Our hearts deny it: and so young, so fair,
Good without effort, great without a
foe;
But now a bride and mother—and now
there!
How many ties did that stern moment
tear!
From thy Sire's to his humblest subject's
breast
Is link'd the electric chain of that despair,
Whose shock was as an earthquake's,
and opprest
The land which loved thee so that none
could love thee best.

CLXXIII

Lo, Nemi! navell'd in the woody hills
So far, that the uprooting wind which
tears
The oak from his foundation, and which
spills
The ocean o'er its boundary, and bears
Its foam against the skies, reluctant
spares
The oval mirror of thy glassy lake;
And calm as cherish'd hate, its surface
wears
A deep cold settled aspect nought can
shake,
All coil'd into itself and round, as sleeps
the snake.

CLXXIV

And near, Albano's scarce divided
waves
Shine from a sister valley;—and afar
The Tiber winds, and the broad ocean
laves
The Latian coast where sprung the Epic
war,

'Arms and the man,' whose re-ascend-
ing star
Rose o'er an empire:—but beneath thy
right
Tully reposed from Rome;—and where
yon bar
Of girdling mountains intercepts the
sight
The Sabine farm was till'd, the weary
bard's delight.

CLXXV

But I forget.—My Pilgrim's shrine is
won,
And he and I must part,—so let it be,—
His task and mine alike are nearly done;
Yet once more let us look upon the sea;
The midland ocean breaks on him and
me,
And from the Alban Mount we now
behold
Our friend of youth, that Ocean, which
when we
Beheld it last by Calpe's rock unfold
Those waves, we follow'd on till the dark
Euxine roll'd

CLXXVI

Upon the blue Symplegades: long
years—
Long, though not very many—since
have done
Their work on both; some suffering and
some tears
Have left us nearly where we had begun:
Yet not in vain our mortal race hath
run;
We have had our reward, and it is
here,—
That we can yet feel gladden'd by the
sun,
And reap from earth, sea, joy almost as
dear
As if there were no man to trouble what is
clear.

CLXXVII

Oh! that the Desert were my dwelling-
place,
With one fair Spirit for my minister,
That I might all forget the human race,
And, hating no one, love but only her!
Ye elements!—in whose ennobling stir
I feel myself exalted—Can ye not
Accord me such a being? Do I err
In deeming such inhabit many a spot?
Though with them to converse can rarely
be our lot.

CLXXVIII

There is a pleasure in the pathless woods,
There is a rapture on the lonely shore,
There is society, where none intrudes
By the deep Sea, and music in its roar:

I love not Man the less, but Nature
    more,
From these our interviews, in which I
    steal
From all I may be, or have been before,
To mingle with the Universe, and feel
What I can ne'er express, yet cannot all
    conceal.

CLXXIX

Roll on, thou deep and dark blue
    Ocean—roll!
Ten thousand fleets sweep over thee in
    vain;
Man marks the earth with ruin—his
    control
Stops with the shore; upon the watery
    plain
The wrecks are all thy deed, nor doth
    remain
A shadow of man's ravage, save his own,
When, for a moment, like a drop of
    rain,
He sinks into thy depths with bubbling
    groan,
Without a grave, unknell'd, uncoffin'd,
    and unknown.

CLXXX

His steps are not upon thy paths,—thy
    fields
Are not a spoil for him,—thou dost
    arise
And shake him from thee; the vile
    strength he wields
For earth's destruction thou dost all de-
    pise,
Spurning him from thy bosom to the
    skies,
And send'st him, shivering in thy play-
    ful spray
And howling, to his Gods, where haply
    lies
His petty hope in some near port or
    bay,
And dashest him again to earth:—there
    let him lay.

CLXXXI

The armaments which thunderstrike
    the walls
Of rock-built cities, bidding nations
    quake,
And monarchs tremble in their capitals,
The oak leviathans, whose huge ribs
    make
Their clay creator the vain title take
Of lord of thee, and arbiter of war—
These are thy toys, and, as the snowy
    flake,
They melt into thy yeast of waves, which
    mar
Alike the Armada's pride or spoils of
    Trafalgar.

CLXXXII

Thy shores are empires, changed in all
    save thee—
Assyria, Greece, Rome, Carthage, what
    are they?
Thy waters wash'd them power while
    they were free,
And many a tyrant since; their shores
    obey
The stranger, slave, or savage; their
    decay
Has dried up realms to deserts:—not so
    thou;—
Unchangeable, save to thy wild waves'
    play,
Time writes no wrinkle on thine azure
    brow:
Such as creation's dawn beheld, thou
    rollest now.

CLXXXIII

Thou glorious mirror, where the Al-
    mighty's form
Glasses itself in tempests; in all time,—
Calm or convulsed, in breeze, or gale, or
    storm,
Icing the pole, or in the torrid clime
Dark-heaving—boundless, endless, and
    sublime,
The image of eternity, the throne
Of the Invisible; even from out thy
    slime
The monsters of the deep are made;
    each zone
Obeys thee; thou goest forth, dread,
    fathomless, alone.

CLXXXIV

And I have loved thee, Ocean! and my
    joy
Of youthful sports was on thy breast to
    be
Borne, like thy bubbles, onward: from
    a boy
I wanton'd with thy breakers—they to
    me
Were a delight; and if the freshening
    sea
Made them a terror—'twas a pleasing
    fear,
For I was as it were a child of thee,
And trusted to thy billows far and near,
And laid my hand upon thy mane—as I do
    here.

CLXXXV

My task is done, my song hath ceased,
    my theme
Has died into an echo; it is fit
The spell should break of this protracted
    dream.
The torch shall be extinguish'd which
    hath lit

My midnight lamp—and what is writ,
   is writ;
Would it were worthier! but I am not
   now
That which I have been—and my visions
   flit
Less palpably before me—and the
   glow
Which in my spirit dwelt is fluttering,
   faint, and low.

CLXXXVI

Farewell! a word that must be, and hath
   been—

A sound which makes us linger;—yet—
   farewell!
Ye! who have traced the Pilgrim to the
   scene
Which is his last, if in your memories
   dwell
A thought which once was his, if on ye
   swell
A single recollection, not in vain
He wore his sandal-shoon and scallop-
   shell;
Farewell! with *him* alone may rest the
   pain,
If such there were—with *you*, the moral of
   his strain.

TALES

THE GIAOUR

A FRAGMENT OF A TURKISH TALE

'One fatal remembrance—one sorrow that throws
Its bleak shade alike o'er our joys and our woes—
To which Life nothing darker nor brighter can bring,
For which joy hath no balm—and affliction no sting.'—MOORE.

TO

SAMUEL ROGERS, ESQ.

AS A SLIGHT BUT MOST SINCERE TOKEN OF ADMIRATION FOR HIS GENIUS, RESPECT FOR
HIS CHARACTER, AND GRATITUDE FOR HIS FRIENDSHIP,

THIS PRODUCTION IS INSCRIBED,

BY HIS OBLIGED AND AFFECTIONATE SERVANT,

LONDON, *May*, 1813.   BYRON.

ADVERTISEMENT

THE tale which these disjointed fragments present is founded upon circumstances now less common
in the East than formerly; either because the ladies are more circumspect than in the 'olden time,'
or because the Christians have better fortune, or less enterprise.

The story, when entire, contained the adventures of a female slave, who was thrown, in the Mussulman manner, into the sea for infidelity, and avenged by a young Venetian, her lover, at the time the
Seven Islands were possessed by the Republic of Venice, and soon after the Arnauts were beaten back
from the Morea, which they had ravaged for some time subsequent to the Russian invasion. The
desertion of the Mainotes, on being refused the plunder of Misitra, led to the abandonment of that
enterprise, and to the desolation of the Morea; during which the cruelty exercised on all sides was
unparalleled even in the annals of the faithful.

No breath of air to break the wave
That rolls below the Athenian's grave,
That tomb which, gleaming o'er the cliff,
First greets the homeward-veering skiff,
High o'er the land he saved in vain;   5
When shall such hero live again?

　　　．　　　．　　　．　　　．

Fair clime! where every season smiles
Benignant o'er those blessed isles,

Which, seen from far Colonna's height,
Make glad the heart that hails the
   sight,   10
And lend to loneliness delight.
There mildly dimpling, Ocean's cheek
Reflects the tints of many a peak
Caught by the laughing tides that lave
These Edens of the eastern wave: 15
And if at times a transient breeze
Break the blue crystal of the seas,

Or sweep one blossom from the trees,
How welcome is each gentle air
That wakes and wafts the odours there!
For there the Rose, o'er crag or vale,   21
Sultana of the Nightingale,
  The maid for whom his melody,
His thousand songs are heard on high,
Blooms blushing to her lover's tale: 25
His queen, the garden queen, his Rose,
Unbent by winds, unchill'd by snows,
Far from the winters of the west,
By every breeze and season blest,
Returns the sweets by nature given   30
In softest incense back to heaven;
And grateful yields that smiling sky
Her fairest hue and fragrant sigh.
And many a summer flower is there,
And many a shade that love might
    share,   35
And many a grotto, meant for rest,
That holds the pirate for a guest;
Whose bark in sheltering cove below
Lurks for the passing peaceful prow,
Till the gay mariner's guitar   40
Is heard, and seen the evening star;
Then stealing with the muffled oar,
Far shaded by the rocky shore,
Rush the night-prowlers on the prey,
And turn to groans his roundelay.   45
Strange—that where Nature loved to
    trace,
As if for gods, a dwelling-place,
And every charm and grace hath mix'd
Within the paradise she fix'd,
There man, enamour'd of distress,   50
Should mar it into wilderness,
And trample, brute-like, o'er each flower
That tasks not one laborious hour;
Nor claims the culture of his hand
To bloom along the fairy land,   55
But springs as to preclude his care,
And sweetly woos him—but to spare!
Strange—that where all is peace beside,
There passion riots in her pride,
And lust and rapine wildly reign   60
To darken o'er the fair domain.
It is as though the fiends prevail'd
Against the seraphs they assail'd,
And, fix'd on heavenly thrones, should
    dwell
The freed inheritors of hell;   65
So soft the scene, so form'd for joy,
So curst the tyrants that destroy!

He who hath bent him o'er the dead
Ere the first day of death is fled,
The first dark day of nothingness,   70
The last of danger and distress,
(Before Decay's effacing fingers
Have swept the lines where beauty lingers,)
And mark'd the mild angelic air,
The rapture of repose that's there,   75
The fix'd yet tender traits that streak
The languor of the placid cheek,

And—but for that sad shrouded eye,
  That fires not, wins not, weeps not, now,
  And but for that chill, changeless brow,
Where cold Obstruction's apathy   81
Appals the gazing mourner's heart,
As if to him it could impart
The doom he dreads, yet dwells upon;
Yes, but for these and these alone,   85
Some moments, ay, one treacherous
    hour,
He still might doubt the tyrant's power;
So fair, so calm, so softly seal'd,
The first, last look by death reveal'd!
Such is the aspect of this shore;   90
'Tis Greece, but living Greece no more!
So coldly sweet, so deadly fair,
We start, for soul is wanting there.
Hers is the loveliness in death,
That parts not quite with parting
    breath;   95
But beauty with that fearful bloom,
That hue which haunts it to the tomb,
Expression's last receding ray,
A gilded halo hovering round decay,
The farewell beam of Feeling pass'd
    away!   100
Spark of that flame, perchance of heavenly
    birth,
Which gleams, but warms no more its
    cherish'd earth!

Clime of the unforgotten brave!
Whose land from plain to mountain-
    cave
Was Freedom's home or Glory's grave!
Shrine of the mighty! can it be,   106
That this is all remains of thee?
Approach, thou craven crouching slave:
Say, is not this Thermopylæ?
These waters blue that round you
    lave,—   110
  Oh servile offspring of the free,
Pronounce what sea, what shore is this?
The gulf, the rock of Salamis!
These scenes, their story not unknown,
Arise, and make again your own;   115
Snatch from the ashes of your sires
The embers of their former fires;
And he who in the strife expires
Will add to theirs a name of fear
That Tyranny shall quake to hear,   120
And leave his sons a hope, a fame,
They too will rather die than shame;
For Freedom's battle once begun,
Bequeath'd by bleeding Sire to Son,
Though baffled oft is ever won.   125
Bear witness, Greece, thy living page!
Attest it many a deathless age!
While kings, in dusty darkness hid,
Have left a nameless pyramid,   129
Thy heroes, though the general doom
Hath swept the column from their tomb,
A mightier monument command,
The mountains of their native land!

THE GIAOUR

There points thy Muse to stranger's eye
The graves of those that cannot die!
'Twere long to tell, and sad to trace, 136
Each step from splendour to disgrace;
Enough—no foreign foe could quell
Thy soul, till from itself it fell;
Yes! Self-abasement paved the way 140
To villain-bonds and despot sway.

What can he tell who treads thy shore?
No legend of thine olden time,
No theme on which the Muse might soar
High as thine own in days of yore, 145
When man was worthy of thy clime.
The hearts within thy valleys bred,
The fiery souls that might have led
Thy sons to deeds sublime,
Now crawl from cradle to the grave, 150
Slaves—nay, the bondsmen of a slave,
And callous, save to crime;
Stain'd with each evil that pollutes
Mankind, where least above the brutes;
Without even savage virtue blest, 155
Without one free or valiant breast,
Still to the neighbouring ports they waft
Proverbial wiles and ancient craft;
In this the subtle Greek is found,
For this, and this alone, renown'd. 160
In vain might Liberty invoke
The spirit to its bondage broke,
Or raise the neck that courts the yoke:
No more her sorrows I bewail,
Yet this will be a mournful tale, 165
And they who listen may believe,
Who heard it first had cause to grieve.

· · · · · ·

Far, dark, along the blue sea glancing,
The shadows of the rocks advancing
Start on the fisher's eye like boat 170
Of island-pirate or Mainote;
And fearful for his light caïque,
He shuns the near but doubtful creek;
Though worn and weary with his toil,
And cumber'd with his scaly spoil, 175
Slowly, yet strongly, plies the oar,
Till Port Leone's safer shore
Receives him by the lovely light
That best becomes an Eastern night.

· · · · · ·

Who thundering comes on blackest
steed, 180
With slacken'd bit and hoof of speed?
Beneath the clattering iron's sound
The cavern'd echoes wake around
In lash for lash, and bound for bound;
The foam that streaks the courser's side
Seems gather'd from the ocean-tide: 186
Though weary waves are sunk to rest,
There's none within his rider's breast;
And though to-morrow's tempest lower,
'Tis calmer than thy heart, young Giaour!
I know thee not, I loathe thy race, 191
But in thy lineaments I trace
What Time shall strengthen, not efface:

Though young and pale, that sallow front
Is scathed by fiery passion's brunt; 195
Though bent on earth thine evil eye,
As meteor-like thou glidest by,
Right well I view and deem thee one
Whom Othman's sons should slay or shun.

On—on he hasten'd, and he drew 200
My gaze of wonder as he flew;
Though like a demon of the night
He pass'd, and vanish'd from my sight,
His aspect and his air impress'd
A troubled memory on my breast, 205
And long upon my startled ear
Rung his dark courser's hoofs of fear.
He spurs his steed; he nears the steep,
That, jutting, shadows o'er the deep;
He winds around; he hurries by; 210
The rock relieves him from mine eye;
For well I ween unwelcome he
Whose glance is fix'd on those that flee;
And not a star but shines too bright
On him who takes such timeless flight.
He wound along; but ere he pass'd, 216
One glance he snatch'd, as if his last,
A moment check'd his wheeling steed,
A moment breathed him from his speed,
A moment on his stirrup stood— 220
Why looks he o'er the olive wood?
The crescent glimmers on the hill,
The Mosque's high lamps are quivering
still:
Though too remote for sound to wake
In echoes of the far tophaike, 225
The flashes of each joyous peal
Are seen to prove the Moslem's zeal.
To-night, set Rhamazani's sun;
To-night, the Bairam feast's begun;
To-night—but who and what art thou 230
Of foreign garb and fearful brow?
And what are these to thine or thee,
That thou shouldst either pause or flee?

He stood—some dread was on his
face,
Soon Hatred settled in its place: 235
It rose not with the reddening flush
Of transient Anger's hasty blush,
But pale as marble o'er the tomb,
Whose ghastly whiteness aids its gloom.
His brow twas bent, his eye was glazed; 240
He raised his arm, and fiercely raised,
And sternly shook his hand on high,
As doubting to return or fly;
Impatient of his flight delay'd,
Here loud his raven charger neigh'd—
Down glanced that hand, and grasp'd his
blade; 246
That sound had burst his waking dream,
As Slumber starts at owlet's scream,
The spur hath lanced his courser's sides;
Away, away, for life he rides: 250
Swift as the hurl'd on high jerreed
Springs to the touch his startled steed:

254

The rock is doubled, and the shore
Shakes with the clattering tramp no more; 255
The crag is won, no more is seen
His Christian crest and haughty mien.
'Twas but an instant he restrain'd
That fiery barb so sternly rein'd;
'Twas but a moment that he stood,
Then sped as if by death pursued; 260
But in that instant o'er his soul
Winters of Memory seem'd to roll,
And gather in that drop of time
A life of pain, an age of crime.
O'er him who loves, or hates, or fears, 265
Such moment pours the grief of years:
What felt *he* then, at once opprest
By all that most distracts the breast?
That pause, which ponder'd o'er his fate,
Oh, who its dreary length shall date! 270
Though in Time's record nearly nought,
It was Eternity to Thought!
For infinite as boundless space
The thought that Conscience must embrace,
Which in itself can comprehend 275
Woe without name, or hope, or end.

The hour is past, the Giaour is gone;
And did he fly or fall alone?
Woe to that hour he came or went!
The curse for Hassan's sin was sent 280
To turn a palace to a tomb;
He came, he went, like the simoom,
That harbinger of fate and gloom,
Beneath whose widely-wasting breath
The very cypress droops to death— 285
Dark tree, still sad when others' grief is
fled,
The only constant mourner o'er the dead!

The steed is vanish'd from the stall;
No serf is seen in Hassan's hall;
The lonely spider's thin gray pall 290
Waves slowly widening o'er the wall;
The bat builds in his haram bower,
And in the fortress of his power
The owl usurps the beacon-tower;
The wild-dog howls o'er the fountain's 295
brim,
With baffled thirst, and famine, grim;
For the stream has shrunk from its marble
bed,
Where the weeds and the desolate dust are
spread.
'Twas sweet of yore to see it play
And chase the sultriness of day, 300
As springing high the silver dew
In whirls fantastically flew,
And flung luxurious coolness round
The air, and verdure o'er the ground.
'Twas sweet, when cloudless stars were
bright, 305
To view the wave of watery light,
And hear its melody by night.
And oft had Hassan's Childhood play'd
Around the verge of that cascade;

And oft upon his mother's breast 310
That sound had harmonized his rest;
And oft had Hassan's Youth along
Its bank been soothed by Beauty's song;
And softer seem'd each melting tone
Of Music mingled with its own. 315
But ne'er shall Hassan's Age repose
Along the brink at twilight's close:
The stream that fill'd that font is fled—
The blood that warm'd his heart is
shed!
And here no more shall human voice
Be heard to rage, regret, rejoice. 321
The last sad note that swell'd the gale
Was woman's wildest funeral wail:
That quench'd in silence, all is still,
But the lattice that flaps when the wind
is shrill; 325
Though raves the gust, and floods the
rain,
No hand shall close its clasp again.
On desert sands 'twere joy to scan
The rudest steps of fellow man,
So here the very voice of Grief 330
Might wake an Echo like relief—
At least 'twould say, 'All are not
gone;
There lingers Life, though but in one'—
For many a gilded chamber 's there,
Which Solitude might well forbear;
Within that dome as yet Decay 336
Hath slowly work'd her cankering
way—
But gloom is gather'd o'er the gate,
Nor there the Fakir's self will wait;
Nor there will wandering Dervise stay.
For bounty cheers not his delay; 341
Nor there will weary stranger halt
To bless the sacred 'bread and salt.'
Alike must Wealth and Poverty
Pass heedless and unheeded by, 345
For Courtesy and Pity died
With Hassan on the mountain side.
His roof, that refuge unto men,
Is Desolation's hungry den.
The guest flies the hall, and the vassal from
labour, 350
Since his turban was cleft by the infidel's
sabre!

. . . . . .

I hear the sound of coming feet,
But not a voice mine ear to greet;
More near—each turban I can scan,
And silver-sheathèd ataghan; 355
The foremost of the band is seen
An Emir by his garb of green:
'Ho! who art thou?'—'This low salam
Replies of Moslem faith I am.
The burthen ye so gently bear 360
Seems one that claims your utmost care,
And, doubtless, holds some precious
freight—
My humble bark would gladly wait.'

THE GIAOUR

'Thou speakest sooth: thy skiff unmoor,
And waft us from the silent shore;   365
Nay, leave the sail still furl'd, and ply
The nearest oar that's scatter'd by,
And midway to those rocks where sleep
The channell'd waters dark and deep.
Rest from your task—so—bravely done,
Our course has been right swiftly run;   371
Yet 'tis the longest voyage, I trow,
That one of—   .   .   .   .   ,'

Sullen it plunged, and slowly sank,
The calm wave rippled to the bank;   375
I watch'd it as it sank, methought
Some motion from the current caught
Bestirr'd it more,—'twas but the beam
That checker'd o'er the living stream:
I gaz'd, till vanishing from view,   380
Like lessening pebble it withdrew;
Still less and less, a speck of white
That gemm'd the tide, then mock'd the
    sight;
And all its hidden secrets sleep,
Known but to Genii of the deep,   385
Which, trembling in their coral caves,
They dare not whisper to the waves.

As rising on its purple wing
The insect queen of eastern spring,
O'er emerald meadows of Kashmeer   390
Invites the young pursuer near,
And leads him on from flower to flower
A weary chase and wasted hour,
Then leaves him as it soars on high,
With panting heart and tearful eye: 395
So Beauty lures the full-grown child,
With hue as bright, and wing as wild;
A chase of idle hopes and fears,
Begun in folly, closed in tears.
If won, to equal ills betray'd,   400
Woe waits the insect and the maid;
A life of pain, the loss of peace,
From infant's play, and man's caprice:
The lovely toy so fiercely sought
Hath lost its charm by being caught,   405
For every touch that woo'd its stay
Hath brush'd its brightest hues away,
Till charm, and hue, and beauty gone,
'Tis left to fly or fall alone.
With wounded wing, or bleeding breast,
Ah! where shall either victim rest?   411
Can this with faded pinion soar
From rose to tulip as before?
Or Beauty, blighted in an hour,
Find joy within her broken bower?   415
No: gayer insects fluttering by
Ne'er droop the wing o'er those that die,
And lovelier things have mercy shown
To every failing but their own,
And every woe a tear can claim   420
Except an erring sister's shame.

The Mind, that broods o'er guilty woes,
Is like the Scorpion girt by fire;
In circle narrowing as it glows,
The flames around their captive close,
Till inly search'd by thousand throes,   426
    And maddening in her ire,
One sad and sole relief she knows,
The sting she nourish'd for her foes,
Whose venom never yet was vain,   430
Gives but one pang and cures all pain,
And darts into her desperate brain:
So do the dark in soul expire,
Or live like Scorpion girt by fire;
So writhes the mind Remorse hath riven,
Unfit for earth, undoom'd for heaven,
Darkness above, despair beneath,   437
Around it flame, within it death!

Black Hassan from the Haram flies,
Nor bends on woman's form his eyes;
The unwonted chase each hour employs,
Yet shares he not the hunter's joys.
Not thus was Hassan wont to fly
When Leila dwelt in his Serai.
Doth Leila there no longer dwell?   445
That tale can only Hassan tell:
Strange rumours in our city say
Upon that eve she fled away
When Rhamazan's last sun was set,
And flashing from each minaret   450
Millions of lamps proclaim'd the feast
Of Bairam through the boundless East.
'Twas then she went as to the bath,
Which Hassan vainly search'd in wrath;
For she was flown her master's rage   455
In likeness of a Georgian page,
And far beyond the Moslem's power
Had wrong'd him with the faithless Giaour.
Somewhat of this had Hassan deem'd;
But still so fond, so fair she seem'd,   460
Too well he trusted to the slave
Whose treachery deserved a grave:
And on that eve had gone to mosque,
And thence to feast in his kiosk.
Such is the tale his Nubians tell,   465
Who did not watch their charge too well;
But others say, that on that night,
By pale Phingari's trembling light,
The Giaour upon his jet-black steed
Was seen, but seen alone to speed   470
With bloody spur along the shore,
Nor maid nor page behind him bore.

Her eye's dark charm 'twere vain to tell,
But gaze on that of the Gazelle,
It will assist thy fancy well;   475
As large, as languishingly dark,
But Soul beam'd forth in every spark
That darted from beneath the lid,
Bright as the jewel of Giamschid.   479
Yea, *Soul*, and should our prophet say
That form was nought but breathing clay,

By Alla! I would answer nay;
Though on Al-Sirat's arch I stood,
Which totters o'er the fiery flood,
With Paradise within my view,   485
And all his Houris beckoning through.
Oh! who young Leila's glance could read
And keep that portion of his creed
Which saith that woman is but dust,
A soulless toy for tyrant's lust?   490
On her might Muftis gaze, and own
That through her eye the Immortal shone;
On her fair cheek's unfading hue
The young pomegranate's blossoms strew
Their bloom in blushes ever new;   495
Her hair in hyacinthine flow,
When left to roll its folds below,
As midst her handmaids in the hall
She stood superior to them all,
Hath swept the marble where her feet   500
Gleam'd whiter than the mountain sleet
Ere from the cloud that gave it birth
It fell, and caught one stain of earth.
The cygnet nobly walks the water;
So moved on earth Circassia's daughter,
The loveliest bird of Franguestan!   506
As rears her crest the ruffled Swan,
    And spurns the waves with wings of pride,
When pass the steps of stranger man
    Along the banks that bound her tide;
Thus rose fair Leila's whiter neck:—   511
Thus arm'd with beauty would she check
Intrusion's glance, till Folly's gaze
Shrunk from the charms it meant to praise.
Thus high and graceful was her gait;   515
Her heart as tender to her mate;
Her mate—stern Hassan, who was he?
Alas! that name was not for thee!

      .   .   .   .   .

Stern Hassan hath a journey ta'en
With twenty vassals in his train,   520
Each arm'd, as best becomes a man,
With arquebuss and ataghan;
The chief before, as deck'd for war,
Bears in his belt the scimitar
Stain'd with the best of Arnaut blood, 525
When in the pass the rebels stood,
And few return'd to tell the tale
Of what befell in Parne's vale.
The pistols which his girdle bore
Were those that once a pasha wore,   530
Which still, though gemm'd and boss'd
    with gold,
Even robbers tremble to behold.
'Tis said he goes to woo a bride
More true than her who left his side;
The faithless slave that broke her bower,
And, worse than faithless, for a Giaour!

      .   .   .   .   .

The sun's last rays are on the hill,
And sparkle in the fountain rill,   538
Whose welcome waters, cool and clear,
Draw blessings from the mountaineer:

Here may the loitering merchant Greek
Find that repose 'twere vain to seek
In cities lodged too near his lord,
And trembling for his secret hoard—
Here may he rest where none can see,   545
In crowds a slave, in deserts free;
And with forbidden wine may stain
The bowl a Moslem must not drain.

The foremost Tartar's in the gap
Conspicuous by his yellow cap;   550
The rest in lengthening line the while
Wind slowly through the long defile:
Above, the mountain rears a peak,
Where vultures whet the thirsty beak,
And theirs may be a feast to-night,   555
Shall tempt them down ere morrow's
    light;
Beneath, a river's wintry stream
Has shrunk before the summer beam,
And left a channel bleak and bare,
Save shrubs that spring to perish there;
Each side the midway path there lay   561
Small broken crags of granite gray,
By time, or mountain lightning, riven
From summits clad in mists of heaven;
For where is he that hath beheld   565
The peak of Liakura unveil'd?

      .   .   .   .   .

They reach the grove of pine at last;
'Bismillah! now the peril 's past;
For yonder view the opening plain,
And there we'll prick our steeds amain:'
The Chiaus spake, and as he said,   571
A bullet whistles o'er his head;
The foremost Tartar bites the ground!
    Scarce had they time to check the rein,
Swift from their steeds the riders bound;
    But three shall never mount again: 576
Unseen the foes that gave the wound,
    The dying ask revenge in vain.
With steel unsheath'd, and carbine bent,
Some o'er their courser's harness leant,
    Half shelter'd by the steed;   581
Some fly behind the nearest rock,
And there await the coming shock,
    Nor tamely stand to bleed
Beneath the shaft of foes unseen,   585
Who dare not quit their craggy screen.
Stern Hassan only from his horse
Disdains to light, and keeps his course,
Till fiery flashes in the van
Proclaim too sure the robber-clan   590
Have well secured the only way
Could now avail the promised prey;
Then curl'd his very beard with ire,
And glared his eye with fiercer fire;
'Though far and near the bullets hiss, 595
I've scaped a bloodier hour than this.'
And now the foe their covert quit,
And call his vassals to submit;
But Hassan's frown and furious word
Are dreaded more than hostile sword,   600

257

Nor of his little band a man
Resign'd carbine or ataghan,
Nor raised the craven cry, Amaun!
In fuller sight, more near and near,
The lately ambush'd foes appear, 605
And issuing from the grove, advance
Some who on battle-charger prance.
Who leads them on with foreign brand
Far flashing in his red right hand?
"Tis he! 'tis he! I know him now; 610
I know him by his pallid brow;
I know him by the evil eye
That aids his envious treachery;
I know him by his jet-black barb;
Though now array'd in Arnaut garb, 615
Apostate from his own vile faith,
It shall not save him from the death:
'Tis he! well met in any hour,
Lost Leila's love, accursèd Giaour!'

As rolls the river into ocean, 620
In sable torrent wildly streaming;
  As the sea-tide's opposing motion,
In azure column proudly gleaming,
Beats back the current many a rood,
In curling foam and mingling flood, 625
While eddying whirl, and breaking wave,
Roused by the blast of winter, rave;
Through sparkling spray, in thundering
    clash,
The lightnings of the waters flash
In awful whiteness o'er the shore, 630
That shines and shakes beneath the roar;
Thus—as the stream and ocean greet,
With waves that madden as they meet—
Thus join the bands, whom mutual wrong,
And fate, and fury, drive along. 635
The bickering sabres' shivering jar;
  And pealing wide or ringing near
Its echoes on the throbbing ear,
The deathshot hissing from afar;
The shock, the shout, the groan of war,
  Reverberate along that vale, 641
  More suited to the shepherd's tale:
Though few the numbers—theirs the
    strife,
That neither spares nor speaks for life!
Ah! fondly youthful hearts can press, 645
To seize and share the dear caress;
But Love itself could never pant
For all that Beauty sighs to grant
With half the fervour Hate bestows
Upon the last embrace of foes, 650
When grappling in the fight they fold
Those arms that ne'er shall lose their hold:
Friends meet to part; Love laughs at faith;
True foes, once met, are join'd till death!

With sabre shiver'd to the hilt, 655
Yet dripping with the blood he spilt;
Yet strain'd within the sever'd hand
Which quivers round that faithless brand;

His turban far behind him roll'd,
And cleft in twain its firmest fold; 660
His flowing robe by falchion torn,
And crimson as those clouds of morn
That, streak'd with dusky red, portend
The day shall have a stormy end;
A stain on every bush that bore 665
A fragment of his palampore;
His breast with wounds unnumber'd riven,
His back to earth, his face to heaven,
Fall'n Hassan lies—his unclosed eye
Yet lowering on his enemy, 670
As if the hour that seal'd his fate
Surviving left his quenchless hate;
And o'er him bends that foe with brow
As dark as his that bled below.—

  ·   ·   ·   ·   ·

'Yes, Leila sleeps beneath the wave, 675
But his shall be a redder grave;
Her spirit pointed well the steel
Which taught that felon heart to feel.
He call'd the Prophet, but his power
Was vain against the vengeful Giaour:
He call'd on Alla, but the word 681
Arose unheeded or unheard.
Thou Paynim fool! could Leila's prayer
Be pass'd, and thine accorded there?
I watch'd my time, I leagued with these,
The traitor in his turn to seize; 686
My wrath is wreak'd, the deed is done,
And now I go—but go alone.'

  ·   ·   ·   ·   ·

  The browsing camels' bells are tinkling:
His mother look'd from her lattice high—
  She saw the dews of eve besprinkling
The pasture green beneath her eye, 692
  She saw the planets faintly twinkling:
"Tis twilight—sure his train is nigh."
She could not rest in the garden-bower,
But gazed through the grate of his steepest
    tower: 696
'Why comes he not? his steeds are fleet,
Nor shrink they from the summer heat;
Why sends not the Bridegroom his prom-
    ised gift?
Is his heart more cold, or his barb less
    swift? 700
Oh, false reproach! yon Tartar now
Has gain'd our nearest mountain's brow,
And warily the steep descends,
And now within the valley bends;
And he bears the gift at his saddle-bow—
How could I deem his courser slow? 706
Right well my largess shall repay
His welcome speed and weary way.'

The Tartar lighted at the gate,
But scarce upheld his fainting weight: 710
His swarthy visage spake distress,
But this might be from weariness;

His garb with sanguine spots was dyed,
But these might be from his courser's side;
He drew the token from his vest—   715
Angel of Death! 'tis Hassan's cloven crest!
His calpac rent—his caftan red—
'Lady, a fearful bride thy son hath wed:
Me, not from mercy, did they spare,
But this empurpled pledge to bear.   720
Peace to the brave! whose blood is spilt:
Woe to the Giaour! for his the guilt.'

   .   .   .   .   .

A turban carved in coarsest stone,
A pillar with rank weeds o'ergrown,
Whereon can now be scarcely read   725
The Koran verse that mourns the dead,
Point out the spot where Hassan fell
A victim in that lonely dell.
There sleeps as true an Osmanlie
As e'er at Mecca bent the knee;   730
As ever scorn'd forbidden wine,
Or pray'd with face towards the shrine,
In orisons resumed anew
At solemn sound of 'Alla Hu!'
Yet died he by a stranger's hand,   735
And stranger in his native land;
Yet died he as in arms he stood,
And unavenged, at least in blood.
But him the maids of Paradise
Impatient to their halls invite,   740
And the dark heaven of Houris' eyes
On him shall glance for ever bright;
They come—their kerchiefs green they wave,
And welcome with a kiss the brave!
Who falls in battle 'gainst a Giaour   745
Is worthiest an immortal bower.

   .   .   .   .   .

But thou, false Infidel! shalt writhe
Beneath avenging Monkir's scythe;
And from its torment 'scape alone
To wander round lost Eblis' throne;   750
And fire unquench'd, unquenchable,
Around, within, thy heart shall dwell;
Nor ear can hear nor tongue can tell
The tortures of that inward hell!
But first, on earth as Vampire sent,   755
Thy corse shall from its tomb be rent:
Then ghastly haunt thy native place,
And suck the blood of all thy race;
There from thy daughter, sister, wife,
At midnight drain the stream of life;   760
Yet loathe the banquet which perforce
Must feed thy livid living corse:
Thy victims ere they yet expire
Shall know the demon for their sire,
As cursing thee, thou cursing them,   765
Thy flowers are wither'd on the stem.
But one that for thy crime must fall,
The youngest, most beloved of all,
Shall bless thee with a *father's* name—
That word shall wrap thy heart in flame!
Yet must thou end thy task, and mark   771
Her cheek's last tinge, her eye's last spark,

And the last glassy glance must view
Which freezes o'er its lifeless blue;
Then with unhallow'd hand shalt tear   775
The tresses of her yellow hair,
Of which in life a lock when shorn,
Affection's fondest pledge was worn,
But now is borne away by thee,
Memorial of thine agony!   780
Wet with thine own best blood shall drip
Thy gnashing tooth and haggard lip;
Then stalking to thy sullen grave,
Go—and with Gouls and Afrits rave;
Till these in horror shrink away   785
From spectre more accursed than they!

   .   .   .   .   .

'How name ye yon lone Caloyer?
His features I have scann'd before
In mine own land: 'tis many a year,
Since, dashing by the lonely shore,   790
I saw him urge as fleet a steed
As ever served a horseman's need.
But once I saw that face, yet then
It was so mark'd with inward pain,
I could not pass it by again;   795
It breathes the same dark spirit now,
As death were stamp'd upon his brow.

''Tis twice three years at summer tide
Since first among our freres he came;
And here it soothes him to abide   800
For some dark deed he will not name.
But never at our vesper prayer,
Nor e'er before confession chair
Kneels he, nor recks he when arise
Incense or anthem to the skies,   805
But broods within his cell alone,
His faith and race alike unknown.
The sea from Paynim land he crost,
And here ascended from the coast;
Yet seems he not of Othman race,   810
But only Christian in his face:
I'd judge him some stray renegade,
Repentant of the change he made,
Save that he shuns our holy shrine,   814
Nor tastes the sacred bread and wine.
Great largess to these walls be brought,
And thus our abbot's favour bought;
But were I prior, not a day
Should brook such stranger's further stay.
Or pent within our penance cell   820
Should doom him there for aye to dwell.
Much in his visions mutters he
Of maiden whelm'd beneath the sea;
Of sabres clashing, foemen flying,
Wrongs avenged, and Moslem dying.   825
On cliff he hath been known to stand,
And rave as to some bloody hand
Fresh sever'd from its parent limb,
Invisible to all but him,
Which beckons onward to his grave,   830
And lures to leap into the wave.'

   .   .   .   .   .

THE GIAOUR

Dark and unearthly is the scowl
That glares beneath his dusky cowl.
The flash of that dilating eye
Reveals too much of times gone by;   835
Though varying, indistinct its hue,
Oft will his glance the gazer rue,
For in it lurks that nameless spell,
Which speaks, itself unspeakable,
A spirit yet unquell'd and high,   840
That claims and keeps ascendency;
And like the bird whose pinions quake,
But cannot fly the gazing snake,
Will others quail beneath his look,
Nor 'scape the glance they scarce can
  brook.   845
From him the half-affrighted Friar
When met alone would fain retire,
As if that eye and bitter smile
Transferr'd to others fear and guile:
Not oft to smile descendeth he,   850
And when he doth 'tis sad to see
That he but mocks at Misery.
How that pale lip will curl and quiver!
Then fix once more as if for ever;
As if his sorrow or disdain   855
Forbade him e'er to smile again.
Well were it so—such ghastly mirth
From joyaunce ne'er derived its birth.
But sadder still it were to trace
What once were feelings in that face: 860
Time hath not yet the features fix'd,
But brighter traits with evil mix'd;
And there are hues not always faded,
Which speak a mind not all degraded
Even by the crimes through which it
  waded: 865
The common crowd but see the gloom
Of wayward deeds, and fitting doom;
The close observer can espy
A noble soul, and lineage high:
Alas! though both bestow'd in vain,   870
Which Grief could change, and Guilt
  could stain,
It was no vulgar tenement
To which such lofty gifts were lent,
And still with little less than dread
On such the sight is riveted.   875
The roofless cot, decay'd and rent,
  Will scarce delay the passer by;
The tower by war or tempest bent,
While yet may frown one battlement,
  Demands and daunts the stranger's
    eye;   880
Each ivied arch, and pillar lone,
Pleads haughtily for glories gone!

His floating robe around him folding,
  Slow sweeps he through the column'd
    aisle;
With dread beheld, with gloom behold-
    ing   885
  The rites that sanctify the pile.
But when the anthem shakes the choir,
And kneel the monks, his steps retire;

By yonder lone and wavering torch
His aspect glares within the porch;   890
There will he pause till all is done—
And hear the prayer, but utter none.
See—by the half-illumined wall
His hood fly back, his dark hair fall,
That pale brow wildly wreathing round,
As if the Gorgon there had bound   896
The sablest of the serpent-braid
That o'er her fearful forehead stray'd:
For he declines the convent oath,
And leaves those locks unhallow'd growth
But wears our garb in all beside;   901
And, not from piety but pride,
Gives wealth to walls that never heard
Of his one holy vow nor word.
Lo!—mark ye, as the harmony   905
Peals louder praises to the sky,
That livid cheek, that stony air
Of mix'd defiance and despair!
Saint Francis, keep him from the shrine!
Else may we dread the wrath divine   910
Made manifest by awful sign.
If ever evil angel bore
The form of mortal, such he wore;
By all my hope of sins forgiven,
Such looks are not of earth nor heaven!'

To love the softest hearts are prone,   916
But such can ne'er be all his own;
Too timid in his woes to share,
Too meek to meet, or brave despair;
And sterner hearts alone may feel   920
The wound that time can never heal.
The rugged metal of the mine
Must burn before its surface shine,
But plunged within the furnace-flame,
It bends and melts—though still the
  same;   925
Then temper'd to thy want, or will,
'Twill serve thee to defend or kill;
A breastplate for thine hour of need,
Or blade to bid thy foeman bleed;
But if a dagger's form it bear,   930
Let those who shape its edge beware!
Thus passion's fire, and woman's art,
Can turn and tame the sterner heart;
From these its form and tone are ta'en,
And what they make it, must remain,   935
But break—before it bend again.

.   .   .   .   .

If solitude succeed to grief,
Release from pain is slight relief;
The vacant bosom's wilderness   939
Might thank the pang that made it less.
We loathe what none are left to share:
Even bliss—'twere woe alone to bear;
The heart once thus left desolate
Must fly at last for ease—to hate.
It is as if the dead could feel   945
The icy worm around them steal,
And shudder, as the reptiles creep
To revel o'er their rotting sleep,

Without the power to scare away
The cold consumers of their clay! 950
It is as if the desert bird,
  Whose beak unlocks her bosom's
    stream
  To still her famish'd nestlings' scream,
Nor mourns a life to them transferr'd,
Should rend her rash devoted breast, 955
And find them flown her empty nest.
The keenest pangs the wretched find
  Are rapture to the dreary void,
  The leafless desert of the mind,
  The waste of feelings unemploy'd. 960
Who would be doom'd to gaze upon
A sky without a cloud or sun?
Less hideous far the tempest's roar
Than ne'er to brave the billows more—
Thrown, when the war of winds is o'er,
A lonely wreck on fortune's shore, 966
'Mid sullen calm, and silent bay,
Unseen to drop by dull decay;—
Better to sink beneath the shock
Than moulder piecemeal on the rock!

    .   .   .   .   .

'Father! thy days have pass'd in peace,
  'Mid counted beads, and countless
    prayer;
To bid the sins of others cease,
  Thyself without a crime or care,
Save transient ills that all must bear, 975
Has been thy lot from youth to age;
And thou wilt bless thee from the rage
Of passions fierce and uncontroll'd,
Such as thy penitents unfold,
Whose secret sins and sorrows rest 980
Within thy pure and pitying breast.
My days, though few, have pass'd below
In much of joy, but more of woe;
Yet still in hours of love or strife,
I've 'scaped the weariness of life: 985
Now leagued with friends, now girt by
    foes,
I loathed the languor of repose.
Now nothing left to love or hate,
No more with hope or pride elate,
I'd rather be the thing that crawls 990
Most noxious o'er a dungeon's walls,
Than pass my dull, unvarying days,
Condemn'd to meditate and gaze.
Yet, lurks a wish within my breast
For rest—but not to feel 'tis rest. 995
Soon shall my fate that wish fulfil;
  And I shall sleep without the dream
Of what I was, and would be still,
  Dark as to thee my deeds may seem:
My memory now is but the tomb 1000
Of joys long dead; my hope, their doom:
Though better to have died with those
Than bear a life of lingering woes.
My spirit shrunk not to sustain
The searching throes of ceaseless pain;
Nor sought the self-accorded grave 1006
Of ancient fool and modern knave:

Yet death I have not fear'd to meet;
And in the field it had been sweet,
Had danger woo'd me on to move 1010
The slave of glory, not of love.
I've braved it—not for honour's boast;
I smile at laurels won or lost;
To such let others carve their way,
For high renown, or hireling pay: 1015
But place again before my eyes
Aught that I deem a worthy prize—
The maid I love, the man I hate—
And I will hunt the steps of fate,
To save or slay, as these require, 1020
Through rending steel and rolling fire:
Nor need'st thou doubt this speech from
    one
Who would but do—what he *hath* done.
Death is but what the haughty brave,
The weak must bear, the wretch must
    crave; 1025
Then let life go to Him who gave:
I have not quail'd to danger's brow
When high and happy—need I *now*?

    .   .   .   .   .

'I loved her, Friar! nay, adored—
  But these are words that all can use—
I proved it more in deed than word; 1031
There's blood upon that dinted sword,
  A stain its steel can never lose:
'Twas shed for her, who died for me,
  It warm'd the heart of one abhorr'd:
Nay, start not—no—nor bend thy knee,
  Nor midst my sins such act record;
Thou wilt absolve me from the deed,
For he was hostile to thy creed!
The very name of Nazarene 1040
Was wormwood to his Paynim spleen.
Ungrateful fool! since but for brands
Well wielded in some hardy hands,
And wounds by Galileans given,
The surest pass to Turkish heaven, 1045
For him his Houris still might wait
Impatient at the Prophet's gate.
I loved her—love will find its way
Through paths where wolves would fear
    to prey;
And if it dares enough, 'twere hard 1050
If passion met not some reward—
No matter how, or where, or why,
I did not vainly seek, nor sigh:
Yet sometimes, with remorse, in vain
I wish she had not loved again. 1055
She died—I dare not tell thee how;
But look—'tis written on my brow!
There read of Cain the curse and crime,
In characters unworn by time: 1059
Still, ere thou dost condemn me, pause;
Not mine the act, though I the cause.
Yet did he but what I had done
Had she been false to more than one,
Faithless to him, he gave the blow;
But true to me, I laid him low: 1065

Howe'er deserved her doom might be,
Her treachery was truth to me;
To me she gave her heart, that all
Which tyranny can ne'er enthral:
And I, alas! too late to save!   1070
Yet all I then could give, I gave,
'Twas some relief, our foe a grave.
His death sits lightly; but her fate
Has made me—what thou well may'st
    hate.

His doom was seal'd—he knew it well,
Warn'd by the voice of stern Taheer,   1076
Deep in whose darkly boding ear
The deathshot peal'd of murder near
As filed the troop to where they fell!
He died too in the battle broil,   1080
A time that heeds nor pain nor toil;
One cry to Mahomet for aid,
One prayer to Alla all he made:
He knew and cross'd me in the fray—
I gazed upon him where he lay,   1085
And watch'd his spirit ebb away;
Though pierced like pard by hunter's steel,
He felt not half that now I feel.
I search'd, but vainly search'd, to find
The workings of a wounded mind;   1090
Each feature of that sullen corse
Betray'd his rage, but no remorse.
Oh, what had Vengeance given to trace
Despair upon his dying face!
The late repentance of that hour,   1095
When Penitence hath lost her power
To tear one terror from the grave,
And will not soothe, and cannot save.

   .   .   .   .   .

'The cold in clime are cold in blood,
Their love can scarce deserve the name;
But mine was like the lava flood   1101
    That boils in Ætna's breast of flame.
I cannot prate in puling strain
Of ladye-love and beauty's chain: 1104
If changing cheek, and scorching vein,
Lips taught to writhe, but not complain,
If bursting heart, and madd'ning brain,
And daring deed, and vengeful steel,
And all that I have felt, and feel,
Betoken love—that love was mine,   1110
And shown by many a bitter sign.
'Tis true, I could not whine nor sigh,
I knew but to obtain or die.
I die—but first I have possess'd,
And come what may, I *have been* bless'd.
Shall I the doom I sought upbraid?   1116
No—reft of all, yet undismay'd
But for the thought of Leila slain,
Give me the pleasure with the pain,
So would I live and love again.   1120
I grieve, but not, my holy guide!
For him who dies, but her who died:
She sleeps beneath the wandering wave—
Ah! had she but an earthly grave,   1124
This breaking heart and throbbing head
Should seek and share her narrow bed.

She was a form of life and light,
That, seen, became a part of sight;
And rose, where'er I turn'd mine eye,
The Morning-star of Memory!   1130

'Yes, Love indeed is light from heaven;
    A spark of that immortal fire
With angels shared, by Alla given,
    To lift from earth our low desire.
Devotion wafts the mind above,   1135
But Heaven itself descends in love;
A feeling from the Godhead caught,
To wean from self each sordid thought;
A Ray of him who form'd the whole;
A Glory circling round the soul!   1140
I grant *my* love imperfect, all
That mortals by the name miscall;
Then deem it evil, what thou wilt;
But say, oh say, *hers* was not guilt!
She was my life's unerring light: 1145
That quench'd, what beam shall break my
    night?
Oh! would it shone to lead me still,
Although to death or deadliest ill!
Why marvel ye, if they who lose
    This present joy, this future hope,   1150
    No more with sorrow meekly cope;
In phrensy then their fate accuse;
In madness do those fearful deeds
    That seem to add but guilt to woe?
Alas! the breast that inly bleeds   1155
    Hath nought to dread from outward
    blow:
Who falls from all he knows of bliss,
Cares little into what abyss.
Fierce as the gloomy vulture's now
    To thee, old man, my deeds appear:
I read abhorrence on thy brow,   1161
    And this too was I born to bear!
'Tis true, that, like that bird of prey,
    With havoc have I mark'd my way:
But this was taught me by the dove,   1165
To die—and know no second love.
This lesson yet hath man to learn,
Taught by the thing he dares to spurn:
The bird that sings within the brake,
The swan that swims upon the lake,   1170
One mate, and one alone, will take.
And let the fool still prone to range,
And sneer on all who cannot change,
Partake his jest with boasting boys;
I envy not his varied joys,   1175
But deem such feeble, heartless man
Less than yon solitary swan;
Far, far beneath the shallow maid
He left believing and betray'd.   1179
Such shame at least was never mine—
Leila! each thought was only thine!
My good, my guilt, my weal, my woe,
My hope on high—my all below.
Earth holds no other like to thee,
Or, if it doth, in vain for me: 1185
For worlds I dare not view the dame
Resembling thee, yet not the same.

The very crimes that mar my youth,
This bed of death—attest my truth!
'Tis all too late—thou wert, thou art
The cherish'd madness of my heart! 1191

'And she was lost—and yet I breathed,
But not the breath of human life:
A serpent round my heart was wreathed,
And stung my every thought to strife.
Alike all time, abhorr'd all place, 1196
Shuddering I shrunk from Nature's face,
Where every hue that charm'd before
The blackness of my bosom wore.
The rest thou dost already know, 1200
And all my sins, and half my woe.
But talk no more of penitence;
Thou seest I soon shall part from hence;
And if thy holy tale were true, 1204
The deed that's done canst *thou* undo?
Think me not thankless—but this grief
Looks not to priesthood for relief.
My soul's estate in secret guess:
But wouldst thou pity more, say less.
When thou canst bid my Leila live, 1210
Then will I sue thee to forgive;
Then plead my cause in that high place
Where purchased masses proffer grace.
Go, when the hunter's hand hath wrung
From forest-cave her shrieking young,
And calm the lonely lioness: 1216
But soothe not—mock not *my* distress!

'In earlier days, and calmer hours,
When heart with heart delights to blend,
Where bloom my native valley's bowers,
I had—Ah! have I now?—a friend!
To him this pledge I charge thee send,
Memorial of a youthful vow; 1223
I would remind him of my end:
Though souls absorb'd like mine allow
Brief thought to distant friendship's claim,
Yet dear to him my blighted name. 1227
'Tis strange—he prophesied my doom,
And I have smiled—I then could smile—
When Prudence would his voice assume,
And warn—I reck'd not what—the
   while: 1231
But now remembrance whispers o'er
Those accents scarcely mark'd before.
Say—that his bodings came to pass,
And he will start to hear their truth,
And wish his words had not been sooth:
Tell him, unheeding as I was, 1237
Through many a busy bitter scene
Of all our golden youth had been,
In pain, my faltering tongue had tried
To bless his memory ere I died; 1241
But Heaven in wrath would turn away
If Guilt should for the guiltless pray.
I do not ask him not to blame,
Too gentle he to wound my name; 1245
And what have I to do with fame?
I do not ask him not to mourn,
Such cold request might sound like scorn;

And what than friendship's manly tear
May better grace a brother's bier? 1250
But bear this ring, his own of old,
And tell him—what thou dost behold!
The wither'd frame, the ruin'd mind,
The wrack by passion left behind,
A shrivell'd scroll, a scatter'd leaf, 1255
Sear'd by the autumn blast of grief!

.   .   .   .   .   .

'Tell me no more of fancy's gleam,
No, father, no, 'twas not a dream;
Alas! the dreamer first must sleep,—
I only watch'd, and wish'd to weep, 1260
But could not, for my burning brow
Throbb'd to the very brain as now:
I wish'd but for a single tear,
As something welcome, new, and dear:
I wish'd it then, I wish it still; 1265
Despair is stronger than my will.
Waste not thine orison, despair
Is mightier than thy pious prayer:
I would not, if I might, be blest;
I want no paradise, but rest. 1270
'Twas then, I tell thee, father! then
I saw her; yes, she lived again;
And shining in her white symar,
As through yon pale gray cloud the
   star
Which now I gaze on, as on her, 1275
Who look'd and looks far lovelier;
Dimly I view its trembling spark;
To-morrow's night shall be more dark;
And I, before its rays appear,
That lifeless thing the living fear. 1280
I wander, father! for my soul
Is fleeting towards the final goal.
I saw her, friar! and I rose
Forgetful of our former woes; 1284
And rushing from my couch, I dart,
And clasp her to my desperate heart;
I clasp—what is it that I clasp?
No breathing form within my grasp,
No heart that beats reply to mine—
Yet, Leila! yet the form is thine! 1290
And art thou, dearest, changed so much
As meet my eye, yet mock my touch?
Ah! were thy beauties e'er so cold,
I care not so my arms enfold
The all they ever wish'd to hold. 1295
Alas! around a shadow prest
They shrink upon my lonely breast;
Yet still 'tis there! In silence stands,
And beckons with beseeching hands!
With braided hair, and bright-black eye—
I knew 'twas false—she could not die!
But he is dead! within the dell 1302
I saw him buried where he fell;
He comes not, for he cannot break
From earth; why then art thou awake?
They told me wild waves roll'd above
The face I view, the form I love; 1307
They told me—'twas a hideous tale!—
I'd tell it, but my tongue would fail:

If true, and from thine ocean-cave   1310
Thou com'st to claim a calmer grave,
Oh! pass thy dewy fingers o'er
This brow that then will burn no more;
Or place them on my hopeless heart:
But, shape or shade! whate'er thou art,
In mercy ne'er again depart!   1316
Or farther with thee bear my soul
Than winds can waft or waters roll!

.   .   .   .   .   .
.   .   .   .   .   .

'Such is my name, and such my tale.
  Confessor! to thy secret ear   1320
I breathe the sorrows I bewail,
  And thank thee for the generous tear
This glazing eye could never shed.
Then lay me with the humblest dead,
And, save the cross above my head,   1325
Be neither name nor emblem spread,
By prying stranger to be read,
Or stay the passing pilgrim's tread.'

  He pass'd—nor of his name and race
Hath left a token or a trace,   1330
Save what the father must not say
Who shrived him on his dying day:
This broken tale was all we knew
Of her he loved, or him he slew.

THE BRIDE OF ABYDOS

A TURKISH TALE,

'Had we never loved so kindly,
Had we never loved so blindly,
Never met or never parted,
We had ne'er been broken-hearted.'—BURNS.

TO

THE RIGHT HON. LORD HOLLAND,

THIS TALE IS INSCRIBED,

WITH EVERY SENTIMENT OF REGARD AND RESPECT,
BY HIS GRATEFULLY OBLIGED AND SINCERE FRIEND,

BYRON.

CANTO THE FIRST

I

KNOW ye the land where the cypress and myrtle
  Are emblems of deeds that are done in their clime?
Where the rage of the vulture, the love of the turtle,
  Now melt into sorrow, now madden to crime!
Know ye the land of the cedar and vine,
Where the flowers ever blossom, the beams ever shine;   6
Where the light wings of Zephyr, oppress'd with perfume,
Wax faint o'er the gardens of Gúl in her bloom;
Where the citron and olive are fairest of fruit,
And the voice of the nightingale never is mute: 10
Where the tints of the earth, and the hues of the sky,
In colour though varied, in beauty may vie,
And the purple of ocean is deepest in dye;
Where the virgins are soft as the roses they twine,   14
And all, save the spirit of man, is divine?
'Tis the clime of the East; 'tis the land of the Sun—
Can he smile on such deeds as his children have done?
Oh! wild as the accents of lovers' farewell
Are the hearts which they bear, and the tales which they tell.

II

Begirt with many a gallant slave,   20
Apparell'd as becomes the brave,
Awaiting each his lord's behest
To guide his steps, or guard his rest,
Old Giaffir sate in his Divan: 24
  Deep thought was in his aged eye;
And though the face of Mussulman
  Not oft betrays to standers by
The mind within, well skill'd to hide
All but unconquerable pride,
His pensive cheek and pondering brow
Did more than he was wont avow.   31

III

'Let the chamber be clear'd.'—The train
disappear'd.—
'Now call me the chief of the Haram
guard.'
With Giaffir is none but his only son,
  And the Nubian awaiting the sire's
award. 35
    'Haroun—when all the crowd that
wait
    Are pass'd beneath the outer gate,
    (Woe to the head whose eye beheld
    My child Zuleika's face unveil'd!)
  Hence, lead my daughter from her
tower; 40
  Her fate is fix'd this very hour:
  Yet not to her repeat my thought;
  By me alone be duty taught!'

'Pacha! to hear is to obey.' 44
No more must slave to despot say—
Then to the tower had ta'en his way,
But here young Selim silence brake,
  First lowly rendering reverence meet;
And downcast look'd, and gently spake,
  Still standing at the Pacha's feet:
For son of Moslem must expire, 51
  Ere dare to sit before his sire!

'Father! for fear that thou shouldst
chide
  My sister, or her sable guide, 54
Know—for the fault, if fault there be,
Was mine, then fall thy frowns on me—
So lovelily the morning shone,
  That—let the old and weary sleep—
I could not; and to view alone 59
  The fairest scenes of land and deep,
With none to listen and reply
To thoughts with which my heart beat
high
Were irksome—for whate'er my mood,
In sooth I love not solitude;
I on Zuleika's slumber broke, 65
  And, as thou knowest that for me
Soon turns the Haram's grating key,
Before the guardian slaves awoke
We to the cypress groves had flown,
And made earth, main, and heaven our
own! 70
There linger'd we, beguiled too long
With Mejnoun's tale, or Sadi's song;
Till I, who heard the deep tambour
Beat thy Divan's approaching hour,
To thee, and to my duty true, 75
Warn'd by the sound, to greet thee flew:
But there Zuleika wanders yet—
Nay, Father, rage not—nor forget
That none can pierce that secret bower
But those who watch the women's
tower.' 80

IV

'Son of a slave'—the Pacha said—
'From unbelieving mother bred,
Vain were a father's hope to see
Aught that beseems a man in thee.
Thou, when thine arm should bend the
bow, 85
  And hurl the dart, and curb the steed,
  Thou, Greek in soul if not in creed,
Must pore where babbling waters flow,
And watch unfolding roses blow.
Would that yon orb, whose matin glow
Thy listless eyes so much admire, 91
Would lend thee something of his fire!
Thou, who wouldst see this battlement
By Christian cannon piecemeal rent;
Nay, tamely view old Stambol's wall
Before the dogs of Moscow fall, 96
Nor strike one stroke for life and death
Against the curs of Nazareth!
Go—let thy less than woman's hand
Assume the distaff—not the brand.
But, Haroun!—to my daughter speed:
And hark—of thine own head take
heed— 102
If thus Zuleika oft takes wing—
Thou see'st yon bow—it hath a string!'

V

No sound from Selim's lip was heard,
  At least that met old Giaffir's ear,
But every frown and every word 107
Pierced keener than a Christian's sword.
  'Son of a slave!—reproach'd with fear!
  Those gibes had cost another dear.
Son of a slave!—and *who* my sire?'
  Thus held his thoughts their dark
career;
And glances ev'n of more than ire
Flash forth, then faintly disappear.
Old Giaffir gazed upon his son 115
  And started; for within his eye
He read how much his wrath had done;
He saw rebellion there begun:
  'Come hither, boy—what, no reply?
I mark thee—and I know thee too; 120
But there be deeds thou dar'st not do:
But if thy beard had manlier length,
And if thy hand had skill and strength,
I'd joy to see thee break a lance,
Albeit against my own perchance.' 125

As sneeringly these accents fell,
On Selim's eye he fiercely gazed:
  That eye return'd him glance for
glance,
And proudly to his sire's was raised,
  Till Giaffir's quail'd and shrunk
askance— 130
And why—he felt, but durst not tell.
'Much I misdoubt this wayward boy
Will one day work me more annoy:
I never loved him from his birth,
And—but his arm is little worth, 135
And scarcely in the chase could cope
With timid fawn or antelope,
Far less would venture into strife

Where man contends for fame and
  life—
I would not trust that look or tone: 140
No—nor the blood so near my own.
That blood—he hath not heard—no
  more—
I'll watch him closer than before.
He is an Arab to my sight, 144
Or Christian crouching in the fight—
But hark!—I hear Zuleika's voice;
  Like Houris' hymn it meets mine ear:
She is the offspring of my choice;
  Oh! more than ev'n her mother dear,
With all to hope, and nought to fear—
My Peri! ever welcome here! 151
Sweet, as the desert fountain's wave
To lips just cool'd in time to save—
  Such to my longing sight art thou;
Nor can they waft to Mecca's shrine
More thanks for life, than I for thine,
  Who blest thy birth and bless thee
    now.'

VI

Fair, as the first that fell of womankind,
  When on that dread yet lovely serpent
    smiling,
Whose image then was stamp'd upon her
  mind— 160
  But once beguil'd—and ever more be-
    guiling;
Dazzling, as that, oh! too transcendent
  vision
To Sorrow's phantom-peopled slumber
  given,
When heart meets heart again in dreams
  Elysian,
  And paints the lost on Earth revived in
    Heaven; 165
Soft, as the memory of buried love;
Pure, as the prayer which Childhood
  wafts above,
Was she—the daughter of that rude old
  Chief,
Who met the maid with tears—but not of
  grief.

Who hath not proved how feebly words
  essay 170
To fix one spark of Beauty's heavenly ray?
Who doth not feel, until his failing sight
Faints into dimness with its own delight,
His changing cheek, his sinking heart
  confess 174
The might, the majesty of Loveliness?
Such was Zuleika, such around her shone
The nameless charms unmark'd by her
  alone—
The light of love, the purity of grace,
The mind, the Music breathing from her
  face,
The heart whose softness harmonized the
  whole, 180
And oh! that eye was in itself a Soul!

Her graceful arms in meekness bending
  Across her gently-budding breast;
At one kind word those arms extending
  To clasp the neck of him who blest
  His child caressing and carest, 186
Zuleika came—and Giaffir felt
His purpose half within him melt:
Not that against her fancied weal
His heart though stern could ever feel;
Affection chain'd her to that heart; 191
Ambition tore the links apart.

VII

'Zuleika! child of gentleness!
How dear this very day must tell,
When I forget my own distress, 195
  In losing what I love so well,
To bid thee with another dwell:
Another! and a braver man
Was never seen in battle's van.
We Moslem reck not much of blood; 200
But yet the line of Carasman
Unchanged, unchangeable hath stood
  First of the bold Timariot bands
That won and well can keep their lands.
Enough that he who comes to woo
Is kinsman of the Bey Oglou: 206
His years need scarce a thought employ:
I would not have thee wed a boy.
And thou shalt have a noble dower:
And his and my united power 210
Will laugh to scorn the death-firman,
Which others tremble but to scan,
And teach the messenger what fate
The bearer of such boon may wait.
And now thou know'st thy father's
  will: 215
  All that thy sex hath need to know:
'Twas mine to teach obedience still—
  The way to love, thy lord may show.'

VIII

In silence bow'd the virgin's head;
  And if her eye was fill'd with tears
That stifled feeling dare not shed, 221
And changed her cheek from pale to
  red,
  And red to pale, as through her ears
Those winged words like arrows sped,
  What could such be but maiden
    fears? 225
So bright the tear in Beauty's eye,
Love half regrets to kiss it dry;
So sweet the blush of Bashfulness,
Even Pity scarce can wish it less!

Whate'er it was the sire forgot; 230
Or if remember'd, mark'd it not;
Thrice clapp'd his hands, and call'd his
  steed,
  Resign'd his gem-adorn'd chibouque,
And mounting featly for the mead,

With Maugrabee and Mamaluke,
His way amid his Delis took,   236
To witness many an active deed
With sabre keen, or blunt jerreed.
The Kislar only and his Moors
Watch well the Haram's massy doors.

IX

His head was leant upon his hand,   241
   His eye look'd o'er the dark blue
      water
That swiftly glides and gently swells
Between the winding Dardanelles;
But yet he saw nor sea nor strand, 245
Nor even his Pacha's turban'd band
   Mix in the game of mimic slaughter,
Careering cleave the folded felt,
With sabre stroke right sharply dealt;
Nor mark'd the javelin-darting crowd
Nor heard their Ollahs wild and loud—
   He thought but of old Giaffir's
      daughter!   252

X

No word from Selim's bosom broke;
One sigh Zuleika's thoughts bespoke:
Still gazed he through the lattice grate,
Pale, mute, and mournfully sedate. 256
To him Zuleika's eye was turn'd,
But little from his aspect learn'd:
Equal her grief, yet not the same;
Her heart confess'd a gentler flame: 260
But yet that heart, alarm'd or weak,
She knew not why, forbade to speak.
Yet speak she must—but when essay?
'How strange he thus should turn away!
Not thus we e'er before have met;   265
Nor thus shall be our parting yet.'
Thrice paced she slowly through the
    room,
   And watch'd his eye—it still was fix'd:
   She snatch'd the urn wherein was
     mix'd
The Persian Atar-gul's perfume,   270
And sprinkled all its odours o'er
The pictured roof and marble floor:
The drops, that through his glittering
    vest
The playful girl's appeal address'd,
Unheeded o'er his bosom flew,   275
As if that breast were marble too.
'What, sullen yet? it must not be—
Oh! gentle Selim, this from thee!'
She saw in curious order set
   The fairest flowers of eastern land—
'He loved them once; may touch them
    yet,   281
   If offer'd by Zuleika's hand.'
The childish thought was hardly
    breathed
Before the rose was pluck'd and
    wreathed;
The next fond moment saw her seat
Her fairy form at Selim's feet: 286

'This rose to calm my brother's cares
A message from the Bulbul bears;
It says to-night he will prolong
For Selim's ear his sweetest song; 290
And though his note is somewhat sad,
He'll try for once a strain more glad,
With some faint hope his alter'd lay
May sing these gloomy thoughts away.

XI

'What! not receive my foolish flower?
   Nay then I am indeed unblest: 296
On me can thus thy forehead lower?
   And know'st thou not who loves thee
    best?
Oh, Selim dear! oh, more than dearest!
Say, is it me thou hat'st or fearest?
Come, lay thy head upon my breast,
And I will kiss thee into rest,
Since words of mine, and songs must
    fail,
Ev'n from my fabled nightingale.
I knew our sire at times was stern, 305
But this from thee had yet to learn:
Too well I know he loves thee not;
But is Zuleika's love forgot?
Ah! deem I right? the Pacha's plan—
This kinsman Bey of Carasman   310
Perhaps may prove some foe of thine.
If so, I swear by Mecca's shrine,—
If shrines that ne'er approach allow
To woman's step admit her vow,—
Without thy free consent, command,
The Sultan should not have my hand!
Think'st thou that I could bear to part
With thee, and learn to halve my heart?
Ah! were I sever'd from thy side,
Where were thy friend—and who my
    guide?   320
Years have not seen, Time shall not see,
The hour that tears my soul from thee:
Ev'n Azrael, from his deadly quiver
   When flies that shaft, and fly it must,
That parts all else, shall doom for ever
   Our hearts to undivided dust!'   326

XII

He lived, he breathed, he moved, he
    felt;
He raised the maid from where she
    knelt;
His trance was gone, his keen eye shone
With thoughts that long in darkness
    dwelt;   330
With thoughts that burn—in rays that
    melt.
As the stream late conceal'd
   By the fringe of its willows,
When it rushes reveal'd
   In the light of its billows;   335
As the bolt bursts on high
   From the black cloud that bound it,
Flash'd the soul of that eye
   Through the long lashes round it.

A war-horse at the trumpet's sound,
A lion roused by heedless hound,   341
A tyrant waked to sudden strife
By graze of ill-directed knife,
Starts not to more convulsive life
Than he, who heard that vow, dis-
    play'd,   345
And all, before repress'd, betray'd:
'Now thou art mine, for ever mine,
With life to keep, and scarce with life
    resign;
Now thou art mine, that sacred oath,
Though sworn by one, hath bound us
    both.   350
Yes, fondly, wisely hast thou done;
That vow hath saved more heads than
    one:
But blench not thou—thy simplest tress
Claims more from me than tenderness;
I would not wrong the slenderest hair
That clusters round thy forehead fair,
For all the treasures buried far   357
Within the caves of Istakar.
This morning clouds upon me lower'd,
Reproaches on my head were shower'd,
And Giaffir almost call'd me coward!
Now I have motive to be brave;   362
The son of his neglected slave,
Nay, start not, 'twas the term he gave,
May show, though little apt to vaunt,
A heart his words nor deeds can
    daunt.   366
His son, indeed!—yet, thanks to thee,
Perchance I am, at least shall be;
But let our plighted secret vow
Be only known to us as now.   370
I know the wretch who dares demand
From Giaffir thy reluctant hand;
More ill-got wealth, a meaner soul
Holds not a Musselim's control:
Was he not bred in Egripo?   375
A viler race let Israel show!
But let that pass—to none be told
Our oath; the rest shall time unfold.
To me and mine leave Osman Bey;
I've partisans for peril's day: 380
Think not I am what I appear;
I've arms, and friends, and vengeance
    near.'

XIII

'Think not thou art what thou appear-
    est!
My Selim, thou art sadly changed:
This morn I saw thee gentlest, dearest;
But now thou'rt from thyself es-
    tranged.   386
My love thou surely knew'st before,
It ne'er was less, nor can be more.
To see thee, hear thee, near thee stay,
    And hate the night I know not why,
Save that we meet not but by day;
    With thee to live, with thee to die,
I dare not to my hope deny:

Thy cheek, thine eyes, thy lips to kiss,
Like this—and this—no more than
    this;   395
For, Allah! sure thy lips are flame:
    What fever in thy veins is flushing?
My own have nearly caught the same,
    At least I feel my cheek, too, blush-
    ing.
To soothe thy sickness, watch thy
    health,   400
Partake, but never waste thy wealth,
Or stand with smiles unmurmuring by,
And lighten half thy poverty;
Do all but close thy dying eye,
For that I could not live to try;   405
To these alone my thoughts aspire:
More can I do? or thou require?
But, Selim, thou must answer why
We need so much of mystery?
The cause I cannot dream nor tell,   410
But be it, since thou say'st 'tis well;
Yet what thou mean'st by "arms" and
    "friends,"
Beyond my weaker sense extends.
I meant that Giaffir should have heard
    The very vow I plighted thee;   415
His wrath would not revoke my word:
    But surely he would leave me free.
Can this fond wish seem strange in
    me,
To be what I have ever been?
What other hath Zuleika seen   420
From simple childhood's earliest hour?
What other can she seek to see
Than thee, companion of her bower,
    The partner of her infancy?
These cherish'd thoughts with life
    begun,   425
    Say, why must I no more avow?
What change is wrought to make me
    shun
    The truth; my pride, and thine till
    now?
To meet the gaze of stranger's eyes
Our law, our creed, our God denies;
Nor shall one wandering thought of
    mine   431
At such, our Prophet's will, repine:
No! happier made by that decree,
He left me all in leaving thee.
Deep were my anguish, thus compell'd
To wed with one I ne'er beheld: 436
This wherefore should I not reveal?
Why wilt thou urge me to conceal?
I know the Pacha's haughty mood
To thee hath never boded good;   440
And he so often storms at nought,
Allah! forbid that e'er he ought!
And why I know not, but within
My heart concealment weighs like sin.
If then such secrecy be crime,   445
    And such it feels while lurking here;
Oh, Selim! tell me yet in time,
    Nor leave me thus to thoughts of fear.

Ah! yonder see the Tchocadar,
My father leaves the mimic war;   450
I tremble now to meet his eye—
Say, Selim, canst thou tell me why?'

XIV

'Zuleika—to thy tower's retreat
Betake thee—Giaffir I can greet:
And now with him I fain must prate
Of firmans, imposts, levies, state.   456
There's fearful news from Danube's
    banks,
Our Vizier nobly thins his ranks,
For which the Giaour may give him
    thanks!
Our Sultan hath a shorter way   460
Such costly triumph to repay.
But, mark me, when the twilight drum
    Hath warn'd the troops to food and
    sleep,
Unto thy cell will Selim come: 464
    Then softly from the Haram creep
    Where we may wander by the deep:
    Our garden battlements are steep;
Nor these will rash intruder climb
To list our words, or stint our time;
And if he doth, I want not steel   470
Which some have felt, and more may
    feel.
Then shalt thou learn of Selim more
Than thou hast heard or thought be-
    fore:
Trust me, Zuleika—fear not me!   474
Thou know'st I hold a Haram key.'
'Fear thee, my Selim! ne'er till now
Did word like this——'
                    'Delay not thou;
I keep the key—and Haroun's guard
Have *some*, and hope of *more* reward.
To-night, Zuleika, thou shalt hear   480
My tale, my purpose, and my fear:
I am not, love! what I appear.'

CANTO THE SECOND

I

THE winds are high on Helle's wave,
    As on that night of stormy water
When Love, who sent, forgot to save
The young, the beautiful, the brave,
    The lonely hope of Sestos' daughter.
Oh! when alone along the sky   6
Her turret-torch was blazing high,
Though rising gale, and breaking foam,
And shrieking sea-birds warn'd him
    home;
And clouds aloft and tides below,   10
With signs and sounds, forbade to go,
He could not see, he would not hear,
Or sound or sign foreboding fear;
His eye but saw that light of love,
The only star it hail'd above;   15
His ear but rang with Hero's song,
'Ye waves, divide not lovers long!'—

That tale is old, but love anew
May nerve young hearts to prove as
    true.   19

II

The winds are high, and Helle's tide
    Rolls darkly heaving to the main;
And Night's descending shadows hide
    That field with blood bedew'd in vain,
The desert of old Priam's pride;   24
    The tombs, sole relics of his reign,
All—save immortal dreams that could
    beguile
The blind old man of Scio's rocky isle!

III

Oh! yet—for there my steps have been;
    These feet have press'd the sacred
    shore,
These limbs that buoyant wave hath
    borne—   30
Minstrel! with thee to muse, to mourn,
    To trace again those fields of yore,
Believing every hillock green
    Contains no fabled hero's ashes,
And that around the undoubted scene
    Thine own 'broad Hellespont' still
    dashes,   36
Be long my lot! and cold were he
Who there could gaze denying thee!

IV

The night hath closed on Helle's
    stream,
    Nor yet hath risen on Ida's hill   40
That moon, which shone on his high
    theme:
No warrior chides her peaceful beam,
    But conscious shepherds bless it still.
Their flocks are grazing on the mound
    Of him who felt the Dardan's arrow:
That mighty heap of gather'd ground
Which Ammon's son ran proudly round
By nations raised, by monarchs crown'd,
    Is now a lone and nameless barrow!
Within—thy dwelling-place how nar-
    row!   50
Without—can only strangers breathe
The name of him that *was* beneath:
Dust long outlasts the storied stone;
But Thou—thy very dust is gone!

V

Late, late to-night will Dian cheer   55
The swain, and chase the boatman's
    fear;
Till then—no beacon on the cliff
May shape the course of struggling
    skiff;
The scatter'd lights that skirt the bay,
All, one by one, have died away;   60
The only lamp of this lone hour
Is glimmering in Zuleika's tower.

Yes! there is light in that lone chamber,
  And o'er her silken ottoman
Are thrown the fragrant beads of
  amber,   65
  O'er which her fairy fingers ran;
Near these, with emerald rays beset,
(How could she thus that gem forget?)
Her mother's sainted amulet,
Whereon engraved the Koorsee text,
Could smooth this life, and win the
  next;   71
And by her comboloio lies
A Koran of illumined dyes;
And many a bright emblazon'd rhyme
By Persian scribes redeem'd from time;
And o'er those scrolls, not oft so
  mute,   76
Reclines her now neglected lute;
And round her lamp of fretted gold
Bloom flowers in urns of China's
  mould;
The richest work of Iran's loom,   80
And Sheeraz' tribute of perfume;
All that can eye or sense delight
  Are gather'd in that gorgeous room:
  But yet it hath an air of gloom.   85
She, of this Peri cell the sprite,
What doth she hence, and on so rude
  a night?

VI

Wrapt in the darkest sable vest,
  Which none save noblest Moslem
    wear,
To guard from winds of heaven the
  breast
  As heaven itself to Selim dear,   90
With cautious steps the thicket thread-
  ing,
  And starting oft, as through the glade
  The gust its hollow moanings made,
Till on the smoother pathway tread-
  ing,
More free her timid bosom beat,   95
  The maid pursued her silent guide;
And though her terror urged retreat,
  How could she quit her Selim's side?
  How teach her tender lips to chide?

VII

They reach'd at length a grotto, hewn
  By nature, but enlarged by art,   101
Where oft her lute she wont to tune,
  And oft her Koran conn'd apart;
And oft in youthful reverie   104
She dream'd what Paradise might be:
Where woman's parted soul shall go
Her Prophet had disdain'd to show;
But Selim's mansion was secure,
Nor deem'd she, could he long endure
His bower in other worlds of bliss   110
Without her, most beloved in this!
Oh! who so dear with him could dwell?
What Houri soothe him half so well?

VIII

Since last she visited the spot
Some change seem'd wrought within
  the grot: 115
It might be only that the night
Disguised things seen by better light:
That brazen lamp but dimly threw
A ray of no celestial hue;
But in a nook within the cell   120
Her eye on stranger objects fell.
There arms were piled, not such as
  wield
The turban'd Delis in the field;
But brands of foreign blade and hilt,
And one was red—perchance with
  guilt!   125
Ah! how without can blood be spilt?
A cup too on the board was set
That did not seem to hold sherbet.
What may this mean? she turn'd to see
Her Selim—'Oh! can this be he?'   130

IX

His robe of pride was thrown aside,
  His brow no high-crown'd turban
    bore,
But in its stead a shawl of red,
  Wreathed lightly round, his temples
    wore: 134
That dagger, on whose hilt the gem
Were worthy of a diadem,
No longer glitter'd at his waist,
Where pistols unadorn'd were braced;
And from his belt a sabre swung,   139
And from his shoulder loosely hung
The cloak of white, the thin capote
That decks the wandering Candiote;
Beneath—his golden plated vest
Clung like a cuirass to his breast;
The greaves below his knee that wound
With silvery scales were sheathed and
  bound.   146
But were it not that high command
Spake in his eye, and tone, and hand,
All that a careless eye could see
In him was some young Galiongée.

X

'I said I was not what I seem'd;   151
  And now thou see'st my words were
    true:
I have a tale thou hast not dream'd,
  If sooth—its truth must others rue.
My story now 'twere vain to hide,   155
I must not see thee Osman's bride:
But had not thine own lips declared
How much of that young heart I shared,
I could not, must not, yet have shown
The darker secret of my own.   160
In this I speak not now of love;
That, let time, truth, and peril prove:
But first—Oh! never wed another—
Zuleika! I am not thy brother!'

XI

'Oh! not my brother!—yet unsay—
    God! am I left alone on earth   166
To mourn—I dare not curse—the day
    That saw my solitary birth?
Oh! thou wilt love me now no more!
    My sinking heart foreboded ill;   170
But know *me* all I was before,
    Thy sister—friend—Zuleika still.
Thou led'st me here perchance to kill;
    If thou hast cause for vengeance, see!
My breast is offer'd—take thy fill!   175
    Far better with the dead to be
Than live thus nothing now to thee!
Perhaps far worse, for now I know
Why Giaffir always seem'd thy foe;
And I, alas! am Giaffir's child,   180
For whom thou wert contemn'd, reviled.
If not thy sister—wouldst thou save
My life, oh! bid me be thy slave!'

XII

'My slave, Zuleika!—nay, I'm thine:
    But, gentle love, this transport calm.
Thy lot shall yet be link'd with mine;
    I swear it by our Prophet's shrine,
    And be that thought thy sorrow's
        balm.
So may the Koran verse display'd
    Upon its steel direct my blade,   190
In danger's hour to guard us both,
    As I preserve that awful oath!
The name in which thy heart hath
        prided
    Must change; but, my Zuleika, know,
That tie is widen'd, not divided,   195
    Although thy Sire's my deadliest foe.
My father was to Giaffir all
    That Selim late was deem'd to thee:
That brother wrought a brother's fall,
    But spared, at least, my infancy;
And lull'd me with a vain deceit   201
    That yet a like return may meet.
He rear'd me, not with tender help,
    But like the nephew of a Cain;
He watch'd me like a lion's whelp,   205
    That gnaws and yet may break his
        chain.
    My father's blood in every vein
Is boiling; but for thy dear sake
No present vengeance will I take;
    Though here I must no more remain.
But first, beloved Zuleika! hear   211
How Giaffir wrought this deed of fear.

XIII

'How first their strife to rancour grew,
    If love or envy made them foes,
It matters little if I knew;   215
    In fiery spirits, slights, though few
    And thoughtless, will disturb repose.
In war Abdallah's arm was strong,
Remember'd yet in Bosniac song,

And Paswan's rebel hordes attest   220
How little love they bore such guest:
His death is all I need relate,
The stern effect of Giaffir's hate;
And how my birth disclosed to me,
Whate'er beside it makes, hath made
    me free.   225

XIV

'When Paswan, after years of strife,
At last for power, but first for life,
In Widdin's walls too proudly sate,
Our Pachas rallied round the state;
Nor last nor least in high command,
Each brother led a separate band;   231
They gave their horse-tails to the
        wind,
    And mustering in Sophia's plain
Their tents were pitch'd, their post
        assign'd;
    To one, alas! assign'd in vain!   235
What need of words! the deadly bowl,
    By Giaffir's order drugged and given,
With venom subtle as his soul,
    Dismiss'd Abdallah's hence to heaven.
Reclined and feverish in the bath,   240
    He, when the hunter's sport was up,
But little deem'd a brother's wrath
    To quench his thirst had such a
        cup:
The bowl a bribed attendant bore;
He drank one draught, nor needed
    more!   245
If thou my tale, Zuleika, doubt,
Call Haroun—he can tell it out.

XV

'The deed once done, and Paswan's
        feud
In part suppress'd, though ne'er sub-
        dued,   249
    Abdallah's Pachalick was gain'd:—
Thou know'st not what in our Divan
Can wealth procure for worse than
        man—
Abdallah's honours were obtain'd
By him a brother's murder stain'd;
'Tis true, the purchase nearly drain'd
His ill-got treasure, soon replaced.   256
Wouldst question whence? Survey the
        waste,
And ask the squalid peasant how
His gains repay his broiling brow!—
Why me the stern usurper spared,   260
Why thus with me his palace shared,
I know not. Shame, regret, remorse,
And little fear from infant's force;
Besides, adoption as a son
By him whom Heaven accorded none,
Or some unknown cabal, caprice,   266
Preserved me thus;—but not in peace:
He cannot curb his haughty mood,
Nor I forgive a father's blood.

XVI

'Within thy father's house are foes;
    Not all who break his bread are
        true: 271
To these should I my birth disclose,
His days, his very hours were few:
They only want a heart to lead,
A hand to point them to the deed. 275
But Haroun only knows, or knew,
    This tale, whose close is almost nigh:
He in Abdallah's palace grew,
    And held that post in his Serai
Which holds he here—he saw him
        die: 280
But what could single slavery do?
Avenge his lord? alas! too late;
Or save his son from such a fate?
He chose the last, and when elate
    With foes subdued, or friends be-
        tray'd,   285
Proud Giaffir in high triumph sate,
He led me helpless to his gate,
    And not in vain it seems essay'd
To save the life for which he pray'd.
The knowledge of my birth secured
    From all and each, but most from
        me;   291
Thus Giaffir's safety was insured.
    Removed he too from Roumelie
To this our Asiatic side,
Far from our seats by Danube's tide,
    With none but Haroun, who retains
Such knowledge—and that Nubian feels
    A tyrant's secrets are but chains,
From which the captive gladly steals,
And this and more to me reveals: 300
Such still to guilt just Allah sends—
Slaves, tools, accomplices—no friends!

XVII

'All this, Zuleika, harshly sounds;
    But harsher still my tale must be:
Howe'er my tongue thy softness
        wounds,   305
    Yet I must prove all truth to thee.
I saw thee start this garb to see,
    Yet is it one I oft have worn,
    And long must wear: this Galiongée,
To whom thy plighted vow is sworn, 311
    Is leader of those pirate hordes,
    Whose laws and lives are on their
        swords;
To hear whose desolating tale
Would make thy waning cheek more
        pale:
Those arms thou see'st my band have
        brought,   315
The hands that wield are not remote;
This cup too for the rugged knaves
    Is fill'd—once quaff'd, they ne'er
        repine:
Our Prophet might forgive the slaves;
    They're only infidels in wine. 320

XVIII

'What could I be? Proscribed at home
And taunted to a wish to roam;
And listless left—for Giaffir's fear
Denied the courser and the spear—
Though oft—Oh, Mahomet! how oft!—
In full Divan the despot scoff'd,   32
As if my weak unwilling hand
Refused the bridle or the brand:
He ever went to war alone,   32
And pent me here untried—unknown
To Haroun's care with women left,
By hope unblest, of fame bereft,
While thou—whose softness long en-
        dear'd,
Though it unmann'd me, still ha
        cheer'd—
To Brusa's walls for safety sent,   33
Awaited'st there the field's event.
Haroun, who saw my spirit pining
    Beneath inaction's sluggish yoke,
His captive, though with dread resign-
        ing,
My thraldom for a season broke,
On promise to return before   34
The day when Giaffir's charge was o'er
'Tis vain—my tongue cannot impart
My almost drunkenness of heart,
When first this liberated eye   34
Survey'd Earth, Ocean, Sun, and Sky,
As if my spirit pierced them through,
And all their inmost wonders knew!
One word alone can paint to thee
That more than feeling—I was Free!
E'en for thy presence ceased to pine;
The World—nay, Heaven itself wa
        mine!

XIX

'The shallop of a trusty Moor
Convey'd me from this idle shore;
I long'd to see the isles that gem 35
Old Ocean's purple diadem:
I sought by turns, and saw them all;
    But when and where I join'd the crew
With whom I'm pledged to rise or fall
    When all that we design to do   36
Is done, 'twill then be time more meet
To tell thee, when the tale's complete

XX

''Tis true, they are a lawless brood,
But rough in form, nor mild in mood
And every creed, and every race,   36
With them hath found—may find a
        place;
But open speech, and ready hand,
Obedience to their chief's command:
A soul for every enterprise,
That never sees with terror's eyes; 370
Friendship for each, and faith to all,
And vengeance vow'd for those who
        fall,

Have made them fitting instruments
For more than ev'n my own intents.
And some—and I have studied all 375
    Distinguish'd from the vulgar rank,
But chiefly to my council call
    The wisdom of the cautious Frank—
And some to higher thoughts aspire,
    The last of Lambro's patriots there
    Anticipated freedom share;   381
And oft around the cavern fire
On visionary schemes debate,
To snatch the Rayahs from their fate.
So let them ease their hearts with prate
Of equal rights, which man ne'er knew;
I have a love for freedom too.   387
Ay! let me like the ocean-Patriarch roam,
Or only know on land the Tartar's home!
My tent on shore, my galley on the sea,
Are more than cities and Serais to me:
Borne by my steed, or wafted by my sail,
Across the desert, or before the gale,
Bound where thou wilt, my barb! or glide,
    my prow!
But be the star that guides the wanderer,
    Thou!   395
Thou, my Zuleika, share and bless my
    bark;
The Dove of peace and promise to mine
    ark!
Or, since that hope denied in worlds of
    strife,
Be thou the rainbow to the storms of
    life!
The evening beam that smiles the clouds
    away,   400
And tints to-morrow with prophetic ray!
Blest—as the Muezzin's strain from
    Mecca's wall
To pilgrims pure and prostrate at his call;
Soft—as the melody of youthful days,
That steals the trembling tear of speech-
    less praise;   405
Dear—as his native song to Exile's ears,
Shall sound each tone thy long-loved
    voice endears.
For thee in those bright isles is built a
    bower
Blooming as Aden in its earliest hour.
A thousand swords, with Selim's heart and
    hand,   410
Wait—wave—defend—destroy—at thy
    command!
Girt by my band, Zuleika at my side,
The spoil of nations shall bedeck my
    bride.
The Haram's languid years of listless ease
Are well resign'd for cares—for joys like
    these;   415
Not blind to fate, I see, where'er I rove,
Unnumber'd perils—but one only love!
Yet well my toils shall that fond breast
    repay,
Though fortune frown, or falser friends
    betray.

How dear the dream in darkest hours of
    ill,   420
Should all be changed, to find thee faithful
    still!
Be but thy soul, like Selim's, firmly shown;
To thee be Selim's tender as thine own;
To soothe each sorrow, share in each
    delight,
Blend every thought, do all—but disunite!
Once free, 'tis mine our horde again to
    guide;   426
Friends to each other, foes to aught be-
    side:
Yet there we follow but the bent assign'd
By fatal Nature to man's warring kind:
Mark! where his carnage and his con-
    quests cease!   430
He makes a solitude, and calls it—peace!
I, like the rest, must use my skill or
    strength,
But ask no land beyond my sabre's
    length:
Power sways but by division—her re-
    source   434
The blest alternative of fraud or force!
Ours be the last; in time deceit may come
When cities cage us in a social home:
There ev'n thy soul might err—how oft
    the heart
Corruption shakes which peril could not
    part!
And woman, more than man, when death
    or woe,   440
Or even Disgrace, would lay her lover low,
Sunk in the lap of Luxury will shame—
Away suspicion!—not Zuleika's name!
But life is hazard at the best; and here
No more remains to win, and much to
    fear: 445
Yes, fear! the doubt, the dread of losing
    thee,
By Osman's power, and Giaffir's stern
    decree.
That dread shall vanish with the favouring
    gale,
Which Love to-night hath promised to my
    sail:
No danger daunts the pair his smile hath
    blest,   450
Their steps still roving, but their hearts at
    rest.
With thee all toils are sweet, each clime
    hath charms;
Earth—sea alike—our world within our
    arms!
Ay—let the loud winds whistle o'er the
    deck,
So that those arms cling closer round my
    neck: 455
The deepest murmur of this lip shall be
No sigh for safety, but a prayer for thee!
The war of elements no fears impart
To Love, whose deadliest bane is human
    Art:

There lie the only rocks our course can
check; 460
Here moments menace—*there* are years
of wreck!
But hence ye thoughts that rise in Horror's
shape!
This hour bestows, or ever bars escape.
Few words remain of mine my tale to
close;
Of thine but *one* to waft us from our foes;
Yea—foes—to me will Giaffir's hate de-
cline? 466
And is not Osman, who would part us,
thine?

XXI

'His head and faith from doubt and
death
Return'd in time my guard to save;
Few heard, none told, that o'er the
wave 470
From isle to isle I roved the while;
And since, though parted from my band
Too seldom now I leave the land,
No deed they've done, nor deed shall
do,
Ere I have heard and doom'd it too:
I form the plan, decree the spoil, 476
'Tis fit I oftener share the toil.
But now too long I've held thine ear;
Time presses, floats my bark, and here
We leave behind but hate and fear.
To-morrow Osman with his train 481
Arrives—to-night must break thy chain:
And wouldst thou save that haughty
Bey,—
Perchance *his* life who gave thee
thine,—
With me this hour away—away! 485
But yet, though thou art plighted
mine,
Wouldst thou recall thy willing vow,
Appall'd by truths imparted now,
Here rest I—not to see thee wed:
But be that peril on *my* head!' 490

XXII

Zuleika, mute and motionless,
Stood like that statue of distress,
When, her last hope for ever gone,
The mother harden'd into stone:
All in the maid that eye could see 495
Was but a younger Niobé.
But ere her lip, or even her eye,
Essay'd to speak, or look reply,
Beneath the garden's wicket porch 499
Far flashed on high a blazing torch!
Another—and another—and another—
'Oh! fly—no more—yet now my more
than brother!'
Far, wide, through every thicket spread
The fearful lights are gleaming red;
Nor these alone—for each right hand
Is ready with a sheathless brand. 506

They part, pursue, return, and wheel
With searching flambeau, shining steel
And last of all, his sabre waving,
Stern Giaffir in his fury raving: 510
And now almost they touch the cave—
Oh! must that grot be Selim's grave?

XXIII

Dauntless he stood—' 'Tis come—soon
past—
One kiss, Zuleika—'tis my last: 514
But yet my band not far from shore
May hear this signal, see the flash;
Yet now too few—the attempt were
rash:
No matter—yet one effort more.'
Forth to the cavern mouth he stept;
His pistol's echo rang on high, 520
Zuleika started not, nor wept,
Despair benumb'd her breast and
eye!—
'They hear me not; or if they ply
Their oars, 'tis but to see me die;
That sound hath drawn my foes more
nigh.
Then forth my father's scimitar, 526
Thou ne'er hast seen less equal war!
Farewell, Zuleika!—sweet! retire:
Yet stay within—here linger safe,
At thee his rage will only chafe. 530
Stir not—lest even to thee perchance
Some erring blade or ball should glance.
Fear'st thou for him?—may I expire
If in this strife I seek thy sire! 534
No—though by him that poison pour'd;
No—though again he call me coward!
But tamely shall I meet their steel?
No—as each crest save *his* may feel!'

XXIV

One bound he made, and gain'd the
sand:
Already at his feet hath sunk 540
The foremost of the prying band,
A gasping head, a quivering trunk:
Another falls—but round him close
A swarming circle of his foes; 544
From right to left his path he cleft,
And almost met the meeting wave:
His boat appears—not five oars'
length—
His comrades strain with desperate
strength—
Oh! are they yet in time to save?
His feet the foremost breakers lave;
His band are plunging in the bay, 551
Their sabres glitter through the spray;
Wet—wild—unwearied to the strand
They struggle—now they touch the
land!
They come—'tis but to add to slaugh-
ter— 555
His heart's best blood is on the water.

XXV

Escaped from shot, unharm'd by steel,
Or scarcely grazed its force to feel,
Had Selim won, betray'd, beset,   559
To where the strand and billows met;
There as his last step left the land—
And the last death-blow dealt his
    hand—
Ah! wherefore did he turn to look
    For her his eye but sought in vain?
That pause, that fatal gaze he took,
    Hath doom'd his death, or fix'd his
    chain.   566
Sad proof, in peril and in pain,
How late will Lover's hope remain!
His back was to the dashing spray;
Behind, but close, his comrades lay,   570
When, at the instant, hiss'd the ball—
'So may the foes of Giaffir fall!'
Whose voice is heard? whose carbine
    rang?
Whose bullet through the night-air
    sang,
Too nearly, deadly aim'd to err?   575
'Tis thine—Abdallah's Murderer!
The father slowly rued his hate,
The son hath found a quicker fate:
Fast from his breast the blood is
    bubbling,
The whiteness of the sea-foam troub-
    ling—   580
If aught his lips essay'd to groan,
The rushing billows choked the tone!

XXVI

Morn slowly rolls the clouds away;
    Few trophies of the fight are there:
The shouts that shook the midnight-bay
Are silent; but some signs of fray   586
    That strand of strife may bear,
And fragments of each shiver'd brand;
Steps stamp'd; and dash'd into the sand
The print of many a struggling hand
    May there be mark'd; nor far remote
A broken torch, an oarless boat;
And tangled on the weeds that heap
The beach where shelving to the deep
    There lies a white capote!   595
'Tis rent in twain—one dark-red stain
The wave yet ripples o'er in vain;
    But where is he who wore?
Ye! who would o'er his relics weep,
Go, seek them where the surges sweep
    Their burthen round Sigæum's steep
And cast on Lemnos' shore:
The sea-birds shriek above the prey,
O'er which their hungry beaks delay,
As shaken on his restless pillow,   605
His head heaves with the heaving
    billow;
That hand, whose motion is not life,
Yet feebly seems to menace strife,
Flung by the tossing tide on high,

Then levell'd with the wave—   610
What recks it, though that corse shall lie
    Within a living grave?
The bird that tears that prostrate form
Hath only robb'd the meaner worm;
The only heart, the only eye   615
Had bled or wept to see him die,
Had seen those scatter'd limbs composed,
    And mourn'd above his turban-stone,
That heart hath burst—that eye was
    closed—
    Yea—closed before his own!   620

XXVII

By Helle's stream there is a voice of wail!
And woman's eye is wet—man's cheek is
    pale:
Zuleika! last of Giaffir's race,
Thy destined lord is come too late:
He sees not—ne'er shall see thy face!
    Can he not hear   626
The loud Wul-wulleh warn his distant ear?
    Thy handmaids weeping at the gate,
    The Koran-chanters of the hymn of fate,
    The silent slaves with folded arms that
        wait,   630
Sighs in the hall, and shrieks upon the gale,
        Tell him thy tale!
Thou didst not view thy Selim fall!
    That fearful moment when he left the
    cave
        Thy heart grew chill: 635
He was thy hope—thy joy—thy love—
    thine all,
And that last thought on him thou couldst
    not save
        Sufficed to kill;
Burst forth in one wild cry—and all was
    still,
    Peace to thy broken heart, and virgin
    grave!   640
Ah! happy! but of life to lose the worst!
That grief—though deep—though fatal—
    was thy first!
Thrice happy ne'er to feel nor fear the force
Of absence, shame, pride, hate, revenge,
    remorse!
And, oh! that pang where more than mad-
    ness lies!   645
The worm that will not sleep—and never
    dies;
Thought of the gloomy day and ghastly
    night,
That dreads the darkness, and yet loathes
    the light,
That winds around, and tears the quiver-
    ing heart!
Ah! wherefore not consume it—and de-
    depart!   650
Woe to thee, rash and unrelenting chief!
    Vainly thou heap'st the dust upon thy
    head,
    Vainly the sackcloth o'er thy limbs dost
    spread:

By that same hand Abdallah—Selim
  bled,
Now let it tear thy beard in idle grief:
Thy pride of heart, thy bride for Osman's
  bed,   656
She, whom thy sultan had but seen to
  wed,
    Thy Daughter's dead!
Hope of thine age, thy twilight's lonely
  beam,
The Star hath set that shone on Helle's
  stream.   660
What quench'd its ray?—the blood that
  thou hast shed!
Hark! to the hurried question of Despair:
'Where is my child?'—an Echo answers—
  'Where?'

XXVIII

Within the place of thousand tombs
  That shine beneath, while dark above
The sad but living cypress glooms 666
  And withers not, though branch and
    leaf
Are stamp'd with an eternal grief,
  Like early unrequited Love,
One spot exists, which ever blooms,
  Ev'n in that deadly grove—   671
A single rose is shedding there
  Its lonely lustre, meek and pale:
It looks as planted by Despair—
  So white—so faint—the slightest gale
Might whirl the leaves on high;   676
  And yet, though storms and blight
    assail,
And hands more rude than wintry sky
  May wring it from the stem—in
    vain—
    To-morrow sees it bloom again: 680
The stalk some spirit gently rears,
And waters with celestial tears;
  For well may maids of Helle deem
That this can be no earthly flower,
Which mocks the tempest's withering
  hour,   685
And buds unshelter'd by a bower;
Nor droops though Spring refuse her
  shower,
Nor woos the summer beam:

To it the livelong night there sings
  A bird unseen—but not remote:
Invisible his airy wings,   691
But soft as harp that Houri strings
  His long entrancing note!
It were the Bulbul; but his throat,
  Though mournful, pours not such a
    strain: 695
For they who listen cannot leave
The spot, but linger there and grieve,
  As if they loved in vain!
And yet so sweet the tears they shed,
'Tis sorrow so unmix'd with dread,
They scarce can bear the morn to break
  That melancholy spell,
And longer yet would weep and wake
  He sings so wild and well!
But when the day-blush bursts from
  high   705
  Expires that magic melody.
And some have been who could believe,
(So fondly youthful dreams deceive,
  Yet harsh be they that blame,)
That note so piercing and profound
Will shape and syllable its sound   710
  Into Zuleika's name.
'Tis from her cypress summit heard,
  That melts in air the liquid word:
'Tis from her lowly virgin earth   715
  That white rose takes its tender birth.
There late was laid a marble stone;
Eve saw it placed—the Morrow gone!
It was no mortal arm that bore
  That deep-fix'd pillar to the shore;
For there, as Helle's legends tell,   721
Next morn 'twas found where Selim fell;
Lash'd by the tumbling tide, whose
  wave
Denied his bones a holier grave:
And there by night, reclin'd, 'tis said,
Is seen a ghastly turban'd head: 726
  And hence extended by the billow,
  'Tis named the 'Pirate-phantom's
    pillow!'
    Where first it lay that mourning flower
    Hath flourish'd; flourisheth this hour,
Alone and dewy, coldly pure and pale:
As weeping Beauty's cheek at Sorrow's
  tale!   732

THE CORSAIR

A TALE

——'I suoi pensieri in lui dormir non ponno.'
TASSO, *Gerusalemne Liberata*, canto X.

TO

THOMAS MOORE, ESQ.

MY DEAR MOORE,

I DEDICATE to you the last production with which I shall trespass on public patience, and your indulgence, for some years; and I own that I feel anxious to avail myself of this latest and only opportunity of adorning my pages with a name, consecrated by unshaken public principle, and the most undoubted and various talents. While Ireland ranks you among the firmest of her patriots; while you stand alone the first of her bards in her estimation, and Britain repeats and ratifies the decree, permit me, whose only regret, since our first acquaintance, has been the years he had lost before it commenced, to add the humble but sincere suffrage of friendship to the voice of more than one nation. It will at least prove to you, that I have neither forgotten the gratification derived from your society, nor abandoned the prospect of its renewal, whenever your leisure or inclination allows you to atone to your friends for too long an absence. It is said among those friends, I trust truly, that you are engaged in the composition of a poem whose scene will be laid in the East; none can do those scenes so much justice. The wrongs of your own country, the magnificent and fiery spirit of her sons, the beauty and feeling of her daughters, may there be found; and Collins, when he denominated his Oriental his Irish Eclogues, was not aware how true, at least, was a part of his parallel. Your imagination will create a warmer sun, and less clouded sky; but wildness, tenderness, and originality, are part of your national claim of oriental descent, to which you have already thus far proved your title more clearly than the most zealous of your country's antiquarians.

May I add a few words on a subject on which all men are supposed to be fluent, and none agreeable?
—Self. I have written much, and published more than enough to demand a longer silence than I now meditate; but, for some years to come, it is my intention to tempt no further the award of 'Gods, men, nor columns.' In the present composition I have attempted not the most difficult, but, perhaps the best adapted measure to our language, the good old and now neglected heroic couplet. The stanza of Spenser is perhaps too slow and dignified for narrative; though, I confess, it is the measure most after my own heart: Scott alone, of the present generation, has hitherto completely triumphed over the fatal facility of the octo-syllabic verse; and this is not the least victory of his fertile and mighty genius: in blank verse, Milton, Thomson, and our dramatists, are the beacons that shine along the deep, but warn us from the rough and barren rock on which they are kindled. The heroic couplet is not the most popular measure certainly; but as I did not deviate into the other from a wish to flatter what is called public opinion, I shall quit it without further apology, and take my chance once more with that versification, in which I have hitherto published nothing but compositions whose former circulation is part of my present, and will be of my future regret.

With regard to my story, and stories in general, I should have been glad to have rendered my personages more perfect and amiable, if possible, inasmuch as I have been sometimes criticised, and considered no less responsible for their deeds and qualities than if all had been personal. Be it so— if I have deviated into the gloomy vanity of 'drawing from self,' the pictures are probably like, since they are unfavourable; and if not, those who know me are undeceived, and those who do not, I have little interest in undeceiving. I have no particular desire that any but my acquaintance should think the author better than the beings of his imagining; but I cannot help a little surprise, and perhaps amusement, at some odd critical exceptions in the present instance, when I see several bards (far more deserving, I allow) in very reputable plight, and quite exempted from all participation in the faults of those heroes, who, nevertheless, might be found with little more morality than 'The Giaour,' and perhaps—but no—I must admit Childe Harold to be a very repulsive personage; and as to his identity, those who like it must give him whatever 'alias' they please.

If, however, it were worth while to remove the impression, it might be of some service to me, that the man who is alike the delight of his readers and his friends, the poet of all circles, and the idol of his own, permits me here and elsewhere to subscribe myself,

Most truly,
And affectionately,
His obedient servant,
BYRON.

January 2, 1814.

THE CORSAIR

CANTO THE FIRST

'————nessun maggior dolore,
Che ricordarsi del tempo felice
Nelle miseria,————'—DANTE.

I

'O'ER the glad waters of the dark blue
sea,
Our thoughts as boundless, and our souls
as free,
Far as the breeze can bear, the billows
foam,
Survey our empire, and behold our home!
These are our realms, no limits to their
sway—   5
Our flag the sceptre all who meet obey.
Ours the wild life in tumult still to range
From toil to rest, and joy in every change.
Oh, who can tell? not thou, luxurious
slave!
Whose soul would sicken o'er the heaving
wave;   10
Not thou, vain lord of wantonness and
ease!
Whom slumber soothes not—pleasure
cannot please—
Oh, who can tell, save he whose heart hath
tried,
And danced in triumph o'er the waters
wide,
The exulting sense—the pulse's madden-
ing play,   15
That thrills the wanderer of that trackless
way?
That for itself can woo the approaching
fight,
And turn what some deem danger to de-
light;
That seeks what cravens shun with more
than zeal,   19
And where the feebler faint can only feel—
Feel—to the rising bosom's inmost core,
Its hope awaken and its spirit soar?
No dread of death if with us die our foes—
Save that it seems even duller than re-
pose:
Come when it will—we snatch the life of
life—   25
When lost—what recks it by disease or
strife?
Let him who crawls enamour'd of decay,
Cling to his couch, and sicken years away:
Heave his thick breath, and shake his
palsied head;
Ours—the fresh turf, and not the feverish
bed.   30
While gasp by gasp he falters forth his
soul,
Ours with one pang—one bound—escapes
control.

His corse may boast its urn and narrow
cave,
And they who loath'd his life may gild his
grave:
Ours are the tears, though few, sincerely
shed,   35
When Ocean shrouds and sepulchres our
dead.
For us, even banquets fond regret supply
In the red cup that crowns our memory;
And the brief epitaph in danger's day,
When those who win at length divide the
prey,   40
And cry, Remembrance saddening o'er
each brow,
How had the brave who fell exulted now!

II

Such were the notes that from the Pirate's
isle
Around the kindling watch-fire rang the
while:
Such were the sounds that thrill'd the
rocks along,   45
And unto ears as rugged seem'd a song!
In scatter'd groups upon the golden sand
They game—carouse—converse—or whet
the brand:
Select the arms—to each his blade assign,
And careless eye the blood that dims its
shine;   50
Repair the boat, replace the helm or oar,
While others straggling muse along the
shore;
For the wild bird the busy springes set,
Or spread beneath the sun the dripping
net:
Gaze where some distant sail a speck
supplies,   55
With all the thirsting eye of Enterprise;
Tell o'er the tales of many a night of toil,
And marvel where they next shall seize a
spoil:
No matter where—their chief's allotment
this;
Theirs, to believe no prey nor plan amiss.
But who that CHIEF? his name on every
shore   61
Is famed and fear'd—they ask and know
no more.
With these he mingles not but to com-
mand;
Few are his words, but keen his eye and
hand.
Ne'er seasons he with mirth their jovial
mess,   65
But they forgive his silence for success.
Ne'er for his lip the purpling cup they
fill,
That goblet passes him untasted still—

278

And for his fare—the rudest of his crew
Would that, in turn, have pass'd untasted
     too;   70
Earth's coarsest bread, the garden's home-
     liest roots,
And scarce the summer luxury of fruits,
His short repast in humbleness supply
With all a hermit's board would scarce
     deny.
But while he shuns the grosser joys of
     sense,   75
His mind seems nourish'd by that absti-
     nence.
'Steer to that shore!'—they sail. 'Do
     this!'—'tis done:
'Now form and follow me!'—the spoil
     is won.
Thus prompt his accents and his actions
     still,
And all obey and few inquire his will;   80
To such, brief answer and contemptuous
     eye
Convey reproof, nor further deign reply.

III

'A sail!—a sail!'—a promised prize to
     Hope!
Her nation—flag—how speaks the tele-
     scope?
No prize, alas! but yet a welcome sail: 85
The blood-red signal glitters in the gale.
Yes—she is ours—a home - returning
     bark—
Blow fair, thou breeze!—she anchors ere
     the dark.
Already doubled is the cape—our bay
Receives that prow which proudly spurns
     the spray.
How gloriously her gallant course she goes!
Her white wings flying—never from her
     foes—
She walks the waters like a thing of life,
And seems to dare the elements to strife.
Who would not brave the battle-fire, the
     wreck,   95
To move the monarch of her peopled
     deck?

IV

Hoarse o'er her side the rustling cable
     rings;
The sails are furl'd; and anchoring round
     she swings;
And gathering loiterers on the land dis-
     cern
Her boat descending from the latticed
     stern.   100
'Tis mann'd—the oars keep concert to the
     strand,
Till grates her keel upon the shallow sand.
Hail to the welcome shout!—the friendly
     speech!
When hand grasps hand uniting on the
     beach;

The smile, the question, and the quick
     reply,   105
And the heart's promise of festivity!

V

The tidings spread, and gathering grows
     the crowd;
The hum of voices, and the laughter loud,
And woman's gentler anxious tone is
     heard—
Friends', husbands', lovers' names in each
     dear word: 110
'Oh! are they safe? we ask not of suc-
     cess—
But shall we see them? will their accents
     bless?
From where the battle roars, the billows
     chafe,
They doubtless boldly did—but who are
     safe?
Here let them haste to gladden and sur-
     prise,   115
And kiss the doubt from these delighted
     eyes!'

VI

'Where is our chief? for him we bear re-
     port—
And doubt that joy—which hails our
     coming—short;
Yet thus sincere, 'tis cheering, though so
     brief;
But, Juan! instant guide us to our chief:
Our greeting paid, we'll feast on our re-
     turn,   121
And all shall hear what each may wish to
     learn.'
Ascending slowly by the rock-hewn way,
To where his watch-tower beetles o'er the
     bay,
By bushy brake, and wild flowers blossom-
     ing,   125
And freshness breathing from each silver
     spring,
Whose scatter'd streams from granite
     basins burst,
Leap into life, and sparkling woo your
     thirst;
From crag to cliff they mount—Near
     yonder cave,
What lonely straggler looks along the
     wave?   130
In pensive posture leaning on the brand,
Not oft a resting-staff to that red hand?
''Tis he—'tis Conrad—here, as wont,
     alone;
On—Juan!—on—and make our purpose
     known.
The bark he views—and tell him we would
     greet   135
His ear with tidings he must quickly meet:
We dare not yet approach—thou know'st
     his mood
When strange or uninvited steps intrude.'

VII

Him Juan sought, and told of their intent;—
He spake not, but a sign express'd assent.
These Juan calls—they come—to their salute   141
He bends him slightly, but his lips are mute.
'These letters, Chief, are from the Greek
—the spy,
Who still proclaims our spoil or peril nigh:
Whate'er his tidings, we can well report,
Much that'—'Peace, peace!'—he cuts their prating short.   146
Wondering they turn, abash'd, while each to each
Conjecture whispers in his muttering speech:
They watch his glance with many a stealing look,
To gather how that eye the tidings took;
But, this as if he guess'd, with head aside,
Perchance from some emotion, doubt, or pride,   152
He read the scroll—'My tablets, Juan, hark—
Where is Gonsalvo?'
                    'In the anchor'd bark.'
'There let him stay—to him this order bear—   155
Back to your duty—for my course prepare:
Myself this enterprise to-night will share.'

'To-night, Lord Conrad!'
                    'Ay! at set of sun:
The breeze will freshen when the day is done.
My corslet, cloak—one hour and we are gone.   160
Sling on thy bugle—see that free from rust
My carbine-lock springs worthy of my trust;
Be the edge sharpen'd of my boarding-brand,
And give its guard more room to fit my hand.
This let the armourer with speed dispose;
Last time, it more fatigued my arm than foes: 166
Mark that the signal-gun be duly fired,
To tell us when the hour of stay's expired.'

VIII

They make obeisance, and retire in haste,
Too soon to seek again the watery waste:
Yet they repine not—so that Conrad guides;   171
And who dare question aught that he decides?
That man of loneliness and mystery
Scarce seen to smile, and seldom heard to sigh;

Whose name appals the fiercest of his crew,   175
And tints each swarthy cheek with sallower hue;
Still sways their souls with that commanding art
That dazzles, leads, yet chills the vulgar heart.
What is that spell, that thus his lawless train
Confess and envy, yet oppose in vain?
What should it be, that thus their faith can bind?   181
The power of Thought—the magic of the Mind!
Link'd with success, assumed and kept with skill,
That moulds another's weakness to its will;
Wields with their hands, but, still to these unknown,   185
Makes even their mightiest deeds appear his own.
Such hath it been—shall be—beneath the sun
The many still must labour for the one!
'Tis Nature's doom—but let the wretch who toils
Accuse not, hate not *him* who wears the spoils.   190
Oh! if he knew the weight of splendid chains,
How light the balance of his humbler pains!

IX

Unlike the heroes of each ancient race,
Demons in act, but Gods at least in face,
In Conrad's form seems little to admire,
Though his dark eyebrow shades a glance of fire: 196
Robust but not Herculean—to the sight
No giant frame sets forth his common height;
Yet, in the whole, who paused to look again,
Saw more than marks the crowd of vulgar men;   200
They gaze and marvel how—and still confess
That thus it is, but why they cannot guess.
Sun-burnt his cheek, his forehead high and pale
The sable curls in wild profusion veil;
And oft perforce his rising lip reveals   205
The haughtier thought it curbs, but scarce conceals.
Though smooth his voice, and calm his general mien,
Still seems there something he would not have seen:
His features' deepening lines and varying hue
At times attracted, yet perplex'd the view,

As if within that murkiness of mind   211
Work'd feelings fearful, and yet unde-
    fined;
Such might it be—that none could truly
    tell—
Too close inquiry his stern glance would
    quell.
There breathe but few whose aspect might
    defy   215
The full encounter of his searching eye;
He had the skill, when Cunning's gaze
    would seek
To probe his heart and watch his chang-
    ing cheek,
At once the observer's purpose to espy,
And on himself roll back his scrutiny,
Lest he to Conrad rather should betray
Some secret thought, than drag that chief's
    to day.
There was a laughing Devil in his sneer,
That raised emotions both of rage and fear;
And where his frown of hatred darkly
    fell,   225
Hope withering fled, and Mercy sigh'd
    farewell!

X

Slight are the outward signs of evil
    thought,
Within—within—'twas there the spirit
    wrought!
Love shows all changes—Hate, Ambition,
    Guile,
Betray no further than the bitter smile;
The lip's least curl, the lightest paleness
    thrown   231
Along the govern'd aspect, speak alone
Of deeper passions; and to judge their
    mien,
He, who would see, must be himself un-
    seen.
Then—with the hurried tread, the up-
    ward eye,   235
The clenchèd hand, the pause of agony,
That listens, starting, lest the step too near
Approach intrusive on that mood of fear;
Then—with each feature working from
    the heart,
With feelings, loosed to strengthen—not
    depart,   240
That rise, convulse, contend—that freeze,
    or glow,
Flush in the cheek, or damp upon the
    brow,
Then, Stranger! if thou canst, and tremb-
    lest not,
Behold his soul—the rest that soothes his
    lot!
Mark how that lone and blighted bosom
    sears   245
The scathing thought of execrated years!
Behold—but who hath seen, or e'er shall
    see,
Man as himself—the secret spirit free?

XI

Yet was not Conrad thus by Nature sent
To lead the guilty—guilt's worse instru-
    ment—   250
His soul was changed, before his deeds
    had driven
Him forth to war with man and forfeit
    heaven.
Warp'd by the world in Disappointment's
    school,
In words too wise, in conduct *there* a fool;
Too firm to yield, and far too proud to
    stoop,   255
Doom'd by his very virtues for a dupe,
He cursed those virtues as the cause of ill,
And not the traitors who betray'd him
    still;
Nor deem'd that gifts bestow'd on better
    men
Had left him joy, and means to give
    again.   260
Fear'd, shunn'd, belied, ere youth had
    lost her force,
He hated man too much to feel remorse,
And thought the voice of wrath a sacred
    call,
To pay the injuries of some on all.
He knew himself a villain—but he deem'd
The rest no better than the thing he
    seem'd;   266
And scorn'd the best as hypocrites who hid
Those deeds the bolder spirit plainly did.
He knew himself detested, but he knew
The hearts that loath'd him, crouch'd
    and dreaded too.   270
Lone, wild, and strange, he stood alike
    exempt
From all affection and from all contempt;
His name could sadden, and his acts sur-
    prise;
But they that fear'd him dared not to
    despise;
Man spurns the worm, but pauses ere he
    wake   275
The slumbering venom of the folded
    snake:
The first may turn, but not avenge the
    blow;
The last expires, but leaves no living foe;
Fast to the doom'd offender's form it
    clings,
And he may crush—not conquer—still it
    stings!   280

XII

None are all evil—quickening round his
    heart
One softer feeling would not yet depart;
Oft could he sneer at others as beguiled
By passions worthy of a fool or child;
Yet 'gainst that passion vainly still he
    strove,   285
And even in him it asks the name of Love!

Yes, it was love—unchangeable—un-
  changed,
Felt but for one from whom he never
  ranged;
Though fairest captives daily met his eye,
He shunn'd, nor sought, but coldly pass'd
  them by;   290
Though many a beauty droop'd in pri-
  son'd bower,
None ever sooth'd his most unguarded
  hour.
Yes—it was Love—if thoughts of tender-
  ness
Tried in temptation, strengthen'd by dis-
  tress,
Unmoved by absence, firm in every clime,
And yet—oh more than all! untired by
  time;   296
Which nor defeated hope, nor baffled
  wile,
Could render sullen were she near to
  smile,
Nor rage could fire, nor sickness fret to
  vent
On her one murmur of his discontent;
Which still would meet with joy, with
  calmness part,   301
Lest that his look of grief should reach
  her heart;
Which nought removed, nor menaced to
  remove—
If there be love in mortals—this was love!
He was a villain—ay, reproaches shower
On him—but not the passion, nor its
  power,   306
Which only proved, all other virtues gone,
Not guilt itself could quench this love-
  liest one!

XIII

He paused a moment—till his hastening
  men
Pass'd the first winding downward to the
  glen.   310
'Strange tidings!—many a peril have I
  pass'd,
Nor know I why this next appears the last!
Yet so my heart forebodes, but must not
  fear,
Nor shall my followers find me falter here.
'Tis rash to meet, but surer death to
  wait   315
Till here they hunt us to undoubted fate;
And, if my plan but hold, and Fortune
  smile,
We'll furnish mourners for our funeral
  pile.
Ay, let them slumber—peaceful be their
  dreams!
Morn ne'er awoke them with such brilliant
  beams   320
As kindle high to-night (but blow, thou
  breeze!)
To warm these slow avengers of the seas.

Now to Medora—Oh! my sinking heart,
Long may her own be lighter than thou
  art!
Yet was I brave—mean boast where all
  are brave!   325
Ev'n insects sting for aught they seek to
  save.
This common courage which with brutes
  we share,
That owes its deadliest efforts to despair,
Small merit claims—but 'twas my nobler
  hope
To teach my few with numbers still to
  cope;   330
Long have I led them—not to vainly
  bleed:
No medium now—we perish or succeed;
So let it be—it irks not me to die;
But thus to urge them whence they cannot
  fly.
My lot hath long had little of my care, 335
But chafes my pride thus baffled in the
  snare:
Is this my skill? my craft? to set at last
Hope, power, and life upon a single cast?
Oh, Fate!—accuse thy folly, not thy fate!
She may redeem thee still, nor yet too
  late.'   340

XIV

Thus with himself communion held he, till
He reach'd the summit of his tower-
  crown'd hill:
There at the portal paused—for wild and
  soft
He heard those accents never heard too
  oft;
Through the high lattice far yet sweet they
  rung,   345
And these the notes his bird of beauty
  sung:

1

'Deep in my soul that tender secret dwells,
  Lonely and lost to light for evermore,
Save when to thine my heart responsive
  swells,   349
  Then trembles into silence as before.

2

'There, in its centre, a sepulchral lamp
  Burns the slow flame, eternal, but un-
    seen;
Which not the darkness of despair can
  damp,
  Though vain its ray as it had never been.

3

'Remember me—Oh! pass not thou my
  grave   355
  Without one thought whose relics there
    recline.
The only pang my bosom dare not brave
  Must be to find forgetfulness in thine.

4

'My fondest, faintest, latest accents
    hear—
    Grief for the dead not virtue can re-
    prove;   360
Then give me all I ever ask'd—a tear,
    The first—last—sole reward of so much
    love!'

He pass'd the portal, cross'd the corridor,
And reach'd the chamber as the strain
    gave o'er—
'My own Medora! sure thy song is
    sad—'   365

'In Conrad's absence wouldst thou have
    it glad!
Without thine ear to listen to my lay,
Still must my song my thoughts, my soul
    betray:
Still must each action to my bosom suit,
My heart unhush'd, although my lips were
    mute!   370
Oh! many a night on this lone couch re-
    clined,
My dreaming fear with storms hath wing'd
    the wind,
And deem'd the breath that faintly fann'd
    thy sail
The murmuring prelude of the ruder gale;
Though soft, it seem'd the low prophetic
    dirge,   375
That mourn'd thee floating on the savage
    surge;
Still would I rise to rouse the beacon fire,
Lest spies less true should let the blaze
    expire;
And many a restless hour outwatch'd each
    star,
And morning came—and still thou wert
    afar.   380
Oh! how the chill blast on my bosom
    blew,
And day broke dreary on my troubled
    view,
And still I gazed and gazed—and not a
    prow
Was granted to my tears, my truth, my
    vow!
At length 'twas noon—I hail'd and blest
    the mast   385
That met my sight—it near'd—Alas! it
    pass'd!
Another came—Oh God! 'twas thine at
    last!
Would that those days were over! wilt
    thou ne'er,
My Conrad! learn the joys of peace to
    share?
Sure thou hast more than wealth, and
    many a home   390
As bright as this invites us not to roam:
Thou know'st it is not peril that I fear,
I only tremble when thou art not here;

Then not for mine, but that far dearer
    life,
Which flies from love and languishes for
    strife—   395
How strange that heart, to me so tender
    still,
Should war with nature and its better
    will!'

'Yea, strange indeed—that heart hath
    long been changed;
Worm-like 'twas trampled, adder-like
    avenged,
Without one hope on earth beyond thy
    love,   400
And scarce a glimpse of mercy from above.
Yet the same feeling which thou dost con-
    demn,
My very love to thee is hate to them,
So closely mingling here, that disen-
    twined,
I cease to love thee when I love mankind:
Yet dread not this—the proof of all the
    past   406
Assures the future that my love will last;
But—oh, Medora! nerve thy gentler heart;
This hour again—but not for long—we
    part.'

'This hour we part—my heart foreboded
    this: 410
Thus ever fade my fairy dreams of bliss.
This hour—it cannot be—this hour
    away!
Yon bark hath hardly anchor'd in the
    bay:
Her consort still is absent, and her crew
Have need of rest before they toil anew:
My love! thou mock'st my weakness; and
    wouldst steel   416
My breast before the time when it must feel;
But trifle now no more with my distress,
Such mirth hath less of play than bitter-
    ness.
Be silent, Conrad!—dearest! come and
    share   420
The feast these hands delighted to pre-
    pare;
Light toil! to cull and dress thy frugal fare!
See, I have pluck'd the fruit that promised
    best,
And where not sure, perplex'd, but pleased,
    I guess'd
At such as seem'd the fairest; thrice the
    hill   425
My steps have wound to try the coolest
    rill;
Yes! thy sherbet to-night will sweetly flow,
See how it sparkles in its vase of snow!
The grapes' gay juice thy bosom never
    cheers;
Thou more than Moslem when the cup
    appears: 430
Think not I mean to chide—for I rejoice
What others deem a penance is thy choice.

But come, the board is spread; our silver
    lamp
Is trimm'd, and heeds not the sirocco's
    damp:
Then shall my handmaids while the time
    along,   435
And join with me the dance, or wake the
    song;
Or my guitar, which still thou lov'st to
    hear,
Shall soothe or lull—or, should it vex
    thine ear,
We'll turn the tale, by Ariosto told,
Of fair Olympia loved and left of old.
Why, thou wert worse than he who broke
    his vow   441
To that lost damsel, shouldst thou leave
    me now;
Or even that traitor chief—I've seen thee
    smile,
When the clear sky show'd Ariadne's
    Isle,
Which I have pointed from these cliffs the
    while;   445
And thus half sportive, half in fear, I
    said,
Lest time should raise that doubt to more
    than dread,
Thus Conrad, too, will quit me for the
    main;
And he deceived me—for he came again!'

'Again, again—and oft again—my love!
If there be life below, and hope above,
He will return—but now, the moments
    bring   452
The time of parting with redoubled wing:
The why, the where—what boots it now
    to tell?
Since all must end in that wild word—
    farewell!
Yet would I fain—did time allow—dis-
    close—   456
Fear not—these are no formidable foes;
And here shall watch a more than wonted
    guard,
For sudden siege and long defence pre-
    pared:
Nor be thou lonely, though thy lord's
    away,   460
Our matrons and thy handmaids with
    thee stay;
And this thy comfort—that, when next
    we meet,
Security shall make repose more sweet.
List!—'tis the bugle!'—Juan shrilly
    blew—
'One kiss—one more—another—Oh!
    Adieu!'   465

She rose—she sprung—she clung to his
    embrace,
Till his heart heaved beneath her hidden
    face:

He dared not raise to his that deep-blue
    eye,
Which downcast droop'd in tearless
    agony.
Her long fair hair lay floating o'er his
    arms,   470
In all the wildness of dishevell'd charms;
Scarce beat that bosom where his image
    bore
So full—*that* feeling seem'd almost un-
    felt!
Hark—peals the thunder of the signal-
    gun!
It told 'twas sunset, and he cursed that
    sun.   475
Again—again—that form he madly
    press'd,
Which mutely clasp'd, imploringly car-
    ess'd!
And tottering to the couch his bride he
    bore,
One moment gazed, as if to gaze no more;
Felt that for him earth held but her
    alone,   480
Kiss'd her cold forehead—turn'd—is Con-
    rad gone?

XV

'And is he gone?' on sudden solitude
How oft that fearful question will intrude!
'Twas but an instant past, and here he
    stood!
And now'—without the portal's porch
    she rush'd,   485
And then at length her tears in freedom
    gush'd;
Big, bright, and fast, unknown to her they
    fell;
But still her lips refused to send—'Fare-
    well!'
For in that word—that fatal word—how-
    e'er
We promise, hope, believe, there breathes
    despair.   490
O'er every feature of that still, pale face,
Had sorrow fix'd what time can ne'er
    erase:
The tender blue of that large loving eye
Grew frozen with its gaze on vacancy,
Till—Oh, how far!—it caught a glimpse
    of him,   495
And then it flow'd, and phrensied seem'd
    to swim,
Through those long, dark, and glistening
    lashes dew'd
With drops of sadness oft to be renew'd.
'He's gone!'—against her heart that
    hand is driven,
Convulsed and quick—then gently raised
    to heaven;   500
She look'd and saw the heaving of the
    main;
The white sail set—she dared not look
    again;

But turn'd with sickening soul within the
    gate—
'It is no dream—and I am desolate!'

XVI

From crag to crag descending, swiftly sped
Stern Conrad down, nor once he turn'd
    his head;   506
But shrunk whene'er the windings of his way
Forced on his eye what he would not
    survey,
His lone but lovely dwelling on the steep,
That hail'd him first when homeward from
    the deep: 510
And she—the dim and melancholy star,
Whose ray of beauty reach'd him from
    afar,
On her he must not gaze, he must not think,
There he might rest—but on Destruction's
    brink:
Yet once almost he stopp'd, and nearly
    gave   515
His fate to chance, his projects to the wave:
But no—it must not be—a worthy chief
May melt, but not betray to woman's
    grief.
He sees his bark, he notes how fair the
    wind,   519
And sternly gathers all his might of mind:
Again he hurries on—and as he hears
The clang of tumult vibrate on his ears,
The busy sounds, the bustle of the shore,
The shout, the signal, and the dashing oar,
As marks his eye the seaboy on the mast,
The anchors rise, the sails unfurling fast,
The waving kerchiefs of the crowd that
    urge
That mute adieu to those who stem the
    surge;
And more than all, his blood-red flag aloft,
He marvell'd how his heart could seem so
    soft.   530
Fire in his glance, and wildness in his
    breast,
He feels of all his former self possest;
He bounds—he flies—until his footsteps
    reach
The verge where ends the cliff, begins the
    beach,
There checks his speed; but pauses less to
    breathe   535
The breezy freshness of the deep beneath,
Than there his wonted statelier step renew;
Nor rush, disturb'd by haste, to vulgar
    view:
For well had Conrad learn'd to curb the
    crowd,
By arts that veil, and oft preserve the proud;
His was the lofty port, the distant mien,
That seems to shun the sight—and awes if
    seen: 542
The solemn aspect, and the high-born pride,
That checks low mirth, but lacks not
    courtesy;

All these he wielded to command assent:
But where he wish'd to win, so well unbent,
That kindness cancell'd fear in those who
    heard,   547
And others' gifts show'd mean beside his
    word,
When echo'd to the heart as from his own
His deep yet tender melody of tone:
But such was foreign to his wonted mood,
He cared not what he soften'd, but sub-
    dued: 552
The evil passions of his youth had made
Him value less who loved—than what
    obey'd.

XVII

Around him mustering ranged his ready
    guard,   555
Before him Juan stands—'Are all pre-
    pared?'

'They are—nay more—embark'd: the
    latest boat
Waits but my Chief——'
            'My sword, and my capote.'
Soon firmly girded on, and lightly slung,
His belt and cloak were o'er his shoulders
    flung: 560
'Call Pedro here!' He comes—and Con-
    rad bends,
With all the courtesy he deign'd his friends;
'Receive these tablets, and peruse with
    care,
Words of high trust and truth are graven
    there;
Double the guard, and when Anselmo's
    bark   565
Arrives, let him alike these orders mark:
In three days (serve the breeze) the sun
    shall shine
On our return—till then all peace be
    thine!'
This said, his brother Pirate's hand he
    wrung,
Then to his boat with haughty gesture
    sprung.   570
Flash'd the dipt oars, and sparkling with
    the stroke,
Around the waves' phosphoric brightness
    broke;
They gain the vessel—on the deck he
    stands,—
Shrieks the shrill whistle, ply the busy
    hands—
He marks how well the ship her helm
    obeys,   575
How gallant all her crew, and deigns to
    praise.
His eyes of pride to young Gonsalvo
    turn—
Why doth he start, and inly seem to
    mourn?
Alas! those eyes beheld his rocky tower
And live a moment o'er the parting hour;

She—his Medora—did she mark the
   prow?   581
Ah! never loved he half so much as now!
But much must yet be done ere dawn of
   day—
Again he mans himself and turns away;
Down to the cabin with Gonsalvo bends,
And there unfolds his plan, his means, and
   ends;   586
Before them burns the lamp, and spreads
   the chart,
And all that speaks and aids the naval art;
They to the midnight watch protract de-
   bate;
To anxious eyes what hour is ever late?
Meantime, the steady breeze serenely
   blew,   591
And fast and falcon-like the vessel flew;
Pass'd the high headlands of each cluster-
   ing isle,
To gain their port—long—long ere morn-
   ing smile:
And soon the night-glass through the
   narrow bay   595
Discovers where the Pacha's galleys lay.
Count they each sail, and mark how there
   supine
The lights in vain o'er heedless Moslem
   shine.
Secure, unnoted, Conrad's prow pass'd by,
And anchor'd where his ambush meant
   to lie;   600
Screen'd from espial by the jutting cape,
That rears on high its rude fantastic shape.
Then rose his band to duty—not from
   sleep—
Equipp'd for deeds alike on land or deep;
While lean'd their leader o'er the fretting
   flood,   605
And calmly talk'd—and yet he talk'd of
   blood!

CANTO THE SECOND

'Conosceste i dubiosi desiri?'—DANTE.

I

IN Coron's bay floats many a galley light,
Through Coron's lattices the lamps are
   bright,
For Seyd, the Pacha, makes a feast to-night:
A feast for promised triumph yet to come,
When he shall drag the fetter'd Rovers
   home;   5
This hath he sworn by Allah and his sword,
And faithful to his firman and his word,
His summon'd prows collect along the coast,
And great the gathering crews, and loud
   the boast;
Already shared the captives and the prize,
Though far the distant foe they thus
   despise;   11
'Tis but to sail—no doubt to-morrow's Sun
Will see the Pirates bound, their haven
   won!

Meantime the watch may slumber, if they
   will,
Nor only wake to war, but dreaming kill.
Though all, who can, disperse on shore
   and seek   16
To flesh their glowing valour on the Greek;
How well such deed becomes the turban'd
   brave—
To bare the sabre's edge before a slave!
Infest his dwelling—but forbear to slay,
Their arms are strong, yet merciful to-day,
And do not deign to smite because they
   may!   22
Unless some gay caprice suggests the blow,
To keep in practice for the coming foe.
Revel and rout the evening hours beguile,
And they who wish to wear a head must
   smile;   26
For Moslem mouths produce their choicest
   cheer,
And hoard their curses, till the coast is
   clear.

II

High in his hall reclines the turban'd Seyd;
Around—the bearded chiefs he came to
   lead.   30
Removed the banquet, and the last pilaff—
Forbidden draughts, 'tis said, he dared to
   quaff,
Though to the rest the sober berry's juice
The slaves bear round for rigid Moslems'
   use;
The long chibouque's dissolving cloud
   supply,   35
While dance the Almas to wild minstrelsy.
The rising morn will view the chiefs em-
   bark;
But waves are somewhat treacherous in
   the dark:
And revellers may more securely sleep
On silken couch than o'er the rugged deep:
Feast there who can—nor combat till they
   must,   41
And less to conquest than to Korans trust:
And yet the numbers crowded in his host
Might warrant more than even the Pacha's
   boast.

III

With cautious reverence from the outer
   gate   45
Slow stalks the slave, whose office there to
   wait,
Bows his bent head, his hand salutes the
   floor,
Ere yet his tongue the trusted tidings bore:
'A captive Dervise, from the Pirate's nest
Escaped, is here—himself would tell the
   rest.'   50
He took the sign from Seyd's assenting eye,
And led the holy man in silence nigh.
His arms were folded on his dark-green vest,
His step was feeble, and his look deprest;

Yet worn he seem'd of hardship more than
  years,   55
And pale his cheek with penance, not from
  fears.
Vow'd to his God—his sable locks he
  wore,
And these his lofty cap rose proudly o'er:
Around his form his loose long robe was
  thrown,
And wrapt a breast bestow'd on heaven
  alone;   60
Submissive, yet with self-possession
  mann'd,
He calmly met the curious eyes that
  scann'd;
And question of his coming fain would
  seek,
Before the Pacha's will allow'd to speak.

IV

'Whence com'st thou, Dervise?'
              'From the outlaw's den,   65
A fugitive—'
      'Thy capture where and when?'
'From Scalanova's port to Scio's isle,
The Saick was bound; but Allah did not
  smile
Upon our course—the Moslem mer-
  chant's gains
The Rovers won; our limbs have worn
  their chains.   70
I had no death to fear, nor wealth to boast,
Beyond the wandering freedom which I
  lost;
At length a fisher's humble boat by night
Afforded hope, and offer'd chance of
  flight;
I seized the hour, and find my safety
  here—   75
With thee—most mighty Pacha! who can
  fear?'

'How speed the outlaws? stand they well
  prepared,
Their plunder'd wealth, and robber's rock,
  to guard?
Dream they of this our preparation,
  doom'd
To view with fire their scorpion nest consumed?'   80

'Pacha! the fetter'd captive's mourning eye,
That weeps for flight, but ill can play the
  spy;
I only heard the reckless waters roar,
Those waves that would not bear me from
  the shore;   84
I only mark'd the glorious sun and sky,
Too bright, too blue, for my captivity;
And felt that all which Freedom's bosom
  cheers,
Must break my chain before it dried my
  tears.

This may'st thou judge, at least, from my
  escape,
They little deem of aught in peril's shape;
Else vainly had I pray'd or sought the
  chance   91
That leads me here—if eyed with vigilance:
The careless guard that did not see me fly
May watch as idly when thy power is nigh.
Pacha! my limbs are faint—and nature
  craves   95
Food for my hunger, rest from tossing
  waves:
Permit my absence—peace be with thee!
  Peace
With all around!—now grant repose—
  release.'

'Stay, Dervise! I have more to question—
  stay,
I do command thee—sit—dost hear?—
  obey!   100
More I must ask, and food the slaves shall
  bring;
Thou shalt not pine where all are ban-
  queting:
The supper done—prepare thee to reply,
Clearly and full—I love not mystery.'
'Twere vain to guess what shook the pious
  man,   105
Who look'd not lovingly on that Divan;
Nor show'd high relish for the banquet
  prest,
And less respect for every fellow guest.
'Twas but a moment's peevish hectic pass'd
Along his cheek, and tranquillised as fast:
He sate him down in silence, and his look
Resumed the calmness which before for-
  sook: 112
The feast was usher'd in, but sumptuous fare
He shunn'd as if some poison mingled
  there.
For one so long condemn'd to toil and
  fast,   115
Methinks he strangely spares the rich re-
  past.

'What ails thee, Dervise? eat—dost thou
  suppose
This feast a Christian's? or my friends thy
  foes?
Why dost thou shun the salt? that sacred
  pledge,
Which, once partaken, blunts the sabre's
  edge,   120
Makes ev'n contending tribes in peace
  unite,
And hated hosts seem brethren to the
  sight!'

'Salt seasons dainties—and my food is still
The humblest root, my drink the simplest
  rill;
And my stern vow and order's laws oppose
To break or mingle bread with friends or
  foes;   126

287   L

It may seem strange—if there be aught to
   dread,
That peril rests upon my single head;
But for thy sway—nay more—thy Sultan's
   throne,
I taste nor bread nor banquet—save alone;
Infringed our order's rule, the Prophet's
   rage   131
To Mecca's dome might bar my pil-
   grimage.'

'Well—as thou wilt—ascetic as thou art—
One question answer; then in peace de-
   part.
How many?—Ha! it cannot sure be day?
What star—what sun is bursting on the
   bay?   136
It shines a lake of fire!—away—away!
Ho! treachery! my guards! my scimitar!
The galleys feed the flames—and I afar!
Accursed Dervise!—these thy tidings—
   thou   140
Some villain spy—seize—cleave him—
   slay him now!'

Up rose the Dervise with that burst of
   light,
Nor less his change of form appall'd the
   sight:
Up rose that Dervise—not in saintly garb,
But like a warrior bounding on his barb,
Dash'd his high cap, and tore his robe
   away—   146
Shone his mail'd breast, and flash'd his
   sabre's ray!
His close but glittering casque, and sable
   plume,
More glittering eye, and black brow's
   sabler gloom,
Glared on the Moslems' eyes some Afrit
   sprite,   150
Whose demon death-blow left no hope for
   fight.
The wild confusion, and the swarthy glow
Of flames on high, and torches from be-
   low;
The shriek of terror, and the mingling
   yell—
For swords began to clash, and shouts to
   swell—   155
Flung o'er that spot of earth the air of hell!
Distracted, to and fro, the flying slaves
Behold but bloody shore and fiery waves;
Nought heeded they the Pacha's angry cry,
They seize that Dervise!—seize on Za-
   tanai!   160
He saw their terror—check'd the first
   despair
That urged him but to stand and perish
   there,
Since far too early and too well obey'd,
The flame was kindled ere the signal made,
He saw their terror—from his baldric
   drew   165

His bugle—brief the blast—but shrilly
   blew;
'Tis answered—'Well ye speed, my gallant
   crew!
Why did I doubt their quickness of career?
And deem design had left me single here?'
Sweeps his long arm—that sabre's whirl-
   ing sway   170
Sheds fast atonement for its first delay;
Completes his fury what their fear begun,
And makes the many basely quail to one.
The cloven turbans o'er the chamber
   spread,
And scarce an arm dare rise to guard its
   head: 175
Even Seyd, convulsed, o'erwhelm'd, with
   rage, surprise,
Retreats before him, though he still defies.
No craven he—and yet he dreads the blow,
So much Confusion magnifies his foe!
His blazing galleys still distract his sight,
He tore his beard, and foaming fled the
   fight;   181
For now the pirates pass'd the Haram gate,
And burst within—and it were death to
   wait;
Where wild Amazement shrieking—kneel-
   ing throws
The sword aside—in vain—the blood o'er-
   flows!   185
The Corsairs pouring, haste to where
   within
Invited Conrad's bugle, and the din
Of groaning victims, and wild cries for life,
Proclaim'd how well he did the work of
   strife.
They shout to find him grim and lonely
   there,   190
A glutted tiger mangling in his lair!
But short their greeting, shorter his reply—
''Tis well—but Seyd escapes, and he must
   die—
Much hath been done, but more remains
   to do—
Their galleys blaze—why not their city
   too?'   195

V

Quick at the word they seized him each a
   torch,
And fire the dome from minaret to porch.
A stern delight was fix'd in Conrad's eye,
But sudden sunk—for on his ear the cry
Of women struck, and like a deadly knell
Knock'd at that heart unmoved by battle's
   yell.   201
'Oh! burst the Haram—wrong not on
   your lives
One female form—remember—*we* have
   wives.
On them such outrage Vengeance will repay;
Man is our foe, and such 'tis ours to slay:
But still we spared—must spare the weaker
   prey.   206

Oh! I forgot—but Heaven will not forgive
If at my word the helpless cease to live;
Follow who will—I go—we yet have time
Our souls to lighten of at least a crime.'
He climbs the crackling stair, he bursts the
    door,   211
Nor feels his feet glow scorching with the
    floor;
His breath choked gasping with the vol-
    umed smoke,
But still from room to room his way he
    broke.
They search—they find—they save: with
    lusty arms   215
Each bears a prize of unregarded charms;
Calm their loud fears; sustain their sinking
    frames
With all the care defenceless beauty
    claims:
So well could Conrad tame their fiercest
    mood,
And check the very hands with gore im-
    brued.   220
But who is she? whom Conrad's arms
    convey
From reeking pile and combat's wreck
    away—
Who but the love of him he dooms to
    bleed?
The Haram queen—but still the slave of
    Seyd!

VI

Brief time had Conrad now to greet
    Gulnare,   225
Few words to re-assure the trembling fair;
For in that pause compassion snatch'd
    from war,
The foe before retiring, fast and far,
With wonder saw their footsteps unpur-
    sued,
First slowlier fled—then rallied—then
    withstood.   230
This Seyd perceives, then first perceives
    how few,
Compared with his, the Corsair's roving
    crew,
And blushes o'er his error, as he eyes
The ruin wrought by panic and surprise.
Alla il Alla! Vengeance swells the cry—
Shame mounts to rage that must atone or
    die!   236
And flame for flame and blood for blood
    must tell,
The tide of triumph ebbs that flow'd too
    well—
When wrath returns to renovated strife,
And those who fought for conquest strike
    for life.   240
Conrad beheld the danger—he beheld
His followers faint by freshening foes re-
    pell'd:
'One effort—one—to break the circling
    host!'

They form—unite—charge—waver—all
    is lost!
Within a narrower ring compress'd, beset,
Hopeless, not heartless, strive and struggle
    yet—   246
Ah! now they fight in firmest file no more,
Hemm'd in, cut off, cleft down, and tram-
    pled o'er,
But each strikes singly, silently, and home,
And sinks outwearied rather than o'er-
    come,   250
His last faint quittance rendering with his
    breath,
Till the blade glimmers in the grasp of
    death!

VII

But first, ere came the rallying host to
    blows,
And rank to rank, and hand to hand
    oppose,
Gulnare and all her Haram handmaids
    freed,   255
Safe in the dome of one who held their
    creed,
By Conrad's mandate safely were be-
    stow'd,
And dried those tears for life and fame that
    flow'd:
And when that dark-eyed lady, young
    Gulnare,
Recall'd those thoughts late wandering in
    despair,   260
Much did she marvel o'er the courtesy
That smooth'd his accents, soften'd in his
    eye:
'Twas strange—that robber thus with gore
    bedew'd
Seem'd gentler then than Seyd in fondest
    mood.
The Pacha woo'd as if he deem'd the slave
Must seem delighted with the heart he
    gave;   266
The Corsair vow'd protection, soothed af-
    fright,
As if his homage were a woman's right.
'The wish is wrong—nay, worse for fe-
    male—vain: 269
Yet much I long to view that chief again;
If but to thank for, what my fear forgot,
The life my loving lord remember'd not!'

VIII

And him she saw, where thickest carnage
    spread,
But gather'd breathing from the happier
    dead;
Far from his band, and battling with a
    host   275
That deem right dearly won the field he lost,
Fell'd—bleeding—baffled of the death he
    sought,
And snatch'd to expiate all the ills he
    wrought;

Preserved to linger and to live in vain,
While Vengeance ponder'd o'er new plans
    of pain,   280
And stanch'd the blood she saves to shed
    again—
But drop for drop, for Seyd's unglutted
    eye
Would doom him ever dying—ne'er to
    die!
Can this be he? triumphant late she saw,
When his red hand's wild gesture waved
    a law!   285
'Tis he indeed—disarm'd but undeprest,
His sole regret the life he still possest;
His wounds too slight, though taken with
    that will,
Which would have kiss'd the hand that
    then could kill.
Oh were there none, of all the many given,
To send his soul—he scarcely ask'd to
    heaven?   291
Must he alone of all retain his breath,
Who more than all had striven and struck
    for death?
He deeply felt—what mortal hearts must
    feel,
When thus reversed on faithless fortune's
    wheel,   295
For crimes committed, and the victor's
    threat
Of lingering tortures to repay the debt—
He deeply, darkly felt; but evil pride
That led to perpetrate, now serves to
    hide.
Still in his stern and self-collected mien
A conqueror's more than captive's air is
    seen,   301
Though faint with wasting toil and stiffen-
    ing wound,
But few that saw—so calmly gazed
    around:
Though the far shouting of the distant
    crowd,   304
Their tremors o'er, rose insolently loud,
The better warriors who beheld him near,
Insulted not the foe who taught them fear;
And the grim guards that to his durance
    led,
In silence eyed him with a secret dread.

IX

The Leech was sent—but not in mercy—
    there,   310
To note how much the life yet left could
    bear;
He found enough to load with heaviest
    chain,
And promise feeling for the wrench of
    pain;
To-morrow—yea—to-morrow's evening
    sun
Will sinking see impalement's pangs
    begun,   315
And rising with the wonted blush of morn

Behold how well or ill those pangs are
    borne.
Of torments this the longest and the worst,
Which adds all other agony to thirst,
That day by day death still forbears to
    slake,   320
While famish'd vultures flit around the
    stake.
'Oh! water—water!'—smiling   Hate
    denies
The victim's prayer, for if he drinks he
    dies.
This was his doom;—the Leech, the guard
    were gone,
And left proud Conrad fetter'd and alone.

X

'Twere vain to paint to what his feelings
    grew—   326
It even were doubtful if their victim knew.
There is a war, a chaos of the mind,
When all its elements convulsed, com-
    bined,
Lie dark and jarring with perturbed force,
And gnashing with impenitent Remorse—
That juggling fiend, who never spake
    before,   332
But cries 'I warn'd thee!' when the deed
    is o'er.
Vain voice! the spirit burning but unbent,
May writhe, rebel—the weak alone repent!
Even in that lonely hour when most it
    feels,   336
And, to itself, all, all that self reveals,—
No single passion, and no ruling thought
That leaves the rest, as once, unseen, un-
    sought,
But the wild prospect when the soul re-
    views,   340
All rushing through their thousand
    avenues—
Ambition's dreams expiring, love's regret,
Endanger'd glory, life itself beset;
The joy untasted, the contempt or hate
'Gainst those who fain would triumph in
    our fate;   345
The hopeless past, the hasting future
    driven
Too quickly on to guess of hell or heaven;
Deeds, thoughts, and words, perhaps re-
    member'd not
So keenly till that hour, but ne'er forgot;
Things light or lovely in their acted time,
But now to stern reflection each a crime;
The withering sense of evil unreveal'd,
Not cankering less because the more con-
    ceal'd—   353
All, in a word, from which all eyes must
    start,
That opening sepulchre—the naked heart
Bares with its buried woes, till Pride
    awake,   356
To snatch the mirror from the soul—and
    break.

Ay, Pride can veil, and Courage brave it
    all—
All—all—before—beyond—the   deadliest
    fall.
Each hath some fear, and he who least
    betrays,   360
The only hypocrite deserving praise:
Not the loud recreant wretch who boasts
    and flies;
But he who looks on death—and silent dies.
So steel'd by pondering o'er his far career,
He half-way meets him should he menace
    near!   365

XI

In the high chamber of his highest tower
Sate Conrad, fetter'd in the Pacha's power.
His palace perish'd in the flame—this fort
Contain'd at once his captive and his
    court.
Not much could Conrad of his sentence
    blame,   370
His foe, if vanquish'd, had but shared the
    same:—
Alone he sate—in solitude had scann'd
His guilty bosom, but that breast he
    mann'd:
One thought alone he could not—dared
    not meet—
'Oh, how these tidings will Medora greet?'
Then—only then—his clanking hands he
    raised,   376
And strain'd with rage the chain on which
    he gazed;
But soon he found, or feign'd, or dream'd
    relief,
And smiled in self-derision of his grief,
'And now come torture when it will—or
    may,   380
More need of rest to nerve me for the day!'
This said, with languor to his mat he crept,
And, whatsoe'er his visions, quickly slept.

'Twas hardly midnight when that fray
    begun,
For Conrad's plans matured, at once were
    done: 385
And Havoc loathes so much the waste of
    time,
She scarce had left an uncommitted crime.
One hour beheld him since the tide he
    stemm'd—
Disguised, discover'd, conquering, ta'en,
    condemn'd—   389
A chief on land, an outlaw on the deep—
Destroying, saving, prison'd, and asleep!

XII

He slept in calmest seeming, for his breath
Was hush'd so deep—Ah! happy if in
    death!
He slept—Who o'er his placid slumber
    bends?
His foes are gone, and here he hath no
    friends;   395

Is it some seraph sent to grant him grace?
No, 'tis an earthly form with heavenly
    face!
Its white arm raised a lamp—yet gently hid,
Lest the ray flash abruptly on the lid
Of that closed eye, which opens but to
    pain,   400
And once unclosed—but once may close
    again.
That form, with eye so dark, and cheek so
    fair,
And auburn waves of gemm'd and braided
    hair;
With shape of fairy lightness—naked foot,
That shines like snow, and falls on earth as
    mute—   405
Through guards and dunnest night how
    came it there?
Ah! rather ask what will not woman dare?
Whom youth and pity lead like thee,
    Gulnare!
She   could   not   sleep—and   while   the
    Pacha's rest
In muttering dreams yet saw his pirate-
    guest,   410
She left his side—his signet-ring she bore,
Which oft in sport adorn'd her hand
    before—
And with it, scarcely question'd, won her
    way
Through drowsy guards that must that
    sign obey.
Worn out with toil, and tired with chang-
    ing blows,   415
Their eyes had envied Conrad his repose;
And chill and nodding at the turret door,
They stretch their listless limbs, and watch
    no more;
Just raised their heads to hail the signet-
    ring,
Nor ask or what or who the sign may
    bring.   420

XIII

She gazed in wonder, 'Can he calmly sleep,
While other eyes his fall or ravage weep?
And mine in restlessness are wandering
    here—
What sudden spell hath made this man so
    dear?
True—'tis to him my life, and more, I owe,
And me and mine he spared from worse
    than woe: 426
'Tis late to think—but soft, his slumber
    breaks—
How   heavily   he   sighs!—he   starts—
    awakes!'
He raised his head, and dazzled with the
    light,
His eye seem'd dubious if it saw aright:
He moved his hand—the grating of his
    chain   431
Too harshly told him that he lived again.

'What is that form? if not a shape of air,
Methinks, my jailor's face shows won-
    drous fair!'

'Pirate! thou know'st me not—but I am
    one,   435
Grateful for deeds thou hast too rarely
    done;
Look on me—and remember her, thy hand
Snatch'd from the flames, and thy more
    fearful band.
I come through darkness—and I scarce
    know why—
Yet not to hurt—I would not see thee die.'

'If so, kind lady! thine the only eye   441
That would not here in that gay hope de-
    light:
Theirs is the chance—and let them use
    their right.
But still I thank their courtesy or thine,
That would confess me at so fair a shrine!'

Strange though it seem—yet with extre-
    mest grief   446
Is link'd a mirth—it doth not bring relief—
That playfulness of Sorrow ne'er beguiles,
And smiles in bitterness—but still it
    smiles;
And sometimes with the wisest and the
    best,   450
Till even the scaffold echoes with their
    jest!
Yet not the joy to which it seems akin—
It may deceive all hearts, save that within.
Whate'er it was that flash'd on Conrad,
    now
A laughing wildness half unbent his brow
And these his accents had a sound of
    mirth,   456
As if the last he could enjoy on earth;
Yet 'gainst his nature—for through that
    short life,
Few thoughts had he to spare from gloom
    and strife.

XIV

'Corsair! thy doom is named—but I have
    power   460
To soothe the Pacha in his weaker hour.
Thee would I spare—nay more—would
    save thee now,
But this—time—hope—nor even thy
    strength allow;
But all I can, I will: at least, delay
The sentence that remits thee scarce a day.
More now were ruin—even thyself were
    loth   466
The vain attempt should bring but doom
    to both.'

'Yes! loth indeed:—my soul is nerved to
    all,
Or fall'n too low to fear a further fall:
Tempt not thyself with peril—me with
    hope   470

Of flight from foes with whom I could no
    cope:
Unfit to vanquish, shall I meanly fly,
The one of all my band that would not die
Yet there is one to whom my memor
    clings,
Till to these eyes her own wild softnes
    springs.   47
My sole resources in the path I trod
Were these—my bark, my sword, my love
    my God!
The last I left in youth!—he leaves m
    now—
And Man but works his will to lay me low
I have no thought to mock his throne wit
    prayer   48
Wrung from the coward crouching o
    despair;
It is enough—I breathe, and I can bear.
My sword is shaken from the worthles
    hand
That might have better kept so true
    brand;
My bark is sunk or captive—but m
    love—   48
For her in sooth my voice would mour
    above:
Oh! she is all that still to earth can bind
And this will break a heart so more tha
    kind,
And blight a form—till thine appear'c
    Gulnare!
Mine eye ne'er ask'd if others were a
    fair.'   49

'Thou lov'st another then?—but what t
    me
Is this—'tis nothing—nothing e'er can be
But yet—thou lov'st—and—Oh! I env
    those
Whose hearts on hearts as faithful ca
    repose,
Who never feel the void—the wanderin
    thought   49
That sighs o'er visions—such as mine hat
    wrought.'

'Lady, methought thy love was his, fo
    whom
This arm redeem'd thee from a fiery tomb.

'My love stern Seyd's! Oh—No—No—
    not my love—
Yet much this heart, that strives no more
    once strove   50
To meet his passion—but it would not be
I felt—I feel—love dwells with—with th
    free.
I am a slave, a favour'd slave at best,
To share his splendour, and seem ver
    blest!
Oft must my soul the question undergo,
Of—'Dost thou love?' and burn t
    answer, 'No!'   50

Oh! hard it is that fondness to sustain,
And struggle not to feel averse in vain;
But harder still the heart's recoil to bear,
And hide from one—perhaps another
    there.   510
He takes the hand I give not, nor with-
    hold—
Its pulse nor check'd, nor quicken'd—
    calmly cold:
And when resign'd, it drops a lifeless
    weight
From one I never loved enough to hate.
No warmth these lips return by his im-
    prest,   515
And chill'd remembrance shudders o'er
    the rest.
Yes—had I ever proved that passion's zeal,
The change to hatred were at least to feel:
But still he goes unmourn'd, returns un-
    sought,
And oft when present—absent from my
    thought.   520
Or when reflection comes—and come it
    must—
I fear that henceforth 'twill but bring dis-
    gust;
I am his slave—but, in despite of pride,
'Twere worse than bondage to become his
    bride.
Oh! that this dotage of his breast would
    cease: 525
Or seek another and give mine release,
But yesterday—I could have said, to
    peace!
Yes, if unwonted fondness now I feign,
Remember; captive! 'tis to break thy chain;
Repay the life that to thy hand I owe; 530
To give thee back to all endear'd below,
Who share such love as I can never know.
Farewell, morn breaks, and I must now
    away:
'Twill cost me dear—but dread no death
    to-day!'

XV

She press'd his fetter'd fingers to her heart,
And bow'd her head, and turn'd her to de-
    part,   536
And noiseless as a lovely dream is gone.
And was she here? and is he now alone?
What gem hath dropp'd and sparkles o'er
    his chain?
The tear most sacred, shed for others'
    pain,   540
That starts at once—bright—pure—from
    Pity's mine,
Already polish'd by the hand divine!
Oh! too convincing—dangerously dear—
In woman's eye the unanswerable tear!
That weapon of her weakness she can
    wield,   545
To save, subdue—at once her spear and
    shield:

Avoid it—Virtue ebbs and Wisdom errs,
Too fondly gazing on that grief of hers!
What lost a world, and bade a hero fly?
The timid tear in Cleopatra's eye.   550
Yet be the soft triumvir's fault forgiven;
By this—how many lose not earth—but
    heaven!
Consign their souls to man's eternal foe,
And seal their own to spare some wanton's
    woe!

XVI

'Tis morn, and o'er his alter'd features
    play   555
The beams—without the hope of yester-
    day.
What shall he be ere night? perchance a
    thing
O'er which the raven flaps her funeral
    wing,
By his closed eye unheeded and unfelt;
While sets that sun, and dews of evening
    melt,   560
Chill, wet, and misty round each stiffen'd
    limb,
Refreshing earth—reviving all but him!

CANTO THE THIRD

'Come vedi—ancor non m'abbandona.'—DANTE.

I

SLOW sinks, more lovely ere his race be run,
Along Morea's hills the setting sun;
Not, as in Northern climes, obscurely
    bright,
But one unclouded blaze of living light!
O'er the hush'd deep the yellow beam he
    throws,   5
Gilds the green wave, that trembles as it
    glows.
On old Ægina's rock and Idra's isle,
The god of gladness sheds his parting
    smile;
O'er his own regions lingering, loves to
    shine,
Though there his altars are no more
    divine.   10
Descending fast the mountain shadows
    kiss
Thy glorious gulf, unconquer'd Salamis!
Their azure arches through the long ex-
    panse
More deeply purpled meet his mellowing
    glance,
And tenderest tints, along their summits
    driven,   15
Mark his gay course, and own the hues of
    heaven;
Till, darkly shaded from the land and deep,
Behind his Delphian cliff he sinks to sleep.

On such an eve, his palest beam he cast,
When—Athens! here thy Wisest look'd
    his last.   20

How watch'd thy better sons his farewell
  ray,
That closed their murder'd sage's latest
  day!
Not yet—not yet—Sol pauses on the hill—
The precious hour of parting lingers still;
But sad his light to agonising eyes,   25
And dark the mountain's once delightful
  dyes:
Gloom o'er the lovely land he seem'd to
  pour,
The land, where Phœbus never frown'd
  before;
But ere he sank below Cithæron's head,
The cup of woe was quaff'd—the spirit
  fled;   30
The soul of him who scorn'd to fear or fly—
Who lived and died, as none can live or die!

But lo! from high Hymettus to the plain,
The queen of night asserts her silent reign.
No murky vapour, herald of the storm,
Hides her fair face, nor girds her glowing
  form: 36
With cornice glimmering as the moon-
  beams play,
There the white column greets her grateful
  ray,
And, bright around with quivering beams
  beset,
Her emblem sparkles o'er the minaret:
The groves of olive scatter'd dark and
  wide   41
Where meek Cephisus pours his scanty
  tide,
The cypress saddening by the sacred
  mosque,
The gleaming turret of the gay kiosk,
And, dun and sombre 'mid the holy calm,
Near Theseus' fane yon solitary palm, 46
All tinged with varied hues arrest the
  eye—
And dull were his that pass'd them heed-
  less by.

Again the Ægean, heard no more afar,
Lulls his chafed breast from elemental
  war;   50
Again his waves in milder tints unfold
Their long array of sapphire and of gold,
Mix'd with the shades of many a distant
  isle,
That frown—where gentler ocean seems
  to smile.

II

Not now my theme—why turn my thoughts
  to thee?   55
Oh! who can look along thy native sea.
Nor dwell upon thy name, whate'er the
  tale,
So much its magic must o'er all prevail?
Who that beheld that Sun upon thee set,
Fair Athens! could thine evening face for-
  get?   60

Not he—whose heart nor time nor distance frees,
Spell-bound within the clustering Cyclades!
Nor seems this homage foreign to its
  strain,
His Corsair's isle was once thine own domain—
Would that with freedom it were thine
  again!   65

III

The Sun hath sunk—and, darker than the
  night,
Sinks with its beam upon the beacon
  height
Medora's heart—the third day's come and
  gone—
With it he comes not—sends not—faith-
  less one!
The wind was fair though light; and storms
  were none.   70
Last eve Anselmo's bark return'd, and yet
His only tidings that they had not met!
Though wild, as now, far different were
  the tale
Had Conrad waited for that single sail.
The night-breeze freshens—she that day
  had pass'd   75
In watching all that Hope proclaim'd a
  mast;
Sadly she sate on high—Impatience bore
At last her footsteps to the midnight shore,
And there she wander'd, heedless of the
  spray
That dash'd her garments oft, and warn'd
  away: 80
She saw not, felt not this—nor dared de-
  part,
Nor deem'd it cold—her chill was at her
  heart;
Till grew such certainty from that sus-
  pense—
His very sight had shock'd from life or
  sense!   84

It came at last—a sad and shatter'd boat,
Whose inmates first beheld whom first
  they sought;
Some bleeding—all most wretched—these
  the few—
Scarce knew they how escaped—*this* all
  they knew.
In silence, darkling, each appear'd to wait
His fellow's mournful guess at Conrad's
  fate: 90
Something they would have said; but
  seem'd to fear
To trust their accents to Medora's ear.
She saw at once, yet sunk not—trembled
  not—
Beneath that grief, that loneliness of lot;

Within that meek fair form were feelings
high,   95
That deem'd not, till they found, their
energy.
While yet was Hope they soften'd, flutter'd,
wept—
All lost—that softness died not—but it
slept;
And o'er its slumber rose that Strength
which said,
'With nothing left to love, there's nought
to dread.'   100
'Tis more than nature's; like the burning
might
Delirium gathers from the fever's height.

'Silent you stand—nor would I hear you
tell
What—speak not—breathe not—for J
know it well—
Yet would I ask—almost my lip denies
The—quick your answer—tell me where
he lies.'   106

'Lady! we know not—scarce with life we
fled;
But here is one denies that he is dead:
He saw him bound: and bleeding—but
alive.'

She heard no further—'twas in vain to
strive—   110
So throbb'd each vein—each thought—
till then withstood;
Her own dark soul—these words at once
subdued:
She totters—falls—and senseless had the
wave
Perchance but snatched her from another
grave,
But that with hands though rude, yet
weeping eyes,   115
They yield such aid as Pity's haste supplies:
Dash o'er her deathlike cheek the ocean dew,
Raise, fan, sustain—till life returns anew;
Awake her handmaids, with the matrons
leave
That fainting form o'er which they gaze
and grieve;   120
Then seek Anselmo's cavern, to report
The tale too tedious—when the triumph
short.

IV

In that wild council words wax'd warm
and strange
With thoughts of ransom, rescue, and revenge;
All, save repose or flight: still lingering
there
Breathed Conrad's spirit, and forbade
despair;   126
Whate'er his fate—the breasts he form'd
and led
Will save him living, or appease him dead.

Woe to his foes! there yet survive a few,
Whose deeds are daring, as their hearts
are true.   130

V

Within the Haram's secret chamber sate
Stern Seyd, still pondering o'er his Cap-
tive's fate:
His thoughts on love and hate alternate
dwell,
Now with Gulnare, and now in Conrad's
cell;
Here at his feet the lovely slave reclined
Surveys his brow—would soothe his gloom
of mind;   136
While many an anxious glance her large
dark eye
Sends in its idle search for sympathy,
His only bends in seeming o'er his beads,
But inly views his victim as he bleeds.
'Pacha! the day is thine; and on thy crest
Sits Triumph—Conrad taken—fall'n the
rest!
His doom is fix'd—he dies: and well his
fate
Was earn'd—yet much too worthless for
thy hate:
Methinks, a short release, for ransom
told   145
With all his treasure, not unwisely sold;
Report speaks largely of his pirate-
hoard—
Would that of this my Pacha were the
lord!
While baffled, weaken'd by this fatal
fray—
Watch'd—follow'd—he were then an
easier prey;   150
But once cut off—the remnant of his band
Embark their wealth, and seek a safer
strand.'

'Gulnare!—if for each drop of blood a
gem
Were offer'd rich as Stamboul's diadem;
If for each hair of his a massy mine   155
Of virgin ore should supplicating shine;
If all our Arab tales divulge or dream
Of wealth were here—that gold should not
redeem!   158
It had not now redeem'd a single hour,
But that I know him fetter'd, in my power;
And, thirsting for revenge, I ponder still
On pangs that longest rack, and latest kill.'

'Nay, Seyd! I seek not to restrain thy
rage,   163
Too justly moved for mercy to assuage;
My thoughts were only to secure for thee
His riches—thus released, he were not free:
Disabled, shorn of half his might and
band,
His capture could but wait thy first com-
mand.'

'His capture *could!*—and shall I then resign
One day to him—the wretch already mine?
Release my foe!—at whose remonstrance?
—thine!   171
Fair suitor!—to thy virtuous gratitude,
That thus repays this Giaour's relenting mood,
Which thee and thine alone of all could spare,
No doubt—regardless if the prize were fair,   175
My thanks and praise alike are due—now hear!
I have a counsel for thy gentler ear:
I do mistrust thee, woman! and each word
Of thine stamps truth on all Suspicion heard.
Borne in his arms through fire from yon Serai—   180
Say, wert thou lingering there with him to fly?
Thou need'st not answer—thy confession speaks,
Already reddening on thy guilty cheeks;
Then, lovely dame, bethink thee! and beware: 184
'Tis not *his* life alone may claim such care!
Another word and—nay—I need no more.
Accursed was the moment when he bore
Thee from the flames, which better far—but no—
I then had mourn'd thee with a lover's woe—
Now 'tis thy lord that warns—deceitful thing!   190
Know'st thou that I can clip thy wanton wing?
In words alone I am not wont to chafe:
Look to thyself, nor deem thy falsehood safe!'

He rose—and slowly, sternly thence withdrew,
Rage in his eye and threats in his adieu:
Ah! little reck'd that chief of womanhood—   196
Which frowns ne'er quell'd, nor menaces subdued;
And little deem'd he what thy heart, Gulnare!
When soft could feel, and when incensed could dare.
His doubts appear'd to wrong—nor yet she knew   200
How deep the root from whence compassion grew—
She was a slave—from such may captives claim
A fellow-feeling, differing but in name;
Still half unconscious—heedless of his wrath,
Again she ventured on the dangerous path,   205

Again his rage repell'd—until arose
That strife of thought, the source of woman's woes!

VI

Meanwhile, long, anxious, weary, still the same
Roll'd day and night: his soul could terror tame—
This fearful interval of doubt and dread,
When every hour might doom him worse than dead,   211
When every step that echo'd by the gate,
Might entering lead where axe and stake await;
When every voice that grated on his ear
Might be the last that he could ever hear;
Could terror tame—that spirit stern and high   216
Had proved unwilling as unfit to die;
'Twas worn—perhaps decay'd—yet silent bore
That conflict, deadlier far than all before:
The heat of fight, the hurry of the gale,
Leave scarce one thought inert enough to quail;   221
But bound and fix'd in fetter'd solitude,
To pine, the prey of every changing mood,
To gaze on thine own heart; and meditate
Irrevocable faults, and coming fate—
Too late the last to shun—the first to mend—   226
To count the hours that struggle to thine end,
With not a friend to animate, and tell
To other ears that death became thee well;
Around thee foes to forge the ready lie,
And blot life's latest scene with calumny;
Before thee tortures, which the soul can dare,
Yet doubts how well the shrinking flesh may bear;
But deeply feels a single cry would shame—
To valour's praise thy last and dearest claim;   235
The life thou leav'st below, denied above
By kind monopolists of heavenly love;
And more than doubtful paradise—thy heaven
Of earthly hope—thy loved one from thee riven.
Such were the thoughts that outlaw must sustain,   240
And govern pangs surpassing mortal pain:
And those sustain'd he—boots it well or ill?
Since not to sink beneath, is something still!

VII

The first day pass'd—he saw not her—Gulnare—
The second, third—and still she came not there;   245

But what her words avouch'd, her charms
  had done,
Or else he had not seen another sun.
The fourth day roll'd along, and with the
  night
Came storm and darkness in their ming-
  ling might.   249
Oh! how he listen'd to the rushing sea,
That ne'er till now so broke upon his sleep;
And his wild spirit wilder wishes sent,
Roused by the roar of his own element!
Oft had he ridden on that winged wave,
And loved its roughness for the speed it
  gave;   255
And now its dashing echo'd on his ear,
A long known voice—alas! too vainly near!
Loud sung the wind above; and, doubly
  loud,
Shook o'er his turret cell the thunder-
  cloud;
And flash'd the lightning by the latticed
  bar,   260
To him more genial than the midnight star:
Close to the glimmering grate he dragg'd
  his chain;
And hoped *that* peril might not prove in
  vain.
He raised his iron hand to Heaven, and
  pray'd
One pitying flash to mar the form it made:
His steel and impious prayer attract
  alike—   266
The storm roll'd onward, and disdain'd to
  strike;
Its peal wax'd fainter—ceased—he felt
  alone,
As if some faithless friend had spurn'd his
  groan!

VIII

The midnight pass'd, and to the massy
  door   270
A light step came—it paused—it moved
  once more;
Slow turns the grating bolt and sullen key:
'Tis as his heart foreboded—that fair she!
Whate'er her sins, to him a guardian saint,
And beauteous still as hermit's hope can
  paint;   275
Yet changed since last within that cell she
  came,
More pale her cheek, more tremulous her
  frame:
On him she cast her dark and hurried eye,
Which spoke before her accents—'Thou
  must die!
Yes, thou must die—there is but one
  resource,   280
The last—the worst—if torture were not
  worse.'

'Lady! I look to none; my lips proclaim
What last proclaim'd they—Conrad still
  the same:

Why shouldst thou seek an outlaw's life to
  spare,
And change the sentence I deserve to bear?
Well have I earn'd—nor here alone—the
  meed   286
Of Seyd's revenge, by many a lawless
  deed.'

'Why should I seek? because—Oh! didst
  thou not
Redeem my life from worse than slavery's
  lot?
Why should I seek?—hath misery made
  thee blind   290
To the fond workings of a woman's mind?
And must I say?—albeit my heart rebel
With all that woman feels, but should not
  tell—
Because, despite thy crimes, that heart is
  moved:
It fear'd thee, thank'd thee, pitied, mad-
  den'd, loved.   295
Reply not, tell not now thy tale again,
Thou lov'st another, and I love in vain:
Though fond as mine her bosom, form
  more fair,
I rush through peril which she would not
  dare.
If that thy heart to hers were truly dear,
Were I thine own thou wert not lonely
  here: 301
An outlaw's spouse and leave her lord to
  roam!
What hath such gentle dame to do with
  home?
But speak not now—o'er thine and o'er
  my head
Hangs the keen sabre by a single thread;
If thou hast courage still, and wouldst be
  free,   306
Receive this poniard—rise and follow me!'

'Ay—in my chains! my steps will gently
  tread,
With these adornments, o'er each slumber-
  ing head!   309
Thou hast forgot—is this a garb for flight?
Or is that instrument more fit for fight?'

'Misdoubting Corsair! I have gain'd the
  guard,
Ripe for revolt, and greedy for reward.
A single word of mine removes that chain:
Without some aid how here could I re-
  main?   315
Well, since we met, hath sped my busy
  time,
If in aught evil, for thy sake the crime:
The crime—'tis none to punish those of
  Seyd.
That hated tyrant, Conrad—he must
  bleed!
I see thee shudder, but my soul is changed—
Wrong'd, spurn'd, reviled, and it shall be
  avenged—   321

Accused of what till now my heart dis-
  dain'd—
Too faithful, though to bitter bondage
  chain'd.
Yes, smile!—but he had little cause to
  sneer,
I was not treacherous then, nor thou too
  dear: 325
But he has said it—and the jealous well—
Those tyrants, teasing, tempting to rebel—
Deserve the fate their fretting lips foretell.
I never loved—he bought me—somewhat
  high—
Since with me came a heart he could not
  buy.   330
I was a slave unmurmuring; he hath said,
But for his rescue I with thee had fled.
'Twas false thou know'st—but let such
  augurs rue,
Their words are omens insult renders true.
Nor was thy respite granted to my prayer;
This fleeting grace was only to prepare
New torments for thy life, and my despair.
Mine too he threatens; but his dotage still
Would fain reserve me for his lordly will:
When wearier of these fleeting charms and
  me,   340
There yawns the sack, and yonder rolls the
  sea!
What, am I then a toy for dotard's play,
To wear but till the gilding frets away?
I saw thee—loved thee—owe thee all—
  would save,
If but to show how grateful is a slave.
But had he not thus menaced fame and
  life—   346
(And well he keeps his oaths pronounced
  in strife)—
I still had saved thee, but the Pacha spared.
Now I am all thine own, for all prepared:
Thou lov'st me not, nor know'st—or but
  the worst.   350
Alas! *this* love—*that* hatred—are the
  first—
Oh! couldst thou prove my truth, thou
  wouldst not start,
Nor fear the fire that lights an Eastern heart;
'Tis now the beacon of thy safety—now
It points within the port a Mainote prow:
But in one chamber, where our path must
  lead,   356
There sleeps—he must not wake—the op-
  pressor Seyd!'

'Gulnare—Gulnare—I never felt till now
My abject fortune, wither'd fame so low:
Seyd is mine enemy; had swept my band
From earth with ruthless but with open
  hand,   361
And therefore came I, in my bark of war,
To smite the smiter with the scimitar;
Such is my weapon—not the secret knife;
Who spares a woman's seeks not slumber's
  life.   365

Thine saved I gladly, Lady—not for this;
Let me not deem that mercy shown amiss.
Now fare thee well—more peace be with
  thy breast!
Night wears apace, my last of earthly
  rest!'

'Rest! rest! by sunrise must thy sinews
  shake,   370
And thy limbs writhe around the ready
  stake.
I heard the order—saw—I will not see—
If thou wilt perish, I will fall with thee.
My life, my love, my hatred—all below
Are on this cast—Corsair! 'tis but a blow!
Without it flight were idle—how evade
His sure pursuit?—my wrongs too un-
  repaid,
My youth disgraced, the long, long wasted
  years,
One blow shall cancel with our future
  fears;
But since the dagger suits thee less than
  brand,   380
I'll try the firmness of a female hand.
The guards are gain'd—one moment all
  were o'er—
Corsair! we meet in safety or no more;
If errs my feeble hand, the morning cloud
Will hover o'er thy scaffold, and my
  shroud.'   385

IX

She turn'd, and vanish'd ere he could re-
  ply,
But his glance follow'd far with eager eye;
And gathering, as he could, the links that
  bound
His form, to curl their length, and curb
  their sound,
Since bar and bolt no more his steps pre-
  clude,   390
He, fast as fetter'd limbs allow, pursued.
'Twas dark and winding, and he knew not
  where
That passage led; nor lamp nor guard was
  there:
He sees a dusky glimmering—shall he seek
Or shun that ray so indistinct and weak?
Chance guides his steps—a freshness seems
  to bear   396
Full on his brow, as if from morning air;
He reach'd an open gallery—on his eye
Gleam'd the last star of night, the clearing
  sky:
Yet scarcely heeded these—another light
From a lone chamber struck upon his
  sight.   401
Towards it he moved; a scarcely closing
  door
Reveal'd the ray within, but nothing more.
With hasty step a figure outward pass'd,
Then paused, and turn'd—and paused—
  'tis she at last!   405

No poniard in that hand, nor sign of ill—
'Thanks to that softening heart—she
　　could not kill!'
Again he look'd, the wildness of her eye
Starts from the day abrupt and fearfully.
She stopp'd—threw back her dark far-
　　floating hair,　　　　　　　　　　410
That nearly veil'd her face and bosom fair,
As if she late had bent her leaning head
Above some object of her doubt or dread.
They meet—upon her brow—unknown,
　　forgot—
Her hurrying hand had left—'twas but a
　　spot—　　　　　　　　　　　　415
Its hue was all he saw, and scarce with-
　　stood—
Oh! slight but certain pledge of crime—
　　'tis blood!

X

He had seen battle—he had brooded lone
O'er promised pangs to sentenced guilt
　　foreshown;
He had been tempted, chasten'd, and the
　　chain　　　　　　　　　　　　420
Yet on his arms might ever there remain:
But ne'er from strife, captivity, remorse—
From all his feelings in their inmost
　　force—
So thrill'd, so shudder'd every creeping
　　vein,
As now they froze before that purple stain.
That spot of blood, that light but guilty
　　streak,　　　　　　　　　　　426
Had banish'd all the beauty from her
　　cheek!
Blood he had view'd, could view un-
　　moved—but then
It flow'd in combat, or was shed by men!

XI

''Tis done—he nearly waked—but it is
　　done.　　　　　　　　　　　　430
Corsair! he perish'd—thou art dearly won.
All words would now be vain—away—
　　away!
Our bark is tossing—'tis already day.
The few gain'd over, now are wholly mine,
And these thy yet surviving band shall
　　join:　　　　　　　　　　　　435
Anon my voice shall vindicate my hand,
When once our sail forsakes this hated
　　strand.'

XII

She clapp'd her hands, and through the
　　gallery pour,
Equipp'd for flight, her vassals—Greek
　　and Moor;
Silent but quick they stoop, his chains un-
　　bind;　　　　　　　　　　　440
Once more his limbs are free as mountain
　　wind!

But on his heavy heart such sadness sate,
As if they there transferr'd that iron
　　weight.
No words are utter'd—at her sign, a door
Reveals the secret passage to the shore:
The city lies behind—they speed, they
　　reach　　　　　　　　　　　446
The glad waves dancing on the yellow
　　beach;
And Conrad following, at her beck, obey'd,
Nor cared he now if rescued or betray'd;
Resistance were as useless as if Seyd
Yet lived to view the doom his ire decreed.

XIII

Embark'd, the sail unfurl'd, the light
　　breeze blew—
How much had Conrad's memory to re-
　　view!
Sunk he in contemplation, till the cape
Where last he anchor'd rear'd its giant
　　shape.　　　　　　　　　　　455
Ah! since that fatal night, though brief the
　　time,
Had swept an age of terror, grief, and
　　crime.
As its far shadow frown'd above the mast,
He veil'd his face, and sorrow'd as he
　　pass'd;
He thought of all—Gonsalvo and his
　　band,　　　　　　　　　　　460
His fleeting triumph and his failing hand;
He thought on her afar, his lonely bride:
He turn'd and saw—Gulnare, the homi-
　　cide!

XIV

She watch'd his features till she could not
　　bear　　　　　　　　　　　464
Their freezing aspect and averted air;
And that strange fierceness, foreign to her
　　eye,
Fell quench'd in tears, too late to shed or
　　dry.
She knelt beside him and his hand she
　　press'd,
'Thou may'st forgive, though Allah's self
　　detest;
But for that deed of darkness what wert
　　thou?　　　　　　　　　　　470
Reproach me—but not yet—Oh! spare me
　　now!
I am not what I seem—this fearful night
My brain bewilder'd—do not madden
　　quite!
If I had never loved, though less my guilt,
Thou hadst not lived to—hate me—if thou
　　wilt.'　　　　　　　　　　　475

XV

She wrongs his thoughts, they more him-
　　self upbraid
Than her, though undesign'd, the wretch
　　he made;

But speechless all, deep, dark, and unex-
　prest,
They bleed within that silent cell—his
　breast.
Still onward, fair the breeze, nor rough the
　surge,　　　　　　　　　　　　　　　480
The blue waves sport around the stern
　they urge,
Far on the horizon's verge appears a speck,
A spot—a mast—a sail—an armed deck!
Their little bark her men of watch descry,
And ampler canvas woos the wind from
　high;　　　　　　　　　　　　　　　485
She bears her down majestically near,
Speed on her prow, and terror in her tier;
A flash is seen—the ball beyond their bow
Booms harmless, hissing to the deep be-
　low.　　　　　　　　　　　　　　　489
Uprose keen Conrad from his silent trance,
A long, long absent gladness in his glance;
"'Tis mine—my blood-red flag! again—
　again—
I am not all deserted on the main!'
They own the signal, answer to the hail,
Hoist out the boat at once, and slacken
　sail.　　　　　　　　　　　　　　　495
"'Tis Conrad! Conrad!' shouting from the
　deck,
Command nor duty could their transport
　check!
With light alacrity and gaze of pride,
They view him mount once more his
　vessel's side;
A smile relaxing in each rugged face,　500
Their arms can scarce forbear a rough
　embrace.
He, half forgetting danger and defeat,
Returns their greeting as a chief may greet,
Wrings with a cordial grasp Anselmo's
　hand,
And feels he yet can conquer and com-
　mand!　　　　　　　　　　　　　　505

XVI

These greetings o'er, the feelings that o'er-
　flow,
Yet grieve to win him back without a
　blow;
They sail'd prepared for vengeance—had
　they known
A woman's hand secured that deed her
　own,
She were their queen—less scrupulous are
　they　　　　　　　　　　　　　　　510
Than haughty Conrad how they win their
　way.
With many an asking smile, and wonder-
　ing stare,
They whisper round, and gaze upon Gul-
　nare;
And her—at once above—beneath her
　sex,
Whom blood appall'd not, their regards
　perplex.　　　　　　　　　　　　　515

To Conrad turns her faint imploring eye,
She drops her veil, and stands in silence
　by;
Her arms are meekly folded on that breast,
Which—Conrad safe—to fate resign'd the
　rest.
Though worse than frenzy could that
　bosom fill,　　　　　　　　　　　　520
Extreme in love or hate, in good or ill,
The worst of crimes had left her woman
　still!

XVII

This Conrad mark'd, and felt—ah! could
　he less?—
Hate of that deed, but grief for her dis-
　tress;
What she has done no tears can wash
　away,　　　　　　　　　　　　　　525
And Heaven must punish on its angry
　day:
But—it was done: he knew, whate'er her
　guilt,
For him that poniard smote, that blood
　was spilt;
And he was free! and she for him had
　given
Her all on earth, and more than all in
　heaven!　　　　　　　　　　　　　530
And now he turn'd him to that dark-eyed
　slave
Whose brow was bow'd beneath the
　glance he gave,
Who now seem'd changed and humbled,
　faint and meek,
But varying oft the colour of her cheek
To deeper shades of paleness—all its
　red　　　　　　　　　　　　　　　535
That fearful spot which stain'd it from the
　dead!
He took that hand—it trembled—now too
　late—
So soft in love, so wildly nerved in hate;
He clasp'd that hand—it trembled—and
　his own
Had lost its firmness, and his voice its
　tone.　　　　　　　　　　　　　　540
'Gulnare!'—but she replied not—'dear
　Gulnare!'
She raised her eye—her only answer
　there—
At once she sought and sunk in his em-
　brace:
If he had driven her from that resting-
　place,
His had been more or less than mortal
　heart,　　　　　　　　　　　　　　545
But—good or ill—it bade her not depart.
Perchance, but for the bodings of his
　breast,
His latest virtue then had join'd the rest.
Yet even Medora might forgive the kiss
That ask'd from form so fair no more
　than this,　　　　　　　　　　　　550

The first, the last that Frailty stole from
   Faith—
To lips where Love had lavish'd all his
   breath,
To lips—whose broken sighs such frag-
   rance fling,
As he had fann'd them freshly with his
   wing!

XVIII

They gain by twilight's hour their lonely
   isle.   555
To them the very rocks appear to smile;
The haven hums with many a cheering
   sound,
The beacons blaze their wonted stations
   round,
The boats are darting o'er the curly bay,
And sportive dolphins bend them through
   the spray;   560
Even the hoarse sea-bird's shrill, dis-
   cordant shriek
Greets like the welcome of his tuneless
   beak!
Beneath each lamp that through its lattice
   gleams,
Their fancy paints the friends that trim
   the beams.
Oh! what can sanctify the joys of home,
Like Hope's gay glance from Ocean's
   troubled foam?   566

XIX

The lights are high on beacon and from
   bower,
And 'midst them Conrad seeks Medora's
   tower:
He looks in vain—'tis strange—and all
   remark,
Amid so many, hers alone is dark.   570
'Tis strange—of yore its welcome never
   fail'd,
Nor now, perchance, extinguish'd, only
   veil'd.
With the first boat descends he for the
   shore,   573
And looks impatient on the lingering oar.
Oh! for a wing beyond the falcon's flight,
To bear him like an arrow to that height!
With the first pause the resting rowers
   gave,
He waits not, looks not—leaps into the
   wave,
Strives through the surge, bestrides the
   beach, and high   579
Ascends the path familiar to his eye.

He reach'd his turret door—he paused—
   no sound
Broke from within; and all was night
   around.
He knock'd, and loudly—footstep nor
   reply
Announced that any heard or deem'd him
   nigh;

He knock'd, but faintly—for his trembling
   hand   585
Refused to aid his heavy heart's demand.
The portal opens—'tis a well-known face,
But not the form he panted to embrace.
Its lips are silent—twice his own essay'd,
And fail'd to frame the question they
   delay'd;   590
He snatch'd the lamp—its light will answer
   all—
It quits his grasp, expiring in the fall.
He would not wait for that reviving ray—
As soon could he have linger'd there for
   day;
But, glimmering through the dusky cor-
   ridor,   595
Another chequers o'er the shadow'd floor;
His steps the chamber gain—his eyes be-
   hold
All that his heart believed not—yet fore-
   told!

XX

He turn'd not—spoke not—sunk not—
   fix'd his look,
And set the anxious frame that lately
   shook: 600
He gazed—how long we gaze despite of
   pain,
And know, but dare not own, we gaze in
   vain!
In life itself she was so still and fair,
That death with gentler aspect wither'd
   there;
And the cold flowers her colder hand con-
   tain'd,   605
In that last grasp as tenderly were strain'd
As if she scarcely felt, but feign'd a sleep,
And made it almost mockery yet to weep:
The long dark lashes fringed her lids of
   snow,
And veil'd—thought shrinks from all that
   lurk'd below—   610
Oh! o'er the eye Death most exerts his
   might,
And hurls the spirit from her throne of
   light;
Sinks those blue orbs in that long last
   eclipse,
But spares, as yet, the charm around her
   lips—
Yet, yet they seem as they forbore to
   smile,   615
And wish'd repose,—but only for a while;
But the white shroud, and each extended
   tress,
Long, fair—but spread in utter lifeless-
   ness,
Which, late the sport of every summer wind,
Escaped the baffled wreath that strove to
   bind;   620
These—and the pale pure cheek, became
   the bier—
But she is nothing—wherefore is he here?

XXI

He ask'd no question—all were answer'd
  now
By the first glance on that still, marble
  brow.
It was enough—she died—what reck'd it
  how ?   625
The love of youth, the hope of better
  years,
The source of softest wishes, tenderest
  fears,
The only living thing he could not hate,
Was reft at once—and he deserved his
  fate,
But did not feel it less;—the good ex-
  plore,   630
For peace, those realms where guilt can
  never soar:
The proud, the wayward—who have fix'd
  below
Their joy, and find this earth enough for
  woe,
Lose in that one their all—perchance a
  mite—
But who in patience parts with all de-
  light?   635
Full many a stoic eye and aspect stern
Mask hearts where grief hath little left to
  learn;
And many a withering thought lies hid,
  not lost,
In smiles that least befit who wear them
  most.   639

XXII

By those, that deepest feel, is ill exprest
The indistinctness of the suffering breast;
Where thousand thoughts begin to end in
  one,
Which seeks from all the refuge found in
  none;
No words suffice the secret soul to show,
For Truth denies all eloquence to Woe.
On Conrad's stricken soul exhaustion
  prest,   646
And stupor almost lull'd it into rest;
So feeble now—his mother's softness crept
To those wild eyes, which like an infant's
  wept:
It was the very weakness of his brain,
Which thus confess'd without relieving
  pain.   651
None saw his trickling tears—perchance,
  if seen,
That useless flood of grief had never been:
Nor long they flow'd—he dried them to
  depart,
In helpless—hopeless—brokenness of
  heart: 655
The sun goes forth, but Conrad's day is
  dim;
And the night cometh—ne'er to pass from
  him.

There is no darkness like the cloud of
  mind,
On Grief's vain eye—the blindest of the
  blind!
Which may not—dare not see—but turns
  aside   660
To blackest shade—nor will endure a
  guide!

XXIII

His heart was form'd for softness—warp'd
  to wrong;
Betray'd too early, and beguiled too long;
Each feeling pure—as falls the dropping
  dew
Within the grot—like that had harden'd
  too;   665
Less clear, perchance, its earthly trials
  pass'd,
But sunk, and chill'd, and petrified at last.
Yet tempests wear, and lightning cleaves
  the rock,
If such his heart, so shatter'd it the
  shock.
There grew one flower beneath its rugged
  brow,   670
Though dark the shade—it shelter'd—
  saved till now.
The thunder came—that bolt hath blasted
  both,
The Granite's firmness, and the Lily's
  growth:
The gentle plant hath left no leaf to tell
Its tale, but shrunk and wither'd where it
  fell;   675
And of its cold protector, blacken round
But shiver'd fragments on the barren
  ground!

XXIV

'Tis morn—to venture on his lonely
  hour
Few dare; though now Anselmo sought
  his tower.
He was not there, nor seen along the
  shore;   680
Ere night, alarm'd, their isle is traversed
  o'er:
Another morn—another bids them seek,
And shout his name till echo waxeth
  weak;
Mount, grotto, cavern, valley search'd in
  vain,
They find on shore a sea-boat's broken
  chain: 685
Their hope revives—they follow o'er the
  main.
'Tis idle all—moons roll on moons away,
And Conrad comes not, came not since
  that day:
Nor trace, nor tidings of his doom de-
  clare
Where lives his grief, or perish'd his
  despair!   690

Long mourn'd his band whom none could
    mourn beside;
And fair the monument they gave his
    bride:
For him they raise not the recording
    stone—

His death yet dubious, deeds too widely
    known;
He left a Corsair's name to other
    times,   695
Link'd with one virtue, and a thousand
    crimes.

LARA

CANTO THE FIRST

I

THE Serfs are glad through Lara's wide
    domain,
And Slavery half forgets her feudal chain;
He, their unhoped, but unforgotten lord,
The long self-exiled chieftain, is restored:
There be bright faces in the busy hall,   5
Bowls on the board, and banners on the
    wall;
Far checkering o'er the pictured window,
    plays
The unwonted faggot's hospitable blaze;
And gay retainers gather round the
    hearth,
With tongues all loudness, and with eyes
    all mirth.   10

II

The chief of Lara is returned again:
And why had Lara cross'd the bounding
    main?
Left by his sire, too young such loss to
    know,
Lord of himself,—that heritage of woe,
That fearful empire which the human
    breast   15
But holds to rob the heart within of rest!—
With none to check, and few to point in
    time
The thousand paths that slope the way to
    crime;
Then, when he most required command-
    ment, then
Had Lara's daring boyhood govern'd
    men.   20
It skills not, boots not step by step to
    trace
His youth through all the mazes of its
    race;
Short was the course his restlessness had
    run,
But long enough to leave him half undone.

III

And Lara left in youth his father-land;
But from the hour he waved his parting
    hand   26
Each trace wax'd fainter of his course, till
    all
Had nearly ceased his memory to recall.

His sire was dust, his vassals could de-
    clare,
'Twas all they knew, that Lara was not
    there;   30
Nor sent, nor came he, till conjecture
    grew
Cold in the many, anxious in the few.
His hall scarce echoes with his wonted
    name,
His portrait darkens in its fading frame,
Another chief consoled his destined bride,
The young forgot him, and the old had
    died;   36
'Yet doth he live!' exclaims the impatient
    heir,
And sighs for sables which he must not
    wear.
A hundred scutcheons deck with gloomy
    grace
The Laras' last and longest dwelling-
    place;   40
But one is absent from the mouldering
    file,
That now were welcome in that Gothic
    pile.

IV

He comes at last in sudden loneliness,
And whence they know not, why they
    need not guess;
They more might marvel, when the greet-
    ing's o'er,   45
Not that he came, but came not long
    before:
No train is his beyond a single page,
Of foreign aspect, and of tender age.
Years had roll'd on, and fast they speed
    away
To those that wander as to those that
    stay;   50
But lack of tidings from another clime
Had lent a flagging wing to weary Time.
They see, they recognise, yet almost deem
The present dubious, or the past a dream.

He lives, nor yet is past his manhood's
    prime,   55
Though sear'd by toil, and something
    touch'd by time;
His faults, whate'er they were, if scarce
    forgot,
Might be untaught him by his varied lot;

Nor good nor ill of late were known, his
   name
Might yet uphold his patrimonial fame:
His soul in youth was haughty, but his
   sins   61
No more than pleasure from the stripling
   wins;
And such, if not yet harden'd in their
   course,
Might be redeem'd, nor ask a long remorse.

V

And they indeed were changed—'tis
   quickly seen,   65
Whate'er he be, 'twas not what he had
   been:
That brow in furrow'd lines had fix'd at
   last,
And spake of passions, but of passion
   past:
The pride, but not the fire, of early days,
Coldness of mien, and carelessness of
   praise;   70
A high demeanour, and a glance that took
Their thoughts from others by a single
   look;
And that sarcastic levity of tongue,
The stinging of a heart the world hath
   stung,
That darts in seeming playfulness around,
And makes those feel that will not own
   the wound;   76
All these seem'd his, and something more
   beneath
Than glance could well reveal, or accent
   breathe.
Ambition, glory, love, the common aim,
That some can conquer, and that all would
   claim,   80
Within his breast appear'd no more to
   strive,
Yet seem'd as lately they had been alive;
And some deep feeling it were vain to
   trace
At moments lighten'd o'er his livid face.

VI

Not much he loved long question of the
   past,   85
Nor told of wondrous wilds, and deserts
   vast,
In those far lands where he had wander'd
   lone,
And—as himself would have it seem—unknown;
Yet these in vain his eye could scarcely
   scan,
Nor glean experience from his fellow
   man;   90
But what he had beheld he shunn'd to
   show,
As hardly worth a stranger's care to
   know;

If still more prying such inquiry grew,
His brow fell darker, and his words mor
   few.

VII

Not unrejoiced to see him once again,
Warm was his welcome to the haunts
   men;   9
Born of high lineage, link'd in high com
   mand,
He mingled with the magnates of his land
Join'd the carousals of the great an
   gay,
And saw them smile or sigh their hour
   away;   10
But still he only saw, and did not share
The common pleasure or the general care
He did not follow what they all pursued
With hope still baffled, still to be renew'd
Nor shadowy honour, nor substantia
   gain,   10
Nor beauty's preference, and the rival'
   pain:
Around him some mysterious circl
   thrown
Repell'd approach, and show'd him stil
   alone;
Upon his eye sat something of reproof,
That kept at least frivolity aloof;   11
And things more timid that beheld hin
   near
In silence gazed, or whisper'd mutual fear
And they the wiser, friendlier few con
   fess'd
They deem'd him better than his air ex
   press'd.

VIII

'Twas strange—in youth all action and al
   life,   11
Burning for pleasure, not averse from
   strife;
Woman, the field, the ocean, all that gav
Promise of gladness, peril of a grave,
In turn he tried—he ransack'd all be-
   low,
And found his recompense in joy or woe
No tame, trite medium; for his feeling
   sought   12
In that intenseness an escape from thought
The tempest of his heart in scorn ha
   gazed
On that the feebler elements had raised;
The rapture of his heart had look'd or
   high,   12
And ask'd if greater dwelt beyond th
   sky:
Chain'd to excess, the slave of each ex
   treme,
How woke he from the wildness of tha
   dream?
Alas! he told not—but he did awake
To curse the wither'd heart that would no
   break.   13

IX

Books, for his volume heretofore was Man,
With eye more curious he appear'd to scan,
And oft, in sudden mood, for many a day,
From all communion he would start away:
And then, his rarely call'd attendants said,
Through night's long hours would sound his hurried tread 136
O'er the dark gallery, where his fathers frown'd
In rude but antique portraiture around:
They heard, but whisper'd—'*that* must not be known—
The sound of words less earthly than his own. 140
Yes, they who chose might smile, but some had seen
They scarce knew what, but more than should have been.
Why gazed he so upon the ghastly head
Which hands profane had gather'd from the dead,
That still beside his open'd volume lay,
As if to startle all save him away? 146
Why slept he not when others were at rest?
Why heard no music, and received no guest?
All was not well, they deem'd—but where the wrong?
Some knew perchance—but 'twere a tale too long; 150
And such besides were too discreetly wise,
To more than hint their knowledge in surmise;
But if they would—they could'—around the board
Thus Lara's vassals prattled of their lord.

X

It was the night—and Lara's glassy stream
The stars are studding, each with imaged beam; 156
So calm, the waters scarcely seem to stray,
And yet they glide like happiness away;
Reflecting far and fairy-like from high
The immortal lights that live along the sky: 160
Its banks are fringed with many a goodly tree,
And flowers the fairest that may feast the bee;
Such in her chaplet infant Dian wove,
And Innocence would offer to her love.
These deck the shore; the waves their channel make 165
In windings bright and mazy like the snake.
All was so still, so soft in earth and air,
You scarce would start to meet a spirit there;

Secure that nought of evil could delight
To walk in such a scene, on such a night!
It was a moment only for the good: 171
So Lara deem'd, nor longer there he stood,
But turn'd in silence to his castle-gate;
Such scene his soul no more could contemplate:
Such scene reminded him of other days,
Of skies more cloudless, moons of purer blaze, 176
Of nights more soft and frequent, hearts that now—
No—no—the storm may beat upon his brow,
Unfelt, unsparing—but a night like this,
A night of beauty, mock'd such breast as his. 180

XI

He turn'd within his solitary hall,
And his high shadow shot along the wall:
There were the painted forms of other times,
'Twas all they left of virtues or of crimes,
Save vague tradition; and the gloomy vaults 185
That hid their dust, their foibles, and their faults;
And half a column of the pompous page,
That speeds the specious tale from age to age;
Where history's pen its praise or blame supplies,
And lies like truth, and still most truly lies. 190
He wandering mused, and as the moon-beam shone
Through the dim lattice o'er the floor of stone,
And the high fretted roof, and saints, that there
O'er Gothic windows knelt in pictured prayer,
Reflected in fantastic figures grew, 195
Like life, but not like mortal life to view:
His bristling locks of sable, brow of gloom,
And the wide waving of his shaken plume,
Glanced like a spectre's attributes, and gave
His aspect all that terror gives the grave.

XII

'Twas midnight—all was slumber; the lone light 201
Dimm'd in the lamp, as loth to break the night.
Hark! there be murmurs heard in Lara's hall—
A sound, a voice, a shriek, a fearful call!
A long, loud shriek—and silence—did they hear 205
That frantic echo burst the sleeping ear?

They heard and rose, and, tremulously
   brave,
Rush where the sound invoked their aid
   to save;
They come with half-lit tapers in their
   hands,
And snatch'd in startled haste unbelted
   brands.   210

XIII

Cold as the marble where his length was
   laid,
Pale as the beam that o'er his features
   play'd,
Was Lara stretch'd; his half-drawn sabre
   near,
Dropp'd it should seem in more than
   nature's fear;
Yet he was firm, or had been firm till
   now,   215
And still defiance knit his gather'd brow;
Though mix'd with terror, senseless as he
   lay,
There lived upon his lip the wish to slay;
Some half-form'd threat in utterance there
   had died,   219
Some imprecation of despairing pride;
His eye was almost seal'd, but not forsook,
Even in its trance, the gladiator's look,
That oft awake his aspect could disclose,
And now was fix'd in horrible repose.
They raise him—bear him:—hush! he
   breathes, he speaks,   225
The swarthy blush recolours in his cheeks,
His lip resumes its red, his eye, though
   dim,
Rolls wide and wild, each slowly quivering
   limb
Recalls its function, but his words are
   strung
In terms that seem not of his native
   tongue;   230
Distinct but strange, enough they under-
   stand
To deem them accents of another land;
And such they were, and meant to meet an
   ear
That hears him not—alas! that cannot
   hear!

XIV

His page approach'd, and he alone ap-
   pear'd   235
To know the import of the words they
   heard;
And, by the changes of his cheek and
   brow,
They were not such as Lara should avow,
Nor he interpret,—yet with less surprise
Than those around their chieftain's state
   he eyes,   240
But Lara's prostrate form he bent beside,
And in that tongue which seem'd his own
   replied,

And Lara heeds those tones that gently
   seem
To soothe away the horrors of his dream—
If dream it were that thus could over
   throw   245
A breast that needed not ideal woe.

XV

Whate'er his frenzy dream'd or eye be-
   held,—
If yet remember'd ne'er to be reveal'd,—
Rests at his heart: the custom'd morning
   came,
And breathed new vigour in his shaken
   frame;   250
And solace sought he none from priest
   nor leech,
And soon the same in movement and in
   speech,
As heretofore he fill'd the passing hours,
Nor less he smiles, nor more his forehead
   lowers,
Than these were wont; and if the coming
   night   255
Appear'd less welcome now to Lara's sight,
He to his marvelling vassals show'd it not,
Whose shuddering proved *their* fear was
   less forgot.
In trembling pairs (alone they dared not)
   crawl
The astonish'd slaves, and shun the fated
   hall;   260
The waving banner, and the clapping
   door,
The rustling tapestry, and the echoing
   floor;
The long dim shadows of surrounding
   trees,
The flapping bat, the night song of the
   breeze;
Aught they behold or hear their thought
   appals,   265
As evening saddens o'er the dark grey walls.

XVI

Vain thought! that hour of ne'er un-
   ravell'd gloom
Came not again, or Lara could assume
A seeming of forgetfulness, that made
His vassals more amazed nor less afraid.
Had memory vanish'd then with sense re-
   stored?   271
Since word, nor look, nor gesture of their
   lord
Betray'd a feeling that recall'd to these
That fever'd moment of his mind's disease.
Was it a dream? was his the voice that
   spoke   275
Those strange wild accents; his the cry
   that broke
Their slumber? his the oppress'd, o'er-
   labour'd heart
That ceased to beat, the look that made
   them start?

ould he who thus had suffer'd so forget,
hen such as saw that suffering shudder
yet?   280
r did that silence prove his memory fix'd
oo deep for words, indelible, unmix'd
that corroding secrecy which gnaws
he heart to show the effect, but not the
cause?
ot so in him; his breast had buried
both,   285
or common gazers could discern the
growth
f thoughts that mortal lips must leave
half told;
hey choke the feeble words that would
unfold.

XVII

him inexplicably mix'd appear'd
uch to be loved and hated, sought and
fear'd;   290
pinion varying o'er his hidden lot,
praise or railing ne'er his name forgot:
is silence form'd a theme for others'
prate—
hey guess'd, they gazed, they fain would
know his fate.
'hat had he been? what was he, thus unknown,   295
'ho walk'd their world, his lineage only
known?
hater of his kind? yet some would
say,
'ith them he could seem gay amidst the
gay;
it own'd that smile, if oft observed and
near,
'aned in its mirth, and wither'd to a
sneer;   300
hat smile might reach his lip, but pass'd
not by,
one e'er could trace its laughter to his
eye:
et there was softness too in his regard,
t times, a heart as not by nature hard,
it once perceived, his spirit seem'd to
chide   305
uch weakness, as unworthy of its pride,
nd steel'd itself, as scorning to redeem
ne doubt from others' half-withheld
esteem;
a self-inflicted penance of a breast
/hich tenderness might once have wrung
from rest;   310
a vigilance of grief that would compel
he soul to hate for having loved too well.

XVIII

here was in him a vital scorn of all:
s if the worst had fall'n which could befall,
e stood a stranger in this breathing
world,   315
n erring spirit from another hurl'd;

A thing of dark imaginings, that shaped
By choice the perils he by chance escaped;
But 'scaped in vain, for in their memory
yet
His mind would half exult and half re-
gret: 320
With more capacity for love than earth
Bestows on most of mortal mould and
birth,
His early dreams of good outstripp'd the
truth,
And troubled manhood follow'd baffled
youth;
With thought of years in phantom chase
mis-spent,   325
And wasted powers for better purpose lent;
And fiery passions that had pour'd their
wrath
In hurried desolation o'er his path,
And left the better feelings all at strife
In wild reflection o'er his stormy life;
But haughty still, and loth himself to blame,
He call'd on Nature's self to share the
shame,
And charged all faults upon the fleshly
form
She gave to clog the soul, and feast the
worm;   334
Till he at last confounded good and ill,
And half mistook for fate the acts of will:
Too high for common selfishness, he could
At times resign his own for others' good,
But not in pity, not because he ought,
But in some strange perversity of thought,
That sway'd him onward with a secret
pride   341
To do what few or none would do beside;
And this same impulse would, in tempting
time,
Mislead his spirit equally to crime;
So much he soar'd beyond, or sunk be-
neath,   345
The men with whom he felt condemn'd to
breathe,
And long'd by good or ill to separate
Himself from all who shared his mortal
state;
His mind abhorring this, had fix'd her
throne
Far from the world, in regions of her
own: 350
Thus coldly passing all that pass'd below,
His blood in temperate seeming now
would flow:
Ah! happier if it ne'er with guilt had
glow'd,
But ever in that icy smoothness flow'd!
'Tis true, with other men their path he
walk'd,   355
And like the rest in seeming did and talk'd,
Nor outraged Reason's rules by flaw nor
start,
His madness was not of the head, but
heart;

And rarely wander'd in his speech, or
    drew
His thoughts so forth as to offend the
    view.   360

XIX

With all that chilling mystery of mien,
And seeming gladness to remain unseen,
He had (if 'twere not nature's boon) an
    art
Of fixing memory on another's heart:
It was not love perchance, nor hate, nor
    aught   365
That words can image to express the
    thought;
But they who saw him did not see in vain,
And once beheld, would ask of him again:
And those to whom he spake remember'd
    well,
And on the words, however light, would
    dwell: 370
None knew nor how, nor why, but he en-
    twined
Himself perforce around the hearer's mind;
There he was stamp'd, in liking, or in hate,
If greeted once; however brief the date
That friendship, pity, or aversion knew,
Still there within the inmost thought he
    grew.   376
You could not penetrate his soul, but
    found,
Despite your wonder, to your own he
    wound;
His presence haunted still; and from the
    breast
He forced an all unwilling interest: 380
Vain was the struggle in that mental net,
His spirit seem'd to dare you to forget!

XX

There is a festival, where knights and
    dames,
And aught that wealth or lofty lineage
    claims,
Appear—a high-born and a welcome
    guest   385
To Otho's hall came Lara with the rest.
The long carousal shakes the illumined
    hall,
Well speeds alike the banquet and the
    ball;
And the gay dance of bounding Beauty's
    train
Links grace and harmony in happiest
    chain: 390
Blest are the early hearts and gentle hands
That mingle there in well according bands;
It is a sight the careful brow might smooth,
And make Age smile, and dream itself to
    youth,
And Youth forget such hour was past on
    earth,   395
So springs the exulting bosom to that
    mirth!

XXI

And Lara gazed on these, sedately gla
His brow belied him if his soul was sa
And his glance follow'd fast each flutter
    fair,
Whose steps of lightness woke no ec
    there:
He lean'd against the lofty pillar nigh
With folded arms and long attentive e
Nor mark'd a glance so sternly fix'd
    his—
Ill brook'd high Lara scrutiny like thi
At length he caught it, 'tis a face
    known,
But seems as searching his, and his alo
Prying and dark, a stranger's by his mi
Who still till now had gazed on him
    seen:
At length encountering meets the mut
    gaze
Of keen inquiry, and of mute amaze;
On Lara's glance emotion gathering gre
As if distrusting that the stranger thre
Along the stranger's aspect, fix'd a
    stern,
Flash'd more than thence the vulgar e
    could learn.

XXII

"Tis he!' the stranger cried, and tho
    that heard
Re-echoed fast and far the whisper
    word.
"Tis he!'—'Tis who?' they question
    and near,
Till louder accents rung on Lara's ear;
So widely spread, few bosoms well cou
    brook
The general marvel, or that single loc
But Lara stirr'd not, changed not, the s
    prise
That sprung at first to his arrested eye
Seem'd now subsided, neither sunk n
    raised
Glanced his eye round, though still t
    stranger gazed;
And drawing nigh, exclaim'd, wi
    haughty sneer,
"Tis he! how came he thence?—wh
    doth he here?'

XXIII

It were too much for Lara to pass by
Such questions, so repeated fierce a
    high;
With look collected, but with accent co
More mildly firm than petulantly bold,
He turn'd, and met the inquisitorial tone-
'My name is Lara!—when thine own
    known,
Doubt not my fitting answer to requite
The unlook'd-for courtesy of such
    knight.

'Tis Lara!—further wouldst thou mark
    or ask?   435
I shun no question, and I wear no mask.'

'Thou shunn'st no question! Ponder—is
    there none
Thy heart must answer, though thine ear
    would shun?
And   deem'st thou me unknown too?
    Gaze again!
At least thy memory was not given in
    vain.   440
Oh! never canst thou cancel half her debt,
Eternity forbids thee to forget.'
With slow and searching glance upon his
    face
Grew Lara's eyes, but nothing there could
    trace
They knew, or chose to know—with
    dubious look   445
He deign'd no answer, but his head he
    shook,
And half contemptuous turn'd to pass
    away;
But the stern stranger motion'd him to
    stay.

'A word!—I charge thee stay, and answer
    here
To one, who, wert thou noble, were thy
    peer,   450
But as thou wast and art—nay, frown not,
    lord,
If false, 'tis easy to disprove the word—
But as thou wast and art, on thee looks
    down,
Distrusts thy smiles, but shakes not at thy
    frown.
Art thou not he? whose deeds——'
          'Whate'er I be,
Words wild as these, accusers like to
    thee,   456
I list no further; those with whom they
    weigh
May hear the rest, nor venture to gainsay
The wondrous tale no doubt thy tongue
    can tell,
Which thus begins so courteously and
    well.   460
Let Otho cherish here his polish'd guest,
To him my thanks and thoughts shall be
    express'd.'
And here their wondering host hath inter-
    posed—
'Whate'er there be between you undis-
    closed,   464
This is no time nor fitting place to mar
The mirthful meeting with a wordy war.
If thou, Sir Ezzelin, hast aught to show
Which it befits Count Lara's ear to know,
To-morrow, here, or elsewhere, as may
    best
Beseem your mutual judgment, speak the
    rest;   470
I pledge myself for thee, as not unknown,

Though, like Count Lara, now return'd
    alone
From other lands, almost a stranger
    grown;
And if from Lara's blood and gentle birth
I augur right of courage and of worth,
He will not that untainted line belie, 476
Nor aught that knighthood may accord,
    deny.'

'To-morrow be it,' Ezzelin replied,
'And here our several worth and truth be
    tried;
I gage my life, my falchion to attest 480
My words, so may I mingle with the blest!'
What answers Lara? to its centre shrunk
His soul, in deep abstraction sudden sunk;
The words of many, and the eyes of all
That there were gather'd, seem'd on him
    to fall;   485
But his were silent, his appear'd to stray
In far forgetfulness away—away—
Alas! that heedlessness of all around
Bespoke remembrance only too profound.

           XXIV

'To-morrow!—ay, to-morrow!' further
    word   490
Than those repeated none from Lara
    heard:
Upon his brow no outward passion spoke;
From his large eye no flashing anger broke;
Yet there was something fix'd in that low
    tone,
Which show'd resolve, determined, though
    unknown.   495
He seized his cloak—his head he slightly
    bow'd,
And passing Ezzelin, he left the crowd;
And as he pass'd him, smiling met the
    frown
With which that chieftain's brow would
    bear him down:
It was nor smile of mirth, nor struggling
    pride   500
That curbs to scorn the wrath it cannot
    hide;
But that of one in his own heart secure
Of all that he would do, or could endure.
Could this mean peace? the calmness of
    the good?
Or guilt grown old in desperate hardi-
    hood?   505
Alas! too like in confidence are each,
For man to trust to mortal look or speech;
From deeds, and deeds alone, may he dis-
    cern
Truths which it wrings the unpractised
    heart to learn.

           XXV

And Lara call'd his page, and went his
    way—   510
Well could that stripling word or sign obey:

His only follower from those climes afar,
Where the soul glows beneath a brighter
    star;
For Lara left the shore from whence he
    sprung,   514
In duty patient, and sedate though young;
Silent as him he served, his faith appears
Above his station, and beyond his years.
Though not unknown the tongue of Lara's
    land,
In such from him he rarely heard com-
    mand;
But fleet his step, and clear his tones
    would come,   520
When Lara's lip breathed forth the words
    of home:
Those accents, as his native mountains
    dear,
Awake their absent echoes in his ear,
Friends', kindred's, parents' wonted voice
    recall,
Now lost, abjured, for one—his friend, his
    all: 525
For him earth now disclosed no other
    guide;
What marvel then he rarely left his side?

XXVI

Light was his form, and darkly delicate
That brow whereon his native sun had
    sate,
But had not marr'd, though in his beams
    he grew,   530
The cheek where oft the unbidden blush
    shone through;
Yet not such blush as mounts when health
    would show
All the heart's hue in that delighted glow;
But 'twas a hectic tint of secret care
That for a burning moment fever'd there;
And the wild sparkle of his eye seem'd
    caught   536
From high, and lighten'd with electric
    thought,
Though its black orb those long low
    lashes' fringe
Had temper'd with a melancholy tinge;
Yet less of sorrow than of pride was there,
Or, if 'twere grief, a grief that none should
    share: 541
And pleased not him the sports that please
    his age,
The tricks of youth, the frolics of the
    page;
For hours on Lara he would fix his glance,
As all-forgotten in that watchful trance;
And from his chief withdrawn, he wan-
    der'd lone,   546
Brief were his answers, and his questions
    none;
His walk the wood, his sport some foreign
    book;
His resting-place the bank that curbs the
    brook;

He seem'd, like him he served, to live
    apart   550
From all that lures the eye, and fills the
    heart;
To know no brotherhood, and take from
    earth
No gift beyond that bitter boon—our birth.

XXVII

If aught he loved, 'twas Lara; but was
    shown
His faith in reverence and in deeds alone;
In mute attention; and his care, which
    guess'd   556
Each wish, fulfill'd it ere the tongue ex-
    press'd.
Still there was haughtiness in all he did,
A spirit deep that brook'd not to be chid;
His zeal, though more than that of servile
    hands,   560
In act alone obeys, his air commands;
As if 'twas Lara's less than *his* desire
That thus he served, but surely not for hire.
Slight were the tasks enjoin'd him by his
    lord,   564
To hold the stirrup, or to bear the sword;
To tune his lute, or, if he will'd it more,
On tomes of other times and tongues to
    pore;
But ne'er to mingle with the menial train,
To whom he show'd nor deference nor dis-
    dain,
But that well-worn reserve which proved
    he knew   570
No sympathy with that familiar crew:
His soul, whate'er his station or his stem,
Could bow to Lara, not descend to them.
Of higher birth he seem'd, and better days,
Nor mark of vulgar toil that hand betrays,
So femininely white it might bespeak 576
Another sex, when match'd with that
    smooth cheek,
But for his garb, and something in his gaze,
More wild and high than woman's eye
    betrays;
A latent fierceness that far more became
His fiery climate than his tender frame:
True, in his words it broke not from his
    breast,   582
But from his aspect might be more than
    guess'd.
Kaled his name, though rumour said he
    bore
Another ere he left his mountain-shore;
For sometimes he would hear, however
    nigh,   586
That name repeated loud without reply,
As unfamiliar, or, if roused again,
Start to the sound, as but remember'd
    then;
Unless 'twas Lara's wonted voice that
    spake,
For then, ear, eyes, and heart would all
    awake.   591

XXVIII

He had look'd down upon the festive
  hall,
And mark'd that sudden strife so mark'd
  of all:
And when the crowd around and near him
  told   594
Their wonder at the calmness of the bold,
Their marvel how the high-born Lara bore
Such insult from a stranger, doubly sore,
The colour of young Kaled went and came,
The lip of ashes, and the cheek of flame;
And o'er his brow the dampening heart-
  drops threw   600
The sickening iciness of that cold dew,
That rises as the busy bosom sinks
With heavy thoughts from which reflection
  shrinks.
Yes—there be things which we must dream
  and dare,   604
And execute ere thought be half aware:
Whate'er might Kaled's be, it was enow
To seal his lip, but agonise his brow.
He gazed on Ezzelin till Lara cast
That sidelong smile upon the knight he
  pass'd;   609
When Kaled saw that smile his visage fell,
As if on something recognised right well:
His memory read in such a meaning more
Than Lara's aspect unto others wore:
Forward he sprung—a moment, both were
  gone,   614
And all within that hall seem'd left alone;
Each had so fix'd his eye on Lara's mien,
All had so mix'd their feelings with that
  scene,
That when his long dark shadow through
  the porch
No more relieves the glare of yon high
  torch,
Each pulse beats quicker, and all bosoms
  seem   620
To bound as doubting from too black a
  dream,
Such as we know is false, yet dread in
  sooth,
Because the worst is ever nearest truth.
And they are gone—but Ezzelin is there,
With thoughtful visage and imperious air;
But long remain'd not; ere an hour expired
He waved his hand to Otho and retired.

XXIX

The crowd are gone, the revellers at rest;
The courteous host, and all-approving
  guest,
Again to that accustom'd couch must
  creep   630
Where joy subsides, and sorrow sighs to
  sleep,
And man, o'erlabour'd with his being's
  strife,
Shrinks to that sweet forgetfulness of life:
There lie love's feverish hope, and cun-
  ning's guile,

Hate's working brain, and lull'd am-
  bition's wile;   635
O'er each vain eye oblivion's pinions wave,
And quench'd existence crouches in a
  grave.
What better name may slumber's bed be-
  come?
Night's sepulchre, the universal home,
Where weakness, strength, vice, virtue,
  sunk supine,   640
Alike in naked helplessness recline;
Glad for a while to heave unconscious
  breath,
Yet wake to wrestle with the dread of
  death,
And shun, though day but dawn on ills in-
  creased,
That sleep, the loveliest, since it dreams
  the least.   645

CANTO THE SECOND

I

NIGHT wanes—the vapours round the
  mountains curl'd
Melt into morn, and Light awakes the
  world,
Man has another day to swell the past,
And lead him near to little but his last:
But mighty Nature bounds as from her
  birth,   5
The sun is in the heavens, and life on
  earth;
Flowers in the valley, splendour in the
  beam,
Health on the gale, and freshness in the
  stream.
Immortal man! behold her glories shine,
And cry, exulting inly, 'They are thine!'
Gaze on, while yet thy gladden'd eye may
  see: 11
A morrow comes when they are not for
  thee:
And grieve what may above thy senseless
  bier,
Nor earth nor sky will yield a single tear;
Nor cloud shall gather more, nor leaf
  shall fall,   15
Nor gale breathe forth one sigh for thee,
  for all;
But creeping things shall revel in their
  spoil,
And fit thy clay to fertilise the soil.

II

'Tis morn—'tis noon—assembled in the
  hall,
The gather'd chieftains come to Otho's
  call;   20
'Tis now the promised hour, that must
  proclaim
The life or death of Lara's future fame;
And Ezzelin his charge may here unfold,
And whatsoe'er the tale, it must be told.

His faith was pledged, and Lara's promise
   given,   25
To meet it in the eye of man and heaven.
Why comes he not? Such truths to be
   divulged,
Methinks the accuser's rest is long indulged.

III

The hour is past and Lara too is there,
With self-confiding, coldly patient air; 30
Why comes not Ezzelin? The hour is past,
And murmurs rise, and Otho's brow's
   o'ercast.
'I know my friend! his faith I cannot fear,
If yet he be on earth, expect him here;
The roof that held him in the valley stands
Between my own and noble Lara's lands;
My halls from such a guest had honour
   gain'd,
Nor had Sir Ezzelin his host disdain'd,
But that some previous proof forbade his
   stay,   39
And urged him to prepare against to-day;
The word I pledged for his I pledge again,
Or will myself redeem his knighthood's
   stain.'   42

He ceased—and Lara answered, 'I am here
To lend at thy demand a listening ear
To tales of evil from a stranger's tongue,
Whose words already might my heart have
   wrung,   46
But that I deem'd him scarcely less than mad,
Or, at the worst, a foe ignobly bad.
I know him not—but me it seems he knew
In lands where—but I must not trifle too:
Produce this babbler—or redeem the
   pledge;   51
Here in thy hold, and with thy falchion's
   edge.'

Proud Otho on the instant, reddening,
   threw
His glove on earth, and forth his sabre flew.
'The last alternative befits me best, 55
And thus I answer for mine absent guest.'

With cheek unchanging from its sallow
   gloom,
However near his own or other's tomb;
With hand, whose almost careless coolness
   spoke
Its grasp well used to deal the sabre-stroke;
With eye, though calm, determin'd not to
   spare,   61
Did Lara too his willing weapon bare.
In vain the circling chieftains round them
   closed,
For Otho's frenzy would not be opposed;
And from his lip those words of insult
   fell—   65
His sword is good who can maintain them
   well.

IV

Short was the conflict; furious, blindly
   rash,
Vain Otho gave his bosom to the gash:
He bled, and fell; but not with deadly
   wound,
Stretch'd by a dexterous sleight along the
   ground.   70
'Demand thy life!' He answer'd not: and
   then
From that red floor he ne'er had risen
   again,
For Lara's brow upon the moment grew
Almost to blackness in its demon hue;
And fiercer shook his angry falchion now
Than when his foe's was levell'd at his
   brow;   76
Then all was stern collectedness and art,
Now rose the unleaven'd hatred of his
   heart;
So little sparing to the foe he fell'd,
That when the approaching crowd his arm
   withheld,   80
He almost turn'd the thirsty point on those
Who thus for mercy dared to interpose;
But to a moment's thought that purpose
   bent;
Yet look'd he on him still with eye intent,
As if he loathed the ineffectual strife 85
That left a foe, howe'er o'ercome, with life;
As if to search how far the wound he gave
Had sent its victim onward to his grave.

V

They raised the bleeding Otho, and the
   Leech
Forbade all present question, sign, and
   speech: 90
The others met within a neighbouring hall,
And he, incensed, and heedless of them
   all,
The cause and conqueror in this sudden
   fray,
In haughty silence slowly strode away;
He back'd his steed, his homeward path he
   took,   95
Nor cast on Otho's towers a single look.

VI

But where was he? that meteor of a night,
Who menaced but to disappear with light.
Where was this Ezzelin? who came and
   went,
To leave no other trace of his intent. 100
He left the dome of Otho long ere morn,
In darkness, yet so well the path was worn
He could not miss it: near his dwelling lay;
But there he was not, and with coming day
Came fast inquiry, which unfolded nought,
Except the absence of the chief it sought.
A chamber tenantless, a steed at rest,
His host alarm'd, his murmuring squires
   distress'd:

Their search extends along, around the
    path,
In dread to meet the marks of prowlers'
    wrath: 110
But none are there, and not a brake hath
    borne
Nor gout of blood, nor shred of mantle
    torn;
Nor fall nor struggle hath defaced the
    grass,
Which still retains a mark where murder
    was;   114
Nor dabbling fingers left to tell the tale,
The bitter print of each convulsive nail,
When agonisèd hands that cease to guard,
Wound in the pang that smoothness of the
    sward.
Some such had been, if here a life was
    reft,
But these were not; and doubting hope is
    left;   120
And strange suspicion, whispering Lara's
    name,
Now daily mutters o'er his blacken'd
    fame;
Then sudden silent when his form ap-
    pear'd,
Awaits the absence of the thing it fear'd,
Again its wonted wondering to renew, 125
And dye conjecture with a darker hue.

VII

Days roll along, and Otho's wounds are
    heal'd,
But not his pride; and hate no more con-
    ceal'd:
He was a man of power, and Lara's foe,
The friend of all who sought to work him
    woe,   130
And from his country's justice now de-
    mands
Account of Ezzelin at Lara's hands.
Who else than Lara could have cause to
    fear
His presence? who had made him dis-
    appear,
If not the man on whom his menaced
    charge   135
Had sate too deeply were he left at large?
The general rumour ignorantly loud,
The mystery dearest to the curious crowd;
The seeming friendlessness of him who
    strove
To win no confidence, and wake no love;
The sweeping fierceness which his soul
    betray'd,   141
The skill with which he wielded his keen
    blade;
Where had his arm unwarlike caught that
    art?
Where had that fierceness grown upon his
    heart?   144
For it was not the blind capricious rage
A word can kindle and a word assuage;

But the deep working of a soul unmix'd
With aught of pity where its wrath had
    fix'd;
Such as long power and overgorged
    success
Concentrates into all that's merciless:
These, link'd with that desire which ever
    sways   151
Mankind, the rather to condemn than
    praise,
'Gainst Lara gathering raised at length a
    storm,
Such as himself might fear, and foes would
    form,   154
And he must answer for the absent head
Of one that haunts him still, alive or dead.

VIII

Within that land was many a malcontent,
Who cursed the tyranny to which he bent;
That soil full many a wringing despot saw
Who work'd his wantonness in form of
    law;   160
Long war without and frequent broil with-
    in
Had made a path for blood and giant sin,
That waited but a signal to begin
New havoc, such as civil discord blends,
Which knows no neuter, owns but foes or
    friends;   165
Fix'd in his feudal fortress each was lord,
In word and deed obey'd, in soul abhorr'd.
Thus Lara had inherited his lands,
And with them pining hearts and sluggish
    hands;
But that long absence from his native
    clime   170
Had left him stainless of oppression's
    crime,
And now, diverted by his milder sway,
All dread by slow degrees had worn away.
The menials felt their usual awe alone,
But more for him than them that fear was
    grown;   175
They deem'd him now unhappy, though at
    first
Their evil judgment augur'd of the worst,
And each long restless night, and silent
    mood,
Was traced to sickness, fed by solitude:
And though his lonely habits threw of
    late   180
Gloom o'er his chamber, cheerful was his
    gate;
For thence the wretched ne'er unsoothed
    withdrew,
For them, at least, his soul compassion
    knew.
Cold to the great, contemptuous to the
    high,
The humble pass'd not his unheeding eye;
Much he would speak not, but beneath his
    roof   186
They found asylum oft, and ne'er reproof.

And they who watch'd might mark that,
   day by day,
Some new retainers gather'd to his sway;
But most of late, since Ezzelin was lost,
He play'd the courteous lord and bounte-
   ous host: 191
Perchance his strife with Otho made him
   dread
Some snare prepared for his obnoxious
   head;
Whate'er his view, his favour more obtains
With these, the people, than his fellow
   thanes.   195
If this were policy, so far 'twas sound,
The million judged but of him as they
   found;
From him by sterner chiefs to exile driven
They but required a shelter, and 'twas given.
By him no peasant mourn'd his rifled cot,
And scarce the Serf could murmur o'er his
   lot;   201
With him old avarice found its hoard secure,
With him contempt forbore to mock the
   poor;
Youth present cheer and promised recom-
   pense
Detain'd, till all too late to part from thence:
To hate he offer'd, with the coming
   change,   206
The deep reversion of delay'd revenge;
To love, long baffled by the unequal match,
The well-won charms success was sure to
   snatch.   209
All now was ripe, he waits but to proclaim
That slavery nothing which was still a name.
The moment came, the hour when Otho
   thought
Secure at last the vengeance which he
   sought: 213
His summons found the destined criminal
Begirt by thousands in his swarming hall,
Fresh from their feudal fetters newly riven,
Defying earth, and confident of heaven.
That morning he had freed the soil-bound
   slaves,
Who dig no land for tyrants but their
   graves!
Such is their cry—some watchword for the
   fight   220
Must vindicate the wrong, and warp the
   right;
Religion — freedom — vengeance — what
   you will,
A word 's enough to raise mankind to kill;
Some factious phrase by cunning caught
   and spread,
That guilt may reign, and wolves and
   worms be fed!   225

IX

Throughout that clime the feudal chiefs
   had gain'd
Such sway, their infant monarch hardly
   reign'd;

Now was the hour for faction's rebel
   growth,
The Serfs contemn'd the one, and hated
   both: 229
They waited but a leader, and they found
One to their cause inseparably bound;
By circumstance compell'd to plunge
   again,
In self-defence, amidst the strife of men.
Cut off by some mysterious fate from those
Whom birth and nature meant not for his
   foes,   235
Had Lara from that night, to him accurst,
Prepared to meet, but not alone, the worst:
Some reason urged, whate'er it was, to
   shun
Inquiry into deeds at distance done;   239
By mingling with his own the cause of all,
E'en if he fail'd, he still delay'd his fall.
The sullen calm that long his bosom kept,
The storm that once had spent itself and
   slept,
Roused by events that seem'd foredoom'd
   to urge
His gloomy fortunes to their utmost verge,
Burst forth, and made him all he once had
   been,   246
And is again; he only changed the scene.
Light care had he for life, and less for fame,
But not less fitted for the desperate game:
He deem'd himself mark'd out for others'
   hate,   250
And mock'd at ruin so they shared his fate.
What cared he for the freedom of the
   crowd?
He raised the humble but to bend the
   proud.
He had hoped quiet in his sullen lair,
But man and destiny beset him there:
Inured to hunters, he was found at bay;
And they must kill, they cannot snare the
   prey.   257
Stern, unambitious, silent, he had been
Henceforth a calm spectator of life's scene;
But dragg'd again upon the arena, stood
A leader not unequal to the feud;   261
In voice, mien, gesture, savage nature
   spoke,
And from his eye the gladiator broke.

X

What boots the oft-repeated tale of strife,
The feast of vultures, and the waste of life?
The varying fortune of each separate field,
The fierce that vanquish, and the faint that
   yield?   267
The smoking ruin, and the crumbled wall?
In this the struggle was the same with all;
Save that distemper'd passions lent their
   force   270
In bitterness that banish'd all remorse.
None sued, for Mercy knew her cry was
   vain,
The captive died upon the battle-plain:

In either cause, one rage alone possess'd
The empire of the alternate victor's breast;
And they that smote for freedom or for
   sway,   276
Deem'd few were slain, while more re-
   main'd to slay.
It was too late to check the wasting brand,
And Desolation reap'd the famish'd land;
The torch was lighted, and the flame was
   spread,   280
And Carnage smiled upon her daily dead.

XI

Fresh with the nerve the new-born impulse
   strung,
The first success to Lara's numbers clung;
But that vain victory hath ruin'd all;
They form no longer to their leader's call:
In blind confusion on the foe they press,
And think to snatch is to secure success.
The lust of booty, and the thirst of hate,
Lure on the broken brigands to their fate:
In vain he doth whate'er a chief may do,
To check the headlong fury of that crew;
In vain their stubborn ardour he would
   tame,   292
The hand that kindles cannot quench the
   flame;
The wary foe alone hath turn'd their
   mood,
And shown their rashness to that erring
   brood: 295
The feign'd retreat, the nightly ambus-
   cade,
The daily harass, and the fight delay'd,
The long privation of the hoped supply,
The tentless rest beneath the humid sky,
The stubborn wall that mocks the leaguer's
   art,   300
And palls the patience of his baffled heart,
Of these they had not deem'd: the battle-
   day
They could encounter as a veteran may;
But more preferr'd the fury of the strife,
And present death, to hourly suffering
   life: 305
And famine wrings, and fever sweeps away
His numbers melting fast from their array;
Intemperate triumph fades to discontent,
And Lara's soul alone seems still unbent:
But few remain to aid his voice and hand,
And thousands dwindled to a scanty band:
Desperate, though few, the last and best
   remain'd   312
To mourn the discipline they late dis-
   dain'd.
One hope survives, the frontier is not far,
And thence they may escape from native
   war;   315
And bear within them to the neighbour-
   ing state
An exile's sorrows, or an outlaw's hate:
Hard is the task their father-land to quit,
But harder still to perish or submit.

XII

It is resolved—they march—consenting
   Night   320
Guides with her star their dim and torch-
   less flight;
Already they perceive its tranquil beam
Sleep on the surface of the barrier stream;
Already they descry—Is yon the bank?
Away! 'tis lined with many a hostile rank.
Return or fly!—What glitters in the rear?
'Tis Otho's banner—the pursuer's spear!
Are those the shepherds' fires upon the
   height?
Alas! they blaze too widely for the flight:
Cut off from hope, and compass'd in the
   toil,   330
Less blood perchance hath bought a
   richer spoil!

XIII

A moment's pause—'tis but to breathe
   their band,
Or shall they onward press, or here with-
   stand?
It matters little—if they charge the foes
Who by their border-stream their march
   oppose,   335
Some few, perchance, may break and pass
   the line,
However link'd to baffle such design.
'The charge be ours! to wait for their
   assault
Were fate well worthy of a coward's halt.'
Forth flies each sabre, rein'd is every steed,
And the next word shall scarce outstrip
   the deed: 341
In the next tone of Lara's gathering
   breath
How many shall but hear the voice of
   death!

XIV

His blade is bared,—in him there is an air
As deep, but far too tranquil for despair;
A something of indifference more than
   then   346
Becomes the bravest, if they feel for men.
He turn'd his eye on Kaled, ever near,
And still too faithful to betray one fear;
Perchance 'twas but the moon's dim twi-
   light threw   350
Along his aspect an unwonted hue
Of mournful paleness, whose deep tint ex-
   press'd
The truth, and not the terror of his breast.
This Lara mark'd, and laid his hand on
   his: 354
It trembled not in such an hour as this;
His lip was silent, scarcely beat his heart,
His eye alone proclaim'd, 'We will not
   part!
Thy band may perish, or thy friends may
   flee,
Farewell to life, but not adieu to thee!'

The word hath pass'd his lips, and onward
  driven,   360
Pours the link'd band through ranks
  asunder riven:
Well has each steed obey'd the armed heel,
And flash the scimitars, and rings the steel;
Outnumber'd, not outbraved, they still
  oppose
Despair to daring, and a front to foes;
And blood is mingled with the dashing
  stream,   366
Which runs all redly till the morning beam.

XV

Commanding, aiding, animating all,
Where foe appear'd to press, or friend to
  fall,
Cheers Lara's voice, and waves or strikes
  his steel,   370
Inspiring hope himself had ceased to feel.
None fled, for well they knew that flight
  were vain;
But those that waver turn to smite again,
While yet they find the firmest of the foe
Recoil before their leader's look and blow:
Now girt with numbers, now almost alone,
He foils their ranks, or re-unites his own;
Himself he spared not—once they seem'd
  to fly—   378
Now was the time, he waved his hand on
  high,
And shook—Why sudden droops that
  plumed crest?   380
The shaft is sped—the arrow's in his
  breast!
That fatal gesture left the unguarded side,
And Death has stricken down yon arm of
  pride.
The word of triumph fainted from his
  tongue;
That hand, so raised, how droopingly it
  hung!   385
But yet the sword instinctively retains,
Though from its fellow shrink the falling
  reins;
These Kaled snatches: dizzy with the blow,
And senseless bending o'er his saddle-bow,
Perceives not Lara that his anxious page
Beguiles his charger from the combat's
  rage: 391
Meantime his followers charge, and
  charge again;
Too mix'd the slayers now to heed the slain!

XVI

Day glimmers on the dying and the dead,
The cloven cuirass and the helmless head;
The war-horse masterless is on the earth,
And that last gasp hath burst his bloody
  girth;   397
And near, yet quivering with what life re-
  main'd,
The heel that urged him and the hand that
  rein'd;

And some too near that rolling torrent lie,
Whose waters mock the lip of those that
  die;   401
That panting thirst which scorches in the
  breath
Of those that die the soldier's fiery death,
In vain impels the burning mouth to crave
One drop—the last—to cool it for the
  grave;   405
With feeble and convulsive effort swept,
Their limbs along the crimson'd turf have
  crept;
The faint remains of life such struggles
  waste,
But yet they reach the stream and bend to
  taste:
They feel its freshness, and almost par-
  take—   410
Why pause? No further thirst have they
  to slake—
It is unquench'd, and yet they feel it not;
It was an agony—but now forgot!

XVII

Beneath a lime, remoter from the scene,
Where but for him that strife had never
  been,   415
A breathing but devoted warrior lay:
'Twas Lara bleeding fast from life away.
His follower once, and now his only guide,
Kneels Kaled watchful o'er his welling
  side,
And with his scarf would stanch the tides
  that rush,   420
With each convulsion, in a blacker gush;
And then, as his faint breathing waxes
  low,
In feebler, not less fatal tricklings flow:
He scarce can speak, but motions him 'tis
  vain,
And merely adds another throb to pain.
He clasps the hand that pang which would
  assuage,   426
And sadly smiles his thanks to that dark
  page,
Who nothing fears, nor feels, nor heeds,
  nor sees,
Save that damp brow which rests upon
  his knees;
Save that pale aspect, where the eye,
  though dim,   430
Held all the light that shone on earth for
  him.

XVIII

The foe arrives, who long had search'd
  the field,
Their triumph nought till Lara too should
  yield;
They would remove him, but they see
  'twere vain,
And he regards them with a calm disdain,
That rose to reconcile him with his fate,
And that escape to death from living hate:

And Otho comes, and leaping from his
    steed,
Looks on the bleeding foe that made him
    bleed,
And questions of his state; he answers
    not,   440
Scarce glances on him as on one forgot,
And turns to Kaled:—each remaining
    word
They understood not, if distinctly heard;
His dying tones are in that other tongue,
To which some strange remembrance
    wildly clung.   445
They spake of other scenes, but what—is
    known
To Kaled, whom their meaning reach'd
    alone;
And he replied, though faintly, to their
    sound,
While gazed the rest in dumb amazement
    round:
They seem'd even then—that twain—unto
    the last   450
To half-forget the present in the past;
To share between themselves some separ-
    ate fate,
Whose darkness none beside should pene-
    trate.

XIX

Their words though faint were many—
    from the tone
Their import those who heard could judge
    alone;   455
From this, you might have deem'd young
    Kaled's death
More near than Lara's by his voice and
    breath,
So sad, so deep, and hesitating broke
The accents his scarce-moving pale lips
    spoke;
But Lara's voice, though low, at first was
    clear   460
And calm, till murmuring death gasp'd
    hoarsely near;
But from his visage little could we guess,
So unrepentant, dark, and passionless,
Save that when struggling nearer to his
    last,
Upon that page his eye was kindly cast;
And once, as Kaled's answering accents
    ceased,   466
Rose Lara's hand, and pointed to the East:
Whether (as then the breaking sun from
    high
Roll'd back the clouds) the morrow caught
    his eye,
Or that 'twas chance, or some remem-
    ber'd scene,   470
That raised his arm to point where such
    had been,
Scarce Kaled seem'd to know, but turn'd
    away,
As if his heart abhorr'd that coming day,

And shrunk his glance before that morn-
    ing light,
To look on Lara's brow—where all grew
    night.   475
Yet sense seem'd left, though better were
    its loss,
For when one near display'd the absolv-
    ing cross,
And proffer'd to his touch the holy bead,
Of which his parting soul might own the
    need,
He look'd upon it with an eye profane,
And smiled—Heaven pardon! if 'twere
    with disdain: 481
And Kaled, though he spoke not, nor
    withdrew
From Lara's face his fix'd despairing view,
With brow repulsive, and with gesture
    swift,
Flung back the hand which held the sacred
    gift,   485
As if such but disturb'd the expiring man,
Nor seem'd to know his life but *then*
    began,
That life of Immortality, secure
To none, save them whose faith in Christ
    is sure.

XX

But gasping heaved the breath that Lara
    drew,   490
And dull the film along his dim eye grew;
His limbs stretch'd fluttering, and his head
    droop'd o'er
The weak yet still untiring knee that bore;
He press'd the hand he held upon his
    heart—
It beats no more, but Kaled will not
    part   495
With the cold grasp, but feels, and feels in
    vain,
For that faint throb which answers not
    again.
'It beats!'—Away, thou dreamer! he is
    gone—
It once was Lara which thou look'st upon.

XXI

He gazed, as if not yet had pass'd away
The haughty spirit of that humbled clay;
And those around have roused him from
    his trance,
But cannot tear from thence his fixed
    glance;
And when, in raising him from where he
    bore
Within his arms the form that felt no
    more,   505
He saw the head his breast would still sus-
    tain,
Roll down like earth to earth upon the
    plain;
He did not dash himself thereby, nor tear
The glossy tendrils of his raven hair,

But strove to stand and gaze, but reel'd
  and fell,   510
Scarce breathing more than that he loved
  so well.
Than that *he* loved! Oh! never yet beneath
The breast of man such trusty love may
  breathe!
That trying moment hath at once reveal'd
The secret long and yet but half conceal'd;
In baring to revive that lifeless breast,   516
Its grief seem'd ended, but the sex con-
  fess'd;
And life return'd, and Kaled felt no
  shame—
What now to her was Womanhood or
  Fame?

XXII

And Lara sleeps not where his fathers
  sleep,   520
But where he died his grave was dug as
  deep;
Nor is his mortal slumber less profound,
Though priest nor bless'd nor marble
  deck'd the mound,
And he was mourn'd by one whose quiet
  grief,
Less loud, outlasts a people's for their
  chief.   525
Vain was all question ask'd her of the past,
And vain e'en menace—silent to the last;
She told nor whence, nor why she left
  behind
Her all for one who seem'd but little kind.
Why did she love him? Curious fool!—be
  still—   530
Is human love the growth of human will?
To her he might be gentleness; the stern
Have deeper thoughts than your dull eyes
  discern,
And when they love, your smilers guess
  not how
Beats the strong heart, though less the lips
  avow.   535
They were not common links, that form'd
  the chain
That bound to Lara Kaled's heart and
  brain;
But that wild tale she brook'd not to un-
  fold,
And seal'd is now each lip that could have
  told.

XXIII

They laid him in the earth, and on his
  breast,   540
Besides the wound that sent his soul to
  rest,
They found the scatter'd dints of many a
  scar,
Which were not planted there in recent war;
Where'er had pass'd his summer years of
  life,
It seems they vanish'd in a land of strife;

But all unknown his glory or his guilt,
These only told that somewhere blood was
  spilt,
And Ezzelin, who might have spoke the
  past,
Return'd no more—that night appear'd
  his last.   549

XXIV

Upon that night (a peasant's is the tale)
A Serf that cross'd the intervening vale,
When Cynthia's light almost gave way to
  morn,
And nearly veil'd in mist her waning horn;
A Serf, that rose betimes to thread the
  wood,
And hew the bough that brought his chil-
  dren's food,   555
Pass'd by the river that divides the plain
Of Otho's lands and Lara's broad domain:
He heard a tramp—a horse and horse-
  man broke
From out the wood—before him was a
  cloak
Wrapt round some burthen at his saddle-
  bow,   560
Bent was his head, and hidden was his
  brow.
Roused by the sudden sight at such a time,
And some foreboding that it might be
  crime,
Himself unheeded watch'd the stranger's
  course,
Who reach'd the river, bounded from his
  horse,   565
And lifting thence the burthen which he
  bore,
Heaved up the bank, and dash'd it from
  the shore,
Then paused, and look'd, and turn'd, and
  seem'd to watch,
And still another hurried glance would
  snatch,
And follow with his step the stream that
  flow'd,   570
As if even yet too much its surface show'd;
At once he started, stoop'd, around him
  strown
The winter floods had scatter'd heaps of
  stone;
Of these the heaviest thence he gather'd
  there,
And slung them with a more than common
  care.   575
Meantime the Serf had crept to where un-
  seen
Himself might safely mark what this might
  mean;
He caught a glimpse, as of a floating breast,
And something glitter'd starlike on the
  vest;
But ere he well could mark the buoyant
  trunk,   580
A massy fragment smote it, and it sunk:

It rose again, but indistinct to view,
And left the waters of a purple hue,
Then deeply disappear'd: the horseman
    gazed   584
Till ebb'd the latest eddy it had raised;
Then turning, vaulted on his pawing steed,
And instant spurr'd him into panting
    speed.
His face was mask'd—the features of the
    dead,
If dead it were, escaped the observer's
    dread;
But if in sooth a star its bosom bore,   590
Such is the badge that knighthood ever
    wore,
And such 'tis known Sir Ezzelin had worn
Upon the night that led to such a morn.
If thus he perish'd, Heaven receive his
    soul!   594
His undiscover'd limbs to ocean roll;
And charity upon the hope would dwell
It was not Lara's hand by which he fell.

XXV

And Kaled—Lara—Ezzelin, are gone,
Alike without their monumental stone!
The first, all efforts vainly strove to wean
From lingering where her chieftain's blood
    had been: 601
Grief had so tamed a spirit once too proud,
Her tears were few, her wailing never loud;
But furious would you tear her from the
    spot

Where yet she scarce believed that he was
    not,   605
Her eye shot forth with all the living fire
That haunts the tigress in her whelpless ire;
But left to waste her weary moments there,
She talk'd all idly unto shapes of air,
Such as the busy brain of Sorrow paints,
And woos to listen to her fond complaints:
And she would sit beneath the very tree
Where lay his drooping head upon her
    knee:
And in that posture where she saw him
    fall,
His words, his looks, his dying grasp re-
    call;   615
And she had shorn, but saved her raven
    hair,
And oft would snatch it from her bosom
    there,
And fold, and press it gently to the ground,
As if she staunch'd anew some phantom's
    wound.   619
Herself would question, and for him reply;
Then rising, start, and beckon him to fly
From some imagined spectre in pursuit;
Then seat her down upon some linden's
    root,
And hide her visage with her meagre hand,
Or trace strange characters along the sand.
This could not last—she lies by him she
    loved;   626
Her tale untold, her truth too dearly
    proved.

THE SIEGE OF CORINTH

TO

JOHN HOBHOUSE, ESQ.,

THIS POEM IS INSCRIBED BY HIS

January 22nd, 1816   FRIEND.

ADVERTISEMENT

'THE grand army of the Turks (in 1715), under the Prime Vizier, to open to themselves a way into the heart of the Morea, and to form the siege of Napoli di Romania, the most considerable place in all that country*, thought it best in the first place to attack Corinth, upon which they made several storms. The garrison being weakened, and the governor seeing it was impossible to hold out against so mighty a force, thought it fit to beat a parley: but while they were treating about the articles, one of the magazines in the Turkish camp, wherein they had six hundred barrels of powder, blew up by accident, whereby six or seven hundred men were killed; which so enraged the infidels, that they would not grant any capitulation, but stormed the place with so much fury, that they took it, and put most of the garrison, with Signior Minotti, the governor, to the sword. The rest, with Antonio Bembo, provedítor extraordinary, were made prisoners of war.'—*History of the Turks*, vol. iii, p. 151.

* Napoli di Romania is not now the most considerable place in the Morea, but Tripolitza, where the Pacha resides, and maintains his government. Napoli is near Argos. I visited all three in 1810–11; and, in the course of journeying through the country from my first arrival in 1809, I crossed the Isthmus eight times in my way from Attica to the Morea, over the mountains; or in the other direction, when passing from the Gulf of Athens to that of Lepanto. Both the routes are picturesque and beautiful, though very different: that by sea has more sameness; but the voyage being always within sight of land, and often very near it, presents many attractive views of the islands Salamis, Ægina, Poros, &c., and the coast of the Continent.

THE SIEGE OF CORINTH

In the year since Jesus died for men,
Eighteen hundred years and ten,
We were a gallant company,
Riding o'er land, and sailing o'er sea.
Oh! but we went merrily! 5
We forded the river, and clomb the high
hill,
Never our steeds for a day stood still;
Whether we lay in the cave or the shed,
Our sleep fell soft on the hardest bed: 9
Whether we couch'd in our rough capote,
On the rougher plank of our gliding boat,
Or stretch'd on the beach, or our saddles
spread
As a pillow beneath the resting head,
Fresh we woke upon the morrow:
All our thoughts and words had scope,
We had health, and we had hope, 16
Toil and travel, but no sorrow.
We were of all tongues and creeds;—
Some were those who counted beads,
Some of mosque, and some of church, 20
And some, or I mis-say, of neither;
Yet through the wide world might ye
search,
Nor find a motlier crew nor blither.

But some are dead, and some are gone,
And some are scattered and alone, 25
And some are rebels on the hills
That look along Epirus' valleys,
Where freedom still at moments rallies,
And pays in blood oppression's ills;
And some are in a far countree, 30
And some all restlessly at home;
But never more, oh! never, we
Shall meet to revel and to roam.

But those hardy days flew cheerily!
And when they now fall drearily, 35
My thoughts, like swallows, skim the
main,
And bear my spirit back again
Over the earth, and through the air,
A wild bird and a wanderer.
'Tis this that ever wakes my strain, 40
And oft, too oft, implores again
The few who may endure my lay,
To follow me so far away.
Stranger—wilt thou follow now,
And sit with me on Acro-Corinth's brow?

I

Many a vanish'd year and age, 46
And tempest's breath, and battle's rage,
Have swept o'er Corinth; yet she stands,
A fortress form'd to Freedom's hands.
The whirlwind's wrath, the earthquake's
shock, 50
Have left untouch'd her hoary rock,
The keystone of a land, which still,
Though fall'n, looks proudly on that hill,

The landmark to the double tide
That purpling rolls on either side, 55
As if their waters chafed to meet,
Yet pause and crouch beneath her feet.
But could the blood before her shed
Since first Timoleon's brother bled,
Or baffled Persia's despot fled, 60
Arise from out the earth which drank
The stream of slaughter as it sank,
That sanguine ocean would o'erflow
Her isthmus idly spread below:
Or could the bones of all the slain, 65
Who perish'd there, be piled again,
That rival pyramid would rise
More mountain-like, through those clear
skies,
Than yon tower-capp'd Acropolis,
Which seems the very clouds to kiss. 70

II

On dun Cithæron's ridge appears
The gleam of twice ten thousand spears;
And downward to the Isthmian plain,
From shore to shore of either main,
The tent is pitch'd, the crescent shines 75
Along the Moslem's leaguering lines;
And the dusk Spahi's bands advance
Beneath each bearded pacha's glance;
And far and wide as eye can reach
The turban'd cohorts throng the beach;
And there the Arab's camel kneels, 81
And there his steed the Tartar wheels;
The Turcoman hath left his herd,
The sabre round his loins to gird;
And there the volleying thunders pour, 85
Till waves grow smoother to the roar.
The trench is dug, the cannon's breath
Wings the far hissing globe of death;
Fast whirl the fragments from the wall,
Which crumbles with the ponderous ball;
And from that wall the foe replies, 91
O'er dusty plain and smoky skies,
With fires that answer fast and well
The summons of the Infidel.

III

But near and nearest to the wall 95
Of those who wish and work its fall,
With deeper skill in war's black art
Than Othman's sons, and high of heart
As any chief that ever stood
Triumphant in the fields of blood; 100
From post to post, and deed to deed,
Fast spurring on his reeking steed,
Where sallying ranks the trench assail,
And make the foremost Moslem quail;
Or where the battery, guarded well, 105
Remains as yet impregnable,
Alighting cheerly to inspire
The soldier slackening in his fire;

320

The first and freshest of the host
Which Stamboul's sultan there can boast,
To guide the follower o'er the field,   111
To point the tube, the lance to wield,
Or whirl around the bickering blade;—
Was Alp, the Adrian renegade!

IV

From Venice—once a race of worth   115
His gentle sires—he drew his birth;
But late an exile from her shore,
Against his countrymen he bore
The arms they taught to bear; and now
The turban girt his shaven brow.   120
Through many a change had Corinth pass'd
With Greece to Venice' rule at last;
And here, before her walls, with those
To Greece and Venice equal foes,
He stood a foe, with all the zeal   125
Which young and fiery converts feel,
Within whose heated bosom throngs
The memory of a thousand wrongs.
To him had Venice ceased to be
Her ancient civic boast—'the Free';   130
And in the palace of St. Mark
Unnamed accusers in the dark
Within the 'Lion's mouth' had placed
A charge against him uneffaced:
He fled in time, and saved his life,   135
To waste his future years in strife,
That taught his land how great her loss
In him who triumph'd o'er the Cross,
'Gainst which he rear'd the Crescent high,
And battled to avenge or die.   140

V

Coumourgi—he whose closing scene
Adorn'd the triumph of Eugene,
When on Carlowitz' bloody plain,
The last and mightiest of the slain,
He sank, regretting not to die,   145
But cursed the Christian's victory—
Coumourgi—can his glory cease,
That latest conqueror of Greece,
Till Christian hands to Greece restore
The freedom Venice gave of yore?   150
A hundred years have roll'd away
Since he refix'd the Moslem's sway;
And now he led the Mussulman,
And gave the guidance of the van
To Alp, who well repaid the trust   155
By cities levell'd with the dust;
And proved, by many a deed of death,
How firm his heart in novel faith.

VI

The walls grew weak; and fast and hot
Against them pour'd the ceaseless shot,
With unabating fury sent   161
From battery to battlement;
And thunder-like the pealing din
Rose from each heated culverin;
And here and there some crackling dome
Was fired before the exploding bomb;   166
And as the fabric sank beneath
The shattering shell's volcanic breath,
In red and wreathing columns flash'd
The flame, as loud the ruin crash'd,   170
Or into countless meteors driven,
Its earth-stars melted into heaven;
Whose clouds that day grew doubly dun,
Impervious to the hidden sun,
With volumed smoke that slowly grew
To one wide sky of sulphurous hue.   176

VII

But not for vengeance, long delay'd,
Alone, did Alp, the renegade,
The Moslem warriors sternly teach
His skill to pierce the promised breach:
Within these walls a maid was pent   181
His hope would win, without consent
Of that inexorable sire,
Whose heart refused him in its ire,
When Alp, beneath his Christian name,
Her virgin hand aspired to claim.
In happier mood, and earlier time,   187
While unimpeach'd for traitorous crime,
Gayest in gondola or hall,
He glitter'd through the Carnival;
And tuned the softest serenade
That e'er on Adria's waters play'd
At midnight to Italian maid.   193

VIII

And many deem'd her heart was won;
For sought by numbers, given to none,
Had young Francesca's hand remain'd
Still by the church's bonds unchain'd:
And when the Adriatic bore
Lanciotto to the Paynim shore,   199
Her wonted smiles were seen to fail,
And pensive wax'd the maid and pale;
More constant at confessional,
More rare at masque and festival;
Or seen at such, with downcast eyes,
Which conquer'd hearts they ceased to prize;   205
With listless look she seems to gaze:
With humbler care her form arrays;
Her voice less lively in the song;
Her step, though light, less fleet among
The pairs, on whom the Morning's glance
Breaks, yet unsated with the dance.   211

IX

Sent by the state to guard the land,
(Which, wrested from the Moslem's hand,
While Sobieski tamed his pride
By Buda's wall and Danube's side,   215
The chiefs of Venice wrung away
From Patra to Euboea's bay,)
Minotti held in Corinth's towers
The Doge's delegated powers,
While yet the pitying eye of Peace   220
Smiled o'er her long forgotten Greece:

And ere that faithless truce was broke
Which freed her from the unchristian yoke,
With him his gentle daughter came;
Nor there, since Menelaus' dame   225
Forsook her lord and land, to prove
What woes await on lawless love,
Had fairer form adorn'd the shore
Than she, the matchless stranger, bore.

X

The wall is rent, the ruins yawn;   230
And with to-morrow's earliest dawn,
O'er the disjointed mass shall vault
The foremost of the fierce assault.
The bands are rank'd; the chosen van
Of Tartar and of Mussulman,   235
The full of hope, misnamed 'forlorn',
Who hold the thought of death in scorn,
And win their way with falchion's force,
Or pave the path with many a corse,
O'er which the following brave may rise,
Their stepping-stone—the last who dies!

XI

'Tis midnight: on the mountains brown
The cold, round moon shines deeply
          down;   243
Blue roll the waters, blue the sky
Spreads like an ocean hung on high,
Bespangled with those isles of light,
So wildly, spiritually bright;
Who ever gazed upon them shining
And turn'd to earth without repining,
Nor wish'd for wings to flee away,   250
And mix with their eternal ray?
The waves on either shore lay there
Calm, clear, and azure as the air;
And scarce their foam the pebbles shook,
But murmur'd meekly as the brook.   255
The winds were pillow'd on the waves;
The banners droop'd along their staves,
And, as they fell around them furling,
Above them shone the crescent curling;
And that deep silence was unbroke,   260
Save where the watch his signal spoke,
Save where the steed neigh'd oft and shrill,
And echo answer'd from the hill,
And the wide hum of that wild host
Rustled like leaves from coast to coast,
As rose the Muezzin's voice in air   266
In midnight call to wonted prayer;
It rose, that chanted mournful strain,
Like some lone spirit's o'er the plain:
'Twas musical, but sadly sweet,   270
Such as when winds and harp-strings
          meet,
And take a long unmeasured tone,
To mortal minstrelsy unknown.
It seem'd to those within the wall
A cry prophetic of their fall:
It struck even the besieger's ear   276
With something ominous and drear,
An undefined and sudden thrill,
Which makes the heart a moment still,

Then beat with quicker pulse, ashamed
Of that strange sense its silence framed;
Such as a sudden passing-bell   282
Wakes, though but for a stranger's knell.

XII

The tent of Alp was on the shore;
The sound was hush'd, the prayer was
          o'er,   285
The watch was set, the night-round made,
All mandates issued and obey'd:
'Tis but another anxious night,
His pains the morrow may requite
With all revenge and love can pay,   290
In guerdon for their long delay.
Few hours remain, and he hath need
Of rest, to nerve for many a deed
Of slaughter; but within his soul   294
The thoughts like troubled waters roll.
He stood alone among the host;
Not his the loud fanatic boast
To plant the crescent o'er the cross,
Or risk a life with little loss,
Secure in paradise to be   300
By Houris loved immortally:
Nor his, what burning patriots feel,
The stern exaltedness of zeal,
Profuse of blood, untired in toil,
When battling on the parent soil.   305
He stood alone—a renegade
Against the country he betray'd;
He stood alone amidst his band,
Without a trusted heart or hand: 309
They follow'd him, for he was brave,
And great the spoil he got and gave;
They crouch'd to him, for he had skill
To warp and wield the vulgar will:
But still his Christian origin
With them was little less than sin.   315
They envied even the faithless fame
He earn'd beneath a Moslem name;
Since he, their mightiest chief, had been
In youth a bitter Nazarene.   319
They did not know how pride can stoop,
When baffled feelings withering droop;
They did not know how hate can burn
In hearts once changed from soft to stern;
Nor all the false and fatal zeal
The convert of revenge can feel.   325
He ruled them—man may rule the worst,
By ever daring to be first:
So lions o'er the jackal sway;
The jackal points, he fells the prey,
Then on the vulgar, yelling, press,   330
To gorge the relics of success.

XIII

His head grows fever'd, and his pulse
The quick successive throbs convulse:
In vain from side to side he throws
His form, in courtship of repose;   335
Or if he dozed, a sound, a start
Awoke him with a sunken heart.

The turban on his hot brow press'd,
The mail weigh'd lead-like on his breast,
Though oft and long beneath its weight
Upon his eyes had slumber sate,   341
Without or couch or canopy,
Except a rougher field and sky
Than now might yield a warrior's bed,
Than now along the heaven was spread.
He could not rest, he could not stay   346
Within his tent to wait for day,
But walk'd him forth along the sand,
Where thousand sleepers strew'd the
      strand.
What pillow'd them? and why should he
More wakeful than the humblest be,
Since more their peril, worse their toil?
And yet they fearless dream of spoil;
While he alone, where thousands pass'd
A night of sleep, perchance their last, 355
In sickly vigil wander'd on,
And envied all he gazed upon.

XIV

He felt his soul become more light
Beneath the freshness of the night.
Cool was the silent sky, though calm, 360
And bathed his brow with airy balm:
Behind, the camp—before him lay,
In many a winding creek and bay,
Lepanto's gulf; and, on the brow
Of Delphi's hill, unshaken snow,   365
High and eternal, such as shone
Through thousand summers brightly
      gone,
Along the gulf, the mount, the clime;
It will not melt, like man, to time;
Tyrant and slave are swept away,   370
Less form'd to wear before the ray;
But that white veil, the lightest, frailest,
Which on the mighty mount thou hailest,
While tower and tree are torn and rent,
Shines o'er its craggy battlement;   375
In form a peak, in height a cloud,
In texture like a hovering shroud,
Thus high by parting Freedom spread,
As from her fond abode she fled,
And linger'd on the spot, where long   380
Her prophet spirit spake in song.
Oh! still her step at moments falters
O'er wither'd fields, and ruin'd altars,
And fain would wake, in souls too broken,
By pointing to each glorious token: 385
But vain her voice, till better days
Dawn in those yet remember'd rays,
Which shone upon the Persian flying,
And saw the Spartan smile in dying.

XV

Not mindless of these mighty times   390
Was Alp, despite his flight and crimes;
And through this night, as on he wander'd,
And o'er the past and present ponder'd,
And thought upon the glorious dead
Who there in better cause had bled,   395

He felt how faint and feebly dim
The fame that could accrue to him,
Who cheer'd the band, and waved the
      sword,
A traitor in a turban'd horde;
And led them to the lawless siege,   400
Whose best success were sacrilege.
Not so had those his fancy number'd,
The chiefs whose dust around him slum-
      ber'd;
Their phalanx marshall'd on the plain,
Whose bulwarks were not then in vain.
They fell devoted, but undying;   406
The very gale their name seem'd sighing;
The waters murmur'd of their name;
The woods were peopled with their fame;
The silent pillar, lone and grey,   410
Claim'd kindred with their sacred clay;
Their spirits wrapp'd the dusky mountain,
Their memory sparkled o'er the fountain;
The meanest rill, the mightiest river
Roll'd mingling with their fame for ever.
Despite of every yoke she bears,   416
That land is glory's still and theirs!
'Tis still a watchword to the earth:
When man would do a deed of worth
He points to Greece, and turns to tread,
So sanction'd, on the tyrant's head: 421
He looks to her, and rushes on
Where life is lost, or freedom won.

XVI

Still by the shore Alp mutely mused,
And woo'd the freshness Night diffused.
There shrinks no ebb in that tideless sea,
Which changeless rolls eternally;   427
So that wildest of waves, in their angriest
      mood,
Scarce break on the bounds of the land
      for a rood;
And the powerless moon beholds them
      flow,   430
Heedless if she come or go:
Calm or high, in main or bay,
On their course she hath no sway.
The rock unworn its base doth bare,
And looks o'er the surf, but it comes not
      there;   435
And the fringe of the foam may be seen
      below,
On the line that it left long ages ago:
A smooth short space of yellow sand
Between it and the greener land.

He wander'd on along the beach,   440
Till within the range of a carbine's reach
Of the leaguer'd wall; but they saw him
      not,
Or how could he 'scape from the hostile
      shot?
Did traitors lurk in the Christians' hold?
Were their hands grown stiff, or their
      hearts wax'd cold?   445

I know not, in sooth; but from yonder
    wall
There flash'd no fire, and there hiss'd no
    ball,
Though he stood beneath the bastion's
    frown,
That flank'd the sea-ward gate of the
    town;
Though he heard the sound, and could
    almost tell   450
The sullen words of the sentinel,
As his measured step on the stone below
Clank'd, as he paced it to and fro;
And he saw the lean dogs beneath the wall
Hold o'er the dead their carnival,   455
Gorging and growling o'er carcass and
    limb;
They were too busy to bark at him!
From a Tartar's skull they had stripp'd
    the flesh,
As ye peel the fig when its fruit is fresh;
And their white tusks crunch'd o'er the
    whiter skull,   460
As it slipp'd through their jaws, when
    their edge grew dull,
As they lazily mumbled the bones of the
    dead,
When they scarce could rise from the spot
    where they fed;
So well had they broken a lingering 'fast
With those who had fallen for that night's
    repast.   465
And Alp knew, by the turbans that roll'd
    on the sand,
The foremost of these were the best of his
    band:
Crimson and green were the shawls of
    their wear,
And each scalp had a single long tuft of
    hair,
All the rest was shaven and bare.   470
The scalps were in the wild dog's maw,
The hair was tangled round his jaw:
But close by the shore, on the edge of the
    gulf,
There sat a vulture flapping a wolf,
Who had stolen from the hills, but kept
    away,   475
Scared by the dogs, from the human
    prey;
But he seized on his share of a steed that
    lay,
Pick'd by the birds, on the sands of the bay.

XVII

Alp turn'd him from the sickening sight:
Never had shaken his nerves in fight;
But he better could brook to behold the
    dying,   481
Deep in the tide of their warm blood lying,
Scorch'd with the death-thirst, and writh-
    ing in vain,
Than the perishing dead who are past all
    pain.

There is something of pride in the perilous
    hour,   485
Whate'er be the shape in which death may
    lower;
For Fame is there to say who bleeds,
And Honour's eye on daring deeds!
But when all is past, it is humbling to
    tread
O'er the weltering field of the tombless
    dead,   490
And see worms of the earth, and fowls of
    the air,
Beasts of the forest, all gathering there;
All regarding man as their prey,
All rejoicing in his decay.

XVIII

There is a temple in ruin stands,   495
Fashion'd by long-forgotten hands;
Two or three columns, and many a stone,
Marble and granite, with grass o'ergrown!
Out upon Time! it will leave no more
Of the things to come than the things
    before!   500
Out upon Time! who for ever will leave
But enough of the past for the future to
    grieve
O'er that which hath been, and o'er that
    which must be:
What we have seen, our sons shall see;
Remnants of things that have pass'd away,
Fragments of stone rear'd by creatures of
    clay!   506

XIX

He sate him down at a pillar's base,
And pass'd his hand athwart his face;
Like one in dreary musing mood,
Declining was his attitude;   510
His head was drooping on his breast,
Fever'd, throbbing, and oppress'd;
And o'er his brow, so downward bent,
Oft his beating fingers went,
Hurriedly, as you may see   515
Your own run over the ivory key,
Ere the measured tone is taken
By the chords you would awaken.
There he sate all heavily,
As he heard the night-wind sigh.   520
Was it the wind through some hollow
    stone
Sent that soft and tender moan?
He lifted his head, and he look'd on the
    sea,
But it was unrippled as glass may be;
He look'd on the long grass—it waved
    not a blade;   525
How was that gentle sound convey'd?
He look'd to the banners—each flag lay
    still,
So did the leaves on Cithæron's hill,
And he felt not a breath come over his
    cheek;
What did that sudden sound bespeak?

He turn'd to the left—is he sure of
   sight?   531
There sate a lady, youthful and bright!

XX

He started up with more of fear
Than if an armed foe were near.
'God of my fathers! what is here? 535
Who art thou? and wherefore sent
So near a hostile armament?'
His trembling hands refused to sign
The cross he deem'd no more divine:
He had resumed it in that hour, 540
But conscience wrung away the power.
He gazed, he saw: he knew the face
Of beauty, and the form of grace;
It was Francesca by his side,
The maid who might have been his
   bride!   545

The rose was yet upon her cheek,
But mellow'd with a tenderer streak:
Where was the play of her soft lips fled?
Gone was the smile that enliven'd their
   red.
The ocean's calm within their view,
Beside her eye had less of blue; 551
But like that cold wave it stood still,
And its glance, though clear, was chill.
Around her form a thin robe twining,
Nought conceal'd her bosom shining;
Through the parting of her hair, 556
Floating darkly downward there,
Her rounded arm show'd white and bare:
And ere yet she made reply,
Once she raised her hand on high; 560
It was so wan, and transparent of hue,
You might have seen the moon shine
   through.

XXI

'I come from my rest to him I love best,
That I may be happy, and he may be
   bless'd,
I have pass'd the guards, the gate, the
   wall;   565
Sought thee in safety through foes and all.
'Tis said the lion will turn and flee
From a maid in the pride of her purity;
And the Power on high, that can shield
   the good
Thus from the tyrant of the wood, 570
Hath extended its mercy to guard me as
   well
From the hands of the leaguering infidel.
I come—and if I come in vain,
Never, oh never, we meet again!
Thou hast done a fearful deed 575
In falling away from thy fathers' creed:
But dash that turban to earth, and sign
The sign of the cross, and for ever be mine;
Wring the black drop from thy heart,
And to-morrow unites us no more to
   part.'   580

'And where should our bridal couch be
   spread?
In the midst of the dying and the dead?
For to-morrow we give to the slaughter
   and flame
The sons and the shrines of the Christian
   name.   584
None, save thou and thine, I've sworn,
Shall be left upon the morn:
But thee will I bear to a lovely spot,
Where our hands shall be join'd, and our
   sorrow forgot.
There thou yet shalt be my bride, 589
When once again I've quell'd the pride
Of Venice; and her hated race
Have felt the arm they would debase
Scourge, with a whip of scorpions, those
Whom vice and envy made my foes.'

Upon his hand she laid her own— 595
Light was the touch, but it thrill'd to the
   bone,
And shot a chillness to his heart,
Which fix'd him beyond the power to
   start.
Though slight was that grasp so mortal
   cold,
He could not loose him from its hold;
But never did clasp of one so dear 601
Strike on the pulse with such feeling of
   fear,
As those thin fingers, long and white,
Froze through his blood by their touch
   that night.
The feverish glow of his brow was gone,
And his heart sank so still that it felt like
   stone,   606
As he look'd on the face, and beheld its
   hue,
So deeply changed from what he knew:
Fair but faint—without the ray
Of mind, that made each feature play
Like sparkling waves on a sunny day;
And her motionless lips lay still as
   death,
And her words came forth without her
   breath,
And there rose not a heave o'er her
   bosom's swell,
And there seem'd not a pulse in her veins
   to dwell.   615
Though her eye shone out, yet the lids
   were fix'd,
And the glance that it gave was wild and
   unmix'd
With aught of change, as the eyes may
   seem
Of the restless who walk in a troubled
   dream;
Like the figures on arras, that gloomily
   glare,   620
Stirr'd by the breath of the wintry air,
So seen by the dying lamp's fitful light,
Lifeless, but life-like, and awful to sight;

As they seem, through the dimness, about
    to come down
From the shadowy wall where their images
    frown;   625
Fearfully flitting to and fro,
As the gusts on the tapestry come and go.

'If not for love of me be given
Thus much, then, for the love of
    heaven,—
Again I say—that turban tear   630
From off thy faithless brow, and swear
Thine injured country's sons to spare,
Or thou art lost; and never shalt see—
Not earth—that's past—but heaven or
    me.
If this thou dost accord, albeit   635
A heavy doom 'tis thine to meet,
That doom shall half absolve thy sin,
And mercy's gate may receive thee within:
But pause one moment more, and take
The curse of Him thou didst forsake;
And look once more to heaven, and see
Its love for ever shut from thee.
There is a light cloud by the moon—
'Tis passing, and will pass full soon—
If, by the time its vapoury sail   645
Hath ceased her shaded orb to veil,
Thy heart within thee is not changed,
Then God and man are both avenged;
Dark will thy doom be, darker still
Thine immortality of ill.'   650

Alp look'd to heaven, and saw on high
The sign she spake of in the sky;
But his heart was swollen, and turn'd aside,
By deep interminable pride.   654
This first false passion of his breast
Roll'd like a torrent o'er the rest.
He sue for mercy! *He* dismay'd
By wild words of a timid maid!
He, wrong'd by Venice, vow to save
Her sons, devoted to the grave!   660
No—though that cloud were thunder's
    worst,
And charged to crush him—let it burst!

He look'd upon it earnestly,
Without an accent of reply;   664
He watch'd it passing; it is flown:
Full on his eye the clear moon shone,
And thus he spake—'Whate'er my fate,
I am no changeling—'tis too late:
The reed in storms may bow and quiver,
Then rise again; the tree must shiver.
What Venice made me, I must be,   671
Her foe in all, save love to thee:
But thou art safe: oh, fly with me!'
He turn'd, but she is gone!
Nothing is there but the column stone.
Hath she sunk in the earth, or melted
    in air?   676
He saw not—he knew not—but nothing
    is there.

XXII

The night is past, and shines the sun
As if that morn were a jocund one.
Lightly and brightly breaks away   680
The Morning from her mantle grey,
And the noon will look on a sultry day.
Hark to the trump, and the drum,
And the mournful sound of the barbarous
    horn,
And the flap of the banners, that flit as
    they're borne,   685
And the neigh of the steed, and the multi-
    tude's hum,
And the clash, and the shout, 'They come!
    they come!'
The horsetails are pluck'd from the
    ground, and the sword
From its sheath; and they form, and but
    wait for the word.
Tartar, and Spahi, and Turcoman,   690
Strike your tents, and throng to the van;
Mount ye, spur ye, skirr the plain,
That the fugitive may flee in vain,
When he breaks from the town; and none
    escape,   694
Aged or young, in the Christian shape;
While your fellows on foot, in a fiery mass,
Bloodstain the breach through which they
    pass.
The steeds are all bridled, and snort to
    the rein;
Curved is each neck, and flowing each
    mane;
White is the foam of their champ on the
    bit;   700
The spears are uplifted; the matches are
    lit;
The cannon are pointed, and ready to
    roar,
And crush the wall they have crumbled
    before:
Forms in his phalanx each janizar;
Alp at their head; his right arm is bare,
So is the blade of his scimitar;   706
The khan and the pachas are all at their
    post;
The vizier himself at the head of the host.
When the culverin's signal is fired, then
    on;
Leave not in Corinth a living one—   710
A priest at her altars, a chief in her halls,
A hearth in her mansions, a stone on her
    walls.
God and the prophet—Alla Hu!
Up to the skies with that wild halloo!
'There the breach lies for passage, the
    ladder to scale;   715
And your hands on your sabres, and how
    should ye fail?
He who first downs with the red cross may
    crave
His heart's dearest wish; let him ask it,
    and have!'

Thus utter'd Coumourgi, the dauntless
    vizier;
The reply was the brandish of sabre and
    spear,   720
And the shout of fierce thousands in joy-
    ous ire:—
Silence—hark to the signal—fire!

XXIII

As the wolves, that headlong go
On the stately buffalo,
Though with fiery eyes, and angry roar,
And hoofs that stamp, and horns that
    gore,   726
He tramples on earth, or tosses on high
The foremost, who rush on his strength
    but to die:
Thus against the wall they went,
Thus the first were backward bent; 730
Many a bosom, sheathed in brass,
Strew'd the earth like broken glass,
Shiver'd by the shot, that tore
The ground whereon they moved no
    more:
Even as they fell, in files they lay, 735
Like the mower's grass at the close of
    day,
When his work is done on the levell'd
    plain;
Such was the fall of the foremost slain.

XXIV

As the spring-tides, with heavy plash,
From the cliffs invading dash   740
Huge fragments, sapp'd by the cease-
    less flow,
Till white and thundering down they go,
Like the avalanche's snow
On the Alpine vales below;   744
Thus at length, outbreathed and worn,
Corinth's sons were downward borne
By the long and oft renew'd
Charge of the Moslem multitude.
In firmness they stood, and in masses
    they fell,
Heap'd by the host of the infidel, 750
Hand to hand, and foot to foot:
Nothing there, save death, was mute:
Stroke, and thrust, and flash, and cry
For quarter or for victory,   754
Mingle there with the volleying thunder,
Which makes the distant cities wonder
How the sounding battle goes,
If with them, or for their foes;
If they must mourn, or may rejoice
In that annihilating voice,   760
Which pierces the deep hills through
    and through
With an echo dread and new:
You might have heard it, on that day,
O'er Salamis and Megara;
(We have heard the hearers say,) 765
Even unto Piræus' bay.

XXV

From the point of encountering blades
    to the hilt,
Sabres and swords with blood were gilt;
But the rampart is won, and the spoil
    begun,
And all but the after carnage done. 770
Shriller shrieks now mingling come
From within the plunder'd dome:
Hark to the haste of flying feet,
That splash in the blood of the slippery
    street;
But here and there, where 'vantage
    ground   775
Against the foe may still be found,
Desperate groups, of twelve or ten,
Make a pause, and turn again—
With banded backs against the wall,
Fiercely stand, or fighting fall. 780
There stood an old man—his hairs were
    white,
But his veteran arm was full of might:
So gallantly bore he the brunt of the
    fray,
The dead before him, on that day,
In a semicircle lay;   785
Still he combated unwounded,
Though retreating, unsurrounded.
Many a scar of former fight
Lurk'd beneath his corslet bright; 789
But of every wound his body bore,
Each and all had been ta'en before:
Though aged, he was so iron of limb,
Few of our youth could cope with
    him,
And the foes, whom he singly kept at
    bay,
Outnumber'd his thin hairs of silver
    grey.   795
From right to left his sabre swept;
Many an Othman mother wept
Sons that were unborn, when dipp'd
His weapon first in Moslem gore,
Ere his years could count a score. 800
Of all he might have been the sire
Who fell that day beneath his ire:
For, sonless left long years ago,
His wrath made many a childless foe;
And since the day, when in the strait
His only boy had met his fate, 806
His parent's iron hand did doom
More than a human hecatomb.
If shades by carnage be appeased,
Patroclus' spirit less was pleased 810
Than his, Minotti's son, who died
Where Asia's bounds and ours divide.
Buried he lay, where thousands be-
    fore
For thousands of years were inhumed
    on the shore;
What of them is left, to tell 815
Where they lie, and how they fell?

Not a stone on their turf, nor a bone in
    their graves;
But they live in the verse that immortally
    saves.

XXVI

Hark to the Allah shout! a band
Of the Mussulman bravest and best is
    at hand;   820
Their leader's nervous arm is bare,
Swifter to smite, and never to spare—
Unclothed to the shoulder it waves
    them on;
Thus in the fight is he ever known:
Others a gaudier garb may show,   825
To tempt the spoil of the greedy foe;
Many a hand's on a richer hilt,
But none on a steel more ruddily gilt;
Many a loftier turban may wear,—
Alp is but known by the white arm
    bare;   830
Look through the thick of the fight,
    'tis there!
There is not a standard on that shore
So well advanced the ranks before;
There is not a banner in Moslem war
Will lure the Delhis half so far;   835
It glances like a falling star!
Where'er that mighty arm is seen,
The bravest be, or late have been;
There the craven cries for quarter
Vainly to the vengeful Tartar;   840
Or the hero, silent lying,
Scorns to yield a groan in dying;
Mustering his last feeble blow
'Gainst the nearest levell'd foe,
Though faint beneath the mutual
    wound,   845
Grappling on the gory ground.

XXVII

Still the old man stood erect,
And Alp's career a moment check'd.
'Yield thee, Minotti; quarter take,
For thine own, thy daughter's sake.'

'Never, renegado, never!   851
Though the life of thy gift would last
    for ever.'

'Francesca!—Oh, my promised bride!
Must she too perish by thy pride?'

'She is safe.'—'Where? where?'—'In
    heaven;   855
From whence thy traitor soul is driven—
Far from thee, and undefiled.'
Grimly then Minotti smiled,
As he saw Alp staggering bow
Before his words, as with a blow.   860

'Oh God! when died she?'—'Yester-
    night—
Nor weep I for her spirit's flight:

None of my pure race shall be
Slaves to Mahomet and thee—
Come on!'—That challenge is in vain—
Alp's already with the slain!   866
While Minotti's words were wreaking
More revenge in bitter speaking
Than his falchion's point had found,
Had the time allow'd to wound,   870
From within the neighbouring porch
Of a long defended church,
Where the last and desperate few
Would the failing fight renew,
The sharp shot dash'd Alp to the
    ground;   875
Ere an eye could view the wound
That crash'd through the brain of the
    infidel,
Round he spun, and down he fell;
A flash like fire within his eyes
Blazed, as he bent no more to rise,   880
And then eternal darkness sunk
Through all the palpitating trunk;
Nought of life left, save a quivering
Where his limbs were slightly shivering:
They turn'd him on his back; his breast
And brow were stain'd with gore and
    dust,   886
And through his lips the life-blood
    oozed,
From its deep veins lately loosed:
But in his pulse there was no throb,
Nor on his lips one dying sob;   890
Sigh, nor word, nor struggling breath
Heralded his way to death;
Ere his very thought could pray,
Unanel'd he pass'd away,
Without a hope from mercy's aid,—
To the last a Renegade.   896

XXVIII

Fearfully the yell arose
Of his followers, and his foes;
These in joy, in fury those:
Then again in conflict mixing,   900
Clashing swords, and spears trans-
    fixing,
Interchanged the blow and thrust,
Hurling warriors in the dust.
Street by street, and foot by foot,
Still Minotti dares dispute   905
The latest portion of the land
Left beneath his high command;
With him, aiding heart and hand,
The remnant of his gallant band.
Still the church is tenable,   910
    Whence issued late the fated ball
    That half avenged the city's fall,
When Alp, her fierce assailant, fell:
Thither bending sternly back,
They leave before a bloody track;   915
And, with their faces to the foe,
Dealing wounds with every blow,
The chief, and his retreating train,
Join to those within the fane:

There they yet may breathe awhile,   920
Shelter'd by the massy pile.

XXIX

Brief breathing-time! the turban'd host,
With added ranks and raging boast,
Press onwards with such strength and
    heat,
Their numbers balk their own retreat;
For narrow the way that led to the
    spot   926
Where still the Christians yielded not;
And the foremost, if fearful, may vainly
    try
Through the massy column to turn and
    fly;
They perforce must do or die.   930
They die; but ere their eyes could close,
Avengers o'er their bodies rose;
Fresh and furious, fast they fill
The ranks unthinn'd, though slaugh-
    ter'd still;   934
And faint the weary Christians wax
Before the still renew'd attacks:
And now the Othmans gain the gate;
Still resists its iron weight,
And still, all deadly aim'd and hot,
From every crevice comes the shot;
From every shatter'd window pour   941
The volleys of the sulphurous shower:
But the portal wavering grows and
    weak—
The iron yields, the hinges creak—
It bends—it falls—and all is o'er;   945
Lost Corinth may resist no more!

XXX

Darkly, sternly, and all alone,
Minotti stood o'er the altar-stone:
Madonna's face upon him shone,
Painted in heavenly hues above,   950
With eyes of light and looks of love;
And placed upon that holy shrine
To fix our thoughts on things divine,
When pictured there, we kneeling see
Her, and the boy-God on her knee,
Smiling sweetly on each prayer   956
To heaven, as if to waft it there.
Still she smiled; even now she smiles,
Though slaughter streams along her
    aisles;
Minotti lifted his aged eye,   960
And made the sign of a cross with a
    sigh,
Then seized a torch which blazed there-
    by;
And still he stood, while with steel and
    flame
Inward and onward the Mussulman
    came.

XXXI

The vaults beneath the mosaic stone
Contain'd the dead of ages gone;   966

Their names were on the graven floor,
But now illegible with gore;
The carved crests, and curious hues
The varied marble's vein diffuse,   970
Were smear'd, and slippery,—stain'd,
    and strown
With broken swords, and helms o'er-
    thrown:
There were dead above, and the dead
    below
Lay cold in many a coffin'd row;
You might see them piled in sable
    state,   975
By a pale light through a gloomy grate;
But War had enter'd their dark caves,
And stored along the vaulted graves
Her sulphurous treasures, thickly
    spread
In masses by the fleshless dead: 980
Here, throughout the siege, had been
The Christians' chiefest magazine;
To these a late-form'd train now led,
Minotti's last and stern resource
Against the foe's o'erwhelming force.

XXXII

The foe came on, and few remain   986
To strive, and those must strive in vain:
For lack of further lives, to slake
The thirst of vengeance now awake,
With barbarous blows they gash the
    dead,   990
And lop the already lifeless head,
And fell the statues from their niche,
And spoil the shrines of offerings rich,
And from each other's rude hands
    wrest
The silver vessels saints had bless'd.
To the high altar on they go;   996
Oh, but it made a glorious show!
On its table still behold
The cup of consecrated gold;
Massy and deep, a glittering prize,   1000
Brightly it sparkles to plunderers' eyes:
That morn it held the holy wine,
Converted by Christ to his blood so
    divine,
Which his worshippers drank at the
    break of day,
To shrive their souls ere they join'd in
    the fray.   1005
Still a few drops within it lay:
And round the sacred table glow
Twelve lofty lamps, in splendid row,
From the purest metal cast;
A spoil—the richest, and the last.

XXXIII

So near they came, the nearest stretch'd
To grasp the spoil he almost reach'd,
    When old Minotti's hand
Touch'd with the torch the train—
    'Tis fired!   1015

Spire, vaults, the shrine, the spoil, the
    slain,
  The turban'd victors, the Christian
    band,
All that of living or dead remain,
Hurl'd on high with the shiver'd fane,
    In one wild roar expired!   1020
The shatter'd town—the walls thrown
    down—
The waves a moment backward bent—
The hills that shake, although unrent,
    As if an earthquake pass'd—
The thousand shapeless things all
    driven   1025
In cloud and flame athwart the heaven,
    By that tremendous blast—
Proclaim'd the desperate conflict o'er
On that too long afflicted shore:
Up to the sky like rockets go   1030
All that mingled there below:
Many a tall and goodly man,
Scorch'd and shrivell'd to a span,
When he fell to earth again
Like a cinder strew'd the plain: 1035
Down the ashes shower like rain;
Some fell in the gulf, which received the
    sprinkles
With a thousand circling wrinkles;
Some fell on the shore, but, far away,
Scatter'd o'er the isthmus lay;   1040
Christian or Moslem, which be they?
Let their mothers seem and say!
When in cradled rest they lay,
And each nursing mother smiled
On the sweet sleep of her child,   1045

Little deem'd she such a day
Would rend those tender limbs away.
Not the matrons that them bore
Could discern their offspring more;
That one moment left no trace   1050
More of human form or face
Save a scatter'd scalp or bone:
And down came blazing rafters, strown
Around, and many a falling stone,
Deeply dinted in the clay,   1055
All blacken'd there and reeking lay.
All the living things that heard
That deadly earth-shock disappear'd:
The wild birds flew; the wild dogs fled,
And howling left the unburied dead;
The camels from their keepers broke;
The distant steer forsook the yoke—
The nearer steed plunged o'er the plain,
And burst his girth, and tore his rein;
The bull-frog's note, from out the
    marsh,   1065
Deep-mouth'd arose, and doubly harsh;
The wolves yell'd on the cavern'd hill
Where echo roll'd in thunder still;
The jackals' troop, in gather'd cry,
Bay'd from afar complainingly,   1070
With a mix'd and mournful sound,
Like crying babe, and beaten hound:
With sudden wing, and ruffled breast,
The eagle left his rocky nest,
And mounted nearer to the sun,   1075
The clouds beneath him seem'd so dun;
Their smoke assail'd his startled beak,
And made him higher soar and shriek—
    Thus was Corinth lost and won!

PARISINA

TO

SCROPE BERDMORE DAVIES, ESQ.

THE FOLLOWING POEM IS INSCRIBED,

BY ONE WHO HAS LONG ADMIRED HIS TALENTS, AND VALUED HIS FRIENDSHIP

January 22, 1816.

ADVERTISEMENT

THE following poem is grounded on a circumstance mentioned in Gibbon's 'Antiquities of the House of Brunswick.' I am aware, that in modern times the delicacy or fastidiousness of the reader may deem such subjects unfit for the purposes of poetry. The Greek dramatists, and some of the best of our old English writers, were of a different opinion: as Alfieri and Schiller have also been, more recently, upon the Continent. The following extract will explain the facts on which the story is founded. The name of *Azo* is substituted for Nicholas, as more metrical.

'Under the reign of Nicholas III. Ferrara was polluted with a domestic tragedy. By the testimony of an attendant, and his own observation, the Marquis of Este discovered the incestuous loves of his wife Parisina, and Hugo his bastard son, a beautiful and valiant youth. They were beheaded in the castle by the sentence of a father and husband, who published his shame, and survived their execution. He was unfortunate, if they were guilty: if they were innocent, he was still more unfortunate; nor is there any possible situation in which I can sincerely approve the last act of the justice of a parent.'— GIBBON'S *Miscellaneous Works*, vol. iii, p. 470.

PARISINA

I

It is the hour when from the boughs
   The nightingale's high note is heard;
It is the hour when lovers' vows
   Seem sweet in every whisper'd word;
And gentle winds, and waters near,   5
Make music to the lonely ear.
Each flower the dews have lightly wet,
And in the sky the stars are met,
And on the wave is deeper blue,
And on the leaf a browner hue,   10
And in the heaven that clear obscure,
So softly dark, and darkly pure,
Which follows the decline of day,
As twilight melts beneath the moon
   away.

II

But it is not to list to the waterfall   15
That Parisina leaves her hall,
And it is not to gaze on the heavenly light
That the lady walks in the shadow of night;
And if she sits in Este's bower,
'Tis not for the sake of its full-blown
   flower;   20
She listens—but not for the nightingale—
Though her ear expects as soft a tale.
There glides a step through the foliage
   thick,
And her cheek grows pale, and her heart
   beats quick.
There whispers a voice through the rust-
   ling leaves,   25
And her blush returns, and her bosom
   heaves:
A moment more and they shall meet—
'Tis past—her lover's at her feet.

III

And what unto them is the world beside,
With all its change of time and tide? 30
Its living things, its earth and sky,
Are nothing to their mind and eye.
And heedless as the dead are they
   Of aught around, above, beneath;
As if all else had pass'd away,   35
   They only for each other breathe;
Their very sighs are full of joy
   So deep, that did it not decay,
That happy madness would destroy
   The hearts which feel its fiery sway:
Of guilt, of peril, do they deem   41
In that tumultuous tender dream?
Who that have felt that passion's power,
Or paused, or fear'd in such an hour?
Or thought how brief such moments
   last?   45
But yet—they are already past!
Alas! we must awake before
We know such vision comes no more.

IV

With many a lingering look they leave
   The spot of guilty gladness past: 50
And though they hope and vow, they
   grieve,
As if that parting were the last.
The frequent sigh—the long embrace—
   The lip that there would cling for ever,
While gleams on Parisina's face   55
   The Heaven she fears will not forgive
   her,
As if each calmly conscious star
Beheld her frailty from afar—
The frequent sigh, the long embrace,
Yet binds them to their trysting place.
But it must come, and they must part
In fearful heaviness of heart,   62
With all the deep and shuddering chill
Which follows fast the deeds of ill.

V

And Hugo is gone to his lonely bed,   65
   To covet there another's bride;
But she must lay her conscious head
   A husband's trusting heart beside.
But fever'd in her sleep she seems,
And red her cheek with troubled
   dreams,   70
   And mutters she in her unrest
A name she dare not breathe by day,
   And clasps her lord unto the breast
Which pants for one away:
And he to that embrace awakes,   75
And, happy in the thought, mistakes
The dreaming sigh, and warm caress,
For such as he was wont to bless;
And could in very fondness weep
O'er her who loves him even in sleep.

VI

He clasp'd her sleeping to his heart,
   And listen'd to each broken word:
He hears—Why doth Prince Azo start,
   As if the Archangel's voice he heard?
And well he may—a deeper doom   85
Could scarcely thunder o'er his tomb,
When he shall wake to sleep no more,
And stand the eternal throne before.
And well he may—his earthly peace
Upon that sound is doom'd to cease. 90
That sleeping whisper of a name
Bespeaks her guilt and Azo's shame.
And whose that name? that o'er his
   pillow
Sounds fearful as the breaking billow,
Which rolls the plank upon the shore,
   And dashes on the pointed rock   96
The wretch who sinks to rise no more,—
   So came upon his soul the shock.

And whose that name? 'tis Hugo's,—
  his—
In sooth he had not deem'd of this!— 99
'Tis Hugo's,—he, the child of one
He loved—his own all-evil son—
The offspring of his wayward youth,
When he betray'd Bianca's truth, 104
The maid whose folly could confide
In him who made her not his bride.

VII

He pluck'd his poniard in its sheath,
  But sheath'd it ere the point was
    bare—
Howe'er unworthy now to breathe,
He could not slay a thing so fair—
At least, not smiling—sleeping—
  there: 111
Nay more:—he did not wake her then,
  But gazed upon her with a glance
  Which, had she roused her from her
    trance,
Had frozen her sense to sleep again; 115
And o'er his brow the burning lamp
Gleam'd on the dew-drops big and
  damp.
She spake no more—but she still slum-
  ber'd—
While, in his thought, her days are
  number'd.

VIII

And with the morn he sought and
  found, 120
In many a tale from those around,
The proof of all he fear'd to know,
Their present guilt, his future woe;
The long-conniving damsels seek
  To save themselves, and would trans-
    fer 125
  The guilt—the shame—the doom—
    to her:
Concealment is no more—they speak
All circumstance which may compel
Full credence to the tale they tell:
And Azo's tortured heart and ear 130
Have nothing more to feel or hear.

IX

He was not one who brook'd delay:
  Within the chamber of his state,
The chief of Este's ancient sway 134
  Upon his throne of judgment sate;
His nobles and his guards are there,—
Before him is the sinful pair;
Both young,—and *one* how passing fair!
With swordless belt, and fetter'd hand,
  Oh, Christ! that thus a son should
    stand 140
  Before a father's face!
Yet thus must Hugo meet his sire,
And hear the sentence of his ire,
  The tale of his disgrace!

And yet he seems not overcome, 145
Although, as yet, his voice be dumb.

X

And still, and pale, and silently
  Did Parisina wait her doom;
How changed since last her speaking
  eye
  Glanced gladness round the glittering
    room, 150
Where high-born men were proud to
  wait,
Where Beauty watch'd to imitate
  Her gentle voice, her lovely mien,
And gather from her air and gait
  The graces of its queen! 155
Then,—had her eye in sorrow wept,
A thousand warriors forth had leapt,
A thousand swords had sheathless
  shone,
And made her quarrel all their own.
Now,—what is she? and what are they?
Can she command, or these obey?
All silent and unheeding now,
With downcast eyes and knitting brow,
And folded arms, and freezing air,
And lips that scarce their scorn for-
  bear, 165
Her knights and dames, her court—is
  there:
And he, the chosen one, whose lance
Had yet been couch'd before her glance,
Who—were his arm a moment free—
Had died or gain'd her liberty; 170
The minion of his father's bride,—
He, too, is fetter'd by her side;
Nor sees her swoln and full eye swim
Less for her own despair than him:
Those lids—o'er which the violet vein
Wandering, leaves a tender stain, 176
Shining through the smoothest white
That e'er did softest kiss invite—
Now seem'd with hot and livid glow
To press, not shade, the orbs below;
Which glance so heavily, and fill, 181
As tear on tear grows gathering still.

XI

And he for her had also wept,
  But for the eyes that on him gazed:
His sorrow, if he felt it, slept; 185
  Stern and erect his brow was raised.
Whate'er the grief his soul avow'd,
He would not shrink before the crowd;
But yet he dared not look on her;
Remembrance of the hours that were—
His guilt, his love, his present state—
His father's wrath, all good men's
  hate— 192
His earthly, his eternal fate—
And hers,—oh, hers! he dared not throw
One look upon that death-like brow!
Else had his rising heart betray'd 196
Remorse for all the wreck it made.

XII

And Azo spake:—'But yesterday
  I gloried in a wife and son;
That dream this morning pass'd away;
  Ere day declines, I shall have none.
My life must linger on alone;   202
Well,—let that pass,—there breathes
      not one
Who would not do as I have done:
Those ties are broken—not by me;
  Let that too pass;—the doom's pre-
      pared!   206
Hugo, the priest awaits on thee,
  And then—thy crime's reward!
Away! address thy prayers to Heaven,
  Before its evening stars are met—
Learn if thou there canst be forgiven;
  Its mercy may absolve thee yet.   212
But here, upon the earth beneath,
  There is no spot where thou and I
Together for an hour could breathe:
  Farewell! I will not see thee die—
But thou, frail thing! shalt view his
      head—   217
  Away! I cannot speak the rest:
Go! woman of the wanton breast;
Not I, but thou his blood dost shed;
Go! if that sight thou canst outlive,
And joy thee in the life I give.'   222

XIII

And here stern Azo hid his face—
  For on his brow the swelling vein
Throbb'd as if back upon his brain
  The hot blood ebb'd and flow'd
      again,   226
And therefore bow'd he for a space,
  And pass'd his shaking hand along
His eye, to veil it from the throng:
While Hugo raised his chainèd hands,
  And for a brief delay demands   231
His father's ear: the silent sire
Forbids not what his words require.

'It is not that I dread the death—
For thou hast seen me by thy side
All redly through the battle ride,
And that—not once a useless brand—
Thy slaves have wrested from my hand
Hath shed more blood in cause of thine,
Than e'er can stain the axe of mine:
  Thou gav'st, and may'st resume my
      breath,   241
A gift for which I thank thee not;
Nor are my mother's wrongs forgot,
Her slighted love and ruin'd name,
Her offspring's heritage of shame;
But she is in the grave, where he,
Her son, thy rival, soon shall be.
Her broken heart—my sever'd head—
Shall witness for thee from the dead
How trusty and how tender were   250
Thy youthful love—paternal care.

'Tis true that I have done thee wrong—
  But wrong for wrong:—this,—
      deem'd thy bride,
The other victim of thy pride,—
Thou know'st for me was destined long;
Thou saw'st, and coveted'st her charms;
  And with thy very crime—my birth—
  Thou tauntedst me, as little worth;
A match ignoble for her arms,   259
Because, forsooth, I could not claim
The lawful heirship of thy name,
Nor sit on Este's lineal throne;
  Yet, were a few short summers mine,
  My name should more than Este's shine
With honours all my own.   265
I had a sword—and have a breast
That should have won as haught a crest
As ever waved along the line
Of all these sovereign sires of thine.
Not always knightly spurs are worn
The brightest by the better born;   271
And mine have lanced my courser's
      flank
Before proud chiefs of princely rank,
When charging to the cheering cry
Of "Este" and of "Victory!"   275
I will not plead the cause of crime,
Nor sue thee to redeem from time
A few brief hours or days that must
At length roll o'er my reckless dust;—
Such maddening moments as my past,
They could not, and they did not, last.
Albeit my birth and name be base,
And thy nobility of race   283
Disdain'd to deck a thing like me—
  Yet in my lineaments they trace
  Some features of my father's face,
And in my spirit—all of thee.
From thee this tamelessness of heart—
From thee—nay, wherefore dost thou
      start?—   289
From thee in all their vigour came
My arm of strength, my soul of flame;
Thou didst not give me life alone,
But all that made me more thine own.
See what thy guilty love hath done!
Repaid thee with too like a son! 295
I am no bastard in my soul,
For that, like thine, abhorr'd control;
And for my breath, that hasty boon
Thou gav'st and wilt resume so soon,
I valued it no more than thou,   300
When rose thy casque above thy brow,
And we, all side by side, have striven,
And o'er the dead our coursers driven:
The past is nothing—and at last
The future can but be the past; 305
Yet would I that I then had died:
  For though thou work'dst my
      mother's ill,
And made thy own my destined bride,
  I feel thou art my father still: 309
And harsh as sounds thy hard decree,
'Tis not unjust, although from thee.

Begot in sin, to die in shame,
My life begun and ends the same:
As err'd the sire, so err'd the son,   314
And thou must punish both in one.
My crime seems worst to human view,
But God must judge between us too!'

XIV

He ceased—and stood with folded
    arms,
    On which the circling fetters sounded;
And not an ear but felt as wounded,
Of all the chiefs that there were
    rank'd,   321
    When those dull chains in meeting
    clank'd:
Till Parisina's fatal charms
Again attracted every eye—
Would she thus hear him doom'd to die!
She stood, I said, all pale and still,
The living cause of Hugo's ill: 327
Her eyes unmoved, but full and wide,
Not once had turn'd to either side—
Nor once did those sweet eyelids close,
Or shade the glance o'er which they
    rose,   331
But round their orbs of deepest blue
The circling white dilated grew—
And there with glassy gaze she stood
As ice were in her curdled blood;
But every now and then a tear   336
    So large and slowly gather'd slid
    From the long dark fringe of that fair
    lid,
It was a thing to see, not hear!
And those who saw, it did surprise,
Such drops could fall from human eyes.
To speak she thought—the imperfect
    note   342
Was choked within her swelling throat,
Yet seem'd in that low hollow groan
Her whole heart gushing in the tone.
It ceased—again she thought to speak,
Then burst her voice in one long shriek,
And to the earth she fell like stone
Or statue from its base o'erthrown,
More like a thing that ne'er had life,—
A monument of Azo's wife,—   351
Than her, that living guilty thing,
Whose every passion was a sting,
Which urged to guilt, but could not
    bear
That guilt's detection and despair.   355
But yet she lived—and all too soon
Recover'd from that death-like swoon—
But scarce to reason—every sense
Had been o'erstrung by pangs intense;
And each frail fibre of her brain   360
(As bowstrings, when relax'd by rain,
The erring arrow launch aside)
Sent forth her thoughts all wild and
    wide—
The past a blank, the future black,
With glimpses of a dreary track,   365

Like lightning on the desert path,
When midnight storms are mustering
    wrath.   367
She fear'd—she felt that something ill
Lay on her soul, so deep and chill;
That there was sin and shame she knew,
That some one was to die—but who?
She had forgotten:—did she breathe?
Could this be still the earth beneath,
The sky above, and men around;   374
Or were they fiends who now so frown'd
On one, before whose eyes each eye
Till then had smiled in sympathy?
All was confused and undefined
To her all-jarr'd and wandering mind;
A chaos of wild hopes and fears: 380
And now in laughter, now in tears,
But madly still in each extreme,
She strove with that convulsive dream;
For so it seem'd on her to break:
Oh! vainly must she strive to wake!

XV

The Convent bells are ringing,   386
    But mournfully and slow;
In the grey square turret swinging,
    With a deep sound, to and fro.
    Heavily to the heart they go!   390
Hark! the hymn is singing—
    The song for the dead below,
Or the living who shortly shall be so!
For a departing being's soul
The death-hymn peals and the hollow
    bells knoll:
He is near his mortal goal;   395
Kneeling at the Friar's knee,
Sad to hear, and piteous to see—
Kneeling on the bare cold ground,
With the block before and the guards
    around—   400
And the headsman with his bare arm
    ready,
That the blow may be both swift and
    steady,
Feels if the axe be sharp and true
Since he set its edge anew:
While the crowd in a speechless circle
    gather   405
To see the Son fall by the doom of the
    Father!

XVI

It is a lovely hour as yet
Before the summer sun shall set,
Which rose upon that heavy day,   409
And mock'd it with his steadiest ray;
And his evening beams are shed
Full on Hugo's fated head,
As his last confession pouring
To the monk, his doom deploring
In penitential holiness,   415
He bends to hear his accents bless
With absolution such as may
Wipe our mortal stains away.

That high sun on his head did glisten
As he there did bow and listen,   420
And the rings of chestnut hair
Curl'd half down his neck so bare;
But brighter still the beam was thrown
Upon the axe which near him shone
With a clear and ghastly glitter——
Oh! that parting hour was bitter!   426
Even the stern stood chill'd with awe:
Dark the crime, and just the law—
Yet they shudder'd as they saw.

XVII

The parting prayers are said and over
Of that false son, and daring lover!   431
His beads and sins are all recounted,
His hours to their last minute mounted;
His mantling cloak before was stripp'd,
His bright brown locks must now be
    clipp'd;   435
'Tis done—all closely are they shorn;
The vest which till this moment worn—
The scarf which Parisina gave—
Must not adorn him to the grave.   439
Even that must now be thrown aside,
And o'er his eyes the kerchief tied;
But no—that last indignity
Shall ne'er approach his haughty eye.
All feelings seemingly subdued,
In deep disdain were half renew'd,
When headsman's hands prepared to bind
Those eyes which would not brook
    such blind,
As if they dared not look on death.
'No—yours my forfeit blood and
    breath;
These hands are chain'd, but let me die
At least with an unshackled eye: 451
Strike:'—and as the word he said,
Upon the block he bow'd his head;
These last accents Hugo spoke:
'Strike'—and flashing fell the stroke—
Roll'd the head—and, gushing, sunk
Back the stain'd and heaving trunk,
In the dust, which each deep vein
Slaked with its ensanguined rain;   459
His eyes and lips a moment quiver,
Convulsed and quick—then fix for ever.

He died, as erring man should die,
    Without display, without parade;
    Meekly had he bow'd and pray'd,
    As not disdaining priestly aid,   465
Nor desperate of all hope on high.
And while before the Prior kneeling,
His heart was wean'd from earthly feeling;
His wrathful sire, his paramour—
What were they in such an hour?   470
No more reproach, no more despair,
No thought but heaven, no word but
    prayer—
Save the few which from him broke,
When, bared to meet the headsman's
    stroke,

He claim'd to die with eyes unbound,
His sole adieu to those around.   476

XVIII

Still as the lips that closed in death,
Each gazer's bosom held his breath:
But yet, afar, from man to man,
A cold electric shiver ran,   480
As down the deadly blow descended
On him whose life and love thus ended;
And, with a hushing sound compress'd,
A sigh shrunk back on every breast;
But no more thrilling noise rose there,
    Beyond the blow that to the block
    Pierced through with forced and
        sullen shock,   487
Save one:—what cleaves the silent air
So madly shrill, so passing wild?
That, as a mother's o'er her child,
Done to death by sudden blow,   491
To the sky these accents go,
Like a soul's in endless woe.
Through Azo's palace-lattice driven,
That horrid voice ascends to heaven,
And every eye is turn'd thereon: 496
But sound and sight alike are gone!
It was a woman's shriek—and ne'er
In madlier accents rose despair;
And those who heard it, as it pass'd,
In mercy wish'd it were the last.   501

XIX

Hugo is fallen; and, from that hour,
No more in palace, hall, or bower,
Was Parisina heard or seen: 504
Her name—as if she ne'er had been—
Was banish'd from each lip and ear,
Like words of wantonness or fear;
And from Prince Azo's voice, by none
Was mention heard of wife or son;
No tomb, no memory had they;   510
Theirs was unconsecrated clay—
At least the knight's who died that day.
But Parisina's fate lies hid
Like dust beneath the coffin lid:
Whether in convent she abode,   515
And won to heaven her dreary road
By blighted and remorseful years
Of scourge, and fast, and sleepless tears;
Or if she fell by bowl or steel,
For that dark love she dared to feel;
Or if, upon the moment smote,   52?
She died by tortures less remote,
Like him she saw upon the block,
With heart that shared the headsman's
    shock,
In quicken'd brokenness that came,
In pity, o'er her shatter'd frame,   526
None knew—and none can ever know:
But whatsoe'er its end below,
Her life began and closed in woe!

XX

And Azo found another bride,   530
And goodly sons grew by his side;

But none so lovely and so brave
As him who wither'd in the grave;
Or if they were—on his cold eye
Their growth but glanced unheeded by,
Or noticed with a smother'd sigh. 536
But never tear his cheek descended,
And never smile his brow unbended;
And o'er that fair broad brow were
  wrought
The intersected lines of thought; 540
Those furrows which the burning share
Of Sorrow ploughs untimely there;
Scars of the lacerating mind
Which the Soul's war doth leave behind.
He was past all mirth or woe:
Nothing more remain'd below 546
But sleepless nights and heavy days,
A mind all dead to scorn or praise,
A heart which shunn'd itself—and yet
That would not yield, nor could forget,
Which, when it least appear'd to melt,
Intently thought, intensely felt: 552
The deepest ice which ever froze
Can only o'er the surface close;
The living stream lies quick below, 555
And flows, and cannot cease to flow.
Still was his seal'd-up bosom haunted
By thoughts which Nature hath im-
  planted; 558
Too deeply rooted thence to vanish,

Howe'er our stifled tears we banish;
When, struggling as they rise to start,
We check those waters of the heart,
They are not dried—those tears unshed
But flow back to the fountain head,
And resting in their spring more pure,
For ever in its depth endure, 566
Unseen, unwept, but uncongeal'd,
And cherish'd most where least reveal'd.
With inward starts of feeling left,
To throb o'er those of life bereft, 570
Without the power to fill again
The desert gap which made his pain;
Without the hope to meet them where
United souls shall gladness share;
With all the consciousness that he
Had only pass'd a just decree; 576
That they had wrought their doom of
  ill;
Yet Azo's age was wretched still.
The tainted branches of the tree,
  If lopp'd with care, a strength may
    give, 580
  By which the rest shall bloom and
    live
All greenly fresh and wildly free:
But if the lightning, in its wrath,
The waving boughs with fury scathe,
The massy trunk the ruin feels, 585
And never more a leaf reveals.

THE PRISONER OF CHILLON

SONNET ON CHILLON

ETERNAL Spirit of the chainless Mind!
  Brightest in dungeons, Liberty! thou art,
  For there thy habitation is the heart—
The heart which love of thee alone can bind;
And when thy sons to fetters are consign'd—
  To fetters, and the damp vault's dayless gloom,
  Their country conquers with their martyrdom,
And Freedom's fame finds wings on every wind.
Chillon! thy prison is a holy place,
  And thy sad floor an altar—for 'twas trod,
Until his very steps have left a trace
  Worn, as if thy cold pavement were a sod,
By Bonnivard! May none those marks efface!
  For they appeal from tyranny to God.

ADVERTISEMENT

WHEN this poem was composed, I was not sufficiently aware of the history of Bonnivard, or I should
have endeavoured to dignify the subject by an attempt to celebrate his courage and his virtues. With
some account of his life I have been furnished, by the kindness of a citizen of that republic, which is
still proud of the memory of a man worthy of the best age of ancient freedom:—

'François de Bonnivard, fils de Louis de Bonnivard, originaire de Seyssel et Seigneur de Lunes,
naquit en 1496. Il fit ses études à Turin: en 1510 Jean Aimé de Bonnivard, son oncle, lui résigna le
Prieuré de St. Victor, qui aboutissait aux murs de Genève, et qui formait un bénéfice considérable.

'Ce grand homme—(Bonnivard mérite ce titre par la force de son âme, la droiture de son cœur,
la noblesse de ses intentions, la sagesse de ses conseils, le courage de ses démarches, l'étendue de ses
connaissances, et la vivacité de son esprit),—ce grand homme, qui excitera l'admiration de tous ceux

qu'une vertu héroïque peut encore émouvoir, inspirera encore la plus vive reconnaissance dans les cœurs des Génévois qui aiment Genève. Bonnivard en fut toujours un des plus fermes appuis: pour assurer la liberté de notre République, il ne craignit pas de perdre souvent la sienne; il oublia son repos; il méprisa ses richesses; il ne négligea rien pour affermir le bonheur d'une patrie qu'il honora de son choix: dès ce moment il la chérit comme le plus zélé de ses citoyens; il la servit avec l'intrépidité d'un héros, et il écrivit son Histoire avec la naïveté d'un philosophe et la chaleur d'un patriote.

'Il dit dans le commencement de son Histoire de Genève, que, *dès qu'il eut commencé de lire l'histoire des nations, il se sentit entraîné par son goût pour les Républiques, dont il épousa toujours les intérêts*: c'est ce goût pour la liberté qui lui fit sans doute adopter Genève pour sa patrie.

'Bonnivard, encore jeune, s'annonça hautement comme le défenseur de Genève contre le Duc de Savoye et l'Evêque.

'En 1519, Bonnivard devient le martyr de sa patrie. Le Duc de Savoye étant entré dans Genève avec cinq cent hommes, Bonnivard craint le ressentiment du Duc; il voulut se retirer à Fribourg pour en éviter les suites; mais il fut trahi par deux hommes qui l'accompagnaient, et conduit par ordre du Prince à Grolée, où il resta prisonnier pendant deux ans. Bonnivard était malheureux dans ses voyages: comme ses malheurs n'avaient point ralenti son zèle pour Genève, il était toujours un ennemi redoutable pour ceux qui la menaçaient, et par conséquent il devait être exposé à leurs coups. Il fut rencontré en 1530 sur le Jura par des voleurs, qui le dépouillèrent et qui le mirent encore entre les mains du Duc de Savoye: ce Prince le fit enfermer dans le Château de Chillon, où il resta sans être interrogé jusques en 1536; il fut alors délivré par les Bernois, qui s'emparèrent du Pays de Vaud.

'Bonnivard, en sortant de sa captivité, eut le plaisir de trouver Genève libre et réformée: la République s'empressa de lui témoigner sa reconnaissance, et de le dédommager des maux qu'il avoit soufferts: elle le reçut Bourgeois de la ville au mois de Juin, 1536; elle lui donna la maison habitée autrefois par le Vicaire-Général, et elle lui assigna une pension de deux cent écus d'or tant qu'il séjournerait à Genève. Il fut admis dans le Conseil de Deux-Cent en 1537.

'Bonnivard n'a pas fini d'être utile: après avoir travaillé à rendre Genève libre, il réussit à la rendre tolérante. Bonnivard engagea le Conseil à accorder aux ecclésiastiques et aux paysans un tems suffisant pour examiner les propositions qu'on leur faisait; il réussit par sa douceur: on prêche toujours le Christianisme avec succès quand on le prêche avec charité.

'Bonnivard fut savant: ses manuscrits, qui sont dans la bibliothèque publique, prouvent qu'il avait bien lu les auteurs classiques Latins, et qu'il avait approfondi la théologie et l'histoire. Ce grand homme aimait les sciences, et il croyait qu'elles pouvaient faire la gloire de Genève; aussi il ne négligea rien pour les fixer dans cette ville naissante; en 1551 il donna sa bibliothèque au public; elle fut le commencement de notre bibliothèque publique; et ces livres sont en partie les rares et belles éditions du quinzième siècle qu'on voit dans notre collection. Enfin, pendant la même année, le bon patriote institua la République son héritière, à condition qu'elle employerait ses biens à entretenir le collège dont on projettait la fondation.

'Il parait que Bonnivard mourut en 1570; mais on ne peut l'assurer, parcequ'il y a une lacune dans le Nécrologe depuis le mois de Juillet, 1570, jusques en 1571.'

I

My hair is grey, but not with years,
   Nor grew it white
   In a single night,
As men's have grown from sudden fears:
My limbs are bow'd, though not with
   toil,   5
   But rusted with a vile repose,
For they have been a dungeon's spoil,
   And mine has been the fate of those
To whom the goodly earth and air
Are bann'd, and barr'd—forbidden
   fare: 10
But this was for my father's faith
I suffer'd chains and courted death;
That father perish'd at the stake
For tenets he would not forsake;
And for the same his lineal race   15
In darkness found a dwelling-place;
We were seven—who now are one,
   Six in youth, and one in age,
Finish'd as they had begun,
   Proud of Persecution's rage;   20
One in fire, and two in field,
Their belief with blood have seal'd,
Dying as their father died,
For the God their foes denied;
Three within a dungeon cast,   25
Of whom this wreck is left the last.

II

There are seven pillars of Gothic mould,
In Chillon's dungeons deep and old,
There are seven columns, massy and
   grey,
Dim with a dull imprison'd ray,   30
A sunbeam which hath lost its way,
And through the crevice and the cleft
Of the thick wall is fallen and left;
Creeping o'er the floor so damp,
Like a marsh's meteor lamp: 35
And in each pillar there is a ring,
   And in each ring there is a chain;
That iron is a cankering thing,
   For in these limbs its teeth remain,
With marks that will not wear away,
Till I have done with this new day,   41
Which now is painful to these eyes,
Which have not seen the sun so rise
For years—I cannot count them o'er,
I lost their long and heavy score,   45
When my last brother droop'd and died,
And I lay living by his side.

III

They chain'd us each to a column stone,
And we were three—yet, each alone;
We could not move a single pace,   50
We could not see each other's face,

But with that pale and livid light
That made us strangers in our sight:
And thus together—yet apart, 54
Fetter'd in hand, but join'd in heart,
'Twas still some solace, in the dearth
Of the pure elements of earth,
To hearken to each other's speech,
And each turn comforter to each
With some new hope, or legend old,
Or song heroically bold; 61
But even these at length grew cold.
Our voices took a dreary tone,
An echo of the dungeon stone,
A grating sound, not full and free, 65
As they of yore were wont to be:
It might be fancy, but to me
They never sounded like our own.

IV

I was the eldest of the three, 69
And to uphold and cheer the rest
I ought to do—and did my best—
And each did well in his degree.
The youngest, whom my father loved,
Because our mother's brow was given
To him, with eyes as blue as heaven—
For him my soul was sorely moved:
And truly might it be distress'd 77
To see such bird in such a nest;
For he was beautiful as day—
(When day was beautiful to me 80
As to young eagles, being free)—
A polar day, which will not see
A sunset till its summer's gone,
Its sleepless summer of long light,
The snow-clad offspring of the sun: 85
And thus he was as pure and bright,
And in his natural spirit gay,
With tears for nought but others' ills,
And then they flow'd like mountain rills,
Unless he could assuage the woe 90
Which he abhorr'd to view below.

V

The other was as pure of mind,
But form'd to combat with his kind;
Strong in his frame, and of a mood
Which 'gainst the world in war had stood, 95
And perish'd in the foremost rank
With joy:—but not in chains to pine:
His spirit wither'd with their clank,
I saw it silently decline—
And so perchance in sooth did mine:
But yet I forced it on to cheer 101
Those relics of a home so dear.
He was a hunter of the hills,
Had follow'd there the deer and wolf;
To him his dungeon was a gulf, 105
And fetter'd feet the worst of ills.

VI

Lake Leman lies by Chillon's walls:
A thousand feet in depth below
Its massy waters meet and flow; 109

Thus much the fathom-line was sent
From Chillon's snow-white battlement,
Which round about the wave in-
thrals:
A double dungeon wall and wave
Have made—and like a living grave
Below the surface of the lake 115
The dark vault lies wherein we lay,
We heard it ripple night and day;
Sounding o'er our heads it knock'd;
And I have felt the winter's spray
Wash through the bars when winds
were high 120
And wanton in the happy sky;
And then the very rock hath rock'd,
And I have felt it shake, unshock'd,
Because I could have smiled to see
The death that would have set me free.

VII

I said my nearer brother pined, 126
I said his mighty heart declined,
He loathed and put away his food;
It was not that 'twas coarse and rude,
For we were used to hunter's fare,
And for the like had little care: 131
The milk drawn from the mountain goat
Was changed for water from the moat,
Our bread was such as captives' tears
Have moisten'd many a thousand years,
Since man first pent his fellow men
Like brutes within an iron den;
But what were these to us or him? 138
These wasted not his heart or limb;
My brother's soul was of that mould
Which in a palace had grown cold,
Had his free breathing been denied
The range of the steep mountain's side;
But why delay the truth?—he died.
I saw, and could not hold his head, 145
Nor reach his dying hand—nor dead,—
Though hard I strove, but strove in vain,
To rend and gnash my bonds in twain.
He died, and they unlock'd his chain,
And scoop'd for him a shallow grave
Even from the cold earth of our cave.
I begg'd them as a boon to lay 152
His corse in dust whereon the day
Might shine—it was a foolish thought,
But then within my brain it wrought,
That even in death his freeborn breast
In such a dungeon could not rest. 157
I might have spared my idle prayer—
They coldly laugh'd, and laid him there:
The flat and turfless earth above
The being we so much did love; 161
His empty chain above it leant,
Such murder's fitting monument!

VIII

But he, the favourite and the flower,
Most cherish'd since his natal hour,
His mother's image in fair face, 166
The infant love of all his race,

His martyr'd father's dearest thought,
My latest care, for whom I sought 169
To hoard my life, that his might be
Less wretched now, and one day free;
He, too, who yet had held untired
A spirit natural or inspired—
He, too, was struck, and day by day
Was wither'd on the stalk away. 175
Oh, God! it is a fearful thing
To see the human soul take wing
In any shape, in any mood:
I've seen it rushing forth in blood,
I've seen it on the breaking ocean
Strive with a swoln convulsive motion,
I've seen the sick and ghastly bed
Of Sin delirious with its dread;
But these were horrors—this was woe
Unmix'd with such—but sure and slow:
He faded, and so calm and meek, 186
So softly worn, so sweetly weak,
So tearless, yet so tender, kind,
And grieved for those he left behind;
With all the while a cheek whose bloom
Was as a mockery of the tomb, 191
Whose tints as gently sunk away
As a departing rainbow's ray;
An eye of most transparent light,
That almost made the dungeon bright,
And not a word of murmur, not 196
A groan o'er his untimely lot,—
A little talk of better days,
A little hope my own to raise,
For I was sunk in silence—lost 200
In this last loss, of all the most;
And then the sighs he would suppress
Of fainting nature's feebleness,
More slowly drawn, grew less and less:
I listen'd, but I could not hear; 205
I call'd, for I was wild with fear;
I knew 'twas hopeless, but my dread
Would not be thus admonished;
I call'd, and thought I heard a sound—
I burst my chain with one strong bound,
And rush'd to him:—I found him not,
I only stirr'd in this black spot, 212
I only lived, *I* only drew
The accursed breath of dungeon-dew;
The last, the sole, the dearest link 215
Between me and the eternal brink,
Which bound me to my failing race,
Was broken in this fatal place.
One on the earth, and one beneath—
My brothers—both had ceased to
    breathe: 220
I took that hand which lay so still,
Alas! my own was full as chill;
I had not strength to stir, or strive,
But felt that I was still alive—
A frantic feeling, when we know 225
That what we love shall ne'er be so.
    I know not why
    I could not die,
I had no earthly hope but faith,
And that forbade a selfish death. 230

IX

What next befell me then and there
    I know not well—I never knew—
First came the loss of light, and air,
    And then of darkness too:
I had no thought, no feeling—none—
Among the stones I stood a stone, 236
And was, scarce conscious what I wist,
As shrubless crags within the mist;
For all was blank, and bleak, and grey;
It was not night, it was not day; 240
It was not even the dungeon-light,
So hateful to my heavy sight,
But vacancy absorbing space,
And fixedness without a place;
There were no stars, no earth, no time,
No check, no change, no good, no
    crime, 246
But silence, and a stirless breath
Which neither was of life nor death;
A sea of stagnant idleness,
Blind, boundless, mute, and motion-
    less! 250

X

A light broke in upon my brain,—
    It was the carol of a bird;
It ceased, and then it came again,
    The sweetest song ear ever heard,
And mine was thankful till my eyes
Ran over with the glad surprise, 256
And they that moment could not see
I was the mate of misery;
But then by dull degrees came back
My senses to their wonted track; 260
I saw the dungeon walls and floor
Close slowly round me as before,
I saw the glimmer of the sun
Creeping as it before had done,
But through the crevice where it came
That bird was perch'd, as fond and
    tame, 266
    And tamer than upon the tree;
A lovely bird, with azure wings,
And song that said a thousand things,
    And seem'd to say them all for me!
I never saw its like before, 271
I ne'er shall see its likeness more:
It seem'd like me to want a mate,
But was not half so desolate,
And it was come to love me when
None lived to love me so again, 276
And cheering from my dungeon's brink,
Had brought me back to feel and think.
I know not if it late were free,
    Or broke its cage to perch on mine,
But knowing well captivity, 281
    Sweet bird! I could not wish for thine!
Or if it were, in winged guise,
A visitant from Paradise;
For—Heaven forgive that thought! the
    while 285
Which made me both to weep and smile—

I sometimes deem'd that it might be
My brother's soul come down to me;
But then at last away it flew,   289
And then 'twas mortal well I knew,
For he would never thus have flown,
And left me twice so doubly lone,
Lone as the corse within its shroud,
Lone as a solitary cloud,—
  A single cloud on a sunny day,   295
While all the rest of heaven is clear,
A frown upon the atmosphere,
That hath no business to appear
  When skies are blue, and earth is gay.

XI

A kind of change came in my fate,
My keepers grew compassionate;   301
I know not what had made them so,
They were inured to sights of woe,
But so it was:—my broken chain
With links unfasten'd did remain,   305
And it was liberty to stride
Along my cell from side to side,
And up and down, and then athwart,
And tread it over every part;
And round the pillars one by one,   310
Returning where my walk begun,
Avoiding only, as I trod,
My brothers' graves without a sod;
For if I thought with heedless tread
My step profaned their lowly bed,   315
My breath came gaspingly and thick,
And my crush'd heart felt blind and sick.

XII

I made a footing in the wall,
  It was not therefrom to escape,
For I had buried one and all   320
  Who loved me in a human shape;
And the whole earth would henceforth be
A wider prison unto me:
No child, no sire, no kin had I,
No partner in my misery;   325
I thought of this, and I was glad,
For thought of them had made me mad;
But I was curious to ascend
To my barr'd windows, and to bend
Once more, upon the mountains high,
The quiet of a loving eye.   331

XIII

I saw them, and they were the same,
They were not changed like me in
  frame;
I saw their thousand years of snow
On high—their wide long lake below,
And the blue Rhone in fullest flow;
I heard the torrents leap and gush   337

O'er channell'd rock and broken bush;
I saw the white-wall'd distant town,
And whiter sails go skimming down;
And then there was a little isle,
Which in my very face did smile,   342
  The only one in view;
A small green isle, it seem'd no more,
Scarce broader than my dungeon floor,
But in it there were three tall trees,
And o'er it blew the mountain breeze,
And by it there were waters flowing,
And on it there were young flowers
  growing,   349
  Of gentle breath and hue.
The fish swam by the castle wall,
And they seem'd joyous each and all;
The eagle rode the rising blast,
Methought he never flew so fast
As then to me he seem'd to fly;   355
And then new tears came in my eye,
And I felt troubled—and would fain
I had not left my recent chain;
And when I did descend again,
The darkness of my dim abode   360
Fell on me as a heavy load;
It was as is a new-dug grave,
Closing o'er one we sought to save,—
And yet my glance, too much opprest,
Had almost need of such a rest.   365

XIV

It might be months, or years, or days,
  I kept no count, I took no note,
I had no hope my eyes to raise,
  And clear them of their dreary mote;
At last men came to set me free;   370
  I ask'd not why, and reck'd not where;
It was at length the same to me,
Fetter'd or fetterless to be,
  I learn'd to love despair.   374
And thus when they appear'd at last,
And all my bonds aside were cast,
These heavy walls to me had grown
A hermitage—and all my own!
And half I felt as they were come
To tear me from a second home: 380
With spiders I had friendship made,
And watch'd them in their sullen trade,
Had seen the mice by moonlight play,
And why should I feel less than they?
We were all inmates of one place,   385
And I, the monarch of each race,
Had power to kill—yet, strange to tell!
In quiet we had learn'd to dwell;
My very chains and I grew friends,
So much a long communion tends   390
To make us what we are:—even I
Regain'd my freedom with a sigh.

MAZEPPA

ADVERTISEMENT

'CELUI qui remplissait alors cette place était un gentilhomme Polonais, nommé Mazeppa, né dans le palatinat de Podolie: il avait été élevé page de Jean Casimir, et avait pris à sa cour quelque teinture des belles-lettres. Une intrigue qu'il eut dans sa jeunesse avec la femme d'un gentilhomme Polonais ayant été découverte, le mari le fit lier tout nu sur un cheval farouche, et le laissa aller en cet état. Le cheval, qui était du pays de l'Ukraine, y retourna, et y porta Mazeppa, demi-mort de fatigue et de faim. Quelques paysans le secoururent: il resta longtems parmi eux, et se signala dans plusieurs courses contre les Tartares. La supériorité de ses lumières lui donna une grande considération parmi les Cosaques: sa réputation s'augmentant de jour en jour obligea le Czar à le faire Prince de l'Ukraine.' —VOLTAIRE, *Hist. de Charles XII.* p. 196.

'Le roi fuyant, et poursuivi, eut son cheval tué sous lui; le Colonel Gieta, blessé, et perdant tout son sang, lui donna le sien. Ainsi on remit deux fois à cheval, dans sa fuite, ce conquérant qui n'avait pu y monter pendant la bataille.'—P. 216.

'Le roi alla par un autre chemin avec quelques cavaliers. Le carrosse, où il était, rompit dans la marche; on le remit à cheval. Pour comble de disgrace, il s'égara pendant la nuit dans un bois; là, son courage ne pouvant plus suppléer à ses forces épuisées, les douleurs de sa blessure devenues plus insupportables par la fatigue, son cheval étant tombé de lassitude, il se coucha quelques heures au pied d'un arbre, en danger d'être surpris à tout moment par les vainqueurs, qui le cherchaient de tous côtés.'—P. 218.

I

'TWAS after dread Pultowa's day,
    When fortune left the royal Swede,
Around a slaughter'd army lay,
    No more to combat and to bleed.
The power and glory of the war,   5
    Faithless as their vain votaries, men,
Had pass'd to the triumphant Czar,
    And Moscow's walls were safe again,
Until a day more dark and drear,
And a more memorable year,   10
Should give to slaughter and to shame
A mightier host and haughtier name;
A greater wreck, a deeper fall,
A shock to one—a thunderbolt to all.

II

Such was the hazard of the die;   15
The wounded Charles was taught to
    fly
By day and night through field and flood,
Stain'd with his own and subjects' blood;
For thousands fell that flight to aid:
And not a voice was heard t' upbraid
Ambition in his humbled hour,   21
When truth had nought to dread from
    power.
His horse was slain, and Gieta gave
His own—and died the Russians' slave.
This too sinks after many a league   25
Of well sustain'd but vain fatigue;
And in the midst of forests darkling,
The watch-fires in the distance spark-
    ling—
The beacons of surrounding foes—
A king must lay his limbs at length.
    Are these the laurels and repose   31
For which the nations strain their
    strength?
They laid him by a savage tree,
In outworn nature's agony;

His wounds were stiff, his limbs were
    stark;   35
The heavy hour was chill and dark;
The fever in his blood forbade
A transient slumber's fitful aid:
And thus it was; but yet through all,
Kinglike the monarch bore his fall,   40
And made, in this extreme of ill,
His pangs the vassals of his will:
All silent and subdued were they,
As once the nations round him lay.

III

A band of chiefs!—alas! how few,
    Since but the fleeting of a day   46
Had thinn'd it; but this wreck was true
    And chivalrous: upon the clay
Each sate him down, all sad and mute,
    Beside his monarch and his steed;
For danger levels man and brute,
    And all are fellows in their need.   52
Among the rest, Mazeppa made
His pillow in an old oak's shade—
Himself as rough, and scarce less old,
The Ukraine's Hetman, calm and bold;
But first, outspent with this long course,
The Cossack prince rubb'd down his
    horse,   58
And made for him a leafy bed,
    And smooth'd his fetlocks and his
        mane,
    And slack'd his girth, and stripp'd his
        rein,
And joy'd to see how well he fed;
For until now he had the dread
His wearied courser might refuse   64
To browse beneath the midnight dews:
But he was hardy as his lord,
And little cared for bed and board;
But spirited and docile too,
Whate'er was to be done, would do.

Shaggy and swift, and strong of limb,
All Tartar-like he carried him;   71
Obey'd his voice, and came to call,
And knew him in the midst of all:
Though thousands were around,—and
    Night,
Without a star, pursued her flight,—
That steed from sunset until dawn   76
His chief would follow like a fawn.

IV

This done, Mazeppa spread his cloak,
And laid his lance beneath his oak,
Felt if his arms in order good   80
The long day's march had well with-
    stood—
If still the powder fill'd the pan,
    And flints unloosen'd kept their lock—
His sabre's hilt and scabbard felt,
And whether they had chafed his belt;
And next the venerable man,   86
From out his havresack and can,
    Prepared and spread his slender stock;
And to the monarch and his men
The whole or portion offer'd then   90
With far less of inquietude
Than courtiers at a banquet would.
And Charles of this his slender share
With smiles partook a moment there,
To force of cheer a greater show,   95
And seem above both wounds and woe;
And then he said—'Of all our band,
Though firm of heart and strong of hand,
In skirmish, march, or forage, none
Can less have said or more have done
Than thee, Mazeppa! on the earth   101
So fit a pair had never birth,
Since Alexander's days till now,
As thy Bucephalus and thou:
All Scythia's fame to thine should yield
For pricking on o'er flood and field.'
Mazeppa answer'd—'Ill betide   107
The school wherein I learn'd to ride!'
Quoth Charles—'Old Hetman, where-
    fore so,
Since thou hast learn'd the art so well?'
Mazeppa said—'Twere long to tell;
And we have many a league to go,
With every now and then a blow,   113
And ten to one at least the foe,
Before our steeds may graze at ease
Beyond the swift Borysthenes:
And, Sire, your limbs have need of rest,
    And I will be the sentinel
Of this your troop.'—'But I request,'
    Said Sweden's monarch, 'thou wilt
        tell   120
This tale of thine, and I may reap,
Perchance, from this the boon of sleep;
For at this moment from my eyes
The hope of present slumber flies.'

'Well, Sire, with such a hope, I'll track
My seventy years of memory back: 126

I think 'twas in my twentieth spring,—
Ay, 'twas,—when Casimir was king—
John Casimir,—I was his page
Six summers, in my earlier age: 130
A learned monarch, faith! was he,
And most unlike your majesty;
He made no wars, and did not gain
New realms to lose them back again;
And (save debates in Warsaw's diet)
He reign'd in most unseemly quiet;
Not that he had no cares to vex;   137
He loved the muses and the sex;
And sometimes these so froward are,
They made him wish himself at war;
But soon his wrath being o'er, he took
Another mistress, or new book: 142
And then he gave prodigious fêtes—
All Warsaw gather'd round his gates
To gaze upon his splendid court,
And dames, and chiefs, of princely port:
He was the Polish Solomon,   147
So sung his poets, all but one,
Who, being unpension'd, made a satire,
And boasted that he could not flatter.
It was a court of jousts and mimes, 151
Where every courtier tried at rhymes;
Even I for once produced some verses,
And sign'd my odes "Despairing Thyrsis."
There was a certain Palatine,   155
    A count of far and high descent,
Rich as a salt or silver mine;
And he was proud, ye may divine,
    As if from heaven he had been sent:
He had such wealth in blood and ore
    As few could match beneath the
        throne;   161
And he would gaze upon his store,
And o'er his pedigree would pore,
    Until by some confusion led,
Which almost look'd like want of head,
    He thought their merits were his own.
His wife was not of this opinion;   167
    His junior she by thirty years,
Grew daily tired of his dominion;
    And, after wishes, hopes, and fears,
To virtue a few farewell tears,   171
A restless dream or two, some glances
At Warsaw's youth, some songs, and
    dances,
Awaited but the usual chances,
Those happy accidents which render
The coldest dames so very tender,   176
To deck her Count with titles given,
'Tis said, as passports into heaven;
But, strange to say, they rarely boast
Of these, who have deserved them most.

V

'I was a goodly stripling then;   181
    At seventy years I so may say,
That there were few, or boys or men,
    Who, in my dawning time of day,
Of vassal or of knight's degree,   185
Could vie in vanities with me;

For I had strength, youth, gaiety,
A port, not like to this ye see,
But smooth, as all is rugged now;
  For time, and care, and war, have
    plough'd   190
My very soul from out my brow;
  And thus I should be disavow'd
By all my kind and kin, could they
Compare my day and yesterday;
This change was wrought, too, long ere
    age   195
Had ta'en my features for his page;
With years, ye know, have not declined
My strength, my courage, or my mind,
Or at this hour I should not be
Telling old tales beneath a tree,   200
With starless skies my canopy.
  But let me on: Theresa's form—
Methinks it glides before me now,
Between me and yon chestnut's bough,
  The memory is so quick and warm;
And yet I find no words to tell   206
The shape of her I loved so well:
She had the Asiatic eye,
  Such as our Turkish neighbourhood
Hath mingled with our Polish blood,
Dark as above us is the sky;   211
But through it stole a tender light,
Like the first moonrise of midnight;
Large, dark, and swimming in the
    stream,   214
Which seem'd to melt to its own beam;
All love, half languor, and half fire,
Like saints that at the stake expire,
And lift their raptured looks on high,
As though it were a joy to die.
A brow like a midsummer lake,   220
  Transparent with the sun therein,
When waves no murmur dare to make,
  And heaven beholds her face within.
A cheek and lip—but why proceed?
  I loved her then, I love her still;
And such as I am, love indeed   226
  In fierce extremes—in good and ill.
But still we love even in our rage,
And haunted to our very age
With the vain shadow of the past,   230
As is Mazeppa to the last.

VI

'We met—we gazed—I saw, and sigh'd,
She did not speak, and yet replied;
There are ten thousand tones and signs
We hear and see, but none defines—
Involuntary sparks of thought,   236
Which strike from out the heart o'er-
    wrought,
And form a strange intelligence,
Alike mysterious and intense,
Which link the burning chain that binds,
Without their will, young hearts and
    minds: 241
Conveying, as the electric wire,
We know not how, the absorbing fire.

I saw, and sigh'd—in silence wept,
And still reluctant distance kept,   245
Until I was made known to her,
And we might then and there confer
Without suspicion—then, even then,
  I long'd, and was resolved to speak;
But on my lips they died again,   250
  The accents tremulous and weak,
Until one hour.—There is a game,
  A frivolous and foolish play,
  Wherewith we while away the day;
It is—I have forgot the name—   255
And we to this, it seems, were set,
By some strange chance, which I forget:
I reck'd not if I won or lost,
  It was enough for me to be
  So near to hear, and oh! to see   260
The being whom I loved the most.
I watch'd her as a sentinel,
(May ours this dark night watch as
    well!)
  Until I saw, and thus it was,
That she was pensive, nor perceived
Her occupation, nor was grieved   266
Nor glad to lose or gain; but still
Play'd on for hours, as if her will
Yet bound her to the place, though not
That hers might be the winning lot.
  Then through my brain the thought
    did pass   271
Even as a flash of lightning there,
That there was something in her air
Which would not doom me to despair;
And on the thought my words broke forth,
  All incoherent as they were;   276
Their eloquence was little worth,
But yet she listen'd—'tis enough—
  Who listens once will listen twice;
  Her heart, be sure, is not of ice,
And one refusal no rebuff.   281

VII

'I loved, and was beloved again—
  They tell me, Sire, you never knew
  Those gentle frailties; if 'tis true,
I shorten all my joy or pain;   285
To you 'twould seem absurd as vain;
But all men are not born to reign,
Or o'er their passions, or as you
Thus o'er themselves and nations too.
I am—or rather *was*—a prince,   290
  A chief of thousands, and could lead
  Them on where each would foremost
    bleed;
But could not o'er myself evince
The like control—But to resume:
  I loved, and was beloved again;   295
In sooth, it is a happy doom,
  But yet it is where happiest ends in pain.
We met in secret, and the hour
Which led me to that lady's bower
Was fiery Expectation's dower.   300
My days and nights were nothing—all
Except that hour, which doth recall,

In the long lapse from youth to age,
    No other like itself: I'd give
    The Ukraine back again to live   305
It o'er once more, and be a page,
The happy page, who was the lord
Of one soft heart, and his own sword,
And had no other gem nor wealth
Save nature's gift of youth and health.
We met in secret—doubly sweet,   311
Some say, they find it so to meet;
I know not that—I would have given
    My life but to have call'd her mine
In the full view of earth and heaven;
    For I did oft and long repine   316
That we could only meet by stealth.

VIII

'For lovers there are many eyes,
    And such there were on us; the devil
    On such occasions should be civil—
The devil!—I'm loth to do him wrong,
    It might be some untoward saint,
Who would not be at rest too long,
    But to his pious bile gave vent—
But one fair night, some lurking spies
Surprised and seized us both.   326
The Count was something more than
        wroth—
I was unarm'd; but if in steel,
All cap-à-pie from head to heel,
What 'gainst their numbers could I do?
'Twas near his castle, far away   331
    From city or from succour near,
And almost on the break of day;
I did not think to see another,
    My moments seem'd reduced to few;
And with one prayer to Mary Mother,
    And, it may be, a saint or two,   337
As I resign'd me to my fate,
They led me to the castle gate:
Theresa's doom I never knew,   340
Our lot was henceforth separate.
An angry man, ye may opine,
Was he, the proud Count Palatine,
And he had reason good to be,   344
    But he was most enraged lest such
    An accident should chance to touch
Upon his future pedigree;
Nor less amazed, that such a blot
His noble 'scutcheon should have got,
While he was highest of his line;   350
    Because unto himself he seem'd
    The first of men, nor less he deem'd
In others' eyes, and most in mine.
'Sdeath! with a page—perchance a king
Had reconciled him to the thing;   355
But with a stripling of a page—
I felt, but cannot paint his rage.

IX

' "Bring forth the horse!"—the horse
        was brought;
    In truth, he was a noble steed,
    A Tartar of the Ukraine breed,   360
Who look'd as though the speed of
        thought
Were in his limbs; but he was wild,
    Wild as the wild deer, and untaught,
With spur and bridle undefiled—
    'Twas but a day he had been caught;
And snorting, with erected mane,   366
And struggling fiercely, but in vain,
In the full foam of wrath and dread
To me the desert-born was led:
They bound me on, that menial throng;
Upon his back with many a thong;   371
Then loosed him with a sudden lash—
Away!—away!—and on we dash!
Torrents less rapid and less rash.

X

'Away!—away! My breath was gone,
I saw not where he hurried on: 376
'Twas scarcely yet the break of day,
And on he foam'd—away!—away!
The last of human sounds which rose,
As I was darted from my foes,   380
Was the wild shout of savage laughter,
Which on the wind came roaring after
A moment from that rabble rout:
With sudden wrath I wrench'd my head,
    And snapp'd the cord, which to the
        mane   385
Had bound my neck in lieu of rein,
And, writhing half my form about,
Howl'd back my curse; but 'midst the
        tread,
The thunder of my courser's speed,
Perchance they did not hear nor heed:
It vexes me—for I would fain   391
Have paid their insult back again.
I paid it well in after days:
There is not of that castle gate,
Its drawbridge and portcullis' weight,
Stone, bar, moat, bridge, or barrier left;
Nor of its fields a blade of grass,   397
    Save what grows on a ridge of wall,
    Where stood the hearth-stone of the
        hall;
And many a time ye there might pass,
Nor dream that e'er the fortress was.
I saw its turrets in a blaze,   402
Their crackling battlements all cleft,
    And the hot lead pour down like rain
From off the scorch'd and blackening
        roof,   405
Whose thickness was not vengeance-
        proof.
    They little thought that day of pain,
When launch'd, as on the lightning's
        flash,
They bade me to destruction dash,   409
    That one day I should come again,
With twice five thousand horse, to thank
    The Count for his uncourteous ride.
They play'd me then a bitter prank,
    When, with the wild horse for my
        guide,   414

They bound me to his foaming flank:
At length I play'd them one as frank
For time at last sets all things even—
 And if we do but watch the hour,
 There never yet was human power
Which could evade, if unforgiven, 420
The patient search and vigil long
Of him who treasures up a wrong.

XI

'Away, away, my steed and I,
 Upon the pinions of the wind,
 All human dwellings left behind;
We sped like meteors through the sky,
When with its crackling sound the night
Is chequer'd with the northern light:
Town—village—none were on our track
 But a wild plain of far extent, 430
And bounded by a forest black;
 And, save the scarce-seen battlement
On distant heights of some strong hold,
Against the Tartars built of old,
No trace of man. The year before 435
A Turkish army had march'd o'er;
And where the Spahi's hoof hath trod,
The verdure flies the bloody sod:
The sky was dull, and dim, and gray,
 And a low breeze crept moaning by—
 I could have answer'd with a sigh—
But fast we fled, away, away, 442
And I could neither sigh nor pray;
And my cold sweat-drops fell like rain
Upon the courser's bristling mane;
But, snorting still with rage and fear,
He flew upon his far career: 447
At times I almost thought, indeed,
He must have slacken'd in his speed;
But no—my bound and slender frame
 Was nothing to his angry might,
And merely like a spur became:
Each motion which I made to free
My swoln limbs from their agony
Increased his fury and affright: 455
I tried my voice,—'twas faint and low,
But yet he swerved as from a blow;
And, starting to each accent, sprang
As from a sudden trumpet's clang:
Meantime my cords were wet with gore,
Which, oozing through my limbs, ran
  o'er; 461
And in my tongue the thirst became
A something fierier far than flame.

XII

'We near'd the wild wood—'twas so
  wide,
I saw no bounds on either side; 465
'Twas studded with old sturdy trees,
That bent not to the roughest breeze
Which howls down from Siberia's waste,
And strips the forest in its haste,—
But these were few and far between,
Set thick with shrubs more young and
  green, 471

Luxuriant with their annual leaves,
Ere strown by those autumnal eves
That nip the forest's foliage dead,
Discolour'd with a lifeless red, 475
Which stands thereon like stiffen'd gore
Upon the slain when battle's o'er,
And some long winter's night hath shed
Its frost o'er every tombless head,
So cold and stark the raven's beak 480
May peck unpierced each frozen cheek:
'Twas a wild waste of underwood,
And here and there a chestnut stood,
The strong oak, and the hardy pine;
 But far apart—and well it were, 485
Or else a different lot were mine—
 The boughs gave way, and did not tear
My limbs; and I found strength to bear
My wounds, already scarr'd with cold;
My bonds forbade to loose my hold.
We rustled through the leaves like wind,
Left shrubs, and trees, and wolves be-
  hind; 492
By night I heard them on the track,
Their troop came hard upon our back,
With their long gallop, which can tire
The hound's deep bate, and hunter's fire:
Where'er we flew they follow'd on, 497
Nor left us with the morning sun;
Behind I saw them, scarce a rood,
At day-break winding through the
  wood, 500
And through the night had heard their
  feet
Their stealing, rustling step repeat.
Oh! how I wish'd for spear or sword,
At least to die amidst the horde,
And perish—if it must be so— 505
At bay, destroying many a foe!
When first my courser's race begun,
I wish'd the goal already won;
But now I doubted strength and speed.
Vain doubt! his swift and savage breed
Had nerved him like the mountain-roe;
Nor faster falls the blinding snow 512
Which whelms the peasant near the door
Whose threshold he shall cross no more,
Bewilder'd with the dazzling blast,
Than through the forest-paths he
  pass'd—
Untired, untamed, and worse than wild;
All furious as a favour'd child
Balk'd of its wish; or fiercer still—
A woman piqued—who has her will.

XIII

'The wood was past; 'twas more than
  noon, 521
But chill the air, although in June;
Or it might be my veins ran cold—
Prolong'd endurance tames the bold;
And I was then not what I seem, 525
But headlong as a wintry stream,
And wore my feelings out before
I well could count their causes o'er:

And what with fury, fear, and wrath,
The tortures which beset my path, 530
Cold, hunger, sorrow, shame, distress,
Thus bound in nature's nakedness;
Sprung from a race whose rising blood,
When stirr'd beyond its calmer mood,
And trodden hard upon, is like 535
The rattle-snake's, in act to strike,
What marvel if this worn-out trunk
Beneath its woes a moment sunk?
The earth gave way, the skies roll'd
    round,
I seem'd to sink upon the ground; 540
But err'd, for I was fastly bound.
My heart turn'd sick, my brain grew
    sore,
And throbb'd awhile, then beat no
    more:
The skies spun like a mighty wheel;
I saw the trees like drunkards reel, 545
And a slight flash sprang o'er my eyes,
Which saw no farther: he who dies
Can die no more than then I died.
O'ertortured by that ghastly ride,
I felt the blackness come and go, 550
    And strove to wake; but could not
    make
My senses climb up from below:
I felt as on a plank at sea,
When all the waves that dash o'er thee,
At the same time upheave and whelm,
And hurl thee towards a desert realm.
My undulating life was as 557
The fancied lights that flitting pass
Our shut eyes in deep midnight, when
Fever begins upon the brain; 560
But soon it pass'd, with little pain,
    But a confusion worse than such:
    I own that I should deem it much,
Dying, to feel the same again;
And yet I do suppose we must 565
Feel far more ere we turn to dust:
No matter; I have bared my brow
Full in Death's face—before—and now.

<h3 style="text-align:center">XIV</h3>

'My thoughts came back; where was I?
    Cold,
And numb, and giddy: pulse by pulse
Life reassumed its lingering hold, 571
And throb by throb,—till grown a pang
Which for a moment would convulse,
My blood reflow'd, though thick and
    chill;
My ear with uncouth noises rang,
    My heart began once more to thrill;
My sight return'd, though dim; alas!
And thicken'd, as it were, with glass.
Methought the dash of waves was nigh;
There was a gleam too of the sky, 580
Studded with stars;—it is no dream;
The wild horse swims the wilder stream!
The bright broad river's gushing tide
Sweeps, winding onward, far and wide,

And we are half-way, struggling o'er
To yon unknown and silent shore. 586
The waters broke my hollow trance,
And with a temporary strength
    My stiffen'd limbs were rebaptized.
My courser's broad breast proudly
    braves, 590
And dashes off the ascending waves,
And onward we advance!
We reach the slippery shore at length,
    A haven I but little prized, 594
For all behind was dark and drear,
And all before was night and fear.
How many hours of night or day
In those suspended pangs I lay,
I could not tell; I scarcely knew
If this were human breath I drew. 600

<h3 style="text-align:center">XV</h3>

'With glossy skin, and dripping mane,
    And reeling limbs, and reeking flank,
The wild steed's sinewy nerves still strain
    Up the repelling bank. 604
We gain the top: a boundless plain
Spreads through the shadow of the
    night,
    And onward, onward, onward, seems,
    Like precipices in our dreams,
To stretch beyond the sight; 609
And here and there a speck of white,
    Or scatter'd spot of dusky green,
In masses broke into the light,
As rose the moon upon my right:
    But nought distinctly seen
In the dim waste would indicate 615
The omen of a cottage gate;
No twinkling taper from afar
Stood like a hospitable star;
Not even an ignis-fatuus rose 619
To make him merry with my woes:
    That very cheat had cheer'd me then!
Although detected, welcome still,
Reminding me, through every ill,
    Of the abodes of men. 624

<h3 style="text-align:center">XVI</h3>

'Onward we went—but slack and slow;
    His savage force at length o'erspent,
The drooping courser, faint and low,
    All feebly foaming went.
A sickly infant had had power 629
To guide him forward in that hour,
    But useless all to me:
His new-born tameness nought avail'd—
My limbs were bound; my force had
    fail'd,
    Perchance, had they been free.
With feeble effort still I tried 635
To rend the bonds so starkly tied,
    But still it was in vain;
My limbs were only wrung the more,
And soon the idle strife gave o'er,
    Which but prolong'd their pain: 640

The dizzy race seem'd almost done,
Although no goal was nearly won:
Some streaks announced the coming
  sun—
  How slow, alas! he came!   644
Methought that mist of dawning gray
Would never dapple into day;
How heavily it roll'd away—
  Before the eastern flame
Rose crimson, and deposed the stars,
And call'd the radiance from their cars,
And fill'd the earth, from his deep
  throne,   651
With lonely lustre, all his own.

XVII

'Up rose the sun; the mists were curl'd
Back from the solitary world
Which lay around, behind, before.
What booted it to traverse o'er   656
Plain, forest, river? Man nor brute,
Nor dint of hoof, nor print of foot,
Lay in the wild luxuriant soil;
No sign of travel, none of toil;   660
The very air was mute;
And not an insect's shrill small horn,
Nor matin bird's new voice was borne
From herb nor thicket. Many a werst,
Panting as if his heart would burst, 665
The weary brute still stagger'd on;
And still we were—or seem'd—alone.
At length, while reeling on our way,
Methought I heard a courser neigh,
From out yon tuft of blackening firs.
Is it the wind those branches stirs? 671
No, no! from out the forest prance
  A trampling troop; I see them come!
In one vast squadron they advance!
I strove to cry—my lips were dumb.
The steeds rush on in plunging pride;
But where are they the reins to guide?
A thousand horse, and none to ride!
With flowing tail, and flying mane,
Wide nostrils never stretch'd by pain,
Mouths bloodless to the bit or rein,
And feet that iron never shod,   682
And flanks unscarr'd by spur or rod,
A thousand horse, the wild, the free,
Like waves that follow o'er the sea,
  Came thickly thundering on,
As if our faint approach to meet;
The sight re-nerved my courser's feet,
A moment staggering, feebly fleet,
A moment, with a faint low neigh,
  He answer'd, and then fell;   691
With gasps and glazing eyes he lay,
  And reeking limbs immoveable,
    His first and last career is done!
On came the troop—they saw him stoop,
  They saw me strangely bound along
  His back with many a bloody thong:
They stop, they start, they snuff the
  air,
Gallop a moment here and there,

Approach, retire, wheel round and
  round,   700
Then plunging back with sudden bound,
Headed by one black mighty steed,
Who seem'd the patriarch of his breed,
Without a single speck or hair
Of white upon his shaggy hide; 705
They snort, they foam, neigh, swerve
  aside,
And backward to the forest fly,
By instinct, from a human eye.
They left me there to my despair,
Link'd to the dead and stiffening wretch,
Whose lifeless limbs beneath me stretch,
Relieved from that unwonted weight,
From whence I could not extricate
Nor him nor me—and there we lay,
  The dying on the dead!   715
I little deem'd another day
  Would see my houseless, helpless
  head.

'And there from morn to twilight
  bound,
I felt the heavy hours toil round,
With just enough of life to see 720
My last of suns go down on me,
In hopeless certainty of mind,
That makes us feel at length resign'd
To that which our foreboding years
Present the worst and last of fears:
Inevitable—even a boon,   726
Nor more unkind for coming soon,
Yet shunn'd and dreaded with such care,
As if it only were a snare
  That prudence might escape: 730
At times both wish'd-for and implored,
At times sought with self-pointed sword,
Yet still a dark and hideous close
To even intolerable woes,
  And welcome in no shape.   735
And, strange to say, the sons of pleasure,
They who have revell'd beyond measure
In beauty, wassail, wine, and treasure,
Die calm, or calmer, oft than he
Whose heritage was misery: 740
For he who hath in turn run through
All that was beautiful and new,
  Hath nought to hope, and nought to
  leave;
And, save the future, (which is view'd
Not quite as men are base or good, 745
But as their nerves may be endued,)
  With nought perhaps to grieve:
The wretch still hopes his woes must end,
And Death, whom he should deem his
  friend,
Appears, to his distemper'd eyes, 750
Arrived to rob him of his prize,
The tree of his new Paradise.
To-morrow would have given him all,
Repaid his pangs, repair'd his fall;
To-morrow would have been the first
Of days no more deplored or curst,

But bright, and long, and beckoning years,
Seen dazzling through the mist of tears,
Guerdon of many a painful hour;
To-morrow would have given him
    power   760
To rule, to shine, to smite, to save—
And must it dawn upon his grave?

XVIII

'The sun was sinking—still I lay
  Chain'd to the chill and stiffening
    steed;
I thought to mingle there our clay, 765
  And my dim eyes of death had need;
  No hope arose of being freed;
I cast my last looks up the sky,
  And there between me and the sun
I saw the expecting raven fly,   770
Who scarce would wait till both should
    die,
  Ere his repast begun;
He flew, and perch'd, then flew once more,
And each time nearer than before;
I saw his wing through twilight flit,
And once so near me he alit   776
  I could have smote, but lack'd the
    strength;
But the slight motion of my hand,
And feeble scratching of the sand,
The exerted throat's faint struggling
    noise,   780
Which scarcely could be called a voice,
  Together scared him off at length.
I know no more—my latest dream
  Is something of a lovely star
  Which fix'd my dull eyes from afar,
And went and came with wandering
    beam,   786
And all the cold, dull, swimming, dense
Sensation of recurring sense,
And then subsiding back to death,
And then again a little breath,   790
A little thrill, a short suspense,
  An icy sickness curdling o'er
My heart, and sparks that cross'd my
    brain—
A gasp, a throb, a start of pain,
  A sigh, and nothing more.   795

XIX

'I woke—where was I?—Do I see
A human face look down on me?
And doth a roof above me close?
Do these limbs on a couch repose?
Is this a chamber where I lie?   800
And is it mortal yon bright eye,
That watches me with gentle glance?
  I closed my own again once more,
As doubtful that my former trance
  Could not as yet be o'er.   805
A slender girl, long-hair'd, and tall,
Sate watching by the cottage wall;
The sparkle of her eye I caught,
Even with my first return of thought;

For ever and anon she threw   810
  A prying, pitying glance on me
  With her black eyes so wild and free:
I gazed, and gazed, until I knew
  No vision it could be,—
But that I lived, and was released 815
From adding to the vulture's feast:
And when the Cossack maid beheld
My heavy eyes at length unseal'd,
She smiled—and I essay'd to speak,
  But fail'd—and she approach'd, and
    made   820
With lip and finger signs that said,
I must not strive as yet to break
The silence, till my strength should be
Enough to leave my accents free; 824
And then her hand on mine she laid,
And smooth'd the pillow for my head,
And stole along on tiptoe tread,
  And gently oped the door, and spake
In whispers—ne'er was voice so sweet!
Even music follow'd her light feet: 830
  But those she call'd were not awake,
And she went forth; but, ere she pass'd,
Another look on me she cast,
  Another sign she made, to say,
That I had nought to fear, that all 835
Were near, at my command or call,
  And she would not delay
Her due return:—while she was gone,
Methought I felt too much alone. 839

XX

'She came with mother and with sire—
What need of more?—I will not tire
With long recital of the rest,
Since I became the Cossack's guest.
They found me senseless on the plain,
  They bore me to the nearest hut, 845
They brought me into life again—
Me—one day o'er their realm to reign!
  Thus the vain fool who strove to glut
His rage, refining on my pain,   849
  Sent me forth to the wilderness,
Bound, naked, bleeding, and alone,
To pass the desert to a throne,—
  What mortal his own doom may guess?
  Let none despond, let none despair!
To-morrow the Borysthenes   855
May see our coursers graze at ease
Upon his Turkish bank, and never
Had I such welcome for a river
  As I shall yield when safely there.
Comrades, good night!'—The Hetman
    threw   860
  His length beneath the oak-tree shade,
  With leafy couch already made,
A bed nor comfortless nor new
To him, who took his rest whene'er
The hour arrived, no matter where:
  His eyes the hastening slumbers steep.
And if ye marvel Charles forgot
To thank his tale, he wonder'd not,—
  The king had been an hour asleep.

THE ISLAND

OR

CHRISTIAN AND HIS COMRADES

ADVERTISEMENT

THE foundation of the following story will be found partly in Lieutenant Bligh's 'Narrative of the Mutiny and Seizure of the Bounty, in the South Seas, in 1789'; and partly in 'Mariner's Account of the Tonga Islands.'

Genoa, 1823.

CANTO THE FIRST

I

THE morning watch was come; the vessel lay
Her course, and gently made her liquid way;
The cloven billow flash'd from off her prow
In furrows form'd by that majestic plough;
The waters with their world were all before;   5
Behind, the South Sea's many an islet shore.
The quiet night, now dappling, 'gan to wane,
Dividing darkness from the dawning main;
The dolphins, not unconscious of the day,   9
Swam high, as eager of the coming ray;
The stars from broader beams began to creep,
And lift their shining eyelids from the deep;
The sail resumed its lately shadow'd white,
And the wind flutter'd with a freshening flight: 14
The purpling ocean owns the coming sun,
But ere he break—a deed is to be done.

II

The gallant chief within his cabin slept,
Secure in those by whom the watch was kept:
His dreams were of Old England's welcome shore,   19
Of toils rewarded, and of dangers o'er;
His name was added to the glorious roll
Of those who search the storm-surrounded Pole.
The worst was over, and the rest seem'd sure,
And why should not his slumber be secure?
Alas! his deck was trod by unwilling feet,
And wilder hands would hold the vessel's sheet;   26
Young hearts, which languish'd for some sunny isle,
Where summer years and summer women smile;
Men without country, who, too long estranged,
Had found no native home, or found it changed,   30
And, half uncivilised, preferr'd the cave
Of some soft savage to the uncertain wave—
The gushing fruits that nature gave untill'd;
The wood without a path but where they will'd;
The field o'er which promiscuous Plenty pour'd   35
Her horn; the equal land without a lord;
The wish—which ages have not yet subdued
In man—to have no master save his mood;
The earth, whose mine was on its face, unsold,
The glowing sun and produce all its gold;
The freedom which can call each grot a home;   41
The general garden, where all steps may roam,
Where Nature owns a nation as her child,
Exulting in the enjoyment of the wild;
Their shells, their fruits, the only wealth they know,   45
Their unexploring navy, the canoe;
Their sport, the dashing breakers and the chase;
Their strangest sight, an European face:—
Such was the country which these strangers yearn'd   49
To see again; a sight they dearly earn'd.

III

Awake, bold Bligh! the foe is at the gate!
Awake! awake!—Alas! it is too late!
Fiercely beside thy cot the mutineer
Stands, and proclaims the reign of rage and fear.
Thy limbs are bound, the bayonet at thy breast;   55
The hands, which trembled at thy voice, arrest;

349

Dragg'd o'er the deck, no more at thy
    command
The obedient helm shall veer, the sail ex-
    pand;
That savage spirit, which would lull by
    wrath   59
Its desperate escape from duty's path,
Glares round thee, in the scarce-believing
    eyes
Of those who fear the chief they sacrifice:
For ne'er can man his conscience all as-
    suage,
Unless he drain the wine of passion—rage.

IV

In vain, not silenced by the eye of death,
Thou call'st the loyal with thy menaced
    breath:—   66
They come not; they are few, and, over-
    awed,
Must acquiesce, while sterner hearts ap-
    plaud.
In vain thou dost demand the cause: a
    curse
Is all the answer, with the threat of worse.
Full in thine eyes is waved the glittering
    blade,   71
Close to thy throat the pointed bayonet
    laid.
The levell'd muskets circle round thy
    breast
In hands as steel'd to do the deadly rest.
Thou dar'st them to their worst, exclaim-
    ing—'Fire!'   75
But they who pitied not could yet admire;
Some lurking remnant of their former
    awe
Restrain'd them longer than their broken
    law;
They would not dip their souls at once in
    blood,   79
But left thee to the mercies of the flood.

V

'Hoist out the boat!' was now the leader's
    cry;
And who dare answer 'No!' to Mutiny,
In the first dawning of the drunken hour,
The Saturnalia of unhoped-for power?
The boat is lower'd with all the haste of
    hate,   85
With its slight plank between thee and thy
    fate;
Her only cargo such a scant supply
As promises the death their hands deny;
And just enough of water and of bread
To keep, some days, the dying from the
    dead: 90
Some cordage, canvas, sails, and lines, and
    twine,
But treasures all to hermits of the brine,
Were added after, to the earnest prayer
Of those who saw no hope, save sea and
    air;

And last, that trembling vassal of the
    Pole—   95
The feeling compass—Navigation's soul.

VI

And now the self-elected chief finds time
To stun the first sensation of his crime,
And raise it in his followers—'Ho! the
    bowl!'
Lest passion should return to reason's
    shoal.   100
'Brandy for heroes!' Burke could once
    exclaim—
No doubt a liquid path to epic fame;
And such the new-born heroes found it
    here,
And drain'd the draught with an applaud-
    ing cheer.
'Huzza! for Otaheite!' was the cry.   105
How strange such shouts from sons of
    Mutiny!
The gentle island, and the genial soil,
The friendly hearts, the feasts without a
    toil,
The courteous manners but from nature
    caught,
The wealth unhoarded, and the love un-
    bought;   110
Could these have charms for rudest sea-
    boys, driven
Before the mast by every wind of heaven?
And now, even now prepared with others'
    woes
To earn mild Virtue's vain desire, repose?
Alas! such is our nature! all but aim
At the same end by pathways not the same;
Our means, our birth, our nation, and our
    name,
Our fortune, temper, even our outward
    frame,
Are far more potent o'er our yielding clay
Than aught we know beyond our little
    day.   120
Yet still there whispers the small voice
    within,
Heard through Gain's silence, and o'er
    Glory's din;
Whatever creed be taught, or land be trod,
Man's conscience is the oracle of God.

VII

The launch is crowded with the faithful
    few   125
Who wait their chief, a melancholy crew:
But some remain'd reluctant on the deck
Of that proud vessel—now a moral
    wreck—
And view'd their captain's fate with piteous
    eyes;   129
While others scoff'd his augur'd miseries,
Sneer'd at the prospect of his pigmy sail,
And the slight bark so laden and so frail.
The tender nautilus, who steers his prow,
The sea-born sailor of his shell canoe,

The ocean Mab, the fairy of the sea,   135
Seems far less fragile, and, alas! more free.
He, when the lightning-wing'd tornados
    sweep
The surge, is safe—his port is in the deep—
And triumphs o'er the armadas of man-
    kind,
Which shake the world, yet crumble in the
    wind.   140

VIII

When all was now prepared, the vessel
    clear
Which hail'd her master in the mutineer,
A seaman, less obdurate than his mates,
Show'd the vain pity which but irritates;
Watch'd his late chieftain with exploring
    eye,   145
And told, in signs, repentant sympathy;
Held the moist shaddock to his parched
    mouth,
Which felt exhaustion's deep and bitter
    drouth.
But soon observed, this guardian was with-
    drawn,
Nor further mercy clouds rebellion's
    dawn,   150
Then forward stepp'd the bold and fro-
    ward boy
His chief had cherish'd only to destroy,
And, pointing to the helpless prow be-
    neath,
Exclaim'd, 'Depart at once! delay is
    death!'
Yet then, even then, his feelings ceased
    not all: 155
In that last moment could a word recall
Remorse for the black deed as yet half
    done,
And what he hid from many show'd to
    one:
When Bligh in stern reproach demanded
    where
Was now his grateful sense of former care?
Where all his hopes to see his name aspire,
And blazon Britain's thousand glories
    higher?   162
His feverish lips thus broke their gloomy
    spell,
''Tis that! 'tis that! I am in hell! in hell!'
No more he said: but urging to the bark
His chief, commits him to his fragile ark;
These the sole accents from his tongue
    that fell,   167
But volumes lurk'd below his fierce fare-
    well.

IX

The arctic sun rose broad above the wave;
The breeze now sank, now whisper'd from
    his cave;   170
As on the Æolian harp, his fitful wings
Now swell'd, now flutter'd o'er his ocean
    strings.

With slow, despairing oar, the abandon'd
    skiff
Ploughs its drear progress to the scarce-
    seen cliff,   174
Which lifts its peak a cloud above the main:
That boat and ship shall never meet again!

But 'tis not mine to tell their tale of grief,
Their constant peril, and their scant relief;
Their days of danger, and their nights of
    pain;
Their manly courage even when deem'd in
    vain;   180
The sapping famine, rendering scarce a son
Known to his mother in the skeleton;
The ills that lessen'd still their little store,
And starved even Hunger till he wrung no
    more;
The varying frowns and favours of the
    deep,   185
That now almost ingulfs, then leaves to
    creep
With crazy oar and shatter'd strength along
The tide that yields reluctant to the strong;
The incessant fever of that arid thirst
Which welcomes, as a well, the clouds that
    burst   190
Above their naked bones, and feels delight
In the cold drenching of the stormy night,
And from the outspread canvas gladly
    wrings
A drop to moisten life's all-gasping
    springs;   194
The savage foe escaped, to seek again
More hospitable shelter from the main;
The ghastly spectres which were doom'd
    at last
To tell as true a tale of dangers past,
As ever the dark annals of the deep
Disclosed for man to dread or woman
    weep.   200

X

We leave them to their fate, but not un-
    known
Nor unredress'd. Revenge may have her
    own:
Roused discipline aloud proclaims their
    cause,
And injured navies urge their broken laws.
Pursue we on his track the mutineer,
Whom distant vengeance had not taught
    to fear.   206
Wide o'er the wave—away! away! away!
Once more his eyes shall hail the welcome
    bay;
Once more the happy shores without a law
Receive the outlaws whom they lately saw;
Nature, and Nature's goddess—woman—
    woos   211
To lands where, save their conscience,
    none accuse;
Where all partake the earth without dispute,
And bread itself is gather'd as a fruit;

Where none contest the fields, the woods,
    the streams:—   215
The goldless age, where gold disturbs no
    dreams,
Inhabits or inhabited the shore,
Till Europe taught them better than be-
    fore:
Bestow'd her customs, and amended
    theirs,
But left her vices also to their heirs,   220
Away with this! behold them as they were,
Do good with Nature, or with Nature err,
'Huzza! for Otaheite!' was the cry,
As stately swept the gallant vessel by.
The breeze springs up; the lately flapping
    sail   225
Extends its arch before the growing gale;
In swifter ripples stream aside the seas,
Which her bold bow flings off with dash-
    ing ease.
Thus Argo plough'd the Euxine's virgin
    foam,
But those she wafted still look'd back to
    home: 230
These spurn their country with their rebel
    bark,
And fly her as the raven fled the ark;
And yet they seek to nestle with the dove,
And tame their fiery spirits down to love.

CANTO THE SECOND

I

How pleasant were the songs of Toobonai,
When summer's sun went down the coral
    bay!
Come, let us to the islet's softest shade,
And hear the warbling birds! the damsels
    said:
The wood-dove from the forest-depth
    shall coo,   5
Like voices of the gods from Bolotoo,
We'll cull the flowers that grow above the
    dead,
For these most bloom where rests the war-
    rior's head;
And we will sit in twilight's face, and see
The sweet moon glancing through the tooa
    tree,   10
The lofty accents of whose sighing bough
Shall sadly please us as we lean below;
Or climb the steep, and view the surf in
    vain
Wrestle with rocky giants o'er the main,
Which spurn in columns back the baffled
    spray.   15
How beautiful are these! how happy they,
Who, from the toil and tumult of their
    lives,
Steal to look down where nought but
    ocean strives!
Even he too loves at times the blue lagoon,
And smoothes his ruffled mane beneath
    the moon.   20

II

Yes—from the sepulchre we'll gather
    flowers,
Then feast like spirits in their promised
    bowers,
Then plunge and revel in the rolling surf,
Then lay our limbs along the tender turf,
And, wet and shining from the sportive
    toil,   25
Anoint our bodies with the fragrant oil,
And plait our garlands gather'd from the
    grave,
And wear the wreaths that sprung from
    out the brave.
But lo! night comes, the Mooa woos us
    back,
The sound of mats are heard along our
    track;
Anon the torchlight dance shall fling its
    sheen   31
In flashing mazes o'er the Marly's green;
And we too will be there; we too recall
The memory bright with many a festival,
Ere Fiji blew the shell of war, when foes
For the first time were wafted in canoes.
Alas! for them the flower of mankind bleeds;
Alas! for them our fields are rank with
    weeds:
Forgotten is the rapture, or unknown,
Of wandering with the moon and love
    alone.   40
But be it so:—*they* taught us how to wield
The club, and rain our arrows o'er the field:
Now let them reap the harvest of their art!
But feast to-night! to-morrow we depart.
Strike up the dance! the cava bowl fill
    high!   45
Drain every drop!—to-morrow we may die.
In summer garments be our limbs array'd;
Around our waists the tappa's white dis-
    play'd;
Thick wreaths shall form our coronal, like
    spring's,
And round our necks shall glance the
    hooni strings;   50
So shall their brighter hues contrast the
    glow
Of the dusk bosoms that beat high below.

III

But now the dance is o'er—yet stay awhile;
Ah, pause! nor yet put out the social smile.
To-morrow for the Mooa we depart,   55
But not to-night—to-night is for the heart.
Again bestow the wreaths we gently woo,
Ye young enchantresses of gay Licoo!
How lovely are your forms! how every
    sense
Bows to your beauties, soften'd, but in-
    tense,   60
Like to the flowers on Mataloco's steep,
Which fling their fragrance far athwart
    the deep!—

We too will see Licoo; but—oh! my
   heart!—
What do I say?—to-morrow we depart!

IV

Thus rose a song—the harmony of times
Before the winds blew Europe o'er these
   climes.   66
True, they had vices—such are Nature's
   growth—
But only the barbarian's—we have both;
The sordor of civilisation, mix'd
With all the savage which man's fall hath
   fix'd.   70
Who hath not seen Dissimulation's reign,
The prayers of Abel link'd to deeds of
   Cain?
Who such would see may from his lattice
   view
The Old World more degraded than the
   New,—
Now *new* no more, save where Columbia
   rears   75
Twin giants, born by Freedom to her
   spheres,
Where Chimborazo, over air, earth, wave,
Glares with his Titan eye, and sees no slave.

V

Such was this ditty of Tradition's days,
Which to the dead a lingering fame con-
   veys   80
In song, where fame as yet hath left no sign
Beyond the sound whose charm is half
   divine;
Which leaves no record to the sceptic eye,
But yields young history all to harmony;
A boy Achilles, with the centaur's lyre 85
In hand, to teach him to surpass his sire.
For one long-cherish'd ballad's simple
   stave,
Rung from the rock, or mingled with the
   wave,
Or from the bubbling streamlet's grassy side,
Or gathering mountain echoes as they
   glide,   90
Hath greater power o'er each true heart
   and ear,
Than all the columns Conquest's minions
   rear;
Invites, when hieroglyphics are a theme
For sages' labours, or the student's dream;
Attracts, when History's volumes are a
   toil,—   95
The first, the freshest bud of Feeling's soil.
Such was this rude rhyme—rhyme is of
   the rude—
But such inspired the Norseman's solitude,
Who came and conquer'd; such, wherever
   rise   99
Lands which no foes destroy or civilise,
Exist: and what can our accomplish'd art
Of verse do more than reach the awaken'd
   heart?

VI

And sweetly now those untaught melodies
Broke the luxurious silence of the skies,
The sweet siesta of a summer day,   105
The tropic afternoon of Toobonai,
When every flower was bloom, and air
   was balm,
And the first breath began to stir the palm,
The first yet voiceless wind to urge the wave
All gently to refresh the thirsty cave,
Where sat the songstress with the stranger
   boy,   111
Who taught her passion's desolating joy,
Too powerful over every heart, but most
O'er those who know not how it may be
   lost;
O'er those who, burning in the new-born
   fire,   115
Like martyrs revel in their funeral pyre,
With such devotion to their ecstasy,
That life knows no such rapture as to die:
And die they do; for earthly life has nought
Match'd with that burst of nature, even
   in thought;   120
And all our dreams of better life above
But close in one eternal gush of love.

VII

There sat the gentle savage of the wild,
In growth a woman, though in years a
   child,
As childhood dates within our colder
   clime,   125
Where nought is ripen'd rapidly save crime;
The infant of an infant world, as pure
From nature—lovely, warm, and pre-
   mature;
Dusky like night, but night with all her
   stars,   129
Or cavern sparkling with its native spars;
With eyes that were a language and a spell,
A form like Aphrodite's in her shell,
With all her loves around her on the deep,
Voluptuous as the first approach of sleep;
Yet full of life—for through her tropic
   cheek   135
The blush would make its way, and all but
   speak:
The sun-born blood suffused her neck, and
   threw
O'er her clear nut-brown skin a lucid hue,
Like coral reddening through the darken'd
   wave,
Which draws the diver to the crimson cave.
Such was this daughter of the southern
   seas,   141
Herself a billow in her energies,
To bear the bark of others' happiness,
Nor feel a sorrow till their joy grew less:
Her wild and warm yet faithful bosom
   knew   145
No joy like what it gave; her hopes ne'er
   drew

Aught from experience, that chill touch-
stone, whose
Sad proof reduces all things from their
hues:
She fear'd no ill, because she knew it not,
Or what she knew was soon—too soon—
forgot: 150
Her smiles and tears had pass'd, as light
winds pass
O'er lakes to ruffle, not destroy, their glass,
Whose depths unsearch'd, and fountains
from the hill,
Restore their surface, in itself so still,
Until the earthquake tear the naiad's cave,
Root up the spring, and trample on the
wave,   156
And crush the living waters to a mass,
The amphibious desert of the dank mo-
rass!
And must their fate be hers? The eternal
change
But grasps humanity with quicker range;
And they who fall but fall as worlds will
fall,   161
To rise, if just, a spirit o'er them all.

VIII

And who is he? the blue-eyed northern child
Of isles more known to man, but scarce
less wild;
The fair-hair'd offspring of the Hebrides,
Where roars the Pentland with its whirling
seas;   166
Rock'd in his cradle by the roaring wind,
The tempest-born in body and in mind,
His young eyes opening on the ocean-
foam,
Had from that moment deem'd the deep
his home,   170
The giant comrade of his pensive moods,
The sharer of his craggy solitudes,
The only Mentor of his youth, where'er
His bark was borne; the sport of wave and
air;
A careless thing, who placed his choice in
chance,   175
Nursed by the legends of his land's ro-
mance;
Eager to hope, but not less firm to bear,
Acquainted with all feelings save despair.
Placed in the Arab's clime, he would have
been
As bold a rover as the sands have seen,
And braved their thirst with as enduring
lip   181
As Ishmael, wafted on his desert-ship;
Fix'd upon Chili's shore, a proud cacique;
On Hellas' mountains, a rebellious Greek;
Born in a tent, perhaps a Tamerlane;
Bred to a throne, perhaps unfit to reign.
For the same soul that rends its path to
sway,   187
If rear'd to such, can find no further prey
Beyond itself, and must retrace its way,

Plunging for pleasure into pain: the same
Spirit which made a Nero, Rome's worst
shame,   191
A humbler state and discipline of heart,
Had form'd his glorious namesake's
counterpart;
But grant his vices, grant them all his own,
How small their theatre without a throne!

IX

Thou smilest:—these comparisons seem
high   196
To those who scan all things with dazzled
eye;
Link'd with the unknown name of one
whose doom
Has nought to do with glory or with Rome,
With Chili, Hellas, or with Araby;   200
Thou smilest?—Smile; 'tis better thus than
sigh;
Yet such he might have been; he was a man,
A soaring spirit, ever in the van,
A patriot hero or despotic chief,
To form a nation's glory or its grief, 205
Born under auspices which make us more
Or less than we delight to ponder o'er.
But these are visions; say, what was he
here?
A blooming boy, a truant mutineer.
The fair-hair'd Torquil, free as ocean's
spray,   210
The husband of the bride of Toobonai.

X

By Neuha's side he sate, and watch'd the
waters,—
Neuha, the sun-flower of the island daugh-
ters,
Highborn, (a birth at which the herald
smiles,
Without a scutcheon for these secret
isles,)   215
Of a long race, the valiant and the free,
The naked knights of savage chivalry,
Whose grassy cairns ascend along the
shore;
And thine—I've seen—Achilles! do no
more.
She, when the thunder-bearing strangers
came,   220
In vast canoes, begirt with bolts of flame,
Topp'd with tall trees, which, loftier than
the palm,
Seem'd rooted in the deep amidst its calm:
But when the winds awaken'd, shot forth
wings
Broad as the cloud along the horizon
flings,   225
And sway'd the waves like cities of the sea,
Making the very billows look less free;—
She, with her paddling oar and dancing
prow,
Shot through the surf, like reindeer
through the snow,

Swift-gliding o'er the breaker's whitening
   edge,   230
Light as a nereid in her ocean sledge,
And gazed and wonder'd at the giant hulk,
Which heaved from wave to wave its
   trampling bulk.
The anchor dropp'd; it lay along the deep,
Like a huge lion in the sun asleep,   235
While round it swarm'd the proas' flitting
   chain,
Like summer bees that hum around his
   mane.

XI

The white man landed! need the rest be
   told?
The New World stretch'd its dusk hand to
   the Old;   239
Each was to each a marvel, and the tie
Of wonder warm'd to better sympathy.
Kind was the welcome of the sun-born
   sires,
And kinder still their daughters' gentler
   fires.
Their union grew: the children of the storm
Found beauty link'd with many a dusky
   form;   245
While these in turn admired the paler
   glow,
Which seem'd so white in climes that knew
   no snow.
The chase, the race, the liberty to roam,
The soil where every cottage show'd a
   home;
The sea-spread net, the lightly launch'd
   canoe,   250
Which stemm'd the studded archipelago,
O'er whose blue blossom rose the starry
   isles;
The healthy slumber, earn'd by sportive
   toils;
The palm, the loftiest dryad of the woods,
Within whose bosom infant Bacchus
   broods,   255
While eagles scarce build higher than the
   crest
Which shadows o'er the vineyard in her
   breast;
The cava feast, the yam, the cocoa's root,
Which bears at once the cup, and milk,
   and fruit;
The bread-tree, which, without the plough-
   share, yields   260
The unreap'd harvest of unfurrow'd fields,
And bakes its unadulterated loaves
Without a furnace in unpurchased groves,
And flings off famine from its fertile breast,
A priceless market for the gathering
   guest;—   265
These, with the luxuries of seas and woods,
The airy joys of social solitudes,
Tamed each rude wanderer to the sympa-
   thies
Of those who were more happy, if less wise,

Did more than Europe's discipline had
   done,   270
And civilised Civilisation's son!

XII

Of these, and there was many a willing pair,
Neuha and Torquil were not the least fair:
Both children of the isles, though distant
   far;
Both born beneath a sea-presiding star;
Both nourish'd amidst nature's native
   scenes,   276
Loved to the last, whatever intervenes
Between us and our childhood's sympathy,
Which still reverts to what first caught the
   eye.
He who first met the Highlands' swelling
   blue   280
Will love each peak that shows a kindred
   hue,
Hail in each crag a friend's familiar face,
And clasp the mountain in his mind's
   embrace.
Long have I roamed through lands which
   are not mine,   284
Adored the Alp, and loved the Apennine,
Revered Parnassus, and beheld the steep
Jove's Ida and Olympus crown the deep:
But 'twas not all long ages' lore, nor all
Their nature held me in their thrilling
   thrall;
The infant rapture still survived the boy,
And Loch-na-gar with Ida look'd o'er
   Troy,   291
Mix'd Celtic memories with the Phrygian
   mount,
And Highland linns with Castalie's clear
   fount.
Forgive me, Homer's universal shade!
Forgive me, Phœbus! that my fancy
   stray'd;   295
The north and nature taught me to adore
Your scenes sublime, from those beloved
   before.

XIII

The love which maketh all things fond and
   fair,
The youth which makes one rainbow of
   the air,
The dangers past, that make even man
   enjoy   300
The pause in which he ceases to destroy,
The mutual beauty, which the sternest feel
Strike to their hearts like lightning to the
   steel,
United the half savage and the whole,
The maid and boy in one absorbing soul.
No more the thundering memory of the
   fight   306
Wrapp'd his wean'd bosom in its dark de-
   light;
No more the irksome restlessness of rest
Disturb'd him like the eagle in her nest,

Whose whetted beak and far-pervading
   eye   310
Darts for a victim over all the sky:
His heart was tamed to that voluptuous
   state,
At once Elysian and effeminate,
Which leaves no laurels o'er the hero's
   urn;—
These wither when for aught save blood
   they burn;   315
Yet when their ashes in their nook are laid,
Doth not the myrtle leave as sweet a shade?
Had Cæsar known but Cleopatra's kiss,
Rome had been free, the world had not
   been his.
And what have Cæsar's deeds and Cæsar's
   fame
Done for the earth? We feel them in our
   shame:
The gory sanction of his glory stains
The rust which tyrants cherish on our
   chains.
Though Glory, Nature, Reason, Freedom,
   bid
Roused millions do what single Brutus
   did—   325
Sweep these mere mock-birds of the des-
   pot's song
From the tall bough where they have
   perch'd so long,—
Still are we hawk'd at by such mousing
   owls,
And take for falcons those ignoble fowls,
When but a word of freedom would dispel
These bugbears, as their terrors show too
   well.   331

XIV

Rapt in the fond forgetfulness of life,
Neuha, the South Sea girl, was all a wife,
With no distracting world to call her off
From love; with no society to scoff   335
At the new transient flame; no babbling
   crowd
Of coxcombry in admiration loud,
Or with adulterous whisper to alloy
Her duty, and her glory, and her joy: 339
With faith and feelings naked as her form,
She stood as stands a rainbow in a storm,
Changing its hues with bright variety,
But still expanding lovelier o'er the sky,
Howe'er its arch may swell, its colours
   move,   344
The cloud-compelling harbinger of love.

XV

Here, in this grotto of the wave-worn shore,
They pass'd the tropic's red meridian o'er;
Nor long the hours—they never paused
   o'er time,
Unbroken by the clock's funereal chime,
Which deals the daily pittance of our span,
And points and mocks with iron laugh at
   man.   351

What deem'd they of the future or the
   past?
The present, like a tyrant, held them fast:
Their hour-glass was the sea-sand, and the
   tide,
Like her smooth billow, saw their mo-
   ments glide;   355
Their clock the sun, in his unbounded
   tow'r;
They reckon'd not, whose day was but an
   hour;
The nightingale, their only vesper-bell,
Sung sweetly to the rose the day's farewell;
The broad sun set, but not with lingering
   sweep,   360
As in the north he mellows o'er the deep;
But fiery, full, and fierce, as if he left
The world for ever, earth of light bereft,
Plunged with red forehead down along the
   wave,   364
As dives a hero headlong to his grave.
Then rose they, looking first along the skies,
And then for light into each other's eyes,
Wondering that summer show'd so brief
   a sun,
And asking if indeed the day were done.

XVI

And let not this seem strange: the devotee
Lives not in earth, but in his ecstasy;
Around him days and worlds are heedless
   driven,
His soul is gone before his dust to heaven.
Is love less potent? No—his path is trod,
Alike uplifted gloriously to God;   375
Or link'd to all we know of heaven below,
The other better self, whose joy or woe
Is more than ours; the all-absorbing flame
Which, kindled by another, grows the
   same,
Wrapt in one blaze; the pure, yet funeral
   pile,   380
Where gentle hearts, like Bramins, sit and
   smile.
How often we forget all time, when lone,
Admiring Nature's universal throne,
Her woods, her wilds, her waters, the in-
   tense
Reply of *hers* to our intelligence!   385
Live not the stars and mountains? Are the
   waves
Without a spirit? Are the dropping caves
Without a feeling in their silent tears?
No, no;—they woo and clasp us to their
   spheres,
Dissolve this clog and clod of clay before
Its hour, and merge our soul in the great
   shore.   391
Strip off this fond and false identity!—
Who thinks of self when gazing on the sky?
And who, though gazing lower, ever
   thought,
In the young moments ere the heart is
   taught   395

Time's lesson, of man's baseness or his
    own?
All nature is his realm, and love his throne.

XVII

Neuha arose, and Torquil: twilight's hour
Came sad and softly to their rocky bower,
Which, kindling by degrees its dewy spars,
Echoed their dim light to the mustering
    stars.   401
Slowly the pair, partaking nature's calm,
Sought out their cottage, built beneath the
    palm;
Now smiling and now silent, as the scene;
Lovely as Love—the spirit!—when serene.
The Ocean scarce spoke louder with his
    swell,   406
Than breathes his mimic murmurer in the
    shell,
As, far divided from his parent deep,
The sea-born infant cries, and will not
    sleep,   409
Raising his little plaint in vain, to rave
For the broad bosom of his nursing wave:
The woods droop'd darkly, as inclined to
    rest,
The tropic bird wheel'd rockward to his
    nest,
And the blue sky spread round them like a
    lake
Of peace, where Piety her thirst might
    slake.   415

XVIII

But through the palm and plantain, hark,
    a voice!
Not such as would have been a lover's
    choice,
In such an hour, to break the air so still;
No dying night-breeze, harping o'er the hill,
Striking the strings of nature, rock and
    tree,   420
Those best and earliest lyres of harmony,
With Echo for their chorus; nor the alarm
Of the loud war-whoop to dispel the charm;
Nor the soliloquy of the hermit owl,
Exhaling all his solitary soul,   425
The dim though large-eyed winged an-
    chorite,
Who peals his dreary pæan o'er the night;
But a loud, long, and naval whistle, shrill
As ever started through a sea-bird's bill;
And then a pause, and then a hoarse,
    'Hillo!   430
Torquil, my boy! what cheer? Ho!
    brother, ho!'
'Who hails?' cried Torquil, following
    with his eye
The sound. 'Here's one,' was all the brief
    reply.

XIX

But here the herald of the self-same mouth
Came breathing o'er the aromatic south,

Not like a 'bed of violets' on the gale,   436
But such as wafts its cloud o'er grog or ale,
Borne from a short frail pipe, which yet
    had blown
Its gentle odours over either zone,
And, puff'd where'er winds rise or waters
    roll,   440
Had wafted smoke from Portsmouth to
    the Pole,
Opposed its vapour as the lightning flash'd,
And reek'd, 'midst mountain-billows, un-
    abash'd,
To Æolus a constant sacrifice,
Through every change of all the varying
    skies.   445
And what was he who bore it?—I may err,
But deem him sailor or philosopher.
Sublime tobacco! which from east to west
Cheers the tar's labour or the Turkman's
    rest;
Which on the Moslem's ottoman divides
His hours, and rivals opium and his
    brides;   451
Magnificent in Stamboul, but less grand,
Though not less loved, in Wapping or the
    Strand;
Divine in hookas, glorious in a pipe,
When tipp'd with amber, mellow, rich,
    and ripe;   455
Like other charmers, wooing the caress,
More dazzlingly when daring in full dress;
Yet thy true lovers more admire by far
Thy naked beauties—Give me a cigar!

XX

Through the approaching darkness of the
    wood   460
A human figure broke the solitude,
Fantastically, it may be, array'd,
A seaman in a savage masquerade;
Such as appears to rise out from the deep
When o'er the line the merry vessels sweep,
And the rough saturnalia of the tar   466
Flock o'er the deck, in Neptune's borrow'd
    car;
And, pleased, the god of ocean sees his
    name
Revive once more, though but in mimic
    game
Of his true sons, who riot in the breeze
Undreamt of in his native Cyclades.   471
Still the old god delights, from out the
    main,
To snatch some glimpses of his ancient
    reign.
Our sailor's jacket, though in ragged trim,
His constant pipe, which never yet burn'd
    dim,   475
His foremast air, and somewhat rolling gait,
Like his dear vessel, spoke his former
    state;
But then a sort of kerchief round his head,
Not over-tightly bound, nor nicely
    spread;

And, 'stead of trowsers (ah! too early
     torn!   480
For even the mildest woods will have their
     thorn),
A curious sort of somewhat scanty mat
Now served for inexpressibles and hat;
His naked feet and neck, and sunburnt face,
Perchance might suit alike with either
     race.   485
His arms were all his own, our Europe's
     growth,
Which two worlds bless for civilising both;
The musket swung behind his shoulders
     broad,
And somewhat stoop'd by his marine
     abode,
But brawny as the boar's; and hung be-
     neath,   490
His cutlass droop'd, unconscious of a
     sheath,
Or lost or worn away; his pistols were
Link'd to his belt, a matrimonial pair—
(Let not this metaphor appear a scoff,
Though one miss'd fire, the other would go
     off);   495
These, with a bayonet, not so free from
     rust
As when the arm-chest held its brighter
     trust,
Completed his accoutrements, as Night
Survey'd him in his garb heteroclite.

XXI

'What cheer, Ben Bunting?' cried (when
     in full view   500
Our new acquaintance) Torquil. 'Aught
     of new?
'Ey, ey!' quoth Ben, 'not new, but news
     enow;
A strange sail in the offing.'—'Sail! and
     how?
What! could you make her out? It cannot
     be;
I've seen no rag of canvas on the sea.'   505
'Belike,' said Ben, 'you might not from the
     bay,
But from the bluff-head, where I watch'd
     to-day,
I saw her in the doldrums; for the wind
Was light and baffling.'—'When the sun
     declined
Where lay she? had she anchor'd?'—'No,
     but still   510
She bore down on us, till the wind grew still.'
'Her flag?'—'I had no glass: but fore and
     aft,
Egad! she seem'd a wicked-looking craft.'
'Arm'd?'—'I expect so;—sent on the
     look-out:
'Tis time, belike, to put our helm about.'
'About?—Whate'er may have us now in
     chase,   516
We'll make no running fight, for that were
     base;

We will die at our quarters, like true men.'
'Ey, ey! for that 'tis all the same to Ben.'
'Does Christian know this?'—'Ay; he
     has piped all hands   520
To quarters. They are furbishing the stands
Of arms; and we have got some guns to
     bear,
And scaled them. You are wanted.'—
     'That's but fair;
And if it were not, mine is not the soul
To leave my comrades helpless on the
     shoal.   525
My Neuha! ah! and must my fate pursue
Not me alone, but one so sweet and true?
But whatsoe'er betide, ah, Neuha! now
Unman me not; the hour will not allow
A tear; I'm thine whatever intervenes!'
'Right,' quoth Ben, 'that will do for the
     marines.'   531

CANTO THE THIRD

I

THE fight was o'er; the flashing through
     the gloom,
Which robes the cannon as he wings a
     tomb,
Had ceased; and sulphury vapours up-
     ward driven
Had left the earth, and but polluted
     heaven:
The rattling roar which rung in every
     volley   5
Had left the echoes to their melancholy;
No more they shriek'd their horror, boom
     for boom;
The strife was done, the vanquish'd had
     their doom;
The mutineers were crush'd, dispers'd, or
     ta'en,
Or lived to deem the happiest were the
     slain.   10
Few, few escaped, and these were hunted
     o'er
The isle they loved beyond their native
     shore.
No further home was theirs, it seem'd, on
     earth,
Once renegades to that which gave them
     birth;
Track'd like wild beasts, like them they
     sought the wild,   15
As to a mother's bosom flies the child;
But vainly wolves and lions seek their den,
And still more vainly men escape from
     men.

II

Beneath a rock whose jutting base pro-
     trudes
Far over ocean in its fiercest moods,   20
When scaling his enormous crag the wave
Is hurl'd down headlong like the foremost
     brave,

And falls back on the foaming crowd
behind,
Which fight beneath the banners of the
wind,   24
But now at rest, a little remnant drew
Together, bleeding, thirsty, faint, and few;
But still their weapons in their hands, and
still
With something of the pride of former will,
As men not all unused to meditate,
And strive much more than wonder at
their fate.   30
Their present lot was what they had fore-
seen,
And dared as what was likely to have been;
Yet still the lingering hope, which deem'd
their lot
Not pardon'd, but unsought for or forgot,
Or trusted that, if sought, their distant
caves   35
Might still be miss'd amidst the world of
waves,
Had wean'd their thoughts in part from
what they saw
And felt, the vengeance of their country's
law.
Their sea-green isle, their guilt-won para-
dise,
No more could shield their virtue or their
vice: 40
Their better feelings, if such were, were
thrown
Back on themselves,—their sins remain'd
alone.
Proscribed even in their second country,
they
Were lost; in vain the world before them
lay;
All outlets seem'd secured. Their new
allies   45
Had fought and bled in mutual sacrifice;
But what avail'd the club and spear, and
arm
Of Hercules, against the sulphury charm,
The magic of the thunder, which destroy'd
The warrior ere his strength could be em-
ploy'd?   50
Dug, like a spreading pestilence, the grave
No less of human bravery than the brave!
Their own scant numbers acted all the
few
Against the many oft will dare and do;
But though the choice seems native to die
free,   55
Even Greece can boast but one Thermo-
pylæ,
Till *now*, when she has forged her broken
chain
Back to a sword, and dies and lives again!

III

Beside the jutting rock the few appear'd,
Like the last remnant of the red-deer's
herd;   60

Their eyes were feverish, and their aspect
worn,
But still the hunter's blood was on their
horn,
A little stream came tumbling from the
height,
And straggling into ocean as it might,
Its bounding crystal frolick'd in the ray,
And gush'd from cliff to crag with saltless
spray;   66
Close on the wild, wide ocean, yet as pure
And fresh as innocence, and more secure,
Its silver torrent glitter'd o'er the deep,
As the shy chamois' eye o'erlooks the
steep,   70
While far below the vast and sullen swell
Of ocean's alpine azure rose and fell.
To this young spring they rush'd,—all
feelings first
Absorb'd in passion's and in nature's
thirst,—
Drank as they do who drink their last, and
threw   75
Their arms aside to revel in its dew;
Cool'd their scorch'd throats, and wash'd
the gory stains
From wounds whose only bandage might
be chains;
Then, when their drought was quench'd,
look'd sadly round,
As wondering how so many still were
found   80
Alive and fetterless:—but silent all,
Each sought his fellow's eyes, as if to call
On him for language which his lips denied,
As though their voices with their cause had
died.

IV

Stern, and aloof a little from the rest,
Stood Christian, with his arms across his
chest.   86
The ruddy, reckless, dauntless hue once
spread
Along his cheek was livid now as lead;
His light-brown locks, so graceful in their
flow,
Now rose like startled vipers o'er his
brow.   90
Still as a statue, with his lips comprest
To stifle even the breath within his breast,
Fast by the rock, all menacing, but mute,
He stood; and, save a slight beat of his
foot,
Which deepen'd now and then the sandy
dint   95
Beneath his heel, his form seem'd turn'd
to flint.
Some paces further Torquil lean'd his head
Against a bank, and spoke not, but he
bled,—
Not mortally:—his worst wound was
within;
His brow was pale, his blue eyes sunken in,

And blood-drops, sprinkled o'er his yellow
   hair, 101
Show'd that his faintness came not from
   despair,
But nature's ebb. Beside him was another,
Rough as a bear, but willing as a brother,—
Ben Bunting, who essay'd to wash, and
   wipe, 105
And bind his wound—then calmly lit his
   pipe,
A trophy which survived a hundred fights,
A beacon which had cheer'd ten thousand
   nights.
The fourth and last of this deserted group
Walk'd up and down—at times would
   stand, then stoop, 110
To pick a pebble up—then let it drop—
Then hurry as in haste—then quickly
   stop—
Then cast his eyes on his companions—
   then
Half whistle half a tune, and pause again—
And then his former movements would
   redouble, 115
With something between carelessness and
   trouble.
This is a long description, but applies
To scarce five minutes pass'd before the
   eyes;
But yet *what* minutes! Moments like to
   these
Rend men's lives into immortalities. 120

V

At length Jack Skyscrape, a mercurial
   man,
Who flutter'd over all things like a fan,
More brave than firm, and more disposed
   to dare
And die at once than wrestle with despair,
Exclaim'd, 'G—d damn!'—those syllables
   intense,— 125
Nucleus of England's native eloquence,
As the Turk's 'Allah!' or the Roman's
   more
Pagan 'Proh Jupiter!' was wont of yore
To give their first impressions such a vent,
By way of echo to embarrassment. 130
Jack was embarrass'd,—never hero more,
And as he knew not what to say, he swore:
Nor swore in vain; the long congenial
   sound
Revived Ben Bunting from his pipe pro-
   found;
He drew it from his mouth, and look'd full
   wise, 135
But merely added to the oath his *eyes*;
Thus rendering the imperfect phrase com-
   plete,
A peroration I need not repeat.

VI

But Christian, of a higher order, stood
Like an extinct volcano in his mood;

Silent, and sad, and savage,—with the
   trace 141
Of passion reeking from his clouded face;
Till lifting up again his sombre eye,
It glanced on Torquil, who lean'd faintly
   by.
'And is it thus?' he cried, 'unhappy boy!
And thee, too, *thee*—my madness must
   destroy!' 146
He said, and strode to where young Tor-
   quil stood,
Yet dabbled with his lately flowing blood;
Seized his hand wistfully, but did not press,
And shrunk as fearful of his own caress;
Inquired into his state; and when he heard
The wound was slighter than he deem'd or
   fear'd, 152
A moment's brightness pass'd along his
   brow,
As much as such a moment would allow.
'Yes,' he exclaim'd, 'we're taken in the
   toil, 155
But not a coward or a common spoil;
Dearly they've bought us—dearly still may
   buy,—
And I must fall; but have you strength to
   fly?
'Twould be some comfort still, could you
   survive;
Our dwindled band is now too few to
   strive. 160
Oh! for a sole canoe! though but a shell,
To bear you hence to where a hope may
   dwell!
For me, my lot is what I sought; to be,
In life or death, the fearless and the free.'

VII

Even as he spoke, around the promontory,
Which nodded o'er the billows high and
   hoary, 166
A dark speck dotted ocean: on it flew
Like to the shadow of a roused sea-mew;
Onward it came—and, lo! a second
   follow'd—
Now seen—now hid—where ocean's vale
   was hollow'd; 170
And near, and nearer, till their dusky crew
Presented well-known aspects to the view,
Till on the surf their skimming paddles play,
Buoyant as wings, and flitting through the
   spray;—
Now perching on the wave's high curl, and
   now 175
Dash'd downward in the thundering foam
   below,
Which flings it broad and boiling sheet on
   sheet,
And slings its high flakes, shiver'd into
   sleet:
But floating still through surf and swell,
   drew nigh
The barks, like small birds through a
   lowering sky. 180

Their art seem'd nature—such the skill to
　　sweep
The wave of these born playmates of the
　　deep.

VIII

And who the first that, springing on the
　　strand,
Leap'd like a nereid from her shell to land,
With dark but brilliant skin, and dewy eye
Shining with love, and hope, and con-
　　stancy?　　　　　　　　　　　　　186
Neuha—the fond, the faithful, the
　　adored—
Her heart on Torquil's like a torrent
　　pour'd;
And smiled, and wept, and near, and
　　nearer clasp'd,
As if to be assured 'twas *him* she grasp'd;
Shudder'd to see his yet warm wound, and
　　then,　　　　　　　　　　　　　　191
To find it trivial, smiled and wept again.
She was a warrior's daughter, and could
　　bear
Such sights, and feel, and mourn, but not
　　despair.
Her lover lived,—nor foes nor fears could
　　blight　　　　　　　　　　　　　　195
That full-blown moment in its all delight:
Joy trickled in her tears, joy fill'd the sob
That rock'd her heart till almost heard to
　　throb;
And paradise was breathing in the sigh
Of nature's child in nature's ecstasy.　200

IX

The sterner spirits who beheld that meet-
　　ing
Were not unmoved; who are, when hearts
　　are greeting?
Even Christian gazed upon the maid and
　　boy
With tearless eye, but yet a gloomy joy
Mix'd with those bitter thoughts the soul
　　arrays　　　　　　　　　　　　　205
In hopeless visions of our better days,
When all's gone—to the rainbow's latest
　　ray.
'And but for me!' he said, and turn'd
　　away;
Then gazed upon the pair, as in his den
A lion looks upon his cubs again;　　210
And then relapsed into his sullen guise,
As heedless of his further destinies.

X

But brief their time for good or evil
　　thought;
The billows round the promontory
　　brought
The plash of hostile oars.—Alas! who
　　made　　　　　　　　　　　　　215
That sound a dread? All around them
　　seem'd array'd

Against them, save the bride of Toobonai:
She, as she caught the first glimpse o'er the
　　bay
Of the arm'd boats, which hurried to
　　complete
The remnant's ruin with their flying feet,
Beckon'd the natives round her to their
　　prows,　　　　　　　　　　　　　221
Embark'd their guests and launch'd their
　　light canoes,
In one placed Christian and his comrades
　　twain;
But she and Torquil must not part again.
She fix'd him in her own.—Away! away!
They clear the breakers, dart along the
　　bay,　　　　　　　　　　　　　226
And towards a group of islets, such as bear
The sea-bird's nest and seal's surf-
　　hollow'd lair,
They skim the blue tops of the billows; fast
They flew, and fast their fierce pursuers
　　chased.　　　　　　　　　　　　230
They gain upon them—now they lose
　　again,—
Again make way and menace o'er the
　　main;
And now the two canoes in chase divide,
And follow different courses o'er the tide,
To baffle the pursuit.—Away! away!
As Life is on each paddle's flight to-day,
And more than Life or lives to Neuha: Love
Freights the frail bark and urges to the
　　cove;
And now the refuge and the foe are nigh—
Yet, yet a moment: Fly, thou light ark,
　　fly!　　　　　　　　　　　　　240

CANTO THE FOURTH

I

WHITE as a white sail on a dusky sea,
When half the horizon's clouded and half
　　free,
Fluttering between the dun wave and the
　　sky,
Is hope's last gleam in man's extremity.
Her anchor parts! but still her snowy sail
Attracts our eye amidst the rudest gale:
Though every wave she climbs divides us
　　more,　　　　　　　　　　　　　7
The heart still follows from the loneliest
　　shore.

II

Not distant from the isle of Toobonai,
A black rock rears its bosom o'er the
　　spray,　　　　　　　　　　　　10
The haunt of birds, a desert to mankind,
Where the rough seal reposes from the
　　wind,
And sleeps unwieldy in his cavern dun,
Or gambols with huge frolic in the sun:
There shrilly to the passing oar is heard
The startled echo of the ocean bird,　16

Who rears on its bare breast her callow
brood,
The feather'd fishers of the solitude.
A narrow segment of the yellow sand
On one side forms the outline of a strand;
Here the young turtle, crawling from his
shell,   21
Steals to the deep wherein his parents dwell;
Chipp'd by the beam, a nursling of the day,
But hatch'd for ocean by the fostering ray;
The rest was one bleak precipice, as e'er
Gave mariners a shelter and despair;   26
A spot to make the saved regret the deck
Which late went down, and envy the lost
wreck.
Such was the stern asylum Neuha chose
To shield her lover from his following
foes;   30
But all its secret was not told; she knew
In this a treasure hidden from the view.

III

Ere the canoes divided, near the spot,
The men that mann'd what held her Tor-
quil's lot,
By her command removed, to strengthen
more   35
The skiff which wafted Christian from the
shore.
This he would have opposed; but with a
smile
She pointed calmly to the craggy isle,
And bade him 'speed and prosper.' *She*
would take   39
The rest upon herself for Torquil's sake.
They parted with this added aid; afar
The proa darted like a shooting star,
And gain'd on the pursuers, who now
steer'd
Right on the rock which she and Torquil
near'd.
They pull'd; her arm, though delicate, was
free   45
And firm as ever grappled with the sea,
And yielded scarce to Torquil's manlier
strength.
The prow now almost lay within its length
Of the crag's steep, inexorable face,
With nought but soundless waters for its
base;   50
Within a hundred boats' length was the foe,
And now what refuge but their frail canoe?
This Torquil ask'd with half-upbraiding
eye,
Which said—'Has Neuha brought me
here to die?
Is this a place of safety, or a grave,   55
And yon huge rock the tombstone of the
wave?'

IV

They rested on their paddles, and uprose
Neuha, and pointing to the approaching
foes,

Cried, 'Torquil, follow me, and fearless
follow!'
Then plunged at once into the ocean's
hollow.   60
There was no time to pause—the foes were
near—
Chains in his eye, and menace in his ear;
With vigour they pull'd on, and as they
came,
Hail'd him to yield, and by his forfeit name.
Headlong he leapt—to him the swimmer's
skill   65
Was native, and now all his hope from ill:
But how, or where? He dived, and rose no
more;
The boat's crew look'd amazed o'er sea
and shore.
There was no landing on that precipice,
Steep, harsh, and slippery as a berg of ice.
They watch'd awhile to see him float again,
But not a trace rebubbled from the main:
The wave roll'd on, no ripple on its face,
Since their first plunge recall'd a single
trace;
The little whirl which eddied, and slight
foam,   75
That whiten'd o'er what seem'd their latest
home,
White as a sepulchre above the pair
Who left no marble (mournful as an heir)
The quiet proa wavering o'er the tide
Was all that told of Torquil and his bride;
And but for this alone the whole might
seem   81
The vanish'd phantom of a seaman's dream.
They paused and search'd in vain, then
pull'd away;
Even superstition now forbade their stay.
Some said he had not plunged into the
wave,   85
But vanish'd like a corpse-light from a
grave;
Others, that something supernatural
Glared in his figure, more than mortal tall;
While all agreed that in his cheek and eye
There was a dead hue of eternity.   90
Still as their oars receded from the crag,
Round every weed a moment would they
lag,
Expectant of some token of their prey;
But no—he had melted from them like the
spray.

V

And where was he the pilgrim of the deep,
Following the nereid? Had they ceased to
weep   96
For ever? or, received in coral caves,
Wrung life and pity from the softening
waves?
Did they with ocean's hidden sovereigns
dwell,
And sound with mermen the fantastic
shell?   100

Did Neuha with the mermaids comb her hair
Flowing o'er ocean as it stream'd in air?
Or had they perish'd, and in silence slept
Beneath the gulf wherein they boldly leapt?

VI

Young Neuha plunged into the deep, and
   he   105
Follow'd: her track beneath her native sea
Was as a native's of the element,
So smoothly, bravely, brilliantly she went,
Leaving a streak of light behind her heel,
Which struck and flash'd like an am-
   phibious steel.   110
Closely, and scarcely less expert to trace
The depths where divers hold the pearl in
   chase,
Torquil, the nursling of the northern seas,
Pursued her liquid steps with heart and
   ease.
Deep—deeper for an instant Neuha led
The way—then upward soar'd—and as
   she spread   116
Her arms, and flung the foam from off her
   locks,
Laugh'd, and the sound was answer'd by
   the rocks.
They had gain'd a central realm of earth
   again,
But look'd for tree, and field, and sky, in
   vain.   120
Around she pointed to a spacious cave,
Whose only portal was the keyless wave,
(A hollow archway by the sun unseen,
Save through the billows' glassy veil of green,
In some transparent ocean holiday, 125
When all the finny people are at play,)
Wiped with her hair the brine from Tor-
   quil's eyes,
And clapp'd her hands with joy at his sur-
   prise;   128
Led him to where the rock appear'd to jut,
And form a something like a Triton's hut;
For all was darkness for a space, till day
Through clefts above let in a sober'd ray;
As in some old cathedral's glimmering
   aisle
The dusty monuments from light recoil,
Thus sadly in their refuge submarine 135
The vault drew half her shadow from the
   scene.

VII

Forth from her bosom the young savage
   drew   137
A pine torch, strongly girded with gnatoo;
A plantain-leaf o'er all, the more to keep
Its latent sparkle from the sapping deep.
This mantle kept it dry; then from a nook
Of the same plantain-leaf a flint she took,
A few shrunk wither'd twigs, and from the
   blade   143
Of Torquil's knife struck fire, and thus
   array'd

The grot with torchlight. Wide it was and
   high,   145
And show'd a self-born Gothic canopy;
The arch uprear'd by nature's architect,
The architrave some earthquake might
   erect;
The buttress from some mountain's
   bosom hurl'd,
When the Poles crash'd, and water was the
   world;   150
Or harden'd from some earth-absorbing
   fire,
While yet the globe reek'd from its funeral
   pyre;
The fretted pinnacle, the aisle, the nave,
Were there, all scoop'd by Darkness from
   her cave.   154
There, with a little tinge of phantasy,
Fantastic faces mop'd and mow'd on high,
And then a mitre or a shrine would fix
The eye upon its seeming crucifix.
Thus Nature play'd with the stalactites,
And built herself a chapel of the seas.

VIII

And Neuha took her Torquil by the hand,
And waved along the vault her kindled
   brand,
And led him into each recess, and show'd
The secret places of their new abode.
Nor these alone, for all had been prepared
Before, to soothe the lover's lot she
   shared: 166
The mat for rest; for dress the fresh gnatoo,
And sandal oil to fence against the dew;
For food the cocoa-nut, the yam, the
   bread
Born of the fruit; for board the plantain
   spread   170
With its broad leaf, or turtle-shell which
   bore
A banquet in the flesh it cover'd o'er;
The gourd with water recent from the rill,
The ripe banana from the mellow hill;
A pine-torch pile to keep undying light,
And she herself, as beautiful as night,
To fling her shadowy spirit o'er the scene,
And make their subterranean world serene.
She had foreseen, since first the stranger's
   sail
Drew to their isle, that force or flight might
   fail,   180
And form'd a refuge of the rocky den
For Torquil's safety from his countrymen.
Each dawn had wafted there her light
   canoe,
Laden with all the golden fruits that grew;
Each eve had seen her gliding through the
   hour   185
With all could cheer or deck their sparry
   bower;
And now she spread her little store with
   smiles,
The happiest daughter of the loving isles.

IX

She, as he gazed with grateful wonder,
    press'd
Her shelter'd love to her impassion'd
    breast;   190
And suited to her soft caresses, told
An olden tale of love,—for love is old,
Old as eternity, but not outworn
With each new being born or to be born:
How a young chief, a thousand moons
    ago,   195
Diving for turtle in the depths below,
Had risen, in tracking fast his ocean prey,
Into the cave which round and o'er them
    lay;
How in some desperate feud of after-time
He shelter'd there a daughter of the clime,   201
A foe beloved, and offspring of a foe;
Saved by his tribe but for a captive's woe;
How, when the storm of war was still'd, he led
His island clan to where the waters spread
Their deep-green shadow o'er the rocky
    door,   205
Then dived—it seem'd as if to rise no more:
His wondering mates, amazed within their
    bark,
Or deem'd him mad, or prey to the blue
    shark;
Row'd round in sorrow the sea-girded
    rock,
Then paused upon their paddles from the
    shock;   210
When, fresh and springing from the deep,
    they saw
A goddess rise—so deem'd they in their
    awe;
And their companion, glorious by her side,
Proud and exulting in his mermaid bride:
And how, when undeceived, the pair they
    bore   215
With sounding conchs and joyous shouts
    to shore;
How they had gladly lived and calmly
    died,
And why not also Torquil and his bride?
Not mine to tell the rapturous caress   219
Which follow'd wildly in that wild recess
This tale; enough that all within that cave
Was love, though buried strong as in the
    grave
Where Abelard, through twenty years of
    death,
When Eloïsa's form was lower'd beneath
Their nuptial vault, his arms outstretch'd,
    and press'd   225
The kindling ashes to his kindled breast.
The waves without sang round their
    couch, their roar
As much unheeded as if life were o'er;
Within, their hearts made all their har-
    mony,
Love's broken murmur and more broken
    sigh.   230

X

And they, the cause and sharers of the
    shock
Which left them exiles of the hollow rock,
Where were they? O'er the sea for life
    they plied,
To seek from Heaven the shelter men
    denied.
Another course had been their choice—
    but where?   235
The wave which bore them still their foes
    would bear,
Who, disappointed of their former chase,
In search of Christian now renew'd their
    race.
Eager with anger, their strong arms made
    way,
Like vultures baffled of their previous
    prey.   240
They gain'd upon them, all whose safety
    lay
In some bleak crag or deeply-hidden bay:
No further chance or choice remain'd;
    and right
For the first further rock which met their
    sight
They steer'd, to take their latest view of
    land,   245
And yield as victims, or die sword in hand;
Dismiss'd the natives and their shallop,
    who
Would still have battled for that scanty
    crew;
But Christian bade them seek their shore
    again,
Nor add a sacrifice which were in vain;
For what were simple bow and savage
    spear   251
Against the arms which must be wielded
    here?

XI

They landed on a wild but narrow scene,
Where few but Nature's footsteps yet had
    been;
Prepared their arms, and with that gloomy
    eye,   255
Stern and sustain'd, of man's extremity,
When hope is gone, nor glory's self remains
To cheer resistance against death or
    chains,—
They stood, the three, as the three hundred
    stood
Who dyed Thermopylæ with holy blood.
But, ah! how different! 'tis the *cause* makes
    all,   261
Degrades or hallows courage in its fall.
O'er them no fame, eternal and intense,
Blazed through the clouds of death and
    beckon'd hence;
No grateful country, smiling through her
    tears,   265
Begun the praises of a thousand years;

No nation's eyes would on their tomb be
    bent,
No heroes envy them their monument;
However boldly their warm blood was
    spilt,
Their life was shame, their epitaph was
    guilt.   270
And this they knew and felt, at least the
    one,
The leader of the band he had undone;
Who, born perchance for better things,
    had set
His life upon a cast which linger'd yet:
But now the die was to be thrown, and all
The chances were in favour of his fall:
And such a fall! But still he faced the
    shock,   277
Obdurate as a portion of the rock
Whereon he stood, and fix'd his levell'd
    gun,
Dark as a sullen cloud before the sun.

XII

The boat drew nigh, well arm'd, and firm
    the crew   281
To act whatever duty bade them do;
Careless of danger, as the onward wind
Is of the leaves it strews, nor looks behind.
And yet perhaps they rather wish'd to go
Against a nation's than a native foe,   286
And felt that this poor victim of self-will,
Briton no more, had once been Britain's
    still.
They hail'd him to surrender—no reply;
Their arms were poised, and glitter'd in
    the sky.   290
They hail'd again—no answer; yet once
    more
They offer'd quarter louder than before.
The echoes only, from the rock's rebound,
Took their last farewell of the dying sound.
Then flash'd the flint, and blazed the
    volleying flame,   295
And the smoke rose between them and
    their aim,
While the rock rattled with the bullets'
    knell,
Which peal'd in vain, and flatten'd as they
    fell;
Then flew the only answer to be given
By those who had lost all hope in earth or
    heaven.   300
After the first fierce peal, as they pull'd
    nigher,
They heard the voice of Christian shout,
    'Now, fire!'
And ere the word upon the echo died,
Two fell; the rest assail'd the rock's rough
    side,   304
And, furious at the madness of their foes,
Disdain'd all further efforts, save to close.
But steep the crag, and all without a path,
Each step opposed a bastion to their
    wrath,

While, placed 'midst clefts the least acces-
    sible,
Which Christian's eye was train'd to mark
    full well,   310
The three maintain'd a strife which must
    not yield,
In spots where eagles might have chosen
    to build.
Their every shot told; while the assailant
    fell,
Dash'd on the shingles like the limpet
    shell;
But still enough survived, and mounted
    still,   315
Scattering their numbers here and there,
    until
Surrounded and commanded, though not
    nigh
Enough for seizure, near enough to die,
The desperate trio held aloof their fate
But by a thread, like sharks who've gorged
    the bait;   320
Yet to the very last they battled well,
And not a groan inform'd their foes *who*
    fell.
Christian died last—twice wounded; and
    once more
Mercy was offer'd when they saw his gore;
Too late for life, but not too late to die,
With, though a hostile hand, to close his
    eye.   326
A limb was broken, and he droop'd along
The crag, as doth a falcon reft of young.
The sound revived him, or appear'd to
    wake
Some passion which a weakly gesture
    spake: 330
He beckon'd to the foremost, who drew
    nigh,
But, as they near'd, he rear'd his weapon
    high—
His last ball had been aim'd, but from his
    breast
He tore the topmost button from his vest,
Down the tube dash'd it, levell'd, fired,
    and smiled   335
As his foe fell; then, like a serpent, coil'd
His wounded, weary form, to where the
    steep
Look'd desperate as himself along the
    deep;
Cast one glance back, and clench'd his
    hand, and shook
His last rage 'gainst the earth which he for-
    sook;   340
Then plunged: the rock below received
    like glass
His body crush'd into one gory mass,
With scarce a shred to tell of human form,
Or fragment for the sea-bird or the worm;
A fair-hair'd scalp, besmear'd with blood
    and weeds,   345
Yet reek'd, the remnant of himself and
    deeds;

Some splinters of his weapons (to the last,
As long as hand could hold, he held them
    fast)
Yet glitter'd, but at distance—hurl'd away
To rust beneath the dew and dashing
    spray.   350
The rest was nothing—save a life mis-
    spent,
And soul—but who shall answer where it
    went?
'Tis ours to bear, not judge the dead; and
    they
Who doom to hell, themselves are on the
    way,
Unless these bullies of eternal pains 355
Are pardon'd their bad hearts for their
    worse brains.

XIII

The deed was over! All were gone or ta'en,
The fugitive, the captive, or the slain.
Chain'd on the deck, where once, a gallant
    crew,
They stood with honour, were the
    wretched few   360
Survivors of the skirmish on the isle;
But the last rock left no surviving spoil.
Cold lay they where they fell, and welter-
    ing,
While o'er them flapp'd the sea-birds'
    dewy wing,
Now wheeling nearer from the neighbour-
    ing surge,   365
And screaming high their harsh and
    hungry dirge:
But calm and careless heaved the wave
    below,
Eternal with unsympathetic flow;
Far o'er its face the dolphins sported on,
And sprung the flying fish against the sun,
Till its dried wing relapsed from its brief
    height,   371
To gather moisture for another flight.

XIV

'Twas morn; and Neuha, who by dawn of
    day
Swam smoothly forth to catch the rising
    ray,
And watch if aught approach'd the am-
    phibious lair   375
Where lay her lover, saw a sail in air:
It flapp'd, it fill'd, and to the growing gale
Bent its broad arch: her breath began to
    fail
With fluttering fear, her heart beat thick
    and high,
While yet a doubt sprung where its course
    might lie.   380

But no! it came not; fast and far away
The shadow lessen'd as it clear'd the bay.
She gazed, and flung the sea-foam from
    her eyes,   383
To watch as for a rainbow in the skies.
On the horizon verged the distant deck,
Diminish'd, dwindled to a very speck—
Then vanish'd. All was ocean, all was joy!
Down plunged she through the cave to
    rouse her boy;   388
Told all she had seen, and all she hoped,
    and all
That happy love could augur or recall;
Sprung forth again, with Torquil follow-
    ing free   391
His bounding nereid over the broad sea;
Swam round the rock, to where a shallow
    cleft
Hid the canoe that Neuha there had left
Drifting along the tide, without an oar,
That eve the strangers chased them from
    the shore;   396
But when these vanish'd, she pursued her
    prow,
Regain'd, and urged to where they found
    it now:
Nor ever did more love and joy embark,
Than now were wafted in that slender
    ark.   400

XV

Again their own shore rises on the view,
No more polluted with a hostile hue;
No sullen ship lay bristling o'er the foam,
A floating dungeon:—all was hope and
    home!
A thousand proas darted o'er the bay,
With sounding shells, and heralded their
    way;   406
The chiefs came down, around the people
    pour'd,
And welcomed Torquil as a son restored;
The women throng'd, embracing and em-
    braced
By Neuha, asking where they had been
    chased,   410
And how escaped? The tale was told; and
    then
One acclamation rent the sky again;
And from that hour a new tradition gave
Their sanctuary the name of 'Neuha's
    Cave.'
A hundred fires, far flickering from the
    height,   415
Blazed o'er the general revel of the night,
The feast in honour of the guest, return'd
To peace and pleasure, perilously earn'd;
A night succeeded by such happy days
As only the yet infant world displays.

THE LAMENT OF TASSO

ADVERTISEMENT

AT Ferrara, in the Library, are preserved the original MSS. of Tasso's Gierusalemme and of Guarini's Pastor Fido, with letters of Tasso, one from Titian to Ariosto, and the inkstand and chair, the tomb and the house, of the latter. But, as misfortune has a greater interest for posterity, and little or none for the cotemporary, the cell where Tasso was confined in the hospital of St. Anna attracts a more fixed attention than the residence or the monument of Ariosto—at least it had this effect on me. There are two inscriptions, one on the outer gate, the second over the cell itself, inviting, unnecessarily, the wonder and the indignation of the spectator. Ferrara is much decayed and de-populated: the castle still exists entire; and I saw the court where Parisina and Hugo were beheaded, according to the annal of Gibbon.

I

Long years!—It tries the thrilling frame
   to bear
And eagle-spirit of a child of Song—
Long years of outrage, calumny, and wrong;
Imputed madness, prison'd solitude,   4
And the mind's canker in its savage mood,
When the impatient thirst of light and air
Parches the heart; and the abhorred grate,
Marring the sunbeams with its hideous
   shade,
Works through the throbbing eyeball to
   the brain,   9
With a hot sense of heaviness and pain;
And bare, at once, Captivity display'd
Stands scoffing through the never-open'd
   gate,
Which nothing through its bars admits,
   save day,
And tasteless food, which I have eat alone
Till its unsocial bitterness is gone;   15
And I can banquet like a beast of prey,
Sullen and lonely, couching in the cave
Which is my lair, and—it may be—my grave.
All this hath somewhat worn me, and may
   wear,
But must be borne. I stoop not to despair;
For I have battled with mine agony,   21
And made me wings wherewith to overfly
The narrow circus of my dungeon wall,
And freed the Holy Sepulchre from thrall;
And revell'd among men and things
   divine,   25
And pour'd my spirit over Palestine,
In honour of the sacred war for Him,
The God who was on earth and is in
   heaven,
For he has strengthen'd me in heart and
   limb.
That through this sufferance I might be
   forgiven,   30
I have employ'd my penance to record
How Salem's shrine was won, and how
   adored.

II

But this is o'er—my pleasant task is
   done:—
My long-sustaining friend of many years!
If I do blot thy final page with tears,   35
Know, that my sorrows have wrung from
   me none.
But thou, my young creation! my soul's
   child!
Which ever playing round me came and
   smiled,
And woo'd me from myself with thy sweet
   sight,   39
Thou too art gone—and so is my delight:
And therefore do I weep and inly bleed
With this last bruise upon a broken reed.
Thou too art ended—what is left me now?
For I have anguish yet to bear—and how?
I know not that—but in the innate force
Of my own spirit shall be found resource.
I have not sunk, for I had no remorse,   47
Nor cause for such: they call'd me mad—
   and why?
Oh Leonora! wilt not thou reply?
I was indeed delirious in my heart   50
To lift my love so lofty as thou art;
But still my frenzy was not of the mind:
I knew my fault, and feel my punishment
Not less because I suffer it unbent.
That thou wert beautiful, and I not blind,
Hath been the sin which shuts me from
   mankind;   56
But let them go, or torture as they will,
My heart can multiply thine image still;
Successful love may sate itself away;
The wretched are the faithful; 'tis their
   fate   60
To have all feeling, save the one, decay,
And every passion into one dilate,
As rapid rivers into ocean pour;
But ours is fathomless, and hath no shore.

III

Above me, hark! the long and maniac cry
Of minds and bodies in captivity.   66
And hark! the lash and the increasing
   howl,
And the half-inarticulate blasphemy!
There be some here with worse than frenzy
   foul,
Some who do still goad on the o'er-
   labour'd mind,   70
And dim the little light that's left behind

THE LAMENT OF TASSO

With needless torture, as their tyrant will
Is wound up to the lust of doing ill:
With these and with their victims am I
    class'd,
'Mid sounds and sights like these long
    years have pass'd;   75
'Mid sights and sounds like these my life
    may close:
So let it be—for then I shall repose.

IV

I have been patient, let me be so yet;
I had forgotten half I would forget,
But it revives—Oh! would it were my lot
To be forgetful as I am forgot!   81
Feel I not wroth with those who bade me
    dwell
In this vast lazar-house of many woes?
Where laughter is not mirth, nor thought
    the mind,
Nor words a language, nor ev'n men man-
    kind;   85
Where cries reply to curses, shrieks to
    blows,
And each is tortured in his separate hell—
For we are crowded in our solitudes—
Many, but each divided by the wall,
Which echoes Madness in her babbling
    moods;   90
While all can hear, none heed his neigh-
    bour's call—
None! save that One, the veriest wretch of
    all,
Who was not made to be the mate of these,
Nor bound between Distraction and Dis-
    ease.
Feel I not wroth with those who placed me
    here?   95
Who have debased me in the minds of men,
Debarring me the usage of my own,
Blighting my life in best of its career,
Branding my thoughts as things to shun
    and fear?
Would I not pay them back these pangs
    again,   100
And teach them inward Sorrow's stifled
    groan?
The struggle to be calm, and cold distress,
Which undermines our Stoical success?
No! still too proud to be vindictive—I
Have pardon'd princes' insults, and would
    die.   105
Yes, Sister of my Sovereign! for thy sake
I weed all bitterness from out my breast,
It hath no business where *thou* art a guest:
Thy brother hates—but I cannot detest;
Thou pitiest not—but I cannot forsake.

V

Look on a love which knows not to despair,
But all unquench'd is still my better part,
Dwelling deep in my shut and silent heart,
As dwells the gather'd lightning in its
    cloud,

Encompass'd with its dark and rolling
    shroud,   115
Till struck,—forth flies the all-ethereal
    dart!
And thus at the collision of thy name,
The vivid thought still flashes through my
    frame,   118
And for a moment all things as they were
Flit by me; they are gone—I am the same.
And yet my love without ambition grew;
I knew thy state, my station, and I knew
A Princess was no love-mate for a bard;
I told it not, I breathed it not, it was
Sufficient to itself, its own reward;   125
And if my eyes reveal'd it, they, alas!
Were punish'd by the silentness of thine,
And yet I did not venture to repine.
Thou wert to me a crystal-girded shrine,
Worshipp'd at holy distance, and around
Hallow'd and meekly kiss'd the saintly
    ground;   131
Not for thou wert a princess, but that Love
Had robed thee with a glory, and array'd
Thy lineaments in beauty that dismay'd—
Oh! not dismay'd—but awed, like One
    above!   135
And in that sweet severity there was
A something which all softness did sur-
    pass;
I know not how—thy genius master'd
    mine;
My star stood still before thee: if it were
Presumptuous thus to love without de-
    sign,   140
That sad fatality hath cost me dear;
But thou art dearest still, and I should be
Fit for this cell, which wrongs me—but for
    thee.
The very love which lock'd me to my chain
Hath lighten'd half its weight; and for the
    rest,   145
Though heavy, lent me vigour to sustain,
And look to thee with undivided breast,
And foil the ingenuity of Pain.

VI

It is no marvel—from my very birth
My soul was drunk with love, which did
    pervade   150
And mingle with whate'er I saw on earth:
Of objects all inanimate I made
Idols, and out of wild and lonely flowers,
And rocks, whereby they grew, a paradise,
Where I did lay me down within the shade
Of waving trees, and dreamed uncounted
    hours,   156
Though I was chid for wandering; and the
    wise
Shook their white aged heads o'er me and
    said,
Of such materials wretched men were
    made,
And such a truant boy would end in woe,
And that the only lesson was a blow;

And then they smote me, and I did not
    weep,
But cursed them in my heart, and to my
    haunt
Return'd and wept alone, and dream'd
    again   164
The visions which arise without a sleep,
And with my years my soul began to pant
With feelings of strange tumult and soft
    pain;
And the whole heart exhaled into One Want,
But undefined and wandering, till the day
I found the thing I sought—and that was
    thee;   170
And then I lost my being, all to be
Absorb'd in thine; the world was past
    away;
Thou didst annihilate the earth to me!

VII

I loved all Solitude, but little thought
To spend I know not what of life, remote
From all communion with existence,
    save   176
The maniac and his tyrant; had I been
Their fellow, many years ere this had seen
My mind like theirs corrupted to its grave.
But who hath seen me writhe, or heard me
    rave?   180
Perchance in such a cell we suffer more
Than the wreck'd sailor on his desert shore;
The world is all before him—*mine* is *here*,
Scarce twice the space they must accord
    my bier.   184
What though *he* perish, he may lift his eye,
And with a dying glance upbraid the sky;
I will not raise my own in such reproof,
Although 'tis clouded by my dungeon roof.

VIII

Yet do I feel at times my mind decline,
But with a sense of its decay: I see   190
Unwonted lights along my prison shine
And a strange demon, who is vexing me
With pilfering pranks and petty pains below
The feeling of the healthful and the free;
But much to One, who long hath suffer'd
    so,   195
Sickness of heart, and narrowness of place,
And all that may be borne, or can debase.
I thought mine enemies had been but Man,
But Spirits may be leagued with them; all
    Earth
Abandons, Heaven forgets me: in the
    dearth   200
Of such defence the Powers of Evil can,
It may be, tempt me further,—and prevail
Against the outworn creature they assail.
Why in this furnace is my spirit proved,
Like steel in tempering fire? because I
    loved?   205
Because I loved what not to love, and see,
Was more or less than mortal, and than
    me.

IX

I once was quick in feeling—that is o'er;
My scars are callous, or I should have
    dash'd
My brain against these bars, as the sun
    flash'd   210
In mockery through them: If I bear and
    bore
The much I have recounted, and the more
Which hath no words,—'tis that I would
    not die
And sanction with self-slaughter the dull
    lie
Which snared me here, and with the brand
    of shame   215
Stamp Madness deep into my memory,
And woo Compassion to a blighted name,
Sealing the sentence which my foes pro-
    claim.
No—it shall be immortal! and I make
A future temple of my present cell,   220
Which nations yet shall visit for my sake.
While thou, Ferrara! when no longer dwell
The ducal chiefs within thee, shalt fall
    down,
And crumbling piecemeal view thy hearth-
    less halls,
A poet's wreath shall be thine only
    crown,—   225
A poet's dungeon thy most far renown,
While strangers wonder o'er thy un-
    peopled walls!
And thou, Leonora! thou—who wert
    ashamed
That such as I could love—who blush'd to
    hear
To less than monarchs that thou couldst
    be dear,   230
Go! tell thy brother, that my heart, un-
    tamed
By grief, years, weariness,—and it may be
A taint of that he would impute to me—
From long infection of a den like this,
Where the mind rots congenial with the
    abyss,—   235
Adores thee still; and add—that when the
    towers
And battlements which guard his joyous
    hours
Of banquet, dance, and revel, are forgot,
Or left untended in a dull repose,—
This, this, shall be a consecrated spot!
But *Thou*—when all that Birth and Beauty
    throws   241
Of magic round thee is extinct—shalt have
One half the laurel which o'ershades my
    grave.
No power in death can tear our names
    apart,
As none in life could rend thee from my
    heart.   245
Yes, Leonora! it shall be our fate
To be entwined for ever—but too late!

THE PROPHECY OF DANTE

"'Tis the sunset of life gives me mystical lore,
And coming events cast their shadows before.'
CAMPBELL.

DEDICATION

LADY! if for the cold and cloudy clime,
  Where I was born, but where I would not die,
  Of the great Poet-Sire of Italy
I dare to build the imitative rhyme,
Harsh Runic copy of the South's sublime,
  THOU art the cause; and howsoever I
  Fall short of his immortal harmony,
Thy gentle heart will pardon me the crime.
Thou, in the pride of Beauty and of Youth,
  Spakest; and for thee to speak and be obey'd
Are one; but only in the sunny South
  Such sounds are uttered, and such charms display'd,
So sweet a language from so fair a mouth—
  Ah! to what effort would it not persuade?

RAVENNA, *June* 21, 1819.

PREFACE

IN the course of a visit to the city of Ravenna in the summer of 1819, it was suggested to the author that having composed something on the subject of Tasso's confinement, he should do the same on Dante's exile,—the tomb of the poet forming one of the principal objects of interest in that city, both to the native and to the stranger.

'On this hint I spake,' and the result has been the following four cantos, in terza rima, now offered to the reader. If they are understood and approved, it is my purpose to continue the poem, in various other cantos, to its natural conclusion in the present age. The reader is requested to suppose that Dante addresses him in the interval between the conclusion of the Divina Commedia and his death, and shortly before the latter event, foretelling the fortunes of Italy in general in the ensuing centuries. In adopting this plan I have had in my mind the Cassandra of Lycophron, and the Prophecy of Nereus by Horace, as well as the Prophecies of Holy Writ. The measure adopted is the terza rima of Dante, which I am not aware to have seen hitherto tried in our language, except it may be by Mr. Hayley, of whose translation I never saw but one extract, quoted in the notes to Caliph Vathek; so that—if I do not err—this poem may be considered as a metrical experiment. The cantos are short, and about the same length of those of the poet, whose name I have borrowed, and most probably taken in vain.

Amongst the inconveniences of authors in the present day, it is difficult for any who have a name, good or bad, to escape translation. I have had the fortune to see the fourth canto of 'Childe Harold' translated into Italian versi sciolti,—that is, a poem written in the *Spenserean stanza* into *blank verse*, without regard to the natural divisions of the stanza or of the sense. If the present poem, being on a national topic, should chance to undergo the same fate, I would request the Italian reader to remember that when I have failed in the imitation of his great 'Padre Alighier,' I have failed in imitating that which all study and few understand, since to this very day it is not yet settled what was the meaning of the allegory in the first canto of the Inferno, unless Count Marchetti's ingenious and probable conjecture may be considered as having decided the question.

He may also pardon my failure the more, as I am not quite sure that he would be pleased with my success, since the Italians, with a pardonable nationality, are particularly jealous of all that is left them as a nation,—their literature; and in the present bitterness of the classic and romantic war, are but ill disposed to permit a foreigner even to approve or imitate them, without finding some fault with his ultramontane presumption. I can easily enter into all this, knowing what would be thought in England of an Italian imitator of Milton, or if a translation of Monti, or Pindemonte, or Arici, should be held up to the rising generation as a model for their future poetical essays. But I perceive that I am deviating into an address to the Italian reader, when my business is with the English one; and be they few or many, I must take my leave of both.

CANTO THE FIRST

ONCE more in man's frail world! which I had left
  So long that 'twas forgotten; and I feel
  The weight of clay again,—too soon bereft
Of the immortal vision which could heal
My earthly sorrows, and to God's own skies
Lift me from that deep gulf without repeal,   5
Where late my ears rung with the damned cries
Of souls in hopeless bale; and from that place

370

Of lesser torment, whence men may arise
Pure from the fire to join the angelic race;
Midst whom my own bright Beatrice
    bless'd   11
My spirit with her light; and to the base
Of the eternal Triad! first, last, best,
Mysterious, three, sole, infinite, great
    God!
Soul universal! led the mortal guest, 15
Unblasted by the glory, though he trod
From star to star to reach the almighty
    throne.
Oh Beatrice! whose sweet limbs the sod
So long hath press'd, and the cold
    marble stone,
Thou sole pure seraph of my earliest
    love,   20
Love so ineffable, and so alone,
That nought on earth could more my
    bosom move,
And meeting thee in heaven was but to
    meet
That without which my soul, like the
    arkless dove,
Had wander'd still in search of, nor her
    feet   25
Relieved her wing till found: without
    thy light
My paradise had still been incomplete.
Since my tenth sun gave summer to my
    sight
Thou wert my life, the essence of my
    thought,
Loved ere I knew the name of love, and
    bright   30
Still in these dim old eyes, now over-
    wrought
With the world's war, and years, and
    banishment,
And tears for thee, by other woes un-
    taught;
For mine is not a nature to be bent
By tyrannous faction, and the brawling
    crowd,   35
And though the long, long conflict hath
    been spent
In vain,—and never more, save when the
    cloud
Which overhangs the Apennine my
    mind's eye
Pierces to fancy Florence, once so proud
Of me, can I return, though but to die,
Unto my native soil,—they have not yet
Quench'd the old exile's spirit, stern and
    high.
But the sun, though not overcast, must set,
And the night cometh; I am old in days,
And deeds, and contemplation, and
    have met   45
Destruction face to face in all his ways.
The world hath left me, what it found
    me, pure,
And if I have not gather'd yet its praise,
I sought it not by any baser lure;

Man wrongs, and Time avenges, and
    my name   50
May form a monument not all obscure,
Though such was not my ambition's end
    or aim,
To add to the vain-glorious list of those
Who dabble in the pettiness of fame,
And make men's fickle breath the wind
    that blows   55
Their sail, and deem it glory to be class'd
With conquerors, and virtue's other
    foes,
In bloody chronicles of ages past.
I would have had my Florence great and
    free;
Oh Florence! Florence! unto me thou
    wast   60
Like that Jerusalem which the Almighty
    He
Wept over, 'but thou wouldst not'; as
    the bird
Gathers its young, I would have
    gather'd thee
Beneath a parent pinion, hadst thou heard
My voice; but as the adder, deaf and
    fierce,   65
Against the breast that cherish'd thee
    was stirr'd
Thy venom, and my state thou didst
    amerce,
And doom this body forfeit to the fire.
Alas! how bitter is his country's curse
To him who for that country would expire,
But did not merit to expire by her,   71
And loves her, loves her even in her ire!
The day may come when she will cease to
    err,
The day may come she would be proud
    to have
The dust she dooms to scatter, and
    transfer   75
Of him, whom she denied a home, the
    grave.
But this shall not be granted; let my
    dust
Lie where it falls; nor shall the soil which
    gave
Me breath, but in her sudden fury thrust
Me forth to breathe elsewhere, so re-
    assume   80
My indignant bones, because her angry
    gust
Forsooth is over, and repeal'd her doom;
No,—she denied me what was mine—
    my roof,
And shall not have what is not hers—
    my tomb.
Too long her armed wrath hath kept aloof
The breast which would have bled for
    her, the heart   86
That beat, the mind that was temptation
    proof,
The man who fought, toil'd, travell'd, and
    each part

371

Of a true citizen fulfill'd, and saw
For his reward the Guelf's ascendant
   art   90
Pass his destruction even into a law.
These things are not made for forget-
   fulness,
Florence shall be forgotten first; too
   raw
The wound, too deep the wrong, and the
   distress
Of such endurance too prolong'd to
   make   95
My pardon greater, her injustice less,
Though late repented; yet—yet for her
   sake
I feel some fonder yearnings, and for
   thine,
My own Beatrice, I would hardly take
Vengeance upon the land which once was
   mine,   100
And still is hallow'd by thy dust's return,
Which would protect the murderess like
   a shrine,
And save ten thousand foes by thy sole
   urn.
Though, like old Marius from Min-
   turnæ's marsh
And Carthage ruins, my lone breast
   may burn   105
At times with evil feelings hot and harsh,
And sometimes the last pangs of a vile
   foe
Writhe in a dream before me, and
   o'erarch
My brow with hopes of triumph,—let
   them go!
Such are the last infirmities of those
Who long have suffer'd more than
   mortal woe,   111
And yet being mortal still have no repose
But on the pillow of Revenge—Revenge,
Who sleeps to dream of blood, and
   waking glows
With the oft-baffled slakeless thirst of
   change,   115
When we shall mount again, and they
   that trod
Be trampled on, while Death and Até
   range
O'er humbled heads and sever'd necks—
   Great God!
Take these thoughts from me—to thy
   hands I yield
My many wrongs, and thine Almighty
   rod   120
Will fall on those who smote me,—be my
   shield!
As thou hast been in peril, and in pain,
In turbulent cities, and the tented field—
In toil, and many troubles borne in vain
For Florence,—I appeal from her to
   Thee!   125
Thee whom I late saw in thy loftiest
   reign,

Even in that glorious vision, which to see
And live was never granted until now,
And yet thou hast permitted this to me.
Alas! with what a weight upon my brow
The sense of earth and earthly things
   come back,   131
Corrosive passions, feelings dull and
   low,
The heart's quick throb upon the mental
   rack,
Long day, and dreary night; the retro-
   spect
Of half a century bloody and black,
And the frail few years I may yet expect
Hoary and hopeless, but less hard to
   bear,
For I have been too long and deeply
   wreck'd
On the lone rock of desolate Despair,
To lift my eyes more to the passing sail
Which shuns that reef so horrible and
   bare;   141
Nor raise my voice—for who would heed
   my wail?
I am not of this people, nor this age,
And yet my harpings will unfold a tale
Which shall preserve these times when not
   a page   145
Of their perturbed annals could attract
An eye to gaze upon their civil rage,
Did not my verse embalm full many an act
Worthless as they who wrought it: 'tis
   the doom
Of spirits of my order to be rack'd
In life, to wear their hearts out, and con-
   sume   151
Their days in endless strife, and die
   alone;
Then future thousands crowd around
   their tomb,
And pilgrims come from climes where
   they have known
The name of him—who now is but a
   name,
And wasting homage o'er the sullen
   stone,   156
Spread his—by him unheard, unheeded—
   fame;
And mine at least hath cost me dear: to
   die
Is nothing; but to wither thus—to tame
My mind down from its own infinity—
To live in narrow ways with little men,
A common sight to every common eye,
A wanderer, while even wolves can find a
   den,   163
Ripp'd from all kindred, from all home,
   all things
That make communion sweet, and
   soften pain—
To feel me in the solitude of kings   166
Without the power that makes them
   bear a crown—
To envy every dove his nest and wings

Which waft him where the Apennine looks
    down
  On Arno, till he perches, it may be,
  Within my all inexorable town,   171
Where yet my boys are, and that fatal she,
  Their mother, the cold partner who hath
    brought
  Destruction for a dowry—this to see
And feel, and know without repair, hath
    taught   175
  A bitter lesson; but it leaves me free:
  I have not vilely found, nor basely
    sought,
They made an Exile—not a slave of me.

CANTO THE SECOND

THE Spirit of the fervent days of Old,
  When words were things that came to
    pass, and thought
  Flash'd o'er the future, bidding men be-
    hold
Their children's children's doom already
    brought
  Forth from the abyss of time which is to
    be   5
  The chaos of events, where lie half-
    wrought
Shapes that must undergo mortality;
  What the great Seers of Israel wore
    within,
  That spirit was on them, and is on me,
And if, Cassandra-like, amidst the din   10
  Of conflict none will hear, or hearing
    heed
  This voice from out the Wilderness, the
    sin
Be theirs, and my own feelings be my meed,
  The only guerdon I have ever known.
  Hast thou not bled? and hast thou still
    to bleed,   15
Italia? Ah! to me such things, foreshown
  With dim sepulchral light, bid me forget
  In thine irreparable wrongs my own;
We can have but one country, and even yet
  Thou'rt mine—my bones shall be within
    thy breast,   20
  My soul within thy language, which
    once set
With our old Roman sway in the wide
    West;
  But I will make another tongue arise
  As lofty and more sweet, in which ex-
    press'd
The hero's ardour, or the lover's sighs,
  Shall find alike such sounds for every
    theme   26
  That every word, as brilliant as thy
    skies,
Shall realise a poet's proudest dream,
  And make thee Europe's nightingale of
    song;
  So that all present speech to thine shall
    seem   30

The note of meaner birds, and every
    tongue
  Confess its barbarism when compared
    with thine.
  This shalt thou owe to him thou didst
    so wrong,
Thy Tuscan bard, the banish'd Ghibelline.
  Woe! woe! the veil of coming centuries
  Is rent,—a thousand years which yet
    supine   36
Lie like the ocean waves ere winds arise,
  Heaving in dark and sullen undulation,
  Float from eternity into these eyes;
The storms yet sleep, the clouds still keep
    their station,   40
  The unborn earthquake yet is in the
    womb,
  The bloody chaos yet expects creation,
But all things are disposing for thy doom;
  The elements await but for the word,
  'Let there be darkness!' and thou
    grow'st a tomb!   45
Yes! thou, so beautiful, shalt feel the sword,
  Thou, Italy! so fair that Paradise,
  Revived in thee, blooms forth to man
    restored:
Ah! must the sons of Adam lose it twice?
  Thou, Italy! whose ever golden fields,
  Plough'd by the sunbeams solely, would
    suffice   51
For the world's granary; thou, whose sky
    heaven gilds
  With brighter stars, and robes with
    deeper blue;
  Thou, in whose pleasant places Summer
    builds
Her palace, in whose cradle Empire grew,
  And form'd the Eternal City's orna-
    ments   56
  From spoils of kings whom freemen
    overthrew;
Birthplace of heroes, sanctuary of saints,
  Where earthly first, then heavenly glory
    made
  Her home; thou, all which fondest fancy
    paints,   60
And finds her prior vision but portray'd
  In feeble colours, when the eye—from
    the Alp
  Of horrid snow, and rock, and shaggy
    shade
Of desert-loving pine, whose emerald scalp
  Nods to the storm—dilates and dotes
    o'er thee,   65
  And wistfully implores, as 'twere for
    help
To see thy sunny fields, my Italy,
  Nearer and nearer yet, and dearer still
  The more approach'd, and dearest were
    they free,
Thou—thou must wither to each tyrant's
    will: 70
  The Goth hath been,—the German,
    Frank, and Hun

Are yet to come,—and on the imperial
    hill
Ruin, already proud of the deeds done
  By the old barbarians, there awaits the
      new,
  Throned on the Palatine, while lost and
      won   75
Rome at her feet lies bleeding; and the hue
Of human sacrifice and Roman slaughter
Troubles the clotted air, of late so blue,
And deepens into red the saffron water
Of Tiber, thick with dead; the helpless
    priest,   80
  And still more helpless nor less holy
      daughter,
Vow'd to their God, have shrieking fled,
    and ceased
  Their ministry: the nations take their
      prey,
  Iberian, Almain, Lombard, and the
      beast
And bird, wolf, vulture, more humane
    than they   85
  Are; these but gorge the flesh and lap
      the gore
Of the departed, and then go their way;
But those, the human savages, explore
  All paths of torture, and insatiate yet,
  With Ugolino hunger prowl for more.
Nine moons shall rise o'er scenes like this
    and set;   91
  The chiefless army of the dead, which
      late
Beneath the traitor Prince's banner met,
Hath left its leader's ashes at the gate;
  Had but the royal Rebel lived, per-
      chance   95
Thou hadst been spared, but his in-
    volved thy fate.
Oh! Rome, the spoiler or the spoil of
    France,
  From Brennus to the Bourbon, never,
      never
Shall foreign standard to thy walls ad-
    vance,
But Tiber shall become a mournful river.
  Oh! when the strangers pass the Alps
      and Po,   101
  Crush them, ye rocks! floods whelm
      them, and for ever!
Why sleep the idle avalanches so,
  To topple on the lonely pilgrim's head?
  Why doth Eridanus but overflow   105
The peasant's harvest from his turbid bed?
Were not each barbarous horde a nobler
    prey?
  Over Cambyses' host the desert spread
Her sandy ocean, and the sea-waves' sway
Roll'd over Pharaoh and his thous-
    ands,—why,   110
  Mountains and waters, do ye not as
      they?
And you, ye men! Romans who dare not
    die,

Sons of the conquerors who overthrew
  Those who o'erthrew proud Xerxes,
      where yet lie
The dead whose tomb Oblivion never
    knew,   115
Are the Alps weaker than Thermopylæ?
Their passes more alluring to the view
Of an invader? is it they, or ye,
  That to each host the mountain-gate
      unbar,
  And leave the march in peace, the
      passage free?   120
Why, Nature's self detains the victor's car,
  And makes your land impregnable, if
      earth
Could be so; but alone she will not war,
Yet aids the warrior worthy of his birth
  In a soil where the mothers bring forth
      men: 125
  Not so with those whose souls are little
      worth;
For them no fortress can avail,—the den
  Of the poor reptile which preserves its
      sting
Is more secure than walls of adamant,
    when
The hearts of those within are quivering.
  Are ye not brave? Yes, yet the Au-
      sonian soil   131
  Hath hearts, and hands, and arms, and
      hosts to bring
Against Oppression; but how vain the toil,
  While still Division sows the seeds of
      woe
And weakness, till the stranger reaps the
    spoil!   135
Oh! my own beauteous land! so long laid
    low,
  So long the grave of thy own children's
      hopes,
When there is but required a single blow
To break the chain, yet—yet the Avenger
    stops,
  And Doubt and Discord step 'twixt
      thine and thee,   140
And join their strength to that which
    with thee copes;
What is there wanting then to set thee free,
  And show thy beauty in its fullest light?
To make the Alps impassable; and we,
Her sons, may do this with *one* deed—
    Unite.   145

CANTO THE THIRD

FROM out the mass of never-dying ill,
  The Plague, the Prince, the Stranger,
    and the Sword,
Vials of wrath but emptied to refill
And flow again, I cannot all record
  That crowds on my prophetic eye: the
      earth   5
  And ocean written o'er would not afford
Space for the annal, yet it shall go forth;

Yes, all, though not by human pen, is
　　graven,
There where the farthest suns and stars
　　have birth,
Spread like a banner at the gate of heaven,
The bloody scroll of our millennial
　　wrongs   11
Waves, and the echo of our groans is
　　driven
Athwart the sound of archangelic songs,
And Italy, the martyr'd nation's gore,
Will not in vain arise to where belongs
Omnipotence and mercy evermore: 16
Like to a harp-string stricken by the wind,
The sound of her lament shall, rising
　　o'er
The seraph voices, touch the Almighty
　　Mind.
Meantime I, humblest of thy sons, and
　　of   20
Earth's dust by immortality refined
To sense and suffering, though the vain
　　may scoff,
And tyrants threat, and meeker victims
　　bow
Before the storm because its breath is
　　rough,
To thee, my country! whom before, as
　　now,   25
I loved and love, devote the mournful
　　lyre
And melancholy gift high powers allow
To read the future; and if now my fire
Is not as once it shone o'er thee, forgive!
I but foretell thy fortunes—then ex-
　　pire;   30
Think not that I would look on them and
　　live.
A spirit forces me to see and speak,
And for my guerdon grants *not* to sur-
　　vive;
My heart shall be pour'd over thee and
　　break: 34
Yet for a moment, ere I must resume
Thy sable web of sorrow, let me take
Over the gleams that flash athwart thy
　　gloom
A softer glimpse; some stars shine
　　through thy night,
And many meteors, and above thy tomb
Leans sculptured Beauty, which Death
　　cannot blight: 40
And from thine ashes boundless spirits
　　rise
To give thee honour, and the earth de-
　　light;
Thy soil shall still be pregnant with the wise,
The gay, the learn'd, the generous, and
　　the brave,
Native to thee as summer to thy skies,
Conquerors on foreign shores, and the far
　　wave,   46
Discoverers of new worlds, which take
　　their name;

For *thee* alone they have no arm to save,
And all thy recompense is in their fame,
A noble one to them, but not to thee—
Shall they be glorious, and thou still the
　　same?   51
Oh! more than these illustrious far shall be
The being—and even yet he may be
　　born—
The mortal saviour who shall set thee
　　free,
And see thy diadem, so changed and
　　worn   55
By fresh barbarians, on thy brow re-
　　placed;
And the sweet sun replenishing thy
　　morn,
Thy moral morn, too long with clouds de-
　　faced,
And noxious vapours from Avernus
　　risen,
Such as all they must breathe who are
　　debased   60
By servitude, and have the mind in prison.
Yet through this centuried eclipse of
　　woe
Some voices shall be heard, and earth
　　shall listen;
Poets shall follow in the path I show,
And make it broader: the same brilliant
　　sky   65
Which cheers the birds to song shall bid
　　them glow,
And raise their notes as natural and high;
Tuneful shall be their numbers; they
　　shall sing
Many of love, and some of liberty,
But few shall soar upon that eagle's wing,
And look in the sun's face with eagle's
　　gaze,   71
All free and fearless as the feather'd
　　king,
But fly more near the earth; how many a
　　phrase
Sublime shall lavish'd be on some small
　　prince
In all the prodigality of praise!   75
And language, eloquently false, evince
The harlotry of genius, which, like
　　beauty,
Too oft forgets its own self-reverence,
And looks on prostitution as a duty.
He who once enters in a tyrant's hall
As guest is slave, his thoughts become
　　a booty,   81
And the first day which sees the chain
　　enthral
A captive, sees his half of manhood
　　gone—
The soul's emasculation saddens all
His spirit; thus the Bard too near the
　　throne   85
Quails from his inspiration, bound to
　　please,—
How servile is the task to please alone!

To smooth the verse to suit his sovereign's
  ease
And royal leisure, nor too much prolong
Aught save his eulogy, and find, and seize,
Or force, or forge fit argument of song!
  Thus trammell'd, thus condemn'd to
    Flattery's trebles,   92
  He toils through all, still trembling to be
    wrong:
For fear some noble thoughts, like heavenly
  rebels,
  Should rise up in high treason to his
    brain,   95
He sings, as the Athenian spoke, with
  pebbles
In 's mouth, lest truth should stammer
  through his strain.
But out of the long file of sonneteers
There shall be some who will not sing in
  vain,
And he, their prince, shall rank among my
  peers,   100
And love shall be his torment; but his
  grief
Shall make an immortality of tears,
And Italy shall hail him as the Chief
  Of Poet-lovers, and his higher song
  Of Freedom wreathe him with as green
    a leaf.   105
But in a farther age shall rise along
  The banks of Po two greater still than he;
  The world which smiled on him shall do
    them wrong
Till they are ashes, and repose with me.
  The first will make an epoch with his
    lyre,   110
And fill the earth with feats of chivalry:
  His fancy like a rainbow, and his fire,
  Like that of Heaven, immortal, and his
    thought
  Borne onward with a wing that cannot
    tire;
Pleasure shall, like a butterfly new caught,
  Flutter her lovely pinions o'er his
    theme,   116
  And Art itself seem into Nature wrought
By the transparency of his bright dream.—
  The second, of a tenderer, sadder mood,
  Shall pour his soul out o'er Jerusalem;
He, too, shall sing of arms, and Christian
  blood   121
  Shed where Christ bled for man; and his
    high harp
  Shall, by the willow over Jordan's flood,
Revive a song of Sion, and the sharp
  Conflict, and final triumph of the brave
  And pious, and the strife of hell to warp
Their hearts from their great purpose,
  until wave   127
  The red-cross banners where the first
    red Cross
  Was crimson'd from his veins who died
    to save,
Shall be his sacred argument; the loss

Of years, of favour, freedom, even of
  fame   131
Contested for a time, while the smooth
  gloss
Of courts would slide o'er his forgotten
  name
And call captivity a kindness, meant
  To shield him from insanity or shame,
Such shall be his meet guerdon! who was sent
  To be Christ's Laureate—they reward
    him well!   137
Florence dooms me but death or banish-
  ment,
Ferrara him a pittance and a cell,
  Harder to bear and less deserved, for I
  Had stung the factions which I strove to
    quell;   141
But this meek man, who with a lover's eye
  Will look on earth and heaven, and who
    will deign
To embalm with his celestial flattery,
As poor a thing as e'er was spawn'd to
  reign,   145
  What will he do to merit such a doom?
  Perhaps he'll love,—and is not love in
    vain
Torture enough without a living tomb?
  Yet it will be so—he and his compeer,
  The Bard of Chivalry, will both con-
    sume   150
In penury and pain too many a year,
  And, dying in despondency, bequeath
  To the kind world, which scarce will
    yield a tear,
A heritage enriching all who breathe
  With the wealth of a genuine poet's
    soul,   155
  And to their country a redoubled
    wreath,
Unmatch'd by time; not Hellas can unroll
  Through her olympiads two such
    names, though one
  Of hers be mighty;—and is this the
    whole
Of such men's destiny beneath the sun?
  Must all the finer thoughts, the thrilling
    sense,   161
  The electric blood with which their
    arteries run,
Their body's self turned soul with the
  intense
  Feeling of that which is, and fancy of
  That which should be, to such a recom-
    pense   165
Conduct? shall their bright plumage on
  the rough
  Storm be still scatter'd? Yes, and it
    must be;
  For, form'd of far too penetrable stuff,
These birds of Paradise but long to flee
  Back to their native mansion, soon they
    find   170
  Earth's mist with their pure pinions not
    agree,

And die or are degraded; for the mind
  Succumbs to long infection, and despair,
  And vulture passions flying close behind,
Await the moment to assail and tear; 175
  And when at length the winged wanderers stoop,
  Then is the prey-birds' triumph, then they share
The spoil, o'erpower'd at length by one fell swoop,
  Yet some have been untouch'd who learn'd to bear,
  Some whom no power could ever force to droop,   180
Who could resist themselves even, hardest care!
  And task most hopeless; but some such have been,
  And if my name amongst the number were,
That destiny austere, and yet serene,
  Were prouder than more dazzling fame unbless'd;   185
  The Alp's snow summit nearer heaven is seen
Than the volcano's fierce eruptive crest,
  Whose splendour from the black abyss is flung,
  While the scorch'd mountain, from whose burning breast
A temporary torturing flame is wrung,
  Shines for a night of terror, then repels
  Its fire back to the hell from whence it sprung,   192
The hell which in its entrails ever dwells.

CANTO THE FOURTH

MANY are poets who have never penn'd
  Their inspiration, and perchance the best:
  They felt, and loved, and died, but would not lend
Their thoughts to meaner beings; they compress'd
  The god within them, and rejoin'd the stars   5
  Unlaurell'd upon earth, but far more bless'd
Than those who are degraded by the jars
  Of passion, and their frailties link'd to fame,
  Conquerors of high renown, but full of scars.
Many are poets but without the name,
  For what is poesy but to create   11
  From overfeeling good or ill; and aim
At an external life beyond our fate,
  And be the new Prometheus of new men,
  Bestowing fire from heaven, and then, too late,   15

Finding the pleasure given repaid with pain,
  And vultures to the heart of the bestower,
  Who, having lavish'd his high gift in vain,
Lies chain'd to his lone rock by the sea-shore?
  So be it: we can bear.—But thus all they
  Whose intellect is an o'ermastering power   21
Which still recoils from its encumbering clay
  Or lightens it to spirit, whatsoe'er
  The form which their creations may essay,
Are bards; the kindled marble's bust may wear   25
  More poesy upon its speaking brow
  Than aught less than the Homeric page may bear;
One noble stroke with a whole life may glow,
  Or deify the canvas till it shine
  With beauty so surpassing all below,
That they who kneel to idols so divine
  Break no commandment, for high heaven is there
  Transfused, transfigurated: and the line
Of poesy, which peoples but the air
  With thought and beings of our thought reflected,   35
  Can do no more: then let the artist share
The palm, he shares the peril, and dejected
  Faints o'er the labour unapproved—Alas!
  Despair and Genius are too oft connected.   39
Within the ages which before me pass
  Art shall resume and equal even the sway
  Which with Apelles and old Phidias
She held in Hellas' unforgotten day.
  Ye shall be taught by Ruin to revive
  The Grecian forms at least from their decay,   45
And Roman souls at last again shall live
  In Roman works wrought by Italian hands,
  And temples, loftier than the old temples, give
New wonders to the world; and while still stands
  The austere Pantheon, into heaven shall soar   50
  A dome, its image, while the base expands
Into a fane surpassing all before,
  Such as all flesh shall flock to kneel in: ne'er
  Such sight hath been unfolded by a door
As this, to which all nations shall repair
  And lay their sins at this huge gate of heaven.   56
  And the bold Architect unto whose care

The daring charge to raise it shall be given,
  Whom all Arts shall acknowledge as
    their lord,   59
Whether into the marble chaos driven
His chisel bid the Hebrew, at whose word
  Israel left Egypt, stop the waves in
    stone,
  Or hues of Hell be by his pencil pour'd
Over the damn'd before the Judgment-
    throne,
  Such as I saw them, such as all shall see,
  Or fanes be built of grandeur yet un-
    known,   66
The stream of his great thoughts shall
    spring from me,
  The Ghibelline, who traversed the three
    realms
  Which form the empire of eternity,
Amidst the clash of swords, and clang of
    helms,   70
  The age which I anticipate, no less
  Shall be the Age of Beauty, and while
    whelms
Calamity the nations with distress,
  The genius of my country shall arise,
  A Cedar towering o'er the Wilderness,
Lovely in all its branches to all eyes, 76
  Fragrant as fair, and recognised afar,
  Wafting its native incense through the
    skies.
Sovereigns shall pause amidst their sport
    of war,
  Wean'd for an hour from blood, to turn
    and gaze   80
  On canvas or on stone; and they who
    mar
All beauty upon earth, compell'd to praise,
  Shall feel the power of that which they
    destroy;
  And Art's mistaken gratitude shall raise
To tyrants who but take her for a toy,
  Emblems and monuments, and prosti-
    tute   86
  Her charms to pontiffs proud, who but
    employ
The man of genius as the meanest brute
  To bear a burthen, and to serve a need,
  To sell his labours, and his soul to boot.
Who toils for nations may be poor indeed,
  But free; who sweats for monarchs is no
    more   92
  Than the gilt chamberlain, who, clothed
    and fee'd,
Stands sleek and slavish, bowing at his
    door.
  Oh, Power that rulest and inspirest! how
     95
  Is it that they on earth, whose earthly
    power
Is likest thine in heaven in outward show,
  Least like to thee in attributes divine,
  Tread on the universal necks that bow,
And then assure us that their rights are
    thine?   100

And how is it that they, the sons of fame,
  Whose inspiration seems to them to
    shine
From high, they whom the nations oftest
    name,
  Must pass their days in penury or pain,
  Or step to grandeur through the paths
    of shame,   105
And wear a deeper brand and gaudier
    chain?
  Or if their destiny be born aloof
  From lowliness, or tempted thence in
    vain,
In their own souls sustain a harder proof,
  The inner war of passions deep and
    fierce?   110
  Florence! when thy harsh sentence
    razed my roof,
I loved thee; but the vengeance of my
    verse,
  The hate of injuries which every year
  Makes greater, and accumulates my
    curse,
Shall live, outliving all thou holdest dear,
  Thy pride, thy wealth, thy freedom, and
    even *that*,   116
  The most infernal of all evils here,
The sway of petty tyrants in a state;
  For such sway is not limited to kings,
  And demagogues yield to them but in
    date,   120
As swept off sooner; in all deadly things,
  Which make men hate themselves, and
    one another,
  In discord, cowardice, cruelty, all that
    springs,
From Death the Sin-born's incest with his
    mother,
  In rank oppression in its rudest shape,
  The faction Chief is but the Sultan's
    brother,   126
And the worst despot's far less human ape:
  Florence! when this lone spirit, which
    so long
  Yearn'd, as the captive toiling at escape,
To fly back to thee in despite of wrong,
  An exile, saddest of all prisoners, 131
  Who has the whole world for a dungeon
    strong,
Seas, mountains, and the horizon's verge
    for bars,
  Which shut him from the sole small spot
    of earth,
  Where—whatsoe'er his fate—he still
    were hers,   135
His country's, and might die where he had
    birth—
  Florence! when this lone spirit shall re-
    turn
  To kindred spirits, thou wilt feel my
    worth,
And seek to honour with an empty urn
  The ashes thou shalt ne'er obtain—
    Alas!   140

'What have I done to thee, my people?'
    Stern
Are all thy dealings, but in this they pass
    The limits of man's common malice, for
All that a citizen could be I was;
Raised by thy will, all thine in peace or war,
    And for this thou hast warr'd with me—
'Tis done: 146
I may not overleap the eternal bar

Built up between us, and will die alone,
    Beholding with the dark eye of a seer
    The evil days to gifted souls foreshown,
Foretelling them to those who will not hear.
    As in the old time, till the hour be come
When Truth shall strike their eyes
    through many a tear,   153
And make them own the Prophet in his
    tomb.

THE MORGANTE MAGGIORE

OF PULCI

ADVERTISEMENT

THE Morgante Maggiore, of the first canto of which this translation is offered, divides with the Orlando Innamorato the honour of having formed and suggested the style and story of Ariosto. The great defects of Boiardo were his treating too seriously the narratives of chivalry, and his harsh style. Ariosto, in his continuation, by a judicious mixture of the gaiety of Pulci, has avoided the one; and Berni, in his reformation of Boiardo's poem, has corrected the other. Pulci may be considered as the precursor and model of Berni altogether, as he has partly been to Ariosto, however inferior to both his copyists. He is no less the founder of a new style of poetry very lately sprung up in England. I allude to that of the ingenious Whistlecraft. The serious poems on Roncesvalles in the same language, and more particularly the excellent one of Mr. Merivale, are to be traced to the same source. It has never yet been decided entirely whether Pulci's intention was or was not to deride the religion which is one of his favourite topics. It appears to me, that such an intention would have been no less hazardous to the poet than to the priest, particularly in that age and country; and the permission to publish the poem, and its reception among the classics of Italy, prove that it neither was nor is so interpreted. That he intended to ridicule the monastic life, and suffered his imagination to play with the simple dulness of his converted giant, seems evident enough; but surely it were as unjust to accuse him of irreligion on this account, as to denounce Fielding for his Parson Adams, Barnabas, Thwackum, Supple, and the Ordinary in Jonathan Wild,—or Scott, for the exquisite use of his Covenanters in the 'Tales of my Landlord.'

In the following translation I have used the liberty of the original with the proper names: as Pulci uses Gan, Ganellon, or Ganellone; Carlo, Carlomagno, or Carlomano; Rondel, or Rondello, &c., as it suits his convenience; so has the translator. In other respects the version is faithful to the best of the translator's ability in combining his interpretation of the one language with the not very easy task of reducing it to the same versification in the other. The reader, on comparing it with the original, is requested to remember that the antiquated language of Pulci, however pure, is not easy to the generality of Italians themselves, from its great mixture of Tuscan proverbs; and he may therefore be more indulgent to the present attempt. How far the translator has succeeded, and whether or no he shall continue the work, are questions which the public will decide. He was induced to make the experiment partly by his love for, and partial intercourse with, the Italian language, of which it is so easy to acquire a slight knowledge, and with which it is so nearly impossible for a foreigner to become accurately conversant. The Italian language is like a capricious beauty, who accords her smiles to all, her favours to few, and sometimes least to those who have courted her longest. The translator wished also to present in an English dress a part at least of a poem never yet rendered into a northern language; at the same time that it has been the original of some of the most celebrated productions on this side of the Alps, as well as of those recent experiments in poetry in England which have been already mentioned.

CANTO THE FIRST

I

IN the beginning was the Word next God;
    God was the Word, the Word no less
    was he:
This was in the beginning, to my mode
    Of thinking, and without him nought
    could be:
Therefore, just Lord! from out thy high abode,
    Benign and pious, bid an angel flee,
One only, to be my companion, who
Shall help my famous, worthy, old song
    through.

II

And thou, oh Virgin! daughter, mother,
    bride
    Of the same Lord, who gave to you each
    key
Of heaven, and hell, and everything beside,
    The day thy Gabriel said 'All hail!' to
    thee,
Since to thy servants pity's ne'er denied,
    With flowing rhymes, a pleasant style
    and free,
Be to my verses then benignly kind,
And to the end illuminate my mind.

III

'Twas in the season when sad Philomel
    Weeps with her sister, who remembers
      and
Deplores the ancient woes which both be-
    fell,
    And makes the nymphs enamour'd, to
      the hand
Of Phaeton by Phœbus loved so well
    His car (but temper'd by his sire's com-
      mand)
Was given, and on the horizon's verge just
    now
Appear'd, so that Tithonus scratch'd his
    brow:

IV

When I prepared my bark first to obey,
    As it should still obey, the helm, my mind,
And carry prose or rhyme, and this my lay
    Of Charles the Emperor, whom you will
      find
By several pens already praised; but they
    Who to diffuse his glory were inclined,
For all that I can see in prose or verse,
Have understood Charles badly, and
    wrote worse.

V

Leonardo Aretino said already,
    That if, like Pepin, Charles had had a
      writer
Of genius quick, and diligently steady,
    No hero would in history look brighter;
He in the cabinet being always ready,
    And in the field a most victorious fighter,
Who for the church and Christian faith
    had wrought,
Certes, far more than yet is said or thought.

VI

You still may see at St. Liberatore,
    The abbey, no great way from Manopell,
Erected in the Abruzzi to his glory,
    Because of the great battle in which fell
A pagan king, according to the story,
    And felon people whom Charles sent to
      hell:
And there are bones so many, and so many,
Near them Giusaffa's would seem few, if
    any.

VII

But the world, blind and ignorant, don't
    prize
    His virtues as I wish to see them: thou,
Florence, by his great bounty don't[1] arise,
    And hast, and may have, if thou wilt
      allow,
All proper customs and true courtesies:
    Whate'er thou hast acquired from then
      till now,
With knightly courage, treasure, or the
    lance,

---

      ¹ don't] dost *conj.*

Is sprung from out the noble blood of
    France.

VIII

Twelve paladins had Charles in court, of
    whom
    The wisest and most famous was Or-
      lando;
Him traitor Gan conducted to the tomb
    In Roncesvalles, as the villain plann'd
      too,
While the horn rang so loud, and knell'd
    the doom
    Of their sad rout, though he did all
      knight can do;
And Dante in his comedy has given
To him a happy seat with Charles in
    heaven.

IX

'Twas Christmas-day; in Paris all his court
    Charles held; the chief, I say, Orlando
      was,
The Dane; Astolfo there too did resort,
    Also Ansuigi, the gay time to pass
In festival and in triumphal sport,
    The much renown'd St. Dennis being
      the cause;
Angiolin of Bayonne, and Oliver,
And gentle Belinghieri too came there:

X

Avolio, and Arino, and Othone
    Of Normandy, and Richard Paladin,
Wise Hamo, and the ancient Salamone,
    Walter of Lion's Mount and Baldovin,
Who was the son of the sad Ganellone,
    Were there, exciting too much gladness
      in
The son of Pepin:—when his knights came
    hither,
    He groan'd with joy to see them all to-
      gether.

XI

But watchful Fortune, lurking, takes good
    heed
    Ever some bar 'gainst our intents to bring,
While Charles reposed him thus, in word
    and deed,
    Orlando ruled court, Charles, and every-
      thing;
Curst Gan, with envy bursting, had such
    need
    To vent his spite, that thus with Charles
      the king
One day he openly began to say,
'Orlando must we always then obey?

XII

'A thousand times I've been about to say,
    Orlando too presumptuously goes on;
Here are we, counts, kings, dukes, to own
    thy sway,
    Hamo, and Otho, Ogier, Solomon,

Each have to honour thee and to obey;
　But he has too much credit near the
　　throne,
Which we won't suffer, but are quite de-
　cided
By such a boy to be no longer guided.

XIII

'And even at Aspramont thou didst begin
　To let him know he was a gallant knight,
And by the fount did much the day to win;
　But I know *who* that day had won the
　　fight
If it had not for good Gherardo been;
　The victory was Almonte's else; his
　　sight
He kept upon the standard, and the laurels
In fact and fairness are his earning,
　Charles.

XIV

'If thou rememberest being in Gascony,
　When there advanced the nations out of
　　Spain,
The Christian cause had suffer'd shame-
　fully,
　Had not his valour driven them back
　　again.
Best speak the truth when there's a reason
　why:
　Know then, oh Emperor! that all com-
　　plain:
As for myself, I shall repass the mounts
O'er which I cross'd with two and sixty
　counts.

XV

''Tis fit thy grandeur should dispense re-
　lief,
　So that each here may have his proper
　　part,
For the whole court is more or less in grief:
　Perhaps thou deem'st this lad a Mars in
　　heart?'
Orlando one day heard this speech in brief,
　As by himself it chanced he sate apart:
Displeased he was with Gan because he
　said it,
But much more still that Charles should
　give him credit.

XVI

And with the sword he would have mur-
　der'd Gan,
　But Oliver thrust in between the pair,
And from his hand extracted Durlindan,
　And thus at length they separated were.
Orlando, angry too with Carloman,
　Wanted but little to have slain him there;
Then forth alone from Paris went the chief,
And burst and madden'd with disdain and
　grief.

XVII

From Ermellina, consort of the Dane,
　He took Cortana, and then took Ron-
　　dell,
And on towards Brara prick'd him o'er the
　plain;
　And when she saw him coming, Alda-
　　belle
Stretch'd forth her arms to clasp her lord
　again:
　Orlando, in whose brain all was not well,
As 'Welcome, my Orlando, home,' she
　said,
Raised up his sword to smite her on the
　head,

XVIII

Like him a fury counsels; his revenge
　On Gan in that rash act he seem'd to
　　take,
Which Aldabella thought extremely strange;
　But soon Orlando found himself awake;
And his spouse took his bridle on this
　change,
　And he dismounted from his horse, and
　　spake
Of everything which pass'd without de-
　mur,
And then reposed himself some days with
　her.

XIX

Then full of wrath departed from the place,
　And far as pagan countries roam'd
　　astray,
And while he rode, yet still at every pace
　The traitor Gan remember'd by the way;
And wandering on in error a long space,
　An abbey which in a lone desert lay,
'Midst glens obscure, and distant lands,
　he found,
Which form'd the Christian's and the
　pagan's bound.

XX

The abbot was call'd Clermont, and by
　blood
　Descended from Anglante: under cover
Of a great mountain's brow the abbey
　stood,
　But certain savage giants look'd him
　　over;
One Passamont was foremost of the brood,
　And Alabaster and Morgante hover
Second and third, with certain slings, and
　throw
In daily jeopardy the place below.

XXI

The monks could pass the convent gate no
　more,
　Nor leave their cells for water or for
　　wood;

Orlando knock'd, but none would ope,
    before
  Unto the prior it at length seem'd good;
Enter'd, he said that he was taught to
    adore
  Him who was born of Mary's holiest
    blood,
And was baptized a Christian; and then
    show'd
How to the abbey he had found his road.

XXII

Said the abbot, 'You are welcome; what
    is mine
  We give you freely, since that you believe
With us in Mary Mother's Son divine;
  And that you may not, cavalier, con-
    ceive
The cause of our delay to let you in
  To be rusticity, you shall receive
The reason why our gate was barr'd to
    you:
Thus those who in suspicion live must do.

XXIII

'When hither to inhabit first we came
  These mountains, albeit that they are
    obscure,
As you perceive, yet without fear or blame
  They seem'd to promise an asylum sure:
From savage brutes alone, too fierce to
    tame,
  'Twas fit our quiet dwelling to secure;
But now, if here we'd stay, we needs must
    guard
Against domestic beasts with watch and
    ward.

XXIV

'These make us stand, in fact, upon the
    watch;
  For late there have appear'd three
    giants rough;
What nation or what kingdom bore the
    batch
  I know not, but they are all of savage
    stuff;
When force and malice with some genius
    match,
  You know, they can do all—we are not
    enough:
And these so much our orisons derange,
I know not what to do, till matters change.

XXV

'Our ancient fathers living the desert in,
  For just and holy works were duly fed;
Think not they lived on locusts sole, 'tis
    certain
  That manna was rain'd down from
    heaven instead;
But here 'tis fit we keep on the alert in
  Our bounds, or taste the stones shower'd
    down for bread,

From off yon mountain daily raining
    faster,
And flung by Passamont and Alabaster.

XXVI

'The third, Morgante, 's savagest by far;
    he
  Plucks up pines, beeches, poplar-trees,
    and oaks,
And flings them, our community to bury;
  And all that I can do but more pro-
    vokes.'
While thus they parley in the cemetery,
  A stone from one of their gigantic
    strokes,
Which nearly crush'd Rondell, came tum-
    bling over,
So that he took a long leap under cover.

XXVII

'For God-sake, cavalier, come in with
    speed;
  The manna's falling now,' the abbot
    cried.
'This fellow does not wish my horse
    should feed,
  Dear Abbot,' Roland unto him replied.
'Of restiveness he'd cure him had he need;
  That stone seems with good will and aim
    applied.'
The holy father said, 'I don't deceive;
They'll one day fling the mountain, I
    believe.'

XXVIII

Orlando bade them take care of Ron-
    dello,
  And also made a breakfast of his own:
'Abbot,' he said, 'I want to find that fellow
  Who flung at my good horse yon corner-
    stone.'
Said the abbot, 'Let not my advice seem
    shallow;
  As to a brother dear I speak alone:
I would dissuade you, baron, from this
    strife,
As knowing sure that you will lose your
    life.

XXIX

'That Passamont has in his hand three
    darts—
  Such slings, clubs, ballast-stones, that
    yield you must:
You know that giants have much stouter
    hearts
  Than us, with reason, in proportion
    just:
If go you will, guard well against their arts,
  For these are very barbarous and ro-
    bust.'
Orlando answer'd, 'This I'll see, be sure,
And walk the wild on foot to be secure.'

XXX

The abbot sign'd the great cross on his
        front,
   'Then go you with God's benison and
        mine:'
Orlando, after he had scaled the mount,
   As the abbot had directed, kept the line
Right to the usual haunt of Passamont;
   Who, seeing him alone in this design,
Survey'd him fore and aft with eyes obser-
        vant,
Then ask'd him, 'If he wish'd to stay as
        servant?'

XXXI

And promised him an office of great ease.
   But said Orlando, 'Saracen insane!
I come to kill you, if it shall so please
   God, not to serve as footboy in your
        train;
You with his monks so oft have broke the
        peace—
      Vile dog! 'tis past his patience to
        sustain.'
The giant ran to fetch his arms, quite
        furious,
When he received an answer so injurious.

XXXII

And being return'd to where Orlando
        stood,
   Who had not moved him from the spot,
        and swinging
The cord, he hurl'd a stone with strength
        so rude,
   As show'd a sample of his skill in sling-
        ing;
It roll'd on Count Orlando's helmet good
   And head, and set both head and helmet
        ringing,
So that he swoon'd with pain as if he died,
But more than dead, he seem'd so stupified.

XXXIII

Then Passamont, who thought him slain
        outright,
   Said, 'I will go, and while he lies along,
Disarm me: why such craven did I fight?'
   But Christ his servants ne'er abandons
        long,
Especially Orlando, such a knight,
   As to desert would almost be a wrong.
While the giant goes to put off his defences,
Orlando has recall'd his force and senses:

XXXIV

And loud he shouted, 'Giant, where dost
        go?
   Thou thought'st me doubtless for the
        bier outlaid;
To the right about—without wings thou'rt
        too slow
   To fly my vengeance—currish rene-
        gade!

'Twas but by treachery thou laid'st me low.'
   The giant his astonishment betray'd,
And turn'd about, and stopp'd his journey
        on,
And then he stoop'd to pick up a great
        stone.

XXXV

Orlando had Cortana bare in hand;
   To split the head in twain was what he
        schemed:
Cortana clave the skull like a true brand
   And pagan Passamont died unredeem'd,
Yet harsh and haughty, as he lay he bann'd,
   And most devoutly Macon still blas-
        phemed;
But while his crude, rude blasphemies he
        heard,
Orlando thank'd the Father and the
        Word,—

XXXVI

Saying, 'What grace to me thou'st this day
        given!
   And I to thee, O Lord! am ever bound.
I know my life was saved by thee from
        heaven,
   Since by the giant I was fairly down'd.
All things by thee are measured just and
        even;
   Our power without thine aid would
        nought be found:
I pray thee take heed of me, till I can
At least return once more to Carloman.'

XXXVII

And having said thus much, he went his
        way;
   And Alabaster he found out below,
Doing the very best that in him lay
   To root from out a bank a rock or two.
Orlando, when he reach'd him, loud 'gan
        say,
   'How think'st thou, glutton, such a
        stone to throw?'
When Alabaster heard his deep voice ring,
He suddenly betook him to his sling,

XXXVIII

And hurl'd a fragment of a size so large,
   That if it had in fact fulfill'd its mission,
And Roland not avail'd him of his targe,
   There would have been no need of a
        physician.
Orlando set himself in turn to charge,
   And in his bulky bosom made incision
With all his sword. The lout fell; but o'er-
        thrown, he
However by no means forgot Macone.

XXXIX

Morgante had a palace in his mode,
   Composed of branches, logs of wood,
        and earth,

And stretch'd himself at ease in this abode,
  And shut himself at night within his
    berth.
Orlando knock'd, and knock'd again, to
  goad
  The giant from his sleep; and he came
    forth,
The door to open, like a crazy thing,
  For a rough dream had shook him
    slumbering.

XL

He thought that a fierce serpent had
  attack'd him;
  And Mahomet he call'd; but Mahomet
Is nothing worth, and not an instant
  back'd him;
  But praying blessed Jesu, he was set
At liberty from all the fears which rack'd
  him;
  And to the gate he came with great re-
    gret—
'Who knocks here?' grumbling all the
  while, said he.
'That,' said Orlando, 'you will quickly
  see:

XLI

'I come to preach to you, as to your
  brothers,
  Sent by the miserable monks—repen-
    tance;
For Providence divine, in you and others,
  Condemns the evil done my new
    acquaintance.
'Tis writ on high—your wrong must pay
  another's:
  From heaven itself is issued out this
    sentence.
Know, then, that colder now than a pilaster
I left your Passamont and Alabaster.'

XLII

Morgante said, 'Oh, gentle cavalier!
  Now by thy God say me no villany:
The favour of your name I fain would
  hear,
  And if a Christian, speak for courtesy.'
Replied Orlando, 'So much to your ear
  I by my faith disclose contentedly;
Christ I adore, who is the genuine Lord,
And, if you please, by you may be adored.'

XLIII

The Saracen rejoin'd in humble tone,
  'I have had an extraordinary vision;
A savage serpent fell on me alone,
  And Macon would not pity my con-
    dition;
Hence to thy God, who for ye did atone
  Upon the cross, preferr'd I my petition;
His timely succour set me safe and free,
And I a Christian am disposed to be.'

XLIV

Orlando answer'd, 'Baron just and pious,
  If this good wish your heart can really
    move
To the true God, who will not then deny us
  Eternal honour, you will go above,
And, if you please, as friends we will ally
  us,
  And I will love you with a perfect love.
Your idols are vain liars, full of fraud:
The only true God is the Christians' God.

XLV

'The Lord descended to the virgin breast
  Of Mary Mother, sinless and divine;
If you acknowledge the Redeemer blest,
  Without whom neither sun nor star can
    shine,
Abjure bad Macon's false and felon test,
  Your renegado god, and worship mine,
Baptize yourself with zeal, since you re-
    pent.'
To which Morgante answer'd, 'I'm con-
  tent.'

XLVI

And then Orlando to embrace him flew,
  And made much of his convert, as he
    cried,
'To the abbey I will gladly marshal you.'
  To whom Morgante, 'Let us go,' re-
    plied;
'I to the friars have for peace to sue.'
  Which thing Orlando heard with in-
    ward pride,
Saying, 'My brother, so devout and good,
Ask the abbot pardon, as I wish you
  would:

XLVII

'Since God has granted your illumination,
  Accepting you in mercy for his own,
Humility should be your first oblation.'
  Morgante said, 'For goodness' sake,
    make known,—
Since that your God is to be mine—your
  station,
  And let your name in verity be shown;
Then will I everything at your command
  do.'
On which the other said, he was Orlando.

XLVIII

'Then,' quoth the giant, 'blessed be Jesu
  A thousand times with gratitude and
    praise!
Oft, perfect baron! have I heard of you
  Through all the different periods of my
    days:
And, as I said, to be your vassal too
  I wish, for your great gallantry always.'
Thus reasoning, they continued much to
  say,
And onwards to the abbey went their way.

XLIX

And by the way about the giants dead
  Orlando with Morgante reason'd: 'Be,
For their decease, I pray you, comforted;
  And, since it is God's pleasure, pardon
    me;
A thousand wrongs unto the monks they
    bred,
  And our true Scripture soundeth openly,
Good is rewarded, and chastised the ill,
Which the Lord never faileth to fulfil:

L

'Because his love of justice unto all
  Is such, he wills his judgment should
    devour
All who have sin, however great or small;
  But good he well remembers to restore.
Nor without justice holy could we call
  Him, whom I now require you to adore.
All men must make his will their wishes
    sway,
And quickly and spontaneously obey.

LI

'And here our doctors are of one accord,
  Coming on this point to the same con-
    clusion,
That in their thoughts who praise in
    heaven the Lord
  If pity e'er was guilty of intrusion
For their unfortunate relations stored
  In hell below, and damn'd in great con-
    fusion,
Their happiness would be reduced to
    nought,
And thus unjust the Almighty's self be
    thought.

LII

'But they in Christ have firmest hope, and
    all
  Which seems to him, to them too must
    appear
Well done; nor could it otherwise befall;
  He never can in any purpose err.
If sire or mother suffer endless thrall,
  They don't disturb themselves for him
    or her:
What pleases God to them must joy in-
    spire;—
Such is the observance of the eternal choir.'

LIII

'A word unto the wise,' Morgante said,
  'Is wont to be enough, and you shall see
How much I grieve about my brethren
    dead;
  And if the will of God seem good to me,
Just, as you tell me, 'tis in heaven obey'd—
  Ashes to ashes,—merry let us be!
I will cut off the hands from both their
    trunks,
And carry them unto the holy monks.

LIV

'So that all persons may be sure and certain
  That they are dead, and have no further
    fear
To wander solitary this desert in,
  And that they may perceive my spirit
    clear
By the Lord's grace, who hath withdrawn
    the curtain
  Of darkness, making his bright realm
    appear.'
He cut his brethren's hands off at these
    words,
And left them to the savage beasts and birds.

LV

Then to the abbey they went on together,
  Where waited them the abbot in great
    doubt.
The monks, who knew not yet the fact, ran
    thither,
  To their superior, all in breathless rout,
Saying with tremor, 'Please to tell us
    whether
  You wish to have this person in or out?'
The abbot, looking through upon the giant,
Too greatly fear'd, at first, to be compliant.

LVI

Orlando, seeing him thus agitated,
  Said quickly, 'Abbot, be thou of good
    cheer;
He Christ believes, as Christian must be
    rated,
  And hath renounced his Macon false';
    which here
Morgante with the hands corroborated,
  A proof of both the giants' fate quite
    clear:
Thence, with due thanks, the abbot God
    adored,
Saying, 'Thou hast contented me, oh Lord!'

LVII

He gazed; Morgante's height he calculated,
  And more than once contemplated his
    size;
And then he said, 'Oh giant celebrated!
  Know, that no more my wonder will
    arise,
How you could tear and fling the trees you
    late did,
  When I behold your form with my own
    eyes.
You now a true and perfect friend will show
Yourself to Christ, as once you were a foe.

LVIII

'And one of our apostles, Saul once
    named,
  Long persecuted sore the faith of Christ,
Till, one day, by the Spirit being inflamed,
  "Why dost thou persecute me thus?"
    said Christ;

And then from his offence he was reclaim'd,
   And went for ever after preaching
     Christ,
And of the faith became a trump, whose
   sounding
O'er the whole earth is echoing and re-
   bounding.

LIX

'So, my Morgante, you may do likewise:
   He who repents—thus writes the Evan-
     gelist—
Occasions more rejoicing in the skies
   Than ninety-nine of the celestial list.
You may be sure, should each desire arise
   With just zeal for the Lord, that you'll
     exist
Among the happy saints for evermore;
But you were lost and damn'd to hell
   before!'

LX

And thus great honour to Morgante paid
   The abbot: many days they did repose.
One day, as with Orlando they both stray'd,
   And saunter'd here and there, where'er
     they chose,
The abbot show'd a chamber, where array'd
   Much armour was, and hung up certain
     bows;
And one of these Morgante for a whim
Girt on, though useless, he believed, to
   him.

LXI

There being a want of water in the place,
   Orlando, like a worthy brother, said,
'Morgante, I could wish you in this case
   To go for water.' 'You shall be obey'd
In all commands,' was the reply, 'straight-
     ways.'
   Upon his shoulder a great tub he laid,
And went out on his way unto a fountain,
Where he was wont to drink below the
   mountain.

LXII

Arrived there, a prodigious noise he hears,
   Which suddenly along the forest spread;
Whereat from out his quiver he prepares
   An arrow for his bow, and lifts his head;
And lo! a monstrous herd of swine appears,
   And onward rushes with tempestuous
     tread,
And to the fountain's brink precisely pours;
So that the giant's join'd by all the boars.

LXIII

Morgante at a venture shot an arrow,
   Which pierced a pig precisely in the ear,
And pass'd unto the other side quite
   thorough;
   So that the boar, defunct, lay tripp'd up
     near.

Another, to revenge his fellow farrow,
   Against the giant rush'd in fierce career,
And reach'd the passage with so swift a
   foot,
Morgante was not now in time to shoot.

LXIV

Perceiving that the pig was on him close,
   He gave him such a punch upon the head,
As floor'd him so that he no more arose,
   Smashing the very bone; and he fell dead
Next to the other. Having seen such blows,
   The other pigs along the valley fled;
Morgante on his neck the bucket took,
Full from the spring, which neither
   swerved nor shook.

LXV

The tub was on one shoulder, and there
   were
   The hogs on t'other, and he brush'd
     apace
On to the abbey, though by no means near,
   Nor spilt one drop of water in his race.
Orlando, seeing him so soon appear
   With the dead boars, and with that
     brimful vase,
Marvell'd to see his strength so very great;
So did the abbot, and set wide the gate.

LXVI

The monks, who saw the water fresh and
   good,
   Rejoiced, but much more to perceive the
     pork;
All animals are glad at sight of food:
   They lay their breviaries to sleep, and
     work
With greedy pleasure, and in such a mood,
   That the flesh needs no salt beneath
     their fork.
Of rankness and of rot there is no fear,
For all the fasts are now left in arrear.

LXVII

As though they wish'd to burst at once,
   they ate;
   And gorged so that, as if the bones had
     been
In water, sorely grieved the dog and cat,
   Perceiving that they all were pick'd too
     clean.
The abbot, who to all did honour great,
   A few days after this convivial scene,
Gave to Morgante a fine horse, well
   train'd,
Which he long time had for himself main-
   tain'd.

LXVIII

The horse Morgante to a meadow led,
   To gallop, and to put him to the proof,
Thinking that he a back of iron had,
   Or to skim eggs unbroke was light
     enough;

But the horse, sinking with the pain, fell dead,
  And burst, while cold on earth lay head and hoof.
Morgante said, 'Get up, thou sulky cur!'
  And still continued pricking with the spur.

LXIX

But finally he thought fit to dismount,
  And said, 'I am as light as any feather,
And he has burst;—to this what say you, count?'
  Orlando answer'd, 'Like a ship's mast rather
You seem to me, and with the truck for front:
  Let him go! Fortune wills that we together
Should march, but you on foot Morgante still.'
  To which the giant answer'd, 'So I will.

LXX

'When there shall be occasion, you will see
  How I approve my courage in the fight.'
Orlando said, 'I really think you'll be,
  If it should prove God's will, a goodly knight;
Nor will you napping there discover me.
  But never mind your horse, though out of sight
'Twere best to carry him into some wood,
  If but the means or way I understood.'

LXXI

The giant said, 'Then carry him I will,
  Since that to carry me he was so slack—
To render, as the gods do, good for ill;
  But lend a hand to place him on my back.'
Orlando answer'd, 'If my counsel still
  May weigh, Morgante, do not undertake
To lift or carry this dead courser, who,
As you have done to him, will do to you.

LXXII

'Take care he don't revenge himself, though dead,
  As Nessus did of old beyond all cure.
I don't know if the fact you've heard or read;
  But he will make you burst, you may be sure.'
'But help him on my back,' Morgante said,
  'And you shall see what weight I can endure.
In place, my gentle Roland, of this palfrey,
With all the bells, I'd carry yonder belfry.'

LXXIII

The abbot said, 'The steeple may do well,
  But, for the bells, you've broken them, I wot.'
Morgante answer'd, 'Let them pay in hell
  The penalty who lie dead in yon grot;'

And hoisting up the horse from where he fell,
  He said, 'Now look if I the gout have got,
Orlando, in the legs—or if I have force;'—
  And then he made two gambols with the horse.

LXXIV

Morgante was like any mountain framed;
  So if he did this 'tis no prodigy;
But secretly himself Orlando blamed,
  Because he was one of his family;
And fearing that he might be hurt or maim'd,
  Once more he bade him lay his burden by:
'Put down, nor bear him further the desert in.'
  Morgante said, 'I'll carry him for certain.'

LXXV

He did; and stow'd him in some nook away,
  And to the abbey then return'd with speed.
Orlando said, 'Why longer do we stay?
  Morgante, here is nought to do indeed.'
The abbot by the hand he took one day,
  And said, with great respect, he had agreed
To leave his reverence; but for this decision
He wish'd to have his pardon and permission.

LXXVI

The honours they continued to receive
  Perhaps exceeded what his merits claim'd:
He said, 'I mean, and quickly, to retrieve
  The lost days of time past, which may be blamed;
Some days ago I should have ask'd your leave,
  Kind father, but I really was ashamed,
And know not how to show my sentiment,
So much I see you with our stay content.

LXXVII

'But in my heart I bear through every clime
  The abbot, abbey, and this solitude—
So much I love you in so short a time;
  For me, from heaven reward you with all good
The God so true, the eternal Lord sublime!
  Whose kingdom at the last hath open stood.
Meantime we stand expectant of your blessing,
And recommend us to your prayers with pressing.'

LXXVIII

Now when the abbot Count Orlando
heard,
  His heart grew soft with inner tender-
  ness,
Such fervour in his bosom bred each word;
  And, 'Cavalier,' he said, 'if I have less
Courteous and kind to your great worth
appear'd,
  Than fits me for such gentle blood to
  express,
I know I have done too little in this case;
But blame our ignorance, and this poor
place.

LXXIX

'We can indeed but honour you with
masses,
  And sermons, thanksgivings, and pater-
  nosters,
Hot suppers, dinners (fitting other places
  In verity much rather than the cloisters);
But such a love for you my heart embraces,
  For thousand virtues which your bosom
  fosters,
That wheresoe'er you go I too shall be,
And, on the other part, you rest with me.

LXXX

'This may involve a seeming contradiction;
  But you I know are sage, and feel, and
  taste,
And understand my speech, with full con-
viction.
  For your just pious deeds may you be
  graced
With the Lord's great reward and bene-
diction,
  By whom you were directed to this
  waste:
To his high mercy is our freedom due,
For which we render thanks to him and
you.

LXXXI

'You saved at once our life and soul: such
fear
  The giants caused us, that the way was
  lost
By which we could pursue a fit career
  In search of Jesus and the saintly host;
And your departure breeds such sorrow
here,
  That comfortless we all are to our cost;
But months and years you would not stay
in sloth,
Nor are you form'd to wear our sober cloth,

LXXXII

'But to bear arms, and wield the lance;
indeed,
  With these as much is done as with this
  cowl;

In proof of which the Scriptures you may
read.
  This giant up to heaven may bear his
  soul
By your compassion: now in peace proceed.
  Your state and name I seek not to unroll;
But, if I'm ask'd, this answer shall be
given,
That here an angel was sent down from
heaven.

LXXXIII

'If you want armour or aught else, go in,
  Look o'er the wardrobe, and take what
  you choose,
And cover with it o'er this giant's skin.'
  Orlando answer'd, 'If there should lie
  loose
Some armour, ere our journey we begin,
  Which might be turn'd to my compan-
  ion's use,
The gift would be acceptable to me.'
The abbot said to him, 'Come in and see.'

LXXXIV

And in a certain closet, where the wall
  Was cover'd with old armour like a
  crust,
The abbot said to them, 'I give you all.'
  Morgante rummaged piecemeal from
  the dust
The whole, which, save one cuirass, was
too small,
  And that too had the mail inlaid with
  rust.
They wonder'd how it fitted him exactly,
Which ne'er has suited others so com-
pactly.

LXXXV

'Twas an immeasurable giant's, who
  By the great Milo of Agrante fell
Before the abbey many years ago.
  The story on the wall was figured well;
In the last moment of the abbey's foe,
  Who long had waged a war implacable:
Precisely as the war occurr'd they drew
him,
And there was Milo as he overthrew him.

LXXXVI

Seeing this history, Count Orlando said
  In his own heart, 'Oh God, who in the sky
Know'st all things! how was Milo hither
led?
  Who caused the giant in this place to
  die?'
And certain letters, weeping, then he read,
  So that he could not keep his visage
  dry,—
As I will tell in the ensuing story.
From evil keep you the high King of glory!

FRANCESCA OF RIMINI

FROM THE INFERNO OF DANTE

CANTO THE FIFTH

'THE land where I was born sits by the seas,
  Upon that shore to which the Po descends,
  With all his followers, in search of peace.
Love, which the gentle heart soon apprehends,
  Seized him for the fair person which was ta'en   5
From me, and me even yet the mode offends.
Love, who to none beloved to love again
  Remits, seized me with wish to please, so strong,
  That, as thou seest, yet, yet it doth remain.
Love to one death conducted us along,
  But Caina waits for him our life who ended:'   11
These were the accents utter'd by her tongue.—
Since I first listen'd to these souls offended,
  I bow'd my visage, and so kept it till—
'What think'st thou,' said the bard; when I unbended,   15
And recommenced: 'Alas! unto such ill
  How many sweet thoughts, what strong ecstasies,
  Led these their evil fortune to fulfil!'
And then I turn'd unto their side my eyes,
  And said, 'Francesca, thy sad destinies
Have made me sorrow till the tears arise.
But tell me, in the season of sweet sighs,   22
  By what and how thy love to passion rose,
  So as his dim desires to recognise?'
Then she to me: 'The greatest of all woes
  Is to remind us of our happy days   26
  In misery, and that thy teacher knows.
But if to learn our passion's first root preys
  Upon thy spirit with such sympathy,
  I will do even as he who weeps and says.
We read one day for pastime, seated nigh,
  Of Lancilot, how love enchain'd him too.   32
  We were alone, quite unsuspiciously.
But oft our eyes met, and our cheeks in hue
  All o'er discolour'd by that reading were;   35
But one point only wholly us o'erthrew;
When we read the long-sigh'd-for smile of her,
  To be thus kiss'd by such devoted lover,
  He who from me can be divided ne'er
Kiss'd my mouth, trembling in the act all over: 40
  Accursed was the book and he who wrote!
That day no further leaf we did uncover.'
While thus one spirit told us of their lot,
  The other wept, so that with pity's thralls
I swoon'd, as if by death I had been smote   45
And fell down even as a dead body falls.

DRAMAS

MANFRED

A DRAMATIC POEM

'There are more things in heaven and earth, Horatio,
Than are dreamt of in your philosophy.'

DRAMATIS PERSONÆ

MANFRED.	WITCH OF THE ALPS.
CHAMOIS HUNTER.	ARIMANES.
ABBOT OF ST. MAURICE.	NEMESIS.
MANUEL.	THE DESTINIES.
HERMAN.	SPIRITS, &c.

*The Scene of the Drama is amongst the Higher Alps—partly in the Castle of Manfred,
and partly in the Mountains.*

ACT I

SCENE I.—MANFRED *alone.—Scene, a
Gothic Gallery.—Time, Midnight.*

Man. The lamp must be replenish'd,
but even then
It will not burn so long as I must watch:
My slumbers—if I slumber—are not sleep,
But a continuance of enduring thought,
Which then I can resist not: in my heart
There is a vigil, and these eyes but close
To look within; and yet I live, and bear
The aspect and the form of breathing men.
But grief should be the instructor of the
wise;
Sorrow is knowledge: they who know the
most   10
Must mourn the deepest o'er the fatal
truth,
The Tree of Knowledge is not that of Life.
Philosophy and science, and the springs
Of wonder, and the wisdom of the world,
I have essay'd, and in my mind there is   15
A power to make these subject to itself—
But they avail not: I have done men good,
And I have met with good even among
men—
But this avail'd not: I have had my foes,
And none have baffled, many fallen before
me—   20
But this avail'd not:—Good, or evil, life,
Powers, passions, all I see in other beings,
Have been to me as rain unto the sands,
Since that all-nameless hour. I have no
dread,
And feel the curse to have no natural fear,
Nor fluttering throb, that beats with hopes
or wishes,   26
Or lurking love of something on the earth.
Now to my task.—

Mysterious agency!
Ye spirits of the unbounded Universe!
Whom I have sought in darkness and in
light—   30
Ye, who do compass earth about, and
dwell
In subtler essence—ye, to whom the tops
Of mountains inaccessible are haunts,
And earth's and ocean's caves familiar
things—
I call upon ye by the written charm   35
Which gives me power upon you—Rise!
Appear!   [*A pause.*
They come not yet.—Now by the voice of
him
Who is the first among you—by this sign,
Which makes you tremble—by the claims
of him
Who is undying,—Rise! Appear!——
Appear!   [*A pause.*
If it be so—Spirits of earth and air,   41
Ye shall not thus elude me: by a power,
Deeper than all yet urged, a tyrant-spell,
Which had its birthplace in a star con-
demn'd,
The burning wreck of a demolish'd world,
A wandering hell in the eternal space;   46
By the strong curse which is upon my
soul,
The thought which is within me and around
me,
I do compel ye to my will—Appear!
[*A star is seen at the darker end of the
gallery: it is stationary; and a voice
is heard singing.*

FIRST SPIRIT

Mortal! to thy bidding bow'd,   50
From my mansion in the cloud,
Which the breath of twilight builds,
And the summer's sunset gilds
With the azure and vermilion,
Which is mix'd for my pavilion;   55

Though thy quest may be forbidden,
On a star-beam I have ridden:
To thine adjuration bow'd,
Mortal—be thy wish avow'd!

Voice of the SECOND SPIRIT

Mont Blanc is the monarch of mountains;
They crown'd him long ago   61
On a throne of rocks, in a robe of clouds,
With a diadem of snow.
Around his waist are forests braced,
The Avalanche in his hand;   65
But ere it fall, that thundering ball
Must pause for my command.
The Glacier's cold and restless mass
Moves onward day by day;
But I am he who bids it pass,   70
Or with its ice delay.
I am the spirit of the place,
Could make the mountain bow
And quiver to his cavern'd base—
And what with me wouldst *Thou*?   75

Voice of the THIRD SPIRIT

In the blue depth of the waters,
Where the wave hath no strife,
Where the wind is a stranger,
And the sea-snake hath life,
Where the Mermaid is decking   80
Her green hair with shells,
Like the storm on the surface
Came the sound of thy spells;
O'er my calm Hall of Coral
The deep echo roll'd—   85
To the Spirit of Ocean
Thy wishes unfold!

FOURTH SPIRIT

Where the slumbering earthquake
Lies pillow'd on fire,
And the lakes of bitumen   90
Rise boilingly higher;
Where the roots of the Andes
Strike deep in the earth,
As their summits to heaven
Shoot soaringly forth;   95
I have quitted my birthplace,
Thy bidding to bide—
Thy spell hath subdued me,
Thy will be my guide!

FIFTH SPIRIT

I am the Rider of the wind,   100
The Stirrer of the storm;
The hurricane I left behind
Is yet with lightning warm;
To speed to thee, o'er shore and sea
I swept upon the blast: 105
The fleet I met sail'd well, and yet
'Twill sink ere night be past.

SIXTH SPIRIT

My dwelling is the shadow of the night,
Why doth thy magic torture me with
light?

SEVENTH SPIRIT

The star which rules thy destiny   110
Was ruled, ere earth began, by me:
It was a world as fresh and fair
As e'er revolved round sun in air;
Its course was free and regular,
Space bosom'd not a lovelier star.   115
The hour arrived—and it became
A wandering mass of shapeless flame,
A pathless comet, and a curse,
The menace of the universe;
Still rolling on with innate force,   120
Without a sphere, without a course,
A bright deformity on high,
The monster of the upper sky!   123
And thou! beneath its influence born—
Thou worm! whom I obey and scorn—
Forced by a power (which is not thine,
And lent thee but to make thee mine)
For this brief moment to descend,
Where these weak spirits round thee
bend   129
And parley with a thing like thee—
What wouldst thou, Child of Clay! with
me?

The SEVEN SPIRITS

Earth, ocean, air, night, mountains,
winds, thy star,
Are at thy beck and bidding, Child of
Clay!
Before thee at thy quest their spirits are—
What wouldst thou with us, son of
mortals—say?   135

Man. Forgetfulness——
First Spirit. Of what—of whom—and
why?
Man. Of that which is within me; read
it there—
Ye know it, and I cannot utter it.
Spirit. We can but give thee that which
we possess:
Ask of us subjects, sovereignty, the power
O'er earth—the whole, or portion—or a
sign   141
Which shall control the elements, whereof
We are the dominators,—each and all,
These shall be thine.
Man.   Oblivion, self-oblivion!
Can ye not wring from out the hidden
realms   145
Ye offer so profusely what I ask?
Spirit. It is not in our essence, in our
skill;
But—thou may'st die.
Man.   Will death bestow it on me?
Spirit. We are immortal, and do not
forget;
We are eternal; and to us the past   150
Is, as the future, present. Art thou an-
swer'd?
Man. Ye mock me—but the power
which brought ye here

Hath made you mine. Slaves, scoff not at
  my will!
The mind, the spirit, the Promethean
  spark,   154
The lightning of my being, is as bright,
Pervading, and far darting as your own,
And shall not yield to yours, though
  coop'd in clay!
Answer, or I will teach you what I am.
  Spirit. We answer as we answer'd; our
    reply
Is even in thine own words.
  Man.   Why say ye so? 160
  Spirit. If, as thou say'st, thine essence
    be as ours,
We have replied in telling thee, the thing
Mortals call death hath nought to do with
  us.
  Man. I then have call'd ye from your
    realms in vain;
Ye cannot, or ye will not, aid me.
  Spirit.   Say, 165
What we possess we offer; it is thine:
Bethink ere thou dismiss us; ask again;
Kingdom, and sway, and strength, and
  length of days——
  Man. Accursed! what have I to do
    with days?
They are too long already.—Hence—be-
  gone!   170
  Spirit. Yet pause: being here, our will
    would do thee service;
Bethink thee, is there then no other gift
Which we can make not worthless in thine
  eyes?
  Man. No, none: yet stay—one mo-
    ment, ere we part,
I would behold ye face to face. I hear
Your voices, sweet and melancholy
  sounds,   176
As music on the waters; and I see
The steady aspect of a clear large star;
But nothing more. Approach me as ye are,
Or one, or all, in your accustom'd forms.
  Spirit. We have no forms, beyond the
    elements   181
Of which we are the mind and principle:
But choose a form—in that we will appear.
  Man. I have no choice; there is no form
    on earth
Hideous or beautiful to me. Let him,
Who is most powerful of ye, take such
  aspect   186
As unto him may seem most fitting—
  Come!
  Seventh Spirit [*appearing in the shape of
    a beautiful female figure*]. Behold!
  Man. Oh God! if it be thus, and *thou*
Art not a madness and a mockery, 189
I yet might be most happy, I will clasp thee,
And we again will be——
           [*The figure vanishes.*
          My heart is crush'd!
          [MANFRED *falls senseless.*

(*A voice is heard in the Incantation which
    follows.*)

When the moon is on the wave,
  And the glow-worm in the grass,
And the meteor on the grave,
  And the wisp on the morass; 195
When the falling stars are shooting,
And the answer'd owls are hooting,
And the silent leaves are still
In the shadow of the hill,
Shall my soul be upon thine, 200
With a power and with a sign.

Though thy slumber may be deep,
Yet thy spirit shall not sleep;
There are shades which will not van-
  ish,
There are thoughts thou canst not ban-
  ish;   205
By a power to thee unknown,
Thou canst never be alone;
Thou art wrapt as with a shroud,
Thou art gather'd in a cloud,
And for ever shalt thou dwell 210
In the spirit of this spell.

Though thou seest me not pass by,
Thou shalt feel me with thine eye
As a thing that, though unseen,
Must be near thee, and hath been; 215
And when in that secret dread
Thou hast turn'd around thy head,
Thou shalt marvel I am not
As thy shadow on the spot,
And the power which thou dost feel
Shall be what thou must conceal. 221

And a magic voice and verse
Hath baptized thee with a curse;
And a spirit of the air
Hath begirt thee with a snare; 225
In the wind there is a voice
Shall forbid thee to rejoice;
And to thee shall night deny
All the quiet of her sky;
And the day shall have a sun, 230
Which shall make thee wish it done.

From thy false tears I did distil
An essence which hath strength to kill;
From thy own heart I then did wring
The black blood in its blackest spring;
From thy own smile I snatch'd the
  snake,   236
For there it coil'd as in a brake;
From thy own lip I drew the charm
Which gave all these their chiefest harm;
In proving every poison known, 240
I found the strongest was thine own.

By thy cold breast and serpent smile,
By thy unfathom'd gulfs of guile,
By that most seeming virtuous eye,
By thy shut soul's hypocrisy; 245

By the perfection of thine art
Which pass'd for human thine own
    heart;
By thy delight in others' pain,
And by thy brotherhood of Cain,
I call upon thee! and compel   250
Thyself to be thy proper Hell!

And on thy head I pour the vial
Which doth devote thee to this trial;
Nor to slumber, nor to die,
Shall be in thy destiny;   255
Though thy death shall still seem near
To thy wish, but as a fear;
Lo! the spell now works around thee,
And the clankless chain hath bound
    thee;
O'er thy heart and brain together   260
Hath the word been pass'd—now
    wither!

SCENE II

*The Mountain of the Jungfrau.—Time,
Morning.*—MANFRED *alone upon the
Cliffs.*

Man. The spirits I have raised abandon
    me,
The spells which I have studied baffle me,
The remedy I reck'd of tortured me;
I lean no more on superhuman aid;
It hath no power upon the past, and for
The future, till the past be gulf'd in dark-
    ness,   6
It is not of my search.—My mother Earth!
And thou fresh breaking Day, and you,
    ye Mountains,
Why are ye beautiful? I cannot love ye.
And thou, the bright eye of the universe,
That openest over all, and unto all   11
Art a delight—thou shin'st not on my
    heart.
And you, ye crags, upon whose extreme
    edge
I stand, and on the torrent's brink beneath
Behold the tall pines dwindled as to shrubs
In dizziness of distance; when a leap,
A stir, a motion, even a breath, would
    bring
My breast upon its rocky bosom's bed
To rest for ever—wherefore do I pause?
I feel the impulse—yet I do not plunge;
I see the peril—yet do not recede;   21
And my brain reels—and yet my foot is
    firm:
There is a power upon me which with-
    holds,
And makes it my fatality to live,—
If it be life to wear within myself   25
This barrenness of spirit, and to be
My own soul's sepulchre, for I have ceased
To justify my deeds unto myself—
The last infirmity of evil. Ay,   29
Thou winged and cloud-cleaving minister,
                    [*An eagle passes.*

Whose happy flight is highest into heaven,
Well may'st thou swoop so near me—I
    should be
Thy prey, and gorge thine eaglets; thou
    art gone
Where the eye cannot follow thee; but
    thine   34
Yet pierces downward, onward, or above,
With a pervading vision.—Beautiful!
How beautiful is all this visible world!
How glorious in its action and itself!
But we, who name ourselves its sovereigns,
    we,
Half dust, half deity, alike unfit   40
To sink or soar, with our mix'd essence
    make
A conflict of its elements, and breathe
The breath of degradation and of pride,
Contending with low wants and lofty will,
Till our mortality predominates,   45
And men are—what they name not to
    themselves,
And trust not to each other. Hark! the
    note,   [*The Shepherd's pipe in the
                    distance is heard.*
The natural music of the mountain reed—
For here the patriarchal days are not
A pastoral fable—pipes in the liberal air,
Mix'd with the sweet bells of the saunter-
    ing herd;   51
My soul would drink those echoes. Oh,
    that I were
The viewless spirit of a lovely sound,
A living voice, a breathing harmony,
A bodiless enjoyment—born and dying
With the blest tone which made me!   56

Enter from below a CHAMOIS HUNTER.

Chamois Hunter.   Even so
This way the chamois leapt: her nimble
    feet
Have baffled me; my gains to-day will
    scarce
Repay my break-neck travail.—What is
    here?
Who seems not of my trade, and yet hath
    reach'd   60
A height which none even of our moun-
    taineers,
Save our best hunters, may attain: his garb
Is goodly, his mien manly, and his air
Proud as a free-born peasant's, at this dis-
    tance:
I will approach him nearer.
Man. [*not perceiving the other*]. To be
    thus—   65
Grey-hair'd with anguish, like these
    blasted pines,
Wrecks of a single winter, barkless,
    branchless,
A blighted trunk upon a cursed root,
Which but supplies a feeling to decay—
And to be thus, eternally but thus,   70
Having been otherwise! Now furrow'd o'er

With wrinkles, plough'd by moments,—
    not by years,—
And hours, all tortured into ages—hours
Which I outlive!—Ye toppling crags of ice!
Ye avalanches, whom a breath draws
    down   75
In mountainous o'erwhelming, come and
    crush me!
I hear ye momently above, beneath,
Crash with a frequent conflict; but ye pass,
And only fall on things that still would live;
On the young flourishing forest, or the hut
And hamlet of the harmless villager. 81
    C. Hun. The mists begin to rise from up
    the valley;
I'll warn him to descend, or he may chance
To lose at once his way and life together.
    Man. The mists boil up around the
    glaciers; clouds   85
Rise curling fast beneath me, white and
    sulphury,
Like foam from the roused ocean of deep
    Hell,
Whose every wave breaks on a living shore,
Heap'd with the damn'd like pebbles.—I
    am giddy.
    C. Hun. I must approach him cautiously;
    if near,   90
A sudden step will startle him, and he
Seems tottering already.
    Man.   Mountains have fallen,
Leaving a gap in the clouds, and with the
    shock
Rocking their Alpine brethren; filling up
The ripe green valleys with destruction's
    splinters;   95
Damming the rivers with a sudden dash,
Which crush'd the waters into mist and
    made
Their fountains find another channel—
    thus,
Thus, in its old age, did Mount Rosen-
    berg—
Why stood I not beneath it?
    C. Hun.   Friend! have a care, 100
Your next step may be fatal!—for the love
Of him who made you, stand not on that
    brink!
    Man. [*not hearing him*]. Such would
    have been for me a fitting tomb;
My bones had then been quiet in their
    depth;
They had not then been strewn upon the
    rocks   105
For the wind's pastime—as thus—thus
    they shall be—
In this one plunge.—Farewell, ye opening
    heavens!
Look not upon me thus reproachfully—
You were not meant for me—Earth! take
    these atoms!
    [*As* MANFRED *is in act to spring from the
    cliff, the* CHAMOIS HUNTER *seizes and
    retains him with a sudden grasp.*

    C. Hun. Hold, madman!—though a-
    weary of thy life,   110
Stain not our pure vales with thy guilty
    blood:
Away with me———I will not quit my
    hold.
    Man. I am most sick at heart—nay,
    grasp me not—
I am all feebleness—the mountains whirl
Spinning around me———I grow blind———
    What art thou?   115
    C. Hun. I'll answer that anon. Away
    with me—
The clouds grow thicker———there—now
    lean on me—
Place your foot here—here, take this staff,
    and cling
A moment to that shrub—now give me
    your hand,
And hold fast by my girdle—softly—
    well—   120
The Chalet will be gain'd within an hour:
Come on, we'll quickly find a surer foot-
    ing,
And something like a pathway, which the
    torrent
Hath wash'd since winter.—Come, 'tis
    bravely done—
You should have been a hunter.—Follow
    me.   125
    [*As they descend the rocks with diffi-
    culty, the scene closes.*

ACT II

SCENE I.—*A Cottage amongst the Bernese
Alps.*

MANFRED *and the* CHAMOIS HUNTER

    C. Hun. No, no—yet pause—thou must
    not yet go forth:
Thy mind and body are alike unfit
To trust each other, for some hours, at
    least;
When thou art better, I will be thy guide—
But whither?
    Man.   It imports not: I do know 5
My route full well, and need no further
    guidance.
    C. Hun. Thy garb and gait bespeak thee
    of high lineage—
One of the many chiefs, whose castled
    crags
Look o'er the lower valleys—which of
    these
May call thee lord? I only know their
    portals;   10
My way of life leads me but rarely down
To bask by the huge hearths of those old
    halls,
Carousing with the vassals; but the paths,
Which step from out our mountains to
    their doors,
I know from childhood—which of these is
    thine?   15

Man. No matter.

C. Hun.   Well, sir, pardon me
  the question,
And be of better cheer. Come, taste my
  wine!
'Tis of an ancient vintage; many a day
'T has thaw'd my veins among our glaciers,
  now
Let it do thus for thine—Come, pledge me
  fairly.   20
Man. Away, away! there's blood upon
  the brim!
Will it then never—never sink in the earth?
C. Hun. What dost thou mean? thy
  senses wander from thee.
Man. I say 'tis blood—my blood! the
  pure warm stream
Which ran in the veins of my fathers, and
  in ours   25
When we were in our youth, and had one
  heart,
And loved each other as we should not
  love,
And this was shed: but still it rises up,
Colouring the clouds, that shut me out
  from heaven,
Where thou art not—and I shall never be.
C. Hun. Man of strange words, and
  some half-maddening sin,   31
Which makes thee people vacancy, whate'er
Thy dread and sufferance be, there's com-
  fort yet—
The aid of holy men, and heavenly pa-
  tience—
Man. Patience and patience! Hence—
  that word was made   35
For brutes of burthen, not for birds of prey;
Preach it to mortals of a dust like thine,—
I am not of thine order.
C. Hun.   Thanks to heaven!
I would not be of thine for the free fame
Of William Tell; but whatsoe'er thine ill,
It must be borne, and these wild starts are
  useless.   41
Man. Do I not bear it?—Look on me—
  I live.
C. Hun. This is convulsion, and no
  healthful life.
Man. I tell thee, man! I have lived many
  years,
Many long years, but they are nothing now
To those which I must number: ages—
  ages—   46
Space and eternity—and consciousness,
With the fierce thirst of death—and still
  unslaked!
C. Hun. Why, on thy brow the seal of
  middle age
Hath scarce been set; I am thine elder far.
Man. Think'st thou existence doth de-
  pend on time?   51
It doth; but actions are our epochs: mine
Have made my days and nights imperish-
  able,

Endless, and all alike, as sands on the
  shore,
Innumerable atoms; and one desert,   55
Barren and cold, on which the wild waves
  break,
But nothing rests, save carcasses and
  wrecks,
Rocks, and the salt-surf weeds of bitter-
  ness.
C. Hun. Alas! he's mad—but yet I
  must not leave him.
Man. I would I were—for then the
  things I see   60
Would be but a distemper'd dream.
C. Hun.   What is it
That thou dost see, or think thou look'st
  upon?
Man. Myself, and thee—a peasant of
  the Alps—
Thy humble virtues, hospitable home,
And spirit patient, pious, proud, and free;
Thy self-respect, grafted on innocent
  thoughts;   66
Thy days of health, and nights of sleep;
  thy toils,
By danger dignified, yet guiltless; hopes
Of cheerful old age and a quiet grave,
With cross and garland over its green
  turf,   70
And thy grandchildren's love for epitaph;
This do I see—and then I look within—
It matters not—my soul was scorch'd al-
  ready!
C. Hun. And wouldst thou then ex-
  change thy lot for mine?
Man. No, friend! I would not wrong
  thee, nor exchange   75
My lot with living being: I can bear—
However wretchedly, 'tis still to bear—
In life what others could not brook to
  dream,
But perish in their slumber.
C. Hun.   And with this—
This cautious feeling for another's pain,
Canst thou be black with evil?—say not
  so.   81
Can one of gentle thoughts have wreak'd
  revenge
Upon his enemies?
Man.   Oh! no, no, no!
My injuries came down on those who loved
  me—
On those whom I best loved: I never quell'd
An enemy, save in my just defence—   86
But my embrace was fatal.
C. Hun.   Heaven give thee rest!
And penitence restore thee to thyself;
My prayers shall be for thee.
Man.   I need them not—
But can endure thy pity. I depart—   90
'Tis time—farewell!—Here's gold, and
  thanks for thee—
No words—it is thy due.—Follow me
  not—

I know my path—the mountain peril's past:
And once again I charge thee, follow not!
[*Exit* MANFRED.

SCENE II.—*A lower Valley in the Alps.—A Cataract.*

Enter MANFRED.

It is not noon—the sunbow's rays still arch
The torrent with the many hues of heaven,
And roll the sheeted silver's waving column
O'er the crag's headlong perpendicular,
And fling its lines of foaming light along,
And to and fro, like the pale courser's tail,
The Giant steed, to be bestrode by Death,
As told in the Apocalypse. No eyes   8
But mine now drink this sight of loveliness;
I should be sole in this sweet solitude,
And with the Spirit of the place divide
The homage of these waters.—I will call
        her.   12
[MANFRED *takes some of the water into
the palm of his hand, and flings it into
the air, muttering the adjuration. After
a pause, the* WITCH OF THE ALPS *rises
beneath the arch of the sunbow of the
torrent.*
Beautiful Spirit! with thy hair of light,
And dazzling eyes of glory, in whose form
The charms of earth's least mortal daugh-
        ters grow   15
To an unearthly stature, in an essence
Of purer elements; while the hues of
        youth,—
Carnation'd like a sleeping infant's cheek,
Rock'd by the beating of her mother's
        heart,
Or the rose tints, which summer's twi-
        light leaves   20
Upon the lofty glacier's virgin snow,
The blush of earth embracing with her
        heaven,—
Tinge thy celestial aspect, and make tame
The beauties of the sunbow which bends
        o'er thee.   24
Beautiful Spirit! in thy calm clear brow,
Wherein is glass'd serenity of soul,
Which of itself shows immortality,
I read that thou wilt pardon to a Son
Of Earth, whom the abstruser powers per-
        mit   29
At times to commune with them—if that he
Avail him of his spells—to call thee thus,
And gaze on thee a moment.
        Witch.   Son of Earth!
I know thee, and the powers which give
        thee power;
I know thee for a man of many thoughts,
And deeds of good and ill, extreme in both,
Fatal and fated in thy sufferings.   36
I have expected this—what wouldst thou
        with me?
        Man. To look upon thy beauty—
        nothing further.

The face of the earth hath madden'd me,
        and I   39
Take refuge in her mysteries, and pierce
To the abodes of those who govern her—
But they can nothing aid me. I have sought
From them what they could not bestow,
        and now
I search no further.
        Witch.   What could be the quest
Which is not in the power of the most
        powerful,   45
The rulers of the invisible?
        Man.   A boon;
But why should I repeat it? 'twere in vain.
        Witch. I know not that; let thy lips
        utter it.
        Man. Well, though it torture me, 'tis
        but the same;
My pang shall find a voice. From my
        youth upwards   50
My spirit walk'd not with the souls of men,
Nor look'd upon the earth with human
        eyes;
The thirst of their ambition was not mine,
The aim of their existence was not mine;
My joys, my griefs, my passions, and my
        powers,   55
Made me a stranger; though I wore the
        form,
I had no sympathy with breathing flesh,
Nor midst the creatures of clay that girded
        me
Was there but one who—but of her anon.
I said with men, and with the thoughts of
        men,   60
I held but slight communion; but instead,
My joy was in the wilderness,—to breathe
The difficult air of the iced mountain's top,
Where the birds dare not build, nor in-
        sect's wing
Flit o'er the herbless granite; or to plunge
Into the torrent, and to roll along   66
On the swift whirl of the new breaking
        wave
Of river-stream, or ocean, in their flow.
In these my early strength exulted; or
To follow through the night the moving
        moon,   70
The stars and their development; or catch
The dazzling lightnings till my eyes grew
        dim;
Or to look, list'ning, on the scatter'd leaves,
While Autumn winds were at their evening
        song.   74
These were my pastimes, and to be alone;
For if the beings, of whom I was one,—
Hating to be so,—cross'd me in my path,
I felt myself degraded back to them,
And was all clay again. And then I dived,
In my lone wanderings, to the caves of
        death,   80
Searching its cause in its effect; and drew
From wither'd bones, and skulls, and
        heap'd up dust,

Conclusions most forbidden. Then I
  pass'd
The nights of years in sciences untaught,
Save in the old time; and with time and
  toil,   85
And terrible ordeal, and such penance
As in itself hath power upon the air,
And spirits that do compass air and earth,
Space, and the peopled infinite, I made
Mine eyes familiar with Eternity,   90
Such as, before me, did the Magi, and
He who from out their fountain dwellings
  raised
Eros and Anteros, at Gadara,
As I do thee;—and with my knowledge
  grew
The thirst of knowledge, and the power
  and joy   95
Of this most bright intelligence, until—
    Witch. Proceed.
    Man.   Oh! I but thus prolong'd
my words,
Boasting these idle attributes, because
As I approach the core of my heart's grief—
But to my task. I have not named to thee
Father or mother, mistress, friend, or
  being,   101
With whom I wore the chain of human
  ties;
If I had such, they seem'd not such to me;
Yet there was one—
    Witch.   Spare not thyself—proceed.
    Man. She was like me in lineaments;
her eyes,   105
Her hair, her features, all, to the very tone
Even of her voice, they said were like to
  mine;
But soften'd all, and temper'd into beauty:
She had the same lone thoughts and
  wanderings,
The quest of hidden knowledge, and a
  mind   110
To comprehend the universe: nor these
Alone, but with them gentler powers than
  mine,
Pity, and smiles, and tears—which I had
  not;
And tenderness—but that I had for her;
Humility—and that I never had.   115
Her faults were mine—her virtues were her
  own—
I loved her, and destroy'd her!
    Witch.   With thy hand?
    Man. Not with my hand, but heart,
which broke her heart;
It gazed on mine, and wither'd. I have
  shed
Blood, but not hers—and yet her blood
  was shed;   120
I saw—and could not stanch it.
    Witch.   And for this—
A being of the race thou dost despise,
The order, which thine own would rise
  above,

Mingling with us and ours,—thou dost
  forego
The gifts of our great knowledge, and
  shrink'st back   125
To recreant mortality—Away!
    Man. Daughter of Air! I tell thee, since
that hour—
But words are breath—look on me in my
  sleep,
Or watch my watchings—Come and sit by
  me!   129
My solitude is solitude no more,
But peopled with the Furies;—I have
  gnash'd
My teeth in darkness till returning morn,
Then cursed myself till sunset;—I have
  pray'd   133
For madness as a blessing—'tis denied me.
I have affronted death—but in the war
Of elements the waters shrunk from me,
And fatal things pass'd harmless; the cold
  hand
Of an all-pitiless demon held me back,
Back by a single hair, which would not
  break.   139
In fantasy, imagination, all
The affluence of my soul—which one day
  was
A Crœsus in creation—I plunged deep,
But, like an ebbing wave, it dash'd me
  back
Into the gulf of my unfathom'd thought.
I plunged amidst mankind—Forgetful-
  ness   145
I sought in all, save where 'tis to be found,
And that I have to learn; my sciences,
My long-pursued and superhuman art,
Is mortal here: I dwell in my despair—
And live—and live for ever.
    Witch.   It may be   150
That I can aid thee.
    Man.   To do this thy power
Must wake the dead, or lay me low with
  them.
Do so—in any shape—in any hour—
With any torture—so it be the last.
    Witch. That is not in my province;
  but if thou   155
Wilt swear obedience to my will, and do
My bidding, it may help thee to thy
  wishes.
    Man. I will not swear—Obey! and
whom? the spirits
Whose presence I command, and be the
  slave
Of those who served me—Never!
    Witch.   Is this all?   160
Hast thou no gentler answer?—Yet be-
  think thee,
And pause ere thou rejectest.
    Man.   I have said it.
    Witch. Enough! I may retire then—say!
    Man.   Retire!
                 [*The* WITCH *disappears.*

Man. [*alone*]. We are the fools of time
  and terror: Days   164
Steal on us, and steal from us; yet we live,
Loathing our life, and dreading still to die.
In all the days of this detested yoke—
This vital weight upon the struggling heart,
Which sinks with sorrow, or beats quick
  with pain,   169
Or joy that ends in agony or faintness—
In all the days of past and future, for
In life there is no present, we can number
How few—how less than few—wherein
  the soul
Forbears to pant for death, and yet draws
  back
As from a stream in winter, though the
  chill   175
Be but a moment's. I have one resource
Still in my science—I can call the dead,
And ask them what it is we dread to be:
The sternest answer can but be the Grave,
And that is nothing. If they answer
  not—   180
The buried Prophet answered to the Hag
Of Endor; and the Spartan Monarch drew
From the Byzantine maid's unsleeping
  spirit
An answer and his destiny—he slew
That which he loved, unknowing what he
  slew,   185
And died unpardon'd—though he call'd in
  aid
The Phyxian Jove, and in Phigalia roused
The Arcadian Evocators to compel
The indignant shadow to depose her wrath,
Or fix her term of vengeance—she replied
In words of dubious import, but fulfill'd.
If I had never lived, that which I love   192
Had still been living; had I never loved,
That which I love would still be beautiful,
Happy and giving happiness. What is she?
What is she now?—a sufferer for my sins—
A thing I dare not think upon—or nothing.
Within few hours I shall not call in vain:
Yet in this hour I dread the thing I dare:
Until this hour I never shrunk to gaze
On spirit, good or evil—now I tremble,
And feel a strange cold thaw upon my
  heart.   202
But I can act even what I most abhor,
And champion human fears.—The night
  approaches.   [*Exit.*

SCENE III.—*The Summit of the Jungfrau
  Mountain.*

Enter FIRST DESTINY.

The moon is rising broad, and round, and
  bright;
And here on snows, where never human
  foot
Of common mortal trod, we nightly tread,
And leave no traces: o'er the savage sea,
The glassy ocean of the mountain ice,   5
We skim its rugged breakers, which put on
The aspect of a tumbling tempest's foam,
Frozen in a moment—a dead whirlpool's
  image:
And this most steep fantastic pinnacle,
The fretwork of some earthquake—where
  the clouds   10
Pause to repose themselves in passing by—
Is sacred to our revels, or our vigils;
Here do I wait my sisters, on our way
To the Hall of Arimanes, for to-night
Is our great festival—'tis strange they
  come not.   15

A Voice without, singing.

The Captive Usurper,
  Hurl'd down from the throne,
Lay buried in torpor,
  Forgotten and lone;
I broke through his slumbers,   20
  I shiver'd his chain,
I leagued him with numbers—
  He's Tyrant again!
With the blood of a million he'll answer
  my care,
With a nation's destruction—his flight and
  despair.   25

Second Voice, without.

The ship sail'd on, the ship sail'd fast,
But I left not a sail, and I left not a mast;
There is not a plank of the hull or the deck,
And there is not a wretch to lament o'er his
  wreck;
Save one, whom I held, as he swam, by the
  hair,   30
And he was a subject well worthy my care;
A traitor on land, and a pirate at sea—
But I saved him to wreak further havoc for
  me!

FIRST DESTINY, *answering.*

The city lies sleeping;
  The morn, to deplore it,   35
May dawn on it weeping:
  Sullenly, slowly,
The black plague flew o'er it—
  Thousands lie lowly;
Tens of thousands shall perish;   40
  The living shall fly from
The sick they should cherish;
  But nothing can vanquish
The touch that they die from.
  Sorrow and anguish,   45
And evil and dread,
  Envelope a nation;
The blest are the dead,
Who see not the sight
  Of their own desolation;   50
This work of a night—
This wreck of a realm—this deed of my
  doing—
For ages I've done, and shall still be re-
  newing!

Enter the SECOND *and* THIRD DESTINIES.

The Three.

Our hands contain the hearts of men,
  Our footsteps are their graves;   55
We only give to take again
  The spirits of our slaves!

First Des. Welcome!—Where's Nemesis?
Second Des.   At some great work;
But what I know not, for my hands were
  full.   59
Third Des. Behold she cometh.

Enter NEMESIS.

First Des. Say, where hast thou been?
My sisters and thyself are slow to-night.
  Nem. I was detain'd repairing shatter'd
    thrones,
Marrying fools, restoring dynasties,
Avenging men upon their enemies,
And making them repent their own re-
  venge;   65
Goading the wise to madness; from the
  dull
Shaping out oracles to rule the world
Afresh, for they were waxing out of date,
And mortals dared to ponder for them-
  selves,
To weigh kings in the balance, and to
  speak   70
Of freedom, the forbidden fruit.—Away!
We have outstay'd the hour—mount we
  our clouds!   [*Exeunt.*

SCENE IV.—*The Hall of Arimanes—*
Arimanes on his Throne, a Globe of
Fire, surrounded by the Spirits.

Hymn of the SPIRITS.

Hail to our Master!—Prince of Earth and
  Air!
  Who walks the clouds and waters—in
    his hand
The sceptre of the elements, which tear
  Themselves to chaos at his high com-
    mand!
He breatheth—and a tempest shakes the
  sea;   5
He speaketh—and the clouds reply in
  thunder;
He gazeth—from his glance the sunbeams
  flee;
He moveth—earthquakes rend the
  world asunder.
Beneath his footsteps the volcanoes rise;
  His shadow is the Pestilence; his path
The comets herald through the crackling
  skies;   11
  And planets turn to ashes at his wrath.
To him War offers daily sacrifice;
  To him Death pays his tribute; Life is
    his,

With all its infinite agonies—   15
  And his the spirit of whatever is!

Enter the DESTINIES *and* NEMESIS.

First Des. Glory to Arimanes! on the
  earth
His power increaseth—both my sisters did
His bidding, nor did I neglect my duty!
  Second Des. Glory to Arimanes! we
    who bow   20
The necks of men, bow down before his
  throne!
  Third Des. Glory to Arimanes! we
    await
His nod!
  Nem. Sovereign of Sovereigns! we are
    thine,
And all that liveth, more or less, is ours,
And most things wholly so; still to in-
  crease   25
Our power, increasing thine, demands our
  care,
And we are vigilant. Thy late commands
Have been fulfill'd to the utmost.

Enter MANFRED.

A Spirit.   What is here?
A mortal!—Thou most rash and fatal
  wretch,   29
Bow down and worship!
  Second Spirit.   I do know the man—
A Magian of great power, and fearful skill!
  Third Spirit. Bow down and worship,
    slave!—
           What, know'st thou not
Thine and our Sovereign?—Tremble, and
  obey!
  All the Spirits. Prostrate thyself, and thy
    condemned clay,
Child of the Earth! or dread the worst.
  Man.   I know it;
And yet ye see I kneel not.
  Fourth Spirit.   'Twill be taught thee.
  Man. 'Tis taught already;—many a
    night on the earth,
On the bare ground, have I bow'd down
  my face,
And strew'd my head with ashes; I have
  known
The fulness of humiliation, for   40
I sunk before my vain despair, and knelt
To my own desolation.
  Fifth Spirit.   Dost thou dare
Refuse to Arimanes on his throne
What the whole earth accords, beholding
  not
The terror of his glory?—Crouch, I say.
  Man. Bid *him* bow down to that which
    is above him,   46
The overruling Infinite—the Maker
Who made him not for worship—let him
  kneel,
And we will kneel together.
  The Spirits.   Crush the worm!

Tear him in pieces!—
 First Des. Hence! avaunt!—he's mine.
Prince of the Powers invisible! This man
Is of no common order, as his port 52
And presence here denote; his sufferings
Have been of an immortal nature, like
Our own; his knowledge, and his powers
 and will, 55
As far as is compatible with clay,
Which clogs the ethereal essence, have
 been such
As clay hath seldom borne; his aspirations
Have been beyond the dwellers of the earth,
And they have only taught him what we
 know— 60
That knowledge is not happiness, and
 science
But an exchange of ignorance for that
Which is another kind of ignorance.
This is not all—the passions, attributes
Of earth and heaven, from which no power,
 nor being, 65
Nor breath from the worm upwards is
 exempt,
Have pierced his heart, and in their con-
 sequence
Made him a thing which I, who pity not,
Yet pardon those who pity. He is mine,
And thine, it may be; be it so, or not,
No other Spirit in this region hath 71
A soul like his—or power upon his soul.
 Nem. What doth he here then?
 First Des. Let him answer that.
 Man. Ye know what I have known; and
 without power
I could not be amongst ye: but there are
Powers deeper still beyond—I come in
 quest 76
Of such, to answer unto what I seek.
 Nem. What wouldst thou?
 Man. Thou canst not reply to me.
Call up the dead—my question is for them.
 Nem. Great Arimanes, doth thy will
 avouch 80
The wishes of this mortal?
 Ari. Yea.
 Nem. Whom wouldst thou
Uncharnel?
 Man. One without a tomb—call up
Astarte.

    NEMESIS.

Shadow! or Spirit!
 Whatever thou art, 85
Which still doth inherit
 The whole or a part
Of the form of thy birth,
 Of the mould of thy clay,
Which return'd to the earth, 90
 Re-appear to the day!
Bear what thou borest,
 The heart and the form,
And the aspect thou worest
 Redeem from the worm. 95

Appear!—Appear!—Appear!
Who sent thee there requires thee here!
 [*The Phantom of* ASTARTE *rises and
 stands in the midst.*
 Man. Can this be death? there's bloom
 upon her cheek;
But now I see it is no living hue,
But a strange hectic—like the unnatural
 red 100
Which Autumn plants upon the perish'd
 leaf.
It is the same! Oh, God! that I should
 dread
To look upon the same—Astarte!—No,
I cannot speak to her—but bid her speak—
Forgive me or condemn me. 105

    NEMESIS.

By the power which hath broken
 The grave which enthrall'd thee,
Speak to him, who hath spoken,
 Or those who have call'd thee!

 Man. She is silent, 110
And in that silence I am more than
 answer'd.
 Nem. My power extends no further.
 Prince of Air!
It rests with thee alone—command her
 voice.
 Ari. Spirit—obey this sceptre!
 Nem. Silent still!
She is not of our order, but belongs 115
To the other powers. Mortal! thy quest
 is vain,
And we are baffled also.
 Man. Hear me, hear me—
Astarte! my beloved! speak to me:
I have so much endured—so much en-
 dure—
Look on me! the grave hath not changed
 thee more 120
Than I am changed for thee. Thou lovedst
 me
Too much, as I loved thee: we were not
 made
To torture thus each other, though it were
The deadliest sin to love as we have loved.
Say that thou loath'st me not—that I do
 bear 125
This punishment for both—that thou wilt
 be
One of the blessed—and that I shall die;
For hitherto all hateful things conspire
To bind me in existence—in a life
Which makes me shrink from immortal-
 ity— 130
A future like the past. I cannot rest.
I know not what I ask, nor what I seek:
I feel but what thou art, and what I am;
And I would hear yet once before I perish
The voice which was my music—Speak to
 me! 135
For I have call'd on thee in the still night,

Startled the slumbering birds from the
   hush'd boughs,
And woke the mountain wolves, and made
   the caves
Acquainted with thy vainly echoed name,
Which answer'd me—many things an-
   swer'd me—   140
Spirits and men—but thou wert silent all.
Yet speak to me! I have outwatch'd the
   stars,
And gazed o'er heaven in vain in search of
   thee.
Speak to me! I have wander'd o'er the
   earth,
And never found thy likeness—Speak to
   me!   145
Look on the fiends around—they feel for
   me:
I fear them not, and feel for thee alone—
Speak to me! though it be in wrath;—but
   say—
I reck not what—but let me hear thee
   once—
This once—once more!
  Phantom of Astarte. Manfred!
  Man.   Say on, say on—   150
I live but in the sound—it is thy voice!
  Phan. Manfred! To-morrow ends
   thine earthly ills.
Farewell!
  Man. Yet one word more—am I for-
   given?
  Phan. Farewell!
  Man.   Say, shall we meet again?
  Phan.   Farewell!
  Man. One word for mercy! Say, thou
   lovest me.   155
  Phan. Manfred!
    [*The Spirit of* ASTARTE *disappears.*
  Nem. She's gone, and will not be re-
   call'd;
Her words will be fulfill'd. Return to the
   earth.
  A Spirit. He is convulsed.—This is to
   be a mortal
And seek the things beyond mortality.
  Another Spirit. Yet, see, he mastereth
   himself, and makes   160
His torture tributary to his will.
Had he been one of us, he would have
   made
An awful spirit.
  Nem.   Hast thou further question
Of our great sovereign, or his worship-
   pers?
  Man. None.
  Nem. Then, for a time, farewell. 165
  Man. We meet then! Where? On the
   earth?—
Even as thou wilt: and for the grace ac-
   corded
I now depart a debtor. Fare ye well!
                   [*Exit* MANFRED.
    (*Scene closes.*)

ACT III

SCENE I.—*A Hall in the Castle of Manfred.*

MANFRED *and* HERMAN.

  Man. What is the hour?
  Her.   It wants but one till sunset,
And promises a lovely twilight.
  Man.   Say,
Are all things so disposed of in the tower
As I directed?
  Her.   All, my lord, are ready:
Here is the key and casket.
  Man.   It is well: 5
Thou may'st retire.   [*Exit* HERMAN.
  Man. [*alone*]. There is a calm upon
   me—
Inexplicable stillness! which till now
Did not belong to what I knew of life.
If that I did not know philosophy 9
To be of all our vanities the motliest,
The merest word that ever fool'd the ear
From out the schoolman's jargon, I should
   deem
The golden secret, the sought 'Kalon',
   found,
And seated in my soul. It will not last,
But it is well to have known it, though but
   once: 15
It hath enlarged my thoughts with a new
   sense,
And I within my tablets would note down
That there is such a feeling. Who is there?

Re-enter HERMAN.

  Her. My lord, the abbot of St. Maurice
   craves
To greet your presence.

Enter the ABBOT OF ST. MAURICE.

  Abbot. Peace be with Count Manfred!
  Man. Thanks, holy father! welcome
   to these walls;   21
Thy presence honours them, and blesseth
   those
Who dwell within them.
  Abbot.   Would it were so, Count!—
But I would fain confer with thee alone.
  Man. Herman, retire.—What would
   my reverend guest?   25
  Abbot. Thus, without prelude:—Age
   and zeal, my office,
And good intent, must plead my privilege;
Our near, though not acquainted neigh-
   bourhood,
May also be my herald. Rumours strange,
And of unholy nature, are abroad,   30
And busy with thy name; a noble name
For centuries: may he who bears it now
Transmit it unimpair'd!
  Man.   Proceed,—I listen.
  Abbot. 'Tis said thou holdest converse
   with the things   34
Which are forbidden to the search of man;

That with the dwellers of the dark abodes,
The many evil and unheavenly spirits
Which walk the valley of the shade of
    death,
Thou communest. I know that with man-
    kind,   39
Thy fellows in creation, thou dost rarely
Exchange thy thoughts, and that thy soli-
    tude
Is as an anchorite's, were it but holy.
  Man. And what are they who do avouch
    these things?
  Abbot. My pious brethren—the scared
    peasantry—
Even thy own vassals—who do look on
    thee   45
With most unquiet eyes. Thy life's in
    peril.
  Man. Take it.
  Abbot. I come to save, and not destroy:
I would not pry into thy secret soul;
But if these things be sooth, there still is
    time
For penitence and pity: reconcile thee
With the true church, and through the
    church to heaven.   51
  Man. I hear thee. This is my reply:
    whate'er
I may have been, or am, doth rest between
Heaven and myself. I shall not choose a
    mortal
To be my mediator. Have I sinn'd   55
Against your ordinances? prove and
    punish!
  Abbot. My son! I did not speak of
    punishment,
But penitence and pardon;—with thyself
The choice of such remains—and for the
    last,   59
Our institutions and our strong belief
Have given me power to smooth the path
    from sin
To higher hope and better thoughts; the
    first
I leave to heaven,—'Vengeance is mine
    alone!'
So saith the Lord, and with all humbleness
His servant echoes back the awful word.
  Man. Old man! there is no power in
    holy'men,   66
Nor charm in prayer, nor purifying form
Of penitence, nor outward look, nor fast,
Nor agony—nor, greater than all these,
The innate tortures of that deep despair,
Which is remorse without the fear of
    hell,   71
But all in all sufficient to itself
Would make a hell of heaven—can exor-
    cise
From out the unbounded spirit the quick
    sense
Of its own sins, wrongs, sufferance, and
    revenge   75
Upon itself; there is no future pang

Can deal that justice on the self-condemn'd
He deals on his own soul.
  Abbot.   All this is well;
For this will pass away, and be succeeded
By an auspicious hope, which shall look up
With calm assurance to that blessed place,
Which all who seek may win, whatever be
Their earthly errors, so they be atoned:
And the commencement of atonement is
The sense of its necessity. Say on—   85
And all our church can teach thee shall be
    taught;
And all we can absolve thee shall be par-
    don'd.
  Man. When Rome's sixth emperor was
    near his last,
The victim of a self-inflicted wound,
To shun the torments of a public death
From senates once his slaves, a certain
    soldier,   91
With show of loyal pity, would have
    stanch'd
The gushing throat with his officious robe;
The dying Roman thrust him back, and
    said—   94
Some empire still in his expiring glance—
'It is too late—is this fidelity?'
  Abbot. And what of this?
  Man.   I answer with the Roman—
'It is too late!'
  Abbot.   It never can be so,
To reconcile thyself with thy own soul,
And thy own soul with heaven. Hast thou
    no hope?   100
'Tis strange—even those who do despair
    above,
Yet shape themselves some fantasy on
    earth,
To which frail twig they cling, like drown-
    ing men.
  Man. Ay—father! I have had those
    earthly visions,   104
And noble aspirations in my youth,
To make my own the mind of other men,
The enlightener of nations; and to rise
I knew not whither—it might be to fall;
But fall, even as the mountain-cataract,
Which having leapt from its more dazzling
    height,   110
Even in the foaming strength of its abyss,
(Which casts up misty columns that be-
    come
Clouds raining from the re-ascended skies,)
Lies low but mighty still.—But this is past,
My thoughts mistook themselves.
  Abbot.   And wherefore so? 115
  Man. I could not tame my nature down;
    for he
Must serve who fain would sway; and
    soothe, and sue,
And watch all time, and pry into all place,
And be a living lie, who would become
A mighty thing amongst the mean, and
    such   120

The mass are; I disdain'd to mingle with
A herd, though to be leader—and of
    wolves.
The lion is alone, and so am I.

   Abbot. And why not live and act with
    other men?

   Man. Because my nature was averse
    from life;   125
And yet not cruel; for I would not make,
But find a desolation. Like the wind,
The red-hot breath of the most lone
    simoom,
Which dwells but in the desert, and sweeps
    o'er
The barren sands which bear no shrubs to
    blast,   130
And revels o'er their wild and arid waves,
And seeketh not, so that it is not sought,
But being met is deadly,—such hath been
The course of my existence; but there came
Things in my path which are no more.

   Abbot.   Alas! 135
I 'gin to fear that thou art past all aid
From me and from my calling; yet so
    young,
I still would—

   Man.   Look on me! there is an order
Of mortals on the earth, who do become
Old in their youth, and die ere middle age,
Without the violence of warlike death;
Some perishing of pleasure, some of study,
Some worn with toil, some of mere weari-
    ness,
Some of disease, and some insanity,
And some of wither'd or of broken hearts;
For this last is a malady which slays 146
More than are number'd in the lists of
    Fate,
Taking all shapes, and bearing many
    names.
Look upon me! for even of all these things
Have I partaken; and of all these things,
One were enough; then wonder not that I
Am what I am, but that I ever was,   152
Or having been, that I am still on earth.

   Abbot. Yet, hear me still——

   Man.   Old man! I do respect
Thine order, and revere thine years; I deem
Thy purpose pious, but it is in vain: 156
Think me not churlish; I would spare thy-
    self,
Far more than me, in shunning at this time
All further colloquy—and so—farewell.

               [*Exit* MANFRED.

   Abbot. This should have been a noble
    creature: he   160
Hath all the energy which would have made
A goodly frame of glorious elements,
Had they been wisely mingled; as it is,
It is an awful chaos—light and darkness,
And mind and dust, and passions and pure
    thoughts   165
Mix'd, and contending without end or
    order,—

All dormant or destructive: he will perish,
And yet he must not; I will try once more,
For such are worth redemption; and my
    duty   169
Is to dare all things for a righteous end.
I'll follow him—but cautiously, though
    surely.   [*Exit* ABBOT.

     SCENE II.—*Another Chamber.*

     MANFRED *and* HERMAN.

   Her. My lord, you bade me wait on you
    at sunset:
He sinks behind the mountain.

   Man.   Doth he so?
I will look on him. [MANFRED *advances
    to the window of the Hall.*
        Glorious Orb! the idol
Of early nature, and the vigorous race
Of undiseased mankind, the giant sons   5
Of the embrace of angels, with a sex
More beautiful than they, which did draw
    down
The erring spirits who can ne'er return.—
Most glorious orb! that wert a worship, ere
The mystery of thy making was reveal'd!
Thou earliest minister of the Almighty,
Which gladden'd, on their mountain tops,
    the hearts   12
Of the Chaldean shepherds, till they pour'd
Themselves in orisons! Thou material
    God!
And representative of the Unknown—
Who chose thee for his shadow! Thou chief
    star!   16
Centre of many stars! which mak'st our
    earth
Endurable, and temperest the hues
And hearts of all who walk within thy rays!
Sire of the seasons! Monarch of the climes,
And those who dwell in them! for near or
    far,   21
Our inborn spirits have a tint of thee
Even as our outward aspects;—thou dost
    rise,
And shine, and set in glory. Fare thee well!
I ne'er shall see thee more. As my first
    glance   25
Of love and wonder was for thee, then take
My latest look; thou wilt not beam on one
To whom the gifts of life and warmth have
    been
Of a more fatal nature. He is gone:
I follow.   [*Exit* MANFRED.

SCENE III.—*The Mountains—The Castle
   of Manfred at some distance—A
   Terrace before a Tower—Time, Twilight.*

HERMAN, MANUEL, *and other Dependants
   of* MANFRED.

   Her. 'Tis strange enough; night after
    night, for years,

He hath pursued long vigils in this tower,
Without a witness. I have been within it,—
So have we all been oft-times; but from it,
Or its contents, it were impossible 5
To draw conclusions absolute, of aught
His studies tend to. To be sure, there is
One chamber where none enter: I would
give
The fee of what I have to come these three
years,
To pore upon its mysteries.
    Manuel.   'Twere dangerous; 10
Content thyself with what thou know'st
already.
    Her. Ah! Manuel! thou art elderly and
wise,
And couldst say much; thou hast dwelt
within the castle—
How many years is't?
    Manuel.   Ere Count Manfred's birth,
I served his father, whom he nought re-
sembles. 15
    Her. There be more sons in like pre-
dicament.
But wherein do they differ?
    Manuel.   I speak not
Of features or of form, but mind and
habits;
Count Sigismund was proud, but gay and
free,—
A warrior and a reveller; he dwelt not
With books and solitude, nor made the
night 21
A gloomy vigil, but a festal time,
Merrier than day; he did not walk the
rocks
And forests like a wolf, nor turn aside
From men and their delights.
    Her.   Beshrew the hour, 25
But those were jocund times! I would that
such
Would visit the old walls again; they look
As if they had forgotten them.
    Manuel.   These walls
Must change their chieftain first. Oh! I
have seen
Some strange things in them, Herman.
    Her.   Come, be friendly; 30
Relate me some to while away our watch:
I've heard thee darkly speak of an event
Which happen'd hereabouts, by this same
tower.
    Manuel. That was a night indeed! I do
remember
'Twas twilight, as it may be now, and such
Another evening;—yon red cloud, which
rests 36
On Eigher's pinnacle, so rested then,
So like that it might be the same; the wind
Was faint and gusty, and the mountain
snows
Began to glitter with the climbing moon;
Count Manfred was, as now, within his
tower,— 41

How occupied, we knew not, but with him
The sole companion of his wanderings
And watchings—her, whom of all earthly
things
That lived, the only thing he seem'd to
love,— 45
As he, indeed, by blood was bound to do,
The lady Astarte, his—
                Hush! who comes here?

Enter the ABBOT.

    Abbot. Where is your master?
    Her.   Yonder in the tower.
    Abbot. I must speak with him.
    Manuel.   'Tis impossible;
He is most private, and must not be thus
Intruded on.
    Abbot.   Upon myself I take
The forfeit of my fault, if fault there be—
But I must see him.
    Her.   Thou hast seen him once
This eve already.
    Abbot.   Herman! I command thee,
Knock, and apprize the Count of my ap-
proach. 55
    Her. We dare not.
    Abbot.   Then it seems I must be herald
Of my own purpose.
    Manuel.   Reverend father, stop—
I pray you pause.
    Abbot.   Why so?
    Manuel.   But step this way,
And I will tell you further.   [*Exeunt.*

SCENE IV.—*Interior of the Tower.*

MANFRED *alone.*

The stars are forth, the moon above the
tops
Of the snow-shining mountains.—Beauti-
ful!
I linger yet with Nature, for the Night
Hath been to me a more familiar face
Than that of man; and in her starry shade
Of dim and solitary loveliness, 6
I learn'd the language of another world.
I do remember me, that in my youth,
When I was wandering,—upon such a night
I stood within the Coliseum's wall, 10
'Midst the chief relics of almighty Rome;
The trees which grew along the broken
arches
Waved dark in the blue midnight, and the
stars
Shone through the rents of ruin; from afar
The watch-dog bay'd beyond the Tiber;
and 15
More near from out the Cæsars' palace
came
The owl's long cry, and, interruptedly,
Of distant sentinels the fitful song
Begun and died upon the gentle wind.
Some cypresses beyond the time-worn
breach 20

Appear'd to skirt the horizon, yet they
    stood
Within a bowshot. Where the Cæsars
    dwelt,
And dwell the tuneless birds of night, amidst
A grove which springs through levell'd
    battlements,
And twines its roots with the imperial
    hearths,   25
Ivy usurps the laurel's place of growth;
But the gladiators' bloody Circus stands,
A noble wreck in ruinous perfection,
While Cæsar's chambers, and the Augus-
    tan halls,
Grovel on earth in indistinct decay.   30
And thou didst shine, thou rolling moon,
    upon
All this, and cast a wide and tender light,
Which soften'd down the hoar austerity
Of rugged desolation, and fill'd up,   34
As 'twere anew, the gaps of centuries;
Leaving that beautiful which still was so,
And making that which was not, till the
    place
Became religion, and the heart ran o'er
With silent worship of the great of old,—
The dead but sceptred sovereigns, who still
    rule   40
Our spirits from their urns.

                 'Twas such a night!
'Tis strange that I recall it at this time;
But I have found our thoughts take wildest
    flight
Even at the moment when they should array
Themselves in pensive order.

       Enter the ABBOT.

  Abbot.   My good lord!   45
I crave a second grace for this approach;
But yet let not my humble zeal offend
By its abruptness—all it hath of ill
Recoils on me; its good in the effect
May light upon your head—could I say
    heart,   50
Could I touch *that*, with words or prayers,
    I should
Recall a noble spirit which hath wander'd;
But is not yet all lost.
  Man.   Thou know'st me not;
My days are number'd, and my deeds re-
    corded: 54
Retire, or 'twill be dangerous—Away!
  Abbot.   Thou dost not mean to menace
    me?
  Man.   Not I;
I simply tell thee peril is at hand,
And would preserve thee.
  Abbot.   What dost thou mean?
  Man.   Look there!
What dost thou see?
  Abbot.   Nothing.
  Man.   Look there I say,
And steadfastly;—now tell me what thou
    seest?   60

  Abbot.   That which should shake me,
    but I fear it not:
I see a dusk and awful figure rise,
Like an infernal god, from out the earth;
His face wrapt in a mantle, and his form
Robed as with angry clouds: he stands be-
    tween   65
Thyself and me—but I do fear him not.
  Man. Thou hast no cause—he shall
    not harm thee—but
His sight may shock thine old limbs into
    palsy.
I say to thee—Retire!
  Abbot.   And I reply—
Never—till I have battled with this
    fiend:—   70
What doth he here?
  Man. Why—ay—what doth he here?
I did not send for him,—he is unbidden.
  Abbot. Alas! lost mortal! what with
    guests like these
Hast thou to do? I tremble for thy sake:
Why doth he gaze on thee, and thou on
    him?   75
Ah! he unveils his aspect: on his brow
The thunder-scars are graven: from his eye
Glares forth the immortality of hell—
Avaunt!—
  Man. Pronounce—what is thy mission?
  Spirit.   Come!
  Abbot. What art thou, unknown be-
    ing? answer!—speak!   80
  Spirit. The genius of this mortal.—
    Come! 'tis time.
  Man. I am prepared for all things, but
    deny
The power which summons me. Who sent
    thee here?
  Spirit. Thou'lt know anon—Come!
    come!
  Man.   I have commanded
Things of an essence greater far than
    thine,   85
And striven with thy masters. Get thee
    hence!
  Spirit. Mortal! thine hour is come—
    Away! I say.
  Man. I knew, and know my hour is
    come, but not
To render up my soul to such as thee:
Away! I'll die as I have lived—alone. 90
  Spirit. Then I must summon up my
    brethren.—Rise!

              [*Other Spirits rise up.*
  Abbot. Avaunt! ye evil ones!—
    Avaunt! I say;
Ye have no power where piety hath power,
And I do charge ye in the name——
  Spirit.   Old man!
We know ourselves, our mission, and
    thine order;   95
Waste not thy holy words on idle uses,
It were in vain: this man is forfeited.
Once more I summon him—Away! Away!

Man. I do defy ye,—though I feel my soul 99
Is ebbing from me, yet I do defy ye;
Nor will I hence, while I have earthly breath
To breathe my scorn upon ye—earthly strength
To wrestle, though with spirits; what ye take 103
Shall be ta'en limb by limb.
    Spirit.   Reluctant mortal!
Is this the Magian who would so pervade
The world invisible, and make himself
Almost our equal? Can it be that thou
Art thus in love with life? the very life
Which made thee wretched!
    Man.   Thou false fiend, thou liest!
My life is in its last hour,—*that* I know,
Nor would redeem a moment of that hour;
I do not combat against death, but thee
And thy surrounding angels; my past power, 113
Was purchased by no compact with thy crew,
But by superior science—penance, daring,
And length of watching, strength of mind, and skill 116
In knowledge of our fathers—when the earth
Saw men and spirits walking side by side,
And gave ye no supremacy: I stand 119
Upon my strength—I do defy—deny—
Spurn back, and scorn ye!—
    Spirit.   But thy many crimes
Have made thee———
    Man.   What are they to such as thee?
Must crimes be punish'd but by other crimes, 123
And greater criminals?—Back to thy hell!
Thou hast no power upon me, *that* I feel;
Thou never shalt possess me, *that* I know:
What I have done is done; I bear within
A torture which could nothing gain from thine; 128

The mind which is immortal makes itself
Requital for its good or evil thoughts,—
Is its own origin of ill and end— 131
And its own place and time: its innate sense,
When stripp'd of this mortality, derives
No colour from the fleeting things without,
But is absorb'd in sufferance or in joy,
Born from the knowledge of its own desert. 136
Thou didst not tempt me, and thou couldst not tempt me;
I have not been thy dupe, nor am thy prey—
But was my own destroyer, and will be
My own hereafter.—Back, ye baffled fiends!— 140
The hand of death is on me—but not yours!
    [*The Demons disappear.*
    Abbot. Alas! how pale thou art—thy lips are white—
And thy breast heaves—and in thy gasping throat
The accents rattle: Give thy prayers to heaven—
Pray—albeit but in thought,—but die not thus. 145
    Man. 'Tis over—my dull eyes can fix thee not;
But all things swim around me, and the earth
Heaves as it were beneath me. Fare thee well!
Give me thy hand.
    Abbot. Cold—cold—even to the heart—
But yet one prayer—Alas! how fares it with thee? 150
    Man. Old man! 'tis not so difficult to die. [MANFRED *expires.*
    Abbot. He's gone—his soul hath ta'en its earthless flight;
Whither? I dread to think—but he is gone.

MARINO FALIERO, DOGE OF VENICE

AN HISTORICAL TRAGEDY IN FIVE ACTS

'*Dux* inquieti turbidus Adriæ.'—HORACE.

PREFACE

THE conspiracy of the Doge Marino Faliero is one of the most remarkable events in the annals of the most singular government, city, and people of modern history. It occurred in the year 1355. Everything about Venice is, or was, extraordinary—her aspect is like a dream, and her history is like a romance. The story of this Doge is to be found in all her Chronicles, and particularly detailed in the 'Lives of the Doges,' by Marin Sanuto, which is given in the Appendix. It is simply and clearly related, and is perhaps more dramatic in itself than any scenes which can be founded upon the subject.

Marino Faliero appears to have been a man of talents and of courage. I find him commander-in-chief of the land forces at the siege of Zara, where he beat the King of Hungary and his army of eighty thousand men, killing eight thousand men, and keeping the besieged at the same time in check; an exploit to which I know none similar in history, except that of Cæsar at Alesia, and of Prince Eugene at Belgrade. He was afterwards commander of the fleet in the same war. He took Capo d'Istria. He was ambassador at Genoa and Rome,—at which last he received the news of his election to the dukedom; his absence being a proof that he sought it by no intrigue, since he was apprised of his predecessor's death and his own succession at the same moment. But he appears to have been of an ungovernable temper. A story is told by Sanuto, of his having, many years before, when podesta and captain at Treviso, boxed the ears of the bishop, who was somewhat tardy in bringing the Host. For this, honest Sanuto 'saddles him with a judgment,' as Thwackum did Square; but he does not tell us whether he was punished or rebuked by the Senate for this outrage at the time of its commission. He seems, indeed, to have been afterwards at peace with the church, for we find him ambassador at Rome, and invested with the fief of Val di Marino, in the march of Treviso, and with the title of count, by Lorenzo Count-bishop of Ceneda. For these facts my authorities are Sanuto, Vettor Sandi, Andrea Navagero, and the account of the siege of Zara, first published by the indefatigable Abate Morelli, in his 'Monumenti Veneziani di varia Letteratura,' printed in 1796, all of which I have looked over in the original language. The moderns, Darù, Sismondi, and Laugier, nearly agree with the ancient chroniclers. Sismondi attributes the conspiracy to his *jealousy*; but I find this nowhere asserted by the national historians. Vettor Sandi, indeed, says, that 'Altri scrissero che . . . . dalla gelosa suspizion di esso Doge siasi fatto (Michel Steno) staccar con violenza,' &c. &c.; but this appears to have been by no means the general opinion, nor is it alluded to by Sanuto, or by Navagero: and Sandi himself adds, a moment after, that 'per altre Veneziane memorie traspiri, che non il *solo* desiderio di vendetta lo dispose alla congiura ma anche la innata abituale ambizion sua, per cui anelava a farsi principe independente.' The first motive appears to have been excited by the gross affront of the words written by Michel Steno on the ducal chair, and by the light and inadequate sentence of the Forty on the offender, who was one of their 'tre Capi.' The attentions of Steno himself appear to have been directed towards one of her damsels, and not to the 'Dogaressa' herself, against whose fame not the slightest insinuation appears, while she is praised for her beauty, and remarked for her youth. Neither do I find it asserted (unless the hint of Sandi be an assertion), that the Doge was actuated by jealousy of his wife; but rather by respect for her, and for his own honour, warranted by his past services and present dignity.

I know not that the historical facts are alluded to in English, unless by Dr. Moore in his View of Italy. His account is false and flippant, full of stale jests about old men and young wives, and wondering at so great an effect from so slight a cause. How so acute and severe an observer of mankind as the author of Zeluco could wonder at this is inconceivable. He knew that a basin of water spilt on Mrs. Masham's gown deprived the Duke of Marlborough of his command, and led to the inglorious peace of Utrecht—that Louis XIV. was plunged into the most desolating wars, because his minister was nettled at his finding fault with a window, and wished to give him another occupation—that Helen lost Troy—that Lucretia expelled the Tarquins from Rome—and that Cava brought the Moors to Spain—that an insulted husband led the Gauls to Clusium, and thence to Rome—that a single verse of Frederick II. of Prussia on the Abbé de Bernis, and a jest on Madame de Pompadour, led to the battle of Rosbach—that the elopement of Dearbhorgil with Mac Murchad conducted the English to the slavery of Ireland—that a personal pique between Maria Antoinette and the Duke of Orleans precipitated the first expulsion of the Bourbons—and, not to multiply instances, that Commodus, Domitian, and Caligula fell victims not to their public tyranny, but to private vengeance—and that an order to make Cromwell disembark from the ship in which he would have sailed to America destroyed both King and Commonwealth. After these instances, on the least reflection, it is indeed extraordinary in Dr. Moore to seem surprised that a man used to command, who had served and swayed in the most important offices, should fiercely resent, in a fierce age, an unpunished affront, the grossest that can be offered to a man, be he prince or peasant. The age of Faliero is little to the purpose, unless to favour it—

'The young man's wrath is like straw on fire,
But like red-hot steel is the old man's ire.'

'Young men soon give and soon forget affronts,
Old age is slow at both.'

Laugier's reflections are more philosophical:—'Tale fù il fine ignominioso di un' uomo, che la sua

407

MARINO FALIERO, DOGE OF VENICE

nascità, la sua età, il suo carattere dovevano tener lontano dalle passioni produttrici di grandi delitti. I suoi *talenti* per lungo tempo esercitati ne' maggiori impieghi, la sua capacità sperimentata ne' governi e nelle ambasciate, gli avevano acquistato la stima e la fiducia de' cittadini, ed avevano uniti i suffragj per collocarlo alla testa della repubblica. Innalzato ad un grado che terminava gloriosamente la sua vita, il resentimento di un' ingiuria leggiera insinuò nel suo cuore tal veleno che bastò a corrompere le antiche sue qualità, e a condurlo al termine dei scellerati; serio esempio, che prova *non esservi età, in cui la prudenza umana sia sicura, e che nell' uomo restano sempre passioni capaci a disonorarlo, quando non invigili sopra se stesso*.'

Where did Dr. Moore find that Marino Faliero begged his life? I have searched the chroniclers, and find nothing of the kind: it is true that he avowed it. He was conducted to the place of torture, but there is no mention made of any application for mercy on his part; and the very circumstance of their having taken him to the rack seems to argue anything but his having shown a want of firmness, which would doubtless have been also mentioned by those minute historians, who by no means favour him: such, indeed, would be contrary to his character as a soldier, to the age in which he lived, and *at* which he died, as it is to the truth of history. I know no justification, at any distance of time, for calumniating an historical character: surely truth belongs to the dead, and to the unfortunate: and they who have died upon a scaffold have generally had faults enough of their own, without a⁺tributing to them that which the very incurring of the perils which conducted them to their violent death renders, of all others, the most improbable. The black veil which is painted over the place of Marino Faliero amongst the Doges, and the Giants' Staircase where he was crowned, and disanowned, and decapitated, struck forcibly upon my imagination; as did his fiery character and strange story. I went, in 1819, in search of his tomb more than once to the church San Giovanni e San Paolo; and, as I was standing before the monument of another family, a priest came up to me and said, 'I can show you finer monuments than that.' I told him that I was in search of that of the Faliero family, and particularly of the Doge Marino's. 'Oh,' said he, 'I will show it you'; and conducting me to the outside, pointed out a sarcophagus in the wall with an illegible inscription. He said that it had been in a convent adjoining, but was removed after the French came, and placed in its present situation; that he had seen the tomb opened at its removal; there were still some bones remaining, but no positive vestige of the decapitation. The equestrian statue of which I have made mention in the third act as before that church is not, however, of a Faliero, but of some other now obsolete warrior, although of a later date. There were two other Doges of this family prior to Marino; Ordelafo, who fell in battle at Zara, in 1117 (where his descendant afterwards conquered the Huns), and Vital Faliero, who reigned in 1082. The family, originally from Fano, was of the most illustrious in blood and wealth in the city of once the most wealthy and still the most ancient families in Europe. The length I have gone into on this subject will show the interest I have taken in it. Whether I have succeeded or not in the tragedy, I have at least transferred into our language an historical fact worthy of commemoration.

It is now four years that I have meditated this work; and before I had sufficiently examined the records, I was rather disposed to have made it turn on a jealousy in Faliero. But, perceiving no foundation for this in historical truth, and aware that jealousy is an exhausted passion in the drama, I have given it a more historical form. I was, besides, well advised by the late Matthew Lewis on that point, in talking with him of my intention at Venice in 1817. 'If you make him jealous,' said he, 'recollect that you have to contend with established writers, to say nothing of Shakspeare, and an exhausted subject:—stick to the old fiery Doge's natural character, which will bear you out, if properly drawn: and make your plot as regular as you can.' Sir William Drummond gave me nearly the same counsel. How far I have followed these instructions, or whether they have availed me, is not for me to decide. I have had no view to the stage; in its present state it is, perhaps, not a very exalted object of ambition; besides, I have been too much behind the scenes to have thought it so at any time. And I cannot conceive any man of irritable feeling putting himself at the mercies of an audience. The sneering reader, and the loud critic, and the tart review, are scattered and distant calamities; but the trampling of an intelligent or of an ignorant audience on a production which, be it good or bad, has been a mental labour to the writer, is a palpable and immediate grievance, heightened by a man's doubt of their competency to judge, and his certainty of his own imprudence in electing them his judges. Were I capable of writing a play which could be deemed stage-worthy, success would give me no pleasure, and failure great pain. It is for this reason that, even during the time of being one of the committee of one of the theatres, I never made the attempt, and never will. But surely there is dramatic power somewhere, where Joanna Baillie, and Milman, and John Wilson exist. The 'City of the Plague' and the 'Fall of Jerusalem' are full of the best *materiel* for tragedy that has been seen since Horace Walpole, except passages of Ethwald and De Montfort. It is the fashion to underrate Horace Walpole; firstly, because he was a nobleman, and secondly, because he was a gentleman; but, to say nothing of the composition of his incomparable letters, and of the 'Castle of Otranto,' he is the 'Ultimus Romanorum,' the author of the 'Mysterious Mother,' a tragedy of the highest order, and not a puling love-play. He is the father of the first romance and of the last tragedy in our language, and surely worthy of a higher place than any living writer, be he who he may.

In speaking of the drama of 'Marino Faliero,' I forgot to mention, that the desire of preserving, though still too remote, a nearer approach to unity than the irregularity, which is the reproach of the English theatrical compositions, permits, has induced me to represent the conspiracy as already formed, and the Doge acceding to it; whereas, in fact, it was of his own preparation, and that of Israel Bertuccio. The other characters (except that of the Duchess), incidents, and almost the time, which was wonderfully short for such a design in real life, are strictly historical, except that all the consultations took place in the palace. Had I followed this, the unity would have been better preserved; but I wished to produce the Doge in the full assembly of the conspirators, instead of mono-tonously placing him always in dialogue with the same individuals. For the real facts, I refer to the Appendix.

* Laugier, Hist. de la Répub. de Venise.

MARINO FALIERO, DOGE OF VENICE

DRAMATIS PERSONÆ

MEN

MARINO FALIERO, *Doge of Venice.*
BERTUCCIO FALIERO, *Nephew of the Doge.*
LIONI, *a Patrician and Senator.*
BENINTENDE, *Chief of the Council of Ten.*
MICHEL STENO, *One of the three Capi of the Forty.*
ISRAEL BERTUCCIO, *Chief of the Arsenal.*
PHILIP CALENDARO,
DAGOLINO,
BERTRAM, } *Conspirators.*

Signor of the Night, } *'Signore di Notte,' one of the Officers belonging to the Republic.*

First Citizen.
Second Citizen.
Third Citizen.
VINCENZO,
PIETRO, } *Officers belonging to the Ducal Palace.*
BATTISTA,
Secretary of the Council of Ten.
Guards, Conspirators, Citizens, the Council of Ten, the Giunta, &c., &c.

WOMEN

ANGIOLINA, *Wife to the Doge.*
MARIANNA, *her Friend.*

Female Attendants, &c.

SCENE,—VENICE *in the year* 1355

ACT I

SCENE I.—*An Antechamber in the Ducal Palace.*

PIETRO *speaks, in entering, to* BATTISTA.

Pie. Is not the messenger return'd?
Bat.   Not yet;
I have sent frequently, as you commanded,
But still the Signory is deep in council,
And long debate on Steno's accusation.
Pie. Too long—at least so thinks the Doge.
Bat.   How bears he   5
These moments of suspense?
Pie.   With struggling patience.
Placed at the ducal table, cover'd o'er
With all the apparel of the state; petitions,
Despatches, judgments, acts, reprieves, reports,
He sits as rapt in duty; but whene'er   10
He hears the jarring of a distant door,
Or aught that intimates a coming step,
Or murmur of a voice, his quick eye wanders,
And he will start up from his chair, then pause,   14
And seat himself again, and fix his gaze
Upon some edict; but I have observed
For the last hour he has not turned a leaf.
Bat. 'Tis said he is much moved,—and doubtless 'twas
Foul scorn in Steno to offend so grossly.
Pie. Ay, if a poor man: Steno's a patrician,   20
Young, galliard, gay, and haughty.
Bat.   Then you think
He will not be judged hardly?
Pie.   'Twere enough
He be judged justly; but 'tis not for us
To anticipate the sentence of the Forty.
Bat. And here it comes.—What news, Vincenzo?

Enter VINCENZO.

Vin.   'Tis   25
Decided; but as yet his doom's unknown:

I saw the president in act to seal
The parchment which will bear the Forty's judgment
Unto the Doge, and hasten to inform him.
                                        [*Exeunt.*

SCENE II.—*The Ducal Chamber.*

MARINO FALIERO, *Doge; and his Nephew,* BERTUCCIO FALIERO.

Ber. F. It cannot be but they will do you justice.
Doge. Ay, such as the Avogadori did,
Who sent up my appeal unto the Forty
To try him by his peers, his own tribunal.
Ber. F. His peers will scarce protect him; such an act   5
Would bring contempt on all authority.
Doge. Know you not Venice? Know you not the Forty?
But we shall see anon.
Ber. F. [*addressing* VINCENZO, *then entering*].   How now—what tidings?
Vin. I am charged to tell his highness that the court
Has pass'd its resolution, and that, soon
As the due forms of judgment are gone through,   11
The sentence will be sent up to the Doge;
In the mean time the Forty doth salute
The Prince of the Republic, and entreat
His acceptation of their duty.
Doge.   Yes—   15
They are wondrous dutiful, and ever humble.
Sentence is pass'd, you say?
Vin.   It is, your highness:
The president was sealing it, when I
Was call'd in, that no moment might be lost
In forwarding the intimation due   20
Not only to the Chief of the Republic,
But the complainant, both in one united.
Ber. F. Are you aware, from aught you have perceived,
Of their decision?
Vin.   No, my lord; you know
The secret custom of the courts in Venice.

409

Ber. F. True; but there still is something given to guess, 26
Which a shrewd gleaner and quick eye would catch at;
A whisper, or a murmur, or an air
More or less solemn spread o'er the tribunal.
The Forty are but men—most worthy men,
And wise, and just, and cautious—this I grant— 31
And secret as the grave to which they doom
The guilty: but with all this, in their aspects—
At least in some, the juniors of the number—
A searching eye, an eye like yours, Vincenzo, 35
Would read the sentence ere it was pronounced.
Vin. My lord, I came away upon the moment,
And had no leisure to take note of that
Which pass'd among the judges, even in seeming;
My station near the accused too, Michel Steno, 40
Made me—
Doge [*abruptly*]. And how look'd *he*? deliver that.
Vin. Calm, but not overcast, he stood resign'd
To the decree, whate'er it were;—but lo!
It comes, for the perusal of his highness.

Enter the SECRETARY *of the Forty.*

Sec. The high tribunal of the Forty sends 45
Health and respect to the Doge Faliero,
Chief magistrate of Venice, and requests
His highness to peruse and to approve
The sentence pass'd on Michel Steno, born
Patrician, and arraign'd upon the charge
Contain'd, together with its penalty, 51
Within the rescript which I now present.
Doge. Retire, and wait without.

Exeunt SECRETARY *and* VINCENZO.

Take thou this paper:
The misty letters vanish from my eyes;
I cannot fix them.
Ber. F. Patience, my dear uncle: 55
Why do you tremble thus?—nay, doubt not, all
Will be as could be wish'd.
Doge. Say on.
Ber. F. [*reading*]. 'Decreed
In council, without one dissenting voice,
That Michel Steno, by his own confession,
Guilty on the last night of Carnival 60
Of having graven on the ducal throne
The following words—'
Doge. Wouldst thou repeat them?
Wouldst *thou* repeat them—*thou*, a Faliero,

Harp on the deep dishonour of our house,
Dishonour'd in its chief—that chief the prince 65
Of Venice, first of cities?—To the sentence.
Ber. F. Forgive me, my good lord; I will obey—
[*Reads*]. 'That Michel Steno be detain'd a month
In close arrest.'
Doge. Proceed.
Ber. F. My Lord, 'tis finish'd.
Doge. How say you?—finish'd! Do I dream?—'tis false— 70
Give me the paper—[*Snatches the paper and reads*]—''Tis decreed in council
That Michael Steno'——Nephew, thine arm!
Ber. F. Nay,
Cheer up, be calm; this transport is uncall'd for—
Let me seek some assistance.
Doge. Stop, sir—Stir not—'Tis past.
Ber. F. I cannot but agree with you 75
The sentence is too slight for the offence;
It is not honourable in the Forty
To affix so slight a penalty to that
Which was a foul affront to you, and even
To them, as being your subjects; but 'tis not 80
Yet without remedy: you can appeal
To them once more, or to the Avogadori,
Who, seeing that true justice is withheld,
Will now take up the cause they once declined,
And do you right upon the bold delinquent. 85
Think you not thus, good uncle? why do you stand
So fix'd? You heed me not:—I pray you, hear me!
Doge [*dashing down the Ducal bonnet, and offering to trample upon it, exclaims, as he is withheld by his nephew*].
Oh! that the Saracen were in St. Mark's!
Thus would I do him homage.
Ber. F. For the sake
Of Heaven and all its saints, my lord——
Doge. Away!
Oh, that the Genoese were in the port!
Oh, that the Huns whom I o'erthrew at Zara 92
Were ranged around the palace!
Ber. F. 'Tis not well
In Venice' Duke to say so.
Doge. Venice' Duke!
Who now is Duke in Venice? let me see him, 95
That he may do me right.
Ber. F. If you forget
Your office, and its dignity and duty,

Remember that of man, and curb this
  passion.
The Duke of Venice ——
  Doge [*interrupting him*]. There is no
    such thing—
It is a word—nay, worse—a worthless by-
    word;   100
The most despised, wrong'd, outraged,
    helpless wretch,
Who begs his bread, if 'tis refused by one,
May win it from another kinder heart:
But he, who is denied his right by those
Whose place it is to do no wrong, is poorer
Than the rejected beggar—he's a slave—
And that am I, and thou, and all our
    house,   107
Even from this hour; the meanest artisan
Will point the finger, and the haughty noble
May spit upon us:—where is our redress?
  Ber. F. The law, my prince——
  Doge [*interrupting him*]. You see what
    it has done;   111
I ask'd no remedy but from the law,
I sought no vengeance but redress by law,
I call'd no judges but those named by law;
As sovereign, I appeal'd unto my subjects,
The very subjects who had made me sove-
    reign,   116
And gave me thus a double right to be so.
The rights of place and choice, of birth and
    service,
Honours and years, these scars, these
    hoary hairs,
The travel, toil, the perils, the fatigues,
The blood and sweat of almost eighty
    years,   121
Were weigh'd i' the balance, 'gainst the
    foulest stain,
The grossest insult, most contemptuous
    crime
Of a rank, rash patrician—and found
    wanting!
And this is to be borne!
  Ber. F.   I say not that:— 125
In case your fresh appeal should be re-
    jected,
We will find other means to make all even.
  Doge. Appeal again! art thou my
    brother's son?
A scion of the house of Faliero?
The nephew of a Doge? and of that blood
Which hath already given three dukes to
    Venice?   131
But thou say'st well—we must be humble
    now.
  Ber. F. My princely uncle! you are too
    much moved;—
I grant it was a gross offence, and grossly
Left without fitting punishment: but still
This fury doth exceed the provocation,
Or any provocation: if we are wrong'd,
We will ask justice; if it be denied,   138
We'll take it; but may do all this in calm-
    ness—

Deep Vengeance is the daughter of deep
    Silence.   140
I have yet scarce a third part of your years,
I love our house, I honour you, its chief,
The guardian of my youth, and its in-
    structor—
But though I understand your grief, and
    enter   144
In part of your disdain, it doth appal me
To see your anger, like our Adrian waves,
O'ersweep all bounds, and foam itself to
    air.
  Doge. I tell thee—*must* I tell thee—
    what thy father
Would have required no words to compre-
    hend?
Hast thou no feeling save the external
    sense   150
Of torture from the touch? hast thou no
    soul—
No pride—no passion—no deep sense of
    honour?
  Ber. F. 'Tis the first time that honour
    has been doubted,
And were the last, from any other sceptic.
  Doge. You know the full offence of this
    born villain,   155
This creeping, coward, rank, acquitted
    felon,
Who threw his sting into a poisonous libel,
And on the honour of—Oh God! my wife,
The nearest, dearest part of all men's
    honour,
Left a base slur to pass from mouth to
    mouth   160
Of loose mechanics, with all coarse foul
    comments,
And villainous jests, and blasphemies ob-
    scene;
While sneering nobles, in more polish'd
    guise,
Whisper'd the tale, and smiled upon the
    lie
Which made me look like them—a cour-
    teous wittol,   165
Patient—ay, proud, it may be, of dis-
    honour.
  Ber. F. But still it was a lie—you knew
    it false
And so did all men.
  Doge.   Nephew, the high Roman
Said, 'Cæsar's wife must not even be sus-
    pected,'
And put her from him.
  Ber. F.   True—but in those days——
  Doge. What is it that a Roman would
    not suffer,   171
That a Venetian prince must bear? old
    Dandolo
Refused the diadem of all the Cæsars,
And wore the ducal cap I trample on,
Because 'tis now degraded.
  Ber. F.   'Tis even so.
  Doge. It is—it is;—I did not visit on

411

The innocent creature thus most vilely
    slander'd
Because she took an old man for her lord,
For that he had been long her father's
    friend
And patron of her house, as if there were
No love in woman's heart but lust of
    youth   181
And beardless faces;—I did not for this
Visit the villain's infamy on her,
But craved my country's justice on his
    head,
The justice due unto the humblest being
Who hath a wife whose faith is sweet to
    him,   186
Who hath a home whose hearth is dear to
    him,
Who hath a name whose honour's all to
    him,
When these are tainted by the accursing
    breath
Of calumny and scorn.
    Ber. F.   And what redress   190
Did you expect as his fit punishment?
    Doge. Death! Was I not the sovereign
    of the state—
Insulted on his very throne, and made
A mockery to the men who should obey
    me?   194
Was I not injured as a husband? scorn'd
As man? reviled, degraded, as a prince?
Was not offence like his a complication
Of insult and of treason?—and he lives!
Had he instead of on the Doge's throne
Stamp'd the same brand upon a peasant's
    stool,   200
His blood had gilt the threshold; for the
    carle
Had stabb'd him on the instant.
    Ber. F.   Do not doubt it,
He shall not live till sunset—leave to me
The means, and calm yourself.
    Doge.   Hold, nephew: this
Would have sufficed but yesterday; at
    present   205
I have no further wrath against this man.
    Ber. F. What mean you? is not the
offence redoubled
By this most rank—I will not say—ac-
    quittal;
For it is worse, being full acknowledgment
Of the offence, and leaving it unpunish'd?
    Doge. It is *redoubled*, but not now by
him: 211
The Forty hath decreed a month's arrest—
We must obey the Forty.
    Ber. F.   Obey *them!*
Who have forgot their duty to the sove-
    reign?
    Doge. Why, yes;—boy, you perceive it
then at last: 215
Whether as fellow citizen who sues
For justice, or as sovereign who com-
    mands it,

They have defrauded me of both my rights
(For here the sovereign is a citizen);
But, notwithstanding, harm not thou a
    hair   220
Of Steno's head—he shall not wear it long.
    Ber. F. Not twelve hours longer, had
you left to me
The mode and means: if you had calmly
    heard me,
I never meant this miscreant should es-
    cape,
But wish'd you to repress such gusts of
    passion,   225
That we more surely might devise to-
    gether
His taking off.
    Doge.   No, nephew, he must live;
At least, just now—a life so vile as his
Were nothing at this hour; in th' olden
    time   229
Some sacrifices ask'd a single victim,
Great expiations had a hecatomb.
    Ber. F. Your wishes are my law: and
yet I fain
Would prove to you how near unto my
    heart
The honour of our house must ever be.
    Doge. Fear not; you shall have time and
place of proof: 235
But be not thou too rash, as I have been.
I am ashamed of my own anger now;
I pray you, pardon me.
    Ber. F.   Why, that's my uncle!
The leader, and the statesman, and the
    chief
Of commonwealths, and sovereign of
    himself!   240
I wonder'd to perceive you so forget
All prudence in your fury at these years,
Although the cause——
    Doge.   Ay, think upon the cause—
Forget it not:—When you lie down to rest,
Let it be black among your dreams; and
    when   245
The morn returns, so let it stand between
The sun and you, as an ill-omen'd cloud
Upon a summer day of festival:
So will it stand to me;—but speak not, stir
    not,—
Leave all to me; we shall have much to do,
And you shall have a part.—But now re-
    tire,   251
'Tis fit I were alone.
    Ber. F. [*taking up and placing the ducal
bonnet on the table*]. Ere I depart,
I pray you to resume what you have
    spurn'd,
Till you can change it haply for a crown.
And now I take my leave, imploring you
In all things to rely upon my duty   256
As doth become your near and faithful
    kinsman,
And not less loyal citizen and subject.
    [*Exit* BERTUCCIO FALIERO.

Doge [*solus*]. Adieu, my worthy
  nephew.—Hollow bauble!
                    [*Taking up the ducal cap.*
Beset with all the thorns that line a crown,
Without investing the insulted brow 261
With the all-swaying majesty of kings;
Thou idle, gilded, and degraded toy,
Let me resume thee as I would a vizor.
                    [*Puts it on.*
How my brain aches beneath thee! and
  my temples   265
Throb feverish under thy dishonest weight.
Could I not turn thee to a diadem?
Could I not shatter the Briarean sceptre
Which in this hundred-handed senate
  rules,
Making the people nothing, and the
  prince   270
A pageant? In my life I have achieved
Tasks not less difficult—achieved for them,
Who thus repay me! Can I not requite
  them?
Oh for one year! Oh! but for even a day
Of my full youth, while yet my body
  served   275
My soul as serves the generous steed his
  lord,
I would have dash'd amongst them, asking
  few
In aid to overthrow these swoln patricians;
But now I must look round for other hands
To serve this hoary head;—but it shall
  plan   280
In such a sort as will not leave the task
Herculean, though as yet 'tis but a chaos
Of darkly brooding thoughts: my fancy is
In her first work, more nearly to the light
Holding the sleeping images of things
For the selection of the pausing judg-
  ment.—   286
The troops are few in——

                Enter VINCENZO.

Vin.   There is one without
Craves audience of your highness.
  Doge.   I'm unwell—
I can see no one, not even a patrician—
Let him refer his business to the council.
  Vin. My lord, I will deliver your reply;
It cannot much import—he's a plebeian,
The master of a galley, I believe.   293
  Doge. How! did you say the patron of
  a galley?
That is—I mean—a servant of the state:
Admit him, he may be on public service.
                    [*Exit* VINCENZO.
  Doge [*solus*]. This patron may be
  sounded; I will try him.   297
I know the people to be discontented:
They have cause, since Sapienza's adverse
  day,
When Genoa conquer'd: they have further
  cause,   300
Since they are nothing in the state, and in

The city worse than nothing—mere
  machines,
To serve the nobles' most patrician plea-
  sure.
The troops have long arrears of pay, oft
  promised,
And murmur deeply—any hope of change
Will draw them forward: they shall pay
  themselves   306
With plunder:—but the priests—I doubt
  the priesthood
Will not be with us; they have hated me
Since that rash hour, when, madden'd
  with the drone,
I smote the tardy bishop at Treviso, 310
Quickening his holy march; yet ne'erthe-
  less,
They may be won, at least their chief at
  Rome,
By some well-timed concessions; but, above
All things, I must be speedy: at my hour
Of twilight little light of life remains. 315
Could I free Venice, and avenge my
  wrongs,
I had lived too long, and willingly would
  sleep
Next moment with my sires; and, wanting
  this,
Better that sixty of my fourscore years
Had been already where—how soon, I
  care not—   320
The whole must be extinguish'd; better that
They ne'er had been, than drag me on to
  be
The thing these arch-oppressors fain
  would make me.
Let me consider—of efficient troops
There are three thousand posted at——

Enter VINCENZO *and* ISRAEL BERTUCCIO.

  Vin.   May it please 325
Your highness, the same patron whom I
  spake of
Is here to crave your patience.
  Doge.   Leave the chamber,
Vincenzo.—   [*Exit* VINCENZO.
              Sir, you may advance—what
  would you?
I. Ber. Redress.
  Doge.   Of whom?
  I. Ber.   Of God and of the Doge.
  Doge. Alas! my friend, you seek it of
  the twain   330
Of least respect and interest in Venice.
You must address the council.
  I. Ber.   'Twere in vain;
For he who injured me is one of them.
  Doge. There's blood upon thy face—
  how came it there?
  I. Ber. 'Tis mine, and not the first I've
  shed for Venice,   335
But the first shed by a Venetian hand:
A noble smote me.
  Doge.   Doth he live?

I. Ber.   Not long—
But for the hope I had and have, that you,
My prince, yourself a soldier, will redress
Him, whom the laws of discipline and
     Venice   340
Permit not to protect himself:—if not—
I say no more.
Doge. But something you would do—
Is it not so?
I. Ber.   I am a man, my lord.
Doge. Why so is he who smote you.
I. Ber.   He is call'd so;
Nay, more, a noble one—at least, in
     Venice: 345
But since he hath forgotten that I am one,
And treats me like a brute, the brute may
     turn—
'Tis said the worm will.
Doge.   Say—his name and lineage?
I. Ber. Barbaro.
Doge.   What was the cause? or
     the pretext?
I. Ber. I am the chief of the arsenal, em-
     ploy'd   350
At present in repairing certain galleys
But roughly used by the Genoese last year.
This morning comes the noble Barbaro
Full of reproof, because our artisans   354
Had left some frivolous order of his house,
To execute the state's decree: I dared
To justify the men—he raised his hand;—
Behold my blood! the first time it e'er
     flow'd
Dishonourably.
Doge.   Have you long time served?
I. Ber. So long as to remember Zara's
     siege,   360
And fight beneath the chief who beat the
     Huns there,
Sometime my general, now the Doge Fa-
     liero.—
Doge. How! are we comrades?—the
     state's ducal robes
Sit newly on me, and you were appointed
Chief of the arsenal ere I came from Rome;
So that I recognised you not. Who placed
     you?   366
I. Ber. The late Doge; keeping still my
     old command
As patron of a galley: my new office
Was given as the reward of certain scars
(So was your predecessor pleased to say):
I little thought his bounty would conduct
     me   371
To his successor as a helpless plaintiff;
At least, in such a cause.
Doge.   Are you much hurt?
I. Ber. Irreparably in my self-esteem.
Doge. Speak out; fear nothing: being
     stung at heart,   375
What would you do to be revenged on this
     man?
I. Ber. That which I dare not name,
     and yet will do.

Doge. Then wherefore came you here?
I. Ber.   I come for justice,
Because my general is Doge, and will not
See his old soldier trampled on. Had any,
Save Faliero, fill'd the ducal throne,
This blood had been wash'd out in other
     blood.
Doge. You come to me for justice—
     unto *me!*
The Doge of Venice, and I cannot give it;
I cannot even obtain it—'twas denied 385
To me most solemnly an hour ago!
I. Ber. How says your highness?
Doge.   Steno is condemn'd
To a month's confinement.
I. Ber.   What! the same who dared
To stain the ducal throne with those foul
     words,
That have cried shame to every ear in
     Venice?   390
Doge. Ay, doubtless they have echo'd
     o'er the arsenal,
Keeping due time with every hammer's
     clink
As a good jest to jolly artisans;
Or making chorus to the creaking oar,
In the vile tune of every galley-slave,
Who, as he sung the merry stave, exulted
He was not a shamed dotard like the Doge.
I. Ber. Is't possible? a month's im-
     prisonment!
No more for Steno?
Doge.   You have heard the offence,
And now you know his punishment; and
     then   400
You ask redress of *me!* Go to the Forty,
Who pass'd the sentence upon Michel
     Steno;
They'll do as much by Barbaro, no doubt.
I. Ber. Ah! dared I speak my feelings!
Doge.   Give them breath.
Mine have no further outrage to endure.
I. Ber. Then in a word, it rests but on
     your word   406
To punish and avenge—I will not say
My petty wrong, for what is a mere blow,
However vile, to such a thing as I am?—
But the base insult done your state and
     person.   410
Doge. You overrate my power, which
     is a pageant.
This cap is not the monarch's crown; these
     robes
Might move compassion, like a beggar's
     rags;
Nay, more, a beggar's are his own, and
     these
But lent to the poor puppet, who must
     play   415
Its part with all its empire in this ermine.
I. Ber. Wouldst thou be king?
Doge.   Yes—of a happy people.
I. Ber. Wouldst thou be sovereign lord
     of Venice?

Doge.   Ay,
If that the people shared that sovereignty,
So that nor they nor I were further slaves
To this o'ergrown aristocratic Hydra,   421
The poisonous heads of whose envenom'd
   body
Have breathed a pestilence upon us all.
   I. Ber. Yet, thou wast born, and still
      hast lived, patrician.
   Doge. In evil hour was I so born; my
      birth   425
Hath made me Doge to be insulted: but
I lived and toil'd a soldier and a servant
Of Venice and her people, not the senate;
Their good and my own honour were my
   guerdon.
I have fought and bled; commanded, ay,
   and conquer'd;   430
Have made and marr'd peace oft in em-
   bassies,
As it might chance to be our country's
   'vantage;
Have traversed land and sea in constant
   duty,
Through almost sixty years, and still for
   Venice,
My fathers' and my birthplace, whose
   dear spires,   435
Rising at distance o'er the blue Lagoon,
It was reward enough for me to view
Once more; but not for any knot of men,
Nor sect, nor faction, did I bleed or sweat!
But would you know why I have done all
   this?   440
Ask of the bleeding pelican why she
Hath ripp'd her bosom? Had the bird a
   voice,
She'd tell thee 'twas for *all* her little ones.
   I. Ber. And yet they made thee duke.
   Doge.   *They made* me so;
I sought it not, the flattering fetters met
   me   445
Returning from my Roman embassy,
And never having hitherto refused
Toil, charge, or duty for the state, I did not,
At these late years, decline what was the
   highest   449
Of all in seeming, but of all most base
In what we have to do and to endure:
Bear witness for me thou, my injured sub-
   ject,
When I can neither right myself nor thee.
   I. Ber. You shall do both, if you possess
      the will;
And many thousands more not less op-
      press'd,   455
Who wait but for a signal—will you give
   it?
   Doge. You speak in riddles.
   I. Ber.   Which shall soon be read
At peril of my life, if you disdain not
To lend a patient ear.
   Doge.   Say on.
   I. Ber.   Not thou,

Nor I alone, are injured and abused,   460
Contemn'd and trampled on; but the
   whole people
Groan with the strong conception of their
   wrongs;
The foreign soldiers in the senate's pay
Are discontented for their long arrears;
The native mariners, and civic troops,
Feel with their friends; for who is he
   amongst them   466
Whose brethren, parents, children, wives,
   or sisters,
Have not partook oppression, or pollu-
   tion,
From the patricians? And the hopeless
   war
Against the Genoese, which is still main-
   tain'd   470
With the plebeian blood, and treasure
   wrung
From their hard earnings, has inflamed
   them further:
Even now—but, I forget that speaking
   thus,
Perhaps I pass the sentence of my death!
   Doge. And suffering what thou hast
      done—fear'st thou death?   475
Be silent then, and live on, to be beaten
By those for whom thou hast bled.
   I. Ber.   No, I will speak
At every hazard; and if Venice' Doge
Should turn delator, be the shame on him,
And sorrow too; for he will lose far more
Than I.
   Doge. From me fear nothing; out with
      it!   481
   I. Ber. Know then, that there are met
      and sworn in secret
A band of brethren, valiant hearts and
   true;
Men who have proved all fortunes, and
   have long
Grieved over that of Venice, and have
   right   485
To do so; having served her in all climes,
And having rescued her from foreign foes,
Would do the same from those within her
   walls.
They are not numerous, nor yet too few
For their great purpose; they have arms,
   and means,   490
And hearts, and hopes, and faith, and
   patient courage.
   Doge. For what then do they pause?
   I. Ber.   An hour to strike.
   Doge [*aside*]. Saint Mark's shall strike
      that hour!
   I. Ber.   I now have placed
My life, my honour, all my earthly hopes
Within thy power, but in the firm belief
That injuries like ours, sprung from one
   cause,   496
Will generate one vengeance: should it
   be so,

415   P

Be our chief now—our sovereign here-
after.
Doge. How many are ye?
I. Ber.   I'll not answer that
Till I am answer'd.
Doge.   How, sir! do you menace?
I. Ber. No; I affirm. I have betray'd
myself;   501
But there's no torture in the mystic wells
Which undermine your palace, nor in those
Not less appalling cells, the 'leaden roofs,'
To force a single name from me of others.
The Pozzi and the Piombi were in vain;
They might wring blood from me, but
treachery never.   507
And I would pass the fearful 'Bridge of
Sighs,'
Joyous that mine must be the last that e'er
Would echo o'er the Stygian wave which
flows   510
Between the murderers and the murder'd,
washing
The prison and the palace walls: there are
Those who would live to think on't, and
avenge me.
Doge. If such your power and purpose,
why come here   514
To sue for justice, being in the course
To do yourself due right?
I. Ber.   Because the man,
Who claims protection from authority,
Showing his confidence and his submission
To that authority, can hardly be   519
Suspected of combining to destroy it.
Had I sate down too humbly with this blow,
A moody brow and mutter'd threats had
made me
A mark'd man to the Forty's inquisition;
But loud complaint, however angrily   524
It shapes its phrase, is little to be fear'd,
And less distrusted. But, besides all this,
I had another reason.
Doge.   What was that?
I. Ber. Some rumours that the Doge
was greatly moved
By the reference of the Avogadori
Of Michel Steno's sentence to the Forty
Had reach'd me. I had served you,
honour'd you,   531
And felt that you were dangerously in-
sulted,
Being of an order of such spirits, as
Requite tenfold both good and evil: 'twas
My wish to prove and urge you to redress.
Now you know all; and that I speak the
truth,   536
My peril be the proof.
Doge.   You have deeply ventured;
But all must do so who would greatly win:
Thus far I'll answer you—your secret's
safe.
I. Ber. And is this all?
Doge.   Unless with all intrusted,
What would you have me answer?

I. Ber.   I would have you
Trust him who leaves his life in trust with
you.
Doge. But I must know your plan, your
names, and numbers;
The last may then be doubled, and the
former
Matured and strengthen'd.
I. Ber.   We're enough already;   545
You are the sole ally we covet now.
Doge. But bring me to the knowledge
of your chiefs.
I. Ber. That shall be done upon your
formal pledge
To keep the faith that we will pledge to
you.
Doge. When? where?
I. Ber.   This night I'll bring to your
apartment   550
Two of the principals: a greater number
Were hazardous.
Doge.   Stay, I must think of this.—
What if I were to trust myself amongst you,
And leave the palace?
I. Ber.   You must come alone.
Doge. With but my nephew.
I. Ber.   Not were he your son.   555
Doge. Wretch! darest thou name my
son? He died in arms
At Sapienza for this faithless state.
Oh! that he were alive, and I in ashes!
Or that he were alive ere I be ashes!
I should not need the dubious aid of
strangers.   560
I. Ber. Not one of all those strangers
whom thou doubtest,
But will regard thee with a filial feeling,
So that thou keep'st a father's faith with
them.
Doge. The die is cast. Where is the
place of meeting?
I. Ber. At midnight I will be alone and
mask'd   565
Where'er your highness pleases to direct
me,
To wait your coming, and conduct you
where
You shall receive our homage, and pro-
nounce
Upon our project.
Doge.   At what hour arises
The moon?
I. Ber. Late, but the atmosphere is
thick and dusky,   570
'Tis a sirocco.
Doge. At the midnight hour, then,
Near to the church where sleep my sires;
the same,
Twin-named from the apostles John and
Paul;
A gondola, with one oar only, will
Lurk in the narrow channel which glides
by.   575
Be there.

I. Ber. I will not fail.
Doge.   And now retire——
I. Ber. In the full hope your highness
  will not falter
In your great purpose. Prince, I take my
  leave.   [*Exit* ISRAEL BERTUCCIO.
Doge [*solus*]. At midnight, by the church
  Saints John and Paul,   579
Where sleep my noble fathers, I repair—
To what? to hold a council in the dark
With common ruffians leagued to ruin
  states!
And will not my great sires leap from the
  vault,
Where lie two doges who preceded me,
And pluck me down amongst them?
  Would they could!   585
For I should rest in honour with the
  honour'd.
Alas! I must not think of them, but those
Who have made me thus unworthy of a
  name
Noble and brave as aught of consular
On Roman marbles; but I will redeem it
Back to its antique lustre in our annals,
By sweet revenge on all that's base in
  Venice,   592
And freedom to the rest, or leave it black
To all the growing calumnies of time,
Which never spare the fame of him who
  fails,
But try the Cæsar, or the Catiline,
By the true touchstone of desert—success.

ACT II

SCENE I.—*An Apartment in the Ducal
  Palace.*

ANGIOLINA (*wife of the* DOGE) *and*
  MARIANNA.

Ang. What was the Doge's answer?
Mar.   That he was
That moment summon'd to a conference.
But 'tis by this time ended. I perceived
Not long ago the senators embarking;
And the last gondola may now be seen
Gliding into the throng of barks which stud
The glittering waters.
Ang.   Would he were return'd!
He has been much disquieted of late;
And Time, which has not tamed his fiery
  spirit,
Nor yet enfeebled even his mortal frame,
Which seems to me more nourish'd by
  a soul   11
So quick and restless that it would con-
  sume
Less hardy clay—Time has but little power
On his resentments or his griefs. Unlike
To other spirits of his order, who,   15
In the first burst of passion, pour away
Their wrath or sorrow, all things wear in
  him

An aspect of eternity: his thoughts,
His feelings, passions, good or evil, all
Have nothing of old age; and his bold
  brow   20
Bears but the scars of mind, the thoughts
  of years,
Not their decrepitude: and he of late
Has been more agitated than his wont.
Would he were come! for I alone have
  power
Upon his troubled spirit.
Mar.   It is true,   25
His highness has of late been greatly
  moved
By the affront of Steno, and with cause:
But the offender doubtless even now
Is doom'd to expiate his rash insult with
Such chastisement as will enforce respect
To female virtue, and to noble blood.   31
Ang. 'Twas a gross insult; but I heed it
  not
For the rash scorner's falsehood in itself,
But for the effect, the deadly deep im-
  pression   34
Which it has made upon Faliero's soul,
The proud, the fiery, the austere—austere
To all save me: I tremble when I think
To what it may conduct.
Mar.   Assuredly
The Doge cannot suspect you?
Ang.   Suspect *me!*
Why Steno dared not: when he scrawl'd
  his lie,   40
Grovelling by stealth in the moon's glim-
  mering light,
His own still conscience smote him for the
  act,
And every shadow on the walls frown'd
  shame
Upon his coward calumny.
Mar.   'Twere fit
He should be punish'd grievously.
Ang.   He is so.
Mar. What! is the sentence pass'd? is
  he condemn'd?   46
Ang. I know not that, but he has been
  detected.
Mar. And deem you this enough for
  such foul scorn?
Ang. I would not be a judge in my own
  cause,
Nor do I know what sense of punishment
May reach the soul of ribalds such as
  Steno;   51
But if his insults sink no deeper in
The minds of the inquisitors than they
Have ruffled mine, he will, for all acquit-
  tance,
Be left to his own shamelessness or shame.
Mar. Some sacrifice is due to slander'd
  virtue.   56
Ang. Why, what is virtue if it needs a
  victim?
Or if it must depend upon men's words?

417

The dying Roman said, ''twas but a name':
It were indeed no more, if human breath
Could make or mar it.   61
    Mar.   Yet full many a dame,
Stainless and faithful, would feel all the
      wrong
Of such a slander; and less rigid ladies,
Such as abound in Venice, would be loud
And all-inexorable in their cry   65
For justice.
    Ang.   This but proves it is the name
And not the quality they prize: the first
Have found it a hard task to hold their
      honour,
If they require it to be blazon'd forth;
And those who have not kept it, seek its
      seeming   70
As they would look out for an ornament
Of which they feel the want, but not be-
      cause
They think it so; they live in others'
      thoughts,
And would seem honest as they must seem
      fair.
    Mar. You have strange thoughts for a
      patrician dame.   75
    Ang. And yet they were my father's;
      with his name,
The sole inheritance he left.
    Mar.   You want none;
Wife to a prince, the chief of the Republic.
    Ang. I should have sought none though
      a peasant's bride,   79
But feel not less the love and gratitude
Due to my father, who bestow'd my hand
Upon his early, tried, and trusted friend,
The Count Val di Marino, now our Doge.
    Mar. And with that hand did he bestow
      your heart?
    Ang. He did so, or it had not been be-
      stow'd.   85
    Mar. Yet this strange disproportion in
      your years,
And, let me add, disparity of tempers,
Might make the world doubt whether such
      an union
Could make you wisely, permanently
      happy.
    Ang. The world will think with world-
      lings; but my heart   90
Has still been in my duties, which are
      many,
But never difficult.
    Mar.   And do you love him?
    Ang. I love all noble qualities which
      merit
Love, and I loved my father, who first
      taught me
To single out what we should love in
      others,   95
And to subdue all tendency to lend
The best and purest feelings of our nature
To baser passions. He bestow'd my hand
Upon Faliero: he had known him noble,

Brave, generous; rich in all the qualities
Of soldier, citizen, and friend; in all   101
Such have I found him as my father said.
His faults are those that dwell in the high
      bosoms
Of men who have commanded; too much
      pride,
And the deep passions fiercely foster'd by
The uses of patricians, and a life   106
Spent in the storms of state and war; and
      also
From the quick sense of honour, which
      becomes
A duty to a certain sign, a vice
When overstrain'd, and this I fear in him.
And then he has been rash from his youth
      upwards,   111
Yet temper'd by redeeming nobleness
In such sort, that the wariest of republics
Has lavish'd all its chief employs upon
      him,
From his first fight to his last embassy,
From which on his return the dukedom
      met him.   116
    Mar. But previous to this marriage,
      had your heart
Ne'er beat for any of the noble youth,
Such as in years had been more meet to
      match
Beauty like yours? or, since, have you
      ne'er seen   120
One, who, if your fair hand were still to
      give,
Might now pretend to Loredano's daugh-
      ter?
    Ang. I answer'd your first question
      when I said
I married.
    Mar.   And the second?
    Ang.   Needs no answer.
    Mar. I pray you pardon, if I have
      offended.   125
    Ang. I feel no wrath, but some surprise:
      I knew not
That wedded bosoms could permit them-
      selves
To ponder upon what they *now* might
      choose,
Or aught save their past choice.
    Mar.   'Tis their past choice
That far too often makes them deem they
      would   130
Now choose more wisely, could they
      cancel it.
    Ang. It may be so. I knew not of such
      thoughts.
    Mar. Here comes the Doge—shall I
      retire?
    Ang.   It may
Be better you should quit me; he seems
      rapt
In thought.—How pensively he takes his
      way!   135
                              [*Exit* MARIANNA.

418

Enter the DOGE *and* PIETRO.

Doge [*musing*]. There is a certain Philip
    Calendaro
Now in the Arsenal, who holds command
Of eighty men, and has great influence
Besides on all the spirits of his comrades:
This man, I hear, is bold and popular,
Sudden and daring, and yet secret; 'twould
Be well that he were won: I needs must
    hope   142
That Israel Bertuccio has secured him,
But fain would be——
Pie.   My lord, pray pardon me
For breaking in upon your meditation;
The Senator Bertuccio, your kinsman,
Charged me to follow and inquire your
    pleasure   147
To fix an hour when he may speak with
    you.
Doge. At sunset.—Stay a moment—let
    me see—
Say in the second hour of night.
                    [*Exit* PIETRO.
Ang.   My lord!
Doge. My dearest child, forgive me—
    why delay   151
So long approaching me?—I saw you not.
Ang. You were absorb'd in thought,
    and he who now
Has parted from you might have words of
    weight
To bear you from the senate.
Doge.   From the senate?
Ang. I would not interrupt him in his
    duty   156
And theirs.
Doge. The senate's duty! you mistake;
'Tis we who owe all service to the senate.
Ang. I thought the Duke had held com-
    mand in Venice.
Doge. He shall.—But let that pass.—
    We will be jocund.   160
How fares it with you? have you been
    abroad?
The day is overcast, but the calm wave
Favours the gondolier's light skimming
    oar;
Or have you held a levee of your friends?
Or has your music made you solitary?
Say—is there aught that you would will
    within   166
The little sway now left the Duke? or aught
Of fitting splendour, or of honest pleasure,
Social or lonely, that would glad your
    heart,
To compensate for many a dull hour,
    wasted   170
On an old man oft moved with many
    cares?
Speak, and 'tis done.
Ang.   You're ever kind to me.
I have nothing to desire, or to request,
Except to see you oftener and calmer.

Doge. Calmer?
Ang. Ay, calmer, my good lord.—Ah,
    why   175
Do you still keep apart, and walk alone,
And let such strong emotions stamp your
    brow,
As not betraying their full import, yet
Disclose too much?
Doge. Disclose too much!—of what?
What is there to disclose?
Ang.   A heart so ill
At ease.
Doge. 'Tis nothing, child.—But in the
    state   181
You know what daily cares oppress all
    those
Who govern this precarious common-
    wealth;
Now suffering from the Genoese without,
And malcontents within—'tis this which
    makes me   185
More pensive and less tranquil than my
    wont.
Ang. Yet this existed long before, and
    never
Till in these late days did I see you thus.
Forgive me; there is something at your
    heart
More than the mere discharge of public
    duties,   190
Which long use and a talent like to yours
Have render'd light, nay, a necessity,
To keep your mind from stagnating. 'Tis
    not
In hostile states, nor perils, thus to shake
    you,—
You, who have stood all storms and never
    sunk,   195
And climb'd up to the pinnacle of power
And never fainted by the way, and stand
Upon it, and can look down steadily
Along the depth beneath, and ne'er feel
    dizzy.   199
Were Genoa's galleys riding in the port,
Were civil fury raging in Saint Mark's,
You are not to be wrought on, but would
    fall,
As you have risen, with an unalter'd brow:
Your feelings now are of a different kind;
Something has stung your pride, not
    patriotism.   205
Doge. Pride! Angiolina? Alas! none
    is left me.
Ang. Yes—the same sin that overthrew
    the angels,
And of all sins most easily besets
Mortals the nearest to the angelic nature:
The vile are only vain; the great are proud.
Doge. I *had* the pride of honour, of *your*
    honour,   211
Deep at my heart—But let us change the
    theme.
Ang. Ah no!—As I have ever shared
    your kindness

419

In all things else, let me not be shut out
From your distress: were it of public im-
     port,   215
You know I never sought, would never
     seek
To win a word from you; but feeling now
Your grief is private, it belongs to me
To lighten or divide it. Since the day
When foolish Steno's ribaldry detected
Unfix'd your quiet, you are greatly
     changed,   221
And I would soothe you back to what you
     were.

  Doge. To what I was!—have you heard
     Steno's sentence?

  Ang. No.

  Doge.   A month's arrest.

  Ang.   Is it not enough?

  Doge. Enough!—yes, for a drunken
     galley slave,   225
Who, stung by stripes, may murmur at his
     master;
But not for a deliberate, false, cool villain,
Who stains a lady's and a prince's honour
Even on the throne of his authority.

  Ang. There seems to me enough in the
     conviction   230
Of a patrician guilty of a falsehood:
All other punishment were light unto
His loss of honour.

  Doge.   Such men have no honour;
They have but their vile lives—and these
     are spared.

  Ang. You would not have him die for
     this offence?   235

  Doge. Not *now*:—being still alive, I'd
     have him live
Long as *he* can; he has ceased to merit
     death;
The guilty saved hath damn'd his hundred
     judges,
And he is pure, for now his crime is theirs.

  Ang. Oh! had this false and flippant
     libeller   240
Shed his young blood for his absurd lam-
     poon,
Ne'er from that moment could this breast
     have known
A joyous hour, or dreamless slumber
     more.

  Doge. Does not the law of Heaven say
     blood for blood?
And he who *taints* kills more than he who
     sheds it.   245
Is it the *pain* of blows, or *shame* of blows,
That makes such deadly to the sense of
     man?
Do not the laws of man say blood for
     honour,—
And, less than honour, for a little gold?
Say not the laws of nations blood for
     treason?   250
Is't nothing to have fill'd these veins with
     poison

For their once healthful current? is it no-
     thing
To have stain'd your name and mine—the
     noblest names?
Is't nothing to have brought into contempt
A prince before his people? to have fail'd
In the respect accorded by mankind   256
To youth in woman, and old age in man?
To virtue in your sex, and dignity
In ours?—But let them look to it who have
     saved him.

  Ang. Heaven bids us to forgive our
     enemies.   260

  Doge. Doth Heaven forgive her own?
     Is there not Hell
For wrath eternal?

  Ang.   Do not speak thus wildly—
Heaven will alike forgive you and your
     foes.

  Doge. Amen! May Heaven forgive
     them!

  Ang.   And will you?

  Doge. Yes, when they are in heaven!

  Ang.   And not till then?

  Doge. What matters my forgiveness?
     an old man's,   266
Worn out, scorn'd, spurn'd, abused; what
     matters then
My pardon more than my resentment,
     both
Being weak and worthless? I have lived
     too long;
But let us change the argument.—My
     child!   270
My injured wife, the child of Loredano,
The brave, the chivalrous, how little
     deem'd
Thy father, wedding thee unto his friend,
That he was linking thee to shame!—Alas!
Shame without sin, for thou art faultless.
     Hadst thou   275
But had a different husband, *any* husband
In Venice save the Doge, this blight, this
     brand,
This blasphemy had never fallen upon
     thee.
So young, so beautiful, so good, so pure,
To suffer this, and yet be unavenged!

  Ang. I am too well avenged, for you
     still love me,   281
And trust, and honour me; and all men
     know
That you are just, and I am true: what more
Could I require, or you command?

  Doge.   'Tis well,
And may be better; but whate'er betide,
Be thou at least kind to my memory. 286

  Ang. Why speak you thus?

  Doge.   It is no matter why;
But I would still, whatever others think,
Have your respect both now and in my
     grave.

  Ang. Why should you doubt it? has it
     ever fail'd?   290

Doge. Come hither, child; I would a
    word with you.
Your father was my friend; unequal for-
    tune
Made him my debtor for some courtesies
Which bind the good more firmly: when,
    oppress'd
With his last malady, he will'd our union,
It was not to repay me, long repaid   296
Before by his great loyalty in friendship;
His object was to place your orphan
    beauty
In honourable safety from the perils
Which, in this scorpion nest of vice, assail
A lonely and undower'd maid. I did not
Think with him, but would not oppose the
    thought   302
Which soothed his death-bed.
    Ang.   I have not forgotten
The nobleness with which you bade me
    speak
If my young heart held any preference
Which would have made me happier; nor
    your offer   306
To make my dowry equal to the rank
Of aught in Venice, and forego all claim
My father's last injunction gave you.
    Doge.   Thus,
'Twas not a foolish dotard's vile caprice,
Nor the false edge of aged appetite,   311
Which made me covetous of girlish beauty,
And a young bride: for in my fieriest youth
I sway'd such passions; nor was this my
    age
Infected with that leprosy of lust   315
Which taints the hoariest years of vicious
    men,
Making them ransack to the very last
The dregs of pleasure for their vanish'd
    joys;
Or buy in selfish marriage some young
    victim,   319
Too helpless to refuse a state that's honest,
Too feeling not to know herself a wretch.
Our wedlock was not of this sort; you had
Freedom from me to choose, and urged in
    answer
Your father's choice.
    Ang.   I did so; I would do so
In face of earth and heaven; for I have
    never   325
Repented for my sake; sometimes for
    yours,
In pondering o'er your late disquietudes.
    Doge. I knew my heart would never
    treat you harshly;
I knew my days could not disturb you
    long;
And then the daughter of my earliest
    friend,   330
His worthy daughter, free to choose again,
Wealthier and wiser, in the ripest bloom
Of womanhood, more skilful to select
By passing these probationary years

Inheriting a prince's name and riches,
Secured, by the short penance of enduring
An old man for some summers, against all
That law's chicane or envious kinsmen
    might
Have urged against her right; my best
    friend's child
Would choose more fitly in respect of
    years,   340
And not less truly in a faithful heart.
    Ang. My lord, I look'd but to my
    father's wishes,
Hallow'd by his last words, and to my
    heart
For doing all its duties, and replying
With faith to him with whom I was
    affianced.   345
Ambitious hopes ne'er cross'd my dreams;
    and should
The hour you speak of come, it will be
    seen so.
    Doge. I do believe you; and I know you
    true:
For love, romantic love, which in my
    youth
I knew to be illusion, and ne'er saw   350
Lasting, but often fatal, it had been
No lure for me, in my most passionate
    days,
And could not be so now, did such exist.
But such respect, and mildly paid regard
As a true feeling for your welfare, and
A free compliance with all honest wishes,—
A kindness to your virtues, watchfulness
Not shown, but shadowing o'er such little
    failings
As youth is apt in, so as not to check
Rashly, but win you from them ere you
    knew   360
You had been won, but thought the change
    your choice;
A pride not in your beauty, but your con-
    duct;
A trust in you; a patriarchal love,
And not a doting homage; friendship,
    faith,—   364
Such estimation in your eyes as these
Might claim, I hoped for.
    Ang.   And have ever had.
    Doge. I think so. For the difference in
    our years
You knew it, choosing me, and chose: I
    trusted
Not to my qualities, nor would have faith
In such, nor outward ornaments of nature,
Were I still in my five and twentieth spring;
I trusted to the blood of Loredano   372
Pure in your veins; I trusted to the soul
God gave you—to the truths your father
    taught you—
To your belief in Heaven—to your mild
    virtues—   375
To your own faith and honour, for my
    own.

421

Ang. You have done well.—I thank you
  for that trust,
Which I have never for one moment ceased
To honour you the more for.
Doge.   Where is honour,
Innate and precept-strengthen'd, 'tis the
  rock   380
Of faith connubial: where it is not—where
Light thoughts are lurking, or the vanities
Of worldly pleasure rankle in the heart,
Or sensual throbs convulse it, well I know
'Twere hopeless for humanity to dream
Of honesty in such infected blood,   386
Although 'twere wed to him it covets
  most:
An incarnation of the poet's god
In all his marble-chisell'd beauty, or
The demi-deity, Alcides, in   390
His majesty of superhuman manhood,
Would not suffice to bind where virtue is
  not;
It is consistency which forms and proves it:
Vice cannot fix, and virtue cannot change.
The once fall'n woman must for ever fall;
For vice must have variety, while virtue
Stands like the sun, and all which rolls
  around   397
Drinks life, and light, and glory from her
  aspect.
Ang. And seeing, feeling thus this truth
  in others,
(I pray you pardon me;) but wherefore
  yield you   400
To the most fierce of fatal passions, and
Disquiet your great thoughts with restless
  hate
Of such a thing as Steno?
Doge.   You mistake me.
It is not Steno who could move me thus;
Had it been so, he should——but let that
  pass.   405
Ang. What is't you feel so deeply, then,
  even now?
Doge. The violated majesty of Venice,
At once insulted in her lord and laws.
Ang. Alas! why will you thus consider
  it?
Doge. I have thought on't till——but
  let me lead you back   410
To what I urged; all these things being
  noted,
I wedded you; the world then did me
  justice
Upon the motive, and my conduct proved
They did me right, while yours was all to
  praise:
You had all freedom, all respect, all trust
From me and mine; and, born of those
  who made   416
Princes at home, and swept kings from
  their thrones
On foreign shores, in all things you ap-
  pear'd
Worthy to be our first of native dames.

Ang. To what does this conduct?
Doge.   To thus much—that
A miscreant's angry breath may blast it
  all—   421
A villain, whom for his unbridled bearing
Even in the midst of our great festival,
I caused to be conducted forth, and taught
How to demean himself in ducal cham-
  bers;   425
A wretch like this may leave upon the wall
The blighting venom of his sweltering
  heart,
And this shall spread itself in general
  poison;
And woman's innocence, man's honour,
  pass
Into a by-word; and the doubly felon
(Who first insulted virgin modesty   431
By a gross affront to your attendant
  damsels
Amidst the noblest of our dames in public)
Requite himself for his most just expulsion
By blackening publicly his sovereign's
  consort,   435
And be absolved by his upright compeers.
Ang. But he has been condemn'd into
  captivity.
Doge. For such as him a dungeon were
  acquittal;
And his brief term of mock-arrest will pass
Within a palace. But I've done with him;
The rest must be with you.
Ang.   With me, my lord?
Doge. Yes, Angiolina. Do not marvel;
  I   442
Have let this prey upon me till I feel
My life cannot be long; and fain would
  have you
Regard the injunctions you will find
  within   445
This scroll [*Giving her a paper*]——Fear
  not; they are for your advantage:
Read them hereafter at the fitting hour.
Ang. My lord, in life, and after life, you
  shall
Be honour'd still by me: but may your
  days
Be many yet—and happier than the
  present!   450
This passion will give way, and you will be
Serene, and what you should be—what
  you were.
Doge. I will be what I should be, or be
  nothing;
But never more—oh! never, never more,
O'er the few days or hours which yet
  await   455
The blighted old age of Faliero, shall
Sweet quiet shed her sunset! Never more
Those summer shadows rising from the
  past
Of a not ill-spent nor inglorious life,
Mellowing the last hours as the night
  approaches,   460

Shall soothe me to my moment of long
   rest.
I had but little more to ask, or hope,
Save the regards due to the blood and
   sweat,
And the soul's labour through which I
   had toil'd
To make my country honour'd. As her
   servant—   465
Her servant, though her chief—I would
   have gone
Down to my fathers with a name serene
And pure as theirs; but this has been de-
   nied me.—
Would I had died at Zara!

   Ang.   There you saved
The state; then live to save her still. A day,
Another day like that would be the best
Reproof to them, and sole revenge for you.

   Doge. But one such day occurs within
   an age;
My life is little less than one, and 'tis
Enough for Fortune to have granted *once*,
That which scarce one more favour'd
   citizen   476
May win in many states and years. But why
Thus speak I? Venice has forgot that
   day—
Then why should I remember it?—Fare-
   well,
Sweet Angiolina! I must to my cabinet;
There's much for me to do—and the hour
   hastens.   481

   Ang. Remember what you were.

   Doge.   It were in vain!
Joy's recollection is no longer joy,
While sorrow's memory is a sorrow still.

   Ang. At least, whate'er may urge, let
   me implore   485
That you will take some little pause of rest:
Your sleep for many nights has been so
   turbid,
That it had been relief to have awaked you,
Had I not hoped that Nature would o'er-
   power
At length the thoughts which shook your
   slumbers thus.   490
An hour of rest will give you to your toils
With fitter thoughts and freshen'd strength.

   Doge.   I cannot—
I must not, if I could; for never was
Such reason to be watchful: yet a few—
Yet a few days and dream-perturbed
   nights,   495
And I shall slumber well—but where?—
   no matter.
Adieu, my Angiolina.

   Ang.   Let me be
An instant—yet an instant your com-
   panion!
I cannot bear to leave you thus.

   Doge.   Come then,
My gentle child—forgive me; thou wert
   made   500

For better fortunes than to share in mine,
Now darkling in their close toward the
   deep vale
Where Death sits robed in his all-sweeping
   shadow.
When I am gone—it may be sooner than
Even these years warrant, for there is that
   stirring   505
Within, above, around, that in this city
Will make the cemeteries populous
As e'er they were by pestilence or war,—
When I *am* nothing, let that which I *was*
Be still sometimes a name on thy sweet
   lips,   510
A shadow in thy fancy, of a thing
Which would not have thee mourn it, but
   remember.
Let us begone, my child—the time is
   pressing.   [*Exeunt.*

   SCENE II.—*A retired spot near the
   Arsenal.*

ISRAEL BERTUCCIO *and* PHILIP CALENDARO.

   Cal. How sped you, Israel, in your late
   complaint?

   I. Ber. Why, well.

   Cal. Is't possible! will he be punish'd?

   I. Ber.   Yes.

   Cal. With what? a mulct or an arrest?

   I. Ber.   With death!

   Cal. Now you rave, or must intend revenge,
Such as I counsell'd you, with your own
   hand.   5

   I. Ber. Yes; and for one sole draught
   of hate, forego
The great redress we meditate for Venice,
And change a life of hope for one of
   exile;
Leaving one scorpion crush'd, and thou-
   sands stinging   9
My friends, my family, my countrymen!
No, Calendaro; these same drops of blood,
Shed shamefully, shall have the whole of
   his
For their requital——but not only his;
We will not strike for private wrongs
   alone: 14
Such are for selfish passions and rash
   men,
But are unworthy a tyrannicide.

   Cal. You have more patience than I
   care to boast.
Had I been present when you bore this
   insult,
I must have slain him, or expired myself
In the vain effort to repress my wrath.

   I. Ber. Thank Heaven you were not—
   all had else been marr'd: 21
As 'tis, our cause looks prosperous still.

   Cal.   You saw
The Doge—what answer gave he?

   I. Ber.   That there **was**

No punishment for such as Barbaro.
  Cal. I told you so before, and that 'twas idle 25
To think of justice from such hands.
  I. Ber.   At least,
It lull'd suspicion, showing confidence.
Had I been silent, not a sbirro but
Had kept me in his eye, as meditating
A silent, solitary, deep revenge. 30
  Cal. But wherefore not address you to the Council?
The Doge is a mere puppet, who can scarce
Obtain right for himself. Why speak to *him*?
  I. Ber. You shall know that hereafter.
  Cal.   Why not now?
  I. Ber. Be patient but till midnight. Get your musters, 35
And bid our friends prepare their companies:
Set all in readiness to strike the blow,
Perhaps in a few hours; we have long waited
For a fit time—that hour is on the dial,
It may be, of to-morrow's sun: delay
Beyond may breed us double danger. See
That all be punctual at our place of meeting,
And arm'd, excepting those of the Sixteen,
Who will remain among the troops to wait
The signal.
  Cal. These brave words have breathed new life 45
Into my veins; I'm sick of these protracted
And hesitating councils: day on day
Crawl'd on, and added but another link
To our long fetters, and some fresher wrong 49
Inflicted on our brethren or ourselves,
Helping to swell our tyrants' bloated strength.
Let us but deal upon them, and I care not
For the result, which must be death or freedom!
I'm weary to the heart of finding neither.
  I. Ber. We will be free in life or death! the grave 55
Is chainless. Have you all the musters ready?
And are the sixteen companies completed
To sixty?
  Cal. All save two, in which there are
Twenty-five wanting to make up the number.
  I. Ber. No matter; we can do without. Whose are they? 60
  Cal. Bertram's and old Soranzo's, both of whom
Appear less forward in the cause than we are.
  I. Ber. Your fiery nature makes you deem all those
Who are not restless cold: but there exists

Oft in concentred spirits not less daring
Than in more loud avengers. Do not doubt them.
  Cal. I do not doubt the elder; but in Bertram
There is a hesitating softness, fatal
To enterprise like ours: I've seen that man
Weep like an infant o'er the misery 70
Of others, heedless of his own, though greater;
And in a recent quarrel I beheld him
Turn sick at sight of blood, although a villain's.
  I. Ber. The truly brave are soft of heart and eyes,
And feel for what their duty bids them do.
I have known Bertram long; there doth not breathe 76
A soul more full of honour.
  Cal.   It may be so:
I apprehend less treachery than weakness;
Yet as he has no mistress, and no wife
To work upon his milkiness of spirit,
He may go through the ordeal; it is well
He is an orphan, friendless save in us:
A woman or a child had made him less
Than either in resolve.
  I. Ber.   Such ties are not
For those who are call'd to the high destinies 85
Which purify corrupted commonwealths;
We must forget all feelings save the *one*,
We must resign all passions save our purpose,
We must behold no object save our country,
And only look on death as beautiful, 90
So that the sacrifice ascend to heaven,
And draw down freedom on her evermore.
  Cal. But if we fail——
  I. Ber.   They never fail who die
In a great cause: the block may soak their gore;
Their heads may sodden in the sun; their limbs 95
Be strung to city gates and castle walls—
But still their spirit walks abroad. Though years
Elapse, and others share as dark a doom,
They but augment the deep and sweeping thoughts
Which overpower all others, and conduct
The world at last to freedom. What were we, 101
If Brutus had not lived? He died in giving
Rome liberty, but left a deathless lesson—
A name which is a virtue, and a soul
Which multiplies itself throughout all time, 105
When wicked men wax mighty, and a state
Turns servile. He and his high friend were styled
'The last of Romans!' Let us be the first

Of true Venetians, sprung from Roman
   sires.   109
   Cal. Our fathers did not fly from Attila
Into these isles, where palaces have sprung
On banks redeem'd from the rude ocean's
   ooze,
To own a thousand despots in his place.
Better bow down before the Hun, and call
A Tartar lord, than these swoln silkworms
   masters!   115
The first at least was man, and used his
   sword
As sceptre: these unmanly creeping things
Command our swords, and rule us with a
   word
As with a spell.
   I. Ber.   It shall be broken soon.
You say that all things are in readiness;
To-day I have not been the usual round,
And why thou knowest; but thy vigilance
Will better have supplied my care: these
   orders
In recent council to redouble now
Our efforts to repair the galleys, have   125
Lent a fair colour to the introduction
Of many of our cause into the arsenal,
As new artificers for their equipment,
Or fresh recruits obtained in haste to man
The hoped-for fleet.—Are all supplied
   with arms?   130
   Cal. All who were deem'd trustworthy:
   there are some
Whom it were well to keep in ignorance
Till it be time to strike, and then supply
   them;
When in the heat and hurry of the hour
They have no opportunity to pause,   135
But needs must on with those who will
   surround them.
   I. Ber. You have said well. Have you
   remark'd all such?
   Cal. I've noted most; and caused the
   other chiefs
To use like caution in their companies.
As far as I have seen, we are enough   140
To make the enterprise secure, if 'tis
Commenced to-morrow; but, till 'tis begun,
Each hour is pregnant with a thousand perils.
   I. Ber. Let the Sixteen meet at the
   wonted hour,
Except Soranzo, Nicoletto Blondo,   145
And Marco Giuda, who will keep their
   watch
Within the arsenal, and hold all ready,
Expectant of the signal we will fix on.
   Cal. We will not fail.
   I. Ber.   Let all the rest be there;
I have a stranger to present to them.   150
   Cal. A stranger! doth he know the
   secret?
   I. Ber.   Yes.
   Cal. And have you dared to peril your
   friends' lives
On a rash confidence in one we know not?

   I. Ber. I have risk'd no man's life ex-
   cept my own—
Of that be certain: he is one who may
Make our assurance doubly sure, accord-
   ing   156
His aid; and if reluctant, he no less
Is in our power: he comes alone with me,
And cannot 'scape us; but he will not
   swerve.
   Cal. I cannot judge of this until I know
   him: 160
Is he one of our order?
   I. Ber.   Ay, in spirit,
Although a child of greatness; he is one—
Who would become a throne, or over-
   throw one—
One who has done great deeds, and seen
   great changes;   164
No tyrant, though bred up to tyranny;
Valiant in war, and sage in council: noble
In nature, although haughty; quick, yet
   wary:
Yet for all this, so full of certain passions,
That if once stirr'd and baffled, as he has
   been
Upon the tenderest points, there is no
   Fury   170
In Grecian story like to that which wrings
His vitals with her burning hands, till he
Grows capable of all things for revenge;
And add too, that his mind is liberal,
He sees and feels the people are oppress'd,
And shares their sufferings. Take him all
   in all,   176
We have need of such, and such have need
   of us.
   Cal. And what part would you have
   him take with us?
   I. Ber. It may be, that of chief.
   Cal.   What! and resign
Your own command as leader?
   I. Ber.   Even so.
My object is to make your cause end well.
And not to push myself to power. Ex-
   perience,   182
Some skill, and your own choice, had
   mark'd me out
To act in trust as your commander, till
Some worthier should appear: if I have
   found such   185
As you yourselves shall own more worthy,
   think you
That I would hesitate from selfishness,
And, covetous of brief authority,
Stake our deep interest on my single
   thoughts,   189
Rather than yield to one above me in
All leading qualities? No, Calendaro,
Know your friend better; but you all shall
   judge.
Away! and let us meet at the fix'd hour.
Be vigilant, and all will yet go well.
   Cal. Worthy Bertuccio, I have known
   you ever   195

425

Trusty and brave, with head and heart to
plan
What I have still been prompt to execute.
For my own part, I seek no other chief;
What the rest will decide I know not, but
I am with YOU, as I have ever been,   200
In all our undertakings. Now farewell,
Until the hour of midnight sees us meet.

[*Exeunt.*

ACT III

SCENE I.—*Scene, the Space between the
Canal and the Church of San Giovanni
e San Paolo. An equestrian Statue
before it.—A Gondola lies in the Canal
at some distance.*

Enter the DOGE *alone, disguised.*

Doge [*solus*]. I am before the hour, the
hour whose voice,
Pealing into the arch of night, might strike
These palaces with ominous tottering,
And rock their marbles to the corner-stone,
Waking the sleepers from some hideous
dream   5
Of indistinct but awful augury
Of that which will befall them. Yes, proud
city!
Thou must be cleansed of the black blood
which makes thee
A lazar-house of tyranny: the task   9
Is forced upon me, I have sought it not;
And therefore was I punish'd, seeing this
Patrician pestilence spread on and on,
Until at length it smote me in my slumbers,
And I am tainted, and must wash away
The plague spots in the healing wave. Tall
fane!   15
Where sleep my fathers, whose dim statues
shadow
The floor which doth divide us from the
dead,
Where all the pregnant hearts of our bold
blood,
Moulder'd into a mite of ashes, hold
In one shrunk heap what once made many
heroes,   20
When what is now a handful shook the
earth—
Fane of the tutelar saints who guard our
house!
Vault where two Doges rest—my sires!
who died
The one of toil, the other in the field,
With a long race of other lineal chiefs
And sages, whose great labours, wounds,
and state   26
I have inherited,—let the graves gape,
Till all thine aisles be peopled with the
dead,
And pour them from thy portals to gaze
on me!
I call them up, and them and thee to wit-
ness   30

What it hath been which put me to this
task—
Their pure high blood, their blazon-roll of
glories,
Their mighty name dishonour'd all *in* me,
Not *by* me, but by the ungrateful nobles
We fought to make our equals, not our
lords: 35
And chiefly thou, Ordelafo the brave,
Who perish'd in the field, where I since
conquer'd,
Battling at Zara, did the hecatombs
Of thine and Venice' foes, there offer'd up
By thy descendant, merit such acquit-
tance?   40
Spirits! smile down upon me; for my cause
Is yours, in all life now can be of yours,—
Your fame, your name, all mingled up in
mine,
And in the future fortunes of our race!
Let me but prosper, and I make this city
Free and immortal, and our house's name
Worthier of what you were, now and here-
after.   47

Enter ISRAEL BERTUCCIO.

I. Ber. Who goes there?
Doge.   A friend to Venice.
I. Ber.   'Tis he.
Welcome, my lord,—you are before the
time.
Doge. I am ready to proceed to your
assembly.   50
I. Ber. Have with you.—I am proud
and pleased to see
Such confident alacrity. Your doubts
Since our last meeting, then, are all dis-
pell'd?
Doge. Not so—but I have set my little
left
Of life upon this cast: the die was thrown
When I first listen'd to your treason.—
Start not!   56
That is the word; I cannot shape my tongue
To syllable black deeds into smooth names,
Though I be wrought on to commit them.
When
I heard you tempt your sovereign, and
forbore   60
To have you dragg'd to prison, I became
Your guiltiest accomplice: now you may,
If it so please you, do as much by me.
I. Ber. Strange words, my lord, and
most unmerited;
I am no spy, and neither are we traitors.
Doge. We—We!—no matter—you have
earn'd the right   66
To talk of *us.*—But to the point.—If this
Attempt succeeds, and Venice, render'd
free
And flourishing, when we are in our graves,
Conducts her generations to our tombs.
And makes her children with their little
hands   71

426

Strew flowers o'er her deliverers' ashes, then
The consequence will sanctify the deed,
And we shall be like the two Bruti in
The annals of hereafter; but if not,   75
If we should fail, employing bloody means
And secret plot, although to a good end,
Still we are traitors, honest Israel;—thou
No less than he who was thy sovereign
Six hours ago, and now thy brother rebel.
    I. Ber. 'Tis not the moment to consider
    thus,   81
Else I could answer.—Let us to the meeting,
Or we may be observed in lingering here.
    Doge. We *are* observed, and have been.
    I. Ber.   We observed!
Let me discover—and this steel——
    Doge.   Put up;
Here are no human witnesses: look there—
What see you?
    I. Ber.   Only a tall warrior's statue
Bestriding a proud steed, in the dim light
Of the dull moon.
    Doge.   That warrior was the sire
Of my sire's fathers, and that statue was
Decreed to him by the twice rescued
    city:—   91
Think you that he looks down on us or no?
    I. Ber. My lord, these are mere fanta-
    sies; there are
No eyes in marble.
    Doge.   But there are in Death.
I tell thee, man, there is a spirit in   95
Such things that acts and sees, unseen,
    though felt;
And, if there be a spell to stir the dead,
'Tis in such deeds as we are now upon.
Deem'st thou the souls of such a race as
    mine
Can rest, when he, their last descendant
    chief,   100
Stands plotting on the brink of their pure
    graves
With stung plebeians?
    I. Ber.   It had been as well
To have pondered this before,—ere you
    embark'd
In our great enterprise.—Do you repent?
    Doge. No—but I *feel*, and shall do to
    the last.   105
I cannot quench a glorious life at once
Nor dwindle to the thing I now must be,
And take men's lives by stealth, without
    some pause;
Yet doubt me not; it is this very feeling,
And knowing *what* has wrung me to be
    thus,   110
Which is your best security. There's not
A roused mechanic in your busy plot
So wrong'd as I, so fall'n, so loudly call'd
To his redress: the very means I am forced
By these fell tyrants to adopt is such,
That I abhor them doubly for the deeds
Which I must do to pay them back for
    theirs.   117

    I. Ber. Let us away—hark—the hour
    strikes.
    Doge.   On—on—
It is our knell, or that of Venice—On.
    I. Ber. Say rather, 'tis her freedom's
    rising peal   120
Of triumph.—This way—we are near the
    place.   [*Exeunt.*

SCENE II.—*The House where the Con-
    spirators meet.*

DAGOLINO, DORO, BERTRAM, FEDELE
TREVISANO,   CALENDARO,   ANTONIO
DELLE BENDE, &c. &c.

    Cal. [*entering*]. Are all here?
    Dag.   All with you; except the three
On duty, and our leader Israel,
Who is expected momently.
    Cal.   Where's Bertram?
    Ber. Here!
    Cal.   Have you not been able to
    complete
The number wanting in your company?
    Ber. I had mark'd out some: but I have
    not dared   6
To trust them with the secret, till assured
That they were worthy faith.
    Cal.   There is no need
Of trusting to their faith; *who*, save our-
    selves
And our more chosen comrades, is aware
Fully of our intent? they think themselves
Engaged in secret to the Signory,   12
To punish some more dissolute young
    nobles
Who have defied the law in their excesses;
But once drawn up, and their new swords
    well flesh'd   15
In the rank hearts of the more odious
    senators,
They will not hesitate to follow up
Their blow upon the others, when they see
The example of their chiefs, and I for one
Will set them such, that they for very
    shame   20
And safety will not pause till all have
    perish'd.
    Ber. How say you? *all!*
    Cal.   Whom wouldst thou spare?
    Ber.   I *spare*?
I have no power to spare. I only question'd,
Thinking that even amongst these wicked
    men
There might be some, whose age and
    qualities   25
Might mark them out for pity.
    Cal.   Yes, such pity
As when the viper hath been cut to pieces,
The separate fragments quivering in the
    sun,
In the last energy of venomous life,
Deserve and have. Why, I should think as
    soon   30

427

Of pitying some particular fang which
  made
One in the jaw of the swoln serpent, as
Of saving one of these: they form but links
Of one long chain; one mass, one breath,
  one body;
They eat, and drink, and live, and breed
  together,   35
Revel, and lie, oppress, and kill in con-
  cert,—
So let them die as *one*!
    Dag.   Should *one* survive,
He would be dangerous as the whole; it is
  not
Their number, be it tens or thousands, but
The spirit of this aristocracy   40
Which must be rooted out; and if there
  were
A single shoot of the old tree in life,
'Twould fasten in the soil, and spring
  again
To gloomy verdure and to bitter fruit.
Bertram, we must be firm!
    Cal.   Look to it well,   45
Bertram; I have an eye upon thee.
    Ber.   Who
Distrusts me?
    Cal.   Not I; for if I did so,
Thou wouldst not now be there to talk of
  trust:
It is thy softness, not thy want of faith,
Which makes thee to be doubted.
    Ber.   You should know   50
Who hear me, who and what I am; a man
Roused like yourselves to overthrow op-
  pression;
A kind man, I am apt to think, as some
Of you have found me; and if brave or no,
You, Calendaro, can pronounce, who
  have seen me   55
Put to the proof; or, if you should have
  doubts,
I'll clear them on your person!
    Cal.   You are welcome,
When once our enterprise is o'er, which
  must not
Be interrupted by a private brawl.
    Ber. I am no brawler; but can bear my-
  self   60
As far among the foe as any he
Who hears me; else why have I been
  selected
To be of your chief comrades? but no less
I own my natural weakness; I have not
Yet learn'd to think of indiscriminate
  murder   65
Without some sense of shuddering; and
  the sight
Of blood which spouts through hoary
  scalps is not
To me a thing of triumph, nor the death
Of men surprised a glory. Well—too well
I know that we must do such things on
  those   70

Whose acts have raised up such avengers;
  but
If there were some of these who could be
  saved
From out this sweeping fate, for our own
  sakes   73
And for our honour, to take off some stain
Of massacre, which else pollutes it wholly,
I had been glad; and see no cause in this
For sneer, nor for suspicion!
    Dag.   Calm thee, Bertram,
For we suspect thee not, and take good
  heart.
It is the cause, and not our will, which asks
Such actions from our hands: we'll wash
  away   80
All stains in Freedom's fountain!

Enter ISRAEL BERTUCCIO, *and the* DOGE,
  disguised.

    Dag.   Welcome, Israel.
    Consp. Most welcome.—Brave Bertuc-
  cio, thou art late—
Who is this stranger?
    Cal.   It is time to name him.
Our comrades are even now prepared to
  greet him
In brotherhood, as I have made it known
That thou wouldst add a brother to our
  cause,   86
Approved by thee, and thus approved by all,
Such is our trust in all thine actions. Now
Let him unfold himself.
    I. Ber.   Stranger, step forth!
          [*The Doge discovers himself.*
    Consp. To arms!—we are betray'd—it
  is the Doge!   90
Down with them both! our traitorous
  captain, and
The tyrant he hath sold us to.
    Cal. [*drawing his sword*]. Hold! hold!
Who moves a step against them dies.
  Hold! hear
Bertuccio—What! are you appall'd to see
A lone, unguarded, weaponless old man
Amongst you?—Israel, speak; what means
  this mystery?   96
    I. Ber. Let them advance and strike at
  their own bosoms,
Ungrateful suicides! for on our lives
Depend their own, their fortunes, and
  their hopes.
    Doge. Strike!—If I dreaded death, a
  death more fearful   100
Than any your rash weapons can inflict,
I should not now be here: Oh, noble
  Courage!
The eldest born of Fear, which makes you
  brave
Against this solitary hoary head!
See the bold chiefs, who would reform a
  state   105
And shake down senates, mad with wrath
  and dread

428

At sight of one patrician! Butcher me!
You can, I care not.—Israel, are these men
The mighty hearts you spoke of? look
    upon them!
    Cal. Faith! he hath shamed us, and
    deservedly.   110
Was this your trust in your true chief
    Bertuccio,
To turn your swords against him and his
    guest?
Sheathe them, and hear him.
    I. Ber.   I disdain to speak.
They might and must have known a heart
    like mine   114
Incapable of treachery; and the power
They gave me to adopt all fitting means
To further their design was ne'er abused.
They might be certain that whoe'er was
    brought
By me into this council had been led
To take his choice—as brother, or as
    victim.   120
    Doge. And which am I to be? your
    actions leave
Some cause to doubt the freedom of the
    choice.
    I. Ber. My lord, we would have perish'd
    here together,
Had these rash men proceeded; but, be-
    hold,
They are ashamed of that mad moment's
    impulse,   125
And droop their heads; believe me, they
    are such
As I described them.—Speak to them.
    Cal.   Ay, speak;
We are all listening in wonder.
    I. Ber. [*addressing the conspirators*].
    You are safe,
Nay, more, almost triumphant—listen
    then,   129
And know my words for truth.
    Doge.   You see me here,
As one of you hath said, an old, unarm'd,
Defenceless man; and yesterday you saw
    me
Presiding in the hall of ducal state,
Apparent sovereign of our hundred isles,
Robed in official purple, dealing out
The edicts of a power which is not mine,
Nor yours, but of our masters—the patri-
    cians.
Why I was there you know, or think you
    know;
Why I am *here*, he who hath been most
    wrong'd,
He who among you hath been most in-
    sulted,   140
Outraged, and trodden on, until he doubt
If he be worm or no, may answer for me,
Asking of his own heart what brought him
    here?
You know my recent story, all men know
    it,

And judge of it far differently from those
Who sate in judgment to heap scorn on
    scorn.   146
But spare me the recital—it is here,
Here at my heart the outrage—but my
    words,
Already spent in unavailing plaints,
Would only show my feebleness the more,
And I come here to strengthen even the
    strong,   151
And urge them on to deeds, and not to war
With woman's weapons; but I need not
    urge you.
Our private wrongs have sprung from
    public vices,
In this—I cannot call it commonwealth,
Nor kingdom, which hath neither prince
    nor people,   156
But all the sins of the old Spartan state
Without its virtues—temperance and va-
    lour.
The Lords of Lacedæmon were true sol-
    diers,   159
But ours are Sybarites, while we are Helots,
Of whom I am the lowest, most enslaved;
Although dress'd out to head a pageant, as
The Greeks of yore made drunk their
    slaves to form
A pastime for their children. You are met
To overthrow this monster of a state,
This mockery of a government, this
    spectre,   166
Which must be exorcised with blood,—
    and then
We will renew the times of truth and justice,
Condensing in a fair free commonwealth
Not rash equality but equal rights,   170
Proportion'd like the columns to the
    temple,
Giving and taking strength reciprocal,
And making firm the whole with grace and
    beauty,   173
So that no part could be removed without
Infringement of the general symmetry.
In operating this great change, I claim
To be one of you—if you trust in me;
If not, strike home,—my life is com-
    promised,   178
And I would rather fall by freemen's hands
Than live another day to act the tyrant
As delegate of tyrants: such I am not,
And never have been—read it in our
    annals;
I can appeal to my past government
In many lands and cities; they can tell you
If I were an oppressor, or a man   185
Feeling and thinking for my fellow men.
Haply had I been what the senate sought,
A thing of robes and trinkets, dizen'd out
To sit in state as for a sovereign's picture;
A popular scourge, a ready sentence-
    signer,   190
A stickler for the Senate and 'the Forty',
A sceptic of all measures which had not

The sanction of 'the Ten', a council-
fawner,
A tool, a fool, a puppet,—they had ne'er
Foster'd the wretch who stung me. What
I suffer 195
Has reach'd me through my pity for the
people;
That many know, and they who know not
yet
Will one day learn: meantime I do devote,
Whate'er the issue, my last days of life—
My present power such as it is, not that
Of Doge, but of a man who has been great
Before he was degraded to a Doge, 202
And still has individual means and mind;
I stake my fame (and I had fame)—my
breath—
(The least of all, for its last hours are nigh)
My heart, my hope, my soul, upon this
cast! 206
Such as I am, I offer me to you
And to your chiefs; accept me or reject me,—
A Prince who fain would be a citizen
Or nothing, and who has left his throne to
be so. 210
    Cal. Long live Faliero!—Venice shall
be free!
    Consp. Long live Faliero!
    I. Ber.   Comrades! did I well?
Is not this man a host in such a cause?
    Doge. This is no time for eulogies, nor
place
For exultation. Am I one of you? 215
    Cal. Ay, and the first among us, as thou
hast been
Of Venice—be our general and chief.
    Doge. Chief!—general!—I was general
at Zara,
And chief in Rhodes and Cyprus, prince
in Venice: 219
I cannot stoop——that is, I am not fit
To lead a band of——patriots: when I lay
Aside the dignities which I have borne,
'Tis not to put on others, but to be
Mate to my fellows—but now to the point;
Israel has stated to me your whole plan—
'Tis bold, but feasible if I assist it, 226
And must be set in motion instantly.
    Cal. E'en when thou wilt. Is it not so,
my friends?
I have disposed all for a sudden blow;
When shall it be then?
    Doge.   At sunrise.
    Ber.   So soon?
    Doge. So soon?—so late—each hour
accumulates 231
Peril on peril, and the more so now
Since I have mingled with you;—know
you not
The Council, and 'the Ten'? the spies, the
eyes
Of the patricians dubious of their slaves,
And now more dubious of the prince they
have made one? 236

I tell you, you must strike, and suddenly,
Full to the Hydra's heart—its heads will
follow.
    Cal. With all my soul and sword, I yield
assent; 239
Our companies are ready, sixty each,
And all now under arms by Israel's order;
Each at their different place of rendezvous,
And vigilant, expectant of some blow;
Let each repair for action to his post!
And now, my lord, the signal?
    Doge.   When you hear
The great bell of St. Mark's, which may
not be 246
Struck without special order of the Doge
(The last poor privilege they leave their
prince),
March on Saint Mark's!
    I. Ber.   And there?—
    Doge.   By different routes
Let your march be directed, every sixty
Entering a separate avenue, and still 251
Upon the way let your cry be of war
And of the Genoese fleet, by the first dawn
Discern'd before the port; form round the
palace,
Within whose court will be drawn out in
arms 255
My nephew and the clients of our house,
Many and martial; while the bell tolls on,
Shout ye, 'Saint Mark!—the foe is on our
waters!'
    Cal. I see it now—but on, my noble lord.
    Doge. All the patricians flocking to the
Council, 260
(Which they dare not refuse, at the dread
signal
Pealing from out their patron saint's proud
tower),
Will then be gather'd in unto the harvest,
And we will reap them with the sword for
sickle.
If some few should be tardy or absent
them, 265
'Twill be but to be taken faint and single,
When the majority are put to rest.
    Cal. Would that the hour were come!
we will not scotch,
But kill.
    Ber. Once more, sir, with your pardon, I
Would now repeat the question which I
ask'd 270
Before Bertuccio added to our cause
This great ally who renders it more sure,
And therefore safer, and as such admits
Some dawn of mercy to a portion of
Our victims—must all perish in this
slaughter? 275
    Cal. All who encounter me and mine,
be sure,
The mercy they have shown, I show.
    Consp.   All! all!
Is this a time to talk of pity? when
Have they e'er shown, or felt, or feign'd it?

430

I. Ber.   Bertram,
This false compassion is a folly, and
Injustice to thy comrades and thy cause!
Dost thou not see, that if we single out
Some for escape, they live but to avenge
The fallen? and how distinguish now the
    innocent
From out the guilty? all their acts are
    one—   285
A single emanation from one body,
Together knit for our oppression! 'Tis
Much that we let their children live; I
    doubt   288
If all of these even should be set apart:
The hunter may reserve some single cub
From out the tiger's litter, but whoe'er
Would seek to save the spotted sire or dam,
Unless to perish by their fangs? however,
I will abide by Doge Faliero's counsel:
Let him decide if any should be saved.
    Doge. Ask me not—tempt me not with
        such a question—
Decide yourselves.   296
    I. Ber. You know their private virtues
Far better than we can, to whom alone
Their public vices, and most foul oppres-
    sion,
Have made them deadly; if there be a-
    mongst them   300
One who deserves to be repeal'd, pro-
    nounce.
    Doge. Dolfino's father was my friend,
        and Lando
Fought by my side, and Marc Cornaro
    shared
My Genoese embassy: I saved the life
Of Veniero—shall I save it twice?   305
Would that I could save them and Venice
    also!
All these men, or their fathers, were my
    friends
Till they became my subjects; then fell
    from me
As faithless leaves drop from the o'er-
    blown flower,   309
All left me a lone blighted thorny stalk,
Which, in its solitude, can shelter nothing;
So, as they let me wither, let them perish.
    Cal. They cannot co-exist with Venice'
        freedom!
    Doge. Ye, though you know and feel
        our mutual mass   314
Of many wrongs, even ye are ignorant
What fatal poison to the springs of life,
To human ties, and all that's good and
    dear,
Lurks in the present institutes of Venice:
All these men were my friends: I loved
    them, they
Requited honourably my regards;   320
We served and fought; we smiled and wept
    in concert;
We revell'd or we sorrow'd side by side:
We made alliances of blood and marriage;

We grew in years and honours fairly,—till
Their own desire, not my ambition, made
Them choose me for their prince, and then
    farewell!   326
Farewell all social memory! all thoughts
In common! and sweet bonds which link
    old friendships,
When the survivors of long years and
    actions,
Which now belong to history, soothe the
    days   330
Which yet remain by treasuring each other,
And never meet, but each beholds the
    mirroi
Of half a century on his brother's brow,
And sees a hundred beings, now in earth,
Flit round them whispering of the days
    gone by,   335
And seeming not all dead, as long as two
Of the brave, joyous, reckless, glorious
    band,
Which once were one and many, still retain
A breath to sigh for them, a tongue to speak
Of deeds that else were silent, save on
    marble——   340
Oimé! Oimé!—and must I do this deed?
    I. Ber. My lord, you are much moved:
        it is not now
That such things must be dwelt upon.
    Doge.   Your patience
A moment—I recede not: mark with me
The gloomy vices of this government.
From the hour they made me Doge, the
    Doge THEY *made* me—
Farewell the past! I died to all that had been,
Or rather they to me: no friends, no kind-
    ness,
No privacy of life—all were cut off:
They came not near me, such approach
    gave umbrage;   350
They could not love me, such was not the
    law;
They thwarted me, 'twas the state's policy;
They baffled me, 'twas a patrician's duty;
They wrong'd me, for such was to right the
    state;
They could not right me, that would give
    suspicion;   355
So that I was a slave to my own subjects;
So that I was a foe to my own friends;
Begirt with spies for guards, with robes for
    power,
With pomp for freedom, gaolers for a
    council,
Inquisitors for friends, and hell for life!
I had one only fount of quiet left,   361
And *that* they poison'd! My pure house-
    hold gods
Were shiver'd on my hearth, and o'er their
    shrine
Sate grinning Ribaldry and sneering Scorn.
    I. Ber. You have been deeply wrong'd,
        and now shall be   365
Nobly avenged before another night.

431

Doge. I had borne all—it hurt me, but
   I bore it—
Till this last running over of the cup
Of bitterness—until this last loud insult,
Not only unredress'd, but sanction'd;
   then,   370
And thus, I cast all further feelings from
   me—
The feelings which they crush'd for me,
   long, long
Before, even in their oath of false allegi-
   ance!
Even in that very hour and vow, they
   abjured
Their friend and made a sovereign, as
   boys make   375
Playthings, to do their pleasure—and be
   broken!
I from that hour have seen but senators
In dark suspicious conflict with the Doge,
Brooding with him in mutual hate and fear;
They dreading he should snatch the
   tyranny   380
From out their grasp, and he abhorring
   tyrants.
To me, then, these men have no *private* life,
Nor claim to ties they have cut off from
   others;
As senators for arbitrary acts
Amenable, I look on them—as such   385
Let them be dealt upon.
   Cal.   And now to action!
Hence, brethren, to our posts, and may
   this be
The last night of mere words: I'd fain be
   doing!
Saint Mark's great bell at dawn shall find
   me wakeful!
   I. Ber. Disperse then to your posts: be
   firm and vigilant;   390
Think on the wrongs we bear, the rights
   we claim.
This day and night shall be the last of
   peril!
Watch for the signal, and then march. I go
To join my band: let each be prompt to
   marshal
His separate charge: the Doge will now
   return   395
To the palace to prepare all for the blow.
We part to meet in freedom and in glory!
   Cal. Doge, when I greet you next, my
   homage to you
Shall be the head of Steno on this sword!
   Doge. No; let him be reserved unto the
   last,   400
Nor turn aside to strike at such a prey,
Till nobler game is quarried: his offence
Was a mere ebullition of the vice,
The general corruption generated   404
By the foul aristocracy: he could not—
He dared not in more honourable days
Have risk'd it. I have merged all private
   wrath

Against him in the thought of our great
   purpose.
A slave insults me—I require his punish-
   ment
From his proud master's hands; if he re-
   fuse it,   410
The offence grows his, and let him answer it.
   Cal. Yet, as the immediate cause of the
   alliance
Which consecrates our undertaking more,
I owe him such deep gratitude, that fain
I would repay him as he merits; may I?
   Doge. You would but lop the hand, and
   I the head;   416
You would but smite the scholar, I the
   master;
You would but punish Steno, I the senate.
I cannot pause on individual hate,
In the absorbing, sweeping, whole revenge,
Which, like the sheeted fire from heaven,
   must blast   421
Without distinction, as it fell of yore,
Where the Dead Sea hath quench'd two
   cities' ashes.
   I. Ber. Away, then, to your posts! I but
   remain
A moment to accompany the Doge   425
To our late place of tryst, to see no spies
Have been upon the scout, and thence I
   hasten
To where my allotted band is under arms.
   Cal. Farewell, then,—until dawn!
   I. Ber.   Success go with you!
   Consp. We will not fail—Away! My
   lord, farewell!   430
   [*The Conspirators salute the* DOGE *and*
     ISRAEL BERTUCCIO, *and retire, headed*
     by PHILIP CALENDARO. *The* DOGE *and*
     ISRAEL BERTUCCIO *remain.*
   I. Ber. We have them in the toil—it can-
   not fail!
Now thou'rt indeed a sovereign, and wilt
   make
A name immortal greater than the greatest.
Free citizens have struck at kings ere now;
Cæsars have fallen, and even patrician
   hands   435
Have crush'd dictators, as the popular steel
Has reach'd patricians: but, until this hour,
What prince has plotted for his people's
   freedom?   438
Or risk'd a life to liberate his subjects?
For ever, and for ever, they conspire
Against the people, to abuse their hands
To chains, but laid aside to carry weapons
Against the fellow nations, so that yoke
On yoke, and slavery and death may whet,
Not glut, the never-gorged Leviathan!
Now, my lord, to our enterprise;—'tis
   great,   446
And greater the reward; why stand you
   rapt?
A moment back, and you were all im-
   patience!

Doge. And is it then decided! must they
　　die?

I. Ber. Who?

Doge.　　　　My own friends by blood
　　and courtesy,　　　　　　　　　450
And many deeds and days—the senators?

I. Ber. You pass'd their sentence, and
　　it is a just one.

Doge. Ay, so it seems, and so it is to
　　you;
You are a patriot, a plebeian Gracchus—
The rebels' oracle, the people's tribune—
I blame you not—you act in your voca-
　　tion;　　　　　　　　　　　　456
They smote you, and oppress'd you, and
　　despised you;
So they have *me;* but *you* ne'er spake with
　　them;
You never broke their bread, nor shared
　　their salt,
You never had their wine-cup at your lips;
You grew not up with them, nor laugh'd,
　　nor wept,　　　　　　　　　　461
Nor held a revel in their company;
Ne'er smiled to see them smile, nor claim'd
　　their smile
In social interchange for yours, nor trusted
Nor wore them in your heart of hearts, as
　　I have:　　　　　　　　　　　465
These hairs of mine are grey, and so are
　　theirs,
The elders of the Council: I remember
When all our locks were like the raven's
　　wing,
As we went forth to take our prey around
The isles wrung from the false Mahome-
　　tan;　　　　　　　　　　　　470
And can I see them dabbled o'er with blood?
Each stab to them will seem my suicide.

I. Ber. Doge! Doge! this vacillation is
　　unworthy
A child; if you are not in second childhood,
Call back your nerves to your own pur-
　　pose, nor　　　　　　　　　　475
Thus shame yourself and me. By heavens!
　　I'd rather
Forego even now, or fail in our intent,
Than see the man I venerate subside
From high resolves into such shallow
　　weakness!
You have seen blood in battle, shed it,
　　both　　　　　　　　　　　　480
Your own and that of others; can you
　　shrink then
From a few drops from veins of hoary
　　vampires,
Who but give back what they have drain'd
　　from millions?

Doge. Bear with me! Step by step, and
　　blow on blow,
I will divide with you; think not I waver:
Ah! no; it is the *certainty* of all　　486
Which I must do doth make me tremble
　　thus.

But let these last and lingering thoughts
　　have way,
To which you only and the night are con-
　　scious,
And both regardless: when the hour
　　arrives,　　　　　　　　　　490
'Tis mine to sound the knell, and strike
　　the blow,
Which shall unpeople many palaces,
And hew the highest genealogic trees
Down to the earth, strew'd with their
　　bleeding fruit,　　　　　　　　494
And crush their blossoms into barrenness:
This will I—must I—have I sworn to do,
Nor aught can turn me from my destiny;
But still I quiver to behold what I
Must be, and think what I have been! Bear
　　with me.

I. Ber. Re-man your breast; I feel no
　　such remorse,　　　　　　　　500
I understand it not: why should you
　　change?
You acted, and you act, on your free will.

Doge. Ay, there it is—*you* feel not, nor
　　do I,
Else I should stab thee on the spot, to save
A thousand lives, and killing, do no mur-
　　der;　　　　　　　　　　　　505
You *feel* not—*you* go to this butcher-work
As if these high-born men were steers for
　　shambles:
When all is over, you'll be free and merry,
And calmly wash those hands incarnadine;
But I, outgoing thee and all thy fellows
In this surpassing massacre, shall be,
Shall see and feel—oh God! oh God! 'tis
　　true,　　　　　　　　　　　　512
And thou dost well to answer that it was
'My own free will and act,' and yet you err,
For I *will* do this! Doubt not—fear not; I
Will be your most unmerciful accomplice!
And yet I act no more on my free will,
Nor my own feelings—both compel me
　　back;
But there is *hell* within me and around,
And like the demon who believes and
　　trembles　　　　　　　　　　520
Must I abhor and do. Away! away!
Get thee unto thy fellows, I will hie me
To gather the retainers of our house.
Doubt not, St. Mark's great bell shall wake
　　all Venice,　　　　　　　　　524
Except her slaughtered senate: ere the sun
Be broad upon the Adriatic there
Shall be a voice of weeping, which shall
　　drown
The roar of waters in the cry of blood!
I am resolved—come on.

I. Ber.　　　　　With all my soul!
Keep a firm rein upon these bursts of
　　passion;　　　　　　　　　　530
Remember what these men have dealt to
　　thee,
And that this sacrifice will be succeeded

By ages of prosperity and freedom
To this unshackled city: a true tyrant
Would have depopulated empires, nor
Have felt the strange compunction which
   hath wrung you   536
To punish a few traitors to the people.
Trust me, such were a pity more misplaced
Than the late mercy of the state to Steno.
   Doge. Man, thou hast struck upon the
      chord which jars   540
All nature from my heart. Hence to our
   task!   [*Exeunt.*

ACT IV

SCENE I.—*Palazzo of the Patrician* LIONI.
  LIONI *laying aside the mask and cloak*
  which the Venetian Nobles wore in
  public, attended by a Domestic.

  Lioni. I will to rest, right weary of this
   revel,
The gayest we have held for many moons,
And yet, I know not why, it cheer'd me not;
There came a heaviness across my heart,
Which, in the lightest movement of the
   dance,   5
Though eye to eye, and hand in hand
   united
Even with the lady of my love, oppress'd
   me,
And through my spirit chill'd my blood,
   until
A damp like death rose o'er my brow; I
   strove
To laugh the thought away, but 'twould
   not be;   10
Through all the music ringing in my ears
A knell was sounding as distinct and clear,
Though low and far, as e'er the Adrian
   wave
Rose o'er the city's murmur in the night,
Dashing against the outward Lido's bul-
   wark: 15
So that I left the festival before
It reach'd its zenith, and will woo my pil-
   low
For thoughts more tranquil, or forgetful-
   ness.
Antonio, take my mask and cloak, and
   light   19
The lamp within my chamber.
  Ant.   Yes, my lord:
Command you no refreshment?
  Lioni.   Nought, save sleep,
Which will not be commanded. Let me
   hope it,   [*Exit* ANTONIO.
Though my breast feels too anxious; I will
   try
Whether the air will calm my spirits: 'tis
A goodly night; the cloudy wind which
   blew   25
From the Levant hath crept into its cave,
And the broad moon hath brighten'd. What
   a stillness! [*Goes to an open lattice.*

And what a contrast with the scene I left,
Where the tall torches' glare, and silver
   lamps'
More pallid gleam along the tapestried
   walls,   30
Spread over the reluctant gloom which
   haunts
Those vast and dimly-latticed galleries
A dazzling mass of artificial light,
Which show'd all things, but nothing as
   they were.   34
There Age essaying to recall the past,
After long striving for the hues of youth
At the sad labour of the toilet, and
Full many a glance at the too faithful
   mirror,
Prank'd forth in all the pride of ornament,
Forgot itself, and trusting to the falsehood
Of the indulgent beams, which show, yet
   hide,   41
Believed itself forgotten, and was fool'd.
There Youth, which needed not, nor
   thought of such
Vain adjuncts, lavish'd its true bloom, and
   health,
And bridal beauty, in the unwholesome
   press   45
Of flush'd and crowded wassailers, and
   wasted
Its hours of rest in dreaming this was
   pleasure,
And so shall waste them till the sunrise
   streams
On sallow cheeks and sunken eyes, which
   should not   49
Have worn this aspect yet for many a year.
The music, and the banquet, and the wine,
The garlands, the rose odours, and the
   flowers,
The sparkling eyes, and flashing orna-
   ments,
The white arms and the raven hair, the
   braids
And bracelets; swanlike bosoms, and the
   necklace,   55
An India in itself, yet dazzling not
The eye like what it circled; the thin robes,
Floating like light clouds 'twixt our gaze
   and heaven;
The many-twinkling feet so small and
   sylph-like,
Suggesting the more secret symmetry 60
Of the fair forms which terminate so well—
All the delusion of the dizzy scene,
Its false and true enchantments—art and
   nature,
Which swam before my giddy eyes, that
   drank
The sight of beauty as the parched pilgrim's
On Arab sands the false mirage, which
   offers   66
A lucid lake to his eluded thirst,
Are gone. Around me are the stars and
   waters—

Worlds mirror'd in the ocean, goodlier
　　sight　　　　　　　　　　　　　　69
Than torches glared back by a gaudy glass;
And the great element, which is to space
What ocean is to earth, spreads its blue
　　depths,
Soften'd with the first breathings of the
　　spring;
The high moon sails upon her beauteous
　　way,　　　　　　　　　　　　　　74
Serenely smoothing o'er the lofty walls
Of those tall piles and sea-girt palaces,
Whose porphyry pillars, and whose costly
　　fronts,
Fraught with the orient spoil of many
　　marbles,
Like altars ranged along the broad canal,
Seem each a trophy of some mighty deed
Rear'd up from out the waters, scarce less
　　strangely　　　　　　　　　　　　81
Than those more massy and mysterious
　　giants
Of architecture, those Titanian fabrics,
Which point in Egypt's plains to times that
　　have　　　　　　　　　　　　　84
No other record. All is gentle: nought
Stirs rudely; but, congenial with the night,
Whatever walks is gliding like a spirit.
The tinklings of some vigilant guitars
Of sleepless lovers to a wakeful mistress,
And cautious opening of the casement,
　　showing　　　　　　　　　　　　90
That he is not unheard; while her young
　　hand,
Fair as the moonlight of which it seems part,
So delicately white, it trembles in
The act of opening the forbidden lattice,
To let in love through music, makes his
　　heart　　　　　　　　　　　　　95
Thrill like his lyre-strings at the sight; the
　　dash
Phosphoric of the oar, or rapid twinkle
Of the far lights of skimming gondolas,
And the responsive voices of the choir
Of boatmen answering back with verse for
　　verse;　　　　　　　　　　　　100
Some dusky shadow checkering the Rialto;
Some glimmering palace roof, or tapering
　　spire,
Are all the sights and sounds which here
　　pervade
The ocean-born and earth-commanding
　　city—
How sweet and soothing is this hour of
　　calm!　　　　　　　　　　　　105
I thank thee, Night! for thou hast chased
　　away
Those horrid bodements which, amidst
　　the throng,
I could not dissipate: and with the blessing
Of thy benign and quiet influence,　　109
Now will I to my couch, although to rest
Is almost wronging such a night as this.—
　　[*A knocking is heard from without.*

Hark! what is that? or who at such a
　　moment?

Enter ANTONIO.

Ant. My lord, a man without, on urgent
　　business,
Implores to be admitted.
　　Lioni.　　　　　　Is he a stranger?
Ant. His face is muffled in his cloak,
　　but both　　　　　　　　　　　115
His voice and gestures seem familiar to
　　me;
I craved his name, but this he seem'd
　　reluctant
To trust, save to yourself; most earnestly
He sues to be permitted to approach you.
Lioni. 'Tis a strange hour, and a suspi-
　　cious bearing!　　　　　　　　120
And yet there is slight peril: 'tis not in
Their houses noble men are struck at; still,
Although I know not that I have a foe
In Venice, 'twill be wise to use some
　　caution.
Admit him, and retire; but call up quickly
Some of thy fellows, who may wait with-
　　out.—　　　　　　　　　　　126
Who can this man be?
　　[*Exit* ANTONIO, *and returns with* BER-
　　TRAM *muffled.*
Ber.　　　　　My good lord Lioni,
I have no time to lose, nor thou,—dismiss
This menial hence; I would be private with
　　you.
　　Lioni. It seems the voice of Bertram—
Go, Antonio.　　　　[*Exit* ANTONIO.
Now, stranger, what would you at such an
　　hour?　　　　　　　　　　　131
Ber. [*discovering himself*]. A boon, my
　　noble patron; you have granted
Many to your poor client, Bertram; add
This one, and make him happy.
　　Lioni.　　　　Thou hast known me
From boyhood, ever ready to assist thee
In all fair objects of advancement, which
Beseem one of thy station; I would promise
Ere thy request was heard, but that the
　　hour,　　　　　　　　　　　138
Thy bearing, and this strange, and hurried
　　mode
Of suing, gives me to suspect this visit
Hath some mysterious import—but say
　　on—　　　　　　　　　　　141
What has occurred, some rash and sudden
　　broil?—
A cup too much, a scuffle, and a stab?—
Mere things of every day; so that thou hast
　　not
Spilt noble blood, I guarantee thy safety;
But then thou must withdraw, for angry
　　friends　　　　　　　　　　　146
And relatives, in the first burst of venge-
　　ance,
Are things in Venice deadlier than the
　　laws.

Ber. My lord, I thank you; but——
Lioni. But what? You have not
Raised a rash hand against one of our
order? 150
If so, withdraw and fly, and own it not;
I would not slay—but then I must not save
thee!
He who has shed patrician blood——
Ber. I come
To save patrician blood, and not to shed it!
And thereunto I must be speedy, for
Each minute lost may lose a life; since
Time
Has changed his slow scythe for the two-
edged sword, 157
And is about to take, instead of sand,
The dust from sepulchres to fill his hour-
glass!—
Go not *thou* forth to-morrow!
Lioni. Wherefore not?
What means this menace?
Ber. Do not seek its meaning,
But do as I implore thee;—stir not forth,
Whate'er be stirring; though the roar of
crowds—
The cry of women, and the shrieks of
babes—
The groans of men—the clash of arms—
the sound 165
Of rolling drum, shrill trump, and hollow
bell,
Peal in one wild alarum!—Go not forth,
Until the tocsin's silent, nor even then
Till I return!
Lioni. Again, what does this mean?
Ber. Again, I tell thee, ask not; but by
all 170
Thou holdest dear on earth or heaven—by
all
The souls of thy great fathers, and thy
hope
To emulate them, and to leave behind
Descendants worthy both of them and
thee—
By all thou hast of bless'd in hope or
memory— 175
By all thou hast to fear here or hereafter—
By all the good deeds thou hast done to
me,
Good I would now repay with greater
good,
Remain within—trust to thy household
gods, 179
And to my word for safety, if thou dost
As I now counsel—but if not, thou art
lost!
Lioni. I am indeed already lost in won-
der;
Surely thou ravest! what have *I* to dread?
Who are my foes? or if there be such, *why*
Art *thou* leagued with them? *thou !* or if so
leagued, 185
Why comest thou to tell me at this hour,
And not before?

Ber. I cannot answer this.
Wilt thou go forth despite of this true
warning?
Lioni. I was not born to shrink from
idle threats, 189
The cause of which I know not: at the hour
Of council, be it soon or late, I shall not
Be found among the absent.
Ber. Say not so!
Once more, art thou determined to go
forth?
Lioni. I am. Nor is there aught which
shall impede me!
Ber. Then, Heaven have mercy on thy
soul!—Farewell! [*Going.*
Lioni. Stay—there is more in this than
my own safety 196
Which makes me call thee back; we must
not part thus:
Bertram, I have known thee long.
Ber. From childhood, signor,
You have been my protector: in the days
Of reckless infancy, when rank forgets,
Or, rather, is not yet taught to remember,
Its cold prerogative, we play'd together;
Our sports, our smiles, our tears, were
mingled oft;
My father was your father's client, I
His son's scarce less than foster-brother;
years 205
Saw us together—happy, heart-full hours!
Oh God! the difference 'twixt those hours
and this!
Lioni. Bertram, 'tis thou who hast for-
gotten them.
Ber. Nor now, nor ever; whatsoe'er be-
tide,
I would have saved you: when to man-
hood's growth 210
We sprung, and you, devoted to the state,
As suits your station, the more humble
Bertram
Was left unto the labours of the humble,
Still you forsook me not; and if my for-
tunes
Have not been towering, 'twas no fault of
him 215
Who ofttimes rescued and supported me,
When struggling with the tides of circum-
stance,
Which bear away the weaker: noble blood
Ne'er mantled in a nobler heart than thine
Has proved to me, the poor plebeian Ber-
tram. 220
Would that thy fellow senators were like
thee!
Lioni. Why, what hast thou to say
against the senate?
Ber. Nothing.
Lioni. I know that there are angry
spirits 223
And turbulent mutterers of stifled treason,
Who lurk in narrow places, and walk out
Muffled to whisper curses to the night;

Disbanded soldiers, discontented ruffians,
And desperate libertines who brawl in
      taverns;
Thou herdest not with such: 'tis true, of late
I have lost sight of thee, but thou wert
      wont   230
To lead a temperate life, and break thy bread
With honest mates, and bear a cheerful
      aspect.
What hath come to thee? in thy hollow eye
And hueless cheek, and thine unquiet
      motions,
Sorrow and shame and conscience seem at
      war   235
To waste thee.
      Ber.   Rather shame and sorrow light
On the accursèd tyranny which rides
The very air in Venice, and makes men
Madden as in the last hours of the plague
Which sweeps the soul deliriously from
      life!   240
      Lioni. Some villains have been tamper-
      ing with thee, Bertram;
This is not thy old language, nor own
      thoughts;
Some wretch has made thee drunk with
      disaffection:
But thou must not be lost so; thou *wert*
      good   244
And kind, and art not fit for such base acts
As vice and villainy would put thee to:
Confess—confide in me—thou know'st
      my nature.   247
What is it thou and thine are bound to do,
Which should prevent thy friend, the only
      son
Of him who was a friend unto thy father,
So that our good-will is a heritage   251
We should bequeath to our posterity
Such as ourselves received it, or aug-
      mented;
I say, what is it thou must do, that I
Should deem thee dangerous, and keep the
      house   255
Like a sick girl?
      Ber.   Nay, question me no further:
I must be gone.——
      Lioni.   And I be murder'd!—say,
Was it not thus thou said'st, my gentle
      Bertram?
      Ber. Who talks of murder? what said I
      of murder?
'Tis false! I did not utter such a word.
      Lioni. Thou didst not; but from out thy
      wolfish eye,   261
So changed from what I knew it, there
      glares forth
The gladiator. If *my* life's thine object,
Take it—I am unarm'd,—and then away!
I would not hold my breath on such a
      tenure   265
As the capricious mercy of such things
As thou and those who have set thee to thy
      taskwork.

      Ber. Sooner than spill thy blood, I peril
      mine;
Sooner than harm a hair of thine, I place
In jeopardy a thousand heads, and some
As noble, nay, even nobler than thine own.
      Lioni. Ay, is it even so? Excuse me,
      Bertram;   272
I am not worthy to be singled out
From such exalted hecatombs—who are
      they
That *are* in danger, and that *make* the
      danger?   275
      Ber. Venice, and all that she inherits,
      are
Divided like a house against itself,
And so will perish ere to-morrow's twi-
      light!
      Lioni. More mysteries, and awful ones!
      But now,
Or thou, or I, or both, it may be, are
Upon the verge of ruin; speak once out,
And thou art safe and glorious; for 'tis
      more   282
Glorious to save than slay, and slay i' the
      dark too—
Fie, Bertram! that was not a craft for thee!
How would it look to see upon a spear
The head of him whose heart was open to
      thee,   286
Borne by thy hand before the shuddering
      people?
And such may be my doom; for here I
      swear,
Whate'er the peril or the penalty
Of thy denunciation, I go forth,   290
Unless thou dost detail the cause, and
      show
The consequence of all which led thee here!
      Ber. Is there no way to save thee?
      minutes fly,
And thou art lost!—*thou!* my sole bene-
      factor,
The only being who was constant to me
Through every change. Yet, make me not
      a traitor!   296
Let me save thee—but spare my honour!
      Lioni.   Where
Can lie the honour in a league of murder?
And who are traitors save unto the
      state?
      Ber. A league is still a compact, and
      more binding   300
In honest hearts when words must stand
      for law;
And in my mind, there is no traitor like
He whose domestic treason plants the
      poniard
Within the breast which trusted to his
      truth.   304
      Lioni. And *who* will strike the steel to
      mine?
      Ber.   Not I;
I could have wound my soul up to all
      things

Save this. *Thou* must not die! and think
  how dear
Thy life is, when I risk so many lives,
Nay, more, the life of lives, the liberty
Of future generations, *not* to be   310
The assassin thou miscall'st me:—once,
  once more
I do adjure thee, pass not o'er thy threshold!
  Lioni. It is in vain—this moment I go
  forth.
  Ber. Then perish Venice rather than my
  friend!
I will disclose—ensnare—betray—des-
  troy—   315
Oh, what a villain I become for thee!
  Lioni. Say, rather, thy friend's saviour
  and the state's!—
Speak—pause not—all rewards, all
  pledges for
Thy safety and thy welfare; wealth such as
The state accords her worthiest servants;
  nay,   320
Nobility itself I guarantee thee,
So that thou art sincere and penitent.
  Ber. I have thought again: it must not
  be—I love thee—
Thou know'st it—that I stand here is the
  proof,
Not least though last; but having done my
  duty   325
By thee, I now must do it by my country!
Farewell—we meet no more in life!—fare-
  well!
  Lioni. What, ho!—Antonio—Pedro—
  to the door!
See that none pass—arrest this man!—

Enter ANTONIO *and other armed Domestics,
  who seize* BERTRAM.

Lioni [*continues*].   Take care
He hath no harm; bring me my sword and
  cloak,   330
And man the gondola with four oars—
  quick—
                    [*Exit* ANTONIO.
We will unto Giovanni Gradenigo's,
And send for Marc Cornaro:—fear not,
  Bertram;   333
This needful violence is for thy safety,
No less than for the general weal.
  Ber.   Where wouldst thou
Bear me a prisoner?
  Lioni.   Firstly to 'the Ten';
Next to the Doge.
  Ber.   To the Doge?
  Lioni.   Assuredly:
Is he not chief of the state?
  Ber.   Perhaps at sunrise—
  Lioni. What mean you?—but we'll
  know anon.
  Ber.   Art sure?
  Lioni. Sure as all gentle means can
  make; and if   340

They fail, you know 'the Ten' and their
  tribunal,
And that St. Mark's has dungeons, and
  the dungeons
A rack.
  Ber. Apply it then before the dawn
Now hastening into heaven.—One more
  such word,
And you shall perish piecemeal, by the
  death   345
You think to doom to me.

                    Re-enter ANTONIO.
  Ant.   The bark is ready,
My lord, and all prepared.
  Lioni.   Look to the prisoner.
Bertram, I'll reason with thee as we go
To the Magnifico's, sage Gradenigo.
                    [*Exeunt.*

SCENE II.—*The Ducal Palace.—The
    Doge's Apartment.*

The DOGE *and his Nephew* BERTUCCIO
    FALIERO.

  Doge. Are all the people of our house
  in muster?
  Ber. F. They are array'd, and eager for
  the signal,
Within our palace precincts at San Polo.
I come for your last orders.
  Doge.   It had been
As well had there been time to have got
  together,   5
From our own fief, Val di Marino, more
Of our retainers—but it is too late.
  Ber. F. Methinks, my lord, 'tis better as
  it is:
A sudden swelling of our retinue
Had waked suspicion; and, though fierce
  and trusty,   10
The vassals of that district are too rude
And quick in quarrel to have long main-
  tain'd
The secret discipline we need for such
A service, till our foes are dealt upon.
  Doge. True; but when once the signal
  has been given,   15
These are the men for such an enterprise;
These city slaves have all their private bias
Their prejudice *against* or *for* this noble,
Which may induce them to o'erdo or spare
Where mercy may be madness; the fierce
  peasants,   20
Serfs of my county of Val di Marino,
Would do the bidding of their lord with-
  out
Distinguishing for love or hate his toes;
Alike to them Marcello or Cornaro,
A Gradenigo or a Foscari;   25
They are not used to start at those vain
  names,
Nor bow the knee before a civic senate;
A chief in armour is their Suzerain,

And not a thing in robes.
   Ber. F.   We are enough;
And for the dispositions of our clients
Against the senate I will answer.
   Doge.   Well,
The die is thrown; but for a warlike ser-
    vice,   32
Done in the field, commend me to my
    peasants:
They made the sun shine through the host
    of Huns
When sallow burghers slunk back to their
    tents,   35
And cower'd to hear their own victorious
    trumpet.
If there be small resistance you will find
These citizens all lions, like their standard;
But if there's much to do, you'll wish,
    with me,
A band of iron rustics at our backs.   40
   Ber. F. Thus thinking, I must marvel
    you resolve
To strike the blow so suddenly.
   Doge.   Such blows
Must be struck suddenly or never. When
I had o'ermaster'd the weak false remorse
Which yearn'd about my heart, too fondly
    yielding   45
A moment to the feelings of old days,
I was most fain to strike; and, firstly, that
I might not yield again to such emotions;
And, secondly, because of all these men,
Save Israel and Philip Calendaro,   50
I know not well the courage or the faith:
To-day might find 'mongst them a traitor
    to us,
As yesterday a thousand to the senate;
But once in, with their hilts hot in their
    hands,
They must *on* for their own sakes: one
    stroke struck,   55
And the mere instinct of the first-born Cain,
Which ever lurks somewhere in human
    hearts,
Though circumstance may keep it in
    abeyance,
Will urge the rest on like to wolves; the
    sight
Of blood to crowds begets the thirst of
    more,   60
As the first wine-cup leads to the long revel;
And you will find a harder task to quell
Than urge them when they *have* com-
    menced, but *till*
That moment, a mere voice, a straw, a
    shadow,
Are capable of turning them aside.—   65
How goes the night?
   Ber. F.   Almost upon the dawn.
   Doge. Then it is time to strike upon the
    bell.
Are the men posted?
   Ber. F.   By this time they are;
But they have orders not to strike, until

They have command from you through
    me in person.   70
   Doge. 'Tis well.—Will the morn never
    put to rest
These stars which twinkle yet o'er all the
    heavens?
I am settled and bound up, and being so,
The very effort which it cost me to
Resolve to cleanse this commonwealth
    with fire,   75
Now leaves my mind more steady. I have
    wept
And trembled at the thought of this dread
    duty;
But now I have put down all idle passion,
And look the growing tempest in the face,
As doth the pilot of an admiral galley:
Yet (wouldst thou think it, kinsman?) it
    hath been   81
A greater struggle to me, than when na-
    tions
Beheld their fate merged in the approach-
    ing fight,
Where I was leader of a phalanx, where
Thousands were sure to perish—Yes, to
    spill   85
The rank polluted current from the veins
Of a few bloated despots needed more
To steel me to a purpose such as made
Timoleon immortal, than to face
The toils and dangers of a life of war.
   Ber. F. It gladdens me to see your for-
    mer wisdom   91
Subdue the furies which so wrung you ere
You were decided.
   Doge.   It was ever thus
With me; the hour of agitation came
In the first glimmerings of a purpose, when
Passion had too much room to sway; but
    in   96
The hour of action I have stood as calm
As were the dead who lay around me: this
They knew who made me what I am, and
    trusted
To the subduing power which I preserved
Over my mood, when its first burst was
    spent.   101
But they were not aware that there are
    things
Which make revenge a virtue by reflection,
And not an impulse of mere anger; though
The laws sleep, justice wakes, and injured
    souls   105
Oft do a public right with private wrong,
And justify their deeds unto themselves.—
Methinks the day breaks—is it not so?
    look,
Thine eyes are clear with youth;—the air
    puts on   109
A morning freshness, and, at least to me,
The sea looks greyer through the lattice.
   Ber. F.   True,
The morn is dappling in the sky.
   Doge.   Away then!

See that they strike without delay, and with
The first toll from St. Mark's, march on the
    palace
With all our house's strength; here I will
    meet you;   115
The Sixteen and their companies will move
In separate columns at the self-same mo-
    ment:
Be sure you post yourself at the great gate:
I would not trust 'the Ten' except to us—
The rest, the rabble of patricians, may
Glut the more careless swords of those
    leagued with us.   121
Remember that the cry is still 'Saint Mark!
The Genoese are come—ho! to the rescue!
Saint Mark and Liberty!'—Now—now to
    action!
    Ber. F. Farewell then, noble uncle! we
    will meet   125
In freedom and true sovereignty, or never!
    Doge. Come hither, my Bertuccio—one
    embrace;
Speed, for the day grows broader; send me
    soon
A messenger to tell me how all goes
When you rejoin our troops, and then
    sound—sound   130
The storm-bell from St. Mark's!
             [*Exit* BERTUCCIO FALIERO.
    Doge [*solus*].   He is gone,
And on each footstep moves a life. 'Tis
    done.
Now the destroying angel hovers o'er
Venice, and pauses ere he pours the vial,
Even as the eagle overlooks his prey,   135
And for a moment, poised in middle air,
Suspends the motion of his mighty wings,
Then swoops with his unerring beak.
    Thou day!
That slowly walk'st the waters! march—
    march on—
I would not smite i' the dark, but rather see
That no stroke errs. And you, ye blue sea
    waves!   141
I have seen you dyed ere now, and deeply
    too,
With Genoese, Saracen, and Hunnish gore,
While that of Venice flow'd too, but vic-
    torious,
Now thou must wear an unmix'd crimson;
    no   145
Barbaric blood can reconcile us now
Unto that horrible incarnadine,
But friend or foe will roll in civic slaughter.
And have I lived to fourscore years for this?
I, who was named Preserver of the City?
I, at whose name the million's caps were
    flung   151
Into the air, and cries from tens of thou-
    sands
Rose up, imploring Heaven to send me
    blessings,
And fame, and length of days—to see this
    day?   154

But this day, black within the calendar,
Shall be succeeded by a bright millennium.
Doge Dandolo survived to ninety summers
To vanquish empires, and refuse their
    crown;
I will resign a crown, and make the state
Renew its freedom—but oh! by what
    means?   160
The noble end must justify them. What
Are a few drops of human blood? 'tis false,
The blood of tyrants is not human; they,
Like to incarnate Molochs, feed on ours,
Until 'tis time to give them to the tombs
Which they have made so populous.—Oh
    world!   166
Oh men! what are ye, and our best designs,
That we must work by crime to punish
    crime?
And slay as if Death had but this one gate,
When a few years would make the sword
    superfluous?   170
And I, upon the verge of th' unknown realm,
Yet send so many heralds on before me?—
I must not ponder this.   [*A pause.*
            Hark! was there not
A murmur as of distant voices, and
The tramp of feet in martial unison?
What phantoms even of sound our wishes
    raise!   176
It cannot be—the signal hath not rung—
Why pauses it? My nephew's messenger
Should be upon his way to me, and he
Himself perhaps even now draws grating
    back   180
Upon its ponderous hinge the steep tower
    portal,
Where swings the sullen huge oracular
    bell,
Which never knells but for a princely
    death,
Or for a state in peril, pealing forth
Tremendous bodements; let it do its office,
And be this peal its awfullest and last
Sound till the strong tower rock!—What!
    silent still?
I would go forth, but that my post is here,
To be the centre of re-union to
The oft discordant elements which form
Leagues of this nature, and to keep com-
    pact   191
The wavering of the weak, in case of con-
    flict;
For if they should do battle, 'twill be here,
Within the palace, that the strife will
    thicken:
Then here must be my station, as becomes
The master-mover.——Hark! he comes—
    he comes,   196
My nephew, brave Bertuccio's messen-
    ger.—
What tidings? Is he marching? hath he
    sped?
They here!—all's lost—yet will I make
    an effort.

Enter a SIGNOR OF THE NIGHT, *with*
Guards, &c. &c.

Sig. Doge, I arrest thee of high treason!
Doge.   Me!
Thy prince, of treason?—Who are they
    that dare   201
Cloak their own treason under such an
    order?
Sig. [*showing his order*]. Behold my
    order from the assembled Ten.
Doge. And *where* are they, and *why*
    assembled? no
Such council can be lawful, till the prince
Preside there, and that duty's mine: on
    thine   206
I charge thee, give me way, or marshal me
To the council chamber.
Sig.   Duke! it may not be:
Nor are they in the wonted Hall of Coun-
    cil,
But sitting in the convent of Saint
    Saviour's.   210
Doge. You dare to disobey me, then?
Sig.   I serve
The state, and needs must serve it faithfully;
My warrant is the will of those who rule it.
Doge. And till that warrant has my sig-
    nature
It is illegal, and, as *now* applied,   215
Rebellious. Hast thou weigh'd well thy
    life's worth,
That thus you dare assume a lawless func-
    tion?
Sig. 'Tis not my office to reply, but act—
I am placed here as guard upon thy person,
And not as judge to hear or to decide.
Doge [*aside*]. I must gain time. So that
    the storm-bell sound,   221
All may be well yet.—Kinsman, speed—
    speed—speed!—
Our fate is trembling in the balance, and
Woe to the vanquish'd! be they prince and
    people,
Or slaves and senate—
    [*The great bell of St. Mark's tolls.*
Lo! it sounds—it tolls!
[*Aloud*]. Hark, Signor of the Night! and
    you, ye hirelings,   226
Who wield your mercenary staves in fear,
It is your knell—Swell on, thou lusty peal!
Now, knaves, what ransom for your lives?
Sig.   Confusion!
Stand to your arms, and guard the door—
    all's lost   230
Unless that fearful bell be silenced soon.
The officer hath miss'd his path or purpose,
Or met some unforeseen and hideous ob-
    stacle.
Anselmo, with thy company proceed
Straight to the tower; the rest remain with
    me.   [*Exit part of the Guard.*
Doge. Wretch! if thou wouldst have thy
    vile life, implore it;   236

It is not now a lease of sixty seconds.
Ay, send thy miserable ruffians forth;
They never shall return.
Sig.   So let it be!
They die then in their duty, as will I.
Doge. Fool! the high eagle flies at
    nobler game   241
Than thou and thy base myrmidons,—live
    on,
So thou provok'st not peril by resistance,
And learn (if souls so much obscured can
    bear   244
To gaze upon the sunbeams) to be free.
Sig. And learn thou to be captive. It
    hath ceased,   [*The bell ceases to toll.*
The traitorous signal, which was to have set
The bloodhound mob on their patrician
    prey—
The knell hath rung, but it is not the
    senate's!   249
Doge [*after a pause*]. All's silent, and
    all's lost!
Sig.   Now, Doge, denounce me
As rebel slave of a revolted council!
Have I not done my duty?
Doge.   Peace, thou thing!
Thou hast done a worthy deed, and earn'd
    the price
Of blood, and they who use thee will re-
    ward thee.
But thou wert sent to watch, and not to
    prate,   255
As thou said'st even now—then do thine
    office,
But let it be in silence, as behoves thee,
Since, though thy prisoner, I am thy prince.
Sig. I did not mean to fail in the respect
Due to your rank: in this I shall obey you.
Doge [*aside*]. There now is nothing left
    me save to die;   261
And yet how near success! I would have
    fallen,
And proudly, in the hour of triumph, but
To miss it thus!——
Enter other SIGNORS OF THE NIGHT, *with*
    BERTUCCIO FALIERO *prisoner.*
2nd Sig.   We took him in the act
Of issuing from the tower, where, at his
    order,   265
As delegated from the Doge, the signal
Had thus begun to sound.
1st Sig.   Are all the passes
Which lead up to the palace well secured?
2nd Sig. They are—besides, it matters
    not; the chiefs
Are all in chains, and some even now on
    trial—   270
Their followers are dispersed, and many
    taken.
Ber. F. Uncle!
Doge. It is in vain to war with Fortune.
The glory hath departed from our house.
Ber. F. Who would have deem'd it?—
    Ah! one moment sooner!

Doge. That moment would have
    changed the face of ages; 275
This gives us to eternity—We'll meet it
As men whose triumph is not in success,
But who can make their own minds all in
    all, 278
Equal to every fortune. Droop not, 'tis
But a brief passage—I would go alone,
Yet if they send us, as 'tis like, together,
Let us go worthy of our sires and selves.
    Ber. F. I shall not shame you, uncle.
    1st Sig. Lords, our orders
Are to keep guard on both in separate
    chambers, 284
Until the council call ye to your trial.
    Doge. Our trial! will they keep their
    mockery up
Even to the last? but let them deal upon us,
As we had dealt on them, but with less
    pomp.
'Tis but a game of mutual homicides,
Who have cast lots for the first death, and
    they 290
Have won with false dice.—Who hath
    been our Judas?
    1st Sig. I am not warranted to answer
    that.
    Ber. F. I'll answer for thee—'tis a cer-
    tain Bertram,
Even now deposing to the secret Giunta.
    Doge. Bertram, the Bergamask! With
    what vile tools 295
We operate to slay or save! This creature,
Black with a double treason, now will earn
Rewards and honours, and be stamp'd in
    story
With the geese in the Capitol, which
    gabbled
Till Rome awoke, and had an annual
    triumph, 300
While Manlius, who hurl'd down the
    Gauls, was cast
From the Tarpeian.
    1st Sig. He aspired to treason,
And sought to rule the state.
    Doge. He saved the state,
And sought but to reform what he re-
    vived—
But this is idle—Come, sirs, do your work.
    1st Sig. Noble Bertuccio, we must now
    remove you 306
Into an inner chamber.
    Ber. F. Farewell, uncle!
If we shall meet again in life I know not,
But they perhaps will let our ashes mingle.
    Doge. Yes, and our spirits, which shall
    yet go forth, 310
And do what our frail clay, thus clogg'd,
    hath fail'd in!
They cannot quench the memory of those
Who would have hurl'd them from their
    guilty thrones,
And such examples will find heirs, though
    distant.

ACT V

SCENE I.—*The Hall of the Council of Ten,
assembled with the additional Senators, who, on the Trials of the Conspirators for the Treason of* MARINO
FALIERO, *composed what was called
the Giunta.*—*Guards, Officers, &c. &c.
*—ISRAEL BERTUCCIO *and* PHILIP CAL-
ENDARO *as Prisoners.*—BERTRAM,
LIONI, *and Witnesses, &c.*

The Chief of the Ten, BENINTENDE.

    Ben. There now rests, after such con-
    viction of
Their manifold and manifest offences,
But to pronounce on these obdurate men
The sentence of the law:—a grievous task
To those who hear, and those who speak.
    Alas! 5
That it should fall to me! and that my days
Of office should be stigmatised through all
The years of coming time, as bearing
    record
To this most foul and complicated treason
Against a just and free state, known to all
The earth as being the Christian bulwark
    'gainst 11
The Saracen and the schismatic Greek,
The savage Hun, and not less barbarous
    Frank;
A city which has open'd India's wealth
To Europe; the last Roman refuge from
O'erwhelming Attila; the ocean's queen;
Proud Genoa's prouder rival! 'Tis to sap
The throne of such a city, these lost men
Have risk'd and forfeited their worthless
    lives— 19
So let them die the death.
    I. Ber. We are prepared;
Your racks have done that for us. Let us
    die.
    Ben. If ye have that to say which would
    obtain
Abatement of your punishment, the Giunta
Will hear you; if you have aught to con-
    fess, 24
Now is your time, perhaps it may avail ye.
    I. Ber. We stand to hear, and not to
    speak.
    Ben. Your crimes
Are fully proved by your accomplices,
And all which circumstance can add to aid
    them;
Yet we would hear from your own lips
    complete 29
Avowal of your treason: on the verge
Of that dread gulf which none repass, the
    truth
Alone can profit you on earth or heaven—
Say, then, what was your motive?
    I. Ber. Justice!
    Ben. What
Your object?

I. Ber.　Freedom!

Ben.　　　　You are brief, sir.

I. Ber.　So my life grows: I　35
Was bred a soldier, not a senator.

Ben.　Perhaps you think by this blunt
　brevity
To brave your judges to postpone the sen-
　tence?

I. Ber.　Do you be brief as I am, and
　believe me,　39
I shall prefer that mercy to your pardon.

Ben. Is this your sole reply to the tribunal?

I. Ber.　Go, ask your racks what they
　have wrung from us,
Or place us there again; we have still some
　blood left,
And some slight sense of pain in these
　wrench'd limbs:
But this ye dare not do; for if we die
　there—　45
And you have left us little life to spend
Upon your engines, gorged with pangs
　already—
Ye lose the public spectacle, with which
You would appal your slaves to further
　slavery!
Groans are not words, nor agony assent,
Nor affirmation truth, if nature's sense
Should overcome the soul into a lie,　52
For a short respite—must we bear or die?

Ben. Say, who were your accomplices?

I. Ber.　　　　　　The Senate.

Ben. What do you mean?

I. Ber.　Ask of the suffering people,
Whom your patrician crimes have driven
　to crime.　56

Ben. You know the Doge?

I. Ber.　　I served with him at Zara
In the field, when *you* were pleading here
　your way
To present office; we exposed our lives,
While you but hazarded the lives of others,
Alike by accusation or defence;　61
And for the rest, all Venice knows her Doge,
Through his great actions, and the Senate's
　insults.

Ben. You have held conference with
　him?

I. Ber.　　　　　I am weary—
Even wearier of your questions than your
　tortures:　65
I pray you pass to judgment.

Ben.　　　　　It is coming.
And you, too, Philip Calendaro, what
Have you to say why you should not be
　doomed?

Cal. I never was a man of many words,
And now have few left worth the utterance.

Ben. A further application of yon en-
　gine　71
May change your tone.

Cal.　　　Most true, it *will* do so;
A former application did so; but
It will not change my words, or, if it did—

Ben. What then?

Cal.　　　Will my avowal on yon rack
Stand good in law?

Ben.　　　　Assuredly.

Cal.　　　　　　Whoe'er
The culprit be whom I accuse of treason?

Ben. Without doubt, he will be brought
　up to trial.　78

Cal. And on this testimony would he
　perish?

Ben. So your confession be detail'd and
　full,
He will stand here in peril of his life.

Cal. Then look well to thy proud self,
　President!　82
For by the eternity which yawns before me,
I swear that *thou*, and only thou, shalt be
The traitor I denounce upon that rack,
If I be stretch'd there for the second time.

One of the Giunta. Lord President,
　'twere best proceed to judgment;
There is no more to be drawn from these
　men.

Ben. Unhappy men! prepare for instant
　death.
The nature of your crime, our law, and
　peril　90
The state now stands in, leave not an hour's
　respite.
Guards! lead them forth, and upon the
　balcony
Of the red columns, where, on festal Thurs-
　day,
The Doge stands to behold the chase of
　bulls,　94
Let them be justified: and leave exposed
Their wavering relics, in the place of judg-
　ment,
To the full view of the assembled people!
And Heaven have mercy on their souls!

The Giunta.　　　　Amen!

I. Ber. Signors, farewell! we shall not
　all again　99
Meet in one place.

Ben.　　And lest they should essay
To stir up the distracted multitude—
Guards! let their mouths be gagg'd even
　in the act
Of execution. Lead them hence!

Cal.　　　　　What! must we
Not even say farewell to some fond friend,
Nor leave a last word with our confessor?

Ben. A priest is waiting in the ante-
　chamber;　106
But, for your friends, such interviews
　would be
Painful to them, and useless all to you.

Cal. I knew that we were gagg'd in life;
　at least
All those who had not heart to risk their
　lives　110
Upon their open thoughts; but still I
　deem'd
That in the last few moments, the same idle

443

Freedom of speech accorded to the dying,
Would not now be denied to us; but
  since——
  I. Ber. Even let them have their way,
    brave Calendaro!   115
What matter a few syllables? let's die
Without the slightest show of favour from
  them;
So shall our blood more readily arise
To Heaven against them, and more testify
To their atrocities, than could a volume
Spoken or written of our dying words!
They tremble at our voices—nay, they
  dread   122
Our very silence—let them live in fear!
Leave them unto their thoughts, and let us
  now
Address our own above!—Lead on; we
  are ready.   125
  Cal. Israel, hadst thou but hearken'd
    unto me
It had not now been thus; and yon pale
  villain,
The coward Bertram, would—
  I. Ber.   Peace, Calendaro!
What brooks it now to ponder upon this?
  Bert. Alas! I fain you died in peace with
    me: 130
I did not seek this task; 'twas forced upon
  me:
Say, you forgive me, though I never can
Retrieve my own forgiveness—frown not
  thus!
  I. Ber. I die and pardon thee!
  Cal. [*spitting at him*].   I die and
    scorn thee!
  [*Exeunt* ISRAEL BERTUCCIO *and* PHILIP
    CALENDARO, *Guards, &c.*
  Ben. Now that these criminals have
    been disposed of,   135
'Tis time that we proceed to pass our
  sentence
Upon the greatest traitor upon record
In any annals, the Doge Faliero!
The proofs and process are complete; the
  time
And crime require a quick procedure:
  shall   140
He now be call'd in to receive the award?
  The Giunta. Ay, ay.
  Ben. Avogadori, order that the Doge
Be brought before the council.
  One of the Giunta.   And the rest,
When shall they be brought up?
  Ben.   When all the chiefs
Have been disposed of. Some have fled to
  Chiozza;   145
But there are thousands in pursuit of
  them,
And such precaution ta'en on terra firma,
As well as in the islands, that we hope
None will escape to utter in strange lands
His libellous tale of treasons 'gainst the
  senate.   150

  Enter the DOGE *as Prisoner, with*
    Guards, &c. &c.

  Ben. Doge—for such still you are, and
    by the law
Must be consider'd, till the hour shall come
When you must doff the ducal bonnet from
That head, which could not wear a crown
  more noble   154
Than empires can confer, in quiet honour,
But it must plot to overthrow your peers,
Who made you what you are, and quench
  in blood
A city's glory—we have laid already
Before you in your chamber at full length,
By the Avogadori, all the proofs   160
Which have appear'd against you; and
  more ample
Ne'er rear'd their sanguinary shadows to
Confront a traitor. What have you to say
In your defence?
  Doge.   What shall I say to ye,
Since my defence must be your condemna-
  tion?   165
You are at once offenders and accusers,
Judges and executioners!—Proceed
Upon your power.
  Ben.   Your chief accomplices
Having confess'd, there is no hope for you.
  Doge. And who be they?
  Ben.   In number many; but
The first now stands before you and the
  court,   171
Bertram, of Bergamo,—would you ques-
  tion him?
  Doge. [*looking at him contemptuously*].
    No.
  Ben. And two others, Israel Bertuccio
And Philip Calendaro, have admitted
Their fellowship in treason with the Doge!
  Doge. And where are they?
  Ben.   Gone to their place, and now
Answering to Heaven for what they did on
  earth.   177
  Doge. Ah! the plebeian Brutus, is he
  gone?
And the quick Cassius of the arsenal?—
How did they meet their doom?
  Ben.   Think of your own:
It is approaching. You decline to plead,
  then?   181
  Doge. I cannot plead to my inferiors,
  nor
Can recognise your legal power to try me.
Show me the law!
  Ben.   On great emergencies
The law must be remodell'd or amended:
Our fathers had not fix'd the punishment
Of such a crime, as on the old Roman
  tables   187
The sentence against parricide was left
In pure forgetfulness; they could not render
That penal, which had neither name nor
  thought   190

In their great bosoms; who would have
    foreseen
That nature could be filed to such a crime
As sons 'gainst sires, and princes 'gainst
    their realms?
Your sin hath made us make a law which
    will
Become a precedent 'gainst such haught
    traitors,   195
As would with treason mount to tyranny;
Not even contented with a sceptre, till
They can convert it to a two-edged sword!
Was not the place of Doge sufficient for ye?
What's nobler than the signory of Venice?
    Doge. The signory of Venice! You be-
    tray'd me—   201
You—*you*, who sit there, traitors as ye are!
From my equality with you in birth,
And my superiority in action,
You drew me from my honourable toils
In distant lands—on flood, in field, in
    cities—   206
You singled me out like a victim to
Stand crown'd, but bound and helpless, at
    the altar
Where you alone could minister. I knew
    not,
I sought not, wish'd not, dream'd not the
    election,   210
Which reach'd me first at Rome, and I
    obey'd;
But on my arrival, that, besides
The jealous vigilance which always led you
To mock and mar your sovereign's best
    intents,   214
You had, even in the interregnum of
My journey to the capital, curtail'd
And mutilated the few privileges
Yet left the duke: all this I bore, and would
Have borne, until my very hearth was
    stain'd
By the pollution of your ribaldry,   220
And he, the ribald, whom I see amongst
    you—
Fit judge in such a tribunal!—
    Ben. [*interrupting him*].   Michel Steno
Is here in virtue of his office, as
One of the Forty; 'the Ten' having craved
A Giunta of patricians from the senate
To aid our judgment in a trial arduous
And novel as the present: he was set
Free from the penalty pronounced upon him,
Because the Doge, who should protect the
    law,   229
Seeking to abrogate all law, can claim
No punishment of others by the statutes
Which he himself denies and violates!
    Doge. *His* PUNISHMENT! I rather see him
    there,
Where he now sits, to glut him with my
    death,   234
Than in the mockery of castigation,
Which your foul, outward, juggling show
    of justice

Decreed as sentence! Base as was his crime,
'Twas purity compared with your protec-
    tion.
    Ben. And can it be, that the great Doge
    of Venice,   239
With three parts of a century of years
And honours on his head, could thus allow
His fury, like an angry boy's, to master
All feeling, wisdom, faith, and fear, on
    such
A provocation as a young man's petu-
    lance?
    Doge. A spark creates the flame—'tis
    the last drop   245
Which makes the cup run o'er, and mine
    was full
Already: you oppress'd the prince and
    people!
I would have freed both, and have fail'd in
    both:
The price of such success would have been
    glory,   249
Vengeance, and victory, and such a name
As would have made Venetian history
Rival to that of Greece and Syracuse
When they were freed, and flourish'd ages
    after,   253
And mine to Gelon and to Thrasybulus:—
Failing, I know the penalty of failure
Is present infamy and death—the future
Will judge, when Venice is no more, or
    free;
Till then, the truth is in abeyance. Pause not;
I would have shown no mercy, and I seek
    none;   259
My life was staked upon a mighty hazard,
And being lost, take what I would have
    taken!
I would have stood alone amidst your
    tombs:
Now you may flock round mine, and
    trample on it,
As you have done upon my heart while
    living.
    Ben. You do confess then, and admit
    the justice   265
Of our tribunal?
    Doge.   I confess to have fail'd;
Fortune is female: from my youth her
    favours
Were not withheld, the fault was mine to
    hope
Her former smiles again at this late hour.
    Ben. You do not then in aught arraign
    our equity?   270
    Doge. Noble Venetians! stir me not
    with questions.
I am resign'd to the worst; but in me still
Have something of the blood of brighter
    days,
And am not over-patient. Pray you, spare
    me
Further interrogation, which boots no-
    thing,   275

445

Except to turn a trial to debate.
I shall but answer that which will offend you,
And please your enemies—a host already;
'Tis true, these sullen walls should yield no
echo:
But walls have ears—nay, more, they have
tongues; and if   280
There were no other way for truth to o'er-
leap them,
You who condemn me, you who fear and
slay me,
Yet could not bear in silence to your graves
What you would hear from me of good or
evil;   284
The secret were too mighty for your souls:
Then let it sleep in mine, unless you court
A danger which would double that you
escape.
Such my defence would be, had I full scope
To make it famous; for true *words* are
things,
And dying men's are things which long
outlive,   290
And oftentimes avenge them; bury mine,
If ye would fain survive me: take this
counsel,
And though too oft ye made me live in
wrath,
Let me die calmly; you may grant me this;
I deny nothing, defend nothing, nothing
I ask of you, but silence for myself,   296
And sentence from the court!
  Ben.   This full admission
Spares us the harsh necessity of ordering
The torture to elicit the whole truth.
  Doge. The torture! you have put me
there already,   300
Daily since I was Doge; but if you will
Add the corporeal rack, you may: these
limbs
Will yield with age to crushing iron; but
There's that within my heart shall strain
your engines.

Enter an OFFICER.

  Officer. Noble Venetians! Duchess Fal-
iero   305
Requests admission to the Giunta's
presence.
  Ben. Say, conscript fathers, shall she be
admitted?
  One of the Giunta. She may have revela-
tions of importance
Unto the state, to justify compliance   309
With her request.
  Ben.   Is this the general will?
  All. It is.
  Doge. Oh! admirable laws of Venice!
Which would admit the wife, in the full
hope
That she might testify against the husband.
What glory to the chaste Venetian dames!
But such blasphemers 'gainst all honour,
as   315

Sit here, do well to act in their vocation.
Now, villain Steno! if this woman fail,
I'll pardon thee thy lie, and thy escape,
And my own violent death, and thy vile life.

The DUCHESS *enters*.

  Ben. Lady! this just tribunal has re-
solved,   320
Though the request be strange, to grant it,
and
Whatever be its purport, to accord
A patient hearing with the due respect
Which fits your ancestry, your rank, and
virtues:
But you turn pale—ho! there, look to the
lady!   325
Place a chair instantly.
  Ang.   A moment's faintness—
'Tis past; I pray you pardon me,—I sit not
In presence of my prince and of my hus-
band,
While he is on his feet.
  Ben.   Your pleasure, lady?
  Ang. Strange rumours, but most true,
if all I hear   330
And see be sooth, have reach'd me, and I
come
To know the worst, even at the worst; for-
give
The abruptness of my entrance and my
bearing.
Is it——I cannot speak—I cannot shape
The question—but you answer it ere
spoken,   335
With eyes averted, and with gloomy
brows—
Oh God! this is the silence of the grave!
  Ben. [*after a pause*]. Spare us, and spare
thyself the repetition
Of our most awful, but inexorable   339
Duty to Heaven and man!
  Ang.   Yet speak; I cannot—
I cannot—no—even now believe these
things.
Is *he* condemned?
  Ben.   Alas!
  Ang.   And was he guilty?
  Ben. Lady! the natural distraction of
Thy thoughts at such a moment makes the
question   344
Merit forgiveness; else a doubt like this
Against a just and paramount tribunal
Were deep offence. But question even the
Doge,
And if he can deny the proofs, believe him
Guiltless as thy own bosom.
  Ang.   Is it so?
My lord, my sovereign, my poor father's
friend,   350
The mighty in the field, the sage in council,
Unsay the words of this man!—Thou art
silent!
  Ben. He hath already own'd to his own
guilt,

Nor, as thou see'st, doth he deny it now.
  Ang. Ay, but he must not die! Spare his
    few years,   355
Which grief and shame will soon cut down
  to days!
One day of baffled crime must not efface
Near sixteen lustres crowded with brave
  acts.
  Ben. His doom must be fulfill'd without
    remission
Of time or penalty—'tis a decree.   360
  Ang. He hath been guilty, but there may
    be mercy.
  Ben. Not in this case with justice.
  Ang.   Alas! signor,
He who is only just is cruel; who
Upon the earth would live were all judged
  justly?
  Ben. His punishment is safety to the
    state.   365
  Ang. He was a subject, and hath served
    the state;
He was your general, and hath saved the
  state;
He is your sovereign, and hath ruled the
  state.
  One of the Council. He is a traitor, and
    betray'd the state.
  Ang. And, but for him, there now had
    been no state   370
To save or to destroy; and you, who sit
There to pronounce the death of your de-
  liverer,
Had now been groaning at a Moslem oar,
Or digging in the Hunnish mines in fetters!
  One of the Council. No, lady, there are
    others who would die   375
Rather than breathe in slavery!
  Ang.   If there are so
Within *these* walls, *thou* art not of the
  number:
The truly brave are generous to the
  fallen!—
Is there no hope?
  Ben.   Lady, it cannot be.
  Ang. [*turning to the Doge*]. Then die,
    Faliero! since it must be so;   380
But with the spirit of my father's friend.
Thou hast been guilty of a great offence,
Half cancell'd by the harshness of these
  men.
I would have sued to them, have pray'd
  to them,
Have begg'd as famish'd mendicants for
  bread,   385
Have wept as they will cry unto their God
For mercy, and be answer'd as they an-
  swer,—
Had it been fitting for thy name or mine,
And if the cruelty in their cold eyes
Had not announced the heartless wrath
  within.   390
Then, as a prince, address thee to thy
  doom!

  Doge. I have lived too long not to know
    how to die!
Thy suing to these men were but the bleat-
  ing
Of the lamb to the butcher, or the cry
Of seamen to the surge: I would not take
A life eternal, granted at the hands   396
Of wretches, from whose monstrous vil-
  lainies
I sought to free the groaning nations!
  Michel Steno.   Doge,
A word with thee, and with this noble
  lady,
Whom I have grievously offended. Would
Sorrow, or shame, or penance on my part,
Could cancel the inexorable past!   402
But since that cannot be, as Christians let
  us
Say farewell, and in peace: with full con-
  trition
I crave, not pardon, but compassion from
  you,   405
And give, however weak, my prayers for
  both.
  Ang. Sage Benintende, now chief judge
    of Venice,
I speak to thee in answer to yon signor.
Inform the ribald Steno, that his words
Ne'er weigh'd in mind with Loredano's
  daughter,   410
Further than to create a moment's pity
For such as he is: would that others had
Despis'd him as I pity! I prefer
My honour to a thousand lives, could such
Be multiplied in mine, but would not have
A single life of others lost for that   416
Which nothing human can impugn—the
  sense
Of virtue, looking not to what is call'd
A good name for reward, but to itself.
To me the scorner's words were as the
  wind   420
Unto the rock: but as there are—alas!
Spirits more sensitive, on which such
  things
Light as the whirlwind on the waters; souls
To whom dishonour's shadow is a sub-
  stance
More terrible than death, here and here-
  after;   425
Men whose vice is to start at vice's scoffing,
And who, though proof against all blan-
  dishments
Of pleasure, and all pangs of pain, are
  feeble
When the proud name on which they pin-
  nacled
Their hopes is breathed on, jealous as the
  eagle   430
Of her high aiery; let what we now
Behold, and feel, and suffer, be a lesson
To wretches how they tamper in their
  spleen
With beings of a higher order. Insects

447

Have made the lion mad ere now; a shaft
I' the heel o'erthrew the bravest of the
    brave; 436
A wife's dishonour was the bane of Troy;
A wife's dishonour unking'd Rome for
    ever;
An injured husband brought the Gauls to
    Clusium,
And thence to Rome, which perish'd for a
    time; 440
An obscene gesture cost Caligula
His life, while Earth yet bore his cruelties;
A virgin's wrong made Spain a Moorish
    province;
And Steno's lie, couch'd in two worthless
    lines, 444
Hath decimated Venice, put in peril
A senate which hath stood eight hundred
    years,
Discrown'd a prince, cut off his crownless
    head,
And forged new fetters for a groaning
    people!
Let the poor wretch, like to the courtesan
Who fired Persepolis, be proud of this,
If it so please him—'twere a pride fit for
    him! 451
But let him not insult the last hours of
Him, who, whate'er he now is, *was* a hero,
By the intrusion of his very prayers;
Nothing of good can come from such a
    source, 455
Nor would we aught with him, nor now,
    nor ever:
We leave him to himself, that lowest depth
Of human baseness. Pardon is for men,
And not for reptiles—we have none for
    Steno,
And no resentment: things like him must
    sting, 460
And higher beings suffer; 'tis the charter
Of life. The man who dies by the adder's
    fang
May have the crawler crush'd, but feels no
    anger:
'Twas the worm's nature; and some men
    are worms
In soul more than the living things of
    tombs. 465
    Doge [*to Ben.*]. Signor! complete that
    which you deem your duty.
    Ben. Before we can proceed upon that
    duty,
We would request the princess to with-
    draw;
'Twill move her too much to be witness to it.
    Ang. I know it will, and yet I must en-
    dure it, 470
For 'tis a part of mine—I will not quit,
Except by force, my husband's side.—
    Proceed!
Nay, fear not either shriek, or sigh, or tear;
Though my heart burst it shall be silent.—
    Speak!

I have that within which shall o'ermaster
    all. 475
    Ben. Marino Faliero, Doge of Venice,
Count of Val di Marino, Senator,
And some time General of the Fleet and
    Army,
Noble Venetian, many times and oft
Intrusted by the state with high employ-
    ments, 480
Even to the highest, listen to the sentence.
Convict by many witnesses and proofs,
And by thine own confession, of the guilt
Of treachery and treason, yet unheard of
Until this trial—the decree is death.
Thy goods are confiscate unto the state,
Thy name is razed from out her records,
    save 487
Upon a public day of thanksgiving
For this our most miraculous deliverance,
When thou art noted in our calendars
With earthquakes, pestilence, and foreign
    foes, 491
And the great enemy of man, as subject
Of grateful masses for Heaven's grace in
    snatching
Our lives and country from thy wickedness.
The place wherein as Doge thou shouldst
    be painted, 495
With thine illustrious predecessors, is
To be left vacant, with a death-black veil
Flung over these dim words engraved be-
    neath,—
'This place is of Marino Faliero, 499
Decapitated for his crimes.'
    Doge.   'His *crimes*!'
But let it be so;—it will be in vain.
The veil which blackens o'er this blighted
    name,
And hides, or seems to hide, these linea-
    ments,
Shall draw more gazers than the thousand
    portraits
Which glitter round it in their pictured
    trappings— 505
Your delegated slaves—the people's ty-
    rants!
'Decapitated for his crimes!'—*What*
    crimes?
Were it not better to record the facts,
So that the contemplator might approve,
Or at the least learn *whence* the crimes
    arose? 510
When the beholder knows a Doge con-
    spired,
Let him be told the cause—it is your history.
    Ben. Time must reply to that; our sons
    will judge
Their fathers' judgment, which I now pro-
    nounce.
As Doge, clad in the ducal robes and cap,
Thou shalt be led hence to the Giant's
    Staircase, 516
Where thou and all our princes are in-
    vested;

And there, the ducal crown being first re-
  sumed
Upon the spot where it was first assumed,
Thy head shall be struck off; and Heaven
  have mercy   520
Upon thy soul!
  Doge. Is this the Giunta's sentence?
  Ben. It is.
  Doge. I can endure it.—And the time?
  Ben. Must be immediate.—Make thy
    peace with God:
Within an hour thou must be in His pre-
  sence.
  Doge. I am *already*; and my blood will
  rise   525
To Heaven before the souls of those who
  shed it.
Are all my lands confiscated?
  Ben.   They are;
And goods, and jewels, and all kind of
  treasure,
Except two thousand ducats—these dis-
  pose of.
  Doge. That's harsh.—I would have
    fain reserved the lands   530
Near to Treviso, which I hold by investment
From Laurence the Count-bishop of
  Ceneda,
In fief perpetual to myself and heirs,
To portion them (leaving my city spoil,
My palace and my treasures, to your for-
  feit)   535
Between my consort and my kinsmen.
  Ben.   These
Lie under the state's ban; their chief, thy
  nephew,
In peril of his own life; but the council
Postpones his trial for the present. If
Thou will'st a state unto thy widow'd prin-
  cess,   540
Fear not, for we will do her justice.
  Ang.   Signors,
I share not in your spoil! From hence-
  forth, know
I am devoted unto God alone,
And take my refuge in the cloister.
  Doge.   Come!
The hour may be a hard one, but 'twill end.
Have I aught else to undergo save death?
  Ben. You have nought to do, except
    confess and die.   547
The priest is robed, the scimitar is bare,
And both await without. But, above all,
Think not to speak unto the people; they
Are now by thousands swarming at the
  gates,   551
But these are closed: the Ten, the Avoga-
  dori,
The Giunta, and the chief men of the Forty,
Alone will be beholders of thy doom,
And they are ready to attend the Doge.
  Doge. The Doge!
  Ben.   Yes, Doge, thou hast lived
    and thou shalt die   556

A sovereign; till the moment which pre-
  cedes
The separation of that head and trunk,
That ducal crown and head shall be united.
Thou hast forgot thy dignity in deigning
To plot with petty traitors; not so we,
Who in the very punishment acknowledge
The prince. Thy vile accomplices have
  died
The dog's death, and the wolf's: but thou
  shalt fall
As falls the lion by the hunters, girt   565
By those who feel a proud compassion for
  thee,
And mourn even the inevitable death
Provoked by thy wild wrath and regal
  fierceness.
Now we remit thee to thy preparation:
Let it be brief, and we ourselves will be
Thy guides unto the place where first we
  were   571
United to thee as thy subjects, and
Thy senate; and must now be parted from
  thee
As such for ever, on the self-same spot.
Guards! form the Doge's escort to his
  chamber.   [*Exeunt.*

SCENE II.—*The Doge's Apartment.*

The DOGE *as Prisoner, and the* DUCHESS
    attending him.

  Doge. Now, that the priest is gone,
    'twere useless all
To linger out the miserable minutes;
But one pang more, the pang of parting
  from thee,
And I will leave the few last grains of sand
Which yet remain of the accorded hour,
Still falling—I have done with Time.
  Ang.   Alas!
And I have been the cause, the unconscious
  cause;
And for this funeral marriage, this black
  union,
Which thou, compliant with my father's
  wish,
Didst promise at *his* death, thou hast
  seal'd thine own.   10
  Doge. Not so; there was that in my
    spirit ever
Which shaped out for itself some great
  reverse;
The marvel is, it came not until now—
And yet it was foretold me.
  Ang.   How foretold you?
  Doge. Long years ago—so long, they
    are a doubt   15
In memory, and yet they live in annals:
When I was in my youth, and served the
  senate
And signory as podesta and captain
Of the town of Treviso, on a day
Of festival, the sluggish bishop who   20

Convey'd the Host aroused my rash
　　young anger
By strange delay, and arrogant reply
To my reproof: I raised my hand and
　　smote him,
Until he reel'd beneath his holy burthen;
And as he rose from earth again, he raised
His tremulous hands in pious wrath to-　26
　　wards Heaven.
Thence pointing to the Host, which had
　　fallen from him,
He turn'd to me, and said, 'The hour will
　　come
When he thou hast o'erthrown shall over-
　　throw thee:
The glory shall depart from out thy house,
The wisdom shall be shaken from thy soul,
And in thy best maturity of mind　　　32
A madness of the heart shall seize upon
　　thee;
Passion shall tear thee when all passions
　　cease
In other men, or mellow into virtues;
And majesty, which decks all other heads,
Shall crown to leave thee headless; honours
　　shall
But prove to thee the heralds of destruc-
　　tion,
And hoary hairs of shame, and both of
　　death,　　　39
But not such death as fits an aged man.'
Thus saying, he pass'd on.—That hour is
　　come.
　　Ang. And with this warning couldst
　　thou not have striven
To avert the fatal moment, and atone,
By penitence, for that which thou hadst
　　done?
　　Doge. I own the words went to my
　　heart, so much　　　45
That I remember'd them amid the maze
Of life, as if they form'd a spectral voice,
Which shook me in a supernatural dream;
And I repented; but 'twas not for me
To pull in resolution: what must be　　50
I could not change, and would not fear.—
　　Nay more,
Thou canst not have forgot, what all re-
　　member,
That on my day of landing here as Doge,
On my return from Rome, a mist of such
Unwonted density went on before　　55
The Bucentaur, like the columnar cloud
Which usher'd Israel out of Egypt, till
The pilot was misled, and disembark'd us
Between the pillars of Saint Mark's, where
　　'tis　　　59
The custom of the state to put to death
Its criminals, instead of touching at
The Riva della Paglia, as the wont is,—
So that all Venice shudder'd at the omen.
　　Ang. Ah! little boots it now to recollect
Such things.
　　Doge. And yet I find a comfort in　65

The thought, that these things are the
　　work of Fate;
For I would rather yield to gods than men,
Or cling to any creed of destiny,
Rather than deem these mortals, most of
　　whom　　　69
I know to be as worthless as the dust,
And weak as worthless, more than instru-
　　ments
Of an o'erruling power; they in themselves
Were all incapable—they could not be
Victors of him who oft had conquer'd for
　　them.
　　Ang. Employ the minutes left in aspira-
　　tions　　　75
Of a more healing nature, and in peace
Even with these wretches take thy flight to
　　heaven.
　　Doge. I *am* at peace: the peace of cer-
　　tainty
That a sure hour will come, when their
　　sons' sons,
And this proud city, and these azure
　　waters,　　　80
And all which makes them eminent and
　　bright,
Shall be a desolation and a curse,
A hissing and a scoff unto the nations,
A Carthage, and a Tyre, an Ocean Babel.
　　Ang. Speak not thus now: the surge of
　　passion still　　　85
Sweeps o'er thee to the last; thou dost
　　deceive
Thyself, and canst not injure them—be
　　calmer.
　　Doge. I stand within eternity, and see
Into eternity, and I behold—
Ay, palpable as I see thy sweet face　　90
For the last time—the days which I de-
　　nounce
Unto all time against these wave-girt walls,
And they who are indwellers.
　　Guard [*coming forward*]. Doge of Venice,
The Ten are in attendance on your high-
　　ness.
　　Doge. Then farewell, Angiolina!—one
　　embrace—　　　95
Forgive the old man who hath been to
　　thee
A fond but fatal husband—love my
　　memory—
I would not ask so much for me still living,
But thou canst judge of me more kindly
　　now,
Seeing my evil feelings are at rest.　　100
Besides, of all the fruit of these long years,
Glory, and wealth, and power, and fame,
　　and name,
Which generally leave some flowers to
　　bloom
Even o'er the grave, I have nothing left,
　　not even　　　104
A little love, or friendship, or esteem,
No, not enough to extract an epitaph

From ostentatious kinsmen; in one hour
I have uprooted all my former life,
And outlived everything, except thy heart,
The pure, the good, the gentle, which will
  oft   110
With unimpair'd but not a clamorous
  grief
Still keep—Thou turn'st so pale!—Alas!
  she faints,
She has no breath, no pulse!—Guards!
  lend your aid—
I cannot leave her thus, and yet 'tis better,
Since every lifeless moment spares a pang.
When she shakes off this temporary death,
I shall be with the Eternal.—Call her
  women—   117
One look!—how cold her hand!—as cold
  as mine
Shall be ere she recovers.—Gently tend
  her,
And take my last thanks——I am ready
  now.   120

[*The Attendants of* ANGIOLINA *enter,
and surround their Mistress, who has
fainted.—Exeunt the* DOGE, *Guards,
&c. &c.*

SCENE III.—*The Court of the Ducal Palace; the outer gates are shut against
the people.—The* DOGE *enters in his
ducal robes, in procession with the
Council of Ten and other Patricians,
attended by the Guards, till they arrive at the top of the 'Giants' Staircase'
(where the Doges took the oaths); the
Executioner is stationed there with his
sword.—On arriving, a Chief of the
Ten takes off the ducal cap from the
Doge's head.*

Doge. So now the Doge is nothing, and
  at last
I am again Marino Faliero:
'Tis well to be so, though but for a
  moment.
Here was I crown'd, and here, bear wit-
  ness, Heaven!
With how much more contentment I
  resign   5
That shining mockery, the ducal bauble,
Than I received the fatal ornament.
  One of the Ten. Thou tremblest, Faliero!
  Doge.   'Tis with age, then.
  Ben. Faliero! hast thou aught further
  to commend,
Compatible with justice, to the senate?
  Doge. I would commend my nephew to
  their mercy,   11
My consort to their justice; for methinks
My death, and such a death, might settle
  all
Between the state and me.
  Ben.   They shall be cared for;
Even notwithstanding thine unheard-of
  crime.   15

Doge. Unheard of! ay, there's not a
  history
But shows a thousand crown'd conspira-
  tors
Against the people; but to set them free,
One sovereign only died, and one is dying.
  Ben. And who were they who fell in
  such a cause?   20
  Doge. The King of Sparta, and the Doge
  of Venice!
Agis and Faliero!
  Ben.   Hast thou more
To utter or to do?
  Doge.   May I speak?
  Ben.   Thou may'st;
But recollect the people are without,   24
Beyond the compass of the human voice.
  Doge. I speak to Time and to Eternity,
Of which I grow a portion, not to man.
Ye elements! in which to be resolved
I hasten, let my voice be as a spirit
Upon you! Ye blue waves! which bore
  my banner,   30
Ye winds! which flutter'd o'er as if you
  loved it,
And fill'd my swelling sails as they were
  wafted
To many a triumph! Thou, my native
  earth,
Which I have bled for! and thou, foreign
  earth,
Which drank this willing blood from many
  a wound!   35
Ye stones, in which my gore will not sink,
  but
Reek up to heaven! Ye skies, which will
  receive it!
Thou sun! which shinest on these things,
  and Thou!
Who kindlest and who quenchest suns!—
  Attest!
I am not innocent—but are these guiltless?
I perish, but not unavenged: far ages   41
Float up from the abyss of time to be,
And show these eyes, before they close,
  the doom
Of this proud city, and I leave my curse
On her and hers for ever!——Yes, the
  hours   45
Are silently engendering of the day,
When she, who built 'gainst Attila a bul-
  wark,
Shall yield, and bloodlessly and basely
  yield,
Unto a bastard Attila, without
Shedding so much blood in her last de-
  fence,   50
As these old veins, oft drain'd in shielding
  her,
Shall pour in sacrifice.—She shall be
  bought
And sold, and be an appanage to those
Who shall despise her!—She shall stoop
  to be   54

A province for an empire, petty town
In lieu of capital, with slaves for senates,
Beggars for nobles, panders for a people!
Then when the Hebrew's in thy palaces,
The Hun in thy high places, and the Greek
Walks o'er thy mart, and smiles on it for
   his: 60
When thy patricians beg their bitter bread
In narrow streets, and in their shameful
   need
Make their nobility a plea for pity;
Then, when the few who still retain a
   wreck
Of their great fathers' heritage shall fawn
Round a barbarian Vice of Kings' Vice-
   gerent, 66
Even in the palace where they sway'd as
   sovereigns,
Even in the palace where they slew their
   sovereign,
Proud of some name they have disgraced,
   or sprung
From an adulteress boastful of her guilt
With some large gondolier or foreign
   soldier, 71
Shall bear about their bastardy in triumph
To the third spurious generation;—when
Thy sons are in the lowest scale of being,
Slaves turn'd o'er to the vanquish'd by the
   victors, 75
Despised by cowards for greater cowar-
   dice,
And scorn'd even by the vicious for such
   vices
As in the monstrous grasp of their con-
   ception
Defy all codes to image or to name them;
Then, when of Cyprus, now thy subject
   kingdom, 80
All thine inheritance shall be her shame
Entail'd on thy less virtuous daughters,
   grown
A wider proverb for worse prostitution;—
When all the ills of conquer'd states shall
   cling thee,
Vice without splendour, sin without relief
Even from the gloss of love to smooth it
   o'er, 86
But in its stead, coarse lusts of habitude,
Prurient yet passionless, cold studied
   lewdness,
Depraving nature's frailty to an art;—
When these and more are heavy on thee,
   when 90
Smiles without mirth, and pastimes with-
   out pleasure,
Youth without honour, age without res-
   pect,
Meanness and weakness, and a sense of
   woe
'Gainst which thou wilt not strive, and
   dar'st not murmur,
Have made thee last and worst of peopled
   deserts, 95

Then, in the last gasp of thine agony,
Amidst thy many murders, think of *mine!*
Thou den of drunkards with the blood of
   princes! 98
Gehenna of the waters! thou sea-Sodom!
Thus I devote thee to the infernal gods!
Thee and thy serpent seed!
   [*Here the* DOGE *turns and addresses the*
                        Executioner.
            Slave, do thine office!
Strike as I struck the foe! Strike as I would
Have struck those tyrants! Strike deep as
   my curse!
Strike—and but once!
   [*The* DOGE *throws himself upon his*
   knees, and as the Executioner raises
   his sword the scene closes.

SCENE IV.—*The Piazza and Piazzetta of*
   St. Mark's.—The people in crowds
   gathered round the grated gates of the
   Ducal Palace, which are shut.

First Citizen. I have gain'd the gate,
   and can discern the Ten,
Robed in their gowns of state, ranged
   round the Doge.
Second. Cit. I cannot reach thee with
   mine utmost effort.
How is it? let us hear at least, since sight
Is thus prohibited unto the people, 5
Except the occupiers of those bars.
First Cit. One has approach'd the
   Doge, and now they strip
The ducal bonnet from his head—and now
He raises his keen eyes to heaven; I see
Them glitter, and his lips move—Hush!
   hush!—no, 10
'Twas but a murmur—Curse upon the dis-
   tance!
His words are inarticulate, but the voice
Swells up like mutter'd thunder; would we
   could
But gather a sole sentence!
Second Cit. Hush! we perhaps may
   catch the sound.
First Cit. 'Tis vain, 15
I cannot hear him.—How his hoary hair
Streams on the wind like foam upon the
   wave!
Now—now—he kneels—and now they
   form a circle
Round him, and all is hidden—but I see
The lifted sword in air——Ah! hark! it
   falls! 20
           [*The people murmur.*
Third Cit. Then they have murder'd
   him who would have freed us.
Fourth Cit. He was a kind man to the
   commons ever.
Fifth Cit. Wisely they did to keep their
   portals barr'd.
Would we had known the work they were
   preparing

Ere we were summon'd here—we would
   have brought   25
Weapons, and forced them!
    Sixth Cit.   Are you sure he 's dead?
    First Cit. I saw the sword fall—Lo!
    what have we here?

*Enter on the Balcony of the Palace which
fronts St. Mark's Place a* CHIEF OF THE
TEN, *with a bloody sword. He waves it
thrice before the People, and exclaims,*

'Justice hath dealt upon the mighty
   Traitor!'

    [*The gates are opened; the populace rush
    in towards the 'Giants' Staircase,'
    where the execution has taken place.
    The foremost of them exclaims to those
    behind,*

'The gory head rolls down the Giants'
   Steps!'   [*The curtain falls.*

SARDANAPALUS

A TRAGEDY

TO

THE ILLUSTRIOUS GOETHE

A STRANGER PRESUMES TO OFFER THE HOMAGE OF A
LITERARY VASSAL TO HIS LIEGE LORD, THE FIRST OF EXISTING WRITERS,
WHO HAS CREATED THE LITERATURE OF HIS OWN COUNTRY,
AND ILLUSTRATED THAT OF EUROPE.

THE UNWORTHY PRODUCTION
WHICH THE AUTHOR VENTURES TO INSCRIBE TO HIM IS ENTITLED,

SARDANAPALUS

PREFACE

IN publishing the following Tragedies* I have only to repeat, that they were not composed with the most remote view to the stage. On the attempt made by the managers in a former instance, the public opinion has been already expressed. With regard to my own private feelings, as it seems that they are to stand for nothing, I shall say nothing.

For the historical foundation of the following compositions the reader is referred to the Notes.

The Author has in one instance attempted to preserve, and in the other to approach, the 'unities'; conceiving that with any very distant departure from them, there may be poetry, but can be no drama. He is aware of the unpopularity of this notion in present English literature; but it is not a system of his own, being merely an opinion, which, not very long ago, was the law of literature throughout the world, and is still so in the more civilized parts of it. But 'nous avons changé tout cela,' and are reaping the advantages of the change. The writer is far from conceiving that anything he can adduce by personal precept or example can at all approach his regular, or even irregular, predecessors: he is merely giving a reason why he preferred the more regular formation of a structure, however feeble, to an entire abandonment of all rules whatsoever. Where he has failed, the failure is in the architect,—and not in the art.

DRAMATIS PERSONÆ

MEN

SARDANAPALUS, *King of Nineveh and Assyria, &c.*
ARBACES, *the Mede who aspired to the Throne.*
BELESES, *a Chaldean and Soothsayer.*
SALEMENES, *the King's Brother-in-Law.*
ALTADA, *an Assyrian Officer of the Palace.*
PANIA.
ZAMES.
SFERO.
BALEA.

WOMEN

ZARINA, *the Queen.*

MYRRHA, *an Ionian female Slave, and the Favourite of* SARDANAPALUS.

Women composing the Harem of SARDANAPALUS, *Guards, Attendants, Chaldean Priests, Medes, &c. &c.*

SCENE.—*A Hall in the Royal Palace of Nineveh*

In this tragedy it has been my intention to follow the account of Diodorus Siculus; reducing it, however, to such dramatic regularity as I best could, and trying to approach the unities. I therefore suppose the rebellion to explode and succeed in one day by a sudden conspiracy, instead of the long war of the history.

ACT I

SCENE I.—*A Hall in the Palace.*
Salemenes [*solus*]. He hath wrong'd his
   queen, but still he is her lord;

He hath wrong'd my sister, still he is my
   brother;
He hath wrong'd his people, still he is
   their sovereign,
And I must be his friend as well as subject:

---

* 'Sardanapalus' and 'The Two Foscari.'

He must not perish thus. I will not see
The blood of Nimrod and Semiramis   6
Sink in the earth, and thirteen hundred
    years
Of empire ending like a shepherd's tale;
He must be roused. In his effeminate heart
There is a careless courage which cor-
    ruption   10
Has not all quench'd, and latent energies,
Repress'd by circumstance, but not de-
    stroy'd—
Steep'd, but not drown'd, in deep volup-
    tuousness.
If born a peasant, he had been a man
To have reach'd an empire: to an empire
    born,   15
He will bequeath none; nothing but a
    name,
Which his sons will not prize in heritage:
Yet, not all lost, even yet he may redeem
His sloth and shame, by only being that
Which he should be, as easily as the thing
He should not be and is. Were it less toil
To sway his nations than consume his life?
To head an army than to rule a harem?
He sweats in palling pleasures, dulls his
    soul,
And saps his goodly strength, in toils
    which yield not   25
Health like the chase, nor glory like the
    war—
He must be roused. Alas! there is no
    sound
    [Sound of soft music heard from within.
To rouse him short of thunder. Hark! the
    lute,
The lyre, the timbrel; the lascivious tink-
    lings
Of lulling instruments, the softening
    voices   30
Of women, and of beings less than women,
Must chime in to the echo of his revel,
While the great king of all we know of earth
Lolls crown'd with roses, and his diadem
Lies negligently by to be caught up   35
By the first manly hand which dares to
    snatch it.
Lo, where they come! already I perceive
The reeking odours of the perfumed trains,
And see the bright gems of the glittering
    girls,   39
At once his chorus and his council, flash
Along the gallery, and amidst the damsels,
As femininely garb'd, and scarce less fe-
    male,
The grandson of Semiramis, the man-
    queen.—
He comes! Shall I await him? yes, and
    front him,
And tell him what all good men tell each
    other,   45
Speaking of him and his. They come, the
    slaves
Led by the monarch subject to his slaves.

SCENE II

Enter SARDANAPALUS *effeminately dressed,
    his Head crowned with Flowers, and
    his Robe negligently flowing, attended
    by a Train of Women and young Slaves.*

Sar. [*speaking to some of his attendants*].
Let the pavilion over the Euphrates
Be garlanded, and lit, and furnish'd forth
For an especial banquet; at the hour
Of midnight we will sup there: see nought
    wanting,   4
And bid the galley be prepared. There is
A cooling breeze which crisps the broad
    clear river:
We will embark anon. Fair nymphs, who
    deign
To share the soft hours of Sardanapalus,
We'll meet again in that the sweetest hour,
When we shall gather like the stars above
    us,   10
And you will form a heaven as bright as
    theirs;
Till then, let each be mistress of her time,
And thou, my own Ionian Myrrha, choose
Wilt thou along with them or me?
    Myr.   My lord——
Sar. My lord!—my life! why answerest
    thou so coldly?   15
It is the curse of kings to be so answer'd.
Rule thy own hours, thou rulest mine—
    say, wouldst thou
Accompany our guests, or charm away
The moments from me?
    Myr.   The king's choice is mine.
Sar. I pray thee say not so: my chiefest
    joy   20
Is to contribute to thine every wish.
I do not dare to breathe my own desire,
Lest it should clash with thine; for thou
    art still
Too prompt to sacrifice thy thoughts for
    others.
    Myr. I would remain: I have no happi-
    ness   25
Save in beholding thine; yet——
    Sar.   Yet! what YET?
Thy own sweet will shall be the only
    barrier
Which ever rises betwixt thee and me.
    Myr. I think the present is the wonted
    hour
Of council; it were better I retire.   30
    Sal. [*comes forward and says*] The
    Ionian slave says well: let her retire.
Sar. Who answers? How now, brother?
    Sal.   The *queen's* brother,
And your most faithful vassal, royal lord.
Sar. [*addressing his train*]. As I have
    said, let all dispose their hours   34
Till midnight, when again we pray your
    presence.   [*The court retiring.*
[*To* MYRRHA, *who is going*]. Myrrha! I
    thought *thou* wouldst remain.

Myr.   Great king,
Thou didst not say so.
Sar.   But *thou* lookedst it:
I know each glance of those Ionic eyes,
Which said thou wouldst not leave me.
Myr.   Sire! your brother——
Sal. His *consort's* brother, minion of
    Ionia!   40
How darest *thou* name *me* and not blush?
Sar.   Not blush!
Thou hast no more eyes than heart to make
    her crimson
Like to the dying day on Caucasus,
Where sunset tints the snow with rosy
    shadows,
And then reproach her with thine own
    cold blindness,   45
Which will not see it. What! in tears, my
    Myrrha?
Sal. Let them flow on; she weeps for
    more than one,
And is herself the cause of bitterer tears.
Sar. Cursed be he who caused those
    tears to flow!
Sal. Curse not thyself—millions do
    that already.   50
Sar. Thou dost forget thee: make me
    not remember
I am a monarch.
Sal.   Would thou couldst!
Myr.   My sovereign,
I pray, and thou, too, prince, permit my
    absence.
Sar. Since it must be so, and this churl
    has check'd   55
Thy gentle spirit, go; but recollect
That we must forthwith meet: I had
    rather lose
An empire than thy presence.
                              [*Exit* MYRRHA.
Sal.   It may be
Thou wilt lose both, and both for ever!
Sar.   Brother!
I can at least command myself, who listen
To language such as this: yet urge me not
Beyond my easy nature.
Sal.   'Tis beyond   61
That easy, far too easy, idle nature,
Which I would urge thee. O that I could
    rouse thee!
Though 'twere against myself.
Sar.   By the god Baal!
The man would make me tyrant.
Sal.   So thou art.
Think'st thou there is no tyranny but that
Of blood and chains? The despotism of
    vice,   67
The weakness and the wickedness of
    luxury,
The negligence, the apathy, the evils
Of sensual sloth—produce ten thousand
    tyrants,
Whose delegated cruelty surpasses   71
The worst acts of one energetic master,

However harsh and hard in his own bear-
    ing.
The false and fond examples of thy lusts
Corrupt no less than they oppress, and
    sap   75
In the same moment all thy pageant power
And those who should sustain it; so that
    whether
A foreign foe invade, or civil broil
Distract within, both will alike prove fatal.
The first thy subjects have no heart to
    conquer;   8c
The last they rather would assist than
    vanquish.
Sar. Why, what makes thee the mouth-
    piece of the people?
Sal. Forgiveness of the queen's, my
    sister's wrongs;
A natural love unto my infant nephews;
Faith to the king, a faith he may need
    shortly,   85
In more than words; respect for Nimrod's
    line;
Also, another thing thou knowest not.
Sar. What's that?
Sal.   To thee an unknown word.
Sar.   Yet speak it;
I love to learn.
Sal.   Virtue.
Sar.   Not know the word!
Never was word yet rung so in my ears—
Worse than the rabble's shout, or splitting
    trumpet: 91
I've heard thy sister talk of nothing else.
Sal. To change the irksome theme, then
    hear of vice.
Sar. From whom?
Sal.   Even from the winds, if thou
    couldst listen
Unto the echoes of the nation's voice.
Sar. Come, I'm indulgent, as thou
    knowest, patient,   96
As thou hast often proved—speak out,
    what moves thee?
Sal. Thy peril.
Sar. Say on.
Sal.   Thus, then: all the nations,
For they are many, whom thy father left
In heritage, are loud in wrath against
    thee.   100
Sar. 'Gainst *me!* What would the
    slaves?
Sal.   A king.
Sar.   And what
Am I then?
Sal.   In their eyes a nothing; but
In mine a man who might be something
    still.
Sar. The railing drunkards! why, what
    would they have?   104
Have they not peace and plenty?
Sal.   Of the first,
More than is glorious; of the last, far less
Than the king recks of.

Sar. Whose then is the crime,
But the false satraps', who provide no
better?
Sal. And somewhat in the monarch
who ne'er looks
Beyond his palace walls, or if he stirs
Beyond them, 'tis but to some mountain
palace,   111
Till summer heats wear down. O glorious
Baal!
Who built up this vast empire, and wert
made
A god, or at the least shinest like a god
Through the long centuries of thy renown,
This, thy presumed descendant, ne'er
beheld   116
As king the kingdoms thou didst leave as
hero,
Won with thy blood, and toil, and time,
and peril!
For what? to furnish imposts for a revel,
Or multiplied extortions for a minion.
Sar. I understand thee—thou wouldst
have me go   121
Forth as a conqueror. By all the stars
Which the Chaldeans read—the restless
slaves
Deserve that I should curse them with
their wishes,
And lead them forth to glory.
Sal. Wherefore not?
Semiramis—a woman only—led   126
These our Assyrians to the solar shores
Of Ganges.
Sar. 'Tis most true. And *how* re-
turn'd?
Sal. Why, like a *man*—a hero; baffled,
but
Not vanquish'd. With but twenty guards,
she made   130
Good her retreat to Bactria.
Sar. And how many
Left she behind in India to the vultures?
Sal. Our annals say not.
Sar. Then I will say for them—
That she had better woven within her
palace
Some twenty garments, than with twenty
guards   135
Have fled to Bactria, leaving to the ravens,
And wolves, and men—the fiercer of the
three,
Her myriads of fond subjects. Is *this*
glory?
Then let me live in ignominy ever.
Sal. All warlike spirits have not the
same fate.   140
Semiramis, the glorious parent of
A hundred kings, although she fail'd in
India,
Brought Persia, Media, Bactria, to the
realm
Which she once sway'd—and thou *might'st*
sway.

Sar. I *sway* them—
She but subdued them.
Sal. It may be ere long
That they will need her sword more than
your sceptre.   146
Sar. There was a certain Bacchus, was
there not?
I've heard my Greek girls speak of such—
they say
He was a god, that is, a Grecian god,
An idol foreign to Assyria's worship,
Who conquer'd this same golden realm
of Ind   151
Thou prat'st of, where Semiramis was
vanquish'd.
Sal. I have heard of such a man; and
thou perceiv'st
That he is deem'd a god for what he did.
Sar. And in his godship I will honour
him—   155
Not much as man. What, ho! my cup-
bearer?
Sal. What means the king?
Sar. To worship your new god
And ancient conqueror. Some wine, I say.

Enter Cupbearer.

Sar. [*addressing the Cupbearer*]. Bring
me the golden goblet, thick with
gems,
Which bears the name of Nimrod's cha-
lice. Hence,   160
Fill full, and bear it quickly.
                               [*Exit Cupbearer.*
Sal. Is this moment
A fitting one for the resumption of
Thy yet unslept-off revels?

Re-enter Cupbearer, with wine.

Sar. [*taking the cup from him*]. Noble
kinsman,
If these barbarian Greeks of the far shores
And skirts of these our realms lie not, this
Bacchus   165
Conquer'd the whole of India, did he not?
Sal. He did, and thence was deem'd a
deity.
Sar. Not so:—of all his conquests a few
columns
Which may be his, and might be mine, if I
Thought them worth purchase and con-
veyance, are   170
The landmarks of the seas of gore he shed,
The realms he wasted, and the hearts he
broke.
But here, here in this goblet is his title
To immortality—the immortal grape
From which he first express'd the soul, and
gave   175
To gladden that of man, as some atone-
ment
For the victorious mischiefs he had done.
Had it not been for this, he would have
been

A mortal still in name as in his grave;
And, like my ancestor Semiramis,   180
A sort of semi-glorious human monster.
Here's that which deified him—let it now
Humanise thee; my surly, chiding brother
Pledge me to the Greek god!

   Sal.   For all thy realms
I would not so blaspheme our country's
   creed.   185

   Sar. That is to say, thou thinkest him
   a hero,
That he shed blood by oceans; and no god,
Because he turn'd a fruit to an enchant-
   ment,
Which cheers the sad, revives the old,
   inspires
The young, makes weariness forget his
   toil,   190
And fear her danger; opens a new world
When this, the present, palls. Well, then
   I pledge thee
And *him* as a true man, who did his utmost
In good or evil to surprise mankind.
                      [Drinks.

   Sal. Wilt thou resume a revel at this
   hour?   195

   Sar. And if I did, 'twere better than a
   trophy,
Being bought without a tear. But that is
   not
My present purpose: since thou wilt not
   pledge me,
Continue what thou pleasest.
       [To the Cupbearer.] Boy, retire.
                    [Exit Cupbearer.

   Sal. I would but have recall'd thee from
   thy dream;   200
Better by me awaken'd than rebellion.

   Sar. Who should rebel? or why? what
   cause? pretext?
I am the lawful king, descended from
A race of kings who knew no predecessors.
What have I done to thee, or to the people,
That thou shouldst rail, or they rise up
   against me?   206

   Sal. Of what thou hast done to me, I
   speak not.

   Sar.   But
Thou think'st that I have wrong'd the
   queen; is't not so?

   Sal. Think! Thou hast wrong'd her!

   Sar. Patience, prince, and hear me.
She has all power and splendour of her
   station,   210
Respect, the tutelage of Assyria's heirs,
The homage and the appanage of sove-
   reignty.
I married her as monarchs wed—for state,
And loved her as most husbands love their
   wives.
If she or thou supposedst I could link me
Like a Chaldean peasant to his mate,
Ye knew nor me, nor monarchs, nor man-
   kind.   217

   Sal. I pray thee, change the theme: my
   blood disdains
Complaint, and Salemenes' sister seeks not
Reluctant love even from Assyria's lord!
Nor would she deign to accept divided
   passion   221
With foreign strumpets and Ionian slaves.
The queen is silent.

   Sar.   And why not her brother?

   Sal. I only echo thee the voice of empires,
Which he who long neglects not long will
   govern.   225

   Sar. The ungrateful and ungracious
   slaves! they murmur
Because I have not shed their blood, nor
   led them
To dry into the desert's dust by myriads,
Or whiten with their bones the banks of
   Ganges;   229
Nor decimated them with savage laws,
Nor sweated them to build up pyramids,
Or Babylonian walls.

   Sal.   Yet these are trophies
More worthy of a people and their prince
Than songs, and lutes, and feasts, and
   concubines,
And lavish'd treasures, and contemned
   virtues.   235

   Sar. Or for my trophies I have founded
   cities:
There's Tarsus and Anchialus, both built
In one day—what could that blood-loving
   beldame,   238
My martial grandam, chaste Semiramis,
Do more, except destroy them?

   Sal.   'Tis most true;
I own thy merit in those founded cities,
Built for a whim, recorded with a verse,
Which shames both them and thee to
   coming ages.

   Sar. Shame me! By Baal, the cities,
   though well built,
Are not more goodly than the verse! Say
   what   245
Thou wilt 'gainst me, my mode of life or
   rule,
But nothing 'gainst the truth of that brief
   record.
Why, those few lines contain the history
Of all things human: hear—'Sardanapalus,
The king, and son of Anacyndaraxes,
In one day built Anchialus and Tarsus.
Eat, drink, and love; the rest's not worth
   a fillip.'

   Sal. A worthy moral, and a wise inscription,
For a king to put up before his subjects!

   Sar. Oh, thou wouldst have me doubtless set up edicts—   255
'Obey the king—contribute to his trea-
   sure—
Recruit his phalanx—spill your blood at
   bidding—

Fall down and worship, or get up and toil.'
Or thus—'Sardanapalus on this spot
Slew fifty thousand of his enemies. 260
These are their sepulchres, and this his
    trophy.'
I leave such things to conquerors; enough
For me, if I can make my subjects feel
The weight of human misery less, and glide
Ungroaning to the tomb: I take no licence
Which I deny to them. We all are men.
    Sal. Thy sires have been revered as
    gods—
    Sar.   In dust
And death, where they are neither gods
    nor men.
Talk not of such to me! the worms are
    gods; 269
At least they banqueted upon your gods,
And died for lack of further nutriment.
Those gods were merely men; look to their
    issue—
I feel a thousand mortal things about me,
But nothing godlike,—unless it may be
The thing which you condemn, a dis-
    position 275
To love and to be merciful, to pardon
The follies of my species, and (that's
    human)
To be indulgent to my own.
    Sal.   Alas!
The doom of Nineveh is seal'd.—Woe—
    woe
To the unrivall'd city!
    Sar.   What dost dread?
    Sal. Thou art guarded by thy foes: in a
    few hours 281
The tempest may break out which over-
    whelms thee,
And thine and mine; and in another day
What *is* shall be the past of Belus' race.
    Sar. What must we dread?
    Sal.   Ambitious treachery,
Which has environ'd thee with snares; but
    yet 286
There is resource: empower me with thy
    signet
To quell the machinations, and I lay
The heads of thy chief foes before thy feet.
    Sar. The heads—how many?
    Sal.   Must I stay to number
When even thine own's in peril? Let me go;
Give me thy signet—trust me with the rest.
    Sar. I will trust no man with unlimited
    lives.
When we take those from others, we nor
    know
What we have taken, nor the thing we
    give. 295
    Sal. Wouldst thou not take their lives
    who seek for thine?
    Sar. That's a hard question—But I
    answer, Yes.
Cannot the thing be done without? Who
    are they

Whom thou suspectest?—Let them be
    arrested.
    Sal. I would thou wouldst not ask me;
    the next moment 300
Will send my answer through thy babbling
    troop
Of paramours, and thence fly o'er the
    palace,
Even to the city, and so baffle all.—
Trust me.
    Sar. Thou knowest I have done so ever;
Take thou the signet. [*Gives the signet.*
    Sal.   I have one more request. 305
    Sar. Name it.
    Sal.   That thou this night forbear the
    banquet
In the pavilion over the Euphrates.
    Sar. Forbear the banquet! Not for all
    the plotters
That ever shook a kingdom! Let them
    come,
And do their worst: I shall not blench for
    them; 310
Nor rise the sooner; nor forbear the gob-
    let;
Nor crown me with a single rose the less;
Nor lose one joyous hour.—I fear them
    not.
    Sal. But thou wouldst arm thee, wouldst
    thou not, if needful?
    Sar. Perhaps. I have the goodliest ar-
    mour, and 315
A sword of such a temper; and a bow
And javelin, which might furnish Nimrod
    forth:
A little heavy, but yet not unwieldy.
And now I think on't, 'tis long since I've
    used them,
Even in the chase. Hast ever seen them,
    brother? 320
    Sal. Is this a time for such fantastic
    trifling?—
If need be, wilt thou wear them?
    Sar.   Will I not?
Oh! if it must be so, and these rash slaves
Will not be ruled with less, I'll use the
    sword
Till they shall wish it turn'd into a distaff.
    Sal. They say thy sceptre's turn'd to
    that already. 326
    Sar. That's false! but let them say so:
    the old Greeks,
Of whom our captives often sing, related
The same of their chief hero, Hercules,
Because he loved a Lydian queen: thou
    seest 330
The populace of all the nations seize
Each calumny they can to sink their sove-
    reigns.
    Sal. They did not speak thus of thy
    fathers.
    Sar.   No;
They dared not. They were kept to toil
    and combat;

And never changed their chains but for
their armour: 335
Now they have peace and pastime, and the
licence
To revel and to rail; it irks me not.
I would not give the smile of one fair girl
For all the popular breath that e'er divided
A name from nothing. What are the rank   340
tongues
Of this vile herd, grown insolent with feed-
ing,
That I should prize their noisy praise, or
dread
Their noisome clamour?
    Sal.   You have said they are men;
As such their hearts are something.
    Sar.   So my dogs' are;
And better, as more faithful:—but, pro-
ceed;   345
Thou hast my signet:—since they are
tumultuous,
Let them be temper'd, yet not roughly, till
Necessity enforce it. I hate all pain,
Given or received; we have enough within us,
The meanest vassal as the loftiest monarch,
Not to add to each other's natural burthen
Of mortal misery, but rather lessen,   352
By mild reciprocal alleviation,
The fatal penalties imposed on life:
But this they know not, or they will not
know.   355
I have, by Baal! done all I could to soothe
them:
I made no wars, I added no new imposts,
I interfered not with their civic lives,
I let them pass their days as best might suit
them: 359
Passing my own as suited me.
    Sal.   Thou stopp'st
Short of the duties of a king; and therefore
They say thou art unfit to be a monarch.
    Sar. They lie.—Unhappily, I am unfit
To be aught save a monarch; else for me
The meanest Mede might be the king in-
stead.   365
    Sal. There is one Mede, at least, who
seeks to be so.
    Sar. What mean'st thou?—'tis thy
secret; thou desirest
Few questions, and I'm not of curious
nature.
Take the fit steps; and, since necessity
Requires, I sanction and support thee.
Ne'er   370
Was man who more desired to rule in peace
The peaceful only: if they rouse me, better
They had conjured up stern Nimrod from
his ashes,
'The mighty hunter.' I will turn these
realms
To one wide desert chase of brutes, who
were,   375
But *would* no more, by their own choice,
be human.

What they have found me, they belie; *that
which*
They yet may find me—shall defy their
wish
To speak it worse; and let them thank
themselves.   379
    Sal. Then thou at last canst feel?
    Sar.   Feel! who feels not
Ingratitude?
    Sal.   I will not pause to answer
With words, but deeds. Keep thou awake
that energy
Which sleeps at times, but is not dead with-
in thee,
And thou may'st yet be glorious in thy
reign,   384
As powerful in thy realm. Farewell!
                                    [*Exit* SALEMENES.
    Sar. [*solus*].   Farewell!
He's gone; and on his finger bears my sig-
net,
Which is to him a sceptre. He is stern
As I am heedless; and the slaves deserve
To feel a master. What may be the danger,
I know not: he hath found it, let him quell
it.   390
Must I consume my life—this little life—
In guarding against all may make it less?
It is not worth so much! It were to die
Before my hour, to live in dread of death,
Tracing revolt; suspecting all about me,
Because they are near; and all who are
remote,   396
Because they are far. But if it should be
so—
If they should sweep me off from earth and
empire,
Why, what is earth or empire of the earth?
I have loved, and lived, and multiplied my
image;   400
To die is no less natural than those
Acts of this clay! 'Tis true I have not shed
Blood as I might have done, in oceans, till
My name became the synonyme of death—
A terror and a trophy. But for this   405
I feel no penitence; my life is love:
If I must shed blood, it shall be by force.
Till now, no drop from an Assyrian vein
Hath flow'd for me, nor hath the smallest
coin
Of Nineveh's vast treasures e'er been
lavish'd   410
On objects which could cost her sons a
tear:
If then they hate me, 'tis because I hate not:
If they rebel, 'tis because I oppress not.
Oh, men! ye must be ruled with scythes,
not sceptres,
And mow'd down like the grass, else all we
reap   415
Is rank abundance, and a rotten harvest
Of discontents infecting the fair soil,
Making a desert of fertility.—
I'll think no more.——Within there, ho!

Enter an ATTENDANT.

Sar.   Slave, tell
The Ionian Myrrha we could crave her
    presence.   420
Attend. King, she is here.

MYRRHA *enters.*

Sar. [apart to Attendant]. Away!
[*Addressing* MYRRHA]. Beautiful being!
Thou dost almost anticipate my heart;
It throbb'd for thee, and here thou comest:
    let me
Deem that some unknown influence, some
    sweet oracle,
Communicates between us, though un-
    seen,   425
In absence, and attracts us to each other.
Myr. There doth.
Sar.   I know there doth, but not its
    name:
What is it?
Myr.   In my native land a God,
And in my heart a feeling like a God's,
Exalted; yet I own 'tis only mortal; 430
For what I feel is humble, and yet happy—
That is, it would be happy; but——
                              [MYRRHA *pauses.*
Sar.   There comes
For ever something between us and what
We deem our happiness: let me remove
The barrier which that hesitating accent
Proclaims to thine, and mine is seal'd.
Myr.   My lord!
Sar. My lord—my king—sire—sove-
    reign; thus it is—   437
For ever thus, address'd with awe. I ne'er
Can see a smile, unless in some broad
    banquet's
Intoxicating glare, when the buffoons
Have gorged themselves up to equality,
Or I have quaff'd me down to their abase-
    ment.   442
Myrrha, I can hear all these things, these
    names,
Lord—king—sire—monarch—nay, time
    was I prized them;
That is, I suffer'd them—from slaves and
    nobles;   445
But when they falter from the lips I love,
The lips which have been press'd to mine,
    a chill
Comes o'er my heart, a cold sense of the
    falsehood
Of this my station, which represses feeling
In those for whom I have felt most, and
    makes me   450
Wish that I could lay down the dull tiara,
And share a cottage on the Caucasus
With thee, and wear no crowns but those
    of flowers.
Myr. Would that we could!
Sar.   And dost *thou* feel this?—Why?
Myr. Then thou wouldst know what
    thou canst never know.   455

Sar. And that is——
Myr.   The true value of a heart;
At least, a woman's.
Sar.   I have proved a thousand—
A thousand, and a thousand.
Myr.   Hearts?
Sar.   I think so.
Myr. Not one! the time may come thou
    may'st.
Sar.   It will.   459
Hear, Myrrha; Salemenes has declared—
Or why or how he hath divined it, Belus,
Who founded our great realm, knows more
    than I—
But Salemenes hath declared my throne
In peril.
Myr. He did well.
Sar.   And say'st *thou* so?
Thou whom he spurn'd so harshly, and
    now dared   465
Drive from our presence with his savage
    jeers,
And made thee weep and blush?
Myr.   I should do both
More frequently, and he did well to call me
Back to my duty. But thou spak'st of
    peril—
Peril to thee——
Sar.   Ay, from dark plots and snares
From Medes—and discontented troops
    and nations,   471
I know not what—a labyrinth of things—
A maze of mutter'd threats and mysteries:
Thou know'st the man—it is his usual
    custom.
But he is honest. Come, we'll think no
    more on't—   475
But of the midnight festival.
Myr.   'Tis time
To think of aught save festivals. Thou hast
    not
Spurn'd his sage cautions?
Sar.   What?—and dost thou fear?
Myr. Fear!—I'm a Greek, and how
    should I fear death?
A slave, and wherefore should I dread my
    freedom?   480
Sar. Then wherefore dost thou turn so
    pale?
Myr. I love.
Sar. And do not I? I love thee far—far
    more
Than either the brief life or the wide realm,
Which, it may be, are menaced;—yet I
    blench not.
Myr. That means thou lovest nor thy-
    self nor me;   485
For he who loves another loves himself,
Even for that other's sake. This is too rash:
Kingdoms and lives are not to be so lost.
Sar. Lost!—why, who is the aspiring
    chief who dared   489
Assume to win them?
Myr.   Who is he should dread

To try so much? When he who is their ruler
Forgets himself, will they remember him?
 Sar. Myrrha!
 Myr. Frown not upon me; you have
  smiled   493
Too often on me not to make those frowns
Bitterer to bear than any punishment
Which they may augur.—King, I am your
 subject!
Master, I am your slave! Man, I have
 loved you!—
Loved you, I know not by what fatal weak-
 ness,
Although a Greek, and born a foe to
 monarchs—   499
A slave, and hating fetters—an Ionian,
And, therefore, when I love a stranger,
 more
Degraded by that passion than by chains!
Still I have loved you. If that love were
 strong
Enough to overcome all former nature,
Shall it not claim the privilege to save you?
 Sar. Save me, my beauty! Thou art
  very fair,   506
And what I seek of thee is love—not safety.
 Myr. And without love where dwells
  security?
 Sar. I speak of woman's love.
 Myr.   The very first
Of human life must spring from woman's
 breast,   510
Your first small words are taught you from
 her lips,
Your first tears quench'd by her, and your
 last sighs
Too often breathed out in a woman's hear-
 ing,
When men have shrunk from the ignoble
 care
Of watching the last hour of him who led
 them.   515
 Sar. My eloquent Ionian! thou speak'st
  music;
The very chorus of the tragic song
I have heard thee talk of as the favourite
 pastime
Of thy far father-land. Nay, weep not—
 calm thee.
 Myr. I weep not.—But I pray thee, do
  not speak   520
About my fathers or their land.
 Sar.   Yet oft
Thou speakest of them.
 Myr. True—true: constant thought
Will overflow in words unconsciously;
But when another speaks of Greece, it
 wounds me.
 Sar. Well, then, how wouldst thou *save*
  me, as thou saidst?   525
 Myr. By teaching thee to save thyself,
  and not
Thyself alone, but these vast realms, from
 all

The rage of the worst war—the war of
 brethren.
 Sar. Why, child, I loathe all war and
  warriors;   529
I live in peace and pleasure: what can man
Do more?
 Myr. Alas! my lord, with common men
There needs too oft the show of war to keep
The substance of sweet peace; and, for a
 king,
'Tis sometimes better to be fear'd than lov'd.
 Sar. And I have never sought but for
  the last.   535
 Myr. And now art neither.
 Sar.   Dost *thou* say so, Myrrha?
 Myr. I speak of civic popular love, *self*-
  love,
Which means that men are kept in awe
 and law,
Yet not oppress'd—at least they must not
 think so,   539
Or if they think so, deem it necessary,
To ward off worse oppression, their own
 passions.
A king of feasts, and flowers, and wine, and
 revel,
And love, and mirth, was never king of
 glory.
 Sar. Glory! what's that?
 Myr.   Ask of the gods thy fathers.
 Sar. They cannot answer; when the
  priests speak for them, 545
'Tis for some small addition to the temple.
 Myr. Look to the annals of thine em-
  pire's founders.
 Sar. They are so blotted o'er with
  blood, I cannot.
But what wouldst have? the empire *has
 been* founded.
I cannot go on multiplying empires. 550
 Myr. Preserve thine own.
 Sar.   At least, I will enjoy it.
Come, Myrrha, let us go on to the Eu-
 phrates:
The hour invites, the galley is prepared,
And the pavilion, deck'd for our return,
In fit adornment for the evening banquet,
Shall blaze with beauty and with light, un-
 til   556
It seems unto the stars which are above us
Itself an opposite star; and we will sit
Crown'd with fresh flowers like—
 Myr.   Victims.
 Sar.   No, like sovereigns,
The shepherd kings of patriarchal times,
Who knew no brighter gems than summer
 wreaths,   561
And none but tearless triumphs. Let us on.

     Enter PANIA.

 Pan. May the king live for ever!
 Sar.   Not an hour
Longer than he can love. How my soul
 hates

This language, which makes life itself a lie,
Flattering dust with eternity! Well, Pania!
Be brief.

 Pan. I am charged by Salemenes to
Reiterate his prayer unto the king, 568
That for this day, at least, he will not quit
The palace: when the general returns,
He will adduce such reasons as will war-
 rant 571
His daring, and perhaps obtain the pardon
Of his presumption.

 Sar. What! am I then coop'd?
Already captive? can I not even breathe
The breath of heaven? Tell prince Salem-
 enes, 575
Were all Assyria raging round the walls
In mutinous myriads, I would still go forth.

 Pan. I must obey you, and yet——

 Myr. Oh, monarch, listen.—
How many a day and moon thou hast re-
 clined
Within these palace walls in silken dalli-
 ance, 580
And never shown thee to thy people's long-
 ing;
Leaving thy subjects' eyes ungratified,
The satraps uncontroll'd, the gods un-
 worshipp'd,
And all things in the anarchy of sloth,
Till all, save evil, slumber'd through the
 realm! 585
And wilt thou not now tarry for a day,—
A day which may redeem thee? Wilt thou
 not
Yield to the few still faithful a few hours,
For them, for thee, for thy past fathers'
 race,
And for thy sons' inheritance?

 Pan. 'Tis true!
From the deep urgency with which the
 prince 591
Despatch'd me to your sacred presence, I
Must dare to add my feeble voice to that
Which now has spoken.

 Sar. No, it must not be.

 Myr. For the sake of thy realm!

 Sar. Away!

 Pan. For that
Of all thy faithful subjects, who will rally
Round thee and thine.

 Sar. These are mere fantasies:
There is no peril:—'tis a sullen scheme
Of Salemenes, to approve his zeal, 599
And show himself more necessary to us.

 Myr. By all that's good and glorious
 take this counsel.

 Sar. Business to-morrow.

 Myr. Ay, or death to-night.

 Sar. Why let it come then unexpectedly,
'Midst joy and gentleness, and mirth and
 love;
So let me fall like the pluck'd rose!—far
 better 605
Thus than be wither'd.

 Myr. Then thou wilt not yield,
Even for the sake of all that ever stirr'd
A monarch into action, to forego 608
A trifling revel.

 Sar. No.

 Myr. Then yield for *mine;*
For my sake!

 Sar. Thine, my Myrrha!

 Myr. 'Tis the first
Boon which I ever ask'd Assyria's king.

 Sar. That's true, and were't my king-
 dom, must be granted.
Well, for thy sake, I yield me. Pania, hence!
Thou hear'st me.

 Pan. And obey. [*Exit* PANIA.

 Sar. I marvel at thee.
What is thy motive, Myrrha, thus to urge
 me? 615

 Myr. Thy safety; and the certainty that
 nought
Could urge the prince thy kinsman to require
Thus much from thee, but some impending
 danger.

 Sar. And if I do not dread it, why
 shouldst thou?

 Myr. Because *thou* dost not fear, I fear
 for *thee.* 620

 Sar. To-morrow thou wilt smile at these
 vain fancies.

 Myr. If the worst come, I shall be where
 none weep,
And that is better than the power to smile.
And thou?

 Sar. I shall be king, as heretofore.

 Myr. Where?

 Sar. With Baal, Nimrod, and Semira-
 mis, 625
Sole in Assyria, or with them elsewhere.
Fate made me what I am—may make me
 nothing—
But either that or nothing must I be:
I will not live degraded.

 Myr. Hadst thou felt
Thus always, none would ever dare degrade thee. 630

 Sar. And who will do so now?

 Myr. Dost thou suspect none?

 Sar. Suspect!—that's a spy's office.
 Oh! we lose
Ten thousand precious moments in vain
 words,
And vainer fears. Within there!—ye
 slaves, deck 634
The hall of Nimrod for the evening revel:
If I must make a prison of our palace,
At least we'll wear our fetters jocundly;
If the Euphrates be forbid us, and
The summer dwelling on its beauteous
 border, 639
Here we are still unmenaced. Ho! within
 there! [*Exit* SARDANAPALUS.

 Myr. [*sola*]. Why do I love this man?
 My country's daughters

Love none but heroes. But I have no
country!
The slave hath lost all save her bonds. I
love him;
And that's the heaviest link of the long
chain—   644
To love whom we esteem not. Be it so:
The hour is coming when he'll need all
love,
And find none. To fall from him now were
baser
Than to have stabb'd him on his throne
when highest
Would have been noble in my country's
creed:
I was not made for either. Could I save
him,   650
I should not love *him* better, but myself;
And I have need of the last, for I have fallen
In my own thoughts, by loving this soft
stranger:
And yet methinks I love him more, per-
ceiving   654
That he is hated of his own barbarians,
The natural foes of all the blood of Greece.
Could I but wake a single thought like those
Which even the Phrygians felt when bat-
tling long
'Twixt Ilion and the sea, within his heart
He would tread down the barbarous
crowds, and triumph.   660
He loves me, and I love him; the slave
loves
Her master, and would free him from his
vices.
If not, I have a means of freedom still,
And if I cannot teach him how to reign,
May show him how alone a king can leave
His throne. I must not lose him from my
sight.   [*Exit.*

ACT II

SCENE I.—*The Portal of the same Hall
of the Palace.*

Beleses [*solus*]. The sun goes down:
methinks he sets more slowly,
Taking his last look of Assyria's empire.
How red he glares amongst those deepen-
ing clouds,
Like the blood he predicts! If not in vain,
Thou sun that sinkest, and ye stars which
rise,   5
I have outwatch'd ye, reading ray by ray
The edicts of your orbs, which make Time
tremble
For what he brings the nations, 'tis the
furthest
Hour of Assyria's years. And yet how
calm!
An earthquake should announce so great
a fall—   10
A summer's sun discloses it. Yon disk,
To the star-read Chaldean, bears upon

Its everlasting page the end of what
Seem'd everlasting; but oh! thou true sun!
The burning oracle of all that live,   15
As fountain of all life, and symbol of
Him who bestows it, wherefore dost thou
limit
Thy lore unto calamity? Why not
Unfold the rise of days more worthy thine
All-glorious burst from ocean? why not
dart   20
A beam of hope athwart the future years,
As of wrath to its days? Hear me! oh, hear
me!
I am thy worshipper, thy priest, thy ser-
vant—
I have gazed on thee at thy rise and fall,
And bow'd my head beneath thy mid-day
beams,   25
When my eye dared not meet thee. I have
watch'd
For thee, and after thee, and pray'd to thee,
And sacrificed to thee, and read, and fear'd
thee,
And ask'd of thee, and thou hast answer'd
—but
Only to thus much: while I speak, he
sinks—   30
Is gone—and leaves his beauty, not his
knowledge,
To the delighted west, which revels in
Its hues of dying glory. Yet what is
Death, so it be but glorious? 'Tis a sunset;
And mortals may be happy to resemble
The gods but in decay.

Enter ARBACES *by an inner door.*

Arb.   Beleses, why   36
So rapt in thy devotions? Dost thou stand
Gazing to trace thy disappearing god
Into some realm of undiscover'd day?
Our business is with night—'tis come.
Bel.   But not
Gone.
Arb. Let it roll on—we are ready.
Bel.   Yes.
Would it were over!
Arb.   Does the prophet doubt,
To whom the very stars shine victory?
Bel. I do not doubt of victory—but the
victor.
Arb. Well, let thy science settle that.
Meantime   45
I have prepared as many glittering spears
As will out-sparkle our allies—your plan-
ets.
There is no more to thwart us. The she-
king,
That less than woman, is even now upon
The waters with his female mates. The
order   50
Is issued for the feast in the pavilion.
The first cup which he drains will be the
last
Quaff'd by the line of Nimrod.

Bel.   'Twas a brave one.
Arb. And is a weak one—'tis worn out
    —we'll mend it.   54
Bel. Art sure of that?
Arb.   Its founder was a hunter—
I am a soldier—what is there to fear?
Bel. The soldier.
Arb.   And the priest, it may be: but
If you thought thus, or think, why not retain
Your king of concubines? why stir me up?
Why spur me to this enterprise? your own
No less than mine?
Bel.   Look to the sky!
Arb.   I look.
Bel. What seest thou?
Arb.   A fair summer's twilight, and
The gathering of the stars.
Bel.   And midst them, mark
Yon earliest, and the brightest, which so
    quivers,   64
As it would quit its place in the blue ether.
    Arb. Well!
    Bel. 'Tis thy natal ruler—thy birth
planet.
    Arb. [*touching his scabbard*]. My star is
    in this scabbard: when it shines,
It shall out-dazzle comets. Let us think
Of what is to be done to justify
Thy planets and their portents. When we
    conquer,   70
They shall have temples—ay, and priests
    —and thou
Shalt be the pontiff of—what gods thou wilt;
For I observe that they are ever just,
And own the bravest for the most devout.
    Bel. Ay, and the most devout for brave
    —thou hast not   75
Seen me turn back from battle.
    Arb.   No; I own thee
As firm in fight as Babylonia's captain,
As skilful in Chaldea's worship: now,
Will it but please thee to forget the priest,
And be the warrior?
    Bel.   Why not both?
    Arb.   The better;
And yet it almost shames me, we shall have
So little to effect. This woman's warfare
Degrades the very conqueror. To have
    pluck'd   83
A bold and bloody despot from his throne,
And grappled with him, clashing steel with
    steel,
That were heroic or to win or fall;
But to upraise my sword against this silk-
    worm,   87
And hear him whine, it may be——
    Bel.   Do not deem it:
He has that in him which may make you
    strife yet;
And were he all you think, his guards are
    hardy,   90
And headed by the cool, stern Salemenes.
    Arb. They'll not resist.
    Bel.   Why not? they are soldiers.

Arb.   True,
And therefore need a soldier to command
    them.
    Bel. That Salemenes is.
    Arb.   But not their king.
Besides, he hates the effeminate thing that
    governs,   95
For the queen's sake, his sister. Mark you
    not
He keeps aloof from all the revels?
    Bel.   But
Not from the council—there he is ever con-
    stant.
    Arb. And ever thwarted: what would
    you have more
To make a rebel out of? A fool reigning,
His blood dishonour'd, and himself dis-
    dain'd: 101
Why, it is *his* revenge we work for.
    Bel.   Could
He but be brought to think so: this I doubt
    of.
    Arb. What, if we sound him?
    Bel.   Yes—if the time served.

Enter BALEA.

    Bal. Satraps! The king commands your
    presence at   105
The feast to-night.
    Bel.   To hear is to obey.
In the pavilion?
    Bal.   No; here in the palace.
    Arb. How! in the palace? it was not
    thus order'd.
    Bal. It is so order'd now.
    Arb.   And why?
    Bal.   I know not.
May I retire?
    Arb.   Stay.
    Bel. [*to Arb. aside*]. Hush! let him go his
    way.   110
[*Alternately to Bal.*]. Yes, Balea, thank the
    monarch, kiss the hem
Of his imperial robe, and say, his slaves
Will take the crumbs he deigns to scatter
    from
His royal table at the hour—was't mid-
    night?
    Bal. It was: the place, the hall of Nim-
    rod. Lords,   115
I humble me before you, and depart,
                    Exit BALEA.
    Arb. I like not this same sudden change
    of place;
There is some mystery: wherefore should
    he change it?
    Bel. Doth he not change a thousand
    times a day?
Sloth is of all things the most fanciful—
And moves more parasangs in its intents
Than generals in their marches, when
    they seek
To leave their foe at fault.—Why dost thou
    muse?

464

Arb. He loved that gay pavilion,—it
was ever
His summer dotage.   124
Bel.   And he loved his queen—
And thrice a thousand harlotry besides—
And he has loved all things by turns, except
Wisdom and glory.
Arb.   Still—I like it not.
If he has changed—why, so must we: the
attack
Were easy in the isolated bower,   130
Beset with drowsy guards and drunken
courtiers;
But in the hall of Nimrod——
Bel.   Is it so?
Methought the haughty soldier fear'd to
mount   133
A throne too easily—does it disappoint thee
To find there is a slipperier step or two
Than what was counted on?
Arb.   When the hour comes,
Thou shalt perceive how far I fear or no.
Thou hast seen my life at stake—and gaily
play'd for:
But here is more upon the die—a kingdom.
Bel. I have foretold already—thou wilt
win it: 140
Then on, and prosper.
Arb.   Now were I a soothsayer,
I would have boded so much to myself.
But be the stars obey'd—I cannot quarrel
With them, nor their interpreter. Who's
here?   144

Enter SALEMENES.

Sal. Satraps!
Bel.   My prince!
Sal.   Well met—I sought ye both,
But elsewhere than the palace.
Arb.   Wherefore so?
Sal. 'Tis not the hour.
Arb.   The hour!—what hour?
Sal.   Of midnight.
Bel. Midnight, my lord!
Sal.   What, are you not invited?
Bel. Oh! yes—we had forgotten.
Sal.   Is it usual
Thus to forget a sovereign's invitation?
Arb. Why—we but now received it.
Sal.   Then why here?
Arb. On duty.
Sal.   On what duty?
Bel.   On the state's.
We have the privilege to approach the
presence;   153
But found the monarch absent.
Sal.   And I too
Am upon duty.
Arb.   May we crave its purport?
Sal. To arrest two traitors. Guards!
Within there!

Enter Guards.

Sal. [*continuing*].   Satraps,

Your swords.
Bel. [*delivering his*]. My lord, behold
my scimitar.
Arb. [*drawing his sword*]. Take mine.
Sal. [*advancing*].   I will.
Arb.   But in your heart the blade—
The hilt quits not this hand.
Sal. [*drawing*]. How! dost thou brave
me?
'Tis well—this saves a trial, and false
mercy.   160
Soldiers, hew down the rebel!
Arb.   Soldiers! Ay—
Alone you dare not.
Sal.   Alone! foolish slave—
What is there in thee that a prince should
shrink from
Of open force? We dread thy treason, not
Thy strength: thy tooth is nought without
its venom—   165
The serpent's, not the lion's. Cut him
down.
Bel. [*interposing*]. Arbaces! are you
mad? Have I not render'd
My sword? Then trust like me our sove-
reign's justice.
Arb. No—I will sooner trust the stars
thou prat'st of,   169
And this slight arm, and die a king at least
Of my own breath and body—so far that
None else shall chain them.
Sal. [*to the guards*]. You hear *him* and
me.
Take him not,—kill.
[*The Guards attack* ARBACES, *who de-
fends himself valiantly and dexter-
ously till they waver.*
Sal.   Is it even so; and must
I do the hangman's office? Recreants! see
How you should fell a traitor.
[SALEMENES *attacks* ARBACES.

Enter SARDANAPALUS *and Train.*

Sar.   Hold your hands—
Upon your lives, I say. What, deaf or
drunken?   176
My sword! O fool, I wear no sword: here,
fellow,
Give me thy weapon.   [*To a Guard.*
[SARDANAPALUS *snatches a sword from
one of the soldiers, and rushes between
the combatants—they separate.*
Sar.   In my very palace!
What hinders me from cleaving you in
twain,   179
Audacious brawlers?
Bel.   Sire, your justice.
Sal.   Or—
Your weakness.
Sar. [*raising the sword*]. How?
Sal.   Strike! so the blow's repeated
Upon yon traitor—whom you spare a
moment,
I trust, for torture—I'm content.

465

Sar.   What—him!
Who dares assail Arbaces?
Sal.   I!
Sar.   Indeed!
Prince, you forget yourself. Upon what
    warrant?   185
Sal. [*showing the signet*]. Thine.
Arb. [*confused*].   The king's!
Sal. Yes! and let the king confirm it.
Sar. I parted not from this for such a
    purpose.
Sal. You parted with it for your safety
    —I
Employ'd it for the best. Pronounce in
    person.
Here I am but your slave—a moment past
I was your representative.   191
Sar.   Then sheathe
Your swords.
    [ARBACES *and* SALEMENES *return
       their swords to the scabbards.*
Sal. Mine's sheathed: I pray you
    sheathe *not* yours:
'Tis the sole sceptre left you now with
    safety.
Sar. A heavy one; the hilt, too, hurts
    my hand.
[*To a Guard*]. Here, fellow, take thy
    weapon back. Well, sirs,   195
What doth this mean?
Bel.   The prince must answer that.
Sal. Truth upon my part, treason upon
    theirs.
Sar. Treason—Arbaces! treachery and
    Beleses!
That were an union I will not believe.
Bel. Where is the proof?
Sal.   I'll answer that, if once
The king demands your fellow-traitor's
    sword.   201
Arb. [*to Sal.*] A sword which hath been
    drawn as oft as thine
Against his foes.
Sal.   And now against his brother,
And in an hour or so against himself.
Sar. That is not possible: he dared not;
    no—   205
No—I'll not hear of such things.—These
    vain bickerings
Are spawn'd in courts by base intrigues,
    and baser
Hirelings, who live by lies on good men's
    lives.
You must have been deceived, my brother.
Sal.   First
Let him deliver up his weapon, and
Proclaim himself your subject by that duty,
And I will answer all.
Sar.   Why, if I thought so—
But no, it cannot be: the Mede Arbaces—
The trusty, rough, true soldier—the best
    captain   214
Of all who discipline our nations——No,
I'll not insult him thus, to bid him render

The scimitar to me he never yielded
Unto our enemies. Chief, keep your
    weapon.   218
Sal. [*delivering back the signet*]. Mon-
    arch, take back your signet.
Sar.   No, retain it;
But use it with more moderation.
Sal.   Sire,
I used it for your honour, and restore it
Because I cannot keep it with my own.
Bestow it on Arbaces.
Sar.   So I should:
He never ask'd it.
Sal.   Doubt not, he will have it,
Without that hollow semblance of respect.
Bel. I know not what hath prejudiced
    the prince   226
So strongly 'gainst two subjects, than
    whom none
Have been more zealous for Assyria's
    weal.
Sal. Peace, factious priest, and faithless
    soldier! thou   229
Unitest in thy own person the worst vices
Of the most dangerous orders of mankind.
Keep thy smooth words and juggling
    homilies
For those who know thee not. Thy fel-
    low's sin   233
Is, at the least, a bold one, and not temper'd
By the tricks taught thee in Chaldea.
Bel.   Hear him,
My liege—the son of Belus! he blasphemes
The worship of the land, which bows the
    knee   237
Before your fathers.
Sar.   Oh! for that I pray you
Let him have absolution. I dispense with
The worship of dead men; feeling that I
Am mortal, and believing that the race
From whence I sprung are—what I see
    them—ashes.   242
Bel. King! do not deem so: they are
    with the stars,
And——
Sar. You shall join them ere they will
    rise,
If you preach further.—Why, *this* is rank
    treason.   245
Sal. My lord!
Sar.   To school me in the worship of
Assyria's idols! Let him be released—
Give him his sword.
Sal.   My lord, and king, and brother,
I pray ye pause.
Sar.   Yes, and be sermonised,
And dinn'd, and deafen'd with dead men
    and Baal,   250
And all Chaldea's starry mysteries.
Bel. Monarch! respect them.
Sar.   Oh! for that—I love them;
I love to watch them in the deep blue vault,
And to compare them with my Myrrha's
    eyes;

I love to see their rays redoubled in   255
The tremulous silver of Euphrates' wave,
As the light breeze of midnight crisps the
    broad
And rolling water, sighing through the
    sedges
Which fringe his banks: but whether they
    may be   259
Gods, as some say, or the abodes of gods,
As others hold, or simply lamps of night,
Worlds, or the lights of worlds, I know nor
    care not.
There's something sweet in my uncer-
    tainty   263
I would not change for your Chaldean lore;
Besides, I know of these all clay can know
Of aught above it, or below it—nothing.
I see their brilliancy and feel their beauty—
When they shine on my grave I shall know
    neither.
    Bel. For *neither*, sire, say *better*.
    Sar.   I will wait,
If it so please you, pontiff, for that know-
    ledge.   270
In the mean time receive your sword, and
    know
That I prefer your service militant
Unto your ministry—not loving either.
    Sal. [*aside*]. His lusts have made him
        mad. Then must I save him,
Spite of himself.
    Sar. Please you to hear me, Satraps!
And chiefly thou, my priest, because I
    doubt thee   276
More than the soldier; and would doubt
    thee all
Wert thou not half a warrior: let us part
In peace—I'll not say pardon—which
    must be
Earn'd by the guilty; this I'll not pro-
    nounce ye,   280
Although upon this breath of mine de-
    pends
Your own; and, deadlier for ye, on my fears.
But fear not—for that I am soft, not fear-
    ful—
And so live on. Were I the thing some
    think me,
Your heads would now be dripping the last
    drops   285
Of their attainted gore from the high gates
Of this our palace, into the dry dust,
Their only portion of the coveted kingdom
They would be crown'd to reign o'er—let
    that pass.   289
As I have said, I will not *deem* ye guilty,
Nor *doom* ye guiltless. Albeit better men
Than ye or I stand ready to arraign you;
And should I leave your fate to sterner
    judges,
And proofs of all kinds, I might sacrifice
Two men, who, whatsoe'er they now are,
    were   295
Once honest. Ye are free, sirs.

    Arb.   Sire, this clemency—
    Bel. [*interrupting him*]. Is worthy of
        yourself; and, although innocent,
We thank——
    Sar. Priest! keep your thanksgivings
        for Belus;
His offspring needs none.
    Bel.   But being innocent——
    Sar. Be silent.—Guilt is loud. If ye are
        loyal,   300
Ye are injured men, and should be sad, not
    grateful.
    Bel. So we should be, were justice
        done
By earthly power omnipotent; but inno-
    cence
Must oft receive her right as a mere favour.
    Sar. That's a good sentence for a
        homily,   305
Though not for this occasion. Prithee keep
    it
To plead thy sovereign's cause before his
    people.
    Bel. I trust there is no cause.
    Sar.   No *cause*, perhaps;
But many causers:—if ye meet with such
In the exercise of your inquisitive function
On earth, or should you read of it in
    heaven   311
In some mysterious twinkle of the stars,
Which are your chronicles, I pray you note,
That there are worse things betwixt earth
    and heaven
Than him who ruleth many and slays
    none;   315
And, hating not himself, yet loves his
    fellows
Enough to spare even those who would not
    spare him
Were they once masters—but that's doubt-
    ful. Satraps!
Your swords and persons are at liberty
To use them as ye will—but from this hour
I have no call for either. Salemenes!
Follow me.
    [*Exeunt* SARDANAPALUS, SALEMENES,
        and the Train, &c., leaving ARBACES
        and BELESES.
    Arb. Beleses!
    Bel.   Now, what think you?
    Arb. That we are lost.
    Bel.   That we have won the kingdom.
    Arb. What? thus suspected—with the
        sword slung o'er us   324
But by a single hair, and that still wavering,
To be blown down by his imperious breath
Which spared us—why, I know not.
    Bel.   Seek not why;
But let us profit by the interval.
The hour is still our own—our power the
    same—
The night the same we destined. He hath
    changed   330
Nothing except our ignorance of all

Suspicion into such a certainty
As must make madness of delay.
 Arb.   And yet—
 Bel. What, doubting still?
 Arb. He spared our lives, nay, more,
Saved them from Salemenes.
 Bel.   And how long
Will he so spare? till the first drunken
 minute.   336
 Arb. Or sober, rather. Yet he did it
 nobly;
Gave royally what we had forfeited
Basely——
 Bel. Say bravely.
 Arb. Somewhat of both, perhaps,
But it has touch'd me, and, whate'er be-
 tide,   340
I will no further on.
 Bel.   And lose the world!
 Arb. Lose anything except my own
 esteem.
 Bel. I blush that we should owe our
 lives to such
A king of distaffs!
 Arb.   But no less we owe them;
And I should blush far more to take the
 grantor's!   345
 Bel. Thou may'st endure whate'er thou
 wilt—the stars
Have written otherwise.
 Arb. Though they came down,
And marshall'd me the way in all their
 brightness,
I would not follow.
 Bel. This is weakness—worse
Than a scared beldam's dreaming of the
 dead,   350
And waking in the dark.—Go to—go to.
 Arb. Methought he look'd like Nimrod
 as he spoke,
Even as the proud imperial statue stands
Looking the monarch of the kings around it,
And sways, while they but ornament, the
 temple.   355
 Bel. I told you that you had too much
 despised him,
And that there was some royalty within
 him—
What then? he is the nobler foe.
 Arb.   But we
The meaner.—Would he had not spared
 us!
 Bel.   So—
Wouldst thou be sacrificed thus readily?
 Arb. No—but it had been better to have
 died   361
Than live ungrateful.
 Bel. Oh, the souls of some men!
Thou wouldst digest what some call trea-
 son, and
Fools treachery—and, behold, upon the
 sudden,
Because for something or for nothing, this
Rash reveller steps, ostentatiously, 366

'Twixt thee and Salemenes, thou art turn'd
Into—what shall I say?—Sardanapalus!
I know no name more ignominious.
 Arb.   But
An hour ago, who dared to term me such
Had held his life but lightly—as it is,
I must forgive you, even as he forgave
 us—
Semiramis herself would not have done it.
 Bel. No—the queen liked no sharers of
 the kingdom,   374
Not even a husband.
 Arb. I must serve him truly——
 Bel. And humbly?
 Arb. No, sir, proudly—being honest.
I shall be nearer thrones than you to heaven;
And if not quite so haughty, yet more lofty.
You may do your own deeming—you have
 codes,
And mysteries, and corollaries of 380
Right and wrong, which I lack for my
 direction,
And must pursue but what a plain heart
 teaches.
And now you know me.
 Bel.   Have you finish'd?
 Arb.   Yes—
With you.
 Bel. And would, perhaps, betray as well
As quit me?
 Arb. That's a sacerdotal thought 385
And not a soldier's.
 Bel. Be it what you will—
Truce with these wranglings, and but hear
 me.
 Arb.   No—
There is more peril in your subtle spirit
Than in a phalanx.
 Bel. If it must be so—
I'll on alone.
 Arb. Alone!
 Bel.   Thrones hold but one.
 Arb. But this is fill'd.
 Bel. With worse than vacancy—
A despised monarch. Look to it, Arbaces:
I have still aided, cherish'd, loved, and
 urged you;   393
Was willing even to serve you, in the hope
To serve and save Assyria. Heaven itself
Seem'd to consent, and all events were
 friendly   396
Even to the last, till that your spirit shrunk
Into a shallow softness; but now, rather
Than see my country languish, I will be
Her saviour or the victim of her tyrant,
Or one or both, for sometimes both are one;
And if I win, Arbaces is my servant. 402
 Arb. Your servant!
 Bel. Why not? better than be slave,
The *pardon'd* slave of *she* Sardanapalus!

Enter PANIA.

 Pan. My lords, I bear an order from the
 king.   405

Arb. It is obey'd ere spoken.
Bel.   Notwithstanding,
Let's hear it.
Pan.   Forthwith, on this very night,
Repair to your respective satrapies   408
Of Babylon and Media.
Bel.   With our troops?
Pan. My order is unto the satraps and
Their household train.
Arb.   But——
Bel.   It must be obey'd:
Say, we depart.
Pan.   My order is to see you
Depart, and not to bear your answer.
Bel. [*aside*].   Ay!
Well, sir, we will accompany you hence.
Pan. I will retire to marshal forth the
      guard   415
Of honour which befits your rank, and wait
Your leisure, so that it the hour exceeds not.
                              [*Exit* PANIA.

Bel. Now then obey!
Arb.   Doubtless.
Bel.   Yes, to the gates
That grate the palace, which is now our
      prison—   419
No further.
Arb. Thou hast harp'd the truth indeed!
The realm itself, in all its wide extension,
Yawns dungeons at each step for thee and
      me.
Bel. Graves!
Arb.   If I thought so, this good
      sword should dig   423
One more than mine.
Bel.   It shall have work enough.
Let me hope better than thou augurest;
At present, let us hence as best we may.
Thou dost agree with me in understanding
This order as a sentence?
Arb.   Why, what other
Interpretation should it bear? it is
The very policy of orient monarchs—   430
Pardon and poison—favours and a
      sword—
A distant voyage, and an eternal sleep.
How many satraps in his father's time—
For he I own is, or at least *was*, bloodless—
Bel. But *will* not, *can* not be so now.
Arb.   I doubt it.
How many satraps have I seen set out
In his sire's day for mighty vice-royalties,
Whose tombs are on their path! I know
      not how,
But they all sicken'd by the way, it was
So long and heavy.
Bel.   Let us but regain   440
The free air of the city, and we'll shorten
The journey.
Arb. 'Twill be shorten'd at the gates,
It may be.
Bel. No; they hardly will risk that.
They mean us to die privately, but not
Within the palace or the city walls,   445

Where we are known, and may have par-
      tisans:
If they had meant to slay us here, we were
No longer with the living. Let us hence.
Arb. If I but thought he did not mean
      my life——
Bel. Fool! hence—what else should
      despotism alarm'd   450
Mean? Let us but rejoin our troops, and
      march.
Arb. Towards our provinces?
Bel.   No; towards your kingdom.
There's time, there's heart, and hope, and
      power, and means,   453
Which their half measures leave us in full
      scope.—
Away!
Arb. And I even yet repenting must
Relapse to guilt!
Bel.   Self-defence is a virtue, 456
Sole bulwark of all right. Away, I say!
Let's leave this place, the air grows thick
      and choking,
And the walls have a scent of night-shade
      —hence!
Let us not leave them time for further
      council.   460
Our quick departure proves our civic zeal;
Our quick departure hinders our good
      escort,
The worthy Pania, from anticipating
The orders of some parasangs from hence:
Nay, there 's no other choice, but—hence,
      I say,   465
   [*Exit with* ARBACES, *who follows re-*
      luctantly.

Enter SARDANAPALUS *and* SALEMENES.

Sar. Well, all is remedied, and without
      bloodshed,
That worst of mockeries of a remedy;
We are now secure by these men's exile.
Sal.   Yes,
As he who treads on flowers is from the
      adder   469
Twined round their roots.
Sar. Why, what wouldst have me do?
Sal. Undo what you have done.
Sar.   Revoke my pardon?
Sal. Replace the crown now tottering
      on your temples.
Sar. That were tyrannical.
Sal.   But sure.
Sar.   We are so.
What danger can they work upon the
      frontier?
Sal. They are not there yet—never
      should they be so,   475
Were I well listen'd to.
Sar.   Nay, I *have* listen'd
Impartially to thee—why not to them?
Sal. You may know that hereafter; as
      it is,
I take my leave to order forth the guard.

Sar. And you will join us at the banquet?
Sal.   Sire,
Dispense with me—I am no wassailer:
Command me in all service save the Bac-
    chant's.   482
Sar. Nay, but 'tis fit to revel now and
    then.
Sal. And fit that some should watch for
    those who revel
Too oft. Am I permitted to depart?
Sar. Yes——Stay a moment, my good
    Salemenes,
My brother, my best subject, better prince
Than I am king. You should have been the
    monarch,
And I—I know not what, and care not; but
Think not I am insensible to all   490
Thine honest wisdom, and thy rough yet
    kind,
Though oft reproving, sufferance of my
    follies.
If I have spared these men against thy
    counsel,
That is, their lives—it is not that I doubt
The advice was sound; but, let them live:
    we will not   495
Cavil about their lives—so let them mend
    them.
Their banishment will leave me still sound
    sleep,
Which their death had not left me.
Sal.   Thus you run
The risk to sleep for ever, to save traitors—
A moment's pang now changed for years
    of crime.   500
Still let them be made quiet.
Sar.   Tempt me not;
My word is past.
Sal.   But it may be recall'd.
Sar. 'Tis royal.
Sal. And should therefore be decisive.
This half indulgence of an exile serves
But to provoke—a pardon should be full,
Or it is none.
Sar.   And who persuaded me   506
After I had repeal'd them, or at least
Only dismiss'd them from our presence,
    who
Urged me to send them to their satrapies?
Sal. True; that I had forgotten; that is,
    sire,   510
If they e'er reach'd their satrapies—why,
    then,
Reprove me more for my advice.
Sar.   And if
They do not reach them—look to it!—in
    safety,
In safety, mark me—and security—   514
Look to thine own.
Sal.   Permit me to depart;
Their *safety* shall be cared for.
Sar.   Get thee hence, then;
And, prithee, think more gently of thy
    brother.

Sal. Sire, I shall ever duly serve my
    sovereign.   [*Exit* SALEMENES.
Sar. [*solus*]. That man is of a temper too
    severe;   519
Hard but as lofty as the rock, and free
From all the taints of common earth—
    while I   521
Am softer clay, impregnated with flowers:
But as our mould is, must the produce be.
If I have err'd this time, 'tis on the side
Where error sits most lightly on that sense,
I know not what to call it; but it reckons
With me ofttimes for pain, and sometimes
    pleasure;   527
A spirit which seems placed about my heart
To count its throbs, not quicken them, and
    ask
Questions which mortal never dared to
    ask me,   530
Nor Baal, though an oracular deity—
Albeit his marble face majestical
Frowns as the shadows of the evening dim
His brows to changed expression, till at
    times
I think the statue looks in act to speak.
Away with these vain thoughts, I will be
    joyous—   536
And here comes Joy's true herald.

Enter MYRRHA.

Myr.   King! the sky
Is overcast, and musters muttering thun-
    der,
In clouds that seem approaching fast, and
    show   539
In forked flashes a commanding tempest.
Will you then quit the palace?
Sar.   Tempest, say'st thou?
Myr. Ay, my good lord.
Sar.   For my own part, I should be
Not ill content to vary the smooth scene,
And watch the warring elements; but this
Would little suit the silken garments and
Smooth faces of our festive friends. Say,
    Myrrha,   546
Art thou of those who dread the roar of
    clouds?
Myr. In my own country we respect
    their voices
As auguries of Jove.
Sar.   Jove!—ay, your Baal—
Ours also has a property in thunder,   550
And ever and anon some falling bolt
Proves his divinity,—and yet sometimes
Strikes his own altars.
Myr.   That were a dread omen.
Sar. Yes—for the priests. Well, we will
    not go forth
Beyond the palace walls to-night, but
    make   555
Our feast within.
Myr.   Now, Jove be praised! that he
Hath heard the prayer thou wouldst not
    hear. The gods

Are kinder to thee than thou to thyself,
And flash this storm between thee and thy
   foes,   559
To shield thee from them.
   Sar.   Child, if there be peril,
Methinks it is the same within these walls
As on the river's brink.
   Myr.   Not so; these walls
Are high and strong, and guarded. Treason
   has   563
To penetrate through many a winding way,
And massy portal; but in the pavilion
There is no bulwark.
   Sar.   No, nor in the palace,
Nor in the fortress, nor upon the top
Of cloud-fenced Caucasus, where the eagle
   sits
Nested in pathless clefts, if treachery be:
Even as the arrow finds the airy king,
The steel will reach the earthly. But be
   calm;   571
The men, or innocent or guilty, are
Banish'd, and far upon their way.
   Myr.   They live, then?
   Sar. So sanguinary? *Thou!*
   Myr.   I would not shrink
From just infliction of due punishment
On those who seek your life: were 't other-
   wise,   576
I should not merit mine. Besides, you heard
The princely Salemenes.
   Sar.   This is strange;
The gentle and the austere are both against me,
And urge me to revenge.
   Myr.   'Tis a Greek virtue.
   Sar. But not a kingly one—I'll none
   on't; or   581
If ever I indulge in't, it shall be
With kings—my equals.
   Myr.   These men sought to be so.
   Sar. Myrrha, this is too feminine, and
   springs
From fear——
   Myr.   For you.
   Sar.   No matter, still 'tis fear.
I have observed your sex, once roused to
   wrath,   586
Are timidly vindictive to a pitch
Of perseverance, which I would not copy.
I thought you were exempt from this, as
   from
The childish helplessness of Asian women.
   Myr. My lord, I am no boaster of my
   love,   591
Nor of my attributes; I have shared your
   splendour,
And will partake your fortunes. You may
   live
To find one slave more true than subject
   myriads: 594
But this the gods avert! I am content
To be beloved on trust for what I feel,
Rather than prove it to you in your griefs,
Which might not yield to any cares of mine.

   Sar. Grief cannot come where perfect
   love exists,   599
Except to heighten it, and vanish from
That which it could not scare away. Let's
   in—
The hour approaches, and we must prepare
To meet the invited guests who grace our
   feast.   [*Exeunt.*

ACT III

SCENE I.—*The Hall of the Palace illumi-*
nated—SARDANAPALUS *and his Guests*
at Table.—A storm without, and Thun-
der occasionally heard during the Ban-
quet.

   Sar. Fill full! why this is as it should be:
   here
Is my true realm, amidst bright eyes and
   faces
Happy as fair! Here sorrow cannot reach.
   Zam. Nor elsewhere—where the king
   is, pleasure sparkles.
   Sar. Is not this better now than Nim-
   rod's huntings,   5
Or my wild grandam's chase in search of
   kingdoms
She could not keep when conquer'd?
   Alt.   Mighty though
They were, as all thy royal line have been,
Yet none of these who went before have
   reach'd
The acmé of Sardanapalus, who   10
Has placed his joy in peace—the sole true
   glory.
   Sar. And pleasure, good Altada, to
   which glory
Is but the path. What is it that we seek?
Enjoyment! We have cut the way short to
   it,
And not gone tracking it through human
   ashes,   15
Making a grave with every footstep.
   Zam.   No;
All hearts are happy, and all voices bless
The king of peace, who holds a world in
   jubilee.
   Sar. Art sure of that? I have heard
   otherwise;   19
Some say that there be traitors.
   Zam.   Traitors they
Who dare to say so!—'Tis impossible.
What cause?
   Sar.   What cause? true,—fill the
   goblet up;
We will not think of them: there are none
   such,
Or if there be, they are gone.
   Alt.   Guests, to my pledge!
Down on your knees, and drink a measure
   to   25
The safety of the king—the monarch, say I!
The god Sardanapalus!

[ZAMES *and the Guests kneel, and ex-*
claim—
                              Mightier than
His father Baal, the god Sardanapalus!
[*It thunders as they kneel; some start up*
in confusion.
Zam. Why do you rise, my friends? in
    that strong peal   29
His father gods consented.
Myr.   Menaced, rather.
King, wilt thou bear this mad impiety?
Sar. Impiety!—nay, if the sires who
    reign'd
Before me can be gods, I'll not disgrace
Their lineage. But arise, my pious friends;
Hoard your devotion for the thunderer
    there: 35
I seek but to be loved, not worshipp'd.
Alt.   Both—
Both you must ever be by all true subjects.
Sar. Methinks the thunders still in-
    crease: it is
An awful night.
Myr.   Oh yes, for those who have
No palace to protect their worshippers.
Sar. That's true, my Myrrha; and could
    I convert   41
My realm to one wide shelter for the
    wretched,
I'd do it.
Myr. Thou'rt no god then, not to be
Able to work a will so good and general,
As thy wish would imply.
Sar.   And your gods, then,
Who can, and do not?
Myr.   Do not speak of that,
Lest we provoke them.
Sar.   True, they love not censure
Better than mortals. Friends, a thought
    has struck me: 48
Were there no temples, would there, think
    ye, be
Air worshippers? that is, when it is angry,
And pelting as even now.
Myr.   The Persian prays
Upon his mountain.
Sar.   Yes, when the sun shines.
Myr. And I would ask if this your
    palace were   53
Unroof'd and desolate, how many flatterers
Would lick the dust in which the king lay
    low?
Alt. The fair Ionian is too sarcastic
Upon a nation whom she knows not well;
The Assyrians know no pleasure but their
    king's,   58
And homage is their pride.
Sar.   Nay, pardon, guests,
The fair Greek's readiness of speech.
Alt.   Pardon! sire:
We honour her of all things next to thee.
Hark! what was that?
Zam.   That! nothing but the jar
Of distant portals shaken by the wind.

Alt. It sounded like the clash of—hark
    again!   64
Zam. The big rain pattering on the
    roof.
Sar.   No more.
Myrrha, my love, hast thou thy shell in
    order?
Sing me a song of Sappho, her, thou
    know'st,
Who in thy country threw—

Enter PANIA, *with his sword and garments*
bloody, and disordered. The guests rise
in confusion.

Pan. [*to the Guards*]. Look to the portals.
And with your best speed to the walls
    without.
Your arms! To arms! The king's in danger.
    Monarch,   70
Excuse this haste,—'tis faith.
Sar.   Speak on.
Pan.   It is
As Salemenes fear'd; the faithless sa-
    traps——
Sar. You are wounded—give some
    wine. Take breath, good Pania.
Pan. 'Tis nothing—a mere flesh wound.
    I am worn   75
More with my speed to warn my sovereign,
Than hurt in his defence.
Myr.   Well, sir, the rebels?
Pan. Soon as Arbaces and Beleses
    reach'd
Their stations in the city, they refused
To march; and on my attempt to use the
    power   79
Which I was delegated with, they call'd
Upon their troops, who rose in fierce de-
    fiance.
Myr. All?
Pan.   Too many.
Sar.   Spare not of thy free speech,
To spare mine ears the truth.
Pan.   My own slight guard
Were faithful, and what's left of it is still
    so.   84
Myr. And are these all the force still
    faithful?
Pan. No—
The Bactrians, now led on by Salemenes,
Who even then was on his way, still urged
By strong suspicion of the Median chiefs,
Are numerous, and make strong head
    against
The rebels, fighting inch by inch, and form-
    ing   90
An orb around the palace, where they mean
To centre all their force, and save the king.
[*He hesitates*]. I am charged to——
Myr.   'Tis no time for hesitation.
Pan. Prince Salemenes doth implore
    the king
To arm himself, although but for a mo-
    ment,   95

And show himself unto the soldiers: his
Sole presence in this instance might do more
Than hosts can do in his behalf.
  Sar.   What, ho!
My armour there.
  Myr.   And wilt thou?
  Sar.   Will I not?
Ho, there!—but seek not for the buckler:
  'tis   100
Too heavy:—a light cuirass and my sword.
Where are the rebels?
  Pan.   Scarce a furlong's length
From the outward wall the fiercest con-
  flict rages.
  Sar. Then I may charge on horseback.
  Sfero, ho!
Order my horse out.—There is space
  enough   105
Even in our courts, and by the outer gate,
To marshal half the horsemen of Arabia.
          [*Exit* SFERO *for the armour.*
  Myr. How I do love thee!
  Sar.   I ne'er doubted it.
  Myr. But now I know thee.
  Sar. [*to his Attendant*]. Bring down
  my spear too.—   109
Where's Salemenes?
  Pan. Where a soldier should be,
In the thick of the fight.
  Sar.   Then hasten to him——Is
The path still open, and communication
Left 'twixt the palace and the phalanx?
  Pan.   'Twas
When I late left him, and I have no fear:
Our troops were steady, and the phalanx
  form'd.   115
  Sar. Tell him to spare his person for the
  present,
And that I will not spare my own—and say,
I come.
  Pan. There's victory in the very word.
                  [*Exit* PANIA.
  Sar. Altada—Zames—forth, and arm
  ye! There
Is all in readiness in the armoury.   120
See that the women are bestow'd in safety
In the remote apartments: let a guard
Be set before them, with strict charge to quit
The post but with their lives—command
  it, Zames.   124
Altada, arm yourself, and return here;
Your post is near our person.
    [*Exeunt* ZAMES, ALTADA, *and all save*
      MYRRHA.

  Enter SFERO *and others with the King's*
      Arms, &c.

  Sfe.   King! your armour.
  Sar. [*arming himself*]. Give me the
  cuirass—so: my baldric; now
My sword: I had forgot the helm—where
  is it?
That's well—no, 'tis too heavy: you mistake, too—

It was not this I meant, but that which
  bears   130
A diadem around it.
  Sfe.   Sire, I deem'd
That too conspicuous from the precious
  stones
To risk your sacred brow beneath—and
  trust me,
This is of better metal, though less rich.
  Sar. You deem'd! Are you too turn'd a
  rebel? Fellow!   135
Your part is to obey: return, and—no—
It is too late—I will go forth without it.
  Sfe. At least, wear this.
  Sar.   Wear Caucasus! why, 'tis
A mountain on my temples.
  Sfe.   Sire, the meanest
Soldier goes not forth thus exposed to
  battle.   140
All men will recognise you—for the storm
Has ceased, and the moon breaks forth in
  her brightness.
  Sar. I go forth to be recognised, and thus
Shall be so sooner. Now—my spear! I'm
  arm'd.   144
  [*In going stops short, and turns to* SFERO.
Sfero—I had forgotten—bring the mirror.
  Sfe. The mirror, sire?
  Sar.   Yes, sir, of polish'd brass,
Brought from the spoils of India!—but be
  speedy.   [*Exit* SFERO.
  Sar. Myrrha, retire unto a place of
  safety.
Why went you not forth with the other
  damsels?   149
  Myr. Because my place is here.
  Sar.   And when I am gone——
  Myr. I follow.
  Sar.   *You!* to battle?
  Myr.   If it were so,
'Twere not the first Greek girl had trod the
  path.
I will await here your *return*.
  Sar.   The place
Is spacious, and the first to be sought out,
If they prevail; and, if it be so,   155
And I return not——
  Myr.   Still we meet again.
  Sar. How?
  Myr. In the spot where all must meet at
  last—
In Hades! if there be, as I believe,
A shore beyond the Styx; and if there be
  not,   159
In ashes.
  Sar. Darest thou so much?
  Myr.   I dare all things
Except survive what I have loved, to be
A rebel's booty: forth, and do your
  bravest.

    Re-enter SFERO *with the mirror.*

  Sar. [*looking at himself*]. This cuirass
  fits me well, the baldric better,

And the helm not at all. Methinks I seem
   [*Flings away the helmet after trying it
      again.*
Passing well in these toys; and now to
   prove them.   165
Altada! Where's Altada?
   Sfe.   Waiting, sire,
Without: he has your shield in readiness.
   Sar. True; I forgot he is my shield-
     bearer
By right of blood, derived from age to age.
Myrrha, embrace me; yet once more—
   once more—   170
Love me, whate'er betide. My chiefest
   glory
Shall be to make me worthier of your love.
   Myr. Go forth, and conquer!
       [*Exeunt* SARDANAPALUS *and* SFERO.
          Now, I am alone,
All are gone forth, and of that all how few
Perhaps return! Let him but vanquish, and
Me perish! If he vanquish not, I perish;
For I will not outlive him. He has wound
About my heart, I know not how nor why.
Not for that he is king; for now his king-
   dom   179
Rocks underneath his throne, and the
   earth yawns
To yield him no more of it than a grave;
And yet I love him more. Oh, mighty
   Jove!
Forgive this monstrous love for a bar-
   barian,
Who knows not of Olympus! yes, I love
   him
Now, now, far more than——Hark—to
   the war shout!   185
Methinks it nears me. If it should be so,
      [*She draws forth a small vial.*
This cunning Colchian poison, which my
   father
Learn'd to compound on Euxine shores,
   and taught me
How to preserve, shall free me! It had
   freed me   189
Long ere this hour, but that I loved, until
I half forgot I was a slave:—where all
Are slaves save one, and proud of servi-
   tude,
So they are served in turn by something
   lower
In the degree of bondage, we forget
That shackles worn like ornaments no
   less   195
Are chains. Again that shout! and now
   the clash
Of arms—and now—and now—

        Enter ALTADA.
   Alt.   Ho, Sfero, ho!
   Myr. He is not here; what wouldst thou
   with him? How
Goes on the conflict?
   Alt.   Dubiously and fiercely.

   Myr. And the king?
   Alt.   Like a king. I must find Sfero,
And bring him a new spear and his own
   helmet.   201
He fights till now bare-headed, and by far
Too much exposed. The soldiers knew
   his face,
And the foe too; and in the moon's broad
   light,
His silk tiara and his flowing hair   205
Make him a mark too royal. Every arrow
Is pointed at the fair hair and fair features,
And the broad fillet which crowns both.
   Myr.   Ye gods,
Who fulminate o'er my father's land, pro-
   tect him!   209
Were you sent by the king?
   Alt.   By Salamenes,
Who sent me privily upon this charge,
Without the knowledge of the careless
   sovereign.
The king! the king fights as he revels! ho!
What, Sfero! I will seek the armoury—
He must be there.   [*Exit* ALTADA.
   Myr.   'Tis no dishonour—no—
'Tis no dishonour to have loved this man.
I almost wish now, what I never wish'd
Before, that he were Grecian. If Alcides
Were shamed in wearing Lydian Om-
   phale's
She-garb, and wielding her vile distaff;
   surely   220
He, who springs up a Hercules at once,
Nursed in effeminate arts from youth to
   manhood,
And rushes from the banquet to the battle,
As though it were a bed of love, deserves
That a Greek girl should be his paramour,
And a Greek bard his minstrel, a Greek
   tomb   226
His monument. How goes the strife, sir?

        Enter an Officer.

   Officer.   Lost,
Lost almost past recovery. Zames!
   Where
Is Zames?
   Myr. Posted with the guard appointed
To watch before the apartment of the
   women.   230
               [*Exit Officer.*
   Myr. [*sola*]. He's gone; and told no
   more than that all's lost!
What need have I to know more? In
   those words,
Those little words, a kingdom and a king,
A line of thirteen ages, and the lives
Of thousands, and the fortune of all left
With life, are merged; and I, too, with the
   great,
Like a small bubble breaking with the
   wave
Which bore it, shall be nothing. At the
   least,   238

My fate is in my keeping: no proud victor
Shall count me with his spoils.

Enter PANIA.

Pan.   Away with me,
Myrrha, without delay; we must not lose
A moment—all that's left us now.
Myr.   The king?
Pan. Sent me here to conduct you
hence beyond
The river, by a secret passage.
Myr.   Then
He lives—
Pan. And charged me to secure your
life,   245
And beg you to live on for his sake, till
He can rejoin you.
Myr.   Will he then give way?
Pan. Not till the last. Still, still he does
whate'er
Despair can do; and step by step disputes
The very palace.
Myr.   They are here, then:—ay,
Their shouts come ringing through the
ancient halls,   251
Never profaned by rebel echoes till
This fatal night. Farewell, Assyria's line!
Farewell to all of Nimrod! Even the name
Is now no more.
Pan.   Away with me—away!
Myr. No: I'll die here!—Away, and
tell your king   256
I loved him to the last.

Enter SARDANAPALUS *and* SALEMENES *with
Soldiers.* PANIA *quits* MYRRHA, *and
ranges himself with them.*

Sar.   Since it is thus,
We'll die where we were born—in our own
halls.
Serry your ranks—stand firm. I have de-
spatch'd   259
A trusty satrap for the guard of Zames,
All fresh and faithful; they'll be here anon.
All is not over.—Pania, look to Myrrha.
*[*PANIA *returns towards* MYRRHA.*
Sal. We have breathing time; yet once
more charge, my friends—
One for Assyria!
Sar.   Rather say for Bactria!
My faithful Bactrians, I will henceforth be
King of your nation, and we'll hold to-
gether   266
This realm as province.
Sal.   Hark! they come—they come.

Enter BELESES *and* ARBACES *with the Rebels.*

Arb. Set on, we have them in the toil.
Charge! charge!
Bel. On! on!—Heaven fights for us,
and with us—On!
*[*They charge the King and* SALEMENES
with their troops, who defend them-

selves till the arrival of* ZAMES *with the
Guard before mentioned. The Rebels
are then driven off, and pursued by*
SALEMENES, &c. *As the King is going
to join the pursuit,* BELESES *crosses him.*
Bel. Ho! tyrant—*I* will end this war.
Sar.   Even so,
My warlike priest, and precious prophet,
and   271
Grateful and trusty subject: yield, I pray
thee.
I would reserve thee for a fitter doom,
Rather than dip my hands in holy blood.
Bel. Thine hour is come.
Sar.   No, thine.—I've lately read,
Though but a young astrologer, the stars;
And ranging round the zodiac, found thy
fate   277
In the sign of the Scorpion, which pro-
claims
That thou wilt now be crush'd.
Bel.   But not by thee.
*[*They fight;* BELESES *is wounded and
disarmed.*
Sar. [*raising his sword to despatch him,
exclaims*]—
Now call upon thy planets, will they shoot
From the sky to preserve their seer and
credit?   281
*[*A party of Rebels enter and rescue* BE-
LESES. *They assail the King, who, in
turn, is rescued by a Party of his
Soldiers, who drive the Rebels off.*
The villain was a prophet after all.
Upon them—ho! there—victory is ours.
*[*Exit in pursuit.*
Myr. [*to Pan.*] Pursue! Why stand'st
thou here, and leav'st the ranks
Of fellow-soldiers conquering without
thee?   285
Pan. The king's command was not to
quit thee.
Myr.   Me!
Think not of me—a single soldier's arm
Must not be wanting now. I ask no guard,
I need no guard: what, with a world at
stake,
Keep watch upon a woman? Hence, I say,
Or thou art shamed! Nay, then, *I* will go
forth,   291
A feeble female, 'midst their desperate
strife,
And bid thee guard me *there*—where thou
shouldst shield
Thy sovereign.   [*Exit* MYRRHA.
Pan. Yet stay, damsel!—She is gone.
If aught of ill betide her, better I   295
Had lost my life. Sardanapalus holds her
Far dearer than his kingdom, yet he fights
For that too; and can I do less than he,
Who never flash'd a scimitar till now?
Myrrha, return, and I obey you, though
In disobedience to the monarch.
*[*Exit* PANIA.

Enter ALTADA *and* SFERO *by an opposite door.*

Alt. Myrrha! 301
What, gone? yet she was here when the
  fight raged,
And Pania also. Can aught have befallen
  them?

Sfe. I saw both safe, when late the
  rebels fled; 304
They probably are but retired to make
Their way back to the harem.

Alt. If the king
Prove victor, as it seems even now he must,
And miss his own Ionian, we are doom'd
To worse than captive rebels.

Sfe. Let us trace them;
She cannot be fled far; and, found, she
  makes 310
A richer prize to our soft sovereign
Than his recover'd kingdom.

Alt. Baal himself
Ne'er fought more fiercely to win empire,
  than
His silken son to save it: he defies
All augury of foes or friends; and like
The close and sultry summer's day, which
  bodes 316
A twilight tempest, bursts forth in such
  thunder
As sweeps the air and deluges the earth.
The man's inscrutable.

Sfe. Not more than others.
All are the sons of circumstance: away—
Let's seek the slave out, or prepare to be
Tortured for his infatuation, and 322
Condemn'd without a crime. [*Exeunt.*

Enter SALEMENES *and Soldiers, &c.*

Sal. The triumph is
Flattering: they are beaten backward from
  the palace,
And we have open'd regular access 325
To the troops station'd on the other side
Euphrates, who may still be true; nay,
  must be,
When they hear of our victory.—But
  where 328
Is the chief victor? where's the king?

Enter SARDANAPALUS, *cum suis, &c. and*
  MYRRHA.

Sar. Here, brother.
Sal. Unhurt, I hope.
Sar. Not quite; but let it pass.
We've clear'd the palace——
Sal. And I trust the city.
Our numbers gather; and I've order'd on-
  ward 332
A cloud of Parthians, hitherto reserved,
All fresh and fiery, to be pour'd upon them
In their retreat, which soon will be a flight.
Sar. It is already, or at least they
  march'd 336

Faster than I could follow with my Bac-
  trians,
Who spared no speed. I am spent: give
  me a seat.
Sal. There stands the throne, sire.
Sar. 'Tis no place to rest on,
For mind nor body: let me have a couch,
                    [*They place a seat.*
A peasant's stool, I care not what: so—
  now 341
I breathe more freely.
Sal. This great hour has proved
The brightest and most glorious of your life.
Sar. And the most tiresome. Where's
  my cupbearer?
Bring me some water.
Sal. [*smiling*]. 'Tis the first time he
Ever had such an order: even I, 346
Your most austere of counsellors, would
  now
Suggest a purpler beverage.
Sar. Blood—doubtless.
But there's enough of that shed; as for
  wine,
I have learn'd to-night the price of the pure
  element: 350
Thrice have I drank of it, and thrice re-
  new'd,
With greater strength than the grape ever
  gave,
My charge upon the rebels. Where's the
  soldier
Who gave me water in his helmet?
One of the Guards. Slain, sire!
An arrow pierced his brain, while, scat-
  tering 355
The last drops from his helm, he stood in
  act
To place it on his brows.
Sar. Slain! unrewarded!
And slain to serve my thirst: that's hard,
  poor slave!
Had he but lived, I would have gorged him
  with
Gold: all the gold of earth could ne'er
  repay 360
The pleasure of that draught; for I was
  parch'd
As I am now. [*They bring water—he drinks.*
                    I live again—from henceforth
The goblet I reserve for hours of love,
But war on water.
Sal. And that bandage, sire,
Which girds your arm?
Sar. A scratch from brave Beleses.
Myr. Oh! he is wounded!
Sar. Not too much of that;
And yet it feels a little stiff and painful,
Now I am cooler.
Myr. You have bound it with—
Sar. The fillet of my diadem: the first
  time 369
That ornament was ever aught to me
Save an encumbrance.

Myr. [*to the Attendants*]. Summon
    speedily
A leech of the most skilful: pray, retire;
I will unbind your wound and tend it.
Sar.   Do so,
For now it throbs sufficiently: but what
Know'st thou of wounds? yet wherefore
    do I ask?   375
Know'st thou, my brother, where I lighted
    on
This minion?
Sal.   Herding with the other females,
Like frighten'd antelopes.
Sar.   No: like the dam
Of the young lion, femininely raging
(And femininely meaneth furiously, 380
Because all passions in excess are female)
Against the hunter flying with her cub,
She urged on with her voice and gesture,
    and
Her floating hair and flashing eyes, the
    soldiers,   314
In the pursuit.
Sal.   Indeed!
Sar.   You see, this night
Made warriors of more than me. I paused
To look upon her, and her kindled cheek;
Her large black eyes, that flash'd through
    her long hair
As it stream'd o'er her; her blue veins that
    rose
Along her most transparent brow; her
    nostril
Dilated from its symmetry; her lips
Apart; her voice that clove through all the
    din,
As a lute pierceth through the cymbals'
    clash,
Jarr'd but not drown'd by the loud bratt-
    ling; her
Waved arms, more dazzling with their own
    born whiteness   395
Than the steel her hand held, which she
    caught up
From a dead soldier's grasp;—all these
    things made
Her seem unto the troops a prophetess
Of victory, or Victory herself,   399
Come down to hail us hers.
Sal. [*aside*].   This is too much.
Again the love-fit's on him, and all's lost,
Unless we turn his thoughts.
            [*Aloud.*] But pray thee, sire,
Think of your wound—you said even now
    'twas painful.
Sar.   That's true, too; but I must not
    think of it.
Sal. I have look'd to all things needful,
    and will now   405
Receive reports of progress made in such
Orders as I had given, and then return
To hear your further pleasure.
Sar.   Be it so.
Sal. [*in retiring*]. Myrrha!

Myr.   Prince!
Sal. You have shown a soul to-night,
Which, were he not my sister's lord—But
    now   410
I have no time: thou lovest the king?
Myr.   I love
Sardanapalus.
Sal. But wouldst have him king still?
Myr. I would not have him less than
    what he should be.
Sal. Well then, to have him king, and
    yours, and all
He should, or should not be; to have him
    live,   415
Let him not sink back into luxury.
You have more power upon his spirit than
Wisdom within these walls, or fierce re-
    bellion
Raging without: look well that he relapse
    not.
Myr. There needed not the voice of
    Salemenes   420
To urge me on to this: I will not fail.
All that a woman's weakness can——
Sal.   Is power
Omnipotent o'er such a heart as his:
Exert it wisely.   [*Exit* SALEMENES.
Sar.   Myrrha! what, at whispers
With my stern brother? I shall soon be
    jealous.   425
Myr. [*smiling*]. You have cause, sire;
    for on the earth there breathes not
A man more worthy of a woman's love,
A soldier's trust, a subject's reverence,
A king's esteem—the whole world's ad-
    miration!
Sar. Praise him, but not so warmly. I
    must not   430
Hear those sweet lips grow eloquent in
    aught
That throws me into shade; yet you speak
    truth.
Myr. And now retire, to have your
    wound look'd to.
Pray lean on me.
Sar.   Yes, love! but not from pain.
               [*Exeunt omnes.*

ACT IV

SCENE I.—SARDANAPALUS *discovered sleep-
    ing upon a Couch, and occasionally dis-
    turbed in his slumbers, with* MYRRHA
    watching.

Myr. [*sola, gazing*]. I have stolen upon
    his rest, if rest it be,
Which thus convulses slumber: shall I
    wake him?
No, he seems calmer. Oh, thou God of
    Quiet!
Whose reign is o'er seal'd eyelids and soft
    dreams,
Or deep, deep sleep, so as to be un-
    fathom'd,   5

Look like thy brother, Death,—so still, so
   stirless—
For then we are happiest, as it may be, we
Are happiest of all within the realm   8
Of thy stern, silent, and unwakening twin.
Again he moves—again the play of pain
Shoots o'er his features, as the sudden gust
Crisps the reluctant lake that lay so calm
Beneath the mountain shadow; or the
   blast
Ruffles the autumn leaves, that drooping
   cling
Faintly and motionless to their loved
   boughs.   15
I must awake him—yet not yet; who
   knows
From what I rouse him? It seems pain;
   but if
I quicken him to heavier pain? The fever
Of this tumultuous night, the grief too of
His wound, though slight, may cause all
   this, and shake   20
Me more to see than him to suffer. No:
Let Nature use her own maternal means,
And I await to second, not disturb her.
  Sar. [*awakening*]. Not so—although ye
   multiplied the stars,
And gave them to me as a realm to share
From you and with you! I would not so
   purchase   26
The empire of eternity. Hence—hence—
Old hunter of the earliest brutes! and ye,
Who hunted fellow-creatures as if brutes!
Once bloody mortals—and now bloodier
   idols,   30
If your priests lie not! And thou, ghastly
   beldame!
Dripping with dusky gore, and trampling
   on
The carcasses of Inde—away! away!
Where am I? Where the spectres?
   Where—No—that
Is no false phantom: I should know it
   'midst   35
All that the dead dare gloomily raise up
From their black gulf to daunt the living.
   Myrrha!
  Myr. Alas! thou art pale, and on thy
   brow the drops
Gather like night dew. My beloved,
   hush—
Calm thee. Thy speech seems of another
   world,   40
And thou art lord of this. Be of good
   cheer;
All will go well.
  Sar. Thy *hand*—so—'tis thy hand;
'Tis flesh; grasp—clasp—yet closer, till I
   feel
Myself that which I was.
  Myr.   At least know me
For what I am, and ever must be—thine.
  Sar. I know it now. I know this life
   again.   46

Ah, Myrrha! I have been where we shall
   be.
  Myr. My lord!
  Sar.   I've been i' the grave—where
   worms are lords,
And kings are——But I did not deem it so;
I thought 'twas nothing.
  Myr.   So it is; except
Unto the timid, who anticipate   51
That which may never be.
  Sar.   Oh, Myrrha! if
Sleep shows such things, what may not
   death disclose?
  Myr. I know no evil death can show,
   which life   54
Has not already shown to those who live
Embodied longest. If there be indeed
A shore where mind survives, 'twill be as
   mind,
All unincorporate: or if there flits
A shadow of this cumbrous clog of clay,
Which stalks, methinks, between our
   souls and heaven,   60
And fetters us to earth—at least the phan-
   tom,
Whate'er it have to fear, will not fear
   death.
  Sar. I fear it not; but I have felt—have
   seen—
A legion of the dead.
  Myr.   And so have I.
The dust we tread upon was once alive,
And wretched. But proceed: what hast
   thou seen?   66
Speak it, 'twill lighten thy dimm'd mind.
  Sar.   Methought——
  Myr. Yet pause, thou art tired—in
   pain—exhausted; all
Which can impair both strength and
   spirit: seek   69
Rather to sleep again.
  Sar.   Not now—I would not
Dream; though I know it now to be a dream
What I have dreamt:—and canst thou
   bear to hear it?
  Myr. I can bear all things, dreams of
   life or death,
Which I participate with you in semblance
Or full reality.
  Sar.   And this look'd real,   75
I tell you: after that these eyes were open,
I saw them in their flight—for then they fled.
  Myr. Say on.
  Sar.   I saw, that is, I dream'd myself
Here—here—even where we are, guests as
   we were,
Myself a host that deem'd himself but
   guest,   80
Willing to equal all in social freedom;
But, on my right hand and my left, instead
Of thee and Zames, and our custom'd
   meeting,
Was ranged on my left hand a haughty,
   dark,   84

And deadly face; I could not recognise it,
Yet I had seen it, though I knew not where:
The features were a giant's, and the eye
Was still, yet lighted; his long locks curl'd
    down
On his vast bust, whence a huge quiver rose
With shaft-heads feather'd from the
    eagle's wing,   90
That peep'd up bristling through his ser-
    pent hair.
I invited him to fill the cup which stood
Between us, but he answer'd not; I fill'd it;
He took it not, but stared upon me, till
I trembled at the fix'd glare of his eye: 95
I frown'd upon him as a king should
    frown;
He frown'd not in his turn, but look'd
    upon me
With the same aspect, which appall'd me
    more,
Because it changed not; and I turn'd for
    refuge
To milder guests, and sought them on the
    right,   100
Where thou wert wont to be. But——
                                  [He pauses.
    Myr.   What instead?
    Sar. In thy own chair—thy own place
    in the banquet—
I sought thy sweet face in the circle—but
Instead—a grey-hair'd, wither'd bloody-
    eyed,
And bloody-handed, ghastly, ghostly
    thing,   105
Female in garb, and crown'd upon the
    brow,
Furrow'd with years, yet sneering with the
    passion
Of vengeance, leering too with that of lust,
Sate:—my veins curdled.
    Myr.   Is this all?
    Sar.   Upon
Her right hand—her lank, bird-like right
    hand—stood   110
A goblet, bubbling o'er with blood; and on
Her left, another, fill'd with—what I saw
    not,
But turn'd from it and her. But all along
The table sate a range of crowned wretches,
Of various aspects, but of one expression.
    Myr. And felt you not this a mere
    vision?
    Sar.   No:
It was so palpable, I could have touch'd
    them.   117
I turn'd from one face to another, in
The hope to find at last one which I knew
Ere I saw theirs: but no—all turn'd upon
    me,   120
And stared, but neither ate nor drank, but
    stared,
Till I grew stone, as they seem'd half to be,
Yet breathing stone, for I felt life in them,
And life in me: there was a horrid kind

Of sympathy between us, as if they   125
Had lost a part of death to come to me,
And I the half of life to sit by them.
We were in an existence all apart
From heaven or earth—And rather let me
    see   129
Death all than such a being!
    Myr.   And the end?
    Sar. At last I sate, marble, as they, when
    rose
The hunter and the crone; and smiling on
    me—
Yes, the enlarged but noble aspect of
The hunter smiled upon me—I should say,
His lips, for his eyes moved not—and the
    woman's   135
Thin lips relax'd to something like a smile.
Both rose, and the crown'd figures on each
    hand
Rose also, as if aping their chief shades—
Mere mimics even in death—but I sate
    still:
A desperate courage crept through every
    limb,   140
And at the last I fear'd them not, but
    laugh'd
Full in their phantom faces. But then—
    then
The hunter laid his hand on mine: I took it,
And grasp'd it—but it melted from my
    own;
While he too vanish'd, and left nothing
    but   145
The memory of a hero, for he look'd so.
    Myr. And was: the ancestor of heroes,
    too,
And thine no less.
    Sar.   Ay, Myrrha, but the woman,
The female who remain'd, she flew upon
    me,
And burnt my lips up with her noisome
    kisses;   150
And, flinging down the goblets on each
    hand,
Methought their poisons flow'd around
    us, till
Each form'd a hideous river. Still she
    clung;
The other phantoms, like a row of statues,
Stood dull as in our temples, but she still
Embraced me, while I shrunk from her,
    as if,   156
In lieu of her remote descendant, I
Had been the son who slew her for her
    incest.
Then—then—a chaos of all loathsome
    things
Throng'd thick and shapeless: I was dead,
    yet feeling—   160
Buried, and raised again—consumed by
    worms,
Purged by the flames, and wither'd in the
    air!
I can fix nothing further of my thoughts,

Save that I long'd for thee, and sought for
    thee,
In all these agonies,—and woke and found
    thee.   165
  Myr. So shalt thou find me ever at thy
    side,
Here and hereafter, if the last may be.
But think not of these things—the mere
    creations
Of late events, acting upon a frame   169
Unused to toil, yet over-wrought by toil
Such as might try the sternest.
  Sar.   I am better.
Now that I see thee once more, what was
    seen   172
Seems nothing.

Enter SALEMENES.

  Sal.   Is the king so soon awake?
  Sar. Yes, brother, and I would I had
    not slept;
For all the predecessors of our line
Rose up, methought, to drag me down to
    them.   176
My father was amongst them, too; but he,
I know not why, kept from me, leaving me
Between the hunter-founder of our race,
And her, the homicide and husband-killer,
Whom you call glorious.
  Sal.   So I term you also,
Now you have shown a spirit like to hers.
By day-break I propose that we set forth,
And charge once more the rebel crew, who
    still
Keep gathering head, repulsed, but not
    quite quell'd.   185
  Sar. How wears the night?
  Sal.   There yet remain some hours
Of darkness: use them for your further rest.
  Sar. No, not to-night, if 'tis not gone:
    methought   188
I pass'd hours in that vision.
  Myr.   Scarcely one;
I watch'd by you: it was a heavy hour,
But an hour only.
  Sar.   Let us then hold council;
To-morrow we set forth.
  Sal.   But ere that time,
I had a grace to seek.
  Sar.   'Tis granted.
  Sal.   Hear it
Ere you reply too readily; and 'tis   194
For *your* ear only.
  Myr.   Prince, I take my leave.
                              [*Exit* MYRRHA.
  Sal. That slave deserves her freedom.
  Sar.   Freedom only!
That slave deserves to share a throne.
  Sal.   Your patience—
'Tis not yet vacant, and 'tis of its partner
I come to speak with you.
  Sar.   How! of the queen?
  Sal. Even so. I judged it fitting for their
    safety   200

That, ere the dawn, she sets forth with her
    children
For Paphlagonia, where our kinsman
    Cotta
Governs; and there at all events secure
My nephews and your sons their lives, and
    with them
Their just pretensions to the crown in
    case——   205
  Sar. I perish—as is probable: well
    thought—
Let them set forth with a sure escort.
  Sal.   That
Is all provided, and the galley ready
To drop down the Euphrates: but ere they
Depart, will you not see——
  Sar.   My sons? It may
Unman my heart, and the poor boys will
    weep;   211
And what can I reply to comfort them,
Save with some hollow hopes and ill-worn
    smiles?
You know I cannot feign.
  Sal.   But you can feel!
At least, I trust so; in a word, the queen
Requests to see you ere you part—for ever.
  Sar. Unto what end? what purpose? I
    will grant   217
Aught—all that she can ask—but such a
    meeting.
  Sal. You know, or ought to know,
    enough of women,
Since you have studied them so steadily,
That what they ask in aught that touches
    on   221
The heart, is dearer to their feelings or
Their fancy than the whole external world.
I think as you do of my sister's wish;
But 'twas her wish—she is my sister—
    you   225
Her husband—will you grant it?
  Sar.   'Twill be useless:
But let her come.
  Sal.   I go.   [*Exit* SALEMENES.
  Sar.   We have lived asunder
Too long to meet again—and *now* to meet!
Have I not cares enow, and pangs enow,
To bear alone, that we must mingle
    sorrows,   230
Who have ceased to mingle love?

Re-enter SALEMENES *and* ZARINA.

  Sal.   My sister! Courage:
Shame not our blood with trembling, but
    remember
From whence we sprung. The queen is
    present, sire.
  Zar. I pray thee, brother, leave me.
  Sal.   Since you ask it.
                              [*Exit* SALEMENES.
  Zar. Alone with him! How many a
    year has pass'd,   235
Though we are still so young, since we
    have met,

Which I have worn in widowhood of
   heart!
He loved me not: yet he seems little
   changed—
Changed to me only—would the change
   were mutual!
He speaks not—scarce regards me—not a
   word,   240
Nor look—yet he *was* soft of voice and
   aspect,
Indifferent, not austere. My lord!
Sar.   Zarina!
  Zar. No, *not* Zarina—do not say
   Zarina.
That tone—that word—annihilate long
   years,
And things which make them longer.
  Sar.   'Tis too late   245
To think of these past dreams. Let's not
   reproach—
That is, reproach me not—for the *last*
   time——
  Zar. And *first.* I ne'er reproach'd you.
  Sar.   'Tis most true;
And that reproof comes heavier on my
   heart
Than——But our hearts are not in our
   own power.   250
  Zar. Nor hands; but I gave both.
  Sar.   Your brother said
It was your will to see me ere you went
From Nineveh with——[*He hesitates*].
  Zar.   Our children: it is true.
I wish'd to thank you that you have not
   divided
My heart from all that's left it now to
   love—   255
Those who are yours and mine, who look
   like you,
And look upon me as you look'd upon me
Once——But they have not changed.
  Sar.   Nor ever will.
I fain would have them dutiful.
  Zar.   I cherish
Those infants, not alone from the blind
   love   260
Of a fond mother, but as a fond woman.
They are now the only tie between us.
  Sar.   Deem not
I have not done you justice: rather make
   them
Resemble your own line than their own
   sire.
I trust them with you—to you: fit them
   for   265
A throne, or, if that be denied——You
   have heard
Of this night's tumults?
  Zar.   I had half forgotten,
And could have welcomed any grief save
   yours,
Which gave me to behold your face again.
  Sar. The throne—I say it not in fear—
   but 'tis   270

In peril: they perhaps may never mount it;
But let them not for this lose sight of it.
I will dare all things to bequeath it them;
But if I fail, then they must win it back
Bravely—and, won, wear it wisely, not as
   I   275
Have wasted down my royalty.
  Zar.   They ne'er
Shall know from me of aught but what
   may honour
Their father's memory.
  Sar.   Rather let them hear
The truth from you than from a trampling
   world.
If they be in adversity, they'll learn 280
Too soon the scorn of crowds for crown-
   less princes,
And find that all their father's sins are
   theirs.
My boys!—I could have borne it were I
   childless.
  Zar. Oh! do not say so—do not poison
   all
My peace left, by unwishing that thou wert
A father. If thou conquerest, they shall
   reign,   286
And honour him who saved the realm for
   them,
So little cared for as his own; and if——
  Sar. 'Tis lost, all earth will cry out,
   thank your father!
And they will swell the echo with a curse.
  Zar. That they shall never do; but
   rather honour   291
The name of him, who, dying like a king,
In his last hours did more for his own
   memory
Than many monarchs in a length of days,
Which date the flight of time, but make no
   annals.   295
  Sar. Our annals draw perchance unto
   their close;
But at the least, whate'er the past, their end
Shall be like their beginning—memorable.
  Zar. Yet be not rash—be careful of
   your life,
Live but for those who love.
  Sar.   And who are they? 300
A slave, who loves from passion—I'll
   not say
Ambition—she has seen thrones shake,
   and loves;
A few friends who have revell'd till we are
As one, for they are nothing if I fall;
A brother I have injured—children whom
I have neglected, and a spouse——
  Zar.   Who loves. 306
  Sar. And pardons?
  Zar.   I have never thought of this,
And cannot pardon till I have condemn'd.
  Sar. My wife!
  Zar.   Now blessings on thee
   for that word!
I never thought to hear it more—from thee.

Sar. Oh! thou wilt hear it from my
  subjects. Yes— 311
These slaves whom I have nurtured, pamper'd, fed,
And swoln with peace, and gorged with plenty, till
They reign themselves—all monarchs in their mansions—
Now swarm forth in rebellion, and demand 315
His death, who made their lives a jubilee;
While the few upon whom I have no claim
Are faithful! This is true, yet monstrous.
Zar.   'Tis
Perhaps too natural; for benefits
Turn poison in bad minds.
Sar.   And good ones make 320
Good out of evil. Happier than the bee,
Which hives not but from wholesome
  flowers.
Zar.   Then reap
The honey, nor inquire whence 'tis derived.
Be satisfied—you are not all abandon'd.
 Sar. My life insures me that. How long,
  bethink you, 325
Were I not yet a king, should I be mortal;
That is, where mortals *are*, not where they
  must be?
Zar. I know not. But yet live for my—
  that is,
Your children's sake!
Sar.   My gentle, wrong'd Zarina!
I am the very slave of circumstance 330
And impulse—borne away with every
  breath!
Misplaced upon the throne—misplaced
  in life.
I know not what I could have been, but feel
I am not what I should be—let it end.
But take this with thee: if I was not form'd
To prize a love like thine, a mind like
  thine, 336
Nor dote even on thy beauty—as I've
  doted
On lesser charms, for no cause save that
  such
Devotion was a duty, and I hated
All that look'd like a chain for me or
  others 340
(This even rebellion must avouch); yet
  hear
These words, perhaps among my last—
  that none
E'er valued more thy virtues, though he
  knew not
To profit by them—as the miner lights
Upon a vein of virgin ore, discovering
That which avails him nothing: he hath
  found it, 346
But 'tis not his—but some superior's, who
Placed him to dig, but not divide the
  wealth
Which sparkles at his feet; nor dare he lift

Nor poise it, but must grovel on, upturning 350
The sullen earth.
Zar.   Oh! if thou hast at length
Discover'd that my love is worth esteem,
I ask no more—but let us hence together,
And *I*—let me say *we*—shall yet be happy.
Assyria is not all the earth—we'll find
A world out of our own—and be more
  bless'd 356
Than I have ever been, or thou, with all
An empire to indulge thee.

Enter SALEMENES.

Sal.   I must part ye—
The moments, which must not be lost, are
  passing.
Zar. Inhuman brother! wilt thou thus
  weigh out 360
Instants so high and blest?
Sal.   Blest!
Zar.   He hath been
So gentle with me, that I cannot think
Of quitting.
Sal.   So—this feminine farewell
Ends as such partings end, in *no* quitting.
I thought as much, and yielded against all
My better bodings. But it must not be.
Zar. Not be?
Sal.   Remain, and perish——
Zar.   With my husband——
Sal. And children.
Zar.   Alas!
Sal.   Hear me, sister, like
My sister:—all's prepared to make your
  safety
Certain, and of the boys too, our last
  hopes; 370
'Tis not a single question of mere feeling,
Though that were much—but 'tis a point
  of state:
The rebels would do more to seize upon
The offspring of their sovereign, and so
  crush——
Zar. Ah! do not name it.
Sal. Well, then, mark me: when
They are safe beyond the Median's grasp,
  the rebels 376
Have miss'd their chief aim—the extinction of
The line of Nimrod. Though the present
  king
Fall, his sons live for victory and vengeance.
Zar. But could not I remain, alone?
Sal.   What! leave
Your children, with two parents and yet
  orphans— 381
In a strange land—so young, so distant?
Zar.   No—
My heart will break.
Sal.   Now you know all—decide.
Sar. Zarina, he hath spoken well, and
  we

Must yield awhile to this necessity. 385
Remaining here, you may lose all; de-
  parting,
You save the better part of what is left,
To both of us, and to such loyal hearts
As yet beat in these kingdoms.
    Sal.   The time presses.
    Sar. Go, then. If e'er we meet again,
      perhaps   390
I may be worthier of you—and, if not,
Remember that my faults, though not
  atoned for,
Are *ended.* Yet, I dread thy nature will
Grieve more about the blighted name and
  ashes
Which once were mightiest in Assyria—
  than—   395
But I grow womanish again, and must not;
I must learn sternness now. My sins have
  all
Been of the softer order——hide thy
  tears—
I do not bid thee *not* to shed them—'twere
Easier to stop Euphrates at its source
Than one tear of a true and tender heart—
But let me not behold them; they unman
  me   402
Here when I had remann'd myself. My
  brother,
Lead her away.
    Zar.   Oh, God! I never shall
Behold him more!
    Sal. [*striving to conduct her*]. Nay,
      sister, I *must* be obey'd.   405
    Zar. I must remain—away! you shall
      not hold me.
What, shall he die alone?—*I* live alone?
    Sal. He shall *not die alone;* but lonely
      you
Have lived for years.
    Zar.   That's false! I knew *he* lived,
And lived upon his image—let me go!
    Sal. [*conducting her off the stage*]. Nay,
      then, I must use some fraternal
      force,   411
Which you will pardon.
    Zar.   Never. Help me! Oh!
Sardanapalus, wilt thou thus behold me
Torn from thee?
    Sal.   Nay—then all is lost again,
If that this moment is not gain'd.
    Zar.   My brain turns—   415
My eyes fail—where is he? [*She faints.*
    Sar. [*advancing*]. No—set her down;
She's dead—and you have slain her.
    Sal.   'Tis the mere
Faintness of o'erwrought passion: in the air
She will recover. Pray, keep back.—
                        [*Aside*] I must
Avail myself of this sole moment to   420
Bear her to where her children are em-
  bark'd,
I' the royal galley on the river.
                [*Salemenes bears her off.*

    Sar. [*solus*].   This, too—
And this too must I suffer—I, who never
Inflicted purposely on human hearts
A voluntary pang! But that is false—
She loved me, and I loved her.—Fatal
  passion!   426
Why dost thou not expire *at once* in hearts
Which thou hast lighted up at once?
  Zarina!
I must pay dearly for the desolation
Now brought upon thee. Had I never
  loved   430
But thee, I should have been an unopposed
Monarch of honouring nations. To what
  gulfs
A single deviation from the track
Of human duties leads even those who
  claim   434
The homage of mankind as their born due,
And find it, till they forfeit it themselves!

Enter Myrrha.

    Sar. You here! Who call'd you?
    Myr.   No one—but I heard
Far off a voice of wail and lamentation,
And thought——
    Sar. It forms no portion of your duties
To enter here till sought for.
    Myr.   Though I might,   440
Perhaps, recall some softer words of yours
(Although they *too were chiding*), which
  reproved
Because I ever dreaded to intrude;
Resisting my own wish and your in-
  junction
To heed no time nor presence, but ap-
  proach you   445
Uncall'd for:—I retire.
    Sar.   Yet stay—being here.
I pray you pardon me: events have sour'd
  me
Till I wax peevish—heed it not: I shall
Soon be myself again.
    Myr.   I wait with patience,
What I shall see with pleasure.
    Sar.   Scarce a moment   450
Before your entrance in this hall, Zarina,
Queen of Assyria, departed hence.
    Myr. Ah!
    Sar. Wherefore do you start?
    Myr.   Did I do so?
    Sar. 'Twas well you enter'd by another
  portal,
Else you had met. That pang at least is
  spared her!   455
    Myr. I know to feel for her.
    Sar.   That is too much,
And beyond nature—'tis nor mutual
Nor possible. You cannot pity her,
Nor she aught but——
    Myr.   Despise the favourite slave?
Not more than I have ever scorn'd myself.
    Sar. Scorn'd! what, to be the envy of
  your sex,   461

483

And lord it o'er the heart of the world's
  lord?
  Myr. Were you the lord of twice ten
  thousand worlds—
As you are like to lose the one you
  sway'd—
I did abase myself as much in being 465
Your paramour, as though you were a
  peasant—
Nay, more, if that the peasant were a
  Greek.
  Sar. You talk it well——
  Myr. And truly.
  Sar. In the hour
Of man's adversity all things grow daring
Against the falling; but as I am not 470
Quite fall'n, nor now disposed to bear
  reproaches,
Perhaps because I merit them too often,
Let us then part while peace is still between
  us.
  Myr. Part!
  Sar. Have not all past human
  beings parted,
And must not all the present one day
  part? 475
  Myr. Why?
  Sar. For your safety, which I
  will have look'd to,
With a strong escort to your native land;
And such gifts, as, if you had not been all
A queen, shall make your dowry worth a
  kingdom.
  Myr. I pray you talk not thus.
  Sar. The queen is gone: 480
You need not shame to follow. I would
  fall
Alone—I seek no partners but in pleasure.
  Myr. And I no pleasure but in parting
  not.
You shall not force me from you.
  Sar. Think well of it—
It soon may be too late.
  Myr. So let it be; 485
For then you cannot separate me from you.
  Sar. And will not; but I thought you
  wish'd it.
  Myr. I!
  Sar. You spoke of your abasement.
  Myr. And I feel it
Deeply—more deeply than all things but
  love. 489
  Sar. Then fly from it.
  Myr. 'Twill not recall the past—
'Twill not restore my honour, nor my
  heart.
No—here I stand or fall. If that you
  conquer,
I live to joy in your great triumph: should
Your lot be different, I'll not weep, but
  share it.
You did not doubt me a few hours ago.
  Sar. Your courage never—nor your
  love till now; 496

And none could make me doubt it save
  yourself.
Those words——
  Myr. Were words. I pray you, let
  the proofs
Be in the past acts you were pleased to
  praise
This very night, and in my further bear-
  ing, 500
Beside, wherever you are borne by fate.
  Sar. I am content: and, trusting in my
  cause,
Think we may yet be victors and return
To peace—the only victory I covet.
To me war is no glory—conquest no
Renown. To be forced thus to uphold my
  right 506
Sits heavier on my heart than all the
  wrongs
These men would bow me down with.
  Never, never
Can I forget this night, even should I live
To add it to the memory of others. 510
I thought to have made mine inoffensive
  rule
An era of sweet peace 'midst bloody
  annals,
A green spot amidst desert centuries,
On which the future would turn back and
  smile, 514
And cultivate, or sigh when it could not
Recall Sardanapalus' golden reign.
I thought to have made my realm a para-
  dise,
And every moon an epoch of new
  pleasures.
I took the rabble's shouts for love—the
  breath
Of friends for truth—the lips of woman
  for 520
My only guerdon—so they are, my
  Myrrha: [*He kisses her.*
Kiss me. Now let them take my realm and
  life!
They shall have both, but never thee!
  Myr. No, never!
Man may despoil his brother man of all
That's great or glittering—kingdoms fall,
  hosts yield, 525
Friends fail, slaves fly, and all betray—
  and, more
Than all, the most indebted—but a heart
That loves without self-love! 'Tis here—
  now prove it.

Enter SALEMENES.

  Sal. I sought you—How! *she* here
  again?
  Sar. Return not
Now to reproof: methinks your aspect
  speaks 530
Of higher matter than a woman's presence.
  Sal. The only woman whom it much
  imports me

At such a moment now is safe in absence—
The queen's embark'd.
 Sar.   And well? say that much.
 Sal.   Yes.
Her transient weakness has pass'd o'er; at
 least,   535
It settled into tearless silence: her
Pale face and glittering eye, after a glance
Upon her sleeping children, were still fix'd
Upon the palace towers as the swift galley
Stole down the hurrying stream beneath
 the starlight;   540
But she said nothing.
 Sar.   Would I felt no more
Than she has said!
 Sal.   'Tis now too late to feel.
Your feelings cannot cancel a sole pang:
To change them, my advices bring sure
 tidings
That the rebellious Medes and Chaldees,
 marshall'd   545
By their two leaders, are already up
In arms again; and, serrying their ranks,
Prepare to attack: they have apparently
Been join'd by other satraps.
 Sar.   What! more rebels?
Let us be first, then.
 Sal.   That were hardly prudent 550
Now, though it was our first intention. If
By noon to-morrow we are join'd by those
I've sent for by sure messengers, we shall
 be
In strength enough to venture an attack,
Ay, and pursuit too; but, till then, my
 voice   555
Is to await the onset.
 Sar.   I detest
That waiting; though it seems so safe to
 fight
Behind high walls, and hurl down foes into
Deep fosses, or behold them sprawl on
 spikes
Strew'd to receive them, still I like it not—
My soul seems lukewarm; but when I set
 on them,   561
Though they were piled on mountains, I
 would have
A pluck at them, or perish in hot blood!—
Let me then charge.
 Sal.   You talk like a young soldier.
 Sar. I am no soldier, but a man: speak
 not   565
Of soldiership, I loathe the word, and
 those
Who pride themselves upon it; but direct
 me
Where I may pour upon them.
 Sal.   You must spare
To expose your life too hastily: 'tis not
Like mine or any other subject's breath;
The whole war turns upon it—with it; this
Alone creates it, kindles, and may quench
 it—   572
Prolong it—end it.

 Sar.   Then let us end both!
'Twere better thus, perhaps, than pro-
 long either;
I'm sick of one, perchance of both.
     [*A trumpet sounds without.*
 Sal.   Hark!
 Sar.   Let us 575
Reply, not listen.
 Sal.   And your wound!
 Sar.   'Tis bound—
'Tis heal'd—I had forgotten it. Away!
A leech's lancet would have scratch'd me
 deeper;
The slave that gave it might be well
 ashamed
To have struck so weakly.
 Sal. Now, may none this hour 580
Strike with a better aim!
 Sar.   Ay, if we conquer;
But if not, they will only leave to me
A task they might have spared their king.
  Upon them! [*Trumpet sounds again.*
 Sal. I am with you.
 Sar. Ho, my arms! again, my arms!
          [*Exeunt.*

ACT V

SCENE I.—*The same Hall in the Palace.*

MYRRHA *and* BALEA.

 Myr. [*at a window*]. The day at last
 has broken. What a night
Hath usher'd it! how beautiful in heaven!
Though varied with a transitory storm,
More beautiful in that variety!
How hideous upon earth! where peace and
 hope,   5
And love and revel, in an hour were
 trampled
By human passions to a human chaos,
Not yet resolved to separate elements—
'Tis warring still! And can the sun so rise,
So bright, so rolling back the clouds into
Vapours more lovely than the unclouded
 sky,   11
With golden pinnacles, and snowy moun-
 tains,
And billows purpler than the ocean's,
 making
In heaven a glorious mockery of the earth,
So like we almost deem it permanent; 15
So fleeting, we can scarcely call it aught
Beyond a vision, 'tis so transiently
Scatter'd along the eternal vault: and yet
It dwells upon the soul, and soothes the
 soul,
And blends itself into the soul, until 20
Sunrise and sunset form the haunted
 epoch
Of sorrow and of love; which they who
 mark not
Know not the realms where those twin
 genii
(Who chasten and who purify our hearts,

So that we would not change their sweet
rebukes   25
For all the boisterous joys that ever shook
The air with clamour) build the palaces
Where their fond votaries repose and
breathe
Briefly;—but in that brief cool calm inhale
Enough of heaven to enable them to bear
The rest of common, heavy, human hours,
And dream them through in placid
sufferance,
Though seemingly employ'd like all the
rest
Of toiling breathers in allotted tasks
Of pain or pleasure, *two* names for *one*
feeling,   35
Which our internal, restless agony
Would vary in the sound, although the
sense
Escapes our highest efforts to be happy.
   Bal. You muse right calmly: and can
you so watch
The sunrise which may be our last?
   Myr.   It is   40
Therefore that I so watch it, and reproach
Those eyes, which never may behold it
more,
For having look'd upon it oft, too oft,
Without the reverence and the rapture due
To that which keeps all earth from being
as fragile   45
As I am in this form. Come, look upon it,
The Chaldee's god, which when I gaze
upon
I grow almost a convert to your Baal.
   Bal. As now he reigns in heaven, so
once on earth
He sway'd.
   Myr.   He sways it now far more,
then; never   50
Had earthly monarch half the power and
glory
Which centres in a single ray of his.
   Bal. Surely he is a god!
   Myr.   So we Greeks deem too;
And yet I sometimes think that gorgeous
orb   54
Must rather be the abode of gods than one
Of the immortal sovereigns. Now he
breaks
Through all the clouds, and fills my eyes
with light
That shuts the world out. I can look no
more.
   Bal. Hark! heard you not a sound?
   Myr.   No, 'twas mere fancy;   59
They battle it beyond the wall, and not
As in late midnight conflict in the very
Chambers: the palace has become a
fortress
Since that insidious hour; and here,
within
The very centre, girded by vast courts   64
And regal halls of pyramid proportions,

Which must be carried one by one before
They penetrate to where they then arrived,
We are as much shut in even from the
sound
Of peril as from glory.
   Bal.   But they reach'd
Thus far before.
   Myr. Yes, by surprise, and were   70
Beat back by valour: now at once we have
Courage and vigilance to guard us.
   Bal.   May they
Prosper!
   Myr. That is the prayer of many, and
The dread of more: it is an anxious hour;
I strive to keep it from my thoughts. Alas!
How vainly!
   Bal.   It is said the king's demeanour
In the late action scarcely more appall'd
The rebels than astonish'd his true subjects.
   Myr. 'Tis easy to astonish or appal
The vulgar mass which moulds a horde of
slaves;   80
But he did bravely.
   Bal.   Slew he not Beleses?
I heard the soldiers say he struck him
down.
   Myr. The wretch was overthrown,
but rescued to
Triumph,   perhaps,   o'er   one   who
vanquish'd him   84
In fight, as he had spared him in his peril;
And by that heedless pity risk'd a crown.
   Bal.   Hark!
   Myr. You are right; some steps
approach, but slowly.

Enter Soldiers, bearing in SALEMENES
*wounded, with a broken javelin in his
side: they seat him upon one of the
couches which furnish the Apartment.*

   Myr. Oh, Jove!
   Bal.   Then all is over.
   Sal.   That is false.
Hew down the slave who says so, if a
soldier.
   Myr. Spare him—he's none: a mere
court butterfly,   90
That flutters in the pageant of a monarch.
   Sal. Let him live on, then.
   Myr.   So wilt thou, I trust.
   Sal. I fain would live this hour out,
and the event,
But doubt it. Wherefore did ye bear me
here?
   Sol. By the king's order. When the
javelin struck you,   95
You fell and fainted: 'twas his strict com-
mand
To bear you to this hall.
   Sal.   'Twas not ill done:
For seeming slain in that cold dizzy trance,
The sight might shake our soldiers—but—
'tis vain,
I feel it ebbing!

Myr.   Let me see the wound;   100
I am not quite skilless: in my native land
'Tis part of our instruction. War being
   constant,
We are nerved to look on such things.
Sol.   Best extract
The javelin.
   Myr.   Hold! no, no, it cannot be.
Sal. I am sped, then!
   Myr. With the blood that fast must
   follow   105
The extracted weapon, I do fear thy life.
Sal. And I *not* death. Where was the
   king when you
Convey'd me from the spot where I was
   stricken?
Sol. Upon the same ground, and en-
   couraging
With voice and gesture the dispirited
   troops   110
Who had seen you fall, and falter'd back.
Sal.   Whom heard ye
Named next to the command?
Sol.   I did not hear.
Sal. Fly then, and tell him, 'twas my
   last request
That Zames take my post until the
   junction,   114
So hoped for, yet delay'd, of Ofratanes,
Satrap of Susa. Leave me here: our troops
Are not so numerous as to spare your
   absence.
   Sol. But, prince——
Sal. Hence, I say! Here's a courtier and
A woman, the best chamber company.
As you would not permit me to expire
Upon the field, I'll have no idle soldiers
About my sick couch. Hence! and do my
   bidding!   [*Exeunt the Soldiers.*
   Myr. Gallant and glorious spirit!
   must the earth
So soon resign thee?
Sal.   Gentle Myrrha, 'tis   124
The end I would have chosen, had I saved
The monarch or the monarchy by this;
As 'tis, I have not outlived them.
   Myr.   You wax paler.
Sal. Your hand; this broken weapon
   but prolongs   128
My pangs, without sustaining life enough
To make me useful: I would draw it forth
And my life with it, could I but hear how
The fight goes.

   Enter SARDANAPALUS *and Soldiers.*

Sar. My best brother!
Sal.   And the battle   132
Is lost?
Sar. [*despondingly*]. You see *me* here.
Sal.   I'd rather see you *thus!*
      [*He draws out the weapon from the
         wound, and dies.*
Sar. And *thus* I will be seen; unless
   the succour,

The last frail reed of our beleaguer'd
   hopes,   135
Arrive with Ofratanes.
   Myr.   Did you not
Receive a token from your dying brother,
Appointing Zames chief?
   Sar.   I did.
   Myr.   Where's Zames?
Sar. Dead.
   Myr.   And Altada?
Sar.   Dying.
   Myr.   Pania? Sfero?
Sar. Pania yet lives: but Sfero's fled
   or captive.   140
I am alone.
   Myr.   And is all lost?
Sar.   Our walls,
Though thinly mann'd, may still hold out
   against
Their present force, or aught save
   treachery:
But i' the field——
   Myr.   I thought 'twas the intent
Of Salemenes not to risk a sally   145
Till ye were strengthen'd by the expected
   succours.
Sar. *I* overruled him.
   Myr. Well, the fault's a brave one.
Sar. But fatal. Oh, my brother! I
   would give
These realms, of which thou wert the orna-
   ment,
The sword and shield, the sole-redeeming
   honour,   150
To call back—But I will not weep for thee;
Thou shalt be mourn'd for as thou wouldst
   be mourn'd.
It grieves me most that thou couldst quit
   this life
Believing that I could survive what thou
Hast died for—our long royalty of race.
If I redeem it, I will give thee blood   156
Of thousands, tears of millions, for atone-
   ment
(The tears of all the good are thine
   already).
If not, we meet again soon,—if the spirit
Within us lives beyond;—thou readest
   mine,   160
And dost me justice now. Let me once
   clasp
That yet warm hand, and fold that throb-
   less heart   [*Embraces the body.*
To this which beats so bitterly. Now, bear
The body hence.
Soldier.   Where?
Sar.   To my proper chamber.
Place it beneath my canopy, as though
The king lay there: when this is done, we
   will   166
Speak further of the rites due to such
   ashes.
      [*Exeunt Soldiers with the body of
         SALEMENES.*

Enter PANIA.

Sar. Well, Pania! have you placed the
    guards, and issued
The orders fix'd on?
    Pan.   Sire, I have obey'd.
    Sar. And do the soldiers keep their
    hearts up?
    Pan.   Sire?   170
    Sar. I'm answer'd! When a king asks
    twice, and has
A question as an answer to *his* question,
It is a portent. What! they are dis-
    hearten'd?
    Pan. The death of Salemenes, and the
    shouts
Of the exulting rebels on his fall,   175
Have made them——
    Sar. Rage—not droop—it should have
    been.
We'll find the means to rouse them.
    Pan.   Such a loss
Might sadden even a victory.
    Sar.   Alas!
Who can so feel it as I feel? but yet,
Though coop'd within these walls, they
    are strong, and we   180
Have those without will break their way
    through hosts,
To make their sovereign's dwelling what
    it was—
A palace; not a prison, nor a fortress.

Enter an Officer, hastily.

    Sar. Thy face seems ominous. Speak!
    Offi.   I dare not.
    Sar.   Dare not?
While millions dare revolt with sword in
    hand!   185
That's strange. I pray thee break that
    loyal silence
Which loathes to shock its sovereign; we
    can hear
Worse than thou hast to tell.
    Pan.   Proceed, thou hearest.
    Offi. The wall which skirted near the
    river's brink   189
Is thrown down by the sudden inundation
Of the Euphrates, which now rolling, swoln
From the enormous mountains where it
    rises,
By the late rains of that tempestuous region,
O'erfloods its banks, and hath destroy'd
    the bulwark.
    Pan. That's a black augury! it has
    been said   195
For ages, 'That the city ne'er should yield
To man, until the river grew its foe.'
    Sar. I can forgive the omen, not the
    ravage.
How much is swept down of the wall?
    Offi.   About
Some twenty stadia.
    Sar.   And all this is left   200
Pervious to the assailants?

    Offi.   For the present
The river's fury must impede the assault;
But when he shrinks into his wonted
    channel,
And may be cross'd by the accustom'd
    barks,
The palace is their own.
    Sar.   That shall be never   205
Though men, and gods, and elements, and
    omens,
Have risen up 'gainst one who ne'er pro-
    voked them,
My fathers' house shall never be a cave
For wolves to horde and howl in.
    Pan.   With your sanction,
I will proceed to the spot, and take such
    measures   210
For the assurance of the vacant space
As time and means permit.
    Sar.   About it straight,
And bring me back, as speedily as full
And fair investigation may permit,   214
Report of the true state of this irruption
Of waters. [*Exeunt* PANIA *and the Officer.*
    Myr. Thus the very waves rise up
Against you.
    Sar. They are not my subjects, girl,
And may be pardon'd, since they can't be
    punish'd
    Myr. I joy to see this portent shakes
    you not.
    Sar. I am past the fear of portents:
    they can tell me   220
Nothing I have not told myself since mid-
    night:
Despair anticipates such things.
    Myr.   Despair!
    Sar. No; not despair precisely. When
    we know
All that can come, and how to meet it, our
Resolves, if firm, may merit a more noble
Word than this is to give it utterance.   226
But what are words to us? we have well
    nigh done
With them and all things.
    Myr.   Save *one deed*—the last
And greatest to all mortals; crowning act
Of all that was, or is, or is to be—   230
The only thing common to all mankind,
So different in their births, tongues, sexes,
    natures,
Hues, features, climes, times, feelings, in-
    tellects,
Without one point of union save in this,
To which we tend, for which we're born,
    and thread   235
The labyrinth of mystery, call'd life.
    Sar. Our clue being well nigh wound
    out, let's be cheerful.
They who have nothing more to fear may
    well
Indulge a smile at that which once
    appall'd;   239
As children at discover'd bugbears.

Re-enter PANIA.

Pan.   'Tis
As was reported: I have order'd there
A double guard, withdrawing from the
    wall
Where it was strongest the required
    addition
To watch the breach occasion'd by the
    waters.
    Sar.   You have done your duty faith-
    fully, and as   245
My worthy Pania! further ties between us
Draw near a close—I pray you take this
    key: [*Gives a key.*
It opens to a secret chamber, placed
Behind the couch in my own chamber
    (now
Press'd by a nobler weight than e'er it
    bore—   250
Though a long line of sovereigns have lain
    down
Along its golden frame—as bearing for
A time what late was Salemenes). Search
The secret covert to which this will lead
    you;   254
'Tis full of treasure; take it for yourself
And your companions: there's enough to
    load ye,
Though ye be many. Let the slaves be
    freed, too;
And all the inmates of the palace, of
Whatever sex, now quit it in an hour.
Thence launch the regal barks, once form'd
    for pleasure,   260
And now to serve for safety, and embark.
The river's broad and swoln, and uncom-
    manded
(More potent than a king) by these
    besiegers.
Fly! and be happy!
    Pan.   Under your protection!
So you accompany your faithful guard.
    Sar.   No, Pania! that must not be; get
    thee hence,   266
And leave me to my fate.
    Pan.   'Tis the first time
I ever disobey'd: but now—
    Sar.   So all men
Dare beard me now, and Insolence within
Apes Treason from without. Question no
    further;   270
'Tis my command, my last command.
    Wilt *thou*
Oppose it? *thou!*
    Pan.   But yet—not yet.
    Sar.   Well, then,
Swear that you will obey when I shall give
The signal.
    Pan.   With a heavy but true heart,
I promise.
    Sar.   'Tis enough. Now order here
Faggots, pine-nuts, and wither'd leaves,
    and such   276

Things as catch fire and blaze with one sole
    spark;
Bring cedar, too, and precious drugs, and
    spices,
And mighty planks, to nourish a tall pile;
Bring frankincense and myrrh, too, for
    it is   280
For a great sacrifice I build the pyre!
And heap them round yon throne.
    Pan.   My lord!
    Sar.   I have said it,
And *you* have sworn.
    Pan.   And could keep my faith
Without a vow.   [*Exit* PANIA.
    Myr.   What mean you?
    Sar.   You shall know
Anon—what the whole earth shall ne'er
    forget.   285

PANIA, *returning with a Herald.*

    Pan.   My king, in going forth upon my
    duty,
This herald has been brought before me,
    craving
An audience.
    Sar.   Let him speak.
    Her.   The *King* Arbaces——
    Sar.   What, crown'd already?—But,
    proceed.
    Her.   Beleses,   289
The anointed high-priest——
    Sar.   Of what god or demon?
With new kings rise new altars. But,
    proceed;
You are sent to prate your master's will,
    and not
Reply to mine.
    Her.   And Satrap Ofratanes—
    Sar.   Why, *he* is ours.
    Her. [*showing a ring*].   Be sure that he
    is now   294
In the camp of the conquerors; behold
His signet ring.
    Sar.   'Tis his. A worthy triad!
Poor Salemenes! thou hast died in time
To see one treachery the less: this man
Was thy true friend and my most|trusted
    subject.
Proceed.
    Her.   They offer thee thy life, and free-
    dom   300
Of choice to single out a residence
In any of the further provinces,
Guarded and watch'd, but not confined
    in person,
Where thou shalt pass thy days in peace;
    but on
Condition that the three young princes
    are   305
Given up as hostages.
    Sar. [*ironically*]. The generous victors!
    Her.   I wait the answer.
    Sar.   Answer, slave! How long
Have slaves decided on the doom of kings?

Her. Since they were free.   308
Sar.   Mouthpiece of mutiny!
Thou at the least shalt learn the penalty
Of treason, though its proxy only. Pania!
Let his head be thrown from our walls
within
The rebels' lines, his carcass down the
river.
Away with him!
          [PANIA *and the Guards seizing him.*
Pan.   I never yet obey'd
Your orders with more pleasure than the
present.   315
Hence with him, soldiers! do not soil this
hall
Of royalty with treasonable gore;
Put him to rest without.
Her.   A single word:
My office, king, is sacred.
Sar.   And what's *mine*?
That thou shouldst come and dare to ask
of me   320
To lay it down?
Her.   I but obey'd my orders,
At the same peril if refused, as now
Incurr'd by my obedience.
Sar.   So there are
New monarchs of an hour's growth as
despotic
As sovereigns swathed in purple, and
enthroned   325
From birth to manhood!
Her.   My life waits your breath.
Yours (I speak humbly)—but it may be—
yours
May also be in danger scarce less
imminent:
Would it then suit the last hours of a line
Such as is that of Nimrod, to destroy
A peaceful herald, unarm'd, in his office;
And violate not only all that man
Holds sacred between man and man—
but that
More holy tie which links us with the gods?
Sar.   He's right.—Let him go free.—
My life's last act   335
Shall not be one of wrath. Here, fellow,
take
    [*Gives him a golden cup from a table near.*
This golden goblet, let it hold your wine,
And think of *me*; or melt it into ingots,
And think of nothing but their weight and
value.
Her.   I thank you doubly for my life,
and this   340
Most gorgeous gift, which renders it more
precious.
But must I bear no answer?
Sar.   Yes,—I ask
An hour's truce to consider.
Her.   But an hour's?
Sar.   An hour's: if at the expiration of
That time your masters hear no further
from me,   345

They are to deem that I reject their terms,
And act befittingly.
Her.   I shall not fail
To be a faithful legate of your pleasure.
Sar.   And hark! a word more.
Her.   I shall not forget it,
Whate'er it be.
Sar.   Commend me to Beleses; 350
And tell him, ere a year expire, I summon
Him hence to meet me.
Her.   Where?
Sar.   At Babylon.
At least from thence he will depart to meet
me.
Her. I shall obey you to the letter.
                    [*Exit Herald.*
Sar.   Pania!—
Now, my good Pania!—quick!—with
what I order'd.   355
Pan. My lord,—the soldiers are
already charged.
And see! they enter.
    [*Soldiers enter, and form a Pile about
    the Throne, &c.*
Sar.   Higher, my good soldiers,
And thicker yet; and see that the founda-
tion
Be such as will not speedily exhaust
Its own too subtle flame; nor yet be
quench'd   360
With aught officious aid would bring to
quell it.
Let the throne form the *core* of it; I would
not
Leave that, save fraught with fire un-
quenchable,
To the new comers. Frame the whole as if
'Twere to enkindle the strong tower of our
Inveterate enemies. Now it bears an
aspect!   366
How say you, Pania, will this pile suffice
For a king's obsequies?
Pan.   Ay, for a kingdom's.
I understand you, now.
Sar.   And blame me?
Pan.   No—
Let me but fire the pile, and share it with
you.   370
Myr. That duty's mine.
Pan.   A woman's!
Myr.   'Tis the soldier's
Part to die *for* his sovereign, and why not
The woman's with her lover?
Pan.   'Tis most strange!
Myr. But not so rare, my Pania, as thou
think'st it.
In the mean time, live thou.—Farewell!
the pile   375
Is ready.
Pan. I should shame to leave my sove-
reign
With but a single female to partake
His death.
Sar.   Too many far have heralded

Me to the dust already. Get thee hence:
Enrich thee.
   Pan.   And live wretched!
   Sar.   Think upon 380
Thy vow:—'tis sacred and irrevocable.
   Pan. Since it is so, farewell.
   Sar.   Search well my chamber,
Feel no remorse at bearing off the gold;
Remember, what you leave you leave the
    slaves
Who slew me: and when you have borne
    away 385
All safe off to your boats, blow one long
    blast
Upon the trumpet as you quit the palace.
The river's brink is too remote, its stream
Too loud at present to permit the echo
To reach distinctly from its banks. Then
    fly,— 390
And as you sail, turn back; but still keep on
Your way along the Euphrates: if you reach
The land of Paphlagonia, where the queen
Is safe with my three sons in Cotta's court,
Say, what you *saw* at parting, and request
That she remember what I *said* at one
Parting more mournful still.
   Pan.   That royal hand!
Let me then once more press it to my lips;
And these poor soldiers who throng round
    you, and
Would fain die with you!
    [*The Soldiers and* PANIA *throng round
    him, kissing his hand and the hem of
    his robe.*
   Sar.   My best! my last friends! 400
Let's not unman each other: part at once:
All farewells should be sudden, when for
    ever,
Else they make an eternity of moments,
And clog the last sad sands of life with tears.
Hence, and be happy: trust me, I am not
Now to be pitied; or far more for what
Is past than present; for the future, 'tis
In the hands of the deities, if such
There be: I shall know soon. Farewell—
    Farewell.
          [*Exeunt* PANIA *and Soldiers.*
   Myr. These men were honest: it is com-
    fort still 410
That our last looks should be on loving
    faces.
   Sar. And *lovely* ones, my beautiful! but
    hear me!
If at this moment—for we now are on
The brink—thou feel'st an inward shrink-
    ing from
This leap through flame into the future,
    say it: 415
I shall not love thee less; nay, perhaps more,
For yielding to thy nature; and there's time
Yet for thee to escape hence.
   Myr.   Shall I light
One of the torches which lie heap'd be-
    neath 419

The ever-burning lamp that burns without,
Before Baal's shrine, in the adjoining hall?
   Sar. Do so. Is that thy answer?
   Myr.   Thou shalt see.
                    [*Exit* MYRRHA.
   Sar. [*solus*]. She's firm. My fathers!
    whom I will rejoin, 423
It may be, purified by death from some
Of the gross stains of too material being,
I would not leave your ancient first abode
To the defilement of usurping bondmen;
If I have not kept your inheritance
As ye bequeath'd it, this bright part of it,
Your treasure, your abode, your sacred
    relics 430
Of arms and records, monuments, and
    spoils,
In which *they* would have revell'd, I bear
    with me
To you in that absorbing element, 433
Which most personifies the soul as leaving
The least of matter unconsumed before
Its fiery workings:—and the light of this
Most royal of funereal pyres shall be
Not a mere pillar form'd of cloud and flame,
A beacon in the horizon for a day,
And then a mount of ashes, but a light
To lesson ages, rebel nations, and 441
Voluptuous princes. Time shall quench
    full many
A people's records, and a hero's acts;
Sweep empire after empire, like this first
Of empires, into nothing; but even then
Shall spare this deed of mine, and hold it up
A problem few dare imitate, and none
Despise—but, it may be, avoid the life
Which led to such a consummation.

    MYRRHA *returns with a lighted Torch in
      one Hand, and a Cup in the other.*
   Myr.   Lo!
I've lit the lamp which lights us to the stars.
   Sar. And the cup?
   Myr.   'Tis my country's custom to
Make a libation to the gods.
   Sar.   And mine
To make libations amongst men. I've not
Forgot the custom; and although alone,
Will drain one draught in memory of
    many 455
A joyous banquet past.
    [SARDANAPALUS *takes the cup, and after
      drinking and tinkling the reversed cup,
      as a drop falls, exclaims*—
                  And this libation
Is for the excellent Beleses.
   Myr.   Why
Dwells thy mind rather upon that man's
    name
Than on his mate's in villainy?
   Sar.   The one
Is a mere soldier, a mere tool, a kind
Of human sword in a friend's hand; the
    other 461

Is master-mover of his warlike puppet;
But I dismiss them from my mind.—Yet
    pause,
My Myrrha! dost thou truly follow me,
Freely and fearlessly?
    Myr.   And dost thou think   465
A Greek girl dare not do for love, that which
An Indian widow braves for custom?
    Sar.   Then
We but await the signal.
    Myr.   It is long
In sounding.
    Sar.   Now, farewell; one last embrace.
    Myr.   Embrace, but *not* the last; there
    is one more.   470
    Sar. True, the commingling fire will
    mix our ashes.
    Myr. And pure as is my love to thee,
        shall they,
Purged from the dross of earth, and earthly
    passion,
Mix pale with thine. A single thought yet
    irks me.
    Sar. Say it.
    Myr.   It is that no kind hand will
    gather   475
The dust of both into one urn.
    Sar.   The better:
Rather let them be borne abroad upon
The winds of heaven, and scatter'd into air,
Than be polluted more by human hands
Of slaves and traitors. In this blazing
    palace,   480
And its enormous walls of reeking ruin,
We leave a nobler monument than Egypt

Hath piled in her brick mountains, o'er
    dead kings,
Or *kine*, for none know whether those
    proud piles   484
Be for their monarch or their ox-god Apis:
So much for monuments that have for-
    gotten
Their very record!
    Myr.   Then farewell, thou earth!
And loveliest spot of earth! farewell,
    Ionia!
Be thou still free and beautiful, and far
Aloof from desolation! My last prayer
Was for thee, my last thoughts, save *one*,
    were of thee!   491
    Sar. And that?
    Myr.   Is yours.
    [*The trumpet of* PANIA *sounds without.*
    Sar.   Hark!
    Myr.   Now!
    Sar.   Adieu, Assyria!
I loved thee well, my own, my father's land,
And better as my country than my king-
    dom.
I sated thee with peace and joys; and this
Is my reward! and now I owe thee nothing,
Not even a grave.   [*He mounts the pile.*
                    Now, Myrrha!
    Myr.   Art thou ready?
    Sar. As the torch in thy grasp.
                [MYRRHA *fires the pile.*
    Myr.   'Tis fired! I come.
    [*As* MYRRHA *springs forward to throw
        herself into the flames, the Curtain
        falls.*

THE TWO FOSCARI

AN HISTORICAL TRAGEDY

'The *father* softens, but the *governor*'s resolved.'—CRITIC.

DRAMATIS PERSONÆ

MEN
FRANCIS FOSCARI, *Doge of Venice.*
JACOPO FOSCARI, *Son of the Doge.*
JAMES LOREDANO, *a Patrician.*
MARCO MEMMO, *a Chief of the Forty.*
BARBARIGO, *a Senator.*

*Other Senators, The Council of Ten, Guards,
    Attendants, &c., &c.*

WOMAN
MARINA, *Wife of young* FOSCARI.

SCENE.—*The Ducal Palace, Venice*

ACT I

SCENE I.—*A Hall in the Ducal Palace.*

Enter LOREDANO *and* BARBARIGO, *meeting.*

    Lor. Where is the prisoner?
    Bar.   Reposing from
The Question.
    Lor. The hour 's past—fix'd yesterday
For the resumption of his trial.—Let us
Rejoin our colleagues in the council, and

Urge his recall.
    Bar.   Nay, let him profit by   5
A few brief minutes for his tortured limbs;
He was o'erwrought by the Question
    yesterday,
And may die under it if now repeated.
    Lor. Well?
    Bar. I yield not to you in love of justice,
Or hate of the ambitious Foscari,   10
Father and son, and all their noxious
    race;

But the poor wretch has suffer'd beyond
  nature's
Most stoical endurance.

Lor.   Without owning
His crime?

Bar. Perhaps without committing any.
But he avow'd the letter to the Duke   15
Of Milan, and his sufferings half atone for
Such weakness.

Lor.   We shall see.

Bar.   You, Loredano,
Pursue hereditary hate too far.

Lor. How far?

Bar.   To extermination.

Lor.   When they are
Extinct, you may say this.—Let's in to
  council.   20

Bar. Yet pause—the number of our
  colleagues is not
Complete yet; two are wanting ere we can
Proceed.

Lor. And the chief judge, the Doge?

Bar.   No—he,
With more than Roman fortitude, is ever
First at the board in this unhappy process
Against his last and only son.

Lor.   True—true—
His *last*.

Bar. Will nothing move you?

Lor.   *Feels he*, think you?

Bar. He shows it not.

Lor. I have mark'd *that*—the wretch!

Bar. But yesterday, I hear, on his return
To the ducal chambers, as he pass'd the
  threshold   30
The old man fainted.

Lor.   It begins to work, then.

Bar. The work is half your own.

Lor.   And should be *all* mine—
My father and my uncle are no more.

Bar. I have read their epitaph, which
  says they died   34
By poison.

Lor. When the Doge declared that he
Should never deem himself a sovereign till
The death of Peter Loredano, both
The brothers sicken'd shortly:—he *is* sove-
  reign.

Bar. A wretched one.

Lor. What should they be who make
Orphans?

Bar. But *did* the Doge make you so?

Lor.   Yes.   40

Bar. What solid proofs?

Lor.   When princes set themselves
To work in secret, proofs and process are
Alike made difficult; but I have such
Of the first, as shall make the second needless.

Bar. But you will move by law?

Lor.   By all the laws   45
Which he would leave us.

Bar.   They are such in this
Our state as render retribution easier
Than 'mongst remoter nations. Is it true

That you have written in your books of
  commerce
(The wealthy practice of our highest
  nobles),   50
'Doge Foscari, my debtor for the deaths
Of Marco and Pietro Loredano,
My sire and uncle?'

Lor.   It is written thus.

Bar. And will it leave it unerased?

Lor.   Till balanced.

Bar. And how?

  [*Two Senators pass over the stage, as in
      their way to 'the Hall of the Council
      of Ten.'*

Lor. You see the number is complete.
Follow me.   [*Exit* LOREDANO.

Bar. [*solus*]. Follow *thee!* I have fol-
  low'd long   56
Thy path of desolation, as the wave
Sweeps after that before it, alike whelming
The wreck that creaks to the wild winds,
  and wretch
Who shrieks within its riven ribs, as gush
The waters through them; but this son and
  sire   61
Might move the elements to pause, and yet
Must I on hardily like them—Oh! would
I could as blindly and remorselessly!—
Lo, where he comes!—Be still, my heart!
  they are   65
Thy foes, must be thy victims: wilt thou
  beat
For those who almost broke thee?

  Enter Guards, with young FOSCARI *as
      prisoner, &c.*

Guard.   Let him rest.
Signor, take time.

Jac. Fos. I thank thee, friend, I'm
  feeble;
But thou may'st stand reproved.

Guard.   I'll stand the hazard.

Jac. Fos. That's kind:—I meet some
  pity, but no mercy;   70
This is the first.

Guard. And might be the last, did they
Who rule behold us.

Bar. [*advancing to the Guard*]. There is
  one who does:
Yet fear not; I will neither be thy judge
Nor thy accuser; though the hour is past,
Wait their last summons—I am of 'the
  Ten',   75
And waiting for that summons, sanction you
Even by my presence: when the last call
  sounds,
We'll in together.—Look well to the
  prisoner!

Jac. Fos. What voice is that?—'Tis
  Barbarigo's! Ah!
Our house's foe, and one of my few judges.

Bar. To balance such a foe, if such there
  be,   81
Thy father sits amongst thy judges.

Jac. Fos.   True,
He judges.

Bar. Then deem not the laws too harsh
Which yield so much indulgence to a sire,
As to allow his voice in such high matter
As the state's safety——

Jac. Fos.   And his son's. I'm faint;
Let me approach, I pray you, for a breath
Of air, yon window which o'erlooks the
waters.

Enter an Officer, who whispers BARBARIGO.

Bar. [*to the Guard*]. Let him approach.
I must not speak with him
Further than thus: I have transgress'd my
duty   90
In this brief parley, and must now redeem it
Within the Council Chamber.
                              [*Exit* BARBARIGO.
[*Guard conducting* JACOPO FOSCARI *to
the window.*
Guard.   There, sir, 'tis
Open.—How feel you?

Jac. Fos.   Like a boy—Oh Venice!
Guard. And your limbs?

Jas. Fos. Limbs! how often have they
borne me
Bounding o'er yon blue tide, as I have
skimm'd   95
The gondola along in childish race,
And, masqued as a young gondolier,
amidst
My gay competitors, noble as I,
Raced for our pleasure, in the pride of
strength;
While the fair populace of crowding beauties,
Plebeian as patrician, cheer'd us on   101
With dazzling smiles, and wishes audible,
And waving kerchiefs, and applauding
hands,
Even to the goal!—How many a time have I
Cloven with arm still lustier, breast more
daring,   105
The wave all roughen'd; with a swimmer's
stroke
Flinging the billows back from my drench'd
hair,
And laughing from my lip the audacious
brine,
Which kiss'd it like a wine-cup, rising o'er
The waves as they arose, and prouder still
The loftier they uplifted me; and oft,
In wantonness of spirit, plunging down
Into their green and glassy gulfs, and
making
My way to shells and sea-weed, all unseen
By those above, till they wax'd fearful;
then   115
Returning with my grasp full of such
tokens
As show'd that I had search'd the deep:
exulting,
With a far-dashing stroke, and drawing
deep

The long-suspended breath, again I
spurn'd
The foam which broke around me, and
pursued   120
My track like a sea-bird.—I was a boy
then.

Guard. Be a man now: there never was
more need
Of manhood's strength.

Jas. Fos. [*looking from the lattice*]. My
beautiful, my own,
My only Venice—*this is breath!* Thy
breeze,
Thine Adrian sea-breeze, how it fans my
face!   125
Thy very winds feel native to my veins,
And cool them into calmness! How
unlike
The hot gales of the horrid Cyclades,
Which howled about my Candiote
dungeon, and
Made my heart sick!

Guard.   I see the colour comes
Back to your cheek: Heaven send you
strength to bear   131
What more may be imposed!—I dread
to think on 't.

Jac. Fos. They will not banish me
again?—No—no,
Let them wring on; I am strong yet.

Guard.   Confess,
And the rack will be spared you.

Jac. Fos.   I confess'd 135
Once—twice before: both times they
exiled me,

Guard. And the third time will slay
you.

Jac. Fos.   Let them do so,
So I be buried in my birth-place: better
Be ashes here than aught that lives else-
where.

Guard. And can you so much love the
soil which hates you?   140

Jac. Fos. The soil!—Oh no, it is the
seed of the soil
Which persecutes me; but my native earth
Will take me as a mother to her arms.
I ask no more than a Venetian grave,
A dungeon, what they will, so it be
here.   145

Enter an Officer.

Offi. Bring in the prisoner!
Guard. Signor, you hear the order.
Jac. Fos. Ay, I am used to such a sum-
mons: 't is
The third time they have tortured me:—
then lend me
Thine arm.   [*To the Guard.*
Offi. Take mine, sir; 'tis my duty to
Be nearest to your person.
Jac. Fos. You!—you are he 150
Who yesterday presided o'er my pangs—
Away!—I'll walk alone.

Offi.   As you please, signor;
The sentence was not of my signing,
  but
I dared not disobey the Council when
  They——
Jac. Fos. Bade thee stretch me on
    their horrid engine.   155
I pray thee touch me not—that is, just
  now;
The time will come they will renew that
  order,
But keep off from me till 'tis issued. As
I look upon thy hands my curdling limbs
Quiver with the anticipated wrench-
  ing,   160
And the cold drops strain through my
  brow, as if——
But onward—I have borne it—I can bear
  it.—
How looks my father?
Offi.   With his wonted aspect.
Jac. Fos. So does the earth, and sky,
  the blue of ocean,
The brightness of our city, and her
  domes,   165
The mirth of her Piazza, even now
Its merry hum of nations pierces here,
Even here, into these chambers of the
  unknown
Who govern, and the unknown and the
  unnumber'd
Judged and destroy'd in silence,—all
  things wear   170
The self-same aspect, to my very sire!
Nothing can sympathise with Foscari,
Not even a Foscari.—Sir, I attend you.
    [*Exeunt* JACOPO FOSCARI, *Officer, &c.*

Enter MEMMO *and another Senator.*

Mem. He's gone—we are too late:—
    think you 'the Ten'   174
Will sit for any length of time to-day?
Sen. They say the prisoner is most
    obdurate,
Persisting in his first avowal; but
More I know not.
Mem.   And that is much; the secrets
Of yon terrific chamber are as hidden
From us, the premier nobles of the
  state,   180
As from the people.
Sen.   Save the wonted rumours,
Which—like the tales of spectres, that
  are rife
Near ruin'd buildings—never have been
  proved,
Nor wholly disbelieved: men know as
  little   184
Of the state's real acts as of the grave's
Unfathom'd mysteries.
Mem.   But with length of time
We gain a step in knowledge, and I look
Forward to be one day of the decemvirs.
Sen. Or Doge?

Mem. Why, no; not if I can avoid it.
Sen. 'Tis the first station of the state,
    and may   190
Be lawfully desired, and lawfully
Attain'd by noble aspirants.
Mem.   To such
I leave it; though born noble, my ambi-
  tion
Is limited: I'd rather be an unit
Of an united and imperial 'Ten,'   195
Than shine a lonely though a gilded
  cipher.—
Whom have we here? the wife of Foscari?

Enter MARINA, *with a female Attendant.*

Mar. What, no one?—I am wrong,
    there still are two;
But they are senators.
Mem.   Most noble lady,
Command us.
Mar. I command!—Alas! my life   200
Has been one long entreaty, and a vain one.
Mem. I understand thee, but I must
    not answer.
Mar. [*fiercely*]. True—none   dare
    answer here save on the rack,
Or question save those——
Mem. [*interrupting her*]. High-born
    dame! bethink thee
Where thou now art.
Mar. Where I now am!—It was   205
My husband's father's palace.
Mem.   The Duke's palace.
Mar. And his son's prison!—True, I
    have not forgot it;
And if there were no other nearer,
  bitterer
Remembrances, would thank the illus-
  trious Memmo
For pointing out the pleasures of the
  place.   210
Mem. Be calm!
Mar. [*looking up towards heaven*]. I
    am; but oh, thou eternal God!
Canst *thou* continue so, with such a
    world?
Mem. Thy husband yet may be ab-
    solved.
Mar.   He is,
In heaven. I pray you, signor senator,
Speak not of that; you are a man of
    office,   215
So is the Doge; he has a son at stake
Now, at this moment, and I have a
    husband,
Or had; they are there within, or were
    at least
An hour since, face to face, as judge and
    culprit:
Will *he* condemn *him*?
Mem.   I trust not.
Mar.   But if
He does not, there are those will sentence
    both.   221

Mem. They can.
Mar.   And with them power and will are one
In wickedness:—my husband's lost!
Mem.   Not so;
Justice is judge in Venice.
Mar.   If it were so,
There now would be no Venice. But let it   225
Live on, so the good die not, till the hour
Of nature's summons; but 'the Ten's' is quicker,
And we must wait on't. Ah! a voice of wail!

[*A faint cry within.*

Sen. Hark!
Mem.   'Twas a cry of—
Mar. No, no; not my husband's—
Not Foscari's.
Mem.   The voice was—
Mar.   *Not his:* no.   230
He shriek! No; that should be his father's part,
Not his—not his—he'll die in silence.

[*A faint groan again within.*

Mem.   What!
Again?
Mar. *His* voice! it seem'd so: I will not
Believe it. Should he shrink, I cannot cease
To love; but—no—no—no—it must have been   235
A fearful pang, which wrung a groan from him.
Sen. And, feeling for thy husband's wrongs, wouldst thou
Have him bear more than mortal pain in silence?
Mar. We all must bear our tortures. I have not
Left barren the great house of Foscari,
Though they sweep both the Doge and son from life;   241
I have endured as much in giving life
To those who will succeed them, as they can
In leaving it: but mine were joyful pangs:
And yet they wrung me till I *could* have shriek'd,   245
But did not; for my hope was to bring forth
Heroes, and would not welcome them with tears.
Mem. All's silent now.
Mar.   Perhaps all's over: but
I will not deem it: he hath nerved himself,
And now defies them.

Enter an Officer hastily.

Mem. How now, friend, what seek you?   250
Offi. A leech. The prisoner has fainted.

[*Exit Officer.*

Mem.   Lady,
'Twere better to retire.

Sen. [*offering to assist her*]. I pray thee do so.
Mar. Off! *I* will tend him.
Mem.   You! Remember, lady!
Ingress is given to none within those chambers,
Except 'the Ten,' and their familiars.
Mar.   Well,
I know that none who enter there return   256
As they have enter'd—many never; but
They shall not balk my entrance.
Mem.   Alas! this
Is but to expose yourself to harsh repulse,
And worse suspense.
Mar.   Who shall oppose me?
Mem.   They
Whose duty 'tis to do so.
Mar.   'Tis *their* duty   261
To trample on all human feelings, all
Ties which bind man to man, to emulate
The fiends who will one day requite them in
Variety of torturing! Yet I'll pass.   265
Mem. It is impossible.
Mar.   That shall be tried.
Despair defies even despotism: there is
That in my heart would make its way through hosts
With levell'd spears; and think you a few jailors
Shall put me from my path? Give me, then, way;   270
This is the Doge's palace; I am wife
Of the Duke's son, the *innocent* Duke's son,
And they shall hear this!
Mem.   It will only serve
More to exasperate his judges.
Mar.   What
Are *judges* who give way to anger? they   275
Who do so are assassins. Give me way.

[*Exit* MARINA.

Sen. Poor lady!
Mem.   'Tis mere desperation: she
Will not be admitted o'er the threshold.
Sen.   And
Even if she be so, cannot save her husband.
But see, the officer returns.

[*The Officer passes over the stage with another person.*

Mem.   I hardly   280
Thought that 'the Ten' had even this touch of pity,
Or would permit assistance to this sufferer.
Sen. Pity! Is't pity to recall to feeling
The wretch too happy to escape to death
By the compassionate trance, poor nature's last   285
Resource against the tyranny of pain?

Mem. I marvel they condemn him
    not at once.
Sen.   That's not their policy: they'd
    have him live,
Because he fears not death; and banish
    him,
Because all earth, except his native
    land,   290
To him is one wide prison, and each
    breath
Of foreign air he draws seems a slow
    poison,
Consuming but not killing.
Mem.   Circumstance
Confirms his crimes, but he avows them
    not.
Sen. None, save the Letter, which he
    says was written,   295
Address'd to Milan's duke, in the full
    knowledge
That it would fall into the senate's
    hands,
And thus he should be re-conveyed to
    Venice.
Mem. But as a culprit.
Sen.   Yes, but to his country;
And that was all he sought,—so he
    avouches.   300
Mem. The accusation of the bribes
    was proved.
Sen. Not clearly, and the charge of
    homicide
Has been annull'd by the death-bed
    confession
Of Nicolas Erizzo, who slew the late
Chief of 'the Ten.'
Mem.   Then why not clear him?
Sen.   That   305
They ought to answer; for it is well
    known
That Almoro Donato, as I said,
Was slain by Erizzo for private vengeance.
Mem. There must be more in this
    strange process than
The apparent crimes of the accused
    disclose—   310
But here come two of 'the Ten;' let us
    retire.

[*Exeunt* MEMMO *and Senator.*

Enter LOREDANO *and* BARBARIGO.

Bar. [*addressing* LOR.]. That were too
    much: believe me, 'twas not
    meet
The trial should go further at this
    moment.
Lor. And so the Council must break
    up, and Justice
Pause in her full career, because a woman
Breaks in on our deliberations?
Bar.   No,   316
That's not the cause; you saw the
    prisoner's state.
Lor. And had he not recover'd?

Bar.   To relapse
Upon the least renewal.
Lor.   'Twas not tried.
Bar. 'Tis vain to murmur; the
    majority   320
In council were against you.
Lor.   Thanks to you, sir,
And the old ducal dotard, who com-
    bined
The worthy voices which o'er-ruled my
    own.
Bar. I am a judge; but must confess
    that part
Of our stern duty, which prescribes the
    Question,   325
And bids us sit and see its sharp in-
    fliction,
Makes me wish——
Lor.   What?
Bar. That *you* would *sometimes* feel,
As I do always.
Lor.   Go to, you're a child,
Infirm of feeling as of purpose, blown
About by every breath, shook by a
    sigh,   330
And melted by a tear—a precious judge
For Venice! and a worthy statesman to
Be partner in my policy.
Bar.   He shed
No tears.
Lor. He cried out twice.
Bar.   A saint had done so,
Even with the crown of glory in his
    eye,   335
At such inhuman artifice of pain
As was forced on him; but he did not
    cry
For pity; not a word nor groan escaped
    him,
And those two shrieks were not in suppli-
    cation,
But wrung from pangs, and follow'd
    by no prayers.   340
Lor. He mutter'd many times between
    his teeth,
But inarticulately.
Bar.   That I heard not;
You stood more near him.
Lor.   I did so.
Bar.   Methought,
To my surprise too, you were touch'd
    with mercy,
And were the first to call out for assis-
    tance   345
When he was failing.
Lor.   I believed that swoon
His last.
Bar. And have I not oft heard thee
    name
His and his father's death your nearest
    wish?
Lor. If he dies innocent, that is to say,
With his guilt unavow'd, he'll be
    lamented.   350

Bar. What, wouldst thou slay his memory?

Lor.   Wouldst thou have His state descend to his children, as it must,
If he die unattainted?

Bar.   War with *them* too?

Lor. With all their house, till theirs or mine are nothing.

Bar. And the deep agony of his pale wife,   355
And the repress'd convulsion of the high
And princely brow of his old father, which
Broke forth in a slight shuddering, though rarely,
Or in some clammy drops, soon wiped away   359
In stern serenity; these moved you not?
                              [*Exit* LOREDANO.
He's silent in his hate, as Foscari
Was in his suffering; and the poor wretch moved me
More by his silence than a thousand outcries
Could have effected. 'Twas a dreadful sight
When his distracted wife broke through into   365
The hall of our tribunal, and beheld
What we could scarcely look upon, long used
To such sights. I must think no more of this,
Lest I forget in this compassion for
Our foes, their former injuries, and lose   370
The hold of vengeance Loredano plans
For him and me; but mine would be content
With lesser retribution than he thirsts for,
And I would mitigate his deeper hatred
To milder thoughts; but for the present, Foscari   375
Has a short hourly respite, granted at
The instance of the elders of the Council,
Moved doubtless by his wife's appearance in
The hall, and his own sufferings.—Lo! they come:
How feeble and forlorn! I cannot bear   380
To look on them again in this extremity:
I'll hence, and try to soften Loredano.
                              [*Exit* BARBARIGO.

ACT II

SCENE I.—*A Hall in the* DOGE's *palace.*
      The DOGE *and a* SENATOR.

Sen. Is it your pleasure to sign the report
Now, or postpone it till to-morrow?

Doge.   Now;
I overlook'd it yesterday: it wants
Merely the signature. Give me the pen—
[*The* DOGE *sits down and signs the paper.*
There, signor.

Sen. [*looking at the paper*]. You have forgot; it is not signed.   5

Doge. Not sign'd? Ah, I perceive my eyes begin
To wax more weak with age. I did not see
That I had dipp'd the pen without effect.

Sen. [*dipping the pen into the ink, and placing the paper before the* DOGE].
Your hand, too, shakes, my lord: allow me, thus—

Doge. 'Tis done, I thank you.

Sen.   Thus the act confirm'd   10
By you and by 'the Ten' gives peace to Venice.

Doge. 'Tis long since she enjoyed it: may it be
As long ere she resume her arms!

Sen.   'Tis almost
Thirty-four years of nearly ceaseless warfare   14
With the Turk, or the powers of Italy:
The state had need of some repose.

Doge.   No doubt:
I found her Queen of Ocean, and I leave her
Lady of Lombardy; it is a comfort
That I have added to her diadem
The gems of Brescia and Ravenna; Crema   20
And Bergamo no less are hers; her realm
By land has grown by thus much in my reign,
While her sea-sway has not shrunk.

Sen.   'Tis most true,
And merits all our country's gratitude.

Doge. Perhaps so.

Sen.   Which should be made manifest.   25

Doge. I have not complain'd, sir.

Sen.   My good lord, forgive me.

Doge. For what?

Sen.   My heart bleeds for you.

Doge.   For me, signor?

Sen. And for your——

Doge.   Stop!

Sen. It must have way, my lord:
I have too many duties towards you
And all your house, for past and present kindness,   30
Not to feel deeply for your son.

Doge.   Was this
In your commission?

Sen.   What, my lord?

Doge.   This prattle
Of things you know not: but the treaty's sign'd;
Return with it to them who sent you.

Sen.   I
Obey. I had in charge, too, from the
Council   35
That you would fix an hour for their
    reunion.
Doge. Say, when they will—now, even
    at this moment,
If it so please them: I am the state's
    servant.
Sen. They would accord some time
    for your repose.
Doge. I have no repose, that is, none
    which shall cause   40
The loss of an hour's time unto the state.
Let them meet when they will, I shall be
    found
Where I should be, and *what* I have been
    ever.   [*Exit* SENATOR. *The* DOGE
                        remains in silence.

Enter an Attendant.

Att. Prince!
Doge. Say on.
Att.   The illustrious lady Foscari
Requests an audience.
Doge.   Bid her enter. Poor 45
Marina!   [*Exit Attendant. The* DOGE
                remains in silence as before.

Enter MARINA.

Mar. I have ventured, father, on
Your privacy.
Doge. I have none from you, my child.
Command my time, when not com-
    manded by
The state.
Mar. I wish'd to speak to you of *him.*
Doge. Your husband?
Mar.   And your son.
Doge.   Proceed, my daughter! 50
Mar. I had obtain'd permission from
    'the Ten'
To attend my husband for a limited
    number
Of hours.
Doge. You had so.
Mar.   'Tis revoked.
Doge.   By whom?
Mar.   'The Ten.'—When we had
    reach'd 'the Bridge of Sighs,'   54
Which I prepared to pass with Foscari,
The gloomy guardian of that passage first
Demurr'd: a messenger was sent back to
'The Ten;'—but as the court no longer
    sate,
And no permission had been given in
    writing,
I was thrust back, with the assurance that
Until that high tribunal re-assembled 61
The dungeon walls must still divide us.
Doge.   True,
The form has been omitted in the haste
With which the court adjourn'd; and till
    it meets,

'Tis dubious.
Mar. Till it meets! and when it
    meets,   65
They'll torture him again; and he and I
Must purchase by renewal of the rack
The interview of husband and of wife,
The holiest tie beneath the heavens!—
    Oh God!
Dost thou see this?
Doge.   Child—child——
Mar. [*abruptly*].   Call *me* not
    'child'!   70
You soon will have no children—you
    deserve none—
You, who can talk thus calmly of a son
In circumstances which would call forth
    tears
Of blood from Spartans! Though these
    did not weep
Their boys who died in battle, is it
    written   75
That they beheld them perish piecemeal,
    nor
Stretch'd forth a hand to save them?
Doge.   You behold me:
I cannot weep—I would I could; but if
Each white hair on this head were a
    young life,
This ducal cap the diadem of earth,   80
This ducal ring with which I wed the
    waves
A talisman to still them—I'd give all
For him.
Mar. With less he surely might be
    saved.
Doge. That answer only shows you
    know not Venice.
Alas! how should you? she knows not
    herself,   85
In all her mystery. Hear me—they who
    aim
At Foscari, aim no less at his father;
The sire's destruction would not save the
    son;
They work by different means to the same
    end,
And that is——but they have not con-
    quer'd yet.   90
Mar. But they have crush'd.
Doge.   Nor crush'd as yet—I live.
Mar. And your son,—how long will
    he live?
Doge.   I trust,
For all that yet is past, as many years
And happier than his father. The rash
    boy,   94
With womanish impatience to return,
Hath ruin'd all by that detected letter:
A high crime, which I neither can deny
Nor palliate, as parent or as Duke:
Had he but borne a little, little longer
His Candiote exile, I had hopes——he
    has quench'd them—   100
He must return.

Mar.   To exile?

Doge.   I have said it.

Mar.   And can I not go with him?

Doge.   You well know
This prayer of yours was twice denied
    before
By the assembled 'Ten,' and hardly now
Will be accorded to a third request,   105
Since aggravated errors on the part
Of your lord renders them still more
    austere.

Mar.   Austere? Atrocious! The old
    human fiends,
With one foot in the grave, with dim eyes,
    strange
To tears save drops of dotage, with long
    white   110
And scanty hairs, and shaking hands, and
    heads
As palsied as their hearts are hard, they
    counsel,
Cabal, and put men's lives out, as if life
Were no more than the feelings long
    extinguish'd
In their accursed bosoms.

Doge.   You know not—   115

Mar.   I do—I do—and so should you,
    methinks—
That these are demons: could it be else
    that
Men, who have been of women born and
    suckled—
Who have loved, or talk'd at least of
    love—have given
Their hands in sacred vows—have danced
    their babes   120
Upon their knees, perhaps have mourn'd
    above them—
In pain, in peril, or in death—who are,
Or were at least in seeming, human,
    could
Do as they have done by yours, and you
    yourself—
You, who abet them?

Doge.   I forgive this, for   125
You know not what you say.

Mar.   *You* know it well,
And feel it nothing.

Doge.   I have borne so much,
That words have ceased to shake me.

Mar.   Oh, no doubt!
You have seen your son's blood flow,
    and your flesh shook not;
And after that, what are a woman's
    words?   130
No more than woman's tears, that they
    should shake you.

Doge.   Woman, this clamorous grief of
    thine, I tell thee,
Is no more in the balance weigh'd with that
Which——but I pity thee, my poor
    Marina:

Mar.   Pity my husband, or I cast it
    from me;   135

Pity thy son! *Thou* pity!—'tis a word
Strange to thy heart—how came it on
    thy lips?

Doge.   I must bear these reproaches,
    though they wrong me.
Couldst thou but read——

Mar.   'Tis not upon thy brow,
Nor in thine eyes, nor in thine acts,—
    where then   140
Should I behold this sympathy? or shall?

Doge (*pointing downwards*).   There.

Mar.   In the earth?

Doge.   To which I am tending: when
It lies upon this heart, far lightlier, though
Loaded with marble, than the thoughts
    which press it
Now, you will know me better.

Mar.   Are you, then,   145
Indeed, thus to be pitied?

Doge.   Pitied! None
Shall ever use that base word, with which
    men
Cloak their soul's hoarded triumph, as a
    fit one
To mingle with my name; that name
    shall be,   149
As far as *I* have borne it, what it was
When I received it.

Mar.   But for the poor children
Of him thou canst not, or thou wilt not
    save
You were the last to bear it.

Doge.   Would it were so!
Better for him he never had been born;
Better for me.—I have seen our house
    dishonour'd.   155

Mar.   That's false! A truer, nobler,
    trustier heart,
More loving, or more loyal, never beat
Within a human breast. I would not
    change
My exiled, persecuted, mangled husband,
Oppress'd but not disgraced, crush'd,
    overwhelm'd,   160
Alive, or dead, for prince or paladin
In story or in fable, with a world
To back his suit. Dishonour'd!—*he*
    dishonour'd!
I tell thee, Doge, 'tis Venice is dis-
    honour'd!
His name shall be her foulest, worst
    reproach,   165
For what he suffers, not for what he did.
'Tis ye who are all traitors, tyrant!—
    ye!
Did you but love your country like this
    victim
Who totters back in chains to tortures,
    and
Submits to all things rather than to
    exile,   170
You'd fling yourselves before him, and
    implore
His grace for your enormous guilt.

Doge.   He was
Indeed all you have said. I better bore
The deaths of the two sons Heaven took
    from me,
Than Jacopo's disgrace.
    Mar.   That word again? 175
    Doge.   Has he not been condemn'd?
    Mar.   Is none but guilt so?
    Doge. Time may restore his memory—
    I would hope so.
He was my pride, my——but 'tis useless
    now—
I am not given to tears, but wept for joy
When he was born: those drops were   180
    ominous.
    Mar. I say he's innocent! And were
    he not so,
Is our own blood and kin to shrink from us
In fatal moments?
    Doge.   I shrank not from him:
But I have other duties than a father's;
The state would not dispense me from   185
    those duties;
Twice I demanded it, but was refused:
They must then be fulfill'd.

Enter an Attendant.

    Att.   A message from
'The Ten.'
    Doge.   Who bears it?
    Att.   Noble Loredano.
    Doge.   He!—but admit him.
                         [*Exit Attendant.*
    Mar.   Must I then retire?
    Doge. Perhaps it is not requisite, if   190
    this
Concerns your husband, and if not——
    Well, signor,
Your pleasure? [*To* LOREDANO *entering.*
    Lor.   I bear that of 'the Ten.'
    Doge.   They
Have chosen well their envoy.
    Lor.   'Tis *their* choice
Which leads me here.
    Doge.   It does their wisdom honour,
And no less to their courtesy.—Proceed.
    Lor. We have decided.
    Doge.   We?
    Lor.   'The Ten' in council.   196
    Doge. What! have they met again, and
    met without
Apprising me?
    Lor. They wish'd to spare your feel-
    ings,
No less than age.
    Doge. That's new—when spared they
    either?
I thank them, notwithstanding.
    Lor.   You know well
That they have power to act at their dis-
    cretion,   201
With or without the presence of the Doge.
    Doge. 'Tis some years since I learn'd
    this, long before

I became Doge, or dream'd of such ad-
    vancement.
You need not school me, signor; I sate in
That council when you were a young   206
    patrician.
    Lor. True, in my father's time; I have
    heard him and
The admiral, his brother, say as much.
Your highness may remember them; they
    both
Died suddenly.
    Doge.   And if they did so, better
So die than live on lingeringly in pain.
    Lor. No doubt: yet most men like to
    live their days out.   212
    Doge. And did not they?
    Lor. The grave knows best: they died,
As I said, suddenly.
    Doge.   Is that so strange,
That you repeat the word emphatically?
    Lor. So far from strange, that never
    was there death   216
In my mind half so natural as theirs.
Think *you* not so?
    Doge. What should I think of mortals?
    Lor. That they have mortal foes.
    Doge.   I understand you;
Your sires were mine, and you are heir in
    all things.   220
    Lor. You best know if I should be so.
    Doge.   I do.
Your fathers were my foes, and I have
    heard
Foul rumours were abroad; I have also
    read   223
Their epitaph, attributing their deaths
To poison. 'Tis perhaps as true as most
Inscriptions upon tombs, and yet no less
A fable.
    Lor. Who dares say so?
    Doge.   I!—'Tis true
Your fathers were mine enemies, as bitter
As their son e'er can be, and I no less
Was theirs; but I was *openly* their foe:
I never work'd by plot in council, nor
Cabal in commonwealth, nor secret
    means
Of practice against life by steel or drug.
The proof is, your existence.
    Lor.   I fear not.
    Doge. You have no cause, being what I
    am; but were I   235
That you would have me thought, you
    long ere now
Were past the sense of fear. Hate on; I
    care not.
    Lor. I never yet knew that a noble's life
In Venice had to dread a Doge's frown,
That is, by open means.
    Doge.   But I, good signor,   240
Am, or at least *was*, more than a mere
    duke,
In blood, in mind, in means; and that
    they know

Who dreaded to elect me, and have since
Striven all they dare to weigh me down:
  be sure,
Before or since that period, had I held
  you   245
At so much price as to require your ab-
  sence,
A word of mine had set such spirits to
  work
As would have made you nothing. But in
  all things
I have observed the strictest reverence;
Not for the laws alone, for those *you* have
  strain'd   250
(I do not speak of *you* but as a single
Voice of the many) somewhat beyond
  what
I could enforce for my authority,
Were I disposed to brawl; but, as I said,
I have observed with veneration, like
A priest's for the high altar, even unto
The sacrifice of my own blood and quiet,
Safety, and all save honour, the decrees,
The health, the pride, and welfare of the
  state.   259
And now, sir, to your business.
  Lor.   'Tis decreed,
That, without further repetition of
The Question, or continuance of the trial,
Which only tends to show how stubborn
  guilt is
('The Ten,' dispensing with the stricter
  law
Which still prescribes the Question till a
  full   265
Confession, and the prisoner partly having
Avow'd his crime in not denying that
The letter to the Duke of Milan's his),
James Foscari return to banishment,
And sail in the same galley which con-
  vey'd him.   270
  Mar. Thank God! At least they will
  not drag him more
Before that horrible tribunal. Would he
But think so, to my mind the happiest
  doom,
Not he alone, but all who dwell here,
  could
Desire, were to escape from such a land.
  Doge. That is not a Venetian thought,
  my daughter.   276
  Mar. No, 'twas too human. May I
  share his exile?
  Lor. Of this 'the Ten' said nothing.
  Mar.   So I thought!
That were too human, also. But it was not
  Inhibited?
  Lor.   It was not named.
  Mar. [*to the Doge*]. Then, father,
Surely you can obtain or grant me thus
  much: [*To* LOREDANO.
And you, sir, not oppose my prayer to be
Permitted to accompany my husband.
  Doge. I will endeavour.

  Mar.   And you, signor?
  Lor.   Lady!
'Tis not for me to anticipate the pleasure
Of the tribunal.
  Mar.   Pleasure! what a word
To use for the decrees of ——
  Doge.   Daughter, know you
In what a presence you pronounce these
  things?   288
  Mar. A prince's and his subject's.
  Lor.   Subject!
  Mar.   Oh!
It galls you:—well, you are his equal, as
You think; but that you are not, nor
  would be,   291
Were he a peasant:—well, then, you're a
  prince,
A princely noble; and what then am I?
  Lor. The offspring of a noble house.
  Mar.   And wedded
To one as noble. What, or whose, then,
  is   295
The presence that should silence my free
  thoughts?
  Lor. The presence of your husband's
  judges.
  Doge.   And
The deference due even to the lightest
  word
That falls from those who rule in Venice.
  Mar.   Keep
Those maxims for your mass of scared
  mechanics,   300
Your merchants, your Dalmatian and
  Greek slaves,
Your tributaries, your dumb citizens,
And mask'd nobility, your sbirri, and
Your spies, your galley and your other
  slaves,
To whom your midnight carryings off and
  drownings,   305
Your dungeons next the palace roofs, or
  under
The water's level; your mysterious meet-
  ings,
And unknown dooms, and sudden execu-
  tions,
Your 'Bridge of Sighs,' your strangling
  chamber, and
Your torturing instruments, have made ye
  seem   310
The beings of another and worse world!
Keep such for them: I fear ye not. I know
  ye;
Have known and proved your worst, in
  the infernal
Process of my poor husband! Treat me as
Ye treated him:—you did so, in so dealing
With him. Then what have I to fear *from*
  you,   316
Even if I were of fearful nature, which
I trust I am not?
  Doge.   You hear, she speaks wildly.
  Mar. Not wisely, yet not wildly.

Lor.   Lady! words   319
Utter'd within these walls I bear no further
Than to the threshold, saving such as pass
Between the Duke and me on the state's
    service.
Doge. have you aught in answer?
    Doge.   Something from
The Doge; it may be also from a parent.
    Lor. My mission *here* is to the *Doge.*
    Doge.   Then say   325
The Doge will choose his own ambassador,
Or state in person what is meet; and for
The father——
    Lor.   I remember *mine.*—Farewell!
I kiss the hands of the illustrious lady,
And bow me to the Duke.
                        [*Exit* LOREDANO.
    Mar.   Are you content?   330
    Doge. I am what you behold.
    Mar.   And that's a mystery.
    Doge. All things are so to mortals;
        who can read them
Save he who made? or, if they can, the few
And gifted spirits, who have studied long
That loathsome volume—man, and pored
        upon   335
Those black and bloody leaves, his heart
        and brain,
But learn a magic which recoils upon
The adept who pursues it: all the sins
We find in others, nature made our own;
All our advantages are those of fortune;
Birth, wealth, health, beauty, are her acci-
        dents,   341
And when we cry out against Fate, 'twere
        well
We should remember Fortune can take
        nought
Save what she *gave*—the rest was naked-
        ness,
And lusts, and appetites, and vanities,
The universal heritage, to battle   346
With as we may, and least in humblest
        stations,
Where hunger swallows all in one low
        want,
And the original ordinance, that man
Must sweat for his poor pittance, keeps all
        passions   350
Aloof, save fear of famine! All is low,
And false, and hollow—clay from first to
        last,
The prince's urn no less than potter's vessel.
Our fame is in men's breath, our lives upon
Less than their breath; our durance upon
        days,   355
Our days on seasons; our whole being on
Something which is not *us*!—So, we are
        slaves,
The greatest as the meanest—nothing rests
Upon our will; the will itself no less
Depends upon a straw than on a storm;
And when we think we lead, we are most
        led,   361

And still towards death, a thing which
        comes as much
Without our act or choice as birth, so that
Methinks we must have sinn'd in some
        old world,   364
And *this* is hell: the best is, that it is not
Eternal.
    Mar. These are things we cannot judge
On earth.
    Doge. And how then shall we judge
        each other,
Who are all earth, and I, who am call'd
        upon
To judge my son? I have administer'd
My country faithfully—victoriously—
I dare them to the proof, the *chart* of what
She was and is: my reign has doubled
        realms;   372
And, in reward, the gratitude of Venice
Has left, or is about to leave, *me* single.
    Mar. And Foscari? I do not think of
        such things,   375
So I be left with him.
    Doge.   You shall be so;
Thus much they cannot well deny.
    Mar.   And if
They should, I will fly with him.
    Doge.   That can ne'er be.
And whither would you fly?
    Mar.   I know not, reck not—
To Syria, Egypt, to the Ottoman—   380
Anywhere, where we might respire
        unfetter'd,
And live nor girt by spies, nor liable
To edicts of inquisitors of state.
    Doge. What, wouldst thou have a
        renegade for husband,
And turn him into traitor?
    Mar.   He is none!   385
The country is the traitress, which thrusts
        forth
Her best and bravest from her. Tyranny
Is far the worst of treasons. Dost thou
        deem
None rebels except subjects? The prince
        who
Neglects or violates his trust is more
A brigand than the robber-chief.
    Doge.   I cannot   391
Charge me with such a breach of faith.
    Mar.   No; thou
Observ'st, obey'st such laws as make old
        Draco's
A code of mercy by comparison.
    Doge. I found the law; I did not make
        it. Were I   395
A subject, still I might find parts and
        portions
Fit for amendment; but as prince, I never
Would change, for the sake of my house,
        the charter
Left by our fathers.
    Mar.   Did they make it for
The ruin of their children?

Doge. Under such laws, Venice
Has risen to what she is—a state to rival
In deeds, and days, and sway, and, let me add,
In glory (for we have had Roman spirits
Amongst us), all that history has
bequeath'd
Of Rome and Carthage in their best times,
when   405
The people swayed by senates.
Mar.   Rather say,
Groan'd under the stern oligarchs.
Doge.   Perhaps so;
But yet subdued the world: in such a state
An individual, be he richest of   409
Such rank as is permitted, or the meanest,
Without a name, is alike nothing, when
The policy, irrevocably tending
To one great end, must be maintain'd in
vigour.
Mar. This means that you are more a
Doge than father.
Doge.   It means, I am more citizen
than either.   415
If we had not for many centuries
Had thousands of such citizens, and shall,
I trust, have still such, Venice were no city.
Mar. Accursed be the city where the laws
Would stifle nature's!
Doge.   Had I as many sons
As I have years, I would have given them
all,   421
Not without feeling, but I would have
given them
To the state's service, to fulfil her wishes
On the flood, in the field, or, if it must be,
As it, alas! has been, to ostracism,   425
Exile, or chains, or whatsoever worse
She might decree.
Mar.   And this is patriotism?
To me it seems the worst barbarity.
Let me seek out my husband: the sage 'Ten,'
With all its jealousy, will hardly war   430
So far with a weak woman as deny me
A moment's access to his dungeon.
Doge.   I'll
So far take on myself, as order that
You may be admitted.
Mar.   And what shall I say
To Foscari from his father?
Doge.   That he obey
The laws.
Mar. And nothing more? Will you
not see him   436
Ere he depart? It may be the last time.
Doge. The last!—my boy!—the last
time I shall see
My last of children! Tell him I will come.
[*Exeunt.*

ACT III

SCENE I.—*The Prison of* JACOPO FOSCARI.

Jac. Fos. [*solus*]. No light, save yon
faint gleam which shows me walls

Which never echo'd but to sorrow's
sounds,
The sigh of long imprisonment, the step
Of feet on which the iron clank'd, the
groan
Of death, the imprecation of despair!   5
And yet for this I have return'd to Venice,
With some faint hope, 'tis true, that time,
which wears
The marble down, had worn away the hate
Of men's hearts; but I knew them not, and
here   9
Must I consume my own, which never beat
For Venice but with such a yearning as
The dove has for her distant nest, when
wheeling
High in the air on her return to greet
Her callow brood. What letters are these
which   [*Approaching the wall.*
Are scrawl'd along the inexorable wall?
Will the gleam let me trace them? Ah! the
names   16
Of my sad predecessors in this place,
The dates of their despair, the brief words
of
A grief too great for many. This stone
page
Holds like an epitaph their history;   20
And the poor captive's tale is graven on
His dungeon barrier, like the lover's
record
Upon the bark of some tall tree, which
bears   23
His own and his beloved's name. Alas!
I recognise some names familiar to me,
And blighted like to mine, which I will add,
Fittest for such a chronicle as this,
Which only can be read, as writ, by
wretches.   [*He engraves his name.*

Enter a Familiar of '*the Ten.*'

Fam. I bring you food.
Jac. Fos. I pray you set it down;   29
I am past hunger: but my lips are parch'd—
The water!
Fam.   There.
Jac. Fos. [*after drinking*]. I thank you:
I am better.
Fam. I am commanded to inform you
that
Your further trial is postponed.
Jac Fos.   Till when?
Fam. I know not.—It is also in my
orders
That your illustrious lady be admitted.   35
Jac. Fos. Ah! they relent, then—I had
ceased to hope it:
'Twas time.

Enter MARINA.

Mar.   My best beloved!
Jac Fos. [*embracing her*].   My true
wife,
And only friend! What happiness!

Mar.   We'll part
No more.
   Jac. Fos.   How! wouldst thou share a
     dungeon?
   Mar.   Ay,   39
The rack, the grave, all—anything with thee,
But the tomb last of all, for there we shall
Be ignorant of each other, yet I will
Share that—all things except new separa-
    tion;
It is too much to have survived the first.
How dost thou? How are those worn
    limbs? Alas!   45
Why do I ask? Thy paleness——
   Jac. Fos.   'Tis the joy
Of seeing thee again so soon, and so
Without expectancy, has sent the blood
Back to my heart, and left my cheeks like
    thine,   49
For thou art pale too, my Marina!
   Mar.   'Tis
The gloom of this eternal cell, which never
Knew sunbeam, and the sallow sullen glare
Of the familiar's torch, which seems akin
To darkness more than light, by lending to
The dungeon vapours its bituminous
    smoke,   55
Which cloud whate'er we gaze on, even
    thine eyes—
No, not thine eyes—they sparkle—how
    they sparkle!
   Jac. Fos.   And thine!—but I am
    blinded by the torch.
   Mar.   As I had been without it.
Couldst thou see here?
   Jac. Fos.   Nothing at first; but use and
    time had taught me   60
Familiarity with what was darkness;
And the grey twilight of such glimmerings as
Glide through the crevices made by the
    winds   63
Was kinder to my eyes than the full sun,
When gorgeously o'ergilding any towers
Save those of Venice: but a moment ere
Thou camest hither I was busy writing.
   Mar.   What?
   Jac. Fos.   My name: look, 'tis there—
    recorded next   68
The name of him who here preceded me,
If dungeon dates say true.
   Mar.   And what of him?
   Jac. Fos.   These walls are silent of
    men's ends; they only
Seem to hint shrewdly of them. Such
    stern walls
Were never piled on high save o'er the
    dead,
Or those who soon must be so.—*What of
    him*?
Thou askest.—What of me? may soon be
    ask'd,   75
With the like answer—doubt and dreadful
    surmise—
Unless thou tell'st my tale.

   Mar.   *I speak* of thee!
   Jac. Fos.   And wherefore not? All then
    shall speak of me:
The tyranny of silence is not lasting,
And, though events be hidden, just men's
    groans   80
Will burst all cerement, even a living
    grave's!
I do not *doubt* my memory, but my life;
And neither do I fear.
   Mar.   Thy life is safe. 83
   Jac. Fos.   And liberty?
   Mar.   The mind should make its own.
   Jac. Fos.   That has a noble sound; but
    'tis a sound,
A music most impressive, but too
    transient:
The mind is much, but is not all. The
    mind
Hath nerved me to endure the risk of
    death,   88
And torture positive, far worse than death
(If death be a deep sleep), without a groan,
Or with a cry which rather shamed my
    judges
Than me; but 'tis not all, for there are
    things
More woful—such as this small dungeon,
    where
I may breathe many years.
   Mar.   Alas! and this   94
Small dungeon is all that belongs to thee
Of this wide realm, of which thy sire is
    prince.
   Jac. Fos.   That thought would scarcely
    aid me to endure it.
My doom is common; many are in
    dungeons,
But none like mine, so near their father's
    palace;
But then my heart is sometimes high, and
    hope   100
Will stream along those moted rays of
    light
Peopled with dusty atoms, which afford
Our only day: for, save the gaoler's torch,
And a strange firefly, which was quickly
    caught   104
Last night in yon enormous spider's net,
I ne'er saw aught here like a ray. Alas!
I know if mind may bear us up, or no,
For I have such, and shown it before men;
It sinks in solitude: my soul is social.
   Mar.   I will be with thee.   110
   Jac. Fos.   Ah! if it were so!
But *that* they never granted—nor will grant,
And I shall be alone: no men; no books—
Those lying likenesses of lying men.
I ask'd for even those outlines of their
    kind,
Which they term annals, history, what you
    will,   115
Which men bequeath as portraits, and
    they were

Refused me,—so these walls have been my
    study,
More faithful pictures of Venetian story,
With all their blank, or dismal stains,
    than is
The Hall not far from hence, which bears
    on high   120
Hundreds of doges, and their deeds and
    dates.
  Mar. I come to tell thee the result of
    their
Last council on thy doom.
  Jac. Fos.   I know it—look!
  [*He points to his limbs, as referring to*
    the Question which he had undergone.
  Mar. No—no—no more of that: even
    they relent   124
From that atrocity.
  Jac. Fos.   What then?
  Mar.   That you
Return to Candia.
  Jac. Fos. Then my last hope's gone.
I could endure my dungeon, for t'was
    Venice;
I could support the torture, there was
    something   128
In my native air that buoy'd my spirits up
Like a ship on the ocean toss'd by storms,
But proudly still bestriding the high waves,
And holding on its course; but *there*,
    afar,
In that accursed isle of slaves and captives,
And unbelievers, like a stranded wreck,
My very soul seem'd mouldering in my
    bosom,   135
And piecemeal I shall perish, if remanded.
  Mar. And *here*?
  Jac. Fos. At once—by better means,
    as briefer.
What! would they even deny me my sire's
    sepulchre,
As well as home and heritage?
  Mar.   My husband!   139
I have sued to accompany thee hence,
And not so hopelessly. This love of thine
For an ungrateful and tyrannic soil
Is passion, and not patriotism; for me,
So I could see thee with a quiet aspect,
And the sweet freedom of the earth and
    air,   145
I would not cavil about climes or regions.
This crowd of palaces and prisons is not
A paradise; its first inhabitants
Were wretched exiles.
  Jac. Fos. Well I know *how* wretched!
  Mar. And yet you see how, from their
    banishment   150
Before the Tartar into these salt isles,
Their antique energy of mind, all that
Remain'd of Rome for their inheritance,
Created by degrees an ocean Rome; 154
And shall an evil, which so often leads
To good, depress thee thus?
  Jac. Fos.   Had I gone forth

From my own land, like the old patriarchs,
    seeking
Another region, with their flocks and
    herds;
Had I been cast out like the Jews from
    Zion,
Or like our fathers, driven by Attila 160
From fertile Italy, to barren islets,
I would have given some tears to my late
    country,
And many thoughts; but afterwards
    address'd
Myself, with those about me, to create
A new home and fresh state: perhaps I
    could   165
Have borne this—though I know not.
  Mar.   Wherefore not?
It was the lot of millions, and must be
The fate of myriads more.
  Jac. Fos.   Ay—we but hear 168
Of the survivors' toil in their new lands,
Their numbers and success; but who can
    number
The hearts which broke in silence at that
    parting,
Or after their departure; of that malady
Which calls up green and native fields to
    view   173
From the rough deep, with such identity
To the poor exile's fever'd eye, that he
Can scarcely be restrained from treading
    them?
That melody, which out of tones and tunes
Collects such pasture for the longing
    sorrow   178
Of the sad mountaineer, when far away
From his snow canopy of cliffs and clouds,
That he feeds on the sweet, but poisonous
    thought,
And dies. You call this *weakness*! It is
    strength,
I say,—the parent of all honest feeling.
He who loves not his country, can love
    nothing.
  Mar. Obey her, then: 'tis she that puts
    thee forth.   185
  Jac. Fos. Ay, there it is; 'tis like a
    mother's curse
Upon my soul—the mark is set upon me.
The exiles you speak of went forth by
    nations,
Their hands upheld each other by the way,
Their tents were pitched together—I'm
    alone.   190
  Mar. You shall be so no more—I will
    go with thee.
  Jac. Fos. My best Marina!—and our
    children?
  Mar.   They,
I fear, by the prevention of the state's
Abhorrent policy (which holds all ties
As threads, which may be broken at her
    pleasure),   195
Will not be suffer'd to proceed with us.

Jac. Fos.   And canst thou leave them?
Mar.   Yes. With many a pang.
But—I *can* leave them, children as they are,
To teach you to be less a child. From this
Learn you to sway your feelings, when
    exacted   200
By duties paramount; and 'tis our first
On earth to bear.
Jac Fos.   Have I not borne?
Mar.   Too much
From tyrannous injustice, and enough
To teach you not to shrink now from a lot,
Which, as compared with what you have
    undergone   205
Of late, is mercy.
Jac. Fos.   Ah! you never yet
Were far away from Venice, never saw
Her beautiful towers in the receding
    distance,
While every furrow of the vessel's track
Seem'd ploughing deep into your heart;
    you never   210
Saw day go down upon your native spires
So calmly with its gold and crimson glory,
And after dreaming a disturbed vision
Of them and theirs, awoke and found them
    not.
Mar.   I will divide this with you. Let
    us think   215
Of our departure from this much-loved
    city
(Since you must *love* it, as it seems), and
    this
Chamber of state, her gratitude allots you.
Our children will be cared for by the Doge,
And by my uncles: we must sail ere night.
Jac. Fos.   That's sudden. Shall I not
    behold my father?   221
Mar. You will.
Jac. Fos.   Where?
Mar. Here, or in the ducal chamber—
He said not which. I would that you could
    bear
Your exile as he bears it.
Jac. Fos.   Blame him not.   224
I sometimes murmur for a moment; but
He could not now act otherwise. A show
Of feeling or compassion on his part
Would have but drawn upon his aged head
Suspicion from 'the Ten,' and upon mine
Accumulated ills.
Mar.   Accumulated!
What pangs are those they have spared
    you?
Jac. Fos.   That of leaving
Venice without beholding him or you,
Which might have been forbidden now,
    as 'twas
Upon my former exile.
Mar.   That is true,   234
And thus far I am also the state's debtor,
And shall be more so when I see us both
Floating on the free waves—away—
    away—

Be it to the earth's end, from this abhorr'd,
Unjust, and—
Jac. Fos.   Curse it not. If I am silent,
Who dares accuse my country?
Mar.   Men and angels!
The blood of myriads reeking up to
    heaven,   241
The groans of slaves in chains, and men in
    dungeons,
Mothers, and wives, and sons, and sires,
    and subjects,
Held in the bondage of ten bald-heads;
    and
Though last, not least, *thy silence! Couldst
    thou* say   245
Aught in its favour, who would praise like
    thee?
Jac. Fos. Let us address us then, since
    so it must be,
To our departure. Who comes here?

Enter LOREDANO, *attended by Familiars.*
Lor. [to the Familiars].   Retire,
But leave the torch.
            [*Exeunt the two Familiars.*
Jac. Fos. Most welcome, noble signor.
I did not deem this poor place could
    have drawn   250
Such presence hither.
Lor.   'Tis not the first time
I have visited these places.
Mar.   Nor would be
The last, were all men's merits well re-
    warded,   253
Came you here to insult us, or remain
As spy upon us, or as hostage for us?
Lor. Neither are of my office, noble
    lady!
I am sent hither to your husband, to
Announce 'the Ten's' decree.
Mar.   That tenderness
Has been anticipated: it is known.
Lor. As how?
Mar. I have inform'd him, not so
    gently,   260
Doubtless, as your nice feelings would
    prescribe,
The indulgence of your colleagues; but he
    knew it.
If you come for our thanks, take them, and
    hence!
The dungeon gloom is deep enough with-
    out you,
And full of reptiles, not less loathsome,
    though   265
Their sting is honester.
Lor.   I pray you, calm you:
Jac. Fos. What can avail such words?
Mar.   To let him know
That he is known.
Lor.   Let the fair dame preserve
Her sex's privilege.
Mar.   I have some sons, sir,   269
Will one day thank you better.

Lor. You do well
To nurse them wisely. Foscari—you know
Your sentence, then?
Jac. Fos. Return to Candia?
Lor. True—
For life.
Jac. Fos. Not long.
Lor. I said—for *life*.
Jac. Fos. And I
Repeat—not long.
Lor. A year's imprisonment 274
In Canea—afterwards the freedom of
The whole isle.
Jac Fos. Both the same to me: the after
Freedom as is the first imprisonment.
Is't true my wife accompanies me?
Lor. Yes,
If she so wills it.
Mar. Who obtain'd that justice?
Lor. One who wars not with women.
Mar. But oppresses
Men: howsoever let him have *my* thanks
For the only boon I would have ask'd or taken
From him or such as he is.
Lor. He receives them
As they are offer'd.
Mar. May they thrive with him
So much!—no more.
Jac. Fos. Is this, sir, your whole mission? 285
Because we have brief time for preparation,
And you perceive your presence doth disquiet
This lady, of a house noble as yours.
Mar. Nobler!
Lor. How nobler?
Mar. As more generous!
We say the 'generous steed' to express the purity 290
Of his high blood. Thus much I've learnt, although
Venetian (who see few steeds save of bronze),
From those Venetians who have skimm'd the coasts
Of Egypt and her neighbour Araby:
And why not say as soon the '*generous man*'? 295
If race be aught, it is in qualities
More than in years; and mine, which is as old
As yours, is better in its product, nay—
Look not so stern—but get you back, and pore 299
Upon your genealogic tree's most green
Of leaves and most mature of fruits, and there
Blush to find ancestors, who would have blush'd
For such a son—thou cold inveterate hater!

Jac. Fos. Again, Marina!
Mar. Again! still, Marina.
See you not, he comes here to glut his hate
With a last look upon our misery?
Let him partake it!
Jac. Fos. That were difficult.
Mar. Nothing more easy. He partakes it now—
Ay, he may veil beneath a marble brow
And sneering lip the pang, but he partakes it. 310
A few brief words of truth shame the devil's servants
No less than master; I have probed his soul
A moment, as the eternal fire, ere long,
Will reach it always. See how he shrinks from me!
With death, and chains, and exile in his hand, 315
To scatter o'er his kind as he thinks fit;
They are his weapons, not his armour, for
I have pierced him to the core of his cold heart. 318
I care not for his frowns! We can but die,
And he but live, for him the very worst
Of destinies: each day secures him more
His tempter's.
Jac. Fos. This is mere insanity.
Mar. It may be so; and *who* hath made us *mad*?
Lor. Let her go on; it irks not me.
Mar. That's false! 324
You came here to enjoy a heartless triumph
Of cold looks upon manifold griefs! You came
To be sued to in vain—to mark our tears,
And hoard our groans—to gaze upon the wreck
Which you have made a prince's son—my husband;
In short, to trample on the fallen—an office 330
The hangman shrinks from, as all men from him!
How have you sped? We are wretched, signor, as
Your plots could make, and vengeance could desire us,
And how *feel you*?
Lor. As rocks.
Mar. By thunder blasted:
They feel not, but no less are shiver'd. Come, 335
Foscari: now let us go, and leave this felon,
The sole fit habitant of such a cell,
Which he has peopled often, but ne'er fitly
Till he himself shall brood in it alone.

Enter the DOGE.

Jac. Fos. My father!
Doge [*embracing him*]. Jacopo! my son—my son! 340
Jac. Fos. My father still! How long it is since I

508

Have heard thee name my name—*our*
name!
Doge.   My boy!
Couldst thou but know——
Jac. Fos. I rarely, sir, have murmur'd.
Doge. I feel too much thou hast not.
Mar.   Doge, look there! 344
          [*She points to* LOREDANO.
Doge. I see the man—what mean'st
thou?
Mar.   Caution!
Lor.   Being
The virtue which this noble lady most
May practise, she doth well to recommend
it.
Mar. Wretch! 'tis no virtue, but the
policy
Of those who fain must deal perforce with
vice:
As such I recommend it, as I would 350
To one whose foot was on an adder's path.
Doge. Daughter, it is superfluous; I
have long
Known Loredano.
Lor.   You may know him better.
Mar. Yes: *worse* he could not.
Jac. Fos.   Father, let not these 354
Our parting hours be lost in listening to
Reproaches, which boot nothing. Is it—
is it,
Indeed, our last of meetings?
Doge.   You behold
These white hairs!
Jac. Fos.   And I feel, besides, that
mine
Will never be so white. Embrace me,
father!   359
I loved you ever—never more than now.
Look to my children—to your last child's
children:
Let them be all to you which he was once,
And never be to you what I am now.
May I not see *them* also?
Mar.   No—not here.
Jac. Fos. They might behold their
parent anywhere.   365
Mar. I would that they beheld their
father in
A place which would not mingle fear with
love,
To freeze their young blood in its natural
current.
They have fed well, slept soft, and knew
not that
Their sire was a mere hunted outlaw.
Well,   370
I know his fate may one day be their
heritage;
But let it only be their *heritage*,
And not their present fee. Their senses,
though
Alive to love, are yet awake to terror;
And these vile damps, too, and yon *thick
green* wave   375

Which floats above the place where we
now stand—
A cell so far below the water's level,
Sending its pestilence through every
crevice,
Might strike them: *this is not their* atmo-
sphere,   379
However you—and you—and most of all,
As worthiest—*you*, sir, noble Loredano!
May breathe it without prejudice.
Jac. Fos.   I have not
Reflected upon this, but acquiesce.
I shall depart, then, without meeting
them?
Doge. Not so: they shall await you in
my chamber.   385
Jac. Fos. And must I leave them—*all*?
Lor.   You must.
Jac. Fos.   Not one?
Lor. They are the state's.
Mar. I thought they had been mine.
Lor. They are, in all maternal things.
Mar.   That is
In all things painful. If they're sick, they
will   389
Be left to me to tend them; should they die,
To me to bury and to mourn; but if
They live, they'll make you soldiers,
senators,
Slaves, exiles—what *you* will; or if they are
Females with portions, brides and *bribes*
for nobles!
Behold the state's care for its sons and
mothers!   395
Lor. The hour approaches, and the
wind is fair.
Jac. Fos. How know you that here,
where the genial wind
Ne'er blows in all its blustering freedom?
Lor.   'Twas so
When I came here. The galley floats
within   399
A bow-shot of the 'Riva di Schiavoni.'
Jac. Fos. Father! I pray you to precede
me, and
Prepare my children to behold their father.
Doge. Be firm, my son!
Jac. Fos.   I will do my endeavour.
Mar. Farewell! at least to this detested
dungeon,   404
And him to whose good offices you owe
In part your past imprisonment.
Lor.   And present
Liberation.
Doge. He speaks truth.
Jac. Fos.   No doubt! but 'tis
Exchange of chains for heavier chains I
owe him.
He knows this, or he had not sought to
change them.   409
But I reproach not.
Lor.   The time narrows, signor.
Jac. Fos. Alas! I little thought so
lingeringly

To leave abodes like this: but when I feel
That every step I take, even from this cell,
Is one away from Venice, I look back   414
Even on these dull damp walls, and——
Doge.   Boy! no tears.
Mar. Let them flow on: he wept not on
    the rack
To shame him, and they cannot shame
    him now.
They will relieve his heart—that too kind
    heart—
And I will find an hour to wipe away
Those tears, or add my own. I could weep
    now,   420
But would not gratify yon wretch so far.
Let us proceed. Doge, lead the way.
Lor. (to the Familiar). The torch, there!
Mar. Yes, light us on, as to a funeral
    pyre,
With Loredano mourning like an heir.
Doge. My son, you are feeble; take
    this hand.
Jac. Fos. Alas!   425
Must youth support itself on age, and I
Who ought to be the prop of yours?
Lor.   Take mine.
Mar. Touch it not, Foscari; 'twill
    sting you. Signor,
Stand off! be sure, that if a grasp of yours
Would raise us from the gulf wherein we
    are plunged,
No hand of ours would stretch itself to
    meet it.   431
Come, Foscari, take the hand the altar
    gave you;
It could not save, but will support you
    ever.   [*Exeunt.*

ACT IV

SCENE I.—*A Hall in the Ducal Palace.*

Enter LOREDANO *and* BARBARIGO.

Bar. And have you confidence in such
    a project?
Lor. I have.
Bar.   'Tis hard upon his years.
Lor.   Say rather
Kind to relieve him from the cares of state.
Bar. 'Twill break his heart.
Lor.   Age has no heart to break.
He has seen his son's half broken, and,
    except   5
A start of feeling in his dungeon, never
Swerved.
Bar. In his countenance, I grant you,
    never;
But I have seen him sometimes in a calm
So desolate, that the most clamorous grief
Had nought to envy him within. Where is
    he?   10
Lor. In his own portion of the palace,
    with
His son, and the whole race of Foscaris.

Bar. Bidding farewell.
Lor.   A last. As soon he shall
Bid to his dukedom.
Bar.   When embarks the son?
Lor. Forthwith—when this long leave
    is taken. 'Tis   15
Time to admonish them again.
Bar.   Forbear;
Retrench not from their moments.
Lor.   Not I, now
We have higher business for our own.
    This day
Shall be the last of the old Doge's reign,
As the first of his son's last banishment,
And that is vengeance.
Bar.   In my mind, too deep.   21
Lor. 'Tis moderate—not even life for
    life, the rule
Denounced of retribution from all time;
They owe me still my father's and my
    uncle's.
Bar. Did not the Doge deny this
    strongly?
Lor.   Doubtless.   25
Bar. And did not this shake your
    suspicion?
Lor.   No.
Bar. But if this deposition should take
    place
By our united influence in the Council,
It must be done with all the deference
Due to his years, his station, and his deeds.
Lor. As much of ceremony as you will,
So that the thing be done. You may, for
    aught
I care, depute the Council on their knees
(Like Barbarossa to the Pope), to beg him
To have the courtesy to abdicate.   35
Bar. What if he will not?
Lor.   We'll elect another,
And make him null.
Bar.   But will the laws uphold us?
Lor. What laws?—'The Ten' are
    laws; and if they were not,
I will be legislator in this business.
Bar. At your own peril?
Lor.   There is none, I tell you,   40
Our powers are such.
Bar.   But he has twice already
Solicited permission to retire,
And twice it was refused.
Lor.   The better reason
To grant it the third time.
Bar.   Unask'd?
Lor.   It shows
The impression of his former instances:
If they were from his heart, he may be
    thankful: 46
If not, 'twill punish his hypocrisy.
Come, they are met by this time; let us
    join them,
And be *thou* fix'd in purpose for this once.
I have prepared such arguments as will
    not   50

Fail to move him, and to remove him:
since
Their thoughts, their objects, have been
sounded, do not
You, with your wonted scruples, teach us
pause,
And all will prosper.
   Bar.   Could I but be certain 54
This is no prelude to such persecution
Of the sire as has fallen upon the son,
I would support you.
   Lor.   He is safe, I tell you;
His fourscore years and five may linger on
As long as he can drag them: 'tis his throne
Alone is aim'd at.
   Bar.   But discarded princes 60
Are seldom long of life.
   Lor.   And men of eighty
More seldom still.
   Bar. And why not wait these few years?
   Lor. Because we have waited long
enough, and he
Lived longer than enough. Hence! in to
council!
   [*Exeunt* LOREDANO *and* BARBARIGO.

Enter MEMMO *and a Senator.*

   Sen. A summons to 'the Ten'! why
so?
   Mem.   'The Ten' 65
Alone can answer; they are rarely wont
To let their thoughts anticipate their
purpose
By previous proclamation. We are sum-
mon'd—
That is enough.
   Sen.   For them, but not for us;
I would know why.
   Mem. You will know why anon,
If you obey: and, if not, you no less 71
Will know why you should have obey'd.
   Sen.   I mean not
To oppose them, *but*——
   Mem. In Venice '*but*''s a traitor.
But me no '*buts*,' unless you would pass
o'er
The Bridge which few repass.
   Sen.   I am silent.
   Mem.   Why 75
Thus hesitate? 'The Ten' have call'd in aid
Of their deliberation five and twenty
Patricians of the senate—you are one,
And I another; and it seems to me
Both honour'd by the choice or chance
which leads us 80
To mingle with a body so august.
   Sen. Most true. I say no more.
   Mem.   As we hope, signor,
And all may honestly, (that is, all those
Of noble blood may,) one day hope to be
Decemvir, it is surely for the senate's 85
Chosen delegates a school of wisdom, to
Be thus admitted, though as novices,
To view the mysteries.

   Sen.   Let us view them: they,
No doubt, are worth it.
   Mem.   Being worth our lives
If we divulge them, doubtless they are
worth 90
Something, at least to you or me.
   Sen.   I sought not
A place within the sanctuary; but being
Chosen, however reluctantly so chosen,
I shall fulfil my office.
   Mem.   Let us not
Be latest in obeying 'the Ten's' summons.
   Sen. All are not met, but I am of your
thought 96
So far—let's in.
   Mem. The earliest are most welcome
In earnest councils—we will not be least
so.   [*Exeunt.*

Enter the DOGE, JACOPO FOSCARI, *and*
MARINA.

   Jac. Fos. Ah, father! though I must
and will depart, 99
Yet—yet—I pray you to obtain for me
That I once more return unto my home,
Howe'er remote the period. Let there be
A point of time, as beacon to my heart,
With any penalty annex'd they please,
But let me still return.
   Doge.   Son Jacopo, 105
Go and obey our country's will: 'tis not
For us to look beyond.
   Jac. Fos.   But still I must
Look back. I pray you think of me.
   Doge.   Alas!
You ever were my dearest offspring, when
They were more numerous, nor can be less
so 110
Now you are last; but did the state demand
The exile of the disinterred ashes
Of your three goodly brothers, now in
earth,
And their desponding shades came flitting
round
To impede the act, I must no less obey
A duty, paramount to every duty. 116
   Mar. My husband! let us on: this but
prolongs
Our sorrow.
   Jac. Fos. But we are not summon'd yet;
The galley's sails are not unfurl'd:—who
knows?
The wind may change.
   Mar.   And if it do, it will not 120
Change *their* hearts, or your lot: the
galley's oars
Will quickly clear the harbour.
   Jac. Fos.   O ye elements!
Where are your storms?
   Mar.   In human breasts. Alas!
Will nothing calm you?
   Jac. Fos.   Never yet did mariner
Put up to patron saint such prayers for
prosperous 125

And pleasant breezes, as I call upon you,
Ye tutelar saints of my own city! which
Ye love not with more holy love than I,
To lash up from the deep the Adrian
   waves,
And waken Auster, sovereign of the 130
   tempest!
Till the sea dash me back on my own shore
A broken corse upon the barren Lido,
Where I may mingle with the sands which
   skirt
The land I love, and never shall see more!
  Mar. And wish you this with *me*
   beside you?
  Jac. Fos. No— 135
No—not for thee, too good, too kind!
  May'st thou
Live long to be a mother to those children
Thy fond fidelity for a time deprives
Of such support! But for myself alone,
May all the winds of heaven howl down 140
   the Gulf,
And tear the vessel, till the mariners,
Appall'd, turn their despairing eyes on me,
As the Phenicians did on Jonah, then
Cast me out from amongst them, as an
   offering
To appease the waves. The billow which
   destroys me 145
Will be more merciful than man, and bear
   me
Dead, but *still bear* me to a native grave,
From fishers' hands, upon the desolate
   strand,
Which, of its thousand wrecks, hath ne'er
   received
One lacerated like the heart which then
Will be.—But wherefore breaks it not? 151
  why live I?
  Mar. To man thyself, I trust, with
  time, to master
Such useless passion. Until now thou wert
A sufferer, but not a loud one: why,
What is this to the things thou hast borne
  in silence— 155
Imprisonment and actual torture?
  Jac. Fos. Double,
Triple, and tenfold torture! But you are
  right,
It must be borne. Father, your blessing.
  Doge. Would
It could avail thee! but no less thou hast it.
  Jac. Fos. Forgive—
  Doge. What?
  Jac. Fos. My poor mother, for my
  birth, 160
And me for having lived, and you yourself
(As I forgive you), for the gift of life,
Which you bestow'd upon me as my sire.
  Mar. What hast thou done?
  Jac. Fos. Nothing. I cannot charge
My memory with much save sorrow: but
I have been so beyond the common lot
Chasten'd and visited, I needs must think

That I was wicked. If it be so, may
What I have undergone here keep me from
A like hereafter!
  Mar. Fear not: *that*'s reserved 170
For your oppressors.
  Jac. Fos. Let me hope not.
  Mar. Hope not?
  Jac. Fos. I cannot wish them *all* they
  have inflicted.
  Mar. *All!* the consummate fiends! A
  thousand-fold
May the worm which ne'er dieth feed upon
  them! 174
  Jac. Fos. They may repent.
  Mar. And if they do, Heaven will not
Accept the tardy penitence of demons.

Enter an Officer and Guards.

  Offi. Signor! the boat is at the shore—
  the wind
Is rising—we are ready to attend you.
  Jac. Fos. And I to be attended. Once
  more, father,
Your hand!
  Doge. Take it. Alas! how thine own
  trembles! 180
  Jac. Fos. No—you mistake; 'tis yours
  that shakes, my father.
Farewell!
  Doge. Farewell! Is there aught else?
  Jac. Fos. No—nothing.
             [To the Officer.
Lend me your arm, good signor.
  Offi. You turn pale—
Let me support you—paler—ho! some
  aid there!
Some water!
  Mar. Ah, he is dying!
  Jac. Fos. Now, I'm ready— 185
My eyes swim strangely—where's the
  door?
  Mar. Away!
Let me support him—my best love! Oh,
  God!
How faintly beats this heart—this pulse!
  Jac. Fos. The light!
Is it the light?—I am faint.
         [Officer presents him with water.
  Offi. He will be better, 189
Perhaps, in the air.
  Jac. Fos. I doubt not. Father—wife—
Your hands!
  Mar. There's death in that damp,
  clammy grasp.
Oh God!—My Foscari, how fare you?
  Jac. Fos. Well! *[He dies.*
  Offi. He's gone!
  Doge. He's free.
  Mar. No—no, he is not dead;
There must be life yet in that heart—he
  could not
Thus leave me.
  Doge. Daughter!
  Mar. Hold thy peace, old man! 195

I am no daughter now—thou hast no son.
Oh, Foscari!

   Offi.   We must remove the body.

   Mar. Touch it not, dungeon miscreants! your base office
Ends with his life, and goes not beyond
murder,
Even by your murderous laws. Leave his
remains   200
To those who know to honour them.

   Offi.   I must
Inform the signory, and learn their
pleasure.

   Doge. Inform the signory from *me*,
the Doge,
They have no further power upon those
ashes:
While he lived, he was theirs, as fits a
subject—   205
Now he is *mine*—my broken-hearted boy!
                       [*Exit Officer.*

   Mar. And I must live!

   Doge.   Your children live, Marina.

   Mar. My children! true—they live,
and I must live
To bring them up to serve the state, and
die
As died their father. Oh! what best of
blessings   210
Were barrenness in Venice! Would my
mother
Had been so!

   Doge.   My unhappy children!

   Mar.   What!
You feel it then at last—*you!*—Where is
now
The stoic of the state?

   Doge [*throwing himself down by the
body*]. Here!

   Mar.   Ay, weep on!
I thought you had no tears—you hoarded
them   215
Until they are useless; but weep on! he
never
Shall weep more—never, never more.

      Enter LOREDANO *and* BARBARIGO.

   Lor.   What's here?

   Mar. Ah! the devil come to insult the
dead! Avaunt!
Incarnate Lucifer! 'tis holy ground.
A martyr's ashes now lie there, which
make it   220
A shrine. Get thee back to thy place of
torment!

   Bar. Lady, we knew not of this sad
event,
But pass'd here merely on our path from
council.

   Mar. Pass on.

   Lor.   We sought the Doge.

   Mar. [*pointing to the Doge, who is still on
the ground by his son's body*].
             He's busy, look,

About the business *you* provided for him,
Are ye content?

   Bar.   We will not interrupt
A parent's sorrows.

   Mar.   No, ye only make them,
Then leave them.

   Doge [*rising*]. Sirs, I am ready.

   Bar.   No—not now.

   Lor. Yet 'twas important.

   Doge.   If 'twas so, I can
Only repeat—I am ready.

   Bar.   It shall not be 230
Just now, though Venice totter'd o'er the
deep
Like a frail vessel. I respect your griefs.

   Doge. I thank you. If the tidings
which you bring
Are evil, you may say them; nothing
further
Can touch me more than him thou look'st
on there;   235
If they be good, say on; you need not *fear*
That they can *comfort* me.

   Bar.   I would they could!

   Doge. I spoke not to *you*, but to
Loredano.
He understands me.

   Mar.   Ah! I thought it would be so.

   Doge. What mean you?

   Mar.   Lo! there is the blood
beginning   240
To flow through the dead lips of Foscari—
The body bleeds in presence of the
assassin.   [*To* LOREDANO.
Thou cowardly murderer by law, behold
How death itself bears witness to thy
deeds!

   Doge. My child! this is a phantasy of
grief.   245
Bear hence the body. [*To his attendants.*]
          Signors, if it please you,
Within an hour I'll hear you.
           [*Exeunt* DOGE, MARINA, *and attendants
           with the body. Manent* LOREDANO
           and* BARBARIGO.

   Bar.   He must not
Be troubled now.

   Lor.   He said himself that nought
Could give him trouble further.

   Bar.   These are words;
But grief is lonely, and the breaking in
Upon it barbarous.

   Lor.   Sorrow preys upon 251
Its solitude, and nothing more diverts it
From its sad visions of the other world,
Than calling it at moments back to this.
The busy have no time for tears.

   Bar.   And therefore 255
You would deprive this old man of all
business?

   Lor. The thing's decreed. The Giunta
and 'the Ten'
Have made it law—who shall oppose that
law?

Bar. Humanity!
Lor. Because his son is dead? 259
Bar. And yet unburied.
Lor. Had we known this when
The act was passing, it might have
suspended
Its passage, but impedes it not—once past.
Bar. I'll not consent.
Lor. You have consented to
All that's essential—leave the rest to me.
Bar. Why press his abdication now?
Lor. The feelings
Of private passion may not interrupt 266
The public benefit; and what the state
Decides to-day must not give way before
To-morrow for a natural accident.
Bar. You have a son.
Lor. I *have*—and *had* a father. 270
Bar. Still so inexorable?
Lor. Still.
Bar. But let him
Inter his son before we press upon him
This edict.
Lor. Let him call up into life
My sire and uncle—I consent. Men may,
Even aged men, be, or appear to be, 275
Sires of a hundred sons, but cannot kindle
An atom of their ancestors from earth.
The victims are not equal; he has seen
His sons expire by natural deaths, and I
My sires by violent and mysterious
maladies. 280
I used no poison, bribed no subtle master
Of the destructive art of healing, to
Shorten the path to the eternal cure.
His sons—and he had four—are dead,
without
My dabbling in vile drugs.
Bar. And art thou sure 285
He dealt in such?
Lor. Most sure.
Bar. And yet he seems
All openness.
Lor. And so he seem'd not long
Ago to Carmagnuola.
Bar. The attainted
And foreign traitor?
Lor. Even so: when *he*, 289
After the very night in which 'the Ten'
(Join'd with the Doge) decided his destruc-
tion,
Met the great Duke at daybreak with a jest,
Demanding whether he should augur him
'The good day or good night'? his Doge-
ship answer'd,
'That he in truth had pass'd a night of
vigil, 295
In which (he added with a gracious smile),
There often has been question about you.'
'Twas true; the question was the death
resolved
Of Carmagnuola, eight months ere he died;
And the old Doge, who knew him doom'd,
smiled on him 300

With deadly cozenage, eight long months
beforehand—
Eight months of such hypocrisy as is
Learnt but in eighty years. Brave Car-
magnuola
Is dead; so is young Foscari and his
brethren—
I never *smiled* on *them*.
Bar. Was Carmagnuola 305
Your friend?
Lor. He was the safeguard of the city.
In early life its foe, but, in his manhood,
Its saviour first, then victim.
Bar. Ah! that seems
The penalty of saving cities. He 309
Whom we now act against not only saved
Our own, but added others to our sway.
Lor. The Romans (and we ape them)
gave a crown
To him who took a city; and they gave
A crown to him who saved a citizen 314
In battle: the rewards are equal. Now,
If we should measure forth the cities taken
By the Doge Foscari, with citizens
Destroy'd by him, or *through* him, the
account
Were fearfully against him, although
narrow'd 319
To private havoc, such as between him
And my dead father.
Bar. Are you then thus fix'd?
Lor. Why, what should change me?
Bar. That which changes me:
But you, I know, are marble to retain
A feud. But when all is accomplish'd,
when
The old man is deposed, his name
degraded, 325
His sons all dead, his family depress'd,
And you and yours triumphant, shall you
sleep?
Lor. More soundly.
Bar. That's an error, and you'll
find it
Ere you sleep with your fathers.
Lor. They sleep not
In their accelerated graves, nor will 330
Till Foscari fills his. Each night I see them
Stalk frowning round my couch, and,
pointing towards
The ducal palace, marshal me to
vengeance.
Bar. Fancy's distemperature! There
is no passion
More spectral or fantastical than Hate;
Not even its opposite, Love, so peoples air
With phantoms, as this madness of the
heart. 337

Enter an Officer.

Lor. Where go you, sirrah?
Offi. By the ducal order
To forward the preparatory rites
For the late Foscari's interment.

Bar.   Their 340
Vault has been often open'd of late years.
Lor. 'Twill be full soon, and may be
    closed for ever.
Offi.   May I pass on?
Lor.   You may.
Bar.   How bears the Doge
This last calamity?
Offi.   With desperate firmness.
In presence of another he says little,   345
But I perceive his lips move now and then;
And once or twice I heard him, from the
    adjoining
Apartment, mutter forth the words—'My
    son!'
Scarce audibly.   I must proceed.
                            [*Exit Officer.*
Bar.   This stroke
Will move all Venice in his favour.
Lor.   Right!   350
We must be speedy: let us call together
The delegates appointed to convey
The Council's resolution.
Bar.   I protest
Against it at this moment.
Lor.   As you please—
I'll take their voices on it ne'ertheless,
And see whose most may sway them,
    yours or mine.   356
    [*Exeunt* BARBARIGO *and* LOREDANO.

ACT V

SCENE I.—*The* DOGE'S *Apartment.*

The DOGE *and Attendants.*

Att. My lord, the deputation is in
    waiting;
But add, that if another hour would better
Accord with your will, they will make it
    theirs.
Doge. To me all hours are like. Let
    them approach.   [*Exit Attendant.*
An Officer. Prince! I have done your
    bidding.
Doge.   What command?   5
Offi. A melancholy one—to call the
    attendance
Of——
Doge. True—true—true; I crave your
    pardon. I
Begin to fail in apprehension, and
Wax very old—old almost as my years.
Till now I fought them off, but they begin
To overtake me.

*Enter the Deputation, consisting of six of
    the Signory and the Chief of the Ten.*

    Noble men, your pleasure!   11
Chief of the Ten. In the first place, the
    Council doth condole
With the Doge on his late and private grief.
Doge. No more—no more of that.
Chief of the Ten. Will not the Duke
Accept the homage of respect?

Doge.   I do   15
Accept it as 'tis given—proceed.
Chief of the Ten.   'The Ten',
With a selected Giunta from the senate
Of twenty-five of the best born patricians,
Having deliberated on the state
Of the republic, and the o'erwhelming
    cares   20
Which, at this moment, doubly must
    oppress
Your years, so long devoted to your
    country,
Have judged it fitting, with all reverence,
Now to solicit from your wisdom (which
Upon reflection must accord in this),   25
The resignation of the ducal ring,
Which you have worn so long and
    venerably:
And to prove that they are not ungrateful,
    nor
Cold to your years and services, they add
An appanage of twenty hundred golden
Ducats, to make retirement not less
    splendid   31
Than should become a sovereign's retreat.
Doge. Did I hear rightly?
Chief of the Ten.   Need I say again?
Doge. No—Have you done?
Chief of the Ten. I have spoken.
    Twenty-four
Hours are accorded you to give an answer.
Doge. I shall not need so many
    seconds.
Chief of the Ten.   We
Will now retire.
Doge.   Stay! four and twenty hours
Will alter nothing which I have to say.
Chief of the Ten. Speak!
Doge.   When I twice before reiterated
My wish to abdicate, it was refused me:
And not alone refused, but ye exacted
An oath from me that I would never more
Renew this instance. I have sworn to die
In full exertion of the functions which
My country call'd me here to exercise,   45
According to my honour and my
    conscience—
I cannot break *my* oath.
Chief of the Ten.   Reduce us not
To the alternative of a decree,
Instead of your compliance.
Doge.   Providence
Prolongs my days to prove and chasten
    me;   50
But ye have no right to reproach my
    length
Of days, since every hour has been the
    country's.
I am ready to lay down my life for her,
As I have laid down dearer things than
    life:
But for my dignity—I hold it of   55
The *whole* republic: when the *general* will
Is manifest, then you shall all be answer'd.

Chief of the Ten. We grieve for such an answer; but it cannot
Avail you aught.
Doge. I can submit to all things,
But nothing will advance; no, not a moment. 60
What you decree—decree.
Chief of the Ten. With this, then, must we
Return to those who sent us?
Doge. You have heard me.
Chief of the Ten. With all due reverence we retire.

[*Exeunt the Deputation, &c.*

Enter an Attendant.

Att. My lord,
The noble dame Marina craves an audience. 64
Doge. My time is hers.

Enter MARINA.

Mar. My lord, if I intrude—
Perhaps you fain would be alone?
Doge. Alone!
Alone, come all the world around me, I
Am now and evermore. But we will bear it.
Mar. We will, and for the sake of those who are,
Endeavour——Oh, my husband!
Doge. Give it way: 70
I cannot comfort thee.
Mar. He might have lived,
So form'd for gentle privacy of life,
So loving, so beloved; the native of
Another land, and who so blest and blessing
As my poor Foscari? Nothing was wanting 75
Unto his happiness and mine save not
To be Venetian.
Doge. Or a prince's son.
Mar. Yes; all things which conduce to other men's
Imperfect happiness or high ambition,
By some strange destiny, to him proved deadly. 80
The country and the people whom he loved,
The prince of whom he was the elder born,
And——
Doge. Soon may be a prince no longer.
Mar. How?
Doge. They have taken my son from me, and now aim
At my too long worn diadem and ring.
Let them resume the gewgaws!
Mar. Oh, the tyrants! 86
In such an hour too!
Doge. 'Tis the fittest time;
An hour ago I should have felt it.
Mar. And
Will you not now resent it?—Oh, for vengeance!

But he, who, had he been enough protected, 90
Might have repaid protection in this moment,
Cannot assist his father.
Doge. Nor should do so
Against his country, had he a thousand lives
Instead of that——
Mar. They tortured from him. This
May be pure patriotism. I am a woman:
To me my husband and my children were
Country and home. I loved *him*—how I loved him! 97
I have seen him pass through such an ordeal as
The old martyrs would have shrunk from:
he is gone,
And I, who would have given my blood for him, 100
Have nought to give but tears! But could I compass
The retribution of his wrongs!—Well, well!
I have sons, who shall be men.
Doge. Your grief distracts you.
Mar. I thought I could have borne it, when I saw him
Bow'd down by such oppression; yes, I thought 105
That I would rather look upon his corse
Than his prolong'd captivity:—I am punish'd
For that thought now. Would I were in his grave!
Doge. I must look on him once more.
Mar. Come with me!
Doge. Is he——
Mar. Our bridal bed is now his bier. 110
Doge. And he is in his shroud!
Mar. Come, come, old man!

[*Exeunt the* DOGE *and* MARINA.

Enter BARBARIGO *and* LOREDANO.

Bar. [*to an Attendant*]. Where is the Doge?
Att. This instant retired hence,
With the illustrious lady his son's widow.
Lor. Where?
Att. To the chamber where the body lies.
Bar. Let us return, then.
Lor. You forget, you cannot. 115
We have the implicit order of the Giunta
To await their coming here, and join them in
Their office: they'll be here soon after us.
Bar. And will they press their answer on the Doge?
Lor. 'Twas his own wish that all should be done promptly. 120
He answer'd quickly, and must so be answer'd;

His dignity is look'd to, his estate
Cared for—what would he more?
   Bar.   Die in his robes:
He could not have lived long; but I have
  done   124
My best to save his honours, and opposed
This proposition to the last, though vainly.
Why would the general vote compel me
  hither?
  Lor. 'Twas fit that some one of such
  different thoughts
From ours should be a witness, lest false
  tongues
Should whisper that a harsh majority 130
Dreaded to have its acts beheld by others.
  Bar. And not less, I must needs think,
  for the sake
Of humbling me for my vain opposition.
You are ingenious, Loredano, in
Your modes of vengeance, nay, poetical,
A very Ovid in the art of *hating*; 136
'Tis thus (although a secondary object,
Yet hate has microscopic eyes), to you
I owe by way of foil to the more zealous,
This undesired association in 140
Your Giunta's duties.
  Lor.   How!—*my* Giunta!
  Bar.   *Yours!*
They speak your language, watch your
  nod, approve
Your plans, and do your work. Are they
  not *yours*?
  Lor. You talk unwarily. 'Twere best
  they hear not
This from you.
  Bar. Oh! they'll hear as much one day
From louder tongues than mine; they have
  gone beyond 146
Even their exorbitance of power: and when
This happens in the most contemn'd and
  abject
States, stung humanity will rise to check it.
  Lor. You talk but idly.
  Bar.   That remains for proof. 150
Here come our colleagues.

Enter the Deputation *as before.*

  Chief of the Ten. Is the Duke aware
We seek his presence?
  Att.   He shall be inform'd.
               [*Exit Attendant.*
  Bar. The Duke is with his son.
  Chief of the Ten.   If it be so,
We will remit him till the rites are over.
Let us return. 'Tis time enough to-
  morrow. 155
  Lor. [*aside to Bar.*] Now the rich
  man's hell-fire upon your tongue,
Unquench'd, unquenchable! I'll have it
  torn
From its vile babbling roots, till you shall
  utter
Nothing but sobs through blood, for this!
  Sage signors,

I pray ye be not hasty.
                 [*Aloud to the others.*
  Bar.   But he human! 160
  Lor. See, the Duke comes!

Enter the DOGE.

  Doge. I have obey'd your summons.
  Chief of the Ten. We come once more
  to urge our past request.
  Doge. And I to answer.
  Chief of the Ten. What?
  Doge.   My only answer.
You have heard it.
  Chief of the Ten. Hear *you* then the
  last decree,
Definitive and absolute!
  Doge.   To the point— 165
To the point! I know of old the forms of
  office,
And gentle preludes to strong acts.—Go on!
  Chief of the Ten. You are no longer
Doge; you are released
From your imperial oath as sovereign;
Your ducal robes must be put off; but for
Your services, the state allots the ap-
  panage 171
Already mention'd in our former congress.
Three days are left you to remove from
  hence,
Under the penalty to see confiscated
All your own private fortune.
  Doge.   That last clause, 175
I am proud to say, would not enrich the
  treasury.
  Chief of the Ten. Your answer, Duke!
  Lor. Your answer, Francis Foscari!
  Doge. If I could have foreseen that my
  old age
Was prejudicial to the state, the chief
Of the republic never would have shown
Himself so far ungrateful, as to place
His own high dignity before his country;
But this *life* having been so many years
Not useless to that country, I would fain
Have consecrated my last moments to her.
But the decree being render'd, I obey. 186
  Chief of the Ten. If you would have the
  three days named extended,
We willingly will lengthen them to eight,
As sign of our esteem.
  Doge.   Not eight hours, signor,
Nor even eight minutes—there's the
  ducal ring 190
          [*Taking off his ring and cap.*
And there the ducal diadem. And so
The Adriatic's free to wed another.
  Chief of the Ten. Yet go not forth so
  quickly.
  Doge.   I am old, sir,
And move to move but slowly must begin
To move betimes. Methinks I see amongst
  you 195
A face I know not.—Senator! your name,
You, by your garb, Chief of the Forty!

Mem. Signor,
I am the son of Marco Memmo.
Doge. Ah!
Your father was my friend.—But *sons* and
fathers!—
What, ho! my servants there!
Atten. My prince!
Doge. No prince— 200
There are the princes of the prince!
[*Pointing to the Ten's Deputation.*]—
Prepare
To part from hence upon the instant.
Chief of the Ten. Why
So rashly? 'twill give scandal.
Doge. Answer that;
[*To the Ten.*
It is your province.—Sirs, bestir your-
selves: [*To the Servants.*
There is one burthen which I beg you bear
With care, although 'tis past all further
harm— 206
But I will look to that myself.
Bar. He means
The body of his son.
Doge. And call Marina,
My daughter!

Enter MARINA.

Doge. Get thee ready, we must mourn
Elsewhere.
Mar. And everywhere.
Doge. True; but in freedom, 210
Without these jealous spies upon the
great.
Signors, you may depart: what would you
more?
We are going: do you fear that we shall bear
The palace with us? Its *old* walls, ten times
As *old* as I am, and I'm very old, 215
Have served you, so have I, and I and they
Could tell a tale; but I invoke them not
To fall upon you! else they would, as erst
The pillars of stone Dagon's temple on
The Israelite and his Philistine foes. 220
Such power I do believe there might exist
In such a curse as mine, provoked by such
As you; but I curse not. Adieu, good
signors!
May the next duke be better than the
present!
Lor. The *present* duke is Paschal
Malipiero. 225
Doge. Not till I pass the threshold of
these doors.
Lor. St. Mark's great bell is soon
about to toll
For his inauguration.
Doge. Earth and heaven!
Ye will reverberate this peal; and I
Live to hear this!—the first Doge who e'er
heard 230
Such sound for his successor: happier he,
My attainted predecessor, stern Faliero—
This insult at the least was spared him.

Lor. What!
Do you regret a traitor?
Doge. No—I merely
Envy the dead.
Chief of the Ten. My lord, if you
indeed 235
Are bent upon this rash abandonment
Of the state's palace, at the least retire
By the private staircase, which conducts
you towards
The landing-place of the canal.
Doge. No. I
Will now descend the stairs by which I
mounted 240
To sovereignty—the Giants' Stairs, on
whose
Broad eminence I was invested duke.
My services have called me up those steps,
The malice of my foes will drive me down
them. 244
There five and thirty years ago was I
Install'd, and traversed these same halls,
from which
I never thought to be divorced except
A corse—a corse, it might be, fighting for
them—
But not push'd hence by fellow-citizens.
But come; my son and I will go together—
He to his grave, and I to pray for him.
Chief of the Ten. What! thus in public?
Doge. I was publicly
Elected, and so will I be deposed.
Marina! art thou willing?
Mar. Here's my arm!
Doge. And here my *staff*: thus
propp'd will I go forth. 255
Chief of the Ten. It must not be—the
people will perceive it.
Doge. The people!—There's no
people, you well know it,
Else you dare not deal thus by them or me.
There is a *populace*, perhaps, whose looks
May shame you; but they dare not groan
nor curse you, 260
Save with their hearts and eyes.
Chief of the Ten. You speak in passion,
Else——
Doge. You have reason. I have
spoken much
More than my wont: it is a foible which
Was not of mine, but more excuses you,
Inasmuch as it shows that I approach
A dotage which may justify this deed
Of yours, although the law does not, nor
will. 267
Farewell, sirs!
Bar. You shall not depart without
An escort fitting past and present rank.
We will accompany, with due respect,
The Doge unto his private palace. Say!
My brethren, will we not?
Different voices. Ay!—Ay!
Doge. You shall not
Stir—in my train, at least. I enter'd here

518

As sovereign—I go out as citizen
By the same impulse, but as citizen.   275
All these vain ceremonies are base insults,
Which only ulcerate the heart the more,
Applying poisons there as antidotes.
Pomp is for princes—I am *none!*—That's
    false,
I *am*, but only to these gates.—Ah!
    Lor.   Hark!   280
    [*The great bell of St. Mark's tolls.*
    Bar. The bell!
    Chief of the Ten. St. Mark's, which
      tolls for the election
Of Malipiero.
    Doge.   Well I recognise
The sound! I heard it once, but once
    before,
And that is five and thirty years ago;
Even *then* I *was not young.*
    Bar.   Sit down, my lord!   285
You tremble.
    Doge. 'Tis the knell of my poor boy!
My heart aches bitterly.
    Bar.   I pray you sit.
    Doge. No; my seat here has been a
    throne till now.
Marina! let us go.
    Mar.   Most readily.   289
    Doge [*walks a few steps, then stops*]. I
    feel athirst—will no one bring me here
A cup of water?
    Bar. I——
    Mar.   And I——
    Lor.   And I——
    [*The Doge takes a goblet from the hand
    of* LOREDANO.
    Doge. I take *yours*, Loredano, from
    the hand
Most fit for such an hour as this.
    Lor.   Why so?
    Doge. 'Tis said that our Venetian
    crystal has   294
Such pure antipathy to poisons as
To burst, if aught of venom touches it.
You bore this goblet, and it is not broken.
    Lor. Well, sir!
    Doge. Then it is false, or you are true.
For my own part, I credit neither; 'tis
An idle legend.
    Mar.   You talk wildly, and   300
Had better now be seated, nor as yet
Depart. Ah! now you look as look'd my
    husband!
    Bar. He sinks!—support him!—quick
    —a chair—support him!
    Doge. The bell tolls on!—let's hence
    —my brain's on fire!
    Bar. I do beseech you, lean upon us!
    Doge.   No!   305
A sovereign should die standing. My poor
    boy!—
Off with your arms!—*That bell!*
    [*The* DOGE *drops down and dies.*
    Mar.   My God! My God!

    Bar. [*to Lor.*]. Behold! your work's
    completed!
    Chief of the Ten. Is there then
No aid? Call in assistance!
    Att.   'Tis all over.
    Chief of the Ten. If it be so, at least his
      obsequies   310
Shall be such as befits his name and nation,
His rank and his devotion to the duties
Of the realm, while his age permitted him
To do himself and them full justice. Breth-
    ren,
Say, shall it not be so?
    Bar.   He has not had   315
The misery to die a subject where
He reign'd: then let his funeral rites be
    princely.
    Chief of the Ten. We are agreed, then?
    All, except Lor., answer.   Yes.
    Chief of the Ten. Heaven's peace be
    with him!
    Mar. Signors, your pardon: this is
    mockery.
Juggle no more with that poor remnant,
    which,   320
A moment since, while yet it had a soul,
(A soul by whom you have increased your
    empire,
And made your power as proud as was his
    glory,)
You banish'd from his palace, and tore
    down
From his high place, with such relentless
    coldness;   325
And now, when he can neither know these
    honours,
Nor would accept them if he could, you,
    signors,
Purpose, with idle and superfluous pomp,
To make a pageant over what you
    trampled.
A princely funeral will be your reproach,
And not his honour.   331
    Chief of the Ten. Lady, we revoke not
Our purposes so readily.
    Mar.   I know it,
As far as touches torturing the living.
I thought the dead had been beyond even
    you,
Though (some, no doubt) consign'd to
    powers which may   335
Resemble that you exercise on earth.
Leave him to me; you would have done so for
His dregs of life, which you have kindly
    shorten'd:
It is my last of duties, and may prove
A dreary comfort in my desolation.   340
Grief is fantastical, and loves the dead,
And the apparel of the grave.
    Chief of the Ten.   Do you
Pretend still to this office?
    Mar.   I do, signor.
Though his possessions have been all con-
    sumed

519

In the state's service, I have still my
   dowry,   345
Which shall be consecrated to his rites,
And those of——
         [*She stops with agitation.*
   Chief of the Ten. Best retain it for
   your children.
   Mar. Ay, they are fatherless, I thank
   you.
   Chief of the Ten.   We
Cannot comply with your request. His
   relics
Shall be exposed with wonted pomp, and
   follow'd   350
Unto their home by the new Doge, not
   clad
As *Doge*, but simply as a senator.
   Mar. I have heard of murderers, who
   have interr'd
Their victims; but ne'er heard, until this
   hour,
Of so much splendour in hypocrisy   355
O'er those they slew. I've heard of
   widows' tears—
Alas! I have shed some—always thanks to
   you!
I've heard of *heirs* in sables—you have
   left none

To the deceased, so you would act the part
Of such. Well, sirs, your will be done! as
   one day,   360
I trust, Heaven's will be done too!
   Chief of the Ten.   Know you, lady,
To whom ye speak, and perils of such
   speech?
   Mar. I know the former better than
   yourselves;
The latter—like yourselves; and can face
   both.
Wish you more funerals?
   Bar.   Heed not her rash words;   365
Her circumstances must excuse her bear-
   ing.
   Chief of the Ten. We will not note
   them down.
   Bar. [*turning to Lor., who is writing upon
   his tablets*].   What art thou writing,
With such an earnest brow, upon thy tab-
   lets?
   Lor. [*pointing to the Doge's body*].
   That *he* has paid me!
   Chief of the Ten.   What debt did he owe
   you?
   Lor. A long and just one; Nature's
   debt and *mine*.   370
                        [*Curtain falls.*

CAIN

A MYSTERY

Now the Serpent was more subtil than any beast of the field which the LORD God had made.—*Gen.* iii. 1.

TO

SIR WALTER SCOTT, BART.,

THIS MYSTERY OF CAIN IS INSCRIBED,

BY HIS OBLIGED FRIEND AND FAITHFUL SERVANT,

THE AUTHOR.

PREFACE

THE following scenes are entitled 'A Mystery', in conformity with the ancient title annexed to dramas upon similar subjects, which were styled 'Mysteries, or Moralities'. The author has by no means taken the same liberties with his subject which were common formerly, as may be seen by any reader curious enough to refer to those very profane productions, whether in English, French, Italian, or Spanish. The author has endeavoured to preserve the language adapted to his characters; and where it is (and this is but rarely) taken from actual *Scripture*, he has made as little alteration, even of words, as the rhythm would permit. The reader will recollect that the book of Genesis does not state that Eve was tempted by a demon, but by 'the Serpent'; and that only because he was 'the most subtil of all the beasts of the field'. Whatever interpretation the Rabbins and the Fathers may have put upon this, I take the words as I find them, and reply, with Bishop Watson upon similar occasions, when the Fathers were quoted to him, as Moderator in the schools of Cambridge, 'Behold the Book!' —holding up the Scripture. It is to be recollected, that my present subject has nothing to do with the *New Testament*, to which no reference can be here made without anachronism. With the poems upon similar topics I have not been recently familiar. Since I was twenty I have never read Milton; but I had read him so frequently before, that this may make little difference. Gesner's 'Death of Abel' I have never read since I was eight years of age, at Aberdeen. The general impression of my recollection is delight; but of the contents I remember only that Cain's wife was called Mahala, and Abel's Thirza; in the following pages I have called them 'Adah' and 'Zillah', the earlier female names which occur in Genesis; they were those of Lamech's wives: those of Cain and Abel are not called by their names. Whether, then, a coincidence of subject may have caused the same in expression, I know nothing, and care as little.

The reader will please to bear in mind (what few choose to recollect), that there is no allusion to a future state in any of the books of Moses, nor indeed in the Old Testament. For a reason for this extraordinary omission he may consult Warburton's 'Divine Legation'; whether satisfactory or not, no better has yet been assigned. I have therefore supposed it new to Cain, without, I hope, any perversion of Holy Writ.

With regard to the language of Lucifer, it was difficult for me to make him talk like a clergyman upon the same subjects; but I have done what I could to restrain him within the bounds of spiritual politeness. If he disclaims having tempted Eve in the shape of the Serpent, it is only because the book of Genesis has not the most distant allusion to anything of the kind, but merely to the Serpent in his serpentine capacity.

Note.—The reader will perceive that the author has partly adopted in this poem the notion of Cuvier, that the world had been destroyed several times before the creation of man. This speculation, derived from the different strata and the bones of enormous and unknown animals found in them, is not contrary to the Mosaic account, but rather confirms it; as no human bones have yet been discovered in those strata, although those of many known animals are found near the remains of the unknown. The assertion of Lucifer, that the pre-Adamite world was also peopled by rational beings much more intelligent than man, and proportionally powerful to the mammoth, &c., &c., is, of course, a poetical fiction to help him to make out his case.

I ought to add, that there is a 'tramelogedia' of Alfieri, called 'Abele'. I have never read that, nor any other of the posthumous works of the writer, except his Life.

RAVENNA, *Sept.* 20, 1821.

DRAMATIS PERSONÆ

MEN	WOMEN	SPIRITS
ADAM	EVE	ANGEL OF THE LORD
CAIN	ADAH	LUCIFER
ABEL	ZILLAH	

ACT I

SCENE I.—*The Land without Paradise.—*
Time, Sunrise.

ADAM, EVE, CAIN, ABEL, ADAH, ZILLAH,
offering a Sacrifice.

Adam. God, the Eternal! Infinite!
    All-wise!—
Who out of darkness on the deep didst
    make
Light on the waters with a word—all hail!
Jehovah, with returning light, all hail!
    Eve. God! who didst name the day,
    and separate   5
Morning from night, till then divided
    never—
Who didst divide the wave from wave, and
    call
Part of thy work the firmament—all hail!
    Abel. God! who didst call the elements
    into
Earth, ocean, air, and fire, and with the
    day   10
And night, and worlds which these
    illuminate,
Or shadow, madest beings to enjoy them,
And love both them and thee—all hail!
    all hail!
    Adah. God, the Eternal! Parent of all
    things!
Who didst create these best and beauteous
    beings   15
To be beloved, more than all, save thee—
Let me love thee and them:—All hail! all
    hail!
    Zillah. Oh, God! who loving, making,
    blessing all,
Yet didst permit the serpent to creep in,
And drive my father forth from Paradise,
Keep us from further evil:—Hail! all hail!
    Adam. Son Cain, my first-born,
    wherefore art thou silent?   22
    Cain. Why should I speak?
    Adam.   To pray.
    Cain.   Have ye not pray'd?
    Adam. We have, most fervently.
    Cain.   And loudly: I
Have heard you.
    Adam.   So will God, I trust.
    Abel.   Amen!   25
    Adam. But thou, my eldest born, art
    silent still.
    Cain. 'Tis better I should be so.
    Adam.   Wherefore so?
    Cain. I have nought to ask.
    Adam.   Nor aught to thank for!
    Cain.   No.
    Adam. Dost thou not live?
    Cain.   Must I not die?
    Eve.   Alas!
The fruit of our forbidden tree begins   30
To fall.
    Adam. And we must gather it again.
Oh, God! why didst thou plant the tree of
    knowledge?
    Cain. And wherefore pluck'd ye not
    the tree of life?
Ye might have then defied him.
    Adam.   Oh! my son,
Blaspheme not: these are serpent's words.
    Cain.   Why not?   35
The snake spoke *truth*; it *was* the tree of
    knowledge;
It *was* the tree of life; knowledge is good,
And life is good; and how can both be evil?

521

Eve. My boy! thou speakest as I
spoke, in sin, 39
Before thy birth: let me not see renew'd
My misery in thine. I have repented.
Let me not see my offspring fall into
The snares beyond the walls of Paradise,
Which e'en in Paradise destroy'd his
parents.
Content thee with what *is.* Had we been
so, 45
Thou now hadst been contented.—Oh,
my son!
Adam. Our orisons completed, let us
hence,
Each to his task of toil—not heavy,
though
Needful: the earth is young, and yields us
kindly
Her fruits with little labour.
Eve. Cain, my son, 50
Behold thy father cheerful and resign'd,
And do as he doth.
[*Exeunt* ADAM *and* EVE.
Zillah. Wilt thou not, my brother?
Abel. Why wilt thou wear this gloom
upon thy brow,
Which can avail thee nothing, save to
rouse
The Eternal anger?
Adah. My beloved Cain, 55
Wilt thou frown even on me?
Cain. No, Adah! no;
I fain would be alone a little while.
Abel, I'm sick at heart; but it will pass;
Precede me, brother—I will follow
shortly. 59
And you, too, sisters, tarry not behind:
Your gentleness must not be harshly met;
I'll follow you anon.
Adah. If not, I will
Return to seek you here.
Abel. The peace of God
Be on your spirit, brother!
[*Exeunt* ABEL, ZILLAH, *and* ADAH.
Cain [*solus*]. And this is
Life!—Toil! and wherefore should I toil?
—because 65
My father could not keep his place in
Eden.
What had *I* done in this?—I was unborn:
I sought not to be born; nor love the state
To which that birth has brought me. Why
did he
Yield to the serpent and the woman? or,
Yielding, why suffer? What was there in
this? 71
The tree was planted, and why not for him?
If not, why place him near it, where it
grew,
The fairest in the centre? They have but
One answer to all questions, "Twas *his*
will, 75
And *he* is good.' How know I that? Be-
cause

He is all-powerful, must all-good, too,
follow?
I judge but by the fruits—and they are
bitter—
Which I must feed on for a fault not mine.
Whom have we here?—A shape like to
the angels, 80
Yet of a sterner and a sadder aspect
Of spiritual essence: why do I quake?
Why should I fear him more than other
spirits,
Whom I see daily wave their fiery swords
Before the gates round which I linger oft,
In twilight's hour, to catch a glimpse of
those 86
Gardens which are my just inheritance,
Ere the night closes o'er the inhibited walls
And the immortal trees which overtop
The cherubim-defended battlements?
If I shrink not from these, the fire-arm'd
angels, 91
Why should I quail from him who now
approaches?
Yet he seems mightier far than them, nor
less
Beauteous, and yet not all as beautiful
As he hath been, and might be: sorrow
seems 95
Half of his immortality. And is it
So? and can aught grieve save humanity?
He cometh.

Enter LUCIFER.

Lucifer. Mortal!
Cain. Spirit, who art thou?
Lucifer. Master of Spirits.
Cain. And being so, canst thou
Leave them, and walk with dust?
Lucifer. I know the thoughts 100
Of dust, and feel for it, and with you.
Cain. How!
You know my thoughts?
Lucifer. They are the thoughts of all
Worthy of thought;—'tis your immortal
part
Which speaks within you.
Cain. What immortal part?
This has not been reveal'd: the tree of life
Was withheld from us by my father's
folly, 106
While that of knowledge, by my mother's
haste,
Was pluck'd too soon; and all the fruit is
death!
Lucifer. They have deceived thee;
thou shalt live.
Cain. I live,
But live to die; and, living, see no thing
To make death hateful, save an innate
clinging, 111
A loathsome, and yet all invincible
Instinct of life, which I abhor, as I
Despise myself, yet cannot overcome—
And so I live. Would I had never lived!

Lucifer. Thou livest, and must live
    for ever: think not   116
The earth, which is thine outward
    cov'ring, is
Existence—it will cease, and thou wilt be
No less than thou art now.
Cain.   No *less!* and why
No more?
Lucifer. It may be thou shalt be as we.
Cain. And ye?
Lucifer.   Are everlasting.
Cain.   Are ye happy? 121
Lucifer. We are mighty.
Cain.   Are ye happy?
Lucifer.   No: art thou?
Cain. How should I be so? Look on
    me!
Lucifer.   Poor clay!
And thou pretendest to be wretched!
    Thou!
Cain. I am:—and thou, with all thy
    might, what art thou?   125
Lucifer. One who aspired to be what
    made thee, and
Would not have made thee what thou art.
Cain.   Ah!
Thou look'st almost a god; and——
Lucifer.   I am none:
And having fail'd to be one, would be
    nought
Save what I am. He conquer'd; let him
    reign!   130
Cain. Who?
Lucifer. Thy sire's Maker, and the
    earth's.
Cain.   And heaven's,
And all that in them is. So I have heard
His seraphs sing; and so my father saith.
Lucifer. They say—what they must
    sing and say, on pain   134
Of being that which I am—and thou art—
Of spirits and of men.
Cain.   And what is that?
Lucifer. Souls who dare use their im-
    mortality—
Souls who dare look the Omnipotent
    tyrant in
His everlasting face, and tell him that
His evil is not good! If he has made,   140
As he saith—which I know not, nor
    believe—
But, if he made us—he cannot unmake:
We are immortal! nay, he'd *have* us so,
That he may torture:—let him! He is
    great—
But, in his greatness, is no happier than
We in our conflict: Goodness would not
    make   146
Evil; and what else hath he made? But
    let him
Sit on his vast and solitary throne,
Creating worlds, to make eternity
Less burthensome to his immense
    existence   150

And unparticipated solitude;
Let him crowd orb on orb: he is alone
Indefinite, indissoluble tyrant;
Could he but crush himself, 'twere the best
    boon
He ever granted: but let him reign on,
And multiply himself in misery!   156
Spirits and Men, at least we sympathise—
And, suffering in concert, make our pangs
Innumerable more endurable,
By the unbounded sympathy of all   160
With all! But *He!* so wretched in his
    height,
So restless in his wretchedness, must still
Create, and re-create——   *
Cain. Thou speak'st to me of things
    which long have swum
In visions through my thought: I never
    could   165
Reconcile what I saw with what I heard.
My father and my mother talk to me
Of serpents, and of fruits and trees: I see
The gates of what they call their Paradise
Guarded by fiery-sworded cherubim,
Which shut them out and me: I feel the
    weight   171
Of daily toil, and constant thought: I look
Around a world where I seem nothing,
    with
Thoughts which arise within me, as if they
Could master all things—but I thought
    alone   175
This misery was *mine*. My father is
Tamed down; my mother has forgot the
    mind
Which made her thirst for knowledge at
    the risk
Of an eternal curse; my brother is   179
A watching shepherd boy, who offers up
The firstlings of the flock to him who bids
The earth yield nothing to us without
    sweat;
My sister Zillah sings an earlier hymn
Than the birds' matins; and my Adah, my
Own and beloved, she, too, understands
    not   185
The mind which overwhelms me: never till
Now met I aught to sympathise with me.
'Tis well—I rather would consort with
    spirits.
Lucifer. And hadst thou not been fit
    by thine own soul
For such companionship, I would not
    now   190
Have stood before thee as I am: a serpent
Had been enough to charm ye, as before.
Cain. Ah! didst *thou* tempt my
    mother?
Lucifer.   I tempt none,
Save with the truth: was not the tree the tree
Of knowledge? and was not the tree of life
Still fruitful? Did *I* bid her pluck them
    not?   196

* [See reviser's Note, p. x.]

Did *I* plant things prohibited within
The reach of beings innocent, and curious
By their own innocence? I would have
   made ye
Gods; and even He who thrust ye forth, so
   thrust ye   200
Because 'ye should not eat the fruits of
   life,
And become gods as we.' Were those his
   words?
   Cain. They were, as I have heard from
   those who heard them,
In thunder.
   Lucifer. Then who was the demon? He
Who would not let ye live, or he who
   would   205
Have made ye live for ever in the joy
And power of knowledge?
   Cain. Would they had snatch'd both
The fruits, or neither!
   Lucifer.   One is yours already,
The other may be still.
   Cain.   How so?
   Lucifer.   By being
Yourselves, in your resistance. Nothing
   can   210
Quench the mind, if the mind will be itself
And centre of surrounding things—'tis
   made
To sway.
   Cain. But didst thou tempt my
   parents?
   Lucifer.   I?
Poor clay! what should I tempt them for,
   or how?
   Cain. They say the serpent was a
   spirit.   215
   Lucifer.   Who
Saith that? It is not written so on high:
The proud One will not so far falsify,
Though man's vast fears and little vanity
Would make him cast upon the spiritual
   nature
His own low failing. The snake *was* the
   snake—   220
No more; and yet not less than those he
   tempted,
In nature being earth also—*more* in
   wisdom,
Since he could overcome them, and fore-
   knew
The knowledge fatal to their narrow joys.
Think'st thou I'd take the shape of things
   that die?   225
   Cain. But the thing had a demon?
   Lucifer.   He but woke one
In those he spake to with his forky tongue.
I tell thee that the serpent was no more
Than a mere serpent: ask the cherubim
Who guard the tempting tree. When thou-
   sand ages   230
Have roll'd o'er your dead ashes, and
   your seed's,
The seed of the then world may thus array

Their earliest fault in fable, and attribute
To me a shape I scorn, as I scorn all
That bows to him, who made things but to
   bend   235
Before his sullen, sole eternity;
But we, who see the truth, must speak it. Thy
Fond parents listen'd to a creeping thing,
And fell. For what should spirits tempt
   them? What
Was there to envy in the narrow bounds
Of Paradise, that spirits who pervade   241
Space——but I speak to thee of what
   thou know'st not,
With all thy tree of knowledge.
   Cain.   But thou canst not
Speak aught of knowledge which I would
   not know,
And do not thirst to know, and bear a
   mind   245
To know.
   Lucifer. And heart to look on?
   Cain.   Be it proved.
   Lucifer. Darest thou look on Death?
   Cain.   He has not yet
Been seen.
   Lucifer. But must be undergone.
   Cain.   My father
Says he is something dreadful, and my
   mother
Weeps when he's named; and Abel lifts
   his eyes   250
To heaven, and Zillah casts hers to the
   earth,
And sighs a prayer; and Adah looks on
   me,
And speaks not.
   Lucifer. And thou?
   Cain.   Thoughts unspeakable
Crowd in my breast to burning, when I
   hear   254
Of this almighty Death, who is, it seems,
Inevitable. Could I wrestle with him?
I wrestled with the lion, when a boy,
In play, till he ran roaring from my gripe.
   Lucifer. It has no shape; but will
   absorb all things
That bear the form of earth-born being.
   Cain.   Ah!   260
I thought it was a being: who could do
Such evil things to beings save a being?
   Lucifer. Ask the Destroyer.
   Cain.   Who?
   Lucifer.   The Maker—call him
Which name thou wilt: he makes but to
   destroy.
   Cain. I knew not that, yet thought it,
   since I heard   265
Of Death: although I know not what it is,
Yet it seems horrible. I have look'd out
In the vast desolate night in search of him;
And when I saw gigantic shadows in
The umbrage of the walls of Eden,
   chequer'd   270

By the far-flashing of the cherubs' swords,
I watch'd for what I thought his coming: for
With fear rose longing in my heart to know
What 'twas which shook us all—but
          nothing came.   274
And then I turn'd my weary eyes from off
Our native and forbidden Paradise,
Up to the lights above us, in the azure,
Which are so beautiful: shall they, too,
          die?
Lucifer. Perhaps—but long outlive
          both thine and thee.
Cain. I'm glad of that: I would not
          have them die—   280
They are so lovely. What is death? I fear,
I feel, it is a dreadful thing; but what,
I cannot compass: 'tis denounced against
          us,
Both them who sinn'd and sinn'd not, as
          an ill—   284
What ill?
Lucifer. To be resolved into the earth.
Cain. But shall I know it?
Lucifer. As I know not death,
I cannot answer.
Cain. Were I quiet earth,
That were no evil: would I ne'er had been
Aught else but dust!
Lucifer. That is a grovelling wish,
Less than thy father's, for he wish'd to
          know.   290
Cain. But not to live, or wherefore
          pluck'd he not
The life-tree?
Lucifer. He was hinder'd.
Cain. Deadly error!
Not to snatch first that fruit:—but ere he
          pluck'd
The knowledge, he was ignorant of death.
Alas! I scarcely now know what it is, 295
And yet I fear it—fear I know not what!
Lucifer. And I, who know all things,
          fear nothing; see
What is true knowledge.
Cain. Wilt thou teach me all?
Lucifer. Ay, upon one condition.
Cain. Name it.
Lucifer. That
Thou dost fall down and worship me—
          thy Lord.   300
Cain. Thou art not the Lord my father
          worships.
Lucifer. No.
Cain. His equal?
Lucifer. No;—I have nought
          in common with him!
Nor would: I would be aught above—
          beneath—
Aught save a sharer or a servant of
His power. I dwell apart; but I am great:—
Many there are who worship me, and
          more   306
Who shall—be thou amongst the first.

Cain. I never
As yet have bow'd unto my father's God,
Although my brother Abel oft implores
That I would join with him in sacrifice:—
Why should I bow to thee?
Lucifer. Hast thou ne'er bow'd   311
To him?
Cain. Have I not said it?—need I say
it?
Could not thy mighty knowledge teach
          thee that?
Lucifer. He who bows not to him has
          bow'd to me.
Cain. But I will bend to neither.
Lucifer. Ne'er the less,   315
Thou art my worshipper; not worshipping
Him makes thee mine the same.
Cain. And what is that?
Lucifer. Thou'lt know here—and
          hereafter.
Cain. Let me but
Be taught the mystery of my being.
Lucifer. Follow
Where I will lead thee.
Cain. But I must retire   320
To till the earth—for I had promised—
Lucifer. What?
Cain. To cull some first-fruits.
Lucifer. Why?
Cain. To offer up
With Abel on an altar.
Lucifer. Said'st thou not
Thou ne'er hadst bent to him who made
          thee?
Cain. Yes—
But Abel's earnest prayer has wrought
          upon me.   325
The offering is more his than mine—and
          Adah——
Lucifer. Why dost thou hesitate?
Cain. She is my sister,
Born on the same day, of the same womb:
          and
She wrung from me, with tears, this
          promise; and
Rather than see her weep, I would, me-
          thinks,   330
Bear all—and worship aught.
Lucifer. Then follow me!
Cain. I will.

                    Enter ADAH.

Adah. My brother, I have come for
          thee;
It is our hour of rest and joy—and we
Have less without thee. Thou hast
          labour'd not
This morn; but I have done thy task: the
          fruits   335
Are ripe, and glowing as the light which
          ripens:
Come away.
Cain. Seest thou not?
Adah. I see an angel;

We have seen many: will he share our hour
Of rest?—he is welcome.
    Cain.   But he is not like
The angels we have seen.
    Adah.   Are there, then, others?   340
But he is welcome, as they were: they deign'd
To be our guests—will he?
    Cain [to Lucifer].   Wilt thou? I ask
    Lucifer.   I ask
Thee to be mine.
    Cain.   I must away with him.
    Adah.   And leave us?
    Cain.   Ay.
    Adah.   And *me?*
    Cain.   Beloved Adah!
    Adah.   Let me go with thee.
    Lucifer.   No, she must not.
    Adah.   Who
Art thou that steppest between heart and
    heart?   346
    Cain.   He is a god.
    Adah.   How know'st thou?
    Cain.   He speaks like
A god.
    Adah.   So did the serpent, and it lied.
    Lucifer.   Thou errest, Adah!—was not
        the tree that   349
Of knowledge?
    Adah.   Ay—to our eternal sorrow.
    Lucifer.   And yet that grief is know-
        ledge—so he lied not:
And if he did betray you, 'twas with truth;
And truth in its own essence cannot be
But good.
    Adah.   But all we know of it has
        gather'd
Evil on ill; expulsion from our home,
And dread, and toil, and sweat, and heavi-
        ness;   356
Remorse of that which was—and hope of
        that
Which cometh not. Cain! walk not with
        this spirit.
Bear with what we have borne, and love
        me—I
Love thee.
    Lucifer.   More than thy mother, and
        thy sire?   360
    Adah.   I do. Is that a sin, too?
    Lucifer.   No, not yet;
It one day will be in your children.
    Adah.   What!
Must not my daughter love her brother
        Enoch?
    Lucifer.   Not as thou lovest Cain.
    Adah.   Oh, my God!
Shall they not love and bring forth things
        that love   365
Out of their love? have they not drawn
        their milk
Out of this bosom? was not he, their
        father,

Born of the same sole womb, in the same
        hour
With me? did we not love each other? and
In multiplying our being multiply   370
Things which will love each other as we
        love
Them?—And as I love thee, my Cain! go
        not
Forth with this spirit; he is not of ours.
    Lucifer.   The sin I speak of is not of
        my making,
And cannot be a sin in you—whate'er
It seem in those who will replace ye in
Mortality.
    Adah.   What is the sin which is not
Sin in itself? Can circumstance make sin
Or virtue?—if it doth, we are the slaves
Of——
    Lucifer.   Higher things than ye are
        slaves: and higher   380
Than them or ye would be so, did they not
Prefer an independency of torture
To the smooth agonies of adulation,
In hymns and harpings, and self-seeking
        prayers,
To that which is omnipotent, because
It is omnipotent, and not from love,   386
But terror and self-hope.
    Adah.   Omnipotence
Must be all goodness.
    Lucifer.   Was it so in Eden?
    Adah.   Fiend! tempt me not with
        beauty; thou art fairer
Than was the serpent, and as false.
    Lucifer.   As true.   390
Ask Eve, your mother: bears she not the
        knowledge
Of good and evil?
    Adah.   Oh, my mother! thou
Hast pluck'd a fruit more fatal to thine off-
        spring
Than to thyself; thou at the least hast
        pass'd
Thy youth in Paradise, in innocent   395
And happy intercourse with happy spirits:
But we, thy children, ignorant of Eden,
Are girt about by demons, who assume
The words of God, and tempt us with our
        own
Dissatisfied and curious thoughts—as
        thou   400
Wert work'd on by the snake, in thy most
        flush'd
And heedless, harmless wantonness of
        bliss.
I cannot answer this immortal thing
Which stands before me; I cannot abhor
        him;   404
I look upon him with a pleasing fear,
And yet I fly not from him: in his eye
There is a fastening attraction which
Fixes my fluttering eyes on his; my heart
Beats quick; he awes me, and yet draws
        me near,

Nearer and nearer:—Cain—Cain—save
  me from him!   410
  Cain. What dreads my Adah? This
is no ill spirit.
  Adah. He is not God—nor God's: I
have beheld
The cherubs and the seraphs; he looks not
Like them.
  Cain   But there are spirits loftier
still—
The archangels.
  Lucifer.   And still loftier than the
  archangels.   415
  Adah. Ay—but not blessed.
  Lucifer.   If the blessedness
Consists in slavery—no.
  Adah.   I have heard it said,
The seraphs *love most*—cherubim *know
  most*—
And this should be a cherub—since he
loves not.
  Lucifer. And if the higher knowledge
  quenches love,   420
What must *he be* you cannot love when
known?
Since the all-knowing cherubim love
least,
The seraphs' love can be but ignorance:
That they are not compatible, the doom
Of thy fond parents, for their daring,
  proves.   425
Choose betwixt love and knowledge—
since there is
No other choice: your sire hath chosen
already:
His worship is but fear.
  Adah.   Oh, Cain! choose love.
  Cain. For thee, my Adah, I choose
not—it was
Born with me—but I love nought else.
  Adah.   Our parents?
  Cain. Did they love us when they
  snatch'd from the tree   431
That which hath driven us all from
Paradise?
  Adah. We were not born then—and
if we had been,
Should we not love them and our children,
Cain?
  Cain. My little Enoch! and his lisping
  sister!   435
Could I but deem them happy, I would
half
Forget——but it can never be forgotten
Through thrice a thousand generations!
never
Shall men love the remembrance of the
man
Who sow'd the seed of evil and mankind
In the same hour! They pluck'd the tree
of science   441
And sin—and, not content with their own
sorrow,
Begot *me*—*thee*—and all the few that are,

And all the unnumber'd and innumerable
Multitudes, millions, myriads, which may
  be,   445
To inherit agonies accumulated
By ages!—and *I* must be sire of such
things!
Thy beauty and thy love—my love and joy,
The rapturous moment and the placid
hour,
All we love in our children and each other,
But lead them and ourselves through many
  years   451
Of sin and pain—or few, but still of
sorrow,
Intercheck'd with an instant of brief
pleasure,
To Death—the unknown! Methinks the
tree of knowledge
Hath not fulfill'd its promise:—if they
  sinn'd,   455
At least they ought to have known all
things that are
Of knowledge—and the mystery of death.
What do they know?—that they are
miserable.
What need of snakes and fruits to teach us
that?
  Adah. I am not wretched, Cain, and if
  thou   460
Wert happy——
  Cain.   Be thou happy, then,
alone—
I will have nought to do with happiness,
Which humbles me and mine.
  Adah.   Alone I could not,
Nor *would* be happy; but with those
around us
I think I could be so, despite of death,
Which, as I know it not, I dread not,
  though   466
It seems an awful shadow—if I may
Judge from what I have heard.
  Lucifer.   And thou couldst not
Alone, thou say'st, be happy?
  Adah.   Alone! Oh, my God!
Who could be happy and alone, or good?
To me my solitude seems sin; unless   471
When I think how soon I shall see my
brother,
His brother, and our children, and our
parents.
  Lucifer. Yet thy God is alone; and is
he happy,
Lonely, and good?
  Adah.   He is not so; he hath   475
The angels and the mortals to make happy,
And thus becomes so in diffusing joy.
What else can joy be, but the spreading
joy?
  Lucifer. Ask of your sire, the exile
fresh from Eden;
Or of his first-born son: ask your own
heart;   480
It is not tranquil.

Adah. Alas! no! and you—
Are you of heaven?
  Lucifer. If I am not, inquire
The cause of this all-spreading happiness
(Which you proclaim) of the all-great and
good 484
Maker of life and living things; it is
His secret, and he keeps it. We must bear,
And some of us resist, and both in vain,
His seraphs say: but it is worth the trial,
Since better may not be without: there is
A wisdom in the spirit, which directs
To right, as in the dim blue air the eye
Of you, young mortals, lights at once upon
The star which watches, welcoming the
morn.
  Adah. It is a beautiful star; I love it for
Its beauty.
  Lucifer. And why not adore?
  Adah. Our father
Adores the Invisible only.
  Lucifer. But the symbols 496
Of the Invisible are the loveliest
Of what is visible; and yon bright star
Is leader of the host of heaven.
  Adah. Our father
Saith that he has beheld the God himself
Who made him and our mother.
  Lucifer. Hast *thou* seen him? 501
  Adah. Yes—in his works.
  Lucifer. But in his being?
  Adah. No—
Save in my father, who is God's own
image;
Or in his angels, who are like to thee—
And brighter, yet less beautiful and
powerful 505
In seeming: as the silent sunny noon,
All light, they look upon us; but thou
seem'st
Like an ethereal night, where long white
clouds
Streak the deep purple, and unnumber'd
stars
Spangle the wonderful mysterious vault
With things that look as if they would be
suns; 511
So beautiful, unnumber'd, and endearing,
Not dazzling, and yet drawing us to them,
They fill my eyes with tears, and so dost
thou.
Thou seem'st unhappy: do not make us so,
And I will weep for thee.
  Lucifer. Alas! those tears! 516
Couldst thou but know what oceans will
be shed—
  Adah. By me?
  Lucifer. By all.
  Adah. What all?
  Lucifer. The million millions—
The myriad myriads—the all-peopled
earth—
The unpeopled earth—and the o'er-
peopled hell, 520

Of which thy bosom is the germ.
  Adah. O Cain!
This spirit curseth us.
  Cain. Let him say on;
Him will I follow.
  Adah. Whither?
  Lucifer. To a place
Whence he shall come back to thee in an
hour;
But in that hour see things of many days.
  Adah. How can that be? 525
  Lucifer. Did not your Maker make
Out of old worlds this new one in few days?
And cannot I, who aided in this work,
Show in an hour what he hath made in
many,
Or hath destroy'd in few?
  Cain. Lead on.
  Adah. Will he,
In sooth, return within an hour?
  Lucifer. He shall. 531
With us acts are exempt from time, and we
Can crowd eternity into an hour,
Or stretch an hour into eternity:
We breathe not by a mortal measure-
ment— 535
But that's a mystery. Cain, come on with
me.
  Adah. Will he return?
  Lucifer. Ay, woman! he alone
Of mortals from that place (the first and
last
Who shall return, save ONE), shall come
back to thee,
To make that silent and expectant world
As populous as this: at present there 541
Are few inhabitants.
  Adah. Where dwellest thou?
  Lucifer. Throughout all space. Where
should I dwell? Where are
Thy God or Gods—there am I: all things
are
Divided with me: life and death—and
time— 545
Eternity—and heaven and earth—and
that
Which is not heaven nor earth, but
peopled with
Those who once peopled or shall people
both—
These are my realms! So that I do divide
His, and possess a kingdom which is not
His. If I were not that which I have
said, 551
Could I stand here? His angels are within
Your vision.
  Adah. So they were when the fair
serpent
Spoke with our mother first.
  Lucifer. Cain! thou hast heard
If thou dost long for knowledge, I can
satiate 555
That thirst; nor ask thee to partake of
fruits

Which shall deprive thee of a single good
The conqueror has left thee. Follow me.
 Cain. Spirit, I have said it.
   [*Exeunt* LUCIFER *and* CAIN.
Adah [*follows exclaiming*]. Cain! my
 brother! Cain!

ACT II

SCENE I.—*The Abyss of Space.*

 Cain. I tread on air, and sink not; yet
 I fear
To sink.
 Lucifer. Have faith in me, and thou
 shalt be
Borne on the air, of which I am the prince.
 Cain. Can I do so without impiety?
 Lucifer. Believe—and sink not!
 doubt—and perish! thus   5
Would run the edict of the other God,
Who names me demon to his angels; they
Echo the sound to miserable things,
Which, knowing nought beyond their
 shallow senses,
Worship the word which strikes their ear,
 and deem   10
Evil or good what is proclaim'd to them
In their abasement. I will have none such:
Worship or worship not, thou shalt behold
The worlds beyond thy little world, nor be
Amerced for doubts beyond thy little life,
With torture of *my* dooming. There will
 come   16
An hour, when, toss'd upon some water-
 drops,
A man shall say to a man, 'Believe in me,
And walk the waters;' and the man shall
 walk
The billows and be safe. *I* will not say,
Believe in *me,* as a conditional creed 21
To save thee; but fly with me o'er the gulf
Of space an equal flight, and I will show
What thou dar'st not deny,—the history
Of past, and present, and of future worlds.
 Cain. Oh, god, or demon, or whate'er
 thou art,   26
Is yon our earth?
 Lucifer. Dost thou not recognise
The dust which form'd your father?
 Cain.   Can it be?
Yon small blue circle, swinging in far
 ether,
With an inferior circlet near it still, 30
Which looks like that which lit our earthly
 night?
Is this our Paradise? Where are its walls,
And they who guard them?
 Lucifer.   Point me out the site
Of Paradise.
 Cain. How should I? As we move
Like sunbeams onward, it grows small and
 smaller,   35
And as it waxes little, and then less,
Gathers a halo round it, like the light

Which shone the roundest of the stars,
 when I
Beheld them from the skirts of Paradise:
Methinks they both, as we recede from
 them,   40
Appear to join the innumerable stars
Which are around us; and, as we move on,
Increase their myriads.
 Lucifer.   And if there should be
Worlds greater than thine own, inhabited
By greater things, and they themselves far
 more   45
In number than the dust of thy dull earth,
Though multiplied to animated atoms,
All living, and all doom'd to death, and
 wretched,
What wouldst thou think?
 Cain. I should be proud of thought
Which knew such things.
 Lucifer. But if that high thought were
Link'd to a servile mass of matter, and,
Knowing such things, aspiring to such
 things,   52
And science still beyond them, were
 chain'd down
To the most gross and petty paltry wants,
All foul and fulsome, and the very best
Of thine enjoyments a sweet degradation,
A most enervating and filthy cheat
To lure thee on to the renewal of
Fresh souls and bodies, all foredoom'd to be
As frail, and few so happy——
 Cain.   Spirit! I 60
Know nought of death, save as a dreadful
 thing
Of which I have heard my parents speak,
 as of
A hideous heritage I owe to them
No less than life; a heritage not happy,
If I may judge, till now. But, spirit! if
It be as thou hast said (and I within 66
Feel the prophetic torture of its truth),
Here let me die: for to give birth to those
Who can but suffer many years, and die,
Methinks is merely propagating death,
And multiplying murder.
 Lucifer.   Thou canst not 71
All die—there is what must survive.
 Cain.   The Other
Spake not of this unto my father, when
He shut him forth from Paradise, with
 death   74
Written upon his forehead. But at least
Let what is mortal of me perish, that
I may be in the rest as angels are.
 Lucifer. *I* am angelic: wouldst thou be
 as I am?
 Cain. I know not what thou art: I see
 thy power,
And see thou show'st me things beyond
 my power,   80
Beyond all power of my born faculties,
Although inferior still to my desires
And my conceptions.

Lucifer. What are they which dwell
So humbly in their pride, as to sojourn
With worms in clay?
Cain. And what art thou who dwellest
So haughtily in spirit, and canst range
Nature and immortality—and yet   87
Seem'st sorrowful?
Lucifer. I seem that which I am;
And therefore do I ask of thee, if thou
Wouldst be immortal?
Cain. Thou hast said, I must be   90
Immortal in despite of me. I knew not
This until lately—but since it must be,
Let me, or happy or unhappy, learn
To anticipate my immortality.
Lucifer. Thou didst before I came
    upon thee.
Cain. How?   95
Lucifer. By suffering.
Cain. And must torture be immortal?
Lucifer. We and thy sons will try.
    But now, behold!
Is it not glorious?
Cain. Oh, thou beautiful
And unimaginable ether! and
Ye multiplying masses of increased   100
And still increasing lights! what are ye?
    what
Is this blue wilderness of interminable
Air, where ye roll along, as I have seen
The leaves along the limpid streams of
    Eden?   104
Is your course measured for ye? Or do ye
Sweep on in your unbounded revelry
Through an aërial universe of endless
Expansion—at which my soul aches to
    think—
Intoxicated with eternity?   109
Oh God! Oh Gods! or whatsoe'er ye are!
How beautiful ye are! how beautiful
Your works, or accidents, or whatsoe'er
They may be! Let me die, as atoms die
(If that they die), or know ye in your might
And knowledge! My thoughts are not in
    this hour   115
Unworthy what I see, though my dust is;
Spirit! let me expire, or see them nearer.
Lucifer. Art thou not nearer? look
    back to thine earth!
Cain. Where is it? I see nothing save a mass
Of most innumerable lights.
Lucifer. Look there!   120
Cain. I cannot see it.
Lucifer. Yet it sparkles still.
Cain. That!—yonder!
Lucifer. Yea.
Cain. And wilt thou tell me so?
Why, I have seen the fire-flies and fire-
    worms
Sprinkle the dusky groves and the green
    banks
In the dim twilight, brighter than yon
    world   125
Which bears them.

Lucifer. Thou hast seen both worms
    and worlds,
Each bright and sparkling—what dost
    think of them?
Cain. That they are beautiful in their
    own sphere,
And that the night, which makes both
    beautiful,
The little shining fire-fly in its flight,   130
And the immortal star in its great course,
Must both be guided.
Lucifer. But by whom or what?
Cain. Show me.
Lucifer. Dar'st thou behold?
Cain. How know I what
I *dare* behold? As yet, thou hast shown
    nought
I dare not gaze on further.
Lucifer. On, then, with me.   135
Wouldst thou behold things mortal or
    immortal?
Cain. Why, what are things?
Lucifer. *Both* partly: but what doth
Sit next thy heart?
Cain. The things I see.
Lucifer. But what
Sate nearest it?
Cain. The things I have not seen,
Nor ever shall—the mysteries of death.
Lucifer. What, if I show to thee things
    which have died,   141
As I have shown thee much which cannot
    die?
Cain. Do so.
Lucifer. Away, then! on our mighty
    wings.
Cain. Oh! how we cleave the blue!
    The stars fade from us!
The earth! where is my earth? Let me
    look on it,   145
For I was made of it.
Lucifer. 'Tis now beyond thee,
Less, in the universe, than thou in it;
Yet deem not that thou canst escape it;
    thou
Shalt soon return to earth, and all its dust:
'Tis part of thy eternity, and mine.   150
Cain. Where dost thou lead me?
Lucifer. To what was before thee!
The phantasm of the world; of which thy
    world
Is but the wreck.
Cain. What! is it not then new?
Lucifer. No more than life is; and that
    was ere thou   154
Or *I* were, or the things which seem to us
Greater than either: many things will have
No end; and some, which would pretend
    to have
Had no beginning, have had one as mean
As thou; and mightier things have been
    extinct
To make way for much meaner than we
    can   160

Surmise; for *moments* only and the *space*
Have been and must be all *unchangeable*.
But changes make not death, except to
    clay;
But thou art clay—and canst but com-
    prehend
That which was clay, and such thou shalt
    behold.   165
  Cain. Clay, spirit! what thou wilt, I
    can survey.
  Lucifer. Away, then!
  Cain. But the lights fade from me fast,
And some till now grew larger as we
    approach'd,
And wore the look of worlds.
  Lucifer.   And such they are.
  Cain. And Edens in them?
  Lucifer.   It may be.
  Cain.   And men? 170
  Lucifer. Yea, or things higher.
  Cain.   Ay? and serpents too?
  Lucifer. Wouldst thou have men with-
    out them? must no reptiles
Breathe, save the erect ones?
  Cain.   How the lights recede!
Where fly we?
  Lucifer. To the world of phantoms,
    which   174
Are beings past, and shadows still to come.
  Cain. But it grows dark, and dark—
    the stars are gone!
  Lucifer. And yet thou seest.
  Cain.   'Tis a fearful light!
No sun, no moon, no lights innumerable,
The very blue of the empurpled night
Fades to a dreary twilight, yet I see 180
Huge dusky masses; but unlike the worlds
We were approaching, which begirt with
    light,
Seem'd full of life even when their
    atmosphere
Of light gave way, and show'd them taking
    shapes
Unequal, of deep valleys and vast moun-
    tains;   185
And some emitting sparks, and some dis-
    playing
Enormous liquid plains, and some begirt
With luminous belts, and floating moons,
    which took,
Like them, the features of fair earth:—
    instead,
All here seems dark and dreadful.
  Lucifer.   But distinct.
Thou seekest to behold death, and dead
    things?   191
  Cain. I seek it not; but as I know there
    are
Such, and that my sire's sin makes him and
    me,
And all that we inherit, liable
To such, I would behold at once, what I
Must one day see perforce.
  Lucifer.   Behold!

  Cain.   'Tis darkness.   196
  Lucifer. And so it shall be ever; but
    we will
Unfold its gates!
  Cain.   Enormous vapours roll
Apart—what's this?
  Lucifer.   Enter!
  Cain.   Can I return?
  Lucifer. Return! be sure: how else
    should death be peopled?   200
Its present realm is thin to what it will be
Through thee and thine.
  Cain.   The clouds still open wide
And wider, and make widening circles
    round us.
  Lucifer. Advance!
  Cain.   And thou!
  Lucifer. Fear not—without me thou
Couldst not have gone beyond thy world.
On! on!   205
    [*They disappear through the clouds.*

SCENE II.—*Hades.*

Enter LUCIFER *and* CAIN.

  Cain. How silent and how vast are
    these dim worlds!
For they seem more than one, and yet
    more peopled
Than the huge brilliant luminous orbs
    which swung
So thickly in the upper air, that I
Had deem'd them rather the bright
    populace   5
Of some all unimaginable Heaven,
Than things to be inhabited themselves,
But that on drawing near them I beheld
Their swelling into palpable immensity
Of matter, which seem'd made for life to
    dwell on,   10
Rather than life itself.   But here, all is
So shadowy, and so full of twilight, that
It speaks of a day past.
  Lucifer.   It is the realm
Of death.—Wouldst have it present?
  Cain.   Till I know 14
That which it really is, I cannot answer.
But if it be as I have heard my father
Deal out in his long homilies, 'tis a thing—
Oh God! I dare not think on't! Cursed be
He who invented life that leads to death!
Or the dull mass of life, that, being life,
Could not retain, but needs must forfeit it—
Even for the innocent!
  Lucifer. Dost thou curse thy father?
  Cain. Cursed he not me in giving me
    my birth?
Cursed he not me before my birth, in
    daring
To pluck the fruit forbidden?
  Lucifer.   Thou say'st well: 25
The curse is mutual 'twixt thy sire and
    thee—
But for thy sons and brother?

Cain.   Let them share it
With me, their sire and brother! What
    else is
Bequeath'd to me? I leave them my
    inheritance.
Oh, ye interminable gloomy realms   30
Of swimming shadows and enormous
    shapes,
Some fully shown, some indistinct, and all
Mighty and melancholy—what are ye?
Live ye, or have ye lived?
Lucifer.   Somewhat of both.
Cain. Then what is death?
Lucifer. What! Hath not he who
    made ye   35
Said 'tis another life?
Cain.   Till now he hath
Said nothing, save that all shall die.
Lucifer.   Perhaps
He one day will unfold that further secret.
Cain. Happy the day!
Lucifer. Yes; happy! when unfolded,
Through agonies unspeakable, and
    clogg'd   40
With agonies eternal, to innumerable
Yet unborn myriads of unconscious
    atoms,
All to be animated for this only!
Cain. What are these mighty
    phantoms which I see
Floating around me?—They wear not the
    form   45
Of the intelligences I have seen
Round our regretted and unenter'd Eden,
Nor wear the form of man as I have view'd
    it
In Adam's and in Abel's, and in mine,
Nor in my sister-bride's, nor in my
    children's: 50
And yet they have an aspect, which,
    though not
Of men nor angels, looks like something
    which
If not the last, rose higher than the first,
Haughty, and high, and beautiful, and
    full
Of seeming strength, but of inexplicable
Shape; for I never saw such. They bear
    not   56
The wing of seraph, nor the face of man,
Nor form of mightiest brute, nor aught
    that is
Now breathing; mighty yet and beautiful
As the most beautiful and mighty which
Live, and yet so unlike them, that I scarce
Can call them living.
Lucifer.   Yet they lived.
Cain.   Where?
Lucifer.   Where
Thou livest.
Cain.   When?
Lucifer.   On what thou callest earth
They did inhabit.
Cain.   Adam is the first.

Lucifer. Of thine, I grant thee—but too
    mean to be   65
The last of these.
Cain.   And what are they?
Lucifer.   That which
Thou shalt be.
Cain.   But what *were* they?
Lucifer.   Living, high,
Intelligent, good, great, and glorious
    things,
As much superior unto all thy sire,   69
Adam, could e'er have been in Eden, as
The sixty-thousandth generation shall be,
In its dull damp degeneracy, to
Thee and thy son;—and how weak they
    are, judge
By thy own flesh.
Cain.   Ah me! and did *they* perish?
Lucifer. Yes, from their earth, as thou
    wilt fade from thine.   75
Cain. But was *mine* theirs?
Lucifer.   It was.
Cain.   But not as now.
It is too little and too lowly to
Sustain such creatures.
Lucifer. True, it was more glorious.
Cain. And wherefore did it fall?
Lucifer.   Ask him who fells.
Cain. But how?
Lucifer. By a most crushing and
    inexorable   80
Destruction and disorder of the elements,
Which struck a world to chaos, as a chaos
Subsiding has struck out a world: such
    things,
Though rare in time, are frequent in
    eternity.—
Pass on, and gaze upon the past.
Cain.   'Tis awful! 85
Lucifer. And true. Behold these
    phantoms! they were once
Material as thou art.
Cain.   And must I be
Like them?
Lucifer. Let Him who made thee
    answer that.
I show thee what thy predecessors are,
And what they *were* thou feelest, in degree
Inferior as thy petty feelings and   91
Thy pettier portion of the immortal part
Of high intelligence and earthly strength.
What ye in common have with what they
    had
Is life, and what ye *shall* have—death: the
    rest   95
Of your poor attributes is such as suits
Reptiles engender'd out of the subsiding
Slime of a mighty universe, crush'd into
A scarcely-yet shaped planet, peopled with
Things whose enjoyment was to be in
    blindness—   100
A Paradise of Ignorance, from which
Knowledge was barr'd as poison. But
    behold

What these superior beings are or were;
Or, if it irk thee, turn thee back and till
The earth, thy task—I'll waft thee there
    in safety.   105
    Cain.   No: I'll stay here.
    Lucifer.   How long?
    Cain.   For ever! Since
I must one day return here from the earth,
I rather would remain; I am sick of all
That dust has shown me—let me dwell in
    shadows.
    Lucifer. It cannot be: thou now
    beholdest as   110
A vision that which is reality.
To make thyself fit for this dwelling, thou
Must pass through what the things thou
    see'st have pass'd—
The gates of death.
    Cain.   By what gate have we enter'd
Even now?
    Lucifer. By mine! But, plighted to
    return,   115
My spirit buoys thee up to breathe in
    regions
Where all is breathless save thyself. Gaze
    on;
But do not think to dwell here till thine
    hour
Is come.
    Cain.   And these, too; can they ne'er
    repass
To earth again?
    Lucifer. Their earth is gone for ever—
So changed by its convulsion, they would
    not   121
Be conscious to a single present spot
Of its new scarcely harden'd surface—
    'twas—
Oh, what a beautiful world it *was!*
    Cain.   And is.
It is not with the earth, though I must till it,
I feel at war, but that I may not profit   126
By what it bears of beautiful, untoiling,
Nor gratify my thousand swelling thoughts
With knowledge, nor allay my thousand
    fears
Of death and life.
    Lucifer. What thy world is thou see'st,
But canst not comprehend the shadow of
That which it was.
    Cain.   And those enormous creatures,
Phantoms inferior in intelligence   133
(At least so seeming) to the things we have
    pass'd,
Resembling somewhat the wild habitants
Of the deep woods of earth, the hugest
    which   136
Roar nightly in the forest, but ten-fold
In magnitude and terror; taller than
The cherub-guarded walls of Eden, with
Eyes flashing like the fiery swords which
    fence them,   140
And tusks projecting like the trees stripp'd
    of

Their bark and branches—what were they?
    Lucifer.   That which
The Mammoth is in thy world;—but
    these lie
By myriads underneath its surface.
    Cain.   But
None on it?
    Lucifer.   No: for thy frail race to war
With them would render the curse on it
    useless—   146
'Twould be destroy'd so early.
    Cain.   But why *war?*
    Lucifer. You have forgotten the
    denunciation
Which drove your race from Eden—war
    with all things,
And death to all things, and disease to
    most things,   150
And pangs, and bitterness; these were the
    fruits
Of the forbidden tree.
    Cain.   But animals—
Did they, too, eat of it, that they must die?
    Lucifer. Your Maker told ye, *they*
    were made for you,
As you for him.—You would not have
    their doom   155
Superior to your own? Had Adam not
Fallen, all had stood.
    Cain.   Alas! the hopeless wretches!
They too must share my sire's fate, like
    his sons;
Like them, too, without having shared the
    apple;
Like them, too, without the so dear-
    bought *knowledge!*   160
It was a lying tree—for we *know* nothing.
At least it *promised* knowledge at the *price*
Of death—but *knowledge* still: but what
    knows man?
    Lucifer. It may be death leads to the
    highest knowledge;
And being of all things the sole thing
    certain,   165
At least leads to the *surest* science: there-
    fore
The tree was true, though deadly.
    Cain.   These dim realms!
I see them, but I know them not.
    Lucifer.   Because
Thy hour is yet afar, and matter cannot
Comprehend spirit wholly—but 'tis some-
    thing   170
To know there are such realms.
    Cain.   We knew already
That there was death.
    Lucifer. But not what was beyond it.
    Cain. Nor know I now.
    Lucifer. Thou knowest that there is
A state, and many states beyond thine
    own—
And this thou knewest not this morn.
    Cain.   But all
Seems dim and shadowy.

Lucifer.   Be content; it will   176
Seem clearer to thine immortality.
   Cain. And yon immeasurable liquid
    space
Of glorious azure which floats on beyond us,
Which looks like water, and which I
   should deem   180
The river which flows out of Paradise
Past my own dwelling, but that it is bank-
   less
And boundless, and of an ethereal hue—
What is it?
   Lucifer. There is still some such on
    earth,
Although inferior, and thy children shall
Dwell near it—'tis the phantasm of an
   ocean.   186
   Cain. 'Tis like another world; a liquid
   sun—
And those inordinate creatures sporting
   o'er
Its shining surface?
   Lucifer.   Are its inhabitants,
The past leviathans.
   Cain.   And yon immense
Serpent, which rears his dripping mane
   and vasty   191
Head ten times higher than the haughtiest
   cedar
Forth from the abyss, looking as he could
   coil
Himself around the orbs we lately look'd
   on—
Is he not of the kind which bask'd beneath
The tree in Eden?
   Lucifer. Eve, thy mother, best 196
Can tell what shape of serpent tempted her.
   Cain. This seems too terrible. No
   doubt the other
Had more of beauty.
   Lucifer. Hast thou ne'er beheld him?
   Cain. Many of the same kind (at least
   so call'd),   200
But never that precisely which persuaded
The fatal fruit, nor even of the same aspect.
   Lucifer. Your father saw him not?
   Cain.   No: 'twas my mother
Who tempted him—she tempted by the
   serpent.
   Lucifer. Good man! whene'er thy wife,
   or thy sons' wives,   205
Tempt thee or them to aught that's new
   or strange,
Be sure thou see'st first who hath tempted
   them.
   Cain. Thy precept comes too late:
   there is no more
For serpents to tempt woman to.
   Lucifer.   But there
Are some things still which woman may
   tempt man to,   210
And man tempt woman:—let thy sons
   look to it!
My counsel is a kind one; for 'tis even

Given chiefly at my own expense; 'tis true,
'Twill not be follow'd, so there's little lost.
   Cain. I understand not this.
   Lucifer.   The happier thou!—
Thy world and thou are still too young!
   Thou thinkest   216
Thyself most wicked and unhappy: is it
   Not so?
   Cain. For crime, I know not; but for
   pain,
I have felt much.
   Lucifer. First-born of the first man!
Thy present state of sin, and thou art evil—
Of sorrow, and thou sufferest—are both
   Eden   221
In all its innocence compared to what
Thou shortly may'st be; and that state
   again,
In its redoubled wretchedness, a Paradise
To what thy sons' sons' sons, accumulating
In generations like to dust (which they
In fact but add to), shall endure and do.—
Now let us back to earth!
   Cain.   And wherefore didst thou
Lead me here only to inform me this?
   Lucifer. Was not thy quest for know-
   ledge?
   Cain. Yes; as being   230
The road to happiness.
   Lucifer.   If truth be so,
Thou hast it.
   Cain. Then my father's God did well
When he prohibited the fatal tree.
   Lucifer. But had done better in not
   planting it.
But ignorance of evil doth not save 235
From evil; it must still roll on the same,
A part of all things.
   Cain.   Not of all things. No:
I'll not believe it—for I thirst for good.
   Lucifer. And who and what doth not?
   Who covets evil
For its own bitter sake?—*None*—nothing!
   'tis   240
The leaven of all life, and lifelessness.
   Cain. Within those glorious orbs
   which we beheld,
Distant, and dazzling, and innumerable,
Ere we came down into this phantom
   realm,
Ill cannot come: they are too beautiful.
   Lucifer. Thou hast seen them from
   afar.
   Cain.   And what of that? 246
Distance can but diminish glory—they,
When nearer, must be more ineffable.
   Lucifer. Approach the things of earth
   most beautiful,
And judge their beauty near.
   Cain.   I have done this—
The loveliest thing I know is loveliest
   nearest.   251
   Lucifer. Then there must be delusion.
   —What is that

Which being nearest to thine eyes is still
More beautiful than beauteous things re-
  mote?
  Cain. My sister Adah.—All the stars
    of heaven,   255
The deep blue noon of night, lit by an orb
Which looks a spirit, or a spirit's world—
The hues of twilight—the sun's gorgeous
  coming—
His setting indescribable, which fills
My eyes with pleasant tears as I behold
Him sink, and feel my heart float softly
  with him   261
Along that western paradise of clouds,
The forest shade, the green bough, the
  bird's voice—
The vesper bird's, which seems to sing of
  love,
And mingles with the song of cherubim,
As the day closes over Eden's walls:—
All these are nothing, to my eyes and
  heart,   267
Like Adah's face: I turn from earth and
  heaven
To gaze on it.
  Lucifer.   'Tis fair as frail mortality,
In the first dawn and bloom of young
  creation,   270
And earliest embraces of earth's parents,
Can make its offspring; still it is delusion.
  Cain. You think so, being not her
    brother.
  Lucifer.   Mortal!
My brotherhood's with those who have
  no children.
  Cain. Then thou canst have no fellow-
    ship with us.   275
  Lucifer. It may be that thine own shall
    be for me.
But if thou dost possess a beautiful
Being beyond all beauty in thine eyes,
Why art thou wretched?
  Cain.   Why do I exist?
Why art *thou* wretched? why are all things
  so?   280
Even he who made us must be, as the
  maker
Of things unhappy! To produce destruc-
  tion
Can surely never be the task of joy,
And yet my sire says he's omnipotent:
Then why is evil—he being good? I ask'd
This question of my father; and he said,
Because this evil only was the path   287
To good. Strange good, that must arise
  from out
Its deadly opposite! I lately saw
A lamb stung by a reptile: the poor
  suckling   290
Lay foaming on the earth, beneath the
  vain
And piteous bleating of its restless dam;
My father pluck'd some herbs, and laid
  them to

The wound; and by degrees the helpless
  wretch
Resumed its careless life, and rose to
  drain   295
The mother's milk, who o'er it tremulous
Stood licking its reviving limbs with joy.
Behold, my son! said Adam, how from
  evil
Springs good!
  Lucifer.   What didst thou answer?
  Cain.   Nothing; for
He is my father: but I thought, that 'twere
A better portion for the animal   301
Never to have been *stung at all*, than to
Purchase renewal of its little life
With agonies unutterable, though
Dispell'd by antidotes.
  Lucifer.   But as thou saidst
Of all beloved things thou lovest her   306
Who shared thy mother's milk, and giveth
  hers
Unto thy children——
  Cain.   Most assuredly:
What should I be without her?
  Lucifer.   What am I?
  Cain. Dost thou love nothing?
  Lucifer.   What does thy God love?
  Cain. All things, my father says; but
  I confess   311
I see it not in their allotment here.
  Lucifer. And, therefore, thou canst
    not see if *I* love
Or no, except some vast and general
  purpose,
To which particular things must melt like
  snows.   315
  Cain. Snows! what are they?
  Lucifer. Be happier in not knowing
What thy remoter offspring must en-
  counter;
But bask beneath the clime which knows
  no winter.
  Cain. But dost thou not love some-
    thing like thyself?   319
  Lucifer. And dost thou love *thyself?*
  Cain.   Yes, but love more
What makes my feelings more endurable,
And is more than myself, because I love it.
  Lucifer. Thou lovest it, because 'tis
    beautiful,
As was the apple in thy mother's eye;
And when it ceases to be so, thy love
Will cease, like any other appetite.   326
  Cain. Cease to be beautiful! how can
    that be?
  Lucifer. With time.
  Cain.   But time has pass'd, and
    hitherto
Even Adam and my mother both are fair:
Not fair like Adah and the seraphim—
But very fair.
  Lucifer. All that must pass away 331
In them and her.
  Cain.   I'm sorry for it; but

535

Cannot conceive my love for her the less:
And when her beauty disappears, me-
    thinks   334
He who creates all beauty will lose more
Than me in seeing perish such a work.
    Lucifer. I pity thee who lovest what
    must perish.
    Cain. And I thee who lov'st nothing.
    Lucifer.   And thy brother—
Sits he not near thy heart?
    Cain.   Why should he not?
    Lucifer. Thy father loves him well—
    so does thy God.   340
    Cain. And so do I.
    Lucifer. 'Tis well and meekly done.
    Cain. Meekly!
    Lucifer. He is the second born of flesh,
And is his mother's favourite.
    Cain.   Let him keep
Her favour, since the serpent was the first
To win it.
    Lucifer. And his father's?
    Cain.   What is that
To me? should I not love that which all
    love?   346
    Lucifer. And the Jehovah—the indul-
    gent Lord,
And bounteous planter of barr'd Para-
    dise—
He, too, looks smilingly on Abel.
    Cain.   I
Ne'er saw him, and I know not if he smiles.
    Lucifer. But you have seen his angels.
    Cain.   Rarely.
    Lucifer.   But   351
Sufficiently to see they love your brother:
His sacrifices are acceptable.
    Cain. So be they! wherefore speak to
    me of this?
    Lucifer. Because thou hast thought of
    this ere now.
    Cain.   And if   355
I *have* thought, why recall a thought
    that—[*he pauses, as agitated*]—Spirit!
Here we are in *thy* world; speak not of
    mine.
Thou hast shown me wonders: thou hast
    shown me those
Mighty pre-Adamites who walk'd the
    earth
Of which ours is the wreck: thou hast
    pointed out   360
Myriads of starry worlds, of which our
    own
Is the dim and remote companion, in
Infinity of life: thou hast shown me
    shadows
Of that existence with the dreaded name
Which my sire brought us—Death; thou
    hast shown me much—   365
But not all: show me where Jehovah
    dwells,
In his especial Paradise—or *thine*:
Where is it?

    Lucifer.   Here, and o'er all space.
    Cain.   But ye
Have some allotted dwelling—as all
    things;
Clay has its earth, and other worlds their
    tenants;   370
All temporary breathing creatures their
Peculiar element; and things which have
Long ceased to breathe *our* breath, have
    theirs, thou say'st;
And the Jehovah and thyself have thine—
Ye do not dwell together?
    Lucifer.   No, we reign   375
Together; but our dwellings are asunder.
    Cain. Would there were only one of
    ye! perchance
An unity of purpose might make union
In elements which seem now jarr'd in
    storms.
How came ye, being spirits, wise and
    infinite,   380
To separate? Are ye not as brethren in
Your essence, and your nature, and your
    glory?
    Lucifer. Art thou not Abel's brother?
    Cain.   We are brethren,
And so we shall remain; but were it not so,
Is spirit like to flesh? can it fall out?
Infinity with Immortality?   386
Jarring and turning space to misery—
For what?
    Lucifer. To reign.
    Cain.   Did ye not tell me that
Ye are both eternal?
    Lucifer.   Yea!
    Cain.   And what I have seen,
Yon blue immensity, is boundless?
    Lucifer.   Ay.
    Cain. And cannot ye both *reign*,
    then?—is there not   391
Enough?—why should ye differ?
    Lucifer.   We *both* reign.
    Cain. But one of you makes evil.
    Lucifer.   Which?
    Cain.   Thou! for
If thou canst do man good, why dost thou
    not?
    Lucifer. And why not he who made?
    I made ye not;   395
Ye are *his* creatures, and not mine.
    Cain.   Then leave us
His creatures, as thou say'st we are, or
    show me
Thy dwelling, or his dwelling.
    Lucifer.   I could show thee
Both; but the time will come thou shalt
    see one
Of them for evermore.
    Cain.   And why not now?
    Lucifer. Thy human mind hath
    scarcely grasp to gather   401
The little I have shown thee into calm
And clear thought; and thou wouldst go
    on aspiring

To the great double mysteries! the *two*
  Principles!
And gaze upon them on their secret
  thrones!   405
Dust! limit thy ambition; for to see
Either of these would be for thee to perish!
  Cain.   And let me perish, so I see them!
  Lucifer.   There
The son of her who snatch'd the apple
  spake!
But thou wouldst only perish, and not see
  them;   410
That sight is for the other state.
  Cain.   Of death?
  Lucifer.   That is the prelude.
  Cain.   Then I dread it less,
Now that I know it leads to something
  definite.
  Lucifer.   And now I will convey thee
  to thy world,
Where thou shalt multiply the race of
  Adam,   415
Eat, drink, toil, tremble, laugh, weep,
  sleep, and die.
  Cain.   And to what end have I beheld
  these things
Which thou hast shown me?
  Lucifer.   Didst thou not require
Knowledge? And have I not, in what I
  show'd,
Taught thee to know thyself?
  Cain.   Alas! I seem
Nothing.
  Lucifer.   And this should be the human
  sum   421
Of knowledge, to know mortal nature's
  nothingness;
Bequeath that science to thy children, and
'Twill spare them many tortures.
  Cain.   Haughty spirit!
Thou speak'st it proudly; but thyself,
  though proud,   425
Hast a superior.
  Lucifer.   No! by heaven, which He
Holds, and the abyss, and the immensity
Of worlds and life, which I hold with him
  —No!
I have a victor—true; but no superior.
Homage he has from all—but none from
  me: 430
I battle it against him, as I battled
In highest heaven. Through all eternity,
And the unfathomable gulfs of Hades,
And the interminable realms of space,
And the infinity of endless ages,   435
All, all, will I dispute! And world by
  world,
And star by star, and universe by universe,
Shall tremble in the balance, till the great
Conflict shall cease, if ever it shall cease,
Which it ne'er shall, till he or I be
  quench'd!   440
And what can quench our immortality,
Our mutual and irrevocable hate?

He as a conqueror will call the conquer'd
  Evil; but what will be the *good* he gives?
Were I the victor, *his* works would be
  deem'd   445
The only evil ones. And you, ye new
And scarce born mortals, what have been
  his gifts
To you already, in your little world?
  Cain.   But few; and some of those but
  bitter.
  Lucifer.   Back
With me, then, to thine earth, and try the
  rest   450
Of his celestial boons to you and yours.
Evil and good are things in their own
  essence,
And not made good or evil by the giver;
But if he gives you good—so call him; if
Evil springs from *him*, do not name it *mine*,
Till ye know better its true fount; and
  judge   456
Not by words, though of spirits, but the
  fruits
Of your existence, such as it must be.
One good gift has the fatal apple given—
Your *reason:*—let it not be over-sway'd
By tyrannous threats to force you into
  faith   461
'Gainst all external sense and inward
  feeling:
Think and endure,—and form an inner
  world
In your own bosom—where the outward
  fails;
So shall you nearer be the spiritual
Nature, and war triumphant with your
  own.   466
                              [*They disappear.*

ACT III

SCENE I.—*The Earth, near Eden, as in Act I.*

Enter CAIN *and* ADAH.

  Adah.   Hush, tread softly, Cain.
  Cain.   I will; but wherefore?
  Adah.   Our little Enoch sleeps upon
  yon bed
Of leaves, beneath the cypress.
  Cain.   Cypress! 'tis
A gloomy tree, which looks as if it
  mourn'd
O'er what it shadows; wherefore didst
  thou choose it   5
For our child's canopy?
  Adah.   Because its branches
Shut out the sun like night, and therefore
  seem'd
Fitting to shadow slumber.
  Cain.   Ay, the last—
And longest; but no matter—lead me to
  him.   [*They go up to the child.*
How lovely he appears! his little cheeks,
In their pure incarnation, vying with   11
The rose leaves strewn beneath them.

537

Adah.   And his lips, too,
How beautifully parted! No; you shall not
Kiss him, at least not now; he will awake
soon.   14
His hour of mid-day rest is nearly over;
But it were pity to disturb him till
'Tis closed.
    Cain. You have said well; I will
contain
My heart till then. He smiles, and
sleeps!—Sleep on,
And smile, thou little, young inheritor
Of a world scarce less young: sleep on, and
smile!   20
Thine are the hours and days when both
are cheering
And innocent! *thou* hast not pluck'd the
fruit—
Thou know'st not thou art naked! Must
the time
Come thou shalt be amerced for sins
unknown,
Which were not thine nor mine? But now
sleep on!   25
His cheeks are reddening into deeper
smiles,
And shining lids are trembling o'er his long
Lashes, dark as the cypress which waves
o'er them;
Half open, from beneath them the clear blue
Laughs out, although in slumber. He
must dream—   30
Of what? Of Paradise!—Ay! dream of it,
My disinherited boy! 'Tis but a dream;
For never more thyself, thy sons, nor
fathers,
Shall walk in that forbidden place of joy!
    Adah. Dear Cain! Nay, do not
whisper o'er our son   35
Such melancholy yearnings o'er the past:
Why wilt thou always mourn for Paradise?
Can we not make another?
    Cain.   Where?
    Adah.   Here, or
Where'er thou wilt: where'er thou art, I
feel not
The want of this so much regretted Eden.
Have I not thee, our boy, our sire, and
brother,   41
And Zillah—our sweet sister, and our Eve,
To whom we owe so much besides our
birth?
    Cain. Yes—death, too, is amongst the
debts we owe her.
    Adah. Cain! that proud spirit, who
withdrew thee hence,   45
Hath sadden'd thine still deeper. I had
hoped
The promised wonders which thou hast
beheld,
Visions, thou say'st, of past and present
worlds,
Would have composed thy mind into the
calm

Of a contented knowledge; but I see   50
Thy guide hath done thee evil: still I thank
him,
And can forgive him all, that he so soon
Hath given thee back to us.
    Cain.   So soon?
    Adah.   'Tis scarcely
Two hours since ye departed: two *long*
hours
To *me*, but only *hours* upon the sun.   55
    Cain. And yet I have approach'd that
sun, and seen
Worlds which he once shone on, and never
more
Shall light; and worlds he never lit: me-
thought
Years had roll'd o'er my absence.
    Adah.   Hardly hours.
    Cain. The mind then hath capacity of
time,   60
And measures it by that which it beholds,
Pleasing or painful; little or almighty.
I had beheld the immemorial works
Of endless beings; skirr'd extinguish'd
worlds;
And, gazing on eternity, methought   65
I had borrow'd more by a few drops of ages
From its immensity: but now I feel
My littleness again. Well said the spirit,
That I was nothing!
    Adah.   Wherefore said he so?
Jehovah said not that.
    Cain.   No: *he* contents him   70
With making us the *nothing* which we are;
And after flattering dust with glimpses of
Eden and Immortality, resolves
It back to dust again—for what?
    Adah.   Thou know'st—
Even for our parents' error.
    Cain.   What is that   75
To us? they sinn'd, then *let them* die!
    Adah. Thou hast not spoken well, nor
is that thought
Thy own, but of the spirit who was with
thee.
Would *I* could die for them, so *they* might
live!
    Cain. Why, so say I—provided that
one victim   80
Might satiate the insatiable of life,
And that our little rosy sleeper there
Might never taste of death nor human
sorrow,
Nor hand it down to those who spring
from him.
    Adah. How know we that some such
atonement one day   85
May not redeem our race?
    Cain.   By sacrificing
The harmless for the guilty? what atone-
ment
Were there? why, *we* are innocent: what
have we
Done, that we must be victims for a deed

Before our birth, or need have victims to
Atone for this mysterious, nameless sin—
If it be such a sin to seek for knowledge?
  Adah. Alas! thou sinnest now, my
Cain: thy words
Sound impious in mine ears.
  Cain.   Then leave me!
  Adah.   Never,
Though thy God left thee.
  Cain.   Say, what have we here? 95
  Adah. Two altars, which our brother
Abel made
During thine absence, whereupon to offer
A sacrifice to God on thy return.
  Cain. And how knew *he,* that *I* would
be so ready
With the burnt offerings, which he daily
brings   100
With a meek brow, whose base humility
Shows more of fear than worship, as a
bribe
To the Creator?
  Adah.   Surely, 'tis well done.
  Cain. One altar may suffice; *I* have no
offering.
  Adah. The fruits of the earth, the
early, beautiful   105
Blossom and bud, and bloom of flowers
and fruits;
These are a goodly offering to the Lord,
Given with a gentle and a contrite spirit.
  Cain. I have toil'd, and till'd, and
sweaten in the sun,
According to the curse:—must I do more?
For what should I be gentle? for a war
With all the elements ere they will yield
The bread we eat? For what must I be
grateful?
For being dust, and grovelling in the dust,
Till I return to dust? If I am nothing—
For nothing shall I be an hypocrite, 116
And seem well-pleased with pain? For
what should I
Be contrite? for my father's sin, already
Expiate with what we all have undergone,
And to be more than expiated by   120
The ages prophesied, upon our seed.
Little deems our young blooming sleeper,
there,
The germs of an eternal misery
To myriads is within him! better 'twere
I snatch'd him in his sleep, and dash'd him
'gainst   125
The rocks, than let him live to——
  Adah.   Oh, my God!
Touch not the child—my child! *thy* child!
Oh, Cain!
  Cain. Fear not! for all the stars, and
all the power
Which sways them, I would not accost
yon infant   129
With ruder greeting than a father's kiss.
  Adah. Then, why so awful in thy
speech?

  Cain.   I said,
'Twere better that he ceased to live, than
give
Life to so much of sorrow as he must
Endure, and, harder still, bequeath; but
since   134
That saying jars you, let us only say—
'Twere better that he never had been born.
  Adah. Oh, do not say so! Where were
then the joys,
The mother's joys of watching, nourish-
ing,
And loving him? Soft! he awakes. Sweet
Enoch!   [*She goes to the child.*
Oh, Cain! look on him; see how full of
life,   140
Of strength, of bloom, of beauty, and of
joy,
How like to me—how like to thee, when
gentle,
For *then* we are *all* alike; is't not so, Cain?
Mother, and sire, and son, our features are
Reflected in each other; as they are 145
In the clear waters, when *they* are *gentle,*
and
When *thou* art *gentle.* Love us, then, my
Cain!
And love thyself for our sakes, for we love
thee.
Look! how he laughs and stretches out
his arms,   149
And opens wide his blue eyes upon thine,
To hail his father; while his little form
Flutters as wing'd with joy. Talk not of
pain!
The childless cherubs well might envy thee
The pleasures of a parent! Bless him,
Cain!
As yet he hath no words to thank thee,
but   155
His heart will, and thine own too.
  Cain.   Bless thee, boy!
If that a mortal blessing may avail thee,
To save thee from the serpent's curse!
  Adah.   It shall.
Surely a father's blessing may avert
A reptile's subtlety.
  Cain.   Of that I doubt; 160
But bless him ne'er the less.
  Adah.   Our brother comes.
  Cain. Thy brother Abel.

Enter ABEL.

  Abel. Welcome, Cain! My brother,
The peace of God be on thee!
  Cain.   Abel, hail!
  Abel. Our sister tells me that thou hast
been wandering,
In high communion with a spirit, far
Beyond our wonted range. Was he of
those   166
We have seen and spoken with, like to our
father?
  Cain. No.

Abel. Why then commune with him? he may be
A foe to the Most High.
Cain. And friend to man.
Has the Most High been so—if so you term him? 170
Abel. *Term him!* your words are strange to-day, my brother.
My sister Adah, leave us for awhile—
We mean to sacrifice.
Adah. Farewell, my Cain;
But first embrace thy son. May his soft spirit, 174
And Abel's pious ministry, recall thee
To peace and holiness!
[*Exit* ADAH, *with her child.*
Abel. Where hast thou been?
Cain. I know not.
Abel. Nor what thou hast seen?
Cain. The dead,
The immortal, the unbounded, the omnipotent,
The overpowering mysteries of space—
The innumerable worlds that were and are— 180
A whirlwind of such overwhelming things,
Suns, moons, and earths, upon their loud-voiced spheres
Singing in thunder round me, as have made me
Unfit for mortal converse: leave me, Abel.
Abel. Thine eyes are flashing with un-natural light— 185
Thy cheek is flush'd with an unnatural hue—
Thy words are fraught with an unnatural sound—
What may this mean?
Cain. It means——I pray thee, leave me.
Abel. Not till we have pray'd and sacrificed together.
Cain. Abel, I pray thee, sacrifice alone— 190
Jehovah loves thee well.
Abel. Both well, I hope.
Cain. But thee the better: I care not for that;
Thou art fitter for his worship than I am;
Revere him, then—but let it be alone—
At least, without me.
Abel. Brother, I should ill 195
Deserve the name of our great father's son,
If, as my elder, I revered thee not,
And in the worship of our God, call'd not
On thee to join me, and precede me in
Our priesthood—'tis thy place.
Cain. But I have ne'er 200
Asserted it.
Abel. The more my grief; I pray thee
To do so now: thy soul seems labouring in
Some strong delusion; it will calm thee.
Cain. No;

Nothing can calm me more. *Calm!* say I?
Never
Knew I what calm was in the soul, although 205
I have seen the elements still'd. My Abel, leave me!
Or let me leave thee to thy pious purpose.
Abel. Neither; we must perform our task together.
Spurn me not.
Cain. If it must be so——well, then,
What shall I do?
Abel. Choose one of those two altars. 210
Cain. Choose for me: they to me are so much turf
And stone.
Abel. Choose thou!
Cain. I have chosen.
Abel. 'Tis the highest,
And suits thee, as the elder. Now prepare
Thine offerings.
Cain. Where are thine?
Abel. Behold them here—
The firstlings of the flock, and fat thereof—
A shepherd's humble offering.
Cain. I have no flocks; 216
I am a tiller of the ground, and must
Yield what it yieldeth to my toil—its fruit:
[*He gathers fruits.*
Behold them in their various bloom and ripeness.
[*They dress their altars, and kindle a flame upon them.*
Abel. My brother, as the elder, offer first 220
Thy prayer and thanksgiving with sacrifice.
Cain. No—I am new to this; lead thou the way,
And I will follow—as I may.
Abel [*kneeling*]. Oh, God!
Who made us, and who breathed the breath of life
Within our nostrils, who hath blessed us,
And spared, despite our father's sin, to make 226
His children all lost, as they might have been,
Had not thy justice been so temper'd with
The mercy which is thy delight, as to
Accord a pardon like a Paradise, 230
Compared with our great crimes:—Sole Lord of light,
Of good, and glory, and eternity!
Without whom all were evil, and with whom
Nothing can err, except to some good end
Of thine omnipotent benevolence— 235
Inscrutable, but still to be fulfill'd—
Accept from out thy humble first of shep-herd's
First of the first-born flocks—an offering,
In itself nothing—as what offering can be

Aught unto thee?—but yet accept it for
The thanksgiving of him who spreads it in
The face of thy high heaven, bowing his
					own			242
Even to the dust, of which he is, in honour
Of thee, and of thy name, for evermore!
	Cain [standing erect during this speech].
Spirit! whate'er or whosoe'er thou art,
Omnipotent, it may be—and, if good,
Shown in the exemption of thy deeds from
	evil;					247
Jehovah upon earth! and God in heaven!
And it may be with other names, because
Thine attributes seem many, as thy works:
If thou must be propitiated with prayers,
Take them! If thou must be induced with
	altars,					252
And soften'd with a sacrifice, receive
	them!
Two beings here erect them unto thee.
If thou lov'st blood, the shepherd's shrine,
	which smokes				255
On my right hand, hath shed it for thy
	service
In the first of his flock, whose limbs now
	reek
In sanguinary incense to thy skies;
Or if the sweet and blooming fruits of
	earth,
And milder seasons, which the unstain'd
	turf					260
I spread them on now offers in the face
Of the broad sun which ripen'd them, may
	seem
Good to thee, inasmuch as they have not
Suffer'd in limb or life, and rather form
A sample of thy works, than supplication
To look on ours! If a shrine without
	victim,				266
And altar without gore, may win thy
	favour,
Look on it! and for him who dresseth it,
He is—such as thou mad'st him; and seeks
	nothing
Which must be won by kneeling: if he's
	evil,				270
Strike him! thou art omnipotent, and
	may'st—
For what can he oppose? If he be good,
Strike him, or spare him, as thou wilt!
	since all
Rests upon thee; and good and evil seem
To have no power themselves, save in thy
	will;				275
And whether that be good or ill I know
	not,
Not being omnipotent, nor fit to judge
Omnipotence, but merely to endure
Its mandate; which thus far I have
	endured.
	[*The fire upon the altar of* ABEL *kindles
	into a column of the brightest flame,
	and ascends to heaven; while a whirl-
	wind throws down the altar of* CAIN,

*and scatters the fruits abroad upon the
	earth.*
Abel [kneeling]. Oh, brother, pray!
	Jehovah's wroth with thee.		280
Cain. Why so?
Abel.				Thy fruits are scatter'd
	on the earth.
Cain. From earth they came, to earth
	let them return;
Their seed will bear fresh fruit there ere
	the summer:
Thy burnt flesh-off'ring prospers better; see
How heaven licks up the flames, when
	thick with blood!			285
Abel. Think not upon my offering's
	acceptance,
But make another of thine own before
It is too late.
Cain.		I will build no more altars,
Nor suffer any——
	Abel [rising]. Cain! what meanest
	thou?
Cain. To cast down yon vile flatt'rer
	of the clouds,			290
The smoky harbinger of thy dull prayers—
Thine altar, with its blood of lambs and
	kids,
Which fed on milk, to be destroy'd in
	blood.
Abel [opposing him]. Thou shalt not:—
	add not impious works to impious
Words! let that altar stand—'tis hallow'd
	now				295
By the immortal pleasure of Jehovah,
In his acceptance of the victims.
Cain.					His!
His pleasure! what was his high pleasure in
The fumes of scorching flesh and smoking
	blood,
To the pain of the bleating mothers,
	which				300
Still yearn for their dead offspring? or the
	pangs
Of the sad ignorant victims underneath
Thy pious knife? Give way! this bloody
	record
Shall not stand in the sun, to shame
	creation!
Abel. Brother, give back! thou shalt
	not touch my altar		305
With violence: if that thou wilt adopt it,
To try another sacrifice, 'tis thine.
Cain. Another sacrifice! Give way, or
	else
That sacrifice may be——
Abel.			What mean'st thou?
Cain.					Give—
Give way!—thy God loves blood!—then
	look to it:—			310
Give way, ere he hath *more!*
Abel.			In *his* great name,
I stand between thee and the shrine which
	hath
Had his acceptance.

Cain.   If thou lov'st thyself,
Stand back till I have strew'd this turf
    along
Its native soil:—else——
   Abel [opposing him]. I love God far
      more   315
Than life.
   *Cain [striking him with a brand, on the
    temples, which he snatches from the
    altar].* Then take thy life unto thy
      God,
Since he loves lives.
   Abel [falls]. What hast thou done, my
    brother?
   Cain. Brother!
   Abel. Oh, God! receive thy servant,
    and
Forgive his slayer, for he knew not what
He did—Cain, give me—give me thy
    hand; and tell   320
Poor Zillah—
   Cain [after a moment's stupefaction]. My
    hand! 'tis all red, and with——
What?
   [*A long pause.—Looking slowly round.*
Where am I? alone! Where's Abel?
    where
Cain? Can it be that I am he? My brother,
Awake!—why liest thou so on the green
    earth?
'Tis not the hour of slumber;—why so
    pale?   325
What hast thou!—thou wert full of life
    this morn!
Abel! I pray thee, mock me not! I smote
Too fiercely, but not fatally. Ah, why
Wouldst thou oppose me? This is
    mockery;
And only done to daunt me:—'twas a
    blow—   330
And but a blow. Stir—stir—nay, only
    stir!
Why, so—that's well!—thou breath'st!
    breathe upon me!
Oh, God! Oh, God!
   Abel [very faintly]. What's he who
    speaks of God?
   Cain. Thy murderer.
   Abel. Then may God forgive him!
    Cain,
Comfort poor Zillah:—she has but one
    brother   335
Now.   [ABEL *dies.*
   Cain. And I none!—Who makes me
    brotherless?
His eyes are open! then he is not dead!
Death is like sleep; and sleep shuts down
    our lids.
His lips, too, are apart; why then he
    breathes;
And yet I feel it not.—His heart!—his
    heart!
Let me see, doth it beat? methinks——   340
No!—no!

This is a vision, else I am become
The native of another and worse world.
The earth swims round me:—what is
    this?—'tis wet;   [*Puts his hand to his
    brow, and then looks at it.*
And yet there are no dews! 'Tis blood—
    my blood—   345
My brother's and my own! and shed by
    me!
Then what have I further to do with life,
Since I have taken life from my own flesh?
But he cannot be dead!—Is silence death?
No; he will wake; then let me watch by
    him.   350
Life cannot be so slight, as to be quench'd
Thus quickly!—he hath spoken to me
    since—
What shall I say to him?—My brother!—
    No:
He will not answer to that name; for
    brethren
Smite not each other. Yet—yet—speak
    to me.   355
Oh! for a word more of that gentle voice,
That I may bear to hear my own again!

Enter ZILLAH.

   Zillah. I heard a heavy sound; what
    can it be?
'Tis Cain; and watching by my husband.
    What
Dost thou there, brother? Doth he sleep?
    Oh, heaven!   360
What means this paleness, and yon
    stream?—No, no!
It is not blood; for who would shed his
    blood?
Abel! what's this?—who hath done this?
    He moves not:
He breathes not: and his hands drop down
    from mine   364
With stony lifelessness! Ah! cruel Cain!
Why cam'st thou not in time to save him
    from
This violence? Whatever hath assail'd
    him,
Thou wert the stronger, and shouldst have
    stepp'd in
Between him and aggression! Father!—
    Eve!—   369
Adah!—come hither! Death is in the
    world!
   [*Exit* ZILLAH, *calling on her Parents,
    &c.*
   Cain [solus]. And who hath brought
    him there?—I—who abhor
The name of Death so deeply, that the
    thought
Empoison'd all my life, before I knew
His aspect—I have led him here, and given
My brother to his cold and still embrace,
As if he would not have asserted his   376
Inexorable claim without my aid.
I am awake at last—a dreary dream

Had madden'd me;—but *he* shall ne'er
  awake!

Enter ADAM, EVE, ADAH, *and* ZILLAH.

  Adam. A voice of woe from Zillah
  brings me here.—   380
What do I see?—'Tis true!—My son!—
  my son!
Woman, behold the serpent's work, and
  thine!   [*To* EVE.
  Eve. Oh! speak not of it now: the ser-
  pent's fangs
Are in my heart. My best beloved, Abel!
Jehovah! this is punishment beyond 385
A mother's sin, to take *him* from me!
  Adam.   Who,
Or what hath done this deed?—speak,
  Cain, since thou
Wert present; was it some more hostile
  angel,
Who walks not with Jehovah? or some
  wild
Brute of the forest?
  Eve.   Ah! a livid light   390
Breaks through, as from a thunder-cloud!
  yon brand
Massy and bloody! snatch'd from off the
  altar,
And black with smoke, and red with—
  Adam.   Speak, my son!
Speak, and assure us, wretched as we are,
That we are not more miserable still. 395
  Adah. Speak, Cain! and say it was
  not *thou!*
  Eve.   It was.
I see it now—he hangs his guilty head,
And covers his ferocious eye with hands
Incarnadine.
  Adah.   Mother, thou dost him
  wrong—   399
Cain! clear thee from this horrible accusal,
Which grief wrings from our parent.
  Eve.   Hear, Jehovah!
May the eternal serpent's curse be on him!
For he was fitter for his seed than ours.
May all his days be desolate! May——
  Adah.   Hold!
Curse him not, mother, for he is thy son—
Curse him not, mother, for he is my
  brother,   406
And my betroth'd.
  Eve.   He hath left thee no brother—
Zillah no husband—me *no son!* for thus
I curse him from my sight for evermore!
All bonds I break between us as he broke
That of his nature, in yon——Oh death!
  death!   411
Why didst thou not take *me*, who first
  incurr'd thee?
Why dost thou not so now?
  Adam.   Eve! let not this,
Thy natural grief, lead to impiety!
A heavy doom was long forespoken to us;
And now that it begins, let it be borne

In such sort as may show our God that we
Are faithful servants to his holy will.
  Eve [*pointing to* Cain]. *His will!* the will
  of yon incarnate spirit
Of death, whom I have brought upon the
  earth   420
To strew it with the dead. May all the
  curses
Of life be on him! and his agonies
Drive him forth o'er the wilderness, like us
From Eden, till his children do by him
As he did by his brother! May the swords
And wings of fiery cherubim pursue him
By day and night—snakes spring up in his
  path—   427
Earth's fruits be ashes in his mouth—the
  leaves
On which he lays his head to sleep be
  strew'd
With scorpions! May his dreams be of his
  victim!   430
His waking a continual dread of death!
May the clear rivers turn to blood as he
Stoops down to stain them with his raging
  lip!
May every element shun or change to him!
May he live in the pangs which others die
  with!   435
And death itself wax something worse
  than death
To him who first acquainted him with man!
Hence, fratricide! henceforth that word is
  Cain,
Through all the coming myriads of man-
  kind,
Who shall abhor thee, though thou wert
  their sire!   440
May the grass wither from thy feet! the
  woods
Deny thee shelter! earth a home! the dust
A grave! the sun his light! and heaven her
  God!   [*Exit* EVE.
  Adam. Cain! get thee forth: we dwell
  no more together.   444
Depart! and leave the dead to me—I am
Henceforth alone—we never must meet
  more.
  Adah. Oh, part not with him thus, my
  father: do not
Add thy deep curse to Eve's upon his
  head!
  Adam. I curse him not: his spirit be his
  curse.
Come, Zillah!
  Zillah.   I must watch my husband's
  corse.   450
  Adam. We will return again, when he
  is gone
Who hath provided for us this dread office.
Come, Zillah!
  Zillah. Yet one kiss on yon pale clay,
And those lips once so warm—my heart!
  my heart!
           [*Exeunt* ADAM *and* ZILLAH, *weeping.*

Adah. Cain! thou hast heard, we must
go forth. I am ready, 455
So shall our children be. I will bear
Enoch,
And you his sister. Ere the sun declines
Let us depart, nor walk the wilderness
Under the cloud of night.—Nay, speak to
me,
To *me—thine own.*
Cain. Leave me!
Adah. Why, all have left thee. 460
Cain. And wherefore lingerest thou?
Dost thou not fear
To dwell with one who hath done this?
Adah. I fear
Nothing except to leave thee, much as I
Shrink from the deed which leaves thee
brotherless.
I must not speak of this—it is between
thee 466
And the great God.
A Voice from within exclaims, Cain! Cain!
Adah. Hear'st thou that voice?
The Voice within. Cain! Cain!
Adah. It soundeth like an angel's tone.

Enter the ANGEL *of the Lord.*

Angel. Where is thy brother Abel?
Cain. Am I then
My brother's keeper?
Angel. Cain! what hast thou done?
The voice of thy slain brother's blood cries
out, 470
Even from the ground, unto the Lord!—
Now art thou
Cursed from the earth, which open'd late
her mouth
To drink thy brother's blood from thy rash
hand.
Henceforth, when thou shalt till the
ground, it shall not
Yield thee her strength; a fugitive shalt
thou 475
Be from this day, and vagabond on earth!
Adah. This punishment is more than
he can bear.
Behold, thou driv'st him from the face of
earth,
And from the face of God shall he be hid.
A fugitive and vagabond on earth, 480
'Twill come to pass, that whoso findeth him
Shall slay him.
Cain. Would they could! but who
are they
Shall slay me? Where are these on the lone
earth
As yet unpeopled?
Angel. Thou hast slain thy brother,
And who shall warrant thee against thy
son? 485
Adah. Angel of Light! be merciful,
nor say
That this poor aching breast now
nourishes

A murderer in my boy, and of his father.
Angel. Then he would but be what his
father is. 489
Did not the milk of Eve give nutriment
To him thou now see'st so besmear'd with
blood?
The fratricide might well engender parri-
cides.—
But it shall not be so—the Lord thy God
And mine commandeth me to set his seal
On Cain, so that he may go forth in safety.
Who slayeth Cain, a sevenfold vengeance
shall 496
Be taken on his head. Come hither!
Cain. What
Wouldst thou with me?
Angel. To mark upon thy brow
Exemption from such deeds as thou hast
done.
Cain. No, let me die!
Angel. It must not be.
[*The* ANGEL *sets the mark on* CAIN'S *brow.*
Cain. It burns 500
My brow, but nought to that which is with-
in it.
Is there more? let me meet it as I may.
Angel. Stern hast thou been and stub-
born from the womb,
As the ground thou must henceforth till;
but he
Thou slew'st was gentle as the flocks he
tended. 505
Cain. After the fall too soon was I be-
gotten;
Ere yet my mother's mind subsided from
The serpent, and my sire still mourn'd for
Eden.
That which I am, I am; I did not seek 510
For life, nor did I make myself; but could I
With my own death redeem him from the
dust—
And why not so? let him return to day,
And I lie ghastly! so shall be restored
By God the life to him he loved; and
taken
From me a being I ne'er loved to bear.
Angel. Who shall heal murder? what
is done, is done;
Go forth! fulfil thy days! and be thy deeds
Unlike the last! [*The* ANGEL *disappears.*
Adah. He's gone, let us go forth;
I hear our little Enoch cry within
Our bower.
Cain. Ah! little knows he what he
weeps for! 520
And I who have shed blood cannot shed
tears!
But the four rivers would not cleanse my
soul.
Think'st thou my boy will bear to look on
me?
Adah. If I thought that he would not, I
would——
Cain [*interrupting her*]. No,

No more of threats: we have had too many
   of them: 525
Go to our children; I will follow thee.
   Adah.   I will not leave thee lonely with
   the dead;
Let us depart together.
   Cain.   Oh! thou dead
And everlasting witness! whose unsinking
Blood darkens earth and heaven! what
   thou *now* art   530
I know not! but if *thou* see'st what *I* am,
I think thou wilt forgive him, whom his
   God
Can ne'er forgive, nor his own soul.—
   Farewell!
I must not, dare not touch what I have
   made thee.
I, who sprung from the same womb with
   thee, drain'd   535
The same breast, clasp'd thee often to my
   own,
In fondness brotherly and boyish, I
Can never meet thee more, nor even dare
To do that for thee, which thou shouldst
   have done
For me—compose thy limbs into their
   grave—   540
The first grave yet dug for mortality.
But who hath dug that grave? Oh, earth!
   Oh, earth!
For all the fruits thou hast render'd to
   me, I
Give thee back this. Now for the wilder-
   ness.

[ADAH *stoops down and kisses the body
                 of* ABEL.
   Adah.   A dreary, and an early doom,
   my brother,   545
Has been thy lot! Of all who mourn for
   thee,
I alone must not weep. My office is
Henceforth to dry up tears, and not to shed
   them;
But yet of all who mourn, none mourn like
   me,
Not only for thyself, but him who slew
   thee.   550
Now, Cain! I will divide thy burden with
   thee.
   Cain.   Eastward from Eden will we
   take our way;
'Tis the most desolate, and suits my steps.
   Adah.   Lead! thou shalt be my guide,
   and may our God
Be thine! Now let us carry forth our
   children.   555
   Cain.   And *he* who lieth there was
   childless. I
Have dried the fountain of a gentle race,
Which might have graced his recent mar-
   riage couch,
And might have temper'd this stern blood
   of mine,
Uniting with our children Abel's offspring!
O Abel!   561
   Adah.   Peace be with him!
   Cain.   But with *me!*——
                         [*Exeunt.*

HEAVEN AND EARTH

A MYSTERY

FOUNDED ON THE FOLLOWING PASSAGE IN GENESIS, CHAP. VI. : 'AND IT CAME TO
PASS . . . THAT THE SONS OF GOD SAW THE DAUGHTERS OF MEN THAT THEY WERE
FAIR ; AND THEY TOOK THEM WIVES OF ALL WHICH THEY CHOSE.'

'And woman wailing for her demon lover.'—COLERIDGE.

DRAMATIS PERSONÆ

ANGELS	MEN	WOMEN
SAMIASA.	NOAH AND HIS SONS.	ANAH.
AZAZIEL.	IRAD.	AHOLIBAMAH.
RAPHAEL, THE ARCHANGEL.	JAPHET.	

Chorus of Spirits of the Earth.   Chorus of Mortals.

PART I

SCENE I.—*A woody and mountainous district near Mount Ararat. Time, Midnight.*

Enter ANAH *and* AHOLIBAMAH.

   Anah.   Our father sleeps: it is the hour
   when they
Who love us are accustom'd to descend
Through the deep clouds o'er rocky
   Ararat:—
How my heart beats!

   Aho.   Let us proceed upon
Our invocation.
   Anah.   But the stars are hidden.
I tremble.   6
   Aho.   So do I, but not with fear
Of aught save their delay.
   Anah.   My sister, though
I love Azaziel more than——oh, too much!
What was I going to say? my heart grows
   impious.
   Aho. And where is the impiety of loving
Celestial natures?   10

Anah. But, Aholibamah,
I love our God less since his angel loved
  me:
This cannot be of good; and though I
  know not
That I do wrong, I feel a thousand fears
Which are not ominous of right.
  Aho. Then wed thee 15
Unto some son of clay, and toil and spin!
There's Japhet loves thee well, hath loved
  thee long:
Marry, and bring forth dust!
  Anah. I should have loved
Azaziel not less were he mortal; yet 19
I am glad he is not. I cannot outlive him.
And when I think that his immortal wings
Will one day hover o'er the sepulchre
Of the poor child of clay which so adored
  him,
As he adores the Highest, death becomes
Less terrible; but yet I pity him: 25
His grief will be of ages, or at least
Mine would be such for him, were I the
  seraph,
And he the perishable.
  Aho. Rather say,
That he will single forth some other
  daughter
Of earth, and love her as he once loved
  Anah. 30
  Anah. And if it should be so, and she
  loved him,
Better thus than that he should weep for
  me.
  Aho. If I thought thus of Samiasa's
  love,
All seraph as he is, I'd spurn him from
  me.
But to our invocation!—'Tis the hour. 35
  Anah. Seraph!
      From thy sphere!
Whatever star contain thy glory;
  In the eternal depths of heaven
  Albeit thou watchest with 'the
    seven,' 40
Though through space infinite and
  hoary
Before thy bright wings worlds be
  driven,
      Yet hear!
Oh! think of her who holds thee dear!
And though she nothing is to thee,
Yet think that thou art all to her. 46
  Thou canst not tell,—and never be
  Such pangs decreed to aught save
    me,—
    The bitterness of tears.
  Eternity is in thine years, 50
Unborn, undying beauty in thine eyes;
  With me thou canst not sympathise,
  Except in love, and there thou must
  Acknowledge that more loving
    dust
Ne'er wept beneath the skies. 55

Thou walk'st thy many worlds, thou
  see'st
  The face of him who made thee
    great,
As he hath made me of the least
  Of those cast out from Eden's gate;
      Yet, Seraph dear! 60
      Oh hear!
For thou hast loved me, and I would
  not die
Until I know what I must die in
  knowing,
That thou forget'st in thine eternity
  Her whose heart death could not
    keep from o'erflowing 65
For thee, immortal essence as thou
  art!
Great is their love who love in sin
  and fear;
And such, I feel, are waging in my
  heart
A war unworthy: to an Adamite
  Forgive, my Seraph! that such
    thoughts appear, 70
      For sorrow is our element;
        Delight
An Eden kept afar from sight,
  Though sometimes with our visions
  blent.
      The hour is near 75
Which tells me we are not abandon'd
  quite.—
      Appear! Appear!
        Seraph!
      My own Azaziel! be but here,
And leave the stars to their own light.
  Aho. Samiasa! 81
        Wheresoe'er
Thou rulest in the upper air—
Or warring with the spirits who may
  dare
        Dispute with him 85
Who made all empires, empire; or recall-
  ing
Some wandering star, which shoots
  through the abyss,
  Whose tenants dying, while their world
  is falling,
Share the dim destiny of clay in this;
  Or joining with the inferior cherubim,
  Thou deignest to partake their hymn—
    Samiasa!
I call thee, I await thee, and I love thee.
  Many may worship thee, that will I not:
If that thy spirit down to mine may move
  thee 95
  Descend and share my lot!
  Though I be form'd of clay,
    And thou of beams
  More bright than those of day
    On Eden's streams, 100
  Thine immortality cannot repay
  With love more warm than mine
My love. There is a ray

In me, which, though forbidden yet to
    shine,   104
I feel was lighted at thy God's and thine.
It may be hidden long: death and decay
Our mother Eve bequeath'd us—but
    my heart
Defies it: though this life must pass away,
Is *that* a cause for thee and me to part?
Thou art immortal—so am I: I feel—   110
I feel my immortality o'ersweep
All pains, all tears, all time, all fears, and
    peal,
Like the eternal thunders of the deep,
Into my ears this truth—'Thou liv'st for
    ever!'
        But if it be in joy   115
I know not, nor would know;
That secret rests with the Almighty giver,
Who folds in clouds the fonts of bliss
    and woe.
But thee and me he never can destroy;
Change us he may, but not o'erwhelm;
    we are   120
Of as eternal essence, and must war
With him if he will war with us: with *thee*
I can share all things, even immortal
    sorrow;
For thou hast ventured to share life with
    me,
And shall *I* shrink from thine eternity?
No! though the serpent's sting should
    pierce me thorough,   126
And thou thyself wert like the serpent,
    coil
Around me still! and I will smile,
    And curse thee not; but hold
    Thee in as warm a fold   130
    As——but descend, and prove
    A mortal's love
For an immortal. If the skies contain
More joy than thou canst give and take,
    remain!
  Anah.   Sister! sister! I view them wing-
    ing   135
Their bright way through the parted night.
  Aho. The clouds from off their pinions
    flinging,
As though they bore to-morrow's light.
  Anah. But if our father see the sight!
  Aho. He would but deem it was the
    moon   140
Rising unto some sorcerer's tune
An hour too soon.
  Anah. They come! *he* comes!—
    Azaziel!
  Aho.   Haste
To meet them! Oh! for wings to bear
My spirit, while they hover there,   145
To Samiasa's breast!
  Anah. Lo! they have kindled all the
    west,
Like a returning sunset;—lo!
    On Ararat's late secret crest
    A mild and many-colour'd bow,   150

The remnant of their flashing path,
Now shines! and now, behold! it hath
Return'd to night, as rippling foam,
    Which the leviathan hath lash'd
From his unfathomable home,   155
When sporting on the face of the calm
    deep,
Subsides soon after he again hath dash'd
Down, down, to where the ocean's
    fountains sleep.
  Aho. They have touch'd earth! Samiasa!
  Anah.   My Azaziel!
                       [*Exeunt.*

SCENE II

Enter IRAD *and* JAPHET.

  Irad. Despond not: wherefore wilt
    thou wander thus
To add thy silence to the silent night,
And lift thy tearful eye unto the stars?
They cannot aid thee.
  Japh.   But they soothe me—now
Perhaps she looks upon them as I look.
Methinks a being that is beautiful   6
Becometh more so as it looks on beauty,
The eternal beauty of undying things.
Oh, Anah!
  Irad.   But she loves thee not.
  Japh.   Alas!
  Irad. And proud Aholibamah spurns
    me also.   10
  Japh. I feel for thee too.
  Irad.   Let her keep her pride,
Mine hath enabled me to bear her scorn;
It may be, time too will avenge it.
  Japh.   Canst thou
Find joy in such a thought?
  Irad.   Nor joy nor sorrow.
I loved her well, I would have loved her
    better,   15
Had love been met with love: as 'tis, I
    leave her
To brighter destinies, if so she deems them.
  Japh. What destinies?
  Irad.   I have some cause to think
She loves another.
  Japh.   Anah!
  Irad.   No; her sister.
  Japh. What other?
  Irad.   That I know not; but her air,
If not her words, tells me she loves
    another.   21
  Japh. Ay, but not Anah: she but
    loves her God.
  Irad. Whate'er she loveth, so she loves
    thee not,
What can it profit thee?
  Japh.   True, nothing; but
I love.
  Irad. And so did I.
  Japh.   And now thou lov'st not,
Or think'st thou lov'st not, art thou
    happier?   26

Irad. Yes.

Japh. I pity thee.

Irad. Me! why?

Japh. For being happy,
Deprived of that which makes my
misery.

Irad. I take thy taunt as part of thy
distemper,
And would not feel as thou dost for more
shekels   30
Than all our father's herds would bring,
if weigh'd
Against the metal of the sons of Cain—
The yellow dust they try to barter with us,
As if such useless and discolour'd trash,
The refuse of the earth, could be received
For milk, and wool, and flesh, and fruits,
and all   36
Our flocks and wilderness afford.—Go,
Japhet,
Sigh to the stars, as wolves howl to the
moon—
I must back to my rest.

Japh. And so would I
If I could rest.

Irad. Thou wilt not to our tents then?

Japh. No, Irad; I will to the cavern,
whose   41
Mouth they say opens from the internal
world
To let the inner spirits of the earth
Forth when they walk its surface.

Irad. Wherefore so?
What wouldst thou there?

Japh. Soothe further my sad spirit 45
With gloom as sad: it is a hopeless spot,
And I am hopeless.

Irad. But 'tis dangerous;
Strange sounds and sights have peopled it
with terrors.
I must go with thee.

Japh. Irad, no; believe me
I feel no evil thought, and fear no evil.

Irad. But evil things will be thy foe
the more   51
As not being of them: turn thy steps aside,
Or let mine be with thine.

Japh. No, neither, Irad;
I must proceed alone.

Irad. Then peace be with thee!
[*Exit* IRAD.

Japh. [*solus*]. Peace! I have sought it
where it should be found,   55
In love—with love, too, which perhaps
deserved it;
And, in its stead, a heaviness of heart,
A weakness of the spirit, listless days,
And nights inexorable to sweet sleep,
Have come upon me. Peace! what peace?
the calm   60
Of desolation, and the stillness of
The untrodden forest, only broken by
The sweeping tempest through its groan-
ing boughs;

Such is the sullen or the fitful state
Of my mind overworn. The earth's grown
wicked,   65
And many signs and portents have
proclaim'd
A change at hand, and an o'erwhelming
doom
To perishable beings. Oh, my Anah!
When the dread hour denounced shall
open wide
The fountains of the deep, how mightest
thou   70
Have lain within this bosom, folded from
The elements; this bosom, which in vain
Hath beat for thee, and then will beat more
vainly,
While thine——Oh, God! at least remit to
her
Thy wrath! for she is pure amidst the
failing   75
As a star in the clouds, which cannot
quench,
Although they obscure it for an hour. My
Anah!
How would I have adored thee, but thou
wouldst not;
And still would I redeem thee—see thee
live
When ocean is earth's grave, and, un-
opposed   80
By rock or shallow, the leviathan,
Lord of the shoreless sea and watery
world,
Shall wonder at his boundlessness of
realm.   [*Exit* JAPHET.

Enter NOAH *and* SHEM.

Noah. Where is thy brother Japhet?

Shem. He went forth,
According to his wont, to meet with Irad,
He said; but, as I fear, to bend his steps
Towards Anah's tents, round which he
hovers nightly,
Like a dove round and round its pillaged
nest;
Or else he walks the wild up to the cavern
Which opens to the heart of Ararat.   90

Noah. What doth he there? It is an
evil spot
Upon an earth all evil; for things worse
Than even wicked men resort there: he
Still loves this daughter of a fated race,
Although he could not wed her if she
loved him,   95
And that she doth not. Oh, the unhappy
hearts
Of men! that one of my blood, knowing
well
The destiny and evil of these days,
And that the hour approacheth, should
indulge
In such forbidden yearnings! Lead the
way;   100
He must be sought for!

Shem.   Go not forward, father:
I will seek Japhet.

Noah.   Do not fear for me:
All evil things are powerless on the man
Selected by Jehovah.—Let us on.

Shem. To the tents of the father of the
    sisters?   105

Noah. No: to the cavern of the
    Caucasus.

                    [*Exeunt* NOAH *and* SHEM.

SCENE III.—*The mountains.—A cavern,
    and the rocks of Caucasus.*

Japh. [*solus*]. Ye wilds, that look
    eternal; and thou cave,
Which seem'st unfathomable; and ye
    mountains,
So varied and so terrible in beauty;
Here, in your rugged majesty of rocks
And toppling trees that twine their roots
    with stone   5
In perpendicular places, where the foot
Of man would tremble, could he reach
    them—yes,
Ye look eternal! Yet, in a few days,
Perhaps even hours, ye will be changed,
    rent, hurl'd   9
Before the mass of waters; and yon cave,
Which seems to lead into a lower world,
Shall have its depths search'd by the
    sweeping wave,
And dolphins gambol in the lion's den!
And man—Oh, men! my fellow-beings!
    Who
Shall weep above your universal grave,
Save I? Who shall be left to weep? My
    kinsmen,   16
Alas! what am I better than ye are,
That I must live beyond ye? Where shall be
The pleasant places where I thought of
    Anah
While I had hope? or the more savage
    haunts,   20
Scarce less beloved, where I despair'd for
    her?
And can it be!—Shall yon exulting peak,
Whose glittering top is like a distant star,
Lie low beneath the boiling of the deep?
No more to have the morning sun break
    forth,   25
And scatter back the mists in floating folds
From its tremendous brow? no more to
    have
Day's broad orb drop behind its head at
    even,
Leaving it with a crown of many hues?
No more to be the beacon of the world,
For angels to alight on, as the spot   31
Nearest the stars? And can those words
    '*no more*'
Be meant for thee, for all things, save for us,
And the predestined creeping things
    reserved   34
By my sire to Jehovah's bidding? May

He preserve *them*, and I *not* have the power
To snatch the loveliest of earth's daughters
    from
A doom which even some serpent, with
    his mate,
Shall 'scape to save his kind to be pro-
    long'd,
To hiss and sting through some emerging
    world,   40
Reeking and dank from out the slime,
    whose ooze
Shall slumber o'er the wreck of this, until
The salt morass subside into a sphere
Beneath the sun, and be the monument,
The sole and undistinguish'd sepulchre,
Of yet quick myriads of all life? How
    much   46
Breath will be still'd at once! All-
    beauteous world!
So young, so mark'd out for destruction, I
With a cleft heart look on thee day by day,
And night by night, thy number'd days
    and nights.   50
I cannot save thee, cannot save even her
Whose love had made me love thee more;
    but as
A portion of thy dust, I cannot think
Upon thy coming doom without a feeling
Such as—Oh God! and canst thou—

                            [*He pauses.*

[*A rushing sound from the cavern is
    heard, and shouts of laughter—after-
    wards a Spirit passes.*

Japh.   In the name 55
Of the Most High, what art thou?

Spirit [*laughs*].   Ha! ha! ha!

Japh. By all that earth holds holiest,
    speak!

Spirit [*laughs*].   Ha! ha!

Japh. By the approaching deluge! by
    the earth
Which will be strangled by the ocean! by
The deep which will lay open all her foun-
    tains!   60
The heaven which will convert her clouds
    to seas,
And the Omnipotent who makes and
    crushes!
Thou unknown, terrible, and indistinct,
Yet awful Thing of Shadows, speak to me!
Why dost thou laugh that horrid laugh?

Spirit.   Why weep'st thou? 65

Japh. For earth and all her children.

Spirit.   Ha! ha! ha!

                            [*Spirit vanishes.*

Japh. How the fiend mocks the
    tortures of a world,
The coming desolation of an orb,
On which the sun shall rise and warm no
    life!
How the earth sleeps! and all that in it is
Sleep too upon the very eve of death! 71
Why should they wake to meet it? What
    are here,

549

Which look like death in life, and speak
 like things
Born ere this dying world? They come like
 clouds!
  [*Various Spirits pass from the cavern.*
Spirit. Rejoice!   75
  The abhorred race
Which could not keep in Eden their high
 place,
  But listen'd to the voice
Of knowledge without power,
  Are nigh the hour   80
   Of death!
Not slow, not single, not by sword, nor
 sorrow,
Nor years, nor heart-break, nor Time's
 sapping motion,
Shall they drop off. Behold their last to-
 morrow!
  Earth shall be ocean! 85
   And no breath,
Save of the winds, be on the unbounded
 wave!
 Angels shall tire their wings, but find no
  spot:
Not even a rock from out the liquid grave
  Shall lift its point to save, 90
Or show the place where strong Despair
 hath died,
After long looking o'er the ocean wide
 For the expected ebb which cometh not:
  All shall be void,
   Destroy'd! 95
Another element shall be the lord
Of life, and the abhorr'd
Children of dust be quench'd; and of each
 hue
Of earth nought left but the unbroken blue;
 And of the variegated mountain 100
  Shall nought remain
  Unchanged, or of the level plain;
 Cedar and pine shall lift their tops in
  vain:
All merged within the universal foun-
 tain,
Man, earth, and fire, shall die, 105
  And sea and sky
Look vast and lifeless in the eternal eye.
  Upon the foam
 Who shall erect a home?
Japh. [*coming forward*]. My sire! 110
  Earth's seed shall not expire;
  Only the evil shall be put away
   From day.
Avaunt! ye exulting demons of the
 waste:
 Who howl your hideous joy 115
When God destroys whom you dare not
 destroy;
  Hence! haste!
 Back to your inner caves!
 Until the waves
Shall search you in your secret place,
 And drive your sullen race 121

Forth, to be roll'd upon the tossing winds,
 In restless wretchedness along all
 space!
Spirit. Son of the saved! 124
 When thou and thine have braved
 The wide and warring element;
 When the great barrier of the deep is rent,
Shall thou and thine be good or happy?—
  No!
Thy new world and new race shall be of
 woe—
 Less goodly in their aspect, in their
  years 130
  Less than the glorious giants, who
  Yet walk the world in pride,
The Sons of Heaven by many a mortal
 bride.
Thine shall be nothing of the past, save
 tears.
  And art thou not ashamed 135
   Thus to survive,
  And eat, and drink, and wive?
With a base heart so far subdued and
 tamed,
As even to hear this wide destruction
 named,
Without such grief and courage, as should
 rather 140
 Bid thee await the world-dissolving wave,
Than seek a shelter with thy favour'd
 father,
 And build thy city o'er the drown'd
 earth's grave?
  Who would outlive their kind,
  Except the base and blind? 145
  Mine
  Hateth thine
As of a different order in the sphere,
  But not our own.
There is not one who hath not left a
 throne 150
Vacant in heaven to dwell in darkness
 here,
Rather than see his mates endure alone.
  Go, wretch! and give
A life like thine to other wretches—live!
 And when the annihilating waters roar
  Above what they have done,
 Envy the giant patriarchs then no more,
And scorn thy sire as the surviving one!
  Thyself for being his son!
Chorus of Spirits issuing from the cavern.
  Rejoice! 160
 No more the human voice
Shall vex our joys in middle air
  With prayer;
  No more
  Shall they adore; 165
And we, who ne'er for ages have adored
 The prayer-exacting Lord,
To whom the omission of a sacrifice
  Is vice;
We, we shall view the deep's salt sources
 pour'd 170

Until one element shall do the work
   Of all in chaos; until they,
  The creatures proud of their poor clay,
Shall perish, and their bleached bones
   shall lurk
In caves, in dens, in clefts of mountains,
   where   175
The deep shall follow to their latest lair;
Where even the brutes, in their despair,
Shall cease to prey on man and on each
   other,
And the striped tiger shall lie down to die
Beside the lamb, as though he were his
   brother;   180
  Till all things shall be as they were,
Silent and uncreated, save the sky:
   While a brief truce
Is made with Death, who shall forbear
The little remnant of the past creation,
  To generate new nations for his use;
This remnant, floating o'er the undulation
Of the subsiding deluge, from its slime,
When the hot sun hath baked the reeking
   soil
Into a world, shall give again to Time
New beings—years, diseases, sorrow,
   crime—   191
With all companionship of hate and toil,
   Until——

Japh. [*interrupting them*]. The eternal
   Will
Shall deign to expound this dream
   Of good and evil; and redeem 195
     Unto himself all times, all things;
     And, gather'd under his almighty
       wings,
       Abolish hell!
   And to the expiated Earth
   Restore the beauty of her birth, 200
     Her Eden in an endless paradise,
   Where man no more can fall as once
   he fell,
   And even the very demons shall do
   well!

Spirits. And when shall take effect this
   wondrous spell?
Japh. When the Redeemer cometh;
   first in pain,   205
     And then in glory.
Spirit. Meantime still struggle in the
   mortal chain,
     Till Earth wax hoary:
War with yourselves, and hell, and heaven,
   in vain,
     Until the clouds look gory 210
With the blood reeking from each battle-
   plain;
New times, new climes, new arts, new
   men; but still,
The same old tears, old crimes, and oldest
   ill,
Shall be amongst your race in different
   forms;
     But the same moral storms 215

Shall oversweep the future, as the waves
In a few hours the glorious giants' graves.

Chorus of Spirits.
   Brethren, rejoice!
     Mortal, farewell!   219
Hark! hark! already we can hear the voice
   Of growing ocean's gloomy swell;
   The winds, too, plume their piercing
   wings;
   The clouds have nearly fill'd their
   springs;
The fountains of the great deep shall be
   broken,
   And heaven set wide her windows;
   while mankind   225
View, unacknowledged, each tremendous
   token—
   Still, as they were from the beginning,
   blind.
   We hear the sound they cannot hear,
   The mustering thunders of the threat-
     ening sphere;
   Yet a few hours their coming is
   delay'd;   230
   Their flashing banners, folded still on
   high,
     Yet undisplay'd,
   Save to the Spirit's all-pervading eye.
   Howl! howl! oh Earth!
Thy death is nearer than thy recent birth;
Tremble, ye mountains, soon to shrink
   below   236
     The ocean's overflow!
The wave shall break upon your cliffs;
   and shells,
The little shells, of ocean's least things be
Deposed where now the eagle's offspring
   dwells—   240
   How shall he shriek o'er the remorseless
   sea!
And call his nestlings up with fruitless yell,
Unanswer'd, save by the encroaching
   swell;—
While man shall long in vain for his broad
   wings,
   The wings which could not save:—
Where could he rest them, while the whole
   space brings   246
Nought to his eye beyond the deep, his
   grave?
     Brethren, rejoice!
And loudly lift each superhuman voice—
     All die,   250
Save the slight remnant of Seth's seed—
   The seed of Seth,
Exempt for future sorrow's sake from
   death,
   But of the sons of Cain
     None shall remain;   255
   And all his goodly daughters
Must lie beneath the desolating waters;
Or, floating upward, with their long hair laid
Along the wave, the cruel heaven upbraid,

Which would not spare 260
Beings even in death so fair.
It is decreed,
All die!
And to the universal human cry
The universal silence shall succeed! 265
Fly, brethren, fly!
But still rejoice!
We fell!
They fall!
So perish all 270
These petty foes of Heaven who shrink
from hell!

[*The Spirits disappear, soaring upwards.*
Japh. [*solus*]. God hath proclaim'd
the destiny of earth;
My father's ark of safety hath announced it;
The very demons shriek it from their
caves;
The scroll of Enoch prophesied it long
In silent books, which, in their silence,
say 276
More to the mind than thunder to the ear:
And yet men listen'd not, nor listen; but
Walk darkling to their doom; which,
though so nigh,
Shakes them no more in their dim dis-
belief, 280
Than their last cries shall shake the
Almighty purpose,
Or deaf obedient ocean, which fulfils it.
No sign yet hangs its banner in the air;
The clouds are few, and of their wonted
texture; 284
The sun will rise upon the earth's last day
As on the fourth day of creation, when
God said unto him, 'Shine!' and he broke
forth
Into the dawn, which lighted not the yet
Unform'd forefather of mankind—but
roused
Before the human orison the earlier 290
Made and far sweeter voices of the birds,
Which in the open firmament of heaven
Have wings like angels, and like them
salute
Heaven first each day before the Adam-
ites:
Their matins now draw nigh—the east is
kindling— 295
And they will sing! and day will break!
Both near,
So near the awful close! For these must
drop
Their outworn pinions on the deep; and
day,
After the bright course of a few brief
morrows,—
Ay, day will rise; but upon what?—a
chaos, 300
Which were day; and which, renew'd,
makes time
Nothing! for, without life, what are the
hours?

No more to dust than is eternity
Unto Jehovah, who created both.
Without him, even eternity would be
A void: without man, time, as made for
man, 306
Dies with man, and is swallow'd in that
deep
Which has no fountain; as his race will be
Devour'd by that which drowns his infant
world.—
What have we here? Shapes of both earth
and air? 310
No—*all* of heaven, they are so beautiful.
I cannot trace their features; but their
forms,
How lovelily they move along the side
Of the grey mountain, scattering its mist!
And after the swart savage spirits, whose
Infernal immortality pour'd forth 316
Their impious hymn of triumph, they shall
be
Welcome as Eden. It may be they come
To tell me the reprieve of our young
world,
For which I have so often pray'd—They
come! 320
Anah! oh, God! and with her——

Enter SAMIASA, AZAZIEL, ANAH, *and*
AHOLIBAMAH.

Anah.   Japhet!
Sam.   Lo!
A son of Adam!
Aza.   What doth the earth-
born here,
While all his race are slumbering?
Japh.   Angel! what
Dost thou on earth when thou shouldst be
on high?
Aza. Know'st thou not, or forgett'st
thou, that a part 325
Of our great function is to guard thine
earth?
Japh. But all good angels have for-
saken earth,
Which is condemn'd; nay, even the evil fly
The approaching chaos. Anah! Anah! my
In vain, and long, and still to be, beloved!
Why walk'st thou with this spirit, in those
hours 331
When no good spirit longer lights below?
Anah. Japhet, I cannot answer thee;
yet, yet
Forgive me——
Japh. May the Heaven, which soon no
more
Will pardon, do so! for thou art greatly
tempted. 335
Aho. Back to thy tents, insulting son
of Noah!
We know thee not.
Japh. The hour may come when thou
May'st know me better; and thy sister
know

552

Me still the same which I have ever been.
   Sam. Son of the patriarch, who hath
     ever been   340
Upright before his God, whate'er thy gifts,
And thy words seem of sorrow, mix'd with
    wrath,
How have Azaziel, or myself, brought on
    thee
Wrong?
   Japh. Wrong! the greatest of all
wrongs; but thou
Say'st well; though she be dust, I did not,
    could not,   345
Deserve her. Farewell, Anah! I have said
That word so often! but now say it, ne'er
To be repeated. Angel! or whate'er
Thou art, or must be soon, hast thou the
    power   349
To save this beautiful—*these* beautiful
Children of Cain?
   Aza.   From what?
   Japh.   And is it so,
That ye too know not? Angels! angels! ye
Have shared man's sin, and, it may be,
    now must
Partake his punishment; or, at the least,
My sorrow.
   Sam.   Sorrow! I ne'er thought till
    now   355
To hear an Adamite speak riddles to me.
   Japh. And hath not the Most High
    expounded them?
Then ye are lost, as they are lost.
   Aho.   So be it!
If they love as they are loved, they will not
    shrink
More to be mortal, than I would to dare
An immortality of agonies   361
With Samiasa!
   Anah.   Sister! sister! speak not
Thus.
   Aza. Fearest thou, my Anah?
   Anah.   Yes, for thee:
I would resign the greater remnant of
This little life of mine, before one hour
Of thine eternity should know a pang.
   Japh. It is for *him*, then! for the seraph
    thou
Hast left me! That is nothing, if thou hast
    not
Left thy God too! for unions like to these,
Between a mortal and an immortal, can-
    not   370
Be happy or be hallow'd. We are sent
Upon the earth to toil and die; and they
Are made to minister on high unto
The Highest: but if he can *save* thee, soon
The hour will come in which celestial aid
Alone can do so.
   Anah.   Ah! he speaks of death.
   Sam. Of death to *us!* and those who
    are with us!
But that the man seems full of sorrow, I
Could smile.

   Japh. I grieve not for myself, nor fear;
I am safe, not for my own deserts, but
    those   380
Of a well-doing sire, who hath been found
Righteous enough to save his children.
    Would
His power was greater of redemption! or
That by exchanging my own life for hers,
Who could alone have made mine happy,
    she,   385
The last and loveliest of Cain's race, could
    share
The ark which shall receive a remnant of
The seed of Seth!
   Aho.   And dost thou think that we,
With Cain's, the eldest born of Adam's,
    blood
Warm in our veins,—strong Cain! who
    was begotten   390
In Paradise,—would mingle with Seth's
    children?
Seth, the last offspring of old Adam's
    dotage?
No, not to save all earth, were earth in
    peril!
Our race hath always dwelt apart from thine
From the beginning, and shall do so ever.
   Japh. I did not speak to thee, Aholi-
    bamah!   396
Too much of the forefather whom thou
    vauntest
Has come down in that haughty blood
    which springs
From him who shed the first, and that a
    brother's!   399
But thou, my Anah! let me call thee mine,
Albeit thou art not; 'tis a word I cannot
Part with, although I must from thee. My
    Anah!
Thou who dost rather make me dream that
    Abel
Had left a daughter, whose pure pious race
Survived in thee, so much unlike thou art
The rest of the stern Cainites, save in
    beauty,   406
For all of them are fairest in their favour——
   Aho. [*interrupting him*]. And wouldst
    thou have her like our father's foe
In mind, in soul? If *I* partook thy thought,
And dream'd that aught of *Abel* was in
    her!—   410
Get thee hence, son of Noah; thou makest
    strife.
   Japh. Offspring of Cain, thy father did
    so!
   Aho.   But
He slew not Seth: and what hast thou to do
With other deeds between his God and
    him?
   Japh. Thou speakest well: his God
    hath judged him, and   415
I had not named his deed, but that thyself
Didst seem to glory in him, nor to shrink
From what he had done.

Aho. He was our fathers' father;
The eldest born of man, the strongest,
    bravest,
And most enduring:—Shall I blush for
    him   420
From whom we had our being? Look
    upon
Our race; behold their stature and their
    beauty,
Their courage, strength, and length of
    days——
    Japh. They are number'd.
    Aho. Be it so! but while yet their hours
    endure,
I glory in my brethren and our fathers.
    Japh. My sire and race but glory in
    their God,   426
Anah! and thou?——
    Anah. Whate'er our God decrees,
The God of Seth, as Cain, I must obey,
And will endeavour patiently to obey.
But could I dare to pray in his dread hour
Of universal vengeance (if such should be),
It would not be to live, alone exempt
Of all my house. My sister! oh, my sister!
What were the world, or other worlds, or
    all
The brightest future, without the sweet
    past—   435
Thy love, my father's, all the life, and all
The things which sprang up with me, like
    the stars,
Making my dim existence radiant with
Soft lights which were not mine? Aholi-
    bamah!
Oh! if there should be mercy—seek it,
    find it: 440
I abhor death, because that thou must die.
    Aho. What, hath this dreamer, with
    his father's ark,
The bugbear he hath built to scare the
    world,
Shaken *my* sister? Are *we* not the loved
Of seraphs? and if we were not, must we
Cling to a son of Noah for our lives? 446
Rather than thus——But the enthusiast
    dreams
The worst of dreams, the fantasies
    engender'd
By hopeless love and heated vigils. Who
Shall shake these solid mountains, this
    firm earth,   450
And bid those clouds and waters take a
    shape
Distinct from that which we and all our
    sires
Have seen them wear on their eternal way?
Who shall do this?
    Japh. He whose one word produced
    them.
    Aho. Who *heard* that word?
    Japh. The universe, which leap'd
To life before it. Ah! smilest thou still in
    scorn?   456

Turn to thy seraphs: if they attest it not,
They are none.
    Sam. Aholibamah, own thy God!
    Aho. I have ever hail'd our Maker,
    Samiasa,
As thine, and mine: a God of love, not
    sorrow.   460
    Japh. Alas! what else is love but
    sorrow? Even
He who made earth in love had soon to
    grieve
Above its first and best inhabitants.
    Aho. 'Tis said so.
    Japh. It is even so.

Enter NOAH *and* SHEM.

    Noah. Japhet! What
Dost thou here with these children of the
    wicked?   465
Dread'st thou not to partake their coming
    doom?
    Japh. Father, it cannot be a sin to seek
To save an earth-born being; and behold,
These are not of the sinful, since they have
The fellowship of angels.
    Noah. These are they, then, 470
Who leave the throne of God, to take
    them wives
From out the race of Cain; the sons of
    heaven,
Who seek earth's daughters for their
    beauty?
    Aza. Patriarch!
Thou hast said it.
    Noah. Woe, woe, woe to such com-
    munion!
Has not God made a barrier between
    earth   475
And heaven, and limited each, kind to kind?
    Sam. Was not man made in high
    Jehovah's image?
Did God not love what he had made? And
    what
Do we but imitate and emulate
His love unto created love?
    Noah. I am 480
But man, and was not made to judge man-
    kind,
Far less the sons of God; but as our God
Has deign'd to commune with me, and
    reveal
His judgments, I reply, that the descent
Of seraphs from their everlasting seat
Unto a perishable and perishing,   486
Even on the very *eve* of *perishing*, world,
Cannot be good.
    Aza. What! though it were
    to save?
    Noah. Not ye in all your glory can
    redeem
What he who made you glorious hath con-
    demn'd.   490
Were your immortal mission safety,
    'twould

Be general, not for two, though beautiful;
And beautiful they are, but not the less
Condemn'd.
  Japh. Oh, father! say it not.
  Noah.   Son! son!
If that thou wouldst avoid their doom,
    forget   495
That they exist: they soon shall cease to be,
While thou shalt be the sire of a new
    world,
And better.
  Japh.   Let me die with *this*, and
    them!
  Noah. Thou *shouldst* for such a
    thought, but shalt not; he
Who *can*, redeems thee.
  Sam.   And why him and thee, 500
More than what he, thy son, prefers to
    both?
  Noah. Ask him who made thee greater
    than myself
And mine, but not less subject to his own
Almightiness. And lo! his mildest and
Least to be tempted messenger appears!

Enter RAPHAEL *the Archangel.*

  Raph.   Spirits!
    Whose seat is near the throne,
        What do ye here?
Is thus a seraph's duty to be shown
    Now that the hour is near   510
    When earth must be alone?
        Return!
        Adore and burn
In glorious homage with the elected
    'seven.'
    Your place is heaven.   515
  Sam. Raphael!
The first and fairest of the sons of God,
    How long hath this been law,
That earth by angels must be left untrod?
    Earth! which oft saw   520
Jehovah's footsteps not disdain her sod!
The world he loved, and made
For love; and oft have we obey'd
His frequent mission with delighted
    pinions:
Adoring him in his least works dis-
    play'd;   525
Watching this youngest star of his
    dominions;
And, as the latest birth of his great word,
Eager to keep it worthy of our Lord.
    Why is thy brow severe?
And wherefore speak'st thou of destruc-
    tion near?   530
  Raph. Had Samiasa and Azaziel been
In their true place, with the angelic choir,
    Written in fire
    They would have seen
    Jehovah's late decree,   535
And not inquired their Maker's breath of
    me:
    But ignorance must ever be

        A part of sin;
And even the spirits' knowledge shall
    grow less
    As they wax proud within; 540
For Blindness is the first-born of Excess.
    When all good angels left the world, ye
    stay'd,
Stung with strange passions, and debased
    By mortal feelings for a mortal maid:
But ye are pardon'd thus far, and
    replaced   545
With your pure equals. Hence! away!
    away!
    Or stay,
    And lose eternity by that delay!
  Aza. And thou! if earth be thus for-
    bidden
    In the decree   550
    To us until this moment hidden,
    Dost thou not err as we
    In being here?
  Raph. I came to call ye back to your
    fit sphere,
    In the great name and at the word of
    God.   555
Dear, dearest in themselves, and scarce
    less dear
    That which I came to do: till now we trod
Together the eternal space; together
Let us still walk the stars. True, earth
    must die!
Her race, return'd into her womb, must
    wither,   560
    And much which she inherits: but oh!
    why
    Cannot this earth be made, or be
    destroy'd,
Without involving ever some vast void
In the immortal ranks? immortal still
    In their immeasurable forfeiture. 565
Our brother Satan fell; his burning will
    Rather than longer worship dared
    endure!
    But ye who still are pure!
Seraphs! less mighty than that mightiest
    one,
    Think how he was undone!   570
And think if tempting man can com-
    pensate
For heaven desired too late?
    Long have I warr'd,
    Long must I war
    With him who deem'd it hard 575
    To be created, and to acknowledge
    him
    Who midst the cherubim
Made him as suns to a dependent star,
Leaving the archangels at his right hand
    dim.
    I loved him—beautiful he was: oh,
    heaven   580
Save *his* who made, what beauty and what
    power
Was ever like to Satan's! Would the hour

In which he fell could ever be forgiven!
The wish is impious: but, oh ye!
Yet undestroy'd, be warn'd! Eternity
   With him, or with his God, is in your
     choice! 586
He hath not tempted you; he cannot tempt
The angels, from his further snares
   exempt:
But man hath listen'd to his voice,
And ye to woman's—beautiful she is,
The serpent's voice less subtle than her
   kiss. 591
The snake but vanquish'd dust; but she
   will draw
A second host from heaven, to break
   heaven's law.
       Yet, yet, oh fly!
      Ye cannot die; 595
      But they
      Shall pass away,
While ye shall fill with shrieks the upper sky
   For perishable clay,
Whose memory in your immortality 600
   Shall long outlast the sun which gave
   them day.
Think how your essence differeth from
   theirs
In all but suffering! why partake
The agony to which they must be heirs—
Born to be plough'd with years, and sown
   with cares, 605
   And reap'd by Death, lord of the human
   soil?
Even had their days been left to toil their
   path
Through time to dust, unshorten'd by
   God's wrath,
   Still they are Evil's prey and Sorrow's
   spoil.
Aho.   Let them fly! 610
I hear the voice which says that all must
   die,
Sooner than our white-bearded patriarchs
   died;
      And that on high
      An ocean is prepared,
      While from below 615
The deep shall rise to meet heaven's over-
   flow.
      Few shall be spared,
It seems; and, of that few, the race of Cain
Must lift their eyes to Adam's God in vain.
      Sister! since it is so, 620
      And the eternal Lord
      In vain would be implored
   For the remission of one hour of woe,
Let us resign even what we have adored,
And meet the wave, as we would meet the
   sword, 625
   If not unmoved, yet undismay'd,
And wailing less for us than those who
   shall
Survive in mortal or immortal thrall,
   And, when the fatal waters are allay'd,

Weep for the myriads who can weep no
   more. 630
Fly, seraphs! to your own eternal shore,
Where winds nor howl nor waters roar.
      Our portion is to die,
     And yours to live for ever:
But which is best, a dead eternity, 635
Or living, is but known to the great Giver.
     Obey him, as we shall obey;
I would not keep this life of mine in clay
     An hour beyond his will; 639
Nor see ye lose a portion of his grace,
For all the mercy which Seth's race
     Find still.
     Fly!
And as your pinions bear ye back to
   heaven,
Think that my love still mounts with thee
   on high, 645
      Samiasa!
And if I look up with a tearless eye,
'Tis that an angel's bride disdains to
   weep,—
Farewell! Now rise, inexorable deep!
Anah.   And must we die? 650
      And must I lose thee too,
      Azaziel?
     Oh, my heart! my heart!
      Thy prophecies were true!
   And yet thou wert so happy too!
The blow, though not unlook'd for, falls
   as new: 656
      But yet depart!
      Ah! why?
   Yet let me not retain thee—fly!
My pangs can be but brief; but thine
   would be 660
Eternal, if repulsed from heaven for me.
   Too much already hast thou deign'd
     To one of Adam's race!
Our doom is sorrow: not to us alone,
But to the spirits who have not disdain'd
To love us, cometh anguish with disgrace.
The first who taught us knowledge hath
   been hurl'd
   From his once archangelic throne
   Into some unknown world:
     And thou, Azaziel! No— 670
     Thou shalt not suffer woe
For me. Away! nor weep!
   Thou canst not weep; but yet
   May'st suffer more, not weeping: then
   forget
Her, whom the surges of the all-strangling
   deep 675
Can bring no pang like this. Fly! fly!
Being gone, 'twill be less difficult to die.
Japh. Oh, say not so!
Father! and thou, archangel, thou!
Surely celestial mercy lurks below 680
   That pure severe serenity of brow:
   Let them not meet this sea without a
   shore,
Save in our ark, or let me be no more!

Noah. Peace, child of passion, peace!
If not within thy heart, yet with thy tongue
    Do God no wrong!   686
Live as he wills it—die, when he ordains,
A righteous death, unlike the seed of
    Cain's.
    Cease, or be sorrowful in silence; cease
To weary Heaven's ear with thy selfish
    plaint.   690
    Wouldst thou have God commit a sin
        for thee?
                    Such would it be
                    To alter his intent
For a mere mortal sorrow. Be a man!
And bear what Adam's race must bear,
    and can.   695
Japh. Ay, father! but when they are
    gone,
        And we are all alone,
Floating upon the azure desert, and
The depth beneath us hides our own dear
    land,
    And dearer, silent friends and brethren,
        all   700
Buried in its immeasurable breast,
Who, who, our tears, our shrieks, shall
    then command?
Can we in desolation's peace have rest?
    Oh God! be thou a God, and spare
        Yet while 'tis time;   705
    Renew not Adam's fall:
Mankind were then but twain,
But they are numerous now as are the waves
    And the tremendous rain,
Whose drops shall be less thick than
    would their graves,   710
Were graves permitted to the seed of
    Cain.
Noah. Silence, vain boy! each word of
    thine's a crime,
Angel! forgive this stripling's fond despair.
Raph. Seraphs! these mortals speak
    in passion: Ye!
Who are, or should be, passionless and
    pure,   715
May now return with me.
Sam.   It may not be:
We have chosen, and will endure.
Raph. Say'st thou?
Aza.   He hath said it, and I say,
    Amen!
Raph.   Again!
        Then from this hour,   720
    Shorn as ye are of all celestial power,
And aliens from your God,
                    Farewell!
Japh. Alas! where shall they dwell?
Hark, hark! Deep sounds, and deeper still,
    Are howling from the mountain's
        bosom: 726
There's not a breath of wind upon the hill,
    Yet quivers every leaf, and drops each
        blossom:
Earth groans as if beneath a heavy load.

Noah. Hark, hark! the sea-birds cry!
In clouds they overspread the lurid sky,
And hover round the mountain, where
    before
    Never a white wing, wetted by the wave,
        Yet dared to soar,
    Even when the waters wax'd too fierce
        to brave.   735
    Soon it shall be their only shore,
        And then, no more!
Japh.   The sun! the sun!
He riseth, but his better light is gone;
        And a black circle, bound   740
        His glaring disk around,
Proclaims earth's last of summer days hath
    shone!
    The clouds return into the hues of
        night,
Save where their brazen-colour'd edges
    streak
The verge where brighter morns were wont
    to break.   745
Noah. And lo! yon flash of light,
The distant thunder's harbinger, appears!
    It cometh! hence, away!
Leave to the elements their evil prey!
Hence to where our all-hallow'd ark up-
    rears   750
        Its safe and wreckless sides!
Japh. Oh, father, stay!
Leave not my Anah to the swallowing tides!
Noah. Must we not leave all life to
    such? Begone!
Japh.   Not I.   755
Noah.   Then die
        With them!
How darest thou look on that prophetic
    sky,
And seek to save what all things now
    condemn,
        In overwhelming unison   760
        With just Jehovah's wrath!
Japh. Can rage and justice join in the
    same path?
Noah. Blasphemer!   darest   thou
    murmur even now?
Raph. Patriarch, be still a father!
    smooth thy brow:
Thy son, despite his folly, shall not sink:
He knows not what he says, yet shall not
    drink   766
    With sobs the salt foam of the swelling
        waters:
But be, when passion passeth, good as
    thou,
    Nor perish like heaven's children with
        man's daughters.
Aho. The tempest cometh; heaven
    and earth unite   770
    For the annihilation of all life.
        Unequal is the strife
Between our strength and the Eternal
    Might!

Sam. But ours is with thee; we will
  bear ye far
To some untroubled star,   775
Where thou, and Anah, shalt partake our
  lot:
And if thou dost not weep for thy lost
  earth,
Our forfeit heaven shall also be forgot.
Anah. Oh! my dear father's tents, my
  place of birth,
And mountains, land, and woods! when
  ye are not,   780
Who shall dry up my tears?
Aza.   Thy spirit-lord.
Fear not; though we are shut from heaven,
Yet much is ours, whence we can not be
  driven.
Raph. Rebel! thy words are wicked,
  as thy deeds
Shall henceforth be but weak: the flaming
  sword,   785
Which chased the first-born out of
  Paradise,
Still flashes in the angelic hands.
Aza. It cannot slay us: threaten dust
  with death,
And talk of weapons unto that which
  bleeds.
What are thy swords in our immortal
  eyes?   790
Raph. The moment cometh to ap-
  prove thy strength;
And learn at length
How vain to war with what thy God com-
  mands:
Thy former force was in thy faith.

Enter Mortals, flying for refuge.
Chorus of Mortals.

The heavens and earth are mingling—
  God! oh God!   795
What have we done? Yet spare!
Hark! even the forest beasts howl forth
  their prayer!
The dragon crawls from out his den,
To herd, in terror, innocent with men;
And the birds scream their agony through
  air.   800
Yet, yet, Jehovah! yet withdraw thy rod
Of wrath, and pity thine own world's
  despair!
Hear not man only but all nature plead!
Raph. Farewell, thou earth! ye
  wretched sons of clay,   804
I cannot, must not, aid you. 'Tis decreed!
              [*Exit* RAPHAEL.
Japh. Some clouds sweep on as
  vultures for their prey,
While others, fix'd as rocks, await the
  word
At which their wrathful vials shall be
  pour'd.
No azure more shall robe the firmament,

Nor spangled stars be glorious: Death
  hath risen: 810
In the sun's place a pale and ghastly glare
Hath wound itself around the dying air.
Aza. Come, Anah! quit this chaos-
  founded prison,
To which the elements again repair,
To turn it into what it was: beneath   815
The shelter of these wings thou shalt be safe,
As was the eagle's nestling once within
Its mother's.—Let the coming chaos chafe
With all its elements! Heed not their din!
A brighter world than this, where thou
  shalt breathe   820
Ethereal life, will we explore:
These darken'd clouds are not the only skies.
  [AZAZIEL *and* SAMIASA *fly off and dis-
    appear with* ANAH *and* AHOLIBAMAH.
Japh. They are gone! They have dis-
  appear'd amidst the roar
Of the forsaken world; and never more,
Whether they live, or die with all earth's
  life,   825
Now near its last, can aught restore
Anah unto these eyes.

Chorus of Mortals.

Oh son of Noah! mercy on thy kind!
What! wilt thou leave us all—all—*all*
  behind?
While safe amidst the elemental strife,
Thou sitt'st within thy guarded ark?   831
  A Mother [*offering her infant to* JAPHET].
    Oh let this child embark!
I brought him forth in woe,
    But thought it joy
  To see him to my bosom clinging so.
    Why was he born?   836
      What hath he done—
      My unwean'd son—
To move Jehovah's wrath or scorn?
What is there in this milk of mine, that
  death   840
  Should stir all heaven and earth up to
    destroy
            My boy?
And roll the waters o'er his placid breath?
Save him, thou seed of Seth!
Or cursed be—with him who made   845
  Thee and thy race, for which we are
    betray'd!
Japh. Peace! 'tis no hour for curses,
  but for prayer!

Chorus of Mortals.

  For prayer!!!
    And where
      Shall prayer ascend,   850
When the swoln clouds unto the moun-
  tains bend
      And burst,
And gushing oceans every barrier rend,
  Until the very deserts know no thirst?
      Accursed   855

Be he who made thee and thy sire!
We deem our curses vain; we must expire;
    But as we know the worst,
Why should our hymn be raised, our knees
        be bent
Before the implacable Omnipotent,   860
Since we must fall the same?
If he hath made earth, let it be his shame,
    To make a world for torture.—Lo! they
        come,
The loathsome waters, in their rage!
And with their roar make wholesome
        nature dumb!   865
    The forests' trees (coeval with the hour
When Paradise upsprung,
    Ere Eve gave Adam knowledge for her
        dower,
Or Adam his first hymn of slavery sung),
    So massy, vast, yet green in their old
        age,   870
        Are overtopp'd,
Their summer blossoms by the surges
        lopp'd,
Which rise, and rise, and rise.
Vainly we look up to the lowering skies—
    They meet the seas,   875
And shut out God from our beseeching
    eyes.
Fly, son of Noah, fly! and take thine
    ease,
In thine allotted ocean-tent;
And view, all floating o'er the element,
The corpses of the world of thy young
    days: 880
        Then to Jehovah raise
        Thy song of praise!
A Mortal.   Blessed are the dead
        Who die in the Lord!
And though the waters be o'er earth out-
        spread,   885
        Yet, as *his* word,
        Be the decree adored!
He gave me life—he taketh but
    The breath which is his own:
And though these eyes should be for ever
    shut,   890
    Nor longer this weak voice before his
        throne
Be heard in supplicating tone,
        Still blessed be the Lord,
        For what is past,
        For that which is: 895
        For all are his,
        From first to last—

Time, space, eternity, life, death—
    The vast known and immeasurable un-
        known.
He made, and can unmake;   900
And shall *I*, for a little gasp of breath,
        Blaspheme and groan?
No; let me die, as I have lived, in faith,
Nor quiver, though the universe may
    quake!

Chorus of Mortals.

        Where shall we fly?   905
        Not to the mountains high;
For now their torrents rush, with double
        roar,
To meet the ocean, which, advancing
        still,
Already grasps each drowning hill,
Nor leaves an unsearch'd cave.   910

Enter a Woman.

Woman.   Oh, save me, save!
Our valley is no more:
    My father and my father's tent,
My brethren and my brethren's herds,
    The pleasant trees that o'er our noon-
        day bent,   915
And sent forth evening songs from
        sweetest birds,
The little rivulet which freshen'd all
        Our pastures green,
        No more are to be seen.
When to the mountain cliff I climb'd this
        morn,   920
    I turn'd to bless the spot,
And not a leaf appear'd about to fall;—
    And now they are not!
Why was I born?
Japh.   To die! in youth to die!
And happier in that doom,   925
Than to behold the universal tomb,
            Which I
Am thus condemn'd to weep above in
    vain.
Why, when all perish, why must I remain?
    [*The waters rise; Men fly in every di-
    rection; many are overtaken by the
    waves; the Chorus of Mortals dis-
    perses in search of safety up the
    mountains: Japhet remains upon a
    rock, while the Ark floats towards him
    in the distance.*

WERNER; OR, THE INHERITANCE:

A TRAGEDY

TO

THE ILLUSTRIOUS GOETHE,

BY ONE OF HIS HUMBLEST ADMIRERS, THIS TRAGEDY IS DEDICATED.

PREFACE

THE following drama is taken entirely from the 'German's Tale, Kruitzner', published many years ago in 'Lee's Canterbury Tales', written (I believe) by two sisters, of whom one furnished only this story and another, both of which are considered superior to the remainder of the collection. I have adopted the characters, plan, and even the language of many parts of this story. Some of the characters are modified or altered, a few of the names changed, and one character (Ida of Stralenheim) added by myself: but in the rest the original is chiefly followed. When I was young (about fourteen, I think), I first read this tale, which made a deep impression upon me; and may, indeed, be said to contain the germ of much that I have since written. I am not sure that it ever was very popular; or, at any rate, its popularity has since been eclipsed by that of other great writers in the same department. But I have generally found that those who *had* read it, agreed with me in their estimate of the singular power of mind and conception which it developes. I should also add *conception,* rather than execution; for the story might, perhaps, have been developed with greater advantage. Amongst those whose opinions agreed with mine upon this story, I could mention some very high names: but it is not necessary, nor indeed of any use; for every one must judge according to his own feelings. I merely refer the reader to the original story, that he may see to what extent I have borrowed from it; and am not unwilling that he should find much greater pleasure in perusing it than the drama which is founded upon its contents.

I had begun a drama upon this tale so far back as 1815 (the first I ever attempted, except one at thirteen years old, called 'Ulric and Ilvina', which I had sense enough to burn), and had nearly completed an act, when I was interrupted by circumstances. This is somewhere amongst my papers in England; but as it has not been found, I have re-written the first, and added the subsequent acts.

The whole is neither intended, nor in any shape adapted, for the stage.

PISA, *February,* 1822.

DRAMATIS PERSONÆ

MEN				WOMEN
WERNER.	IDENSTEIN.	HENRICK.	MEISTER.	JOSEPHINE.
ULRIC.	GABOR.	ERIC.	RODOLPH.	IDA STRALENHEIM.
STRALENHEIM.	FRITZ.	ARNHEIM.	LUDWIG.	

SCENE.—*Partly on the frontier of Silesia, and partly in Siegendorf Castle, near Prague.*

TIME.—The Close of the Thirty Years' War.

ACT I

SCENE I.—*The Hall of a decayed Palace near a small Town on the Northern Frontier of Silesia—the Night tempestuous.*

WERNER *and* JOSEPHINE, *his Wife.*

Jos. My love, be calmer!
Wer.   I am calm.
Jos.   To me—
Yes, but not to thyself: thy pace is hurried,
And no one walks a chamber like to ours
With steps like thine when his heart is at
  rest.
Were it a garden, I should deem thee
  happy,   5
And stepping with the bee from flower to
  flower;
But *here!*

Wer. 'Tis chill; the tapestry lets
  through
The wind to which it waves: my blood is
  frozen.
Jos. Ah, no!
Wer. [*smiling*]. Why! wouldst thou
  have it so?
Jos.   I would
Have it a healthful current.
Wer.   Let it flow 10
Until 'tis spilt or check'd—how soon, I
  care not.
Jos. And am I nothing in thy heart?
Wer.   All—all.
Jos. Then canst thou wish for that
  which must break mine?
Wer. [*approaching her slowly*]. But for
  thee I had been—no matter what,
But much of good and evil; what I
  am,   15

560

Thou knowest; what I might or should
  have been,
Thou knowest not: but still I love thee, nor
Shall aught divide us.
        [WERNER *walks on abruptly, and then*
              approaches JOSEPHINE.
              The storm of the night
Perhaps affects me; I'm a thing of feelings,
And have of late been sickly, as, alas!   20
Thou know'st by sufferings more than
  mine, my love!
In watching me.
    Jos.   To see thee well is much—
To see thee happy—
    Wer.   Where hast thou seen such?
Let me be wretched with the rest!
    Jos.   But think
How many in this hour of tempest shiver
Beneath the biting wind and heavy rain,
Whose every drop bows them down nearer
  earth,
Which hath no chamber for them save
  beneath
Her surface.
    Wer.   And that's not the worst: who
  cares
For chambers? rest is all. The wretches
  whom   30
Thou namest—ay, the wind howls round
  them, and
The dull and dropping rain saps in their
  bones
The creeping marrow. I have been a
  soldier,
A hunter, and a traveller, and am
A beggar, and should know the thing thou
  talk'st of.   35
    Jos.   And art thou not now shelter'd
  from them all?
    Wer.   Yes. And from these alone.
    Jos.   And that is something.
    Wer.   True—to a peasant.
    Jos.   Should the nobly born
Be thankless for that refuge which their
  habits
Of early delicacy render more   40
Needful than to the peasant, when the ebb
Of fortune leaves them on the shoals of
  life?
    Wer.   It is not that, thou know'st it is
  not: we
Have borne all this, I'll not say patiently,
Except in thee—but we have borne it.
    Jos.   Well?
    Wer.   Something beyond our outward
  sufferings (though
These were enough to gnaw into our souls)
Hath stung me oft, and, more than ever,
  now,
When, but for this untoward sickness,
  which   49
Seized me upon this desolate frontier, and
Hath wasted, not alone my strength, but
  means,

And leaves us—no! this is beyond me!—
  but
For this I had been happy—*thou* been
  happy—
The splendour of my rank sustain'd—my
  name—
My father's name—been still upheld; and,
  more   55
Than those——
    Jos. [*abruptly*]. My son—our son—
  our Ulric,
Been clasp'd again in these long-empty
  arms,
And all a mother's hunger satisfied.
Twelve years! he was but eight then:—
  beautiful
He was, and beautiful he must be now,
My Ulric! my adored!   61
    Wer.   I have been full oft
The chase of Fortune; now she hath
  o'ertaken
My spirit where it cannot turn at bay,—
Sick, poor, and lonely.
    Jos.   Lonely! my dear husband?
    Wer.   Or worse—involving all I love,
  in this   65
Far worse than solitude. *Alone*, I had
  died,
And all been over in a nameless grave.
    Jos.   And I had not outlived thee; but
  pray take
Comfort! We have struggled long; and
  they who strive   69
With Fortune win or weary her at last,
So that they find the goal or cease to feel
Further. Take comfort,—we shall find
  our boy.
    Wer.   We were in sight of him, of
  everything
Which could bring compensation for past
  sorrow—
And to be baffled thus!
    Jos.   We are not baffled.   75
    Wer.   Are we not penniless?
    Jos.   We ne'er were wealthy.
    Wer.   But I was born to wealth, and
  rank, and power;
Enjoy'd them, loved them, and, alas!
  abused them,
And forfeited them by my father's wrath,
In my o'er-fervent youth: but for the
  abuse   80
Long sufferings have atoned. My father's
  death
Left the path open, yet not without snares.
This cold and creeping kinsman, who so
  long
Kept his eye on me, as the snake upon
The fluttering bird, hath ere this time out-
  stept me,   85
Become the master of my rights, and lord
Of that which lifts him up to princes in
Dominion and domain.
    Jos.   Who knows? our son

May have return'd back to his grandsire,
and
Even now uphold thy rights for thee?
  Wer.   'Tis hopeless.   90
Since his strange disappearance from my
father's,
Entailing, as it were, my sins upon
Himself, no tidings have reveal'd his
course.
I parted with him to his grandsire, on
The promise that his anger would stop
short   95
Of the third generation; but Heaven seems
To claim her stern prerogative, and visit
Upon my boy his father's faults and follies.
  Jos.   I must hope better still,—at least
we have yet
Baffled the long pursuit of Stralenheim.
  Wer.   We should have done, but for
this fatal sickness;   101
More fatal than a mortal malady,
Because it takes not life, but life's sole
solace:
Even now I feel my spirit girt about
By the snares of this avaricious fiend:—
How do I know he hath not track'd us
here?   106
  Jos.   He does not know thy person;
and his spies,
Who so long watch'd thee, have been left
at Hamburgh.
Our unexpected journey, and this change
Of name, leaves all discovery far behind:
None hold us here for aught save what we
seem.   111
  Wer.   Save what we seem! save what
we *are*—sick beggars,
Even to our very hopes.—Ha! ha!
  Jos.   Alas!
That bitter laugh!
  Wer.   Who would read in this form
The high soul of the son of a long line?
Who, in this garb, the heir of princely
lands?   116
Who, in this sunken, sickly eye, the pride
Of rank and ancestry? In this worn cheek
And famine-hollow'd brow, the lord of
halls
Which daily feast a thousand vassals?
  Jos.   You   120
Ponder'd not thus upon these worldly
things,
My Werner! when you deign'd to choose
for bride
The foreign daughter of a wandering exile.
  Wer.   An exile's daughter with an out-
cast son,   124
Were a fit marriage: but I still had hopes
To lift thee to the state we both were born
for.
Your father's house was noble, though
decay'd;
And worthy by its birth to match with
ours.

  Jos.   Your father did not think so,
though 'twas noble;
But had my birth been all my claim to
match   130
With thee, I should have deem'd it what
it is.
  Wer.   And what is that in thine eyes?
  Jos.   All which it
Has done in our behalf,—nothing?
  Wer.   How,—nothing?
  Jos.   Or worse; for it has been a canker in
Thy heart from the beginning: but for this,
We had not felt our poverty but as   136
Millions of myriads feel it, cheerfully;
But for these phantoms of thy feudal
fathers,
Thou might'st have earn'd thy bread, as
thousands earn it;
Or, if that seem too humble, tried by
commerce,   140
Or other civic means, to amend thy
fortunes.
  Wer. [*ironically*].   And been an Han-
seatic burgher? Excellent!
  Jos   Whate'er thou might'st have
been, to me thou art
What no state high or low can ever change,
My heart's first choice; which chose thee,
knowing neither   145
Thy birth, thy hopes, thy pride; nought,
save thy sorrows:
While they last, let me comfort or divide
them:
When they end, let mine end with them,
or thee!
  Wer.   My better angel! Such I have
ever found thee;
This rashness, or this weakness of my
temper,   150
Ne'er raised a thought to injure thee or
thine.
Thou didst not mar my fortunes: my own
nature
In youth was such as to unmake an empire,
Had such been my inheritance; but now,
Chasten'd, subdued, out-worn, and taught
to know   155
Myself,—to lose this for our son and thee!
Trust me, when, in my two-and-twentieth
spring,
My father barr'd me from my fathers'
house,
The last sole scion of a thousand sires
(For I was then the last), it hurt me less
Than to behold my boy and my boy's
mother   161
Excluded in their innocence from what
My faults deserved—exclusion; although
then
My passions were all living serpents, and
Twined like the Gorgon's round me.
            [*A loud knocking is heard.*
  Jos.   Hark!
  Wer.   A knocking!   165

Jos. Who can it be at this lone hour?
   We have
Few visitors.
  Wer.   And poverty hath none,
Save those who come to make it poorer
  still.
Well, I am prepared.
   [WERNER *puts his hand into his bosom,*
     as if to search for some weapon.
  Jos.   Oh! do not look so. I
Will to the door. It cannot be of import
In this lone spot of wintry desolation:—
The very desert saves man from mankind.
                [*She goes to the door.*

      Enter IDENSTEIN.

  Iden. A fair good evening to my fairer
   hostess
And worthy——What's your name, my
  friend?
  Wer.   Are you
Not afraid to demand it?
  Iden.   Not afraid? 175
Egad! I am afraid. You look as if
I ask'd for something better than your
  name,
By the face you put on it.
  Wer.   Better, sir!
  Iden. Better or worse, like matrimony:
  what
Shall I say more? You have been a guest
  this month   180
Here in the prince's palace—(to be sure,
His highness had resign'd it to the ghosts
And rats these twelve years—but 'tis still
  a palace)—
I say you have been our lodger, and as yet
We do not know your name.
  Wer.   My name is Werner. 185
  Iden. A goodly name, a very worthy
  name,
As e'er was gilt upon a trader's board:
I have a cousin in the lazaretto
Of Hamburgh, who has got a wife who bore
The same. He is an officer of trust, 190
Surgeon's assistant (hoping to be surgeon),
And has done miracles i' the way of
  business.
Perhaps you are related to my relative?
  Wer. To yours?
  Jos.   Oh, yes; we are, but distantly.
[*Aside to* WERNER]. Cannot you humour
  the dull gossip till   195
We learn his purpose?
  Iden.   Well, I'm glad of that;
I thought so all along, such natural yearn-
  ings
Play'd round my heart:—blood is not
  water, cousin;
And so let's have some wine, and drink
  unto
Our better acquaintance: relatives should
  be   200
Friends.

Wer. You appear to have drank
  enough already;
And if you have not, I've no wine to offer,
Else it were yours: but this you know, or
  should know:
You see I am poor, and sick, and will not
  see
That I would be alone; but to your
  business!   205
What brings you here?
  Iden.   Why, what should bring me
  here?
  Wer. I know not, though I think that
  I could guess
That which will send you hence.
  Jos. [*aside*]. Patience, dear Werner!
  Iden. You don't know what has
  happen'd, then?
  Jos.   How should we?
  Iden. The river has o'erflow'd.
  Jos.   Alas! we have known 210
That to our sorrow for these five days;
  since
It keeps us here.
  Iden.   But what you don't know is,
That a great personage, who fain would
  cross
Against the stream and three postilions'
  wishes,
Is drown'd below the ford, with five post-
  horses,   215
A monkey, and a mastiff, and a valet.
  Jos. Poor creatures! are you sure?
  Iden.   Yes, of the monkey,
And the valet, and the cattle; but as yet
We know not if his excellency's dead 219
Or no; your noblemen are hard to drown,
As it is fit that men in office should be;
But what is certain is, that he has
  swallow'd
Enough of the Oder to have burst two
  peasants;
And now a Saxon and Hungarian
  traveller,
Who, at their proper peril, snatch'd him
  from   225
The whirling river, have sent on to crave
A lodging, or a grave, according as
It may turn out with the live or dead body.
  Jos. And where will you receive him?
  here, I hope,
If we can be of service—say the word.
  Iden. Here? no; but in the prince's
  own apartment,   231
As fits a noble guest:—'tis damp, no
  doubt,
Not having been inhabited these twelve
  years;
But then he comes from a much damper
  place,
So scarcely will catch cold in't, if he be
Still liable to cold—and if not, why 236
He'll be worse lodged to-morrow:
  ne'ertheless,

I have order'd fire and all appliances
To be got ready for the worst—that is,
In case he should survive.
 Jos.   Poor gentleman, 240
I hope he will, with all my heart.
 Wer.   Intendant,
Have you not learn'd his name? My Jose-
 phine,   [*Aside to his wife.*
Retire: I'll sift this fool.

       [*Exit* JOSEPHINE.
 Iden.   His name? oh Lord!
Who knows if he hath now a name or no?
'Tis time enough to ask it when he's able
To give an answer; or if not, to put 246
His heir's upon his epitaph. Methought
Just now you chid me for demanding
 names?
 Wer. True, true, I did so: you say well
 and wisely.

    Enter GABOR.

 Gab. If I intrude, I crave—
 Iden.   Oh, no intrusion! 250
This is the palace; this a stranger like
Yourself; I pray you make yourself at
 home:
But where's his excellency? and how fares he?
 Gab. Wetly and wearily, but out of
 peril:
He paused to change his garments in a
 cottage   255
(Where I doff'd mine for these, and came
 on hither),
And has almost recover'd from his drench-
 ing.
He will be here anon.
 Iden.   What ho, there! bustle!
Without there, Herman, Weilburg, Peter,
 Conrad!   259
 [*Gives directions to different servants
        who enter.*
A nobleman sleeps here to-night—see that
All is in order in the damask chamber—
Keep up the stove—I will myself to the
 cellar—
And Madame Idenstein (my consort,
 stranger)
Shall furnish forth the bed-apparel; for,
To say the truth, they are marvellous
 scant of this   265
Within the palace precincts, since his high-
 ness
Left it some dozen years ago. And then
His excellency will sup, doubtless?
 Gab.   Faith!
I cannot tell; but I should think the pillow
Would please him better than the table,
 after   270
His soaking in your river: but for fear
Your viands should be thrown away, I
 mean
To sup myself, and have a friend without
Who will do honour to your good cheer with
A traveller's appetite.

 Iden.   But are you sure 275
His excellency——But his name: what is it?
 Gab. I do not know.
 Iden. And yet you saved his life.
 Gad. I help'd my friend to do so.
 Iden.   Well, that's strange,
To save a man's life whom you do not
 know.
 Gab. Not so; for there are some I
 know so well,   280
I scarce should give myself the trouble.
 Iden.   Pray,
Good friend, and who may you be?
 Gab.   By my family,
Hungarian.
 Iden. Which is call'd?
 Gab.   It matters little.
 Iden. [*aside*]. I think that all the world
 are grown anonymous,
Since no one cares to tell me what he's
 call'd!   285
Pray, has his excellency a large suite?
 Gab.   Sufficient.
 Iden. How many?
 Gab.   I did not count them.
We came up by mere accident, and just
In time to drag him through his carriage
 window.
 Iden. Well, what would I give to save
 a great man!   290
No doubt you'll have a swingeing sum as
 recompense.
 Gab. Perhaps.
 Iden. Now, how much do you reckon
 on?
 Gab. I have not yet put up myself to
 sale:
In the mean time, my best reward would be
A glass of your Hockcheimer—a *green*
 glass,   295
Wreath'd with rich grapes and Bacchanal
 devices,
O'erflowing with the oldest of your
 vintage:
For which I promise you, in case you e'er
Run hazard of being drown'd (although I
 own
It seems, of all deaths, the least likely, for
 you),   300
I'll pull you out for nothing. Quick, my
 friend,
And think, for every bumper I shall quaff,
A wave the less may roll above your head.
 Iden. [*aside*]. I don't much like this
 fellow—close and dry
He seems,—two things which suit me not;
 however,   305
Wine he shall have; if that unlock him not,
I shall not sleep to-night for curiosity.

       [*Exit* IDENSTEIN.
 Gab. [*to* WERNER]. This master of the
 ceremonies is
The intendant of the palace, I presume:
'Tis a fine building, but decay'd.

Wer.   The apartment
Design'd for him you rescued will be
    found   311
In fitter order for a sickly guest.
    Gab. I wonder then you occupied it
    not,
For you seem delicate in health.
    Wer. [*quickly*].   Sir!
    Gab.   Pray
Excuse me: have I said aught to offend
    you?   315
    Wer. Nothing: but we are strangers to
    each other.
    Gab. And that's the reason I would
    have us less so:
I thought our bustling host without had
    said
You were a chance and passing guest, the
    counterpart
Of me and my companions.
    Wer.   Very true. 320
    Gab. Then, as we never met before,
    and never,
It may be, may again encounter, why,
I thought to cheer up this old dungeon
    here
(At least to me) by asking you to share
The fare of my companions and myself.
    Wer. Pray, pardon me; my health——
    Gab.   Even as you please.
I have been a soldier, and perhaps am
    blunt
In bearing.
    Wer. I have also served, and can
Requite a soldier's greeting.
    Gab.   In what service?
The Imperial?
    Wer. [*quickly, and then interrupting him-
    self*]. I commanded—no—I mean
I served; but it is many years ago,   331
When first Bohemia raised her banner
    'gainst
The Austrian.
    Gab. Well, that's over now, and
    peace
Has turn'd some thousand gallant hearts
    adrift
To live as they best may: and, to say
    truth,   335
Some take the shortest.
    Wer.   What is that?
    Gab.   Whate'er
They lay their hands on. All Silesia and
Lusatia's woods are tenanted by bands
Of the late troops, who levy on the
    country
Their maintenance: the Chatelains must
    keep   340
Their castle walls—beyond them 'tis but
    doubtful
Travel for your rich count or full-blown
    baron.
My comfort is that, wander where I may,
I've little left to lose now.

Wer.   And I—nothing.
    Gab. That's harder still. You say you
    were a soldier.   345
    Wer. I was.
    Gab. You look one still. All soldiers
    are
Or should be comrades, even though
    enemies.
Our swords when drawn must cross, our
    engines aim
(While levell'd) at each other's hearts; but
    when   349
A truce, a peace, or what you will, remits
The steel into its scabbard, and lets sleep
The spark which lights the matchlock, we
    are brethren.
You are poor and sickly—I am not rich,
    but healthy;
I want for nothing which I cannot want;
You seem devoid of this—wilt share it?
                [GABOR *pulls out his purse.*
    Wer.   Who 355
Told you I was a beggar?
    Gab.   You yourself,
In saying you were a soldier during peace-
    time.
    Wer. [*looking at him with suspicion*].
    You know me not?
    Gab.   I know no man, not even
Myself: how should I then know one I
    ne'er
Beheld till half an hour since?
    Wer.   Sir, I thank you. 360
Your offer's noble were it to a friend,
And not unkind as to an unknown
    stranger,
Though scarcely prudent; but no less I
    thank you.
I am a beggar in all save his trade;   364
And when I beg of any one, it shall be
Of him who was the first to offer what
Few can obtain by asking. Pardon me.
                        [*Exit* WERNER.
    Gab. [*solus*]. A goodly fellow by his
    looks, though worn,
As most good fellows are, by pain or
    pleasure,   369
Which tear life out of us before our time;
I scarce know which most quickly: but he
    seems   371
To have seen better days, as who has not
Who has seen yesterday?—But here ap-
    proaches
Our sage intendant, with the wine: how-
    ever,   374
For the cup's sake I'll bear the cupbearer.

                Enter IDENSTEIN.

    Iden. 'Tis here! the supernaculum!
    twenty years
Of age, if 'tis a day.
    Gab.   Which epoch makes
Young women and old wine; and 'tis great
    pity,

                        565

Of two such excellent things, increase of
   years,
Which still improves the one, should spoil
   the other.   380
Fill full—Here's to our hostess!—your
   fair wife!   [*Takes the glass.*
   Iden. Fair!—Well, I trust your taste
   in wine is equal
To that you show for beauty; but I pledge you
Nevertheless.
   Gab.   Is not the lovely woman
I met in the adjacent hall, who, with   385
An air, and port, and eye, which would
   have better
Beseem'd this palace in its brightest days
(Though in a garb adapted to its present
Abandonment), return'd my salutation—
Is not the same your spouse?
   Iden.   I would she were! 390
But   you're   mistaken:—that's   the
   stranger's wife.
   Gab. And by her aspect she might be
   a prince's;
Though time hath touch'd her too, she
   still retains
Much beauty, and more majesty.
   Iden.   And that
Is more than I can say for Madame
   Idenstein,   395
At least in beauty: as for majesty,
She has some of its properties which might
Be spared—but never mind!
   Gab.   I don't. But who
May be this stranger? He too hath a bear-
   ing
Above his outward fortunes.
   Iden.   There I differ. 400
He's poor as Job, and not so patient; but
Who he may be, or what, or aught of him,
Except his name (and that I only learn'd
To-night), I know not.
   Gab.   But how came he here?
   Iden. In a most miserable old caleche,
About a month since, and immediately
Fell sick, almost to death. He should have
   died.
   Gab. Tender and true!—but why?
   Iden.   Why, what is life
Without a living? He has not a stiver.
   Gab. In that case, I much wonder that
   a person   410
Of your apparent prudence should admit
Guests so forlorn into this noble mansion.
   Iden. That's true: but pity, as you
   know, *does* make
One's heart commit these follies; and
   besides,   414
They had some valuables left at that time,
Which paid their way up to the present
   hour;
And so I thought they might as well be
   lodged
Here as at the small tavern, and I gave
   them

The run of some of the oldest palace
   rooms.
They served to air them, at the least as
   long   420
As they could pay for firewood.
   Gab.   Poor souls!
   Iden.   Ay,
Exceeding poor.
   Gab.   And yet unused to poverty,
If I mistake not. Whither were they
   going?
   Iden. Oh! Heaven knows where, unless
   to heaven itself.
Some days ago that look'd the likeliest
   journey   425
For Werner.
   Gab. Werner! I have heard the name:
But it may be a feign'd one.
   Iden.   Like enough!
But hark! a noise of wheels and voices,
   and
A blaze of torches from without. As sure
As destiny, his excellency 's come.   430
I must be at my post; will you not join me,
To help him from his carriage, and
   present
Your humble duty at the door?
   Gab.   I dragg'd him
From out that carriage when he would
   have given
His barony or county to repel   435
The rushing river from his gurgling throat.
He has valets now enough: they stood
   aloof then,
Shaking their dripping ears upon the
   shore,
All roaring 'Help!' but offering none; and as
For *duty* (as you call it)—I did mine *then*,
Now do *yours*. Hence, and bow and
   cringe him here!   441
   Iden. *I* cringe!—but I shall lose the
   opportunity—
Plague take it! he'll be *here*, and I *not
   there*!   [*Exit* IDENSTEIN *hastily.*

                Re-enter WERNER.

Wer. [*to himself*]. I heard a noise of
   wheels and voices. How
All sounds now jar me!
                Still here! Is he not 445
                      [*Perceiving* GABOR.
A spy of my pursuer's? His frank offer
So suddenly, and to a stranger, wore
The aspect of a secret enemy;
For friends are slow at such.
   Gab.   Sir, you seem rapt;
And yet the time is not akin to thought.
These old walls will be noisy soon. The
   baron,   451
Or count (or whatsoe'er this half drown'd
   noble
May be), for whom this desolate village
   and

Its lone inhabitants show more respect
Than did the elements, is come.
    Iden. [*without*].   This way— 455
This way, your excellency:—have a care,
The staircase is a little gloomy, and
Somewhat decay'd; but if we had expected
So high a guest—Pray take my arm, my
    lord!

Enter STRALENHEIM, IDENSTEIN, *and*
    Attendants,—partly his own, and partly
    Retainers of the Domain of which
    IDENSTEIN *is Intendant.*

    Stral. I'll rest here a moment.
    Iden. [*to the servants*].   Ho! a chair!
Instantly, knaves!   461
          [STRALENHEIM *sits down.*
    Wer. [*aside*].   'Tis he!
    Stral.   I'm better now.
Who are these strangers?
    Iden.   Please you, my good lord,
One says he is no stranger.
    Wer. [*aloud and hastily*]. *Who* says
    that?
        [*They look at him with surprise.*
    Iden. Why, no one spoke *of you*, or *to*
    you!—but
Here 's one his excellency may be pleased
To recognise.   [*Pointing to* GABOR.
    Gab.   I seek not to disturb 466
His noble memory.
    Stral.   I apprehend
This is one of the strangers to whose aid
I owe my rescue. Is not that the other?
          [*Pointing to* WERNER.
My state when I was succour'd must
    excuse   470
My uncertainty to whom I owe so much.
    Iden. He!—no, my lord! he rather
wants for rescue
Than can afford it. 'Tis a poor sick man,
Travel-tired, and lately risen from a bed
From whence he never dream'd to rise.
    Stral.   Methought
That there were two.
    Gab.   There were, in company;
But, in the service render'd to your lord-
    ship
I needs must say but *one*, and he is absent.
The chief part of whatever aid was
    render'd   479
Was *his*: it was his fortune to be first.
My will was not inferior, but his strength
And youth outstripp'd me; therefore do
    not waste
Your thanks on me. I was but a glad
    second
Unto a nobler principal.
    Stral.   Where is he?
    An Atten. My lord, he tarried in the
    cottage where   485
Your excellency rested for an hour,
And said he would be here to-morrow.
    Stral.   Till

That hour arrives, I can but offer thanks,
And then——
    Gab. I seek no more, and scarce
    deserve
So much. My comrade may speak for
    himself.   490
    Stral. [*fixing his eyes upon* WERNER:
    then aside].
It cannot be! and yet he must be look'd to.
'Tis twenty years since I beheld him with
These eyes; and, though my agents still
    have kept
Theirs on him, policy has held aloof
My own from his, not to alarm him into
Suspicion of my plan. Why did I leave
At Hamburgh those who would have
    made assurance
If this be he or no? I thought, ere now,
To have been lord of Siegendorf, and
    parted   499
In haste, though even the elements appear
To fight against me, and this sudden flood
May keep me prisoner here till——
    [*He pauses and looks at* WERNER; *then*
                    resumes.
               This man must
Be watch'd. If it is he, he is so changed,
His father, rising from his grave again,
Would pass him by unknown. I must be
    wary: 505
An error would spoil all.
    Iden.   Your lordship seems
Pensive. Will it not please you to pass on?
    Stral. 'Tis past fatigue, which gives
    my weigh'd-down spirit
An outward show of thought. I will to rest.
    Iden. The prince's chamber is pre-
    pared, with all   510
The very furniture the prince used when
Last here, in its full splendour.
           [*Aside*]. Somewhat tatter'd,
And devilish damp, but fine enough by
    torchlight;
And that's enough for your right noble
    blood
Of twenty quarterings upon a hatchment;
So let their bearer sleep 'neath something
    like one   516
Now, as he one day will for ever lie.
    Stral. [*rising and turning to* GABOR].
    Good night, good people! Sir, I
    trust to-morrow
Will find me apter to requite your service.
In the mean time I crave your company
A moment in my chamber.   521
    Gab.   I attend you.
    Stral. [*after a few steps, pauses, and calls*
    WERNER]. Friend!
    Wer.   Sir!
    Iden.   Sir! Lord—oh Lord! Why
    don't you say
His lordship, or his excellency? Pray,
My lord, excuse this poor man's want of
    breeding:

He hath not been accustom'd to admission
To such a presence.   526
   Stral. [*to* IDENSTEIN]. Peace, intendant!
   Iden.   Oh!
I am dumb.
   Stral. [*to* WERNER]. Have you been
    long here?
   Wer.   Long?
   Stral.   I sought
An answer, not an echo.
   Wer.   You may seek
Both from the walls. I am not used to
    answer
Those whom I know not.
   Stral.   Indeed! Ne'er the less,   530
You might reply with courtesy to what
Is ask'd in kindness.
   Wer.   When I know it such,
I will requite—that is, *reply*—in unison.
   Stral. The intendant said you had
    been detain'd by sickness—
If I could aid you—journeying the same
    way?   535
   Wer. [*quickly*]. I am not journeying
    the same way.
   Stral.   How know ye
That, ere you know my route?
   Wer.   Because there is
But one way that the rich and poor must
    tread
Together. You diverged from that dread
    path
Some hours ago, and I some days: hence-
    forth   540
Our roads must lie asunder, though they
    tend
All to one home.
   Stral.   Your language is above
Your station.
   Wer. [*bitterly*]. Is it?
   Stral.   Or, at least, beyond
Your garb.
   Wer.   'Tis well that it is not beneath it,
As sometimes happens to the better clad.
But, in a word, what would you with me?
   Stral. [*startled*].   I?
   Wer. Yes—you! You know me not,
    and question me,
And wonder that I answer not—not know-
    ing
My inquisitor. Explain what you would
    have,   549
And then I'll satisfy yourself, or me.
   Stral. I knew not that you had reasons
    for reserve.
   Wer. Many have such:—Have you
    none?
   Stral.   None which can
Interest a mere stranger.
   Wer.   Then forgive
The same unknown and humble stranger, if
He wishes to remain so to the man
Who can have nought in common with
    him.

   Stral.   Sir,
I will not balk your humour, though un-
    toward:
I only meant you service—but good night!
Intendant, show the way! [*To* GABOR.
   Sir, you will with me?
    [*Exeunt* STRALENHEIM *and Attendants*,
             IDENSTEIN *and* GABOR.
   Wer. [*solus*]. 'Tis he! I am taken in
    the toils. Before   560
I quitted Hamburgh, Giulio, his late
    steward,
Inform'd me, that he had obtain'd an
    order
From Brandenburg's elector, for the arrest
Of Kruitzner (such the name I then bore)
    when   564
I came upon the frontier; the free city
Alone preserved my freedom—till I left
Its walls—fool that I was to quit them!
    But
I deem'd this humble garb, and route
    obscure,
Had baffled the slow hounds in their
    pursuit.
What's to be done? He knows me not by
    person;   570
Nor could aught, save the eye of appre-
    hension,
Have recognised *him*, after twenty years,
We met so rarely and so coldly in
    Our youth. But those about him! Now
    I can
Divine the frankness of the Hungarian,
    who   575
No doubt is a mere tool and spy of
    Stralenheim's,
To sound and to secure me. Without
    means!
Sick, poor—begirt too with the flooding
    rivers,   578
Impassable even to the wealthy, with
All the appliances which purchase modes
Of overpowering peril, with men's lives,—
How can I hope? An hour ago methought
My state beyond despair; and now, 'tis
    such,
The past seems paradise. Another day,
And I'm detected,—on the very eve
Of honours, rights, and my inheritance,
When a few drops of gold might save me
    still
In favouring an escape.

   Enter IDENSTEIN *and* FRITZ *in conversation.*

   Fritz.   Immediately.
   Iden. I tell you, 'tis impossible.
   Fritz.   It must
Be tried, however; and if one express
Fail, you must send on others, till the
    answer   591
Arrives from Frankfort, from the com-
    mandant.
   Iden. I will do what I can.

Fritz.   And recollect
To spare no trouble; you will be repaid
Tenfold.
   Iden.   The baron is retired to rest?
   Fritz.   He hath thrown himself into an
easy chair   596
Beside the fire, and slumbers; and has
   order'd
He may not be disturb'd until eleven,
When he will take himself to bed.
   Iden.   Before
An hour is past I'll do my best to serve
   him.   600
   Fritz.   Remember!   [*Exit* FRITZ.
   Iden.   The devil take these great
   men! they
Think all things made for them. Now here
   must I
Rouse up some half a dozen shivering
   vassals
From their scant pallets, and, at peril of
Their lives, despatch them o'er the river
   towards   605
Frankfort. Methinks the baron's own
   experience
Some hours ago might teach him fellow-
   feeling:
But no, 'it *must*,' and there's an end. How
   now?
Are you there, Mynheer Werner?
   Wer.   You have left
Your noble guest right quickly.
   Iden.   Yes—he's dozing,   610
And seems to like that none should sleep
   besides.
Here is a packet for the commandant
Of Frankfort, at all risks and all expenses;
But I must not lose time: Good night!
                                          [*Exit*.
   Wer.   'To Frankfort!'
So, so, it thickens! Ay, 'the com-
   mandant.'   615
This tallies well with all the prior steps
Of this cool, calculating fiend, who walks
Between me and my father's house. No
   doubt
He writes for a detachment to convey me
Into some secret fortress.—Sooner than
This——   621
   [WERNER *looks around, and snatches up
      a knife lying on a table in a recess.*
Now I am master of myself at least.
Hark,—footsteps! How do I know that
   Stralenheim
Will wait for even the show of that authority
Which is to overshadow usurpation?
That he suspects me's certain. I'm alone;
He with a numerous train. I weak;
   he strong   626
In gold, in numbers, rank, authority.
I nameless, or involving in my name
Destruction, till I reach my own domain;
He full-blown with his titles, which
   impose   630

Still further on these obscure petty
   burghers
Than they could do elsewhere. Hark!
   nearer still!
I'll to the secret passage, which communi-
   cates
With the——No! all is silent—'twas my
   fancy!—   634
Still as the breathless interval between
The flash and thunder:—I must hush my
   soul
Amidst its perils. Yet I will retire,
To see if still be unexplored the passage
I wot of: it will serve me as a den   639
Of secrecy for some hours, at the worst.
   [WERNER *draws a panel, and exit, closing
                                 it after him.*

Enter GABOR *and* JOSEPHINE.

   Gab.   Where is your husband?
   Jos.   *Here*, I thought: I left him
Not long since in his chamber. But these
   rooms
Have many outlets, and he may be gone
To accompany the intendant.   644
   Gab.   Baron Stralenheim
Put many questions to the intendant on
The subject of your lord, and, to be plain,
I have my doubts if he means well.
   Jos.   Alas!
What can there be in common with the
   proud
And wealthy baron, and the unknown
   Werner?
   Gab.   That you know best.
   Jos.   Or, if it were so, how   650
Come you to stir yourself in his behalf,
Rather than that of him whose life you
   saved?
   Gab.   I help'd to save him, as in peril;
   but
I did not pledge myself to serve him in
Oppression. I know well these nobles,
   and   655
Their thousand modes of trampling on the
   poor.
I have proved them; and my spirit boils
   up when
I find them practising against the weak:—
This is my only motive.
   Jos.   It would be
Not easy to persuade my consort of   660
Your good intentions.
   Gab.   Is he so suspicious?
   Jos.   He was not once; but time and
   troubles have
Made him what you beheld.
   Gab.   I'm sorry for it.
Suspicion is a heavy armour, and
With its own weight impedes more than
   protects.   665
Good night! I trust to meet with him at
   daybreak.   [*Exit* GABOR.

Re-enter IDENSTEIN *and some Peasants.*
JOSEPHINE *retires up the Hall.*

First Peasant. But if I'm drown'd?
Iden. Why, you will be well paid for't,
And have risk'd more than drowning for
as much,
I doubt not.
Second Peasant. But our wives and
families?
Iden. Cannot be worse off than they
are, and may 670
Be better.
Third Peasant. I have neither, and will
venture.
Iden. That's right. A gallant carle,
and fit to be
A soldier. I'll promote you to the ranks
In the prince's body-guard—if you
succeed:
And you shall have besides, in sparkling
coin, 675
Two thalers.
Third Peasant. No more!
Iden. Out upon your avarice!
Can that low vice alloy so much ambition?
I tell thee, fellow, that two thalers in
Small change will subdivide into a
treasure.
Do not five hundred thousand heroes
daily 680
Risk lives and souls for the tithe of one
thaler?
When had you half the sum?
Third Peasant. Never—but ne'er
The less I must have three.
Iden. Have you forgot
Whose vassal you were born, knave?
Third Peasant. No—the prince's,
And not the stranger's.
Iden. Sirrah! in the prince's 685
Absence, I am sovereign; and the baron is
My intimate connexion;—'Cousin Iden-
stein!
(Quoth he) you'll order out a dozen
villains.'
And so, you villains! troop—march—
march, I say; 689
And if a single dog's ear of this packet
Be sprinkled by the Oder—look to it!
For every page of paper, shall a hide
Of yours be stretch'd as parchment on a
drum,
Like Ziska's skin, to beat alarm to all
Refractory vassals, who can not effect
Impossibilities.—Away, ye earth-worms!
[*Exit, driving them out.*
Jos. [*coming forward*]. I fain would
shun these scenes, too oft repeated,
Of feudal tyranny o'er petty victims;
I cannot aid, and will not witness such.
Even here, in this remote, unnamed, dull
spot, 700
The dimmest in the district's map, exist

The insolence of wealth in poverty
O'er something poorer still—the pride of
rank
In servitude, o'er something still more ser-
vile;
And vice in misery affecting still 705
A tatter'd splendour. What a state of
being!
In Tuscany, my own dear sunny land,
Our nobles were but citizens and mer-
chants,
Like Cosmo. We had evils, but not such
As these; and our all-ripe and gushing
valleys 710
Made poverty more cheerful, where each
herb
Was in itself a meal, and every vine
Rain'd, as it were, the beverage which
makes glad
The heart of man; and the ne'er unfelt sun
(But rarely clouded, and when clouded,
leaving 715
His warmth behind in memory of his
beams)
Makes the worn mantle, and the thin robe,
less
Oppressive than an emperor's jewell'd
purple.
But, here! the despots of the north appear
To imitate the ice-wind of their clime,
Searching the shivering vassal through
his rags, 721
To wring his soul—as the bleak elements
His form. And 'tis to be amongst these
sovereigns
My husband pants! and such his pride of
birth— 724
That twenty years of usage, such as no
Father born in a humble state could nerve
His soul to persecute a son withal,
Hath changed no atom of his early nature;
But I, born nobly also, from my father's
Kindness was taught a different lesson.
Father! 730
May thy long-tried and now rewarded
spirit
Look down on us and our so long desired
Ulric! I love my son, as thou didst me!
What's that? Thou, Werner! can it be?
and thus?

Enter WERNER *hastily, with the knife in his
hand, by the secret panel, which he closes
hurriedly after him.*

Wer. [*not at first recognising her*]. Dis-
cover'd! then I'll stab——[*recognis-
ing her*].
Ah! Josephine, 735
Why art thou not at rest?
Jos. What rest? My God!
What doth this mean?
Wer. [*showing a rouleau*]. Here's *gold*—
gold, Josephine,
Will rescue us from this detested dungeon.

Jos. And how obtain'd?—that knife!
Wer. 'Tis bloodless—*yet.*
Away—we must to our chamber.
Jos. But whence comest thou? 740
Wer. Ask not! but let us think where
we shall go—
This—this will make us way—[*showing
the gold*]—I'll fit them now.
Jos. I dare not think thee guilty of
dishonour.
Wer. Dishonour!
Jos. I have said it.
Wer. Let us hence:
'Tis the last night, I trust, that we need pass
here. 745
Jos. And not the worst, I hope.
Wer. Hope! I make *sure.*
But let us to our chamber.
Jos. Yet one question—
What hast thou *done?*
Wer. [*fiercely*]. Left one thing *undone,*
which
Had made all well: let me not think of it!
Away! 749
Jos. Alas, that I should doubt of thee!
[*Exeunt.*

ACT II

SCENE I.—*A Hall in the same Palace.*

Enter IDENSTEIN *and Others.*

Iden. Fine doings! goodly doings!
honest doings!
A baron pillaged in a prince's palace!
Where, till this hour, such a sin ne'er was
heard of.
Fritz. It hardly could, unless the rats
despoil'd
The mice of a few shreds of tapestry. 5
Iden. Oh! that I e'er should live to see
this day!
The honour of our city's gone for ever.
Fritz. Well, but now to discover the
delinquent:
The baron is determined not to lose
This sum without a search.
Iden. And so am I. 10
Fritz. But whom do you suspect?
Iden. Suspect! all people
Without — within — above — below —
Heaven help me!
Fritz. Is there no other entrance to the
chamber?
Iden. None whatsoever.
Fritz. Are you sure of that?
Iden. Certain. I have lived and served
here since my birth, 15
And if there were such, must have heard
of such,
Or seen it.
Fritz. Then it must be some one who
Had access to the antechamber.
Iden. Doubtless.
Fritz. The man call'd *Werner*'s poor!

Iden. Poor as a miser. 19
But lodged so far off, in the other wing,
By which there's no communication with
The baron's chamber, that it can't be he.
Besides, I bade him 'good night' in the
hall,
Almost a mile off, and which only leads
To his own apartment, about the same
time 25
When this burglarious, larcenous felony
Appears to have been committed.
Fritz. There's another,
The stranger——
Iden. The Hungarian?
Fritz. He who help'd
To fish the baron from the Oder.
Iden. Not
Unlikely. But, hold—might it not have
been 30
One of the suite?
Fritz. How? *We,* sir!
Iden. No—not *you,*
But some of the inferior knaves. You say
The baron was asleep in the great chair—
The velvet chair—in his embroider'd
nightgown;
His toilet spread before him, and upon it
A cabinet with letters, papers, and 36
Several rouleaux of gold; of which *one*
only
Has disappear'd:—the door unbolted,
with
No difficult access to any.
Fritz. Good sir,
Be not so quick! the honour of the corps
Which forms the baron's household's
unimpeach'd 41
From steward to scullion, save in the fair
way
Of peculation; such as in accompts,
Weights, measures, larder, cellar, buttery,
Where all men take their prey; as also in
Postage of letters, gathering of rents,
Purveying feasts, and understanding with
The honest trades who furnish noble
masters;
But for your petty, picking, downright
thievery, 49
We scorn it as we do board-wages. Then
Had one of our folks done it, he would not
Have been so poor a spirit as to hazard
His neck for *one* rouleau, but have
swoop'd all;
Also the cabinet, if portable.
Iden. There is some sense in that——
Fritz. No, sir, be sure 55
'Twas none of our corps; but some petty,
trivial
Picker and stealer, without art or genius.
The only question is—Who else could have
Access, save the Hungarian and yourself?
Iden. You don't mean me?
Fritz. No, sir; I honour more 60
Your talents——

Iden. And my principles, I hope.
Fritz. Of course. But to the point:
What's to be done?
Iden. Nothing—but there's a good
deal to be said.
We'll offer a reward; move heaven and
earth,
And the police (though there's none
nearer than 65
Frankfort); post notices in manuscript
(For we've no printer); and set by my
clerk
To read them (for few can, save he and I);
We'll send out villains to strip beggars,
and
Search empty pockets; also to arrest 70
All gipsies, and ill-clothed and sallow
people.
Prisoners we'll have at least, if not the
culprit;
And for the baron's gold—if 'tis not
found,
At least he shall have the full satisfaction
Of melting twice its substance in the
raising 75
The ghost of this rouleau. Here's alchemy
For your Lord's losses!
Fritz. He hath found a better.
Iden. Where?
Fritz. In a most immense inheritance.
The late Count Siegendorf, his distant
kinsman,
Is dead near Prague, in his castle, and my
lord 80
Is on his way to take possession.
Iden. Was there
No heir?
Fritz. Oh, yes; but he has disappear'd
Long from the world's eye, and perhaps
the world.
A prodigal son, beneath his father's ban
For the last twenty years: for whom his
sire 85
Refused to kill the fatted calf; and, there-
fore,
If living, he must chew the husks still.
But
The baron would find means to silence
him,
Were he to re-appear: he's politic,
And has much influence with a certain
court. 90
Iden. He's fortunate.
Fritz. 'Tis true, there is a grandson,
Whom the late count reclaim'd from his
son's hands,
And educated as his heir; but then
His birth is doubtful.
Iden. How so?
Fritz. His sire made
A left-hand, love, imprudent sort of
marriage, 95
With an Italian exile's dark-eyed
daughter:

Noble, they say, too; but no match for
such
A house as Siegendorf's. The grandsire ill
Could brook the alliance; and could ne'er
be brought
To see the parents, though he took the
son. 100
Iden. If he's a lad of mettle, he may
yet
Dispute your claim, and weave a web that
may
Puzzle your baron to unravel.
Fritz. Why,
For mettle, he has quite enough: they say,
He forms a happy mixture of his sire 105
And grandsire's qualities,—impetuous as
The former, and deep as the latter; but
The strangest is, that he too disappear'd
Some months ago.
Iden. The devil he did!
Fritz. Why, yes:
It must have been at his suggestion, at
An hour so critical as was the eve 111
Of the old man's death, whose heart was
broken by it.
Iden. Was there no cause assign'd?
Fritz. Plenty, no doubt,
And none, perhaps, the true one. Some
averr'd 114
It was to seek his parents; some because
The old man held his spirit in so strictly
(But that could scarce be, for he doted on
him):
A third believed he wish'd to serve in war,
But peace being made soon after his de-
parture,
He might have since return'd, were that
the motive; 120
A fourth set charitably have surmised
As there was something strange and mystic
in him,
That in the wild exuberance of his nature
He had join'd the black bands, who lay
waste Lusatia,
The mountains of Bohemia and Silesia,
Since the last years of war had dwindled
into 126
A kind of general condottiero system
Of bandit warfare; each troop with its
chief,
And all against mankind.
Iden. That cannot be,
A young heir, bred to wealth and luxury,
To risk his life and honours with dis-
banded 131
Soldiers and desperadoes!
Fritz. Heaven best knows!
But there are human natures so allied
Unto the savage love of enterprise,
That they will seek for peril as a pleasure.
I've heard that nothing can reclaim your
Indian, 136
Or tame the tiger, though their infancy
Were fed on milk and honey. After all,

Your Wallenstein, your Tilly and
   Gustavus,
Your Bannier, and your Torstenson and
   Weimar,   140
Were but the same thing upon a grand
   scale;
And now that they are gone, and peace
   proclaim'd,
They who would follow the same pastime
   must
Pursue it on their own account. Here
   comes   144
The baron, and the Saxon stranger, who
Was his chief aid in yesterday's escape,
But did not leave the cottage by the Oder
Until this morning.

       Enter STRALENHEIM *and* ULRIC.

   Stral.   Since you have refused
All compensation, gentle stranger, save
Inadequate thanks, you almost check even
   them,   150
Making me feel the worthlessness of
   words,
And blush at my own barren gratitude,
They seem so niggardly, compared with
   what
Your courteous courage did in my
   behalf——
   Ulr. I pray you press the theme no
   further.
   Stral.   But   155
Can I not serve you? You are young, and
   of
That mould which throws out heroes; fair
   in favour;
Brave, I know, by my living now to say so;
And, doubtlessly, with such a form and
   heart,
Would look into the fiery eyes of war,
As ardently for glory as you dared   161
An obscure death to save an unknown
   stranger,
In an as perilous, but opposite, element.
You are made for the service: I have
   served;
Have rank by birth and soldiership, and
   friends,   165
Who shall be yours. 'Tis true this pause of
   peace
Favours such views at present scantily;
But 'twill not last, men's spirits are too
   stirring;
And, after thirty years of conflict, peace
Is but a petty war, as the time shows us
In every forest, or a mere arm'd truce.
War will reclaim his own; and, in the
   mean time,
You might obtain a post, which would
   insure
A higher soon, and, by my influence, fail
   not   174
To rise. I speak of Brandenburg, wherein
I stand well with the Elector; in Bohemia,

Like you, I am a stranger, and we are now
Upon its frontier.
   Ulr.   You perceive my garb
Is Saxon, and of course my service due
To my own sovereign. If I must decline
Your offer, 'tis with the same feeling which
Induced it.
   Stral. Why, this is mere usury!
I owe my life to you, and you refuse
The acquittance of the interest of the debt,
To heap more obligations on me, till
I bow beneath them.   186
   Ulr.   You shall say so when
I claim the payment.
   Stral. Well, sir, since you will not—
You are nobly born?
   Ulr. I have heard my kinsmen say so.
   Stral. Your actions show it. Might I
   ask your name?
   Ulr. Ulric.
   Stral.   Your house's?
   Ulr.   When I'm worthy of it,   190
I'll answer you.
   Stral. [*aside*]. Most probably an
   Austrian,
Whom these unsettled times forbid to
   boast
His lineage on these wild and dangerous
   frontiers,
Where the name of his country is abhorr'd.
       [*Aloud to* FRITZ *and* IDENSTEIN.
So, sirs! how have ye sped in your re-
   searches?   195
   Iden. Indifferent well, your excellency.
   Stral.   Then
I am to deem the plunderer is caught?
   Iden. Humph!—not exactly.
   Stral.   Or at least suspected?
   Iden. Oh! for that matter, very much
   suspected.
   Stral. Who may he be?
   Iden.   Why, don't *you* know, my
   lord?   200
   Stral. How should I? I was fast asleep.
   Iden.   And so
Was I, and that's the cause I know no
   more
Than does your excellency.
   Stral.   Dolt!
   Iden.   Why, if
Your lordship, being robb'd, don't
   recognise
The rogue; how should I, not being robb'd,
   identify   205
The thief among so many? In the crowd,
May it please your excellency, your thief
   looks
Exactly like the rest, or rather better:
'Tis only at the bar and in the dungeon,
That wise men know your felon by his
   features;   210
But I'll engage, that if seen there but once,
Whether he be found criminal or no,
His face shall be so.

Stral. [*to* FRITZ]. Prithee, Fritz, inform
  me
What hath been done to trace the fellow?
Fritz. Faith!
My lord, not much as yet, except con-
  jecture. 215
  Stral. Besides the loss (which, I must
  own, affects me
Just now materially), I needs would find
The villain out of public motives; for
So dexterous a spoiler, who could creep
Through my attendants, and so many
  peopled 220
And lighted chambers, on my rest, and
  snatch
The gold before my scarce-closed eyes,
  would soon
Leave bare your borough, Sir Intendant!
  Iden. True!
If there were aught to carry off, my lord.
  Ulr. What is all this?
  Stral. You join'd us but this morning,
And have not heard that I was robb'd last
  night. 226
  Ulr. Some rumour of it reach'd me as
  I pass'd
The outer chambers of the palace, but
I know no further.
  Stral. It is a strange business;
The intendant can inform you of the facts.
  Iden. Most willingly. You see——
  Stral. [*impatiently*]. Defer your tale,
Till certain of the hearer's patience.
  Iden. That
Can only be approved by proofs. You
  see——
  Stral. [*again interrupting him, and
  addressing* ULRIC]. In short, I was
  asleep upon my chair, 234
My cabinet before me, with some gold
Upon it (more than I much like to lose,
Though in part only): some ingenious
  person
Contrived to glide through all my own
  attendants,
Besides those of the place, and bore away
A hundred golden ducats, which to find
I would be fain, and there's an end.
  Perhaps 241
You (as I still am rather faint) would add
To yesterday's great obligation, this,
Though slighter, yet not slight, to aid
  these men
(Who seem but lukewarm) in recovering
  it? 245
  Ulr. Most willingly, and without loss
  of time—
[*To* IDENSTEIN]. Come hither, mynheer!
  Iden. But so much haste bodes
Right little speed, and——
  Ulr. Standing motionless
None; so let's march; we'll talk as we go
  on.
  Iden. But——

Ulr. Show the spot, and then I'll
  answer you. 250
Fritz. I will, sir, with his excellency's
  leave.
Stral. Do so, and take yon old ass
  with you.
Fritz. Hence!
Ulr. Come on, old oracle, expound
  thy riddle!
  [*Exit with* IDENSTEIN *and* FRITZ.
Stral. [*solus*]. A stalwart, active,
  soldier-looking stripling,
Handsome as Hercules ere his first labour,
And with a brow of thought beyond his
  years 256
When in repose, till his eye kindles up
In answering yours. I wish I could engage
  him:
I have need of some such spirits near me
  now,
For this inheritance is worth a struggle.
And though I am not the man to yield
  without one, 261
Neither are they who now rise up between
  me
And my desire. The boy, they say, 's a
  bold one;
But he hath play'd the truant in some hour
Of freakish folly, leaving fortune to 265
Champion his claims. That's well. The
  father, whom
For years I've track'd, as does the blood-
  hound, never
In sight, but constantly in scent, had put
  me
To fault; but *here* I *have* him, and that's
  better.
It must be *he!* All circumstance proclaims
  it; 270
And careless voices, knowing not the
  cause
Of my inquiries, still confirm it.—Yes,
The man, his bearing, and the mystery
Of his arrival, and the time; the account,
  too,
The intendant gave (for I have not beheld
  her) 275
Of his wife's dignified but foreign aspect;
Besides the antipathy with which we met,
As snakes and lions shrink back from each
  other
By secret instinct that both must be foes
Deadly, without being natural prey to
  either; 280
All—all—confirm it to my mind. How-
  ever,
We'll grapple, ne'ertheless. In a few hours
The order comes from Frankfort, if these
  waters
Rise not the higher (and the weather
  favours
Their quick abatement), and I'll have
  him safe 285
Within a dungeon, where he may avouch

His real estate and name; and there's no
    harm done,
Should he prove other than I deem. This
    robbery
(Save for the actual loss) is lucky also;
He's poor, and that's suspicious—he's
    unknown,   290
And that's defenceless.—True, we have
    no proofs
Of guilt,—but what hath he of innocence?
Were he a man indifferent to my prospects,
In other bearings, I should rather lay
The inculpation on the Hungarian, who
Hath something which I like not; and
    alone   296
Of all around, except the intendant, and
The prince's household and my own, had
    ingress
Familiar to the chamber.

Enter GABOR.

                    Friend, how fare you?
Gab. As those who fare well every-
    where, when they   300
Have supp'd and slumber'd, no great
    matter how—
And you, my lord?
Stral.   Better in rest than purse:
Mine inn is like to cost me dear.
Gab.   I heard
Of your late loss; but 'tis a trifle to
One of your order.
Stral.   You would hardly think so,
Were the loss yours.
Gab.   I never had so much
(At once) in my whole life, and therefore
    am not
Fit to decide. But I came here to seek you.
Your couriers are turn'd back—I have
    outstripp'd them,   309
In my return.
Stral.   You!—Why?
Gab.   I went at daybreak,
To watch for the abatement of the river,
As being anxious to resume my journey.
Your messengers were all check'd like
    myself;
And, seeing the case hopeless, I await
The current's pleasure.   315
Stral.   Would the dogs were in it!
Why did they not, at least, attempt the
    passage?
I order'd this at all risks.
Gab.   Could you order
The Oder to divide, as Moses did
The Red Sea (scarcely redder than the flood
Of the swoln stream), and be obey'd,
    perhaps   320
They might have ventured.
Stral.   I must see to it:
The knaves! the slaves!—but they shall
    smart for this. [*Exit* STRALENHEIM.
Gab. [*solus*]. There goes my noble,
    feudal, self-will'd baron!

Epitome of what brave chivalry
The preux chevaliers of the good old times
Have left us. Yesterday he would have
    given   326
His lands (if he hath any), and, still dearer,
His sixteen quarterings, for as much fresh
    air
As would have fill'd a bladder, while he lay
Gurgling and foaming halfway through
    the window   330
Of his o'erset and water-logg'd con-
    veyance;
And now he storms at half a dozen
    wretches
Because they love their lives too! Yet, he's
    right:
'Tis strange they should, when such as he
    may put them
To hazard at his pleasure. Oh, thou
    world!   335
Thou art indeed a melancholy jest!
                                    [*Exit* GABOR.

SCENE II.—*The Apartment of* WERNER, *in
    the Palace.*

Enter JOSEPHINE *and* ULRIC.

Jos. Stand back, and let me look on
    thee again!
My Ulric!—my beloved!—can it be—
After twelve years?
Ulr.   My dearest mother!
Jos.   Yes!
My dream is realised—how beautiful!—
How more than all I sigh'd for! Heaven
    receive   5
A mother's thanks! a mother's tears of joy!
This is indeed thy work!—At such an
    hour, too,
He comes not only as a son, but saviour.
Ulr. If such a joy await me, it must
    double
What I now feel, and lighten from my
    heart   10
A part of the long debt of duty, not
Of love (for that was ne'er withheld)—
    forgive me!
This long delay was not my fault.
Jos.   I know it,
But cannot think of sorrow now, and
    doubt
If I e'er felt it, 'tis so dazzled from   15
My memory by this oblivious transport!—
My son!

Enter WERNER.

Wer. What have we here,—more
    strangers?
Jos.   No!
Look upon him! What do you see?
Wer.   A stripling,
For the first time—
Ulr. [*kneeling*]. For twelve long years,
    my father!

575   U

Wer. Oh, God!
Jos. He faints!
Wer. No—I am better now— 20
Ulric! [*Embraces him*].
Ulr. My father, Siegendorf!
Wer. [*starting*]. Hush! boy—
The walls may hear that name!
Ulr. What then?
Wer. Why, then—
But we will talk of that anon. Remember,
I must be known here but as Werner. Come!
Come to my arms again! Why, thou look'st all 25
I should have been, and was not.
Josephine!
Sure 'tis no father's fondness dazzles me;
But, had I seen that form amid ten thousand
Youth of the choicest, my heart would have chosen
This for my son!
Ulr. And yet you knew me not! 30
Wer. Alas! I have had that upon my soul
Which makes me look on all men with an eye
That only knows the evil at first glance.
Ulr. My memory served me far more fondly: I
Have not forgotten aught; and oft-times in 35
The proud and princely halls of—(I'll not name them,
As you say that 'tis perilous)—but i' the pomp
Of your sire's feudal mansion, I look'd back
To the Bohemian mountains many a sunset,
And wept to see another day go down
O'er thee and me, with those huge hills between us. 41
They shall not part us more.
Wer. I know not that.
Are you aware my father is no more?
Ulr. Oh, heavens! I left him in a green old age,
And looking like the oak, worn, but still steady 45
Amidst the elements, whilst younger trees
Fell fast around him. 'Twas scarce three months since.
Wer. Why did you leave him?
Jos. [*embracing* ULRIC]. Can you ask that question?
Is he not *here*?
Wer. True; he hath sought his parents,
And found them; but oh! *how*, and in what state! 50
Ulr. All shall be better'd. What we have to do
Is to proceed, and to assert our rights,
Or rather yours; for I waive all, unless
Your father has disposed in such a sort
Of his broad lands as to make mine the foremost, 55
So that I must prefer my claim for form:
But I trust better, and that all is yours.
Wer. Have you not heard of Stralenheim?
Ulr. I saved
His life but yesterday; he's here.
Wer. You saved
The serpent who will sting us all!
Ulr. You speak 60
Riddles: what is this Stralenheim to us?
Wer. Everything. One who claims our father's lands:
Our distant kinsman, and our nearest foe.
Ulr. I never heard his name till now. The count,
Indeed, spoke sometimes of a kinsman, who, 65
If his own line should fail, might be remotely
Involved in the succession; but his titles
Were never named before me—and what then?
His right must yield to ours.
Wer. Ay, if at Prague;
But here he is all-powerful; and has spread 70
Snares for thy father, which, if hitherto
He hath escaped them, is by fortune, not
By favour.
Ulr. Doth he personally know you?
Wer. No; but he guesses shrewdly at my person,
As he betray'd last night; and I, perhaps,
But owe my temporary liberty 76
To his uncertainty.
Ulr. I think you wrong him
(Excuse me for the phrase); but Stralenheim
Is not what you prejudge him, or, if so,
He owes me something both for past and present. 80
I saved his life, he therefore trusts in me.
He hath been plunder'd too, since he came hither:
Is sick; a stranger; and as such not now
Able to trace the villain who hath robb'd him:
I have pledged myself to do so; and the business 85
Which brought me here was chiefly that: but I
Have found, in searching for another's dross,
My own whole treasure—you, my parents!
Wer. [*agitatedly*]. Who
Taught you to mouth that name of 'villain'?
Ulr. What
More noble name belongs to common thieves? 90

Wer. Who taught you thus to brand
an unknown being
With an infernal stigma?
Ulr.   My own feelings
Taught me to name a ruffian from his
deeds.
Wer. Who taught you, long-sought
and ill-found boy! that
It would be safe for my own son to insult
me?   95
Ulr. I named a villain. What is there
in common
With such a being and my father?
Wer.   Everything!
That ruffian is thy father!
Jos.   Oh, my son!
Believe him not—and yet!——[*her voice
falters*].
Ulr. [*starts, looks earnestly at* WERNER
and then says slowly,] And you
avow it?
Wer. Ulric, before you dare despise
your father,   100
Learn to divine and judge his actions.
Young,
Rash, new to life, and rear'd in luxury's
lap,
Is it for you to measure passion's force,
Or misery's temptation? Wait—(not
long,
It cometh like the night, and quickly)—
Wait!—   105
Wait till, like me, your hopes are blighted
—till
Sorrow and shame are handmaids of your
cabin;
Famine and poverty your guests at table;
Despair your bed-fellow—then rise, but
not
From sleep, and judge! Should that day
e'er arrive—   110
Should you see then the serpent, who hath
coil'd
Himself around all that is dear and noble
Of you and yours, lie slumbering in your
path,
With but *his* folds between your steps and
happiness,
When *he*, who lives but to tear from you
name,   115
Lands, life itself, lies at your mercy, with
Chance your conductor—midnight for
your mantle—
The bare knife in your hand, and earth
asleep,
Even to your deadliest foe; and he as
'twere
Inviting death, by looking like it, while
His death alone can save you:—Thank
your God!   121
If then, like me, content with petty
plunder,
You turn aside——I did so.
Ulr.   But——

Wer. [*abruptly*].   Hear me!
I will not brook a human voice—scarce
dare   124
Listen to my own (if that be human still)—
Hear me! you do not know this man—I do.
He's mean, deceitful, avaricious. You
Deem yourself safe, as young and brave;
but learn
None are secure from desperation, few
From subtilty. My worst foe, Stralen-
heim,   130
Housed in a prince's palace, couch'd
within
A prince's chamber, lay below my knife!
An instant—a mere motion—the least
impulse—
Had swept him and all fears of mine from
earth.
He was within my power—my knife was
raised—   135
Withdrawn—and I'm in his:—are you
not so?
Who tells you that he knows you *not*?
Who says
He hath not lured you here to end you? or
To plunge you, with your parents, in a
dungeon?   [*He pauses.*
Ulr. Proceed—proceed!
Wer.   *Me* he hath ever known, 140
And hunted through each change of
time—name—fortune—
And why not *you*? Are you more versed
in men?
He wound snares round me; flung along
my path
Reptiles, whom, in my youth, I would
have spurn'd
Even from my presence; but, in spurning
now,   145
Fill only with fresh venom. Will you be
More patient? Ulric!—Ulric!—there are
crimes
Made venial by the occasion, and tempta-
tions
Which nature cannot master or forbear.
Ulr. [*who looks first at him, and then at*
JOSEPHINE].   My mother!
Wer. Ah! I thought so: you have now
Only one parent. I have lost alike 151
Father and son, and stand alone.
Ulr.   But stay!
[WERNER *rushes out of the chamber.*
Jos. [*to* ULRIC]. Follow him not, until
this storm of passion
Abates. Think'st thou, that were it well
for him,
I had not follow'd?
Ulr.   I obey you, mother, 155
Although reluctantly. My first act shall
not
Be one of disobedience.
Jos.   Oh! he is good!
Condemn him not from his own mouth,
but trust

577

To me, who have borne so much with him,
and for him,   159
That this is but the surface of his soul,
And that the depth is rich in better things.
  Ulr. These then are but my father's
    principles?
My mother thinks not with him?
  Jos.   Nor doth he
Think as he speaks. Alas! long years of
    grief
Have made him sometimes thus.
  Ulr.   Explain to me 165
More clearly, then, these claims of Stralen-
    heim,
That, when I see the subject in its bearings,
I may prepare to face him, or at least
To extricate you from your present perils.
I pledge myself to accomplish this—but
    would   170
I had arrived a few hours sooner!
  Jos.   Ay!
Hadst thou but done so!

Enter GABOR *and* IDENSTEIN, *with
      Attendants.*

  Gab. [*to* ULRIC]. I have sought you,
    comrade.
So this is my reward!
  Ulr.   What do you mean?
  Gab. 'Sdeath! have I lived to these
    years, and for this!
[*To* IDENSTEIN]. But for your age and
    folly, I would——
  Iden.   Help!   175
Hands off! Touch an intendant!
  Gab.   Do not think
I'll honour you so much as save your
    throat
From the Ravenstone by choking you
    myself.
  Iden. I thank you for the respite: but
    there are
Those who have greater need of it than
    me.   180
  Ulr. Unriddle this vile wrangling,
    or——
  Gab.   At once, then,
The baron has been robbed, and upon me
This worthy personage has deign'd to fix
His kind suspicions—me! whom he ne'er
    saw
Till yester evening.
  Iden. Wouldst have me suspect 185
My own acquaintances? You have to
    learn
That I keep better company.
  Gab.   You shall
Keep the best shortly, and the last for all
    men,
The worms! you hound of malice!
          [GABOR *seizes on him.*
  Ulr. [*interfering*]. Nay, no violence:
He's old, unarm'd—be temperate, Gabor!
  Gab. [*letting go* IDENSTEIN]. True:

I am a fool to lose myself because 191
Fools deem me knave: it is their homage.
  Ulr. [*to* IDENSTEIN].   How
Fare you?
  Iden. Help!
  Ulr.   I *have* help'd you.
  Iden.   Kill him! then
I'll say so.
  Gab.   I am calm—live on!
  Iden.   That's more
Than you shall do, if there be judge or
    judgment   195
In Germany. The baron shall decide!
  Gab. Does *he* abet you in your
    accusation?
  Iden. Does he not?
  Gab. Then next time let him go sink
Ere I go hang for snatching him from
    drowning.
But here he comes!

Enter STRALENHEIM.

  Gab. [*goes up to him*]. My noble lord,
    I'm here!   200
  Stral. Well, sir!
  Gab.   Have you aught with me?
  Stral.   What should I
Have with you?
  Gab.   You know best, if yesterday's
Flood has not wash'd away your memory;
But that's a trifle. I stand here accused,
In phrases not equivocal, by yon 205
Intendant, of the pillage of your person
Or chamber:—is the charge your own or
    his?
  Stral. I accuse no man.
  Gab.   Then you acquit me, baron?
  Stral. I know not whom to accuse, or
    to acquit,
Or scarcely to suspect.
  Gab.   But you at least 210
Should know whom *not* to suspect. I am
    insulted—
Oppress'd here by these menials, and I
    look
To you for remedy—teach them their
    duty!
To look for thieves at home were part of it,
If duly taught; but, in one word, if I 215
Have an accuser, let it be a man
Worthy to be so of a man like me.
I am your equal.
  Stral.   You!
  Gab.   Ay, sir; and, for
Aught that you know, superior; but
    proceed—
I do not ask for hints, and surmises, 220
And circumstance, and proof: I know
    enough
Of what I have done for you, and what
    you owe me,
To have at least waited your payment rather
Than paid myself, had I been eager of
Your gold. I also know, that were I even

The villain I am deem'd, the service
   render'd   226
So recently would not permit you to
Pursue me to the death, except through
   shame,
Such as would leave your scutcheon but a
   blank.
But this is nothing: I demand of you   230
Justice upon your unjust servants, and
From your own lips a disavowal of
All sanction of their insolence: thus much
You owe to the unknown, who asks no
   more,
And never thought to have ask'd so much.
   Stral.   This tone   235
May be of innocence.
   Gab.   'Sdeath! who dare doubt it,
Except such villains as ne'er had it?
   Stral.   You
Are hot, sir.
   Gab.   Must I turn an icicle
Before the breath of menials, and their
   master?
   Stral. Ulric! you know this man; I
   found him in   240
Your company.
   Gab.   We found *you* in the Oder,
Would we had left you there!
   Stral.   I give you thanks, sir.
   Gab. I've earned them; but might
   have earn'd more from others,
Perchance, if I had left you to your fate.
   Stral. Ulric! you know this man?
   Gab.   No more than you do   245
If he avouches not my honour.
   Ulr.   I
Can vouch your courage, and, as far as my
Own brief connexion led me, honour.
   Stral.   Then
I'm satisfied.
   Gab. [*ironically*]. Right easily, methinks.
What is the spell in his asseveration   250
More than in mine?
   Stral.   I merely said that *I*
Was satisfied—not that you are absolved.
   Gab. Again! Am I accused or no?
   Stral.   Go to!
You wax too insolent. If circumstance
And general suspicion be against you,
Is the fault mine? Is't not enough that I
Decline all question of your guilt or inno-
   cence?   257
   Gab. My lord, my lord, this is mere
   cozenage,
A vile equivocation; you well know
Your doubts are certainties to all around
   you—   260
Your looks a voice—your frowns a
   sentence; you
Are practising your power on me—
   because
You have it; but beware! you know not
   whom
You strive to tread on.

   Stral.   Threat'st thou?
   Gab.   Not so much   264
As you accuse. You hint the basest injury.
And I retort it with an open warning.
   Stral. As you have said, 'tis true I owe
   you something,
For which you seem disposed to pay
   yourself.
   Gab. Not with your gold.
   Stral.   With bootless insolence.
     [*To his Attendants and* IDENSTEIN.
You need not further to molest this man,
But let him go his way. Ulric, good
   morrow!   271
     [*Exit* STRALENHEIM, IDENSTEIN, *and
     Attendants.*
   Gab. [*following*]. I'll after him and—
   Ulr. [*stopping him*].   Not a step.
   Gab.   Who shall
Oppose me?
   Ulr.   Your own reason, with a
   moment's
Thought.
   Gab.   Must I bear this?
   Ulr.   Pshaw! we all must bear
The arrogance of something higher than
Ourselves—the highest cannot temper
   Satan,   276
Nor the lowest his vicegerents upon earth.
I've seen you brave the elements, and bear
Things which had made this silkworm cast
   his skin—
And shrink you from a few sharp sneers
   and words?   280
   Gab. Must I bear to be deem'd a thief?
If 'twere
A bandit of the woods, I could have borne
   it—
There's something daring in it:—but to
   steal
The moneys of a slumbering man!—
   Ulr.   It seems, then,
You are *not* guilty.
   Gab.   Do I hear aright?   285
You too!
   Ulr. I merely ask'd a simple question.
   Gab. If the judge ask'd me, I would
   answer 'No'—
To you I answer *thus*.   [*He draws.*
   Ulr. [*drawing*].   With all my heart!
   Jos. Without there! Ho! help! help!—
Oh, God! here's murder!
     [*Exit* JOSEPHINE, *shrieking.*

GABOR *and* ULRIC *fight.* GABOR *is dis-
   armed just as* STRALENHEIM, JOSEPHINE,
   IDENSTEIN, &c., *re-enter.*
   Jos. Oh! glorious heaven! He's safe!
   Stral. [*to* JOSEPHINE].   *Who's* safe?
   Jos.   My——
   Ulr. [*interrupting her with a stern look,
   and turning afterwards to* STRALEN-
   HEIM].
                 Both!   290
Here's no great harm done.

Stral.   What hath caused all this?
Ulr.   *You*, baron, I believe; but as the
        effect
Is harmless, let it not disturb you.—
        Gabor!
There is your sword; and when you bare
        it next,
Let it not be against your *friends*.
        [ULRIC *pronounces the last words slowly*
        and emphatically in a low voice to
        GABOR.
Gab.   I thank you 295
Less for my life than for your counsel.
Stral.   These
Brawls must end here.
Gab. [*taking his sword*]. They *shall*.
        You've wrong'd me, Ulric,
More with your unkind thoughts than
        sword: I would
The last were in my bosom rather than
The first in yours. I could have borne yon
        noble's   300
Absurd insinuations—ignorance
And dull suspicion are a part of his
Entail will last him longer than his
        lands.—
But I may fit *him* yet:—you have van-
        quish'd me.
I was the fool of passion to conceive 305
That I could cope with you, whom I had
        seen
Already proved by greater perils than
Rest in this arm. We may meet by and by,
However—but in friendship.
                        [*Exit* GABOR.
Stral.   I will brook
No more! This outrage following upon his
        insults,   310
Perhaps his guilt, has cancell'd all the little
I owed him heretofore for the so-vaunted
Aid which he added to your abler succour.
Ulric, you are not hurt?—
Ulr.   Not even by a scratch.
Stral. [*to* IDENSTEIN]. Intendant! take
        your measures to secure 315
Yon fellow: I revoke my former lenity.
He shall be sent to Frankfort with an
        escort,
The instant that the waters have abated.
Iden. Secure him! He hath got his
        sword again—
And seems to know the use on't; 'tis his
        trade,   320
Belike;—*I'm* a civilian.
Stral.   Fool! are not
Yon score of vassals dogging at your heels
Enough to seize a dozen such? Hence!
        after him!
Ulr. Baron, I do beseech you!
Stral.   I must be
Obey'd. No words!
Iden.   Well, if it must be so— 325
March, vassals! I'm your leader, and will
        bring

The rear up: a wise general never should
Expose his precious life—on which all
        rests.
I like that article of war.
                [*Exit* IDENSTEIN *and Attendants.*
Stral.   Come hither,
Ulric; what does that woman here? Oh!
        now   330
I recognise her, 'tis the stranger's wife
Whom they *name* 'Werner.'
Ulr.   'Tis his name.
Stral.   Indeed!
Is not your husband visible, fair dame?—
Jos.   Who seeks him?
Stral.   No one—for the present: but
I fain would parley, Ulric, with yourself
Alone.
Ulr.   I will retire with you.
Jos.   Not so: 336
You are the latest stranger, and com-
        mand
All places here.
[*Aside to* ULRIC, *as she goes out*]. O Ulric!
        have a care—
Remember what depends on a rash word!
Ulr. [*to* JOSEPHINE].   Fear not!—
                            [*Exit* JOSEPHINE.
Stral. Ulric, I think that I may trust
        you;   340
You saved my life—and acts like these
        beget
Unbounded confidence.
Ulr.   Say on.
Stral.   Mysterious
And long-engender'd circumstances (not
To be now fully enter'd on) have made
This man obnoxious—perhaps fatal to
        me.   345
Ulr. Who? Gabor, the Hungarian?
Stral.   No—this 'Werner'—
With the false name and habit.
Ulr.   How can this be?
He is the poorest of the poor—and yellow
Sickness sits cavern'd in his hollow eye:
The man is helpless.
Stral.   He is—'tis no matter;— 350
But if he be the man I deem (and that
He is so, all around us here—and much
That is not here—confirm my appre-
        hension),
He must be made secure ere twelve hours
        further.   354
Ulr.   And what have I to do with this?
Stral.   I have sent
To Frankfort, to the governor, my friend,
(I have the authority to do so by
An order of the house of Brandenburg),
For a fit escort—but this cursed flood
Bars all access, and may do for some
        hours.   360
Ulr. It is abating.
Stral.   That is well.
Ulr.   But how
Am I concern'd?

Stral.   As one who did so much
For me, you cannot be indifferent to
That which is of more import to me than
The life you rescued.—Keep your eye on
      him!   365
The man avoids me, knows that I now
      know him.—
Watch him!—as you would watch the
      wild boar when
He makes against you in the hunter's
      gap—
Like him he must be spear'd.
      Ulr.   Why so?
      Stral.   He stands
Between me and a brave inheritance!   370
Oh! could you see it! But you shall.
      Ulr.   I hope so.
      Stral. It is the richest of the rich
      Bohemia,
Unscathed by scorching war. It lies so
      near
The strongest city, Prague, that fire and
      sword
Have skimm'd it lightly: so that now,
      besides   375
Its own exuberance, it bears double value
Confronted with whole realms far and
      near
Made deserts.
      Ulr.   You describe it faithfully.
      Stral. Ay—could you see it, you
      would say so—but,   379
As I have said, you shall.
      Ulr.   I accept the omen.
      Stral. Then claim a recompense from
      it and me,
Such as *both* may make worthy your
      acceptance
And services to me and mine for ever.
      Ulr. And this sole, sick, and miserable
      wretch—
This way-worn stranger—stands between
      you and   385
This Paradise?—(As Adam did between
The devil and his)—[*Aside*].
      Stral.   He doth.
      Ulr.   Hath he no right?
      Stral. Right! none. A disinherited
      prodigal,
Who for these twenty years disgraced his
      lineage   389
In all his acts—but chiefly by his marriage,
And living amidst commerce-fetching
      burghers,
And dabbling merchants, in a mart of
      Jews.
      Ulr. He has a wife, then?
      Stral.   You'd be sorry to
Call such your mother. You have seen
      the woman   394
He *calls* his wife.
      Ulr.   Is she not so?
      Stral.   No more
Than he's your father:—an Italian girl,

The daughter of a banish'd man, who lives
On love and poverty with this same
      Werner.
      Ulr. They are childless, then?
      Stral.   There is or was a bastard,
Whom the old man—the grandsire (as
      old age   400
Is ever doting) took to warm his bosom,
As it went chilly downward to the grave:
But the imp stands not in my path—he
      has fled,
No one knows whither; and if he had not,
His claims alone were too contemptible
To stand.—Why do you smile?
      Ulr.   At your vain fears:
A poor man almost in his grasp—a child
Of doubtful birth—can startle a grandee!
      Stral. All's to be fear'd, where all is to
      be gain'd.
      Ulr. True; and aught done to save or
      to obtain it.   410
      Stral. You have harp'd the very string
next to my heart.
I may depend upon you?
      Ulr.   'Twere too late
To doubt it.
      Stral.   Let no foolish pity shake
Your bosom (for the appearance of the
      man
Is pitiful)—he is a wretch, as likely   415
To have robb'd me as the fellow more
      suspected,
Except that circumstance is less against
      him;
He being lodged far off, and in a chamber
Without approach to mine; and, to say
      truth,   419
I think too well of blood allied to mine,
To deem he would descend to such an
      act:
Besides, he was a soldier, and a brave one
Once—though too rash.
      Ulr.   And they, my lord, we know
By our experience, never plunder till
They knock the brains out first—which
      makes them heirs,   425
Not thieves. The dead, who feel nought,
      can lose nothing,
Nor e'er be robb'd: their spoils are a be-
      quest—
No more.
      Stral. Go to! you are a wag. But say
I may be sure you'll keep an eye on this
      man,
And let me know his slightest movement
      towards   430
Concealment or escape?
      Ulr.   You may be sure
You yourself could not watch him more
      than I
Will be his sentinel.
      Stral.   By this you make me
Yours, and for ever.
      Ulr. Such is my intention. [*Exeunt.*

ACT III

Scene I.—*A Hall in the same Palace, from whence the secret passage leads.*

Enter WERNER *and* GABOR.

Gab. Sir, I have told my tale: if it so please you
To give me refuge for a few hours, well—
If not, I'll try my fortune elsewhere.
Wer. How
Can I, so wretched, give to Misery
A shelter?—wanting such myself as much
As e'er the hunted deer a covert——
Gab. Or   6
The wounded lion his cool cave. Methinks
You rather look like one would turn at bay,
And rip the hunter's entrails.
Wer. Ah!
Gab. I care not
If it be so, being much disposed to do
The same myself. But will you shelter me?
I am oppress'd like you—and poor like you—
Disgraced——
Wer. [*abruptly*]. Who told you that I was disgraced?
Gab. No one; nor did I say *you* were so: with
Your poverty my likeness ended; but   15
I said *I* was so—and would add, with truth,
As undeservedly as *you*.
Wer. Again!
As *I*?
Gab. Or any other honest man.
What the devil would you have? You don't believe me
Guilty of this base theft?
Wer. No, no—I cannot.   20
Gab. Why that's my heart of honour! yon young gallant—
Your miserly intendant and dense noble—
All—all suspected me; and why? because
I am the worst clothed and least named amongst them;
Although, were Momus' lattice in your breasts,   25
My soul might brook to open it more widely
Than theirs: but thus it is—you poor and helpless—
Both still more than myself.
Wer. How knew you that?
Gab. You're right: I ask for shelter at the hand
Which I call helpless; if you now deny it,
I were well paid. But you, who seem to have proved   31
The wholesome bitterness of life, know well,
By sympathy, that all the outspread gold

Of the New World the Spaniard boasts about,
Could never tempt the man who knows its worth   35
Weigh'd at its proper value in the balance,
Save in such guise (and there I grant its power,
Because I feel it) as may leave no nightmare
Upon his heart o' nights.
Wer. What do you mean?
Gab. Just what I say; I thought my speech was plain;   40
You are no thief—nor I—and, as true men,
Should aid each other.
Wer. It is a damn'd world, sir.
Gab. So is the nearest of the two next, as
The priests say (and no doubt they should know best),   44
Therefore I'll stick by this—as being loth
To suffer martyrdom, at least with such
An epitaph as larceny upon my tomb.
It is but a night's lodging which I crave;
To-morrow I will try the waters, as
The dove did, trusting that they have abated.   50
Wer. Abated? Is there hope of that?
Gab. There was
At noontide.
Wer. Then we may be safe.
Gab. Are *you*
In peril?
Wer. Poverty is ever so.
Gab. That I know by long practice. Will you not
Promise to make mine less?
Wer. Your poverty?   55
Gab. No—you don't look a leech for that disorder;
I meant my peril only: you've a roof,
And I have none; I merely seek a covert.
Wer. Rightly; for how should such a wretch as I
Have gold?
Gab. Scarce honestly, to say the truth on't,   60
Although I almost wish you had the baron's.
Wer. Dare you insinuate?
Gab. What?
Wer. Are you aware
To whom you speak?
Gab. No; and I am not used
Greatly to care. [*A noise heard without.*]
But hark! they come!
Wer. Who come?
Gab. The intendant and his manhounds after me: 65
I'd face them—but it were in vain to expect
Justice at hands like theirs. Where shall I go?
But show me any place. I do assure you,
If there be faith in man, I am most guiltless:
Think if it were your own case!

Wer. [*aside*].   Oh, just God!   70
Thy hell is not hereafter! Am I dust still?
Gab. I see you're moved; and it shows
      well in you:
I may live to requite it.
Wer.   Are you not
A spy of Stralenheim's?
Gab.   Not I! and if
I were, what is there to espy in you?   75
Although, I recollect, his frequent
      question
About you and your spouse might lead to
      some
Suspicion; but you best know—what—
      and why.
I am his deadliest foe.
Wer.   You?
Gab.   After such
A treatment for the service which in part
I render'd him, I am his enemy: 81
If you are not his friend, you will assist me.
Wer. I will.
Gab.   But how?
Wer. [*showing the panel*]. There is a
      secret spring:
Remember, I discover'd it by chance,
And used it but for safety.
Gab.   Open it,   85
And I will use it for the same.
Wer.   I found it,
As I have said: it leads through winding
      walls
(So thick as to bear paths within their ribs,
Yet lose no jot of strength or stateliness),
And hollow cells, and obscure niches, to
I know not whither; you must not
      advance: 91
Give me your word.
Gab.   It is unnecessary:
How should I make my way in darkness
      through
A Gothic labyrinth of unknown wind-
      ings?
Wer. Yes, but who knows to what
      place it may lead?   95
I know not—(mark you!)—but who
      knows it might not
Lead even into the chamber of your foe?
So strangely were contrived these galleries
By our Teutonic fathers in old days,
When man built less against the elements
Than his next neighbour. You must not
      advance   101
Beyond the two first windings; if you do
(Albeit I never pass'd them), I'll not
      answer
For what you may be led to.
Gab.   But I will.
A thousand thanks!
Wer. You'll find the spring more
      obvious   105
On the other side; and, when you would
      return,
It yields to the least touch.

Gab.   I'll in—farewell!
   [GABOR *goes in by the secret panel.*
Wer. [*solus*]. What have I done? Alas!
      what *had* I done
Before to make this fearful? Let it be
Still some atonement that I save the man,
Whose sacrifice had saved perhaps my
      own—   111
They come! to seek elsewhere what is
      before them!

           Enter IDENSTEIN *and Others.*
Iden. Is he not here? He must have
      vanish'd then
Through the dim Gothic glass by pious aid
Of pictured saints upon the red and yellow
Casements, through which the sunset
      streams like sunrise   116
On long pearl-colour'd beards and
      crimson crosses,
And gilded crosiers, and cross'd arms,
      and cowls,
And helms, and twisted armour, and long
      swords,
All the fantastic furniture of windows
Dim with brave knights and holy hermits,
      whose   121
Likeness and fame alike rest in some panes
Of crystal, which each rattling wind pro-
      claims
As frail as any other life or glory.
He's gone, however.
Wer.   Whom do you seek?
Iden.   A villain.   125
Wer. Why need you come so far, then?
Iden.   In the search
Of him who robb'd the baron.
Wer.   Are you sure
You have divined the man?
Iden.   As sure as you
Stand there: but where's he gone?
Wer.   Who?
Iden.   He we sought.
Wer. You see he is not here.
Iden.   And yet we traced him   130
Up to this hall. Are you accomplices?
Or deal you in the black art?
Wer.   I deal plainly,
To many men the blackest.
Iden.   It may be
I have a question or two for yourself
Hereafter; but we must continue now
Our search for t'other.   135
Wer.   You had best begin
Your inquisition now: I may not be
So patient always.
Iden.   I should like to know,
In good sooth, if you really are the man
That Stralenheim's in quest of.
Wer.   Insolent!   140
Said you not that he was not here?
Iden.   Yes, *one*;
But there's another whom he tracks more
      keenly,

And soon, it may be, with authority
Both paramount to his and mine. But
   come!
Bustle, my boys! we are at fault.
    [*Exit* IDENSTEIN *and Attendants.*
  Wer. In what 145
A maze hath my dim destiny involved me!
And one base sin hath done me less ill than
The leaving undone one far greater.
   Down,
Thou busy devil, rising in my heart!
Thou art too late! I'll nought to do with
   blood. 150

Enter ULRIC.

  Ulr. I sought you, father.
  Wer. Is't not dangerous?
  Ulr. No; Stralenheim is ignorant of all
Or any of the ties between us: more—
He sends me here a spy upon your actions,
Deeming me wholly his.
  Wer. I cannot think it: 155
'Tis but a snare he winds about us both,
To swoop the sire and son at once.
  Ulr. I cannot
Pause in each petty fear, and stumble at
The doubts that rise like briers in our path,
But must break through them, as an
   unarm'd carle 160
Would, though with naked limbs, were
   the wolf rustling
In the same thicket where he hew'd for
   bread.
Nets are for thrushes, eagles are not caught
   so:
We'll overfly or rend them.
  Wer. Show me *how?*
  Ulr. Can you not guess?
  Wer. I cannot.
  Ulr. That is strange. 165
Came the thought ne'er into your mind
  last night?
  Wer. I understand you not.
  Ulr. Then we shall never
More understand each other. But to
  change
The topic——
  Wer. You mean to *pursue* it, as
'Tis of our safety.
  Ulr. Right; I stand corrected. 170
I see the subject now more clearly, and
Our general situation in its bearings.
The waters are abating; a few hours
Will bring his summon'd myrmidons
  from Frankfort,
When you will be a prisoner, perhaps
  worse, 175
And I an outcast, bastardised by practice
Of this same baron to make way for him.
  Wer. And now your remedy! I
  thought to escape
By means of this accursed gold; but now
I dare not use it, show it, scarce look on it.
Methinks it wears upon its face my guilt

For motto, not the mintage of the state;
And, for the sovereign's head, my own
  begirt
With hissing snakes, which curl around
  my temples, 184
And cry to all beholders, Lo! a villain!
  Ulr. You must not use it, at least now;
  but take
This ring. [*He gives* WERNER *a jewel.*
  Wer. A gem! It was my father's!
  Ulr. And
As such is now your own. With this you
  must
Bribe the intendant for his old caleche
And horses to pursue your route at sun-
  rise, 190
Together with my mother.
  Wer. And leave you,
So lately found, in peril too?
  Ulr. Fear nothing!
The only fear were if we fled together,
For that would make our ties beyond all
  doubt.
The waters only lie in flood between 195
This burgh and Frankfort; so far's in our
  favour.
The route on to Bohemia, though encum-
  ber'd,
Is not impassable; and when you gain
A few hours' start, the difficulties will be
The same to your pursuers. Once beyond
The frontier, and you're safe.
  Wer. My noble boy!
  Ulr. Hush! hush! no transports: we'll
  indulge in them
In Castle Siegendorf! Display no gold!
Show Idenstein the gem (I know the man,
And have look'd through him): it will
  answer thus 205
A double purpose. Stralenheim lost
  gold—
No jewel; therefore it could *not* be his;
And then the man who was possest of this
Can hardly be suspected of abstracting
The baron's coin, when he could thus
  convert 210
This ring to more than Stralenheim has
  lost
By his last night's slumber. Be not over
  timid
In your address, nor yet too arrogant,
And Idenstein will serve you.
  Wer. I will follow
In all things your direction.
  Ulr. I would have 215
Spared you the trouble; but had I appear'd
To take an interest in you, and still more
By dabbling with a jewel in your favour,
All had been known at once.
  Wer. My guardian angel!
This overpays the past. But how wilt thou
Fare in our absence? 221
  Ulr. Stralenheim knows nothing
Of me as aught of kindred with yourself.

I will but wait a day or two with him
To lull all doubts, and then rejoin my
  father.
Wer. To part no more!
Ulr.   I know not that; but at   225
The least we'll meet again once more.
Wer.					My boy!
My friend! my only child, and sole pre-
  server!
Oh, do not hate me!
Ulr.				Hate my father!
Wer.				Ay,
My father hated me. Why not my son?
Ulr. Your father knew you not as I do.
Wer.				Scorpions
Are in thy words! Thou know me? in this
  guise					231
Thou canst not know me, I am not myself;
Yet (hate me not) I will be soon.
Ulr.					I'll *wait!*
In the mean time be sure that all a son
Can do for parents shall be done for mine.
Wer. I see it, and I feel it; yet I feel
Further—that you despise me.
Ulr.			Wherefore should I?
Wer. Must I repeat my humiliation?
Ulr.				No! 238
I have fathom'd it and you. But let us talk
Of this no more. Or if it must be ever,
Not *now.* Your error has redoubled all
The present difficulties of our house,
At secret war with that of Stralenheim:
All we have now to think of is to baffle
HIM. I have shown *one* way.
Wer.		The only one, 245
And I embrace it, as I did my son,
Who show'd *himself* and father's *safety* in
One day.
Ulr.	You *shall* be safe; let that suffice.
Would Stralenheim's appearance in
  Bohemia
Disturb your right, or mine, if once we
  were					250
Admitted to our lands?
Wer.			Assuredly,
Situate as we are now; although the first
Possessor might, as usual, prove the
  strongest,
Especially the next in blood.
Ulr.		Blood! 'tis 254
A word of many meanings; in the veins,
And out of them, it is a different thing—
And so it should be, when the same in
  blood
(As it is call'd) are aliens to each other,
Like Theban brethren: when a part is bad,
A few spilt ounces purify the rest.   260
Wer. I do not apprehend you.
Ulr.			That may be—
And should, perhaps—and yet—but get
  ye ready;
You and my mother must away to-night.
Here comes the intendant: sound him with
  the gem;					264

'Twill sink into his venal soul like lead
Into the deep, and bring up slime and mud,
And ooze too, from the bottom, as the lead
  doth
With its greased understratum; but no less
Will serve to warn our vessels through
  these shoals.
The freight is rich, so heave the line in
  time!					270
Farewell! I scarce have time, but yet your
  hand,
My father!——
Wer.		Let me embrace thee!
Ulr.				We may be
Observed: subdue your nature to the
  hour!
Keep off from me as from your foe!
Wer.				Accursed
Be he who is the stifling cause which
  smothers				275
The best and sweetest feeling of our hearts;
At such an hour too!
Ulr.		Yes, curse—it will ease you!
Here is the intendant.

Enter IDENSTEIN.
				Master Idenstein,
How fare you in your purpose? Have you
  caught					279
The rogue?
Iden.	No, faith!
Ulr.		Well, there are plenty more:
You may have better luck another chase.
Where is the baron?
Iden.	Gone back to his chamber:
And now I think on't, asking after you
With nobly-born impatience.
Ulr.			Your great men
Must be answer'd on the instant, as the
  bound					285
Of the stung steed replies unto the spur:
'Tis well they have horses, too; for, if they
  had not,
I fear that men must draw their chariots,
  as
They say kings did Sesostris.
Iden.			Who was he?
Ulr. An old Bohemian—an imperial
  gipsy.					290
Iden. A gipsy or Bohemian, 'tis the
  same,
For they pass by both names. And was
  he one?
Ulr. I've heard so; but I must take
  leave. Intendant,
Your servant!—Werner [*to* WERNER
  slightly], if that be your name,
Yours.				[*Exit* ULRIC.
Iden. A well-spoken pretty-faced
  young man!				295
And prettily behaved! He knows his
  station,
You see, sir: how he gave to each his due
Precedence!

Wer. I perceived it, and applaud
His just discernment and your own.
Iden. That's well—
That's very well. You also know your
place, too; 300
And yet I don't know that *I* know your
place.
Wer. [*showing the ring*]. Would this
assist your knowledge?
Iden. How!—What!—Eh?
A jewel.
Wer. 'Tis your own on one condition.
Iden. Mine!—Name it!
Wer. That hereafter you permit me
At thrice its value to redeem it: 'tis 305
A family ring.
Iden. A family!—*yours!*—a gem!
I'm breathless!
Wer. You must also furnish me,
An hour ere daybreak, with all means to quit
This place.
Iden. But is it real? Let me look on it:
Diamond, by all that's glorious!
Wer. Come, I'll trust you: 310
You have guess'd, no doubt, that I was
born above
My present seeming.
Iden. I can't say I did,
Though this looks like it: this is the true
breeding
Of gentle blood!
Wer. I have important reasons
For wishing to continue privily 315
My journey hence.
Iden. So then *you are* the man
Whom Stralenheim's in quest of?
Wer. I am not;
But being taken for him might conduct
So much embarrassment to me just now,
And to the baron's self hereafter—'tis
To spare both that I would avoid all bustle.
Iden. Be you the man or no, 'tis not
my business;
Besides, I never could obtain the half
From this proud, niggardly noble, who
would raise 324
The country for some missing bits of coin,
And never offer a precise reward—
But *this!*—another look!
Wer. Gaze on it freely;
At day-dawn it is yours.
Iden. Oh, thou sweet sparkler!
Thou more than stone of the philosopher!
Thou touchstone of Philosophy herself!
Thou bright eye of the Mine! thou loadstar
of 331
The Soul! the true magnetic Pole to which
All hearts point duly north, like trembling
needles!
Thou flaming Spirit of the Earth! which,
sitting
High on the monarch's diadem, attractest
More worship than the majesty who
sweats 336

Beneath the crown which makes his head
ache, like
Millions of hearts which bleed to lend it
lustre!
Shalt thou be mine? I am, methinks, already
A little king, a lucky alchymist!— 340
A wise magician, who has bound the devil
Without the forfeit of his soul. But come,
Werner, or what else?
Wer. Call me Werner still;
You may yet know me by a loftier title.
Iden. I do believe in thee! thou art the
spirit 345
Of whom I long have dream'd in a low
garb.—
But come, I'll serve thee: thou shalt be as
free
As air, despite the waters; let us hence:
I'll show thee I am honest—(oh, thou
jewel!)
Thou shalt be furnish'd, Werner, with such
means 350
Of flight, that if thou wert a snail, not birds
Should overtake thee.—Let me gaze
again!
I have a foster-brother in the mart
Of Hamburgh skill'd in precious stones.
How many
Carats may it weigh?—Come, Werner, I
will wing thee. [*Exeunt.* 355

SCENE II.—STRALENHEIM'S *Chamber.*

STRALENHEIM *and* FRITZ.

Fritz. All's ready, my good lord!
Stral. I am not sleepy,
And yet I must to bed; I fain would say
To rest, but something heavy on my spirit,
Too dull for wakefulness, too quick for
slumber,
Sits on me as a cloud along the sky, 5
Which will not let the sunbeams through,
nor yet
Descend in rain and end, but spreads itself
'Twixt earth and heaven, like envy between
man
And man, an everlasting mist:—I will
Unto my pillow.
Fritz. May you rest there well! 10
Stral. I feel, and fear, I shall.
Fritz. And wherefore fear?
Stral. I know not why, and therefore
do fear more,
Because an undescribable——but 'tis
All folly. Were the locks (as I desired)
Changed, to-day, of this chamber? for
last night's 15
Adventure makes it needful.
Fritz. Certainly,
According to your order, and beneath
The inspection of myself and the young
Saxon
Who saved your life. I think they call him
'Ulric.'

Stral. You *think!* you supercilious
　slave! what right　　　　　　　　　20
Have you to *tax your* memory, which
　should be
Quick, proud, and happy to retain the
　name
Of him who saved your master, as a litany
Whose daily repetition marks your
　duty?—
Get hence! '*You think,*' indeed! you, who
　stood still　　　　　　　　　　　　25
Howling and dripping on the bank, whilst
　I
Lay dying, and the stranger dash'd aside
The roaring torrent, and restored me to
Thank him—and despise you. '*You
　think!*' and scarce　　　　　　　29
Can recollect his name! I will not waste
More words on you. Call me betimes.
　Fritz.　　　　　　　　　Good night!
I trust to-morrow will restore your lord-
　ship
To renovated strength and temper.
　　　　　　　　　　[*The scene closes.*

SCENE III.—*The secret Passage.*

　Gab. [*solus*].　　　　　　　　Four—
Five—six hours have I counted, like the
　guard
Of outposts on the never-merry clock;
That hollow tongue of time, which, even
　when
It sounds for joy, takes something from
　enjoyment　　　　　　　　　　　5
With every clang. 'Tis a perpetual knell,
Though for a marriage feast it rings: each
　stroke
Peals for a hope the less; the funeral note
Of Love deep-buried without resurrection
In the grave of Possession; while the knoll
Of long-lived parents finds a jovial echo
To triple time in the son's ear.
　　　　　　　　　　　　I'm cold—
I'm dark;—I've blown my fingers—num-
　ber'd o'er
And o'er my steps—and knock'd my head
　against
Some fifty buttresses—and roused the
　rats　　　　　　　　　　　　　15
And bats in general insurrection, till
Their cursed pattering feet and whirling
　wings
Leave me scarce hearing for another sound.
A light! It is at distance (if I can
Measure in darkness distance): but it
　blinks　　　　　　　　　　　　20
As through a crevice or a key-hole, in
The inhibited direction: I must on,
Nevertheless, from curiosity.
A distant lamp-light is an incident
In such a den as this. Pray Heaven it lead
　me　　　　　　　　　　　　　25
To nothing that may tempt me! Else—
　Heaven aid me

To obtain or to escape it! Shining still!
Were it the star of Lucifer himself,
Or he himself girt with its beams, I could
Contain no longer. Softly: mighty well!
That corner's turn'd—so—ah! no:—
　right! it draws　　　　　　　　31
Nearer. Here is a darksome angle—so,
That's weather'd.—Let me pause.—
　Suppose it leads
Into some greater danger than that which
I have escaped—no matter, 'tis a new one;
And novel perils, like fresh mistresses,
Wear more magnetic aspects:—I will on,
And be it where it may—I have my
　dagger,
Which may protect me at a pinch.—Burn
　still,
Thou little light! Thou art my *ignis
　fatuus!*　　　　　　　　　　　40
My stationary Will-o'-the-wisp!—So! so!
He hears my invocation, and fails not.
　　　　　　　　　　[*The scene closes.*

SCENE IV.—*A Garden.*

Enter WERNER.

　Wer. I could not sleep—and now the
　hour's at hand;
All's ready. Idenstein has kept his word;
And station'd in the outskirts of the town,
Upon the forest's edge, the vehicle
Awaits us. Now the dwindling stars be-
　gin　　　　　　　　　　　　　5
To pale in heaven; and for the last time I
Look on these horrible walls. Oh! never,
　never
Shall I forget them. Here I came most
　poor,
But not dishonour'd: and I leave them
　with　　　　　　　　　　　　9
A stain,—if not upon my name, yet in
My heart!—a never-dying canker-worm,
Which all the coming splendour of the
　lands,
And rights, and sovereignty of Siegendorf
Can scarcely lull a moment. I must find
Some means of restitution, which would
　ease　　　　　　　　　　　　15
My soul in part: but how, without dis-
　covery?—
It must be done, however; and I'll pause
Upon the method the first hour of safety.
The madness of my misery led to this
Base infamy; repentance must retrieve it:
I will have nought of Stralenheim's upon
My spirit, though he would grasp all of
　mine;
Lands, freedom, life,—and yet he sleeps
　as soundly,
Perhaps, as infancy, with gorgeous
　curtains　　　　　　　　　　　24
Spread for his canopy, o'er silken pillows,
Such as when——Hark! what noise is
　that? Again!

587

The branches shake; and some loose
    stones have fallen
From yonder terrace.
    [ULRIC *leaps down from the terrace.*
                Ulric! ever welcome!
Thrice welcome now! this filial——
Ulr.   Stop! Before
We approach, tell me——
Wer.   Why look you so?
Ulr.   Do I 30
Behold my father, or——
Wer.   What?
Ulr.   An assassin?
Wer.   Insane or insolent!
Ulr.   Reply, sir, as
You prize your life, or mine!
Wer.   To what must I
Answer?
Ulr.   Are you or are you not the
    assassin
Of Stralenheim?
Wer.   I never was as yet 35
The murderer of any man. What mean you?
Ulr.   Did not you *this* night (as the
    night before)
Retrace the secret passage? Did you not
Again revisit Stralenheim's chamber?
    and——
             [ULRIC *pauses.*
Wer.   Proceed.
Ulr.   *Died* he not by your hand?
Wer.   Great God! 40
Ulr.   You are innocent, then! my
    father's innocent!
Embrace me! Yes,—your tone—your
    look—yes, yes,—
Yet *say* so.
Wer.   If I e'er, in heart or mind,
Conceived deliberately such a thought,
But rather strove to trample back to hell
Such thoughts—if e'er they glared a
    moment through 46
The irritation of my oppressed spirit—
May heaven be shut for ever from my
    hopes,
As from mine eyes!
Ulr.   But Stralenheim is dead.
Wer.   'Tis horrible! 'tis hideous, as
    'tis hateful!—   50
But what have I to do with this?
Ulr.   No bolt
Is forced; no violence can be detected,
Save on his body. Part of his own house-
    hold
Have been alarm'd; but as the intendant is
Absent, I took upon myself the care 55
Of mustering the police. His chamber has,
Past doubt, been enter'd secretly. Excuse
    me,
If nature——
Wer.   Oh, my boy! what unknown
    woes
Of dark fatality, like clouds, are gathering
Above our house!

Ulr.   My father! I acquit you! 60
But will the world do so? will even the
    judge,
If——But you must away this instant.
Wer.   No!
I'll face it. Who shall dare suspect me?
Ulr.   Yet
You had *no* guests—*no* visitors—no life
Breathing around you, save my mother's?
Wer.   Ah! 65
The Hungarian!
Ulr.   He is gone! he disappear'd
Ere sunset.
Wer.   No; I hid him in that very
Conceal'd and fatal gallery.
Ulr.   There I'll find him.
                [ULRIC *is going.*
Wer.   It is too late: he had left the
    palace ere
I quitted it. I found the secret panel 70
Open, and the doors which lead from that
    hall
Which masks it: I but thought he had
    snatch'd the silent
And favourable moment to escape
The myrmidons of Idenstein, who were
Dogging him yester-even.
Ulr.   You reclosed 75
The panel?
Wer.   Yes; and not without reproach
(And inner trembling for the avoided
    peril)
At his dull heedlessness, in leaving thus
His shelterer's asylum to the risk
Of a discovery.
Ulr.   You are sure you closed it? 80
Wer.   Certain.
Ulr.   That's well; but had been better,
    if
You ne'er had turn'd it to a den for——
                [He *pauses.*
Wer.   Thieves!
Thou wouldst say: I must bear it, and
    deserve it;
But not—
Ulr.   No, father; do not speak of this:
This is no hour to think of petty crimes,
But to prevent the consequence of great
    ones.   86
Why would you shelter this man?
Wer.   Could I shun it?
A man pursued by my chief foe; disgraced
For my own crime: a victim to *my* safety,
Imploring a few hours' concealment from
The very wretch who was the cause he
    needed   91
Such refuge. Had he been a wolf, I could not
Have in such circumstances thrust him
    forth.
Ulr.   And like the wolf he hath repaid
    you. But
It is too late to ponder thus:—you must
Set out ere dawn. I will remain here to
Trace the murderer, if 'tis possible. 97

Wer. But this my sudden flight will give the Moloch
Suspicion: two new victims in the lieu
Of one, if I remain. The fled Hungarian,
Who seems the culprit, and——
Ulr.   Who *seems? Who* else   101
Can be so?
Wer.   Not *I*, though just now you doubted—
You, my *son!*—doubted—
Ulr.   And do you doubt of him
The fugitive?
Wer.   Boy! since I fell into
The abyss of crime (though not of *such* crime), I,   105
Having seen the innocent oppress'd for me,
May doubt even of the guilty's guilt. Your heart
Is free, and quick with virtuous wrath to accuse
Appearances; and views a criminal
In Innocence's shadow, it may be,   110
Because 'tis dusky.
Ulr.   And if I do so,
What will mankind, who know you not, or knew
But to oppress? You must not stand the hazard.
Away!—I'll make all easy. Idenstein
Will for his own sake and his jewel's hold
His peace—he also is a partner in   116
Your flight—moreover——
Wer.   Fly! and leave my name
Link'd with the Hungarian's, or preferr'd as poorest,
To bear the brand of bloodshed?
Ulr.   Pshaw! leave anything
Except our fathers' sovereignty and castles,
For which you have so long panted, and in vain!   121
What *name?* You have *no name*, since that you bear
Is feign'd.
Wer. Most true: but still I would not have it
Engraved in crimson in men's memories,
Though in this most obscure abode of men——   125
Besides, the search——
Ulr.   I will provide against
Aught that can touch you. No one knows you here
As heir of Siegendorf: if Idenstein
Suspects, 'tis *but suspicion*, and he is
A fool: his folly shall have such employment,   130
Too, that the unknown Werner shall give way
To nearer thoughts of self. The laws (if e'er
Laws reach'd this village) are all in abeyance
With the late general war of thirty years,
Or crush'd, or rising slowly from the dust,
To which the march of armies trampled them.   136

Stralenheim, although noble, is unheeded
Here, save as *such*—without lands, influence,
Save what hath perish'd with him. Few prolong
A week beyond their funeral rites their sway   140
O'er men, unless by relatives, whose interest
Is roused: such is not here the case; he died
Alone, unknown,—a solitary grave,
Obscure as his deserts, without a scutcheon,
Is all he'll have, or wants. If *I* discover
The assassin, 'twill be well—if not, believe me,   146
None else; though all the full-fed train of menials
May howl above his ashes (as they did
Around him in his danger on the Oder),
Will no more stir a finger *now* than *then.*
Hence! hence! I must not hear your answer.—Look!   151
The stars are almost faded, and the grey
Begins to grizzle the black hair of night.
You shall not answer:—Pardon me that I
Am peremptory; 'tis your son that speaks,
Your long-lost, late-found son.—Let's call my mother!   156
Softly and swiftly step, and leave the rest
To me: I'll answer for the event as far
As regards *you*, and that is the chief point,
As my first duty, which shall be observed.
We'll meet in Castle Siegendorf—once more   161
Our banners shall be glorious! Think of that
Alone, and leave all other thoughts to me,
Whose youth may better battle with them—Hence!
And may your age be happy!—I will kiss
My mother once more, then Heaven's speed be with you!   166
Wer. This counsel's safe—but is it honourable?
Ulr. To save a father is a child's chief honour.   [*Exeunt.*

ACT IV

SCENE I.—*A Gothic Hall in the Castle of Siegendorf, near Prague.*

Enter ERIC *and* HENRICK, *Retainers of the Count.*

Eric. So, better times are come at last; to these
Old walls new masters and high wassail—both
A long desideratum.
Hen.   Yes, for *masters*,
It might be unto those who long for novelty,

Though made by a new grave: but as for
    wassail, 5
Methinks the old Count Siegendorf main-
    tain'd
His feudal hospitality as high
As e'er another prince of the empire.
  Eric.   Why
For the mere cup and trencher, we no
    doubt
Fared passing well; but as for merriment
And sport, without which salt and sauces
    season 11
The cheer but scantily, our sizings were
Even of the narrowest.
  Hen.   The old count loved not
The roar of revel; are you sure that *this*
    does?
  Eric. As yet he hath been courteous as
    he's bounteous, 15
And we all love him.
  Hen.   His reign is as yet
Hardly a year o'erpast its honey-moon,
And the first year of sovereigns is bridal:
Anon, we shall perceive his real sway
And moods of mind.
  Eric. Pray Heaven he keep the
    present! 20
Then his brave son, Count Ulric—there's
    a knight!
Pity the wars are o'er!
  Hen.   Why so?
  Eric.   Look on him!
And answer that yourself.
  Hen.   He's very youthful,
And strong and beautiful as a young tiger.
  Eric. That's not a faithful vassal's
    likeness.
  Hen.   But 25
Perhaps a true one.
  Eric.   Pity, as I said,
The wars are over: in the hall, who like
Count Ulric for a well-supported pride,
Which awes, but yet offends not? in the
    field,
Who like him with his spear in hand,
    when, gnashing 30
His tusks, and ripping up from right to left
The howling hounds, the boar makes for
    the thicket?
Who backs a horse, or bears a hawk, or
    wears
A sword like him? Whose plume nods
    knightlier?
  Hen. No one's, I grant you. Do not
    fear, if war 35
Be long in coming, he is of that kind
Will make it for himself, if he hath not
Already done as much.
  Eric.   What do you mean?
  Hen. You can't deny his train of
    followers
(But few our native fellow-vassals born
On the domain) are such a sort of knaves
As——   [*Pauses.*

  Eric. What?
  Hen.   The war (you love so
    much) leaves living.
Like other parents, she spoils her worst
    children.
  Eric. Nonsense! they are all brave
    iron-visaged fellows,
Such as old Tilly loved.
  Hen.   And who loved Tilly? 45
Ask that at Magdebourg—or for that
    matter
Wallenstein either;—they are gone to——
  Eric.   Rest!
But what beyond, 'tis not ours to pro-
    nounce.
  Hen. I wish they had left us something
    of their rest:
The country (nominally now at peace)
Is over-run with—God knows who: they
    fly 51
By night, and disappear with sunrise; but
Leave us no less desolation, nay, even
    more,
Than the most open warfare.
  Eric.   But Count Ulric—
What has all this to do with him?
  Hen.   With him! 55
He——might prevent it. As you say he's
    fond
Of war, why makes he it not on those
    marauders?
  Eric. You'd better ask himself.
  Hen.   I would as soon
Ask the lion why he laps not milk.
  Eric. And here he comes!
  Hen.   The devil! you'll hold your
    tongue? 60
  Eric. Why do you turn so pale?
  Hen.   'Tis nothing—but
Be silent.
  Eric. I will, upon what you have said.
  Hen. I assure you I meant nothing,—
    a mere sport
Of words, no more; besides, had it been
    otherwise,
He is to espouse the gentle Baroness 65
Ida of Stralenheim, the late baron's heiress;
And she, no doubt, will soften whatsoever
Of fierceness the late long intestine wars
Have given all natures, and most unto
    those
Who were born in them, and bred up
    upon 70
The knees of Homicide; sprinkled, as it
    were,
With blood even at their baptism. Prithee,
    peace
On all that I have said!

Enter ULRIC *and* RODOLPH.

                Good morrow, Count.
  Ulr. Good morrow, worthy Henrick.
    Eric, is
All ready for the chase?

Eric.   The dogs are order'd 75
Down to the forest, and the vassals out
To beat the bushes, and the day looks
   promising.
Shall I call forth your excellency's suite?
What courser will you please to mount?
   Ulr.   The dun,
Walstein.
   Eric.   I fear he scarcely has
   recover'd   80
The toils of Monday: 'twas a noble chase:
You spear'd *four* with your own hand.
   Ulr.   True, good Eric;
I had forgotten—let it be the grey, then,
Old Ziska: he has not been out this fort-
   night.
   Eric. He shall be straight caparison'd.
   How many   85
Of your immediate retainers shall
Escort you?
   Ulr.   I leave that to Weilburgh, our
Master of the horse.   [*Exit* ERIC.
                    Rodolph!
   Rod.   My lord!
   Ulr.   The news
Is awkward from the——
                  [RODOLPH *points to* HENRICK.
           How now, Henrick? why
Loiter you here?
   Hen.   For your commands, my lord.
   Ulr.   Go to my father, and present my
   duty,   91
And learn if he would aught with me
   before
I mount.   [*Exit* HENRICK.
   Rodolph, our friends have had a check
Upon the frontiers of Franconia, and
'Tis rumour'd that the column sent
   against them   95
Is to be strengthen'd. I must join them soon.
   Rod. Best wait for further and more
   sure advices.
   Ulr. I mean it—and indeed it could
   not well
Have fallen out at a time more opposite
To all my plans.
   Rod.   It will be difficult 100
To excuse your absence to the count your
   father.
   Ulr. Yes, but the unsettled state of our
   domain
In high Silesia will permit and cover
My journey. In the mean time, when we are
Engaged in the chase, draw off the eighty
   men   105
Whom Wolffe leads—keep the forests on
   your route:
You know it well?
   Rod.   As well as on that night
When we——
   Ulr. We will not speak of that until
We can repeat the same with like success:
And when you have join'd, give Rosen-
   berg this letter.   [*Gives a letter.*

Add further, that I have sent this slight
   addition   111
To our force with you and Wolffe, as
   herald of
My coming, though I could but spare
   them ill
At this time, as my father loves to keep
Full numbers of retainers round the castle,
Until this marriage, and its feasts and
   fooleries,   116
Are rung out with its peal of nuptial non-
   sense.
   Rod. I thought you loved the lady Ida?
   Ulr.   Why,
I do so—but it follows not from that
I would bind in my youth and glorious
   years,   120
So brief and burning, with a lady's zone,
Although 'twere that of Venus:—but I
   love her,
As woman should be loved, fairly and
   solely.
   Rod. And constantly?
   Ulr.   I think so; for I love
Nought else.—But I have not the time to
   pause   125
Upon these gewgaws of the heart. Great
   things
We have to do ere long. Speed! speed!
   good Rodolph!
   Rod. On my return, however, I shall
   find
The Baroness Ida lost in Countess
   Siegendorf?
   Ulr. Perhaps: my father wishes it; and
   sooth   130
'Tis no bad policy: this union with
The last bud of the rival branch at once
Unites the future and destroys the past.
   Rod. Adieu.
   Ulr.   Yet hold—we had better
   keep together
Until the chase begins; then draw thou
   off,   135
And do as I have said.
   Rod.   I will. But to
Return—'twas a most kind act in the
   count
Your father to send up to Konigsberg
For this fair orphan of the baron, and
To hail her as his daughter.
   Ulr.   Wondrous kind! 140
Especially as little kindness till
Then grew between them.
   Rod.   The late baron died
Of a fever, did he not?
   Ulr.   How should I know?
   Rod. I have heard it whisper'd there
   was something strange
About his death—and even the place of
   it   145
Is scarcely known.
   Ulr.   Some obscure village on
The Saxon or Silesian frontier.

Rod.   He
Has left no testament—no farewell words?
Ulr. I am neither confessor nor notary,
So cannot say.
Rod.   Ah! here's the lady Ida. 150

Enter IDA STRALENHEIM.

Ulr. You are early, my sweet cousin!
Ida.   Not *too* early,
Dear Ulric, if I do not interrupt you.
Why do you call me 'cousin'?
Ulr. [*smiling*].   Are we not so?
Ida. Yes, but I do not like the name;
    methinks   154
It sounds so cold, as if you thought upon
Our pedigree, and only weigh'd our blood.
Ulr. [*starting*].   Blood!
Ida. Why does yours start from your
    cheeks?
Ulr.   Ay! doth it?
Ida. It doth—but no! it rushes like a
    torrent
Even to your brow again.
Ulr. [*recovering himself*]. And if it fled,
It only was because your presence sent it
Back to my heart, which beats for you,
    sweet cousin!   161
Ida. 'Cousin' again.
Ulr.   Nay, then, I'll call you sister.
Ida. I like that name still worse.—
Would we had ne'er
Been aught of kindred!
Ulr. [*gloomily*]. Would we never had!
Ida. Oh, heavens! and can *you* wish
    that?
Ulr.   Dearest Ida! 165
Did I not echo your own wish?
Ida.   Yes, Ulric,
But then I wish'd it not with such a glance,
And scarce knew what I said; but let me be
Sister or cousin, what you will, so that
I still to you am something.
Ulr.   You shall be 170
All—all——
Ida.   And you to *me are* so already;
But I can wait.
Ulr.   Dear Ida!
Ida.   Call me Ida,
Your Ida, for I would be yours, none
    else's—
Indeed I have none else left, since my poor
    father—   [*She pauses.*
Ulr. You have *mine*—you have *me.*
Ida.   Dear Ulric, how I wish 175
My father could but view my happiness,
Which wants but this!
Ulr.   Indeed!
Ida.   You would have loved him,
He you; for the brave ever love each other:
His manner was a little cold, his spirit
Proud (as is birth's prerogative); but
    under   180
This grave exterior——Would you had
    known each other!

Had such as you been near him on his
    journey,
He had not died without a friend to soothe
His last and lonely moments.
Ulr.   Who says *that?*
Ida. What?
Ulr.   That he *died alone.*
Ida.   The general rumour 185
And disappearance of his servants, who
Have ne'er return'd: that fever was most
    deadly
Which swept them all away.
Ulr.   If they were near him,
He could not die neglected or alone.
Ida. Alas! what is a menial to a death-
    bed,   190
When the dim eye rolls vainly round for
    what
It loves?—They say he died of a fever.
Ulr.   Say!
It *was* so.
Ida.   I sometimes dream otherwise.
Ulr. All dreams are false.
Ida.   And yet I see him as
I see you.
Ulr.   Where?
Ida.   In sleep—I see him lie 195
Pale, bleeding, and a man with a raised
    knife
Beside him.
Ulr.   But you do not see his *face!*
Ida [*looking at him*]. No! Oh, my
    God! do *you?*
Ulr.   Why do you ask?
Ida. Because you look as if you saw a
    murderer!
Ulr. [*agitatedly*]. Ida, this is mere child-
    ishness; your weakness   200
Infects me, to my shame: but as all feelings
Of yours are common to me, it affects me.
Prithee, sweet child, change——
Ida.   Child, indeed! I have
Full fifteen summers!   [*A bugle sounds.*
Rod.   Hark, my lord, the bugle!
Ida [*peevishly to* RODOLPH]. Why need
    you tell him that? Can he not hear it
Without your echo?
Rod.   Pardon me, fair baroness!
Ida. I will not pardon you, unless you
    earn it
By aiding me in my dissuasion of
Count Ulric from the chase to-day.
Rod.   You will not,
Lady, need aid of mine.
Ulr.   I must not now 210
Forgo it.
Ida. But you shall!
Ulr.   Shall!
Ida.   Yes, or be
No true knight.—Come, dear Ulric! yield
    to me
In this, for this one day: the day looks
    heavy,
And you are turn'd so pale and ill.

Ulr.   You jest.
Ida. Indeed I do not:—ask of Rodolph.
Rod.   Truly, 215
My lord, within this quarter of an hour
You have changed more than e'er I saw you change
In years.
Ulr. 'Tis nothing; but if 'twere, the air
Would soon restore me. I'm the true chameleon,
And live but on the atmosphere; your feasts 220
In castle halls, and social banquets, nurse not
My spirit—I'm a forester and breather
Of the steep mountain-tops, where I love all
The eagle loves.
Ida.   Except his prey, I hope.
Ulr. Sweet Ida, wish me a fair chase, and I 225
Will bring you six boars' heads for trophies home.
Ida. And will you not stay, then? You shall not go!
Come! I will sing to you.
Ulr.   Ida, you scarcely
Will make a soldier's wife.
Ida.   I do not wish
To be so; for I trust these wars are over,
And you will live in peace on your domains. 231

Enter WERNER *as* COUNT SIEGENDORF.

Ulr. My father, I salute you, and it grieves me
With such brief greeting.—You have heard our bugle;
The vassals wait.
Sieg.   So let them.—You forget
To-morrow is the appointed festival 235
In Prague for peace restored. You are apt to follow
The chase with such an ardour as will scarce
Permit you to return to-day, or if
Return'd, too much fatigued to join to-morrow
The nobles in our marshall'd ranks.
Ulr.   You, count, 240
Will well supply the place of both—I am not
A lover of these pageantries.
Sieg.   No, Ulric:
It were not well that you alone of all
Our young nobility——
Ida.   And far the noblest
In aspect and demeanour.
Sieg. [*to* IDA]. True, dear child, 245
Though somewhat frankly said for a fair damsel.—
But, Ulric, recollect too our position,
So lately reinstated in our honours.
Believe me, 'twould be mark'd in any house,

But most in *ours*, that ONE should be found wanting 250
At such a time and place. Besides, the Heaven
Which gave us back our own, in the same moment
It spread its peace o'er all, hath double claims
On us for thanksgiving: first, for our country;
And next, that we are here to share its blessings. 255
Ulr. [*aside*]. Devout, too! Well, sir, I obey at once.
[*Then aloud to a Servant*]. Ludwig, dismiss the train without!
[*Exit* LUDWIG.
Ida.   And so
You yield at once to him what I for hours
Might supplicate in vain.
Sieg. [*smiling*].   You are not jealous
Of me, I trust, my pretty rebel! who 260
Would sanction disobedience against all
Except thyself? But fear not; thou shalt rule him
Hereafter with a fonder sway and firmer.
Ida. But I should like to govern *now*.
Sieg.   You shall,
Your *harp*, which by the way awaits you with 265
The countess in her chamber. She complains
That you are a sad truant to your music:
She attends you.
Ida. Then good morrow, my kind kinsmen!
Ulric, you'll come and hear me?
Ulr.   By and by.
Ida. Be sure I'll sound it better than your bugles; 270
Then pray you be as punctual to its notes:
I'll play you King Gustavus' march.
Ulr.   And why not Old Tilly's?
Ida. Not that monster's! I should think
My harp-strings rang with groans, and not with music,
Could aught of *his* sound on it:—but come quickly; 275
Your mother will be eager to receive you.
[*Exit.*
Sieg. Ulric, I wish to speak with you alone.
Ulr. My time's your vassal.—
[*Aside to* RODOLPH]. Rodolph, hence! and do
As I directed: and by his best speed
And readiest means let Rosenberg reply.
Rod. Count Siegendorf, command you aught? I am bound 281
Upon a journey past the frontier.
Sieg. [*starts*].   Ah!—
Where? on *what* frontier?

Rod. The Silesian, on—
My way—[*Aside to* ULRIC].—*Where* shall
I say?
Ulr. [*aside to* RODOLPH]. To Ham-
burgh.
[*Aside to himself.*] That
Word will, I think, put a firm padlock on
His further inquisition.
Rod. Count, to Hamburgh. 286
Sieg. [*agitated*]. Hamburgh! No, I
have nought to do there, nor
Am aught connected with that city. Then
God speed you!
Rod. Fare ye well, Count Siegendorf!
[*Exit* RODOLPH.
Sieg. Ulric, this man, who has just
departed, is 290
One of those strange companions whom I
fain
Would reason with you on.
Ulr. My lord, he is
Noble by birth, of one of the first houses
In Saxony.
Sieg. I talk not of his birth,
But of his bearing. Men speak lightly of
him. 295
Ulr. So they will do of most men.
Even the monarch
Is not fenced from his chamberlain's
slander, or
The sneer of the last courtier whom he has
made
Great and ungrateful.
Sieg. If I must be plain,
The world speaks more than lightly of this
Rodolph: 300
They say he is leagued with the 'black
bands' who still
Ravage the frontier.
Ulr. And will you believe
The world?
Sieg. In this case—yes.
Ulr. In *any* case,
I thought you knew it better than to take
An accusation for a sentence.
Sieg. Son! 305
I understand you: you refer to——but
My destiny has so involved about me
Her spider web, that I can only flutter
Like the poor fly, but break it not. Take
heed,
Ulric; you have seen to what the passions
led me: 310
Twenty long years of misery and famine
Quench'd them not—twenty thousand
more, perchance,
Hereafter (or even here in *moments* which
Might date for years, did Anguish make
the dial)
May not obliterate or expiate 315
The madness and dishonour of an instant.
Ulric, be warn'd by a father!—I was not
By mine, and you behold me!
Ulr. I behold

The prosperous and beloved Siegendorf,
Lord of a prince's appanage, and honour'd
By those he rules and those he ranks with.
Sieg. Ah! 321
Why wilt thou call me prosperous, while
I fear
For thee? Beloved, when thou lovest me not!
All hearts but one may beat in kindness
for me—
But if my son's is cold!——
Ulr. Who *dare* say that? 325
Sieg. None else but I, who see it—*feel*
it—keener
Than would your adversary, who dared
say so,
Your sabre in his heart! But mine
survives
The wound.
Ulr. You err. My nature is not given
To outward fondling: how should it be
so, 330
After twelve years' divorcement from my
parents?
Sieg. And did not *I* too pass those
twelve torn years
In a like absence? But 'tis vain to urge
you—
Nature was never call'd back by remon-
strance.
Let's change the theme. I wish you to
consider 335
That these young violent nobles of high
name,
But dark deeds (ay, the darkest, if all
Rumour
Reports be true), with whom thou con-
sortest,
Will lead thee——
Ulr. [*impatiently*]. I'll be *led* by no
man.
Sieg. Nor 339
Be leader of such, I would hope: at once
To wean thee from the perils of thy youth
And haughty spirit, I have thought it well
That thou shouldst wed the lady Ida—
more
As thou appear'st to love her.
Ulr. I have said
I will obey your orders, were they to 345
Unite with Hecate—can a son say more?
Sieg. He says too much in saying this.
It is not
The nature of thine age, nor of thy blood,
Nor of thy temperament, to talk so coolly,
Or act so carelessly, in that which is 350
The bloom or blight of all men's happiness,
(For Glory's pillow is but restless, if
Love lay not down his cheek there): some
strong bias,
Some master fiend is in thy service, to
Misrule the mortal who believes him
slave, 355
And makes his every thought sub-
servient; else

Thou'dst say at once—'I love young Ida,
and
Will wed her;' or, 'I love her not, and
all
The powers of earth shall never make me.'
—So
Would *I* have answer'd.
   Ulr.   Sir, *you* wed for love. 360
   Sieg. I did, and it has been my only
refuge
In many miseries.
   Ulr.   Which miseries
Had never been but for this love-match.
   Sieg.   Still
Against your age and nature! Who at
twenty
E'er answer'd thus till now?
   Ulr.   Did you not warn me 365
Against your own example?
   Sieg.   Boyish sophist!
In a word, do you love, or love not, Ida?
   Ulr. What matters it, if I am ready to
Obey you in espousing her?
   Sieg.   As far
As you feel, nothing, but all life for her.
She's young—all-beautiful—adores you
—is 371
Endow'd with qualities to give happiness,
Such as rounds common life into a dream
Of something which your poets cannot
paint,
And (if it were not wisdom to love virtue)
For which Philosophy might barter
Wisdom; 376
And giving so much happiness, deserves
A little in return. I would not have her
Break her heart for a man who has none
to break;
Or wither on her stalk like some pale rose
Deserted by the bird she thought a nightin-
gale, 381
According to the Orient tale. She is——
   Ulr. The daughter of dead Stralen-
heim, your foe:
I'll wed her, ne'ertheless; though, to say
truth,
Just now I am not violently transported
In favour of such unions.
   Sieg.   But she loves you. 386
   Ulr. And I love her, and therefore
would think *twice*.
   Sieg. Alas! Love never did so.
   Ulr.   Then 'tis time
He should begin, and take the bandage
from
His eyes, and look before he leaps; till
now 390
He hath ta'en a jump i' the dark.
   Sieg.   But you consent?
   Ulr. I did, and do.
   Sieg.   Then fix the day.
   Ulr.   'Tis usual,
And certes courteous, to leave that to the
lady.

   Sieg. *I* will engage for *her*.
   Ulr.   So will not *I*
For any woman: and as what I fix, 395
I fain would see unshaken, when she gives
Her answer, I'll give mine.
   Sieg.   But 'tis your office
To woo.
   Ulr. Count, 'tis a marriage of your
making,
So be it of your wooing; but to please you,
I will now pay my duty to my mother,
With whom, you know, the lady Ida is.—
What would you have? You have forbid
my stirring
For manly sports beyond the castle walls,
And I obey; you bid me turn a chamberer,
To pick up gloves, and fans, and knitting-
needles, 405
And list to songs and tunes, and watch for
smiles,
And smile at pretty prattle, and look into
The eyes of feminine, as though they were
The stars receding early to our wish
Upon the dawn of a world-winning
battle— 410
What can a son or man do more?
                     [*Exit* ULRIC.
   Sieg. [*solus*].   Too much!—
Too much of duty, and too little love!
He pays me in the coin he owes me not:
For such hath been my wayward fate, I
could not
Fulfil a parent's duties by his side 415
Till now; but love he owes me, for my
thoughts
Ne'er left him, nor my eyes long'd with-
out tears
To see my child again, and now I have
found him!
But how—obedient, but with coldness;
duteous
In my sight, but with carelessness; mys-
terious— 420
Abstracted—distant—much given to long
absence,
And where—none know—in league with
the most riotous
Of our young nobles; though, to do him
justice,
He never stoops down to their vulgar
pleasures;
Yet there's some tie between them which
I cannot 425
Unravel. They look up to him—consult
him—
Throng round him as a leader: but with
me
He hath no confidence! Ah! can I hope it
After—what! doth my father's curse
descend
Even to my child? Or is the Hungarian
near 430
To shed more blood? or—Oh! if it should
be!

Spirit of Stralenheim, dost thou walk
  these walls
To wither him and his—who, though they
  slew not,
Unlatch'd the door of death for thee?
  'Twas not
Our fault, nor is our sin: thou wert our
  foe,   435
And yet I spared thee when my own
  destruction
Slept with thee, to awake with thine
  awakening!
And only took—Accursed gold! thou liest
Like poison in my hands; I dare not use
  thee,
Nor part from thee; thou camest in such
  a guise,   440
Methinks thou wouldst contaminate all
  hands
Like mine. Yet I have done, to atone for
  thee,
Thou villainous gold! and thy dead
  master's doom,
Though he died not by me or mine, as
  much   444
As if he were my brother! I have ta'en
His orphan Ida—cherish'd her as one
Who will be mine.

Enter an ATTENDANT.

  Atten.   The abbot, if it please
Your excellency, whom you sent for, waits
Upon you.   [*Exit* ATTENDANT.

Enter the PRIOR ALBERT.

  Prior. Peace be with these walls, and
  all
Within them!
  Sieg.   Welcome, welcome, holy
  father!   450
And may thy prayer be heard!—all men
  have need
Of such, and I——
  Prior.   Have the first claim to all
The prayers of our community. Our
  convent,
Erected by your ancestors, is still
Protected by their children.
  Sieg.   Yes, good father; 455
Continue daily orisons for us
In these dim days of heresies and blood,
Though the schismatic Swede, Gustavus,
  is
Gone home.
  Prior. To the endless home of un-
  believers,
Where there is everlasting wail and woe,
Gnashing of teeth, and tears of blood, and
  fire   461
Eternal, and the worm which dieth not!
  Sieg. True, father: and to avert those
  pangs from one,
Who, though of our most faultless holy
  church,

Yet died without its last and dearest
  offices,   465
Which smooth the soul through purga-
  torial pains,
I have to offer humbly this donation
In masses for his spirit.
  [SIEGENDORF *offers the gold which he
    had taken from* STRALENHEIM.
  Prior.   Count, if I
Receive it, 'tis because I know too well
Refusal would offend you. Be assured
The largess shall be only dealt in alms,
And every mass no less sung for the dead.
Our house needs no donations, thanks to
  yours,
Which has of old endow'd it; but from you
And yours in all meet things 'tis fit we
  obey.   475
For whom shall mass be said?
  Sieg. [*faltering*]. For—for—the dead.
  Prior. His name?
  Sieg.   'Tis from a soul, and not a
  name,
I would avert perdition.
  Prior.   I meant not
To pry into your secret. We will pray
For one unknown, the same as for the
  proudest.   480
  Sieg. Secret! I have none: but, father,
  he who's gone
Might *have* one; or, in short, he did
  bequeath—
No, not bequeath—but I bestow this sum
For pious purposes.
  Prior.   A proper deed
In the behalf of our departed friends.
  Sieg. But he who's gone was not my
  friend, but foe,   486
The deadliest and the stanchest.
  Prior.   Better still!
To employ our means to obtain heaven
  for the souls
Of our dead enemies is worthy those
Who can forgive them living.
  Sieg.   But I did not 490
Forgive this man. I loathed him to the
  last,
As he did me. I do not love him now,
But——
  Prior. Best of all! for this is pure
  religion!
You fain would rescue him you hate from
  hell—
An evangelical compassion—with 495
Your own gold too!
  Sieg.   Father, 'tis not my gold.
  Prior. Whose then? You said it was
  no legacy.
  Sieg. No matter whose—of this be
  sure, that he
Who own'd it never more will need it, save
In that which it may purchase from your
  altars: 500
'Tis yours, or theirs.

Prior.   Is there no blood upon it?
Sieg. No; but there's worse than blood—eternal shame!
Prior. Did he who own'd it die in his bed?
Sieg.   Alas!
He did.
Prior. Son! you relapse into revenge,
If you regret your enemy's bloodless death.   505
Sieg. His death was fathomlessly deep in blood.
Prior. You said he died in his bed, not battle.
Sieg.   He
Died, I scarce know—but—he was stabb'd i' the dark,
And now you have it—perish'd on his pillow
By a cut-throat!—Ay!—you may look upon me!   510
I am *not* the man. I'll meet your eye on that point,
As I can one day God's.
Prior.   Nor did he die
By means, or men, or instrument of yours?
Sieg. No! by the God who sees and strikes!
Prior.   Nor know you
Who slew him?
Sieg. I could only guess at *one*,   515
And he to me a stranger, unconnected,
As unemploy'd. Except by one day's knowledge,
I never saw the man who was suspected.
Prior. Then you are free from guilt.
Sieg. [*eagerly*].   Oh! *am* I?—say!
Prior. You have said so, and know best.
Sieg.   Father! I have spoken   520
The truth, and nought but truth, if *not* the whole;
Yet say I am *not* guilty! for the blood
Of this man weighs on me, as if I shed it,
Though, by the Power who abhorreth human blood,
I did not!—nay, once spared it, when I might   525
And *could*—ay, perhaps, *should* (if our self-safety
Be e'er excusable in such defences
Against the attacks of over-potent foes):
But pray for him, for me, and all my house;   529
For, as I said, though I be innocent,
I know not why, a like remorse is on me,
As if he had fallen by me or mine. Pray for me,
Father! I have pray'd myself in vain.
Prior.   I will.
Be comforted! You are innocent, and should
Be calm as innocence.
Sieg.   But calmness is not   535

Always the attribute of innocence.
I feel it is not.
Prior.   But it will be so,
When the mind gathers up its truth within it.
Remember the great festival to-morrow,
In which you rank amidst our chiefest nobles,   540
As well as your brave son; and smooth your aspect,
Nor in the general orison of thanks
For bloodshed stopt, let blood you shed not rise,
A cloud, upon your thoughts. This were to be
Too sensitive. Take comfort, and forget
Such things, and leave remorse unto the guilty.   [*Exeunt.*

ACT V

Scene I.—*A large and magnificent Gothic Hall in the Castle of Siegendorf, decorated with Trophies, Banners, and Arms of that family.*

Enter ARNHEIM *and* MEISTER, *Attendants of* COUNT SIEGENDORF.

Arn. Be quick! the count will soon return: the ladies
Already are at the portal. Have you sent
The messengers in search of him he seeks for?
Meis. I have, in all directions, over Prague,
As far as the man's dress and figure could
By your description track him. The devil take   6
These revels and processions! All the pleasure
(If such there be) must fall to the spectators.
I'm sure none doth to us who make the show.
Arn. Go to! my lady countess comes.
Meis.   I'd rather   10
Ride a day's hunting on an outworn jade,
Than follow in the train of a great man,
In these dull pageantries.
Arn.   Begone! and rail
Within.   [*Exeunt.*

Enter the COUNTESS JOSEPHINE SIEGENDORF *and* IDA STRALENHEIM.

Jos. Well, Heaven be praised! the show is over.
Ida. How can you say so? Never have I dreamt   15
Of aught so beautiful. The flowers, the boughs,
The banners, and the nobles, and the knights,
The gems, the robes, the plumes, the happy faces,

The coursers, and the incense, and the sun
Streaming through the stain'd windows,
   even the *tombs*,   20
Which look'd so calm, and the celestial
   hymns,
Which seem'd as if they rather came from
   heaven
Than mounted there. The bursting
   organ's peal
Rolling on high like an harmonious
   thunder;
The white robes and the lifted eyes; the
   world   25
At peace! and all at peace with one
   another!
Oh, my sweet mother!
           [*Embracing* JOSEPHINE.
  Jos.   My beloved child!
For such, I trust, thou shalt be shortly.
  Ida.   Oh!
I am so already. Feel how my heart beats!
  Jos. It does, my love; and never may
   it throb   30
With aught more bitter.
  Ida.   Never shall it do so!
How should it? What should make us
   grieve? I hate
To hear of sorrow: how can we be sad,
Who love each other so entirely? You,
The count, and Ulric, and your daughter
   Ida.   35
  Jos. Poor child!
  Ida.   Do you pity me?
  Jos.   No: I but envy,
And that in sorrow, not in the world's
   sense
Of the universal vice, if one vice be
More general than another.
  Ida.   I'll not hear
A word against a world which still
   contains   40
You and my Ulric. Did you ever see
Aught like him? How he tower'd
   amongst them all!
How all eyes follow'd him! The flowers
   fell faster—
Rain'd from each lattice at his feet, me-
   thought,
Than before all the rest; and where he
   trod   45
I dare be sworn that they grow still, nor
   e'er
Will wither.
  Jos. You will spoil him, little flatterer,
If he should hear you.
  Ida.   But he never will.
I dare not say so much to him—I fear
   him.
  Jos. Why so? he loves you well.
  Ida.   But I can never 50
Shape my thoughts *of* him into words *to*
   him:
Besides, he sometimes frightens me.
  Jos.   How so?

  Ida. A cloud comes o'er his blue eyes
   suddenly,
Yet he says nothing.
  Jos.   It is nothing: all men, 54
Especially in these dark troublous times,
Have much to think of.
  Ida.   But I cannot think
Of aught save him.
  Jos.   Yet there are other men,
In the world's eye, as goodly. There's,
   for instance,
The young Count Waldorf, who scarce
   once withdrew
His eyes from yours to-day.
  Ida.   I did not see him 60
But Ulric. Did you not see at the moment
When all knelt, and I wept? and yet me-
   thought,
Through my fast tears, though they were
   thick and warm,
I saw him smiling on me.
  Jos.   I could not
See aught save heaven, to which my eyes
   were rais'd,   65
Together with the people's.
  Ida.   I thought too
Of heaven, although I look'd on Ulric.
  Jos.   Come,
Let us retire! they will be here anon
Expectant of the banquet. We will lay
Aside these nodding plumes and dragging
   trains.   70
  Ida. And, above all, these stiff and
   heavy jewels,
Which make my head and heart ache, as
   both throb
Beneath their glitter o'er my brow and
   zone.
Dear mother, I am with you.

Enter COUNT SIEGENDORF, *in full dress,*
  from the solemnity, and LUDWIG.

  Sieg.   Is he not found?
  Lud. Strict search is making every-
   where; and if   75
The man be in Prague, be sure he will be
   found.
  Sieg. Where's Ulric?
  Lud.   He rode round the other way
With some young nobles; but he left them
   soon;
And, if I err not, not a minute since
I heard his excellency, with his train, 80
Gallop o'er the west drawbridge.

     Enter ULRIC, *splendidly dressed.*

  Sieg. [*to* LUDWIG]. See they cease not
Their quest of him I have described.
               [*Exit* LUDWIG.
                Oh, Ulric!
How have I long'd for thee!
  Ulr.   Your wish is granted—
Behold me!
  Sieg. I have seen the murderer.

Ulr. Whom? Where?

Sieg. The Hungarian, who slew
Stralenheim.   85

Ulr. You dream.

Sieg. I live! and as I live, I saw him—
Heard him! he dared to utter even my
name.

Ulr. What name?

Sieg.   Werner! *'twas* mine.

Ulr.   It must be so
No more: forget it.

Sieg.   Never! never! all
My destinies were woven in that name:
It will not be engraved upon my tomb,
But it may lead me there.

Ulr. To the point——the Hungarian?

Sieg. Listen!—The church was
throng'd: the hymn was raised;
'*Te Deum*' peal'd from nations rather
than
From choirs, in one great cry of 'God be
praised'   95
For one day's peace, after thrice ten dread
years,
Each bloodier than the former: I arose,
With all the nobles, and as I look'd down
Along the lines of lifted faces,—from
Our banner'd and escutcheon'd gallery, I
Saw, like a flash of lightning (for I saw
A moment and no more), what struck me
sightless
To all else—the Hungarian's face! I grew
Sick; and when I recover'd from the mist
Which curl'd about my senses, and again
Look'd down, I saw him not. The thanks-
giving   106
Was over, and we march'd back in pro-
cession.

Ulr. Continue.

Sieg.   When we reach'd the
Muldau's bridge,
The joyous crowd above, the numberless
Barks mann'd with revellers in their best
garbs,   110
Which shot along the glancing tide below,
The decorated street, the long array,
The clashing music, and the thundering
Of far artillery, which seem'd to bid
A long and loud farewell to its great
doings,   115
The standards o'er me, and the tramplings
round,
The roar of rushing thousands,—all—all
could not
Chase this man from my mind, although
my senses
No longer held him palpable.

Ulr.   You saw him
No more, then?

Sieg. I look'd, as a dying soldier   120
Looks at a draught of water, for this man;
But still I saw him not; but in his stead——

Ulr. What in his stead?

Sieg.   My eye for ever fell

Upon your dancing crest; the loftiest,
As on the loftiest and the loveliest head,
It rose the highest of the stream of plumes,
Which overflow'd the glittering streets of
Prague.

Ulr. What's this to the Hungarian?

Sieg.   Much; for I
Had almost then forgot him in my son;
When just as the artillery ceased, and
paused   130
The music, and the crowd embraced in lieu
Of shouting, I heard in a deep, low voice,
Distinct and keener far upon my ear
Than the late cannon's volume, this
word—'*Werner!*'

Ulr. Utter'd by——

Sieg.   HIM! I turn'd—and saw—
and fell.   135

Ulr. And wherefore? Were you seen?

Sieg.   The officious care
Of those around me dragg'd me from the
spot,
Seeing my faintness, ignorant of the cause:
You, too, were too remote in the pro-
cession
(The old nobles being divided from their
children)   140
To aid me.

Ulr.   But I'll aid you now.

Sieg.   In what?

Ulr. In searching for this man, or——
When he's found.
What shall we do with him?

Sieg.   I know not that.

Ulr. Then wherefore seek?

Sieg.   Because I cannot rest
Till he is found. His fate, and Stralen-
heim's,   145
And ours, seem intertwisted! nor can be
Unravell'd, till——

                    Enter an ATTENDANT

Atten.   A stranger to wait on
Your excellency.

Sieg.   Who?

Atten.   He gave no name.

Sieg. Admit him, ne'ertheless.
[*The* ATTENDANT *introduces* GABOR,
and afterwards exit.

                    Ah!

Gab.   'Tis then Werner!

Sieg. [*haughtily*]. The same you knew,
sir, by that name; and *you!*   150

Gab. [*looking round*]. I recognise you
both: father and son,
It seems. Count, I have heard that you,
or yours,
Have lately been in search of me: I am
here.

Sieg. I have sought you, and have
found you: you are charged
(Your own heart may inform you why)
with such   155
A crime as——   [*He pauses.*

Gab. Give it utterance, and then I'll meet the consequences.

Sieg. You shall do so—Unless——

Gab. First, who accuses me?

Sieg. All things, If not all men: the universal rumour—My own presence on the spot—the place—the time— 160 And every speck of circumstance unite To fix the blot on you.

Gab. And on *me only*? Pause ere you answer: is no other name Save mine, stain'd in this business?

Sieg. Trifling villain! Who play'st with thine own guilt! Of all that breathe 165 Thou best dost know the innocence of him 'Gainst whom thy breath would blow thy bloody slander. But I will talk no further with a wretch, Further than justice asks. Answer at once, And without quibbling, to my charge.

Gab. 'Tis false! 170

Sieg. Who says so?

Gab. I,

Sieg. And how disprove it?

Gab. By The presence of the murderer.

Sieg. Name him.

Gab. He May have more names than one. Your lordship had so Once on a time.

Sieg. If you mean me, I dare Your utmost.

Gab. You may do so, and in safety; I know the assassin.

Sieg. Where is he?

Gab. [*pointing to* ULRIC]. Beside you!

[ULRIC *rushes forward to attack* GABOR; SIEGENDORF *interposes*.

Sieg. Liar and fiend! but you shall not be slain; These walls are mine, and you are safe within them. [*He turns to* ULRIC. Ulric, repel this calumny, as I Will do. I avow it is a growth so monstrous, 180 I could not deem it earth-born: but be calm; It will refute itself. But touch him not.

[ULRIC *endeavours to compose himself*.

Gab. Look at *him*, count, and then hear me.

Sieg. [*first to* GABOR, *and then looking at* ULRIC]. I hear thee. My God! you look——

Ulr. How?

Sieg. As on that dread night, When we met in the garden.

Ulr. [*composes himself*]. It is nothing.

Gab. Count, you are bound to hear me. I came hither 186

Not seeking you, but sought. When I knelt down Amidst the people in the church, I dream'd not To find the beggar'd Werner in the seat Of senators and princes; but you have call'd me, 190 And we have met.

Sieg. Go on, sir.

Gab. Ere I do so, Allow me to inquire, who profited By Stralenheim's death? Was't I—as poor as ever; And poorer by suspicion on my name! The baron lost in that last outrage neither Jewels nor gold; his life alone was sought,— A life which stood between the claims of others To honours and estates scarce less than princely.

Sieg. These hints, as vague as vain, attach no less To me than to my son.

Gab. I can't help that. 200 But let the consequence alight on him Who feels himself the guilty one among us. I speak to you, Count Siegendorf, because I know you innocent, and deem you just. But ere I can proceed—*dare* you protect me? 205 *Dare* you command me?

[SIEGENDORF *first looks at the Hungarian, and then at* ULRIC, *who has unbuckled his sabre, and is drawing lines with it on the floor—still in its sheath.*

Ulr. [*looks at his father, and says,*] Let the man go on!

Gab. I am unarm'd, count—bid your son lay down His sabre.

Ulr. [*offers it to him contemptuously*]. Take it.

Gab. No, sir, 'tis enough That we are both unarm'd—I would not choose To wear a steel which may be stain'd with more 210 Blood than came there in battle.

Ulr. [*casts the sabre from him in contempt*]. It—or some Such other weapon, in my hand—spared yours Once, when disarm'd and at my mercy.

Gab. True— I have not forgotten it: you spared me for Your own especial purpose—to sustain An ignominy not my own.

Ulr. Proceed. The tale is doubtless worthy the relater. But is it of my father to hear further?

[*To* SIEGENDORF.

Sieg. [*takes his son by the hand*]. My son, I know my own innocence, and doubt not

Of yours—but I have promised this man
   patience;   220
Let him continue.
    Gab.   I will not detain you,
By speaking of myself much: I began
Life early—and am what the world has
   made me.
At Frankfort on the Oder, where I pass'd
A winter in obscurity, it was   225
My chance at several places of resort
(Which I frequented sometimes, but not
   often)
To hear related a strange circumstance
In February last. A martial force,
Sent by the state, had, after strong re-
   sistance,   230
Secured a band of desperate men, sup-
   posed
Marauders from the hostile camp.—They
   proved,
However, not to be so—but banditti
Whom either accident or enterprise
Had carried from their usual haunt—the
   forests   235
Which skirt Bohemia—even into Lusatia.
Many amongst them were reported of
High rank—and martial law slept for a
   time.
At last they were escorted o'er the
   frontiers,
And placed beneath the civil jurisdiction
Of the free town of Frankfort. Of *their*
   fate   241
I know no more.
    Sieg.   And what is this to Ulric?
    Gab. Amongst them there was said to
   be one man
Of wonderful endowments:—birth and
   fortune,
Youth, strength, and beauty, almost
   superhuman,   245
And courage as unrivall'd, were pro-
   claim'd
His by the public rumour; and his sway,
Not only over his associates, but
His judges, was attributed to witchcraft,
Such was his influence: I have no great
   faith   250
In any magic save that of the mine—
I therefore deem'd him wealthy.—But my
   soul
Was roused with various feelings to seek
   out
This prodigy, if only to behold him.
    Sieg. And did you so?
    Gab. You'll hear. Chance favour'd
   me: 255
A popular affray in the public square
Drew crowds together—it was one of
   those
Occasions where men's souls look out of
   them,
And show them as they are—even in their
   faces:

The moment my eye met his, I exclaim'd,
'This is the man!' though he was then, as
   since,   261
With the nobles of the city. I felt sure
I had not err'd, and watch'd him long and
   nearly;
I noted down his form—his gesture—
   features,
Stature, and bearing—and amidst them
   all,   265
'Midst every natural and acquired distinc-
   tion,
I could discern, methought, the assassin's
   eye
And gladiator's heart.
    Ulr. [*smiling*].   The tale sounds well.
    Gab. And may sound better.—He ap-
   pear'd to me
One of those beings to whom Fortune
   bends,   270
As she doth to the daring—and on whom
The fates of others oft depend; besides,
An indescribable sensation drew me
Near to this man, as if my point of fortune
Was to be fix'd by him.—There I was
   wrong.   275
    Sieg. And may not be right now.
    Gab.   I follow'd him,
Solicited his notice—and obtain'd it—
Though not his friendship:—it was his in-
   tention
To leave the city privately—we left it
Together—and together we arrived   280
In the poor town where Werner was con-
   ceal'd,
And Stralenheim was succour'd——Now
   we are on
The verge—*dare* you hear further?
    Sieg.   I must do so—
Or I have heard too much.
    Gab.   I saw in you
A man above his station—and if not   285
So high, as now I find you, in my then
Conceptions, 'twas that I had rarely seen
Men such as you appear'd in height of
   mind,
In the most high of worldly rank; you
   were
Poor, even to all save rags: I would have
   shared   290
My purse, though slender, with you—you
   refused it.
    Sieg. Doth my refusal make a debt to
   you,
That thus you urge it?
    Gab.   Still you owe me something,
Though not for that; and I owed you my
   safety,   294
At least my seeming safety, when the slaves
Of Stralenheim pursued me on the grounds
That *I* had robb'd him.
    Sieg.   *I* conceal'd you—I,
Whom and whose house you arraign, re-
   viving viper!

Gab. I accuse no man—save in my defence.

You, count, have made yourself accuser—
judge: 300

Your hall's my court, your heart is my
tribunal.

Be just, and *I*'ll be merciful!

Sieg. You merciful?—
You! Base calumniator!

Gab. I. 'Twill rest
With me at last to be so. You conceal'd
me—

In secret passages known to yourself, 305

You said, and to none else. At dead of
night,

Weary with watching in the dark, and
dubious

Of tracing back my way, I saw a glimmer,

Through distant crannies, of a twinkling
light:

I follow'd it, and reach'd a door—a secret

Portal—which open'd to the chamber,
where, 311

With cautious hand and slow, having first
undone

As much as made a crevice of the fastening,

I look'd through and beheld a purple bed,

And on it Stralenheim!—

Sieg. Asleep! And yet
You slew him!—Wretch!

Gab. He was already slain, 316
And bleeding like a sacrifice. My own
Blood became ice.

Sieg. But he was all alone!
You saw none else? You did not see the——
[*He pauses from agitation.*]

Gab. No,
He, whom you dare not name, nor even I
Scarce dare to recollect, was not then in
The chamber.

Sieg. [*to* ULRIC]. Then, my boy! thou
art guiltless still— 322

Thou bad'st me say *I* was so once—Oh!
now
Do thou as much!

Gab. Be patient! I can *not*
Recede now, though it shake the very walls
Which frown above us. You remember,—
or 326

If not, your son does,—that the locks were
changed

Beneath *his* chief inspection on the morn

Which led to this same night: how he had
enter'd

He best knows—but within an antechamber, 330

The door of which was half ajar, I saw

A man who wash'd his bloody hands, and
oft

With stern and anxious glance gazed back
upon

The bleeding body—but it moved no more.

Sieg. Oh! God of fathers!

Gab. I beheld his features

As I see yours—but yours they were not,
though 336

Resembling them—behold them in Count
Ulric's!

Distinct as I beheld them, though the expression

Is not now what it then was!—but it was so

When I first charged him with the crime—
so lately. 340

Sieg. This is so——

Gab. [*interrupting him*]. Nay—but hear
me to the end!

Now you must do so.—I conceived myself

Betray'd by you and *him* (for now I saw

There was some tie between you) into this

Pretended den of refuge, to become 345

The victim of your guilt; and my first
thought

Was vengeance: but, though arm'd with a
short poniard

(Having left my sword without), I was no
match

For him at any time, as had been proved

That morning—either in address or force.

I turn'd and fled—i' the dark: chance rather
than 351

Skill made me gain the secret door of the
hall,

And thence the chamber where you slept:
if I

Had found you *waking*, Heaven alone can
tell

What vengeance and suspicion might have
prompted; 355

But ne'er slept guilt as Werner slept that
night.

Sieg. And yet I had horrid dreams! and
such brief sleep,

The stars had not gone down when I awoke.

Why didst thou spare me? I dreamt of my
father—

And now my dream is out!

Gab. 'Tis not my fault,
If I have read it.—Well! I fled and hid
me— 361

Chance led me here after so many moons—

And show'd me Werner in Count Siegendorf!

Werner, whom I had sought in huts in vain,

Inhabited the palace of a sovereign! 365

You sought me and have found me—now
you know

My secret, and may weigh its worth.

Sieg. [*after a pause*]. Indeed!

Gab. Is it revenge or justice which inspires

Your meditation?

Sieg. Neither—I was weighing
The value of your secret.

Gab. You shall know it
At once:—When you were poor, and I,
though poor, 371

Rich enough to relieve such poverty

As might have envied mine, I offer'd you

My purse—you would not share it:—I'll
  be franker
With you: you are wealthy, noble, trusted
  by   375
The imperial powers—you understand me?
  Sieg.   Yes.
Gab. Not quite. You think me venal,
  and scarce true:
'Tis no less true, however, that my fortunes
Have made me both at present. You shall
  aid me:
I would have aided you—and also have
Been somewhat damaged in my name to
  save   381
Yours and your son's. Weigh well what I
  have said.
  Sieg. Dare you await the event of a few
  minutes'
  Deliberation?
  Gab. [*casts his eyes on* ULRIC, *who is lean-
  ing against a pillar*]. If I should do so?
  Sieg. I pledge my life for yours. With-
  draw into   385
This tower.   [*Opens a turret door.*
  Gab. [*hesitatingly*]. This is the second
  safe asylum
You have offer'd me.
  Sieg.   And was not the first so?
  Gab. I know not that even now—but
  will approve
The second. I have still a further shield.—
I did not enter Prague alone; and should I
Be put to rest with Stralenheim, there are
Some tongues without will wag in my be-
  half.
Be brief in your decision!
  Sieg.   I will be so.—
My word is sacred and irrevocable
Within *these* walls, but it extends no fur-
  ther.   395
  Gab. I'll take it for so much.
  Sieg. [*points to* ULRIC's *sabre, still upon
  the ground*].   Take also *that*—
I saw you eye it eagerly, and him
Distrustfully.
  Gab. [*takes up the sabre*]. I will; and so
  provide
To sell my life—not cheaply.
  [GABOR *goes into the turret, which*
     SIEGENDORF *closes.*
  Sieg. [*advances to* ULRIC]. Now, Count
  Ulric!
For son I dare not call thee—What say'st
  thou?   400
  Ulr. His tale is true.
  Sieg.   True, monster!
  Ulr.   Most true, father!
And you did well to listen to it: what
We know, we can provide against. He
  must
Be silenced.
  Sieg.   Ay, with half of my domains;
And with the other half, could he and thou
Unsay this villany.

  Ulr.   It is no time   406
For trifling or dissembling. I have said
His story's true; and he too must be
  silenced.
  Sieg. How so?
  Ulr.   As Stralenheim is. Are you
  so dull
As never to have hit on this before?   410
When we met in the garden, what except
Discovery in the act could make me know
His death? Or had the prince's household
  been
Then summon'd, would the cry for the
  police   414
Been left to such a stranger? Or should I
Have loiter'd on the way? Or could *you,*
  Werner,
The object of the baron's hate and fears,
Have fled, unless by many an hour before
Suspicion woke? I sought and fathom'd
  you,
Doubting if you were false or feeble: I   420
Perceived you were the latter: and yet so
Confiding have I found you, that I doubted
At times your weakness.
  Sieg.   Parricide! no less
Than common stabber! What deed of my
  life,
Or thought of mine, could make you deem
  me fit   425
For your accomplice?
  Ulr.   Father, do not raise
The devil you cannot lay between us. This
Is time for union and for action, not
For family disputes. While *you* were tor-
  tured,
Could *I* be calm? Think you that I have
  heard   430
This fellow's tale without some feeling?—
  You
Have taught me feeling for *you* and myself;
For whom or what else did you ever teach
  it?
  Sieg. Oh! my dead father's curse! 'tis
  working now.
  Ulr. Let it work on! the grave will keep
  it down!   435
Ashes are feeble foes: it is more easy
To baffle such, than countermine a mole,
Which winds its blind but living path
  beneath you.
Yet hear me still!—If *you* condemn me, yet
Remember *who* hath taught me once too
  often   440
To listen to him! *Who* proclaim'd to me
That *there were crimes* made venial by the
  occasion?
That *passion was our nature?* that the
  goods   443
Of Heaven waited on the goods of fortune?
Who show'd me his humanity secured
By his *nerves* only? *Who* deprived me of
All power to vindicate myself and race
In open day? By his disgrace which stamp'd

(It might be) bastardy on me, and on
Himself—a *felon's* brand! The man who is
At once both warm and weak invites to
deeds   451
He longs to do, but dare not. Is it strange
That I should *act* what you could *think?*
We have done
With right and wrong: and now must only
ponder
Upon effects, not causes. Stralenheim,
Whose life I saved from impulse, as, *un-
known*,   456
I would have saved a peasant's or a dog's,
I slew
Known as our foe—but not from venge-
ance. He
Was a rock in our way which I cut through
As doth the bolt, because it stood between
us   460
And our true destination—but not idly.
As stranger I preserved him, and he *owed me*
His *life*: when due, I but resumed the debt.
He, you, and I stood o'er a gulf wherein
I have plunged our enemy. *You* kindled
first   465
The torch—*you* show'd the path: now
trace me that
Of safety—or let me!
    Sieg.   I have done with life!
    Ulr. Let us have done with that which
cankers life—
Familiar feuds and vain recriminations
Of things which cannot be undone. We
have   470
No more to learn or hide: I know no fear,
And have within these very walls men who
(Although you know them not) dare ven-
ture all things.
You stand high with the state; what passes
here
Will not excite her too great curiosity: 475
Keep your own secret, keep a steady eye,
Stir not, and speak not;—leave the rest to
me:
We must have no *third* babblers thrust be-
tween us.   [*Exit* ULRIC.
    Sieg. [*solus*]. Am I awake? are these my
father's halls?
And *you*—my son! *My* son! *mine!* who
have ever   480
Abhorr'd both mystery and blood, and yet
Am plunged into the deepest hell of both!
I must be speedy, or more will be shed—
The Hungarian's!—Ulric—he hath parti-
sans,
It seems: I might have guess'd as much.
Oh fool!   485
Wolves prowl in company. He hath the key
(As I too) of the opposite door which leads
Into the turret. Now then! or once more
To be the father of fresh crimes, no less
Than of the criminal! Ho! Gabor! Gabor!
    [*Exit into the turret, closing the
        door after him.*

SCENE II.—*The Interior of the Turret.*

GABOR *and* SIEGENDORF.

Gab. Who calls?
Sieg. I—Siegendorf! Take these and
fly!
Lose not a moment!
    [*Tears off a diamond star and other jewels,
        and thrusts them into* GABOR'S *hand.*
Gab.   What am I to do
With these?
Sieg. Whate'er you will: sell them,
or hoard,
And prosper; but delay not, or you are lost!
Gab. You pledged your honour for my
safety!
Sieg.   And   5
Must thus redeem it. Fly! I am not master,
It seems, of my own castle—of my own
Retainers—nay, even of these very walls,
Or I would bid them fall and crush me! Fly!
Or you will be slain by——
Gab.   Is it even so?   10
Farewell, then! Recollect, however, count,
You sought this fatal interview!
Sieg.   I did:
Let it not be more fatal still!—Begone!
Gab. By the same path I enter'd?
Sieg.   Yes; that's safe still!
But loiter not in Prague;—you do not
know   15
With whom you have to deal.
Gab.   I know too well—
And knew it ere yourself, unhappy sire!
Farewell!   [*Exit* GABOR.
Sieg. [*solus and listening*]. He hath
clear'd the staircase. Ah! I hear
The door sound loud behind him! He is
safe!
Safe!—Oh, my father's spirit!—I am
faint—   20
    [*He leans down upon a stone seat, near the
        wall of the tower, in a drooping posture.*

Enter ULRIC, *with others armed, and with
        weapons drawn.*

Ulr. Despatch!—he's there!
Lud.   The count, my lord!
Ulr. [*recognising* SIEGENDORF]. *You*
here, sir!
Sieg. Yes; if you want another victim,
strike!
Ulr. [*seeing him stript of his jewels*].
Where is the ruffian who hath plunder'd
you?
Vassals, despatch in search of him! You see
'Twas as I said—the wretch hath stript my
father   25
Of jewels which might form a prince's heir-
loom!
Away. I'll follow you forthwith.
    [*Exeunt all but* SIEGENDORF *and* ULRIC.
                        What's this?
Where is the villain?

Sieg. There are *two*, sir: which Are you in quest of?

Ulr. Let us hear no more Of this: he must be found. You have not let him Escape? 30

Sieg. He's gone.

Ulr. With your connivance?

Sieg. With My fullest, freest aid.

Ulr. Then fare you well! [ULRIC *is going.*

Sieg. Stop! I command—entreat—implore! Oh, Ulric! Will you then leave me?

Ulr. What! remain to be Denounced—dragg'd, it may be, in chains; and all 35 By your inherent weakness, half-humanity, Selfish remorse, and temporising pity, That sacrifices your whole race to save A wretch to profit by our ruin! No, count, Henceforth you have no son!

Sieg. I never had one; 40 And would you ne'er had borne the useless name! Where will you go? I would not send you forth Without protection.

Ulr. Leave that unto me. I am not alone; nor merely the vain heir Of your domains; a thousand, ay, ten thousand 45 Swords, hearts, and hands are mine.

Sieg. The foresters! With whom the Hungarian found you first at Frankfort!

Ulr. Yes—men—who are worthy of the name! Go tell Your senators that they look well to Prague;

Their feast of peace was early for the times; There are more spirits abroad than have been laid 51 With Wallenstein!

Enter JOSEPHINE *and* IDA.

Jos. What is't we hear? My Siegendorf! Thank Heaven. I see you safe!

Sieg. Safe!

Ida. Yes, dear father!

Sieg. No, no; I have no children: never more 54 Call me by that worst name of parent.

Jos. What Means my good lord?

Sieg. That you have given birth To a demon!

Ida [*taking* ULRIC'S *hand*]. Who shall dare say this of Ulric?

Sieg. Ida, beware! there's blood upon that hand.

Ida [*stooping to kiss it*]. I'd kiss it off, though it were mine.

Sieg. It is so! 59

Ulr. Away! it is your father's! [*Exit* ULRIC.

Ida. Oh, great God! And I have loved this man!

[IDA *falls senseless—*JOSEPHINE *stands speechless with horror.*

Sieg. The wretch hath slain Them both!—My Josephine! we are now alone! Would we had ever been so!—All is over For me!—Now open wide, my sire, thy grave; 64 Thy curse hath dug it deeper for thy son In mine!—The race of Siegendorf is past!

THE DEFORMED TRANSFORMED

A DRAMA

ADVERTISEMENT

THIS production is founded partly on the story of a novel called 'The Three Brothers', published many years ago, from which M. G. Lewis's 'Wood Demon' was also taken; and partly on the 'Faust' of the great Goethe. The present publication contains the two first Parts only, and the opening chorus of the third. The rest may perhaps appear hereafter.

DRAMATIS PERSONÆ

STRANGER, *afterwards* CÆSAR.
ARNOLD.
BOURBON.
PHILIBERT.
CELLINI.

BERTHA.
OLIMPIA.

Spirits, Soldiers, Citizens of Rome, Priests, Peasants, &c.

PART I

SCENE I.—*A Forest.*

Enter ARNOLD *and his mother* BERTHA.

Bert. Out, hunchback!

Arn. I was born so, mother!

Bert. Out, Thou incubus! Thou nightmare! Of seven sons, The sole abortion!

Arn. Would that I had been so, And never seen the light!

Bert. I would so, too!

But as thou *hast*—hence, hence—and do
thy best!   5
That back of thine may bear its burthen;
'tis   .
More high, if not so broad as that of others.
  Arn. It *bears* its burthen;—but, my
heart! Will it
Sustain that which you lay upon it, mother?
I love, or, at the least, I loved you: nothing
Save you, in nature, can love aught like me.
You nursed me—do not kill me!
  Bert.   Yes—I nursed thee,
Because thou wert my first-born, and I
knew not
If there would be another unlike thee,
That monstrous sport of nature. But get
hence,   15
And gather wood!
  Arn.   I will: but when I bring it,
Speak to me kindly. Though my brothers
are
So beautiful and lusty, and as free
As the free chase they follow, do not spurn
me:
Our milk has been the same.
  Bert.   As is the hedgehog's,
Which sucks at midnight from the whole-
some dam   21
Of the young bull, until the milkmaid finds
The nipple next day sore and udder dry.
Call not thy brothers brethren! Call me not
Mother; for if I brought thee forth, it was
As foolish hens at times hatch vipers, by
Sitting upon strange eggs. Out, urchin,
out!   [*Exit* BERTHA.
  Arn. [*solus*]. Oh, mother!——She is
gone, and I must do
Her bidding;—wearily but willingly
I would fulfil it, could I only hope   30
A kind word in return. What shall I do?
  [ARNOLD *begins to cut wood: in doing
this he wounds one of his hands.*
My labour for the day is over now.
Accursed be this blood that flows so fast;
For double curses will be my meed now
At home—What home? I have no home,
no kin,   35
No kind—not made like other creatures, or
To share their sports or pleasures. Must I
bleed, too,
Like them? Oh, that each drop which falls
to earth
Would rise a snake to sting them, as they
have stung me!
Or that the devil, to whom they liken me,
Would aid his likeness! If I must partake
His form, why not his power? Is it because
I have not his will too? For one kind word
From her who bore me would still recon-
cile me
Even to this hateful aspect. Let me wash
The wound.
  [ARNOLD *goes to a spring, and stoops to
wash his hand: he starts back.*

They are right; and Nature's mirror
shows me   46
What she hath made me. I will not look on
it
Again, and scarce dare think on't. Hideous
wretch
That I am! The very waters mock me with
My horrid shadow—like a demon placed
Deep in the fountain to scare back the cattle
From drinking therein.   [*He pauses.*
            And shall I live on,
A burden to the earth, myself, and shame
Unto what brought me into life! Thou
blood,
Which flow'st so freely from a scratch, let
me   55
Try if thou wilt not in a fuller stream
Pour forth my woes for ever with thyself
On earth, to which I will restore at once
This hateful compound of her atoms, and
Resolve back to her elements, and take
The shape of any reptile save myself,
And make a world for myriads of new
worms!
This knife! now let me prove if it will sever
This wither'd slip of nature's nightshade—
my   64
Vile form—from the creation, as it hath
The green bough from the forest.
  [ARNOLD *places the knife in the ground,
with the point upwards.*
             Now 'tis set,
And I can fall upon it. Yet one glance
On the fair day, which sees no foul thing
like
Myself, and the sweet sun which warm'd
me, but   69
In vain. The birds—how joyously they sing!
So let them, for I would not be lamented:
But let their merriest notes be Arnold's
knell;
The fallen leaves my monument; the mur-
mur
Of the near fountain my sole elegy.
Now, knife, stand firmly, as I fain would
fall!   75
  [*As he rushes to throw himself upon the
knife, his eye is suddenly caught by the
fountain, which seems in motion.*
The fountain moves without a wind: but
shall
The ripple of a spring change my resolve?
No. Yet it moves again! The waters stir,
Not as with air, but by some subterrane
And rocking power of the internal world.
What's here? A mist! No more?—
  [*A cloud comes from the fountain. He
stands gazing upon it: it is dispelled,
and a tall black man comes towards
him.*
  Arn.   What would you? Speak!   81
Spirit or man?
  Stran.   As man is both, why not
Say both in one?

Arn.   Your form is man's, and yet
You may be devil.
    Stran.   So many men are that
Which is so call'd or thought, that you may
    add me   85
To which you please, without much wrong
    to either.
But come: you wish to kill yourself;—
    pursue
Your purpose.
    Arn.   You have interrupted me.
    Stran. What is that resolution which
    can e'er
Be interrupted? If I be the devil   90
You deem, a single moment would have
    made you
Mine, and for ever, by your suicide;
And yet my coming saves you.
    Arn.   I said not
You *were* the demon, but that your ap-
    proach
Was like one.   95
    Stran.   Unless you keep company
With him (and you seem scarce used to
    such high
Society), you can't tell how he approaches;
And for his aspect, look upon the fountain,
And then on me, and judge which of us
    twain   99
Looks likest what the boors believe to be
Their cloven-footed terror.
    Arn.   Do you—dare *you*
To taunt me with my born deformity?
    Stran. Were I to taunt a buffalo with this
Cloven foot of thine, or the swift drome-
    dary   104
With thy sublime of humps, the animals
Would revel in the compliment. And yet
Both beings are more swift, more strong,
    more mighty
In action and endurance than thyself,
And all the fierce and fair of the same kind
With thee. Thy form is natural: 'twas only
Nature's mistaken largess to bestow
The gifts which are of others upon man.
    Arn. Give me the strength then of the
    buffalo's foot,   113
When he spurs high the dust, beholding his
Near enemy; or let me have the long
And patient swiftness of the desert-ship,
The helmless dromedary!—and I'll bear
Thy fiendish sarcasm with a saintly pa-
    tience.   118
    Stran. I will.
    Arn. [*with surprise*]. Thou *canst?*
    Stran. Perhaps. Would you aught else?
    Arn. Thou mockest me.
    Stran.   Not I. Why should I mock
What all are mocking? That's poor sport,
    methinks.   121
To talk to thee in human language (for
Thou canst not yet speak mine), the forester
Hunts not the wretched coney, but the boar,
Or wolf, or lion, leaving paltry game   125

To petty burghers, who leave once a year
Their walls, to fill their household caldrons
    with
Such scullion prey. The meanest gibe at
    thee,—   128
Now *I* can mock the mightiest.
    Arn.   Then waste not
Thy time on me: I seek thee not.
    Stran.   Your thoughts
Are not far from me. Do not send me back:
I'm not so easily recall'd to do
Good service.
    Arn.   What wilt thou do for me?
    Stran.   Change
Shapes with you, if you will, since yours so
    irks you;   134
Or form you to your wish in any shape.
    Arn. Oh! then you are indeed the demon,
    for
Nought else would wittingly wear mine.
    Stran.   I'll show thee
The brightest which the world e'er bore,
    and give thee   138
Thy choice.
    Arn.   On what condition?
    Stran.   There's a question!
An hour ago you would have given your soul
To look like other men, and now you pause
To wear the form of heroes.
    Arn.   No; I will not.
I must not compromise my soul.
    Stran.   What soul,
Worth naming so, would dwell in such a
    carcass?
    Arn. 'Tis an aspiring one, whate'er the
    tenement   145
In which it is mislodged. But name your
    compact:
Must it be sign'd in blood?
    Stran.   Not in your own.
    Arn. Whose blood then?
    Stran. We will talk of that hereafter.
But I'll be moderate with you, for I see
Great things within you. You shall have
    no bond   150
But your own will, no contract save your
    deeds.
Are you content?
    Arn.   I take thee at thy word.
    Stran. Now then!
[*The Stranger approaches the fountain,
    and turns to* ARNOLD.
                A little of your blood.
    Arn.   For what?
    Stran. To mingle with the magic of the
    waters,
And make the charm effective.
    Arn. [*holding out his wounded arm*]. Take
    it all.   155
    Stran. Not now. A few drops will suf-
    fice for this.
[*The Stranger takes some of* ARNOLD'S
    *blood in his hand, and casts it into the
    fountain.*

607   X

Shadows of beauty!
　Shadows of power!
Rise to your duty—
　This is the hour!   160
Walk lovely and pliant
　From the depth of this fountain,
As the cloud-shapen giant
　Bestrides the Hartz Mountain.
Come as ye were,   165
　That our eyes may behold
The model in air
　Of the form I will mould,
Bright as the Iris
　When ether is spann'd;—   170
Such *his* desire is, [*Pointing to* ARNOLD.
　Such my command!
Demons heroic—
　Demons who wore
The form of the stoic   175
　Or sophist of yore—
Or the shape of each victor,
　From Macedon's boy,
To each high Roman's picture,
　Who breathed to destroy—   180
Shadows of beauty!
　Shadows of power!
Up to your duty—
　This is the hour!   184

[*Various phantoms arise from the waters,
and pass in succession before the Stranger and* ARNOLD.

Arn. What do I see?
Stran.　　The black-eyed Roman, with
The eagle's beak between those eyes which
　　ne'er
Beheld a conqueror, or look'd along
The land he made not Rome's, while Rome
　　became
His, and all theirs who heir'd his very name.
Arn. The phantom's bald; my quest is
　　beauty. Could I   190
Inherit but his fame with his defects!
Stran. His brow was girt with laurels
　　more than hairs.
You see his aspect—choose it, or reject.
I can but promise you his form; his fame
Must be long sought and fought for.
Arn.　　I will fight, too.   195
But not as a mock Cæsar. Let him pass;
His aspect may be fair, but suits me not.
Stran. Then you are far more difficult
　　to please
Than Cato's sister, or than Brutus's mother,
Or Cleopatra at sixteen—an age   200
When love is not less in the eye than heart.
But be it so! Shadow, pass on!

[*The phantom of Julius Cæsar disappears.*
Arn.　　　　　And can it
Be, that the man who shook the earth is
　　gone,
And left no footstep?
Stran.　　There you err. His substance
Left graves enough, and woes enough, and
　　fame   205

More than enough to track his memory;
But for his shadow, 'tis no more than yours,
Except a little longer and less crooked
I' the sun. Behold another!
　　　　　　　　[*A second phantom passes.*
Arn.　　　　　　　Who is he?
Stran. He was the fairest and the bravest
　　of   210
Athenians. Look upon him well.
Arn.　　　　　　　　He is
More lovely than the last. How beautiful!
Stran. Such was the curled son of Clini-
　　as;—Wouldst thou
Invest thee with his form?
Arn.　　　Would that I had
Been born with it! But since I may choose
　　further,   215
I will *look* further.
　　　　　　[*The shade of Alcibiades disappears.*
Stran.　　　Lo! behold again!
Arn. What! that low, swarthy, short-
　　nosed, round-eyed satyr,
With the wide nostrils and Silenus' aspect,
The splay feet and low stature! I had better
Remain that which I am.
Stran.　　　And yet he was
The earth's perfection of all mental beauty,
And personification of all virtue.   222
But you reject him?
Arn.　　If his form could bring me
That which redeem'd it—no.
Stran.　　　I have no power
To promise that; but you may try, and find it
Easier in such a form, or in your own.
Arn. No. I was not born for philosophy,
Though I have that about me which has
　　need on 't.   228
Let him fleet on.
Stran.　　Be air, thou hemlock-drinker!
　　　[*The shadow of Socrates disappears: an-
other rises.*
Arn. What's here? whose broad brow
　　and whose curly beard
And manly aspect look like Hercules,
Save that his jocund eye hath more of
　　Bacchus   232
Than the sad purger of the infernal world,
Leaning dejected on his club of conquest,
As if he knew the worthlessness of those
For whom he had fought.
Stran.　　It was the man who lost
The ancient world for love.
Arn.　　　I cannot blame him,
Since I have risk'd my soul because I find
　　not   238
That which he exchanged the earth for.
Stran.　　　Since so far
You seem congenial, will you wear his
　　features?
Arn. No. As you leave me choice, I am
　　difficult,
If but to see the heroes I should ne'er
Have seen else on this side of the dim shore
Whence they float back before us.

Stran.   Hence, triumvir,
Thy Cleopatra's waiting.
  [*The shade of Antony disappears: another
    rises.*
  Arn.   Who is this?
Who truly looketh like a demigod,
Blooming and bright, with golden hair, and
  stature,
If not more high than mortal, yet immortal
In all that nameless bearing of his limbs,
Which he wears as the sun his rays—a some-
  thing   250
Which shines from him, and yet is but the
  flashing
Emanation of a thing more glorious still.
Was *he e'er human only*?
  Stran.   Let the earth speak,
If there be atoms of him left, or even   254
Of the more solid bearing of that form'd his urn.
  Arn. Who was this glory of mankind?
  Stran.   The shame
Of Greece in peace, her thunderbolt in
  war—
Demetrius the Macedonian, and
Taker of cities.
  Arn.   Yet one shadow more.
  Stran. [*addressing the shadow*]. Get thee
    to Lamia's lap!
  [*The shade of Demetrius Poliorcetes
    vanishes: another rises.*
                        I'll fit you still,
Fear not, my hunchback: if the shadows of
That which existed please not your nice taste,
I'll animate the ideal marble, till
Your soul be reconciled to her new gar-
  ment.   264
  Arn. Content! I will fix here.
  Stran.   I must commend
Your choice. The god-like son of the sea-
  goddess,
The unshorn boy of Peleus, with his locks
As beautiful and clear as the amber waves
Of rich Pactolus, roll'd o'er sands of gold,
Soften'd by intervening crystal, and   270
Rippled like flowing waters by the wind,
All vow'd to Sperchius as they were—be-
  hold them!
And *him*—as he stood by Polixena,
With sanction'd and with soften'd love, be-
  fore
The altar, gazing on his Trojan bride,   275
With some remorse within for Hector slain
And Priam weeping, mingled with deep
  passion
For the sweet downcast virgin, whose
  young hand
Trembled in *his* who slew her brother. So
He stood i' the temple! Look upon him as
Greece look'd her last upon her best, the
  instant   281
Ere Paris' arrow flew.
  Arn.   I gaze upon him
As if I were his soul, whose form shall soon
Envelope mine.

Stran. You have done well. The greatest
Deformity should only barter with   285
The extremest beauty, if the proverb's true
Of mortals, that extremes meet.
  Arn.   Come! Be quick!
I am impatient.
  Stran.   As a youthful beauty
Before her glass. *You both* see what is not,
But dream it is what must be.
  Arn.   Must I wait?
  Stran. No; that were a pity. But a word
  or two:
His stature is twelve cubits; would you so far
Outstep these times, and be a Titan? Or
(To talk canonically) wax a son   294
Of Anak?
  Arn. Why not?
  Stran.   Glorious ambition!
I love thee most in dwarfs! A mortal of
Philistine stature would have gladly pared
His own Goliath down to a slight David:
But thou, my manikin, wouldst soar a show
Rather than hero. Thou shalt be indulged,
If such be thy desire; and yet, by being
A little less removed from present men
In figure, thou canst sway them more; for all
Would rise against thee now, as if to hunt
A new-found mammoth: and their cursed
  engines,   305
Their culverins, and so forth, would find
  way
Through our friend's armour there, with
  greater ease
Than the adulterer's arrow through his heel,
Which Thetis had forgotten to baptize   309
In Styx.
  Arn. Then let it be as thou deem'st best.
  Stran. Thou shalt be beauteous as the
  thing thou seest,
And strong as what it was, and——
  Arn.   I ask not
For valour, since deformity is daring.
It is its essence to o'ertake mankind
By heart and soul, and make itself the
  equal—   315
Ay, the superior of the rest. There is
A spur in its halt movements, to become
All that the others cannot, in such things
As still are free to both, to compensate
For stepdame Nature's avarice at first.
They woo with fearless deeds the smiles of
  fortune,
And oft, like Timour the lame Tartar, win
  them.
  Stran. Well spoken! and thou doubtless
  wilt remain
Form'd as thou art. I may dismiss the
  mould
Of shadow, which must turn to flesh, to
  incase   325
This daring soul, which could achieve no less
Without it.
  Arn.   Had no power presented me
The possibility of change, I would

Have done the best which spirit may to
    make   329
Its way with all deformity's dull, deadly
Discouraging weight upon me, like a moun-
    tain,
In feeling, on my heart as on my shoulders—
A hateful and unsightly molehill, to
The eyes of happier men. I would have
    look'd   334
On beauty in that sex which is the type
Of all we know or dream of beautiful
Beyond the world they brighten, with a
    sigh—
Not of love, but despair; nor sought to win,
Though to a heart all love, what could not
    love me   339
In turn, because of this vile crooked clog,
Which makes me lonely. Nay, I could have
    borne
It all, had not my mother spurn'd me from
    her.
The she-bear licks her cubs into a sort
Of shape;—my dam beheld my shape was
    hopeless.   344
Had she exposed me, like the Spartan, ere
I knew the passionate part of life, I had
Been a clod of the valley,—happier nothing
Than what I am. But even thus, the lowest,
Ugliest, and meanest of mankind, what
    courage
And perseverance could have done, per-
    chance   350
Had made me something—as it has made
    heroes
Of the same mould as mine. You lately
    saw me
Master of my own life, and quick to quit it;
And he who is so is the master of   354
Whatever dreads to die.
    Stran.   Decide between
What you have been, or will be.
    Arn.   I have done so.
You have open'd brighter prospects to my
    eyes,
And sweeter to my heart. As I am now,
I might be fear'd, admired, respected, loved
Of all save those next to me, of whom I
Would be beloved. As thou showest me
A choice of forms, I take the one I view.
Haste! haste!
    Stran.   And what shall *I* wear?
    Arn.   Surely, he
Who can command all forms will choose
    the highest,   364
Something superior even to that which was
Pelides now before us. Perhaps *his*
Who slew him, that of Paris: or—still
    higher—
The poet's god, clothed in such limbs as are
Themselves a poetry.
    Stran.   Less will content me;   369
For I, too, love a change.
    Arn.   Your aspect is
Dusky, but not uncomely.

    Stran.   If I chose,
I might be whiter; but I have a penchant
For black—it is so honest, and besides
Can neither blush with shame nor pale
    with fear;   374
But I have worn it long enough of late,
And now I'll take your figure.
    Arn.   Mine!
    Stran.   Yes. You
Shall change with Thetis' son, and I with
    Bertha,
Your mother's offspring.   People have
    their tastes:
You have yours—I mine.
    Arn.   Despatch! Despatch!
    Stran.   Even so.
[*The Stranger takes some earth and
    moulds it along the turf, and then
    addresses the phantom of Achilles.*
Beautiful shadow
    Of Thetis's boy!
Who sleeps in the meadow
    Whose grass grows o'er Troy:
From the red earth, like Adam,
    Thy likeness I shape,   385
As the being who made him,
    Whose actions I ape.
Thou clay, be all glowing,
    Till the rose in his cheek
Be as fair as, when blowing,   390
    It wears its first streak!
Ye violets, I scatter,
    Now turn into eyes!
And thou, sunshiny water,
    Of blood take the guise!   395
Let these hyacinth boughs
    Be his long flowing hair,
And wave o'er his brows
    As thou wavest in air!
Let his heart be this marble   400
    I tear from the rock!
But his voice as the warble
    Of birds on yon oak!
Let his flesh be the purest
    Of mould, in which grew   405
The lily-root surest,
    And drank the best dew!
Let his limbs be the lightest
    Which clay can compound,
And his aspect the brightest   410
    On earth to be found!
Elements, near me,
    Be mingled and stirr'd,
Know me, and hear me,
    And leap to my word!   415
Sunbeams, awaken
    This earth's animation!
'Tis done! He hath taken
    His stand in creation!
[ARNOLD *falls senseless; his soul passes
    into the shape of Achilles, which rises
    from the ground; while the phantom
    has disappeared, part by part, as the
    figure was formed from the earth.*

Arn. [*in his new form*]. I love, and I shall
  be beloved! O, life!
At last I feel thee! Glorious spirit!
  Stran.   Stop!
What shall become of your abandon'd gar-
  ment,
Yon hump, and lump, and clod of ugliness,
Which late you wore, or were?
  Arn.   Who cares? Let wolves
And vultures take it, if they will.
  Stran.   And if
They do, and are not scared by it, you'll say
It must be peace-time, and no better fare
Abroad i' the fields.
  Arn.   Let us but leave it there
No matter what becomes on't.
  Stran.   That's ungracious,
If not ungrateful. Whatso'er it be,
It hath sustain'd your soul full many a day.
  Arn. Ay, as the dunghill may conceal a
  gem
Which is now set in gold, as jewels should be.
  Stran. But if I give another form, it must
  be   434
By fair exchange, not robbery. For they
Who make men without women's aid have
  long
Had patents for the same, and do not love
Your interlopers. The devil may take men,
Not make them,—though he reap the
  benefit
Of the original workmanship: and there-
  fore   440
Some one must be found to assume the
  shape
You have quitted.
  Arn.   Who would do so?
  Stran.   That I know not,
And therefore I must.
  Arn.   You!
  Stran.   I said it ere
You inhabited your present dome of
  beauty.
  Arn. True. I forget all things in the new
  joy   445
Of this immortal change.
  Stran.   In a few moments
I will be as you were, and you shall see
Yourself for ever by you, as your shadow.
  Arn. I would be spared this.
  Stran.   But it cannot be.
What! shrink already, being what you are,
From seeing what you were?
  Arn.   Do as thou wilt.
  Stran. [*to the late form of* ARNOLD, *ex-
  tended on the earth*].
Clay, not dead, but soul-less!
  Though no man would choose thee,
An immortal no less
  Deigns not to refuse thee.   455
Clay thou art; and unto spirit
All clay is of equal merit.
Fire! *without* which nought can live;
Fire! but *in* which nought can live,

Save the fabled salamander,   460
Or immortal souls which wander,
Praying what doth not forgive,
Howling for a drop of water,
Burning in a quenchless lot,
Fire! the only element   465
  Where nor fish, beast, bird, nor worm,
  Save the worm which dieth not,
Can preserve a moment's form,
But must with thyself be blent:
Fire! man's safeguard and his slaughter:
Fire! Creation's first-born daughter,
  And Destruction's threaten'd son,
  When heaven with the world hath done:
Fire! assist me to renew
Life in what lies in my view   475
  Stiff and cold!
His resurrection rests with me and you!
One little, marshy spark of flame—
And he again shall seem the same;
  But I his spirit's place shall hold!   480
[*An ignis-fatuus flits through the wood
  and rests on the brow of the body. The
  Stranger disappears: the body rises.*
  Arn. [*in his new form*]. Oh! horrible!
  Stran. [*in* ARNOLD'S *late shape*]. What!
  tremblest thou?
  Arn.   Not so—
I merely shudder. Where is fled the shape
Thou lately worest?
  Stran.   To the world of shadows.
But let us thread the present. Whither wilt
  thou?   484
  Arn. Must thou be my companion?
  Stran.   Wherefore not?
Your betters keep worse company.
  Arn.   My betters!
  Stran. Oh! you wax proud, I see, of
  your new form:
I'm glad of that. Ungrateful too! That's
  well;
You improve apace;—two changes in an
  instant,   489
And you are old in the world's ways already.
But bear with me: indeed you'll find me
  useful
Upon your pilgrimage. But come, pro-
  nounce
Where shall we now be errant?
  Arn.   Where the world
Is thickest, that I may behold it in   494
Its workings.
  Stran. That's to say, where there is war
And woman in activity. Let's see!
Spain—Italy—the new Atlantic world—
Afric, with all its Moors. In very truth,
There is small choice: the whole race are
  just now   499
Tugging as usual at each other's hearts.
  Arn. I have heard great things of Rome.
  Stran.   A goodly choice—
And scarce a better to be found on earth,
Since Sodom was put out. The field is wide
  too;

For now the Frank, and Hun, and Spanish
    scion   504
Of the old Vandals, are at play along
The sunny shores of the world's garden.
    Arn.   How
Shall we proceed?
    Stran. Like gallants, on good coursers.
What, ho! my chargers! Never yet were
    better,
Since Phaeton was upset into the Po.   509
Our pages too!

*Enter two Pages, with four coal-black
        horses.*

    Arn.   A noble sight!
    Stran.   And of
A nobler breed. Match me in Barbary,
Or your Kochlini race of Araby,
With these!
    Arn. The mighty steam, which volumes
    high
From their proud nostrils, burns the very
    air;
And sparks of flame, like dancing fire-flies,
    wheel   515
Around their manes, as common insects
    swarm
Round common steeds towards sunset.
    Stran.   Mount, my lord:
They and I are your servitors.
    Arn.   And these
Our dark-eyed pages—what may be their
    names?   519
    Stran. You shall baptize them.
    Arn.   What! in holy water?
    Stran. Why not? The deeper sinner,
    better saint.
    Arn. They are beautiful, and cannot,
    sure, be demons.
    Stran. True; the devil's always ugly;
    and your beauty
Is never diabolical.
    Arn.   I'll call him
Who bears the golden horn, and wears
    such bright   525
And blooming aspect, *Huon;* for he looks
Like to the lovely boy lost in the forest,
And never found till now. And for the
    other
And darker, and more thoughtful, who
    smiles not,   529
But looks as serious though serene as night,
He shall be *Memnon,* from the Ethiop king
Whose statue turns a harper once a day.
And you?
    Stran. I have ten thousand names, and
    twice
As many attributes: but as I wear   534
A human shape, will take a human name.
    Arn. More human than the shape
    (though it was mine once)
I trust.
    Stran. Then call me Cæsar.
    Arn.   Why, that name

Belongs to empires, and has been but
    borne   538
By the world's lords.
    Stran.   And therefore fittest for
The devil in disguise—since so you deem
    me,
Unless you call me pope instead.
    Arn.   Well, then,
Cæsar thou shalt be. For myself, my name
Shall be plain Arnold still.
    Cæs.   We'll add a title—
'Count Arnold': it hath no ungracious
    sound,   544
And will look well upon a billet-doux.
    Arn. Or in an order for a battle-field.
    Cæs. [*sings*]. To horse! to horse! my
    coal-black steed
Paws the ground, and snuffs the air!
There's not a foal of Arab's breed
More knows whom he must bear;   550
On the hill he will not tire,
Swifter as it waxes higher;
In the marsh he will not slacken,
On the plain be overtaken;
In the wave he will not sink,   555
Nor pause at the brook's side to drink;
In the race he will not pant,
In the combat he'll not faint;
On the stones he will not stumble,   559
Time nor toil shall make him humble;
In the stall he will not stiffen,
But be winged as a griffin,
Only flying with his feet:
And will not such a voyage be sweet?
Merrily! merrily! never unsound,   565
Shall our bonny black horses skim over
    the ground!
From the Alps to the Caucasus, ride we,
    or fly!
For we'll leave them behind in the glance
    of an eye.
        [*They mount their horses, and disappear.*

[SCENE II.—*A Camp before the Walls
            of Rome*

ARNOLD and CÆSAR.

    Cæs. You are well enter'd now.
    Arn.   Ay; but my path
Has been o'er carcasses: mine eyes are full
Of blood.
    Cæs. Then wipe them, and see clearly.
    Why!
Thou art a conqueror; the chosen knight
And free companion of the gallant Bour-
    bon,   5
Late constable of France: and now to be
Lord of the city which hath been earth's
    lord
Under its emperors, and—changing sex,
Not sceptre, an hermaphrodite of empire—
Lady of the old world.
    Arn.   How *old*? What! are there
New worlds?

Cæs. To *you.* You'll find there are such
    shortly,
By its rich harvests, new disease, and gold;
From one *half* of the world named a *whole*
    new one,
Because you know no better than the dull
And dubious notice of your eyes and ears.
    Arn. I'll trust them.   16
    Cæs. Do! they will deceive you sweetly,
And that is better than the bitter truth.
    Arn. Dog!
    Cæs.   Man!
    Arn.   Devil!
    Cæs. Your obedient humble servant.
    Arn. Say *master* rather. Thou hast lured
    me on,
Through scenes of blood and lust, till I am
    here.   20
    Cæs. And where wouldst thou be?
    Arn.   Oh, at peace—in peace.
    Cæs. And where is that which is so?
    From the star
To the winding worm, all life is motion;
    and
In life *commotion* is the extremest point
Of life. The planet wheels till it becomes
A comet, and destroying as it sweeps
The stars, goes out. The poor worm
    winds its way,
Living upon the death of other things,
But still, like them, must live and die, the
    subject
Of something which has made it live and
    die.   30
You must obey what all obey, the rule
Of fix'd necessity: against her edict
Rebellion prospers not.
    Arn.   And when it prospers——
    Cæs. 'Tis no rebellion.
    Arn.   Will it prosper now?
    Cæs. The Bourbon hath given orders
    for the assault,   35
And by the dawn there will be work.
    Arn.   Alas!
And shall the city yield? I see the giant
Abode of the true God, and his true saint,
Saint Peter, rear its dome and cross into
That sky whence Christ ascended from
    the cross,   40
Which his blood made a badge of glory
    and
Of joy (as once of torture unto him,
God and God's Son, man's sole and only
    refuge).
    Cæs. 'Tis there, and shall be.
    Arn.   What?
    Cæs.   The crucifix
Above, and many altar shrines below.
Also some culverins upon the walls,   46
And harquebusses, and what not; besides
The men who are to kindle them to death
Of other men.
    Arn. And those scarce mortal arches,
Pile above pile of everlasting wall,   50

The theatre where emperors and their
    subjects
(Those subjects *Romans*) stood at gaze
    upon
The battles of the monarchs of the wild
And wood, the lion and his tusky rebels
Of the then untamed desert, brought to
    joust   55
In the arena (as right well they might,
When they had left no human foe uncon-
    quer'd);
Made even the forest pay its tribute of
Life to their amphitheatre, as well   59
As Dacia men to die the eternal death
For a sole instant's pastime, and 'Pass on
To a new gladiator!'—Must it fall?
    Cæs. The city, or the amphitheatre?
The church, or one, or all? for you con-
    found
Both them and me.
    Arn.   To-morrow sounds the assault
With the first cock-crow.
    Cæs.   Which, if it end with
The evening's first nightingale, will be
Something new in the annals of great
    sieges;
For men must have their prey after long toil.
    Arn. The sun goes down as calmly,
    and perhaps   70
More beautifully, than he did on Rome
On the day Remus leapt her wall.
    Cæs.   I saw him.
    Arn. You!
    Cæs. Yes, sir. You forget I am or was
Spirit, till I took up with your cast shape,
And a worse name. I'm Cæsar and a
    hunchback   75
Now. Well! the first of Cæsars was a
    baldhead,
And loved his laurels better as a wig
(So history says) than as a glory. Thus
The world runs on, but we'll be merry still.
I saw your Romulus (simple as I am)   80
Slay his own twin, quick-born of the same
    womb,
Because he leapt a ditch ('twas then no
    wall,
Whate'er it now be); and Rome's earliest
    cement
Was brother's blood; and if its native
    blood   84
Be spilt till the choked Tiber be as red
As e'er 'twas yellow, it will never wear
The deep hue of the ocean and the earth,
Which the great robber sons of fratricide
Have made their never-ceasing scene of
    slaughter
For ages.
    Arn. But what have these done, their
    far   90
Remote descendants, who have lived in
    peace,
The peace of heaven, and in her sunshine of
Piety?

Cæs. And what had *they* done, whom
    the old
Romans o'erswept?—Hark!
    Arn.   They are soldiers singing
A reckless roundelay, upon the eve   95
Of many deaths, it may be of their own.
    Cæs. And why should they not sing
    as well as swans?
They are black ones, to be sure.
    Arn.   So, you are learn'd,
I see, too?
    Cæs.   In my grammar, certes. I
Was educated for a monk of all times,
And once I was well versed in the for-
    gotten   101
Etruscan letters, and—were I so minded—
Could make their hieroglyphics plainer
    than
Your alphabet.
    Arn.   And wherefore do you not?
    Cæs. It answers better to resolve the
    alphabet   105
Back into hieroglyphics. Like your states-
    man,
And prophet, pontiff, doctor, alchymist,
Philosopher, and what not, they have
    built
More Babels, without new dispersion, than
The stammering young ones of the flood's
    dull ooze,   110
Who fail'd and fled each other. Why?
    why, marry,
Because no man could understand his
    neighbour.
They are wiser now, and will not separate
For nonsense. Nay, it is their brother-
    hood,
Their Shibboleth, their Koran, Talmud,
    their   115
Cabala; their best brick-work, where-
    withal
They build more——
    Arn. [*interrupting him*]. Oh, thou ever-
    lasting sneerer!
Be silent! How the soldier's rough strain
    seems
Soften'd by distance to a hymn-like
    cadence!
Listen!
    Cæs. Yes. I have heard the angels
    sing.   120
    Arn. And demons howl.
    Cæs.   And man, too. Let us listen:
I love all music.

    Song of the Soldiers within.

The black bands came over
    The Alps and their snow;
With Bourbon, the rover,   125
    They pass'd the broad Po.
We have beaten all foemen,
    We have captured a king,
We have turn'd back on no men,
    And so let us sing!   130

Here's the Bourbon for ever!
    Though penniless all,
We'll have one more endeavour
    At yonder old wall.
With the Bourbon we'll gather   135
    At day-dawn before
The gates, and together
    Or break or climb o'er
The wall: on the ladder
    As mounts each firm foot,   140
Our shout shall grow gladder,
    And death only be mute.
With the Bourbon we'll mount o'er
    The walls of old Rome,
And who then shall count o'er   145
    The spoils of each dome?
Up! up with the lily!
    And down with the keys!
In old Rome, the seven-hilly,
    We'll revel at ease.   150
Her streets shall be gory,
    Her Tiber all red,
And her temples so hoary
    Shall clang with our tread.
Oh, the Bourbon! the Bourbon!   155
    The Bourbon for aye!
Of our song bear the burden!
    And fire, fire away!
With Spain for the vanguard,
    Our varied host comes;   160
And next to the Spaniard
    Beat Germany's drums;
And Italy's lances
    Are couch'd at their mother;
But our leader from France is,   165
    Who warr'd with his brother.
Oh, the Bourbon! the Bourbon!
    Sans country or home,
We'll follow the Bourbon,
    To plunder old Rome.   170
    Cæs.   An indifferent song
For those within the walls, methinks, to
    hear.
    Arn. Yes, if they keep to their chorus.
    But here comes
The general with his chiefs and men of
    trust.
A goodly rebel!

Enter the Constable BOURBON '*cum suis,*'
    &c. &c.

    Phil. How now, noble prince,   175
You are not cheerful?
    Bourb.   Why should I be so?
    Phil. Upon the eve of conquest, such
    as ours,
Most men would be so.
    Bourb.   If I were secure!
    Phil. Doubt not our soldiers. Were
    the walls of adamant,
They'd crack them. Hunger is a sharp
    artillery.   180
    Bourb. That they will falter is my
    least of fears.

That they will be repulsed, with Bourbon for
Their chief, and all their kindled appetites
To marshal them on—were those hoary
  walls
Mountains, and those who guard them
  like the gods   185
Of the old fables, I would trust my
  Titans;—
But now——
  Phil.   They are but men who war with
    mortals.
  Bourb.   True: but those walls have
    girded in great ages,
And sent forth mighty spirits. The past
  earth
And present phantom of imperious Rome
Is peopled with those warriors; and me-
  thinks   191
They flit along the eternal city's rampart,
And stretch their glorious, gory, shadowy
  hands,
And beckon me away!
  Phil.   So let them! Wilt thou
Turn back from shadowy menaces of
  shadows?   195
  Bourb.   They do not menace me. I
    could have faced,
Methinks, a Sylla's menace; but they clasp,
And raise, and wring their dim and death-
  like hands,
And with their thin aspen faces and fix'd
  eyes
Fascinate mine. Look there!
  Phil.   I look upon   200
A lofty battlement.
  Bourb.   And there!
  Phil.   Not even
A guard in sight; they wisely keep below,
Shelter'd by the grey parapet from some
Stray bullet of our lansquenets, who might
Practise in the cool twilight.
  Bourb.   You are blind.   205
  Phil.   If seeing nothing more than may
    be seen
Be so.
  Bourb.   A thousand years have mann'd
    the walls
With all their heroes,—the last Cato stands
And tears his bowels, rather than survive
The liberty of that I would enslave,   210
And the first Cæsar with his triumphs flits
From battlement to battlement.
  Phil.   Then conquer
The walls for which he conquer'd, and be
  greater!
  Bourb.   True: so I will, or perish.
  Phil.   You can *not.*
In such an enterprise to die is rather   215
The dawn of an eternal day, than death.
      [*Count* ARNOLD *and* CÆSAR *advance.*
  Cæs.   And the mere men—do they too
    sweat beneath
The noon of this same ever-scorching
  glory?

  Bourb.   Ah!
Welcome the bitter hunchback! and his
  master,
The beauty of our host, and brave as
  beauteous,   220
And generous as lovely. We shall find
Work for you both ere morning.
  Cæs.   You will find,
So please your highness, no less for your-
  self.
  Bourb.   And if I do, there will not be a
    labourer
More forward, hunchback!
  Cæs.   You may well say so, 225
For *you* have seen that back—as general,
Placed in the rear in action—but your foes
Have never seen it.
  Bourb.   That's a fair retort,
For I provoked it:—but the Bourbon's
  breast
Has been, and ever shall be, far advanced
In danger's face as yours, were you the
  devil.   231
  Cæs.   And if I were, I might have saved
    myself
The toil of coming here.
  Phil.   Why so?
  Cæs.   One half
Of your brave bands of their own bold
  accord   234
Will go to him, the other half be sent,
More swiftly, not less surely.
  Bourb.   Arnold, your
Slight crooked *friend*'s as snake-like in his
  words
As his deeds.
  Cæs.   Your highness much mistakes me.
The first snake was a flatterer—I am none;
And for my deeds, I only sting when
  stung.   240
  Bourb.   You are brave, and that's
    enough for me; and quick
In speech as sharp in action—and *that*'s
  more.
I am not alone a soldier, but the soldiers'
  Comrade.
  Cæs.   They are but bad company, your
    highness;
And worse even for their friends than foes,
  as being   245
More permanent acquaintance.
  Phil.   How now, fellow!
Thou waxest insolent, beyond the privilege
Of a buffoon.
  Cæs.   You mean I speak the truth.
I'll lie—it is as easy: then you'll praise me
For calling you a hero.
  Bourb.   Philibert!   250
Let him alone; he's brave, and ever has
Been first, with that swart face and
  mountain shoulder,
In field or storm, and patient in starvation;
And for his tongue, the camp is full of
  licence,

And the sharp stinging of a lively rogue
Is, to my mind, far preferable to   256
The gross, dull, heavy, gloomy execration
Of a mere famish'd, sullen, grumbling slave,
Whom nothing can convince save a full
  meal,
And wine, and sleep, and a few maravedis,
With which he deems him rich.
  Cæs.   It would be well
If the earth's princes ask'd no more.
  Bourb.   Be silent!
  Cæs. Ay, but not idle. Work yourself
  with words!
You have few to speak.
  Phil. What means the audacious
  prater?
  Cæs. To prate, like other prophets.
  Bourb.   Philibert!   265
Why will you vex him? Have we not
  enough
To think on? Arnold! I will lead the attack
To-morrow.
  Arn. I have heard as much, my lord.
  Bourb. And you will follow?
  Arn.   Since I must not lead.
  Bourb. 'Tis necessary for the further
  daring   270
Of our too needy army, that their chief
Plant the first foot upon the foremost
  ladder's
First step.
  Cæs. Upon its topmost, let us hope:
So shall he have his full deserts.
  Bourb.   The world's
Great capital perchance is ours to-
  morrow.   275
Through every change the seven-hill'd
  city hath
Retain'd her sway o'er nations, and the
  Cæsars
But yielded to the Alarics, the Alarics
Unto the pontiffs. Roman, Goth, or
  priest,
Still the world's masters! Civilized, bar-
  barian,   280
Or saintly, still the walls of Romulus
Have been the circus of an empire. Well!
'Twas *their* turn—now 'tis ours; and let
  us hope
That we will fight as well, and rule much
  better.
  Cæs. No doubt, the camp's the school
  of civic rights.   285
What would you make of Rome?
  Bourb.   That which it was.
  Cæs. In Alaric's time?
  Bourb. No, slave! in the first Cæsar's,
Whose name you bear like other curs——
  Cæs.   And kings!
'Tis a great name for blood-hounds.
  Bourb.   There's a demon
In that fierce rattlesnake thy tongue. Wilt
  never   290
Be serious?

  Cæs. On the eve of battle, no;—
That were not soldier-like. 'Tis for the
  general
To be more pensive: we adventurers
Must be more cheerful. Wherefore should
  we think?
Our tutelar deity, in a leader's shape,   295
Takes care of us. Keep thought aloof
  from hosts!
If the knaves take to thinking, you will
  have
To crack those walls alone.
  Bourb.   You may sneer, since
'Tis lucky for you that you fight no worse
  for't.
  Cæs. I thank you for the freedom; 'tis
  the only   300
Pay I have taken in your highness' service.
  Bourb. Well, sir, to-morrow you shall
  pay yourself.
Look on those towers; they hold my
  treasury;
But, Philibert, we'll in to council. Arnold,
We would request your presence.
  Arn.   Prince, my service   305
Is yours, as in the field.
  Bourb.   In both we prize it,
And yours will be a post of trust at day-
  break.
  Cæs. And mine?
  Bourb. To follow glory with the
  Bourbon.
Good night!
  Arn. [*to* CÆSAR]. Prepare our armour
  for the assault,
And wait within my tent.
  [*Exeunt* BOURBON, ARNOLD, PHILIBERT,
  &c.
  Cæs. [*solus*].   Within thy tent!   310
Think'st thou that I pass from thee with
  my presence?
Or that this crooked coffer, which con-
  tain'd
Thy principle of life, is aught to me
Except a mask? And these are men, for-
  sooth!
Heroes and chiefs, the flower of Adam's
  bastards!   315
This is the consequence of giving matter
The power of thought. It is a stubborn
  substance,
And thinks chaotically, as it acts,
Ever relapsing into its first elements.
Well! I must play with these poor puppets:
  'tis   320
The spirit's pastime in his idler hours.
When I grow weary of it, I have business
Amongst the stars, which these poor
  creatures deem
Were made for them to look at. 'Twere a
  jest now
To bring one down amongst them, and
  set fire   325
Unto their anthill: how the pismires then

Would scamper o'er the scalding soil, and,
　　ceasing
From tearing down each other's nests,
　　pipe forth
One universal orison! Ha! ha!
　　　　　　　　　　　　　　　[*Exit* CÆSAR.

PART II

SCENE I.—*Before the walls of Rome.*—*The
Assault: the Army in motion, with
ladders to scale the walls;* BOURBON,
*with a white scarf over his armour, fore-
most.*

Chorus of Spirits in the air.

I

'Tis the morn, but dim and dark.
Whither flies the silent lark?
Whither shrinks the clouded sun?
Is the day indeed begun?
Nature's eye is melancholy　　　　　　5
O'er the city high and holy:
But without there is a din
Should arouse the saints within,
And revive the heroic ashes
Round which yellow Tiber dashes.　　10
Oh, ye seven hills! awaken,
Ere your very base be shaken!

II

Hearken to the steady stamp!
Mars is in their every tramp!
Not a step is out of tune,　　　　　　15
As the tides obey the moon!
On they march, though to self-slaughter,
Regular as rolling water,
Whose high waves o'ersweep the border
Of huge moles, but keep their order,　20
Breaking only rank by rank.
Hearken to the armour's clank!
Look down o'er each frowning warrior,
How he glares upon the barrier:
Look on each step of each ladder,　　25
As the stripes that streak an adder.

III

Look upon the bristling wall,
Mann'd without an interval!
Round and round, and tier on tier,
Cannon's black mouth, shining spear,　30
Lit match, bell-mouth'd musquetoon,
Gaping to be murderous soon;
All the warlike gear of old,
Mix'd with what we now behold,
In this strife 'twixt old and new,　　35
Gather like a locusts' crew.
Shade of Remus! 'tis a time
Awful as thy brother's crime!
Christians war against Christ's shrine:—
Must its lot be like to thine?　　　　40

IV

Near—and near—and nearer still,
As the earthquake saps the hill,
First with trembling, hollow motion,
Like a scarce awaken'd ocean,　　　　44
Then with stronger shock and louder,
Till the rocks are crush'd to powder,—
Onward sweeps the rolling host!
Heroes of the immortal boast!
Mighty chiefs! eternal shadows!
First flowers of the bloody meadows　50
Which encompass Rome, the mother
Of a people without brother!
Will you sleep when nations' quarrels
Plough the root up of your laurels?
Ye who weep o'er Carthage burning,
Weep not—*strike!* for Rome is mourning!

V

Onward sweep the varied nations!
Famine long hath dealt their rations.
To the wall, with hate and hunger,
Numerous as wolves, and stronger,　　60
On they sweep. Oh, glorious city!
Must thou be a theme for pity?
Fight, like your first sire, each Roman!
Alaric was a gentle foeman,
Match'd with Bourbon's black banditti!
Rouse thee, thou eternal city;　　　66
Rouse thee! Rather give the torch
With thine own hand to thy porch,
Than behold such hosts pollute
Your worst dwelling with their foot.　70

VI

Ah! behold yon bleeding spectre!
Ilion's children find no Hector;
Priam's offspring loved their brother;
Rome's great sire forgot his mother,
When he slew his gallant twin,　　　75
With inexpiable sin.
See the giant shadow stride
O'er the ramparts high and wide!
When the first o'erleapt thy wall,
Its foundation mourn'd thy fall.　　80
Now, though towering like a Babel,
Who to stop his steps are able?
Stalking o'er thy highest dome,
Remus claims his vengeance, Rome!

VII

Now they reach thee in their anger:　85
Fire and smoke and hellish clangour
Are around thee, thou world's wonder!
Death is in thy walls and under.
Now the meeting steel first clashes,
Downward then the ladder crashes,　90
With its iron load all gleaming,
Lying at its foot blaspheming!
Up again! for every warrior
Slain, another climbs the barrier.
Thicker grows the strife: thy ditches　95
Europe's mingling gore enriches.

Rome! although thy wall may perish,
Such manure thy fields will cherish,
Making gay the harvest-home;
But thy hearths, alas! oh, Rome!—   100
Yet be Rome amidst thine anguish,
Fight as thou wast wont to vanquish!

VIII

Yet once more, ye old Penates!
Let not your quench'd hearths be Até's!
Yet again, ye shadowy heroes,   105
Yield not to these stranger Neros!
Though the son who slew his mother
Shed Rome's blood, he was your brother;
'Twas the Roman curb'd the Roman;—
Brennus was a baffled foeman.   110
Yet again, ye saints and martyrs,
Rise! for yours are holier charters!
Mighty gods of temples falling,
Yet in ruin still appalling!
Mightier founders of those altars,   115
True and Christian,—strike the assaulters!
Tiber! Tiber! let thy torrent
Show even nature's self abhorrent.
Let each breathing heart dilated
Turn, as doth the lion baited!   120
Rome be crush'd to one wide tomb,
But be still the Roman's Rome!

BOURBON, ARNOLD, CÆSAR, *and others,*
   arrive at the foot of the wall. ARNOLD
   is about to plant his ladder.

Bourb. Hold, Arnold! I am first.
Arn.   Not so, my lord.
Bourb. Hold, sir, I charge you!
   Follow! I am proud
Of such a follower, but will brook no
   leader.   125
   [BOURBON *plants his ladder, and begins
   to mount.*
Now, boys! On! on!
   [*A shot strikes him, and* BOURBON *falls.*
Cæs.   And off!
Arn.   Eternal powers!
The host will be appall'd,—but vengeance!
   vengeance!
Bourb. 'Tis nothing—lend me your
   hand.
   [BOURBON *takes* ARNOLD *by the hand,
   and rises; but as he puts his foot on
   the step, falls again.*
                   Arnold! I am sped.
Conceal my fall—all will go well—conceal
   it!
Fling my cloak o'er what will be dust
   anon;   130
Let not the soldiers see it.
Arn.   You must be
Removed; the aid of——
Bourb.   No, my gallant boy!
Death is upon me. But what is *one* life?
The Bourbon's spirit shall command them
   still.

Keep them yet ignorant that I am but
   clay,   135
Till they are conquerors—then do as you
   may.
Cæs. Would not your highness choose
   to kiss the cross?
We have no priest here, but the hilt of
   sword
May serve instead:—it did the same for
   Bayard.
Bourb. Thou bitter slave! to name
   him at this time!   140
But I deserve it.
Arn. [*to* CÆSAR]. Villain, hold your
   peace!
Cæs. What, when a Christian dies?
   Shall I not offer
A Christian 'Vade in pace'?
Arn.   Silence! Oh!
Those eyes are glazing which o'erlook'd
   the world,
And saw no equal.
Bourb.   Arnold, shouldst thou see
France—But hark! hark! the assault
   grows warmer—Oh!   146
For but an hour, a minute more of life,
To die within the wall! Hence, Arnold,
   hence!
You lose time—they will conquer Rome
   without thee.
Arn. And without *thee.*
Bourb.   Not so; I'll lead them still
In spirit. Cover up my dust, and breathe
   not   151
That I have ceased to breathe. Away!
   and be
Victorious.
Arn. But I must not leave thee thus.
Bourb. You must—farewell—Up! up!
   the world is winning.
                   [BOURBON *dies.*
Cæs. [*to* ARNOLD]. Come, count, to
   business.
Arn. True. I'll weep hereafter.   155
   [ARNOLD *covers* BOURBON'S *body with a
   mantle, mounts the ladder, crying*
The Bourbon! Bourbon! On, boys! Rome
   is ours!
Cæs. Good night, lord constable! thou
   wert a man.
   [CÆSAR *follows* ARNOLD; *they reach
   the battlement;* ARNOLD *and* CÆSAR
   are struck down.
Cæs. A precious somerset! Is your
   countship injured?
Arn. No.   [*Remounts the ladder.*
Cæs. A rare blood-hound, when his
   own is heated!
And 'tis no boy's play. Now he strikes
   them down!   160
His hand is on the battlement—he grasps it
As though it were an altar; now his foot
Is on it, and——What have we here?—a
                   Roman?   [*A man falls.*

The first bird of the covey! he has fallen
On the outside of the nest. Why, how
    now, fellow?   165
Wounded Man.   A drop of water!
Cæs.   Blood's the only liquid
Nearer than Tiber.
Wounded Man.   I have died for Rome.
                                            [*Dies.*

Cæs.   And so did Bourbon, in another
    sense.
Oh, these immortal men! and their great
    motives!   169
But I must after my young charge. He is
By this time i' the forum. Charge! charge!
    [CÆSAR *mounts the ladder; the scene
    closes.*

SCENE II.—*The City.—Combats between
    the Besiegers and Besieged in the streets.
    Inhabitants flying in confusion.*

            Enter CÆSAR.

Cæs.   I cannot find my hero; he is
    mix'd
With the heroic crowd that now pursue
The fugitives, or battle with the desperate.
What have we here? A cardinal or two
That do not seem in love with martyrdom.
How the old red-shanks scamper! Could
    they doff   6
Their hose as they have doff'd their hats,
    'twould be
A blessing, as a mark the less for plunder.
But let them fly; the crimson kennels now
Will not much stain their stockings, since
    the mire   10
Is of the self-same purple hue.

Enter a party fighting—ARNOLD *at the
    head of the Besiegers.*

                              He comes,
Hand in hand with the mild twins—Gore
    and Glory.
Holla! hold, count!
Arn.   Away! they must not rally.
Cæs.   I tell thee, be not rash; a golden
    bridge
Is for a flying enemy. I gave thee   15
A form of beauty, and an
Exemption from some maladies of body,
But not of mind, which is not mine to give.
But though I gave the form of Thetis' son,
I dipt thee not in Styx; and 'gainst a foe
I would not warrant thy chivalric heart
More than Pelides' heel; why, then, be
    cautious,   22
And know thyself a mortal still.
Arn.   And who
With aught of soul would combat if he were
Invulnerable? That were pretty sport.
Think'st thou I beat for hares when lions
    roar?   [ARNOLD *rushes into the
                                        combat.*

Cæs.   A precious sample of humanity!

Well, his blood's up; and if a little's shed,
'Twill serve to curb his fever.
    [ARNOLD *engages with a Roman, who
    retires towards a portico.*
Arn.   Yield thee, slave!
I promise quarter.
Rom.   That's soon said.
Arn.   And done—   30
My word is known.
Rom.   So shall be my deeds.
            [*They re-engage.* CÆSAR *comes
                                        forward.*

Cæs.   Why, Arnold! hold thine own:
    thou hast in hand
A famous artisan, a cunning sculptor;
Also a dealer in the sword and dagger.
Not so, my musqueteer; 'twas he who slew
The Bourbon from the wall.
Arn.   Ay, did he so?   36
Then he hath carved his monument.
Rom.   I yet
May live to carve your better's.
Cæs.   Well said, my man of marble!
    Benvenuto,
Thou hast some practice in both ways;
    and he   40
Who slays Cellini will have work'd as hard
As e'er thou didst upon Carrara's blocks.
    [ARNOLD *disarms and wounds* CELLINI,
    *but slightly: the latter draws a pistol,
    and fires; then retires, and disappears
    through the portico.*
Cæs.   How farest thou? Thou hast a
    taste, methinks,
Of red Bellona's banquet.
Arn. [*staggers*].   'Tis a scratch.
Lend me thy scarf. He shall not 'scape me
    thus.   45
Cæs.   Where is it?
Arn.   In the shoulder, not the sword
    arm—
And that's enough. I am thirsty: would I
    had
A helm of water!
Cæs.   That's a liquid now
In requisition, but by no means easiest
To come at.
Arn.   And my thirst increases;—but
I'll find a way to quench it.
Cæs.   Or be quench'd
Thyself.
Arn.   The chance is even; we will throw
The dice thereon. But I lose time in pra-
    ting;
Prithee be quick.   [CÆSAR *binds on the
                                        scarf.*
                    And what dost thou so idly?
Why dost not strike?
Cæs.   Your old philosophers   55
Beheld mankind, as mere spectators of
The Olympic games. When I behold a
    prize
Worth wrestling for, I may be found a
    Milo.

Arn. Ay, 'gainst an oak.
Cæs.   A forest, when it suits me:
I combat with a mass, or not at all.   60
Meantime, pursue thy sport as I do mine;
Which is just now to gaze, since all these
    labourers
Will reap my harvest gratis.
Arn.   Thou art still
A fiend!
Cæs. And thou—a man.
Arn. Why, such I fain would show me.
Cæs.   True—as men are.   65
Arn. And what is that?
Cæs.   Thou feelest and thou see'st.
[*Exit* ARNOLD, *joining in the combat,
    which still continues between detached
    parties. The scene closes.*

SCENE III.—*St. Peter's—The Interior of
    the Church—The Pope at the Altar—
    Priests, &c., crowding in confusion,
    and Citizens flying for refuge, pursued
    by Soldiery.*

Enter CÆSAR.

A Spanish Soldier. Down with them,
    comrades! seize upon those lamps!
Cleave yon bald-pated shaveling to the
    chine!
His rosary's of gold!
Lutheran Soldier. Revenge! revenge!
Plunder hereafter, but for vengeance
    now—
Yonder stands Anti-Christ!
Cæs. [*interposing*]. How now, schis-
    matic?   5
What wouldst thou?
Luth. Sold. In the holy name of Christ,
Destroy proud Anti-Christ. I am a
    Christian.
Cæs. Yes, a disciple that would make
    the founder
Of your belief renounce it, could he see
Such proselytes. Best stint thyself to
    plunder.   10
Luth. Sold. I say he is the devil.
Cæs.   Hush! keep that secret,
Lest he should recognise you for his own.
Luth. Sold. Why would you save him?
    I repeat he is
The devil, or the devil's vicar upon earth.
Cæs. And that's the reason: would you
    make a quarrel   15
With your best friends? You had far best
    be quiet;
His hour is not yet come.
Luth. Sold. That shall be seen!
[*The Lutheran Soldier rushes forward:
    a shot strikes him from one of the
    Pope's Guards, and he falls at the foot
    of the Altar.*
Cæs. [*to the Lutheran*]. I told you so.
Luth. Sold. And will you not avenge
    me?

Cæs. Not I! You know that 'Vengeance
    is the Lord's':
You see he loves no interlopers.
Luth. Sold. [*dying*].   Oh!   20
Had I but slain him, I had gone on high,
Crown'd with eternal glory! Heaven, for-
    give
My feebleness of arm that reach'd him not,
And take thy servant to thy mercy. 'Tis
A glorious triumph still; proud Babylon's
No more; the Harlot of the Seven Hills
Hath changed her scarlet raiment for sack-
    cloth   27
And ashes!   [*The Lutheran dies.*
Cæs. Yes, thine own amidst the rest.
Well done, old Babel!
[*The Guards defend themselves desper-
    ately, while the Pontiff escapes, by a
    private passage, to the Vatican and the
    Castle of St. Angelo.*
Cæs.   Ha! right nobly battled!
Now, priest! now, soldier! the two great
    professions,   30
Together by the ears and hearts! I have
    not
Seen a more comic pantomime since Titus
Took Jewry. But the Romans had the
    best then;
Now they must take their turn.
Soldiers.   He hath escaped!
Follow!
Another Sold. They have barr'd the
    narrow passage up,   35
And it is clogg'd with dead even to the
    door.
Cæs. I am glad he hath escaped: he
    may thank me for't
In part. I would not have his bulls
    abolish'd—
'Twere worth one half our empire: his
    indulgences
Demand some in return,—no, no, he must
    not   40
Fall;—and, besides, his now escape may
    furnish
A future miracle, in future proof
Of his infallibility.
                        [*To the Spanish Soldiery.*
                        Well, cut-throats!
What do you pause for? If you make not
    haste,   44
There will not be a link of pious gold left.
And you, too, Catholics! Would ye return
From such a pilgrimage without a relic?
The very Lutherans have more true devo-
    tion:
See how they strip the shrines!
Soldiers.   By holy Peter!
He speaks the truth; the heretics will bear
The best away.
Cæs. And that were shame! Go to!
Assist in their conversion. [*The Soldiers
    disperse; many quit the Church, others
    enter.*

Cæs.   They are gone,
And others come: so flows the wave on
          wave
Of what these creatures call eternity,
Deeming themselves the breakers of the
          ocean,   55
While they are but its bubbles, ignorant
That foam is their foundation. So another!

Enter OLIMPIA, *flying from the pursuit—*
          She springs upon the Altar.
Sold.   She's mine!
Another Sold. [opposing the former].
          You lie, I track'd her first: and were
          she
The Pope's niece, I'll not yield her.
                                        [*They fight.*
3d Sold. [advancing towards OLIMPIA].
          You may settle
Your claims; I'll make mine good.
Olimp.   Infernal slave!   60
You touch me not alive.
3d Sold.   Alive or dead!
Olimp. [embracing a massive crucifix].
          Respect your God!
3d Sold.   Yes, when he shines in gold.
Girl, you but grasp your dowry.
     [*As he advances,* OLIMPIA, *with a strong
          and sudden effort, casts down the cru-
          cifix; it strikes the Soldier, who falls.*
3d Sold.   Oh, great God!
Olimp. Ah! now you recognise him.
3d Sold.   My brain's crush'd!
Comrades, help, ho! All's darkness!
                                        [*He dies.*
Other Soldiers [coming up].   Slay her,
     although she had a thousand lives:
She hath kill'd our comrade.
Olimp.   Welcome such a death!
You have no life to give, which the worst
          slave
Would take.   Great God! through thy
          redeeming Son,
And thy Son's Mother, now receive me as
I would approach thee, worthy her, and
          him,   71
And thee!

          Enter ARNOLD.

Arn. What do I see? Accursed jackals!
Forbear!
Cæs. [aside and laughing]. Ha! ha!
     here's equity! The dogs
Have as much right as he. But to the issue!
Soldiers. Count, she hath slain our
     comrade.
Arn.   With what weapon?   75
Sold. The cross, beneath which he is
     crush'd; behold him
Lie there, more like a worm than man; she
     cast it
Upon his head.
Arn.   Even so; there is a woman
Worthy a brave man's liking. Were ye
          such,

Ye would have honour'd her. But get ye
          hence,   80
And thank your meanness, other God you
          have none,
For your existence. Had you touch'd a hair
Of those dishevell'd locks, I would have
          thinn'd
Your ranks more than the enemy. Away!
Ye jackals! gnaw the bones the lion leaves
But not even these till he permits.
A Sold. [murmuring].   The lion
Might conquer for himself then.
Arn. [cuts him down].   Mutineer!
Rebel in hell—you shall obey on earth!
                         [*The Soldiers assault* ARNOLD.
Arn. Come on! I'm glad on 't! I will
          show you, slaves,
How you should be commanded, and who
          led you   90
First o'er the wall you were so shy to scale,
Until I waved my banners from its height,
As you are bold within it.
          [ARNOLD *mows down the foremost; the
                rest throw down their arms.*
Soldiers.   Mercy! mercy!
Arn. Then learn to grant it. Have I
          taught you who
Led you o'er Rome's eternal battlements?
Soldiers. We saw it, and we know it;
          yet forgive   96
A moment's error in the heat of conquest—
The conquest which you led to.
Arn.   Get you hence!
Hence to your quarters! you will find them
          fix'd
In the Colonna palace.
Olimp. [aside].   In my father's   100
House!
Arn. [to the Soldiers]. Leave your arms;
          ye have no further need
Of such: the city's render'd. And mark
          well
You keep your hands clean, or I'll find out
          a stream
As red as Tiber now runs, for your baptism.
*Soldiers [deposing their arms and depart-
          ing].* We obey!
Arn. [to OLIMPIA]. Lady, you are safe.
Olimp.   I should be so,   105
Had I a knife even; but it matters not—
Death hath a thousand gates; and on the
          marble,
Even at the altar foot, whence I look down
Upon destruction, shall my head be dash'd,
Ere thou ascend it. God forgive thee,
          man!   110
Arn. I wish to merit his forgiveness, and
Thine own, although I have not injured
          thee.
Olimp. No! Thou hast only sack'd my
          native land,—
No injury!—and made my father's house
A den of thieves! No injury!—this
          temple—   115

Slippery with Roman and with holy gore!
No injury! And now thou wouldst pre-
    serve me,
To be——but that shall never be!

[*She raises her eyes to heaven, folds her
robe round her, and prepares to dash
herself down on the side of the Altar
opposite to that where* ARNOLD *stands.*

Arn.   Hold! hold!
I swear.

Olimp. Spare thine already forfeit soul
A perjury for which even hell would loathe
    thee.   120
I know thee.

Arn. No, thou know'st me not; I am not
Of these men, though——

Olimp.   I judge thee by thy mates;
It is for God to judge thee as thou art.
I see thee purple with the blood of Rome;
Take mine, 'tis all thou e'er shalt have of
    me,   125
And here, upon the marble of this temple,
Where the baptismal font baptized me
    God's,
I offer him a blood less holy
But not less pure (pure as it left me then,
A redeemed infant) than the holy water
The saints have sanctified!

[OLIMPIA *waves her hand to* ARNOLD *with
disdain, and dashes herself on the
pavement from the Altar.*

Arn.   Eternal God!
I feel thee now! Help! help! She's gone.
Cæs. [*approaches*].   I am here.
Arn. Thou! but oh, save her!
Cæs. [*assisting him to raise* OLIMPIA].
She hath done it well!
The leap was serious.
Arn.   Oh! she is lifeless!
Cæs.   If
She be so, I have nought to do with that:
The resurrection is beyond me.
Arn.   Slave!
Cæs. Ay, slave or master, 'tis all one:
    methinks
Good words, however, are as well at times.
Arn. Words!—Canst thou aid her?
Cæs.   I will try. A sprinkling
Of that same holy water may be useful.

[*He brings some in his helmet from the
font.*

Arn. 'Tis mix'd with blood.
Cæs.   There is no cleaner now
In Rome.
Arn. How pale! how beautiful! how
    lifeless!
Alive or dead, thou essence of all beauty,
I love but thee!
Cæs.   Even so Achilles loved
Penthesilea: with his form it seems   145
You have his heart, and yet it was no soft one.
Arn. She breathes! But no, 'twas
    nothing, or the last
Faint flutter life disputes with death.

Cæs.   She breathes.
Arn. Thou say'st it? Then 'tis truth.
Cæs.   You do me right—
The devil speaks truth much oftener than
    he's deem'd: 150
He hath an ignorant audience.
Arn. [*without attending to him*]. Yes!
    her heart beats.
Alas! that the first beat of the only heart
I ever wish'd to beat with mine should
    vibrate
To an assassin's pulse.
Cæs.   A sage reflection,
But somewhat late i' the day. Where shall
    we bear her?   155
I say she lives.
Arn.   And will she live?
Cæs.   As much
As dust can.
Arn.   Then she is dead!
Cæs.   Bah! bah! You are so,
And do not know it. She will come to life—
Such as you think so, such as you now are:
But we must work by human means.
Arn.   We will   160
Convey her unto the Colonna palace,
Where I have pitch'd my banner.
Cæs.   Come then! raise her up!
Arn. Softly!
Cæs.   As softly as they bear the dead,
Perhaps because they cannot feel the
    jolting.
Arn. But doth she live indeed?
Cæs.   Nay, never fear! 165
But, if you rue it after, blame not me.
Arn. Let her but live!
Cæs.   The spirit of her life
Is yet within her breast, and may revive.
Count! count! I am your servant in all
    things,
And this is a new office:—'tis not oft 170
I am employ'd in such; but you perceive
How stanch a friend is what you call a
    fiend.
On earth you have often only fiends for
    friends;
Now *I* desert not mine. Soft! bear her
    hence.
The beautiful half-clay, and nearly spirit!
I am almost enamour'd of her, as 176
Of old the angels of her earliest sex.
Arn. Thou!
Cæs.   I! But fear not. I'll not be
    your rival.
Arn. Rival!
Cæs. I could be one right formidable;
But since I slew the seven husbands of 180
Tobias' future bride (and after all
Was smoked out by some incense), I have
    laid
Aside intrigue: 'tis rarely worth the trouble
Of gaining, or—what is more difficult—
Getting rid of your prize again; for there's
The rub! at least to mortals.

Arn.   Prithee, peace!
Softly! methinks her lips move, her eyes
    open!
  Cæs.   Like stars, no doubt; for that's a
    metaphor
For Lucifer and Venus.
  Arn.   To the palace
Colonna, as I told you!
  Cæs.   Oh! I know
My way through Rome.
  Arn.   Now onward, onward! Gently!
[*Exeunt, bearing* OLIMPIA. *The scene
    closes.*

PART III

SCENE I.—*A Castle in the Apennines, sur-
rounded by a wild but smiling Country.
Chorus of Peasants singing before the
Gates.*

Chorus.

I

The wars are over,
    The spring is come;
The bride and her lover
    Have sought their home:
They are happy, we rejoice;
Let their hearts have an echo in every voice!

II

The spring is come; the violet's gone,
The first-born child of the early sun:
With us she is but a winter's flower,
The snow on the hills cannot blast her
    bower,   10
And she lifts up her dewy eye of blue
To the youngest sky of the self-same hue.

III

And when the spring comes with her host
Of flowers, that flower beloved the most
Shrinks from the crowd that may confuse
Her heavenly odour and virgin hues.   16

IV

Pluck the others, but still remember
Their herald out of dim December—
The morning star of all the flowers,
The pledge of daylight's lengthen'd hours;
Nor, midst the roses, e'er forget   21
The virgin—virgin violet.

Enter CÆSAR.

Cæs. [*singing*]. The wars are all over,
    Our swords are all idle,
    The steed bites the bridle.   25
The casque's on the wall.
There's rest for the rover;
    But his armour is rusty,
    And the veteran grows crusty,
As he yawns in the hall.   30
    He drinks—but what's drinking?
    A mere pause from thinking!
No bugle awakes him with life-and-
    death call.

Chorus.

But the hound bayeth loudly,
    The boar's in the wood,   35
And the falcon longs proudly
    To spring from her hood:
On the wrist of the noble
    She sits like a crest,
And the air is in trouble   40
    With birds from their nest.

Cæs. Oh! shadow of glory!
    Dim image of war!
But the chase hath no story,
    Her hero no star,   45
Since Nimrod, the founder
    Of empire and chase,
Who made the woods wonder
    And quake for their race.
When the lion was young,   50
    In the pride of his might,
Then 'twas sport for the strong
    To embrace him in fight;
To go forth, with a pine
    For a spear, 'gainst the mammoth,
Or strike through the ravine   56
    At the foaming behemoth;
While man was in stature
    As towers in our time,
The first-born of Nature,   60
    And, like her, sublime!

Chorus.

But the wars are over,
    The spring is come;
The bride and her lover
    Have sought their home;   65
They are happy, and we rejoice;
Let their hearts have an echo from every
    voice! [*Exeunt the Peasantry, singing.*

BEPPO

A VENETIAN STORY

Rosalind. Farewell, Monsieur Traveller: Look you lisp, and wear strange suits: disable all the benefits of your own country; be out of love with your Nativity, and almost chide God for making you that countenance you are; or I will scarce think that you have swam in a *Gondola.—As You Like It,* Act IV., Scene i.

Annotation of the Commentators.

That is, been at *Venice,* which was much visited by the young English gentlemen of those times, and was then what *Paris* is *now*—the seat of all dissoluteness.—S.A.

I

'Tis known, at least it should be, that throughout
    All countries of the Catholic persuasion,
Some weeks before Shrove Tuesday comes about,
    The people take their fill of recreation,
And buy repentance, ere they grow devout,
    However high their rank, or low their station,
With fiddling, feasting, dancing, drinking, masking,
And other things which may be had for asking.

II

The moment night with dusky mantle covers
    The skies (and the more duskily the better),
The time less liked by husbands than by lovers
    Begins, and prudery flings aside her fetter;
And gaiety on restless tiptoe hovers,
    Giggling with all the gallants who beset her;
And there are songs and quavers, roaring, humming,
Guitars, and every other sort of strumming.

III

And there are dresses splendid, but fantastical,
    Masks of all times and nations, Turks and Jews,
And harlequins and clowns, with feats gymnastical,
    Greeks, Romans, Yankee-doodles, and Hindoos;
All kinds of dress, except the ecclesiastical,
    All people, as their fancies hit, may choose,
But no one in these parts may quiz the clergy,—
Therefore take heed, ye Freethinkers! I charge ye.

IV

You'd better walk about begirt with briars,
    Instead of coat and smallclothes, than put on
A single stitch reflecting upon friars,
    Although you swore it only was in fun;
They'd haul you o'er the coals, and stir the fires
    Of Phlegethon with every mother's son,
Nor say one mass to cool the caldron's bubble
That boil'd your bones, unless you paid them double.

V

But saving this, you may put on whate'er
    You like by way of doublet, cape, or cloak,
Such as in Monmouth-street, or in Rag Fair,
    Would rig you out in seriousness or joke;
And even in Italy such places are,
    With prettier name in softer accents spoke,
For, bating Covent Garden, I can hit on
No place that's called 'Piazza' in Great Britain.

VI

This feast is named the Carnival, which being
    Interpreted, implies 'farewell to flesh':
So call'd, because the name and thing agreeing,
    Through Lent they live on fish both salt and fresh.
But why they usher Lent with so much glee in,
    Is more than I can tell, although I guess
'Tis as we take a glass with friends at parting,
In the stage-coach or packet, just at starting.

VII

And thus they bid farewell to carnal
dishes,
And solid meats, and highly spiced rag-
outs,
To live for forty days on ill-dress'd fishes,
Because they have no sauces to their
stews;
A thing which causes many 'poohs' and
'pishes,'
And several oaths (which would not
suit the Muse),
From travellers accustom'd from a boy
To eat their salmon, at the least, with soy;

VIII

And therefore humbly I would recom-
mend
'The curious in fish-sauce,' before they
cross
The sea, to bid their cook, or wife, or
friend,
Walk or ride to the Strand, and buy in
gross
(Or if set out beforehand, these may send
By any means least liable to loss)
Ketchup, Soy, Chili-vinegar, and Harvey,
Or by the Lord! a Lent will well nigh
starve ye;

IX

That is to say, if your religion's Roman,
And you at Rome would do as Romans
do,
According to the proverb,—although no
man,
If foreign, is obliged to fast; and you
If Protestant, or sickly, or a woman,
Would rather dine in sin on a ragout—
Dine and be d—d! I don't mean to be
coarse,
But that's the penalty, to say no worse.

X

Of all the places where the Carnival
Was most facetious in the days of yore,
For dance, and song, and serenade, and
ball,
And masque, and mime, and mystery,
and more
Than I have time to tell now, or at all,
Venice the bell from every city bore,—
And at the moment when I fix my story,
That sea-born city was in all her glory.

XI

They've pretty faces yet, those same Vene-
tians,
Black eyes, arch'd brows, and sweet ex-
pressions still;
Such as of old were copied from the
Grecians,
In ancient arts by moderns mimick'd ill;

And like so many Venuses of Titian's
(The best's at Florence—see it, if ye
will),
They look when leaning over the balcony,
Or stepp'd from out a picture by Gior-
gione;

XII

Whose tints are truth and beauty at their
best;
And when you to Manfrini's palace go,
That picture (howsoever fine the rest)
Is loveliest to my mind of all the show;
It may perhaps be also to *your* zest,
And that's the cause I rhyme upon it so:
'Tis but a portrait of his son, and wife,
And self; but *such* a woman! love in life!

XIII

Love in full life and length, not love ideal,
No, nor ideal beauty, that fine name,
But something better still, so very real,
That the sweet model must have been
the same;
A thing that you would purchase, beg, or
steal,
Were't not impossible, besides a shame:
The face recalls some face, as 'twere with
pain,
You once have seen, but ne'er will see
again.

XIV

One of those forms which flit by us, when
we
Are young, and fix our eyes on every
face;
And, oh! the loveliness at times we see
In momentary gliding, the soft grace,
The youth, the bloom, the beauty which
agree,
In many a nameless being we retrace,
Whose course and home we knew not, nor
shall know,
Like the lost Pleiad seen no more below.

XV

I said that like a picture by Giorgione
Venetian women were, and so they *are*,
Particularly seen from a balcony
(For beauty's sometimes best set off
afar),
And there, just like a heroine of Goldoni,
They peep from out the blind, or o'er
the bar;
And truth to say, they're mostly very
pretty,
And rather like to show it, more's the
pity!

XVI

For glances beget ogles, ogles sighs,
  Sighs wishes, wishes words, and words a
    letter,
Which flies on wings of light-heel'd Mer-
    curies,
  Who do such things because they know
    no better;
And then, God knows what mischief may
    arise,
  When love links two young people in
    one fetter,
Vile assignations, and adulterous beds,
Elopements, broken vows, and hearts, and
    heads.

XVII

Shakspeare described the sex in Desde-
    mona
  As very fair, but yet suspect in fame,
And to this day from Venice to Verona
  Such matters may be probably the same,
Except that since those times was never
    known a
  Husband whom mere suspicion could
    inflame
To suffocate a wife no more than twenty,
Because she had a 'cavalier servente.'

XVIII

Their jealousy (if they are ever jealous)
  Is of a fair complexion altogether,
Not like that sooty devil of Othello's,
  Which smothers women in a bed of
    feather,
But worthier of these much more jolly fellows,
  When weary of the matrimonial tether
His head for such a wife no mortal bothers,
But takes at once another, or another's.

XIX

Didst ever see a Gondola? For fear
  You should not, I'll describe it you
    exactly:
'Tis a long cover'd boat that's common here
  Carved at the prow, built lightly, but
    compactly,
Row'd by two rowers, each call'd 'Gon-
    dolier,'
  It glides along the water looking blackly.
Just like a coffin clapt in a canoe,
Where none can make out what you say
    or do.

XX

And up and down the long canals they go,
  And under the Rialto shoot along,
By night and day, all paces, swift or slow,
  And round the theatres, a sable throng,
They wait in their dusk livery of woe,—
  But not to them do woeful things belong,
For sometimes they contain a deal of fun,
Like mourning coaches when the funeral's
    done.

XXI

But to my story.—'Twas some years ago,
  It may be thirty, forty, more or less,
The Carnival was at its height, and so
  Were all kinds of buffoonery and dress;
A certain lady went to see the show,
  Her real name I know not, nor can guess,
And so we'll call her Laura, if you please,
Because it slips into my verse with ease.

XXII

She was not old, nor young, nor at the
    years
  Which certain people call a 'certain age,'
Which yet the most uncertain age appears,
  Because I never heard, nor could engage
A person yet by prayers, or bribes, or tears,
  To name, define by speech, or write on
    page,
The period meant precisely by that word,—
Which surely is exceedingly absurd.

XXIII

Laura was blooming still, had made the
    best
  Of time, and time return'd the compli-
    ment,
And treated her genteelly, so that, dress'd,
  She look'd extremely well where'er she
    went;
A pretty woman is a welcome guest,
  And Laura's brow a frown had rarely
    bent;
Indeed, she shone all smiles, and seem'd to
    flatter
Mankind with her black eyes for looking
    at her.

XXIV

She was a married woman; 'tis convenient,
  Because in Christian countries 'tis a rule
To view their little slips with eyes more
    lenient;
  Whereas if single ladies play the fool
(Unless within the period intervenient
  A well-timed wedding makes the scandal
    cool),
I don't know how they ever can get over it,
Except they manage never to discover it.

XXV

Her husband sail'd upon the Adriatic,
  And made some voyages, too, in other
    seas,
And when he lay in quarantine for pratique
  (A forty days' precaution 'gainst disease),
His wife would mount, at times, her high-
    est attic,
  For thence she could discern the ship
    with ease:
He was a merchant trading to Aleppo,
His name Giuseppe, call'd more briefly,
    Beppo.

XXVI

He was a man as dusky as a Spaniard,
  Sunburnt with travel, yet a portly figure;
Though colour'd, as it were, within a tan-
  yard,
  He was a person both of sense and
  vigour—
A better seaman never yet did man yard;
  And she, although her manners show'd
  no rigour,
Was deem'd a woman of the strictest
  principle,
So much as to be thought almost invin-
  cible.

XXVII

But several years elapsed since they had
  met;
  Some people thought the ship was lost,
  and some
That he had somehow blunder'd into debt,
  And did not like the thought of steering
  home;
And there were several offer'd any bet,
  Or that he would, or that he would not
  come;
For most men (till by losing render'd
  sager)
Will back their own opinions with a wager.

XXVIII

'Tis said that their last parting was pathetic,
  As partings often are, or ought to be,
And their presentiment was quite pro-
  phetic,
  That they should never more each other
  see,
(A sort of morbid feeling, half poetic,
  Which I have known occur in two or
  three,)
When kneeling on the shore upon her sad
  knee
He left this Adriatic Ariadne.

XXIX

And Laura waited long, and wept a little,
  And thought of wearing weeds, as well
  she might;
She almost lost all appetite for victual,
  And could not sleep with ease alone at
  night;
She deem'd the window-frames and shut-
  ters brittle
  Against a daring housebreaker or sprite,
And so she thought it prudent to connect
  her
With a vice-husband, *chiefly* to *protect her.*

XXX

She chose, (and what is there they will not
  choose,
  If only you will but oppose their choice?)
Till Beppo should return from his long
  cruise,

And bid once more her faithful heart re-
  joice,
A man some women like, and yet abuse—
  A coxcomb was he by the public voice;
A Count of wealth, they said, as well as
  quality,
And in his pleasures of great liberality.

XXXI

And then he was a Count, and then he
  knew
  Music, and dancing, fiddling, French
  and Tuscan;
The last not easy, be it known to you,
  For few Italians speak the right Etruscan.
He was a critic upon operas, too,
  And knew all niceties of sock and
  buskin;
And no Venetian audience could endure a
Song, scene, or air, when he cried 'secca-
  tura!'

XXXII

His 'bravo' was decisive, for that sound
  Hush'd 'Academie' sigh'd in silent awe;
The fiddlers trembled as he look'd around,
  For fear of some false note's detected
  flaw;
The 'prima donna's' tuneful heart would
  bound,
  Dreading the deep damnation of his
  'bah!'
Soprano, basso, even the contra-alto,
Wish'd him five fathom under the Rialto.

XXXIII

He patronised the Improvisatori,
  Nay, could himself extemporise some
  stanzas,
Wrote rhymes, sang songs, could also tell
  a story,
  Sold pictures, and was skilful in the
  dance as
Italians can be, though in this their glory
  Must surely yield the palm to that which
  France has;
In short, he was a perfect cavaliero,
And to his very valet seem'd a hero.

XXXIV

Then he was faithful too, as well as amor-
  ous;
  So that no sort of female could com-
  plain,
Although they're now and then a little
  clamorous,
  He never put the pretty souls in pain;
His heart was one of those which most
  enamour us,
  Wax to receive, and marble to retain:
He was a lover of the good old school,
Who still become more constant as they
  cool.

BEPPO

XXXV

No wonder such accomplishments should turn
  A female head, however sage and steady—
With scarce a hope that Beppo could return,
  In law he was almost as good as dead, he
Nor sent, nor wrote, nor show'd the least concern,
  And she had waited several years already;
And really if a man won't let us know
That he's alive, he's *dead*, or should be so.

XXXVI

Besides, within the Alps, to every woman,
  (Although, God knows, it is a grievous sin,)
'Tis, I may say, permitted to have *two* men;
  I can't tell who first brought the custom in,
But 'Cavalier Serventes' are quite common,
  And no one notices or cares a pin;
And we may call this (not to say the worst)
A *second* marriage which corrupts the *first*.

XXXVII

The word was formerly a 'Cicisbeo,'
  But *that* is now grown vulgar and indecent;
The Spaniards call the person a '*Cortejo*,'
  For the same mode subsists in Spain, though recent;
In short, it reaches from the Po to Teio,
  And may perhaps at last be o'er the sea sent:
But Heaven preserve Old England from such courses!
Or what becomes of damage and divorces?

XXXVIII

However, I still think, with all due deference
  To the fair *single* part of the creation,
That married ladies should preserve the preference
  In *tête-à-tête* or general conversation—
And this I say without peculiar reference
  To England, France, or any other nation—
Because they know the world, and are at ease,
And being *natural*, naturally please.

XXXIX

'Tis true, your budding Miss is very charming,
  But shy and awkward at first coming out,
So much alarm'd, that she is quite alarming,
  All Giggle, Blush; half Pertness, and half Pout;
And glancing at *Mamma*, for fear there's harm in
  What you, she, it, or they, may be about,
The nursery still lisps out in all they utter—
Besides, they always smell of bread and butter.

XL

But 'Cavalier Servente' is the phrase
  Used in politest circles to express
This supernumerary slave, who stays
  Close to the lady as a part of dress,
Her word the only law which he obeys.
  His is no sinecure, as you may guess;
Coach, servants, gondola, he goes to call,
And carries fan and tippet, gloves and shawl.

XLI

With all its sinful doings, I must say,
  That Italy's a pleasant place to me,
Who love to see the Sun shine every day,
  And vines (not nail'd to walls) from tree to tree
Festoon'd, much like the back scene of a play,
  Or melodrame, which people flock to see,
When the first act is ended by a dance
In vineyards copied from the south of France.

XLII

I like on Autumn evenings to ride out,
  Without being forced to bid my groom be sure
My cloak is round his middle strapp'd about,
  Because the skies are not the most secure;
I know too that, if stopp'd upon my route,
  Where the green alleys windingly allure,
Reeling with grapes red waggons choke the way,—
In England 'twould be dung, dust, or a dray.

XLIII

I also like to dine on becaficas,
  To see the Sun set, sure he'll rise tomorrow,
Not through a misty morning twinkling weak as
  A drunken man's dead eye in maudlin sorrow,
But with all Heaven t'himself; the day will break as
  Beauteous as cloudless, nor be forced to borrow
That sort of farthing candlelight which glimmers
Where reeking London's smoky caldron simmers.

XLIV

I love the language, that soft bastard Latin,
  Which melts like kisses from a female
    mouth,
And sounds as if it should be writ on satin,
  With syllables which breathe of the
    sweet South,
And gentle liquids gliding all so pat in,
  That not a single accent seems uncouth,
Like our harsh northern whistling, grunt-
    ing guttural,
Which we're obliged to hiss, and spit, and
    sputter all.

XLV

I like the women too (forgive my folly),
  From the rich peasant cheek of ruddy
    bronze,
And large black eyes that flash on you a
    volley
  Of rays that say a thousand things at once,
To the high dama's brow, more melan-
    choly,
  But clear, and with a wild and liquid
    glance,
Heart on her lips, and soul within her eyes,
Soft as her clime, and sunny as her skies.

XLVI

Eve of the land which still is Paradise!
  Italian beauty! didst thou not inspire
Raphael, who died in thy embrace, and vies
  With all we know of Heaven, or can
    desire,
In what he hath bequeath'd us?—in what
    guise,
  Though flashing from the fervour of the
    lyre,
Would *words* describe thy past and present
    glow,
While yet Canova can create below?

XLVII

'England! with all thy faults I love thee
    still,'
  I said at Calais, and have not forgot it;
I like to speak and lucubrate my fill;
  I like the government (but that is not it);
I like the freedom of the press and quill;
  I like the Habeas Corpus (when we've
    got it);
I like a parliamentary debate,
Particularly when 'tis not too late;

XLVIII

I like the taxes, when they're not too many;
  I like a seacoal fire, when not too dear;
I like a beef-steak, too, as well as any;
  Have no objection to a pot of beer;
I like the weather, when it is not rainy,
  That is, I like two months of every year,
And so God save the Regent, Church, and
    King!
Which means that I like all and everything.

XLIX

Our standing army, and disbanded sea-
    men,
  Poor's rate, Reform, my own, the
    nation's debt,
Our little riots just to show we are free
    men,
  Our trifling bankruptcies in the Gazette,
Our cloudy climate, and our chilly women,
  All these I can forgive, and those forget,
And greatly venerate our recent glories,
And wish they were not owing to the
    Tories.

L

But to my tale of Laura,—for I find
  Digression is a sin, that by degrees
Becomes exceeding tedious to my mind,
  And, therefore, may the reader too dis-
    please—
The gentle reader, who may wax unkind,
  And caring little for the author's ease,
Insist on knowing what he means, a hard
And hapless situation for a bard.

LI

Oh that I had the art of easy writing
  What should be easy reading! could I
    scale
Parnassus, where the Muses sit inditing
  Those pretty poems never known to fail,
How quickly would I print (the world de-
    lighting)
  A Grecian, Syrian, or Assyrian tale;
And sell you, mix'd with western senti-
    mentalism,
Some samples of the finest Orientalism!

LII

But I am but a nameless sort of person,
  (A broken Dandy lately on my travels)
And take for rhyme, to hook my rambling
    verse on,
  The first that Walker's Lexicon unravels,
And when I can't find that, I put a worse
    on,
  Not caring as I ought for critics' cavils;
I've half a mind to tumble down to prose,
But verse is more in fashion—so here goes.

LIII

The Count and Laura made their new
    arrangement,
  Which lasted, as arrangements some-
    times do,
For half a dozen years without estrange-
    ment;
  They had their little differences, too;
Those jealous whiffs, which never any
    change meant;
  In such affairs there probably are few
Who have not had this pouting sort of
    squabble,
From sinners of high station to the rabble.

LIV

But, on the whole, they were a happy pair,
  As happy as unlawful love could make
    them;
The gentleman was fond, the lady fair,
  Their chains so slight, 'twas not worth
    while to break them;
The world beheld them with indulgent air;
  The pious only wish'd 'the devil take
    them!'
He took them not; he very often waits,
And leaves old sinners to be young ones'
  baits.

LV

But they were young: Oh! what without
  our youth
  Would love be! What would youth be
    without love!
Youth lends it joy, and sweetness, vigour,
  truth,
  Heart, soul, and all that seems as from
    above;
But, languishing with years, it grows un-
  couth—
  One of few things experience don't im-
    prove,
Which is, perhaps, the reason why old
  fellows
Are always so preposterously jealous.

LVI

It was the Carnival, as I have said
  Some six and thirty stanzas back, and so
Laura the usual preparations made,
  Which you do when your mind's made
    up to go
To-night to Mrs. Boehm's masquerade,
  Spectator, or partaker in the show;
The only difference known between the
  cases
Is—*here*, we have six weeks of 'varnish'd
  faces.'

LVII

Laura, when dress'd, was (as I sang before)
  A pretty woman as was ever seen,
Fresh as the Angel o'er a new inn door,
  Or frontispiece of a new Magazine,
With all the fashions which the last month
  wore,
  Colour'd, and silver paper leaved be-
    tween
That and the title-page, for fear the press
Should soil with parts of speech the parts
  of dress.

LVIII

They went to the Ridotto;—'tis a hall
  Where people dance, and sup, and dance
    again;
Its proper name, perhaps, were a masqued
  ball,

But that's of no importance to my
  strain;
'Tis (on a smaller scale) like our Vauxhall,
  Excepting that it can't be spoilt by rain;
The company is 'mix'd' (the phrase I
  quote is
As much as saying they're below your
  notice);

LIX

For a 'mix'd company' implies that, save
  Yourself and friends, and half a hun-
    dred more,
Whom you may bow to without looking
  grave,
  The rest are but a vulgar set, the bore
Of public places, where they basely brave
  The fashionable stare of twenty score
Of well-bred persons, call'd '*The World*;'
  but I,
Although I know them, really don't know
  why.

LX

This is the case in England; at least was
  During the dynasty of Dandies, now
Perchance succeeded by some other class
  Of imitated imitators:—how
Irreparably soon decline, alas!
  The demagogues of fashion: all below
Is frail; how easily the world is lost
By love, or war, and now and then by frost!

LXI

Crush'd was Napoleon by the northern
  Thor,
  Who knock'd his army down with icy
    hammer,
Stopp'd by the *elements*, like a whaler, or
  A blundering novice in his new French
    grammar;
Good cause had he to doubt the chance of
  war,
  And as for Fortune—but I dare not
    d—n her,
Because, were I to ponder to infinity,
The more I should believe in her divinity.

LXII

She rules the present, past, and all to be yet,
  She gives us luck in lotteries, love, and
    marriage;
I cannot say that she's done much for me
  yet;
  Not that I mean her bounties to dis-
    parage,
We've not yet closed accounts, and we
  shall see yet
  How much she'll make amends for past
    miscarriage.
Meantime the Goddess I'll no more impor-
  tune,
Unless to thank her when she's made my
  fortune.

LXIII

To turn,—and to return;—the devil take it!
  This story slips for ever through my
    fingers,
Because, just as the stanza likes to make it,
  It needs must be, and so it rather lingers:
This form of verse began, I can't well
    break it,
  But must keep time and tune like public
    singers;
But if I once get through my present measure,
I'll take another when I'm next at leisure.

LXIV

They went to the Ridotto ('tis a place
  To which I mean to go myself to-morrow,
Just to divert my thoughts a little space,
  Because I'm rather hippish, and may
    borrow
Some spirits, guessing at what kind of face
  May lurk beneath each mask; and as
    my sorrow
Slackens its pace sometimes, I'll make, or
    find,
Something shall leave it half an hour
    behind).

LXV

Now Laura moves along the joyous crowd,
  Smiles in her eyes, and simpers on her
    lips;
To some she whispers, others speaks
    aloud;
  To some she curtsies, and to some she
    dips,
Complains of warmth, and this complaint
    avow'd,
  Her lover brings the lemonade, she sips;
She then surveys, condemns, but pities still
Her dearest friends for being dress'd so ill.

LXVI

One has false curls, another too much
    paint,
  A third—where did she buy that fright-
    ful turban?
A fourth's so pale she fears she's going to
    faint,
  A fifth's look's vulgar, dowdyish, and
    suburban,
A sixth's white silk has got a yellow taint,
  A seventh's thin muslin surely will be
    her bane,
And lo! an eighth appears,—'I'll see no
    more!'
For fear, like Banquo's kings, they reach
    a score.

LXVII

Meantime, while she was thus at others
    gazing,
  Others were levelling their looks at her;
She heard the men's half-whisper'd mode
    of praising,

And, till 'twas done, determined not to
    stir;
The women only thought it quite amazing
  That, at her time of life, so many were
Admirers still,—but 'Men are so debased,
Those brazen creatures always suit their
    taste.'

LXVIII

For my part, now, I ne'er could under-
    stand
  Why naughty women—but I won't dis-
    cuss
A thing which is a scandal to the land,
  I only don't see why it should be thus;
And if I were but in a gown and band,
  Just to entitle me to make a fuss,
I'd preach on this till Wilberforce and
    Romilly
Should quote in their next speeches from
    my homily.

LXIX

While Laura thus was seen, and seeing,
    smiling,
  Talking, she knew not why, and cared
    not what,
So that her female friends, with envy broil-
    ing,
  Beheld her airs and triumph, and all
    that;
And well-dress'd males still kept before
    her filing,
  And passing bow'd and mingled with
    her chat;
More than the rest one person seem'd to
    stare
With pertinacity that's rather rare.

LXX

He was a Turk, the colour of mahogany;
  And Laura saw him, and at first was
    glad,
Because the Turks so much admire philo-
    gyny,
  Although their usage of their wives is
    sad;
'Tis said they use no better than a dog any
  Poor woman, whom they purchase like
    a pad;
They have a number, though they ne'er
    exhibit 'em,
Four wives by law, and concubines 'ad
    libitum.'

LXXI

They lock them up, and veil, and guard
    them daily,
  They scarcely can behold their male re-
    lations,
So that their moments do not pass so gaily
  As is supposed the case with northern
    nations;

Confinement, too, must make them look
    quite palely;
  And as the Turks abhor long conversa-
    tions,
Their days are either pass'd in doing
    nothing,
Or bathing, nursing, making love, and
    clothing.

LXXII

They cannot read, and so don't lisp in
    criticism;
  Nor write, and so they don't affect the
    muse;
Were never caught in epigram or witticism,
  Have no romances, sermons, plays, re-
    views,—
In harams learning soon would make a
    pretty schism,
  But luckily these beauties are no 'Blues;'
No bustling Botherby have they to show
    'em
'That charming passage in the last new
    poem:'

LXXIII

No solemn, antique gentleman of rhyme,
  Who having angled all his life for fame,
And getting but a nibble at a time,
  Still fussily keeps fishing on, the same
Small 'Triton of the minnows,' the sublime
  Of mediocrity, the furious tame,
The echo's echo, usher of the school
Of female wits, boy bards—in short, a
    fool!

LXXIV

A stalking oracle of awful phrase,
  The approving 'Good!' (by no means
    GOOD in law),
Humming like flies around the newest
    blaze,
  The bluest of bluebottles you e'er saw,
Teasing with blame, excruciating with
    praise,
  Gorging the little fame he gets all raw,
Translating tongues he knows not even by
    letter,
And sweating plays so middling, bad were
    better.

LXXV

One hates an author that's *all author*,
    fellows
  In foolscap uniforms turn'd up with ink,
So very anxious, clever, fine, and jealous,
  One don't know what to say to them, or
    think,
Unless to puff them with a pair of bellows;
  Of coxcombry's worst coxcombs e'en
    the pink
Are preferable to these shreds of paper,
These unquench'd snuffings of the mid-
    night taper.

LXXVI

Of these same we see several, and of others,
  Men of the world, who know the world
    like men,
Scott, Rogers, Moore, and all the better
    brothers,
  Who think of something else besides the
    pen;
But for the children of the 'mighty mo-
    ther's,'
  The would-be wits, and can't-be gentle-
    men,
I leave them to their daily 'tea is ready,'
Smug coterie, and literary lady.

LXXVII

The poor dear Mussulwomen whom I
    mention
  Have none of these instructive pleasant
    people,
And *one* would seem to them a new inven-
    tion,
  Unknown as bells within a Turkish
    steeple;
I think 'twould almost be worth while to
    pension
  (Though best-sown projects very often
    reap ill)
A missionary author, just to preach
Our Christian usage of the parts of speech.

LXXVIII

No chemistry for them unfolds her gases,
  No metaphysics are let loose in lectures,
No circulating library amasses
  Religious novels, moral tales, and stric-
    tures
Upon the living manners, as they pass us;
  No exhibition glares with annual pic-
    tures;
They stare not on the stars from out their
    attics,
Nor deal (thank God for that!) in mathe-
    matics.

LXXIX

Why I thank God for that is no great
    matter,
  I have my reasons, you no doubt sup-
    pose,
And as, perhaps, they would not highly
    flatter,
  I'll keep them for my life (to come) in
    prose;
I fear I have a little turn for satire,
  And yet methinks the older that one
    grows
Inclines us more to laugh than scold,
    though laughter
Leaves us so doubly serious shortly after.

LXXX

Oh, mirth and innocence! Oh, milk and
water!
Ye happy mixtures of more happy days!
In these sad centuries of sin and slaughter,
Abominable Man no more allays
His thirst with such pure beverage. No
matter,
I love you both, and both shall have my
praise:
Oh, for old Saturn's reign of sugar candy!—
Meantime I drink to your return in brandy.

LXXXI

Our Laura's Turk still kept his eyes upon
her,
Less in the Mussulman than Christian
way,
Which seems to say, 'Madam, I do you
honour,
And while I please to stare, you'll please
to stay.'
Could staring win a woman, this had won
her,
But Laura could not thus be led astray;
She had stood fire too long and well, to
boggle
Even at this stranger's most outlandish ogle.

LXXXII

The morning now was on the point of
breaking,
A turn of time at which I would advise
Ladies who have been dancing, or partaking
In any other kind of exercise,
To make their preparations for forsaking
The ball-room ere the sun begins to rise,
Because when once the lamps and candles
fail,
His blushes make them look a little pale.

LXXXIII

I've seen some balls and revels in my time,
And stay'd them over for some silly
reason,
And then I look'd (I hope it was no crime)
To see what lady best stood out the
season,
And though I've seen some thousands in
their prime,
Lovely and pleasing, and who still may
please on,
I never saw but one (the stars withdrawn)
Whose bloom could after dancing dare
the dawn.

LXXXIV

The name of this Aurora I'll not mention,
Although I might, for she was nought
to me
More than that patent work of God's
invention,
A charming woman, whom we like to
see;
But writing names would merit repre-
hension,
Yet if you like to find out this fair *she*,
At the next London or Parisian ball
You still may mark her cheek out-bloom-
ing all.

LXXXV

Laura, who knew it would not do at all
To meet the daylight after seven hours'
sitting
Among three thousand people at a ball,
To make her curtsy thought it right and
fitting;
The Count was at her elbow with her
shawl,
And they the room were on the point of
quitting,
When lo! those cursed gondoliers had got
Just in the very place where they *should not*.

LXXXVI

In this they're like our coachmen, and the
cause
Is much the same—the crowd, and pull-
ing, hauling,
With blasphemies enough to break their
jaws,
They make a never intermitted bawling,
At home, our Bow-street gemmen keep
the laws,
And here a sentry stands within your
calling;
But for all that, there is a deal of swearing,
And nauseous words past mentioning or
bearing.

LXXXVII

The Count and Laura found their boat at
last,
And homeward floated o'er the silent
tide,
Discussing all the dances gone and past;
The dancers and their dresses, too,
beside;
Some little scandals eke; but all aghast
(As to their palace-stairs the rowers
glide)
Sate Laura by the side of her Adorer,
When lo! the Mussulman was there before
her.

LXXXVIII

'Sir,' said the Count, with brow exceeding
grave,
'Your unexpected presence here will
make
It necessary for myself to crave
Its import? But perhaps 'tis a mistake;
I hope it is so; and, at once to waive
All compliment, I hope so for *your* sake;
You understand my meaning, or you *shall*.'
'Sir,' (quoth the Turk) ''tis no mistake at
all:

LXXXIX

'That lady is *my wife!*' Much wonder paints
  The lady's changing cheek, as well it
    might;
But where an Englishwoman sometimes
    faints,
  Italian females don't do so outright;
They only call a little on their saints,
  And then come to themselves, almost or
    quite;
Which saves much hartshorn, salts, and
    sprinkling faces,
And cutting stays, as usual in such cases.

XC

She said,—what could she say? Why, not
    a word:
  But the Count courteously invited in
The stranger, much appeased by what he
    heard:
  'Such things, perhaps, we'd best discuss
    within,'
Said he; 'don't let us make ourselves absurd
In public, by a scene, nor raise a din,
For then the chief and only satisfaction
Will be much quizzing on the whole trans-
    action.'

XCI

They enter'd, and for coffee call'd—it came,
  A beverage for Turks and Christians
    both,
Although the way they make it's not the
    same.
  Now Laura, much recover'd, or less loth
To speak, cries 'Beppo! what's your pagan
    name?
  Bless me! your beard is of amazing
    growth!
And how came you to keep away so long?
Are you not sensible 'twas very wrong?

XCII

'And are you *really*, *truly*, now a Turk?
  With any other women did you wive?
Is't true they use their fingers for a fork?
  Well, that's the prettiest shawl—as I'm
    alive!
You'll give it me? They say you eat no
    pork.
  And how so many years did you con-
    trive
To—Bless me! did I ever? No, I never
Saw a man grown so yellow! How's your
    liver?

XCIII

'Beppo! that beard of yours becomes you
    not;
  It shall be shaved before you're a day
    older:
Why do you wear it? Oh! I had forgot—
  Pray don't you think the weather here
    is colder?

How do I look? You shan't stir from this
    spot
  In that queer dress, for fear that some
    beholder
Should find you out, and make the story
    known.
How short your hair is! Lord! how grey
    it's grown!'

XCIV

What answer Beppo made to these de-
    mands
  Is more than I know. He was cast away
About where Troy stood once, and
    nothing stands;
  Became a slave of course, and for his pay
Had bread and bastinadoes, till some
    bands
  Of pirates landing in a neighbouring bay,
He join'd the rogues and prosper'd, and
    became
A renegado of indifferent fame.

XCV

But he grew rich, and with his riches grew
    so
  Keen the desire to see his home again,
He thought himself in duty bound to do so,
  And not be always thieving on the main;
Lonely he felt, at times, as Robin Crusoe,
  And so he hired a vessel come from
    Spain,
Bound for Corfu: she was a fine polacca,
Mann'd with twelve hands, and laden with
    tobacco.

XCVI

Himself, and much (Heaven knows how
    gotten!) cash,
  He then embark'd, with risk of life and
    limb,
And got clear off, although the attempt
    was rash;
  He said that *Providence* protected him—
For my part, I say nothing—lest we clash
  In our opinions:—well, the ship was trim,
Set sail, and kept her reckoning fairly on,
Except three days of calm when off Cape
    Bonn.

XCVII

They reach'd the island, he transferr'd his
    lading
  And self and live stock to another bottom,
And pass'd for a true Turkey-merchant,
    trading
  With goods of various names, but I've
    forgot 'em.
However, he got off by this evading,
  Or else the people would perhaps have
    shot him;
And thus at Venice landed to reclaim
His wife, religion, house, and Christian
    name.

XCVIII

His wife received, the patriarch re-baptized him
  (He made the church a present, by the way);
He then threw off the garments which disguised him,
  And borrow'd the Count's smallclothes for a day:
His friends the more for his long absence prized him,
  Finding he'd wherewithal to make them gay,
With dinners, where he oft became the laugh of them,
'For stories—but *I* don't believe the half of them.

XCIX

Whate'er his youth had suffer'd, his old age
  With wealth and talking made him some amends;
Though Laura sometimes put him in a rage,
  I've heard the Count and he were always friends.
My pen is at the bottom of a page,
  Which being finish'd, here the story ends;
'Tis to be wish'd it had been sooner done,
But stories somehow lengthen when begun.

DON JUAN

'Difficile est propriè communia dicere.'—HORACE.

'Dost thou think, because thou art virtuous, there shall be no more cakes and ale? Yes, by Saint Anne, and ginger shall be hot i' the mouth, too!'—SHAKESPEARE, *Twelfth Night, or What You Will.*

CANTO THE FIRST*

FRAGMENT

On the back of the Poet's MS. of Canto I.

I WOULD to heaven that I were so much clay,
  As I am blood, bone, marrow, passion, feeling—
Because at least the past were pass'd away—
  And for the future—(but I write this reeling,
Having got drunk exceedingly to-day,
  So that I seem to stand upon the ceiling)
I say—the future is a serious matter—
And so—for God's sake—hock and soda-water!

DEDICATION

I

BOB SOUTHEY! You're a poet—Poet-laureate,
  And representative of all the race;
Although 'tis true that you turn'd out a Tory at
  Last,—yours has lately been a common case;
And now, my Epic Renegade! what are ye at?
  With all the Lakers, in and out of place?
A nest of tuneful persons, to my eye
Like 'four and twenty Blackbirds in a pye;

II

'Which pye being open'd they began to sing'
  (This old song and new simile holds good),
'A dainty dish to set before the King,'
  Or Regent, who admires such kind of food;—
And Coleridge, too, has lately taken wing,
  But like a hawk encumber'd with his hood,—
Explaining metaphysics to the nation—
I wish he would explain his Explanation.

III

You, Bob! are rather insolent, you know,
  At being disappointed in your wish
To supersede all warblers here below,
  And be the only Blackbird in the dish;
And then you overstrain yourself, or so,
  And tumble downward like the flying fish
Gasping on deck, because you soar too high, Bob,
And fall, for lack of moisture quite a-dry, Bob!

IV

And Wordsworth, in a rather long 'Excursion'
  (I think the quarto holds five hundred pages),
Has given a sample from the vasty version
  Of his new system to perplex the sages;

* ['Begun at Venice September 6; finished Nov. 1, 1818.'—B.]

635

'Tis poetry—at least by his assertion,
   And may appear so when the dog-star
      rages—
And he who understands it would be able
To add a story to the Tower of Babel.

V

You—Gentlemen! by dint of long se-
    clusion
   From better company, have kept your
     own
At Keswick, and, through still continued
    fusion
   Of one another's minds, at last have
     grown
To deem as a most logical conclusion,
   That Poesy has wreaths for you alone:
There is a narrowness in such a notion,
Which makes me wish you'd change your
    lakes for ocean.

VI

I would not imitate the petty thought,
   Nor coin my self-love to so base a vice,
For all the glory your conversion brought,
   Since gold alone should not have been
    its price.
You have your salary: was't for that you
    wrought?
   And Wordsworth has his place in the
    Excise.
You're shabby fellows—true—but poets
    still,
And duly seated on the immortal hill.

VII

Your bays may hide the baldness of your
    brows—
   Perhaps some virtuous blushes;—let
    them go—
To you I envy neither fruit nor boughs—
   And for the fame you would engross
    below,
The field is universal, and allows
   Scope to all such as feel the inherent
    glow:
Scott, Rogers, Campbell, Moore, and
    Crabbe, will try
'Gainst you the question with posterity.

VIII

For me, who, wandering with pedestrian
    Muses,
   Contend not with you on the winged
    steed,
I wish your fate may yield ye, when she
    chooses,
   The fame you envy, and the skill you
    need;
And recollect a poet nothing loses
   In giving to his brethren their full meed
Of merit, and complaint of present days
Is not the certain path to future praise.

IX

He that reserves his laurels for posterity
   (Who does not often claim the brigth
    reversion)
Has generally no great crop to spare it, he
   Being only injured by his own assertion;
And although here and there some
    glorious rarity
   Arise like Titan from the sea's immersion,
The major part of such appellants go
To—God knows where—for no one else
    can know.

X

If, fallen in evil days on evil tongues,
   Milton appealed to the Avenger, Time,
If Time, the Avenger, execrates his wrongs,
   And makes the word 'Miltonic' mean
    '*sublime*,'
He deign'd not to belie his soul in songs,
   Nor turn his very talent to a crime;
He did not loathe the Sire to laud the Son,
But closed the tyrant-hater he begun.

XI

Think'st thou, could he—the blind Old
    Man—arise,
   Like Samuel from the grave, to freeze
    once more
The blood of monarchs with his prophecies,
   Or be alive again—again all hoar
With time and trials, and those helpless
    eyes,
   And heartless daughters—worn—and
    pale—and poor;
Would *he* adore a sultan? *he* obey
The intellectual eunuch Castlereagh?

XII

Cold-blooded, smooth-faced, placid mis-
    creant!
   Dabbling its sleek young hands in Erin's
    gore,
And thus for wider carnage taught to pant,
   Transferr'd to gorge upon a sister shore,
The vulgarest tool that Tyranny could want,
   With just enough of talent, and no more,
To lengthen fetters by another fix'd,
And offer poison long already mix'd.

XIII

An orator of such set trash of phrase
   Ineffably—legitimately vile,
That even its grossest flatterers dare not
    praise,
   Nor foes—all nations—condescend to
    smile;
Not even a sprightly blunder's spark can
    blaze
   From that Ixion grindstone's ceaseless
    toil,
That turns and turns to give the world a
    notion
Of endless torments and perpetual motion.

XIV

A bungler even in its disgusting trade,
    And botching, patching, leaving still be-
        hind
Something of which its masters are afraid,
    States to be curb'd, and thoughts to be
        confined,
Conspiracy or Congress to be made—
    Cobbling at manacles for all mankind—
A tinkering slave-maker, who mends old
        chains,
With God and man's abhorrence for its
        gains.

XV

If we may judge of matter by the mind,
    Emasculated to the marrow *It*
Hath but two objects, how to serve, and
        bind,
    Deeming the chain it wears even men]
        may fit,
Eutropius of its many masters,—blind
    To worth as freedom, wisdom as to wit,
Fearless—because *no* feeling dwells in ice,
Its very courage stagnates to a vice.

XVI

Where shall I turn me not to *view* its bonds,
    For I will never *feel* them;—Italy!
Thy late reviving Roman soul desponds
    Beneath the lie this State-thing breathed
        o'er thee—
Thy clanking chain, and Erin's yet green
        wounds,
    Have voices—tongues to cry aloud for
        me.
Europe has slaves, allies, kings, armies still,
And Southey lives to sing them very ill.

XVII

Meantime, Sir Laureate, I proceed to
        dedicate,
    In honest simple verse, this song to you.
And, if in flattering strains I do not predi-
        cate,
    'Tis that I still retain my 'buff and blue;'
My politics as yet are all to educate:
    Apostasy's so fashionable, too,
To keep *one* creed's a task grown quite
        Herculean:
Is it not so, my Tory, ultra-Julian?
                    VENICE, *September* 16, 1818.

I

I WANT a hero: an uncommon want,
    When every year and month sends forth
        a new one,
Till, after cloying the gazettes with cant,
    The age discovers he is not the true one:
Of such as these I should not care to vaunt,
    I'll therefore take our ancient friend
        Don Juan—
We all have seen him, in the pantomime,
Sent to the devil somewhat ere his time.

II

Vernon, the butcher Cumberland, Wolfe,
        Hawke,
    Prince Ferdinand, Granby, Burgoyne,
        Keppel, Howe,
Evil and good, have had their tithe of talk,
    And fill'd their sign-posts then, like
        Wellesley now;
Each in their turn like Banquo's monarchs
        stalk,
    Followers of fame, 'nine farrow' of that
        sow:
France, too, had Buonaparté and Du-
        mourier
Recorded in the Moniteur and Courier.

III

Barnave, Brissot, Condorcet, Mirabeau,
    Pétion, Clootz, Danton, Marat, La
        Fayette,
Were French, and famous people, as we
        know;
    And there were others, scarce forgotten
        yet,
Joubert, Hoche, Marceau, Lannes, De-
        saix, Moreau,
    With many of the military set,
Exceedingly remarkable at times,
But not at all adapted to my rhymes.

IV

Nelson was once Britannia's god of war,
    And still should be so, but the tide is
        turn'd;
There's no more to be said of Trafalgar,
    'Tis with our hero quietly inurn'd;
Because the army's grown more popular,
    At which the naval people are con-
        cern'd,
Besides, the prince is all for the land-
        service,
Forgetting Duncan, Nelson, Howe, and
        Jervis.

V

Brave men were living before Agamemnon
    And since, exceeding valorous and sage,
A good deal like him too, though quite the
        same none;
    But then they shone not on the poet's
        page,
And so have been forgotten:—I condemn
        none,
    But can't find any in the present age
Fit for my poem (that is, for my new one);
So, as I said, I'll take my friend Don Juan.

VI

Most epic poets plunge 'in medias res'
    (Horace makes this the heroic turnpike
        road),
And then your hero tells, whene'er you
        please,
    What went before—by way of episode,

637

While seated after dinner at his ease,
  Beside his mistress in some soft abode,
Palace, or garden, paradise, or cavern,
Which serves the happy couple for a tavern.

VII

That is the usual method, but not mine—
  My way is to begin with the beginning;
The regularity of my design
  Forbids all wandering as the worst of
    sinning,
And therefore I shall open with a line
  (Although it cost me half an hour in
    spinning)
Narrating somewhat of Don Juan's father,
And also of his mother, if you'd rather.

VIII

In Seville was he born, a pleasant city,
  Famous for oranges and women—he
Who has not seen it will be much to pity,
  So says the proverb—and I quite agree;
Of all the Spanish towns is none more
    pretty,
  Cadiz, perhaps—but that you soon may
    see:—
Don Juan's parents lived beside the river,
A noble stream, and call'd the Guadal-
    quivir.

IX

His father's name was José—*Don*, of
    course,
  A true Hidalgo, free from every stain
Of Moor or Hebrew blood, he traced his
    source
  Through the most Gothic gentlemen of
    Spain;
A better cavalier ne'er mounted horse,
  Or, being mounted, e'er got down again,
Than José, who begot our hero, who
Begot—but that's to come——Well, to
    renew:

X

His mother was a learned lady, famed
  For every branch of every science
    known—
In every Christian language ever named,
  With virtues equall'd by her wit alone:
She made the cleverest people quite
    ashamed,
  And even the good with inward envy
    groan,
Finding themselves so very much exceeded
In their own way by all the things that
  she did.

XI

Her memory was a mine: she knew by heart
  All Calderon and greater part of Lopé,
So that if any actor miss'd his part
  She could have served him for the
    prompter's copy;

For her Feinagle's were an useless art,
  And he himself obliged to shut up shop
    —he
Could never make a memory so fine as
That which adorn'd the brain of Donna
  Inez.

XII

Her favourite science was the mathe-
    matical,
  Her noblest virtue was her magnanim-
    ity;
Her wit (she sometimes tried at wit) was
    Attic all,
  Her serious sayings darken'd to sub-
    limity;
In short, in all things she was fairly what
    I call
  A prodigy—her morning dress was
    dimity,
Her evening silk, or, in the summer,
    muslin,
And other stuffs, with which I won't stay
  puzzling.

XIII

She knew the Latin—that is, 'the Lord's
    prayer,'
  And Greek—the alphabet—I'm nearly
    sure;
She read some French romances here and
    there,
  Although her mode of speaking was not
    pure;
For native Spanish she had no great care,
  At least her conversation was obscure;
Her thoughts were theorems, her words a
    problem,
As if she deem'd that mystery would en-
  noble 'em.

XIV

She liked the English and the Hebrew
    tongue,
  And said there was analogy between
    'em;
She proved it somehow out of sacred song,
  But I must leave the proofs to those
    who've seen 'em,
But this I heard her say, and can't be wrong,
  And all may think which way their judg-
    ments lean 'em,
"'Tis strange—the Hebrew noun which
    means "I am,"
The English always use to govern d—n.'

XV

Some women use their tongues—she
    look'd a lecture,
  Each eye a sermon, and her brow a
    homily,
An all-in-all sufficient self-director,
  Like the lamented late Sir Samuel
    Romilly,

The Law's expounder, and the State's corrector,
    Whose suicide was almost an anomaly—
One sad example more, that 'All is vanity,'—
(The jury brought their verdict in 'Insanity.')

XVI

In short, she was a walking calculation,
  Miss Edgeworth's novels stepping from
    their covers,
Or Mrs. Trimmer's books on education,
  Or 'Cœlebs' Wife' set out in quest of
    lovers,
Morality's prim personification,
  In which not Envy's self a flaw discovers;
To others' share let 'female errors fall,'
For she had not even one—the worst of all.

XVII

Oh! she was perfect past all parallel—
  Of any modern female saint's com-
    parison;
So far above the cunning powers of hell,
  Her guardian angel had given up his
    garrison;
Even her minutest motions went as well
  As those of the best time-piece made by
    Harrison:
In virtues nothing earthly could surpass her,
Save thine 'incomparable oil,' Macassar!

XVIII

Perfect she was, but as perfection is
  Insipid in this naughty world of ours,
Where our first parents never learn'd to
    kiss
  Till they were exiled from their earlier
    bowers,
Where all was peace, and innocence, and
    bliss
  (I wonder how they got through the
    twelve hours),
Don José, like a lineal son of Eve,
Went plucking various fruit without her
    leave.

XIX

He was a mortal of the careless kind,
  With no great love for learning, or the
    learn'd,
Who chose to go where'er he had a mind,
  And never dream'd his lady was con-
    cern'd;
The world, as usual, wickedly inclined
  To see a kingdom or a house o'erturn'd,
Whisper'd he had a mistress, some said
    two,
But for domestic quarrels *one* will do.

XX

Now Donna Inez had, with all her merit,
  A great opinion of her own good
    qualities;
Neglect, indeed, requires a saint to bear it,
  And such, indeed, she was in her moral-
    ities;
But then she had a devil of a spirit,
  And sometimes mix'd up fancies with
    realities,
And let few opportunities escape
Of getting her liege lord into a scrape.

XXI

This was an easy matter with a man
  Oft in the wrong, and never on his
    guard;
And even the wisest, do the best they can,
  Have moments, hours, and days, so un-
    prepared,
That you might 'brain them with their
    lady's fan';
  And sometimes ladies hit exceeding
    hard,
And fans turn into falchions in fair hands,
And why and wherefore no one under-
    stands.

XXII

'Tis pity learned virgins ever wed
  With persons of no sort of education,
Or gentlemen, who, though well born and
    bred,
  Grow tired of scientific conversation;
I don't choose to say much upon this head,
  I'm a plain man, and in a single station,
But—Oh! ye lords of ladies intellectual,
Inform us truly have they not hen-peck'd
    you all?

XXIII

Don José and his lady quarrell'd—*why*,
  Not any of the many could divine,
Though several thousand people chose to
    try,
  'Twas surely no concern of theirs nor
    mine;
I loathe that low vice—curiosity;
  But if there's anything in which I shine,
'Tis in arranging all my friends' affairs,
Not having, of my own, domestic cares.

XXIV

And so I interfered, and with the best
  Intentions, but their treatment was not
    kind;
I think the foolish people were possess'd,
  For neither of them could I ever find,
Although their porter afterwards con-
    fess'd—
  But that's no matter, and the worst's
    behind,
For little Juan o'er me threw, down stairs,
A pail of housemaid's water unawares.

xxv

A little curly-headed, good-for-nothing,
  And mischief-making monkey from his
    birth;
His parents ne'er agreed except in doting
  Upon the most unquiet imp on earth;
Instead of quarrelling, had they been but
    both in
  Their senses, they'd have sent young
    master forth
To school, or had him soundly whipp'd at
    home,
To teach him manners for the time to
    come.

xxvi

Don José and the Donna Inez led
  For some time an unhappy sort of life,
Wishing each other, not divorced, but
    dead;
  They lived respectably as man and wife,
Their conduct was exceedingly well-bred,
  And gave no outward signs of inward
    strife,
Until at length the smother'd fire broke out,
And put the business past all kind of doubt.

xxvii

For Inez call'd some druggists and phy-
    sicians,
  And tried to prove her loving lord was
    mad,
But as he had some lucid intermissions,
  She next decided he was only *bad*;
Yet when they ask'd her for her deposi-
    tions,
  No sort of explanation could be had,
Save that her duty both to man and God
Required this conduct—which seem'd very
    odd.

xxviii

She kept a journal, where his faults were
    noted,
  And open'd certain trunks of books and
    letters,
All which might, if occasion served, be
    quoted;
  And then she had all Seville for abettors,
Besides her good old grandmother (who
    doted);
  The hearers of her case became re-
    peaters,
Then advocates, inquisitors, and judges,
Some for amusement, others for old
    grudges.

xxix

And then this best and meekest woman
    bore
  With such serenity her husband's woes,
Just as the Spartan ladies did of yore,
  Who saw their spouses kill'd, and nobly
    chose

Never to say a word about them more—
  Calmly she heard each calumny that
    rose,
And saw *his* agonies with such sublimity,
That all the world exclaim'd, 'What mag-
    nanimity!'

xxx

No doubt this patience, when the world is
    damning us,
  Is philosophic in our former friends;
'Tis also pleasant to be deem'd magnani-
    mous,
  The more so in obtaining our own ends;
And what the lawyers call a '*malus
    animus*'
  Conduct like this by no means compre-
    hends:
Revenge in person's certainly no virtue,
But then 'tis not *my* fault, if *others* hurt
    you.

xxxi

And if our quarrels should rip up old
    stories,
  And help them with a lie or two addi-
    tional,
I'm not to blame, as you well know—no
    more is
  Any one else—they were become tradi-
    tional;
Besides, their resurrection aids our glories
  By contrast, which is what we just were
    wishing all:
And science profits by this resurrection—
Dead scandals form good subjects for dis-
    section.

xxxii

Their friends had tried at reconciliation,
  Then their relations, who made matters
    worse,
('Twere hard to tell upon a like occasion
  To whom it may be best to have re-
    course—
I can't say much for friend or yet relation):
  The lawyers did their utmost for divorce,
But scarce a fee was paid on either side
Before, unluckily, Don José died.

xxxiii

He died: and most unluckily, because,
  According to all hints I could collect
From counsel learned in those kinds of
    laws
  (Although their talk's obscure and cir-
    cumspect),
His death contrived to spoil a charming
    cause;
  A thousand pities also with respect
To public feeling, which on this occasion
Was manifested in a great sensation.

XXXIV

But ah! he died; and buried with him lay
  The public feeling and the lawyers' fees:
His house was sold, his servants sent
    away,
  A Jew took one of his two mistresses,
A priest the other—at least so they say:
  I ask'd the doctors after his disease—
He died of the slow fever called the
    tertian,
And left his widow to her own aversion.

XXXV

Yet José was an honourable man,
  That I must say, who knew him very
    well;
Therefore his frailties I'll no further scan,
  Indeed there were not many more to
    tell:
And if his passions now and then outran
  Discretion, and were not so peaceable
As Numa's (who was also named Pompi-
    lius),
He had been ill brought up, and was born
    bilious.

XXXVI

Whate'er might be his worthlessness or
    worth,
  Poor fellow! he had many things to
    wound him,
Let's own—since it can do no good on
    earth—
  It was a trying moment that which
    found him
Standing alone beside his desolate hearth,
  Where all his household gods lay
    shiver'd round him:
No choice was left his feelings or his pride,
Save death or Doctors' Commons—so he
    died.

XXXVII

Dying intestate, Juan was sole heir
  To a chancery suit, and messuages and
    lands,
Which, with a long minority and care,
  Promised to turn out well in proper
    hands:
Inez became sole guardian, which was fair,
  And answer'd but to nature's just de-
    mands;
An only son left with an only mother
Is brought up much more wisely than
    another.

XXXVIII

Sagest of women, even of widows, she
  Resolved that Juan should be quite a
    paragon,
And worthy of the noblest pedigree:
  (His sire was of Castile, his dam from
    Aragon).

Then for accomplishments of chivalry,
  In case our lord the king should go to
    war again,
He learn'd the arts of riding, fencing, gun-
    nery,
And how to scale a fortress—or a nunnery.

XXXIX

But that which Donna Inez most desired,
  And saw into herself each day before all
The learned tutors whom for him she
    hired,
  Was, that his breeding should be strictly
    moral:
Much into all his studies she inquired,
  And so they were submitted first to her,
    all,
Arts, sciences, no branch was made a
    mystery
To Juan's eyes, excepting natural history.

XL

The languages, especially the dead,
  The sciences, and most of all the
    abstruse,
The arts, at least all such as could be said
  To be the most remote from common
    use,
In all these he was much and deeply read:
  But not a page of anything that's loose,
Or hints continuation of the species,
Was ever suffer'd, lest he should grow
    vicious.

XLI

His classic studies made a little puzzle,
  Because of filthy loves of gods and god-
    desses,
Who in the earlier ages raised a bustle,
  But never put on pantaloons or bodices;
His reverend tutors had at times a tussle,
  And for their Æneids, Iliads, and
    Odysseys,
Were forced to make an odd sort of
    apology,
For Donna Inez dreaded the Mythology.

XLII

Ovid's a rake, as half his verses show him,
  Anacreon's morals are a still worse
    sample,
Catullus scarcely has a decent poem,
  I don't think Sappho's Ode a good
    example,
Although Longinus tells us there is no
    hymn
  Where the sublime soars forth on wings
    more ample;
But Virgil's songs are pure, except that
    horrid one
Beginning with 'Formosum Pastor Cory-
    don.'

XLIII

Lucretius' irreligion is too strong
  For early stomachs, to prove whole-
    some food;
I can't help thinking Juvenal was wrong,
  Although no doubt his real intent was
    good,
For speaking out so plainly in his song,
  So much indeed as to be downright
    rude;
And then what proper person can be
    partial
To all those nauseous epigrams of Martial?

XLIV

Juan was taught from out the best edition,
  Expurgated by learned men, who place,
Judiciously, from out the schoolboy's
    vision,
  The grosser parts; but, fearful to deface
Too much their modest bard by this
    omission,
  And pitying sore his mutilated case,
They only add them all in an appendix,
Which saves, in fact, the trouble of an
    index;

XLV

For there we have them all 'at one fell
    swoop,'
  Instead of being scatter'd through the
    pages;
They stand forth marshall'd in a handsome
    troop,
  To meet the ingenuous youth of future
    ages,
Till some less rigid editor shall stoop
  To call them back into their separate
    cages,
Instead of standing staring all together,
Like garden gods—and not so decent
    either.

XLVI

The Missal too (it was the family Missal)
  Was ornamented in a sort of way
Which ancient mass-books often are, and
    this all
  Kinds of grotesques illumined; and how
    they,
Who saw those figures on the margin kiss
    all,
  Could turn their optics to the text and
    pray,
Is more than I know—But Don Juan's
    mother
Kept this herself, and gave her son another.

XLVII

Sermons he read, and lectures he endured,
  And homilies, and lives of all the saints;
To Jerome and to Chrysostom inured,
  He did not take such studies for re-
    straints;

But how faith is acquired, and then in-
    sured,
  So well not one of the aforesaid paints
As Saint Augustine in his fine Confessions,
Which make the reader envy his trans-
    gressions.

XLVIII

This, too, was a seal'd book to little Juan—
  I can't but say that his mamma was right,
If such an education was the true one.
  She scarcely trusted him from out her
    sight;
Her maids were old, and if she took a new
    one,
  You might be sure she was a perfect
    fright,
She did this during even her husband's
    life—
I recommend as much to every wife.

XLIX

Young Juan wax'd in godliness and grace;
  At six a charming child, and at eleven
With all the promise of as fine a face
  As e'er to man's maturer growth was
    given.
He studied steadily and grew apace,
  And seem'd, at least, in the right road to
    heaven,
For half his days were pass'd at church,
    the other
Between his tutors, confessor, and mother.

L

At six, I said, he was a charming child,
  At twelve he was a fine, but quiet boy;
Although in infancy a little wild,
  They tamed him down amongst them:
    to destroy
His natural spirit not in vain they toil'd,
  At least it seem'd so; and his mother's
    joy
Was to declare how sage, and still, and
    steady,
Her young philosopher was grown already.

LI

I had my doubts, perhaps I have them still,
  But what I say is neither here nor there:
I knew his father well, and have some skill
  In character—but it would not be fair
From sire to son to augur good or ill:
  He and his wife were an ill sorted pair—
But scandal's my aversion—I protest
Against all evil speaking, even in jest.

LII

For my part I say nothing—nothing—but
  This I will say—my reasons are my
    own—
That if I had an only son to put
  To school (as God be praised that I have
    none),

'Tis not with Donna Inez I would shut
　　Him up to learn his catechism alone,
No—no—I'd send him out betimes to
　　college,
For there it was I pick'd up my own know-
　　ledge.

LIII

For there one learns—'tis not for me to
　　boast,
　　Though I acquired—but I pass over
　　　that,
As well as all the Greek I since have lost:
　　I say that there's the place—but '*Verb-
　　　um sat*,'
I think I pick'd up too, as well as most,
　　Knowledge of matters—but no matter
　　　what—
I never married—but, I think, I know
That sons should not be educated so.

LIV

Young Juan now was sixteen years of age,
　　Tall, handsome, slender, but well knit:
　　　he seem'd
Active, though not so sprightly, as a page;
　　And everybody but his mother deem'd
Him almost man; but she flew in a rage
　　And bit her lips (for else she might have
　　　scream'd)
If any said so, for to be precocious
Was in her eyes a thing the most atrocious.

LV

Amongst her numerous acquaintance, all
　　Selected for discretion and devotion,
There was the Donna Julia, whom to call
　　Pretty were but to give a feeble notion
Of many charms in her as natural
　　As sweetness to the flower, or salt to
　　　ocean,
Her zone to Venus, or his bow to Cupid
(But this last simile is trite and stupid).

LVI

The darkness of her Oriental eye
　　Accorded with her Moorish origin;
(Her blood was not all Spanish, by the by;
　　In Spain, you know, this is a sort of sin).
When proud Granada fell, and, forced to
　　fly,
　　Boabdil wept, of Donna Julia's kin
Some went to Africa, some stay'd in Spain,
Her great great grandmamma chose to re-
　　main.

LVII

She married (I forget the pedigree)
　　With an Hidalgo, who transmitted down
His blood less noble than such blood
　　should be;
　　At such alliances his sires would frown,
In that point so precise in each degree
　　That they bred *in and in*, as might be
　　　shown,
Marrying their cousins—nay, their aunts,
　　and nieces,
Which always spoils the breed, if it in-
　　creases.

LVIII

This heathenish cross restored the breed
　　again,
　　Ruin'd its blood, but much improved
　　　its flesh;
For from a root the ugliest in old Spain
　　Sprung up a branch as beautiful as
　　　fresh;
The sons no more were short, the daughters
　　plain:
　　But there's a rumour which I fain would
　　　hush,
'Tis said that Donna Julia's grandmamma
Produced her Don more heirs at love than
　　law.

LIX

However this might be, the race went on
　　Improving still through every genera-
　　　tion,
Until it centred in an only son,
　　Who left an only daughter: my narra-
　　　tion
May have suggested that this single one
　　Could be but Julia (whom on this
　　　occasion
I shall have much to speak about), and she
Was married, charming, chaste, and
　　twenty-three.

LX

Her eye (I'm very fond of handsome eyes)
　　Was large and dark, suppressing half its
　　　fire
Until she spoke, then through its soft dis-
　　guise
　　Flash'd an expression more of pride
　　　than ire,
And love than either; and there would
　　arise
　　A something in them which was not
　　　desire,
But would have been, perhaps, but for the
　　soul
Which struggled through and chasten'd
　　down the whole.

LXI

Her glossy hair was cluster'd o'er a brow
　　Bright with intelligence, and fair, and
　　　smooth;
Her eyebrow's shape was like the aërial
　　bow,
　　Her cheek all purple with the beam of
　　　youth,

643

Mounting, at times, to a transparent glow,
　As if her veins ran lightning; she, in
　　sooth,
Possess'd an air and grace by no means
　common:
Her stature tall—I hate a dumpy woman.

LXII

Wedded she was some years, and to a man
　Of fifty, and such husbands are in
　　plenty;
And yet, I think, instead of such a ONE
　'Twere better to have TWO of five-and-
　　twenty,
Especially in countries near the sun:
　And now I think on't, 'mi vien in mente,'
Ladies even of the most uneasy virtue
Prefer a spouse whose age is short of thirty.

LXIII

'Tis a sad thing, I cannot choose but say,
　And all the fault of that indecent sun,
Who cannot leave alone our helpless clay,
　But will keep baking, broiling, burning
　　on,
That howsoever people fast and pray,
　The flesh is frail, and so the soul undone:
What men call gallantry, and gods
　adultery,
Is much more common where the climate's
　sultry.

LXIV

Happy the nations of the moral North!
　Where all is virtue, and the winter season
Sends sin, without a rag on, shivering forth
　('Twas snow that brought St. Anthony
　　to reason);
Where juries cast up what a wife is worth,
　By laying whate'er sum, in mulct, they
　　please on
The lover, who must pay a handsome price,
Because it is a marketable vice.

LXV

Alfonso was the name of Julia's lord,
　A man well looking for his years, and
　　who
Was neither much beloved nor yet
　abhorr'd:
　They lived together as most people do,
Suffering each other's foibles by accord,
　And not exactly either *one* or *two*;
Yet he was jealous, though he did not
　show it,
For jealousy dislikes the world to know it.

LXVI

Julia was—yet I never could see why—
　With Donna Inez quite a favourite
　　friend;
Between their tastes there was small sym-
　pathy,
　For not a line had Julia ever penn'd:

Some people whisper (but, no doubt, they
　lie,
　For malice still imputes some private
　　end)
That Inez had, ere Don Alfonso's mar-
　riage,
Forgot with him her very prudent carriage;

LXVII

And that still keeping up the old con-
　nexion,
　Which time had lately render'd much
　　more chaste,
She took his lady also in affection,
　And certainly this course was much the
　　best:
She flatter'd Julia with her sage protection,
　And complimented Don Alfonso's
　　taste;
And if she could not (who can?) silence
　scandal,
At least she left it a more slender handle.

LXVIII

I can't tell whether Julia saw the affair
　With other people's eyes, or if her own
Discoveries made, but none could be
　aware
　Of this, at least no symptom e'er was
　　shown;
Perhaps she did not know, or did not care,
　Indifferent from the first, or callous
　　grown:
I'm really puzzled what to think or say,
She kept her counsel in so close a way.

LXIX

Juan she saw, and, as a pretty child,
　Caress'd him often—such a thing might
　　be
Quite innocently done, and harmless
　styled,
　When she had twenty years, and thirteen
　　he;
But I am not so sure I should have smiled
　When he was sixteen, Julia twenty-
　　three;
These few short years make wondrous
　alterations,
Particularly amongst sun-burnt nations.

LXX

Whate'er the cause might be, they had be-
　come
Changed; for the dame grew distant, the
　youth shy,
Their looks cast down, their greetings
　almost dumb,
　And much embarrassment in either eye;
There surely will be little doubt with some
　That Donna Julia knew the reason why,
But as for Juan, he had no more notion
Than he who never saw the sea of ocean.

LXXI

Yet Julia's very coldness still was kind,
  And tremulously gentle her small hand
Withdrew itself from his, but left behind
  A little pressure, thrilling, and so bland
And slight, so very slight, that to the mind
  'Twas but a doubt; but ne'er magician's
      wand
Wrought change with all Armida's fairy
      art
Like what this light touch left on Juan's
      heart.

LXXII

And if she met him, though she smiled no
      more,
  She look'd a sadness sweeter than her
      smile,
As if her heart had deeper thoughts in
      store
  She must not own, but cherish'd more
      the while
For that compression in its burning core;
  Even innocence itself has many a wile,
And will not dare to trust itself with truth,
And love is taught hypocrisy from youth.

LXXIII

But passion most dissembles, yet betrays
  Even by its darkness; as the blackest sky
Foretells the heaviest tempest, it displays
  Its workings through the vainly guarded
      eye,
And in whatever aspect it arrays
  Itself, 'tis still the same hypocrisy:
Coldness or anger, even disdain or hate,
Are masks it often wears, and still too late.

LXXIV

Then there were sighs, the deeper for sup-
      pression,
  And stolen glances, sweeter for the theft,
And burning blushes, though for no trans-
      gression,
  Tremblings when met, and restlessness
      when left;
All these are little preludes to possession,
  Of which young passion cannot be be-
      reft,
And merely tend to show how greatly love is
Embarrass'd at first starting with a novice.

LXXV

Poor Julia's heart was in an awkward
      state;
  She felt it going, and resolved to make
The noblest efforts for herself and mate,
  For honour's, pride's, religion's, vir-
      tue's sake.
Her resolutions were most truly great,
  And almost might have made a Tarquin
      quake:
She pray'd the Virgin Mary for her grace,
As being the best judge of a lady's case.

LXXVI

She vow'd she never would see Juan more,
  And next day paid a visit to his mother,
And look'd extremely at the opening door,
  Which, by the Virgin's grace, let in
      another;
Grateful she was, and yet a little sore—
  Again it opens, it can be no other,
'Tis surely Juan now—No! I'm afraid
That night the Virgin was no further
      pray'd.

LXXVII

She now determined that a virtuous
      woman
  Should rather face and overcome
      temptation,
That flight was base and dastardly, and no
      man
  Should ever give her heart the least sen-
      sation;
That is to say, a thought beyond the com-
      mon
  Preference, that we must feel upon occa-
      sion,
For people who are pleasanter than others,
But then they only seem so many brothers.

LXXVIII

And even if by chance—and who can tell?
  The devil's so very sly—she should dis-
      cover
That all within was not so very well,
  And, if still free, that such or such a
      lover
Might please perhaps, a virtuous wife can
      quell
  Such thoughts, and be the better when
      they're over;
And if the man should ask, 'tis but denial:
I recommend young ladies to make trial.

LXXIX

And then there are such things as love
      divine,
  Bright and immaculate, unmix'd and
      pure,
Such as the angels think so very fine,
  And matrons, who would be no less
      secure,
Platonic, perfect, 'just such love as mine':
  Thus Julia said—and thought so, to be
      sure;
And so I'd have her think, were I the man
On whom her reveries celestial ran.

LXXX

Such love is innocent, and may exist
  Between young persons without any
      danger:
A hand may first, and then a lip be kist;
  For my part, to such doings I'm a
      stranger,

But *hear* these freedoms form the utmost
list
   Of all o'er which such love may be a
ranger:
If people go beyond, 'tis quite a crime,
But not my fault—I tell them all in time.

LXXXI

Love, then, but love within its proper
limits
   Was Julia's innocent determination
In young Don Juan's favour, and to him
its
   Exertion might be useful on occasion;
And, lighted at too pure a shrine to dim its
   Ethereal lustre, with what sweet persua-
sion
He might be taught, by love and her to-
gether—
I really don't know what, nor Julia either.

LXXXII

Fraught with this fine intention, and well
fenced
   In mail of proof—her purity of soul,
She, for the future of her strength con-
vinced,
   And that her honour was a rock, or mole,
Exceeding sagely from that hour dispensed
   With any kind of troublesome control;
But whether Julia to the task was equal
Is that which must be mention'd in the
sequel.

LXXXIII

Her plan she deem'd both innocent and
feasible,
   And, surely, with a stripling of sixteen
Not scandal's fangs could fix on much
that's seizable,
   Or if they did so, satisfied to mean
Nothing but what was good, her breast
was peaceable:
   A quiet conscience makes one so serene!
Christians have burnt each other, quite
persuaded
That all the Apostles would have done as
they did.

LXXXIV

And if in the mean time her husband died,
   But Heaven forbid that such a thought
should cross
Her brain, though in a dream! (and then
she sigh'd)
   Never could she survive that common
loss;
But just suppose that moment should be-
tide,
   I only say suppose it—*inter nos.*
(This should be *entre nous*, for Julia
thought
In French, but then the rhyme would go
for nought.)

LXXXV

I only say, suppose this supposition:
   Juan being then grown up to man's
estate
Would fully suit a widow of condition,
   Even seven years hence it would not be
too late;
And in the interim (to pursue this vision)
   The mischief, after all, could not be
great,
For he would learn the rudiments of love,
I mean the seraph way of those above.

LXXXVI

So much for Julia. Now we'll turn to Juan.
   Poor little fellow! he had no idea
Of his own case, and never hit the true one;
   In feelings quick as Ovid's Miss Medea,
He puzzled over what he found a new one,
   But not as yet imagined it could be a
Thing quite in course, and not at all alarm-
ing,
Which, with a little patience, might grow
charming.

LXXXVII

Silent and pensive, idle, restless, slow,
   His home deserted for the lonely wood,
Tormented with a wound he could not
know,
   His, like all deep grief, plunged in soli-
tude:
I'm fond myself of solitude or so,
   But then, I beg it may be understood,
By solitude I mean a Sultan's, not
A hermit's, with a haram for a grot.

LXXXVIII

'Oh Love! in such a wilderness as this,
   Where transport and security entwine,
Here is the empire of thy perfect bliss,
   And here thou art a god indeed divine.'
The bard I quote from does not sing amiss,
   With the exception of the second line,
For that same twining 'transport and
security'
Are twisted to a phrase of some obscurity.

LXXXIX

The poet meant, no doubt, and thus ap-
peals
   To the good sense and senses of man-
kind,
The very thing which everybody feels,
   As all have found on trial, or may find,
That no one likes to be disturb'd at meals
   Or love.—I won't say more about 'en-
twined'
Or 'transport,' as we knew all that before,
But beg 'Security' will bolt the door.

XC

Young Juan wander'd by the glassy brooks,
　　Thinking unutterable things; he threw
Himself at length within the leafy nooks
　　Where the wild branch of the cork
　　　forest grew;
There poets find materials for their books,
　　And every now and then we read them
　　　through,
So that their plan and prosody are eligible,
Unless, like Wordsworth, they prove unin-
　　telligible.

XCI

He, Juan (and not Wordsworth), so pur-
　　sued
　　His self-communion with his own high
　　　soul,
Until his mighty heart, in its great mood,
　　Had mitigated part, though not the whole
Of its disease; he did the best he could
　　With things not very subject to control,
And turn'd, without perceiving his con-
　　dition,
Like Coleridge, into a metaphysician.

XCII

He thought about himself, and the whole
　　earth,
　　Of man the wonderful, and of the stars,
And how the deuce they ever could have
　　birth;
　　And then he thought of earthquakes,
　　　and of wars,
How many miles the moon might have in
　　girth,
　　Of air-balloons, and of the many bars
To perfect knowledge of the boundless
　　skies;—
And then he thought of Donna Julia's eyes.

XCIII

In thoughts like these true wisdom may
　　discern
　　Longings sublime, and aspirations high,
Which some are born with, but the most
　　part learn
　　To plague themselves withal, they know
　　　not why:
'Twas strange that one so young should
　　thus concern
　　His brain about the action of the sky;
If you think 'twas philosophy that this did,
I can't help thinking puberty assisted.

XCIV

He pored upon the leaves, and on the
　　flowers,
　　And heard a voice in all the winds; and
　　　then
He thought of wood-nymphs and im-
　　mortal bowers,
　　And how the goddesses came down to
　　　men:

He miss'd the pathway, he forgot the
　　hours,
　　And when he look'd upon his watch
　　　again,
He found how much old Time had been a
　　winner—
He also found that he had lost his dinner.

XCV

Sometimes he turn'd to gaze upon his
　　book,
　　Boscan, or Garcilasso;—by the wind
Even as the page is rustled while we look,
　　So by the poesy of his own mind
Over the mystic leaf his soul was shook,
　　As if 'twere one whereon magicians bind
Their spells, and give them to the passing
　　gale
According to some good old woman's tale.

XCVI

Thus would he while his lonely hours away
　　Dissatisfied, nor knowing what he
　　　wanted;
Nor glowing reverie, nor poet's lay,
　　Could yield his spirit that for which it
　　　panted,
A bosom whereon he his head might lay,
　　And hear the heart beat with the love it
　　　granted,
With——several other things, which I for-
　　get,
Or which, at least, I need not mention yet.

XCVII

Those lonely walks, and lengthening reve-
　　ries,
　　Could not escape the gentle Julia's eyes;
She saw that Juan was not at his ease;
　　But that which chiefly may, and must
　　　surprise,
Is, that the Donna Inez did not tease
　　Her only son with question or surmise;
Whether it was she did not see, or would
　　not,
Or, like all very clever people, could not.

XCVIII

This may seem strange, but yet 'tis very
　　common;
　　For instance—gentlemen, whose ladies
　　　take
Leave to o'erstep the written rights of
　　woman,
　　And break the——Which command-
　　　ment is't they break?
(I have forgot the number, and think no
　　man
　　Should rashly quote, for fear of a mis-
　　　take.)
I say, when these same gentlemen are
　　jealous,
They make some blunder, which their
　　ladies tell us.

XCIX

A real husband always is suspicious,
  But still no less suspects in the wrong
    place,
Jealous of some one who had no such
    wishes,
  Or pandering blindly to his own disgrace,
By harbouring some dear friend extremely
    vicious,
  The last indeed's infallibly the case:
And when the spouse and friend are gone
    off wholly,
He wonders at their vice, and not his folly.

C

Thus parents also are at times short-
    sighted;
  Though watchful as the lynx, they ne'er
    discover,
The while the wicked world beholds de-
    lighted,
  Young Hopeful's mistress, or Miss
    Fanny's lover,
Till some confounded escapade has blighted
  The plan of twenty years, and all is over;
And then the mother cries, the father
    swears,
And wonders why the devil he got heirs.

CI

But Inez was so anxious, and so clear
  Of sight, that I must think, on this occa-
    sion,
She had some other motive much more
    near
  For leaving Juan to this new temptation,
But what that motive was, I shan't say
    here;
  Perhaps to finish Juan's education,
Perhaps to open Don Alfonso's eyes,
In case he thought his wife too great a
    prize.

CII

It was upon a day, a summer's day;—
  Summer's indeed a very dangerous
    season,
And so is spring about the end of May;
  The sun, no doubt, is the prevailing
    reason;
But whatsoe'er the cause is, one may say,
  And stand convicted of more truth than
    treason,
That there are months which nature grows
    more merry in,—
March has its hares, and May must have
    its heroine.

CIII

'Twas on a summer's day—the sixth of
    June:—
  I like to be particular in dates,
Not only of the age, and year, but moon;
  They are a sort of post-house, where the
    Fates

Change horses, making history change its
    tune,
  Then spur away o'er empires and o'er
    states,
Leaving at last not much besides chrono-
    logy,
Excepting the post-obits of theology.

CIV

'Twas on the sixth of June, about the hour
  Of half-past six—perhaps still nearer
    seven—
When Julia sate within as pretty a bower
  As e'er held houri in that heathenish
    heaven
Described by Mahomet, and Anacreon
    Moore,
  To whom the lyre and laurels have been
    given,
With all the trophies of triumphant song—
He won them well, and may he wear them
    long!

CV

She sate, but not alone; I know not well
  How this same interview had taken
    place,
And even if I knew, I should not tell—
  People should hold their tongues in any
    case;
No matter how or why the thing befell,
  But there were she and Juan, face to
    face—
When two such faces are so, 'twould be
    wise,
But very difficult, to shut their eyes.

CVI

How beautiful she look'd! her conscious
    heart
  Glow'd in her cheek, and yet she felt no
    wrong,
Oh Love! how perfect is thy mystic art,
  Strengthening the weak, and trampling
    on the strong!
How self-deceitful is the sagest part
  Of mortals whom thy lure hath led
    along!—
The precipice she stood on was immense,
So was her creed in her own innocence.

CVII

She thought of her own strength, and
    Juan's youth,
  And of the folly of all prudish fears,
Victorious virtue, and domestic truth,
  And then of Don Alfonso's fifty years:
I wish these last had not occurr'd, in sooth,
  Because that number rarely much en-
    dears,
And through all climes, the snowy and the
    sunny,
Sounds ill in love, whate'er it may in
    money.

CVIII

When people say, 'I've told you *fifty*
    times,'
    They mean to scold, and very often do;
When poets say, 'I've written *fifty*
    rhymes,'
    They make you dread that they'll recite
        them too;
In gangs of *fifty*, thieves commit their
    crimes;
At *fifty* love for love is rare, 'tis true,
But then, no doubt, it equally as true is,
A good deal may be bought for *fifty* Louis.

CIX

Julia had honour, virtue, truth, and love
    For Don Alfonso; and she inly swore,
By all the vows below to powers above,
    She never would disgrace the ring she
        wore,
Nor leave a wish which wisdom might re-
    prove;
    And while she ponder'd this, besides
        much more,
One hand on Juan's carelessly was thrown,
Quite by mistake—she thought it was her
    own;

CX

Unconsciously she lean'd upon the other,
    Which play'd within the tangles of her
        hair;
And to contend with thoughts she could
    not smother
    She seem'd, by the distraction of her air.
'Twas surely very wrong in Juan's mother
    To leave together this imprudent pair,
She who for many years had watch'd her
    son so—
I'm very certain *mine* would not have done
    so.

CXI

The hand which still held Juan's, by de-
    grees
Gently, but palpably confirm'd its grasp,
As if it said, 'Detain me, if you please';
    Yet there's no doubt she only meant to
        clasp
His fingers with a pure Platonic squeeze;
    She would have shrunk as from a toad,
        or asp,
Had she imagined such a thing could
    rouse
A feeling dangerous to a prudent spouse.

CXII

I cannot know what Juan thought of this,
    But what he did, is much what you
        would do;
His young lip thank'd it with a grateful
    kiss,
    And then, abash'd at its own joy, with-
        drew

In deep despair, lest he had done amiss,—
    Love is so very timid when 'tis new:
She blush'd, and frown'd not, but she
    strove to speak,
And held her tongue, her voice was grown
    so weak.

CXIII

The sun set, and up rose the yellow moon:
    The devil's in the moon for mischief;
        they
Who call'd her CHASTE, methinks, began
    too soon
    Their nomenclature; there is not a day,
The longest, not the twenty-first of June,
    Sees half the business in a wicked way,
On which three single hours of moonshine
    smile—
And then she looks so modest all the while.

CXIV

There is a dangerous silence in that hour,
    A stillness, which leaves room for the
        full soul
To open all itself, without the power
    Of calling wholly back its self-control;
The silver light which, hallowing tree and
    tower,
    Sheds beauty and deep softness o'er the
        whole,
Breathes also to the heart, and o'er it throws
A loving languor, which is not repose.

CXV

And Julia sate with Juan, half embraced
    And half retiring from the glowing arm,
Which trembled like the bosom where
    'twas placed;
    Yet still she must have thought there
        was no harm,
Or else 'twere easy to withdraw her waist;
    But then the situation had its charm,
And then——God knows what next—I
    can't go on;
I'm almost sorry that I e'er begun.

CXVI

Oh Plato! Plato! you have paved the way,
    With your confounded fantasies, to more
Immoral conduct by the fancied sway
    Your system feigns o'er the controlless
        core
Of human hearts, than all the long array
    Of poets and romancers:—You're a bore,
A charlatan, a coxcomb—and have been,
At best, no better than a go-between.

CXVII

And Julia's voice was lost, except in sighs,
    Until too late for useful conversation;
The tears were gushing from her gentle
    eyes,
    I wish, indeed, they had not had occa-
        sion;

But who, alas! can love, and then be wise?
　　Not that remorse did not oppose temptation;
A little still she strove, and much repented,
And whispering 'I will ne'er consent'—
　　consented.

CXVIII

'Tis said that Xerxes offer'd a reward
　　To those who could invent him a new pleasure.
Methinks the requisition's rather hard,
　　And must have cost his majesty a treasure:
For my part, I'm a moderate-minded bard,
　　Fond of a little love (which I call leisure);
I care not for new pleasures, as the old
Are quite enough for me, so they but hold.

CXIX

Oh Pleasure! you're indeed a pleasant thing,
　　Although one must be damn'd for you, no doubt:
I make a resolution every spring
　　Of reformation, ere the year run out,
But somehow, this my vestal vow takes wing,
　　Yet still, I trust, it may be kept throughout:
I'm very sorry, very much ashamed,
And mean, next winter, to be quite reclaim'd.

CXX

Here my chaste Muse a liberty must take—
　　Start not! still chaster reader—she'll be nice hence—
Forward, and there is no great cause to quake;
　　This liberty is a poetic licence,
Which some irregularity may make
　　In the design, and as I have a high sense
Of Aristotle and the Rules, 'tis fit
To beg his pardon when I err a bit.

CXXI

This licence is to hope the reader will
　　Suppose from June the sixth (the fatal day
Without whose epoch my poetic skill
　　For want of facts would all be thrown away),
But keeping Julia and Don Juan still
　　In sight, that several months have pass'd; we'll say
'Twas in November, but I'm not so sure
About the day—the era's more obscure.

CXXII

We'll talk of that anon.—'Tis sweet to hear
　　At midnight on the blue and moonlit deep
The song and oar of Adria's gondolier,
　　By distance mellow'd, o'er the waters sweep;
'Tis sweet to see the evening star appear;
　　'Tis sweet to listen as the night-winds creep
From leaf to leaf; 'tis sweet to view on high
The rainbow, based on ocean, span the sky.

CXXIII

'Tis sweet to hear the watch-dog's honest bark
　　Bay deep-mouth'd welcome as we draw near home;
'Tis sweet to know there is an eye will mark
　　Our coming, and look brighter when we come;
'Tis sweet to be awaken'd by the lark,
　　Or lull'd by falling waters; sweet the hum
Of bees, the voice of girls, the song of birds,
The lisp of children, and their earliest words.

CXXIV

Sweet is the vintage, when the showering grapes
　　In Bacchanal profusion reel to earth,
Purple and gushing; sweet are our escapes
　　From civic revelry to rural mirth;
Sweet to the miser are his glittering heaps,
　　Sweet to the father is his first-born's birth,
Sweet is revenge—especially to women,
Pillage to soldiers, prize-money to seamen.

CXXV

Sweet is a legacy, and passing sweet
　　The unexpected death of some old lady
Or gentleman of seventy years complete,
　　Who've made 'us youth' wait too—too long already
For an estate, or cash, or country seat,
　　Still breaking, but with stamina so steady
That all the Israelites are fit to mob its
Next owner for their double-damn'd post-obits.

CXXVI

'Tis sweet to win, no matter how, one's laurels,
　　By blood or ink; 'tis sweet to put an end
To strife; 'tis sometimes sweet to have our quarrels,
　　Particularly with a tiresome friend:
Sweet is old wine in bottles, ale in barrels;
　　Dear is the helpless creature we defend
Against the world; and dear the schoolboy spot
We ne'er forget, though there we are forgot.

CXXVII

But sweeter still than this, than these, than all,
  Is first and passionate love—it stands alone,
Like Adam's recollection of his fall;
  The tree of knowledge has been pluck'd—all's known—
And life yields nothing further to recall
  Worthy of this ambrosial sin, so shown,
No doubt in fable, as the unforgiven
Fire which Prometheus filch'd for us from heaven.

CXXVIII

Man's a strange animal, and makes strange use
  Of his own nature, and the various arts,
And likes particularly to produce
  Some new experiment to show his parts;
This is the age of oddities let loose,
  Where different talents find their different marts;
You'd best begin with truth, and when you've lost your
Labour, there's a sure market for imposture.

CXXIX

What opposite discoveries we have seen!
  (Signs of true genius, and of empty pockets.)
One makes new noses, one a guillotine,
  One breaks your bones, one sets them in their sockets;
But vaccination certainly has been
  A kind antithesis to Congreve's rockets,
With which the Doctor paid off an old pox,
By borrowing a new one from an ox.

CXXX

Bread has been made (indifferent) from potatoes;
  And galvanism has set some corpses grinning,
But has not answer'd like the apparatus
  Of the Humane Society's beginning,
By which men are unsuffocated gratis:
  What wondrous new machines have late been spinning!
I said the small pox has gone out of late;
Perhaps it may be follow'd by the great.

CXXXI

'Tis said the great came from America;
  Perhaps it may set out on its return,—
The population there so spreads, they say
  'Tis grown high time to thin it in its turn,
With war, or plague, or famine, any way,
  So that civilisation they may learn;
And which in ravage the more loathsome evil is—
Their real lues, or our pseudo-syphilis?

CXXXII

This is the patent age of new inventions
  For killing bodies, and for saving souls,
All propagated with the best intentions;
  Sir Humphry Davy's lantern, by which coals
Are safely mined for in the mode he mentions,
  Tombuctoo travels, voyages to the Poles,
Are ways to benefit mankind, as true,
Perhaps, as shooting them at Waterloo.

CXXXIII

Man's a phenomenon, one knows not what,
  And wonderful beyond all wondrous measure;
'Tis pity though, in this sublime world, that
  Pleasure's a sin, and sometimes sin's a pleasure;
Few mortals know what end they would be at,
  But whether glory, power, or love, or treasure,
The path is through perplexing ways, and when
The goal is gain'd, we die, you know—and then——

CXXXIV

What then?—I do not know, no more do you—
  And so good night.—Return we to our story:
'Twas in November, when fine days are few,
  And the far mountains wax a little hoary,
And clap a white cape on their mantles blue;
  And the sea dashes round the promontory,
And the loud breaker boils against the rock,
And sober suns must set at five o'clock.

CXXXV

'Twas, as the watchmen say, a cloudy night;
  No moon, no stars, the wind was low or loud
By gusts, and many a sparkling hearth was bright
  With the piled wood, round which the family crowd;
There's something cheerful in that sort of light,
  Even as a summer sky's without a cloud:
I'm fond of fire, and crickets, and all that,
A lobster salad, and champagne, and chat.

CXXXVI

'Twas midnight—Donna Julia was in bed,
  Sleeping, most probably,—when at her
    door
Arose a clatter might awake the dead,
  If they had never been awoke before,
And that they have been so we all have
    read,
  And are to be so, at the least, once
    more;—
The door was fasten'd, but with voice and
    fist
First knocks were heard, then 'Madam—
    Madam—hist!

CXXXVII

'For God's sake, Madam—Madam—
    here's my master,
  With more than half the city at his
    back—
Was ever heard of such a curst disaster!
  'Tis not my fault—I kept good watch—
    Alack!
Do pray undo the bolt a little faster—
  They're on the stair just now, and in a
    crack
Will all be here; perhaps he yet may fly—
Surely the window's not so *very* high!'

CXXXVIII

By this time Don Alfonso was arrived,
  With torches, friends, and servants in
    great number;
The major part of them had long been
    wived,
  And therefore paused not to disturb the
    slumber
Of any wicked woman, who contrived
  By stealth her husband's temples to
    encumber:
Examples of this kind are so contagious,
Were *one* not punish'd, *all* would be out-
    rageous.

CXXXIX

I can't tell how, or why, or what suspicion
  Could enter into Don Alfonso's head;
But for a cavalier of his condition
  It surely was exceedingly ill-bred,
Without a word of previous admonition,
  To hold a levee round his lady's bed,
And summon lackeys, arm'd with fire and
    sword,
To prove himself the thing he most
    abhorr'd.

CXL

Poor Donna Julia! starting as from sleep
  (Mind—that I do not say—she had not
    slept),
Began at once to scream, and yawn, and
    weep;
  Her maid, Antonia, who was an adept,

Contrived to fling the bed-clothes in a
    heap,
  As if she had just now from out them
    crept:
I can't tell why she should take all this
    trouble
To prove her mistress had been sleeping
    double.

CXLI

But Julia mistress, and Antonia maid,
  Appear'd like two poor harmless
    women, who
Of goblins, but still more of men afraid,
  Had thought one man might be deterr'd
    by two,
And therefore side by side were gently laid,
  Until the hours of absence should run
    through,
And truant husband should return, and
    say,
'My dear, I was the first who came away.'

CXLII

Now Julia found at length a voice, and
    cried,
  'In heaven's name, Don Alfonso, what
    d'ye mean?
Has madness seized you? would that I had
    died
  Ere such a monster's victim I had been!
What may this midnight violence betide,
  A sudden fit of drunkenness or spleen?
Dare you suspect me, whom the thought
    would kill?
Search, then, the room!'—Alfonso said,
    'I will.'

CXLIII

He search'd, *they* search'd, and rummaged
    everywhere,
  Closet and clothes-press, chest and
    window-seat,
And found much linen, lace, and several
    pair
  Of stockings, slippers, brushes, combs,
    complete,
With other articles of ladies fair,
  To keep them beautiful, or leave them
    neat:
Arras they prick'd and curtains with their
    swords,
And wounded several shutters, and some
    boards.

CXLIV

Under the bed they search'd, and there
    they found—
  No matter what—it was not that they
    sought:
They open'd windows, gazing if the
    ground
  Had signs or footmarks, but the earth
    said nought;

And then they stared each others' faces
   round;
'Tis odd, not one of all these seekers
   thought,
And seems to me almost a sort of blunder,
Of looking *in* the bed as well as under.

CXLV

During this inquisition Julia's tongue
   Was not asleep—'Yes, search and
   search,' she cried,
'Insult on insult heap, and wrong on wrong!
   It was for this that I became a bride!
For this in silence I have suffer'd long
   A husband like Alfonso at my side;
But now I'll bear no more, nor here
   remain,
If there be law or lawyers in all Spain.

CXLVI

'Yes, Don Alfonso! husband! now no more,
   If ever you indeed deserved the name,
Is't worthy of your years?—you have
   threescore—
Fifty, or sixty, it is all the same—
Is't wise or fitting, causeless to explore
   For facts against a virtuous woman's
   fame?
Ungrateful, perjured, barbarous Don
   Alfonso,
How dare you think your lady would go
   on so?

CXLVII

'Is it for this I have disdain'd to hold
   The common privileges of my sex?
That I have chosen a confessor so old
   And deaf, that any other it would vex,
And never once he has had cause to scold,
   But found my very innocence perplex
So much, he always doubted I was
   married—
How sorry you will be when I've mis-
   carried!

CXLVIII

'Was it for this that no Cortejo e'er
   I yet have chosen from out the youth of
   Seville?
Is it for this I scarce went anywhere,
   Except to bull-fights, mass, play, rout,
   and revel?
Is it for this, whate'er my suitors were,
   I favour'd none—nay, was almost
   uncivil?
Is it for this that General Count O'Reilly,
Who took Algiers, declares I used him vilely?

CXLIX

'Did not the Italian Musico Cazzani
   Sing at my heart six months at least in
   vain?
Did not his countryman, Count Corniani,
   Call me the only virtuous wife in Spain?

Were there not also Russians, English,
   many?
The Count Strongstroganoff I put in
   pain,
And Lord Mount Coffeehouse, the Irish
   peer,
Who kill'd himself for love (with wine) last
   year.

CL

'Have I not had two bishops at my feet?
   The Duke of Ichar, and Don Fernan
   Nunez?
And is it thus a faithful wife you treat?
   I wonder in what quarter now the moon
   is:
I praise your vast forbearance not to beat
   Me also, since the time so opportune
   is—
Oh, valiant man! with sword drawn and
   cock'd trigger,
Now, tell me, don't you cut a pretty
   figure?

CLI

'Was it for this you took your sudden
   journey,
   Under pretence of business in-
   dispensable,
With that sublime of rascals your attorney,
   Whom I see standing there, and looking
   sensible
Of having play'd the fool? though both I
   spurn, he
   Deserves the worst, his conduct's less
   defensible,
Because, no doubt, 'twas for his dirty fee,
And not from any love to you nor me.

CLII

'If he comes here to take a deposition,
   By all means let the gentleman proceed;
You've made the apartment in a fit con-
   dition:—
   There's pen and ink for you, sir, when
   you need—
Let everything be noted with precision,
   I would not you for nothing should be
   fee'd—
But as my maid's undrest, pray turn your
   spies out.'
'Oh!' sobb'd Antonia, 'I could tear their
   eyes out.'

CLIII

'There is the closet, there the toilet, there
   The antechamber—search them under,
   over;
There is the sofa, there the great arm-
   chair,
   The chimney—which would really hold
   a lover.

I wish to sleep, and beg you will take care
  And make no further noise, till you
    discover
The secret cavern of this lurking treasure—
And when 'tis found, let me, too, have that
  pleasure.

CLIV

'And now, Hidalgo! now that you have
  thrown
  Doubt upon me, confusion over all,
Pray have the courtesy to make it known
  Who is the man you search for? how
    d'ye call
Him? what's his lineage? let him but be
  shown—
  I hope he's young and handsome—is he
    tall?
Tell me—and be assured, that since you
  stain
Mine honour thus, it shall not be in vain.

CLV

'At least, perhaps, he has not sixty years,
  At that age he would be too old for
    slaughter,
Or for so young a husband's jealous
  fears—
  (Antonia! let me have a glass of water.)
I am ashamed of having shed these tears,
  They are unworthy of my father's
    daughter;
My mother dream'd not in my natal hour,
That I should fall into a monster's power.

CLVI

'Perhaps 'tis of Antonia you are jealous,
  You saw that she was sleeping by my
    side,
When you broke in upon us with your
  fellows;
  Look where you please—we've nothing,
    sir, to hide;
Only another time, I trust, you'll tell us,
  Or for the sake of decency abide
A moment at the door, that we may be
Drest to receive so much good company.

CLVII

'And now, sir, I have done, and say no
  more;
  The little I have said may serve to show
The guileless heart in silence may grieve
  o'er
  The wrongs to whose exposure it is
    slow:—
I leave you to your conscience as before,
  'Twill one day ask you, *why* you used me
    so?
God grant you feel not then the bitterest
  grief!
Antonia! where's my pocket-handker-
  chief?'

CLVIII

She ceased, and turn'd upon her pillow;
  pale
  She lay, her dark eyes flashing through
    their tears,
Like skies that rain and lighten; as a veil,
  Waved and o'ershading her wan cheek,
    appears
Her streaming hair; the black curls strive,
  but fail,
  To hide the glossy shoulder, which
    uprears
Its snow through all;—her soft lips lie
  apart,
And louder than her breathing beats her
  heart.

CLIX

The Senhor Don Alfonso stood confused;
  Antonia bustled round the ransack'd
    room,
And, turning up her nose, with looks
  abused
  Her master, and his myrmidons, of
    whom
Not one, except the attorney, was amused;
  He, like Achates, faithful to the tomb,
So there were quarrels, cared not for the
  cause,
Knowing they must be settled by the laws.

CLX

With prying snub-nose, and small eyes,
  he stood,
  Following Antonia's motions here and
    there,
With much suspicion in his attitude;
  For reputations he had little care;
So that a suit or action were made good,
  Small pity had he for the young and fair,
And ne'er believed in negatives, till these
Were proved by competent false witnesses.

CLXI

But Don Alfonso stood with downcast
  looks,
  And, truth to say, he made a foolish
    figure;
When, after searching in five hundred
  nooks,
  And treating a young wife with so much
    rigour,
He gain'd no point, except some self-
  rebukes,
  Added to those his lady with such
    vigour
Had pour'd upon him for the last half
  hour,
Quick, thick, and heavy—as a thunder-
  shower.

CLXII

At first he tried to hammer an excuse,
  To which the sole reply were tears and
    sobs,
And indications of hysterics, whose
  Prologue is always certain throes, and
    throbs,
Gasps, and whatever else the owners
    choose:
  Alfonso saw his wife, and thought of
    Job's;
He saw too, in perspective, her relations,
And then he tried to muster all his patience.

CLXIII

He stood in act to speak, or rather stammer,
  But sage Antonia cut him short before
The anvil of his speech received the
    hammer,
  With 'Pray, sir, leave the room, and say
    no more,
Or madam dies.'—Alfonso mutter'd,
    'D—n her,'
  But nothing else, the time of words was
    o'er;
He cast a rueful look or two, and did,
He knew not wherefore, that which he was
    bid.

CLXIV

With him retired his '*posse comitatus*,'
  The attorney last, who linger'd near the
    door
Reluctantly, still tarrying there as late as
  Antonia let him—not a little sore
At this most strange and unexplain'd
    '*hiatus*'
  In Don Alfonso's facts, which just now
    wore
An awkward look; as he revolved the case,
The door was fasten'd in his legal face.

CLXV

No sooner was it bolted, than—Oh shame!
  Oh sin! Oh sorrow! and Oh woman-
    kind!
How can you do such things and keep your
    fame,
  Unless this world, and t'other too, be
    blind?
Nothing so dear as an unfilch'd good name!
  But to proceed—for there is more
    behind:
With much heartfelt reluctance be it said,
Young Juan slipp'd, half-smother'd, from
    the bed.

CLXVI

He had been hid—I don't pretend to say
  How, nor can I indeed describe the
    where—
Young, slender, and pack'd easily, he lay,
  No doubt, in little compass, round or
    square;

But pity him I neither must nor may
  His suffocation by that pretty pair;
'Twere better, sure, to die so, than be shut
With maudlin Clarence in his Malmsey
    butt.

CLXVII

And, secondly, I pity not, because
  He had no business to commit a sin,
Forbid by heavenly, fined by human
    laws;
  At least 'twas rather early to begin;
But at sixteen the conscience rarely gnaws
  So much as when we call our old debts in
At sixty years, and draw the accompts of
    evil,
And find a deuced balance with the devil.

CLXVIII

Of his position I can give no notion:
  'Tis written in the Hebrew Chronicle,
How the physicians, leaving pill and potion,
  Prescribed, by way of blister, a young
    belle,
When old King David's blood grew dull
    in motion,
  And that the medicine answer'd very
    well;
Perhaps 'twas in a different way applied,
For David lived, but Juan nearly died.

CLXIX

What's to be done? Alfonso will be back
  The moment he has sent his fools away.
Antonia's skill was put upon the rack,
  But no device could be brought into
    play—
And how to parry the renew'd attack?
  Besides, it wanted but few hours of day:
Antonia puzzled; Julia did not speak,
But press'd her bloodless lip to Juan's
    cheek.

CLXX

He turn'd his lip to hers, and with his hand
  Call'd back the tangles of her wandering
    hair;
Even then their love they could not all
    command,
  And half forgot their danger and
    despair:
Antonia's patience now was at a stand—
  'Come, come, 'tis no time now for fool-
    ing there,'
She whisper'd, in great wrath—'I must
    deposit
This pretty gentleman within the closet:

CLXXI

'Pray, keep your nonsense for some
    luckier night—
  Who can have put my master in this
    mood?
What will become on't—I'm in such a
    fright,
  The devil's in the urchin, and no good—

Is this a time for giggling? this a plight?
  Why, don't you know that it may end
    in blood?
You'll lose your life, and I shall lose my
    place,
  My mistress all, for that half-girlish face.

CLXXII

'Had it but been for a stout cavalier
  Of twenty-five or thirty—(come, make
    haste)
But for a child, what piece of work is here!
  I really, madam, wonder at your taste—
(Come, sir, get in)—my master must be
    near:
  There, for the present, at the least, he's
    fast,
And if we can but till the morning keep
Our counsel—(Juan, mind, you must not
    sleep).'

CLXXIII

Now, Don Alfonso entering, but alone,
  Closed the oration of the trusty maid:
She loiter'd, and he told her to be gone,
  An order somewhat sullenly obey'd;
However, present remedy was none,
  And no great good seem'd answer'd if
    she staid:
Regarding both with slow and sidelong
    view,
She snuff'd the candle, curtsied, and with-
    drew.

CLXXIV

Alfonso paused a minute—then begun
  Some strange excuses for his late pro-
    ceeding:
He would not justify what he had done,
  To say the best, it was extreme ill-
    breeding;
But there were ample reasons for it, none
  Of which he specified in this his plead-
    ing:
His speech was a fine sample, on the whole,
Of rhetoric, which the learn'd call
  'rigmarole.'

CLXXV

Julia said nought; though all the while
    there rose
  A ready answer, which at once enables
A matron, who her husband's foible
    knows,
  By a few timely words to turn the tables,
Which, if it does not silence, still must
    pose,
  Even if it should comprise a pack of
    fables;
'Tis to retort with firmness, and when he
Suspects with *one*, do you reproach with
  three.

CLXXVI

Julia, in fact, had tolerable grounds,—
  Alfonso's loves with Inez were well
    known;
But whether 'twas that one's own guilt
    confounds—
  But that can't be, as has been often
    shown,
A lady with apologies abounds;—
  It might be that her silence sprang alone
From delicacy to Don Juan's ear,
To whom she knew his mother's fame was
  dear.

CLXXVII

There might be one more motive, which
    makes two,
  Alfonso ne'er to Juan had alluded,—
Mentioned his jealousy, but never who
  Had been the happy lover, he con-
    cluded,
Conceal'd amongst his premises; 'tis true,
  His mind the more o'er this its mystery
    brooded
To speak of Inez now were, one may say,
Like throwing Juan in Alfonso's way.

CLXXVIII

A hint, in tender cases, is enough;
  Silence is best: besides there is a *tact*—
(That modern phrase appears to me sad
    stuff,
  But it will serve to keep my verse com-
    pact)—
Which keeps, when push'd by questions
    rather rough,
  A lady always distant from the fact:
The charming creatures lie with such a
    grace,
There's nothing so becoming to the face.

CLXXIX

They blush, and we believe them, at least I
  Have always done so; 'tis of no great
    use,
In any case, attempting a reply,
  For then their eloquence grows quite
    profuse;
And when at length they're out of breath,
    they sigh,
  And cast their languid eyes down, and
    let loose
A tear or two, and then we make it up:
And then—and then—and then—sit
  down and sup.

CLXXX

Alfonso closed his speech, and begg'd her
    pardon,
  Which Julia half withheld, and then
    half granted,
And laid conditions, he thought very hard,
    on,
  Denying several little things he wanted:

He stood like Adam lingering near his
　　garden,
　　With useless penitence perplex'd and
　　　haunted,
Beseeching she no further would refuse,
When, lo! he stumbled o'er a pair of shoes.

CLXXXI

A pair of shoes!—what then? not much,
　　if they
　　Are such as fit with ladies' feet, but these
(No one can tell how much I grieve to say)
　　Were masculine; to see them, and to
　　　seize,
Was but a moment's act.—Ah! well-a-
　　day!
　　My teeth begin to chatter, my veins
　　　freeze—
Alfonso first examined well their fashion,
And then flew out into another passion.

CLXXXII

He left the room for his relinquish'd
　　sword,
　　And Julia instant to the closet flew.
'Fly, Juan, fly! for heaven's sake—not a
　　word—
　　The door is open—you may yet slip
　　　through
The passage you so often have explored—
　　Here is the garden-key—Fly—fly—
　　　Adieu!
Haste—haste! I hear Alfonso's hurrying
　　feet—
Day has not broke—there's no one in the
　　street.'

CLXXXIII

None can say that this was not good
　　advice,
　　The only mischief was, it came too late;
Of all experience 'tis the usual price,
　　A sort of income-tax laid on by fate:
Juan had reach'd the room-door in a trice,
　　And might have done so by the garden-
　　　gate,
But met Alfonso in his dressing-gown,
Who threaten'd death—so Juan knock'd
　　him down.

CLXXXIV

Dire was the scuffle, and out went the
　　light;
　　Antonia cried out 'Rape!' and Julia
　　　'Fire!'
But not a servant stirr'd to aid the fight.
　　Alfonso, pommell'd to his heart's
　　　desire,
Swore lustily he'd be revenged this night;
　　And Juan, too, blasphemed an octave
　　　higher;
His blood was up: though young, he was
　　a Tartar,
And not at all disposed to prove a martyr.

CLXXXV

Alfonso's sword had dropp'd ere he could
　　draw it,
　　And they continued battling hand to
　　　hand,
For Juan very luckily ne'er saw it;
　　His temper not being under great com-
　　　mand,
If at that moment he had chanced to claw
　　it,
　　Alfonso's days had not been in the land
Much longer.—Think of husbands',
　　lovers' lives!
And how ye may be doubly widows—
　　wives!

CLXXXVI

Alfonso grappled to detain the foe,
　　And Juan throttled him to get away,
And blood ('twas from the nose) began to
　　flow;
　　At last, as they more faintly wrestling
　　　lay,
Juan contrived to give an awkward blow,
　　And then his only garment quite gave
　　　way;
He fled, like Joseph, leaving it; but there,
I doubt, all likeness ends between the pair.

CLXXXVII

Lights came at length, and men, and
　　maids, who found
　　An awkward spectacle their eyes before;
Antonia in hysterics, Julia swoon'd,
　　Alfonso leaning, breathless, by the
　　　door;
Some half-torn drapery scatter'd on the
　　ground,
　　Some blood, and several footsteps, but
　　　no more:
Juan the gate gain'd, turn'd the key about,
And liking not the inside, lock'd the out.

CLXXXVIII

Here ends this canto.—Need I sing, or say,
　　How Juan, naked, favour'd by the
　　　night,
Who favours what she should not, found
　　his way,
　　And reach'd his home in an unseemly
　　　plight?
The pleasant scandal which arose next day,
　　The nine days' wonder which was
　　　brought to light,
And how Alfonso sued for a divorce,
Were in the English newspapers, of course.

CLXXXIX

If you would like to see the whole proceed-
　　ings,
　　The depositions and the cause at full,
The names of all the witnesses, the plead-
　　ings
　　Of counsel to nonsuit, or to annul,

There's more than one edition, and the readings
  Are various, but they none of them are dull;
The best is that in short-hand ta'en by Gurney,
Who to Madrid on purpose made a journey.

CXC

But Donna Inez, to divert the train
  Of one of the most circulating scandals
That had for centuries been known in Spain,
  At least since the retirement of the Vandals,
First vow'd (and never had she vow'd in vain)
  To Virgin Mary several pounds of candles;
And then, by the advice of some old ladies,
She sent her son to be shipp'd off from Cadiz.

CXCI

She had resolved that he should travel through
  All European climes, by land or sea,
To mend his former morals, and get new,
  Especially in France and Italy
(At least this is the thing most people do).
  Julia was sent into a convent: she
Grieved, but, perhaps, her feelings may be better
Shown in the following copy of her Letter:—

CXCII

'They tell me 'tis decided; you depart:
  'Tis wise—'tis well, but not the less a pain;
I have no further claim on your young heart,
  Mine is the victim, and would be again:
To love too much has been the only art
  I used;—I write in haste, and if a stain
Be on this sheet, 'tis not what it appears;
My eyeballs burn and throb, but have no tears.

CXCIII

'I loved, I love you, for this love have lost
  State, station, heaven, mankind's, my own esteem,
And yet cannot regret what it hath cost,
  So dear is still the memory of that dream;
Yet, if I name my guilt, 'tis not to boast,
  None can deem harshlier of me than I deem:
I trace this scrawl because I cannot rest—
I've nothing to reproach or to request.

CXCIV

'Man's love is of man's life a thing apart,
  'Tis woman's whole existence; man may range

The court, camp, church, the vessel, and the mart;
  Sword, gown, gain, glory, offer in exchange
Pride, fame, ambition, to fill up his heart,
  And few there are whom these cannot estrange;
Men have all these resources, we but one,
To love again, and be again undone.

CXCV

'You will proceed in pleasure, and in pride,
  Beloved and loving many; all is o'er
For me on earth, except some years to hide
  My shame and sorrow deep in my heart's core:
These I could bear, but cannot cast aside
  The passion which still rages as before,—
And so farewell—forgive me, love me—No,
That word is idle now—but let it go.

CXCVI

'My breast has been all weakness, is so yet;
  But still I think I can collect my mind;
My blood still rushes where my spirit's set,
  As roll the waves before the settled wind;
My heart is feminine, nor can forget—
  To all, except one image, madly blind;
So shakes the needle, and so stands the pole,
As vibrates my fond heart to my fix'd soul.

CXCVII

'I have no more to say, but linger still,
  And dare not set my seal upon this sheet,
And yet I may as well the task fulfil.
  My misery can scarce be more complete:
I had not lived till now, could sorrow kill;
  Death shuns the wretch who fain the blow would meet,
And I must even survive this last adieu,
And bear with life to love and pray for you!'

CXCVIII

This note was written upon gilt-edged paper
  With a neat little crow-quill, slight and new;
Her small white hand could hardly reach the taper,
  It trembled as magnetic needles do,
And yet she did not let one tear escape her;
  The seal a sun-flower; 'Elle vous suit partout,'
The motto, cut upon a white cornelian;
The wax was superfine, its hue vermilion.

CXCIX

This was Don Juan's earliest scrape; but whether
  I shall proceed with his adventures is
Dependent on the public altogether;
  We'll see, however, what they say to this,

Their favour in an author's cap's a feather,
    And no great mischief's done by their
        caprice;
And if their approbation we experience,
Perhaps they'll have some more about a
    year hence.

CC

My poem's epic, and is meant to be
    Divided in twelve books; each book
        containing,
With love, and war, a heavy gale at sea,
    A list of ships, and captains, and kings
        reigning,
New characters; the episodes are three:
    A panoramic view of hell's in training,
After the style of Virgil and of Homer,
So that my name of Epic's no misnomer.

CCI

All these things will be specified in time,
    With strict regard to Aristotle's rules,
The *Vade Mecum* of the true sublime,
    Which makes so many poets, and some
        fools:
Prose poets like blank-verse, I'm fond of
    rhyme,
    Good workmen never quarrel with their
        tools,
I've got new mythological machinery,
And very handsome supernatural scenery.

CCII

There's only one slight difference between
    Me and my epic brethren gone before,
And here the advantage is my own, I ween
    (Not that I have not several merits more,
But this will more peculiarly be seen);
    They so embellish, that 'tis quite a bore
Their labyrinth of fables to thread through,
Whereas this story's actually true.

CCIII

If any person doubt it, I appeal
    To history, tradition, and to facts,
To newspapers, whose truth all know and
    feel,
    To plays in five, and operas in three acts;
All these confirm my statement a good deal,
    But that which more completely faith
        exacts
Is, that myself, and several now in Seville,
Saw Juan's last elopement with the devil.

CCIV

If ever I should condescend to prose,
    I'll write poetical commandments, which
Shall supersede beyond all doubt all those
    That went before; in these I shall enrich
My text with many things that no one
    knows,
    And carry precept to the highest pitch:
I'll call the work 'Longinus o'er a Bottle,
Or, Every Poet his *own* Aristotle.'

CCV

Thou shalt believe in Milton, Dryden, Pope;
    Thou shalt not set up Wordsworth, Cole-
        ridge, Southey;
Because the first is crazed beyond all hope,
    The second drunk, the third so quaint
        and mouthy:
With Crabbe it may be difficult to cope,
    And Campbell's Hippocrene is some-
        what drouthy:
Thou shalt not steal from Samuel Rogers,
    nor
Commit—flirtation with the muse of Moore.

CCVI

Thou shalt not covet Mr. Sotheby's Muse,
    His Pegasus, nor anything that's his;
Thou shalt not bear false witness like 'the
    Blues'—
    (There's *one*, at least, is very fond of
        this);
Thou shalt not write, in short, but what I
    choose:
    This is true criticism, and you may kiss—
Exactly as you please, or not,—the rod;
But if you don't, I'll lay it on, by G—d!

CCVII

If any person should presume to assert
    This story is not moral, first, I pray,
That they will not cry out before they're
    hurt,
    Then that they'll read it o'er again, and
        say
(But, doubtless, nobody will be so pert),
    That this is not a moral tale, though gay;
Besides, in Canto Twelfth, I mean to show
The very place where wicked people go.

CCVIII

If, after all, there should be some so blind
    To their own good this warning to de-
        spise,
Let by some tortuosity of mind,
    Not to believe my verse and their own
        eyes,
And cry that they 'the moral cannot find,'
    I tell him, if a clergyman, he lies;
Should captains the remark, or critics, make,
They also lie too—under a mistake.

CCIX

The public approbation I expect,
    And beg they'll take my word about the
        moral,
Which I with their amusement will connect
    (So children cutting teeth receive a coral);
Meantime they'll doubtless please to recol-
    lect
    My epical pretensions to the laurel:
For fear some prudish readers should grow
    skittish,
I've bribed my Grandmother's Review—
    the British.

CCX

I sent it in a letter to the Editor,
    Who thank'd me duly by return of post—
I'm for a handsome article his creditor;
    Yet, if my gentle Muse he please to roast,
And break a promise after having made it
        her,
    Denying the receipt of what it cost,
And smear his page with gall instead of
        honey,
All I can say is—that he had the money.

CCXI

I think that with this holy new alliance
    I may ensure the public, and defy
All other magazines of art or science,
    Daily, or monthly, or three monthly; I
Have not essay'd to multiply their clients,
    Because they tell me 'twere in vain to try,
And that the Edinburgh Review and Quar-
        terly
Treat a dissenting author very martyrly.

CCXII

'Non ego hoc ferrem calida juventa
    Consule Planco,' Horace said, and so
Say I; by which quotation there is meant a
    Hint that some six or seven good years
        ago
(Long ere I dreamt of dating from the
        Brenta)
    I was most ready to return a blow,
And would not brook at all this sort of
        thing
In my hot youth—when George the Third
        was King.

CCXIII

But now at thirty years my hair is gray—
    (I wonder what it will be like at forty?
I thought of a peruke the other day—)
    My heart is not much greener; and, in
        short, I
Have squander'd my whole summer while
        'twas May,
    And feel no more the spirit to retort; I
Have spent my life, both interest and
        principal,
And deem not, what I deem'd, my soul
        invincible.

CCXIV

No more—no more—Oh! never more on
        me
    The freshness of the heart can fall like
        dew,
Which out of all the lovely things we see
    Extracts emotions beautiful and new;
Hived in our bosoms like the bag o' the
        bee.
    Think'st thou the honey with those ob-
        jects grew?
Alas! 'twas not in them, but in thy power
To double even the sweetness of a flower.

CCXV

No more—no more—Oh! never more, my
        heart,
    Canst thou be my sole world, my uni-
        verse!
Once all in all, but now a thing apart,
    Thou canst not be my blessing or my
        curse:
The illusion's gone for ever, and thou art
    Insensible, I trust, but none the worse,
And in thy stead I've got a deal of judg-
        ment,
Though heaven knows how it ever found
        a lodgment.

CCXVI

My days of love are over; me no more
    The charms of maid, wife, and still less
        of widow,
Can make the fool of which they made
        before,—
    In short, I must not lead the life I did do;
The credulous hope of mutual minds is
        o'er,
    The copious use of claret is forbid too,
So for a good old-gentlemanly vice,
I think I must take up with avarice.

CCXVII

Ambition was my idol, which was broken
    Before the shrines of Sorrow, and of
        Pleasure;
And the two last have left me many a token
    O'er which reflection may be made at
        leisure:
Now, like Friar Bacon's brazen head, I've
        spoken,
    'Time is, Time was, Time's past':—a
        chymic treasure
Is glittering youth, which I have spent be-
        times—
My heart in passion, and my head on
        rhymes.

CCXVIII

What is the end of fame? 'tis but to fill
    A certain portion of uncertain paper:
Some liken it to climbing up a hill,
    Whose summit, like all hills, is lost in
        vapour;
For this men write, speak, preach, and
        heroes kill,
    And bards burn what they call their
        'midnight taper,'
To have, when the original is dust,
A name, a wretched picture, and worse bust.

CCXIX

What are the hopes of man? Old Egypt's
        King
    Cheops erected the first pyramid
And largest, thinking it was just the thing
    To keep his memory whole, and mummy
        hid:

But somebody or other rummaging,
  Burglariously broke his coffin's lid:
Let not a monument give you or me hopes,
Since not a pinch of dust remains of Cheops.

CCXX

But I, being fond of true philosophy,
  Say very often to myself, 'Alas!
All things that have been born were born
    to die,
  And flesh (which Death mows down to
    hay) is grass;
You've pass'd your youth not so unpleas-
    antly,
  And if you had it o'er again—'twould
    pass—
So thank your stars that matters are no
    worse,
And read your Bible, sir, and mind your
    purse.'

CCXXI

But for the present, gentle reader! and
  Still gentler purchaser! the bard—that's
    I—
Must, with permission, shake you by the
    hand,
  And so your humble servant, and good-
    bye!
We meet again, if we should understand
  Each other; and if not, I shall not try
Your patience further than by this short
    sample—
'Twere well if others follow'd my example.

CCXXII

'Go, little book, from this my solitude!
  I cast thee on the waters—go thy ways!
And if, as I believe, thy vein be good,
  The world will find thee after many days.'
When Southey's read, and Wordsworth
    understood,
  I can't help putting in my claim to praise—
The four first rhymes are Southey's, every
    line:
For God's sake, reader! take them not for
    mine!

CANTO THE SECOND*

I

OH ye! who teach the ingenuous youth of
    nations,
  Holland, France, England, Germany, or
    Spain,
I pray ye flog them upon all occasions,
  It mends their morals, never mind the
    pain:
The best of mothers and of educations
  In Juan's case were but employ'd in vain,
Since, in a way that's rather of the oddest, he
Became divested of his native modesty.

* ['Begun at Venice, December 13, 1818,—
finished January 20, 1819.'—B.]

II

Had he but been placed at a public school,
  In the third form, or even in the fourth,
His daily task had kept his fancy cool,
  At least, had he been nurtured in the
    north;
Spain may prove an exception to the rule,
  But then exceptions always prove its
    worth—
A lad of sixteen causing a divorce
Puzzled his tutors very much, of course.

III

I can't say that it puzzles me at all,
  If all things be consider'd; first, there
    was
His lady-mother, mathematical,
  A —— never mind; his tutor, an old
    ass;
A pretty woman—(that's quite natural,
  Or else the thing had hardly come to
    pass)
A husband rather old, not much in unity
With his young wife—a time, and oppor-
    tunity.

IV

Well—well; the world must turn upon its
    axis,
  And all mankind turn with it, heads or
    tails,
And live and die, make love and pay our
    taxes,
  And as the veering wind shifts, shift our
    sails;
The king commands us, and the doctor
    quacks us,
  The priest instructs, and so our life ex-
    hales,
A little breath, love, wine, ambition, fame,
Fighting, devotion, dust,—perhaps a name.

V

I said, that Juan had been sent to Cadiz—
  A pretty town, I recollect it well—
'Tis there the mart of the colonial trade is,
  (Or was, before Peru learn'd to rebel,)
And such sweet girls—I mean, such grace-
    ful ladies,
  Their very walk would make your bosom
    swell;
I can't describe it, though so much it strike,
Nor liken it—I never saw the like:

VI

An Arab horse, a stately stag, a barb
  New broke, a cameleopard, a gazelle,
No—none of these will do;—and then their
    garb,
  Their veil and petticoat—Alas! to dwell

Upon such things would very near absorb
    A canto—then their feet and ankles,—
        well,
Thank Heaven I've got no metaphor quite
    ready,
(And so, my sober Muse—come, let's be
    steady—

VII

Chaste Muse!—well, if you must, you
    must)—the veil
    Thrown back a moment with the glanc-
        ing hand,
While the o'erpowering eye, that turns you
    pale,
    Flashes into the heart:—All sunny land
Of love! when I forget you, may I fail
    To—say my prayers—but never was
        there plann'd
A dress through which the eyes give such
    a volley,
Excepting the Venetian Fazzioli.

VIII

But to our tale: the Donna Inez sent
    Her son to Cadiz only to embark;
To stay there had not answer'd her intent,
    But why?—we leave the reader in the
        dark—
'Twas for a voyage the young man was
    meant,
    As if a Spanish ship were Noah's ark,
To wean him from the wickedness of earth,
And send him like a dove of promise forth.

IX

Don Juan bade his valet pack his things
    According to direction, then received
A lecture and some money: for four springs
    He was to travel; and though Inez grieved
(As every kind of parting has its stings),
    She hoped he would improve—perhaps
        believed:
A letter, too, she gave (he never read it)
Of good advice—and two or three of credit.

X

In the mean time, to pass her hours away,
    Brave Inez now set up a Sunday school
For naughty children, who would rather
    play
    (Like truant rogues) the devil, or the
        fool;
Infants of three years old were taught that
    day,
    Dunces were whipt, or set upon a stool:
The great success of Juan's education
Spurr'd her to teach another generation.

XI

Juan embark'd—the ship got under way,
    The wind was fair, the water passing
    rough;

A devil of a sea rolls in that bay,
    As I, who've cross'd it oft, know well
        enough;
And, standing upon deck, the dashing
    spray
    Flies in one's face, and makes it weather-
        tough:
And there he stood to take, and take again,
His first—perhaps his last—farewell of
    Spain.

XII

I can't but say it is an awkward sight
    To see one's native land receding through
The growing waters; it unmans one quite,
    Especially when life is rather new:
I recollect Great Britain's coast looks
    white,
    But almost every other country's blue,
When gazing on them, mystified by dis-
    tance,
We enter on our nautical existence.

XIII

So Juan stood, bewilder'd on the deck:
    The wind sung, cordage strain'd, and
        sailors swore,
And the ship creak'd, the town became a
    speck,
    From which away so fair and fast they
        bore.
The best of remedies is a beef-steak
    Against sea-sickness: try it, sir, before
You sneer, and I assure you this is true,
For I have found it answer—so may you.

XIV

Don Juan stood, and, gazing from the
    stern,
    Beheld his native Spain receding far:
First partings form a lesson hard to learn,
    Even nations feel this when they go to
        war;
There is a sort of unexprest concern,
    A kind of shock that sets one's heart
        ajar:
At leaving even the most unpleasant people
And places, one keeps looking at the
    steeple.

XV

But Juan had got many things to leave,
    His mother, and a mistress, and no wife,
So that he had much better cause to grieve
    Than many persons more advanced in
        life;
And if we now and then a sigh must heave
    At quitting even those we quit in strife,
No doubt we weep for those the heart en-
    dears—
That is, till deeper griefs congeal our tears.

XVI

So Juan wept, as wept the captive Jews
   By Babel's waters, still remembering
      Sion:
I'd weep,—but mine is not a weeping
      Muse,
   And such light griefs are not a thing to
      die on;
Young men should travel, if but to amuse
   Themselves; and the next time their ser-
      vants tie on
Behind their carriages their new portman-
      teau,
Perhaps it may be lined with this my canto.

XVII

And Juan wept, and much he sigh'd and
      thought,
   While his salt tears dropp'd into the salt
      sea,
'Sweets to the sweet;' (I like so much to
      quote;
   You must excuse this extract,—'tis where
      she,
The Queen of Denmark, for Ophelia
      brought
   Flowers to the grave;) and, sobbing
      often, he
Reflected on his present situation,
And seriously resolved on reformation.

XVIII

'Farewell, my Spain! a long farewell!' he
      cried,
   'Perhaps I may revisit thee no more,
But die, as many an exiled heart hath died,
   Of its own thirst to see again thy shore:
Farewell, where Guadalquivir's waters
      glide!
   Farewell, my mother! and, since all is
      o'er,
Farewell, too, dearest Julia!—(here he
      drew
Her letter out again, and read it through.)

XIX

And oh! if e'er I should forget, I swear—
   But that's impossible, and cannot be—
Sooner shall this blue ocean melt to air,
   Sooner shall earth resolve itself to sea,
Than I resign thine image, oh, my fair!
   Or think of anything, excepting thee;
A mind diseased no remedy can physic—
(Here the ship gave a lurch, and he grew
      sea-sick.)

XX

'Sooner shall heaven kiss earth—(here he
      fell sicker)
   Oh, Julia! what is every other woe?—
(For God's sake let me have a glass of
      liquor;
   Pedro, Battista, help me down below.)
Julia, my love!—(you rascal, Pedro, quick-
      er)—
   Oh, Julia!—(this curst vessel pitches
      so)—
Beloved Julia, hear me still beseeching!'
(Here he grew inarticulate with retching.)

XXI

He felt that chilling heaviness of heart,
   Or rather stomach, which, alas! attends,
Beyond the best apothecary's art,
   The loss of love, the treachery of friends,
Or death of those we dote on, when a part
   Of us dies with them as each fond hope
      ends:
No doubt he would have been much more
      pathetic,
But the sea acted as a strong emetic.

XXII

Love's a capricious power: I've known it
      hold
   Out through a fever caused by its own
      heat,
But be much puzzled by a cough and cold,
   And find a quinsy very hard to treat;
Against all noble maladies he's bold,
   But vulgar illnesses don't like to meet,
Nor that a sneeze should interrupt his sigh,
Nor inflammations redden his blind eye.

XXIII

But worst of all is nausea, or a pain
   About the lower region of the bowels;
Love, who heroically breathes a vein,
   Shrinks from the application of hot
      towels,
And purgatives are dangerous to his reign,
   Sea-sickness death: his love was perfect,
      how else
Could Juan's passion, while the billows
      roar,
Resist his stomach, ne'er at sea before?

XXIV

The ship, call'd the most holy 'Trinidada,'
   Was steering duly for the port Leghorn;
For there the Spanish family Moncada
   Were settled long ere Juan's sire was
      born:
They were relations, and for them he had a
   Letter of introduction, which the morn
Of his departure had been sent him by
His Spanish friends for those in Italy.

XXV

His suite consisted of three servants and
   A tutor, the licentiate Pedrillo,
Who several languages did understand,
   But now lay sick and speechless on his
      pillow,

And, rocking in his hammock, long'd for
    land,
  His headache being increased by every
    billow;
And the waves oozing through the port-
    hole made
His berth a little damp, and him afraid.

XXVI

'Twas not without some reason, for the
    wind
  Increased at night, until it blew a gale;
And though 'twas not much to a naval
    mind,
  Some landsmen would have look'd a
    little pale,
For sailors are, in fact, a different kind:
  At sunset they began to take in sail,
For the sky show'd it would come on to
    blow,
And carry away, perhaps, a mast or so.

XXVII

At one o'clock the wind with sudden shift
  Threw the ship right into the trough of
    the sea,
Which struck her aft, and made an awk-
    ward rift,
  Started the stern-post, also shatter'd the
Whole of her stern-frame, and, ere she
    could lift
  Herself from out her present jeopardy,
The rudder tore away: 'twas time to sound
The pumps, and there were four feet water
    found.

XXVIII

One gang of people instantly was put
  Upon the pumps, and the remainder set
To get up part of the cargo, and what not;
  But they could not come at the leak as
    yet;
At last they did get at it really, but
  Still their salvation was an even bet:
The water rush'd through in a way quite
    puzzling,
While they thrust sheets, shirts, jackets,
    bales of muslin,

XXIX

Into the opening; but all such ingredients
  Would have been vain, and they must
    have gone down,
Despite of all their efforts and expedients,
  But for the pumps: I'm glad to make
    them known
To all the brother tars who may have need
    hence,
  For fifty tons of water were upthrown
By them per hour, and they all had been
    undone,
But for the maker, Mr. Mann, of London.

XXX

As day advanced the weather seem'd to
    abate,
  And then the leak they reckon'd to re-
    duce,
And keep the ship afloat, though three feet
    yet
  Kept two hand- and one chain-pump
    still in use.
The wind blew fresh again: as it grew late
  A squall came on, and while some guns
    broke loose,
A gust—which all descriptive power tran-
    scends—
Laid with one blast the ship on her beam
    ends.

XXXI

There she lay, motionless, and seem'd up-
    set;
  The water left the hold, and wash'd the
    decks,
And made a scene men do not soon forget;
  For they remember battles, fires, and
    wrecks,
Or any other thing that brings regret,
  Or breaks their hopes, or hearts, or
    heads, or necks;
Thus drownings are much talk'd of by the
    divers,
And swimmers, who may chance to be
    survivors.

XXXII

Immediately the masts were cut away,
  Both main and mizen: first the mizen
    went,
The main-mast follow'd; but the ship still
    lay
  Like a mere log, and baffled our intent.
Foremast and bowsprit were cut down,
    and they
  Eased her at last (although we never
    meant
To part with all till every hope was
    blighted),
And then with violence the old ship righted.

XXXIII

It may be easily supposed, while this
  Was going on, some people were un-
    quiet,
That passengers would find it much amiss
  To lose their lives, as well as spoil their
    diet;
That even the able seaman, deeming his
  Days nearly o'er, might be disposed to
    riot,
As upon such occasions tars will ask
For grog, and sometimes drink rum from
    the cask.

XXXIV

There's nought, no doubt, so much the
  spirit calms
As rum and true religion: thus it was,
Some plunder'd, some drank spirits, some
  sung psalms,
  The high wind made the treble, and as
  bass
The hoarse harsh waves kept time; fright
  cured the qualms
  Of all the luckless landsmen's sea-sick
  maws:
Strange sounds of wailing, blasphemy, de-
  votion,
Clamour'd in chorus to the roaring ocean.

XXXV

Perhaps more mischief had been done, but
  for
  Our Juan, who, with sense beyond his
  years,
Got to the spirit-room, and stood before
  It with a pair of pistols; and their fears,
As if Death were more dreadful by his door
  Of fire than water, spite of oaths and
  tears,
Kept still aloof the crew, who, ere they sunk,
Thought it would be becoming to die drunk.

XXXVI

'Give us more grog,' they cried, 'for it
  will be
  All one an hour hence.' Juan answer'd,
  'No!
'Tis true that death awaits both you and
  me,
  But let us die like men, not sink below
Like brutes':—and thus his dangerous post
  kept he,
  And none liked to anticipate the blow;
And even Pedrillo, his most reverend tutor,
Was for some rum a disappointed suitor.

XXXVII

The good old gentleman was quite aghast,
  And made a loud and pious lamenta-
  tion;
Repented all his sins, and made a last
  Irrevocable vow of reformation;
Nothing should tempt him more (this peril
  past)
  To quit his academic occupation,
In cloisters of the classic Salamanca,
To follow Juan's wake, like Sancho Panca.

XXXVIII

But now there came a flash of hope once
  more;
  Day broke, and the wind lull'd: the
  masts were gone;
The leak increased; shoals round her, but
  no shore,
  The vessel swam, yet still she held her
  own.

They tried the pumps again, and though
  before
  Their desperate efforts seem'd all useless
  grown,
A glimpse of sunshine set some hands to
  bale—
The stronger pump'd, the weaker thrumm'd
  a sail.

XXXIX

Under the vessel's keel the sail was pass'd,
  And for a moment it had some effect;
But with a leak, and not a stick of mast,
  Nor rag of canvas, what could they ex-
  pect?
But still 'tis best to struggle to the last,
  'Tis never too late to be wholly wreck'd:
And though 'tis true that man can only die
  once,
'Tis not so pleasant in the Gulf of Lyons.

XL

There winds and waves had hurl'd them,
  and from thence,
  Without their will, they carried them
  away;
For they were forced with steering to dis-
  pense,
  And never had as yet a quiet day
On which they might repose, or even com-
  mence
  A jurymast or rudder, or could say
The ship would swim an hour, which, by
  good luck,
Still swam—though not exactly like a duck.

XLI

The wind, in fact, perhaps, was rather less,
  But the ship labour'd so, they scarce
  could hope
To weather out much longer; the distress
  Was also great with which they had to
  cope
For want of water, and their solid mess
  Was scant enough: in vain the telescope
Was used—nor sail nor shore appear'd in
  sight,
Nought but the heavy sea, and coming
  night.

XLII

Again the weather threaten'd,—again blew
  A gale, and in the fore and after hold
Water appear'd; yet, though the people
  knew
  All this, the most were patient, and some
  bold,
Until the chains and leathers were worn
  through
  Of all our pumps:—a wreck complete
  she roll'd,
At mercy of the waves, whose mercies are
Like human beings during civil war.

XLIII

Then came the carpenter, at last, with tears
 In his rough eyes, and told the captain, he
Could do no more: he was a man in years,
 And long had voyaged through many a stormy sea,
And if he wept at length, they were not fears
 That made his eyelids as a woman's be,
But he, poor fellow, had a wife and children,
Two things for dying people quite bewildering.

XLIV

The ship was evidently settling now
 Fast by the head; and, all distinction gone,
Some went to prayers again, and made a vow
 Of candles to their saints—but there were none
To pay them with; and some look'd o'er the bow;
 Some hoisted out the boats; and there was one
That begg'd Pedrillo for an absolution,
Who told him to be damn'd—in his confusion.

XLV

Some lash'd them in their hammocks; some put on
 Their best clothes, as if going to a fair;
Some cursed the day on which they saw the sun,
 And gnash'd their teeth, and howling, tore their hair;
And others went on as they had begun,
 Getting the boats out, being well aware
That a tight boat will live in a rough sea,
Unless with breakers close beneath her lee.

XLVI

The worst of all was, that in their condition,
 Having been several days in great distress,
'Twas difficult to get out such provision
 As now might render their long suffering less:
Men, even when dying, dislike inanition;
 Their stock was damaged by the weather's stress:
Two casks of biscuit, and a keg of butter,
Were all that could be thrown into the cutter.

XLVII

But in the long-boat they contrived to stow
 Some pounds of bread, though injured by the wet;
Water, a twenty-gallon cask or so;
 Six flasks of wine: and they contrived to get
A portion of their beef up from below,
 And with a piece of pork, moreover, met,
But scarce enough to serve them for a luncheon—
Then there was rum, eight gallons in a puncheon.

XLVIII

The other boats, the yawl and pinnace, had
 Been stove in the beginning of the gale;
And the long-boat's condition was but bad,
 As there were but two blankets for a sail,
And one oar for a mast, which a young lad
 Threw in by good luck over the ship's rail;
And two boats could not hold, far less be stored,
To save one half the people then on board.

XLIX

'Twas twilight, and the sunless day went down
 Over the waste of waters; like a veil,
Which, if withdrawn, would but disclose the frown
 Of one whose hate is mask'd but to assail.
Thus to their hopeless eyes the night was shown,
 And grimly darkled o'er the faces pale,
And the dim desolate deep: twelve days had Fear
Been their familiar, and now Death was here.

L

Some trial had been making at a raft,
 With little hope in such a rolling sea,
A sort of thing at which one would have laugh'd,
 If any laughter at such times could be,
Unless with people who too much have quaff'd,
 And have a kind of wild and horrid glee,
Half epileptical, and half hysterical:—
Their preservation would have been a miracle.

LI

At half-past eight o'clock, booms, hen-coops, spars,
 And all things, for a chance, had been cast loose
That still could keep afloat the struggling tars,
 For yet they strove, although of no great use:
There was no light in heaven but a few stars,
 The boats put off o'ercrowded with their crews;
She gave a heel, and then a lurch to port,
And, going down head foremost—sunk, in short.

LII

Then rose from sea to sky the wild fare-
        well—
    Then shriek'd the timid, and stood still
        the brave—
Then some leap'd overboard with dread-
        ful yell,
    As eager to anticipate their grave;
And the sea yawn'd around her like a hell,
    And down she suck'd with her the whirl-
        ing wave,
Like one who grapples with his enemy,
And strives to strangle him before he die.

LIII

And first one universal shriek there rush'd,
    Louder than the loud ocean, like a crash
Of echoing thunder; and then all was
        hush'd,
    Save the wild wind and the remorseless
        dash
Of billows; but at intervals there gush'd,
    Accompanied with a convulsive splash,
A solitary shriek, the bubbling cry
Of some strong swimmer in his agony.

LIV

The boats, as stated, had got off before,
    And in them crowded several of the
        crew;
And yet their present hope was hardly
        more
    Than what it had been, for so strong it
        blew
There was slight chance of reaching any
        shore;
    And then they were too many, though
        so few—
Nine in the cutter, thirty in the boat,
Were counted in them when they got afloat.

LV

All the rest perish'd; near two hundred
        souls
    Had left their bodies; and what's worse,
        alas!
When over Catholics the ocean rolls,
    They must wait several weeks before a
        mass
Takes off one peck of purgatorial coals,
    Because, till people know what's come
        to pass,
They won't lay out their money on the
        dead—
It costs three francs for every mass that's
        said.

LVI

Juan got into the long-boat, and there
    Contrived to help Pedrillo to a place;
It seem'd as if they had exchanged their
        care,
    For Juan wore the magisterial face

Which courage gives, while poor Pedrillo's
        pair
    Of eyes were crying for their owner's
        case:
Battista, though (a name call'd shortly
        Tita),
Was lost by getting at some aqua-vita.

LVII

Pedro, his valet, too, he tried to save,
    But the same cause, conducive to his loss,
Left him so drunk, he jump'd into the
        wave,
    As o'er the cutter's edge he tried to cross,
And so he found a wine-and-watery grave;
    They could not rescue him although so
        close,
Because the sea ran higher every minute,
And for the boat—the crew kept crowding
        in it.

LVIII

A small old spaniel—which had been Don
        José's,
    His father's, whom he loved, as ye may
        think,
For on such things the memory reposes
    With tenderness—stood howling on the
        brink,
Knowing, (dogs have such intellectual
        noses!)
    No doubt, the vessel was about to sink;
And Juan caught him up, and ere he
        stepp'd
Off threw him in, then after him he leap'd.

LIX

He also stuff'd his money where he could
    About his person, and Pedrillo's too,
Who let him do, in fact, whate'er he would,
    Not knowing what himself to say, or do,
As every rising wave his dread renew'd;
    But Juan, trusting they might still get
        through,
And deeming there were remedies for any
        ill,
Thus re-embark'd his tutor and his spaniel.

LX

'Twas a rough night, and blew so stiffly
        yet,
    That the sail was becalm'd between the
        seas,
Though on the wave's high top too much
        to set,
    They dared not take it in for all the
        breeze:
Each sea curl'd o'er the stern, and kept
        them wet,
    And made them bale without a moment's
        ease,
So that themselves as well as hopes were
        damp'd,
And the poor little cutter quickly swamp'd.

LXI

Nine souls more went in her: the long-boat still
  Kept above water, with an oar for mast,
Two blankets stitch'd together, answering ill
  Instead of sail, were to the oar made fast:
Though every wave roll'd menacing to fill,
  And present peril all before surpass'd,
They grieved for those who perish'd with the cutter,
And also for the biscuit-casks and butter.

LXII

The sun rose red and fiery, a sure sign
  Of the continuance of the gale: to run
Before the sea until it should grow fine,
  Was all that for the present could be done:
A few tea-spoonfuls of their rum and wine
  Was served out to the people, who begun
To faint, and damaged bread wet through the bags,
And most of them had little clothes but rags.

LXIII

They counted thirty, crowded in a space
  Which left scarce room for motion or exertion;
They did their best to modify their case,
  One half sate up, though numb'd with the immersion,
While t'other half were laid down in their place,
  At watch and watch; thus, shivering like the tertian
Ague in its cold fit, they fill'd their boat,
With nothing but the sky for a great coat.

LXIV

'Tis very certain the desire of life
  Prolongs it: this is obvious to physicians,
When patients, neither plagued with friends nor wife,
  Survive through very desperate conditions,
Because they still can hope, nor shines the knife
  Nor shears of Atropos before their visions:
Despair of all recovery spoils longevity,
And makes men's miseries of alarming brevity.

LXV

'Tis said that persons living on annuities
  Are longer lived than others,—God knows why,
Unless to plague the grantors,—yet so true it is,
  That some, I really think, *do* never die;

Of any creditors the worst a Jew it is,
  And *that*'s their mode of furnishing supply:
In my young days they lent me cash that way,
Which I found very troublesome to pay.

LXVI

'Tis thus with people in an open boat,
  They live upon the love of life, and bear
More than can be believed, or even thought,
  And stand like rocks the tempest's wear and tear;
And hardship still has been the sailor's lot,
  Since Noah's ark went cruising here and there;
She had a curious crew as well as cargo,
Like the first old Greek privateer, the Argo.

LXVII

But man is a carnivorous production,
  And must have meals, at least one meal a day;
He cannot live, like woodcocks, upon suction,
  But, like the shark and tiger, must have prey;
Although his anatomical construction
  Bears vegetables, in a grumbling way,
Your labouring people think beyond all question
Beef, veal, and mutton, better for digestion.

LXVIII

And thus it was with this our hapless crew;
  For on the third day there came on a calm,
And though at first their strength it might renew,
  And lying on their weariness like balm,
Lull'd them like turtles sleeping on the blue
  Of ocean, when they woke they felt a qualm,
And fell all ravenously on their provision,
Instead of hoarding it with due precision.

LXIX

The consequence was easily foreseen—
  They ate up all they had, and drank their wine,
In spite of all remonstrances, and then
  On what, in fact, next day were they to dine?
They hoped the wind would rise, these foolish men!
  And carry them to shore; these hopes were fine,
But as they had but one oar, and that brittle,
It would have been more wise to save their victual.

LXX

The fourth day came, but not a breath of
    air,
  And Ocean slumber'd like an unwean'd
    child:
The fifth day, and their boat lay floating
    there,
  The sea and sky were blue, and clear,
    and mild—
With their one oar (I wish they had had a
    pair)
  What could they do? and hunger's rage
    grew wild:
So Juan's spaniel, spite of his entreating,
Was kill'd, and portion'd out for present
    eating.

LXXI

On the sixth day they fed upon his hide,
  And Juan, who had still refused, because
The creature was his father's dog that died,
  Now feeling all the vulture in his jaws,
With some remorse received (though first
    denied)
  As a great favour one of the fore-paws,
Which he divided with Pedrillo, who
Devour'd it, longing for the other too.

LXXII

The seventh day, and no wind—the burn-
    ing sun
  Blister'd and scorch'd, and, stagnant on
    the sea,
They lay like carcasses; and hope was none,
  Save in the breeze that came not: sav-
    agely
They glared upon each other—all was done,
  Water, and wine, and food,—and you
    might see
The longings of the cannibal arise
(Although they spoke not) in their wolfish
    eyes.

LXXIII

At length one whisper'd his companion,
    who
  Whisper'd another, and thus it went
    round,
And then into a hoarser murmur grew,
  An ominous, and wild, and desperate
    sound;
And when his comrade's thought each
    sufferer knew,
  'Twas but his own, suppress'd till now,
    he found:
And out they spoke of lots for flesh and
    blood,
And who should die to be his fellow's food.

LXXIV

But ere they came to this, they that day
    shared
  Some leathern caps, and what remain'd
    of shoes;

And then they look'd around them, and
    despair'd,
  And none to be the sacrifice would
    choose;
At length the lots were torn up, and pre-
    pared,
  But of materials that must shock the
    Muse—
Having no paper, for the want of better,
They took by force from Juan Julia's letter.

LXXV

Then lots were made, and mark'd, and
    mix'd, and handed
  In silent horror, and their distribution
Lull'd even the savage hunger which de-
    manded,
  Like the Promethean vulture, this pollu-
    tion;
None in particular had sought or plann'd it,
  'Twas Nature gnaw'd them to this reso-
    lution,
By which none were permitted to be
    neuter—
And the lot fell on Juan's luckless tutor.

LXXVI

He but requested to be bled to death:
  The surgeon had his instruments, and
    bled
Pedrillo, and so gently ebb'd his breath,
  You hardly could perceive when he was
    dead.
He died as born, a Catholic in faith,
  Like most in the belief in which they're
    bred,
And first a little crucifix he kiss'd,
And then held out his jugular and wrist.

LXXVII

The surgeon, as there was no other fee,
  Had his first choice of morsels for his
    pains;
But being thirstiest at the moment, he
  Preferr'd a draught from the fast-flow-
    ing veins:
Part was divided, part thrown in the sea,
  And such things as the entrails and the
    brains
Regaled two sharks, who follow'd o'er the
    billow—
The sailors ate the rest of poor Pedrillo.

LXXVIII

The sailors ate him, all save three or four,
  Who were not quite so fond of animal
    food;
To these was added Juan, who, before
  Refusing his own spaniel, hardly could
Feel now his appetite increased much more;
  'Twas not to be expected that he should,
Even in extremity of their disaster,
Dine with them on his pastor and his
    master.

LXXIX

'Twas better that he did not; for, in fact,
  The consequence was awful in the extreme;
For they, who were most ravenous in the act,
  Went raging mad—Lord! how they did blaspheme!
And foam, and roll, with strange convulsions rack'd,
  Drinking salt-water like a mountain-stream;
Tearing, and grinning, howling, screeching, swearing,
And, with hyæna-laughter, died despairing.

LXXX

Their numbers were much thinn'd by this infliction,
  And all the rest were thin enough, Heaven knows;
And some of them had lost their recollection,
  Happier than they who still perceived their woes;
But others ponder'd on a new dissection,
  As if not warn'd sufficiently by those
Who had already perish'd, suffering madly,
For having used their appetites so sadly.

LXXXI

And next they thought upon the master's mate,
  As fattest; but he saved himself, because,
Besides being much averse from such a fate,
  There were some other reasons: the first was,
He had been rather indisposed of late;
  And that which chiefly proved his saving clause,
Was a small present made to him at Cadiz,
By general subscription of the ladies.

LXXXII

Of poor Pedrillo something still remain'd,
  But was used sparingly,—some were afraid,
And others still their appetites constrain'd,
  Or but at times a little supper made;
All except Juan, who throughout abstain'd,
  Chewing a piece of bamboo, and some lead:
At length they caught two boobies, and a noddy,
And then they left off eating the dead body.

LXXXIII

And if Pedrillo's fate should shocking be,
  Remember Ugolino condescends
To eat the head of his arch-enemy
  The moment after he politely ends

His tale: if foes be food in hell, at sea
  'Tis surely fair to dine upon our friends,
When shipwreck's short allowance grows too scanty,
Without being much more horrible than Dante.

LXXXIV

And the same night there fell a shower of rain,
  For which their mouths gaped, like the cracks of earth
When dried to summer dust; till taught by pain,
  Men really know not what good water's worth;
If you had been in Turkey or in Spain,
  Or with a famish'd boat's-crew had your berth,
Or in the desert heard the camel's bell,
You'd wish yourself where Truth is—in a well.

LXXXV

It pour'd down torrents, but they were no richer,
  Until they found a ragged piece of sheet,
Which served them as a sort of spongy pitcher,
  And when they deem'd its moisture was complete,
They wrung it out, and though a thirsty ditcher
  Might not have thought the scanty draught so sweet
As a full pot of porter, to their thinking
They ne'er till now had known the joys of drinking.

LXXXVI

And their baked lips, with many a bloody crack,
  Suck'd in the moisture, which like nectar stream'd;
Their throats were ovens, their swoln tongues were black
  As the rich man's in hell, who vainly scream'd
To beg the beggar, who could not rain back
  A drop of dew, when every drop had seem'd
To taste of heaven—If this be true, indeed,
Some Christians have a comfortable creed.

LXXXVII

There were two fathers in this ghastly crew,
  And with them their two sons, of whom the one
Was more robust and hardy to the view,
  But he died early; and when he was gone,

His nearest messmate told his sire, who
    threw
  One glance at him, and said, 'Heaven's
    will be done!
I can do nothing,' and he saw him thrown
Into the deep without a tear or groan.

LXXXVIII

The other father had a weaklier child,
  Of a soft cheek, and aspect delicate;
But the boy bore up long, and with a mild
  And patient spirit held aloof his fate;
Little he said, and now and then he smiled,
  As if to win a part from off the weight
He saw increasing on his father's heart,
  With the deep deadly thought, that they
    must part.

LXXXIX

And o'er him bent his sire, and never raised
  His eyes from off his face, but wiped the
    foam
From his pale lips, and ever on him gazed,
  And when the wish'd-for shower at
    length was come,
And the boy's eyes, which the dull film
    half glazed,
  Brighten'd, and for a moment seem'd
    to roam,
He squeezed from out a rag some drops
    of rain
Into his dying child's mouth—but in vain.

XC

The boy expired—the father held the clay,
  And look'd upon it long, and when at
    last
Death left no doubt, and the dead burthen
    lay
  Stiff on his heart, and pulse and hope
    were past,
He watch'd it wistfully, until away
  'Twas borne by the rude wave wherein
    'twas cast;
Then he himself sunk down all dumb and
    shivering,
And gave no sign of life, save his limbs
    quivering.

XCI

Now overhead a rainbow, bursting through
  The scattering clouds, shone, spanning
    the dark sea,
Resting its bright base on the quivering
    blue;
  And all within its arch appear'd to be
Clearer than that without, and its wide hue
  Wax'd broad and waving, like a banner
    free,
Then changed like to a bow that's bent,
    and then
Forsook the dim eyes of these shipwreck'd
    men.

XCII

It changed, of course; a heavenly chame-
    leon,
  The airy child of vapour and the sun,
Brought forth in purple, cradled in
    vermilion,
  Baptized in molten gold, and swathed
    in dun,
Glittering like crescents o'er a Turk's
    pavilion,
  And blending every colour into one,
Just like a black eye in a recent scuffle
(For sometimes we must box without the
    muffle).

XCIII

Our shipwreck'd seamen thought it a
    good omen—
  It is as well to think so, now and then;
'Twas an old custom of the Greek and
    Roman,
  And may become of great advantage
    when
Folks are discouraged; and most surely
    no men
  Had greater need to nerve themselves
    again
Than these, and so this rainbow look'd
    like hope—
Quite a celestial kaleidoscope.

XCIV

About this time a beautiful white bird,
  Web-footed, not unlike a dove in size
And plumage (probably it might have
    err'd
  Upon its course), pass'd oft before their
    eyes,
And tried to perch, although it saw and
    heard
  The men within the boat, and in this
    guise
It came and went, and flutter'd round
    them till
Night fell:—this seem'd a better omen
    still.

XCV

But in this case I also must remark,
  'Twas well this bird of promise did not
    perch,
Because the tackle of our shatter'd bark
  Was not so safe for roosting as a church;
And had it been the dove from Noah's
    ark,
  Returning there from her successful
    search,
Which in their way that moment chanced
    to fall,
They would have eat her, olive-branch
    and all.

XCVI

With twilight it again came on to blow,
  But not with violence; the stars shone
    out,
The boat made way; yet now they were so
    low,
  They knew not where nor what they
    . were about;
Some fancied they saw land, and some
    said 'No!'
  The frequent fog-banks gave them cause
    to doubt—
Some swore that they heard breakers,
    others guns,
And all mistook about the latter once.

XCVII

As morning broke, the light wind died
    away,
  When he who had the watch sung out
    and swore,
If 'twas not land that rose with the sun's
    ray,
  He wish'd that land he never might see
    more:
And the rest rubb'd their eyes, and saw
    a bay,
  Or thought they saw, and shaped their
    course for shore;
For shore it was, and gradually grew
Distinct, and high, and palpable to view.

XCVIII

And then of these some part burst into
    tears,
  And others, looking with a stupid stare,
Could not yet separate their hopes from
    fears,
  And seem'd as if they had no further
    care;
While a few pray'd—(the first time for
    some years)—
  And at the bottom of the boat three
    were
Asleep: they shook them by the hand and
    head,
And tried to awaken them, but found them
    dead.

XCIX

The day before, fast sleeping on the water,
  They found a turtle of the hawk's-bill
    kind,
And by good fortune, gliding softly,
    caught her,
  Which yielded a day's life, and to their
    mind
Proved even still a more nutritious matter,
  Because it left encouragement be-
    hind:
They thought that in such perils, more
    than chance
Had sent them this for their deliverance.

C

The land appear'd a high and rocky coast,
  And higher grew the mountains as they
    drew,
Set by a current, toward it: they were lost
  In various conjectures, for none knew
To what part of the earth they had been
    tost,
  So changeable had been the winds that
    blew;
Some thought it was Mount Ætna, some
    the highlands
Of Candia, Cyprus, Rhodes, or other
    islands.

CI

Meantime the current, with a rising gale,
  Still set them onwards to the welcome
    shore,
Like Charon's bark of spectres, dull and
    pale:
  Their living freight was now reduced to
    four,
And three dead, whom their strength
    could not avail
To heave into the deep with those before,
Though the two sharks still follow'd them,
    and dash'd
The spray into their faces as they splash'd.

CII

Famine, despair, cold, thirst, and heat,
    had done
  Their work on them by turns, and
    thinn'd them to
Such things a mother had not known her
    son
  Amidst the skeletons of that gaunt
    crew;
By night chill'd, by day scorch'd, thus one
    by one
  They perish'd, until wither'd to these
    few,
But chiefly by a species of self-slaughter,
In washing down Pedrillo with salt water.

CIII

As they drew nigh the land, which now
    was seen
  Unequal in its aspect here and there,
They felt the freshness of its growing
    green,
  That waved in forest-tops, and
    smooth'd the air,
And fell upon their glazed eyes like a
    screen
  From glistening waves, and skies so hot
    and bare—
Lovely seem'd any object that should
    sweep
Away the vast, salt, dread, eternal deep.

CIV

The shore look'd wild, without a trace of
    man,
    And girt by formidable waves; but they
Were mad for land, and thus their course
    they ran,
    Though right ahead the roaring
    breakers lay:
A reef between them also now began
    To show its boiling surf and bounding
    spray,
But finding no place for their landing
    better,
They ran the boat for shore,—and overset
    her.

CV

But in his native stream, the Guadalquivir,
    Juan to lave his youthful limbs was
    wont;
And having learnt to swim in that sweet
    river,
    Had often turn'd the art to some
    account:
A better swimmer you could scarce see
    ever,
    He could, perhaps, have pass'd the
    Hellespont,
As once (a feat on which ourselves we
    prided)
Leander, Mr. Ekenhead, and I did.

CVI

So here, though faint, emaciated, and
    stark,
    He buoy'd his boyish limbs, and strove
    to ply
With the quick wave, and gain, ere it was
    dark,
    The beach which lay before him, high
    and dry:
The greatest danger here was from a shark,
    That carried off his neighbour by the
    thigh;
As for the other two, they could not swim,
So nobody arrived on shore but him.

CVII

Nor yet had he arrived but for the oar,
    Which, providentially for him, was
    wash'd
Just as his feeble arms could strike no
    more,
    And the hard wave o'erwhelm'd him
    as 'twas dash'd
Within his grasp; he clung to it, and sore
    The waters beat while he thereto was
    lash'd:
At last, with swimming, wading, scram-
    bling, he
Roll'd on the beach, half senseless, from
    the sea:

CVIII

There, breathless, with his digging nails
    he clung
Fast to the sand, lest the returning wave,
From whose reluctant roar his life he
    wrung,
    Should suck him back to her insatiate
    grave:
And there he lay, full length, where he was
    flung,
Before the entrance of a cliff-worn cave,
With just enough of life to feel its pain,
And deem that it was saved, perhaps in
    vain.

CIX

With slow and staggering effort he arose,
    But sunk again upon his bleeding knee
And quivering hand; and then he look'd
    for those
Who long had been his mates upon the
    sea;
But none of them appear'd to share his
    woes,
    Save one, a corpse, from out the
    famish'd three,
Who died two days before, and now had
    found
An unknown barren beach for burial-
    ground.

CX

And as he gazed, his dizzy brain spun fast,
    And down he sunk; and as he sunk, the
    sand
Swam round and round, and all his senses
    pass'd:
    He fell upon his side, and his stretch'd
    hand
Droop'd dripping on the oar (their jury-
    mast),
    And, like a wither'd lily, on the land
His slender frame and pallid aspect lay,
As fair a thing as e'er was form'd of clay.

CXI

How long in his damp trance young Juan
    lay
    He knew not, for the earth was gone
    for him,
And time had nothing more of night nor
    day
    For his congealing blood, and senses
    dim;
And how this heavy faintness pass'd away
    He knew not, till each painful pulse and
    limb,
And tingling vein, seem'd throbbing back
    to life,
For Death, though vanquish'd, still
    retired with strife.

CXII

His eyes he open'd, shut, again unclosed,
    For all was doubt and dizziness; he
        thought
He still was in the boat, and had but dozed,
    And felt again with his despair o'er-
        wrought,
And wish'd it death in which he had
        reposed,
    And then once more his feelings back
        were brought,
And slowly by his swimming eyes was
        seen
A lovely female face of seventeen.

CXIII

'Twas bending close o'er his, and the
        small mouth
    Seem'd almost prying into his for
        breath;
And chafing him, the soft warm hand of
        youth
    Recall'd his answering spirits back
        from death;
And, bathing his chill temples, tried to
        soothe
    Each pulse to animation, till beneath
Its gentle touch and trembling care, a sigh
To these kind efforts made a low reply.

CXIV

Then was the cordial pour'd, and mantle
        flung
    Around his scarce-clad limbs; and the
        fair arm
Raised higher the faint head which o'er it
        hung;
    And her transparent cheek, all pure and
        warm,
Pillow'd his death-like forehead; then she
        wrung
    His dewy curls, long drench'd by every
        storm;
And watch'd with eagerness each throb
        that drew
A sigh from his heaved bosom—and hers,
        too.

CXV

And lifting him with care into the cave,
    The gentle girl, and her attendant,—
        one
Young, yet her elder, and of brow less
        grave,
    And more robust of figure—then begun
To kindle fire, and as the new flames gave
    Light to the rocks that roof'd them,
        which the sun
Had never seen, the maid, or whatsoe'er
She was, appear'd distinct, and tall, and
        fair.

CXVI

Her brow was overhung with coins of gold,
    That sparkled o'er the auburn of her hair,
Her clustering hair, whose longer locks
        were roll'd
    In braids behind; and though her
        stature were
Even of the highest for a female mould,
    They nearly reach'd her heel; and in her
        air
There was a something which bespoke
        command,
As one who was a lady in the land.

CXVII

Her hair, I said, was auburn; but her eyes
    Were black as death, their lashes the
        same hue,
Of downcast length, in whose silk shadow
        lies
    Deepest attraction; for when to the view
Forth from its raven fringe the full glance
        flies,
    Ne'er with such force the swiftest arrow
        flew;
'Tis as the snake late coil'd, who pours his
        length,
And hurls at once his venom and his
        strength.

CXVIII

Her brow was white and low, her cheek's
        pure dye
    Like twilight rosy still with the set sun;
Short upper lip—sweet lips! that make us
        sigh
    Ever to have seen such; for she was one
Fit for the model of a statuary
    (A race of mere impostors, when all's
        done—
I've seen much finer women, ripe and real,
Than all the nonsense of their stone ideal).

CXIX

I'll tell you why I say so, for 'tis just
    One should not rail without a decent
        cause:
There was an Irish lady, to whose bust
    I ne'er saw justice done, and yet she was
A frequent model; and if e'er she must
    Yield to stern Time and Nature's
        wrinkling laws,
They will destroy a face which mortal
        thought
Ne'er compass'd, nor less mortal chisel
        wrought.

CXX

And such was she, the lady of the cave,
    Her dress was very different from the
        Spanish,
Simpler, and yet of colours not so grave;
    For, as you know, the Spanish women
        banish

Bright hues when out of doors, and yet,
　　while wave
　Around them (what I hope will never
　　vanish)
The basquina and the mantilla, they
Seem at the same time mystical and gay.

CXXI

But with our damsel this was not the case:
　Her dress was many-colour'd, finely
　　spun;
Her locks curl'd negligently round her
　　face,
　But through them gold and gems pro-
　　fusely shone:
Her girdle sparkled, and the richest lace
Flow'd in her veil, and many a precious
　　stone
Flash'd on her little hand; but, what was
　　shocking,
Her small snow feet had slippers, but no
　　stocking.

CXXII

The other female's dress was not unlike,
　But of inferior materials: she
Had not so many ornaments to strike,
　Her hair had silver only, bound to be
Her dowry; and her veil, in form alike,
　Was coarser; and her air, though firm,
　　less free;
Her hair was thicker, but less long; her eyes
As black, but quicker, and of smaller size.

CXXIII

And these two tended him, and cheer'd
　　him both
　With food and raiment, and those soft
　　attentions,
Which are—(as I must own)—of female
　　growth,
　And have ten thousand delicate inven-
　　tions:
They made a most superior mess of broth,
　A thing which poesy but seldom men-
　　tions,
But the best dish that e'er was cook'd
　　since Homer's
Achilles order'd dinner for new comers.

CXXIV

I'll tell you who they were, this female
　　pair,
　Lest they should seem princesses in
　　disguise;
Besides, I hate all mystery, and that air
　Of clap-trap, which your recent poets
　　prize;
And so, in short, the girls they really were
　They shall appear before your curious
　　eyes,
Mistress and maid; the first was only
　　daughter
Of an old man, who lived upon the water.

CXXV

A fisherman he had been in his youth,
　And still a sort of fisherman was he;
But other speculations were, in sooth,
　Added to his connexion with the sea,
Perhaps not so respectable, in truth:
　A little smuggling, and some piracy,
Left him, at last, the sole of many masters
Of an ill-gotten million of piastres.

CXXVI

A fisher, therefore, was he,—though of
　　men,
　Like Peter the Apostle,—and he fish'd
For wandering merchant vessels, now and
　　then,
　And sometimes caught as many as he
　　wish'd;
The cargoes he confiscated, and gain
　He sought in the slave-market too, and
　　dish'd
Full many a morsel for that Turkish trade,
By which, no doubt, a good deal may be
　　made.

CXXVII

He was a Greek, and on his isle had built
　(One of the wild and smaller Cyclades)
A very handsome house from out his guilt,
　And there he lived exceedingly at ease;
Heaven knows what cash he got, or blood
　　he spilt,
　A sad old fellow was he, if you please;
But this I know, it was a spacious building,
Full of barbaric carving, paint, and gilding.

CXXVIII

He had an only daughter, call'd Haidée,
　The greatest heiress of the Eastern Isles;
Besides, so very beautiful was she,
　Her dowry was as nothing to her smiles:
Still in her teens, and like a lovely tree
　She grew to womanhood, and between
　　whiles
Rejected several suitors, just to learn
How to accept a better in his turn.

CXXIX

And walking out upon the beach, below
　The cliff,—towards sunset, on that day
　　she found,
Insensible,—not dead, but nearly so,—
　Don Juan, almost famish'd, and half
　　drown'd;
But being naked, she was shock'd, you know,
　Yet deem'd herself in common pity bound,
As far as in her lay, 'to take him in,
A stranger' dying, with so white a skin.

CXXX

But taking him into her father's house
　Was not exactly the best way to save,
But like conveying to the cat the mouse,
　Or people in a trance into their grave;

Because the good old man had so much
'*vous*,'
  Unlike the honest Arab thieves so
    brave,
He would have hospitably cured the
  stranger
And sold him instantly when out of
  danger.

CXXXI

And therefore, with her maid, she thought
  it best
  (A virgin always on her maid relies)
To place him in the cave for present rest:
  And when, at last, he open'd his black
    eyes,
Their charity increased about their guest;
  And their compassion grew to such a
    size,
It open'd half the turnpike gates to
  heaven—
(St. Paul says, 'tis the toll which must be
  given).

CXXXII

They made a fire,—but such a fire as they
  Upon the moment could contrive with
    such
Materials as were cast up round the
    bay,—
  Some broken planks, and oars, that to
    the touch
Were nearly tinder, since so long they lay,
  A mast was almost crumbled to a
    crutch;
But, by God's grace, here wrecks were in
  such plenty,
That there was fuel to have furnish'd
  twenty.

CXXXIII

He had a bed of furs, and a pelisse,
  For Haidée stripp'd her sables off to
    make
His couch; and, that he might be more at
    ease,
  And warm, in case by chance he should
    awake,
They also gave a petticoat apiece,
  She and her maid,—and promised by
    daybreak
To pay him a fresh visit, with a dish
For breakfast, of eggs, coffee, bread, and
  fish.

CXXXIV

And thus they left him to his lone repose:
  Juan slept like a top, or like the dead,
Who sleep at last, perhaps (God only
    knows),
  Just for the present; and in his lull'd
    head
Not even a vision of his former woes
  Throbb'd in accursed dreams, which
    sometimes spread

Unwelcome visions of our former years,
Till the eye, cheated, opens thick with
  tears.

CXXXV

Young Juan slept all dreamless:—but the
  maid,
  Who smooth'd his pillow, as she left the
    den
Look'd back upon him, and a moment
    stayed,
  And turn'd, believing that he call'd again.
He slumber'd; yet she thought, at least she
    said
  (The heart will slip, even as the tongue
    and pen),
He had pronounced her name—but she
  forgot
That at this moment Juan knew it not.

CXXXVI

And pensive to her father's house she
  went,
  Enjoining silence strict to Zoe, who
Better than her knew what, in fact, she
  meant,
  She being wiser by a year or two:
A year or two's an age when rightly spent,
  And Zoe spent hers, as most women do,
In gaining all that useful sort of knowledge
Which is acquired in Nature's good old
  college.

CXXXVII

The morn broke, and found Juan slumber-
  ing still
  Fast in his cave, and nothing clash'd
    upon
His rest: the rushing of the neighbouring
  rill,
  And the young beams of the excluded
    sun,
Troubled him not, and he might sleep his
  fill;
  And need he had of slumber yet, for
    none
Had suffer'd more—his hardships were
  comparative
To those related in my grand-dad's
  'Narrative.'

CXXXVIII

Not so Haidée: she sadly toss'd and
  tumbled,
  And started from her sleep, and,
    turning o'er,
Dream'd of a thousand wrecks, o'er which
  she stumbled,
  And handsome corpses strew'd upon
    the shore;
And woke her maid so early that she
  grumbled,
  And call'd her father's old slaves up,
    who swore

In several oaths—Armenian, Turk, and
    Greek—
They knew not what to think of such a
    freak.

CXXXIX

But up she got, and up she made them get,
    With some pretence about the sun, that
    makes
Sweet skies just when he rises, or is set;
    And 'tis, no doubt, a sight to see when
    breaks
Bright Phœbus, while the mountains still
    are wet
    With mist, and every bird with him
    awakes,
And night is flung off like a mourning suit
Worn for a husband,—or some other
    brute.

CXL

I say, the sun is a most glorious sight:
    I've seen him rise full oft, indeed of late
I have sat up on purpose all the night,
    Which hastens, as physicians say, one's
    fate;
And so all ye, who would be in the right
    In health and purse, begin your day to
    date
From daybreak, and when coffin'd at four-
    score
Engrave upon the plate, you rose at four.

CXLI

And Haidée met the morning face to face;
    Her own was freshest, though a feverish
    flush
Had dyed it with the headlong blood,
    whose race
    From heart to cheek is curb'd into a
    blush,
Like to a torrent which a mountain's base,
    That overpowers some Alpine river's
    rush,
Checks to a lake, whose waves in circles
    spread;
Or the Red Sea—but the sea is not red.

CXLII

And down the cliff the island virgin came,
    And near the cave her quick light foot-
    steps drew,
While the sun smiled on her with his first
    flame,
    And young Aurora kiss'd her lips with
    dew,
Taking her for a sister; just the same
    Mistake you would have made on see-
    ing the two,
Although the mortal, quite as fresh and
    fair,
Had all the advantage, too, of not being
    air.

CXLIII

And when into the cavern Haidée stepp'd
    All timidly, yet rapidly, she saw
That like an infant Juan sweetly slept;
    And then she stopp'd, and stood as if
    in awe
(For sleep is awful), and on tiptoe crept
    And wrapt him closer, lest the air, too
    raw,
Should reach his blood, then o'er him still
    as death
Bent, with hush'd lips, that drank his
    scarce-drawn breath.

CXLIV

And thus like to an angel o'er the dying
    Who die in righteousness, she lean'd;
    and there
All tranquilly the shipwreck'd boy was
    lying,
    As o'er him lay the calm and stirless air:
But Zoe the meantime some eggs was
    frying,
    Since, after all, no doubt the youthful
    pair
Must breakfast, and betimes—lest they
    should ask it,
She drew out her provision from the
    basket.

CXLV

She knew that the best feelings must have
    victual,
    And that a shipwreck'd youth would
    hungry be;
Besides, being less in love, she yawn'd a
    little,
    And felt her veins chill'd by the neigh-
    bouring sea;
And so, she cook'd their breakfast to a
    tittle;
    I can't say that she gave them any tea,
But there were eggs, fruit, coffee, bread,
    fish, honey,
With Scio wine,—and all for love, not
    money.

CXLVI

And Zoe, when the eggs were ready, and
    The coffee made, would fain have
    waken'd Juan;
But Haidée stopp'd her with her quick
    small hand,
    And without word, a sign her finger
    drew on
Her lip, which Zoe needs must under-
    stand;
    And, the first breakfast spoilt, prepared
    a new one,
Because her mistress would not let her
    break
That sleep which seem'd as it would ne'er
    awake.

CXLVII

For still he lay, and on his thin worn cheek
　A purple hectic play'd like dying day
On the snow-tops of distant hills; the
　　streak
　Of sufferance yet upon his forehead lay,
Where the blue veins look'd shadowy,
　　shrunk, and weak;
　　And his black curls were dewy with the
　　　spray,
Which weigh'd upon them yet, all damp
　　and salt,
Mix'd with the stony vapours of the vault.

CXLVIII

And she bent o'er him, and he lay beneath,
　Hush'd as the babe upon its mother's
　　breast,
Droop'd as the willow when no winds can
　　breathe,
　Lull'd like the depth of ocean when at
　　rest,
Fair as the crowning rose of the whole
　　wreath,
　Soft as the callow cygnet in its nest;
In short, he was a very pretty fellow,
Although his woes had turn'd him rather
　　yellow.

CXLIX

He woke and gazed, and would have slept
　　again,
　But the fair face which met his eyes
　　forbade
Those eyes to close, though weariness and
　　pain
　Had further sleep a further pleasure
　　made;
For woman's face was never form'd in
　　vain
　For Juan, so that even when he pray'd
He turn'd from grisly saints, and martyrs
　　hairy,
To the sweet portraits of the Virgin Mary.

CL

And thus upon his elbow he arose,
　And look'd upon the lady, in whose
　　cheek
The pale contended with the purple rose,
　As with an effort she began to speak;
Her eyes were eloquent, her words would
　　pose,
　Although she told him, in good modern
　　Greek,
With an Ionian accent, low and sweet,
That he was faint, and must not talk, but
　　eat.

CLI

Now Juan could not understand a word,
　Being no Grecian; but he had an ear,
And her voice was the warble of a bird,
　So soft, so sweet, so delicately clear,
That finer, simpler music ne'er was heard;
　The sort of sound we echo with a tear,
Without knowing why—an overpowering
　　tone,
Whence melody descends as from a
　　throne.

CLII

And Juan gazed as one who is awoke
　By a distant organ, doubting if he be
Not yet a dreamer, till the spell is broke
　By the watchman, or some such reality,
Or by one's early valet's cursed knock;
　At least it is a heavy sound to me,
Who like a morning slumber—for the night
Shows stars and women in a better light.

CLIII

And Juan, too, was help'd out from his
　　dream,
　Or sleep, or whatsoe'er it was, by feeling
A most prodigious appetite; the steam
　Of Zoe's cookery no doubt was stealing
Upon his senses, and the kindling beam
　Of the new fire, which Zoe kept up,
　　kneeling,
To stir her viands, made him quite awake
And long for food, but chiefly a beef-steak.

CLIV

But beef is rare within these oxless isles;
　Goat's flesh there is, no doubt, and kid,
　　and mutton,
And, when a holiday upon them smiles,
　A joint upon their barbarous spits they
　　put on:
But this occurs but seldom, between
　　whiles,
　For some of these are rocks with scarce
　　a hut on;
Others are fair and fertile, among which
This, though not large, was one of the
　　most rich.

CLV

I say that beef is rare, and can't help thinking
　That the old fable of the Minotaur—
From which our modern morals, rightly
　　shrinking,
　Condemn the royal lady's taste who
　　wore
A cow's shape for a mask—was only
　　(sinking
　The allegory) a mere type, no more,
That Pasiphae promoted breeding cattle,
To make the Cretans bloodier in battle.

CLVI

For we all know that English people are
　Fed upon beef—I won't say much of
　　beer,
Because 'tis liquor only, and being far
　From this my subject, has no business
　　here;

We know, too, they are very fond of war,
　　A pleasure—like all pleasures—rather
　　　dear;
So were the Cretans—from which I infer
That beef and battles both were owing to
　　her.

CLVII

But to resume. The languid Juan raised
　　His head upon his elbow, and he saw
A sight on which he had not lately gazed,
　　As all his latter meals had been quite
　　　raw,
Three or four things, for which the Lord
　　he praised,
　　And, feeling still the famish'd vulture
　　　gnaw,
He fell upon whate'er was offer'd, like
A priest, a shark, an alderman, or pike.

CLVIII

He ate, and he was well supplied; and she,
　　Who watch'd him like a mother, would
　　　have fed
Him past all bounds, because she smiled
　　to see
　　Such appetite in one she had deem'd
　　　dead:
But Zoe, being older than Haidée,
　　Knew (by tradition, for she ne'er had
　　　read)
That famish'd people must be slowly
　　nurst,
And fed by spoonfuls, else they always
　　burst.

CLIX

And so she took the liberty to state,
　　Rather by deeds than words, because
　　　the case
Was urgent, that the gentleman, whose
　　fate
　　Had made her mistress quit her bed to
　　　trace
The sea-shore at this hour, must leave his
　　plate,
　　Unless he wish'd to die upon the place—
She snatch'd it, and refused another
　　morsel,
Saying, he had gorged enough to make a
　　horse ill.

CLX

Next they—he being naked, save a tatter'd
　　Pair of scarce decent trowsers—went to
　　　work,
And in the fire his recent rags they
　　scatter'd,
　　And dress'd him, for the present, like a
　　　Turk,
Or Greek—that is, although it not much
　　matter'd,
　　Omitting turban, slippers, pistols,
　　　dirk,—

They furnish'd him, entire, except some
　　stitches,
With a clean shirt, and very spacious
　　breeches.

CLXI

And then fair Haidée tried her tongue at
　　speaking,
　　But not a word could Juan comprehend,
Although he listen'd so that the young
　　Greek in
　　Her earnestness would ne'er have made
　　　an end;
And, as he interrupted not, went eking
　　Her speech out to her protégé and
　　　friend,
Till pausing at the last her breath to take,
She saw he did not understand Romaic.

CLXII

And then she had recourse to nods, and
　　signs,
　　And smiles, and sparkles of the speaking
　　　eye,
And read (the only book she could) the
　　lines
　　Of his fair face, and found, by sympathy,
The answer eloquent, where the soul
　　shines
　　And darts in one quick glance a long
　　　reply;
And thus in every look she saw exprest
A world of words, and things at which she
　　guess'd.

CLXIII

And now, by dint of fingers and of eyes,
　　And words repeated after her, he took
A lesson in her tongue; but by surmise,
　　No doubt, less of her language than her
　　　look:
As he who studies fervently the skies
　　Turns oftener to the stars than to his
　　　book,
Thus Juan learn'd his alpha beta better
From Haidée's glance than any graven
　　letter.

CLXIV

'Tis pleasing to be school'd in a strange
　　tongue
　　By female lips and eyes—that is, I mean,
When both the teacher and the taught are
　　young,
　　As was the case, at least, where I have
　　　been;
They smile so when one's right, and when
　　one's wrong
　　They smile still more, and then there
　　　intervene
Pressure of hands, perhaps even a chaste
　　kiss;—
I learn'd the little that I know by this:

CLXV

That is, some words of Spanish, Turk, and
    Greek,
  Italian not at all, having no teachers;
Much English I cannot pretend to speak,
    Learning that language chiefly from its
    preachers,
Barrow, South, Tillotson, whom every
    week
  I study, also Blair, the highest reachers
Of eloquence in piety and prose—
I hate your poets, so read none of those.

CLXVI

As for the ladies, I have nought to say,
  A wanderer from the British world of
    fashion,
Where I, like other 'dogs, have had my
    day,'
  Like other men, too, may have had my
    passion—
But that, like other things, has pass'd away,
  And all her fools whom I *could* lay the
    lash on:
Foes, friends, men, women, now are
    nought to me
But dreams of what has been, no more to
    be.

CLXVII

Return we to Don Juan. He begun
  To hear new words, and to repeat them;
    but
Some feelings, universal as the sun,
  Were such as could not in his breast be
    shut
More than within the bosom of a nun:
  He was in love,—as you would be, no
    doubt,
With a young benefactress,—so was she,
Just in the way we very often see.

CLXVIII

And every day by daybreak—rather early
  For Juan, who was somewhat fond of
    rest—
She came into the cave, but it was merely
  To see her bird reposing in his nest;
And she would softly stir his locks so
    curly,
  Without disturbing her yet slumbering
    guest,
Breathing all gently o'er his cheek and
    mouth,
As o'er a bed of roses the sweet south.

CLXIX

And every morn his colour freshlier came,
  And every day help'd on his con-
    valescence;
'Twas well, because health in the human
    frame
  Is pleasant, besides being true love's
    essence,

For health and idleness to passion's flame
  Are oil and gunpowder; and some good
    lessons
Are also learnt from Ceres and from
    Bacchus,
Without whom Venus will not long attack
    us.

CLXX

While Venus fills the heart (without heart
    really
  Love, though good always, is not quite
    so good),
Ceres presents a plate of vermicelli,—
  For love must be sustain'd like flesh and
    blood,
While Bacchus pours out wine, or hands a
    jelly:
  Eggs, oysters, too, are amatory food;
But who is their purveyor from above
Heaven knows,—it may be Neptune, Pan,
    or Jove.

CLXXI

When Juan woke he found some good
    things ready,
  A bath, a breakfast, and the finest eyes
That ever made a youthful heart less
    steady,
  Besides her maid's, as pretty for their
    size;
But I have spoken of all this already—
  And repetition's tiresome and unwise,—
Well—Juan, after bathing in the sea,
Came always back to coffee and Haidée.

CLXXII

Both were so young, and one so innocent,
  That bathing pass'd for nothing: Juan
    seem'd
To her, as 'twere, the kind of being sent,
  Of whom these two years she had
    nightly dream'd,
A something to be loved, a creature
    meant
  To be her happiness, and whom she
    deem'd
To render happy: all who joy would win
Must share it,—Happiness was born a
    twin.

CLXXIII

It was such pleasure to behold him, such
  Enlargement of existence to partake
Nature with him, to thrill beneath his
    touch,
  To watch him slumbering, and to see
    him wake;
To live with him for ever were too much;
  But then the thought of parting made
    her quake:
He was her own, her ocean-treasure, cast
Like a rich wreck—her first love, and her
    last.

CLXXIV

And thus a moon roll'd on, and fair
  Haidée
Paid daily visits to her boy, and took
Such plentiful precautions, that still he
  Remain'd unknown within his craggy
  nook;
At last her father's prows put out to sea,
  For certain merchantmen upon the
  look,
Not as of yore to carry off an Io,
But three Ragusan vessels bound for Scio.

CLXXV

Then came her freedom, for she had no
  mother,
  So that, her father being at sea, she was
Free as a married woman, or such other
  Female, as where she likes may freely
  pass,
Without even the encumbrance of a
  brother,
  The freest she that ever gazed on glass:
I speak of Christian lands in this com-
  parison,
Where wives, at least, are seldom kept in
  garrison.

CLXXVI

Now she prolong'd her visits and her talk
  (For they must talk), and he had learnt
  to say
So much as to propose to take a walk,—
  For little had he wander'd since the day
On which, like a young flower snapp'd
  from the stalk,
  Drooping and dewy on the beach he
  lay,—
And thus they walk'd out in the afternoon,
And saw the sun set opposite the moon.

CLXXVII

It was a wild and breaker-beaten coast,
  With cliffs above, and a broad sandy
  shore,
Guarded by shoals and rocks as by an
  host,
  With here and there a creek, whose
  aspect wore
A better welcome to the tempest-tost;
  And rarely ceased the haughty billow's
  roar,
Save on the dead long summer days,
  which make
The outstretch'd ocean glitter like a lake.

CLXXVIII

And the small ripple spilt upon the beach
  Scarcely o'erpass'd the cream of your
  champagne,
When o'er the brim the sparkling bumpers
  reach,
  That spring-dew of the spirit! the heart's
  rain!

Few things surpass old wine; and they
  may preach
Who please,—the more because they
  preach in vain,—
Let us have wine and women, mirth and
  laughter,
Sermons and soda-water the day after.

CLXXIX

Man, being reasonable, must get drunk;
  The best of life is but intoxication:
Glory, the grape, love, gold, in these are
  sunk
  The hopes of all men, and of every
  nation;
Without their sap, how branchless were
  the trunk
  Of life's strange tree, so fruitful on
  occasion!
But to return,—Get very drunk; and when
You wake with headache, you shall see
  what then.

CLXXX

Ring for your valet—bid him quickly bring
  Some hock and soda-water, then you'll
  know
A pleasure worthy Xerxes the great king;
  For not the blest sherbet, sublimed with
  snow,
Nor the first sparkle of the desert spring,
  Nor Burgundy in all its sunset glow,
After long travel, ennui, love, or slaughter,
Vie with that draught of hock and soda-
  water.

CLXXXI

The coast—I think it was the coast that I
  Was just describing—Yes, it *was* the
  coast—
Lay at this period quiet as the sky,
  The sands untumbled, the blue waves
  untost,
And all was stillness, save the sea-bird's cry,
  And dolphin's leap, and little billow
  crost
By some low rock or shelve, that made it fret
Against the boundary it scarcely wet.

CLXXXII

And forth they wander'd, her sire being
  gone,
  As I have said, upon an expedition;
And mother, brother, guardian, she had
  none,
  Save Zoe, who, although with due pre-
  cision
She waited on her lady with the sun,
  Thought daily service was her only
  mission,
Bringing warm water, wreathing her long
  tresses,
And asking now and then for cast-off
  dresses.

CLXXXIII

It was the cooling hour, just when the rounded
  Red sun sinks down behind the azure hill,
Which then seems as if the whole earth it bounded,
  Circling all nature, hush'd, and dim, and still,
With the far mountain-crescent half surrounded
  On one side, and the deep sea calm and chill,
Upon the other, and the rosy sky,
With one star sparkling through it like an eye.

CLXXXIV

And thus they wander'd forth, and hand in hand,
  Over the shining pebbles and the shells,
Glided along the smooth and harden'd sand,
  And in the worn and wild receptacles
Work'd by the storms, yet work'd as it were plann'd,
  In hollow halls, with sparry roofs and cells,
They turn'd to rest; and, each clasp'd by an arm,
Yielded to the deep twilight's purple charm.

CLXXXV

They look'd up to the sky, whose floating glow
  Spread like a rosy ocean, vast and bright;
They gazed upon the glittering sea below,
  Whence the broad moon rose circling into sight;
They heard the waves splash, and the wind so low,
  And saw each other's dark eyes darting light
Into each other—and, beholding this,
Their lips drew near, and clung into a kiss;

CLXXXVI

A long, long kiss, a kiss of youth, and love,
  And beauty, all concentrating like rays
Into one focus, kindled from above;
  Such kisses as belong to early days,
Where heart, and soul, and sense, in concert move,
  And the blood's lava, and the pulse a blaze,
Each kiss a heart-quake,—for a kiss's strength,
I think it must be reckon'd by its length.

CLXXXVII

By length I mean duration; theirs endured
  Heaven knows how long—no doubt they never reckon'd;

And if they had, they could not have secured
  The sum of their sensations to a second:
They had not spoken; but they felt allured,
  As if their souls and lips each other beckon'd,
Which, being join'd, like swarming bees they clung—
Their hearts the flowers from whence the honey sprung.

CLXXXVIII

They were alone, but not alone as they
  Who shut in chambers think it loneliness;
The silent ocean, and the starlight bay,
  The twilight glow, which momently grew less,
The voiceless sands, and dropping caves, that lay
  Around them, made them to each other press,
As if there were no life beneath the sky
Save theirs, and that their life could never die.

CLXXXIX

They fear'd no eyes nor ears on that lone beach,
  They felt no terrors from the night; they were
All in all to each other; though their speech
  Was broken words, they *thought* a language there,—
And all the burning tongues the passions teach
  Found in one sigh the best interpreter
Of nature's oracle—first love,—that all
Which Eve has left her daughters since her fall.

CXC

Haidée spoke not of scruples, ask'd no vows,
  Nor offer'd any; she had never heard
Of plight and promises to be a spouse,
  Or perils by a loving maid incurr'd;
She was all which pure ignorance allows,
  And flew to her young mate like a young bird,
And never having dreamt of falsehood, she
Had not one word to say of constancy.

CXCI

She loved, and was beloved—she adored,
  And she was worshipp'd; after nature's fashion,
Their intense souls, into each other pour'd,
  If souls could die, had perish'd in that passion,—

But by degrees their senses were restored,
  Again to be o'ercome, again to dash
    on;
And, beating 'gainst *his* bosom, Haidée's
    heart
Felt as if never more to beat apart.

CXCII

Alas! they were so young, so beautiful,
  So lonely, loving, helpless, and the hour
Was that in which the heart is always full,
  And, having o'er itself no further
    power,
Prompts deeds eternity cannot annul,
  But pays off moments in an endless
    shower
Of hell-fire—all prepared for people
    giving
Pleasure or pain to one another living.

CXCIII

Alas! for Juan and Haidée! they were
  So loving and so lovely—till then never,
Excepting our first parents, such a pair
  Had run the risk of being damn'd for
    ever:
And Haidée, being devout as well as fair,
  Had, doubtless, heard about the
    Stygian river,
And hell and purgatory—but forgot
Just in the very crisis she should not.

CXCIV

They look upon each other, and their eyes
  Gleam in the moonlight; and her white
    arm clasps
Round Juan's head, and his around her
    lies
  Half buried in the tresses which it
    grasps;
She sits upon his knee, and drinks his
    sighs,
  He hers, until they end in broken gasps;
And thus they form a group that's quite
    antique,
Half naked, loving, natural, and Greek.

CXCV

And when those deep and burning
    moments pass'd,
  And Juan sunk to sleep within her arms,
She slept not, but all tenderly, though
    fast,
  Sustain'd his head upon her bosom's
    charms;
And now and then her eye to heaven is
    cast,
  And then on the pale cheek her breast
    now warms,
Pillow'd on her o'erflowing heart, which
    pants
With all it granted, and with all it grants.

CXCVI

An infant when it gazes on a light,
  A child the moment when it drains the
    breast,
A devotee when soars the Host in sight,
  An Arab with a stranger for a guest,
A sailor when the prize has struck in fight,
  A miser filling his most hoarded chest,
Feel rapture; but not such true joy are
    reaping
As they who watch o'er what they love
    while sleeping.

CXCVII

For there it lies so tranquil, so beloved,
  All that it hath of life with us is living;
So gentle, stirless, helpless, and unmoved,
  And all unconscious of the joy 'tis
    giving;
All it hath felt, inflicted, pass'd, and
    proved,
  Hush'd into depths beyond the
    watcher's diving;
There lies the thing we love with all its
    errors
And all its charms, like death without its
    terrors.

CXCVIII

The lady watch'd her lover—and that hour
  Of Love's, and Night's, and Ocean's
    solitude,
O'erflow'd her soul with their united
    power;
  Amidst the barren sand and rocks so
    rude
She and her wave-worn love had made
    their bower,
  Where nought upon their passion could
    intrude,
And all the stars that crowded the blue
    space
Saw nothing happier than her glowing
    face.

CXCIX

Alas! the love of women! it is known
  To be a lovely and a fearful thing;
For all of theirs upon that die is thrown,
  And if 'tis lost, life hath no more to
    bring
To them but mockeries of the past alone,
  And their revenge is as the tiger's spring,
Deadly, and quick, and crushing; yet, as
    real
Torture is theirs, what they inflict they feel.

CC

They are right; for man, to man so oft
    unjust,
  Is always so to women; one sole bond
Awaits them, treachery is all their trust;
  Taught to conceal, their bursting hearts
    despond

Over their idol, till some wealthier lust
  Buys them in marriage—and what rests
    beyond?
A thankless husband, next a faithless
    lover,
Then dressing, nursing, praying, and all 's
    over.

CCI

Some take a lover, some take drams or
    prayers,
  Some mind their household, others dis-
    sipation,
Some run away, and but exchange their
    cares,
  Losing the advantage of a virtuous
    station;
Few changes e'er can better their affairs,
  Theirs being an unnatural situation,
From the dull palace to the dirty hovel:
Some play the devil, and then write a
    novel.

CCII

Haidée was Nature's bride, and knew not
    this:
  Haidée was Passion's child, born where
    the sun
Showers triple light, and scorches even
    the kiss
  Of his gazelle-eyed daughters; she was
    one
Made but to love, to feel that she was his
  Who was her chosen: what was said or
    done
Elsewhere was nothing. She had nought
    to fear,
Hope, care, nor love beyond,—her heart
    beat *here*.

CCIII

And oh! that quickening of the heart, that
    beat!
  How much it costs us! yet each rising
    throb
Is in its cause as its effect so sweet,
  That Wisdom, ever on the watch to rob
Joy of its alchemy, and to repeat
  Fine truths; even Conscience, too, has
    a tough job
To make us understand each good old
    maxim,
So good—I wonder Castlereagh don't tax
    'em.

CCIV

And now 'twas done—on the lone shore
    were plighted
  Their hearts; the stars, their nuptial
    torches, shed
Beauty upon the beautiful they lighted:
  Ocean their witness, and the cave their
    bed,

By their own feelings hallow'd and united,
  Their priest was Solitude, and they were
    wed:
And they were happy, for to their young
    eyes
Each was an angel, and earth paradise.

CCV

Oh, Love! of whom great Cæsar was the
    suitor,
  Titus the master, Antony the slave,
Horace, Catullus, scholars, Ovid tutor,
  Sappho the sage blue-stocking, in whose
    grave
All those may leap who rather would be
    neuter—
  (Leucadia's rock still overlooks the
    wave)—
Oh, Love! thou art the very god of evil,
For, after all, we cannot call thee devil.

CCVI

Thou mak'st the chaste connubial state
    precarious,
  And jestest with the brows of mightiest
    men:
Cæsar and Pompey, Mahomet, Belisarius,
  Have much employ'd the muse of
    history's pen:
Their lives and fortunes were extremely
    various,
  Such worthies Time will never see again;
Yet to these four in three things the same
    luck holds,
They all were heroes, conquerors, and
    cuckolds.

CCVII

Thou mak'st philosophers; there's
    Epicurus
  And Aristippus, a material crew!
Who to immoral courses would allure us
  By theories quite practicable too;
If only from the devil they would insure
    us,
  How pleasant were the maxim (not
    quite new),
'Eat, drink, and love; what can the rest
    avail us?'
So said the royal sage Sardanapalus.

CCVIII

But Juan! had he quite forgotten Julia?
  And should he have forgotten her so
    soon?
I can't but say it seems to me most truly a
  Perplexing question; but, no doubt,
    the moon
Does these things for us, and whenever
    newly a
  Strong palpitation rises, 'tis her boon,
Else how the devil is it that fresh features
Have such a charm for us poor human
    creatures?

CCIX

I hate inconstancy—I loathe, detest,
  Abhor, condemn, abjure the mortal
      made
Of such quicksilver clay that in his breast
  No permanent foundations can be laid;
Love, constant love, has been my constant
    guest,
  And yet last night, being at a masquer-
    ade,
I saw the prettiest creature, fresh from
    Milan,
Which gave me some sensations like a
    villain.

CCX

But soon Philosophy came to my aid,
  And whisper'd, 'Think of every sacred
      tie!'
'I will, my dear Philosophy!' I said,
  'But then her teeth, and then, oh,
      Heaven! her eye!
I'll just inquire if she be wife or maid,
  Or neither—out of curiosity.'
'Stop!' cried Philosophy, with air so
    Grecian
(Though she was masqued then as a fair
    Venetian);

CCXI

'Stop!' so I stopp'd.—But to return: that
    which
  Men call inconstancy is nothing more
Than admiration due where nature's rich
  Profusion with young beauty covers
      o'er
Some favour'd object; and as in the niche
  A lovely statue we almost adore,
This sort of adoration of the real
Is but a heightening of the *beau idéal.*

CCXII

'Tis the perception of the beautiful,
  A fine extension of the faculties,
Platonic, universal, wonderful,
  Drawn from the stars, and filter'd
      through the skies,
Without which life would be extremely
    dull;
  In short, it is the use of our own eyes,
With one or two small senses added, just
To hint that flesh is form'd of fiery dust.

CCXIII

Yet 'tis a painful feeling, and unwilling,
  For surely if we always could perceive
In the same object graces quite as killing
  As when she rose upon us like an Eve,
'Twould save us many a heart-ache, many
    a shilling
  (For we must get them any how, or
      grieve),
Whereas, if one sole lady pleased for ever,
How pleasant for the heart, as well as liver!

CCXIV

The heart is like the sky, a part of heaven,
  But changes night and day, too, like the
      sky;
Now o'er it clouds and thunder must be
    driven,
  And darkness and destruction as on high:
But when it hath been scorch'd, and
    pierced, and riven,
  Its storms expire in water-drops; the eye
Pours forth at last the heart's blood turn'd
    to tears,
Which make the English climate of our
    years.

CCXV

The liver is the lazaret of bile,
  But very rarely executes its function,
For the first passion stays there such a while,
  That all the rest creep in and form a
      junction,
Like knots of vipers on a dunghill's soil,
  Rage, fear, hate, jealousy, revenge, com-
      punction,
So that all mischiefs spring up from this
    entrail,
Like earthquakes from the hidden fire
    call'd 'central.'

CCXVI

In the mean time, without proceeding more
  In this anatomy, I've finish'd now
Two hundred and odd stanzas as before,
  That being about the number I'll allow
Each canto of the twelve, or twenty-four;
  And, laying down my pen, I make my bow,
Leaving Don Juan and Haidée to plead
For them and theirs with all who deign to
    read.

CANTO THE THIRD

I

Hail, Muse! *et cætera.*—We left Juan
    sleeping,
  Pillow'd upon a fair and happy breast,
And watch'd by eyes that never yet knew
    weeping,
  And loved by a young heart, too deeply
      blest
To feel the poison through her spirit
    creeping,
  Or know who rested there, a foe to rest,
Had soil'd the current of her sinless years,
And turn'd her pure heart's purest blood
    to tears!

II

Oh, Love! what is it in this world of ours
  Which makes it fatal to be loved? Ah
      why
With cypress branches hast thou wreathed
    thy bowers,
  And made thy best interpreter a sigh?

As those who dote on odours pluck the flowers,
    And place them on their breast—but place to die—
Thus the frail beings we would fondly cherish
Are laid within our bosoms but to perish.

III

In her first passion woman loves her lover,
    In all the others all she loves is love,
Which grows a habit she can ne'er get over
    And fits her loosely—like an easy glove,
As you may find, whene'er you like to prove her:
    One man alone at first her heart can move;
She then prefers him in the plural number,
Not finding that the additions much encumber.

IV

I know not if the fault be men's or theirs;
    But one thing's pretty sure; a woman planted
(Unless at once she plunge for life in prayers)—
    After a decent time must be gallanted;
Although, no doubt, her first of love affairs
    Is that to which her heart is wholly granted;
Yet there are some, they say, who have had *none*,
But those who have ne'er end with only *one*.

V

'Tis melancholy, and a fearful sign
    Of human frailty, folly, also crime,
That love and marriage rarely can combine,
    Although they both are born in the same clime;
Marriage from love, like vinegar from wine—
    A sad, sour, sober beverage—by time
Is sharpen'd from its high celestial flavour,
Down to a very homely household savour.

VI

There's something of antipathy, as 'twere,
    Between their present and their future state;
A kind of flattery that's hardly fair
    Is used until the truth arrives too late—
Yet what can people do, except despair?
    The same things change their names at such a rate;
For instance—passion in a lover's glorious,
But in a husband is pronounced uxorious.

VII

Men grow ashamed of being so very fond;
    They sometimes also get a little tired

(But that, of course, is rare), and then despond:
    The same things cannot always be admired,
Yet 'tis 'so nominated in the bond,'
    That both are tied till one shall have expired.
Sad thought! to lose the spouse that was adorning
Our days, and put one's servants into mourning.

VIII

There's doubtless something in domestic doings
    Which forms, in fact, true love's antithesis;
Romances paint at full length people's wooings,
    But only give a bust of marriages;
For no one cares for matrimonial cooings,
    There's nothing wrong in a connubial kiss:
Think you, if Laura had been Petrarch's wife,
He would have written sonnets all his life?

IX

All tragedies are finish'd by a death,
    All comedies are ended by a marriage;
The future states of both are left to faith,
    For authors fear description might disparage
The worlds to come of both, or fall beneath,
    And then both worlds would punish their miscarriage;
So leaving each their priest and prayer-book ready,
They say no more of Death or of the Lady.

X

The only two that in my recollection
    Have sung of heaven and hell, or marriage, are
Dante and Milton, and of both the affection
    Was hapless in their nuptials, for some bar
Of fault or temper ruin'd the connexion
    (Such things, in fact, it don't ask much to mar);
But Dante's Beatrice and Milton's Eve
Were not drawn from their spouses, you conceive.

XI

Some persons say that Dante meant theology
    By Beatrice, and not a mistress—I,
Although my opinion may require apology,
    Deem this a commentator's phantasy,

Unless indeed it was from his own know-
  ledge he
  Decided thus, and show'd good reason
      why;
I think that Dante's more abstruse ecsta-
  tics
Meant to personify the mathematics.

XII

Haidée and Juan were not married, but
  The fault was theirs, not mine: it is not
      fair,
Chaste reader, then, in any way to put
  The blame on me, unless you wish they
      were;
Then if you'd have them wedded, please
      to shut
  The book which treats of this erroneous
      pair,
Before the consequences grow too awful;
'Tis dangerous to read of loves unlawful.

XIII

Yet they were happy,—happy in the illicit
  Indulgence of their innocent desires;
But more imprudent grown with every
      visit,
  Haidée forgot the island was her sire's:
When we have what we like, 'tis hard to
      miss it,
  At least in the beginning, ere one tires;
Thus she came often, not a moment losing,
Whilst her piratical papa was cruising.

XIV

Let not his mode of raising cash seem
      strange,
  Although he fleeced the flags of every
      nation,
For into a prime minister but change
  His title, and 'tis nothing but taxation;
But he, more modest, took an humbler
      range
  Of life, and in an honester vocation
Pursued o'er the high seas his watery
      journey,
And merely practised as a sea-attorney.

XV

The good old gentleman had been detain'd
  By winds and waves, and some impor-
      tant captures;
And, in the hope of more, at sea remain'd,
  Although a squall or two had damp'd
      his raptures,
By swamping one of the prizes; he had
      chain'd
  His prisoners, dividing them like chap-
      ters
In number'd lots; they all had cuffs and
      collars,
And averaged each from ten to a hundred
      dollars.

XVI

Some he disposed of off Cape Matapan,
  Among his friends the Mainots; some
      he sold
To his Tunis correspondents, save one man
  Toss'd overboard unsaleable (being
      old);
The rest—save here and there some richer
      one,
  Reserved for future ransom—in the hold,
Were link'd alike, as for the common
      people he
Had a large order from the Dey of Tripoli.

XVII

The merchandise was served in the same
      way,
  Pieced out for different marts in the
      Levant,
Except some certain portions of the prey,
  Light classic articles of female want,
French stuffs, lace, tweezers, toothpicks,
      teapot, tray,
  Guitars and castanets from Alicant,
All which selected from the spoil he
      gathers,
Robb'd for his daughter by the best of
      fathers.

XVIII

A monkey, a Dutch mastiff, a mackaw,
  Two parrots, with a Persian cat and
      kittens,
He chose from several animals he saw—
  A terrier, too, which once had been a
      Briton's,
Who dying on the coast of Ithaca,
  The peasants gave the poor dumb thing
      a pittance.
These to secure in this strong blowing
      weather,
He caged in one huge hamper all together.

XIX

Then having settled his marine affairs,
  Despatching single cruisers here and
      there,
His vessel having need of some repairs,
  He shaped his course to where his
      daughter fair
Continued still her hospitable cares;
  But that part of the coast being shoal
      and bare,
And rough with reefs which ran out many
      a mile,
His port lay on the other side o' the isle.

XX

And there he went ashore without delay,
  Having no custom-house nor quaran-
      tine
To ask him awkward questions on the way,
  About the time and place where he had
      been:

He left his ship to be hove down next day,
  With orders to the people to careen;
So that all hands were busy beyond
    measure,
In getting out goods, ballast, guns, and
    treasure.

XXI

Arriving at the summit of a hill
  Which overlook'd the white walls of his
    home,
He stopp'd.—What singular emotions fill
  Their bosoms who have been induced to
    roam!
With fluttering doubts if all be well or ill—
  With love for many, and with fears for
    some;
All feelings which o'erleap the years long
    lost,
And bring our hearts back to their start-
    ing-post.

XXII

The approach of home to husbands and to
    sires,
  After long travelling by land or water,
Most naturally some small doubt in-
    spires—
  A female family's a serious matter;
(None trusts the sex more, or so much
    admires—
  But they hate flattery, so I never flatter;)
Wives in their husbands' absences grow
    subtler,
And daughters sometimes run off with the
    butler.

XXIII

An honest gentleman at his return
  May not have the good fortune of
    Ulysses;
Not all lone matrons for their husbands
    mourn,
  Or show the same dislike to suitors'
    kisses;
The odds are that he finds a handsome urn
  To his memory—and two or three
    young misses
Born to some friend, who holds his wife
    and riches;—
And that *his* Argus bites him by—the
    breeches.

XXIV

If single, probably his plighted fair
  Has in his absence wedded some rich
    miser;
But all the better, for the happy pair
  May quarrel, and the lady growing wiser,
He may resume his amatory care
  As cavalier servente, or despise her;
And that his sorrow may not be a dumb
    one,
Write odes on the Inconstancy of Woman.

XXV

And oh! ye gentlemen who have already
  Some chaste *liaison* of the kind—I
    mean
An honest friendship with a married
    lady—
  The only thing of this sort ever seen
To last—of all connexions the most
    steady,
  And the true Hymen, (the first's but a
    screen)—
Yet for all that keep not too long away;
I've known the absent wrong'd four times
    a day.

XXVI

Lambro, our sea-solicitor, who had
  Much less experience of dry land than
    ocean,
On seeing his own chimney-smoke, felt
    glad;
  But not knowing metaphysics, had no
    notion
Of the true reason of his not being sad,
  Or that of any other strong emotion;
He loved his child, and would have wept
    the loss of her,
But knew the cause no more than a philo-
    sopher.

XXVII

He saw his white walls shining in the sun,
  His garden trees all shadowy and green;
He heard his rivulet's light bubbling run,
  The distant dog-bark; and perceived
    between
The umbrage of the wood so cool and dun,
  The moving figures, and the sparkling
    sheen
Of arms (in the East all arm)—and various
    dyes
Of colour'd garbs, as bright as butterflies.

XXVIII

And as the spot where they appear he
    nears,
  Surprised at these unwonted signs of
    idling,
He hears—alas! no music of the spheres,
  But an unhallow'd, earthly sound of
    fiddling!
A melody which made him doubt his ears,
  The cause being past his guessing or un-
    riddling;
A pipe, too, and a drum, and shortly after,
A most unoriental roar of laughter.

XXIX

And still more nearly to the place ad-
    vancing,
  Descending rather quickly the declivity,
Through the waved branches, o'er the
    greensward glancing,
  'Midst other indications of festivity,

Seeing a troop of his domestics dancing
　　Like dervises, who turn as on a pivot, he
Perceived it was the Pyrrhic dance so martial,
To which the Levantines are very partial.

XXX

And further on a group of Grecian girls,
　　The first and tallest her white kerchief waving,
Were strung together like a row of pearls,
　　Link'd hand in hand, and dancing: each too having
Down her white neck long floating auburn curls—
　　(The least of which would set ten poets raving);
Their leader sang—and bounded to her song,
With choral step and voice, the virgin throng.

XXXI

And here, assembled cross-legg'd round their trays,
　　Small social parties just begun to dine;
Pilaus and meats of all sorts met the gaze,
　　And flasks of Samian and of Chian wine,
And sherbet cooling in the porous vase;
　　Above them their dessert grew on its vine,
The orange and pomegranate nodding o'er
Dropp'd in their laps, scarce pluck'd, their mellow store.

XXXII

A band of children, round a snow-white ram,
　　There wreathe his venerable horns with flowers;
While peaceful as if still an unwean'd lamb,
　　The patriarch of the flock all gently cowers
His sober head, majestically tame,
　　Or eats from out the palm, or playful lowers
His brow, as if in act to butt, and then
Yielding to their small hands, draws back again.

XXXIII

Their classical profiles, and glittering dresses,
　　Their large black eyes, and soft seraphic cheeks,
Crimson as cleft pomegranates, their long tresses,
　　The gesture which enchants, the eye that speaks,
The innocence which happy childhood blesses,
　　Made quite a picture of these little Greeks;

So that the philosophical beholder
Sigh'd for their sakes—that they should e'er grow older.

XXXIV

Afar, a dwarf buffoon stood telling tales
　　To a sedate grey circle of old smokers,
Of secret treasures found in hidden vales,
　　Of wonderful replies from Arab jokers,
Of charms to make good gold and cure bad ails,
　　Of rocks bewitch'd that open to the knockers,
Of magic ladies who, by one sole act,
Transform'd their lords to beasts (but that's a fact).

XXXV

Here was no lack of innocent diversion
　　For the imagination or the senses,
Song, dance, wine, music, stories from the Persian,
　　All pretty pastimes in which no offence is;
But Lambro saw all these things with aversion,
　　Perceiving in his absence such expenses,
Dreading that climax of all human ills
The inflammation of his weekly bills.

XXXVI

Ah! what is man? what perils still environ
　　The happiest mortals even after dinner!
A day of gold from out an age of iron
　　Is all that life allows the luckiest sinner;
Pleasure (whene'er she sings, at least)'s a siren,
　　That lures, to flay alive, the young beginner;
Lambro's reception at his people's banquet
Was such as fire accords to a wet blanket.

XXXVII

He—being a man who seldom used a word
　　Too much, and wishing gladly to surprise
(In general he surprised men with the sword)
　　His daughter—had not sent before to advise
Of his arrival, so that no one stirr'd;
　　And long he paused to reässure his eyes,
In fact much more astonish'd than delighted,
To find so much good company invited.

XXXVIII

He did not know (alas! how men will lie!)
　　That a report (especially the Greeks)
Avouch'd his death (such people never die),
　　And put his house in mourning several weeks,—

But now their eyes and also lips were dry;
  The bloom, too, had return'd to
    Haidée's cheeks.
Her tears, too, being return'd into their
    fount,
She now kept house upon her own ac-
    count.

XXXIX

Hence all this rice, meat, dancing, wine,
    and fiddling,
  Which turn'd the isle into a place of
    pleasure;
The servants all were getting drunk or
    idling,
  A life which made them happy beyond
    measure.
Her father's hospitality seem'd middling,
  Compared with what Haidée did with
    his treasure;
'Twas wonderful how things went on im-
    proving,
While she had not one hour to spare from
    loving.

XL

Perhaps you think, in stumbling on this
    feast,
  He flew into a passion, and in fact
There was no mighty reason to be pleased;
  Perhaps you prophesy some sudden act,
The whip, the rack, or dungeon at the
    least,
  To teach his people to be more exact,
And that, proceeding at a very high rate,
He show'd the royal *penchants* of a pirate.

XLI

You're wrong.—He was the mildest man-
    ner'd man
  That ever scuttled ship or cut a throat,
With such true breeding of a gentleman,
  You never could divine his real thought;
No courtier could, and scarcely woman can
  Gird more deceit within a petticoat;
Pity he loved adventurous life's variety,
He was so great a loss to good society.

XLII

Advancing to the nearest dinner tray,
  Tapping the shoulder of the nighest
    guest,
With a peculiar smile, which, by the way,
  Boded no good, whatever it express'd,
He asked the meaning of this holiday;
  The vinous Greek to whom he had ad-
    dress'd
His question, much too merry to divine
The questioner, fill'd up a glass of wine,

XLIII

And without turning his facetious head,
  Over his shoulder, with a Bacchant air,
Presented the o'erflowing cup, and said,
  'Talking's dry work, I have no time to
    spare.'

A second hiccup'd, 'Our old master's
    dead,
  You'd better ask our mistress who's his
    heir.'
'Our mistress!' quoth a third: 'Our mis-
    tress!—pooh—
You mean our master—not the old, but
    new.'

XLIV

These rascals, being new comers, knew
    not whom
  They thus address'd—and Lambro's
    visage fell—
And o'er his eye a momentary gloom
  Pass'd, but he strove quite courteously
    to quell
The expression, and endeavouring to re-
    sume
  His smile, requested one of them to tell
The name and quality of his new patron,
Who seem'd to have turn'd Haidée into
    a matron.

XLV

'I know not,' quoth the fellow, 'who or
    what
  He is, nor whence he came—and little
    care;
But this I know, that this roast capon's fat,
  And that good wine ne'er wash'd down
    better fare;
And if you are not satisfied with that,
  Direct your questions to my neighbour
    there;
He'll answer all for better or for worse,
For none likes more to hear himself con-
    verse.'

XLVI

I said that Lambro was a man of patience,
  And certainly he show'd the best of
    breeding,
Which scarce even France, the paragon of
    nations,
  E'er saw her most polite of sons ex-
    ceeding;
He bore these sneers against his near rela-
    tions,
  His own anxiety, his heart, too, bleed-
    ing,
The insults, too, of every servile glutton,
Who all the time was eating up his mutton.

XLVII

Now in a person used to much com-
    mand—
  To bid men come, and go, and come
    again—
To see his orders done, too, out of hand—
  Whether the word was death, or but the
    chain—

It may seem strange to find his manners
bland;
  Yet such things are, which I cannot explain,
Though doubtless he who can command
himself
Is good to govern—almost as a Guelf.

XLVIII

Not that he was not sometimes rash or so,
  But never in his real and serious mood;
Then calm, concentrated, and still, and
slow,
  He lay coil'd like the boa in the wood;
With him it never was a word and blow,
  His angry word once o'er, he shed no
blood,
But in his silence there was much to rue,
And his *one* blow left little work for *two*.

XLIX

He ask'd no further questions, and pro-
ceeded
  On to the house, but by a private way,
So that the few who met him hardly
heeded,
  So little they expected him that day;
If love paternal in his bosom pleaded
  For Haidée's sake, is more than I can
say,
But certainly to one deem'd dead return-
ing,
This revel seem'd a curious mode of
mourning.

L

If all the dead could now return to life,
  (Which God forbid!) or some, or a
great many,
For instance, if a husband or his wife
  (Nuptial examples are as good as any),
No doubt, whate'er might be their former
strife,
  The present weather would be much
more rainy—
Tears shed into the grave of the connexion
Would share most probably its resur-
rection.

LI

He enter'd in the house no more his home,
  A thing to human feelings the most
trying,
And harder for the heart to overcome,
  Perhaps, than even the mental pangs of
dying;
To find our hearthstone turn'd into a
tomb,
  And round its once warm precincts
palely lying
The ashes of our hopes, is a deep grief,
Beyond a single gentleman's belief.

LII

He enter'd in the house—his home no
more,
  For without hearts there is no home;—
and felt
The solitude of passing his own door
  Without a welcome: *there* he long had
dwelt,
There his few peaceful days Time had
swept o'er,
  There his worn bosom and keen eye
would melt
Over the innocence of that sweet child,
His only shrine of feelings undefiled.

LIII

He was a man of a strange temperament,
  Of mild demeanour though of savage
mood,
Moderate in all his habits, and content
  With temperance in pleasure, as in food,
Quick to perceive, and strong to bear, and
meant
  For something better, if not wholly
good;
His country's wrongs and his despair to
save her
Had stung him from a slave to an enslaver.

LIV

The love of power, and rapid gain of gold,
  The hardness by long habitude pro-
duced,
The dangerous life in which he had grown
old,
  The mercy he had granted oft abused,
The sights he was accustom'd to behold,
  The wild seas, and wild men with whom
he cruised,
Had cost his enemies a long repentance,
And made him a good friend, but bad
acquaintance.

LV

But something of the spirit of old Greece
  Flash'd o'er his soul a few heroic rays,
Such as lit onward to the Golden Fleece
  His predecessors in the Colchian days;
'Tis true he had no ardent love for peace—
  Alas! his country show'd no path to
praise:
Hate to the world and war with every
nation
He waged, in vengeance of her degrada-
tion.

LVI

Still o'er his mind the influence of the
clime
  Shed its Ionian elegance, which show'd
Its power unconsciously full many a
time,—
  A taste seen in the choice of his abode,

A love of music and of scenes sublime,
  A pleasure in the gentle stream that
      flow'd
Past him in crystal, and a joy in flowers,
Bedew'd his spirit in his calmer hours.

LVII

But whatsoe'er he had of love reposed
  On that beloved daughter; she had been
The only thing which kept his heart un-
    closed
  Amidst the savage deeds he had done and
    seen,
A lonely pure affection unopposed:
  There wanted but the loss of this to wean
His feelings from all milk of human kind-
    ness,
And turn him like the Cyclops mad with
    blindness.

LVIII

The cubless tigress in her jungle raging
  Is dreadful to the shepherd and the
    flock;
The ocean when its yeasty war is waging
  Is awful to the vessel near the rock;
But violent things will sooner bear as-
    suaging,
  Their fury being spent by its own shock,
Than the stern, single, deep, and wordless ire
Of a strong human heart, and in a sire.

LIX

It is a hard although a common case
  To find our children running restive—
    they
In whom our brightest days we would re-
    trace,
  Our little selves re-formed in finer clay,
Just as old age is creeping on apace,
  And clouds come o'er the sunset of our
    day,
They kindly leave us, though not quite
    alone,
But in good company—the gout or stone.

LX

Yet a fine family is a fine thing
  (Provided they don't come in after
    dinner);
'Tis beautiful to see a matron bring
  Her children up (if nursing them don't
    thin her);
Like cherubs round an altar-piece they
    cling
  To the fire-side (a sight to touch a sinner).
A lady with her daughters or her nieces
Shine like a guinea and seven-shilling
    pieces.

LXI

Old Lambro pass'd unseen a private gate,
  And stood within his hall at eventide;
Meantime the lady and her lover sate
  At wassail in their beauty and their pride:

An ivory inlaid table spread with state
  Before them, and fair slaves on every
    side;
Gems, gold, and silver, form'd the service
    mostly,
Mother of pearl and coral the less costly.

LXII

The dinner made about a hundred dishes;
  Lamb and pistachio nuts—in short, all
    meats,
And saffron soups, and sweetbreads; and
    the fishes
  Were of the finest that e'er flounced in
    nets,
Drest to a Sybarite's most pamper'd wishes;
  The beverage was various sherbets
Of raisin, orange, and pomegranate juice,
Squeezed through the rind, which makes
    it best for use.

LXIII

These were ranged round, each in its
    crystal ewer,
  And fruits, and date-bread loaves
    closed the repast,
And Mocha's berry, from Arabia pure,
  In small fine China cups, came in at last;
Gold cups of filigree made to secure
  The hand from burning underneath
    them placed;
Cloves, cinnamon, and saffron too were
    boil'd
Up with the coffee, which (I think) they
    spoil'd.

LXIV

The hangings of the room were tapestry,
    made
  Of velvet panels, each of different hue,
And thick with damask flowers of silk
    inlaid;
  And round them ran a yellow border
    too;
The upper border, richly wrought, dis-
    play'd,
  Embroider'd delicately o'er with blue,
Soft Persian sentences, in lilac letters,
From poets, or the moralists their betters.

LXV

These Oriental writings on the wall,
  Quite common in those countries, are a
    kind
Of monitors adapted to recall,
  Like skulls at Memphian banquets, to
    the mind
The words which shook Belshazzar in his
    hall,
  And took his kingdom from him: You
    will find,
Though sages may pour out their wisdom's
    treasure,
There is no sterner moralist than Pleasure.

LXVI

A beauty at the season's close grown hectic,
  A genius who has drunk himself to death,
A rake turn'd methodistic, or Eclectic—
  (For that's the name they like to pray
    beneath)—
But most, an alderman struck apoplectic,
  Are things that really take away the
    breath,—
And show that late hours, wine, and love
    are able
To do not much less damage than the table.

LXVII

Haidée and Juan carpeted their feet
  On crimson satin, border'd with pale
    blue;
Their sofa occupied three parts complete
  Of the apartment—and appear'd quite
    new;
The velvet cushions (for a throne more
    meet)
  Were scarlet, from whose glowing centre
    grew
A sun emboss'd in gold, whose rays of tissue,
Meridian-like, were seen all light to issue.

LXVIII

Crystal and marble, plate and porcelain,
  Had done their work of splendour;
    Indian mats
And Persian carpets, which the heart bled
    to stain,
  Over the floors were spread; gazelles
    and cats,
And dwarfs and blacks, and such like
    things that gain
  Their bread as ministers and favourites
    —(that's
To say, by degradation)—mingled there
As plentiful as in a court or fair.

LXIX

There was no want of lofty mirrors, and
  The tables, most of ebony inlaid
With mother of pearl or ivory, stood at
    hand,
  Or were of tortoise-shell or rare woods
    made,
Fretted with gold or silver:—by command,
  The greater part of these were ready
    spread
With viands and sherbets in ice—and
    wine—
Kept for all comers at all hours to dine.

LXX

Of all the dresses I select Haidée's:
  She wore two jelicks—one was of pale
    yellow;
Of azure, pink, and white was her
    chemise—
  'Neath which her breast heaved like a
    little billow,

With buttons form'd of pearls as large as
    peas,
  All gold and crimson shone her jelick's
    fellow,
And the striped white gauze baracan that
    bound her,
Like fleecy clouds about the moon, flow'd
    round her.

LXXI

One large gold bracelet clasp'd each lovely
    arm,
  Lockless—so pliable from the pure gold
That the hand stretch'd and shut it without
    harm,
  The limb which it adorn'd its only
    mould;
So beautiful—its very shape would charm,
  And clinging as if loath to lose its hold,
The purest ore enclosed the whitest skin
That e'er by precious metal was held in.

LXXII

Around, as princess of her father's land,
  A like gold bar above her instep roll'd
Announced her rank; twelve rings were on
    her hand;
  Her hair was starr'd with gems; her
    veil's fine fold
Below her breast was fasten'd with a band
  Of lavish pearls, whose worth could
    scarce be told;
Her orange silk full Turkish trousers
    furl'd
About the prettiest ankle in the world.

LXXIII

Her hair's long auburn waves down to her
    heel
  Flow'd like an Alpine torrent which
    the sun
Dyes with his morning light,—and would
    conceal
  Her person if allow'd at large to run,
And still they seem resentfully to feel
  The silken fillet's curb, and sought to
    shun
Their bonds whene'er some Zephyr caught
    began
To offer his young pinion as her fan.

LXXIV

Round her she made an atmosphere of
    life,
  The very air seem'd lighter from her
    eyes,
They were so soft and beautiful, and rife
  With all we can imagine of the skies,
And pure as Psyche ere she grew a wife—
  Too pure even for the purest human
    ties;
Her overpowering presence made you feel
It would not be idolatry to kneel.

LXXV

Her eyelashes, though dark as night,
were tinged
(It is the country's custom), but in vain;
For those large black eyes were so blackly
fringed,
The glossy rebels mock'd the jetty stain,
And in their native beauty stood avenged:
Her nails were touch'd with henna; but
again
The power of art was turn'd to nothing,
for
They could not look more rosy than before.

LXXVI

The henna should be deeply dyed to make
The skin relieved appear more fairly
fair;
She had no need of this, day ne'er will
break
On mountain-tops more heavenly white
than her:
The eye might doubt if it were well awake,
She was so like a vision; I might err,
But Shakspeare also says, 'tis very silly
'To gild refined gold, or paint the lily.'

LXXVII

Juan had on a shawl of black and gold,
But a white baracan, and so transparent
The sparkling gems beneath you might
behold,
Like small stars through the milky way
apparent;
His turban furl'd in many a graceful fold,
An emerald aigrette with Haidée's hair
in't
Surmounted, as its clasp, a glowing
crescent,
Whose rays shone ever trembling, but in-
cessant.

LXXVIII

And now they were diverted by their suite,
Dwarfs, dancing-girls, black eunuchs,
and a poet,
Which made their new establishment com-
plete;
The last was of great fame, and liked to
show it;
His verses rarely wanted their due feet—
And for his theme—he seldom sung
below it,
He being paid to satirise or flatter,
As the psalm says, 'inditing a good
matter.'

LXXIX

He praised the present, and abused the
past,
Reversing the good custom of old days,
An Eastern anti-jacobin at last
He turn'd, preferring pudding to *no*
praise—

For some few years his lot had been o'er-
cast
By his seeming independent in his lays,
But now he sung the Sultan and the Pacha
With truth like Southey, and with verse
like Crashaw.

LXXX

He was a man who had seen many changes,
And always changed as true as any
needle;
His polar star being one which rather
ranges,
And not the fix'd—he knew the way to
wheedle:
So vile he 'scaped the doom which oft
avenges;
And being fluent (save indeed when
fee'd ill),
He lied with such a fervour of intention—
There was no doubt he earn'd his laureate
pension.

LXXXI

But he had genius,—when a turncoat has it,
The 'Vates irritabilis' takes care
That without notice few full moons shall
pass it;
Even good men like to make the public
stare:—
But to my subject—let me see—what was
it?—
Oh!—the third canto—and the pretty
pair—
Their loves, and feasts, and house, and
dress, and mode
Of living in their insular abode.

LXXXII

Their poet, a sad trimmer, but no less
In company a very pleasant fellow,
Had been the favourite of full many a mess
Of men, and made them speeches when
half mellow;
And though his meaning they could rarely
guess,
Yet still they deign'd to hiccup or to
bellow
The glorious meed of popular applause,
Of which the first ne'er knows the second
cause.

LXXXIII

But now being lifted into high society,
And having pick'd up several odds and
ends
Of free thoughts in his travels, for variety,
He deem'd, being in a lone isle, among
friends,
That without any danger of a riot, he
Might for long lying make himself
amends;
And singing as he sung in his warm youth,
Agree to a short armistice with truth.

LXXXIV

He had travell'd 'mongst the Arabs,
        Turks, and Franks,
    And knew the self-loves of the different
        nations;
And having lived with people of all ranks,
    Had something ready upon most occa-
        sions—
Which got him a few presents and some
        thanks.
    He varied with some skill his adulations;
To 'do at Rome as Romans do,' a piece
Of conduct was which he observed in
        Greece.

LXXXV

Thus, usually, when he was asked to sing,
    He gave the different nations something
        national;
'Twas all the same to him—'God save the
        king,'
Or 'Ça ira,' according to the fashion all:
His muse made increment of anything,
    From the high lyric down to the low
        rational:
If Pindar sang horse-races, what should
        hinder
Himself from being as pliable as Pindar?

LXXXVI

In France, for instance, he would write a
        chanson;
    In England a six-canto quarto tale;
In Spain he'd make a ballad or romance on
    The last war—much the same in Portu-
        gal;
In Germany, the Pegasus he'd prance on
    Would be old Goethe's—(see what says
        De Staël);
In Italy he'd ape the 'Trecentisti';
In Greece, he'd sing some sort of hymn
        like this t' ye:

1

The isles of Greece, the isles of Greece!
    Where burning Sappho loved and
        sung,
Where grew the arts of war and peace,
    Where Delos rose, and Phœbus
        sprung!
Eternal summer gilds them yet,
But all, except their sun, is set.

2

The Scian and the Teian muse,
    The hero's harp, the lover's lute,
Have found the fame your shores refuse:
    Their place of birth alone is mute
To sounds which echo further west
Than your sires' 'Islands of the Blest.'

3

The mountains look on Marathon—
    And Marathon looks on the sea;
And musing there an hour alone,
    I dream'd that Greece might still be
        free;
For standing on the Persians' grave,
I could not deem myself a slave.

4

A king sate on the rocky brow
    Which looks o'er sea-born Salamis;
And ships, by thousands, lay below,
    And men in nations;—all were his!
He counted them at break of day—
And when the sun set where were they?

5

And where are they? and where art thou,
    My country? On thy voiceless shore
The heroic lay is tuneless now—
    The heroic bosom beats no more!
And must thy lyre, so long divine,
Degenerate into hands like mine?

6

'Tis something, in the dearth of fame,
    Though link'd among a fetter'd race,
To feel at least a patriot's shame,
    Even as I sing, suffuse my face;
For what is left the poet here?
For Greeks a blush—for Greece a tear.

7

Must we but weep o'er days more blest?
    Must we but blush?—Our fathers bled.
Earth! render back from out thy breast
    A remnant of our Spartan dead!
Of the three hundred grant but three,
To make a new Thermopylæ!

8

What, silent still? and silent all?
    Ah! no;—the voices of the dead
Sound like a distant torrent's fall,
    And answer, 'Let one living head,
But one arise,—we come, we come!'
'Tis but the living who are dumb.

9

In vain—in vain: strike other chords;
    Fill high the cup with Samian wine!
Leave battles to the Turkish hordes,
    And shed the blood of Scio's vine!
Hark! rising to the ignoble call—
How answers each bold Bacchanal!

10

You have the Pyrrhic dance as yet;
    Where is the Pyrrhic phalanx gone?
Of two such lessons, why forget
    The nobler and the manlier one?
You have the letters Cadmus gave—
Think ye he meant them for a slave?

11

Fill high the bowl with Samian wine!
    We will not think of themes like these!
It made Anacreon's song divine:
    He served—but served Polycrates—
A tyrant; but our masters then
Were still, at least, our countrymen.

12

The tyrant of the Chersonese
    Was freedom's best and bravest
        friend;
That tyrant was Miltiades!
    Oh! that the present hour would lend
Another despot of the kind!
Such chains as his were sure to bind.

13

Fill high the bowl with Samian wine:
    On Suli's rock, and Parga's shore,
Exists the remnant of a line
    Such as the Doric mothers bore;
And there, perhaps, some seed is sown,
The Heracleidan blood might own.

14

Trust not for freedom to the Franks—
    They have a king who buys and sells;
In native swords, and native ranks,
    The only hope of courage dwells:
But Turkish force, and Latin fraud,
Would break your shield, however
    broad.

15

Fill high the bowl with Samian wine!
    Our virgins dance beneath the shade—
I see their glorious black eyes shine;
    But gazing on each glowing maid,
My own the burning tear-drop laves,
To think such breasts must suckle slaves.

16

Place me on Sunium's marbled steep,
    Where nothing, save the waves and I,
May hear our mutual murmurs sweep;
    There, swan-like, let me sing and die:
A land of slaves shall ne'er be mine—
Dash down yon cup of Samian wine!

LXXXVII

Thus sung, or would, or could, or should
    have sung,
    The modern Greek, in tolerable verse;
If not like Orpheus quite, when Greece
    was young,
    Yet in these times he might have done
        much worse:
His strain display'd some feeling—right or
    wrong;
And feeling, in a poet, is the source
Of others' feeling; but they are such liars,
And take all colours—like the hands of
    dyers.

LXXXVIII

But words are things, and a small drop of
    ink,
    Falling like dew, upon a thought, pro-
        duces
That which makes thousands, perhaps
    millions, think;
    'Tis strange, the shortest letter which
    man uses
Instead of speech, may form a lasting link
    Of ages; to what straits old Time re-
        duces
Frail man, when paper—even a rag like
    this,
Survives himself, his tomb, and all that's
    his!

LXXXIX

And when his bones are dust, his grave a
    blank,
    His station, generation, even his nation,
Become a thing, or nothing, save to rank
    In chronological commemoration,
Some dull MS. oblivion long has sank,
    Or graven stone found in a barrack's
        station
In digging the foundation of a closet,
May turn his name up, as a rare deposit.

XC

And glory long has made the sages smile;
    'Tis something, nothing, words, illusion,
        wind—
Depending more upon the historian's style
    Than on the name a person leaves be-
        hind:
Troy owes to Homer what whist owes to
    Hoyle:
    The present century was growing blind
To the great Marlborough's skill in giving
    knocks,
Until his late Life by Archdeacon Coxe.

XCI

Milton's the prince of poets—so we say;
    A little heavy, but no less divine:
An independent being in his day—
    Learn'd, pious, temperate in love and
    wine;
But his life falling into Johnson's way,
    We're told this great high priest of all
    the Nine
Was whipt at college—a harsh sire—odd
    spouse,
For the first Mrs. Milton left his house.

XCII

All these are, *certes*, entertaining facts,
    Like Shakspeare's stealing deer, Lord
    Bacon's bribes;
Like Titus' youth, and Cæsar's earliest
    acts;
    Like Burns (whom Doctor Currie well
    describes);

Like Cromwell's pranks;—but although
    truth exacts
      These amiable descriptions from the
      scribes,
As most essential to their hero's story,
They do not much contribute to his glory.

XCIII

All are not moralists, like Southey, when
    He prated to the world of 'Pantiso-
    cracy';
Or Wordsworth unexcised, unhired, who
    then
      Season'd his pedlar poems with de-
      mocracy;
Or Coleridge, long before his flighty pen
    Let to the Morning Post its aristocracy;
When he and Southey, following the same
    path,
Espoused two partners (milliners of Bath).

XCIV

Such names at present cut a convict figure,
    The very Botany Bay in moral geo-
    graphy;
Their loyal treason, renegado rigour,
    Are good manure for their more bare
    biography,
Wordsworth's last quarto, by the way, is
    bigger
    Than any since the birthday of typo-
    graphy;
A drowsy frowzy poem, call'd the 'Excur-
    sion,'
Writ in a manner which is my aversion.

XCV

He there builds up a formidable dyke
    Between his own and others' intellect:
But Wordsworth's poem, and his fol-
    lowers, like
Joanna Southcote's Shiloh, and her sect,
    Are things which, in this century don't
    strike
      The public mind,—so few are the elect;
And the new births of both their stale
    virginities
Have proved but dropsies, taken for divi-
    nities.

XCVI

But let me to my story: I must own,
    If I have any fault, it is digression,
Leaving my people to proceed alone,
    While I soliloquize beyond expression:
But these are my addresses from the throne,
    Which put off business to the ensuing
    session:
Forgetting each omission is a loss to
The world, not quite so great as Ariosto.

XCVII

I know that what our neighbours call
    'longueurs,'
    (We've not so good a *word*, but have the
    thing,

In that complete perfection which insures
    An epic from Bob Southey every
    Spring—)
Form not the true temptation which allures
    The reader; but 'twould not be hard to
    bring
Some fine examples of the *epopée*,
To prove its grand ingredient is *ennui*.

XCVIII

We learn from Horace, 'Homer some-
    times sleeps;'
    We feel without him, Wordsworth
    sometimes wakes,—
To show with what complacency he creeps,
    With his dear '*Waggoners*,' around his
    lakes.
He wishes for 'a boat' to sail the deeps—
    Of ocean?—No, of air; and then he
    makes
Another outcry for 'a little boat,'
And drivels seas to set it well afloat.

XCIX

If he must fain sweep o'er the ethereal
    plain,
    And Pegasus runs restive in his 'Waggon',
    Could he not beg the loan of Charles's
    Wain?
Or pray Medea for a single dragon?
    Or if, too classic for his vulgar brain,
    He fear'd his neck to venture such a nag
    on,
And he must needs mount nearer to the
    moon,
Could not the blockhead ask for a balloon?

C

'Pedlars,' and 'Boats,' and 'Waggons!'
    Oh! ye shades
    Of Pope and Dryden, are we come to
    this?
That trash of such sort not alone evades
    Contempt, but from the bathos' vast abyss
Floats scumlike uppermost, and these
    Jack Cades
    Of sense and song above your graves
    may hiss—
The 'little boatman' and his 'Peter Bell'
Can sneer at him who drew 'Achitophel'!

CI

T' our tale.—The feast was over, the slaves
    gone,
    The dwarfs and dancing girls had all
    retired;
The Arab lore and poet's song were done,
    And every sound of revelry expired;
The lady and her lover, left alone,
    The rosy flood of twilight's sky ad-
    mired;—
Ave Maria! o'er the earth and sea,
That heavenliest hour of Heaven is worth-
    iest thee!

CII

Ave Maria! blessed be the hour!
　The time, the clime, the spot, where I so
　　oft
Have felt that moment in its fullest power
Sink o'er the earth so beautiful and soft,
While swung the deep bell in the distant
　　tower,
　Or the faint dying day-hymn stole aloft,
And not a breath crept through the rosy
　　air,
And yet the forest leaves seem'd stirr'd
　with prayer.

CIII

Ave Maria! 'tis the hour of prayer!
　Ave Maria! 'tis the hour of love!
Ave Maria! may our spirits dare
　Look up to thine and to thy Son's above!
Ave Maria! oh that face so fair!
　Those downcast eyes beneath the Al-
　　mighty dove—
What though 'tis but a pictured image?
　　—strike,
That painting is no idol,—'tis too like.

CIV

Some kinder casuists are pleased to say,
　In nameless print—that I have no devo-
　　tion;
But set those persons down with me to
　　pray,
　And you shall see who has the properest
　　notion
Of getting into heaven the shortest way;
　My altars are the mountains and the
　　ocean,
Earth, air, stars,—all that springs from the
　　great Whole,
Who hath produced, and will receive the
　soul.

CV

Sweet hour of twilight!—in the solitude
　Of the pine forest, and the silent shore
Which bounds Ravenna's immemorial
　　wood,
　Rooted where once the Adrian wave
　　flow'd o'er,
To where the last Cæsarean fortress stood,
　Evergreen forest! which Boccaccio's lore
And Dryden's lay made haunted ground
　to me,
How have I loved the twilight hour and
　thee!

CVI

The shrill cicalas, people of the pine,
　Making their summer lives one cease-
　　less song,
Were the sole echoes, save my steed's and
　　mine,
　And vesper bell's that rose the boughs
　　along;

The spectre huntsman of Onesti's line,
　His hell-dogs, and their chase, and the
　　fair throng
Which learn'd from this example not to fly
From a true lover,—shadow'd my mind's
　eye.

CVII

Oh, Hesperus! thou bringest all good
　　things—
　Home to the weary, to the hungry cheer,
To the young bird the parent's brooding
　　wings,
　The welcome stall to the o'erlabour'd
　　steer;
Whate'er of peace about our hearthstone
　　clings,
　Whate'er our household gods protect of
　　dear,
Are gather'd round us by thy look of rest;
Thou bring'st the child, too, to the
　mother's breast.

CVIII

Soft hour! which wakes the wish and melts
　　the heart
　Of those who sail the seas, on the first
　　day
When they from their sweet friends are
　　torn apart;
　Or fills with love the pilgrim on his way
As the far bell of vesper makes him start,
　Seeming to weep the dying day's decay;
Is this a fancy which our reason scorns?
Ah! surely nothing dies but something
　mourns!

CIX

When Nero perish'd by the justest doom
　Which ever the destroyer yet destroy'd,
Amidst the roar of liberated Rome,
　Of nations freed, and the world over-
　　joy'd,
Some hands unseen strew'd flowers upon
　his tomb:
　Perhaps the weakness of a heart not void
Of feeling for some kindness done, when
　　power
Had left the wretch an uncorrupted hour.

CX

But I'm digressing; what on earth has
　　Nero,
　Or any such like sovereign buffoons,
To do with the transactions of my hero,
　More than such madmen's fellow man
　　—the moon's?
Sure my invention must be down at zero,
　And I grown one of many 'wooden
　　spoons'
Of verse (the name with which we Cantabs
　please
To dub the last of honours in degrees).

CXI

I feel this tediousness will never do—
    'Tis being *too* epic, and I must cut down
(In copying) this long canto into two;
    They'll never find it out, unless I own
The fact, excepting some experienced few;
    And then as an improvement 'twill be
        shown:
I'll prove that such the opinion of the
    critic is
From Aristotle *passim.*—See Ποιητικης.

CANTO THE FOURTH

I

NOTHING so difficult as a beginning
    In poesy, unless perhaps the end;
For oftentimes when Pegasus seems win-
        ning
    The race, he sprains a wing, and down
        we tend,
Like Lucifer when hurl'd from heaven for
    sinning;
    Our sin the same, and hard as his to
        mend,
Being pride, which leads the mind to soar
    too far,
Till our own weakness shows us what we are.

II

But time, which brings all beings to their
    level,
    And sharp Adversity, will teach at last
Man,—and, as we would hope,—perhaps
    the devil,
    That neither of their intellects are vast:
While youth's hot wishes in our red veins
    revel,
    We know not this—the blood flows on
        too fast:
But as the torrent widens towards the ocean,
We ponder deeply on each past emotion.

III

As boy, I thought myself a clever fellow,
    And wish'd that others held the same
        opinion;
They took it up when my days grew more
    mellow,
    And other minds acknowledged my
        dominion:
Now my sere fancy 'falls into the yellow
    Leaf,' and Imagination droops her
        pinion,
And the sad truth which hovers o'er my
    desk
Turns what was once romantic to bur-
    lesque.

IV

And if I laugh at any mortal thing,
    'Tis that I may not weep; and if I weep,
'Tis that our nature cannot always bring
    Itself to apathy, for we must steep

Our hearts first in the depths of Lethe's
    spring,
    Ere what we least wish to behold will
        sleep:
Thetis baptized her mortal son in Styx;
A mortal mother would on Lethe fix.

V

Some have accused me of a strange design
    Against the creed and morals of the
        land,
And trace it in this poem every line;
    I don't pretend that I quite understand
My own meaning when I would be *very* fine;
    But the fact is that I have nothing plann'd,
Unless it were to be a moment merry,
A novel word in my vocabulary.

VI

To the kind reader of our sober clime
    This way of writing will appear exotic;
Pulci was sire of the half-serious rhyme,
    Who sang when chivalry was more
        Quixotic,
And revell'd in the fancies of the time,
    True knights, chaste dames, huge giants,
        kings despotic:
But all these, save the last, being obsolete,
I chose a modern subject as more meet.

VII

How I have treated it, I do not know;
    Perhaps no better than they have treated
        me,
Who have imputed such designs as show
    Not what they saw, but what they
        wish'd to see;
But if it gives them pleasure, be it so,
    This is a liberal age, and thoughts are
        free:
Meantime Apollo plucks me by the ear,
And tells me to resume my story here.

VIII

Young Juan and his lady-love were left
    To their own hearts' most sweet society;
Even Time the pitiless in sorrow cleft
    With his rude scythe such gentle
        bosoms; he
Sigh'd to behold them of their hours bereft,
    Though foe to love; and yet they could
        not be
Meant to grow old, but die in happy spring,
Before one charm or hope had taken wing.

IX

Their faces were not made for wrinkles,
    their
    Pure blood to stagnate, their great
        hearts to fail;
The blank grey was not made to blast their
    hair,
    But like the climes that know nor snow
        nor hail,

They were all summer; lightning might
    assail
    And shiver them to ashes, but to trail
A long and snake-like life of dull decay
Was not for them—they had too little clay.

X

They were alone once more; for them to be
    Thus was another Eden; they were never
Weary, unless when separate: the tree
    Cut from its forest root of years—the
    river
Damm'd from its fountain—the child from
    the knee
    And breast maternal wean'd at once for
    ever,—
Would wither less than these two torn apart;
Alas! there is no instinct like the heart—

XI

The heart—which may be broken: happy
    they!
    Thrice fortunate! who of that fragile
    mould,
The precious porcelain of human clay,
    Break with the first fall: they can ne'er
    behold
The long year link'd with heavy day on day,
    And all which must be borne, and never
    told;
While life's strange principle will often lie
Deepest in those who long the most to die.

XII

'Whom the gods love die young' was said
    of yore,
    And many deaths do they escape by this:
The death of friends, and that which slays
    even more—
    The death of friendship, love, youth, all
    that is,
Except mere breath; and since the silent
    shore
    Awaits at last even those who longest
    miss
The old archer's shafts, perhaps the early
    grave
Which men weep over may be meant to
    save.

XIII

Haidée and Juan thought not of the dead.
    The heavens, and earth, and air, seem'd
    made for them:
They found no fault with Time, save that
    he fled;
    They saw not in themselves aught to
    condemn;
Each was the other's mirror, and but read
    Joy sparkling in their dark eyes like a
    gem,
And knew such brightness was but the
    reflection
Of their exchanging glances of affection.

XIV

The gentle pressure, and the thrilling
    touch,
    The least glance better understood than
    words,
Which still said all, and ne'er could say
    too much;
    A language, too, but like to that of birds,
Known but to them, at least appearing
    such
    As but to lovers a true sense affords;
Sweet playful phrases, which would seem
    absurd
To those who have ceased to hear such, or
    ne'er heard.

XV

All these were theirs, for they were children
    still,
    And children still they should have ever
    been;
They were not made in the real world to fill
    A busy character in the dull scene,
But like two beings born from out a rill,
    A nymph and her beloved, all unseen
To pass their lives in fountains and on
    flowers,
And never know the weight of human
    hours.

XVI

Moons changing had roll'd on, and
    changeless found
    Those their bright rise had lighted to
    such joys
As rarely they beheld throughout their
    round;
    And these were not of the vain kind
    which cloys,
For theirs were buoyant spirits, never
    bound
    By the mere senses; and that which de-
    stroys
Most love, possession, unto them appear'd
A thing which each endearment more en-
    dear'd.

XVII

Oh beautiful! and rare as beautiful!
    But theirs was love in which the mind
    delights
To lose itself, when the old world grows
    dull,
    And we are sick of its hack sounds and
    sights,
Intrigues, adventures of the common
    school,
    Its petty passions, marriages, and flights,
Where Hymen's torch but brands one
    strumpet more,
Whose husband only knows her not a
    whore.

XVIII

Hard words; harsh truth; a truth which
    many know.
Enough.—The faithful and the fairy
    pair,
Who never found a single hour too slow,
    What was it made them thus exempt
      from care?
Young innate feelings all have felt below,
    Which perish in the rest, but in them
      were
Inherent; what we mortals call romantic,
And always envy, though we deem it frantic.

XIX

This is in others a factitious state,
    An opium dream of too much youth and
      reading,
But was in them their nature or their fate:
    No novels e'er had set their young hearts
      bleeding,
For Haidée's knowledge was by no means
    great,
And Juan was a boy of saintly breeding;
So that there was no reason for their loves
More than for those of nightingales or doves.

XX

They gazed upon the sunset; 'tis an hour
    Dear unto all, but dearest to *their* eyes,
For it had made them what they were: the
    power
    Of love had first o'erwhelm'd them from
      such skies,
When happiness had been their only dower,
    And twilight saw them link'd in
      passion's ties;
Charm'd with each other, all things
    charm'd that brought
The past still welcome as the present thought.

XXI

I know not why, but in that hour to-night,
    Even as they gazed, a sudden tremor
      came,
And swept, as 'twere, across their hearts'
    delight,
    Like the wind o'er a harp-string, or a
      flame,
When one is shook in sound, and one in
    sight:
    And thus some boding flash'd through
      either frame,
And call'd from Juan's breast a faint low
    sigh,
While one new tear arose in Haidée's eye.

XXII

That large black prophet eye seem'd to
    dilate
    And follow far the disappearing sun,
As if their last day of a happy date
    With his broad, bright, and dropping
      orb were gone.

Juan gazed on her as to ask his fate—
    He felt a grief, but knowing cause for
      none,
His glance inquired of hers for some excuse
For feelings causeless, or at least abstruse.

XXIII

She turn'd to him, and smiled, but in that
    sort
    Which makes not others smile; then
      turn'd aside:
Whatever feeling shook her, it seem'd
    short,
    And master'd by her wisdom or her
      pride;
When Juan spoke, too—it might be in
    sport—
    Of this their mutual feeling, she re-
      plied—
'If it should be so,—but—it cannot be—
Or I at least shall not survive to see.'

XXIV

Juan would question further, but she
    press'd
His lips to hers, and silenced him with
    this,
And then dismiss'd the omen from her
    breast,
    Defying augury with that fond kiss;
And no doubt of all methods 'tis the best:
    Some people prefer wine—'tis not
      amiss;
I have tried both; so those who would a
    part take
May choose between the headache and the
    heartache.

XXV

One of the two according to your choice,
    Woman or wine, you'll have to undergo;
Both maladies are taxes on our joys:
    But which to choose, I really hardly
      know;
And if I had to give a casting voice,
    For both sides I could many reasons
      show,
And then decide, without great wrong to
    either,
It were much better to have both than
    neither.

XXVI

Juan and Haidée gazed upon each other
    With swimming looks of speechless
      tenderness,
Which mix'd all feelings, friend, child,
    lover, brother;
All that the best can mingle and express
When two pure hearts are pour'd in one
    another,
    And love too much, and yet cannot love
      less;
But almost sanctify the sweet excess
By the immortal wish and power to bless.

XXVII

Mix'd in each other's arms, and heart in
    heart,
  Why did they not then die?—they had
    lived too long
Should an hour come to bid them breathe
    apart;
  Years could but bring them cruel things
    or wrong;
The world was not for them, nor the
    world's art
  For beings passionate as Sappho's song;
Love was born *with* them, *in* them, so
    intense,
It was their very spirit—not a sense.

XXVIII

They should have lived together deep in
    woods,
  Unseen as sings the nightingale; they
    were
Unfit to mix in these thick solitudes
  Call'd social, haunts of Hate, and Vice,
    and Care;
How lonely every freeborn creature
    broods!
  The sweetest song-birds nestle in a pair;
The eagle soars alone; the gull and crow
Flock o'er their carrion, just like men below.

XXIX

Now pillow'd cheek to cheek, in loving
    sleep,
  Haidée and Juan their siesta took,
A gentle slumber, but it was not deep,
  For ever and anon a something shook
Juan, and shuddering o'er his frame would
    creep;
  And Haidée's sweet lips murmur'd like
    a brook
A wordless music, and her face so fair
Stirr'd with her dream, as rose-leaves with
    the air;

XXX

Or as the stirring of a deep clear stream
  Within an Alpine hollow, when the wind
Walks o'er it, was she shaken by the dream,
  The mystical usurper of the mind—
O'erpowering us to be whate'er may seem
  Good to the soul which we no more can
    bind:
Strange state of being! (for 'tis still to be),
Senseless to feel, and with seal'd eyes to
    see.

XXXI

She dream'd of being alone on the sea-shore,
  Chain'd to a rock; she knew not how,
    but stir
She could not from the spot, and the loud
    roar
  Grew, and each wave rose roughly,
    threatening her;

And o'er her upper lip they seem'd to pour,
  Until she sobb'd for breath, and soon
    they were
Foaming o'er her lone head, so fierce and
    high—
Each broke to drown her, yet she could
    not die.

XXXII

Anon—she was released, and then she
    stray'd
  O'er the sharp shingles with her bleed-
    ing feet,
And stumbled almost every step she made;
  And something roll'd before her in a
    sheet,
Which she must still pursue howe'er afraid:
  'Twas white and indistinct, nor stopp'd
    to meet
Her glance nor grasp, for still she gazed
    and grasp'd,
And ran, but it escaped her as she clasp'd.

XXXIII

The dream changed:—in a cave she stood,
    its walls
  Were hung with marble icicles; the work
Of ages on its water-fretted halls,
  Where waves might wash, and seals
    might breed and lurk;
Her hair was dripping, and the very balls
  Of her black eyes seem'd turn'd to tears,
    and mirk
The sharp rocks look'd below each drop
    they caught,
Which froze to marble as it fell,—she
    thought.

XXXIV

And wet, and cold, and lifeless at her feet,
  Pale as the foam that froth'd on his dead
    brow,
Which she essay'd in vain to clear, (how
    sweet
  Were once her cares, how idle seem'd
    they now!)
Lay Juan, nor could aught renew the beat
  Of his quench'd heart; and the sea dirges
    low
Rang in her sad ears like a mermaid's song,
And that brief dream appear'd a life too long.

XXXV

And gazing on the dead, she thought his face
  Faded, or alter'd into something new—
Like to her father's features, till each trace
  More like and like to Lambro's aspect
    grew—
With all his keen worn look and Grecian
    grace;
  And starting, she awoke, and what to
    view?
Oh! Powers of Heaven! what dark eye
    meets she there?
'Tis—'tis her father's—fix'd upon the pair!

XXXVI

Then shrieking, she arose, and shrieking
fell,
  With joy and sorrow, hope and fear, to
  see
Him whom she deem'd a habitant where
dwell
  The ocean-buried, risen from death, to
  be
Perchance the death of one she loved too
well:
  Dear as her father had been to Haidée,
It was a moment of that awful kind——
I have seen such—but must not call to
mind.

XXXVII

Up Juan sprung to Haidée's bitter shriek,
  And caught her falling, and from off the
  wall
Snatch'd down his sabre, in hot haste to
wreak
  Vengeance on him who was the cause of
  all:
Then Lambro, who till now forbore to
speak,
  Smiled scornfully, and said, 'Within my
  call,
A thousand scimitars await the word;
Put up, young man, put up your silly
sword.'

XXXVIII

And Haidée clung around him; 'Juan,
'tis—
  'Tis Lambro—'tis my father! Kneel
  with me—
He will forgive us—yes—it must be—yes.
  Oh! dearest father, in this agony
Of pleasure and of pain—even while I kiss
  Thy garment's hem with transport, can
  it be
That doubt should mingle with my filial
joy?
Deal with me as thou wilt, but spare this
boy.'

XXXIX

High and inscrutable the old man stood,
  Calm in his voice, and calm within his
  eye—
Not always signs with him of calmest
mood:
  He look'd upon her, but gave no reply;
Then turn'd to Juan, in whose cheek the
blood
  Oft came and went, as there resolved to
  die;
In arms, at least, he stood, in act to spring
On the first foe whom Lambro's call might
bring.

XL

'Young man, your sword;' so Lambro
once more said:
  Juan replied, 'Not while this arm is
  free.'
The old man's cheek grew pale, but not
with dread,
  And drawing from his belt a pistol, he
Replied, 'Your blood be then on your own
head.'
  Then look'd close at the flint, as if to see
'Twas fresh—for he had lately used the
lock—
And next proceeded quietly to cock.

XLI

It has a strange quick jar upon the ear,
  That cocking of a pistol, when you know
A moment more will bring the sight to bear
  Upon your person, twelve yards off, or
  so;
A gentlemanly distance, not too near,
  If you have got a former friend for foe;
But after being fired at once or twice,
The ear becomes more Irish, and less nice.

XLII

Lambro presented, and one instant more
  Had stopp'd this Canto, and Don Juan's
  breath,
When Haidée threw herself her boy be-
fore;
  Stern as her sire: 'On me,' she cried,
  'let death
Descend—the fault is mine; this fatal
shore
  He found—but sought not. I have
  pledged my faith;
I love him—I will die with him: I knew
Your nature's firmness—know your daugh-
ter's too.'

XLIII

A minute past, and she had been all tears,
  And tenderness, and infancy; but now
She stood as one who champion'd human
fears—
  Pale, statue-like, and stern, she woo'd
  the blow;
And tall beyond her sex, and their com-
peers,
  She drew up to her height, as if to show
A fairer mark; and with a fix'd eye scann'd
Her father's face—but never stopp'd his
hand.

XLIV

He gazed on her, and she on him; 'twas
strange
  How like they look'd! the expression
  was the same;
Serenely savage, with a little change
  In the large dark eye's mutual-darted
  flame;

For she, too, was as one who could
  avenge,
  If cause should be—a lioness, though
    tame;
Her father's blood before her father's face
Boil'd up, and proved her truly of his race.

XLV

I said they were alike, their features and
  Their stature, differing but in sex and
    years:
Even to the delicacy of their hand
  There was resemblance, such as true
    blood wears;
And now to see them, thus divided, stand
  In fix'd ferocity, when joyous tears,
And sweet sensations, should have wel-
  comed both,
Show what the passions are in their full
  growth.

XLVI

The father paused a moment, then with-
  drew
  His weapon, and replaced it; but stood
    still,
And looking on her, as to look her through,
  'Not I,' he said, 'have sought this
    stranger's ill;
Not I have made this desolation: few
  Would bear such outrage, and forbear
    to kill;
But I must do my duty—how thou hast
Done thine, the present vouches for the
  past.

XLVII

'Let him disarm; or, by my father's head,
  His own shall roll before you like a
    ball!'
He raised his whistle as the word he said,
  And blew; another answer'd to the call,
And rushing in disorderly, though led,
  And arm'd from boot to turban, one
    and all,
Some twenty of his train came, rank on
  rank;
He gave the word, 'Arrest or slay the
  Frank.'

XLVIII

Then, with a sudden movement, he with-
  drew
  His daughter; while compress'd within
    his clasp,
'Twixt her and Juan interposed the crew;
  In vain she struggled in her father's
    grasp—
His arms were like a serpent's coil: then
  flew
Upon their prey, as darts an angry asp,
The file of pirates: save the foremost, who
Had fallen, with his right shoulder half cut
  through.

XLIX

The second had his cheek laid open; but
  The third, a wary, cool old sworder,
    took
The blows upon his cutlass, and then put
  His own well in; so well, ere you could
    look,
His man was floor'd, and helpless at his
  foot,
  With the blood running like a little
    brook
From two smart sabre gashes, deep and
  red—
One on the arm, the other on the head.

L

And then they bound him where he fell,
  and bore
  Juan from the apartment: with a sign
Old Lambro bade them take him to the
  shore,
  Where lay some ships which were to sail
    at nine.
They laid him in a boat, and plied the oar
  Until they reach'd some galliots, placed
    in line;
On board of one of these, and under
  hatches,
They stow'd him, with strict orders to the
  watches.

LI

The world is full of strange vicissitudes,
  And here was one exceedingly un-
    pleasant:
A gentleman so rich in the world's goods,
  Handsome and young, enjoying all the
    present,
Just at the very time when he least broods
  On such a thing, is suddenly to sea sent,
Wounded and chain'd, so that he cannot
  move,
And all because a lady fell in love.

LII

Here I must leave him, for I grow pathetic,
  Moved by the Chinese nymph of tears,
    green tea!
Than whom Cassandra was not more pro-
  phetic;
  For if my pure libations exceed three,
I feel my heart become so sympathetic,
  That I must have recourse to black
    Bohea:
'Tis pity wine should be so deleterious,
For tea and coffee leave us much more
  serious,

LIII

Unless when qualified with thee, Cogniac!
Sweet Naïad of the Phlegethontic rill!
Ah! why the liver wilt thou thus attack,
  And make, like other nymphs, thy lovers
    ill?

I would take refuge in weak punch, but
    rack
    (In each sense of the word), whene'er I
    fill
My mild and midnight beakers to the brim,
Wakes me next morning with its synonym.

LIV

I leave Don Juan for the present, safe—
    Not sound, poor fellow, but severely
    wounded;
Yet could his corporal pangs amount to
    half
    Of those with which his Haidée's bosom
    bounded!
She was not one to weep, and rave, and
    chafe,
    And then give way, subdued because
    surrounded;
Her mother was a Moorish maid from Fez,
Where all is Eden, or a wilderness.

LV

There the large olive rains its amber store
    In marble fonts; there grain, and flower,
    and fruit,
Gush from the earth until the land runs
    o'er;
    But there, too, many a poison-tree has
    root,
And midnight listens to the lion's roar,
    And long, long deserts scorch the
    camel's foot,
Or heaving whelm the helpless caravan;
And as the soil is, so the heart of man.

LVI

Afric is all the sun's, and as her earth
    Her human clay is kindled; full of power
For good or evil, burning from its birth,
    The Moorish blood partakes the planet's
    hour,
And like the soil beneath it will bring
    forth:
    Beauty and love were Haidée's mother's
    dower;
But her large dark eye show'd deep
    Passion's force,
Though sleeping like a lion near a source.

LVII

Her daughter, temper'd with a milder ray,
    Like summer clouds all silvery, smooth,
    and fair,
Till slowly charged with thunder they dis-
    play
    Terror to earth, and tempest to the air,
Had held till now her soft and milky way;
    But overwrought with passion and des-
    pair,
The fire burst forth from her Numidian
    veins,
Even as the Simoom sweeps the blasted
    plains.

LVIII

The last sight which she saw was Juan's
    gore,
    And he himself o'ermaster'd and cut
    down;
His blood was running on the very floor
    Where late he trod, her beautiful, her
    own;
Thus much she view'd an instant and no
    more,—
    Her struggles ceased with one convul-
    sive groan;
On her sire's arm, which until now scarce
    held
Her writhing, fell she like a cedar fell'd.

LIX

A vein had burst, and her sweet lips' pure
    dyes
    Were dabbled with the deep blood
    which ran o'er;
And her head droop'd, as when the lily lies
    O'ercharged with rain: her summon'd
    handmaids bore
Their lady to her couch with gushing eyes;
    Of herbs and cordials they produced
    their store,
But she defied all means they could em-
    ploy,
Like one life could not hold, nor death
    destroy.

LX

Days lay she in that state unchanged,
    though chill—
    With nothing livid, still her lips were
    red;
She had no pulse, but death seem'd absent
    still;
    No hideous sign proclaim'd her surely
    dead;
Corruption came not in each mind to kill
    All hope; to look upon her sweet face
    bred
New thoughts of life, for it seem'd full of
    soul—
She had so much, earth could not claim
    the whole.

LXI

The ruling passion, such as marble shows
    When exquisitely chisell'd, still lay
    there,
But fix'd as marble's unchanged aspect
    throws
    O'er the fair Venus, but for ever fair;
O'er the Laocoön's all eternal throes,
    And ever-dying Gladiator's air,
Their energy like life forms all their fame,
Yet looks not life, for they are still the
    same.

LXII

She woke at length, but not as sleepers
     wake,
  Rather the dead, for life seem'd some-
     thing new,
A strange sensation which she must par-
     take
  Perforce, since whatsoever met her view
Struck not on memory, though a heavy
     ache
  Lay at her heart, whose earliest beat
     still true
Brought back the sense of pain without the
     cause,
For, for a while, the furies made a pause.

LXIII

She look'd on many a face with vacant eye,
  On many a token without knowing
     what;
She saw them watch her without asking
     why,
  And reck'd not who around her pillow
     sat;
Not speechless, though she spoke not; not
     a sigh
  Relieved her thoughts; dull silence and
     quick chat
Were tried in vain by those who served;
     she gave
No sign, save breath, of having left the
     grave.

LXIV

Her handmaids tended, but she heeded
     not;
  Her father watch'd, she turn'd her eyes
     away;
She recognised no being, and no spot,
  However dear or cherish'd in their day;
They changed from room to room, but all
     forgot,
  Gentle, but without memory she lay;
At length those eyes, which they would
     fain be weaning
Back to old thoughts, wax'd full of fearful
     meaning.

LXV

And then a slave bethought her of a harp;
  The harper came, and tuned his instru-
     ment;
At the first notes, irregular and sharp,
  On him her flashing eyes a moment bent,
Then to the wall she turn'd as if to warp
  Her thoughts from sorrow through her
     heart re-sent;
And he begun a long low island song
Of ancient days, ere tyranny grew strong.

LXVI

Anon her thin wan fingers beat the wall
  In time to his old tune; he changed the
     theme,

And sung of love; the fierce name struck
     through all
  Her recollection; on her flash'd the
     dream
Of what she was, and is, if ye could call
  To be so being; in a gushing stream
The tears rush'd forth from her o'erclouded
     brain,
Like mountain mists at length dissolved
     in rain.

LXVII

Short solace, vain relief!—thought came
     too quick,
  And whirl'd her brain to madness; she
     arose
As one who ne'er had dwelt among the
     sick,
  And flew at all she met, as on her foes;
But no one ever heard her speak or shriek,
  Although her paroxysm drew towards
     its close;—
Hers was a phrensy which disdain'd to
     rave,
Even when they smote her, in the hope to
     save.

LXVIII

Yet she betray'd at times a gleam of sense;
  Nothing could make her meet her
     father's face,
Though on all other things with looks
     intense
  She gazed, but none she ever could re-
     trace;
Food she refused, and raiment; no pre-
     tence
  Avail'd for either; neither change of
     place,
Nor time, nor skill, nor remedy, could give
     her
Senses to sleep—the power seem'd gone
     for ever.

LXIX

Twelve days and nights she wither'd thus;
     at last,
  Without a groan, or sigh, or glance, to
     show
A parting pang, the spirit from her passed:
  And they who watch'd her nearest
     could not know
The very instant, till the change that cast
  Her sweet face into shadow, dull and
     slow,
Glazed o'er her eyes—the beautiful, the
     black—
Oh! to possess such lustre—and then lack!

LXX

She died, but not alone; she held within
  A second principle of life, which might
Have dawn'd a fair and sinless child of sin;
  But closed its little being without light,

And went down to the grave unborn, wherein
Blossom and bough lie wither'd with one blight;
In vain the dews of Heaven descend above
The bleeding flower and blasted fruit of love.

LXXI

Thus lived—thus died she; never more on her
Shall sorrow light, or shame. She was not made
Through years or moons the inner weight to bear,
Which colder hearts endure till they are laid
By age in earth: her days and pleasures were
Brief, but delightful—such as had not stayed
Long with her destiny; but she sleeps well
By the sea-shore, whereon she loved to dwell.

LXXII

That isle is now all desolate and bare,
Its dwellings down, its tenants pass'd away;
None but her own and father's grave is there,
And nothing outward tells of human clay;
Ye could not know where lies a thing so fair,
No stone is there to show, no tongue to say,
What was; no dirge, except the hollow sea's,
Mourns o'er the beauty of the Cyclades.

LXXIII

But many a Greek maid in a loving song
Sighs o'er her name; and many an islander
With her sire's story makes the night less long;
Valour was his, and beauty dwelt with her:
If she loved rashly, her life paid for wrong—
A heavy price must all pay who thus err,
In some shape; let none think to fly the danger,
For soon or late Love is his own avenger.

LXXIV

But let me change this theme, which grows too sad,
And lay this sheet of sorrows on the shelf;
I don't much like describing people mad,
For fear of seeming rather touch'd my-self—

Besides, I've no more on this head to add;
And as my Muse is a capricious elf,
We'll put about, and try another tack
With Juan, left half-kill'd some stanzas back.

LXXV

Wounded and fetter'd, 'cabin'd, cribb'd, confined,'
Some days and nights elapsed before that he
Could altogether call the past to mind;
And when he did, he found himself at sea,
Sailing six knots an hour before the wind;
The shores of Ilion lay beneath their lee—
Another time he might have liked to see 'em,
But now was not much pleased with Cape Sigæum.

LXXVI

There, on the green and village-cotted hill, is
(Flank'd by the Hellespont, and by the sea)
Entomb'd the bravest of the brave, Achilles;
They say so—(Bryant says the contrary):
And further downward, tall and towering still, is
The tumulus—of whom? Heaven knows; 't may be
Patroclus, Ajax, or Protesilaus;
All heroes, who if living still would slay us.

LXXVII

High barrows, without marble, or a name,
A vast, untill'd, and mountain-skirted plain,
And Ida in the distance, still the same,
And old Scamander (if 'tis he) remain;
The situation seems still form'd for fame—
A hundred thousand men might fight again
With ease; but where I sought for Ilion's walls,
The quiet sheep feeds, and the tortoise crawls;

LXXVIII

Troops of untended horses; here and there,
Some little hamlets, with new names un-couth;
Some shepherds (unlike Paris), led to stare
A moment at the European youth
Whom to the spot their school-boy feelings bear;
A Turk, with beads in hand, and pipe in mouth,
Extremely taken with his own religion,
Are what I found there—but the devil a Phrygian.

LXXIX

Don Juan, here permitted to emerge
    From his dull cabin, found himself a
      slave;
Forlorn, and gazing on the deep blue surge,
    O'ershadow'd there by many a hero's
      grave;
Weak still with loss of blood, he scarce
    could urge
    A few brief questions; and the answers
      gave
No very satisfactory information
About his past or present situation.

LXXX

He saw some fellow-captives, who ap-
    pear'd
    To be Italians, as they were in fact;
From them, at least, *their* destiny he
    heard,
    Which was an odd one; a troop going
      to act
In Sicily—all singers, duly rear'd
    In their vocation; had not been attack'd
In sailing from Livorno by the pirate,
But sold by the impresario at no high rate.

LXXXI

By one of these, the buffo of the party,
    Juan was told about their curious case;
For although destined to the Turkish
    mart, he
    Still kept his spirits up—at least his face;
The little fellow really look'd quite hearty,
    And bore him with some gaiety and
      grace,
Showing a much more reconciled de-
    meanour,
Than did the prima-donna and the tenor.

LXXXII

In a few words he told their hapless story,
    Saying, 'Our Machiavelian impresario,
Making a signal off some promontory,
    Hail'd a strange brig; Corpo di Caio
      Mario!
We were transferr'd on board her in a
    hurry,
    Without a single scudo of salario;
But if the Sultan has a taste for song,
We will revive our fortunes before long.

LXXXIII

'The prima-donna, though a little old,
    And haggard with a dissipated life,
And subject, when the house is thin, to
    cold,
    Has some good notes; and then the
    tenor's wife,
With no great voice, is pleasing to behold;
    Last carnival she made a deal of strife,
By carrying off Count Cesare Cicogna
From an old Roman princess at Bologna.

LXXXIV

'And then there are the dancers; there's
    the Nini,
    With more than one profession gains
      by all;
Then there's that laughing slut the Pele-
    grini,
She, too, was fortunate last carnival,
    And made at least five hundred good
      zecchini,
    But spends so fast, she has not now a
      paul;
And then there's the Grotesca—such a
    dancer!
Where men have souls or bodies she must
    answer.

LXXXV

'As for the figuranti, they are like
    The rest of all that tribe; with here and
      there
A pretty person, which perhaps may strike,
    The rest are hardly fitted for a fair;
There's one, though tall and stiffer than a
    pike,
    Yet has a sentimental kind of air
Which might go far, but she don't dance
    with vigour;
The more's the pity, with her face and
    figure.

LXXXVI

'As for the men, they are a middling set;
    The musico is but a crack'd old basin,
But being qualified in one way yet,
    May the seraglio do to set his face in,
And as a servant some preferment get;
    His singing I no further trust can place
     in:
From all the Pope makes yearly 'twould
    perplex
To find three perfect pipes of the *third* sex.

LXXXVII

'The tenor's voice is spoilt by affectation,
    And for the bass, the beast can only
     bellow;
In fact, he had no singing education,
    An ignorant, noteless, timeless, tuneless
     fellow;
But being the prima-donna's near relation,
    Who swore his voice was very rich and
    mellow,
They hired him, though to hear him you'd
    believe
An ass was practising recitative.

LXXXVIII

''Twould not become myself to dwell upon
    My own merits, and though young—
     I see, sir—you
Have got a travell'd air, which shows you
    one
To whom the opera is by no means new:

You've heard of Raucocanti?—I'm the
    man:
    The time may come when you may hear
    me too;
You was not last year at the fair of Lugo,
But next, when I'm engaged to sing there—
    do go.

LXXXIX

'Our baritone I almost had forgot,
    A pretty lad, but bursting with conceit;
With graceful action, science not a jot,
    A voice of no great compass, and not
    sweet,
He always is complaining of his lot,
    Forsooth, scarce fit for ballads in the
    street;
In lovers' parts his passion more to
    breathe,
Having no heart to show, he shows his
    teeth.'

XC

Here Raucocanti's eloquent recital
    Was interrupted by the pirate crew,
Who came at stated moments to invite all
    The captives back to their sad berths;
    each threw
A rueful glance upon the waves, (which
    bright all
    From the blue skies derived a double
    blue,
Dancing all free and happy in the sun,)
And then went down the hatchway one by
    one.

XCI

They heard next day—that in the Darda-
    nelles,
    Waiting for his Sublimity's firmān,
The most imperative of sovereign spells,
    Which everybody does without who can,
More to secure them in their naval cells,
    Lady to lady, well as man to man,
Were to be chain'd and lotted out per
    couple,
For the slave-market of Constantinople.

XCII

It seems when this allotment was made
    out,
    There chanced to be an odd male, and
    odd female,
Who (after some discussion and some doubt,
    If the soprano might be deem'd to be
    male,
They placed him o'er the women as a
    scout)
    Were link'd together, and it happen'd
    the male
Was Juan, who,—an awkward thing at
    his age,
Pair'd off with a Bacchante blooming
    visage.

XCIII

With Raucocanti lucklessly was chain'd
    The tenor; these two hated with a hate
Found only on the stage, and each more
    pain'd
    With this his tuneful neighbour than his
    fate:
Sad strife arose, for they were so cross-
    grain'd,
    Instead of bearing up without debate,
That each pull'd different ways with many
    an oath,
'Arcades ambo,' *id est*—blackguards both.

XCIV

Juan's companion was a Romagnole,
    But bred within the March of old Ancona,
With eyes that look'd into the very soul
    (And other chief points of a 'bella
    donna'),
Bright—and as black and burning as a coal;
    And through her clear brunette com-
    plexion shone a
Great wish to please—a most attractive
    dower,
Especially when added to the power.

XCV

But all that power was wasted upon him,
    For sorrow o'er each sense held stern
    command;
Her eye might flash on his, but found it dim:
    And though thus chain'd, as natural her
    hand
Touch'd his, nor that—nor any handsome
    limb
    (And she had some not easy to with-
    stand)
Could stir his pulse, or make his faith feel
    brittle;
Perhaps his recent wounds might help a
    little.

XCVI

No matter; we should ne'er too much
    inquire,
    But facts are facts: no knight could be
    more true,
And firmer faith no ladye-love desire;
    We will omit the proofs, save one or two:
'Tis said no one in hand 'can hold a fire
    By thought of frosty Caucasus;' but
    few,
I really think; yet Juan's then ordeal
Was more triumphant, and not much less
    real.

XCVII

Here I might enter on a chaste description,
    Having withstood temptation in my
    youth,
But hear that several people take exception
    At the first two books having too much
    truth;

Therefore I'll make Don Juan leave the
    ship soon,
    Because the publisher declares, in sooth,
Through needles' eyes it easier for the
    camel is
To pass, than those two cantos into
    families.

XCVIII

'Tis all the same to me; I'm fond of yield-
    ing,
    And therefore leave them to the purer
        page
Of Smollett, Prior, Ariosto, Fielding,
    Who say strange things for so correct an
        age;
I once had great alacrity in wielding
    My pen, and liked poetic war to wage,
And recollect the time when all this cant
Would have provoked remarks which
    now it shan't.

XCIX

As boys love rows, my boyhood liked a
    squabble;
    But at this hour I wish to part in peace,
Leaving such to the literary rabble,
    Whether my verse's fame be doom'd to
        cease
While the right hand which wrote it still is
    able,
    Or of some centuries to take a lease;
The grass upon my grave will grow as long,
And sigh to midnight winds, but not to
    song.

C

Of poets who come down to us through
    distance
    Of time and tongues, the foster-babes of
        Fame,
Life seems the smallest portion of exist-
    ence;
    Where twenty ages gather o'er a name,
'Tis as a snow-ball which derives assistance
    From every flake, and yet rolls on the
        same,
Even till an iceberg it may chance to grow;
But, after all, 'tis nothing but cold snow.

CI

And so great names are nothing more than
    nominal,
    And love of glory's but an airy lust,
Too often in its fury overcoming all
    Who would as 'twere identify their dust
From out the wide destruction, which,
    entombing all,
    Leaves nothing till 'the coming of the
        just'—
Save change: I've stood upon Achilles'
    tomb,
And heard Troy doubted; time will
    doubt of Rome.

CII

The very generations of the dead
    Are swept away, and tomb inherits tomb,
Until the memory of an age is fled,
    And, buried, sinks beneath its off-
        spring's doom:
Where are the epitaphs our fathers read?
    Save a few glean'd from the sepulchral
        gloom
Which once-named myriads nameless lie
    beneath,
And lose their own in universal death.

CIII

I canter by the spot each afternoon
    Where perish'd in his fame the hero-
        boy,
Who lived too long for men, but died too
    soon
    For human vanity, the young De Foix!
A broken pillar, not uncouthly hewn,
    But which neglect is hastening to de-
        stroy,
Records Ravenna's carnage on its face,
While weeds and ordure rankle round the
    base.

CIV

I pass each day where Dante's bones are
    laid:
    A little cupola, more neat than solemn,
Protects his dust, but reverence here is paid
    To the bard's tomb, and not the
        warrior's column:
The time must come, when both alike
    decay'd,
    The chieftain's trophy, and the poet's
        volume,
Will sink where lie the songs and wars of
    earth,
Before Pelides' death, or Homer's birth.

CV

With human blood that column was
    cemented,
    With human filth that column is defiled,
As if the peasant's coarse contempt were
    vented
    To show his loathing of the spot he
        soil'd:
Thus is the trophy used, and thus lamented
    Should ever be those blood-hounds,
        from whose wild
Instinct of gore and glory earth has known
Those sufferings Dante saw in hell alone.

CVI

Yet there will still be bards: though fame
    is smoke,
    Its fumes are frankincense to human
        thought;
And the unquiet feelings, which first woke
    Song in the world, will seek what then
        they sought:

As on the beach the waves at last are broke,
  Thus to their extreme verge the passions
    brought
Dash into poetry, which is but passion,
  Or at least was so ere it grew a fashion.

CVII

If in the course of such a life as was
  At once adventurous and contemplative,
Men who partake all passions as they pass,
  Acquire the deep and bitter power to give
Their images again as in a glass,
  And in such colours that they seem to
    live;
You may do right forbidding them to show
    'em,
  But spoil (I think) a very pretty poem.

CVIII

Oh! ye, who make the fortunes of all books!
  Benign Ceruleans of the second sex!
Who advertise new poems by your looks,
  Your 'imprimatur' will ye not annex?
What! must I go to the oblivious cooks,
  Those Cornish plunderers of Parnassian
    wrecks?
Ah! must I then the only minstrel be,
Proscribed from tasting your Castalian tea?

CIX

What! can I prove 'a lion' then no more?
  A ball-room bard, a foolscap, hot-press
    darling?
To bear the compliments of many a bore,
  And sigh, 'I can't get out,' like Yorick's
    starling;
Why then I'll swear, as poet Wordy swore
  (Because the world won't read him,
    always snarling),
That taste is gone, that fame is but a
    lottery,
Drawn by the blue-coat misses of a coterie.

CX

Oh! 'darkly, deeply, beautifully blue,'
  As some one somewhere sings about the
    sky,
And I, ye learned ladies, say of you;
  They say your stockings are so—
    (Heaven knows why,
I have examined few pair of that hue);
  Blue as the garters which serenely lie
Round the patrician left-legs, which adorn
The festal midnight, and the levée morn.

CXI

Yet some of you are most seraphic crea-
    tures—
  But times are alter'd since, a rhyming
    lover,
You read my stanzas, and I read your
    features:
  And—but no matter, all those things
    are over;

Still I have no dislike to learned natures,
  For sometimes such a world of virtues
    cover;
I know one woman of that purple school,
  The loveliest, chastest, best, but—quite a
    fool.

CXII

Humboldt, 'the first of travellers,' but not
  The last, if late accounts be accurate,
Invented, by some name I have forgot,
  As well as the sublime discovery's date,
An airy instrument, with which he sought
  To ascertain the atmospheric state,
By measuring 'the *intensity of blue*':
Oh, Lady Daphne! let me measure you!

CXIII

But to the narrative:—The vessel bound
  With slaves to sell off in the capital,
After the usual process, might be found
  At anchor under the seraglio wall;
Her cargo, from the plague being safe and
    sound,
  Were landed in the market, one and all,
And there with Georgians, Russians, and
    Circassians,
Bought up for different purposes and
    passions.

CXIV

Some went off dearly; fifteen hundred
    dollars
  For one Circassian, a sweet girl, were
    given,
Warranted virgin; beauty's brightest
    colours
  Had deck'd her out in all the hues of
    heaven:
Her sale sent home some disappointed
    bawlers,
  Who bade on till the hundreds reached
    eleven;
But when the offer went beyond, they
    knew
'Twas for the Sultan, and at once with-
    drew.

CXV

Twelve negresses from Nubia brought a
    price
  Which the West Indian market scarce
    would bring,
Though Wilberforce, at last, has made it
    twice
  What 'twas ere Abolition; and the thing
Need not seem very wonderful, for vice
  Is always much more splendid than a
    king:
The virtues, even the most exalted,
    Charity,
Are saving—vice spares nothing for a
    rarity.

CXVI

But for the destiny of this young troop,
　How some were bought by pachas,
　　some by Jews,
How some to burdens were obliged to
　stoop,
　And others rose to the command of
　　crews
As renegadoes; while in hapless group,
　Hoping no very old vizier might choose,
The females stood, as one by one they
　pick'd 'em,
To make a mistress, or fourth wife, or
　victim:

CXVII

All this must be reserved for further song;
　Also our hero's lot, howe'er unpleasant
(Because this Canto has become too long),
　Must be postponed discreetly for the
　　present;
I'm sensible redundancy is wrong,
　But could not for the muse of me put
　　less in't:
And now delay the progress of Don Juan,
Till what is call'd in Ossian the fifth Duan.

CANTO THE FIFTH

I

WHEN amatory poets sing their loves
　In liquid lines mellifluously bland,
And pair their rhymes as Venus yokes her
　doves,
　They little think what mischief is in
　　hand;
The greater their success the worse it
　proves,
　As Ovid's verse may give to understand;
Even Petrarch's self, if judged with due
　severity,
Is the Platonic pimp of all posterity.

II

I therefore do denounce all amorous writ-
　ing,
　Except in such a way as not to attract;
Plain—simple—short, and by no means
　inviting,
　But with a moral to each error tack'd,
Form'd rather for instructing than de-
　lighting,
　And with all passions in their turn
　　attack'd;
Now, if my Pegasus should not be shod ill,
This poem will become a moral model.

III

The European with the Asian shore
　Sprinkled with palaces; the Ocean
　　stream
Here and there studded with a seventy-
　four;
　Sophia's cupola with golden gleam;

The cypress groves; Olympus high and
　hoar;
　The twelve isles, and the more than I
　　could dream,
Far less describe, present the very view
Which charm'd the charming Mary
　Montagu.

IV

I have a passion for the name of 'Mary,'
　For once it was a magic sound to me;
And still it half calls up the realms of fairy,
　Where I beheld what never was to be;
All feelings changed, but this was last to
　vary,
　A spell from which even yet I am not
　　quite free:
But I grow sad—and let a tale grow cold,
Which must not be pathetically told.

V

The wind swept down the Euxine, and the
　wave
　Broke foaming o'er the blue Symple-
　　gades;
'Tis a grand sight from off 'the Giant's
　Grave'
　To watch the progress of those rolling
　　seas
Between the Bosphorus, as they lash and
　lave
　Europe and Asia, you being quite at ease:
There's not a sea the passenger e'er pukes
　in,
Turns up more dangerous breakers than
　the Euxine.

VI

'Twas a raw day of Autumn's bleak begin-
　ning,
　When nights are equal, but not so the
　　days:
The Parcæ then cut short the further
　spinning
　Of seamen's fates, and the loud tempests
　　raise
The waters, and repentance for past sin-
　ning
　In all, who o'er the great deep take their
　　ways:
They vow to amend their lives, and yet
　they don't;
Because if drown'd, they can't—if spared,
　they won't.

VII

A crowd of shivering slaves of every
　nation,
　And age, and sex, were in the market
　　ranged;
Each bevy with the merchant in his sta-
　tion:
　Poor creatures! their good looks were
　　sadly changed.

All save the blacks seem'd jaded with
    vexation,
    From friends, and home, and freedom
      far estranged;
The negroes more philosophy display'd,—
Used to it, no doubt, as eels are to be
    flay'd.

VIII

Juan was juvenile, and thus was full,
    As most at his age are, of hope, and
      health;
Yet I must own, he look'd a little dull,
    And now and then a tear stole down by
      stealth;
Perhaps his recent loss of blood might pull
    His spirit down; and then the loss of
      wealth,
A mistress, and such comfortable quarters,
To be put up for auction amongst Tartars,

IX

Were things to shake a stoic; ne'ertheless,
    Upon the whole his carriage was serene:
His figure, and the splendour of his dress,
    Of which some gilded remnants still
      were seen,
Drew all eyes on him, giving them to guess
    He was above the vulgar by his mien;
And then, though pale, he was so very
    handsome;
And then—they calculated on his ransom.

X

Like a backgammon board the place was
    dotted
    With whites and blacks, in groups on
      show for sale,
Though rather more irregularly spotted:
    Some bought the jet, while others chose
      the pale.
It chanced amongst the other people
    lotted,
    A man of thirty, rather stout and hale,
With resolution in his dark grey eye,
Next Juan stood, till some might choose
    to buy.

XI

He had an English look; that is, was
    square
    In make, of a complexion white and
      ruddy,
Good teeth, with curling rather dark
    brown hair,
    And, it might be from thought, or toil,
      or study,
An open brow a little mark'd with care:
    One arm had on a bandage rather
      bloody;
And there he stood with such *sang froid*,
    that greater
Could scarce be shown even by a mere
    spectator.

XII

But seeing at his elbow a mere lad,
    Of a high spirit evidently, though
At present weigh'd down by a doom which
    had
    O'erthrown even men, he soon began to
      show
A kind of blunt compassion for the sad
    Lot of so young a partner in the woe,
Which for himself he seem'd to deem no
    worse
Than any other scrape, a thing of course.

XIII

'My boy!'—said he, 'amidst this motley
    crew
    Of Georgians, Russians, Nubians, and
      what not,
All ragamuffins differing but in hue,
    With whom it is our luck to cast our lot,
The only gentlemen seem I and you;
    So let us be acquainted, as we ought:
If I could yield you any consolation,
'Twould give me pleasure.—Pray, what is
    your nation?'

XIV

When Juan answer'd—'Spanish!' he re-
    plied,
    'I thought, in fact, you could not be a
      Greek;
Those servile dogs are not so proudly eyed:
    Fortune has play'd you here a pretty
      freak,
But that's her way with all men, till they're
    tried;
    But never mind,—she'll turn, perhaps,
      next week;
She has served me also much the same as
    you,
Except that I have found it nothing new.'

XV

'Pray, sir,' said Juan, 'if I may presume,
    What brought you here?'—'Oh! no-
      thing very rare—
Six Tartars and a drag-chain——'—'To
    this doom
    But what conducted, if the question's fair,
Is that which I would learn.'—'I served
    for some
    Months with the Russian army here and
      there;
And taking lately, by Suwarrow's bidding,
A town, was ta'en myself instead of Widdin.'

XVI

'Have you no friends?'—'I had—but, by
    God's blessing,
    Have not been troubled with them
      lately. Now
I have answer'd all your questions without
    pressing,
    And you an equal courtesy should show.'

'Alas!' said Juan, ''twere a tale distress-
      ing,
   And long besides.'—'Oh! if 'tis really
      so,
You're right on both accounts to hold
      your tongue;
A sad tale saddens doubly when 'tis long.

XVII

'But droop not: Fortune at your time of
      life,
   Although a female moderately fickle,
Will hardly leave you (as she's not your
      wife)
   For any length of days in such a pickle.
To strive, too, with our fate were such a
      strife
   As if the corn-sheaf should oppose the
      sickle:
Men are the sport of circumstances, when
The circumstances seem the sport of men.'

XVIII

''Tis not,' said Juan, 'for my present doom
   I mourn, but for the past;—I loved a
      maid:'—
He paused, and his dark eye grew full of
      gloom;
   A single tear upon his eyelash stayed
A moment, and then dropp'd; 'but to re-
      sume,
   'Tis not my present lot, as I have said,
Which I deplore so much; for I have borne
Hardships which have the hardiest over-
      worn,

XIX

'On the rough deep. But this last blow—'
      and here
   He stopp'd again, and turn'd away his
      face.
'Ay,' quoth his friend, 'I thought it would
      appear
   That there had been a lady in the case;
And these are things which ask a tender
      tear,
   Such as I, too, would shed if in your
      place:
I cried upon my first wife's dying day,
And also when my second ran away:

XX

'My third——'—'Your third!' quoth
      Juan, turning round;
   'You scarcely can be thirty: have you
      three?'
'No—only two at present above ground:
   Surely, 'tis nothing wonderful to see
One person thrice in holy wedlock bound!'
   'Well, then, your third,' said Juan;
      'what did she?'
She did not run away, too,—did she, sir?'
'No, faith.'—'What then?'—'I ran away
      from her.'

XXI

'You take things coolly, sir,' said Juan.
      'Why,'
   Replied the other, 'what can a man do?
There still are many rainbows in your sky,
   But mine have vanish'd. All, when life
      is new,
Commence with feelings warm, and pros-
      pects high;
   But time strips our illusions of their hue,
And one by one in turn, some grand mis-
      take
Casts off its bright skin yearly like the
      snake.

XXII

''Tis true, it gets another bright and fresh,
   Or fresher, brighter; but the year gone
      through,
This skin must go the way, too, of all flesh,
   Or sometimes only wear a week or
      two;—
Love's the first net which spreads its
      deadly mesh;
   Ambition, Avarice, Vengeance, Glory,
      glue
The glittering lime-twigs of our latter days,
Where still we flutter on for pence or
      praise.'

XXIII

'All this is very fine, and may be true,'
   Said Juan, 'but I really don't see how
It betters present times with me or you.'
   'No?' quoth the other; 'yet you will allow
By setting things in their right point of view,
   Knowledge, at least, is gain'd; for in-
      stance, now,
We know what slavery is, and our disasters
May teach us better to behave when masters.'

XXIV

'Would we were masters now, if but to try
   Their present lessons on our Pagan
      friends here,'
Said Juan—swallowing a heart-burning
      sigh:
   'Heaven help the scholar, whom his
      fortune sends here!'
'Perhaps we shall be one day, by and by,'
   Rejoin'd the other, 'when our bad luck
      mends here;
Meantime (yon old black eunuch seems to
      eye us)
I wish to G—d that somebody would buy
      us!

XXV

'But after all, what is our present state?
   'Tis bad, and may be better—all men's
      lot:
Most men are slaves, none more so than
      the great,
   To their own whims and passions, and
      what not;

Society itself, which should create
  Kindness, destroys what little we had
    got:
To feel for none is the true social art
Of the world's stoics—men without a
    heart.'

XXVI

Just now a black old neutral personage
  Of the third sex stept up, and peering
    over
The captives, seem'd to mark their looks
    and age,
  And capabilities, as to discover
If they were fitted for the purposed cage:
  No lady e'er is ogled by a lover,
Horse by a blackleg, broadcloth by a
    tailor,
Fee by a counsel, felon by a jailor,

XXVII

As is a slave by his intended bidder.
  'Tis pleasant purchasing our fellow-
    creatures;
And all are to be sold, if you consider
  Their passions, and are dext'rous; some
    by features
Are bought up, others by a warlike leader,
  Some by a place—as tend their years or
    natures;
The most by ready cash—but all have
    prices,
From crowns to kicks, according to their
    vices.

XXVIII

The eunuch, having eyed them o'er with
    care,
  Turn'd to the merchant, and began to
    bid
First but for one, and after for the pair;
  They haggled, wrangled, swore, too—so
    they did!
As though they were in a mere Christian
    fair,
  Cheapening an ox, an ass, a lamb, or
    kid;
So that their bargain sounded like a battle
For this superior yoke of human cattle.

XXIX

At last they settled into simple grumbling,
  And pulling out reluctant purses, and
Turning each piece of silver o'er, and
    tumbling
  Some down, and weighing others in
    their hand,
And by mistake sequins with paras jumb-
    ling,
  Until the sum was accurately scann'd,
And then the merchant giving change, and
    signing
Receipts in full, began to think of dining.

XXX

I wonder if his appetite was good?
  Or, if it were, if also his digestion?
Methinks at meals some odd thoughts
    might intrude,
  And conscience ask a curious sort of
    question,
About the right divine how far we should
  Sell flesh and blood. When dinner has
    opprest one,
I think it is perhaps the gloomiest hour
Which turns up out of the sad twenty-four.

XXXI

Voltaire says 'No'; he tells you that
    Candide
  Found life most tolerable after meals;
He's wrong—unless man were a pig, in-
    deed,
  Repletion rather adds to what he feels,
Unless he's drunk, and then no doubt he's
    freed
  From his own brain's oppression while
    it reels.
Of food I think with Philip's son, or rather
Ammon's (ill pleased with one world and
    one father);

XXXII

I think with Alexander, that the act
  Of eating, with another act or two,
Makes us feel our mortality in fact
  Redoubled; when a roast and a ragout,
And fish, and soup, by some side dishes
    back'd,
  Can give us either pain or pleasure, who
Would pique himself on intellects, whose
    use
Depends so much upon the gastric juice?

XXXIII

The other evening ('twas on Friday last)—
  This is a fact, and no poetic fable—
Just as my great coat was about me cast,
  My hat and gloves still lying on the table,
I heard a shot—'twas eight o'clock scarce
    past—
  And, running out as fast as I was able,
I found the military commandant
Stretch'd in the street, and able scarce to
    pant.

XXXIV

Poor fellow! for some reason, surely bad,
  They had slain him with five slugs; and
    left him there
To perish on the pavement: so I had
  Him borne into the house and up the stair,
And stripp'd, and look'd to,—But why
    should I add
  More circumstances? vain was every
    care;
The man was gone: in some Italian quarrel
Kill'd by five bullets from an old gun-barrel.

XXXV

I gazed upon him, for I knew him well;
   And though I have seen many corpses, never
Saw one, whom such an accident befell,
   So calm; though pierced through stomach, heart, and liver,
He seem'd to sleep,—for you could scarcely tell
   (As he bled inwardly, no hideous river
Of gore divulged the cause) that he was dead:
So as I gazed on him, I thought or said—

XXXVI

'Can this be death? then what is life or death?
   Speak!' but he spoke not: 'wake!' but still he slept:—
'But yesterday, and who had mightier breath?
   A thousand warriors by his word were kept
In awe: he said, as the centurion saith,
   "Go," and he goeth; "come," and forth he stepp'd.
The trump and bugle till he spake were dumb—
And now nought left him but the muffled drum.'

XXXVII

And they who waited once and worshipp'd—they
   With their rough faces throng'd about the bed
To gaze once more on the commanding clay
   Which for the last, though not the first, time bled;
And such an end! that he who many a day
   Had faced Napoleon's foes until they fled,—
The foremost in the charge or in the sally,
Should now be butcher'd in a civic alley.

XXXVIII

The scars of his old wounds were near his new,
   Those honourable scars which brought him fame;
And horrid was the contrast to the view——
   But let me quit the theme; as such things claim
Perhaps even more attention than is due
   From me: I gazed (as oft I have gazed the same)
To try if I could wrench aught out of death
Which should confirm, or shake, or make a faith;

XXXIX

But it was all a mystery. Here we are,
   And there we go:—but *where?* five bits of lead,
Or three, or two, or one, send very far!
   And is this blood, then, form'd but to be shed?
Can every element our elements mar?
   And air—earth—water—fire live—and we dead?
We, whose minds comprehend all things. No more;
But let us to the story as before.

XL

The purchaser of Juan and acquaintance
   Bore off his bargains to a gilded boat,
Embark'd himself and them, and off they went thence
   As fast as oars could pull and water float;
They look'd like persons being led to sentence,
   Wond'ring what next, till the caïque was brought
Up in a little creek below a wall
O'ertopp'd with cypresses, dark-green and tall.

XLI

Here their conductor tapping at the wicket
   Of a small iron door, 'twas open'd, and
He led them onward, first through a low thicket
   Flank'd by large groves, which tower'd on either hand:
They almost lost their way, and had to pick it—
   For night was closing ere they came to land.
The eunuch made a sign to those on board,
Who row'd off, leaving them without a word.

XLII

As they were plodding on their winding way
   Through orange bowers, and jasmine, and so forth:
(Of which I might have a good deal to say,
   There being no such profusion in the North
Of oriental plants, 'et cetera,'
   But that of late your scribblers think it worth
Their while to rear whole hotbeds in *their* works,
Because one poet travell'd 'mongst the Turks:)

XLIII

As they were threading on their way, there came
   Into Don Juan's head a thought, which he
Whisper'd to his companion:—'twas the same
   Which might have then occurr'd to you or me.

'Methinks,'—said he,—'it would be no
    great shame
If we should strike a stroke to set us free;
Let's knock that old black fellow on the
    head,
And march away—'twere easier done than
    said.'

XLIV

'Yes,' said the other, 'and when done,
    what then?
    How get out? how the devil got we in?
And when we once were fairly out, and
    when
    From Saint Bartholomew we have
      saved our skin,
To-morrow'd see us in some other den,
    And worse off than we hitherto have been;
Besides, I'm hungry, and just now would
    take,
Like Esau, for my birthright a beef-steak.

XLV

'We must be near some place of man's
    abode;—
    For the old negro's confidence in creep-
      ing,
With his two captives, by so queer a road,
    Shows that he thinks his friends have
      not been sleeping;
A single cry would bring them all abroad:
    'Tis better therefore looking before
      leaping—
And there, you see, this turn has brought
    us through,
By Jove, a noble palace!—lighted too.'

XLVI

It was indeed a wide extensive building
    Which open'd on their view, and o'er the
    front
There seem'd to be besprent a deal of
    gilding
    And various hues, as is the Turkish
    wont,—
A gaudy taste, for they are little skill'd in
    The arts of which these lands were once
    the font:
Each villa on the Bosphorus looks a screen
New painted, or a pretty opera-scene.

XLVII

And nearer as they came, a genial savour
    Of certain stews, and roast-meats, and
    pilaus,
Things which in hungry mortals' eyes find
    favour,
    Made Juan in his harsh intentions pause,
And put himself upon his good behaviour:
    His friend, too, adding a new saving
    clause,
Said, 'In Heaven's name let's get some
    supper now,
And then I'm with you, if you're for a row.'

XLVIII

Some talk of an appeal unto some passion,
    Some to men's feelings, others to their
    reason;
The last of these was never much the
    fashion,
    For reason thinks all reasoning out of
    season:
Some speakers whine, and others lay the
    lash on,
    But more or less continue still to tease
    on,
With arguments according to their 'forte';
But no one ever dreams of being short.—

XLIX

But I digress: of all appeals,—although
    I grant the power of pathos, and of gold,
Of beauty, flattery, threats, a shilling,—no
    Method's more sure at moments to
    take hold
Of the best feelings of mankind, which grow
    More tender, as we every day behold,
Than that all-softening, overpowering
    knell,
The tocsin of the soul—the dinner-bell.

L

Turkey contains no bells, and yet men
    dine;
    And Juan and his friend, albeit they
    heard
No Christian knoll to table, saw no line
    Of lackeys usher to the feast prepared,
Yet smelt roast-meat, beheld a huge fire
    shine,
    And cooks in motion with their clean
    arms bared,
And gazed around them to the left and
    right,
With the prophetic eye of appetite.

LI

And giving up all notions of resistance,
    They follow'd close behind their sable
    guide,
Who little thought that his own crack'd
    existence
    Was on the point of being set aside:
He motion'd them to stop at some small
    distance,
    And knocking at the gate, 'twas open'd
    wide,
And a magnificent large hall display'd
The Asian pomp of Ottoman parade.

LII

I won't describe; description is my forte,
    But every fool describes in these bright
    days
His wondrous journey to some foreign
    court,
    And spawns his quarto, and demands
    your praise—

Death to his publisher, to him 'tis sport;
    While Nature, tortured twenty thou-
        sand ways,
Resigns herself with exemplary patience
    To guide-books, rhymes, tours, sketches,
        illustrations.

LIII

Along this hall, and up and down, some,
        squatted
    Upon their hams, were occupied at
        chess;
Others in monosyllable talk chatted,
    And some seem'd much in love with
        their own dress;
And divers smoked superb pipes,
        decorated
    With amber mouths of greater price or
        less;
And several strutted, others slept, and
        some
Prepared for supper with a glass of rum.

LIV

As the black eunuch enter'd with his
        brace
    Of purchased Infidels, some raised
        their eyes
A moment, without slackening from their
        pace;
    But those who sate, ne'er stirr'd in any
        wise:
One or two stared the captives in the face,
    Just as one views a horse to guess his
        price;
Some nodded to the negro from their
        station,
But no one troubled him with conversa-
        tion.

LV

He leads them through the hall, and, with-
        out stopping,
    On through a farther range of goodly
        rooms,
Splendid but silent, save in *one*, where,
        dropping,
    A marble fountain echoes through the
        glooms
Of night, which robe the chamber, or
        where popping
    Some female head most curiously
        presumes
To thrust its black eyes through the door
        or lattice,
As wondering what the *devil* noise that is.

LVI

Some faint lamps gleaming from the lofty
        walls
    Gave light enough to hint their farther
        way,
But not enough to show the imperial halls
    In all the flashing of their full array;

Perhaps there's nothing—I'll not say
        appals,
    But saddens more by night as well as
        day,
Than an enormous room without a soul
    To break the lifeless splendour of the
        whole.

LVII

Two or three seem so little, *one* seems
        nothing:
    In deserts, forests, crowds, or by the
        shore,
There solitude, we know, has her full
        growth in
    The spots which were her realms for
        evermore;
But in a mighty hall or gallery, both in
    More modern buildings and those built
        of yore,
A kind of death comes o'er us all alone,
Seeing what's meant for many with but
        one.

LVIII

A neat, snug study on a winter's night,
    A book, friend, single lady, or a glass
Of claret, sandwich, and an appetite,
    Are things which make an English
        evening pass;
Though *certes* by no means so grand a
        sight
    As is a theatre lit up by gas.
I pass my evenings in long galleries solely,
And that's the reason I'm so melancholy.

LIX

Alas! man makes that great which makes
        him little:
    I grant you in a church 'tis very well:
What speaks of heaven should by no
        means be brittle,
    But strong and lasting, till no tongue
        can tell
Their names who rear'd it; but huge
        houses fit ill—
    And huge tombs worse—mankind,
        since Adam fell:
Methinks the story of the tower of Babel
Might teach them this much better than
        I'm able.

LX

Babel was Nimrod's hunting-box, and then
    A town of gardens, walls, and wealth
        amazing,
Where Nebuchadonosor, king of men,
    Reign'd, till one summer's day he took
        to grazing,
And Daniel tamed the lions in their den,
    The people's awe and admiration raising;
'Twas famous, too, for Thisbe and for
        Pyramus,
And the calumniated queen Semiramis.—

LXI

That injured Queen, by chroniclers so
    coarse,
  Has been accused (I doubt not by
    conspiracy)
Of an improper friendship for her horse
  (Love, like religion, sometimes runs to
    heresy):
This monstrous tale had probably its source
  (For such exaggerations here and there
    I see)
In writing 'Courser' by mistake for 'Cou-
    rier;'
I wish the case would come before a jury
    here.

LXII

But to resume,—should there be (what may
    not
  Be in these days?) some infidels, who
    don't,
Because they can't, find out the very spot
  Of that same Babel, or because they won't
(Though Claudius Rich, Esquire, some
    bricks has got,
  And written lately two memoirs upon't)
Believe the Jews, those unbelievers, who
Must be believed, though they believe not
    you,

LXIII

Yet let them think that Horace has exprest
  Shortly and sweetly the masonic place of
    rest,
Of those, forgetting the great place of rest,
  Who give themselves to architecture
    wholly;
We know where things and men must end
    at best:
  A moral (like all morals) melancholy,
And 'Et sepulchri immemor struis domos'
Shows that we build when we should but
    entomb us.

LXIV

At last they reach'd a quarter most retired,
  Where echo woke as if from a long
    slumber;
Though full of all things which could be
    desired,
  One wonder'd what to do with such a
    number
Of articles which nobody required;
  Here wealth had done its utmost to en-
    cumber
With furniture an exquisite apartment,
Which puzzled Nature much to know what
    Art meant.

LXV

It seem'd, however, but to open on
  A range or suite of further chambers,
    which
Might lead to heaven knows where; but in
    this one
  The moveables were prodigally rich:

Sofas 'twas half a sin to sit upon,
  So costly were they; carpets every stitch
Of workmanship so rare, they made you
    wish
You could glide o'er them like a golden
    fish.

LXVI

The black, however, without hardly deign-
    ing
  A glance at that which wrapt the slaves
    in wonder,
Trampled what they scarce trod for fear
    of staining,
  As if the milky way their feet was under
With all its stars; and with a stretch attain-
    ing
  A certain press or cupboard niched in
    yonder,
In that remote recess which you may see—
Or if you don't the fault is not in me,—

LXVII

I wish to be perspicuous; and the black,
  I say, unlocking the recess, pull'd forth
A quantity of clothes fit for the back
  Of any Mussulman, whate'er his worth;
And of variety there was no lack—
  And yet, though I have said there was
    no dearth,—
He chose himself to point out what he
    thought
Most proper for the Christians he had
    bought.

LXVIII

The suit he thought most suitable to each
  Was, for the elder and the stouter, first
A Candiote cloak, which to the knee
    might reach,
  And trousers not so tight that they
    would burst,
But such as fit an Asiatic breech;
  A shawl, whose folds in Cashmire had
    been nurst,
Slippers of saffron, dagger rich and handy;
In short, all things which form a Turkish
    dandy.

LXIX

While he was dressing, Baba, their black
    friend,
  Hinted the vast advantages which they
Might probably obtain both in the end,
  If they would but pursue the proper
    way
Which Fortune plainly seem'd to re-
    commend;
  And then he added, that he needs must
    say,
''Twould greatly tend to better their con-
    dition,
If they would condescend to circumcision.

719

LXX

'For his own part, he really should rejoice
    To see them true believers, but no less
Would leave his proposition to their
        choice.'
The other, thanking him for this excess
Of goodness, in thus leaving them a voice
    In such a trifle, scarcely could express
'Sufficiently' (he said) 'his approbation
Of all the customs of this polish'd nation.

LXXI

'For his own share—he saw but small
        objection
    To so respectable an ancient rite;
And, after swallowing down a slight
        refection,
    For which he own'd a present appetite,
He doubted not a few hours of reflection
    Would reconcile him to the business
        quite.'
'Will it?' said Juan, sharply: 'Strike me
        dead,
But they as soon shall circumcise my head!

LXXII

'Cut off a thousand heads, before——'—
        'Now, pray,'
Replied the other, 'do not interrupt.
You put me out in what I had to say.
Sir!—as I said, as soon as I have supped,
I shall perpend if your proposal may
    Be such as I can properly accept;
Provided always your great goodness still
Remits the matter to our own free-will.'

LXXIII

Baba eyed Juan, and said, 'Be so good
    As dress yourself—' and pointed out a
        suit
In which a Princess with great pleasure
        would
    Array her limbs; but Juan standing mute,
As not being in a masquerading mood,
    Gave it a slight kick with his Christian
        foot;
And when the old negro told him to 'Get
        ready,'
Replied, 'Old gentleman, I'm not a lady.'

LXXIV

'What you may be, I neither know nor
        care,'
    Said Baba; 'but pray do as I desire:
I have no more time nor many words to
        spare.
    'At least,' said Juan, 'sure I may inquire
The cause of this odd travesty?'—'For-
        bear,'
    Said Baba, 'to be curious; 'twill
        transpire,
No doubt, in proper place, and time, and
        season:
I have no authority to tell the reason.'

LXXV

'Then if I do,' said Juan, 'I'll be——'—
        'Hold!'
Rejoin'd the negro, 'pray be not pro-
        voking;
This spirit's well, but it may wax too bold,
    And you will find us not too fond of
        joking.'
'What, sir,' said Juan, 'shall it e'er be told
    That I unsex'd my dress?' But Baba,
        stroking
The things down, said, 'Incense me, and I
        call
Those who will leave you of no sex at all.

LXXVI

'I offer you a handsome suit of clothes:
    A woman's, true; but then there is a
        cause
Why you should wear them.'—'What,
        though my soul loathes
    The effeminate garb?'—thus, after a
        short pause,
Sigh'd Juan, muttering also some slight
        oaths,
    'What the devil shall I do with all this
        gauze?'
Thus he profanely term'd the finest lace
Which e'er set off a marriage-morning face.

LXXVII

And then he swore; and, sighing, on he
        slipp'd
    A pair of trousers of flesh-colour'd silk;
Next with a virgin zone he was equipp'd,
    Which girt a slight chemise as white as
        milk;
But tugging on his petticoat, he tripp'd,
    Which—as we say—or as the Scotch
        say, whilk,
(The rhyme obliges me to this; sometimes
Monarchs are less imperative than
        rhymes)—

LXXVIII

Whilk, which (or what you please), was
        owing to
    His garment's novelty, and his being
        awkward:
And yet at last he managed to get through
    His toilet, though no doubt a little back-
        ward:
The negro Baba help'd a little too,
    When some untoward part of raiment
        stuck hard;
And, wrestling both his arms into a gown,
He paused, and took a survey up and down.

LXXIX

One difficulty still remain'd—his hair
    Was hardly long enough; but Baba found
So many false long tresses all to spare,
    That soon his head was most completely
        crown'd,

After the manner then in fashion there;
  And this addition with such gems was
    bound
As suited the *ensemble* of his toilet,
While Baba made him comb his head and
    oil it.

LXXX

And now being femininely all array'd,
  With some small aid from scissors,
    paint, and tweezers,
He look'd in almost all respects a maid,
  And Baba smilingly exclaim'd, 'You
    see, sirs,
A perfect transformation here display'd;
  And now, then, you must come along
    with me, sirs,
That is—the Lady:' clapping his hands
    twice,
Four blacks were at his elbow in a trice.

LXXXI

'You, sir,' said Baba, nodding to the one,
  'Will please to accompany those gentle-
    men
To supper; but you, worthy Christian nun,
  Will follow me: no trifling, sir; for
    when
I say a thing, it must at once be done.
  What fear you? think you this a lion's
    den?
Why, 'tis a palace; where the truly wise
Anticipate the Prophet's paradise.

LXXXII

'You fool! I tell you no one means you
    harm.'
  'So much the better,' Juan said, 'for
    them;
Else they shall feel the weight of this my
    arm,
  Which is not quite so light as you may
    deem.
I yield thus far; but soon will break the
    charm,
  If any take me for that which I seem:
So that I trust for everybody's sake,
That this disguise may lead to no mistake.'

LXXXIII

'Blockhead! come on, and see,' quoth
    Baba; while
  Don Juan, turning to his comrade, who
Though somewhat grieved, could scarce
    forbear a smile
  Upon the metamorphosis in view,—
'Farewell!' they mutually exclaim'd: 'this
    soil
  Seems fertile in adventures strange and
    new;
One's turn'd half Mussulman, and one a
    maid,
  By this old black enchanter's unsought
    aid.'

LXXXIV

'Farewell!' said Juan: 'should we meet
    no more,
  I wish you a good appetite.'—'Farewell!'
Replied the other; 'though it grieves me
    sore:
  When we next meet, we'll have a tale to
    tell:
We needs must follow when Fate puts
    from shore.
  Keep your good name; though Eve
    herself once fell.'
'Nay,' quoth the maid, 'the Sultan's self
    shan't carry me,
Unless his highness promises to marry me.'

LXXXV

And thus they parted, each by separate
    doors;
  Baba led Juan onward room by room
Through glittering galleries, and o'er
    marble floors,
  Till a gigantic portal through the gloom,
Haughty and huge, along the distance
    lowers;
  And wafted far arose a rich perfume:
It seem'd as though they came upon a
    shrine,
For all was vast, still, fragrant, and divine.

LXXXVI

The giant door was broad, and bright,
    and high,
  Of gilded bronze, and carved in curious
    guise;
Warriors thereon were battling furiously;
  Here stalks the victor, there the van-
    quish'd lies;
There captives led in triumph droop the eye,
  And in perspective many a squadron flies:
It seems the work of times before the line
Of Rome transplanted fell with Con-
    stantine.

LXXXVII

This massy portal stood at the wide close
  Of a huge hall, and on its either side
Two little dwarfs, the least you could
    suppose,
  Were sate, like ugly imps, as if allied
In mockery to the enormous gate which
    rose
  O'er them in almost pyramidic pride:
The gate so splendid was in all its *features*,
You never thought about those little
    creatures,

LXXXVIII

Until you nearly trod on them, and then
  You started back in horror to survey
The wondrous hideousness of those small
    men,
  Whose colour was not black, nor white,
    nor grey,

But an extraneous mixture, which no pen
  Can trace, although perhaps the pencil
    may;
They were mis-shapen pigmies, deaf and
    dumb,—
Monsters, who cost a no less monstrous
    sum.

LXXXIX

Their duty was—for they were strong, and
    though
  They look'd so little, did strong things
    at times—
To ope this door, which they could really do,
  The hinges being as smooth as Rogers'
    rhymes;
And now and then, with tough strings of
    the bow,
  As is the custom of those Eastern climes,
To give some rebel Pacha a cravat;
For mutes are generally used for that.

XC

They spoke by signs—that is, not spoke
    at all;
  And looking like two incubi, they glared
As Baba with his fingers made them fall
  To heaving back the portal folds: it
    scared
Juan a moment, as this pair so small,
  With shrinking serpent optics on him
    stared;
It was as if their little looks could poison
Or fascinate whome'er they fix'd their eyes
    on.

XCI

Before they enter'd, Baba paused to hint
  To Juan some slight lessons as his guide:
'If you could just contrive,' he said, 'to
    stint
  That somewhat manly majesty of stride,
'Twould be as well, and—(though there's
    not much in't),
  To swing a little less from side to side,
Which has at times an aspect of the
    oddest:—
And also could you look a little modest,

XCII

''Twould be convenient; for these mutes
    have eyes
  Like needles, which may pierce those
    petticoats;
And if they should discover your disguise,
  You know how near us the deep
    Bosphorus floats;
And you and I may chance, ere morning
    rise,
  To find our way to Marmora without
    boats,
Stitch'd up in sacks—a mode of navigation
A good deal practised here upon
    occasion.'

XCIII

With this encouragement, he led the way
  Into a room still nobler than the last;
A rich confusion form'd a disarray
  In such sort, that the eye along it cast
Could hardly carry anything away,
  Object on object flash'd so bright and
    fast;
A dazzling mass of gems, and gold, and
    glitter,
Magnificently mingled in a litter.

XCIV

Wealth had done wonders—taste not
    much; such things
  Occur in Orient palaces, and even
In the more chasten'd domes of Western
    kings
  (Of which I have also seen some six or
    seven),
Where I can't say or gold or diamond
    flings
  Great lustre, there is much to be for-
    given;
Groups of bad statues, tables, chairs, and
    pictures,
On which I cannot pause to make my
    strictures.

XCV

In this imperial hall, at distance lay
  Under a canopy, and there reclined
Quite in a confidential queenly way,
  A lady; Baba stopp'd, and kneeling
    sign'd
To Juan, who, though not much used to
    pray,
  Knelt down by instinct, wondering in
    his mind
What all this meant: while Baba bow'd
    and bended
His head, until the ceremony ended.

XCVI

The lady rising up with such an air
  As Venus rose with from the wave, on
    them
Bent like an antelope a Paphian pair
  Of eyes, which put out each surround-
    ing gem;
And raising up an arm as moonlight fair,
  She sign'd to Baba, who first kiss'd the
    hem
Of her deep purple robe, and speaking
    low,
Pointed to Juan, who remain'd below.

XCVII

Her presence was as lofty as her state;
  Her beauty of that overpowering kind,
Whose force description only would
    abate:
  I'd rather leave it much to your own
    mind,

Than lessen it by what I could relate
  Of forms and features; it would strike
      you blind
Could I do justice to the full detail;
So, luckily for both, my phrases fail.

XCVIII

This much however I may add,—her years
  Were ripe, they might make six-and-
      twenty springs,
But there are forms which Time to touch
      forbears,
  And turns aside his scythe to vulgar
      things:
Such as was Mary's Queen of Scots; true—
      tears
  And love destroy; and sapping sorrow
      wrings
Charms from the charmer, yet some
      never grow
Ugly; for instance—Ninon de l'Enclos.

XCIX

She spake some words to her attendants,
      who
  Composed a choir of girls, ten or a
      dozen,
And were all clad alike; like Juan, too,
  Who wore their uniform, by Baba
      chosen:
They form'd a very nymph-like looking
      crew,
  Which might have called Diana's
      chorus 'cousin,'
As far as outward show may correspond;
I won't be bail for anything beyond.

C

They bow'd obeisance and withdrew,
      retiring,
  But not by the same door through
      which came in
Baba and Juan, which last stood admiring,
  At some small distance, all he saw within
This strange saloon, much fitted for
      inspiring
  Marvel and praise; for both or none
      things win;
And I must say, I ne'er could see the very
Great happiness of the 'Nil Admirari.'

CI

'Not to admire is all the art I know
  (Plain truth, dear Murray, needs few
      flowers of speech)
To make men happy, or to keep them so'
  (So take it in the very words of Creech)—
Thus Horace wrote we all know long ago;
  And thus Pope quotes the precept to
      re-teach
From his translation; but had *none*
      admired,
Would Pope have sung, or Horace been
      inspired?

CII

Baba, when all the damsels were with-
      drawn,
  Motion'd to Juan to approach, and then
A second time desired him to kneel down,
  And kiss the lady's foot; which maxim
      when
He heard repeated, Juan with a frown
  Drew himself up to his full height again,
And said, 'It grieved him, but he could
      not stoop
To any shoe, unless it shod the Pope.'

CIII

Baba, indignant at this ill-timed pride,
  Made fierce remonstrances, and then
      a threat
He mutter'd (but the last was given aside)
  About a bow-string—quite in vain;
      not yet
Would Juan bend, though 'twere to
      Mahomet's bride:
  There's nothing in the world like
      etiquette
In kingly chambers or imperial halls,
As also at the race and county balls.

CIV

He stood like Atlas, with a world of words
  About his ears, and nathless would not
      bend:
The blood of all his line's Castilian lords
  Boil'd in his veins, and rather than
      descend
To stain his pedigree, a thousand swords
  A thousand times of him had made an
      end;
At length perceiving the '*foot*' could not
      stand,
Baba proposed that he should kiss the
      hand.

CV

Here was an honourable compromise,
  A half-way house of diplomatic rest,
Where they might meet in much more
      peaceful guise;
  And Juan now his willingness exprest
To use all fit and proper courtesies,
  Adding, that this was commonest and
      best,
For through the South, the custom still
      commands
The gentleman to kiss the lady's hands.

CVI

And he advanced, though with but a bad
      grace,
  Though on more *thorough-bred* or
      fairer fingers
No lips e'er left their transitory trace:
  On such as these the lip too fondly
      lingers,

And for one kiss would fain imprint a brace,
  As you will see, if she you love shall bring hers
In contact; and sometimes even a fair stranger's
An almost twelvemonth's constancy endangers.

CVII

The lady eyed him o'er and o'er, and bade
  Baba retire, which he obey'd in style,
As if well used to the retreating trade;
  And taking hints in good part all the while,
He whisper'd Juan not to be afraid,
  And looking on him with a sort of smile,
Took leave, with such a face of satisfaction,
As good men wear who have done a virtuous action.

CVIII

When he was gone, there was a sudden change:
  I know not what might be the lady's thought,
But o'er her bright brow flash'd a tumult strange,
  And into her clear cheek the blood was brought,
Blood-red as sunset summer clouds which range
  The verge of Heaven; and in her large eyes wrought,
A mixture of sensations might be scann'd,
Of half-voluptuousness and half-command.

CIX

Her form had all the softness of her sex,
  Her features all the sweetness of the devil,
When he put on the cherub to perplex
  Eve, and paved (God knows how) the road to evil;
The sun himself was scarce more free from specks
  Than she from aught at which the eye could cavil;
Yet, somehow, there was something somewhere wanting,
As if she rather *order'd* than was *granting*.—

CX

Something imperial, or imperious, threw
  A chain o'er all she did; that is, a chain
Was thrown as 'twere about the neck of you,—
  And rapture's self will seem almost a pain
With aught which looks like despotism in view;
  Our souls at least are free, and 'tis in vain

We would against them make the flesh obey—
The spirit in the end will have its way.

CXI

Her very smile was haughty, though so sweet;
  Her very nod was not an inclination:
There was a self-will even in her small feet,
  As though they were quite conscious of her station—
They trod as upon necks; and to complete
  Her state (it is the custom of her nation),
A poniard deck'd her girdle, as the sign
She was a sultan's bride (thank Heaven, not mine!)

CXII

'To hear and to obey' had been from birth
  The law of all around her; to fulfil
All phantasies which yielded joy or mirth,
  Had been her slaves' chief pleasure, as her will;
Her blood was high, her beauty scarce of earth:
  Judge, then, if her caprices e'er stood still;
Had she but been a Christian, I've a notion
We should have found out the 'perpetual motion.'

CXIII

Whate'er she saw and coveted was brought;
  Whate'er she did *not* see, if she supposed
It might be seen, with diligence was sought,
  And when 'twas found straightway the bargain closed:
There was no end unto the things she bought,
  Nor to the trouble which her fancies caused:
Yet even her tyranny had such a grace,
The women pardon'd all except her face.

CXIV

Juan, the latest of her whims, had caught
  Her eye in passing on his way to sale;
She order'd him directly to be bought,
  And Baba, who had ne'er been known to fail
In any kind of mischief to be wrought,
  At all such auctions knew how to prevail:
She had no prudence, but he had; and this
Explains the garb which Juan took amiss.

CXV

His youth and features favour'd the disguise,
  And should you ask how she, a sultan's bride,
Could risk or compass such strange phantasies,
  This I must leave sultanas to decide:

724

Emperors are only husbands in wives'
        eyes,
    And kings and consorts oft are
        mystified,
As we may ascertain with due precision,
Some by experience, others by tradition.

CXVI

But to the main point, where we have been
        tending:—
    She now conceived all difficulties past,
And deem'd herself extremely con-
        descending
    When, being made her property at last,
Without more preface, in her blue eyes
        blending
    Passion and power, a glance on him she
        cast,
    And merely saying, 'Christian, canst thou
        love?'
Conceived that phrase was quite enough
        to move.

CXVII

And so it was, in proper time and place;
    But Juan, who had still his mind o'er-
        flowing
With Haidée's isle and soft Ionian face,
    Felt the warm blood, which in his face
        was glowing,
Rush back upon his heart, which fill'd
        apace,
    And left his cheeks as pale as snow-
        drops blowing:
These words went through his soul like
        Arab spears,
So that he spoke not, but burst into tears.

CXVIII

She was a good deal shock'd; not shock'd
        at tears,
    For women shed and use them at their
        liking;
But there is something when man's eye
        appears
    Wet, still more disagreeable and strik-
        ing:
A woman's tear-drop melts, a man's half
        sears,
    Like molten lead, as if you thrust a pike
        in
His heart to force it out, for (to be shorter)
To them 'tis a relief, to us a torture.

CXIX

And she would have consoled, but knew
        not how:
    Having no equals, nothing which had
        e'er
Infected her with sympathy till now,
    And never having dreamt what 'twas
        to bear

Aught of a serious, sorrowing kind,
        although
    There might arise some pouting petty
        care
To cross her brow, she wonder'd how so
        near
Her eyes another's eye could shed a tear.

CXX

But nature teaches more than power can
        spoil,
    And, when a *strong* although a strange
        sensation
Moves—female hearts are such a genial
        soil
    For kinder feelings, whatsoe'er their
        nation,
They naturally pour the 'wine and oil,'
    Samaritans in every situation;
And thus Gulbeyaz, though she knew not
        why,
Felt an odd glistening moisture in her eye.

CXXI

But tears must stop like all things else;
        and soon
    Juan, who for an instant had been
        moved
To such a sorrow by the intrusive tone
    Of one who dared to ask if 'he *had*
        loved,'
Call'd back the stoic to his eyes, which
        shone
    Bright with the very weakness he re-
        proved;
And although sensitive to beauty, he
Felt most indignant still at not being free.

CXXII

Gulbeyaz, for the first time in her days,
    Was much embarrass'd, never having
        met
In all her life with aught save prayers and
        praise;
    And as she also risk'd her life to get
Him whom she meant to tutor in love's
        ways,
    Into a comfortable tête-à-tête,
To lose the hour would make her quite a
        martyr,
And they had wasted now almost a
        quarter.

CXXIII

I also would suggest the fitting time,
    To gentlemen in any such like case,
That is to say—in a meridian clime,
    With us there is more law given to the
        chase,
But here a small delay forms a great crime:
    So recollect that the extremest grace
Is just two minutes for your declaration—
A moment more would hurt your
        reputation.

CXXIV

Juan's was good; and might have been
 still better,
But he had got Haidée into his head:
However strange, he could not yet forget
 her,
Which made him seem exceedingly ill-
 bred.
Gulbeyaz, who look'd on him as her debtor
For having had him to her palace led,
Began to blush up to the eyes, and then
Grow deadly pale, and then blush back
 again.

CXXV

At length, in an imperial way, she laid
 Her hand on his, and bending on him
 eyes,
Which needed not an empire to persuade,
 Look'd into his for love, where none
 replies:
Her brow grew black, but she would not
 upbraid,
 That being the last thing a proud
 woman tries;
She rose, and pausing one chaste moment,
 threw
Herself upon his breast, and there she grew.

CXXVI

This was an awkward test, as Juan found,
 But he was steel'd by sorrow, wrath,
 and pride:
With gentle force her white arms he
 unwound,
 And seated her all drooping by his side,
Then rising haughtily he glanced around,
 And looking coldly in her face, he cried,
'The prison'd eagle will not pair, nor I
Serve a sultana's sensual phantasy.

CXXVII

'Thou ask'st, if I can love? be this the
 proof
 How much I *have* loved—that I love
 not *thee*!
In this vile garb, the distaff, web, and woof,
 Were fitter for me: Love is for the free!
I am not dazzled by this splendid roof;
 Whate'er thy power, and great it seems
 to be,
Heads bow, knees bend, eyes watch
 around a throne,
And hands obey—our hearts are still our
 own.'

CXXVIII

This was a truth to us extremely trite;
 Not so to her, who ne'er had heard such
 things:
She deem'd her least command must
 yield delight,
 Earth being only made for queens and
 kings.

If hearts lay on the left side or the right
 She hardly knew, to such perfection
 brings
Legitimacy its born votaries, when
Aware of their due royal rights o'er men.

CXXIX

Besides, as has been said, she was so fair
 As even in a much humbler lot had
 made
A kingdom or confusion anywhere,
 And also, as may be presumed, she laid
Some stress on charms, which seldom are,
 if e'er,
 By their possessors thrown into the
 shade:
She thought hers gave a double 'right
 divine';
And half of that opinion's also mine.

CXXX

Remember, or (if you can not) imagine,
 Ye! who have kept your chastity when
 young,
While some more desperate dowager has
 been waging
 Love with you, and been in the dog-
 days stung
By your refusal, recollect her raging!
 Or recollect all that was said or sung
On such a subject; then suppose the
 face
Of a young downright beauty in this
 case.

CXXXI

Suppose,—but you already have sup-
 posed,
 The spouse of Potiphar, the Lady
 Booby,
Phædra, and all which story has disclosed
 Of good examples; pity that so few by
Poets and private tutors are exposed,
 To educate—ye youth of Europe—
 you by!
But when you have supposed the few we
 know,
You can't suppose Gulbeyaz' angry brow.

CXXXII

A tigress robb'd of young, a lioness,
 Or any interesting beast of prey,
Are similes at hand for the distress
 Of ladies who cannot have their own
 way;
But though my turn will not be served
 with less,
 These don't express one half what I
 should say:
For what is stealing young ones, few or
 many,
To cutting short their hopes of having
 any?

CXXXIII

The love of offspring's nature's general
      law,
  From tigresses and cubs to ducks and
      ducklings;
There's nothing whets the beak, or arms
      the claw,
  Like an invasion of their babes and
      sucklings;
And all who have seen a human nursery,
      saw
  How mothers love their children's
      squalls and chucklings:
This strong extreme effect (to tire no
      longer
Your patience) shows the cause must still
      be stronger.

CXXXIV

If I said fire flash'd from Gulbeyaz' eyes,
  'Twere nothing—for her eyes flash'd
      always fire;
Or said her cheeks assumed the deepest
      dyes,
  I should but bring disgrace upon the
      dyer,
So supernatural was her passion's rise;
  For ne'er till now she knew a check'd
      desire:
Even ye who know what a check'd woman
      is
(Enough, God knows!) would much fall
      short of this.

CXXXV

Her rage was but a minute's, and 'twas
      well—
  A moment's more had slain her; but
      the while
It lasted 'twas like a short glimpse of hell:
  Nought's more sublime than energetic
      bile,
Though horrible to see, yet grand to tell,
  Like ocean warring 'gainst a rocky isle;
And the deep passions flashing through
      her form
Made her a beautiful embodied storm.

CXXXVI

A vulgar tempest 'twere to a typhoon
  To match a common fury with her rage,
And yet she did not want to reach the
      moon,
  Like moderate Hotspur on the immortal
      page;
Her anger pitch'd into a lower tune,
  Perhaps the fault of her soft sex and
      age—
Her wish was but to 'kill, kill, kill,' like
      Lear's,
And then her thirst of blood was quench'd
      in tears.

CXXXVII

A storm it raged, and like the storm it
      pass'd,
  Pass'd without words—in fact she
      could not speak;
And then her sex's shame broke in at last,
  A sentiment till then in her but weak,
But now it flow'd in natural and fast,
  As water through an unexpected leak;
For she felt humbled—and humiliation
Is sometimes good for people in her
      station.

CXXXVIII

It teaches them that they are flesh and blood
  It also gently hints to them that others,
Although of clay, are yet not quite of mud;
  That urns and pipkins are but fragile
      brothers,
And works of the same pottery, bad or
      good,
  Though not all born of the same sires
      and mothers,
It teaches—Heaven knows only what it
      teaches,
But sometimes it may mend, and often
      reaches.

CXXXIX

Her first thought was to cut off Juan's
      head;
  Her second, to cut only his—acquain-
      tance;
Her third, to ask him where he had been
      bred;
  Her fourth, to rally him into re-
      pentance;
Her fifth, to call her maids and go to bed;
  Her sixth, to stab herself; her seventh,
      to sentence
The lash to Baba:—but her grand resource
Was to sit down again, and cry of course.

CXL

She thought to stab herself, but then she
      had
  The dagger close at hand, which made
      it awkward;
For Eastern stays are little made to pad,
  So that a poniard pierces if 'tis stuck
      hard:
She thought of killing Juan—but, poor lad!
  Though he deserved it well for being so
      backward,
The cutting off his head was not the art
Most likely to attain her aim—his heart.

CXLI

Juan was moved: he had made up his mind
  To be impaled, or quarter'd as a dish
For dogs, or to be slain with pangs
      refined,
  Or thrown to lions, or made baits for
      fish,

And thus heroically stood resign'd,
 Rather than sin—except to his own
  wish:
But all his great preparatives for dying
Dissolved like snow before a woman
 crying.

CXLII

As through his palms Bob Acres' valour
 oozed,
 So Juan's virtue ebb'd, I know not how;
And first he wonder'd why he had refused;
 And then, if matters could be made up
  now;
And next his savage virtue he accused,
 Just as a friar may accuse his vow,
Or as a dame repents her of her oath,
Which mostly ends in some small breach
 of both.

CXLIII

So he began to stammer some excuses;
 But words are not enough in such a
  matter,
Although you borrow'd all that e'er the
 muses
 Have sung, or even a Dandy's dandiest
  chatter,
Or all the figures Castlereagh abuses;
 Just as a languid smile began to flatter
His peace was making, but before he
 ventured
Further, old Baba rather briskly enter'd.

CXLIV

'Bride of the Sun! and Sister of the
 Moon!'
 ('Twas thus he spake,) 'and Empress of
  the Earth!
Whose frown would put the spheres all
 out of tune,
 Whose smile makes all the planets
  dance with mirth,
Your slave brings tidings—he hopes not
 too soon—
 Which your sublime attention may be
  worth:
The Sun himself has sent me like a ray,
To hint that he is coming up this way.'

CXLV

'Is it,' exclaim'd Gulbeyaz, 'as you say?
 I wish to heaven he would not shine till
  morning!
But bid my women form the Milky-way.
 Hence, my old comet! give the stars due
  warning—
And, Christian! mingle with them as you
 may,
 And as you'd have me pardon your past
  scorning'—
Here they were interrupted by a humming
Sound, and then by a cry, 'The Sultan's
 coming!'

CXLVI

First came her damsels, a decorous file,
 And then his Highness' eunuchs, black
  and white;
The train might reach a quarter of a mile:
 His majesty was always so polite
As to announce his visits a long while
 Before he came, especially at night;
For being the last wife of the Emperor,
She was of course the favourite of the four.

CXLVII

His Highness was a man of solemn port,
 Shawl'd to the nose, and bearded to the
  eyes,
Snatch'd from a prison to preside at court,
 His lately bowstrung brother caused
  his rise;
He was as good a sovereign of the sort
 As any mentioned in the histories
Of Cantemir, or Knöllës, where few shine
Save Solyman, the glory of their line.

CXLVIII

He went to mosque in state, and said his
 prayers
 With more than 'Oriental scrupulosity';
He left to his vizier all state affairs,
 And show'd but little royal curiosity:
I know not if he had domestic cares—
 No process proved connubial ani-
  mosity;
Four wives and twice five hundred maids,
 unseen,
Were ruled as calmly as a Christian queen.

CXLIX

If now and then there happen'd a slight
 slip,
 Little was heard of criminal or crime;
The story scarcely pass'd a single lip—
 The sack and sea had settled all in time,
From which the secret nobody could rip:
 The public knew no more than does this
  rhyme;
No scandals made the daily press a
 curse—
Morals were better, and the fish no worse.

CL

He saw with his own eyes the moon was
 round,
 Was also certain that the earth was
  square,
Because he had journey'd fifty miles, and
 found
 No sign that it was circular anywhere:
His empire also was without a bound:
 'Tis true, a little troubled here and there,
By rebel pachas, and encroaching giaours,
But then they never came to 'the Seven
 Towers';

CLI

Except in shape of envoys, who were sent
　　To lodge there when a war broke out,
　　　　according
To the true law of nations, which ne'er
　　meant
　　　　Those scoundrels, who have never had
　　　　　a sword in
Their dirty diplomatic hands, to vent
　　Their spleen in making strife, and
　　　　safely wording
Their lies, yclept despatches, without risk
　　or
The singeing of a single inky whisker.

CLII

He had fifty daughters and four dozen sons,
　　Of whom all such as came of age were
　　　　stow'd,
The former in a palace, where like nuns
　　They lived till some Bashaw was sent
　　　　abroad,
When she, whose turn it was, was wed at
　　once,
　　　　Sometimes at six years old—though
　　　　　this seems odd,
'Tis true; the reason is, that the Bashaw
Must make a present to his sire-in-law.

CLIII

His sons were kept in prison, till they grew
　　Of years to fill a bowstring or the throne,
One or the other, but which of the two
　　Could yet be known unto the fates alone;
Meantime the education they went
　　through
　　　　Was princely, as the proofs have always
　　　　　shown;
So that the heir-apparent still was found
No less deserving to be hang'd than
　　crown'd.

CLIV

His Majesty saluted his fourth spouse
　　With all the ceremonies of his rank,
Who clear'd her sparkling eyes and
　　smooth'd her brows,
　　　　As suits a matron who has play'd a
　　　　　prank;
These must seem doubly mindful of their
　　vows,
　　　　To save the credit of their breaking bank:
To no men are such cordial greetings given
As those whose wives have made them fit
　　for heaven.

CLV

His Highness cast around his great black
　　eyes,
　　　　And looking, as he always look'd,
　　　　　perceived
Juan amongst the damsels in disguise,
　　At which he seem'd no whit surprised
　　　　nor grieved,

But just remark'd with air sedate and wise,
　　While still a fluttering sigh Gulbeyaz
　　　　heaved,
'I see you've bought another girl; 'tis pity
That a mere Christian should be half so
　　pretty.'

CLVI

This compliment, which drew all eyes
　　upon
　　　　The new-bought virgin, made her blush
　　　　　and shake.
Her comrades, also, thought themselves
　　undone:
　　　　Oh! Mahomet! that his Majesty should
　　　　　take
Such notice of a giaour, while scarce to
　　one
　　　　Of them his lips imperial ever spake!
There was a general whisper, toss, and
　　wriggle,
But etiquette forbade them all to giggle.

CLVII

The Turks do well to shut—at least, some-
　　times—
　　　　The women up—because, in sad reality,
Their chastity in these unhappy climes
　　Is not a thing of that astringent quality
Which in the north prevents precocious
　　crimes,
　　　　And makes our snow less pure than our
　　　　　morality;
The sun, which yearly melts the polar ice,
Has quite the contrary effect on vice.

CLVIII

Thus in the East they are extremely strict,
　　And wedlock and a padlock mean the
　　　　same:
Excepting only when the former's pick'd
　　It ne'er can be replaced in proper frame;
Spoilt, as a pipe of claret is when prick'd:
　　But then their own polygamy's to
　　　　blame;
Why don't they knead two virtuous souls
　　for life
Into that moral centaur, man and wife?

CLIX

Thus far our chronicle; and now we pause,
　　Though not for want of matter; but 'tis
　　　　time,
According to the ancient epic laws,
　　To slacken sail, and anchor with our
　　　　rhyme.
Let this fifth canto meet with due applause,
　　The sixth shall have a touch of the sub-
　　　　lime;
Meanwhile, as Homer sometimes sleeps,
　　perhaps
You'll pardon to my Muse a few short
　　naps.

PREFACE TO
CANTOS VI, VII, AND VIII

THE details of the siege of Ismail in two of the following cantos (*i.e.* the seventh and eighth) are taken from a French Work, entitled 'Histoire de la Nouvelle Russie.' Some of the incidents attributed to Don Juan really occurred, particularly the circumstance of his saving the infant, which was the actual case of the late Duc de Richelieu, then a young volunteer in the Russian service, and afterward the founder and benefactor of Odessa, where his name and memory can never cease to be regarded with reverence.

In the course of these cantos, a stanza or two will be found relative to the late Marquis of Londonderry, but written some time before his decease. Had that person's oligarchy died with him, they would have been suppressed; as it is, I am aware of nothing in the manner of his death or of his life to prevent the free expression of the opinions of all whom his whole existence was consumed in endeavouring to enslave. That he was an amiable man in *private* life, may or may not be true: but with this the public have nothing to do; and as to lamenting his death, it will be time enough when Ireland has ceased to mourn for his birth. As a minister, I, for one of millions, looked upon him as the most despotic in intention, and the weakest in intellect, that ever tyrannised over a country. It is the first time indeed since the Normans that England has been insulted by a *minister* (at least) who could not speak English, and that parliament permitted itself to be dictated to in the language of Mrs. Malaprop.

Of the manner of his death little need be said, except that if a poor radical, such as Waddington or Watson, had cut his throat, he would have been buried in a cross-road, with the usual appurtenances of the stake and mallet. But the minister was an elegant lunatic—a sentimental suicide—he merely cut the 'carotid artery,' (blessings on their learning!) and lo! the pageant, and the Abbey! and 'the syllables of dolour yelled forth' by the newspapers—and the harangue of the Coroner in a eulogy over the bleeding body of the deceased—(an Anthony worthy of such a Cæsar)—and the nauseous and atrocious cant of a degraded crew of conspirators against all that is sincere and honourable. In his death he was necessarily one of two things by the *law**—a felon or a madman—and in either case no great subject for panegyric. In his life he was—what all the world knows, and half of it will feel for years to come, unless his death prove a 'moral lesson' to the surviving† Sejani of Europe. It may at least serve as some consolation to the nations, that their oppressors are not happy, and in some instances judge so justly of their own actions as to anticipate the sentence of mankind.—Let us hear no more of this man; and let Ireland remove the ashes of her Grattan from the sanctuary of Westminster. Shall the patriot of humanity repose by the Werther of politics!!!

* I say by the *law* of the *land*—the laws of humanity judge more gently; but as the legitimates have always the *law* in their mouths, let them here make the most of it.

† From this number must be excepted Canning. Canning is a genius, almost a universal one, an orator, a wit, a poet, a statesman; and no man of talent can long pursue the path of his late predecessor, Lord C. If ever man saved his country, Canning *can;* but *will* he? I, for one, hope so.

With regard to the objections which have been made on another score to the already published cantos of this poem, I shall content myself with two quotations from Voltaire:—'La pudeur s'est enfuite des cœurs, et s'est refugiée sur les lèvres.' . . . . . 'Plus les mœurs sont dépravés, plus les expressions deviennent mesurées; on croit regagner en langage ce qu'on a perdu en vertu.'

This is the real fact, as applicable to the degraded and hypocritical mass which leavens the present English generation, and is the only answer they deserve. The hackneyed and lavished title of Blasphemer—which, with Radical, Liberal, Jacobin, Reformer, &c., are the changes which the hirelings are daily ringing in the ears of those who will listen—should be welcome to all who recollect on *whom* it was originally bestowed. Socrates and Jesus Christ were put to death publicly as *blasphemers*, and so have been and may be many who dare to oppose the most notorious abuses of the name of God and the mind of man. But persecution is not refutation, nor even triumph: the 'wretched infidel,' as he is called, is probably happier in his prison than the proudest of his assailants. With his opinions I have nothing to do—they may be right or wrong—but he has suffered for them, and that very suffering for conscience' sake will make more proselytes to deism than the example of heterodox prelates to Christianity, suicide statesmen to oppression, or overpensioned homicides to the impious alliance which insults the world with the name of 'Holy'! I have no wish to trample on the dishonoured or the dead; but it would be well if the adherents to the classes from whence those persons sprung should abate a little of the *cant* which is the crying sin of this double-dealing and false-speaking time of selfish spoilers, and—but enough for the present.

PISA, *July*, 1822.

CANTO THE SIXTH

I

'THERE is a tide in the affairs of men,
　Which, taken at the flood,'—you know
　　the rest,
And most of us have found it now and
　　then:
　At least we think so, though but few
　　have guess'd
The moment, till too late to come again.
　But no doubt everything is for the best—
Of which the surest sign is in the end:
When things are at the worst they some-
　　times mend.

II

There is a tide in the affairs of women,
　Which, taken at the flood, leads—God
　　knows where:
Those navigators must be able seamen
　Whose charts lay down its currents to a
　　hair,
Not all the reveries of Jacob Behmen
　With its strange whirls and eddies can
　　compare:
Men with their heads reflect on this and
　　that—
But women with their hearts or heaven
　　knows what!

III

And yet a headlong, headstrong, downright she,
  Young, beautiful, and daring—who
   would risk
A throne, the world, the universe, to be
  Beloved in her own way, and rather
   whisk
The stars from out the sky, than not be
  free
As are the billows when the breeze is
  brisk—
Though such a she's a devil (if there be
  one),
Yet she would make full many a Mani-
  chean.

IV

Thrones, worlds, et cetera, are so oft up-
 set
  By commonest ambition, that when
   passion
O'erthrows the same, we readily forget,
  Or at the least forgive, the loving rash
   one.
If Anthony be well remember'd yet,
  'Tis not his conquests keep his name in
   fashion,
But Actium lost, for Cleopatra's eyes
Outbalance all the Cæsar's victories.

V

He died at fifty for a queen of forty;
  I wish their years had been fifteen and
   twenty,
For then wealth, kingdoms, worlds are
  but a sport—I
  Remember when, though I had no great
   plenty
Of worlds to lose, yet still, to pay my court, I
  Gave what I had—a heart; as the world
   went, I
Gave what was worth a world; for worlds
  could never
Restore me those pure feelings, gone for
  ever.

VI

'Twas the boy's 'mite,' and, like the
 'widow's,' may
  Perhaps be weigh'd hereafter, if not
   now;
But whether such things do or do not
  weigh,
  All who have loved, or love, will still
   allow
Life has nought like it. God is love, they
  say,
  And Love's a god, or was before the
   brow
Of earth was wrinkled by the sins and
  tears
Of—but Chronology best knows the
  years.

VII

We left our hero and third heroine in
  A kind of state more awkward than un-
   common,
For gentlemen must sometimes risk their
  skin
  For that sad tempter, a forbidden
   woman:
Sultans too much abhor this sort of sin,
  And don't agree at all with the wise
   Roman,
Heroic, stoic Cato, the sententious,
Who lent his lady to his friend Hortensius.

VIII

I know Gulbeyaz was extremely wrong;
  I own it, I deplore it, I condemn it;
But I detest all fiction even in song,
  And so must tell the truth, howe'er you
   blame it.
Her reason being weak, her passions
  strong,
  She thought that her lord's heart (even
   could she claim it)
Was scarce enough; for he had fifty-nine
Years, and a fifteen-hundredth con-
  cubine.

IX

I am not, like Cassio, 'an arithmetician,'
  But by the 'bookish theoric' it appears,
If 'tis summ'd up with feminine precision,
  That, adding to the account his High-
   ness' years,
The fair Sultana erred from inanition;
  For, were the Sultan just to all his dears,
She could but claim the fifteen-hundredth
  part
Of what should be monopoly—the heart.

X

It is observed that ladies are litigious
  Upon all legal objects of possession,
And not the least so when they are
  religious,
  Which doubles what they think of the
   transgression:
With suits and prosecutions they besiege
  us,
  As the tribunals show through many a
   session,
When they suspect that any one goes
  shares
In that to which the law makes them sole
  heirs.

XI

Now, if this holds good in a Christian land,
  The heathen also, though with lesser
   latitude,
Are apt to carry things with a high hand,
  And take, what kings call 'an imposing
   attitude';

And for their rights connubial make a
stand,
    When their liege husbands treat them
      with ingratitude;
And as four wives must have quadruple
claims,
    The Tigris hath its jealousies like Thames.

XII

Gulbeyaz was the fourth, and (as I said)
    The favourite; but what's favour
      amongst four?
Polygamy may well be held in dread,
    Not only as a sin, but as a *bore:*
Most wise men with *one* moderate
      woman wed,
    Will scarcely find philosophy for more;
And all (except Mahometans) forbear
To make the nuptial couch a 'Bed of
Ware.'

XIII

His Highness, the sublimest of man-
kind,—
    So styled according to the usual forms
Of every monarch, till they are consign'd
    To those sad hungry Jacobins the
      worms,
Who on the very loftiest kings have
dined,—
    His Highness gazed upon Gulbeyaz'
      charms,
Expecting all the welcome of a lover
(A 'Highland welcome' all the wide world
over).

XIV

Now here we should distinguish; for
howe'er
    Kisses, sweet words, embraces, and all
      that,
May look like what is—neither here nor
there,
    They are put on as easily as a hat,
Or rather bonnet, which the fair sex wear,
    Trimm'd either heads or hearts to
      decorate,
Which form an ornament, but no more
part
Of heads, than their caresses of the heart.

XV

A slight blush, a soft tremor, a calm kind
    Of gentle feminine delight, and shown
More in the eyelids than the eyes, resign'd
    Rather to hide what pleases most
      unknown,
Are the best tokens (to a modest mind)
    Of love, when seated on his loveliest
      throne,
A sincere woman's breast,—for over-
warm
Or over-*cold* annihilates the charm.

XVI

For over-warmth, if false, is worse than
truth;
    If true, 'tis no great lease of its own fire;
For no one, save in very early youth,
    Would like (I think) to trust all to desire,
Which is but a precarious bond, in sooth,
    And apt to be transferr'd to the first
      buyer
At a sad discount: while your over-chilly
Women, on t'other hand, seem somewhat
silly.

XVII

That is, we cannot pardon their bad taste,
    For so it seems to lovers swift or slow,
Who fain would have a mutual flame
confess'd,
    And see a sentimental passion glow,
Even were St. Francis' paramour their guest,
    In his monastic concubine of snow;—
In short, the maxim for the amorous tribe is
Horatian, 'Medio tu tutissimus ibis.'

XVIII

The 'tu' 's *too* much,—but let it stand,—
the verse
    Requires it, that's to say, the English
      rhyme,
And not the pink of old hexameters;
    But, after all, there's neither tune nor
      time
In the last line, which cannot well be worse,
    And was thrust in to close the octave's
      chime:
I own no prosody can ever rate it
As a rule, but *truth* may, if you translate it.

XIX

If fair Gulbeyaz overdid her part,
    I know not—it succeeded, and success
Is much in most things, not less in the
heart
    Than other articles of female dress.
Self-love in man, too, beats all female art;
    They lie, we lie, all lie, but love no less:
And no one virtue yet, except starvation,
Could stop that worst of vices—pro-
pagation.

XX

We leave this royal couple to repose:
    A bed is not a throne, and they may
      sleep,
Whate'er their dreams be, if of joys or
woes:
    Yet disappointed joys are woes as deep
As any man's clay mixture undergoes.
    Our least of sorrows are such as we
      weep;
'Tis the vile daily drop on drop which
wears
The soul out (like the stone) with petty
cares.

XXI

A scolding wife, a sullen son, a bill
  To pay, unpaid, protested or discounted
At a per-centage; a child cross, dog ill,
  A favourite horse fallen lame just as he's
    mounted,
A bad old woman making a worse will,
  Which leaves you minus of the cash you
    counted
As certain;—these are paltry things, and
    yet
I've rarely seen the man they did not fret.

XXII

I'm a philosopher; confound them all!
  Bills, beasts, and men, and—no! *not*
    womankind!
With one good hearty curse I vent my gall,
  And then my stoicism leaves nought
    behind
Which it can either pain or evil call,
  And I can give my whole soul up to
    mind;
Though what *is* soul, or mind, their birth
    or growth,
Is more than I know—the deuce take
    them both!

XXIII

So now all things are damn'd one feels at
    ease,
  As after reading Athanasius' curse,
Which doth your true believer so much
    please:
  I doubt if any now could make it worse
O'er his worst enemy when at his knees,
  'Tis so sententious, positive, and terse,
And decorates the Book of Common
    Prayer,
As doth a rainbow the just clearing air.

XXIV

Gulbeyaz and her lord were sleeping, or
  At least one of them!—Oh, the heavy
    night,
When wicked wives, who love some
    bachelor,
  Lie down in dudgeon to sigh for the
    light
Of the grey morning, and look vainly for
  Its twinkle through the lattice dusky
    quite—
To toss, to tumble, doze, revive, and quake
Lest their too lawful bed-fellow should
    wake!

XXV

These are beneath the canopy of heaven,
  Also beneath the canopy of beds
Four-posted and silk-curtain'd, which are
    given
  For rich men and their brides to lay
    their heads

Upon, in sheets white as what bards call
    'driven
  Snow.' Well! 'tis all hap-hazard when
    one weds.
Gulbeyaz was an empress, but had been
Perhaps as wretched if a *peasant's quean.*

XXVI

Don Juan in his feminine disguise,
  With all the damsels in their long array,
Had bow'd themselves before th' imperial
    eyes,
  And at the usual signal ta'en their way
Back to their chambers, those long
    galleries
  In the seraglio, where the ladies lay
Their delicate limbs; a thousand bosoms
    there
Beating for love, as the caged birds for
    air.

XXVII

I love the sex, and sometimes would
    reverse
  The tyrant's wish, 'that mankind only
    had
One neck, which he with one fell stroke
    might pierce:'
  My wish is quite as wide, but not so bad,
And much more tender on the whole than
    fierce;
  It being (not *now,* but only while a lad)
That womankind had but one rosy
    mouth,
To kiss them all at once from North to
    South.

XXVIII

Oh, enviable Briareus! with thy hands
  And heads, if thou hadst all things
    multiplied
In such proportion!—But my Muse with-
    stands
  The giant thought of being a Titan's
    bride,
Or travelling in Patagonian lands;
  So let us back to Lilliput, and guide
Our hero through the labyrinth of love
In which we left him several lines above.

XXIX

He went forth with the lovely Odalisques,
  At the given signal join'd to their array;
And though he certainly ran many risks,
  Yet he could not at times keep, by the
    way,
(Although the consequences of such frisks
  Are worse than the worst damages men
    pay
In moral England, where the thing's a
    tax,)
From ogling all their charms from breasts
    to backs.

XXX

Still he forgot not his disguise:—along
  The galleries from room to room they
    walk'd,
A virgin-like and edifying throng,
  By eunuchs flank'd; while at their head
    there stalk'd
A dame who kept up discipline among
  The female ranks, so that none stirr'd
    or talk'd,
Without her sanction on their she-
    parades:
Her title was 'the Mother of the Maids.'

XXXI

Whether she was a 'mother,' I know not,
  Or whether they were 'maids' who
    call'd her mother;
But this is her seraglio title, got
  I know not how, but good as any other;
So Cantemir can tell you, or De Tott:
  Her office was to keep aloof or smother
All bad propensities in fifteen hundred
Young women, and correct them when
    they blunder'd.

XXXII

A goodly sinecure, no doubt! but made
  More easy by the absence of all men—
Except his majesty,—who, with her aid,
  And guards, and bolts, and walls, and
    now and then,
A slight example, just to cast a shade
  Along the rest, contrived to keep this
    den
Of beauties cool as an Italian convent,
Where all the passions have, alas! but one
    vent.

XXXIII

And what is that? Devotion, doubtless—
    how
  Could you ask such a question?—but
    we will
Continue. As I said, this goodly row
  Of ladies of all countries at the will
Of one good man, with stately march and
    slow,
  Like water-lilies floating down a rill—
Or rather lake—for *rills* do *not* run
    slowly,—
Paced on most maiden-like and melan-
    choly.

XXXIV

But when they reach'd their own apart-
    ments, there,
  Like birds, or boys, or bedlamites
    broke loose,
Waves at spring-tide, or women any-
    where
  When freed from bonds (which are of
    no great use

After all), or like Irish at a fair,
  Their guards being gone, and as it were
    a truce
Establish'd between them and bondage,
    they
Began to sing, dance, chatter, smile, and
    play.

XXXV

Their talk, of course, ran most on the new
    comer;
  Her shape, her hair, her air, her every-
    thing:
Some thought her dress did not so much
    become her,
  Or wonder'd at her ears without a ring;
Some said her years were getting nigh
    their summer,
  Others contended they were but in
    spring;
Some thought her rather masculine in
    height,
While others wish'd that she had been so
    quite.

XXXVI

But no one doubted on the whole, that she
  Was what her dress bespoke, a damsel
    fair,
And fresh, and 'beautiful exceedingly,'
  Who with the brightest Georgians
    might compare:
They wonder'd how Gulbeyaz, too, could
    be
  So silly as to buy slaves who might share
(If that his Highness wearied of his bride)
Her throne and power, and everything
    beside.

XXXVII

But what was strangest in this virgin crew,
  Although her beauty was enough to vex,
After the first investigating view,
  They all found out as few, or fewer,
    specks
In the fair form of their companion new,
  Than is the custom of the gentle sex,
When they survey, with Christian eyes or
    Heathen,
In a new face 'the ugliest creature breath-
    ing.'

XXXVIII

And yet they had their little jealousies,
  Like all the rest; but upon this occasion,
Whether there are such things as
    sympathies
  Without our knowledge or our appro-
    bation,
Although they could not see through his
    disguise,
  All felt a soft kind of concatenation,
Like magnetism, or devilism, or what
You please—we will not quarrel about
    that:

XXXIX

But certain 'tis they all felt for their new
　　Companion something newer still, as
　　　'twere
A sentimental friendship through and
　　through,
　　Extremely pure, which made them all
　　　concur
In wishing her their sister, save a few
　　Who wish'd they had a brother just like
　　　her,
Whom, if they were at home in sweet
　　Circassia,
They would prefer to Padisha or Pacha.

XL

Of those who had most genius for this
　　sort
　　Of sentimental friendship, there were
　　　three,
Lolah, Katinka, and Dudù; in short
　　(To save description), fair as fair can be
Were they, according to the best report,
　　Though differing in stature and degree,
And clime and time, and country and
　　complexion;
They all alike admired their new con-
　　nexion.

XLI

Lolah was dusk as India and as warm;
　　Katinka was a Georgian, white and red,
With great blue eyes, a lovely hand and
　　arm,
　　And feet so small they scarce seem'd
　　　made to tread,
But rather skim the earth; while Dudù's
　　form
　　Look'd more adapted to be put to bed,
Being somewhat large, and languishing,
　　and lazy,
Yet of a beauty that would drive you crazy.

XLII

A kind of sleepy Venus seem'd Dudù,
　　Yet very fit to 'murder sleep' in those
Who gazed upon her cheek's trans-
　　cendent hue,
　　Her Attic forehead, and her Phidian
　　　nose:
Few angles were there in her form, 'tis true,
　　Thinner she might have been, and yet
　　　scarce lose:
Yet, after all, 'twould puzzle to say where
It would not spoil some separate charm
　　to pare.

XLIII

She was not violently lively, but
　　Stole on your spirit like a May-day
　　　breaking;
Her eyes were not too sparkling, yet, half-
　　shut,
　　They put beholders in a tender taking;

She look'd (this simile's quite new) just cut
　　From marble, like Pygmalion's statue
　　　waking,
The mortal and the marble still at strife,
And timidly expanding into life.

XLIV

Lolah demanded the new damsel's
　　name—
　　'Juanna,'—Well, a pretty name enough.
Katinka ask'd her also whence she came—
　　'From Spain.'—'But where is
　　　Spain?'—'Don't ask such stuff,
Nor show your Georgian ignorance—for
　　shame!'
　　Said Lolah, with an accent rather rough,
To poor Katinka: 'Spain's an island near
Morocco, betwixt Egypt and Tangier.'

XLV

Dudù said nothing, but sat down beside
　　Juanna, playing with her veil or hair;
And looking at her stedfastly, she sigh'd,
　　As if she pitied her for being there,
A pretty stranger, without friend or guide,
　　And all abash'd, too, at the general stare
Which welcomes hapless strangers in all
　　places,
With kind remarks upon their mien and
　　faces.

XLVI

But here the Mother of the Maids drew
　　near,
　　With 'Ladies, it is time to go to rest:
I'm puzzled what to do with you, my
　　dear,'
　　She added to Juanna, their new guest:
'Your coming has been unexpected here,
　　And every couch is occupied; you had
　　　best
Partake of mine; but by to-morrow early
We will have all things settled for you
　　fairly.'

XLVII

Here Lolah interposed—'Mamma, you
　　know
　　You don't sleep soundly, and I cannot
　　　bear
That anybody should disturb you so;
　　I'll take Juanna; we're a slenderer pair
Than you would make the half of;—don't
　　say no;
　　And I of your young charge will take due
　　　care.'
But here Katinka interfered, and said,
'She also had compassion and a bed.'

XLVIII

'Besides, I hate to sleep alone,' quoth she.
　　The matron frown'd: 'Why so?'—
　　　'For fear of ghosts,'
Replied Katinka; 'I am sure I see
　　A phantom upon each of the four posts;

And then I have the worst dreams that
   can be,
   Of Guebres, Giaours, and Ginns, and
      Gouls in hosts.'
The dame replied, 'Between your dreams
   and you,
I fear Juanna's dreams would be but few.

XLIX

'You, Lolah, must continue still to lie
   Alone, for reasons which don't matter;
      you
The same, Katinka, until by and by:
   And I shall place Juanna with Dudù,
Who's quiet, inoffensive, silent, shy,
   And will not toss and chatter the night
      through.
What say you, child?'—Dudù said
      nothing, as
Her talents were of the more silent class;

L

But she rose up, and kiss'd the matron's
      brow
   Between the eyes, and Lolah on both
      cheeks,
Katinka too; and with a gentle bow
   (Curt'sies are neither used by Turks nor
      Greeks)
She took Juanna by the hand to show
   Their place of rest, and left to both
      their piques,
The others pouting at the matron's
      preference
Of Dudù, though they held their tongues
      from deference.

LI

It was a spacious chamber (Oda is
   The Turkish title), and ranged round
      the wall
Were couches, toilets—and much more
      than this
   I might describe, as I have seen it all,
But it suffices—little was amiss;
   'Twas on the whole a nobly furnish'd
      hall,
With all things ladies want, save one or
      two,
And even those were nearer than they
      knew.

LII

Dudù, as has been said, was a sweet
      creature,
   Not very dashing, but extremely
      winning,
With the most regulated charms of feature,
   Which painters cannot catch like faces
      sinning
Against proportion—the wild strokes of
      nature
   Which they hit off at once in the
      beginning,

Full of expression, right or wrong, that
      strike,
And pleasing, or unpleasing, still are like.

LIII

But she was a soft landscape of mild earth,
   Where all was harmony, and calm, and
      quiet,
Luxuriant, budding; cheerful without
      mirth,
   Which, if not happiness, is much more
      nigh it
Than are your mighty passions and so
      forth,
   Which some call 'the sublime': I wish
      they'd try it:
I've seen your stormy seas and stormy
      women,
And pity lovers rather more than seamen.

LIV

But she was pensive more than melan-
      choly,
   And serious more than pensive, and
      serene,
It may be, more than either—not unholy
   Her thoughts, at least till now, appear
      to have been.
The strangest thing was, beauteous, she
      was wholly
   Unconscious, albeit turn'd of quick
      seventeen,
That she was fair, or dark, or short, or
      tall;
She never thought about herself at all.

LV

And therefore was she kind and gentle as
   The Age of Gold (when gold was yet
      unknown,
By which its nomenclature came to pass;
   Thus most appropriately has been
      shown
'Lucus à non lucendo,' not what was,
   But what was not; a sort of style that's
      grown
Extremely common in this age, whose
      metal
The devil may decompose, but never
      settle:

LVI

I think it may be of 'Corinthian Brass,'
   Which was a mixture of all metals, but
The brazen uppermost). Kind reader!
      pass
   This long parenthesis: I could not shut
It sooner for the soul of me, and class
   My faults even with your own! which
      meaneth, Put
A kind construction upon them and me:
   But that you won't—then don't—I am
      not less free.

LVII

'Tis time we should return to plain narration,
  And thus my narrative proceeds:—Dudù,
With every kindness short of ostentation,
  Show'd Juan, or Juanna, through and through
This labyrinth of females, and each station
  Described—what's strange—in words extremely few:
I have but one simile, and that's a blunder,
For wordless woman, which is *silent* thunder.

LVIII

And next she gave her (I say *her*, because
  The gender still was epicene, at least
In outward show, which is a saving clause)
  An outline of the customs of the East,
With all their chaste integrity of laws,
  By which the more a harem is increased,
The stricter doubtless grow the vestal duties
Of any supernumerary beauties.

LIX

And then she gave Juanna a chaste kiss:
  Dudù was fond of kissing—which I'm sure
That nobody can ever take amiss,
  Because 'tis pleasant, so that it be pure,
And between females means no more than this—
  That they have nothing better near, or newer.
'Kiss' rhymes to 'bliss' in fact as well as verse—
I wish it never led to something worse.

LX

In perfect innocence she then unmade
  Her toilet, which cost little, for she was
A child of Nature carelessly array'd:
  If fond of a chance ogle at her glass,
'Twas like the fawn, which, in the lake display'd,
  Beholds her own shy, shadowy image pass,
When first she starts, and then returns to peep,
Admiring this new native of the deep.

LXI

And one by one her articles of dress
  Were laid aside; but not before she offer'd
Her aid to fair Juanna, whose excess
  Of modesty declined the assistance proffer'd:

Which pass'd well off—as she could do no less;
  Though by this *politesse* she rather suffer'd,
Pricking her fingers with those cursed pins,
Which surely were invented for our sins,—

LXII

Making a woman like a porcupine,
  Not to be rashly touch'd. But still more dread,
Oh, ye! whose fate it is, as once 'twas mine,
  In early youth, to turn a lady's maid;—
I did my very boyish best to shine
  In tricking her out for a masquerade:
The pins were placed sufficiently, but not
Stuck all exactly in the proper spot.

LXIII

But these are foolish things to all the wise,
  And I love wisdom more than she loves me;
My tendency is to philosophise
  On most things, from a tyrant to a tree;
But still the spouseless virgin *Knowledge* flies.
  What are we? and whence came we? what shall be
Our *ultimate* existence? what's our present?
Are questions answerless, and yet incessant.

LXIV

There was deep silence in the chamber: dim
  And distant from each other burn'd the lights,
And slumber hover'd o'er each lovely limb
  Of the fair occupants: if there be sprites,
They should have walk'd there in their sprightliest trim,
  By way of change from their sepulchral sites,
And shown themselves as ghosts of better taste
Than haunting some old ruin or wild waste.

LXV

Many and beautiful lay those around,
  Like flowers of different hue, and clime, and root,
In some exotic garden sometimes found,
  With cost, and care, and warmth, induced to shoot.
One with her auburn tresses lightly bound,
  And fair brows gently drooping, as the fruit
Nods from the tree, was slumbering with soft breath,
And lips apart, which show'd the pearls beneath.

LXVI

One with her flush'd cheek laid on her
    white arm,
    And raven ringlets gather'd in dark
      crowd
Above her brow, lay dreaming soft and
    warm;
    And smiling through her dream, as
      through a cloud
The moon breaks, half unveil'd each
    further charm,
As, slightly stirring in her snowy shroud,
Her beauties seized the unconscious hour
    of night
All bashfully to struggle into light.

LXVII

This is no bull, although it sounds so; for
    'Twas night, but there were lamps, as
      hath been said.
A third's all pallid aspect offer'd more
    The traits of sleeping sorrow, and
      betray'd
Through the heaved breast the dream of
    some far shore
    Beloved and deplored; while slowly
      stray'd
(As night-dew, on a cypress glittering,
    tinges
The black bough) tear-drops through her
    eyes' dark fringes.

LXVIII

A fourth as marble, statue-like and still,
    Lay in a breathless, hush'd, and stony
      sleep;
White, cold, and pure, as looks a frozen rill,
    Or the snow minaret on an Alpine steep,
Or Lot's wife done in salt,—or what you
    will;—
    My similes are gather'd in a heap,
So pick and choose—perhaps you'll be
    content
With a carved lady on a monument.

LXIX

And lo! a fifth appears;—and what is she?
    A lady of a 'certain age,' which means
Certainly aged—what her years might be
    I know not, never counting past their
      teens;
But there she slept, not quite so fair to see,
    As ere that awful period intervenes
Which lays both men and women on the
    shelf,
To meditate upon their sins and self.

LXX

But all this time how slept, or dream'd,
    Dudù?
    With strict inquiry I could ne'er discover,
And scorn to add a syllable untrue;
    But ere the middle watch was hardly
      over,

Just when the fading lamps waned dim
    and blue,
    And phantoms hover'd, or might seem
      to hover,
To those who like their company, about
The apartment, on a sudden she scream'd
    out:

LXXI

And that so loudly, that upstarted all
    The Oda, in a general commotion:
Matron and maids, and those whom you
    may call
    Neither, came crowding like the waves
      of ocean,
One on the other, throughout the whole
    hall,
    All trembling, wondering, without the
      least notion
More than I have myself of what could
    make
The calm Dudù so turbulently wake.

LXXII

But wide awake she was, and round her bed
    With floating draperies and with flying
      hair,
With eager eyes, and light but hurried
    tread,
    And bosoms, arms, and ankles glancing
      bare,
And bright as any meteor ever bred
    By the North Pole,—they sought her
      cause of care,
For she seem'd agitated, flush'd, and
    frighten'd,
Her eye dilated, and her colour heighten'd.

LXXIII

But what is strange—and a strong proof
    how great
    A blessing is sound sleep—Juanna lay
As fast as ever husband by his mate
    In holy matrimony snores away.
Not all the clamour broke her happy state
    Of slumber, ere they shook her,—so
      they say
At least,—and then she, too, unclosed
    her eyes,
And yawned a good deal with discreet
    surprise.

LXXIV

And now commenced a strict investigation,
    Which, as all spoke at once, and more
      than once
Conjecturing, wondering, asking a narra-
    tion,
    Alike might puzzle either wit or dunce
To answer in a very clear oration.
    Dudù had never pass'd for wanting
      sense,
But being 'no orator as Brutus is,'
Could not at first expound what was
    amiss.

LXXV

At length she said, that in a slumber
sound
  She dream'd a dream, of walking in a
  wood—
A 'wood obscure,' like that where Dante
found
  Himself in at the age when all grow
  good;
Life's half-way house, where dames with
virtue crown'd
  Run much less risk of lovers turning
  rude;
And that this wood was full of pleasant
fruits,
And trees of goodly growth and spreading
roots;

LXXVI

And in the midst a golden apple grew,—
  A most prodigious pippin—but it
  hung
Rather too high and distant; that she threw
  Her glances on it, and then, longing,
  flung
Stones and whatever she could pick up, to
  Bring down the fruit, which still
  perversely clung
To its own bough, and dangled yet in sight,
But always at a most provoking height;—

LXXVII

That on a sudden, when she least had hope,
  It fell down of its own accord before
Her feet; that her first movement was to
stoop
  And pick it up, and bite it to the core;
That just as her young lip began to ope
  Upon the golden fruit the vision bore,
A bee flew out, and stung her to the heart,
And so—she woke with a great scream
and start.

LXXVIII

All this she told with some confusion and
  Dismay, the usual consequence of
  dreams
Of the unpleasant kind, with none at hand
  To expound their vain and visionary
  gleams.
I've known some odd ones which seem'd
really plann'd
  Prophetically, or that which one deems
A 'strange coincidence,' to use a phrase
By which such things are settled now-a-
days.

LXXIX

The damsels, who had thoughts of some
great harm,
  Began, as is the consequence of fear,
To scold a little at the false alarm
  That broke for nothing on their sleep-
  ing ear.

The matron, too, was wroth to leave her
warm
  Bed for the dream she had been obliged
  to hear,
And chafed at poor Dudù, who only
sigh'd,
And said, that she was sorry she had cried.

LXXX

'I've heard of stories of a cock and bull;
  But visions of an apple and a bee,
To take us from our natural rest, and pull
  The whole Oda from their beds at half-
  past three,
Would make us think the moon is at its
full.
  You surely are unwell, child! we must
  see,
To-morrow,   what   his   Highness's
physician
Will say to this hysteric of a vision.

LXXXI

'And poor Juanna, too, the child's first
night
  Within these walls, to be broke in upon
With such a clamour—I had thought it
right
  That the young stranger should not lie
  alone,
And, as the quietest of all, she might
  With you, Dudù, a good night's rest
  have known:
But now I must transfer her to the charge
Of Lolah—though her couch is not so
large.'

LXXXII

Lolah's eyes sparkled at the proposition;
  But poor Dudù, with large drops in her
  own,
Resulting from the scolding or the vision,
  Implored that present pardon might be
  shown
For this first fault, and that on no condi-
tion
  (She added in a soft and piteous tone)
Juanna should be taken from her, and
Her future dreams should all be kept in
hand.

LXXXIII

She promised never more to have a dream,
  At least to dream so loudly as just now;
She wonder'd at herself how she could
scream—
  'Twas foolish, nervous, as she must
  allow,
A fond hallucination, and a theme
  For laughter—but she felt her spirits
  low,
And begg'd they would excuse her; she'd
get over
This weakness in a few hours, and recover.

LXXXIV

And here Juanna kindly interposed,
  And said she felt herself extremely well
Where she then was, as her sound sleep
    disclosed,
  When all around rang like a tocsin bell;
She did not find herself the least disposed
  To quit her gentle partner, and to dwell
Apart from one who had no sin to show,
Save that of dreaming once 'mal-à-propos.'

LXXXV

As thus Juanna spoke, Dudù turn'd round
  And hid her face within Juanna's
    breast:
Her neck alone was seen, but that was
    found
  The colour of a budding rose's crest.
I can't tell why she blush'd, nor can
    expound
  The mystery of this rupture of their rest;
All that I know is, that the facts I state
Are true as truth has ever been of late.

LXXXVI

And so good night to them—or, if you will,
  Good morrow—for the cock had
    crown, and light
Began to clothe each Asiatic hill,
  And the mosque crescent struggled
    into sight
Of the long caravan, which in the chill
  Of dewy dawn wound slowly round each
    height
That stretches to the stony belt, which girds
Asia, where Kaff looks down upon the
    Kurds.

LXXXVII

With the first ray, or rather grey of morn,
  Gulbeyaz rose from restlessness; and
    pale
As Passion rises, with its bosom worn,
  Array'd herself with mantle, gem, and
    veil.
The nightingale that sings with the deep
    thorn,
  Which fable places in her breast of wail,
Is lighter far of heart and voice than those
Whose headlong passions form their
    proper woes.

LXXXVIII

And that's the moral of this composition,
  If people would but see its real drift;—
But *that* they will not do without suspicion,
  Because all gentle readers have the gift
Of closing 'gainst the light their orbs of
    vision;
  While gentle writers also love to lift
Their voices 'gainst each other, which is
    natural,
The numbers are too great for them to
    flatter all.

LXXXIX

Rose the sultana from a bed of splendour,
  Softer than the soft Sybarite's, who
    cried
Aloud because his feelings were too tender
  To brook a ruffled rose-leaf by his
    side,—
So beautiful that art could little mend her,
  Though pale with conflicts between love
    and pride;
So agitated was she with her error,
She did not even look into the mirror.

XC

Also arose about the self-same time,
  Perhaps a little later, her great lord,
Master of thirty kingdoms so sublime,
  And of a wife by whom he was abhorr'd;
A thing of much less import in that
    clime—
  At least to those of incomes which
    afford
The filling up their whole connubial
    cargo—
Than where two wives are under an
    embargo.

XCI

He did not think much on the matter, nor
  Indeed on any other: as a man
He liked to have a handsome paramour
  At hand, as one may like to have a fan,
And therefore of Circassians had good
    store,
  As an amusement after the Divan;
Though an unusual fit of love, or duty,
Had made him lately bask in his bride's
    beauty.

XCII

And now he rose; and after due ablutions
  Exacted by the customs of the East,
And prayers and other pious evolutions,
  He drank six cups of coffee at the least,
And then withdrew to hear about the
    Russians,
  Whose victories had recently increased
In Catherine's reign, whom glory still
    adores,
As greatest of all sovereigns and w——s.

XCIII

But oh, thou grand legitimate Alexander!
  Her son's, let not this last phrase
    offend
Thine ear, if it should reach—and now
    rhymes wander
  Almost as far as Petersburgh, and lend
A dreadful impulse to each loud meander
  Of murmuring Liberty's wide waves,
    which blend
Their roar even with the Baltic's—so you
    be
Your father's son, 'tis quite enough for me.

XCIV

To call men love-begotten, or proclaim
　　Their mothers as the antipodes of
　　　Timon,
That hater of mankind, would be a shame,
　　A libel, or whate'er you please to
　　　rhyme on:
But people's ancestors are history's game;
　　And if one lady's slip could leave a
　　　crime on
All generations, I should like to know
What pedigree the best would have to
　　show?

XCV

Had Catherine and the sultan understood
　　Their own true interests, which kings
　　　rarely know,
Until 'tis taught by lessons rather rude,
　　There was a way to end their strife,
　　　although
Perhaps precarious, had they but thought
　　good,
　　Without the aid of prince or plenipo:
She to dismiss her guards and he his
　　harem,
And for their other matters, meet and
　　share 'em.

XCVI

But as it was, his Highness had to hold
　　His daily council upon ways and means
How to encounter with this martial scold,
　　This modern Amazon and queen of
　　　queans;
And the perplexity could not be told
　　Of all the pillars of the state, which
　　　leans
Sometimes a little heavy on the backs
Of those who cannot lay on a new tax.

XCVII

Meantime Gulbeyaz, when her king was
　　gone,
　　Retired into her boudoir, a sweet place
For love or breakfast; private, pleasing,
　　lone,
　　And rich with all contrivances which
　　　grace
Those gay recesses:—many a precious
　　stone
　　Sparkled along its roof, and many a
　　　vase
Of porcelain held in the fetter'd flowers
Those captive soothers of a captive's hours.

XCVIII

Mother of pearl, and porphyry, and
　　marble,
　　Vied with each other on this costly spot;
And singing birds without were heard to
　　warble;
　　And the stain'd glass which lighted this
　　　fair grot

Varied each ray;—but all descriptions
　　garble
　　The true effect, and so we had better
　　　not
Be too minute; an outline is the best,—
A lively reader's fancy does the rest.

XCIX

And here she summon'd Baba, and
　　required
　　Don Juan at his hands, and information
Of what had pass'd since all the slaves
　　retired,
　　And whether he had occupied their
　　　station:
If matters had been managed as desired,
　　And his disguise with due consideration
Kept up; and above all, the where and
　　how
He had pass'd the night, was what she
　　wish'd to know.

C

Baba, with some embarrassment, replied
　　To this long catechism of questions,
　　　ask'd
More easily than answer'd,—that he had
　　tried
　　His best to obey in what he had been
　　　task'd;
But there seem'd something that he
　　wish'd to hide,
　　Which hesitation more betray'd than
　　　mask'd;
He scratch'd his ear, the infallible resource
To which embarrass'd people have
　　recourse.

CI

Gulbeyaz was no model of true patience,
　　Nor much disposed to wait in word or
　　　deed;
She liked quick answers in all conversa-
　　tions;
　　And when she saw him stumbling like a
　　　steed
In his replies, she puzzled him for fresh
　　ones;
　　And as his speech grew still more
　　　broken-kneed,
Her cheek began to flush, her eyes to
　　sparkle,
And her proud brow's blue veins to swell
　　and darkle.

CII

When Baba saw these symptoms, which
　　he knew
　　To bode him no great good, he depre-
　　　cated
Her anger, and beseech'd she 'd hear him
　　through—
　　He could not help the thing which he
　　　related:

Then out it came at length, that to Dudù
   Juan was given in charge, as hath been
   stated;
But not by Baba's fault, he said, and
   swore on
The holy camel's hump, besides the
   Koran.

CIII

The chief dame of the Oda, upon whom
   The discipline of the whole harem bore,
As soon as they reënter'd their own room,
   For Baba's function stopt short at the
   door,
Had settled all; nor could he then pre-
   sume
   (The aforesaid Baba) just then to do more,
Without exciting such suspicion as
Might make the matter still worse than it
   was.

CIV

He hoped, indeed he thought, he could be
   sure,
   Juan had not betray'd himself; in fact
'Twas certain that his conduct had been
   pure,
   Because a foolish or imprudent act
Would not alone have made him insecure,
   But ended in his being found out and
   sack'd,
And thrown into the sea.—Thus Baba
   spoke
Of all save Dudù's dream, which was no
   joke.

CV

This he discreetly kept in the back ground,
   And talk'd away—and might have
   talk'd till now,
For any further answer that he found,
   So deep an anguish wrung Gulbeyaz'
   brow:
Her cheek turn'd ashes, ears rung, brain
   whirl'd round,
   As if she had received a sudden blow,
And the heart's dew of pain sprang fast
   and chilly
O'er her fair front, like Morning's on a lily.

CVI

Although she was not of the fainting sort,
   Baba thought she would faint, but
   there he err'd—
It was but a convulsion, which though
   short
   Can never be described; we all have
   heard,
And some of us have felt thus 'all amort,'
   When things beyond the common have
   occurr'd;—
Gulbeyaz proved in that brief agony
What she could ne'er express—then how
   should I?

CVII

She stood a moment as a Pythoness
   Stands on her tripod, agonised, and full
Of inspiration gather'd from distress,
   When all the heart-strings like wild
   horses pull
The heart asunder;—then, as more or
   less
   Their speed abated or their strength
   grew dull,
She sunk down on her seat by slow
   degrees,
And bow'd her throbbing head o'er
   trembling knees.

CVIII

Her face declined and was unseen; her
   hair
   Fell in long tresses like the weeping
   willow,
Sweeping the marble underneath her
   chair,
   Or rather sofa (for it was all pillow,
A low, soft ottoman), and black despair
   Stirr'd up and down her bosom like a
   billow,
Which rushes to some shore whose
   shingles check
Its farther course, but must receive its
   wreck.

CIX

Her head hung down, and her long hair
   in stooping
   Conceal'd her features better than a
   veil;
And one hand o'er the ottoman lay
   drooping,
   White, waxen, and as alabaster pale:
Would that I were a painter! to be group-
   ing
   All that a poet drags into detail!
Oh that my words were colours! but their
   tints
May serve perhaps as outlines or slight
   hints.

CX

Baba, who knew by experience when to
   talk
   And when to hold its tongue, now held
   it till
This passion might blow o'er, nor dared
   to balk
   Gulbeyaz' taciturn or speaking will.
At length she rose up, and began to walk
   Slowly along the room, but silent still,
And her brow clear'd, but not her
   troubled eye;
The wind was down but still the sea ran
   high.

CXI

She stopp'd, and raised her head to
    speak—but paused,
    And then moved on again with rapid
    pace;
Then slacken'd it, which is the march
    most caused
    By deep emotion:—you may some-
    times trace
A feeling in each footstep, as disclosed
    By Sallust in his Catiline, who, chased
By all the demons of all passions, show'd
Their work even by the way in which he
    trode.

CXII

Gulbeyaz stopp'd and beckon'd Baba:—
    'Slave!
    Bring the two slaves!' she said in a low
    tone,
But one which Baba did not like to brave,
    And yet he shudder'd, and seem'd
    rather prone
To prove reluctant, and begg'd leave to
    crave
    (Though he well knew the meaning) to
    be shown
What slaves her highness wish'd to
    indicate,
For fear of any error, like the late.

CXIII

'The Georgian and her paramour,'
    replied
    The imperial bride—and added, 'Let
    the boat
Be ready by the secret portal's side:
    You know the rest.' The words stuck
    in her throat,
Despite her injured love and fiery pride;
    And of this Baba willingly took note,
And begg'd by every hair of Mahomet's
    beard,
She would revoke the order he had heard.

CXIV

'To hear is to obey,' he said; 'but still,
    Sultana, think upon the consequence:
It is not that I shall not all fulfil
    Your orders, even in their severest
    sense;
But such precipitation may end ill,
    Even at your own imperative expense:
I do not mean destruction and exposure,
In case of any premature disclosure;

CXV

'But your own feelings. Even should all
    the rest
    Be hidden by the rolling waves, which
    hide
Already many a once love-beaten breast
    Deep in the caverns of the deadly tide—

You love this boyish, new, seraglio
    guest,
    And if this violent remedy be tried—
Excuse my freedom, when I here assure
    you,
That killing him is not the way to cure you.'

CXVI

'What dost thou know of love or feel-
    ing!—Wretch!
    Begone!' she cried, with kindling eyes—
    'and do
My bidding!' Baba vanish'd, for to
    stretch
    His own remonstrance further he well
    knew
Might end in acting as his own 'Jack
    Ketch';
    And though he wish'd extremely to get
    through
This awkward business without harm to
    others,
He still preferr'd his own neck to another's.

CXVII

Away he went then upon his commission,
    Growling and grumbling in good
    Turkish phrase
Against all women of whate'er condition,
    Especially sultanas and their ways;
Their obstinacy, pride, and indecision,
    Their never knowing their own mind
    two days,
The trouble that they gave, their immorality,
Which made him daily bless his own
    neutrality.

CXVIII

And then he call'd his brethren to his aid,
    And sent one on a summons to the pair,
That they must instantly be well array'd,
    And above all be comb'd even to a hair,
And brought before the empress, who had
    made
    Inquiries after them with kindest care:
At which Dudù look'd strange, and Juan
    silly;
But go they must at once, and will I—
    nill I.

CXIX

And here I leave them at their preparation
    For the imperial presence, wherein
    whether
Gulbeyaz show'd them both com-
    miseration,
    Or got rid of the parties altogether,
Like other angry ladies of her nation,—
    Are things the turning of a hair or
    feather
May settle; but far be't from me to antici-
    pate
In what way feminine caprice may
    dissipate.

CXX

I leave them for the present with good
   wishes,
   Though doubts of their well doing, to
     arrange
Another part of history; for the dishes
   Of this our banquet we must some-
     times change;
And trusting Juan may escape the fishes,
   Although his situation now seems
     strange,
And scarce secure, as such digressions
   are fair,
The Muse will take a little touch at war-
   fare.

CANTO THE SEVENTH

I

O LOVE! O Glory! what are ye who fly
   Around us ever, rarely to alight?
There's not a meteor in the Polar sky
   Of such transcendent and more fleeting
     flight.
Chill, and chain'd to cold earth, we lift on
   high
   Our eyes in search of either lovely light;
A thousand and a thousand colours they
Assume, then leave us on our freezing way.

II

And such as they are, such my present
   tale is,
   A nondescript and ever-varying rhyme,
A versified Aurora Borealis,
   Which flashes o'er a waste and icy clime.
When we know what all are, we must
   bewail us,
   But ne'ertheless I hope it is no crime
To laugh at *all* things—for I wish to know
What, after *all*, are *all* things—but a *show?*

III

They accuse me—*Me*—the present writer
   of
   The present poem—of—I know not
     what—
A tendency to under-rate and scoff
   At human power and virtue, and all that;
And this they say in language rather
   rough.
   Good God! I wonder what they would
     be at!
I say no more than has been said in
   Dante's
Verse, and by Solomon and by Cervantes;

IV

By Swift, by Machiavel, by Roche-
   foucault,
   By Fénelon, by Luther, and by Plato;
By Tillotson, and Wesley, and Rousseau,
   Who knew this life was not worth a
     potato.

'Tis not their fault, nor mine, if this be
   so,—
   For my part, I pretend not to be Cato,
Nor even Diogenes.—We live and die,
But which is best, you know no more
   than I.

V

Socrates said, our only knowledge was
   'To know that nothing could be
     known'; a pleasant
Science enough, which levels to an ass
   Each man of wisdom, future, past, or
     present.
Newton (that proverb of the mind), alas!
   Declared, with all his grand discoveries
     recent,
That he himself felt only 'like a youth
Picking up shells by the great ocean—
   Truth.'

VI

Ecclesiastes said, 'that all is vanity'—
   Most modern preachers say the same,
     or show it
By their examples of true Christianity:
   In short, all know, or very soon may
     know it;
And in this scene of all-confess'd inanity,
   By saint, by sage, by preacher, and by
     poet,
Must I restrain me, through the fear of
   strife,
From holding up the nothingness of life?

VII

Dogs, or men!—for I flatter you in saying
   That ye are dogs—your betters far—ye
     may
Read, or read not, what I am now essay-
   ing
   To show ye what ye are in every way.
As little as the moon stops for the baying
   Of wolves, will the bright Muse with-
     draw one ray
From out her skies—then howl your idle
   wrath!
While she still silvers o'er your gloomy
   path.

VIII

'Fierce loves and faithless wars'—I am
   not sure
   If this be the right reading—'tis no
     matter;
The fact's about the same, I am secure;
   I sing them both, and am about to
     batter
A town which did a famous siege endure,
   And was beleaguer'd both by land and
     water
By Souvaroff, or Anglicè Suwarrow,
Who loved blood as an alderman loves
   marrow.

IX

The fortress is call'd Ismail, and is placed
  Upon the Danube's left branch and left
    bank,
With buildings in the Oriental taste,
  But still a fortress of the foremost rank,
Or was at least, unless 'tis since defaced,
  Which with your conquerors is a com-
    mon prank:
It stands some eighty versts from the high
    sea,
And measures round of toises thousands
    three.

X

Within the extent of this fortification
  A borough is comprised along the
    height
Upon the left, which from its loftier
    station
  Commands the city, and upon its site
A Greek had raised around this elevation
  A quantity of palisades *upright*,
So placed as to *impede* the fire of those
Who held the place, and to *assist* the foe's.

XI

This circumstance may serve to give a
    notion
  Of the high talents of this new Vauban:
But the town ditch below was deep as
    ocean,
  The rampart higher than you'd wish to
    hang:
But there was a great want of pre-
    caution
  (Prithee, excuse this engineering slang),
Nor work advanced, nor cover'd way was
    there,
To hint at least 'Here is no thoroughfare.'

XII

But a stone bastion, with a narrow gorge,
  And walls as thick as most skulls born
    as yet;
Two batteries, cap-à-pie, as our St.
    George,
  Casemated one, and t'other 'à bar-
    bette,'
Of Danube's bank took formidable
    charge;
  While two-and-twenty cannon duly set
Rose over the town's right side, in brist-
    ling tier,
Forty feet high, upon a cavalier.

XIII

But from the river the town's open quite,
  Because the Turks could never be per-
    suaded
A Russian vessel e'er would heave in
    sight;
  And such their creed was till they were
    invaded,

When it grew rather late to set things right:
  But as the Danube could not well be
    waded,
They look'd upon the Muscovite flotilla,
And only shouted, 'Allah!' and 'Bis Millah!'

XIV

The Russians now were ready to attack:
  But oh, ye goddesses of war and glory!
How shall I spell the name of each
    Cossacque
  Who were immortal, could one tell
    their story?
Alas! what to their memory can lack?
  Achilles' self was not more grim and
    gory
Than thousands of this new and polish'd
    nation,
Whose names want nothing but—pro-
    nunciation.

XV

Still I'll record a few, if but to increase
  Our euphony: there was Strongenoff,
    and Strokonoff,
Meknop, Serge Lwow, Arséniew of modern
    Greece,
  And Tschitsshakoff, and Roguenoff,
    and Chokenoff,
And others of twelve consonants apiece;
  And more might be found out, if I
    could poke enough
Into gazettes; but Fame (capricious
    strumpet),
It seems, has got an ear as well as trumpet,

XVI

And cannot tune those discords of narra-
    tion,
  Which may be names at Moscow, into
    rhyme;
Yet there were several worth commemora-
    tion,
  As e'er was virgin of a nuptial chime;
Soft words, too, fitted for the peroration
  Of Londonderry drawling against time,
Ending in 'ischskin,' 'ousckin,' 'iffskchy,'
    'ouski,'
Of whom we can insert but Rousamouski,

XVII

Scherematoff and Chrematoff, Koklophti,
  Koclobski, Kourakin, and Mouskin
    Pouskin,
All proper men of weapons, as e'er scoff'd
    high
  Against a foe, or ran a sabre through
    skin:
Little cared they for Mahomet or Mufti,
  Unless to make their kettle-drums a
    new skin
Out of their hides, if parchment had
    grown dear,
And no more handy substitute been near.

XVIII

Then there were foreigners of much
renown,
  Of various nations, and all volunteers;
Not fighting for their country or its crown,
  But wishing to be one day brigadiers;
Also to have the sacking of a town;
  A pleasant thing to young men at their
  years.
'Mongst them were several Englishmen
  of pith,
Sixteen call'd Thomson, and nineteen
  named Smith.

XIX

Jack Thomson and Bill Thomson;—all
  the rest
  Had been call'd '*Jemmy*,' after the
  great bard;
I don't know whether they had arms or
  crest,
  But such a godfather's as good a card.
Three of the Smiths were Peters; but the
  best
  Amongst them all, hard blows to inflict
  or ward,
Was *he*, since so renown'd 'in country
  quarters
At Halifax'; but now he served the Tartars.

XX

The rest were Jacks and Gills and Wills
  and Bills,
  But when I've added that the elder Jack
  Smith
Was born in Cumberland among the hills,
  And that his father was an honest black-
  smith,
I've said all *I* know of a name that fills
  Three lines of the despatch in taking
  'Schmacksmith,'
A village of Moldavia's waste, wherein
He fell, immortal in a bulletin.

XXI

I wonder (although Mars no doubt's a
  god I
  Praise) if a man's name in a *bulletin*
May make up for a *bullet in* his body?
  I hope this little question is no sin,
Because, though I am but a simple noddy,
  I think one Shakespeare puts the same
  thought in
The mouth of some one in his plays so
  doting,
Which many people pass for wits by
  quoting.

XXII

Then there were Frenchmen, gallant,
  young, and gay;
  But I'm too great a patriot to record
Their Gallic names upon a glorious day;
  I'd rather tell ten lies than say a word

Of truth;—such truths are treason; they
  betray
  Their country; and as traitors are ab-
  horr'd,
Who name the French in English, save to
  show
How Peace should make John Bull the
  Frenchman's foe.

XXIII

The Russians, having built two batteries
  on
  An isle near Ismail, had two ends in
  view;
The first was to bombard it, and knock
  down
  The public buildings and the private
  too,
No matter what poor souls might be
  undone.
  The city's shape suggested this, 'tis
  true;
Form'd like an amphitheatre, each dwelling
Presented a fine mark to throw a shell in.

XXIV

The second object was to profit by
  The moment of the general con-
  sternation,
To attack the Turk's flotilla, which lay
  nigh,
  Extremely tranquil, anchor'd at its
  station:
But a third motive was as probably
  To frighten them into capitulation;
A phantasy which sometimes seizes
  warriors,
Unless they are game as bull-dogs and
  fox-terriers.

XXV

A habit rather blameable, which is
  That of despising those we combat with,
Common in many cases, was in this
  The cause of killing Tchitchitzkoff and
  Smith;
One of the valorous 'Smiths' whom we
  shall miss
  Out of those nineteen who late rhymed
  to 'pith';
But 'tis a name so spread o'er 'Sir' and
  'Madam,'
That one would think the *first* who bore
  it '*Adam*'.

XXVI

The Russian batteries were incomplete,
  Because they were constructed in a
  hurry;
Thus the same cause which makes a verse
  want feet,
  And throws a cloud o'er Longman and
  John Murray,

When the sale of new books is not so fleet
　As they who print them think is
　　necessary,
May likewise put off for a time what story
Sometimes calls 'murder,' and at others
　'glory.'

XXVII

Whether it was their engineer's stupidity,
　Their haste, or waste, I neither know
　　nor care,
Or some contractor's personal cupidity,
　Saving his soul by cheating in the ware
Of homicide, but there was no solidity
　In the new batteries erected there;
They either miss'd, or they were never miss'd,
And added greatly to the missing list.

XXVIII

A sad miscalculation about distance
　Made all their naval matters incorrect;
Three fireships lost their amiable existence
　Before they reach'd a spot to take effect;
The match was lit too soon, and no
　　assistance
　Could remedy this lubberly defect;
They blew up in the middle of the river,
While, though 'twas dawn, the Turks
　slept fast as ever.

XXIX

At seven they rose, however, and survey'd
　The Russ flotilla getting under way;
'Twas nine, when still advancing un-
　　dismay'd,
　Within a cable's length their vessels lay
Off Ismail, and commenced a cannonade,
　Which was return'd with interest, I may
　　say,
And by a fire of musketry and grape,
And shells and shot of every size and shape.

XXX

For six hours bore they without inter-
　　mission
　The Turkish fire, and, aided by their own
Land batteries, work'd their guns with
　　great precision;
　At length they found mere cannonade
　　alone
By no means would produce the town's
　　submission,
　And made a signal to retreat at one.
One bark blew up, a second near the works
Running aground, was taken by the Turks.

XXXI

The Moslem, too, had lost both ships and
　　men;
　But when they saw the enemy retire,
Their Delhis mann'd some boats, and
　　sail'd again,
　And gall'd the Russians with a heavy
　　fire,

And tried to make a landing on the main;
　But here the effect fell short of their
　　desire:
Count Damas drove them back into the
　　water
Pell-mell, and with a whole gazette of
　slaughter.

XXXII

'If' (says the historian here) 'I could report
　All that the Russians did upon this day,
I think that several volumes would fall short,
　And I should still have many things to
　　say';
And so he says no more—but pays his
　　court
　To some distinguish'd strangers in that
　　fray;
The Prince de Ligne, and Langeron, and
　Damas,
Names great as any that the roll of Fame
　has.

XXXIII

This being the case, may show us what
　Fame *is:*
　For out of these three '*preux Cheva-
　liers,*' how
Many of common readers give a guess
　That such existed? (and they may live
　　now
For aught we know.) Renown's all hit or
　　miss;
　There's fortune even in fame, we must
　　allow.
'Tis true, the Memoirs of the Prince de
　Ligne
Have half withdrawn from *him* oblivion's
　screen.

XXXIV

But here are men who fought in gallant
　　actions
　As gallantly as ever heroes fought,
But buried in the heap of such trans-
　　actions
　Their names are rarely found, nor often
　　sought.
Thus even good fame may suffer sad con-
　　tractions,
　And is extinguish'd sooner than she
　　ought:
Of all our modern battles, I will bet
You can't repeat nine names from each
　Gazette.

XXXV

In short, this last attack, though rich in
　glory,
　Show'd that *somewhere, somehow,*
　　there was a fault,
And Admiral Ribas (known in Russian
　story)
　Most strongly recommended an assault;

In which he was opposed by young and
    hoary,
  Which made a long debate; but I must
    halt,
For if I wrote down every warrior's speech,
  I doubt few readers e'er would mount the
    breach.

XXXVI

There was a man, if that he was a man,
  Not that his manhood could be call'd
    in question,
For had he not been Hercules, his span
  Had been as short in youth as indiges-
    tion
Made his last illness, when, all worn and
    wan,
  He died beneath a tree, as much unblest
    on
The soil of the green province he had
    wasted,
As e'er was locust on the land it blasted.

XXXVII

This was Potemkin—a great thing in days
  When homicide and harlotry made
    great;
If stars and titles could entail long praise,
  His glory might half equal his estate.
This fellow, being six foot high, could
    raise
  A kind of phantasy proportionate
In the then sovereign of the Russian people,
Who measured men as you would do a
    steeple.

XXXVIII

While things were in abeyance, Ribas sent
  A courier to the prince, and he suc-
    ceeded
In ordering matters after his own bent;
  I cannot tell the way in which he
    pleaded,
But shortly he had cause to be content.
  In the mean time the batteries pro-
    ceeded,
And fourscore cannon on the Danube's
    border
Were briskly fired and answer'd in due
    order.

XXXIX

But on the thirteenth, when already part
  Of the troops were embark'd, the siege
    to raise,
A courier on the spur inspired new heart
  Into all panters for newspaper praise,
As well as dilettanti in war's art,
  By his despatches couch'd in pithy
    phrase;
Announcing the appointment of that
    lover of
Battles to the command, Field-Marshal
    Souvaroff.

XL

The letter of the prince to the same
    marshal
Was worthy of a Spartan, had the cause
Been one to which a good heart could be
    partial—
  Defence of freedom, country, or of laws;
But as it was mere lust of power to o'er-
    arch all
  With its proud brow, it merits slight
    applause,
Save for its style, which said, all in a trice,
'You will take Ismail at whatever price.'

XLI

'Let there be light!' said God, 'and there
    was light!'
  'Let there be blood!' says man, and
    there's a sea!
The fiat of this spoil'd child of the Night
  (For Day ne'er saw his merits) could
    decree
More evil in an hour, than thirty bright
  Summers could renovate, though they
    should be
Lovely as those which ripen'd Eden's fruit;
For war cuts up not only branch, but root.

XLII

Our friends, the Turks, who with loud
    'Allahs' now
  Began to signalise the Russ retreat,
Were damnably mistaken; few are slow
  In thinking that their enemy is beat,
(Or *beaten*, if you insist on grammar,
    though
  I never think about it in a heat,)
But here I say the Turks were much mis-
    taken,
Who hating hogs, yet wish'd to save their
    bacon.

XLIII

For, on the sixteenth, at full gallop, drew
  In sight two horsemen, who were
    deem'd Cossacques
For some time, till they came in nearer
    view.
  They had but little baggage at their
    backs,
For there were but three shirts between
    the two;
  But on they rode upon two Ukraine
    hacks,
Till, in approaching, were at length descried
In this plain pair, Suwarrow and his guide.

XLIV

'Great joy to London now!' says some
    great fool,
  When London had a grand illumina-
    tion,
Which to that bottle-conjurer, John Bull,
  Is of all dreams the first hallucination;

So that the streets of colour'd lamps are
        full,
    That sage (*said* John) surrenders at
        discretion
His purse, his soul, his sense, and even his
        nonsense.
To gratify, like a huge moth, this *one*
        sense.

XLV

'Tis strange that he should further 'Damn
        his eyes,'
    For they are damn'd; that once all-
        famous oath
Is to the devil now no further prize,
    Since John has lately lost the use of
        both.
Debt he calls wealth, and taxes Paradise;
    And Famine, with her gaunt and bony
        growth,
Which stare him in the face, he won't
        examine,
Or swears that Ceres hath begotten
        Famine.

XLVI

But to the tale;—great joy unto the camp!
    To Russian, Tartar, English, French,
        Cossacque,
O'er whom Suwarrow shone like a gas
        lamp,
    Presaging a most luminous attack;
Or like a wisp along the marsh so damp,
    Which leads beholders on a boggy
        walk,
He flitted to and fro a dancing light,
Which all who saw it follow'd, wrong or
        right.

XLVII

But certes matters took a different face;
    There was enthusiasm and much
        applause,
The fleet and camp saluted with great
        grace,
    And all presaged good fortune to their
        cause.
Within a cannon-shot length of the place
    They drew, constructed ladders, repair'd
        flaws
In former works, made new, prepared
        fascines,
And all kinds of benevolent machines.

XLVIII

'Tis thus the spirit of a single mind
    Makes that of multitudes take one
        direction,
As roll the waters to the breathing wind,
    Or roams the herd beneath the bull's
        protection;
Or as a little dog will lead the blind,
    Or a bell-wether form the flock's con-
        nexion

By tinkling sounds, when they go forth to
        victual;
Such is the sway of your great men o'er
        little.

XLIX

The whole camp rung with joy; you
        would have thought
    That they were going to a marriage
        feast
(This metaphor, I think, holds good as
        aught,
    Since there is discord after both at
        least):
There was not now a luggage boy but
        sought
    Danger and spoil with ardour much
        increased;
And why? because a little—odd—old
        man,
Stript to his shirt, was come to lead the
        van.

L

But so it was; and every preparation
    Was made with all alacrity: the first
Detachment of three columns took its
        station,
    And waited but the signal's voice to
        burst
Upon the foe: the second's ordination
    Was also in three columns, with a thirst
For glory gaping o'er a sea of slaughter:
The third, in columns two, attack'd by
        water.

LI

New batteries were erected, and was held
    A general council, in which unanimity,
That stranger to most councils, here
        prevail'd,
    As sometimes happens in a great
        extremity;
And every difficulty being dispell'd,
    Glory began to dawn with due sub-
        limity,
While Souvaroff, determined to obtain it,
Was teaching his recruits to use the
        bayonet.

LII

It is an actual fact, that he, commander
    In chief, in proper person deign'd to
        drill
The awkward squad, and could afford to
        squander
    His time, a corporal's duty to fulfil;
Just as you'd break a sucking sala-
        mander
    To swallow flame, and never take it ill:
He show'd them how to mount a ladder
        (which
Was not like Jacob's) or to cross a ditch.

LIII

Also he dress'd up, for the nonce, fascines
  Like men with turbans, scimitars, and
    dirks,
And made them charge with bayonet these
  machines,
  By way of lesson against actual Turks;
And when well practised in these mimic
  scenes,
  He judged them proper to assail the
    works;
At which your wise men sneer'd in phrases
  witty:
He made no answer; but he took the city.

LIV

Most things were in this posture on the eve
  Of the assault, and all the camp was in
A stern repose; which you would scarce
  conceive;
  Yet men resolved to dash through thick
    and thin
Are very silent when they once believe
  That all is settled:—there was little din,
For some were thinking of their home and
  friends,
And others of themselves and latter ends.

LV

Suwarrow chiefly was on the alert,
  Surveying, drilling, ordering, jesting,
    pondering,
For the man was, we safely may assert,
  A thing to wonder at beyond most
    wondering;
Hero, buffoon, half-demon, and half-dirt,
  Praying, instructing, desolating, plunder-
    ing;
Now Mars, now Momus; and when bent
  to storm
A fortress, Harlequin in uniform.

LVI

The day before the assault, while upon
  drill—
  For this great conqueror play'd the
    corporal—
Some Cossacques, hovering like hawks
  round a hill,
  Had met a party towards the twilight's
    fall,
One of whom spoke their tongue—or
  well or ill,
  'Twas much that he was understood at
    all;
But whether from his voice, or speech, or
  manner,
They found that he had fought beneath
  their banner.

LVII

Whereon immediately at his request
  They brought him and his comrades to
    head-quarters;

Their dress was Moslem, but you might
  have guess'd
  That these were merely masquerading
    Tartars,
And that beneath each Turkish-fashion'd
  vest
  Lurk'd Christianity; which sometimes
    barters
Her inward grace for outward show, and
  makes
It difficult to shun some strange mistakes.

LVIII

Suwarrow, who was standing in his shirt
  Before a company of Calmucks, drilling,
Exclaiming, fooling, swearing at the inert,
  And lecturing on the noble art of
    killing,—
For deeming human clay but common dirt,
  This great philosopher was thus
    instilling
His maxims, which to martial compre-
  hension
Proved death in battle equal to a pen-
  sion;—

LIX

Suwarrow, when he saw this company
  Of Cossacques and their prey, turn'd
    round and cast
Upon them his slow brow and piercing
  eye:—
  'Whence come ye?'—'From Constanti-
    nople last,
Captives just now escaped,' was the reply.
  'What are ye?'—'What you see us.'
    Briefly pass'd
This dialogue; for he who answer'd knew
To whom he spoke, and made his words
  but few.

LX

'Your names?'—'Mine's Johnson, and
  my comrade's Juan;
  The other two are women, and the third
Is neither man nor woman.' The chief
  threw on
  The party a slight glance, then said, 'I
  have heard
Your name before, the second is a new
  one:
  To bring the other three here was absurd:
But let that pass:—I think I have heard
  your name
In the Nikolaiew regiment?'—'The same.'

LXI

'You served at Widdin?'—'Yes.'—'You
  led the attack?'
  'I did.'—'What next?'—'I really hardly
    know.'
'You were the first i' the breach?'—'I was
  not slack
  At least to follow those who might be so.'

'What follow'd?'—'A shot laid me on my
    back,
And I became a prisoner to the foe.'
'You shall have vengeance, for the town
    surrounded
Is twice as strong as that where you were
    wounded.

LXII

'Where will you serve?'—'Where'er you
    please.'—'I know
    You like to be the hope of the forlorn,
And doubtless would be foremost on the
    foe
    After the hardships you've already
    borne.
And this young fellow—say what can he do?
    He with the beardless chin and gar-
    ments torn?'
'Why, general, if he hath no greater fault
In war than love, he had better lead the
    assault.'

LXIII

'He shall if that he dare.' Here Juan bow'd
    Low as the compliment deserved. Su-
    warrow
Continued: 'Your old regiment's allow'd,
    By special providence, to lead to-
    morrow,
Or it may be to-night, the assault: I have
    vow'd
    To several saints, that shortly plough or
    harrow
Shall pass o'er what was Ismail, and its
    tusk
Be unimpeded by the proudest mosque.

LXIV

'So now, my lads, for glory!'—Here he
    turn'd
    And drill'd away in the most classic
    Russian,
Until each high, heroic bosom burn'd
    For cash and conquest, as if from a
    cushion
A preacher had held forth (who nobly
    spurn'd
    All earthly goods save tithes) and bade
    them push on
To slay the Pagans who resisted, battering
The armies of the Christian Empress
    Catherine.

LXV

Johnson, who knew by this long colloquy
    Himself a favourite, ventured to address
Suwarrow, though engaged with accents
    high
    In his resumed amusement. 'I confess
My debt in being thus allow'd to die
    Among the foremost; but if you'd ex-
    press
Explicitly our several posts, my friend
And self would know what duty to attend.'

LXVI

'Right! I was busy, and forgot. Why, you
    Will join your former regiment, which
    should be
Now under arms. Ho! Katskoff, take him
    to—
    (Here he call'd up a Polish orderly)
His post, I mean the regiment Nikolaiew:
    The stranger stripling may remain with
    me;
He's a fine boy. The women may be sent
To the other baggage, or to the sick tent.'

LXVII

But here a sort of scene began to ensue:
    The ladies,—who by no means had been
    bred
To be disposed of in a way so new,
    Although their harem education led
Doubtless to that of doctrines the most
    true,
    Passive obedience,—now raised up the
    head,
With flashing eyes and starting tears, and
    flung,
Their arms, as hens their wings about
    their young,

LXVIII

O'er the promoted couple of brave men
    Who were thus honour'd by the greatest
    chief
That ever peopled hell with heroes slain,
    Or plunged a province or a realm in
    grief.
Oh, foolish mortals! Always taught in
    vain!
    Oh, glorious laurel! since for one sole
    leaf
Of thine imaginary deathless tree,
Of blood and tears must flow the unebbing
    sea.

LXIX

Suwarrow, who had small regard for tears,
    And not much sympathy for blood, sur-
    vey'd
The women with their hair about their ears
    And natural agonies, with a slight shade
Of feeling: for however habit sears
    Men's hearts against whole millions,
    when their trade
Is butchery, sometimes a single sorrow
Will touch even heroes—and such was
    Suwarrow.

LXX

He said,—and in the kindest Calmuck
    tone,—
    'Why, Johnson, what the devil do you
    mean
By bringing women here? They shall be
    shown
    All the attention possible, and seen

In safety to the waggons, where alone
  In fact they can be safe. You should
    have been
Aware this kind of baggage never thrives;
Save wed a year, I hate recruits with wives.'

LXXI

'May it please your excellency,' thus replied
  Our British friend, 'these are the wives
    of others,
And not our own. I am too qualified
  By service with my military brothers
To break the rules by bringing one's own
    bride
    Into a camp: I know that nought so
      bothers
The hearts of the heroic on a charge,
As leaving a small family at large.

LXXII

'But these are but two Turkish ladies, who
  With their attendant aided our escape,
And afterwards accompanied us through
  A thousand perils in this dubious shape.
To me this kind of life is not so new;
  To them, poor things, it is an awkward
    step.
I therefore, if you wish me to fight freely,
Request that they may both be used gen-
  teelly.'

LXXIII

Meantime these two poor girls, with swim-
  ming eyes,
  Look'd on as if in doubt if they could
    trust
Their own protectors; nor was their sur-
  prise
  Less than their grief (and truly not less
    just)
To see an old man, rather wild than wise
  In aspect, plainly clad, besmear'd with
    dust,
Stript to his waistcoat, and that not too
  clean,
More fear'd than all the sultans ever seen.

LXXIV

For everything seem'd resting on his nod,
  As they could read in all eyes. Now to
    them,
Who were accustom'd, as a sort of god,
  To see the sultan, rich in many a gem,
Like an imperial peacock stalk abroad
  (That royal bird, whose tail's a diadem)
With all the pomp of power, it was a doubt
How power could condescend to do with-
  out.

LXXV

John Johnson, seeing their extreme dismay,
  Though little versed in feelings oriental,
Suggested some slight comfort in his way:
  Don Juan, who was much more senti-
    mental,

Swore they should see him by the dawn of
  day,
  Or that the Russian army should repent
    all:
And, strange to say, they found some con-
  solation
In this—for females like exaggeration.

LXXVI

And then with tears, and sighs, and some
  slight kisses,
  They parted for the present—these to
    await,
According to the artillery's hits or misses,
  What sages call Chance, Providence, or
    Fate—
(Uncertainty is one of many blisses,
  A mortgage on Humanity's estate)—
While their beloved friends began to arm,
To burn a town which never did them
  harm.

LXXVII

Suwarrow,—who but saw things in the
  gross,
  Being much too gross to see them in
    detail,
Who calculated life as so much dross,
  And as the wind a widow'd nation's
    wail,
And cared as little for his army's loss
  (So that their efforts should at length
    prevail)
As wife and friends did for the boils of
  Job,—
What was't to him to hear two women sob?

LXXVIII

Nothing.—The work of glory still went on
  In preparations for a cannonade
As terrible as that of Ilion,
  If Homer had found mortars ready
    made;
But now, instead of slaying Priam's son,
  We only can but talk of escalade,
Bombs, drums, guns, bastions, batteries,
  bayonets, bullets;
Hard words, which stick in the soft
  Muses' gullets.

LXXIX

Oh, thou eternal Homer! who couldst charm
  All ears, though long; all ages, though
    so short,
By merely wielding with poetic arm
  Arms to which men will never more
    resort,
Unless gunpowder should be found to
  harm
  Much less than is the hope of every
    court,
Which now is leagued young Freedom to
  annoy;
But they will not find Liberty a Troy:—

LXXX

Oh, thou eternal Homer! I have now
    To paint a siege, wherein more men
        were slain,
With deadlier engines and a speedier blow,
    Than in thy Greek gazette of that cam-
        paign;
And yet, like all men else, I must allow,
    To vie with thee would be about as vain
As for a brook to cope with ocean's flood;
But still we moderns equal you in blood;

LXXXI

If not in poetry, at least in fact;
    And fact is truth, the grand desidera-
        tum!
Of which, howe'er the Muse describes
      each act,
    There should be ne'ertheless a slight
      substratum.
But now the town is going to be attack'd;
    Great deeds are doing—how shall I re-
      late 'em?
Souls of immortal generals! Phœbus
      watches
To colour up his rays from your des-
      patches.

LXXXII

Oh, ye great bulletins of Bonaparte!
    Oh, ye less grand long lists of kill'd and
      wounded!
Shade of Leonidas, who fought so hearty,
    When my poor Greece was once, as
      now, surrounded!
Oh, Cæsar's Commentaries! now impart,
    ye
    Shadows of glory! (lest I be con-
      founded),
A portion of your fading twilight hues,
So beautiful, so fleeting, to the Muse.

LXXXIII

When I call 'fading' martial immortality,
    I mean, that every age and every year,
And almost every day, in sad reality,
    Some sucking hero is compell'd to rear,
Who, when we come to sum up the totality
    Of deeds to human happiness most dear,
Turns out to be a butcher in great business,
Afflicting young folks with a sort of dizzi-
    ness.

LXXXIV

Medals, ranks, ribands, lace, embroidery,
    scarlet,
    Are things immortal to immortal man,
As purple to the Babylonian harlot:
    An uniform to boys is like a fan
To women; there is scarce a crimson varlet
    But deems himself the first in Glory's van.
But Glory's glory; and if you would find
What *that* is—ask the pig who sees the
    wind!

LXXXV

At least *he feels it*, and some say he *sees*,
    Because he runs before it like a pig;
Or, if that simple sentence should dis-
    please,
    Say, that he scuds before it like a brig,
A schooner, or—but it is time to ease
    This Canto, ere my Muse perceives
      fatigue.
The next shall ring a peal to shake all
    people,
Like a bob-major from a village steeple.

LXXXVI

Hark! through the silence of the cold, dull
    night,
    The hum of armies gathering rank on
      rank!
Lo! dusky masses steal in dubious sight
    Along the leaguer'd wall and bristling
      bank
Of the arm'd river, while with straggling
    light
    The stars peep through the vapours dim
      and dank,
Which curl in curious wreaths:—how soon
    the smoke
Of Hell shall pall them in a deeper cloak!

LXXXVII

Here pause we for the present—as even
    then
    That awful pause, dividing life from
      death,
Struck for an instant on the hearts of
    men,
    Thousands of whom were drawing their
      last breath!
A moment—and all will be life again!
    The march! the charge! the shouts of
      either faith,
Hurrah! and Allah! and—one moment
    more—
The death-cry drowning in the battle's
    roar.

CANTO THE EIGHTH

I

Oh, blood and thunder! and oh, blood and
    wounds!
    These are but vulgar oaths, as you may
      deem,
Too gentle reader! and most shocking
    sounds:
    And so they are; yet thus is Glory's
      dream
Unriddled, and as my true Muse expounds
    At present such things, since they are
      her theme,
So be they her inspirers! Call them Mars,
Bellona, what you will—they mean but
    wars.

II

All was prepared—the fire, the sword, the men
    To wield them in their terrible array.
The army, like a lion from his den,
    March'd forth with nerve and sinews bent to slay,—
A human Hydra, issuing from its fen
    To breathe destruction on its winding way,
Whose heads were heroes, which, cut off in vain,
Immediately in others grew again.

III

History can only take things in the gross;
    But could we know them in detail, perchance
In balancing the profit and the loss,
    War's merit it by no means might enhance,
To waste so much gold for a little dross,
    As hath been done, mere conquest to advance.
The drying up a single tear has more
Of honest fame, than shedding seas of gore.

IV

And why?—because it brings self-approbation;
    Whereas the other, after all its glare,
Shouts, bridges, arches, pensions from a nation,
    Which (it may be) has not much left to spare,
A higher title, or a loftier station,
    Though they may make Corruption gape or stare,
Yet, in the end, except in freedom's battles,
Are nothing but a child of Murder's rattles.

V

And such they are—and such they will be found:
    Not so Leonidas and Washington,
Whose every battle-field is holy ground,
    Which breathes of nations saved, not worlds undone.
How sweetly on the ear such echoes sound!
    While the mere victor's may appal or stun
The servile and the vain, such names will be
A watchword till the future shall be free.

VI

The night was dark, and the thick mist allow'd
    Nought to be seen save the artillery's flame,
Which arch'd the horizon like a fiery cloud,
    And in the Danube's waters shone the same—

A mirror'd hell! the volleying roar, and loud
    Long booming of each peal on peal, o'ercame
The ear far more than thunder; for Heaven's flashes
Spare, or smite rarely—man's make millions ashes!

VII

The column order'd on the assault scarce pass'd
    Beyond the Russian batteries a few toises,
When up the bristling Moslem rose at last,
    Answering the Christian thunders with like voices:
Then one vast fire, air, earth, and stream embraced,
    Which rock'd as 'twere beneath the mighty noises;
While the whole rampart blazed like Etna, when
The restless Titan hiccups in his den;

VIII

And one enormous shout of 'Allah!' rose
    In the same moment, loud as even the roar
Of war's most mortal engines, to their foes
    Hurling defiance: city, stream, and shore
Resounded 'Allah!' and the clouds which close
    With thick'ning canopy the conflict o'er,
Vibrate to the Eternal name. Hark! through
All sounds it pierceth, 'Allah! Allah! Hu!'

IX

The columns were in movement one and all,
    But of the portion which attack'd by water,
Thicker than leaves the lives began to fall,
    Though led by Arseniew, that great son of slaughter,
As brave as ever faced both bomb and ball.
    'Carnage, (so Wordsworth tells you) is God's daughter:'
If he speak truth, she is Christ's sister, and
Just now behaved as in the Holy Land.

X

The Prince de Ligne was wounded in the knee;
    Count Chapeau-Bras, too, had a ball between
His cap and head, which proves the head to be
    Aristocratic as was ever seen,
Because it then received no injury
    More than the cap; in fact, the ball could mean
No harm unto a right legitimate head;
'Ashes to ashes'—why not lead to lead?

XI

Also the General Markow, Brigadier,
  Insisting on removal of the *prince*
Amidst some groaning thousands dying
    near,—
  All common fellows, who might writhe
    and wince,
And shriek for water into a deaf ear,—
  The General Markow, who could thus
    evince
His sympathy for rank, by the same token,
To teach him greater, had his own leg
  broken.

XII

Three hundred cannon threw up their
    emetic,
  And thirty thousand muskets flung their
    pills
Like hail, to make a bloody diuretic.
  Mortality! thou hast thy monthly bills:
Thy plagues, thy famines, thy physicians,
    yet tick,
  Like the death-watch, within our ears
    the ills
Past, present, and to come;—but all may
    yield
To the true portrait of one battle-field;

XIII

There the still varying pangs, which multi-
    ply
  Until their very number makes men hard
By the infinities of agony,
  Which meet the gaze, whate'er it may
    regard—
The groan, the roll in dust, the all-*white* eye
  Turn'd back within its socket,—these
    reward
Your rank and file by thousands, while the
    rest
May win perhaps a riband at the breast!

XIV

Yet I love glory;—glory's a great thing:-
  Think what it is to be in your old age
Maintain'd at the expense of your good
    king:
  A moderate pension shakes full many a
    sage,
And heroes are but made for bards to sing,
  Which is still better; thus in verse to
    wage
Your wars eternally, besides enjoying
Half-pay for life, make mankind worth
  destroying.

XV

The troops, already disembark'd, push'd on
  To take a battery on the right: the others,
Who landed lower down, their landing
    done,
  Had set to work as briskly as their
    brothers:
Being grenadiers, they mounted one by
    one,
  Cheerful as children climb the breasts of
    mothers,
O'er the intrenchment and the palisade,
Quite orderly, as if upon parade.

XVI

And this was admirable; for so hot
  The fire was, that were red Vesuvius
    loaded,
Besides its lava, with all sorts of shot
  And shells or hells, it could not more
    have goaded.
Of officers a third fell on the spot,
  A thing which victory by no means
    boded
To gentlemen engaged in the assault:
Hounds, when the huntsman tumbles, are
  at fault.

XVII

But here I leave the general concern,
  To track our hero on his path of fame:
He must his laurels separately earn;
  For fifty thousand heroes, name by
    name,
Though all deserving equally to turn
  A couplet, or an elegy to claim,
Would form a lengthy lexicon of glory,
And what is worse still, a much longer
  story:

XVIII

And therefore we must give the greater
    number
  To the Gazette—which doubtless fairly
    dealt
By the deceased, who lie in famous
    slumber
  In ditches, fields, or wheresoe'er they felt
Their clay for the last time their souls
    encumber;—
  Thrice happy he whose name has been
    well spelt
In the despatch: I knew a man whose loss
Was printed *Grove*, although his name was
  Grose.

XIX

Juan and Johnson join'd a certain corps,
  And fought away with might and main,
    not knowing
The way which they had never trod before,
  And still less guessing where they might
    be going;
But on they march'd, dead bodies tramp-
    ling o'er,
  Firing, and thrusting, slashing, sweat-
    ing, glowing,
But fighting thoughtlessly enough to win,
To their *two* selves, *one* whole bright
  bulletin.

XX

Thus on they wallow'd in the bloody mire
  Of dead and dying thousands,—some-
      times gaining
A yard or two of ground, which brought
      them nigher
  To some odd angle for which all were
      straining;
At other times, repulsed by the close fire,
  Which really pour'd as if all hell were
      raining
Instead of heaven, they stumbled back-
      wards o'er
A wounded comrade, sprawling in his gore.

XXI

Though 'twas Don Juan's first of fields,
      and though
  The nightly muster and the silent march
In the chill dark, when courage does not
      glow
  So much as under a triumphal arch,
Perhaps might make him shiver, yawn, or
      throw
  A glance on the dull clouds (as thick as
      starch,
Which stiffen'd heaven) as if he wish'd for
      day;—
Yet for all this he did not run away.

XXII

Indeed he could not. But what if he had?
  There *have been* and *are* heroes who
      begun
With something not much better, or as
      bad:
  Frederick the Great from Molwitz
      deign'd to run,
For the first and last time; for, like a pad,
  Or hawk, or bride, most mortals after
      one
Warm bout are broken in to their new
      tricks,
And fight like fiends for pay or politics.

XXIII

He was what Erin calls, in her sublime
  Old Erse or Irish, or it may be *Punic*;—
(The antiquarians who can settle time,
  Which settles all things, Roman, Greek,
      or Runic,
Swear that Pat's language sprung from the
      same clime
  With Hannibal, and wears the Tyrian
      tunic
Of Dido's alphabet; and this is rational
As any other notion, and not national;)—

XXIV

But Juan was quite 'a broth of a boy,'
  A thing of impulse and a child of song;
Now swimming in the sentiment of joy,
  Or the *sensation* (if that phrase seem
      wrong),

And afterward, if he must needs destroy,
  In such good company as always throng
To battles, sieges, and that kind of
      pleasure,
No less delighted to employ his leisure;

XXV

But always without malice: if he warr'd
  Or loved, it was with what we call 'the
      best
Intentions,' which form all mankind's
      trump card,
  To be produced when brought up to the
      test.
The statesman, hero, harlot, lawyer—ward
  Off each attack, when people are in quest
Of their designs, by saying they *meant
      well*;
'Tis pity 'that such meaning should pave
      hell.'

XXVI

I almost lately have begun to doubt
  Whether hell's pavement—if it be so
      paved—
Must not have latterly been quite worn out,
  Not by the numbers good intent hath
      saved,
But by the mass who go below without
  Those ancient good intentions, which
      once shaved
And smooth'd the brimstone of that street
      of hell
Which bears the greatest likeness to Pall
      Mall.

XXVII

Juan, by some strange chance, which oft
      divides
  Warrior from warrior in their grim
      career,
Like chastest wives from constant hus-
      bands' sides
  Just at the close of the first bridal year,
By one of those odd turns of Fortune's
      tides,
  Was on a sudden rather puzzled here,
When, after a good deal of heavy firing,
He found himself alone, and friends retir-
      ing.

XXVIII

I don't know how the thing occurr'd—it
      might
  Be that the greater part were kill'd or
      wounded,
And that the rest had faced unto the right
  About; a circumstance which has con-
      founded
Cæsar himself, who, in the very sight
  Of his whole army, which so much
      abounded
In courage, was obliged to snatch a shield,
And rally back his Romans to the field.

XXIX

Juan, who had no shield to snatch, and
was
   No Cæsar, but a fine young lad, who
   fought
He knew not why, arriving at this pass,
   Stopp'd for a minute, as perhaps he
   ought
For a much longer time; then, like an ass
   (Start not, kind reader, since great
   Homer thought
This simile enough for Ajax, Juan
Perhaps may find it better than a new
   one);

XXX

Then, like an ass, he went upon his way,
   And, what was stranger, never look'd
   behind;
But seeing, flashing forward, like the day
   Over the hills, a fire enough to blind
Those who dislike to look upon a fray,
   He stumbled on, to try if he could find
A path, to add his own slight arm and
   forces
To corps, the greater part of which were
   corses.

XXXI

Perceiving then no more the commandant
   Of his own corps, nor even the corps,
   which had
Quite disappear'd—the gods know how!
   (I can't
   Account for everything which may look
   bad
In history; but we at least may grant
   It was not marvellous that a mere lad,
In search of glory, should look on before,
Nor care a pinch of snuff about his
   corps:)—

XXXII

Perceiving nor commander nor com-
   manded,
   And left at large, like a young heir, to
   make
His way to—where he knew not—single-
   handed;
   As travellers follow over bog and brake
An 'ignis fatuus'; or as sailors stranded
   Unto the nearest hut themselves betake;
So Juan, following honour and his nose,
Rush'd where the thickest fire announced
   most foes.

XXXIII

He knew not where he was, nor greatly
   cared,
   For he was dizzy, busy, and his veins
Fill'd as with lightning—for his spirit
   shared
   The hour, as is the case with lively
   brains;

And where the hottest fire was seen and
   heard,
   And the loud cannon peal'd his hoarsest
   strains,
He rush'd, while earth and air were sadly
   shaken
By thy humane discovery, Friar Bacon!

XXXIV

And as he rush'd along, it came to pass he
   Fell in with what was late the second
   column,
Under the orders of the General Lascy,
   But now reduced, as is a bulky volume
Into an elegant extract (much less massy)
   Of heroism, and took his place with
   solemn
Air 'midst the rest, who kept their valiant
   faces
And levell'd weapons still against the
   glacis.

XXXV

Just at this crisis up came Johnson too,
   Who had 'retreated,' as the phrase is
   when
Men run away much rather than go
   through
   Destruction's jaws into the devil's den;
But Johnson was a clever fellow, who
   Knew when and how 'to cut and come
   again,'
And never ran away, except when running
Was nothing but a valorous kind of cun-
   ning.

XXXVI

And so, when all his corps were dead or
   dying,
   Except Don Juan, a mere novice, whose
More virgin valour never dreamt of flying,
   From ignorance of danger, which in-
   dues
Its votaries, like innocence relying
   On its own strength, with careless
   nerves and thews,—
Johnson retired a little, just to rally
Those who catch cold in 'shadows of
   death's valley.'

XXXVII

And there, a little shelter'd from the shot,
   Which rain'd from bastion, battery,
   parapet,
Rampart, wall, casement, house—for there
   was not
   In this extensive city, sore beset
By Christian soldiery, a single spot
   Which did not combat like the devil, as
   yet,—
He found a number of Chasseurs, all
   scatter'd
By the resistance of the chase they batter'd.

XXXVIII

And these he call'd on; and, what's
    strange, they came
Unto his call, unlike 'the spirits from
The vasty deep,' to whom you may ex-
    claim,
    Says Hotspur, long ere they will leave
    their home.
Their reasons were uncertainty, or shame
    At shrinking from a bullet or a bomb,
And that odd impulse, which in wars or
    creeds
Makes men, like cattle, follow him who
    leads.

XXXIX

By Jove! he was a noble fellow, Johnson,
    And though his name, than Ajax or
    Achilles,
Sounds less harmonious, underneath the
    sun soon
    We shall not see his likeness: he could
    kill his
Man quite as quietly as blows the monsoon
    Her steady breath (which some months
    the same *still* is):
Seldom he varied feature, hue, or muscle,
And could be very busy without bustle;

XL

And therefore, when he ran away, he did so
    Upon reflection, knowing that behind
He would find others who would fain be
    rid so
Of idle apprehensions, which like wind
Trouble heroic stomachs. Though their
    lids so
    Oft are soon closed, all heroes are not
    blind,
But when they light upon immediate
    death,
Retire a little, merely to take breath.

XLI

But Johnson only ran off, to return
    With many other warriors, as we said,
Unto that rather somewhat misty bourne,
    Which Hamlet tells us is a pass of dread.
To Jack, howe'er, this gave but slight con-
    cern:
    His soul (like galvanism upon the dead)
Acted upon the living as on wire,
And led them back into the heaviest fire.

XLII

Egad! they found the second time what
    they
    The first time thought quite terrible
    enough
To fly from, malgré all which people say
    Of glory, and all that immortal stuff
Which fills a regiment (besides their pay,
    That daily shilling which makes war-
    riors tough)—

They found on their return the self-same
    welcome,
Which made some *think*, and others *know*,
    a *hell* come.

XLIII

They fell as thick as harvests beneath hail,
    Grass before scythes, or corn below the
    sickle,
Proving that trite old truth, that life's as
    frail
    As any other boon for which men
    stickle.
The Turkish batteries thrash'd them like a
    flail,
    Or a good boxer, into a sad pickle
Putting the very bravest, who were knock'd
Upon the head before their guns were
    cock'd.

XLIV

The Turks behind the traverses and flanks
    Of the next bastion, fired away like
    devils,
And swept, as gales sweep foam away,
    whole ranks:
    However, Heaven knows how, the Fate
    who levels
Towns, nations, worlds, in her revolving
    pranks,
    So order'd it, amid these sulphury
    revels,
That Johnson, and some few who had not
    scamper'd,
Reach'd the interior talus of the rampart.

XLV

First one or two, then five, six, and a
    dozen
    Came mounting quickly up, for it was
    now
All neck or nothing, as, like pitch or rosin,
    Flame was shower'd forth above, as
    well's below,
So that you scarce could say who best had
    chosen,
    The gentlemen that were the first to show
Their martial faces on the parapet,
Or those who thought it brave to wait as
    yet.

XLVI

But those who scaled found out that their
    advance
    Was favour'd by an accident or blunder:
The Greek or Turkish Cohorn's ignor-
    ance
    Had palisado'd in a way you'd wonder
To see in forts of Netherlands or France—
    (Though these to our Gibraltar must
    knock under)—
Right in the middle of the parapet
Just named, these palisades were primly
    set:

XLVII

So that on either side some nine or ten
    Paces were left, whereon you could con-
      trive
To march; a great convenience to our men,
    At least to all those who were left alive,
Who thus could form a line and fight again;
    And that which further aided them to
      strive
Was, that they could kick down the pali-
      sades,
Which scarcely rose much higher than
    grass blades.

XLVIII

Among the first—I will not say the *first*,
    For such precedence upon such occa-
      sions
Will oftentimes make deadly quarrels burst
    Out between friends as well as allied
      nations:
The Briton must be bold who really durst
    Put to such trial John Bull's partial
      patience,
As say that Wellington at Waterloo
Was beaten,—though the Prussians say so
    too;—

XLIX

And that if Blücher, Bulow, Gneisenau,
    And God knows who besides in 'au'
      and 'ow,'
Had not come up in time to cast an awe
    Into the hearts of those who fought till
      now
As tigers combat with an empty craw,
    The Duke of Wellington had ceased to
      show
His orders, also to receive his pensions;
Which are the heaviest that our history
    mentions.

L

But never mind;—'God save the king!'
    and *kings!*
    For if *he* don't, I doubt if *men* will
      longer—
I think I hear a little bird, who sings
    The people by and by will be the
      stronger:
The veriest jade will wince whose harness
    wrings
    So much into the raw as quite to wrong
      her
Beyond the rules of posting,—and the mob
At last fall sick of imitating Job.

LI

At first it grumbles, then it swears, and
    then,
    Like David, flings smooth pebbles
      'gainst a giant;
At last it takes to weapons such as men
    Snatch when despair makes human
      hearts less pliant.

Then comes the 'tug of war';—'twill come
    again,
    I rather doubt; and I would fain say 'fie
      on 't,'
If I had not perceived that revolution
Alone can save the earth from hell's pollu-
    tion.

LII

But to continue:—I say not *the* first,
    But of the first, our little friend Don
      Juan,
Walk'd o'er the walls of Ismail, as if
    nursed
    Amidst such scenes—though this was
      quite a new one
To him, and I should hope to *most*. The
    thirst
    Of glory, which so pierces through and
      through one,
Pervaded him—although a generous crea-
    ture,
As warm in heart as feminine in feature.

LIII

And here he was—who upon woman's
    breast,
    Even from a child, felt like a child;
      howe'er
The man in all the rest might be confest,
    To him it was Elysium to be there;
And he could even withstand that awk-
      ward test
    Which Rousseau points out to the
      dubious fair,
'Observe your lover when he *leaves* your
    arms';
But Juan never *left* them while they had
    charms,

LIV

Unless compell'd by fate, or wave, or
    wind,
    Or near relations, who are much the
      same.
But *here* he was!—where each tie that can
    bind
    Humanity must yield to steel and flame:
And *he* whose very body was all mind,
    Flung here by fate or circumstance,
      which tame
The loftiest, hurried by the time and place,
Dash'd on like a spurr'd blood-horse in a
    race.

LV

So was his blood stirr'd while he found
    resistance,
    As is the hunter's at the five-bar gate,
Or double post and rail, where the exis-
    tence
    Of Britain's youth depends upon their
      weight,

The lightest being the safest: at a distance
　He hated cruelty, as all men hate
Blood, until heated—and even there his own
At times would curdle o'er some heavy groan.

LVI

The General Lascy, who had been hard press'd,
　Seeing arrive an aid so opportune
As were some hundred youngsters all abreast,
　Who came as if just dropp'd down from the moon,
To Juan, who was nearest him, address'd
　His thanks, and hopes to take the city soon,
Not reckoning him to be a 'base Bezonian'
(As Pistol calls it), but a young Livonian.

LVII

Juan, to whom he spoke in German, knew
　As much of German as of Sanscrit, and
In answer made an inclination to
　The general who held him in command:
For seeing one with ribands, black and blue,
　Stars, medals, and a bloody sword in hand,
Addressing him in tones which seem'd to thank,
He recognised an officer of rank.

LVIII

Short speeches pass between two men who speak
　No common language; and besides, in time
Of war and taking towns, when many a shriek
　Rings o'er the dialogue, and many a crime
Is perpetrated ere a word can break
　Upon the ear, and sounds of horror chime
In like church-bells, with sigh, howl, groan, yell, prayer,
There cannot be much conversation there.

LIX

And therefore all we have related in
　Two long octaves, pass'd in a little minute;
But in the same small minute, every sin
　Contrived to get itself comprised within it.
The very cannon, deafen'd by the din,
　Grew dumb, for you might almost hear a linnet,
As soon as thunder, 'midst the general noise
Of human nature's agonising voice!

LX

The town was enter'd. Oh eternity!—
　'God made the country, and man made the town,'
So Cowper says—and I begin to be
　Of his opinion, when I see cast down
Rome, Babylon, Tyre, Carthage, Nineveh,
　All walls men know, and many never known;
And pondering on the present and the past,
To deem the woods shall be our home at last:—

LXI

Of all men, saving Sylla the man-slayer,
　Who passes for in life and death most lucky,
Of the great names which in our faces stare,
　The General Boon, back-woodsman of Kentucky,
Was happiest amongst mortals anywhere,
　For killing nothing but a bear or buck, he
Enjoy'd the lonely, vigorous, harmless days
Of his old age in wilds of deepest maze.

LXII

Crime came not near him—she is not the child
　Of solitude; Health shrank not from him—for
Her home is in the rarely trodden wild,
　Where if men seek her not, and death be more
Their choice than life, forgive them, as beguiled
　By habit to what their own hearts abhor—
In cities caged. The present case in point I
Cite is, that Boon lived hunting up to ninety;

LXIII

And what's still stranger, left behind a name
　For which men vainly decimate the throng,
Not only famous, but of that *good* fame
　Without which glory's but a tavern song—
Simple, serene, the *antipodes* of shame,
　Which hate nor envy e'er could tinge with wrong;
An active hermit, even in age the child
Of Nature, or the Man of Ross run wild.

LXIV

'Tis true he shrank from men even of his nation,
　When they built up unto his darling trees,—
He moved some hundred miles off, for a station
　Where there were fewer houses and more ease;

The inconvenience of civilisation
  Is, that you neither can be pleased nor
      please;
But where he met the individual man,
He show'd himself as kind as mortal can.

LXV

He was not all alone: around him grew
  A sylvan tribe of children of the chase,
Whose young, unwaken'd world was
    ever new,
  Nor sword nor sorrow yet had left a
    trace
On her unwrinkled brow, nor could you
    view
  A frown on Nature's or on human face;
The free-born forest found and kept them
    free,
And fresh as is a torrent or a tree.

LXVI

And tall, and strong, and swift of foot
    were they,
  Beyond the dwarfing city's pale abor-
    tions,
Because their thoughts had never been the
    prey
  Of care or gain: the green woods were
    their portions;
No sinking spirits told them they grew grey,
  No fashion made them apes of her dis-
    tortions;
Simple they were, not savage; and their
    rifles,
Though very true, were not yet used for
    trifles.

LXVII

Motion was in their days, rest in their
    slumbers,
  And cheerfulness the handmaid of their
    toil;
Nor yet too many nor too few their
    numbers;
  Corruption could not make their hearts
    her soil;
The lust which stings, the splendour which
    encumbers,
  With the free foresters divide no spoil;
Serene, not sullen, were the solitudes
Of this unsighing people of the woods.

LXVIII

So much for Nature:—by way of variety,
  Now back to thy great joys, Civilisation!
And the sweet consequence of large
    society,
  War, pestilence, the despot's desolation,
The kingly scourge, the lust of notoriety,
  The millions slain by soldiers for their
    ration,
The scenes like Catherine's boudoir at
    three-score,
With Ismail's storm to soften it the more.

LXIX

The town was enter'd: first one column
    made
  Its sanguinary way good—then another;
The reeking bayonet and the flashing blade
  Clash'd 'gainst the scimitar, and babe
    and mother
With distant shrieks were heard Heaven to
    upbraid:—
  Still closer sulphury clouds began to
    smother
The breath of morn and man, where foot
    by foot
The madden'd Turks their city still dis-
    pute.

LXX

Koutousow, he who afterwards beat back
  (With some assistance from the frost
    and snow)
Napoleon on his bold and bloody track,
  It happen'd was himself beat back just
    now:
He was a jolly fellow, and could crack
  His jest alike in face of friend or foe,
Though life, and death, and victory were
    at stake;
But here it seem'd his jokes had ceased to
    take:

LXXI

For having thrown himself into a ditch,
  Follow'd in haste by various grenadiers,
Whose blood the puddle greatly did en-
    rich,
  He climb'd to where the parapet ap-
    pears;
But there his project reach'd its utmost
    pitch
  ('Mongst other deaths the General
    Ribaupierre's
Was much regretted), for the Moslem men
Threw them all down into the ditch again.

LXXII

And had it not been for some stray troops
    landing
  They knew not where, being carried by
    the stream
To some spot, where they lost their under-
    standing,
  And wander'd up and down as in a
    dream,
Until they reach'd, as daybreak was ex-
    panding,
  That which a portal to their eyes did
    seem,—
The great and gay Koutousow might have
    lain
Where three parts of his column yet re-
    main.

LXXIII

And scrambling round the rampart, these
  same troops,
  After the taking of the 'Cavalier,'
Just as Koutousow's most 'forlorn' of
  'hopes'
  Took, like chameleons, some slight
    tinge of fear,
Open'd the gate call'd 'Kilia,' to the groups
  Of baffled heroes, who stood shyly near,
Sliding knee-deep in lately frozen mud,
Now thaw'd into a marsh of human blood.

LXXIV

The Kozacks, or, if so you please, Cos-
    sacques—
  (I don't much pique myself upon ortho-
    graphy,
So that I do not grossly err in facts,
  Statistics, tactics, politics, and geo-
    graphy)—
Having been used to serve on horses' backs,
  And no great dilettanti in topography
Of fortresses, but fighting where it pleases
Their chiefs to order,—were all cut to pieces.

LXXV

Their column, though the Turkish bat-
    teries thunder'd
  Upon them, ne'ertheless had reach'd
    the rampart,
And naturally thought they could have
    plunder'd
  The city, without being further ham-
    per'd;
But as it happens to brave men, they
    blunder'd—
  The Turks at first pretended to have
    scamper'd,
Only to draw them 'twixt two bastion
    corners,
From whence they sallied on those Chris-
  tian scorners.

LXXVI

Then being taken by the tail—a taking
  Fatal to bishops as to soldiers—these
Cossacques were all cut off as day was
    breaking,
  And found their lives were let at a short
    lease—
But perish'd without shivering or shaking,
  Leaving as ladders their heap'd car-
    casses,
O'er which Lieutenant-Colonel Yesouskoi
March'd with the brave battalion of Po-
  louzki:—

LXXVII

This valiant man kill'd all the Turks he met,
  But could not eat them, being in his turn
Slain by some Mussulmans, who would
    not yet,
  Without resistance, see their city burn.

The walls were won, but 'twas an even bet
  Which of the armies would have cause
    to mourn:
'Twas blow for blow, disputing inch by inch,
For one would not retreat, nor t' other flinch.

LXXVIII

Another column also suffer'd much:—
  And here we may remark with the his-
    torian,
You should but give few cartridges to such
  Troops as are meant to march with
    greatest glory on:
When matters must be carried by the touch
  Of the bright bayonet, and they all
    should hurry on,
They sometimes, with a hankering for
    existence,
Keep merely firing at a foolish distance.

LXXIX

A junction of the General Meknop's men
  (Without the General, who had fallen
    some time
Before, being badly seconded just then)
  Was made at length with those who
    dared to climb
The death-disgorging rampart once again;
  And though the Turks' resistance was
    sublime,
They took the bastion, which the Seraskier
Defended at a price extremely dear.

LXXX

Juan and Johnson, and some volunteers
  Among the foremost, offer'd him good
    quarter,
A word which little suits with Seraskiers,
  Or at least suited not this valiant Tartar.
He died, deserving well his country's tears,
  A savage sort of military martyr.
An English naval officer, who wish'd
To make him prisoner, was also dish'd:

LXXXI

For all the answer to his proposition
  Was from a pistol-shot that laid him dead;
On which the rest, without more intermis-
    sion,
  Began to lay about with steel and lead—
The pious metals most in requisition
  On such occasions: not a single head
Was spared;—three thousand Moslems
    perish'd here,
And sixteen bayonets pierced the Seraskier.

LXXXII

The city's taken—only part by part—
  And death is drunk with gore: there's
    not a street
Where fights not to the last some desperate
    heart
  For those for whom it soon shall cease
    to beat.

Here War forgot his own destructive art
  In more destroying Nature; and the heat
Of carnage, like the Nile's sun-sodden slime,
Engender'd monstrous shapes of every crime.

LXXXIII

A Russian officer, in martial tread
  Over a heap of bodies, felt his heel
Seized fast, as if 'twere by the serpent's head
  Whose fangs Eve taught her human seed to feel:
In vain he kick'd, and swore, and writhed, and bled,
  And howl'd for help as wolves do for a meal—
The teeth still kept their gratifying hold,
As do the subtle snakes described of old.

LXXXIV

A dying Moslem, who had felt the foot
  Of a foe o'er him, snatch'd at it, and bit
The very tendon which is most acute—
  (That which some ancient Muse or modern wit
Named after thee, Achilles) and quite through 't
  He made the teeth meet, nor relinquish'd it
Even with his life—for (but they lie) 'tis said
To the live leg still clung the sever'd head.

LXXXV

However this may be, 'tis pretty sure
  The Russian officer for life was lamed,
For the Turk's teeth stuck faster than a skewer,
  And left him 'midst the invalid and maim'd:
The regimental surgeon could not cure
  His patient, and perhaps was to be blamed
More than the head of the inveterate foe,
Which was cut off, and scarce even then let go.

LXXXVI

But then the fact's a fact—and 'tis the part
  Of a true poet to escape from fiction
Whene'er he can; for there is little art
  In leaving verse more free from the restriction
Of truth than prose, unless to suit the mart
  For what is sometimes call'd poetic diction
And that outrageous appetite for lies
Which Satan angles with for souls, like flies.

LXXXVII

The city's taken, but not render'd!—No!
  There's not a Moslem that hath yielded sword:
The blood may gush out, as the Danube's flow
  Rolls by the city wall; but deed nor word
Acknowledge aught of dread of death or foe:
  In vain the yell of victory is roar'd
By the advancing Muscovite—the groan
Of the last foe is echoed by his own.

LXXXVIII

The bayonet pierces and the sabre cleaves,
  And human lives are lavish'd everywhere,
As the year closing whirls the scarlet leaves
  When the stripp'd forest bows to the bleak air,
And groans; and thus the peopled city grieves,
  Shorn of its best and loveliest, and left bare;
But still it falls with vast and awful splinters,
As oaks blown down with all their thousand winters.

LXXXIX

It is an awful topic—but 'tis not
  My cue for any time to be terrific:
For checker'd as is seen our human lot
  With good, and bad, and worse, alike prolific
Of melancholy merriment, to quote
  Too much of one sort would be soporific;—
Without, or with, offence to friends or foes,
I sketch your world exactly as it goes.

XC

And one good action in tne midst of crimes
  Is 'quite refreshing,' in the affected phrase
Of these ambrosial, Pharisaic times,
  With all their pretty milk-and-water ways,
And may serve therefore to bedew these rhymes,
  A little scorch'd at present with the blaze
Of conquest and its consequences, which
Make epic poesy so rare and rich.

XCI

Upon a taken bastion, where there lay
  Thousands of slaughter'd men, a yet warm group
Of murder'd women, who had found their way
  To this vain refuge, made the good heart droop

And shudder;—while, as beautiful as May,
  A female child of ten years tried to stoop
And hide her little palpitating breast
Amidst the bodies lull'd in bloody rest.

XCII

Two villainous Cossacques pursued the
    child
  With flashing eyes and weapons:
    match'd with *them*,
The rudest brute that roams Siberia's wild
  Has feelings pure and polish'd as a
    gem,—
The bear is civilised, the wolf is mild:
  And whom for this at last must we con-
    demn?
Their natures? or their sovereigns, who
    employ
All arts to teach their subjects to destroy?

XCIII

Their sabres glitter'd o'er her little head,
  Whence her fair hair rose twining with
    affright,
Her hidden face was plunged amidst the
    dead:
  When Juan caught a glimpse of this sad
    sight,
I shall not say exactly what he *said*,
  Because it might not solace 'ears polite';
But what he *did*, was to lay on their backs,
The readiest way of reasoning with Cos-
    sacques.

XCIV

One's hip he slash'd, and split the other's
    shoulder,
  And drove them with their brutal yells
    to seek
If there might be chirurgeons who could
    solder
  The wounds they richly merited, and
    shriek
Their baffled rage and pain; while waxing
    colder
  As he turn'd o'er each pale and gory
    cheek,
Don Juan raised his little captive from
The heap a moment more had made her
    tomb.

XCV

And she was chill as they, and on her face
  A slender streak of blood announced
    how near
Her fate had been to that of all her race;
  For the same blow which laid her
    mother here
Had scarr'd her brow, and left its crimson
    trace,
  As the last link with all she had held
    dear;
But else unhurt, she open'd her large eyes,
And gazed on Juan with a wild surprise.

XCVI

Just at this instant, while their eyes were
    fix'd
  Upon each other, with dilated glance,
In Juan's look, pain, pleasure, hope, fear,
    mix'd
  With joy to save, and dread of some mis-
    chance
Unto his protégée; while hers, transfix'd
  With infant terrors, glared as from a
    trance,
A pure, transparent, pale, yet radiant face,
Like to a lighted alabaster vase;—

XCVII

Up came John Johnson (I will not say '*Jack*,'
  For that were vulgar, cold, and com-
    monplace
On great occasions, such as an attack
  On cities, as hath been the present case):
Up Johnson came, with hundreds at his
    back,
  Exclaiming—'Juan! Juan! On, boy!
    brace
Your arm, and I'll bet Moscow to a dollar,
That you and I will win St. George's collar.

XCVIII

'The Seraskier is knock'd upon the head,
  But the stone bastion still remains, wherein
The old Pacha sits among some hundreds
    dead,
  Smoking his pipe quite calmly 'midst
    the din
Of our artillery and his own: 'tis said
  Our kill'd, already piled up to the chin,
Lie round the battery; but still it batters,
And grape in volleys, like a vineyard,
    scatters.

XCIX

'Then up with me!'—But Juan answer'd,
    'Look
  Upon this child—I saved her—must
    not leave
Her life to chance; but point me out some
    nook
  Of safety, where she less may shrink and
    grieve,
And I am with you.'—Whereon Johnson
    took
  A glance around—and shrugg'd—and
    twitch'd his sleeve
And black silk neckcloth—and replied,
    'You're right;
Poor thing! what's to be done? I'm
    puzzled quite.'

C

Said Juan—'Whatsoever is to be
  Done, I'll not quit her till she seems
    secure
Of present life a good deal more than
    we.'—
  Quoth Johnson—'*Neither* will I quite
    insure;

But at the least *you* may die gloriously.'—
Juan replied—'At least I will endure
Whate'er is to be borne—but not resign
This child, who is parentless, and therefore
  mine.'

CI

Johnson said—'Juan, we've no time to
  lose;
  The child's a pretty child—a very
  pretty—
I never saw such eyes—but hark! now
  choose
  Between your fame and feelings, pride
  and pity:—
Hark! how the roar increases!—no excuse
Will serve when there is plunder in a
  city;—
I should be loth to march without you, but,
By God! we'll be too late for the first cut.'

CII

But Juan was immovable; until
  Johnson, who really loved him in his
  way,
Pick'd out amongst his followers with
  some skill
  Such as he thought the least given up to
  prey;
And swearing if the infant came to ill
  That they should all be shot on the next
  day;
But if she were deliver'd safe and sound,
They should at least have fifty rubles
  round,

CIII

And all allowances besides of plunder
  In fair proportion with their com-
  rades;—then
Juan consented to march on through
  thunder,
  Which thinn'd at every step their ranks
  of men:
And yet the rest rush'd eagerly—no
  wonder,
  For they were heated by the hope of
  gain,
A thing which happens everywhere each
  day—
No hero trusteth wholly to half pay.

CIV

And such is victory, and such is man!
  At least nine-tenths of what we call
  so:—God
May have another name for half we scan
  As human beings, or his ways are odd.
But to our subject: a brave Tartar khan—
  Or 'sultan,' as the author (to whose nod
In prose I bend my humble verse) doth call
This chieftain—somehow would not yield
  at all:

CV

But flank'd by *five* brave sons (such is
  polygamy,
  That she spawns warriors by the score,
  where none
Are prosecuted for that false crime
  bigamy),
  He never would believe the city won
While courage clung but to a single twig.—
  Am I
  Describing Priam's, Peleus', or Jove's
  son?
Neither—but a good, plain, old, temperate
  man,
Who fought with his five children in the
  van.

CVI

To *take* him was the point. The truly brave,
  When they behold the brave oppress'd
  with odds,
Are touch'd with a desire to shield and
  save:—
  A mixture of wild beasts and demi-gods
Are they—now furious as the sweeping
  wave,
  Now moved with pity; even as some-
  times nods
The rugged tree unto the summer wind,
Compassion breathes along the savage
  mind.

CVII

But he would *not* be *taken*, and replied
  To all the propositions of surrender
By mowing Christians down on every side,
  As obstinate as Swedish Charles at
  Bender.
His five brave boys no less the foe defied;
  Whereon the Russian pathos grew less
  tender,
As being a virtue, like terrestrial patience,
Apt to wear out on trifling provocations.

CVIII

And spite of Johnson and of Juan, who
  Expended all their Eastern phraseology
In begging him, for God's sake, just to show
  So much less fight as might form an
  apology
For *them* in saving such a desperate foe—
  He hew'd away, like doctors of theology
When they dispute with sceptics; and with
  curses
Struck at his friends, as babies beat their
  nurses.

CIX

Nay, he had wounded, though but slightly,
  both
  Juan and Johnson; whereupon they fell,
The first with sighs, the second with an
  oath,
  Upon his angry sultanship, pell-mell,

And all around were grown exceeding wroth
  At such a pertinacious infidel,
And pour'd upon him and his sons like rain,
  Which they resisted like a sandy plain

CX

That drinks and still is dry. At last they
  perish'd—
  His second son was levell'd by a shot;
His third was sabred; and the fourth, most
  cherish'd
  Of all the five, on bayonets met his lot;
The fifth, who, by a Christian mother
  nourish'd,
  Had been neglected, ill-used, and what
    not,
Because deform'd, yet died all game and
  bottom,
To save a sire, who blush'd that he begot
  him.

CXI

The eldest was a true and tameless Tartar,
  As great a scorner of the Nazarene
As ever Mahomet pick'd out for a martyr,
  Who only saw the black-eyed girls in
    green,
Who make the beds of those who won't
  take quarter
  On earth, in Paradise; and when once
    seen,
Those houris, like all other pretty crea-
  tures,
Do just whate'er they please, by dint of
  features.

CXII

And what they pleased to do with the
  young khan
  In heaven I know not, nor pretend to
    guess;
But doubtless they prefer a fine young man
  To tough old heroes, and can do no less;
And that's the cause no doubt why, if we
  scan
  A field of battle's ghastly wilderness,
For one rough, weather-beaten, veteran
  body,
You'll find ten thousand handsome cox-
  combs bloody.

CXIII

Your houris also have a natural pleasure
  In lopping off your lately married men,
Before the bridal hours have danced their
  measure,
  And the sad, second moon grows dim
    again,
Or dull repentance hath had dreary leisure
  To wish him back a bachelor now and
    then:
And thus your houri (it may be) disputes
Of these brief blossoms the immediate
  fruits.

CXIV

Thus the young khan, with houris in his
  sight,
  Thought not upon the charms of four
    young brides,
But bravely rush'd on his first heavenly
  night.
  In short, howe'er *our* better faith de-
    rides,
These black-eyed virgins make the Mos-
  lems fight,
  As though there were one heaven and
    none besides—
Whereas, if all be true we hear of heaven
And hell, there must at least be six or seven.

CXV

So fully flash'd the phantom on his eyes,
  That when the very lance was in his heart,
He shouted 'Allah!' and saw Paradise
  With all its veil of mystery drawn apart,
And bright eternity without disguise
  On his soul, like a ceaseless sunrise,
    dart:—
With prophets, houris, angels, saints, de-
  scried
In one voluptuous blaze,—and then he died:

CXVI

But with a heavenly rapture on his face,
  The good old khan, who long had
    ceased to see
Houris, or aught except his florid race
  Who grew like cedars round him glori-
    ously—
When he beheld his latest hero grace
  The earth, which he became like a fell'd
    tree,
Paused for a moment from the fight, and
  cast
A glance on that slain son, his first and last.

CXVII

The soldiers, who beheld him drop his point,
  Stopp'd as if once more willing to con-
    cede
Quarter, in case he bade them not 'aroynt!'
  As he before had done. He did not heed
Their pause nor signs: his heart was out of
  joint,
  And shook (till now unshaken) like a
    reed,
As he look'd down upon his children gone,
And felt—though done with life—he was
  alone.

CXVIII

But 'twas a transient tremor:—with a
  spring
  Upon the Russian steel his breast he
    flung,
As carelessly as hurls the moth her wing
  Against the light wherein she dies: he
    clung

Closer, that all the deadlier they might
wring,
  Unto the bayonets which had pierced
his young;
And throwing back a dim look on his sons,
In one wide wound pour'd forth his soul
at once.

CXIX

'Tis strange enough—the rough, tough
soldiers who
  Spared neither sex nor age in their
career
Of carnage, when this old man was pierced
through,
  And lay before them with his children
near,
Touch'd by the heroism of him they slew,
  Were melted for a moment; though no
tear
Flow'd from their bloodshot eyes, all red
with strife,
They honour'd such determined scorn of
life.

CXX

But the stone bastion still kept up its fire,
  Where the chief pacha calmly held his
post:
Some twenty times he made the Russ re-
tire,
  And baffled the assaults of all their host;
At length he condescended to inquire,
  If yet the city's rest were won or lost;
And being told the latter, sent a bey
To answer Ribas' summons to give way.

CXXI

In the mean time, cross-legg'd, with great
sang-froid,
  Among the scorching ruins he sat
smoking
Tobacco on a little carpet;—Troy
  Saw nothing like the scene around;—yet
looking
With martial stoicism, nought seem'd to
annoy
  His stern philosophy; but gently strok-
ing
His beard, he puff'd his pipe's ambrosial
gales,
As if he had three lives, as well as tails.

CXXII

The town was taken—whether he might
yield
  Himself or bastion, little matter'd now:
His stubborn valour was no future shield.
  Ismail's no more! The crescent's silver
bow
Sunk, and the crimson cross glared o'er
the field,
  But red with no *redeeming* gore: the
glow

Of burning streets, like moonlight on the
water,
Was imaged back in blood, the sea of
slaughter.

CXXIII

All that the mind would shrink from ot
excesses;
  All that the body perpetrates of bad;
All that we read, hear, dream, of man's
distresses;
  All that the devil would do if run stark
mad;
All that defies the worst which pen ex-
presses;
  All by which hell is peopled, or as sad
As hell—mere mortals who their power
abuse—
Was here (as heretofore and since) let loose.

CXXIV

If here and there some transient trait of
pity
  Was shown, and some more noble heart
broke through
Its bloody bond, and saved, perhaps, some
pretty
  Child, or an aged, helpless man or two—
What's this in one annihilated city,
  Where thousand loves, and ties, and
duties grew?
Cockneys of London! Muscadins of
Paris!
Just ponder what a pious pastime war is.

CXXV

Think how the joys of reading a Gazette
  Are purchased by all agonies and
crimes;
Or if these do not move you, don't forget
  Such doom may be your own in after-
times.
Meantime the Taxes, Castlereagh, and
Debt,
  Are hints as good as sermons, or as
rhymes.
Read your own hearts and Ireland's
present story,
Then feed her famine fat with Wellesley's
glory.

CXXVI

But still there is unto a patriot nation,
  Which loves so well its country and its
king,
A subject of sublimest exultation—
  Bear it, ye Muses, on your brightest wing!
Howe'er the mighty locust, Desolation,
  Strip your green fields, and to your
harvest cling,
Gaunt famine never shall approach the
throne—
Though Ireland starve, great George
weighs twenty stone.

CXXVII

But let me put an end unto my theme:
  There was an end of Ismail—hapless
    town!
Far flash'd her burning towers o'er
  Danube's stream,
  And redly ran his blushing waters down.
The horrid war-whoop and the shriller
  scream
    Rose still; but fainter were the thunders
    grown:
Of forty thousand who had mann'd the wall,
Some hundreds breathed—the rest were
  silent all!

CXXVIII

In one thing ne'ertheless 'tis fit to praise
  The Russian army upon this occasion,
A virtue much in fashion now-a-days,
  And therefore worthy of commemora-
    tion:
The topic's tender, so shall be my phrase—
  Perhaps the season's chill, and their long
    station
In winter's depth, or want of rest and victual,
Had made them chaste;—they ravish'd
  very little.

CXXIX

Much did they slay, more plunder, and no
  less
    Might here and there occur some viola-
    tion
In the other line;—but not to such excess
  As when the French, that dissipated
    nation,
Take towns by storm: no causes can I guess,
  Except cold weather and commiseration;
But all the ladies, save some twenty score,
Were almost as much virgins as before.

CXXX

Some odd mistakes, too, happen'd in the
  dark,
    Which show'd a want of lanterns, or of
    taste—
Indeed the smoke was such they scarce
  could mark
    Their friends from foes,—besides, such
    things from haste
Occur, though rarely, when there is a spark
  Of light to save the venerably chaste:
But six old damsels, each of seventy years,
Were all deflower'd by different grena-
  diers.

CXXXI

But on the whole their continence was great;
  So that some disappointment there en-
    sued
To those who had felt the inconvenient
  state
    Of 'single blessedness,' and thought it
    good

(Since it was not their fault, but only fate,
  To bear these crosses) for each waning
    prude
To make a Roman sort of Sabine wedding,
Without the expense and the suspense of
  bedding.

CXXXII

Some voices of the buxom middle-aged
  Were also heard to wonder in the din
(Widows of forty were these birds long
  caged)
    'Wherefore the ravishing did not be-
    gin!'
But while the thirst for gore and plunder
  raged,
  There was small leisure for superfluous
    sin;
But whether they escaped or no, lies hid
In darkness—I can only hope they did.

CXXXIII

Suwarrow now was conqueror—a match
  For Timour or for Zinghis in his trade.
While mosques and streets, beneath his
  eyes, like thatch
    Blazed, and the cannon's roar was
    scarce allay'd,
With bloody hands he wrote his first de-
  spatch;
    And here exactly follows what he
    said:—
'Glory to *God* and to the Empress!'
  (*Powers*
Eternal! such names mingled!) 'Ismail's
  ours.'

CXXXIV

Methinks these are the most tremendous
  words,
    Since 'Mené, Mené, Tekel,' and 'Uphar-
    sin,'
Which hands or pens have ever traced of
  swords.
    Heaven help me! I'm but little of a
    parson:
What Daniel read was short-hand of the
  Lord's,
    Severe, sublime; the prophet wrote no
    farce on
The fate of nations;—but this Russ so
  witty
Could rhyme, like Nero, o'er a burning
  city.

CXXXV

He wrote this Polar melody, and set it,
  Duly accompanied by shrieks and
    groans,
Which few will sing, I trust, but none
  forget it—
    For I will teach, if possible, the stones

To rise against earth's tyrants. Never let it
  Be said that we still truckle unto
    thrones;—
But ye—our children's children! think
    how we
Show'd *what things were* before the world
    was free!

CXXXVI

That hour is not for us, but 'tis for you.
  And as, in the great joy of your millen-
    nium,
You hardly will believe such things were
    true
    As now occur, I thought that I would
    pen you 'em;
But may their very memory perish too!—
    Yet if perchance remember'd, still dis-
    dain you 'em
More than you scorn the savages of yore,
Who *painted* their *bare* limbs, but *not* with
    gore.

CXXXVII

And when you hear historians talk of
    thrones,
  And those that sate upon them, let it be
As we now gaze upon the mammoth's
    bones,
  And wonder what old world such things
    could see,
Or hieroglyphics on Egyptian stones,
  The pleasant riddles of futurity—
Guessing at what shall happily be hid,
As the real purpose of a pyramid.

CXXXVIII

Reader! I have kept my word,—at least so
    far
  As the first canto promised. You have
    now
Had sketches of love, tempest, travel,
    war,—
  All very accurate, you must allow,
And *epic*, if plain truth should prove no
    bar;
  For I have drawn much less with a long
    bow
Than my forerunners. Carelessly I sing,
But Phœbus lends me now and then a string,

CXXXIX

With which I still can harp, and carp, and
    fiddle.
  What further hath befallen or may be-
    fall
The hero of this grand poetic riddle,
  I by and by may tell you, if at all:
But now I choose to break off in the
    middle,
  Worn out with battering Ismail's stub-
    born wall,
While Juan is sent off with the despatch,
For which all Petersburgh is on the watch.

CXL

This special honour was conferr'd, be-
    cause
He had behaved with courage and hu-
    manity—
Which *last* men like, when they have time
    to pause
From their ferocities produced by
    vanity.
His little captive gain'd him some ap-
    plause
For saving her amidst the wild insanity
Of carnage,—and I think he was more
    glad in her
Safety, than his new order of St. Vladimir.

CXLI

The Moslem orphan went with her pro-
    tector,
  For she was homeless, houseless, help-
    less; all
Her friends, like the sad family of Hector,
  Had perish'd in the field or by the
    wall:
Her very place of birth was but a spectre
  Of what it had been; there the Muezzin's
    call
To prayer was heard no more! and Juan
    wept,
And made a vow to shield her, which he
    kept.

CANTO THE NINTH

I

Oh, Wellington! (or 'Vilainton'—for
    Fame
  Sounds the heroic syllables both ways;
France could not even conquer your great
    name,
  But punn'd it down to this facetious
    phrase—
Beating or beaten she will laugh the same)
  You obtain'd great pensions and
    much praise:
Glory like yours should any dare gainsay,
Humanity would rise, and thunder 'Nay!'

II

I don't think that you used Kinnaird quite
    well
  In Marinet's affair—in fact 'twas
    shabby,
And like some other things won't do to tell
  Upon your tomb in Westminster's old
    abbey.
Upon the rest 'tis not worth while to
    dwell,
  Such tales being for the tea-hours of
    some tabby;
But though your years as *man* tend fast to
    zero,
In fact your grace is still but a *young hero*.

III

Though Britain owes (and pays you too)
    so much
    Yet Europe doubtless owes you greatly
    more:
You have repair'd Legitimacy's crutch,
    A prop not quite so certain as before:
The Spanish, and the French, as well as
    Dutch,
    Have seen, and felt, how strongly you
    restore;
And Waterloo has made the world your
    debtor
(I wish your bards would sing it rather
    better).

IV

You are 'the best of cut-throats':—do not
    start;
    The phrase is Shakspeare's, and not
    misapplied:—
War's a brain-spattering, windpipe-slit-
    ting art,
    Unless her cause by right be sanctified.
If you have acted *once* a generous part,
    The world, not the world's masters, will
    decide,
And I shall be delighted to learn who,
Save you and yours, have gain'd by Water-
    loo?

V

I am no flatterer—you've supp'd full of
    flattery:
    They say you like it too—'tis no great
    wonder.
He whose whole life has been assault and
    battery,
    At last may get a little tired of thunder;
And swallowing eulogy much more than
    satire, he
    May like being praised for every lucky
    blunder,
Call'd 'Saviour of the Nations'—not yet
    saved,
And 'Europe's Liberator'—still enslaved.

VI

I've done. Now go and dine from off the
    plate
    Presented by the Prince of the Brazils,
And send the sentinel before your gate
    A slice or two from your luxurious meals:
He fought, but has not fed so well of late.
    Some hunger, too, they say the people
    feels:—
There is no doubt that you deserve your
    ration,
But pray give back a little to the nation.

VII

I don't mean to reflect—a man so great as
    You, my lord duke! is far above re-
    flection:

The high Roman fashion, too, of Cincin-
    natus,
    With modern history has but small con-
    nexion:
Though as an Irishman you love potatoes,
    You need not take them under your
    direction;
And half a million for your Sabine farm
Is rather dear!—I'm sure I mean no harm.

VIII

Great men have always scorn'd great
    recompenses:
    Epaminondas saved his Thebes, and
    died,
Not leaving even his funeral expenses:
    George Washington had thanks, and
    nought beside,
Except the all-cloudless glory (which few
    men's is)
    To free his country: Pitt too had his
    pride,
And as a high-soul'd minister of state is
Renown'd for ruining Great Britain gratis.

IX

Never had mortal man such opportunity,
    Except Napoleon, or abused it more:
You might have freed fallen Europe from
    the unity
    Of tyrants, and been blest from shore to
    shore:
And *now*—what *is* your fame? Shall the
    Muse tune it ye?
    Now—that the rabble's first vain shouts
    are o'er?
Go! hear it in your famish'd country's
    cries!
Behold the world! and curse your vic-
    tories!

X

As these new cantos touch on warlike feats,
    To *you* the unflattering Muse deigns to
    inscribe
Truths, that you will not read in the
    Gazettes,
    But which 'tis time to teach the hireling
    tribe
Who fatten on their country's gore, and
    debts,
    Must be recited—and without a bribe.
You *did great* things: but not being *great*
    in mind,
Have left *undone* the *greatest*—and man-
    kind.

XI

Death laughs—Go ponder o'er the skele-
    ton
    With which men image out the unknown
    thing
That hides the past world, like to a set sun
    Which still elsewhere may rouse a
    brighter spring—

Death laughs at all you weep for:—look
  upon
  This hourly dread of all! whose *threat-
  en'd sting*
Turns life to terror, even though in its
  sheath:
Mark! how its lipless mouth grins without
  breath!

XII

Mark! how it laughs and scorns at all you
  are!
  And yet *was* what you are; from *ear* to
  ear
It *laughs not*—there is now no fleshy bar
  So call'd; the Antic long hath ceased to
  hear,
But still he *smiles;* and whether near or far
  He strips from man that mantle (far
  more dear
Than even the tailor's), his incarnate skin,
White, black, or copper—the dead bones
  will grin.

XIII

And thus Death laughs,—it is sad merri-
  ment,
  But still it *is* so; and with such example
Why should not Life be equally content
  With his superior, in a smile to trample
Upon the nothings which are daily spent
  Like bubbles on an ocean much less
  ample
Than the eternal deluge, which devours
Suns as rays—worlds like atoms—years
  like hours?

XIV

'To be, or not to be? *that* is the question,'
  Says Shakspeare, who just now is much
  in fashion.
I am neither Alexander nor Hephæstion,
  Nor ever had for *abstract* fame much
  passion;
But would much rather have a sound
  digestion,
  Than Buonaparte's cancer:—could I
  dash on
Through fifty victories to shame or fame,
Without a stomach—what were a good
  name?

XV

'*O dura ilia messorum!*'—'Oh
  Ye rigid guts of reapers!' I translate
For the great benefit of those who know
  What indigestion is—that inward fate
Which makes all Styx through one small
  liver flow.
  A peasant's sweat is worth his lord's
  estate:
Let *this* one toil for bread—*that* rack for
  rent,
He who sleeps best may be the most con-
  tent.

XVI

'To be, or not to be?'—Ere I decide,
  I should be glad to know that which *is
  being;*
'Tis true we speculate both far and wide,
  And deem, because we *see*, we are *all-
  seeing:*
For my part, I'll enlist on neither side,
  Until I see both sides for once agreeing.
For me, I sometimes think that life is
  death,
Rather than life a mere affair of breath.

XVII

'*Que sçais-je?*' was the motto of Mon-
  taigne,
  As also of the first academicians;
That all is dubious which man may attain,
  Was one of their most favourite posi-
  tions.
There's no such thing as certainty, that's
  plain
  As any of Mortality's conditions;
So little do we know what we're about in
This world, I doubt if doubt itself be
  doubting.

XVIII

It is a pleasant voyage perhaps to float,
  Like Pyrrho, on a sea of speculation;
But what if carrying sail capsize the boat?
  Your wise men don't know much of
  navigation;
And swimming long in the abyss of thought
  Is apt to tire: a calm and shallow station
Well nigh the shore, where one stoops
  down and gathers
Some pretty shell, is best for moderate
  bathers.

XIX

'But heaven,' as Cassio says, 'is above
  all—
  No more of this, then, let us pray!' We
  have
Souls to save, since Eve's slip and Adam's
  fall,
  Which tumbled all mankind into the grave,
Besides fish, beasts, and birds. 'The
  sparrow's fall
  Is special providence,' though how *it*
  gave
Offence, we know not; probably it perch'd
Upon the tree which Eve so fondly
  search'd.

XX

Oh! ye immortal Gods! what is theogony?
  Oh! thou too mortal man! what is
  philanthropy?
Oh! world, which was and is, what is
  cosmogony?
  Some people have accused me of misan-
  thropy;

And yet I know no more than the ma-
    hogany
    That forms this desk, of what they
      mean; *lykanthropy*
I comprehend, for without transformation
Men become wolves on any slight occa-
    sion.

XXI

But I, the mildest, meekest of mankind,
    Like Moses, or Melancthon, who have
      ne'er
Done anything exceedingly unkind,—
    And (though I could not now and then
      forbear
Following the bent of body or of mind)
    Have always had a tendency to spare,—
Why do they call me misanthrope? Be-
    cause
They hate me, not I them:—and here we'll
    pause.

XXII

'Tis time we should proceed with our good
    poem,—
    For I maintain that it is really good,
Not only in the body but the proem,
    However little both are understood
Just now,—but by and by the Truth will
    show 'em
    Herself in her sublimest attitude:
And till she doth, I fain must be content
To share her beauty and her banishment.

XXIII

Our hero (and, I trust, kind reader! yours)
    Was left upon his way to the chief city
Of the immortal Peter's polish'd boors,
    Who still have shown themselves more
      brave than witty.
I know its mighty empire now allures
    Much flattery—even Voltaire's, and
      that's a pity.
For me, I deem an absolute autocrat
Not a barbarian, but much worse than
    that.

XXIV

And I will war, at least in words (and—
    should
    My chance so happen—deeds), with all
      who war
With Thought;—and of Thought's foes
    by far most rude,
    Tyrants and sycophants have been and
      are.
I know not who may conquer: if I could
    Have such a prescience, it should be no
      bar
To this my plain, sworn, downright de-
    testation
Of every despotism in every nation.

XXV

It is not that I adulate the people:
    Without *me*, there are demagogues
      enough,
And infidels, to pull down every steeple,
    And set up in their stead some proper
      stuff.
Whether they may sow scepticism to reap
    hell,
    As is the Christian dogma rather rough,
I do not know;—I wish men to be free
As much from mobs as kings—from you
    as me.

XXVI

The consequence is, being of no party,
    I shall offend all parties:—never mind!
My words, at least, are more sincere and
    hearty
    Than if I sought to sail before the wind.
He who has nought to gain can have small
    art: he
    Who neither wishes to be bound nor
      bind,
May still expatiate freely, as will I,
Nor give my voice to slavery's jackal cry.

XXVII

That's an appropriate simile, *that jack-
    al*:—
    I've heard them in the Ephesian ruins
      howl
By night, as do that mercenary pack all,
    Power's base purveyors, who for pick-
      ings prowl,
And scent the prey their masters would
    attack all.
However, the poor jackals are less foul
(As being the brave lions' keen providers)
Than human insects, catering for spiders.

XXVIII

Raise but an arm! 'twill brush their web
    away,
    And without *that*, their poison and their
      claws
Are useless. Mind, good people! what I
    say—
    (Or rather peoples)—*go on* without
      pause!
The web of these tarantulas each day
    Increases, till you shall make common
      cause:
None, save the Spanish fly and Attic bee,
As yet are strongly stinging to be free.

XXIX

Don Juan, who had shone in the late
    slaughter,
    Was left upon his way with the despatch,
Where blood was talk'd of as we would of
    water;
    And carcasses that lay as thick as thatch

O'er silenced cities, merely served to flatter
  Fair Catherine's pastime—who look'd
      on the match
Between these nations as a main of cocks,
Wherein she liked her own to stand like
      rocks.

XXX

And there in a *kibitka* he roll'd on,
  (A cursèd sort of carriage without
      springs,
Which on rough roads leaves scarcely a
      whole bone,)
Pondering on glory, chivalry, and kings,
And orders, and on all that he had done—
  And wishing that post-horses had the
      wings
Of Pegasus, or at the least post-chaises
Had feathers, when a traveller on deep
      ways is.

XXXI

At every jolt—and they were many—still
  He turn'd his eyes upon his little charge,
As if he wish'd that she should fare less ill
  Than he, in these sad highways left at
      large
To ruts, and flints, and lovely Nature's skill,
  Who is no paviour, nor admits a barge
On *her* canals, where God takes sea and
      land,
Fishery and farm, both into his own hand.

XXXII

At least he pays no rent, and has best right
  To be the first of what we used to call
'Gentlemen farmers', a race worn out quite,
  Since lately there have been no rents at all,
And 'gentlemen' are in a piteous plight,
  And 'farmers' can't raise Ceres from
      her fall:
She fell with Buonaparte—What strange
      thoughts
Arise, when we see emperors fall with oats!

XXXIII

But Juan turn'd his eyes on the sweet child
  Whom he had saved from slaughter—
      what a trophy!
Oh! ye who build up monuments, defiled
  With gore, like Nadir Shah, that costive
      sophy,
Who, after leaving Hindostan a wild,
  And scarce to the Mogul a cup of coffee
To soothe his woes withal, was slain, the
      sinner!
Because he could no more digest his
      dinner;—

XXXIV

Oh ye! or we! or he! or she! reflect,
  That *one* life saved, especially if young
Or pretty, is a thing to recollect
  Far sweeter than the greenest laurels
      sprung

From the manure of human clay, though
      deck'd
With all the praises ever said or sung:
Though hymn'd by every harp, unless within
Your heart joins chorus, Fame is but a din.

XXXV

Oh! ye great authors luminous, volumin-
      ous!
  Ye twice ten hundred thousand daily
      scribes!
Whose pamphlets, volumes, newspapers,
      illumine us!
  Whether you're paid by government in
      bribes,
To prove the public debt is not consuming
      us—
  Or, roughly treading on the 'courtier's
      kibes'
With clownish heel, your popular circulation
Feeds you by printing half the realm's
      starvation;—

XXXVI

Oh, ye great authors!—*Apropos des
      bottes*,—
  I have forgotten what I meant to say,
As sometimes have been greater sages'
      lots;—
  'Twas something calculated to allay
All wrath in barracks, palaces, or cots:
  Certes it would have been but thrown
      away,
And that's one comfort for my lost advice,
Although no doubt it was beyond all price.

XXXVII

But let it go:—it will one day be found
  With other relics of 'a former world,'
When this world shall be *former*, under-
      ground,
  Thrown topsy-turvy, twisted, crisp'd,
      and curl'd,
Baked, fried, or burnt, turn'd inside-out,
      or drown'd,
  Like all the worlds before, which have
      been hurl'd
First out of, and then back again to chaos,
The superstratum which will overlay us.

XXXVIII

So Cuvier says:—and then shall come
      again
  Unto the new creation, rising out
From our old crash, some mystic, ancient
      strain
  Of things destroy'd and left in airy
      doubt;
Like to the notions we now entertain
  Of Titans, giants, fellows of about
Some hundred feet in height, *not* to say
      miles,
And mammoths, and your wingèd croco-
      diles.

XXXIX

Think if then George the Fourth should
    be dug up,
  How the new worldlings of the then new
    East
Will wonder where such animals could
    sup!
  (For they themselves will be but of the
    least:
Even worlds miscarry, when too oft they
    pup,
  And every new creation hath decreased
In size, from overworking the material—
Men are but maggots of some huge
    Earth's burial).

XL

How will—to these young people, just
    thrust out
  From some fresh Paradise, and set to
    plough,
And dig, and sweat, and turn themselves
    about,
  And plant, and reap, and spin, and
    grind, and sow,
Till all the arts at length are brought about,
  Especially of war and taxing,—*how*,
I say, will these great relics, when they
    see 'em,
Look like the monsters of a new museum!

XLI

But I am apt to grow too metaphysical:
  'The time is out of joint,'—and so am I;
I quite forget this poem's merely quizzical,
  And deviate into matters rather dry.
I ne'er decide what I shall say, and this I
    call
  Much too poetical: men should know
    why
They write, and for what end; but, note or
    text,
I never know the word which will come
    next.

XLII

So on I ramble, now and then narrating,
  Now pondering:—it is time we should
    narrate.
I left Don Juan with his horses baiting—
  Now we'll get o'er the ground at a great
    rate.
I shall not be particular in stating
  His journey, we've so many tours of
    late:
Suppose him then at Petersburgh; suppose
That pleasant capital of painted snows;

XLIII

Suppose him in a handsome uniform;
  A scarlet coat, black facings, a long
    plume,
Waving, like sails new shiver'd in a storm,
  Over a cock'd hat in a crowded room,

And brilliant breeches, bright as a Cairn
    Gorme,
  Of yellow casimere we may presume,
White stockings drawn uncurdled as new
    milk
O'er limbs whose symmetry set off the silk;

XLIV

Suppose him sword by side, and hat in
    hand,
  Made up by youth, fame, and an army
    tailor—
That great enchanter, at whose rod's com-
    mand
  Beauty springs forth, and Nature's self
    turns paler,
Seeing how Art can make her work more
    grand
  (When she don't pin men's limbs in like
    a gaoler),—
Behold him placed as if upon a pillar! He
Seems Love turn'd a lieutenant of artillery!

XLV

His bandage slipp'd down into a cravat;
  His wings subdued to epaulettes; his
    quiver
Shrunk to a scabbard, with his arrows at
  His side as a small sword, but sharp as
    ever;
His bow converted into a cock'd hat;
  But still so like, that Psyche were more
    clever
Than some wives (who make blunders no
    less stupid),
If she had not mistaken him for Cupid.

XLVI

The courtiers stared, the ladies whisper'd,
    and
  The empress smiled: the reigning favour-
    ite frown'd—
I quite forget which of them was in hand
  Just then, as they are rather numerous
    found,
Who took by turns that difficult command
  Since first her majesty was singly
    crown'd:
But they were mostly nervous six-foot
    fellows,
All fit to make a Patagonian jealous.

XLVII

Juan was none of these, but slight and slim,
  Blushing and beardless; and yet ne'er-
    theless
There was a something in his turn of limb,
  And still more in his eye, which seem'd
    to express,
That though he look'd one of the sera-
    phim,
  There lurk'd a man beneath the spirit's
    dress.
Besides, the empress sometimes liked a boy,
And had just buried the fair-faced Lanskoi.

774

XLVIII

No wonder then that Yermoloff, or Mo-
  monoff,
  Or Scherbatoff, or any other *off*
Or *on*, might dread her majesty had not
  room enough
Within her bosom (which was not too
  tough)
For a new flame; a thought to cast of
  gloom enough
  Along the aspect, whether smooth or
    rough,
Of him who, in the language of his station,
Then held that 'high official situation.'

XLIX

Oh, gentle ladies! should you seek to know
  The import of this diplomatic phrase,
Bid Ireland's Londonderry's Marquess
  show
  His parts of speech; and in the strange
    displays
Of that odd string of words, all in a row,
  Which none divine, and every one obeys,
Perhaps you may pick out some queer *no*
  meaning,
Of that weak wordy harvest the sole glean-
  ing.

L

I think I can explain myself without
  That sad inexplicable beast of prey—
That Sphinx, whose words would ever be
  a doubt,
  Did not his deeds unriddle them each
    day—
That monstrous hieroglyphic—that long
  spout
  Of blood and water, leaden Castle-
    reagh!
And here I must an anecdote relate,
But luckily of no great length or weight.

LI

An English lady ask'd of an Italian,
  What were the actual and official duties
Of the strange thing, some women set a
  value on,
  Which hovers oft about some married
    beauties,
Call'd 'Cavalier servente'? a Pygmalion
  Whose statues warm (I fear, alas! too
    true 'tis)
Beneath his art. The dame, press'd to dis-
  close them,
Said—'Lady, I beseech you to *suppose
  them.*'

LII

And thus I supplicate your supposition,
  And mildest, matron-like interpretation,
Of the imperial favourite's condition.
  'Twas a high place, the highest in the
    nation

In fact, if not in rank! and the suspicion
  Of any one's attaining to his station
No doubt gave pain, where each new pair
  of shoulders,
If rather broad, made stocks rise and their
  holders.

LIII

Juan, I said, was a most beauteous boy,
  And had retain'd his boyish look be-
    yond
The usual hirsute seasons which destroy,
  With beards and whiskers, and the like,
    the fond
Parisian aspect, which upset old Troy
  And founded Doctors' Commons:—I
    have conn'd
The history of divorces, which, though
  chequer'd,
Calls Ilion's the first damages on record.

LIV

And Catherine, who loved all things (save
  her lord,
  Who was gone to his place), and pass'd
    for much,
Admiring those (by dainty dames ab-
  horr'd)
  Gigantic gentlemen, yet had a touch
Of sentiment: and he she most adored
  Was the lamented Lanskoi, who was
    such
A lover as had cost her many a tear,
And yet but made a middling grenadier.

LV

Oh thou '*teterrima causa*' of all '*belli*'—
  Thou gate of life and death—thou non-
    descript!
Whence is our exit and our entrance, well I
  May pause in pondering how all souls
    are dipt
In thy perennial fountain: how man *fell* I
  Know not, since knowledge saw her
    branches stript
Of her first fruit; but how he *falls* and
  rises
Since, *thou* hast settled beyond all sur-
  mises.

LVI

Some call thee 'the *worst* cause of war,'
  but I
  Maintain thou art the *best*: for after all,
From thee we come, to thee we go, and
  why
  To get at thee not batter down a wall,
Or waste a world? since no one can deny
  Thou dost replenish worlds both great
    and small:
With, or without thee, all things at a stand
Are, or would be, thou sea of life's dry
  land!

LVII

Catherine, who was the grand epitome
    Of that great cause of war, or peace, or
        what
You please (it causes all the things which be,
    So you may take your choice of this or
        that)—
Catherine, I say, was very glad to see
    The handsome herald, on whose plum-
        age sat
Victory; and, pausing as she saw him kneel
With his despatch, forgot to break the seal.

LVIII

Then recollecting the whole empress, nor
    Forgetting quite the woman (which
        composed
At least three parts of this great whole),
        she tore
    The letter open with an air which posed
The court, that watch'd each look her
        visage wore,
    Until a royal smile at length disclosed
Fair weather for the day. Though rather
        spacious,
Her face was noble, her eyes fine, mouth
        gracious.

LIX

Great joy was hers, or rather joys: the first
    Was a ta'en city, thirty thousand slain.
Glory and triumph o'er her aspect burst,
    As an East Indian sunrise on the main.
These quench'd a moment her ambition's
        thirst—
    So Arab deserts drink in summer's rain:
In vain!—As fall the dews on quenchless
        sands,
Blood only serves to wash Ambition's
        hands!

LX

Her next amusement was more fanciful;
    She smiled at mad Suwarrow's rhymes,
        who threw
Into a Russian couplet rather dull
    The whole gazette of thousands whom
        he slew.
Her third was feminine enough to annul
    The shudder which runs naturally
        through
Our veins, when things call'd sovereigns
        think it best
To kill, and generals turn it into jest.

LXI

The two first feelings ran their course com-
        plete,
    And lighted first her eye, and then her
        mouth:
The whole court look'd immediately most
        sweet,
    Like flowers well water'd after a long
        drouth:—

But when on the lieutenant at her feet
    Her majesty, who liked to gaze on youth
Almost as much as on a new despatch,
Glanced mildly, all the world was on the
        watch.

LXII

Though somewhat large, exuberant, and
        truculent,
    When *wroth*—while *pleased*, she was as
        fine a figure
As those who like things rosy, ripe, and
        succulent,
    Would wish to look on, while they are in
        vigour.
She could repay each amatory look you
        lent
    With interest, and in turn was wont with
        rigour
To exact of Cupid's bills the full amount
At sight, nor would permit you to dis-
        count.

LXIII

With her the latter, though at times con-
        venient,
    Was not so necessary; for they tell
That she was handsome, and though fierce
        look'd lenient,
    And always used her favourites too well.
If once beyond her boudoir's precincts in
        ye went,
    Your 'fortune' was in a fair way 'to
        swell
A man' (as Giles says); for though she
        would widow all
Nations, she liked man as an individual.

LXIV

What a strange thing is man! and what a
        stranger
    Is woman! What a whirlwind is her
        head,
And what a whirlpool full of depth and
        danger
    Is all the rest about her! Whether wed,
Or widow, maid, or mother, she can
        change her
    Mind like the wind: whatever she has
        said
Or done, is light to what she'll say or do;—
The oldest thing on record, and yet new!

LXV

Oh Catherine! (for of all interjections,
    To thee both *oh!* and *ah!* belong of right
In love and war) how odd are the con-
        nexions
    Of human thoughts, which jostle in their
        flight!
Just now *yours* were cut out in different
        sections:
    First Ismail's capture caught your fancy
        quite;

Next of new knights, the fresh and glorious
    batch;
And *thirdly* he who brought you the des-
    patch!

LXVI

Shakespeare talks of 'the herald Mercury
    New lighted on a heaven-kissing hill':
And some such visions cross'd her majesty,
    While her young herald knelt before her
        still.
'Tis very true the hill seem'd rather high,
    For a lieutenant to climb up; but skill
Smooth'd even the Simplon's steep, and
    by God's blessing,
With youth and health all kisses are
    'heaven-kissing.'

LXVII

Her majesty look'd down, the youth look'd
    up—
And so they fell in love:—she with his face,
    His grace, his God-knows-what: for
        Cupid's cup
    With the first draught intoxicates apace,
A quintessential laudanum or 'black drop,'
    Which makes one drunk at once, with-
        out the base
Expedient of full bumpers; for the eye
In love drinks all life's fountains (save
    tears) dry.

LXVIII

He, on the other hand, if not in love,
    Fell into that no less imperious passion,
Self-love—which, when some sort of
    thing above
    Ourselves, a singer, dancer, much in
        fashion,
Or duchess, princess, empress, 'deigns to
    prove'
    ('Tis Pope's phrase) a great longing,
        though a rash one,
For one especial person out of many,
Makes us believe ourselves as good as any.

LXIX

Besides, he was of that delighted age
    Which makes all female ages equal—
        when
We don't much care with whom we may
    engage,
    As bold as Daniel in the lions' den,
So that we can our native sun assuage
    In the next ocean, which may flow just
        then,
To make a *twilight* in, just as Sol's heat is
Quench'd in the lap of the salt sea, or
    Thetis.

LXX

And Catherine (we must say thus much
    for Catherine),
    Though bold and bloody, was the kind
        of thing

Whose temporary passion was quite
    flattering,
    Because each lover look'd a sort of king,
Made up upon an amatory pattern,
    A royal husband in all save the *ring*—
Which, being the damn'dest part of matri-
    mony,
Seem'd taking out the sting to leave the
    honey.

LXXI

And when you add to this, her womanhood
    In its meridian, her blue eyes or gray—
(The last, if they have soul, are quite as good,
    Or better, as the best examples say:
Napoleon's, Mary's (queen of Scotland),
    should
    Lend to that colour a transcendent ray;
And Pallas also sanctions the same hue,
Too wise to look through optics black or
    blue)—

LXXII

Her sweet smile, and her then majestic
    figure,
    Her plumpness, her imperial condescen-
        sion,
Her preference of a boy to men much
    bigger
    (Fellows whom Messalina's self would
        pension),
Her prime of life, just now in juicy vigour,
    With other *extras*, which we need not
        mention,—
All these, or any one of these, explain
Enough to make a stripling very vain.

LXXIII

And that's enough, for love is vanity,
    Selfish in its beginning as its end,
Except where 'tis a mere insanity,
    A maddening spirit which would strive
        to blend
Itself with beauty's frail inanity,
    On which the passion's self seems to
        depend;
And hence some heathenish philosophers
Make love the main-spring of the universe.

LXXIV

Besides Platonic love, besides the love
    Of God, the love of sentiment, the loving
Of faithful pairs—(I needs must rhyme
    with dove,
    That good old steam-boat which keeps
        verses moving
'Gainst reason—Reason ne'er was hand-
    and-glove
    With rhyme, but always leant less to im-
        proving
The sound than sense) besides all these
    pretences
To love, there are those things which
    words name senses;

LXXV

Those movements, those improvements in
    our bodies
    Which make all bodies anxious to get
      out
Of their own sand-pits, to mix with a god-
    dess,
    For such all women are at first no doubt.
How beautiful that moment! and how
    odd is
    That fever which precedes the languid
      rout
Of our sensations! What a curious way
The whole thing is of clothing souls in clay!

LXXVI

The noblest kind of love is love Platonical,
    To end or to begin with; the next grand
Is that which may be christen'd love
    canonical,
    Because the clergy take the thing in
      hand;
The third sort to be noted in our chronicle
    As flourishing in every Christian land,
Is, when chaste matrons to their other ties
Add what may be call'd *marriage in dis-
guise.*

LXXVII

Well, we won't analyse—our story must
    Tell for itself: the sovereign was smitten,
Juan much flatter'd by her love, or lust;—
    I cannot stop to alter words once writ-
      ten,
And the *two* are so mix'd with human dust,
    That he who *names one*, both perchance
      may hit on:
But in such matters Russia's mighty em-
    press
Behaved no better than a common semp-
    stress.

LXXVIII

The whole court melted into one wide
    whisper,
    And all lips were applied unto all ears!
The elder ladies' wrinkles curl'd much
    crisper
    As they beheld; the younger cast some
    leers
On one another, and each lovely lisper
    Smiled as she talk'd the matter o'er; but
    tears
Of rivalship rose in each clouded eye
Of all the standing army who stood by.

LXXIX

All the ambassadors of all the powers
    Inquired, Who was this very new young
    man,
Who promised to be great in some few
    hours?
    Which is full soon (though life is but a
    span).

Already they beheld the silver showers
    Of rubles rain, as fast as specie can,
Upon his cabinet, besides the presents
Of several ribands, and some thousand
    peasants.

LXXX

Catherine was generous,—all such ladies
    are:
    Love—that great opener of the heart
    and all
The ways that lead there, be they near or
    far,
    Above, below, by turnpikes great or
    small,—
Love—(though she had a cursed taste for
    war,
    And was not the best wife, unless we
    call
Such Clytemnestra, though perhaps 'tis
    better
That one should die, than two drag on the
    fetter)—

LXXXI

Love had made Catherine make each
    lover's fortune,
    Unlike our own half-chaste Elizabeth,
Whose avarice all disbursements did im-
    portune,
    If history, the grand liar, ever saith
The truth; and though grief her old age
    might shorten,
    Because she put a favourite to death,
Her vile, ambiguous method of flirtation,
And stinginess, disgrace her sex and sta-
    tion.

LXXXII

But when the levée rose, and all was bustle
    In the dissolving circle, all the nations'
Ambassadors began as 'twere to hustle
    Round the young man with their con-
    gratulations.
Also the softer silks were heard to rustle
    Of gentle dames, among whose recrea-
    tions
It is to speculate on handsome faces,
Especially when such lead to high places.

LXXXIII

Juan, who found himself, he knew not
    how,
    A general object of attention, made
His answers with a very graceful bow,
    As if born for the ministerial trade.
Though modest, on his unembarrass'd
    brow
    Nature had written 'gentleman.' He
    said
Little, but to the purpose; and his manner
Flung hovering graces o'er him like a
    banner.

LXXXIV

An order from her majesty consign'd
  Our young lieutenant to the genial care
Of those in office: all the world look'd kind,
  (As it will look sometimes with the first
    stare,
Which youth would not act ill to keep in
    mind,)
  As also did Miss Protasoff then there,
Named from her mystic office 'l'Eprou-
    veuse,'
A term inexplicable to the Muse.

LXXXV

With *her* then, as in humble duty bound,
  Juan retired,—and so will I, until
My Pegasus shall tire of touching ground.
  We have just lit on a 'heaven-kissing hill,'
So lofty that I feel my brain turn round,
  And all my fancies whirling like a mill;
Which is a signal to my nerves and brain,
To take a quiet ride in some green lane.

CANTO THE TENTH

I

WHEN Newton saw an apple fall, he found
  In that slight startle from his contem-
    plation—
'Tis *said* (for I'll not answer above ground
  For any sage's creed or calculation)—
A mode of proving that the earth turn'd
    round
  In a most natural whirl, called 'gravi-
    tation';
And this is the sole mortal who could
    grapple,
Since Adam, with a fall, or with an apple.

II

Man fell with apples, and with apples rose,
  If this be true; for we must deem the
    mode
In which Sir Isaac Newton could disclose
  Through the then unpaved stars the
    turnpike road,
A thing to counterbalance human woes:
  For ever since immortal man hath
    glow'd
With all kinds of mechanics, and full soon
Steam-engines will conduct him to the
    moon.

III

And wherefore this exordium?—Why,
    just now,
  In taking up this paltry sheet of paper,
My bosom underwent a glorious glow,
  And my internal spirit cut a caper:
And though so much inferior, as I know,
  To those who, by the dint of glass and
    vapour,
Discover stars, and sail in the wind's eye,
I wish to do as much by poesy.

IV

In the wind's eye I have sail'd, and sail;
    but for
  The stars, I own my telescope is dim;
But at the least I have shunn'd the com-
    mon shore,
  And leaving land far out of sight, would
    skim
The ocean of eternity: the roar
  Of breakers has not daunted my slight,
    trim,
But *still* sea-worthy skiff; and she may
    float
Where ships have founder'd, as doth many
  a boat.

V

We left our hero, Juan, in the *bloom*
  Of favouritism, but not yet in the
    blush:—
And far be it from my *Muses* to pre-
    sume
  (For I have more than one Muse at a
    push)
To follow him beyond the drawing-room:
  It is enough that Fortune found him
    flush
Of youth, and vigour, beauty, and those
    things
Which for an instant clip enjoyment's
    wings.

VI

But soon they grow again and leave their
    nest.
  'Oh!' saith the Psalmist, 'that I had a
    dove's
Pinions to flee away, and be at rest!'
  And who that recollects young years
    and loves,—
Though hoary now, and with a withering
    breast,
  And palsied fancy, which no longer roves
Beyond its dimm'd eye's sphere,—but
    would much rather
Sigh like his son, than cough like his
  grandfather?

VII

But sighs subside, and tears (even widows')
    shrink,
  Like Arno in the summer, to a shallow,
So narrow as to shame their wintry brink,
  Which threatens inundations deep and
    yellow!
Such difference doth a few months make.
    You'd think
  Grief a rich field which never would lie
    fallow;
No more it doth, its ploughs but change
    their boys,
Who furrow some new soil to sow for
  joys.

VIII

But coughs will come when sighs depart—
and now
    And then before sighs cease; for oft the
one
Will bring the other, ere the lake-like brow
    Is ruffled by a wrinkle, or the sun
Of life reach ten o'clock: and while a glow,
    Hectic and brief as summer's day nigh
done,
O'erspreads the cheek which seems too
pure for clay,
Thousands blaze, love, hope, die,—how
happy they!—

IX

But Juan was not meant to die so soon.
    We left him in the focus of such glory
As may be won by favour of the moon
    Or ladies' fancies—rather transitory
Perhaps; but who would scorn the month
of June,
    Because December, with his breath so
hoary,
Must come? Much rather should he court
the ray,
To hoard up warmth against a wintry day.

X

Besides, he had some qualities which fix
    Middle-aged ladies even more than
young:
The former know what's what; while new-
fledged chicks
    Know little more of love than what is
sung
In rhymes, or dreamt (for fancy will play
tricks)
    In visions of those skies from whence
Love sprung.
Some reckon women by their suns or years,
I rather think the moon should date the
dears.

XI

And why? because she's changeable and
chaste.
    I know no other reason, whatsoe'er
Suspicious people, who find fault in haste,
    May choose to tax me with; which is
not fair,
Nor flattering to 'their temper or their taste,'
    As my friend Jeffrey writes with such an
air:
However, I forgive him, and I trust
He will forgive himself;—if not, I must.

XII

Old enemies who have become new friends
    Should so continue—'tis a point of
honour;
And I know nothing which could make
amends
For a return to hatred: I would shun her

Like garlic, howsoever she extends
    Her hundred arms and legs, and fain
outrun her.
Old flames, new wives, become our bitterest foes—
Converted foes should scorn to join with
those.

XIII

This were the worst desertion:—renegadoes,
    Even shuffling Southey, that incarnate lie,
Would scarcely join again the 'reformadoes',
    Whom he forsook to fill the laureate's
sty:
And honest men from Iceland to Bar-
badoes,
    Whether in Caledon or Italy,
Should not veer round with every breath,
nor seize
To pain, the moment when you cease to
please.

XIV

The lawyer and the critic but behold
    The baser sides of literature and life,
And nought remains unseen, but much
untold,
    By those who scour those double vales
of strife.
While common men grow ignorantly old,
    The lawyer's brief is like the surgeon's
knife,
Dissecting the whole inside of a question,
And with it all the process of digestion.

XV

A legal broom's a moral chimney-sweeper,
    And that's the reason he himself 's so
dirty!
The endless soot bestows a tint far deeper
    Than can be hid by altering his shirt; he
Retains the sable stains of the dark
creeper,
    At least some twenty-nine do out of
thirty,
In all their habits;—not so *you*, I own;
As Cæsar wore his robe you wear your
gown.

XVI

And all our little feuds, at least all *mine*,
    Dear Jeffrey, once my most redoubted
foe
(As far as rhyme and criticism combine
    To make such puppets of us things
below),
Are over: Here's a health to 'Auld Lang
Syne!'
    I do not know you, and may never know
Your face—but you have acted on the
whole
Most nobly, and I own it from my soul.

XVII

And when I use the phrase of 'Auld Lang
    Syne!'
    'Tis not address'd to you—the more's
    the pity
For me, for I would rather take my wine
    With you, than aught (save Scott) in
    your proud city.
But somehow—it may seem a schoolboy's
    whine,
    And yet I seek not to be grand nor witty,
But I am half a Scot by birth, and bred
A whole one, and my heart flies to my
    head,—

XVIII

As 'Auld Lang Syne' brings Scotland, one
    and all,
    Scotch plaids, Scotch snoods, the blue
    hills, and clear streams,
The Dee, the Don, Balgounie's brig's *black
    wall*,
    All my boy feelings, all my gentler dreams
Of what I *then dreamt*, clothed in their own
    pall,
    Like Banquo's offspring:—floating past
    me seems
My childhood in this childishness of mine:
I care not—'tis a glimpse of '*Auld Lang Syne.*'

XIX

And though, as you remember, in a fit
    Of wrath and rhyme, when juvenile and
    curly,
I rail'd at Scots to show my wrath and wit,
    Which must be own'd was sensitive and
    surly,
Yet 'tis in vain such sallies to permit,
    They cannot quench young feelings
    fresh and early:
I '*scotch*'d not kill'd' the Scotchman in my
    blood,
And love the land of 'mountain and of
    flood.'

XX

Don Juan, who was real, or ideal,—
    For both are much the same, since what
    men think
Exists when the once thinkers are less real
    Than what they thought, for mind can
    never sink,
And 'gainst the body makes a strong appeal;
    And yet 'tis very puzzling on the brink
Of what is call'd eternity, to stare,
And know no more of what is *here*, than
    there;—

XXI

Don Juan grew a very polish'd Russian—
    How we won't mention, *why* we need
    not say:
Few youthful minds can stand the strong
    concussion
    Of any slight temptation in their way;

But *his* just now were spread as is a cushion
    Smooth'd for a monarch's seat of
    honour: gay
Damsels, and dances, revels, ready money,
Made ice seem paradise, and winter sunny.

XXII

The favour of the empress was agreeable;
    And though the duty wax'd a little hard,
Young people at his time of life should be
    able
    To come off handsomely in that regard.
He was now growing up like a green tree,
    able
    For love, war, or ambition, which reward
Their luckier votaries, till old age's tedium
Make some prefer the circulating medium.

XXIII

About this time, as might have been antici-
    pated,
    Seduced by youth and dangerous examples,
Don Juan grew, I fear, a little dissipated;
    Which is a sad thing, and not only
    tramples
On our fresh feelings, but—as being par-
    ticipated
    With all kinds of incorrigible samples
Of frail humanity—must make us selfish,
And shut our souls up in us like a shell-fish.

XXIV

This we pass over. We will also pass
    The usual progress of intrigues between
Unequal matches, such as are, alas!
    A young lieutenant's with a *not old* queen,
But one who is not so youthful as she was
    In all the royalty of sweet seventeen.
Sovereigns may sway materials, but not
    matter,
And wrinkles, the d——d democrats,
    won't flatter.

XXV

And death, the sovereign's sovereign,
    though the great
    Gracchus of all mortality, who levels,
With his *Agrarian* laws, the high estate
    Of him who feasts, and fights, and roars,
    and revels,
To one small grass-grown patch (which
    must await
    Corruption for its crop) with the poor
    devils
Who never had a foot of land till now,—
Death's a reformer, all men must allow.

XXVI

He lived (not Death, but Juan) in a hurry
    Of waste, and haste, and glare, and
    gloss, and glitter,
In this gay clime of bear-skins black and
    furry—
    Which (though I hate to say a thing
    that's bitter)

781

Peep out sometimes, when things are in a
     flurry,
   Through all the 'purple and fine linen,'
     fitter
For Babylon's than Russia's royal har-
     lot—
And neutralise her outward show of
     scarlet.

XXVII

And this same state we won't describe: we
     could
   Perhaps from hearsay, or from recollec-
     tion;
But getting nigh grim Dante's 'obscure
     wood,'
   That horrid equinox, that hateful section
Of human years, that half-way house, that
     rude
   Hut, whence wise travellers drive with
     circumspection
Life's sad post-horses o'er the dreary
     frontier
Of age, and looking back to youth, give
     one tear;—

XXVIII

I won't describe,—that is, if I can help
   Description; and I won't reflect,—that
     is,
If I can stave off thought, which—as a
     whelp
   Clings to its teat—sticks to me through
     the abyss
Of this odd labyrinth; or as the kelp
   Holds by the rock; or as a lover's kiss
Drains its first draught of lips:—but, as I
     said,
I *won't* philosophise, and *will* be read.

XXIX

Juan, instead of courting courts, was
     courted,—
   A thing which happens rarely: this he
     owed
Much to his youth, and much to his re-
     ported
   Valour; much also to the blood he
     show'd,
Like a race-horse; much to each dress he
     sported,
   Which set the beauty off in which he
     glow'd,
As purple clouds befringe the sun; but
     most
He owed to an old woman and his post.

XXX

He wrote to Spain;—and all his near re-
     lations,
   Perceiving he was in a handsome way
Of getting on himself, and finding stations
   For cousins also, answer'd the same day.

Several prepared themselves for emigra-
     tions;
   And eating ices, were o'erheard to say,
That with the addition of a slight pelisse,
Madrid's and Moscow's climes were of a
     piece.

XXXI

His mother, Donna Inez, finding, too,
   That in the lieu of drawing on his banker,
Where his assets were waxing rather few,
   He had brought his spending to a hand-
     some anchor,—
Replied, 'that she was glad to see him
     through
   Those pleasures after which wild youth
     will hanker;
As the sole sign of man's being in his
     senses
Is, learning to reduce his past expenses.

XXXII

'She also recommended him to God,
   And no less to God's Son, as well as
     Mother,
Warn'd him against Greek worship, which
     looks odd
   In Catholic eyes; but told him, too, to
     smother
Outward dislike, which don't look well
     abroad;
   Inform'd him that he had a little brother
Born in a second wedlock; and above
All, praised the empress's *maternal* love.

XXXIII

'She could not too much give her appro-
     bation
   Unto an empress, who preferr'd young
     men
Whose age, and what was better still,
     whose nation
   And climate, stopp'd all scandal (now
     and then);—
At home it might have given her some
     vexation;
   But where thermometers sunk down to
     ten,
Or five, or one, or zero, she could never
Believe that virtue thaw'd before the
     river.'

XXXIV

Oh for a *forty-parson power* to chant
   Thy praise, Hypocrisy! Oh for a hymn
Loud as the virtues thou dost loudly vaunt,
   Not practise! Oh for trumps of cheru-
     bim!
Or the ear-trumpet of my good old aunt,
   Who, though her spectacles at last grew
     dim,
Drew quiet consolation through its hint,
When she no more could read the pious
     print.

XXXV

She was no hypocrite at least, poor soul,
　But went to heaven in as sincere a way
As anybody on the elected roll,
　Which portions out upon the judgment
　　day
Heaven's freeholds, in a sort of doomsday
　scroll,
　Such as the conqueror William did re-
　　pay
His knights with, lotting others' properties
Into some sixty thousand new knights'
　fees.

XXXVI

I can't complain, whose ancestors are
　there,
　Erneis,　　Radulphus—eight-and-forty
　　manors
(If that my memory doth not greatly err)
　Were their reward for following Billy's
　　banners:
And though I can't help thinking 'twas
　scarce fair
　To strip the Saxons of their *hydes*, like
　　tanners;
Yet as they founded churches with the
　produce,
You'll deem, no doubt, they put it to a
　good use.

XXXVII

The gentle Juan flourish'd, though at times
　He felt like other plants call'd sensitive,
Which shrink from touch, as monarchs do
　from rhymes,
　Save such as Southey can afford to give.
Perhaps he long'd in bitter frosts for climes
　In which the Neva's ice would cease to
　　live
Before May-day: perhaps, despite his duty,
In royalty's vast arms he sigh'd for beauty:

XXXVIII

Perhaps—but, sans perhaps, we need not
　seek
　For causes young or old: the canker-
　　worm
Will feed upon the fairest, freshest cheek,
　As well as further drain the wither'd
　　form:
Care, like a housekeeper, brings every week
　His bills in, and however we may storm,
They must be paid: though six days
　smoothly run,
The seventh will bring blue devils or a dun.

XXXIX

I don't know how it was, but he grew sick:
　The empress was alarm'd, and her phy-
　　sician
(The same who physick'd Peter) found the
　tick
　Of his fierce pulse betoken a condition
Which augur'd of the dead, however
　quick
　Itself, and show'd a feverish disposi-
　　tion;
At which the whole court was extremely
　troubled,
The sovereign shock'd, and all his medi-
　cines doubled.

XL

Low were the whispers, manifold the
　rumours,
　Some said he had been poison'd by
　　Potemkin;
Others talk'd learnedly of certain tumours,
　Exhaustion, or disorders of the same
　　kin;
Some said 'twas a concoction of the
　humours,
　Which with the blood too readily will
　　claim kin;
Others again were ready to maintain,
''Twas only the fatigue of last campaign.'

XLI

But here is one prescription out of many:
　'*Sodæ sulphat. ʒvj. ʒfs. Mannæ optim.*
Aq. fervent. f. ʒ ifs. ʒij. tinct. Sennæ
　Haustus' (and here the surgeon came
　　and cupp'd him),
'*R. Pulv. Com. gr. iij. Ipecacuanhæ*'
　(With more beside if Juan had not
　　stopp'd 'em).
'*Bolus Potassæ Sulphuret. sumendus,*
Et haustus ter in die capiendus.'

XLII

This is the way physicians mend or end
　us,
　Secundum artem: but although we
　　sneer
In health—when ill, we call them to attend
　us,
　Without the least propensity to jeer:
While that '*hiatus maxime deflendus,*'
　To be fill'd up by spade or mattock,
　　's near,
Instead of gliding graciously down Lethe,
We tease mild Baillie, or soft Abernethy.

XLIII

Juan demurr'd at this first notice to
　Quit; and though death had threaten'd
　　an ejection,
His youth and constitution bore him
　through,
　And sent the doctors in a new direction.
But still his state was delicate: the hue
　Of health but flicker'd with a faint re-
　　flection
Along his wasted cheek, and seem'd to
　gravel
The faculty—who said that he must travel.

XLIV

The climate was too cold, they said, for
    him,
  Meridian-born, to bloom in. This
    opinion
Made the chaste Catherine look a little
    grim,
  Who did not like at first to lose her
    minion:
But when she saw his dazzling eye wax
    dim,
  And drooping like an eagle's with clipt
    pinion,
She then resolved to send him on a mission,
But in a style becoming his condition.

XLV

There was just then a kind of a discussion,
  A sort of treaty or negotiation,
Between the British cabinet and Russian,
  Maintain'd with all the due prevarica-
    tion
With which great states such things are
    apt to push on;
  Something about the Baltic's naviga-
    tion,
Hides, train-oil, tallow, and the rights of
    Thetis,
Which Britons deem their *uti possidetis*.

XLVI

So Catherine, who had a handsome way
  Of fitting out her favourites, conferr'd
This secret charge on Juan, to display
  At once her royal splendour, and reward
His services. He kiss'd hands the next day,
  Received instructions how to play his
    card,
Was laden with all kinds of gifts and
    honours,
Which show'd what great discernment
    was the donor's.

XLVII

But she was lucky, and luck's all. Your
    queens
  Are generally prosperous in reigning;
Which puzzles us to know what Fortune
    means:
  But to continue: though her years were
    waning,
Her climacteric teased her like her teens;
  And though her dignity brook'd no
    complaining,
So much did Juan's setting off distress her,
She could not find at first a fit successor.

XLVIII

But time, the comforter, will come at last;
  And four-and-twenty hours, and twice
    that number
Of candidates requesting to be placed,
  Made Catherine taste next night a quiet
    slumber:—

Not that she meant to fix again in haste,
  Nor did she find the quantity encumber,
But always choosing with deliberation,
Kept the place open for their emulation.

XLIX

While this high post of honour's in
    abeyance,
  For one or two days, reader, we request
You'll mount with our young hero the
    conveyance
  Which wafted him from Petersburgh:
    the best
Barouche, which had the glory to display
    once
  The fair Czarina's autocratic crest
When, a new Iphigene, she went to Tauris,
Was given to her favourite, and now *bore
    his*.

L

A bull-dog, and a bull-finch, and an
    ermine,
  All private favourites of Don Juan;—
    for
(Let deeper sages the true cause determine)
  He had a kind of inclination, or
Weakness, for what most people deem
    mere vermin,
  Live animals: an old maid of threescore
For cats and birds more penchant ne'er
    display'd,
Although he was not old, nor even a
    maid;—

LI

The animals aforesaid occupied
  Their station: there were valets, secre-
    taries,
In other vehicles; but at his side
  Sat little Leila, who survived the
    parries
He made 'gainst Cossacque sabres in the
    wide
  Slaughter of Ismail. Though my wild
    Muse varies
Her note, she don't forget the infant girl
Whom he preserved, a pure and living
    pearl.

LII

Poor little thing! She was as fair as docile,
  And with that gentle, serious character,
As rare in living beings as a fossile
  Man, 'midst thy mouldy mammoths,
    'grand Cuvier!'
Ill fitted was her ignorance to jostle
  With this o'erwhelming world, where
    all must err:
But she was yet but ten years old, and
    therefore
Was tranquil, though she knew not why
    or wherefore.

LIII

Don Juan loved her, and she loved him, as
  Nor brother, father, sister, daughter
    love.
I cannot tell exactly what it was;
  He was not yet quite old enough to
    prove
Parental feelings, and the other class,
  Call'd brotherly affection, could not
    move
His bosom,—for he never had a sister:
Ah! if he had, how much he would have
  miss'd her!

LIV

And still less was it sensual; for besides
  That he was not an ancient debauchee,
(Who like sour fruit, to stir their veins'
    salt tides,
  As acids rouse a dormant alkali,)
Although ('twill happen as our planet
    guides)
  His youth was not the chastest that
    might be,
There was the purest Platonism at bottom
Of all his feelings—only he forgot 'em.

LV

Just now there was no peril of temptation;
  He loved the infant orphan he had saved,
As patriots (now and then) may love a
    nation,
  His pride, too, felt that she was not
    enslaved
Owing to him;—as also her salvation
  Through his means and the church's
    might be paved.
But one thing's odd, which here must be
    inserted,
The little Turk refused to be converted.

LVI

'Twas strange enough she should retain
    the impression
  Through such a scene of change, and
    dread, and slaughter;
But though three bishops told her the
    transgression,
  She show'd a great dislike to holy water:
She also had no passion for confession;
  Perhaps she had nothing to confess:—
    no matter
Whate'er the cause, the church made little
    of it—
She still held out that Mahomet was a
    prophet.

LVII

In fact, the only Christian she could bear
  Was Juan; whom she seem'd to have
    selected
In place of what her home and friends
    once *were*.
  He naturally loved what he protected:

And thus they form'd a rather curious
    pair,
  A guardian green in years, a ward con-
    nected
In neither clime, time, blood, with her
    defender;
And yet this want of ties made theirs more
    tender.

LVIII

They journey'd on through Poland and
    through Warsaw,
  Famous for mines of salt and yokes of
    iron:
Through Courland also, which that
    famous farce saw
  Which gave her dukes the graceless
    name of 'Biron.'
'Tis the same landscape which the
    modern Mars saw
  Who march'd to Moscow, led by Fame,
    the siren!
To lose by one month's frost some twenty
    years
Of conquest, and his guard of grenadiers.

LIX

Let not this seem an anti-climax:—'Oh!
  My guard! my old guard!' exclaim'd
    that god of clay.
Think of the Thunderer's falling down
    below
  Carotid-artery-cutting Castlereagh!
Alas! that glory should be chill'd by
    snow!
  But should we wish to warm us on our
    way
Through Poland, there is Kosciusko's name
Might scatter fire through ice, like Hecla's
    flame.

LX

From Poland they came on through
    Prussia Proper.
  And Königsberg, the capital, whose
    vaunt,
Besides some veins of iron, lead, or
    copper,
  Has lately been the great Professor Kant.
Juan, who cared not a tobacco-stopper
  About philosophy, pursued his jaunt
To Germany, whose somewhat tardy
    millions
Have princes who spur more than their
    postilions.

LXI

And thence through Berlin, Dresden, and
    the like,
  Until he reach'd the castellated
    Rhine:—
Ye glorious Gothic scenes! how much ye
    strike
  All phantasies, not even excepting mine!

A grey wall, a green ruin, rusty pike,
　Make my soul pass the equinoctial line
Between the present and past worlds, and
　　hover
Upon their airy confine, half-seas-over.

LXII

But Juan posted on through Mannheim,
　　Bonn,
　Which Drachenfels frowns over like a
　　spectre
Of the good feudal times for ever gone,
　On which I have not time just now to
　　lecture.
From thence he was drawn onwards to
　　Cologne,
　A city which presents to the inspector
Eleven thousand maidenheads of bone,
The greatest number flesh hath ever known.

LXIII

From thence to Holland's Hague and
　　Helvoetsluys,
　That water-land of Dutchmen and of
　　ditches,
Where juniper expresses its best juice,
　The poor man's sparkling substitute
　　for riches.
Senates and sages have condemn'd its use—
　But to deny the mob a cordial, which is
Too often all the clothing, meat, or fuel,
Good government has left them, seems
　　but cruel.

LXIV

Here he embark'd, and with a flowing sail
　Went bounding for the island of the free,
Towards which the impatient wind blew
　　half a gale;
　High dash'd the spray, the bows dipp'd
　　in the sea,
And sea-sick passengers turn'd somewhat
　　pale;
　But Juan, season'd, as he well might be,
By former voyages, stood to watch the
　　skiffs,
Which pass'd, or catch the first glimpse of
　　the cliffs.

LXV

At length they rose, like a white wall
　　along
　The blue sea's border; and Don Juan
　　felt—
What even young strangers feel a little
　　strong
　At the first sight of Albion's chalky
　　belt—
A kind of pride that he should be among
　Those haughty shopkeepers, who
　　sternly dealt
Their goods and edicts out from pole to
　　pole
And made the very billows pay them toll.

LXVI

I've no great cause to love that spot of
　　earth,
　Which holds what *might have been* the
　　noblest nation;
But though I owe it little but my birth,
　I feel a mix'd regret and veneration
For its decaying fame and former worth.
　Seven years (the usual term of trans-
　　portation)
Of absence lay one's old resentments level,
When a man's country's going to the devil.

LXVII

Alas! could she but fully, truly, know
　How her great name is now through-
　　out abhorr'd;
How eager all the earth is for the blow
　Which shall lay bare her bosom to the
　　sword;
How all the nations deem her their worst
　　foe,
　That worse than *worst of foes*, the once
　　adored
False friend, who held out freedom to
　　mankind,
And now would chain them, to the very
　　mind;—

LXVIII

Would she be proud, or boast herself the
　　free,
　Who is but first of slaves? The nations are
In prison,—but the gaoler, what is he?
　No less a victim to the bolt and bar.
Is the poor privilege to turn the key
　Upon the captive, freedom? He's as far
From the enjoyment of the earth and air
Who watches o'er the chain, as they who
　　wear.

LXIX

Don Juan now saw Albion's earliest
　　beauties,
　Thy cliffs, *dear* Dover! harbour, and
　　hotel;
Thy custom-house, with all its delicate
　　duties;
　Thy waiters running mucks at every bell;
Thy packets, all whose passengers are
　　booties
　To those who upon land or water dwell;
And last, not least, to strangers unin-
　　structed,
Thy long, long bills, whence nothing is
　　deducted.

LXX

Juan, though careless, young, and
　　magnifique,
　And rich in rubles, diamonds, cash, and
　　credit,
Who did not limit much his bills per week,
　Yet stared at this a little, though he paid
　　it—

(His Maggior Duomo, a smart, subtle
  Greek,
    Before him summ'd the awful scroll and
      read it):
But, doubtless, as the air, though seldom
  sunny,
Is free, the respiration's worth the money.

LXXI

On with the horses! Off to Canterbury!
  Tramp, tramp o'er pebble, and splash,
    splash through puddle;
Hurrah! how swiftly speeds the post so
  merry!
    Not like slow Germany, wherein they
      muddle
Along the road, as if they went to bury
  Their fare; and also pause besides, to
    fuddle,
With 'schnapps'—sad dogs! whom
  'Hundsfot,' or 'Verflucter,'
Affect no more than lightning a conductor.

LXXII

Now there is nothing gives a man such
  spirits,
    Leavening his blood as cayenne doth a
      curry,
As going at full speed—no matter where its
  Direction be, so 'tis but in a hurry,
And merely for the sake of its own merits;
  For the less cause there is for all this
    flurry,
The greater is the pleasure in arriving
And the great *end* of travel—which is
  driving.

LXXIII

They saw at Canterbury the cathedral;
  Black Edward's helm, and Becket's
    bloody stone,
Were pointed out as usual by the bedral,
  In the same quaint, uninterested tone:—
There's glory again for you, gentle reader!
  All
Ends in a rusty casque and dubious bone,
Half-solved into these sodas or magnesias,
Which form that bitter draught, the
  human species.

LXXIV

The effect on Juan was of course sublime:
  He breathed a thousand Cressys, as he
    saw
That casque, which never stoop'd except
  to Time.
    Even the bold Churchman's tomb
      excited awe,
Who died in the then great attempt to climb
  O'er kings, who *now* at least *must talk*
    of law
Before they butcher. Little Leila gazed,
And ask'd why such a structure had been
  raised;

LXXV

And being told it was 'God's house,' she
  said
    He was well lodged, but only wonder'd
      how
He suffer'd Infidels in his homestead,
  The cruel Nazarenes, who had laid low
His holy temples in the lands which bred
  The True Believers;—and her infant
    brow
Was bent with grief that Mahomet should
  resign
A mosque so noble, flung like pearls to
  swine.

LXXVI

On! on! through meadows, managed like
  a garden,
    A paradise of hops and high pro-
      duction;
For, after years of travel by a bard in
  Countries of greater heat, but lesser
    suction,
A green field is a sight which makes him
  pardon
    The absence of that more sublime con-
      struction
Which mixes up vines, olives, precipices,
Glaciers, volcanos, oranges, and ices.

LXXVII

And when I think upon a pot of beer—
  But I won't weep!—and so drive on,
    postilions!
As the smart boys spurr'd fast in their career,
  Juan admired these highways of free
    millions;
A country in all senses the most dear
  To foreigner or native, save some silly
    ones,
Who 'kick against the pricks' just at this
  juncture,
And for their pains get only a fresh puncture.

LXXVIII

What a delightful thing's a turnpike road!
  So smooth, so level, such a mode of
    shaving
The earth, as scarce the eagle in the broad
  Air can accomplish, with his wide wings
    waving.
Had such been cut in Phaeton's time, the god
  Had told his son to satisfy his craving
With the York mail;—but onward as we
  roll,
Surgit amari aliquid—the toll!

LXXIX

Alas! how deeply painful is all payment!
  Take lives, take wives, take aught except
    men's purses.
As Machiavel shows those in purple
  raiment,
    Such is the shortest way to general curses.

They hate a murderer much less than a claimant
  On that sweet ore which everybody nurses.—
Kill a man's family, and he may brook it,
But keep your hands out of his breeches' pocket:

LXXX

So said the Florentine; ye monarchs, hearken
  To your instructor. Juan now was borne,
Just as the day began to wane and darken,
  O'er the high hill, which looks with pride or scorn
Toward the great city.—Ye who have a spark in
  Your veins of Cockney spirit, smile or mourn
According as you take things well or ill;
Bold Britons, we are now on Shooter's Hill!

LXXXI

The sun went down, the smoke rose up, as from
  A half-unquench'd volcano, o'er a space
Which well beseem'd the 'Devil's drawing-room,'
  As some have qualified that wondrous place:
But Juan felt, though not approaching home,
  As one who, though he were not of the race,
Revered the soil, of those true sons the mother,
Who butcher'd half the earth, and bullied t'other.

LXXXII

A mighty mass of brick, and smoke, and shipping,
  Dirty and dusky, but as wide as eye
Could reach, with here and there a sail just skipping
  In sight, then lost amidst the forestry
Of masts; a wilderness of steeples peeping
  On tiptoe through their sea-coal canopy;
A huge, dun cupola, like a foolscap crown
On a fool's head—and there is London Town.

LXXXIII

But Juan saw not this: each wreath of smoke
  Appear'd to him but as the magic vapour
Of some alchymic furnace, from whence broke
  The wealth of worlds (a wealth of tax and paper):

The gloomy clouds, which o'er it as a yoke
  Are bow'd, and put the sun out like a taper,
Were nothing but the natural atmosphere,
Extremely wholesome, though but rarely clear.

LXXXIV

He paused—and so will I; as doth a crew
  Before they give their broadside. By and by,
My gentle countrymen, we will renew
  Our old acquaintance; and at least I'll try
To tell you truths *you* will not take as true,
  Because they are so;—a male Mrs. Fry,
With a soft besom will I sweep your halls,
And brush a web or two from off the walls.

LXXXV

Oh Mrs. Fry! Why go to Newgate? Why
  Preach to *poor* rogues? And wherefore not begin
With Carlton, or with other houses? Try
  Your hand at harden'd and imperial sin.
To mend the people's an absurdity,
  A jargon, a mere philanthropic din,
Unless you make their betters better:—Fy!
I thought you had more religion, Mrs. Fry.

LXXXVI

Teach *them* the decencies of good three-score;
  Cure *them* of tours, hussar and high-land dresses;
Tell *them* that youth once gone returns no more,
  That hired huzzas redeem no land's distresses;
Tell them Sir William Curtis is a bore,
  Too dull even for the dullest of excesses,
The witless Falstaff of a hoary Hal,
A fool whose bells have ceased to ring at all.

LXXXVII

Tell them, though it may be perhaps too late
  On life's worn confine, jaded, bloated, sated,
To set up vain pretences of being *great*,
  'Tis not so to be *good*; and be it stated,
The worthiest kings have ever loved least state;
  And tell them——But you won't, and I have prated
Just now enough; but by and by I'll prattle
Like Roland's horn in Roncesvalles' battle.

CANTO THE ELEVENTH

I

WHEN Bishop Berkeley said 'there was no
        matter,'
    And proved it—'twas no matter what
        he said:
They say his system 'tis in vain to batter,
    Too subtle for the airiest human head;
And yet who can believe it? I would
        shatter
    Gladly all matters down to stone or
        lead,
Or adamant, to find the world a spirit,
And wear my head, denying that I wear
        it.

II

What a sublime discovery 'twas to make
        the
    Universe universal egotism,
That all's ideal—*all ourselves!* I'll stake
        the
    World (be it what you will) that *that's*
        no schism:
Oh Doubt!—if thou be'st Doubt, for
        which some take thee,
    But which I doubt extremely—thou
        sole prism
Of the Truth's rays, spoil not my draught
        of spirit!
Heaven's brandy, though our brain can
        hardly bear it.

III

For ever and anon comes Indigestion
    (Not the most 'dainty Ariel'), and per-
        plexes
Our soarings with another sort of
        question:
    And that which after all my spirit vexes,
Is, that I find no spot where man can rest
        eye on,
    Without confusion of the sorts and
        sexes,
Of beings, stars, and this unriddled
        wonder,
The world, which at the worst's a *glorious*
        blunder—

IV

If it be chance; or if it be according
    To the old text, still better:—lest it
        should
Turn out so, we'll say nothing 'gainst the
        wording,
    As several people think such hazards
        rude.
They're right; our days are too brief for
        affording
    Space to dispute what *no one* ever could
Decide, and *everybody one day* will
Know very clearly—or at least lie still.

V

And therefore will I leave off meta-
        physical
    Discussion, which is neither here nor
        there:
If I agree that what is, is; then this I call
    Being quite perspicuous and extremely
        fair;
The truth is, I've grown lately rather
        phthisical:
    I don't know what the reason is—the air
Perhaps; but as I suffer from the shocks
Of illness, I grow much more orthodox.

VI

The first attack at once proved the
        Divinity
    (But *that* I never doubted, nor theDevil);
The next, the Virgin's mystical virginity;
    The third, the usual Origin of Evil;
The fourth at once establish'd the whole
        Trinity
    On so uncontrovertible a level,
That I devoutly wish'd the three were four
On purpose to believe so much the more.

VII

To our theme.—The man who has stood
        on the Acropolis
    And look'd down over Attica; or he
Who has sail'd where picturesque Con-
        stantinople is,
    Or seen Timbuctoo, or hath taken tea
In small-eyed China's crockery-ware
        metropolis,
    Or sat amidst the bricks of Nineveh,
May not think much of London's first
        appearance—
But ask him what he thinks of it a year
        hence?

VIII

Don Juan had got out on Shooter's Hill;
    Sunset the time, the place the same
        declivity
Which looks along that vale of good and
        ill
    Where London streets ferment in full
        activity;
While everything around was calm and
        still,
    Except the creak of wheels, which on
        their pivot he
Heard,—and that bee-like, bubbling,
        busy hum
Of cities, that boils over with their scum:—

IX

I say, Don Juan, wrapt in contemplation,
    Walk'd on behind his carriage, o'er the
        summit,
And lost in wonder of so great a nation,
    Gave way to't, since he could not over-
        come it.

'And here,' he cried, 'is Freedom's
    chosen station;
  Here peals the people's voice, nor can
    entomb it
Racks, prisons, inquisitions; resurrection
Awaits it, each new meeting or election.

                    X

'Here are chaste wives, pure lives; here
    people pay
  But what they please; and if that things
    be dear,
'Tis only that they love to throw away
  Their cash, to show how much they
    have a year.
Here laws are all inviolate; none lay
  Traps for the traveller; every highway's
    clear;
Here'—he was interrupted by a knife,
  With—'Damn your eyes! your money or
    your life!'—

                    XI

These freeborn sounds proceeded from
    four pads
  In ambush laid, who had perceived him
    loiter
Behind his carriage; and, like handy lads,
  Had seized the lucky hour to recon-
    noitre,
In which the heedless gentleman who
    gads
  Upon the road, unless he prove a fighter,
May find himself within that isle of riches
Exposed to lose his life as well as breeches.

                    XII

Juan, who did not understand a word
  Of English, save their shibboleth, 'God
    damn!'
And even that he had so rarely heard,
  He sometimes thought 'twas only their
    'Salām,'
Or 'God be with you!'—and 'tis not
    absurd
  To think so: for half English as I am
(To my misfortune), never can I say
I heard them wish 'God with you,' save
    that way;—

                    XIII

Juan yet quickly understood their gesture,
  And being somewhat choleric and
    sudden,
Drew forth a pocket-pistol from his
    vesture,
  And fired it into one assailant's
    pudding—
Who fell, as rolls an ox o'er in his pasture,
  And roar'd out, as he writhed his native
    mud in,
Unto his nearest follower or henchman,
'Oh Jack! I'm floor'd by that 'ere bloody
    Frenchman!'

                    XIV

On which Jack and his train set off at
    speed,
  And Juan's suite, late scatter'd at a
    distance,
Came up, all marvelling at such a deed,
  And offering, as usual, late assistance.
Juan, who saw the moon's late minion
    bleed
  As if his veins would pour out his exis-
    tence,
Stood calling out for bandages and lint,
And wish'd he had been less hasty with
    his flint.

                    XV

'Perhaps,' thought he, 'it is the country's
    wont
  To welcome foreigners in this way: now
I recollect some innkeepers who don't
  Differ, except in robbing with a bow,
In lieu of a bare blade and brazen front.
  But what is to be done? I can't allow
The fellow to lie groaning on the road:
So take him up; I'll help you with the
    load.'

                    XVI

But ere they could perform this pious
    duty,
  The dying man cried, 'Hold! I've got
    my gruel!
Oh! for a glass of *max*! We've miss'd our
    booty;
  Let me die where I am!' And as the
    fuel
Of life shrunk in his heart, and thick and
    sooty
  The drops fell from his death-wound,
    and he drew ill
His breath,—he from his swelling throat
    untied
A kerchief, crying 'Give Sal that!'—and
    died.

                    XVII

The cravat stain'd with bloody drops fell
    down
  Before Don Juan's feet: he could not
    tell
Exactly why it was before him thrown,
  Nor what the meaning of the man's
    farewell.
Poor Tom was once a kiddy upon town,
  A thorough varmint, and a *real* swell,
Full flash, all fancy, until fairly diddled,
His pockets first and then his body riddled.

                    XVIII

Don Juan, having done the best he could
  In all the circumstances of the case,
As soon as 'Crowner's quest' allow'd,
    pursued
  His travels to the capital apace;—

Esteeming it a little hard he should
   In twelve hours' time, and very little
      space,
Have been obliged to slay a free-born
      native
In self-defence: this made him meditative.

XIX

He from the world had cut off a great man,
   Who in his time had made heroic bustle.
Who in a row like Tom could lead the
      van,
   Booze in the ken, or at the spellken
      hustle?
Who queer a flat? Who (spite of Bow-
      street's ban)
   On the high toby-spice so flash the
      muzzle?
Who on a lark, with black-eyed Sal (his
      blowing),
So prime, so swell, so nutty, and so
      knowing?

XX

But Tom's no more—and so no more of
      Tom.
   Heroes must die; and by God's blessing
      'tis
Not long before the most of them go home.
   Hail! Thamis, hail! Upon thy verge it is
That Juan's chariot, rolling like a drum
   In thunder, holds the way it can't well
      miss,
Through Kennington and all the other
      'tons,'
Which make us wish ourselves in town at
      once;—

XXI

Through Groves, so call'd as being void of
      trees,
   (Like lucus from no light); through
      prospects named
Mount Pleasant, as containing nought to
      please,
   Nor much to climb; through little boxes
      framed
Of bricks, to let the dust in at your ease,
   With 'To be let,' upon their doors pro-
      claim'd;
Through 'Rows' most modestly call'd
      'Paradise,'
Which Eve might quit without much
      sacrifice;—

XXII

Through coaches, drays, choked turn-
      pikes, and a whirl
   Of wheels, and roar of voices, and con-
      fusion;
Here taverns wooing to a pint of 'purl,'
   There mails fast flying off like a
      delusion;

There barbers' blocks with periwigs in
      curl
   In windows; here the lamplighter's
      infusion
Slowly distill'd into the glimmering glass
   (For in those days we had not got to
      gas—);

XXIII

Through this, and much, and more, is the
      approach
   Of travellers to mighty Babylon:
Whether they come by horse, or chaise,
      or coach,
   With slight exceptions, all the ways seem
      one.
I could say more, but do not choose to
      encroach
   Upon the Guide-book's privilege. The
      sun
Had set some time, and night was on the
      ridge
Of twilight, as the party cross'd the bridge.

XXIV

That's rather fine, the gentle sound of
      Thamis—
   Who vindicates a moment, too, his
      stream—
Though hardly heard through multi-
      farious 'damme's.'
   The lamps of Westminster's more
      regular gleam,
The breadth of pavement, and yon shrine
      where fame is
   A spectral resident—whose pallid beam
In shape of moonshine hovers o'er the
      pile—
Make this a sacred part of Albion's isle.

XXV

The Druid's groves are gone—so much
      the better:
   Stonehenge is not—but what the devil
      is it?—
But Bedlam still exists with its sage fetter,
   That madmen may not bite you on a
      visit;
The Bench too seats or suits full many a
      debtor;
   The Mansion-House, too (though some
      people quiz it),
To me appears a stiff yet grand erection;
But then the Abbey's worth the whole
      collection.

XXVI

The line of lights, too, up to Charing
      Cross,
   Pall Mall, and so forth, have a corusca-
      tion
Like gold as in comparison to dross,
   Match'd with the Continent's illumina-
      tion,

Whose cities Night by no means deigns to
  gloss.
    The French were not yet a lamp-
      lighting nation,
And when they grew so—on their new-
      found lantern,
    Instead of wicks, they made a wicked man
      turn.

XXVII

A row of gentlemen along the streets
  Suspended, may illuminate mankind,
As also bonfires made of country-seats;
  But the old way is best for the purblind:
The other looks like phosphorus on sheets,
  A sort of *ignis fatuus* to the mind,
Which, though 'tis certain to perplex and
      frighten,
Must burn more mildly ere it can en-
      lighten.

XXVIII

But London's so well lit, that if Diogenes
  Could recommence to hunt his *honest
      man*,
And found him not amidst the various
      progenies
Of this enormous city's spreading spawn,
'Twere not for want of lamps to aid his
      dodging his
Yet undiscover'd treasure. What *I* can,
I've done to find the same throughout
      life's journey,
But see the world is only one attorney.

XXIX

Over the stones still rattling, up Pall Mall,
  Through crowds and carriages, but
      waxing thinner
As thunder'd knockers broke the long-
      seal'd spell
  Of doors 'gainst duns, and to an early
      dinner
Admitted a small party as night fell,—
  Don Juan, our young diplomatic
      sinner,
Pursued his path, and drove past some
      hotels,
St. James's Palace and St. James's 'Hells.'

XXX

They reach'd the hotel: forth stream'd
      from the front door
  A tide of well-clad waiters, and around
The mob stood, and as usual several score
  Of those pedestrian Paphians who
      abound
In decent London when the daylight's
      o'er;
  Commodious but immoral, they are
      found
Useful, like Malthus, in promoting mar-
      riage.—
But Juan now is stepping from his carriage

XXXI

Into one of the sweetest of hotels,
  Especially for foreigners—and mostly
For those whom favour or whom fortune
      swells,
  And cannot find a bill's small items
      costly.
There many an envoy either dwelt or
      dwells
  (The den of many a diplomatic lost lie),
Until to some conspicuous square they
      pass,
And blazon o'er the door their names in
      brass.

XXXII

Juan, whose was a delicate commission,
  Private, though publicly important,
      bore
No title to point out with due precision
  The exact affair on which he was sent
      o'er.
'Twas merely known, that on a secret
      mission
  A foreigner of rank had graced our
      shore,
Young, handsome, and accomplish'd,
      who was said
(In whispers) to have turn'd his sovereign's
      head.

XXXIII

Some rumour also of some strange adven-
      tures
  Had gone before him, and his wars and
      loves;
And as romantic heads are pretty painters,
  And, above all, an Englishwoman's
      roves
Into the excursive, breaking the indentures
  Of sober reason, wheresoe'er it moves,
He found himself extremely in the fashion,
Which serves our thinking people for a
      passion.

XXXIV

I don't mean that they are passionless,
      but quite
  The contrary; but then 'tis in the head;
Yet as the consequences are as bright
  As if they acted with the heart instead,
What after all can signify the site
  Of ladies' lucubrations? So they lead
In safety to the place for which you start,
What matters if the road be head or
      heart?

XXXV

Juan presented in the proper place,
  To proper placemen, every Russ
      credential,
And was received with all the due grimace
  By those who govern in the mood
      potential,

Who, seeing a handsome stripling with
   smooth face,
   Thought (what in state affairs is most
    essential)
That they as easily might *do* the youngster,
As hawks may pounce upon a woodland
   songster.

XXXVI

They err'd, as aged men will do; but by
   And by we'll talk of that; and if we
    don't,
'Twill be because our notion is not high
   Of politicians and their double front,
Who live by lies, yet dare not boldly lie:—
   Now what I love in women is, they
    won't
Or can't do otherwise than lie, but do it
So well, the very truth seems falsehood to
   it.

XXXVII

And, after all, what is a lie? 'Tis but
   The truth in masquerade; and I defy
Historians, heroes, lawyers, priests, to put
   A fact without some leaven of a lie.
The very shadow of true Truth would shut
   Up annals, revelations, poesy,
And prophecy—except it should be dated
Some years before the incidents related.

XXXVIII

Praised be all liars and all lies! Who now
   Can tax my mild Muse with mis-
    anthropy?
She rings the world's 'Te Deum,' and her
   brow
   Blushes for those who will not:—but
    to sigh
Is idle; let us like most others bow,
   Kiss hands, feet, any part of majesty,
After the good example of 'Green Erin,'
Whose Shamrock now seems rather worse
   for wearing.

XXXIX

Don Juan was presented, and his dress
   And mien excited general admiration—
I don't know which was most admired or
   less:
   One monstrous diamond drew much
    observation,
Which Catherine in a moment of '*ivresse*'
   (In love or brandy's fervent fermenta-
    tion)
Bestow'd upon him, as the public learn'd;
And, to say truth, it had been fairly earn'd.

XL

Besides the ministers and underlings,
   Who must be courteous to the
    accredited
Diplomatists of rather wavering kings,
   Until their royal riddle's fully read,

The very clerks,—those somewhat dirty
   springs
Of office, or the house of office, fed
By foul corruption into streams,—even
   they
Were hardly rude enough to earn|their pay:

XLI

And insolence no doubt is what they are
   Employ'd for, since it is their daily
    labour,
In the dear offices of peace or war;
   And should you doubt, pray ask of your
    next neighbour,
When for a passport, or some other bar
   To freedom, he applied (a grief and *a*
    bore),
If he found not in this spawn of taxborn
   riches,
Like lap-dogs, the least civil sons of
   b——s.

XLII

But Juan was received with much '*em-
   pressement*:'—
   These phrases of refinement I must
    borrow
From our next neighbour's land, where,
   like a chessman,
   There is a move set down for joy or
    sorrow,
Not only in mere talking, but the press. Man
   In islands is, it seems, downright and
    thorough,
More than on continents—as if the sea
(See Billingsgate) made even the tongue
   more free.

XLIII

And yet the British 'Damme''s rather
   Attic;
   Your continental oaths are but inconti-
    nent,
And turn on things which no aristocratic
   Spirit would name, and therefore even
    I won't anent
This subject quote; as it would be schis-
   matic
   In *politesse*, and have a sound affronting
    in't;—
But 'Damme''s quite ethereal, though too
   daring—
Platonic blasphemy, the soul of swearing.

XLIV

For downright rudeness, ye may stay at
   home;
   For true or false politeness (and scarce
    that
Now) you may cross the blue deep and
   white foam—
   The first the emblem (rarely though) of
    what

You leave behind, the next of much you
  come
  To meet. However, 'tis no time to chat
On general topics: poems must confine
Themselves to unity, like this of mine.

XLV

In the great world,—which, being inter-
  preted,
  Meaneth the west or worst end of a
  city,
And about twice two thousand people
  bred
  By no means to be very wise or witty,
But to sit up while others lie in bed,
  And look down on the universe with
  pity,—
Juan, as an inveterate patrician,
Was well received by persons of condition.

XLVI

He was a bachelor, which is a matter
  Of import both to virgin and to bride,
The former's hymeneal hopes to flatter;
  And (should she not hold fast by love
  or pride)
'Tis also of some moment to the latter:
  A rib's a thorn in a wed gallant's side,
Requires decorum, and is apt to double
The horrid sin—and what's still worse,
  the trouble.

XLVII

But Juan was a bachelor—of arts,
  And parts, and hearts: he danced and
  sung, and had
An air as sentimental as Mozart's
  Softest of melodies; and could be sad
Or cheerful, without any 'flaws or starts,'
  Just at the proper time: and though a lad,
Had seen the world—which is a curious
  sight,
And very much unlike what people write.

XLVIII

Fair virgins blush'd upon him; wedded
  dames
  Bloom'd also in less transitory hues;
For both commodities dwell by the
  Thames,
  The painting and the painted; youth,
  ceruse,
Against his heart preferr'd their usual
  claims,
  Such as no gentleman can quite refuse;
Daughters admired his dress, and pious
  mothers
Inquired his income, and if he had
  brothers.

XLIX

The milliners who furnish 'drapery Misses'
  Throughout the season, upon speculation

Of payment ere the honeymoon's last
  kisses
  Have waned into a crescent's corusca-
  tion,
Thought such an opportunity as this is,
  Of a rich foreigner's initiation,
Not to be overlook'd—and gave such
  credit,
That future bridegrooms swore, and
  sigh'd, and paid it.

L

The Blues, that tender tribe, who sigh o'er
  sonnets,
  And with the pages of the last Review
Line the interior of their heads or bonnets,
  Advanced in all their azure's highest
  hue:
They talk'd bad French of Spanish, and
  upon its
  Late authors ask'd him for a hint or
  two;
And which was softest, Russian or
  Castilian?
And whether in his travels he saw Ilion?

LI

Juan, who was a little superficial,
  And not in literature a great Draw-
  cansir,
Examined by this learned and especial
  Jury of matrons, scarce knew what to
  answer:
His duties warlike, loving, or official,
  His steady application as a dancer,
Had kept him from the brink of Hippo-
  crene,
Which now he found was blue instead of
  green.

LII

However, he replied at hazard, with
  A modest confidence and calm as-
  surance,
Which lent his learned lucubrations pith,
  And pass'd for arguments of good
  endurance.
That prodigy, Miss Araminta Smith
  (Who at sixteen translated 'Hercules
  Furens'
Into as furious English), with her best
  look,
Set down his sayings in her common-
  place book.

LIII

Juan knew several languages—as well
  He might—and brought them up with
  skill, in time
To save his fame with each accomplish'd
  belle,
  Who still regretted that he did not
  rhyme.

There wanted but this requisite to swell
  His qualities (with them) into sublime:
Lady Fitz-Frisky, and Miss Mævia
  Mannish,
Both long'd extremely to be sung in
  Spanish.

LIV

However, he did pretty well, and was
  Admitted as an aspirant to all
The coteries, and, as in Banquo's glass,
  At great assemblies or in parties small,
He saw ten thousand living authors pass,
  That being about their average numeral;
Also the eighty 'greatest living poets,'
As every paltry magazine can show it's.

LV

In twice five years the 'greatest living
  poet,'
  Like to the champion in the fisty ring,
Is call'd on to support his claim, or show it,
  Although 'tis an imaginary thing.
Even I—albeit I'm sure I did not know it,
  Nor sought of foolscap subjects to be
  king,—
Was reckon'd, a considerable time,
The grand Napoleon of the realms of
  rhyme.

LVI

But Juan was my Moscow, and Faliero
  My Leipsic, and my Mont Saint Jean
  seems Cain:
La Belle Alliance of dunces down at zero,
  Now that the Lion's fall'n, may rise
  again:
But I will fall at least as fell my hero;
  Nor reign at all, or as a monarch reign;
Or to some lonely isle of gaolers go,
With turncoat Southey for my turnkey
  Lowe.

LVII

Sir Walter reign'd before me; Moore and
  Campbell
  Before and after: but now grown more
  holy,
The Muses upon Sion's hill must ramble
  With poets almost clergymen, or
  wholly:
And Pegasus hath a psalmodic amble
  Beneath the very Reverend Rowley
  Powley,
Who shoes the glorious animal with stilts,
A modern Ancient Pistol—by the hilts!

LVIII

Still he excels that artificial hard
  Labourer in the same vineyard, though
  the vine
Yields him but vinegar for his reward,—
  That neutralised dull Dorus of the
  Nine;

That swarthy Sporus, neither man nor bard;
  That ox of verse, who ploughs for every
  line:—
Cambyses' roaring Romans beat at least
The howling Hebrews of Cybele's priest.—

LIX

Then there's my gentle Euphues; who,
  they say,
  Sets up for being a sort of moral me;
He'll find it rather difficult some day
  To turn out both, or either, it may be.
Some persons think that Coleridge hath
  the sway;
  And Wordsworth has supporters, two
  or three;
And that deep-mouth'd Bœotian 'Savage
  Landor'
Has taken for a swan rogue Southey's
  gander.

LX

John Keats, who was kill'd off by one
  critique,
  Just as he really promised something
  great,
If not intelligible, without Greek
  Contrived to talk about the Gods of late,
Much as they might have been supposed
  to speak.
  Poor fellow! His was an untoward fate;
'Tis strange the mind, that very fiery particle,
Should let itself be snuff'd out by an article.

LXI

The list grows long of live and dead pretenders
  To that which none will gain—or none
  will know
The conqueror at least; who, ere Time
  renders
  His last award, will have the long grass
  grow
Above his burnt-out brain, and sapless
  cinders.
  If I might augur, I should rate but low
Their chances;—they're too numerous,
  like the thirty
Mock tyrants, when Rome's annals wax'd
  but dirty.

LXII

This is the literary lower empire,
  Where the prætorian bands take up the
  matter;—
A 'dreadful trade,' like his who 'gathers
  samphire,'
  The insolent soldiery to soothe and
  flatter,
With the same feelings as you'd coax a
  vampire.
  Now, were I once at home, and in good
  satire,
I'd try conclusions with those Janizaries,
And show them what an intellectual war is.

LXIII

I think I know a trick or two, would turn
    Their flanks;—but it is hardly worth
    my while
With such small gear to give myself
    concern:
Indeed I've not the necessary bile;
My natural temper's really aught but
    stern,
    And even my Muse's worst reproof 's
    a smile;
And then she drops a brief and modern
    curtsy,
And glides away, assured she never hurts
    ye.

LXIV

My Juan, whom I left in deadly peril
    Amongst live poets and *blue* ladies,
    pass'd
With some small profit through that field
    so sterile,
    Being tired in time, and neither least
    nor last,
Left it before he had been treated very
    ill;
    And henceforth found himself more
    gaily class'd
Amongst the higher spirits of the day,
The sun's true son, no vapour, but a
    ray.

LXV

His morns he pass'd in business—which
    dissected,
    Was like all business, a laborious
    nothing
That leads to lassitude, the most infected
    And Centaur Nessus garb of mortal
    clothing,
And on our sofas makes us lie dejected,
    And talk in tender horrors of our
    loathing
All kinds of toil, save for our country's
    good—
Which grows no better, though 'tis time
    it should.

LXVI

His afternoons he pass'd in visits,
    luncheons,
    Lounging, and boxing; and the twilight
    hour
In riding round those vegetable puncheons
Call'd 'Parks,' where there is neither
    fruit nor flower
Enough to gratify a bee's slight munch-
    ings;
    But after all it is the only 'bower'
(In Moore's phrase) where the fashionable
    fair
Can form a slight acquaintance with fresh
    air.

LXVII

Then dress, then dinner, then awakes the
    world!
    Then glare the lamps, then whirl the
    wheels, then roar
Through street and square fast flashing
    chariots hurl'd
    Like harness'd meteors; then along the
    floor
Chalk mimics painting; then festoons are
    twirl'd;
    Then roll the brazen thunders of the
    door,
Which opens to the thousand happy few
An earthly Paradise of *Or Molu*.

LXVIII

There stands the noble hostess, nor shall
    sink
    With the three-thousandth curtsy;
    there the waltz,
The only dance which teaches girls to
    think,
    Makes one in love even with its very
    faults.
Saloon, room, hall, o'erflow beyond their
    brink,
    And long the latest of arrivals halts,
'Midst royal dukes and dames condemn'd
    to climb,
And gain an inch of staircase at a time.

LXIX

Thrice happy he who, after a survey
    Of the good company, can win a corner,
A door that's *in* or boudoir *out* of the way,
    Where he may fix himself like small
    'Jack Horner,'
And let the Babel round run as it may,
    And look on as a mourner, or a scorner,
Or an approver, or a mere spectator,
Yawning a little as the night grows later.

LXX

But this won't do, save by and by; and he
    Who, like Don Juan, takes an active
    share,
Must steer with care through all that
    glittering sea
    Of gems and plumes and pearls and
    silks, to where
He deems it is his proper place to be;
    Dissolving in the waltz to some soft air,
Or proudlier prancing with mercurial skill,
Where Science marshals forth her own
    quadrille.

LXXI

Or, if he dance not, but hath higher views
    Upon an heiress or his neighbour's
    bride,
Let him take care that that which he
    pursues
    Is not at once too palpably descried.

Full many an eager gentleman oft rues
  His haste; impatience is a blundering
    guide,
Amongst a people famous for reflection,
Who like to play the fool with circumspec-
    tion.

LXXII

But, if you can contrive, get next at
    supper;
  Or if forestall'd, get opposite and
    ogle:—
Oh, ye ambrosial moments! always upper
In mind, a sort of sentimental bogle,
Which sits for ever upon memory's
    crupper,
  The ghost of vanish'd pleasures once in
    vogue! Ill
Can tender souls relate the rise and fall
Of hopes and fears which shake a single
    ball.

LXXIII

But these precautionary hints can touch
  Only the common run, who must
    pursue,
And watch, and ward; whose plans a word
    too much
  Or little overturns; and not the few
Or many (for the number's sometimes
    such)
  Whom a good mien, especially if new,
Or fame, or name, for wit, war, sense, or
    nonsense,
Permits whate'er they please, or *did* not
    long since.

LXXIV

Our hero, as a hero, young and handsome,
  Noble, rich, celebrated, and a stranger,
Like other slaves of course must pay his
    ransom,
  Before he can escape from so much
    danger
As will environ a conspicuous man. Some
  Talk about poetry, and 'rack and man-
    ger,'
And ugliness, disease, as toil and
    trouble;—
I wish they knew the life of a young noble.

LXXV

They are young, but know not youth—it
    is anticipated;
  Handsome but wasted, rich without a
    sou;
Their vigour in a thousand arms is dissi-
    pated;
  Their cash comes *from*, their wealth
    goes *to* a Jew;
Both senates see their nightly votes par-
    ticipated
  Between the tyrant's and the tribunes'
    crew;

And having voted, dined, drank, gamed,
    and whored,
The family vault receives another lord.

LXXVI

'Where is the world,' cries Young, 'at
    eighty? Where
  The world in which a man was born?'
    Alas!
Where is the world of *eight* years past?
    'Twas there—
  I look for it—'tis gone, a globe of glass!
Crack'd, shiver'd, vanish'd, scarcely
    gazed on, ere
  A silent change dissolves the glittering
    mass.
Statesmen, chiefs, orators, queens,
    patriots, kings,
And dandies, all are gone on the wind's
    wings.

LXXVII

Where is Napoleon the Grand? God
    knows:
  Where little Castlereagh? The devil
    can tell:
Where Grattan, Curran, Sheridan, all
    those
  Who bound the bar or senate in their
    spell?
Where is the unhappy Queen, with all her
    woes?
  And where the Daughter, whom the
    Isles loved well?
Where are those martyr'd saints the Five
    per Cents?
And where—oh, where the devil are the
    Rents?

LXXVIII

Where's Brummel? Dish'd. Where's Long
    Pole Wellesley? Diddled.
  Where's Whitbread? Romilly? Where's
    George the Third?
Where is his will? (That's not so soon
    unriddled.)
  And where is 'Fum' the Fourth, our
    'royal bird'?
Gone down, it seems, to Scotland to be
    fiddled
  Unto by Sawney's violin, we have heard:
'Caw me, caw thee'—for six months hath
    been hatching
This scene of royal itch and loyal scratch-
    ing.

LXXIX

Where is Lord This? And where my Lady
    That?
  The Honourable Mistresses and
    Misses?
Some laid aside like an old Opera hat,
  Married, unmarried, and remarried
    (this is

An evolution oft performed of late).
 Where are the Dublin shouts—and London hisses?
Where are the Grenvilles? Turn'd as usual. Where
My friends the Whigs? Exactly where they were.

LXXX

Where are the Lady Carolines and Franceses?
 Divorced or doing thereanent. Ye annals
So brilliant, where the list of routs and dances is,—
 Thou Morning Post, sole record of the panels
Broken in carriages, and all the phantasies
 Of fashion,—say what streams now fill those channels?
Some die, some fly, some languish on the Continent,
Because the times have hardly left them *one* tenant.

LXXXI

Some who once set their caps at cautious dukes,
 Have taken up at length with younger brothers:
Some heiresses have bit at sharpers' hooks:
 Some maids have been made wives, some merely mothers:
Others have lost their fresh and fairy looks:
 In short, the list of alterations bothers.
There's little strange in this, but something strange is
The unusual quickness of these common changes.

LXXXII

Talk not of seventy years as age; in seven
 I have seen more changes, down from monarchs to
The humblest individual under heaven,
 Than might suffice a moderate century through.
I knew that nought was lasting, but now even
 Change grows too changeable, without being new:
Nought's permanent among the human race,
Except the Whigs *not* getting into place.

LXXXIII

I have seen Napoleon, who seem'd quite a Jupiter,
 Shrink to a Saturn. I have seen a Duke
(No matter which) turn politician stupider,
 If that can well be, than his wooden look;

But it is time that I should hoist my 'blue Peter,'
 And sail for a new theme:—I have seen—and shook
To see it—the king hiss'd, and then caressed;
But don't pretend to settle which was best.

LXXXIV

I have seen the Landholders without a rap—
 I have seen Joanna Southcote—I have seen
The House of Commons turn'd to a tax-trap—
 I have seen that sad affair of the late Queen—
I have seen crowns worn instead of a fool's cap—
 I have seen a Congress doing all that's mean—
I have seen some nations, like o'erloaded asses,
Kick off their burthens—meaning the high classes.

LXXXV

I have seen small poets, and great prosers, and
 Interminable—*not eternal*—speakers—
I have seen the funds at war with house and land—
 I have seen the country gentlemen turn squeakers—
I have seen the people ridden o'er like sand
 By slaves on horseback—I have seen malt liquors
Exchanged for 'thin potations' by John Bull—
I have seen John half detect himself a fool.—

LXXXVI

But '*carpe diem*,' Juan, '*carpe, carpe!*'
 To-morrow sees another race as gay
And transient, and devour'd by the same harpy.
 'Life's a poor player,'—then 'play out the play,
Ye villains!' and above all keep a sharp eye
 Much less on what you do than what you say:
Be hypocritical, be cautious, be
Not what you *seem*, but always what you *see*.

LXXXVII

But how shall I relate in other cantos
 Of what befell our hero in the land,
Which 'tis the common cry and lie to vaunt as
 A moral country? But I hold my hand—

For I disdain to write an Atalantis;
But 'tis as well at once to understand
You are *not* a moral people, and you know
    it
Without the aid of too sincere a poet.

LXXXVIII

What Juan saw and underwent shall be
    My topic, with of course the due
    restriction
Which is required by proper courtesy;
    And recollect the work is only fiction,
And that I sing of neither mine nor me,
    Though every scribe, in some slight
    turn of diction,
Will hint allusions never *meant*. Ne'er
    doubt
This—when I speak, I *don't hint*, but
    speak out.

LXXXIX

Whether he married with the third or
    fourth
    Offspring of some sage husband-
    hunting countess,
Or whether with some virgin of more
    worth
    (I mean in Fortune's matrimonial
    bounties),
He took to regularly peopling Earth,
    Of which your lawful, awful wedlock
    fount is,—
Or whether he was taken in for damages,
For being too excursive in his homages,—

XC

Is yet within the unread events of time.
    Thus far, go forth, thou lay, which I will
    back
Against the same given quantity of rhyme,
    For being as much the subject of attack
As ever yet was any work sublime,
    By those who love to say that white is
    black.
So much the better!—I may stand alone,
But would not change my free thoughts
    for a throne.

CANTO THE TWELFTH

I

Of all the barbarous middle ages, that
    Which is most barbarous is the middle
    age
Of man! it is—I really scarce know what;
    But when we hover between fool and
    sage,
And don't know justly what we would be
    at—
A period something like a printed page,
Black letter upon foolscap, while our hair
Grows grizzled, and we are not what we
    were;—

II

Too old for youth,—too young, at thirty-
    five,
    To herd with boys, or hoard with good
    threescore,—
I wonder people should be left alive;
    But since they are, that epoch is a bore:
Love lingers still, although 'twere late to
    wive:
    And as for other love, the illusion's
    o'er;
And money, that most pure imagina-
    tion,
Gleams only through the dawn of its
    creation.

III

O Gold! Why call we misers miserable?
    Theirs is the pleasure that can never
    pall;
Theirs is the best bower anchor, the chain
    cable
    Which holds fast other pleasures great
    and small.
Ye who but see the saving man at table,
    And scorn his temperate board, as none
    at all,
And wonder how the wealthy can be
    sparing,
Know not what visions spring from each
    cheeseparing.

IV

Love or lust makes man sick, and wine
    much sicker;
    Ambition rends, and gaming gains a
    loss;
But making money, slowly first, then
    quicker,
    And adding still a little through each
    cross
(Which *will* come over things), beats love
    or liquor,
    The gamester's counter, or the states-
    man's *dross*.
O Gold! I still prefer thee unto paper,
Which makes bank credit like a bark of
    vapour.

V

Who hold the balance of the world? Who
    reign
    O'er congress, whether royalist or
    liberal?
Who rouse the shirtless patriots of Spain
    (That make old Europe's journals
    squeak and gibber all)?
Who keep the world, both old and new,
    in pain
    Or pleasure? Who make politics run
    glibber all?
The shade of Buonaparte's noble daring?
Jew Rothschild, and his fellow-Christian,
    Baring.

VI

Those, and the truly liberal Lafitte,
  Are the true lords of Europe. Every
     loan
Is not a merely speculative hit,
  But seats a nation or upsets a throne.
Republics also get involved a bit;
    Columbia's stock hath holders not
     unknown
On 'Change, and even thy silver soil, Peru,
Must get itself discounted by a Jew.

VII

Why call the miser miserable? as
  I said before: the frugal life is his,
Which in a saint or cynic ever was
    The theme of praise: a hermit would
     not miss
Canonization for the self-same cause,
    And wherefore blame gaunt wealth's
     austerities?
Because, you'll say, nought calls for such
  a trial;—
Then there's more merit in his self-denial.

VIII

He is your only poet;—passion, pure
    And sparkling on from heap to heap,
     displays,
Possess'd, the ore, of which *mere hopes*
  allure
    Nations athwart the deep: the golden
     rays
Flash up in ingots from the mine obscure:
  On him the diamond pours its brilliant
    blaze,
While the mild emerald's beam shades
  down the dies
Of other stones, to soothe the miser's eyes.

IX

The lands on either side are his; the ship
    From Ceylon, Inde, or far Cathay,
     unloads
For him the fragrant produce of each trip;
    Beneath his cars of Ceres groan the
     roads,
And the vine blushes like Aurora's lip;
    His very cellars might be kings' abodes;
While he, despising every sensual call,
Commands—the intellectual lord of *all*.

X

Perhaps he hath great projects in his mind,
  To build a college, or to found a race,
A hospital, a church,—and leave behind
    Some dome surmounted by his meagre
    face:
Perhaps he fain would liberate mankind
    Even with the very ore which makes
    them base;
Perhaps he would be wealthiest of his
  nation,
Or revel in the joys of calculation.

XI

But whether all, or each, or none of
  these
    May be the hoarder's principle of
    action,
The fool will call such mania a disease:—
    What is his *own*? Go—look at each
    transaction,
Wars, revels, loves—do these bring men
  more ease
    Than the mere plodding through each
    'vulgar fraction'?
Or do they benefit mankind? Lean miser!
Let spendthrifts' heirs inquire of yours—
  who's wiser?

XII

How beauteous are rouleaus! how charm-
  ing chests
    Containing ingots, bags of dollars, coins
(Not of old victors, all whose heads and
  crests
    Weigh not the thin ore where their
    visage shines,
But) of fine unclipt gold, where dully rests
    Some likeness, which the glittering
    cirque confines,
Of modern, reigning, sterling, stupid
  stamp:
Yes! ready money *is* Aladdin's lamp.

XIII

'Love rules the camp, the court, the grove,
   —for love
    Is heaven, and heaven is love':—so
    sings the bard;
Which it were rather difficult to prove
    (A thing with poetry in general hard).
Perhaps there may be something in 'the
  grove,'
    At least it rhymes to 'love:' but I'm
    prepared
To doubt (no less than landlords of their
  rental)
If 'courts' and 'camps' be quite so sentimental.

XIV

But if Love don't, *Cash* does, and Cash
  alone:
    Cash rules the grove, and fells it too
    beside;
Without cash, camps were thin, and
  courts were none;
    Without cash, Malthus tells you—
    'take no brides.'
So Cash rules Love the ruler, on his own
    High ground, as virgin Cynthia sways
    the tides:
And as for 'Heaven being Love,' why not
  say honey
Is wax? Heaven is not Love, 'tis Matrimony.

XV

Is not all love prohibited whatever,
  Excepting marriage? which is love, no
    doubt,
After a sort; but somehow people never
  With the same thought the two words
    have help'd out.
Love may exist *with* marriage, and *should*
    ever,
  And marriage also may exist without;
But love *sans* banns is both a sin and shame,
And ought to go by quite another name.

XVI

Now if the 'court,' and 'camp,' and
    'grove,' be not
  Recruited all with constant married men,
Who never coveted their neighbour's lot,
  I say *that* line's a lapsus of the pen;—
Strange too in my *buon camerado* Scott,
  So celebrated for his morals, when
My Jeffrey held him up as an example
To me;—of which these morals are a sample.

XVII

Well, if I don't succeed, I *have* succeeded,
  And that's enough; succeeded in my
    youth,
The only time when much success is
    needed:
  And my success produced what I, in
    sooth,
Cared most about; it need not now be
    pleaded—
  Whate'er it was, 'twas mine; I've paid,
    in truth,
Of late, the penalty of such success,
But have not learn'd to wish it any less.

XVIII

That suit in Chancery,—which some
    persons plead
  In an appeal to the unborn, whom they,
In the faith of their procreative creed,
  Baptize posterity, or future clay,—
To me seems but a dubious kind of reed
  To lean on for support in any way;
Since odds are that posterity will know
No more of them, than they of her, I trow.

XIX

Why, I'm posterity—and so are you;
  And whom do we remember? Not a
    hundred.
Were every memory written down all true,
  The tenth or twentieth name would be
    but blundered;
Even Plutarch's Lives have but pick'd out
    a few,
  And 'gainst those few your annalists
    have thunder'd;
And Mitford in the nineteenth century
Gives, with Greek truth, the good old
    Greek the lie.

XX

Good people all, of every degree,
  Ye gentle readers and ungentle writers,
In this twelfth Canto 'tis my wish to be
  As serious as if I had for inditers
Malthus and Wilberforce:—the last set
    free
  The Negroes, and is worth a million
    fighters;
While Wellington has but enslaved the
    Whites,
And Malthus does the thing 'gainst which
    he writes.

XXI

I'm serious—so are all men upon paper;
  And why should I not form my specula-
    tion,
And hold up to the sun my little taper?
  Mankind just now seem wrapt in
    meditation
On constitutions and steam-boats of
    vapour;
  While sages write against all pro-
    creation,
Unless a man can calculate his means
Of feeding brats the moment his wife
    weans.

XXII

That's noble! That's romantic! For my
    part,
  I think that 'Philo-genitiveness' is—
(Now here's a word quite after my own
    heart,
  Though there's a shorter a good deal
    than this
If that politeness set it not apart;
  But I'm resolved to say nought that's
    amiss)—
I say, methinks that 'Philo-genitiveness'
Might meet from men a little more forgive-
    ness.

XXIII

And now to business.—O my gentle Juan!
  Thou art in London—in that pleasant
    place,
Where every kind of mischief's daily brew-
    ing,
  Which can await warm youth in its wild
    race.
'Tis true, that thy career is not a new one;
  Thou art no novice in the headlong
    chase
Of early life; but this is a new land,
Which foreigners can never understand.

XXIV

What with a small diversity of climate,
  Of hot or cold, mercurial or sedate,
I could send forth my mandate like a
    primate
  Upon the rest of Europe's social state;

But thou art the most difficult to rhyme at,
  Great Britain, which the Muse may
    penetrate.
All countries have their 'Lions,' but in
  thee
There is but one superb menagerie.

XXV

But I am sick of politics. Begin,
  '*Paulo Majora*.' Juan, undecided
Amongst the paths of being 'taken in,'
  Above the ice had like a skater glided:
When tired of play, he flirted without sin
  With some of those fair creatures who
    have prided
Themselves on innocent tantalisation,
And hate all vice except its reputation.

XXVI

But these are few, and in the end they
  make
  Some devilish escapade or stir, which
    shows
That even the purest people may mistake
  Their way through virtue's primrose
    paths of snows;
And then men stare, as if a new ass spake
  To Balaam, and from tongue to ear
    o'erflows
Quicksilver small talk, ending (if you note
  it)
With the kind world's amen—'Who
  would have thought it?'

XXVII

The little Leila, with her Orient eyes,
  And taciturn Asiatic disposition,
(Which saw all Western things with small
  surprise,
To the surprise of people of condition,
  Who think that novelties are butterflies
    To be pursued as food for inanition,)
Her charming figure and romantic history
Became a kind of fashionable mystery.

XXVIII

The women much divided—as is usual
  Amongst the sex in little things or great.
Think not, fair creatures, that I mean to
  abuse you all—
  I have always liked you better than I
    state:
Since I've grown moral, still I must accuse
  you all
  Of being apt to talk at a great rate;
And now there was a general sensation
Amongst you, about Leila's education.

XXIX

In one point only were you settled—and
  You had reason; 'twas that a young
    child of grace,
As beautiful as her own native land,
  And far away, the last bud of her race,

Howe'er our friend Don Juan might com-
  mand
  Himself for five, four, three, or two
    years' space,
Would be much better taught beneath the
  eye
Of peeresses whose follies had run dry.

XXX

So first there was a generous emulation,
  And then there was a general competi-
    tion,
To undertake the orphan's education.
  As Juan was a person of condition,
It had been an affront on this occasion
  To talk of a subscription or petition;
But sixteen dowagers, ten unwed she
  sages,
Whose tale belongs to 'Hallam's Middle
  Ages,'

XXXI

And one or two sad, separate wives, with-
  out
  A fruit to bloom upon their withering
    bough—
Begg'd to bring *up* the little girl, and
  '*out*,'—
  For that's the phrase that settles all
    things now,
Meaning a virgin's first blush at a rout,
  And all her points as thorough-bred to
    show:
And I assure you, that like virgin honey
Tastes their first season (mostly if they
  have money).

XXXII

How all the needy honourable misters,
  Each out-at-elbow peer, or desperate
    dandy,
The watchful mothers, and the careful
  sisters,
  (Who, by the by, when clever, are more
    handy
At making matches, where ''tis gold that
  glisters,'
  Than their *he* relatives), like flies o'er
    candy
Buzz round 'the Fortune' with their busy
  battery,
To turn her head with waltzing and with
  flattery!

XXXIII

Each aunt, each cousin, hath her specula-
  tion;
  Nay, married dames will now and then
    discover
Such pure disinterestedness of passion,
  I've known them court an heiress for
    their lover.

'*Tantæne!*' Such the virtues of high
        station,
    Even in the hopeful Isle, whose outlet's
        'Dover!'
While the poor rich wretch, object of these
        cares,
    Has cause to wish her sire had had male
        heirs.

XXXIV

Some are soon bagg'd, and some reject
        three dozen.
    'Tis fine to see them scattering refusals
And wild dismay o'er every angry cousin
    (Friends of the party), who begin
        accusals
Such as—'Unless Miss (Blank) meant to
        have chosen
    Poor Frederick, why did she accord
        perusals
To his billets? *Why* waltz with him? Why,
        I pray,
Look *yes* last night, and yet say *no* to-day?'

XXXV

'Why?—Why?—Besides, Fred really was
        attach'd;
    'Twas not her fortune—he has enough
        without:
The time will come she'll wish that she
        had snatch'd
    So good an opportunity, no doubt:—
But the old Marchioness some plan had
        hatch'd,
    As I'll tell Aurea at to-morrow's rout:
And after all poor Frederick may do
        better—
Pray did you see her answer to his letter?'

XXXVI

Smart uniforms and sparkling coronets
    Are spurn'd in turn, until her turn arrives,
After male loss of time, and hearts, and bets
    Upon the sweepstakes for substantial
        wives;
And when at last the pretty creature gets
    Some gentleman, who fights, or writes,
        or drives,
It soothes the awkward squad of the rejected
To find how very badly she selected.

XXXVII

For sometimes they accept some long
        pursuer,
    Worn out with importunity; or fall
(But here perhaps the instances are fewer)
    To the lot of him who scarce pursued
        at all.
A hazy widower turn'd of forty's sure
    (If 'tis not vain examples to recall)
To draw a high prize: now, howe'er he got
        her, I
See nought more strange in this than
        t'other lottery.

XXXVIII

I, for my part—(one 'modern instance'
        more,
    'True, 'tis a pity—pity 'tis, 'tis true')—
Was chosen from out an amatory score,
    Albeit my years were less discreet than
        few;
But though I also had reform'd before
    Those became one who soon were to be
        two,
I'll not gainsay the generous public's
        voice,
That the young lady made a monstrous
        choice.

XXXIX

Oh, pardon me digression—or at least
    Peruse! 'Tis always with a moral end
That I dissert, like grace before a feast:
    For like an aged aunt, or tiresome
        friend,
A rigid guardian, or a zealous priest,
    My Muse by exhortation means to
        mend
All people, at all times, and in most places,
Which puts my Pegasus to these grave
        paces.

XL

But now I'm going to be immoral; now
    I mean to show things really as they are,
Not as they ought to be: for I avow,
    That till we see what's what in fact,
        we're far
From much improvement with that
        virtuous plough
    Which skims the surface, leaving scarce
        a scar
Upon the black loam long manured by
        Vice,
Only to keep its corn at the old price.

XLI

But first of little Leila we'll dispose;
    For like a day-dawn she was young and
        pure,
Or like the old comparison of snows,
    Which are more pure than pleasant to
        be sure.
Like many people everybody knows,
    Don Juan was delighted to secure
A goodly guardian for his infant charge,
Who might not profit much by being at
        large.

XLII

Besides, he had found out that he was no
        tutor
    (I wish that others would find out the
        same),
And rather wish'd in such things to stand
        neuter,
    For silly wards will bring their
        guardians blame:

So when he saw each ancient dame a
    suitor
  To make his little wild Asiatic tame,
Consulting 'the Society for Vice
Suppression,' Lady Pinchbeck was his
    choice.

XLIII

Olden she was—but had been very young:
  Virtuous she was—and had been, I
    believe;
Although the world has such an evil
    tongue
  That——but my chaster ear will not
    receive
An echo of a syllable that's wrong;
  In fact, there's nothing makes me so
    much grieve,
As that abominable tittle-tattle,
Which is the cud eschew'd by human cattle.

XLIV

Moreover I've remark'd (and I was once
  A slight observer in a modest way),
And so may every one except a dunce,
  That ladies in their youth a little gay,
Besides their knowledge of the world, and
    sense
  Of the sad consequence of going astray,
Are wiser in their warnings 'gainst the woe
Which the mere passionless can never
    know.

XLV

While the harsh prude indemnifies her
    virtue
  By railing at the unknown and envied
    passion,
Seeking far less to save you than to hurt
    you,
  Or, what's still worse, to put you out of
    fashion,—
The kinder veteran with calm words will
    court you,
  Entreating you to pause before you
    dash on;
Expounding and illustrating the riddle
Of epic Love's beginning, end, and middle.

XLVI

Now whether it be thus, or that they are
    stricter,
  As better knowing why they should be so,
I think you'll find from many a family
    picture,
  That daughters of such mothers as may
    know
The world by experience rather than by
    lecture,
  Turn out much better for the Smithfield
    Show
Of vestals brought into the marriage mart,
Than those bred up by prudes without a
    heart.

XLVII

I said that Lady Pinchbeck had been talk'd
    about—
  As who has not, if female, young, and
    pretty?
But now no more the ghost of Scandal
    stalk'd about;
  She merely was deem'd amiable and
    witty,
And several of her best *bons-mots* were
    hawk'd about:
  Then she was given to charity and pity,
And pass'd (at least the latter years of life)
For being a most exemplary wife.

XLVIII

High in high circles, gentle in her own,
  She was the mild reprover of the young,
Whenever—which means every day—
    they'd shown
  An awkward inclination to go wrong.
The quantity of good she did's unknown,
  Or at the least would lengthen out my
    song:
In brief, the little orphan of the East
Had raised an interest in her, which
    increased.

XLIX

Juan, too, was a sort of favourite with her,
  Because she thought him a good heart
    at bottom,
A little spoil'd, but not so altogether;
  Which was a wonder, if you think who
    got him,
And how he had been toss'd, he scarce
    knew whither:
  Though this might ruin others, it did
    not him,
At least entirely—for he had seen too
    many
Changes in youth, to be surprised at any.

L

And these vicissitudes tell best in youth;
  For when they happen at a riper age,
People are apt to blame the Fates, for-
    sooth,
  And wonder Providence is not more
    sage.
Adversity is the first path to truth:
  He who hath proved war, storm, or
    woman's rage,
Whether his winters be eighteen or eighty,
Hath won the experience which is deem'd
    so weighty.

LI

How far it profits is another matter.—
  Our hero gladly saw his little charge
Safe with a lady, whose last grown-up
    daughter
  Being long married, and thus set at
    large,

Had left all the accomplishments she
    taught her
  To be transmitted, like the Lord
    Mayor's barge,
To the next comer; or—as it will tell
More Muse-like—like to Cytherea's shell.

LII

I call such things transmission; for there is
  A floating balance of accomplishment,
Which forms a pedigree from Miss to Miss,
  According as their minds or backs are
    bent.
Some waltz; some draw; some fathom the
    abyss
  Of metaphysics; others are content
With music; the most moderate shine as
    wits;
While others have a genius turn'd for fits.

LIII

But whether fits, or wits, or harpsichords,
  Theology, fine arts, or finer stays,
May be the baits for gentlemen or lords
  With regular descent, in these our days,
The last year to the new transfers its
    hoards;
  New vestals claim men's eyes with the
    same praise
Of 'elegant' et cætera, in fresh batches—
All matchless creatures, and yet bent on
    matches.

LIV

But now I will begin my poem. 'Tis
  Perhaps a little strange, if not quite new,
That from the first of Cantos up to this
  I've not begun what we have to go
    through.
These first twelve books are merely
    flourishes,
  Preludios, trying just a string or two
Upon my lyre, or making the pegs sure;
And when so, you shall have the overture.

LV

My Muses do not care a pinch of rosin
  About what's call'd success, or not
    succeeding:
Such thoughts are quite below the strain
    they have chosen;
  'Tis a 'great moral lesson' they are
    reading.
I thought, at setting off, about two dozen
  Cantos would do; but at Apollo's
    pleading,
If that my Pegasus should not be
    founder'd,
I think to canter gently through a hundred.

LVI

Don Juan saw that microcosm on stilts,
  Yclept the Great World; for it is the
    least,

Although the highest: but as swords have
    hilts
  By which their power of mischief is
    increased,
When man in battle or in quarrel tilts,
  Thus the low world, north, south, or
    west, or east,
Must still obey the high—which is their
    handle,
Their moon, their sun, their gas, their
    farthing candle.

LVII

He had many friends who had many wives,
    and was
  Well look'd upon by both, to that extent
Of friendship which you may accept or
    pass,
  It does nor good, nor harm: being
    merely meant
To keep the wheels going of the higher
    class,
  And draw them nightly when a ticket's
    sent;
And what with masquerades, and fêtes,
    and balls,
For the first season such a life scarce palls.

LVIII

A young unmarried man, with a good name
    And fortune, has an awkward part to
    play;
For good society is but a game,
  'The royal game of Goose,' as I may
    say,
Where everybody has some separate aim,
  An end to answer, or a plan to lay—
The single ladies wishing to be double,
The married ones to save the virgins
    trouble.

LIX

I don't mean this as general, but particular
  Examples may be found of such
    pursuits:
Though several also keep their perpendi-
    cular
  Like poplars, with good principles for
    roots;
Yet many have a method more reticular—
  'Fishers for men,' like sirens with soft
    lutes:
For talk six times with the same single lady,
And you may get the wedding dresses ready.

LX

Perhaps you'll have a letter from the
    mother,
  To say her daughter's feelings are tre-
    pann'd;
Perhaps you'll have a visit from the
    brother,
  All strut, and stays, and whiskers, to
    demand

What 'your intentions are?'—One way
    or other
  It seems the virgin's heart expects your
    hand:
And between pity for her case and yours,
You'll add to Matrimony's list of cures.

LXI

I've known a dozen weddings made even
    thus,
  And some of them high names: I have
    also known
Young men who—though they hated to
    discuss
  Pretensions which they never dream'd
    to have shown—
Yet neither frighten'd by a female fuss,
  Nor by mustachios moved, were let alone,
And lived, as did the broken-hearted fair,
In happier plight than if they form'd a pair.

LXII

There's also nightly, to the uninitiated,
  A peril—not indeed like love or
    marriage,
But not the less for this to be depreciated:
  It is—I meant and mean not to dis-
    parage
The show of virtue even in the vitiated—
  It adds an outward grace unto their
    carriage—
But to denounce the amphibious sort of
    harlot,
Couleur de rose, who's neither white nor
    scarlet.

LXIII

Such is your cold coquette, who can't say
    'No,'
  And won't say 'Yes,' and keeps you on
    and off-ing
On a lee-shore, till it begins to blow—
  Then sees your heart wreck'd with an
    inward scoffing.
This works a world of sentimental woe,
  And sends new Werters yearly to their
    coffin;
But yet is merely innocent flirtation,
Not quite adultery, but adulteration.

LXIV

'Ye gods, I grow a talker!' Let us prate.
  The next of perils, though I place it
    *stern*est,
Is when, without regard to 'church or state,'
  A wife makes or takes love in upright
    earnest.
Abroad, such things decide few women's
    fate—
  (Such, early traveller! is the truth thou
    learnest)—
But in old England, when a young bride
    errs,
Poor thing! Eve's was a trifling case to
    hers.

LXV

For 'tis a low, newspaper, humdrum, law-
    suit
  Country, where a young couple of the
    same ages
Can't form a friendship, but the world
    o'erawes it.
  Then there's the vulgar trick of those
    d——d damages!
A verdict—grievous foe to those who
    cause it!—
  Forms a sad climax to romantic
    homages;
Besides those soothing speeches of the
    pleaders,
And evidences which regale all readers.

LXVI

But they who blunder thus are raw
    beginners;
  A little genial sprinkling of hypocrisy
Has saved the fame of thousand splendid
    sinners,
  The loveliest oligarchs of our gyno-
    cracy;
You may see such at all the balls and
    dinners,
  Among the proudest of our aristocracy,
So gentle, charming, charitable, chaste—
And all by having *tact* as well as taste.

LXVII

Juan, who did not stand in the predica-
    ment
  Of a mere novice, had one safeguard
    more;
For he was sick—no, 'twas not the word
    sick I meant—
  But he had seen so much good love
    before,
That he was not in heart so very weak;—
    I meant
  But thus much, and no sneer against the
    shore
Of white cliffs, white necks, blue eyes,
    bluer stockings,
Tithes, taxes, duns, and doors with double
    knockings.

LXVIII

But coming young from lands and scenes
    romantic,
  Where lives, not lawsuits, must be
    risk'd for Passion,
And Passion's self must have a spice of
    frantic,
  Into a country where 'tis half a fashion,
Seem'd to him half commercial, half
    pedantic,
  Howe'er he might esteem this moral
    nation:
Besides (alas! his taste—forgive and pity!)
At *first* he did not think the women pretty.

LXIX

I say at *first*—for he found out at *last*,
　But by degrees, that they were fairer far
Than the more glowing dames whose lot
　　is cast
Beneath the influence of the eastern star.
A further proof we should not judge in
　　haste;
　Yet inexperience could not be his bar
To taste:—the truth is, if men would con-
　　fess,
That novelties *please* less than they
　impress.

LXX

Though travell'd, I have never had the
　　luck to
Trace up those shuffling negroes, Nile
　　or Niger,
To that impracticable place Timbuctoo,
　Where Geography finds no one to oblige
　her
With such a chart as may be safely stuck
　　to—
　For Europe ploughs in Afric like '*bos
　piger*';
But if I *had been* at Timbuctoo, there
No doubt I should be told that black is
　fair.

LXXI

It is. I will not swear that black is white;
　But I suspect in fact that white is black,
And the whole matter rests upon eye-
　sight.
　Ask a blind man, the best judge. You'll
　attack
Perhaps this new position—but I'm right;
　Or if I'm wrong, I'll not be ta'en
　aback:—
He hath no morn nor night, but all is dark
Within; and what seest thou? A dubious
　spark.

LXXII

But I'm relapsing into metaphysics,
　That labyrinth, whose clue is of the same
Construction as your cures for hectic
　phthisics,
　Those bright moths fluttering round a
　dying flame:
And this reflection brings me to plain
　physics,
　And to the beauties of a foreign dame,
Compared with those of our pure pearls of
　price,
Those polar summers, *all* sun, and some
　ice.

LXXIII

Or say they are like virtuous mermaids,
　whose
　Beginnings are fair faces, ends mere
　fishes;—

Not that there's not a quantity of those
　Who have a due respect for their own
　wishes.
Like Russians rushing from hot baths to
　snows
　Are they, at bottom virtuous even when
　vicious;
They warm into a scrape, but keep of course,
As a reserve, a plunge into remorse.

LXXIV

But this has nought to do with their out-
　sides.
　I said that Juan did not think them pretty
At the first blush; for a fair Briton hides
　Half her attractions—probably from
　pity—
And rather calmly into the heart glides,
　Than storms it as a foe would take a
　city;
But once *there* (if you doubt this, prithee try)
She keeps it for you like a true ally.

LXXV

She cannot step as does an Arab barb,
　Or Andalusian girl from mass returning,
Nor wear as gracefully as Gauls her garb,
　Nor in her eye Ausonia's glance is burn-
　ing;
Her voice, though sweet, is not so fit to warb-
　le those *bravuras* (which I still am
　learning
To like, though I have been seven years in
　Italy,
And have, or had, an ear that served me
　prettily);—

LXXVI

She cannot do these things, nor one or two
　Others, in that off-hand and dashing
　style
Which takes so much—to give the devil
　his due;
　Nor is she quite so ready with her smile,
Nor settles all things in one interview
　(A thing approved as saving time and
　toil);—
But though the soil may give you time and
　trouble,
Well cultivated, it will render double.

LXXVII

And if in fact she takes to a *grande
　passion*,
　It is a very serious thing indeed:
Nine times in ten 'tis but caprice or
　fashion,
　Coquetry, or a wish to take the lead,
The pride of a mere child with a new sash
　on,
　Or wish to make a rival's bosom bleed:
But the *tenth* instance will be a tornado,
For there's no saying what they will or
　may do.

LXXVIII

The reason's obvious: if there's an *éclat*,
　They lose their caste at once, as do the
　　Parias;
And when the delicacies of the law
　Have fill'd their papers with their com-
　　ments various,
Society, that china without flaw,
　(The hypocrite!) will banish them like
　　Marius,
To sit amidst the ruins of their guilt:
For Fame's a Carthage not so soon
　rebuilt.

LXXIX

Perhaps this is as it should be;—it is
　A comment on the Gospel's 'Sin no
　　more,
And be thy sins forgiven';—but upon this
　I leave the saints to settle their own
　　score.
Abroad, though doubtless they do much
　amiss,
　An erring woman finds an opener door
For her return to Virtue—as they call
That lady, who should be at home to all.

LXXX

For me, I leave the matter where I find it,
　Knowing that such uneasy virtue leads
People some ten times less in fact to mind
　it,
　And care but for discoveries, and not
　　deeds.
And as for chastity, you'll never bind it
　By all the laws the strictest lawyer
　　pleads,
But aggravate the crime you have not
　prevented,
By rendering desperate those who had
　else repented.

LXXXI

But Juan was no casuist, nor had ponder'd
　Upon the moral lessons of mankind:
Besides, he had not seen of several
　hundred
　A lady altogether to his mind.
A little *blasé*—'tis not to be wonder'd
　At, that his heart had got a tougher
　　rind:
And though not vainer from his past
　success,
No doubt his sensibilities were less.

LXXXII

He also had been busy seeing sights—
　The Parliament and all the other
　　houses;
Had sat beneath the gallery at nights,
　To hear debates whose thunder *roused*
　　(not *rouses*)

The world to gaze upon those northern
　lights,
　Which flash'd as far as where the musk-
　　bull browses;
He had also stood at times behind the
　throne—
But Grey was not arrived, and Chatham
　gone.

LXXXIII

He saw, however, at the closing session,
　That noble sight, when *really* free the
　　nation,
A king in constitutional possession
　Of such a throne as is the proudest
　　station,
Though despots know it not—till the pro-
　gression
　Of freedom shall complete their educa-
　　tion.
'Tis not mere splendour makes the show
　august
To eye or heart—it is the people's trust.

LXXXIV

There, too, he saw (whate'er he may be
　now)
　A Prince, the prince of princes at the
　　time,
With fascination in his very bow,
　And full of promise, as the spring of
　　prime.
Though royalty was written on his brow,
　He had *then* the grace, too, rare in
　　every clime,
Of being, without alloy of fop or beau,
A finish'd gentleman from top to toe.

LXXXV

And Juan was received, as hath been said,
　Into the best society; and there
Occurr'd what often happens, I'm afraid,
　However disciplined and debonnaire:—
The talent and good humour he display'd,
　Besides the mark'd distinction of his
　　air,
Exposed him, as was natural, to tempta-
　tion,
Even though himself avoided the occasion.

LXXXVI

But what, and where, with whom, and
　when, and why,
　Is not to be put hastily together;
And as my object is morality
　(Whatever people say), I don't know
　　whether
I'll leave a single reader's eyelid dry,
　But harrow up his feelings till they
　　wither,
And hew out a huge monument of pathos,
As Philip's son proposed to do with Athos.

LXXXVII

Here the twelfth Canto of our introduction
    Ends. When the body of the book's
    begun,
You'll find it of a different construction
    From what some people say 'twill be
    when done;
The plan at present's simply in concoction.
    I can't oblige you, reader, to read on;
That's your affair, not mine: a real spirit
Should neither court neglect, nor dread
    to bear it.

LXXXVIII

And if my thunderbolt not always rattles,
    Remember, reader! you have had
    before
The worst of tempests and the best of
    battles,
    That e'er were brew'd from elements or
    gore,
Besides the most sublime of—Heaven
    knows what else;
    An usurer could scarce expect much
    more—
But my best canto, save one on astronomy,
Will turn upon 'political economy.'

LXXXIX

That is your present theme for popularity:
    Now that the public hedge hath scarce
    a stake,
It grows an act of patriotic charity,
    To show the people the best way to
    break.
My plan (but I, if but for singularity,
    Reserve it) will be very sure to take.
Meantime, read all the national-debt
    sinkers,
And tell me what you think of your great
    thinkers.

CANTO THE THIRTEENTH

I

I NOW mean to be serious;—it is time,
    Since laughter now-a-days is deem'd
    too serious;
A jest at Vice by Virtue's call'd a crime,
    And critically held as deleterious:
Besides, the sad's a source of the sublime,
    Although when long a little apt to
    weary us;
And therefore shall my lay soar high and
    solemn,
As an old temple dwindled to a column.

II

The Lady Adeline Amundeville
    ('Tis an old Norman name, and to be
    found
In pedigrees, by those who wander still
    Along the last fields of that Gothic
    ground)

Was high-born, wealthy by her father's
    will,
    And beauteous, even where beauties
    most abound,
In Britain—which of course true patriots
    find
The goodliest soil of body and of mind.

III

I'll not gainsay them; it is not my cue;
    I'll leave them to their taste, no doubt
    the best:
An eye's an eye, and whether black or
    blue,
    Is no great matter, so 'tis in request;
'Tis nonsense to dispute about a hue—
    The kindest may be taken as a test.
The fair sex should be always fair; and no
    man
Till thirty, should perceive there's a plain
    woman.

IV

And after that serene and somewhat dull
    Epoch, that awkward corner turn'd for
    days
More quiet, when our moon's no more at
    full,
    We may presume to criticise or praise;
Because indifference begins to lull
    Our passions, and we walk in wisdom's
    ways;
Also because the figure and the face
Hint, that 'tis time to give the younger
    place.

V

I know that some would fain postpone
    this era,
    Reluctant as all placemen to resign
Their post; but theirs is merely a chimera,
    For they have pass'd life's equinoctial
    line:
But then they have their claret and
    Madeira
    To irrigate the dryness of decline;
And county meetings, and the parliament,
And debt, and what not, for their solace
    sent.

VI

And is there not religion, and reform,
    Peace, war, the taxes, and what's called
    the 'Nation'?
The struggle to be pilots in a storm?
    The landed and the monied specula-
    tion?
The joys of mutual hate to keep them
    warm,
    Instead of love, that mere hallucina-
    tion?
Now hatred is by far the longest pleasure;
Men love in haste, but they detest at
    leisure.

VII

Rough Johnson, the great moralist, profess'd,
  Right honestly, 'he liked an honest hater!'—
The only truth that yet has been confest
  Within these latest thousand years or later.
Perhaps the fine old fellow spoke in jest:—
  For my part, I am but a mere spectator,
And gaze where'er the palace or the hovel is,
Much in the mode of Goethe's Mephistopheles;

VIII

But neither love nor hate in much excess;
  Though 'twas not once so. If I sneer sometimes,
It is because I cannot well do less,
  And now and then it also suits my rhymes.
I should be very willing to redress
  Men's wrongs, and rather check than punish crimes,
Had not Cervantes, in that too true tale
Of Quixote, shown how all such efforts fail.

IX

Of all tales 'tis the saddest—and more sad,
  Because it makes us smile: his hero's right,
And still pursues the right;—to curb the bad
  His only object, and 'gainst odds to fight
His guerdon: 'tis his virtue makes him mad!
  But his adventures form a sorry sight;—
A sorrier still is the great moral taught
By that real epic unto all who have thought.

X

Redressing injury, revenging wrong,
  To aid the damsel and destroy the caitiff;
Opposing singly the united strong,
  From foreign yoke to free the helpless native:—
Alas! must noblest views, like an old song,
  Be for mere fancy's sport a theme creative,
A jest, a riddle, Fame through thin and thick sought!
And Socrates himself but Wisdom's Quixote?

XI

Cervantes smiled Spain's chivalry away;
  A single laugh demolish'd the right arm
Of his own country;—seldom since that day
  Has Spain had heroes. While Romance could charm,

The world gave ground before her bright array;
  And therefore have his volumes done such harm,
That all their glory, as a composition,
Was dearly purchased by his land's perdition.

XII

I'm 'at my old lunes'—digression, and forget
  The Lady Adeline Amundeville;
The fair most fatal Juan ever met,
  Although she was not evil nor meant ill;
But Destiny and Passion spread the net
  (Fate is a good excuse for our own will),
And caught them;—what do they not catch methinks?
But I'm not Œdipus, and life's a Sphinx.

XIII

I tell the tale as it is told, nor dare
  To venture a solution: '*Davus sum!*'
And now I will proceed upon the pair.
  Sweet Adeline, amidst the gay world's hum,
Was the Queen-Bee, the glass of all that's fair;
  Whose charms made all men speak, and women dumb.
The last's a miracle, and such was reckon'd,
And since that time there has not been a second.

XIV

Chaste was she, to detraction's desperation,
  And wedded unto one she had loved well—
A man known in the councils of the nation,
  Cool, and quite English, imperturbable,
Though apt to act with fire upon occasion,
  Proud of himself and her: the world could tell
Nought against either, and both seem'd secure—
She in her virtue, he in his hauteur.

XV

It chanced some diplomatical relations,
  Arising out of business, often brought
Himself and Juan in their mutual stations
  Into close contact. Though reserved, nor caught
By specious seeming, Juan's youth, and patience,
  And talent, on his haughty spirit wrought,
And form'd a basis of esteem, which ends
In making men what courtesy calls friends.

XVI

And thus Lord Henry, who was cautious as
    Reserve and pride could make him, and
      full slow
In judging men—when once his judgment
    was
    Determined, right or wrong, on friend
      or foe,
Had all the pertinacity pride has,
    Which knows no ebb to its imperious
      flow,
And loves or hates, disdaining to be guided,
Because its own good pleasure hath
    decided.

XVII

His friendships, therefore, and no less
    aversions,
    Though oft well founded, which con-
      firm'd but more
His prepossessions, like the laws of
    Persians
    And Medes, would ne'er revoke what
      went before.
His feelings had not those strange fits, like
    tertians,
    Of common likings, which make some
      deplore
What they should laugh at—the mere ague
    still
Of men's regard, the fever or the chill.

XVIII

''Tis not in mortals to command success:
    But *do you more*, Sempronius—*don't*
      deserve it,'
And take my word, you won't have any less.
    Be wary, watch the time, and always
      serve it;
Give gently way, when there's too great a
    press;
    And for your conscience only learn to
      nerve it,
For, like a racer, or a boxer training,
'Twill make, if proved, vast efforts without
    paining.

XIX

Lord Henry also liked to be superior,
    As most men do, the little or the great;
The very lowest find out an inferior,
    At least they think so, to exert their state
Upon: for there are very few things wearier
    Than solitary Pride's oppressive weight,
Which mortals generously would divide,
By bidding others carry while they ride.

XX

In birth, in rank, in fortune likewise equal,
    O'er Juan he could no distinction claim;
In years he had the advantage of time's
    sequel;
    And, as he thought, in country much
    the same—

Because bold Britons have a tongue and
    free quill,
    At which all modern nations vainly aim;
And the Lord Henry was a great debater,
So that few members kept the House up
    later.

XXI

These were advantages: and then he
    thought—
    It was his foible, but by no means sinis-
      ter—
That few or none more than himself had
    caught
    Court mysteries, having been himself a
      minister:
He liked to teach that which he had been
    taught,
    And greatly shone whenever there had
      been a stir;
And reconciled all qualities which grace
    man,
Always a patriot, and sometimes a place-
    man.

XXII

He liked the gentle Spaniard for his
    gravity;
    He almost honour'd him for his
      docility;
Because, though young, he acquiesced
    with suavity,
    Or contradicted but with proud
      humility.
He knew the world, and would not see
    depravity
    In faults which sometimes show the
      soil's fertility,
If that the weeds o'erlive not the first
    crop—
For then they are very difficult to stop.

XXIII

And then he talk'd with him about
    Madrid,
    Constantinople, and such distant
      places;
Where people always did as they were bid,
    Or did what they should not with
      foreign graces.
Of coursers also spake they: Henry rid
    Well, like most Englishmen, and loved
      the races;
And Juan, like a true-born Andalusian,
Could back a horse, as despots ride a
    Russian.

XXIV

And thus acquaintance grew, at noble
    routs,
    And diplomatic dinners, or at other—
For Juan stood well both with Ins and
    Outs,
    As in freemasonry a higher brother.

Upon his talent Henry had no doubts;
  His manner show'd him sprung from a
    high mother;
And all men like to show their hospitality
  To him whose breeding matches with his
    quality.

XXV

At Blank-Blank Square;—for we will
    break no squares
  By naming streets: since men are so
    censorious,
And apt to sow an author's wheat with
    tares,
  Reaping allusions private and in-
    glorious,
Where none were dreamt of, unto love's
    affairs,
  Which were, or are, or are to be
    notorious,
That therefore do I previously declare,
Lord Henry's mansion was in Blank-
    Blank Square.

XXVI

Also there bin another pious reason
  For making squares and streets
    anonymous;
Which is, that there is scarce a single
    season
  Which doth not shake some very
    splendid house
With some slight heart-quake of domestic
    treason—
  A topic scandal doth delight to rouse:
Such I might stumble over unawares,
Unless I knew the very chastest squares.

XXVII

'Tis true, I might have chosen Piccadilly,
  A place where peccadillos are unknown;
But I have motives, whether wise or silly,
  For letting that pure sanctuary alone.
Therefore I name not square, street, place,
    until I
  Find one where nothing naughty can be
    shown,
A vestal shrine of innocence of heart:
Such are—but I have lost the London
    Chart.

XXVIII

At Henry's mansion then, in Blank-Blank
    Square,
  Was Juan a *recherché*, welcome guest,
As many other noble scions were;
  And some who had but talent for their
    crest;
Or wealth, which is a passport everywhere;
  Or even mere fashion, which indeed's
    the best
Recommendation; and to be well drest
Will very often supersede the rest.

XXIX

And since 'there's safety in a multitude
  Of counsellors,' as Solomon has said,
Or some one for him, in some sage,
    grave mood;—
  Indeed we see the daily proof display'd
In senates, at the bar, in wordy feud,
  Where'er collective wisdom can parade,
Which is the only cause that we can guess
Of Britain's present wealth and happi-
    ness;—

XXX

But as 'there's safety' grafted in the number
  'Of counsellors' for men,—thus for the
    sex
A large acquaintance lets not Virtue
    slumber;
  Or should it shake, the choice will more
    perplex—
Variety itself will more encumber.
  'Midst many rocks we guard more
    against wrecks;
And thus with women: howsoe'er it
    shocks some's
Self-love, there's safety in a crowd of
    coxcombs.

XXXI

But Adeline had not the least occasion
  For such a shield, which leaves but little
    merit
To virtue proper, or good education.
  Her chief resource was in her own high
    spirit,
Which judged mankind at their due
    estimation;
  And for coquetry, she disdain'd to wear
    it:
Secure of admiration, its impression
Was faint as of an every-day possession.

XXXII

To all she was polite without parade;
  To some she show'd attention of that kind
Which flatters, but is flattery convey'd
  In such a sort as cannot leave behind
A trace unworthy either wife or maid;—
  A gentle, genial courtesy of mind,
To those who were, or pass'd for meri-
    torious,
Just to console sad glory for being glorious;

XXXIII

Which is in all respects, save now and then,
  A dull and desolate appendage. Gaze
Upon the shades of those distinguish'd men
  Who were or are the puppet-shows of
    praise,
The praise of persecution. Gaze again
  On the most favour'd; and amidst the
    blaze
Of sunset halos o'er the laurel-brow'd,
What can ye recognize?—a gilded cloud.

XXXIV

There also was of course in Adeline
  That calm patrician polish in the
    address,
Which ne'er can pass the equinoctial line
  Of anything which nature would express;
Just as a mandarin finds nothing fine,—
  At least his manner suffers not to guess,
That anything he views can greatly please.
Perhaps we have borrow'd this from the
    Chinese—

XXXV

Perhaps from Horace: his '*Nil admirari*'
  Was what he call'd the 'Art of Happi-
    ness'—
An art on which the artists greatly vary,
  And have not yet attain'd to much
    success.
However, 'tis expedient to be wary:
  Indifference certes don't produce dis-
    tress;
And rash enthusiasm in good society
Were nothing but a moral inebriety.

XXXVI

But Adeline was not indifferent: for
  (*Now* for a common-place!) beneath the
    snow,
As a volcano holds the lava more
  Within—*et cætera*. Shall I go on?—No,
I hate to hunt down a tired metaphor,
  So let the often-used volcano go.
Poor thing! How frequently, by me and
    others,
It hath been stirr'd up till its smoke quite
    smothers!

XXXVII

I'll have another figure in a trice:—
  What say you to a bottle of champagne?
Frozen into a very vinous ice,
  Which leaves few drops of that
    immortal rain,
Yet in the very centre, past all price,
  About a liquid glassful will remain;
And this is stronger than the strongest grape
Could e'er express in its expanded shape:

XXXVIII

'Tis the whole spirit brought to a quint-
    essence;
  And thus the chilliest aspects may
    concentre
A hidden nectar under a cold presence.
  And such are many—though I only
    meant her
From whom I now deduce these moral
    lessons,
  On which the Muse has always sought
    to enter.
And your cold people are beyond all price,
When once you have broken their con-
    founded ice.

XXXIX

But after all they are a North-West
    Passage
  Unto the glowing India of the soul;
And as the good ships sent upon that
    message
  Have not exactly ascertain'd the Pole
(Though Parry's efforts look a lucky
    presage),
  Thus gentlemen may run upon a shoal;
For if the Pole's not open, but all frost
(A chance still), 'tis a voyage or vessel lost.

XL

And young beginners may as well com-
    mence
  With quiet cruising o'er the ocean
    Woman;
While those who are not beginners should
    have sense
  Enough to make for port, ere Time
    shall summon
With his grey signal-flag; and the past
    tense,
  The dreary '*Fuimus*' of all things
    human,
Must be declined, while life's thin thread's
    spun out
Between the gaping heir and gnawing
    gout.

XLI

But heaven must be diverted; its diversion
  Is sometimes truculent—but never
    mind;
The world upon the whole is worth the
    assertion
  (If but for comfort) that all things are
    kind:
And that same devilish doctrine of the
    Persian,
  Of the 'Two Principles', but leaves behind
As many doubts as any other doctrine
Has ever puzzled faith withal, or yoked
    her in.

XLII

The English winter—ending in July,
  To recommence in August—now was
    done.
'Tis the postilion's paradise: wheels fly;
  On roads, east, south, north, west, there
    is a run.
But for post-horses who finds sympathy?
  Man's pity for himself, or for his son,
Always premising that said son at college
Has not contracted much more debt than
    knowledge.

XLIII

The London winter's ended in July—
  Sometimes a little later. I don't err
In this: whatever other blunders lie
  Upon my shoulders, here I must aver

My Muse a glass of *Weatherology*;
  For parliament is our barometer:
Let radicals its other acts attack,
Its sessions form our only almanack.

XLIV

When its quicksilver's down at zero,—lo!
  Coach, chariot, luggage, baggage,
    equipage!
Wheels whirl from Carlton palace to
    Soho,
  And happiest they who horses can
    engage;
The turnpikes glow with dust; and Rotten
    Row
  Sleeps from the chivalry of this bright
    age;
And tradesmen, with long bills and longer
    faces,
Sigh—as the postboys fasten on the traces.

XLV

They and their bills, 'Arcadians both,' are
    left
  To the Greek kalends of another session.
Alas! to them of ready cash bereft,
  What hope remains? Of *hope* the full
    possession
Or generous draft, conceded as a gift,
  At a long date—till they can get a fresh
    one—
Hawk'd about at a discount, small or
    large;
Also the solace of an overcharge.

XLVI

But these are trifles. Downward flies my
    lord,
  Nodding beside my lady in his carriage.
Away! away! 'Fresh horses!' are the
    word,
  And changed as quickly as hearts after
    marriage;
The obsequious landlord hath the change
    restored;
  The postboys have no reason to
    disparage
Their fee; but ere the water'd wheels may
    hiss hence,
The ostler pleads for a small reminiscence.

XLVII

'Tis granted; and the valet mounts the
    dickey,
  That gentleman of lords and gentlemen;
Also my lady's gentlewoman, tricky,
  Trick'd out, but modest more than
    poet's pen
Can paint,—' *Cosi viaggino i Ricchi!*'
  (Excuse a foreign slipslop now and then,
If but to show I've travell'd: and what's
    travel,
Unless it teaches one to quote and cavil?)

XLVIII

The London winter and the country
    summer
  Were well nigh over. 'Tis perhaps a
    pity,
When nature wears the gown that doth
    become her.
  To lose those best months in a sweaty
    city,
And wait until the nightingale grows
    dumber,
  Listening debates not very wise or
    witty,
Ere patriots their true *country* can remem-
    ber;—
But there's no shooting (save grouse) till
    September.

XLIX

I've done with my tirade. The world was
    gone;
  The twice two thousand, for whom
    earth was made,
Were vanish'd to be what they call alone—
  That is, with thirty servants for parade,
As many guests, or more; before whom
    groan
  As many covers, duly, daily laid.
Let none accuse old England's hospi-
    tality—
Its quantity is but condensed to quality.

L

Lord Henry and the Lady Adeline
  Departed like the rest of their compeers,
The peerage, to a mansion very fine;
  The Gothic Babel of a thousand years.
None than themselves could boast a
    longer line,
  Where time through heroes and through
    beauties steers;
And oaks as olden as their pedigree
Told of their sires, a tomb in every tree.

LI

A paragraph in every paper told
  Of their departure: such is modern
    fame:
'Tis pity that it takes no further hold
  Than an advertisement, or much the
    same;
When, ere the ink be dry, the sound grows
    cold.
  The Morning Post was foremost to
    proclaim—
'Departure, for his country seat, to-day,
Lord H. Amundeville and Lady A.

LII

'We understand the splendid host intends
  To entertain, this autumn, a select
And numerous party of his noble friends;
  'Midst whom we have heard, from
    sources quite correct,

The Duke of D—— the shooting season
　　spends,
　　With many more by rank and fashion
　　　　deck'd;
Also a foreigner of high condition,
　　The envoy of the secret Russian mission.'

LIII

And thus we see—who doubts the Morn-
　　ing Post?
　　(Whose articles are like the 'Thirty-
　　　　nine,'
Which those most swear to who believe
　　them most)—
　　Our gay Russ Spaniard was ordain'd
　　　　to shine,
Deck'd by the rays reflected from his host,
　　With those who, Pope says, 'greatly
　　　　daring dine.'—
'Tis odd, but true,—last war the News
　　abounded
More with these dinners than the kill'd or
　　wounded;—

LIV

As thus: 'On Thursday there was a grand
　　dinner:
　　Present, Lords A.B.C.'—Earls, dukes,
　　　　by name
Announced with no less pomp than
　　victory's winner:
　　Then underneath, and in the very same
Column: date, 'Falmouth. There has
　　lately been here
　　The Slap-dash regiment, so well known
　　　　to fame,
Whose loss in the late action we regret:
The vacancies are fill'd up—see Gazette.'

LV

To Norman Abbey whirl'd the noble
　　pair,—
　　An old, old monastery once, and now
Still older mansion,—of a rich and rare
　　Mix'd Gothic, such as artists all allow
Few specimens yet left us can compare
　　Withal: it lies perhaps a little low,
Because the monks preferr'd a hill behind,
To shelter their devotion from the wind.

LVI

It stood embosom'd in a happy valley,
　　Crown'd by high woodlands, where the
　　　　Druid oak
Stood, like Caractacus in act to rally
　　His host, with broad arms 'gainst the
　　　　thunderstroke,
And from beneath his boughs were seen
　　to sally
　　The dappled foresters; as day awoke,
The branching stag swept down with all
　　his herd,
To quaff a brook which murmur'd like a
　　bird.

LVII

Before the mansion lay a lucid lake,
　　Broad as transparent, deep, and
　　　　freshly fed
By a river, which its soften'd way did take
　　In currents through the calmer water
　　　　spread
Around: the wildfowl nestled in the brake
　　And sedges, brooding in their liquid
　　　　bed:
The woods sloped downwards to its brink,
　　and stood
With their green faces fix'd upon the flood.

LVIII

Its outlet dash'd into a deep cascade,
　　Sparkling with foam, until again sub-
　　　　siding,
Its shriller echoes—like an infant made
　　Quiet—sank into softer ripples, gliding
Into a rivulet: and thus allay'd,
　　Pursued its course, now gleaming, and
　　　　now hiding
Its windings through the woods; now
　　clear, now blue,
According as the skies their shadows
　　threw.

LIX

A glorious remnant of the Gothic pile
　　(While yet the church was Rome's)
　　　　stood half apart
In a grand arch, which once screen'd
　　many an aisle.
　　These last had disappear'd—a loss to
　　　　art:
The first yet frown'd superbly o'er the soil,
　　And kindled feelings in the roughest
　　　　heart,
Which mourn'd the power of time's or
　　tempest's march,
In gazing on that venerable arch.

LX

Within a niche, nigh to its pinnacle,
　　Twelve saints had once stood sanctified
　　　　in stone;
But these had fallen, not when the friars
　　fell,
　　But in the war which struck Charles
　　　　from his throne,
When each house was a fortalice—as tell
　　The annals of full many a line undone,—
The gallant cavaliers, who fought in vain
For those who knew not to resign or reign.

LXI

But in a higher niche, alone, but crown'd,
　　The Virgin-Mother of the God-born
　　　　Child,
With her Son in her blessed arms, look'd
　　round;
　　Spared by some chance when all beside
　　　　was spoil'd;

She made the earth below seem holy
 ground.
  This may be superstition, weak or wild,
But even the faintest relics of a shrine
Of any worship wake some thoughts divine.

LXII

A mighty window, hollow in the centre,
  Shorn of its glass of thousand colour-
   ings,
Through which the deepen'd glories once
  could enter,
  Streaming from off the sun like seraph's
   wings,
Now yawns all desolate: now loud, now
  fainter,
  The gale sweeps through its fretwork,
   and oft sings
The owl his anthem, where the silenced
  quire
Lie with their hallelujahs quench'd like
  fire.

LXIII

But in the noontide of the moon, and when
  The wind is wingèd from one point of
   heaven,
There moans a strange unearthly sound,
  which then
  Is musical—a dying accent driven
Through the huge arch, which soars and
  sinks again.
  Some deem it but the distant echo given
Back to the night wind by the waterfall,
And harmonised by the old choral wall:

LXIV

Others, that some original shape, or form
  Shaped by decay perchance, hath given
   the power
(Though less than that of Memnon's
  statue, warm
  In Egypt's rays, to harp at a fix'd hour)
To this grey ruin, with a voice to charm
  Sad, but serene, it sweeps o'er tree or
   tower;
The cause I know not, nor can solve; but
  such
The fact:—I've heard it,—once perhaps
  too much.

LXV

Amidst the court a Gothic fountain play'd,
  Symmetrical, but deck'd with carvings
   quaint—
Strange faces, like to men in masquerade,
  And here perhaps a monster, there a
   saint:
The spring gush'd through grim mouths
  of granite made,
  And sparkled into basins, where it spent
Its little torrent in a thousand bubbles,
Like man's vain glory, and his vainer
  troubles.

LXVI

The mansion's self was vast and venerable,
  With more of the monastic than has
   been
Elsewhere preserved: the cloisters still
  were stable,
  The cells, too, and refectory, I ween:
An exquisite small chapel had been able,
  Still unimpair'd, to decorate the scene;
The rest had been reform'd, replaced, or
  sunk,
And spoke more of the baron than the
  monk.

LXVII

Huge halls, long galleries, spacious
  chambers, join'd
  By no quite lawful marriage of the arts,
Might shock a connoisseur; but when
  combined,
  Form'd a whole which, irregular in parts,
Yet left a grand impression on the mind,
  At least of those whose eyes are in their
   hearts:
We gaze upon a giant for his stature,
Nor judge at first if all be true to nature.

LXVIII

Steel barons, molten the next generation
  To silken rows of gay and garter'd earls,
Glanced from the walls in goodly pre-
  servation:
  And Lady Marys blooming into girls,
With fair long locks, had also kept their
  station:
  And countesses mature in robes and
   pearls:
Also some beauties of Sir Peter Lely,
Whose drapery hints we may admire
  them freely.

LXIX

Judges in very formidable ermine
  Were there, with brows that did not
   much invite
The accused to think their lordships would
  determine
  His cause by leaning much from might
   to right:
Bishops, who had not left a single sermon;
  Attorneys-general, awful to the sight,
As hinting more (unless our judgments
  warp us)
Of the 'Star Chamber' than of 'Habeas
  Corpus.'

LXX

Generals, some all in armour, of the old
  And iron time, ere lead had ta'en the
   lead;
Others in wigs of Marlborough's martial
  fold,
  Huger than twelve of our degenerate
   breed:

816

Lordlings, with staves of white or keys of
    gold:
  Nimrods, whose canvas scarce con-
    tain'd the steed;
And here and there some stern high
    patriot stood,
Who could not get the place for which he
    sued.

LXXI

But ever and anon, to soothe your vision,
  Fatigued with these hereditary glories,
There rose a Carlo Dolce or a Titian,
  Or wilder group of savage Salvatore's:
Here danced Albano's boys, and here the
    sea shone
  In Vernet's ocean lights; and there the
    stories
Of martyrs awed, as Spagnoletto tainted
His brush with all the blood of all the
    sainted.

LXXII

Here sweetly spread a landscape of Lor-
    raine;
  There Rembrandt made his darkness
    equal light,
Or gloomy Caravaggio's gloomier stain
  Bronzed o'er some lean and stoic
    anchorite:—
But, lo! a Teniers woos, and not in vain,
  Your eyes to revel in a livelier sight:
His bell-mouth'd goblet makes me feel
    quite Danish
Or Dutch with thirst—What, ho! a flask of
    Rhenish.

LXXIII

O reader! if that thou canst read,—and
    know,
  'Tis not enough to spell, or even to read,
To constitute a reader; there must go
  Virtues of which both you and I have
    need.
Firstly, begin with the beginning—(though
  That clause is hard); and secondly, pro-
    ceed:
Thirdly, commence not with the end—or,
    sinning
In this sort, end at least with the beginning.

LXXIV

But reader, thou hast patient been of late,
  While I, without remorse of rhyme, or
    fear,
Have built and laid out ground at such a
    rate,
  Dan Phœbus takes me for an auctioneer.
That poets were so from their earliest date,
  By Homer's 'Catalogue of ships' is
    clear;
But a mere modern must be moderate—
I spare you then the furniture and plate.

LXXV

The mellow autumn came, and with it
    came
  The promised party, to enjoy its sweets.
The corn is cut, the manor full of game;
  The pointer ranges, and the sportsman
    beats
In russet jacket:—lynx-like is his aim;
  Full grows his bag, and wonder*ful* his
    feats.
Ah, nutbrown partridges! Ah, brilliant
    pheasants!
And ah, ye poachers!—'Tis no sport for
    peasants.

LXXVI

An English autumn, though it hath no
    vines,
  Blushing with Bacchant coronals along
The paths, o'er which the far festoon
    entwines
  The red grape in the sunny lands of
    song,
Hath yet a purchased choice of choicest
    wines;
  The claret light, and the Madeira strong;
If Britain mourn her bleakness, we can tell
    her,
The very best of vineyards is the cellar.

LXXVII

Then, if she hath not that serene decline
  Which makes the southern autumn's
    day appear
As if 'twould to a second spring resign
  The season, rather than to winter
    drear,—
Of in-door comforts still she hath a mine,—
  The sea-coal fires, the 'earliest of the
    year';
Without doors, too, she may compete in
    mellow,
As what is lost in green is gain'd in yellow.

LXXVIII

And for the effeminate *villeggiatura*—
  Rife with more horns than hounds—she
    hath the chase,
So animated that it might allure a
  Saint from his beads to join the jocund
    race;
Even Nimrod's self might leave the plains
    of Dura,
  And wear the Melton jacket for a space:
If she hath no wild boars, she hath a tame
Preserve of bores, who ought to be made
    game.

LXXIX

The noble guests, assembled at the Abbey,
  Consisted of—we give the sex the *pas*—
The Duchess of Fitz-Fulke; the Countess
    Crabby;
  The Ladies Scilly, Busey;—Miss Eclat,

Miss Bombazeen, Miss Mackstay, Miss
  O'Tabby,
  And Mrs. Rabbi, the rich banker's
  squaw;
Also the honourable Mrs. Sleep,
Who look'd a white lamb, yet was a black
  sheep:

LXXX

With other Countesses of Blank—but
  rank;
  At once the 'lie' and the *élite* of
  crowds;
Who pass like water filter'd in a tank,
  All purged and pious from their native
  clouds;
Or paper turn'd to money by the Bank:
  No matter how or why, the passport
  shrouds
The *passée* and the past; for good
  society
Is no less famed for tolerance than piety,—

LXXXI

That is, up to a certain point; which point
  Forms the most difficult in punctua-
  tion.
Appearances appear to form the joint
  On which it hinges in a higher station;
And so that no explosion cry 'Aroint
  Thee, witch!' or each Medea has her
  Jason;
Or (to the point with Horace and with
  Pulci)
'*Omne tulit punctum, quæ miscuit utile
  dulci.*'

LXXXII

I can't exactly trace their rule of right,
  Which hath a little leaning to a lottery.
I've seen a virtuous woman put down
  quite
  By the mere combination of a coterie;
Also a so-so matron boldly fight
  Her way back to the world by dint of
  plottery,
And shine the very *Siria* of the spheres,
Escaping with a few slight, scarless sneers.

LXXXIII

I have seen more than I'll say:—but we
  will see
  How *our* '*villeggiatura*' will get on.
The party might consist of thirty-three
  Of highest caste—the Brahmins of the
  ton.
I have named a few, not foremost in
  degree,
  But ta'en at hazard as the rhyme may
  run,
By way of sprinkling, scatter'd amongst
  these
There also were some Irish absentees.

LXXXIV

There was Parolles, too, the legal bully,
  Who limits all his battles to the bar
And senate: when invited elsewhere, truly,
  He shows more appetite for words than
  war.
There was the young bard Rackrhyme,
  who had newly
  Come out and glimmer'd as a six weeks'
  star.
There was Lord Pyrrho, too, the great
  freethinker;
And Sir John Pottledeep, the mighty
  drinker.

LXXXV

There was the Duke of Dash, who was a—
  duke,
  'Ay, every inch a' duke; there were
  twelve peers
Like Charlemagne's—and all such peers
  in *look*
  And *intellect*, that neither eyes nor
  ears
For commoners had ever them mistook.
  There were the six Miss Rawbolds—
  pretty dears!
All song and sentiment; whose hearts were
  set
Less on a convent than a coronet.

LXXXVI

There were four Honourable Misters,
  whose
  Honour was more before their names
  than after;
There was the *preux Chevalier de la
  Ruse*,
  Whom France and Fortune lately
  deign'd to waft here,
Whose chiefly harmless talent was to
  amuse;
  But the clubs found it rather serious
  laughter,
Because—such was his magic power to
  please—
The dice seem'd charm'd, too, with his re-
  partees.

LXXXVII

There was Dick Dubious, the metaphysi-
  cian,
  Who loved philosophy and a good
  dinner;
Angle, the *soi-disant* mathematician;
  Sir Henry Silvercup, the great race-
  winner.
There was the Reverend Rodomont Pre-
  cisian,
  Who did not hate so much the sin as
  sinner;
And Lord Augustus Fitz-Plantagenet,
Good at all things, but better at a bet.

LXXXVIII

There was Jack Jargon, the gigantic
 guardsman;
 And General Fireface, famous in the
 field,
A great tactician, and no less a swordsman,
 Who ate, last war, more Yankees than
 he kill'd.
There was the waggish Welsh Judge,
 Jefferies Hardsman,
 In his grave office so completely skill'd,
That when a culprit came for condemna-
 tion,
He had his judge's joke for consolation.

LXXXIX

Good company's a chess-board—there
 are kings,
 Queens, bishops, knights, rooks, pawns;
 the world's a game;
Save that the puppets pull at their own
 strings,
 Methinks gay Punch hath something
 of the same.
My Muse, the butterfly hath but her wings,
 Not stings, and flits through ether with-
 out aim,
Alighting rarely:—were she but a hornet,
 Perhaps there might be vices which would
 mourn it.

XC

I had forgotten—but must not forget—
 An orator, the latest of the session,
Who had deliver'd well a very set
 Smooth speech, his first and maidenly
 transgression
Upon debate: the papers echoed yet
 With this *début*, which made a strong
 impression,
And rank'd with what is every day dis-
 play'd—
'The best first speech that ever yet was made.'

XCI

Proud of his 'Hear hims!' proud, too, of
 his vote
 And lost virginity of oratory,
Proud of his learning (just enough to quote),
 He revell'd in his Ciceronian glory:
With memory excellent to get by rote,
 With wit to hatch a pun or tell a story,
Graced with some merit, and with more
 effrontery,
'His country's pride,' he came down to the
 country.

XCII

There also were two wits by acclamation,
 Longbow from Ireland, Strongbow
 from the Tweed,
Both lawyers and both men of education;
 But Strongbow's wit was of more
 polish'd breed;

Longbow was rich in an imagination
 As beautiful and bounding as a steed,
But sometimes stumbling over a potato,—
 While Strongbow's best things might have
 come from Cato.

XCIII

Strongbow was like a new-tuned harpsi-
 chord;
 But Longbow wild as an Æolian harp,
With which the winds of heaven can claim
 accord,
 And make a music, whether flat or
 sharp.
Of Strongbow's talk you would not change
 a word:
 At Longbow's phrases you might some-
 times carp:
Both wits—one born so, and the other
 bred,
This by his heart—his rival by his head.

XCIV

If all these seem an heterogeneous mass
 To be assembled at a country seat,
Yet think, a specimen of every class
 Is better than an humdrum tête-à-tête.
The days of Comedy are gone, alas!
 When Congreve's fool could vie with
 Molière's *bête:*
Society is smooth'd to that excess,
That manners hardly differ more than
 dress.

XCV

Our ridicules are kept in the back ground—
 Ridiculous enough, but also dull;
Professions, too, are no more to be found
 Professional; and there is nought to
 cull
Of folly's fruit; for though your fools
 abound,
 They're barren, and not worth the pains
 to pull.
Society is now one polish'd horde,
Form'd of two mighty tribes, the *Bores*
 and *Bored.*

XCVI

But from being farmers, we turn gleaners,
 gleaning
 The scanty but right-well thresh'd ears
 of truth;
And, gentle reader! when you gather
 meaning,
 You may be Boaz, and I—modest Ruth.
Further I'd quote, but Scripture inter-
 vening
 Forbids. A great impression in my
 youth
Was made by Mrs. Adams, where she cries
'That Scriptures out of church are blas-
 phemies.'

XCVII

But what we can we glean in this vile age
  Of chaff, although our gleanings be not
  grist.
I must not quite omit the talking sage,
  Kit-Cat, the famous Conversationist,
Who, in his common-place book, had a
  page
  Prepared each morn for evenings.
  'List, oh list!'
'Alas, poor ghost!'—What unexpected
  woes
Await those who have studied their *bons-
  mots!*

XCVIII

Firstly, they must allure the conversation
  By many windings to their clever clinch;
And secondly, must let slip no occasion,
  Nor *bate* (abate) their hearers of an *inch*,
But take an ell—and make a great sensation,
  If possible; and thirdly, never flinch
When some smart talker puts them to the
  test,
But seize the last word, which no doubt's
  the best.

XCIX

Lord Henry and his lady were the hosts;
  The party we have touch'd on were the
  guests.
Their table was a board to tempt even
  ghosts
  To pass the Styx for more substantial
  feasts.
I will not dwell upon *ragoûts* or roasts,
  Albeit all human history attests
That happiness for man—the hungry sin-
  ner!—
Since Eve ate apples, much depends on
  dinner.

C

Witness the lands which 'flow'd with milk
  and honey,'
  Held out unto the hungry Israelites:
To this we have added since, the love of
  money,
  The only sort of pleasure which requites.
Youth fades, and leaves our days no
  longer sunny;
  We tire of mistresses and parasites;
But oh, ambrosial cash! Ah! who would
  lose thee?
When we no more can use, or even abuse
  thee!

CI

The gentlemen got up betimes to shoot,
  Or hunt: the young, because they liked
  the sport—
The first thing boys like after play and fruit;
  The middle-aged, to make the day more
  short;

For *ennui* is a growth of English root,
  Though nameless in our language:—we
  retort
The fact for words, and let the French
  translate
That awful yawn which sleep cannot abate.

CII

The elderly walk'd through the library,
  And tumbled books, or criticised the
  pictures,
Or saunter'd through the gardens piteous-
  ly,
  And made upon the hot-house several
  strictures,
Or rode a nag which trotted not too high,
  Or on the morning papers read their
  lectures,
Or on the watch their longing eyes would fix,
Longing at sixty for the hour of six.

CIII

But none were *gêné*: the great hour of
  union
  Was rung by dinner's knell; till then all
  were
Masters of their own time—or in communion,
  Or solitary, as they chose to bear
The hours, which how to pass is but to few
  known.
  Each rose up at his own, and had to
  spare
What time he chose for dress, and broke
  his fast
When, where, and how he chose for that
  repast.

CIV

The ladies—some rouged, some a little
  pale—
  Met the morn as they might. If fine,
  they rode,
Or walk'd; if foul, they read, or told a tale,
  Sung, or rehearsed the last dance from
  abroad;
Discuss'd the fashion which might next
  prevail,
  And settled bonnets by the newest code,
Or cramm'd twelve sheets into one little
  letter,
To make each correspondent a new debtor.

CV

For some had absent lovers, all had friends.
  The earth has nothing like a she epistle,
And hardly heaven—because it never ends.
  I love the mystery of a female missal,
Which, like a creed, ne'er says all it in-
  tends,
  But full of cunning as Ulysses' whistle,
When he allured poor Dolon:—you had
  better
Take care what you reply to such a letter.

CVI

Then there were billiards; cards, too, but
          _no_ dice;—
    Save in the clubs no man of honour
        plays;—
Boats when 'twas water, skating when
        'twas ice,
    And the hard frost destroy'd the scent-
        ing days:
And angling, too, that solitary vice,
    Whatever Izaak Walton sings or says:
The quaint, old, cruel coxcomb, in his
        gullet
Should have a hook, and a small trout to
        pull it.

CVII

With evening came the banquet and the
        wine;
    The conversazione; the duet,
Attuned by voices more or less divine
    (My heart or head aches with the mem-
        ory yet).
The four Miss Rawbolds in a glee would
        shine;
    But the two youngest loved more to be
        set
Down to the harp—because to music's
        charms
They added graceful necks, white hands
        and arms.

CVIII

Sometimes a dance (though rarely on field
        days,
    For then the gentlemen were rather
        tired)
Display'd some sylph-like figures in its
        maze;
    Then there was small-talk ready when
        required;
Flirtation—but decorous; the mere praise
    Of charms that should or should not be
        admired.
The hunters fought their fox-hunt o'er
        again,
And then retreated soberly—at ten.

CIX

The politicians, in a nook apart,
    Discuss'd the world, and settled all the
        spheres;
The wits watch'd every loophole for their
        art,
    To introduce a _bon-mot_ head and
        ears;
Small is the rest of those who would be
        smart,
    A moment's good thing may have cost
        them years
Before they find an hour to introduce it;
And then, even _then_, some bore may make
        them lose it.

CX

But all was gentle and aristocratic
    In this our party; polish'd, smooth, and
        cold,
As Phidian forms cut out of marble Attic.
    There now are no Squire Westerns as
        of old;
And our Sophias are not so emphatic,
    But fair as then, or fairer to behold.
We have no accomplish'd blackguards,
        like Tom Jones,
But gentlemen in stays, as stiff as stones.

CXI

They separated at an early hour;
    That is, ere midnight—which is Lon-
        don's noon;
But in the country ladies seek their bower
    A little earlier than the waning moon.
Peace to the slumbers of each folded
        flower—
    May the rose call back its true colours
        soon!
Good hours of fair cheeks are the fairest
        tinters,
And lower the price of rouge—at least
        some winters.

CANTO THE FOURTEENTH

I

If from great nature's or our own abyss
    Of thought we could but snatch a cer-
        tainty,
Perhaps mankind might find the path they
        miss—
    But then 'twould spoil much good philo-
        sophy.
One system eats another up, and this
    Much as old Saturn ate his progeny;
For when his pious consort gave him
        stones
In lieu of sons, of these he made no bones.

II

But System doth reverse the Titan's break-
        fast,
    And eats her parents, albeit the digestion
Is difficult. Pray tell me, can you make fast,
    After due search, your faith to any
        question?
Look back o'er ages, ere unto the stake fast
    You bind yourself, and call some mode
        the best one.
Nothing more true than _not_ to trust your
        senses;
And yet what are your other evidences?

III

For me, I know nought; nothing I deny,
    Admit, reject, contemn; and what know
        you,
Except perhaps that you were born to die?
    And both may after all turn out untrue.

An age may come, Font of Eternity,
  When nothing shall be either old or new.
Death, so call'd, is a thing which makes
    men weep,
And yet a third of life is pass'd in sleep.

IV

A sleep without dreams, after a rough day
  Of toil, is what we covet most; and yet
How clay shrinks back from more quies-
    cent clay!
  The very Suicide that pays his debt
At once without instalments (an old way
  Of paying debts, which creditors regret),
Lets out impatiently his rushing breath,
Less from disgust of life than dread of
    death.

V

'Tis round him, near him, here, there,
    everywhere,
  And there's a courage which grows out
    of fear,
Perhaps of all most desperate, which will
    dare
  The worst to *know* it:—when the moun-
    tains rear
Their peaks beneath your human foot, and
    there
  You look down o'er the precipice, and
    drear
The gulf of rock yawns,—you can't gaze a
    minute,
Without an awful wish to plunge within it.

VI

'Tis true, you don't—but, pale and struck
    with terror,
  Retire: but look into your past im-
    pression!
And you will find, though shuddering at
    the mirror
  Of your own thoughts, in all their self-
    confession,
The lurking bias, be it truth or error,
  To the *unknown;* a secret prepossession,
To plunge with all your fears—but where?
    You know not,
And that's the reason why you do—or
    do not.

VII

But what's this to the purpose? you will say.
  Gent. reader, nothing; a mere specula-
    tion,
For which my sole excuse is—'tis my way;
  Sometimes *with* and sometimes without
    occasion,
I write what's uppermost, without delay;
  This narrative is not meant for narra-
    tion,
But a mere airy and fantastic basis,
To build up common things with common
    places.

VIII

You know, or don't know, that great
    Bacon saith,
  'Fling up a straw, 'twill show the way
    the wind blows;'
And such a straw, borne on by human
    breath,
  Is poesy, according as the mind glows;
A paper kite which flies 'twixt life and
    death,
  A shadow which the onward soul be-
    hind throws:
And mine's a bubble, not blown up for
    praise,
But just to play with, as an infant plays.

IX

The world is all before me—or behind;
  For I have seen a portion of that same,
And quite enough for me to keep in
    mind;—
  Of passions, too, I have proved enough
    to blame,
To the great pleasure of our friends, man-
    kind,
  Who like to mix some slight alloy with
    fame;
For I was rather famous in my time,
Until I fairly knock'd it up with rhyme.

X

I have brought this world about my ears,
    and eke
  The other; that's to say, the clergy—
    who
Upon my head have bid their thunders
    break
  In pious libels by no means a few.
And yet I can't help scribbling once a week,
  Tiring old readers, nor discovering new.
In youth I wrote because my mind was full,
And *now* because I feel it growing dull.

XI

But 'why then publish?'—There are no
    rewards,
  Of fame or profit when the world grows
    weary.
I ask in turn,—Why do you play at cards?
  Why drink? Why read?—To make
    some hour less dreary.
It occupies me to turn back regards
  On what I've seen or ponder'd, sad or
    cheery;
And what I write I cast upon the stream,
To swim or sink—I have had at least my
    dream.

XII

I think that were I *certain* of success,
  I hardly could compose another line:
So long I've battled either more or less,
  That no defeat can drive me from the
    Nine.

This feeling 'tis not easy to express,
  And yet 'tis not affected, I opine.
In play, there are two pleasures for your
      choosing—
The one is winning, and the other losing.

XIII

Besides, my Muse by no means deals in
      fiction:
  She gathers a repertory of facts,
Of course with some reserve and slight
      restriction,
  But mostly sings of human things and
      acts—
And that's one cause she meets with con-
      tradiction;
  For too much truth, at first sight, ne'er
      attracts;
And were her object only what's call'd
      glory,
With more ease too she'd tell a different
      story.

XIV

Love, war, a tempest—surely there's
      variety:
  Also a seasoning slight of lucubration;
A bird's-eye-view, too, of that wild,
      Society;
  A slight glance thrown on men of every
      station.
If you have nought else, here's at least
      satiety,
  Both in performance and in prepara-
      tion;
And though these lines should only line
      portmanteaus,
Trade will be all the better for these
      Cantos.

XV

The portion of this world which I at
      present
  Have taken up to fill the following ser-
      mon,
Is one of which there's no description
      recent:
  The reason why, is easy to determine:
Although it seems both prominent and
      pleasant,
  There is a sameness in its gems and
      ermine,
A dull and family likeness through all
      ages,
Of no great promise for poetic pages.

XVI

With much to excite, there's little to exalt;
  Nothing that speaks to all men and all
      times;
A sort of varnish over every fault;
  A kind of common-place, even in their
      crimes;

Factitious passions, wit without much salt,
  A want of that true nature which
      sublimes
Whate'er it shows with truth; a smooth
      monotony
Of character, in those at least who have
      got any.

XVII

Sometimes, indeed, like soldiers off parade,
  They break their ranks and gladly leave
      the drill;
But then the roll-call draws them back
      afraid,
  And they must be or seem what they
      were: still
Doubtless it is a brilliant masquerade:
  But when of the first sight you have had
      your fill,
It palls—at least it did so upon me,
This paradise of pleasure and *ennui*.

XVIII

When we have made our love, and gamed
      our gaming,
  Drest, voted, shone, and, may be, some-
      thing more;
With dandies dined; heard senators de-
      claiming;
  Seen beauties brought to market by the
      score,
Sad rakes to sadder husbands chastely
      taming;
  There's little left but to be bored or
      bore.
Witness those *ci-devant jeunes hommes*
      who stem
The stream, nor leave the world which
      leaveth them.

XIX

'Tis said—indeed a general complaint—
  That no one has succeeded in describing
The *monde*, exactly as they ought to paint:
  Some say, that authors only snatch, by
      bribing
The porter, some slight scandals strange
      and quaint,
  To furnish matter for their moral
      gibing;
And that their books have but one style in
      common—
My lady's prattle, filter'd through her
      woman.

XX

But this can't well be true, just now; for
      writers
  Are grown of the *beau monde* a part
      potential:
I've seen them balance even the scale with
      fighters,
  Especially when young, for that's essen-
      tial.

Why do their sketches fail them as inditers
  Of what they deem themselves most
    consequential,
The *real* portrait of the highest tribe?
'Tis that, in fact, there's little to describe.

XXI

'*Haud ignara loquor;*' these are *Nugæ,*
    '*quarum*
  Pars parva *fui,*' but still art and part.
Now I could much more easily sketch a
    harem,
  A battle, wreck, or history of the heart,
Than these things; and besides, I wish to
    spare 'em,
  For reasons which I choose to keep
    apart.
'*Vetabo Cereris sacrum qui vulgarit*'—
  Which means, that vulgar people must
    not share it.

XXII

And therefore what I throw off is ideal—
  Lower'd, leaven'd, like a history of free-
    masons,
Which bears the same relation to the real,
  As Captain Parry's voyage may do to
    Jason's.
The grand *arcanum's* not for men to see
    all;
  My music has some mystic diapasons;
And there is much which could not be
    appreciated
In any manner by the uninitiated.

XXIII

Alas! worlds fall—and woman, since she
    fell'd
  The world (as, since that history, less
    polite
Than true, hath been a creed so strictly
    held),
  Has not yet given up the practice quite.
Poor thing of usages! coerced, compell'd,
  Victim when wrong, and martyr oft
    when right,
Condemn'd to child-bed, as men for their
    sins
Have shaving too entail'd upon their
    chins,—

XXIV

A daily plague, which in the aggregate
  May average on the whole with parturi-
    tion.
But as to women, who can penetrate
  The real sufferings of their she con-
    dition?
Man's very sympathy with their estate
  Has much of selfishness, and more sus-
    picion.
Their love, their virtue, beauty, education,
But form good housekeepers, to breed a
    nation.

XXV

All this were very well, and can't be better;
  But even this is difficult, Heaven knows,
So many troubles from her birth beset her,
  Such small distinction between friends
    and foes,
The gilding wears so soon from off her
    fetter,
  That——but ask any woman if she'd
    choose
(Take her at thirty, that is) to have been
Female or male? a schoolboy or a queen?

XXVI

'Petticoat influence' is a great reproach,
  Which even those who obey would fain
    be thought
To fly from, as from hungry pikes a roach;
  But since beneath it upon earth we are
    brought,
By various joltings of life's hackney coach,
  I for one venerate a petticoat—
A garment of a mystical sublimity,
No matter whether russet, silk, or dimity.

XXVII

Much I respect, and much I have adored,
  In my young days, that chaste and
    goodly veil,
Which holds a treasure, like a miser's
    hoard,
    And more attracts by all it doth con-
      ceal—
A golden scabbard on a Damasque sword,
  A loving letter with a mystic seal,
A cure for grief—for what can ever rankle
Before a petticoat and peeping ankle?

XXVIII

And when upon a silent, sullen day,
  With a sirocco, for example, blowing,
When even the sea looks dim with all its
    spray,
  And sulkily the river's ripple's flowing,
And the sky shows that very ancient gray,
  The sober, sad antithesis to glowing,—
'Tis pleasant, if *then* anything is pleasant,
To catch a glimpse even of a pretty
    peasant.

XXIX

We left our heroes and our heroines
  In that fair clime which don't depend on
    climate,
Quite independent of the Zodiac's signs,
  Though certainly more difficult to
    rhyme at,
Because the sun, and stars, and aught that
    shines,
  Mountains, and all we can be most
    sublime at,
Are there oft dull and dreary as a *dun*—
Whether a sky's or tradesman's is all one.

XXX

And in-door life is less poetical;
   And out-of-door hath showers, and
      mists, and sleet,
With which I could not brew a pastoral.
   But be it as it may, a bard must meet
All difficulties, whether great or small,
   To spoil his undertaking, or complete,
And work away like spirit upon matter,
Embarrass'd somewhat both with fire and
      water.

XXXI

Juan—in this respect, at least, like saints—
   Was all things unto people of all sorts,
And lived contentedly, without com-
      plaints,
   In camps, in ships, in cottages, or
      courts—
Born with that happy soul which seldom
      faints,
   And mingling modestly in toils or
      sports.
He likewise could be most things to all
      women,
Without the coxcombry of certain *she*
      men.

XXXII

A fox-hunt to a foreigner is strange;
   'Tis also subject to the double danger
Of tumbling first, and having in exchange
   Some pleasant jesting at the awkward
      stranger;
But Juan had been early taught to range
   The wilds, as doth an Arab turn'd
      avenger,
So that his horse, or charger, hunter, hack,
Knew that he had a rider on his back.

XXXIII

And now in this new field, with some ap-
      plause,
   He clear'd hedge, ditch, and double
      post, and rail,
And never *craned*, and made but few '*faux
      pas*,'
   And only fretted when the scent 'gan
      fail.
He broke, 'tis true, some statutes of the
      laws
   Of hunting—for the sagest youth is
      frail;
Rode o'er the hounds, it may be, now and
      then,
And once o'er several country gentlemen.

XXXIV

But on the whole, to general admiration
   He acquitted both himself and horse:
      the squires
Marvell'd at merit of another nation;
   The boors cried 'Dang it! who'd have
      thought it?'—Sires,

The Nestors of the sporting generation,
   Swore praises, and recall'd their former
      fires;
The huntsman's self relented to a grin,
And rated him almost a whipper-in.

XXXV

Such were his trophies—not of spear and
      shield,
   But leaps, and bursts, and sometimes
      foxes' brushes;
Yet I must own,—although in this I yield
   To patriot sympathy a Briton's blush-
      es,—
He thought at heart like courtly Chester-
      field,
   Who, after a long chase o'er hills, dales,
      bushes,
And what not, though he rode beyond all
      price,
Ask'd next day, 'If men ever hunted
      twice?'

XXXVI

He also had a quality uncommon
   To early risers after a long chase,
Who wake in winter ere the cock can sum-
      mon
   December's drowsy day to his dull
      race,—
A quality agreeable to woman,
   When her soft, liquid words run on
      apace,
Who likes a listener, whether saint or sin-
      ner,—
He did not fall asleep just after dinner;

XXXVII

But, light and airy, stood on the alert,
   And shone in the best part of dialogue,
By humouring always what they might
      assert,
   And listening to the topics most in
      vogue,—
Now grave, now gay, but never dull or
      pert;
   And smiling but in secret—cunning
      rogue!—
He ne'er presumed to make an error
      clearer;—
In short, there never was a better hearer.

XXXVIII

And then he danced,—all foreigners excel
   The serious Angles in the eloquence
Of pantomime,—he danced, I say, right
      well,
   With emphasis, and also with good
      sense—
A thing in footing indispensable;
   He danced without theatrical pretence,
Not like a ballet-master in the van
Of his drill'd nymphs, but like a gentle-
      man.

XXXIX

Chaste were his steps, each kept within
    due bound,
    And elegance was sprinkled o'er his
    figure;
Like swift Camilla, he scarce skimm'd the
    ground,
    And rather held in than put forth his
    vigour;
And then he had an ear for music's sound,
    Which might defy a crotchet critic's
    rigour.
Such classic *pas*—sans flaws—set off our
    hero,
He glanced like a personified Bolero;

XL

Or, like a flying Hour before Aurora,
    In Guido's famous fresco, which alone
Is worth a tour to Rome, although no
    more a
    Remnant were there of the old world's
    sole throne.
The '*tout ensemble*' of his movements
    wore a
    Grace of the soft ideal, seldom shown,
And ne'er to be described; for to the dolour
Of bards and prosers, words are void of
    colour.

XLI

No marvel then he was a favourite;
    A full-grown Cupid, very much ad-
    mired;
A little spoilt, but by no means so quite;
    At least he kept his vanity retired.
Such was his tact, he could alike delight
    The chaste, and those who are not so
    much inspired.
The Duchess of Fitz-Fulke, who loved
    tracasserie,
Began to treat him with some small *aga-*
    cerie.

XLII

She was a fine and somewhat full-blown
    blonde,
    Desirable, distinguish'd, celebrated
For several winters in the grand, *grand*
    monde.
    I'd rather not say what might be related
Of her exploits, for this were ticklish
    ground;
    Besides there might be falsehood in
    what's stated;
Her late performance had been a dead set
At Lord Augustus Fitz-Plantagenet.

XLIII

This noble personage began to look
    A little black upon this new flirtation;
But such small licences must lovers brook,
    Mere freedoms of the female corpora-
    tion.

Woe to the man who ventures a rebuke!
    'Twill but precipitate a situation
Extremely disagreeable, but common
To calculators when they count on woman.

XLIV

The circle smiled, then whisper'd, and then
    sneer'd;
    The misses bridled, and the matrons
    frown'd;
Some hoped things might not turn out as
    they fear'd;
    Some would not deem such women
    could be found;
Some ne'er believed one half of what they
    heard;
    Some look'd perplex'd, and others look'd
    profound;
And several pitied with sincere regret
Poor Lord Augustus Fitz-Plantagenet.

XLV

But what is odd, none ever named the
    duke,
    Who, one might think, was something
    in the affair:
True, he was absent, and, 'twas rumour'd,
    took
    But small concern about the when, or
    where,
Or what his consort did: if he could brook
    Her gaieties, none had a right to stare:
Theirs was that best of unions, past all
    doubt,
Which never meets, and therefore can't fall
    out.

XLVI

But, oh! that I should ever pen so sad a line!
    Fired with an abstract love of virtue, she,
My Dian of the Ephesians, Lady Adeline,
    Regretting much that she had chosen so
    bad a line,
    And waxing chiller in her courtesy,
Look'd grave and pale to see her friend's
    fragility,
For which most friends reserve their sensi-
    bility.

XLVII

There's nought in this bad world like
    sympathy;
    'Tis so becoming to the soul and face,
Sets to soft music the harmonious sigh,
    And robes sweet friendship in a Brussels
    lace.
Without a friend, what were humanity,
    To hunt our errors up with a good grace?
Consoling us with—'Would you had
    thought twice!
Ah! if you had but follow'd my advice!'

XLVIII

O Job! you had two friends: one's quite
      enough,
   Especially when we are ill at ease;
They are but bad pilots when the weather's
      rough,
   Doctors less famous for their cures than
      fees.
Let no man grumble when his friends fall off,
   As they will do like leaves at the first
      breeze:
When your affairs come round, one way
      or t'other,
Go to the coffee-house, and take another.

XLIX

But this is not my maxim: had it been,
   Some heart-aches had been spared me:
      yet I care not—
I would not be a tortoise in his screen
   Of stubborn shell, which waves and
      weather wear not;
'Tis better on the whole to have felt and
      seen
   That which humanity may bear, or bear
      not:
'Twill teach discernment to the sensitive,
And not to pour their ocean in a sieve.

L

Of all the horrid, hideous notes of woe,
   Sadder than owl-songs or the midnight
      blast,
Is that portentous phrase, 'I told you so,'
   Utter'd by friends, those prophets of the
      past,
Who, 'stead of saying what you *now*
      should do,
   Own they foresaw that you would fall
      at last,
And solace your slight lapse 'gainst *bonos
      mores*,
With a long memorandum of old stories.

LI

The Lady Adeline's serene severity
   Was not confined to feeling for her
      friend,
Whose fame she rather doubted with pos-
      terity,
   Unless her habits should begin to mend:
But Juan also shared in her austerity,
   But mix'd with pity, pure as e'er was
      penn'd:
His inexperience moved her gentle ruth,
And (as her junior by six weeks) his youth.

LII

These forty days' advantage of her years—
   And hers were those which can face cal-
      culation,
Boldly referring to the list of peers
   And noble births, nor dread the enume-
      ration—

Gave her a right to have maternal fears
   For a young gentleman's fit education;
Though she was far from that leap year,
      whose leap,
In female dates, strikes Time all of a
      heap.

LIII

This may be fix'd at somewhere before
      thirty—
   Say seven-and-twenty; for I never knew
The strictest in chronology and virtue
   Advance beyond, while they could pass
      for new.
O Time! why dost not pause? Thy scythe,
      so dirty
   With rust, should surely cease to hack
      and hew.
Reset it: shave more smoothly, also
      slower,
If but to keep thy credit as a mower.

LIV

But Adeline was far from that ripe age,
   Whose ripeness is but bitter at the best:
'Twas rather her experience made her sage,
   For she had seen the world and stood
      its test,
As I have said in—I forget what page;
   My Muse despises reference, as you
      have guess'd
By this time;—but strike six from seven-
      and-twenty,
And you will find her sum of years in
      plenty.

LV

At sixteen she came out; presented,
      vaunted,
   She put all coronets into commotion:
At seventeen, too, the world was still en-
      chanted
   With the new Venus of their brilliant
      ocean:
At eighteen, though below her feet still
      panted
   A hecatomb of suitors with devotion,
She had consented to create again
That Adam, call'd 'the happiest of men.'

LVI

Since then she had sparkled through three
      glowing winters,
   Admired, adored; but also so correct,
That she had puzzled all the acutest hinters,
   Without the apparel of being circum-
      spect:
They could not even glean the slightest
      splinters
   From off the marble, which had no defect.
She had also snatch'd a moment since her
      marriage
To bear a son and heir—and one miscar-
      riage.

LVII

Fondly the wheeling fire-flies flew around
  her,
  Those little glitterers of the London night;
But none of these possess'd a sting to
    wound her—
  She was a pitch beyond a coxcomb's
    flight.
Perhaps she wish'd an aspirant pro-
    founder;
  But whatsoe'er she wish'd, she acted right;
And whether coldness, pride, or virtue,
    dignify
A woman, so she's good, what *does* it signify?

LVIII

I hate a motive, like a lingering bottle
  Which with the landlord makes too long
    a stand,
Leaving all claretless the unmoisten'd
    throttle,
  Especially with politics on hand;
I hate it, as I hate a drove of cattle,
  Who whirl the dust as simooms whirl
    the sand;
I hate it, as I hate an argument,
A laureate's ode, or servile peer's 'Con-
    tent.'

LIX

'Tis sad to hack into the roots of things,
  They are so much intertwisted with the
    earth;
So that the branch a goodly verdure flings,
  I reck not if an acorn gave it birth.
To trace all actions to their secret springs
  Would make indeed some melancholy
    mirth;
But this is not at present my concern,
And I refer you to wise Oxenstiern.

LX

With the kind view of saving an *éclat*,
  Both to the duchess and diplomatist,
The Lady Adeline, as soon's she saw
  That Juan was unlikely to resist—
(For foreigners don't know that a *faux pas*
  In England ranks quite on a different list
From those of other lands unblest with
    juries,
Whose verdict for such sin a certain cure
    is;—)

LXI

The Lady Adeline resolved to take
  Such measures as she thought might
    best impede
The further progress of this sad mistake.
  She thought with some simplicity indeed;
But innocence is bold even at the stake,
  And simple in the world, and doth not
    need
Nor use those palisades by dames erected,
Whose virtue lies in never being detected.

LXII

It was not that she fear'd the very worst:
  His Grace was an enduring, married
    man,
And was not likely all at once to burst
  Into a scene, and swell the clients' clan
Of Doctors' Commons: but she dreaded
    first
  The magic of her Grace's talisman,
And next a quarrel (as he seem'd to fret)
With Lord Augustus Fitz-Plantagenet.

LXIII

Her Grace, too, pass'd for being an *intri-
    gante*,
  And somewhat *méchante* in her amor-
    ous sphere:
One of those pretty, precious plagues,
    which haunt
  A lover with caprices soft and dear,
That like to *make* a quarrel, when they can't
  Find one, each day of the delightful year;
Bewitching, torturing, as they freeze or
    glow,
And—what is worst of all—won't let you
    go;

LXIV

The sort of thing to turn a young man's
    head,
  Or make a Werter of him in the end.
No wonder then a purer soul should dread
  This sort of chaste *liaison* for a friend;
It were much better to be wed or dead,
  Than wear a heart a woman loves to
    rend.
'Tis best to pause, and think, ere you rush
    on,
If that a '*bonne fortune*' be really '*bonne*.'

LXV

And first, in the o'erflowing of her heart,
  Which really knew or thought it knew
    no guile,
She call'd her husband now and then apart,
  And bade him counsel Juan. With a
    smile
Lord Henry heard her plans of artless art
  To wean Don Juan from the siren's wile;
And answer'd, like a statesman or a
    prophet,
In such guise that she could make nothing
    of it.

LXVI

Firstly, he said, 'he never interfered
  In anybody's business but the king's':
Next, that 'he never judged from what
    appear'd,
  Without strong reason, of those sorts of
    things':
Thirdly, that 'Juan had more brain than
    beard,
  And was not to be held in leading-
    strings';

And fourthly, what need hardly be said
twice,
'That good but rarely came from good
advice.'

LXVII

And, therefore, doubtless to approve the
truth
Of the last axiom, he advised his spouse
To leave the parties to themselves, for-
sooth—
At least as far as *bienséance* allows:
That time would temper Juan's faults of
youth;
That young men rarely made monastic
vows;
That opposition only more attaches——
But here a messenger brought in des-
patches:

LXVIII

And being of the council call'd 'the Privy,'
Lord Henry walk'd into his cabinet,
To furnish matter for some future Livy
To tell how he reduced the nation's
debt;
And if their full contents I do not give ye,
It is because I do not know them yet;
But I shall add them in a brief appendix,
To come between mine epic and its index.

LXIX

But ere he went, he added a slight hint,
Another gentle common-place or two,
Such as are coin'd in conversation's mint,
And pass, for want of better, though
not new:
Then broke his packet, to see what was
in't,
And having casually glanced it through,
Retired: and, as he went out, calmly kiss'd
her,
Less like a young wife than an aged sister.

LXX

He was a cold, good, honourable man,
Proud of his birth, and proud of every-
thing;
A goodly spirit for a state divan,
A figure fit to walk before a king;
Tall, stately, form'd to lead the courtly van
On birthdays, glorious with a star and
string;
The very model of a chamberlain—
And such I mean to make him when I
reign.

LXXI

But there was something wanting on the
whole—
I don't know what, and therefore cannot tell—
Which pretty women—the sweet souls!—
call *soul*.
Certes it was not body; he was well

Proportion'd, as a poplar or a pole,
A handsome man, that human miracle;
And in each circumstance of love or war
Had still preserved his perpendicular.

LXXII

Still there was something wanting, as I've
said—
That undefinable '*Je ne sçais quoi,*'
Which, for what I know, may of yore have
led
To Homer's Iliad, since it drew to Troy
The Greek Eve, Helen, from the Spartan's
bed;
Though on the whole, no doubt, the
Dardan boy
Was much inferior to King Menelaüs:—
But thus it is some women will betray us.

LXXIII

There is an awkward thing which much
perplexes,
Unless like wise Tiresias we had proved
By turns the difference of the several sexes;
Neither can show quite *how* they would
be loved.
The sensual for a short time but connects
us—
The sentimental boasts to be unmoved;
But both together form a kind of centaur,
Upon whose back 'tis better not to venture.

LXXIV

A something all-sufficient for the *heart*
Is that for which the sex are always seeking:
But how to fill up that same vacant part?
There lies the rub—and this they are but
weak in.
Frail mariners afloat without a chart,
They run before the wind through high
seas breaking;
And when they have made the shore
through every shock,
'Tis odd, or odds, it may turn out a rock.

LXXV

There is a flower call'd 'Love in Idleness,'
For which see Shakespeare's ever-
blooming garden;—
I will not make his great description less,
And beg his British godship's humble
pardon,
If, in my extremity of rhyme's distress,
I touch a single leaf where he is war-
den;—
But though the flower is different, with the
French
Or Swiss Rousseau, cry '*Voilà la Per-
venche!*'

LXXVI

Eureka! I have found it! What I mean
To say is, not that love is idleness,
But that in love such idleness has been
An accessory, as I have cause to guess.

Hard labour's an indifferent go-between;
  Your men of business are not apt to express
Much passion, since the merchant-ship,
    the Argo,
Convey'd Medea as her supercargo.

LXXVII

'*Beatus ille procul!*' from '*negotiis,*'
  Saith Horace: the great little poet's wrong;
His other maxim, '*Noscitur à sociis,*'
  Is much more to the purpose of his song;
Though even that were sometimes too ferocious,
  Unless good company be kept too long;
But, in his teeth, whate'er their state or station,
Thrice happy they who *have* an occupation!

LXXVIII

Adam exchanged his Paradise for ploughing,
  Eve made up millinery with fig leaves—
The earliest knowledge from the tree so knowing,
  As far as I know, that the church receives:
And since that time it need not cost much showing,
  That many of the ills o'er which man grieves,
And still more women, spring from not employing
Some hours to make the remnant worth enjoying.

LXXIX

And hence high life is oft a dreary void,
  A rack of pleasures, where we must invent
A something wherewithal to be annoy'd.
  Bards may sing what they please about *Content;*
Contented, when translated, means but cloy'd;
  And hence arise the woes of sentiment,
Blue-devils, and blue-stockings, and romances
Reduced to practice, and perform'd like dances.

LXXX

I do declare, upon an affidavit,
  Romances I ne'er read like those I have seen;
Nor, if unto the world I ever gave it,
  Would some believe that such a tale had been:
But such intent I never had, nor have it;
  Some truths are better kept behind a screen,
Especially when they would look like lies;
I therefore deal in generalities.

LXXXI

'An oyster may be cross'd in love,'—and why?
  Because he mopeth idly in his shell,
And heaves a lonely subterraqueous sigh,
  Much as a monk may do within his cell:
And *à-propos* of monks, their piety
  With sloth hath found it difficult to dwell;
Those vegetables of the Catholic creed
Are apt exceedingly to run to seed.

LXXXII

O Wilberforce! thou man of black renown,
  Whose merit none enough can sing or say,
Thou hast struck one immense Colossus down,
  Thou moral Washington of Africa!
But there's another little thing, I own,
  Which you should perpetrate some summer's day,
And set the other half of earth to rights;
You have freed the *blacks*—now pray shut up the whites.

LXXXIII

Shut up the bald-coot bully Alexander!
  Ship off the Holy Three to Senegal;
Teach them that 'sauce for goose is sauce for gander,'
  And ask them how *they* like to be in thrall?
Shut up each high heroic salamander,
  Who eats fire gratis (since the pay's but small);
Shut up—no, *not* the King, but the Pavilion,
Or else 'twill cost us all another million.

LXXXIV

Shut up the world at large, let Bedlam out;
  And you will be perhaps surprised to find
All things pursue exactly the same route,
  As now with those of *soi-disant* sound mind.
This I could prove beyond a single doubt,
  Were there a jot of sense among mankind;
But till that *point d'appui* is found, alas!
Like Archimedes, I leave earth as 'twas.

LXXXV

Our gentle Adeline had one defect—
  Her heart was vacant, though a splendid mansion;
Her conduct had been perfectly correct,
  As she had seen nought claiming its expansion.
A wavering spirit may be easier wreck'd,
  Because 'tis frailer, doubtless, than a stanch one;
But when the latter works its own undoing,
Its inner crash is like an earthquake's ruin.

LXXXVI

She loved her lord, or thought so; but *that*
        love
    Cost her an effort, which is a sad toil,
The stone of Sysiphus, if once we move
    Our feelings 'gainst the nature of the
        soil.
She had nothing to complain of, or re-
        prove,
    No bickerings, no connubial turmoil:
Their union was a model to behold,
Serene and noble,—conjugal, but cold.

LXXXVII

There was no great disparity of years,
    Though much in temper; but they never
        clash'd:
They moved like stars united in their
        spheres,
    Or like the Rhone by Leman's waters
        wash'd,
Where mingled, and yet separate appears
    The river from the lake, all bluely dash'd
Through the serene and placid glassy
        deep,
Which fain would lull its river-child to
        sleep.

LXXXVIII

Now when she once had ta'en an interest
    In anything, however she might flatter
Herself that her intentions were the best,
    Intense intentions are a dangerous
        matter:
Impressions were much stronger than she
        guess'd,
    And gather'd as they run like growing
        water
Upon her mind: the more so, as her breast
Was not at first too readily impress'd.

LXXXIX

But when it was, she had that lurking
        demon
    Of double nature, and thus doubly
        named—
Firmness yclept in heroes, kings, and sea-
        men,
    That is, when they succeed; but greatly
        blamed
As *obstinacy*, both in men and women,
    Whene'er their triumph pales, or star is
        tamed:—
And 'twill perplex the casuist in morality
To fix the due bounds of this dangerous
        quality.

XC

Had Buonaparte won at Waterloo,
    It had been firmness; now 'tis perti-
        nacity:
Must the event decide between the two?
    I leave it to your people of sagacity
To draw the line between the false and
        true,
    If such can e'er be drawn by man's
        capacity:
My business is with Lady Adeline,
Who in her way too was a heroine.

XCI

She knew not her own heart; then how
        should I?
    I think not she was *then* in love with
        Juan:
If so, she would have had the strength to fly
    The wild sensation, unto her a new one:
She merely felt a common sympathy
    (I will not say it was a false or true one)
In him, because she thought he was in
        danger,—
Her husband's friend, her own, young,
        and a stranger.

XCII

She was, or thought she was, his friend—
        and this
    Without the farce of friendship, or ro-
        mance
Of platonism, which leads so oft amiss
    Ladies who have studied friendship but
        in France,
Or Germany, where people *purely* kiss.
    To thus much Adeline would not ad-
        vance;
But of such friendship as man's may to
        man be
She was as capable as woman can be.

XCIII

No doubt the secret influence of the sex
    Will there, as also in the ties of blood,
An innocent predominance annex,
    And tune the concord to a finer mood.
If free from passion, which all friendship
        checks,
    And your true feelings fully understood,
No friend like to a woman earth discovers,
So that you have not been nor will be
        lovers.

XCIV

Love bears within its breast the very
        germ
    Of change; and how should this be
        otherwise?
That violent things more quickly find a
        term
    Is shown through nature's whole analo-
        gies;
And how should the most fierce of all be
        firm?
    Would you have endless lightning in the
        skies?
Methinks Love's very title says enough:
How should 'the *tender* passion' e'er be
        tough?

XCV

Alas! by all experience, seldom yet
  (I merely quote what I have heard from
      many)
Had lovers not some reason to regret
  The passion which made Solomon a
      zany.
I've also seen some wives (not to forget
  The marriage state, the best or worst of
      any)
Who were the very paragons of wives,
Yet made the misery of at least two lives.

XCVI

I've also seen some female *friends* ('tis odd,
  But true—as, if expedient, I could prove)
That faithful were through thick and thin,
      abroad,
  At home, far more than ever yet was
      Love—
Who did not quit me when Oppression trod
  Upon me; whom no scandal could re-
      move;
Who fought, and fight, in absence, too,
      my battles,
Despite the snake Society's loud rattles.

XCVII

Whether Don Juan and chaste Adeline
  Grew friends in this or any other sense,
Will be discuss'd hereafter, I opine:
  At present I am glad of a pretence
To leave them hovering, as the effect is fine,
  And keeps the atrocious reader in *sus-
      pense*:
The surest way for ladies and for books
To bait their tender or their tenter hooks.

XCVIII

Whether they rode, or walk'd, or studied
      Spanish,
  To read Don Quixote in the original,
A pleasure before which all others vanish;
  Whether their talk was of the kind call'd
      'small,'
Or serious, are the topics I must banish
  To the next Canto; where perhaps I shall
Say something to the purpose, and display
Considerable talent in my way.

XCIX

Above all, I beg all men to forbear
  Anticipating aught about the matter:
They'll only make mistakes about the fair,
  And Juan too, especially the latter.
And I shall take a much more serious air
  Than I have yet done, in this epic satire.
It is not clear that Adeline and Juan
Will fall; but if they do, 'twill be their ruin.

C

But great things spring from little:—
      Would you think,
That in our youth, as dangerous a passion

As e'er brought man and woman to the
      brink
Of ruin, rose from such a slight occasion,
As few would ever dream could form the
      link
Of such a sentimental situation?
You'll never guess, I'll bet you millions,
      milliards—
It all sprung from a harmless game at
      billiards.

CI

'Tis strange,—but true; for truth is always
      strange;
  Stranger than fiction: if it could be told,
How much would novels gain by the ex-
      change!
  How differently the world would men
      behold!
How oft would vice and virtue places change!
  The new world would be nothing to the
      old,
If some Columbus of the moral seas
Would show mankind their souls' anti-
      podes.

CII

What 'antres vast and deserts idle' then
  Would be discover'd in the human soul!
What icebergs in the hearts of mighty men,
  With self-love in the centre as their pole!
What Anthropophagi in nine of ten
  Of those who hold the kingdoms in
      control!
Were things but only call'd by their right
      name,
Cæsar himself would be ashamed of fame.

CANTO THE FIFTEENTH

I

AH!—What should follow slips from my
      reflection;
  Whatever follows ne'ertheless may be
As *à-propos* of hope or retrospection,
  As though the lurking thought had
      follow'd free.
All present life is but an interjection,
  An 'Oh!' or 'Ah!' of joy or misery,
Or a 'Ha! ha!' or 'Bah!'—a yawn, or
      'Pooh!'
Of which perhaps the latter is most true.

II

But, more or less, the whole's a syncopé
  Or a *singultus*—emblems of emotion,
That grand antithesis to great *ennui*,
  Wherewith we break our bubbles on the
      ocean,
That watery outline of eternity,
  Or miniature at least, as is my notion,
Which ministers unto the soul's delight,
In seeing matters which are out of sight.

III

But all are better than the sigh supprest,
  Corroding in the cavern of the heart,
Making the countenance a masque of rest,
  And turning human nature to an art.
Few men dare show their thoughts of
    worst or best;
  Dissimulation always sets apart
A corner for herself; and therefore fiction
Is that which passes with least contradiction.

IV

Ah! who can tell? Or rather, who cannot
  Remember, without telling, passion's
    errors?
The drainer of oblivion, even the sot,
  Hath got *blue devils* for his morning
    mirrors:
What though on Lethe's stream he seem to
    float,
  He cannot sink his tremours or his terrors:
The ruby glass that shakes within his hand
Leaves a sad sediment of Time's worst
    sand.

V

And as for love—O love!—We will pro-
    ceed.
  The Lady Adeline Amundeville,
A pretty name as one would wish to read,
  Must perch harmonious on my tuneful
    quill.
There's music in the sighing of a reed;
  There's music in the gushing of a rill;
There's music in all things, if men had
    ears:
Their earth is but an echo of the spheres.

VI

The Lady Adeline, right honourable,
  And honour'd, ran a risk of growing less
    so;
For few of the soft sex are very stable
  In their resolves—alas! that I should
    say so;
They differ as wine differs from its label,
  When once decanted;—I presume to
    guess so,
But will not swear: yet both upon occasion,
Till old, may undergo adulteration.

VII

But Adeline was of the purest vintage,
  The unmingled essence of the grape;
    and yet
Bright as a new napoleon from its mintage,
  Or glorious as a diamond richly set;
A page where Time should hesitate to
    print age,
  And for which Nature might forego her
    debt—
Sole creditor whose process doth involve
    in't
The luck of finding everybody solvent.

VIII

O Death! thou dunnest of all duns! thou
    daily
  Knockest at doors, at first with modest
    tap,
Like a meek tradesman when, approach-
    ing palely,
  Some splendid debtor he would take by
    sap:
But oft denied, as patience 'gins to fail, he
  Advances with exasperated rap,
And (if let in) insists, in terms unhandsome,
On ready money, or 'a draft on Ransom.'

IX

Whate'er thou takest, spare awhile poor
    Beauty!
  She is so rare, and thou hast so much
    prey.
What though she now and then may slip
    from duty,
  The more 's the reason why you ought to
    stay:
Gaunt Gourmand! with whole nations for
    your booty,
  You should be civil in a modest way:
Suppress, then, some slight feminine dis-
    eases,
And take as many heroes as Heaven pleases.

X

Fair Adeline, the more ingenuous
  Where she was interested (as was said),
Because she was not apt, like some of us,
  To like too readily, or too high bred
To show it—(points we need not now dis-
    cuss)—
  Would give up artlessly both heart and
    head
Unto such feelings as seem'd innocent,
For objects worthy of the sentiment.

XI

Some parts of Juan's history, which
    Rumour,
  That live gazette, had scatter'd to dis-
    figure,
She had heard; but women hear with more
    good humour
  Such aberrations than we men of rigour:
Besides, his conduct, since in England,
    grew more
  Strict, and his mind assumed a manlier
    vigour;
Because he had, like Alcibiades,
The art of living in all climes with ease.

XII

His manner was perhaps the more seduc-
    tive,
  Because he ne'er seem'd anxious to
    seduce;
Nothing affected, studied, or constructive
  Of coxcombry or conquest: no abuse

Of his attractions marr'd the fair per-
    spective,
  To indicate a Cupidon broke loose,
And seem to say, 'Resist us if you can'—
Which makes a dandy while it spoils a
    man.

XIII

They are wrong—that's not the way to set
    about it;
  As, if they told the truth, could well be
    shown.
But, right or wrong, Don Juan was with-
    out it;
  In fact, his manner was his own alone:
Sincere he was—at least you could not
    doubt it,
  In listening merely to his voice's tone.
The devil hath not in all his quiver's choice
An arrow for the heart like a sweet voice.

XIV

By nature soft, his whole address held off
  Suspicion; though not timid, his regard
Was such as rather seem'd to keep aloof,
  To shield himself than put you on your
    guard:
Perhaps 'twas hardly quite assured enough,
  But modesty's at times its own reward,
Like virtue; and the absence of pretension
Will go much farther than there's need to
    mention.

XV

Serene, accomplish'd, cheerful but not
    loud;
  Insinuating without insinuation;
Observant of the foibles of the crowd,
  Yet ne'er betraying this in conversation;
Proud with the proud, yet courteously
    proud,
  So as to make them feel he knew his
    station
And theirs:—without a struggle for prior-
    ity,
He neither brook'd nor claim'd superior-
    ity—

XVI

That is, with men: with women he was what
  They pleased to make or take him for;
    and their
Imagination's quite enough for that:
  So that the outline's tolerably fair,
They fill the canvas up—and 'verbum sat.'
  If once their phantasies be brought to
    bear
Upon an object, whether sad or playful,
They can transfigure brighter than a
    Raphael.

XVII

Adeline, no deep judge of character,
  Was apt to add a colouring from her
    own:

'Tis thus the good will amiably err,
  And eke the wise, as has been often
    shown.
Experience is the chief philosopher,
  But saddest when his science is well
    known:
And persecuted sages teach the schools
Their folly in forgetting there are fools.

XVIII

Was it not so, great Locke? and greater
    Bacon?
  Great Socrates? And thou, Diviner still,
Whose lot it is by man to be mistaken,
  And thy pure creed made sanction of all
    ill?
Redeeming worlds to be by bigots shaken,
  How was thy toil rewarded? We might
    fill
Volumes with similar sad illustrations,
But leave them to the conscience of the
    nations.

XIX

I perch upon an humbler promontory,
  Amidst life's infinite variety:
With no great care for what is nicknamed
    glory,
  But speculating as I cast mine eye
On what may suit or may not suit my story,
  And never straining hard to versify,
I rattle on exactly as I'd talk
With anybody in a ride or walk.

XX

I don't know that there may be much ability
  Shown in this sort of desultory rhyme;
But there's a conversational facility,
  Which may round off an hour upon a
    time.
Of this I'm sure at least, there's no ser-
    vility
  In mine irregularity of chime,
Which rings what's uppermost of new or
    hoary,
Just as I feel the *Improvvisatore*.

XXI

'*Omnia vult belle Matho dicere—dic ali-
    quando*
  Et bene, dic neutrum, dic aliquando male.'
The first is rather more than mortal can do;
  The second may be sadly done or gaily;
The third is still more difficult to stand to;
  The fourth we hear, and see, and say
    too, daily:
The whole together is what I could wish
To serve in this conundrum of a dish.

XXII

A modest hope—but modesty's my forte,
  And pride my feeble:—let us ramble on.
I meant to make this poem very short,
  But now I can't tell where it may not run.

No doubt, if I had wish'd to pay my court
  To critics, or to hail the *setting* sun
Of tyranny of all kinds, my concision
  Were more;—but I was born for opposi-
    tion.

XXIII

But then 'tis mostly on the weaker side;
  So that I verily believe if they
Who now are basking in their full-blown
    pride
  Were shaken down and 'dogs had had
    their day,'
Though at the first I might perchance deride
  Their tumble, I should turn the other
    way,
And wax an ultra-royalist in loyalty,
Because I hate even democratic royalty.

XXIV

I think I should have made a decent spouse,
  If I had never proved the soft condition;
I think I should have made monastic vows,
  But for my own peculiar superstition:
'Gainst rhyme I never should have knock'd
    my brows,
  Nor broken my own head, nor that of
    Priscian,
Nor worn the motley mantle of a poet,
If some one had not told me to forego it.

XXV

But *laissez aller*—knights and dames I
    sing,
  Such as the times may furnish. 'Tis a
    flight
Which seems at first to need no lofty wing,
  Plumed by Longinus or the Stagyrite:
The difficulty lies in colouring
  (Keeping the due proportions still in sight)
With nature manners which are artificial,
And rend'ring general that which is especial.

XXVI

The difference is, that in the days of old
  Men made the manners; manners now
    make men—
Pinn'd like a flock, and fleeced too in their
    fold,
  At least nine, and a ninth beside of ten.
Now this at all events must render cold
  Your writers, who must either draw again
Days better drawn before, or else assume
The present, with their common-place cos-
    tume.

XXVII

We'll do our best to make the best on't:—
    March!
  March, my Muse! If you cannot fly,
    yet flutter;
And when you may not be sublime, be
    arch,
  Or starch, as are the edicts statesmen
    utter.

We surely shall find something worth re-
    search:
  Columbus found a new world in a
    cutter,
Or brigantine, or pink, of no great ton-
    nage,
While yet America was in her non-age.

XXVIII

When Adeline, in all her growing sense
  Of Juan's merits and his situation,—
Felt on the whole an interest intense,—
  Partly perhaps because a fresh sensa-
    tion,
Or that he had an air of innocence,
  Which is for innocence a sad tempta-
    tion—
As women hate half measures, on the whole,
She 'gan to ponder how to save his soul.

XXIX

She had a good opinion of advice,
  Like all who give and eke receive it gratis,
For which small thanks are still the market
    price,
  Even where the article at highest rate is:
She thought upon the subject twice or
    thrice,
  And morally decided, the best state is
For morals, marriage; and this question
    carried,
She seriously advised him to get married.

XXX

Juan replied, with all becoming deference,
  He had a predilection for that tie;
But that, at present, with immediate refer-
    ence
  To his own circumstances, there might
    lie
Some difficulties, as in his own preference,
  Or that of her to whom he might apply:
That still he'd wed with such or such a lady,
If that they were not married all already.

XXXI

Next to the making matches for herself,
  And daughters, brothers, sisters, kith or
    kin,
Arranging them like books on the same
    shelf,
  There's nothing women love to dabble in
More (like a stock-holder in growing pelf)
  Than match-making in general: 'tis no
    sin
Certes, but a preventative, and therefore
That is, no doubt, the only reason where-
    fore.

XXXII

But never yet (except of course a miss
  Unwed, or mistress never to be wed,
Or wed already, who object to this)
  Was there chaste dame who had not in
    her head

Some drama of the marriage unities,
  Observed as strictly both at board and
    bed
As those of Aristotle, though sometimes
They turn out melodrames or pantomimes

XXXIII

They generally have some only son
  Some heir to a large property, some
    friend
Of an old family, some gay Sir John,
  Or grave Lord George, with whom per-
    haps might end
A line, and leave posterity undone,
  Unless a marriage was applied to mend
The prospect and their morals: and be-
    sides,
  They have at hand a blooming glut of
    brides.

XXXIV

From these they will be careful to select,
  For this an heiress, and for that a
    beauty;
For one a songstress who hath no defect,
  For t'other one who promises much duty;
For this a lady no one can reject,
  Whose sole accomplishments were quite
    a booty;
A second for her excellent connexions;
A third, because there can be no objec-
    tions.

XXXV

When Rapp the Harmonist embargo'd
    marriage
  In his harmonious settlement—(which
    flourishes
Strangely enough as yet without mis-
    carriage,
  Because it breeds no more mouths than
    it nourishes,
Without those sad expenses which dis-
    parage
  What Nature naturally most encour-
    ages)—
Why call'd he 'Harmony' a state sans
    wedlock?
Now here I have got the preacher at a dead
    lock.

XXXVI

Because he either meant to sneer at har-
    mony
  Or marriage, by divorcing them thus
    oddly.
But whether reverend Rapp learn'd this in
    Germany
  Or no, 'tis said his sect is rich and godly,
Pious and pure, beyond what I can term
    any
  Of ours, although they propagate more
    broadly.
My objection's to his title, not his ritual,
Although I wonder how it grew habitual.

XXXVII

But Rapp is the reverse of zealous matrons,
  Who favour, *malgré* Malthus, genera-
    tion—
Professors of that genial art, and patrons
  Of all the modest part of propagation;
Which after all at such a desperate rate
    runs,
  That half its produce tends to emigra-
    tion,
That sad result of passions and potatoes—
Two weeds which pose our economic
    Catos.

XXXVIII

Had Adeline read Malthus? I can't tell;
  I wish she had: his book's the eleventh
    commandment,
Which says, 'Thou shalt not marry,' un-
    less *well*:
  This he (as far as I can understand)
    meant.
'Tis not my purpose on his views to dwell,
  Nor canvass what 'so eminent a hand'
    meant;
But certes it conducts to lives ascetic,
Or turning marriage into arithmetic.

XXXIX

But Adeline, who probably presumed
  That Juan had enough of maintenance,
Or *separate* maintenance, in case 'twas
    doom'd—
  As on the whole it is an even chance
That bridegrooms, after they are fairly
    groom'd,
  May retrograde a little in the dance
Of marriage—(which might form a
    painter's fame,
Like Holbein's 'Dance of Death'—but
    'tis the same);—

XL

But Adeline determined Juan's wedding
  In her own mind, and that's enough for
    woman;
But then, with whom? There was the sage
    Miss Reading,
  Miss Raw, Miss Flaw, Miss Showman,
    and Miss Knowman,
And the two fair co-heiresses Giltbedding.
  She deem'd his merits something more
    than common:
All these were unobjectionable matches,
And might go on, if well wound up, like
    watches.

XLI

There was Miss Millpond, smooth as
    summer's sea,
  That usual paragon, an only daughter,
Who seem'd the cream of equanimity,
  Till skimm'd—and then there was some
    milk and water,

With a slight shade of blue too, it might be
  Beneath the surface; but what did it
    matter?
Love's riotous, but marriage should have
  quiet,
And being consumptive, live on a milk diet.

XLII

And then there was the Miss Audacia
  Shoestring,
  A dashing *demoiselle* of good estate,
Whose heart was fix'd upon a star or blue
  string;
  But whether English dukes grew rare of
    late,
Or that she had not harp'd upon the true
  string,
  By which such sirens can attract our great,
She took up with some foreign younger
  brother,
A Russ or Turk—the one's as good as
  t'other.

XLIII

And then there was—but why should I go
  on,
  Unless the ladies should go off?—there
    was
Indeed a certain fair and fairy one,
  Of the best class, and better than her
    class,—
Aurora Raby, a young star who shone
  O'er life, too sweet an image for such
    glass,
A lovely being, scarcely form'd or moulded,
A rose with all its sweetest leaves yet folded;

XLIV

Rich, noble, but an orphan; left an only
  Child to the care of guardians good and
    kind;
But still her aspect had an air so lonely!
  Blood is not water; and where shall we
    find
Feelings of youth like those which over-
    thrown lie
By death, when we are left, alas! behind,
To feel, in friendless palaces, a home
Is wanting, and our best ties in the tomb?

XLV

Early in years, and yet more infantine
  In figure, she had something of sublime
In eyes which sadly shone, as seraphs'
  shine.
  All youth—but with an aspect beyond
    time;
Radiant and grave—as pitying man's de-
    cline;
  Mournful—but mournful of another's
    crime,
She look'd as if she sat by Eden's door,
And grieved for those who could return no
  more.

XLVI

She was a Catholic, too, sincere, austere,
  As far as her own gentle heart allow'd,
And deem'd that fallen worship far more
  dear
  Perhaps because 'twas fallen: her sires
    were proud
Of deeds and days when they had fill'd the
  ear
  Of nations, and had never bent or bow'd
To novel power; and as she was the last,
She held their old faith and old feelings fast.

XLVII

She gazed upon a world she scarcely knew,
  As seeking not to know it; silent, lone,
As grows a flower, thus quietly she grew,
  And kept her heart serene within its
    zone.
There was awe in the homage which she
  drew;
  Her spirit seem'd as seated on a throne
Apart from the surrounding world, and
  strong
In its own strength—most strange in one
  so young!

XLVIII

Now it so happen'd, in the catalogue
  Of Adeline, Aurora was omitted,
Although her birth and wealth had given
  her vogue,
  Beyond the charmers we have already
    cited;
Her beauty also seem'd to form no clog
  Against her being mention'd as well fitted,
By many virtues, to be worth the trouble
Of single gentlemen who would be double.

XLIX

And this omission, like that of the bust
  Of Brutus at the pageant of Tiberius,
Made Juan wonder, as no doubt he must.
  This he express'd half smiling and half
    serious;
When Adeline replied with some disgust,
  And with an air, to say the least, im-
    perious,
She marvell'd 'what he saw in such a baby
As that prim, silent, cold Aurora Raby?'

L

Juan rejoin'd—'She was a Catholic,
  And therefore fittest, as of his persuasion;
Since he was sure his mother would fall
  sick,
  And the Pope thunder excommunication,
If——' But here Adeline, who seem'd to
  pique
  Herself extremely on the inoculation
Of others with her own opinions, stated—
As usual—the same reason which she late
  did.

LI

And wherefore not? A reasonable reason,
  If good, is none the worse for repetition;
If bad, the best way's certainly to tease on,
  And amplify: you lose much by con-
    cision,
Whereas insisting in or out of season
  Convinces all men, even a politician;
Or—what is just the same—it wearies out.
So the end's gain'd, what signifies the
    route?

LII

Why Adeline had this slight prejudice—
  For prejudice it was—against a creature
As pure as sanctity itself from vice,
  With all the added charm of form and
    feature,
For me appears a question far too nice,
  Since Adeline was liberal by nature;
But nature's nature, and has more caprices
Than I have time, or will, to take to pieces.

LIII

Perhaps she did not like the quiet way
  With which Aurora on those baubles
    look'd,
Which charm most people in their earlier
    day:
  For there are few things by mankind less
    brook'd,
And womankind too, if we so may say,
  Than finding thus their genius stand
    rebuked,
Like 'Antony's by Cæsar,' by the few
Who look upon them as they ought to do.

LIV

It was not envy—Adeline had none;
  Her place was far beyond it, and her
    mind.
It was not scorn—which could not light on
    one
  Whose greatest *fault* was leaving few to
    find.
It was not jealousy, I think: but shun
  Following the *ignes fatui* of mankind.
It was not——but 'tis easier far, alas!
To say what it was *not* than what it was.

LV

Little Aurora deem'd she was the theme
  Of such discussion. She was there a
    guest;
A beauteous ripple of the brilliant stream
  Of rank and youth, though purer than
    the rest,
Which flow'd on for a moment in the beam
  Time sheds a moment o'er each spark-
    ling crest.
Had she known this, she would have
    calmly smiled—
She had so much, or little, of the child.

LVI

The dashing and proud air of Adeline
  Imposed not upon her: she saw her
    blaze
Much as she would have seen a glow-
    worm shine,
  Then turn'd unto the stars for loftier rays.
Juan was something she could not divine,
  Being no sibyl in the new world's ways;
Yet she was nothing dazzled by the meteor,
Because she did not pin her faith on fea-
    ture.

LVII

His fame too,—for he had that kind of fame
  Which sometimes plays the deuce with
    womankind,
A heterogeneous mass of glorious blame,
  Half virtues and whole vices being com-
    bined;
Faults which attract because they are not
    tame;
  Follies trick'd out so brightly that they
    blind:—
These seals upon her wax made no im-
    pression,
Such was her coldness or her self-posses-
    sion.

LVIII

Juan knew nought of such a character—
  High, yet resembling not his lost Haidée;
Yet each was radiant in her proper sphere:
  The island girl, bred up by the lone sea,
More warm, as lovely, and not less sin-
    cere,
  Was Nature's all: Aurora could not be,
Nor would be thus:—the difference in
    them
Was such as lies between a flower and gem.

LIX

Having wound up with this sublime com-
    parison,
  Methinks we may proceed upon our
    narrative,
And, as my friend Scott says, 'I sound my
    warison';
  Scott, the superlative of my compara-
    tive—
Scott, who can paint your Christian knight
    or Saracen,
  Serf, lord, man, with such skill as none
    would share it, if
There had not been one Shakspeare and
    Voltaire,
Of one or both of whom he seems the heir.

LX

I say, in my slight way I may proceed
  To play upon the surface of humanity.
I write the world, nor care if the world
    read,
  At least for this I cannot spare its vanity.

My Muse hath bred, and still perhaps may
      breed
  More foes by this same scroll: when I
      began it, I
Thought that it might turn out so—*now*
      I *know* it,
But still I am, or was, a pretty poet.

LXI

The conference or congress (for it ended
  As congresses of late do) of the Lady
Adeline and Don Juan rather blended
  Some acids with the sweets—for she was
      heady;
But, ere the matter could be marr'd or
      mended,
  The silvery bell rung, not for 'dinner
      ready,'
But for that hour, call'd *half-hour*, given
      to dress,
Though ladies' robes seem scant enough
      for less.

LXII

Great things were now to be achieved at
      table,
  With massy plate for armour, knives
      and forks
For weapons; but what Muse since
      Homer's able
  (His feasts are not the worst part of his
      works)
To draw up in array a single day-bill
  Of modern dinners? where more mystery
      lurks,
In soups or sauces, or a sole *ragoût*,
Than witches, b—ches, or physicians, brew.

LXIII

There was a goodly 'soupe à la *bonne femme*,'
  Though God knows whence it came
      from; there was, too,
A turbot for relief of those who cram,
  Relieved with 'dindon à la Périgueux:'
There also was——the sinner that I am!
  How shall I get this gourmand stanza
      through?—
'Soupe à la Beauveau,' whose relief was
      dory,
Relieved itself by pork, for greater glory.

LXIV

But I must crowd all into one grand mess,
  Or mass; for should I stretch into detail,
My Muse would run much more into excess,
  Than when some squeamish people
      deem her frail;
But though a 'bonne vivante,' I must
      confess
  Her stomach's not her peccant part;
      this tale
However doth require some slight refec-
      tion,
Just to relieve her spirits from dejection.

LXV

Fowls 'à la Condé,' slices eke of salmon,
  With 'sauces Génévoises,' and haunch
      of venison:
Wines, too, which might again have slain
      young Ammon—
  A man like whom I hope we sha'n't see
      many soon;
They also set a glazed Westphalian ham
      on,
  Whereon Apicius would bestow his
      benison;
And then there was champagne with foam-
      ing whirls,
As white as Cleopatra's melted pearls.

LXVI

Then there was God knows what 'à l'Alle-
      mande,'
  'A l'Espagnole,' 'timballe,' and 'sal-
      picon'—
With things I can't withstand or under-
      stand,
  Though swallow'd with much zest upon
      the whole;
And '*entremets*' to piddle with at hand,
  Gently to lull down the subsiding soul;
While great Lucullus' *Robe triumphal*
      muffles—
(*There's fame*)—young partridge fillets,
      deck'd with truffles.

LXVII

What are the *fillets* on the victor's brow
  To these? They are rags or dust. Where
      is the arch
Which nodded to the nation's spoils below?
  Where the triumphal chariots' haughty
      march?
Gone to where victories must like dinners
      go.
  Farther I shall not follow the research:
But oh! ye modern heroes with your car-
      tridges,
When will your names lend lustre even to
      partridges?

LXVIII

Those truffles too are no bad accessaries,
  Follow'd by 'petits puits d'amour'—a
      dish
Of which perhaps the cookery rather
      varies,
  So every one may dress it to his wish,
According to the best of dictionaries,
  Which encyclopedise both flesh and fish;
But even sans *confitures*, it no less true is,
There's pretty picking in those *petits puits*.

LXIX

The mind is lost in mighty contemplation
  Of intellect expended on two courses;
And indigestion's grand multiplication
  Requires arithmetic beyond my forces.

Who would suppose, from Adam's simple
   ration,
   That cookery could have call'd forth
      such resources,
As form a science and a nomenclature
From out the commonest demands of
   nature?

LXX

The glasses jingled, and the palates tingled;
   The diners of celebrity dined well;
The ladies with more moderation mingled
   In the feast, pecking less than I can tell;
Also the younger men too: for a springald
   Can't, like ripe age, in *gourmandise* excel,
But thinks less of good eating than the
      whisper
(When seated next him) of some pretty
      lisper.

LXXI

Alas! I must leave undescribed the *gibier*,
   The *salmi*, the *consommé*, the *purée*,
All which I use to make my rhymes run
      glibber
   Than could roast beef in our rough
      John Bull way:
I must not introduce even a spare rib here,
   'Bubble and squeak' would spoil my
      liquid lay,
But I have dined, and must forego, alas!
The chaste description even of a 'bécasse;'

LXXII

And fruits, and ice, and all that art refines
   From nature for the service of the
      goût—
Taste or the *gout*,—pronounce it as in-
      clines
   Your stomach! Ere you dine, the
      French will do;
But *after*, there are sometimes certain signs
   Which prove plain English truer of the
      two.
Hast ever *had* the *gout*? I have not had it—
But I may have, and you too, reader,
      dread it.

LXXIII

The simple olives, best allies of wine,
   Must I pass over in my bill of fare?
I must, although a favourite *plat* of mine
   In Spain, and Lucca, Athens, every-
      where:
On them and bread 'twas oft my luck to dine,
   The grass my table-cloth, in open air,
On Sunium or Hymettus, like Diogenes,
Of whom half my philosophy the progeny is.

LXXIV

Amidst this tumult of fish, flesh, and fowl,
   And vegetables, all in masquerade,
The guests were placed according to their
      roll,
   But various as the various meats dis-
      play'd:

Don Juan sat next an 'à l'Espagnole'—
   No damsel, but a dish, as hath been said:
But so far like a lady, that 'twas drest
   Superbly, and contain'd a world of zest.

LXXV

By some odd chance too, he was placed
      between
   Aurora and the Lady Adeline—
A situation difficult, I ween,
   For man therein, with eyes and heart, to
      dine.
Also the conference which we have seen
   Was not such as to encourage him to
      shine,
For Adeline, addressing few words to him,
With two transcendent eyes seem'd to look
      through him.

LXXVI

I sometimes almost think that eyes have
      ears:
   This much is sure, that, out of earshot,
      things
Are somehow echoed to the pretty dears,
   Of which I can't tell whence their know-
      ledge springs.
Like that same mystic music of the spheres,
   Which no one hears, so loudly though
      it rings,
'Tis wonderful how oft the sex have heard
Long dialogues—which pass'd without a
      word!

LXXVII

Aurora sat with that indifference
   Which piques a *preux chevalier*—as it
      ought:
Of all offences that's the worst offence,
   Which seems to hint you are not worth
      a thought.
Now Juan, though no coxcomb in pretence,
   Was not exactly pleased to be so caught;
Like a good ship entangled among ice,
And after so much excellent advice.

LXXVIII

To his gay nothings, nothing was replied,
   Or something which was nothing, as
      urbanity
Required. Aurora scarcely look'd aside,
   Nor even smiled enough for any vanity.
The devil was in the girl! Could it be
      pride?
   Or modesty, or absence, or inanity?
Heaven knows! But Adeline's malicious
      eyes
Sparkled with her successful prophecies,

LXXIX

And look'd as much as if to say, 'I said it';
   A kind of triumph I'll not recommend,
Because it sometimes, as I've seen or
      read it,
   Both in the case of lover and of friend,

Will pique a gentleman, for his own credit,
  To bring what was a jest to a serious end :
For all men prophesy what *is* or *was*,
  And hate those who won't let them come
    to pass.

LXXX

Juan was drawn thus into some attentions,
  Slight but select, and just enough to
    express,
To females of perspicuous comprehen-
    sions,
  That he would rather make them more
    than less.
Aurora at the last (so history mentions,
  Though probably much less a fact than
    guess)
So far relax'd her thoughts from their
    sweet prison,
  As once or twice to smile, if not to listen.

LXXXI

From answering she began to question:
    this
  With her was rare; and Adeline, who
    as yet
Thought her predictions went not much
    amiss,
  Began to dread she'd thaw to a co-
    quette—
So very difficult, they say, it is
  To keep extremes from meeting, when
    once set
In motion; but she here too much refined—
Aurora's spirit was not of that kind.

LXXXII

But Juan had a sort of winning way,
  A proud humility, if such there be,
Which show'd such deference to what
    females say,
  As if each charming word were a decree.
His tact, too, temper'd him from grave to
    gay,
  And taught him when to be reserved or
    free :
He had the art of drawing people out,
Without their seeing what he was about.

LXXXIII

Aurora, who in her indifference
  Confounded him in common with the
    crowd
Of flutterers, though she deem'd he had
    more sense
  Than whispering foplings, or than wit-
    lings loud—
Commenced (from such slight things will
    great commence)
  To feel that flattery which attracts the
    proud
Rather by deference than compliment,
And wins even by a delicate dissent.

LXXXIV

And then he had good looks;—that point
    was carried
  Nem. con. amongst the women, which I
    grieve
To say leads oft to *crim. con.* with the
    married—
  A case which to the juries we may leave,
Since with digressions we too long have
    tarried.
  Now though we know of old that looks
    deceive,
And always have done, somehow these
    good looks
Make more impression than the best of
    books.

LXXXV

Aurora, who look'd more on books than
    faces,
  Was very young, although so very sage,
Admiring more Minerva than the Graces,
  Especially upon a printed page.
But Virtue's self, with all her tightest laces,
  Has not the natural stays of strict old
    age;
And Socrates, that model of all duty,
Own'd to a *penchant*, though discreet, for
    beauty.

LXXXVI

And girls of sixteen are thus far Socratic,
  But innocently so, as Socrates;
And really, if the sage sublime and Attic
  At seventy years had phantasies like
    these,
Which Plato in his dialogues dramatic
  Has shown, I know not why they should
    displease
In virgins—always in a modest way,
Observe; for that with me 's a *sine quâ*.

LXXXVII

Also observe, that, like the great Lord Coke
  (See Littleton), whene'er I have ex-
    press'd
Opinions two, which at first sight may look
  Twin opposites, the second is the best.
Perhaps I have a third too, in a nook,
  Or none at all—which seems a sorry jest :
But if a writer should be quite consistent,
How could he possibly show things exis-
    tent?

LXXXVIII

If people contradict themselves, can I
  Help contradicting them, and everybody,
Even my veracious self?—But that 's a lie :
  I never did so, never will—how should I ?
He who doubts all things nothing can
    deny :
  Truth's fountains may be clear—her
    streams are muddy,
And cut through such canals of contra-
    diction,
That she must often navigate o'er fiction.

LXXXIX

Apologue, fable, poesy, and parable,
  Are false, but may be render'd also true,
By those who sow them in a land that's
    arable.
  'Tis wonderful what fable will not do!
'Tis said it makes reality more bearable:
  But what's reality? Who has its clue?
Philosophy? No; she too much rejects.
Religion? *Yes;* but which of all her sects?

XC

Some millions must be wrong, that's
    pretty clear;
  Perhaps it may turn out that all were
    right.
God help us! Since we have need on our
    career
  To keep our holy beacons always bright,
'Tis time that some new prophet should
    appear,
  Or *old* indulge man with a second sight.
Opinions wear out in some thousand
    years,
Without a small refreshment from the
    spheres.

XCI

But here again, why will I thus entangle
  Myself with metaphysics? None can
    hate
So much as I do any kind of wrangle;
  And yet, such is my folly, or my fate,
I always knock my head against some
    angle
  About the present, past, or future state:
Yet I wish well to Trojan and to Tyrian,
For I was bred a moderate Presbyterian.

XCII

But though I am a temperate theologian,
  And also meek as a metaphysician,
Impartial between Tyrian and Trojan
  As Eldon on a lunatic commission,
In politics my duty is to show John
  Bull something of the lower world's con-
    dition.
It makes my blood boil like the springs of
    Hecla,
To see men let these scoundrel sovereigns
    break law.

XCIII

But politics, and policy, and piety,
  Are topics which I sometimes introduce,
Not only for the sake of their variety,
  But as subservient to a moral use;
Because my business is to *dress* society,
  And stuff with *sage* that very verdant
    goose.
And now, that we may furnish with some
    matter all
Tastes, we are going to try the super-
    natural.

XCIV

And now I will give up all argument;
  And positively henceforth no tempta-
    tion
Shall 'fool me to the top up of my bent';—
  Yes, I'll begin a thorough reformation.
Indeed, I never knew what people meant
  By deeming that my Muse's conversa-
    tion
Was dangerous;—I think she is as harm-
    less
As some who labour more and yet may
    charm less.

XCV

Grim reader! did you ever see a ghost?
  No; but you have heard—I understand
    —be dumb!
And don't regret the time you may have
    lost,
  For you have got that pleasure still to
    come:
And do not think I mean to sneer at most
  Of these things, or by ridicule benumb
That source of the sublime and the mys-
    terious:—
For certain reasons my belief is serious.

XCVI

Serious? You laugh;—you may; that will
    I not;
  My smiles must be sincere or not at all.
I say I do believe a haunted spot
  Exists—and where? That shall I not
    recall,
Because I'd rather it should be forgot,
  'Shadows the soul of Richard' may
    appal.
In short, upon that subject I've some
    qualms very
Like those of the philosopher of Malms-
    bury.

XCVII

The night—(I sing by night—sometimes
    an owl,
  And now and then a nightingale)—is dim,
And the loud shriek of sage Minerva's fowl
  Rattles around me her discordant hymn:
Old portraits from old walls upon me
    scowl—
  I wish to heaven they would not look so
    grim;
The dying embers dwindle in the grate—
I think too that I have sat up too late:

XCVIII

And therefore, though 'tis by no means
    my way
  To rhyme at noon—when I have other
    things
To think of, if I ever think—I say
  I feel some chilly midnight shudderings,

And prudently postpone, until mid-day,
  Treating a topic which, alas! but brings
Shadows;—but you must be in my con-
    dition
Before you learn to call this superstition.

XCIX

Between two worlds life hovers like a star,
  'Twixt night and morn, upon the hori-
    zon's verge.
How little do we know that which we are!
  How less what we may be! The eternal
    surge
Of time and tide rolls on, and bears afar
  Our bubbles; as the old burst, new emerge,
Lash'd from the foam of ages; while the
    graves
Of empires heave but like some passing
    waves.

CANTO THE SIXTEENTH

I

THE antique Persians taught three useful
    things,
  To draw the bow, to ride, and speak the
    truth.
This was the mode of Cyrus, best of
    kings—
  A mode adopted since by modern youth.
Bows have they, generally with two strings,
  Horses they ride without remorse or
    ruth;
At speaking truth perhaps they are less
    clever,
But draw the long bow better now than
    ever.

II

The cause of this effect, or this defect,—
  'For this effect defective comes by
    cause,'
Is what I have not leisure to inspect;
  But this I must say in my own applause,
Of all the Muses that I recollect,
  Whate'er may be her follies or her flaws,
In some things, mine's beyond all contra-
    diction
The most sincere that ever dealt in fiction.

III

And as she treats all things, and ne'er re-
    treats
  From anything, this epic will contain
A wilderness of the most rare conceits,
  Which you might elsewhere hope to
    find in vain.
'Tis true there be some bitters with the
    sweets,
  Yet mix'd so slightly, that you can't
    complain,
But wonder they so few are, since my tale is
'De rebus cunctis et quibusdam aliis.'

IV

But of all truths which she has told, the
    most
  True is that which she is about to tell.
I said it was a story of a ghost—
  What then? I only know it so befell.
Have you explored the limits of the coast,
  Where all the dwellers of the earth must
    dwell?
'Tis time to strike such puny doubters
    dumb as
The sceptics who would not believe
    Columbus.

V

Some people would impose now with
    authority,
  Turpin's or Monmouth Geoffry's
    Chronicle;
Men whose historical superiority
  Is always greatest at a miracle.
But Saint Augustine has the great priority,
  Who bids all men believe the impossible,
Because 'tis so. Who nibble, scribble,
    quibble, he
Quiets at once with 'quia impossibile.'

VI

And therefore, mortals, cavil not at all;
  Believe:—if 'tis improbable, you must,
And if it is impossible, you shall:
  'Tis always best to take things upon
    trust.
I do not speak profanely, to recall
  Those holier mysteries which the wise
    and just
Receive as gospel, and which grow more
    rooted,
As all truths must, the more they are dis-
    puted:

VII

I merely mean to say what Johnson said,
  That in the course of some six thousand
    years,
All nations have believed that from the
    dead
  A visitant at intervals appears;
And what is strangest upon this strange
    head,
  Is, that whatever bar the reason rears
'Gainst such belief, there's something
    stronger still
In its behalf, let those deny who will.

VIII

The dinner and the soirée too were done,
  The supper too discuss'd, the dames
    admired,
The banqueteers had dropp'd off one by
    one—
  The song was silent, and the dance ex-
    pired:

The last thin petticoats were vanish'd, gone
  Like fleecy clouds into the sky retired,
And nothing brighter gleam'd through the
    saloon
Than dying tapers—and the peeping moon.

IX

The evaporation of a joyous day
  Is like the last glass of champagne,
    without
The foam which made its virgin bumper
    gay;
  Or like a system coupled with a doubt;
Or like a soda bottle when its spray
  Has sparkled and let half its spirit out;
Or like a billow left by storms behind,
Without the animation of the wind;

X

Or like an opiate, which brings troubled
    rest,
  Or none; or like—like nothing that I
    know
Except itself;—such is the human breast;
  A thing, of which similitudes can show
No real likeness,—like the old Tyrian vest
  Dyed purple, none at present can tell
    how,
If from a shell-fish or from cochineal.
So perish every tyrant's robe piece-meal!

XI

But next to dressing for a rout or ball,
  Undressing is a woe; our *robe de
    chambre*
May sit like that of Nessus, and recall
  Thoughts quite as yellow, but less clear
    than amber.
Titus exclaim'd, 'I've lost a day!' Of all
  The nights and days most people can
    remember,
(I have had of both, some not to be dis-
    dain'd,)
I wish they'd state how many they have
    gain'd.

XII

And Juan, on retiring for the night,
  Felt restless, and perplex'd, and com-
    promised:
He thought Aurora Raby's eyes more
    bright
  Than Adeline (such is advice) advised;
If he had known exactly his own plight,
  He probably would have philosophised;
A great resource to all, and ne'er denied
Till wanted; therefore Juan only sigh'd.

XIII

He sigh'd;—the next resource is the full
    moon,
  Where all sighs are deposited; and now
It happen'd luckily, the chaste orb shone
  As clear as such a climate will allow;

And Juan's mind was in the proper tone
  To hail her with the apostrophe—'O
    thou!'
Of amatory egotism the *Tuism*,
Which further to explain would be a truism.

XIV

But lover, poet, or astronomer,
  Shepherd, or swain, whoever may be-
    hold,
Feel some abstraction when they gaze on
    her;
  Great thoughts we catch from thence
    (besides a cold
Sometimes, unless my feelings rather
    err);
  Deep secrets to her rolling light are
    told;
The ocean's tides and mortals' brains she
    sways,
And also hearts, if there be truth in lays.

XV

Juan felt somewhat pensive, and disposed
  For contemplation rather than his pil-
    low:
The Gothic chamber, where he was en-
    closed,
  Let in the rippling sound of the lake's
    billow,
With all the mystery by midnight caused:
  Below his window waved (of course) a
    willow;
And he stood gazing out on the cascade
That flash'd and after darken'd in the
    shade.

XVI

Upon his table or his toilet,—*which
  Of these is not exactly ascertain'd,—
(I state this, for I am cautious to a pitch
  Of nicety, where a fact is to be gain'd,)
A lamp burn'd high, while he leant from
    a niche,
  Where many a Gothic ornament re-
    main'd,
In chisell'd stone and painted glass, and
    all
That time has left our fathers of their hall.

XVII

Then, as the night was clear though cold,
    he threw
  His chamber door wide open—and
    went forth
Into a gallery, of a sombre hue,
  Long, furnish'd with old pictures of
    great worth,
Of knights and dames heroic and chaste too,
  As doubtless should be people of high
    birth.
But by dim lights the portraits of the dead
Have something ghastly, desolate, and
    dread.

XVIII

The forms of the grim knight and pictured
        saint
    Look living in the moon; and as you turn
Backward and forward to the echoes faint
    Of your own footsteps—voices from the
        urn
Appear to wake, and shadows wild and
        quaint
    Start from the frames which fence their
        aspects stern,
As if to ask how you can dare to keep
A vigil there, where all but death should
        sleep.

XIX

And the pale smile of beauties in the grave,
    The charms of other days, in starlight
        gleams,
Glimmer on high; their buried locks still
        wave
    Along the canvas; their eyes glance like
        dreams
On ours, or spars within some dusky cave,
    But death is imaged in their shadowy
        beams.
A picture is the past; even ere its frame
Be gilt, who sate hath ceased to be the same.

XX

As Juan mused on mutability,
    Or on his mistress—terms synony-
        mous—
No sound except the echo of his sigh
    Or step ran sadly through that antique
        house;
When suddenly he heard, or thought so,
        nigh,
    A supernatural agent—or a mouse,
Whose little nibbling rustle will embarrass
Most people as it plays along the arras.

XXI

It was no mouse, but lo! a monk, array'd
    In cowl and beads, and dusky garb,
        appear'd,
Now in the moonlight, and now lapsed in
        shade,
    With steps that trod as heavy, yet un-
        heard;
His garments only a slight murmur made;
    He moved as shadowy as the sisters
        weird,
But slowly; and as he passed Juan by,
Glanced, without pausing, on him a bright
        eye.

XXII

Juan was petrified; he had heard a hint
    Of such a spirit in these halls of old,
But thought, like most men, there was no-
        thing in 't
    Beyond the rumour which such spots
        unfold,

Coin'd from surviving superstition's mint,
    Which passes ghosts in currency like gold,
But rarely seen, like gold compared with
        paper.
And did he see this? or was it a vapour?

XXIII

Once, twice, thrice pass'd, repass'd—the
        thing of air,
    Or earth beneath, or heaven, or t'other
        place;
And Juan gazed upon it with a stare,
    Yet could not speak or move; but, on
        its base
As stands a statue, stood: he felt his hair
    Twine like a knot of snakes around his
        face;
He tax'd his tongue for words, which were
        not granted,
To ask the reverend person what he wanted.

XXIV

The third time, after a still longer pause,
    The shadow pass'd away—but where?
        the hall
Was long, and thus far there was no great
        cause
    To think his vanishing unnatural:
Doors there were many, through which,
        by the laws
    Of physics, bodies whether short or tall
Might come or go; but Juan could not
        state
Through which the spectre seem'd to
        evaporate.

XXV

He stood—how long he knew not, but it
        seem'd
    An age—expectant, powerless, with his
        eyes
Strain'd on the spot where first the figure
        gleam'd,
    Then by degrees recall'd his energies,
And would have pass'd the whole off as a
        dream,
    But could not wake; he was, he did sur-
        mise,
Waking already, and return'd at length
Back to his chamber, shorn of half his
        strength.

XXVI

All there was as he left it: still his taper
    Burnt, and not *blue*, as modest tapers
        use,
Receiving sprites with sympathetic va-
        pour;
    He rubb'd his eyes, and they did not
        refuse
Their office; he took up an old newspaper;
    The paper was right easy to peruse;
He read an article the king attacking,
And a long eulogy of 'patent blacking.'

XXVII

This savour'd of this world; but his hand
    shook:
He shut his door, and after having read
A paragraph, I think about Horne Tooke,
    Undrest, and rather slowly went to bed.
There, couch'd all snugly on his pillow's
    nook,
    With what he had seen his phantasy he
        fed;
And though it was no opiate, slumber
    crept
Upon him by degrees, and so he slept.

XXVIII

He woke betimes; and, as may be sup-
    posed,
    Ponder'd upon his visitant or vision,
And whether it ought not to be disclosed,
    At risk of being quizz'd for superstition.
The more he thought, the more his mind
    was posed;
    In the mean time, his valet, whose pre-
        cision
Was great, because his master brook'd no
    less,
Knock'd to inform him it was time to
    dress.

XXIX

He dress'd; and like young people he was
    wont
    To take some trouble with his toilet,
        but
This morning rather spent less time upon 't;
    Aside his very mirror soon was put;
His curls fell negligently o'er his front,
    His clothes were not curb'd to their
        usual cut,
His very neckcloth's Gordian knot was
    tied
Almost an hair's breadth too much on one
    side.

XXX

And when he walk'd down into the saloon,
    He sate him pensive o'er a dish of tea,
Which he perhaps had not discover'd
    soon,
    Had it not happen'd scalding hot to be,
Which made him have recourse unto his
    spoon;
    So much *distrait* he was, that all could see
That something was the matter—Adeline
The first—but *what* she could not well
    divine.

XXXI

She look'd, and saw him pale, and turn'd
    as pale
    Herself; then hastily look'd down, and
        mutter'd
Something, but what's not stated in my tale.
    Lord Henry said, his muffin was ill-
        butter'd;

The Duchess of Fitz-Fulke play'd with her
    veil,
    And look'd at Juan hard, but nothing
        utter'd.
Aurora Raby with her large dark eyes
Survey'd him with a kind of calm surprise.

XXXII

But seeing him all cold and silent still,
    And everybody wondering more or
        less,
Fair Adeline inquired 'If he were ill?'
    He started, and said, 'Yes—no—rather
        —yes.'
The family physician had great skill,
    And being present, now began to ex-
        press
His readiness to feel his pulse and tell
The cause, but Juan said, 'He was quite
    well.'

XXXIII

'Quite well; yes,—no.'—These answers
    were mysterious,
    And yet his looks appear'd to sanction
        both,
However they might savour of delirious;
    Something like illness of a sudden
        growth
Weigh'd on his spirit, though by no means
    serious:
    But for the rest, as he himself seem'd
        loth
To state the case, it might be ta'en for
    granted
It was not the physician that he wanted.

XXXIV

Lord Henry, who had now discuss'd his
    chocolate,
    Also the muffin whereof he complain'd,
Said, Juan had not got his usual look
    elate,
    At which he marvell'd, since it had not
        rain'd;
Then ask'd her Grace what news were of
    the duke of late?
    Her Grace replied, *his* Grace was rather
        pain'd
With some slight, light, hereditary twinges
Of gout, which rusts aristocratic hinges.

XXXV

Then Henry turn'd to Juan, and address'd
    A few words of condolence on his state:
'You look,' quoth he, 'as if you had had
    your rest
    Broke in upon by the Black Friar of late.'
'What Friar?' said Juan; and he did his
    best
    To put the question with an air sedate,
Or careless; but the effort was not valid
To hinder him from growing still more
    pallid.

XXXVI

'Oh! have you never heard of the Black
    Friar?
    The spirit of these walls?'—'In truth
      not I.'
'Why Fame—but Fame you know's some-
    times a liar—
Tells an odd story, of which by and by:
Whether with time the spectre has grown
    shyer,
    Or that our sires had a more gifted eye
For such sights, though the tale is half
    believed,
The Friar of late has not been oft perceived.

XXXVII

'The last time was——'—'I pray,' said
    Adeline—
    (Who watch'd the changes of Don
      Juan's brow,
And from its context thought she could
    divine
    Connexions stronger than he chose to
      avow
With this same legend)—'if you but design
    To jest, you'll choose some other theme
      just now,
Because the present tale has oft been told,
And is not much improved by growing old.'

XXXVIII

'Jest!' quoth Milor; 'why, Adeline, you
    know
    That we ourselves—'twas in the honey-
      moon—
Saw——'—'Well, no matter, 'twas so
    long ago;
    But, come, I'll set your story to a tune.'
Graceful as Dian when she draws her bow,
    She seiz'd her harp, whose strings were
    kindled soon
As touch'd, and plaintively began to play
The air of ''Twas a Friar of Orders Gray.'

XXXIX

'But add the words,' cried Henry, 'which
    you made;
    For Adeline is half a poetess,'
Turning round to the rest, he smiling said.
    Of course the others could not but
    express
In courtesy their wish to see display'd
    By one *three* talents, for there were no
    less—
The voice, the words, the harper's skill, at
    once,
Could hardly be united by a dunce.

XL

After some fascinating hesitation,—
    The charming of these charmers, who
    seem bound,
I can't tell why, to this dissimulation,—
    Fair Adeline, with eyes fix'd on the
    ground

At first, then kindling into animation,
    Added her sweet voice to the lyric
    sound,
And sang with much simplicity,—a merit
Not the less precious, that we seldom hear
    it.

1

Beware! beware! of the Black Friar,
    Who sitteth by Norman stone,
For he mutters his prayer in the midnight
    air,
    And his mass of the days that are gone.
When the Lord of the Hill, Amundeville,
    Made Norman Church his prey,
And expell'd the friars, one friar still
    Would not be driven away.

2

Though he came in his might, with King
    Henry's right,
    To turn church lands to lay,
With sword in hand, and torch to light
    Their walls, if they said nay;
A monk remain'd, unchased, unchain'd,
    And he did not seem form'd of clay,
For he's seen in the porch, and he's seen
    in the church,
    Though he is not seen by day.

3

And whether for good, or whether for ill,
    It is not mine to say;
But still to the house of Amundeville
    He abideth night and day.
By the marriage-bed of their lords, 'tis said,
    He flits on the bridal eve;
And 'tis held as faith, to their bed of death
    He comes—but not to grieve.

4

When an heir is born, he is heard to mourn,
    And when aught is to befall
That ancient line, in the pale moonshine
    He walks from hall to hall.
His form you may trace, but not his face,
    'Tis shadow'd by his cowl;
But his eyes may be seen from the folds
    between,
    And they seem of a parted soul.

5

But beware! beware! of the Black Friar,
    He still retains his sway,
For he is yet the Church's heir,
    Whoever may be the lay.
Amundeville is lord by day,
    But the monk is lord by night;
Nor wine nor wassail could raise a vassal
    To question that friar's right.

6

Say nought to him as he walks the hall,
    And he'll say nought to you;
He sweeps along in his dusky pall,
    As o'er the grass the dew.

Then grammercy! for the Black Friar;
  Heaven sain him! fair or foul,
And whatsoe'er may be his prayer,
  Let ours be for his soul.

XLI

The lady's voice ceased, and the thrilling
    wires
  Died from the touch that kindled them
    to sound;
And the pause follow'd, which when song
    expires
  Pervades a moment those who listen
    round;
And then of course the circle much admires,
  Nor less applauds, as in politeness bound,
The tones, the feeling, and the execution,
To the performer's diffident confusion.

XLII

Fair Adeline, though in a careless way,
  As if she rated such accomplishment
As the mere pastime of an idle day,
  Pursued an instant for her own content,
Would now and then, as 'twere *without*
    display,
  Yet *with* display in fact, at times relent
To such performances with haughty smile,
To show she *could*, if it were worth her
    while.

XLIII

Now this (but we will whisper it aside)
  Was—pardon the pedantic illustra-
    tion—
Trampling on Plato's pride with greater
    pride,
  As did the Cynic on some like occasion:
Deeming the sage would be much morti-
    fied,
  Or thrown into a philosophic passion,
For a spoilt carpet—but the 'Attic bee'
Was much consoled by his own repartee.

XLIV

Thus Adeline would throw into the shade
  (By doing easily, whene'er she chose,
What dilettanti do with vast parade)
  Their sort of *half profession*; for it grows
To something like this when too oft dis-
    play'd;
  And that it is so, everybody knows,
Who have heard Miss That or This, or
    Lady T'other,
Show off—to please their company or
    mother.

XLV

Oh! the long evenings of duets and trios!
  The admirations and the speculations;
The 'Mamma Mia's!' and the 'Amor
    Mio's!'
  The 'Tanti palpiti's' on such occasions:

The 'Lasciami's,' and quavering 'Ad-
    dio's!'
  Amongst our own most musical of
    nations;
With 'Tu mi chamas's' from Portingale,
To soothe our ears, lest Italy should fail.

XLVI

In Babylon's *bravuras*—as the home
  Heart-ballads of Green Erin or Gray
    Highlands,
That bring Lochaber back to eyes that
    roam
  O'er far Atlantic continents or islands,
The calentures of music which o'ercome
  All mountaineers with dreams that they
    are nigh lands,
No more to be beheld but in such visions—
Was Adeline well versed, as compositions.

XLVII

She also had a twilight tinge of '*Blue*,'
  Could write rhymes, and compose more
    than she wrote,
Made epigrams occasionally too
  Upon her friends, as everybody ought.
But still from that sublimer azure hue,
  So much the present dye, she was remote;
Was weak enough to deem Pope a great
    poet,
And what was worse, was not ashamed to
    show it.

XLVIII

Aurora—since we are touching upon taste,
  Which now-a-days is the thermometer
By whose degrees all characters are
    class'd—
  Was more Shaksperian, if I do not err.
The worlds beyond this world's perplex-
    ing waste
  Had more of her existence, for in her
There was a depth of feeling to embrace
Thoughts, boundless, deep, but silent too
    as Space.

XLIX

Not so her gracious, graceful, graceless
    Grace,
  The full-grown Hebe of Fitz-Fulke,
    whose mind,
If she had any, was upon her face,
  And that was of a fascinating kind.
A little turn for mischief you might trace
  Also thereon,—but that's not much;
    we find
Few females without some such gentle
    leaven,
For fear we should suppose us quite in
    heaven.

L

I have not heard she was at all poetic,
  Though once she was seen reading the
    Bath Guide,
And Hayley's *Triumphs*, which she deem'd
    pathetic,

Because she said *her temper* had been
    tried
So much, the bard had really been pro-
    phetic
Of what she had gone through with—
    since a bride.
But of all verse, what most insured her
    praise
Were sonnets to herself, or *bouts rimés*.

LI

'Twere difficult to say what was the object
Of Adeline, in bringing this same lay
To bear on what appear'd to her the sub-
    ject
Of Juan's nervous feelings on that day.
Perhaps she merely had the simple project
    To laugh him out of his supposed dis-
    may;
Perhaps she might wish to confirm him
    in it,
Though why I cannot say—at least this
    minute.

LII

But so far the immediate effect
    Was to restore him to his self-propriety,
A thing quite necessary to the elect,
    Who wish to take the tone of their
    society:
In which you cannot be too circumspect,
    Whether the mode be persiflage or piety,
But wear the newest mantle of hypocrisy,
On pain of much displeasing the gyno-
    cracy.

LIII

And therefore Juan now began to rally
    His spirits, and without more explana-
    tion
To jest upon such themes in many a sally.
    Her Grace, too, also seized the same
    occasion,
With various similar remarks to tally,
    But wish'd for a still more detail'd
    narration
Of this same mystic friar's curious doings,
About the present family's deaths and
    wooings.

LIV

Of these few could say more than has been
    said;
    They pass'd as such things do, for
    superstition
With some, while others, who had more
    in dread
    The theme, half credited the strange
    tradition;
And much was talk'd on all sides on that
    head:
    But Juan, when cross-question'd on the
    vision,
Which some supposed (though he had not
    avow'd it)
Had stirr'd him, answer'd in a way to
    cloud it.

LV

And then, the mid-day having worn to
    one,
    The company prepared to separate;
Some to their several pastimes, or to none,
    Some wondering 'twas so early, some
    so late.
There was a goodly match too, to be run
    Between some greyhounds on my lord's
    estate,
And a young race-horse of old pedigree,
Match'd for the spring, whom several
    went to see.

LVI

There was a picture-dealer who had
    brought
    A special Titian, warranted original,
So precious that it was not to be bought,
    Though princes the possessor were
    besieging all.
The king himself had cheapen'd it, but
    thought
    The civil list he deigns to accept (oblig-
    ing all
His subjects by his gracious acceptation)—
Too scanty, in these times of low taxation.

LVII

But as Lord Henry was a connoisseur,—
    The friend of artists, if not arts,—the
    owner,
With motives the most classical and pure,
    So that he would have been the very
    donor,
Rather than seller, had his wants been fewer,
    So much he deem'd his patronage an
    honour,
Had brought the *capo d'opera*, not for sale,
But for his judgment—never known to fail.

LVIII

There was a modern Goth, I mean a
    Gothic
Bricklayer of Babel, call'd an architect,
    Brought to survey these grey walls, which
    though so thick,
    Might have from time acquired some
    slight defect;
Who, after rummaging the Abbey through
    thick
    And thin, produced a plan whereby to
    erect
New buildings of correctest conformation,
And throw down old, which he call'd
    restoration.

LIX

The cost would be a trifle—an 'old song,'
    Set to some thousands ('tis the usual
    burden
Of that same tune, when people hum it
    long)—
    The price would speedily repay its
    worth in

An edifice no less sublime than strong,
  By which Lord Henry's good taste
    would go forth in
Its glory, through all ages shining sunny,
For Gothic daring shown in English money.

LX

There were two lawyers busy on a
    mortgage
  Lord Henry wish'd to raise for a new
    purchase;
Also a lawsuit upon tenures burgage,
  And one on tithes, which sure are
    Discord's torches,
Kindling Religion till she throws down
    her gage,
  'Untying' squires 'to fight against the
    churches';
There was a prize ox, a prize pig, and
    ploughman,
For Henry was a sort of Sabine showman.

LXI

There were two poachers caught in a steel
    trap,
  Ready for gaol, their place of con-
    valescence;
There was a country girl in a close cap
  And scarlet cloak (I hate the sight to
    see, since—
Since—since—in youth, I had the sad
    mishap—
  But luckily I have paid few parish fees
    since):
That scarlet cloak, alas! unclosed with
    rigour
Presents the problem of a double figure.

LXII

A reel within a bottle is a mystery,
  One can't tell how it e'er got in or out;
Therefore the present piece of natural
    history
  I leave to those who are fond of solving
    doubt;
And merely state, though not for the con-
    sistory,
  Lord Henry was a justice, and that Scout
The constable, beneath a warrant's banner,
Had bagg'd this poacher upon Nature's
    manor.

LXIII

Now justices of peace must judge all pieces
  Of mischief of all kinds, and keep the
    game
And morals of the country from caprices
  Of those who have not a licence for the
    same;
And of all things, excepting tithes and leases,
  Perhaps these are most difficult to tame:
Preserving partridges and pretty wenches
Are puzzles to the most precautious
benches.

LXIV

The present culprit was extremely pale,
  Pale as if painted so; her cheek being red
By nature, as in higher dames less hale
  'Tis white, at least when they just rise
    from bed.
Perhaps she was ashamed of seeming frail,
  Poor soul! for she was country born
    and bred,
And knew no better in her immorality
Than to wax white—for blushes are for
    quality.

LXV

Her black, bright, downcast, yet *espiègle*
    eye,
  Had gather'd a large tear into its corner,
Which the poor thing at times essay'd to
    dry,
  For she was not a sentimental mourner
Parading all her sensibility,
  Nor insolent enough to scorn the
    scorner,
But stood in trembling, patient tribula-
    tion,
To be call'd up for her examination.

LXVI

Of course these groups were scatter'd here
    and there,
  Not nigh the gay saloon of ladies gent.
The lawyers in the study; and in air
  The prize pig, ploughman, poachers;
    the men sent
From town, viz. architect and dealer, were
  Both busy (as a general in his tent
Writing despatches) in their several
    stations,
Exulting in their brilliant lucubrations.

LXVII

But this poor girl was left in the great hall,
  While Scout, the parish guardian of the
    frail,
Discuss'd (he hated beer yclept the
    'small')
  A mighty mug of *moral* double ale.
She waited until Justice could recall
  Its kind attentions to their proper pale,
To name a thing in nomenclature rather
Perplexing for most virgins—a child's
    father.

LXVIII

You see here was enough of occupation
  For the Lord Henry, link'd with dogs
    and horses.
There was much bustle too, and prepara-
    tion
  Below stairs on the score of second
    courses;
Because, as suits their rank and situation,
  Those who in counties have great land
    resources

Have 'public days,' when all men may
    carouse,
Though not exactly what's call'd 'open
    house.'

LXIX

But once a week or fortnight, *un*invited
    (Thus we translate a *general invitation*),
All country gentlemen, esquired or
    knighted,
    May drop in without cards, and take
    their station
At the full board, and sit alike delighted
    With fashionable wines and conversa-
    tion;
And, as the isthmus of the grand con-
    nexion,
Talk o'er themselves the past and next
    election.

LXX

Lord Henry was a great electioneerer,
    Burrowing for boroughs like a rat or
    rabbit.
But county contests cost him rather
    dearer,
    Because the neighbouring Scotch Earl
    of Giftgabbit
Had English influence, in the self-same
    sphere here;
    His son, the Honourable Dick Diced-
    rabbit,
Was member for the 'other interest' (meaning
The same self-interest, with a different
    leaning).

LXXI

Courteous and cautious therefore in his
    county,
    He was all things to all men, and
    dispensed
To some civility, to others bounty,
    And promises to all—which last com-
    menced
To gather to a somewhat large amount, he
    Not calculating how much they con-
    densed;
But what with keeping some, and break-
    ing others,
His word had the same value as another's.

LXXII

A friend to freedom and freeholders—yet
    No less a friend to government—he
    held,
That he exactly the just medium hit
    'Twixt place and patriotism—albeit
    compell'd,
Such was his sovereign's pleasure, (though
    unfit,
    He added modestly, when rebels rail'd,)
To hold some sinecures he wish'd abolish'd,
But that with them all law would be
    demolish'd.

LXXIII

He was 'free to confess'—(whence comes
    this phrase?
    Is't English? No—'tis only parlia-
    mentary)
That innovation's spirit now-a-days
    Had made more progress than for the
    last century.
He would not tread a factious path to
    praise,
    Though for the public weal disposed to
    venture high;
As for his place, he could but say this of it,
That the fatigue was greater than the profit.

LXXIV

Heaven, and his friends, knew that a
    private life
    Had ever been his sole and whole
    ambition;
But could he quit his king in times of
    strife,
    Which threaten'd the whole country
    with perdition?
When demagogues would with a butcher's
    knife
    Cut through and through (oh! damnable
    incision!)
The Gordian or the Geordi-an knot,
    whose strings
Have tied together commons, lords, and
    kings.

LXXV

Sooner 'come Place into the Civil List
    And champion him to the utmost—'
    he would keep it,
Till duly disappointed or dismiss'd:
    Profit he cared not for, let others reap
    it;
But should the day come when place
    ceased to exist,
    The country would have far more cause
    to weep it:
For how could it go on? Explain who
    can!
He gloried in the name of Englishman.

LXXVI

He was as independent—ay, much more—
    Than those who were not paid for
    independence,
As common soldiers, or a common——
    shore,
    Have in their several arts or parts
    ascendance
O'er the irregulars in lust or gore,
    Who do not give professional atten-
    dance.
Thus on the mob all statesmen are as eager
To prove their pride, as footmen to a
    beggar.

LXXVII

All this (save the last stanza) Henry said,
And thought. I say no more—I've said
  too much;
For all of us have either heard or read—
Off—or *upon* the hustings—some slight
  such
Hints from the independent heart or head
Of the official candidate. I'll touch
No more on this—the dinner-bell hath
  rung.
And grace is said; the grace I *should* have
  sung—

LXXVIII

But I'm too late, and therefore must make
  play.
  'Twas a great banquet, such as Albion
  old
Was wont to boast—as if a glutton's tray
  Were something very glorious to behold.
But 'twas a public feast and public day,—
  Quite full, right dull, guests hot, and
  dishes cold,
Great plenty, much formality, small cheer,
And everybody out of their own sphere.

LXXIX

The squires familiarly formal, and
  My lords and ladies proudly con-
  descending;
The very servants puzzling how to hand
  Their plates—without it might be too
  much bending
From their high places by the sideboard's
  stand—
  Yet, like their masters, fearful of
  offending.
For any deviation from the graces
Might cost both man and master too—
  their *places*.

LXXX

There were some hunters bold, and
  coursers keen,
  Whose hounds ne'er err'd, nor grey-
  hounds deign'd to lurch;
Some deadly shots too, Septembrizers, seen
  Earliest to rise, and last to quit the search
Of the poor partridge through his stubble
  screen.
  There were some massy members of the
  church,
Takers of tithes, and makers of good
  matches,
And several who sung fewer psalms than
  catches.

LXXXI

There were some country wags too—and,
  alas!
  Some exiles from the town, who had
  been driven
To gaze, instead of pavement, upon grass,
  And rise at nine in lieu of long eleven.

And lo! upon that day it came to pass,
  I sate next that o'erwhelming son of
  heaven,
The very powerful parson, Peter Pith,
The loudest wit I e'er was deafen'd with.

LXXXII

I knew him in his livelier London days,
  A brilliant diner-out, though but a
  curate;
And not a joke he cut but earn'd its praise,
  Until preferment, coming at a sure rate,
(O Providence! how wondrous are thy ways!
  Who would suppose thy gifts some-
  times obdurate?)
Gave him, to lay the devil who looks o'er
  Lincoln,
A fat fen vicarage, and nought to think on.

LXXXIII

His jokes were sermons, and his sermons
  jokes;
  But both were thrown away amongst
  the fens;
For wit hath no great friend in aguish folks.
  No longer ready ears and short-hand
  pens
Imbibed the gay *bon-mot*, or happy hoax:
  The poor priest was reduced to com-
  mon sense,
Or to coarse efforts very loud and long,
To hammer a hoarse laugh from the thick
  throng.

LXXXIV

There *is* a difference, says the song, 'be-
  tween
  A beggar and a queen,' or *was* (of late
The latter worse used of the two we've
  seen—
  But we'll say nothing of affairs of
  state);
A difference ''twixt a bishop and a dean,'
  A difference between crockery ware and
  plate,
As between English beef and Spartan
  broth—
And yet great heroes have been bred by
  both.

LXXXV

But of all nature's discrepancies, none
  Upon the whole is greater than the
  difference
Beheld between the country and the town,
  Of which the latter merits every preference
From those who have few resources of
  their own,
  And only think, or act, or feel, with
  reference
To some small plan of interest or ambi-
  tion—
Both which are limited to no condition.

LXXXVI

But *En avant!* The light loves languish
 o'er
 Long banquets and too many guests,
  although
A slight repast makes people love much
 more,
 Bacchus and Ceres being, as we know,
Even from our grammar upwards, friends
 of yore
 With vivifying Venus, who doth owe
To these the invention of champagne and
 truffles:
Temperance delights her, but long fasting
 ruffles.

LXXXVII

Dully pass'd o'er the dinner of the day;
 And Juan took his place, he knew not
  where,
Confused, in the confusion, and *distrait*,
 And sitting as if nail'd upon his chair:
Though knives and forks clang'd round
 as in a fray,
 He seem'd unconscious of all passing
  there,
Till some one, with a groan, exprest a wish
(Unheeded twice) to have a fin of fish.

LXXXVIII

On which, at the *third* asking of the banns,
 He started; and perceiving smiles around
Broadening to grins, he colour'd more
 than once,
 And hastily—as nothing can confound
A wise man more than laughter from a
 dunce—
 Inflicted on the dish a deadly wound,
And with such hurry, that, ere he could
 curb it,
He had paid his neighbour's prayer with
 half a turbot.

LXXXIX

This was no bad mistake, as it occurr'd,
 The supplicator being an amateur;
But others, who were left with scarce a
 third,
 Were angry—as they well might, to be
  sure.
They wonder'd how a young man so absurd
 Lord Henry at his table should endure;
And this, and his not knowing how much
 oats
Had fall'n last market, cost his host three
 votes.

XC

They little knew, or might have sympa-
 thised,
 That he the night before had seen a
  ghost,
A prologue which but slightly harmonised
 With the substantial company engross'd

By matter, and so much materialised,
 That one scarce knew at what to marvel
  most
Of two things—how (the question rather
 odd is)
Such bodies could have souls, or souls
 such bodies.

XCI

But what confused him more than smile or
 stare,
 From all the 'squires and 'squiresses
  around,
Who wonder'd at the abstraction of his air,
 Especially as he had been renown'd
For some vivacity among the fair,
 Even in the country circle's narrow
  bound—
(For little things upon my lord's estate
Were good small talk for others still less
 great)—

XCII

Was, that he caught Aurora's eye on his,
 And something like a smile upon her
  cheek.
Now this he really rather took amiss;
 In those who rarely smile, their smiles
  bespeak
A strong external motive; and in this
 Smile of Aurora's there was nought to
  pique,
Or hope, or love, with any of the wiles
Which some pretend to trace in ladies'
 smiles.

XCIII

'Twas a mere quiet smile of contempla-
 tion,
 Indicative of some surprise and pity;
And Juan grew carnation with vexation,
 Which was not very wise, and still less
  witty,
Since he had gain'd at least her observa-
 tion,
 A most important outwork of the city—
As Juan should have known, had not his
 senses
By last night's ghost been driven from
 their defences.

XCIV

But what was bad, she did not blush in
 turn,
 Nor seem embarrass'd—quite the con-
  trary;
Her aspect was as usual, still—*not* stern—
 And she withdrew, but cast not down,
  her eye,
Yet grew a little pale—with what? con-
 cern?
 I know not; but her colour ne'er was
  high—
Though sometimes faintly flush'd—and
 always clear,
As deep seas in a sunny atmosphere.

XCV

But Adeline was occupied by fame
   This day; and watching, witching, con-
      descending
To the consumers of fish, fowl, and game,
   And dignity with courtesy so blending,
As all must blend whose part it is to aim
   (Especially as the sixth year is ending)
At their lord's, son's, or similar con-
     nexion's
Safe conduct through the rocks of re-
   ëlections.

XCVI

Though this was most expedient on the
   whole,
   And usual—Juan, when he cast a glance
On Adeline while playing her grand *rôle*,
   Which she went through as though it
     were a dance,
Betraying only now and then her soul
   By a look scarce perceptibly askance
(Of weariness or scorn), began to feel
Some doubt how much of Adeline was
   real;

XCVII

So well she acted all and every part
   By turns—with that vivacious versatility,
Which many people take for want of
   heart.
   They err—'tis merely what is call'd
     mobility,
A thing of temperament and not of art,
   Though seeming so, from its supposed
     facility;
And false—though true; for surely they're
   sincerest
Who are strongly acted on by what is
   nearest.

XCVIII

This makes your actors, artists, and
   romancers,
   Heroes sometimes, though seldom—
     sages never:
But speakers, bards, diplomatists, and
   dancers,
   Little that's great, but much of what is
     clever;
Most orators, but very few financiers,
   Though all Exchequer chancellors
     endeavour,
Of late years, to dispense with Cocker's
   rigours,
And grow quite figurative with their
   figures.

XCIX

The poets of arithmetic are they
   Who, though they prove not two and
     two to be
Five, as they might do in a modest way,
   Have plainly made it out that four are
   three,

Judging by what they take, and what they
   pay.
   The Sinking Fund's unfathomable sea,
That most unliquidating liquid, leaves
The debt unsunk, yet sinks all it receives.

C

While Adeline dispensed her airs and
   graces,
   The fair Fitz-Fulke seem'd very much
     at ease;
Though too well bred to quiz men to their
   faces,
   Her laughing blue eyes with a glance
     could seize
The ridicules of people in all places—
   That honey of your fashionable bees—
And store it up for mischievous enjoy-
   ment;
And this at present was her kind employ-
   ment.

CI

However, the day closed, as days must
   close;
   The evening also waned—and coffee
     came.
Each carriage was announced, and ladies
   rose,
   And curtsying off, as curtsies country
     dame,
Retired: with most unfashionable bows
   Their docile esquires also did the same,
Delighted with the dinner and their host,
But with the Lady Adeline the most.

CII

Some praised her beauty: others her great
   grace;
   The warmth of her politeness, whose
     sincerity
Was obvious in each feature of her face,
   Whose traits were radiant with the rays
     of verity.
Yes: *she* was truly worthy *her* high place!
   No one could envy her deserved
     prosperity.
And then her dress—what beautiful
   simplicity
Draperied her form with curious felicity!

CIII

Meanwhile sweet Adeline deserved their
   praises,
   By an impartial indemnification
For all her past exertion and soft phrases,
   In a most edifying conversation,
Which turn'd upon their late guests'
   miens and faces,
   And families, even to the last relation;
Their hideous wives, their horrid selves
   and dresses,
And truculent distortion of their tresses.

CIV

True, *she* said little—'twas the rest that
    broke
Forth into universal epigram;
But then 'twas to the purpose what she
    spoke:
    Like Addison's 'faint praise,' so wont
        to damn,
Her own but served to set off every joke,
    As music chimes in with a melodrame.
How sweet the task to shield an absent
    friend!
I ask but this of mine, to——*not* defend.

CV

There were but two exceptions to this keen
    Skirmish of wits o'er the departed; one
Aurora, with her pure and placid mien;
    And Juan, too, in general behind none
In gay remark on what he had heard or
    seen,
    Sate silent now, his usual spirits gone:
In vain he heard the others rail or rally,
He would not join them in a single sally.

CVI

'Tis true he saw Aurora look as though
    She approved his silence; she perhaps
        mistook
Its motive for that charity we owe
    But seldom pay the absent, nor would
        look
Farther; it might or it might not be so.
    But Juan, sitting silent in his nook,
Observing little in his reverie,
Yet saw this much, which he was glad to
    see.

CVII

The ghost at least had done him this much
    good,
    In making him as silent as a ghost,
If in the circumstances which ensued
    He gain'd esteem where it was worth
        the most;
And certainly Aurora had renew'd
    In him some feelings he had lately lost,
Or harden'd; feelings which, perhaps ideal,
Are so divine, that I must deem them
    real:—

CVIII

The love of higher things and better days;
    The unbounded hope, and heavenly
        ignorance
Of what is call'd the world, and the world's
    ways;
    The moments when we gather from a
        glance
More joy than from all future pride or praise,
    Which kindle manhood, but can ne'er
        entrance
The heart in an existence of its own,
Of which another's bosom is the zone.

CIX

Who would not sigh Αἴ αἴ τὰν Κυθέρειαν
    That *hath* a memory, or that *had* a heart?
Alas! *her* star must wane like that of Dian:
    Ray fades on ray, as years on years depart.
Anacreon only had the soul to tie an
    Unwithering myrtle round the un-
        blunted dart
Of Eros: but though thou hast play'd us
        many tricks,
Still we respect thee, '*Alma Venus Gene-*
    trix!'

CX

And full of sentiments, sublime as billows
    Heaving between this world and worlds
        beyond,
Don Juan, when the midnight hour of
        pillows
    Arrived, retired to his; but to despond
Rather than rest. Instead of poppies,
        willows
    Waved o'er his couch; he meditated,
        fond
Of those sweet bitter thoughts which
        banish sleep,
And make the worldling sneer, the young-
        ling weep.

CXI

The night was as before: he was undrest,
    Saving his night-gown, which is an
        undress;
Completely *sans culotte*, and without
        vest;
    In short, he hardly could be clothed with
        less:
But apprehensive of his spectral guest,
    He sate with feelings awkward to
        express
(By those who have not had such visita-
        tions),
Expectant of the ghost's fresh operations.

CXII

And not in vain he listen'd;—Hush!
        what's that?
    I see—I see—Ah, no!—'tis not—yet 'tis—
Ye powers! it is the—the—the—Pooh!
        the cat!
    The devil may take that stealthy pace
        of his!
So like a spiritual pit-a-pat,
    Or tiptoe of an amatory Miss,
Gliding the first time to a *rendezvous*,
And dreading the chaste echoes of her
    shoe.

CXIII

Again—what is 't? The wind? No, no,—
        this time
    It is the sable Friar as before,
With awful footsteps regular as rhyme,
    Or (as rhymes may be in these days)
        much more.

Again through shadows of the night sublime,
　When deep sleep fell on men, and the
　　world wore
The starry darkness round her like a girdle
Spangled with gems—the monk made his
　blood curdle.

CXIV

A noise like to wet fingers drawn on glass,
　Which sets the teeth on edge; and a
　　slight clatter
Like showers which on the midnight gusts
　will pass,
　Sounding like very supernatural water,
Came over Juan's ear, which throbb'd, alas!
　For immaterialism's a serious matter;
So that even those whose faith is the most
　great
In souls immortal, shun them *tête-à-tête*.

CXV

Were his eyes open?—Yes! and his mouth
　too.
　Surprise has this effect—to make one
　　dumb,
Yet leave the gate which eloquence slips
　through
　As wide, as if a long speech were to
　　come.
Nigh and more nigh the awful echoes
　drew,
　Tremendous to a mortal tympanum:
His eyes were open, and (as was before
Stated) his mouth. What open'd next?—
　the door.

CXVI

It open'd with a most infernal creak,
　Like that of hell. 'Lasciate ogni
　　speranza
Voi ch' entrate!' The hinge seem'd to
　speak,
　Dreadful as Dante's rima, or this
　　stanza;
Or—but all words upon such themes are
　weak:
　A single shade's sufficient to entrance a
Hero—for what is substance to a spirit?
Or how is't *matter* trembles to come near
　it?

CXVII

The door flew wide, not swiftly,—but, as
　fly
　The sea-gulls, with a steady, sober
　　flight—
And then swung back; nor close—but
　stood awry,
　Half letting in long shadows on the
　　light,
Which still in Juan's candlesticks burn'd
　high,
　For he had two, both tolerably bright,
And in the doorway, darkening darkness,
　stood
The sable Friar in his solemn hood.

CXVIII

Don Juan shook, as erst he had been shaken
　The night before; but being sick of
　　shaking,
He first inclined to think he had been mis-
　taken;
　And then to be ashamed of such
　　mistaking;
His own internal ghost began to awaken
　Within him, and to quell his corporal
　　quaking—
Hinting that soul and body on the whole
Were odds against a disembodied soul.

CXIX

And then his dread grew wrath, and his
　wrath fierce,
　And he arose, advanced—the shade
　　retreated;
But Juan, eager now the truth to pierce,
　Followed, his veins no longer cold, but
　　heated,
Resolved to thrust the mystery *carte* and
　tierce,
　At whatsoever risk of being defeated:
The ghost stopp'd, menaced, then retired,
　until
He reach'd the ancient wall, then stood
　stone still.

CXX

Juan put forth one arm—Eternal powers!
　It touch'd no soul, nor body, but the
　　wall,
On which the moonbeams fell in silvery
　showers,
　Chequer'd with all the tracery of the
　　hall;
He shudder'd, as no doubt the bravest
　cowers
　When he can't tell what 'tis that doth
　　appal.
How odd, a single hobgoblin's nonentity
Should cause more fear than a whole
　host's identity!

CXXI

But still the shade remain'd: the blue eyes
　glared,
　And rather variably for stony death;
Yet one thing rather good the grave had
　spared,
　The ghost had a remarkably sweet
　　breath:
A straggling curl show'd he had been
　fairhair'd;
　A red lip, with two rows of pearls beneath,
Gleam'd forth, as through the casement's
　ivy shroud
The moon peep'd, just escaped from a
　grey cloud.

CXXII

And Juan, puzzled, but still curious, thrust
His other arm forth—Wonder upon wonder!
It press'd upon a hard but glowing bust,
Which beat as if there was a warm heart under.
He found, as people on most trials must,
That he had made at first a silly blunder,
And that in his confusion he had caught
Only the wall, instead of what he sought.

CXXIII

The ghost, if ghost it were, seem'd a sweet soul
As ever lurk'd beneath a holy hood:
A dimpled chin, a neck of ivory, stole
Forth into something much like flesh and blood;
Back fell the sable frock and dreary cowl,
And they reveal'd—alas! that e'er they should!
In full, voluptuous, but *not* o'ergrown bulk,
The phantom of her frolic Grace—Fitz-Fulke!

CANTO THE SEVENTEENTH

I

The world is full of orphans: firstly, those
Who are so in the strict sense of the phrase;
But many a lonely tree the loftier grows
Than others crowded in the Forest's maze—
The next are such as are not doomed to lose
Their tender parents, in their budding days,
But, merely, their parental tenderness,
Which leaves them orphans of the heart no less.

II

The next are 'only' Children,' as they are styled,
Who grow up Children only, since th' old saw
Pronounces that an 'only"'s a spoilt child—
But not to go too far, I hold it law,
That where their education, harsh or mild,
Transgresses the great bounds of love or awe,
The sufferers—be 't in heart or intellect—
Whate'er the *cause*, are orphans in *effect*.

III

But to return unto the stricter rule—
As far as words make rules—our common notion
Of orphans paints at once a parish school,
A half-starved babe, a wreck upon Life's ocean,
A human (what the Italians nickname) 'Mule!'
A theme for Pity or some worse emotion;
Yet, if examined, it might be admitted
The wealthiest orphans are to be more pitied.

IV

Too soon they are Parents to themselves: for what
Are Tutors, Guardians, and so forth, compared
With Nature's genial Genitors? so that
A child of Chancery, that Star-Chamber ward,
(I'll take the likeness I can first come at,)
Is like—a duckling by Dame Partlett reared,
And frights—especially if 't is a daughter,
Th' old Hen—by running headlong to the water.

V

There is a common-place book argument,
Which glibly glides from every vulgar tongue;
When any dare a new light to present,
'If you are right, then everybody's wrong!'
Suppose the converse of this precedent
So often urged, so loudly and so long;
'If you are wrong, then everybody's right!'
Was ever everybody yet so quite?

VI

Therefore I would solicit free discussion
Upon all points—no matter what, or whose—
Because as Ages upon Ages push on,
The last is apt the former to accuse
Of pillowing its head on a pin-cushion,
Heedless of pricks because it was obtuse:
What was a paradox becomes a truth or
A something like it—as bear witness Luther!

VII

The Sacraments have been reduced to two,
And Witches unto none, though somewhat late
Since burning agéd women (save a few—
Not witches only b—ches —who create
Mischief in families, as some know or knew,
Should still be singed, but slightly, let me state,)
Has been declared an act of inurbanity,
Malgré Sir Matthew Hales's great humanity.

VIII

Great Galileo was debarred the Sun,
　　Because he fixed it; and, to stop his
　　　talking,
How Earth could round the solar orbit run,
　　Found his own legs embargoed from
　　　mere walking:
The man was well-nigh dead, ere men begun
　　To think his skull had not some need of
　　　caulking;
But now, it seems, he's right—his notion
　　just:
No doubt a consolation to his dust.

IX

Pythagoras, Locke, Socrates—but pages
　　Might be filled up, as vainly as before,
With the sad usage of all sorts of sages,
　　Who in his life-time, each, was deemed a
　　　Bore!
The loftiest minds outrun their tardy ages:
　　This they must bear with and, perhaps,
　　　much more;
The wise man's sure when he no more can
　　share it, he
Will have a firm Post Obit on posterity.

X

If such doom waits each intellectual Giant,
　　We little people in our lesser way,
In Life's small rubs should surely be more
　　pliant,
　　And so for one will I—as well I may—
Would that I were less bilious—but, oh,
　　fie on 't!
Just as I make my mind up every day,
To be a '*totus, teres,*' Stoic, Sage,
The wind shifts and I fly into a rage.

XI

Temperate I am—yet never had a temper;
　　Modest I am—yet with some slight
　　　assurance;
Changeable too—yet somehow '*Idem
　　semper:*'
　　Patient—but not enamoured of endur-
　　　ance;

Cheerful—but, sometimes, rather apt to
　　whimper:
　　Mild—but at times a sort of '*Hercules
　　　furens:*'
So that I almost think that the same skin
For one without—has two or three within.

XII

Our Hero was, in Canto the Sixteenth,
　　Left in a tender moonlight situation,
Such as enables Man to show his strength
　　Moral or physical: on this occasion
Whether his virtue triumphed—or, at
　　length,
　　His vice—for he was of a kindling nation—
Is more than I shall venture to describe;—
Unless some Beauty with a kiss should bribe.

XIII

I leave the thing a problem, like all things:—
　　The morning came—and breakfast, tea
　　　and toast,
Of which most men partake, but no one
　　sings.
　　The company whose birth, wealth, worth,
　　　have cost
My trembling Lyre already several strings,
　　Assembled with our hostess, and mine
　　　host;
The guests dropped in—the last but one,
　　Her Grace,
The latest, Juan, with his virgin face.

XIV

Which best it is to encounter—Ghost, or
　　none,
　　'Twere difficult to say—but Juan looked
As if he had combated with more than one,
　　Being wan and worn, with eyes that hardly
　　　brooked
The light, that through the Gothic windows
　　shone:
　　Her Grace, too, had a sort of air
　　　rebuked—
Seemed pale and shivered, as if she had kept
A vigil, or dreamt rather more than slept.

Notes and Index

NOTES

HOURS OF IDLENESS

Page 2, col. 1.

'ON THE DEATH OF A YOUNG LADY.'] The author claims the indulgence of the reader more for this piece than, perhaps, any other in the collection; but as it was written at an earlier period than the rest (being composed at the age of fourteen), and his first essay, he preferred submitting it to the indulgence of his friends in its present state, to making either addition or alteration.

Page 3, col. 2.

'On Marston.'] The battle of Marston Moor, where the adherents of Charles I. were defeated.

Page 3, col. 2.

'With Rupert, 'gainst traitors contending.'] Son of the Elector Palatine, and nephew to Charles I. He afterwards commanded the fleet in the reign of Charles II.

Page 9, col. 1.

TO THE DUKE OF DORSET.] In looking over my papers to select a few additional poems for this second edition, I found the above lines, which I had totally forgotten, composed in the summer of 1805, a short time previous to my departure from Harrow. They were addressed to a young schoolfellow of high rank, who had been my frequent companion in some rambles through the neighbouring country: however, he never saw the lines, and most probably never will. As, on a re-perusal, I found them not worse than some other pieces in the collection, I have now published them, for the first time, after a slight revision.

Page 9, col. 1.

'Bade *thee* obey, and gave *me* to command.'] At every public school the junior boys are completely subservient to the upper forms till they attain a seat in the higher classes. From this state of probation, very properly, no rank is exempt; but after a certain period, they command in turn those who succeed.

Page 9, col. 1.

'Though passive tutors, fearful to dispraise.'] Allow me to disclaim any personal allusions, even the most distant. I merely mention generally what is too often the weakness of preceptors.

Page 10, col. 2.

'Oh! could Le Sage's demon's gift.'] The Diable Boiteux of Le Sage, where Asmodeus, the demon, places Don Cleofas on an elevated situation, and unroofs the houses for inspection.

Page 11, col. 1.

'Who reads false quantities in Seale.'] Seale's publication on Greek Metres displays considerable talent and ingenuity, but, as might be expected in so difficult a work, is not remarkable for accuracy.

Page 11, col. 1.

'In barbarous Latin doom'd to wrangle.'] The Latin of the schools is of the *canine species*, and not very intelligible.

Page 11, col. 1.

'The square of the hypothenuse.'] The discovery of Pythagoras, that the square of the hypothenuse is equal to the squares of the other two sides of a right-angled triangle.

Page 11, col. 1.

'A numerous crowd, array'd in white.'] On a saint's day the students wear surplices in chapel.

Page 12, col. 1.

'I fancied that Mossop himself was outshone.'] Mossop, a contemporary of Garrick, famous for his performance of Zanga.

Page 12, col. 2.

'Would twinkle dimly through their sphere.']
'Two of the fairest stars in all the heaven,
  Having some business, do intreat her eyes
  To twinkle in their spheres till they return.'
                                        SHAKESPEARE.

Page 12, col. 2.

'Woman, thy vows are traced in sand.'] The last line is almost a literal translation from a Spanish proverb.

Page 13, col. 2.

'And hurtling o'er thy lovely head.'] This word is used by Gray in his poem to the Fatal Sisters:—

'Iron-sleet of arrowy shower
  Hurtles in the darken'd air.'

Page 14, col. 2.

'In law an infant, and in years a boy.'] In law every person is an infant who has not attained the age of twenty-one.

Page 15, col. 2.

'To form the place of assignation.'] In the above little piece the author has been accused by some *candid readers* of introducing the name of a lady from whom he was some hundred miles distant at the time this was written; and poor Juliet, who has slept so long in 'the tomb of all the Capulets,' has been converted, with a trifling alteration of her name, into an English damsel walking in a garden of their own creation, during the month of *December*, in a village where the author never passed a winter. Such has been the candour of some ingenious critics. He would advise these *liberal* commentators on taste and arbiters of decorum to read *Shakespeare*.

Page 16, col. 1.

'But curse my fate for ever after.'] Having heard that a very severe and indelicate censure has been passed on the above poem, I beg leave to reply in a quotation from an admired work, 'Carr's Stranger in France:'—'As we were contemplating a painting on a large scale, in which, among other figures, is the uncovered whole length of a warrior, a prudish-looking lady, who seemed to have touched the age of desperation, after having attentively surveyed it through her glass, observed to her party, that there was a great deal of indecorum ín that picture. Madame S. shrewdly whispered in my ear "that the indecorum was in the remark."'

Page 16, col. 1.

'OSCAR OF ALVA.'] The catastrophe of this tale was suggested by the story of 'Jeronyme and Lorenzo,' in the first volume of Schiller's 'Armenian, or the Ghost-Seer.' It also bears some resemblance to a scene in the third act of 'Macbeth.'

Page 21, col. 2.

'Creusa's style but wanting to the dame.'] The mother of Iulus, lost on the night when Troy was taken.

Page 24, col. 2.

'Ah! hapless dame! no sire bewails.'] Medea, who accompanied Jason to Corinth, was deserted by him for the daughter of Creon, king of that city. The chorus, from which this is taken, here addresses Medea; though a considerable liberty is taken with the original, by expanding the idea, as also in some other parts of the translation.

Page 24, col. 2.

'Who ne'er unlocks with silver key.'] The original is 'Καθαρὰν ἀνοίξαντι κλῆρα φρενῶν;' literally 'disclosing the bright key of the mind.'

Page 24, col. 2.

'MAGNUS his ample front sublime uprears.'] No reflection is here intended against the person mentioned under the name of Magnus. He is merely represented as performing an unavoidable function of his office. Indeed, such an attempt could only recoil upon myself; as that gentleman is now as much distinguished by his eloquence, and the dignified propriety with which he fills his situation, as he was in his younger days for wit and conviviality.

Page 25, col. 1.

'Th' ATHENIAN's glowing style, or Tully's fire.'] Demosthenes.

Page 25, col. 2.

'Yet prizing Bentley's, Brunck's, or Porson's note.'] The present Greek professor at Trinity College, Cambridge; a man whose powers of mind and writings may, perhaps, justify their preference.

Page 25, col. 2.

'Whether 'tis Pitt or Petty rules the hour.'] Since this was written, Lord Henry Petty [now Marquis of Lansdowne] has lost his place, and subsequently (I had almost said consequently) the honour of representing the University. A fact so glaring requires no comment.

Page 28, col. 1.

'Sweet scene of my youth! seat of Friendship and Truth.'] Harrow.

Page 29, col. 2.

'LACHIN Y GAIR.'] Lachin y Gair, or, as it is pronounced in the Erse, Loch na Garr, towers proudly pre-eminent in the Northern Highlands, near Invercauld. One of our modern tourists mentions it as the highest mountain, perhaps, in Great Britain. Be this as it may, it is certainly one of the most sublime and picturesque amongst our 'Caledonian Alps.' Its appearance is of a dusky hue, but the summit is the seat of eternal snows. Near Lachin y Gair I spent some of the early part

of my life, the recollection of which has given birth to these stanzas.

Page 29, col. 2.

'My cap was the bonnet, my cloak was the plaid.'] This word is erroneously pronounced plad: the proper pronunciation (according to the Scotch) is shown by the orthography.

Page 29, col. 2.

'Ill-starr'd, though brave, did no visions foreboding.'] I allude here to my maternal ancestors, 'the Gordons,' many of whom fought for the unfortunate Prince Charles, better known by the name of the Pretender. This branch was nearly allied by blood, as well as attachment, to the Stuarts. George, the second Earl of Huntley, married the Princess Annabella Stuart, daughter of James I. of Scotland. By her he left four sons: the third, Sir William Gordon, I have the honour to claim as one of my progenitors.

Page 29, col. 2.

'Ah! were you destined to die at Culloden.'] Whether any perished in the battle of Culloden, I am not certain; but, as many fell in the insurrection, I have used the name of the principal action, 'pars pro toto.'

Page 29, col. 2.

'You rest with your clan in the caves of Braemar.'] A tract of the Highlands so called. There is also a Castle of Braemar.

Page 30, col. 1.

'A Pylades in every friend?'] It is hardly necessary to add, that Pylades was the companion of Orestes, and a partner in one of those friendships which, with those of Achilles and Patroclus, Nisus and Euryalus, Damon and Pythias, have been handed down to posterity as remarkable instances of attachments, which in all probability never existed beyond the imagination of the poet, or the page of an historian, or modern novelist.

Page 31, col. 1.

'ELEGY ON NEWSTEAD ABBEY.'] As one poem on this subject is already printed, the author had, originally, no intention of inserting the following. It is now added at the particular request of some friends.

Page 31, col. 1.

'Religion's shrine! repentant HENRY's pride!'] Henry II. founded Newstead soon after the murder of Thomas à Becket.

Page 31, col. 2.

'No mail-clad serfs, obedient to their lord.'] This word is used by Walter Scott, in his poem, 'The Wild Huntsman;' synonymous with vassal.

Page 31, col. 2.

'In grim array the crimson cross demand.'] The red cross was the badge of the Crusaders.

Page 31, col. 2.

'Soon as the gloaming spreads her waning shade.'] As 'gloaming,' the Scottish word for twilight, is far more poetical, and has been recommended by many eminent literary men, particularly by Dr. Moore in his Letters to Burns, I have ventured to use it on account of its harmony.

Page 31, col. 2.

'Or matin orisons to Mary paid.'] The priory was dedicated to the Virgin.

Page 32, col. 1.

'Another HENRY the kind gift recalls.'] At the dissolution of the monasteries, Henry VIII. bestowed Newstead Abbey on Sir John Byron.

Page 32, col. 1.

'An abbey once, a regal fortress now.'] Newstead sustained a considerable siege in the war between Charles I. and his parliament.

Page 32, col. 1.

'Trembling she snatch'd him from th' unequal strife.'] Lord Byron and his brother Sir William held high commands in the royal army. The former was general-in-chief in Ireland, lieutenant of the Tower, and governor to James, Duke of York, afterwards the unhappy James II.; the latter had a principal share in many actions.

Page 32, col. 1.

'To lead the band where godlike FALKLAND fell.'] Lucius Cary, Lord Viscount Falkland, the most accomplished man of his age, was killed at the Battle of Newbury, charging in the ranks of Lord Byron's regiment of Cavalry.

Page 32, col. 2.

'Loathing the offering of so dark a death.'] This is an historical fact. A violent tempest occurred immediately subsequent to the death or interment of Cromwell, which occasioned many disputes between his partisans and the cavaliers: both interpreted the circumstance into divine interposition; but whether as approbation or condemnation, we leave to the casuists of that age to decide. I have made such use of the occurrence as suited the subject of my poem.

Page 33, col. 1.

'The legal ruler now resumes the helm.'] Charles II.

Page 35, col. 1.

'PROBUS, the pride of science, and the boast.'] Dr. Drury. This most able and excellent man retired from his situation in March, 1805, after having resided thirty-five years at Harrow; the last twenty as head-master; an office he held with equal honour to himself and advantage to the very extensive school over which he presided. Panegyric would here be superfluous: it would be useless to enumerate qualifications which were never doubted. A considerable contest took place between three rival candidates for his vacant chair: of this I can only say,

Si mea cum vestris valuissent vota, Pelasgi?
Non foret ambiguus tanti certaminis hæres.

Page 37, col. 2.

'As speakers each supports an equal name.'] This alludes to the public speeches delivered at the school where the author was educated.

Page 38, col. 2.

'And Love, without his pinion, smiled on Youth.'] 'L'Amitié est l'Amour sans ailes,' is a French proverb.

Page 38, col. 2.

ENTITLED 'THE COMMON LOT.'] Written by James Montgomery, author of the 'Wanderer in Switzerland,' &c.

Page 38, col. 2.

'The hero rolls the tide of war.'] No particular hero is here alluded to. The exploits of Bayard, Nemours, Edward the Black Prince, and, in more modern times, the fame of Marlborough, Frederick the Great, Count Saxe, Charles of Sweden, &c., are familiar to every historical reader, but the exact places of their birth are known to a very small proportion of their admirers.

Page 40, col. 1.

'AN IMITATION OF MACPHERSON'S OSSIAN.'] It may be necessary to observe, that the story, though considerably varied in the catastrophe, is taken from 'Nisus and Euryalus,' of which episode a translation is already given in the present volume.

Page 41, col. 2.

'Tears of the storm.'] I fear Laing's late edition has completely overthrown every hope that Macpherson's Ossian might prove the translation of a series of poems complete in themselves; but, while the imposture is discovered, the merit of the work remains undisputed, though not without faults—particularly, in some parts, turgid and bombastic diction.—The present humble imitation will be pardoned by the admirers of the original as an attempt, however inferior, which evinces an attachment to their favourite author.

Page 42, col. 1.

'Seat of my youth! thy distant spire.'] Harrow.

Page 44, col. 2.

'The cumbrous pomp of Saxon pride.'] Sassenach or Saxon, a Gaelic word, signifying either Lowland or English.

Page 45, col. 1.

'To flee away, and be at rest.'] 'And I said, Oh! that I had wings like a dove; for then would I fly away and be at rest.'—Psalm lv. 6. This verse also constitutes a part of the most beautiful anthem in our language.

Page 45, col. 1.

'And climb'd thy steep summit, oh Morven of snow!'] Morven, a lofty mountain in Aberdeenshire. 'Gormal of snow' is an expression frequently to be found in Ossian.

Page 45, col. 1.

'Or the mist of the tempest that gather'd below.'] This will not appear extraordinary to those who have been accustomed to the mountains. It is by no means uncommon, on attaining the top of Ben-e-vis, Ben-y-bourd, &c., to perceive, between the summit and the valley, clouds pouring down rain, and occasionally accompanied by lightning, while the spectator literally looks down upon the storm, perfectly secure from its effects.

Page 45, col. 1.

'I breasted the billows of Dee's rushing tide.'] The Dee is a beautiful river, which rises near Mar Lodge, and falls into the sea at New Aberdeen.

Page 45, col. 2.

'I think of the rocks that o'ershadow Colbleen.'] Colbleen is a mountain near the verge of the Highlands, not far from the ruins of Dee Castle.

Page 46, col. 2.

'As void of wit and moral.'] These stanzas were written soon after the appearance of a severe critique in a northern review on a new publication of the British Anacreon.

Page 47, col. 1.

'I really will not fight them.'] A bard [Moore] (horresco referens) defied his reviewer [Jeffrey] to mortal combat. If this example becomes prevalent, our periodical censors must be dipped in the river Styx: for what else can secure them from the numerous host of their enraged assailants?

OCCASIONAL PIECES

Page 48, col. 1.

'Adieu, thou Hill! where early joy.'] Harrow.

Page 51, col. 2.

'ON REVISITING HARROW.'] Some years ago, when at Harrow, a friend of the author engraved on a particular spot the names of both, with a few additional words, as a memorial. Afterwards, on receiving some real or imagined injury, the author destroyed the frail record before he left Harrow. On revisiting the place in 1807, he wrote under it these stanzas.

Page 59, col. 2.

'WRITTEN AFTER SWIMMING FROM SESTOS TO ABYDOS.'] On the 3rd of May, 1810, while the Salsette (Captain Bathurst) was lying in the Dardanelles, Lieutenant Ekenhead, of that frigate, and the writer of these rhymes, swam from the European shore to the Asiatic—by the by, from Abydos to Sestos would have been more correct. The whole distance, from the place whence we started to our landing on the other side, including the length we were carried by the current, was computed by those on board the frigate at upwards of four English miles, though the actual breadth is barely one. The rapidity of the current is such that no boat can row directly across, and it may, in some measure be estimated from the circumstance of the whole distance being accomplished by one of the parties, in an hour and five, and by the other in an hour and ten minutes. The water was extremely cold, from the melting of the mountain snows. About three weeks before, in April, we had made an attempt; but, having ridden all the way from the Troad the same morning, and the water being of an icy chillness, we found it necessary to postpone the completion till the frigate anchored below the castles, when we swam the straits, as just stated, entering a considerable way above the European, and landing below the Asiatic, fort. Chevalier says that a young Jew swam the same distance for his mistress; and Oliver mentions its having been done by a Neapolitan; but our consul, Tarragona, remembered neither of these circumstances, and tried to dissuade us from the attempt. A number of the Salsette's crew were known to have accomplished a greater distance; and the only thing that surprised me was that, as doubts had been entertained of the truth of Leander's story, no traveller had ever endeavoured to ascertain its practicability.

Page 60, col. 1.

'Ζώη μοῦ, σᾶς ἀγαπῶ.'] Romaic expression of tenderness: If I translate it, I shall affront the gentlemen, as it may seem that I supposed they could not; and if I do not, I may affront the ladies.

For fear of any misconstruction on the part of the latter, I shall do so, begging pardon of the learned. It means, 'My life, I love you!' which sounds very prettily in all languages, and is as much in fashion in Greece at this day as, Juvenal tells us, the two first words were amongst the Roman ladies, whose erotic expressions were all Hellenised.

Page 60, col. 1.

'By all the token-flowers that tell.'] In the East (where ladies are not taught to write, lest they should scribble assignations) flowers, cinders, pebbles, &c. convey the sentiments of the parties by that universal deputy of Mercury—an old woman. A cinder says, 'I burn for thee;' a bunch of flowers tied with hair, 'Take me and fly;' but a pebble declares—what nothing else can.

Page 60, col. 1.

'Though I fly to Istambol.'] Constantinople.

Page 60, col. 1.

'Δεῦτε παῖδες τῶν 'Ελλήνων.'] The song Δεῦτε παῖδες, &c. was written by Riga, who perished in the attempt to revolutionise Greece. This translation is as literal as the author could make it in verse. It is of the same measure as that of the original.

Page 60, col. 2.

'And the seven-hill'd city seeking.'] Constantinople, ''Επτάλοφος.'

Page 61, col. 2.

'Ὡραιότατη Χάηδή, &c.'] The song from which this is taken is a great favourite with the young girls of Athens of all classes. Their manner of singing it is by verses in rotation, the whole number present joining in the chorus. I have heard it frequently at our 'χόροι,' in the winter of 1810–11. The air is plaintive and pretty.

Page 68, col. 1.

'VERSES FOUND IN A SUMMER-HOUSE AT HALESOWEN.'] In Warwickshire.

Page 68, col. 1.

'His hours in whistling spent, "for want of thought."'] See Cymon and Iphigenia.

Page 73, col. 2.

'The rapture of the strife.'] 'Certaminis gaudia.' The expression of Attila in his harangue to his army previous to the battle of Chalons, given in Cassiodorus.

Page 74, col. 2.

'Thou Timour! in his captive's cage.'] The cage of Bajazet, by order of Tamerlane.

Page 74, col. 2.

'Or, like the thief of fire from heaven.'] Prometheus.

Page 74, col. 2.

'The very Fiend's arch mock.']

      ——'The very fiend's arch mock—
To lip a wanton and suppose her chaste.'
                SHAKESPEARE.

Page 84, col. 2.

'Turning rivers into blood.'] See Rev. chap. viii. ver. 7, &c. 'The first angel sounded, and there followed hail and fire mingled with blood,' &c.

Ver. 8, 'And the second angel sounded, and as it were a great mountain burning with fire was cast into the sea; and the third part of the sea became blood,' &c. Ver. 10, 'And the third angel sounded, and there fell a great star from heaven, burning as it were a lamp: and it fell upon the third part of the rivers, and upon the fountains of waters.' Ver. 11, 'And the name of the star is called *Wormwood:* and the third part of the waters became *wormwood;* and many men died of the waters because they were made bitter.'

Page 84, col. 2.

'Whose realm refused thee ev'n a tomb.'] Murat's remains are said to have been torn from the grave and burnt.

Page 85, col. 2.

'FROM THE FRENCH.] 'All wept, but particularly Savary, and a Polish officer who had been exalted from the ranks by Buonaparte. He clung to his master's knees; wrote a letter to Lord Keith, entreating permission to accompany him, even in the most menial capacity, which could not be admitted.'

Page 85, col. 2.

'Blessing him they served so well.'] 'At Waterloo one man was seen, whose left arm was shattered by a cannon ball, to wrench it off with the other, and throwing it up in the air, exclaimed to his comrades, "Vive l'Empereur, jusqu' à la mort!" There were many other instances of the like: this you may, however, depend on as true.'—*Private Letter from Brussels.*

Page 86, col. 1.

'Of three bright colours, each divine.'] The tricolour.

Page 94, col. 1.

'Like to the Pontic monarch of old days.'] Mithridates of Pontus.

Page 97, col. 1.

'The worthy rival of the wondrous *Three!*'] Fox—Pitt—Burke.

Page 99, col. 1.

'Leman! these names are worthy of thy shore.'] Geneva, Ferney, Copet, Lausanne.

Page 99, col. 1.

'ROMANCE MUY DOLOROSO DEL SITIO Y TOMA DE ALHAMA.'] The effect of the original ballad—which existed both in Spanish and Arabic—was such, that it was forbidden to be sung by the Moors, on pain of death, within Granada.

Page 103, col. 2.

'For the man, "poor and shrewd."'] *Vide* your letter.

ENGLISH BARDS AND SCOTCH REVIEWERS

Page 113, col. 1.

'His creaking couplets in a tavern hall.']

IMIT. 'Semper ego auditor tantum? nunquamne, reponam,
　　Vexatus toties rauci Theseide Codri?'—
　　　　　　　　　　　　　　　　Juv. Sat. I.
Mr. Fitzgerald, facetiously termed by Cobbett the 'Small-Beer Poet,' inflicts his annual tribute of verse on the Literary Fund: not content with writing, he spouts in person, after the company have imbibed a reasonable quantity of bad port, to enable them to sustain the operation.

Page 114, col. 1.

'Our task complete, like Hamet's shall be free.'] Cid Hamet Benengeli promises repose to his pen, in the last chapter of Don Quixote. Oh! that our voluminous gentry would follow the example of Cid Hamet Benengeli!

Page 114, col. 1.

'Fail'd to preserve the spurious farce from shame.'] This ingenious youth is mentioned more particularly, with his production, in another place.

Page 114, col. 1.

'No matter, George continues still to write.'] In the Edinburgh Review.

Page 114, col. 2.

'By Jeffrey's heart, or Lambe's Bœotian head.'] Messrs. Jeffrey and Lambe are the alpha and omega, the first and last, of the Edinburgh Review; the others are mentioned hereafter.

Page 114, col. 2.

'While these are censors, 'twould be sin to spare.']

IMIT. 'Stulta est Clementia, cum tot ubique
　　——occurras periturae parcere chartae.'
　　　　　　　　　　　　　　　Juv. Sat. I.

Page 114, col. 2.

'Then should you ask me, why I venture o'er.']
IMIT. 'Cur tamen hoc libeat potius decurrere campo
　　　Per quem magnus equos Auruncae flexit alumnus:
　　　Si vacat, et placidi rationem admittitis edam.'　　　　　　*Juv.* Sat. I.

Page 115, col. 2.

'From soaring Southey down to grovelling Stott.'] Stott, better known in the 'Morning Post' by the name of Hafiz. This personage is at present the most profound explorer of the bathos. I remember, when the reigning family left Portugal, a special Ode of Master Stott's, beginning thus:—
(*Stott loquitur quoad Hibernia*)—

　　'Princely offspring of Braganza,
　　　Erin greets thee with a stanza,' &c.

Also a Sonnet to Rats, well worthy of the subject, and a most thundering Ode, commencing as follows:—

　　'Oh! for a Lay! loud as the surge
　　　That lashes Lapland's sounding shore.'

Lord have mercy on us! the 'Lay of the Last Minstrel' was nothing to this.

Page 115, col. 2.

'Thus Lays of Minstrels—may they be the last!']—See the 'Lay of the Last Minstrel,' *passim.* Never was any plan so incongruous and absurd as the groundwork of this production. The entrance of Thunder and Lightning, prologuising to Bayes' tragedy, unfortunately takes away the merit of originality from the dialogue between Messieurs the Spirits of Flood and Fell in the first canto. Then we have the amiable William of Deloraine, 'a stark moss-trooper,' videlicet, a happy compound of poacher, sheep-stealer, and highwayman. The propriety of his magical lady's injunction not to read can only be equalled by his candid acknowledgment of his independence of the trammels of spelling, although, to use his own elegant phrase, ''twas his neck-verse at Harribee,' i.e. the gallows. —The biography of Gilpin Horner, and the marvellous pedestrian page, who travelled twice as fast as his master's horse, without the aid of seven-leagued boots, are *chefs-d'œuvre* in the improvement of taste. For incident we have the invisible, but by no means sparing, box on the ear bestowed on the page, and the entrance of a knight and charger into the castle, under the very natural disguise of a wain of hay. Marmion, the hero of the latter romance, is exactly what William of Deloraine would have been, had he been able to read and write. The poem was manufactured for Messrs. Constable, Murray, and Miller, worshipful booksellers, in consideration of the receipt of a sum of money; and truly, considering the inspiration, it is a very creditable production. If Mr. Scott will write for hire, let him do his best for his paymasters, but not disgrace his genius, which is undoubtedly great, by a repetition of black-letter ballad imitations.

Page 116, col. 1.

'And bid a long "good night to Marmion."'] 'Good night to Marmion'—the pathetic and also prophetic exclamation of Henry Blount, Esquire, on the death of honest Marmion.

Page 116, col. 1.

'The single wonder of a thousand years.'] As the Odyssey is so closely connected with the story of the Iliad, they may almost be classed as one grand historical poem. In alluding to Milton and Tasso, we consider the 'Paradise Lost,' and 'Gierusalemme Liberata,' as their standard efforts; since neither the 'Jerusalem Conquered' of the Italian, nor the 'Paradise Regained' of the English bard, obtained a proportionate celebrity to their former poems. Query: Which of Mr. Southey's will survive?

Page 116, col. 1.

'Next see tremendous Thalaba come on.'] 'Thalaba,' Mr. Southey's second poem, is written in open defiance of precedent and poetry. Mr. S. wished to produce something novel, and succeeded to a miracle. 'Joan of Arc' was marvellous enough, but 'Thalaba' was one of those poems 'which,' in the words of Porson, 'will be read when Homer and Virgil are forgotten, but—*not till then.*'

Page 116, col. 2.

'Oh! Southey! Southey! cease thy varied song!'] We beg Mr. Southey's pardon: 'Madoc disdains the degrading title of epic.' See his preface. Why is epic degraded? and by whom? Certainly the late romaunts of Masters Cottle, Laureat Pye, Ogilvy, Hole, and gentle Mistress Cowley, have not exalted the epic muse; but, as Mr. Southey's poem 'disdains the appellation,' allow us to ask—has he substituted anything better in its stead? or must he be content to rival Sir Richard Blackmore in the quantity as well as quality of his verse?

Page 116, col. 2.

'Thou wilt devote old women to the devil.'] See 'The Old Woman of Berkeley,' a ballad, by Mr. Southey, wherein an aged gentlewoman is carried away by Beelzebub, on a 'high-trotting horse.'

Page 116, col. 2.

'"God help thee," Southey, and thy readers too.'] The last line, 'God help thee,' is an evident plagiarism from the Anti-jacobin to Mr. Southey, on his Dactylics.

Page 116, col. 2.

'And quit his books, for fear of growing double.'] Lyrical Ballads, p. 4.—'The Tables Turned.' Stanza 1.

'Up, up, my friend, and clear your looks;
    Why all this toil and trouble?
Up, up, my friend, and quit your books,
    Or surely you'll grow double.'

Page 116, col. 2.

'And, like his bard, confounded night with day.'] Mr. W. in his preface labours hard to prove, that prose and verse are much the same; and certainly his precepts and practice are strictly conformable:—

'And thus to Betty's questions he
    Made answer, like a traveller bold,
The cock did crow, to-whoo, to-whoo,
And the sun did shine so cold,' &c. &c.,
                                                    p. 129.

Page 116, col. 2.

'To him who takes a pixy for a muse.'] Coleridge's Poems, p. 11, 'Songs of the Pixies, i.e. Devonshire Fairies;' p. 42 we have 'Lines to a young Lady;' and p. 52, 'lines to a young Ass.'

Page 117, col. 1.

'All hail, M.P.! from whose infernal brain.'] 'For every one knows little Matt's an M.P.' See a poem to Mr. Lewis, in 'The Statesman,' supposed to be written by Mr. Jekyll.

Page 117, col. 1.

'Hibernian Strangford! with thine eyes of blue.'] The reader, who may wish for an explanation of this, may refer to 'Strangford's Camoëns,' p. 127, note to p. 56, or to the last page of the Edinburgh Review of Strangford's Camoëns.

Page 117, col. 1.

By dressing Camoëns in a suit of lace?'] It is also to be remarked, that the things given to the public as poems of Camoëns are no more to be found in the original Portuguese than in the Song of Solomon.

Page 117, col. 2.

'That luckless music never triumph'd there.'] Hayley's two most notorious verse productions are 'Triumphs of Temper,' and 'The Triumph of Music.' He has also written much comedy in rhyme, epistles, &c. &c. As he is rather an elegant writer of notes and biography, let us recommend Pope's advice to Wycherley to Mr. H's consideration, viz. 'to convert poetry into prose,' which may be easily done by taking away the final syllable of each couplet.

Page 117, col. 2.

Sepulchral Grahame, pours his notes sublime.'] Mr. Grahame has poured forth two volumes of cant, under the name of 'Sabbath Walks' and 'Biblical Pictures.'

Page 117, col. 2.

What merry sounds proceed from Oxford bells.'] See Bowles's 'Sonnet to Oxford,' and 'Stanzas on hearing the Bells of Ostend.'

NOTES TO ENGLISH BARDS AND SCOTCH REVIEWERS

Page 118, col. 1.

'Awake a louder and a loftier strain.'] 'Awake a louder,' &c., is the first line in Bowles's 'Spirit of Discovery;' a very spirited and pretty dwarf-epic. Among other exquisite lines we have the following

——'A kiss
Stole on the list'ning silence, never yet
Here heard; they trembled even as if the power,'
&c. &c.

That is, the woods of Madeira trembled to a kiss; very much astonished, as well they might be, at such a phenomenon.

Page 118, col. 1.

'The bard sighs forth a gentle episode.'] The episode above alluded to is the story of 'Robert à Machin' and 'Anna d' Arfet,' a pair of constant lovers, who performed the kiss above mentioned, that startled the woods of Madeira.

Page 118, col. 1.

'Consult Lord Fanny, and confide in Curll.'] Curll is one of the heroes of the Dunciad, and was a bookseller. Lord Fanny is the poetical name of Lord Hervey, author of 'Lines to the Imitator of Horace.'

Page 118, col. 1.

'And do from hate what Mallet did for hire.'] Lord Bolingbroke hired Mallet to traduce Pope after his decease, because the poet had retained some copies of a work by Lord Bolingbroke—the 'Patriot King,'—which that splendid but malignant genius had ordered to be destroyed.

Page 118, col. 1.

'To rave with Dennis, and with Ralph to rhyme.'] Dennis the critic, and Ralph the rhymester.—

'Silence, ye wolves! while Ralph to Cynthia howls,
Making night hideous: answer him, ye owls!'
DUNCIAD.

Page 118, col. 1.

'And link'd thee to the Dunciad for thy pains.'] See Bowles's late edition of Pope's works, for which he received three hundred pounds. Thus Mr. B. has experienced how much easier it is to profit by the reputation of another, than to elevate his own.

Page 118, col. 2.

'Had Cottle still adorn'd the counter's side.'] Mr. Cottle, Amos, Joseph, I don't know which, but one or both, once sellers of books they did not write, and now writers of books they do not sell, have published a pair of epics—'Alfred,' (poor Alfred! Pye has been at him too!)—'Alfred,' and the 'Fall of Cambria.'

Page 118, col. 2.

'Dull Maurice all his granite weight of leaves.'] Mr. Maurice hath manufactured the component parts of a ponderous quarto, upon the beauties of 'Richmond Hill,' and the like:—it also takes in a charming view of Turnham Green, Hammersmith, Brentford, Old and New, and the parts adjacent.

Page 118, col. 2.

'May no rude hand disturb their early sleep!'] Poor Montgomery, though praised by every English Review, has been bitterly reviled by the Edinburgh. After all, the bard of Sheffield is a man of considerable genius. His 'Wanderer of Switzerland' is worth a thousand 'Lyrical Ballads,' and at least fifty 'degraded epics.'

Page 119, col. 1.

'Nor hunt the blood-hounds back to Arthur's seat?'] Arthur's Seat; the hill which overhangs Edinburgh.

Page 119, col. 1.

'When Little's leadless pistol met his eye.'] In 1806, Messrs. Jeffrey and Moore met at Chalk-Farm. The duel was prevented by the interference of the magistracy; and, on examination, the balls of the pistols were found to have evaporated. This incident gave occasion to much waggery in the daily prints.

Page 119, col. 2.

'The other half pursued its calm career.'] The Tweed here behaved with proper decorum; it would have been highly reprehensible in the English half of the river to have shown the smallest symptom of apprehension.

Page 119, col. 2.

'If Jeffrey died, except within her arms.'] This display of sympathy on the part of the Tolbooth (the principal prison in Edinburgh), which truly seems to have been most affected on this occasion, is much to be commended. It was to be apprehended, that the many unhappy criminals executed in the front might have rendered the edifice more callous. She is said to be of the softer sex, because her delicacy of feeling on this day was truly feminine, though, like most feminine impulses, perhaps a little selfish.

Page 119, col. 2.

'The travell'd thane, Athenian Aberdeen.'] His lordship has been much abroad, is a member of the Athenian Society, and reviewer of 'Gell's Topography of Troy.'

Page 119, col. 2.

'Herbert shall wield Thor's hammer, and sometimes.'] Mr. Herbert is a translator of Icelandic and other poetry. One of the principal pieces is a 'Song on the Recovery of Thor's Hammer:' the translation is a pleasant chant in the vulgar tongue, and endeth thus:—

'Instead of money and rings, I wot,
The hammer's bruises were her lot.
Thus Odin's son his hammer got.'

Page 119, col. 2.

'Smug Sydney too thy bitter page shall seek.'] The Rev. Sydney Smith, the reputed author of Peter Plymley's Letters, and sundry criticisms.

Page 119, col. 2.

'And classic Hallam, much renown'd for Greek.'] Mr. Hallam reviewed Payne Knight's 'Taste,' and was exceedingly severe on some Greek verses therein. It was not discovered that the lines were Pindar's till the press rendered it impossible to cancel the critique, which still stands an everlasting monument of Hallam's ingenuity.—*Note added to second edition.* The said Hallam is incensed because he is falsely accused, seeing that he never dineth at Holland House. If this be true, I am sorry—not for having said so, but on his account, as I understand his lordship's feasts are preferable to his compositions. If he did not review Lord

Holland's performance, I am glad; because it must have been painful to read, and irksome to praise it. If Mr. Hallam will tell me who did review it, the real name shall find a place in the text; provided, nevertheless, the said name be of two orthodox musical syllables, and will come into the verse: till then, Hallam must stand for want of a better.

Page 119, col. 2.

'And paltry Pillans shall traduce his friend.']
Pillans is a tutor at Eton.

Page 120, col. 1.

'While gay Thalia's luckless votary, Lambe.']
The Hon. George Lambe reviewed 'Beresford's Miseries,' and is, moreover, author of a farce enacted with much applause at the Priory, Stanmore; and damned with great expedition at the late theatre, Covent Garden. It was entitled, 'Whistle for it.'

Page 120, col. 1.

'Beware lest blundering Brougham destroy the sale.'] Mr. Brougham, in No. XXV of the Edinburgh Review, throughout the article concerning Don Pedro de Cevallos, has displayed more politics than policy; many of the worthy burgesses of Edinburgh being so incensed at the infamous principles it evinces, as to have withdrawn their subscriptions.—Here followed in the first edition, —'The name of this personage is pronounced Broom in the south, but the truly northern and *musical* pronunciation is BROUGH-AM, in two syllables;' but for this, Lord B. substituted in the second edition:—'It seems that Mr. Brougham is not a Pict, as I supposed, but a Borderer, and his name is pronounced Broom from Trent to Tay:— so be it.'

Page 120, col. 1.

'Her son, and vanish'd in a Scottish mist.'] I ought to apologise to the worthy deities for introducing a new goddess with short petticoats to their notice: but, alas! what was to be done? I could not say Caledonia's genius, it being well known there is no such genius to be found from Clackmannan to Caithness; yet, without supernatural agency, how was Jeffrey to be saved? The national 'kelpies' are too unpoetical, and the 'brownies' and 'gude neighbours' (spirits of a good disposition) refused to extricate him. A goddess, therefore, has been called for the purpose; and great ought to be the gratitude of Jeffrey, seeing it is the only communication he ever held, or is likely to hold, with anything heavenly.

Page 120, col. 1.

'This scents its pages, and that gilds its rear.']
See the colour of the back binding of the Edinburgh Review.

Page 120, col. 1.

'Declare his landlord can at least translate!']
Lord Holland has translated some specimens of Lope de Vega, inserted in his life of the author. Both are bepraised by his *disinterested* guests.

Page 120, col. 2.

'Reforms each error, and refines the whole.']
Certain it is, her ladyship is suspected of having displayed her matchless wit in the Edinburgh Review. However that may be, we know from good authority that the manuscripts are submitted to her perusal—no doubt, for correction.

Page 120, col. 2.

'Puns, and a prince within a barrel pent.'] In the melo-drama of Tekeli, that heroic prince is clapt into a barrel on the stage; a new asylum for distressed heroes.

Page 120, col. 2.

'While Reynolds vents his "dammes!" "poohs!" and "zounds!"'] All these are favourite expressions of Mr. Reynolds, and prominent in his comedies, living and defunct.

Page 120, col. 2.

'A tragedy complete in all but words?'] Mr. T. Sheridan, the new manager of Drury Lane theatre, stripped the tragedy of Bonduca of the dialogue, and exhibited the scenes as the spectacle of Caractacus. Was this worthy of his sire? or of himself?

Page 121, col. 1.

'Her flight to garnish Greenwood's gay designs.'] Mr. Greenwood is, we believe, scenepainter to Drury Lane theatre—as such, Mr. Skeffington is much indebted to him.

Page 121, col. 1.

'In five facetious acts comes thundering on.'] Mr. [afterwards Sir Lumley] Skeffington is the illustrious author of the 'Sleeping Beauty;' and some comedies, particularly 'Maids and Bachelors:' Baccalaurii baculo magis quam lauro digni.

Page 121, col. 1.

'And worship Catalani's pantaloons.'] Naldi and Catalani require little notice; for the visage of the one, and the salary of the other, will enable us long to recollect these amusing vagabonds. Besides, we are still black and blue from the squeeze on the first night of the lady's appearance in trousers.

Page 121, col. 2.

'Of vice and folly, Greville and Argyle!'] To prevent any blunder, such as mistaking a street for a man, I beg leave to state that it is the institution, and not the Duke of that name, which is here alluded to. A gentleman, with whom I am slightly acquainted, lost in the Argyle Rooms several thousand pounds at backgammon. It is but justice to the manager in this instance to say, that some degree of misapprobation was manifested: but why are the implements of gaming allowed in a place devoted to the society of both sexes? A pleasant thing for the wives and daughters of those who are blest or cursed with such connexions, to hear the billiard-tables rattling in one room, and the dice in another! That this is the case I myself can testify, as a late unworthy member of an institution which materially affects the morals of the higher orders, while the lower may not even move to the sound of a tabor and fiddle without a chance of indictment for riotous behaviour.

Page 121, col. 2.

'Behold the new Petronius of the day.'] Petronius, 'Arbiter elegantiarum' to Nero, 'and a very pretty fellow in his day,' as Mr. Congreve's 'Old Bachelor' saith of Hannibal.

Page 122, col. 1.

'To live like Clodius, and like Falkland fall.']
I knew the late Lord Falkland well. On Sunday night I beheld him presiding at his own table, in all the honest pride of hospitality; on Wednesday

morning, at three o'clock, I saw stretched before me all that remained of courage, feeling, and a host of passions. He was a gallant and successful officer: his faults were the faults of a sailor [those of dissipation]—as such, Britons will forgive them. He died like a brave man in a better cause; for had he fallen in like manner on the deck of the frigate to which he was just appointed, his last moments would have been held up by his countrymen as an example to succeeding heroes.

Page 122, col. 1.

'From silly Hafiz up to simple Bowles.'] What would be the sentiments of the Persian Anacreon, Hafiz, could he rise from his splendid sepulchre at Sheeraz (where he reposes with Ferdousi and Sadi, the oriental Homer and Catullus), and behold his name assumed by one Stott of Dromore, the most impudent and execrable of literary poachers for the daily prints?

Page 122, col. 2.

'Lord, rhymester, petit-maître, and pamphlet-eer!'] The Earl of Carlisle has lately published an eighteenpenny pamphlet on the state of the stage, and offers his plan for building a new theatre. It is to be hoped his lordship will be permitted to bring forward anything for the stage—except his own tragedies.

Page 122, col. 2.

'And hang a calf-skin on those recreant lines.']
'Doff that lion's hide,
And hang a calf-skin on those recreant limbs.'
Shak. King John.
Lord Carlisle's works, most resplendently bound, form a conspicuous ornament to his book-shelves:—
'The rest is all but leather and prunella.'

Page 122, col. 2.

'And Melville's Mantle prove a blanket too!']
'Melville's Mantle,' a parody on 'Elijah's Mantle,' a poem.

Page 123, col. 1.

'Leave wondering comprehension far behind.'] This lovely little Jessica, the daughter of the noted Jew King, seems to be a follower of the Della Crusca school, and has published two volumes of very respectable absurdities in rhyme, as times go; besides sundry novels in the style of the first edition of the Monk.

Page 123, col. 1.

'Chain'd to the signature of O. P. Q.'] These are the signatures of various worthies who figure in the poetical departments of the newspapers.

Page 123, col. 1.

'And Capel Lofft declares 'tis quite sublime.'] Capel Lofft, Esq., the Mæcenas of shoemakers, and preface-writer-general to distressed versemen; a kind of gratis accoucheur to those who wish to be delivered of rhyme, but do not know how to bring forth.

Page 123, col. 1.

'Bloomfield! why not on brother Nathan too?'] See Nathaniel Bloomfield's ode, elegy, or whatever he or any one else chooses to call it, on the enclosures of 'Honington Green.'

Page 123, col. 2.

'May Moorland weavers boast Pindaric skill.'] Vide 'Recollections of a Weaver in the Moorlands of Staffordshire.'

Page 123, col. 2.

'Recall the pleasing memory of the past.'] It would be superfluous to recall to the mind of the reader the authors of 'The Pleasures of Memory' and 'The Pleasures of Hope,' the most beautiful didactic poems in our language, if we except Pope's 'Essay on Man:' but so many poetasters have started up, that even the names of Campbell and Rogers are become strange.

Page 123, col. 2.

'Bear witness, Gifford.'] Gifford, author of the Baviad and Mæviad, the first satires of the day, and translator of Juvenal.

Page 123, col. 2.

'Sotheby.'] Sotheby, translator of Wieland's Oberon and Virgil's Georgics, and author of 'Saul,' an epic poem.

Page 123, col. 2.

'Macneil.'] Macneil, whose poems are deservedly popular, particularly 'Scotland's Scaith,' and the 'Waes of War,' of which ten thousand copies were sold in one month.

Page 123, col. 2.

'Why slumbers Gifford? let us ask again.'] Mr. Gifford promised publicly that the Baviad and Mæviad should not be his last original works: let him remember, 'Mox in reluctantes dracones.'

Page 124, col. 1.

'Unhappy White! while life was in its spring.'] Henry Kirke White died at Cambridge, in October, 1806, in consequence of too much exertion in the pursuit of studies that would have matured a mind which disease and poverty could not impair, and which death itself destroyed rather than subdued. His poems abound in such beauties as must impress the reader with the liveliest regret that so short a period was allotted to talents which would have dignified even the sacred functions he was destined to assume.

Page 124, col. 1.

'And here let Shee and Genius find a place.'] Mr. Shee [afterwards President of the Royal Academy], author of 'Rhymes on Art,' and 'Elements of Art.'

Page 124, col. 2.

'Wright! 'twas thy happy lot at once to view.'] Walter Rodwell Wright, late consul-general for the Seven Islands, is author of a very beautiful poem, just published: it is entitled 'Horæ Ionicæ,' and is descriptive of the isles and the adjacent coast of Greece.

Page 124, col. 2.

'And you, associate bards! who snatch'd to light.'] The translators of the Anthology, Bland and Merivale, have since published separate poems, which evince genius that only requires opportunity to attain eminence.

Page 124, col. 2.

'False glare attracts, but more offends the eye.'] The neglect of the 'Botanic Garden' is some proof of returning taste. The scenery is its sole recommendation.

Page 125, col. 1.

Seems blessed harmony to Lamb and Lloyd.'] Messrs. Lamb and Lloyd, the most ignoble followers of Southey and Co.

NOTES TO HINTS FROM HORACE

Page 125, col. 1.

'And thou, too, Scott! resign to minstrels rude.']
By the bye, I hope that in Mr. Scott's next poem,
his hero or heroine will be less addicted to
'Gramarye,' and more to grammar, than the Lady
of the Lay and her bravo, William of Deloraine.

Page 125, col. 1.

'Let Stott, Carlisle, Matilda, and the rest.'] It
may be asked, why I have censured the Earl of
Carlisle, my guardian and relative, to whom I
dedicated a volume of puerile poems a few years
ago?—The guardianship was nominal, at least as
far as I have been able to discover; the relationship
I cannot help, and am very sorry for it; but as his
lordship seemed to forget it on a very essential
occasion to me, I shall not burden my memory
with the recollection. I do not think that personal
differences sanction the unjust condemnation of
a brother scribbler; but I see no reason why they
should act as a preventive, when the author, noble
or ignoble, has, for a series of years, beguiled a
'discerning public' (as the advertisements have it)
with divers reams of most orthodox, imperial nonsense. Besides, I do not step aside to vituperate
the earl: no—his works come fairly in review with
those of other patrician literati. If, before I escaped
from my teens, I said anything in favour of his
lordship's paper books, it was in the way of dutiful
dedication, and more from the advice of others
than my own judgment, and I seize the first opportunity of pronouncing my sincere recantation. I
have heard that some persons conceive me to be
under obligations to Lord Carlisle: if so, I shall
be most particularly happy to learn what they are,
and when conferred, that they may be duly appre-
ciated and publicly acknowledged. What I have
humbly advanced as an opinion on his printed
things, I am prepared to support, if necessary, by
quotations from elegies, eulogies, odes, episodes,
and certain facetious and dainty tragedies bearing
his name and mark:—

'What can ennoble knaves, or fools, or cowards?
Alas! not all the blood of all the Howards.'

So says Pope. Amen!

Page 125, col. 2.

'Requires no sacred theme to bid us list.'] The
'Games of Hoyle,' well known to the votaries of
whist, chess, &c., are not to be superseded by the
vagaries of his poetical namesake, whose poem
comprised, as expressly stated in the advertisement,
all the 'plagues of Egypt.'

Page 126, col. 1.

'Himself a living libel on mankind.'] This
person, who has lately betrayed the most rabid
symptoms of confirmed authorship, is writer of a
poem denominated the 'Art of Pleasing,' as 'lucus
a non lucendo,' containing little pleasantry and
less poetry. He also acts as monthly stipendiary
and collector of calumnies for the 'Satirist.' If this
unfortunate young man would exchange the magazines for the mathematics, and endeavour to take a
decent degree in his university, it might eventually
prove more serviceable than his present salary.

Page 126, col. 1.

'Oh! dark asylum of a Vandal race!'] 'Into
Cambridgeshire the Emperor Probus transported a
considerable body of Vandals.'—Gibbon's Decline
and Fall, vol. ii. p. 83. There is no reason to doubt
the truth of this assertion; the breed is still in high
perfection.

Page 126, col. 1.

'So lost to Phœbus, that nor Hodgson's verse.']
This gentleman's name requires no praise: the
man who in translation displays unquestionable
genius may be well expected to excel in original
composition, of which, it is to be hoped, we shall
soon see a splendid specimen.

Page 126, col. 1.

'Can make thee better, nor poor Hewson's
worse.'] Hewson Clarke, Esq., as it is written.

Page 126, col. 1.

'And modern Britons glory in their sires.'] The
'Aboriginal Britons,' an excellent poem, by Richards.

Page 126, col. 1.

'And old dame Portland fills the place of Pitt.']
A friend of mine being asked, why his Grace of
Portland was likened to an old woman? replied,
'he supposed it was because he was past bearing.'
—His Grace is now gathered to his grandmothers,
where he sleeps as sound as ever; but even his sleep
was better than his colleagues' waking. 1811.

Page 126, col. 2.

'Thence shall I stray through beauty's native
clime.'] Georgia.

Page 126, col. 2.

'Where Kaff is clad in rocks, and crown'd with
snows sublime.'] Mount Caucasus.

Page 126, col. 2.

'Let Aberdeen and Elgin still pursue.'] Lord
Elgin would fain persuade us that all the figures,
with and without noses, in his stoneshop, are the
works of Phidias! 'Credat Judæus!'

Page 126, col. 2.

'Gell.'] Mr. Gell's Topography of Troy and
Ithaca cannot fail to insure the approbation of
every man possessed of classical taste, as well for
the information Mr. Gell conveys to the mind of
the reader, as for the ability and research the respective works display.

HINTS FROM HORACE

Page 128, col. 1.

'Or low Dubost—as once the world has seen.']
—In an English newspaper, which finds its way
abroad wherever there are Englishmen, I read an
account of this dirty dauber's caricature of Mr.
H—— as a 'beast,' and the consequent action, &c.
The circumstance is, probably, too well known to
require further comment.

Page 128, col. 2.

'To paint a rainbow, or—the river Thames.']
'Where pure description held the place of sense.'—
POPE.

Page 129, col. 1.

'But coats must claim another artisan.'] Mere
common mortals were commonly content with one
tailor and with one bill, but the more particular
gentlemen found it impossible to confide their
lower garments to the makers of their body clothes.
I speak of the beginning of 1809: what reform may
have since taken place I neither know, nor desire
to know.

NOTES TO HINTS FROM HORACE

Page 129, col. 2.

'As Pitt has furnish'd us a word or two.']
Mr. Pitt was liberal in his additions to our parliamentary tongue; as may be seen in many publications, particularly the Edinburgh Review.

Page 129, col. 2.

'True, some decay, yet not a few revive.'] Old ballads, old plays, and old women's stories, are at present in as much request as old wine or new speeches. In fact, this is the millennium of black letter; thanks to our Hebers, Webers, and Scotts!

Page 130, col. 1.

'You doubt—see Dryden, Pope, St. Patrick's dean,'] 'Mac Flecknoe,' the 'Dunciad,' and all Swift's lampooning ballads. Whatever their other works may be, these originated in personal feelings, and angry retort on unworthy rivals; and though the ability of these satires elevates the poetical, their poignancy detracts from the personal character of the writers.

Page 130, col. 1.

'For jest and *pun* in very middling prose.'] With all the vulgar applause and critical abhorrence of *puns*, they have Aristotle on their side; who permits them to orators, and gives them consequence by a grave disquisition.

Page 130, col. 2.

'To "hollowing Hotspur" and the sceptred sire.'] 'And in his ear I'll hollow, Mortimer!'— 1 *Henry IV.*

Page 131, col. 1.

'Difficile est proprie communia dicere: tuque.']
Mde. Dacier, Mde. de Sévigné, Boileau, and others, have left their dispute on the meaning of this passage in a tract considerably longer than the poem of Horace. It is printed at the close of the eleventh volume of Madame de Sévigné's Letters, edited by Grouvelle, Paris, 1806. Presuming that all who *can* construe may venture an opinion on such subjects, particularly as so many who can *not* have taken the same liberty, I should have held my 'farthing candle' as awkwardly as another, had not my respect for the wits of Louis the Fourteenth's Augustan siècle induced me to subjoin these illustrious authorities. 1st, Boileau: 'Il est difficile de traiter des sujets qui sont à la portée de tout le monde d'une manière qui vous les rende propres, ce qui s'appelle s'approprier un sujet par le tour qu'on y donne.' 2ndly, Batteux: 'Mais il est bien difficile de donner des traits propres et individuels aux êtres purement possibles.' 3rdly, Dacier: 'Il est difficile de traiter convenablement ces caractères que tout le monde peut inventer.' Mde. de Sévigné's opinion and translation, consisting of some thirty pages, I omit, particularly as M. Grouvelle observes, 'La chose est bien remarquable, aucune de ces diverses interprétations ne parait être la véritable.' But, by way of comfort, it seems, fifty years afterwards, 'Le lumineux Dumarsais' made his appearance, to set Horace on his legs again, 'dissiper tous les nuages, et concilier tous les dissentimens;' and some fifty years hence, somebody, still more luminous, will doubtless start up and demolish Dumarsais and his system on this weighty affair, as if he were no better than Ptolemy and Tycho, or his comments of no more consequence than astronomical calculations on the present comet. I am happy to say, 'la longueur de la dissertation' of M. D. prevents M. G. from saying

any more on the matter. A better poet than Boileau, and at least as good a scholar as Sévigné, has said,

'A little learning is a dangerous thing.'
And by this comparison of comments, it may be perceived how a good deal may be rendered as perilous to the proprietors.

Page 131, col. 2.

'Beware—for God's sake, don't begin like Bowles!'] About two years ago a young man, named Townsend, was announced by Mr. Cumberland, in a review (since deceased) as being engaged in an epic poem to be entitled 'Armageddon.' The plan and specimen promise much; but I hope neither to offend Mr. Townsend, nor his friends, by recommending to his attention the lines of Horace to which these rhymes allude. If Mr. Townsend succeeds in his undertaking, as there is reason to hope, how much will the world be indebted to Mr. Cumberland for bringing him before the public! But, till that eventful day arrives, it may be doubted whether the premature display of his plan (sublime as the ideas confessedly are) has not,—by raising expectations too high, or diminishing curiosity, by developing his argument,—rather incurred the hazard of injuring Mr. Townsend's future prospects. Mr. Cumberland (whose talents I shall not depreciate by the humble tribute of my praise) and Mr. Townsend must not suppose me actuated by unworthy motives in this suggestion. I wish the author all the success he can wish himself, and shall be truly happy to see epic poetry weighed up from the bathos where it lies sunken with Southey, Cottle, Cowley (Mrs. or Abraham), Ogilvy, Wilkie, Pye, and all the 'dull of past and present days.' Even if he is not a *Milton*, he may be better than *Blackmore*; if not a *Homer*, an *Antimachus*. I should deem myself presumptuous, as a young man, in offering advice, were it not addressed to one still younger. Mr. Townsend has the greatest difficulties to encounter: but in conquering them he will find employment; in having conquered them, his reward. I know too well 'the scribbler's scoff, the critic's contumely;' and I am afraid time will teach Mr. Townsend to know them better. Those who succeed, and those who do not, must bear this alike, and it is hard to say which have most of it. I trust that Mr. Townsend's share will be from *envy*; he will soon know mankind well enough not to attribute this expression to malice.

Page 132, col. 1.

'O'er Virgil's devilish verses and his own.']
Harvey, the *circulator* of the *circulation* of the blood, used to fling away Virgil in his ecstasy of admiration and say, 'the book had a devil.' Now, such a character as I am copying would probably fling it away also, but rather wish that the devil had the book; not from dislike to the poet, but a well-founded horror of hexameters. Indeed, the public school penance of 'Long and Short' is enough to beget an antipathy to poetry for the residue of a man's life, and, perhaps, so far may be an advantage.

Page 132, col. 1.

'Unlucky Tavell! doom'd to daily cares.'] 'Infandum, regina, jubes renovare dolorem.' I dare say Mr. Tavell (to whom I mean no affront) will understand me; and it is no matter whether any one else does or no.—To the above events, 'quæque ipse miserrima vidi, et quorum pars magna fui,' all *times* and *terms* bear testimony.

Page 132, col. 2.

'Master of arts! as *hells* and *clubs* proclaim.']
'Hell,' a gaming-house so called, where you risk
little, and are cheated a good deal. 'Club,' a
pleasant purgatory, where you lose more, and are
not supposed to be cheated at all.

Page 133, col. 1.

'A halter'd heroine Johnson sought to slay.']
'Irene had to speak two lines with the bow-string
round her neck; but the audience cried out
"Murder!" and she was obliged to go off the stage
alive.'—*Boswell's Johnson.*

Page 133, col. 1.

'Whose postscripts prate of dyeing "heroines
blue"?'] In the postscript to the 'Castle Spectre,'
Mr. Lewis tells us, that though blacks were unknown in England at the period of his action, yet
he has made the anachronism to set off the scene:
and if he could have produced the effect 'by
making his heroine blue,'—I quote him—'blue he
would have made her!'

Page 133, col. 2.

'Ere scenes were play'd by many a reverend
clerk.'] 'The first theatrical representations, entitled "Mysteries and Moralities," were generally
enacted at Christmas, by monks (as the only persons who could read), and latterly by the clergy
and students of the universities. The dramatis
personæ were usually Adam, Pater Cœlestis, Faith,
Vice,' &c. &c.—See Warton's History of English
Poetry.

Page 133, col. 2.

''Tis strange Benvolio suffers such a show.']
Benvolio does not bet: but every man who maintains race-horses is a promoter of all the concomitant evils of the turf. Avoiding to bet is a little
pharisaical. Is it an exculpation? I think not.
I never yet heard a bawd praised for chastity,
because *she herself* did not commit fornication.

Page 134, col. 1.

'But find in thine, like pagan Plato's bed.']
Under Plato's pillow a volume of the *Mimes* of
Sophron was found the day he died.—*Vide* Barthé-
lémi, De Pauw, or Diogenes Laertius, if agreeable.
De Pauw calls it a jest-book. Cumberland, in his
Observer, terms it moral, like the sayings of
Publius Syrus.

Page 134, col. 1.

'Yet Chesterfield, whose polish'd pen inveighs.']
His speech on the Licensing Act is one of his most
eloquent efforts.

Page 134, col. 1.

'And "Estifania" gull her "Copper" spouse.']
Michael Perez, the Copper Captain, in 'Rule a
Wife and have a Wife.'

Page 134, col. 1.

'And, spite of puritans and Collier's curse.']
Jerry Collier's controversy with Congreve, &c. on
the subject of the drama, is too well known to
require further comment.

Page 134, col. 2.

'And Simeon kicks.'] Mr. Simeon is the very
bully of beliefs, and castigator of 'good works.'
He is ably supported by John Stickles, a labourer
in the same vineyard:—but I say no more, for,

according to Johnny in full congregation, 'No
hopes for them as laughs.'

Page 134, col. 2.

'Where Baxter only "shoves."'] 'Baxter's Shove
to heavy-a—d Christians,' the veritable title of a
book once in good repute, and likely enough to be
so again.

Page 136, col. 1.

'And keep your bushy locks a year from Blake.']
As famous a tonsor as Licinus himself, and better
paid, and may, like him, be one day a senator,
having a better qualification than one half of the
heads he crops, viz.—independence.

Page 137, col. 1.

'For poets (says this sage and many more).'] I
have not the original by me, but the Italian translation runs as follows:—'E una cosa a mio credere
molto stravagante, che un padre desideri, o per-
metta, che suo figliuolo coltivi e perfezioni questo
talento.' A little further on: 'Si trovano di rado
nel Parnaso le miniere d' oro e d' argento.'—*Edu-
cazione dei Fanciulli del Signor Locke.*

Page 137, col. 1.

'Is poor as Irus.'] 'Iro pauperior:' this is the
same beggar who boxed with Ulysses for a pound
of kid's fry, which he lost, and half a dozen teeth
besides.—See Odyssey, b. 18.

Page 137, col. 1.

'Or an Irish mine.'] The Irish gold mine of
Wicklow, which yields just ore enough to swear
by, or gild a bad guinea.

Page 137, col. 2.

'And double-barrels (damn them!) miss their
mark.'] As Mr. Pope took the liberty of damning
Homer, to whom he was under great obligations—
'*And Homer (damn him!) calls*'—it may be presumed that anybody or anything may be damned
in verse by poetical license; and, in case of accident,
I beg leave to plead so illustrious a precedent.

Page 137, col. 2.

'Let Havard's fate o'ertake him, who, for once.']
For the story of Billy Havard's tragedy, see
'Davies's Life of Garrick.' I believe it is 'Regulus,'
or 'Charles the First.' The moment it was known
to be his the theatre thinned, and the bookseller refused to give the customary sum for the copyright.

Page 138, col. 1.

'Or mild Eclectics, when some, worse than
Turks.'] To the Eclectic or Christian Reviewers
I have to return thanks for the fervour of that
charity which, in 1809, induced them to express a
hope that a thing then published by me might lead
to certain consequences, which, although natural
enough, surely came but rashly from reverend lips.
I refer them to their own pages, where they con-
gratulated themselves on the prospect of a tilt
between Mr. Jeffrey and myself, from which some
great good was to accrue, provided one or both
were knocked on the head. Having survived two
years and a half those 'Elegies' which they were
kindly preparing to review, I have no peculiar
gusto to give them 'so joyful a trouble,' except
indeed 'upon compulsion, Hal;' but if, as David
says in the 'Rivals,' it should come to 'bloody
sword and gun fighting,' we 'won't run, will we,
Sir Lucius?' I do not know what I had done to

871

these Eclectic gentlemen: my works are their lawful perquisite, to be hewn in pieces like Agag, if it seem meet unto them: but why they should be in such a hurry to kill off their author, I am ignorant. 'The race is not always to the swift, nor the battle to the strong:' and now, as these Christians have 'smote me on one cheek,' I hold them up the other; and, in return for their good wishes, give them an opportunity of repeating them. Had any other set of men expressed such sentiments, I should have smiled, and left them to the 'recording angel;' but from the pharisees of Christianity decency might be expected. I can assure these brethren, that, publican and sinner as I am, I would not have treated 'mine enemy's dog thus.' To show them the superiority of my brotherly love, if ever the Reverend Messrs. Simeon or Ramsden should be engaged in such a conflict as that in which they requested me to fall, I hope they may escape with being 'winged' only, and that Heaviside may be at hand to extract the ball.

Page 138, col. 2.

'From Corydon unkind Alexis turns.'] Invenies alium, si te hic fastidit, Alexin.

Page 139, col. 1.

'And hark 'ye, Southey! pray—but don't be vex'd.'] Mr. Southey has lately tied another canister to his tail in the 'Curse of Kehama,' maugre the neglect of Madoc, &c., and has in one instance had a wonderful effect. A literary friend of mine, walking out one lovely evening last summer, on the eleventh bridge of the Paddington canal, was alarmed by the cry of 'one in jeopardy:' he rushed along, collected a body of Irish haymakers (supping on butter-milk in an adjacent paddock), procured three rakes, one eel-spear, and a landing-net, and at last (horresco referens) pulled out—his own publisher. The unfortunate man was gone for ever, and so was a large quarto wherewith he had taken the leap, which proved, on inquiry, to have been Mr. Southey's last work. Its 'alacrity of sinking' was so great, that it has never since been heard of; though some maintain that it is at this moment concealed at Alderman Birch's pastry premises, Cornhill. Be this as it may, the coroner's inquest brought in a verdict of 'Felo de bibliopolâ' against a 'quarto unknown;' and circumstantial evidence being since strong against the 'Curse of Kehama' (of which the above words are an exact description), it will be tried by its peers next session, in Grub-street—Arthur, Alfred, Davideis, Richard Cœur de Lion, Exodus Exodia, Epigoniad, Calvary, Fall of Cambria, Siege of Acre, Don Roderick, and Tom Thumb the Great, are the names of the twelve jurors. The judges are Pye, Bowles, and the bellman of St. Sepulchre's. The same advocates, pro and con, will be employed as are now engaged in Sir F. Burdett's celebrated cause in the Scotch courts. The public anxiously await the result, and all *live* publishers will be subpœnaed as witnesses.—But Mr. Southey has published the 'Curse of Kehama,'—an inviting title to quibblers. By-the-by, it is a good deal beneath Scott and Campbell, and not much above Southey, to allow the booby Ballantyne to entitle them, in the Edinburgh Annual Register (of which, by-the-by, Southey is editor), 'the grand poetical triumvirate of the day.' But, on second thoughts, it can be no great degree of praise to be the one-eyed leaders of the blind, though they might as well keep to themselves 'Scott's thirty thousand copies sold,' which must sadly discomfit poor Southey's unsale-

ables. Poor Southey, it should seem, is the 'Lepidus' of this poetical triumvirate. I am only surprised to see him in such good company.

'Such things, we know, are neither rich nor rare, But wonder how the devil *he* came there.'

The trio are well defined in the sixth proposition of Euclid:—'Because, in the triangles D B C, A C B, D B is equal to A C, and B C common to both; the two sides D B, B C, are equal to the two A C, C B, each to each, and the angle D B C is equal to the angle A C B: therefore, the base D C is equal to the base A B, and the triangle D B C (Mr. Southey) is equal to the triangle A C B, the *less* to the *greater*, which is *absurd*,' &c.—The editor of the Edinburgh Register will find the rest of the theorem hard by his stabling; he has only to cross the river; 'tis the first turnpike t'other side 'Pons Asinorum.'*

Page 139, col. 1.

'Though "Madoc," with "Pucelle," instead of punk.'] Voltaire's 'Pucelle' is not quite so immaculate as Mr. Southey's 'Joan of Arc,' and yet I am afraid the Frenchman has both more truth and poetry too on his side—(they rarely go together)—than our patriotic minstrel, whose first essay was in praise of a fanatical French strumpet, whose title of witch would be correct with the change of the first letter.

Page 139, col. 1.

'May travel back to Quito—on a trunk.'] Like Sir Bland Burgess's 'Richard;' the tenth book of which I read at Malta, on a trunk of Eyre's, 19, Cockspur-street. If this be doubted, I shall buy a portmanteau to quote from.

Page 140, col. 1.

'Fool on, as fluent as an Orpheus' head.']
'Tum quoque marmorea caput a cervice revulsum,
Gurgite cum medio portans Œagrius Hebrus,
Volveret Eurydicen vox ipsa, et frigida lingua,
Ah, miseram Eurydicen! anima fugiente vocabat;
Eurydicen toto referebant flumine ripæ.'
                    Georgic., iv. 523.

Page 140, col. 1.

'The cobbler-laureats.'] I beg Nathaniel's pardon: he is not a cobbler; *it* is a *tailor*, but begged Capel Lofft to sink the profession in his preface to two pair of panta—psha!—of cantos, which he wished the public to try on; but the sieve of a patron let it out, and so far saved the expense of an advertisement to his country customers.—Merry's 'Moorfields whine' was nothing to all this. The 'Della Cruscans' were people of some education, and no profession: but these Arcadians ('Arcades ambo'—bumpkins both) send out their native nonsense without the smallest alloy, and leave all the shoes and smallclothes in the parish unrepaired, to patch up Elegies on Enclosures, and Pæans to Gunpowder. Sitting on a shopboard, they describe the fields of battle, when the only blood they ever saw was shed from the finger; and an 'Essay on War' is produced by the ninth part of a 'poet.'

* This Latin has sorely puzzled the University of Edinburgh. Ballantyne said it meant the 'Bridge of Berwick.' but Southey claimed it as half English; Scott swore it was the 'Brig o' Stirling:' he had just passed two king Jameses and a dozen Douglases over it. At last it was decided by Jeffrey that it meant nothing more nor less than the 'counter of Archy Constable's shop.'

'And own that *nine* such poets made a Tate.'
Did Nathan ever read that line of Pope? and if he
did, why not take it as his motto?

Page 140, col. 1.

'Sing to Capel Lofft!'] This well-meaning gentleman has spoiled some excellent shoemakers, and
been accessory to the poetical undoing of many of
the industrious poor. Nathaniel Bloomfield and
his brother Bobby have set all Somersetshire singing; nor has the malady confined itself to one
county. Pratt too (who once was wiser) has caught
the contagion of patronage, and decoyed a poor
fellow named Blackett into poetry: but he died
during the operation, leaving one child and two
volumes of 'Remains' utterly destitute. The girl,
if she don't take a poetical twist, and come forth
as a shoe-making Sappho, may do well; but the
'tragedies' are as rickety as if they had been the
offspring of an Earl or a Seatonian prize poet. The
patrons of this poor lad are certainly answerable
for his end; and it ought to be an indictable
offence. But this is the least they have done: for,
by a refinement of barbarity, they have made the
(late) man posthumously ridiculous, by printing
what he would have had sense enough never to
print himself. Certes these rakers of 'Remains'
come under the statute against 'resurrection men.'
What does it signify whether a poor dear dead
dunce is to be stuck up in Surgeons' or in Sta-
tioners' Hall? Is it so bad to unearth his bones as
his blunders? Is it not better to gibbet his body on
a heath, than his soul in an octavo? 'We know
what we are, but we know not what we may be;'
and it is to be hoped we never shall know, if a man
who has passed through life with a sort of éclat is
to find himself a mountebank on the other side of
Styx, and made, like poor Blackett, the laughing-
stock of purgatory. The plea of publication is to
provide for the child; now, might not some of this
'Sutor ultra Crepidam's' friends and seducers have
done a decent action without inveigling Pratt into
biography? And then his inscription split into so
many modicums!—'To the Duchess of So-much,
the Right Hon. So-and-So, and Mrs. and Miss
Somebody, these volumes are,' &c. &c.—why, this
is doling out the 'soft milk of dedication' in gills,—
there is but a quart, and he divides it among a
dozen. Why, Pratt, hadst thou not a puff left?
Dost thou think six families of distinction can
share this in quiet? There is a child, a book, and
a dedication: send the girl to her grace, the volumes
to the grocer, and the dedication to the devil.

Page 140, col. 2.

'There's plenty of the sort.']—Here will Mr.
Gifford allow me to introduce once more to his
notice the sole survivor, the 'ultimus Romanorum,'
the last of the Crusca[dì]—'Edwin' the 'profound,'
by our Lady of Punishment! here he is, as lively
as in the days of 'well said Baviad the Correct.'
I thought Fitzgerald had been the tail of poesy;
but, alas! he is only the penultimate.

A FAMILIAR EPISTLE TO THE EDITOR OF THE
MORNING CHRONICLE.

'What reams of paper, floods of ink,'
Do some men spoil, who never think!
And so perhaps you'll say of me,
In which your readers may agree.

Still I write on, and tell you why;
Nothing's so bad, you can't deny,
But may instruct or entertain
Without the risk of giving pain, &c. &c.

ON SOME MODERN QUACKS AND REFORMERS.

In tracing of the human mind
Through all its various courses,
Though strange, 'tis true, we often find
It knows not its resources:

And men through life assume a part
For which no talents they possess,
Yet wonder that, with all their art,
They meet no better with success, &c. &c.

Page 141, col. 1.

'If you will breed this bastard of your brains.']
Minerva being the first by Jupiter's head-piece, and
a variety of equally unaccountable parturitions
upon earth, such as Madoc, &c. &c.

Page 141, col. 1.

'And furnish food for critics, or their quills.'
'A crust for the critics.'—*Bayes, in the 'Rehearsal.'*

Page 141, col. 1.

'As yawning waiters fly.'] And the 'waiters'
are the only fortunate people who can 'fly' from
them; all the rest, viz. the sad subscribers to the
'Literary Fund,' being compelled, by courtesy, to
sit out the recitation without a hope of exclaiming,
'Sic' (that is, by choking Fitz. with bad wine, or
worse poetry) 'me servavit Apollo!'

Page 141, col. 2.

'"To die like Cato," leapt into the Thames!'
On his table were found these words: 'What Cato
did, and Addison approved, cannot be wrong.'
But Addison did not 'approve;' and if he had,
it would not have mended the matter. He had
invited his daughter on the same water-party; but
Miss Budgell, by some accident, escaped this last
paternal attention. Thus fell the sycophant of
'Atticus,' and the enemy of Pope.

Page 141, col. 2.

'Dosed with vile drams on Sunday he was
found.'] If 'dosed with,' &c. be censured as low,
I beg leave to refer to the original for something
still lower; and if any reader will translate 'Minxerit in patrios cineres,' &c. into a decent couplet,
I will insert said couplet in lieu of the present.

THE CURSE OF MINERVA

Page 142, col. 1.

'That closed their murder'd sage's latest day!']
Socrates drank the hemlock a short time before
sunset (the hour of execution), notwithstanding the
entreaties of his disciples to wait till the sun went
down.

Page 142, col. 2.

'The queen of night asserts her silent reign.']
The twilight in Greece is much shorter than in our
own country; the days in winter are longer, but in
summer of less duration.

Page 142, col. 2.

'The gleaming turret of the gay kiosk.'] The
kiosk is a Turkish summer-house; the palm is
without the present walls of Athens, not far from
the Temple of Theseus, between which and the tree
the wall intervenes. Cephisus' stream is indeed
scanty, and Ilissus has no stream at all.

Page 143, col. 1.

'*These* Cecrops placed, *this* Pericles adorn'd.']
This is spoken of the city in general, and not of the

NOTES TO THE WALTZ

Acropolis in particular. The temple of Jupiter Olympius, by some supposed the Pantheon, was finished by Hadrian; sixteen columns are standing, of the most beautiful marble and architecture.

Page 143, col. 2.

'When Venus half avenged Minerva's shame.']
His lordship's name, and that of one who no longer bears it, are carved conspicuously on the Parthenon; above, in a part not far distant, are the torn remnants of the basso-relievos, destroyed in a vain attempt to remove them.

Page 143, col. 2.

'And well I know within that bastard land.']
'Irish bastards,' according to Sir Callaghan O'Brallaghan.

Page 144, col. 1.

'And own himself an infant of fourscore.'] Mr. West, on seeing the 'Elgin Collection' (I suppose we shall hear of the 'Abershaw' and 'Jack Sheppard' collection) declared himself 'a mere tyro' in art.

Page 144, col. 1.

'And marvel at his lordship's "stone shop" there.'] Poor Cribb was sadly puzzled when the marbles were first exhibited at Elgin House; he asked if it was not 'a stone shop?'—He was right; it *is* a shop.

Page 145, col. 1.

'"Blest paper credit;" who shall dare to sing?']
'Blest paper credit! last and best supply,
That lends Corruption lighter wings to fly.'—
POPE.

Page 145, col. 1.

'And pirates barter all that's left behind.'] The Deal and Dover traffickers in specie.

THE WALTZ

Page 146, col. 1.

'Muse of the many-twinkling feet! whose charms.']
'Glance their many-twinkling feet.'—GRAY.

Page 147, col. 1.

'On Hounslow's heath to rival Wellesley's fame.'] To rival Lord Wellesley's, or his nephew's, as the reader pleases:—the one gained a pretty woman, whom he deserved, by fighting for, and the other has been fighting in the Peninsula many a long day, 'by Shrewsbury clock,' without gaining anything in *that* country but the title of 'the Great Lord,' and 'the Lord;' which savours of profanation, having been hitherto applied only to that Being to whom '*Te Deums*' for carnage are the rankest blasphemy.—It is to be presumed the general will one day return to his Sabine farm: there

'To tame the genius of the stubborn plain,
  Almost as quickly as he conquer'd Spain!'

The Lord Peterborough conquered continents in a summer; we do more—we contrive both to conquer and lose them in a shorter season. If the 'Great Lord's' *Cincinnatus* progress in agriculture be no speedier than the proportional average of time in Pope's couplet, it will, according to the farmer's proverb, be 'ploughing with dogs.'

By-the-bye—one of this illustrious person's new titles is forgotten—it is, however, worth remembering—'*Salvador del mundo!*' *credite, posteri!* If this be the appellation annexed by the inhabitants of the Peninsula to the name of a *man* who has not yet saved them—query—are they worth saving, even in this world? for, according to the mildest modifications of any Christian creed, those three words make the odds much against them in the next—'Saviour of the world,' quotha!—it were to be wished that he, or any one else, could save a corner of it—his country. Yet this stupid misnomer, although it shows the near connexion between superstition and impiety, so far has its use, that it proves there can be little to dread from those Catholics (inquisitorial Catholics too) who can confer such an appellation on a *Protestant*. I suppose next year he will be entitled the 'Virgin Mary:' if so, Lord George Gordon himself would have nothing to object to such liberal bastards of our Lady of Babylon.

Page 147, col. 2.

'While unburnt Moscow yet had news to send.'] The patriotic arson of our amiable allies cannot be sufficiently commended—nor subscribed for. Amongst other details omitted in the various despatches of our eloquent ambassador, he did not state (being too much occupied with the exploits of Colonel C——, in swimming rivers frozen, and galloping over roads impassable) that one entire province perished by famine in the most melancholy manner, as follows:—In General Rostopchin's consummate conflagration, the consumption of tallow and train oil was so great, that the market was inadequate to the demand: and thus one hundred and thirty-three thousand persons were starved to death, by being reduced to wholesome diet! The lamplighters of London have since subscribed a pint (of oil) a piece, and the tallow-chandlers have unanimously voted a quantity of best moulds (four to the pound), to the relief of the surviving Scythians;—the scarcity will soon, by such exertions, and a proper attention to the *quality* rather than the quantity of provision, be totally alleviated. It is said, in return, that the untouched Ukraine has subscribed sixty thousand beeves for a day's meal to our suffering manufacturers.

Page 148, col. 1.

'Can Egypt's Almas—tantalising group.'] Dancing girls—who do for hire what Waltz doth gratis.

Page 148, col. 2.

'Goats in their visage, women in their shape.'] It cannot be complained now, as in the Lady Baussière's time, of the 'Sieur de la Croix,' that there be 'no whiskers;' but how far these are indications of valour in the field, or elsewhere, may *still* be questionable. Much may be, and hath been, avouched on both sides. In the olden time philosophers had whiskers, and soldiers none—Scipio himself was shaven—Hannibal thought his one eye handsome enough without a beard; but Adrian, the emperor, wore a beard (having warts on his chin, which neither the Empress Sabina nor even the courtiers could abide)—Turenne had whiskers, Marlborough none—Buonaparte is unwhiskered, the Regent whiskered; '*argal*' greatness of mind and whiskers may or may not go together; but certainly the different occurrences, since the growth of the last mentioned, go further in behalf of whiskers than the anathema of Anselm did *against* long hair in the reign of Henry I.—Formerly *red* was a favourite colour. See Lodowick Barrey's comedy of Ram Alley, 1661; Act I, Scene I.

'*Taffeta*. Now for a wager—What coloured beard comes next by the window?
'*Adriana*. A black man's, I think.
'*Taffeta*. I think not so: I think a *red*, for that is most in fashion.'
There is 'nothing new under the sun;' but *red*, then a *favourite*, has now subsided into *favourite's* colour.

Page 148, col. 2.

'The court, the Regent, like herself were new.'] An anachronism—Waltz and the battle of Austerlitz are before said to have opened the ball together; the bard means (if he means anything), Waltz was not so much in vogue till the Regent attained the acmé of his popularity. Waltz, the comet, whiskers, and the new government, illuminated heaven and earth, in all their glory, much about the same time: of these the comet only has disappeared; the other three continue to astonish us still.—*Printer's Devil.*

Page 148, col. 2.

'New coins (most new) to follow those that fled.'] Amongst others a new ninepence—a creditable coin now forthcoming, worth a pound, in paper, at the fairest calculation.

Page 149, col. 1.

'Each new, quite new—(except some ancient tricks).']
'Oh that *right* should thus overcome *might!*' Who does not remember the 'delicate investigation' in the 'Merry Wives of Windsor?'—
'*Ford.* Pray you, come near; if I suspect without cause, why then make sport at me; then let me be your jest; I deserve it. How now? whither bear you this?
'*Mrs. Ford.* What have you to do whither they bear it?—you were best meddle with buckwashing.'

Page 149, col. 1.

'So saith the muse: my ——, what say you?'] The gentle, or ferocious, reader may fill up the blank as he pleases—there are several dissyllabic names at *his* service (being already in the Regent's): it would not be fair to back any peculiar initial against the alphabet, as every month will add to the list now entered for the sweepstakes;— a distinguished consonant is said to be the favourite, much against the wishes of the *knowing ones.*

Page 149, col. 1.

'That spot where hearts were once supposed to be.'] 'We have changed all that,' says the Mock Doctor—'tis all gone—Asmodeus knows where. After all, it is of no great importance how women's hearts are disposed of; they have nature's privilege to distribute them as absurdly as possible. But there are also some men with hearts so thoroughly bad, as to remind us of those phenomena often mentioned in natural history; viz. a mass of solid stone—only to be opened by force—and when divided, you discover a toad in the centre, lively, and with the reputation of being venomous.

Page 149, col. 1.

'If "nothing follows all this palming work?"'] In Turkey a pertinent, here an impertinent and superfluous, question—literally put, as in the text, by a Persian to Morier, on seeing a Waltz in Pera.—*Vide* Morier's Travels.

NOTES TO THE BLUES, ETC.

THE BLUES

Page 154, col. 1.

'*Ink.* I shan't go so far—I can have them at Grange's.'] Grange is or was a famous pastry-cook and fruiterer in Piccadilly.

Page 155, col. 1.

'I feel so elastic—"*so buoyant—so buoyant!*"'] Fact from life, with the *words.*

THE VISION OF JUDGMENT

Page 168, col. 1.

'Reviewing "the ungentle craft," and then.'] See 'Life of Henry Kirke White.'

Page 168, col. 2.

'Like King Alfonso. When I thus see double.'] Alfonso, speaking of the Ptolemean system, said that 'had he been consulted at the creation of the world, he would have spared the Maker some absurdities.'

Page 168, col. 2.

'Like lightning, off from his "melodious twang."'] See Aubrey's account of the apparition which disappeared 'with a curious perfume, and a *most melodious twang*;' or see the '*Antiquary*,' vol. i. p. 225.

Page 169, col. 1.

'For all corrupted things are buoy'd like corks.'] A drowned body lies at the bottom till rotten; it then floats, as most people know.

THE AGE OF BRONZE

Page 172, col. 1.

'Hear! hear Prometheus from his rock appeal.'] I refer the reader to the first address of Prometheus in Æschylus, when he is left alone by his attendants, and before the arrival of the chorus of Sea-nymphs.

Page 173, col. 2.

'The knife of Arragon, Toledo's steel.'] The Arragonians are peculiarly dexterous in the use of this weapon, and displayed it particularly in former French wars.

Page 174, col. 2.

'Many an old woman, but no Catherine.'] The dexterity of Catherine extricated Peter (called the Great by courtesy), when surrounded by the Mussulmans on the banks of the river Pruth.

Page 175, col. 2.

'That nose, the hook where he suspends the world!']
'Naso suspendit adunco.'—HORACE.

The Roman applies it to one who merely was imperious to his acquaintance.

Page 178, col.1.

'There Chateaubriand forms new books of martyrs.'] Monsieur Chateaubriand, who has not forgotten the author in the minister, received a handsome compliment at Verona from a literary sovereign: 'Ah! Monsieur C., are you related to that Chateaubriand who—who—who has written *something?*' (*écrit quelque chose!*) It is said that the author of Atala repented him for a moment of his legitimacy.

CHILDE HAROLD'S PILGRIMAGE

Page 180, col. 2.

'Yes! sigh'd o'er Delphi's long deserted shrine.'] The little village of Castri stands partly on the site of Delphi. Along the path of the mountain, from Chrysso, are the remains of sepulchres hewn in and from the rock:—'One,' said the guide, 'of a king who broke his neck hunting.' His majesty had certainly chosen the fittest spot for such an achievement. A little above Castri is a cave, supposed the Pythian, of immense depth; the upper part of it is paved, and now a cowhouse. On the other side of Castri stands a Greek monastery; some way above which is the cleft in the rock, with a range of caverns difficult of ascent, and apparently leading to the interior of the mountain; probably to the Corycian Cavern mentioned by Pausanias. From this part descend the fountain and the 'Dews of Castalie.'

Page 184, col. 1.

'And rest ye at "Our Lady's house of woe."'] The convent of 'Our Lady of Punishment,' *Nossa Señora de Pena*, on the summit of the rock. Below, at some distance, is the Cork Convent, where St. Honorius dug his den, over which is his epitaph. From the hills, the sea adds to the beauty of the view.—*Note to 1st Edition.* Since the publication of this poem, I have been informed [by Walter Scott] of the misapprehension of the term *Nossa Señora de Pena*. It was owing to the want of the *tilde* or mark over the *ñ*, which alters the signification of the word: with it, *Peña* signifies a rock; without it, *Pena* has the sense I adopted. I do not think it necessary to alter the passage; as though the common acceptation affixed to it is 'Our Lady of the Rock,' I may well assume the other sense from the severities practised there.—*Note to 2nd Edition.*

Page 184, col. 1.

'Throughout this purple land, where law secures not life.'] It is a well-known fact, that in the year 1809, the assassinations in the streets of Lisbon and its vicinity were not confined to the Portuguese to their countrymen; but that Englishmen were daily burchered: and so far from redress being obtained, we were requested not to interfere if we perceived any compatriot defending himself against his allies. I was once stopped in the way to the theatre at eight o'clock in the evening, when the streets were not more empty than they generally are at that hour, opposite to an open shop, and in a carriage with a friend: had we not fortunately been armed, I have not the least doubt that we should have 'adorned a tale' instead of telling one.

Page 184, col. 2.

'Behold the hall where chiefs were late convened!'] The Convention of Cintra was signed in the palace of the Marchese Marialva.

Page 185, col. 1.

'But here the Babylonian whore hath built.'] The extent of Mafra is prodigious; it contains a palace, convent, and most superb church. The six organs are the most beautiful I ever beheld, in point of decoration: we did not hear them, but were told that their tones were correspondent to their splendour. Mafra is termed the Escurial of Portugal.

Page 186, col. 1.

''Twixt him and Lusian slave, the lowest of the low.'] As I found the Portuguese, so I have characterized them. That they are since improved, at least in courage, is evident. The late exploits of Lord Wellington have effaced the follies of Cintra. He has, indeed, done wonders: he has, perhaps, changed the character of a nation, reconciled rival superstitions, and baffled an enemy who never retreated before his predecessors.—1812.

Page 186, col. 1.

'That dyed thy mountain streams with Gothic gore?'] Count Julian's daughter, the Helen of Spain. Pelagius preserved his independence in the fastnesses of the Asturias, and the descendants of his followers, after some centuries, completed their struggle by the conquest of Granada.

Page 188, col. 1.

'No! as he speeds, he chants "Vivā el Rey!"'] 'Vivā el Rey Fernando!' Long live King Ferdinand! is the chorus of most of the Spanish patriotic songs. They are chiefly in dispraise of the old King Charles, the Queen, and the Prince of Peace. I have heard many of them: some of the airs are beautiful. Godoy, the *Principe de la Paz*, of an ancient but decayed family, was born at Badajoz, on the frontiers of Portugal, and was originally in the ranks of the Spanish guards; till his person attracted the queen's eyes, and raised him to the dukedom of Alcudia, &c. &c. It is to this man that the Spaniards universally impute the ruin of their country.

Page 188, col. 1.

'Which tells you whom to shun and whom to greet.'] The red cockade, with 'Fernando Septimo' in the centre.

Page 188, col. 2.

'The ball-piled pyramid, the ever-blazing match,'] All who have seen a battery will recollect the pyramidal form in which shot and shells are piled. The Sierra Morena was fortified in every defile through which I passed in my way to Seville.

Page 189, col. 1.

'Foil'd by a woman's hand, before a batter'd wall?'] Such were the exploits of the Maid of Saragoza, who by her valour elevated herself to the highest rank of heroines. When the author was at Seville, she walked daily on the Prado, decorated with medals and orders, by command of the Junta.

Page 189, col. 2.

'Denotes how soft that chin which bears his touch.']
'Sigilla in mento impressa Amoris digitulo
Vestigio demonstrant mollitudinem.—
AUL. GEL.

Page 189, col. 2.

'Match me, ye harems of the land! where now.'] This stanza was written in Turkey.

Page 189, col. 2.

'Oh, thou Parnassus! whom I now survey.'] These stanzas were written in Castri (Delphos), at the foot of Parnassus, now called Λιακυρά (Liakura), Dec. 1809.

Page 190, col. 1.

'Her strength, her wealth, her site of ancient days.'] Seville was the Hispalis of the Romans.

Page 191, col. 1.

'Ask ye, Bœotian shades! the reason why?'] This was written at Thebes, and consequently in the best situation for asking and answering such a question;

not as the birthplace of Pindar, but as the capital of Bœotia, where the first riddle was propounded and solved.

Page 192, col. 2.

'Full from the fount of Joy's delicious springs.']
'Medio de fonte leporum
Surgit amari aliquid quod in ipsis floribus angat.'
Luc.

Page 193, col. 2.

'A traitor only fell beneath the feud.'] Alluding to the conduct and death of Solano, the governor of Cadiz, in May, 1809.

Page 193, col. 2.

'War, war is still the cry, "War even to the knife!"'] 'War to the knife.' Palafox's answer to the French general at the siege of Saragoza.

Page 194, col. 2.

'And thou, my friend!—since unavailing woe.']
The Honourable John Wingfield of the Guards, who died of a fever at Coimbra (May 14, 1811). I had known him ten years, the better half of his life, and the happiest part of mine. In the short space of one month I have lost *her* who gave me being, and most of those who had made that being tolerable. To me the lines of Young are no fiction:

'Insatiate archer! could not one suffice?
Thy shaft flew thrice, and thrice my peace was slain,
And thrice ere thrice yon moon had fill'd her horn.'

I should have ventured a verse to the memory of the late Charles Skinner Matthews, Fellow of Downing College, Cambridge, were he not too much above all praise of mine. His powers of mind, shown in the attainment of greater honours, against the ablest candidates, than those of any graduate on record at Cambridge, have sufficiently established his fame on the spot where it was acquired; while his softer qualities live in the recollection of friends who loved him too well to envy his superiority.

Page 195, col. 1.

'And is, despite of war and wasting fire.'] Part of the Acropolis was destroyed by the explosion of a magazine during the Venetian siege.

Page 195, col. 1.

'That thoughts of thee and thine on polish'd breasts bestow.'] We can all feel, or imagine, the regret with which the ruins of cities, once the capitals of empires, are beheld: the reflections suggested by such objects are too trite to require recapitulation. But never did the littleness of man, and the vanity of his very best virtues, of patriotism to exalt, and of valour to defend, his country, appear more conspicuous than in the record of what Athens was, and the certainty of what she now is. This theatre of contention between mighty factions, of the struggles of orators, the exaltation and deposition of tyrants, the triumph and punishment of generals, is now become a scene of petty intrigue and perpetual disturbance, between the bickering agents of certain British nobility and gentry. 'The wild foxes, the owls and serpents in the ruins of Babylon,' were surely less degrading than such inhabitants. The Turks have the plea of conquest for their tyranny, and the Greeks have only suffered the fortune of war, incidental to the bravest; but how are the mighty fallen, when two painters contest the privilege of plundering the Parthenon, and triumph in turn, according to the tenor of each succeeding firman! Sylla could but punish, Philip subdue, and Xerxes burn Athens; but it remained for the paltry antiquarian, and his despicable agents, to render her contemptible as himself and his pursuits. The Parthenon, before its destruction, in part, by fire during the Venetian siege, had been a temple, a church, and a mosque. In each point of view it is an object of regard: it changed its worshippers; but still it was a place of worship thrice sacred to devotion: its violation is a triple sacrifice. But—

'Man, proud man,
Drest in a little brief authority,
Plays such fantastic tricks before high Heaven
As make the angels weep.'

Page 195, col. 2.

'Far on the solitary shore he sleeps.'] It was not always the custom of the Greeks to burn their dead; the greater Ajax, in particular, was interred entire. Almost all the chiefs became gods after their decease; and he was indeed neglected, who had not annual games near his tomb, or festivals in honour of his memory by his countrymen, as Achilles, Brasidas, &c., and at last even Antinous, whose death was as heroic as his life was infamous.

Page 196, col. 1.

'Here, son of Saturn! was thy fav'rite throne.']
The temple of Jupiter Olympius, of which sixteen columns, entirely of marble, yet survive; originally there were one hundred and fifty. These columns, however, are by many supposed to have belonged to the Pantheon.

Page 196, col. 2.

'And bear these altars o'er the long-reluctant brine.'] The ship was wrecked in the Archipelago.

Page 196, col. 2.

'To rive what Goth, and Turk, and Time hath spared.'] At this moment (January 3, 1810), besides what has been already deposited in London, an Hydriot vessel is in the Pyræus to receive every portable relic. Thus, as I heard a young Greek observe, in common with many of his countrymen —for, lost as they are, they yet feel on this occasion—thus may Lord Elgin boast of having ruined Athens. An Italian painter of the first eminence, named Lusieri, is the agent of devastation; and like the Greek *finder* of Verres in Sicily, who followed the same profession, he has proved the able instrument of plunder. Between this artist and the French Consul Fauvel, who wishes to rescue the remains for his own government, there is now a violent dispute concerning a car employed in their conveyance, the wheel of which—I wish they were both broken upon it!—has been locked up by the Consul, and Lusieri has laid his complaint before the Waywode. Lord Elgin has been extremely happy in his choice of Signor Lusieri. During a residence of ten years in Athens, he never had the curiosity to proceed as far as Sunium (now Cape Colonna), till he accompanied us in our second excursion. However, his works, as far as they go, are most beautiful; but they are almost all unfinished. While he and his patrons confine themselves to tasting medals, appreciating cameos, sketching columns, and cheapening gems, their little absurdities are as harmless as insect or fox-hunting, maiden speechifying, barouche-driving, or any such pastime; but when they carry away three or four shiploads of the most valuable and massy relics that time and barbarism have left to the most injured and most celebrated of cities: when they destroy, in a vain attempt to tear down, those works which have been the admiration of ages, I know no motive which can excuse, no name which can designate, the perpetrators of this dastardly devastation. It was not the least of the crimes laid to the charge of Verres, that he had plundered Sicily, in the manner since imitated at Athens. The most unblushing impudence could hardly go further than to affix the name of its plunderer to the walls of the Acropolis; while the wanton and useless defacement of the whole range of the basso-relievos, in one compartment of the temple, will never permit that name to be pronounced by an observer without execration.

On this occasion I speak impartially: I am not a collector or admirer of collections, consequently no rival; but I have some early prepossession in favour of Greece, and do not think the honour of England advanced by plunder, whether of India or Attica.

Another noble Lord has done better, because he has done less: but some others, more or less noble, yet 'all honourable men,' have done *best*, because, after a deal of excavation and execration, bribery to the Waywode, mining and countermining, they have done nothing at all. We had such ink-shed, and wine-shed, which almost ended in bloodshed! Lord E.'s 'prig'—see Jonathan Wild for the definition of 'priggism'—quarrelled with another *Gropius** by name (a very good name too for his business), and muttered something about satisfaction, in a verbal answer to a note of the poor Prussian: this was stated at table to Gropius, who laughed, but could eat no dinner afterwards. The rivals were not reconciled when I left Greece. I have reason to remember their squabble, for they wanted to make me their arbitrator.

Page 196, col. 2.

'Yet felt some portion of their mother's pains.'] I cannot resist availing myself of the permission of my friend Dr. Clarke, whose name requires no comment with the public, but whose sanction will add tenfold weight to my testimony, to insert the following extract from a very obliging letter of his to me, as a note to the above lines:—'When the last of the Metopes was taken from the Parthenon, and, in moving of it, great part of the superstructure with one of the triglyphs was thrown down by the workmen whom Lord Elgin employed, the Disdar, who beheld the mischief done to the building, took his pipe from his mouth, dropped a tear, and, in a

* This Sr. Gropius was employed by a noble Lord for the sole purpose of sketching, in which he excels; but I am sorry to say, that he has, through the abused sanction of that most respectable name, been treading at humble distance in the steps of Sr. Lusieri.—A shipful of his trophies was detained, and I believe confiscated, at Constantinople, in 1810. I am most happy to be now enabled to state, that 'this was not in his bond;' that he was employed solelyas a painter,and that his noble patron disavows all connexion with him, except as an artist. If the error in the first and second edition of this poem has given the noble Lord a moment's pain, I am very sorry for it: Sr. Gropius has assumed for years the name of his agent; and though I cannot much condemn myself for sharing in the mistake of so many, I am happy in being one of the first to be undeceived. Indeed, I have as much pleasure in contradicting this as I felt regret in stating it.—*Note to third edition.*

supplicating tone of voice, said to Lusieri, Τελος!—I was present.' The Disdar alluded to was the father of the present Disdar.

Page 196, col. 2.

'Stern Alaric and Havoc on their way?'] According to Zosimus, Minerva and Achilles frightened Alaric from the Acropolis; but others relate that the Gothic king was nearly as mischievous as the Scottish peer.—See Chandler.

Page 197, col. 1.

'The well-reeved guns, the netted canopy.'] To prevent blocks or splinters from falling on deck during action.

Page 199, col. 1.

'But not in silence pass Calypso's isles.'] Goza is said to have been the island of Calypso.

Page 200, col. 1.

'Land of Albania! let me bend mine eyes.'] Albania comprises part of Macedonia, Illyria, Chaonia, and Epirus. Iskander is the Turkish word for Alexander; and the celebrated Scanderbeg (Lord Alexander) is alluded to in the third and fourth lines of the thirty-eighth stanza. I do not know whether I am correct in making Scanderbeg the countryman of Alexander, who was born at Pella in Macedon, but Mr. Gibbon terms him so, and adds Pyrrhus to the list, in speaking of his exploits.

Of Albania Gibbon remarks that a country 'within sight of Italy is less known than the interior of America.' Circumstances, of little consequence to mention, led Mr. Hobhouse and myself into that country before we visited any other part of the Ottoman dominions; and with the exception of Major Leake, then officially resident at Joannina, no other Englishmen have ever advanced beyond the capital into the interior, as that gentleman very lately assured me. Ali Pacha was at that time (October, 1809) carrying on war against Ibrahim Pacha, whom he had driven to Berat, a strong fortress, which he was then besieging: on our arrival at Joannina we were invited to Tepaleni, his highness's birthplace, and favourite Serai, only one day's distance from Berat; at this juncture the Vizier had made it his head-quarters. After some stay in the capital, we accordingly followed; but though furnished with every accommodation, and escorted by one of the Vizier's secretaries, we were nine days (on account of the rains) in accomplishing a journey which, on our return, barely occupied four. On our route we passed two cities, Argyrocastro and Libochabo, apparently little inferior to Yanina in size; and no pencil or pen can ever do justice to the scenery in the vicinity of Zitza and Delvinachi, the frontier village of Epirus and Albania Proper.

On Albania and its inhabitants I am unwilling to descant, because this will be done so much better by my fellow-traveller, in a work which may probably precede this in publication, that I as little wish to follow as I would to anticipate him. But some few observations are necessary to the text. The Arnaouts, or Albanese, struck me forcibly by their resemblance to the Highlanders of Scotland, in dress, figure, and manner of living. Their very mountains seemed Caledonian, with a kinder climate. The kilt, though white; the spare, active form; their dialect, Celtic in its sound, and their hardy habits, all carried me back to Morven. No nation are so detested and dreaded by their neighbours as the Albanese; the Greeks hardly regard them as Christians, or the Turks as Moslems; and in fact they are a mixture of both, and sometimes neither. Their habits are predatory—all are armed; and the red-shawled Arnaouts, the Montenegrins, Chimariots, and Gegdes, are treacherous; the others differ somewhat in garb, and essentially in character. As far as my own experience goes, I can speak favourably. I was attended by two, an Infidel and a Mussulman, to Constantinople and every other part of Turkey which came within my observation; and more faithful in peril, or indefatigable in service, are rarely to be found. The Infidel was named Basilius, the Moslem, Dervish Tahiri; the former a man of middle age, and the latter about my own. Basili was strictly charged by Ali Pacha in person to attend us; and Dervish was one of fifty who accompanied us through the forests of Acarnania to the banks of Achelous, and onward to Messalonghi in Ætolia. There I took him into my own service, and never had occasion to repent it till the moment of my departure.

When, in 1810, after the departure of my friend Mr. Hobhouse for England, I was seized with a severe fever in the Morea, these men saved my life by frightening away my physician, whose throat they threatened to cut if I was not cured within a given time. To this consolatory assurance of posthumous retribution, and a resolute refusal of Dr. Romanelli's prescriptions, I attributed my recovery. I had left my last remaining English servant at Athens; my dragoman was as ill as myself, and my poor Arnaouts nursed me with an attention which would have done honour to civilisation. They had a variety of adventures; for the Moslem, Dervish, being a remarkably handsome man, was always squabbling with the husbands of Athens; insomuch that four of the principal Turks paid me a visit of remonstrance at the Convent, on the subject of his having taken a woman from the bath—whom he had lawfully bought, however—a thing quite contrary to etiquette. Basili also was extremely gallant amongst his own persuasion, and had the greatest veneration for the church, mixed with the highest contempt of churchmen, whom he cuffed upon occasion in a most heterodox manner. Yet he never passed a church without crossing himself; and I remember the risk he ran in entering St. Sophia, in Stambol, because it had once been a place of his worship. On remonstrating with him on his inconsistent proceedings, he invariably answered, 'Our church is holy, our priests are thieves:' and then he crossed himself as usual, and boxed the ears of the first 'papas' who refused to assist in any required operation, as was always found to be necessary where a priest had any influence with the Cogia Bashi of his village. Indeed, a more abandoned race of miscreants cannot exist than the lower orders of the Greek clergy.

When preparations were made for my return, my Albanians were summoned to receive their pay. Basili took his with an awkward show of regret at my intended departure, and marched away to his quarters with his bag of piastres. I sent for Dervish, but for some time he was not to be found; at last he entered, just as Signor Logotheti, father to the ci-devant Anglo-consul of Athens, and some other of my Greek acquaintances, paid me a visit. Dervish took the money, but on a sudden dashed it to the ground; and clasping his hands, which he raised to his forehead, rushed out of the room weeping bitterly. From that moment to the hour of my embarkation, he continued his lamentations, and all our efforts to console him only produced this answer, '*Μ'ἀφείνει*,' 'He leaves me.' Signor Logotheti, who never wept before for anything less than the loss of a para (about the fourth of a farthing), melted; the padre of the convent, my attendants, my visitors—and I verily believe that even Sterne's 'foolish fat scullion' would have left her 'fishkettle' to sympathise with the unaffected and unexpected sorrow of this barbarian.

For my own part, when I remembered that, a short time before my departure from England, a noble and most intimate associate had excused himself from taking leave of me because he had to attend a relation 'to a milliner's,' I felt no less surprised than humiliated by the present occurrence and the past recollection. That Dervish would leave me with some regret was to be expected; when master and man have been scrambling over the mountains of a dozen provinces together, they are unwilling to separate; but his present feelings, contrasted with his native ferocity, improved my opinion of the human heart. I believe this almost feudal fidelity is frequent amongst them. One day, on our journey over Parnassus, an Englishman in my service gave him a push in some dispute about the baggage, which he unluckily mistook for a blow; he spoke not, but sat down leaning his head upon his hands. Foreseeing the consequences, we endeavoured to explain away the affront, which produced the following answer:—'I *have been* a robber: I *am* a soldier: no captain ever struck me: *you* are my master, I have eaten your bread, but by *that* bread! (a usual oath,) had it been otherwise, I would have stabbed the dog, your servant, and gone to the mountains.' So the affair ended, but from that day forward he never thoroughly forgave the thoughtless fellow who insulted him. Dervish excelled in the dance of his country, conjectured to be a remnant of the ancient Pyrrhic: be that as it may, it is manly, and requires wonderful agility. It is very distinct from the stupid Romaika, the dull round-about of the Greeks, of which our Athenian party had so many specimens. The Albanians in general (I do not mean the cultivators of the earth in the provinces, who have also that appellation, but the mountaineers) have a fine cast of countenance; and the most beautiful women I ever beheld, in stature and in features, we saw *levelling* the *road* broken down by the torrents between Delvinachi and Libochabo. Their manner of walking is truly theatrical; but this strut is probably the effect of the capote, or cloak, depending from one shoulder. Their long hair reminds you of the Spartans, and their courage in desultory warfare is unquestionable. Though they have some cavalry amongst the Gegdes, I never saw a good Arnaout horseman; my own preferred the English saddles, which, however, they could never keep. But on foot they are not to be subdued by fatigue.

Page 200, col. 1.

'Where sad Penelope o'erlook'd the wave.'] Ithaca.

Page 200, col. 1.

'Childe Harold hail'd Leucadia's cape afar.'] Leucadia, now Santa Maura. From the promontory (the Lover's Leap) Sappho is said to have thrown herself.

Page 200, col. 2.

'Actium, Lepanto, fatal Trafalgar.'] Actium and Trafalgar need no further mention. The battle of Lepanto, equally bloody and considerable, but less known, was fought in the Gulf of Patras. Here the author of Don Quixote lost his left hand.

Page 201, col. 1.

'Did many a Roman chief and Asian king.'] It is said, that, on the day previous to the battle of Actium, Antony had thirteen kings at his levee.

Page 201, col. 1.

'Look where the second Cæsar's trophies rose.'] Nicopolis, whose ruins are most extensive, is at some distance from Actium, where the wall of the Hippodrome survives in a few fragments. These ruins are large masses of brickwork, the bricks of which are joined by interstices of mortar, as large as the bricks themselves, and equally durable.

Page 201, col. 2.

'He pass'd bleak Pindus, Acherusia's lake.'] According to Pouqueville, the lake of Yanina: but Pouqueville is always out.

Page 201, col. 2.

'To greet Albania's chief, whose dread command.'] The celebrated Ali Pacha. Of this extraordinary man there is an incorrect account in Pouqueville's Travels.

Page 201, col. 2.

'Hurl their defiance far, nor yield, unless to gold.'] Five thousand Suliotes, among the rocks and in the castle of Suli, withstood thirty thousand Albanians for eighteen years; the castle at last was taken by bribery. In this contest there were several acts performed not unworthy of the better days of Greece.

Page 201, col. 2.

'Monastic Zitza! from thy shady brow.'] The convent and village of Zitza are four hours journey from Joannina, or Yanina, the capital of the Pachalick. In the valley the river Kalamas (once the Acheron) flows, and, not far from Zitza, forms a fine cataract. The situation is perhaps the finest in Greece, though the approach to Delvinachi and parts of Acarnania and Ætolia may contest the palm. Delphi, Parnassus, and, in Attica, even Cape Colonna and Port Raphti, are very inferior: as also every scene in Ionia, or the Troad: I am almost inclined to add the approach to Constantinople; but, from the different features of the last, a comparison can hardly be made.

Page 201, col. 2.

'Here dwells the caloyer, nor rude is he.'] The Greek monks are so called.

Page 202, col. 1.

'Nature's volcanic amphitheatre.'] The Chimariot mountains appear to have been volcanic.

Page 202, col. 1.

'Nodding above; behold black Acheron!'] Now called Kalamas.

Page 202, col. 1.

'The little shepherd in his white capote.'] Albanese cloak.

Page 202, col. 2.

'The sun had sunk behind vast Tomerit.'] Anciently Mount Tomarus.

Page 202, col. 2.

'And Laos wide and fierce came roaring by.'] The river Laos was full at the time the author passed it; and, immediately above Tepaleen, was to the eye as wide as the Thames at Westminster;

at least in the opinion of the author and his fellow-traveller. In the summer it must be much narrower. It certainly is the finest river in the Levant; neither Achelous, Alpheus, Acheron, Scamander, nor Cayster, approached it in breadth or beauty.

Page 204, col. 1.

'And fellow-countrymen have stood aloof—'] Alluding to the wreckers of Cornwall.

Page 204, col. 2.

'The feast was done, the red wine circling fast.' The Albanian Mussulmans do not abstain from wine, and, indeed, very few of the others.

Page 204, col. 2.

'Each Palikar his sabre from him cast.'] Palikar, shortened when addressed to a single person, from Παλικάρι, a general name for a soldier amongst the Greeks and Albanese, who speak Romaic: it means, properly, 'a lad.'

Page 205, col. 1.

'While thus in concert they this lay half sang, half scream'd.'] As a specimen of the Albanian or Arnaout dialect of the Illyric, I here insert two of their most popular choral songs, which are generally chanted in dancing by men or women indiscriminately. The first words are merely a kind of chorus without meaning, like some in our own and all other languages.

1. Bo, Bo, Bo, Bo, Bo, Bo,
   Naciarura, popuso.
2. Naciarura na civin
   Ha pen derini ti hin.
3. Ha pe uderi escrotini
   Ti vin ti mar servetini.
4. Caliriote me surme
   Ea ha pe pse dua tive.
5. Buo, Bo, Bo, Bo, Bo,
   Gi egem spirta esimiro
6. Caliriote vu le funde
   Ede vete tunde tunde.
7. Caliriote me surme
   Ti mi put e poi mi le.
8. Se ti puta citi mora
   Si mi ri ni veti udo gia.
9. Va le ni il che cadale
   Celo more, more celo.
10. Plu hari ti tirete
    Plu huron cia pra seti.

1. Lo, Lo, I come, I come; be thou silent.

2. I come, I run; open the door that I may enter.

3. Open the door by halves, that I may take my turban.

4. Caliriotes* with the dark eyes, open the gate that I may enter.

5. Lo, Lo, I hear thee, my soul.

6. An Arnaout girl, in costly garb, walks with graceful pride.

7. Caliriot maid of the dark eyes, give me a kiss.

8. If I have kissed thee, what hast thou gained? My soul is consumed with fire.

9. Dance lightly, more gently, and gently still.

10. Make not so much dust to destroy your embroidered hose.

* The Albanese, particularly the women, are frequently termed 'Caliriotes,' for what reason I inquired in vain.

The last stanza would puzzle a commentator; the men have certainly buskins of the most beautiful texture, but the ladies (to whom the above is supposed to be addressed) have nothing under their little yellow boots and slippers but a well-turned and sometimes very white ankle. The Arnaout girls are much handsomer than the Greeks, and their dress is far more picturesque. They preserve

1. Ndi sefda tinde ulavossa
   Vettimi upri vi lofsa.
2. Ah vaisisso mi privi lofse
   Si mi rini mi la vosse.
3. Uti tasa roba stua
   Sitti eve tulati dua.
4. Roba stinori ssidua
   Qu mi sini vetti dua.
5. Qurmini dua civileni
   Roba ti siarmi tildi eni.
6. Utara pisa vaisisso me simi rin ti hapti
   Eti mi bire a piste si gui dendroi tiltati.
7. Udi vura udorini udiri cicova cilti mora
   Udorini talti hollna u ede caimoni mora.

their shape much longer also, from being always in the open air. It is to be observed, that the Arnaout is not a *written* language: the words of this song, therefore, as well as the one which follows, are spelt according to their pronunciation. They are copied by one who speaks and understands the dialect perfectly, and who is a native of Athens.

1. I am wounded by thy love, and have loved but to scorch myself.
2. Thou hast consumed me! Ah, maid! thou hast struck me to the heart.
3. I have said I wish no dowry, but thine eyes and eyelashes.
4. The accursed dowry I want not, but thee only.
5. Give me thy charms, and let the portion feed the flames.
6. I have loved thee, maid, with a sincere soul, but thou hast left me like a withered tree.
7. If I have placed my hand on thy bosom, what have I gained? my hand is withdrawn, but retains the flame.

I believe the two last stanzas, as they are in a different measure, ought to belong to another ballad. An idea something similar to the thought in the last lines was expressed by Socrates, whose arm having come in contact with one of his '*ὑποκόλπιοι*,' Critobulus or Cleobulus, the philosopher complained of a shooting pain as far as his shoulder for some days after, and therefore very properly resolved to teach his disciples in future without touching them.

Page 205, col. 1.

'TAMBOURGI! Tambourgi! thy 'larum afar.'] Drummer.

Page 205, col. 1.

'Chimariot, Illyrian, and dark Suliote!'] These stanzas are partly taken from different Albanese songs, as far as I was able to make them out by the exposition of the Albanese in Romaic and Italian.

Page 205, col. 2.

'Remember the moment when Previsa fell.'] It was taken by storm from the French.

Page 205, col. 2.

'Let the yellow-hair'd.'] Yellow is the epithet given to the Russians.

Page 205, col. 2.

'Giaours.'] Infidels.

Page 205, col. 2.

'View his horsetail with dread.'] The insignia of a Pacha.

Page 205, col. 2.

'When his Delhis come dashing in blood o'er the banks.'] Horsemen, answering to our forlorn hope.

Page 205, col. 2.

'Selictar! unsheathe then our chief's scimitar.'] Sword-bearer.

Page 205, col. 2.

I.

'Fair Greece! sad relic of departed worth!'] Before I say anything about a city of which everybody, traveller or not, has thought it necessary to say something, I will request Miss Owenson, when she next borrows an Athenian heroine for her four volumes, to have the goodness to marry her to

somebody more of a gentleman than a 'Disdar Aga' (who by the by is not an Aga), the most impolite of petty officers, the greatest patron of larceny Athens ever saw (except Lord E.), and the unworthy occupant of the Acropolis, on a handsome annual stipend of 150 piastres (eight pounds sterling), out of which he has only to pay his garrison, the most ill-regulated corps in the ill-regulated Ottoman Empire. I speak it tenderly, seeing I was once the cause of the husband of 'Ida of Athens' nearly suffering the bastinado; and because the said 'Disdar' is a turbulent husband, and beats his wife; so that I exhort and beseech Miss Owenson to sue for a separate maintenance in behalf of 'Ida.' Having premised thus much, on a matter of such import to the readers of romances, I may now leave Ida, to mention her birthplace.

Setting aside the magic of the name, and all those associations which it would be pedantic and superfluous to recapitulate, the very situation of Athens would render it the favourite of all who have eyes for art or nature. The climate, to me at least, appeared a perpetual spring; during eight months I never passed a day without being as many hours on horseback: rain is extremely rare, snow never lies in the plains, and a cloudy day is an agreeable rarity. In Spain, Portugal, and every part of the East which I visited, except Ionia and Attica, I perceived no such superiority of climate to our own; and at Constantinople, where I passed May, June, and part of July (1810), you might 'damn the climate, and complain of spleen,' five days out of seven.

The air of the Morea is heavy and unwholesome, but the moment you pass the isthmus in the direction of Megara the change is strikingly perceptible. But I fear Hesiod will still be found correct in his description of a Bœotian winter.

We found at Livadia an 'esprit fort' in a Greek bishop, of all free-thinkers! This worthy hypocrite rallied his own religion with great intrepidity (but not before his flock), and talked of a mass as a 'coglioneria.' It was impossible to think better of him for this; but, for a Bœotian, he was brisk with all his absurdity. This phenomenon (with the exception indeed of Thebes, the remains of Chæronea, the plain of Platea, Orchomenus, Livadia, and its nominal cave of Trophonius) was the only remarkable thing we saw before we passed Mount Cithæron.

The fountain of Dirce turns a mill: at least my companion (who, resolving to be at once cleanly and classical, bathed in it) pronounced it to be the fountain of Dirce, and anybody who thinks it worth while may contradict him. At Castri we drank of half a dozen streamlets, some not of the purest, before we decided to our satisfaction which was the true Castalian, and even that had a villainous twang, probably from the snow, though it did not throw us into an epic fever, like poor Dr. Chandler.

From Fort Phyle, of which large remains still exist, the Plain of Athens, Pentelicus, Hymettus, the Ægean, and the Acropolis, burst upon the eye at once; in my opinion, a more glorious prospect than even Cintra or Istambol. Not the view from the Troad, with Ida, the Hellespont, and the more distant Mount Athos, can equal it, though so superior in extent.

I heard much of the beauty of Arcadia, but excepting the view from the Monastery of Megaspelion (which is inferior to Zitza in a command of country), and the descent from the mountains on the way from Tripolitza to Argos, Arcadia has little to recommend it beyond the name.

'Sternitur, et *dulces* moriens reminiscitur Argos.' Virgil could have put this into the mouth of none but an Argive, and (with reverence be it spoken) it does not deserve the epithet. And if the Polynices of Statius, 'In mediis audit duo litora campis,' did actually hear both shores in crossing the isthmus of Corinth, he had better ears than have ever been worn in such a journey since.

'Athens,' says a celebrated topographer, 'is still the most polished city of Greece.' Perhaps it may be of *Greece*, but not of the *Greeks*; for Joannina in Epirus is universally allowed, amongst themselves, to be superior in the wealth, refinement, learning, and dialect of its inhabitants. The Athenians are remarkable for their cunning; and the lower orders are not improperly characterised in that proverb, which classes them with the 'Jews of Salonica, and the Turks of the Negropont.'

Among the various foreigners resident in Athens, French, Italians, Germans, Ragusans, &c., there was never a difference of opinion in their estimate of the Greek character, though on all other topics they disputed with great acrimony.

M. Fauvel, the French consul, who has passed thirty years principally at Athens, and to whose talents as an artist, and manners as a gentleman, none who have known him can refuse their testimony, has frequently declared in my hearing, that the Greeks do not deserve to be emancipated; reasoning on the grounds of their 'national and individual depravity!' while he forgot that such depravity is to be attributed to causes which can only be removed by the measure he reprobates.

M. Roque, a French merchant of respectability long settled in Athens, asserted with the most amusing gravity, 'Sir, they are the same *canaille* that existed *in the days of Themistocles!*' an alarming remark to the 'Laudator temporis acti.' The ancients banished Themistocles; the moderns cheat Monsieur Roque; thus great men have ever been treated!

In short, all the Franks who are fixtures, and most of the Englishmen, Germans, Danes, &c. of passage, came over by degrees to their opinion, on much the same grounds that a Turk in England would condemn the nation by wholesale, because he was wronged by his lacquey, and overcharged by his washerwoman.

Certainly it was not a little staggering when the Sieurs Fauvel and Lusieri, the two greatest demagogues of the day, who divide between them the power of Pericles and the popularity of Cleon, and puzzle the poor Waywode with perpetual differences, agreed in the utter condemnation, 'nulla virtute redemptum,' of the Greeks in general, and of the Athenians in particular.

For my own humble opinion, I am loth to hazard it, knowing as I do, that there be now in MS. no less than five tours of the first magnitude and of the most threatening aspect, all in typographical array, by persons of wit and honour, and regular commonplace books: but, if I may say this without offence, it seems to me rather hard to declare so positively and pertinaciously, as almost everybody has declared, that the Greeks, because they are very bad, will never be better.

Eton and Sonnini have led us astray by their panegyrics and projects: but, on the other hand, De Pauw and Thornton have debased the Greeks beyond their demerits.

The Greeks will never be independent: they will never be sovereigns as heretofore, and God forbid they ever should! but they may be subjects without being slaves. Our colonies are not independent, but they are free and industrious, and such may Greece be hereafter.

At present, like the Catholics of Ireland and the Jews throughout the world, and such other cudgelled and heterodox people, they suffer all the moral and physical ills that can afflict humanity. Their life is a struggle against truth; they are vicious in their own defence. They are so unused to kindness, that when they occasionally meet with it they look upon it with suspicion, as a dog often beaten snaps at your fingers if you attempt to caress him. 'They are ungrateful, notoriously, abominably ungrateful!'—this is the general cry. Now, in the name of Nemesis! for what are they to be grateful? Where is the human being that ever conferred a benefit on Greek or Greeks? They are to be grateful to the Turks for their fetters, and to the Franks for their broken promises and lying counsels. They are to be grateful to the artist who engraves their ruins, and to the antiquary who carries them away; to the traveller whose janissary flogs them, and to the scribbler whose journal abuses them. This is the amount of their obligations to foreigners.

II.

FRANCISCAN CONVENT, ATHENS, *January* 23, 1811.

Amongst the remnants of the barbarous policy of the earlier ages, are the traces of bondage which yet exist in different countries; whose inhabitants, however divided in religion and manners, almost all agree in oppression.

The English have at last compassionated their negroes, and under a less bigoted government, may probably one day release their Catholic brethren; but the interposition of foreigners alone can emancipate the Greeks, who, otherwise, appear to have as small a chance of redemption from the Turks, as the Jews have from mankind in general.

Of the ancient Greeks we know more than enough; at least the younger men of Europe devote much of their time to the study of the Greek writers and history, which would be more usefully spent in mastering their own. Of the moderns, we are perhaps more neglectful than they deserve; and while every man of any pretensions to learning is tiring out his youth, and often his age, in the study of the language and of the harangues of the Athenian demagogues in favour of freedom, the real or supposed descendants of these sturdy republicans are left to the actual tyranny of their masters, although a very slight effort is required to strike off their chains.

To talk, as the Greeks themselves do, of their rising again to their pristine superiority, would be ridiculous: as the rest of the world must resume its barbarism, after re-asserting the sovereignty of Greece; but there seems to be no very great obstacle, except in the apathy of the Franks, to their becoming an useful dependency, or even a free state, with a proper guarantee;—under correction, however, be it spoken, for many and well-informed men doubt the practicability even of this.

The Greeks have never lost their hope, though they are now more divided in opinion on the subject of their probable deliverers. Religion recommends the Russians; but they have twice been deceived and abandoned by that power, and the dreadful lesson they received after the Muscovite desertion in the Morea has never been forgotten. The French they dislike; although the subjugation of the rest of Europe will, probably, be attended by the deliverance of continental Greece. The islanders look to the English for succour, as they have very lately possessed themselves of the Ionian republic, Corfu excepted. But whoever appear with arms in their hands will be welcome; and when that day arrives, Heaven have mercy on the Ottomans; they cannot expect it from the Giaours.

But instead of considering what they have been, and speculating on what they may be, let us look at them as they are.

And here it is impossible to reconcile the contrariety of opinions: some, particularly the merchants, decrying the Greeks in the strongest language; others, generally travellers, turning periods in their eulogy, and publishing very curious speculations grafted on their former state, which can have no more effect on their present lot, than the existence of the Incas on the future fortunes of Peru.

One very ingenious person terms them the 'natural allies of Englishmen;' another, no less ingenious, will not allow them to be the allies of anybody, and denies their very descent from the ancients; a third, more ingenious than either, builds a Greek empire on a Russian foundation, and realises (on paper) all the chimeras of Catherine II. As to the question of their descent, what can it import whether the Mainotes are the lineal Laconians or not? or the present Athenians as indigenous as the bees of Hymettus, or as the grasshoppers, to which they once likened themselves? What Englishman cares if he be of a Danish, Saxon, Norman, or Trojan blood? or who, except a Welshman, is afflicted with a desire of being descended from Caractacus?

The poor Greeks do not so much abound in the good things of this world, as to render even their claims to antiquity an object of envy; it is very cruel, then, in Mr. Thornton to disturb them in the possession of all that time has left them; viz. their pedigree, of which they are the more tenacious, as it is all they can call their own. It would be worth while to publish together, and compare, the works of Messrs. Thornton and De Pauw, Eton and Sonnini; paradox on one side, and prejudice on the other. Mr. Thornton conceives himself to have claims to public confidence from a fourteen years' residence at Pera; perhaps he may on the subject of the Turks, but this can give him no more insight into the real state of Greece and her inhabitants, than as many years spent in Wapping into that of the Western Highlands.

The Greeks of Constantinople live in Fanal; and if Mr. Thornton did not oftener cross the Golden Horn than his brother merchants are accustomed to do, I should place no great reliance on his information. I actually heard one of these gentlemen boast of their little general intercourse with the city, and assert of himself, with an air of triumph, that he had been but four times at Constantinople in as many years.

As to Mr. Thornton's voyages in the Black Sea with Greek vessels, they gave him the same idea of Greece as a cruise to Berwick in a Scotch smack would of Johnny Groat's house. Upon what grounds then does he arrogate the right of condemning by wholesale a body of men, of whom he can know little? It is rather a curious circumstance that Mr. Thornton, who so lavishly dispraises Pouqueville on every occasion of mentioning the Turks, has yet recourse to him as authority on the Greeks, and terms him an impartial observer. Now, Dr. Pouqueville is as little entitled to that appellation as Mr. Thornton to confer it on him.

The fact is, we are deplorably in want of information on the subject of the Greeks, and in particular their literature, nor is there any probability of our being better acquainted, till our intercourse becomes more intimate, or their independence confirmed. The relations of passing travellers are as little to be depended on as the invectives of angry factors; but till something more can be attained, we must be content with the little to be acquired from similar sources.*

However defective these may be, they are preferable to the paradoxes of men who have read superficially of the ancients, and seen nothing of the moderns, such as De Pauw; who, when he asserts that the British breed of horses is ruined by Newmarket, and that the Spartans were cowards in the field, betrays an equal knowledge of English horses and Spartan men. His 'philosophical observations' have a much better claim to the title of 'poetical.' It could not be expected that he who so liberally

---

* A word *en passant* with Mr. Thornton and Dr. Pouqueville, who have been guilty between them of sadly clipping the Sultan's Turkish.

Dr. Pouqueville tells a long story of a Moslem who swallowed corrosive sublimate in such quantities that he acquired the name of 'Suleyman Yeyen,' i.e. quoth the Doctor, 'Suleyman, the eater of corrosive sublimate.' 'Aha,' thinks Mr. Thornton, (angry with the Doctor for the fiftieth time,) have I caught you?'— Then, in a note twice the thickness of the Doctor's anecdote, he questions the Doctor's proficiency in the Turkish tongue, and his veracity in his own.— 'For,' observes Mr. Thornton (after inflicting on us the tough participle of a Turkish verb), 'it means nothing more than "*Suleyman the eater*," ' and quite cashiers the supplementary '*sublimate.*' Now both are right, and both are wrong. If Mr. Thornton, when he next resides 'fourteen years in the factory,' will consult his Turkish dictionary, or ask any of his Stamboline acquaintance, he will discover that '*Suleyma'n yeyen,*' put together discreetly, mean the '*Swallower of sublimate,*' without any '*Suleyman*' in the case: '*Suleyma*' signifying '*corrosive sublimate,*' and not being a proper name on this occasion, although it be an orthodox name enough with the addition of *n*. After Mr. Thornton's frequent hints of profound Orientalism, he might have found this out before he sang such pæans over Dr. Pouqueville.

After this, I think 'Travellers *versus* Factors' shall be our motto, though the above Mr. Thornton has condemned 'hoc genus omne,' for mistake and misrepresentation. 'Ne Sutor ultra crepidam,' 'No merchant beyond his bales.' N.B. For the benefit of Mr. Thornton 'Sutor' is not a proper name.

condemns some of the most celebrated institutions of the ancient, should have mercy on the modern Greeks; and it fortunately happens, that the absurdity of his hypothesis on their forefathers refutes his sentence on themselves.

Let us trust, then, that in spite of the prophecies of De Pauw, and the doubts of Mr. Thornton, there is a reasonable hope of the redemption of a race of men, who, whatever may be the errors of their religion and policy, have been amply punished by three centuries and a half of captivity.

III.

ATHENS, FRANCISCAN CONVENT, *March* 17, 1811.

'I must have some talk with this learned Theban.'

Some time after my return from Constantinople to this city I received the thirty-first number of the Edinburgh Review as a great favour, and certainly at this distance an acceptable one, from the captain of an English frigate off Salamis. In that number, Art. 3, containing the review of a French translation of Strabo, there are introduced some remarks on the modern Greeks and their literature, with a short account of Coray, a co-translator in the French version. On those remarks I mean to ground a few observations; and the spot where I now write will, I hope, be sufficient excuse for introducing them in a work in some degree connected with the subject. Coray, the most celebrated of living Greeks, at least among the Franks, was born at Scio (in the Review, Smyrna is stated, I have reason to think, incorrectly), and besides the translation of Beccaria and other works mentioned by the Reviewer, has published a lexicon in Romaic and French, if I may trust the assurance of some Danish travellers lately arrived from Paris; but the latest we have seen here in French and Greek is that of Gregory Zolikogloou.* Coray has recently been involved in an unpleasant controversy with M. Gail,† a Parisian commentator and editor of some translations from the Greek poets, in consequence of the Institute having awarded him the prize for his version of Hippocrates '*Περὶ ὑδάτων*,' &c., to the disparagement, and consequently displeasure, of the said Gail. To his exertions, literary and patriotic, great praise is undoubtedly due; but a part of that praise ought not to be withheld from the two brothers Zosimado (merchants settled in Leghorn), who sent him to Paris, and maintained him, for the express purpose of elucidating the ancient, and adding to the modern, researches of his countrymen. Coray, however, is not considered by his countrymen equal to some who lived in the two last centuries; more particularly Dorotheus of Mitylene, whose Hellenic writings are so much esteemed by the Greeks, that Meletius terms him '*Μετὰ τὸν Θουκυδίδην καὶ Ξενοφῶντα ἄριστος Ἑλλήνων.*' (P. 224, Ecclesiastical History, vol. iv.)

Panagiotes Kodrikas, the translator of Fonte-

nelle, and Kamarases, who translated Ocellus Lucanus on the Universe into French, Christodoulus, and more particularly Psalida, whom I have conversed with in Joannina, are also in high repute among their literati. The last-mentioned has published in Romaic and Latin a work on 'True Happiness,' dedicated to Catherine II. But Polyzois, who is stated by the Reviewer to be the only modern except Coray who has distinguished himself by a knowledge of Hellenic, if he be the Polyzois Lampanitziotes of Yanina, who has published a number of editions in Romaic, was neither more nor less than an itinerant vender of books; with the contents of which he had no concern beyond his name on the title page, placed there to secure his property in the publication; and he was, moreover, a man utterly destitute of scholastic acquirements. As the name, however, is not uncommon, some other Polyzois may have edited the Epistles of Aristaenetus.

It is to be regretted that the system of continental blockade has closed the few channels through which the Greeks received their publications, particularly Venice and Trieste. Even the common grammars for children are become too dear for the lower orders. Amongst their original works the Geography of Meletius, Archbishop of Athens, and a multitude of theological quartos and poetical pamphlets, are to be met with; their grammars and lexicons of two, three, and four languages are numerous and excellent. Their poetry is in rhyme. The most singular piece I have lately seen is a satire in dialogue between a Russian, English, and French traveller, and the Waywode of Wallachia (or Black-bey, as they term him), an archbishop, a merchant, and Cogia Bachi (or primate), in succession; to all of whom under the Turks the writer attributes their present degeneracy. Their songs are sometimes pretty and pathetic, but their tunes generally unpleasing to the ear of a Frank; the best is the famous '*Δεῦτε παῖδες τῶν Ἑλλήνων*', by the unfortunate Riga. But from a catalogue of more than sixty authors, now before me, only fifteen can be found who have touched on any theme except theology.

I am intrusted with a commission by a Greek of Athens named Marmarotouri to make arrangements, if possible, for printing in London a translation of Barthelemi's Anacharsis in Romaic, as he has no other opportunity, unless he despatches the MS. to Vienna by the Black Sea and Danube.

The Reviewer mentions a school established at Hecatonesi, and suppressed at the instigation of Sebastiani: he means Cidonies, or, in Turkish, Haivali; a town on the continent, where that institution for a hundred students and three professors still exists. It is true that this establishment was disturbed by the Porte, under the ridiculous pretext that the Greeks were constructing a fortress instead of a college: but on investigation, and the payment of some purses to the Divan, it has been permitted to continue. The principal professor, named Ueniamin, (i.e. Benjamin), is stated to be a man of talent, but a freethinker. He was born in Lesbos, studied in Italy, and is master of Hellenic, Latin, and some Frank languages: besides a smattering of the sciences.

Though it is not my intention to enter farther on this topic than may allude to the article in question, I cannot but observe that the Reviewer's lamentation over the fall of the Greeks appears singular, when he closes it with these words: '*The change is to be attributed to their misfortunes rather than to any "physical degradation."*' It may be true

---

* I have in my possession an excellent lexicon '*τρί-γλωσσον*,' which I received in exchange from S. G——, Esq. for a small gem: my antiquarian friends have never forgotten it, or forgiven me.

† In Gail's pamphlet against Coray, he talks of 'throwing the insolent Hellenist out of the windows.' On this a French critic exclaims, 'Ah, my God! throw an Hellenist out of the window! what sacrilege!' It certainly would be a serious business for those authors who dwell in the attics: but I have quoted the passage merely to prove the similarity of style among the controversialists of all polished countries; London and Edinburgh could hardly parallel this Parisian ebullition.

that the Greeks are not physically degenerated, and that Constantinople contained on the day when it changed masters as many men of six feet and upwards as in the hour of prosperity; but ancient history and modern politics instruct us that something more than physical perfection is necessary to preserve a state in vigour and independence; and the Greeks, in particular, are a melancholy example of the near connexion between moral degradation and national decay.

The Reviewer mentions a plan '*we believe*' by Potemkin for the purification of the Romaic; and I have endeavoured in vain to procure any tidings or traces of its existence. There was an academy in St. Petersburg for the Greeks; but it was suppressed by Paul, and has not been revived by his successor.

There is a slip of the pen, and it can only be a slip of the pen, in p. 58, No. 31 of the 'Edinburgh Review,' where these words occur:—'We are told that when the capital of the East yielded to *Solyman*.'—It may be presumed that this last word will, in a future edition, be altered to Mahomet II.* The 'ladies of Constantinople,' it seems, at that period spoke a dialect, 'which would not have disgraced the lips of an Athenian.' I do not know how that might be, but am sorry to say the ladies in general, and the Athenians in particular, are much altered; being far from choice either in their dialect or expressions, as the whole Attic race are barbarous to a proverb:—

'Ὦ Ἀθήνα, πρότη χώρα,
Τί γαιδάρους τρέφεις τώρα.'

In Gibbon, vol. x. p. 161, is the following sentence:—'The vulgar dialect of the city was gross and barbarous, though the compositions of the church and palace sometimes affected to copy the purity of the Attic models.' Whatever may be asserted on the subject, it is difficult to conceive that the 'ladies of Constantinople,' in the reign of the last Cæsar, spoke a purer dialect than Anna Comnena wrote three centuries before: and those royal pages are not esteemed the best models of composition, although the princess γλῶτταν εἶχεν ἈΚΡΙΒΩΣ Ἀττικίζουσαν. In the Fanal, and in Yanina, the best Greek is spoken: in the latter there is a flourishing school under the direction of Psalida.

There is now in Athens a pupil of Psalida's, who is making a tour of observation through Greece: he is intelligent, and better educated than a fellow-commoner of most colleges. I mention this as a proof that the spirit of inquiry is not dormant among the Greeks.

* In a former number of the Edinburgh Review, 1808, it is observed: 'Lord Byron passed some of his early years in Scotland, where he might have learned that *pibroch* does not mean a *bagpipe*, any more than *duet* means a *fiddle*.' Query,—Was it in Scotland that the young gentlemen of the Edinburgh Review *learned* that *Solyman* means *Mahomet II.* any more than *criticism* means *infallibility?*—but thus it is,
'Cædimus inque vicem præbemus crura sagittis.'
The mistake seemed so completely a lapse of the pen (from the great *similarity* of the two words, and the *total absence of error* from the former pages of the literary leviathan) that I should have passed it over as in the text, had I not perceived in the Edinburgh Review much facetious exultation on all such detections, particularly a recent one, where words and syllables are subjects of disquisition and transposition; and the above-mentioned parallel passage in my own case irresistibly propelled me to hint how much easier it is to be critical than correct. The *gentlemen*, having enjoyed many a *triumph* on such victories, will hardly begrudge me a slight *ovation* for the present.

The Reviewer mentions Mr. Wright, the author of the beautiful poem 'Horæ Ionicæ,' as qualified to give details of these nominal Romans and degenerate Greeks; and also of their language: but Mr. Wright, though a good poet and an able man, has made a mistake where he states the Albanian dialect of the Romaic to approximate nearest to the Hellenic; for the Albanians speak a Romaic as notoriously corrupt as the Scotch of Aberdeenshire, or the Italian of Naples. Yanina, (where, next to the Fanal, the Greek is purest,) although the capital of Ali Pacha's dominions, is not in Albania, but Epirus; and beyond Delvinachi in Albania Proper up to Argyrocastro and Tepaleen (beyond which I did not advance) they spoke worse Greek than even the Athenians. I was attended for a year and a half by two of these singular mountaineers, whose mother tongue is Illyric, and I never heard them or their countrymen (whom I have seen, not only at home, but to the amount of twenty thousand in the army of Vely Pacha) praised for their Greek, but often laughed at for their provincial barbarisms.

I have in my possession about twenty-five letters, amongst which some from the Bey of Corinth, written to me by Notaras, the Cogia Bachi, and others by the dragoman of the Caimacam of the Morea (which last governs in Vely Pacha's absence), are said to be favourable specimens of their epistolary style. I also received some at Constantinople from private persons, written in a most hyperbolical style, but in the true antique character.

The Reviewer proceeds, after some remarks on the tongue in its past and present state, to a paradox (page 59) on the great mischief the knowledge of his own language has done to Coray, who, it seems, is less likely to understand the ancient Greek, because he is perfect master of the modern! This observation follows a paragraph, recommending, in explicit terms, the study of the Romaic, as 'a powerful auxiliary,' not only to the traveller and foreign merchant, but also to the classical scholar; in short, to everybody except the only person who can be thoroughly acquainted with its uses; and by a parity of reasoning, our old language is conjectured to be probably more attainable by 'foreigners' than by ourselves! Now, I am inclined to think, that a Dutch Tyro in our tongue, (albeit himself of Saxon blood) would be sadly perplexed with 'Sir Tristrem,' or any other given 'Auchinleck MS.,' with or without a grammar or glossary; and to most apprehensions it seems evident, that none but a native can acquire a competent, far less complete, knowledge of our obsolete idioms. We may give the critic credit for his ingenuity, but no more believe him than we do Smollet's Lismahago, who maintains that the purest English is spoken in Edinburgh. That Coray may err is very possible; but if he does, the fault is in the man rather than in his mother tongue, which is, as it ought to be, of the greatest aid to the native student.—Here the Reviewer proceeds to business on Strabo's translators, and here I close my remarks.

Sir W. Drummond, Mr. Hamilton, Lord Aberdeen, Dr. Clarke, Captain Leake, Mr. Gell, Mr. Walpole, and many others now in England, have all the requisites to furnish details of this fallen people. The few observations I have offered I should have left where I made them, had not the article in question, and above all the spot where I read it, induced me to advert to those pages, which the advantage of my present situation enabled me to clear, or at least to make the attempt.

I have endeavoured to waive the personal feelings which rise in despite of me in touching upon any part of the Edinburgh Review; not from a wish to conciliate the favour of its writers, or to cancel the remembrance of a syllable I have formerly published, but simply from a sense of the impropriety of mixing up private resentments with a disquisition of the present kind, and more particularly at this distance of time and place.

Amongst an enslaved people, obliged to have recourse to foreign presses even for their books of religion, it is less to be wondered at that we find so few publications on general subjects than that we find any at all. The whole number of the Greeks, scattered up and down the Turkish empire and elsewhere, may amount, at most, to three millions; and yet, for so scanty a number, it is impossible to discover any nation with so great a proportion of books and their authors as the Greeks of the present century. 'Ay,' but say the generous advocates of oppression, who, while they assert the ignorance of the Greeks, wish to prevent them from dispelling it, 'ay, but these are mostly, if not all, ecclesiastical tracts, and consequently good for nothing.' Well! and pray what else can they write about? It is pleasant enough to hear a Frank, particularly an Englishman, who may abuse the government of his own country; or a Frenchman, who may abuse every government except his own, and who may range at will over every philosophical, religious, scientific, sceptical, or moral subject, sneering at the Greek legends. A Greek must not write on politics, and cannot touch on science for want of instruction; if he doubts, he is excommunicated and damned; therefore his countrymen are not poisoned with modern philosophy; and as to morals, thanks to the Turks! there are no such things. What then is left him, if he has a turn for scribbling? Religion and holy biography: and it is natural enough that those who have so little in this life should look to the next. It is no great wonder, then, that in a catalogue now before me of fifty-five Greek writers, many of whom were lately living, not above fifteen should have touched on anything but religion. The catalogue alluded to is contained in the twenty-sixth chapter of the fourth volume of Meletius' Ecclesiastical History.

Page 206, col. 1.

'Spirit of freedom! when on Phyle's brow.'] Phyle, which commands a beautiful view of Athens, has still considerable remains: it was seized by Thrasybulus, previous to the expulsion of the Thirty.

Page 206, col. 1.

'Trembling beneath the scourge of Turkish hand.'] The difficulties of travelling in Turkey have been much exaggerated, or rather have considerably diminished, of late years. The Mussulmans have been beaten into a kind of sullen civility very comfortable to voyagers.

It is hazardous to say much on the subject of Turks and Turkey; since it is possible to live amongst them twenty years without acquiring information, at least from themselves. As far as my own slight experience carried me, I have no complaint to make; but am indebted for many civilities (I might also say for friendship), and much hospitality, to Ali Pacha, his son Veli Pacha of the Morea, and several others of high rank in the provinces. Suleyman Aga, late Governor of Athens, and now of Thebes, was a *bon vivant*, and

as social a being as ever sat cross-legged at a tray or a table. During the carnival, when our English party were masquerading, both himself and his successor were more happy to 'receive masks,' than any dowager in Grosvenor-square.

On one occasion of his supping at the convent, his friend and visitor, the Cadi of Thebes, was carried from table perfectly qualified for any club in Christendom; while the worthy Waywode himself triumphed in his fall.

In all money transactions with the Moslems, I ever found the strictest honour, the highest disinterestedness. In transacting business with them, there are none of those dirty peculations, under the name of interest, difference of exchange, commission, &c. &c., uniformly found in applying to a Greek consul to cash bills, even on the first houses in Pera.

With regard to presents, an established custom in the East, you will rarely find yourself a loser; as one worth acceptance is generally returned by another of similar value—a horse, or a shawl.

In the capital and at court the citizens and courtiers are formed in the same school with those of Christianity; but there does not exist a more honourable, friendly, and high-spirited character than the true Turkish provincial Aga, or Moslem country gentleman. It is not meant here to designate the governors of towns, but those Agas who, by a kind of feudal tenure, possess lands and houses, of more or less extent, in Greece and Asia Minor.

The lower orders are in as tolerable discipline as the rabble in countries with greater pretensions to civilization. A Moslem, in walking the streets of our country-towns, would be more incommoded in England than a Frank in a similar situation in Turkey. Regimentals are the best travelling dress.

The best accounts of the religion and different sects of Islamism, may be found in D'Ohsson's French; of their manners, &c. perhaps in Thornton's English. The Ottomans, with all their defects, are not a people to be despised. Equal, at least, to the Spaniards, they are superior to the Portuguese. If it be difficult to pronounce what they are, we can at least say what they are *not;* they are *not* treacherous, they are *not* cowardly, they do *not* burn heretics, they are *not* assassins, nor has an enemy advanced to *their* capital. They are faithful to their sultan till he becomes unfit to govern, and devout to their God without an inquisition. Were they driven from St. Sophia to-morrow, and the French or Russians enthroned in their stead, it would become a question whether Europe would gain by the exchange. England would certainly be the loser.

With regard to that ignorance of which they are so generally, and sometimes justly, accused, it may be doubted, always excepting France and England, in what useful points of knowledge they are excelled by other nations. Is it in the common arts of life? In their manufactures? Is a Turkish sabre inferior to a Toledo? or is a Turk worse clothed, or lodged, or fed and taught, than a Spaniard? Are their Pachas worse educated than a Grandee? or an Effendi than a Knight of St. Jago? I think not.

I remember Mahmout, the grandson of Ali Pacha, asking whether my fellow-traveller and myself were in the upper or lower House of Parliament. Now, this question from a boy of ten years old proved that his education had not been neglected. It may be doubted if an English boy at that age knows the difference of the Divan from a College of Dervises; but I am very sure a Spaniard does not. How little Mahmout, surrounded, as he had been, entirely by his Turkish tutors, had learned that there was such a thing as a Parliament, it were useless to conjecture, unless we suppose that his instructors did not confine his studies to the Koran.

In all the mosques there are schools established, which are very regularly attended; and the poor are taught without the church of Turkey being put into peril. I believe the system is not yet printed (though there is such a thing as a Turkish press, and books printed on the late military institution of the Nizam Gedidd); nor have I heard whether the Mufti and the Mollas have subscribed, or the Caimacan and the Tefterdar taken the alarm, for fear the ingenuous youth of the turban should be taught not to 'pray to God their way.' The Greeks also—a kind of Eastern Irish papists—have a college of their own at Maynooth,—no, at Haivali; where the heterodox receive much the same kind of countenance from the Ottoman as the Catholic college from the English legislature. Who shall then affirm that the Turks are ignorant bigots, when they thus evince the exact proportion of Christian charity which is tolerated in the most prosperous and orthodox of all possible kingdoms? But though they allow all this, they will not suffer the Greeks to participate in their privileges: no, let them fight their battles, and pay their haratch (taxes), be drubbed in this world, and damned in the next. And shall we then emancipate our Irish Helots? Mahomet forbid! We should then be bad Mussulmans, and worse Christians: at present we unite the best of both—jesuitical faith, and something not much inferior to Turkish toleration.

Page 206, col. 1.

'Receive the fiery Frank, her former guest.'] When taken by the Latins, and retained for several years.

Page 206, col. 2.

'The prophet's tomb of all its pious spoil.'] Mecca and Medina were taken some time ago by the Wahabees, a sect yearly increasing.

Page 207, col. 2.

'Thy vales of evergreen, thy hills of snow.'] On many of the mountains, particularly Liakura, the snow never is entirely melted, notwithstanding the intense heat of the summer; but I never saw it lie on the plains, even in winter.

Page 207, col. 2.

'Above its prostrate brethren of the cave.'] Of Mount Pentelicus, from whence the marble was dug that constructed the public edifices of Athens. The modern name is Mount Mendeli. An immense cave, formed by the quarries, still remains, and will till the end of time.

Page 207, col. 2.

'Colonna's cliff, and gleams along the wave.'] In all Attica, if we except Athens itself and Marathon, there is no scene more interesting than Cape Colonna. To the antiquary and artist, sixteen columns are an inexhaustible source of observation and design; to the philosopher, the supposed scene of some of Plato's conversations will not be unwelcome; and the traveller will be struck with the beauty of the prospect over 'Isles that crown the Ægean deep;' but, for an Englishman, Colonna has yet an additional interest, as the actual spot of Falconer's shipwreck. Pallas and Plato are forgotten, in the recollection of Falconer and Campbell:—

'Here in the dead of night by Lonna's steep,
The seaman's cry was heard along the deep.'

This temple of Minerva may be seen at sea from a great distance. In two journeys which I made, and one voyage to Cape Colonna, the view from either side, by land, was less striking than the approach from the isles. In our second land excursion, we had a narrow escape from a party of Mainotes, concealed in the caverns beneath. We were told afterwards, by one of their prisoners, subsequently ransomed, that they were deterred from attacking us by the appearance of my two Albanians: conjecturing very sagaciously, but falsely, that we had a complete guard of these Arnaouts at hand, they remained stationary, and thus saved our party, which was too small to have opposed any effectual resistance. Colonna is no less a resort of painters than of pirates; there

'The hireling artist plants his paltry desk,
And makes degraded nature picturesque.'
(See Hodgson's Lady Jane Grey, &c.)

But there Nature, with the aid of Art, has done that for herself. I was fortunate enough to engage a very superior German artist; and hope to renew my acquaintance with this and many other Levantine scenes, by the arrival of his performances.

Page 208, col. 1.

'When Marathon became a magic word.'] 'Siste Viator—heroa calcas!' was the epitaph on the famous Count Merci;—what then must be our feelings when standing on the tumulus of the two hundred (Greeks) who fell on Marathon? The principal barrow has recently been opened by Fauvel: few or no relics, as vases, &c. were found by the excavator. The plain of Marathon was offered to me for sale at the sum of sixteen thousand piastres, about nine hundred pounds! Alas! —'Expende—quot *libras* in duce summo—invenies!'—was the dust of Miltiades worth no more? It could scarcely have fetched less if sold by *weight*.

Page 212, col. 1.

'In "pride of place" here last the eagle flew.'] 'Pride of place' is a term of falconry, and means the highest pitch of flight. See Macbeth, &c.:—

'An eagle towering in his pride of place,' &c.

Page 212, col. 1.

'Such as Harmodius drew on Athens' tyrant lord.'] See the famous song on Harmodius and Aristogiton. The best English translation is in Bland's Anthology, by Mr. (since Lord Chief Justice) Denman:—

'With myrtle my sword will I wreathe,' &c.

Page 212, col. 2.

'And all went merry as a marriage-bell.'] On the night previous to the action, it is said that a ball was given at Brussels.

Page 213, col. 1.

'And Evan's, Donald's fame rings in each clansman's ears!'] Sir Evan Cameron, and his descendant Donald, the 'gentle Lochiel' of the 'forty-five.'

Page 213, col. 1.

'And Ardennes waves above them her green leaves.'] The wood of Soignies is supposed to be a remnant of the forest of Ardennes, famous in

Boiardo's Orlando, and immortal in Shakespeare's 'As You Like It.' It is also celebrated in Tacitus, as being the spot of successful defence by the Germans against the Roman encroachments. I have ventured to adopt the name connected with nobler associations than those of mere slaughter.

Page 213, col. 2.

'I turn'd from all she brought to those she coula not bring.'] My guide from Mount St. Jean over the field seemed intelligent and accurate. The place where Major Howard fell was not far from two tall and solitary trees (there was a third cut down, or shivered in the battle), which stand a few yards from each other at a pathway's side. Beneath these he died and was buried. The body has since been removed to England. A small hollow for the present marks where it lay, but will probably soon be effaced; the plough has been upon it, and the grain is. After pointing out the different spots where Picton and other gallant men had perished, the guide said, 'Here Major Howard lay: I was near him when wounded.' I told him my relationship, and he seemed then still more anxious to point out the particular spot and circumstances. The place is one of the most marked in the field, from the peculiarity of the two trees above mentioned. I went on horseback twice over the field, comparing it with my recollection of similar scenes. As a plain, Waterloo seems marked out for the scene of some great action, though this may be mere imagination: I have viewed with attention those of Platea, Troy, Mantinea, Leuctra, Chæronea, and Marathon: and the field around Mount St. Jean and Hougoumont appears to want little but a better cause, and that undefinable but impressive halo which the lapse of ages throws around a celebrated spot, to vie in interest with any or all of these, except, perhaps, the last mentioned.

Page 214, col. 1.

'Like to the apples on the Dead Sea's shore.'] The (fabled) apples on the brink of the lake Asphaltites were said to be fair without, and, within, ashes. Vide Tacitus, Histor. lib. v. 7.

Page 215, col. 1.

'For sceptred cynics earth were far too wide a den.'] The great error of Napoleon, 'if we have writ our annals true,' was a continued obtrusion on mankind of his want of all community of feeling for or with them; perhaps more offensive to human vanity than the active cruelty of more trembling and suspicious tyranny. Such were his speeches to public assemblies as well as individuals; and the single expression which he is said to have used on returning to Paris after the Russian winter had destroyed his army, rubbing his hands over a fire, 'This is pleasanter than Moscow,' would probably alienate more favour from his cause than the destruction and reverses which led to the remark.

Page 216, col. 1.

'What want these outlaws conquerors should have?'] 'What wants that knave that a king should have?' was King James's question on meeting Johnny Armstrong and his followers in full accoutrements.—See the Ballad.

Page 217, col. 1.

'The castled crag of Drachenfels.'] The castle of Drachenfels stands on the highest summit of 'the Seven Mountains, over the Rhine banks; it is in ruins, and connected with some singular traditions. It is the first in view on the road from Bonn, but on the opposite side of the river; on this bank, nearly facing it, are the remains of another, called the Jew's Castle, and a large cross, commemorative of the murder of a chief by his brother. The number of castles and cities along the course of the Rhine on both sides is very great, and their situations remarkably beautiful.

Page 218, col. 1.

'The whiteness of his soul, and thus men o'er him wept.'] The monument of the young and lamented General Marceau (killed by a rifle-ball at Alterkirchen, on the last day of the fourth year of the French republic) still remains as described. The inscriptions on his monument are rather too long, and not required: his name was enough; France adored, and her enemies admired; both wept over him. His funeral was attended by the generals and detachments from both armies. In the same grave General Hoche is interred, a gallant man also in every sense of the word; but though he distinguished himself greatly in battle, *he* had not the good fortune to die there: his death was attended by suspicions of poison. A separate monument (not over his body, which is buried by Marceau's) is raised for him near Andernach, opposite to which one of his most memorable exploits was performed, in throwing a bridge to an island on the Rhine. The shape and style are different from that of Marceau's, and the inscription more simple and pleasing:—'The Army of the Sambre and Meuse to its Commander-in-Chief Hoche.' This is all, and as it should be. Hoche was esteemed among the first of France's earlier generals, before Buonaparte monopolised her triumphs. He was the destined commander of the invading army of Ireland.

Page 218, col. 1.

'Here Ehrenbreitstein, with her shatter'd wall.'] Ehrenbreitstein, *i.e.* 'the broad stone of honour,' one of the strongest fortresses in Europe, was dismantled and blown up by the French at the truce of Leoben. It had been, and could only be, reduced by famine or treachery. It yielded to the former, aided by surprise. After having seen the fortifications of Gibraltar and Malta, it did not much strike by comparison; but the situation is commanding. General Marceau besieged it in vain for some time, and I slept in a room where I was shown a window at which he is said to have been standing observing the progress of the siege by moonlight, when a ball struck immediately below it.

Page 218, col. 2.

'Unsepulchred they roam'd, and shriek'd each wandering ghost.'] The chapel is destroyed, and the pyramid of bones diminished to a small number by the Burgundian legion in the service of France; who anxiously effaced this record of their ancestors' less successful invasions. A few still remain, notwithstanding the pains taken by the Burgundians for ages (all who passed that way removing a bone to their own country), and the less justifiable larcenies of the Swiss postilions, who carried them off to sell for knife-handles; a purpose for which the whiteness imbibed by the bleaching of years had rendered them in great request. Of these relics I ventured to bring away as much as may have made a quarter of a hero, for which the sole excuse is, that if I had not, the next passer-by might have perverted them to worse uses than the careful preservation which I intend for them.

Page 219, col. 1.

'Levell'd Aventicum, hath strew'd her subject lands.'] Aventicum, near Morat, was the Roman capital of Helvetia, where Avenches now stands.

Page 219, col. 1.

'And held within their urn one mind, one heart, one dust.'] Julia Alpinula, a young Aventian priestess, died soon after a vain endeavour to save her father, condemned to death as a traitor by Aulus Cæcina. Her epitaph was discovered many years ago;—it is thus:—'Julia Alpinula: Hic jaceo. Infelicis patris, infelix proles. Deæ Aventiæ Sacerdos. Exorare patris necem non potui: Male mori in fatis ille erat. Vixi annos XXIII.'—I know of no human composition so affecting as this, nor a history of deeper interest. These are the names and actions which ought not to perish, and to which we turn with a true and healthy tenderness, from the wretched and glittering detail of a confused mass of conquests and battles, with which the mind is roused for a time to a false and feverish sympathy, from whence it recurs at length with all the nausea consequent on such intoxication.

Page 219, col. 1.

'In the sun's face, like yonder Alpine snow.'] This is written in the eye of Mont Blanc (June 3rd, 1816), which even at this distance dazzles mine.—(July 20th.) I this day observed for some time the distinct reflection of Mont Blanc and Mont Argentière in the calm of the lake, which I was crossing in my boat; the distance of these mountains from their mirror is sixty miles.

Page 219, col. 2.

'By the blue rushing of the arrowy Rhone.'] The colour of the Rhone at Geneva is blue, to a depth of tint which I have never seen equalled in water, salt or fresh, except in the Mediterranean and Archipelago.

Page 220, col. 2.

'This hallow'd, too, the memorable kiss.'] This refers to the account in his 'Confessions' of his passion for the Comtesse d'Houdetot (the mistress of St. Lambert), and his long walk every morning, for the sake of the single kiss which was the common salutation of French acquaintance. Rousseau's description of his feelings on this occasion may be considered as the most passionate, yet not impure, description and expression of love that ever kindled into words; which, after all, must be felt, from their very force, to be inadequate to the delineation; a painting can give no sufficient idea of the ocean.

Page 222, col. 1.

'Of earth-o'ergazing mountains, and thus take.'] It is to be recollected, that the most beautiful and impressive doctrines of the divine Founder of Christianity were delivered, not in the *Temple*, but on the *Mount*. To waive the question of devotion, and turn to human eloquence,—the most effectual and splendid specimens were not pronounced within walls. Demosthenes addressed the public and popular assemblies. Cicero spoke in the forum. That this added to their effect on the mind of both orator and hearers, may be conceived from the difference between what we read of the emotions then and there produced, and those we ourselves experience in the perusal in the closet. It is one thing to read the Iliad at Sigæum and on the tumuli, or by the springs with Mount Ida above, and the plain and rivers and Archipelago around you; and another to trim your taper over it in a snug library—*this* I know. Were the early and rapid progress of what is called Methodism to be attributed to any cause beyond the enthusiasm excited by its vehement faith and doctrines (the truth or error of which I presume neither to canvass nor to question), I should venture to ascribe it to the practice of preaching in the *fields*, and the unstudied and extemporaneous effusions of its teachers. The Mussulmans, whose erroneous devotion (at least in the lower orders) is most sincere, and therefore impressive, are accustomed to repeat their prescribed orisons and prayers, wherever they may be, at the stated hours—of course, frequently in the open air, kneeling upon a light mat (which they carry for the purpose of a bed or cushion as required); the ceremony lasts some minutes, during which they are totally absorbed, and only living in their supplication: nothing can disturb them. On me the simple and entire sincerity of these men, and the spirit which appeared to be within and upon them, made a far greater impression than any general rite which was ever performed in places of worship, of which I have seen those of almost every persuasion under the sun; including most of our own sectaries, and the Greek, the Catholic, the Armenian, the Lutheran, the Jewish, and the Mahometan. Many of the negroes of whom there are numbers in the Turkish empire, are idolaters, and have free exercise of their belief and its rites; some of these I had a distant view of at Patras; and, from what I could make out of them, they appeared to be of a truly Pagan description, and not very agreeable to a spectator.

Page 222, col. 2.

'The sky is changed!—and such a change! Oh night.'] The thunder-storm to which these lines refer occurred on the 13th of June, 1816, at midnight. I have seen, among the Acroceraunian mountains of Chimari, several more terrible, but none more beautiful.

Page 223, col. 2.

'And sun-set into rose-hues sees them wrought.'] Rousseau's Héloïse, Lettre 17, Part IV., note. 'Ces montagnes sont si hautes qu'une demi-heure après le soleil couche, leurs sommets sont éclairés de ses rayons; dont le rouge forme sur ces cimes blanches *une belle couleur de rose*, qu'on aperçoit de fort loin.'—This applies more particularly to the heights over Meillerie.—'J'allai à Vevay loger à la Clef, et pendant deux jours que j'y restai sans voir personne, je pris pour cette ville un amour qui m'a suivi dans tous mes voyages, et qui m'y a fait établir enfin les héros de mon roman. Je dirais volontiers à ceux qui ont du goût et qui sont sensibles: Allez à Vevay—visitez le pays, examinez les sites, promenez-vous sur le lac, et dites si la Nature n'a pas fait ce beau pays pour une Julie, pour une Claire, et pour un St. Preux; mais ne les y cherchez pas.'—*Les Confessions*, livre iv. p. 306, Lyon, ed. 1796.—In July, 1816, I made a voyage round the Lake of Geneva: and, as far as my own observations have led me in a not uninterested nor inattentive survey of all the scenes most celebrated by Rousseau in his 'Héloïse,' I can safely say, that in this there is no exaggeration. It would be difficult to see Clarens (with the scenes around it, Vevay, Chillon, Bôveret, St. Gingo, Meillerie, Eivan, and the entrances of the Rhone) without being forcibly struck with its peculiar adaptation to the persons and events with which it has been peopled. But this is not all; the feeling with which all around Clarens, and the

NOTES TO CHILDE HAROLD'S PILGRIMAGE

opposite rocks of Meillerie, is invested, is of a still higher and more comprehensive order than the mere sympathy with individual passion; it is a sense of the existence of love in its most extended and sublime capacity, and of our own participation of its good and of its glory: it is the great principle of the universe, which is there more condensed, but not less manifested; and of which, though knowing ourselves a part, we lose our individuality, and mingle in the beauty of the whole.—If Rousseau had never written, nor lived, the same associations would not less have belonged to such scenes. He has added to the interest of his works by their adoption; he has shown his sense of their beauty by the selection; but they have done that for him which no human being could do for them.—I had the fortune (good or evil as it might be) to sail from Meillerie (where we landed for some time) to St. Gingo during a lake storm, which added to the magnificence of all around, although occasionally accompanied by danger to the boat, which was small and overloaded. It was over this very part of the lake that Rousseau has driven the boat of St. Preux and Madame Wolmar to Meillerie for shelter during a tempest. On gaining the shore at St. Gingo, I found that the wind had been sufficiently strong to blow down some fine old chestnut trees on the lower part of the mountains. On the opposite height of Clarens is a château. The hills are covered with vineyards, and interspersed with some small but beautiful woods; one of these was named the 'Bosquet de Julie;' and it is remarkable that, though long ago cut down by the brutal selfishness of the monks of St. Bernard (to whom the land appertained), that the ground might be enclosed into a vineyard for the miserable drones of an execrable superstition, the inhabitants of Clarens still point out the spot where its trees stood, calling it by the name which consecrated and survived them. Rousseau has not been particularly fortunate in the preservation of the 'local habitations' he has given to 'airy nothings.' The Prior of Great St. Bernard has cut down some of his woods for the sake of a few casks of wine, and Buonaparte has levelled part of the rocks of Meillerie in improving the road to the Simplon. The road is an excellent one; but I cannot quite agree with a remark which I heard made, that 'La route vaut mieux que les souvenirs.'

Page 224, col. 1.

'Of names which unto you bequeath'd a name.']
Voltaire and Gibbon.

Page 225, col. 2.

'Had I not filed my mind, which thus itself subdued.']
—'If it be thus,
For Banquo's issue have I *filed* my mind.'—
MACBETH.

Page 225, col. 2.

'O'er others' griefs that some sincerely grieve.']
It is said by Rochefoucault that 'there is *always* something in the misfortunes of men's best friends not displeasing to them.'

Page 227, col. 2.

'She looks a sea Cybele, fresh from ocean.']
Sabellicus, describing the appearance of Venice, has made use of the above image, which would not be poetical were it not true.—'Quo fit ut qui superne urbem contempletur, turritam telluris imaginem medio Oceano figuratam se putet inspicere.'

Page 228, col. 2.

'Sparta hath many a worthier son than he.']
The answer of the mother of Brasidas, the Lacedæmonian general, to the strangers who praised the memory of her son.

Page 229, col. 1.

'The "Planter of the Lion," which through fire.']
That is, the Lion of St. Mark, the standard of the republic, which is the origin of the word Pantaloon—Piantaleone, Pantaleon, Pantaloon.

Page 229, col. 2.

'Redemption rose up in the Attic Muse.']
The story is told in Plutarch's Life of Nicias.

Page 229, col. 2.

'And Otway, Radcliffe, Schiller, Shakespeare's art.']
'Venice Preserved;' 'Mysteries of Udolpho;' 'The Ghost-Seer, or Armenian;' 'The Merchant of Venice;' 'Othello.'

Page 230, col. 1.

'But from their nature will the tannen grow.']
Tannen is the plural of *tanne*, a species of fir peculiar to the Alps, which only thrives in very rocky parts, where scarcely soil sufficient for its nourishment can be found. On these spots it grows to a greater height than any other mountain tree.

Page 231, col. 1.

'Floats through the azure air—an island of the blest!']
The above description may seem fantastical or exaggerated to those who have never seen an Oriental or an Italian sky, yet it is but a literal and hardly sufficient delineation of an August evening (the eighteenth), as contemplated in one of many rides along the banks of the Brenta, near La Mira.

Page 231, col. 2.

'Or, it may be, with demons, who impair.']
The struggle is to the full as likely to be with demons as with our better thoughts. Satan chose the wilderness for the temptation of our Saviour. And our unsullied John Locke preferred the presence of a child to complete solitude.

Page 233, col. 1.

'Victor or vanquish'd, thou the slave of friend or foe.']
The two stanzas XLII. and XLIII. are, with the exception of a line or two, a translation of the famous sonnet of Filicaja:—'Italia, Italia, O tu cui feo la sorte!'

Page 233, col. 1.

'Wandering in youth, I traced the path of him.']
The celebrated letter of Servius Sulpicius to Cicero, on the death of his daughter, describes as it then was, and now is, a path which I often traced in Greece, both by sea and land, in different journeys and voyages. 'On my return from Asia, as I was sailing from Ægina towards Megara, I began to contemplate the prospect of the countries around me: Ægina was behind, Megara before me; Piræus on the right, Corinth on the left: all which towns, once famous and flourishing, now lie overturned and buried in their ruins. Upon this sight, I could not but think presently within myself, Alas! how do we poor mortals fret and vex ourselves if any of our friends happen to die or be killed, whose life is yet so short, when the carcasses of so many noble cities lie here exposed before me in one view.'—See Middleton's Cicero, vol. ii, p. 371.

Page 233, col. 2.

'The skeleton of her Titanic form.'] It is Poggio, who, looking from the Capitoline hill upon ruined Rome, breaks forth into the exclamation, 'Ut nunc omni decore nudata, prostrata jacet, instar gigantei cadaveris corrupti atque undique exesi.'

Page 234, col. 1.

'Feeding on thy sweet cheek! while thy lips are.']

'Οφθαλμοὺς ἐστιᾶν.

'Atque oculos pascat uterque suos.'—OVID. *Amor*. lib. ii.

Page 236, col. 2.

'Charming the eye with dread,—a matchless cataract.'] I saw the Cascata del Marmore of Terni twice, at different periods—once from the summit of the precipice, and again from the valley below. The lower view is far to be preferred, if the traveller has time for one only; but in any point of view, either from above or below, it is worth all the cascades and torrents of Switzerland put together: the Staubach, Reichenbach, Pisse Vache, fall of Arpenaz, &c. are rills in comparative appearance. Of the fall of Schaffhausen I cannot speak, not yet having seen it.

Page 236, col. 2.

'An Iris sits, amidst the infernal surge.'] Of the time, place, and qualities of this kind of iris, the reader will see a short account in a note to *Manfred*. The fall looks so much like 'the hell of waters,' that Addison thought the descent alluded to by the gulf in which Alecto plunged into the infernal regions. It is singular enough, that two of the finest cascades in Europe should be artificial—this of the Velino, and the one at Tivoli. The traveller is strongly recommended to trace the Velino, at least as high as the little lake called *Pie'* *di Lup*. The Reatine territory was the classic Tempe (Cicer. Epist. ad Attic. xv. lib. iv.), and the ancient naturalists (Plin. Hist. Nat. lib. ii. cap. lxii), amongst other beautiful varieties, remarked the daily rainbows of the lake Velinus. A scholar of great name has devoted a treatise to this district alone. See Ald. Manut. 'De Reatina Urbe Agroque,' ap. Sallengre, Thesaur. tom. i. p. 773.

Page 237, col. 1.

'Sits on more shaggy summits, and where roar.'] In the greater part of Switzerland, the avalanches are known by the name of lauwine.

Page 237, col. 1.

'The drill'd dull lesson, forced down word by word.'] These stanzas may probably remind the reader of Ensign Northerton's remarks, 'D—n Homo,' &c.; but the reasons for our dislike are not exactly the same. I wish to express, that we become tired of the task before we can comprehend the beauty; that we learn by rote before we can get by heart; that the freshness is worn away, and the future pleasure and advantage deadened and destroyed, by the didactic anticipation, at an age when we can neither feel nor understand the power of compositions which it requires an acquaintance with life, as well as Latin and Greek, to relish, or to reason upon. For the same reason, we never can be aware of the fulness of some of the finest passages of Shakespeare ('To be, or not to be,' for instance), from the habit of having them hammered into us at eight years old, as an exercise, not of mind, but of memory: so that when we are old enough to enjoy them, the taste is gone, and the appetite

palled. In some parts of the continent, young persons are taught from more common authors, and do not read the best classics till their maturity. I certainly do not speak on this point from any pique or aversion towards the place of my education. I was not a slow, though an idle boy; and I believe no one could, or can be, more attached to Harrow than I have always been, and with reason; —a part of the time passed there was the happiest of my life; and my preceptor, the Rev. Dr. Joseph Drury, was the best and worthiest friend I ever possessed, whose warnings I have remembered but too well, though too late, when I have erred,—and whose counsels I have but followed when I have done well or wisely. If ever this imperfect record of my feelings towards him should reach his eyes, let it remind him of one who never thinks of him but with gratitude and veneration—of one who would more gladly boast of having been his pupil, if, by more closely following upon his injunctions, he could reflect any honour upon his instructor.

Page 237, col. 2.

'The Scipios' tomb contains no ashes now.'] For a comment on this and the two following stanzas, the reader may consult 'Historical Illustrations,' p. 46.

Page 238, col. 1.

'The trebly hundred triumphs! and the day.'] Orosius gives 320 for the number of triumphs. He is followed by Panvinius; and Panvinius by Mr. Gibbon and the modern writers.

Page 238, col. 2.

'Beheld him win two realms, and, happier, yield his breath.'] On the 3rd of September Cromwell gained the victory of Dunbar; a year afterwards he obtained 'his crowning mercy' of Worcester; and a few years after, on the same day, which he had ever esteemed the most fortunate for him, died.

Page 239, col. 2.

'Our senses narrow, and our reason frail.']—— 'Omnes pene veteres; qui nihil cognosci, nihil percepi, nihil sciri posse dixerunt; angustos sensus; imbecillos animos, brevia curricula vitæ; in profundo veritatem demersam; opinionibus et institutis omnia teneri; nihil veritati relinqui: deinceps omnia tenebris circumfusa esse dixerunt.'—Academ. l. 13. The eighteen hundred years which have elapsed since Cicero wrote this have not removed any of the imperfections of humanity: and the complaints of the ancient philosophers may, without injustice or affectation, be transcribed in a poem written yesterday.

Page 240, col. 1.

'There is a stern round tower of other days.'] Alluding to the tomb of Cecilia Metella, called Capo di Bove. See 'Historical Illustrations,' p.200.

Page 240, col. 2.

'Heaven gives its favourites—early death; yet shed.']

'῍Ον οἱ θεοὶ φιλοῦσιν, ἀποθνήσκει νέος·
Τὸ γὰρ θανεῖν οὐκ αἰσχρὸν ἀλλ' αἰσχρῶς θανεῖν.'

Rich. Franc. Phil. Brunck. Poetæ Gnomici, p. 231, edit. 1784.

Page 241, col. 2.

'There is the moral of all human tales.'] The author of the Life of Cicero, speaking of the opinion entertained of Britain by that orator and his contemporary Romans, has the following eloquent passage:—'From their railleries of this kind, on the barbarity and misery of our island, one cannot help reflecting on the surprising fate and revolutions of kingdoms; how Rome, once the mistress of the world, the seat of arts, empire, and glory, now lies sunk in sloth, ignorance, and poverty, enslaved to the most cruel as well as to the most contemptible of tyrants, superstition and religious imposture; while this remote country, anciently the jest and contempt of the polite Romans, is become the happy seat of liberty, plenty, and letters; flourishing in all the arts and refinements of civil life; yet running, perhaps, the same course which Rome itself had run before it, from virtuous industry to wealth; from wealth to luxury; from luxury to an impatience of discipline, and corruption of morals: till, by a total degeneracy and loss of virtue, being grown ripe for destruction, it falls a prey at last to some hardy oppressor, and, with the loss of liberty, losing everything that is valuable, sinks gradually again into its original barbarism.' (See 'History of the life of M. Tullius Cicero, sect. vi. vol. ii. p. 102.)

Page 242, col. 1.

'To crush the imperial urn, whose ashes slept sublime.'] The column of Trajan is surmounted by St. Peter; that of Aurelius by St. Paul. See 'Historical Illustrations,' p. 214.

Page 242, col. 2.

'Rienzi! last of Romans! While the tree.'] The name and exploits of Rienzi must be familiar to the reader of Gibbon. Some details and inedited manuscripts, relative to this unhappy hero, will be seen in the 'Historical Illustrations of the Fourth Canto,' p. 248.

Page 244, col. 1.

'Yet let us ponder boldly—'tis a base.'] 'At all events,' says the author of the 'Academical Questions,' 'I trust, whatever may be the fate of my own speculations, that philosophy will regain that estimation which it ought to possess. The free and philosophic spirit of our nation has been the theme of admiration to the world. This was the proud distinction of Englishmen, and the luminous source of all their glory. Shall we then forget the manly and dignified sentiments of our ancestors, to prate in the language of the mother or the nurse about our good old prejudices? This is not the way to defend the cause of truth. It was not thus that our fathers maintained it in the brilliant periods of our history. Prejudice may be trusted to guard the outworks for a short space of time, while reason slumbers in the citadel; but if the latter sink into a lethargy, the former will quickly erect a standard for herself. Philosophy, wisdom, and liberty support each other: he who will not reason is a bigot; he who cannot is a fool; and he who dares not is a slave.'—Vol. i, pref., pp. 14, 15.

Page 246, col. 1.

'Like laurels on the bald first Cæsar's head.'] Suetonius informs us that Julius Cæsar was particularly gratified by that decree of the senate which enabled him to wear a wreath of laurel on all occasions. He was anxious, not to show that he was the conqueror of the world, but to hide that he was bald. A stranger at Rome would hardly have guessed at the motive, nor should we without the help of the historian.

Page 246, col. 2.

'While stands the Coliseum, Rome shall stand.'] This is quoted in the 'Decline and Fall of the Roman Empire,' as a proof that the Coliseum was entire, when seen by the Anglo-Saxon pilgrims at the end of the seventh, or the beginning of the eighth, century. A notice on the Coliseum may be seen in the 'Historical Illustrations,' p. 263.

Page 246, col. 2.

'From Jove to Jesus—spared and blest by time.'] 'Though plundered of all its brass, except the ring which was necessary to preserve the aperture above; though exposed to repeated fires; though sometimes flooded by the river, and always open to the rain, no monument of equal antiquity is so well preserved as this rotundo. It passed with little alteration from the Pagan into the present worship; and so convenient were its niches for the Christian altar, that Michael Angelo, ever studious of ancient beauty, introduced their design as a model in the Catholic church.'—*Forsyth's Italy*, p. 137, 2nd edit.

Page 246, col. 2.

'Their eyes on honour'd forms, whose busts around them close.'] The Pantheon has been made a receptacle for the busts of modern great, or, at least, distinguished men. The flood of light which once fell through the large orb above on the whole circle of divinities, now shines on a numerous assemblage of mortals, some one or two of whom have been almost deified by the veneration of their countrymen. For a notice of the Pantheon, see 'Historical Illustrations,' p. 287.

Page 246, col. 2.

'There is a dungeon, in whose dim drear light.'] This and the three next stanzas allude to the story of the Roman daughter, which is recalled to the traveller by the site, or pretended site, of that adventure, now shown at the church of St. Nicholas *in Carcere*. The difficulties attending the full belief of the tale are stated in 'Historical Illustrations,' p. 295.

Page 247, col. 2.

'Turn to the mole which Hadrian rear'd on high.'] The castle of St. Angelo. See 'Historical Illustrations.'

Page 247, col. 2.

'But lo! the dome—the vast and wondrous dome.'] This and the six stanzas have a reference to the church of St. Peter's. For a measurement of the comparative length of this basilica and the other great churches of Europe, see the pavement of St. Peter's, and the 'Classical Tour through Italy,' vol. ii. p. 125 et seq., chap. iv.

Page 250, col. 1.

'Nations have arm'd in madness, the strange fate.'] Mary died on the scaffold; Elizabeth of a broken heart; Charles V. a hermit; Louis XIV. a bankrupt in means and glory; Cromwell of anxiety and, 'the greatest is behind,' Napoleon lives a prisoner. To these sovereigns a long but superfluous list might be added of names equally illustrious and unhappy.

Page 250, col. 1.

'Lo, Nemi! navell'd in the woody hills.'] The village of Nemi was near the Arician retreat of Egeria, and, from the shades which embosomed the temple of Diana, has preserved to this day its distinctive appellation of *The Grove*. Nemi is but an evening's ride from the comfortable inn of Albano.

THE GIAOUR

Page 252, col. 1.

'That tomb which, gleaming o'er the cliff.'] A tomb above the rocks on the promontory, by some supposed the sepulchre of Themistocles.

Page 253, col. 1.

'Sultana of the Nightingale.'] The attachment of the nightingale to the rose is a well-known Persian fable. If I mistake not, the 'Bulbul of a thousand tales' is one of his appellations.

Page 253, col. 1.

'Till the gay mariner's guitar.'] The guitar is the constant amusement of the Greek sailor by night; with a steady fair wind, and during a calm, it is accompanied always by the voice, and often by dancing.

Page 253, col. 2.

'Where cold Obstruction's apathy.']

'Ay, but to die and go we know not where,
To lie in cold obstruction?'
Measure for Measure, Act iii. sc. 1.

Page 253, col. 2.

'The first, last look by death reveal'd!'] I trust that few of my readers have ever had an opportunity of witnessing what is here attempted in description; but those who have will probably retain a painful remembrance of that singular beauty which pervades, with few exceptions, the features of the dead, a few hours, and but for a few hours, after 'the spirit is not there.' It is to be remarked in cases of violent death by gun-shot wounds, the expression is always that of languor, whatever the natural energy of the sufferer's character; but in death from a stab the countenance preserves its traits of feeling or ferocity, and the mind its bias, to the last.

Page 254, col. 1.

'Slaves—nay, the bondsmen of a slave.'] Athens is the property of the Kislar Aga (the slave of the seraglio and guardian of the women), who appoints the Waywode. A pander and eunuch—these are not polite, yet true appellations—now *governs* the *governor* of Athens!

Page 254, col. 2.

'In echoes of the far tophaike.'] 'Tophaike,' musket. The Bairam is announced by the cannon at sunset: the illumination of the mosques, and the firing of all kinds of small arms, loaded with *ball*, proclaim it during the night.

Page 254, col. 2.

'Swift as the hurl'd on high jerreed.'] Jerreed, or Djerrid, a blunted Turkish javelin, which is darted from horseback with great force and precision. It is a favourite exercise of the Mussulmans; but I know not if it can be called a *manly* one, since the most expert in the art are the Black Eunuchs of Constantinople. I think, next to these, a Mamlouk at Smyrna was the most skilful that came within my observation.

Page 255, col. 1.

'He came, he went, like the simoom.'] The blast of the desert, fatal to every thing living, and often alluded to in eastern poetry.

Page 255, col. 2.

'To bless the sacred "bread and salt."'] To partake of food, to break bread and salt with your host, insures the safety of the guest: even though an enemy, his person from that moment is sacred.

Page 255, col. 2.

'Since his turban was cleft by the infidel's sabre!'] I need hardly observe, that Charity and Hospitality are the first duties enjoined by Mahomet; and to say truth, very generally practised by his disciples. The first praise that can be bestowed on a chief is a panegyric on his bounty; the next, on his valour.

Page 255, col. 2.

'And silver-sheathed ataghan.'] The ataghan, a long dagger worn with pistols in the belt, in a metal scabbard, generally of silver; and, among the wealthier, gilt, or of gold.

Page 255, col. 2.

'An Emir by his garb of green.'] Green is the privileged colour of the prophet's numerous pretended descendants; with them, as here, faith (the family inheritance) is supposed to supersede the necessity of good works: they are the worst of a very indifferent brood.

Page 255, col. 2.

'"Ho! who art thou?"—"This low salam."'] 'Salam aleikoum! aleikoum salam!' peace be with you; be with you peace—the salutation reserved for the faithful:—to a Christian, 'Urlarula,'[a good journey; or 'saban hiresem, saban serula;' good morn, good even; and sometimes, 'may your end be happy;' are the usual salutes.

Page 256, col. 1.

'The insect queen of eastern spring.'] The blue-winged butterfly of Kashmeer, the most rare and beautiful of the species.

Page 256, col. 2.

'Is like the Scorpion girt by fire.'] Alluding to the dubious suicide of the scorpion, so placed for experiment by gentle philosophers. Some maintain that the position of the sting, when turned towards the head, is merely a convulsive movement; but others have actually brought in the verdict 'Felo de se.' The scorpions are surely interested in a speedy decision of the question; as, if once fairly established as insect Catos, they will probably be allowed to live as long as they think proper, without being martyred for the sake of an hypothesis.

Page 256, col. 2.

'When Rhamazan's last sun was set.'] The cannon at sunset close the Rhamazan.

Page 256, col. 2.

By pale Phingari's trembling light.'] Phingari, the moon.

Page 256, col. 2.

'Bright as the jewel of Giamschid.'] The celebrated fabulous ruby of Sultan Giamschid, the embellisher of Istakhar; from its splendour, named Schebgerag, 'the torch of night;' also 'the cup of the sun,' &c. In the first edition, 'Giamschid' was written as a word of three syllables; so D'Herbelot has it; but I am told Richardson reduces it to a dissyllable, and writes 'Jamshid.' I have left in the text the orthography of the one with the pronunciation of the other.

Page 257, col. 1.

'Though on Al-Sirat's arch I stood.'] Al-Sirat, the bridge of breath, narrower than the thread of a famished spider, and sharper than the edge of a sword, over which the Mussulmans must *skate* into Paradise, to which it is the only entrance; but this is not the worst, the river beneath being hell itself, into which, as may be expected, the unskilful and tender of foot contrive to tumble with a 'facilis descensus Averni,' not very pleasing in prospect to the next passenger. There is a shorter cut downwards for the Jews and Christians.

Page 257, col. 1.

'A soulless toy for tyrant's lust?'] A vulgar error; the Koran allots at least a third of Paradise to well-behaved women; but by far the greater number of Mussulmans interpret the text their own way, and exclude their moieties from heaven. Being enemies to Platonics, they cannot discern 'any fitness of things' in the souls of the other sex, conceiving them to be superseded by the Houris.

Page 257, col. 1.

'The young pomegranate's blossoms strew.'] An oriental simile, which may, perhaps, though fairly stolen, be deemed 'plus Arabe qu'en Arabie.'

Page 257, col. 1.

'Her hair in hyacinthine flow.'] Hyacinthine, in Arabic 'Sunbul;' as common a thought in the eastern poets as it was among the Greeks.

Page 257, col. 1.

'The loveliest bird of Franguestan!'] 'Franguestan,' Circassia.

Page 257, col. 2.

'Bismillah! now the peril's past.'] 'In the name of God;' the commencement of all the chapters of the Koran but one, and of prayer and thanksgiving.

Page 257, col. 2.

'Then curl'd his very beard with ire.'] A phenomenon not uncommon with an angry Mussulman. In 1809, the Capitan Pacha's whiskers at a diplomatic audience were no less lively with indignation than a tiger cat's, to the horror of all the dragomans; the portentous mustachios twisted, they stood erect of their own accord, and were expected every moment to change their colour, but at last condescended to subside, which, probably, saved more heads than they contained hairs.

Page 258, col. 1.

'Nor raised the craven cry, Amaun!'] 'Amaun,' quarter, pardon.

Page 258, col. 1.

'I know him by the evil eye.'] The 'evil eye,' a common superstition in the Levant, and of which the imaginary effects are yet very singular on those who conceive themselves affected.

Page 258, col. 2.

'A fragment of his palampore.'] The flowered shawls generally worn by persons of rank.

Page 259, col. 1.

'His calpac rent—his caftan red.'] The calpac is the solid cap or centre part of the head-dress; the shawl is wound round it, and forms the turban.

Page 259, col. 1.

'A turban carved in coarsest stone.'] The turban, pillar, and inscriptive verse, decorate the tombs of the Osmanlies, whether in the cemetery or the wilderness. In the mountains you frequently pass similar mementos; and on inquiry you are informed that they record some victim of rebellion, plunder, or revenge.

Page 259, col. 1.

'At solemn sound of "Alla Hu!"'] 'Alla Hu!' the concluding words of the Muezzin's call to prayer from the highest gallery on the exterior of the Minaret. On a still evening, when the Muezzin has a fine voice, which is frequently the case, the effect is solemn and beautiful beyond all the bells in Christendom.

Page 259, col. 1.

'They come—their kerchiefs green they wave.'] The following is part of a battle song of the Turks: —'I see—I see a dark-eyed girl of Paradise, and she waves a handkerchief, a kerchief of green; and cries aloud, "Come, kiss me, for I love thee,"' &c.

Page 259, col. 1.

'Beneath avenging Monkir's scythe.'] Monkir and Nekir are the inquisitors of the dead, before whom the corpse undergoes a slight noviciate and preparatory training for damnation. If the answers are none of the clearest, he is hauled up with a scythe and thumped down with a red-hot mace till properly seasoned, with a variety of subsidiary probations. The office of these angels is no sinecure; there are but two, and the number of orthodox deceased being in a small proportion to the remainder, their hands are always full. See Relig. Ceremon. and Sale's Koran.

Page 259, col. 1.

'To wander round lost Eblis' throne.'] Eblis, the Oriental Prince of Darkness.

Page 259, col. 1.

'But first, on earth as Vampire sent.'] The Vampire superstition is still general in the Levant. Honest Tournefort tells a long story, which Mr. Southey, in the notes on Thalaba, quotes, about these 'Vroucolochas,' as he calls them. The Romaic term is 'Vardoulacha.' I recollect a whole family being terrified by the scream of a child, which they imagined must proceed from such a visitation. The Greeks never mention the word without horror. I find that 'Broucolokas' is an old legitimate Hellenic appellation—at least is so applied to Arsenius, who, according to the Greeks, was after his death animated by the Devil. The moderns, however, use the word I mention.

Page 259, col. 2.

'Thy gnashing tooth and haggard lip.'] The freshness of the face, and the wetness of the lip with blood, are the never-failing signs of a Vampire. The stories told in Hungary and Greece of these foul feeders are singular, and some of them most *incredibly* attested.

Page 261, col. 1.

'It is as if the desert bird.'] The pelican is, I believe, the bird so libelled, by the imputation of feeding her chickens with her blood.

Page 262, col. 1.

'Deep in whose darkly boding ear.'] This superstition of a second-hearing (for I never met with downright second-sight in the East) fell once under my own observation. On my third journey to Cape Colonna, early in 1811, as we passed through the defile that leads from the hamlet between Keratia and Colonna, I observed Dervish Tahiri riding rather out of the path, and leaning his head upon his hand, as if in pain. I rode up and inquired. 'We are in peril,' he answered. 'What peril? we are not now in Albania, nor in the passes to Ephesus, Messalunghi, or Lepanto; there are plenty of us, well armed, and the Choriates have not courage to be thieves.'—'True, Affendi, but nevertheless the shot is ringing in my ears.'—'The shot! not a top-haike has been fired this morning.'—'I hear it not-withstanding—Bom—Bom—as plainly as I hear your voice.'—'Psha!'—'As you please, Affendi; if it is written, so will it be.'—I left this quick-eared predestinarian, and rode up to Basili, his Christian compatriot, whose ears, though not at all pro-phetic, by no means relished the intelligence. We all arrived at Colonna, remained some hours, and returned leisurely, saying a variety of brilliant things, in more languages than spoiled the building of Babel, upon the mistaken seer. Romaic, Arna-out, Turkish, Italian, and English, were all exer-cised, in various conceits, upon the unfortunate Mussulman. While we were contemplating the beautiful prospect, Dervish was occupied about the columns. I thought he was deranged into an antiquarian, and asked him if he had become a '*Palaocastro*' man? 'No,' said he, 'but these pillars will be useful in making a stand;' and added other remarks, which at least evinced his own belief in his troublesome faculty of *forehearing*. On our return to Athens we heard from Leoné (a prisoner set ashore some days after) of the intended attack of the Mainotes, mentioned, with the cause of its not taking place, in the notes to Childe Harold, Canto 2nd. I was at some pains to question the man, and he described the dresses, arms, and marks of the horses of our party so accurately, that, with other circumstances, we could not doubt of *his* having been in 'villainous company,' and ourselves in a bad neighbourhood. Dervish became a sooth-sayer for life, and I dare say is now hearing more musketry than ever will be fired, to the great re-freshment of the Arnaouts of Berat, and his native mountains.—I shall mention one trait more of this singular race. In March, 1811, a remarkably stout and active Arnaout came (I believe the fiftieth on the same errand) to offer himself as an attendant, which was declined: 'Well, Affendi,' quoth he, 'may you live!—you would have found me useful. I shall leave the town for the hills to-morrow; in the winter I return, perhaps you will then receive me,'—Dervish, who was present, remarked as a thing of course, and of no consequence, 'in the mean time he will join the Klephtes' (robbers), which was true to the letter. If not cut off, they come down in the winter, and pass it unmolested in some town, where they are often as well known as their exploits.

Page 263, col. 1.

'Looks not to priesthood for relief.'] The monk's sermon is omitted. It seems to have had so little effect upon the patient, that it could have no hopes from the reader. It may be sufficient to say, that it was of a customary length (as may be perceived from the interruptions and uneasiness of the patient), and was delivered in the usual tone of all orthodox preachers.

Page 263, col. 2.

'And shining in her white symar.'] 'Symar,' a shroud.

Page 264, col. 2.

'Or stay the passing pilgrim's tread.'] The cir-cumstance to which the above story relates was not very uncommon in Turkey. A few years ago the wife of Muchtar Pacha complained to his father of his son's supposed infidelity; he asked with whom, and she had the barbarity to give in a list of the twelve handsomest women in Yanina. They were seized, fastened up in sacks, and drowned in the lake the same night! One of the guards who was present informed me, that not one of the victims uttered a cry, or showed a symptom of terror, at so sudden a 'wrench from all we know, from all we love.' The fate of Phrosine, the fairest of this sacrifice, is the subject of many a Romaic and Arnaout ditty. The story in the text is one told of a young Venetian many years ago, and now nearly forgotten. I heard it by accident recited by one of the coffee-house story-tellers who abound in the Levant, and sing or recite their narratives. The additions and interpolations by the translator will be easily distinguished from the rest, by the want of Eastern imagery; and I regret that my memory has retained so few fragments of the ori-ginal. For the contents of some of the notes I am indebted partly to D'Herbelot, and partly to that most Eastern, and, as Mr. Weber justly entitles it, 'sublime tale,' the 'Caliph Vathek.' I do not know from what source the author of that singular volume may have drawn his materials; some of his incidents are to be found in the 'Bibliothèque Orientale;' but for correctness of costume, beauty of description, and power of imagination, it far surpasses all European imitations: and bears such marks of originality, that those who have visited the East will find some difficulty in believing it to be more than a translation. As an Eastern tale, even Rasselas must bow before it; his 'Happy Valley' will not bear a comparison with the 'Hall of Eblis.'

THE BRIDE OF ABYDOS

Page 264, col. 1.

'Wax faint o'er the gardens of Gúl in her bloom.'] 'Gúl,' the rose.

Page 264, col. 2.

'Can he smile on such deeds as his children have done?']

'Souls made of fire, and children of the Sun,
With whom revenge is virtue.'—
                           YOUNG's *Revenge*.

Page 265, col. 1.

'With Mejnoun's tale, or Sadi's song.'] Mejnoun and Leila, the Romeo and Juliet of the East. Sadi, the moral poet of Persia.

Page 265, col. 1.

'Till I, who heard the deep tambour.'] Tam-bour, Turkish drum, which sounds at sunrise, noon, and twilight.

Page 266, col. 1.

'He is an Arab to my sight.'] The Turks abhor the Arabs (who return the compliment a hundred-fold) even more than they hate the Christians.

Page 266, col. 1.

'The mind, the Music breathing from her face.'] This expression has met with objections. I will not refer to 'Him who hath not Music in his soul,' but merely request the reader to recollect, for ten seconds, the features of the woman whom he be-lieves to be the most beautiful; and, if he then does not comprehend fully what is feebly expressed in the above line, I shall be sorry for us both. For

NOTES TO THE BRIDE OF ABYDOS

an eloquent passage in the latest work of the first female writer of this, perhaps of any age, on the analogy (and the immediate comparison excited by that analogy) between 'painting and music,' see vol. iii. cap. 10, DE L'ALLEMAGNE. And is not this connexion still stronger with the original than the copy? with the colouring of Nature than of Art? After all, this is rather to be felt than described; still I think there are some who will understand it, at least they would have done had they beheld the countenance whose speaking harmony suggested the idea; for this passage is not drawn from imagination but memory, that mirror which Affliction dashes to the earth, and looking down upon the fragments, only beholds the reflection multiplied!

Page 266, col. 2.

'But yet the line of Carasman.'] Carasman Oglou, or Kara Osman Oglou, is the principal land-holder in Turkey; he governs Magnesia: those who, by a kind of feudal tenure, possess land on condition of service, are called Timariots: they serve as Spahis, according to the extent of territory, and bring a certain number into the field, generally cavalry.

Page 266, col. 2.

'And teach the messenger what fate.'] When a Pacha is sufficiently strong to resist, the single messenger, who is always the first bearer of the order for his death, is strangled instead, and sometimes five or six, one after the other, on the same errand, by command of the refractory patient; if, on the contrary, he is weak or loyal, he bows, kisses the Sultan's respectable signature, and is bow-strung with great complacency. In 1810, several of these presents were exhibited in the niche of the Seraglio gate; among others the head of the Pacha of Bagdat, a brave young man, cut off by treachery, after a desperate resistance.

Page 266, col. 2.

'Thrice clapp'd his hands, and call'd his steed.'] Clapping of the hands calls the servants. The Turks hate a superfluous expenditure of voice, and they have no bells.

Page 266, col. 2.

'Resign'd his gem-adorn'd chibouque.'] 'Chibouque,' the Turkish pipe, of which the amber mouth-piece, and sometimes the ball which contains the leaf, is adorned with precious stones, if in possession of the wealthier orders.

Page 267, col. 1.

'With Maugrabee and Mamaluke.'] 'Maugrabee,' Moorish mercenaries.

Page 267, col. 1.

'His way amid his Delis took.'] 'Delis,' bravos who form the forlorn hope of the cavalry, and always begin the action.

Page 267, col. 1.

'Careering cleave the folded felt.'] A twisted fold of *felt* is used for scimitar practice by the Turks, and few but Mussulman arms can cut through it at a single stroke: sometimes a tough turban is used for the same purpose. The jerreed is a game of blunt javelins, animated and graceful.

Page 267, col. 1.

'Nor heard their Ollahs wild and loud.'] 'Ollahs,' Alla il Allah, the 'Leilies,' as the Spanish poets call them, the sound is Ollah; a cry of which the Turks, for a silent people, are somewhat profuse, particularly during the jerreed, or in the chase, but mostly in battle. Their animation in the field, and gravity in the chamber, with their pipes and comboloios, form an amusing contrast.

Page 267, col. 1.

'The Persian Atar-gul's perfume.'] 'Atar-gul,' ottar of roses. The Persian is the finest.

Page 267, col. 1.

'The pictured roof and marble floor.'] The ceiling and wainscots, or rather walls, of the Mussulman apartments are generally painted, in great houses, with one eternal and highly-coloured view of Constantinople, wherein the principal feature is a noble contempt of perspective; below, arms, scimitars, &c., are, in general, fancifully and not inelegantly disposed.

Page 267, col. 2.

'A message from the Bulbul bears.'] It has been much doubted whether the notes of this 'Lover of the rose' are sad or merry; and Mr. Fox's remarks on the subject have provoked some learned controversy as to the opinions of the ancients on the subject. I dare not venture a conjecture on the point, though a little inclined to the 'errare mallem,' &c., *if* Mr. Fox *was* mistaken.

Page 267, col. 2.

'Ev'n Azrael, from his deadly quiver.'] 'Azrael,' the angel of death.

Page 268, col. 1.

'Within the caves of Istakar.'] The treasures of the Pre-Adamite Sultans. See D'Herbelot, article *Istakar.*

Page 268, col. 1.

'Holds not a Musselim's control.'] 'Musselim,' a governor, the next in rank after a Pacha; a Waywode is the third; and then come the Agas.

Page 268, col. 1.

'Was he not bred in Egripo?'] 'Egripo,' the Negropont. According to the proverb, the Turks of Egripo, the Jews of Salonica, and the Greeks of Athens, are the worst of their respective races.

Page 269, col. 1.

'Ah! yonder see the Tchocadar.'] 'Tchocadar' —one of the attendants who precedes a man of authority.

Page 269, col. 2.

'Thine own "broad Hellespont" still dashes.'] The wrangling about this epithet, 'the broad Hellespont' or the 'boundless Hellespont,' whether it means one or the other, or what it means at all, has been beyond all possibility of detail. I have even heard it disputed on the spot; and not foreseeing a speedy conclusion to the controversy, amused myself with swimming across it in the mean time; and probably may again, before the point is settled. Indeed, the question as to the truth of 'the tale of Troy divine' still continues, much of it resting upon the talismanic word 'ἄπειρος:' probably Homer had the same notion of distance that a coquette has of time; and when he talks of boundless, means half a mile; as the latter, by a like figure, when she says *eternal* attachment simply specifies three weeks.

Page 269, col. 2.

'Which Ammon's son ran proudly round.'] Before his Persian invasion, and crowned the altar with laurels, &c. He was afterwards imitated by Caracalla in his race. It is believed that the last also poisoned a friend, named Festus, for the sake of new Patroclan games. I have seen the sheep feeding on the tombs of Æsietes and Antilochus: the first is in the centre of the plain.

Page 270, col. 1.

'O'er which her fairy fingers ran.'] When rubbed, the amber is susceptible of a perfume, which is slight, but *not* disagreeable.

Page 270, col. 1.

'Her mother's sainted amulet.'] The belief in amulets engraved on gems, or enclosed in gold boxes, containing scraps from the Koran, worn round the neck, wrist, or arm, is still universal in the East. The Koorsee (throne) verse in the second cap. of the Koran describes the attributes of the Most High, and is engraved in this manner, and worn by the pious, as the most esteemed and sublime of all sentences.

Page 270, col. 1.

'And by her comboloio lies.'] 'Comboloio'—a Turkish rosary. The MSS., particularly those of the Persians, are richly adorned and illuminated. The Greek females are kept in utter ignorance; but many of the Turkish girls are highly accomplished, though not actually qualified for a Christian coterie. Perhaps some of our own '*blues*' might not be the worse for *bleaching*.

Page 270, col. 2.

'In him was some young Galiongée.'] 'Galiongée'—or Galiongi, a sailor, that is, a Turkish sailor; the Greeks navigate, the Turks work the guns. Their dress is picturesque; and I have seen the Capitan Pacha, more than once, wearing it as a kind of *incog*. Their legs, however, are generally naked. The buskins described in the text are sheathed behind with silver are those of an Arnaut robber, who was my host (he had quitted the profession) at his Pyrgo, near Gastouni in the Morea; they were plated in scales one over the other, like the back of an armadillo.

Page 271, col. 1.

'So may the Koran verse display'd.'] The characters on all Turkish scimitars contain sometimes the name of the place of their manufacture, but more generally a text from the Koran, in letters of gold. Amongst those in my possession is one with a blade of singular construction: it is very broad, and the edge notched into serpentine curves like the ripple of water, or the wavering of flame. I asked the Armenian who sold it, what possible use such a figure could add: he said, in Italian, that he did not know; but the Mussulmans had an idea that those of this form gave a severer wound; and liked it because it was 'piu feroce.' I did not much admire the reason, but bought it for its peculiarity.

Page 271, col. 1.

'But like the nephew of a Cain.'] It is to be observed, that every allusion to any thing or personage in the Old Testament, such as the Ark, or Cain, is equally the privilege of Mussulman and Jew: indeed, the former profess to be much better acquainted with the lives, true and fabulous, of the patriarchs, than is warranted by our own sacred writ; and not content with Adam, they have a biography of Pre-Adamites. Solomon is the monarch of all necromancy, and Moses a prophet inferior only to Christ and Mahomet. Zuleika is the Persian name of Potiphar's wife; and her amour with Joseph constitutes one of the finest poems in their language. It is, therefore, no violation of costume to put the names of Cain, or Noah, into the mouth of a Moslem.

Page 271, col. 2.

'And Paswan's rebel hordes attest.'] Paswan Oglou, the rebel of Widdin: who, for the last years of his life, set the whole power of the Porte at defiance.

Page 271, col. 2.

'They gave their horse-tails to the wind.'] Horse-tail,' the standard of a Pacha.

Page 271, col. 2.

'He drank one draught, nor needed more!'] Giaffir, Pacha of Argyro Castro, or Scutari, I am not sure which, was actually taken off by the Albanian Ali, in the manner described in the text. Ali Pacha, while I was in the country, married the daughter of his victim, some years after the event had taken place at a bath in Sophia, or Adrianople. The poison was mixed in the cup of coffee, which is presented before the sherbet by the bath keeper, after dressing.

Page 272, col. 2.

'I sought by turns, and saw them all.'] The Turkish notions of almost all islands are confined to the Archipelago, the sea alluded to.

Page 273, col. 1.

'The last of Lambro's patriots there.'] Lambro Canzani, a Greek, famous for his efforts, in 1789–90, for the independence of his country. Abandoned by the Russians, he became a pirate, and the Archipelago was the scene of his enterprises. He is said to be still alive at Petersburg. He and Riga are the two most celebrated of the Greek revolutionists.

Page 273, col. 1.

'To snatch the Rayahs from their fate.'] 'Rayahs,'—all who pay the capitation tax, called the 'Haratch.'

Page 273, col. 1.

'Ay! let me like the ocean-Patriarch roam.'] This first of voyages is one of the few with which the Mussulmans profess much acquaintance.

Page 273, col. 1.

'Or only know on land the Tartar's home!'] The wandering life of the Arabs, Tartars, and Turkomans, will be found well detailed in any book of Eastern travels. That it possesses a charm peculiar to itself, cannot be denied. A young French renegado confessed to Chateaubriand, that he never found himself alone, galloping in the desert, without a sensation approaching to rapture which was indescribable.

Page 273, col. 1.

'Blooming as Aden in its earliest hour.'] 'Jannat al Aden,' the perpetual abode, the Mussulman paradise.

Page 275, col. 2.

'And mourn'd above his turban-stone.'] A turban is carved in stone above the graves of *men* only.

897

Page 275, col. 2.

'The loud Wul-wulleh warn his distant ear?']
The death-song of the Turkish women. The 'silent
slaves' are the men, whose notions of decorum forbid complaint in *public*.

Page 276, col. 1.

'"Where is my child?"—an Echo answers—
"Where?"'] 'I came to the place of my birth, and
cried, "The friends of my youth, where are they?"
and an Echo answered, "Where are they?"'—
From an Arabic MS. The above quotation (from
which the idea in the text is taken) must be already
familiar to every reader; it is given in the first annotation, p. 67, of 'The Pleasures of Memory;'
a poem so well known as to render a reference
almost superfluous; but to whose pages all will be
delighted to recur.

Page 276, col. 2.

'Will shape and syllable its sound.']

'And airy tongues that *syllable* men's names.'
                                    MILTON.

For a belief that the souls of the dead inhabit the
form of birds, we need not travel to the East. Lord
Lyttelton's ghost story, the belief of the Duchess of
Kendal, that George I. flew into her window in the
shape of a raven (see 'Orford's Reminiscences'),
and many other instances, bring this superstition
nearer home. The most singular was the whim of
a Worcester lady, who, believing her daughter to
exist in the shape of a singing bird, literally furnished her pew in the cathedral with cages full of
the kind; and as she was rich, and a benefactress in
beautifying the church, no objection was made to
her harmless folly. For this anecdote, see 'Orford's
Letters.'

THE CORSAIR

Page 277.

'The Corsair.'] The time in this poem may seem
too short for the occurrences, but the whole of
the Ægean isles are within a few hours' sail of the
continent, and the reader must be kind enough to
take the *wind* as I have often found it.

Page 281, col. 1.

'Hope withering fled, and Mercy sigh'd farewell!'] That Conrad is a character not altogether
out of nature, I shall attempt to prove by some
historical coincidences which I have met with since
writing 'The Corsair.'

'Eccelin prisonnier,' dit Rolandini, 's'enfermoit
dans un silence menaçant, il fixoit sur la terre son
visage féroce, et ne donnoit point d'essor à sa pro-
fonde indignation. De toutes partes cependant les
soldats et les peuples accouroient; ils vouloient voir
cet homme, jadis si puissant, et la joie universelle
éclatoit de toutes partes. * * * * Eccelin étoit d'une
petite taille; mais tout l'aspect de sa personne, tous
ses mouvemens, indiquoient un soldat.—Son langage étoit amer, son déportement superbe—et par
son seul égard, il faisoit trembler les plus hardis.'
—*Sismondi*, tome iii. p. 219.

Again, 'Gizericus (Genseric, king of the Vandals, the conqueror of both Carthage and Rome),
staturâ mediocris, et equi casu claudicans, animo
profundus, sermone rarus, luxuriæ contemptor, irâ
turbidus, habendi cupidus, ad solicitandas gentes
providentissimus,' &c. &c.—*Jornandes de Rebus
Geticis*, c. 33.

I beg leave to quote these gloomy realities to
keep in countenance my Giaour and Corsair.

Page 284, col. 1.

'Of fair Olympia loved and left of old.'] Orlando
Furioso, Canto x.

Page 285, col. 2.

'Around the waves' phosphoric brightness
broke.'] By night, particularly in a warm latitude,
every stroke of the oar, every motion of the boat
or ship, is followed by a slight flash like sheet
lightning from the water.

Page 286, col. 2.

'Though to the rest the sober berry's juice.']
Coffee.

Page 286, col. 2.

'The long chibouque's dissolving cloud supply.']
'Chibouque,' pipe.

Page 286, col. 2.

'While dance the Almas to wild minstrelsy.']
Dancing girls.

Page 286, col. 2.

'Escaped, is here—himself would tell the rest.']
It has been observed, that Conrad's entering disguised as a spy is out of nature. Perhaps so. I find
something not unlike it in history.—'Anxious to
explore with his own eyes the state of the Vandals,
Majorian ventured, after disguising the colour of
his hair, to visit Carthage in the character of his
own ambassador; and Genseric was afterwards
mortified by the discovery, that he had entertained
and dismissed the Emperor of the Romans. Such
an anecdote may be rejected as an improbable fiction: but it is a fiction which would not have been
imagined unless in the life of a hero.'—See GIB-
BON's Decline and Fall, vol. vi. p. 180.

Page 287, col. 1.

'And my stern vow and order's laws oppose.']
The Dervises are in colleges, and of different
orders, as the monks.

Page 288, col. 1.

'*They* seize that Dervise!—seize on Zatanai!']
'Zatanai,' Satan.

Page 288, col. 2.

'He tore his beard, and foaming fled the fight.']
A common and not very novel effect of Mussulman
anger. See Prince Eugene's Memoirs, page 24.
'The Seraskier received a wound in the thigh; he
plucked up his beard by the roots, because he was
obliged to quit the field.'

Page 289, col. 1.

'Brief time had Conrad now to greet Gulnare.']
Gulnare, a female name; it means, literally, the
flower of the pomegranate.

Page 292, col. 1.

'Till even the scaffold echoes with their jest!']
In Sir Thomas More, for instance, on the scaffold,
and Anne Boleyn, in the Tower, when, grasping
her neck, she remarked, that it 'was too slender to
trouble the headsman much.' During one part of
the French Revolution, it became a fashion to
leave some '*mot*' as a legacy; and the quantity of
facetious last words spoken during that period
would form a melancholy jest-book of a considerable size.

Page 293, col. 1.

'Slow sinks, more lovely ere his race be run.']
The opening lines, as far as section ii., have, perhaps, little business here, and were annexed to an
unpublished (though printed) poem ['The Curse
of Minerva']; but they were written on the spot, in
the Spring of 1814, and—I scarce know why—the
reader must excuse their appearance here—if he
can.

Page 294, col. 1.

'That closed their murder'd sage's latest day!']
Socrates drank the hemlock a short time before
sunset (the hour of execution), notwithstanding the
entreaties of his disciples to wait till the sun went
down.

Page 294, col. 1.

'The queen of night asserts her silent reign.']
The twilight in Greece is much shorter than in our
own country; the days in winter are longer, but in
summer of shorter duration.

Page 294, col. 1.

'The gleaming turret of the gay kiosk.'] The
Kiosk is a Turkish summer-house: the palm is
without the present walls of Athens, not far from
the temple of Theseus, between which and the tree
the wall intervenes.—Cephisus' stream is indeed
scanty, and Ilissus has no stream at all.

Page 295, col. 2.

'His only bends in seeming o'er his beads.'] The
comboloio, or Mahometan rosary; the beads are
in number ninety-nine.

Page 301, col. 2.

'And the cold flowers her colder hand contain'd.'] In the Levant it is the custom to strew
flowers on the bodies of the dead, and in the hands
of young persons to place a nosegay.

Page 303, col. 2.

'Link'd with one virtue, and a thousand crimes.']
That the point of honour which is represented in
one instance of Conrad's character has not been
carried beyond the bounds of probability, may perhaps be in some degree confirmed by the following
anecdote of a brother buccaneer in the year 1814:
—'Our readers have all seen the account of the
enterprise against the pirates of Barrataria; but
few, we believe, were informed of the situation,
history, or nature of that establishment. For the
information of such as were unacquainted with it,
we have procured from a friend the following interesting narrative of the main facts, of which he
has personal knowledge, and which cannot fail to
interest some of our readers:—Barrataria is a bay,
or a narrow arm, of the Gulf of Mexico; it runs
through a rich but very flat country, until it reaches
within a mile of the Mississippi river, fifteen miles
below the city of New Orleans. The bay has
branches almost innumerable, in which persons
can lie concealed from the severest scrutiny. It
communicates with three lakes which lie on the
south-west side, and these, with the lake of the
same name, and which lies contiguous to the sea,
where there is an island formed by the two arms of
this lake and the sea. The east and west points of
this island were fortified, in the year 1811, by a
band of pirates, under the command of one Monsieur La Fitte. A large majority of these outlaws
are of that class of the population of the state of
Louisiana who fled from the island of St. Domingo

during the troubles there, and took refuge in the
island of Cuba; and when the last war between
France and Spain commenced, they were compelled to leave that island with the short notice of
a few days. Without ceremony they entered the
United States, the most of them the state of Louisiana, with all the negroes they had possessed in
Cuba. They were notified by the Governor of that
State of the clause in the constitution which forbade the importation of slaves; but, at the same
time, received the assurance of the Governor that
he would obtain, if possible, the approbation of the
General Government for their retaining this property.—The island of Barrataria is situated about
lat. 29 deg. 15 min., lon. 92. 30.; and is as remarkable for its health as for the superior scale and shell
fish with which its waters abound. The chief of this
horde, like Charles de Moor, had, mixed with his
many vices, some virtues. In the year 1813, this
party had, from its turpitude and boldness, claimed
the attention of the Governor of Louisiana; and
to break up the establishment he thought proper to
strike at the head. He therefore offered a reward
of 500 dollars for the head of Monsieur La Fitte,
who was well known to the inhabitants of the city
of New Orleans, from his immediate connexion,
and his once having been a fencing-master in that
city of great reputation, which art he learnt in
Buonaparte's army, where he was a captain. The
reward which was offered by the Governor for the
head of La Fitte was answered by the offer of a
reward from the latter of 15,000 for the head of the
Governor. The Governor ordered out a company
to march from the city to La Fitte's island, and to
burn and destroy all the property, and to bring to
the city of New Orleans all his banditti. This company, under the command of a man who had been
the intimate associate of this bold Captain, approached very near to the fortified island, before
he saw a man, or heard a sound, until he heard a
whistle, not unlike a boatswain's call. Then it was
he found himself surrounded by armed men who
had emerged from the secret avenues which led
into Bayou. Here it was that the modern Charles
de Moor developed his few noble traits; for to this
man, who had come to destroy his life and all that
was dear to him, he not only spared his life, but
offered him that which would have made the honest
soldier easy for the remainder of his days; which
was indignantly refused. He then, with the approbation of his captor, returned to the city. This circumstance, and some concomitant events, proved
that this band of pirates was not to be taken by
land. Our naval force having always been small in
that quarter, exertions for the destruction of this
illicit establishment could not be expected from
them until augmented: for an officer of the navy,
with most of the gun-boats on that station, had to
retreat from an overwhelming force of La Fitte's.
So soon as the augmentation of the navy author-
ized an attack, one was made; the overthrow of this
banditti has been the result: and now this almost
invulnerable point and key to New Orleans is clear
of an enemy, it is to be hoped the government will
hold it by a strong military force.'—American
Newspaper.

In Noble's continuation of 'Granger's Biogra-
phical History' there is a singular passage in his
account of Archbishop Blackbourne; and as in
some measure connected with the profession of the
hero of the foregoing poem, I cannot resist the
temptation of extracting it.—'There is something
mysterious in the history and character of Dr.

Blackbourne. The former is but imperfectly known; and report has even asserted he was a buccaneer; and that one of his brethren in that profession having asked, on his arrival in England, what had become of his old chum, Blackbourne, was answered, he is Archbishop of York. We are informed that Blackbourne was installed sub-dean of Exeter in 1694, which office he resigned in 1702; but after his successor Lewis Barnet's death, in 1704, he regained it. In the following year he became dean; and in 1714 held with it the archdeaconry of Cornwall. He was consecrated bishop of Exeter, February 24, 1716; and translated to York, November 28, 1724, as a reward, according to court scandal, for uniting George I. to the Duchess of Munster. This, however, appears to have been an unfounded calumny. As archbishop he behaved with great prudence, and was equally respectable as the guardian of the revenues of the see. Rumour whispered he retained the vices of his youth, and that a passion for the fair sex formed an item in the list of his weaknesses; but so far from being convicted by seventy witnesses, he does not appear to have been directly criminated by one. In short, I look upon these aspersions as the effects of mere malice. How is it possible a buccaneer should have been so good a scholar as Blackbourne certainly was? He who had so perfect a knowledge of the classics (particularly of the Greek tragedians), as to be able to read them with the same ease as he could Shakespeare, must have taken great pains to acquire the learned languages; and have had both leisure and good masters. But he was undoubtedly educated at Christ-church College, Oxford. He is allowed to have been a pleasant man; this, however, was turned against him, by its being said, "he gained more hearts than souls."'

'The only voice that could soothe the passions of the savage (Alphonso III.) was that of an amiable and virtuous wife, the sole object of his love; the voice of Donna Isabella, the daughter of the Duke of Savoy, and the grand-daughter of Philip II. King of Spain.—Her dying words sunk deep into his memory; his fierce spirit melted into tears; and, after the last embrace, Alphonso retired into his chamber to bewail his irreparable loss, and to meditate on the vanity of human life.'—*Gibbon's Miscellaneous Works*, vol. iii. p. 473.

LARA

Page 303, col. 1.

'The Serfs are glad through Lara's wide domain.'] The reader is apprised, that the name of Lara being Spanish, and no circumstance of local and natural description fixing the scene or hero of the poem to any country or age, the word 'Serf,' which could not be correctly applied to the lower classes in Spain, who were never vassals of the soil, has nevertheless been employed to designate the followers of our fictitious chieftain.

Page 318, col. 2.

'A Serf that cross'd the intervening vale.'] The event in this section was suggested by the description of the death, or rather burial, of the Duke of Gandia. The most interesting and particular account of it is given by Burchard, and is in substance as follows:—'On the eighth day of June, the Cardinal of Valenza and the Duke of Gandia, sons of the pope, supped with their mother, Vanozza, near the church of *S. Pietro ad vincula*; several other persons being present at the entertainment. A late

hour approaching, and the cardinal having reminded his brother that it was time to return to the apostolic palace, they mounted their horses or mules, with only a few attendants, and proceeded together as far as the Palace of Cardinal Ascanio Sforza, when the duke informed the cardinal that, before he returned home, he had to pay a visit of pleasure. Dismissing therefore all his attendants, excepting his *staffiero*, or footman, and a person in a mask, who had paid him a visit whilst at supper, and who, during the space of a month or thereabouts, previous to this time, had called upon him almost daily at the apostolic palace, he took this person behind him on his mule, and proceeded to the street of the Jews, where he quitted his servant, directing him to remain there until a certain hour; when, if he did not return, he might repair to the palace. The duke then seated the person in the mask behind him, and rode, I know not whither; but in that night he was assassinated, and thrown into the river. The servant, after having been dismissed, was also assaulted and mortally wounded; and although he was attended with great care, yet such was his situation, that he could give no intelligible account of what had befallen his master. In the morning, the duke not having returned to the palace, his servants began to be alarmed; and one of them informed the pontiff of the evening excursion of his sons, and that the duke had not yet made his appearance. This gave the pope no small anxiety; but he conjectured that the duke had been attracted by some courtesan to pass the night with her, and not choosing to quit the house in open day, had waited till the following evening to return home. When, however, the evening arrived, and he found himself disappointed in his expectations, he became deeply afflicted, and began to make inquiries from different persons, whom he ordered to attend him for that purpose. Amongst these was a man named Giorgio Schiavoni, who, having discharged some timber from a bark in the river, had remained on board the vessel to watch it; and being interrogated whether he had seen any one thrown into the river on the night preceding, he replied, that he saw two men on foot, who came down the street, and looked diligently about, to observe whether any person was passing. That seeing no one, they returned, and a short time afterwards two others came, and looked around in the same manner as the former: no person still appearing, they gave a sign to their companions, when a man came, mounted on a white horse, having behind him a dead body, the head and arms of which hung on one side, and the feet on the other side of the horse; the two persons on foot supporting the body, to prevent its falling. They thus proceeded towards that part where the filth of the city is usually discharged into the river, and turning the horse, with his tail towards the water, the two persons took the dead body by the arms and feet, and with all their strength flung it into the river. The person on horseback then asked if they had thrown it in; to which they replied, *Signor sì* (yes, Sir). He then looked towards the river, and seeing a mantle floating on the stream, he inquired what it was that appeared black, to which they answered, it was a mantle; and one of them threw stones upon it, in consequence of which it sunk. The attendants of the pontiff then inquired from Giorgio, why he had not revealed this to the governor of the city; to which he replied, that he had seen in his time a hundred dead bodies thrown into the river at the same place, without any inquiry being made respecting them; and that he had not, therefore, considered it as a matter of any importance. The fishermen and seamen were then collected, and ordered to search the river, where, on the following evening, they found the body of the duke, with his habit entire, and thirty ducats in his purse. He was pierced with nine wounds, one of which was in his throat, the others in his head, body, and limbs. No sooner was the pontiff informed of the death of his son, and that he had been thrown, like filth, into the river, than, giving way to his grief, he shut himself up in a chamber, and wept bitterly. The Cardinal of Segovia, and other attendants on the pope, went to the door, and after many hours spent in persuasions and exhortations, prevailed upon him to admit them. From the evening of Wednesday till the following Saturday the pope took no food; nor did he sleep from Thursday morning till the same hour on the ensuing day. At length, however, giving way to the entreaties of his attendants, he began to restrain his sorrow, and to consider the injury which his own health might sustain by the further indulgence of his grief.'—ROSCOE'S *Leo Tenth*, vol. i. p. 265.

THE SIEGE OF CORINTH

Page 320, col. 1.

'And some are rebels on the hills.'] The last tidings recently heard of Dervish (one of the Arnaouts who followed me) state him to be in revolt upon the mountains, at the head of some of the bands common in that country in times of trouble.

Page 320, col. 1.

'The Turcoman hath left his herd.'] The life of the Turcomans is wandering and patriarchal: they dwell in tents.

Page 321, col. 1.

'Coumourgi—he whose closing scene.'] Ali Coumourgi, the favourite of three Sultans, and Grand Vizier to Achmet III., after recovering Peloponnesus from the Venetians in one campaign, was mortally wounded in the next, against the Germans, at the battle of Peterwaradin (in the plain of Carlowitz), in Hungary, endeavouring to rally his guards. He died of his wounds next day. His last order was the decapitation of General Breuner, and some other German prisoners; and his last words, 'Oh that I could thus serve all the Christian dogs!' a speech and act not unlike one of Caligula. He was a young man of great ambition and unbounded presumption: on being told that Prince Eugene, then opposed to him, 'was a great general,' he said, 'I shall become a greater, and at his expense.'

Page 323, col. 2.

'There shrinks no ebb in that tideless sea.'] The reader need hardly be reminded that there are no perceptible tides in the Mediterranean.

Page 324, col. 1.

'And their white tusks crunch'd o'er the whiter skull.'] This spectacle I have seen, such as described, beneath the wall of the Seraglio at Constantinople, in the little cavities worn by the Bosphorus in the rock, a narrow terrace of which projects between the wall and the water. I think the fact is also mentioned in Hobhouse's Travels. The bodies were probably those of some refractory Janizaries.

Page 324, col. 1.

'And each scalp had a single long tuft of hair.'] This tuft, or long lock, is left from a superstition that Mahomet will draw them into Paradise by it.

Page 324, col. 2.

'Sent that soft and tender moan?'] I must here acknowledge a close, though unintentional, resemblance in these twelve lines to a passage in an unpublished poem of Mr. Coleridge, called 'Christabel.' It was not till after these lines were written that I heard that wild and singularly original and beautiful poem recited; and the MS. of that production I never saw till very recently, by the kindness of Mr. Coleridge himself, who, I hope, is convinced that I have not been a wilful plagiarist. The original idea undoubtedly pertains to Mr. Coleridge, whose poem has been composed above fourteen years. Let me conclude by a hope that he will not longer delay the publication of a production, of which I can only add my mite of approbation to the applause of far more competent judges.

Page 326, col. 1.

'There is a light cloud by the moon.'] I have been told that the idea expressed in this and the five following lines has been admired by those whose approbation is valuable. I am glad of it: but it is not original—at least not mine; it may be found much better expressed in pages 182–3–4 of the English version of 'Vathek' (I forget the precise page of the French), a work to which I have before referred; and never recur to, or read, without a renewal of gratification.

Page 326, col. 2.

'The horsetails are pluck'd from the ground, and the sword.'] The horsetails, fixed upon a lance, a pacha's standard.

Page 327, col. 2.

'And since the day, when in the strait.'] In the naval battle at the mouth of the Dardanelles, between the Venetians and Turks.

Page 330, col. 2.

'The jackals' troop, in gather'd cry.'] I believe I have taken a poetical licence to transplant the jackal from Asia. In Greece I never saw nor heard these animals; but among the ruins of Ephesus I have heard them by hundreds. They haunt ruins, and follow armies.

PARISINA

Page 331.

'Parisina.'] This turned out a calamitous year for the people of Ferrara, for there occurred a very tragical event in the court of their sovereign. Our annals, both printed and in manuscript, with the exception of the unpolished and negligent work of Sardi, and one other, have given the following relation of it,—from which, however, are rejected many details, and especially the narrative of Bandelli, who wrote a century afterwards, and who does not accord with the contemporary historians.

'By the above-mentioned Stella dell' Assassino, the Marquis, in the year 1405, had a son called Ugo, a beautiful and ingenuous youth. Parisina Malatesta, second wife of Niccolo, like the generality of step-mothers, treated him with little kindness, to the infinite regret of the Marquis, who regarded him with fond partiality. One day she asked leave of her husband to undertake a certain journey, to which he consented, but upon condition that Ugo should bear her company; for he hoped by these means to induce her, in the end, to lay aside the obstinate aversion which she had conceived against him. And indeed his intent was accomplished but too well, since, during the journey, she not only divested herself of all her hatred, but fell into the opposite extreme. After their return, the Marquis had no longer any occasion to renew his former reproofs. It happened one day that a servant of the Marquis, named Zoese, or, as some call him, Giorgio, passing before the apartments of Parisina, saw going out from them one of her chamber-maids, all terrified and in tears. Asking the reason, she told him that her mistress, for some slight offence, had been beating her; and giving vent to her rage, she added, that she could easily be revenged, if she chose to make known the criminal familiarity which subsisted between Parisina and her step-son. The servant took note of the words, and related them to his master. He was astounded thereat, but, scarcely believing his ears, he assured himself of the fact, alas! too clearly, on the 18th of May, by looking through a hole made in the ceiling of his wife's chamber. Instantly he broke into a furious rage, and arrested both of them, together with Aldobrandino Rangoni, of Modena, her gentleman, and also, as some say, two of the women of her chamber, as abettors of this sinful act. He ordered them to be brought to a hasty trial, desiring the judges to pronounce sentence, in the accustomed forms, upon the culprits. This sentence was death. Some there were that bestirred themselves in favour of the delinquents, and amongst others, Ugoccion Contrario, who was all-powerful with Niccolo, and also his aged and much-deserving minister Alberto dal Sale. Both of these, their tears flowing down their cheeks, and upon their knees, implored him for mercy; adducing whatever reasons they could suggest for sparing the offenders, besides those motives of honour and decency which might persuade him to conceal from the public so scandalous a deed. But his rage made him inflexible, and, on the instant, he commanded that sentence should be put in execution.

'It was, then, in the prisons of the castle, and exactly in those frightful dungeons which are seen at this day beneath the chamber called the Aurora, at the foot of the Lion's tower, at the top of the street Giovecca, that on the night of the 21st of May were beheaded, first Ugo, and afterwards Parisina. Zoese, he that accused her, conducted the latter under his arm to the place of punishment. She, all along, fancied that she was to be thrown into a pit, and asked at every step, whether she was yet come to the spot? She was told that her punishment was the axe. She inquired what was become of Ugo, and received for answer, that he was already dead; at the which, sighing grievously, she exclaimed, "Now, then, I wish not myself to live;" and, being come to the block, she stripped herself with her own hands of all her ornaments, and, wrapping a cloth round her head, submitted to the fatal stroke, which terminated the cruel scene. The same was done with Rangoni, who, together with the others, according to two calendars in the library of St. Francesco, was buried in the cemetery of that convent. Nothing else is known respecting the women.

'The Marquis kept watch the whole of that dreadful night, and, as he was walking backwards and forwards, inquired of the captain of the castle if Ugo was dead yet? who answered him, Yes. He then gave himself up to the most desperate lamentations, exclaiming, "Oh that I too were dead, since I have been hurried on to resolve thus against my own Ugo!" And then gnawing with his teeth a cane which he had in his hand, he passed the rest of the night in sighs and in tears, calling frequently upon his own dear Ugo. On the following day, calling to mind that it would be necessary to make public his justification, seeing that the transaction could not be kept secret, he ordered the narrative to be drawn out upon paper, and sent it to all the courts of Italy.

'On receiving this advice, the Doge of Venice, Francesco Foscari, gave orders, but without publishing his reasons, that stop should be put to the preparations for a tournament, which, under the auspices of the Marquis, and at the expense of the city of Padua, was about to take place, in the square of St. Mark, in order to celebrate his advancement to the ducal chair.

'The Marquis, in addition to what he had already done, from some unaccountable burst of vengeance, commanded that as many of the married women as were well known to him to be faithless, like his Parisina, should, like her, be beheaded. Amongst others, Barberina, or, as some call her, Laodamia Romei, wife of the court judge, underwent this sentence at the usual place of execution; that is to say, in the quarter of St. Giacomo, opposite the present fortress, beyond St. Paul's. It cannot be told how strange appeared this proceeding in a prince, who, considering his own disposition, should, as it seemed, have been in such cases most indulgent. Some, however, there were who did not fail to commend him.'*

Page 331, col. 1.

'As twilight melts beneath the moon away.'] The lines contained in this section were printed as set to music some time since, but belonged to the poem where they now appear; the greater part of which was composed prior to 'Lara.'

Page 333, col. 2.

'That should have won as haught a crest.'] Haught—haughty—'Away, *haught* man, thou art insulting me.'—SHAKESPEARE.

THE PRISONER OF CHILLON

Page 337, col. 1.

'In a single night.'] Ludovico Sforza, and others. —The same is asserted of Marie Antoinette's, the wife of Louis the Sixteenth, though not in quite so short a period. Grief is said to have the same effect: to such, and not to fear, this change in *hers* was to be attributed.

Page 338, col. 2.

'From Chillon's snow-white battlement.'] The Château de Chillon is situated between Clarens and Villeneuve, which last is at one extremity of the Lake of Geneva. On its left are the entrances of the Rhone, and opposite are the heights of Meillerie and the range of Alps above Boveret and St. Gingo. Near it, on a hill behind, is a torrent: below it, washing its walls, the lake has a depth fathomed to the depth of 800 feet French measure: within it are a range of dungeons, in which the early reformers, and subsequently prisoners of state, were confined. Across one of the vaults is

* FRIZZI—'History of Ferrara.'

a beam black with age, on which we were informed that the condemned were formerly executed. In the cells are seven pillars, or, rather, eight, one being half merged in the wall; in some of these are rings for the fetters and the fettered: in the pavement the steps of Bonnivard have left their traces. He was confined here several years. It is by this castle that Rousseau has fixed the catastrophe of his Héloïse, in the rescue of one of her children by Julie from the water; the shock of which, and the illness produced by the immersion, is the cause of her death. The château is large, and seen along the lake for a great distance. The walls are white.

Page 340, col. 2.

'And then there was a little isle.'] Between the entrances of the Rhone and Villeneuve, not far from Chillon, is a very small island; the only one I could perceive, in my voyage round and over the lake, within its circumference. It contains a few trees (I think not above three), and from its single-ness and diminutive size has a peculiar effect upon the view.

MAZEPPA

Page 342, col. 2.

'Rich as a salt or silver mine.'] This comparison of a 'salt' mine' may, perhaps, be permitted to a Pole, as the wealth of the country consists greatly in the salt mines.

THE ISLAND

Page 351, col. 2.

'And bread itself is gather'd as a fruit.'] The now celebrated bread-fruit, to transplant which Captain Bligh's expedition was undertaken.

Page 352, col. 1.

'How pleasant were the songs of Toobonai.'] The first three sections are taken from an actual song of the Tonga Islanders, of which a prose translation is given in 'Mariner's Account of the Tonga Islands.' Toobonai is *not* however one of them; but was one of those where Christian and the mutineers took refuge. I have altered and added, but have retained as much as possible of the original.

Page 354, col. 1.

'As Ishmael, wafted on his desert-ship.'] The 'ship of the desert' is the Oriental figure for the camel or dromedary; and they deserve the metaphor well,—the former for his endurance, the latter for his swiftness.

Page 354, col. 1.

'Beyond itself, and must retrace its way.']

'Lucullus, when frugality could charm,
Had roasted turnips in the Sabine farm.'—
POPE.

Page 354, col. 2.

'Had formed his glorious namesake's counter-part.'] The consul Nero, who made the unequalled march which deceived Hannibal, and defeated Asdrubal; thereby accomplishing an achievement almost unrivalled in military annals. The first intelligence of his return, to Hannibal, was the sight of Asdrubal's head thrown into his camp. When Hannibal saw this, he exclaimed with a sigh, that 'Rome would now be the mistress of the world.' And yet to this victory of Nero's it might

be owing that his imperial namesake reigned at all. But the infamy of the one has eclipsed the glory of the other. When the name of 'Nero' is heard, who thinks of the consul?—But such are human things!

Page 355, col. 2.

'And Loch-na-gar with Ida held o'er Troy.'] When very young, about eight years of age, after an attack of the scarlet fever at Aberdeen, I was removed by medical advice into the Highlands. Here I passed occasionally some summers, and from this period I date my love of mountainous countries. I can never forget the effect, a few years afterwards, in England, of the only thing I had long seen, even in miniature, of a mountain, in the Malvern Hills. After I returned to Cheltenham, I used to watch them every afternoon, at sunset, with a sensation which I cannot describe. This was boyish enough; but I was then only thirteen years of age, and it was in the holidays.

Page 356, col. 2.

'Sung sweetly to the rose the day's farewell.'] The now well-known story of the loves of the nightingale and rose need not be more than alluded to, being sufficiently familiar to the Western as to the Eastern reader.

Page 357, col. 1.

'Than breathes his mimic murmurer in the shell.'] If the reader will apply to his ear the sea-shell on his chimney-piece, he will be aware of what is alluded to. If the text should appear obscure, he will find in 'Gebir' the same idea better expressed in two lines. The poem I never read, but have heard the lines quoted by a more recondite reader—who seems to be of a different opinion from the editor of the Quarterly Review, who qualified it, in his answer to the Critical Reviewer of his Juvenal, as trash of the worst and most insane description. It is to Mr. Landor, the author of 'Gebir,' so qualified, and of some Latin poems, which vie with Martial or Catullus in obscenity, that the immaculate Mr. Southey addresses his declamation against impurity!

Page 357, col. 2.

'But deem him sailor or philosopher.'] Hobbes, the father of Locke's and other philosophy, was an inveterate smoker,—even to pipes beyond computation.

Page 357, col. 2.

'Flock o'er the deck, in Neptune's borrow'd car.'] This rough but jovial ceremony, used in crossing the line, has been so often and so well described, that it need not be more than alluded to.

Page 358, col. 2.

'"Right," quoth Ben, "that will do for the marines."'] 'That will do for the marines, but the sailors won't believe it,' is an old saying; and one of the few fragments of former jealousies which still survive (in jest only) between these gallant services.

Page 359, col. 1.

'No less of human bravery than the brave!'] Archidamus, king of Sparta, and son of Agesilaus, when he saw a machine invented for the casting of stones and darts, exclaimed that it was the 'grave of valour.' The same story has been told of some knights on the first application of gunpowder; but the original anecdote is in Plutarch.

NOTES TO THE ISLAND

Page 363, col. 1.

'Whose only portal was the keyless wave.'] Of this cave (which is no fiction) the original will be found in the ninth chapter of 'Mariner's Account of the Tonga Islands.' I have taken the poetical liberty to transplant it to Toobonai, the last island where any distinct account is left of Christian and his comrades.

Page 363, col. 2.

'The fretted pinnacle, the aisle, the nave.'] This may seem too minute for the general outline (in Mariner's Account) from which it is taken. But few men have travelled without seeing something of the kind—on *land*, that is. Without adverting to Ellora, in Mungo Park's last journal, he mentions having met with a rock or mountain so exactly resembling a Gothic cathedral, that only minute inspection could convince him that it was a work of nature.

Page 364, col. 1.

'With each new being born or to be born.'] The reader will recollect the epigram of the Greek anthology, or its translation into most of the modern languages:—

'Whoe'er thou art, thy master see—
He was, or is, or is to be.'

Page 364, col. 1.

'The kindling ashes to his kindled breast.'] The tradition is attached to the story of Eloisa, that when her body was lowered into the grave of Abelard (who had been buried twenty years), he opened his arms to receive her.

Page 365, col. 2.

'He tore the topmost button from his vest.'] In Thibault's account of Frederic the Second of Prussia, there is a singular relation of a young Frenchman, who with his mistress appeared to be of some rank. He enlisted and deserted at Schweidnitz; and after a desperate resistance was retaken, having killed an officer, who attempted to seize him after he was wounded, by the discharge of his musket loaded with a *button* of his uniform. Some circumstances on his court-martial raised a great interest amongst his judges, who wished to discover his real situation in life, which he offered to disclose, but to the *king* only, to whom he requested permission to write. This was refused, and Frederic was filled with the greatest indignation, from baffled curiosity or some other motive, when he understood that his request had been denied.

THE PROPHECY OF DANTE

Page 371, col. 1.

''Midst whom my own bright Beatrice bless'd.'] The reader is requested to adopt the Italian pronunciation of Beatricĕ, sounding all the syllables.

Page 371, col. 1.

'My paradise had still been incomplete.']

'Che sol per le belle opre
Che fanno in Cielo il sole a l' altre stelle
Dentro di lui' *si crede il Paradiso*,
Cosi se guardi fiso
Pensar ben dèi ch' ogni terren' piacere.'

Canzone, in which Dante describes the person of Beatrice, Strophe third.

Page 371, col. 2.

'I would have had my Florence great and free.']

'L'Esilio che m' è dato onor mi tegno
*   *   *   *   *
Cader tra' buoni è pur il lode degno.'
Sonnet of Dante,

in which he represents Right, Generosity, and Temperance as banished from among men, and seeking refuge from Love, who inhabits his bosom.

Page 371, col. 2.

'And doom this body forfeit to the fire.'] 'Ut si quis predictorum ullo tempore in fortiam dicti communis pervenerit, *talis perveniens igne comburatur, sic quod moriatur.*' Second sentence of Florence against Dante, and the fourteen accused with him. The Latin is worthy of the sentence.

Page 373, col. 1.

'Where yet my boys are, and that fatal she.'] This lady, whose name was *Gemma*, sprung from one of the most powerful Guelph families named Donati. Corso Donati was the principal adversary of the Ghibellines. She is described as being '*Admodum morosa, ut de Xantippe Socratis philosophi conjuge scriptum esse legimus*,' according to Giannozzo Manetti. But Lionardo Aretino is scandalised with Boccace, in his Life of Dante, for saying that literary men should not marry. 'Qui il Boccaccio non ha pazienza, e dice, le mogli esser contrarie agli studj; e non si ricorda che Socrate il più nobile filosofo che mai fosse, ebbe moglie e figliuoli e uffici della Repubblica nella sua Città; e Aristotele che, &c. &c., ebbe due mogli in varj tempi, ed ebbe figliuoli, e ricchezze assai.—E Marco Tullio—e Catone—e Varrone—e Seneca—ebbero moglie,' &c. &c. It is odd that honest Lionardo's examples, with the exception of Seneca, and, for anything I know, of Aristotle, are not the most felicitous. Tully's Terentia, and Socrates' Xantippe, by no means contributed to their husbands' happiness, whatever they might do to their philosophy—Cato gave away his wife—of Varro's we know nothing—and of Seneca's, only that she was disposed to die with him, but recovered and lived several years afterwards. But says Lionardo, 'L'uomo è *animale civile*, secondo piace a tutti i filosofi.' And thence concludes that the greatest proof of the *animal's civism* is 'la prima congiunzione, dalla quale multiplicata nasce la Città.'

Page 374, col. 1.

'Nine moons shall rise o'er scenes like this and set.'] See 'Sacco di Roma,' generally attributed to Guicciardini. There is another written by a Jacopo *Buonaparte*.

Page 375, col. 1.

'Conquerors on foreign shores, and the far wave.'] Alexander of Parma, Spinola, Pescara, Eugene of Savoy, Montecucco.

Page 375, col. 1.

'Discoverers of new worlds, which take their name.'] Columbus, Americus Vespusius, Sebastian Cabot.

Page 375, col. 2.

'He who once enters in a tyrant's hall.'] A verse from the Greek tragedians, with which Pompey took leave of Cornelia on entering the boat in which he was slain.

Page 375, col. 2.

'A captive, sees his half of manhood gone.'] The verse and sentiment are taken from Homer.

Page 376, col. 1.

'And he, their prince, shall rank among my peers.'] Petrarch.

Page 377, col. 2.

'A dome, its image, while the base expands.'] The Cupola of St. Peter's.

Page 378, col. 1.

'His chisel bid the Hebrew, at whose word.'] The statue of Moses on the monument of Julius II.

SONETTO

Di Giovanni Battista Zappi

Chi è costui, che in dura pietra scolto,
Siede gigante; e le più illustre, e conte
Opre dell' arte avvanza, e ha vive, e pronte
Le labbia sì, che le parole ascolto?
Quest' è Mosè; ben me 'l diceva il folto
Onor del mento, e 'l doppio raggio in fronte,
Quest' è Mosè, quando scendea del monte,
E gran parte del Nume avea nel volto.
Tal era allor, che le sonanti, e vaste
Acque ei sospese a se d' intorno, e tale
Quando il mar chiuse, e ne fè tomba altrui.
E voi sue turbe un rio vitello alzaste?
Alzata aveste imago a questa eguale!
Ch' era men fallo l' adorar costui.

Page 378, col. 1.

'Over the damn'd before the Judgment-throne.'] The Last Judgment, in the Sistine Chapel.

Page 378, col. 1.

'The stream of his great thoughts shall spring from me.'] I have read somewhere (if I do not err, for I cannot recollect where), that Dante was so great a favourite of Michael Angelo's, that he had designed the whole of the Divina Commedia: but that the volume containing these studies was lost by sea.

Page 378, col. 1.

'Her charms to pontiffs proud, who but employ.'] See the treatment of Michael Angelo by Julius II., and his neglect by Leo X.

Page 379, col. 1.

'"What have I done to thee, my people?" Stern.'] 'E scrisse più volte non solamente a particolari cittadini del reggimento, ma ancora al popolo, e intra l' altre una Epistola assai lunga che comincia: "*Popule mi, quid feci tibi?*"' *Vita di Dante scritta da Lionardo Aretino.*

THE MORGANTE MAGGIORE

Page 386, col. 2.

'He gave him such a punch upon the head.'] 'Gli dette in su la testa un gran punzone.' It is strange that Pulci should have literally anticipated the technical terms of my old friend and master, Jackson, and the art which he has carried to its highest pitch. '*A punch on the head*,' or '*a punch in the head*,'—'un punzone in su la testa,'—is the exact and frequent phrase of our best pugilists, who little dream that they are talking the purest Tuscan.

MANFRED

Page 396, col. 1.

'It is not noon—the sunbow's rays still arch.'] This iris is formed by the rays of the sun over the lower part of the Alpine torrents: it is exactly like a rainbow come down to pay a visit, and so close that you may walk into it: this effect lasts till noon.

Page 397, col. 1.

'Eros and Anteros, at Gadara.'] The philosopher Jamblicus. The story of the raising of Eros and Anteros may be found in his Life by Eunapius. It is well told.

Page 398, col. 1.

'In words of dubious import, but fulfill'd.'] The story of Pausanias, king of Sparta (who commanded the Greeks at the battle of Platea, and afterwards perished for an attempt to betray the Lacedæmonians), and Cleonice, is told in Plutarch's Life of Cimon; and in the Laconics of Pausanias the sophist, in his description of Greece.

Page 403, col. 2.

'Of undiseased mankind, the giant sons.'] 'And it came to pass, that the *Sons of God* saw the daughters of men, that they were fair,' &c.—'There were giants in the earth in those days; and also after that, when the *Sons of God* came in unto the daughters of men, and they bare children to them, the same became mighty men which were of old, men of renown.'—*Genesis*, ch. vi. verses 2 and 4.

MARINO FALIERO, DOGE OF VENICE

APPENDIX

NOTE A

I am obliged for the following excellent translation of the old Chronicle to Mr. F. Cohen, to whom the reader will find himself indebted for a version that I could not myself—though after many years' intercourse with Italian—have given by any means so purely and so faithfully.

STORY OF MARINO FALIERO, DOGE XLIX. MCCCLIV

On the eleventh day of September, in the year of our Lord 1354, Marino Faliero was elected and chosen to be the Duke of the Commonwealth of Venice. He was Count of Valdemarino, in the Marches of Treviso, and a knight, and a wealthy man to boot. As soon as the election was completed, it was resolved in the Great Council, that a deputation of twelve should be despatched to Marino Faliero the Duke, who was then on his way from Rome; for when he was chosen, he was ambassador at the court of the Holy Father, at Rome,—the Holy Father himself held his court at Avignon. When Messer Marino Faliero the Duke was about to land in this city, on the 5th day of October, 1354, a thick haze came on and darkened the air: and he was enforced to land on the place of St. Mark, between the two columns, on the spot where evil-doers are put to death; and all thought that this was the worst of tokens.—Nor must I forget to write that which I have read in a chronicle. When Messer Marino Faliero was Podesta and Captain of Treviso, the Bishop delayed coming in with the holy sacrament, on a day when a procession was to take place. Now, the said Marino Faliero was so very proud and wrathful, that he buffeted the Bishop, and almost struck him to the ground: and, therefore, Heaven allowed Marino Faliero to go out of his right senses, in order that he might bring himself to an evil death.

When this Duke had held the dukedom during nine months and six days, he, being wicked and ambitious, sought to make himself Lord of Venice, in the manner which I have read in an ancient chronicle. When the Thursday arrived upon which they were wont to hunt the bull, the bull hunt took place as usual; and, according to the usage of those times, after the bull hunt had ended, they all proceeded unto the palace of the Duke, and assembled together in one of his halls; and they disported themselves with the women. And until the first bell tolled they danced, and then a banquet was served up. My Lord the Duke paid the expenses thereof, provided he had a Duchess, and after the banquet they all returned to their homes.

Now to this feast there came a certain Ser Michele Steno, a gentleman of poor estate and very young, but crafty and daring, and who loved one of the damsels of the Duchess. Ser Michele stood amongst the women upon the solajo; and he behaved indiscreetly, so that my Lord the Duke ordered that he should be kicked off the solajo; and the esquires of the Duke flung him down from the solajo accordingly. Ser Michele thought that such an affront was beyond all bearing; and when the feast was over, and all other persons had left the palace, he, continuing heated with anger, went to the hall of audience, and wrote certain unseemly words relating to the Duke and the Duchess upon the chair in which the Duke was used to sit; for in those days the Duke did not cover his chair with cloth of sendal, but he sat in a chair of wood. Ser Michele wrote thereon—'*Marin Falier, the husband of the fair wife; others kiss her, but he keeps her.*' In the morning the words were seen, and the matter was considered to be very scandalous; and the Senate commanded the Avogadori of the Commonwealth to proceed therein with the greatest diligence. A largess of great amount was immediately proffered by the Avogadori, in order to discover who had written these words. And at length it was known that Michele Steno had written them. It was resolved in the Council of Forty that he should be arrested; and he then confessed that in the fit of vexation and spite, occasioned by his being thrust off the solajo in the presence of his mistress, he had written the words. Therefore the Council debated thereon. And the Council took his youth into consideration, and that he was a lover; and therefore they adjudged that he should be kept in close confinement during two months, and that afterwards he should be banished from Venice and the state during one year. In consequence of this merciful sentence the Duke became exceedingly wroth, it appearing to him, that the Council had not acted in such a manner as was required by the respect due to his ducal dignity; and he said that they ought to have condemned Ser Michele to be hanged by the neck, or at least to be banished for life.

Now it was fated that my Lord Duke Marino was to have his head cut off. And as it is necessary when any effect is to be brought about, that the cause of such effect must happen, it therefore came to pass, that on the very day after sentence had been pronounced on Ser Michele Steno, being the first day of Lent, a gentleman of the house of Barbaro, a choleric gentleman, went to the arsenal, and required certain things of the masters of the galleys. This he did in the presence of the Admiral of the arsenal, and he, hearing the request, answered,—No, it cannot be done. High words arose between the gentleman and the Admiral, and the gentleman struck him with his fist just above the eye; and as he happened to have a ring on his finger, the ring cut the Admiral and drew blood. The Admiral, all bruised and bloody, ran straight to the Duke to complain, and with the intent of praying him to inflict some heavy punishment upon the gentleman of Cà Barbaro.—'What wouldst thou have me do for thee?' answered the Duke:—'think upon the shameful gibe which hath been written concerning me: and think on the manner in which they have punished that ribald Michele Steno, who wrote it; and see how the Council of Forty respect our person.'—Upon this the Admiral answered,—'My Lord Duke, if you would wish to make yourself a prince, and to cut all those cuckoldy gentlemen to pieces, I have the heart, if you do but help me, to make you prince of all this state; and then you may punish them all.' Hearing this, the Duke said,—'How can such a matter be brought about?'—and so they discoursed thereon.

The Duke called for his nephew, Ser Bertuccio Faliero, who lived with him in the palace, and they communed about this plot. And without leaving the place, they sent for Philip Calendaro, a seaman of great repute, and for Bertuccio Israello, who was exceedingly wily and cunning. Then taking counsel amongst themselves, they agreed to call in some others; and so, for several nights successively, they met with the Duke at home in his palace. And the following men were called in singly; to wit:—Niccolo Fagiuolo, Giovanni da Corfu, Stefano Fagiono, Niccolo dalle Bende, Niccolo Biondo, and Stefano Trivisano.—It was concerted that sixteen or seventeen leaders should be stationed in various parts of the city, each being at the head of forty men, armed and prepared; but the followers were not to know their destination. On the appointed day they were to make affrays amongst themselves here and there, in order that the Duke might have a pretence for tolling the bells of San Marco; these bells are never rung but by the order of the Duke. And at the sound of the bells, these sixteen or seventeen, with their followers, were to come to San Marco, through the streets which open upon the Piazza. And when the noble and leading citizens should come into the Piazza, to know the cause of the riot, then the conspirators were to cut them in pieces; and this work being finished, my Lord Marino Faliero the Duke was to be proclaimed the Lord of Venice. Things having been thus settled, they agreed to fulfil their intent on Wednesday, the 15th day of April, in the year 1355. So covertly did they plot, that no one ever dreamt of their machinations.

But the Lord, who hath always helped this most glorious city, and who, loving its righteousness and holiness, hath never forsaken it, inspired one Beltramo Bergamasco to be the cause of bringing the plot to light, in the following manner. This Beltramo, who belonged to Ser Niccolo Lioni of Santo Stefano, had heard a word or two of what was to take place; and so, in the above-mentioned month of April, he went to the house of the aforesaid Ser Niccolo Lioni, and told him all the particulars of the plot. Ser Niccolo, when he heard all these things, was struck dead, as it were, with affright. He heard all the particulars; and Beltramo prayed him to keep it all secret; and if he told Ser Niccolo, it was in order that Ser Niccolo might stop at home on the 15th of April, and thus save his life. Beltramo was going, but Ser Niccolo ordered his servants to lay hands upon him, and lock him up. Ser Niccolo then went to the house of Messer Giovanni Gradenigo Nasoni, who afterwards became Duke, and who also lived at Santo Stefano, and told him all. The matter seemed to him to be of the very greatest importance, as indeed it was; and they two went to the house of Ser Marco Cornaro, who lived at San Felice; and, having spoken with him, they all three then determined to go back to the house of Ser Niccolo Lioni, to examine the said Beltramo; and having questioned him, and heard all that he had to say, they left him in confinement. And then they all three went into the sacristy of San Salvatore, and sent their men to summon the Councillors, the Avogadori, the Capi de' Dieci, and those of the Great Council.

When all were assembled, the whole story was told to them. They were struck dead, as it were, with affright. They determined to send for Beltramo. He was brought in before them. They examined him, and ascertained that the matter was true; and, although they were exceedingly troubled, yet they determined upon their measures. And they sent for the Capi de' Quarante, the Signori di Notte, the Capi de' Sestieri, and the Cinque della Pace; and they were ordered to associate to their men other good men and true, who were to proceed to the houses of the ringleaders of the conspiracy, and secure them. And they secured the foreman of the arsenal, in order that the conspirators might not do mischief. Towards nightfall they assembled in the palace. When they were assembled in the palace, they caused the gates of the quadrangle of the palace to be shut. And they sent to the keeper of the Bell-tower, and forbade the tolling of the bells. All this was carried into effect. The before-mentioned conspirators were secured, and they were brought to the palace; and, as the Council of Ten saw that the Duke was in the plot, they resolved that twenty of the leading men of the state should be associated to them, for the purpose of consultation and deliberation, but that they should not be allowed to ballot.

The counsellors were the following:—Ser Giovanni Mocenigo, of the Sestiero of San Marco; Ser Almoro Veniero da Santa Marina, of the Sestiero of Castello; Ser Tomaso Viadro, of the Sestiero of Canaregio; Ser Giovanni Sanudo, of the Sestiero of Santa Croce; Ser Pietro Trivisano, of the Sestiero of San Paolo; Ser Pantalione Barbo il Grando, of the Sestiero of Ossoduro. The Avogadori of the Commonwealth were Zufredo Morosini, and Ser Orio Pasqualigo; and these did not ballot. Those of the Council of Ten were Ser Giovanni Marcello, Ser Tomaso Sanudo, and Ser Micheletto Dolfino, the heads of the aforesaid Council of Ten. Ser Luca da Legge, and Ser Pietro da Mosto, inquisitors of the aforesaid Council. And Ser Marco Polani, Ser Marino Veniero, Ser Lando Lombardo, and Ser Nicoletto Trivisano, of Sant' Angelo.

Late in the night, just before the dawning, they chose a junta of twenty noblemen of Venice from amongst the wisest, and the worthiest, and the oldest. They were to give counsel, but not to ballot. And they would not admit any one of Cà Faliero. And Niccolo Faliero, and another Niccolo Faliero, of San Tomaso, were expelled from the Council, because they belonged to the family of the Doge. And this resolution of creating the junta of twenty was much praised throughout the state. The following were the members of the junta of twenty:—Ser Marco Giustiniani, Procuratore, Ser Andrea Erizzo, Procuratore, Ser Lionardo Giustiniani, Procuratore, Ser Andrea Contarini,

Ser Simone Dandolo, Ser Niccolo Volpe, Ser Giovanni Loredano, Ser Marco Diedo, Ser Giovanni Gradenigo, Ser Andrea Cornaro, Cavaliere, Ser Marco Soranzo, Ser Rinieri du Mosto, Ser Gazano Marcello, Ser Marino Morosini, Ser Stefano Belegno, Ser Niccolo Lioni, Ser Filippo Orio, Ser Marco Trivisano, Ser Jacopo Bragadino, Ser Giovanni Foscarini.

These twenty were accordingly called in to the Council of Ten; and they sent for my Lord Marino Faliero, the Duke: and my Lord Marino was then consorting in the palace with people of great estate, gentlemen, and other good men, none of whom knew yet how the fact stood.

At the same time Bertuccio Israello, who, as one of the ringleaders, was to head the conspirators in Santa Croce, was arrested and bound, and brought before the Council. Zanello del Brin, Nicoletto di Rosa, Nicoletto Alberto, and the Guardiaga, were also taken, together with several seamen, and people of various ranks. These were examined, and the truth of the plot was ascertained.

On the 16th of April judgment was given in the Council of Ten, that Filippo Calendaro and Bertuccio Israello should be hanged upon the red pillars of the balcony of the palace, from which the Duke is wont to look at the bull hunt: and they were hanged with gags in their mouths.

The next day the following were condemned:— Niccolo Zuccuolo, Niccolo Biondo, Nicoletto Doro, Marco Giuda, Jacomello Dagolino, Nicoletto Fidele, the son of Filippo Calendaro, Marco Torello, called Israello, Stefano Trivisano, the money-changer of Santa Margherita, and Antonio dalle Bende. These were all taken at Chiozza, for they were endeavouring to escape. Afterwards, by virtue of the sentence which was passed upon them in the Council of Ten, they were hanged on successive days; some singly and some in couples, upon the columns of the palace, beginning from the red columns, and so going onwards towards the canal, And other prisoners were discharged, because, although they had been involved in the conspiracy, yet they had not assisted in it: for they were given to understand by some of the heads of the plot, that they were to come armed and prepared for the service of the state, and in order to secure certain criminals; and they knew nothing else. Nicoletto Alberto, the Guardiaga, and Bartolommeo Ciricolo and his son, and several others, who were not guilty, were discharged.

On Friday, the 16th day of April, judgment was also given in the aforesaid Council of Ten, that my Lord Marino Faliero, the Duke, should have his head cut off; and that the execution should be done on the landing-place of the stone staircase, where the Dukes take their oath when they first enter the palace. On the following day, the 17th of April, the doors of the palace being shut, the Duke had his head cut off, about the hour of noon. And the cap of estate was taken from the Duke's head before he came down-stairs. When the execution was over, it is said that one of the Council of Ten went to the columns of the palace over against the place of St. Mark, and that he showed the bloody sword unto the people, crying out with a loud voice—'The terrible doom hath fallen upon the traitor!'—and the doors were opened, and the people all rushed in, to see the corpse of the Duke, who had been beheaded.

It must be known that Ser Giovanni Sanudo, the councillor, was not present when the aforesaid sentence was pronounced; because he was unwell and remained at home. So that only fourteen balloted; that is to say, five councillors, and nine of the Council of Ten. And it was adjudged, that all the lands and chattels of the Duke, as well as of the other traitors, should be forfeited to the state. And as a grace to the Duke, it was resolved in the Council of Ten, that he should be allowed to dispose of two thousand ducats out of his own property. And it was resolved, that all the councillors, and all the Avogadori of the Commonwealth, those of the Council of Ten, and the members of the junta, who had assisted in passing sentence on the Duke and the other traitors, should have the privilege of carrying arms both by day and by night in Venice, and from Grado to Cavazere. And they were also to be allowed two footmen carrying arms, the aforesaid footmen living and boarding with them in their own houses. And he who did not keep two footmen might transfer the privilege to his sons or his brothers; but only to two. Permission of carrying arms was also granted to the four Notaries of the Chancery, that is to say, of the Supreme Court, who took the depositions; and they were, Amedio, Nicoletto di Lorino, Steffanello, and Pietro de Compostelli, the secretaries of the Signori di Notte.

After the traitors had been hanged, and the Duke had had his head cut off, the state remained in great tranquillity and peace. And, as I have read in a Chronicle, the corpse of the Duke was removed in a barge, with eight torches, to his tomb in the church of San Giovanni e Paolo, where it was buried. The tomb is now in that aisle in the middle of the little church of Santa Maria della Pace which was built by Bishop Gabriel of Bergamo. It is a coffin of stone, with these words engraven thereon: 'Heic jacet Dominus Marinus Faletro Dux.'—And they did not paint his portrait in the hall of the Great Council:—but in the place where it ought to have been, you see these words:— 'Hic est locus Marini Faletro, decapitati pro criminibus.'—And it is thought that his house was granted to the church of Sant' Apostoli; it was that great one near the bridge. Yet this could not be the case, or else the family bought it back from the church; for it still belongs to Cà Faliero. I must not refrain from noting, that some wished to write the following words in the place where his portrait ought to have been, as aforesaid:—'Marinus Faletro Dux, temeritas me cepit. Pœnas lui, decapitatus pro criminibus.'—Others, also, indited a couplet, worthy of being inscribed upon his tomb.

'Dux Venetum jacet heic, patriam qui prodere tentans,
Sceptra, decus, censum perdidit, atque caput.'

NOTE B

PETRARCH ON THE CONSPIRACY OF MARINO FALIERO

'Al giovane Doge Andrea Dandolo succedette un vecchio, il quale tardi si pose al timone della repubblica, ma sempre prima di quel, che facea d' uopo a lui, ed alla patria: egli è Marino Faliero, personaggio a me noto per antica dimestichezza. Falsa era l' opinione intorno a lui, giacchè egli si mostrò fornito più di coraggio, che di senno. Non pago della prima dignità, entro con sinistro piede nel pubblico Palazzo: imperciocchè questo Doge dei Veneti, magistrato sacro in tutti i secoli, che dagli antichi fù sempre venerato qual nume in quella città, l' altr' jeri fù decollato nel vestibolo dell' istesso Palazzo. Discorrerei fin dal principio le cause di un tale evvento, e così vario, ed ambiguo non ne fosse il grido. Nessuno però lo scusa, tutti affermano, che egli abbia voluto cangiar qualche cosa nell' ordine della repubblica a lui tramandato dai maggiori. Che desiderava egli di più? Io son d' avviso, che egli abbia ottenuto ciò, che non si concedette a nessun altro: mentre adempiva gli uffici di legato presso il Pontefice, e sulle rive del Rodano trattava la pace, che io prima di lui avevo indarno tentato di conchiudere, gli fù conferito l' onore del Ducato, che ne chiedeva, ne s' aspettava. Tornato in patria, pensò a quello, cui nessuno non pose mente giammai, e soffrì quello che a niuno accadde mai di soffrire: giacchè in quel luogo celeberrimo, e chiarissimo, e bellissimo infra tutti quelli, che io vidi, ove i suoi antenati avevano ricevuti grandissimi onori in mezzo alle pompe trionfali, ivi egli fù trascinato in modo servile, e spogliato delle insegne ducali, perdette la testa, e macchiò col proprio sangue le soglie del tempio, l' atrio del Palazzo, e le scale marmoree rendute spesse volte illustri o dalle solenni festività, o dalle ostili spoglie. Hò notato il luogo, ora noto il tempo: è l' anno del Natale di Cristo, 1355, fù il giorno 18 d' Aprile. Si alto è il grido sparso, che se alcuno esaminerà la disciplina, e le costumanze di quella città, e quanto mutamento di cose venga minacciato dalla morte di un sol uomo (quantunque molti altri, come narrano, essendo complici, o subirono l' istesso supplicio, o lo aspettano) si accorgerà, che nulla di più grande avvenne ai nostri tempi nella Italia. Tu forse qui attendi il mio giudizio: assolvo il popolo, se credere alla fama, benchè abbia potuto e castigare più mitemente, e con maggior dolcezza vendicare il suo dolore: ma non cosi facilmente, si modera un' ira giusta insieme, e grande in un numeroso popolo principalmente, nel quale il precipitoso, ed instabile volgo aguzza gli stimoli dell' irracondia con rapidi, e sconsigliati clamori. Compatisco, e nell' istesso tempo mi adiro con quell' infelice uomo, il quale adorno di un' insolito onore, non so, che cosa si volesse negli estremi anni della sua vita: la calamità di lui diviene sempre più grave, perchè dalla sentenza contra di esso promulgata aperirà, che egli fù non solo misero, ma insano, e demente, e che con vane arti si usurpò per tanti anni una falsa fama di sapienza. Ammonisco i Dogi, i quali gli succederano, che questo e un' esempio posto innanzi ai loro occhj, quale specchio, nel quale veggano d' essere non Signori, ma Duci, anzi nemmeno Duci, ma onorati servi della Repubblica. Tu sta sano; e giacchè fluttuano le pubbliche cose, sforsiamosi di governar modestissimamente i privati nostri affari.'—LEVATI, Viaggi di Petrarca, vol. iv. p. 323.

The above Italian translation from the Latin epistles of Petrarch proves—1stly, That Marino Faliero was a personal friend of Petrarch's; 'antica dimestichezza,' old intimacy, is the phrase of the poet. 2ndly, That Petrarch thought that he had more courage than conduct, 'più di corraggio che di senno.' 3rdly, That there was some jealousy on the part of Petrarch; for he says that Marino Faliero was treating of the peace which he himself had 'vainly attempted to conclude.' 4thly, That the honour of the Dukedom was conferred upon him, which he neither sought nor expected, 'che nè chiedeva nè aspettava,' and which had never been granted to any other in like circumstances, 'ciò che non si concedette a nessun altro,' a proof of the high esteem in which he must have been held. 5thly, That he had a reputation for wisdom, only forfeited by the last enterprise of his life, 'si usurpò per tanti anni una falsa fama di sapienza.'—'He had usurped for so many years a false fame of wisdom,' rather a difficult task, I should think. People are generally found out before eighty years of age, at least in a republic.—From these, and the other historical notes which I have collected, it may be inferred, that Marino Faliero possessed many of the qualities, but not the success of a hero; and that his passions were too violent. The paltry and ignorant account of Dr. Moore falls to the ground. Petrarch says, 'that there had been no greater event in his times' (*our times* literally), 'nostri tempi,' in Italy. He also differs from the historian in saying that Faliero was 'on the banks of the *Rhone*,' instead of at Rome, when elected: the other accounts say, that the deputation of the Venetian senate met him at Ravenna. How this may have been, it is not for me to decide, and is of no great importance. Had the man succeeded, he would have changed the face of Venice, and perhaps of Italy. As it is, what *are* they both?

NOTE C

VENETIAN SOCIETY AND MANNERS

'Vice without splendour, sin without relief
Even from the gloss of love to smooth it o'er;
But, in its stead, coarse lusts of habitude,' &c.
[*See* p. 452.]

'To these attacks so frequently pointed by the government against the clergy,—to the continual struggles between the different constituted bodies, —to these enterprises carried on by the mass of the nobles against the depositaries of power,—to all those projects of innovation, which always ended by a stroke of state policy, we must add a cause not less fitted to spread contempt for ancient doctrines; *this was the excess of corruption.*

'That freedom of manners, which had been long boasted of as the principal charm of Venetian society, had degenerated into scandalous licentiousness: the tie of marriage was less sacred in that Catholic country, than among those nations where the laws and religion admit of its being dissolved. Because they could not break the contract, they feigned that it had not existed; and the ground of nullity, immodestly alleged by the married pair, was admitted with equal facility by priests and magistrates, alike corrupt. These divorces, veiled under another name, became so frequent that the most important act of civil society was discovered to be amenable to a tribunal of exceptions; and to restrain the open scandal of such proceedings became the office of the police. In 1782 the Council of Ten decreed, that every woman who should sue for a dissolution of her marriage should be compelled to await the decision of the judges in some convent, to be named by the court.* Soon afterwards the same council summoned all causes of that nature before itself.† This infringement on ecclesiastical jurisdiction having occasioned some remonstrance from Rome, the council retained only the right of rejecting the petition of the married persons, and consented to refer such causes to the holy office as it should not previously have rejected.‡

'There was a moment in which, doubtless, the destruction of private fortunes, the ruin of youth, the domestic discord occasioned by these abuses,

determined the government to depart from its established maxims concerning the freedom of manners allowed the subject. All the courtesans were banished from Venice; but their absence was not enough to reclaim and bring back good morals to a whole people brought up in the most scandalous licentiousness. Depravity reached the very bosom of private families, and even into the cloister; and they found themselves obliged to recall, and even to indemnify,§ women who sometimes gained possession of important secrets, and who might be usefully employed in the ruin of men whose fortunes might have rendered them dangerous. Since that time licentiousness has gone on increasing; and we have seen mothers, not only selling the innocence of their daughters, but selling it by a contract, authenticated by the signature of a public officer, and the performance of which was secured by the protection of the laws.||

'The parlours of the convents of noble ladies and the houses of the courtesans, though the police carefully kept up a number of spies about them, were the only assemblies for society in Venice; and in these two places, so different from each other, there was equal freedom. Music, collations, gallantry, were not more forbidden in the parlours than at the casinos. There were a number of casinos for the purpose of public assemblies, where gaming was the principal pursuit of the company. It was a strange sight to see persons of either sex masked, or grave in their magisterial robes, round a table, invoking chance, and giving way at one instant to the agonies of despair, at the next to the illusions of hope, and that without uttering a single word.

'The rich had private casinos, but they lived *incognito* in them; and the wives whom they abandoned found compensation in the liberty they enjoyed. The corruption of morals had deprived them of their empire. We have just reviewed the whole history of Venice, and we have not once seen them exercise the slightest influence.'—DARU: *Hist. de la Répub. de Venise*, vol. v. p. 95.

NOTES

Page 413, col. 2.

'I smote the tardy bishop at Treviso.'] An historical fact. See Marin Sanuto's 'Lives of the Doges.'

Page 415, col. 2.

'*Doge* (*aside*). Saint Mark's shall strike that hour!'] The bells of San Marco were never rung but by order of the Doge. One of the pretexts for ringing this alarm was to have been an announcement of the appearance of a Genoese fleet off the Lagune.

Page 416, col. 2.

'A gondola, with one oar only, will.'] A gondola is not like a common boat, but is as easily rowed with one oar as with two (though, of course, not so swiftly), and often is so from motives of privacy; and, since the decay of Venice, of economy.

Page 427, col. 2.

'Engaged in secret to the Signory.'] An historical fact. See APPENDIX, Note A.

---

* Correspondence of M. Schlick, French chargé d'affaires. Despatch of 24th August, 1782.
† *Ibid.* Despatch 31st August.
‡ *Ibid.* Despatch of 3rd September, 1785.

§ The decree for their recall designates them as *nostre benemerite meretrici;* a fund and some houses, called *Case rampane*, were assigned to them; hence the opprobrious appellation of *Carampane.*
|| Mayer, Description of Venice, vol. ii.; and M. Archenholz, Picture of Italy, vol. i. ch. 2.

NOTES TO MARINO FALIERO

Page 438, col. 2.

'Within our palace precincts at San Polo.'] The Doge's family palace.

Page 443, col. 2.

'Of the red columns, where, on festal Thursday.'] 'Giovedi grasso,'—'fat or greasy Thursday,' —which I cannot literally translate in the text, was the day.

Page 443, col. 2.

'Guards! let their mouths be gagg'd even in the act.'] Historical fact. See Sanuto, APPENDIX, Note A.

Page 446, col. 1.

'*Ben.* Say, conscript fathers, shall she be admitted?'] The Venetian senate took the same title as the Roman, of 'conscript fathers.'

Page 451, col. 1.

'*Doge.* 'Tis with age, then.'] This was the actual reply of Bailli, maire of Paris, to a Frenchman who made him the same reproach on his way to execution, in the earliest part of their revolution. I find in reading over (since the completion of this tragedy), for the first time these six years, 'Venice Preserved,' a similar reply on a different occasion by Renault, and other coincidences arising from the subject. I need hardly remind the gentlest reader, that such coincidences must be accidental, from the very facility of their detection by reference to so popular a play on the stage and in the closet as Otway's chef-d'œuvre.

Page 451, col. 2.

'Who shall despise her!—She shall stoop to be.'] Should the dramatic picture seem harsh, let the reader look to the historical, of the period prophesied, or rather of the few years preceding that period. Voltaire calculated their 'nostre bene merite Meretrici' at 12,000 of regulars, without including volunteers and local militia, on what authority I know not; but it is, perhaps, the only part of the population not decreased. Venice once contained two hundred thousand inhabitants: there are now about ninety thousand; and THESE!! few individuals can conceive, and none could describe, the actual state into which the more than infernal tyranny of Austria has plunged this unhappy city. From the present decay and degeneracy of Venice under the Barbarians, there are some honourable individual exceptions. There is Pasqualigo, the last, and, alas! *posthumous* son of the marriage of the Doges with the Adriatic, who fought his frigate with far greater gallantry than any of his French coadjutors in the memorable action off Lissa. I came home in the squadron with the prizes in 1811, and recollect to have heard Sir William Hoste, and the other officers engaged in that glorious conflict, speak in the highest terms of Pasqualigo's behaviour. There is the Abbate Morelli. There is Alvise Querini, who, after a long and honourable diplomatic career, finds some consolation for the wrongs of his country, in the pursuits of literature with his nephew, Vittor Benzon, the son of the celebrated beauty, the heroine of 'La Biondina in Gondoletta.' There are the patrician poet Morosini, and the poet Lamberti, the author of the 'Biondina,' &c., and many other estimable productions; and, not least in an Englishman's estimation, Madame Michelli, the translator of Shakspeare. There are the young Dandolo and the improvvisatore Carrer, and Giuseppe Albrizzi, the accomplished son of an accomplished mother. There is Aglietti, and, were

there nothing else, there is the immortality of Canova. Cicognara, Mustoxithi, Bucati, &c. &c., I do not reckon, because the one is a Greek, and the others were born at least a hundred miles off, which, throughout Italy, constitutes, if not a *foreigner*, at least a *stranger* (*forestiére*).

Page 452, col. 1.

'Then when the Hebrew's in thy palaces.'] The chief palaces on the Brenta now belong to the Jews; who in the earlier times of the republic were only allowed to inhabit Mestri, and not to enter the city of Venice. The whole commerce is in the hands of the Jews and Greeks, and the Huns form the garrison.

Page 452, col. 1.

'But in its stead, coarse lusts of habitude.'] [See APPENDIX, Note C.]

Page 452, col. 1.

''Gainst which thou wilt not strive, and dar'st not murmur.'] If the Doge's prophecy seem remarkable, look to the following, made by Alamanni two hundred and seventy years ago:—'There is one very singular prophecy concerning Venice: "If thou dost not change," it says to that proud republic, "thy liberty, which is already on the wing, will not reckon a century more than the thousandth year." If we carry back the epocha of Venetian freedom to the establishment of the government under which the republic flourished, we shall find that the date of the election of the first Doge is 697; and if we add one century to a thousand, that is, eleven hundred years, we shall find the sense of the prediction to be literally this: "Thy liberty will not last till 1797." Recollect that Venice ceased to be free in the year 1796, the fifth year of the French republic; and you will perceive that there never was prediction more pointed, or more exactly followed by the event. You will, therefore, note as very remarkable the three lines of Alamanni addressed to Venice; which, however, no one has pointed out:—

"Se non cangi pensier, un secol solo
    Non conterà sopra 'l millesimo anno
    Tua libertà, che va fuggendo a volo."

Many prophecies have passed for such, and many men have been called prophets for much less.'— GINGUENÉ, *Hist. Lit. de l' Italie*, t. ix. p. 144.

Page 452, col. 2.

'Thou den of drunkards with the blood of princes!'] Of the first fifty Doges, *five* abdicated— *five* were banished with their eyes put out—*five* were MASSACRED—and *nine* deposed—so that *nineteen* out of fifty lost the throne by violence, besides two who fell in battle: this occurred long previous to the reign of Marino Faliero. One of his more immediate predecessors, Andrea Dandolo, died of vexation. Marino Faliero himself perished as related. Amongst his successors, *Foscari*, after seeing his son repeatedly tortured and banished, was deposed, and died of breaking a blood-vessel, on hearing the bell of Saint Mark's toll for the election of his successor. Morosini was impeached for the loss of Candia; but this was previous to his dukedom, during which he conquered the Morea, and was styled the Peloponnesian. Faliero might truly say,—

'Thou den of drunkards with the blood of princes!'

Page 453, col. 1.

'Chief of the Ten.'] 'Un Capo de' Diece' are the words of Sanuto's Chronicle.

SARDANAPALUS

Page 454, col. 2.

'And thou, my own Ionian Myrrha, choose'] 'The Ionian name had been still more comprehensive, having included the Achaians and the Bœotians, who, together with those to whom it was afterwards confined, would make nearly the whole of the Greek nation; and among the Orientals it was always the general name for the Greeks.'— MITFORD'S *Greece*, vol. i. p. 199.

Page 457, col. 2.

'Eat, drink, and love; the rest's not worth a fillip.'] 'For this expedition he took only a small chosen body of the phalanx, but all his light troops. In the first day's march he reached Anchialus, a town said to have been founded by the king of Assyria, Sardanapalus. The fortifications, in their magnitude and extent, still in Arrian's time, bore the character of greatness, which the Assyrians appear singularly to have affected in works of the kind. A monument representing Sardanapalus was found there, warranted by an inscription in Assyrian characters, of course in the old Assyrian language, which the Greeks, whether well or ill, interpreted thus: 'Sardanapalus, son of Anacyndaraxes, in one day founded Anchialus and Tarsus. Eat, drink, play; all other human joys are not worth a fillip.' Supposing this version nearly exact (for Arrian says it was not quite so), whether the purpose has not been to invite to civil order a people disposed to turbulence, rather than to recommend immoderate luxury, may perhaps reasonably be questioned. What, indeed, could be the object of a king of Assyria in founding such towns in a country so distant from his capital, and so divided from it by an immense extent of sandy deserts and lofty mountains, and, still more, how the inhabitants could be at once in circumstances to abandon themselves to the intemperate joys which their prince has been supposed to have recommended, is not obvious; but it may deserve observation that, in that line of coast, the southern of Lesser Asia, ruins of cities, evidently of an age after Alexander, yet barely named in history, at this day astonish the adventurous traveller by their magnificence and elegance. Amid the desolation which, under a singularly barbarian government, has for so many centuries been daily spreading in the finest countries of the globe, whether more from soil and climate, or from opportunities for commerce, extraordinary means must have been found for communities to flourish there; whence it may seem that the measures of Sardanapalus were directed by juster views than have been commonly ascribed to him; but that monarch having been the last of a dynasty ended by a revolution, obloquy on his memory would follow of course from the policy of his successors and their partisans. The inconsistency of traditions concerning Sardanapalus is striking in Diodorus's account of him.'—MITFORD'S *Greece*, vol. ix. p. 311.

Page 488, col. 1.

'Some twenty stadia.'] About two miles and a half.

THE TWO FOSCARI

Page 506, col. 1.

'Created by degrees an ocean Rome.'] In Lady Morgan's fearless and excellent work upon Italy,

I perceive the expression of 'Rome of the Ocean' applied to Venice. The same phrase occurs in the 'Two Foscari.' My publisher can vouch for me, that the tragedy was written and sent to England some time before I had seen Lady Morgan's work, which I only received on the 16th of August. I hasten, however, to notice the coincidence, and to yield the originality of the phrase to her who first placed it before the public.

Page 506, col. 2.

'That melody, which out of tones and tunes.' Alluding to the Swiss air and its effects.

Page 514, col. 1.

'There often has been question about you.'] An historical fact. See DARU, tom. ii.

Page 520, col. 1.

'O'er those they slew. I've heard of widows' tears.']—The Venetians appear to have had a particular turn for breaking the hearts of their Doges. The following is another instance of the kind in the Doge Marco Barbarigo: he was succeeded by his brother Agostino Barbarigo, whose chief merit is here mentioned.—'Le doge, blessé de trouver constamment un contradicteur et un censeur si amer dans son frère, lui dit un jour en plein conseil; "Messire Augustin, vous faites tout votre possible pour hâter ma mort; vous vous flattez de me succéder; mais, si les autres vous connaissent aussi bien que je vous connais, ils n'auront garde de vous élire." Là-dessus il se leva, ému de colère, rentra dans son appartement, et mourut quelques jours après. Ce frère, contre lequel il s'était emporté, fut précisément le successeur qu'on lui donna. C'était un mérite dont on aimait à tenir compte; surtout à un parent, de s'être mis en opposition avec le chef de la républi-que.'—DARU, *Hist. de Venise*, t. ii. p. 533.

Page 520, col. 2.

'*Lor.* (*pointing to the Doge's body*). That *he* has paid me!'] '*L'ha pagata.*' An historical fact. See *Hist. de Venise*, par P. DARU, t. ii. p. 411.

CAIN

Page 544, col. 2.

'But the four rivers would not cleanse my soul.'] The 'four rivers' which flowed round Eden, and consequently the only waters with which Cain was acquainted upon earth.

HEAVEN AND EARTH

Page 546, col. 1.

'Albeit thou watchest with "the seven."'] The archangels, said to be seven in number, and to occupy the eighth rank in the celestial hierarchy.

Page 551, col. 2.

'In a few hours the glorious giants' graves.'] 'And there were giants in the earth in those days, and after, mighty men, which were of old, men of renown.'—*Genesis.*

Page 551, col. 2.

'And heaven set wide her windows; while mankind.'] 'The same day were all the fountains of the great deep broken up, and the windows of heaven were opened.'—*Ibid.*

NOTES TO WERNER, ETC.

Page 552, col. 1.

'The scroll of Enoch prophesied it long.'] The book of Enoch, preserved by the Ethiopians, is said by them to be anterior to the flood.

WERNER

Page 578, col. 1.

'From the Ravenstone by choking you myself.'] The Ravenstone, 'Rabenstein,' is the *stone gibbet* of Germany, and so called from the ravens perching on it.

DEFORMED TRANSFORMED

Page 608, col. 1.

'Bestrides the Hartz Mountain.'] This is a well-known German superstition—a gigantic shadow produced by reflection on the Brocken.

Page 610, col. 2.

'From the red earth, like Adam.'] Adam means '*red earth*,' from which the first man was formed.

Page 617, col. 2.

'Weep not—*strike!* for Rome is mourning!'] Scipio, the second Africanus, is said to have repeated a verse of Homer, and wept over the burning of Carthage. He had better have granted it a capitulation.

BEPPO

Page 628, col. 1.

'The Spaniards call the person a "*Cortejo.*"'] Corte*h*o is pronounced Corte*h*o, with an aspirate, according to the Arabesque guttural. It means what there is as yet no precise name for in England, though the practice is as common as in any tramontane country whatever.

Page 629, col. 1.

'Raphael, who died in thy embrace, and vies.'] For the received accounts of the cause of Raphael's death, see his Lives.

Page 629, col. 1.

'While yet Canova can create below?'']

(In talking thus, the writer, more especially
  Of women, would be understood to say,
He speaks as a spectator, not officially,
  And always, reader, in a modest way;
Perhaps, too, in no very great degree shall he
  Appear to have offended in this lay,
Since, as all know, without the sex, our sonnets
Would seem unfinish'd, like their untrimm'd
  bonnets.)

(Signed) PRINTER'S DEVIL.

DON JUAN

Page 636, col. 1.

'And Wordsworth has his place in the Excise.'] Wordsworth's place may be in the Customs—it is, I think, in that or the Excise—besides another at Lord Lonsdale's table, where this poetical charlatan and political parasite licks up the crumbs with a hardened alacrity; the converted Jacobin having long subsided into the clownish sycophant of the worst prejudices of the aristocracy.

Page 636, col. 2.

'And heartless daughters—worn—and pale—and poor.'] 'Pale, but not cadaverous:'—Milton's two elder daughters are said to have robbed him of his books, besides cheating and plaguing him in the economy of his house, &c. &c. His feelings on such an outrage, both as a parent and a scholar, must have been singularly painful. Hayley compares him to Lear. See part third, Life of Milton, by W. Hayley (or Hailey, as spelt in the edition before me).

Page 636, col. 2.

'The intellectual eunuch Castlereagh?'] Or,—

'Would *he* subside into a hackney Laureate—
  A scribbling, self-sold, soul-hired, scorn'd Iscariot?'

I doubt if 'Laureate' and 'Iscariot' be good rhymes, but must say, as Ben Jonson did to Sylvester, who challenged him to rhyme with—

'I, John Sylvester,
  Lay with your sister.'

Jonson answered,—'I, Ben Jonson, lay with your wife.' Sylvester answered,—'That is not rhyme.'—'No,' said Ben Jonson; 'but it is *true.*'

Page 637, col. 1.

'Eutropius of its many masters,—blind.'] For the character of Eutropius, the eunuch and minister at the court of Arcadius, see Gibbon.

Page 637, col. 1.

'Is it not so, my Tory, Ultra-Julian?'] I allude not to our friend Landor's hero, the traitor Count Julian, but to Gibbon's hero, vulgarly yclept 'The Apostate.'

Page 639, col. 1.

'Save thine "incomparable oil," Macassar!'] Description des *vertus incomparables* de l'Huile de Macascar.'—See the Advertisement.

Page 641, col. 1.

'As Numa's (who was also named Pompilius).']

——'primus qui legibus urbem
Fundabit, curibus parvis et paupere terrâ
Missus in imperium magnum.'—VIRG.

Page 641, col. 2.

'Although Longinus tells us there is no hymn.'] See Longinus, Section 10, 'ἵνα μὴ ἕν τι περὶ αὐτὴν πάθος φαίνηται, παθῶν δὲ σύνοδος.'

Page 642, col. 1.

'They only add them all in an appendix.'] Fact! There is, or was, such an edition, with all the obnoxious epigrams of Martial placed by themselves at the end.

Page 642, col. 2.

'Which make the reader envy his transgressions.'] See his Confessions, l. i. c. ix. By the representation which Saint Augustine gives of himself in his youth, it is easy to see that he was what we should call a rake. He avoided the school as the plague; he loved nothing but gaming and public shows; he robbed his father of everything he could find; he invented a thousand lies to escape the rod, which they were obliged to make use of to punish his irregularities.

Page 644, col. 1.

'('Twas snow that brought St. Anthony to reason).'] For the particulars of St. Anthony's recipe for hot blood in cold weather, see Mr. Alban Butler's 'Lives of the Saints.'

Page 646, col. 2.

'In feelings quick as Ovid's Miss Medea.'] See Ovid. de Art. Amand. l. ii.

Page 646, col. 2.

'The bard I quote from does not sing amiss.'] Campbell's Gertrude of Wyoming—(I think)—the opening of Canto Second—but quote from memory.

Page 653, col. 1.

'Was it for this that no Cortejo e'er.'] The Spanish 'Cortejo' is much the same as the Italian 'Cavalier Servente.'

Page 653, col. 1.

'Who took Algiers, declares I used him vilely?'] Donna Julia here made a mistake. Count O'Reilly did not take Algiers—but Algiers very nearly took him: he and his army and fleet retreated with great loss, and not much credit, from before that city, in the year 1775.

Page 660, col. 2.

'My days of love are over; me no more.']

'Me nec femina, nec puer
Jam, nec spes animi credula mutui,
Nec certare juvat mero;
Nec vincire novis tempora floribus.'—Hor.

Page 662, col. 1.

'Excepting the Venetian Fazzioli.'] *Fazzioli*—literally, the little handkerchiefs—the veils most availing of St. Mark.

Page 670, col. 1.

'Remember Ugolino condescends.']

'Quandò ebbe detto ciò, con gli occhi torti
Riprese il teschio misero co' denti,
Che furo all' osso, come d'un can forti.'

Page 686, col. 2.

'Dante.'] Dante calls his wife, in the 'Inferno,' 'la fiera moglie.'

Page 686, col. 2.

'Milton.'] Milton's first wife ran away from him within the first month. If she had not, what would John Milton have done?

Page 690, col. 2.

'For none likes more to hear himself converse.']

'Rispone allor' Margutte, a dir tel tosto,
Io non credo piu al nero ch' all' azzurro:
Ma nel cappone, o lesso, o vuogli arrosto,
E credo alcuna volta anco nel burro;
Nella cervigia, e quando io n' ho nel mosto,
E molto più nell' espro che il mangurro;
Ma sopra tutto nel buon vino ho fede,
E credo che sia salvo chi gli crede.'—
Pulci, *Morgante Maggiore*, ca. 18, st. 151.

Page 693, col. 2.

'That e'er by precious metal was held in.'] The dress is Moorish, and the bracelets and bar are worn in the manner described. The reader will perceive hereafter, that as the mother of Haidée was of Fez, her daughter wore the garb of the country.

Page 693, col. 2.

'A like gold bar above her instep roll'd.'] The bar of gold above the instep is a mark of sovereign rank in the women of the families of the deys, and is worn as such by their female relatives.

Page 693, col. 2.

'Her person if allow'd at large to run.'] This is no exaggeration: there were four women whom I remember to have seen, who possessed their hair in this profusion; of these, three were English, the other was a Levantine. Their hair was of that length and quantity, that, when let down, it almost entirely shaded the person, so as nearly to render dress a superfluity. Of these, only one had dark hair; the Oriental had, perhaps, the lightest colour of the four.

Page 695, col. 1.

'Than your sires' "Islands of the Blest."'] The νῆσοι μακάρων of the Greek poets were supposed to have been the Cape de Verd islands or the Canaries.

Page 695, col. 2.

'And when the sun set where were they?']

'Deep were the groans of Xerxes, when he saw
This havoc; for his seat, a lofty mound
Commanding the wide sea, o'erlook'd the hosts.
With rueful cries he rent his royal robes,
And through his troops embattled on the shore
Gave signal of retreat; then started wild
And fled disorder'd.'—Æschylus.

Page 696, col. 1.

'There, swan-like, let me sing and die.']

. . . 'Γενοίμαν
ἵν' ὑλᾶεν ἔπεστι πόντου
πρόβλημ' ἁλίκλυστον, ἄκραν
ὑπὸ πλάκα Σουνίου.' κ.τ.λ.—Soph. *Ajax*, v. 1217.

Page 696, col. 2.

'For the first Mrs. Milton left his house.'] See Johnson's Life of Milton.

Page 697, col. 2.

'Can sneer at him who drew "Achitophel!"'] 'The verses of Dryden, once highly celebrated, are forgotten.'—Mr. W. Wordsworth's *Preface*.

Page 698, col. 2.

'Oh, Hesperus! thou bringest all good things.']

' Ἕσπερε πάντα φέρεις,
Φέρεις οἰνον—φέρεις αἰνα,
Φέρεις ματέρι παῖδα.'—*Fragment of Sappho.*

Page 698, col. 2.

'Ah! surely nothing dies but something mourns!']

'Era gia l' ora che volge 'l disio,
A' naviganti, e 'ntenerisce il cuore,
Lo di ch' han detto a' dolci amici a dio;
E che lo nuovo peregrin' d' amore
Punge, se ode Squilla di lontano,
Che paia 'l giorno pianger che si muore.'—
Dante's *Purgatory*, canto viii.

This last line is the first of Gray's Elegy, taken by him [not] without acknowledgment.

Page 698, col. 2.

'Some hands unseen strewed flowers upon his tomb.'] See Suetonius for this fact.

Page 700, col. 1.

'"Whom the gods love die young," was said of yore.'] See Herodotus (Cleobis and Biton). The sentiment is in a fragment of Menander.

Page 705, col. 2.

'A vein had burst, and her sweet lips' pure dyes.'] This is no very uncommon effect of the violence of conflicting and different passions. The Doge Francis Foscari, on his deposition in 1457, hearing the bells of St. Mark announce the election of his successor, 'mourut subitement d'une hémorragie causée par une veine qui s'éclata dans sa poitrine,' (see Sismondi and Daru, vols. i. and ii.) at the age of eighty years, when '*Who would have thought the old man had so much blood in him?*' Before I was sixteen years of age, I was witness to a melancholy instance of the same effect of mixed passions upon a young person, who, however, did not die in consequence, at that time, but fell a victim some years afterwards to a seizure of the same kind, arising from causes intimately connected with agitation of mind.

Page 708, col. 1.

'But sold by the impresario at no high rate.'] This is a fact. A few years ago a man engaged a company for some foreign theatre, embarked them at an Italian port, and carrying them to Algiers, sold them all. One of the women, returned from her captivity, I heard sing, by a strange coincidence, in Rossini's opera of 'L' Italiana in Algieri,' at Venice, in the beginning of 1817.

Page 708, col. 2.

'From all the Pope makes yearly 'twould perplex.'] It is strange that it should be the Pope and the Sultan who are the chief encouragers of this branch of trade—women being prohibited as singers at St. Peter's, and not deemed trustworthy as guardians of the harem.

Page 712, col. 1.

'Sprinkled with palaces; the Ocean stream.'] 'Ωκεανοῖο ῥέογιο. This expression of Homer has been much criticised. It hardly answers to our Atlantic ideas of the ocean, but is sufficiently applicable to the Hellespont, and the Bosphorus, with the Ægean intersected with islands.

Page 712, col. 2.

'"Tis a grand sight from off "the Giant's Grave."'] The 'Giant's Grave' is a height on the Asiatic shore of the Bosphorus, much frequented by holiday parties; like Harrow and Highgate.

Page 715, col. 2.

'Of food I think with Philip's son, or rather.'] See Plutarch in Alex., Q. Curt. Hist. Alex., and Sir Richard Clayton's 'Critical Inquiry into the Life of Alexander the Great.'

Page 715, col. 2.

'Stretch'd in the street, and able scarce to pant.'] The assassination alluded to took place on the 8th of December, 1820, in the streets of Ravenna, not a hundred paces from the residence of the writer. The circumstances were as described.

Page 716, col. 2.

'Wond'ring what next, till the caïque was brought.'] The light and elegant wherries plying about the quays of Constantinople are so called.

Page 717, col. 1.

'From Saint Bartholomew we have saved our skin.'] St. Bartholomew is said to have been flayed alive.

Page 718, col. 1.

'Prepared for supper with a glass of rum.'] In Turkey nothing is more common than for the Mussulmans to take several glasses of strong spirits by way of appetizer. I have seen them take as many as six of raki before dinner, and swear that they dined the better for it: I tried the experiment, but fared like the Scotchman, who having heard that the birds called kittiwakes were admirable whets, ate six of them, and complained that 'he was no hungrier than when he began.'

Page 718, col. 1.

'Splendid but silent, save in *one*, where a dropping.'] A common furniture. I recollect being received by Ali Pacha, in a large room, paved with marble, containing a marble basin, and fountain playing in the centre, &c. &c.

Page 718, col. 2.

'And the calumniated queen Semiramis.'] Babylon was enlarged by Nimrod, strengthened and beautified by Nabuchadonosor, and rebuilt by Semiramis.

Page 721, col. 2.

'The gate so splendid was in all its *features*.'] *Features* of a gate—a ministerial metaphor: 'the *feature* upon which this question *hinges*.' See the 'Fudge Family,' or hear Castlereagh.

Page 722, col. 1.

'A good deal practised here upon occasion.'] A few years ago the wife of Muchtar Pacha complained to his father of his son's supposed infidelity: he asked with whom, and she had the barbarity to give in a list of the twelve handsomest women in Yanina. They were seized, fastened up in sacks, and drowned in the lake the same night. One of the guards who was present informed me, that not one of the victims uttered a cry, or showed a symptom of terror at so sudden a 'wrench from all we know, from all we love.'

Page 723, col. 2.

'Though on more *thorough-bred* or fairer fingers.'] There is nothing, perhaps, more distinctive of birth than the hand. It is almost the only sign of blood which aristocracy can generate.

Page 728, col. 2.

'Save Solyman, the glory of their line.'] It may not be unworthy of remark, that Bacon, in his essay on 'Empire,' hints that Solyman was the last of his line; on what authority, I know not. These are his words:—'The destruction of Mustapha was so fatal to Solyman's line, as the succession of the Turks from Solyman until this day is suspected to be untrue, and of strange blood; for that Selymus the second was thought to be supposititious.' But Bacon, in his historical authorities, is often inaccurate. I could give half-a-dozen instances from his Apophthegms only.

BACON'S APOPHTHEGMS.	OBSERVATIONS.

91.

Michael Angelo, the famous painter, painting in the Pope's chapel the portraiture of hell

This was *not* the portrait of a cardinal, but of the

and damned souls, made one of the damned souls so like a cardinal that was his enemy, as everybody at first sight knew it: whereupon the cardinal complained to Pope Clement, humbly praying it might be defaced. The Pope said to him, Why, you know very well I have power to deliver a soul out of purgatory, but not out of hell.

Pope's master of the ceremonies.

155.

Alexander, after the battle of Granicum, had very great offers made him by Darius. Consulting with his captains concerning them, Parmenio said, Sure, I would accept of these offers, if I were as Alexander. Alexander answered, So would I, if I were as Parmenio.

It was after the battle of Issus and during the siege of Tyre, and *not* immediately after the passage of the Granicus, that this is said to have occurred.

158.

Antigonus, when it was told him that the enemy had such volleys of arrows that they did hide the sun, said, That falls out well, for it is hot weather, and so we shall fight in the shade.

This was *not* said by Antigonus, but by a Spartan, previously to the battle of Thermopylæ.

162.

There was a philosopher that disputed with Adrian the Emperor, and did it but weakly. One of his friends that stood by afterwards said unto him, Methinks you were not like yourself last day, in argument with the Emperor: I could have answered better myself. Why, said the philosopher, would you have me contend with him that commands thirty legions?

This happened under Augustus Cæsar, and *not* during the reign of Adrian.

164.

There was one that found a great mass of money, digging underground in his grandfather's house, and being somewhat doubtful of the case signified it to the emperor that he had found such treasure. The emperor made a rescript thus: Use it. He writ back again, that the sum was greater than his state or condition could use. The emperor writ a new rescript thus: Abuse it.

This happened to the father of Herodes Atticus, and the answer was made by the Emperor Nerva, who deserved that his name should have been stated by the 'greatest — wisest —meanest of mankind.'

178.

One of the seven was wont to say, that laws were like cobwebs: where the small flies were caught, and the great break through.

This was said by Anacharsis the Scythian, and *not* by a Greek.

209.

An orator of Athens said to Demosthenes, The Athenians

This was *not* said *by* Demosthenes,

will kill you if they wax mad. Demosthenes replied, And they will kill you if they be in good sense.

but *to* Demosthenes by *Phocion*.

221.

There was a philosopher about Tiberius that, looking into the nature of Caius, said of him, That he was mire mingled with blood.

This was not said of Caius (Caligula, I presume, is intended by Caius), but of *Tiberius* himself.

97.

There was a king of Hungary took a bishop in battle, and kept him prisoner: whereupon the Pope writ a monitory to him, for that he had broken the privilege of holy church, and taken his son: the king sent an embassage to him, and sent withal the armour wherein the bishop was taken, and this only in writing—*Vide num hæc sit vestis filii tui?* Know now whether this be thy son's coat?

This reply was *not* made by a king of *Hungary*, but sent by Richard the First, Cœur de Lion, of England, to the Pope with the breast-plate of the bishop of Beauvais.

267.

Demetrius, king of Macedon, had a petition offered him divers times by an old woman, and answered he had no leisure; whereupon the woman said aloud, Why then give over to be king.

This did *not* happen to Demetrius, but to *Philip*, King of Macedon.

VOLTAIRE

Having stated that Bacon was frequently incorrect in his citations from history, I have thought it necessary in what regards so great a name (however trifling), to support the assertion by such facts as more immediately occur to me. They are but trifles, and yet for such trifles a school-boy would be whipped (if still in the fourth form); and Voltaire for half-a-dozen similar errors has been treated as a superficial writer, notwithstanding the testimony of the learned Warton:—'Voltaire, a writer of *much deeper research* than is imagined, and the *first* who has displayed the literature and customs of the dark ages with *any degree of penetration* and comprehension.'* For another distinguished testimony to Voltaire's merits in literary research, see also Lord Holland's excellent Account of the Life and Writings of Lope de Vega, vol. i. p. 215, edition of 1817.

Voltaire has even been termed a 'shallow fellow,' by some of the same school who called Dryden's Ode 'a drunken song;'—a *school* (as it is called, I presume, from their education being still incomplete) the whole of whose filthy trash of Epics, Excursions, &c. &c. &c., is not worth the two words in Zaïre, '*Vous pleurez*,'† or a single speech of Tancred:—a *school*, the apostate lives of whose renegadoes, with their tea-drinking neutrality of morals, and their convenient treachery in politics—in the record of their accumulated pretences to virtue can produce no *actions* (were all their good

* Dissertation I.
† ——'Il est trop vrai que l'honneur me l'ordonne,
Que je vous adorai, que je vous abandonne,
Que je renonce à vous, que vous le désirez,
Que sous une autre loi . . . Zaïre, VOUS PLEUREZ?'
—*Zaïre*, acte iv, sc. ii.

deeds drawn up in array) to equal or approach the sole defence of the family of Calas, by that great and unequalled genius—the universal Voltaire.

I have ventured to remark on these little inaccuracies of 'the greatest genius that England, or perhaps any other country, ever produced,'* merely to show our national injustice in condemning *generally* the greatest genius of France for such inadvertencies as these, of which the highest of England has been no less guilty. Query, was Bacon a greater intellect than Newton?

CAMPBELL

Being in the humour of criticism, I shall proceed, after having ventured upon the slips of Bacon, to touch upon one or two as trifling in the edition of the British Poets, by the justly celebrated Campbell. But I do this in good will, and trust it will be so taken. If anything could add to my opinion of the talents and true feeling of that gentleman, it would be his classical, honest, and triumphant defence of Pope, against the vulgar cant of the day, and its existing Grub Street.

The inadvertencies to which I allude are—

Firstly, in speaking of *Anstey*, whom he accuses of having taken 'his leading characters from *Smollett*.' Anstey's Bath Guide was published in 1766. Smollett's Humphrey Clinker (the only work of Smollett's from which Tabitha, &c. &c. *could* have been taken) was written during *Smollett's last residence* at Leghorn in 1770—'*Argal*,' if there has been any borrowing, Anstey must be the creditor, and not the debtor. I refer Mr. Campbell to his *own* data in his Lives of Smollett and Anstey.

Secondly, Mr. Campbell says in the Life of Cowper (note to page 358, vol. vii.) that he knows not to whom Cowper alludes in these lines,—

'Nor he who, for the bane of thousands born,
Built *God* a *church*, and laugh'd his word to scorn.'

The Calvinist meant Voltaire, and the church of Ferney, with its inscription 'Deo erexit Voltaire.'

Thirdly, in the Life of Burns, Mr. Campbell quotes Shakspeare thus,—

'To gild refined gold, to paint *the rose*,
Or *add fresh* perfume *to* the violet.'

This version by no means improves the original, which is as follows—

'To gild refined gold, to paint the *lily*,
To *throw a perfume on* the violet,' &c.—*King John.*

A great poet quoting another should be correct; he should also be accurate, when he accuses a Parnassian brother of that dangerous charge 'borrowing:' a poet had better borrow anything (excepting money) than the thoughts of another—they are always sure to be reclaimed; but it is very hard, having been the *lender*, to be denounced as the debtor, as is the case of Anstey *versus* Smollett. As there is 'honour amongst thieves,' let there be some amongst poets, and give each his due,—none can afford to give it more than Mr. Campbell himself, who, with a high reputation for originality, and a fame which cannot be shaken, is the only poet of the times (except Rogers) who can be reproached (and *in him* it is indeed a reproach) with having written *too little*.

Ravenna, Jan. 5, 1821.

* Pope, in Spencer's Anecdotes, p. 158. Malone's edition.

Page 730, col. 2.

'"Which, taken at the flood,"—you know the rest.'] See Shakspeare, Julius Cæsar, act iv. sc. iii.

Page 731, col. 2.

'Who lent his lady to his friend Hortensius.'] Cato gave up his wife, Martia, to his friend Hortensius; but, on the death of the latter, took her back again. This conduct was ridiculed by the Romans, who observed, that Martia entered the house of Hortensius very poor, but returned to the bed of Cato loaded with treasures.—PLUTARCH.

Page 732, col. 1.

'(A "Highland welcome" all the wide world over.)'] See Waverley.

Page 732, col. 2.

'In his monastic concubine of snow.'] 'The blessed Francis, being strongly solicited one day by the emotions of the flesh, pulled off his clothes and scourged himself soundly: being after this inflamed with a wonderful fervour of mind, he plunged his naked body into a great heap of snow. The devil, being overcome, retired immediately, and the holy man returned victorious into his cell.'—See BUTLER's *Lives of the Saints*.

Page 733, col. 2.

'The tyrant's "wish, that mankind only had."'] Caligula—See Suetonius. 'Being in a rage at the people, for favouring a party in the Circensian games in opposition to him, he cried out, "I wish the Roman people had but one neck."'

Page 733, col. 2.

'He went forth with the lovely Odalisques.'] The ladies of the seraglio.

Page 734, col. 2.

'Who with the brightest Georgians might compare.'] 'It is in the adjacent climates of Georgia, Mingrelia, and Circassia, that nature has placed, at least to our eyes, the model of beauty, in the shape of the limbs, the colour of the skin, the symmetry of the features, and the expression of the countenance; the men are formed for action, the women for love.'—GIBBON.

Page 735, col. 1.

'They would prefer to Padisha or Pacha.'] Padisha is the Turkish title of the Grand Signior.

Page 739, col. 1.

'A "wood obscure," like that where Dante found.']

'Nell' mezzo del' cammin' di nostra vita
Mi ritrovai per una selva oscura,' &c.—*Inferno.*

Page 749, col. 2.

'Was teaching his recruits to use the bayonet.'] Fact: Souwarrow did this in person.

Page 754, col. 2.

'All sounds it pierceth, "Allah! Allah! Hu!"'] Allah Hu! is properly the war-cry of the Mussulmans, and they dwell on the last syllable, which gives it a wild and peculiar effect.

Page 754, col. 2.

'Carnage, (so Wordsworth tells you) is God's daughter.']

> 'But *Thy** most dreaded instrument
> In working out a pure intent,
> Is man array'd for mutual slaughter;
> Yea, *Carnage is thy daughter!'*
> WORDSWORTH'S *Thanksgiving Ode.*

Page 755, col. 2.

'Was printed *Grove*, although his name was Grose.'] A fact: see the Waterloo Gazettes. I recollect remarking at the time to a friend:— *There is fame!* a man is killed, his name is Grose, and they print it Grove.' I was at college with the deceased, who was a very amiable and clever man, and his society in great request for his wit, gaiety, and 'Chansons à boire.'

Page 756, col. 1.

'(The antiquarians who can settle time.'] See General Valancey and Sir Lawrence Parsons.

Page 756, col. 2.

''Tis pity "that such meaning should pave hell."'] The Portuguese proverb says, that 'hell is paved with good intentions.'

Page 757, col. 2.

'By thy humane discovery, Friar Bacon!'] Gunpowder is said to have been discovered by this friar.

Page 764, col. 2.

'That you and I will win St. George's collar.'] A Russian military order.

Page 769, col. 2.

'Humanity would rise, and thunder "Nay!"'] Query, *Ney?*—Printer's Devil.

Page 770, col. 1.

'And "Europe's Liberator"—still enslaved.'] Vide Speeches in Parliament, after the battle of Waterloo.

Page 771, col. 2.

'"But heaven," as Cassio says, "is above all."'] See Othello.

Page 772, col. 2.

'I've heard them in the Ephesian ruins howl.'] In Greece I never saw or heard these animals; but among the ruins of Ephesus I have heard them by hundreds.

Page 773, col. 1.

'Because he could no more digest his dinner.'] He was killed in a conspiracy, after his temper had been exasperated by his extreme costivity to a degree of insanity.

Page 774, col. 2.

'And had just buried the fair-faced Lanskoi.'] He was the grande passion of the grande Catherine. See her Lives under the head of 'Lanskoi.'

Page 775, col. 1.

'Bid Ireland's Londonderry's Marquess show.'] This was written long before the suicide of that person.

Page 775, col. 2.

'Oh thou "teterrima causa" of all "belli."'] Hor. Sat. lib. i. sat. iii.

* To wit, the Deity's; this is perhaps as pretty a pedigree for murder as ever was found out by Garter King at Arms.—What would have been said, had any free-spoken people discovered such a lineage?

Page 776, col. 2.

'"A man" (as Giles says): for though she would widow all.'] 'His fortune swells him, it is rank, he's married.'—*Sir Giles Overreach;* MASSINGER'S *New Way to Pay Old Debts.*

Page 778, col. 2.

'Of several ribands, and some thousand peasants.'] A Russian estate is always valued by the number of the slaves upon it.

Page 780, col. 2.

'Would scarcely join again the "reformadoes."'] 'Reformers,' or rather 'Reformed.' The Baron Bradwardine, in Waverley, is authority for the word.

Page 780, col. 2.

'The endless soot bestows a tint far deeper.'] Query, *suit?*—Printer's Devil.

Page 781, col. 1.

'The Dee, the Don, Balgounie's brig's *black wall.*'] The brig of Don, near the 'auld toun' of Aberdeen, with its one arch, and its black deep salmon-stream below, is in my memory as yesterday. I still remember, though perhaps I may misquote, the awful proverb which made me pause to cross it, and yet lean over it with childish delight, being an only son, at least by the mother's side. The saying as recollected by me was this, but I have never heard or seen it since I was nine years of age:—

> 'Brig of Balgounie, *black's* your *wa'*,
> Wi' a wife's *ae son*, and a mear's *ae foal*,
> Doun ye shall fa'!'

Page 781, col. 2.

'With his *Agrarian* laws, the high estate.'] Tiberius Gracchus, being tribune of the people, demanded in their name the execution of the Agrarian law; by which all persons possessing above a certain number of acres were to be deprived of the surplus for the benefit of the poor citizens.

Page 782, col. 1.

'But getting nigh grim Dante's "obscure wood."'] 'Mi retrovai per un selva oscura.'—*Inferno, Canto I.*

Page 782, col. 2.

'Oh for a *forty-parson power* to chant.'] A metaphor taken from the 'forty-horse power' of a steam-engine. That mad wag the Reverend Sydney Smith, sitting by a brother clergyman at dinner, observed afterwards, that his dull neighbour had a '*twelve-parson power*' of conversation.

Page 783, col. 1.

'To strip the Saxons of their *hydes*, like tanners.'] 'Hyde.'—I believe a hyde of land to be a legitimate word, and, as such, subject to the tax of a quibble.

Page 784, col. 2.

'Was given to her favourite, and now *bore his.*'] The empress went to the Crimea, accompanied by the emperor Joseph, in the year—I forget which.

Page 785, col. 1.

'Which gave her dukes the graceless name of "Biron."'] In the Empress Anne's time, Biren, her favourite, assumed the name and arms of the 'Birons' of France, which families are yet extant

917

with that of England. There are still the daughters of Courland of that name; one of them I remember seeing in England in the blessed year of the Allies (1814)—the Duchess of S.—to whom the English Duchess of Somerset presented me as a namesake.

Page 786, col. 1.

'The greatest number flesh hath ever known.'] St. Ursula and her eleven thousand virgins were still extant in 1816, and may be so yet, as much as ever.

Page 791, col. 1.

'And so knowing?'] The advance of science and of language has rendered it unnecessary to translate the above true and good English, spoken in its original purity by the select mobility and their patrons. The following is a stanza of a song which was very popular, at least in my early days:—

'On the high toby-spice flash the muzzle, In spite of each gallows old scout; If you at the spellken can't hustle, You'll be hobbled in making a Clout.

Then your Blowing will wax gallows haughty, When she hears of your scaly mistake, She'll surely turn snitch for the forty— That her Jack may be regular weight.'

If there be any gemman so ignorant as to require a traduction, I refer him to my old friend and corporeal pastor and master, John Jackson, Esq., Professor of Pugilism; who, I trust, still retains the strength and symmetry of his model of a form, together with his good-humour and athletic as well as mental accomplishments.

Page 792, col. 1.

'St. James's Palace and St. James's "Hells."'] 'Hells,' gaming-houses. What their number may now be, in this life, I know not. Before I was of age I knew them pretty accurately, both 'gold' and 'silver.' I was once nearly called out by a acquaintance, because when he asked me where I thought that his soul would be found hereafter, I answered, 'In Silver Hell.'

Page 793, col. 2.

'Spirit would name, and therefore even I won't anent.'] 'Anent' was a Scotch phrase meaning 'concerning'—'with regard to:' it has been made English by the Scotch novels; and, as the Frenchman said, 'If it be not, ought to be English.'

Page 794, col. 1.

'The milliners who furnish "drapery Misses."'] 'Drapery Misses.'—This term is probably anything now but a *mystery*. It was, however, almost so to me when I first returned from the East in 1811–1812. It means a pretty, a high-born, a fashionable young female, well instructed by her friends, and furnished by her milliner with a wardrobe upon credit, to be repaid, when married, by the *husband*. The riddle was first read to me by a young and pretty heiress, on my praising the 'drapery' of the '*untochered*' but 'pretty virginities' (like Mrs. Anne Page) of the *then* day, which has now been some years yesterday; she assured me that the thing was common in London; and as her own thousands, and blooming looks, and rich simplicity of array, put any suspicion in her own case out of the question, I confess I gave some credit to the allegation. If necessary, authorities might be cited; in which case I could quote both 'drapery'

and the wearers. Let us hope, however, that it is now obsolete.

Page 795, col. 2.

''Tis strange the mind, that fiery particle.'] 'Divinæ particulum auræ.'

Page 796, col. 1.

'And Centaur Nessus garb of mortal clothing.'] 'Illita Nesseo tibi texta veneno.'—OVID, Epist. ix.

Page 797, col. 1.

'In mind, a sort of sentimental bogle.'] Scotch for goblin.

Page 799, col. 2.

'Who rouse the shirtless patriots of Spain.'] The Descamisados.

Page 801, col. 1.

'And Mitford in the nineteenth century.'] See Mitford's Greece. 'Græcia *Verax*.' His great pleasure consists in praising tyrants, abusing Plutarch, spelling oddly, and writing quaintly; and what is strange, after all *his* is the best modern history of Greece in any language, and he is perhaps the best of all modern historians whatsoever. Having named his sins, it is but fair to state his virtues—learning, labour, research, wrath, and partiality. I call the latter virtues in a writer, because they make him write in earnest.

Page 803, col. 1.

'A hazy widower turn'd of forty's sure.'] This line may puzzle the commentators more than the present generation.

Page 807, col. 2.

'Like Russians rushing from hot baths to snows.'] The Russians, as is well known, run out from their hot baths to plunge into the Neva; a pleasant practical antithesis, which it seems does them no harm.

Page 808, col. 2.

'Which flash'd as far as where the musk-bull browses.'] For a description and print of this inhabitant of the polar region and native country of the Auroræ Boreales, see Parry's Voyage in search of a North-west Passage.

Page 808, col. 2.

'As Philip's son proposed to do with Athos.'] A sculptor projected to hew Mount Athos into a statue of Alexander, with a city in one hand, and, I believe, a river in his pocket, with various other similar devices. But Alexander's gone, and Athos remains, I trust ere long to look over a nation of freemen.

Page 812, col. 1.

'Also there bin another pious reason.']

'With everything that pretty *bin*, My lady sweet, arise.'—SHAKSPEARE.

Page 814, col. 1.

'They and their bills, "Arcadians both," are left.'] 'Arcades ambo.'

Page 817, col. 1.

'Or wilder group of savage Salvatore's.'] Salvator Rosa.

Page 817, col. 1.

'His bell-mouth'd goblet makes me feel quite Danish.'] If I err not, 'your Dane' is one of Iago's catalogue of nations 'exquisite in their drinking.'

Page 817, col. 2.

'Even Nimrod's self might leave the plains of Dura.'] In Assyria.

Page 818, col. 1.

'And shine the very *Siria* of the spheres.'] Siria, i.e., bitch-star.

Page 819, col. 2.

'That Scriptures out of church are blasphemies.'] 'Mrs. Adams answered Mr. Adams, that it was blasphemous to talk of Scripture out of church.' This dogma was broached to her husband—the best Christian in any book.—See *Joseph Andrews*.

Page 821, col. 1.

'Should have a hook, and a small trout to pull it.'] It would have taught him humanity at least. This sentimental savage, whom it is a mode to quote (amongst the novelists) to show their sympathy for innocent sports and old songs, teaches how to sew up frogs, and break their legs by way of experiment, in addition to the art of angling, the cruelest, the coldest, and the stupidest of pretended sports. They may talk about the beauties of nature, but the angler merely thinks of his dish of fish; he has no leisure to take his eyes from off the streams, and a single *bite* is worth to him more than all the scenery around. Besides, some fish bite best on a rainy day. The whale, the shark, and the tunny fishery have somewhat of noble and perilous in them; even net fishing, trawling, &c., are more humane and useful. But angling!—No angler can be a good man.

'One of the best men I ever knew,—as humane, delicate-minded, generous, and excellent a creature as any in the world,—was an angler: true, he angled with painted flies, and would have been incapable of the extravagances of I. Walton.'

The above addition was made by a friend in reading over the MS.:—'Audi alteram partem.'— I leave it to counterbalance my own observation.

Page 825, col. 1.

'And never *craned*, and made but few "*faux pas*."'] *Craning.*—'To *crane*' is, or was, an expression used to denote a gentleman's stretching out his neck over a hedge, 'to look before he leaped:'—a pause in his 'vaulting ambition,' which in the field doth occasion some delay and execration in those who may be immediately behind the equestrian sceptic. 'Sir, if you don't choose to take the leap, let me!'—was a phrase which generally sent the aspirant on again; and to good purpose: for though 'the horse and rider' might fall, they made a gap through which, and over him and his steed, the field might follow.

Page 825, col. 2.

'Ask'd next day, "If men ever hunted *twice?*"'] See his Letters to his Son.

Page 827, col. 1.

'Go to the coffee-house, and take another.'] In Swift's or Horace Walpole's letters I think it is mentioned that somebody, regretting the loss of a friend, was answered by an universal Pylades: 'When I lose one, I go to the Saint James's Coffee-house, and take another.' I recollect having heard an anecdote of the same kind. Sir W. D. was a great gamester. Coming in one day to the club of which he was a member, he was observed to look melancholy. 'What is the matter, Sir William?' cried Hare, of facetious memory. 'Ah!' replied

Sir W., 'I have just *lost* poor Lady D.'—'*Lost!* What at? *Quinze* or *Hazard?*' was the consolatory rejoinder of the querist.

Page 828, col. 1.

'And I refer you to wise Oxenstiern.'] The famous Chancellor Oxenstiern said to his son, on the latter expressing his surprise upon the great effects arising from petty causes in the presumed mystery of politics: 'You see by this, my son, with how little wisdom the kingdoms of the world are governed.'

Page 829, col. 2.

'Or Swiss Rousseau, cry " *Voilà la Pervenche!* "'] See 'La Nouvelle Héloïse.'

Page 830, col. 1.

'" *Beatus ille procul!* " from "*negotiis.*"'] Hor. Epod. Od. ii.

Page 834, col. 2.

'Great Socrates? And thou, Diviner still.'] As it is necessary in these times to avoid ambiguity, I say that I mean, by 'Diviner still,' CHRIST. If ever God was man—or man God—he was *both*. I never arraigned his creed, but the use, or abuse—made of it. Mr. Canning one day quoted Christianity to sanction negro slavery, and Mr. Wilberforce had little to say in reply. And was Christ crucified that black men might be scourged? If so, he had better been born a Mulatto, to give both colours an equal chance of freedom, or at least salvation.

Page 836, col. 1.

'When Rapp the Harmonist embargo'd marriage.'] This extraordinary and flourishing German colony in America does not entirely exclude matrimony, as the 'Shakers' do; but lays such restrictions upon it as prevents more than a certain quantum of births within a certain number of years; which births (as Mr. Hulme observes) generally arrive 'in a little flock like those of a farmer's lambs, all within the same month perhaps.' These Harmonists (so called from the name of their settlement) are represented as a remarkably flourishing, pious, and quiet people. See the various recent writers on America.

Page 836, col. 2.

'Nor canvass what "so eminent a hand" meant.'] Jacob Tonson, according to Mr. Pope, was accustomed to call his writers 'able pens,' 'persons of honour,' and especially 'eminent hands.' Vide Correspondence, &c. &c.

Page 837, col. 2.

'Of Brutus at the pageant of Tiberius.'] See Tacitus, b. vi.

Page 839, col. 2.

'(*There's fame*)—young partridge fillets, deck'd with truffles.'] A dish 'à la Lucullus.' This hero, who conquered the East, has left his more extended celebrity to the transplantation of cherries (which he first brought into Europe), and the nomenclature of some very good dishes:—and I am not sure that (barring indigestion) he has not done more service to mankind by his cookery than by his conquests. A cherry-tree may weigh against a bloody laurel: besides, he has contrived to earn celebrity from both.

Page 839, col. 2.

'There's pretty picking in those "petits puits." ']
'Petits puits d'amour garnis des confitures,'—a classical and well-known dish for part of the flank of a second course.

Page 841, col. 2.

'Observe; for that with me's a "sine quâ." ']
Subauditur '*non*;' omitted for the sake of euphony.

Page 842, col. 1.

'It makes my blood boil like the springs of Hecla.'] Hecla is a famous hot-spring in Iceland.

Page 842, col. 2.

'Shall "fool me to the top up of my bent." ']
Hamlet, Act iii. sc. 2.

Page 842, col. 2.

'Like those of the philosopher of Malmsbury.']
Hobbes: who, doubting of his own soul, paid that compliment to the souls of other people as to decline their visits, of which he had some apprehension.

Page 843, col. 1.

'To draw the bow, to ride, and speak the truth.']
Xenophon, Cyrop.

Page 843, col. 1.

' "For this effect defective comes by cause." '
Hamlet, Act ii, sc. 2.

Page 844, col. 1.

'If from a shell-fish or from cochineal.'] The composition of the old Tyrian purple, whether from a shell-fish, or from cochineal, or from kermes, is still an article of dispute: and even its colour—some say purple, others scarlet: I say nothing.

Page 848, col. 1.

'Was much consoled by his own repartee.'] I think that it *was* a *carpet* on which Diogenes trod, with—'Thus I trample on the pride of Plato!'—'With greater pride,' as the other replied. But as *carpets* are *meant* to be trodden upon, my memory probably misgives me, and it might be a robe, or tapestry, or a tablecloth, or some other expensive and uncynical piece of furniture.

Page 848, col. 2.

'To soothe our ears, lest Italy should fail.'] I remember that the mayoress of a provincial town, somewhat surfeited with a similar display from foreign parts, did rather indecorously break through the applause of an intelligent audience—intelligent, I mean, as to music—for the words, besides being in recondite languages (it was some years before the peace, ere all the world had travelled, and while I was a collegian), were sorely disguised by the performers:—this mayoress, I say, broke out with, 'Rot your Italianos! for my part, I loves a simple ballat!' Rossini will go a good way to bring most people to the same opinion, some day. Who would imagine that he was to be the successor of Mozart? However, I state this with diffidence, as a liege and loyal admirer of Italian music in general, and of much of Rossini's; but we may say, as the connoisseur did of painting, in 'The Vicar of Wakefield,' 'that the picture would be better painted if the painter had taken more pains.'

Page 850, col. 1.

'For Gothic daring shown in English money.']
'Ausu Romano ære Veneto' is the inscription (and well inscribed in this instance) on the sea walls between the Adriatic and Venice. The walls were a republican work of the Venetians; the inscription, I believe, imperial; and inscribed by Napoleon the *First*. It is time to continue to him that title—there will be a second by and by, 'Spes altera mundi,' *if he live*; let him not defeat it like his father. But, in any case, he will be preferable to Imbeciles. There is a glorious field for him, if he know how to cultivate it.—[Napoleon, Duke of Reichstadt, died at Vienna, July 22, 1832—to the disappointment of many prophets. He had just completed his twenty-first year.]

Page 850, col. 1.

' "Untying" squires "to fight against the churches." ']
'I conjure you, by that which you profess
(Howe'er you come to know it), answer me:
Though ye *untie* the winds, and let them fight
Against the *churches*.'—*Macbeth*.

Page 851, col. 2.

' "And champion him to the utmost—" ' he would keep it.']
'Rather than so, come, fate, into the list,
And champion me to the utterance.'—*Macbeth.*

Page 854, col. 1.

'They err—'tis merely what is call'd mobility.']
In French '*mobilité*.' I am not sure that mobility is English; but it is expressive of a quality which rather belongs to other climates, though it is sometimes seen to a great extent in our own. It may be defined as an excessive susceptibility of immediate impressions—at the same time without *losing* the past; and is, though sometimes apparently useful to the possessor, a most painful and unhappy attribute.

Page 854, col. 2.

'Draperied her form with curious felicity!']
'Curiosa felicitas.'—PETRONIUS ARBITER.

Page 856, col. 1.

'A noise like to wet fingers drawn on glass.']
See the account of the ghost of the uncle of Prince Charles of Saxony, raised by Schroepfer—'Karl—Karl—was willst du mit mir?'

Page 856, col. 2.

'Should cause more fear than a whole host's identity!']
'*Shadows* to-night
Have struck more terror to the soul of Richard,
Than oan the *substance* of ten thousand soldiers,' &c.   *Richard III.*

Page 857, col. 2.

'A human (what the Italians nickname) "Mule!" '] The Italians, at least in some parts of Italy, call bastards and foundlings the *mules*—why, I cannot see, unless they mean to infer that the offspring of matrimony are asses.

INDEX OF TITLES AND FIRST LINES

(The titles are printed in italics)

INDEX OF TITLES AND FIRST LINES

INDEX OF TITLES AND FIRST LINES

SET IN
GREAT BRITAIN
AT THE
UNIVERSITY PRESS
OXFORD
REPRINTED BY
NEILL AND CO. LTD.
EDINBURGH